Artificial Intelligence and the Rule of Law

Artificial intelligence is an important driving force of the new round of technological revolution and industrial change. Artificial intelligence and blockchain have risen to the level of national policy. While the rapid development of AI brings convenience to people's lives, it also poses challenges to global changes and the development of human society, social governance and legal regulation, such as the leakage of personal privacy, frequent data security problems, and prejudice and discrimination caused by algorithms. AI is profoundly changing the world, and it is necessary to think about how to promote the construction of responsible AI from the perspective of global governance in the future.

In response to these issues, this series aims to explore and study the new situations and new issues at the intersection of AI, law and political science all over the world, to provide a legal basis for the development of AI-related frontier fields and to limit the development of AI within the framework of law to promote the harmonious and orderly construction of AI and legal systems. Based on the above purpose, this series is selected and integrated with multidisciplinary strengths to strengthen the research on legal, ethical, and social issues related to AI, focusing on laws, regulations, institutional systems, and ethics for the healthy development of AI. The authors of this series are all top authoritative experts and scholars in AI, law, political science, and other disciplines in China, and they have already made considerable achievements and social reputations in this field of research.

This series has a clear awareness of the problem and proposes specific solutions for the implementation and implementation of AI governance from a multidisciplinary and multidisciplinary perspective, covering AI, blockchain, algorithms, digital currency and other specific segments closely related to law, with cutting-edge, academic and theoretical value.

Hugo Luz dos Santos

Controllable Artificial Intelligence and the Future of Law

Set 1

Springer

Hugo Luz dos Santos
Faculty of Humanities
City University of Macau
Macao, Macao

ISSN 2731-6238 ISSN 2731-6246 (electronic)
Artificial Intelligence and the Rule of Law
ISBN 978-981-95-0507-4 ISBN 978-981-95-0508-1 (eBook)
https://doi.org/10.1007/978-981-95-0508-1

This Springer imprint is published by the registered company Springer Nature Singapore Pte Ltd.
The registered company address is: 152 Beach Road, #21-01/04 Gateway East, Singapore 189721, Singapore

Foreword by Professor Nuno Garoupa

The rapid emergence of artificial intelligence (AI) has prompted a tectonic shift in how modern societies conceive of regulation, individual autonomy, and the infrastructure of justice. In *Controllable Artificial Intelligence and the Future of Law*, Professor Hugo Luz dos Santos confronts this transformation with urgency and intellectual clarity. From the standpoint of law and economics, which is my field of interest, the issues raised by this work are not merely academic—they are foundational. They concern the allocation of rights, the minimization of social costs, and the preservation of legal predictability in the face of computational opacity.

The economic analysis of law proceeds from the idea that legal institutions serve to allocate entitlements in a way that promotes efficiency, minimizes transaction costs, and addresses externalities. From Coase to Calabresi, legal economists have emphasized how rules should be structured to guide behavior in ways that reflect rational incentives and information availability. AI disrupts these assumptions. When algorithms act as opaque intermediaries between individual action and legal consequence—when decisions are made by systems whose internal logic is inaccessible even to their designers—traditional economic models of law lose traction. As Professor Hugo dos Santos illustrates, this loss of traction is not a theoretical problem alone: it has immediate repercussions for equality, accountability, and access to justice.

One of the central themes of the book is the erosion of the rule of law under what the author terms "algorithmic dictatorship." In economic terms, this phenomenon can be described as a massive informational asymmetry: individuals subject to algorithmic decision-making cannot observe, audit, or contest the criteria by which decisions are made. The result is not only a breakdown in procedural fairness but an increase in systemic risk—one that undermines trust in legal institutions and generates externalities that ripple across markets and societies.

The law and economics tradition has long emphasized the importance of predictability and transparency in legal rules. Hayek, for instance, viewed the rule of law as the precondition for any functioning price system. In that view, when law becomes unpredictable, individuals cannot plan, contracts become less reliable, and economic coordination breaks down. Professor Hugo dos Santos forcefully argues

that many AI systems today, particularly black-box models, are incompatible with these foundational principles. They cannot be interpreted, contested, or understood by those subject to their authority. In this way, they represent not a continuation but a negation of the liberal legal tradition.

And yet, as the author rightly observes, AI also presents opportunities—if we are willing to reform our institutional frameworks accordingly. From a law and economics perspective, the challenge is to design rules and architectures that realign the incentives of AI developers, regulators, and users with the principles of procedural integrity and distributive fairness. Professor Hugo dos Santos's notion of a "Controllable Artificial Intelligence" is central in this regard. Rather than rejecting algorithmic tools wholesale, he proposes a governance framework that makes AI systems interpretable, auditable, and amenable to legal scrutiny. In economic terms, this is a call to reduce the transaction costs of contesting algorithmic decisions, to create liability structures that internalize the risks of faulty predictions, and to establish a legal infrastructure that rewards transparency.

A particularly powerful insight of the book lies in its critique of algorithmic decision-making in domains characterized by moral hazard and adverse selection—two concepts central to economic theory. Consider credit scoring, insurance pricing, or criminal sentencing: in each case, the use of predictive algorithms risks compounding the informational disadvantages of the most vulnerable. If these systems rely on biased or incomplete data—and if their users cannot detect or correct those flaws—the result is not efficiency but perpetuation of structural inequality. In such cases, the economic justification for algorithmic deployment collapses. Instead of promoting allocative efficiency, AI tools become instruments of statistical discrimination.

Professor dos Santos also engages seriously with the empirical literature on predictive policing and recidivism assessment. These are areas where machine learning models have been marketed as tools to improve resource allocation—an ostensibly economic rationale. But as he shows, these systems often replicate past biases, undermine individual rights, and decouple legal sanctions from actual behavior. From a law and economics perspective, the purported gains in efficiency are illusory if they are achieved at the cost of legitimacy, accuracy, or equality before the law.

At its best, the economic analysis of law promotes institutions that channel behavior in socially beneficial ways. It recognizes that regulation is not free, that information is costly, and that legal design involves trade-offs. What Professor Hugo dos Santos brings to this discussion is a rich and multidisciplinary understanding of how AI reshapes those trade-offs. He highlights, for instance, the "measurement bias" and "dimensionality curse" that plague even the most sophisticated machine learning models. He draws attention to the "automation bias" that infects human reliance on AI-generated recommendations. And he articulates a theory of "algorithmic common good" that reintroduces normative considerations—fairness, dignity, reason-giving—into a field too often obsessed with optimization alone.

For legal economists, the book offers several important lessons. First, it underscores the need to revise our models of information and incentives when dealing with autonomous systems. Second, it cautions against the uncritical importation of market

analogies into legal contexts where power, rights, and identity are at stake. Third, it challenges the field to think more rigorously about the normative infrastructure required to make AI-compatible with legal values.

There is, in this book, a kind of moral urgency—an insistence that legal theory must not lag behind technological practice. Professor Hugo dos Santos makes clear that the stakes are existential: algorithmic opacity and unaccountability are not abstract concerns, but mechanisms that can silently erode democratic governance. Law, in his view, must remain not merely a tool of order or economic efficiency, but a bulwark against domination—especially in an era when computational systems increasingly mediate access to housing, employment, healthcare, and justice itself.

In sum, *Controllable Artificial Intelligence and the Future of Law* is a landmark contribution to the emerging literature on AI governance. It blends doctrinal insight with philosophical depth and technological fluency. For scholars and students of law and economics, it offers both a warning and a blueprint. The warning: that without legal safeguards, AI may exacerbate the very problems it purports to solve. The blueprint: that through accountability, interpretability, and careful institutional design, we can harness computational power without sacrificing the values that make law legitimate in the first place.

As we stand at the frontier of algorithmic governance, this book reminds us that efficiency is not enough. Justice demands that the systems we create—no matter how complex—remain under human control, subject to legal reasoning, and responsive to the values of an open society. The economic analysis of law, updated for the age of AI, must rise to that challenge.

Professor Nuno Garoupa
Professor of Law and Faculty Director
of Graduate Studies, George Mason
University, Antonin Scalia Law School
Fairfax, USA

Foreword by Professor Ronald Montague Silley

As the proliferation of artificial intelligence accelerates in every part of our modern world, this presents a defining challenge for our systems of law, governance and justice. In *Controllable Artificial Intelligence and the Future of Law*, Prof. Hugo Luz dos Santos not only gives us a scholarly and philosophical treatise on this phenomenon, but an essential and practical reckoning that our legal institutions must face during such a significant technological transformation.

This is a book precisely written at a pivotal time of change, when our legal practices must catch-up to scientific innovations and our ethical concepts must keep-up with the power of computers. With little public awareness and even less oversight, we are entering an era where machines do more than just assist human decision-making, they are increasingly replacing it. As human judgment is subordinated to machine learning, and moral accountability is displaced by statistical inferences, Prof. Hugo Luz dos Santos not only asks whether machines can be made to follow the law, he confronts the more profound, difficult and urgent questions, of what becomes of law, and indeed our society itself, when our most important deliberations are increasingly outsourced to computer systems? As these operate without transparency and often without scrutiny, he sounds an alarm on what he terms the rise of an "Algorithmic Dictatorship".

In the powerfully interdisciplinary style for which he is known, Prof. Hugo Luz dos Santos meticulously connects classical legal theory, ethics and critical studies, with novel social and technological analysis. The result is an original and pragmatic investigation that elevates our understanding of AI in jurisprudence. This book's contributions are wide-ranging and, in many respects, groundbreaking. It masterfully illuminates the underexplored intersections between AI and critical legal studies. By mapping practices from predictive policing and algorithmic credit scoring, to automated tenant screening and the hallucinatory risks of generative AI, this book shows how supposedly neutral tools are in fact embedded with the beliefs and inequalities of the societies that have created them. As these opaque systems are carriers of both values and assumptions, encoded with prejudices and inherited biases, they not only replicate historical inequities under a guise of impartial computation, but may even exacerbate discriminatory and exclusionary consequences.

While Prof. Hugo Luz dos Santos reminds us that law must not abdicate its normative authority to data-driven systems for efficiency, this book is also not fatalist in despair nor Luddite in its resistance to new technology. It never loses sight of justice as law's fundamental aim and calls for the law to not only be reactive but also resilient. It offers a practical framework for reform and provides a blueprint for an "Algorithmic Common Good", anchored by principles that are rooted in the rule of law, distributive justice and procedural integrity. As a guide to inspire all to recognize that the future of law cannot be written by machines alone, this helps bridge the gap for those who build the tools of tomorrow and those who struggle with their applications today.

Informed by history and driven by urgency, this is a book of uncommon clarity and consequence. The issues raised will not go away, but only grow more pressing as the use of AI becomes more prevalent. This book not only speaks to scholars and students, lawmakers and judges, regulators and technologists, but to all people having an interest in technology's disruptions and society's ethical imperatives for upholding human dignity, fairness, legal equality, procedural justice and the rule of law in the future.

Professor Ronald Montague Silley
European Executive Co-Dean
China-EU School of Law at the China
University of Political Science
and Law Hamburg
Germany/Beijing, China

Foreword by Professor Tu Guangjian

Human beings' lives have been improving by tools and technologies invented by themselves since they came to this planet. In the history of humankind, each time when there is a new "big" invention, people's life style may change, for example electricity, cars, trains, airplanes, computers and internet etc. have fundamentally changed our life. Online life is a natural extension of offline life while a life with AI i.e. AI life is also a natural extension of online life after big data is usable because of internet and computer.

We are in an era of big data and AI now. AI is a far-reaching, pervasive, cutting-through and penetrating technology. AI can perform many functions that are beneficial to us such as predicting, decision-making and information (answer)-providing etc. Whether you like it or not, sooner or later, we are going to live in a world full of AI and AI is increasingly being full of our life from your household appliances to your workstation, from what you eat to what your wear and almost everywhere you can see so that it is not exaggerating that everybody has an AI life.

"Rule by law" is the human wisdom distilled from many years' experiences and 'bloody" history of countries and the common belief of civilized societies nowadays. As the train can only run well on the railway, the society can only be run well on the proper framework of law and so are AI and people's AI life. AI can be related to different areas of laws: It can be used for concluding a contract by the parties; police can make use of it to identify the suspect; court and tribunals can rely on it to deal with evidences and draft legal documents in the procedures ...... Few laws, however, have been made by few jurisdictions for this new phenomenon so far. We need to study its impact on the different aspects of laws and how the laws can accommodate it and may have to adapt to it in details when its functions unfold in judicial practices. Hugo's book is a timely legal research and publication that can provide answers to many of our queries and obliviate our doubts when encountered with AI and living an AI life.

Human inventions can never be as perfect as what has been made by the Almighty God. The author has demonstrated a very healthy attitude towards AI. To any technology, one must face its risks and harness it. As with the nuclear technology which can be utilized to develop nuclear medicine but can also be applied to make nuclear

bomb, AI, for the use of humankind, also has potential risks. The author rightly called for "AI should be thing-centred and trustworthy". Although the use of AI is hailed and highly expected by many, the author is sober to point out the possible problems that could even be exacerbated and the potential risks that could happen by the use of AI including the danger of losing rule of law.

In the book, the author highlighted the problem of algorithmic dictatorship and argued that "many lasting problems in our traditional society will continue to last, even more entrenched into the modern and future society of AI, due to algorithmic dictatorship". Of course, nobody can shrug away from the history. When AI is largely used, the past and ingrained hallmarks will continue and even become deeper owing to the fact that AI is based on big data that is "previous and past". We must still be alert to the problem of racial and gender discrimination under the seemingly neutral data-driven framework. However, the author does not lose heart and find out meaningful and valuable ways from algorithmic dictatorship to algorithmic common good, which is worth commending indeed. The author also warned us against making high-stake decisions by using AI. Although AI can be more "objective" and "efficient" than human beings, AI can have "hallucination" besides "black box". The author advocated "a controllable AI amenable to be interpretable, accountable and fair" and "relevant stakeholders must track the quality of the dataset from which machine learning algorithms were built to foster algorithmic fairness" and "to audit the pearls of algorithmic wisdom", which is applaudable to me.

Moreover, this book not only deals with AI & Law but also deeper problem of society with law (criminology) and how they can be further reflected and dealt with by law when assisted with AI.

This book is a very good exploration of what has been done and may do in the future when AI is still a fast-moving and developing area. To be better prepared for an AI era, this is a book I would like to highly recommend.

Professor Tu Guangjian
Professor of Law, Faculty of Law
of the University of Macau
Macao, Macao

Foreword by Professor Peter Chi Hin Chan

Artificial intelligence is transforming nearly every aspect of modern life, from how we communicate to how we make decisions. Yet for all its promises, AI also poses unprecedented challenges to our legal systems. We live in an era when algorithms can influence judicial outcomes, enforce regulations, and even shape public opinion. As we stand at this crossroad, a pressing question emerges: how do we ensure that these powerful technologies remain **controllable**, aligned with the rule of law and the common good? In *Controllable Artificial Intelligence and the Future of Law*, Hugo Luz dos Santos tackles this question head-on, offering a timely and incisive exploration of the legal world's response to the rise of advanced AI. This book could not come at a more crucial moment. It speaks to the significance of its topic with clarity and urgency, illuminating why *controlling* AI is not just a technical matter but a fundamental legal and ethical imperative for society.

The book unfolds in **five well-organized parts**, each addressing a crucial facet of the AI-law relationship. **Part I** serves as a wake-up call: it articulates why society must not be complacent about algorithmic decision-making. Here, the author probes whether advances in AI have swung the "pendulum" of power too far, edging us toward an era where algorithms exercise disproportionate control. This opening part frames the core concern that resonates throughout the book—if we do nothing, are we tacitly accepting a form of digital dictatorship governed by algorithms? **Part II** titled *The History of Artificial Intelligence*, takes a step back and provides a brief historical account of AI's evolution. In these chapters, we are reminded that understanding where AI comes from—its origins, its development, and past attempts at regulation—is essential to grasp why the notion of making AI "controllable" arose in the first place. By tracing AI's journey from a speculative idea to a reality embedded in everyday life, the author underscores how past developments have led to present dilemmas.

Building on this foundation, **Part III: Critical Artificial Intelligence Studies (CAIS)** brings a rigorous analytical lens to the interplay between technology and society. In this section, Santos engages with contemporary philosophical and critical frameworks to dissect how AI systems can inadvertently entrench bias and inequality. By the end of Part III, the reader gains a sobering understanding: the potential for

an algorithmic dictatorship is not a distant science-fiction threat, but a tangible risk already perceptible in today's biased algorithms and data-driven decisions. If Part III diagnoses the problem, **Part IV** titled *Algorithmic Dictatorship and the Chilling Effect on Democracy* confronts its consequences for our legal and democratic institutions. Here, Santos goes so far as to brand the unchecked proliferation of algorithm-driven power as a "**devilishly harmful virus**" attacking the rule of law, asking pointedly whether the Rule of Law is "backsliding beyond repair" under this onslaught. This vivid metaphor captures the book's central worry: that without intervention, AI could erode the foundations of justice in ways that may be difficult to reverse. Through a series of well-chosen examples, the author illustrates how this erosion is already underway. He enumerates a litany of what he calls the "**unpalatable byproducts**" of unchecked algorithms—from predictive policing and discriminatory credit scoring to phenomena like *"algorithmic Jim Crow"*—even noting the troubling emergence of falsehoods or "hallucinations" in large language models like ChatGPT. By cataloguing these real-world issues, Part IV paints a comprehensive picture of the stakes: *algorithmic decision-making is not just a technical progression, it is a force that can either undermine or uphold our most cherished legal principles.*

Yet, this book does not stop at critique. **Part V: Algorithmic Common Good to Oust Algorithmic Dictatorship** marks the transition from diagnosis to prescription. In these final chapters, the author puts forward a constructive vision for reining in AI and aligning it with our highest legal and ethical values. The very notion of an "**Algorithmic Common Good**" is a scholarly innovation that this book develops—it encapsulates the idea that we must reorient AI design and governance toward shared human values and societal well-being, rather than allowing profit or efficiency alone to dictate outcomes. Santos argues that by embedding principles of justice, transparency, and accountability into the fabric of AI systems, we can **oust** the looming algorithmic dictatorship and replace it with a form of algorithmic governance that serves everyone. To build this argument, he draws on the rich heritage of legal thought and philosophy. By reviving the classic ideas in the context of AI, the author shows that our modern challenges can still be guided by enduring values. Impressively, Santos even proposes using AI tools to monitor and correct other AI systems, a creative approach to harnessing technology against its own potential abuses. This blending of legal theory, ethical principles, and practical policy proposals showcases the book's most important contribution: it moves the conversation from what is wrong to what can be done.

Reflecting on the entirety of this book, one cannot help but appreciate the scholarly rigor and passion that underlie its pages. *Controllable Artificial Intelligence and the Future of Law* is both a comprehensive academic study and a call to action. It spans an impressive range—from recounting the early history of AI to dissecting the latest controversies over algorithms in the courtroom, all while maintaining a clear focus on the future of law in an AI-driven world. The key themes of the book—**accountability in AI**, **preservation of the rule of law**, **prevention of algorithmic tyranny**, **and the pursuit of an algorithmic common good**—are interwoven into a coherent narrative that advances our understanding of each. Legal scholars will value the depth of research, and policymakers will find concrete ideas on practically

regulating AI. Technologists, too, can glean insight from this work about the societal and legal context in which their creations will operate. On a more personal note, as a friend of the author, I have observed Santos' abiding commitment to justice in the face of technological change. This book is a testament to that commitment. There is a palpable passion in these chapters—a determination to ensure that our future with AI is one where **human dignity and rights are upheld rather than trampled by cold algorithms**. And yet, the tone of the book remains measured and reasoned, reflecting the balance of an academic who is keenly aware of both the potentials and pitfalls of AI.

Controllable Artificial Intelligence and the Future of Law is a landmark contribution to the ongoing conversation about AI's place in our legal order. It challenges us to recognize the stakes: if we value democracy, equality, and the rule of law, we cannot afford to leave AI unchecked. But more importantly, it lights the way forward by outlining how we can **controllably integrate** AI into our legal frameworks without sacrificing our core values. I have no doubt that readers will find it as illuminating and thought-provoking as I did. As we grapple with the future of law in an age of intelligent machines, Hugo Luz dos Santos has given us not only a warning of the specter of an "algorithmic dictatorship", but also a vision of hope—a future where artificial intelligence is harnessed in service of a just and orderly society, under the steadfast guidance of the law.

Professor Peter Chi Hin Chan
Associate Professor at the School of Law
of City University of Hong Kong
Kowloon Tong, Hong Kong

Competing Interests The author has no competing interests to declare that are relevant to the content of this manuscript.

Praise for Controllable Artificial Intelligence and the Future of Law

"Professor Hugo Luz dos Santos's notion of a "Controllable Artificial Intelligence" is central in this regard. Rather than rejecting algorithmic tools wholesale, he proposes a governance framework that makes AI systems interpretable, auditable, and amenable to legal scrutiny.

In sum, *Controllable Artificial Intelligence and the Future of Law* is a landmark contribution to the emerging literature on AI governance. It blends doctrinal insight with philosophical depth and technological fluency. For scholars and students of law and economics, it offers both a warning and a blueprint. The warning: that without legal safeguards, AI may exacerbate the very problems it purports to solve. The blueprint: that through accountability, interpretability, and careful institutional design, we can harness computational power without sacrificing the values that make law legitimate in the first place."

—Professor Nuno Garoupa, *Professor of Law and Faculty Director of Graduate Studies, George Mason University, Antonin Scalia Law School*

"In *Controllable Artificial Intelligence and the Future of Law*, Prof. Hugo Luz dos Santos not only gives us a scholarly and philosophical treatise on this phenomenon, but an essential and practical reckoning that our legal institutions must face during such a significant technological transformation.

This is a book precisely written at a pivotal time of change, when our legal practices must catch-up to scientific innovations and our ethical concepts must keep-up with the power of computers.

In the powerfully interdisciplinary style for which he is known, Prof. Hugo Luz dos Santos meticulously connects classical legal theory, ethics and critical studies, with novel social and technological analysis. The result is an original and pragmatic investigation that elevates our understanding of AI in jurisprudence. This book's contributions are wide-ranging and, in many respects, groundbreaking. It masterfully illuminates the underexplored intersections between AI and critical legal studies."

—Prof. Ronald Montague Silley, *European Executive Co-Dean China-EU School of Law at the China University of Political Science and Law, Hamburg, Germany/Beijing, China*

"This book could not come at a more crucial moment. It speaks to the significance of its topic with clarity and urgency, illuminating why *controlling* AI is not just a technical matter but a fundamental legal and ethical imperative for society.

There is a palpable passion in these chapters—a determination to ensure that our future with AI is one where **human dignity and rights are upheld rather than trampled by cold algorithms**. And yet, the tone of the book remains measured and reasoned, reflecting the balance of an academic who is keenly aware of both the potentials and pitfalls of AI.

Controllable Artificial Intelligence and the Future of Law is a landmark contribution to the ongoing conversation about AI's place in our legal order. It challenges us to recognize the stakes: if we value democracy, equality, and the rule of law, we cannot afford to leave AI unchecked. But more importantly, it lights the way forward by outlining how we can **controllably integrate** AI into our legal frameworks without sacrificing our core values. I have no doubt that readers will find it as illuminating and thought-provoking as I did".

—Peter Chi Hin Chan, *Associate Professor at School of Law of City University of Hong Kong*

"Hugo's book is a timely legal research and publication that can provide answers to many of our queries and obliviate our doubts when encountered with AI and living an AI life.

The author advocated "a controllable AI amenable to be interpretable, accountable and fair" and "relevant stakeholders must track the quality of the dataset from which machine learning algorithms were built to foster algorithmic fairness" and "to audit the pearls of algorithmic wisdom", which is applaudable to me.

This book is a very good exploration of what has been done and may do in the future when AI is still a fast-moving and developing area. To be better prepared for an AI era, this is a book I would like to highly recommend."

—Guangjian Tu, *Professor of Law, Faculty of Law of the University of Macau*

Contents

Part I
Has the Pendulum Swung Too Far? Towards an Algorithmic Dictatorship?

Chapter 1
Why You Should Be Worried with a Looming *Algorithmic Dictatorship*

1.1 Introduction

§§ Regulating Artificial Intelligence through the lens of predictability is a vital, but rather elusive,[1] task.[2] Tellingly, the extent to which Artificial Intelligence—which sifts through reams of data to ferret out meaningful patterns[3]—is controllable[4]/predictable[5] is widely contested.[6]

---

[1] Yeung, Karen, "Algorithmic Regulation: A Critical Interrogation", *Regulation & Governance*, Volume 12, 2018, pp. 505 and ff and passim (on the sweltering challenges posed by algorithmic regulation).

[2] See: Brownsword, Roger, *Law, Technology and Society: Re-Imagining the Regulatory Environment*, London: Routledge, 2020, pp. 1–361 (passim) (broaches the interplay between law, technology, and society with a sharper focus in the era of smart regulatory technologies).

[3] The issue of a digital reality fed by a data-driven world has been shrewdly portrayed by renowned scholars, whom offer gripping examples of it: Suzor, Nicolas P., *Lawless: The Secret Rules that Govern our Digital Lives*. Cambridge, United Kingdom: Cambridge University Press, 2019, pp. 1–218 (passim).

[4] Weizenbaum, Joseph, *Computer Power and Human Reason: From Judgment to Calculation*, 1st edition, New York, W. H. Freeman & Co, 1976, pp. 1–300 (227) ("examines the sources of the computer's powers and offers evaluative explorations of what computers can do, cannot do, and should not be employed to do") (this founding father of Artificial Intelligence presciently noted that we should not entrust Artificial Intelligence-embedded technologies with "tasks that demand wisdom"). Italics added. The approval of rental applications is arguably one of those tasks that should never be entrusted to machines). More on this on Part IV, Chap. 4, Sects. 4.4. to 4.4.2.1 of this book.

[5] See: Rudin, Cynthia, "A process for predicting manhole events in Manhattan", *Machine Learning*, Volume 80, 2018, pp. 1–31.

[6] About this daunting reality, see, in broad strokes: Géron, Aurélien, *Hands-On Machine Learning with Scikit-Learn, Keras, and TensorFlow: Concepts, Tools, and Techniques to Build Intelligent Systems*. Sebastopol, California: O'Reilly Media, 2019, pp. 1–856.

H. L. dos Santos, *Controllable Artificial Intelligence and the Future of Law*, Artificial Intelligence and the Rule of Law, https://doi.org/10.1007/978-981-95-0508-1_1

§§ On the heels of such axiom, the legal framework for Artificial Intelligence is not as extensively developed[7]/regulated[8] yet as that which exists for Tort Law.[9]

§§ To add to our woes, a growing literature stream discusses[10] whether and to what extent the Artificial Intelligence is amenable to be trusted[11]

---

[7] Leslie, David/Burr, Christopher/Aitken, Mhairi/Cowls, Josh/Katell, Mike/Briggs, Morgan, "Artificial Intelligence, Human Rights, Democracy, and the Rule of Law: A Primer", prepared to support the feasibility study by the Council of Europe's Ad Hoc Committee on Artificial Intelligence, Council of Europe, The Alan Turing Institute, 2025, pp. 1–46 (5) ("*The Study examines how the fundamental rights and freedoms that are already codified in international human rights law can be used as the basis for such a legal framework. It proposes nine principles and priorities that are fitted to the novel challenges posed by the design, development, and deployment of AI systems. When codified into law, these principles and priorities create a set of interlocking rights and obligations that will work towards ensuring that the design and use of AI technologies conform to the values of human rights, democracy, and the rule of law. The Feasibility Study concludes that current rules and legal regimes are neither adequate for safeguarding these basic values as they pertain to AI, nor suitable, in and of themselves, for creating an AI innovation environment that can be deemed sufficiently trustworthy for steering AI and data intensive technologies in the right direction. A new legal framework is needed*"). Italics added.

[8] Boden, Margaret A., *Artificial Intelligence: A Very Short Introduction*. Oxford: Oxford University Press, 2018.

[9] Coleman, J. L., *Practice of Principle*, Oxford, Oxford University Press, 2001, *passim* (at the heart of the fabric of tort law lies the assertion according to which the tortfeasor or the wrongdoer must be held accountable for the damages inflicted upon the plaintiff); Morgan, Jonathan, "Tort. Insurance and Incoherence", *The Modern Law Review*, Volume 67, Issue 3, 2004, 84–401 (392); Calabresi, Guido, *The Costs of Accidents: A Legal and Economic Analysis*, New Haven, Yale University Press, 1970, pp. 1–350 (passim) (argues that one of the overriding goals of tort law is award to plaintiff's justice, *fairness*, and redress from wrongs); Blum, W. J./Kalven, H., "The Empty Cabinet of Dr. Calabresi—Auto Accidents and General Deterrence", *University of Chicago Law Review*, 34, 1967, pp. 268 ff (averring that tort law also pursues the goal of, and resonates with, allaying victim's feeling of utter indignation); Goldberg, John C. P., "The Constitutional Status of Tort Law: Due Process and the Right to a Law for the Redress of wrongs", *The Yale Law Journal*, 115 (3), 2005, p. 597; Green, Michael D., *Comparative Stimulations for Developing Tort Law*, Helmut Koziol (ed.), European Centre of Tort Law and Insurance Law, Jan Sramek Verlag, Wien, Austria, 2015, 35 (argues that "one who has harmed by the wrongdoing of another might justifiably appeal to *fairness* in righting a wrong as the basis for demanding recompense from the wrongdoer"). Italics added.

[10] Laudably and timely enough, a strand of Spanish doctrine is making rapid strides in unveiling/unravelling/unlocking the dire need to award/afford/grant protection to the circle of fundamental rights affected by artificial intelligence within the purview of criminal procedure law. See: Beriain, Iñigo de/Estrada/Pérez, M. Josune, "La inteligencia artificial en el proceso penal español: un análisis de su admisibilidad sobre la base de los derechos fundamentales implicados", *Revista de derecho UNED (RDUNED)*, Volume 25, 2019, pp. 531–561.

[11] Assessment List for Trustworthy Artificial Intelligence (ALTAI) for self-assessment, 17 Jul 2020, available at: https://digital-strategy.ec.europa.eu/en/library/assessment-list-trustworthy-artificial-intelligence-altai-self-assessment (access: 16.12.2024). See also: Bengio, Y., Hinton, G., Yao, A., Song, D., Abbeel, P., Harari, Y. N., Hadfield, G., Russell, S., Kahneman, D., & Mindermann, S., *Managing ai risks in an era of rapid progress*, arXiv preprint arXiv:2310.17688, 2023.

upon.[12] Which is nothing but formulaic: the boundaries between humans[13] and machines[14] are becoming increasingly blurred,[15] thus playing havoc with our ability

[12] See: O'Neil, Cathy, "When Not to Trust the Algorithm", *Interview published in the Harvard Business Review's Ideacast*, 2016, passim. See also: O'Neill, Cathy, *Weapons of Math Destruction. How Big Data Increases Inequality and Threatens Democracy*. London: Penguin Random House, 2016, passim.

[13] Tegmark, Max, *Life 3.0: Being Human in the Age of Artificial Intelligence*. New York: Knopf, 2018, pp. 1–384 (pp. 24 and ff) (charts the path ahead for a wide range of intelligences, including artificial intelligence in the digital age). There is a handful of authors that wonder if artificial intelligence can mimic not only human intelligence but, and foremost, human behaviour. Amongst whom stands: Russel, Stuart, Norvig, Peter, *Artificial Intelligence: A Modern Approach*. London: United Kingdom, Pearson, 2018, passim.

[14] Against the backdrop of which humans and machines are poised to dovetail seamlessly. This turbid reality—although difficult to depict at this moment—will be inevitably morphed into a disturbingly dystopic reality sooner rather than later. See: Remus, Dana/Levy, Frank, "Can Robots be Lawyers? Computers, Lawyers, and the Practice of Law", *Georgetown Journal of Legal Ethics*, Volume 30, 2018, pp. 501 and ff and passim.

[15] See: Cuellar, Mariano-Florentino, "A Common Law for the Age of Artificial Intelligence: Incremental Adjudication, Institutions, and Relational Non-Arbitrariness", *Columbia Law Review*, Volume 119, 2020, pp. 1773–1775 (this author presciently posits that "(t)he coevolution of human and artificial intelligence—what we could call our dance with machines—is well on its way to becoming routine"). See also: Cataleta, Maria Stefania/Cataleta, Anna, "Artificial Intelligence and Human Rights: An Unequal Struggle", *CIFILE Journal of International Law*, Volume 1, N. º 2, 2020 ("*Artificial Intelligence (AI) is a kind of intelligence that was born in the 1950s and is an integral part of the digital revolution. Progress made by AI has permitted the birth of systems capable of rivalling human capacities or, in some cases, surpassing them.* The progress of the intellectual capacities of AI will change the way of life for human beings and will revolutionise the world of employment. *Intelligent systems present problems regarding individual rights and responsibilities, because as technology replaces more and more of what humans have typically done, our individual roles will become more blurred.*"). Italics added. Converging: Cataleta, Maria Stefania, "Artificial Intelligence vs Human Intelligence", in: Martin, L. Miraut/Zalucki, M. (editors), *Artificial intelligence and Human Rights, Dickinson eBook*. Krakow: AFM Krakow University, 2021, pp. 117–127 (on the slew of both moral, ethical, and legal issues with which jurists will grapple in the forthcoming future due to the rise of artificial intelligence in legal arena).

to grasp the inner workings of Artificial Intelligence[16] while toiling towards a near future whereby humans and machines are poised to haggle[17] to share[18] the same space.[19] This assertion is neither unwarranted[20] nor uncalled for.[21]

---

[16] As we throw ourselves in the boundless arena of automated processes powered by Artificial Intelligence, the difficulties to grasp its delicate intricacies mount exponentially. See: Cohen, Julien E., *Between Truth and Power: The Legal Constructions of Informational Capitalism*. Oxford: Oxford University Press, 2019, pp. 1–376 (p. 192) (asserts adamantly that "*automated processes* have *obvious efficiency advantages, but such processes may not align well (or well at all) with applicable legal requirements that are couched in shades of gray*"). Italics added.

[17] Buolamwini, Joy, Unmasking AI: My Mission to Protect What Is Human in a World of Machines, New York, Random House, 2023, pp. 1–336 ("*The conscience of the AI revolution" (Fortune) explains how we've arrived at an era of AI harms and oppression, and what we can do to avoid its pitfalls.* "AI is not coming, it's here. If we answer the beautiful call inside these pages, *we can decide who we are going to be and how we're going to use technology in service of what it means to be fully human.*"—Brené Brown, #1 *New York Times* bestselling author of *Dare to Lead*. A *LOS ANGELES TIMES* BEST BOOK OF THE YEAR • Shortlisted for the *Inc.* Non-Obvious Book Award. *To most of us, it seems like recent developments in artificial intelligence emerged out of nowhere to pose unprecedented threats to humankind. But to Dr. Joy Buolamwini, who has been at the forefront of AI research, this moment has been a long time in the making*"). Italics added.

[18] Raisch, S., & Fomina, K., "Combining human and artificial intelligence: Hybrid problem-solving in organizations", *Academy of Management Review*, 2023.

[19] Levin, M., "AI: A bridge toward diverse intelligence and humanity's future", *Tufts University Working Paper*, 2024, passim.

[20] But see: Roli, A., Jaeger, J. and Kauffman, S.A., "How organisms come to know the world: Fundamental limits on artificial general intelligence", *Frontiers in Ecology and Evolution*, 2022, pp. 1035–1050.

[21] See: Part III, Chap. 3, Sects. 3.5.4 to 3.5.4.1.1 of this book (on the functional aspects of Critical Artificial Intelligence Studies, with a sharper focus on the harmful effects of Artificial Intelligence-embedded technologies, namely Large Language Models and its multifarious downsides and shortcomings). See also: Part IV, Chap. 4, Sects. 4.9.1 to 4.9.2 (on ChatGPT's functional abilities). See also: Part IV, Chap. 4, Sects. 4.9 to 4.9.7 (on ChatGPT's functional drawbacks and pitfalls, including, but no limited to, "hallucinations").

§§ Fast-paced strides in Artificial Intelligence are burgeoningly giving rise to a plethora of AI-entrenched technologies[22] that are bound to sway[23] a myriad of aspects[24] of modern societies,[25] which will accordingly catalyse a slew of

---

[22] See: Hu, Margaret, "From the National Surveillance State to the Cybersurveillance State", *The Annual Review of Law and Social Science*, Volume 13, 2017, p. 163 ("*Biometric identification and identity assessments are becoming essential tools for multiple preventive purposes in criminal, military, and intelligence contexts.* The third part addresses how precrime policy rationales are now informed by biometric-based analysis. *In short, biometrics is the means by which analysis of a citizenry's data, and any resulting decisions based on that analysis, can be connected back to a physical person in the real world*—whether to approve that person as eligible for a job, *as some employment eligibility database screening systems like E-Verify are, by moving toward biometrics through adopting the E-Verify photo tool* (Hu 2013), *or to determine whether that person is eligible to fly on a commercial airline. The No Fly List and digital watchlisting systems are increasingly biometrically centered (Tau 2015). These types of governance assessments, however, fall within the civil law and administrative law structure. Biometric cybersurveillance systems can inform targeted killing decisions and other lethal consequences. Often in the service of precrime/counterterrorism policies, biometric cybersurveillance, therefore, is becoming a linchpin for broader policymaking and decisionmaking*"). Italics added.

[23] See: Hu, Margaret, "From the National Surveillance State to the Cybersurveillance State", *The Annual Review of Law and Social Science*, Volume 13, 2017, p. 163 ("*collect-it-all efforts like TIA embody a philosophy that aspires to preventive policing.* Mass data collection is construed as a tool to assess and prevent future threats (Murray 2010). *In TIA and other programs tested or adopted after 9/11, biometric database screening and analysis have emerged as a preferred method for tracking, identifying, and establishing identity-based inferences in counterterrorism*"). Italics added.

[24] On algorithmic big data biometric governance: Hu, Margaret, "From the National Surveillance State to the Cybersurveillance State", *The Annual Review of Law and Social Science*, Volume 13, 2017, p. 169 ("*as a result of big data biometric governance trends, meaningful distinctions between biometric credentialing for identification and behavioral biometric profiling are disappearing. The objectives are merging: Reliable credentialing is used to advance security and precrime policy rationales. Biometric data mission creep occurs by necessity in a big data world because the cybersurveillance systems are often designed to engage in mass data integration and analysis and predictive policing. Biometric surveillance serves two purposes in preventive policing: It increases identity transparency, and the biometric data categorize identity through cataloging behavioral and physical characteristics and assess these characteristics for risk. Contrasting small data biometric credentialing protocols with big data credentialing protocols is useful. It illustrates how biometric surveillance fits within the Cybersurveillance State. In a small data world, paper-based passports and nondigitized photographs are examples of a small data biometric-based identification system*"). Italics added.

[25] Amongst which stands arguably cybersurveillance, which is an outgrowth of National Surveillance State: Hu, Margaret, "From the National Surveillance State to the Cybersurveillance State", *The Annual Review of Law and Social Science*, Volume 13, 2017, p. 168 ("*as a result, the Cybersurveillance State, as a technological successor to the National Surveillance State, will execute bureaucratized biometric cybersurveillance in ways that are largely invisible and that appear routinized when technologically embedded within biometric identification technologies harnessed by the Administrative State. The normalization of day-to-day cybersurveillance will be achieved largely through governing functions that appear purely administrative (e.g., identity assessments for the granting of welfare, rights, privileges, and governing incentives).* Because of the routinized and administrative nature of the government-led big data program or *data surveillance (dataveillance) program, contemporary cybersurveillance is likely to be viewed as justified under crime,*

challenges[26] in the legal arena[27] that are not amenable to be glossed over.[28] Which begs the vexing questions: will law keep abreast with the newest developments[29]

---

immigration control, and counterterrorism policy rationales"). Italics added. Balkin, Jack M., "The Constitution in the National Surveillance State", *Minnesota Law Review*, Volume 93, Issue 1, 2008, pp. 17 and ff; Christopher Slobogin, "Panvasive Surveillance, Political Process Theory, and the Nondelegation Doctrine", *Georgetown Law Journal*, Volume 102, 2014, pp. 1721–1775.

[26] Weizenbaum, Joseph, *Computer Power and Human Reason: From Judgment to Calculation*, 1st edition, New York, W. H. Freeman & Co, 1976, pp. 1–300 (227) ("examines the sources of the computer's powers and offers evaluative explorations of what computers can do, cannot do, and should not be employed to do") (this founding father of Artificial Intelligence presciently noted that we should not entrust Artificial Intelligence-embedded technologies with "tasks that demand wisdom"). Italics added. The approval of rental applications is arguably one of those tasks that should never be entrusted to machines). More on this on Part IV, Chap. 4, Sects. 4.4 to 4.4.2.1 of this book.

[27] Hu, Margaret, "From the National Surveillance State to the Cybersurveillance State", *The Annual Review of Law and Social Science*, Volume 13, 2017, p. 169 ("*the potential for mass surveillance is part of the problematic nature of biometric credentialing and identification practices. Like most digital data, biometric identification data are not restricted to the purpose for which they were originally collected.* Biometric data can be repurposed for secondary uses, such as identification of potential suspects or victims through real-time analytics, assessment of threats of terrorism, tactical decisionmaking, or behavioral and genetic research (Duster 2003). Beyond secondary—and tertiary, quaternary, and quinary—uses, biometric data become a part of population-wide *risk assessments that incorporate bureaucratized surveillance into governing decisions, policing, and threat assessments. Through big data tools, precrime governance models are increasingly reflected in collect-it-all cybersurveillance systems. In these systems, biometric data is a surveillance axis that can be used to track, identify, and isolate suspicious persons, digital data, or devices*"). Italics added. See also on mass surveillance: Bentham, Jeremy, *Panopticon: Or, the inspection-house*, Thomas Byrne, 1787. See also: Balkin, Jack M./Levinson, Sanford, "The Processes of Constitutional Change: From Partisan Entrenchment to the National Surveillance State", *Fordham Law Review*, Volume 75, 2006, pp. 489 and ff; Slogogin, Christopher, "Public Privacy: Camera Surveillance of Public Places and the Right to Anonymity", *Mississippi Law Journal*, Volume 72, 2002, pp. 213–251.

[28] Candent challenges that come under the yoke of intelligent automation, which is shaping up to morph the legal arena beyond recognition. See: Bornet, Pascal/Barkin, Ian/Wirtz, Jochen, *Intelligent Automation: Learn how to harness Artificial Intelligence to boost business and make out world more human*, 2020, pp. 1–432.

[29] The newest developments arising out of the "collect-it-all" technologies are slated to create a spate of sizzling hot challenges to the sustainability of the Rule of Law. See: Hu, Margaret, "From the National Surveillance State to the Cybersurveillance State", *The Annual Review of Law and Social Science*, Volume 13, 2017, pp. 162–163 ("*policymakers view these technological developments, including biometric technologies, as tools with the potential to identify individuals who may pose a threat to national and homeland security and to prevent crime and terrorism. One example of technology intended for risk assessment and threat management is the post-9/11 program Total Information Awareness (TIA).* TIA was the progeny of the Defense Advanced Research Projects Agency (DARPA) in the US Department of Defense. *TIA can be understood as a "collect-it-all" data surveillance program. TIA was not explicitly identified as a collect-it-all program—this phrase originated with the Snowden disclosures.* One National Security Agency (NSA) slide described the NSA's procedure as "collect-it-all" (Greenwald 2014b). *Collect-it-all efforts like TIA embody a philosophy that aspires to preventive policing. Mass data collection is construed as a tool to assess and prevent future threats (Murray 2010). In TIA and other programs tested or adopted after 9/*

in the camp of the ever-evolving[30] artificial intelligence?[31] Will law keep pace with scorching challenges brought to bear by inscrutable[32] artificial intelligence?[33] Will law lag behind instead? If law keeps apace with the newest developments

11, biometric database screening and analysis have emerged as a preferred method for tracking, identifying, and establishing identity-based inferences in counterterrorism"). Italics added.

[30] Hu, Margaret, "From the National Surveillance State to the Cybersurveillance State", *The Annual Review of Law and Social Science*, Volume 13, 2017, p. 169 ("*Facial recognition technology drawing upon a photo database could potentially link a plethora of digital images of a person, including social media, the internet, photo databases like driver's licenses, live-streaming video, CCTV surveillance, and images obtained from hacking cameras on laptops and digital devices.* Biometric data collection and storage are becoming increasingly compulsory through either government identification requirements, *such as digital photo requirements for passports and driver's licenses, or corporate identification requirements, such as biometric access to digital devices*"). Italics added.

[31] Bengio, Y., Hinton, G., Yao, A., Song, D., Abbeel, P., Harari, Y. N., Hadfield, G., Russell, S., Kahneman, D., & Mindermann, S., *Managing ai risks in an era of rapid progress*, arXiv preprint arXiv:2310.17688, 2023.

[32] For an on-point breakdown of the distinct levels of opacity arising out of machine learning algorithms: Selbst, Andrew D./Barocas, Solon, "The Intuitive Appeal of Explainable Machines", *Fordham Law Review*, Volume 87, 2018, pp. 1085, 1089–99 (holding that there are plenty reasons for the insurer's ignorance. To begin with, the algorithm entails specialized knowledge to understand. That is, the insurer's employees may lack sufficient knowledge to understand the rationale behind the reasons in view of which the algorithm is producing prices for different customers—personalized pricing. Lastly, even if the insurer himself comprehends how the model operates, it may nonetheless lack expertise to comprehend why it operates the way it does. For that reason, the explainability of machines is a vital, but rather elusive, task. Thence, the famed authors deem it as the "nonintuitive" nature of algorithms. For purposes here, the insurer himself might indeed understand that its Artificial Intelligence-embedded technology formulates higher prices for those who actually access the website at hand, but may fail to come to terms with the fact that the explanation for this fact arises from the website's capacity to proxy for genetic information). See also: Scherer, Matthew U. Scherer, "Regulating Artificial Intelligence Systems: Risks, Challenges, Competencies, and Strategies", *Harvard Journal of Law and Technology*, Volume 29, 2016, pp. 353–369 (frames the crippling problem of opacity as "the possibility that the inner workings of an AI system may be kept secret and may not be susceptible to reverse engineering").

[33] See in French doctrine: Baller, Stéphane/Deffains, Bruno, "Intelligence artificielle et devenir de la professions d'avocat; l'avenir est présent», *Revue pratique de la prospective et de innovation*, Volume 1, 2018, pp. 14 and ff (canvass the foundations of deep-rooted concerns regarding the irruption of artificial intelligence in the legal arena).

sprang into action by an unstoppable Artificial Intelligence[34] will accordingly lose its moral standing? Will a fast-paced Artificial Intelligence[35] devour a sluggish law instead?[36]

---

[34] Hu, Margaret, "From the National Surveillance State to the Cybersurveillance State", *The Annual Review of Law and Social Science*, Volume 13, 2017, p. 168 ("*currently, biometric verification and identification technologies are not commonly perceived to be surveillance technologies—the public and private sectors typically treat them as a benign and useful form of digitized identification. Such automated biometric screening is considered to be a more efficient form of small data verification technologies, such as human screening or human-driven practices involving assessments of biometric or forensic data. Small data biometric verification could include comparing a passport photo against the person holding the passport. Big data biometric identification, however, has a distinct impact from that of small data biometric investigation because it can facilitate surveillance. Big data photo screening may entail the collection of digital photographs. This in turn can lead to facilitating facial recognition technology through the mass digitization of photo databases, potentially including billions of facial images.* One Snowden disclosure noted that the NSA collects millions of digital photographs from internet and social media sources and uses facial recognition technology to identify individuals"). Italics added.

[35] Fergus, Rachel, "Biased Technology: The Automated Discrimination of Facial Recognition", *ACLU Minnesota*, February 29, 2024, available at: https://www.aclu-mn.org/en/news/biased-technology-automated-discrimination-facial-recognition (access: 20.09.2024) ("*Technology is developing much more quickly than the laws we need to protect our rights. Anyone with a smartphone or social media account knows how rapidly technology changes, while legislating can take a long, long time. It is essential to proactively put policies into place that will protect our rights as new and more advanced technology is constantly released. Especially when that technology—and law enforcement members using it—have been shown over and over to be biased toward marginalized groups*"). Italics added. See also: Hu, Margaret, "From the National Surveillance State to the Cybersurveillance State", *The Annual Review of Law and Social Science*, Volume 13, 2017, p. 169 ("*in a big data world, a digitized passport system can link to multiple other sources, such as license plate readers, No Fly Lists, and Terrorist Watchlists. Facial recognition technology drawing upon a photo database could potentially link a plethora of digital images of a person, including social media, the internet, photo databases like driver's licenses, live-streaming video, CCTV surveillance, and images obtained from hacking cameras on laptops and digital devices. Biometric data collection and storage are becoming increasingly compulsory through either government identification requirements*, such as digital photo requirements for passports and driver's licenses, or corporate identification requirements, such as biometric access to digital devices"). Italics added.

[36] Scholars haven't been neither coy nor bashful in pinpointing the drawbacks and downsides concerning the unbridled and rampant rise of the Artificial Intelligence in the legal arena. See: Wu, Tim, "Will Artificial Intelligence Eat the Law? The Rise of Hybrid Social-Ordering Systems", *Columbia Law Review*, Volume 119, 2019, pp. 2001 and ff and passim.

§§ To the extent law is woefully ill-prepared to tackle a conglomeration of sizzling hot topics arising out of artificial intelligence,[37] befitted legal measures are in dire need of being enacted.[38] Take the example of criminal procedure law, which is shaping up to be at loggerheads with its fundamental tenets amidst the unbridled rise of Artificial Intelligence.

---

[37] Take the example of biometric surveillance, which is very hard to shy away from nowadays. See: Hu, Margaret, "From the National Surveillance State to the Cybersurveillance State", *The Annual Review of Law and Social Science*, Volume 13, 2017, p. 169 ("*because of technological developments and trends in governance, it is challenging, if not impossible, to prevent biometric data capture and collection. Biometric surveillance systems increasingly require opting in as the price of social, economic, and political participation.* Biometric data capture is difficult to resist because it is simultaneously compulsory and transparent. Biometric data collection is often compulsory because it is increasingly mandatory to establish identity. *Biometrics are transparent qualities because it is very difficult to hide biometrics; an individual's face, iris, or fingerprint can be digitally captured in any public place. Because biometric data support larger big data programs, such as No Fly List–type risk assessments, it is extraordinarily difficult, if not impossible, to opt out*"). Italics added.

[38] Hu, Margaret, "From the National Surveillance State to the Cybersurveillance State", *The Annual Review of Law and Social Science*, Volume 13, 2017, p. 169 ("*the potential for mass surveillance is part of the problematic nature of biometric credentialing and identification practices. Like most digital data, biometric identification data are not restricted to the purpose for which they were originally collected*. Biometric data can be repurposed for secondary uses, such as identification of potential suspects or victims through real-time analytics, assessment of threats of terrorism, tactical decisionmaking, or behavioral and genetic research (Duster 2003). Beyond secondary—and tertiary, quaternary, and quinary—uses, biometric data become a part of population-wide *risk assessments that incorporate bureaucratized surveillance into governing decisions, policing, and threat assessments. Through big data tools, precrime governance models are increasingly reflected in collect-it-all cybersurveillance systems. In these systems, biometric data is a surveillance axis that can be used to track, identify, and isolate suspicious persons, digital data, or devices*"). Italics added.

§§ As we hurdle[39] into[40] a digital[41] future,[42] the candent[43] challenges[44] posed[45] by a burgeoningly[46] pervasive[47] technology[48] loom

---

[39] See: Santos, Hugo Luz dos, “"Brain-Computer Interfaces, Generative Artificial Intelligence (ChatGPT and Deep Fakes) and Criminal Procedure Law: what’s at stake?”, *Journal of Research in E. and Computer Science*, Edinburgh, United Kingdom, June 2024, Volume 2, 2024, pp. 39–78, which I will follow closely in this regard.

[40] As we throw ourselves in the immense arena of automated processes powered by Artificial Intelligence, the difficulties to grasp its delicate intricacies mount exponentially. See: Cohen, Julien E., *Between Truth and Power: The Legal Constructions of Informational Capitalism.* Oxford: Oxford University Press, 2019, pp. 1–376 (p. 192) (asserts adamantly that “*automated processes* have obvious efficiency advantages, *but such processes may not align well (or well at all) with applicable legal requirements that are couched in shades of gray*”). Italics added.

[41] Digital future which will ineluctably give rise to a “Artificial Intelligent Justice”. See: Re, Richard M./Solow-Niederman, Alicia, “Developing Artificially Intelligent”, *Stanford Technology Law Review*, Volume 22, 2019, pp. 242 ff and passim. But see: Part V, Chap. 5, Sect. 5.8.5 of this book (on law number five to interpret algorithmic decision-making, which mandates that robot-judges, robot-prosecutors and robot-lawyers must not enter the courtroom for they are utterly incapable of making sound and interpretable value judgements).

[42] Tegmark, Max, *Life 3.0: Being Human in the Age of Artificial Intelligence.* New York: Knopf, 2018, pp. 1–384 (pp. 24 and ff) (charts the path ahead for a wide range of intelligences, including artificial intelligence in the digital age). There is a handful of authors that wonder if artificial intelligence can mimic not only human intelligence but, and foremost, human behaviour. Amongst whom stands: Russel, Stuart, Norvig, Peter, *Artificial Intelligence: A Modern Approach.* London: United Kingdom, Pearson, 2018, passim.

[43] Candent challenges that come under the yoke of intelligent automation, which is shaping up to morph the legal arena in an overarching sense. See: Bornet, Pascal/Barkin, Ian/Wirtz, Jochen, *Intelligent Automation: Learn how to harness Artificial Intelligence to boost business and make out world more human*, 2020, pp. 1–432.

[44] Amongst which stands arguably social cleavages spawned by a technology that fondly includes the rich and outrightly excludes the poor, thereby compounding social issues with which modern have been grappling/tussling/scuffling/floundering since immemorial times. Social cleavages—a cloak under which mounting social outcry is often wrapped—that threaten to crumble the foundations upon which stands the linchpin of western societies. See in general: Abramsky, Sasha, *Jumping at Shadows: The Triumph of Fear and the End of the American Dream.* New York: Bold Type Books, 2017, pp. 1–272 (passim).

[45] Sivarajah, Uthayasnkar et al., “Critical Analysis of Big Data Challenges and Analytical Methods”, *Journal of Business Research*, Volume 70, 2017, pp. 263 and ff and passim; Jetten, Lieke /Sharon, Stephen, “Selected Issues concerning the Ethical Use of Big Data Health Analytics”, *Washington & Lee Law Review Online*, Volume 72, 2016, passim.

[46] See in Italian doctrine: Quintarelli, Stefano, *Capitalismo Immateriale—Le tecnologie digitali ed il nuovo conflito sociale*, 7ª edizione. Turin: Bollati Boringhieri, 2019, pp. 1–198.

[47] Of which robot-lawyers and robot-judges are a living—yet heinous and disturbing—testament. See: Davis, Joshua P., “Of Robolawyers and robojudges”, *Hastings Law Journal*, Volume 73, Issue 5, 2022, pp. 1176–1201; Davis, Joshua P., *Unnatural Law: AI, Consciousness, Ethics, and Legal Theory*. Cambridge: Cambridge University Press, 2023. But see: Part V, Chap. 5, Sect. 5.8.5 of this book (on law number five to interpret algorithmic decision-making, which mandates that robot-judges, robot-prosecutors and robot-lawyers must not enter the courtroom for they are utterly incapable of making sound and interpretable value judgements).

[48] Ver: Scherer, Maxi, “Artificial Intelligence and Legal Decision-Making: The Wide Open?”, *Journal of International Arbitration*, Volume 36, 2019, passim.

large[49] and lurk[50] ahead.[51] Lest criminal procedure law[52] endeavours to eschew the peril of legal tokenism[53]—which would produce deleterious[54]

[49] Lauritsen, Marc, "Towards a Phenomenology of Machine-Assisted Legal Work", *Journal of Robotics, Artificial Intelligence & Law*, Volume 1, Issue 2, 2018, pp. 67–79.

[50] The liability of artificial-intelligence-based robots is a challenge that not only lurks ahead, but, and foremost, is something that future lawmakers and policymakers should never lose sight of. See: Rachum-Twaig, Omri, "Whose robot anyway?: liability for artificial-intelligence-based robots", *University of Illinois Law Review*, Volume 4, 2020, pp. 1141–1175. See: Part V, Chap. 5, Sect. 5.7.1 of this book (on law number one to control algorithmic decision-making, which mandates that whoever develops and/or deploys machines to undertake a given task must be held criminal accountable for the Hard-AI crimes the latter perpetrates).

[51] The worrisome challenges posed by the up-and-coming and rough around the edges self-driving cars. See: Teoh, Eric/Kidd, David G., "Rage Against the Machine? Google's Self-Driving Versus Human Drivers", *Journal of Safety Research*, Volume 63, 2019, pp. 57–59 and passim (on the legal quandaries laid bare by the self-driving cars). See: Part III, Chap. 3, Sects. 3.5.9 to 3.5.9.3 of this book (devoted to Critical Artificial Intelligence Studies, with a sharper focus on the pressing challenges facing self-driving vehicles).

[52] Pagallo, Ugo/Quattrocolo, Serena, "The Impact of AI on Criminal Law and its twofold procedures", Barfield, W./Pagallo, Ugo (Editors), *Research Handbook on the Law of Artificial Intelligence,* 2018. Cheltenham: Edward Elgar, 2018, pp. 385–409.

[53] Amongst the main grievances brought forth by the movement of Critical Legal Studies stand both legal tokenism and legal indeterminacy, which, taken together, sap the overall functionality of a given legal system. See: Hutchinson, Alan C./Monahan, Patrick J., "Law, Politics and the Critical Legal Scholars: The Unfolding Drama of American Legal Thought", *Stanford Law Review*, Volume 36, 1984, 199–245 (pp. 200–202) (on law's indeterminacy, which would eventually merit vitriolic remarks from other Critical Legal Scholars). Soon enough, the grievances toward law's indeterminacy were to be levelled up. Critical legal scholars not only debunked the indeterminacy of law, but also the facts 'nagging—and, foremost, unsettling—uncertainty regarding legal decision-making. See: McLeod, Ian, *Legal Theory*, 3rd Edition. New York: Palgrave Macmillan Law Masters, 2005, pp. 140–150 (decrying law's and facts 'indeterminacy, especially in cases in which legal decision-making is to rely upon witnesses 'flawed and skewed memory, which is to cast doubts on the witnesses' ability to aid judges in attaining the arduous task to serve justice in the first place). But see: Weizenbaum, Joseph, *Computer Power and Human Reason: From Judgment to Calculation*, 1st edition, New York, W. H. Freeman & Co, 1976, pp. 1–300 (227) ("examines the sources of the computer's powers and offers evaluative explorations of what computers can do, cannot do, and should not be employed to do") (this founding father of Artificial Intelligence presciently noted that we should not entrust Artificial Intelligence-embedded technologies with "tasks that demand wisdom"). Italics added. The approval of rental applications is arguably one of those tasks that should never be entrusted to machines). More on this on Part IV, Chap. 4, Sects. 4.4 to 4.4.2.1 of this book. See also: Part V, Chap. 5, Sect. 5.7.2 of this book (on law number two to control algorithmic decision-making, which mandates that black box models must not be entrusted with the task of making high stake decisions—v.g. health and freedom).

[54] Deleterious effects that can take the shape of a predictive criminal justice run by machines accountable to no one. See in French doctrine: Brigant, Jean-Marie, "Les risques accentués d'une justice pénale prédictive», *Archives de Philosophie du Droit*, Volume 60, 2018, pp. 238 and ff and passim. See: Part V, Chap. 5, Sect. 5.7.1 of this book (on law number one to control algorithmic decision-making, which mandates that whoever develops and/or deploys machines to undertake a given task must be held criminal accountable for the Hard-AI crimes the latter perpetrates).

ripple[55] effects[56] throughout the globe[57]—, such challenges[58] must neither go unaddressed[59] nor poorly latched on.[60] For a simple reason:

[55] Ripple effects arising out challenges that are neither amenable to be shrugged off nor relinquished. Let alone unduly forsaken. The challenges catalysed by an ever-evolving and far-reaching "Blockchain digital society" should urge the legal community to rattle off a wide range of actionable solutions to tackle this issue of paramount importance. See: De Filippi/Primavera/Wright, Aaron, *Blockchain and the Law. Rule of Code.* Cambridge: Harvard University Press, 2019, pp. 196–200 (presciently addresses the hazard of the data collated by enterprises that fall prey to decontextualization). If lawmakers fail to entertain proficiently this issue, somewhere along the line the data fed into the machines will spawn algorithmic discrimination or algorithmic biases in criminal justice. Which means that algorithmic biases—caused by data decontextualization—will ripple forward to the detriment of a sought-after algorithmic fairness. See: Part IV, Chap. 4, Sects. 4.10.1 to 4.10.6 of this book (on biased algorithmic risk assessment in criminal procedure law settings, with a sharper focus on COMPAS). See: Part IV, Chap. 4, Sects. 4.1 to 4.1.1 of this book (on biased predictive policing).

[56] Such as a yawning gap between rich—that can adroitly harness artificial intelligence to advance their goals and shady agendas—and poor—that grapple to meet basic needs and are automatically excluded from the equation of digital society powered by Artificial Intelligence—which will directly impact the fabric of societies worldwide, thereby augmenting the chasm between the «digitally-chosen» and the «digitally-outcast» enabled by a algorithmic discrimination that does nothing but irreparable harm. See: Yu, Peter K., "The Algorithmic Divide and Equality in the Age of Artificial Intelligence", *Florida Law Review*, Volume 72, 2020, pp. 355–360 (addresses the issue of algorithmic discrimination).

[57] Thereby catalysing drastic changes in the cultural matrix that constitute the backbone of a given society. See: Vance, J.D., *A Memoir of a Family and Culture in Crisis.* New York: Harper, 2016, passim.

[58] Such as those arising out an unpalatable and unsavoury *cyborg justice* in which both *robots-lawyers* and *robots-judges* play a pivotal—yet somewhat unsettling—role. See: Crootof, Rebecca, "Cyborg Justice" and the Risk of Technological-Legal Lock-In", *Columbia Law Review*, Volume 119, 2019, pp. 233 and ff. See also: Markovic, Milan, "Rise of the Robot Lawyers?", *Arizona Law Review*, Volume 61, 2019, pp. 325 and ff and passim. See: Part V, Chap. 5, Sect. 5.8.5 of this book (on law number five to interpret algorithmic decision-making, which mandates that robot-judges, robot-prosecutors and robot-lawyers must not enter the courtroom for they are utterly incapable of making sound and interpretable value judgements).

[59] See: Lee, Kai-Fu, *AI Superpowers: China, Silicon Valley, and the New World.* New York: Harper Business, 2018, pp. 3 (talks about the *Google Deepmind*, which has catalyzed the tagged «Sputnik moment» across Asia).

[60] See: Cataleta, Maria Stefania/Cataleta, Anna, "Artificial Intelligence and Human Rights: An Unequal Struggle", *CIFILE Journal of International Law*, Volume 1, N. ° 2, 2020 ("*Artificial Intelligence (AI) is a kind of intelligence that was born in the 1950s and is an integral part of the digital revolution. Progress made by AI has permitted the birth of systems capable of rivalling human capacities or, in some cases, surpassing them.* The progress of the intellectual capacities of AI will change the way of life for human beings and will revolutionise the world of employment. *Intelligent systems present problems regarding individual rights and responsibilities, because as technology replaces more and more of what humans have typically done, our individual roles will become more blurred.*"). Italics added. Converging: Cataleta, Maria Stefania, "Artificial Intelligence vs Human Intelligence", in: Martin, L. Miraut/Zalucki, M. (editors), *Artificial intelligence and Human Rights, Dickinson eBook.* Krakow: AFM Krakow University, 2021, pp. 117–127 (on the slew of both moral,

normative underpinnings abhor the shifting sands of legal insecurity,[61] which runs afoul of a sought-after legal certainty[62]

ethical, and legal issues with which jurists will grapple in the forthcoming future due to the rise of artificial intelligence in legal arena).

[61] Take the example of Rule of Law. This concept is of overriding importance in modern democracies. Regrettably, the Rule of Law is backsliding worldwide. Especially in Central and Eastern Europe. See: Avbelj, Matej, "The Rule of Law, Comprehensive Doctrines, Overlapping Consensus, and the Future of Europe", *Ratio Juris*, Volume 36, Issue 3, September, 2023, pp. 242–258. The Rule of Law is not a «one size fits all» format nonetheless. But see: Chesterman, Simon, "An International Rule of Law", *The American Journal of Comparative Law*, Volume 56, 2008, pp. 331–362 (on the thrust to grasp (?) a catch-all International Rule of Law). See: Peari, Sagi, "Better Law as a Better Outcome", *The American Journal of Comparative Law*, Volume 63, Issue 1, 2015, pp. 155–195 (156) (on Leflar's stance on «better rule of law»). For the purposes of this piece, Rule of Law amounts to a lighthouse of procedural fairness to which citizens, regardless of where they are, resort to upon gaining access to a given system of administration of criminal justice. Whilst further utterances on the fabric of Rule of Law fall well outside the scope and breadth of this book, one must not be oblivious of the fact that the thrust to Deglobalizing Rule of Law is underway. See: Bussani, Mauro, "Deglobalizing Rule of Law and Democracy: Hunting Down Rhetoric Through Comparative Law", *The American Journal of Comparative Law*, Volume 67, 2019, pp. 701–744 (701) (contending that the thrust to Deglobalizing Rule of Law is interwoven with thrust to take heed of «well-known differences that run through cultures and traditions». In spite of which, «the West has never stopped trying to export its own law into the rest of the world»). Unsurprisingly, there have been educated calls to take heed of the pinpointed cultural and legal differences by, in the case of China, allow for a «Socialist Rule of Law». See: Chinese Common Law Guiding Cases, *Harvard Law Review*, Volume 129, 2016, p. 2213. We will come back to this issue further down is this paper. More on this later. See: Part V, Chap. 5, Sect. 5.1.1 of this book (on the central tenets of Rule of Law that lends itself to a beacon of justice amidst the sepulchral darkness that is about to take hold). See: Part V, Chap. 5, Sect. 5.1.2 of this book (on the central tenets of Procedural Rule of Law that lends itself to a lighthouse of justice that allows citizens to challenge the pearls of algorithmic wisdom in a court of law).

[62] Ironically, the quest for legal certainty is shaping up to have a detrimental effect on criminal procedure law in the forthcoming future. The rise of digital justice—or algorithmic justice—is set to beget the absolute power of algorithms, which will make judges 'life considerably easier. Soon enough, judges will blindly follow the pearls of wisdom breed by inscrutable algorithms which will—keenly and promptly—point out to them the best course of action to be taken in a given procedure. See: Millar, Jason/Kerr, Ian, "Delegation, Relinquishment and Responsibility: The Prospect of Expert Robots", *Robot Law*, Ryan Calo/Froomkin, A. Michael/Kerr, Ian. Cheltenham: Edward Elgar Publishing, 2016, pp. 102, 106–107 (as these authors aptly put it "*We will rely on robots without really knowing why—simply because their algorithms provide the greatest number of successful outcomes.* We have already seen this in Google's search approach. Neither Larry (Page) nor Sergey (Brin) (nor any other Google employee) knowns exactly why one particular web page is a better result than another. *When the click patterns say it is, that's good enough.* No semantic or causal analysis is required...*Like the ancients, we will, quite rationally, come to rely upon them, knowing full well that we cannot necessarily explain the reasons for their decisions*"). Italics added. Converging: Casey, Anthony J./Niblett, Anthony, "Self-driving Laws", *University of Toronto Law Journal*, Volume 66, 2016, pp. 429–435 (contend that "as more information is generated, and the evolutionary algorithm updates and become a better forecaster, *we imagine that judges will increasingly rely on the advice of the algorithm*"). Italics added. The danger of *automation bias* looms nonetheless large. Which is already happening in the realm of rental housing, thereby exacting a toll on members of communities of colour (Blacks and Latinos). See: Wonyoung, So, "Which

that forms part of a broader legal apparatus[63] within which criminal procedure law operates.

§§ There is a plethora of bigoted,[64] flawed,[65] and biased[66] algorithms[67] that fall readily under the catch-all umbrella encompassing a myriad of sweltering challenges[68] brought to bear by Artificial Intelligence,[69] which has arguably

---

Information Matters? Measuring Landlord Assessment of Tenant Screening Reports", *Housing Policy Debate*, Volume 33, n. ° 6, 2023, pp. 1484–1510 (1484) ("*Through a behavioral experiment with landlords using simulated tenant screening reports, this study shows that landlords use blanket screening policies, that they conflate the existence of tenant records with outcomes (e.g., eviction filings with executed evictions), and that they display, on average, tendencies toward automation bias that are influenced by the risk assessments and scores presented by tenant screening reports.* I argue that maintaining blanket screening policies and automation bias, combined with the downstream effects of creating and *using racially biased eviction and criminal records, means that people of color will inevitably experience disproportionate exclusion from rental housing due to perceived "risk" on the part of landlords*"). Italics added. Bu see: Part V, Chap. 5, Sect. 5.8.5 of this book (on law number five to interpret algorithmic decision-making, which mandates that robot-judges, robot-prosecutors and robot-lawyers must not enter the courtroom for they are utterly incapable of making sound and interpretable value judgements).

[63] That is why the German doctrine of *Wesensgehaltsgarantie* is so cherished in the ambit of both constitutional law and criminal procedure law: Mayer, Mathias, *Untermaß, Übermaß und Wesensgehaltsgarantie. Die Bedeutung staatlicher Schutzpflichten für den Gesetzgebers im Grundrechtsbereich.* Baden-Baden: Nomos, 2005, passim.

[64] See: Nutter, Patrick W., "Machine Learning Evidence: Admissibility and Weight", *Penn Law Journal, Constitutional Law*, Volume 21, 2019, pp. 919 and ff and passim.

[65] See: Osaba, Osonde/Welser, William IV, *An Intelligence in Our Image—The Risk of Bias and Errors in Artificial Intelligence*, Santa Monica, California, Rand, 2018, passim.

[66] See: Chandler, Anupam, "The Racist Algorithm", *Michigan Law Review*, Volume 115, n. ° 6, 2018, p. 1026 (on racist algorithms, noting that "the possibilities for discriminatory manipulation are legion"). But see: Altenburger, Kristen M./Ho, Daniel E., "When Algorithms Import Private Bias into Public Enforcement: The Promise and Limitations of Statistical Debiasing Solutions", *Journal of Institutional & Theoretical Economics*, Volume 175, 2019, pp. 97–98 (calls for a "debias predictive algorithms" to assuage racist and/or biased, doctored and bigoted algorithms nevertheless). See: Part IV, Chap. 4, Sects. 4.10.1 to 4.10.6 of this book (on biased algorithmic risk assessment in criminal procedure law settings, with a sharper focus on COMPAS). See: Part IV, Chap. 4, Sects. 4.1 to 4.1.1 of this book (on biased predictive policing).

[67] See: Hamilton, Melissa, "The Biased Algorithm: Evidence of Disparate Impact on Hispanics", *American Criminal Law Review*, Volume 56, 2019, pp. 1553 and ff and passim. See: Part IV, Chap. 4, Sects. 4.10.1 to 4.10.6 of this book (on biased algorithmic risk assessment in criminal procedure law settings, with a sharper focus on COMPAS). See: Part IV, Chap. 4, Sects. 4.1 to 4.1.1 of this book (on biased predictive policing).

[68] Wachter, S/Mittelstadt. B., "A right to Reasonable Inferences: Re-thinking Data Protection Law in the Age of Big Data and AI", *Columbia Business Law Review*, 2019, pp. 1 and ff and passim.

[69] Artificial intelligence, like everything else, is not without sizable drawbacks and shortcomings though. The most menacing of which happens to be flawed or biased algorithms, which are bound to mar a sought-after bias-free decision making in dispute resolution. See: Sternlight, Jean, "Pouring a Little Psychological Cold Water on Online Dispute Resolution", *Journal of Dispute Resolution*, 1, 2020, pp. 23 ff (raises awareness to the perils of biased algorithms on online dispute resolution). Converging: Schmitz, Amy, "Expanding Access to Remedies Through E-Court Initiatives", *Buffalo Law Review*, Volume 67, 2019, pp. 90–100 (showing concerns that e-courts might

turbocharged[70] the concerns around the skewed data[71] that algorithms operate upon.[72] Such concerns are not to be swept aside: the warped data[73] that feeds into the algorithms are often suffused with invidious discrimination that further entrenches and compounds a jarring racial bias with which minorities[74] have been tussling for a long-winded span of time.[75] The hazard of «automation bias»[76] therefore lurks ahead.

---

be premising their decisions on flawed and bigoted algorithms). Which is something to be frowned upon. Why? Most likely, flawed or biased algorithms will deepen the chasm between rich and poor. See: Eubanks, Virginia, *Automating Inequality: How High-Tech Tools Profile, Police and Punish the Poor*. New York: St. Martin's Press, 2018, 1–272 (1 ff and passim) (coining the expression «automating inequality» to vividly portray the downsides of using high-technology to compound the yawning gap between rich and poor against the backdrop of biased algorithms). See also: Soss, Joe, Richard C. Fording, and Sanford F. Schram, *Disciplining the Poor: Neoliberal Paternalism and the Persistent Power of Race*. Chicago: University of Chicago Press, 2011. See: Part IV, Chap. 4, Sects. 4 to 4.10.6 of this book (on Algorithmic Dictatorship and its chilling effect on democracy).

[70] See: Roth, Andrea, "Machine Testimony", *Yale Law Journal*, Volume 126, 2017, pp. 1972 and ff and passim.

[71] *Tech, Bias and Housing Initiative, the Promise and Perils of Residential Proptech, Year 1, Research Summary Report, April 2023, TechEquity Collaborative*, p. 11, available at: https://techequity.us/wp-content/uploads/2023/04/TBHI-Y1-Research-Summary-Report.pdf (28.11.2024). ("*Once bad data enters the analysis of one factor, it gets baked into the subsequent process, multiplying the effect that one disadvantageous data point can have on someone's overall housing determination*"). Italics added.

[72] See: Grimm, Paul W., "Practical Considerations for the Admissibility of Artificial Intelligence Evidence", *Maryland Bar Journal*, Volume 2, Issue 3, 2021, pp. 39 and ff and passim (pinpoints that challenges posed by Artificial Intelligence in the camp of law for years to come). See: Part V, Chap. 5, Sect. 5.8.5 of this book (on law number five to interpret algorithmic decision-making, which mandates that robot-judges, robot-prosecutors and robot-lawyers must not enter the courtroom for they are utterly incapable of making sound and interpretable value judgements).

[73] Sivarajah, Uthayasnkar et al., "Critical Analysis of Big Data Challenges and Analytical Methods", *Journal of Business Research*, Volume 70, 2017; Jetten, Lieke /Sharon, Stephen, "Selected Issues concerning the Ethical Use of Big Data Health Analytics", *Washington & Lee Law Review Online*, Volume 72, 2016, passim.

[74] *Tech, Bias and Housing Initiative, the Promise and Perils of Residential Proptech, Year 1, Research Summary Report, April 2023, TechEquity Collaborative*, p. 5 available at: https://techequity.us/wp-content/uploads/2023/04/TBHI-Y1-Research-Summary-Report.pdf (28.11.2024). ("*Residential Proptech also has the potential to exacerbate the bias inherent in our housing system. Its rise is due, in part, to the desperation felt by average home seekers. With a severely constrained housing supply, companies offering an easier pathway to homeownership may exploit communities that have been harmed by housing discrimination in the past. Opaque algorithms incorporate biased data into their decision-making processes, making it harder to enforce fair housing laws.* Residential Proptech companies often operate in a regulatory gray area, leaving consumers without the protections they would have from traditional housing regulatory systems. *As unprecedented capital investment flows into this space, venture-backed companies' winner-take-all approach to growth has the potential to exacerbate inequality rather than combat it*"). Italics added.

[75] See: Dong et al., Qi,, "Imbalanced deep learning by minority class incremental rectification, *IEEE Transactions on Pattern Analysis & Machine Intelligence*, Volume 41, 2019, p. 1367 (posit that "*most existing learning algorithms produce inductive bias (learning bias)* towards the frequent (majority) classes if training data are not balanced, *resulting in poor minority class recognition performance*"). Italics added.

[76] See: Wonyoung, So, "Which Information Matters? Measuring Landlord Assessment of Tenant Screening Reports", *Housing Policy Debate*, Volume 33, n. ° 6, 2023, pp. 1484–1510 (1484)

§§ No surprise stems from the fact that such challenges[77] are in dire need of being adroitly[78] addressed[79] sooner rather than later. A staggering amount of effort[80] must therefore be poured in to shrewdly solve the great bulk of issues[81] arisen from the

(*"Through a behavioral experiment with landlords using simulated tenant screening reports, this study shows that landlords use blanket screening policies, that they conflate the existence of tenant records with outcomes (e.g., eviction filings with executed evictions), and that they display, on average, tendencies toward automation bias that are influenced by the risk assessments and scores presented by tenant screening reports.* I argue that maintaining blanket screening policies and automation bias, combined with the downstream effects of creating and *using racially biased eviction and criminal records, means that people of color will inevitably experience disproportionate exclusion from rental housing due to perceived "risk" on the part of landlords*"). Italics added. See: Part IV, Chap. 4, Sects. 4.4 to 4.4.2.3 of this book. But see: Weizenbaum, Joseph, *Computer Power and Human Reason: From Judgment to Calculation*, 1st edition, New York, W. H. Freeman & Co, 1976, pp. 1–300 (227) ("examines the sources of the computer's powers and offers evaluative explorations of what computers can do, cannot do, and should not be employed to do") (this founding father of Artificial Intelligence presciently noted that we should not entrust Artificial Intelligence-embedded technologies with "tasks that demand wisdom"). Italics added. The approval of rental applications is arguably one of those tasks that should never be entrusted to machines). More on this on Part IV, Chap. 4, Sects. 4.4 to 4.4.2.1 of this book. Kleinberg, Jon/Lakkaraju, Himabindu/Leskovec, Jure/Ludwig, Jens/Mullainathan, Sendhil, "Human Decisions and Machine Predictions", *Quarterly Journal of Economics*, Volume 133, 2018, passim.

[77] A challenge amenable to be fetched out from the bucket of concerns to be keenly addressed is the role that technology plays in predicting recidivism. See: Zhu, Mirilla, "Jury, Using Artificial Intelligence to Predict Recidivism Rates", *Yale Scientific*, 2020, passim. See also: Chasemi et al., Medhi, "The application of Machine Learning to a General Risk-Need Assessment Instrument in the Prediction of Criminal Recidivism", *Criminal Justice and Behavior*, Volume 48, 2020, pp. 518–538. See: Part IV, Chap. 4, Sects. 4.10.1 to 4.10.6 of this book (on biased algorithmic risk assessment in criminal procedure law settings, with a sharper focus on COMPAS). See: Part IV, Chap. 4, Sect. 4.1 to 4.1.1 of this book (on biased predictive policing).

[78] See: Pasquale, Frank, "A Rule of Persons, Not Machines: The Limits of Legal Automation", *George Washington Law Review*, Volume 87, 2019, pp. 1 and ff and passim. See: Part V, Chap. 5, Sect. 5.8.5 of this book (on law number five to interpret algorithmic decision-making, which mandates that robot-judges, robot-prosecutors and robot-lawyers must not enter the courtroom for they are utterly incapable of making sound and interpretable value judgements).

[79] Yet these challenges are not amenable to be addressed within the purview of law and economics. But see in French doctrine: Ferey, Samuel, « Analyse économique du droit, big data et justice prédictive», *Archives de Philosophie du Droit*, Volume 60, 2018, pp. 68–81.

[80] Whooping efforts that should also be poured in as to ascertain the extent to which algorithms can usher in an era of fair use in the realm of law. See: Yu, Peter K, "Can Algorithms Promote Fair Use?", *Fiu Law Review*, Volume 14, 2020, pp. 328 and ff and passim.

[81] One can single out the worrisome issue of "predictive machines" in this regard. See: Agrawal, Ajay/Gans, Joshua/Goldfarb, Avi, *Prediction Machines: The Simple Economics of Artificial Intelligence*, 2nd Edition. Massachusetts: Harvard Business Review Press, 2022, pp. 1–304.

harmful[82] effects[83] of technology[84] or avoidable mishaps will otherwise occur.[85] Amongst which stands arguably a bevy of algorithmic biases[86] within the remit of criminal justice,[87] which boasts a heightened likelihood to emit ripples across jurisdictions.[88]

---

[82] Amongst which stands the insurmountable barriers disadvantaged parties—*pro se* disputants that cannot afford to pay a well-adjusted and seasoned lawyer—face when they access judicial courts. This problem will only get worse as technology gains traction in criminal procedure law settings. An empirical research premises such an assertion. See: Kroeper, Kathryn/Quintanilla, Victor D./Frisby, Michael/Yel, Nedim/Applegate, Amy G./Sherman, Steven J./Murphy, Mary C., "Underestimating the Unrepresented: Cognitive Biases Disadvantage Pro Se Litigants in Family Law Cases", *Psychology, Public Policy, and Law*, Volume 26, n.º 2, 2020, pp. 198–212 (211) (emphazise "*the present research suggests that the mere presence or absence of pro se status affects the inferences that legal officials make about parties in the civil justice system.* Legal officials appraised the cases of counselled parties as less meritorious the cases of counselled parties and predicted the *unrepresented persons would experience the civil justice system as less fair and satisfying the counselled litigants, even when all case facts were held constant, and especially when trial (vs. mediation) was considered to be the dispute resolution mechanism*"). Italics added. See also: Quintanilla, Victor/ Allen, R. A./Hirt, E. R., "The signalling effect of pro se status", *Law & Social Inquiry*, Volume 42, 2018, pp. 1092–1120.

[83] Michaels, Andrew C., "Artificial Intelligence, Legal Change, and Separation of Powers, *University of Cincinnati Law Review*, 2020, pp. 1083 and ff and passim.

[84] Davis, Joshua P. "Law Without Mind: AI, Ethics, and Jurisprudence", *California Western Law Review*, Volume 55, 2018, pp. 181 e ss and passim (deals with an agreed-upon Artificial opacity while emphasizing a sought-after transparency to trounce it).

[85] Mishaps that may give to punitive damages that give rise to exemplary punishments. In French doctrine, Juen, Emmanuelle, "Vers la consecrâtion des dommages-intérêts punitifs en droit français. Présentation d'un regime", *Revue trimestrielle de droit civil*, juillet-septembre de 2017, 2017, pp. 565–585 (defending the consecration of punitive damages in France amidst a hotly debated tort law reform). But see Italian doctrine: Rodotá, Stefano, "Technische Rissarcitorie e nuovi interessi", *Tutela dell'onore e mezzi di communicazione di massa*, Milano, Giufrè, 1979, 52 ff (harshly criticizes *punitive damages* for symbolizing a capitalist logic in tort law—especially in litigation related with personality rights within the realm of social mass media and the tutelage of honour).

[86] Baeza-Yates, R., "Bias on the web", *Communications of the ACM*, 61 (6), June 2018, 2018, pp. 54–61 (argues that "*algorithmic bias is when the bias is not present in the input data* and is added *purely by the algorithm*"). Italics added.

[87] See: Osaba, Osonde/Welser, William IV, *An Intelligence in Our Image—The Risk of Bias and Errors in Artificial Intelligence*, Santa Monica, California, Rand, 2018, passim.

[88] Ripple effects arising out challenges that are neither amenable to be shrugged off nor relinquished. Let alone unduly forsaken. The challenges brought forth by an ever-evolving and far-reaching "Blockchain digital society" should urge the legal community to rattle off a wide range of actionable solutions to tackle this issue of paramount importance. See: De Filippi/Primavera/ Wright, Aaron, *Blockchain and the Law. Rule of Code*. Cambridge: Harvard University Press, 2019, pp. 196–200 (presciently addresses the hazard of the data collated by enterprises that falls prey to decontextualization). If lawmakers fail to entertain proficiently this issue, somewhere along the line the data fed into the machines will spawn algorithmic discrimination or algorithmic biases in criminal justice. Which means that *algorithmic biases*—caused by data decontextualization—will ripple forward to the detriment of a sought-after algorithmic fairness. See: Baeza-Yates, R., "Bias on the web", *Communications of the ACM*, 61 (6), June 2018, 2018, pp. 54–61 (argues that "*algorithmic bias is when the bias is not present in the input data* and is added *purely by the algorithm*"). Italics added.

§§ To the extent criminal procedure law should strive[89] to keep its core[90] unscathed[91] while avoiding to careening into the chaos of irrelevance,[92] the scourge of legal insecurity[93] must be disfranchised[94] with no qualms whatsoever.[95] Truth be

[89] Strive to uphold a flawless reputation amidst the arrival of artificial intelligence in the realm of criminal procedure law in the first place. This an endeavour that criminal justice should take very seriously indeed. See: Edmond, Gary/Martire, Kristy A., "Just Cognition: Scientific Research on Bias and Some Implications for Legal Procedure and Decision-Making", *The Modern Law Review*, Volume 82, n. ° 4, 2019, p. 664 (on the dire need of keeping "good reputation (…) "and the appearance of justice").

[90] Few to none can bode—let alone portend or forecast—the future accurately. But make no mistake: the future of courts rests upon its ability—or lack thereof—to adapt to the ceaseless stream of changes that will keep coming its way. Or else. By else I mean its core will change beyond recognition. See: Susskind, Richard, "The Future of Courts", *Remote Courts*, Volume 6, n.º 5, July/August 2020, 2020, pp. 1 and ff and passim (contending that "in the middle of March 2020, court buildings around the world began to close in response to the rapid spread of a newly identified coronavirus, SARS-CoV-2 (the "virus"). Within days, alternative ways of delivering court service were put in place in many jurisdictions. The uptake of various technologies, especially video, was accelerated in the justice systems of numerous countries. There remain some skeptics and critics, but in light of the experience during the crisis, there is certainly greater acceptance now than in February 2020—amongst lawyers, judges, officials, and court users—that judicial and court work might be undertaken very differently in years to come. Minds have been opened and changed over the past few months. Many assumptions have been swept aside. We remain in an era of threat, with risks of barely functioning court systems, greatly reduced access to justice, and, in turn, a potential weakening of the rule of law. We are also in an era of opportunity—the chance to build boldly on the shift of attitude and on demonstrable recent successes with technology, and to put in place improved, sustainable court services that are much more accessible than today's"). Future—as may know—is not up for grabs. See in Italian doctrine: Irti, Natalino, *Un Diritto Incalcolabile*. Torino: G. Giappichelli Editore, 2016, pp. 20 and ff and passim.

[91] Recall, criminal procedure law's foundations—and fundamental tenets—are set to wobble if a keen attention is not paid to the underlying human dignity from which the former derives. See Spanish doctrine: Laukyte, Migle, "Dignidad humana y nuevos derechos: el derecho a la inteligencia artificial", *Inteligencia Artificial y Derecho. El jurista ante los retos de la era digital*, AAVV. Navarra: Aranzadi, 2021, passim.

[92] Laudably and timely enough, a branch of Spanish doctrine is making rapid strides in unveiling/unravelling/unlocking the dire need to award/afford/grant protection to the circle of fundamental rights affected by artificial intelligence within the purview of criminal procedure law. See: Beriain, Iñigo de/Estrada/ Pérez, M. Josune, "La inteligencia artificial en el proceso penal español: un análisis de su admisibilidad sobre la base de los derechos fundamentales implicados", *Revista de derecho UNED (RDUNED),* Volume 25, 2019, pp. 531–561.

[93] See: Volokh, Eugene, "Chief Justice Robots", *Duke Law Journal*, Volume 68, 2019, pp. 1135 and ff and passim (on the sizzling hot challenges that the legal community is shaping up to face further the rise of Chief Justice Robots). See: Part V, Chap. 5, Sect. 5.8.5 of this book (on law number five to interpret algorithmic decision-making, which mandates that robot-judges, robot-prosecutors and robot-lawyers must not enter the courtroom for they are utterly incapable of making sound and interpretable value judgements).

[94] Or the mayhem of math destruction—powered by a far-reaching Artificial Intelligence—may just otherwise ensue: O'Neill, C., *Weapons of Math Destruction*. London: Penguin Random House, 2016, passim.

[95] See: Ward, Jeff, "10 Things Judges Should Know About AI", *Judicature*, Volume 12, 2019, passim.

told, public law[96] is already lagging far behind[97] the ever-evolving[98]

[96] See: Williams, Rebecca, "Accountable Algorithms: Adopting the Public Law Toolbox Outside the Realm of Public Law", *Current Legal Problems,* Vol. 75, 2022, pp. 237–263.

[97] See in the purview of Administrative Law: Williams, Rebecca, "Rethinking Administrative Law for Algorithmic Decision-Making", *Oxford Journal of Legal Studies,* Volume 42, 2021, pp. 468 e ff and passim.

[98] Unbeknownst to the cohort of insouciant and nonchalant, a full-blown criminal-digital justice—powered by an omnipotent artificial intelligence prosecutor—is currently being served/deployed in China. Which means that China is spearheading a digital transformation which will catalyse a paradigm shift in the remit of criminal procedure law. See: "The Chinese government has developed the AI system 206, an *artificial intelligence prosecutor designed to alleviate the workload of prosecutors in China.* The system is allegedly capable of prosecuting "Shanghai's eight most common crimes." The AI was 'trained' using *"17,000 real-life cases from 2015 to 2020."* Fears abound that the technology could be weaponized by the state, potentially charging citizens for political dissent. According to a Dailyalts.com story in 2019, the AI was first officially tested in a Shanghai court in early 2019. It was also trialed in several provinces in 2018. The system can perform the following tasks with an alleged 97% accuracy: *Transcribe testimony*; *Transfer physical data and documents to electronic databases*; *Display relevant parameters immediately, such as time, place, people, behavior, and consequences*; *Identify defective or contradicting evidence*; *Respond to oral commands to display evidence and information on screens around the courtroom*; *Inter-connect with judicial, procuratorial, public security authorities and courts.* The crimes that the AI can prosecute *"include 'provoking trouble' —a term used to stifle dissent in China, credit card fraud, gambling crimes, dangerous driving, theft, fraud, intentional injury, and obstructing official duties."* In February of 2017, the Political and Judiciary Commission under the Central Committee of the Communist Party of China tasked courts in Shanghai to develop and test an AI system to assist with prosecutions. Between 2017 and 2019, Shanghai allocated more than *"400 people from courts, procuratorates, and public security bureaus, working with more than 300 IT staff from tech giant iFLYTEK"* to develop the technology. The company was established in 1999 and is a well-known speech recognition and artificial intelligence developer. From the iFLYTEK website: *"Since its establishment, the company is devoted to cornerstone technological research in speech and languages, natural language understanding, machine learning, machine reasoning, adaptive learning, and has maintained the world-leading position in those domains. The company actively promotes the development of AI products and their sector-based applications, with visions of enabling machines to listen and speak, understand and think, creating a better world with artificial intelligence."* The system runs on a standard computer that employs algorithms based on evidence collection from "102 common cases" programmed into the system. The AI can pull up questioning models for law enforcement and *"can help the judge find fact, authenticate evidence[s], protect the right to appeal and judge impartially on the trial, so as to prevent wrongfully convicted cases,"* according to Guo Weiqing, president of Shanghai No 2 Intermediate People's Court. It translates voice into characters and *"can distinguish between questioner and responder."* The software captures salient elements of cases from electronic files. According to NotTheBee, some cities in China have used AI *"to monitor government employees' social circles and activities to detect corruption."* Italics added. Ver: https://uncoverdc.com/2022/01/10/ai-system-206-replacing-human-prosecutors-in-china (acesso: 23.09.2023). United States of America—while trying to keep pace with China—is not lagging far behind in this regard. Leveraging on the advantageous conditions brought about by Covid-19, United States of America is currently relying upon *forensic algorithms* to curb/ebb/assuage overburdened dockets, soothe out overcrowded criminal courts, and, foremost, allay courts 'backlogs of cases. See: "*The technology is also being used in the U.S., according to InterestingEngineering.com. With the backlog of cases piling up due to COVID*, the

challenges[99] posed by an omnipotent[100] Artificial[101] Intelligence[102] that never[103] ceases[104] to amaze.[105,106]

use of AI has picked up to "streamline" judicial processes. The use of *forensic algorithms* is particularly popular in the collection of evidence: *"U.S. Fingerprint matching software aims to correctly identify suspects with staggering speed and precision, facial recognition helps law enforcement agencies track people down, and probabilistic genotyping can work wonders to assist investigators in determining if a genetic sample from a crime scene is linked to a person of interest or not."*. Italics added and italics on the original. See: https://uncoverdc.com/2022/01/10/ai-system-206-replacing-human-prosecutors-in-china (access: 23.09.2023). Bu see: Part V, Chap. 5, Sect. 5.8.5 of this book (on law number five to interpret algorithmic decision-making, which mandates that robot-judges, robot-prosecutors and robot-lawyers must not enter the courtroom for they are utterly incapable of making sound and interpretable value judgements).

99 Callaway, E, "'It will change everything": DeepMind's AI makes gigantic leap in solving protein structures", *Nature*, 2020, passim.

100 Lauritsen, Marc, "Towards a Phenomenology of Machine-Assisted Legal Work", in: *Journal of Robotics, Artificial Intelligence & Law*, Volume 1, Issue 2, 2018, pp. 67–79.

101 See: Ashley, Kevin D., *Artificial Intelligence and Legal Analytics. New Tools for Law Practice in the Digital Age*. Cambridge: Cambridge University Press, 2018, pp. 108 and ff and passim.

102 Against the background of which an eerily predictive criminal law is unfolding in France. See: Brigant, Jean-Marie, "Les risques accentués d'une justice pénale predictive", *Archives de Philosophie du Droit*, Volume 60, 2018, p. 239 (on the so-called predictable criminal justice). See: Part IV, Chap. 4, Sects. 4.10.1 to 4.10.6 of this book (on biased algorithmic risk assessment in criminal procedure law settings, with a sharper focus on COMPAS). See: Part IV, Chap. 4, Sects. 4.1 to 4.1.1 of this book (on biased predictive policing).

103 Susskind, Richard, *Tomorrow's Lawyers: An Introduction to your Future*, 2d edition, Oxford, Oxford University Press, 2018, passim; Hanke, Philip, "Computers with Law Degrees? The Role of Artificial Intelligence in Transnational Dispute Resolution, and Its Implications of the Legal Profession", *Transnational Dispute Management*, Volume 14, Issue 2, 2018, passim.

104 One of the developments that must not go unchecked are the ones related with transhumanism; epiphenomenon that is keeping the French doctrine quite occupied indeed. See: Lassere, Valérie, "Justice prédictive et transhumanisme", *Archives de Philosophie du Droit*, Volume 60, 2018, pp. 311 and ff and passim. See: Part III, Chap. 3, Sect. 3.5.11 of this book (on the functional aspects of Critical Artificial Intelligence Studies, with a sharper focus on the harmful effects of Artificial Intelligence-embedded technologies, namely, Genetic Algorithms that can write DNA on demand, thereby ushering the age of Transhumanism, Genetic Darwinism and Genetic Plutocracy, which, taken together, are poised to create layers of distinction between citizens).

105 Pham, TV/Luong, CM/Hoang, VD and al., "AI outperformed every dermatologist in dermoscopic melanoma diagnosis, using an optimized deep-CNN architecture with custom mini-batch logic and loss function", *Nature Science*, Vol 17, 2021, passim. But see: Part III, Chap. 3, Sect. 3.5.6 (on Critical Artificial Intelligence Studies, with a sharper focus on the harmful effects of Large Language Models 'medical hallucinations that are poised to undermine its overall trustworthiness).

106 Killock, 'AI Outperforms radiologists in mammographic screening, *National Review of Clinical Oncology*, Volume 17, 2020, pp. 134 and ff and passim. But see: Part III, Chap. 3, Sects. 3.5.6 to 3.5.6.1 of this book (on Critical Artificial Intelligence Studies, with a sharper focus on the harmful effects of Large Language Models 'medical hallucinations that are poised to undermine its overall trustworthiness).

§§ Make no mistake: the clout that Artificial Intelligence is shaping up to have in the forthcoming years[107] must not to be narrowed down to doctored algorithms that hamper its fair use.[108] Rather, there is a batch of other pressing legal challenges that must neither be forsaken[109] nor glossed over in this regard. Let alone brushed aside

---

[107] But see: Dahl, Matthew/Magesh, Varun/Suzgun, Mirac/Ho, Daniel E., "Large Legal Fictions: Profiling Legal Hallucinations in Large Language Models", *Journal of Legal Analysis*, Volume 16, 2024, 64–93 (64) ("*Do large language models (LLMs) know the law? LLMs are increasingly being used to augment legal practice, education, and research, yet their revolutionary potential is threatened by the presence of "hallucinations"—textual output that is not consistent with legal facts.* We present the first systematic evidence of these hallucinations in public-facing LLMs, documenting trends across jurisdictions, courts, time periods, and cases. *Using OpenAI's ChatGPT 4 and other public models, we show that LLMs hallucinate at least 58% of the time, struggle to predict their own hallucinations, and often uncritically accept users' incorrect legal assumptions. We conclude by cautioning against the rapid and unsupervised integration of popular LLMs into legal tasks*"). Italics added. For further developments: See: Part III, Chap. 3, Sects. 3.5.4 to 3.5.4.1.1 of this book (on the functional aspects of Critical Artificial Intelligence Studies, with a sharper focus on the harmful effects of Artificial Intelligence-embedded technologies, namely Large Language Models and its multifarious downsides and shortcomings). See also: Part IV, Chap. 4, Sects. 4.9.1 to 4.9.2 (on ChatGPT's functional abilities). See also: Part IV, Chap. 4, Sects. 4.9 to 4.9.7 (on ChatGPT's functional drawbacks and pitfalls, including, but no limited to, "hallucinations"). See: Part IV, Chap. 4, Sects. 4.5 to 4.5.2 of this book (on "algorithmic Jim Crow", a travel ban issued during the first Trump Administration to prevent certain individuals from entering the United States of America, which, given its racial undertones, stands as an outgrowth of congeries of laws enacted during the Jim Crow epoch). See: Part III, Chap. 3, Sects. 3.5.7 to 3.5.8.1 of this book (on the functional aspects of Critical Artificial Intelligence Studies, with a sharper focus on the perils concerning the deployment of facial recognition technology). See: Part III, Chap. 3, Sects. 3.5.6 to 3.5.6.1 of this book (on Critical Artificial Intelligence Studies, with a sharper focus on the harmful effects of Large Language Models 'medical hallucinations that are poised to undermine its overall trustworthiness). See: Part III, Chap. 3, Sects. 3.5.9 to 3.5.9.3 of this book (devoted to Critical Artificial Intelligence Studies, with a sharper focus on the pressing challenges facing self-driving vehicles).

[108] See: Burk, Dan L., "Algorithmic Fair Use", *University of Chicago Law Review*, Volume 86, 2019, pp. 283–288 (asserts that "*fair use carries with it the disadvantage of ex ante uncertainty*; no one can be entirely certain in advance how a court will weigh the four factors, *and hence there is always some apprehension that a use may be found infringing rather than fair*"). Italics added.

[109] Amongst the most worrisome issues stands arguably the impervious communication codes that machines use to communicate with each other. This problem is in dire need of quashing—even quelching. See: Ver: Wilson, Mark, "AI is Inventing Languages Humans Can't Understand. Should We Stop It?", *Fast Company*, 2018, passim.

to the unheeded bucket of legal oblivion[110] that pesters society in an overarching sense.[111] Or legal havoc[112] may otherwise ensue.[113]

§§ Holistic in scope and boundless in outreach, Artificial Intelligence—which is currently divided into a subset of disciplines, like machine learning[114] and deep

---

[110] Legal oblivion that derails the collective efforts to deal with deep-seated social maladies while hindering a sought-after primacy of narrative agency in the legal arena. See: Lucas, Sarah Drew, "Re-reading Seyla Benhabib on narrativity", *Feminist Theory*, Volume 19, Issue 2, 2018, pp. 123–143 (noting that "by self I mean the unique confluence of narratives and norms that make up each individual. These norms and narratives are always changing, but the individual's uniqueness is constant").

[111] On legal oblivion in the remit of philosophy: Lucas, Sarah Drew, "Loneliness and appearance: Toward a concept of ontological agency", *European Journal of Philosophy*, 2019, pp. 1–14 (noting that "even in a world with robust public sphere, loneliness is a possible result of depression, homelessness, social marginalisation, displacement, extreme pain, illnesses, and the inability to overcome pats trauma").

[112] Legal havoc that will take the shape of bad laws that do nothing but to further compound the state of overall disbelief on the lawmakers 'ability to tackle candent issues brought to bear—and laid bare—by the pervasiveness of Artificial Intelligence. As a result, bad laws will inevitably become evil laws that must not be obeyed. In this vein, Professor H. L. Hart asserts that "*laws may be law but too evil to be obeyed*. This is a moral condemnation which everyone can understand and it makes an immediate and obvious claim to moral attention. If, on the other hand, we formulate our objection as an assertion that these evil things are not law, here is an assertion which many people do not believe, and if they are disposed to consider it at all, it would seem to raise a whole host philosophical issues before it can be solves". Italics added. See: Hart, H. L., "Positivism and the Separation of Law and Morals", *Harvard Law Review*, Volume 71, Issue 4, 1958, pp. 598 ff (this amounts to a glimpse of the incorporation of the moral concept of law in Hart's conception of law).

[113] Thus thwarting the basic tenets of society as we know, which are set to fall apart, thereby dragging the sacrosanct Rule of Law—and the law as a social fact—to the abandoned streets of recklessness. See: Tyler, Tom R., *Why People Obey the Law*. New Jersey, United States of America: Princeton University Press, 2006, pp. 1–320 (92–110) (Professor Tom R. Tyler contends that lawmakers and law enforcers should make legal systems worthy of respect instead of trying to instil fear of punishment onto citizens. He finds that laypeople obey law primarily because they believe in respecting legitimate authority when such respect is due. Which means that legal systems must be worthy of respect before demanding for respect). See: Part V, Chap. 5, Sect. 5.1.1 of this book (on the central tenets of Rule of Law that lends itself to a beacon of justice amidst the sepulchral darkness that is about to take hold). See: Part V, Chap. 5, Sect. 5.1.2 of this book (on the central tenets of Procedural Rule of Law that lends itself to a lighthouse of justice that allows citizens to challenge the pearls of algorithmic wisdom in a court of law).

[114] See: Murphy, Kevin P., *Machine Learning: A Probabilistic Perspective (Adaptive Computation and Machine Learning series)*. Massachusetts: The MIT Press, 2012, pp. 1–1104 (states avowedly that "machine Learning attempts to combine deductive, inductive, and abductive reasoning to make person-like reasoning in AI Entities possible. Machine-learning AI Entities initially learn in the same way a human child learns. First, they notice details and patterns in shapes, sounds, and behaviors; then put them together to distinguish one person from another, or a dog from a cat. Eventually, the AI can recognize and identify" common objects). See also: Hutto-Schultz, Jess, "Dicitur Ex Machina: Artificial Intelligence and the Hearsay Rule", *George Mason Law Review*, Volume 27, n.° 2, 2020, pp. 684–718 (689).

learning[115]—is not amenable to be bogged down to warped[116] or prejudiced[117] algorithms though, which are just the first-generation byproducts of Artificial Intelligence. Artificial Intelligence extends far beyond them as we are about to find out. Its effects can be pernicious if befitted legal safeguards fail to be put in place in a timely manner.[118]

115 See: Chollet, François, *Deep Learning with Python*. Shelter Island, Nova Iorque: Manning, 2018, pp. 1–384 (passim). *Deep Learning* stands as a byproduct of *Machine Learning*. *Machine Learning*, a subset of Artificial Intelligence, unfolds itself in *Deep Learning*, which "involves computer algorithms that have the ability to "learn" or improve in performance over time on some task". See: Surden, Harry, "Machine Learning and Law", *Washington Law Review*, Volume 89, 2015, pp. 87 and ff.

116 From the social psychology, warped algorithms accomplish nothing but the impairment of procedural justice. See: Thibaut, John/ Walker, Laurens, *Procedural Justice: A Psychological Analysis*. Hillsdale, N.J.: Lawrence Erlbaum Associates, 1975, pp. 1–150 (procedural justice is tightly interlocked to raising the levels of fairness in criminal procedure law settings. Absent of which procedural fairness is to mar. Criminal procedure law must not lose sight of such assertion). Converging: Lind, Edgar Allan/Tyler, Tom R., *The Social Psychology of Procedural Justice*. New York: Springer, 1988, pp. 208 ff (emphasizing that perceptions of justice being justly and correctly served enhances exponentially citizens' perception of provider legitimacy). Tyler, Tom R., "The Psychology of Procedural Justice: A Test of the Group-Value Model", *Journal of Personality and Social Psychology*, Volume 57, 1989, p. 830 (reports that in any procedure "several non-control issues—the *neutrality* of the decision-making procedure, trust in the 3rd party, and the information the experience communicates about social standing—influence both procedural preferences and judgments of procedural justice"). See also: Simmons, Ric, "Big Data and Procedural Justice: Legitimizing Algorithms in the Criminal Justice System", *Ohio State Journal of Criminal Law*, Volume 15, 2018, pp. 576 and ff and passim.

117 Note, though, that prejudiced algorithms are set to be brought to the limelight as they are one foundational basis of *justice prédictive* so voguish in France. No surprise stems from the fact that prejudiced algorithms will feed *justice prédictive*—and that is something quite unsavoury and unpalatable in criminal justice indeed. See: Garapon, Antoine, "Les enjeux de la justice predictive", *Juris-Classeur périodique*, Volume 31, 2018, passim. See also: Larret-Chahine, Louis, "Le droit isométrique: un nouveau paradigme juridique né de la justice prédictive», *Archives de Philosophie du Droit*, Volume 60, 2018, pp. 287 and ff and passim. See: Part IV, Chap. 4, Sects. 4.10.1 to 4.10.6 of this book (on biased algorithmic risk assessment in criminal procedure law settings, with a sharper focus on COMPAS). See: Part IV, Chap. 4, Sects. 4.1 to 4.1.1 of this book (on biased predictive policing).

118 See: Bar-Gill, Oren/Sunstein, Cass R./Talgam-Cohen, Inbal, "Algorithmic Harm in Consumer Markets", *Journal of Legal Analysis*, Volume 15, n. ° 1, 2023, pp. 1–47.

§§ Which is why Rule of Law[119] is so dearly needed by criminal procedure law.[120] The latter—criminal procedure law[121]—is set to be plunged into the chaos of tokenism if the former—Rule of Law[122]—fails to uphold its fundamental

---

[119] See: Raz, Joseph, "The Rule of Law and its Virtue", *The Authority of Law: Essays on Law and Morality*. Oxford: Clarendon Press, 1979, pp. 210–214 (on the quintessential value of Rule of Law).

[120] Waldron, Jeremy, "The Rule of Law and the Importance of Procedure", *New York Public Law and Legal Theory*, 2010, p. 4 (notes that "the Rule of Law is violated when due attention is not paid to these procedural matters or when the institutions that are supposed to embody this procedure are undermined or interfered with". Further down this author would admit that there are some substantive dimensions of Rule of Law, such as respect for right for property and presumption of liberty and so forth). See: Part V, Chap. 5, Sect. 5.1.1 of this book (on the central tenets of Rule of Law that lends itself to a beacon of justice amidst the sepulchral darkness that is about to take hold). See: Part V, Chap. 5, Sect. 5.1.2 of this book (on the central tenets of Procedural Rule of Law that lends itself to a lighthouse of justice that allows citizens to challenge the pearls of algorithmic wisdom in a court of law).

[121] Taekema, Sanne, "The Procedural Rule of Law: Examining Waldron's Argument on Dignity and Agency", *Jahrbuch für Recht und Ethik*, Band 21, 2013, pp. 133 ff (contends that "Waldron's understanding of the Rule of Law as procedural which demands the opportunity for individuals to contest legal decisions in the formalized processes of courts and tribunals"). See: Part V, Chap. 5, Sect. 5.1.1 of this book (on the central tenets of Rule of Law that lends itself to a beacon of justice amidst the sepulchral darkness that is about to take hold). See: Part V, Chap. 5, Sect. 5.1.2 of this book (on the central tenets of Procedural Rule of Law that lends itself to a lighthouse of justice that allows citizens to challenge the pearls of algorithmic wisdom in a court of law).

[122] Cass, Ronald A., *The Rule of Law in America*. Baltimore, Maryland: The Johns Hopkins University Press, 2001, p. 17 (noting that a "central element of the Rule of law, constraint from external authority…helps assure that the process of government, *rather than the predilections of the individual decision-maker*") Italics added. See: Part V, Chap. 5, Sect. 5.1.1 of this book (on the central tenets of Rule of Law that lends itself to a beacon of justice amidst the sepulchral darkness that is about to take hold). See: Part V, Chap. 5, Sect. 5.1.2 of this book (on the central tenets of Procedural Rule of Law that lends itself to a lighthouse of justice that allows citizens to challenge the pearls of algorithmic wisdom in a court of law).

tenets amidst the age of *weaponization of Artificial Intelligence*[123] that lurks[124] ahead.[125]

---

[123] Which is why the onset of the age of Artificial Intelligence is set to put the Rule of Law to the test like never before. Recall, the Rule of Law is a functional barrier—aimed at clamping down a host of unlawful deeds undertaken by those in power—that must not be teared apart or criminal procedure law will be otherwise despoiled from its intrinsic validity and vitality. See: Raz, Joseph, "The Rule of Law and its Virtue", *The Authority of Law: Essays on Law and Morality, cit.*, p. 224 (asserts adamantly that the Rule of Law is aimed at cushioning the hazards of abuse perpetrated by those in power. In this vein, Raz contends that "the law inevitably creates a great danger of arbitrary power—the Rule of Law is designed to minimize the danger created by the law itself...*Thus the (R)ule of (L)aw is designed to minimize the danger created by law itself...Thus the (R)ule of (L)aw is a negative virtue...the evil which is avoided is evil which could only have been caused by the law itself*"). Italics added. See: *Tech, Bias and Housing Initiative, the Promise and Perils of Residential Proptech, Year 1, Research Summary Report, April 2023, TechEquity Collaborative*, p. 11, available at: https://techequity.us/wp-content/uploads/2023/04/TBHI-Y1-Research-Summary-Report.pdf (28.11.2024). ("*From information on company websites, it is not clear what analysis or data is behind subjective determinations like "suitability" to a unit or what the nexus between an individual's characteristics and a unit's characteristics is that indicates the likelihood for property damage. Based on sample reports, even landlords are not privy to how the determinations are made. Instead, they receive a risk score out of 100 simplified into green, yellow, and red recommendations.* What companies withhold in terms of how it works, they make up for with the extent to which they tell landlords it works: Naborly claims their predictions reduce lease defaults by up to 89%. 15 *As Naborly's sample report demonstrates, its property damage assessment is then used as an input to determine its projected eviction outcomes; its early vacancy prediction, in turn, is based on "all assessment factors.*"). Italics added.

[124] McAfee, Andrew/Brynjolfsson, *Machine, Platform, Crowd: Harnessing our Digital Future*, London: Brilliance Audio; Unabridged edition, 2017 (pores over a myriad of automatic biases displayed by artificial intelligence).

[125] The inception of the era of omnipotent Artificial Intelligence is about to revive the overriding importance of the dichotomy between *censory jurisprudence* (what law actually is and/or looks like) and *expository jurisprudence* (what law should do and/or be to halt the weaponization of Artificial Intelligence by those in power). This dyad has been created by Jeremy Bentham. See: Bentham, Jeremy, *An Introduction to the Principles of Morals and Legislation.* London: Great Books in Philosophy, Prometheus Books, 1988, 1–352 (293–294) (Jeremy Bentham's work on "the Principles of Morals and Legislation emerges from its historic roots in hedonism and teleology as a scientific attempt to assess the moral content of human action by focusing on its results or consequences. Proceeding from the assumption that human beings desire pleasure (and avoid pain), Bentham's unique perspective, known as utilitarianism, is used to construct a fascinating calculus for determining which action to perform when confronted with situations requiring moral decision-making the goal of which is to arrive at the "*greatest happiness of the greatest number.*" Toward this end, he endeavours to delineate the sources and kinds of pleasure and pain and how they can be measured when assessing one's moral options. Bentham supports his arguments with discussions of intentionality, consciousness, motives, and dispositions"). This is not to say that we embrace Bentham's utilitarianism—so harshly criticized in Hart's *Concept of Law*—or the claim according to which an understanding of the Rule of Law presupposes a good understanding of law in a given country or community. Yet, there is a high degree of academic accuracy in Bentham's distinction when it comes to differentiating *expository jurisprudence—explaining what law is*—and *censorial jurisprudence—explaining what law ought to be.* As for effective access to justice and the procedural approach to the Rule of Law in the purview of criminal procedure law, there is markedly clear line between what legal officials are—purveyors of procedural fairness—and what an effective access

§§ Rule of Law[126] is thus a beacon of justice that should illuminate criminal procedure law in the midst of sepulchral darkness that is about to take hold of the data-driven world[127] we are engulfed in.[128] Attaining a (mirific?) *fair machine learning*[129] therefore stands as an overriding goal that criminal procedural law should bear very firmly in mind.

§§ Whilst some scholars are reasonably bullish when it comes to extolling the superpowers of artificial intelligence[130] in dealing with complex social problems,[131] I keenly believe that criminal procedure law is woefully ill-prepared to deal with the second (*Generative Artificial Intelligence*) and third generation (*Brain-Computer Interfaces*) outgrowths of Artificial Intelligence, which, taken together, are shaping up to transform the gist of criminal procedure law beyond recognition. This is one central claim of this book, which will merit our undivided attention in the next chapters.

---

to justice ought to be—a place whereby social inequalities caused by the era of artificial intelligence are to be buffered (criminal procedure law settings) in a swift, prompt, and streamlined manner. Or irreparable damages may otherwise occur. See: Part V, Chap. 5, Sect. 5.1.1 of this book (on the central tenets of Rule of Law that lends itself to a beacon of justice amidst the sepulchral darkness that is about to take hold). See: Part V, Chap. 5, Sect. 5.1.2 of this book (on the central tenets of Procedural Rule of Law that lends itself to a lighthouse of justice that allows citizens to challenge the pearls of algorithmic wisdom in a court of law). See: Part IV, Chap. 4, Sects. 4.10.1 to 4.10.6 of this book (on biased algorithmic risk assessment in criminal procedure law settings, with a sharper focus on COMPAS). See: Part IV, Chap. 4, Sects. 4.1 to 4.1.1 of this book (on biased predictive policing).

126 Dino, Dylan, "The Rule of Law and the Rule of Empire: A. V. Dicey in Imperial Context", *The Modern Law Review*, Volume 81, Issue 5, 2018, pp. 739–764 (739–741) (highlights that "*the idea of the rule of law, more ubiquitous globally than ever before*, owes a lasting debt to the work of Victorian legal theorist A.V. Dicey (...) To Dicey we owe not only the phrase "the rule of law" but also one of the most influential expositions. Dicey's account of the rule of law emphasised three elements: first, government through legal norms and *procedures rather than unrestrained discretion; second, formal equality before the law*; and third, the establishment of individual rights through gradual, bottom-up (common-law) development"). Italics added.

127 But see: Hardt, Moritz, "How big data is unfair: Understanding sources of unfairness in data driven decision making", *Medium*, Archived on Oct. 8, 2014, available at: https://web.archive.org/web/20141008185829/ https://medium.com/@mrtz/how-big-data-is-unfair-9aa544d739de. (access: 17.12.2024).

128 The issue of a digital reality fed by a data-driven world has been shrewdly portrayed by renowned scholars, which offer gripping examples of it: Suzor, Nicolas P., *Lawless: The Secret Rules that Govern our Digital Lives*. Cambridge, United Kingdom: Cambridge University Press, 2019, pp. 1–218 (passim).

129 See: Corbett-Davies, Sam/Goel, Sharad, "The Measure and Mismeasure of Fairness: a critical Review of Fair Machine Learning", *Cornell University Library*, 2018, pp. 3 and ff and passim (undertake laudable efforts to debunk algorithm biases that primarily target ethnic minorities, such as Hispanics and coloured people).

130 But see: Segran, G., "The complexity of artificial intelligence", *Singapore Management University*, 2021, passim (on the elaborate and complex trappings of Artificial Intelligence).

131 Maxwell, J./Tomlinson, J., *Experiments in Automating Immigration Systems*. Bristol: Bristol University Press, 2022, passim.

§§ Although there have been whopping efforts to smooth out the harmful effects of first-generation byproducts of artificial intelligence (biased,[132] warped, or bigoted[133] algorithms)[134,135,136] through the fulfilment[137] of the *right to explanation*[138]—that has given rise to the movement[139] of *Explainable Artificial Intelligence*[140] (XAI for

[132] Borgesius, FJ Zuiderveen, "Strengthening legal protection against discrimination by algorithms and artificial intelligence", *International Journal of Human Rights*, Volume 24, Issue 10, 2020, pp. 1573 and ff and passim.

[133] Van Bueren, G., "Inclusivity and the law: do we need to prohibit class discrimination", *European Human Rights Law Review*, Volume 3, 2021, pp. 273 and ff and passim.

[134] Chesterman, Simon, "Artificial Intelligence and the Problem of Autonomy", *Notre Dame Journal on Emerging Technologies*, Volume 1, 2019, pp. 2 e ss e passim.

[135] See in Italian doctrine: Maranella, Stefano: "La protezione dei dati personali contro un uso distopico dell'AI, Il diritto nell'era digitale", *Persona, Mercato, Amministrazione Giustizia*. Milano: Giuffrè, 2022, pp. 51–69 (pp. 52–56 and ff and passim).

[136] See: Aggarwal, N., "The Norms of Algorithmic Credit Scoring", *Cambridge Law Journal*, Volume 80, Issue 1, 2021, pp. 43–71.

[137] On the challenges arisen from an algorithm-driven economy: Ezrachi, A./Stucke, M., *Virtual Competition—The Promise and Perils of the Algorithm-Driven Economy*. Cambridge, Massachusetts: Harvard University Press, 2016, passim; Ezrachi, A., "Is This a Competition Problem?—The Challenge of Digitalisation and the Limits of Enforcement", *Keele Law Review*, Volume 1, 2020, pp. 59 and ff and passim.

[138] See: Goodman/Flaxman, S., "EU Regulations on Algorithmic Decision-making and a "right to explanation", *Artificial Intelligence Magazine*, Volume 38, Issue 3, 2017, pp. 50 and ff and passim.

[139] See: Kaminski, M., "The Right to Explanation, Explained", *Berkeley Technology Law Journal*, Volume 34, 2019, pp. 189 and ff and passim. See: Part V, Chap. 5, Sects. 5.2 to Sect. 5.6.2.1 of this book (on the thing-centred algorithmic decision-making propelled by a *Controllable* and *Interpretable* Machine Learning that weeds out *Algorithmic Dictatorship* and secures *Algorithmic Common Good*. It is worth recalling that the **thing-centred algorithmic decision-making** seeks to unwind the perils arising out of the lack of theoretical underpinnings facing the **human-centred algorithmic decision-making**, as extensively fleshed out Part III, Chap. 3, Sects. 3.4.3 to 3.4.4 of this book). See also: Part V, Chap. 5, Sects. 5.7 to 5.7.5 of this book (on the five laws to control algorithmic decision-making). See: Part V, Chap. 5, Sects. 5.8 to 5.8.5 of this book (on the five laws to interpret algorithmic decision-making).

[140] See: Samek, Wojciech/Müller, Klaus-Robert, "Explainable AI: interpreting, explaining and visualizing deep learning", *Towards Explainable Artificial Intelligence*, Samek, Wojciech/Montavon, Grégoire/ Vedaldi, Andrea/Hansen, Lars Kai/ Müller, Klaus-Robert (Editors). Heidelberg/Berlin/ New York: Springer, 2019, pp. 5–22 ("in recent years, machine learning (ML) has become a key enabling technology for the sciences and industry. Especially through improvements in methodology, the availability of large databases and increased computational power, *today's ML algorithms are able to achieve excellent performance (at times even exceeding the human level) on an increasing number of complex tasks. Deep learning models are at the forefront of this development. However, due to their nested non-linear structure, these powerful models have been generally considered "black boxes", not providing any information about what exactly makes them arrive at their predictions*. Since in many applications, e.g., in the medical domain, *such lack of transparency may be not acceptable, the development of methods for visualizing, explaining and interpreting deep learning models has recently attracted increasing attention. This introductory paper presents recent developments and applications in this field and makes a plea for a wider use of explainable learning algorithms in practice*."). Italics added.

short)[141]—such piecemeal measures fall short of matching the theoretical underpinnings of a *Controllable*[142] and *Interpretable*[143] *Artificial Intelligence*[144] amenable to bestow upon citizens the rationale behind a given automated[145] decision.[146]

§§ There is still plenty to be done when it comes to weeding out/uprooting biases, which are often wrapped under a patina of inevitability. Undertaking a much-needed cleansing on the data that algorithms operate upon[147] is thus a herculean task that should spare no one.[148] Which should not come as a surprise at this juncture: rigged

---

141 See: Selbst, A./Powles, J., "Meaningful information and the right to explanation", *International Data Privacy Law*, Volume 7, 2018, pp. 233 and ff and passim.

142 See: Part V, Chap. 5, Sects. 5.7 to 5.7.5 of this book (on the five laws to control algorithmic decision-making).

143 See: Part V, Chap. 5, Sects. 5.8 to 5.8.5 of this book (on the five laws to interpret algorithmic decision-making).

144 See: Freitas, A.A., "Comprehensible classification models: a position paper", *ACM SIGKDD Explorations Newsletter*, Volume 15, 2014, passim.

145 Weizenbaum, Joseph, *Computer Power and Human Reason: From Judgment to Calculation*, 1st edition, New York, W. H. Freeman & Co, 1976, pp. 1–300 (227) ("examines the sources of the computer's powers and offers evaluative explorations of what computers can do, cannot do, and should not be employed to do") (this founding father of Artificial Intelligence presciently noted that we should not entrust Artificial Intelligence-embedded technologies with with with "tasks that demand wisdom"). Italics added. The approval of rental applications is arguably one of those tasks that should never be entrusted to machines). More on this on Part IV, Chap. 4, Sects. 4.4 to 4.4.2.1 of this book. See: Part V, Chap. 5, Sect. 5.7.2 of this book (on law number two to control algorithmic decision-making, which mandates that black box models must not be entrusted with the task of making high stake decisions—v.g. health and freedom). See: Part V, Chap. 5, Sect. 5.8.5 of this book (on law number five to interpret algorithmic decision-making, which mandates that robot-judges, robot-prosecutors and robot-lawyers must not enter the courtroom for they are utterly incapable of making sound and interpretable value judgements).

146 See: Huysmans, J./Dejaeger, K./Mues, C./Vanthienen, J./Baesens, B, "An empirical evaluation of the comprehensibility of decision table, tree and rule based predictive models", *Decision Support Systems*, Volume 51, 2011, pp. 141–154.

147 *Tech, Bias and Housing Initiative, the Promise and Perils of Residential Proptech, Year 1, Research Summary Report, April 2023, TechEquity Collaborative*, p. 5 available at: https://techequity.us/wp-content/uploads/2023/04/TBHI-Y1-Research-Summary-Report.pdf (28.11.2024). ("*Residential Proptech also has the potential to exacerbate the bias inherent in our housing system. Its rise is due, in part, to the desperation felt by average home seekers. With a severely constrained housing supply, companies offering an easier pathway to homeownership may exploit communities that have been harmed by housing discrimination in the past. Opaque algorithms incorporate biased data into their decision-making processes, making it harder to enforce fair housing laws.* Residential Proptech companies often operate in a regulatory gray area, leaving consumers without the protections they would have from traditional housing regulatory systems. *As unprecedented capital investment flows into this space, venture-backed companies' winner-take-all approach to growth has the potential to exacerbate inequality rather than combat it*"). Italics added.

148 See: Angelino, E./Larus-Stone, N./Alabi, D./Seltzer, M./Rudin, C., "Learning certifiability optimal rule lists for categorical data", *Journal of Machine Learning Research*, Volume 18, 2018, pp. 1–78.

data[149] may contain deep-rooted biases that we may not wish to re-entrench into computer-generated algorithms[150] that will decide our future.[151] But there is more to it.

§§ Compellingly, a string of mind-boggling questions crops up with unshakeable unease: why is the public sector still using black box[152] systems[153] whose inner

[149] Barocas, Solon/Selbst, Andrew D., "Big Data's Disparate Impact", *California Law Review*, Volume 104, 2016, pp. 671–682 (discussing how data is often flawed, rigged, incomplete, imperfect, and therefore algorithms inherit the prejudice of the original decision makers). But see: Citron, Danielle Keats/Pasquale, Frank, "The Scored Society: Due Process for Automated Predictions", *Washington Law Review*, Volume 89, 2014, pp. 1, 4–5 (highlighting how human beings programming automated systems is directly conducive to, and leads, to fundamentally inaccurate results since the source code, predictive algorithms and datasets may encompass human biases which, in turn, have a disparate impact on historically disadvantaged groups). But see: Bornstein, Stepanhie, "Antidiscriminatory Algorithms", *Alabama Law Review*, Volume 70, 2018, pp. 519, 524–528 (contending, however, that the tagged "facially neutral" algorithms producing discriminatory outcomes should be quashed).

[150] Balkin, Jack M., "The Three Laws of Robotics in the Age of Big Data", *Ohio State Law Journal*, Volume 78, Issue 5, 2017, pp. 1217–1241.

[151] *Tech, Bias and Housing Initiative, the Promise and Perils of Residential Proptech, Year 1, Research Summary Report, April 2023, TechEquity Collaborative*, p. 11, available at: https://techequity.us/wp-content/uploads/2023/04/TBHI-Y1-Research-Summary-Report.pdf (28.11.2024). ("*Once bad data enters the analysis of one factor, it gets baked into the subsequent process, multiplying the effect that one disadvantageous data point can have on someone's overall housing determination*"). Italics added.

[152] Rudin, C., & Radin, J., "Why are we using black box models in AI when we don't need to? A lesson from an explainable AI competition", *Harvard Data Science Review*, 2019, Volume 1, Issue 2, passim.

[153] See: Pasquale, Frank, *The Black Box Society: The Secret Algorithms that Control Money and Information*. Cambridge, Massachusetts: Harvard University Press, 2015, 1–320 (pp. 8–10 and passim) (noting that biased algorithms, which have underlying discrimination problems, contribute exponentially to further social biases. His most intriguing claim is that such biased algorithms have been logded/etched/steeped in the bulk of the corporations' informatic system, to the detriment of human kind in an overarching sense). See: Part V, Chap. 5, Sect. 5.7.2 of this book (on law number two to control algorithmic decision-making, which mandates that black box models must not be entrusted with the task of making high stake decisions—v.g. health and freedom). See: Part V, Chap. 5, Sects. 5.7 to 5.7.5 of this book (on the five laws to control algorithmic decision-making).

workings[154] are eerily inscrutable[155] to the citizens?[156] Shouldn't Artificial Intelligence—as a befitted tool to advance the goals of society while bettering its overall quality of life—be *interpretable*[157] instead of a gruesomely vague *explainable*[158] machine hemmed in opaqueness?[159] Put differently, shouldn't Artificial Intelligence

---

[154] Tan, S., Caruana, R., Hooker, G., and Lou, Y., "Distill-and-compare: Auditing blackbox models using transparent model distillation", *Proceedings of the 2018 AAAI/ACM Conference on AI, Ethics, and Society, Association for Computing Machinery*, 2018, pp. 303–310. See: Part V, Chap. 5, Sect. 5.7.2 of this book (on law number two to control algorithmic decision-making, which mandates that black box models must not be entrusted with the task of making high stake decisions—v.g. health and freedom). See: Part V, Chap. 5, Sects. 5.7 to 5.7.5 of this book (on the five laws to control algorithmic decision-making).

[155] See: Rudin, Cynthia, "Please stop explaining black box models for high stakes decisions", *Proceedings of NeurIPS 2018 Workshop on Critiquing and Correcting Trends in Machine Learning (NIPS 2018)*, 2018, passim. See: Part V, Chap. 5, Sect. 5.7.2 of this book (on law number two to control algorithmic decision-making, which mandates that black box models must not be entrusted with the task of making high stake decisions—v.g. health and freedom). See: Part V, Chap. 5, Sects. 5.7 to 5.7.5 of this book (on the five laws to control algorithmic decision-making).

[156] There are far more unsettling issues with which criminal justice flounders with. To begin with, the inscrutable way algorithms make their correlations and draw their inferences accordingly—which is eerily unbeknownst even for the cohort of programmers that designed them—stand out. This is deemed *black box*, that further enhances the shroud of mystery under which algorithms are cloaked. See, for a compelling account of AI black box: See: Bathaee, Yavar, "The Artificial Intelligence Black Box and the Failure of Intent and Causation", *Harvard Journal of Law and Technology*, n.º 37, 2018, p. 901 (adduces that "*one possible reason AI may be a black box to humans is that it relies on machine-learning algorithms that internalize data in ways that are not easily audited or understood by humans* (...) "*first, a lack may arise from the complexity of the algorithm's structure, such as with deep neural network, which consists of thousands of artificial neurons working together in a diffuse way to solve a problem. This reason for AI being a black box is referred to as "complexity". Second, the lack of transparency may arise because the AI is using a machine-learning algorithm that relies on geometric relationships that humans cannot visualize, such as with support vector machines. This reason for AI being a black box is referred to as "dimensionality"*"). Italics added. But see: Pearl, Judea, *Causality*, 2nd edition, Cambridge, Cambridge University Press, 2009 (on the fundamental tenets of causality). But see: Kilbertus, Niki/Carulla, Mateo Rojas/Parascandolo, Giambattista/Hardt, Moritz/Janzing, Dominik/ Schoellkopf, Bernhard, "Avoiding Discrimination through Causal Reasoning", *Advances in Neural Information Processing Systems*, I. Guyon, U. V. Luxburg, S. Bengio, H. Wallach, R. Fergus, S. Vishwanathan, and R. Garnett (Eds.), Vol. 30. Curran Associates, Inc., 2017, pp. 656–666 (arguing that is feasible to avoiding discrimination through a granular and fine-grained causal reasoning).

[157] See: Part V, Chap. 5, Sects. 5.8 to 5.8.5 of this book (on the five laws to interpret algorithmic decision-making).

[158] Mittelstadt, B./Russell, C./Watcher, S., "Explaining explanations in AI", *Proceedings of Fairness, Accountability, and Transparency (FAT) (ACM)*, 2019, passim.

[159] Watcher, S./Mittelstadt, B./Russell, C., "Counterfactual explanations without opening the black box: automated decisions and the GDPR", *Harvard Journal of Law & Technology*, Volume 1, 2018, passim. See: *Tech, Bias and Housing Initiative, the Promise and Perils of Residential Proptech, Year 1, Research Summary Report, April 2023, TechEquity Collaborative*, p. 11, available at: https://techequity.us/wp-content/uploads/2023/04/TBHI-Y1-Research-Summary-Report.pdf (28.11.2024). ("*From information on company websites, it is not clear what analysis or data is behind subjective determinations like "suitability" to a unit or what the nexus between an individual's characteristics and a unit's characteristics is that indicates the likelihood for property damage. Based on sample reports, even landlords are not privy to how the determinations are made.*

be both *interpretable*[160] and *controllable*[161] to instil trust upon stakeholders within, say, the purview of credit scoring?[162,163]

Instead, they receive a risk score out of 100 simplified into green, yellow, and red recommendations. What companies withhold in terms of how it works, they make up for with the extent to which they tell landlords it works: Naborly claims their predictions reduce lease defaults by up to 89%. 15 *As Naborly's sample report demonstrates, its property damage assessment is then used as an input to determine its projected eviction outcomes; its early vacancy prediction, in turn, is based on "all assessment factors."*). Italics added. See also: *Tech, Bias and Housing Initiative, the Promise and Perils of Residential Proptech, Year 1, Research Summary Report, April 2023, TechEquity Collaborative*, p. 5 available at: https://techequity.us/wp-content/uploads/2023/04/TBHI-Y1-Research-Summary-Report.pdf (28.11.2024). ("*Residential Proptech also has the potential to exacerbate the bias inherent in our housing system. Its rise is due, in part, to the desperation felt by average home seekers. With a severely constrained housing supply, companies offering an easier pathway to homeownership may exploit communities that have been harmed by housing discrimination in the past. Opaque algorithms incorporate biased data into their decision-making processes, making it harder to enforce fair housing laws.* Residential Proptech companies often operate in a regulatory gray area, leaving consumers without the protections they would have from traditional housing regulatory systems. *As unprecedented capital investment flows into this space, venture-backed companies' winner-take-all approach to growth has the potential to exacerbate inequality rather than combat it*"). Italics added. See: Part IV, Chap. 4, Sects. 4.4 to 4.4.2.3 of this book.

160 See: Part V, Chap. 5, Sects. 5.8 to 5.8.5 of this book (on the five laws to interpret algorithmic decision-making). See also: Chen, C./Rudin, C., "An optimization approach to learning falling rule lists", *Proceedings of Machine Learning Research, Artificial Intelligence and Statistics*, Volume 84, 2018, pp. 604–612.

161 See: Part V, Chap. 5, Sects. 5.7 to 5.7.5 of this book (on the five laws to control algorithmic decision-making).

162 See: Sokolovska, N./Chevaleyre, Y./Zucker, J.D., "A provable algorithm for learning interpretable scoring systems", *Proceedings of Machine Learning Research, Artificial Intelligence and Statistics*, Volume 84, pp. 566–574. But see: Einav, Liran/Jenkins, Mark/Levin, Jonathan, "The Impact of Credit Scoring on Consumer Lending", *The RAND Journal of Economics*, Volume 44, 2013, p. 249 (showing unequivocally that the adoption of computer-run algorithmic credit scoring led to conspicuously higher-risk applicant lending).

163 But see: Wonyoung, So, "Which Information Matters? Measuring Landlord Assessment of Tenant Screening Reports", *Housing Policy Debate*, Volume 33, n. ° 6, 2023, pp. 1484–1510 (1502) ("*One additional finding of the experiment is that algorithmic scoring can exacerbate this racially unequal landscape in rental agreements not just because the algorithm may be inaccurate, but because landlords may want to follow the risk assessment made by the tenant screening report. This is alarming for low-income tenants, particularly housing voucher holders. Security deposits are one of the most significant barriers to obtaining housing for voucher holders, because vouchers do not pay security deposits but most private landlords require them (Rosenblatt & Cossyleon, 2018).* Given that voucher holders have exceptionally low income (usually less than 50% of area median income) and might experience more housing insecurity (rental debts and eviction-related experiences), *imposing greater security deposits on voucher holders almost equates to denying them housing—yet these decisions could be justified by algorithmic scoring if tenant screening services employ it*"). Italics added.

§§ Crucially, and perhaps disturbingly, the very fact that black box systems[164]—whose inner workings are conveniently wrapped under a veneer of unimpeachable objectivity[165]—are tasked with the duty to make high stake decisions (e.g. those related with your freedom,[166] your youth,[167] your future,[168] your health,[169] your credit scoring,[170] your money,[171] and your property) defies common sense[172] and accordingly raises eyebrows.[173] Furthermore, it makes you feel clueless about *what*

[164] See: Part V, Chap. 5, Sect. 5.7.2 of this book (on law number two to control algorithmic decision-making, which mandates that black box models must not be entrusted with the task of making high stake decisions—v.g. health and freedom).

[165] Benjamin, Ruha, *Race After Technology: Abolitionist Tools for the New Jim Code*, New York, Polity, 2019, pp. 1–172 (7) (discussing that Artificial Intelligence-embedded technologies are viewed as iron-clad tools of objectivity and devoid of any biases whatsoever). Ruha Benjamin contends that "the employment of new technologies that reflect and reproduce existing inequities but that are promoted and perceived as more objective or progressive than the discriminatory systems of a previous era").

[166] Crow, M. S., "The complexities of prior record, race, ethnicity, and policy: Interactive effects in sentencing", *Criminal Justice Review*, Volume 33, Issue 4, 2008, pp. 502–523; Fornili, K. S., "Racialized mass incarceration and the war on drugs: A critical race theory appraisal", *Journal of Addictions Nursing*, Volume 29, Issue 1, 2018, 65–72.

[167] Andersen, T. S, "Race, Ethnicity, and Structural Variations in Youth Risk of Arrest: Evidence from a National Longitudinal Sample", *Criminal Justice and Behavior*, Volume 42, Issue 9, 2015, pp. 900–916.

[168] Stevenson, M. T./Slobogin, C., "Algorithmic risk assessments and the double-edged sword of youth", *Washington University Law Review*, Volume 96, 2018, passim.

[169] See: Rudin, Cynthia/Ustun, B., "Optimized scoring systems: toward trust in machine learning for healthcare and criminal justice", *Interfaces*, Volume 48, 2018, pp. 399–486.

[170] Hurley, Mikella/Adebayo, Julius, "Credit Scoring in the Era of Big Data", *Yale Journal of Law and Technology*, Volume 18, 2016, pp. 148–168.

[171] Bruckner, Matthew Adam, "The Promise and Perils of Algorithmic Lenders' Use of Big Data", *Chicago-Kent Law Review*, Volume 93, 2018, pp. 25–29.

[172] O'Neil, Cathy, "When Not to Trust the Algorithm", *Interview published in the Harvard Business Review's Ideacast*, 2016, passim.

[173] See: Weizenbaum, Joseph, *Computer Power and Human Reason: From Judgment to Calculation*, 1st edition, New York, W. H. Freeman & Co, 1976, pp. 1–300 (227) ("examines the sources of the computer's powers and offers evaluative explorations of what computers can do, cannot do, and should not be employed to do") (this founding father of Artificial Intelligence presciently noted that we should not entrust Artificial Intelligence-embedded technologies with with with "tasks that demand wisdom"). Italics added. The approval of rental applications is arguably one of those tasks that should never be entrusted to machines). More on this on Part IV, Chap. 4, Sects. 4.4 to 4.4.2.1 of this book.

comes next;[174] *who* should be jailed;[175] who should be granted parole;[176] *who* should be granted a rental[177] agreement;[178] *who* should live; *who* should be given a flawless credit scoring[179] and *who* should be unlawfully deprived from his property. Think about that for a moment and ask yourself, dear reader, if Artificial Intelligence should

---

[174] See: Buolamwini, Joy, Unmasking AI: My Mission to Protect What Is Human in a World of Machines, New York, Random House, 2023, pp. 1–336 ("*The conscience of the AI revolution" (Fortune) explains how we've arrived at an era of AI harms and oppression, and what we can do to avoid its pitfalls.* "AI is not coming, it's here. If we answer the beautiful call inside these pages, *we can decide who we are going to be and how we're going to use technology in service of what it means to be fully human.*"—Brené Brown, #1 *New York Times* bestselling author of *Dare to Lead.* A *LOS ANGELES TIMES* BEST BOOK OF THE YEAR • Shortlisted for the *Inc.* Non-Obvious Book Award. *To most of us, it seems like recent developments in artificial intelligence emerged out of nowhere to pose unprecedented threats to humankind. But to Dr. Joy Buolamwini, who has been at the forefront of AI research, this moment has been a long time in the making*"). Italics added.

[175] Patrick, Keith (2018, August 14), "Should an algorithm determine whether a criminal gets bail?" *Inside Sources.* See: https://insidesources.com/algorithm-determine-whether-criminal-gets-bail. Access: 10.07.2024. See also: Wexler, R., "Code of silence: How private companies hide flaws in the software that governments use to decide who goes to prison and who gets out", *Washington Monthly*, 2017, https://washingtonmonthly.com/2017/06/11/code-of-silence/. Access: 10.07.2024.

[176] See: Kleinberg, Jon/Lakkaraju, Himabindu/Leskovec, Jure/Ludwig, Jens/Mullainathan, Sendhil, "Human Decisions and Machine Predictions", *Quarterly Journal of Economics*, Volume 133, 2018, passim.

[177] *Tech, Bias and Housing Initiative, the Promise and Perils of Residential Proptech, Year 1, Research Summary Report, April 2023, TechEquity Collaborative*, p. 11, available at: https://techequity.us/wp-content/uploads/2023/04/TBHI-Y1-Research-Summary-Report.pdf (28.11.2024). ("*From information on company websites, it is not clear what analysis or data is behind subjective determinations like "suitability" to a unit or what the nexus between an individual's characteristics and a unit's characteristics is that indicates the likelihood for property damage. Based on sample reports, even landlords are not privy to how the determinations are made. Instead, they receive a risk score out of 100 simplified into green, yellow, and red recommendations.* What companies withhold in terms of how it works, they make up for with the extent to which they tell landlords it works: Naborly claims their predictions reduce lease defaults by up to 89%. 15 *As Naborly's sample report demonstrates, its property damage assessment is then used as an input to determine its projected eviction outcomes; its early vacancy prediction, in turn, is based on "all assessment factors.*"). Italics added.

[178] *Tech, Bias and Housing Initiative, the Promise and Perils of Residential Proptech, Year 1, Research Summary Report, April 2023, TechEquity Collaborative*, p. 10, available at: https://techequity.us/wp-content/uploads/2023/04/TBHI-Y1-Research-Summary-Report.pdf (28.11.2024). ("**Opaque, Predictive Algorithms Determine Who Gets What Housing Unlike Analog Models**, *Algorithmic Tenant Screening Tools Predict Future Behavior To Determine Housing Access As landlord tech took hold, more property managers of all sizes came to rely on it to interface with tenants. One key feature of landlord tech is the use of algorithms to screen rental applicants and assess their suitability as tenants. The tenant screening industry, which pulls a wide array of information about potential tenants to inform landlords' decisions, is now valued at $1.3 billion with as many as two thousand screening companies vying for market share.*10 11 *Such companies include Equifax, TransUnion, and Experian (commonly known as "The Big Three"), as well as smaller startup companies that apply algorithms to make those determinations faster*"). Italics added.

[179] Chen, C. et al., "An interpretable model with globally consistent explanations for credit risk", *Proceedings of NeurIPS 2018 Workshop on Critiquing and Correcting Trends in Machine Learning (NIPS 2018)*, 2018, passim.

be entrusted with the duty to make all those high stake decisions that will decide the course of your life.

§§ This is the kernel of my newly-crafted concept of *algorithmic dictatorship*[180] that draws on a plethora of human biases that disgracefully creep into the algorithm[181] and feeds into an automated decision that comes to the expense of one's freedom,[182] health, property, and credit scoring. Thereby creating a haze of ambiguity that obfuscates automated decision-making while propelling a façade of neutrality[183] that should keep us eagerly awaken at night.[184] The pinpointed issues will be extensively broached throughout this book.[185]

---

[180] See: Part IV, Chap. 4, Sects. 4 to 4.10.6 of this book (on algorithmic dictatorship and its chilling effect on democracy).

[181] Citron, Danielle Keats/Pasquale, Frank A., "The Scored Society: Due Process for Automated Predictions", *Washington Law Review*, Volume 89, 2014, pp. 1–34 (arguing that "[a]*dvocates applaud the removal of human beings and their flaws from the assessment process*," but arguing that bias remains "[*b]ecause human beings program predictive algorithms, their biases and values are embedded into the software's instructions*"). Italics added.

[182] Wexler, R., "When a computer program keeps you in jail: How computers are harming criminal justice", *New York Times*, 2017, June 13.

[183] Farina, M., & Lavazza, A., *Philosophy, expertise, and the myth of neutrality. Routledge Studies in Contemporary Philosophy*, London, Routledge, 2024. See also: Tyler, Tom R., "The Psychology of Procedural Justice: A Test of the Group-Value Model", *Journal of Personality and Social Psychology*, Volume 57, 1989, p. 830 (reports that in any procedure "several non-control issues—the *neutrality* of the decision-making procedure, trust in the 3rd party, and the information the experience communicates about social standing—influence both procedural preferences and judgments of procedural justice").

[184] Balkin, Jack M., "The Three Laws of Robotics in the Age of Big Data", *cit.*, pp. 1217–1241.

[185] See: Part IV, Chap. 4, Sects. 4 to 4.10.6 of this book (on algorithmic dictatorship and its chilling effect on democracy).

§§ But for the sake of the argument, why should Artificial Intelligence be both *interpretable*[186] and *controllable*?[187] The skewed data[188] baked into the bigoted algorithms—machine learning[189] biases[190]—spawns harrowing effects with which modern societies[191] have been grappling with[192] for a long-haul[193]/drawn-out.[194]

---

[186] See: Part V, Chap. 5, Sects. 5.8 to 5.8.5 of this book (on the five laws to interpret algorithmic decision-making). See also: Wang, J./Oh, J./Wang, H./Wiens, J., "Learning credible models", *Proceedings of 24th ACM SIGKDD International Conference on Knowledge Discovery and Data Mining*, ACM, 2018, pp. 2417–2426. But see: Balkin, Jack, "Constitution in the National Surveillance State", *Minnesota Law Review*, Volume 93, 2008, p. 13 (*data mining* allows inferences not only about the direct subject of surveillance, but about other people with whom they live, work and communicate"). But see: Pedreshi, Dino/Ruggieri, Salvatore/Turini, Franco, "Discrimination-aware Data Mining", *Proceedings of the 14th ACM SIGKDD International Conference on Knowledge Discovery and Data Mining (Las Vegas, Nevada, USA), ACM*, 2008, pp. 560–568 (arguing that one should shift its gaze downstream by putting in place discrimination-aware algorithmic tools while performing data mining).

[187] See: Part V, Chap. 5, Sects. 5.7 to 5.7.5 of this book (on the five laws to control algorithmic decision-making).

[188] *Tech, Bias and Housing Initiative, the Promise and Perils of Residential Proptech, Year 1, Research Summary Report, April 2023, TechEquity Collaborative*, p. 11, available at: https://techequity.us/wp-content/uploads/2023/04/TBHI-Y1-Research-Summary-Report.pdf (28.11.2024). ("*Once bad data enters the analysis of one factor, it gets baked into the subsequent process, multiplying the effect that one disadvantageous data point can have on someone's overall housing determination*"). Italics added.

[189] Sun, R. (Ed.), *The Cambridge Handbook of Computational Cognitive Sciences*, Cambridge, Cambridge University Press, 2023.

[190] Fisher, A., Rudin, C., & Dominici, F., "All models are wrong, but many are useful: Learning a variable's importance by studying an entire class of prediction models simultaneously", *Journal of Machine Learning Research*, 20, 2019, pp. 1–81.

[191] Annamma, S. A., Jackson, D. D., & Morrison, D., "Conceptualizing color-evasiveness: Using dis/ability critical race theory to expand a color-blind racial ideology in education and society", *Race Ethnicity and Education*, Volume 20, Issue 2, 2017, pp. 147–162.

[192] See: Alcalá, H. E., & Montoya, M. F. L., "Association of skin color and generation on arrests among Mexican-origin latinos", *Race and Justice*, Volume 8, Issue 2, 2018, pp. 178–193.

[193] Brewer, R. M./Heitzeg, N. A., "The racialization of crime and punishment: Criminal justice, Color-Blind racism, and the political economy of the prison industrial complex", *American Behavioral Scientist*, Volume 51, Issue 5, 2008, pp. 625–644.

[194] Flores, A.W./Lowenkamp, C.T./Bechtel, K., "False positives, false negatives, and false analyses: a rejoinder to "machine bias: there's software used across the country to predict future criminal", *Federal Probation Journal*, Volume 80, 2016, pp. 38–46. Sun, R. (Ed.), *The Cambridge Handbook of Computational Cognitive Sciences*, Cambridge, Cambridge University Press, 2023.

§§ Tellingly, and perhaps unsurprisingly, law enforcement evinces biases[195] that run along both gender[196] and race[197] lines.[198] No surprise springs from the fact that computer-generated algorithms that underpin *predictive policing*[199]

---

[195] Brayne, S., "The criminal law and law enforcement implications of big data", *Annual Review of Law and Social Science*, Volume 14, 2018, pp. 293–308.

[196] Hamilton, Melissa, "The sexist algorithm", *Behavioral Sciences and the Law*, Volume 37, Issue 2, Special Issue: the Use of Statistics in Criminal Cases, March–April 2019, 2019, pp. 1 and ff ("*Algorithmic risk assessment tools are informed by scientific research concerning which factors are predictive of recidivism and thus support the evidence-based practice movement in criminal justice.* Automated assessments of individualized risk (low, medium, high) *permit officials to make more effective management decisions. Computer-generated algorithms appear to be objective and neutral. But are these algorithms actually fair? The focus herein is on gender equity.* Studies confirm that women typically have far lower recidivism rates than men. *This differential raises the question of how well algorithmic outcomes fare in terms of predictive parity by gender.* This essay reports original research using a large dataset of offenders who were scored on the popular risk assessment tool COMPAS. *Findings indicate that COMPAS performs reasonably well at discriminating between recidivists and non-recidivists for men and women. Nonetheless, COMPAS algorithmic outcomes systemically overclassify women in higher risk groupings. Multiple measures of algorithmic equity and predictive accuracy are provided to support the conclusion that this algorithm is sexist.*"). Italics added.

[197] Crutchfield, J., Fisher, A., & Webb, S. L., "Colorism and police killings", *The Western Journal of Black Studies*, 41 (3–4), 2017, 81; Dottolo, A. L., & Stewart, A. J. (2008). "Don't ever forget now, you're a Black man in America": Intersections of race, class and gender in encounters with the police", *Sex Roles*, 59(5–6), 2008, pp. 350–364.

[198] Baradan, S., "Race, prediction, and discretion", *The George Washington Law Review*, Volume 81, Issue 1, 2013, pp. 157–222.

[199] Hardyns, W./Rummens, A., "Predictive policing as a new tool for law enforcement? recent developments and challenges", *European Journal on Criminal Policy and Research*, Volume 24, Issue 3, 2018, pp. 201–218. A feted scholar (Bernard Harcourt) adamantly contends that (1) predictive crime control efforts may produce more harm than good; (2) they may engender a "ratchet effect" in which the disparate impact of forecast on black folks worsens over time; and (3) the technological allure of prediction can both besmirch and mar deep-rooted moral conceptions of justice. See: Harcourt, Bernard E., *Against Prediction: Profiling, Policing, and Punishing in An Actuarial Age*, Chicago, Illinois, University of Chicago Press, 2007, pp. 7–18 and passim. Converging: Ensign, Danielle, "Runaway Feedback Loops in Predictive Policing", *Proceedings of Machine Learning Research*, Volume 81, 2018, p. 1; Starr, Sonja B., "Evidence-Based Sentencing and the Scientific Rationalization of Discrimination", *Stanford Law Review*, Volume 66, 2014, pp. 804–06 (arguing that that risk assessment during sentencing may derail deep-seated concepts of justice that we hold so dear). In addition to this line of reasoning, Professor Sandra Mayson avers that, because any extant racial disparity in crime risk is the byproduct of a long-haul historical oppression, it is therefore an unfitting basis for coercive state action. To put it bluntly, it is unfair for the state to condition coercion on crime risk that modern societies have unjustly created. Put another way, one may be led to believe that the data are simply warped and that the risk at hand is fundamentally uniform across racial lines. Understandably, though not laudably, one may be also led to believe that crime risk is a fundamentally haphazard and incoherent concept, owing to the fact that all people who are self-determining agents have an equal capacity to eschew flagitious behaviour or engaging in criminal activities. See: Mayson, Sandra G., "Bias In, Bias Out", *cit.*, pp. 2218–2300. See: Part IV, Chap. 4, Sects. 4.10.1 to 4.10.6 of this book (on biased algorithmic risk assessment in criminal procedure law settings, with a sharper focus on COMPAS). See: Part IV, Chap. 4, Sects. 4.1 to 4.1.1 of this book (on biased predictive policing).

are often flagged as tools[200] whereby[201] racial[202] discrimination[203] abounds.[204]

[200] Fielding-Miller, R., Cooper, H. L. F., Caslin, S./Raj, A., "The Interaction of Race and Gender as a Significant Driver of Racial Arrest Disparities for African American Men", *Journal of Urban Health*, Volume 97, 2020, pp. 112–122. See also: See: Hu, Margaret, "From the National Surveillance State to the Cybersurveillance State", *The Annual Review of Law and Social Science*, Volume 13, 2017, p. 166 (argues that ubiquitous and ever-present surveillance of socially undesirables remains at a pitch of degradation of fundamental rights in that Artificial Intelligence-embedded technologies—propelled by tools like Social Radar and Total Information Awareness, TIA, can capture "a *pictorial depiction of the comprehensive cybersurveillance anticipated through the Social Radar system, which anticipated the full integration of drone footage, biometrric data signatures, econometrics, and other intelligence sources to achieve higher-order cybersurveillance inferences. Social Radar appears to trace its philosophical origins to TIA.* The development of TIA after the 9/11 terrorist attacks was guided under the leadership of the newly created Information Awareness Office within DARPA (Harris 2012, Murray 2010). Within this office, TIA was an effort led by retired Navy Vice Admiral John M. Poindexter (Murray 2010), who served as a national security advisor to President Reagan (Harris 2012). *TIA was informed by a philosophy of "predictive policing," which "focuses not on collecting evidence about actual wrongdoing but on the broad collection of information about everyday activities with the intention of detecting (and preventing) future behavior*" (Murray 2010, p. 5). Congress officially defunded TIA in late 2003 (Murray 2010, Slobogin 2008, USA Today 2003). *Experts have nonetheless noted that remnants of the TIA program and its philosophy have persisted*"). Italics added. See: Part IV, Chap. 4, Sects. 4.5 to 4.5.2 of this book (on "algorithmic Jim Crow", which stands as an outgrowth of congeries of laws enacted during the Jim Crow epoch).

[201] Fagan, J., "Race and the new policing", *Columbia Public Law Research Paper*, 2 (14–561), 2017, 83–116.

[202] Barrett, L, "Reasonably suspicious algorithms: Predictive policing at the United States border", *New York Review of Law and Social Change*, Volume 41, 2017, pp. 327–365. See: Part IV, Chap. 4, Sects. 4.1 to 4.1.1 of this book (on biased predictive policing).

[203] Brayne, S., "Big data surveillance: The case of policing", *American Sociological Review*, Volume 82, Issue 5, 2017, pp. 977–1008. See: Part IV, Chap. 4, Sects. 4.1 to 4.1.1 of this book (on biased predictive policing).

[204] Berk, R./Heidari, H./Jabbari, S./Kearns, M./Roth, A., "Fairness in criminal justice risk assessments: The state of the art", Sociological Methods & Research, Volume 50, Issue 1, 2018, passim.

§§ Compellingly, the relationship between skewed data (*inputs*) and inferences (*outputs*) has shown to be reciprocal.[205] Put simply, the relationship that a given algorithm uses to make a prediction[206] reflects hidden correlations[207] in the data as opposed to a causal connection[208] to the outcome/prediction.[209] A vicious cycle inevitably unfolds: biased data[210] that feeds into the algorithm begets equally biased

---

205 *Tech, Bias and Housing Initiative, the Promise and Perils of Residential Proptech, Year 1, Research Summary Report, April 2023, TechEquity Collaborative*, p. 11, available at: https://techequity.us/wp-content/uploads/2023/04/TBHI-Y1-Research-Summary-Report.pdf (28.11.2024). ("*Once bad data enters the analysis of one factor, it gets baked into the subsequent process, multiplying the effect that one disadvantageous data point can have on someone's overall housing determination*"). Italics added.

206 Agrawal, A., Gans, J., & Goldfarb, A., "Prediction machines (updated and expanded): The simple economics of artificial intelligence", *Harvard Business Review Press*, 2022.

207 See: Part V, Chap. 5, Sects. 5.1.5.2.2 to 5.1.5.2.2.1.4 of this book (on the fundamental shift away from causation to correlations in algorithmic decision-making).

208 But see: Kilbertus, Niki/Carulla, Mateo Rojas/Parascandolo, Giambattista/Hardt, Moritz/ Janzing, Dominik/ Schoellkopf, Bernhard, "Avoiding Discrimination through Causal Reasoning", *Advances in Neural Information Processing Systems*, I. Guyon, U. V. Luxburg, S. Bengio, H. Wallach, R. Fergus, S. Vishwanathan, and R. Garnett (Eds.), Vol. 30. Curran Associates, Inc., 2017, pp. 656–666 (arguing that is feasible to avoiding discrimination through a granular and fine-grained causal reasoning). See: Part V, Chapt. 5, Sects. 5.1.5.2.2 to 5.1.5.2.2.1.4 of this book (on the fundamental shift away from causation to correlations in algorithmic decision-making).

209 Gillis, Talia B., "The Input Data Fallacy", *Minnesota Law Review*, Volume 106, 2022, pp. 1176–1263 (p. 1244).

210 *Tech, Bias and Housing Initiative, the Promise and Perils of Residential Proptech, Year 1, Research Summary Report, April 2023, TechEquity Collaborative*, p. 5, available at: https://techequity.us/wp-content/uploads/2023/04/TBHI-Y1-Research-Summary-Report.pdf (28.11.2024). ("*Residential Proptech also has the potential to exacerbate the bias inherent in our housing system. Its rise is due, in part, to the desperation felt by average home seekers. With a severely constrained housing supply, companies offering an easier pathway to homeownership may exploit communities that have been harmed by housing discrimination in the past. Opaque algorithms incorporate biased data into their decision-making processes, making it harder to enforce fair housing laws.* Residential Proptech companies often operate in a regulatory gray area, leaving consumers without the protections they would have from traditional housing regulatory systems. *As unprecedented capital investment flows into this space, venture-backed companies' winner-take-all approach to growth has the potential to exacerbate inequality rather than combat it*"). Italics added.

predictions,[211] thereby further compounding a jarring tapestry of racial discrimination that besets modern societies.[212] This is epiphenomenon has been tagged as «runaway feedback loops»[213] that re-entrench existing biases in predictive policing,[214] which primarily targets racial minorities.

---

[211] Agrawal, A., Gans, J., & Goldfarb, A., "Power and prediction: The disruptive economics of artificial intelligence", *Harvard Business Review Press*, 2022.

[212] *Tech, Bias and Housing Initiative, the Promise and Perils of Residential Proptech, Year 1, Research Summary Report, April 2023, TechEquity Collaborative*, p. 11, available at: https://techequity.us/wp-content/uploads/2023/04/TBHI-Y1-Research-Summary-Report.pdf (28.11.2024). ("*Once bad data enters the analysis of one factor, it gets baked into the subsequent process, multiplying the effect that one disadvantageous data point can have on someone's overall housing determination*"). Italics added.

[213] Ensign, Danielle/Friedler, Sorelle A./Neville, Scott/Scheidegger, Carlos/ Venkatasubramanian, Suresh, "Runaway Feedback Loops in Predictive Policing", *Proceedings of Machine Learning Research, Conference on Fairness, Accountability, and Transparency*, Volume 81, 2018, pp. 1–12 (1) ("Predictive policing systems are increasingly used to determine how to allocate police across a city in order to best prevent crime. *Discovered crime data (e.g., arrest counts) are used to help update the model, and the process is repeated. Such systems have been empirically shown to be susceptible to runaway feedback loops, where police are repeatedly sent back to the same neighborhoods regardless of the true crime rate*"). Italics added. See: Part IV, Chap. 4, Sects. 4.1 to 4.1.1 of this book (on biased predictive policing).

[214] See: Hu, Margaret, "From the National Surveillance State to the Cybersurveillance State", *The Annual Review of Law and Social Science*, Volume 13, 2017, p. 166 (argues that ubiquitous and ever-present surveillance of socially undesirables remains at a pitch of degradation of fundamental rights in that Artificial Intelligence-embedded technologies—propelled by tools like Social Radar and Total Information Awareness, TIA, can capture "a *pictorial depiction of the comprehensive cybersurveillance anticipated through the Social Radar system, which anticipated the full integration of drone footage, biometrric data signatures, econometrics, and other intelligence sources to achieve higher-order cybersurveillance inferences. Social Radar appears to trace its philosophical origins to TIA.* The development of TIA after the 9/11 terrorist attacks was guided under the leadership of the newly created Information Awareness Office within DARPA (Harris 2012, Murray 2010). Within this office, TIA was an effort led by retired Navy Vice Admiral John M. Poindexter (Murray 2010), who served as a national security advisor to President Reagan (Harris 2012). *TIA was informed by a philosophy of "predictive policing," which "focuses not on collecting evidence about actual wrongdoing but on the broad collection of information about everyday activities with the intention of detecting (and preventing) future behavior*" (Murray 2010, p. 5). Congress officially defunded TIA in late 2003 (Murray 2010, Slobogin 2008, USA Today 2003). *Experts have nonetheless noted that remnants of the TIA program and its philosophy have persisted*"). Italics added. See: Part IV, Chap. 4, Sects. 4.5 to 4.5.2 of this book (on "algorithmic Jim Crow", a travel ban issued during the first Trump Administration to prevent certain individuals from entering the United States of America, which, given its racial undertones, stands as an outgrown of congeries of laws enacted during the Jim Crow epoch).

§§ It should not therefore come as a surprise that this sort of *shady algorithmic governance*[215] is a byproduct of a gruelling *algorithmic dictatorship*[216] that is shaping up to topple the foundations of Rule of Law[217] upon which stands modern societies.[218] Insofar humans[219] refrain themselves from standing up for their swiftly dwindling fundamental rights, that is exactly what will happen in the forthcoming future. This is one of the key takeaways of this book.

---

[215] Jefferson, B., *Digitize and Punish: Racial Criminalization in the Digital Age*, Minnesota, University of Minnesota Press, 2020.

[216] See: Part IV, Chap. 4, Sects. 4 to 4.10.6 of this book (on algorithmic dictatorship and its chilling effect on democracy).

[217] Ferreri, Mara/Sanyal, Romola, "Digital informalisation: rental housing, platforms, and the management of risk", *Housing Studies*, Volume 37, Issue 6, 2022, pp. 1035–1053 ("*The eruption of disruptive digital platforms is reshaping geographies of housing under the gaze of corporations and through the webs of algorithms.* Engaging with interdisciplinary scholarship on informal housing across the Global North and South, we propose the term *'digital informalisation' to examine how digital platforms are engendering new and opaque ways of governing housing,* presenting a theoretical and political blind spot. Focusing on *rental housing, our paper unpacks the ways in which new forms of digital management of risk control access and filter populations. In contrast to progressive imaginaries of 'smart' technological mediation, practices of algorithmic redlining, biased tenant profiling and the management of risk in private tenancies and in housing welfare both introduce and extend discriminatory and exclusionary housing practices*"). Italics added. See: Part IV, Chap. 4, Sects. 4.4 to 4.4.2.3 of this book.

[218] *Tech, Bias and Housing Initiative, the Promise and Perils of Residential Proptech, Year 1, Research Summary Report, April 2023, TechEquity Collaborative*, p. 11, available at: https://techequity.us/wp-content/uploads/2023/04/TBHI-Y1-Research-Summary-Report.pdf (28.11.2024). ("*From information on company websites, it is not clear what analysis or data is behind subjective determinations like "suitability" to a unit or what the nexus between an individual's characteristics and a unit's characteristics is that indicates the likelihood for property damage. Based on sample reports, even landlords are not privy to how the determinations are made. Instead, they receive a risk score out of 100 simplified into green, yellow, and red recommendations.* What companies withhold in terms of how it works, they make up for with the extent to which they tell landlords it works: Naborly claims their predictions reduce lease defaults by up to 89%. 15 *As Naborly's sample report demonstrates, its property damage assessment is then used as an input to determine its projected eviction outcomes; its early vacancy prediction, in turn, is based on "all assessment factors.*"). Italics added.

[219] Pasquale, Frank, "A Rule of Persons, Not Machines: The Limits of Legal Automation", *George Washington Law Review*, Volume 87, 2019, passim. See: Part V, Chap. 5, Sect. 5.8.5 of this book (on law number five to interpret algorithmic decision-making, which mandates that robot-judges, robot-prosecutors and robot-lawyers must not enter the courtroom for they are utterly incapable of making sound and interpretable value judgements).

§§ In an earnest attempt to allay the unbecoming effects of Artificial Intelligence,[220] Computer Science pundits[221] have neither been coy nor bashful in overtly decrying/ bemoaning—a trenchant criticism that has been deployed with a crushing lack of subtlety—the impermissible disparities of treatment[222] that dispiritingly run along[223] race[224] lines.[225] Especially, but not exclusively, regarding algorithmic risk assessment[226] aimed at predicting criminal recidivism.[227] I accordingly aver that *algorithmic dictatorship* is the primary lens through which racial disparities can be seen in the remit of predictive policing.[228]

---

220 Hu, Margaret, "From the National Surveillance State to the Cybersurveillance State", *The Annual Review of Law and Social Science*, Volume 13, 2017, p. 169 ("*as a result of big data biometric governance trends, meaningful distinctions between biometric credentialing for identification and behavioral biometric profiling are disappearing. The objectives are merging: Reliable credentialing is used to advance security and precrime policy rationales. Biometric data mission creep occurs by necessity in a big data world because the cybersurveillance systems are often designed to engage in mass data integration and analysis and predictive policing. Biometric surveillance serves two purposes in preventive policing: It increases identity transparency, and the biometric data categorize identity through cataloging behavioral and physical characteristics and assess these characteristics for risk. Contrasting small data biometric credentialing protocols with big data credentialing protocols is useful. It illustrates how biometric surveillance fits within the Cybersurveillance State. In a small data world, paper-based passports and nondigitized photographs are examples of a small data biometric-based identification system*"). Italics added.

221 Brennan, T., Dieterich, W., & Ehret, B., "Evaluating the predictive validity of the COMPAS risk and needs assessment system", *Criminal Justice and Behavior*, Volume 36, Issue 1, 2009, pp. 21–40.

222 Coglianese, C., & Lehr, D., "Transparency and algorithmic governance". *Working Paper. Penn Program on Regulation, University of Pennsylvania Law School*, 2018.

223 Delgado, R./Stefancic, J., "Critical race theory and criminal justice", *Humanity & Society*, Volume 31, 2007, pp. 133–145.

224 Gottfredson, S. D., & Jarjoura, G. R., "Race, gender, and guidelines-based decision making", *Journal of Research in Crime and Delinquency*, Volume 33, Issue 1, 1996, pp. 49–69.

225 Rudin, Cynthia/Wang, Caroline/Coker, Beau, "The Age of Secrecy and Unfairness in Recidivism Prediction", *Harvard Data Science Review*, Issue 2.1. Winter 2020, 2020, passim.

226 See: Part IV, Chap. 4, Sects. 4.10.1 to 4.10.6 of this book (on biased algorithmic risk assessment in criminal procedure law settings). See also: Eckhouse, L., Lum, K., Conti-Cook, C./Ciccolini, J., "Layers of bias: A unified approach for understanding problems with risk assessment", *Criminal Justice and Behavior*, Volume 46, Issue 2, 2019, pp. 185–209.

227 Tollenaar, N., & van der Heijden, P., "Which method predicts recidivism best? A comparison of statistical, machine learning and data mining predictive models", *Journal of the Royal Statistical Society: Series A*, Volume 176, Issue 2, 2013, pp. 565–584. Zhu, Mirilla, "Jury, Using Artificial Intelligence to Predict Recidivism Rates", *Yale Scientific*, 2020, passim. See also: Chasemi et al., Medhi, "The application of Machine Learning to a General Risk-Need Assessment Instrument in the Prediction of Criminal Recidivism", *Criminal Justice and Behavior*, Volume 48, 2020, pp. 518–538.

228 See: Hu, Margaret, "From the National Surveillance State to the Cybersurveillance State", *The Annual Review of Law and Social Science*, Volume 13, 2017, p. 166 (argues that ubiquitous and ever-present surveillance of socially undesirables remains at a pitch of degradation of fundamental rights in that Artificial Intelligence-embedded technologies—propelled by tools like Social Radar and Total Information Awareness, TIA, can capture "a *pictorial depiction of the comprehensive cybersurveillance anticipated through the Social Radar system, which anticipated the full integration of drone footage, biometrric data signatures, econometrics, and other intelligence sources to achieve higher-order cybersurveillance inferences. Social Radar appears to trace its philosophical*

§§ Bearing this truism very firmly in mind, we must be chary of computer-generated algorithms if they entrench or worsen existing biases.[229] Under either approach, the wedge between the socially acceptable and the legally permissible should not be behemoth or disparate impact[230] on racial minorities[231] may otherwise ratchet up[232] in the purview of predictive[233] policing.[234]

---

origins to TIA. The development of TIA after the 9/11 terrorist attacks was guided under the leadership of the newly created Information Awareness Office within DARPA (Harris 2012, Murray 2010). Within this office, TIA was an effort led by retired Navy Vice Admiral John M. Poindexter (Murray 2010), who served as a national security advisor to President Reagan (Harris 2012). *TIA was informed by a philosophy of "predictive policing," which "focuses not on collecting evidence about actual wrongdoing but on the broad collection of information about everyday activities with the intention of detecting (and preventing) future behavior*" (Murray 2010, p. 5). Congress officially defunded TIA in late 2003 (Murray 2010, Slobogin 2008, USA Today 2003). *Experts have nonetheless noted that remnants of the TIA program and its philosophy have persisted*"). Italics added.

229 Gillis, Talia B., "The Input Data Fallacy", *Minnesota Law Review*, Volume 106, 2022, pp. 1176–1263.

230 Barocas, Solon/Selbst, Andrew D., "Big Data's Disparate Impact", *California Law Review*, Volume 104, 2016, pp. 671 and ff and passim.

231 Robinson, M. A., "Black bodies on the ground: Policing disparities in the African American Community-An analysis of newsprint from January 1, 2015, through December 31, 2015", *Journal of Black Studies*, Volume 48, Issue 6, pp. 551–571. See: Part IV, Chap. 4, Sects. 4.10.1 to 4.10.6 of this book (on biased algorithmic risk assessment in criminal procedure law settings, with a sharper focus on COMPAS). See: Part IV, Chap. 4, Sects. 4.1 to 4.1.1 of this book (on biased predictive policing).

232 Browne, S., *Dark matters: on the surveillance of blackness*, Duke University Press, 2015, passim.

233 See: Part IV, Chap. 4, Sects. 4.1 to 4.1.1 of this book (on biased predictive policing). See also: DaViera, A. L./Uriostegui, M., Gottlieb/A./Onyeka, O, "Risk, race, and predictive policing: A critical race theory analysis of the strategic subject list", *American Journal of Community Psychology*, Volume 73, 2024, pp. 91–103. See: Part IV, Chap. 4, Sects. 4.10.1 to 4.10.6 of this book (on biased algorithmic risk assessment in criminal procedure law settings, with a sharper focus on COMPAS). See: Part IV, Chap. 4, Sects. 4.10.6 to 4.1.1 of this book (on biased predictive policing).

234 Jefferson, B. J., "Predictable policing: Predictive crime mapping and geographies of policing and race", *Annals of the American Association of Geographers*, Volume 108, Issue 1, 2018, 1–16. See: Part IV, Chap. 4, Sects. 4.10.1 to 4.10.6 of this book (on biased algorithmic risk assessment in criminal procedure law settings, with a sharper focus on COMPAS). See: Part IV, Chap. 4, Sects. 4.1 to 4.1.1 of this book (on biased predictive policing).

§§ To cater for that, algorithms that bolster/propel predictive policing must be held to normative standards that should be even harsher than extant benchmarks that govern other areas (e.g. fair lending[235] or credit scoring[236]). Absent/bereft of which, criminal

---

[235] It is crucially important to note, though, that the very fact that only certain types of behaviours are assessed and gauged by credit scores leads to the conclusion that some borrowers are not scored at all. The overwhelming majority of consumers boast meagre, if any, credit files owing to the fact that the likelihood to access to the sort of financial services that actually report to the orthodox credit bureaus scattered across modern economies is exceedingly low, which, in turn, morphs them into credit invisible persons. See: Yu, Persis/McLaughlin, Jilian/Levy, Marina, "Big Data: A Big Disappointment for Scoring Consumer Creditworthiness", *The National Consumer Law Center*, 2 (Mar. 14, 2014), available at: https://www.nclc.org/images/pdf/pr-reports/ report-big-data.pdf [https://perma.cc/W4SK-NXD5] (access: 21.12.2024). See: Part IV, Chap. 4, Sects. 4.4 to 4.4.2.1 of this book (on mortgage redlining). See: Part IV, Chap. 4, Sects. 4.2 to 4.4.3 of this book (on algorithmic credit scoring, consumer racism and credit card redlining). See: Part IV, Chap. 4, Sects. 4.4 to 4.4.2.3 of this book (on algorithmic redlining). See: Part IV, Chap. 4, Sect. 4.4.3 of this book (on "algorithmic redliking"). See: Part IV, Chap. 4, Sect. 4.3 of this book (on algorithmic prime-lining).

[236] Havard, Cassandra Jones, "On The Take": The Black Box of Credit Scoring and Mortgage Discrimination", *Boston University Public Interest Law Journal*, Volume 20, 2011, pp. 241–247 (highlighting that credit scoring, if unchecked, is an intrinsic, encroached, deep-rooted form of racial discrimination akin to mortgage redlining); Pasquale, Frank, *The Black Box Society: The Secret Algorithms that Control Money and Information.* Cambridge, Massachusetts: Harvard University Press, 2015, 1–320 (8–10 and passim); Watcher, S./Mittelstadt, B./Russell, C., "Counterfactual explanations without opening the black box: automated decisions and the GDPR", *Harvard Journal of Law & Technology*, Volume 1, 2018, passim; Rudin, C./Radin, J., "Why are we using black box models in AI when we don't need to? A lesson from an explainable AI competition", *Harvard Data Science Review*, 2019, Volume 1, Issue 2, passim; Tan, S., Caruana, R., Hooker, G., and Lou, Y., "Distill-and-compare: Auditing blackbox models using transparent model distillation". *Proceedings of the 2018 AAAI/ACM Conference on AI, Ethics, and Society, Association for Computing Machinery*, 2018, pp. 303–310; Rudin, Cynthia, "Please stop explaining black box models for high stakes decisions", *Proceedings of NeurIPS 2018 Workshop on Critiquing and Correcting Trends in Machine Learning (NIPS 2018)*, 2018, passim. See also: *Tech, Bias and Housing Initiative, the Promise and Perils of Residential Proptech, Year 1, Research Summary Report, April 2023, TechEquity Collaborative*, p. 10, available at: https://techequity.us/wp-content/uploads/2023/04/TBHI-Y1-Research-Summary-Report.pdf (28.11.2024). ("*Tenant screening tools are often packaged as part of a larger suite of property management tools for landlords. Unlike Analog Models, Algorithmic Tenant Screening Tools Predict Future Behavior To Determine Housing Access.* Before the advent of algorithmic tenant screening, landlords vetted tenants by having them submit their own records and references from previous landlords or others who could vouch for their trustworthiness. During an analog rental application process, a prospective tenant provides certain personal information and then gives consent for the landlord to run a background check to verify their information. *The landlord, housing provider, or property manager then pays a third-party entity such as TransUnion to pull information that gives a sense of whether the applicant will be a trustworthy renter. In analog screening, those reports return information from an applicant's credit, eviction, and criminal histories. There are many inequities with this analog model. Eviction and criminal records are often wrong or lack important context. 12 13 Credit scoring techniques are notoriously biased*"). Italics added. See: Part IV, Chap. 4, Sects. 4.4 to 4.4.2.3 of this book. See: Part IV, Chap. 4, Sects. 4.4 to 4.4.2.1 of this book (on mortgage redlining). See: Part IV, Chap. 4, Sects. 4.2 to 4.4.3 of this book (on algorithmic credit scoring, consumer racism and credit card redlining). See: Part IV, Chap. 4, Sects. 4.4 to 4.4.2.3 of this book (on algorithmic redlining). See: Part IV, Chap. 4, Sect. 4.4.3 of this book (on "algorithmic redliking"). See: Part IV, Chap. 4, Sect. 4.3 of this book (on algorithmic prime-lining).

justice is bound to careen into chaos of ever-lasting *selective police*[237] *surveillance*[238] that will widen the yawning gap between racialized citizens and law enforcement.[239] In that case, *algorithmic surveillance*[240] will rise and the remnants of the worst of human nature will be accordingly laid bare.[241]

§§ That is why computer-generated algorithms should abide by stringent requirements of *Algorithmic Common Good*[242] The rationale behind this seemingly lopsided yardstick is straightforward: avoid at any cost unlawful «arrests by skin colour»,[243]

---

[237] Toro, J. D./Lloyd, T., Buchanan/K. S., Robins/S. J., Bencharit/L. Z., Smiedt/M. G., Reddy/K. S., Pouget, E. R./Kerrison, E. M./Goff, P. A., "The criminogenic and psychological effects of police stops on adolescent black and Latino boys", *Proceedings of the National Academy of Sciences of the United States of America*, Volume 116, Issue 17, 2019, pp. 8261–8268. See: Part IV, Chap. 4, Sects. 4.10.1 to 4.10.6 of this book (on biased algorithmic risk assessment in criminal procedure law settings, with a sharper focus on COMPAS). See: Part IV, Chap. 4, Sect. 4.1 to Sect. 4.1.1 of this book (on biased predictive policing).

[238] See: Hu, Margaret, "From the National Surveillance State to the Cybersurveillance State", *The Annual Review of Law and Social Science*, Volume 13, 2017, pp. 162–163 ("*policymakers view these technological developments, including biometric technologies, as tools with the potential to identify individuals who may pose a threat to national and homeland security and to prevent crime and terrorism. One example of technology intended for risk assessment and threat management is the post-9/11 program Total Information Awareness (TIA). (….) Collect-it-all efforts like TIA embody a philosophy that aspires to preventive policing. Mass data collection is construed as a tool to assess and prevent future threats (Murray 2010). In TIA and other programs tested or adopted after 9/11, biometric database screening and analysis have emerged as a preferred method for tracking, identifying, and establishing identity-based inferences in counterterrorism*"). Italics added. See also: Ball, Kirstie, and Frank Webster (Eds.), *The Intensification of Surveillance: Crime, Terrorism & Warfare in the Information Age*, London, UK: Pluto Press, 2007; Guzik, Keith, "Discrimination by Design: Predictive Data Mining as Security Practice in the United States' 'War on Terrorism.'", *Surveillance and Society*, 7 (1), 2009, pp. 1–17. See: Part IV, Chap. 4, Sects. 4.5 to 4.5.2 of this book (on "algorithmic Jim Crow", which stands as an outgrowth of congeries of laws enacted during the Jim Crow epoch).

[239] Benjamin, R., *Race After Technology: Abolitionist Tools for the New Jim Code*, John Wiley & Sons, 2019, passim. See also: Epp, Charles R., Steven Maynard-Moody, and Donald P. Haider-Markel, *Pulled Over: How Police Stops Define Race and Citizenship*, Chicago: University of Chicago Press, 2014.

[240] Abdillahi, I., "Algorithmic surveillance in the era of the appsphere", *American Journal of Community Psychology*, Volume 73, 2024, passim.

[241] See: Part III, Chap. 3, Sect. 3.1 of this book (that discusses the issue of "inequality in application" facing Artificial Intelligence-embedded technologies).

[242] See: Part V, Chap. 5, Sects. 5.2 to 5.6.2.1 of this book (on the thing-centred algorithmic decision-making propelled by a *Controllable* and *Interpretable* Machine Learning that weeds out *Algorithmic Dictatorship* and secures *Algorithmic Common Good*).

[243] Kizer, J. M., "Arrested by skin color: Evidence from siblings and a nationally representative sample", *Socius: Sociological Research for a Dynamic World*, 3, 2017, passim; Kochel, T. R., Wilson, D. B./Mastrofski, S. D., "Effect of suspect race on officers' arrest decisions", *Criminology*, Volume 49, Issue 2, 2011, pp. 473–512. Mitchell, O./Caudy, M. S., "Examining racial disparities in drug arrests", *Justice Quarterly*, Volume 32, Issue 2, 2015, pp. 288–313; Kirk, D. S., "The neighborhood context of racial and ethnic disparities in arrest", *Demography*, 45, 2008, pp. 55–77.

flagitious arrests by age[244] or spirited off arrests by transgender[245] in the remit of algorithmic predictive policing.[246] Which should not strike anyone as odd: predictive policing[247]—and criminal justice in an overarching sense—should be much

---

[244] McCauley, E. J., "The cumulative probability of arrest by age 28 years in the United States by disability status, race/ethnicity, and gender", *American Journal of Public Health*, Volume 107, Issue 12, 2017, pp. 1977–1981.

[245] Stotzer, R. L., "Law enforcement and criminal justice personnel interactions with transgender people in the United States: A literature review", *Aggression and Violent Behavior*, Volume 19, Issue 3, 2014, 263–277; Furman, E./Singh, A. K./Darko, N. A./Wilson, C. L., "Activism, intersectionality, and community psychology: The way in which Black Lives Matter Toronto helps us to examine white supremacy in Canada's LGBTQ community. Community Psychology in Global Perspective, Volume 4, Issue 2, 34–54. See: Part IV, Chap. 4, Sects. 4.10.1 to 4.10.6 of this book (on biased algorithmic risk assessment in criminal procedure law settings, with a sharper focus on COMPAS). See: Part IV, Chap. 4, Sects. 4.1 to 4.1.1 of this book (on biased predictive policing).

[246] Saunders, J., Hunt, P., & Hollywood, J. S., "Predictions put into practice: A quasi-experimental evaluation of Chicago's predictive policing pilot", *Journal of Experimental Criminology*, Volume 12, Issue 3, 2016, pp. 347–371. See: Part IV, Chap. 4, Sects. 4.1 to 4.1.1 of this book (on biased predictive policing).

[247] Meijer, A., & Wessels, M., "Predictive policing: Review of benefits and drawbacks", *International Journal of Public Administration*, Volume 42, Issue 12, 2019, pp. 1031–1039. See also: See: Hu, Margaret, "From the National Surveillance State to the Cybersurveillance State", *The Annual Review of Law and Social Science*, Volume 13, 2017, p. 166 (argues that ubiquitous and ever-present surveillance of socially undesirables remains at a pitch of degradation of fundamental rights in that Artificial Intelligence-embedded technologies—propelled by tools like Social Radar and Total Information Awareness, TIA, can capture "a *pictorial depiction of the comprehensive cybersurveillance anticipated through the Social Radar system, which anticipated the full integration of drone footage, biometrric data signatures, econometrics, and other intelligence sources to achieve higher-order cybersurveillance inferences. Social Radar appears to trace its philosophical origins to TIA.* The development of TIA after the 9/11 terrorist attacks was guided under the leadership of the newly created Information Awareness Office within DARPA (Harris 2012, Murray 2010). Within this office, TIA was an effort led by retired Navy Vice Admiral John M. Poindexter (Murray 2010), who served as a national security advisor to President Reagan (Harris 2012). *TIA was informed by a philosophy of "predictive policing," which "focuses not on collecting evidence about actual wrongdoing but on the broad collection of information about everyday activities with the intention of detecting (and preventing) future behavior*" (Murray 2010, p. 5). Congress officially defunded TIA in late 2003 (Murray 2010, Slobogin 2008, USA Today 2003). *Experts have nonetheless noted that remnants of the TIA program and its philosophy have persisted*"). Italics added. See: Part IV, Chap. 4, Sects. 4.1 to 4.1.1 of this book (on biased predictive policing).

more than a canopied tool to stamp out the socially[248] undesirables[249] after all.[250] Books like this one should spearhead, and be at the forefront of, efforts to lead the way towards *Algorithmic Common Good*[251] that allows you, dear reader, to sleep peacefully at night.

§§ *Algorithmic fairness*, albeit a bedazzling gift, is not without sizable hurdles though. The most prominent of which is that Artificial Intelligence, to produce algorithmic fairness, must be fundamentally *interpretable*[252] by citizens.[253] Intent and causation—agreed-upon benchmarks to gauge the extent to which the computer-generated conclusions are fair and reasonable—are utterly incapable of explaining the complex world of AI-powered black box.[254]

---

[248] Darden, T. M., & Godsay, S., "Hands up, don't shoot: A community psychology perspective on unarmed police shootings of Black people in America", *Community Psychology in Global Perspective*, Volume 4, Issue 2, 2018, pp. 9–21. See: Part IV, Chap. 4, Sects. 4.1 to 4.1.1 of this book (on biased predictive policing).

[249] Monk, E. P., "The color of punishment: African Americans, skin tone, and the criminal justice system", *Ethnic and Racial Studies*, Volume 42, Issue 10, 2019, pp. 1593–1612; Agung-Igusti, R. P., "Raced and risky subjects: The interplay of racial and managerial ideologies as an expression of "colorblind" racism", *American Journal of Community Psychology*, Volume 73, 2024, passim; Alexander, M., *The new Jim Crow: Mass incarceration in the age of colorblindness*, The New Press, 2012. See: Part IV, Chap. 4, Sects. 4.10.1 to 4.10.6 of this book (on biased algorithmic risk assessment in criminal procedure law settings, with a sharper focus on COMPAS). See: Part IV, Chap. 4, Sects. 4.1 to 4.1.1 of this book (on biased predictive policing).

[250] Schenwar, M./Law, V., *Prison by any other name: The harmful consequences of popular reforms*, 2020, The New Press.

[251] See: Part V, Chap. 5, Sects. 5.2 to 5.6.2.1 of this book (on the thing-centred algorithmic decision-making propelled by a *Controllable* and *Interpretable* Machine Learning that weeds out *Algorithmic Dictatorship* and secures *Algorithmic Common Good*).

[252] See: Part V, Chap. 5, Sects. 5.8 to 5.8.5 of this book (on the five laws to interpret algorithmic decision-making).

[253] Citron, Danielle K., "Technological Due Process", *Washington University Law Review*, Volume 85, 2008, pp. 1249–1253 ("Computer programs seamlessly combine rulemaking and individual adjudications without the critical procedural protections owed either of them."). See: Part V, Chap. 5, Sects. 5.2 to 5.6.2.1 of this book (on the thing-centred algorithmic decision-making propelled by a *Controllable* and *Interpretable* Machine Learning that weeds out *Algorithmic Dictatorship* and secures *Algorithmic Common Good*).

[254] As hinted above, algorithms make their inferences and draw their conclusions in a way difficult to understand, even for the cohort of programmers that designed them. This is deemed *black box*, that further enhances the shroud of mystery under which algorithms are cloaked. See, for a compelling account of AI black box: Ver: Bathaee, Yavar, "The Artificial Intelligence Black Box and the Failure of Intent and Causation", *Harvard Journal of Law and Technology*, n.º 37, 2018, p. 901 (adduces that "*one possible reason AI may be a black box to humans is that it relies on machine-learning algorithms that internalize data in ways that are not easily audited or understood by humans (…) "first, a lack may arise from the complexity of the algorithm's structure, such as with deep neural network, which consists of thousands of artificial neurons working together in a diffuse way to solve a problem. This reason for AI being a black box is referred to as "complexity". Second, the lack of transparency may arise because the AI is using a machine-learning algorithm that relies on geometric relationships that humans cannot visualize, such as with support vector machines.*

§§ For a simple reason: machine learning[255]—and, especially, deep learning[256]—is a world of hidden *correlations* embedded in the data that has been fed into the computer-generated algorithms, as opposed to a world of *causation* that currently reigns[257] in the legal arena.[258] To bypass/circumvent this perceived

---

This reason for AI being a black box is referred to as "dimensionality"). Italics added. See also: Mittelstadt, B./Russell, C./Watcher, S., "Explaining explanations in AI", *Proceedings of Fairness, Accountability, and Transparency (FAT) (ACM)*, 2019, passim. But see: Pearl, Judea, *Causality*, 2nd edition, Cambridge, Cambridge University Press, 2009 (on the fundamental tenets of causality). But see: Kilbertus, Niki/Carulla, Mateo Rojas/Parascandolo, Giambattista/Hardt, Moritz/Janzing, Dominik/ Schoellkopf, Bernhard, "Avoiding Discrimination through Causal Reasoning", *Advances in Neural Information Processing Systems*, I. Guyon, U. V. Luxburg, S. Bengio, H. Wallach, R. Fergus, S. Vishwanathan, and R. Garnett (Eds.), Vol. 30. Curran Associates, Inc., 2017, pp. 656–666 (arguing that is feasible to avoiding discrimination through a granular and fine-grained causal reasoning). See: Part V, Chap. 5, Sects. 5.2 to Sect. 5.6.2.1 of this book (on the thing-centred algorithmic decision-making propelled by a *Controllable* and *Interpretable* Machine Learning that weeds out *Algorithmic Dictatorship* and secures *Algorithmic Common Good*. It is worth recalling that the **thing-centred algorithmic decision-making** seeks to unwind the perils arising out of the lack of theoretical underpinnings facing the **human-centred algorithmic decision-making**, as extensively fleshed out Part III, Chap. 3, Sects. 3.4.3 to 3.4.4 of this book).

255 Machine learning "involves computer algorithms *that have the ability to "learn" or improve in performance over time on some task*". Ver: Surden, Harry, "Machine Learning and Law", in: *Washington Law Review*, Volume 89, 2014, pp. 87 e ss; Murphy, Kevin P., *Machine Learning: A Probabilistic Perspective (Adaptive Computation and Machine Learning series)*, Massachusetts, The MIT Press, 2012, pp. 1–1104. Machine learning "*attempts to combine deductive, inductive, and abductive reasoning to make person-like reasoning in AI Entities possible. Machine-learning AI Entities initially learn in the same way a human child learns. First, they notice details and patterns in shapes, sounds, and behaviors*; then put them together to distinguish one person from another, or a dog from a cat. Eventually, the AI can recognize and identify" common objects. See: Hutto-Schultz, Jess, "Dicitur Ex Machina: Artificial Intelligence and the Hearsay Rule", *George Mason Law Review*, Volume 27, n. ° 2, 2020, pp. 684–718 (689).

256 See: Goodfellow, Ian/Bengio, Yoshua/Courville, Aaron, *Deep Learning (Adaptive Computation and Machine Learning series)*, Massachusetts, The MIT Press, 2016, pp. 1–800 ("*Deep learning is a form of machine learning that enables computers to learn from experience and understand the world in terms of a hierarchy of concepts.* Because *the computer gathers knowledge from experience, there is no need for a human computer operator to formally specify all the knowledge that the computer needs. The hierarchy of concepts allows the computer to learn complicated concepts by building them out of simpler ones; a graph of these hierarchies would be many layers deep*"). See also: Chollet, François, *Deep Learning with Python*, Shelter Island, New York, Manning, 2017, pp. 1–384; Franceschetti, Donald R. (Editor), *Principles of Robotics and Artificial Intelligence*, New York, Salem Press, 2018, pp. 1–399. Deep learning is capable of recommending meaningful legal materials. See: Huang, Zihan/Low/Charles/Teng, Mengqiu/Zhang, Hongyi/Ho, Daniel E./ Krass, Mark S. et al., "Context-Aware Legal Citation Recommendation Using Deep Learning", *Proceedings of the 18th ACM Internationational Conference on Artificial Intelligence and Law*, 79, 2021.

257 Pearl, Judea, *Causality*, 2nd edition, Cambridge, Cambridge University Press, 2009.

258 Bibal, A., Lognoul, M/De Streel/A., Frénay B, "Legal requirements on explainability in machine learning", *Artificial Intelligence and Law*, Volume 29, 2021, pp. 149–169; Ashley, KD, *Artificial Intelligence and Legal Analytics: New Tools for Law Practice in the Digital Age*, Cambridge, Cambridge University Press, 2017.

quandary,[259] poignant calls have been made to keep «humans in the loop»[260] as far as the emission of automated decisions is concerned.[261]

§§ Notwithstanding, the turn towards *Algorithmic Common Good*[262] entails, and fundamentally requires, a shift away from a legal analysis that haphazardly seeks to uncover/unlock/unveil/unearth causal connections[263] between inputs and outputs.[264] This book therefore proposes that *Algorithmic Common Good* must shift its gaze

---

[259] See: Chap. 4 of this book.

[260] Saxena, Devansh/Badillo-Urquiola, Karla/Wisniewski, Pamela J./Guha, Shion, "A Human-Centered Review of the Algorithms Used Within the U.S. Child Welfare System", *2020 Proceedings of Conference on Human Factors in Computing Systems*, Apr. 2020, 2020, passim.

[261] Almada, M., "Human intervention in automated decision-making: toward the construction of contestable systems", *Proceedings of the Seventeenth International Conference on Artificial Intelligence and Law*, 2019, pp. 2–11; Williams, Rebecca, "Rethinking Administrative Law for Algorithmic Decision-Making", *Oxford Journal of Legal Studies*, Volume 42, 2021, pp. 468 e ff and passim.

[262] See: Part V, Chap. 5, Sects. 5.2 to 5.6.2.1 of this book (on the thing-centred algorithmic decision-making propelled by a *Controllable* and *Interpretable* Machine Learning that weeds out *Algorithmic Dictatorship* and secures *Algorithmic Common Good*).

[263] See: Kilbertus, Niki/Carulla, Mateo Rojas/Parascandolo, Giambattista/Hardt, Moritz/Janzing, Dominik/ Schoellkopf, Bernhard, "Avoiding Discrimination through Causal Reasoning", *Advances in Neural Information Processing Systems*, I. Guyon, U. V. Luxburg, S. Bengio, H. Wallach, R. Fergus, S. Vishwanathan, and R. Garnett (Eds.), Vol. 30. Curran Associates, Inc., 2017, pp. 656–666 (arguing that is feasible to avoiding discrimination through a granular and fine-grained causal reasoning).

[264] Gillis, Talia B., "The Input Data Fallacy", *Minnesota Law Review*, Volume 106, 2022, pp. 1176–1263 (p. 1257).

downstream to the predictions[265] (outputs)[266] made by computer-generated algorithms[267] to usher in, and pave the way to, a new[268] era[269] of automation[270]

[265] See: Part V, Chap. 5, Sects. 5.1.5.2.2 to 5.1.5.2.2.1.4 of this book (on the fundamental shift away from causation to correlations in algorithmic decision-making).

[266] Chander, Anupam, "The Racist Algorithm?", *Michigan Law Review*, Volume 115, 2017, pp. 1023–1039 ("The focus on outcomes rather than how an algorithm operates seems especially useful as algorithms become increasingly complicated, even able to modify themselves."). See: Part V, Chap. 5, Sects. 5.1.5.2.2 to 5.1.5.2.2.1.4 of this book (on the fundamental shift away from causation to correlations in algorithmic decision-making).

[267] Gillis, Talia B., "The Input Data Fallacy", *cit.* p. 1257.

[268] In Italian doctrine, on the challenges law may face in the forthcoming future: Irti, Natalino, *Un Diritto Incalcolabile*, Torino, G. Giappichelli Editore, 2016, passim.

[269] See: Susskind, Richard, "The Future of Courts", in: *Remote Courts*, Volume 6, n.° 5, July/August 2020, 2020, pp. 1 e ss ("The uptake of various technologies, especially video, was accelerated in the justice systems of numerous countries. There remain some skeptics and critics, but in light of the experience during the crisis, there is certainly greater acceptance now than in February 2020—amongst lawyers, judges, officials, and court users—that judicial and court work might be undertaken very differently in years to come. Minds have been opened and changed over the past few months. Many assumptions have been swept aside. We remain in an era of threat, with risks of barely functioning court systems, greatly reduced access to justice, and, in turn, a potential weakening of the rule of law. We are also in an era of opportunity—the chance to build boldly on the shift of attitude and on demonstrable recent successes with technology, and to put in place improved, sustainable court services that are much more accessible than today's").

[270] Weizenbaum, Joseph, *Computer Power and Human Reason: From Judgment to Calculation*, 1st edition, New York, W. H. Freeman & Co, 1976, pp. 1–300 (227) ("examines the sources of the computer's powers and offers evaluative explorations of what computers can do, cannot do, and should not be employed to do") (this founding father of Artificial Intelligence presciently noted that we should not entrust Artificial Intelligence-embedded technologies with with "tasks that demand wisdom"). Italics added. The approval of rental applications is arguably one of those tasks that should never be entrusted to machines). More on this on Part IV, Chap. 4, Sects. 4.4 to 4.4.2.1 of this book. See: Part V, Chap. 5, Sect. 5.7.2 of this book (on law number two to control algorithmic decision-making, which mandates that black box models must not be entrusted with the task of making high stake decisions—v.g. health and freedom).

brimming with both procedural fairness[271] and algorithmic accountability.[272] More on this later.[273]

§§ *Algorithmic Common Good*—a byproduct of a much-acclaimed evidence-based approach to law—shies away from whimsical intuitions,[274] which run afoul of a

---

[271] Tyler, Tom, "What is procedural justice?", *Law and Society Review*, Volume 22, 1988, pp. 301–355; Tyler, Tom, "The Psychology of procedural justice: A test of the group value model.", in: *Journal of Personality and Social Psychology*, Volume 57, 1989, 830–838; Tyler, Tom, *Why people obey the law*, New Haven, CT, Yale University Press, 1990, 1–320 (premising his conclusions on a sound body of empirical research, the author states that "*people obey the law if they believe it's legitimate*, not because they fear punishment-this is the startling conclusion of Tom Tyler's classic study. Tyler suggests that lawmakers and law enforcers would do much better to make legal systems worthy of respect than to try to instill fear of punishment. *He finds that people obey law primarily because they believe in respecting legitimate authority*"). Italics added. Tyler, Tom, "Legitimizing unpopular public policies: Does procedure matter?", *Zeitschrift für Reichssoziologie*, Volume 14, 1993, pp. 47–54; Tyler, Tom, "Governing amid diversity: can fair decision-making procedures bridge competing public interests and values?", *Law and Society Review*, Volume 28, 1994, pp. 701–722; Tyler, Tom, "Psychological models of the justice motive", *Journal of Personality and Social Psychology*, Volume 67, 1994, 850–863; Tyler, Tom, "The relationship of the outcome and procedural fairness: How does knowing the outcome influences judgments about the procedure?", *Social Justice and Research*, Volume 9, 1996, pp. 311–325; Tyler, Tom, "Compliance with intellectual property laws", in: *Journal of International Law and Politics*, Volume 28, 1997, pp. 101–116; Tyler, Tom, "Justice and power in civil dispute processing", in: *Sociolegal studies*, Evanston, IL, Northwestern University Press, 1997; Tor, A./Gazal-Ayal, O./Garcia, S. M., "Fairness and willingness to accept plea bargain offers", *Journal of Empirical Legal Studies*, Volume 7, 2010, pp. 97–116 (drawing upon a body of empirical evidence the authors made an the interplay between overall fairness of the proceedings and the disputant's willingness to accept plea bargain offers made by the Government). But see: Guha, Neel/Henderson, Peter/Zambrano, Diego, "Vulnerabilities in Discovery Tech", *Harvard Journal of Law and Technology*, Volume 35, 2022, passim.

[272] Zarsky, Tal, "Transparency in Data Mining: From Theory to Practice", *Discrimination and Privacy in the Information Society: Data Mining and Profiling in Large Databases*, Bart Custers et al. eds., Belin, Springer, 2013; Kroll, Joshua A. et al., "Accountable Algorithms", *University of Pennsylvania Law Review*, Volume 165, 2017, passim. But see: Balkin, Jack, "Constitution in the National Surveillance State", *Minnesota Law Review*, Volume 93, 2008, p. 13 (*data mining* allows inferences not only about the direct subject of surveillance, but about other people with whom they live, work and communicate"); Pearl, Judea, "Causal inference in statistics: An overview", *Statistics Surveys*, Volume 3, 2009, pp. 96–146. But see: Pedreshi, Dino/Ruggieri, Salvatore/Turini, Franco, "Discrimination-aware Data Mining", *Proceedings of the 14th ACM SIGKDD International Conference on Knowledge Discovery and Data Mining (Las Vegas, Nevada, USA), ACM*, 2008, pp. 560–568 (arguing that one should shift its gaze downstream by putting in place discrimination-aware algorithmic tools while performing data mining).

[273] See: Part V, Chap. 5, Sects. 5.2 to 5.6.2.1 of this book (on the thing-centred algorithmic decision-making propelled by a *Controllable* and *Interpretable* Machine Learning that weeds out *Algorithmic Dictatorship* and secures *Algorithmic Common Good*. It is worth recalling that the **thing-centred algorithmic decision-making** seeks to unwind the perils arising out of the lack of theoretical underpinnings facing the **human-centred algorithmic decision-making**, as extensively fleshed out Part III, Chap. 3, Sects. 3.4.3 to 3.4.4 of this book).

[274] Tyler, Tom, "Methodology in Legal Research", in: *Utrecht Law Review*, Volume 13, Issue 3, 2017, pp. 130–131 ("*Accurate facts plus good legal rules lead to substantive justice.* This is the normative framework of right and wrong defined by traditional legal analysis. *Risk analysis is a nice example of the benefits of empiricism because studies suggest that the use of empirical methods to*

sought-after objectivity[275] that should pervade the realm of[276] «technological due process».[277] That is the only way forward when it comes to bestow *trust in the law*[278] upon citizens. Unsurprisingly, procedural justice[279]—a beacon of hope in the age of

---

assess future dangerousness is more accurate than is the use of human intuition. It is better to use a formula when making a legal decision that involves estimates of someone's likely future conduct than it is to rely upon the impressions of judges or prosecutors" (...) "*The legal system relies on predictions about people's likely future behaviour at many points in the system*: pretrial detention; sentencing; parole and probation; etc. And it has been used with a variety of special populations, including juveniles; the mentally ill; and sexual predators. A key reason to use such quantitative methods is that they are better able to predict future behaviour and as a consequence the many points in the system at which judgments are made—pre-trial detention; sentencing; parole—are better able to enact justice for both the innocent and the guilty. *The focus by social scientists upon helping to identify and use facts in ways that produce more accurate decisions fits well with the argument that the aims of justice are best served when they are based upon accurate factual information. Accuracy, in turn is enhanced by the use of empirical methods. Facts are sought that can guide the application of normative legal principles*"). Italics added.

[275] But see: Benjamin, Ruha, *Race After Technology: Abolitionist Tools for the New Jim Code*, New York, Polity, 2019, pp. 1–172 (7) (discussing that Artificial Intelligence-embedded technologies are viewed as iron-clad tools of objectivity and devoid of any biases whatsoever). Ruha Benjamin contends that "the employment of new technologies that reflect and reproduce existing inequities but that are promoted and perceived as more objective or progressive than the discriminatory systems of a previous era").

[276] But see: Hamilton, Melissa, "The sexist algorithm", *Behavioral Sciences and the Law*, Volume 37, Issue 2, Special Issue: the Use of Statistics in Criminal Cases, March–April 2019, 2019, pp. 1 and ff ("*Algorithmic risk assessment tools are informed by scientific research concerning which factors are predictive of recidivism and thus support the evidence-based practice movement in criminal justice.* Automated assessments of individualized risk (low, medium, high) *permit officials to make more effective management decisions. Computer-generated algorithms appear to be objective and neutral. But are these algorithms actually fair? The focus herein is on gender equity.* Studies confirm that women typically have far lower recidivism rates than men. *This differential raises the question of how well algorithmic outcomes fare in terms of predictive parity by gender.* This essay reports original research using a large dataset of offenders who were scored on the popular risk assessment tool COMPAS. *Findings indicate that COMPAS performs reasonably well at discriminating between recidivists and non-recidivists for men and women. Nonetheless, COMPAS algorithmic outcomes systemically overclassify women in higher risk groupings. Multiple measures of algorithmic equity and predictive accuracy are provided to support the conclusion that this algorithm is sexist.*"). Italics added. See: Part IV, Chap. 4, Sects. 4.10.1 to 4.10.6 of this book (on biased algorithmic risk assessment in criminal procedure law settings, with a sharper focus on COMPAS). See: Part IV, Chap. 4, Sects. 4.1 to 4.1.1 of this book (on biased predictive policing).

[277] Citron, Danielle K., "Technological Due Process", *Washington University Law Review*, Volume 85, 2008, pp. 1249–1253 ("Computer programs seamlessly combine rulemaking and individual adjudications without the critical procedural protections owed either of them."). See: Part V, Chap. 5, Sects. 5.7 to 5.7.5 of this book (on the five laws to control algorithmic decision-making). See: Part V, Chap. 5, Sects. 5.8 to 5.8.5 of this book (on the five laws to interpret algorithmic decision-making).

[278] Tyler, Tom, *Trust in the Law*, New York, NY: Russell-Sage, 2002, passim.

[279] See: Zimmerman, Nourit/Tyler, Tom R., "Between Access to Counsel and Access to Justice: A Psychological Perspective", *Fordham Urban Law Journal*, Volume 37, 2010, pp. 473–488 (contends that "evaluations about neutrality, *trust*, and respect for the legal system as a whole"—satisfaction with the *procedural fairness* and *procedural justice* will not lag far behind); Tyler, Tom R./Lind, Edgar Allan, "Procedural justice", *Handbook of law and social science*, J. Sanders/V.L. Hamilton

Algorithmic Dictatorship[280] that looms large[281]—lies at heart of a «technological due process»[282] that should breed legitimization[283] to automated decisions.

(Eds.), New York, Plenum Press, 2001, pp. 65–92; Tyler, Tom R./Smith, H. J./Huo, Y. J., "Member diversity and leadership effectiveness: Procedural justice, social identity, and group dynamics", *Advances in group processes*, B. Markovsky (Ed.), Greenwich, CT: JAI Press, Volume 13, 1996, pp. 33–68; Tyler, Tom R./Lind, Edgar Allan/Huo, Yuen J., "Cultural Values and Authority Relations: The Psychology of Conflict Resolution Across Cultures", in: *Psychology, Public Policy and Law*, Volume 6, n.º 4, 2000, pp. 1138–1163 (parsing the relationship between high and low levels of power distance values and the relational model of authority); Leung, K./Lind, Edgar Allan, "Procedural justice and culture: Effects of culture, gender, and investigator status on procedural preferences", *Journal of Personality and Social Psychology*, Volume 50, 1986, pp. 1134–1140; Leung, K./Morris, K. W., "Justice through the lens of culture and ethnicity", *Handbook of Law and Social Science: Justice*, Sanders, J./Hamilton, V. L., (Eds.), New York, Plenum, 2001, pp. 343–378; Lind, Edgar Allan/ Tyler, Tom R., *The social psychology of procedural justice*, New York, Plenum Press, 1988, passim; Lind, Edgar Allan/ Tyler, Tom R./Huo, Y.J., "Procedural context and culture: Variation in the antecedents of procedural justice judgments", *Journal of Personality and Social Psychology*, Volume 73, 1997, pp. 767–780.

280 See: Part IV, Chap. 4, Sects. 4 to 4.10.6 of this book (on Algorithmic Dictatorship and its chilling effect on democracy).

281 *Tech, Bias and Housing Initiative, the Promise and Perils of Residential Proptech, Year 1, Research Summary Report, April 2023, TechEquity Collaborative*, p. 10, available at: https://techequity.us/wp-content/uploads/2023/04/TBHI-Y1-Research-Summary-Report.pdf (28.11.2024). ("**Opaque, Predictive Algorithms Determine Who Gets What Housing Unlike Analog Models**, *Algorithmic Tenant Screening Tools Predict Future Behavior To Determine Housing Access As landlord tech took hold, more property managers of all sizes came to rely on it to interface with tenants. One key feature of landlord tech is the use of algorithms to screen rental applicants and assess their suitability as tenants. The tenant screening industry, which pulls a wide array of information about potential tenants to inform landlords' decisions, is now valued at $1.3 billion with as many as two thousand screening companies vying for market share.*10 11 *Such companies include Equifax, TransUnion, and Experian (commonly known as "The Big Three"), as well as smaller startup companies that apply algorithms to make those determinations faster*"). Italics added.

282 Citron, Danielle K., "Technological Due Process", *Washington University Law Review*, Volume 85, 2008, pp. 1249–1253 ("Computer programs seamlessly combine rulemaking and individual adjudications without the critical procedural protections owed either of them."). See: Part V, Chap. 5, Sects. 5.7 to 5.7.5 of this book (on the five laws to control algorithmic decision-making). See: Part V, Chap. 5, Sects. 5.8 to 5.8.5 of this book (on the five laws to interpret algorithmic decision-making).

283 Tyler, Tom R., "Psychological perspectives on legitimacy and legitimation", in: *Annual Review of Psychology*, Volume 57, 2006, pp. 375–400 (on the role that perceived legitimacy plays in everyday life); Tyler, Tom R., *Why people cooperate: The role of social motivations*, Princeton, New Jersey, Princeton University Press, 2011; Robbins, J. M./M.T. Ford/L.E. Tetrick, "Perceived unfairness and employee health: A meta-analytic integration", in: *Journal of Applied Psychology*, Volume 97, 2012, pp. 235–272; Tyler, Tom R., "What is procedural justice? Criteria used by citizens to assess the fairness of legal procedures", *Law and Society Review*, Volume 22, 1988, pp. 103–135 (on the interplay between fairness of legal procedures and procedural justice. Unsurprisingly, the lack of fairness of legal procedures impacts the procedural justice -or the lack thereof -); Sunshine, J./Tyler, Tom R., "The role of procedural justice and legitimacy in shaping public support for policing", *Law & Society Review*, Volume 37, 2003, pp. 513–548 (on the role of procedural justice to enhance/boost legitimacy); Bies, Robert J., "Are Procedural Justice and Interactional Justice

§§ However, the unshattered hope that spurs the potential of *Algorithmic Common Good*[284] to instil trust upon the «technological due process»[285] must not overshadow the assertion according to which the pendulum may have already swung too far. This time around, the matrix in which the Rule of Law[286] rests upon may well wobble after all. Take the example of deep learning cutting-edge techniques[287] which have spawned Invasive Brain-Computer Interfaces[288], that are fundamentally brain implants.[289]

§§ Leveraging on the «extended mind thesis»,[290] the fourth industrial revolution brought about a mesmerizing promise: the scientific project that long sought to

---

Conceptually Distinct?", *Handbook of Organizational Justice*, Greenberg, Jerald/Colquitt, Jason, (Editors), New Jersey, Lawrence Erlbaum Associates Publishers, 2005, pp. 85–86 (arguing that a respectful treatment is an important part of, and the linchpin of a much-needed, procedural justice, which also plays an pivotal role in the remit of interactional justice).

[284] See: Part V, Chap. 5, Sects. 5.2 to 5.6.2.1 of this book (on the thing-centred algorithmic decision-making propelled by a *Controllable* and *Interpretable* Machine Learning that weeds out *Algorithmic Dictatorship* and secures *Algorithmic Common Good*).

[285] Citron, Danielle K., "Technological Due Process", *Washington University Law Review*, Volume 85, 2008, pp. 1249–1253.

[286] See: Sempill, J.A., "Ruler's Sword, Citizen's Shield: The Rule of Law and the Constitution of Power", *Journal of Law and Politics*, Volume 31, 2018, pp. 333 ff; McArthur, N., "Laws Not Men: Hume's Distinction Between Barbarous and Civilized Government", *Hume Studies*, Volume 31, 2005, pp. 123 ff; Stromseth, J./Wippman, D./Brooks, R., *Can Might Make Rights? Building the Rule of Law After Military Interventions.* Cambridge: Cambridge University Press, 2006, pp. 28 ff; Humphreys, S., *Theatre of the Rule of Law: Transnational Legal Intervention in Theory and* Practice. Cambridge: Cambridge University Press, 2020, passim; Farrall, J./Charlesworth, H. (eds), *Strengthening the Rule of Law Through the UN Security* Council. Abingdon: Routledge, 2018; Rajagopal, B., "Invoking the Rule of Law in Post-Conflict Rebuilding: A Critical Examination", *William and Mary Law Review*, Volume 49, 2008, pp. 1347 ff; Trubek, D. M./Santos (eds), *The New Law and Development: A Critical Appraisal.* Cambridge: Cambridge University Press, 2012, passim (all essays converge in one direction: the rule of law—chiefly its reinstatement—is paramount despite gruesome circumstance).

[287] Schirrmeister, RT/Springenberg, JT/Fiederer, LDJ, et al., "Deep learning with convolutional neural networks for EEG decoding and visualization", *Human Brain Mapp.*, Volume 38, Issue 11, 2017, pp. 5391–5420. See: Part II, Chap. 2, Sects. 2 and 2.1 of this book (for further insights on how the human brain and deep neural network function, respectively).

[288] See: Part III, Chap. 3, Sect. 3.4.5 of this book (on Critical Artificial Intelligence Studies, with a sharper focus on the harmful effects of Brain-Computer Interfaces). See: Lawhern VJ, Solon AJ, Waytowich NR, et al. Eegnet, "A compact convolutional neural network for EEG-based brain-computer interfaces", *J Neural Eng.*, Volume 15, Issue 5, 2018, passim.

[289] Ieracitano, C., Mammone, N./Bramanti, A., et al., "A convolutional neural network approach for classification of dementia stages based on 2D-spectral representation of EEG recordings", *Neurocomputing*, 2019, pp. 96–107.

[290] Clark, Andy/Chalmers, David, "The Extended Mind", *Analysis*, Volume 58, Issue 1, January 1998. Oxford: Oxford University Press, 1998, pp. 7–19 (passim). See: Part III, Chap. 3, Sect. 3.4.5 of this book (on Critical Artificial Intelligence Studies, with a sharper focus on the harmful effects of Brain-Computer Interfaces). See: Part III, Chap. 3, Sect. 3.5.10 of this book (on the functional aspects of Critical Artificial Intelligence Studies, with a sharper focus on the harmful effects of Artificial Intelligence-embedded technologies, namely, Brain-Computer Interfaces that can read and control your mind and behaviour).

accomplish a once mirific functional convergence between humans and machines would be finally off the ground.[291] Before long, science has accordingly made rapid strides in attaining such a «laudable» goal.[292]

§§ Drawing on a portmanteau of both machine learning algorithms[293] and deep learning algorithms,[294] there is an unremitting thrust to dovetail seamlessly a machine with a human being with a view to restore both physical[295] and mental prowess[296]

---

[291] See: Santos, Hugo Luz dos, *Inteligência Artificial e Processo Penal*, Braga, NovaCausa Edições Jurídicas, 2022. See: Santos, Hugo Luz dos, “"Brain-Computer Interfaces, Generative Artificial Intelligence (ChatGPT and Deep Fakes) and Criminal Procedure Law: what’s at stake?”, *Journal of Research in E. and Computer Science*, Edinburgh, United Kingdom, June 2024, Volume 2, 2024, pp. 39–78, which I will follow closely in this regard.

[292] See: Margaret, M. Jehosheba/Banu, N.M. Masoodhu, “Performance analysis of EEG based emotion recognition using deep learning models”, *Brain-Computer Interfaces*, Taylor & Francis Group, Volume 10, n. ° 2–4, 2023, pp. 79–98 (79) (“*recent advances in the field of Neuroscience Engineering have made the idea of interfacing the machine with human into a reality*. This has opened the door for restoring the physical and mental activities of human beings. This technology contributes for medical applications like rehabilitation, *medical equipment, and neuro feedback systems in control of prosthetics and diseases like Parkinson’s disease that uses deep brain simulation*”). Italics added. See also: Baker, B., Lansdell, B., & Kording, K. P., “Three aspects of representation in neuroscience”, *Trends in Cognitive Sciences*, 2022.

[293] Bălan O, Moise G, Petrescu L, et al., “Emotion classification based on biophysical signals and machine learning techniques”, *Symmetry* 2020, Issue 1, 2020, pp. 1–22.

[294] Yang Y./Sun, Y., “Facial expression recognition based on arousal-valence emotion model and deep learning method,” *Proc.—2017 Int. Conf. Computer Technol. Electron Commun, ICCTEC*, 2017, pp. 59–62; Li, M., Chen, “W. FFT-based deep feature learning method for EEG classification”, *Biomedical Signal Processing and Control*, 2021; Chao, H., Zhi, H., Dong, L., et al., “Recognition of Emotions Using Multichannel EEG Data and DBN-GC-Based Ensemble Deep Learning Framework”, *Computer Intelligence Neuroscience*, 2018; Garg, D, Verma, GK, “Emotion Recognition in Valence-Arousal Space from Multi-channel EEG data and Wavelet based Deep Learning Framework”, *Procedia Computer Science*, 2020, pp. 857–867.

[295] Tien-Thong Nguyen Do/Ngoc My Hanh Duong/Chin-Teng Lin, “Integrating Sensing Devices for Human-Brain Interfaces”, *More-than-Moore Devices and Integration for Semiconductors*, Iacopi, Francesca/Balestra, Francis (Editors), New York/Berlin, Springer, 2023, pp. 241–258 (“*Brain-computer interfaces (BCI) help users to interact with machines* via *brain activity and without the use of muscles. Among the many components of BCI frameworks, sensor technology helps to make the systems highly efficient and robust. As a source of input for BCI systems, sensors also provide high-quality signals that can support downstream tasks, such as noise removal and feature extraction*. This book chapter explores the fundamental concepts and configurations of the non-invasive sensor technology that are commonly used in BCI systems”). See: Part III, Chap. 3, Sect. 3.4.5 of this book (on Critical Artificial Intelligence Studies, with a sharper focus on the harmful effects of Brain-Computer Interfaces). See: Part III, Chap. 3, Sect. 3.5.10 of this book (on the functional aspects of Critical Artificial Intelligence Studies, with a sharper focus on the harmful effects of Artificial Intelligence-embedded technologies, namely, Brain-Computer Interfaces that can read and control your mind and behaviour).

[296] Gupta, Bishal Kumar/Koirala, Tawal Kumar/Rai, Jyoti/Panda, Baidyanath/Bhoi, Akash Kumar, “A Review of Brain-Computer Interface (BCI) System: Advancement and Applications”, *Enabling Person-Centric Healthcare Using Ambient Assistive Technology*, Barsocchi, Paolo/Parvathaneni, Naga Srinivasu/ Garg, Amik/Bhoi, Akash Kumar/ Palumbo, Filippo (Editors), New York/Berlin, Springer, 2023, pp. 199–226 (“Brain-Computer Interface (BCI) is a cutting-edge and diverse area of ongoing research based on neuroscience, signal processing, biomedical sensors, and hardware.

to those who have been deprived from them.[297] But these are hardly uplifting news. Sooner rather than later, you, dear reader, will be thrust headlong into a dystopian reality whereby your thoughts[298] will be at arms 'length just as buying groceries at the supermarket is.

§§ Brain-Computer Interfaces[299]—originally designed as a device to improve disabled people's quality of life[300]—are therefore poised to be converted into

---

Numerous ground-breaking studies have been conducted in this area over the last few decades. However, the BCI domain has yet to be the subject of a thorough examination. As a result, this study provides an in-depth analysis of the BCI issue"). See also: Baker, B., Lansdell, B., & Kording, K. P., "Three aspects of representation in neuroscience", *Trends in Cognitive Sciences*, 2022.

[297] Rao, RPN, *Brain-computer interfacing: An Introduction*, New York, USA: Cambridge University Press, 2013.

[298] See: Part III, Chap. 3, Sect. 3.5.10 of this book (on the functional aspects of Critical Artificial Intelligence Studies, with a sharper focus on the harmful effects of Artificial Intelligence-embedded technologies, namely, Brain-Computer Interfaces that can read and control your mind and behaviour).

[299] Bin, He/Han, Yuan/Jianjun, Meng/Shangkai, Gao, "Brain-Computer Interfaces", *Neural Engineering*, Bin, He (Editor), New York/Berlin, Springer, 2020, pp. 131–183 ("*Brain–computer interfaces (BCIs) have emerged as a novel technology that bridges the brain with external devices. BCIs have been developed to decode human's intention, leading to direct brain control of a computer or device without going through the neuromuscular pathway. Bidirectional brain–computer interfaces not only allow brain control but also open the door for modulating the central nervous system through neural interfacing. We review the concepts, principles, and various building blocks of BCIs, from signal acquisition, signal processing, feature extraction, feature translation, to device control, and various applications*. The performance assessment and challenges of BCIs are also discussed. Examples of noninvasive BCIs are discussed to aid readers for an in-depth understanding of the noninvasive BCI technology, although this chapter is aimed at providing a general introduction to brain–computer interfaces").

[300] See: Margaret, M. Jehosheba/Banu, N.M. Masoodhu, Performance analysis of EEG based emotion recognition using deep learning models, *cit.*, pp. 79–98 (79) ("quality life is essential for people with cognitive deficit, and when it seems difficult for them, they must be cared by caretakers. In order to provide such quality life to the those people, a study of human emotion is needed which in turn needs machine interface [2]. *Hence, affective computing is necessary to improve the quality of life as it studies about the devices that are capable of stimulating, processing, and identifying emotions* [3]. Autism kids are one such example where we need the services of affective computing to understand their emotion [4]."). Internal citations omitted. Italics added.

shady tools to collate/gauge thoughts,[301] emotions,[302] sentiments[303] and crime-related information[304,305] that would be otherwise inaccessible to the governments', rogue nations' or unscrupulous actors' prying eyes. But not just that though: Brain-Computer Interfaces[306] with the right settings, are amenable to control your mind.[307] Much to our dismay, an eerily dystopian world is unfolding before our very eyes.

---

301 Schirrmeister, RT/Springenberg, JT/Fiederer, LDJ, et al., "Deep learning with convolutional neural networks for EEG decoding and visualization", *Human Brain Mapp.*, Volume 38, Issue 11, 2017, pp. 5391–5420; Joshi, VM, Ghongade, RB, "IDEA: intellect database for emotion analysis using EEG signal", *J King Saud University Computer Inf Sci*, 2020;

302 Bo, Pan WZ/Zheng W., "Emotion Recognition Based on EEG using Generative Adversarial Nets and Convolutional Neural Network", *Comput Math Methods Med*, 2021; Houssein, EH/Hammad A., Ali AA, Human emotion recognition from EEG-based brain–computer interface using machine learning: a comprehensive review, London, Springer, 2022;

303 Priyadarshini I, Cotton C., "A novel LSTM–CNN–grid search-based deep neural network for sentiment analysis", *J Supercomputer*, Volume 77, Issue 12, 2021, pp. 13911–13932.

304 Sakhavi, S./Guan C./Yan S., "Learning temporal information for brain-computer interface using convolutional neural networks", *IEEE Trans Neural Netw Learning Systems*, Volume 29, Issue 11, 2018, 5619–5629; Jeon, E, Ko, W, Yoon, JS, et al., "Mutual information-driven subject-invariant and class-relevant deep representation learning in BCI", *IEEE Trans Neural Netw Learn Syst.*, Volume 34, Issue 2, 2021–Feb 2023, pp. 739–749.

305 Wronkiewicz, M., Larson E., Lee, AKC, "Leveraging anatomical information to improve transfer learning in brain–computer interfaces", *J Neural Eng.*, Volume 12, Issue 4, 2015, passim; Sakhavi, S./Guan C, "Convolutional neural network-based transfer learning and knowledge distillation using multi-subject data in motor imagery BCI", *8th International IEEE/EMBS Conference on Neural Engineering* (NER), Shanghai, China, 2017. See: Part III, Chap. 3, Sect. 3.4.5 of this book (on Critical Artificial Intelligence Studies, with a sharper focus on the harmful effects of Brain-Computer Interfaces). See: Part III, Chap. 3, Sect. 3.5.10 of this book (on the functional aspects of Critical Artificial Intelligence Studies, with a sharper focus on the harmful effects of Artificial Intelligence-embedded technologies, namely, Brain-Computer Interfaces that can read and control your mind and behaviour).

306 Graimann, Bernhard/Pfurtscheller, Gert/ (Editors), *Brain-Computer Interfaces—Revolutionizing Human-Computer Interaction*, New York/Berlin, Springer, 2010, pp. 1–357 ("*A brain-computer interface (BCI) establishes a direct output channel between the human brain and external devices. BCIs infer user intent* via *direct measures of brain activity and thus enable communication and control without movement.* This book, authored by experts in the field, provides an accessible introduction to the neurophysiological and signal-processing background required for BCI, presents state-of-the-art non-invasive and invasive approaches, gives an overview of current hardware and software solutions, and reviews the most interesting as well as new, emerging BCI applications. The book is intended not only for students and young researchers, but also for newcomers and other readers from diverse backgrounds keen to learn about this vital scientific endeavour"). Italics added.

307 Wolpaw, JR/Birbaumer, N./McFarland, DJ, et al., "Brain-computer interfaces for communication and control", *Clin Neurophysiology*, Volume 113, Issue 6, 2002, pp. 767–791. See: Part III, Chap. 3, Sect. 3.4.5 of this book (on Critical Artificial Intelligence Studies, with a sharper focus on the harmful effects of Brain-Computer Interfaces). See: Part III, Chap. 3, Sect. 3.5.10 of this book (on the functional aspects of Critical Artificial Intelligence Studies, with a sharper focus on the harmful effects of Artificial Intelligence-embedded technologies, namely, Brain-Computer Interfaces that can read and control your mind and behaviour).

§§ Brain-Computer Interfaces (BCI),[308] as hinted above, spottily mirror the trotted-out theory of «extended mind thesis»[309] against the backdrop of which humans and machines should be weaved together. It is neither flabbergasting nor flummoxing that the sought-after fusion between humans and machines will accordingly create a new set of challenges[310] for both Rule of Law and Criminal Procedure Law. A war for everyone's brains[311] and underlying wired emotions[312]—under the gloss/veneer/facade of intellectual[313] enhancement[314,315]—is underway and yet few to none have come to terms with the fact that Brain-Computer Interfaces is a game-changer in the remit of law (in general) and criminal procedure law (in particular).

§§ Criminal procedure law, in turn, is likely to be a central battleground on which the boundaries of «technological due process»[316] and invidiousness will be fiercely fought. Red lines are accordingly in dire need of being drawn or an unavoidable clash between titans («technological due process» and a shady social engineering) may otherwise occur.

§§ This topic should neither be downplayed nor forsaken: there is so much at stake in this regard. Starting with your beloved freedom of thought[317] that no government has yet got a hold of. The sway of Brain-Computer Interfaces in the purview of law

---

308 Li, Y, Guo, L, Liu Y, et al., "A temporal-spectral-based squeeze-and- excitation feature fusion network for motor imagery EEG decoding", *IEEE Trans Neural System Rehabil Eng.*, Volume 29, 2021, pp. 1534–1545.

309 Clark, Andy/Chalmers, David, "The Extended Mind", *Analysis*, Volume 58, Issue 1, January 1998. Oxford: Oxford University Press, 1998, pp. 7–19 (passim).

310 Amongst which stands arguably "biometric privacy". See: Levin, Daniel, "Face the Fact, or is the Face a Fact?: Biometric Privacy in Publicly Available Information", *Fordham Intellectual Media and Entertainment Law Journal*, Volume 32, 2022, pp. 1010–1015.

311 Called "Neural Battlefield". See: Dunker, Anders, "The Neural Battlefield of Cognitive Capitalism", *L. A. Review of Books*, 2020, passim.

312 Steinert, Steffen/Orsolya, Friedrich, "Wired Emotions: Ethical Issues of Affective Brain-Computer Interfaces", *Science and Engineering Ethics*, Volume 26, 2020, pp. 351 and ff and passim.

313 See: Castanheira, Jason da Silva/Perez, Hector Domingo Orozco/Misic, Bratislav/Baillet, Sylvain, "Brief Segments of Neurophysiological Activity Enable Individual Differentiation", *Nature Commc'ns*, Volume 12, 2021, pp. 1 and ff and passim.

314 See: Polizzotto, Riccardo Nicola/Ramakrishnan, Nithya/Cho, Y. Raymond, "Is It Possible to Improve Working Memory with Prefrontal tDCS? Bridging Currents to Working Memory Models", *Frontiers of Psychology*, Volume 1, Issue 1, 2020, pp. 11 and ff and passim.

315 See: Alimardani, Maryam/Hiraki, Kazuo, "Passive Brain-Computer Interfaces for Enhanced Human–Robot Interaction", *Frontiers of Robotics and Artificial Intelligence*, Volume 7, 2020, pp. 1 and ff and passim.

316 Citron, Danielle K., "Technological Due Process", *Washington University Law Review*, Volume 85, 2008, pp. 1249–1253.

317 See: Klein, Eran/Goering, Sara/Gagne, John/Shea, Conor V./Franklin, Rachel/Zorowitz, Samuel/Dougherty, Darin D./Widge, Alik S., "Brain-Computer Interface-Based Control of Closed-Loop Brain Stimulation: Attitudes and Ethical Considerations", *Brain-Computer Interfaces*, Volume 3, 2016, p. 140 (argue that Brain-Computer Interfaces—BCI for short—erode citizens 'mental privacy while depriving them from thinking "for themselves").

maps seamlessly onto, and neatly fits, hands-in-glove, the taxonomy of a pandora box that is not amenable to be jettisoned to the unheeded bucket of legal oblivion.

§§ Lest we forget, freedom of thought is what set us apart from animals. If we are to be unlawfully disfranchised from this paramount tool that enable us to carry ourselves forward, our uniqueness will peter out in the process. Our humanity will be accordingly trounced. In addition to that, our human dignity will be inevitably vanquished. No surprise stems from the fact that scholars have not refrained themselves from pouring in trenchant criticism on the lack of a full-fledged and comprehensive legal framework to govern this sizzling hot topic.[318]

§§ Law is, once again, sorely slipping behind the newest technological developments brought forth/sprang into action by an ever-evolving science that shows no conspicuous signs of slowing down. Law, an invaluable tool to infuse social stability into a given jurisdiction, should not be so sluggish in deftly addressing this gamut of pressing issues—especially, when there is so much at stake.[319]

§§ This book accordingly proposes a batch/cluster of legal measures to protect citizens' fundamental rights against the mayhem of procedural unfairness that tags along with a disheartening social engineering under which Brain-Computer Interfaces[320] are wrapped.[321]

§§ Notwithstanding, the influence that an unfettered Artificial Intelligence is set to boast in the forthcoming future is not amenable to be bogged down to what has been previously written in this book though. Quite the opposite, it uncannily stretches far beyond that.

---

[318] Khan, Sadia/Cole, Daniel/Ekbia, Hamid,", Autonomy and Free Thought in Brain-Computer Interactions: Review of Legal Precedent for Precautionary Regulation of Consumer Products", *Hastings Science & Technology Law Journal*, Volume 15, Number 1, Article 5, 2024, pp. 95–130 (95) ("*The expanding use of neurotechnologies in consumer products increases the risks to human rights such as autonomy and free thought. While potentially beneficial in clinical applications, technologies such as brain implants and EEG-enabled wearable devices pose serious concerns about mental and psychological manipulation of human beings. In the US in particular, law and policy are lagging behind technical developments, thereby increasing the risks of abuse and misuse from commercial neurotechnologies*"). Italics added.

[319] Fergus, Rachel, "Biased Technology: The Automated Discrimination of Facial Recognition", *ACLU Minnesota*, February 29, 2024, available at: https://www.aclu-mn.org/en/news/biased-technology-automated-discrimination-facial-recognition (access: 20.09.2024) ("*Technology is developing much more quickly than the laws we need to protect our rights. Anyone with a smartphone or social media account knows how rapidly technology changes, while legislating can take a long, long time. It is essential to proactively put policies into place that will protect our rights as new and more advanced technology is constantly released. Especially when that technology—and law enforcement members using it—have been shown over and over to be biased toward marginalized groups*"). Italics added.

[320] Nagarajan, A./Robinson, N./Guan, C., "Relevance-based channel selection in motor imagery brain–computer interface", *J Neural Eng.*, Volume 20, Issue 1, 2023, passim.

[321] See: Chap. 5 of this book.

§§ Imagine, if you will, that computer-generated genetic algorithms[322] are suitably equipped to write human DNA[323] on demand,[324] thereby enabling wealthy parents to handpick fitter, taller, healthier, brighter siblings, whom are fundamentally immune to a slew of diseases that accordingly augments their span of life. This is the gist of *Transhumanism*, *Genetic Darwinism*, and *Genetic Plutocracy*[325]—a byproduct of convolutional neural networks[326] that centre around deep learning genetic algorithms[327]—that will overhaul the current legal landscape beyond recognition.

§§ On the heels of the rampant rise of genetic[328] algorithms[329]—which, in turn, relies upon deep learning[330]—human beings will be irresistibly tempted to grasp the holy

---

322 Sun, Y, Xue, B, Zhang, M, et al., "Automatically designing CNN architectures using the genetic algorithm for image classification", *IEEE Trans Cybern.*, Volume 50, Issue 9, 2020, pp. 3840–3854.

323 Gowda, CC, Mayya, SG, "Comparison of back propagation neural network and genetic algorithm neural network for stream flow prediction", *Journal of Computer Environment Science*, 2014, pp. 1–6.

324 See: Part III, Chap. 3, Sect. 3.5.11 of this book (on the functional aspects of Critical Artificial Intelligence Studies, with a sharper focus on the harmful effects of Artificial Intelligence-embedded technologies, namely, Genetic Algorithms that can write DNA on demand, thereby ushering the age of Transhumanism, Genetic Darwinism and Genetic Plutocracy, which, taken together, are poised to create layers of distinction between citizens).

325 See: Part III, Chap. 3, Sect. 3.5.11 of this book (on the functional aspects of Critical Artificial Intelligence Studies, with a sharper focus on the harmful effects of Artificial Intelligence-embedded technologies, namely, Genetic Algorithms that can write DNA on demand, thereby ushering the age of Transhumanism, Genetic Darwinism and Genetic Plutocracy, which, taken together, are poised to create layers of distinction between citizens).

326 Krizhevsky, A., Sutskever, I., & Hinton, G. E., "Imagenet classification with deep convolutional neural networks", *Advances in Neural Information Processing Systems*, Volume 25, 2012. Lake, B. M., & Baroni, M., "Human-like systematic generalization through a meta-learning neural network", *Nature*, 623 (7985), 2023, pp. 115–121.

327 Rikhtegar A, Pooyan M, Manzuri-Shalmani MT, "Genetic algorithm-optimised structure of convolutional neural network for face recognition applications", *IET Computer Vision*, Volume 10, Issue 6, 2016, pp. 559–566.

328 In general: Zhangyu Wang/Benjamin Gregg/Li Du, "Regulatory barriers to US-China collaboration for generative AI development in genomic research", *Cell Genomics*, https://doi.org/10.1016/j.xgen.2024.100564, 2024, pp. 1–5 (1) ("*The application of generative AI has shown potential in advancing scientific knowledge, including genomic research, which relies on the effective processing and analysis of large genomic and health datasets. The development of generative-AI-assisted genomic research is still in its early stages. It confronts challenges concerning access to highly sensitive personal data, such as genomic data and patients' health records, as well as to more diverse datasets under different legal and governmental jurisdictions.* In particular, data diver sity and quality play decisive roles in reducing AI bias and improving prediction accuracy. Consequently, access to and sharing of genomic data are crucial for the two leading players in genomic research—China and the United States, each possessing some of the largest active genomic databases"). Internal citation omitted and italics added.

329 Sun, Y., Xue, B., Zhang, M, et al., "Automatically designing CNN architectures using the genetic algorithm for image classification", *EEE Trans Cybern*, Volume 50, Issue 9, 2020, pp. 3840–3854.

330 Vishnupriya R./Neethu, Robinson/Ramasubba, Reddy M., "Genetic algorithm based deep learning model adaptation for improvising the motor imagery classification", *Brain-Computer Interfaces*, May 2024, 2024, pp. 1–12 (3–4) ("*Genetic algorithms (GAs) are search techniques based on*

grail of immortality, thereby posing both ethical[331] and legal challenges, which boast an exceedingly high likelihood to throw the extant legal framework into a frenzy.

§§ Which begs the questions: Are we on the cusp of a *Genetic Darwinism* that is poised to create (additional) layers of distinction between citizens? If so, how should law respond to these unprecedented challenges brought forth by a burgeoning

---

natural genetics and evolutionary principles that can generate optimal solutions to optimization and search problems. The search process is carried out by GAs in four stages: initialization, selection, crossover, and mutation [20]. The first step is to generate an initial population of solutions to the problem. These solutions are not the best for the problem, and as a result, they must be evolved. *The evolution process begins by selecting a few fittest solutions as parents. From the selected set of parents, each pair of parents mate in order to produce one or more children.* Using the crossover operation, each child inherits genes from both parents. Selective mutation is introduced to make random changes to the children to alter the inherited capabilities. Because of these random changes, some children may be fitter or weaker than their parents. *These generated children and their parents form the evolved population for the next generation. The fittest solutions from the evolved population are selected as parents and better solutions will likely be found by mating the best parents and producing more children. The process is repeated for a fixed number of generations or until the desired solution is found that does not require further optimization*"). Italics added. On randomness: Teigena, Halvor/Kanten, Alf Børre, "Out of the blue: on the suddenness of perceived chance events", *Thinking & Reasoning*, Volume 29, n. ° 1, 2023, pp. 137–175 (137) ("*people commonly use terms like 'random', 'by chance', or 'accidentally' when they describe occurrences that sidestep the normal course of events, with no apparent causal link to ongoing activities. Such intrusive events are typically perceived as happening all of a sudden.* This was demonstrated in seven experiments (N ¼ 1299) by asking people to identify statements they believed belonged to stories about chance events, and by comparing chance vs. nonchance events from their own life and from the lives of others. Suddenness also appeared to be more strongly associated with beginnings than with endings of an episode. Thus, statements about sudden beginnings of a career or a relationship were more readily believed to happen 'by chance' than 'not by chance'. *But life-changing events did not become more accidental simply by being placed in the beginning of a 'life chapter'. These studies highlight a central but neglected feature of perceived randomness*"). Italics added.

[331] On the dire need of creation of an ethical-fraught landscape within the remit of algorithmic decision-making: Upreti, Nijesh/Jessica Ciupa/Vaishak Belle "Towards Developing Ethical Reasoners: Integrating Probabilistic Reasoning and Decision-Making for Complex AI Systems", arXiv:2502.21250v1 [cs.AI] 28 Feb 2025, 2025, p. 1 ("*A computational ethics framework is essential for AI and autonomous systems operating in complex, real world environments. Existing approaches often lack the adaptability needed to integrate ethical principles into dynamic and ambiguous contexts, limiting their effectiveness across diverse scenarios. To address these challenges, we outline the necessary ingredients for building a holistic, meta-level framework that combines intermediate representations, probabilistic reasoning, and knowledge representation. The specifications therein emphasize scalability, supporting ethical reasoning at both individual decision-making levels and within the collective dynamics of multi-agent systems. By integrating theoretical principles with contextual factors, it facilitates structured and context-aware decision-making, ensuring alignment with overarching ethical standards.* We further explore proposed theorems outlining how ethical reasoners should operate, *offering a foundation for practical implementation. These constructs aim to support the development of robust and ethically reliable AI systems capable of navigating the complexities of real-world moral decision-making scenarios.*"). Italics added.

field such genetic algorithms[332]? This book charts the path ahead as to draw set-in-stone boundaries to prevent jurisdictions from careening into the chaos of *Genetic Plutocracy.*[333]

§§ Moving along, robotics has earned praise amongst legal pundits. Broadly speaking, this subject is all the rage in the criminal justice system.[334] Pundits are adamant in averring that robots are about to take over the criminal justice system.[335] The sobriquet of «digital justice» suits, hands-in-glove, the undeterred hype surrounding robotics.[336]

---

[332] Boyabatli, O., "Parameter selection in genetic algorithms parameter selection in genetic algorithms parameter selection in genetic algorithms", *Ihsan Param Sel Genetic Algorithms*, Volume 4, Issue 2, 2004, pp. 78–83.

[333] See: Part III, Chap. 3, Sect. 3.5.11 of this book (on the functional aspects of Critical Artificial Intelligence Studies, with a sharper focus on the harmful effects of Artificial Intelligence-embedded technologies, namely, Genetic Algorithms that can write DNA on demand, thereby ushering the age of Transhumanism, Genetic Darwinism and Genetic Plutocracy, which, taken together, are poised to create layers of distinction between citizens).

[334] But see: Newell, Lauren A., "Rebooting Empathy for the Digital Generation Lawyer", *Ohio State Journal on Dispute Resolution*, Volume 34, Issue 1, 2019, 1–96 (4–6) (contending that empathy is now needed more than ever amidst a digital world in which people somewhere along the line ceased to communicate "face to face". Rebooting empathy in the remit of administration of justice is the way forward in this scholar's insightful view). See: Part V, Chap. 5, Sect. 5.8.5 of this book (on law number five to interpret algorithmic decision-making, which mandates that robot-judges, robot-prosecutors and robot-lawyers must not enter the courtroom for they are utterly incapable of making sound and interpretable value judgements).

[335] The rise of digital justice—or algorithmic justice—is set to beget the absolute power of algorithms, which will make judges 'life considerably easier. Soon enough, judges will blindly follow the pearls of wisdom breed by inscrutable algorithms which will—keenly and promptly—point out to them the best course of action to be taken in a given procedure. See: Millar, Jason/Kerr, Ian, "Delegation, Relinquishment and Responsibility: The Prospect of Expert Robots", *Robot Law*, Ryan Calo/Froomkin, A. Michael/Kerr, Ian. Cheltenham: Edward Elgar Publishing, 2016, pp. 102, 106–107 (as these authors aptly put it "*We will rely on robots without really knowing why—simply because their algorithms provide the greatest number of successful outcomes.* We have already seen this in Google's search approach. Neither Larry (Page) nor Sergey (Brin) (nor any other Google employee) knowns exactly why one particular web page is a better result than another. *When the click patterns say it is, that's good enough.* No semantic or causal analysis is required...*Like the ancients, we will, quite rationally, come to rely upon them, knowing full well that we cannot necessarily explain the reasons for their decisions*"). Italics added. Converging: Casey, Anthony J./Niblett, Anthony, "Self-driving Laws", *University of Toronto Law Journal*, Volume 66, 2016, pp. 429–435 (contend that "as more information is generated, and the evolutionary algorithm updates and become a better forecaster, we imagine that judges will increasingly rely on the advice of the algorithm"). But see: Part V, Chap. 5, Sect. 5.8.5 of this book (on law number five to interpret algorithmic decision-making, which mandates that robot-judges, robot-prosecutors and robot-lawyers must not enter the courtroom for they are utterly incapable of making sound and interpretable value judgements).

[336] The literature on robotics law is endless and countless. The sizzling hot topics of transparency and liability of the creators of robots is in the limelight in the United States of America. See, amongst many other authors,: Abbott, Ryan, "I Think, Therefore I Invent: Creative Computers and the Future of Patent Law", *Boston College Law Review*, Volume 57, 2016, pp. 1078 ff; Calo, Ryan, "Robotics and the Lessons of Cyberlaw", *California Law Review*, Volume 103, 2015, pp. 512 ff; Casey, Bryan, "Amoral Machines, or: How Robotics Can Learn to Stop Worrying and Love the Law", *New York*

§§ Yet, this tool—a robot-judge or a robot-prosecutor, which should never be used in judicial settings[337]—should be pulled from use until it is duly tested and adroitly calibrated or avoidable mishaps are slated to otherwise occur.[338] For purposes here, who should be held accountable[339] if a robot-judge renders a decision that purposefully/callously harms others? By the same token, who should be held accountable if a robot-judge or a robot-prosecutor kills someone in a court of law owing to an unforeseen malfunction?[340]

University Law Review, Volume 111, 2017, pp. 1346 ff; Balkin, Jack M., "The Path of Robotics Law", *California Law Review*, Volume 6, 2015, pp. 44 ff. But see: Part V, Chap. 5, Sect. 5.8.5 of this book (on law number five to interpret algorithmic decision-making, which mandates that robot-judges, robot-prosecutors and robot-lawyers must not enter the courtroom for they are utterly incapable of making sound and interpretable value judgements).

[337] See: Part V, Chap. 5, Sect. 5.8.5 of this book (on law number five to interpret algorithmic decision-making, which mandates that robot-judges, robot-prosecutors and robot-lawyers must not enter the courtroom for they are utterly incapable of making sound and interpretable value judgements).

[338] See: Part III, Chap. 3, Sect. 3.5.1.1 of this book (on the functional aspects of Critical Artificial Intelligence Studies, with a sharper focus on the harmful effects of Artificial Intelligence-embedded technologies, namely, perpetuation technologies—griefbots, avatars and robots—that are slated to dehumanize human-laden emotions).

[339] The liability of artificial-intelligence-based robots is a challenge that not only lurks ahead, but, and foremost, is something that future lawmakers and policymakers should never lose sight of. See: Rachum-Twaig, Omri, "Whose robot anyway? Liability for artificial-intelligence-based robots", *University of Illinois Law Review*, Volume 4, 2020, pp. 1141–1175. See: Part V, Chap. 5, Sect. 5.7.1 of this book (on law number one to control algorithmic decision-making, which mandates that whoever develops and/or deploys machines to undertake a given task must be held criminal accountable for the Hard-AI crimes the latter perpetrates).

[340] Artificial Intelligence in criminal procedure law settings is not without drawbacks and shortcomings though. One which is the use of robots to commit crimes in its functional compass. Who should be held accountable in that case: the designer or the robot? This holds relevance in criminal procedure law settings in cases in which the robot causes physical harm to one of the disputants during the court hearings or court sessions. See: McAllister, Amanda, "Stranger Than Science Fiction: The Rise of A.I. Interrogation in the Dawn of Autonomous Robots and the Need for an Additional Protocol to the U.N. Convention against Torture", *Minnesota Law Review*, Volume 101, 2018, pp. 2566–2569 (on the guidelines to use robots to perform human tasks). But there is more to it. Just think of the hotly debated biased-bigoted algorithms. Which begs the question: what if a robot that happens to be helping the judge to decide a case in criminal procedure law settings suggests an outcome based on a racist or gender-biased algorithm? Future policymakers and lawmakers must pay close attention to these pressing issues upon stocking their options as to allow (or not) the use of technology at the table of criminal procedure law. See: Lemley, Mark A./Casey, Bryan, "Remedies for Robots", *The University of Chicago Law Review*, Volume 86, Issue 5, 2019, pp. 1311–1396 (1376) (alerting to the perils of algorithmic bias). See also: Chandler, Anupam, "The Racist Algorithm", *Michigan Law Review*, Volume 115, Issue 6, 2018, p. 1026 (noting that, in the terrain of racist algorithm, "the possibilities for discriminatory manipulation are legion"). See also: Baeza-Yates, R., "Bias on the web", *Communications of the ACM*, 61 (6), June 2018, 2018, pp. 54–61 (argues that "*algorithmic bias is when the bias is not present in the input data* and is added *purely by the algorithm*"). Italics added. See: Part V, Chap. 5, Sect. 5.7.1 of this book (on law number one to control algorithmic decision-making, which mandates that whoever develops and/or deploys machines to undertake a given task must be held criminal accountable for the Hard-AI crimes the latter perpetrates).

§§ This book offers a useful template to avoid liability gaps in this regard while expressing the unease with which computer-generated algorithms can be deployed to target *socially undesirables*,[341] thereby compounding extant social cleavages.

§§ Last but not least, this book addresses one of most pressing issues facing modern societies: *Quantum Technology* that can not only solve the most complex equations at a lightning speed but, and foremost, can gain access to any electronic device only to decrypt the data enshrined in it. It will be the demise of privacy as we know. A worrying question arises: if this state-of-the-art technology falls in the wrong hands, can they (*Quantum Algorithms*) bypass/circumvent virtually impenetrable military security systems only to trigger weapons of mass destruction, thus wiping out the overwhelming majority of human race? Food for thoughts that, in the meantime, should keep you, dear reader, eagerly awaken at night.[342]

§§ This book unfolds as follows. Part II provides, in very broad strokes, an historical account on Artificial Intelligence. Part III introduces the blazingly new concept of *Critical Artificial Intelligence Studies* (CAIS). Part IV pores over the unsavoury byproducts of *algorithmic dictatorship*, such as predictive policing,[343] biased algorithmic credit

[341] See: Part V, Chap. 5, Sect. 5.7.1 of this book (on law number one to control algorithmic decision-making, which mandates that whoever develops and/or deploys machines to undertake a given task must be held criminal accountable for the Hard-AI crimes the latter perpetrates).

[342] See: Part III, Chap. 3, Sect. 3.5.11 of this book (on the functional aspects of Critical Artificial Intelligence Studies, with a sharper focus on the harmful effects of Artificial Intelligence-embedded technologies, namely, Quantum Technology, which will bring entire industries to their knees while allowing unscrupulous actors to get a hold of, and whimsically activate, weapons of mass destruction).

[343] See: Part IV, Chap. 4, Sects. 4.1 to 4.1.1 of this book (on biased predictive policing). See also: Hu, Margaret, "From the National Surveillance State to the Cybersurveillance State", *The Annual Review of Law and Social Science*, Volume 13, 2017, p. 166 (argues that ubiquitous and ever-present surveillance of socially undesirables remains at a pitch of degradation of fundamental rights in that Artificial Intelligence-embedded technologies—propelled by tools like Social Radar and Total Information Awareness, TIA, can capture "a *pictorial depiction of the comprehensive cyber-surveillance anticipated through the Social Radar system, which anticipated the full integration of drone footage, biometrric data signatures, econometrics, and other intelligence sources to achieve higher-order cybersurveillance inferences. Social Radar appears to trace its philosophical origins to TIA.* The development of TIA after the 9/11 terrorist attacks was guided under the leadership of the newly created Information Awareness Office within DARPA (Harris 2012, Murray 2010). Within this office, TIA was an effort led by retired Navy Vice Admiral John M. Poindexter (Murray 2010), who served as a national security advisor to President Reagan (Harris 2012). *TIA was informed by a philosophy of "predictive policing," which "focuses not on collecting evidence about actual wrongdoing but on the broad collection of information about everyday activities with the intention of detecting (and preventing) future behavior*" (Murray 2010, p. 5). Congress officially defunded TIA in late 2003 (Murray 2010, Slobogin 2008, USA Today 2003). *Experts have nonetheless noted that remnants of the TIA program and its philosophy have persisted*"). Italics added.

scoring,[344] mortgage redlining,[345] algorithmic redliking,[346] «algorithmic Jim Crow»,[347] proxy discrimination,[348] and biased algorithmic risk assessment.[349] Part V seeks to outline concluding remarks to capture the gist of the book while bringing forth a cluster of actionable proposals to surpass the perceived bottlenecks that forestall the normal flow of *Procedural Rule of Law*[350] within the purview of algorithmic decision-making. To cater for that, the newly-crafted concept of *Algorithmic Common Good* will be sketched out.[351]

---

[344] See: Part IV, Chap. 4, Sects. 4.2 to 4.4.3 of this book (on algorithmic credit scoring, consumer racism and credit card redlining). But see: Hurley, Mikella/Adebayo, Julius, "Credit Scoring in the Era of Big Data", *Yale Journal of Law and Technology*, Volume 18, 2016, pp. 148, 151–156, 172 (averring that FICO scoring boasts a redoubtable capacity to routinely weed out some populations that have been historically and systematically underrepresented or grossly unfairly represented in the credit industry market). Tellingly, by 2016, ten states had disavowed the unlawful practice of employers using shady algorithmic credit scores due to their perceived disparate impact on low-income applicants and members of racialized communities (mostly Black folks). See: O'Neill, Cathy, *Weapons of Math Destruction. How Big Data Increases Inequality and Threatens Democracy*. London: Penguin Random House, 2016, pp. 128 and ff and passim.

[345] See: Part IV, Chap. 4, Sects. 4.4 to 4.4.2.1 of this book (on mortgage redlining). In spite of its deep-seated racial bias, decision-makers continue to deploy redlining tactics through big data and may even justify such unlawful practices by claiming that the latter abide by cost-effectiveness. See: Humber, Nadiyah J., "A Home for Digital Equity: Algorithmic Redlining and Property Technology", *California Law Review*, Volume 111, Issue 5, 2023, pp. 1421–1484. Allen, James, "The Color of Algorithms: An Analysis and Proposed Research Agenda Deterring Algorithmic Redlining", *Fordham Urban Law Journal*, Volume 46, 2019, pp. 219–234 (229–234) (discussing how historical mortgage redlining greatly swayed modern algorithms generated by massive batches of data sets that consist of decades of information built on exclusion and racial discrimination in the purview of financing, marketing, and housing). See also: Part IV, Chap. 4, Sects. 4.4 to 4.4.2.3 of this book. See: Part IV, Chap. 4, Sects. 4.4 to 4.4.2.1 of this book (on mortgage redlining). See: Part IV, Chap. 4, Sects. 4.2 to 4.4.3 of this book (on algorithmic credit scoring, consumer racism and credit card redlining). See: Part IV, Chap. 4, Sects. 4.4 to 4.4.2.3 of this book (on algorithmic redlining). See: Part IV, Chap. 4, Sect. 4.4.3 of this book (on "algorithmic redliking"). See: Part IV, Chap. 4, Sect. 4.3 of this book (on algorithmic prime-lining).

[346] See: Part IV, Chap. 4, Sect. 4.4.3 of this book (on "algorithmic redliking").

[347] See: Part IV, Chap. 4, Sects. 4.5 to 4.5.2 of this book (on "algorithmic Jim Crow", which stands as an outgrowth of congeries of laws enacted during the long-haul Jim Crow epoch).

[348] See: Part IV, Chap. 4, Sect. 4.6.3 of this book (on proxy discrimination).

[349] See: Part IV, Chap. 4, Sects. 4.10.1 to 4.10.6 of this book (on biased algorithmic risk assessment in criminal procedure law settings).

[350] See: Part V, Chap. 5, Sect. 5.1.2 of this book (on the central tenets of Procedural Rule of Law that bestows upon citizens the fundamental right to challenge the pearls of algorithmic wisdom—outputs—offered by algorithmic decision-making).

[351] See: Part V, Chap. 5, Sects. 5.2 to 5.6.2.1 of this book (on the thing-centred algorithmic decision-making propelled by a *Controllable* and *Interpretable* Machine Learning that weeds out *Algorithmic Dictatorship* and secures *Algorithmic Common Good*).

Part II
The History of Artificial Intelligence

Chapter 2
Why Do We Need a *Controllable Artificial Intelligence*: Brief Historical Account

2.1 Setting the Stage[1]

§§ Scholars are fundamentally tasked with the duty of furnishing baselines for a full-fledged interaction between humans and machines. Casts broadly, scholars are to be accordingly allotted the incumbency to prevent that the Rule of Law falls into abeyance amidst the rise of an unbridled/unfettered Artificial Intelligence.[2] Not just that though: pundits must not shy away from pouring in staggering efforts to prevent Rule of Law[3] goes berserk in the midst the unbidden irruption of Artificial

[1] Part II, Chap. 2 of this book has been written by Leong Cheng Hang.

[2] Of which big data biometric verification and identification technologies—a.k.a. surveillance technologies—stand as a capstone. See: Hu, Margaret, "From the National Surveillance State to the Cybersurveillance State", *The Annual Review of Law and Social Science*, Volume 13, 2017, p. 168 ("*currently, biometric verification and identification technologies are not commonly perceived to be surveillance technologies—the public and private sectors typically treat them as a benign and useful form of digitized identification. Such automated biometric screening is considered to be a more efficient form of small data verification technologies, such as human screening or human-driven practices involving assessments of biometric or forensic data. Small data biometric verification could include comparing a passport photo against the person holding the passport. Big data biometric identification, however, has a distinct impact from that of small data biometric investigation because it can facilitate surveillance. Big data photo screening may entail the collection of digital photographs. This in turn can lead to facilitating facial recognition technology through the mass digitization of photo databases, potentially including billions of facial images.* One Snowden disclosure noted that the NSA collects millions of digital photographs from internet and social media sources and *uses facial recognition technology to identify individuals*"). Italics added. See: Part IV, Chap. 4, Sects. 4.5 to 4.5.2 of this book (on "algorithmic Jim Crow", which stands as an outgrowth of congeries of laws enacted during the Jim Crow epoch).

[3] See: Part V, Chap. 5, Sect. 5.1.1 of this book (on the central tenets of Rule of Law that lends itself to a beacon of justice amidst the sepulchral darkness that is about to take hold).

H. L. dos Santos, *Controllable Artificial Intelligence and the Future of Law*, Artificial Intelligence and the Rule of Law, https://doi.org/10.1007/978-981-95-0508-1_2

Intelligence in our daily lives.[4] This assertion, albeit seemingly trivial/nugatory, has never been so pressing as we steadfastly head towards the mayhem of *Algorithmic Dictatorship.*[5]

§§ Scholars should therefore spearhead efforts to outline the foundations upon which should stand the interaction between humans and machines.[6] There is no way around this: humans should get to terms with the fact that Artificial Intelligence is not going anywhere. Humans should accordingly be prepared to share the limelight with machines[7] in a not-so-distant future.[8]

§§ Failing which, humans better brace themselves to be engulfed in a drawn-out affray that is bound to cast a vast array of harms onto citizens, which is nothing but bemoaning. It follows that the general furore over Artificial Intelligence should halted or inordinate damages are shaping up to be externalized onto innocent others. This axiom, dear reader, is neither unwarranted nor uncalled for. For a simple reason:

---

[4] See: Ting-an Lin, "Democratizing AI" and the Concern of Algorithmic Injustice", *Philosophy and Technology*, Volume 37 (103), 2024, pp. 3–27. See also: Birhane, A., "Algorithmic injustice: A relational ethics approach", *Patterns*, 2 (2), 2021, pp. 1–9. Završnik, A. "Algorithmic justice: Algorithms and big data in criminal justice settings", *European Journal of Criminology*, 2019, passim.

[5] See: Part IV, Chap. 4, Sects. 4 to 4.10.6 of this book (on Algorithmic Dictatorship and its chilling effect on democracy).

[6] Buolamwini, Joy, Unmasking AI: My Mission to Protect What Is Human in a World of Machines, New York, Random House, 2023, pp. 1–336 ("*The conscience of the AI revolution" (Fortune) explains how we've arrived at an era of AI harms and oppression, and what we can do to avoid its pitfalls.* "AI is not coming, it's here. If we answer the beautiful call inside these pages, *we can decide who we are going to be and how we're going to use technology in service of what it means to be fully human.*"—Brené Brown, #1 *New York Times* bestselling author of *Dare to Lead*. A *LOS ANGELES TIMES* BEST BOOK OF THE YEAR • Shortlisted for the *Inc.* Non-Obvious Book Award. *To most of us, it seems like recent developments in artificial intelligence emerged out of nowhere to pose unprecedented threats to humankind. But to Dr. Joy Buolamwini, who has been at the forefront of AI research, this moment has been a long time in the making*"). Italics added.

[7] But see: Pasquale, Frank, "A Rule of Persons, Not Machines: The Limits of Legal Automation", *George Washington Law Review*, Volume 87, 2019, passim.

[8] See: Liu, Hin-Yan/Zawieska, Karolina, "From responsible robotics towards a human rights regime oriented to the challenges of robotics and artificial intelligence", *Ethics Information Technology*, Volume 22, Issue 4, 2020, pp. 321–333.

decisions vital to our collective welfare appallingly leverage on rigged data[9] baked into databases[10] scattered across the data-driven world[11] we live in.

---

[9] *Tech, Bias and Housing Initiative, the Promise and Perils of Residential Proptech, Year 1, Research Summary Report, April 2023, TechEquity Collaborative*, p. 11, available at: https://techequity.us/wp-content/uploads/2023/04/TBHI-Y1-Research-Summary-Report.pdf (28.11.2024). ("*Once bad data enters the analysis of one factor, it gets baked into the subsequent process, multiplying the effect that one disadvantageous data point can have on someone's overall housing determination*"). Italics added. See: Part IV, Chap. 4, Sects. 4.4 to 4.4.2.1 of this book (on mortgage redlining). See: Part IV, Chap. 4, Sects. 4.2 to 4.4.3 of this book (on algorithmic credit scoring, consumer racism and credit card redlining). See: Part IV, Chap. 4, Sects. 4.4 to 4.4.2.3 of this book (on algorithmic redlining). See: Part IV, Chap. 4, Sect. 4.4.3 of this book (on "algorithmic redliking"). See: Part IV, Chap. 4, Sect. 4.3 of this book (on algorithmic prime-lining).

[10] Balkin, Jack M., "The Three Laws of Robotics in the Age of Big Data", *Ohio State Law Journal*, Volume 78, Issue 5, 2017, pp. 1217–1241, whose research I have been following closely. See also: See: Hu, Margaret, "From the National Surveillance State to the Cybersurveillance State", *The Annual Review of Law and Social Science*, Volume 13, 2017, p. 165 ("*Datafication, like most big data processes, requires increasing amounts of digital data to support or construct cybersurveillance.* It empowers government actions that are based on digital data collection, data processing protocols, and bulk data analyses (Mayer-Schonberger & Cukier ¨ 2013). *Another way to characterize datafication is as a governmental policy interest that both transforms analog data (PCAST 2014) into searchable, centralized digital databases and develops new forms of stored data*"). Italics added.

[11] Hardt, Moritz, "How big data is unfair: Understanding sources of unfairness in data driven decision making", *Medium*, Archived on Oct. 8, 2014, available at: https://web.archive.org/web/20141008185829/ https://medium.com/@mrtz/how-big-data-is-unfair-9aa544d739de (access: 17.12.2024).

§§ Disturbingly enough, the foregoing rigged data[12] contains the residue of deeply entrenched discriminations and injustice[13] of which we should be keenly chary of.[14] It follows machines—which, recall, have been previously fed with data riddled with deep-seated residues of invidiousness[15] and racial discrimination[16]—will

---

[12] But see: Barocas, Solon/Selbst, Andrew D., "Big Data's Disparate Impact", *California Law Review*, Volume 104, 2016, pp. 671–682 (discussing how data is often flawed, rigged, incomplete, imperfect and therefore algorithms inherit the prejudice of the original decision makers). But see: Citron, Danielle Keats/Pasquale, Frank, "The Scored Society: Due Process for Automated Predictions", *Washington Law Review*, Volume 89, 2014, pp. 1, 4–5 (highlighting how human beings programming automated systems is directly conducive to, and leads, to fundamentally inaccurate results since the source code, predictive algorithms and datasets may encompass human biases which, in turn, have a disparate impact on historically disadvantaged groups). But see: Bornstein, Stepanhie, "Antidiscriminatory Algorithms", *Alabama Law Review*, Volume 70, 2018, pp. 519, 524–528 (contending, however, that the tagged "facially neutral" algorithms producing discriminatory outcomes should be quashed).

[13] Balkin, Jack M., "The Three Laws of Robotics in the Age of Big Data", *cit.*, pp. 1217–1241.

[14] Wonyoung, So, "Which Information Matters? Measuring Landlord Assessment of Tenant Screening Reports", *Housing Policy Debate*, Volume 33, n. ° 6, 2023, pp. 1484–1510 (1502) ("*One additional finding of the experiment is that algorithmic scoring can exacerbate this racially unequal landscape in rental agreements not just because the algorithm may be inaccurate, but because landlords may want to follow the risk assessment made by the tenant screening report. This is alarming for low-income tenants, particularly housing voucher holders. Security deposits are one of the most significant barriers to obtaining housing for voucher holders, because vouchers do not pay security deposits but most private landlords require them (Rosenblatt & Cossyleon, 2018).* Given that voucher holders have exceptionally low income (usually less than 50% of area median income) and might experience more housing insecurity (rental debts and eviction-related experiences), *imposing greater security deposits on voucher holders almost equates to denying them housing—yet these decisions could be justified by algorithmic scoring if tenant screening services employ it*"). Italics added. See: Part IV, Chap. 4, Sects. 4.4 to 4.4.2.3 of this book. See: Part IV, Chap. 4, Sects. 4.4 to 4.4.2.1 of this book (on mortgage redlining). See: Part IV, Chap. 4, Sects. 4.2 to 4.4.3 of this book (on algorithmic credit scoring, consumer racism and credit card redlining). See: Part IV, Chap. 4, Sects. 4.4 to 4.4.2.3 of this book (on algorithmic redlining). See: Part IV, Chap. 4, Sect. 4.4.3 of this book (on "algorithmic redliking"). See: Part IV, Chap. 4, Sect. 4.3 of this book (on algorithmic prime-lining).

[15] Dong et al., Qi, "Imbalanced deep learning by minority class incremental rectification, *IEEE Transactions on Pattern Analysis & Machine Intelligence*, Volume 41, 2019, p. 1367 (posit that "*most existing learning algorithms produce inductive bias (learning bias)* towards the frequent (majority) classes if training data are not balanced, *resulting in poor minority class recognition performance*"). Italics added. See: Part V, Chapter 5, Sect. 5.7.4 of this book (on one of the laws to control algorithmic decision-making, namely, law number four: data partitioning must be performed—i.e. randomly split an entire dataset into the «training dataset» and the «test dataset»—to accurately predict outcomes in the real world while forestalling «inductive bias» (learning bias)).

[16] Packard, Jerald M., *American Nightmare: The History of Jim Crow*, Broadway, New York, St. Martin's Press; First Edition, 2002, pp. 1–304 (vii–viii) ("[A*] structure of exclusion and discrimination devised by white Americans to be employed principally against black Americans.... Its central purpose was to maintain a second-class social and economic status for blacks while upholding a first-class social and economic status for whites.... In the South, Jim Crow discrimination at its height existed not only by statute but by custom and racial 'etiquette,' and it was rigidly enforced by both the law enforcement agencies* and courts as well as by ordinary white citizens who were neither policemen nor judges but who often took the law into their own hands as though they were"). Italics added. See: Part IV, Chap. 4, Sects. 4.4 to 4.4.2.3 of this book. See: Part IV, Chap. 4, Sects. 4.4 to

accordingly spawn a cascade of biased judgments which will inevitably come to the expense of citizens' fundamental rights.[17] Hence the overriding importance of a *Controllable Artificial Intelligence*.[18] This is a central contention of book that must not fall into the shady depths of oblivion.

§§ Mind you, dear reader, that the unshakable hopes of being in control of Artificial Intelligence have so far been dashed by its murkiness,[19] its unfathomable ubiquity,

---

4.4.2.1 of this book (on mortgage redlining). See: Part IV, Chap. 4, Sects. 4.2 to 4.4.3 of this book (on algorithmic credit scoring, consumer racism and credit card redlining). See: Part IV, Chap. 4, Sects. 4.4 to 4.4.2.3 of this book (on algorithmic redlining). See: Part IV, Chap. 4, Sect. 4.4.3 of this book (on "algorithmic redliking"). See: Part IV, Chap. 4, Sect. 4.3 of this book (on algorithmic prime-lining).

[17] *Tech, Bias and Housing Initiative, the Promise and Perils of Residential Proptech, Year 1, Research Summary Report, April 2023, TechEquity Collaborative*, p. 5 available at: https://techequity.us/wp-content/uploads/2023/04/TBHI-Y1-Research-Summary-Report.pdf (28.11.2024). ("*Residential Proptech also has the potential to exacerbate the bias inherent in our housing system. Its rise is due, in part, to the desperation felt by average home seekers. With a severely constrained housing supply, companies offering an easier pathway to homeownership may exploit communities that have been harmed by housing discrimination in the past. Opaque algorithms incorporate biased data into their decision-making processes, making it harder to enforce fair housing laws.* Residential Proptech companies often operate in a regulatory gray area, leaving consumers without the protections they would have from traditional housing regulatory systems. *As unprecedented capital investment flows into this space, venture-backed companies' winner-take-all approach to growth has the potential to exacerbate inequality rather than combat it*"). Italics added. See: Part IV, Chap. 4, Sects. 4.4 to 4.4.2.3 of this book.

[18] See: Part V, Chap. 5, Sects. 5.2 to 5.6.2.1 of this book (on the thing-centred algorithmic decision-making propelled by a *Controllable* and *Interpretable* Machine Learning that weeds out *Algorithmic Dictatorship* and secures *Algorithmic Common Good*).

[19] Ferreri, Mara/Sanyal, Romola, "Digital informalisation: rental housing, platforms, and the management of risk", *Housing Studies*, Volume 37, Issue 6, 2022, pp. 1035–1053 (1035) ("*The eruption of disruptive digital platforms is reshaping geographies of housing under the gaze of corporations and through the webs of algorithms.* Engaging with interdisciplinary scholarship on informal housing across the Global North and South, we propose the term *'digital informalisation' to examine how digital platforms are engendering new and opaque ways of governing housing,* presenting a theoretical and political blind spot. Focusing on *rental housing, our paper unpacks the ways in which new forms of digital management of risk control access and filter populations. In contrast to progressive imaginaries of 'smart' technological mediation, practices of algorithmic redlining, biased tenant profiling and the management of risk in private tenancies and in housing welfare both introduce and extend discriminatory and exclusionary housing practices*"). Italics added. See: Part IV, Chap. 4, Sects. 4.4 to 4.4.2.3 of this book. See: Part IV, Chap. 4, Sects. 4.4 to 4.4.2.3 of this book. See: Part IV, Chap. 4, Sects. 4.4 to 4.4.2.1 of this book (on mortgage redlining). See: Part IV, Chap. 4, Sects. 4.2 to 4.4.3 of this book (on algorithmic credit scoring, consumer racism and credit card redlining). See: Part IV, Chap. 4, Sects. 4.4 to 4.4.2.3 of this book (on algorithmic redlining). See: Part IV, Chap. 4, Sect. 4.4.3 of this book (on "algorithmic redliking"). See: Part IV, Chap. 4, Sect. 4.3 of this book (on algorithmic prime-lining).

and its unbearable opacity[20,21] that stymie any endeavour to grasp its inner workings.[22] These are hardly uplifting news: zero control over Artificial Intelligence begets zero accountability.

§§ Worse still: bereft of an actionable course of algorithmic action to be taken, the dearth/paucity of pathways to challenge the «pearls of algorithmic wisdom» produced by Artificial Intelligence is nothing but dispiriting, to say the very least.[23] It follows that *Algorithmic Dictatorship*[24] is shaping up to redoubtably dictate the course of your lives with little to none accountability whatsoever. To add to our woes, along with zero actionable lines of action to *challenge* its pearls of algorithmic wisdom

[20] Balkin, Jack M., "The Three Laws of Robotics in the Age of Big Data", *cit.*, pp. 1217–1241.

[21] For an on-point breakdown of the distinct levels of opacity arising out of machine learning algorithms: Selbst, Andrew D./Barocas, Solon, "The Intuitive Appeal of Explainable Machines", *Fordham Law Review*, Volume 87, 2018, pp. 1085, 1089–99 (holding that there are plenty reasons for the insurer's ignorance. To begin with, the algorithm entails specialized knowledge to understand. That is, the insurer's employees may lack sufficient knowledge to understand the rationale behind the reasons in view of which the algorithm is producing prices for different customers—personalized pricing. Lastly, even if the insurer himself comprehends how the model operates, it may nonetheless lack expertise to comprehend why it operates the way it does. For that reason, the explainability of machines is a vital, but rather elusive, task. Thence, the famed authors deem it as the "nonintuitive" nature of algorithms. For purposes here, the insurer himself might indeed understand that its Artificial Intelligence-embedded technology formulates higher prices for those who actually access the website at hand, but may fail to come to terms with the fact that the explanation for this fact arises from the website's capacity to proxy for genetic information).

[22] *Tech, Bias and Housing Initiative, the Promise and Perils of Residential Proptech, Year 1, Research Summary Report, April 2023, TechEquity Collaborative*, p. 11, available at: https://techequity.us/wp-content/uploads/2023/04/TBHI-Y1-Research-Summary-Report.pdf (28.11.2024). ("*From information on company websites, it is not clear what analysis or data is behind subjective determinations like "suitability" to a unit or what the nexus between an individual's characteristics and a unit's characteristics is that indicates the likelihood for property damage. Based on sample reports, even landlords are not privy to how the determinations are made. Instead, they receive a risk score out of 100 simplified into green, yellow, and red recommendations.* What companies withhold in terms of how it works, they make up for with the extent to which they tell landlords it works: Naborly claims their predictions reduce lease defaults by up to 89%. 15 *As Naborly's sample report demonstrates, its property damage assessment is then used as an input to determine its projected eviction outcomes; its early vacancy prediction, in turn, is based on "all assessment factors.*"). Italics added. See: Part IV, Chap. 4, Sects. 4.4 to 4.4.2.3 of this book. See: Part IV, Chap. 4, Sects. 4.4 to 4.4.2.3 of this book. See: Part IV, Chap. 4, Sects. 4.4 to 4.4.2.1 of this book (on mortgage redlining). See: Part IV, Chap. 4, Sects. 4.2 to 4.4.3 of this book (on algorithmic credit scoring, consumer racism and credit card redlining). See: Part IV, Chap. 4, Sects. 4.4 to 4.4.2.3 of this book (on algorithmic redlining). See: Part IV, Chap. 4, Sect. 4.4.3 of this book (on "algorithmic redliking"). See: Part IV, Chap. 4, Sect. 4.3 of this book (on algorithmic prime-lining).

[23] See: Part III, Chap. 3, Sects. 3.5.2 to 3.5.3.1 of this book (on the functional aspects of Critical Artificial Intelligence Studies, with a sharper focus on the harmful effects of Artificial Intelligence-embedded technologies, namely, Generative Artificial Intelligence and its offsprings—deepfakes and its deleterious effects on human memory).

[24] See: Part IV, Chap. 4, Sects. 4 to 4.10.6 of this book (on Algorithmic Dictatorship and its chilling effect on democracy).

comes the perpetuation of long-standing discrimination and gruelling injustice.[25] It will be the demise of two of the greatest beacons of fairness there is: Rule of Law[26] and Procedural Rule of Law.[27] For that reason, the world sorely needs *Algorithmic Common Good*[28]

§§ Whilst this book is not by any means a foray to miraculously solve hitherto unassailable quandaries that pester/beset modern societies, it surely stands as an earnest attempt to chart the path ahead for a peaceful and fuss-free interaction between humans and machines. This book, if nothing else, seeks to set a high bar for academic debate for centuries to come.

2.1.1 Brief (Thumbnail Sketch) Historical Account on the Rise of Artificial Intelligence

§§ Artificial Intelligence, often wrapped under the shroud of a bedazzling gift, is all but blazingly new. Which should not come as a surprise for anyone who hasn't lived under a rock for the last 50 years or so.[29] Put otherwise, Artificial Intelligence has always been a flurry of interest for the legal community and for a long-winded span of time.[30]

---

[25] See: Part III, Chap. 3, Sect. 3.1 of this book (that discusses the issue of "inequality in application" facing Artificial Intelligence-embedded technologies).

[26] See: Part V, Chap. 5, Sect. 5.1.1 of this book (on the central tenets of Rule of Law that lends itself to a beacon of justice amidst the sepulchral darkness that is about to take hold).

[27] See: Part V, Chap. 5, Sect. 5.1.2 of this book (on the central tenets of Procedural Rule of Law that bestows upon citizens the fundamental right to challenge the pearls of algorithmic wisdom—outputs—offered by algorithmic decision-making).

[28] See: Part V, Chap. 5, Sects. 5.2 to 5.6.2.1 of this book (on the thing-centred algorithmic decision-making propelled by a *Controllable* and *Interpretable* Machine Learning that weeds out *Algorithmic Dictatorship* and secures *Algorithmic Common Good*).

[29] See: Cataleta, Maria Stefania/Cataleta, Anna, "Artificial Intelligence and Human Rights: An Unequal Struggle", *CIFILE Journal of International Law*, Volume 1, N. ° 2, 2020 ("*Artificial Intelligence (AI) is a kind of intelligence that was born in the 1950s and is an integral part of the digital revolution. Progress made by AI has permitted the birth of systems capable of rivalling human capacities or, in some cases, surpassing them.* The progress of the intellectual capacities of AI will change the way of life for human beings and will revolutionise the world of employment. *Intelligent systems present problems regarding individual rights and responsibilities, because as technology replaces more and more of what humans have typically done, our individual roles will become more blurred.*"). Italics added. Converging: Cataleta, Maria Stefania, "Artificial Intelligence vs Human Intelligence", in: Martin, L. Miraut/Zalucki, M. (editors), *Artificial intelligence and Human Rights, Dickinson eBook*. Krakow: AFM Krakow University, 2021, pp. 117–127 (on the slew of both moral, ethical and legal issues with which jurists will tussle/flounder in the forthcoming future due to the rise of artificial intelligence in legal arena).

[30] See in Italian doctrine: Quintarelli, Stefano, *Capitalismo Immateriale—Le tecnologie digitali ed il nuovo conflito sociale*, 7ª edizione. Turin: Bollati Boringhieri, 2019, pp. 1–198.

§§ It follows that to frame the social, theoretical, and legal discussions that are about to be unlocked throughout this book, a brief historical account is in dire need of being skeletally sketched out. The overriding goal is to find out how did we get to the point where algorithmic systems can cleanse bigoted data into eerily «powerful stigmatizing scores»[31] that boast a high likelihood to mimic discrimination[32] deeply steeped in past decision-making.[33]

§§ Put it bluntly, how did things look like before rigged data and input variables were fed into an algorithm, which currently boasts the capability to briskly learn from reams of data? On the other hand, how did things pan out before algorithmic decisions were made underpinned by warped/rigged data that often contains harmful correlations[34] we may not wish to perpetuate, recreate, exacerbate,[35] and re-entrench?[36] Conversely, has the legal playing field already been unfairly tilted against the poor,[37]

---

[31] Citron, Danielle K./Pasquale, Frank, "The Scored Society: Due Process for Automated Predictions", *Washington Law Review*, Volume 89, Issue 1, 2014, pp. 1–34.

[32] See: Griemmelmann, James/Westreich, Daniel, "Incomprehensible Discrimination ", *California Law Review Online*, Volume 7, 2018, pp. 164–171.

[33] Balkin, Jack M., "The Three Laws of Robotics in the Age of Big Data", *cit.*, pp. 1217–1241.

[34] *Tech, Bias and Housing Initiative, the Promise and Perils of Residential Proptech, Year 1, Research Summary Report, April 2023, TechEquity Collaborative*, p. 11, available at: https://techequity.us/wp-content/uploads/2023/04/TBHI-Y1-Research-Summary-Report.pdf (28.11.2024). ("*Once bad data enters the analysis of one factor, it gets baked into the subsequent process, multiplying the effect that one disadvantageous data point can have on someone's overall housing determination*"). Italics added. See: Part IV, Chap. 4, Sects. 4.4 to 4.4.2.3 of this book. See: Part IV, Chap. 4, Sects. 4.4 to 4.4.2.3 of this book. See: Part IV, Chap. 4, Sects. 4.4 to 4.4.2.1 of this book (on mortgage redlining). See: Part IV, Chap. 4, Sects. 4.2 to 4.4.3 of this book (on algorithmic credit scoring, consumer racism and credit card redlining). See: Part IV, Chap. 4, Sects. 4.4 to 4.4.2.3 of this book (on algorithmic redlining). See: Part IV, Chap. 4, Sect. 4.4.3 of this book (on "algorithmic redliking"). See: Part IV, Chap. 4, Sect. 4.3 of this book (on algorithmic prime-lining).

[35] *Tech, Bias and Housing Initiative, the Promise and Perils of Residential Proptech, Year 1, Research Summary Report, April 2023, TechEquity Collaborative*, p. 5 available at: https://techequity.us/wp-content/uploads/2023/04/TBHI-Y1-Research-Summary-Report.pdf (28.11.2024). ("*Residential Proptech also has the potential to exacerbate the bias inherent in our housing system. Its rise is due, in part, to the desperation felt by average home seekers. With a severely constrained housing supply, companies offering an easier pathway to homeownership may exploit communities that have been harmed by housing discrimination in the past. Opaque algorithms incorporate biased data into their decision-making processes, making it harder to enforce fair housing laws.* Residential Proptech companies often operate in a regulatory gray area, leaving consumers without the protections they would have from traditional housing regulatory systems. *As unprecedented capital investment flows into this space, venture-backed companies' winner-take-all approach to growth has the potential to exacerbate inequality rather than combat it*"). Italics added. See: Part IV, Chap. 4, Sects. 4.4 to 4.4.2.3 of this book.

[36] Balkin, Jack M., "The Three Laws of Robotics in the Age of Big Data", *cit.*, pp. 1217–1241.

[37] See: Eubanks, Virginia, *Automating Inequality: How High-Tech Tools Profile, Police and Punish the Poor*, New York: St. Martin's Press, 2018, 1–272 (1 ff and passim) (coining the expression «automating inequality» to vividly portray the downsides of using high-technology to further compound the yawning gap between rich and poor against the backdrop of biased algorithms).

the outcast,[38] the coloured,[39] and the *socially undesirables* beyond repair? If so, how did we get here? To forestall these definitional quandaries, Rule of Law[40] must claw its way back to the limelight when its empire is poised to crumble/fall apart[41] amidst the rise of an undeterred *Algorithmic Dictatorship*.[42] There is no way around this.

See also: Soss, Joe, Richard C. Fording, and Sanford F. Schram, *Disciplining the Poor: Neoliberal Paternalism and the Persistent Power of Race*. Chicago: University of Chicago Press, 2011.

[38] Becker, Howard S., *Outsiders: Studies in the Sociology of Deviance*. New York: Free Press, 1963.

[39] Allen, James, "The Color of Algorithms: An Analysis and Proposed Research Agenda Deterring Algorithmic Redlining", *Fordham Urban Law Journal*, Volume 46, 2019, pp. 219–234 (229–234) (discussing how historical mortgage redlining greatly swayed modern algorithms generated by massive batches of data sets that consist of decades of information built on exclusion and racial discrimination in the purview of financing, marketing, and housing). See: Part IV, Chap. 4, Sects. 4.4 to 4.4.2.3 of this book. See: Part IV, Chap. 4, Sects. 4.4 to 4.4.2.3 of this book. See: Part IV, Chap. 4, Sects. 4.4 to 4.4.2.1 of this book (on mortgage redlining). See: Part IV, Chap. 4, Sects. 4.2 to 4.4.3 of this book (on algorithmic credit scoring, consumer racism and credit card redlining). See: Part IV, Chap. 4, Sects. 4.4 to 4.4.2.3 of this book (on algorithmic redlining). See: Part IV, Chap. 4, Sect. 4.4.3 of this book (on "algorithmic redliking"). See: Part IV, Chap. 4, Sect. 4.3 of this book (on algorithmic prime-lining).

[40] See: Part V, Chap. 5, Sect. 5.1.1 of this book (on the central tenets of Rule of Law that lends itself to a beacon of justice amidst the sepulchral darkness that is about to take hold).

[41] Recall, the Rule of Law is languishing. This concept is of overriding importance in modern democracies. Regrettably, the Rule of Law is backsliding worldwide. Especially in Central and Eastern Europe. See: Avbelj, Matej, "The Rule of Law, Comprehensive Doctrines, Overlapping Consensus, and the Future of Europe", *Ratio Juris*, Volume 36, Issue 3, September, 2023, pp. 242–258. The Rule of Law is not a «one size fits all» format nonetheless. But see: Chesterman, Simon, "An International Rule of Law", *The American Journal of Comparative Law*, Volume 56, 2008, pp. 331–362 (on the thrust to grasp (?) a catch-all International Rule of Law). See: Peari, Sagi, "Better Law as a Better Outcome", *The American Journal of Comparative Law*, Volume 63, Issue 1, 2015, pp. 155–195 (156) (on Leflar's stance on «better rule of law»). For the purposes of this piece, Rule of Law amounts to a lighthouse of procedural fairness to which citizens, regardless of where they are, resort to upon gaining access to a given system of administration of criminal justice. Whilst further utterances on the fabric of Rule of Law fall well outside the scope and breadth of this paper, one must not be oblivious of the fact that the thrust to Deglobalizing Rule of Law is underway. See: Bussani, Mauro, "Deglobalizing Rule of Law and Democracy: Hunting Down Rhetoric Through Comparative Law", *The American Journal of Comparative Law*, Volume 67, 2019, pp. 701–744 (701) (contending that the thrust to Deglobalizing Rule of Law is interwoven with thrust to take heed of «well-known differences that run through cultures and traditions». In spite of which, «the West has never stopped trying to export its own law into the rest of the world»). Unsurprisingly, there have been educated calls to take heed of the pinpointed cultural and legal differences by, in the case of China, allow for a «Socialist Rule of Law». See: Chinese Common Law Guiding Cases, *Harvard Law Review*, Volume 129, 2016, p. 2213. We will come back to this issue further down is this paper. More on this later.

[42] See: Part IV, Chap. 4, Sects. 4 to 4.10.6 of this book (on Algorithmic Dictatorship and its chilling effect on democracy).

§§ Why is this crucially important? Seldom have scholars been busier, yet scarcely ever have laypeople seemed so distraught about holding the programmers accountable[43] for the hideous acts perpetrated by an unbridled artificial intelligence as abuses pile up.[44]

§§ The time is now ripe to take a step back in a bid to gauge how did we get to the point of the so-called unmooring of the machines that looms large in the discussion we are about to kick-off. Which begs the question: are we on the verge of the *Algorithmic Dictatorship*[45] that is shaping up to throw traditional concepts—such as the Rule of Law[46]—into a frenzy?

§§ As of now, the technological underpinnings of Artificial Intelligence are capable of performing behavioural analytics at more granular levels.[47] As hinted above,[48] Artificial Intelligence may avail humans' experiences[49] that way transcends having a body.[50]

---

[43] But see: Citron, Danielle Keats/Pasquale, Frank, "The Scored Society: Due Process for Automated Predictions", *Washington Law Review*, Volume 89, 2014, pp. 1, 4–5 (highlighting how human beings programming automated systems is directly conducive to, and leads, to fundamentally inaccurate results since the source code, predictive algorithms and datasets may encompass human biases which, in turn, have a disparate impact on historically disadvantaged groups).

[44] See: Part V, Chap. 5, Sect. 5.7.1 of this book (on law number one to control algorithmic decision-making, which mandates that whoever develops and/or deploys machines to undertake a given task must be held criminal accountable for the Hard-AI crimes the latter perpetrates).

[45] See: Part IV, Chap. 4, Sects. 4 to 4.10.6 of this book (on Algorithmic Dictatorship and its chilling effect on democracy).

[46] See: Part V, Chap. 5, Sect. 5.1.1 of this book (on the central tenets of Rule of Law that lends itself to a beacon of justice amidst the sepulchral darkness that is about to take hold).

[47] But see: *Tech, Bias and Housing Initiative, the Promise and Perils of Residential Proptech, Year 1, Research Summary Report, April 2023, TechEquity Collaborative*, p. 11, available at: https://techequity.us/wp-content/uploads/2023/04/TBHI-Y1-Research-Summary-Report.pdf (28.11.2024). ("*From information on company websites, it is not clear what analysis or data is behind subjective determinations like "suitability" to a unit or what the nexus between an individual's characteristics and a unit's characteristics is that indicates the likelihood for property damage. Based on sample reports, even landlords are not privy to how the determinations are made. Instead, they receive a risk score out of 100 simplified into green, yellow, and red recommendations.* What companies withhold in terms of how it works, they make up for with the extent to which they tell landlords it works: Naborly claims their predictions reduce lease defaults by up to 89%. 15 *As Naborly's sample report demonstrates, its property damage assessment is then used as an input to determine its projected eviction outcomes; its early vacancy prediction, in turn, is based on "all assessment factors.*"). Italics added.

[48] See: Part I of this book (Introduction).

[49] See generally: Waytowhich, N./Lawhern, VJ/Garcia, JO, et al., "Compact Convolutional neural networks for classification of asynchronous steady-state visual evoked potentials", *Journal of Neural Engineering*, Volume 15, Issue 6, 2018, passim.

[50] See: Levin, Daniel, "Are you out of your mind? Neurotechnologies and the Making of Disembodied Agency", *Berkeley Technology Law Journal*, Volume 38, 2023, pp. 232–252. See: Part III, Chap. 3, Sect. 3.4.5 of this book (on Critical Artificial Intelligence Studies, with a sharper focus on the harmful effects of Brain-Computer Interfaces). See: Part III, Chap. 3, Sect. 3.5.10 of this book (on the functional aspects of Critical Artificial Intelligence Studies, with a sharper focus

§§ Artificial Intelligence is not only capable of using past decisions as proxies for future[51] decisions[52] but, and foremost, can translate your thoughts[53] into texts.[54] Yet underlying these ground-breaking milestones is a burning question: will our freedom of thought survive these technological developments[55] that draw human–machine

---

on the harmful effects of Artificial Intelligence-embedded technologies, namely, Brain-Computer Interfaces that can read and control your mind and behaviour).

[51] But see: *Tech, Bias and Housing Initiative, the Promise and Perils of Residential Proptech, Year 1, Research Summary Report, April 2023, TechEquity Collaborative*, p. 5 available at: https://techequity.us/wp-content/uploads/2023/04/TBHI-Y1-Research-Summary-Report.pdf (28.11.2024). ("*Residential Proptech also has the potential to exacerbate the bias inherent in our housing system. Its rise is due, in part, to the desperation felt by average home seekers. With a severely constrained housing supply, companies offering an easier pathway to homeownership may exploit communities that have been harmed by housing discrimination in the past. Opaque algorithms incorporate biased data into their decision-making processes, making it harder to enforce fair housing laws.* Residential Proptech companies often operate in a regulatory gray area, leaving consumers without the protections they would have from traditional housing regulatory systems. *As unprecedented capital investment flows into this space, venture-backed companies' winner-take-all approach to growth has the potential to exacerbate inequality rather than combat it*"). Italics added.

[52] Campisi, Natalie, From Inherent Racial Bias to Incorrect Data The Problems With Current Credit Scoring Models, Forbes (Feb. 26, 2021), https://www.forbes.com/advisor/creditcards/from-inherent-racial-bias-to-incorrect-data-the-problems-with-current-credit-scoring-models/ [https://perma.cc/EWA4-CS8E] (highlighting rampant racial bias in credit scoring systems); Oyama, Rebecca, "Do Not (Re)Enter: the Rise of Criminal Background Tenant Screening as a Violation of the Fair Housing Act", *Michigan Journal of Race and Law*, Volume 15, 2009, pp. 181, 184–93 (discussing a broad range of historical/criminal accounts as a way to screen undesirable tenants, such as Blacks and Latinos); Statement of Interest of the United States at 12, *Louis v. SafeRent Sols., LLC, No. 1:22-cv-10800* (D. Mass. Jan. 9, 2023) (holding that the Fair Housing Act liability stretches far and beyond, thus encompassing a vast assortment of entities providing housing-related services, including corporations that offer tenant screening services). See: Massey, Douglas S., "The Legacy of the 1968 Fair Housing Act", *Social Forces*, Volume 30, 2015, pp. 571, 575–76, 578 ("[*The FHA] outlawed the refusal to rent or sell to someone because of race; it prohibited racial discrimination in the terms and conditions of rental or sale; it barred discrimination in real estate advertising; it banned agents from making untrue statements about a dwelling's availability in order to deny access to blacks*; and it enjoined real estate agents from making comments about the race of neighbors or in-movers in order to promote panic selling. Although the new law applied only to around 80% of the nation's housing stock, a Supreme Court decision adjudicated just two months later extended its reach to all housing in the United States"). Italics added. Internal citations omitted. See: Part IV, Chap. 4, Sects. 4.4 to 4.4.2.1 of this book (on mortgage redlining). See: Part IV, Chap. 4, Sects. 4.2 to 4.4.3 of this book (on algorithmic credit scoring, consumer racism and credit card redlining). See: Part IV, Chap. 4, Sects. 4.4 to 4.4.2.3 of this book (on algorithmic redlining). See: Part IV, Chap. 4, Sect. 4.4.3 of this book (on "algorithmic redliking"). See: Part IV, Chap. 4, Sect. 4.3 of this book (on algorithmic prime-lining).

[53] See generally: Steinhert, Steffen/Bublitz, Christoph/Jox, Ralf/Friedrich, Orsolya, "Doing Things with Thoughts: Brain-Computer Interfaces and Disembodied Agency", *Philosophy and Technology*, Volume 32, 2018, pp. 458 and ff and passim.

[54] See: Zhang, X./Sheng, QZ et al., "Converting your thoughts to texts: enabling brain typing via deep feature learning of eeg signals", *IEEE International Conference on Pervasive Computing and Communications*. Athens: IEEE, 2018, passim.

[55] See generally: Oikonomou, VP/Nikolopoulos, S./Kompatsiaris, I., "A Bayesian multiple kernel learning algorithm for SSVEP BCI detection", *Institute of Electrical and Electronical Engineers (IEEE), Journal of Biomedical and Health Informatics*, Volume 23, Issue 5, 2018, pp. 1990–2001.

synergies[56] eerily nearer?[57] My point is both straightforward and clear-cut: gloomier as it currently seems, Artificial Intelligence hasn't always looked this scary. There was a time—a long time ago—in which law did not always lag behind emerging technologies.[58]

§§ The birth of Artificial Intelligence can be traced back to a seminal paper penned by Warren McCulloch and Walter Pitts titled «A logical calculus of the ideas immanent

[56] See: Saffari, Farzad/Khadem, Ali, "A deep learning method for classification of steady-state visual evoked potentials in a brain-computer interface speller", *Brain-Computer Interfaces*, 2023, p. 1 (state avowedly that "Brain-computer interfaces (AKA Brain-Machine Interface) yield an alternative communication pathway especially for people with severe neuromuscular disability (e.g. ALS or brainstem stroke) to communicate with the environment").

[57] See: Levin, Daniel, "Are you out of your mind? Neurotechnologies and the Making of Disembodied Agency", *Berkeley Technology Law Journal*, Volume 38, 2023, pp. 232–252. See: Part III, Chap. 3, Sect. 3.4.5 of this book (on Critical Artificial Intelligence Studies, with a sharper focus on the harmful effects of Brain-Computer Interfaces). See: Part III, Chap. 3, Sect. 3.5.10 of this book (on the functional aspects of Critical Artificial Intelligence Studies, with a sharper focus on the harmful effects of Artificial Intelligence-embedded technologies, namely, Brain-Computer Interfaces that can read and control your mind and behaviour).

[58] Fergus, Rachel, "Biased Technology: The Automated Discrimination of Facial Recognition", *ACLU Minnesota*, February 29, 2024, available at: https://www.aclu-mn.org/en/news/biased-technology-automated-discrimination-facial-recognition (access: 20.09.2024) ("*Technology is developing much more quickly than the laws we need to protect our rights. Anyone with a smartphone or social media account knows how rapidly technology changes, while legislating can take a long, long time. It is essential to proactively put policies into place that will protect our rights as new and more advanced technology is constantly released. Especially when that technology—and law enforcement members using it—have been shown over and over to be biased toward marginalized groups*"). Italics added. Hu, Margaret, "From the National Surveillance State to the Cybersurveillance State", *The Annual Review of Law and Social Science*, Volume 13, 2017, p. 169 ("*in a big data world, a digitized passport system can link to multiple other sources, such as license plate readers, No Fly Lists, and Terrorist Watchlists. Facial recognition technology drawing upon a photo database could potentially link a plethora of digital images of a person, including social media, the internet, photo databases like driver's licenses, live-streaming video, CCTV surveillance, and images obtained from hacking cameras on laptops and digital devices. Biometric data collection and storage are becoming increasingly compulsory through either government identification requirements*, such as digital photo requirements for passports and driver's licenses, or corporate identification requirements, such as biometric access to digital devices"). Italics added. See: Part III, Chap. 3, Sects. 3.5.7 to 3.5.8.1 of this book (on the functional aspects of Critical Artificial Intelligence Studies, with a sharper focus on the perils concerning the deployment of facial recognition technology).

in nervous activity».[59] This path-breaking paper accurately described the way human neurons worked.[60]

§§ For that reason alone, this paper has been deemed as the forebear—the harbinger or the precursor—of modern Artificial Intelligence.[61] From this point onwards, the research about neural networks[62] were to revolve around the inner workings of human brain, with a sharper focus on grasping the intricate and complex biologic process that underpins its functioning.[63]

§§ Conversely, the research on neural networks was geared towards grasping the inner working of human brain, which neatly consisted of a computational reasoning bolstered by a pervasive «artificial neuronal network».[64]

§§ Casts broadly, these renowned scholars contended that the research on neural network should be broken down into two different—yet tightly interlocked—hemispheres.[65] On one hand, one should be focused on clutching the inner workings of human brain. On the other hand, one should be equally focused on grasping the computational reasoning propelled by a neuronal artificial network.[66]

---

[59] See: McCulloch, Warren/Pitts, Walter, "A logical calculus of the ideas immanent in nervous activity", *The bulletin of mathematical biophysics*, Volume 5, 1943, pp. 115–143 ("because of the "all-or-none" character of nervous activity, neural events and the relations among them can be treated by means of propositional logic. It is found that the behavior of every net can be described in these terms, with the addition of more complicated logical means for nets containing circles; and that for any logical expression satisfying certain conditions, one can find a net behaving in the fashion it describes. It is shown that many particular choices among possible neurophysiological assumptions are equivalent, in the sense that for every net behaving under one assumption, there exists another net which behaves under the other and gives the same results, although perhaps not in the same time. Various applications of the calculus are discussed").

[60] Alves, Jones Figueirêdo/Pimentel, Alexandre Freire, "Breves notas sobre os preconceitos decisionais judiciais produzidos por redes neurais artificiais (Brief notes about the judicial decisional prejudices produced by artificial neural networks), *Lisbon Law Review*, Thematic Issue: Law and Technology, Year LXII, Numbers 1 and 2, 2022, pp. 555–577 (558).

[61] Alves, Jones Figueirêdo/Pimentel, Alexandre Freire, "Breves notas sobre os preconceitos decisionais judiciais produzidos por redes neurais artificiais (Brief notes about the judicial decisional prejudices produced by artificial neural networks), *cit.*, pp. 555–577 (558).

[62] Aggarwal, C. C., *Neural networks and deep learning*, Heidelberg, Springer, 2018, passim.

[63] Alves, Jones Figueirêdo/Pimentel, Alexandre Freire, "Breves notas sobre os preconceitos decisionais judiciais produzidos por redes neurais artificiais (Brief notes about the judicial decisional prejudices produced by artificial neural networks), *cit.*, pp. 555–577 (558).

[64] Alves, Jones Figueirêdo/Pimentel, Alexandre Freire, "Breves notas sobre os preconceitos decisionais judiciais produzidos por redes neurais artificiais (Brief notes about the judicial decisional prejudices produced by artificial neural networks), *cit.*, pp. 555–577 (558).

[65] McCulloch, Warren/Pitts, Walter, "A logical calculus of the ideas immanent in nervous activity", *The bulletin of mathematical biophysics*, *cit.*, pp. 115–143.

[66] McCulloch, Warren/Pitts, Walter, "A logical calculus of the ideas immanent in nervous activity", *The bulletin of mathematical biophysics*, *cit.*, pp. 115–143; Alves, Jones Figueirêdo/Pimentel, Alexandre Freire, "Breves notas sobre os preconceitos decisionais judiciais produzidos por redes neurais artificiais (Brief notes about the judicial decisional prejudices produced by artificial neural networks), *cit.*, pp. 555–577 (558).

§§ Put otherwise, according to these pundits, the inner working of the human brain is akin/tantamount to the inner working of an artificial neuronal network. The latter would give rise to the birth of Artificial Intelligence, brimming with both endless opportunities and sweltering challenges.[67]

§§ Notwithstanding, and just as posited above,[68] artificial intelligence is a world of both correlations and hidden patterns deeply ingrained on the data[69] on which machine learning[70] leverages on.[71]

---

[67] Amongst which stands arguably social cleavages spawned by a technology that fondly includes the rich and outrightly excludes the poor, thereby compounding social issues with which modern have been grappling/tussling/scuffling/floundering since immemorial times. Social cleavages—a cloak under which mounting social outcry is often wrapped—that threaten to crumble the foundations upon which stands the linchpin of western societies. See in general: Abramsky, Sasha, *Jumping at Shadows: The Triumph of Fear and the End of the American Dream.* New York: Bold Type Books, 2017, pp. 1–272 (passim).

[68] See: Part I of this book (Introduction).

[69] As hinted above, algorithms make their inferences and draw their conclusions in a way difficult to understand, even for the cohort of programmers that designed them. This is deemed *black box*, that further enhances the shroud of mystery under which algorithms are cloaked. See, for a compelling account of AI black box: Ver: Bathaee, Yavar, "The Artificial Intelligence Black Box and the Failure of Intent and Causation", *Harvard Journal of Law and Technology*, n.º 37, 2018, p. 901 (adduces that "*one possible reason AI may be a black box to humans is that it relies on machine-learning algorithms that internalize data in ways that are not easily audited or understood by humans* (…) "*first, a lack may arise from the complexity of the algorithm's structure, such as with deep neural network, which consists of thousands of artificial neurons working together in a diffuse way to solve a problem. This reason for AI being a black box is referred to as "complexity""*. *Second, the lack of transparency may arise because the AI is using a machine-learning algorithm that relies on geometric relationships that humans cannot visualize, such as with support vector machines. This reason for AI being a black box is referred to as "dimensionality"*). Italics added. But see: Pearl, Judea, *Causality*, 2nd edition, Cambridge, Cambridge University Press, 2009 (on the fundamental tenets of causality). But see: Kilbertus, Niki/Carulla, Mateo Rojas/Parascandolo, Giambattista/ Hardt, Moritz/Janzing, Dominik/ Schoellkopf, Bernhard, "Avoiding Discrimination through Causal Reasoning", *Advances in Neural Information Processing Systems*, I. Guyon, U. V. Luxburg, S. Bengio, H. Wallach, R. Fergus, S. Vishwanathan, and R. Garnett (Eds.), Vol. 30. Curran Associates, Inc., 2017, pp. 656–666 (arguing that is feasible to avoiding discrimination through a granular and fine-grained causal reasoning). See: Part V, Chap. 5, Sects. 5.1.5.2.2 to 5.1.5.2.2.1.4 of this book (on the fundamental shift away from causation to correlations in algorithmic decision-making). See also: Part V, Chap. 5, Sect. 5.7.2 of this book (on law number two to control algorithmic decision-making, which mandates that black box models must not be entrusted with the task of making high stake decisions—v.g. health and freedom).

[70] Sivarajah, Uthayasnkar et al., "Critical Analysis of Big Data Challenges and Analytical Methods", *Journal of Business Research*, Volume 70, 2017, pp. 263 and ff and passim; Jetten, Lieke /Sharon, Stephen, "Selected Issues concerning the Ethical Use of Big Data Health Analytics", *Washington & Lee Law Review Online*, Volume 72, 2016, passim.

[71] Gillis, Talia B., "The Input Data Fallacy", *Minnesota Law Review*, Volume 106, 2022, pp. 1176–1263 (p. 1244). Machine learning "involves computer algorithms *that have the ability to "learn" or improve in performance over time on some task*". See: Surden, Harry, "Machine Learning and Law", in: *Washington Law Review*, Volume 89, 2014, pp. 87 e ss; Murphy, Kevin P., *Machine Learning: A Probabilistic Perspective (Adaptive Computation and Machine Learning series)*, Massachusetts, The MIT Press, 2012, pp. 1–1104. Machine learning "*attempts to combine deductive, inductive, and abductive reasoning to make person-like reasoning in AI Entities possible. Machine-learning AI*

§§ Deep learning, a byproduct of machine learning,[72] enables the machine to improve its performance over the course of time.[73] On the opposite pole, human legal reasoning is a world of causation[74] that seldom chimes in with hidden correlations.[75] They are poles apart. This mismatch is set to put law at loggerheads with its fundamental tenets. Amongst which stands legal security. Especially, albeit not

---

Entities initially learn in the same way a human child learns. First, they notice details and patterns in shapes, sounds, and behaviors; then put them together to distinguish one person from another, or a dog from a cat. Eventually, the AI can recognize and identify" common objects. See also: Hutto-Schultz, Jess, "Dicitur Ex Machina: Artificial Intelligence and the Hearsay Rule", *George Mason Law Review*, Volume 27, n. ° 2, 2020, pp. 684–718 (689).

[72] See: Chollet, François, *Deep Learning with Python*. Shelter Island, Nova Iorque: Manning, 2018, pp. 1–384 (passim). *Deep Learning* stands as a byproduct of *Machine Learning*. *Machine Learning*, a subset of Artificial Intelligence, unfolds itself in *Deep Learning*, which "involves computer algorithms that have the ability to "learn" or improve in performance over time on some task". See: Surden, Harry, "Machine Learning and Law", *Washington Law Review*, Volume 89, 2015, pp. 87 and ff.

[73] See: Samek, Wojciech/Müller, Klaus-Robert, "Explainable AI: interpreting, explaining and visualizing deep learning", *Towards Explainable Artificial Intelligence*, Samek, Wojciech/Montavon, Grégoire/ Vedaldi, Andrea/Hansen, Lars Kai/Müller, Klaus-Robert (Editors). Heidelberg/Berlin/ New York: Springer, 2019, pp. 5–22 ("in recent years, machine learning (ML) has become a key enabling technology for the sciences and industry. Especially through improvements in methodology, the availability of large databases and increased computational power, *today's ML algorithms are able to achieve excellent performance (at times even exceeding the human level) on an increasing number of complex tasks. Deep learning models are at the forefront of this development. However, due to their nested non-linear structure, these powerful models have been generally considered "black boxes", not providing any information about what exactly makes them arrive at their predictions*. Since in many applications, e.g., in the medical domain, *such lack of transparency may be not acceptable, the development of methods for visualizing, explaining and interpreting deep learning models has recently attracted increasing attention. This introductory paper presents recent developments and applications in this field and makes a plea for a wider use of explainable learning algorithms in practice*."). Italics added. See: Part V, Chap. 5, Sects. 5.7 to 5.7.5 of this book (on the five laws to control algorithmic decision-making). See: Part V, Chap. 5, Sects. 5.8 to 5.8.5 of this book (on the five laws to interpret algorithmic decision-making). See: Part V, Chap. 5, Sects. 5.2 to 5.6.2.1 of this book (on the thing-centred algorithmic decision-making propelled by a *Controllable* and *Interpretable* Machine Learning that weeds out *Algorithmic Dictatorship* and secures *Algorithmic Common Good*. It is worth recalling that the thing-centred algorithmic decision-making seeks to unwind the perils arising out of the lack of theoretical underpinnings facing the human-centred algorithmic decision-making, as extensively fleshed out Part III, Chap. 3, Sects. 3.4.3 to 3.4.4 of this book).

[74] But see: Pearl, Judea, *Causality*, 2nd edition, Cambridge, Cambridge University Press, 2009 (on the fundamental tenets of causality).

[75] As we throw ourselves in the immense arena of automated processes powered by Artificial Intelligence, the difficulties to grasp its delicate intricacies mount exponentially. See: Cohen, Julien E., *Between Truth and Power: The Legal Constructions of Informational Capitalism*. Oxford: Oxford University Press, 2019, pp. 1–376 (p. 192) (asserts adamantly that "*automated processes* have obvious efficiency advantages, *but such processes may not align well (or well at all) with applicable legal requirements that are couched in shades of gray*"). Italics added. See: Part V, Chap. 5, Sects. 5.1.5.2.2 to 5.1.5.2.2.1.4 of this book (on the fundamental shift away from causation to correlations in algorithmic decision-making).

exclusively, when artificial intelligence[76] is deployed to assist judges[77] in performing legal reasoning[78] underpinning a legal decision[79] making.[80] More on this later.[81]

---

[76] This is the gist of a digital future, which will ineluctably give rise to a "Artificial Intelligent Justice". See: Re, Richard M./Solow-Niederman, Alicia, "Developing Artificially Intelligent", *Stanford Technology Law Review*, Volume 22, 2019, pp. 242 ff and passim. See: Part V, Chap. 5, Sect. 5.7.2 of this book (on law number two to control algorithmic decision-making, which mandates that black box models must not be entrusted with the task of making high stake decisions—v.g. health and freedom).

[77] There is an excellent body of empirical research that shows that a poor judicial performance spawns low trust in legal systems. See: Magalhães, Pedro C./Garoupa, Nuno, "Judicial Performance and Trust in Legal Systems: Findings from a Decade of Surveys in 20 European Countries", *Social Science Quarterly*, 2020, 1 (the main goal of this exciting piece of research was «determining the existence of a relationship between judicial performance and citizens 'trust in the legal system». To cater for that, the methodology used «cross-classified multilevel models, using data from more than 20 European countries, 80 surveys, and 100, 000 respondents, over a decade». Regarding the results, «the longer the time that lower courts take, on average, to dispose of pending cases, the lower is the public's trust in their legal system». As an upshot, «judicial performance, operationalized as the ability of courts to avoid delays in the delivery of justice, is a significant correlate of citizens'evalatuations of their country's legal system»). Tyler, Tom R., "Trust and Law Abidingness: A Proactive Model of Social Regulation", *Boston University Law Review*, Volume 81, 2001, pp. 361 ff; Barbalet, Jack, "A Characterization of Trust, and Its Consequences", *Theory and Society*, Volume 38, 2009, pp. 367–372; Farrell, Henry, "Institutions and Midlevel Explanations of Trust", Cook, Karen S./Levi, Margaret/Hardin, Russell (Eds.), *Whom can We Trust? How Groups, Networks, and Institutions Make Trust Possible.* Manhattan, New York City: Russell Sage Publication, 2010, pp. 128–129; Cross, Frank B., "Law and Trust", *Georgetown Law Journal*, Volume 93, 2005, pp. 1457 ff (parsing the relationship between the concept of trust in the realm of groups and trust networks in Western cultures). Trust plays a pivotal role in catering for the citizen's confidence in a given jurisdiction. This is something that prospective lawmakers and policymakers should never lose sight of. Especially in the realm of criminal procedure law.

[78] See in French doctrine: Baller, Stéphane/Deffains, Bruno, "Intelligence artificielle et devenir de la professions d'avocat; l'avenir est présent», *Revue pratique de la prospective et de innovation*, Volume 1, 2018, pp. 14 and ff (canvass the foundations of deep-rooted concerns regarding the irruption of artificial intelligence in the legal arena). Scholars haven't been neither coy nor bashful in pinpointing the drawbacks and downsides concerning the unbridled and rampant rise of the Artificial Intelligence in the legal arena. See: Wu, Tim, "Will Artificial Intelligence Eat the Law? The Rise of Hybrid Social-Ordering Systems", *Columbia Law Review*, Volume 119, 2019, pp. 2001 and ff and passim.

[79] See: Scherer, Maxi, "Artificial Intelligence and Legal Decision-Making: The Wide Open?", *Journal of International Arbitration*, Volume 36, 2019, passim. See: Weizenbaum, Joseph, *Computer Power and Human Reason: From Judgment to Calculation*, 1st edition, New York, W. H. Freeman & Co, 1976, pp. 1–300 (227) ("examines the sources of the computer's powers and offers evaluative explorations of what computers can do, cannot do, and should not be employed to do") (this founding father of Artificial Intelligence presciently noted that we should not entrust Artificial Intelligence-embedded technologies with with "tasks that demand wisdom"). Italics added. The approval of rental applications is arguably one of those tasks that should never be entrusted to machines). More on this on Part IV, Chap. 4, Sects. 4.4 to 4.4.2.1 of this book.

[80] For a perspective on the changes that the legal arena in currently undergoing, see in French doctrine: Deffains, Bruno, "Le monde du droit face à la transformation numérique", *Revue Française d'Études Constitutionnelles et Politiques*, Volume 170, 2019, pp. 49 and ff and passim.

[81] See: Part V, Chap. 5, Sect. 5.8.5 of this book (on law number five to interpret algorithmic decision-making, which mandates that robot-judges, robot-prosecutors and robot-lawyers must not enter the

§§ From the breakdown painstakingly outlined by McCulloch and Pitts arose a computational model of neural artificial network which received inputs signals, multiplied by a given measure and compared the result against a given benchmark.[82] Underpinned by these seminal concepts, the logical-binary model has surfaced, thereby giving rise to the very first neuronal network[83] comprised by a sole and square neuronal layer,[84] which is far cry from the billions of neuronal layers encompassing a modern neuronal[85] network.[86]

§§ The blazingly new developments regarding Artificial Intelligence did not stave off here. Nor could anyone upend the inexorable marching of time. Before long, the polymath Alan Turing built—alongside David Champernowne—a top-notch system of machine learning, which has greatly contributed to the overall advancement of Artificial Intelligence. It bears mentioning that the overriding goal underpinning such

---

courtroom for they are utterly incapable of making sound and interpretable value judgements). See: Part V, Chap. 5, Sects. 5.2 to 5.6.2.1 of this book (on the thing-centred algorithmic decision-making propelled by a *Controllable* and *Interpretable* Machine Learning that weeds out *Algorithmic Dictatorship* and secures *Algorithmic Common Good*). See: Part III, Chap. 3, Sect. 3.5.1.1 of this book (on the functional aspects of Critical Artificial Intelligence Studies, with a sharper focus on the harmful effects of Artificial Intelligence-embedded technologies, namely, perpetuation technologies—griefbots, avatars and robots—that are slated to dehumanize human-laden emotions).

[82] McCulloch, Warren/Pitts, Walter, "A logical calculus of the ideas immanent in nervous activity", *The bulletin of mathematical biophysics, cit.*, pp. 115–143; Alves, Jones Figueirêdo/Pimentel, Alexandre Freire, "Breves notas sobre os preconceitos decisionais judiciais produzidos por redes neurais artificiais (Brief notes about the judicial decisional prejudices produced by artificial neural networks), *cit.*, pp. 555–577 (558).

[83] Aggarwal, C. C., *Neural networks and deep learning*, Heidelberg, Springer, 2018, passim; Agrawal, A., Gans, J., & Goldfarb, A., "Prediction machines (updated and expanded): The simple economics of artificial intelligence", *Harvard Business Review Press*, 2022; Agrawal, A., Gans, J., & Goldfarb, A., "Power and prediction: The disruptive economics of artificial intelligence", *Harvard Business Review Press*, 2022; Bengio, Y., Hinton, G., Yao, A., Song, D., Abbeel, P., Harari, Y. N., Hadfield, G., Russell, S., Kahneman, D., & Mindermann, S., *Managing ai risks in an era of rapid progress*, arXiv preprint arXiv:2310.17688, 2023, passim (on neural networks and deep learning that operate jointly in the age of Artificial Intelligence-embedded technologies).

[84] McCulloch, Warren/Pitts, Walter, "A logical calculus of the ideas immanent in nervous activity", *The bulletin of mathematical biophysics, cit.*, pp. 115–143; Alves, Jones Figueirêdo/Pimentel, Alexandre Freire, "Breves notas sobre os preconceitos decisionais judiciais produzidos por redes neurais artificiais (Brief notes about the judicial decisional prejudices produced by artificial neural networks), *cit.*, pp. 555–577 (558).

[85] Aggarwal, C. C., *Neural networks and deep learning*, Heidelberg, Springer, 2018, passim; Agrawal, A., Gans, J., & Goldfarb, A., "Prediction machines (updated and expanded): The simple economics of artificial intelligence", *Harvard Business Review Press*, 2022; Agrawal, A., Gans, J., & Goldfarb, A., "Power and prediction: The disruptive economics of artificial intelligence", *Harvard Business Review Press*, 2022; Bengio, Y., Hinton, G., Yao, A., Song, D., Abbeel, P., Harari, Y. N., Hadfield, G., Russell, S., Kahneman, D., & Mindermann, S., *Managing ai risks in an era of rapid progress*, arXiv preprint arXiv:2310.17688, 2023, passim (on neural networks and deep learning that operate jointly in the age of Artificial Intelligence-embedded technologies).

[86] See generally: Podmore, J.J./Breckon, TP/Aznan, NKN, et al., "On the relative contribution of deep convulational neural networks for SSVEP-based bio-signal decoding in BCI speller applications", *Institute of Electrical and Electronic Engineers (IEEE), Transactions on Neural System and Rehabilitation Engineering*, Volume 27, Issue 4, 2019, pp. 611–618.

state-of-the-art system of machine learning was to create an algorithm to play chess. This algorithm was tagged as "Turochamp", which comprised the creators 'names.[87]

§§ The algorithm itself was not able-bodied until 1950 though. Yet, dispiritingly, the then technological developments did not keep pace with their new-fangled algorithm, thus hindering its full-fledged implementation.[88] For an unfortunate reason: back then, people fought shy of technology as the world was emerging from a protracted and blood-soaked second world war, which has arguably taken a toll on their willingness to embrace the sappiness of the new.

§§ As the outreach of the pinpointed algorithm was conspicuously meagre, Alan Turing,[89] awash with exceedingly high creative vibrations, brought forth a theoretical matrix for the betterment of Artificial Intelligence, which, in turn, has not only fallen in sharp alignment with the overall advancement of humanity, but, and foremost, has unleashed the potential of machines to vie with human beings for the control of the world we live in.

§§ Imbued with both ambrosial aims and a propelling force, Alan Turing[90] engendered an earth-shattering paper titled «Computing Machinery and Intelligence»,[91] which comprised an introductory chapter («The imitation game»).[92] This introductory chapter laced itself with luck as gave rise to a movie, which, in truth, has been heaped worldwide praise.

---

[87] Alves, Jones Figueirêdo/Pimentel, Alexandre Freire, "Breves notas sobre os preconceitos decisionais judiciais produzidos por redes neurais artificiais (Brief notes about the judicial decisional prejudices produced by artificial neural networks), *cit.*, pp. 555–577 (558).

[88] Alves, Jones Figueirêdo/Pimentel, Alexandre Freire, "Breves notas sobre os preconceitos decisionais judiciais produzidos por redes neurais artificiais (Brief notes about the judicial decisional prejudices produced by artificial neural networks), *cit.*, pp. 555–577 (558).

[89] Turing, A. M., "Intelligent Machinery, in Mechanical Intelligence", Collected Works of A. M. Turing. D. C. Ince, ed. North Holland, 1948/1992, pp. 107–127.

[90] "When we talk about the history of AI we must refer to the 1940s, the Second World War and the advent of the first computers. It was at that time that the idea of the human–machine analogy was born, that human intelligence could be simulated through the use of machines, an essential condition for the development of AI. In this period, one of the greatest thinkers to explore this theme was Alan Turing." See: https://www.klondike.ai/en/ai-history-the-dartmouth-conference/ (access: 09.09.2024).

[91] Turing, Alan M., "Computing Machinery and Intelligence", *Mind*, Volume LIX, Issue 236, October 1950, 1950, pp. 433–460.

[92] Alves, Jones Figueirêdo/Pimentel, Alexandre Freire, "Breves notas sobre os preconceitos decisionais judiciais produzidos por redes neurais artificiais (Brief notes about the judicial decisional prejudices produced by artificial neural networks), *cit.*, pp. 555–577 (558).

§§ Set against the background of a convoluted world[93] that mercilessly/ruthlessly clamped down those who dared to stand out, Alan Turing, overcome with a bursting ingenious force, penned a mesmerizing paper[94] whereby he grappled with the dilemma of whether and to what extent machines were amenable to develop an autonomous thinking on their own akin to that of humans.[95]

§§ He went on to set in stone an emblematic paragraph that arguably constitutes the hallmark of his stance in this regard. It reads as follows: «we may hope that machines will eventually compete with men in all purely intellectual fields (…) This process could follow the normal teaching of a child. Things would be pointed out and named, etc.».[96]

§§ Turing's paper has been deemed as one of the foundational pillars of modern Artificial Intelligence[97] as set the tone for modern discussions[98] on the extent to which machines[99] will trounce/vanquish humans[100] in the forthcoming future.[101] No

---

[93] Against the backdrop of which people often tussle – in that they flounder – to understand each other amidst an increasingly conflict-prone world. See: Menkel-Meadow, Carrie, "Why We can't "Just All Get Along: Dysfunction in the Polity and Conflict Resolution and What We Might do About It", *Journal of Dispute Resolution*, Volume 1, Issue 5, 2018, pp. 6 and ff and passim (this lauded scholar notes, however, that inequality, social cleavages, and lack of tolerance beset the globalized world).

[94] Turing, Alan M., "Computing Machinery and Intelligence", *cit.*, pp. 433–460.

[95] Alves, Jones Figueirêdo/Pimentel, Alexandre Freire, "Breves notas sobre os preconceitos decisionais judiciais produzidos por redes neurais artificiais (Brief notes about the judicial decisional prejudices produced by artificial neural networks), *cit.*, pp. 555–577 (559).

[96] Turing, Alan M., "Computing Machinery and Intelligence", *cit.*, pp. 433–460.

[97] Santos, Hugo Luz dos, *Direito Contratual do Jogo: Um Olhar Bifronte*, Braga, NovaCausa Edições Jurídicas, 2023, pp. 1–760.

[98] "If in previous centuries the conditions for the study of human intelligence and its possible artificializations were created with scientific and mathematical studies, it was only with the advent of the first electronic computers in the 1940s that this interest took a concrete path. A further decisive step was taken thanks to the work of Alan Turing. The British scientist Alan Turing is considered one of the fathers of modern computer science and was among the first to take an interest in the subject. His work was not only theoretical, but had very important applications especially in the field of cryptography. In fact, Turing made a fundamental contribution to the success of the allies in Second World War: thanks to his collaboration with the British government, the code behind the Enigma device and the German military transmissions were cracked." See: https://www.klondike.ai/en/ai-history-the-dartmouth-conference/ (access: 09.09.2024).

[99] Boden, Margaret A., *Artificial Intelligence: A Very Short Introduction*. Oxford: Oxford University Press, 2018, pp. 26–28 (fleshes out both *expert systems* and *rule-based programmes*).

[100] See: Tegmark, Max, *Life 3.0: Being Human in the Age of Artificial Intelligence*. New York: Knopf, 2018, pp. 1–384 (pp. 24 and ff) (charts the path ahead for a wide range of intelligences, including artificial intelligence in the digital age). There is a handful of authors that wonder if artificial intelligence can mimic not only human intelligence but, and foremost, human behaviour. Amongst whom stands: Russel, Stuart, Norvig, Peter, *Artificial Intelligence: A Modern Approach*. London: United Kingdom, Pearson, 2018, passim.

[101] See: Cuellar, Mariano-Florentino, "A Common Law for the Age of Artificial Intelligence: Incremental Adjudication, Institutions, and Relational Non-Arbitrariness", *Columbia Law Review*, Volume 119, 2020, pp. 1773–1775 (this author presciently posits that "(t)he coevolution of human

surprise stems for the fact that Turing's stance on the unbridled potential of Artificial Intelligence[102] still ripples forward.[103] Which, in turn, are hardly elating news for humans[104] as we are about to find out on the chapters to come.

§§ History, in spite of its wrenching pain, is neither amenable to be unlived nor whimsically upended. We are keenly aware of that by now. Consistent with the laudable truism according to which no one is redoubtable enough to hobble the unremitting marching of time, another paramount contribute to the overall betterment of Artificial Intelligence has surfaced.

§§ This time around, the mathematician Claude Elwood Shannon published an erudite paper whereby he laid down the foundations upon which digital codification would brawnily stand. This paper[105] has been lavished a sheer amount of praise.

§§ Claude Elwood Shannon trounced his internal squabbles only to lay down the groundwork for codification. Drawing on the seminal work of Norbert Wiener,

---

and artificial intelligence—what we could call our dance with machines—is well on its way to becoming routine"). See also: Cataleta, Maria Stefania/Cataleta, Anna, "Artificial Intelligence and Human Rights: An Unequal Struggle", *CIFILE Journal of International Law*, Volume 1, N. ° 2, 2020 ("*Artificial Intelligence (AI) is a kind of intelligence that was born in the 1950s and is an integral part of the digital revolution. Progress made by AI has permitted the birth of systems capable of rivalling human capacities or, in some cases, surpassing them.* The progress of the intellectual capacities of AI will change the way of life for human beings and will revolutionise the world of employment. *Intelligent systems present problems regarding individual rights and responsibilities, because as technology replaces more and more of what humans have typically done, our individual roles will become more blurred.*"). Italics added. Converging: Cataleta, Maria Stefania, "Artificial Intelligence vs Human Intelligence", in: Martin, L. Miraut/Zalucki, M. (editors), *Artificial intelligence and Human Rights, Dickinson eBook*. Krakow: AFM Krakow University, 2021, pp. 117–127 (on the slew of both moral, ethical and legal issues with which jurists will grapple in the forthcoming future due to the rise of artificial intelligence in legal arena).

[102] Such as the potential to perform heightened security that allows permanent digital surveillance of individuals deemed socially unfit or—worse yet—biologically or mentally prone to engage in flagitious and unlawful activities. The German doctrine has fleshed out this topic in depth. See: Müller, Helmut, "Europäische Rechtssicherheit gegen Deutsches Sicherheitsrecht? Zur EGMR-Entscheidung in Sachen nachträgliche (Verlängerung der) Sicherungsverwahrung", *Kritische Justiz*, Volume 43, Issue 3, 2010, pp. 256–268. This topic—although enthralling/besotting/buoying—falls conspicuously outside the breadth and scope of this essay.

[103] Candent challenges that come under the yoke of intelligent automation, which is shaping up to morph the legal arena beyond recognition. See: Bornet, Pascal/Barkin, Ian/Wirtz, Jochen, *Intelligent Automation: Learn how to harness Artificial Intelligence to boost business and make out world more human*, 2020, pp. 1–432.

[104] Against the backdrop of which there will be a seamless meld of humans and machines. This turbid reality—although difficult to depict at this moment—will be inevitably morphed into a disturbingly dystopic reality sooner rather than later. See: Remus, Dana/Levy, Frank, "Can Robots be Lawyers? Computers, Lawyers, and the Practice of Law", *Georgetown Journal of Legal Ethics*, Volume 30, 2018, pp. 501 and ff and passim.

[105] Shannon, Claude Elwood, "Mathematical Theory of Communication", *The Bell System Technical Journal*, Vol. 27, July–October 1948, 1948, pp. 379–423, 623–656.

Claude Elwood Shannon intrepidly delved into the depths of a hitherto inscrutable issue: how to meaningfully ferret out the best way to codify an information.[106]

§§ For purposes here, his overriding goal was to conceive a digital bit amenable to convey/relay an information from one end (sender) to another end[107] (receiver).[108] The up until then blurred boundaries between information and digital information were finally belched out and accordingly swept aside. The world back then—so dither and dilly-dally in embracing the vibrant contours of the blazingly new—was finally steadfast in keeping abreast with the newest developments in science to retain efficacy.

§§ The previously mentioned digital breakthrough spawned a technology which has fallen neatly onto the dazzling category of turnkey. Put simply, this digital breakthrough enhanced, rather than degraded, the social relations back then. From this point onwards, the digital bit became a propelling force, and a crowning achievement, with which to reckon in science. But not just that though: this digital breakthrough carried forward a rivetingly promising omen: digital communications would be possible, thereby revolutionizing human interaction for decades to come.

§§ Bearing this backdrop very firmly in mind, Claude Elwood Shannon was unsurprisingly hailed as one of the founding fathers of digital communications.[109] The digital bit was deployed in ways that make us feel comfortable with, not creep out by, digital communications. E-mail and the World Wide Web[110] stand as both capstones/flagship achievements in this regard.

§§ All humans were left to do was to spotlight violations stemming from the misuse of digital communications, and accordingly assume an all-encompassing watchdog role to stymie abuses—those laid bare by cyber hacking and deep fake technology—arising out of the dingiest corners of modern internet.[111] A both herculean and gargantuan task that is far from being completed nonetheless. Which is something that

---

106 Alves, Jones Figueirêdo/Pimentel, Alexandre Freire, "Breves notas sobre os preconceitos decisionais judiciais produzidos por redes neurais artificiais (Brief notes about the judicial decisional prejudices produced by artificial neural networks), *cit.*, pp. 555–577 (559).

107 Alves, Jones Figueirêdo/Pimentel, Alexandre Freire, "Breves notas sobre os preconceitos decisionais judiciais produzidos por redes neurais artificiais (Brief notes about the judicial decisional prejudices produced by artificial neural networks), *cit.*, pp. 555–577 (559).

108 Shannon, Claude Elwood, "Mathematical Theory of Communication", *cit.*, pp. 379–423, 623–656.

109 Alves, Jones Figueirêdo/Pimentel, Alexandre Freire, "Breves notas sobre os preconceitos decisionais judiciais produzidos por redes neurais artificiais (Brief notes about the judicial decisional prejudices produced by artificial neural networks), *cit.*, pp. 555–577 (559).

110 Alves, Jones Figueirêdo/Pimentel, Alexandre Freire, "Breves notas sobre os preconceitos decisionais judiciais produzidos por redes neurais artificiais (Brief notes about the judicial decisional prejudices produced by artificial neural networks), *cit.*, pp. 555–577 (559).

111 See: Luguri, Jamie/Lior, Jacob Strahilevitz, "Shining a Light on Dark Patterns", *Journal of Legal Analytics*, Volume 13, 2021, pp. 43–109.

should warrant deep concerns from all stakeholders as the deepfake technology[112] gains traction and gathers pace. The flurry of concern about the deepfake technology is accordingly mounting. From where we stand, the malady will only expand. More on this later.[113]

§§ The unrelenting drive of history knowingly snowballs as the cycle of innovation repeats itself; the cascade inevitably strengthens and the plot accordingly thickens: this is the perpetual cycle of innovation that ushers in, and paves the way to, the greatest leaps forward in human history.

§§ Law, however, is despairingly sluggish—even glacially slow—in that often keeps apace with the newest technological developments.[114] Concisely, law proverbially lags behind emerging technologies. Strikingly, that is the rationale behind patching social problems with far-fetched digital solutions, which is far easier than mustering

---

[112] Dean, Ashley, "Deepfakes, Pose Detection, and the Death of "Seeing is believing", *Law and Technology Today*, 2019; Maras, Marie-Helen/Alexandrou, "Determining Authenticity of Video Evidence in the Age of Artificial Intelligence and in the Wake of Deepfake Videos", *International Journal of Evidence and Proof*, Volume 23, Issue 3, 2019, pp. 255–262.

[113] See: Part III, Chap. 3, Sects. 3.5.2 to 3.5.3.1 of this book (on the functional aspects of Critical Artificial Intelligence Studies, with a sharper focus on the harmful effects of Artificial Intelligence-embedded technologies, namely, Generative Artificial Intelligence and its offsprings—deepfakes and its deleterious effects on human memory).

[114] Fergus, Rachel, "Biased Technology: The Automated Discrimination of Facial Recognition", *ACLU Minnesota*, February 29, 2024, available at: https://www.aclu-mn.org/en/news/biased-technology-automated-discrimination-facial-recognition (access: 20.09.2024) ("*Technology is developing much more quickly than the laws we need to protect our rights. Anyone with a smartphone or social media account knows how rapidly technology changes, while legislating can take a long, long time. It is essential to proactively put policies into place that will protect our rights as new and more advanced technology is constantly released. Especially when that technology—and law enforcement members using it—have been shown over and over to be biased toward marginalized groups*"). Italics added. Hu, Margaret, "From the National Surveillance State to the Cybersurveillance State", *The Annual Review of Law and Social Science*, Volume 13, 2017, p. 169 ("*in a big data world, a digitized passport system can link to multiple other sources, such as license plate readers, No Fly Lists, and Terrorist Watchlists. Facial recognition technology drawing upon a photo database could potentially link a plethora of digital images of a person, including social media, the internet, photo databases like driver's licenses, live-streaming video, CCTV surveillance, and images obtained from hacking cameras on laptops and digital devices. Biometric data collection and storage are becoming increasingly compulsory through either government identification requirements*, such as digital photo requirements for passports and driver's licenses, or corporate identification requirements, such as biometric access to digital devices"). Italics added.

the unshakeable resolve to deftly tackle the deep-rooted legal issues about invidiousness, callousness and inequity that beset the data-driven world we live in.[115] More on this later.[116]

§§ Turning to the topic at hand, 1949 was an auspicious year for science. 1949 was a year in which Donald Hebb successfully sprang into action his take on computational reasoning.[117] This technology was brought to bear with a sweeping objective: laying out the fundamental tenets of the neurological pathways taken by the brain prior to engaging in any type of fruit-bearing reasoning. To cater for that, Donald Hebb wrote an influential book whereby he outlined the foundational pillars of his neuropsychological theory.[118]

§§ Donald Olding Hebb shrewdly created a behavioural thesis against the backdrop of which there is a perceived correlation between neurological and psychological

---

[115] The issue of a digital reality fed by a data-driven world has been shrewdly portrayed by renowned scholars, which offer gripping examples of it: Suzor, Nicolas P., *Lawless: The Secret Rules that Govern our Digital Lives*. Cambridge, United Kingdom: Cambridge University Press, 2019, pp. 1–218 (passim). But see: Hardt, Moritz, "How big data is unfair: Understanding sources of unfairness in data driven decision making", *Medium*, Archived on Oct. 8, 2014, available at: https://web.archive.org/web/20141008185829/ https://medium.com/@mrtz/how-big-data-is-unfair-9aa544d739de. (access: 17.12.2024).

[116] See: Part IV, Chap. 4, Sects. 4 to 4.10.6 of this book (on Algorithmic Dictatorship and its chilling effect on democracy).

[117] Alves, Jones Figueirêdo/Pimentel, Alexandre Freire, "Breves notas sobre os preconceitos decisionais judiciais produzidos por redes neurais artificiais (Brief notes about the judicial decisional prejudices produced by artificial neural networks), *cit.*, pp. 555–577 (559).

[118] Donald Olding Hebb, *The Organization of Behavior: A Neuropsychological Theory*, Psychology Press, 2002, pp. 1–378 ("since its publication in 1949, D.O. Hebb's, *The Organization of Behavior* has been one of the most influential books in the fields of psychology and neuroscience. However, the original edition has been unavailable since 1966, ensuring that Hebb's comment that a classic normally means "cited but not read" is true in his case. This new edition rectifies a long-standing problem for behavioral neuroscientists–the inability to obtain one of the most cited publications in the field. *The Organization of Behavior* played a significant part in stimulating the investigation of the neural foundations of behavior and continues to be inspiring because it provides a general framework for relating behavior to synaptic organization through the dynamics of neural networks.

D.O. Hebb was also the first to examine the mechanisms by which environment and experience can influence brain structure and function, and his ideas formed the basis for work on enriched environments as stimulants for behavioral development. References to Hebb, the Hebbian cell assembly, the Hebb synapse, and the Hebb rule increase each year. These forceful ideas of 1949 are now applied in engineering, robotics, and computer science, as well as neurophysiology, neuroscience, and psychology–a tribute to Hebb's foresight in developing a foundational neuropsychological theory of the organization of behavior"). See also: Baker, B., Lansdell, B., & Kording, K. P., "Three aspects of representation in neuroscience", *Trends in Cognitive Sciences*, 2022.

conceptions arising out of perception,[119] motivation and learning.[120] But there is so much more to be remarked upon in this regard though.

§§ Compellingly, Donald Olding Hebb deftly carved out the concept of reverberation circuit in an earnest attempt to accurately understand the procedure that leads to the growth of neuronal networks.[121] The latter—neuronal networks—are the byproduct of the intrinsic linkage between metabolic changes and repeated transmission through neuronal synapses.[122]

§§ Setting aside the overhyped/overblown promises to grasp the inner workings of the brain—which remains an insurmountable task to this day—, Donald Olding Hebb's work has nevertheless sent ripple effects throughout the globe. Tellingly, his trailblazing research mapped out the pathways through which neuronal networks can be reinforced.[123]

§§ Conversely, Hebb has adamantly shown that neuronal networks[124] are buttressed through repetition.[125] The more a given learning path is repeated, the more proficient that learning curve will be.[126] A widely known quote is in dire need of being brought to the fore in this regard: «an excited neuron tends to decrease its discharge to inactive neurons, and increase this discharge to any active neuron, and therefore to form a

[119] Hebb, Donald Olding, *The Organization of Behavior: A Neuropsychological Theory*, *cit.*, pp. 1–378.

[120] Alves, Jones Figueirêdo/Pimentel, Alexandre Freire, "Breves notas sobre os preconceitos decisionais judiciais produzidos por redes neurais artificiais (Brief notes about the judicial decisional prejudices produced by artificial neural networks), *cit.*, pp. 555–577 (559).

[121] Alves, Jones Figueirêdo/Pimentel, Alexandre Freire, "Breves notas sobre os preconceitos decisionais judiciais produzidos por redes neurais artificiais (Brief notes about the judicial decisional prejudices produced by artificial neural networks), *cit.*, pp. 555–577 (559). Hebb, Donald Olding, *The Organization of Behavior: A Neuropsychological Theory*, *cit.*, pp. 1–378.

[122] Alves, Jones Figueirêdo/Pimentel, Alexandre Freire, "Breves notas sobre os preconceitos decisionais judiciais produzidos por redes neurais artificiais (Brief notes about the judicial decisional prejudices produced by artificial neural networks), *cit.*, pp. 555–577 (559); Hebb, Donald Olding, *The Organization of Behavior: A Neuropsychological Theory*, *cit.*, pp. 1–378.

[123] Alves, Jones Figueirêdo/Pimentel, Alexandre Freire, "Breves notas sobre os preconceitos decisionais judiciais produzidos por redes neurais artificiais (Brief notes about the judicial decisional prejudices produced by artificial neural networks), *cit.*, pp. 555–577 (559); Hebb, Donald Olding, *The Organization of Behavior: A Neuropsychological Theory*, *cit.*, pp. 1–378.

[124] Aggarwal, C. C., *Neural networks and deep learning*, Heidelberg, Springer, 2018, passim.

[125] Alves, Jones Figueirêdo/Pimentel, Alexandre Freire, "Breves notas sobre os preconceitos decisionais judiciais produzidos por redes neurais artificiais (Brief notes about the judicial decisional prejudices produced by artificial neural networks), *cit.*, pp. 555–577 (559); Hebb, Donald Olding, *The Organization of Behavior: A Neuropsychological Theory*, *cit.*, pp. 1–378.

[126] Alves, Jones Figueirêdo/Pimentel, Alexandre Freire, "Breves notas sobre os preconceitos decisionais judiciais produzidos por redes neurais artificiais (Brief notes about the judicial decisional prejudices produced by artificial neural networks), *cit.*, pp. 555–577 (559); Hebb, Donald Olding, *The Organization of Behavior: A Neuropsychological Theory*, *cit.*, pp. 1–378.

route to it, whether there are intervening neurons between the two or not. With repetition this tendency is prepotent in the formation of neural routes».[127]

§§ Albeit Donald Olding Hebb's work—who was a psychologist in Canada[128]—seems wholly unrelated with Artificial Intelligence, this fallacious averment could not be farther away from the truth. His disruptive research falls squarely within the breadth and scope of both deep learning and machine learning. To begin with, Donald Olding Hebb's work was instrumental in acutely unveiling the inner working of electrical circuits which, in many ways, mimic/mirror the overall functional of human neuronal networks.[129]

§§ Donald Olding Hebb's research therefore falls readily under the catch-all umbrella of a dashing technological innovation for the bulk of reasons I have skeletally rattled off. Put another way, his unprecedented/unheard of work bridged the gap between practice and theory while clearly showing that humans and machines boast more similarities than one could possibly fathom at first blush.

§§ Donald Olding Hebb's research accomplished much more than that though. By tracing the similarities between the inner working of human neuronal networks and the elaborate trappings of machine neuronal networks,[130] Hebb has successfully disentangled/unpacked the sapid ingredients of both human intelligence and machine learning. A breakthrough that still resonates today.[131]

§§ Recall, machine learning, just like human learning, leverages on, and erupts on the heels of, repeated patterns of cognition: the more the process of cognition is repeated, the greater is the learning curve that leads, in the case of machines, to both

---

[127] Alves, Jones Figueirêdo/Pimentel, Alexandre Freire, "Breves notas sobre os preconceitos decisionais judiciais produzidos por redes neurais artificiais (Brief notes about the judicial decisional prejudices produced by artificial neural networks), *cit.*, pp. 555–577 (560); Hebb, Donald Olding, *The Organization of Behavior: A Neuropsychological Theory*, *cit.*, pp. 1–378.

[128] Alves, Jones Figueirêdo/Pimentel, Alexandre Freire, "Breves notas sobre os preconceitos decisionais judiciais produzidos por redes neurais artificiais (Brief notes about the judicial decisional prejudices produced by artificial neural networks), *cit.*, pp. 555–577 (560); Hebb, Donald Olding, *The Organization of Behavior: A Neuropsychological Theory*, *cit.*, pp. 1–378.

[129] Alves, Jones Figueirêdo/Pimentel, Alexandre Freire, "Breves notas sobre os preconceitos decisionais judiciais produzidos por redes neurais artificiais (Brief notes about the judicial decisional prejudices produced by artificial neural networks), *cit.*, pp. 555–577 (560); Hebb, Donald Olding, *The Organization of Behavior: A Neuropsychological Theory*, *cit.*, pp. 1–378.

[130] Aggarwal, C. C., *Neural networks and deep learning*, Heidelberg, Springer, 2018, passim.

[131] Since it has come to our attention that *machine-learning algorithms "are capable of making intuitive decisions based in newly learned information, much like humans*. The new wave of AI developments will generate powerful AI that is capable of improvising itself, *perhaps even by rewriting its own algorithms, advancing its intelligence beyond that of humans*". Italics added. See: Hutto-Schultz, Jess, "Dicitur Ex Machina: Artificial Intelligence and the Hearsay Rule", *George Mason Law Review*, Volume 27, n. ° 2, 2020, pp. 684–718 (684).

machine learning and deep learning.[132] The assertion according to which Donald Olding Hebb's work was mould-breaking is neither unwarranted nor uncalled for.[133]

§§ Although pundits seldom refrain themselves from spitting out accurate suggestions for the next technological trends, Marvin Lee Minsky, who was a promising student of both McCulloch and Pitts,[134] had no qualms whatsoever in kick-starting the next phase of technological innovation that brought us one step closer to where we stand now.

§§ Marvin Lee Minsky[135] accordingly pushed the boundaries of research in devising a much-acclaimed SNARC (*Stochastic*[136] *Neural Analog Reinforcement Calculator*)[137] which, much like machine learning, could greatly enhance its overall performance through a process akin/tantamount to trial and error (*reinforcement learning*). It is often tagged as the first neural network computer.[138]

---

[132] See: Chollet, François, *Deep Learning with Python*. Shelter Island, Nova Iorque: Manning, 2018, pp. 1–384 (passim). *Deep Learning* stands as a byproduct of *Machine Learning*. *Machine Learning*, a subset of Artificial Intelligence, unfolds itself in *Deep Learning*, which "involves computer algorithms that have the ability to "learn" or improve in performance over time on some task". See: Surden, Harry, "Machine Learning and Law", *Washington Law Review*, Volume 89, 2015, pp. 87 and ff. But see: Dong et al., Qi,, "Imbalanced deep learning by minority class incremental rectification, *IEEE Transactions on Pattern Analysis & Machine Intelligence*, Volume 41, 2019, p. 1367 (posit that "*most existing learning algorithms produce inductive bias (learning bias)* towards the frequent (majority) classes if training data are not balanced, *resulting in poor minority class recognition performance*"). Italics added.

[133] See loosely on how machines really learn: Lapuschkin, Sebastian, "Unmasking Clever Hans Predictors and Assessing what Machines Really Learn", *Nature Community*, Volume 10, Issue 1, 2019, pp. 1096 and passim.

[134] Alves, Jones Figueirêdo/Pimentel, Alexandre Freire, "Breves notas sobre os preconceitos decisionais judiciais produzidos por redes neurais artificiais (Brief notes about the judicial decisional prejudices produced by artificial neural networks), *cit.*, pp. 555–577 (560).

[135] "In January 1952 Marvin Minsky, a graduate student at Harvard University Psychological Laboratories implemented the SNARC (*S*tochastic *N*eural *A*nalog *R*einforcement *C*alculator). This randomly connected network of Hebb synapses was the first connectionist neural network learning machine that when "rewarded" facilitated recently-used pathways. The SNARC, implemented using vacuum tubes, was possibly the first artificial self-learning machine." See: https://www.historyofinformation.com/detail.php?id=3884 (access: 07.09.2024).

[136] But see: Bender, E. M., Gebru, T., McMillan-Major, A., & Shmitchell, S., "On the dangers of stochastic parrots: Can language models be too big?", *Proceedings of the 2021 ACM conference on fairness, accountability, and transparency*, 2021, pp. 610–623.

[137] Alves, Jones Figueirêdo/Pimentel, Alexandre Freire, "Breves notas sobre os preconceitos decisionais judiciais produzidos por redes neurais artificiais (Brief notes about the judicial decisional prejudices produced by artificial neural networks), *cit.*, pp. 555–577 (560).

[138] "The Stochastic Neural Analog Reinforcement Calculator (SNARC) embodied a type of neural network that is designed to learn from experience and improve its performance through a process of trial and error (similar to reinforcement learning). This machine was well suited for problems that involved sequential decision-making and made use of prior experience, for example—navigating out of a maze. In fact this is the problem Minsky had set out to solve. The original SNARC system consisted of a set of 40 artificial neurons (specifically Hebb synapses) that are connected to each other in a network. Each neuron receives input from other neurons and produces an output that is passed on to other neurons in the network. The network is trained by adjusting the strengths of the

§§ Marvin Lee Minsky built the very first simulator, which formed part of a broader technological apparatus within which an artificial neuronal network[139] operates. The latter not only set the tone for ulterior technological developments,[140] but, and foremost, set a scientific high bar for the neophyte that appears to be impossible to wean itself off. In many ways, SNARC (*Stochastic Neural Analog Reinforcement Calculator*) represents the dawn of a blazingly new era teeming with enrapturing technological developments that seemingly knows no bounds.

§§ Marvin Lee Minsky's besotting/buoying invention was capable of both learning and moulding a given brain activity.[141] In his insightful view, intelligence is a byproduct of the ceaseless interaction between non-intelligent components,[142] like small-scaled computers connected by ginormous/behemoth networks.[143] In so doing, Marvin Lee Minsky's dispelled the yawning gulf between shapeless dream-like inventions and telluric technological breakthroughs that impel human kind forward.

§§ As the year of 1956 wore on, an enthralling headway came to fruition: the hitherto amorphous expression «Artificial Intelligence» gained currency at a conference held at the University of Darthmouth, New Hampshire, United States of America.[144] The

connections between neurons based on the outcomes of previous trials. The training of this network was manually done by the operator who would provide feedback to the machine when it produced the right outcome." See: https://zahid-parvez.medium.com/history-of-ai-the-first-neural-network-computer-marvin-minsky-231c8bd58409 (access: 06.09.2024).

139 Alves, Jones Figueirêdo/Pimentel, Alexandre Freire, "Breves notas sobre os preconceitos decisionais judiciais produzidos por redes neurais artificiais (Brief notes about the judicial decisional prejudices produced by artificial neural networks), *cit.*, pp. 555–577 (560).

140 See generally: Waytowhich, N./Lawhern, VJ/Garcia, JO, et al., "Compact Convolutional neural networks for classification of asynchronous steady-state visual evoked potentials", *Journal of Neural Engineering*, Volume 15, Issue 6, 2018, passim. See generally: Kwak, N-S/Müller, K-R/Lee, S-W., "A Convolutional neural network for steady state visual evoked potential classification under ambulatory environment", *PloS one*, Volume 12, Issue 2, 2017, passim.

141 Alves, Jones Figueirêdo/Pimentel, Alexandre Freire, "Breves notas sobre os preconceitos decisionais judiciais produzidos por redes neurais artificiais (Brief notes about the judicial decisional prejudices produced by artificial neural networks), *cit.*, pp. 555–577 (560).

142 Alves, Jones Figueirêdo/Pimentel, Alexandre Freire, "Breves notas sobre os preconceitos decisionais judiciais produzidos por redes neurais artificiais (Brief notes about the judicial decisional prejudices produced by artificial neural networks), *cit.*, pp. 555–577 (560).

143 Alves, Jones Figueirêdo/Pimentel, Alexandre Freire, "Breves notas sobre os preconceitos decisionais judiciais produzidos por redes neurais artificiais (Brief notes about the judicial decisional prejudices produced by artificial neural networks), *cit.*, pp. 555–577 (560).

144 Alves, Jones Figueirêdo/Pimentel, Alexandre Freire, "Breves notas sobre os preconceitos decisionais judiciais produzidos por redes neurais artificiais (Brief notes about the judicial decisional prejudices produced by artificial neural networks), *cit.*, pp. 555–577 (560).

hosts of that glistening academic event were the likes of Professors John McCarty,[145] Marvin Minsky, Nathaniel Rochester, and Claude Shannon.[146,147]

§§ The foregoing cohort of top-notch scholars had already partaken in a mould-breaking academic event (1955)[148] whereby they laid the groundwork upon which Artificial Intelligence would sturdily stand. The byproduct of that joint academic endeavour was a peerless paper named «A Proposal[149] for the Dartmouth Summer Research Project on Artificial Intelligence».[150]

---

[145] See: McCarthy, John, Compt. Scientist, Stanford University, Stanford University, in: http://jmc.stanford.edu/artificial-intelligence/what-is-ai/index.html (Nov. 12, 2007) (according to the so-called father of Artificial Intelligence, AI is "the science and engineering of making intelligent machines, especially intelligent computer programs. It is related to the similar task of using computers to understand human intelligence"). Access: 24.9.2024. Converging: Chabert, J.L. et al., *A History of Algorithms: From the Pebble to the Microchip*. New York/Heidelberg: Springer, 2013, p. 2.

[146] Alves, Jones Figueirêdo/Pimentel, Alexandre Freire, "Breves notas sobre os preconceitos decisionais judiciais produzidos por redes neurais artificiais (Brief notes about the judicial decisional prejudices produced by artificial neural networks), *cit*., pp. 555–577 (560).

[147] "The following summer, the group of scholars met at "Dartmouth College for the Dartmouth Summer Research Project on Artificial Intelligence". 1956 thus marks the official beginning of a new field of research that the mathematician John McCarthy, a professor at Dartmouth and major promoter of this event, proposed to call Artificial Intelligence. Among the other organizers were all great personalities of the time: Marvin Minsky, a researcher in mathematics and neurology at Harvard; Nathaniel Rochester, director of information research at an IBM research center; Claude Shannon, a mathematician already famous for information theory, then at the Bell telephone laboratories." See: https://www.klondike.ai/en/ai-history-the-dartmouth-conference (access: 09.09.2024).

[148] "The following summer, the group of scholars met at "Dartmouth College for the Dartmouth Summer Research Project on Artificial Intelligence". 1956 thus marks the official beginning of a new field of research that the mathematician John McCarthy, a professor at Dartmouth and major promoter of this event, proposed to call Artificial Intelligence. Among the other organizers were all great personalities of the time: Marvin Minsky, a researcher in mathematics and neurology at Harvard; Nathaniel Rochester, director of information research at an IBM research center; Claude Shannon, a mathematician already famous for information theory, then at the Bell telephone laboratories." See: https://www.klondike.ai/en/ai-history-the-dartmouth-conference (access: 09.09.2024).

[149] The proposal begins with the following statement: *"We propose that a 2 month, 10 man study of artificial intelligence be carried out during the summer of 1956 at Dartmouth College in Hanover, New Hampshire. The study is to proceed on the basis of the conjecture that every aspect of learning or any other feature of intelligence can in principle be so precisely described that a machine can be made to simulate it. An attempt will be made to find how to make machines use language, form abstractions and concepts, solve kinds of problems now reserved for humans, and improve themselves. We think that a significant advance can be made in one or more of these problems if a carefully selected group of scientists work on it together for a summer"*. See: https://www.klondike.ai/en/ai-history-the-dartmouth-conference (access: 09.09.2024).

[150] McCarthy, John/Minsky, Marvin/Rochester, Nathaniel/Shannon, Claude, "A Proposal for the Dartmouth Summer Research Project on Artificial Intelligence", *AI Magazine*, Volume 27 Number 4 (2006) (© AAAI), 2006 "The 1956 Dartmouth summer research project on artificial intelligence was initiated by this August 31, 1955 proposal, authored by John McCarthy, Marvin Minsky, Nathaniel Rochester, and Claude Shannon. The original typescript consisted of 17 pages plus a title page. Copies of the typescript are housed in the archives at Dartmouth College and Stanford

§§ A slew of forward-looking aspects regarding Artificial Intelligence were timely set out in this valiant proposal. Amongst which stands: **(1) what can automatic computers do?** «If a machine can do a job, then an automatic calculator can be programmed to simulate the machine. The speeds and memory capacities of present computers may be insufficient to simulate many of the higher functions of the human brain, but the major obstacle is not lack of machine capacity, but our inability to write programs taking full advantage of what we have»[151].

§§ **(2) How can a computer be programmed to use a language?** «It may be speculated that a large part of human thought consists of manipulating words according to rules of reasoning and rules of conjecture. From this point of view, forming a generalization consists of admitting a new word and some rules whereby sentences containing it imply and are implied by others. This idea has never been very precisely formulated nor have examples been worked out».[152]

§§ ((**3) How do Neuron Nets behave?** «How can a set of (hypothetical) neurons be arranged so as to form concepts. Considerable theoretical and experimental work has been done on this problem by Uttley, Rashevsky and his group, Farley and Clark, Pitts and McCulloch, Minsky, Rochester and Holland, and others. Partial results have been obtained but the problem needs more theoretical work».[153]

§§ ((**4) Theory of the Size of a Calculation**: «If we are given a well-defined problem (one for which it is possible to test mechanically whether or not a proposed answer is a valid answer) one way of solving it is to try all possible answers in order. This method is inefficient, and to exclude it one must have some criterion for efficiency of calculation. Some consideration will show that to get a measure of the efficiency of a calculation it is necessary to have on hand a method of measuring the complexity of calculating devices which in turn can be done if one has a theory of the complexity of

University. The first 5 papers state the proposal, and the remaining pages give qualifications and interests of the four who proposed the study. In the interest of brevity, this article reproduces only the proposal itself, along with the short autobiographical statements of the proposers". See: "In August 1955 a document, known as the "Dartmouth proposal", was drawn up by four academics. It examines some main themes of fields of research of the period, including neural networks, the theory of computability, creativity and natural language processing and recognition. These topics would be discussed the following summer." See: https://www.klondike.ai/en/ai-history-the-dartmouth-conference (access: 09.09.2024).

[151] McCarthy, John/Minsky, Marvin/Rochester, Nathaniel/Shannon, Claude, "A Proposal for the Dartmouth Summer Research Project on Artificial Intelligence", http://jmc.stanford.edu/articles/dartmouth/dartmouth.pdf (access: 07.09.2024).

[152] McCarthy, John/Minsky, Marvin/Rochester, Nathaniel/Shannon, Claude, "A Proposal for the Dartmouth Summer Research Project on Artificial Intelligence", http://jmc.stanford.edu/articles/dartmouth/dartmouth.pdf (access: 07.09.2024).

[153] McCarthy, John/Minsky, Marvin/Rochester, Nathaniel/Shannon, Claude, "A Proposal for the Dartmouth Summer Research Project on Artificial Intelligence", http://jmc.stanford.edu/articles/dartmouth/dartmouth.pdf (access: 07.09.2024).

functions.[154] Some partial results on this problem have been obtained by Shannon, and also by McCarthy».[155]

§§ ((5) **The forebear of machine learning and deep learning, which has received the baptism of machine self-improvement**: «Probably a truly intelligent machine will carry out activities which may best be described as self-improvement. Some schemes for doing this have been proposed and are worth further study. It seems likely that this question can be studied abstractly as well».[156]

§§ **(6) Abstractions: «**A number of types of "abstraction" can be distinctly defined and several others less distinctly. A direct attempt to classify these and to describe machine methods of forming abstractions from sensory and other data would seem worthwhile».[157]

§§ **(7) Randomness[158] and Creativity:** «A fairly attractive and yet clearly incomplete conjecture is that the difference between creative thinking and unimaginative competent thinking lies in the injection of a some randomness. The randomness must be guided by intuition to be efficient. In other words, the educated guess or the hunch include controlled randomness in otherwise orderly thinking».[159]

§§ Strikingly, finding number 4 enshrined in the Proposal for the Dartmouth Summer Research Project on Artificial Intelligence (*how can a computer be programmed*

---

[154] See: Segran, G., "The complexity of artificial intelligence", *Singapore Management University*, 2021, passim (on the elaborate and complex trappings of Artificial Intelligence).

[155] McCarthy, John/Minsky, Marvin/Rochester, Nathaniel/Shannon, Claude, "A Proposal for the Dartmouth Summer Research Project on Artificial Intelligence", http://jmc.stanford.edu/articles/dartmouth/dartmouth.pdf (access: 07.09.2024).

[156] McCarthy, John/Minsky, Marvin/Rochester, Nathaniel/Shannon, Claude, "A Proposal for the Dartmouth Summer Research Project on Artificial Intelligence", http://jmc.stanford.edu/articles/dartmouth/dartmouth.pdf (access: 07.09.2024).

[157] McCarthy, John/Minsky, Marvin/Rochester, Nathaniel/Shannon, Claude, "A Proposal for the Dartmouth Summer Research Project on Artificial Intelligence", http://jmc.stanford.edu/articles/dartmouth/dartmouth.pdf (access: 07.09.2024).

[158] Teigena, Halvor/Kanten, Alf Børre, "Out of the blue: on the suddenness of perceived chance events", *Thinking & Reasoning*, Volume 29, n. º 1, 2023, pp. 137–175 (137) ("*people commonly use terms like 'random', 'by chance', or 'accidentally' when they describe occurrences that sidestep the normal course of events, with no apparent causal link to ongoing activities. Such intrusive events are typically perceived as happening all of a sudden.* This was demonstrated in seven experiments (N ¼ 1299) by asking people to identify statements they believed belonged to stories about chance events, and by comparing chance vs. nonchance events from their own life and from the lives of others. Suddenness also appeared to be more strongly associated with beginnings than with endings of an episode. Thus, statements about sudden beginnings of a career or a relationship were more readily believed to happen 'by chance' than 'not by chance'. *But life-changing events did not become more accidental simply by being placed in the beginning of a 'life chapter'. These studies highlight a central but neglected feature of perceived randomness*"). Italics added.

[159] McCarthy, John/Minsky, Marvin/Rochester, Nathaniel/Shannon, Claude, "A Proposal for the Dartmouth Summer Research Project on Artificial Intelligence", http://jmc.stanford.edu/articles/dartmouth/dartmouth.pdf (access: 07.09.2024).

to use a language[160]) bears a striking resemblance with the basic tenets of Large Language Models against the backdrop of which ChatGPT and DeepSeek unfold.[161]

§§ ChatGPT[162] can be deployed to perform a portmanteau of wearisome tasks and accordingly accomplish a paraphernalia of meaningful goals. People are increasingly relying upon Large Language Models (LLM's) to run seemingly anodyne errands.[163] So, what are Large Language Models of which ChatGPT is part of?[164] Large Language Model are tools built to help people to undertake a series of boresome chores, which are both time-consuming and energy-draining. How are LLM's fuelled? For the sake of brevity, Large Language Models ingest reams of data and text—gleaned from the internet—to predict the next word in a bid to form a meaningful sentence or a flawless essay.[165]

---

[160] Which reads as follows: "It may be speculated that a *large part of human thought consists of manipulating words according to rules of reasoning and rules of conjecture*. From this point of view, *forming a generalization consists of admitting a new word and some rules whereby sentences containing it imply and are implied by others*. This idea has never been very precisely formulated nor have examples been worked out". See: McCarthy, John/Minsky, Marvin/Rochester, Nathaniel/Shannon, Claude, "A Proposal for the Dartmouth Summer Research Project on Artificial Intelligence", http://jmc.stanford.edu/articles/dartmouth/dartmouth.pdf (access: 07.09.2024). Italics added.

[161] See: Part III, Chap. 3, Sects. 3.5.4 to 3.5.4.1.1 of this book (on the functional aspects of Critical Artificial Intelligence Studies, with a sharper focus on the harmful effects of Artificial Intelligence-embedded technologies, namely Large Language Models and its multifarious downsides and shortcomings). See also: Part IV, Chap. 4, Sects. 4.9 to 4.9.7 (on ChatGPT's functional drawbacks and pitfalls, including, but no limited to, "hallucinations").

[162] "The first wave of excitement about generative artificial intelligence (ai) was like nothing else the world had seen. Within two months of its launch in November 2022, Chatgpt had racked up 100 m users. Internet searches for "artificial intelligence" surged; more than $40bn in venture capital flowed into ai firms in the first half of this year alone. The craze for consumer experimentation has since cooled a little: Chatgpt use has fallen and fewer people are Googling "ai". Son Masayoshi, a Japanese investor notorious for diving into already frothy markets, is thought to be interested in investing in Openai, Chatgpt's creator. But a second, more serious phase is beginning. An entirely new industry centred on supercharged ai models is taking shape. Three forces will determine what it eventually looks like—and whether Openai stays dominant, or other players prevail.". See: https://www.economist.com/leaders/2023/09/21/chatgpt-mania-may-be-cooling-but-a-serious-new-industry-is-taking-shape?utm_medium=social (access: 25.09.2023).

[163] Santos, Hugo Luz dos, *Inteligência Artificial (ChatGPT/AutoGPT/Robots-Advogados/Robots Proceduradores/Robots-Juízes) e Responsabilidade Penal das Pessoas Colectivas*, Braga, NovaCausa Edições Jurídicas, 2023, pp. 1–108. See: Santos, Hugo Luz dos, *Inteligência Artificial e Processo Penal*, Braga, NovaCausa Edições Jurídicas, 2022. See: Santos, Hugo Luz dos, ""Brain-Computer Interfaces, Generative Artificial Intelligence (ChatGPT and Deep Fakes) and Criminal Procedure Law: what's at stake?", *Journal of Research in E. and Computer Science*, Edinburgh, United Kingdom, June 2024, Volume 2, 2024, pp. 39–78, which I will follow closely in this regard.

[164] See also: Part IV, Chap. 4, Sects. 4.9.1 to 4.9.2 (on ChatGPT's functional abilities).

[165] Santos, Hugo Luz dos, ""Brain-Computer Interfaces, Generative Artificial Intelligence (ChatGPT and Deep Fakes) and Criminal Procedure Law: what's at stake?", *Journal of Research in E. and Computer Science*, Edinburgh, United Kingdom, June 2024, Volume 2, 2024, pp. 39–78.

§§ A perceived peril lurks ahead: before long, key stakeholders in corporate law[166]—amongst whom the company directors[167]—will increasingly resort to Artificial Intelligence and Large Language Models to perform, for example, corporate internal investigations (*investigaciones*[168] *internas*)[169] to ferret out the culprit of a poor decision that paved the way to a crime of which the corporation is to be held accountable in criminal procedural law settings. Which will not only impact the fundamental rights of those targeted by the corporate internal investigations,[170] but, and foremost, will also bring to the fore the exclusionary rules[171] (*prueba ilícita*)[172] around which both criminal compliance[173] and criminal procedure law[174] revolve. More on this later.[175]

§§ Turning to the topic at hand, and for purposes here, there is a point that not only deserves to be remarked upon, but, and foremost, be fetched out from the Proposal for the Dartmouth Summer Research Project on Artificial: Professors John McCarty, Marvin Minsky, Nathaniel Rochester and Claude Shannon came to terms with the fact that, to some extent, artificial intelligence tallies with, and is fundamentally commensurate with, human intelligence.

---

166 Goshen, Zohar/ Squire, Richard, "Principal Costs: A New Theory for Corporate Law and Governance", *Columbia Law Review*, Volume 117, 2018, pp. 766 ff and passim.

167 Soltes, Eugene, *Why They Do It: Inside the Mind of the White-Collar Criminal*. New York: Public Affairs, 2018, pp. 1–464.

168 Martín Nieto, Ádan, "Investigaciones internas", *Manual de cumplimiento en la empresa*, Martín Nieto, Ádan (Coord.). Valência: Tirant lo Blanch, 2015.

169 Martín, Ádan Nieto, "Investigaciones internas, whistleblowing y cooperación: la lucha por la información en el proceso penal", *La Ley, 3823/2013*, 2013, pp. 1 e ss e passim.

170 See in Spanish doctrine: Duro Carrión, Susana, "El deber de información en el artículo 87 y 89 LOPDGDD. La quiebra de la expectativa de privacidad vinculada al derecho a la intimidad y otros derechos fundamentales en liza en la relación laboral", Revista de Derecho Laboral, N. 3, 2021, pp. 70–93.

171 See in Spanish doctrine: Colomer Hernández, Ignacio. "Derechos fundamentales y valor probatorio en el proceso penal de las evidencias obtenidas en investigaciones internas en un sistema de compliance". Madrid Boquín, Christa María; Gómez Colomer, Juan Luis. *Tratado sobre Compliance Penal: responsabilidad penal de las personas jurídicas y modelos de organización y gestión*. Valencia: Tirant lo Blanch, 2019, pp. 609–652.

172 See in Spanish doctrine: Gómez Amigo, Luis, "Tratamiento procesal de la prueba ilícita en el proceso penal: del régimen actual al Anteproyecto de Ley de Enjuiciamiento Criminal de 2020", *Revista Asociación de profesores de Derecho Procesal de las Universidades Españolas*, n.º 4, 2021, pp. 201–232 (passim).

173 See in Spanish doctrine: Gimeno Beviá, Jordi, *Compliance y proceso penal. El proceso penal de las personas jurídicas: adaptada a las reformas del CP y LECrim de 2015, Circular FGE 1–2016 y jurisprudencia del TS*. Madrid: Civitas, 2016, passim.

174 See in Spanish doctrine: Carrillo Del Teso, Ana. "La prueba ilícita aportada por particulares: ¿admisión o exclusión? Fundamentos y soluciones jurisprudenciales", *La Ley Penal*, n.º 159, 2022, pp. 1–24.

175 See: Part V, Chapter 5 of this book.

§§ A finding that would pave the way to the emergence of Brain-Computer Interfaces[176] which draw on, and spottily mirror, the well-known theory of «extended mind thesis»[177] against the backdrop of which humans and machines should dovetail seamlessly. It is neither baffling nor befuddling that the sought-after fusion between humans and machines[178] will inevitably create new set of challenges[179] for both Rule of Law and Criminal Procedure Law. More on this later.[180]

§§ All in all, the Darthmouth Proposal for Artificial Intelligence is often coined as the first event whereby the terms «Artificial» and «Intelligence» were cobbled together.[181] By the same token, the Darthmouth Proposal for Artificial Intelligence

[176] See: Part III, Chap. 3, Sect. 3.4.5 of this book (on Critical Artificial Intelligence Studies, with a sharper focus on the harmful effects of Brain-Computer Interfaces). See: Part III, Chap. 3, Sect. 3.5.10 of this book (on the functional aspects of Critical Artificial Intelligence Studies, with a sharper focus on the harmful effects of Artificial Intelligence-embedded technologies, namely, Brain-Computer Interfaces that can read and control your mind and behaviour).

[177] Clark, Andy/Chalmers, David, "The Extended Mind", *Analysis*, Volume 58, Issue 1, January 1998. Oxford: Oxford University Press, 1998, pp. 7–19 (passim).

[178] See: Klein, Eran/Goering, Sara/Gagne, John/Shea, Conor V./Franklin, Rachel/Zorowitz, Samuel/ Dougherty, Darin D./Widge, Alik S., "Brain-Computer Interface-Based Control of Closed-Loop Brain Stimulation: Attitudes and Ethical Considerations", *Brain-Computer Interfaces*, Volume 3, 2016, p. 140 (argue that Brain-Computer Interfaces—BCI for short—erode citizens 'mental privacy while depriving them from thinking "for themselves").

[179] Amongst which stands arguably "biometric privacy". See: Levin, Daniel, "Face the Fact, or is the Face a Fact?: Biometric Privacy in Publicly Available Information", *Fordham Intellectual Media and Entertainment Law Journal*, Volume 32, 2022, pp. 1010–1015. Citron; Danielle Keats Citron/ Pasquale, Frank, "Network Accountability for the Domestic Intelligence Apparatus", *Hasting Law Journal*, Volume 62, 2011, 1441, 1444–45; Gray, David/Citron, Danielle Keats, "The Right to Quantitative Privacy", *Minnesota Law Review*, Volume 98, 2013, pp. 62–81.

[180] See: Part III, Chap. 3, Sect. 3.4.5 of this book (on Critical Artificial Intelligence Studies, with a sharper focus on the harmful effects of Brain-Computer Interfaces). See: Part III, Chap. 3, Sect. 3.5.10 of this book (on the functional aspects of Critical Artificial Intelligence Studies, with a sharper focus on the harmful effects of Artificial Intelligence-embedded technologies, namely, Brain-Computer Interfaces that can read and control your mind and behaviour).

[181] "Artificial Intelligence (AI) is officially born in 1956, the year of a highly notable summer conference held at Dartmouth College in Hanover, New Hampshire, USA. On this occasion this new discipline was founded. The scientific community agrees on this date, as it was the first time the terms "Intelligence" and "Artificial" were coined together. Yet the origins of AI can also be traced to the contributions of researchers in previous years." See: https://www.klondike.ai/en/ai-history-the-dartmouth-conference/ (access: 09.09.2024).

kicked-off the heated debate about a sough-after fusion between humans and machines,[182] which still ripples forward.[183]

§§ This pioneering academic event, which was funded by the Rockefeller foundation, had the core features of brainstorming whereby researchers would freely exude their views on the future of artificial intelligence. Tellingly, the scientists were asked to openly convey their stances on whether and to what extent machines were to perform like humans in the forthcoming future.[184]

§§ Discussions were also held about the materialistic vision of human mind paired with the extent to which machines could trump humans in the decades to come.[185] To cater for that, light has been cast upon the machines 'computational capacity to

---

[182] "When we talk about the history of AI we must refer to the 1940s, the Second World War and the advent of the first computers. It was at that time that the idea of the human–machine analogy was born, that human intelligence could be simulated through the use of machines, an essential condition for the development of AI. In this period, one of the greatest thinkers to explore this theme was Alan Turing." See: https://www.klondike.ai/en/ai-history-the-dartmouth-conference/ (access: 09.09.2024).

[183] Santos, Hugo Luz dos, *Inteligência Artificial (ChatGPT/AutoGPT/Robots-Advogados/Robots Proceduradores/Robots-Juízes) e Responsabilidade Penal das Pessoas Colectivas*, Braga, Nova-Causa Edições Jurídicas, 2023, pp. 1–108; Santos, Hugo Luz dos, ""Brain-Computer Interfaces, Generative Artificial Intelligence (ChatGPT and Deep Fakes) and Criminal Procedure Law: what's at stake?", *Journal of Research in E. and Computer Science*, Edinburgh, United Kingdom, June 2024, Volume 2, 2024, pp. 39–78.

[184] "The event, funded by the Rockefeller Foundation, had the characteristics of brainstorming, that is an open debate with little structure, with the purpose of understanding whether it was possible to for machines to perform like humans. The challenge that pushed the group was precisely the attempt to demonstrate that every aspect of learning and characteristic of human intelligence could be simulated by a machine." See: https://www.klondike.ai/en/ai-history-the-dartmouth-conference/ (access: 09.09.2024).

[185] "Many different questions and ideological positions emerged from the common discussions: on the one hand a materialistic vision of the human mind, on the other a conception that attempts to highlight the peculiar and unavoidable traits of man compared to any machine." See: https://www.klondike.ai/en/ai-history-the-dartmouth-conference/ (access: 09.09.2024).

attain such seemingly untenable result (supersede human intelligence[186] in the years to come).[187]

§§ In spite of all the hype surrounding this laudable initiative, the findings arising out of this earth-shattering academic event fell short of matching its overblown expectations. Strikingly, the findings arisen from this event were tagged as «somewhat inconclusive».[188]

§§ All things considered, the foregoing academic event set the tone for subsequent discussions on the breadth and scope of Artificial Intelligence. On the account, the Darthmouth Proposal for Artificial Intelligence of 1956 was the launching pad for major breakthroughs in this regard. Great leaps forward were accordingly accomplished by either the scientists that partook in this highly inspiring meeting or by their students.[189]

§§ Cogently, and more in tune with the overriding goal from which it was borne, the Dartmouth Proposal for Artificial Intelligence of 1956 carved out a sentence

---

[186] See: Cuellar, Mariano-Florentino, "A Common Law for the Age of Artificial Intelligence: Incremental Adjudication, Institutions, and Relational Non-Arbitrariness", *Columbia Law Review*, Volume 119, 2020, pp. 1773–1775 (this author presciently posits that "(t)he coevolution of human and artificial intelligence—what we could call our dance with machines—is well on its way to becoming routine"). See also: Cataleta, Maria Stefania/Cataleta, Anna, "Artificial Intelligence and Human Rights: An Unequal Struggle", *CIFILE Journal of International Law*, Volume 1, N. ° 2, 2020 ("*Artificial Intelligence (AI) is a kind of intelligence that was born in the 1950s and is an integral part of the digital revolution. Progress made by AI has permitted the birth of systems capable of rivalling human capacities or, in some cases, surpassing them.* The progress of the intellectual capacities of AI will change the way of life for human beings and will revolutionise the world of employment. *Intelligent systems present problems regarding individual rights and responsibilities, because as technology replaces more and more of what humans have typically done, our individual roles will become more blurred.*"). Italics added. Converging: Cataleta, Maria Stefania, "Artificial Intelligence vs Human Intelligence", in: Martin, L. Miraut/Zalucki, M. (editors), *Artificial intelligence and Human Rights, Dickinson eBook*. Krakow: AFM Krakow University, 2021, pp. 117–127 (on the slew of both moral, ethical and legal issues with which jurists will grapple in the forthcoming future due to the rise of artificial intelligence in legal arena).

[187] "Another problem was related to the machinery of the time, which did not have adequate computational capacity." See: https://www.klondike.ai/en/ai-history-the-dartmouth-conference/ (access: 09.09.2024).

[188] "The conference did not go as planned and the results were somewhat inconclusive. Furthermore, several names indicated by McCarthy did not show up and, in the end, there were only ten participants." See: https://www.klondike.ai/en/ai-history-the-dartmouth-conference/ (access: 09.09.2024).

[189] "Still, the historical importance of the conference is unquestionable. Many experts met in Dartmouth for the first time and this was a highly inspiring meeting. In fact, for a whole subsequent period, the main achievements in the field of AI have been obtained by these same scientists or by their students. It was therefore after the Dartmouth Conference that AI became in effect an intellectual research field, even if controversial, and from that moment it began to progress more and more rapidly." See: https://www.klondike.ai/en/ai-history-the-dartmouth-conference/ (access: 09.09.2024).

packed/crammed with both truthfulness and accuracy[190]: «for the present purpose the artificial intelligence problem is taken to be that of making a machine behave in ways that would be called intelligent if a human were so behaving».[191]

§§ Compellingly, the much-acclaimed Dartmouth Congress had a lasting effect: it set in motion a private investment spree that was the propelling force behind rapid strides in the remit of Artificial Intelligence.[192] The ARPA movement[193]—which would eventually be the founding father of Internet—deftly harnessed the unfading enthusiasm catalysed by Darthmouth Proposal for Artificial Intelligence.[194]

§§ From this event onwards, Artificial Intelligence gained a momentum that shows no conspicuous signs of petering out anytime soon. Something that deserves nothing

---

[190] See: McCarthy, John, Compt. Scientist, Stanford University, Stanford University, in: http://jmc.stanford.edu/artificial-intelligence/what-is-ai/index.html (Nov. 12, 2007) (according to the so-called father of Artificial Intelligence, AI is "the science and engineering of making intelligent machines, especially intelligent computer programs. It is related to the similar task of using computers to understand human intelligence"). Access: 24.9.2023. Converging: Chabert, J.L. et al., *A History of Algorithms: From the Pebble to the Microchip*. New York/Heidelberg: Springer, 2013, p. 2.

[191] McCarthy, John/Minsky, Marvin/Rochester, Nathaniel/Shannon, Claude, "A Proposal for the Dartmouth Summer Research Project on Artificial Intelligence", http://jmc.stanford.edu/articles/dartmouth/dartmouth.pdf (access: 09.09.2024).

[192] Alves, Jones Figueirêdo/Pimentel, Alexandre Freire, "Breves notas sobre os preconceitos decisionais judiciais produzidos por redes neurais artificiais (Brief notes about the judicial decisional prejudices produced by artificial neural networks), *cit.*, pp. 555–577 (561).

[193] The newest developments posed by the "collect-it-all" technologies are slated to create a slew of sizzling hot challenges to the sustainability of the Rule of Law. See: Hu, Margaret, "From the National Surveillance State to the Cybersurveillance State", *The Annual Review of Law and Social Science*, Volume 13, 2017, pp. 162–163 ("*policymakers view these technological developments, including biometric technologies, as tools with the potential to identify individuals who may pose a threat to national and homeland security and to prevent crime and terrorism. One example of technology intended for risk assessment and threat management is the post-9/11 program Total Information Awareness (TIA).* TIA was the progeny of the Defense Advanced Research Projects Agency (DARPA) in the US Department of Defense. *TIA can be understood as a "collect-it-all" data surveillance program. TIA was not explicitly identified as a collect-it-all program—this phrase originated with the Snowden disclosures.* One National Security Agency (NSA) slide described the NSA's procedure as "collect-it-all" (Greenwald 2014b). *Collect-it-all efforts like TIA embody a philosophy that aspires to preventive policing. Mass data collection is construed as a tool to assess and prevent future threats (Murray 2010). In TIA and other programs tested or adopted after 9/11, biometric database screening and analysis have emerged as a preferred method for tracking, identifying, and establishing identity-based inferences in counterterrorism*"). Italics added. See also: Ball, Kirstie, and Frank Webster (Eds.), *The Intensification of Surveillance: Crime, Terrorism & Warfare in the Information Age*, London, UK: Pluto Press, 2007; Guzik, Keith, "Discrimination by Design: Predictive Data Mining as Security Practice in the United States' 'War on Terrorism.'", *Surveillance and Society*, 7 (1), 2009, pp. 1–17. See: Part IV, Chap. 4, Sects. 4.5 to 4.5.2 of this book (on "algorithmic Jim Crow", a travel ban issued during the first Trump Administration to prevent certain individuals from entering the United States of America, which, given its racial undertones, stands as an outgrown of congeries of laws arising out Jim Crow epoch).

[194] Alves, Jones Figueirêdo/Pimentel, Alexandre Freire, "Breves notas sobre os preconceitos decisionais judiciais produzidos por redes neurais artificiais (Brief notes about the judicial decisional prejudices produced by artificial neural networks), *cit.*, pp. 555–577 (561).

but unfettered plaudits as the headways made by Artificial Intelligence since then have been nothing but astonishing.[195] For that reason, Law must be eagerly watchful of its undying development.

§§ Lest we forget, Law must keep abreast with the newest developments in technology or the grievances against its proverbial sluggishness will only flare up.[196] Law must fly in the face of belatedness and lethargy. Law must accordingly keep pace with the blazingly new or may otherwise find itself on the brink of a gruelling legal tokenism.[197] Put otherwise, Artificial Intelligence threatens to entrench an eerily

---

[195] Since it has come to our attention that *machine-learning algorithms "are capable of making intuitive decisions based in newly learned information, much like humans.* The new wave of AI developments will generate powerful AI that is capable of improvising itself, *perhaps even by rewriting its own algorithms, advancing its intelligence beyond that of humans*". Italics added. See: Hutto-Schultz, Jess, "Dicitur Ex Machina: Artificial Intelligence and the Hearsay Rule", *George Mason Law Review*, Volume 27, n. ° 2, 2020, pp. 684–718 (684).

[196] Fergus, Rachel, "Biased Technology: The Automated Discrimination of Facial Recognition", *ACLU Minnesota*, February 29, 2024, available at: https://www.aclu-mn.org/en/news/biased-technology-automated-discrimination-facial-recognition (access: 20.09.2024) ("*Technology is developing much more quickly than the laws we need to protect our rights. Anyone with a smartphone or social media account knows how rapidly technology changes, while legislating can take a long, long time. It is essential to proactively put policies into place that will protect our rights as new and more advanced technology is constantly released. Especially when that technology—and law enforcement members using it—have been shown over and over to be biased toward marginalized groups*"). Italics added. See: Part III, Chap. 3, Sects. 3.5.7 to 3.5.8.1 of this book (on the functional aspects of Critical Artificial Intelligence Studies, with a sharper focus on the perils concerning the deployment of facial recognition technology).

[197] Recall, the public outcry catalyzed by the movement of Critical Legal Studies was underpinned by two foundational pillars: legal tokenism and legal indeterminacy, which, taken together, derail the overall functionality of a given legal system. See: Hutchinson, Alan C./Monahan, Patrick J., "Law, Politics and the Critical Legal Scholars: The Unfolding Drama of American Legal Thought", *Stanford Law Review*, Volume 36, 1984, 199–245 (pp. 200–202) (on law's indeterminacy, which would eventually merit vitriolic remarks from other Critical Legal Scholars). Soon enough, the grievances toward law's indeterminacy were to be levelled up. Critical legal scholars not only decried/bemoaned the indeterminacy of law, but also the facts 'nagging—and, foremost, unsettling—uncertainty regarding legal decision-making. See: McLeod, Ian, *Legal Theory*, 3rd Edition. New York: Palgrave Macmillan Law Masters, 2005, pp. 140–150 (decrying law's and facts 'indeterminacy, especially in cases in which legal decision-making is to rely upon witnesses 'flawed and skewed memory, which is to cast doubts on the witnesses' ability to aid judges in attaining the arduous task to serve justice in the first place). The sizzling hot challenges posed by an ever-evolving Artificial Intelligence are bound to further compound the abhorrent phenomenon of legal tokenism that shows no signs of fizzling out anytime soon. Like a full-fledged and full-bodied legal apparatus comprising algorithmic fairness that casts aside algorithmic discrimination in criminal procedure law settings. See on algorithmic discrimination: Kleinberg, Jon, et al., "Discrimination in the Age of Algorithms", *Journal of Legal Analysis*, 2018, pp. 114–174; See: Kleinberg, Jon, et al., "Algorithms as Discrimination Detectors", *Proceeds of the National Academy of Science*, Volume 117, 2020, pp. 30096–30110; Huq, Aziz, "Racial Equity in Algorithmic Criminal Justice", *Duke Law Journal*, Volume 68, 2022, pp. 1076–1134.

On a different note, criminal judges yearn for ways to reduce their overburdened dockets and their clogged backlogs of cases through the settlement of disputes. There is a piece of empirical evidence that disavows such judicial practice. Stating that such judicial practice disfigures core judicial values, thereby contributing exponentially to the appalling phenomenon of vanishing trials.

narrow eliminatory vision of human dignity that should accordingly raise a lot of eyebrows.

§§ Bereft of robust legal oversight,[198] Artificial Intelligence will be left to develop to its own accord. Humans may accordingly find themselves cluelessly adrift in the complex trappings of technology, which will ineluctably prove detrimental to their fundamental rights of which they are so keenly fond of. For that reason, Artificial Intelligence must be much more than merely *Explainable*.[199] Instead, advanced

---

See: Sela, Ayelet/Zimerman, Nourit/ Alberstein, Michal, "Judges as Gatekeepers and the Dismaying Shadow of the Law: Courtroom Observations of Judicial Settlement Practices", *Harvard Negotiation Law Review*, Volume 24, 2018, p. 83 (noting that "judges engage in case management and settlement promotion more than do in trials and judgments" thus couching the concerns with the rampant phenomenon of vanishing trials). See on the phenomenon of vanishing trials: Galanter, Marc, "The Vanishing Trial: An Examination of Trials and Related Matters in Federal and State Courts", *Journal of Empirical Legal Studies*, Volume 1, 2004, pp. 459 ff (on the perils of the vanishing trials). But see: Hadfield, Gillian K./Heine, Jamie, "Life in the Law-Thick World: Legal Resources for Ordinary Americans", Estreicher, Sam/Radice, Joy (Eds.), *Beyond Elite Law: Access to Civil Justice in America*. New York: Cambridge University Press, 2016, pp. 23–51 (this is consistent with the perceived high costs associated to litigation in courts). Unsurprisingly, Governments worldwide have been pledging themselves to look for other mechanisms to solving disputes. Amicable mechanisms of settling disputes stand out from the crowd. Which should not come as a surprise to anyone committed to afford disputants both a *formal access to justice* and an *effective access to justice* as an extension of Rule of Law. Like we do.

[198] See: Part V, Chap. 5, Sects. 5.2 to 5.6.2.1 of this book (on the thing-centred algorithmic decision-making propelled by a *Controllable* and *Interpretable* Machine Learning that weeds out *Algorithmic Dictatorship* and secures *Algorithmic Common Good*). See: Part V, Chap. 5, Sect. 5.7.2 of this book (on law number two to control algorithmic decision-making, which mandates that black box models must not be entrusted with the task of making high stake decisions—v.g. health and freedom). See: Part V, Chap. 5, Sects. 5.7 to 5.7.5 of this book (on the five laws to control algorithmic decision-making). See: Part V, Chap. 5, Sect. 5.8.5 of this book (on law number five to interpret algorithmic decision-making, which mandates that robot-judges, robot-prosecutors and robot-lawyers must not enter the courtroom for they are utterly incapable of making sound and interpretable value judgements).

[199] See: Deeks, Ahsley, "The Judicial Demand for Explainable Artificial Intelligence", *Columbia Law Review*, Volume 119, 2019, pp. 1829 and ff and passim. See: Hacker, Phillip/Passoth, Jan-Hendrick, "Varieties of AI Explanations under the Law: From the GDPR to the AIA, and Beyond", *XxAI Beyond Explainable AI, International Workshop on Extending Explainable AI Beyond Deep Models and Classifiers*. Berlin/New York/Singapore/Beijing: Springer, 2021, pp. 343–373 ("the quest to explain the output of artificial intelligence systems has clearly moved from a mere technical to a highly legally and politically relevant endeavor. In this paper, we provide an overview of legal obligations to explain AI and evaluate current policy proposals. In this, we distinguish between different functional varieties of AI explanations—such as multiple forms of enabling, technical and protective transparency—and show how different legal areas engage with and mandate such different types of explanations to varying degrees. Starting with the rights-enabling framework of the GDPR, we proceed to uncover technical and protective forms of explanations owed under contract, tort and banking law. Moreover, we discuss what the recent EU proposal for an Artificial Intelligence Act means for explainable AI, and review the proposal's strengths and limitations in this respect. Finally, from a policy perspective, we advocate for moving beyond mere explainability towards a more encompassing framework for trustworthy and responsible AI that includes actionable explanations, values-in-design and co-design methodologies, interactions with algorithmic fairness, and quality benchmarking.").

technology should be both *Interpretable*[200] and *Controllable.*[201] This one of the key takeaways of this book that should be bore very firmly in mind. More on this later.[202]

§§ Time inexorably went by, so too did the headways made by a cohort of researchers that pledged themselves to the overall advancement of Artificial Intelligence. At that juncture, the name that deserves to be remarked upon is John von Neumann, who was one the forebears of theory of games of strategy.[203]

§§ John von Neumann—unlike Donald Olding Hebb and Marvin Lee Minsky, who avowedly claimed that machines learn in a manner tantamount to that of humans—adamantly contended that the human brain works in a manner radically different to that of machines.[204] Casts broadly, the human brain does not operate in a way commensurate with digital procedures.[205]

§§ As far as he was concerned, digital computers deal with precise units of measure whereas the human brain operates upon an endless pool of possibilities that seemingly knows no bounds.[206]

§§ John von Neumann's stance is that which the quest to grasp intelligent computation entails the dereliction of a solely digital approach while upholding the creation of

---

200 See: Part V, Chap. 5, Sects. 5.8 to 5.8.5 of this book (on the five laws to interpret algorithmic decision-making).

201 See: Part V, Chap. 5, Sects. 5.7 to 5.7.5 of this book (on the five laws to control algorithmic decision-making).

202 See: Part V, Chap. 5, Sects. 5.2 to 5.6.2.1 of this book (on the thing-centred algorithmic decision-making propelled by a *Controllable* and *Interpretable* Machine Learning that weeds out *Algorithmic Dictatorship* and secures *Algorithmic Common Good*).

203 Von Neumann, John/Morgenstern, Oskar, *Theory of Games and Economic Behavior*, 1st edition (1944), 60th Anniversary Commemorative Edition (April 2007), Princeton Classic Editions, New Jersey, Princeton University Press 2007, pp. 1–786 (*passim*) (John von Neumann and Oskar Morgenstern have conceived a groundbreaking mathematical theory of economic and social organization, based on a theory of games of strategy). See also: Schelling, Thomas C., *The Strategy of Conflict,* Cambridge, Massachusetts, *Harvard University* Press, 1980, pp. 1–328 (*passim*) ("Schelling's work prompted new developments in game theory and accelerated its use and application throughout the social sciences. Notably, his analysis of strategic commitments has explained a wide range of phenomena, from the competitive strategies of firms to the delegation of political decision power"). Self-evidently, zero-sum mind-set and positive sum mind-set derived from the mathematical language and it is inextricably linked to the field of game theory. Put differently, the zero-sum mind-set and positive sum mind-set have been harvested from the fertile soil of mathematics. It is pure mathematical parlance. Mathematical jargon in light of which the game theory accrues academic plausibility.

204 Alves, Jones Figueirêdo/Pimentel, Alexandre Freire, "Breves notas sobre os preconceitos decisionais judiciais produzidos por redes neurais artificiais (Brief notes about the judicial decisional prejudices produced by artificial neural networks), *cit.*, pp. 555–577 (561).

205 Alves, Jones Figueirêdo/Pimentel, Alexandre Freire, "Breves notas sobre os preconceitos decisionais judiciais produzidos por redes neurais artificiais (Brief notes about the judicial decisional prejudices produced by artificial neural networks), *cit.*, pp. 555–577 (561).

206 Alves, Jones Figueirêdo/Pimentel, Alexandre Freire, "Breves notas sobre os preconceitos decisionais judiciais produzidos por redes neurais artificiais (Brief notes about the judicial decisional prejudices produced by artificial neural networks), *cit.*, pp. 555–577 (561).

hybrid pathways to process information through a patchwork of digital and analogic structures.[207] According to John von Neumann, this neat method would streamline intelligent computation in ways hardly unforeseen back then.

§§ Neumann upheld his stance with steadfast resolve until the twilight of his life.[208] Hardly any surprise springs form the fact that John von Neumann's take has somewhat swayed one of his most devoted acolytes: Frank Rosenblatt.

§§ Yet, bafflingly, Frank Rosenblatt has introduced a cluster of changes that did nothing but to disfigure the core features of John von Neumann's theory on the inner working of human brain. Recall, John von Neumann posited that the human brain and artificial neuronal networks work in a radically different manner. In a nutshell, both process information in different ways.

§§ On the opposite pole, and building on Warren McCulloch's and Walter Pitts' take on the inner workings of the human brain, Frank Rosenblatt outlined a network model comprised of multiple neurons against the backdrop of which a slew of algorithms would seamlessly operate in a manner tantamount to that of the human brain.[209]

§§ The foregoing model was so advanced that was capable of processing visual information: the ancestor of modern computer vision and its sibling facial recognition.[210] The pinpointed neuronal network was coined as *Perceptron*,[211] which, much to Frank

[207] Alves, Jones Figueirêdo/Pimentel, Alexandre Freire, "Breves notas sobre os preconceitos decisionais judiciais produzidos por redes neurais artificiais (Brief notes about the judicial decisional prejudices produced by artificial neural networks), *cit.*, pp. 555–577 (561).

[208] Alves, Jones Figueirêdo/Pimentel, Alexandre Freire, "Breves notas sobre os preconceitos decisionais judiciais produzidos por redes neurais artificiais (Brief notes about the judicial decisional prejudices produced by artificial neural networks), *cit.*, pp. 555–577 (561).

[209] Alves, Jones Figueirêdo/Pimentel, Alexandre Freire, "Breves notas sobre os preconceitos decisionais judiciais produzidos por redes neurais artificiais (Brief notes about the judicial decisional prejudices produced by artificial neural networks), *cit.*, pp. 555–577 (561).

[210] See: Part III, Chap. 3, Sects. 3.5.7 to 3.5.8.1 of this book (on the functional aspects of Critical Artificial Intelligence Studies, with a sharper focus on the perils concerning the deployment of facial recognition technology). But see: Hu, Margaret, "From the National Surveillance State to the Cybersurveillance State", *The Annual Review of Law and Social Science*, Volume 13, 2017, p. 169 ("*in a big data world, a digitized passport system can link to multiple other sources, such as license plate readers, No Fly Lists, and Terrorist Watchlists. Facial recognition technology drawing upon a photo database could potentially link a plethora of digital images of a person, including social media, the internet, photo databases like driver's licenses, live-streaming video, CCTV surveillance, and images obtained from hacking cameras on laptops and digital devices. Biometric data collection and storage are becoming increasingly compulsory through either government identification requirements*, such as digital photo requirements for passports and driver's licenses, or corporate identification requirements, such as biometric access to digital devices"). Italics added. See: Part IV, Chap. 4, Sects. 4.5 to 4.5.2 of this book (on "algorithmic Jim Crow", a travel ban issued during the first Trump Administration to prevent certain individuals from entering the United States of America, which, given its racial undertones, stands as an outgrowth of congeries of laws enacted during the Jim Crow epoch).

[211] Alves, Jones Figueirêdo/Pimentel, Alexandre Freire, "Breves notas sobre os preconceitos decisionais judiciais produzidos por redes neurais artificiais (Brief notes about the judicial decisional prejudices produced by artificial neural networks), *cit.*, pp. 555–577 (561).

Rosenblatt's overwhelming joy, was fully funded by the United States of America's Navy.[212] But Frank Rosenblatt's delight did not last long though.

§§ To the extent this project was fraught with a potential threat to citizens 'mental privacy, a public outcry was triggered whereby the latter openly showed their discontent.[213] *Perceptron*[214] sparked widespread howls of protest across the United States of America. The country was steadfastly careening into chaos against backdrop of which a seething social uproar unfolded.

§§ Back then, citizens were neither bashful nor coy in openly upbraiding this looming threat to their mental privacy. Nor should they. Tellingly, the grievances brought forth by the citizens back then bear a striking resemblance with the whinges echoed by the nowadays citizens. On that account, it should not come as a surprise that they somewhat imbricate/overlap.

§§ To be fair, the citizens were distraught for a good reason. *Perceptron* was the encapsulation of an omnipotent computer that had the ability to walk, talk, see, write, and reproduce itself[215] while being fully aware of its own existence.[216]

§§ *Perceptron,* as its name implies, had the ability to mimic—even reproduce—human thinking.[217] There were accordingly mounting concerns that *Perceptron*—which was wrapped under the veneer of a bedazzling gift to human kind—could surpass human kind in a not-so-distant future. Citizens were verklempt for a good reason after all: Perceptron embodied the core features of a seemingly anodyne tool that blatantly threatened to fray the fabric of both their mental privacy and

[212] Alves, Jones Figueirêdo/Pimentel, Alexandre Freire, "Breves notas sobre os preconceitos decisionais judiciais produzidos por redes neurais artificiais (Brief notes about the judicial decisional prejudices produced by artificial neural networks), *cit.*, pp. 555–577 (561).

[213] Alves, Jones Figueirêdo/Pimentel, Alexandre Freire, "Breves notas sobre os preconceitos decisionais judiciais produzidos por redes neurais artificiais (Brief notes about the judicial decisional prejudices produced by artificial neural networks), *cit.*, pp. 555–577 (561).

[214] Rosenblatt, F., "The perceptron: a probabilistic model for information storage and organization in the brain", *Psychological Review*, Volume 65, Issue 6, 1958, passim.

[215] Rosenblatt, F., *Principles of neurodynamics: Perceptrons and the theory of brain mechanisms*, Washington, DC: Spartan Books, 1962.

[216] Alves, Jones Figueirêdo/Pimentel, Alexandre Freire, "Breves notas sobre os preconceitos decisionais judiciais produzidos por redes neurais artificiais (Brief notes about the judicial decisional prejudices produced by artificial neural networks), *cit.*, pp. 555–577 (562).

[217] Alves, Jones Figueirêdo/Pimentel, Alexandre Freire, "Breves notas sobre os preconceitos decisionais judiciais produzidos por redes neurais artificiais (Brief notes about the judicial decisional prejudices produced by artificial neural networks), *cit.*, pp. 555–577 (562).

biometric[218] privacy.[219] An unrivalled lesson that nowadays citizens should not lose sight of.[220]

§§ Notwithstanding, in spite of all the staggering efforts to stymie *Perceptron's* rise to prominence, this ghastly tool has already entered our daily lives.[221] Take the example of Brain-Computer Interfaces[222] which, as captioned above,[223] seeks to gain access to our brains while wiping out our uniqueness in the process. Back then, just like nowadays, our beloved mental privacy[224] faces a tangible threat to its survival. A

[218] Which, I may venture to add, is something—*biometric surveillance*—that amounts to nothing but to the price of partaking in social settings, which is very hard to shy away from nowadays. See: Hu, Margaret, "From the National Surveillance State to the Cybersurveillance State", *The Annual Review of Law and Social Science*, Volume 13, 2017, p. 169 ("*because of technological developments and trends in governance, it is challenging, if not impossible, to prevent biometric data capture and collection. Biometric surveillance systems increasingly require opting in as the price of social, economic, and political participation.* Biometric data capture is difficult to resist because it is simultaneously compulsory and transparent. Biometric data collection is often compulsory because it is increasingly mandatory to establish identity. *Biometrics are transparent qualities because it is very difficult to hide biometrics; an individual's face, iris, or fingerprint can be digitally captured in any public place. Because biometric data support larger big data programs, such as No Fly List–type risk assessments, it is extraordinarily difficult, if not impossible, to opt out*"). Italics added. See: Part IV, Chap. 4, Sects. 4.5 to 4.5.2 of this book (on "algorithmic Jim Crow", a travel ban issued during the first Trump Administration to prevent certain individuals from entering the United States of America, which, given its racial undertones, stands as an outgrowth of congeries of laws enacted during the Jim Crow epoch).

[219] Levin, Daniel, "Face the Fact, or is the Face a Fact?: Biometric Privacy in Publicly Available Information", *Fordham Intellectual Media and Entertainment Law Journal*, Volume 32, 2022, pp. 1010–1015. Citron; Danielle Keats Citron/Pasquale, Frank, "Network Accountability for the Domestic Intelligence Apparatus", *Hasting Law Journal*, Volume 62, 2011, 1441, 1444–45; Gray, David/Citron, Danielle Keats, "The Right to Quantitative Privacy", *Minnesota Law Review*, Volume 98, 2013, pp. 62–81.

[220] About mental privacy: See: Greenberg, Jeremy/Ringrose, Katelyn/Berger, Sara/VanDodick/Rossi, Francesca/New, Joshua, "Privacy and the Connected Mind", *The Future Privacy Forum*, 2021.

[221] Steinert, Steffen/Orsolya, Friedrich, "Wired Emotions: Ethical Issues of Affective Brain-Computer Interfaces", *Science and Engineering Ethics*, Volume 26, 2020, pp. 351 and ff and passim.

[222] See: Santos, Hugo Luz dos, ""Brain-Computer Interfaces, Generative Artificial Intelligence (ChatGPT and Deep Fakes) and Criminal Procedure Law: what's at stake?", *Journal of Research in E. and Computer Science*, Edinburgh, United Kingdom, June 2024, Volume 2, 2024, pp. 39–78.

[223] Part I of this book (Introduction). See: Part III, Chap. 3, Sect. 3.4.5 of this book (on Critical Artificial Intelligence Studies, with a sharper focus on the harmful effects of Brain-Computer Interfaces). See: Part III, Chap. 3, Sect. 3.5.10 of this book (on the functional aspects of Critical Artificial Intelligence Studies, with a sharper focus on the harmful effects of Artificial Intelligence-embedded technologies, namely, Brain-Computer Interfaces that can read and control your mind and behaviour).

[224] Klein, Eran/Goering, Sara/Gagne, John/Shea, Conor V./Franklin, Rachel/Zorowitz, Samuel/Dougherty, Darin D./Widge, Alik S., "Brain-Computer Interface-Based Control of Closed-Loop Brain Stimulation: Attitudes and Ethical Considerations", *Brain-Computer Interfaces*, Volume 3, 2016, p. 140 (argue that Brain-Computer Interfaces—BCI for short—erode citizens 'mental privacy while depriving them from thinking "for themselves").

battle for our brains is underway and yet few to none seem to have even noticed.[225] More on this later.[226]

§§ With this context in place, Artificial Intelligence was all the rage in the late 1950's.[227] But the hype surrounding AI swiftly dwindled. Before long, a harsh winter downed on Artificial Intelligence. Suddenly, the rapid strides made in the 1950's were a glimpse of a distant past. The scant computer memory—which has fallen short of matching the ginormous computational capacity boasted by the extant computers—was to blame.[228]

§§ Artificial Intelligence—a burgeoning field that used to move faster than a speeding bullet in the 1950's—was now moving at a snail's pace in the 1960's. Given the paucity of computer memory, the ulterior developments in the remit of Artificial Intelligence were as scarce as hen's teeth. The dearth of computer memory has nonetheless showed that Artificial Intelligence is not a field amenable to be approached in a piecemeal and haphazard manner. Rather, its continuous advance hinges upon a wide range of electronic components that enable its seamless inner working.

§§ To cut to the chase, Artificial Intelligence is a multidisciplinary science that not only requires an all-hands-on-deck approach but, and foremost, an integrated vision to steadily buttress its sought-after progress. Failing which, the headways will be glacially slow. Worse still, all the stakeholders will sorely feel its lethargy, thereby impairing the overall advancement of society. This is a gloomy reality that hovered the purview of Artificial Intelligence back in the 1960's.

§§ Worryingly, there were no noticeable signs that Artificial Intelligence would be able to bounce back anytime soon. Which was a vivid source of disenchantment to the scientific community in an overarching sense.

§§ Earnest attempts have been made to remedy this dispiriting situation, but to no avail. It seemed as though this gruesome was seemingly unsurpassable. The clouds of uncertainty accordingly hovered in the sky of Artificial Intelligence. Much to the dismay of its staunch supporters, this standoff was not showing signs of petering out anytime soon.

§§ To make things worse, people flocked to rallies to voice their vehement concerns over the unbridled rise of Artificial Intelligence. The bulwark supporters of Artificial

---

[225] Called "Neural Battlefield". See: Dunker, Anders, "The Neural Battlefield of Cognitive Capitalism", *L. A. Review of Books*, 2020, passim.

[226] See: Part III, Chap. 3, Sect. 3.4.5 of this book (on Critical Artificial Intelligence Studies, with a sharper focus on the harmful effects of Brain-Computer Interfaces). See: Part III, Chap. 3, Sect. 3.5.10 of this book (on the functional aspects of Critical Artificial Intelligence Studies, with a sharper focus on the harmful effects of Artificial Intelligence-embedded technologies, namely, Brain-Computer Interfaces that can read and control your mind and behaviour).

[227] Russell, S. J., & Norvig, P., *Artificial intelligence a modern approach*, London: Pearson, 2022.

[228] Alves, Jones Figueirêdo/Pimentel, Alexandre Freire, "Breves notas sobre os preconceitos decisionais judiciais produzidos por redes neurais artificiais (Brief notes about the judicial decisional prejudices produced by artificial neural networks), *cit.*, pp. 555–577 (562).

Intelligence, in turn, gave a lacklustre performance when they were summoned to explain the basic tenets of this technology to citizens.

§§ The boat (Artificial Intelligence) was stranded in shallow waters after all. Scientists thronged to academic conferences to untie this stalemate. But these initiatives were, at best, seldom fruit-bearing. At its worst, were brazenly inconclusive. Even outright fruitless.

§§ The crux of the quagmire was that the algorithms that have been painstakingly devised to propel *Perceptron* lacked a robust database[229] to operate upon.[230] Bereft a brawny database,[231] the living dream to process data and convert it into actionable information that could be used to solve problems while advancing society in an overarching sense[232] was inexorably hampered.

§§ *Perceptron*, which has endured both trenchant criticism and vitriolic remarks during its short span of life, was about to be brushed aside to unheeded bucket of

---

[229] See: Hu, Margaret, "From the National Surveillance State to the Cybersurveillance State", *The Annual Review of Law and Social Science*, Volume 13, 2017, p. 165 ("*Datafication, like most big data processes, requires increasing amounts of digital data to support or construct cybersurveillance*". It empowers government actions that are based on *digital data collection, data processing protocols, and bulk data analyses* (Mayer-Schonberger & Cukier 2013). Italics added. See: Part IV, Chap. 4, Sects. 4.5 to 4.5.2 of this book (on "algorithmic Jim Crow", a travel ban issued during the first Trump Administration to prevent certain individuals from entering the United States of America, which, given its racial undertones, stands as an outgrowth of congeries of laws enacted during the Jim Crow epoch).

[230] But see: *Tech, Bias and Housing Initiative, the Promise and Perils of Residential Proptech, Year 1, Research Summary Report, April 2023, TechEquity Collaborative*, p. 5 available at: https://techequity.us/wp-content/uploads/2023/04/TBHI-Y1-Research-Summary-Report.pdf (28.11.2024). ("*Residential Proptech also has the potential to exacerbate the bias inherent in our housing system. Its rise is due, in part, to the desperation felt by average home seekers. With a severely constrained housing supply, companies offering an easier pathway to homeownership may exploit communities that have been harmed by housing discrimination in the past. Opaque algorithms incorporate biased data into their decision-making processes, making it harder to enforce fair housing laws.* Residential Proptech companies often operate in a regulatory gray area, leaving consumers without the protections they would have from traditional housing regulatory systems. *As unprecedented capital investment flows into this space, venture-backed companies' winner-take-all approach to growth has the potential to exacerbate inequality rather than combat it*"). Italics added.

[231] *Tech, Bias and Housing Initiative, the Promise and Perils of Residential Proptech, Year 1, Research Summary Report, April 2023, TechEquity Collaborative*, p. 11, available at: https://techequity.us/wp-content/uploads/2023/04/TBHI-Y1-Research-Summary-Report.pdf (28.11.2024). ("*Once bad data enters the analysis of one factor, it gets baked into the subsequent process, multiplying the effect that one disadvantageous data point can have on someone's overall housing determination*"). Italics added. See: Part IV, Chap. 4, Sects. 4.4 to 4.4.2.3 of this book. See: Part IV, Chap. 4, Sects. 4.4 to 4.4.2.1 of this book (on mortgage redlining). See: Part IV, Chap. 4, Sects. 4.2 to 4.4.3 of this book (on algorithmic credit scoring, consumer racism and credit card redlining). See: Part IV, Chap. 4, Sects. 4.4 to 4.4.2.3 of this book (on algorithmic redlining). See: Part IV, Chap. 4, Sect. 4.4.3 of this book (on "algorithmic redliking"). See: Part IV, Chap. 4, Sect. 4.3 of this book (on algorithmic prime-lining).

[232] Alves, Jones Figueirêdo/Pimentel, Alexandre Freire, "Breves notas sobre os preconceitos decisionais judiciais produzidos por redes neurais artificiais (Brief notes about the judicial decisional prejudices produced by artificial neural networks), *cit.*, pp. 555–577 (562).

oblivion. Apparently, a flagship of algorithmic wisdom was on the verge of being cast off. Only this time for good.

§§ To add to their woes, the shifting sands in which Artificial Intelligence was engulfed in dragged everyone down. It seemed as though this limbic stage spared no one. Including two of the founding fathers of Artificial Intelligence: Marvin Minsky and Seymour Papert. These two pundits penned an essay titled «Perceptron» against the backdrop of which they adamantly claimed that Frank Rosenblatt's groundbreaking creation (*Perceptron*) lacked bespoke settings to be successfully implemented.[233] *Perceptron*, to be seamlessly implemented, required a larger technological apparatus, which did not exist back then.[234]

§§ The foregoing essay further compounded the dreary atmosphere of disgruntlement with which Artificial Intelligence was tussling for a long-winded span of time. On the heels of the pinpointed atmosphere of chagrin and disbelief, a plethora of promising projects were accordingly discontinued.[235]

§§ The essay «Perceptron» has catalysed a slew of shockwaves—which echoed across the whole country—while inflicting a toll on the momentum that Artificial Intelligence had back then. None of which gleeful news for the overall advancement of Artificial Intelligence.[236]

§§ Altogether, the 1960's were utterly unpalatable—some lads would say unsavoury or even hideous—for the overall improvement of Artificial Intelligence.[237] There were three overriding factors that were slowing Artificial Intelligence down. The first of which was the technological limitations of the extant computers that lacked enough computational memory to perform tasks that would render their existence socially useful.[238]

---

[233] Alves, Jones Figueirêdo/Pimentel, Alexandre Freire, "Breves notas sobre os preconceitos decisionais judiciais produzidos por redes neurais artificiais (Brief notes about the judicial decisional prejudices produced by artificial neural networks), *cit.*, pp. 555–577 (562).

[234] Alves, Jones Figueirêdo/Pimentel, Alexandre Freire, "Breves notas sobre os preconceitos decisionais judiciais produzidos por redes neurais artificiais (Brief notes about the judicial decisional prejudices produced by artificial neural networks), *cit.*, pp. 555–577 (562).

[235] Alves, Jones Figueirêdo/Pimentel, Alexandre Freire, "Breves notas sobre os preconceitos decisionais judiciais produzidos por redes neurais artificiais (Brief notes about the judicial decisional prejudices produced by artificial neural networks), *cit.*, pp. 555–577 (562).

[236] Alves, Jones Figueirêdo/Pimentel, Alexandre Freire, "Breves notas sobre os preconceitos decisionais judiciais produzidos por redes neurais artificiais (Brief notes about the judicial decisional prejudices produced by artificial neural networks), *cit.*, pp. 555–577 (562).

[237] Alves, Jones Figueirêdo/Pimentel, Alexandre Freire, "Breves notas sobre os preconceitos decisionais judiciais produzidos por redes neurais artificiais (Brief notes about the judicial decisional prejudices produced by artificial neural networks), *cit.*, pp. 555–577 (562).

[238] Alves, Jones Figueirêdo/Pimentel, Alexandre Freire, "Breves notas sobre os preconceitos decisionais judiciais produzidos por redes neurais artificiais (Brief notes about the judicial decisional prejudices produced by artificial neural networks), *cit.*, pp. 555–577 (562).

§§ The second of which was the paucity of storage capability to keep the information that would spur the processing of information through computational means.[239] The third of which was the shortfall of data to prop Artificial Intelligence up.[240] There was nothing but a surfeit of reasons to falloff/taper off the overall betterment of Artificial Intelligence after all. Yet, mind-bogglingly, circumstances were to alter.

§§ In a fortunate stroke of serendipity, and undeterred by the widespread atmosphere of discontentedness facing Artificial Intelligence, Joseph Weizenbaum made a significant headway in 1964 amidst a bursting disbelief. Humanity was about to be thrust headlong a period crammed with mesmerizing strides that were to follow suit.

§§ 1964 was a felicitous year for the overall advancement of Artificial Intelligence. Joseph Weizenbaum,[241] filled with an overwhelming ingenious force, laid down the brawny upon which the first chatbot in human history would stand.[242] The chatbot was named ELIZA. This chatbot, which was created in MIT by the pansophic Joseph Weizenbaum, who sought to pay an homage to George Bernard Shaw's fictional character «Pygmalion», Eliza Doolittle,[243] of whom he was keenly fond of.

§§ Eliza was fully capable of engaging in meaningful dialogues with human beings. Eliza's demeanour was akin to that of humans insofar she could behave in a way a human would. Eliza was fully equipped to shrewdly use expressions, mannerisms,

---

[239] Alves, Jones Figueirêdo/Pimentel, Alexandre Freire, "Breves notas sobre os preconceitos decisionais judiciais produzidos por redes neurais artificiais (Brief notes about the judicial decisional prejudices produced by artificial neural networks), *cit.*, pp. 555–577 (562).

[240] But see: *Tech, Bias and Housing Initiative, the Promise and Perils of Residential Proptech, Year 1, Research Summary Report, April 2023, TechEquity Collaborative*, p. 11, available at: https://techequity.us/wp-content/uploads/2023/04/TBHI-Y1-Research-Summary-Report.pdf (28.11.2024). ("*Once bad data enters the analysis of one factor, it gets baked into the subsequent process, multiplying the effect that one disadvantageous data point can have on someone's overall housing determination*"). Italics added. See: Part IV, Chap. 4, Sects. 4.4 to 4.4.2.3 of this book.

[241] But see: Weizenbaum, Joseph, *Computer Power and Human Reason: From Judgment to Calculation*, 1st edition, New York, W. H. Freeman & Co, 1976, pp. 1–300 (227) ("examines the sources of the computer's powers and offers evaluative explorations of what computers can do, cannot do, and should not be employed to do") (this founding father of Artificial Intelligence presciently noted that we should not entrust Artificial Intelligence-embedded technologies with with "tasks that demand wisdom"). Italics added. The approval of rental applications is arguably one of those tasks that should never be entrusted to machines). More on this on Part IV, Chap. 4, Sects. 4.4 to 4.4.2.1 of this book. See: Part V, Chap. 5, Sect. 5.7.2 of this book (on law number two to control algorithmic decision-making, which mandates that black box models must not be entrusted with the task of making high stake decisions—v.g. health and freedom). See: Part V, Chap. 5, Sects. 5.7 to 5.7.5 of this book (on the five laws to control algorithmic decision-making).

[242] Alves, Jones Figueirêdo/Pimentel, Alexandre Freire, "Breves notas sobre os preconceitos decisionais judiciais produzidos por redes neurais artificiais (Brief notes about the judicial decisional prejudices produced by artificial neural networks), *cit.*, pp. 555–577 (562).

[243] Alves, Jones Figueirêdo/Pimentel, Alexandre Freire, "Breves notas sobre os preconceitos decisionais judiciais produzidos por redes neurais artificiais (Brief notes about the judicial decisional prejudices produced by artificial neural networks), *cit.*, pp. 555–577 (562).

emotions, and archaisms that a human would.[244] Hardly any surprise stems from the fact that Eliza was designed to mimic human behaviour while appearing to be one. Eliza would have passed the Turing Test[245] with flying colours.

§§ Eliza has nevertheless been originally built to accomplish a far more arduous task: to perform the duty of psychologist, which, until then, was proverbially allotted to humans only.[246] It seems as though Eliza had been purposefully built to not only mirror human behaviour but, and foremost, to have a human-like consciousness.[247]

§§ Unbeknownst to both the nonchalant and the insouciant—who often display a dishevelled stance on the origins of Artificial Intelligence—Eliza embodied the onset of a sheer amount of concerns related with the possibility (or lack thereof) to implant a human-like consciousness onto machines[248] and, especially, onto human organoids.[249]

---

[244] Alves, Jones Figueirêdo/Pimentel, Alexandre Freire, "Breves notas sobre os preconceitos decisionais judiciais produzidos por redes neurais artificiais (Brief notes about the judicial decisional prejudices produced by artificial neural networks), *cit.*, pp. 555–577 (562).

[245] About the Turing test: Russel, Stuart J./Norvig, Peter, "Artificial Intelligence: a modern approach", Prentice-Hall, Inc. A Simon & Schuster Company, 1995 (The Turing Test aims to evaluate intelligent behaviour [1]. To proficiently evaluate intelligent behaviour, the computer should be interrogated by a human via a teletype, and passes the test if the interrogator cannot tell if there is a computer or a human at the other end [1]. The framework of Turing Test lies in the following and successive phases: the computer would need to possess the following capabilities: 0 natural language processing to enable it to communicate successfully in English (or some other human language); moreover, < C > knowledge representation to store information provided before or during the interrogation; furthermore, <) automated reasoning to use the stored information to answer questions and to draw new conclusions; another feature needed is <) machine learning to adapt to new circumstances and to detect and extrapolate patterns [1]. Finally, to pass the total Turing Test, the computer will need computer vision <) computer vision to perceive objects and robotics (> robotics to move them about [1]. See also: Santos, Hugo Luz dos, *Direito Contratual do Jogo: Um Olhar Bifronte*, Braga, NovaCausa Edições Jurídicas, 2023, pp. 1–760; Simon, Herbert, *Artificial intelligence: Current status and future potential*, National Research Council Report – Office of Naval Research, 1985.

[246] Alves, Jones Figueirêdo/Pimentel, Alexandre Freire, "Breves notas sobre os preconceitos decisionais judiciais produzidos por redes neurais artificiais (Brief notes about the judicial decisional prejudices produced by artificial neural networks), *cit.*, pp. 555–577 (562).

[247] See about human consciousness: Feinberg, Todd E./Mallatt, Jon M., *Consciousness Demystified*. Cambridge, Massachusetts: The MIT Press, 2018, passim. See generally on human consciousness: Michel, M., "Consciousness Science Undetermined Ergo, an Open Access", *Journal of Philosophy*, Volume 6, 2019, passim. Shepherd, Lois/Pike, Williams C./Persily, Jesse B./Marshall, Mary Faith, "The Case of Hannah Capes: How Much Does Consciousness Matter?", *Neuroethics*, Volume 15, Issue 14, 2022, pp. 1–16. See generally on human consciousness: Fins, Joseph J., *Rights come to mind: Brain Injury, Ethics, and the Struggle for Consciousness*. Cambridge: Cambridge University Press, 2015, pp. 1–394.

[248] See: McCorduck, P., *Machines who think: A personal inquiry into the history and prospects of artificial intelligence*, Cleveland, CRC Press Books, 2004.

[249] The worries can be packaged in the following manner: is it possible to implant other's minds? Implant other's mindsets? Implant unbending obedience? See generally: Sebo, J., "The Moral Problem of Other Minds", *Harvard Review of Philosophy*, Volume 25, 2018, pp. 51–70.

§§ Underlying this sweltering issue is a burning question: should laypeople allow scientists to brew human organoids[250] only to implant[251] them onto a machine in due course? To put it bluntly, should they be allowed to use human organoids[252] to bestow upon machines a human-like consciousness only to instil unfaltering obedience onto them?[253]

§§ This drawn-out topic loosely consists of leveraging on a human brain[254] organoid[255] to create a surrogate brain,[256] which raises multiple ethical issues[257] with which the scientific community has been floundering with for a long-winded span of time.

§§ This sizzling hot topic will knock on criminal justice's[258] door eventually.[259] It can nonetheless be encapsulated in a couple of vexing questions: will machines have

[250] See generally on the transplantation of human cerebral humanoids: Kitahar, T./Sakaguchi, H./ Morizane, A./Kikuchi, T./Miyamoto, S./Takahashi, J. "Axonal Extensions along Corticospinal Tracts from Transplanted Human Cerebral Organoids", *Stem Cells Report*, Volume 15, 2020, pp. 467–481.

[251] See generally on the operation through which human cerebral organoids can be successfully transplanted: Daviaud, N./Friedel, R.H./Zou, H., "Vascularization and Engraftment of Transplanted Human Cerebral Organoids in Mouse Cortex, *eNeuro*, Volume 5, 2019, passim.

[252] See generally on human brain organoids: Seto, Y./Eiraku, M., "Toward the formation of neural circuits in human brain organoids", *Current Opinion in Cell Biology*, Volume 61, 2019, pp. 86–91. Would that amount to panpsychism? See about this sizzling hot topic: Seager, W.E., *The Routledge Handbook of Panpsychism*. New York: Routledge, 2020. See: Shepherd, J., *Consciousness and Moral Status*. Oxford: Routledge, 2020.

[253] While reaping both their minds and consciousness: Shepherd, J., *Consciousness and Moral Status*. Oxford: Routledge, 2020.

[254] See generally on human brain surrogacy for living human brains: Zuradzki, T., "Against the Precautionary Approach to Moral Status: The Case of Surrogates for Living Human Brains", *The American Journal of Bioethics*, Volume 21, 2021, pp. 53–56.

[255] See generally on the transplantation of human brain organoids: Sakaguchi, H./Ozaki, Y./Ashida, T./Matsubara, N./Oishi, S./Kihara/Takahashi, "Self-Organized Synchronous Calcium Transients in a Cultured Human Network Derived from Cerebral Organoids", *Stem Cell Reports*, Volume 13, 2020, pp. 458–473.

[256] See: Greely, H.T., "Human Brain Surrogates Research: The Onrushing Ethical Dilemma", *The American Journal of Bioethics*, Volume 21, 2021, pp. 34–45.

[257] See on human consciousness coupled with the multiple ethical issues surrounding it: Lavazza, A./Massimini, M., "Cerebral organoids. Ethical issues and consciousness assessment", *Journal of Medical Ethics*, Volume 44, 2019, pp. 606–610.

[258] That forms part of a broader legal apparatus according to which "Law is an Artifact". See: Burazin, Luka/Himma, Keneth Heinar/Roversi, Corrado (Editors), *Law as an Artifact*. Oxford: Oxford University Press, 2018, pp. 1–304.

[259] See generally: Hyun, I/Scharf-Deering, J.C./Lunshof, J.E., "Ethical issues related to brain organoid research", *Brain Research*, 2020, passim. Information loosely amounts to awareness. See generally: Bayne, T./Seth, A.K./Massimini, M., "Are There Islands of Awareness?", *Trends in Neurosciences*, Volume 43, 2020, pp. 6–16.

a human-like consciousness[260] in the future?[261] Will this render machines eligible to face criminal charges for the misdeeds they commit? More on this later.[262]

§§ Fast forward to the gist of this brief historical account, the 1970's are often dubbed as the second era of Artificial Intelligence, cramming with a vast assortment of opportunities to grow exponentially.[263] The 1970's were the years in which the plight—technical limitations,[264] which were rattled off earlier—that hobbled the development of Artificial Intelligence was finally swept aside.

§§ The operational quandaries that once threatened to wobble the foundations upon which the growth of Artificial Intelligence stood were now a glimpse of a caliginous past that left nothing to long for. The internal squabbles to oust doubt were accordingly vanquished.

§§ The long-haul agony of a then languishing and feeble Artificial Intelligence was on its final throes. Disbelief and unease—thieves of unshakeable hopes—were accordingly disfranchised.

§§ The 1970's were the break of a new dawn for Artificial Intelligence. Although there was no such thing as big data[265] back then,[266] the pundits ferreted out a way to pull through nonetheless. The 1970's were buoying years for Artificial Intelligence. Back

---

260 See on human consciousness coupled with the multiple ethical issues surrounding it: Lavazza, A./Massimini, M., "Cerebral organoids. Ethical issues and consciousness assessment", *Journal of Medical Ethics*, Volume 44, 2019, pp. 606–610.

261 See generally on human consciousness: Lee, A.Y., "Is Consciousness Intrinsically Valuable?", *Philosophical Studies*, Volume 175, 2018, pp. 1–17. See generally on human consciousness: Frith, C.D., "The neural basis of consciousness", *Psychological Medicine*, 2019, pp. 1–13.

262 See: Part III, Chap. 3, Sect. 3.4.5 of this book (on Critical Artificial Intelligence Studies, with a sharper focus on the harmful effects of Brain-Computer Interfaces). See: Part III, Chap. 3, Sect. 3.5.10 of this book (on the functional aspects of Critical Artificial Intelligence Studies, with a sharper focus on the harmful effects of Artificial Intelligence-embedded technologies, namely, Brain-Computer Interfaces that can read and control your mind and behaviour).

263 Alves, Jones Figueirêdo/Pimentel, Alexandre Freire, "Breves notas sobre os preconceitos decisionais judiciais produzidos por redes neurais artificiais (Brief notes about the judicial decisional prejudices produced by artificial neural networks), *cit.*, pp. 555–577 (563).

264 Alves, Jones Figueirêdo/Pimentel, Alexandre Freire, "Breves notas sobre os preconceitos decisionais judiciais produzidos por redes neurais artificiais (Brief notes about the judicial decisional prejudices produced by artificial neural networks), *cit.*, pp. 555–577 (563).

265 But see: See: Simmons, Ric, "Big Data and Procedural Justice: Legitimizing Algorithms in the Criminal Justice System", *Ohio State Journal of Criminal Law*, Volume 5, 2018, pp. 573 and ff and passim (argues, however, that too much AI in criminal procedure law settings can backfire, thereby hindering citizens 'trust on the criminal system of justice). Big data that is in the limelight these days. See: Sivarajah, Uthayasnkar et al., "Critical Analysis of Big Data Challenges and Analytical Methods", *Journal of Business Research*, Volume 70, 2017, pp. 263 and ff and passim; Jetten, Lieke /Sharon, Stephen, "Selected Issues concerning the Ethical Use of Big Data Health Analytics", *Washington & Lee Law Review Online*, Volume 72, 2016, passim.

266 Alves, Jones Figueirêdo/Pimentel, Alexandre Freire, "Breves notas sobre os preconceitos decisionais judiciais produzidos por redes neurais artificiais (Brief notes about the judicial decisional prejudices produced by artificial neural networks), *cit.*, pp. 555–577 (563).

then, polymaths thronged to Silicon Valley[267] to showcase their technical expertise in an earnest attempt to contribute to the overall advance of Artificial Intelligence.

§§ Two names come across as crucially important in this regard: Marshall McLuhan and Stewart Brand. They attained a remarkable milestone back then: miniaturization of computers,[268] which became then amenable to be depicted in a brief (thumbnail sketch).

§§ University of Stanford made significant strides regarding the creation of MYCIN (in 1972), which consisted of an algorithm fully capable of performing accurate medical diagnoses through the analysis of patients 'blood samples.[269] But not just that though. The foregoing algorithm was also capable of identifying harmful bacteria while prescribing the befitted medication[270] to fight the disease with which the patient was grappling with.

§§ In many ways, MYCIN was the forebear of the state-of-the-art machine learning algorithms that are equally capable of identifying a vast array of harmful diseases. Such as skin cancer.[271] As of now, Artificial Intelligence outperforms radiologists in identifying harmful diseases.[272] Which is nothing but formulaic: experts have long forecasted that machine learning algorithms would bode exceedingly well provided

---

[267] Alves, Jones Figueirêdo/Pimentel, Alexandre Freire, "Breves notas sobre os preconceitos decisionais judiciais produzidos por redes neurais artificiais (Brief notes about the judicial decisional prejudices produced by artificial neural networks), *cit.*, pp. 555–577 (563).

[268] Alves, Jones Figueirêdo/Pimentel, Alexandre Freire, "Breves notas sobre os preconceitos decisionais judiciais produzidos por redes neurais artificiais (Brief notes about the judicial decisional prejudices produced by artificial neural networks), *cit.*, pp. 555–577 (563).

[269] Alves, Jones Figueirêdo/Pimentel, Alexandre Freire, "Breves notas sobre os preconceitos decisionais judiciais produzidos por redes neurais artificiais (Brief notes about the judicial decisional prejudices produced by artificial neural networks), *cit.*, pp. 555–577 (563).

[270] Alves, Jones Figueirêdo/Pimentel, Alexandre Freire, "Breves notas sobre os preconceitos decisionais judiciais produzidos por redes neurais artificiais (Brief notes about the judicial decisional prejudices produced by artificial neural networks), *cit.*, pp. 555–577 (563).

[271] Pham, TV/Luong, CM/Hoang, VD and al., "AI outperformed every dermatologist in dermoscopic melanoma diagnosis, using an optimized deep-CNN architecture with custom mini-batch logic and loss function", *Nature Science*, Vol 17, 2021, passim. But see: Part III, Chap. 3, Sects. 3.5.6 to 3.5.6.1 of this book (on Critical Artificial Intelligence Studies, with a sharper focus on the harmful effects of Large Language Models 'medical hallucinations that are poised to undermine its overall trustworthiness).

[272] Killock, 'AI Outperforms radiologists in mammographic screening, *National Review of Clinical Oncology*, Volume 17, 2020, pp. 134 and ff and passim. But see: Part III, Chap. 3, Sect. 3.5.6 (on Critical Artificial Intelligence Studies, with a sharper focus on the harmful effects of Large Language Models 'medical hallucinations that are poised to undermine its overall trustworthiness).

they could leverage on behemoth databases.[273] In such cases, machines would surpass humans in the medical[274] domain.[275]

§§ It seems as though the apprentice (machine learning algorithms) outshined the master (humans) whom both taught and programmed them.[276] Which begs the vexing question: to what cost? More on this later.[277]

§§ For purposes here, there was a staggering outpouring of inventions of so-called software of routine automation.[278] Today, these expert systems that would not be deemed as Artificial Intelligence systems, because the latter did not hinge upon

---

[273] But see: *Tech, Bias and Housing Initiative, the Promise and Perils of Residential Proptech, Year 1, Research Summary Report, April 2023, TechEquity Collaborative*, p. 11, available at: https://techequity.us/wp-content/uploads/2023/04/TBHI-Y1-Research-Summary-Report.pdf (28.11.2024). ("*Once bad data enters the analysis of one factor, it gets baked into the subsequent process, multiplying the effect that one disadvantageous data point can have on someone's overall housing determination*"). Italics added. See: Part IV, Chap. 4, Sects. 4.4 to 4.4.2.3 of this book.

[274] But see: Part III, Chap. 3, Sects. 3.5.6 to 3.5.6.1 of this book (on Critical Artificial Intelligence Studies, with a sharper focus on the harmful effects of Large Language Models 'medical hallucinations that are poised to undermine its overall trustworthiness).

[275] See: Samek, Wojciech/Müller, Klaus-Robert, "Explainable AI: interpreting, explaining and visualizing deep learning", *Towards Explainable Artificial Intelligence*, Samek, Wojciech/Montavon, Grégoire/ Vedaldi, Andrea/Hansen, Lars Kai/ Müller, Klaus-Robert (Editors). Heidelberg/Berlin/ New York: Springer, 2019, pp. 5–22 ("*in recent years, machine learning (ML) has become a key enabling technology for the sciences and industry. Especially through improvements in methodology, the availability of large databases and increased computational power, today's ML algorithms are able to achieve excellent performance (at times even exceeding the human level) on an increasing number of complex tasks. Deep learning models are at the forefront of this development. However, due to their nested non-linear structure, these powerful models have been generally considered "black boxes", not providing any information about what exactly makes them arrive at their predictions.* Since in many applications, e.g., in the *medical domain, such lack of transparency may be not acceptable, the development of methods for visualizing, explaining and interpreting deep learning models has recently attracted increasing attention. This introductory paper presents recent developments and applications in this field and makes a plea for a wider use of explainable learning algorithms in practice.*"). Italics and bold added.

[276] But see: Barocas, Solon/Selbst, Andrew D., "Big Data's Disparate Impact", *California Law Review*, Volume 104, 2016, pp. 671–682 (discussing how data is often flawed, rigged, incomplete, imperfect and therefore algorithms inherit the prejudice of the original decision makers). But see: Citron, Danielle Keats/Pasquale, Frank, "The Scored Society: Due Process for Automated Predictions", *Washington Law Review*, Volume 89, 2014, pp. 1, 4–5 (highlighting how human beings programming automated systems is directly conducive to, and leads, to fundamentally inaccurate results since the source code, predictive algorithms and datasets may encompass human biases which, in turn, have a disparate impact on historically disadvantaged groups). But see: Bornstein, Stepanhie, "Antidiscriminatory Algorithms", *Alabama Law Review*, Volume 70, 2018, pp. 519, 524–528 (contending, however, that the tagged "facially neutral" algorithms producing discriminatory outcomes should be quashed).

[277] But see: Part III, Chap. 3, Sects. 3.5.6 to 3.5.6.1 of this book (on Critical Artificial Intelligence Studies, with a sharper focus on the harmful effects of Large Language Models 'medical hallucinations that are poised to undermine its overall trustworthiness).

[278] Alves, Jones Figueirêdo/Pimentel, Alexandre Freire, "Breves notas sobre os preconceitos decisionais judiciais produzidos por redes neurais artificiais (Brief notes about the judicial decisional prejudices produced by artificial neural networks), *cit.*, pp. 555–577 (563).

machine learning algorithms to operate.[279] The mode of operation that propelled these expert systems was commensurate with a human expert that is trained to solve highly complex problems based on the knowledge and experience garnered over the course of years.[280]

§§ Put otherwise, these were systems of automatic computation that made reasonable inferences[281] premised on a batch of information provided by the end-users.[282] Machine learning algorithms—that are fully equipped to solve problems based on the cluster of information provided by the citizens—were not deployed back then.[283]

§§ Time is a sledgehammer that weeds out the old while opening the hallowed door of the new. Bearing this axiom very firmly in mind, 2010 kicked-off the third era of Artificial Intelligence that still stands.[284] The third era of Artificial Intelligence

---

[279] Alves, Jones Figueirêdo/Pimentel, Alexandre Freire, "Breves notas sobre os preconceitos decisionais judiciais produzidos por redes neurais artificiais (Brief notes about the judicial decisional prejudices produced by artificial neural networks), *cit.*, pp. 555–577 (563).

[280] Alves, Jones Figueirêdo/Pimentel, Alexandre Freire, "Breves notas sobre os preconceitos decisionais judiciais produzidos por redes neurais artificiais (Brief notes about the judicial decisional prejudices produced by artificial neural networks), *cit.*, pp. 555–577 (563).

[281] Wachter, S./Mittelstadt. B., "A right to Reasonable Inferences: Re-thinking Data Protection Law in the Age of Big Data and AI", *Columbia Business Law Review*, 2019, pp. 1 and ff and passim. The issue of judicial inferences is a hot topic in the realm of *pro se* disputants. There is a perceived impression that there are insurmountable barriers created to disadvantaged parties—*pro se* disputants that cannot afford to pay a well-adjusted and seasoned lawyer—as they access judicial courts. This problem will only get worse as technology gains traction in criminal procedure law settings. An empirical research premises such assertion. See: Kroeper, Kathryn/Quintanilla, Victor D./Frisby, Michael/Yel, Nedim/Applegate, Amy G./Sherman, Steven J./Murphy, Mary C., "Underestimating the Unrepresented: Cognitive Biases Disadvantage Pro Se Litigants in Family Law Cases", *Psychology, Public Policy, and Law*, Volume 26, n.º 2, 2020, pp. 198–212 (211) (emphazise "*the present research suggests that the mere presence or absence of pro se status affects the inferences that legal officials make about parties in the civil justice system.* Legal officials appraised the cases of counselled parties as less meritorious the cases of counselled parties and predicted the *unrepresented persons would experience the civil justice system as less fair and satisfying the counselled litigants, even when all case facts were held constant, and especially when trial (vs. mediation) was considered to be the dispute resolution mechanism*"). Italics added. See also: Quintanilla, Victor/ Allen, R. A./Hirt, E. R., "The signalling effect of pro se status", *Law & Social Inquiry*, Volume 42, 2018, pp. 1092–1120.

Michaels, Andrew C., "Artificial Intelligence, Legal Change, and Separation of Powers, *University of Cincinnati Law Review*, 2020, pp. 1083 and ff and passim.

[282] Alves, Jones Figueirêdo/Pimentel, Alexandre Freire, "Breves notas sobre os preconceitos decisionais judiciais produzidos por redes neurais artificiais (Brief notes about the judicial decisional prejudices produced by artificial neural networks), *cit.*, pp. 555–577 (563).

[283] Alves, Jones Figueirêdo/Pimentel, Alexandre Freire, "Breves notas sobre os preconceitos decisionais judiciais produzidos por redes neurais artificiais (Brief notes about the judicial decisional prejudices produced by artificial neural networks), *cit.*, pp. 555–577 (563).

[284] Alves, Jones Figueirêdo/Pimentel, Alexandre Freire, "Breves notas sobre os preconceitos decisionais judiciais produzidos por redes neurais artificiais (Brief notes about the judicial decisional prejudices produced by artificial neural networks), *cit.*, pp. 555–577 (563).

veered off towards the massive usage of data.[285] For that reason alone, it was tagged

[285] Unbeknownst to the cohort of insouciant and nonchalant, a full-blown criminal-digital justice—powered by an omnipotent artificial intelligence prosecutor—is currently being served/deployed in China. Which means that China is spearheading a digital transformation which will catalyse a paradigm shift in the remit of criminal procedure law. See: "The Chinese government has developed the AI system 206, an *artificial intelligence prosecutor designed to alleviate the workload of prosecutors in China.* The system is allegedly capable of prosecuting "Shanghai's eight most common crimes." The AI was 'trained' using *"17,000 real-life cases from 2015 to 2020."* Fears abound that the technology could be weaponized by the state, potentially charging citizens for political dissent. According to a Dailyalts.com story in 2019, the AI was first officially tested in a Shanghai court in early 2019. It was also trialed in several provinces in 2018. The system can perform the following tasks with an alleged 97% accuracy: *Transcribe testimony*; *Transfer physical data and documents to electronic databases*; *Display relevant parameters immediately, such as time, place, people, behavior, and consequences*; *Identify defective or contradicting evidence*; *Respond to oral commands to display evidence and information on screens around the courtroom*; *Inter-connect with judicial, procuratorial, public security authorities and courts.* The crimes that the AI can prosecute *"include 'provoking trouble' —a term used to stifle dissent in China, credit card fraud, gambling crimes, dangerous driving, theft, fraud, intentional injury, and obstructing official duties."* In February of 2017, the Political and Judiciary Commission under the Central Committee of the Communist Party of China tasked courts in Shanghai to develop and test an AI system to assist with prosecutions. Between 2017 and 2019, Shanghai allocated more than *"400 people from courts, procuratorates, and public security bureaus, working with more than 300 IT staff from tech giant iFLYTEK"* to develop the technology. The company was established in 1999 and is a well-known speech recognition and artificial intelligence developer. From the iFLYTEK website: *"Since its establishment, the company is devoted to cornerstone technological research in speech and languages, natural language understanding, machine learning, machine reasoning, adaptive learning, and has maintained the world-leading position in those domains. The company actively promotes the development of AI products and their sector-based applications, with visions of enabling machines to listen and speak, understand and think, creating a better world with artificial intelligence."* The system runs on a standard computer that employs algorithms based on evidence collection from "102 common cases" programmed into the system. The AI can pull up questioning models for law enforcement and *"can help the judge find fact, authenticate evidence[s], protect the right to appeal and judge impartially on the trial, so as to prevent wrongfully convicted cases,"* according to Guo Weiqing, president of Shanghai No 2 Intermediate People's Court. It translates voice into characters and *"can distinguish between questioner and responder."* The software captures salient elements of cases from electronic files. According to NotTheBee, some cities in China have used AI *"to monitor government employees' social circles and activities to detect corruption."* Italics added. Ver: https://uncoverdc.com/2022/01/10/ai-system-206-replacing-human-prosecutors-in-china (acesso: 23.08.2024). United States of America—while trying to keep pace with China—is not lagging far behind in this regard. Leveraging on the advantageous conditions brought about by Covid-19, United States of America is currently relying upon *forensic algorithms* to curb/ebb/assuage overburdened dockets, soothe out overcrowded criminal courts, and, foremost, allay courts 'backlogs of cases. See: "*The technology is also being used in the U.S., according to InterestingEngineering.com. With the backlog of cases piling up due to COVID*, the use of AI has picked up to "streamline" judicial processes. The use of *forensic algorithms* is particularly popular in the collection of evidence: *"U.S. Fingerprint matching software aims to correctly identify suspects with staggering speed and precision, facial recognition helps law enforcement agencies track people down, and probabilistic genotyping can work wonders to assist investigators in determining if a genetic sample from a crime scene is linked to a person of*

as the era of Big Data[286] that fuels Artificial Intelligence (in general) and machine learning and deep learning (in particular). More on this later.[287]

§§ The third era of Artificial Intelligence stands tall before our very eyes and is poised to become a rule of machines, as opposed to a rule of persons.[288] Before long, machines alone will decide who should be jailed, who should be given a house,[289] who should walk free, and who should be afforded credit.[290] Just take heed of what is currently happening in the remit of predictive[291] recidivism.[292] Grudgingly, one

interest or not.". Italics added and italics on the original. See: https://uncoverdc.com/2022/01/10/ai-system-206-replacing-human-prosecutors-in-china (access: 23.08.2024).

286 See in French doctrine: Ferey, Samuel, « Analyse économique du droit, big data et justice prédictive», *Archives de Philosophie du Droit*, Volume 60, 2018, pp. 68–81.

287 See: Part IV of this book.

288 See: Pasquale, Frank, "A Rule of Persons, Not Machines: The Limits of Legal Automation", *George Washington Law Review*, Volume 87, 2019, pp. 1 and ff and passim.

289 *Tech, Bias and Housing Initiative, the Promise and Perils of Residential Proptech, Year 1, Research Summary Report, April 2023, TechEquity Collaborative*, p. 10, available at: https://techequity.us/wp-content/uploads/2023/04/TBHI-Y1-Research-Summary-Report.pdf (28.11.2024). ("Opaque, Predictive Algorithms Determine Who Gets What Housing Unlike Analog Models, *Algorithmic Tenant Screening Tools Predict Future Behavior To Determine Housing Access As landlord tech took hold, more property managers of all sizes came to rely on it to interface with tenants. One key feature of landlord tech is the use of algorithms to screen rental applicants and assess their suitability as tenants. The tenant screening industry, which pulls a wide array of information about potential tenants to inform landlords' decisions, is now valued at $1.3 billion with as many as two thousand screening companies vying for market share.*10 11 *Such companies include Equifax, TransUnion, and Experian (commonly known as "The Big Three"), as well as smaller startup companies that apply algorithms to make those determinations faster*"). Italics added. See: Part IV, Chap. 4 of this book.

290 See: Part IV, Chap. 4, Sects. 4.4 to 4.4.2.1 of this book (on mortgage redlining). See: Part IV, Chap. 4, Sects. 4.2 to 4.4.3 of this book (on algorithmic credit scoring, consumer racism and credit card redlining).

291 See: Part IV, Chap. 4, Sects. 4.10.1 to 4.10.6 of this book (on biased algorithmic risk assessment in criminal procedure law settings). See: Part IV, Chap. 4, Sects. 4.1 to 4.1.1 of this book (on biased predictive policing). See: Part V, Chap. 5, Sect. 5.7.2 of this book (on law number two to control algorithmic decision-making, which mandates that black box models must not be entrusted with the task of making high stake decisions—v.g. health and freedom). See: Part V, Chap. 5, Sect. 5.8.5 of this book (on law number five to interpret algorithmic decision-making, which mandates that robot-judges, robot-prosecutors and robot-lawyers must not enter the courtroom for they are utterly incapable of making sound and interpretable value judgements).

292 A challenge amenable to be fetched out from the bucket of concerns to be keenly addressed is the role that technology plays in predicting recidivism. See: Zhu, Mirilla, "Jury, Using Artificial Intelligence to Predict Recidivism Rates", *Yale Scientific*, 2020, passim. See also: Chasemi et al., Medhi, "The application of Machine Learning to a General Risk-Need Assessment Instrument in the Prediction of Criminal Recidivism", *Criminal Justice and Behavior*, Volume 48, 2020, pp. 518–538. See: Part IV, Chap. 4, Sects. 4.10.1 to 4.10.6 of this book (on biased algorithmic risk assessment in criminal procedure law settings). See: Part IV, Chap. 4, Sects. 4.1 to 4.1.1 of this book (on biased predictive policing).

must aver that the door of *Algorithmic Dictatorship* is already ajar slightly. More on this later.[293]

§§ The third era of Artificial Intelligence is not to be bogged down to big data nevertheless. One of the propelling forces of, and of the crowning achievements arising out of, the big data era is the creation, from scratch, of a broader technological apparatus encompassing cutting-edge software and hardware[294] to spur the seamless functioning of Artificial Intelligence amidst the data-driven world we currently live in.[295]

§§ Recall, the third era of Artificial Intelligence is not to be narrowed down to big data though. Machine learning algorithms—that were once used just to solve a tiny fraction of problems—are now used to sway citizens'lives in a regular basis.[296] Put another way, machine learning algorithms, if shrewdly used, are amenable to steer citizens towards a direction social engineers see fit. The potential that machine learning algorithms boast to influence people in social media[297] is walloping.

§§ Tellingly, machine learning algorithms draw on thumping great databases that feed into the pearls of wisdom offered by a pervasive Artificial Intelligence that rules our

---

[293] See: Part IV, Chap. 4, Sects. 4 to 4.10.6 of this book (on Algorithmic Dictatorship and its chilling effect on democracy). See: Part V, Chap. 5, Sect. 5.8.5 of this book (on law number five to interpret algorithmic decision-making, which mandates that robot-judges, robot-prosecutors and robot-lawyers must not enter the courtroom for they are utterly incapable of making sound and interpretable value judgements).

[294] Alves, Jones Figueirêdo/Pimentel, Alexandre Freire, "Breves notas sobre os preconceitos decisionais judiciais produzidos por redes neurais artificiais (Brief notes about the judicial decisional prejudices produced by artificial neural networks), *cit.*, pp. 555–577 (564).

[295] But see: Hardt, Moritz, "How big data is unfair: Understanding sources of unfairness in data driven decision making", *Medium*, Archived on Oct. 8, 2014, available at: https://web.archive.org/web/20141008185829/, https://medium.com/@mrtz/how-big-data-is-unfair-9aa544d739de. (access: 17.12.2024).

[296] Alves, Jones Figueirêdo/Pimentel, Alexandre Freire, "Breves notas sobre os preconceitos decisionais judiciais produzidos por redes neurais artificiais (Brief notes about the judicial decisional prejudices produced by artificial neural networks), *cit.*, pp. 555–577 (564).

[297] Alves, Jones Figueirêdo/Pimentel, Alexandre Freire, "Breves notas sobre os preconceitos decisionais judiciais produzidos por redes neurais artificiais (Brief notes about the judicial decisional prejudices produced by artificial neural networks), *cit.*, pp. 555–577 (564).

daily lives[298] with nearly absolute power.[299] Artificial Intelligence-powered systems with manifold expertise[300] keep popping up like mushrooms.

§§ The third era of Artificial Intelligence catalysed fast-paced strides[301] in the remit of digital capitalism[302] which, in turn, spawned both the age of surveillance capitalism[303] and informational capitalism.[304] The United States of America government

---

[298] It is crucially important to note, though, that the very fact that only certain types of behaviours are assessed and gauged by credit scores leads to the conclusion some borrowers are not scored at all. The overwhelming majority of consumers boast meagre, if any, credit files owing to the fact that the likelihood to access to the sort of financial services that actually report to the orthodox credit bureaus scattered across modern economies is exceedingly low, which, in turn, morphs them into credit invisible persons. See: Yu, Persis/McLaughlin, Jilian/Levy, Marina, "Big Data: A Big Disappointment for Scoring Consumer Creditworthiness,", *The National Consumer Law Center,* 2 (Mar. 14, 2014), available at: https://www.nclc.org/images/pdf/pr-reports/ report-big-data.pdf [https://perma.cc/W4SK-NXD5] (access: 21.12.2024).

[299] But see: *Tech, Bias and Housing Initiative, the Promise and Perils of Residential Proptech, Year 1, Research Summary Report, April 2023, TechEquity Collaborative,* p. 11, available at: https://techequity.us/wp-content/uploads/2023/04/TBHI-Y1-Research-Summary-Report.pdf (28.11.2024). ("*Once bad data enters the analysis of one factor, it gets baked into the subsequent process, multiplying the effect that one disadvantageous data point can have on someone's overall housing determination*"). Italics added. See: Part IV, Chap. 4, Sects. 4.4 to 4.4.2.3 of this book.

[300] Alves, Jones Figueirêdo/Pimentel, Alexandre Freire, "Breves notas sobre os preconceitos decisionais judiciais produzidos por redes neurais artificiais (Brief notes about the judicial decisional prejudices produced by artificial neural networks), *cit.*, pp. 555–577 (564).

[301] Fergus, Rachel, "Biased Technology: The Automated Discrimination of Facial Recognition", *ACLU Minnesota*, February 29, 2024, available at: https://www.aclu-mn.org/en/news/biased-technology-automated-discrimination-facial-recognition (access: 20.09.2024) ("*Technology is developing much more quickly than the laws we need to protect our rights. Anyone with a smartphone or social media account knows how rapidly technology changes, while legislating can take a long, long time. It is essential to proactively put policies into place that will protect our rights as new and more advanced technology is constantly released. Especially when that technology—and law enforcement members using it—have been shown over and over to be biased toward marginalized groups*"). Italics added. See also: Hu, Margaret, "From the National Surveillance State to the Cybersurveillance State", *The Annual Review of Law and Social Science*, Volume 13, 2017, p. 169 ("*in a big data world, a digitized passport system can link to multiple other sources, such as license plate readers, No Fly Lists, and Terrorist Watchlists. Facial recognition technology drawing upon a photo database could potentially link a plethora of digital images of a person, including social media, the internet, photo databases like driver's licenses, live-streaming video, CCTV surveillance, and images obtained from hacking cameras on laptops and digital devices. Biometric data collection and storage are becoming increasingly compulsory through either government identification requirements*, such as digital photo requirements for passports and driver's licenses, or corporate identification requirements, such as biometric access to digital devices"). Italics added. See: Part III, Chap. 3, Sects. 3.5.7 to 3.5.8.1 of this book (on the functional aspects of Critical Artificial Intelligence Studies, with a sharper focus on the perils concerning the deployment of facial recognition technology).

[302] See in Italian doctrine: Quintarelli, Stefano, *Capitalismo Immateriale—Le tecnologie digitali ed il nuovo conflito sociale*, 7ª edizione. Turin: Bollati Boringhieri, 2019, pp. 1–198.

[303] See: Zuboff, Zhoshana, *The Age of Surveillance Capitalism, The Fight for a Human Future at the New Frontier of Power*. New Yor City: PublicAffairs Books, 2019, pp. 1–704 (360) (argues that we are indomitably heading towards a "instrumentarianism" that draws on "totalitarianism").

[304] See: Cohen, Julien E., *Between Truth and Power: The Legal Constructions of Informational Capitalism*. Oxford: Oxford University Press, 2019, pp. 1–376 (p. 192) (asserts adamantly that

made massive investments in the aftermath of a gruelling financial crisis (2008 and 2012)[305] that frayed the fabric of its economy.

"*automated processes* have obvious efficiency advantages, *but such processes may not align well (or well at all) with applicable legal requirements that are couched in shades of gray*"). Italics added.

[305] On the causes that set in motion those economic crisis: See: CORDEIRO, ANTÓNIO MENEZES, "A crise planetária de 2007/2010 e o governo das sociedades", *Revista de Direito das Sociedades* (*RDS*), I (2009), 2, Coimbra, Almedina, 2009, pp. 268–271; CORDEIRO, António BARRETO MENEZES, "Organização e supervisão dos mercados financeiros", *Revista de Direito das Sociedades* (*RDS*), Ano VI (2014), Números 3/4, Coimbra, Almedina, 2015, pp. 581 e ss; SILVA, JOÃO CALVÃO DA, "*Fair value* ou valor de mercado: multiplicador da primeira crise financeira global", *Revista de Legislação e de Jurisprudência* (*RLJ*), ano 141.°, n.° 3974, Maio-Junho 2012, Coimbra, Coimbra Editora, 2012, pp. 280 e ss; OLIVEIRA, ANA PERESTRELO DE/OLIVEIRA, MADALENA PERESTRELO DE, "Derivados Financeiros e governo societário: a propósito da nova regulação mobiliária europeia e da consulta pública da ESMA", *Revista de Direito das Sociedades em Revista* (*RDS*), Ano IV (2012), Número I, Coimbra, Almedina, 2012, pp. 59–61; MURDOCK, CHARLES, "The Dodd—Frank Wall Street Reform and Consumer Protection Act: What Caused The Financial Crisis and Will Dodd—Frank Prevent Future Crisis?", in: *S.M.U. Law Review*, 1243, 2011, pp. 138 e ss; SANTOS, HUGO LUZ DOS, "O contrato de swap de taxas de juro e os instrumentos derivados financeiros à luz do recente Acórdão do Supremo Tribunal de Justiça, de 10 de Outubro de 2013: a "Alteração Anormal das Circunstâncias" e as categorias doutrinais norte-americanas da "Unconscionability" e a "Bounded Rationality": Um estranho caso de aliança luso-americana?", *Revista de Direito das Sociedades* (*RDS*), Ano VI (2014), Número 2, Coimbra, Almedina, 2014, pp. 411–433; OLIVEIRA, MADALENA PERESTRELO DE, "Instrumentos financeiros com fins de garantia e exercício de direitos sociais", *Revista de Direito das Sociedades* (RDS), Ano V (2013), Número III, Coimbra, Almedina, 2013, pp. 537–604; BESSA, TIAGO, "Crise, Regulação e Supervisão de Hedge Funds", *Revista de Direito das Sociedades* (*RDS*), Ano II (2010)—Número 3–4, Coimbra, Almedina, 2011, pp. 853–869; DIAS, GABRIELA FIGUEIREDO, "Regulação e Supervisão de Hedge Funds: Percurso, Oportunidade e Tendências", in: AAVV, *Direitos dos Valores Mobiliários*, Volume VIII, 2008, em especial, pp. 65–81; CULLEN, Ian, "Hedge Funds: Structure and Documentation", in: AAVV, *Hedge Funds: Law and Regulation*, coord., Iain Cullen e Helen Parry, 2001, pp. 141–157; ANTUNES, JOSÉ ENGRÁCIA, "Os "Hedge Funds" e o Governo das Sociedades", AAVV, *Direitos dos Valores Mobiliários*, Volume IX, 2010, pp. 9–70; GHOSCH, DILI/CLARCK, EPHRAIM, *Arbitrage, Hedging, and Speculation: The Foreign Exchange Market*, Praeger, New York, 2004, pp. 8 e ss; MATOS, INÊS SERRANO DE, "Hedge Fund: o Accionista que nunca dorme?", in: *Homenagem ao Prof. Doutor António José Avelãs Nunes*, *Boletim de Ciências Económicas*, Volume II, Coimbra, Universidade de Coimbra, 2014, pp. 2233 e ss; ROTHLEY, OLIVER, "Aufgabe der Macroton-Grundsätze", in: *GWR*, 2013, pp. 489 e ss; ARNOLD, MICHAEL/ ROTHENBERG, VERA, "BGH-Entscheidung zum Delisting: Alle Fragen geklärt?", in: *DStR*, 2014, pp. 144–161; KLHÖN, LARS, "Delisting- Zehn Jahre später/Die Auswirkungen von BVerfGE," in: *NZG*, 2012, pp. 821 e ss; SANTOS, HUGO LUZ DOS, "A perda da qualidade de sociedade aberta (*delisting* de participações sociais): a tutela dos sócios minoritários, o direito de propriedade, e o dever de lealdade dos administradores das sociedades comerciais (com uma breve paragem em Macau e em Hong Kong)", *Revista de Direito das Sociedades* (*RDS*), Coimbra, Almedina, Ano 8 (2016), N.° 4, Coimbra, Almedina, 2016, pp. 893–929.

§§ Suffice to say that the tidal wave of digital capitalism was deftly ridden by corporate moguls the likes of Google, Facebook, Tencent,[306] which have created a sort-of digital bubble that permanently embroils/ensnares citizens in a haze hovering over their inner workings. The assertion according to which these corporate moguls play by their own rules while controlling the digital economy[307] is neither unwarranted nor uncalled for.

§§ It has been said that Artificial Intelligence is currently equipped to perform three highly complex tasks.[308] On one hand, Artificial Intelligence can create meaningful patterns arising out of equally meaningful information. On the other hand, Artificial Intelligence is suitably tailored to analyse massive amounts of raw data[309] while drawing meaningful inferences related with the topic at hand—the nub of data mining.[310]

[306] Alves, Jones Figueirêdo/Pimentel, Alexandre Freire, "Breves notas sobre os preconceitos decisionais judiciais produzidos por redes neurais artificiais (Brief notes about the judicial decisional prejudices produced by artificial neural networks), *cit.*, pp. 555–577 (564).

[307] Alves, Jones Figueirêdo/Pimentel, Alexandre Freire, "Breves notas sobre os preconceitos decisionais judiciais produzidos por redes neurais artificiais (Brief notes about the judicial decisional prejudices produced by artificial neural networks), *cit.*, pp. 555–577 (564).

[308] See: Sadin, Éric, "La inteligencia artificial: el superyó del siglo XXI", *Revista Nueva Sociedad*, n.º 279, enero-febrero 2019, 2019, pp. 142 and ff and passim.

[309] Kleinberg, Jon/Ludwig, Jens/Mullainathan, Sendhil/Sunstein Cass R., "Discrimination in the Age of Algorithms", *Journal of Legal Analysis*, Volume 10, 1, 2018, pp. 28–29, 33–34 (draw a distinction between "group differences in the raw data" and biases for the "choice of predictors.").

[310] Balkin, Jack, "Constitution in the National Surveillance State", *Minnesota Law Review*, Volume 93, 2008, p. 13 (note, though, that "*data mining* allows inferences not only about the direct subject of surveillance, but about other people with whom they live, work and communicate"). It bears mentioning that pundits have neither been coy nor bashful in strongly highlighting the perceived peril—consumer harm—of monetizing the data harvested/gleaned by Artificial Intelligence-embedded technologies while performing data mining. See: Yang/Kai Hao, "Selling Consumer Data for Profit: Optimal Market-Segmentation Design and its Consequences", *American Economic Review*, Volume 112, Issue 4, April 2022, 2022, pp. 1364–1393.

§§ This operation is called data mining[311] and puts in jeopardy a plethora of citizens 'fundamental rights[312] whose violations must neither go unnoticed[313] nor unpunished.[314]

§§ Data mining is an operation through which machines can process information—at a lighting speed—while capturing meaningful correlations entrenched in the rigged data baked into databases[315] in ways that are utterly impossible to grasp by humans.[316]

---

[311] Kamatkar, S.J./Tayade, A./Viloria, A./Hernández-Chacín, A., "Application of classification technique of data mining for employee management system", *Lecture Notes in Computer Science (including subseries Lecture Notes in Artificial Intelligence and Lecture Notes in Bioinformatics*, Vol. 10943 LNCS, Springer Verlag, 2018, pp. 434–444; Grimm, Paul W., "Practical Considerations for the Admissibility of Artificial Intelligence Evidence", in: *Sedona Conference Journal*, Volume 2, 2021, p. 30 (alludes to *data analytics* and *data mining*, which "refer to processes for harvesting previously unknown information from a vast sea of raw data, while data science refers to the practice of performing data analytics or *data mining*". Itálicos nossos.

[312] Wagner/Gerhard/Eidenmuller, Horst, "Down by Algorithms? Siphoning Rents, Exploiting Biases, and Shaping Preferences: Regulating the Dark Side of Targeted Transactions", *University of Chicago Law Review*, Volume 86, 2019, pp. 581–609; Wallheimer, Brian, "Are you Ready for Personalized Pricing? Companies Are Figuring out What Individual Customers Will Pay-and Charging Accordingly", *Chicago Booth Review*, 2018, passim.

[313] Balkin, Jack, "Constitution in the National Surveillance State", *Minnesota Law Review*, Volume 93, 2008, p. 13 ("*data mining* allows inferences not only about the direct subject of surveillance, but about other people with whom they live, work and communicate"). Pearl, Judea, "Causal inference in statistics: An overview", *Statistics Surveys*, Volume 3, 2009, pp. 96–146. But see: Pedreshi, Dino/Ruggieri, Salvatore/Turini, Franco, "Discrimination-aware Data Mining", *Proceedings of the 14th ACM SIGKDD International Conference on Knowledge Discovery and Data Mining (Las Vegas, Nevada, USA), ACM*, 2008, pp. 560–568 (arguing that one should shift its gaze downstream by putting in place discrimination-aware algorithmic tools while performing data mining). See: Part III, Chap. 3, Sects. 3.5.7 to 3.5.8.1 of this book (on the functional aspects of Critical Artificial Intelligence Studies, with a sharper focus on the perils concerning the deployment of facial recognition technology).

[314] But see: Posner, Richard A., "Privacy, Surveillance, and Law", in: *University of Chicago Law Review*, Volume 75, 2008, p. 251 ("Privacy is the terrorist's best friend"). See also on the tradeoff between privacy and security: Solove, Daniel J., *Nothing to Hide: The False Tradeoff Between privacy and security*, New Haven/London, Yale University Press, 2013, pp. 101–110; Santos, Hugo Luz dos, "They See You and yet you don't see them: Privacy in the Multilayered National Surveillance State Realm: a Dystopian Digital Society?", *Journal of Computer Science & Systems Biology*, Volume 11, n.º 3, New York, United States of America, 2018, pp. 200–216. Citron; Danielle Keats/Pasquale, Frank, "Network Accountability for the Domestic Intelligence Apparatus", *Hasting Law Journal*, Volume 62, 2011, 1441, 1444–45; Gray, David/Citron, Danielle Keats, "The Right to Quantitative Privacy", *Minnesota Law Review*, Volume 98, 2013, pp. 62–81.

[315] *Tech, Bias and Housing Initiative, the Promise and Perils of Residential Proptech, Year 1, Research Summary Report, April 2023, TechEquity Collaborative*, p. 11, available at: https://techequity.us/wp-content/uploads/2023/04/TBHI-Y1-Research-Summary-Report.pdf (28.11.2024). ("*Once bad data enters the analysis of one factor, it gets baked into the subsequent process, multiplying the effect that one disadvantageous data point can have on someone's overall housing determination*"). Italics added.

[316] Sadin, Éric, "La inteligencia artificial: el superyó del siglo XXI", *cit.*, pp. 142 and ff and passim; Alves, Jones Figueirêdo/Pimentel, Alexandre Freire, "Breves notas sobre os preconceitos decisionais judiciais produzidos por redes neurais artificiais (Brief notes about the judicial decisional prejudices produced by artificial neural networks), *cit.*, pp. 555–577 (564).

§§ The data that was once hunkered down in a position sheltered by a number of legal guardrails, is a now a commodity[317] in the data-driven world we live in.[318] Laypeople's pleas to safeguard their data have fallen in deaf ears after all. Data should be looked up, not laughed at. Regrettably, the whopping effort to keep data safe is laughed at given the ease with which criminals get a hold of sensitive information these days.[319]

§§ This sizzling hot topic needs to be governed owing to its swift diffusion in that boasts every likelihood to throw extant normative underpinnings out of balance. All of which, understandably, has led citizens to probe other ways to protect[320] their sensitive data.[321]

---

[317] Yang/Kai Hao, "Selling Consumer Data for Profit: Optimal Market-Segmentation Design and its Consequences", *American Economic Review*, Volume 112, Issue 4, April 2022, 2022, pp. 1364–1393.

[318] The issue of a digital reality fed by a data-driven world has been shrewdly portrayed by renowned scholars, which offer gripping examples of it: Suzor, Nicolas P., *Lawless: The Secret Rules that Govern our Digital Lives*. Cambridge, United Kingdom: Cambridge University Press, 2019, pp. 1–218 (passim). But see: Hardt, Moritz, "How big data is unfair: Understanding sources of unfairness in data driven decision making", *Medium*, Archived on Oct. 8, 2014, available at: https://web.archive.org/web/20141008185829/ https://medium.com/@mrtz/how-big-data-is-unfair-9aa544d739de. (access: 17.12.2024).

Brownsword, Roger, *Law, Technology and Society: Re-Imagining the Regulatory Environment*, London: Routledge, 2020, pp. 1–361 (passim) (broaches the interplay law, technology and society with a sharper focus in the era of smart regulatory technologies). See: Part III, Chap. 3, Sects. 3.5.7 to 3.5.8.1 of this book (on the functional aspects of Critical Artificial Intelligence Studies, with a sharper focus on the perils concerning the deployment of facial recognition technology).

[319] Yang/Kai Hao, "Selling Consumer Data for Profit: Optimal Market-Segmentation Design and its Consequences", *cit.*, pp. 1364–1393.

[320] Waldman, Ari Ezra, "Privacy, Practice, and Performance", *California Law Review*, Volume 110, 2022, pp. 1221–1227 (contend, however, that we have all been cunningly schooled to "thinking that managing our privacy is an individual responsibility"); Citron; Danielle Keats Citron/Pasquale, Frank, "Network Accountability for the Domestic Intelligence Apparatus", *Hasting Law Journal*, Volume 62, 2011, 1441, 1444–45; Gray, David/Citron, Danielle Keats, "The Right to Quantitative Privacy", *Minnesota Law Review*, Volume 98, 2013, pp. 62–81.

[321] Recall, from the social psychology, warped algorithms—that draw on rigged data—accomplish nothing but the impairment of procedural justice. See: Thibaut, John/ Walker, Laurens, *Procedural Justice: A Psychological Analysis*. Hillsdale, N.J.: Lawrence Erlbaum Associates, 1975, pp. 1–150 (procedural justice is tightly interlocked to raising the levels of fairness in criminal procedure law settings. Absent of which procedural fairness is to mar. Criminal procedure law must not lose sight of such assertion). Converging: Lind, Edgar Allan/Tyler, Tom R., *The Social Psychology of Procedural Justice*. New York: Springer, 1988, pp. 208 ff (emphasizing that perceptions of justice being justly and correctly served enhances exponentially citizens' perception of provider legitimacy). Tyler, Tom R., "The Psychology of Procedural Justice: A Test of the Group-Value Model", *Journal of Personality and Social Psychology*, Volume 57, 1989, p. 830 (reports that in any procedure "several non-control issues—the *neutrality* of the decision-making procedure, trust in the 3rd party, and the information the experience communicates about social standing—influence both procedural preferences and judgments of procedural justice"). See also: Simmons, Ric, "Big Data and Procedural Justice: Legitimizing Algorithms in the Criminal Justice System", *Ohio State Journal of Criminal Law*, Volume 15, 2018, pp. 576 and ff and passim.

§§ Which is nothing but formulaic: rapid advances in Artificial Intelligence are paving the way for a plethora of AI-embedded technologies that are burgeoningly swaying a multitude of aspects of nowadays societies.[322] Yet, dispiritingly, there is a perceived dearth of in-depth research that advances an accurate understanding of when, and which type of, befitted legal measures can be enacted to adroitly tackle

[322] Chopra, Samir/White, Laurence F., *A Legal Theory of Autonomous Artificial Agents*, Michigan, University of Michigan Press, 2011, pp. 1–264 (5) (2011) ("There are two views of the goals of artificial intelligence. From an engineering perspective, as Marvin Minsky noted, it is the 'science of making machines do things that would require intelligence if done by men.' *From a cognitive science perspective, it is to design and build systems that work the way the human mind does. In the former perspective, artificial intelligence is deemed successful along a performative dimension; in the latter, along a theoretical one.* The latter embodies Giambattista Vico's perspective of verum et factum convertuntur, 'the true and the made are... convertible'; *in such a view, artificial intelligence would be reckoned the laboratory that validates our best science of the human mind. This perspective sometimes shades into the claim artificial intelligence's success lies in the replication of human capacities such as emotions, the sensations of taste, and self-consciousness. Here, artificial intelligence is conceived of as building artificial persons, not just designing systems that are 'intelligent*'") ("*As an example of how agent technologies might evolve to incorporate learning, autonomy, and discretion, consider a hypothetical agent designed to find used books on the Internet. The agent is provided with a list of websites to scour, sample titles with abstracts as learning data to recognize other titles in the genre, and electronic cash accounts with which to make purchases.* The agent is allowed to purchase books within a preset spending limit with discretion in the number, subjects, and individual prices of books bought. Such an agent has a broadly defined goal with enough executive discretion in the choices it makes to optimize satisfaction of that goal. The agent is able to interact with its environment by reading and scanning information at the sites it visits; it interacts with other agents such as selling agents deployed by other users. The agent "moves" from site to site, makes purchases, and reads recommendations provided by book-selling agents. The agent checks recommendations for matches on parameters of interest, and then depending on the outcome, buys more books or declines offers. *It is able to buy titles not on its original list, and to proactively make the decision to buy a new title. Such an agent is able to decide to take an action, in response to inputs it decides to focus on; its interactions on the Internet, in a world populated by other shopping agents and sometimes humans, exemplify autonomous, goal-directed, proactive behavior*"). Italics added.

this worrisome issue that should keep citizens eagerly awaken at night.[323] Failing which, the Rule of Law[324] hangs on the balance.[325]

§§ Las but not least, Artificial Intelligence boasts a hardly unforeseen autonomy to make decisions on its own.[326] Artificial Intelligence accordingly waives human supervision to attain a given goal.[327] The best example is the high-frequency trading

---

[323] McAfee, Andrew/Brynjolfsson, *Machine, Platform, Crowd: Harnessing our Digital Future*, London: Brilliance Audio; Unabridged edition, 2017 (pore over a myriad of automatic biases displayed by artificial intelligence).

[324] See: Raz, Joseph, "The Rule of Law and its Virtue", *The Authority of Law: Essays on Law and Morality*. Oxford: Clarendon Press, 1979, pp. 210–214 (on the quintessential value of Rule of Law); Waldron, Jeremy, "The Rule of Law and the Importance of Procedure", *New York Public Law and Legal Theory*, 2010, p. 4 (notes that "the Rule of Law is violated when due attention is not paid to these procedural matters or when the institutions that are supposed to embody this procedure are undermined or interfered with". Further down this author would admit that there are some substantive dimensions of Rule of Law, such as respect for right for property and presumption of liberty and so forth). Taekema, Sanne, "The Procedural Rule of Law: Examining Waldron's Argument on Dignity and Agency", *Jahrbuch für Recht und Ethik*, Band 21, 2013, pp. 133 ff (contends that "Waldron's understanding of the Rule of Law as procedural which demands the opportunity for individuals to contest legal decisions in the formalized processes of courts and tribunals"); Cass, Ronald A., *The Rule of Law in America*. Baltimore, Maryland: The Johns Hopkins University Press, 2001, p. 17 (noting that a "central element of the Rule of law, constraint from external authority...helps assure that the process of government, *rather than the predilections of the individual decision-maker*") Italics added.

[325] Which is why the onset of the age of Artificial Intelligence will put the Rule of Law to the test like never before. Recall, the Rule of Law is a functional barrier—aimed at clamping down a host of unlawful deeds undertaken by those in power—that must not be teared apart or criminal procedure law will be otherwise despoiled from its intrinsic validity and vitality. See: Raz, Joseph, "The Rule of Law and its Virtue", *The Authority of Law: Essays on Law and Morality*, *cit.*, p. 224 (asserts adamantly that the Rule of Law is aimed at cushioning the hazards of abuse perpetrated by those in power. In this vein, Raz contends that "the law inevitably creates a great danger of arbitrary power—the Rule of Law is designed to minimize the danger created by the law itself...*Thus the (R)ule of (L)aw is designed to minimize the danger created by law itself...Thus the (R)ule of (L)aw is a negative virtue...the evil which is avoided is evil which could only have been caused by the law itself*"). Italics added. See: Part V, Chap. 5, Sect. 5.1.1 of this book (on the central tenets of Rule of Law that lends itself to a beacon of justice amidst the sepulchral darkness that is about to take hold). See: Part V, Chap. 5, Sect. 5.1.2 of this book (on the central tenets of Procedural Rule of Law that lends itself to a lighthouse of justice that allows citizens to challenge the pearls of algorithmic wisdom in a court of law).

[326] Since it has come to our attention that *machine-learning algorithms "are capable of making intuitive decisions based in newly learned information, much like humans*. The new wave of AI developments will generate powerful AI that is capable of improvising itself, *perhaps even by rewriting its own algorithms, advancing its intelligence beyond that of humans*". Italics added. See: Hutto-Schultz, Jess, "Dicitur Ex Machina: Artificial Intelligence and the Hearsay Rule", *George Mason Law Review*, Volume 27, n. ° 2, 2020, pp. 684–718 (684).

[327] Sadin, Éric, "La inteligencia artificial: el superyó del siglo XXI", *cit.*, pp. 142 and ff and passim; Alves, Jones Figueirêdo/Pimentel, Alexandre Freire, "Breves notas sobre os preconceitos decisionais judiciais produzidos por redes neurais artificiais (Brief notes about the judicial decisional prejudices produced by artificial neural networks), *cit.*, pp. 555–577 (564).

robots[328] that can buy and sell stocks in the stock exchange with minimum or inexistent human oversight.[329]

§§ Against this background, hardly any surprise springs from the fact that Artificial Intelligence's humongous skills can only be brought to bear if apposite conditions are timely put in place. Put otherwise, Artificial Intelligence, to be fully functional, relies heavily on both the dimension and quality[330] of the database[331] that is intended to operate upon.[332]

---

[328] See: Millar, Jason/Kerr, Ian, "Delegation, Relinquishment and Responsibility: The Prospect of Expert Robots", *Robot Law*, Calo, Ryan /Froomkin, A. Michael/Kerr, Ian, Cheltenham, Edward Elgar Publishing, 2016, pp. 102, 106–107 (as these authors aptly put it "*we will rely on robots without really knowing why—simply because their algorithms provide the greatest number of successful outcomes.* We have already seen this in Google's search approach. Neither Larry (Page) nor Sergey (Brin) (nor any other Google employee) knowns exactly why one particular web page is a better result than another. *When the click patterns say it is, that's good enough.* No semantic or causal analysis is required…*Like the ancients, we will, quite rationally, come to rely upon them, knowing full well that we cannot necessarily explain the reasons for their decisions*"). Italics added. Converging: Casey, Anthony J./Niblett, Anthony, "Self-driving Laws", *University of Toronto Law Journal*, Volume 66, 2016, pp. 429–435 (contend that "as more information is generated, and the evolutionary algorithm updates and become a better forecaster, we imagine that judges will increasingly rely on the advice of the algorithm").

[329] Sadin, Éric, "La inteligencia artificial: el superyó del siglo XXI", *cit.*, pp. 142 and ff and passim; Alves, Jones Figueirêdo/Pimentel, Alexandre Freire, "Breves notas sobre os preconceitos decisionais judiciais produzidos por redes neurais artificiais (Brief notes about the judicial decisional prejudices produced by artificial neural networks), *cit.*, pp. 555–577 (564).

[330] See: *Tech, Bias and Housing Initiative, the Promise and Perils of Residential Proptech, Year 1, Research Summary Report, April 2023, TechEquity Collaborative*, p. 11, available at: https://techequity.us/wp-content/uploads/2023/04/TBHI-Y1-Research-Summary-Report.pdf (28.11.2024). ("*Once bad data enters the analysis of one factor, it gets baked into the subsequent process, multiplying the effect that one disadvantageous data point can have on someone's overall housing determination*"). Italics added. See: Part IV, Chap. 4, Sects. 4.4 to 4.4.2.3 of this book.

[331] But see: *Tech, Bias and Housing Initiative, the Promise and Perils of Residential Proptech, Year 1, Research Summary Report, April 2023, TechEquity Collaborative*, p. 5 available at: https://techequity.us/wp-content/uploads/2023/04/TBHI-Y1-Research-Summary-Report.pdf (28.11.2024). ("*Residential Proptech also has the potential to exacerbate the bias inherent in our housing system. Its rise is due, in part, to the desperation felt by average home seekers. With a severely constrained housing supply, companies offering an easier pathway to homeownership may exploit communities that have been harmed by housing discrimination in the past. Opaque algorithms incorporate biased data into their decision-making processes, making it harder to enforce fair housing laws.* Residential Proptech companies often operate in a regulatory gray area, leaving consumers without the protections they would have from traditional housing regulatory systems. *As unprecedented capital investment flows into this space, venture-backed companies' winner-take-all approach to growth has the potential to exacerbate inequality rather than combat it*"). Italics added. See: Part IV, Chap. 4, Sects. 4.4 to 4.4.2.1 of this book (on mortgage redlining). See: Part IV, Chap. 4, Sects. 4.2 to 4.4.3 of this book (on algorithmic credit scoring, consumer racism and credit card redlining). See: Part IV, Chap. 4, Sects. 4.4 to 4.4.2.3 of this book (on algorithmic redlining). See: Part IV, Chap. 4, Sect. 4.4.3 of this book (on "algorithmic redliking"). See: Part IV, Chap. 4, Sect. 4.3 of this book (on algorithmic prime-lining).

[332] Alves, Jones Figueirêdo/Pimentel, Alexandre Freire, "Breves notas sobre os preconceitos decisionais judiciais produzidos por redes neurais artificiais (Brief notes about the judicial decisional prejudices produced by artificial neural networks), *cit.*, pp. 555–577 (565).

§§ Not in the least surprising, machine learning algorithms boast remarkable skills in that they are fully capable to accomplish a series of tasks with an impressive degree of proficiency/accuracy.[333]

§§ Amongst those remarkable functionalities stand four features that merit a bunch of utterances. Overall, the foregoing features—that deserve to be both accounted for and remarked upon—read as follows: (i) behavioural surveillance[334] that draws on the accumulation of big data;[335] (ii) citizens 'behavioural perception;[336] (iii) forecasting

---

[333] Alves, Jones Figueirêdo/Pimentel, Alexandre Freire, "Breves notas sobre os preconceitos decisionais judiciais produzidos por redes neurais artificiais (Brief notes about the judicial decisional prejudices produced by artificial neural networks), *cit.*, pp. 555–577 (565).

[334] See: Hu, Margaret, "From the National Surveillance State to the Cybersurveillance State", *The Annual Review of Law and Social Science*, Volume 13, 2017, pp. 162–163 ("*policymakers view these technological developments, including biometric technologies, as tools with the potential to identify individuals who may pose a threat to national and homeland security and to prevent crime and terrorism. One example of technology intended for risk assessment and threat management is the post-9/11 program Total Information Awareness (TIA). (….) Collect-it-all efforts like TIA embody a philosophy that aspires to preventive policing. Mass data collection is construed as a tool to assess and prevent future threats (Murray 2010). In TIA and other programs tested or adopted after 9/11, biometric database screening and analysis have emerged as a preferred method for tracking, identifying, and establishing identity-based inferences in counterterrorism*"). Italics added. See also: Ball, Kirstie, and Frank Webster (Eds.), *The Intensification of Surveillance: Crime, Terrorism & Warfare in the Information Age*, London, UK: Pluto Press, 2007; Guzik, Keith, "Discrimination by Design: Predictive Data Mining as Security Practice in the United States' 'War on Terrorism.'", *Surveillance and Society*, 7 (1), 2009, pp. 1–17. See: Part III, Chap. 3, Sects. 3.5.7 to 3.5.8.1 of this book (on the functional aspects of Critical Artificial Intelligence Studies, with a sharper focus on the perils concerning the deployment of facial recognition technology).

[335] Brayne, S., "Big data surveillance: The case of policing", *American Sociological Review*, Volume 82, Issue 5, 2017, pp. 977–1008; Robinson, M. A., "Black bodies on the ground: Policing disparities in the African American Community-An analysis of newsprint from January 1, 2015, through December 31, 2015", *Journal of Black Studies*, Volume 48, Issue 6, pp. 551–571; Browne, S., *Dark matters: on the surveillance of blackness*, Duke University Press, 2015, passim. Toro, J. D./Lloyd, T., Buchanan/K. S., Robins/S. J., Bencharit/L. Z., Smiedt/M. G., Reddy/K. S., Pouget, E. R./Kerrison, E. M./Goff, P. A., "The criminogenic and psychological effects of police stops on adolescent black and Latino boys", *Proceedings of the National Academy of Sciences of the United States of America*, Volume 116, Issue 17, 2019, pp. 8261–8268; Sewell, A. A., Jefferson, K. A./Lee, H., "Living under surveillance: Gender, psychological distress, and stop-question- and-frisk policing in New York city", *Social Science & Medicine*, Volume 159, 2016, pp. 1–13; Benjamin, Ruha, *Race After Technology: Abolitionist Tools for the New Jim Code*, John Wiley & Sons, 2019, passim; Abdillahi, I., "Algorithmic surveillance in the era of the appsphere", *American Journal of Community Psychology*, Volume 73, 2024, passim; Zuboff, Zhoshana, *The Age of Surveillance Capitalism, The Fight for a Human Future at the New Frontier of Power*. New Yor City: PublicAffairs Books, 2019, pp. 1–704 (360) (argues that we are indomitably heading towards a "instrumentarianism" that draws on "totalitarianism"). See: Part IV, Chap. 4, Sects. 4.10.1 to 4.10.6 of this book (on biased algorithmic risk assessment in criminal procedure law settings, with a sharper focus on COMPAS). See: Part IV, Chap. 4, Sects. 4.1 to 4.1.1 of this book (on biased predictive policing).

[336] On algorithmic big data biometric governance: Hu, Margaret, "From the National Surveillance State to the Cybersurveillance State", *The Annual Review of Law and Social Science*, Volume 13, 2017, p. 169 ("*as a result of big data biometric governance trends, meaningful distinctions between biometric credentialing for identification and behavioral biometric profiling are disappearing. The objectives are merging: Reliable credentialing is used to advance security and precrime policy*

human behaviour[337] and, finally, (iv) modulation of human behaviour[338] that are capable of subtly steer citizens towards a given direction. Out of accuracy, they should be fleshed out separately.

§§ Digital surveillance—or *behavioural surveillance* undertaken through *surveillance capitalism*[339]—stands for an intrusive activity by means of which Artificial Intelligence gleans information through a ubiquitous surveillance.[340] An all-pervasive and far-reaching surveillance[341] that captures both the citizens' online

---

rationales. Biometric data mission creep occurs by necessity in a big data world because the cybersurveillance systems are often designed to engage in mass data integration and analysis and predictive policing. Biometric surveillance serves two purposes in preventive policing: It increases identity transparency, and the biometric data categorize identity through cataloging behavioral and physical characteristics and assess these characteristics for risk. Contrasting small data biometric credentialing protocols with big data credentialing protocols is useful. It illustrates how biometric surveillance fits within the Cybersurveillance State. In a small data world, paper-based passports and nondigitized photographs are examples of a small data biometric-based identification system"). Italics added. See: Part IV, Chap. 4, Sects. 4.5 to 4.5.2 of this book (on "algorithmic Jim Crow", a travel ban issued during the first Trump Administration to prevent certain individuals from entering the United States of America, which, given its racial undertones, stands as an outgrowth of congeries of laws enacted during the Jim Crow epoch).

337 It is often contended that machine learning algorithms engender their own models to forecast future outcomes on the basis of analysis of training data. See: Mittelstadt, Brent Daniel/Taddeo, Patrick Allo, Mariarosaria/Wachter, Sandra/Floridi, Luciano, "The Ethics of Algorithms: Mapping the Debate", *Big Data & Society*, July–Dec. 2016, 2016, p. 3. See also: Rudin, Cynthia, "A process for predicting manhole events in Manhattan", *Machine Learning*, Volume 80, 2018, pp. 1–31. See also: Berk, R., *Criminal Justice Forecasts of Risk: A Machine Learning Approach*, New York, Springer Science & Business Media, 2012, passim; Kehl, D. L., Guo, P., and Kessler, S. A., *Algorithms in the Criminal Justice System: Assessing the Use of Risk Assessments in Sentencing*, 2017, accessed at https://dash.harvard.edu/bitstream/handle/1/33746041/2017-07_responsivecommunities_2.pdf?sequence¼1 on October 24, 2024.

338 Alves, Jones Figueirêdo/Pimentel, Alexandre Freire, "Breves notas sobre os preconceitos decisionais judiciais produzidos por redes neurais artificiais (Brief notes about the judicial decisional prejudices produced by artificial neural networks), *cit.*, pp. 555–577 (565).

339 See: Zuboff, Zhoshana, *The Age of Surveillance Capitalism, The Fight for a Human Future at the New Frontier of Power*. New Yor City: PublicAffairs Books, 2019, pp. 1–704 (360) (argues that we are indomitably heading towards a "instrumentarianism" that draws on "totalitarianism"). See: Part IV, Chap. 4, Sects. 4.5 to 4.5.2 of this book (on "algorithmic Jim Crow", a travel ban issued during the first Trump Administration to prevent certain individuals from entering the United States of America, which, given its racial undertones, stands as an outgrowth of congeries of laws enacted during the Jim Crow epoch).

340 Alves, Jones Figueirêdo/Pimentel, Alexandre Freire, "Breves notas sobre os preconceitos decisionais judiciais produzidos por redes neurais artificiais (Brief notes about the judicial decisional prejudices produced by artificial neural networks), *cit.*, pp. 555–577 (565).

341 Which, I may venture to add, amounts to something—*biometric surveillance*—that equals nothing but to the price of partaking in public affairs, which is very hard to shy away from nowadays. See: Hu, Margaret, "From the National Surveillance State to the Cybersurveillance State", *The Annual Review of Law and Social Science*, Volume 13, 2017, p. 169 ("*because of technological developments and trends in governance, it is challenging, if not impossible, to prevent biometric data capture and collection. Biometric surveillance systems increasingly require opting in as the price of social, economic, and political participation.* Biometric data capture is difficult to resist

and offline activities,[342] thereby bearing an eerily striking resemblance with an ever-present *Panopticon.*[343]

§§ It is worth recalling that digital surveillance gave rise to a multitude of Artificial Intelligence-embedded technologies[344] that are shaping up to jettison a bevy of

---

because it is simultaneously compulsory and transparent. Biometric data collection is often compulsory because it is increasingly mandatory to establish identity. *Biometrics are transparent qualities because it is very difficult to hide biometrics; an individual's face, iris, or fingerprint can be digitally captured in any public place. Because biometric data support larger big data programs, such as No Fly List–type risk assessments, it is extraordinarily difficult, if not impossible, to opt out*"). Italics added. See: Part IV, Chap. 4, Sects. 4.5 to 4.5.2 of this book (on "algorithmic Jim Crow", a travel ban issued during the first Trump Administration to prevent certain individuals from entering the United States of America, which, given its racial undertones, stands as an outgrowth of congeries of laws enacted during the Jim Crow epoch).

342 Alves, Jones Figueirêdo/Pimentel, Alexandre Freire, "Breves notas sobre os preconceitos decisionais judiciais produzidos por redes neurais artificiais (Brief notes about the judicial decisional prejudices produced by artificial neural networks), *cit.*, pp. 555–577 (565).

343 Recall, first-generation of Artificial Intelligence—comprised by bigoted or doctored algorithms—that relies heavily on citizens' personal information gleaned in digital contexts, thus bearing a striking resemblance with an eerily *Panopticon.* For an economic approach of this epiphenomenon: Gandy, O., *The Panoptic Sort: A Political Economy of Personal Information.* Oxford: Oxford University Press, 2021, Chap. 2.

344 Chopra, Samir/White, Laurence F., *A Legal Theory of Autonomous Artificial Agents*, Michigan, University of Michigan Press, 2011, pp. 1–264 (5) (2011) ("There are two views of the goals of artificial intelligence. From an engineering perspective, as Marvin Minsky noted, it is the 'science of making machines do things that would require intelligence if done by men.' *From a cognitive science perspective, it is to design and build systems that work the way the human mind does. In the former perspective, artificial intelligence is deemed successful along a performative dimension; in the latter, along a theoretical one.* The latter embodies Giambattista Vico's perspective of verum et factum convertuntur, 'the true and the made are... convertible'; *in such a view, artificial intelligence would be reckoned the laboratory that validates our best science of the human mind. This perspective sometimes shades into the claim artificial intelligence's success lies in the replication of human capacities such as emotions, the sensations of taste, and self-consciousness. Here, artificial intelligence is conceived of as building artificial persons, not just designing systems that are 'intelligent'*") ("*As an example of how agent technologies might evolve to incorporate learning, autonomy, and discretion, consider a hypothetical agent designed to find used books on the Internet. The agent is provided with a list of websites to scour, sample titles with abstracts as learning data to recognize other titles in the genre, and electronic cash accounts with which to make purchases.* The agent is allowed to purchase books within a preset spending limit with discretion in the number, subjects, and individual prices of books bought. Such an agent has a broadly defined goal with enough executive discretion in the choices it makes to optimize satisfaction of that goal. The agent is able to interact with its environment by reading and scanning information at the sites it visits; it interacts with other agents such as selling agents deployed by other users. The agent "moves" from site to site, makes purchases, and reads recommendations provided by book-selling agents. The agent checks recommendations for matches on parameters of interest, and then depending on the outcome, buys more books or declines offers. *It is able to buy titles not on its original list, and to proactively make the decision to buy a new title. Such an agent is able to decide to take an action, in response to inputs it decides to focus on; its interactions on the Internet, in a world populated by other shopping agents and sometimes humans, exemplify autonomous, goal-directed, proactive behavior*"). Italics added.

fundamental rights into a frenzy.[345] Which is wholly unbecoming in that could end up helping maintain, perpetuate, recreate, and exacerbate social maladies with which societies have been scuffling for a long-winded span of time.[346] Not that just that though: inordinate harms may accordingly be caused in the process.

§§ Succinctly portray, digital surveillance grew into a high-octane intrusive force with deep-rooted restrictive underpinnings. Digital surveillance channels seemingly benign behaviour (fend off citizens from their own misgivings) toward *Algorithmic Dictatorship*.[347] An eerily ever-present blazingly new world of digital repression blossoms spontaneously from Artificial Intelligence-embedded technologies before our very eyes.

§§ Put otherwise, a brave new world of permanent surveillance is unfolding before our very eyes. Citizens must decide what type of Artificial Intelligence they want to avoid further misapprehensions that might cost them dearly along the line. This vexing question has always struck me as absolutely ineluctable. More on this later.[348]

---

[345] Such as heightened security that allows permanent digital surveillance of individuals deemed socially unfit or—worse yet—biologically or mentally prone to engage in flagitious and unlawful activities. The German doctrine has fleshed out this topic in depth. See: Müller, Helmut, "Europäische Rechtssicherheit gegen Deutsches Sicherheitsrecht? Zur EGMR-Entscheidung in Sachen nachträgliche (Verlängerung der) Sicherungsverwahrung", *Kritische Justiz*, Volume 43, Issue 3, 2010, pp. 256–268. This topic—although enthralling/besotting/buoying—falls conspicuously outside the breadth and scope of this essay. See: Part IV, Chap. 4, Sects. 4.5 to 4.5.2 of this book (on "algorithmic Jim Crow", a travel ban issued during the first Trump Administration to prevent certain individuals from entering the United States of America, which, given its racial undertones, stands as an outgrowth of congeries of laws enacted during the Jim Crow epoch).

[346] *Tech, Bias and Housing Initiative, the Promise and Perils of Residential Proptech, Year 1, Research Summary Report, April 2023, TechEquity Collaborative*, p. 5 available at: https://techequity.us/wp-content/uploads/2023/04/TBHI-Y1-Research-Summary-Report.pdf (28.11.2024). ("*Residential Proptech also has the potential to exacerbate the bias inherent in our housing system. Its rise is due, in part, to the desperation felt by average home seekers. With a severely constrained housing supply, companies offering an easier pathway to homeownership may exploit communities that have been harmed by housing discrimination in the past. Opaque algorithms incorporate biased data into their decision-making processes, making it harder to enforce fair housing laws.* Residential Proptech companies often operate in a regulatory gray area, leaving consumers without the protections they would have from traditional housing regulatory systems. *As unprecedented capital investment flows into this space, venture-backed companies' winner-take-all approach to growth has the potential to exacerbate inequality rather than combat it*"). Italics added. See: Part IV, Chap. 4, Sects. 4.4 to 4.4.2.1 of this book (on mortgage redlining). See: Part IV, Chap. 4, Sects. 4.2 to 4.4.3 of this book (on algorithmic credit scoring, consumer racism and credit card redlining). See: Part IV, Chap. 4, Sects. 4.4 to 4.4.2.3 of this book (on algorithmic redlining). See: Part IV, Chap. 4, Sect. 4.4.3 of this book (on "algorithmic redliking"). See: Part IV, Chap. 4, Sect. 4.3 of this book (on algorithmic prime-lining).

[347] See: Part IV, Chap. 4, Sects. 4 to 4.10.6 of this book (on Algorithmic Dictatorship and its chilling effect on democracy).

[348] See: Part V, Chap. 5, Sects. 5.2 to Sect. 5.6.2.1 of this book (on the thing-centred algorithmic decision-making propelled by a *Controllable* and *Interpretable* Machine Learning that weeds out *Algorithmic Dictatorship* and secures *Algorithmic Common Good*).

§§ As noted above, the uptake of Artificial Intelligence heavily relies upon the type of AI-entrenched technologies—more or less invasive—employed to achieve a given goal. Yet Artificial Intelligence constitutes a blazingly new world unto itself, thereby rendering futile any attempts to pin a definition down onto a page when it comes to drawing its agreed-upon frontiers. This unease finds echoes in a broader perception of AI-embedded technologies[349] that citizens should look askance at. This brings us to the second feature of the third era of Artificial Intelligence: citizens 'behavioural perception.

§§ Citizens 'behavioural perception is not to be confounded with, nor mistaken by, digital surveillance[350]/behavioural surveillance.[351] The merest glance at the overriding principles of the former elicits the vividly clear impression that it boils down

---

[349] Chopra, Samir/White, Laurence F., *A Legal Theory of Autonomous Artificial Agents*, Michigan, University of Michigan Press, 2011, pp. 1–264 (5) (2011) ("*There are two views of the goals of artificial intelligence. From an engineering perspective, as Marvin Minsky noted, it is the 'science of making machines do things that would require intelligence if done by men.' From a cognitive science perspective, it is to design and build systems that work the way the human mind does. In the former perspective, artificial intelligence is deemed successful along a performative dimension; in the latter, along a theoretical one.* The latter embodies Giambattista Vico's perspective of verum et factum convertuntur, 'the true and the made are... convertible'; *in such a view, artificial intelligence would be reckoned the laboratory that validates our best science of the human mind. This perspective sometimes shades into the claim artificial intelligence's success lies in the replication of human capacities such as emotions, the sensations of taste, and self-consciousness. Here, artificial intelligence is conceived of as building artificial persons, not just designing systems that are 'intelligent*") ("*As an example of how agent technologies might evolve to incorporate learning, autonomy, and discretion, consider a hypothetical agent designed to find used books on the Internet. The agent is provided with a list of websites to scour, sample titles with abstracts as learning data to recognize other titles in the genre, and electronic cash accounts with which to make purchases.* The agent is allowed to purchase books within a preset spending limit with discretion in the number, subjects, and individual prices of books bought. Such an agent has a broadly defined goal with enough executive discretion in the choices it makes to optimize satisfaction of that goal. The agent is able to interact with its environment by reading and scanning information at the sites it visits; it interacts with other agents such as selling agents deployed by other users. The agent "moves" from site to site, makes purchases, and reads recommendations provided by book-selling agents. The agent checks recommendations for matches on parameters of interest, and then depending on the outcome, buys more books or declines offers. *It is able to buy titles not on its original list, and to proactively make the decision to buy a new title. Such an agent is able to decide to take an action, in response to inputs it decides to focus on; its interactions on the Internet, in a world populated by other shopping agents and sometimes humans, exemplify autonomous, goal-directed, proactive behavior*"). Italics added.

[350] Which is all but joyful news. Germany, for example, allows forms of heightened security which, in turn, gives rise to permanent digital surveillance of individuals deemed socially unfit or—worse yet—biologically or mentally prone to engage in flagitious/unlawful activities. The German doctrine has fleshed out this topic in depth. See: Müller, Helmut, "Europäische Rechtssicherheit gegen Deutsches Sicherheitsrecht? Zur EGMR-Entscheidung in Sachen nachträgliche (Verlängerung der) Sicherungsverwahrung", *Kritische Justiz*, Volume 43, Issue 3, 2010, pp. 256–268. This topic—although enthralling/besotting/buoying—falls conspicuously outside the breadth and scope of this essay.

[351] Hu, Margaret, "From the National Surveillance State to the Cybersurveillance State", *The Annual Review of Law and Social Science*, Volume 13, 2017, p. 169 ("*as a result of big data biometric governance trends, meaningful distinctions between biometric credentialing for identification and*

to tools aimed at parsing citizens 'behaviour in the internet,[352] which, in turn, has transmogrified itself into a mighty force riddled with *dictatorial undertones*. Hence the paramount importance of my newly crafted concept of *Algorithmic Dictatorship* that wishes fundamental rights away.[353]

§§ More to the point, AI-powered technologies parse the citizens' behaviour in the Internet only to grasp their behavioural patterns of which the latter are often unbeknownst of. To cater for that, this batch of silent tools draw on whopping amounts of both raw data,[354] personal data[355] and big data[356] that offers information about other correlated personal data, but not the concrete content of the personal data itself (metadata). That bundle of data is subsequently converted into meaningful

---

behavioral biometric profiling are disappearing. The objectives are merging: Reliable credentialing is used to advance security and precrime policy rationales. Biometric data mission creep occurs by necessity in a big data world because the cybersurveillance systems are often designed to engage in mass data integration and analysis and predictive policing. Biometric surveillance serves two purposes in preventive policing: It increases identity transparency, and the biometric data categorize identity through cataloging behavioral and physical characteristics and assess these characteristics for risk. Contrasting small data biometric credentialing protocols with big data credentialing protocols is useful. It illustrates how biometric surveillance fits within the Cybersurveillance State. In a small data world, paper-based passports and nondigitized photographs are examples of a small data biometric-based identification system"). Italics added.

352 Alves, Jones Figueirêdo/Pimentel, Alexandre Freire, "Breves notas sobre os preconceitos decisionais judiciais produzidos por redes neurais artificiais (Brief notes about the judicial decisional prejudices produced by artificial neural networks), *cit.*, pp. 555–577 (565).

353 See: Part IV, Chap. 4, Sects. 4 to 4.10.6 of this book (on Algorithmic Dictatorship and its chilling effect on democracy). See: Part V, Chap. 5, Sects. 5.2 to 5.6.2.1 of this book (on the thing-centred algorithmic decision-making propelled by a *Controllable* and *Interpretable* Machine Learning that weeds out *Algorithmic Dictatorship* and secures *Algorithmic Common Good*).

354 Kleinberg, Jon/Ludwig, Jens/Mullainathan, Sendhil/Sunstein Cass R., "Discrimination in the Age of Algorithms", *Journal of Legal Analysis*, Volume 10, 1, 2018, pp. 28–29, 33–34 (draw a distinction between "group differences in the raw data" and biases for the "choice of predictors.").

355 Alves, Jones Figueirêdo/Pimentel, Alexandre Freire, "Breves notas sobre os preconceitos decisionais judiciais produzidos por redes neurais artificiais (Brief notes about the judicial decisional prejudices produced by artificial neural networks), *cit.*, pp. 555–577 (565).

356 Big data that is in the limelight these days. See: Sivarajah, Uthayasnkar et al., "Critical Analysis of Big Data Challenges and Analytical Methods", *Journal of Business Research*, Volume 70, 2017, pp. 263 and ff and passim; Jetten, Lieke /Sharon, Stephen, "Selected Issues concerning the Ethical Use of Big Data Health Analytics", *Washington & Lee Law Review Online*, Volume 72, 2016, passim; Wachter, S./Mittelstadt. B., "A right to Reasonable Inferences: Re-thinking Data Protection Law in the Age of Big Data and AI", *Columbia Business Law Review*, 2019, pp. 1 and ff and passim; See in French doctrine: Ferey, Samuel, « Analyse économique du droit, big data et justice prédictive», *Archives de Philosophie du Droit*, Volume 60, 2018, pp. 68–81; Završnik, A. "Algorithmic justice: Algorithms and big data in criminal justice settings", *European Journal of Criminology*, 2019, passim; Joh, Elizabeth E., "The New Surveillance Discretion: Automated Suspicion, Big Data, and Policing." *Harvard Law and Policy Review*, 10 (1), 2016, pp. 15–42.

information[357] that may purportedly serve the pleasure of a hidden agenda of which citizens are gleefully incognizant of.

§§ This sheer amount of personal data is clustered by machine learning algorithms[358] that are noticeably forestalling fairness efforts.[359] Often, the data collated by corporate moguls falls prey to decontextualization,[360] thereby sending ripples

[357] Alves, Jones Figueirêdo/Pimentel, Alexandre Freire, "Breves notas sobre os preconceitos decisionais judiciais produzidos por redes neurais artificiais (Brief notes about the judicial decisional prejudices produced by artificial neural networks), *cit.*, pp. 555–577 (565).

[358] But see: O'Neil, Cathy, *Weapons of Math Destruction. How Big Data Increases Inequality and Threatens Democracy*, London, Penguin Random House, 2016, passim (showing how algorithms utilized in modern societies are amenable to perpetuate racial discrimination, partially through perpetuation of social disadvantage and wealth divides). See also: O'Neil, Cathy, "When Not to Trust the Algorithm", *Interview published in the Harvard Business Review's Ideacast*, 2016, passim; O' Neil, Cathy, "Amazon's Gender-Biased Algorithm Is Not Alone", 2018, accessed 2 January 2025 (on gender-related algorithmic biases).

[359] Such as a yawning gap between rich—that can adroitly harness artificial intelligence to advance their goals and shady agendas—and poor—that grapple to meet basic needs and are automatically excluded from the equation of digital society powered by Artificial Intelligence—which will directly impact the fabric of societies worldwide, thereby augmenting the chasm between the «digitally-chosen» and the «digitally-outcast» enabled by a algorithmic discrimination that does nothing but irreparable harm. See: Yu, Peter K., "The Algorithmic Divide and Equality in the Age of Artificial Intelligence", *Florida Law Review*, Volume 72, 2020, pp. 355–360 (addresses the issue of algorithmic discrimination).

[360] Ripple effects arising out challenges that are neither amenable to be shrugged off nor relinquished. Let alone unduly forsaken. The challenges brought forth by an ever-evolving and far-reaching "Blockchain digital society" should urge the legal community to rattle off a wide range of actionable solutions to tackle this issue of paramount importance. See: De Filippi/Primavera/Wright, Aaron, *Blockchain and the Law. Rule of Code.* Cambridge: Harvard University Press, 2019, pp. 196–200 (presciently addresses the hazard of the data collated by enterprises fall prey to decontextualization). If lawmakers fail to entertain proficiently this issue, somewhere along the line the data fed into the machines will spawn algorithmic discrimination or algorithmic biases in criminal justice. Which means that algorithmic biases—caused by data decontextualization—will ripple forward to the detriment of a sought-after algorithmic fairness.

across the data-driven world that will ultimately prove detrimental to citizens' fundamental rights. Algorithmic fairness[361] measures are therefore in dire need of being implemented or inordinate damages may otherwise occur. More on this later.[362]

§§ Fearsomely enough, these tools can also cast a keen light upon citizens 'future behaviour—a sort-of predictive tool that points which behavioural direction a given citizen will pursue in the forthcoming future. Which brings us to the third feature of the third era of Artificial Intelligence: forecasting human behaviour that bears a striking resemblance with a predictive social justice that lurks ahead. That is, a predictive[363] justice[364] carried out by predictive[365] machines.[366]

---

[361] Corbett-Davies, Sam/Pierson, Emma/Feller, Avi/Goel, Sharad/Huq, Aziz, "Algorithmic Decision Making and the Cost of Fairness", *KDD '17: Proceedings of the 23rd ACM SIGKDD International Conference on Knowledge Discovery and Data Mining*, 2017, pp. 797–806 ("*Algorithms are now regularly used to decide whether defendants awaiting trial are too dangerous to be released back into the community. In some cases, black defendants are substantially more likely than white defendants to be incorrectly classified as high risk. To mitigate such disparities, several techniques have recently been proposed to achieve algorithmic fairness.* Here we reformulate *algorithmic fairness* as constrained optimization: the objective is to maximize public safety while satisfying formal fairness constraints designed to reduce racial disparities. We show that for several past definitions of fairness, the optimal algorithms that result require detaining defendants above race-specific risk thresholds. *We further show that the optimal unconstrained algorithm requires applying a single, uniform threshold to all defendants.* The unconstrained algorithm thus maximizes public safety while also satisfying one important understanding of equality: that all individuals are held to the same standard, irrespective of race. Because the optimal constrained and unconstrained algorithms generally differ, there is tension between improving public safety and satisfying prevailing notions of algorithmic fairness. *By examining data from Broward County, Florida, we show that this trade-off can be large in practice. We focus on algorithms for pretrial release decisions, but the principles we discuss apply to other domains, and also to human decision makers carrying out structured decision rules*". Italics added. This paper also deals with the topic of "predictive equality" (p. 798); Kleinberg, Jon, et al., "Inherent Trade-offs in the Fair Determination of Risk Scores", *Leibniz International Proceedings in Informatics*, Jan. 2017, 2017, at 43:1, 43:4; at 4 ("balance for the negative class"). See: Mayson, Sandra G., "Bias In, Bias Out", *cit.*, pp. 2218–2300.

[362] See: Part V, Chap. 5, Sects. 5.2 to 5.6.2.1 of this book (on the thing-centred algorithmic decision-making propelled by a *Controllable* and *Interpretable* Machine Learning that weeds out *Algorithmic Dictatorship* and secures *Algorithmic Common Good*).

[363] *Tech, Bias and Housing Initiative, the Promise and Perils of Residential Proptech, Year 1, Research Summary Report, April 2023, TechEquity Collaborative*, p. 11, available at: https://techequity.us/wp-content/uploads/2023/04/TBHI-Y1-Research-Summary-Report.pdf (28.11.2024). ("And while we know that the *data is predictive, meaning it has little to do with demonstrated behavior of the applicant themself, we do not know exactly where companies get their data.*"). Italics added. See: Part IV, Chap. 4, Sects. 4.4 to 4.4.2.3 of this book.

[364] See: Part IV, Chap. 4, Sects. 4.10.1 to 4.10.6 of this book (on biased algorithmic risk assessment in criminal procedure law settings). See: Part IV, Chapt. 4, Sects. 4.1 to 4.1.1 of this book (on biased predictive policing).

[365] Karnow, Curtis E. A., "The Opinion of Machines", *The Cambridge Handbook of the Law of Algorithms*, Bartfield, Woodrow (Editor), Cambridge, United Kingdom: Cambridge University Press, 2021, pp. 15 and ff and passim.

[366] Agrawal, Ajay/Gans, Joshua/Goldfarb, Avi, *Prediction Machines: The Simple Economics of Artificial Intelligence*, 2nd Edition. Massachusetts: Harvard Business Review Press, 2022, pp. 1–304. Aggarwal, C. C., *Neural networks and deep learning*, Heidelberg, Springer, 2018, passim;

§§ Forecasting human behaviour is all predicting citizens 'next move. Hence the sobriquet predictive social justice.[367] These predictive tools aim to predict citizens 'social and political preferences and act accordingly. Bigoted machine learning[368] algorithms[369] will subsequently adjust the ads—and related commercial offers—to the citizens 'social and political leanings. Consumer preferences[370] will not lag far behind.

§§ It should not come as a bewildering surprise that these predictive[371] tools[372] tend, if anything, to reify,[373] compound and exacerbate deep-seated social and ethnic concerns with which modern societies have been tussling for a long-winded span of

Agrawal, A., Gans, J., & Goldfarb, A., "Prediction machines (updated and expanded): The simple economics of artificial intelligence", *Harvard Business Review Press*, 2022; Agrawal, A., Gans, J., & Goldfarb, A., "Power and prediction: The disruptive economics of artificial intelligence", *Harvard Business Review Press*, 2022; Bengio, Y., Hinton, G., Yao, A., Song, D., Abbeel, P., Harari, Y. N., Hadfield, G., Russell, S., Kahneman, D., & Mindermann, S., *Managing ai risks in an era of rapid progress*, arXiv preprint arXiv:2310.17688, 2023, passim (on neural networks and deep learning that operate jointly in the age of Artificial Intelligence-embedded technologies).

[367] Which can give rise to deleterious effects that can take the shape of a predictive criminal justice run by machines accountable to no one. See in French doctrine: Brigant, Jean-Marie, "Les risques accentués d'une justice pénale prédictive», *Archives de Philosophie du Droit*, Volume 60, 2018, pp. 238 and ff and passim.

[368] See on algorithmic discrimination: Kleinberg, Jon, et al., "Discrimination in the Age of Algorithms", *Journal of Legal Analysis*, 2018, pp. 114–174; See: Kleinberg, Jon, et al., "Algorithms as Discrimination Detectors", *Proceeds of the National Academy of Science*, Volume 117, 2020, pp. 30,096–30,110; Griemmelmann, James/Westreich, Daniel, "Incomprehensible Discrimination ", *California Law Review Online*, Volume 7, 2018, pp. 164–171; Xiang, Alice, "Reconciling Legal and Technical Approaches to Algorithmic Bias", *Tennessee Law Review*, Volume 88, 2021, passim.

[369] Prejudiced algorithms are set to be brought to the fore as they are one foundational basis of *justice prédictive* so voguish in France. No surprise stems from the fact that prejudiced algorithms will feed *justice prédictive*—and that is something quite unsavoury and unpalatable in criminal justice indeed. See: Garapon, Antoine, "Les enjeux de la justice predictive", *Juris-Classeur périodique*, Volume 31, 2018, passim. See also: Larret-Chahine, Louis, "Le droit isométrique: un nouveau paradigme juridique né de la justice prédictive», *Archives de Philosophie du Droit*, Volume 60, 2018, pp. 287 and ff and passim.

[370] Alves, Jones Figueirêdo/Pimentel, Alexandre Freire, "Breves notas sobre os preconceitos decisionais judiciais produzidos por redes neurais artificiais (Brief notes about the judicial decisional prejudices produced by artificial neural networks), *cit.*, pp. 555–577 (565).

[371] *Tech, Bias and Housing Initiative, the Promise and Perils of Residential Proptech, Year 1, Research Summary Report, April 2023, TechEquity Collaborative*, p. 11, available at: https://techequity.us/wp-content/uploads/2023/04/TBHI-Y1-Research-Summary-Report.pdf (28.11.2024). ("And while we know that the *data is predictive, meaning it has little to do with demonstrated behavior of the applicant themself, we do not know exactly where companies get their data.*"). Italics added. See: Part IV, Chap. 4, Sects. 4.4 to 4.4.2.3 of this book.

[372] Against the background of which an eerily predictive criminal law is unfolding in France. See: Brigant, Jean-Marie, "Les risques accentués d'une justice pénale predictive", *Archives de Philosophie du Droit*, Volume 60, 2018, p. 239 (on the so-called predictable criminal justice).

[373] Duster, Troy, "Race and Reification in Science." *Science*, 307, 2005, passim.

time,[374] such as misogyny, racism,[375] xenophobe and political hatred which, taken together, are rife for misfire, social unrest, and upheaval.

§§ As far as the fourth feature of the third era of Artificial Intelligence is concerned, decisional autonomy is the taxonomy that bears mentioning in this regard. It boils down to a warrant (or lack thereof) given by the programmer to the machines to make autonomous decisions.[376] Notwithstanding, it is often averred that machines are not really ascribed the task to decide on their own.[377] Rather, they are given a

---

[374] *Tech, Bias and Housing Initiative, the Promise and Perils of Residential Proptech, Year 1, Research Summary Report, April 2023, TechEquity Collaborative*, p. 5 available at: https://techequity.us/wp-content/uploads/2023/04/TBHI-Y1-Research-Summary-Report.pdf (28.11.2024). ("*Residential Proptech also has the potential to exacerbate the bias inherent in our housing system. Its rise is due, in part, to the desperation felt by average home seekers. With a severely constrained housing supply, companies offering an easier pathway to homeownership may exploit communities that have been harmed by housing discrimination in the past. Opaque algorithms incorporate biased data into their decision-making processes, making it harder to enforce fair housing laws.* Residential Proptech companies often operate in a regulatory gray area, leaving consumers without the protections they would have from traditional housing regulatory systems. *As unprecedented capital investment flows into this space, venture-backed companies' winner-take-all approach to growth has the potential to exacerbate inequality rather than combat it*"). Italics added. See: Part IV, Chap. 4, Sect. 4.4 to 4.4.2.3 of this book.

[375] For a simple reason: Dong et al., Qi,, "Imbalanced deep learning by minority class incremental rectification, *IEEE Transactions on Pattern Analysis & Machine Intelligence*, Volume 41, 2019, p. 1367 (posit that "*most existing learning algorithms produce inductive bias (learning bias)* towards the frequent (majority) classes if training data are not balanced, *resulting in poor minority class recognition performance*"). Italics added. See: Chandler, Anupam, "The Racist Algorithm", *Michigan Law Review*, Volume 115, n. ° 6, 2018, p. 1026 (on racist algorithms, noting that "the possibilities for discriminatory manipulation are legion"). But see: Altenburger, Kristen M./Ho, Daniel E., "When Algorithms Import Private Bias into Public Enforcement: The Promise and Limitations of Statistical Debiasing Solutions", *Journal of Institutional & Theoretical Economics*, Volume 175, 2019, pp. 97–98 (calls for a "debias predictive algorithms" to assuage racist and/or biased, doctored and bigoted algorithms nevertheless). See: Hamilton, Melissa, "The Biased Algorithm: Evidence of Disparate Impact on Hispanics", *American Criminal Law Review*, Volume 56, 2019, pp. 1553 and ff and passim.

[376] Alves, Jones Figueirêdo/Pimentel, Alexandre Freire, "Breves notas sobre os preconceitos decisionais judiciais produzidos por redes neurais artificiais (Brief notes about the judicial decisional prejudices produced by artificial neural networks), *cit.*, pp. 555–577 (565). See: Part V, Chap. 5, Sect. 5.7.4 of this book (on one of the laws to control algorithmic decision-making, namely, law number four: data partitioning must be performed—i.e. randomly split an entire dataset into the «training dataset» and the «test dataset»—to accurately predict outcomes in the real world while forestalling «inductive bias» (learning bias)).

[377] However, it has come to our attention that *machine-learning algorithms "are capable of making intuitive decisions based in newly learned information, much like humans.* The new wave of AI developments will generate powerful AI that is capable of improvising itself, *perhaps even by rewriting its own algorithms, advancing its intelligence beyond that of humans*". Italics added. See: Hutto-Schultz, Jess, "Dicitur Ex Machina: Artificial Intelligence and the Hearsay Rule", *George Mason Law Review*, Volume 27, n. ° 2, 2020, pp. 684–718 (684).

discretionary power to decide[378] the best course of action to be taken, subject to human oversight.[379]

§§ The worst part is that machines will make decisions that will directly influence one's freedom, credit scoring,[380] job opportunities and the list goes on. That is why a brawny set of philosophical principles are in dire need of being implemented to forestall a looming *Algorithmic Dictatorship* that may cost us dearly along the line.[381]

---

[378] Strandburg, Katherine J., "Rulemaking and Inscrutable Decision Tools", *Columbia Law Review*, Volume 119, 2019, passim.

[379] Alves, Jones Figueirêdo/Pimentel, Alexandre Freire, "Breves notas sobre os preconceitos decisionais judiciais produzidos por redes neurais artificiais (Brief notes about the judicial decisional prejudices produced by artificial neural networks), *cit.*, pp. 555–577 (565).

[380] See: Part IV, Chap. 4, Sects. 4.4 to 4.4.2.1 of this book (on mortgage redlining). See: Part IV, Chap. 4, Sects. 4.2 to 4.4.3 of this book (on algorithmic credit scoring, consumer racism and credit card redlining). It is crucially important to note, though, that the very fact that only certain types of behaviours are assessed and gauged by credit scores leads to the conclusion some borrowers are not scored at all. The overwhelming majority of consumers boast meagre, if any, credit files owing to the fact that the likelihood to access to the sort of financial services that actually report to the orthodox credit bureaus scattered across modern economies is exceedingly low, which, in turn, morphs them into credit invisible persons. See: Yu, Persis/McLaughlin, Jilian/Levy, Marina, "Big Data: A Big Disappointment for Scoring Consumer Creditworthiness", *The National Consumer Law Center,* 2 (Mar. 14, 2014), available at: https://www.nclc.org/images/pdf/pr-reports/report-big-data.pdf [https://perma.cc/W4SK-NXD5] (access: 21.12.2024).

[381] See: Part IV, Chap. 4, Sects. 4 to 4.10.6 of this book (on Algorithmic Dictatorship and its chilling effect on democracy).

Part III
Critical Artificial Intelligence Studies (CAIS)

Chapter 3
Philosophy and Technology

3.1 Laying Down the Groundwork

§§ Artificial Intelligence lies at the crossroads between the perennial quest for the overall betterment of society and the undeterred yearn to grasp Algorithmic Fairness/*Algorithmic Common Good*.[1] It is thus imperative to thoroughly address a bevy of social situations against the backdrop of which Artificial Intelligence-entrenched technologies exacerbate longstanding implicit biases with which modern societies have been persistently grappling.[2]

---

[1] Stevenson, Megan T./Slogobin, Christopher, "Algorithmic Risk Assessments and the Double-Edged Sword of Youth", *Behavioural Sciences and the Law*, Volume 36, 2018, pp. 638–639. But see: Tutt, Andrew, "An FDA for Algorithms", *Administrative Law Review*, Volume 69, 2018, pp. 83–109 (proposes a federal statutory benchmark/yardstick with regard to algorithms' explainability). See: Part V, Chap. 5, Sects. 5.1.7–.5.1.7.5 of this book (on the five laws to control algorithmic decision-making). See: Part V, Chap. 5, Sects. 5.1.8–5.1.8.5 of this book (on the five laws to interpret algorithmic decision-making). See: Part V, Chap. 5, Sects. 5.1.2–5.1.6.2.1 of this book (on the thing-centred algorithmic decision-making propelled by a *Controllable* and *Interpretable* Machine Learning that weeds out *Algorithmic Dictatorship* and secures *Algorithmic Common Good*. It is worth recalling that the **thing-centred algorithmic decision-making** seeks to unwind the perils arising out of the lack of theoretical underpinnings facing the **human-centred algorithmic decision-making**, as extensively fleshed out Part III, this chapter, Sects. 3.1.4.3 and 3.1.4.4 of this book). See: Part V, Chap. 5, Sect. 5.1.7.5 of this book (on *Algorithmic Common Good*, with a sharper focus on the dire need of algorithmic auditing, undertaken by external auditors that must be given full access to the dataset used to train the running models).

[2] *Tech, Bias and Housing Initiative, the Promise and Perils of Residential Proptech, Year 1, Research Summary Report, April 2023, TechEquity Collaborative*, p. 5, available at: https://techequity.us/wp-content/uploads/2023/04/TBHI-Y1-Research-Summary-Report.pdf (28.11.2024) ("*Residential Proptech also has the potential to exacerbate the bias inherent in our housing system. Its rise is due, in part, to the desperation felt by average home seekers. With a severely constrained housing supply, companies offering an easier pathway to homeownership may exploit communities that have been harmed by housing discrimination in the past. Opaque algorithms incorporate biased data into their decision-making processes, making it harder to enforce fair housing laws.* Residential Proptech companies often operate in a regulatory gray area, leaving

H. L. dos Santos, *Controllable Artificial Intelligence and the Future of Law*, Artificial Intelligence and the Rule of Law, https://doi.org/10.1007/978-981-95-0508-1_3

§§ Staggering efforts are therefore in dire need of being poured in to stymie the perceived hazards arising out of Artificial Intelligence-entrenched technologies that might be more noticeably pre-empting the central thrust of dispelling invidiousness, callousness, and flagitiousness.[3]

---

consumers without the protections they would have from traditional housing regulatory systems. *As unprecedented capital investment flows into this space, venture-backed companies' winner-take-all approach to growth has the potential to exacerbate inequality rather than combat it*"). Italics added. See: Part IV, Chap. 4, Sects. 4.1.4–4.1.4.2.3 of this book. See: Part IV, Chap. 4, Sects.4.1.4–4.1.4.2.1 of this book (on mortgage redlining). See: Part IV, Chap. 4, Sects. 4.1.2–4.1.4.3 of this book (on algorithmic credit scoring, consumer racism and credit card redlining). See: Part IV, Chap. 4, Sects. 4.1.4–4.1.4.2.3 of this book (on algorithmic redlining). See: Part IV, Chap. 4, Sects. 4.1.4.3 of this book (on "algorithmic redliking"). See: Part IV, Chap. 4, Sect. 4.1.1.3 of this book (on algorithmic prime-lining).

[3] The newest developments posed by the "collect-it-all" technologies are slated to create a slew of sizzling hot challenges to the sustainability of the Rule of Law. See: Hu, Margaret, "From the National Surveillance State to the Cybersurveillance State", *The Annual Review of Law and Social Science*, Volume 13, 2017, pp. 162–163 ("*policymakers view these technological developments, including biometric technologies, as tools with the potential to identify individuals who may pose a threat to national and homeland security and to prevent crime and terrorism. One example of technology intended for risk assessment and threat management is the post-9/11 program Total Information Awareness (TIA).* TIA was the progeny of the Defense Advanced Research Projects Agency (DARPA) in the US Department of Defense. *TIA can be understood as a "collect-it-all" data surveillance program. TIA was not explicitly identified as a collect-it-all program—this phrase originated with the Snowden disclosures.* One National Security Agency (NSA) slide described the NSA's procedure as "collect-it-all" (Greenwald 2014b). *Collect-it-all efforts like TIA embody a philosophy that aspires to preventive policing. Mass data collection is construed as a tool to assess and prevent future threats* (Murray 2010). *In TIA and other programs tested or adopted after 9/11, biometric database screening and analysis have emerged as a preferred method for tracking, identifying, and establishing identity-based inferences in counterterrorism*"). Italics added. See also: Ball, Kirstie, and Frank Webster (Eds.), *The Intensification of Surveillance: Crime, Terrorism & Warfare in the Information Age*, London, UK: Pluto Press, 2007; Guzik, Keith, "Discrimination by Design: Predictive Data Mining as Security Practice in the United States' 'War on Terrorism'", *Surveillance and Society*, 7 (1), 2009, pp. 1–17. See: Part IV, Chap. 4, Sects. 4.1.5–4.1.5.2 of this book (on "algorithmic Jim Crow", a travel ban issued during the first Trump Administration to prevent certain individuals from entering the United States of America, which, given its racial undertones, stands as an outgrowth of congeries of laws enacted during the Jim Crow epoch). See: Part III, this chapter, Sects. 3.1.5.7–3.1.5.8.1 of this book (on the functional aspects of Critical Artificial Intelligence Studies, with a sharper focus on the perils concerning the deployment of facial recognition technology).

§§ Time-hallowed fundamental rights (amongst which stands the right to privacy,[4] the right to mental privacy[5] and the right of freedom[6]) hang on the balance amidst the unbridled rise of *Uncontrollable Artificial Intelligence*. Yet the remedy to allay these technology-borne hazards should be more much effective than merely providing an explanation[7] on the inner workings of Artificial Intelligence as citizens are woefully ill-prepared to grasp its essence.[8]

---

[4] Waldman, Ari Ezra, "Privacy, Practice, and Performance", *California Law Review*, Volume 110, 2022, pp. 1221–1227 (contend, however, that we have all been cunningly schooled to "thinking that managing our privacy is an individual responsibility"). Citron; Danielle Keats/Pasquale, Frank, "Network Accountability for the Domestic Intelligence Apparatus", *Hasting Law Journal*, Volume 62, 2011, 1441, 1444–45; Gray, David/Citron, Danielle Keats, "The Right to Quantitative Privacy", *Minnesota Law Review*, Volume 98, 2013, pp. 62–81.

[5] Santos, Hugo Luz dos, "Brain-Computer Interfaces, Generative Artificial Intelligence (ChatGPT and Deep Fakes) and Criminal Procedure Law: what's at stake?", *Journal of Research in E. and Computer Science*, Edinburgh, United Kingdom, June 2024, Volume 2, 2024, pp. 39–78; Santos, Hugo Luz dos, *Programas de Compliance e Inteligência Artificial: Consequências ao nível da Law and Economics, do Direito Penal, do Processo Penal e da Behavioral Law and Economics*, Braga, NovaCausa Edições Jurídicas, 2024, pp. 1–330; Santos, Hugo Luz dos, *Inteligência Artificial (ChatGPT/AutoGPT/Robots-Advogados/RobotsProceduradores/Robots-Juízes) e Responsabilidade Penal das Pessoas Colectivas*, Braga, NovaCausa Edições Jurídicas, 2023, pp. 1–108; Santos, Hugo Luz dos, *Inteligência Artificial e Processo Penal*, Braga, NovaCausa Edições Jurídicas, 2022, pp. 1–256; Santos, Hugo Luz dos, *Inteligência Artificial e Processo Penal*, Braga, NovaCausa Edições Jurídicas, 2022, pp. 1–256; Santos, Hugo Luz dos, *Inteligência Artificial e Processo Civil na Era do Metaverse e dos Machine Learning Algorithms*, Braga, NovaCausa Edições Jurídicas, 2022, pp. 1–264.

[6] Crow, M. S., "The complexities of prior record, race, ethnicity, and policy: Interactive effects in sentencing", *Criminal Justice Review*, Volume 33, Issue 4, 2008, pp. 502–523; Fornili, K. S., "Racialized mass incarceration and the war on drugs: A critical race theory appraisal", *Journal of Addictions Nursing*, Volume 29, Issue 1, 2018, 65–72. See: Part IV, Chap. 4, Sects. 4.1.10.1–4.1.10.6 of this book (on biased algorithmic risk assessment in criminal procedure law settings, with a sharper focus on COMPAS). See: Part IV, Chap. 4, Sects. 4.1.1–4.1.1.1 of this book (on biased predictive policing).

[7] Adadi, Amina/Berrada, Mohammed, "Peeking Inside the Black-Box: A Survey on Explainable Artificial Intelligence (XAI)", *Institute of Electrical and Electronics Engineers*, Volume 6, 2018, passim. But see: Part V, Chap. 5, Sect. 5.1.7.2 of this book (on law number two to control algorithmic decision-making, which mandates that black box models must not be entrusted with the task of making high stake decisions—v.g. health and freedom).

[8] Edwards, Lilian/Veale, Michael, "Slave to the Algorithm? Why a "Right to an Explanation" is Probably not the Remedy You are Looking for", *Duke Law and Technology Review*, Volume 16, 2018, pp. 18–67 (pondering whether and to what extent XAI will come in handy because citizens are woefully ill-prepared to "make use of the kind of algorithmic explanations they are likely to be offered"); Miller, Tim, "Explanations in Artificial Intelligence: Insights from Social Sciences", *Artificial Intelligence*, Volume 267, 2019, pp. 1–38. See: Part V, Chap. 5, Sects. 5.1.7–5.1.7.5 of this book (on the five laws to control algorithmic decision-making). See: Part V, Chap. 5, Sects. 5.1.8–5.1.8.5 of this book (on the five laws to interpret algorithmic decision-making). See: Part V, Chap. 5, Sects. 5.1.2–5.1.6.2.1 of this book (on the thing-centred algorithmic decision-making propelled by a *Controllable* and *Interpretable* Machine Learning that weeds out *Algorithmic Dictatorship* and secures *Algorithmic Common Good*. It is worth recalling that the **thing-centred algorithmic decision-making** seeks to unwind the perils arising out of the lack of theoretical underpinnings facing the **human-centred algorithmic decision-making**, as extensively fleshed out Part III, this

§§ Which is nothing but formulaic: machines and humans[9]—albeit poised to haggle for the social limelight in the forthcoming future[10]—have radically different ways of processing information. Tellingly, humans and machines follow markedly different pathways to come up with a decision.[11] Law must accordingly keep pace with this burgeoning reality[12] or will dispiritingly lag behind.[13]

chapter, Sects. 3.1.4.3 and 3.1.4.4 of this book). See: Part V, Chap. 5, Sect. 5.1.7.5 of this book (on Algorithmic Common Good, with a sharper focus on the dire need of algorithmic auditing, undertaken by external auditors that must be given full access to the dataset used to train the running models).

[9] Against the backdrop of which there will be a seamless meld of humans and machines. This turbid reality—although difficult to depict at this moment—will be inevitably morphed into a disturbingly dystopic reality sooner rather than later. See: Remus, Dana/Levy, Frank, "Can Robots be Lawyers? Computers, Lawyers, and the Practice of Law", *Georgetown Journal of Legal Ethics*, Volume 30, 2018, pp. 501 and ff and passim. See: Part III, this chapter, Sect. 3.1.4.5 of this book (on Critical Artificial Intelligence Studies, with a sharper focus on the harmful effects of Brain-Computer Interfaces). See: Part III, this chapter, Sect. 3.1.5.10 of this book (on the functional aspects of Critical Artificial Intelligence Studies, with a sharper focus on the harmful effects of Artificial Intelligence-embedded technologies, namely, Brain-Computer Interfaces that can read and control your mind and behaviour).

[10] Cuellar, Mariano-Florentino, "A Common Law for the Age of Artificial Intelligence: Incremental Adjudication, Institutions, and Relational Non-Arbitrariness", *Columbia Law Review*, Volume 119, 2020, pp. 1773–1775 (this author presciently posits that "(t)he coevolution of human and artificial intelligence – what we could call our dance with machines – is well on its way to becoming routine").

[11] Vera-Cruz Pinto, Eduardo, "Filosofia do Direito Digital: pensar juridicamente a relação entre Direito e tecnologia no ciberespaço", *Lisbon Law Review*, Thematic Issue: Law and Technology, Year LXII, Numbers 1 and 2, 2022, pp. 297–340 (298), which I will follow closely.

[12] Fergus, Rachel, "Biased Technology: The Automated Discrimination of Facial Recognition", *ACLU Minnesota*, February 29, 2024, available at: https://www.aclu-mn.org/en/news/biased-technology-automated-discrimination-facial-recognition (access: 20.09.2024) ("*Technology is developing much more quickly than the laws we need to protect our rights. Anyone with a smartphone or social media account knows how rapidly technology changes, while legislating can take a long, long time. It is essential to proactively put policies into place that will protect our rights as new and more advanced technology is constantly released. Especially when that technology – and law enforcement members using it - have been shown over and over to be biased toward marginalized groups*"). Italics added. See: Part IV, Chap. 4, Sects. 4.1.5–4.1.5.2 of this book (on "algorithmic Jim Crow", a travel ban issued during the first Trump Administration to prevent certain individuals from entering the United States of America, which, given its racial undertones, stands as an outgrowth of congeries of laws enacted during the Jim Crow epoch). See: Part III, this chapter, Sects. 3.1.5.7–3.1.5.8.1 of this book (on the functional aspects of Critical Artificial Intelligence Studies, with a sharper focus on the perils concerning the deployment of facial recognition technology).

[13] As adumbrated, scholars haven't been neither coy nor bashful in pinpointing the drawbacks and downsides concerning the unbridled and rampant rise of the Artificial Intelligence in the legal arena. See: Wu, Tim, "Will Artificial Intelligence Eat the Law? The Rise of Hybrid Social-Ordering Systems", *Columbia Law Review*, Volume 119, 2019, pp. 2001 and ff and passim. See: Part V, Chap. 5, Sect. 5.1.8.5 of this book (on law number five to interpret algorithmic decision-making, which mandates that robot-judges, robot-prosecutors and robot-lawyers must not enter the courtroom for they are utterly incapable of making sound and interpretable value judgements).

§§ Although science—and loosely technology—is neither good nor bad,[14] caution must be exercised before its deployment.[15] Crucially, it comes down to whom[16] uses the technology[17] and for what ends.[18] Put differently, technology, albeit neutral,[19]

---

[14] Barthes, Roland, *The Neutral*, Krauss, Rosalind E./Hollier, Denis (Translators), New York, Columbia University Press, 2005, passim.

[15] See in French doctrine: Baller, Stéphane/Deffains, Bruno, "Intelligence artificielle et devenir de la professions d'avocat; l'avenir est présent», *Revue pratique de la prospective et de innovation*, Volume 1, 2018, pp. 14 and ff (canvass the foundations of deep-rooted concerns regarding the irruption of artificial intelligence in the legal arena). See: Part V, Chap. 5, Sect. 5.1.8.5 of this book (on law number five to interpret algorithmic decision-making, which mandates that robot-judges, robot-prosecutors and robot-lawyers must not enter the courtroom for they are utterly incapable of making sound and interpretable value judgements).

[16] Christian, Brian, *The Most Human: What Artificial Intelligence teaches us about being alive*, London, Penguin, 2012, pp. 1–320.

[17] Like tools that can debias racial discrimination within the remit of criminal justice—the essence of racial equity in criminal justice. See: Huq, Aziz, "Racial Equity in Algorithmic Criminal Justice", *Duke Law Journal*, Volume 68, 2022, pp. 1076–1134. See: Part IV, Chap. 4, Sects. 4.1.10.1–4.1.10.6 of this book (on biased algorithmic risk assessment in criminal procedure law settings, with a sharper focus on COMPAS). See: Part IV, Chap. 4, Sects. 4.1.1–4.1.1.1 of this book (on biased predictive policing).

[18] Wiener, N., *The Human Use of Human Beings. Cybertics and Society*, London, Free Association Books, 1989, passim.

[19] Barthes, Roland, *The Neutral*, *cit.*, passim. But see: Hamilton, Melissa, "The sexist algorithm", *Behavioral Sciences and the Law*, Volume 37, Issue 2, Special Issue: The Use of Statistics in Criminal Cases, March–April 2019, 2019, pp. 1 and ff ("*Algorithmic risk assessment tools are informed by scientific research concerning which factors are predictive of recidivism and thus support the evidence-based practice movement in criminal justice* (….) *Computer-generated algorithms appear to be objective and neutral. But are these algorithms actually fair? The focus herein is on gender equity*. Studies confirm that women typically have far lower recidivism rates than men. *This differential raises the question of how well algorithmic outcomes fare in terms of predictive parity by gender*. This essay reports original research using a large dataset of offenders who were scored on the popular risk assessment tool COMPAS. *Findings indicate that COMPAS performs reasonably well at discriminating between recidivists and non-recidivists for men and women. Nonetheless, COMPAS algorithmic outcomes systemically overclassify women in higher risk groupings. Multiple measures of algorithmic equity and predictive accuracy are provided to support the conclusion that this algorithm is sexist*"). Italics added. See: Part IV, Chap. 4, Sects. 4.1.10.1–4.1.10.6 of this book (on biased algorithmic risk assessment in criminal procedure law settings, with a sharper focus on COMPAS). See: Part IV, Chap. 4, Sects. 4.1.1–4.1.1.1 of this book (on biased predictive policing).

can be used to attain either socially valuable goals[20] or utterly bemoaning[21] ones.[22] This statement finds echoes in a broader view about law and technology.[23]

---

[20] Like an automatic discrimination detector in criminal procedure law settings. See: Kleinberg, Jon, et al., "Algorithms as Discrimination Detectors", *Proceeds of the National Academy of Science*, Volume 117, 2020, pp. 30096–30110.

[21] For instance, technology can bestow upon criminal judges a pathway to allay their overburdened dockets and their backlog of cases through the settlement of disputes. There is a piece of empirical evidence that disavows such judicial practice though. Stating that such judicial practice disfigures core judicial values, thereby contributing exponentially to the appalling phenomenon of vanishing trials. See: Sela, Ayelet/Zimerman, Nourit/Alberstein, Michal, "Judges as Gatekeepers and the Dismaying Shadow of the Law: Courtroom Observations of Judicial Settlement Practices", *Harvard Negotiation Law Review*, Volume 24, 2018, p. 83 (noting that "judges engage in case management and settlement promotion more than do in trials and judgments" thus couching the concerns with the rampant phenomenon of vanishing trials). See on the phenomenon of vanishing trials: Galanter, Marc, "The Vanishing Trial: An Examination of Trials and Related Matters in Federal and State Courts", *Journal of Empirical Legal Studies*, Volume 1, 2004, p. 459 ff (on the perils of the vanishing trials). But see: Hadfield, Gillian K./Heine, Jamie, "Life in the Law-Thick World: Legal Resources for Ordinary Americans", Estreicher, Sam/Radice, Joy (Eds.), *Beyond Elite Law: Access to Civil Justice in America*. New York: Cambridge University Press, 2016, pp. 23–51 (this is consistent with the perceived high costs associated to litigation in courts). Unsurprisingly, Governments worldwide have been pledging themselves to look for other mechanisms to solving disputes. Amicable mechanisms of settling disputes stand out from the crowd. Which should not come as a surprise to anyone committed to afford disputants both a *formal access to justice* and an *effective access to justice* as an extension of Rule of Law. Like we do.

[22] See: McAllister, Amanda, "Stranger Than Science Fiction: The Rise of A.I. Interrogation in the Dawn of Autonomous Robots and the Need for an Additional Protocol to the U.N. Convention against Torture", *Minnesota Law Review*, Volume 101, 2018, pp. 2566–2569 (on the guidelines to use robots to perform human tasks).

[23] See: Hurley, Mikella/Adebayo, Julius, "Credit Scoring in the Era of Big Data", *Yale Journal of Law and Technology*, Volume 18, 2016, p. 149 ("*these tools may furthermore obscure discriminatory and subjective lending policies behind a single "objective" score* (...) *sophisticated algorithms may combine facially neutral data points and treat them as proxies for immutable characteristics such as race or gender, thereby circumventing existing non-discrimination laws and systematically denying credit access to certain groups. Finally, big-data tools may allow online payday lenders to target the most vulnerable consumers and lure them into debt traps*"). Italics added. See also: Farina, M./Lavazza, A., *Philosophy, expertise, and the myth of* neutrality, Routledge Studies in Contemporary Philosophy, London, Routledge, 2024. See: Part IV, Chap. 4, Sects. 4.1.4–4.1.4.2.1 of this book (on mortgage redlining). See: Part IV, Chap. 4, Sects. 4.1.2–4.1.4.3 of this book (on algorithmic credit scoring, consumer racism and credit card redlining). See: Part IV, Chap. 4, Sects. 4.1.4–4.1.4.2.3 of this book (on algorithmic redlining). See: Part IV, Chap. 4, Sect. 4.1.4.3 of this book (on "algorithmic redliking"). See: Part IV, Chap. 4, Sect. 4.1.3 of this book (on algorithmic prime-lining).

§§ A key takeaway accordingly jumps out as ripe in this regard: AI-embedded technologies,[24] if nothing else, are prone to reify,[25] compound and exacerbate deep-seated social and ethnic concerns with which modern societies have been scuffling

---

[24] Chopra, Samir/White, Laurence F., *A Legal Theory of Autonomous Artificial Agents*, Michigan, University of Michigan Press, 2011, pp. 1–264 (5) (2011) ("There are two views of the goals of artificial intelligence. From an engineering perspective, as Marvin Minsky noted, it is the 'science of making machines do things that would require intelligence if done by men.' *From a cognitive science perspective, it is to design and build systems that work the way the human mind does. In the former perspective, artificial intelligence is deemed successful along a performative dimension; in the latter, along a theoretical one.* The latter embodies Giambattista Vico's perspective of verum et factum convertuntur, 'the true and the made are... convertible'; *in such a view, artificial intelligence would be reckoned the laboratory that validates our best science of the human mind. This perspective sometimes shades into the claim artificial intelligence's success lies in the replication of human capacities such as emotions, the sensations of taste, and self-consciousness. Here, artificial intelligence is conceived of as building artificial persons, not just designing systems that are 'intelligent'*") ("*As an example of how agent technologies might evolve to incorporate learning, autonomy, and discretion, consider a hypothetical agent designed to find used books on the Internet. The agent is provided with a list of websites to scour, sample titles with abstracts as learning data to recognize other titles in the genre, and electronic cash accounts with which to make purchases.* The agent is allowed to purchase books within a preset spending limit with discretion in the number, subjects, and individual prices of books bought. Such an agent has a broadly defined goal with enough executive discretion in the choices it makes to optimize satisfaction of that goal. The agent is able to interact with its environment by reading and scanning information at the sites it visits; it interacts with other agents such as selling agents deployed by other users. The agent "moves" from site to site, makes purchases, and reads recommendations provided by book-selling agents. The agent checks recommendations for matches on parameters of interest, and then depending on the outcome, buys more books or declines offers. *It is able to buy titles not on its original list, and to proactively make the decision to buy a new title. Such an agent is able to decide to take an action, in response to inputs it decides to focus on; its interactions on the Internet, in a world populated by other shopping agents and sometimes humans, exemplify autonomous, goal-directed, proactive behavior*"). Italics added. See: Part V, Chap. 5, Sect. 5.1.7.2 of this book (on law number two to control algorithmic decision-making, which mandates that black box models must not be entrusted with the task of making high stake decisions—v.g. health and freedom). See: Part V, Chap. 5, Sects. 5.1.7–5.1.7.5 of this book (on the five laws to control algorithmic decision-making).

[25] Duster, Troy, "Race and Reification in Science", *Science*, 307, 2005, passim.

for a long-drawn-out,[26] such as misogyny,[27] racism,[28] xenophobe and political hatred which, taken together, are rife for misfire, social outcry, uproar, and a plethora of grievances alike. The time to forestall jarring outcomes arising out of the intersection between law and technology is right now.

§§ Lawmakers and policymakers must be ready to lay down the groundwork encompassing Artificial Intelligence-embedded technologies before it is too late. If they intervene too little or too late, technology will have already created deep-seated roots that will prove impossible to unwind or to uproot.

§§ Lawmakers and policymakers should act now before they run out of time. Failing which, harmful technology will become mainstream and there will be no shortage of deep-seated interests to forcefully oppose any meaningful changes.[29] The more entrenched Artificial Intelligence-embedded technologies[30] become, the harder

---

[26] *Tech, Bias and Housing Initiative, the Promise and Perils of Residential Proptech, Year 1, Research Summary Report, April 2023, TechEquity Collaborative*, p. 5 available at: https://techequity.us/wp-content/uploads/2023/04/TBHI-Y1-Research-Summary-Report.pdf (28.11.2024) ("*Residential Proptech also has the potential to exacerbate the bias inherent in our housing system. Its rise is due, in part, to the desperation felt by average home seekers. With a severely constrained housing supply, companies offering an easier pathway to homeownership may exploit communities that have been harmed by housing discrimination in the past. Opaque algorithms incorporate biased data into their decision-making processes, making it harder to enforce fair housing laws.* Residential Proptech companies often operate in a regulatory gray area, leaving consumers without the protections they would have from traditional housing regulatory systems. *As unprecedented capital investment flows into this space, venture-backed companies' winner-take-all approach to growth has the potential to exacerbate inequality rather than combat it*"). Italics added. See: Part IV, Chap. 4, Sects. 4.1.4–4.1.4.2.3 of this book.

[27] Avery, Mallory/Leibbrandt, Andreas/Vecci, Joseph, "Does Artificial Intelligence Help or Hurt Gender Diversity? Evidence from Two Field Experiments on Recruitment on Tech", *Monash University, Monash Business School*, 2023, pp. 1–70.

[28] Here is a tool to dispel the rampant racism that besets the criminal system of justice: Huq, Aziz, "Racial Equity in Algorithmic Criminal Justice", *Duke Law Journal*, Volume 68, 2022, pp. 1076–1134.

[29] Just take a hard look of what is already happening with the monetization of data. Corporate moguls are making large tons of money with it. They will not relinquish control over data—nor will they willingly cede control over its monetization—without a protracted, public, and bloody fight. The earlier the intervention is, the easier it gets to unseat vested private interests that often run afoul with the public interest. Like monetizing the data harvested/gleaned by Artificial Intelligence while performing data mining. See: Yang/Kai Hao, "Selling Consumer Data for Profit: Optimal Market-Segmentation Design and its Consequences", *American Economic Review*, Volume 112, Issue 4, April 2022, 2022, pp. 1364–1393. Wagner/Gerhard/Eidenmuller, Horst, "Down by Algorithms? Siphoning Rents, Exploiting Biases, and Shaping Preferences: Regulating the Dark Side of Targeted Transactions", *University of Chicago Law Review*, Volume 86, 2019, pp. 581–609; Wallheimer, Brian, "Are you Ready for Personalized Pricing? Companies Are Figuring out What Individual Customers Will Pay-and Charging Accordingly", *Chicago Booth Review*, 2018, passim.

[30] Chopra, Samir/White, Laurence F., *A Legal Theory of Autonomous Artificial Agents*, Michigan, University of Michigan Press, 2011, pp. 1–264 (5) ("*There are two views of the goals of artificial intelligence. From an engineering perspective, as Marvin Minsky noted, it is the 'science of making machines do things that would require intelligence if done by men.' From a cognitive science perspective, it is to design and build systems that work the way the human mind does. In*

will be to outline brawny normative underpinnings to govern this quickly-shifting field.

§§ Although technology should be shrewdly harnessed,[31] its multifarious pitfalls[32] must be equally taken into account.[33] That is the only way forward when it comes to shore up **Algorithmic Common**[34] within the remit of Artificial Intelligence-entrenched technologies.[35]

---

the former perspective, artificial intelligence is deemed successful along a performative dimension; in the latter, along a theoretical one. The latter embodies Giambattista Vico's perspective of verum et factum convertuntur, 'the true and the made are... convertible'; *in such a view, artificial intelligence would be reckoned the laboratory that validates our best science of the human mind. This perspective sometimes shades into the claim artificial intelligence's success lies in the replication of human capacities such as emotions, the sensations of taste, and self-consciousness. Here, artificial intelligence is conceived of as building artificial persons, not just designing systems that are 'intelligent'*") ("*As an example of how agent technologies might evolve to incorporate learning, autonomy, and discretion, consider a hypothetical agent designed to find used books on the Internet. The agent is provided with a list of websites to scour, sample titles with abstracts as learning data to recognize other titles in the genre, and electronic cash accounts with which to make purchases.* The agent is allowed to purchase books within a preset spending limit with discretion in the number, subjects, and individual prices of books bought. Such an agent has a broadly defined goal with enough executive discretion in the choices it makes to optimize satisfaction of that goal. The agent is able to interact with its environment by reading and scanning information at the sites it visits; it interacts with other agents such as selling agents deployed by other users. The agent "moves" from site to site, makes purchases, and reads recommendations provided by book-selling agents. The agent checks recommendations for matches on parameters of interest, and then depending on the outcome, buys more books or declines offers. *It is able to buy titles not on its original list, and to proactively make the decision to buy a new title. Such an agent is able to decide to take an action, in response to inputs it decides to focus on; its interactions on the Internet, in a world populated by other shopping agents and sometimes humans, exemplify autonomous, goal-directed, proactive behavior*"). Italics added.

[31] Sternlight, Jean R., "Justice in a Brave New World?", *Connecticut Law Review*, Volume 52, Issue 1, 2020, p. 232 (on the possibility to harness technology to "whether voice recognition, analysis of facial expressions, or measurements of body twitches may provide better insight into truthfulness"); Sela, Ayelet, "The Effect of Technologies on Dispute Resolution System Design: Antecedents, Current Trends, and Future Directions", *Lewis and Clark Law Review*, Volume 21, 2018, pp. 634 ff and passim (arguing that the widespread use of technology has beget the turn to online dispute resolution).

[32] Jackson, Maya C., "Artificial Intelligence and Algorithmic Bias: The Issues with Technology Reflecting History and Humans", *Journal of Business Technology Law*, Volume 16, 2021, pp. 299–316; West, Sarah Myers/Whittaker, Meredith/Crawford, Kate, *Discriminating Systems. Gender, Race and Power in AI*. New York: AI Now Institute, 2019, pp. 15 and ff and passim.

[33] Like an automatic discrimination detector in criminal procedure law settings. See: Kleinberg, Jon, et al., "Algorithms as Discrimination Detectors", *Proceeds of the National Academy of Science*, Volume 117, 2020, pp. 30096–30110.

[34] See: Part V, Chap. 5, Sects. 5.1.2–5.1.6.2.1 of this book (on the thing-centred algorithmic decision-making propelled by a *Controllable* and *Interpretable* Machine Learning that weeds out *Algorithmic Dictatorship* and secures *Algorithmic Common Good*).

[35] Like tools that can debias racial discrimination within the remit of criminal justice—the essence of racial equity in criminal justice. See: Huq, Aziz, "Racial Equity in Algorithmic Criminal Justice", *Duke Law Journal*, Volume 68, 2022, pp. 1076–1134. See: Part IV, Chap. 4, Sects. 4.1.10.1–4.1.10.6 of this book (on biased algorithmic risk assessment in criminal procedure law settings, with a sharper

§§ To cater for that, algorithmic black box[36] must be belched out, as opposed to just whimsically wished away.[37] But not just that though: the gruelling phenomenon of «deception by design»[38] is in dire need of quashing. So too is the unpalatable phenomenon of «input fallacy».[39]

§§ Tools of algorithmic fairness are therefore sorely needed—like algorithmic bias[40] detection[41]—to ebb the darkest patterns[42] of Artificial Intelligence[43]-embedded technologies arising out of the dingiest corners of the digital reality.[44]

§§ Little we knew that Artificial Intelligence might have a hidden agenda on its own.[45] But, indeed, it might have one after all. And that is wholly unbecoming in this regard. For a simple reason: machines should not get to decide who lives and who

focus on COMPAS). See: Part IV, Chap. 4, Sects. 4.1.1–4.1.1.1 of this book (on biased predictive policing).

36 See: Part V, Chap. 5, Sect. 5.1.7.2 of this book (on law number two to control algorithmic decision-making, which mandates that black box models must not be entrusted with the task of making high stake decisions—v.g. health and freedom). See: Wisser, Leah, "Pandora's Algorithmic Black Box: The Challenges of Using Algorithmic Risk Assessments in Sentencing", *American Criminal Law Review*, Volume 56, 2019, pp. 1811–1832.

37 Fisher, Aaron et al., "All Models are Wrong, but Many are Useful", *Journal of Machine Learning Research*, Volume 20, 2019, pp. 1 and ff.

38 Willis, Lauren, "Deception by Design", *Harvard Journal Law and Technology*, Volume 34, 2020, pp. 115–190.

39 Gillis, Talia, "The Input Fallacy", *Minnesota Law Review*, Volume 106, 2022, pp. 1184–1266.

40 Baeza-Yates, R., "Bias on the web", *Communications of the ACM*, 61 (6), June 2018, 2018, pp. 54–61 (argues that "*algorithmic bias is when the bias is not present in the input data* and is added *purely by the algorithm*"). Italics added.

41 Lee, Nicole Turner/Resnick, Paul/Barton, Genie, *Algorithmic Bias Detection and Mitigation: Best Practices and Policies to Reduce Consumer Harms*. Washington, DC: Brookings Institution, 2019, passim.

42 Luguri, Jamie/Lior, Jacob Strahilevitz, "Shining a Light on Dark Patterns", *Journal of Legal Analytics*, Volume 13, 2021, pp. 43–109.

43 For a concise definition of Artificial Intelligence: Kaplan, Jerry, *Intelligenza artificiale. Guida al futuro prossimo*, 2nd Edition. Roma: Luiss University Press, 2018, pp. 1–198 (pp. 28 and ff and passim). See also: McCarthy, John, Compt. Scientist, Stanford University, Stanford University, in: https://jmc.stanford.edu/artificial-intelligence/what-is-ai/index.html (Nov. 12, 2007) (according to the so-called father of Artificial Intelligence, AI is "the science and engineering of making intelligent machines, especially intelligent computer programs. It is related to the similar task of using computers to understand human intelligence"). Access: 24.8.2024. Converging: Chabert, J.L. et al., *A History of Algorithms: From the Pebble to the Microchip*. New York/Heidelberg: Springer, 2013, p. 2.

44 Digital future which will ineluctably give rise to a "Artificial Intelligent Justice". See: Re, Richard M./Solow-Niederman, Alicia, "Developing Artificially Intelligent", *Stanford Technology Law Review*, Volume 22, 2019, pp. 242 ff and passim.

45 Assad, Stephanie et al., "Autonomous Algorithmic Collusion", *Oxford Review of Economic Policy*, Volume 37, 2021, pp. 459–478.

dies; who gets help[46] and who does not; who gets appropriate medical care and who does not[47]; who gets expedited access to credit and who should be prevented from gaining access to credit[48]; which neighbourhoods should constantly be targeted by law enforcement agencies and which ones should not.[49]

§§ To prevent that jarring scenario from coming to fruition, society should roll up its collective sleeves in a bid to chart the path ahead for a *Controllable Artificial Intelligence*[50] amenable to be *interpretable, controllable, accountable,* and *fair*. Lest we endeavour to eschew the labyrinthic rule of machines,[51] this is the pathway forward that both lawmakers and policymakers should choose to pursue.[52]

§§ This assertion rests upon the premise according to which cryptic algorithms will, in all likelihood, undercut laypeople's deep-rooted sense of algorithmic fairness. But something else is at stake: the trust citizens place upon algorithmic justice. Which is of acute importance as machines are poised to take over the judicial system.[53]

---

[46] Sorenson, S. B./L. Sinko/R. A. Berk, "The Endemic Amid the Pandemic: Seeking Help for Violence against Women in the Initial Phases of COVID-19", *Journal of Interpersonal Violence*, 2021.

[47] See: Bartlett, Robert/Morse, Adair/Wallace, Nancy/Stanton, Richard, "Algorithmic Discrimination and Input Accountability Under the Civil Rights Acts", *Berkeley Technology Law Journal*, Volume 36, 2021, pp. 675–736 (675) ("the disproportionate burden of COVID-19 among communities of color and a necessary renewed attention to racial inequalities have lent new urgency to concerns that algorithmic decision-making can lead to unintentional discrimination against members of historically marginalized groups").

[48] See: Part IV, Chap. 4, Sects. 4.1.4–4.1.4.2.1 of this book (on mortgage redlining). See: Part IV, Chap. 4, Sects. 4.1.2–4.1.4.3 of this book (on algorithmic credit scoring, consumer racism and credit card redlining). But see: Havard, Cassandra Jones, "'On The Take': The Black Box of Credit Scoring and Mortgage Discrimination", *Boston University Public Interest Law Journal*, Volume 20, 2011, pp. 241–247 (highlighting that credit scoring if unchecked is an intrinsic, encroached, deep-rooted form of racial discrimination akin to mortgage redlining); Watcher, S./Mittelstadt, B./Russell, C., "Counterfactual explanations without opening the black box: automated decisions and the GDPR", *Harvard Journal of Law & Technology*, Volume 1, 2018, passim.

[49] See: Part IV, Chap. 4, Sects. 4.1.1–4.1.1.1 of this book (on biased predictive policing).

[50] See: Part V, Chap. 5, Sects. 5.1.2–5.1.6.2.1 of this book (on the thing-centred algorithmic decision-making propelled by a *Controllable* and *Interpretable* Machine Learning that weeds out *Algorithmic Dictatorship* and secures *Algorithmic Common Good*).

[51] Tegmark, Max, *Life 3.0: Being Human in the Age of Artificial Intelligence*. New York: Knopf, 2018, pp. 1–384 (pp. 24 and ff) (charts the path ahead for a wide range of intelligences, including artificial intelligence in the digital age). There is a handful of authors that wonder if artificial intelligence can mimic not only human intelligence but, and foremost, human behaviour. Amongst whom stands: Russel, Stuart/Norvig, Peter, *Artificial Intelligence: A Modern Approach*. London: United Kingdom, Pearson, 2018, passim; Boden, Margaret A., *Artificial Intelligence: A Very Short Introduction*. Oxford: Oxford University Press, 2018, passim.

[52] Cohen, Julien E., *Between Truth and Power: The Legal Constructions of Informational Capitalism*. Oxford: Oxford University Press, 2019, pp. 1–376 (p. 192) (contends presciently that "*automated processes* have obvious efficiency advantages, *but such processes may not align well (or well at all) with applicable legal requirements that are couched in shades of gray*"). Italics added.

[53] But see: Part V, Chap. 5, Sect. 5.1.8.5 of this book (on law number five to interpret algorithmic decision-making, which mandates that robot-judges, robot-prosecutors and robot-lawyers must

§§ The lack of trust on the justice[54] rendered by machines[55]—accompanied by a more than certain lacklustre performance regarding **Algorithmic Common Good**[56] while doing so[57]—will most likely beget both the lack of legitimacy[58] and

---

not enter the courtroom for they are utterly incapable of making sound and interpretable value judgements).

But see: Millar, Jason/Kerr, Ian, "Delegation, Relinquishment and Responsibility: The Prospect of Expert Robots", *Robot Law*, Calo, Ryan/Froomkin, A. Michael/Kerr, Ian (Editors), Cheltenham, Edward Elgar Publishing, 2016, pp. 102, 106–107 (as these authors aptly put it "*we will rely on robots without really knowing why – simply because their algorithms provide the greatest number of successful outcomes.* We have already seen this in Google's search approach. Neither Larry (Page) nor Sergey (Brin) (nor any other Google employee) knowns exactly why one particular web page is a better result than another. *When the click patterns say it is, that's good enough.* No semantic or causal analysis is required…*Like the ancients, we will, quite rationally, come to rely upon them, knowing full well that we cannot necessarily explain the reasons for their decisions*"). Italics added. Converging: Casey, Anthony J./Niblett, Anthony, "Self-driving Laws", *University of Toronto Law Journal*, Volume 66, 2016, pp. 429–435 (contend that "as more information is generated, and the evolutionary algorithm updates and become a better forecaster, *we imagine that judges will increasingly rely on the advice of the algorithm*"). But see: Weizenbaum, Joseph, *Computer Power and Human Reason: From Judgment to Calculation*, 1st edition, New York, W. H. Freeman & Co, 1976, pp. 1–300 (227) ("examines the sources of the computer's powers and offers evaluative explorations of what computers can do, cannot do, and should not be employed to do") (this founding father of Artificial Intelligence presciently noted that we should not entrust Artificial Intelligence-embedded technologies with with "tasks that demand wisdom"). Italics added. The approval of rental applications is arguably one of those tasks that should never be entrusted to machines. More on this on Part IV, Chap. 4, Sects. 4.1.4–4.1.4.2.1 of this book. See also: Cohen, Julien E., *Between Truth and Power: The Legal Constructions of Informational Capitalism*. Oxford: Oxford University Press, 2019, pp. 1–376 (p. 192) (contends presciently that "*automated processes* have obvious efficiency advantages, *but such processes may not align well (or well at all) with applicable legal requirements that are couched in shades of gray*"). Italics added.

[54] Tyler, Tom, *Trust in the Law*, New York, NY: Russell-Sage, 2002, passim.

[55] Simmons, Ric, "Big Data and Procedural Justice: Legitimizing Algorithms in the Criminal Justice System", *Ohio State Journal of Criminal Law*, Volume 5, 2018, pp. 573 and ff and passim (argues that too much AI in criminal procedure law settings can backfire, thereby hindering citizens 'trust on the criminal system of justice').

[56] See: Part V, Chap. 5, Sects. 5.1.2–5.1.6.2.1 of this book (on the thing-centred algorithmic decision-making propelled by a *Controllable* and *Interpretable* Machine Learning that weeds out *Algorithmic Dictatorship* and secures *Algorithmic Common Good*).

[57] See: Part V, Chap. 5, Sect. 5.1.8.5 of this book (on law number five to interpret algorithmic decision-making, which mandates that robot-judges, robot-prosecutors and robot-lawyers must not enter the courtroom for they are utterly incapable of making sound and interpretable value judgements).

[58] Tyler, Tom R., "Psychological perspectives on legitimacy and legitimation", in: *Annual Review of Psychology*, Volume 57, 2006, pp. 375–400 (on the role that perceived legitimacy plays in everyday life); Tyler, Tom R., *Why people cooperate: The role of social motivations*, Princeton, New Jersey, Princeton University Press, 2011; Robbins, J. M./M.T. Ford/L.E. Tetrick, "Perceived unfairness and employee health: A meta-analytic integration", in: *Journal of Applied Psychology*, Volume 97, 2012, pp. 235–272; Tyler, Tom R., "What is procedural justice? Criteria used by citizens to assess the fairness of legal procedures", *Law and Society Review*, Volume 22, 1988, pp. 103–135 (on the interplay between fairness of legal procedures and procedural justice. Unsurprisingly, the lack of fairness of legal procedures impacts the procedural justice -or the lack thereof -); Sunshine,

the lack of procedural justice[59] of algorithmic justice[60]—two of the most prominent cornerstones/linchpins/mainstays/bedrocks of any system of administration of justice[61] worthy of such a haughty sobriquet.

§§ The system of administration of justice—especially, criminal justice—will accordingly careen into the chaos of *Algorithmic Dictatorship* accountable to no one.[62] The promise of a technological due process[63] will accordingly flounder.

J./Tyler, Tom R., "The role of procedural justice and legitimacy in shaping public support for policing", *Law & Society Review*, Volume 37, 2003, pp. 513–548 (on the role of procedural justice to enhance/boost legitimacy); Bies, Robert J., "Are Procedural Justice and Interactional Justice Conceptually Distinct?", *Handbook of Organizational Justice*, Greenberg, Jerald/Colquitt, Jason, (Editors), New Jersey, Lawrence Erlbaum Associates Publishers, 2005, pp. 85–86 (arguing that a respectful treatment is an important part of, and the linchpin of a much-needed, procedural justice, which also plays an pivotal role in the remit of interactional justice).

[59] Zimmerman, Nourit/Tyler, Tom R., "Between Access to Counsel and Access to Justice: A Psychological Perspective", *Fordham Urban Law Journal*, Volume 37, 2010, pp. 473–488 (contends that "evaluations about neutrality, *trust*, and respect for the legal system as a whole"—satisfaction with the *procedural fairness* and *procedural justice* will not lag far behind); Tyler, Tom R./Lind, Edgar Allan, "Procedural justice", *Handbook of law and social science*, J. Sanders/V.L. Hamilton (Eds.), New York, Plenum Press, 2001, pp. 65–92; Tyler, Tom R./Smith, H. J./Huo, Y. J., "Member diversity and leadership effectiveness: Procedural justice, social identity, and group dynamics", *Advances in group processes*, B. Markovsky (Ed.), Greenwich, CT: JAI Press, Volume 13, 1996, pp. 33–68; Tyler, Tom R./Lind, Edgar Allan/Huo, Yuen J., "Cultural Values and Authority Relations: The Psychology of Conflict Resolution Across Cultures", in: *Psychology, Public Policy and Law*, Volume 6, n.º 4, 2000, pp. 1138–1163 (parsing the relationship between high and low levels of power distance values and the relational model of authority); Leung, K./Lind, Edgar Allan, "Procedural justice and culture: Effects of culture, gender, and investigator status on procedural preferences", *Journal of Personality and Social Psychology,* Volume 50, 1986, pp. 1134–1140; Leung, K./Morris, K. W., "Justice through the lens of culture and ethnicity", *Handbook of Law and Social Science: Justice,* Sanders, J./Hamilton, V. L., (Eds.), New York, Plenum, 2001, pp. 343–378; Lind, Edgar Allan/Tyler, Tom R., *The social psychology of procedural justice*, New York, Plenum Press, 1988, passim; Lind, Edgar Allan/Tyler, Tom R./Huo, Y.J., "Procedural context and culture: Variation in the antecedents of procedural justice judgments", *Journal of Personality and Social Psychology,* Volume 73, 1997, pp. 767–780.

[60] There is an excellent body of empirical research that shows that a poor judicial performance spawns low trust in legal systems. See: Magalhães, Pedro C./Garoupa, Nuno, "Judicial Performance and Trust in Legal Systems: Findings from a Decade of Surveys in 20 European Countries", *Social Science Quarterly*, 2020, 1 (the main goal of this exciting piece of research was «determining the existence of a relationship between judicial performance and citizens' trust in the legal system». To cater for that, the methodology used «cross-classified multilevel models, using data from more than 20 European countries, 80 surveys, and 100,000 respondents, over a decade». Regarding the results, «the longer the time that lower courts take, on average, to dispose of pending cases, the lower is the public's trust in their legal system». As an upshot, «judicial performance, operationalized as the ability of courts to avoid delays in the delivery of justice, is a significant correlate of citizens' evalatuations of their country's legal system»).

[61] Calo, Ryan/Citron, Danielle Keats, "The Automated Administrative State: A Crisis of Legitimacy", *Emory Law Journal*, Volume 70, 2021, passim.

[62] See: Part IV, Chap. 4, Sects. 4.1–4.1.10.6 of this book (on Algorithmic Dictatorship and its chilling effect on democracy).

[63] Citron, Danielle Keats, "Technological Due Process", *Washington University Law Review*, Volume 85, 2008, pp. 1256–1257.

§§ Against this long-winded backdrop, this section seeks to offer insights on the harmful effects of advanced technology while keeping citizens 'fundamental rights front of mind. To cater for that, red lines are in dire need of being swiftly drawn. To that end, *Critical Artificial Intelligence Studies* will prove paramount in opening windows through which the light can pass unscathed.

3.1.1 Artificial Intelligence-Embedded Technologies and the Pressing Issue of «Inequality in Application» (Ryan Calo) That Paves the Way to **Algorithmic Dictatorship**

§§ Artificial Intelligence and Rule of Law are shaping up to be inversely correlated. Artificial Intelligence will inevitably stifle vested fundamental rights that we, collectively, hold so dear. The unbridled rise of Artificial Intelligence[64] will accordingly fray the fabric of Rule of Law,[65] which is already backsliding in some parts of the world.[66]

---

[64] Fergus, Rachel, "Biased Technology: The Automated Discrimination of Facial Recognition", *ACLU Minnesota*, February 29, 2024, available at: https://www.aclu-mn.org/en/news/biased-technology-automated-discrimination-facial-recognition (access: 20.09.2024) ("*Technology is developing much more quickly than the laws we need to protect our rights. Anyone with a smartphone or social media account knows how rapidly technology changes, while legislating can take a long, long time. It is essential to proactively put policies into place that will protect our rights as new and more advanced technology is constantly released. Especially when that technology – and law enforcement members using it - have been shown over and over to be biased toward marginalized groups*"). Italics added.

[65] See: Part V, Chap. 5, Sect. 5.1.1.1 of this book (on the central tenets of Rule of Law that lends itself to a beacon of justice amidst the sepulchral darkness that is about to take hold). See: Part V, Chap. 5, Sect. 5.1.1.2 of this book (on the central tenets of Procedural Rule of Law that bestows upon citizens the fundamental right to challenge the pearls of algorithmic wisdom—outputs—offered by algorithmic decision-making).

[66] Regrettably, the Rule of Law is backsliding worldwide. Especially in Central and Eastern Europe. See: Avbelj, Matej, "The Rule of Law, Comprehensive Doctrines, Overlapping Consensus, and the Future of Europe", *Ratio Juris*, Volume 36, Issue 3, September, 2023, pp. 242–258. The Rule of Law is not a «one size fits all» format nonetheless. But see: Chesterman, Simon, "An International Rule of Law", *The American Journal of Comparative Law*, Volume 56, 2008, pp. 331–362 (on the thrust to grasp (?) a catch-all International Rule of Law). See: Peari, Sagi, "Better Law as a Better Outcome", *The American Journal of Comparative Law*, Volume 63, Issue 1, 2015, pp. 155–195 (156) (on Leflar's stance on «better rule of law»). For the purposes of this piece, Rule of Law amounts to a lighthouse of procedural fairness to which citizens, regardless of where they are, resort to upon gaining access to a given system of administration of criminal justice. Whilst further utterances on the fabric of Rule of Law fall well outside the scope and breadth of this paper, one must not be oblivious of the fact that the thrust to Deglobalizing Rule of Law is underway. See: Bussani, Mauro, "Deglobalizing Rule of Law and Democracy: Hunting Down Rhetoric Through Comparative Law", *The American Journal of Comparative Law*, Volume 67, 2019, pp. 701–744 (701) (contending that the thrust to Deglobalizing Rule of Law is interwoven with thrust to take heed of «well-known differences that run through cultures and traditions». In spite of which, «the

§§ Setting aside the more than overhyped promises of a brave new world for the filthy rich and endless throes to the less fortunate ones[67]—which is already a plight that beleaguers modern societies[68]—a burning question that often goes unanswered is the extent to which citizens should entrust technology with deciding their lives.[69]

West has never stopped trying to export its own law into the rest of the world»). Unsurprisingly, there have been educated calls to take heed of the pinpointed cultural and legal differences by, in the case of China, allow for a «Socialist Rule of Law». See: Chinese Common Law Guiding Cases, *Harvard Law Review*, Volume 129, 2016, p. 2213. We will come back to this issue further down is this paper. More on this later.

[67] This problem is neither new nor easy to solve. Whilst the effects of technology—digital justice—on the courtroom have been previously broached by the doctrine, few to none consensus has been reached about actionable lines of action to be taken. See: Donoghue, Jane, "The Rise of Digital Justice: Courtroom Technology, Public Participation and Access to Justice", *The Modern Law Review*, Volume 80, Issue 6, 2018, p. 995 (noting that technology in the courtroom might widen the gap between the rich and the poor. In this vein, this renowned author has contended that "*legal reforms have omitted any detailed consideration of the type and quality of citizen participation in newly digitised court processes which have fundamental implications for the legitimacy and substantive outcomes of court-based processes; and for enhancing democratic procedure through improved access to justice.* It is argued that although digital court tools and systems offer great promise for enhancing efficiency, participation and accessibility, they *simultaneously have the potential to amplify the scope for injustice, and to attenuate central principles of the legal system, including somewhat paradoxically, access to justice*"). Italics added. See also: Heintz, M.E., "The digital divide and courtroom technology: Can David keep up with Goliath", *Federal Communications Law Journal*, Volume 54, 2002, pp. 566 ff and passim. The great bulk of these assertions has been anticipated by an iconic piece of research. See: Galanter, Marc, "Why the "Haves" Come Out Ahead: Speculations on the Limits of Legal Change", *Law & Society Review*, Volume 9, 1974, pp. 98–103 (this renowned author talks about a *social reality* in which the dubbed «repeat players»—which go by the name of «haves»—tend to «to come out ahead» by putting their knowledge and vast resources to good use. This perceived advantage will not only impact the choice on the procedures but will ultimately benefit their interests as opposed to the deemed «one-shot» players (the «have nots») that will have slimmer and fewer chances to get palpable results in dispute resolution). Technology in the courtroom—that includes the rich and excludes the poor—will make this problem considerably worse. But see: Bailey, J./Burkell, J./Reynolds, G. "Access to Justice for All: Towards an "Expansive Vision" of Justice and Technology", *Windsor Yearbook of Access to Justice*, Volume 31, 2013, pp. 183–201 (in stark contrast, these authors stress that the digital and technological apparatus can indeed spawn a both time-effective and streamlined access to justice in a given jurisdiction).

[68] Amongst which stands arguably social cleavages spawned by a technology that fondly includes the rich and outrightly excludes the poor, thereby compounding social issues with which modern have been grappling/tussling/scuffling/floundering since immemorial times. Social cleavages—a cloak under which mounting social outcry is often wrapped—that threaten to crumble the foundations upon which stands the linchpin of western societies. See in general: Abramsky, Sasha, *Jumping at Shadows: The Triumph of Fear and the End of the American Dream*. New York: Bold Type Books, 2017, pp. 1–272 (passim).

[69] But see: Weizenbaum, Joseph, *Computer Power and Human Reason: From Judgment to Calculation*, 1st edition, New York, W. H. Freeman & Co, 1976, pp. 1–300 (227) ("examines the sources of the computer's powers and offers evaluative explorations of what computers can do, cannot do, and should not be employed to do") (this founding father of Artificial Intelligence presciently noted that we should not entrust Artificial Intelligence-embedded technologies with with "tasks that demand wisdom"). Italics added. The approval of rental applications is arguably one of those tasks that should never be entrusted to machines. More on this on Part IV, Chap. 4, Sects. 4.1.4–4.1.4.2.1 of this book.

This vexing question is frequently passed over. It is unfortunate that such is the case: a pressing question of this magnitude should not be glossed over.[70]

§§ This one of those critical questions that should be hardened into binding law if necessary. Which begs the questions: should citizens trust the technology deployed to decide their lives[71]? It is often averred that easy-to-follow explanations describe

---

[70] See: *Tech, Bias and Housing Initiative, the Promise and Perils of Residential Proptech, Year 1, Research Summary Report, April 2023, TechEquity Collaborative*, p. 5 available at: https://techequity.us/wp-content/uploads/2023/04/TBHI-Y1-Research-Summary-Report.pdf (28.11.2024) ("*Residential Proptech also has the potential to exacerbate the bias inherent in our housing system. Its rise is due, in part, to the desperation felt by average home seekers. With a severely constrained housing supply, companies offering an easier pathway to homeownership may exploit communities that have been harmed by housing discrimination in the past. Opaque algorithms incorporate biased data into their decision-making processes, making it harder to enforce fair housing laws.* Residential Proptech companies often operate in a regulatory gray area, leaving consumers without the protections they would have from traditional housing regulatory systems. *As unprecedented capital investment flows into this space, venture-backed companies' winner-take-all approach to growth has the potential to exacerbate inequality rather than combat it*"). Italics added. See: Part IV, Chap. 4, Sects. 4.1.4–4.1.4.2.3 of this book. See: Part IV, Chap. 4, Sects. 4.1.4–4.1.4.2.1 of this book (on mortgage redlining). See: Part IV, Chap. 4, Sects. 4.1.2–4.1.4.3 of this book (on algorithmic credit scoring, consumer racism and credit card redlining). See: Part IV, Chap. 4, Sects. 4.1.4–4.1.4.2.3 of this book (on algorithmic redlining). See: Part IV, Chap. 4, Sect. 4.1.4.3 of this book (on "algorithmic redliking"). See: Part IV, Chap. 4, Sect. 4.1.3 of this book (on algorithmic prime-lining).

[71] Chopra, Samir/White, Laurence F., *A Legal Theory of Autonomous Artificial Agents*, Michigan, University of Michigan Press, 2011, pp. 1–264 (5) (2011) ("*There are two views of the goals of artificial intelligence. From an engineering perspective, as Marvin Minsky noted, it is the 'science of making machines do things that would require intelligence if done by men.' From a cognitive science perspective, it is to design and build systems that work the way the human mind does. In the former perspective, artificial intelligence is deemed successful along a performative dimension; in the latter, along a theoretical one.* The latter embodies Giambattista Vico's perspective of verum et factum convertuntur, 'the true and the made are... convertible'; *in such a view, artificial intelligence would be reckoned the laboratory that validates our best science of the human mind. This perspective sometimes shades into the claim artificial intelligence's success lies in the replication of human capacities such as emotions, the sensations of taste, and self-consciousness. Here, artificial intelligence is conceived of as building artificial persons, not just designing systems that are 'intelligent'*") ("*As an example of how agent technologies might evolve to incorporate learning, autonomy, and discretion, consider a hypothetical agent designed to find used books on the Internet. The agent is provided with a list of websites to scour, sample titles with abstracts as learning data to recognize other titles in the genre, and electronic cash accounts with which to make purchases.* The agent is allowed to purchase books within a preset spending limit with discretion in the number, subjects, and individual prices of books bought. Such an agent has a broadly defined goal with enough executive discretion in the choices it makes to optimize satisfaction of that goal. The agent is able to interact with its environment by reading and scanning information at the sites it visits; it interacts with other agents such as selling agents deployed by other users. The agent "moves" from site to site, makes purchases, and reads recommendations provided by book-selling agents. The agent checks recommendations for matches on parameters of interest, and then depending on the outcome, buys more books or declines offers. *It is able to buy titles not on its original list, and to proactively make the decision to buy a new title. Such an agent is able to decide to take an action, in response to inputs it decides to focus on; its interactions on the Internet, in a world populated by other shopping agents and sometimes humans, exemplify autonomous, goal-directed, proactive behavior*"). Italics added. See: Part V, Chap. 5, Sect. 5.1.7.2 of this book (on law number two to control algorithmic decision-making, which mandates that black box models must not be entrusted with the task of making high

succinctly the inner workings of technology on the balance of probabilities. It is often posited that those explanations suffice to meet the criteria of transparency.[72]

§§ However, do these easy-to-follow explanations suffice when technology is entrusted with making high stake decisions? More to the point, are algorithms capable to reflect agreed-upon «human values such as fairness, accountability, and transparency («FAT»)»,[73] which are vital in making decisions[74] about citizens 'life, health, liberty, and financial affairs?[75] The answer is a resounding «no».

§§ Lest we forget, my newly-crafted concept of *Algorithmic Dictatorship*[76] arises out of discriminatory algorithmic decision-making undertaken by Artificial Intelligence[77] that affects the fundamental rights of citizens devoid of, and fundamentally

---

stake decisions—v.g. health and freedom). See: Part V, Chap. 5, Sects. 51..7–5.1.7.5 of this book (on the five laws to control algorithmic decision-making).

[72] See: Tyler, Tom R., "Does the American Public Accept the Rule of Law? The Findings of Psychological Research on Deference to Authority", *De Paul Law Review*, 56, 2007, pp. 661–664 (stating that "transparency and openness foster the belief that decision-making procedures are neutral"). See also: Coglianese, Cary/Lehr, David, "Transparency and Algorithmic Governance", *Administrative Law Review*, Volume 71, 2019, passim. See also: Doherty, Joseph W./Reville, Robert T./Zakaras, Laura(ed.), *Introduction to Confidentiality, Transparency, and the U.S. Civil Justice System*, Oxford, Oxford University Press, 2012, 1–258 (passim) (noting that the lack of transparency yields sizable social costs). But see: Weizenbaum, Joseph, *Computer Power and Human Reason: From Judgment to Calculation*, 1st edition, New York, W. H. Freeman & Co, 1976, pp. 1–300 (227) ("examines the sources of the computer's powers and offers evaluative explorations of what computers can do, cannot do, and should not be employed to do") (this founding father of Artificial Intelligence presciently noted that we should not entrust Artificial Intelligence-embedded technologies with with "tasks that demand wisdom"). Italics added. The approval of rental applications is arguably one of those tasks that should never be entrusted to machines. More on this on Part IV, Chap. 4, Sects. 4.1.4–4.1.4.2.1 of this book. See: Part V, Chap. 5, Sect. 5.1.7.2 of this book (on law number two to control algorithmic decision-making, which mandates that black box models must not be entrusted with the task of making high stake decisions—v.g. health and freedom). See: Part V, Chap. 5, Sects. 5.1.7–5.1.7.5 of this book (on the five laws to control algorithmic decision-making).

[73] Calo, Ryan, "Artificial Intelligence Policy: Primer and Roadmap", *University of California*, Davis, Volume 51, 2017, pp. 399–435 (411).

[74] Candent challenges that come under the yoke of intelligent automation, which is shaping up to morph the legal arena in an overarching sense. See: Bornet, Pascal/Barkin, Ian/Wirtz, Jochen, *Intelligent Automation: Learn how to harness Artificial Intelligence to boost business and make out world more human*, 2020, pp. 1–432. See: Part V, Chap. 5, Sect. 5.1.8.5 of this book (on law number five to interpret algorithmic decision-making, which mandates that robot-judges, robot-prosecutors and robot-lawyers must not enter the courtroom for they are utterly incapable of making sound and interpretable value judgements).

[75] Calo, Ryan, "Artificial Intelligence Policy: Primer and Roadmap", *cit.*, pp. 399–435 (411).

[76] See: Part IV, Chap. 4, Sects. 4.1–4.1.10.6 of this book (on Algorithmic Dictatorship and its chilling effect on democracy).

[77] Such as heightened security that allows permanent digital surveillance of individuals deemed socially unfit or—worse yet—biologically/mentally prone to engage in flagitious and unlawful activities. The German doctrine has fleshed out this topic in depth. See: Müller, Helmut, „Europäische Rechtssicherheit gegen Deutsches Sicherheitsrecht? Zur EGMR-Entscheidung in Sachen nachträgliche (Verlängerung der) Sicherungsverwahrung", *Kritische Justiz*, Volume 43, Issue 3, 2010, pp. 256–268. This topic—although enthralling/besotting/buoying—falls conspicuously outside the breadth and scope of our essay.

decoupled of, any reasonable grounds to do so. Which means that the pinpointed algorithmic life-changing decisions (those pertaining to citizens' health, wealth, freedom, and credit scoring) should be subject to stringent scrutiny or inordinate damages may otherwise occur.

§§ This is the kernel of «inequality in application»[78] that consists of Artificial Intelligence-embedded technologies that seemingly works well for everyone,[79] when such is not the case. The paradigmatic examples of errors-fraught evaluations undertaken by machine learning algorithms are legion.

§§ The examples flow from watered down computer vision that features black African Americans as gorillas[80]; botched computer vision that is incapable of recognizing the prototypical physical features of Asian people[81] to software that biasedly associates certain occupations with certain genders (v.g. machine learning algorithms associate the role of an engineer to a male, whereas the same technology associates the role of a nurse[82] to a female).[83] Dispiritingly, though, the list goes on.[84]

§§ Strikingly, and more in tune with the *Algorithmic Dictatorship* from which biased algorithms were borne,[85] black African Americans have fewer opportunities on Facebook than do members from other ethnicities owing to blatantly discriminatory[86] allowances.[87] Amongst whom white.[88] In the same vein, algorithms openly

[78] Calo, Ryan, "Artificial Intelligence Policy: Primer and Roadmap", *cit.*, pp. 399–435 (411).

[79] Calo, Ryan, "Artificial Intelligence Policy: Primer and Roadmap", *cit.*, pp. 399–435 (411).

[80] Calo, Ryan, "Artificial Intelligence Policy: Primer and Roadmap", *cit.*, pp. 399–435 (411).

[81] Calo, Ryan, "Artificial Intelligence Policy: Primer and Roadmap", *cit.*, pp. 399–435 (411).

[82] Caliskan, Aylin et al., "Semantics Derived Automatically from Language Corpora Contain Human-Like Biases", *Science*, 356, 2017, pp. 183 and ff and passim.

[83] Calo, Ryan, "Artificial Intelligence Policy: Primer and Roadmap", *cit.*, pp. 399–435 (411).

[84] See: Part IV, Chap. 4, Sect. 4.1.8 of this book (on biased word embeddings with an entrenched presence on search engines run by tech moguls).

[85] See: Part IV, Chap. 4, Sects. 4.1–4.1.10.6 of this book (on Algorithmic Dictatorship and its chilling effect on democracy).

[86] Menasce, Juliana Horowitz/Brown, Anna/Cox, Kiana, "Views of Racial Inequality", *Pew Research Center*, April 9, 2019, available at: https://www.pewresearch.org/social-trends/2019/04/09/views-of-racial-inequality/ (access: 2.12.2024) ("*more than four-in-ten Americans say the country still has work to do to give black people equal rights with whites. Blacks, in particular, are skeptical that black people will ever have equal rights in this country* (….) *A majority of adults say that being white helps people's ability to get ahead in the country at least a little (59%); 28% say being white neither helps nor hurts and 12% say it hurts.* On the flip side, a majority (56%) sees being black as a disadvantage, with 25% saying it hurts people's ability to get ahead a lot. *About a quarter (26%) say being black neither helps nor hurts and 17% say it helps at least a little. More also say that being Hispanic hurts people's ability to get ahead in this country (51%) than say it helps (18%) or that it neither helps nor hurts (30%).* Opinions are more split when it comes to the impact of being Native American – about the same shares say this hurts as say it neither helps nor hurts, while a smaller share says it helps. *And while a plurality says being Asian neither helps nor hurts, more say it helps (34%) than hurts (21%) people's ability to get ahead*"). Italics added.

[87] Calo, Ryan, "Artificial Intelligence Policy: Primer and Roadmap", *cit.*, pp. 399–435 (411).

[88] Angwin, Julia/Parris Jr, Terry, "Facebook Lets Advertisers Exclude Users by Race", *ProPublica*, October 28, 2016, available at: https://www.propublica.org/article/facebook-lets-advertisers-exclude-users-by-race (access: 19.09.2024) ("*Imagine if, during the Jim Crow era, a newspaper*

discriminate Asian Americans, whom are charged exceedingly higher prices for test preparation than do members than other ethnicities.[89] Amongst whom whites.[90]

---

offered advertisers the option of placing ads only in copies that went to white readers. That's basically what Facebook is doing nowadays. The ubiquitous social network not only allows advertisers to target users by their interests or background, it also gives advertisers the ability to exclude specific groups it calls "Ethnic Affinities." *Ads that exclude people based on race, gender and other sensitive factors are prohibited by federal law in housing and employment*"). Italics added. Packard, Jerald M., *American Nightmare: The History of Jim Crow*, Broadway, New York, St. Martin's Press; First Edition, 2002, pp. 1–304 ("*For a hundred years after the end of the Civil War, a quarter of all Americans lived under a system of legalized segregation called Jim Crow. Together with its rigidly enforced canon of racial "etiquette," these rules governed nearly every aspect of life-and outlined draconian punishments for infractions. The purpose of Jim Crow was to keep African Americans subjugated at a level as close as possible to their former slave status. Exceeding even South Africa's notorious apartheid in the humiliation, degradation, and suffering it brought, Jim Crow left scars on the American psyche that are still felt today. American Nightmare* examines and explains Jim Crow from its beginnings to its end: how it came into being, how it was lived, how it was justified, and how, at long last, it was overcome only a few short decades ago. *Most importantly, this book reveals how a nation founded on principles of equality and freedom came to enact as law a pervasive system of inequality and virtual slavery.* Although America has finally consigned Jim Crow to the historical graveyard, *Jerrold Packard shows why it is important that this scourge-and an understanding of how it happened-remain alive in the nation's collective memory*"). Italics added.

[89] Calo, Ryan, "Artificial Intelligence Policy: Primer and Roadmap", *cit.*, pp. 399–435 (412).

[90] Angwin, Julia/Larson, Jeff, "The Tiger Mom Tax: Asians Are Nearly Twice as Likely to Get a Higher Price from Princeton Review", September 1, 2015, available at: https://www.propublica.org/article/asians-nearly-twice-as-likely-to-get-higher-price-from-princeton-review ("Every year, thousands of high school students get ready for the SAT by using The Princeton Review's test preparation services. But few, if any, realize that the prices for The Princeton Review's online SAT tutoring packages vary substantially depending on where customers live. If they type some ZIP codes into the company's website, they are offered The Princeton Review's Premier course for as little as $6,600. For other ZIP codes, the same course costs as much as $8,400. One unexpected effect of the company's geographic approach to pricing is that Asians are almost twice as likely to be offered a higher price than non-Asians, an analysis by ProPublica shows. The gap remains even for Asians in lower income neighborhoods. Consider a ZIP code in Flushing, a neighborhood in Queens, New York. Asians make up 70.5 percent of the population in this ZIP code. According to the U.S. Census, the median household income in the ZIP code, $41,884, is lower than most, yet The Princeton Review customers there are quoted the highest price. The Princeton Review said in a statement that its pricing is based on the "costs of running our business and the competitive attributes of the given market," and that the company charges the same price everywhere in New York City. Although the test prep service markets its service as "24-hr Online Tutoring," the company says the tutoring is done in one-on-one sessions in person or online and that the tutors typically live in the same areas as their students. "The areas that experience higher prices will also have a disproportionately higher population of members of the financial services industry, people who tend to vote Democratic, journalists and any other group that is more heavily concentrated in areas like New York City," The Princeton Review's statement said. These types of price differences are not illegal, and the consequences are not intentional, but researchers say they are likely to become more common in the age of services like Uber, which set prices by computer algorithms. The Princeton Review says its prices are simply determined by geographic region. Last year, a (White House report on "Big Data" cautioned that the "algorithmic decisions raise the specter of 'redlining' in the digital economy – the potential to discriminate against the most vulnerable classes of our society under the guise of neutral algorithms." In 2012, the Wall Street Journal reported that the online office

retailer Staples was varying prices by ZIP code. Staples appeared to be calculating prices based on the user's distance from a rival store, but the inadvertent effect was that people in lower-income ZIP codes saw the higher prices. In 2014, researchers at Northeastern University found that top Web sites, such as Home Depot, Orbitz and Travelocity, were steering some users toward more expensive products. And this year, another study found that users who were identified by Google as female received fewer ads for a high-paying job. Offline, the practice of offering different prices for the same product in different places is fairly common—gasoline or a gallon of milk can be priced differently just a few blocks apart. But as long as there is no intent to racially discriminate, it is generally legal, says Andrew Selbst, an attorney who co-authored a paper on the biases that can be inherent in Big Data. "If you are open for business, you can't discriminate against certain protected classes," Selbst said. *Unintentional racial discrimination is illegal in housing and employment under the legal doctrine known as "disparate impact," which prohibits inadvertent actions that hurt people in a protected class. But the disparate impact doctrine does not apply to the online world, where it's often difficult to determine how and why different prices are being offered.* Earlier this year, Harvard undergraduate Christian Haigh stumbled on The Princeton Review's variable prices doing research for a class he was taking called "Data Science to Save the World." Haigh had been looking for price differences in hotel rooms if he booked from different locations around the world. But he wasn't finding much. So he looked for websites that required entering a ZIP code. "We thought maybe if you have to put in the ZIP code, they were trying to discriminate," Haigh said. Today, Haigh and three fellow students are publishing their findings that The Princeton Review's higher prices correlate to areas with higher income. ProPublica reviewed the code that one of Haigh's fellow students posted on a public web site and collected its own data in July, and again on Monday. The data showed that The Princeton Review offered four different prices for the same "Premier Level" online tutoring package. Many of the prices are regional. *For instance, the entire New York City area, including Long Island, receives the highest possible price, $8,400. Much of California, except San Diego, is offered the second-highest price, $7,200, while ZIP codes in San Diego are charged the lowest price. Because the pricing regions are large, sometimes spanning multiple states, they are different than the personalized tech algorithms used by some web sites, which make real-time decisions about which advertisements to show to a particular visitor.* ProPublica tested whether The Princeton Review prices were tied to different characteristics of each ZIP code, including income, race and education level. When it came to getting the highest prices, living in a ZIP code with a high median income or a large Asian population seemed to make the greatest difference. The analysis showed that higher income areas are twice as likely to receive higher prices than the general population. For example, wealthy suburbs of Washington D.C. are charged higher prices. But that isn't always the case: Residents of affluent neighborhoods in Dallas are charged the lowest price, $6,600. *Customers in areas with a high density of Asian residents were 1.8 times as likely to be offered higher prices, regardless of income.* For instance, residents of the gritty industrial city of Westminster, California, which is half Asian with a median income below most, were charged the second-highest price for the Premier tutoring service. The Princeton Review said it would be a mistake to call its pricing practices discrimination. "To equate the incidental differences in impact that occur from this type of geographic based pricing that pervades all American commerce with discrimination misconstrues both the literal, legal and moral meaning of the word," the company said in its statement. The company said the prices of its online tutoring services are based on the prices of local tutors, which vary "just as virtually every good or service does, be it gasoline, rent or eggs." *Even if the price differences were unintentional, the Harvard students said they found them disturbing. Haigh, the student who discovered the variations, is an economics major and said he's not generally against price differences unless particular demographic groups are affected. "It's*

§§ Conversely, *datafication*[91]—that draws on the gargantuan batches of data that feed into the databases that will eventually produce the pearls of algorithmic wisdom[92] that will exact a toll on[93] «inequality in application»—empowers the rich while disfranchising the poor.[94]

---

something that makes a very small impact on one individual's life but can make a big impact to large groups," Haigh said. Italics added.

[91] Viljoen, Salomé, "A Relational Theory of Data Governance", *Yale Law Journal*, Volume 131, 2021, pp. 573–653 ("*[D]atafication may be wrong not only because it manipulates people, but also because the social effects it produces or materializes violate standards of equality.* As an economic process, datafication *may lead to unfair wealth inequality that violates distributive ideals of justice.* As a social process, *datafication may reproduce and amplify forms of social hierarchy that violate relational standards of justice*"). Italics added.

[92] *Tech, Bias and Housing Initiative, the Promise and Perils of Residential Proptech, Year 1, Research Summary Report, April 2023, TechEquity Collaborative*, p. 11, available at: https://techequity.us/wp-content/uploads/2023/04/TBHI-Y1-Research-Summary-Report.pdf (28.11.2024) ("*Once bad data enters the analysis of one factor, it gets baked into the subsequent process, multiplying the effect that one disadvantageous data point can have on someone's overall housing determination*"). Italics added. See: Part IV, Chap. 4, Sects. 4.1.4–4.1.4.2.3 of this book. See: Part IV, Chap. 4, Sects. 4.1.4–4.1.4.2.1 of this book (on mortgage redlining). See: Part IV, Chap. 4, Sects. 4.1.2–4.1.4.3 of this book (on algorithmic credit scoring, consumer racism and credit card redlining). See: Part IV, Chap. 4, Sects. 4.1.4–4.1.4.2.3 of this book (on algorithmic redlining). See: Part IV, Chap. 4, Sect. 4.1.4.3 of this book (on "algorithmic redliking"). See: Part IV, Chap. 4, Sect. 4.1.3 of this book (on algorithmic prime-lining).

[93] Ferreri, Mara/Sanyal, Romola, "Digital informalisation: rental housing, platforms, and the management of risk", *Housing Studies*, Volume 37, Issue 6, 2022, pp. 1035–1053 (1035) ("*The eruption of disruptive digital platforms is reshaping geographies of housing under the gaze of corporations and through the webs of algorithms.* Engaging with interdisciplinary scholarship on informal housing across the Global North and South, we propose the term *'digital informalisation' to examine how digital platforms are engendering new and opaque ways of governing housing*, presenting a theoretical and political blind spot. Focusing on *rental housing, our paper unpacks the ways in which new forms of digital management of risk control access and filter populations. In contrast to progressive imaginaries of 'smart' technological mediation, practices of algorithmic redlining, biased tenant profiling and the management of risk in private tenancies and in housing welfare both introduce and extend discriminatory and exclusionary housing practices*"). Italics added. See: Part IV, Chap. 4, Sects. 4.1.4–4.1.4.2.3 of this book. See: Part IV, Chap. 4, Sects. 4.1.4–4.1.4.2.1 of this book (on mortgage redlining). See: Part IV, Chap. 4, Sects. 4.1.2–4.1.4.3 of this book (on algorithmic credit scoring, consumer racism and credit card redlining). See: Part IV, Chap. 4, Sects. 4.1.4–4.1.4.2.3 of this book (on algorithmic redlining). See: Part IV, Chap. 4, Sect. 4.1.4.3 of this book (on "algorithmic redliking"). See: Part IV, Chap. 4, Sect. 4.1.3 of this book (on algorithmic prime-lining).

[94] Angel, María P./Calo, Ryan, "Distinguishing Privacy Law: A Critique of Privacy as Social Taxonomy", *Columbia Law Review*, Volume 124, 2024, pp. 507–551 ("*Privacy disempowers marginalized populations, for example, by rendering their oppression less visible, but empowers these populations to resist unequal treatments* that result from the misuse of their information... [h]ow do we balance privacy against privacy?"). Citron; Danielle Keats Citron/Pasquale, Frank, "Network Accountability for the Domestic Intelligence Apparatus", *Hasting Law Journal*, Volume 62, 2011, 1441, 1444–45; Gray, David/Citron, Danielle Keats, "The Right to Quantitative Privacy", *Minnesota Law Review*, Volume 98, 2013, pp. 62–81.

§§ In many ways, these are «algorithms of oppression»[95] that not only further compound the yawning gap between the rich[96] and the poor,[97] but, and foremost,

[95] Noble, Safiya Umoja, *Algorithms of Oppression*: *How search engines reinforce racism*, New York, New University Press, 2018, pp. 1–248 ("*Run a Google search for "Black girls"—what will you find? "Big Booty" and other sexually explicit terms are likely to come up as top search terms. But, if you type in "white girls," the results are radically different.* The suggested porn sites and unmoderated discussions about "why Black women are so sassy" or "why Black women are so angry" presents a disturbing portrait of Black womanhood in modern society. In *Algorithms of Oppression*, Safiya Umoja Noble challenges the idea that search engines like Google offer an equal playing field for all forms of ideas, identities, and activities. *Data discrimination is a real social problem; Noble argues that the combination of private interests in promoting certain sites, along with the monopoly status of a relatively small number of Internet search engines, leads to a biased set of search algorithms that privilege whiteness and discriminate against people of color, specifically women of color*"). Italics added. See: Part IV, Chap. 4, Sect. 4.1.8 of this book (on biased word embeddings with an entrenched presence on search engines run by tech moguls).

[96] Derenoncourt, Ellora/Kim, Chi Hyun/Kuhn, Moritz/Schularik, Moritz, "The Wealth of Two Nations: The U.S. Racial Wealth Gap, 1860–2020", *The Quarterly Journal of Economics*, Volume 139, Issue 2, 2024, p. 741 ("A large class of commonly discussed policies for reducing racial wealth inequality seeks to reduce gaps in income, savings, and capital gains. These include policies that encourage financial diversification or stock equity holdings among Black households; policies aimed at financial literacy and retirement or savings behavior; or policies aimed at improving educational and labor market outcomes of Black Americans through improved school quality or reductions in discrimination. *Yet on a realistic note, our simulation in Section IV.A shows that even if wealth accumulation conditions had been equal since 1870, the wealth gap would still be 3 to 1 today, and full convergence would be more than 200 years away. Put differently: to close the racial wealth gap in the immediate term via flow parameters, Black Americans would need a substantial positive lead over whites, not "just" more equality*"). Italics added.

[97] Edick, Cole, "Opt-out Privacy Policy Worsens Algorithmic Price Discrimination: The Case of the American Privacy Rights Act", *Minnesota Journal of Law & Inequality*, 2024, p. 1 ("In a data-driven world, data governance has serious implications for social inequality—from civil rights to consumer protection. [1] But the current approach to data governance in the United States may overemphasize *individual* privacy choice at the cost of *collective* approaches to inequality that better mitigate the harms inherent in the datafication of an already-unequal society. [2] This blog post examines that tension, critiquing the exceptions and opt-out mechanisms present in the recently announced American Privacy Rights Act of 2024 (APRA), arguing that such provisions fail to adequately address inequality—in particular, the potential exacerbation of algorithm-powered price discrimination through APRA's loyalty program exception"). But see: Hardt, Moritz, "How big data is unfair: Understanding sources of unfairness in data driven decision making", *Medium*, Archived on Oct. 8, 2014, available at: https://web.archive.org/web/20141008185829/, https://medium.com/@mrtz/how-big-data-is-unfair-9aa544d739de (access: 17.12.2024).

re-entrench deep-seated biases against racial minorities[98] (*bias in, bias out*).[99] Hence the taxonomy of *Algorithmic Dictatorship*, which seamlessly encapsulates both the *algorithmic invidiousness* and *algorithmic unfairness* against the backdrop of which extant machine learning algorithms unfold.[100]

§§ *Algorithmic Dictatorship*[101]—a newly-crafted taxonomy that comprises the hazards of trusting too much on the opinion of machines[102]—equally boasts downstream policy implications.[103] Yet these policy ramifications are anything but elating news. For example, Asians endure gruelling hurdles to renew their passport owing to their cultural heritage.[104]

---

[98] Menasce, Juliana Horowitz/Brown, Anna/Cox, Kiana, "Views of Racial Inequality", *Pew Research Center*, April 9, 2019, available at: https://www.pewresearch.org/social-trends/2019/04/09/views-of-racial-inequality/ (access: 2.12.2024) ("*more than four-in-ten Americans say the country still has work to do to give black people equal rights with whites. Blacks, in particular, are skeptical that black people will ever have equal rights in this country (….) A majority of adults say that being white helps people's ability to get ahead in the country at least a little (59%); 28% say being white neither helps nor hurts and 12% say it hurts.* On the flip side, a majority (56%) sees being black as a disadvantage, with 25% saying it hurts people's ability to get ahead a lot. *About a quarter (26%) say being black neither helps nor hurts and 17% say it helps at least a little. More also say that being Hispanic hurts people's ability to get ahead in this country (51%) than say it helps (18%) or that it neither helps nor hurts (30%).* Opinions are more split when it comes to the impact of being Native American – about the same shares say this hurts as say it neither helps nor hurts, while a smaller share says it helps. *And while a plurality says being Asian neither helps nor hurts, more say it helps (34%) than hurts (21%) people's ability to get ahead*"). Italics added.

[99] Fundamental rights often besmeared further the so-called "Bias in, Bias out". See: Mayson, Sandra G., "Bias In, Bias Out", *Yale Law Journal*, Volume 128, 2019, pp. 2218 and ff and passim. See: Part IV, Chap. 4, Sects. 4.1.10.1–4.1.10.6 of this book (on biased algorithmic risk assessment in criminal procedure law settings). See: Part IV, Chap. 4, Sects. 4.1.1–4.1.1.1 of this book (on biased predictive policing).

[100] Havard, Cassandra Jones, "On The Take": The Black Box of Credit Scoring and Mortgage Discrimination", *Boston University Public Interest Law Journal*, Volume 20, 2011, pp. 241–247 (highlighting that credit scoring if unchecked is an intrinsic, encroached, deep-rooted form of racial discrimination akin to mortgage redlining). See: Part IV, Chap. 4, Sects. 4.1.4–4.1.4.2.1 of this book (on mortgage redlining). See: Part IV, Chap. 4, Sects. 4.1.2–4.1.4.3 of this book (on algorithmic credit scoring, consumer racism and credit card redlining). See: Part IV, Chap. 4, Sects. 4.1.4–4.1.4.2.3 of this book (on algorithmic redlining). See: Part IV, Chap. 4, Sect. 4.1.4.3 of this book (on "algorithmic redliking"). See: Part IV, Chap. 4, Sect. 4.1.3 of this book (on algorithmic prime-lining).

[101] See: Part IV, Chap. 4, Sects. 4.1–4.1.10.6 of this book (on Algorithmic Dictatorship and its chilling effect on democracy).

[102] Karnow, Curtis E. A., "The Opinion of Machines", *The Cambridge Handbook of the Law of Algorithms*, Bartfield, Woodrow (Editor), Cambridge, United Kingdom: Cambridge University Press, 2021, pp. 15 and ff and passim.

[103] Calo, Ryan, "Artificial Intelligence Policy: Primer and Roadmap", *cit.*, pp. 399–435 (412).

[104] Cheng, Selina, "An Algorithm Rejected an Asian Man's Passport Photo for Having "Closed Eyes", December 7, 2016, available at: https://qz.com/857122/an-algorithm-rejected-an-asian-mans-passport-photo-for-having-closed-eyes (access: 19.09.2024) ("Another knock against the robots. Earlier this week, an Asian New Zealander posted a screenshot to Facebook showing his passport photo being rejected for having closed eyes, even though they are visibly open. Twenty-two-year-old Richard Lee—an engineer student from New Zealand who was born in Taiwan and

§§ Worryingly, Turkish women canvassing international opportunities in education are unable to ferret out opportunities[105] other than nursing and gender-related positions alike.[106] Compellingly, unlawful behaviour—or downright unsavoury behaviour—is invariably associated with racial minorities. Especially, albeit not exclusively, to African Americans.[107]

---

is currently studying in Melbourne, Australia—was trying to renew his passport online using an algorithm-based photo-checker operated by New Zealand's department of internal affairs. Lee took the mess-up in stride. "No hard feelings on my part," he told Reuters. *"I've always had very small eyes and facial recognition technology is relatively new and unsophisticated." He also told Mashable that he ended up taking more photos, one of which was accepted by the system.* Passport-photo errors are common—as many as 20% of photos submitted to the system Lee used are rejected, most often for closed eyes—but the complexities are indicative of broader issues with facial-recognition technology. As far back as 2010, Time magazine reported) that people using digital cameras equipped with similar algorithms had similar issues: Cameras would warn that people's eyes (particularly people of Asian descent) were closed when they weren't." Italics added.

[105] Calo, Ryan, "Artificial Intelligence Policy: Primer and Roadmap", *cit.*, pp. 399–435 (412).

[106] Hadzy, Adam, "Biased Bots: Artificial-Intelligence Systems Echo Human Prejudices", *Princeton University*, December 7, 2016, available at: https://www.princeton.edu/news/2017/04/18/biased-bots-artificial-intelligence-systems-echo-human-prejudices (access: 19.09.2024) ("For instance, the machine-learning program associated female names more than male names with familial attributes such as "parents" and "wedding." Male names had stronger associations with career-related words such as "professional" and "salary." Of course, results such as these are often just objective reflections of the true, unequal distributions of occupation types with respect to gender—like how 77 percent of computer programmers are male, according to the U.S. Bureau of Labor Statistics. *This bias about occupations can end up having pernicious, sexist effects.* For example, machine-learning programs can translate foreign languages into sentences that reflect or reinforce gender stereotypes. *Turkish uses a gender-neutral, third person pronoun, "o." Plugged into the online translation service Google Translate, however, the Turkish sentences "o bir doktor" and "o bir hemşire" are translated into English as "he is a doctor" and "she is a nurse"*"). Italics added. See: Part IV, Chap. 4, Sect. 4.1.8 of this book (on biased word embeddings with an entrenched presence on search engines run by tech moguls).

[107] Hadzy, Adam, "Biased Bots: Artificial-Intelligence Systems Echo Human Prejudices", *Princeton University*, December 7, 2016, available at: https://www.princeton.edu/news/2017/04/18/biased-bots-artificial-intelligence-systems-echo-human-prejudices (access: 19.09.2024) ("This paper reiterates the important point that machine-learning methods are not 'objective' or 'unbiased' just because they rely on mathematics and algorithms," said Hanna Wallach, a senior researcher at Microsoft Research New York City, who is familiar with the study but was not involved in it. "Rather, as long as they are trained using data from society, and as long as society exhibits biases, these methods will likely reproduce these biases." *The researchers also found that machine-learning programs more often associated African American names with unpleasantness than European American names.* Again, this bias plays out in people. A well-known 2004 paper by Marianne Bertrand from the University of Chicago and Sendhil Mullainathan of Harvard University sent out close to 5,000 identical resumes to 1,300 job advertisements, changing only the applicants' names to be either traditionally European American or African American. The former group was 50% more likely to be offered an interview than the latter. *Computer programmers might hope to prevent the perpetuation of cultural stereotypes through the development of explicit, mathematics-based instructions for the machine learning programs underlying AI systems. Not unlike how parents and mentors try to instill concepts of fairness and equality in children and students, coders could endeavor to make machines reflect the better angels of human nature.* "The biases that we studied in the paper are easy to overlook when designers are creating systems," Narayanan said. "The biases and stereotypes in our society reflected in our language are complex and longstanding. Rather than

§§ Artificial Intelligence is bound to exact a toll on society far greater than its most immediate repercussions. The shallow, deceitful, hollow, and nomadic promise of algorithmic fairness for all populations stands as the shiniest example. The merest glance at the basic tenets that underpin computer vision—and within which core, facial recognition[108]—elicits the vividly clear impression that such is not the case though.

§§ To begin with, there is a shroud of secrecy[109] around which the source codes[110] that propel Artificial Intelligence[111] revolve.[112] The long overdue promise of *algorithmic democracy* may never see the light of day after all.[113] Bearing those

trying to sanitize or eliminate them, we should treat biases as part of the language and establish an explicit way in machine learning of determining what we consider acceptable and unacceptable"). Italics added.

108 See: Part III, this chapter, Sects. 3.1.5.7–3.1.5.8.1 of this book (on the functional aspects of Critical Artificial Intelligence Studies, with a sharper focus on the perils concerning the deployment of facial recognition technology). See also: Hu, Margaret, "From the National Surveillance State to the Cybersurveillance State", *The Annual Review of Law and Social Science*, Volume 13, 2017, p. 169 ("*in a big data world, a digitized passport system can link to multiple other sources, such as license plate readers, No Fly Lists, and Terrorist Watchlists. Facial recognition technology drawing upon a photo database could potentially link a plethora of digital images of a person, including social media, the internet, photo databases like driver's licenses, live-streaming video, CCTV surveillance, and images obtained from hacking cameras on laptops and digital devices. Biometric data collection and storage are becoming increasingly compulsory through either government identification requirements*, such as digital photo requirements for passports and driver's licenses, or corporate identification requirements, such as biometric access to digital devices"). Italics added.

109 Deeks, Ahsley, "Secret Reason-Giving", *Yale Law Journal*, Volume 129, 2019, passim.

110 Katyal, Sonia K, "The Paradox of Source Code Secrecy", *Cornell Law Review*, Volume 104, 2019, pp. 1183–1236.

111 Pasquale, Frank, *The Black Box Society: The Secret Algorithms that Control Money and Information*. Cambridge, Massachusetts: Harvard University Press, 2015, 1–320 (pp. 8–10 and passim) (noting that biased algorithms, which have underlying discrimination problems, contribute exponentially to further social biases. His most intriguing claim is that such biased algorithms have been incorporated/etched in the bulk of the corporations' informatic system, to the detriment of human kind in an overarching sense).

112 Wexler, Rebecca, "Life, Liberty, and Trade Secrets: Intellectual Property in the Criminal Justice System", *Stanford Law Review*, Volume 70, 2018, pp. 1343 and ff.

113 Okidegbe, Ngozi, "The Democratizing Potential of Algorithms?", *Connecticut Law Review*, Volume 54, 2021, passim.

misgivings very firmly in mind, pundits accordingly aver that *algorithmic transparency* is not only needed,[114] but, and foremost, utterly indispensable.[115] Which is nothing but formulaic: impervious—or shady—algorithmic decision-making breeds inscrutable[116] decisions[117] that serve the pleasure of a hidden agenda.[118]

---

[114] See: Tyler, Tom R., "Does the American Public Accept the Rule of Law? The Findings of Psychological Research on Deference to Authority", *De Paul Law Review*, 56, 2007, pp. 661–664 (stating that "transparency and openness foster the belief that decision-making procedures are neutral"). See also: Coglianese, Cary/Lehr, David, "Transparency and Algorithmic Governance", *Administrative Law Review*, Volume 71, 2019, passim. See also: Doherty, Joseph W./Reville, Robert T./Zakaras, Laura(ed.), *Introduction to Confidentiality, Transparency, and the U.S. Civil Justice System*, Oxford, Oxford University Press, 2012, 1–258 (passim) (noting that the lack of transparency yields sizable social costs). But see: Weizenbaum, Joseph, *Computer Power and Human Reason: From Judgment to Calculation*, 1st edition, New York, W. H. Freeman & Co, 1976, pp. 1–300 (227) ("examines the sources of the computer's powers and offers evaluative explorations of what computers can do, cannot do, and should not be employed to do") (this founding father of Artificial Intelligence presciently noted that we should not entrust Artificial Intelligence-embedded technologies with "tasks that demand wisdom"). Italics added. The approval of rental applications is arguably one of those tasks that should never be entrusted to machines). More on this on Part IV, Chap. 4, Sects. 4.1.4–4.1.4.2.1 of this book.

[115] Brauneis, Robert/Goodman, Ellen P. "Algorithmic Transparency for the Smart City", *Yale Journal of Law and Technology*, Volume 20, 2018, pp. 103–109.

[116] For an on-point breakdown of the distinct levels of opacity arising out of machine learning algorithms: Selbst, Andrew D./Barocas, Solon, "The Intuitive Appeal of Explainable Machines", *Fordham Law Review*, Volume 87, 2018, pp. 1085, 1089–99 (holding that there are plenty reasons for the insurer's ignorance. To begin with, the algorithm entails specialized knowledge to understand. That is, the insurer's employees may lack sufficient knowledge to understand the rationale behind the reasons in view of which the algorithm is producing prices for different customers—personalized pricing. Lastly, even if the insurer himself comprehends how the model operates, it may nonetheless lack expertise to comprehend why it operates the way it does. For that reason, the explainability of machines is a vital, but rather elusive, task. Thence, the famed authors deem it as the "nonintuitive" nature of algorithms. For purposes here, the insurer himself might indeed understand that its Artificial Intelligence-embedded technology formulates higher prices for those who actually access the website at hand, but may fail to come to terms with the fact that the explanation for this fact arises from the website's capacity to proxy for genetic information). See also: Scherer, Matthew U. Scherer, "Regulating Artificial Intelligence Systems: Risks, Challenges, Competencies, and Strategies", *Harvard Journal of Law and Technology*, Volume 29, 2016, pp. 353–369 (frames the crippling problem of opacity as "the possibility that the inner workings of an AI system may be kept secret and may not be susceptible to reverse engineering").

[117] Strandburg, Katherine J., "Rulemaking and Inscrutable Decision Tools", *Columbia Law Review*, Volume 119, 2019, passim.

[118] See: Part V, Chap. 5, Sects. 5.1.2–5.1.6.2.1 of this book (on the thing-centred algorithmic decision-making propelled by a *Controllable* and *Interpretable* Machine Learning that weeds out *Algorithmic Dictatorship* and secures *Algorithmic Common Good*).

§§ More to the point, the rigged data[119] that feeds into the algorithms is often suffused with invidious[120] discrimination[121] that further entrenches and compounds a jarring racial bias[122] with which minorities have been scuffling[123] for a long-winded

---

[119] Sivarajah, Uthayasnkar et al., "Critical Analysis of Big Data Challenges and Analytical Methods", *Journal of Business Research*, Volume 70, 2017; Jetten, Lieke/Sharon, Stephen, "Selected Issues concerning the Ethical Use of Big Data Health Analytics", *Washington & Lee Law Review Online*, Volume 72, 2016, passim.

[120] Griemmelmann, James/Westreich, Daniel, "Incomprehensible Discrimination", *California Law Review Online*, Volume 7, 2018, pp. 164–171.

[121] Prejudiced algorithms are set to be brought to the limelight as they are one foundational basis of *justice prédictive* so voguish in France. No surprise stems from the fact that prejudiced algorithms will feed *justice predictive*—and that is something quite unsavoury and unpalatable in criminal justice indeed. See: Garapon, Antoine, "Les enjeux de la justice predictive", *Juris-Classeur périodique*, Volume 31, 2018, passim. See also: Larret-Chahine, Louis, "Le droit isométrique: un nouveau paradigme juridique né de la justice prédictive», *Archives de Philosophie du Droit*, Volume 60, 2018, pp. 287 and ff and passim. See: Part IV, Chap. 4, Sects. 4.1.10.1–4.1.10.6 of this book (on biased algorithmic risk assessment in criminal procedure law settings, with a sharper focus on COMPAS). See: Part IV, Chap. 4, Sects. 4.1.1–4.1.1.1 of this book (on biased predictive policing).

[122] See: Wonyoung, So, "Which Information Matters? Measuring Landlord Assessment of Tenant Screening Reports", *Housing Policy Debate*, Volume 33, n.º 6, 2023, pp. 1484–1510 (1502) ("*One additional finding of the experiment is that algorithmic scoring can exacerbate this racially unequal landscape in rental agreements not just because the algorithm may be inaccurate, but because landlords may want to follow the risk assessment made by the tenant screening report. This is alarming for low-income tenants, particularly housing voucher holders*"). Italics added.

[123] *Tech, Bias and Housing Initiative, the Promise and Perils of Residential Proptech, Year 1, Research Summary Report, April 2023, TechEquity Collaborative*, p. 11, available at: https://techequity.us/wp-content/uploads/2023/04/TBHI-Y1-Research-Summary-Report.pdf (28.11.2024) ("*Once bad data enters the analysis of one factor, it gets baked into the subsequent process, multiplying the effect that one disadvantageous data point can have on someone's overall housing determination*"). Italics added. See: Part IV, Chap. 4, Sects. 4.1.4–4.1.4.2.1 of this book (on mortgage redlining). See: Part IV, Chap. 4, Sects. 4.1.2–4.1.4.3 of this book (on algorithmic credit scoring, consumer racism and credit card redlining). See: Part IV, Chap. 4, Sects. 4.1.4–4.1.4.2.3 of this book (on algorithmic redlining). See: Part IV, Chap. 4, Sects. 4.1.4.3 of this book (on "algorithmic redliking"). See: Part IV, Chap. 4, Sects. 4.1.3 of this book (on algorithmic prime-lining).

span of time.[124] Just take a step back have a hard look on the multifarious mishaps[125] arising out of facial[126] recognition.[127]

§§ As captioned, technology does not work well for certain racial groups or populations. The pendulum may have already swung too far after all. Tellingly, machine learning algorithms are frequently trained on data where a particular demographic group is underrepresented.[128] This is called *inductive bias*—or *learning bias*[129]—that

---

124 See: Dong et al., Qi, "Imbalanced deep learning by minority class incremental rectification", *IEEE Transactions on Pattern Analysis & Machine Intelligence*, Volume 41, 2019, p. 1367 (posit that "*most existing learning algorithms produce inductive bias (learning bias)* towards the frequent (majority) classes if training data are not balanced, *resulting in poor minority class recognition performance*"). Italics added. See: Part V, Chap. 5, Sect. 5.1.7.4 of this book (on one of the law to control algorithmic decision-making, namely, law number four: data partitioning must be performed—i.e. randomly split an entire dataset into the «training dataset» and the «test dataset»—to accurately predict outcomes in the real world while forestalling «inductive bias» [learning bias]).

125 Is facial recognition helping or hurting law enforcement? Available at: https://innovatrics.com/trustreport/is-facial-recognition-helping-or-hurting-law-enforcement/ (access: 20.09.2024) ("In 2018, a man was accused of stealing a pair of socks from a department store in New York. The man was first identified by a facial recognition algorithm fed with a security camera image. Officer Jones then sent the match to a security guard working at the store. Is this the guy? she asked. The guard confirmed it. The suspect was arrested. However, he could not have stolen the socks. At the time of the theft, he was at the hospital where his son was being born").

126 Facial recognition issues, available at: https://www.thalesgroup.com/en/markets/digital-identity-and-security/government/inspired/facial-recognition-issues (access: 20.09.2034) ("*At its core, facial recognition technology is a form of biometric authentication that uses unique facial features to identify individuals.* It's a powerful tool that offers convenience and security, streamlining processes that once required manual intervention. However, this convenience doesn't come without its share of controversies"). Italics added.

127 Fergus, Rachel, "Biased Technology: The Automated Discrimination of Facial Recognition", *ACLU Minnesota*, February 29, 2024, available at: https://www.aclu-mn.org/en/news/biased-technology-automated-discrimination-facial-recognition (access: 20.09.2024) ("Facial recognition technology is everywhere. We use it to unlock our phones, prove our identity before boarding a plane, and send money from our virtual wallets to buy groceries and baseball tickets. *Because this technology is nearly unavoidable in today's world, it is logical to assume that it is rigorously monitored and regulated. It is not. In fact, the technology is deeply flawed and mostly unregulated. Technology does not exist outside of the biases and racism that are prevalent in our society. Studies show that facial recognition is least reliable for people of color, women, and nonbinary individuals. And that can be life-threatening when the technology is in the hands of law enforcement*"). Italics added. See: Part III, this chapter, Sects. 3.1.5.7–3.1.5.8.1 of this book (on the functional aspects of Critical Artificial Intelligence Studies, with a sharper focus on the perils concerning the deployment of facial recognition technology).

128 Calo, Ryan, "Artificial Intelligence Policy: Primer and Roadmap", *cit.*, pp. 399–435 (412).

129 See: Dong et al., Qi, "Imbalanced deep learning by minority class incremental rectification", *IEEE Transactions on Pattern Analysis & Machine Intelligence*, Volume 41, 2019, p. 1367 (posit that "*most existing learning algorithms produce inductive bias (learning bias)* towards the frequent (majority) classes if training data are not balanced, *resulting in poor minority class recognition performance*"). Italics added. See also: Chandler, Anupam, "The Racist Algorithm", *Michigan Law Review*, Volume 115, n.º 6, 2018, p. 1026 (on racist algorithms, noting that "the possibilities for discriminatory manipulation are legion"). But see: Altenburger, Kristen M./Ho, Daniel E., "When Algorithms Import Private Bias into Public Enforcement: The Promise and Limitations of Statistical Debiasing Solutions", *Journal of Institutional & Theoretical Economics*, Volume 175, 2019,

inordinately befalls members of communities of colour. As a result, machine learning algorithms will fare better recognizing white faces than black or Asian faces. To put it bluntly, facial recognition technology[130] works best on white faces.[131]

---

pp. 97–98 (calls for a "debias predictive algorithms" to assuage racist and/or biased, doctored and bigoted algorithms nevertheless). See also: Hamilton, Melissa, "The Biased Algorithm: Evidence of Disparate Impact on Hispanics", *American Criminal Law Review*, Volume 56, 2019, pp. 1553 and ff and passim. See: Part V, Chap. 5, Sect. 5.1.7.4 of this book (on one of the law to control algorithmic decision-making, namely, law number four: data partitioning must be performed—i.e. randomly split an entire dataset into the «training dataset» and the «test dataset»—to accurately predict outcomes in the real world while forestalling «inductive bias» [learning bias]).

[130] Hu, Margaret, "From the National Surveillance State to the Cybersurveillance State", *The Annual Review of Law and Social Science*, Volume 13, 2017, p. 169 ("*in a big data world, a digitized passport system can link to multiple other sources, such as license plate readers, No Fly Lists, and Terrorist Watchlists. Facial recognition technology drawing upon a photo database could potentially link a plethora of digital images of a person, including social media, the internet, photo databases like driver's licenses, live-streaming video, CCTV surveillance, and images obtained from hacking cameras on laptops and digital devices. Biometric data collection and storage are becoming increasingly compulsory through either government identification requirements*, such as digital photo requirements for passports and driver's licenses, or corporate identification requirements, such as biometric access to digital devices"). Italics added. See: Part IV, Chap. 4, Sects. 4.1.5–4.1.5.2 of this book (on "algorithmic Jim Crow", a travel ban issued during the first Trump Administration to prevent certain individuals from entering the United States of America, which, given its racial undertones, stands as an outgrowth of congeries of laws enacted during the Jim Crow epoch).

[131] Fergus, Rachel, "Biased Technology: The Automated Discrimination of Facial Recognition", *ACLU Minnesota*, February 29, 2024, available at: https://www.aclu-mn.org/en/news/biased-technology-automated-discrimination-facial-recognition (access: 20.09.2024) ("*Studies show that facial recognition technology is biased. The error rate for light-skinned men is 0.8%, compared to 34.7% for darker-skinned women, according to a 2018 study titled "Gender Shades" by Joy Buolamwini and Timnit Gebru, published by MIT Media Lab. A 2019 test by the federal government concluded the technology works best on middle-age white men.* The accuracy rates weren't impressive for people of color, women, children, and elderly individuals"). Italics added.

§§ Why? Quite simply because the training data[132] on which machine learning algorithms leverage on to produce outputs is overrepresented with white faces[133] while falling short of matching the criteria of racial diversity.[134]

§§ It boils down to simple math: more white faces on the training data will equal higher accuracy levels when recognizing white faces. Such as the opposite: less black and yellow faces on the training data will equal lower accuracy when recognizing

---

[132] On the quality—or lack thereof—of training data in the remit of real estate and beyond. See: Wonyoung, So, "Which Information Matters? Measuring Landlord Assessment of Tenant Screening Reports", *Housing Policy Debate*, Volume 33, n.° 6, 2023, pp. 1484–1510 (1501–1502) ("*Algorithmic scoring using criminal records is problematic because training data—a data set that is used to train a machine learning model—is inaccurate and the outcome variable ("desirable tenants") is unclear. For instance, the tenant screening company RealPage produces 11,000 reports using "abbreviated" criminal records, which are cheaper to acquire than full criminal records but do not include details of the resolution* (Kirchner and Goldstein 2020). *An inaccurate model is highly likely to result from tenant screening services using these kinds of abbreviated data, given that it is important to include the final resolution of criminal justice procedures for proper assessment. Moreover, it would be challenging to set an outcome variable for developing this kind of algorithm because it is hard to project a certain criminal outcome into "good" tenant behaviors*"). Italics added. For further developments: Part IV, Chap. 4, Sects. 4.1.4–4.1.4.2.2 of this book. Note, though, that the training of machine learning is long and tedious in that is an error-prone procedure than can ultimately impair future algorithmic decision-making: Price, W. Nicholson Price II, "Regulating Black-Box Medicine", *Michigan Law Review*, Volume 116, 2017, pp. 421–431 (leverages on Google Image's image recognition learning algorithm to shed light on the four-step process by which some algorithms are thoroughly trained. First, the algorithm is shown "a set of known images ('Here are 10,000 pictures of ducks')." Second, the algorithm "develops complex internal rules based on nonlinear processes." Third, the algorithm "tests those rules on a test set ('Which of these are ducks?')." And fourth, the algorithm accordingly adjusts its "internal rules based on the success of the test." These steps are trotted out and repeated many times "until it can accurately and consistently classify the images").

[133] Is facial recognition helping or hurting law enforcement? Available at: https://innovatrics.com/trustreport/is-facial-recognition-helping-or-hurting-law-enforcement/ (access: 20.09.2024) ("*Because facial recognition is a multi-step process, many variables come into play: how new and accurate is the algorithm being used by the police department? What input photo is fed into the algorithm?* How is the list of suspects presented to witnesses for their confirmation or identification? The public tends to focus solely on how accurate the software is").

[134] See: Dong et al., Qi, "Imbalanced deep learning by minority class incremental rectification, *IEEE Transactions on Pattern Analysis & Machine Intelligence*, Volume 41, 2019, p. 1367 (posit that "*most existing learning algorithms produce inductive bias (learning bias)* towards the frequent (majority) *classes if training data are not balanced, resulting in poor minority class recognition performance*"). Italics added. Note, though, that the training of machine learning is long and tedious in that is an error-prone procedure than can ultimately impair future algorithmic decision-making: Price, W. Nicholson Price II, "Regulating Black-Box Medicine", *Michigan Law Review*, Volume 116, 2017, pp. 421–431 (leverages on Google Image's image recognition learning algorithm to shed light on the four-step process by which some algorithms are thoroughly trained. First, the algorithm is shown "a set of known images ('Here are 10,000 pictures of ducks')." Second, the algorithm "develops complex internal rules based on nonlinear processes." Third, the algorithm "tests those rules on a test set ('Which of these are ducks?')." And fourth, the algorithm accordingly adjusts its "internal rules based on the success of the test." These steps are trotted out and repeated many times "until it can accurately and consistently classify the images").

black and yellow faces, thereby compounding both longstanding racial biases[135] and the disparate treatment inflicted upon both racial minorities[136] and vulnerable groups,[137] which are disproportionately targeted by law enforcement agencies.[138]

---

[135] Fergus, Rachel, "Biased Technology: The Automated Discrimination of Facial Recognition", *ACLU Minnesota*, February 29, 2024, available at: https://www.aclu-mn.org/en/news/biased-technology-automated-discrimination-facial-recognition (access: 20.09.2024) ("*Facial recognition automates discrimination. The ACLU-MN is fighting to end law enforcement's use of facial recognition technology in Minnesota. More than a dozen large cities have banned the technology, including Minneapolis, Boston, and San Francisco.* If Minnesota adopts a policy to ban the technology, it would be the first state to do so. Here's why the ACLU-MN will fight this legislative session to ban facial recognition tech:

1. *It gives blanketed and indiscriminate surveillance to authorities to track you.*
2. *It is inaccurate and intensifies racial and gender biases that already exist in law enforcement, which lead to disparate treatment.*
3. It can be used to target and identify vulnerable groups, *such as immigrants and refugees.*
4. It can be used to track your personal movements, including going to abortion clinics or drug treatment.
5. Facial recognition technology violates our Constitutional rights"). Italics added.

[136] Is facial recognition helping or hurting law enforcement? Available at: https://innovatrics.com/trustreport/is-facial-recognition-helping-or-hurting-law-enforcement/ (access: 20.09.2024) ("*An algorithm's reliability depends on many factors. These include the way the neural network was constructed, the choices made by the developer, the dataset used to train the algorithm and how the training has been carried out.* The result also depends on the quality of the input photo. *Some algorithms also perform better or worse depending on the race, gender and age of the person being searched. One of the biggest concerns at present is that algorithms could disproportionately harm black people, as the technology often has higher error rates for people with dark skin*"). Italics added.

[137] Fergus, Rachel, "Biased Technology: The Automated Discrimination of Facial Recognition", *ACLU Minnesota*, February 29, 2024, available at: https://www.aclu-mn.org/en/news/biased-technology-automated-discrimination-facial-recognition (access: 20.09.2024) ("*It's no secret that the Department of Homeland Security and its sub-agencies ICE and Customs and Border Protection have already committed horrific abuses – the ACLU sees the tragic consequences. With facial recognition, these agencies could potentially pinpoint the location of immigrants across the country, marking them for detention and deportation on an unprecedented scale.* In 2017 alone, ICE, DHS and other government agencies used this technology to locate and arrest 400 family members and caregivers of unaccompanied migrant children, separating families and leaving children in detention"). Italics added.

[138] Fergus, Rachel, "Biased Technology: The Automated Discrimination of Facial Recognition", *ACLU Minnesota*, February 29, 2024, available at: https://www.aclu-mn.org/en/news/biased-technology-automated-discrimination-facial-recognition (access: 20.09.2024) ("*Law enforcement and the criminal justice system already disproportionately target and incarcerate people of color. Using technology that has documented problems with correctly identifying people of color is dangerous.* The ACLU-MN has an appalling firsthand example here in Minnesota: We sued on behalf of Kylese Perryman, an innocent young man who was falsely arrested and detained based solely on incorrect facial identification. The injustice does not stop there. A 2020 ACLU study found that since Black people are more likely to be arrested than white people for minor crimes, their faces and personal data are more likely to be in mugshot databases. *That makes them more likely to be misidentified as suspects and forced to sit in lineups – despite the documented lack of accuracy behind all these means*

§§ This turbid digital reality—a black box[139] that spurs invidious Artificial Intelligence-embedded technologies[140]—will further compound the behemoth gulf between the «digitally-chosen» (whom are bound to receive a lenient treatment from law enforcement agencies) and the «digitally-outcast» (whom are poised to be permanently targeted by law enforcement agencies).[141]

---

of supposed identification. The ACLU found that police surveillance cameras are disproportionately installed in Black and Brown neighborhoods, which again exacerbates systematic racism. It is a common assumption that technology is unbiased, and thus infallible. This simply isn't true. All technology is created by people and people are biased"). Italics added.

139 Pasquale, Frank, *The Black Box Society: The Secret Algorithms that Control Money and Information*. Cambridge, Massachusetts: Harvard University Press, 2015, 1–320 (pp. 8–10 and passim) (noting that biased algorithms, which have underlying discrimination problems, contribute exponentially to further social biases. His most intriguing claim is that such biased algorithms have been incorporated/etched in the bulk of the corporations' informatic system, to the detriment of human kind in an overarching sense). See: Part V, Chap. 5, Sect. 5.1.7.2 of this book (on law number two to control algorithmic decision-making, which mandates that black box models must not be entrusted with the task of making high stake decisions—v.g. health and freedom).

140 Chopra, Samir/White, Laurence F., *A Legal Theory of Autonomous Artificial Agents*, Michigan, University of Michigan Press, 2011, pp. 1–264 (5) (2011) ("*There are two views of the goals of artificial intelligence. From an engineering perspective, as Marvin Minsky noted, it is the 'science of making machines do things that would require intelligence if done by men.' From a cognitive science perspective, it is to design and build systems that work the way the human mind does. In the former perspective, artificial intelligence is deemed successful along a performative dimension; in the latter, along a theoretical one.* The latter embodies Giambattista Vico's perspective of verum et factum convertuntur, 'the true and the made are... convertible'; *in such a view, artificial intelligence would be reckoned the laboratory that validates our best science of the human mind. This perspective sometimes shades into the claim artificial intelligence's success lies in the replication of human capacities such as emotions, the sensations of taste, and self-consciousness. Here, artificial intelligence is conceived of as building artificial persons, not just designing systems that are 'intelligent'*") ("*As an example of how agent technologies might evolve to incorporate learning, autonomy, and discretion, consider a hypothetical agent designed to find used books on the Internet. The agent is provided with a list of websites to scour, sample titles with abstracts as learning data to recognize other titles in the genre, and electronic cash accounts with which to make purchases.* The agent is allowed to purchase books within a preset spending limit with discretion in the number, subjects, and individual prices of books bought. Such an agent has a broadly defined goal with enough executive discretion in the choices it makes to optimize satisfaction of that goal. The agent is able to interact with its environment by reading and scanning information at the sites it visits; it interacts with other agents such as selling agents deployed by other users. The agent "moves" from site to site, makes purchases, and reads recommendations provided by book-selling agents. The agent checks recommendations for matches on parameters of interest, and then depending on the outcome, buys more books or declines offers. *It is able to buy titles not on its original list, and to proactively make the decision to buy a new title. Such an agent is able to decide to take an action, in response to inputs it decides to focus on; its interactions on the Internet, in a world populated by other shopping agents and sometimes humans, exemplify autonomous, goal-directed, proactive behavior*"). Italics added. See: Part V, Chap. 5, Sect. 5.1.7.2 of this book (on law number two to control algorithmic decision-making, which mandates that black box models must not be entrusted with the task of making high stake decisions—v.g. health and freedom).

141 The digital society powered by Artificial Intelligence—which will directly impact the fabric of societies worldwide, thereby augmenting the chasm between the «digitally-chosen» and the «digitally-outcast» enabled by a algorithmic discrimination that does nothing but irreparable harm—will compound social stratification. See: Yu, Peter K., "The Algorithmic Divide and Equality in the

§§ On that account, technology is amenable to be weaponized against a thicket of socially undesirables: «the marginalized populations».[142] This stance on the uses of technology will have, in all likelihood, a chilling effect on democracy.[143] Hence, once more, the paramount importance of putting in place befitted legal guardrails to stymie a looming *Algorithmic Dictatorship*[144].

§§ There is therefore a heightened risk of unlawful arrests[145] facing racial minorities. To forestall this harrowing, and gruesome, scenario there is a perceived need to resort to tools that evaluate the degree to which algorithms are biased against marginalized populations, such as the Facial Recognition Vendor Test

---

Age of Artificial Intelligence", *Florida Law Review*, Volume 72, 2020, pp. 355–360 (addresses the issue of algorithmic discrimination).

142 Calo, Ryan, "Artificial Intelligence Policy: Primer and Roadmap", *cit.*, pp. 399–435 (412).

143 Fergus, Rachel, "Biased Technology: The Automated Discrimination of Facial Recognition", *ACLU Minnesota*, February 29, 2024, available at: https://www.aclu-mn.org/en/news/biased-technology-automated-discrimination-facial-recognition (access: 20.09.2024) ("*Facial recognition technology could have a chilling effect on democracy: People may decide not to protest out of fear they'll be documented by this technology.* The Fourth Amendment protects against unreasonable searches and seizures, and it's getting an unnecessary workout. *Faulty facial recognition already has led to searches and arrests of innocent people. "The criminal justice system can really trap people into false arrest, false identification," said Mohamed. "You have to prove that you're innocent because a computer said that you're guilty."* Facial recognition technology isn't all bad. For example, it's been helpful in missing persons cases, and identifying victims of natural disasters and at crash scenes. *But technology is developing much more quickly than the laws we need to protect our rights. Anyone with a smartphone or social media account knows how rapidly technology changes, while legislating can take a long, long time. It is essential to proactively put policies into place that will protect our rights as new and more advanced technology is constantly released. Especially when that technology – and law enforcement members using it - have been shown over and over to be biased toward marginalized groups*"). Italics added.

144 See: Part IV, Chap. 4, Sects. 4.1–4.1.10.6 of this book (on Algorithmic Dictatorship and its chilling effect on democracy).

145 Is facial recognition helping or hurting law enforcement? Available at: https://innovatrics.com/trustreport/is-facial-recognition-helping-or-hurting-law-enforcement/ (access: 20.09.2024) ("*The risk of wrongful arrest is one of the main concerns surrounding the use of facial recognition by law enforcement.* Yet on the other hand, the technology has helped law enforcement to speed up investigations, accurately identify criminals and prevent crimes on countless occasions"). Italics added.

(FRVT).[146] In addition to that, human oversight is duly needed to offset the multiple pitfalls[147] facing facial recognition[148] technology.[149]

---

[146] Is facial recognition helping or hurting law enforcement? Available at: https://innovatrics.com/trustreport/is-facial-recognition-helping-or-hurting-law-enforcement/ (access: 20.09.2024) ("To evaluate the role of bias in facial recognition algorithms, we need relevant data coming from trustworthy sources. *One such source is the Facial Recognition Vendor Test (FRVT) developed by the National Institute of Standards and Technology (NIST). FRVT is one of the world's most respected evaluators of facial recognition algorithms.* It evaluates the accuracy of algorithms submitted by vendors around the world in terms of both verification and identification, and challenges the software with demanding tests that involve using different demographic groups or poor-quality images. Every month, the FRVT releases a report from its Ongoing series, which assesses the performance of facial recognition algorithms across different demographic groups, such as race and gender. *Based on the most recent evaluation , each of the top 150 algorithms are over 99% accurate across black male, white male, black female and white female demographics. Of the top 20 algorithms, accuracy of the highest performing demographic versus the lowest varies by just 0.1%, from 99.8% to 99.7%.* Unexpectedly, white male was the lowest performing of the four demographic groups in the top 20 algorithms. *Not only have NIST evaluations shown that the accuracy of algorithms has improved dramatically in recent years, but they also provide the public and law enforcement agencies with a ranking of the algorithms that perform best in certain areas*"). Italics added.

[147] Is facial recognition helping or hurting law enforcement? Available at: https://innovatrics.com/trustreport/is-facial-recognition-helping-or-hurting-law-enforcement/ (access: 20.09.2024) ("However, at the same time, cities such as San Francisco, Oakland and Boston have banned the use of facial recognition technology by public agencies in order to avoid any of its potential pitfalls. It's clear technology alone cannot be the only source of identifying criminals, but is an all-or-nothing approach really the right answer? *According to many observers, there is another option: increase the transparency on how the technology is used in criminal investigations, and educate communities to its value and risks. That means building better governance for the use of facial recognition systems in law enforcement, to ensure that society as a whole can benefit*"). Italics added.

[148] Hu, Margaret, "From the National Surveillance State to the Cybersurveillance State", *The Annual Review of Law and Social Science*, Volume 13, 2017, p. 169 ("*Facial recognition technology drawing upon a photo database could potentially link a plethora of digital images of a person, including social media, the internet, photo databases like driver's licenses, live-streaming video, CCTV surveillance, and images obtained from hacking cameras on laptops and digital devices.* Biometric data collection and storage are becoming increasingly compulsory through either government identification requirements, *such as digital photo requirements for passports and driver's licenses, or corporate identification requirements, such as biometric access to digital devices*"). Italics added.

[149] Is facial recognition helping or hurting law enforcement?, available at: https://innovatrics.com/trustreport/is-facial-recognition-helping-or-hurting-law-enforcement/ (access: 20.09.2024) ("A recent report by the Georgetown Law Center on Privacy & Technology lists all the shortcomings of the use of facial recognition in law enforcement. The authors claim that both the agencies and the public underestimate the significant degree of human judgement involved. *Before and after the input photo is fed to the algorithm, human operators have to select, edit and review the image, all of which can have a significant impact on the reliability of the algorithm's results. The leads generated by the technology then require further human involvement, whether from the officers or from witnesses who may be required to make a positive identification.* Buy how reliable is this aspect of human identification? Research has shown that an untrained eye – such as that of a witness or even a police officer – can have error rates varying from around 10 to 60% (page 22–23). *However, a 2015 study showed that trained facial forensic examiners – personnel with many years' experience of comparing face images for law enforcement and government agencies – have significantly*

§§ Turning to predictive[150] policing,[151] law enforcement agencies heavily rely upon «heat maps»[152] that seek to predict areas whereby a myriad of criminal activities[153] are most likely to occur.[154] Notwithstanding the ambrosial aims with which these tools are steeped, predictive policing exacts a toll on member of racialized communities.[155]

§§ All too often, African Americans are unlawfully harassed by law enforcement agencies[156] owing to the exceedingly higher likelihood to engage in flagitious activities when compared to white Americans. Predictive policing,[157] to abide by the

---

lower error rates. The way forward, according to some experts, is thus to combine algorithms with conscious human input that is controlled by robust policies and transparent workflows"). Italics added.

[150] *Tech, Bias and Housing Initiative, the Promise and Perils of Residential Proptech, Year 1, Research Summary Report, April 2023, TechEquity Collaborative*, p. 11, available at: https://techequity.us/wp-content/uploads/2023/04/TBHI-Y1-Research-Summary-Report.pdf (28.11.2024) ("And while we know that the *data is predictive, meaning it has little to do with demonstrated behavior of the applicant themself, we do not know exactly where companies get their data*"). Italics added. See: Part IV, Chap. 4, Sects. 4.1.4–4.1.4.2.3 of this book.

[151] See: Part IV, Chap. 4, Sects. 4.1.1–4.1.1.1 of this book (on biased predictive policing).

[152] Calo, Ryan, "Artificial Intelligence Policy: Primer and Roadmap", *cit.*, pp. 399–435 (412).

[153] Predictive Policing Using Machine Learning (with examples), available at: https://www.cogentinfo.com/resources/predictive-policing-using-machine-learning-with-examples (access: 20.09.2024) ("*Trying to predict the patterns of crime and criminal behavior is very effective but challenging to execute in the traditional framework. A few years ago, Crime analysts were expected to go through a large volume of data to understand the underlying patterns and use that information to prevent crimes in the future.* A report by the RAND Corporation found that predictive policing can effectively reduce crime rates. With technologies like machine learning and artificial intelligence, predictive policing has got a new lease on life. *As crime patterns can be automatically identified using this technology, police departments across the world can get to stopping them rather than sifting through a database to identify patterns. The mathematically principled approach is useful in discovering patterns quickly and helping to catch offenders*"). Italics added.

[154] Predictive Policing Using Machine Learning (with examples), available at: https://www.cogentinfo.com/resources/predictive-policing-using-machine-learning-with-examples (access: 20.09.2024) ("*Machine learning plays a crucial role in predictive policing by enabling law enforcement to analyze large amounts of data quickly and accurately.* Machine learning algorithms can identify patterns and trends in crime data that may not be immediately apparent to human analysts. *By analyzing these patterns, machine learning algorithms can make predictions about where and when crimes are most likely to occur, enabling law enforcement to take preventive action*"). Italics added.

[155] Predictive Policing Using Machine Learning (with examples), available at: https://www.cogentinfo.com/resources/predictive-policing-using-machine-learning-with-examples (access: 20.09.2024) ("A report by the University of Chicago found that the machine learning algorithm model developed by the University was able to predict crimes one week before with 90% accuracy. *The model also suggested bias in police response as crimes in wealthy areas led to more arrests while arrests in poor areas dropped. The report further added that the advanced in machine learning and artificial intelligence had generated interest from several governments to use these technologies for predictive policing*"). Italics added.

[156] Calo, Ryan, "Artificial Intelligence Policy: Primer and Roadmap", *cit.*, pp. 399–435 (412).

[157] See: Hu, Margaret, "From the National Surveillance State to the Cybersurveillance State", *The Annual Review of Law and Social Science*, Volume 13, 2017, p. 166 (argues that ubiquitous and

fundamental tenets of algorithmic fairness, should be more much more than a tool to check the box of cost-effectiveness[158] and preventive action.[159] At the end of the

ever-present surveillance of socially undesirables remains at a pitch of degradation of fundamental rights in that Artificial Intelligence-embedded technologies—propelled by tools like Social Radar and Total Information Awareness, TIA, can capture "a *pictorial depiction of the comprehensive cybersurveillance anticipated through the Social Radar system, which anticipated the full integration of drone footage, biometrric data signatures, econometrics, and other intelligence sources to achieve higher-order cybersurveillance inferences. Social Radar appears to trace its philosophical origins to TIA.* The development of TIA after the 9/11 terrorist attacks was guided under the leadership of the newly created Information Awareness Office within DARPA (Harris 2012; Murray 2010). Within this office, TIA was an effort led by retired Navy Vice Admiral John M. Poindexter (Murray 2010), who served as a national security advisor to President Reagan (Harris 2012). *TIA was informed by a philosophy of "predictive policing," which "focuses not on collecting evidence about actual wrongdoing but on the broad collection of information about everyday activities with the intention of detecting (and preventing) future behavior"* (Murray 2010, p. 5). Congress officially defunded TIA in late 2003 (Murray 2010; Slobogin 2008; USA Today 2003). *Experts have nonetheless noted that remnants of the TIA program and its philosophy have persisted*"). Italics added.

[158] Predictive Policing Using Machine Learning (with examples), available at: https://www.cogentinfo.com/resources/predictive-policing-using-machine-learning-with-examples (access: 20.09.2024) ("*Another advantage of predictive policing using machine learning is that it can be cost-effective. By using machine learning algorithms to analyze data, law enforcement agencies can identify areas and times where crimes are most likely to occur.* This can help to reduce the overall cost of policing by reducing the need for patrol officers to be present in all areas at all times. While this may seem not aligned with the mission of reducing crime rates, it is important to consider *that police departments across the world are dealing with increasing crime rates and, as a result, increasing costs*"). Italics added.

[159] Predictive Policing Using Machine Learning (with examples), available at: https://www.cogentinfo.com/resources/predictive-policing-using-machine-learning-with-examples (access: 21.09.2024) ("Machine learning plays a crucial role in predictive policing by enabling law enforcement to analyze large amounts of data quickly and accurately. Machine learning algorithms can identify patterns and trends in crime data that may not be immediately apparent to human analysts. *By analyzing these patterns, machine learning algorithms can make predictions about where and when crimes are most likely to occur, enabling law enforcement to take preventive action*"). Italics added.

day, it boils down to doing the right thing for the right reasons: the gist of both wealth maximization[160] and procedural fairness[161] that should make everyone better off.[162]

§§ Predictive policing, to meet the stringent requirements of procedural fairness,[163] must not lose sight of the fact that the quality of the data[164] that feeds

---

[160] "Wealth maximization provides an ethically attractive norm for social and political choices, such as those made by courts asked to determine whether negligence or strict liability should be the rule for deciding whether an injurer must compensate his victim. Wealth, in a broad sense, is not confined to money. Rather, wealth is fundamentally linked to a utility that enshrines people's preference aversion to risk, being that utility the access to justice system". Itálicos nossos. Seguimos textualmente: Posner, Richard, "Wealth Maximization Revisited", *Notre Dame Journal of Law Ethics & Public Policy*, 2 1987, pp. 85–89; Posner, Richard, *The Problems of Jurisprudence*, Massachusetts, Harvard University Press, 1990, pp. 18–98.

[161] Tyler, Tom R., *Why people obey the law*, New Haven, CT, Yale University Press, 1990, 1–320 (premising his conclusions on a sound body of empirical research, the author states that "*people obey the law if they believe it's legitimate, not because they fear punishment-this is the startling conclusion of Tom Tyler's classic study. Tyler suggests that lawmakers and law enforcers would do much better to make legal systems worthy of respect* than to try to instil fear of punishment. *He finds that people obey law primarily because they believe in respecting legitimate authority*"). Italics added. Tyler, Tom R., "Legitimizing unpopular public policies: Does procedure matter?", in: *Zeitschrift für Reichssoziologie*, Volume 14, 1993, pp. 47–54; Tyler, Tom R., "Governing amid diversity: can fair decision-making procedures bridge competing public interests and values?", in: *Law and Society Review*, Volume 28, 1994, pp. 701–722; Tyler, Tom R., "Psychological models of the justice motive", *Journal of Personality and Social Psychology*, Volume 67, 1994, 850–863; Tyler, Tom R. "The relationship of the outcome and procedural fairness: How does knowing the outcome influences judgments about the procedure?", in: *Social Justice and Research*, Volume 9, 1996, pp. 311–325; Tyler, Tom R. "Compliance with intellectual property laws", in: *Journal of International Law and Politics*, Volume 28, 1997, pp. 101–116; Tyler, Tom R., "Justice and power in civil dispute processing", in: *Sociolegal studies*, Evanston, IL, Northwestern University Press, 1997.

[162] Kaplow, Louis/Shavell, Stephen, Fairness versus Welfare, Cambridge (Massachusetts), Harvard University Press, 2002, pp. 1–578 (the authors, drawing on the Pareto principle, aver that "what makes everyone better off should be preferred").

[163] Tor, A./Gazal-Ayal, O./Garcia, S. M., "Fairness and willingness to accept plea bargain offers", in: *Journal of Empirical Legal Studies*, Volume 7, 2010, pp. 97–116 (drawing upon a body of empirical evidence the authors made the interplay between *overall fairness* of the proceedings and the disputant's willingness to accept plea bargain offers made by the Government). Tyler, Tom R./Smith, H. J./Huo, Y. J., "Member diversity and leadership effectiveness: Procedural justice, social identity, and group dynamics", in: Advances in group processes, B. Markovsky (Ed.), Greenwich, CT: JAI Press, Volume 13, 1996, pp. 33–68. Tyler, Tom R./Lind, Edgar Allan/Huo, Yuen J., "Cultural Values and Authority Relations: The Psychology of Conflict Resolution Across Cultures", in: Psychology, Public Policy and Law, Volume 6, n.º 4, 2000, pp. 1138–1163 (parsing the relationship between high and low levels of power distance values and the relational model of authority); Zimmerman, Nourit/ Tyler, Tom R., "Between Access to Counsel and Access to Justice: A Psychological Perspective", in: Fordham Urban Law Journal, Volume 37, 2010, pp. 473–488 (broaches the "evaluations about neutrality, trust, and respect for the legal system as a whole"—*satisfaction with both procedural fairness and procedural justice* will not lag far behind).

[164] Predictive Policing Using Machine Learning (with examples), available at: https://www.cogentinfo.com/resources/predictive-policing-using-machine-learning-with-examples (access: 21.09.2024) ("Once the data has been preprocessed and the features have been selected, the machine learning model can be trained. The model is trained using labeled data, where the correct outputs are known. *During training, the model adjusts its parameters to minimize the error between*

into the algorithms[165] is conducive to procedural fairness that no evidence-informed law[166] can possibly shrug off. This is the only way forward as to beget both trust in the law[167] and law abidingness[168] of which citizens—law abiding citizens—are so fond of.[169]

---

its predicted outputs and the actual outputs. The accuracy of the model depends on the quality and quantity of the data used for training"). Italics added. Note, though, that the training of machine learning is long and tedious in that is an error-prone procedure than can ultimately impair future algorithmic decision-making: Price, W. Nicholson Price II, "Regulating Black-Box Medicine", *Michigan Law Review*, Volume 116, 2017, pp. 421–431 (leverages on Google Image's image recognition learning algorithm to shed light on the four-step process by which some algorithms are thoroughly trained. First, the algorithm is shown "a set of known images ('Here are 10,000 pictures of ducks')." Second, the algorithm "develops complex internal rules based on nonlinear processes." Third, the algorithm "tests those rules on a test set ('Which of these are ducks?')." And fourth, the algorithm accordingly adjusts its "internal rules based on the success of the test." These steps are trotted out and repeated many times "until it can accurately and consistently classify the images").

165 But see: Kirkpatrick, Keith, "It's not the Algorithm, it's the Data", *Communications of the ACM*, February 2017, Volume 60, n.° 2, 2017 ("critics, however, say tools such as PredPol and CommandCentral *are inherently biased since they rely heavily on reported crimes data, which is often concentrated in areas that are heavily policed, thereby skewing statistics to overrepresent poor or minority communities.* "*We know that we have a history of racially biased policing in the United States, and that has fed into all the data that we have on where arrests have occurred, which crimes are more likely to occur in specific communities, and at which particular times,*" says Jennifer Lynch, senior staff attorney at the Electronic Frontier Foundation. "*That's the data that's being fed into predictive policing algorithms*""). Italics added. See also: Kirkpatrick, Keith, "Battling Algorithmic Bias: How Do We Ensure Algorithms Treat Us Fairly?" *Commun. ACM 59*, Volume 10, 2016, p. 1 and ff and passim.

166 Tyler, Tom, "Methodology in Legal Research", Utrecht Law Review, Volume 13, Issue 3, 2017, pp. 130–131 ("*empirical models have become increasingly popular with the increasing availability of large data sets and the growth in familiarity both with quantitative regression models and qualitative methods for research.* Empirical research has value and it is much better to base policy on evidence than on hunches. In this article it is suggested that the benefits of an empirical approach are enhanced not simply by the use of data, but in particular by drawing upon the power of social science theories. A number of social science theories might potentially be relevant. Because my own background is in psychology, I focus on psychological theories. *These theories allow the law to expand the framework within which issues of law are considered. It is in drawing upon theoretically based social science models of human nature that the law has been especially weak and has a great deal to gain, and not just in the widespread use of research instead of intuition, hunch and supposition*"). Italics added.

167 Tyler, Tom R., Trust in the Law, New York, NY: Russell-Sage, 2002, passim.

168 Tyler, Tom R., "Trust and Law Abidingness: A Proactive Model of Social Regulation", Boston University Law Review, Volume 81, 2001, pp. pp. 359 and ff and passim.

169 Tyler, Tom R., *Why People Obey the Law*. New Jersey, United States of America: Princeton University Press, 2006, pp. 1–320 (92–110) (Professor Tom R. Tyler contends that lawmakers and law enforcers should make legal systems worthy of respect instead of trying to instil fear of punishment onto disputants. He finds that laypeople obey law primarily because they believe in respecting legitimate authority when such respect is due. Which means that legal systems must be worthy of respect before demanding for respect).

§§ Predictive policing, if nothing else, should hold citizens to the same standards or the Rule of Law will otherwise backslide[170] beyond repair.[171] Predictive policing,[172] if anything, should be underpinned by procedural fairness that forms part of a broader legal apparatus. For a very straightforward reason: procedural fairness is deeply woven into the fabric of Rule of Law.[173]

[170] Strikingly, the newest developments posed by the "collect-it-all" technologies are slated to create a slew of sizzling hot challenges to the sustainability of the Rule of Law. See: Hu, Margaret, "From the National Surveillance State to the Cybersurveillance State", *The Annual Review of Law and Social Science*, Volume 13, 2017, pp. 162–163 ("*policymakers view these technological developments, including biometric technologies, as tools with the potential to identify individuals who may pose a threat to national and homeland security and to prevent crime and terrorism. One example of technology intended for risk assessment and threat management is the post-9/11 program Total Information Awareness (TIA).* TIA was the progeny of the Defense Advanced Research Projects Agency (DARPA) in the US Department of Defense. *TIA can be understood as a "collect-it-all" data surveillance program. TIA was not explicitly identified as a collect-it-all program—this phrase originated with the Snowden disclosures.* One National Security Agency (NSA) slide described the NSA's procedure as "collect-it-all" (Greenwald 2014b). *Collect-it-all efforts like TIA embody a philosophy that aspires to preventive policing. Mass data collection is construed as a tool to assess and prevent future threats* (Murray 2010). *In TIA and other programs tested or adopted after 9/11, biometric database screening and analysis have emerged as a preferred method for tracking, identifying, and establishing identity-based inferences in counterterrorism*"). Italics added. See also: Ball, Kirstie, and Frank Webster (Eds.), *The Intensification of Surveillance: Crime, Terrorism & Warfare in the Information Age*, London, UK: Pluto Press, 2007; Guzik, Keith, "Discrimination by Design: Predictive Data Mining as Security Practice in the United States' 'War on Terrorism'", *Surveillance and Society*, 7 (1), 2009, pp. 1–17.

[171] See: Raz, Joseph, "The Rule of Law and its Virtue", *The Authority of Law: Essays on Law and Morality*. Oxford: Clarendon Press, 1979, pp. 210–214 (on the quintessential value of Rule of Law); Cass, Ronald A., *The Rule of Law in America*. Baltimore, Maryland: The Johns Hopkins University Press, 2001, p. 17 (noting that a "central element of the Rule of law, constraint from external authority…helps assure that the process of government, *rather than the predilections of the individual decision-maker*") Italics added.

[172] But see: Cappers, Ben, "Afroturism, Critical Race Theory, and Policing in the year of 2044", *The New York Law Review*, Volume 94, Number 1, April 2019, 2029, p. 1 ("*In 2044, the United States is projected to become a "majority-minority" country, with people of color making up more than half of the population. And yet in the public imagination—from Robocop to Minority Report, from Star Trek to Star Wars, from A Clockwork Orange to 1984 to Brave New World—the future is usu ally envisioned as majority white. What might the future look like in year 2044, when people of color make up the majority in terms of numbers, or in the ensuing years, when they also wield the majority of political and economic power? And specifically, what might policing look like? This Article attempts to answer these questions by examining how artists, cybertheorists, and speculative scholars of color—Afrofuturists and Critical Race Theorists—have imagined the future.* What can we learn from Afrofuturism, the term given to "speculative fiction that treats African-American themes and addresses African-American concerns [in the con text of] techno culture?" And what can we learn from Critical Race Theory and its "father" Derrick Bell, who famously wrote of space explorers to examine issues of race and law? *What do they imagine policing to be, and what can we imagine policing to be in a brown and black world?*"). Italics added.

[173] Waldron, Jeremy, "The Rule of Law and the Importance of Procedure", *New York Public Law and Legal Theory*, 2010, p. 4 (notes that "*the Rule of Law is violated when due attention is not paid to these procedural matters or when the institutions that are supposed to embody this procedure are undermined or interfered with*". Further down this author would admit that there are some substantive dimensions of Rule of Law, such as respect for right for property and presumption of liberty and so

§§ Predictive policing, to be even-handed, must treat citizens just the same.[174] Predictive policing, which is eerily undergirded by Artificial Intelligence-powered technologies,[175] must accordingly fight shy of the remnants of the worst of human

---

forth); Taekema, Sanne, "The Procedural Rule of Law: Examining Waldron's Argument on Dignity and Agency", *Jahrbuch für Recht und Ethik*, Band 21, 2013, pp. 133 ff (contends that "Waldron's understanding of the Rule of Law as procedural which demands the opportunity for individuals to contest legal decisions in the formalized processes of courts and tribunals").

174 Which is why the onset of the age of Artificial Intelligence will put the Rule of Law to the test like never before. Recall, the Rule of Law is a functional barrier—aimed at clamping down a host of unlawful deeds undertaken by those in power—that must not be teared apart or criminal procedure law will be otherwise despoiled from its intrinsic validity and vitality. See: Raz, Joseph, "The Rule of Law and its Virtue", *The Authority of Law: Essays on Law and Morality*, *cit.*, p. 224 (asserts adamantly that the Rule of Law is aimed at cushioning the hazards of abuse perpetrated by those in power. In this vein, Raz contends that "the law inevitably creates a great danger of arbitrary power – the Rule of Law is designed to minimize the danger created by the law itself…*Thus the (R)ule of (L)aw is designed to minimize the danger created by law itself…Thus the (R)ule of (L)aw is a negative virtue…the evil which is avoided is evil which could only have been caused by the law itself*"). Italics added. See: Part V, Chap. 5, Sect. 5.1.1.1 of this book (on the central tenets of Rule of Law that lends itself to a beacon of justice amidst the sepulchral darkness that is about to take hold). See: Part V, Chap. 5, Sect. 5.1.1.2 of this book (on the central tenets of Procedural Rule of Law that lends itself to a lighthouse of justice that allows citizens to challenge the pearls of algorithmic wisdom in a court of law).

175 The inception of the era of omnipotent Artificial Intelligence is about to revive the overriding importance of the dichotomy between *censory jurisprudence* (what law actually is and/or looks like) and *expository jurisprudence* (what law should do and/or be to halt the weaponization of Artificial Intelligence by those in power against *socially undesirables*). This dyad has been suitably tailored by Jeremy Bentham. See: Bentham, Jeremy, *An Introduction to the Principles of Morals and Legislation.* London: Great Books in Philosophy, Prometheus Books, 1988, 1–352 (293–294) (Jeremy Bentham's work on "the Principles of Morals and Legislation emerges from its historic roots in hedonism and teleology as a scientific attempt to assess the moral content of human action by focusing on its results or consequences. Proceeding from the assumption that human beings desire pleasure (and avoid pain), Bentham's unique perspective, known as utilitarianism, is used to construct a fascinating calculus for determining which action to perform when confronted with situations requiring moral decision-making the goal of which is to arrive at the "*greatest happiness of the greatest number*." Toward this end, he endeavours to delineate the sources and kinds of pleasure and pain and how they can be measured when assessing one's moral options. Bentham supports his arguments with discussions of intentionality, consciousness, motives, and dispositions"). This is not to say that we embrace Bentham's utilitarianism—so harshly criticized in Hart's *Concept of Law*—or the claim according to which an understanding of the Rule of Law presupposes a good understanding of law in a given country or community. Yet, there is a high degree of academic accuracy in Bentham's distinction when it comes to differentiating *expository jurisprudence—explaining what law is*—and *censorial jurisprudence—explaining what law ought to be.* As for effective access to justice and the procedural approach to the Rule of Law in the purview of criminal procedure law, there is markedly clear line between what legal officials are—purveyors of procedural fairness—and what an effective access to justice ought to be—a place whereby social inequalities caused by the era of artificial intelligence are to be buffered (criminal procedure law settings) in a swift, prompt, and streamlined manner. Or irreparable damages may otherwise occur. See: Part V, Chap. 5, Sect. 5.1.1.1 of this book (on the central tenets of Rule of Law that lends itself to a beacon of justice amidst the sepulchral darkness that is about to take hold). See: Part V, Chap. 5, Sect. 5.1.1.2 of this book (on the central tenets of Procedural Rule of Law that lends itself to a lighthouse of justice that allows citizens to challenge the pearls of algorithmic wisdom in a court of law).

nature. The way forward is the creation of anti-discriminatory algorithms[176] that weeds out both invidiousness and discrimination[177] while breeding algorithmic fairness in the remit of predictive policing. Yet there is plenty to be done to attain this encomiastic goal.[178]

§§ Although the interaction between humans and machines[179] is shaping up to becoming a routine[180] and as the heated debate on how to shrewdly regulate predictive policing trudges on, few, if any, befitted measures have been taken to level the playing field between races.

§§ To illustrate, law enforcement agencies have refrained themselves from engaging in bespoke inward techniques to predict which police officers have higher likelihood to engage in flagitious behaviour under the guise of either police brutality[181] or unjustified use of force by police officers[182], race wise.

§§ There is therefore a perceived paucity of cutting-edge proposals to ameliorate predictive policing and crime prevention in an overarching sense.[183] The kerfuffle around which inscrutable technology[184] revolves is not to be bogged down to the shortfall of innovative approaches to entertain the pinpointed issues nonetheless.

---

[176] Bornstein, Stephane, "Antidiscriminatory Algorithms", *Alabama Law Review*, Volume 70, 2018, pp. 519–570.

[177] Ifeoma, Ajunwa, "The Paradox of Automation as Anti-Bias Intervention", *Cardozo Law Review*, Volume 41, 2020, pp. 1672, 1726–1727 (on the unwanted effects of automation, which can also be transplanted to criminal justice).

[178] *Tech, Bias and Housing Initiative, the Promise and Perils of Residential Proptech, Year 1, Research Summary Report, April 2023, TechEquity Collaborative*, p. 11, available at: https://techequity.us/wp-content/uploads/2023/04/TBHI-Y1-Research-Summary-Report.pdf (28.11.2024) ("And while we know that the *data is predictive, meaning it has little to do with demonstrated behavior of the applicant themself, we do not know exactly where companies get their data*"). Italics added. See: Part IV, Chap. 4, Sects. 4.1.4–4.1.4.2.3 of this book.

[179] Tegmark, Max, *Life 3.0: Being Human in the Age of Artificial Intelligence*. New York: Knopf, 2018, pp. 1–384 (pp. 24 and ff) (charts the path ahead for a wide range of intelligences, including artificial intelligence in the digital age). There is a handful of authors that wonder if artificial intelligence can mimic not only human intelligence but, and foremost, human behaviour. Amongst whom stands: Russel, Stuart, Norvig, Peter, *Artificial Intelligence: A Modern Approach*. London: United Kingdom, Pearson, 2018, passim.

[180] Cuellar, Mariano-Florentino, "A Common Law for the Age of Artificial Intelligence: Incremental Adjudication, Institutions, and Relational Non-Arbitrariness", *Columbia Law Review*, Volume 119, 2020, pp. 1773–1775 (this author presciently posits that "(t)he coevolution of human and artificial intelligence – what we could call our dance with machines – is well on its way to becoming routine"); Remus, Dana/Levy, Frank, "Can Robots be Lawyers? Computers, Lawyers, and the Practice of Law", *Georgetown Journal of Legal Ethics*, Volume 30, 2018, pp. 501 and ff and passim.

[181] Calo, Ryan, "Artificial Intelligence Policy: Primer and Roadmap", *cit.*, pp. 399–435 (412).

[182] Crawford, Kate/Calo, Ryan, "There is a Blind Spot in AI Research", *Nature*, Volume 538, 2016, pp. 311 and ff and passim.

[183] See: Part IV of this book.

[184] For an on-point breakdown of the distinct levels of opacity arising out of machine learning algorithms: Selbst, Andrew D./Barocas, Solon, "The Intuitive Appeal of Explainable Machines", *Fordham Law Review*, Volume 87, 2018, pp. 1085, 1089–99 (holding that there are plenty reasons for the insurer's ignorance. To begin with, the algorithm entails specialized knowledge to understand. That is, the insurer's employees may lack sufficient knowledge to understand the rationale

§§ Tellingly, only rarely since the emergence of Artificial Intelligence-embedded technologies have policymakers deftly used the redoubtable power to urge industry stakeholders to shed a keen light around which the construction of those invasive technologies revolves. Which, I may venture to add, is wholly unbecoming in this regard. Absent such a brawny intervention, citizens 'lives, freedom, property, and healthcare[185] hangs on the balance.[186]

§§ To put it bluntly, lawmakers' grudging reluctance to pin down a definition onto page with regard to Artificial Intelligence-embedded technologies that may incur on the hazard of fraying the fabric of citizens' fundamental rights should be looked askance. Especially, albeit not exclusively, when it comes to the use of force—likewise, the affordance of healthcare to patients in dire need of receiving one—arising out of Artificial Intelligence-borne decision-making.

---

behind the reasons in view of which the algorithm is producing prices for different customers—personalized pricing. Lastly, even if the insurer himself comprehends how the model operates, it may nonetheless lack expertise to comprehend why it operates the way it does. For that reason, the explainability of machines is a vital, but rather elusive, task. Thence, the famed authors deem it as the "nonintuitive" nature of algorithms. For purposes here, the insurer himself might indeed understand that its Artificial Intelligence-embedded technology formulates higher prices for those who actually access the website at hand, but may fail to come to terms with the fact that the explanation for this fact arises from the website's capacity to proxy for genetic information). See also: Scherer, Matthew U. Scherer, "Regulating Artificial Intelligence Systems: Risks, Challenges, Competencies, and Strategies", *Harvard Journal of Law and Technology*, Volume 29, 2016, pp. 353–369 (frames the crippling problem of opacity as "the possibility that the inner workings of an AI system may be kept secret and may not be susceptible to reverse engineering").

[185] See: Bartlett, Robert/Morse, Adair/Wallace, Nancy/Stanton, Richard, "Algorithmic Discrimination and Input Accountability Under the Civil Rights Acts", *Berkeley Technology Law Journal*, Volume 36, 2021, pp. 675–736 (675) ("the disproportionate burden of COVID-19 among communities of color and a necessary renewed attention to racial inequalities have lent new urgency to concerns that algorithmic decision-making can lead to unintentional discrimination against members of historically marginalized groups").

[186] Cracking the Code: the Black Box Problem of Ai, available at: https://scads.ai/cracking-the-code-the-black-box-problem-of-ai/ (access: 21.09.2024) ("Artificial intelligence (AI) is increasingly becoming integrated into our daily lives, from virtual assistants to self-driving cars. Despite AI having the potential to revolutionize the way we live and work, it also presents unique challenges. One of the most significant challenges is the "black box" problem. *The black box problem refers to the lack of transparency and interpretability of AI algorithms. As a matter of fact, it is difficult to understand how an AI system arrives at its conclusions or predictions. This poses a significant challenge. Decisions made by AI can have serious consequences, such as in healthcare or financial sectors*"). Italics added. See: Part V, Chap. 5, Sects. 5.1.7–5.1.7.5 of this book (on the five laws to control algorithmic decision-making). See: Part V, Chap. 5, Sects. 5.1.8–5.1.8.5 of this book (on the five laws to interpret algorithmic decision-making). See: Part V, Chap. 5, Sects. 5.1.2–5.1.6.2.1 of this book (on the thing-centred algorithmic decision-making propelled by a *Controllable* and *Interpretable* Machine Learning that weeds out *Algorithmic Dictatorship* and secures *Algorithmic Common Good*. It is worth recalling that the **thing-centred algorithmic decision-making** seeks to unwind the perils arising out of the lack of theoretical underpinnings facing the **human-centred algorithmic decision-making**, as extensively fleshed out Part III, this chapter, Sects. 3.1.4.3 and 3.1.4.4 of this book). See: Part V, Chap. 5, Sect. 5.1.7.5 of this book (on Algorithmic Common Good, with a sharper focus on the dire need of algorithmic auditing, undertaken by external auditors that must be given full access to the dataset used to train the running models).

§§ More to the point, what is the benchmark to gauge the extent to which the AI-enabled decision that led to the use of force is warranted? Relatedly, what is the yardstick used by AI-embedded technologies to ascertain whether and to what extent a patient should be granted appropriated healthcare?[187]

§§ Conversely, what is the touchstone used by AI-entrenched technologies to grant loans to some citizens while downrightly spurning to grant loans to other citizens?[188] Casts broadly, what are the guidelines,[189] if any, that enable AI-embedded technologies (e.g. self-driving cars)[190] to timely identify pawns that intend to cross the

---

[187] Cracking the Code: the Black Box Problem of Ai, available at: https://scads.ai/cracking-the-code-the-black-box-problem-of-ai/ (access: 21.09.2024) ("*The black box problem has significant implications for AI's use in healthcare. AI algorithms are increasingly used to diagnose diseases and recommend treatments.* For instance, AI-based diagnostic tools can identify patterns in medical images such as X-rays, MRIs, and CT scans. *However, the lack of transparency in the algorithm's decision-making process makes it difficult to validate the tool's accuracy and understand how it arrives at its diagnosis*"). Italics added. But see: Weizenbaum, Joseph, *Computer Power and Human Reason: From Judgment to Calculation*, 1st edition, New York, W. H. Freeman & Co, 1976, pp. 1–300 (227) ("examines the sources of the computer's powers and offers evaluative explorations of what computers can do, cannot do, and should not be employed to do") (this founding father of Artificial Intelligence presciently noted that we should not entrust Artificial Intelligence-embedded technologies with with "tasks that demand wisdom"). Italics added. The approval of rental applications is arguably one of those tasks that should never be entrusted to machines. More on this on Part IV, Chap. 4, Sects. 4.1.4–4.1.4.2.1 of this book. See: Part V, Chap. 5, Sect. 5.1.7.2 of this book (on law number two to control algorithmic decision-making, which mandates that black box models must not be entrusted with the task of making high stake decisions—v.g. health and freedom).

[188] Cracking the Code: the Black Box Problem of Ai, available at: https://scads.ai/cracking-the-code-the-black-box-problem-of-ai/ (access: 21.09.2024) ("*Similarly, in finance, AI algorithms are used for fraud detection, credit scoring, and trading decisions.* The lack of transparency and interpretability makes it difficult to understand how the algorithm arrived at a particular decision. It also makes it challenging to identify and rectify errors or biases"). Italics added. See: Part IV, Chap. 4, Sects. 4.1.4–4.1.4.2.1 of this book (on mortgage redlining). See: Part IV, Chap. 4, Sects. 4.1.2–4.1.4.3 of this book (on algorithmic credit scoring, consumer racism and credit card redlining). See: Part IV, Chap. 4, Sects. 4.1.4–4.1.4.2.3 of this book (on algorithmic redlining). See: Part IV, Chap. 4, Sects. 4.1.4.3 of this book (on "algorithmic redliking"). See: Part IV, Chap. 4, Sect. 4.1.3 of this book (on algorithmic prime-lining).

[189] The worrisome challenges posed by the up-and-coming and rough around the edges self-driving cars are legion. See: Teoh, Eric/Kidd, David G., "Rage Against the Machine? Google's Self-Driving Versus Human Drivers", *Journal of Safety Research*, Volume 63, 2019, pp. 57–59 and passim (on the legal quandaries laid bare by the self-driving cars).

[190] Cracking the Code: the Black Box Problem of Ai, available at: https://scads.ai/cracking-the-code-the-black-box-problem-of-ai/ (access: 21.09.2024) ("*To understand the black box problem, let's take an example of a self-driving car. The car's AI system is designed to make decisions based on various inputs such as road signs, sensors, and cameras. As a result, if the car gets into an accident, it may be challenging to determine what went wrong and why the AI system made a particular decision additionally.* The AI algorithm's decision-making process is often opaque and may involve complex calculations, making it difficult for humans to interpret"). Italics added. See: Part III, this chapter, Sects. 3.1.5.9–3.1.5.9.3 of this book (on Critical Artificial Intelligence Studies, with a sharper focus on the functional shortcomings facing self-driving vehicles).

road and stop accordingly?[191] What are the foundations upon which stands the storage and processing of citizens' personal data by corporations, mostly from the standpoint of data-contextualization[192]? Last but not least, what are the stringent requirements, if any, used by Artificial Intelligence-embedded technologies to suggest[193] to the sitting judge[194] that one citizen should be jailed while another should walk free?

§§ The answer to the foregoing cluster of questions is an unsettling «we don't really know». Which, if nothing else, beckons a harshly unpleasant distrust on AI-embedded technologies[195] that currently run afoul with the shallowest level of

[191] See: Part III, this chapter, Sects. 3.1.5.9–3.1.5.9.3 of this book (on Critical Artificial Intelligence Studies, with a sharper focus on the functional shortcomings of self-driving vehicles). See also: Gless, Sabine/Silvermann, Emile/Weigend, Thomas, "If Robots Cause Harm, Who Is to Blame? Self-Driving Cars and Criminal Liability", *New Criminal Law Review: An International and Interdisciplinary Journal*, Volume 19, No. 3 (Summer 2016), 2016, pp. 412–436.

[192] See: De Filippi/Primavera/Wright, Aaron, *Blockchain and the Law. Rule of Code.* Cambridge: Harvard University Press, 2019, pp. 196–200 (presciently addresses the hazard of the data collated by enterprises fall prey to decontextualization). If lawmakers fail to entertain proficiently this issue, somewhere along the line the data fed into the machines will spawn algorithmic discrimination or algorithmic biases in criminal justice. Which means that algorithmic biases—caused by data decontextualization—will ripple forward to the detriment of a sought-after algorithmic fairness.

[193] Casey, Anthony J./Niblett, Anthony, "Self-driving Laws", *University of Toronto Law Journal*, Volume 66, 2016, pp. 429–435 (contend that "as more information is generated, and the evolutionary algorithm updates and become a *better forecaster, we imagine that judges will increasingly rely on the advice of the algorithm*").

[194] The rise of digital justice—or algorithmic justice—is set to usher in the absolute power of algorithms, which will make judges' life considerably easier. Soon enough, judges will blindly follow the pearls of wisdom breed by inscrutable algorithms which will—keenly and promptly—point out to them the best course of action to be taken in a given procedure. See: Millar, Jason/Kerr, Ian, "Delegation, Relinquishment and Responsibility: The Prospect of Expert Robots", *Robot Law*, Ryan Calo/Froomkin, A. Michael/Kerr, Ian. Cheltenham: Edward Elgar Publishing, 2016, pp. 102, 106–107 (as these authors aptly put it "*we will rely on robots without really knowing why – simply because their algorithms provide the greatest number of successful outcomes.* We have already seen this in Google's search approach. Neither Larry (Page) nor Sergey (Brin) (nor any other Google employee) knowns exactly why one particular web page is a better result than another. *When the click patterns say it is, that's good enough. No semantic or causal analysis is required...Like the ancients, we will, quite rationally, come to rely upon them, knowing full well that we cannot necessarily explain the reasons for their decisions*"). Italics added. See: Part V, Chap. 5, Sect. 5.1.7.1 of this book (on law number one to control algorithmic decision-making, which mandates that whoever develops and/or deploys machines to undertake a given task must be held criminal accountable for the Hard-AI crimes the latter perpetrates).

[195] Ashley, Kevin D., *Artificial Intelligence and Legal Analytics. New Tools for Law Practice in the Digital Age.* Cambridge: Cambridge University Press, 2018, passim.

predictability[196] and accuracy.[197] The doors of *Algorithmic Dictatorship*—for which I have been iteratively drawing a keen attention to—are ajar slightly.[198]

§§ To stave off such a loathsome scenario, there have been ongoing efforts to deftly tackle the nuances of this sweltering topic, but—despite the groundswell of angelical intentions with which the great bulk of these staggering efforts are soaked—to no avail.[199] Some pundits accordingly contend that we are steadfastly heading towards a predictive digital justice[200] against the backdrop of which criminal cases will be briskly dealt with.[201]

§§ But make no mistake: predictive digital justice will introduce a *Digital Darwinism* against the backdrop of which the survival of the economically fittest[202] will unfold. *Digital Darwinism*, which, in turn, is poised to usher in, and herald, a

---

[196] Recall, algorithms make their inferences and draw their conclusions in a manner eerily unknown, even for the cohort of programmers that designed them. This is deemed *black box*, that further enhances the shroud of mystery under which algorithms are cloaked. See, for a compelling account of AI black box: Ver: Bathaee, Yavar, "The Artificial Intelligence Black Box and the Failure of Intent and Causation", *Harvard Journal of Law and Technology*, n.º 37, 2018, p. 901 (adduces that "*one possible reason AI may be a black box to humans is that it relies on machine-learning algorithms that internalize data in ways that are not easily audited or understood by humans* (...)" "*first, a lack may arise from the complexity of the algorithm's structure, such as with deep neural network, which consists of thousands of artificial neurons working together in a diffuse way to solve a problem. This reason for AI being a black box is referred to as "complexity". Second, the lack of transparency may arise because the AI is using a machine-learning algorithm that relies on geometric relationships that humans cannot visualize, such as with support vector machines. This reason for AI being a black box is referred to as "dimensionality"*"). Italics added. But see: Pearl, Judea, *Causality*, 2nd edition, Cambridge, Cambridge University Press, 2009 (on the fundamental tenets of causality). But see: Kilbertus, Niki/Carulla, Mateo Rojas/Parascandolo, Giambattista/Hardt, Moritz/Janzing, Dominik/Schoellkopf, Bernhard, "Avoiding Discrimination through Causal Reasoning", *Advances in Neural Information Processing Systems*, I. Guyon, U. V. Luxburg, S. Bengio, H. Wallach, R. Fergus, S. Vishwanathan, and R. Garnett (Eds.), Vol. 30. Curran Associates, Inc., 2017, pp. 656–666 (arguing that is feasible to avoiding discrimination through a granular and fine-grained causal reasoning). See: Part V, Chap. 5, Sects. 5.1.1.5.2.2–5.1.1.5.2.2.1.4 of this book (on the fundamental shift away from causation to correlations in algorithmic decision-making).

[197] Lauritsen, Marc, "Towards a Phenomenology of Machine-Assisted Legal Work", *Journal of Robotics, Artificial Intelligence & Law*, Volume 1, Issue 2, 2018, pp. 67–79.

[198] See: Part IV, Chap. 4, Sects. 4.1–4.1.10.6 of this book (on Algorithmic Dictatorship and its chilling effect on democracy).

[199] Whooping efforts that should also be poured in as to ascertain the extent to which algorithms can usher in an era of fair use in the realm of law. See: Yu, Peter K, "Can Algorithms Promote Fair Use?", *Fiu Law Review*, Volume 14, 2020, pp. 328 and ff and passim.

[200] Against the background of which an eerily predictive criminal law is unfolding in France. See: Brigant, Jean-Marie, "Les risques accentués d'une justice pénale predictive", *Archives de Philosophie du Droit*, Volume 60, 2018, p. 239 (on the so-called predictable criminal justice).

[201] Such a tournant towards a predictive justice will spawn deleterious effects that can take the shape of a predictive criminal justice run by machines accountable to no one. See in French doctrine: Brigant, Jean-Marie, "Les risques accentués d'une justice pénale prédictive», *Archives de Philosophie du Droit*, Volume 60, 2018, pp. 238 and ff and passim.

[202] One of the burgeoning developments that must not go unchecked is the one posed by transhumanism—a symbol of economic prowess that enable the wealthy to enhance their lifespan while bettering their overall conditions of life—, which is an epiphenomenon that has been timely parsed

criminal justice than leans toward the rich and privileged[203] while disfranchising the poor[204] and less fortunate from their inalienable fundamental rights.[205] The mayhem of an abhorring plutocracy will therefore ensue while dragging the criminal system of justice to the shifting sands of gruelling injustice that will further chastise the impecunious.[206]

§§ Against this background, lifechanging decisions—those intrinsically related to citizens' lives and freedom—should never be commissioned to machines alone.[207]

---

by the French doctrine. See: Lassere, Valérie, "Justice prédictive et transhumanisme", *Archives de Philosophie du Droit*, Volume 60, 2018, pp. 311 and ff and passim.

[203] As a result, prejudiced algorithms are set to be brought to the limelight as they are one foundational basis of *justice prédictive* so voguish in France. No surprise stems from the fact that prejudiced algorithms will feed *justice predictive*—and that is something quite unsavoury and unpalatable in criminal justice indeed. See: Garapon, Antoine, "Les enjeux de la justice predictive", *Juris-Classeur périodique*, Volume 31, 2018, passim. See also: Larret-Chahine, Louis, "Le droit isométrique: un nouveau paradigme juridique né de la justice prédictive», *Archives de Philosophie du Droit*, Volume 60, 2018, pp. 287 and ff and passim.

[204] Soss, Joe, Richard C. Fording, and Sanford F. Schram, *Disciplining the Poor: Neoliberal Paternalism and the Persistent Power of Race*. Chicago: University of Chicago Press, 2011.

[205] Thereby furthering the yawning gap between rich—that can adroitly harness artificial intelligence to advance their goals and shady agendas—and poor—that grapple to meet basic needs and are automatically excluded from the equation of digital society powered by Artificial Intelligence—which will directly impact the fabric of societies worldwide, thereby augmenting the chasm between the «digitally-chosen» and the «digitally-outcast» enabled by a algorithmic discrimination that does nothing but irreparable harm. See: Yu, Peter K., "The Algorithmic Divide and Equality in the Age of Artificial Intelligence", *Florida Law Review*, Volume 72, 2020, pp. 355–360 (addresses the issue of algorithmic discrimination).

[206] Disadvantaged parties—*pro se* disputants that cannot afford to pay a well-adjusted and seasoned lawyer—already face insurmountable hurdles when they access judicial courts. This problem will only get worse as technology gains traction in criminal procedure law settings. An empirical research premises such assertion. See: Kroeper, Kathryn/Quintanilla, Victor D./Frisby, Michael/Yel, Nedim/Applegate, Amy G./Sherman, Steven J./Murphy, Mary C., "Underestimating the Unrepresented: Cognitive Biases Disadvantage Pro Se Litigants in Family Law Cases", *Psychology, Public Policy, and Law*, Volume 26, n.º2, 2020, pp. 198–212 (211) (emphazise "*the present research suggests that the mere presence or absence of pro se status affects the inferences that legal officials make about parties in the civil justice system.* Legal officials appraised the cases of counselled parties as less meritorious the cases of counselled parties and predicted the *unrepresented persons would experience the civil justice system as less fair and satisfying the counselled litigants, even when all case facts were held constant, and especially when trial (vs. mediation) was considered to be the dispute resolution mechanism*"). Italics added. See also: Quintanilla, Victor/ Allen, R. A./Hirt, E. R., "The signalling effect of pro se status", *Law & Social Inquiry*, Volume 42, 2018, pp. 1092–1120.

Michaels, Andrew C., "Artificial Intelligence, Legal Change, and Separation of Powers", *University of Cincinnati Law Review*, 2020, pp. 1083 and ff and passim.

[207] See: Part V, Chap. 5, Sect. 5.1.7.2 of this book (on law number two to control algorithmic decision-making, which mandates that black box models must not be entrusted with the task of making high stake decisions—v.g. health and freedom). See also: Kleinberg, Jon/Lakkaraju, Himabindu/Leskovec, Jure/Ludwig, Jens/Mullainathan, Sendhil, "Human Decisions and Machine Predictions", *Quarterly Journal of Economics*, Volume 133, 2018, passim. See: Weizenbaum, Joseph, *Computer Power and Human Reason: From Judgment to Calculation*, 1st edition, New York, W. H. Freeman & Co, 1976, pp. 1–300 (227) ("examines the sources of the computer's powers and offers evaluative explorations of what computers can do, cannot do, and should not be

Put otherwise, lawmakers and policymakers should never entrust machines[208] with making lifechanging decisions that may either cause a citizen's death or the deprivation of his/her freedom.[209]

§§ There are lifechanging decisions that, given its utmost importance, should always be made by humans only.[210] This is a feasible way to forestall *Algorithmic Dictatorship*[211] while preventing the criminal system of justice from either falling prey to *Digital Darwinism* or careening into the chaos of *Digital Plutocracy*. With regard to lifechanging decisions in criminal procedure law settings, «predictive machines»[212] should be accordingly kept at bay.

§§ Relatedly, the decision to deploy weapons of mass destruction should never rest upon machines' whimsical, and foremost inscrutable, discretion.[213]

---

employed to do") (*this founding father of Artificial Intelligence presciently noted that we should not entrust Artificial Intelligence-embedded technologies* with with "tasks that demand wisdom"). Italics added. The approval of rental applications is arguably one of those tasks that should never be entrusted to machines). More on this on Part IV, Chap. 4, Sects. 4.1.4–4.1.4.2.1 of this book. On the use of algorithms to undertake risk assessment in sentencing: Gialuz, M., "Quando la giustizia penale encontra l'intelligenza artificiale: luci e e ombre di risk assessment tools tra Stati Uniti ed Europa", 2019, available at: www.penalecontemporaneo.it.d/6702-quando-la-giustizia-penale-encontra-l'intelligenz-artificiale-luci-e-ombre-di-risk-assessment-tools (access: 03.07.2024); Peeters, R./Schuilenburg, M., "Machine Justice: Governing Security through Bureaucracy of Algorithms", *Information Polity*, Volume 23, 2018, pp. 267–274; Hamilton, Melissa, "Sentencing Disparities", *British Journal of American Legal Studies*, Volume 6, Issue 2, 2017, pp. 181 ff; Rodrigues, Anabela Miranda, "Medida da pena de prisão – desafios da era da inteligência artificial", *Revista de Legislação e de Jurisprudência*, Março-Abril de 2020, Ano 149.º, N.º 4021, 2020, pp. 258 ff; Santos, Hugo Luz dos, "Brain-Computer Interfaces, Generative Artificial Intelligence (ChatGPT and Deep Fakes) and Criminal Procedure Law: what's at stake?", *Journal of Research in E. and Computer Science*, Edinburgh, United Kingdom, June 2024, Volume 2, 2024, pp. 39–78; Santos, Hugo Luz dos, *Programas de Compliance e Inteligência Artificial: Consequências ao nível da Law and Economics, do Direito Penal, do Processo Penal e da Behavioral Law and Economics*, Braga, NovaCausa Edições Jurídicas, 2024, pp. 1–330; Santos, Hugo Luz dos, *Inteligência Artificial (ChatGPT/AutoGPT/Robots-Advogados/RobotsProceduradores/Robots-Juízes) e Responsabilidade Penal das Pessoas Colectivas*, Braga, NovaCausa Edições Jurídicas, 2023, pp. 1–108; Santos, Hugo Luz dos, *Inteligência Artificial e Processo Penal*, Braga, NovaCausa Edições Jurídicas, 2022, pp. 1–256; Santos, Hugo Luz dos, *Inteligência Artificial e Processo Penal*, Braga, NovaCausa Edições Jurídicas, 2022, pp. 1–256; Santos, Hugo Luz dos, *Inteligência Artificial e Processo Civil na Era do Metaverse e dos Machine Learning Algorithms*, Braga, NovaCausa Edições Jurídicas, 2022, pp. 1–264.

208 Calo, Ryan, "Artificial Intelligence Policy: Primer and Roadmap", *cit.*, pp. 399–435 (415).

209 Allan, T. R. S., *The Sovereignty of Law: Freedom, Constitution, and the Common* Law. Oxford: Oxford University Press, 2018 (especially this chapter).

210 Pasquale, Frank, "A Rule of Persons, Not Machines: The Limits of Legal Automation", *George Washington Law Review*, Volume 87, 2019, pp. 1 and ff and passim. See: Part V, Chap. 5, Sect. 5.1.7.2 of this book (on law number two to control algorithmic decision-making, which mandates that black box models must not be entrusted with the task of making high stake decisions—v.g. health and freedom).

211 See: Part IV, Chap. 4, Sects. 4.1–4.1.10.6 of this book (on Algorithmic Dictatorship and its chilling effect on democracy).

212 See: Agrawal, Ajay/Gans, Joshua/Goldfarb, Avi, *Prediction Machines: The Simple Economics of Artificial Intelligence*, 2nd Edition. Massachusetts: Harvard Business Review Press, 2022, pp. 1–304.

213 Calo, Ryan, "Artificial Intelligence Policy: Primer and Roadmap", *cit.*, pp. 399–435 (415).

§§ To add to our woes, an unbeknownst to both the insouciant and the nonchalant, neurotechnological devices are beginning to dovetail seamlessly the porous concepts of mind and machine in ways hitherto foreseen.[214]

§§ As time inexorably marches on, so too does the rampant developments in Artificial Intelligence-embedded technologies.[215] Brain-Computer Interfaces[216] are fully equipped to convert thoughts into texts.[217] Miraculously, Brain-Computer Interfaces can restore vision to blind people,[218] which is something that deserves nothing but unfettered plaudits.

§§ Notwithstanding, a robust legal[219] framework[220] to upend «incomprehensible discrimination»[221] is therefore needed[222] to protect citizens' privacy[223] while beefing

---

[214] Levin, Daniel, "Are you out of your mind? Neurotechnologies and the Making of Disembodied Agency", *Berkeley Technology Law Journal*, Volume 38, 2023, pp. 232–252, which we have been following closely.

[215] Waytowhich, N./Lawhern, VJ/Garcia, JO, et al., "Compact Convolutional neural networks for classification of asynchronous steady-state visual evoked potentials", *Journal of Neural Engineering*, Volume 15, Issue 6, 2018, passim; Kwak, N-S/Müller, K-R/Lee, S-W., "A Convolutional neural network for steady state visual evoked potential classification under ambulatory environment", *PloS One*, Volume 12, Issue 2, 2017, passim.

[216] See: Part III, this chapter, Sect. 3.1.4.5 of this book (on Critical Artificial Intelligence Studies, with a sharper focus on the harmful effects of Brain-Computer Interfaces). See: Part III, this chapter, Sect. 3.1.5.10 of this book (on the functional aspects of Critical Artificial Intelligence Studies, with a sharper focus on the harmful effects of Artificial Intelligence-embedded technologies, namely, Brain-Computer Interfaces that can read and control your mind and behaviour). See also: AAVV, "Deep Brain Stimulation (DBS) for the Treatment of Parkinson's Disease and Other Movement Disorders", *National Institute of Neurological Disorders and Stroke*, 2022, passim; Saha, S./Baumert, M., "Intra-and-inter subject variability in EEG-based sensorimotor brain computer interface: a review", *Frontiers of Computer Neuroscience*, Volume 87, 2020, passim.

[217] Zhang, X./Sheng, QZ et al., "Converting your thoughts to texts: enabling brain typing via deep feature learning of eeg signals", *IEEE International Conference on Pervasive Computing and Communications*. Athens: IEEE, 2018, passim; Dockrill, Peter, "Brain Implant Translates Paralyzed Man's Thoughts into Text With 94% Accuracy", *SCI Alert*, 2021, passim.

[218] Cassella, Carly, "Brain Implant Gives Blind Woman Artificial Vision in Scientific First", *SCI Alert*, 2021, passim.

[219] See loosely on this subject: Strandburg, Katherine J., "Rulemaking and Inscrutable Decision Tools", *Columbia Law Review*, Volume 119, 2019, passim.

[220] That hopefully breeds explainability as opposed to idleness. See: Watcher, Sandra/Mittelstadt, Brent/Russell, Chris, "Counterfactual Explanations Without Opening the Black Box: Automated Decisions and the GDPR", *Harvard Journal of Law and Technology*, Volume 31, 2018, pp. 841 e ss and passim.

[221] See: Griemmelmann, James/Westreich, Daniel, "Incomprehensible Discrimination", *California Law Review Online*, Volume 7, 2018, pp. 164–171. In the same vein, see also.

[222] See: Xiang, Alice, "Reconciling Legal and Technical Approaches to Algorithmic Bias", *Tennessee Law Review*, Volume 88, 2021, passim.

[223] See: Waldman, Ezra, "Privacy, Practice, and Performance", *California Law Review*, Volume 110, 2021, passim. Citron; Danielle Keats Citron/Pasquale, Frank, "Network Accountability for the Domestic Intelligence Apparatus", *Hasting Law Journal*, Volume 62, 2011, 1441, 1444–45; Gray, David/Citron, Danielle Keats, "The Right to Quantitative Privacy", *Minnesota Law Review*, Volume 98, 2013, pp. 62–81.

up their fundamental rights[224] through «private accountability in the Age of Artificial Intelligence».[225] To cater for that, both «algorithmic injustice»[226] and *Algorithmic Dictatorship* must be trounced. Even vanquished.

3.1.2 *The Rationale Behind the Creation and Deployment of Artificial Intelligence-Embedded Technologies That Propel* Algorithmic Dictatorship

§§ The deftness with which Artificial Intelligence-embedded technologies strike back at both the *socially undesirables* and racialized people is astounding.[227] In spite of the heavy praise of an algorithmic tool of risk assessment,[228] the rotten

---

[224] Fundamental rights often besmeared further the so-called "Bias in, Bias out". See: Mayson, Sandra G., "Bias In, Bias Out", *Yale Law Journal*, Volume 128, 2019, pp. 2218 and ff and passim.

[225] See: Katyal, Sonia, "Private Accountability in the Age of Artificial Intelligence", *UCLA Law Review*, Volume 66, 2019, pp. 54–99.

[226] See: Ting-an Lin, "Democratizing AI" and the Concern of Algorithmic Injustice", *Philosophy and Technology*, Volume 37 (103), 2024, pp. 3–27. See also: Birhane, A., "Algorithmic injustice: A relational ethics approach", *Patterns*, 2 (2), 2021, pp. 1–9. Završnik, A. "Algorithmic justice: Algorithms and big data in criminal justice settings", *European Journal of Criminology*, 2019, passim.

[227] Noble, Safiya Umoja, *Algorithms of Oppression: How search engines reinforce racism*, New York, New University Press, 2018, pp. 1–248 ("*Run a Google search for "Black girls"—what will you find? "Big Booty" and other sexually explicit terms are likely to come up as top search terms. But, if you type in "white girls," the results are radically different*. The suggested porn sites and unmoderated discussions about "why Black women are so sassy" or "why Black women are so angry" presents a disturbing portrait of Black womanhood in modern society. In *Algorithms of Oppression*, Safiya Umoja Noble challenges the idea that search engines like Google offer an equal playing field for all forms of ideas, identities, and activities. *Data discrimination is a real social problem; Noble argues that the combination of private interests in promoting certain sites, along with the monopoly status of a relatively small number of Internet search engines, leads to a biased set of search algorithms that privilege whiteness and discriminate against people of color, specifically women of color*"). Italics added. See: Part IV, Chap. 4, Sect. 4.1.8 of this book (on biased word embeddings with an entrenched presence on search engines run by tech moguls).

[228] See: Part IV, Chap. 4, Sects. 4.1.10.1–4.1.10.6 of this book (on biased algorithmic risk assessment in criminal procedure law settings). See also: Mohler, G. O., Short, M. B., Malinowski, S., Johnson, M., Tita, G. E., Bertozzi, A. L., & Brantingham, P. J., "Randomized controlled field trials of predictive policing", *Journal of the American Statistical Association*, 110 (512), 2015, 1399–1411.

apple (predictive policing[229]) does not fall far from its tree though: a social construction that builds on, and seeks to forcefully maintain, White privilege[230] and White supremacy.[231] The overriding goal underpinning these racially motivated policies was

---

[229] See: Part IV, Chap. 4, Sects. 4.1.1–4.1.1.1 of this book (on biased predictive policing). See also: Hu, Margaret, "From the National Surveillance State to the Cybersurveillance State", *The Annual Review of Law and Social Science*, Volume 13, 2017, p. 169 ("*as a result of big data biometric governance trends, meaningful distinctions between biometric credentialing for identification and behavioral biometric profiling are disappearing. The objectives are merging: Reliable credentialing is used to advance security and precrime policy rationales. Biometric data mission creep occurs by necessity in a big data world because the cybersurveillance systems are often designed to engage in mass data integration and analysis and predictive policing. Biometric surveillance serves two purposes in preventive policing: It increases identity transparency, and the biometric data categorize identity through cataloging behavioral and physical characteristics and assess these characteristics for risk. Contrasting small data biometric credentialing protocols with big data credentialing protocols is useful. It illustrates how biometric surveillance fits within the Cybersurveillance State*"). Italics added.

[230] Roithmayr, Daria, *Reproducing Racism: How everyday choices lock in White Advantage*, New York, New York University Press, 2014, pp. 1–272 ("*Argues that racial inequality reproduces itself automatically over time because early unfair advantage for whites has paved the way for continuing advantage. This book is designed to change the way we think about racial inequality (…) Legal scholar Daria Roithmayr provocatively argues that racial inequality lives on because white advantage functions as a powerful self-reinforcing monopoly, reproducing itself automatically from generation to generation even in the absence of intentional discrimination. Drawing on work in antitrust law and a range of other disciplines, Roithmayr brilliantly compares the dynamics of white advantage to the unfair tactics of giants like AT&T and Microsoft.* With penetrating insight, Roithmayr *locates the engine of white monopoly in positive feedback loops that connect the dramatic disparity of Jim Crow to modern racial gaps in jobs, housing and education. Wealthy white neighborhoods fund public schools that then turn out wealthy white neighbors. Whites with lucrative jobs informally refer their friends, who refer their friends, and so on. Roithmayr concludes that racial inequality might now be locked in place, unless policymakers immediately take drastic steps to dismantle this oppressive system*"). Italics added. This book points out how White privilege is perpetuated throughout generations through residential segregation (*mortgage redlining*), abhorrent nepotism, and other bemoaning social practices that pester modern societies). See: Part IV, Chap. 4, Sects. 4.1.4–4.1.4.2.3 of this book. See: Part IV, Chap. 4, Sects. 4.1.4–4.1.4.2.1 of this book (on mortgage redlining). See: Part IV, Chap. 4, Sects. 4.1.2–4.1.4.3 of this book (on algorithmic credit scoring, consumer racism and credit card redlining). See: Part IV, Chap. 4, Sects. 4.1.4–4.1.4.2.3 of this book (on algorithmic redlining). See: Part IV, Chap. 4, Sect. 4.1.4.3 of this book (on "algorithmic redliking"). See: Part IV, Chap. 4, Sect. 4.1.3 of this book (on algorithmic prime-lining).

[231] See: Perea, Juan F., "Doctrines of Delusion: How the History of the G.I. Bill and Other Inconvenient Truths Undermind the Supreme Court's Affirmative Action Jurisprudence", *University of Pittsburgh Law Review*, Volume 75, 1995, pp. 583, 586–89 (establishes a liaison between Jim Crow laws, the G.I. Bill, and the Social Security Act and White supremacy); Milligan, Joy, "Protecting Disfavored Minorities: Towards Institutional Realism", *UCLA Law Review*, Volume 63, 2016, pp. 894, pp. 918–21 (shedding a keen light on racial inequality in U.S. Department of Agriculture farm assistance); Robinson, Reginald Leamon, "The Racial Limits of the Fair Housing Act: The Intersection of Dominant White Images, the Violence of Neighborhood Purity, and the Master Narrative of Black Inferiority", *William & Mary Law Review*, Volume 37, 1995, pp. 69, 71–74 (establishes a connection between the failures of the FHA and White supremacy). But see: Wormser, Richard, *The Rise and Fall of Jim Crow*, Manhattan, New York City, St Martin's Press, 2014, pp. 1–222 ("*White supremacy prevailed, but it did not destroy the spirit of the black community*"). Italics added.

squeaky clear: the bevy of privileges should belong jointly to all (whites) and severally to each (white).[232] To cater for that, several tools of social control[233] regarding *social undesirables* have been shrewdly devised and subsequently deployed.

§§ Congeries of rules have been accordingly created[234] to keep the *social undesirables* at the outskirts of modern societies.[235] Ranging from warped data

---

[232] O'Neil, Cathy, *Weapons of Math Destruction. How Big Data Increases Inequality and Threatens Democracy*, London, Penguin Random House, 2016, passim (showing how algorithms utilized in modern societies are amenable to perpetuate racial discrimination, partially through perpetuation of social disadvantage and wealth divides). See: Part IV, Chap. 4, Sects. 4.1.4–4.1.4.2.1 of this book (on mortgage redlining). See: Part IV, Chap. 4, Sects. 4.1.2–4.1.4.3 of this book (on algorithmic credit scoring, consumer racism and credit card redlining). See: Part IV, Chap. 4, Sects. 4.1.4–4.1.4.2.3 of this book (on algorithmic redlining). See: Part IV, Chap. 4, Sect. 4.1.4.3 of this book (on "algorithmic redliking"). See: Part IV, Chap. 4, Sect. 4.1.3 of this book (on algorithmic prime-lining).

[233] Brewer, R. M., & Heitzeg, N. A., "The racialization of crime and punishment: Criminal justice, Color-Blind racism, and the political economy of the prison industrial complex", *American Behavioral Scientist*, 51 (5), 2008, 625–644.

[234] Quadagno, Jill, *The Color of Welfare: How Racism Undermined the War on Poverty*, Oxford, Oxford University Press, 1994, pp. 1–272 ("*From Reconstruction to Lyndon Johnson and beyond, Quadagno reveals how American social policy has continually foundered on issues of race. Drawing on extensive primary research, Quadagno shows, for instance, how Roosevelt, in need of support from southern congressmen, excluded African Americans from the core programs of the Social Security Act. Turning to Lyndon Johnson's "unconditional war on poverty," she contends that though anti-poverty programs for job training, community action, health care, housing, and education have accomplished much, they have not been fully realized because they became inextricably intertwined with the civil rights movement of the 1960s, which triggered a white backlash*"). Italics added. See: Part IV, Chap. 4, Sects. 4.1.4–4.1.4.2.3 of this book. See: Part IV, Chap. 4, Sects. 4.1.4–4.1.4.2.1 of this book (on mortgage redlining). See: Part IV, Chap. 4, Sects. 4.1.2–4.1.4.3 of this book (on algorithmic credit scoring, consumer racism and credit card redlining). See: Part IV, Chap. 4, Sects. 4.1.4–4.1.4.2.3 of this book (on algorithmic redlining). See: Part IV, Chap. 4, Sect. 4.1.4.3 of this book (on "algorithmic redliking"). See: Part IV, Chap. 4, Sect. 4.1.3 of this book (on algorithmic prime-lining).

[235] Katznelson, Ira, *When Affirmative Action Was White: An Untold History of Racial Inequality in Twentieth-Century America*, New York, W. W. Norton & Company; Reprint edition (August 17, 2006), 2006, pp. 1–272 ("In this "penetrating new analysis" (*New York Times Book Review*) *Ira Katznelson fundamentally recasts our understanding of twentieth-century American history and demonstrates that all the key programs passed during the New Deal and Fair Deal era of the 1930s and 1940s were created in a deeply discriminatory manner. Through mechanisms designed by Southern Democrats that specifically excluded maids and farm workers, the gap between blacks and whites actually widened despite postwar prosperity. In the words of noted historian Eric Foner*, "Katznelson's incisive book should change the terms of debate about affirmative action, and about the last seventy years of American history""). Italics added. This book parses the impact of several racially motivated laws—Social Security Act, G: I. Bill, and labour laws implementing unemployment stipends, minimum wages, and union protection—in the history of United States of America). Italics added. See: Part IV, Chap. 4, Sects. 4.1.4–4.1.4.2.1 of this book (on mortgage redlining). See: Part IV, Chap. 4, Sects. 4.1.2–4.1.4.3 of this book (on algorithmic credit scoring, consumer racism and credit card redlining). See: Part IV, Chap. 4, Sects. 4.1.4–4.1.4.2.3 of this book (on algorithmic redlining). See: Part IV, Chap. 4, Sect. 4.1.4.3 of this book (on "algorithmic redliking"). See: Part IV, Chap. 4, Sect. 4.1.3 of this book (on algorithmic prime-lining).

that impairs the access to credit[236] (biased credit scoring,[237] fair lending[238]

[236] But see: Atkinson, Abbye, "Rethinking Credit as a Social Provision", *Stanford Law Review*, Volume 71, 2019, pp. 1093–1099 (contending that credit, which shifts consumption temporally, is only beneficial insofar income ratchets up in the forthcoming future. As of now, though, "credit is fundamentally incompatible with the entrenched intergenerational poverty that plagues low-income Americans." Id. Notably, it is crucially important to come to terms with the fact that credit is not a panacea for the great bulk of economic struggles, and concretely wage stagnation. Although credit is not befitted to all consumers at all prices, affordable credit can nonetheless play a pivotal role in the creation of wealth). See: Part IV, Chap. 4, Sects. 4.1.4–4.1.4.2.1 of this book (on mortgage redlining). See: Part IV, Chap. 4, Sects. 4.1.2–4.1.4.3 of this book (on algorithmic credit scoring, consumer racism and credit card redlining). See: Part IV, Chap. 4, Sects. 4.1.4–4.1.4.2.3 of this book (on algorithmic redlining). See: Part IV, Chap. 4, Sect. 4.1.4.3 of this book (on "algorithmic redliking"). See: Part IV, Chap. 4, Sect. 4.1.3 of this book (on algorithmic prime-lining).

[237] Note, though, that certain types of racial discrimination may not be fully intentional. More likely than not, it can be related with the perils of big data colour-blindness that nonetheless relies on proxies to race and gender to make algorithmic decisions. Another problem is the one related with "creditworthiness by association" that causes more problems than it solves. Hurley, Mikella/Adebayo, Julius, "Credit Scoring in the Era of Big Data", *Yale Journal of Law and Technology*, Volume 18, 2016, p. 149 ("*recent studies have also questioned the accuracy of the data used by these tools, in some cases identifying serious flaws that have a substantial bearing on lending decisions. Big-data tools may also risk creating a system of "creditworthiness by association" in which consumers' familial, religious, social, and other affiliations determine their eligibility for an affordable loan. These tools may furthermore obscure discriminatory and subjective lending policies behind a single "objective" score. Such discriminatory scoring may not be intentional; instead, sophisticated algorithms may combine facially neutral data points and treat them as proxies for immutable characteristics such as race or gender, thereby circumventing existing non-discrimination laws and systematically denying credit access to certain groups. Finally, big-data tools may allow online payday lenders to target the most vulnerable consumers and lure them into debt traps*"). Italics added. See: Part IV, Chap. 4, Sects. 4.1.2–4.1.2.3 of this book. See: Part IV, Chap. 4, Sects. 4.1.4–4.1.4.2.1 of this book (on mortgage redlining). See: Part IV, Chap. 4, Sects. 4.1.2–4.1.4.3 of this book (on algorithmic credit scoring, consumer racism and credit card redlining). See: Part IV, Chap. 4, Sects. 4.1.4–4.1.4.2.3 of this book (on algorithmic redlining). See: Part IV, Chap. 4, Sect. 4.1.4.3 of this book (on "algorithmic redliking"). See: Part IV, Chap. 4, Sect. 4.1.3 of this book (on algorithmic prime-lining).

[238] Allen, James, "The Color of Algorithms: An Analysis and Proposed Research Agenda Deterring Algorithmic Redlining", *Fordham Urban Law Journal*, Volume 46, 2019, pp. 219–234 (229–234) (discussing how historical mortgage redlining greatly swayed modern algorithms generated by massive batches of data sets that consist of decades of information built on exclusion and racial discrimination in the purview of financing, marketing, and housing). See: Part IV, Chap. 4, Sects. 4.1.4–4.1.4.2.3 of this book. See: Part IV, Chap. 4, Sects. 4.1.4–4.1.4.2.1 of this book (on mortgage redlining). See: Part IV, Chap. 4, Sects. 4.1.2–4.1.4.3 of this book (on algorithmic credit scoring, consumer racism and credit card redlining). See: Part IV, Chap. 4, Sects. 4.1.4–4.1.4.2.3 of this book (on algorithmic redlining). See: Part IV, Chap. 4, Sect. 4.1.4.3 of this book (on "algorithmic redliking"). See: Part IV, Chap. 4, Sect. 4.1.3 of this book (on algorithmic prime-lining).

and fair housing[239]) to algorithmic redlining.[240] More on this later.[241]

[239] Wonyoung, So, "Which Information Matters? Measuring Landlord Assessment of Tenant Screening Reports", *Housing Policy Debate*, Volume 33, n.º 6, 2023, pp. 1484–1510 (1502) (arguing that landlords display automation bias as the "*study finds that landlords tend to rely more on the automated system's judgment: when a report noted that a tenant was either medium or high risk, landlords showed a higher tendency toward rejection, or, if conditionally accepted, they imposed a higher security deposit. This indicates that tenant screening services' risk scoring may critically affect landlords' decision-making.* Given that there is no regulation pertaining to producing and deploying such algorithms, and 1502 W. SO given the inherent inaccuracies of eviction data (Porton et al. 2021) and widespread, serial eviction filings (Garboden and Rosen 2019), particularly automatic eviction filings activated by digitized property management systems and large, corporate landlords (Fields 2022; Gomory 2022; Immergluck et al. 2020), *tenant screening services very likely contribute to perpetuating algorithmic inequality* (Eubanks 2018) *by denying qualified applicants—disproportionately from protected groups—access to housing*"). Italics added. See: Part IV, Chap. 4, Sects. 4.1.4–4.1.4.2.3 of this book. See: Part IV, Chap. 4, Sects. 4.1.4–4.1.4.2.1 of this book (on mortgage redlining). See: Part IV, Chap. 4, Sects. 4.1.2–4.1.4.3 of this book (on algorithmic credit scoring, consumer racism and credit card redlining). See: Part IV, Chap. 4, Sects. 4.1.4–4.1.4.2.3 of this book (on algorithmic redlining). See: Part IV, Chap. 4, Sect. 4.1.4.3 of this book (on "algorithmic redliking"). See: Part IV, Chap. 4, Sect. 4.1.3 of this book (on algorithmic prime-lining).

[240] In spite of its deep-seated racial bias, decision-makers continue to deploy redlining tactics through big data and may even justify such unlawful practices by claiming that the latter abide by cost-effectiveness. See: Humber, Nadiyah J., "A Home for Digital Equity: Algorithmic Redlining and Property Technology", *California Law Review*, Volume 111, Issue 5, 2023, pp. 1421–1484. See also: Hurley, Mikella/Adebayo, Julius, "Credit Scoring in the Era of Big Data", *Yale Journal of Law and Technology*, Volume 18, 2016, pp. 148, 151–156, 172 (averring that FICO scoring boasts a redoubtable capacity to routinely weed out some populations that have been historically and systematically underrepresented or grossly unfairly represented in the credit industry market). Tellingly, by 2016, ten states had disavowed the unlawful practice of employers using shady algorithmic credit scores due to their perceived disparate impact on low-income applicants and members of racialized communities (mostly Black folks). See: O'Neill, Cathy, *Weapons of Math Destruction. How Big Data Increases Inequality and Threatens Democracy*. London: Penguin Random House, 2016, pp. 128 and ff and passim. See: Part IV, Chap. 4, Sects. 4.1.4–4.1.4.2.3 of this book. See: Part IV, Chap. 4, Sects. 4.1.4–4.1.4.2.1 of this book (on mortgage redlining). See: Part IV, Chap. 4, Sects. 4.1.2–4.1.4.3 of this book (on algorithmic credit scoring, consumer racism and credit card redlining). See: Part IV, Chap. 4, Sects. 4.1.4–4.1.4.2.3 of this book (on algorithmic redlining). See: Part IV, Chap. 4, Sect. 4.1.4.3 of this book (on "algorithmic redliking"). See: Part IV, Chap. 4, Sect. 4.1.3 of this book (on algorithmic prime-lining).

[241] See: Part IV, Chap. 4, Sects. 4.1.4–4.1.4.2.1 of this book (on mortgage redlining). See: Part IV, Chap. 4, Sects. 4.1.2–4.1.4.3 of this book (on algorithmic credit scoring, consumer racism and credit card redlining).

3.1.3 Critical Artificial Intelligence Studies (CAIS) and Algorithmic Common Good (ACG) to Cast off Algorithmic Dictatorship: Introduction

§§ As hinted above, the great bulk of Artificial Intelligence-embedded technologies are tools that reify,[242] compound, and exacerbate[243] deep-seated social and ethnic concerns with which modern societies have been wrestling for a long-winded span of time,[244] such as misogyny,

[242] Duster, Troy, "Race and Reification in Science." *Science*, 307, 2005, passim.

[243] *Tech, Bias and Housing Initiative, the Promise and Perils of Residential Proptech, Year 1, Research Summary Report, April 2023, TechEquity Collaborative*, p. 5, available at: https://techequity.us/wp-content/uploads/2023/04/TBHI-Y1-Research-Summary-Report.pdf (28.11.2024) ("*Residential Proptech also has the potential to exacerbate the bias inherent in our housing system. Its rise is due, in part, to the desperation felt by average home seekers. With a severely constrained housing supply, companies offering an easier pathway to homeownership may exploit communities that have been harmed by housing discrimination in the past. Opaque algorithms incorporate biased data into their decision-making processes, making it harder to enforce fair housing laws.* Residential Proptech companies often operate in a regulatory gray area, leaving consumers without the protections they would have from traditional housing regulatory systems. *As unprecedented capital investment flows into this space, venture-backed companies' winner-take-all approach to growth has the potential to exacerbate inequality rather than combat it*"). Italics added. See: Part IV, Chap. 4, Sects. 4.1.4–4.1.4.2.3 of this book.

[244] See: Wonyoung, So, "Which Information Matters? Measuring Landlord Assessment of Tenant Screening Reports", *Housing Policy Debate*, Volume 33, n.º 6, 2023, pp. 1484–1510 (1502) ("*One additional finding of the experiment is that algorithmic scoring can exacerbate this racially unequal landscape in rental agreements not just because the algorithm may be inaccurate, but because landlords may want to follow the risk assessment made by the tenant screening report. This is alarming for low-income tenants, particularly housing voucher holders. Security deposits are one of the most significant barriers to obtaining housing for voucher holders, because vouchers do not pay security deposits but most private landlords require them* (Rosenblatt and Cossyleon 2018). Given that voucher holders have exceptionally low income (usually less than 50% of area median income) and might experience more housing insecurity (rental debts and eviction-related experiences), *imposing greater security deposits on voucher holders almost equates to denying them housing—yet these decisions could be justified by algorithmic scoring if tenant screening services employ it*"). Italics added. See: Part IV, Chap. 4, Sects. 4.1.4–4.1.4.2.1 of this book (on mortgage redlining). See: Part IV, Chap. 4, Sects. 4.1.2–4.1.4.3 of this book (on algorithmic credit scoring, consumer racism and credit card redlining). See: Part IV, Chap. 4, Sects. 4.1.4–4.1.4.2.3 of this book (on algorithmic redlining). See: Part IV, Chap. 4, Sect. 4.1.4.3 of this book (on "algorithmic redliking"). See: Part IV, Chap. 4, Sect. 4.1.3 of this book (on algorithmic prime-lining).

sexism,[245] racism,[246] xenophobe and political hatred which, taken together, are rife for misfire, social unrest, public outcry, upheaval, and grievances of any kind. Bereft of actionable ideas to abrogate this gruelling scenario, social mayhem may otherwise ensue.

---

245 Hamilton, Melissa, "The sexist algorithm", *Behavioral Sciences and the Law*, Volume 37, Issue 2, Special Issue: the Use of Statistics in Criminal Cases, March-April 2019, 2019, pp. 1 and ff ("Algorithmic risk assessment tools are informed by scientific research concerning which factors are predictive of recidivism and thus support the evidence-based practice movement in criminal justice. Automated assessments of individualized risk (low, medium, high) permit officials to make more effective management decisions. Computer-generated algorithms appear to be objective and neutral. But are these algorithms actually fair? The focus herein is on gender equity. Studies confirm that women typically have far lower recidivism rates than men. *This differential raises the question of how well algorithmic outcomes fare in terms of predictive parity by gender*. This essay reports original research using a large dataset of offenders who were scored on the popular risk assessment tool COMPAS. *Findings indicate that COMPAS performs reasonably well at discriminating between recidivists and non-recidivists for men and women. Nonetheless, COMPAS algorithmic outcomes systemically overclassify women in higher risk groupings. Multiple measures of algorithmic equity and predictive accuracy are provided to support the conclusion that this algorithm is sexist*"). Italics added. See: Part IV, Chap. 4, Sects. 4.1.10.1–4.1.10.6 of this book (on biased algorithmic risk assessment in criminal procedure law settings, with a sharper focus on COMPAS). See: Part IV, Chap. 4, Sects. 4.1.1–4.1.1.1 of this book (on biased predictive policing).

246 For a simple reason: Dong et al., Qi, "Imbalanced deep learning by minority class incremental rectification, *IEEE Transactions on Pattern Analysis & Machine Intelligence*, Volume 41, 2019, p. 1367 (posit that "*most existing learning algorithms produce inductive bias (learning bias)* towards the frequent (majority) classes if training data are not balanced, *resulting in poor minority class recognition performance*"). Italics added. See: Chandler, Anupam, "The Racist Algorithm", *Michigan Law Review*, Volume 115, n. ° 6, 2018, p. 1026 (on racist algorithms, noting that "the possibilities for discriminatory manipulation are legion"). But see: Altenburger, Kristen M./Ho, Daniel E., "When Algorithms Import Private Bias into Public Enforcement: The Promise and Limitations of Statistical Debiasing Solutions", *Journal of Institutional & Theoretical Economics*, Volume 175, 2019, pp. 97–98 (calls for a "debias predictive algorithms" to assuage racist and/or biased, doctored and bigoted algorithms nevertheless). See: Hamilton, Melissa, "The Biased Algorithm: Evidence of Disparate Impact on Hispanics", *American Criminal Law Review*, Volume 56, 2019, pp. 1553 and ff and passim. Note, though, that the training of machine learning is long and tedious in that is an error-prone procedure than can ultimately impair future algorithmic decision-making: Price, W. Nicholson Price II, "Regulating Black-Box Medicine", *Michigan Law Review*, Volume 116, 2017, pp. 421–431 (leverages on Google Image's image recognition learning algorithm to shed light on the four-step process by which some algorithms are thoroughly trained. First, the algorithm is shown "a set of known images ('Here are 10,000 pictures of ducks')." Second, the algorithm "develops complex internal rules based on nonlinear processes." Third, the algorithm "tests those rules on a test set ('Which of these are ducks?')." And fourth, the algorithm accordingly adjusts its "internal rules based on the success of the test." These steps are trotted out and repeated many times "until it can accurately and consistently classify the images"). See: Part V, Chap. 5, Sect. 5.1.7.4 of this book (on one of the law to control algorithmic decision-making, namely, law number four: data partitioning must be performed—i.e. randomly split an entire dataset into the «training dataset» and the «test dataset»—to accurately predict outcomes in the real world while forestalling «inductive bias» [learning bias]).

§§ The time is right now as to quash the harmful effects of Artificial Intelligence-embedded technologies on both race and gender. To cater for that, I will briefly introduce the concept of *Critical Artificial Intelligence Studies* (CAIS), which is tightly interlocked with the concept of *Algorithmic Common Good* (ACG), whose fundamental tenets will be fleshed out in due course.[247]

§§ *Critical Artificial Intelligence Studies* (CAIS) consists of a tool that aims to combat any dollop of discrimination enabled by Artificial Intelligence-embedded technologies. By the same token, CAIS seeks to halt both *digital racism* and *digital sexism* that arise out of an all-out deployment of Artificial Intelligence. Not just that though. CAIS upholds the use of Artificial Intelligence-embedded technologies, but only to the extent that it doesn't further the yawning gap between races and genders. Hence the overriding importance of *Algorithmic Common Good* (ACG). More on this later.[248]

§§ *Critical Artificial Intelligence Studies* (CAIS) lends itself to a frame of reference that seeks to strenuously combat any forms of discrimination enabled by a pervasive technology that begets both oppression and social divide between citizens.

§§ *Critical Artificial Intelligence Studies* (CAIS) picks out the central or focal point of Artificial Intelligence-embedded technologies (its perceived potential to aggrandize both racial and wealth divides[249]) while striving to bringing a legal framework into being and sustaining it over time, as opposed to merely opting for other types of social ordering that would yield meagre tangible results along the line.

§§ *Critical Artificial Intelligence Studies* (CAIS) thus endeavours to pinpoint—and, foremost, unseat, unwind, and tail off—the harmful effects of Artificial Intelligence-embedded technologies that propel forward the unfettered rise of *Algorithmic Dictatorship* that further compounds the disheartening tapestry of decades-long of racial discrimination.

---

[247] See: Part V, Chap. 5, Sects. 5.1.2–5.1.6.2.1 of this book (on the thing-centred algorithmic decision-making propelled by a *Controllable* and *Interpretable* Machine Learning that weeds out *Algorithmic Dictatorship* and secures *Algorithmic Common Good*).

[248] See: Part V, Chap. 5, Sects. 5.1.7–5.1.7.5 of this book (on the five laws to control algorithmic decision-making). See: Part V, Chap. 5, Sects. 5.1.8–5.1.8.5 of this book (on the five laws to interpret algorithmic decision-making).

[249] Derenoncourt, Ellora/Kim, Chi Hyun/Kuhn, Moritz/Schularik, Moritz, "The Wealth of Two Nations: The U.S. Racial Wealth Gap, 1860-2020", *The Quarterly Journal of Economics*, Volume 139, Issue 2, 2024, p. 741 ("A large class of commonly discussed policies for reducing racial wealth inequality seeks to reduce gaps in income, savings, and capital gains. These include policies that encourage financial diversification or stock equity holdings among Black households; policies aimed at financial literacy and retirement or savings behavior; or policies aimed at improving educational and labor market outcomes of Black Americans through improved school quality or reductions in discrimination. *Yet on a realistic note, our simulation in Section IV.A shows that even if wealth accumulation conditions had been equal since 1870, the wealth gap would still be 3 to 1 today, and full convergence would be more than 200 years away. Put differently: to close the racial wealth gap in the immediate term via flow parameters, Black Americans would need a substantial positive lead over whites, not "just" more equality*"). Italics added.

§§ To forestall such a jarring reality, CAIS draws on Critical Race Theory (CRT) to canvass the foundations of *systemic racism* while pitching a handful of actionable ideas that will contribute exponentially to uproot racial discrimination carried out by Artificial Intelligence-embedded technologies. It is pivotally important to note that the functional aspects of Critical Artificial Intelligence Studies[250] exhibit an inextricable link to *Algorithmic Common Good* (ACG),[251] will be sketched out throughout this book.[252]

3.1.4 Foundations of Critical Artificial Intelligence Studies *(CAIS)*

3.1.4.1 Critical Race Theory (CRT) to Shine a Keen Light on the Hidden Agenda Underpinning Predictive Policing

§§ Artificial Intelligence-embedded technologies drift so far away from the core of human dignity[253] that are shaping up to put law at loggerheads with its fundamental

---

[250] See: Part III, this chapter, Sect. 3.1.5.10 of this book (on the functional aspects of Critical Artificial Intelligence Studies, with a sharper focus on the harmful effects of Artificial Intelligence-embedded technologies, namely, Brain-Computer Interfaces that can read and control your mind and behaviour). See: Part III, this chapter, Sect. 3.1.5.11 of this book (on the functional aspects of Critical Artificial Intelligence Studies, with a sharper focus on the harmful effects of Artificial Intelligence-embedded technologies, namely, Genetic Algorithms that can write DNA on demand, thereby ushering the age of Transhumanism, Genetic Darwinism and Genetic Plutocracy, which, taken together, are poised to create layers of distinction between citizens). See: Part III, this chapter, Sect. 3.1.5.11 of this book (on the functional aspects of Critical Artificial Intelligence Studies, with a sharper focus on the harmful effects of Artificial Intelligence-embedded technologies, namely, Quantum Technology, which will bring entire industries to its knees while allowing unscrupulous actors to get a hold of, and whimsically activate, weapons of mass destruction). See: Part III, this chapter, Sect. 3.1.5.1.1 of this book (on the functional aspects of Critical Artificial Intelligence Studies, with a sharper focus on the harmful effects of Artificial Intelligence-embedded technologies, namely, perpetuation technologies—griefbots, avatars and robots—that are slated to dehumanize human-laden emotions). See: Part III, this chapter, Sects. 3.1.5.2–3.1.5.3.1 of this book (on the functional aspects of Critical Artificial Intelligence Studies, with a sharper focus on the harmful effects of Artificial Intelligence-embedded technologies, namely, Generative Artificial Intelligence and its offsprings—deepfakes and its deleterious effects on human memory).

[251] See: Part V, Chap. 5, Sects. 5.1.2–5.1.6.2.1 of this book (on the thing-centred algorithmic decision-making propelled by a *Controllable* and *Interpretable* Machine Learning that weeds out *Algorithmic Dictatorship* and secures *Algorithmic Common Good*).

[252] See: Part V, Chap. 5, Sects. 5.1.7–5.1.7.5 of this book (on the five laws to control algorithmic decision-making). See: Part V, Chap. 5, Sects. 5.1.8–5.1.8.5 of this book (on the five laws to interpret algorithmic decision-making).

[253] Human dignity is a Kantian-inspired notion which were to send ripples across cultures of dignity, mainly from the fundamental rights standpoint. In German doctrine: Ramm, Thilo, "Die sozialen Grundrechte im Verfassungsgefüge", in: *Soziale Grundrechte – 5. Rechtspolitischer Kongress der SPD vom 29. Februar bis 2. März 1980 in Saarbrüchen*, Heidelberg/Karlsruhe, 1981, pp. 28–32; in Portuguese doctrine, Botelho, Catarina Santos, "40 anos de Direitos Sociais: uma reflexão

tenets: the agreed-upon axiom that citizens must obey the law[254] on the heels of a brawny and sturdy Rule of Law[255] Which begs the question: should citizens[256] obey the law amidst a decaying Rule of Law[257] owing to the dissemination of Artificial Intelligence-embedded technologies?

---

sobre o papel dos Direitos Fundamentais Sociais no Século XXI", *Julgar*, 29, 2016, pp. 197 ff. In French doctrine: Fierens, Jacques, "La dignitè humaine comme concept juridique", *Journal des tribunaux*, 121, 2002, pp. 578–580; Carvalho, Natalia Brigagão Ferrer Alves, "Catholic Social Thought, Politics and Human Dignity in the Brazilian Constitutional Assembly of 1987–1988", *The American Journal of Legal History*, 1, 2019, 1–30; Taekema, Sanne, "The Procedural Rule of Law: Examining Waldron's Argument on Dignity and Agency", *cit.*: 140 ff (arguing that the «Rule of Law serves the value of human dignity»).

[254] Fuller, Lon L., "A Reply to Professors Cohen and Dworkin", *Villanova Law Review*, 10, 1965, 657 (noting that «it is generally accepted that the citizen has, under ordinary circumstances and subject to exceptions, a moral duty to obey the law»); Fuller, Lon L., *The Morality of Law*, Revised Edition, New Haven, Yale University Press, 1969, 39–42; 81–90 (on citizen's moral duty to obey the law, which is not to be confounded with judges' fidelity as a «species of congruence between official action and the law»).

[255] The concept of Rule of Law is of paramount importance in modern democracies. Regrettably, the Rule of Law is backsliding worldwide. Especially in Central and Eastern Europe. See: Avbelj, Matej, "The Rule of Law, Comprehensive Doctrines, Overlapping Consensus, and the Future of Europe", *Ratio Juris*, Volume 36, Issue 3, September, 2023, pp. 242–258. The Rule of Law is not a «one size fits all» format nonetheless. But see: Chesterman, Simon, "An International Rule of Law", *The American Journal of Comparative Law*, Volume 56, 2008, pp. 331–362 (on the thrust to grasp (?) a catch-all International Rule of Law). See: Peari, Sagi, "Better Law as a Better Outcome", *The American Journal of Comparative Law*, Volume 63, Issue 1, 2015, pp. 155–195 (156) (on Leflar's stance on «better rule of law»). For the purposes of this piece, Rule of Law amounts to a lighthouse of procedural fairness to which citizens, regardless of where they are, resort to upon gaining access to a given system of administration of criminal justice. Whilst further utterances on the fabric of Rule of Law fall well outside the scope and breadth of this paper, one must not be oblivious of the fact that the thrust to Deglobalizing Rule of Law is underway. See: Bussani, Mauro, "Deglobalizing Rule of Law and Democracy: Hunting Down Rhetoric Through Comparative Law", *The American Journal of Comparative Law*, Volume 67, 2019, pp. 701–744 (701) (contending that the thrust to Deglobalizing Rule of Law is interwoven with thrust to take heed of «well-known differences that run through cultures and traditions». In spite of which, «the West has never stopped trying to export its own law into the rest of the world»). Unsurprisingly, there have been educated calls to take heed of the pinpointed cultural and legal differences by, in the case of China, allow for a «Socialist Rule of Law». See: Chinese Common Law Guiding Cases, *Harvard Law Review*, Volume 129, 2016, p. 2213.

[256] See: Amigud, Alexander, "The Age of the Intelligent Machine: Singularity, Efficiency, and Existential Peril", *Philosophy & Technology*, 37:49, 2024, p. 1 ("*many of the externalities, such as security risks, loss of privacy, and economic instability will result from trying to fit the emerging technologies into the existing frame of efficiency and utility, by redefining the notions of human value, identity, autonomy, purity, and truth*, among others. *The age of the intelligent machine is elevating alienation to new levels, treating the individual as mere patterns in data-its primary commodity*"). Italics added.

[257] See: Part V, Chap. 5, Sect. 5.1.1.1 of this book (on the central tenets of Rule of Law that lends itself to a beacon of justice amidst the sepulchral darkness that is about to take hold). See: Part V, Chap. 5, Sect. 5.1.1.2 of this book (on the central tenets of Procedural Rule of Law that lends itself to a lighthouse of justice that allows citizens to challenge the pearls of algorithmic wisdom in a court of law).

§§ It boils down to an unvarnished truth deeply woven into the fabric of cost-benefit analysis[258]: the continuous deployment of invasive[259] technology[260] begets citizens' distrust on the law.[261] Especially, albeit not exclusively, from

[258] *Cost-benefit Analysis* is in the limelight. Its development falls conspicuously outside the scope and aim of this book though. See: Sunstein, Cass R., "The Real World of Cost-Benefits Analysis: Thirty-Six Questions (and almost as many answers)", *Columbia Law Review*, 114 (1), 2014, 177; Bayefsky, Rachel, "Dignity as a value in Agency Cost-Benefit Analysis", *Yale Law Journal*, 123, 2014, 1740; Sunstein, Cass R., *Valuing Life: Humanizing the Regulatory State*, 2014, 8 ff; Gordon, Jeffrey, "The Empty Call for Cost-Benefits Analysis for Financial Regulators", *Journal of Legal Studies*, 43, 2014, 351; Sunstein, Cass R., "The Limits of Quantification", *California Law Review*, 103, 2014, 1369; Adler, Mathew/Posner, Eric A., "New Foundations of Cost-Benefit Analysis", *Regulation & Governance*, 3, 2006, 72; Thomas J. Miles/Sunstein, Cass R., "The Real World of Arbitrariness Review", *University of Chicago Law Review*, 75, 2008, 761; Coates, John C. IV, "Cost-Benefit Analysis of Financial Regulation: Case Studies and Implications", *Yale Law Journal*, 124, 2015, pp. 882–911; Posner, Eric A./Weyl E. Glen, "Cost-Benefit Analysis of Financial Regulations: Response to Criticisms", *Yale Law Journal*, 124, 2015, pp. 246–265 (parsing the relationship between agency cost-benefit analysis and human dignity).

[259] See: Part III, this chapter, Sect. 3.1.4.5 of this book (on Critical Artificial Intelligence Studies, with a sharper focus on the harmful effects of Brain-Computer Interfaces). See: Part III, this chapter, Sect. 3.1.5.10 of this book (on the functional aspects of Critical Artificial Intelligence Studies, with a sharper focus on the harmful effects of Artificial Intelligence-embedded technologies, namely, Brain-Computer Interfaces that can read and control your mind and behaviour).

[260] The newest developments posed by the "collect-it-all" technologies are slated to create a slew of sizzling hot challenges to the sustainability of the Rule of Law. See: Hu, Margaret, "From the National Surveillance State to the Cybersurveillance State", *The Annual Review of Law and Social Science*, Volume 13, 2017, pp. 162–163 ("*policymakers view these technological developments, including biometric technologies, as tools with the potential to identify individuals who may pose a threat to national and homeland security and to prevent crime and terrorism. One example of technology intended for risk assessment and threat management is the post-9/11 program Total Information Awareness (TIA).* TIA was the progeny of the Defense Advanced Research Projects Agency (DARPA) in the US Department of Defense. *TIA can be understood as a "collect-it-all" data surveillance program. TIA was not explicitly identified as a collect-it-all program—this phrase originated with the Snowden disclosures.* One National Security Agency (NSA) slide described the NSA's procedure as "collect-it-all" (Greenwald 2014b). *Collect-it-all efforts like TIA embody a philosophy that aspires to preventive policing. Mass data collection is construed as a tool to assess and prevent future threats* (Murray 2010). *In TIA and other programs tested or adopted after 9/11, biometric database screening and analysis have emerged as a preferred method for tracking, identifying, and establishing identity-based inferences in counterterrorism*"). Italics added. See also: Ball, Kirstie, and Frank Webster (Eds.), *The Intensification of Surveillance: Crime, Terrorism & Warfare in the Information Age*, London, UK: Pluto Press, 2007; Guzik, Keith, "Discrimination by Design: Predictive Data Mining as Security Practice in the United States' 'War on Terrorism'", *Surveillance and Society*, 7 (1), 2009, pp. 1–17. See: Part IV, Chap. 4, Sects. 4.1.5–4.1.5.2 of this book (on "algorithmic Jim Crow", a travel ban issued during the first Trump Administration to prevent certain individuals from entering the United States of America, which, given its racial undertones, stands as an outgrowth of congeries of laws enacted during the Jim Crow epoch).

[261] Tyler, Tom R., *Trust in the Law*. New York, NY: Russell-Sage, 2002, *passim* (on the paramount importance of trust in law); See: Magalhães, Pedro C./Garoupa, Nuno, "Judicial Performance and Trust in Legal Systems: Findings from a Decade of Surveys in 20 European Countries", *Social Science Quarterly*, 2020, p. 1 (the main goal of this exciting piece of research was "determining the existence of a relationship between judicial performance and citizens' trust in the legal system";

racial minorities whom have been floundering with hideous oppression,[262] structural disadvantage,[263] and gruelling racial discrimination for a long-haul.[264]

§§ On the heels of a sweeping system of racism laid down in vast swathes of the data-driven world we live in,[265] racialized people are far more likely to

---

Tyler, Tom R., "Psychological perspectives on legitimacy and legitimation", *Annual Review of Psychology*, Volume 57, 2006, pp. 375–400 (on the role that perceived legitimacy plays in everyday life); Tyler, Tom R., *Why people cooperate: The role of social motivations*. Princeton, New Jersey: Princeton University Press, 2011, passim (the author establishes a parallelism between underlying social motivations—such as trust and perceived legitimacy—to engage in cooperation with the authorities in legal settings).

262 Packard, Jerald M., *American Nightmare: The History of Jim Crow*, Broadway, New York, St. Martin's Press; First Edition, 2002, pp. 1–304 (vii–viii) ("[A*] structure of exclusion and discrimination devised by white Americans to be employed principally against black Americans.... Its central purpose was to maintain a second-class social and economic status for blacks while upholding a first-class social and economic status for whites.... In the South, Jim Crow discrimination at its height existed not only by statute but by custom and racial 'etiquette,' and it was rigidly enforced by both the law enforcement agencies* and courts as well as by ordinary white citizens who were neither policemen nor judges but who often took the law into their own hands as though they were"). Italics added.

263 See: Barocas, Solon/Selbst, Andrew, "Big Data's Disparate Impact", *California Law Review*, Volume 104, pp. 2016, p. 691 (highlighting the worrisome, and gruesome, issue of "structural disadvantage" with which racialized communities have been tussling for centuries). See also: Powell, Richard/Porter, Jeremy, "Redlining, Concentrated Disadvantage and Crime: The Effects of Discriminatory Government Policies on Violent Crime", *American Journal of Criminal Justice*, Volume 48, 2023, pp. 1132–1156 ("*Redlining and other discriminatory government policies enacted during the first half of the Twentieth Century have had long-lasting negative effects on neighborhoods, especially those inhabited by people of color. This study attempts to link the practice of redlining to current-day indicators of neighborhood concentrated disadvantage and violent crime using spatio-temporal data from Chicago (…) In addition, it seeks to determine whether redlining was associated with violent crime, and if that association was mediated by redlining's effect on concentrated disadvantage. The results indicate that redlining was associated with increases in both concentrated disadvantage and violent crime, and that redlining's relationship with violent crime was, indeed, partially mediated by its relationship with concentrated disadvantage*"). Italics added. See also: Gandy, Oscar H., *Coming to Terms with Chance: Engaging Rational Discrimination and Cumulative Disadvantage*, Farnham, UK: Ashgate Publishing, 2009. See: Part IV, Chap. 4, Sects. 4.1.4–4.1.4.2.1 of this book (on mortgage redlining). See: Part IV, Chap. 4, Sects. 4.1.2–4.1.4.3 of this book (on algorithmic credit scoring, consumer racism and credit card redlining). See: Part IV, Chap. 4, Sects. 4.1.4–4.1.4.2.3 of this book (on algorithmic redlining). See: Part IV, Chap. 4, Sect. 4.1.4.3 of this book (on "algorithmic redliking"). See: Part IV, Chap. 4, Sect. 4.1.3 of this book (on algorithmic prime-lining).

264 Gandy, Oscar H., *Coming to Terms with Chance: Engaging Rational Discrimination and Cumulative Disadvantage*, Farnham, UK: Ashgate Publishing, 2009.

265 But see: BALKIN, JACK, "Constitution in the National Surveillance State", *Minnesota Law Review*, Volume 93, 2008, p. 13 ("*data mining* allows inferences not only about the direct subject of surveillance, but about other people with whom they live, work and communicate"). Pearl, Judea, "Causal inference in statistics: An overview", *Statistics Surveys*, Volume 3, 2009, pp. 96–146. But see: Pedreshi, Dino/Ruggieri, Salvatore/Turini, Franco, "Discrimination-aware Data Mining", *Proceedings of the 14th ACM SIGKDD International Conference on Knowledge Discovery and Data Mining (Las Vegas, Nevada, USA), ACM*, 2008, pp. 560–568 (arguing that one should shift its gaze downstream by putting in place discrimination-aware algorithmic tools while performing data mining).

be surveilled,[266] controlled[267] and arrested[268] than white[269] folks.[270] Racism—and sexism[271]—is firmly rooted in a social construction against the backdrop of which ever-lasting surveillance,[272] unfaltering obedience and social control[273] unfolds.[274]

---

[266] Gandy, Oscar H., "Data Mining and Surveillance in the Post-9.11 Environment." *Presentation to the Political Economy Section, International Association for Media and Communication Research*, 2002.

[267] Garland, David, *The Culture of Control: Crime and Social Order in Contemporary Society*, New York: Oxford University Press, 2001; Kohler-Hausmann, Issa, "Misdemeanor Justice: Control without Conviction", *American Journal of Sociology*, 119 (2), 2013, pp. 351–93.

[268] Beckett, Katherine, Kris Nyrop, Lori Pfingst, and Melissa Bowen, "Drug Use, Drug Possession Arrests, and the Question of Race: Lessons from Seattle", *Social Problems* (52), 3, 2005, pp. 419–441.

[269] See: Connecticut Fair Housing Center, et al. v. CoreLogic Rental Property Solutions - Cohen Milstein (access: 20.11.2024) ("*The U.S. Department of Housing & Urban Development observed in 2016 that excluding rental applicants because of their criminal records disproportionately harms Latinos and African Americans, who are significantly more likely than whites to be arrested or convicted. Studies show such disparities are linked to differential enforcement rather than to differences in likelihood of engaging in criminal activity.* HUD advised that to avoid discriminating, an "individualized review" should be conducted considering the nature of the offense, how long ago it occurred, intervening changed circumstances, and other relevant factors to avoid denying housing to an applicant who does not pose a genuine and ongoing threat to persons or property. *Further, HUD's guidance specifically advises landlords not to consider arrests that did not result in a conviction in making their evaluations*"). Italics added. See: Part IV, Chap. 4, Sects. 4.1.4–4.1.4.2.1 of this book (on mortgage redlining). See: Part IV, Chap. 4, Sects. 4.1.2–4.1.4.3 of this book (on algorithmic credit scoring, consumer racism and credit card redlining). See: Part IV, Chap. 4, Sects. 4.1.4–4.1.4.2.3 of this book (on algorithmic redlining). See: Part IV, Chap. 4, Sect. 4.1.4.3 of this book (on "algorithmic redliking"). See: Part IV, Chap. 4, Sect. 4.1.3 of this book (on algorithmic prime-lining).

[270] Capers, I. B., "Policing, race, and place", *Harvard Civil Rights-Civil Liberties Law Review*, Volume 44, 2009, pp. 43–78.

[271] Hamilton, Melissa, "The sexist algorithm", *Behavioral Sciences and the Law*, Volume 37, Issue 2, Special Issue: the Use of Statistics in Criminal Cases, March-April 2019, 2019, pp. 1 and ff ("*Findings indicate that COMPAS performs reasonably well at discriminating between recidivists and non-recidivists for men and women. Nonetheless, COMPAS algorithmic outcomes systemically overclassify women in higher risk groupings. Multiple measures of algorithmic equity and predictive accuracy are provided to support the conclusion that this algorithm is sexist*"). Italics added. See: Part IV, Chap. 4, Sects. 4.1.10.1–4.1.10.6 of this book (on biased algorithmic risk assessment in criminal procedure law settings, with a sharper focus on COMPAS).

[272] Browne, Simone, *Dark Matters: On the Surveillance of Blackness*, Durham, NC: Duke University Press, 2015; Brayne, Sarah, "Surveillance and System Avoidance: Criminal Justice Contact and Institutional Attachment", *American Sociological Review*, 79 (3), 2014, pp. 367–391.

[273] Cohen, Stanley, *Visions of Social Control: Crime, Punishment and Classification*, Malden, MA: Polity Press, 1985.

[274] Brewer, R. M., & Heitzeg, N. A., "The racialization of crime and punishment: Criminal justice, Color-Blind racism, and the political economy of the prison industrial complex", *American Behavioral Scientist*, 51 (5), 2008, pp. 625–644.

§§ Which begs the vexing questions: what is the rationale behind the «racialization of crime»[275] and the deployment of cutting-edge technology to advance the hidden agenda of digital racism? Critical Race Theory (CRT)—one of the bedrocks of *Critical Artificial Intelligence Studies*—offers invaluable insights in this regard.

§§ Racism[276] is so deeply ingrained within the foundations of modern societies[277] that scholars often posit that the former is on the brink of a dispiriting normalcy.[278] The overriding goal of CRT is to challenge deep-seated racial inequalities[279] that beleaguers/pesters modern societies while fraying its fabric.[280] More to the point, CRT seeks to instil racial consciousness onto citizens[281] in an earnest attempt to unwind the gruelling effects of racial discrimination.[282]

§§ CRT contends that racism was created to maintain racial privileges for White folks.[283] The constant oppression of Blacks[284] amounts to the flagship of this abhorrent policy of divide and conquer. CRT accordingly seeks to canvass the foundations upon which stands this policy of divide and conquer while highlighting the racial inequality that besets modern societies.

---

[275] Brewer, R. M., & Heitzeg, N. A., "The racialization of crime and punishment: Criminal justice, Color-Blind racism, and the political economy of the prison industrial complex", *cit.*, pp. 625–644.

[276] Epp, Charles R., Steven Maynard-Moody, and Donald P. Haider-Markel, *Pulled Over: How Police Stops Define Race and Citizenship*, Chicago: University of Chicago Press, 2014.

[277] DaViera, A. L./Uriostegui, M., Gottlieb/A./Onyeka, O, "Risk, race, and predictive policing: A critical race theory analysis of the strategic subject list", *cit.*, pp. 91–103.

[278] Delgado, R., & Stefancic, J., "Critical race theory and criminal justice", *Humanity & Society*, 31, 2007, 133–145.

[279] Menasce, Juliana Horowitz/Brown, Anna/Cox, Kiana, "Views of Racial Inequality", *Pew Research Center*, April 9, 2019, 2919, available at: https://www.pewresearch.org/social-trends/2019/04/09/views-of-racial-inequality/ (access: 2.12.2024) ("*more than four-in-ten Americans say the country still has work to do to give black people equal rights with whites. Blacks, in particular, are skeptical that black people will ever have equal rights in this country (….) A majority of adults say that being white helps people's ability to get ahead in the country at least a little (59%); 28% say being white neither helps nor hurts and 12% say it hurts.* On the flip side, a majority (56%) sees being black as a disadvantage, with 25% saying it hurts people's ability to get ahead a lot. *About a quarter (26%) say being black neither helps nor hurts and 17% say it helps at least a little. More also say that being Hispanic hurts people's ability to get ahead in this country (51%) than say it helps (18%) or that it neither helps nor hurts (30%).* Opinions are more split when it comes to the impact of being Native American – about the same shares say this hurts as say it neither helps nor hurts, while a smaller share says it helps. *And while a plurality says being Asian neither helps nor hurts, more say it helps (34%) than hurts (21%) people's ability to get ahead*"). Italics added.

[280] Fiske, John, "Surveilling the City: Whiteness, the Black Man and Democratic Totalitarianism.", *Theory, Culture and Society*, 15 (2), 1998, pp. 67–88 (on the overhyped surveillance on black people as a byproduct of systemic racism).

[281] Capers, I. B., "Policing, race, and place", *Harvard Civil Rights-Civil Liberties Law Review*, Volume 44, 2009, pp. 43–78.

[282] DaViera, A. L./Uriostegui, M., Gottlieb/A./Onyeka, O, "Risk, race, and predictive policing: A critical race theory analysis of the strategic subject list", *cit.*, pp. 91–103.

[283] DaViera, A. L./Uriostegui, M., Gottlieb/A./Onyeka, O, "Risk, race, and predictive policing: A critical race theory analysis of the strategic subject list", *cit.*, pp. 91–103.

[284] Crutchfield, J., Fisher, A., & Webb, S. L., "Colorism and police killings", *The Western Journal of Black Studies*, 41 (3–4), 2017, 81.

§§ To cater for that, CRT leverages on a propelling force (the unshakeable goal to highlight the multifarious sub-systems of oppression and subordination arising out of racism, like poverty[285]) to gauge the extent to which the pendulum (systemic racism[286] and White supremacy,[287] which, taken together, spur racial disparities[288]) has swung too far. As it turns out, it did.

---

[285] Gilliom, John, *Overseers of the Poor: Surveillance, Resistance, and the Limits of Privacy*, Chicago: University of Chicago Press, 2001. Soss, Joe, Richard C. Fording, and Sanford F. Schram, *Disciplining the Poor: Neoliberal Paternalism and the Persistent Power of Race*. Chicago: University of Chicago Press, 2011.

[286] See: Feagin, J. R., *Systemic racism: a theory of oppression*, New York: Routledge, 2006. See also: Fiske, John, "Surveilling the City: Whiteness, the Black Man and Democratic Totalitarianism", *Theory, Culture and Society*, 15 (2), 1998, pp. 67–88 (on the overhyped surveillance on black people as a byproduct of systemic racism). See: Part IV, Chap. 4, Sects. 4.1.4–4.1.4.2.1 of this book (on mortgage redlining). See: Part IV, Chap. 4, Sects. 4.1.2–4.1.4.3 of this book (on algorithmic credit scoring, consumer racism and credit card redlining). See: Part IV, Chap. 4, Sects. 4.1.4–4.1.4.2.3 of this book (on algorithmic redlining). See: Part IV, Chap. 4, Sect. 4.1.4.3 of this book (on "algorithmic redliking"). See: Part IV, Chap. 4, Sect. 4.1.3 of this book (on algorithmic prime-lining).

[287] See: Perea, Juan F., "Doctrines of Delusion: How the History of the G.I. Bill and Other Inconvenient Truths Undermind the Supreme Court's Affirmative Action Jurisprudence", *University of Pittsburgh Law Review*, Volume 75, 1995, pp. 583, 586–89 (establishes a liaison between Jim Crow laws, the G.I. Bill, and the Social Security Act and White supremacy); Milligan, Joy, "Protecting Disfavored Minorities: Towards Institutional Realism", *UCLA Law Review*, Volume 63, 2016, pp. 894, pp. 918–21 (shedding a keen light on racial inequality in U.S. Department of Agriculture farm assistance); Robinson, Reginald Leamon, "The Racial Limits of the Fair Housing Act: The Intersection of Dominant White Images, the Violence of Neighborhood Purity, and the Master Narrative of Black Inferiority", *William & Mary Law Review*, Volume 37, 1995, pp. 69, 71–74 (establishes a connection between the failures of the FHA and White supremacy). But see: Wormser, Richard, *The Rise and Fall of Jim Crow*, Manhattan, New York City, St Martin's Press, 2014, pp. 1–222 ("*White supremacy prevailed, but it did not destroy the spirit of the black community*"). Italics added. See: Part IV, Chap. 4, Sects. 4.1.4–4.1.4.2.1 of this book (on mortgage redlining). See: Part IV, Chap. 4, Sects. 4.1.2–4.1.4.3 of this book (on algorithmic credit scoring, consumer racism and credit card redlining). See: Part IV, Chap. 4, Sects. 4.1.4–4.1.4.2.3 of this book (on algorithmic redlining). See: Part IV, Chap. 4, Sect. 4.1.4.3 of this book (on "algorithmic redliking"). See: Part IV, Chap. 4, Sect. 4.1.3 of this book (on algorithmic prime-lining).

[288] Berg, M. T., "Accounting for racial disparities in the nature of violent victimization", *Journal of Quantitative Criminology*, 30 (4), 2014, 629–650.

§§ The chief aim of, and the central tenet of, CRT is to shine a keen light upon the racial social hierarchy, which is underpinned by, and revolves around of, a multi-layered system of racial oppression[289] that purposefully creates a racial wedge[290] between White folks[291] and Blacks.[292]

§§ Race therefore amounts to the intellectual lodestar of CRT in that the former is the linchpin of the latter. Put otherwise, race is the guiding concept, and the propelling force, around which CRT revolves.[293] In many ways, CRT holds race[294] at the fulcrum of its granular analysis.[295]

§§ CRT accordingly delves into controversies surrounding racialized communities[296] in a bid to grasp, parse and flesh out the harrowing experiences[297] of those unlawfully targeted by an oppressive system[298] that begets widespread discrimination[299] and racial prejudice[300] that, if nothing else, is difficult to allay.[301]

---

[289] Rios, Victor M., *Punished: Policing the Lives of Black and Latino Boys*, New York: NYU Press, 2011.

[290] Western, Bruce, and Becky, Pettit, "Black-White Wage Inequality, Employment Rates, and Incarceration", *American Journal of Sociology*, 111 (2), 2005, 553 78.

[291] DaViera, A. L./Uriostegui, M., Gottlieb/A./Onyeka, O, "Risk, race, and predictive policing: A critical race theory analysis of the strategic subject list", *cit.*, pp. 91–103. See: Part IV, Chap. 4, Sects. 4.1.10.1–4.1.10.6 of this book (on biased algorithmic risk assessment in criminal procedure law settings, with a sharper focus on COMPAS).

[292] Gross, Samuel R., Maurice Possley, and Kalara Stephens, "Race and Wrongful Convictions in the United States." National Registry of Exonerations, Newkirk Centre for Science and Society, University of California-Irvine, 2017.

[293] DaViera, A. L./Uriostegui, M., Gottlieb/A./Onyeka, O, "Risk, race, and predictive policing: A critical race theory analysis of the strategic subject list", *cit.*, pp. 91–103.

[294] Pager, Devah, Marked: Race, Crime, and Finding Work in an Era of Mass Incarceration, Chicago: University of Chicago Press, 2007.

[295] Bonilla-Silva, E., "The linguistics of color blind racism: How to talk nasty about blacks without sounding 'racist'", *Critical Sociology*, 28 (2), 2002, 41–64.

[296] DaViera, A. L./Uriostegui, M., Gottlieb/A./Onyeka, O, "Risk, race, and predictive policing: A critical race theory analysis of the strategic subject list", *cit.*, pp. 91–103.

[297] Crutchfield, J., Fisher, A., & Webb, S. L., "Colorism and police killings", *The Western Journal of Black Studies*, 41 (3–4), 2017, 81.

[298] Arnold, David, Will Dobbie, and Peter Hull, "Measuring Racial Discrimination in Bail Decisions," *American Economic Review*, 112, 2022, pp. 2992–3038.

[299] Sampson, Robert J., and Dawn J. Bartusch, "Legal Cynicism and (Subcultural?) Tolerance of Deviance: The Neighbourhood Context of Racial Differences", *Law and Society Review*, 32, 1998, pp. 777–804.

[300] Eckhouse, L., Lum, K., Conti-Cook, C., & Ciccolini, J., "Layers of bias: A unified approach for understanding problems with risk assessment", *Criminal Justice and Behavior*, 46 (2), 2019, 185–209.

[301] Dobbie, Will, Jacob Goldin, and Crystal S. Yang, "The Effects of Pretrial Detention on Conviction, Future Crime, and Employment: Evidence from Randomly Assigned Judges," *American Economic Review*, 108 2018, 201–240.

§§ Marginalized communities[302]—amongst whom Blacks,[303] Latinos[304] and Native Americans—are lodged at CRT's centre of analysis. Marginalized communities that, unbewilderingly, have been grappling with multiple layers of both deep-seated racial[305] biases[306] and gruesome discrimination[307] for a long-winded span of time.[308]

§§ In addition to that, CRT argues that modern societies laws are undergirded by, and thus revolve around of, the maintenance of White privilege,[309] fundamentally aimed at maximizing White folks benefits while minimizing the universe of rights pertaining to Blacks,[310] Latinos[311] and «risky subjects»[312] alike.[313]

§§ CRT furthermore argues that the structural racism upholds an agreed-upon policy that jettisons non-White communities to suburban areas.[314] This is the gist of a disheartening policy called *mortgage redlining*, which will merit our undivided attention later in this book.[315]

---

[302] Braga, Anthony A., and David L. Weisburd, *Policing Problem Places: Crime Hot Spots and Effective Prevention*, New York: Oxford University Press, 2010.

[303] Dottolo, A. L., & Stewart, A. J., ""Don't ever forget now, you're a Black man in America": Intersections of race, class and gender in encounters with the police", *Sex Roles*, 59 (5–6), 2008, 350–364.

[304] Rios, Victor M., *Punished: Policing the Lives of Black and Latino Boys*. New York: NYU Press, 2011.

[305] Abdillahi, I., "Algorithmic surveillance in the era of the appsphere", *American Journal of Community Psychology*, 2024, 73.

[306] Fagan, J., "Race and the new policing", *Columbia Public Law Research Paper*, 2 (14–561), 2017, pp. 83–116.

[307] Becker, Gary, *The Economics of Discrimination*, Chicago: University of Chicago Press, 1957.

[308] Henne, K., & Troshynski, E. I., "Intersectional criminologies for the contemporary moment: Crucial questions of power, praxis and technologies of control", *Critical Criminology*, 27 (1), 2019, 55–71.

[309] Fornili, K. S., "Racialized mass incarceration and the war on drugs: A critical race theory appraisal", *Journal of Addictions Nursing*, 29 (1), 2018, pp. 65–72.

[310] Arnold, David, Will Dobbie, and Crystal S. Yang, "Racial Bias in Bail Decisions," *Quarterly Journal of Economics*, 133, 2018, pp. 1885–1932.

[311] Rios, Victor M, *Punished: Policing the Lives of Black and Latino Boys*, New York: NYU Press, 2011.

[312] Agung-Igusti, R. P., "Raced and risky subjects: The interplay of racial and managerial ideologies as an expression of "colorblind" racism", *American Journal of Community Psychology*, 2024, 73.

[313] DaViera, A. L./Uriostegui, M., Gottlieb/A./Onyeka, O, "Risk, race, and predictive policing: A critical race theory analysis of the strategic subject list", *cit.*, pp. 91–103. See also: Alexander, M., *The new Jim Crow: Mass incarceration in the age of colorblindness*, The New Press, 2012. See: Part IV, Chap. 4, Sects. 4.1.10.1–4.1.10.6 of this book (on biased algorithmic risk assessment in criminal procedure law settings, with a sharper focus on COMPAS).

[314] Du Bois, W. E. B., *Black Reconstruction in America: Toward a history of the part which black folk played in the attempt to reconstruct democracy in America*, London, Routledge, 2017.

[315] See: Part IV, Chap. 4, Sects. 4.1.4–4.1.4.2.1 of this book (on mortgage redlining). See: Part IV, Chap. 4, Sects. 4.1.2–4.1.4.3 of this book (on algorithmic credit scoring, consumer racism and credit card redlining). See: Part IV, Chap. 4, Sects. 4.1.4–4.1.4.2.3 of this book (on algorithmic redlining). See: Part IV, Chap. 4, Sect. 4.1.4.3 of this book (on "algorithmic redliking"). See: Part

§§ The overriding goal of this initiative—*mortgage redlining*,[316] which boiled down to a policy according to which non-White communities should be thrown to the outskirts of urban cities—was clear-cut: cast a shady shadow on racialized people, thereby creating a bespoke connection between race,[317] class, crime hot spots,[318] income,[319] proclivity to engage in flagitious activities,[320] syndicates of organized crime,[321] gang violence,[322] and crime-ridden neighbourhoods[323] that still reverberates,[324] and ripples forward,[325] across generations.[326] The rate and pace at which non-White are incarcerated gives credence to this main contention.[327]

§§ CRT adamantly contents that modern societies are left largely tethered to outdated structures that prevent non-White communities from both vindicate their rights or forgo their enforcement.

IV, Chap. 4, Sect. 4.1.3 of this book (on algorithmic prime-lining). See: Part IV, Chap. 4, Sects. 4.1.10.1–4.1.10.6 of this book (on biased algorithmic risk assessment in criminal procedure law settings, with a sharper focus on COMPAS).

[316] See: Part IV, Chap. 4, Sects. 4.1.4–4.1.4.2.1 of this book (on mortgage redlining). See: Part IV, Chap. 4, Sects. 4.1.2–4.1.4.3 of this book (on algorithmic credit scoring, consumer racism and credit card redlining). See: Part IV, Chap. 4, Sects. 4.1.4–4.1.4.2.3 of this book (on algorithmic redlining). See: Part IV, Chap. 4, Sect. 4.1.4.3 of this book (on "algorithmic redliking"). See: Part IV, Chap. 4, Sect. 4.1.3 of this book (on algorithmic prime-lining).

[317] Pager, Devah, *Marked: Race, Crime, and Finding Work in an Era of Mass Incarceration*, Chicago: University of Chicago Press, 2007.

[318] Braga, Anthony A., and David L. Weisburd, *Policing Problem Places: Crime Hot Spots and Effective Prevention*, New York: Oxford University Press, 2010.

[319] Gustafson, Kaaryn S, *Cheating Welfare: Public Assistance and the Criminalization of Poverty*, New York: NYU Press, 2011.

[320] DaViera, A. L./Uriostegui, M., Gottlieb/A./Onyeka, O, "Risk, race, and predictive policing: A critical race theory analysis of the strategic subject list", *cit.*, pp. 91–103.

[321] Papachristos, Andrew V., David M. Hureau, and Anthony A. Braga, "The Corner and the Crew: The Influence of Geography and Social Networks on Gang Violence", *American Sociological Review*, 78 (3), 2013, pp. 417–47.

[322] Quillian, Lincoln, and Devah Pager, "Black Neighbors, Higher Crime? The Role of Racial Stereotypes in Evaluations of Neighborhood Crime", *American Journal of Sociology*, 107 (3), 2001, 717–67.

[323] Brewer, R. M., & Heitzeg, N. A., "The racialization of crime and punishment: Criminal justice, Color-Blind racism, and the political economy of the prison industrial complex", *American Behavioral Scientist*, 51 (5), 2008, 625–644; Sampson, Robert J., and Dawn J. Bartusch, "Legal Cynicism and (Subcultural?) Tolerance of Deviance: The Neighborhood Context of Racial Differences", *Law and Society Review*, 32, 1998, pp. 777–804.

[324] Skogan, Wesley G., *Police and Community in Chicago: A Tale of Three Cities*, New York: Oxford University Press, 2006.

[325] Sherman, Lawrence W., Patrick R. Gartin, and Michael E. Buerger, "Hot Spots of Predatory Crime: Routine Activities and the Criminology of Place", *Criminology*, 27 (1), 1989, pp. 27–55.

[326] Jacoby, S. F., Dong, B., Beard, J. H., Wiebe, D. J., & Morrison, C. N., "The enduring impact of historical and structural racism on urban violence in Philadelphia", *Social Science & Medicine*, 1982/2018, 199, 2018, pp. 87–95.

[327] Travis, Jeremy, Bruce Western, and Steve Redburn (Eds.), *Growth of Incarceration in the United States: Exploring Causes and Consequences*, Washington, DC: National Academy of Science, 2014.

§§ Stated differently, modern societies are underpinned by the foundational pillars of systemic racism[328] whose overriding goal is to uphold White supremacy[329]/ White privilege[330] while consistently downplaying the rights and needs of non-White communities, whom are deemed as inferior forms of life. The unsavoury encounters with law enforcement agencies[331] add plausibility to this sweeping claim.[332]

§§ The «racialization of crime»[333] process accordingly lends itself to racialized defendants' earnest attempts to fend off attacks perpetrated by law enforcement agencies. The soared/ballooned figures of wrong convictions lend weight to this overriding claim.[334]

---

[328] Chafe, William H./Gavins, Raymond/Korstad, Robert (Editors), *Remembering Jim Crow: African Americans Tell About Life in the Segregated South*, Revised Edition, New York, The New Press, 2014, pp. 1–448 ("based on interviews collected by the Behind the Veil Project at Duke University's Center for Documentary Studies, this remarkable book presents for the first time the most extensive oral history ever compiled of African American life under segregation. *Men and women from all walks of life tell how their most ordinary activities were subjected to profound and unrelenting racial oppression.* Yet *Remembering Jim Crow is also a testament to how black southerners fought back against systemic racism—building churches and schools, raising children, running businesses, and struggling for respect in a society that denied them the most basic rights. The result is a powerful story of individual and community survival*"). Italics added.

[329] See: Perea, Juan F., "Doctrines of Delusion: How the History of the G.I. Bill and Other Inconvenient Truths Undermind the Supreme Court's Affirmative Action Jurisprudence", *University of Pittsburgh Law Review*, Volume 75, 1995, pp. 583, 586–89 (establishes a liaison between Jim Crow laws, the G. I. Bill, and the Social Security Act and White supremacy); Milligan, Joy, "Protecting Disfavored Minorities: Towards Institutional Realism", *UCLA Law Review*, Volume 63, 2016, pp. 894, 918–21 (shedding a keen light on racial inequality in U.S. Department of Agriculture farm assistance); Robinson, Reginald Leamon, "The Racial Limits of the Fair Housing Act: The Intersection of Dominant White Images, the Violence of Neighborhood Purity, and the Master Narrative of Black Inferiority", *William & Mary Law Review*, Volume 37, 1995, pp. 69, 71–74 (establishes a connection between the failures of the FHA and White supremacy). But see: Wormser, Richard, *The Rise and Fall of Jim Crow*, Manhattan, New York City, St Martin's Press, 2014, pp. 1–222 ("*White supremacy prevailed, but it did not destroy the spirit of the black community*"). Italics added. See: Part IV, Chap. 4, Sects. 4.1.4–4.1.4.2.1 of this book (on mortgage redlining). See: Part IV, Chap. 4, Sects. 4.1.2–4.1.4.3 of this book (on algorithmic credit scoring, consumer racism and credit card redlining). See: Part IV, Chap. 4, Sects. 4.1.4–4.1.4.2.3 of this book (on algorithmic redlining). See: Part IV, Chap. 4, Sect. 4.1.4.3 of this book (on "algorithmic redliking"). See: Part IV, Chap. 4, Sect. 4.1.3 of this book (on algorithmic prime-lining).

[330] Bhopal, K., *White Privilege: The Myth of a Post-Racial Society*, Bristol, Policy Press Bristol University Press, 2018.

[331] Western, Bruce, *Punishment and Inequality in America*, New York: Russell Sage Foundation, 2006.

[332] Soss, Joe, Richard C. Fording, and Sanford F. Schram, *Disciplining the Poor: Neoliberal Paternalism and the Persistent Power of Race*, Chicago: University of Chicago Press, 2011.

[333] Brewer, R. M., & Heitzeg, N. A., "The racialization of crime and punishment: Criminal justice, Color-Blind racism, and the political economy of the prison industrial complex", *cit.*, pp. 625–644.

[334] Gross, Samuel R., Maurice Possley, and Kalara Stephens, "Race and Wrongful Convictions in the United States" National Registry of Exonerations, Newkirk Centre for Science and Society, University of California-Irvine, 2017.

§§ On the heels of, and fundamentally building on, the structural racism[335] against the backdrop of which White privilege unfolds,[336] CRT avowedly contents that the newest technological developments (e.g. predictive policing[337]) amount to the crowning achievement of an agreed-upon strategy according to which non-White communities (chiefly, Black, and Latino[338]) should be become enmeshed in criminal justice system.[339] Especially, albeit not exclusively, young black men.[340]

---

[335] Packard, Jerald M., *American Nightmare: The History of Jim Crow*, Broadway, New York, St. Martin's Press; First Edition, 2002, pp. 1–304 (vii–viii) ("[A*] structure of exclusion and discrimination devised by white Americans to be employed principally against black Americans.... Its central purpose was to maintain a second-class social and economic status for blacks while upholding a first-class social and economic status for whites.... In the South, Jim Crow discrimination at its height existed not only by statute but by custom and racial 'etiquette,' and it was rigidly enforced by both the law enforcement agencies* and courts as well as by ordinary white citizens who were neither policemen nor judges but who often took the law into their own hands as though they were"). Italics added.

[336] Laub, John H., "Understanding Inequality and the Justice System Response: Charting a New Way Forward." New York: William T. Grant Foundation, 2014. See: Part IV, Chap. 4, Sects. 4.1.10.1–4.1.10.6 of this book (on biased algorithmic risk assessment in criminal procedure law settings, with a sharper focus on COMPAS).

[337] See: Part IV, Chap. 4, Sects. 4.1.1–4.1.1.1 of this book (on biased predictive policing). See: Part IV, Chap. 4, Sects. 4.1.10.1–4.1.10.6 of this book (on biased algorithmic risk assessment in criminal procedure law settings, with a sharper focus on COMPAS). See: Hu, Margaret, "From the National Surveillance State to the Cybersurveillance State", *The Annual Review of Law and Social Science*, Volume 13, 2017, p. 166 (argues that ubiquitous and ever-present surveillance of socially undesirables remains at a pitch of degradation of fundamental rights in that Artificial Intelligence-embedded technologies—propelled by tools like Social Radar and Total Information Awareness, TIA—can capture "a *pictorial depiction of the comprehensive cybersurveillance anticipated through the Social Radar system, which anticipated the full integration of drone footage, biometrric data signatures, econometrics, and other intelligence sources to achieve higher-order cybersurveillance inferences. Social Radar appears to trace its philosophical origins to TIA.* The development of TIA after the 9/11 terrorist attacks was guided under the leadership of the newly created Information Awareness Office within DARPA (Harris 2012; Murray 2010). Within this office, TIA was an effort led by retired Navy Vice Admiral John M. Poindexter (Murray 2010), who served as a national security advisor to President Reagan (Harris 2012). *TIA was informed by a philosophy of "predictive policing," which "focuses not on collecting evidence about actual wrongdoing but on the broad collection of information about everyday activities with the intention of detecting (and preventing) future behavior"* (Murray 2010, p. 5). Congress officially defunded TIA in late 2003 (Murray 2010; Slobogin 2008; USA Today 2003). *Experts have nonetheless noted that remnants of the TIA program and its philosophy have persisted*"). Italics added. See: Part IV, Chap. 4, Sects. 4.1.5–4.1.5.2 of this book (on "algorithmic Jim Crow", a travel ban issued during the first Trump Administration to prevent certain individuals from entering the United States of America, which, given its racial undertones, stands as an outgrowth of congeries of laws enacted during the Jim Crow epoch).

[338] Rios, Victor M., *Punished: Policing the Lives of Black and Latino Boys*, New York: NYU Press, 2011.

[339] Duster, Troy, "Pattern, Purpose and Race in the Drug War", *Crack in America: Demon Drugs and Social Justice*, Reinarman and H. G. Levine (Editors), Berkeley: University of California Press, 1997.

[340] Epp, Charles R., Steven Maynard-Moody, and Donald P. Haider-Markel, *Pulled Over: How Police Stops Define Race and Citizenship*, Chicago: University of Chicago Press, 2014.

§§ To put it bluntly, Blacks and Latinos should be permanently targeted, harassed, arrested,[341] and convicted[342] by law enforcement.[343] Predictive policing—to which a fine-grained attention will be paid in this book[344]—therefore *automates suspicion,*[345] which unlawfully befalls racialized people. On that account, predictive policing has been enduring both trenchant criticism and vitriolic remarks.[346] More on this later.[347]

§§ Against this background, there has been a *punitive turn* steered by an inscrutable «Intelligence-led Policing»[348] aimed at further chastising racialized

---

[341] See: Connecticut Fair Housing Center, et al. v. CoreLogic Rental Property Solutions - Cohen Milstein (access: 20.11.2024) ("*The U.S. Department of Housing & Urban Development observed in 2016 that excluding rental applicants because of their criminal records disproportionately harms Latinos and African Americans, who are significantly more likely than whites to be arrested or convicted. Studies show such disparities are linked to differential enforcement rather than to differences in likelihood of engaging in criminal activity.* HUD advised that to avoid discriminating, an "individualized review" should be conducted considering the nature of the offense, how long ago it occurred, intervening changed circumstances, and other relevant factors to avoid denying housing to an applicant who does not pose a genuine and ongoing threat to persons or property. *Further, HUD's guidance specifically advises landlords not to consider arrests that did not result in a conviction in making their evaluations*"). Italics added.

[342] Gross, Samuel R., Maurice Possley, and Kalara Stephens, "Race and Wrongful Convictions in the United States." National Registry of Exonerations, Newkirk Centre for Science and Society, University of California-Irvine, 2017.

[343] Rios, Victor M., *Punished: Policing the Lives of Black and Latino Boys*, New York: NYU Press, 2011.

[344] See: Part IV, Chap. 4, Sects. 4.1.1–4.1.1.1 of this book (on biased predictive policing).

[345] Joh, Elizabeth E., "The New Surveillance Discretion: Automated Suspicion, Big Data, and Policing", *Harvard Law and Policy Review*, 10 (1), 2016, pp. 15–42.

[346] Harcourt, Bernard E. 2006, *Against Prediction: Profiling, Policing, and Punishing in an Actuarial Age*, Chicago: University of Chicago Press, 2006.

[347] See: Part IV, Chap. 4, Sects. 4.1.1–4.1.1.1 of this book (on biased predictive policing).

[348] Ratcliffe, Jerry, *Intelligence-Led Policing*, Cullompton, UK: Willan Publishing, 2008.

people under a patina of objectivity (foremost, wrapped in the opaqueness[349] of catch-all concepts of *trust in science*[350] and *trust in numbers*[351]).

§§ The rationale behind the creation of this «Intelligence-led Policing» was nonetheless straightforward: over-policing the so-called crime-ridden neighbourhoods[352] fraught with *socially undesirables* (Blacks and Latinos). Especially, albeit not exclusively, young black men.[353]

§§ Hardly any surprise stems from the fact that technological developments (v.g. *predictive policing*,[354] *algorithmic prime-lining*,[355] *algorithmic redlining*,[356] *credit card redlining*,[357] *algorithmic redliking*,[358] «algorithmic Jim Crow»,[359] *proxy*

---

349 *Tech, Bias and Housing Initiative, the Promise and Perils of Residential Proptech, Year 1, Research Summary Report, April 2023, TechEquity Collaborative*, p. 11, available at: https://techequity.us/wp-content/uploads/2023/04/TBHI-Y1-Research-Summary-Report.pdf (28.11.2024) ("*From information on company websites, it is not clear what analysis or data is behind subjective determinations like "suitability" to a unit or what the nexus between an individual's characteristics and a unit's characteristics is that indicates the likelihood for property damage. Based on sample reports, even landlords are not privy to how the determinations are made. Instead, they receive a risk score out of 100 simplified into green, yellow, and red recommendations.* What companies withhold in terms of how it works, they make up for with the extent to which they tell landlords it works: Naborly claims their predictions reduce lease defaults by up to 89%. 15 *As Naborly's sample report demonstrates, its property damage assessment is then used as an input to determine its projected eviction outcomes; its early vacancy prediction, in turn, is based on "all assessment factors*"). Italics added.

350 Sherman, Lawrence W., "Targeting, Testing and Tracking Police Services: The Rise of Evidence Based Policing, 1975–2025", *Crime and Justice*, 42 (1), 2013, pp. 377–451; Lavender III, I., *Race in American science fiction*, Bloomington: Indiana University Press, 2011.

351 Porter, Theodore M., *Trust in Numbers: The Pursuit of Objectivity in Science and Public Life*, Princeton, NJ: Princeton University Press, 1995.

352 DaViera, A. L./Uriostegui, M., Gottlieb/A./Onyeka, O, "Risk, race, and predictive policing: A critical race theory analysis of the strategic subject list", *cit.*, pp. 91–103.

353 Fagan, J., "Race and the new policing", *Columbia Public Law Research Paper*, 2 (14–561), 2017, 83–116.

354 See: Part IV, Chap. 4, Sects. 4.1.1–4.1.1.1 of this book.

355 See: Part IV, Chap. 4, Sect. 4.1.3 of this book.

356 See: Part IV, Chap. 4, Sects. 4.1.4–4.1.4.2.3 of this book.

357 See: Part IV, Chap. 4, Sect. 4.1.2.3 of this book.

358 See: Part IV, Chap. 4, Sect. 4.1.4.3 of this book.

359 See: Part IV, Chap. 4, Sects. 4.1.5–4.1.5.1 of this book.

discrimination,[360] *algorithmic credit scoring,*[361] *facial recognition*[362] and so forth) are tools suitably tailored to assist the Government-run entities (police, public bureaus, and law enforcement agencies alike) in advancing a hidden agenda of social

---

360 See: Part IV, Chap. 4, Sect. 4.1.6 of this book. See also: Campisi, Natalie, From Inherent Racial Bias to Incorrect Data The Problems With Current Credit Scoring Models, Forbes (Feb. 26, 2021), https://www.forbes.com/advisor/creditcards/from-inherent-racial-bias-to-incorrect-data-the-problems-with-current-credit-scoring-models/ [https://perma.cc/EWA4-CS8E] (highlighting rampant racial bias in credit scoring systems); Oyama, Rebecca, "Do Not (Re)Enter: the Rise of Criminal Background Tenant Screening as a Violation of the Fair Housing Act", *Michigan Journal of Race and Law*, Volume 15, 2009, pp. 181, 184–93 (discussing a broad range of historical/criminal accounts as a way to screen undesirable tenants, such as Blacks and Latinos); Statement of Interest of the United States at 12, *Louis v. SafeRent Sols., LLC, No. 1:22-cv-10800* (D. Mass. Jan. 9, 2023) (holding that the Fair Housing Act liability stretches far and beyond, thus encompassing a vast assortment of entities providing housing-related services, including corporations that offer tenant screening services). See also: Massey, Douglas S., "The Legacy of the 1968 Fair Housing Act", *Social Forces*, Volume 30, 2015, pp. 571, 575–76, 578 ("*[The FHA] outlawed the refusal to rent or sell to someone because of race; it prohibited racial discrimination in the terms and conditions of rental or sale; it barred discrimination in real estate advertising; it banned agents from making untrue statements about a dwelling's availability in order to deny access to blacks*; and it enjoined real estate agents from making comments about the race of neighbors or in-movers in order to promote panic selling. Although the new law applied only to around 80% of the nation's housing stock, a Supreme Court decision adjudicated just two months later extended its reach to all housing in the United States"). Italics added. Internal citations omitted.

361 See: Part IV, Chap. 4, Sect. 4.1.4.2.2 of this book. But see: Wonyoung, So, "Which Information Matters? Measuring Landlord Assessment of Tenant Screening Reports", *Housing Policy Debate*, Volume 33, n.º 6, 2023, pp. 1484–1510 (1502) ("*One additional finding of the experiment is that algorithmic scoring can exacerbate this racially unequal landscape in rental agreements not just because the algorithm may be inaccurate, but because landlords may want to follow the risk assessment made by the tenant screening report. This is alarming for low-income tenants, particularly housing voucher holders. Security deposits are one of the most significant barriers to obtaining housing for voucher holders, because vouchers do not pay security deposits but most private landlords require them* (Rosenblatt and Cossyleon 2018). Given that voucher holders have exceptionally low income (usually less than 50% of area median income) and might experience more housing insecurity (rental debts and eviction-related experiences), *imposing greater security deposits on voucher holders almost equates to denying them housing—yet these decisions could be justified by algorithmic scoring if tenant screening services employ it*"). Italics added.

362 See: Part III, this chapter, Sects. 3.1.5.7–3.1.5.8.1 of this book (on the functional aspects of Critical Artificial Intelligence Studies, with a sharper focus on the perils concerning the deployment of facial recognition technology). See: Hu, Margaret, "From the National Surveillance State to the Cybersurveillance State", *The Annual Review of Law and Social Science*, Volume 13, 2017, p. 169 ("*in a big data world, a digitized passport system can link to multiple other sources, such as license plate readers, No Fly Lists, and Terrorist Watchlists. Facial recognition technology drawing upon a photo database could potentially link a plethora of digital images of a person, including social media, the internet, photo databases like driver's licenses, live-streaming video, CCTV surveillance, and images obtained from hacking cameras on laptops and digital devices. Biometric data collection and storage are becoming increasingly compulsory through either government identification requirements*, such as digital photo requirements for passports and driver's licenses, or corporate identification requirements, such as biometric access to digital devices"). Italics added. See: Part IV, Chap. 4, Sects. 4.1.5–4.1.5.2 of this book (on "algorithmic Jim Crow", a travel ban issued during the first Trump Administration to prevent certain individuals from entering the United States of

control[363] that strives to maintain both White supremacy[364] and White privilege[365] while further chastising non-White communities.

America, which, given its racial undertones, stands as an outgrowth of congeries of laws enacted during the Jim Crow epoch).

363 Garland, David, *The Culture of Control: Crime and Social Order in Contemporary Society*, New York: Oxford University Press, 2001; Kohler-Hausmann, Issa, "Misdemeanor Justice: Control without Conviction", *American Journal of Sociology*, 119 (2), 2013, pp. 351–93; Cohen, Stanley, *Visions of Social Control: Crime, Punishment and Classification*, Malden, MA: Polity Press, 1985.

364 Daley, Jane/Gimore, Glenda Elizabeth/Simon, Bryant (Editors), Jumpin' *Jim Crow: Southern Politics from Civil War to Civil Rights*, Princeton, Princeton University Press, 2020, pp. 1–331 ("*White supremacy shaped all aspects of post-Civil War southern life, yet its power was never complete or total. The form of segregation and subjection nicknamed Jim Crow constantly had to remake itself over time even as white southern politicians struggled to extend its grip.* Here, some of the most innovative scholars of southern history question Jim Crow's sway, evolution, and methods over the course of a century. These essays bring to life the southern men and women-some heroic and decent, others mean and sinister, most a mixture of both-who supported and challenged Jim Crow, showing that white supremacy always had to prove its power. *Jim Crow was always in motion, always adjusting to meet resistance and defiance by both African Americans and whites. Sometimes white supremacists responded with increased ferocity, sometimes with more subtle political and legal ploys. Jumpin' Jim Crow presents a clear picture of this complex negotiation. For example, even as some black and white women launched the strongest attacks on the system, other white women nurtured myths glorifying white supremacy.* Even as elite whites blamed racial violence on poor whites, they used Jim Crow to dominate poor whites as well as blacks. Most important, the book portrays change over time, suggesting that Strom Thurmond is not a simple reincarnation of Ben Tillman and that Rosa Parks was not the first black woman to say no to Jim Crow"). Italics added. See also: Rich, Camille Gear, "Marginal Whiteness", *California Law Review*, Volume 98, 2010, passim; Smångs, Mattias, "Doing Violence, Making Race: Southern Lynching and White Racial Group Formation, *American Journal of Sociology*, Volume 121, 2016.

365 Roithmayr, Daria, *Reproducing Racism: How everyday choices lock in White Advantage*, New York, New York University Press, 2014, pp. 1–272 ("*Argues that racial inequality reproduces itself automatically over time because early unfair advantage for whites has paved the way for continuing advantage. This book is designed to change the way we think about racial inequality (...) Legal scholar Daria Roithmayr provocatively argues that racial inequality lives on because white advantage functions as a powerful self-reinforcing monopoly, reproducing itself automatically from generation to generation even in the absence of intentional discrimination. Drawing on work in antitrust law and a range of other disciplines, Roithmayr brilliantly compares the dynamics of white advantage to the unfair tactics of giants like AT&T and Microsoft.* With penetrating insight, Roithmayr *locates the engine of white monopoly in positive feedback loops that connect the dramatic disparity of Jim Crow to modern racial gaps in jobs, housing and education. Wealthy white neighborhoods fund public schools that then turn out wealthy white neighbors. Whites with lucrative jobs informally refer their friends, who refer their friends, and so on. Roithmayr concludes that racial inequality might now be locked in place, unless policymakers immediately take drastic steps to dismantle this oppressive system*"). Italics added. This book points out how White privilege is perpetuated throughout generations through residential segregation (*mortgage redlining*), abhorrent nepotism, and other bemoaning social practices that pester modern societies). See: Part IV, Chap. 4, Sects. 4.1.4–4.1.4.2.3 of this book.

§§ By the same token, the foregoing tools (especially, predictive policing) enable the police to over-patrol the «hot spots of predatory crime»[366] (the tagged crime-ridden neighbourhoods allegedly infested by drugs and gang violence[367]) for the benefit and convenience[368] of White folks[369] coupled with a group of privileged people alike.[370] Here lies the cardinal importance of predictive policing.[371]

§§ Predictive policing has been hailed as, and has been lavished praise for, being a cost-effective solution[372] to quell crime. A stance that bears a striking resemblance with one of the central tenets of law and economics,[373] which upholds a wealth

---

[366] Sherman, Lawrence W., Patrick R. Gartin, and Michael E. Buerger, "Hot Spots of Predatory Crime: Routine Activities and the Criminology of Place", *Criminology*, 27 (1), 1989, pp. 27–55; Skogan, Wesley G., *Police and Community in Chicago: A Tale of Three Cities*, New York: Oxford University Press, 2006.

[367] Robinson, M. A., "Black bodies on the ground: Policing disparities in the African American Community—An analysis of newsprint from January 1, 2015, through December 31, 2015", *Journal of Black Studies*, 48 (6), 2017, pp. 551–571.

[368] Frankenberg, Ruth, *Introduction: local whitenesses, localizing whiteness', Displacing whiteness*, Ruth Frankenberg (Editor), Durham, NC: Duke University Press, 1997, pp. 1–33; Garner, S., *Whiteness: an introduction*, Abingdon: Routledge, 2007.

[369] DaViera, A. L./Uriostegui, M., Gottlieb/A./Onyeka, O, "Risk, race, and predictive policing: A critical race theory analysis of the strategic subject list", *cit.*, pp. 91–103.

[370] Vargas, J. C., & Amparo Alves, J., "Geographies of death: An intersectional analysis of police lethality and the racialized regimes of citizenship in São Paulo", *Ethnic and Racial Studies*, 33 (4), 2010, pp. 611–636.

[371] See: Part IV, Chap. 4, Sects. 4.1.1–4.1.1.1 of this book (on biased predictive policing). But see: Wang, Jackie, *Carceral Capitalism, Massachusetts*, MIT Press, 2018, passim ("Essays on the contemporary continuum of incarceration: the biopolitics of *juvenile delinquency, predatory policing*, the *political economy of fees and fines, and algorithmic policing*. What we see happening in Ferguson and other cities around the country is not the creation of livable spaces, but the *creation of living hells. When people are trapped in a cycle of debt it also can affect their subjectivity and how they temporally inhabit the world by making it difficult for them to imagine and plan for the future. What psychic toll does this have on residents? How does it feel to be routinely dehumanized and exploited by the police*?"). Italics added.

[372] Solution that strikingly resembles an ancient idea of administrating justice through the lens of cost-effectiveness, which has been heaped praise by French doctrine: Severin, E. "Comment Esprit du management est venu à l'administration de la justice", *La Nouveau Management de la Justice et l'indépendance des juges*, Paris, Dalloz, 2011.

[373] Posner, Richard, "Values and Consequences: as an introduction to economic analysis of Law", in: John M. Olin Law & Economics Working Paper, 53, 1998, p. 2 e ss e passim; Calabresi, Guido, "Some Thoughts on Risk Distribution and the Law of Torts," *Yale Law Journal*, Volume 70, 1961, passim; Posner, Richard, "The Decline of Law as an Autonomous Discipline: 1962–1987", *Harvard Law Review*, 80, 1987; Posner, Richard, *El Análisis Económico del Derecho*, México, Fondo de Cultura Económico, 1998; Posner, Richard, *Overcoming Law*, Cambridge, Harvard University Press, 1995, 1–608 (passim).

maximization of the criminal judicial system.[374] But this truism, although enthralling, is beside the point here.

§§ The point is that predictive policing is not just a mere tool to attain socially valid goals (squelch crime while keeping populations safe). Rather, predictive policing is a customized algorithmic tool to exert social control over, and employ a hard oversight on, *socially undesirables* (non-White communities) with a gloss of, and under a patina of, science-based objectivity.

§§ Hence the paramount importance of *Critical Artificial Intelligence Studies* (CAIS) to instil consciousness onto citizens on the dire need to exercise caution when deploying Artificial Intelligence-embedded technologies that boast an exceedingly high likelihood to further compound the racial wedge between White folks and racialized communities. More on this later.[375]

§§ On that note, scholars have neither been coy nor bashful in bringing to the fore the propelling force behind algorithmic tools like predictive policing[376]: reinforce White supremacy[377] over non-White communities[378] while keeping the latter

---

[374] "*Wealth maximization provides an ethically attractive norm for social and political choices*, such as those made by courts asked to determine whether negligence or strict liability should be the rule for deciding whether an injurer must compensate his victim. Wealth, in a broad sense, is not confined to money. *Rather, wealth is fundamentally linked to a utility that enshrines people's preference aversion to risk, being that utility the access to justice system*". Italics added. See: Posner, Richard, "Wealth Maximization Revisited", *Notre Dame Journal of Law Ethics & Public Policy*, 2, 1987, pp. 85–89; Posner, Richard, *The Problems of Jurisprudence*, Massachusetts, Harvard University Press, 1990, pp. 18–98; Posner, Richard, *Economic Analysis of Law*, Aspen, Aspen Publishers, 7th edition, 2007, pp. 1–816.

[375] See Part IV, Chap. 4, Sects. 4.1–4.1.1.1 of this book.

[376] See: Part IV, Chap. 4, Sects. 4.1.1–4.1.1.1 of this book (on biased predictive policing). See: Eckhouse, L., Lum, K., Conti-Cook, C., & Ciccolini, J., "Layers of bias: A unified approach for understanding problems with risk assessment", *Criminal Justice and Behavior*, 46 (2), 2019, pp. 185–209.

[377] Feagin, J. R., *The white racial frame: centuries of racial framing and counter-framing*, 2nd edition, New York: Routledge, 2013.

[378] Daley, Jane/Gimore, Glenda Elizabeth/Simon, Bryant (Editors), Jumpin' Jim Crow: Southern Politics from Civil War to Civil Rights, Princeton, Princeton University Press, 2020, pp. 1–331 ("*White supremacy shaped all aspects of post-Civil War southern life, yet its power was never complete or total. The form of segregation and subjection nicknamed Jim Crow constantly had to remake itself over time even as white southern politicians struggled to extend its grip.* Here, some of the most innovative scholars of southern history question Jim Crow's sway, evolution, and methods over the course of a century. These essays bring to life the southern men and women-some heroic and decent, others mean and sinister, most a mixture of both-who supported and challenged Jim Crow, showing that white supremacy always had to prove its power. *Jim Crow was always in motion, always adjusting to meet resistance and defiance by both African Americans and whites. Sometimes white supremacists responded with increased ferocity, sometimes with more subtle political and legal ploys. Jumpin' Jim Crow presents a clear picture of this complex negotiation. For example, even as some black and white women launched the strongest attacks on the system, other white women nurtured myths glorifying white supremacy.* Even as elite whites blamed racial violence on poor whites, they used Jim Crow to dominate poor whites as well as blacks. Most important, the book portrays change over time, suggesting that Strom Thurmond is not a simple reincarnation of Ben Tillman and that Rosa Parks was not the first black woman to say no to Jim Crow"). Italics added. See also: Rich, Camille Gear, "Marginal Whiteness", *California Law Review*, Volume 98,

at bay.[379] Take the example of the seemingly anodyne the Strategic Subject List (SSL),[380] which will be fleshed out at the proper time.[381]

§§ Scholars rightly aver that SSL does not build on race, nor does use race as a predictor in their built-in machine learning algorithm.[382] Handpicked variables are nonetheless used as proxies for[383] race,[384] thereby leading to an unsavoury *selective*

2010, passim; Smångs, Mattias, "Doing Violence, Making Race: Southern Lynching and White Racial Group Formation, *American Journal of Sociology*, Volume 121, 2016.

379 Benjamin, Ruha, *Race After Technology: Abolitionist Tools for the New Jim Code*, New York, Polity, 2019, pp. 1–172 ("*From everyday apps to complex algorithms, Ruha Benjamin cuts through tech-industry hype to understand how emerging technologies can reinforce White supremacy and deepen social inequity.* Benjamin argues that automation, far from being a sinister story of racist programmers scheming on the dark web, has the potential to hide, speed up, *and deepen discrimination while appearing neutral and even benevolent when compared to the racism of a previous era.* Presenting the concept of the "New Jim Code," she shows how a range of discriminatory designs encode inequity by explicitly amplifying racial hierarchies; by ignoring but thereby replicating social divisions; or by aiming to fix racial bias but ultimately doing quite the opposite. *Moreover, she makes a compelling case for race itself as a kind of technology, designed to stratify and sanctify social injustice in the architecture of everyday life.* This illuminating guide provides conceptual tools for decoding tech promises with sociologically informed skepticism. In doing so, it challenges us to question not only the technologies we are sold but also the ones we ourselves manufacture"). Italics added.

380 See: Part IV, Chap. 4, Sects. 4.1.1–4.1.1.1 of this book (on biased predictive policing).

381 See: Part IV, Chap. 4, Sects. 4.1.1–4.1.1.1 of this book (on biased predictive policing). See also: DaViera, A. L./Uriostegui, M., Gottlieb/A./Onyeka, O, "Risk, race, and predictive policing: A critical race theory analysis of the strategic subject list", *cit.*, pp. 91–103.

382 DaViera, A. L./Uriostegui, M., Gottlieb/A./Onyeka, O, "Risk, race, and predictive policing: A critical race theory analysis of the strategic subject list", *cit.*, pp. 91–103.

383 Campisi, Natalie, From Inherent Racial Bias to Incorrect Data The Problems With Current Credit Scoring Models, Forbes (Feb. 26, 2021), https://www.forbes.com/advisor/creditcards/from-inherent-racial-bias-to-incorrect-data-the-problems-with-current-credit-scoring-models/ [https://perma.cc/EWA4-CS8E] (highlighting rampant racial bias in credit scoring systems); Oyama, Rebecca, "Do Not (Re)Enter: the Rise of Criminal Background Tenant Screening as a Violation of the Fair Housing Act", *Michigan Journal of Race and Law*, Volume 15, 2009, pp. 181, 184–93 (discussing a broad range of historical/criminal accounts as a way to screen undesirable tenants, such as Blacks and Latinos); Statement of Interest of the United States at 12, *Louis v. SafeRent Sols., LLC, No. 1:22-cv-10800* (D. Mass. Jan. 9, 2023) (holding that the Fair Housing Act liability stretches far and beyond, thus encompassing a vast assortment of entities providing housing-related services, including corporations that offer tenant screening services). See also: Massey, Douglas S., "The Legacy of the 1968 Fair Housing Act", *Social Forces*, Volume 30, 2015, pp. 571, 575–76, 578 ("*[The FHA] outlawed the refusal to rent or sell to someone because of race; it prohibited racial discrimination in the terms and conditions of rental or sale; it barred discrimination in real estate advertising; it banned agents from making untrue statements about a dwelling's availability in order to deny access to blacks*; and it enjoined real estate agents from making comments about the race of neighbors or in-movers in order to promote panic selling. Although the new law applied only to around 80% of the nation's housing stock, a Supreme Court decision adjudicated just two months later extended its reach to all housing in the United States"). Italics added. Internal citations omitted.

384 DaViera, A. L./Uriostegui, M., Gottlieb/A./Onyeka, O, "Risk, race, and predictive policing: A critical race theory analysis of the strategic subject list", *cit.*, pp. 91–103.

surveillance on racialized communities[385] that draws on a purely whimsical choice of «potentially threatening individuals».[386]

§§ Predictive policing, if nothing else, amounts to an algorithmic tool[387] that «automates inequality»[388] while buttressing and augmenting racial inequalities.[389] Worse still: predictive policing hides the racist agenda behind the veneer of science-based objectivity.[390]

§§ It should not therefore come as a bewildering surprise that pundits have been rallying around the idea that predictive policing is awash with a hidden/shady

[385] Schenwar, M., & Law, V., *Prison by any other name: The harmful consequences of popular reforms*, New York, The New Press, 2020.

[386] Correll, J., Park, B., Judd, C. M., & Wittenbrink, B., "The police officer's dilemma: using ethnicity to disambiguate potentially threatening individuals", *Journal of Personality and Social Psychology*, 83 (6), 2002, pp. 1314–1329.

[387] See: Hu, Margaret, "From the National Surveillance State to the Cybersurveillance State", *The Annual Review of Law and Social Science*, Volume 13, 2017, p. 166 (argues that ubiquitous and ever-present surveillance of socially undesirables remains at a pitch of degradation of fundamental rights in that Artificial Intelligence-embedded technologies—propelled by tools like Social Radar and Total Information Awareness, TIA, can capture "a *pictorial depiction of the comprehensive cybersurveillance anticipated through the Social Radar system, which anticipated the full integration of drone footage, biometrric data signatures, econometrics, and other intelligence sources to achieve higher-order cybersurveillance inferences. Social Radar appears to trace its philosophical origins to TIA.* The development of TIA after the 9/11 terrorist attacks was guided under the leadership of the newly created Information Awareness Office within DARPA (Harris 2012; Murray 2010). Within this office, TIA was an effort led by retired Navy Vice Admiral John M. Poindexter (Murray 2010), who served as a national security advisor to President Reagan (Harris 2012). *TIA was informed by a philosophy of "predictive policing," which "focuses not on collecting evidence about actual wrongdoing but on the broad collection of information about everyday activities with the intention of detecting (and preventing) future behavior*" (Murray 2010, p. 5). Congress officially defunded TIA in late 2003 (Murray 2010; Slobogin 2008; USA Today 2003). *Experts have nonetheless noted that remnants of the TIA program and its philosophy have persisted*"). Italics added.

[388] Eubanks, Virginia, *Automating inequality: how high-tech tools profile, police, and punish the poor*, New York: St. Martin's Press, 2017. Gilliom, John, *Overseers of the Poor: Surveillance, Resistance, and the Limits of Privacy*, Chicago: University of Chicago Press, 2001. Soss, Joe, Richard C. Fording, and Sanford F. Schram, *Disciplining the Poor: Neoliberal Paternalism and the Persistent Power of Race*. Chicago: University of Chicago Press, 2011.

[389] Noble, S. U., *Algorithms of oppression: how search engines reinforce racism*, New York: New York University Press, 2018.

[390] DaViera, A. L./Uriostegui, M., Gottlieb/A./Onyeka, O, "Risk, race, and predictive policing: A critical race theory analysis of the strategic subject list", *cit.*, pp. 91–103. Saini, A., *Superior: The Return of Race Science*, London: 4th Estate, 2019; Sinclair, B., "Integrating the histories of race and technology", *Technology and the African-American Experience: Needs and Opportunities for Study*, Bruce Sinclair (Editor), Cambridge, MA: MIT Press, 2004.

agenda[391] that awards a free pass to White folks while consistently marginalizing the non-White community.[392]

§§ More to the point, this shady agenda of social control[393] leverages on the uses of «science»[394] to legitimize the algorithmic recommendations[395] around which

---

391 See: Hu, Margaret, "From the National Surveillance State to the Cybersurveillance State", *The Annual Review of Law and Social Science*, Volume 13, 2017, p. 166 (argues that ubiquitous and ever-present surveillance of socially undesirables remains at a pitch of degradation of fundamental rights in that Artificial Intelligence-embedded technologies—propelled by tools like Social Radar and Total Information Awareness, TIA, can capture "a *pictorial depiction of the comprehensive cybersurveillance anticipated through the Social Radar system, which anticipated the full integration of drone footage, biometrric data signatures, econometrics, and other intelligence sources to achieve higher-order cybersurveillance inferences. Social Radar appears to trace its philosophical origins to TIA*. The development of TIA after the 9/11 terrorist attacks was guided under the leadership of the newly created Information Awareness Office within DARPA (Harris 2012; Murray 2010). Within this office, TIA was an effort led by retired Navy Vice Admiral John M. Poindexter (Murray 2010), who served as a national security advisor to President Reagan (Harris 2012). *TIA was informed by a philosophy of "predictive policing," which "focuses not on collecting evidence about actual wrongdoing but on the broad collection of information about everyday activities with the intention of detecting (and preventing) future behavior*" (Murray 2010, p. 5). Congress officially defunded TIA in late 2003 (Murray 2010; Slobogin 2008; USA Today 2003). *Experts have nonetheless noted that remnants of the TIA program and its philosophy have persisted*"). Italics added. See: Part IV, Chap. 4, Sects. 4.1.5–4.1.5.2 of this book (on "algorithmic Jim Crow", a travel ban issued during the first Trump Administration to prevent certain individuals from entering the United States of America, which, given its racial undertones, stands as an outgrowth of congeries of laws enacted during the Jim Crow epoch).

392 Menasce, Juliana Horowitz/Brown, Anna/Cox, Kiana, "Views of Racial Inequality", *Pew Research Center*, April 9, 2019, 2919, available at: https://www.pewresearch.org/social-trends/2019/04/09/views-of-racial-inequality/ (access: 2.12.2024) ("*more than four-in-ten Americans say the country still has work to do to give black people equal rights with whites. Blacks, in particular, are skeptical that black people will ever have equal rights in this country* (….) *A majority of adults say that being white helps people's ability to get ahead in the country at least a little (59%); 28% say being white neither helps nor hurts and 12% say it hurts*. On the flip side, a majority (56%) sees being black as a disadvantage, with 25% saying it hurts people's ability to get ahead a lot. *About a quarter (26%) say being black neither helps nor hurts and 17% say it helps at least a little. More also say that being Hispanic hurts people's ability to get ahead in this country (51%) than say it helps (18%) or that it neither helps nor hurts (30%)*. Opinions are more split when it comes to the impact of being Native American – about the same shares say this hurts as say it neither helps nor hurts, while a smaller share says it helps. *And while a plurality says being Asian neither helps nor hurts, more say it helps (34%) than hurts (21%) people's ability to get ahead*"). Italics added.

393 Jefferson, B., *Digitize and Punish: Racial Criminalization in the Digital Age*, Minnesota, University of Minnesota Press, 2020.

394 DaViera, A. L./Uriostegui, M., Gottlieb/A./Onyeka, O, "Risk, race, and predictive policing: A critical race theory analysis of the strategic subject list", *cit.*, pp. 91–103.

395 Wang, Jackie, *Carceral Capitalism, Massachusetts*, MIT Press, 2018, passim ("Essays on the contemporary continuum of incarceration: the biopolitics of juvenile delinquency, *predatory policing, the political economy of fees and fines, and algorithmic policing*. What we see happening in Ferguson and other cities around the country is not the creation of livable spaces, but the creation of living hells. When people are trapped in a cycle of debt it also can affect their subjectivity and how they temporally inhabit the world by making it difficult for them to imagine and plan for the future. *What psychic toll does this have on residents? How does it feel to be routinely dehumanized and exploited by the police*?"). Italics added.

predictive policing revolves,[396] which, given its lack of transparency, legitimacy, and intrinsic goodness, has every likelihood to fray the fabric of Rule of Law[397]

§§ To forestall such a wholly unbecoming scenario, *Critical Artificial Intelligence Studies* (CAIS) avers that extreme caution must be exercised prior to deploying Artificial Intelligence-embedded technologies, which may otherwise flare up the racial divide between White folks and racialized communities in modern societies.

3.1.4.2 «Engineered Inequity», «Default Discrimination», and «Coded Exposure» (Ruha Benjamin)

§§ *Critical Artificial Intelligence Studies* (CAIS) aims to set out a broad roadmap for the safe use of technology in an overarching sense. To cater for that, I will strive to chart a course, and map out a pathway, forward with a view to anticipating how Artificial Intelligence-embedded technologies may fare in the long-term. I accordingly query how central are the principles underpinning the brawny exercise of authority to secure *Algorithmic Common Good* (ACG).[398]

§§ The great bulk of issues concerning Artificial Intelligence-embedded technologies are familiar, well-worn, and well-canvassed in, which yields further insights on the potential of technology to contribute exponentially to the overall betterment of humankind.

[396] Jefferson, B. J., "Predictable policing: Predictive crime mapping and geographies of policing and race", Annals of the American Association of Geographers, 108 (1), 2018, pp. 1–16.

[397] See: Part V, Chap. 5, Sect. 5.1.1.1 of this book (on the central tenets of Rule of Law that lends itself to a beacon of justice amidst the sepulchral darkness that is about to take hold). See: Part V, Chap. 5, Sect. 5.1.1.2 of this book (on the central tenets of Procedural Rule of Law that lends itself to a lighthouse of justice that allows citizens to challenge the pearls of algorithmic wisdom in a court of law). See also: Tyler, Tom R., "Does the American Public Accept the Rule of Law? The Findings of Psychological Research on Deference to Authority", *De Paul Law Review*, 56, 2007, pp. 661–664 (stating that «transparency and openness foster the belief that decision-making procedures are neutral»). See also: Doherty, Joseph W./Reville, Robert T./Zakaras, Laura(ed.), *Introduction to Confidentiality, Transparency, and the U.S. Civil Justice System*, Oxford, Oxford University Press, 2012, 1–258 (passim) (noting that the lack of transparency yields sizable social costs). But see: Weizenbaum, Joseph, *Computer Power and Human Reason: From Judgment to Calculation*, 1st edition, New York, W. H. Freeman & Co, 1976, pp. 1–300 (227) ("examines the sources of the computer's powers and offers evaluative explorations of what computers can do, cannot do, and should not be employed to do") (this founding father of Artificial Intelligence presciently noted that we should not entrust Artificial Intelligence-embedded technologies with with "tasks that demand wisdom"). Italics added. The approval of rental applications is arguably one of those tasks that should never be entrusted to machines). More on this on Part IV, Chap. 4, Sects. 4.1.4–4.1.4.2.1 of this book.

[398] See: Part V, Chap. 5, Sects. 5.1.2–5.1.6.2.1 of this book (on the thing-centred algorithmic decision-making propelled by a *Controllable* and *Interpretable* Machine Learning that weeds out *Algorithmic Dictatorship* and secures *Algorithmic Common Good*).

§§ However, whilst the legal community is rallying around the idea according to which technology *must* be timely regulated[399] it remains nonetheless deeply divided and unclear on *how* should technology be regulated. This is a pressing issue that is in dire need of being shrewdly addressed or inordinate damages may otherwise occur.[400] Spoiler alert: piecemeal, patchwork and haphazard measures (such the right to explanation[401]) will not suffice in this regard.[402] We already know why: citizens are woefully ill-equipped to understand the multiple correlations made by machine learning algorithms.

§§ Citizens will not candidly accept pearls of algorithmic wisdom that they are utterly unable to understand, which will accordingly undermine the much-needed

---

[399] Suzor, Nicolas P., *Lawless: The Secret Rules that Govern our Digital Lives*, Cambridge, United Kingdom: Cambridge University Press, 2019, pp. 1–218 (passim); Brownsword, Roger, *Law, Technology and Society: Re-Imagining the Regulatory Environment*, London: Routledge, 2020, pp. 1–361 (passim) (broaches the interplay law, technology, and society with a sharper focus in the era of smart regulatory technologies); Wagner, Gerhard/Eidenmuller, Horst, "Down by Algorithms? Siphoning Rents, Exploiting Biases, and Shaping Preferences: Regulating the Dark Side of Targeted Transactions", *University of Chicago Law Review*, Volume 86, 2019, pp. 581–609.

[400] Bar-Gill, Oren/Sunstein, Cass R./Talgam-Cohen, Inbal, "Algorithmic Harm in Consumer Markets", *Journal of Legal Analysis*, Volume 15, n.º 1, 2023, pp. 1–47.

[401] Goodman/Flaxman, S., "EU Regulations on Algorithmic Decision-making and a "right to explanation"", *Artificial Intelligence Magazine*, Volume 38, Issue 3, 2017, pp. 50 and ff and passim; Kaminski, M., "The Right to Explanation, Explained", *Berkeley Technology Law Journal*, Volume 34, 2019, pp. 189 and ff and passim; Samek, Wojciech/Müller, Klaus-Robert, "Explainable AI: interpreting, explaining and visualizing deep learning", *Towards Explainable Artificial Intelligence*, Samek, Wojciech/Montavon, Grégoire/Vedaldi, Andrea/Hansen, Lars Kai/Müller, Klaus-Robert (Editors). Heidelberg/Berlin/New York: Springer, 2019, pp. 5–22 ("in recent years, machine learning (ML) has become a key enabling technology for the sciences and industry. Especially through improvements in methodology, the availability of large databases and increased computational power, *today's ML algorithms are able to achieve excellent performance (at times even exceeding the human level) on an increasing number of complex tasks. Deep learning models are at the forefront of this development. However, due to their nested non-linear structure, these powerful models have been generally considered "black boxes", not providing any information about what exactly makes them arrive at their predictions.* Since in many applications, e.g., in the medical domain, *such lack of transparency may be not acceptable, the development of methods for visualizing, explaining and interpreting deep learning models has recently attracted increasing attention. This introductory paper presents recent developments and applications in this field and makes a plea for a wider use of explainable learning algorithms in practice*"). Italics added; Selbst, A./Powles, J., "Meaningful information and the right to explanation", *International Data Privacy Law*, Volume 7, 2018, pp. 233 and ff and passim; Adadi, Amina/Berrada, Mohammed, "Peeking Inside the Black-Box: A Survey on Explainable Artificial Intelligence (XAI), *Institute of Electrical and Electronics Engineers*, Volume 6, 2018, passim; Miller, Tim, "Explanations in Artificial Intelligence: Insights from Social Sciences", *Artificial Intelligence*, Volume 267, 2019, pp. 1–38; Avery, Mallory/Leibbrandt, Andreas/Vecci, Joseph, "Does Artificial Intelligence Help or Hurt Gender Diversity? Evidence from Two Field Experiments on Recruitment on Tech", *Monash University, Monash Business School*, 2023, pp. 1–70. Blattner, Laura/Nelson, Scott/Spiess, Jann, *Unpacking the Black Box: Regulating Algorithmic Decisions.*

[402] See: Part V, Chap. 5, Sects. 5.1.2–5.1.6.2.1 of this book (on the thing-centred algorithmic decision-making propelled by a *Controllable* and *Interpretable* Machine Learning that weeds out *Algorithmic Dictatorship* and secures *Algorithmic Common Good*).

legitimacy[403] of algorithmic decision-making. As a result, the lack of trust on algorithmic decision-making will give rise to an ebbed law abidingness.[404]

§§ *Critical Artificial Intelligence Studies* (CAIS) therefore seeks to shine a keen light on the harmful effects of advanced technology and the extent to which the latter degrade, rather than enhance, human flourishing.

§§ Here lies the pivotal importance of *Critical Artificial Intelligence Studies* (CAIS), which seeks to foster a *safe* and *controllable* environment whereby humans can *trust* and *interpret* the pearls of algorithmic wisdom spawned by Artificial Intelligence-embedded technologies. This is the nub of *Interpretable* and *Controllable* Artificial Intelligence, which forms part of a broader technological apparatus within which *Algorithmic Common Good* (ACG) operates. More on this later.[405]

§§ *Critical Artificial Intelligence Studies* (CAIS) accordingly frames Artificial Intelligence-embedded technologies as an *interpretable* and *controllable* environment against the backdrop of which *Algorithmic Dictatorship*-borne racial disparities are to be both dwindled and brushed aside. Which brings us one step closer to the second pillar of CAIS: the *social engineering* behind the racial disparities in modern societies, which are in dire need of quashing.

§§ It bears mentioning that algorithmic decisions often obscure the core determinations of fairness that they are entrusted to make. Why? The unbalanced

---

[403] Tyler, Tom R., *Trust in the Law*. New York, NY: Russell-Sage, 2002, *passim* (on the paramount importance of trust in law). There is an excellent body of empirical research that shows that a shoddy, botched and watered-down judicial performance spawns low trust in legal systems. See: Magalhães, Pedro C./Garoupa, Nuno, "Judicial Performance and Trust in Legal Systems: Findings from a Decade of Surveys in 20 European Countries", *Social Science Quarterly*, 2020, p. 1 (the main goal of this exciting piece of research was "determining the existence of a relationship between judicial performance and citizens 'trust in the legal system". To cater for that, the methodology used "cross-classified multilevel models, using data from more than 20 European countries, 80 surveys, and 100, 000 respondents, over a decade». Regarding the results, "the longer the time that lower courts take, on average, to dispose of pending cases, the lower is the public's trust in their legal system". As an upshot, "judicial performance, operationalized as the ability of courts to avoid delays in the delivery of justice, is a significant correlate of citizens' evalatuations of their country's legal system"). Converging: Tyler, Tom R., "Psychological perspectives on legitimacy and legitimation", *Annual Review of Psychology*, Volume 57, 2006, pp. 375–400 (on the role that perceived legitimacy plays in everyday life); Tyler, Tom R., *Why people cooperate: The role of social motivations*. Princeton, New Jersey: Princeton University Press, 2011, passim (the author establishes a parallelism between underlying social motivations—such as trust and perceived legitimacy—to engage in cooperation with the authorities in legal settings).

[404] Tyler, Tom R., "Trust and Law Abidingness: A Proactive Model of Social Regulation", *Boston University Law Review*, Volume 81, 2001; Barbalet, Jack, "A Characterization of Trust, and Its Consequences", *Theory and Society*, Volume 38, 2009; Farrell, Henry, "Institutions and Midlevel Explanations of Trust", Cook, Karen S./Levi, Margaret/Hardin, Russell (Eds.), *Whom can We Trust? How Groups, Networks, and Institutions Make Trust Possible*. Manhattan, New York City: Russell Sage Publication, 2010; Cross, Frank B., "Law and Trust", *Georgetown Law Journal*, Volume 93, 2005, pp. 1457 ff (on the interplay between trust and law abidingness).

[405] See: Part V, Chap. 5, Sects. 5.1.2–5.1.6.2.1 of this book (on the thing-centred algorithmic decision-making propelled by a *Controllable* and *Interpretable* Machine Learning that weeds out *Algorithmic Dictatorship* and secures *Algorithmic Common Good*).

and unrepresentative training data[406] is to blame.[407] The pearls of algorithmic

[406] But see: Dong et al., Qi, "Imbalanced deep learning by minority class incremental rectification, *IEEE Transactions on Pattern Analysis & Machine Intelligence*, Volume 41, 2019, p. 1367 (posit that "*most existing learning algorithms produce inductive bias (learning bias)* towards the frequent (majority) classes if training data are not balanced, *resulting in poor minority class recognition performance*"). Italics added. See: Chandler, Anupam, "The Racist Algorithm", *Michigan Law Review*, Volume 115, n.º 6, 2018, p. 1026 (on racist algorithms, noting that "the possibilities for discriminatory manipulation are legion"). But see: Altenburger, Kristen M./Ho, Daniel E., "When Algorithms Import Private Bias into Public Enforcement: The Promise and Limitations of Statistical Debiasing Solutions", *Journal of Institutional & Theoretical Economics*, Volume 175, 2019, pp. 97–98 (calls for a "debias predictive algorithms" to assuage racist and/or biased, doctored and bigoted algorithms nevertheless). See also: Hamilton, Melissa, "The Biased Algorithm: Evidence of Disparate Impact on Hispanics", *American Criminal Law Review*, Volume 56, 2019, pp. 1553 and ff and passim. Note, though, that the training of machine learning is long and tedious in that is an error-prone procedure than can ultimately impair future algorithmic decision-making: Price, W. Nicholson Price II, "Regulating Black-Box Medicine", *Michigan Law Review*, Volume 116, 2017, pp. 421–431 (leverages on Google Image's image recognition learning algorithm to shed light on the four-step process by which some algorithms are thoroughly trained. First, the algorithm is shown "a set of known images ('Here are 10,000 pictures of ducks')." Second, the algorithm "develops complex internal rules based on nonlinear processes." Third, the algorithm "tests those rules on a test set ('Which of these are ducks?')." And fourth, the algorithm accordingly adjusts its "internal rules based on the success of the test." These steps are trotted out and repeated many times "until it can accurately and consistently classify the images"). See: Part V, Chap. 5, Sect. 5.1.7.4 of this book (on one of the law to control algorithmic decision-making, namely, law number four: data partitioning must be performed—i.e. randomly split an entire dataset into the «training dataset» and the «test dataset»—to accurately predict outcomes in the real world while forestalling «inductive bias» [learning bias]).

[407] *Tech, Bias and Housing Initiative, the Promise and Perils of Residential Proptech, Year 1, Research Summary Report, April 2023, TechEquity Collaborative*, p. 11, available at: https://techequity.us/wp-content/uploads/2023/04/TBHI-Y1-Research-Summary-Report.pdf (28.11.2024) ("And while we know that the *data is predictive, meaning it has little to do with demonstrated behavior of the applicant themself, we do not know exactly where companies get their data*"). Italics added. See: Part IV, Chap. 4, Sects. 4.1.4–4.1.4.2.3 of this book. See: Part IV, Chap. 4, Sects. 4.1.4–4.1.4.2.1 of this book (on mortgage redlining). See: Part IV, Chap. 4, Sect. 4.1.2–4.1.4.3 of this book (on algorithmic credit scoring, consumer racism and credit card redlining). See: Part IV, Chap. 4, Sects. 4.1.4–4.1.4.2.3 of this book (on algorithmic redlining). See: Part IV, Chap. 4, Sect. 4.1.4.3 of this book (on "algorithmic redliking"). See: Part IV, Chap. 4, Sect. 4.1.3 of this book (on algorithmic prime-lining).

wisdom are as good as the training data[408] they operate[409] upon.[410] Warped—or

[408] *Tech, Bias and Housing Initiative, the Promise and Perils of Residential Proptech, Year 1, Research Summary Report, April 2023, TechEquity Collaborative*, p. 11, available at: https://techequity.us/wp-content/uploads/2023/04/TBHI-Y1-Research-Summary-Report.pdf (28.11.2024) ("*Once bad data enters the analysis of one factor, it gets baked into the subsequent process, multiplying the effect that one disadvantageous data point can have on someone's overall housing determination*"). Italics added. See: Part IV, Chap. 4, Sects. 4.1.4–4.1.4.2.1 of this book (on mortgage redlining). See: Part IV, Chap. 4, Sects. 4.1.2–4.1.4.3 of this book (on algorithmic credit scoring, consumer racism and credit card redlining). See: Part IV, Chap. 4, Sects. 4.1.4–4.1.4.2.3 of this book (on algorithmic redlining). See: Part IV, Chap. 4, Sect. 4.1.4.3 of this book (on "algorithmic redliking"). See: Part IV, Chap. 4, Sect. 4.1.3 of this book (on algorithmic prime-lining).

[409] See: Kirkpatrick, Keith, "It's not the Algorithm, it's the Data", *Communications of the ACM*, February 2017, Volume 60, n.º 2, 2017 ("critics, however, say tools such as PredPol and CommandCentral *are inherently biased since they rely heavily on reported crimes data, which is often concentrated in areas that are heavily policed, thereby skewing statistics to overrepresent poor or minority communities. "We know that we have a history of racially biased policing in the United States, and that has fed into all the data that we have on where arrests have occurred, which crimes are more likely to occur in specific communities, and at which particular times*," says Jennifer Lynch, senior staff attorney at the Electronic Frontier Foundation. "*That's the data that's being fed into predictive policing algorithms*"). Italics added. See also: Kirkpatrick, Keith, "Battling Algorithmic Bias: How Do We Ensure Algorithms Treat Us Fairly?" *Commun. ACM 59*, Volume 10, 2016, pp. 1 and ff and passim.

[410] Dong et al., Qi, "Imbalanced deep learning by minority class incremental rectification, *IEEE Transactions on Pattern Analysis & Machine Intelligence*, Volume 41, 2019, p. 1367 (posit that "*most existing learning algorithms produce inductive bias (learning bias)* towards the frequent (majority) classes if training data are not balanced, *resulting in poor minority class recognition performance*"). Italics added. Note, though, that the training of machine learning is long and tedious in that is an error-prone procedure than can ultimately impair future algorithmic decision-making: Price, W. Nicholson Price II, "Regulating Black-Box Medicine", *Michigan Law Review*, Volume 116, 2017, pp. 421–431 (leverages on Google Image's image recognition learning algorithm to shed light on the four-step process by which some algorithms are thoroughly trained. First, the algorithm is shown "a set of known images ('Here are 10,000 pictures of ducks')." Second, the algorithm "develops complex internal rules based on nonlinear processes." Third, the algorithm "tests those rules on a test set ('Which of these are ducks?')." And fourth, the algorithm accordingly adjusts its "internal rules based on the success of the test." These steps are trotted out and repeated many times "until it can accurately and consistently classify the images").

rigged[411]—data contain residues of deep-rooted biases[412] that we may not wish to re-entrench into computer-generated algorithms[413] entrusted with deciding[414] our future.[415]

---

[411] But see: Barocas, Solon/Selbst, Andrew D., "Big Data's Disparate Impact", *California Law Review*, Volume 104, 2016, pp. 671–682 (discussing how data is often flawed, rigged, incomplete, imperfect and therefore algorithms inherit the prejudice of the original decision makers). But see: Citron, Danielle Keats/Pasquale, Frank, "The Scored Society: Due Process for Automated Predictions", *Washington Law Review*, Volume 89, 2014, pp. 1, 4–5 (highlighting how human beings programming automated systems is directly conducive to, and leads, to fundamentally inaccurate results since the source code, predictive algorithms and datasets may encompass human biases which, in turn, have a disparate impact on historically disadvantaged groups). But see: Bornstein, Stepanhie, "Antidiscriminatory Algorithms", *Alabama Law Review*, Volume 70, 2018, pp. 519, 524–528 (contending, however, that the tagged "facially neutral" algorithms producing discriminatory outcomes should be quashed).

[412] *Tech, Bias and Housing Initiative, the Promise and Perils of Residential Proptech, Year 1, Research Summary Report, April 2023, TechEquity Collaborative*, p. 5 available at: https://techequity.us/wp-content/uploads/2023/04/TBHI-Y1-Research-Summary-Report.pdf (28.11.2024) ("*Residential Proptech also has the potential to exacerbate the bias inherent in our housing system. Its rise is due, in part, to the desperation felt by average home seekers. With a severely constrained housing supply, companies offering an easier pathway to homeownership may exploit communities that have been harmed by housing discrimination in the past. Opaque algorithms incorporate biased data into their decision-making processes, making it harder to enforce fair housing laws.* Residential Proptech companies often operate in a regulatory gray area, leaving consumers without the protections they would have from traditional housing regulatory systems. *As unprecedented capital investment flows into this space, venture-backed companies' winner-take-all approach to growth has the potential to exacerbate inequality rather than combat it*"). Italics added.

[413] Balkin, Jack M., "The Three Laws of Robotics in the Age of Big Data", *Ohio State Law Journal*, Volume 78, Issue 5, 2017, pp. 1217–1241. But see: O'Neil, Cathy, *Weapons of Math Destruction. How Big Data Increases Inequality and Threatens Democracy*, London, Penguin Random House, 2016, passim (showing how algorithms utilized in modern societies are amenable to perpetuate racial discrimination, partially through perpetuation of social disadvantage and wealth divides). See: Part V, Chap. 5, Sect. 5.1.7.2 of this book (on law number two to control algorithmic decision-making, which mandates that black box models must not be entrusted with the task of making high stake decisions—v.g. health and freedom). See: Part V, Chap. 5, Sects. 5.1.7–5.1.7.5 of this book (on the five laws to control algorithmic decision-making).

[414] But see: Rudin, Cynthia, "Please stop explaining black box models for high stakes decisions", *Proceedings of NeurIPS 2018 Workshop on Critiquing and Correcting Trends in Machine Learning (NIPS 2018)*, 2018, passim.

[415] But see: Weizenbaum, Joseph, *Computer Power and Human Reason: From Judgment to Calculation*, 1st edition, New York, W. H. Freeman & Co, 1976, pp. 1–300 (227) ("examines the sources of the computer's powers and offers evaluative explorations of what computers can do, cannot do, and should not be employed to do") (this founding father of Artificial Intelligence presciently noted that we should not entrust Artificial Intelligence-embedded technologies with with "tasks that demand wisdom"). Italics added. The approval of rental applications is arguably one of those tasks that should never be entrusted to machines). More on this on Part IV, Chap. 4, Sects. 4.1.4–4.1.4.2.1 of this book. See: Part V, Chap. 5, Sect. 5.1.7.2 of this book (on law number two to control algorithmic decision-making, which mandates that black box models must not be entrusted with the task of making high stake decisions—v.g. health and

§§ *Critical Artificial Intelligence Studies* (CAIS) accordingly contends that Artificial Intelligence-embedded technologies should evolve exponentially to become increasingly attuned with *Algorithmic Common Good* (ACG) or conditions conducive to *human flourishing* will be accordingly hindered. This also includes, but is not limited to, robotics,[416] which is also an Artificial Intelligence-embedded technology. More on this later.[417]

§§ Closely related with the question of whether and to what extent human rights are decided or limited by algorithmic decision-making is the question of the degree to which rigged data that contains residues of deep-rooted biases feeds into computer-generated algorithms. Most importantly, under whose behest and to what ends.

§§ As captioned, CRT offers a pathway forward as to grasp the rationale behind the deployment of Artificial Intelligence-embedded technologies. So too does the underlying *social engineering*—that underpins the usage of technology to maintain White privilege[418]—that propels Professor Ruha Benjamin's insightful offering.

---

freedom). See: Part V, Chap. 5, Sects. 5.1.7–5.1.7.5 of this book (on the five laws to control algorithmic decision-making).

[416] See: Part V, Chap. 5, Sect. 5.1.8.5 of this book (on law number five to interpret algorithmic decision-making, which mandates that robot-judges, robot-prosecutors and robot-lawyers must not enter the courtroom for they are utterly incapable of making sound and interpretable value judgements). The literature on robotics law is endless and countless. The sizzling hot topics of transparency and liability of the creators of robots is in the limelight in the United States of America. See, amongst many other authors,: Abbott, Ryan, "I Think, Therefore I Invent: Creative Computers and the Future of Patent Law", *Boston College Law Review*, Volume 57, 2016, pp. 1078 ff; Calo, Ryan, "Robotics and the Lessons of Cyberlaw", *California Law Review*, Volume 103, 2015, pp. 512 ff; Casey, Bryan, "Amoral Machines, or: How Robotics Can Learn to Stop Worrying and Love the Law", *New York University Law Review*, Volume 111, 2017, pp. 1346 ff; Balkin, Jack M., "The Path of Robotics Law", *California Law Review*, Volume 6, 2015, pp. 44 ff.

[417] See: Part V, Chap. 5, Sects. 5.1.2–5.1.6.2.1 of this book (on the thing-centred algorithmic decision-making propelled by a *Controllable* and *Interpretable* Machine Learning that weeds out *Algorithmic Dictatorship* and secures *Algorithmic Common Good*).

[418] See: Roithmayr, Daria, *Reproducing Racism: How everyday choices lock in White Advantage*, New York, New York University Press, 2014, pp. 1–272 ("*Argues that racial inequality reproduces itself automatically over time because early unfair advantage for whites has paved the way for continuing advantage. This book is designed to change the way we think about racial inequality* (…) *Legal scholar Daria Roithmayr provocatively argues that racial inequality lives on because white advantage functions as a powerful self-reinforcing monopoly, reproducing itself automatically from generation to generation even in the absence of intentional discrimination. Drawing on work in antitrust law and a range of other disciplines, Roithmayr brilliantly compares the dynamics of white advantage to the unfair tactics of giants like AT&T and Microsoft.* With penetrating insight, Roithmayr *locates the engine of white monopoly in positive feedback loops that connect the dramatic disparity of Jim Crow to modern racial gaps in jobs, housing and education. Wealthy white neighborhoods fund public schools that then turn out wealthy white neighbors. Whites with lucrative jobs informally refer their friends, who refer their friends, and so on. Roithmayr concludes that racial inequality might now be locked in place, unless policymakers immediately take drastic steps to dismantle this oppressive system*"). Italics added. This book points out how White privilege is perpetuated throughout generations through residential segregation (*mortgage redlining*), abhorrent nepotism, and other bemoaning social practices that pester modern societies). See: Part IV, Chap. 4, Sects. 4.1.4–4.1.4.2.3 of this book.

§§ Recall, the crux of this legal quagmire—capture the rationale behind the deployment of Artificial Intelligence-embedded technologies within the remit of predictive policing—raises a multitude of value-laden scenarios. Amongst which stands the perceived imbalances between various axes of social actors with race looming large in the discussion. These are the baselines from which Professor Ruha Benjamin kick-starts her insightful essay.

§§ Ruha Benjamim echoes the concerns voiced by a wide range of pundits: Artificial Intelligence-embedded technologies, if nothing else, are deployed only to broaden the racial wedge—and the social divide—between Whites and non-Whites. Put differently, Artificial Intelligence-embedded technologies were created to maintain White supremacy[419] under a facade of a science-based objectivity[420] that casts a shady shadow on these algorithmic tools.[421] But much more lies beyond that.

§§ Ruha Benjamim,[422] amongst many other scholars,[423] posits that modern societies are underpinned by a tyrannical system that mimics, reproduces, and unduly

[419] DaViera, A. L./Uriostegui, M., Gottlieb/A./Onyeka, O, "Risk, race, and predictive policing: A critical race theory analysis of the strategic subject list", *American Journal of Community Psychology*, Volume 73, 2024, pp. 91–103. See also: Daley, Jane/Gimore, Glenda Elizabeth/Simon, Bryant (Editors), Jumpin' *Jim Crow: Southern Politics from Civil War to Civil Rights*, Princeton, Princeton University Press, 2020, pp. 1–331 ("*White supremacy shaped all aspects of post-Civil War southern life, yet its power was never complete or total. The form of segregation and subjection nicknamed Jim Crow constantly had to remake itself over time even as white southern politicians struggled to extend its grip.* Here, some of the most innovative scholars of southern history question Jim Crow's sway, evolution, and methods over the course of a century. These essays bring to life the southern men and women-some heroic and decent, others mean and sinister, most a mixture of both-who supported and challenged Jim Crow, showing that white supremacy always had to prove its power. *Jim Crow was always in motion, always adjusting to meet resistance and defiance by both African Americans and whites. Sometimes white supremacists responded with increased ferocity, sometimes with more subtle political and legal ploys. Jumpin' Jim Crow presents a clear picture of this complex negotiation. For example, even as some black and white women launched the strongest attacks on the system, other white women nurtured myths glorifying white supremacy.* Even as elite whites blamed racial violence on poor whites, they used Jim Crow to dominate poor whites as well as blacks. Most important, the book portrays change over time, suggesting that Strom Thurmond is not a simple reincarnation of Ben Tillman and that Rosa Parks was not the first black woman to say no to Jim Crow"). Italics added. See also: Rich, Camille Gear, "Marginal Whiteness", *California Law Review*, Volume 98, 2010, passim; Smångs, Mattias, "Doing Violence, Making Race: Southern Lynching and White Racial Group Formation", *American Journal of Sociology*, Volume 121, 2016.

[420] Benjamin, Ruha, *Race After Technology: Abolitionist Tools for the New Jim Code*, New York, Polity, 2019, pp. 1–172.

[421] Eckhouse, L., Lum, K., Conti-Cook, C./Ciccolini, J., "Layers of bias: A unified approach for understanding problems with risk assessment", *Criminal Justice and Behavior*, Volume 46, Issue 2, 2019, pp. 185–209.

[422] Benjamin, Ruha, *Race After Technology: Abolitionist Tools for the New Jim Code, cit.*, pp. 1–172.

[423] Fagan, J., "Race and the new policing", *Columbia Public Law Research Paper*, 2 (14–561), 2017, 83–116; Brewer, R. M./Heitzeg, N. A., "The racialization of crime and punishment: Criminal justice, Color-Blind racism, and the political economy of the prison industrial complex", *American Behavioral Scientist*, Volume 51, Issue 5, 2008, pp. 625–644; Robinson, M. A., "Black bodies on the ground: Policing disparities in the African American Community—An analysis of newsprint from January 1, 2015, through December 31, 2015", *Journal of Black Studies*, 48 (6), 2017, pp. 551–571.

exacerbates inordinate harm, social divide, social stratification, and racial segregation through criminal system of justice that unlawfully limits the fundamental rights of the poor and non-white dwelling in racialized communities.[424] Artificial Intelligence-embedded technologies only worsen this *Algorithmic Dictatorship*[425].

§§ All too often racialized communities are subject to unlawful, unfair,[426] lopsided, unhinged, and unequal treatment.[427] More to the point, racialized communities endure harrowing ordeals against the backdrop of which unequal violence,[428] enhanced surveillance and scarce protection from law enforcement[429] agencies[430] unfold.[431]

§§ There is accordingly a bespoke connection between the deployment of Artificial Intelligence-embedded technologies (v.g. predictive policing[432]), land, gentrification, and state violence[433] against racialized[434] communities,[435] which can be broken down as follows: **(i)** ***«banishment»***[436] (unlawful displacement of communities and homes); **(ii)** ***«containment»***[437] (either narrowing down the precinct in which

[424] DaViera, A. L./Uriostegui, M., Gottlieb/A./Onyeka, O, "Risk, race, and predictive policing: A critical race theory analysis of the strategic subject list", *cit.*, pp. 91–103.

[425] See: Part IV, Chap. 4, Sects. 4.1–4.1.10.6 of this book (on Algorithmic Dictatorship and its chilling effect on democracy).

[426] Kochel, T. R., Wilson, D. B., & Mastrofski, S. D., "Effect of suspect race on officers' arrest decisions", *Criminology*, 49 (2), 2011, pp. 473–512.

[427] Kirk, D. S., "The neighborhood context of racial and ethnic disparities in arrest", *Demography*, 45, 2008, pp. 55–77.

[428] Langley, M., & Sugarmann, J., Hispanic victims of lethal firearms violence in the United States. Violence Policy Center (Report No. February 2018), 2018.

[429] Brewer, R. M./Heitzeg, N. A., "The racialization of crime and punishment: Criminal justice, Color-Blind racism, and the political economy of the prison industrial complex", *American Behavioral Scientist*, Volume 51, Issue 5, 2008, pp. 625–644.

[430] Gottlieb, A., & Wilson, R., "The effect of direct and vicarious police contact on the educational achievement of urban teens", *Children and Youth Services Review*, 103, 2019, pp. 190–199.

[431] DaViera, A. L./Uriostegui, M., Gottlieb/A./Onyeka, O, "Risk, race, and predictive policing: A critical race theory analysis of the strategic subject list", *cit.*, pp. 91–103 (94).

[432] See: Part IV, Chap. 4, Sects. 4.1.1–4.1.1.1 of this book (on biased predictive policing).

[433] Davies, E. J., Jackson, J. M., & Streeter, S., "Bringing abolition in: Addressing carceral logics in social science research", *Social Science Quarterly*, 102 (7), 2021, pp. 1–8.

[434] Perry, B., "Nobody trusts them! under- and over-policing Native American communities", *Critical Criminology*, 14 (4), 2006, pp. 411–444.

[435] Monk, E. P., "The color of punishment: African Americans, skin tone, and the criminal justice system", *Ethnic and Racial Studies*, 42 (10), 2019, pp. 1593–1612.

[436] DaViera, A. L./Uriostegui, M., Gottlieb/A./Onyeka, O, "Risk, race, and predictive policing: A critical race theory analysis of the strategic subject list", *cit.*, pp. 91–103 (94).

[437] DaViera, A. L./Uriostegui, M., Gottlieb/A./Onyeka, O, "Risk, race, and predictive policing: A critical race theory analysis of the strategic subject list", *cit.*, pp. 91–103 (94).

people can live and «thrive» or forbid people from accessing certain places altogether); **(iii)** ***«blight»***[438] (utterly neglecting vast swathes of territory in a bid to maintain both social divides and racial segregation while assuring that racial hierarchies are kept unscathed); **(iv)** ***«extraction»***[439] (siphoning wealth and funnelling natural resources from one place onto another, while withdrawing both attention and investment from racialized communities); **(v)** ***«elimination»***[440] (taking people out—or murdering them on sight—arrest[441]/[442] or incarcerate[443] racialized people[444]).

§§ Bearing the foregoing background very firmly in mind, Ruha Benjamin adamantly avers that the rationale behind the deployment of «technological

---

[438] DaViera, A. L./Uriostegui, M., Gottlieb/A./Onyeka, O, "Risk, race, and predictive policing: A critical race theory analysis of the strategic subject list", *cit.*, pp. 91–103 (94).

[439] DaViera, A. L./Uriostegui, M., Gottlieb/A./Onyeka, O, "Risk, race, and predictive policing: A critical race theory analysis of the strategic subject list", *cit.*, pp. 91–103 (94).

[440] DaViera, A. L./Uriostegui, M., Gottlieb/A./Onyeka, O, "Risk, race, and predictive policing: A critical race theory analysis of the strategic subject list", *cit.*, pp. 91–103 (94).

[441] Gaston, S., "Producing race disparities: A study of drug arrests across place and race", *Criminology*, 5793, 2019, pp. 424–451; Gaston, S., "Enforcing Race: A Neighborhood-Level Explanation of Black–White Differences in Drug Arrests", *Crime & Delinquency*, 65 (4), 2019, pp. 499–526.

[442] Mitchell, O., & Caudy, M. S., "Examining racial disparities in drug arrests", *Justice Quarterly*, 32 (2), 2015, pp. 288–313.

[443] Gottlieb, A., & Flynn, K., "The Legacy of Slavery and Mass Incarceration: Evidence from Felony Case Outcomes", *Social Service Review*, 95 (1), 2021, pp. 3–35.

[444] Fornili, K. S., "Racialized mass incarceration and the war on drugs: A critical race theory appraisal", *Journal of Addictions Nursing*, 29 (1), 2018, pp. 65–72.

advances» is clear: buttress White supremacy[445] while maintaining extant racial disparities between White[446] and non-White communities.[447]

§§ But not that just that though: the pearls of algorithmic wisdom spawned by Artificial Intelligence-embedded technologies are conveniently wrapped under a patina of objectivity.[448] The endgame is to make those science-based pearls of

---

[445] Daley, Jane/Gimore, Glenda Elizabeth/Simon, Bryant (Editors), *Jumpin' Jim Crow: Southern Politics from Civil War to Civil Rights*, Princeton, Princeton University Press, 2020, pp. 1–331 ("*White supremacy shaped all aspects of post-Civil War southern life, yet its power was never complete or total. The form of segregation and subjection nicknamed Jim Crow constantly had to remake itself over time even as white southern politicians struggled to extend its grip.* Here, some of the most innovative scholars of southern history question Jim Crow's sway, evolution, and methods over the course of a century. These essays bring to life the southern men and women-some heroic and decent, others mean and sinister, most a mixture of both-who supported and challenged Jim Crow, showing that white supremacy always had to prove its power. *Jim Crow was always in motion, always adjusting to meet resistance and defiance by both African Americans and whites. Sometimes white supremacists responded with increased ferocity, sometimes with more subtle political and legal ploys. Jumpin' Jim Crow presents a clear picture of this complex negotiation. For example, even as some black and white women launched the strongest attacks on the system, other white women nurtured myths glorifying white supremacy.* Even as elite whites blamed racial violence on poor whites, they used Jim Crow to dominate poor whites as well as blacks. Most important, the book portrays change over time, suggesting that Strom Thurmond is not a simple reincarnation of Ben Tillman and that Rosa Parks was not the first black woman to say no to Jim Crow"). Italics added. See also: Rich, Camille Gear, "Marginal Whiteness", *California Law Review*, Volume 98, 2010, passim; Smångs, Mattias, "Doing Violence, Making Race: Southern Lynching and White Racial Group Formation", *American Journal of Sociology*, Volume 121, 2016.

[446] Cole, Stephanie/Ring, Natalie et al. (Editors), *The Folly of Jim Crow: Rethinking the Segregated South (Walter Prescott Webb Memorial Lectures, published for the University of Texas at Arlington by Texas A&M University Press Book 43)*, Texas, Texas A&M University Press (April 3, 2012), 2012 ("*The studies in this collection incorporate important perspectives that have developed during the past two decades among scholars interested in gender and politics, the culture of resistance, and "the hegemonic function of 'whiteness.'*" By asking fresh questions and critically examining long-held beliefs, the new studies contained in *The Folly of Jim Crow* will, ironically, reinforce at least one of the key observations made in C. Vann Woodward's landmark 1955 study: *In its idiosyncratic, contradictory, and multifaceted development and application, the career of Jim Crow was, indeed, strange. Further, as these studies demonstrate—and as alluded to in the title—it is folly to attempt to locate the genesis of the South's institutional racial segregation in any single event, era, or policy. "Instead," as W. Fitzhugh Brundage notes in his introduction to the volume*, "formal segregation evolved through an untidy process of experimentation and adaptation"). Italics added.

[447] See: Lipsitz, George, *The Possessive Investment in Whiteness: How White People Profit from Identity Politics*, Philadelphia, Pennsylvania, Temple University Press; 1st edition (July 13, 2018), 2018, pp. 1–448 ("*George Lipsitz's classic book The Possessive Investment in Whiteness argues that public policy and private prejudice work together to create a possessive investment in whiteness that is responsible for the racialized hierarchies of our society*"). Italics added. See: Part IV, Chap. 4, Sects. 4.1.4–4.1.4.2.3 of this book.

[448] Christin, Angèle, "From Daguerreotypes to Algorithms: Machines, Expertise, and Three Forms of Objectivity." *ACM Computers & Society*, 46 (1), 2016, pp. 27–32 (on the multifarious facets of algorithmic objectivity).

algorithmic wisdom appear as more objective than the blatantly discriminatory legal frameworks[449] of the gruelling past.[450]

§§ To the extent that the aims with which those pearls of algorithmic wisdom have been suffused by are far from being angelical, there has been a seething public outcry on whether and to what extent the data around which predictive policing[451] revolves is fraught with racial[452] bias.[453] This is the gist of the «New Jim Code»[454] that seeks to discriminate racialized people with a gloss of science-based objectivity.

---

[449] Eckhouse, L., Lum, K., Conti-Cook, C., & Ciccolini, J., "Layers of bias: A unified approach for understanding problems with risk assessment", *Criminal Justice and Behavior*, 46 (2), 2019, pp. 185–209.

[450] Benjamin, Ruha, *Race After Technology: Abolitionist Tools for the New Jim Code, cit.*, pp. 1–172 (9 and ff and passim).

[451] See: Hu, Margaret, "From the National Surveillance State to the Cybersurveillance State", *The Annual Review of Law and Social Science*, Volume 13, 2017, p. 166 (argues that ubiquitous and ever-present surveillance of socially undesirables remains at a pitch of degradation of fundamental rights in that Artificial Intelligence-embedded technologies—propelled by tools like Social Radar and Total Information Awareness, TIA—can capture "a *pictorial depiction of the comprehensive cybersurveillance anticipated through the Social Radar system, which anticipated the full integration of drone footage, biometrric data signatures, econometrics, and other intelligence sources to achieve higher-order cybersurveillance inferences. Social Radar appears to trace its philosophical origins to TIA.* The development of TIA after the 9/11 terrorist attacks was guided under the leadership of the newly created Information Awareness Office within DARPA (Harris 2012; Murray 2010). Within this office, TIA was an effort led by retired Navy Vice Admiral John M. Poindexter (Murray 2010), who served as a national security advisor to President Reagan (Harris 2012). *TIA was informed by a philosophy of "predictive policing," which "focuses not on collecting evidence about actual wrongdoing but on the broad collection of information about everyday activities with the intention of detecting (and preventing) future behavior"* (Murray 2010, p. 5). Congress officially defunded TIA in late 2003 (Murray 2010; Slobogin 2008; USA Today 2003). *Experts have nonetheless noted that remnants of the TIA program and its philosophy have persisted*"). Italics added. See: Part IV, Chap. 4, Sects. 4.1.5–4.1.5.2 of this book (on "algorithmic Jim Crow", a travel ban issued during the first Trump Administration to prevent certain individuals from entering the United States of America, which, given its racial undertones, stands as an outgrowth of congeries of laws enacted during the Jim Crow epoch).

[452] Browne, Simone, *Dark Matters: On the Surveillance of Blackness*. Durham, NC: Duke University Press, 2015.

[453] Jefferson, B. J., "Predictable policing: Predictive crime mapping and geographies of policing and race". *Annals of the American Association of Geographers*, 108 (1), 2018, pp. 1–16. See: Part IV, Chap. 4, Sects. 4.1.10.1–4.1.10.6 of this book (on biased algorithmic risk assessment in criminal procedure law settings, with a sharper focus on COMPAS). See: Part IV, Chap. 4, Sects. 4.1.1–4.1.1.1 of this book (on biased predictive policing).

[454] Benjamin, Ruha, *Race After Technology: Abolitionist Tools for the New Jim Code, cit.*, pp. 1–172 (9 and ff and passim).

§§ The «New Jim Code» stands for an artful wordplay that seeks to establish an intrinsic connection between the Jim[455] Crow[456] era[457]—against the backdrop of which modern societies (v.g. the United States of America)[458] enforced[459] racial

---

455 Wormser, Richard, *The Rise and Fall of Jim Crow*, Manhattan, New York City, St Martin's Press, 2014, pp. 1–222 ("*between 1880 and 1954, African Americans dedicated their energies, and sometimes their lives, to defeating segregation. During these difficult decades, they acquired education and land and built businesses, churches, and communities, despite laws designed to isolate and disenfranchise them. White supremacy prevailed, but it did not destroy the spirit of the black community*. Incorporating first-person accounts and never-before-seen images and graphics, *The Rise and Fall of Jim Crow* is the story of this long struggle for freedom after the Civil War. The book documents the work of such figures as the activist and separatist Benjamin "Pap" Singleton, anti-lynching crusader Ida B. Wells, and W.E.B. Du Bois and Booker T. Washington. It examines the emergence of the black middle class and intellectual elite, and the birth of the NAACP. Above all, it tells the stories of ordinary heroes who accomplished extraordinary things: Charlotte Hawkins Brown, a teacher who founded the Palmer Memorial Institute, a private black high school in North Carolina; Ned Cobb, an Alabama tenant farmer who became a union organizer; Isaiah Montgomery, who founded Mound Bayou, an all-black town in Mississippi; Charles Evers, brother of civil rights leader Medgar Evers, who fought for voter registration in 1940s Mississippi; and Barbara Johns, a sixteen-year-old who organized a student strike in 1951 Virginia. *That strike led to a lawsuit that became one of the five cases the Supreme Court reviewed when it declared segregation in education illegal. Rich in historical commentary and eyewitness testimony by blacks and whites who lived through the period, The Rise and Fall of Jim Crow is a poignant record of a time when indignity and terror constantly faced off against courage and accomplishment*"). Italics added.

456 Pierce, C., "W.E.B. du bois and caste education: Racial capitalist schooling from reconstruction to Jim Crow", *American Educational Research Journal*, 54 (1_Suppl.), 2017, pp. 23S–47S. Packard, Jerald M., *American Nightmare: The History of Jim Crow*, Broadway, New York, St. Martin's Press; First Edition, 2002, pp. 1–304 (vii–viii) ("[A*] structure of exclusion and discrimination devised by white Americans to be employed principally against black Americans.... Its central purpose was to maintain a second-class social and economic status for blacks while upholding a first-class social and economic status for whites.... In the South, Jim Crow discrimination at its height existed not only by statute but by custom and racial 'etiquette,' and it was rigidly enforced by both the law enforcement agencies* and courts as well as by ordinary white citizens who were neither policemen nor judges but who often took the law into their own hands as though they were"). Italics added.

457 Benjamin, Ruha, *Race After Technology: Abolitionist Tools for the New Jim Code*, *cit.*, pp. 1–172.

458 See: Part IV, Chap. 4, Sects. 4.1.5–4.1.5.2 of this book (on "algorithmic Jim Crow", which stands as an outgrown of congeries of laws arising out Jim Crow epoch).

459 Packard, Jerald M., *American Nightmare: The History of Jim Crow*, Broadway, New York, St. Martin's Press; First Edition, 2002, pp. 1–304 ("*For a hundred years after the end of the Civil War, a quarter of all Americans lived under a system of legalized segregation called Jim Crow. Together with its rigidly enforced canon of racial "etiquette," these rules governed nearly every aspect of life-and outlined draconian punishments for infractions. The purpose of Jim Crow was to keep African Americans subjugated at a level as close as possible to their former slave status. Exceeding even South Africa's notorious apartheid in the humiliation, degradation, and suffering it brought, Jim Crow left scars on the American psyche that are still felt today. American Nightmare* examines and explains Jim Crow from its beginnings to its end: how it came into being, how it was lived, how it was justified, and how, at long last, it was overcome only a few short decades ago. *Most importantly, this book reveals how a nation founded on principles of equality and freedom came to enact as law a pervasive system of inequality and virtual slavery*. Although America has finally consigned Jim Crow to the historical graveyard, *Jerrold Packard shows why it is important that this*

segregation[460]—and the *Black Codes*,[461] which consisted of a compilation of laws that severely limited the rights of Black folks in the aftermath of the long-haul slavery[462] epoch.[463]

§§ All things considered, the Artificial Intelligence-embedded technologies amount to nothing but old wine (racial segregation) in new bottles (science-based objectivity that breeds pearls of algorithmic wisdom that nonetheless worsens the racial wedge between citizens while maintaining White supremacy).

---

scourge-and an understanding of how it happened-remain alive in the nation's collective memory"). Italics added.

460 Benjamin, Ruha, *Race After Technology: Abolitionist Tools for the New Jim Code*, *cit.*, pp. 1–172.

461 DaViera, A. L./Uriostegui, M., Gottlieb/A./Onyeka, O, "Risk, race, and predictive policing: A critical race theory analysis of the strategic subject list", *cit.*, pp. 91–103.

462 Klarman, Michael J., *From Jim Crow to Civil Rights: The Supreme Court and the Struggle for Racial Equality*, Oxford, Oxford University Press, 2006, pp. 1–655 ("*A monumental investigation of the Supreme Court's rulings on race, From Jim Crow To Civil Rights* spells out in compelling detail the political and social context within which the Supreme Court Justices operate and the consequences of their decisions for American race relations. *In a highly provocative interpretation of the decision's connection to the civil rights movement, Klarman argues that Brown was more important for mobilizing southern white opposition to racial change than for encouraging direct-action protest. Brown* unquestioningly had a significant impact-it brought race issues to public attention and it mobilized supporters of the ruling. *It also, however, energized the opposition. In this authoritative account of constitutional law concerning race, Michael Klarman details, in the richest and most thorough discussion to date, how and whether Supreme Court decisions do, in fact, matter*"). Italics added. See also: Schmidt, Benno C., Jr., "Principle and Prejudice: The Supreme Court and Race in the Progressive Era. Part 1: The Heyday of Jim Crow", *Columbia Law Review*, Volume 82, 1982. Fox, James W., Jr., "Doctrinal Myths and the Management of Cognitive Dissonance: Race, Law, and the Supreme Court's Doctrinal Support of Jim Crow", *Stetson Law Review*, Volume 34, 2005. See: Part IV, Chap. 4, Sects. 4.1.5–4.1.5.2 of this book (on "algorithmic Jim Crow", a travel ban issued during the first Trump Administration to prevent certain individuals from entering the United States of America, which, given its racial undertones, stands as an outgrowth of congeries of laws enacted during the Jim Crow epoch).

463 Higginbotham, Michael F., *Ghosts of Jim Crow: Ending Racism in Post-Racial America*, New York, New York University Press, 2015, pp. 1–352 ("*when America inaugurated its first African American president, in 2009, many wondered if the country had finally become a "post-racial" society.* Was this the dawning of a new era, in which America, a nation nearly severed in half by slavery, and whose racial fault lines are arguably among its most enduring traits, would at last move beyond race with the election of Barack Hussein Obama? In *Ghosts of Jim Crow*, F. *Michael Higginbotham convincingly argues that America remains far away from that imagined utopia. Indeed, the shadows of Jim Crow era laws and attitudes continue to perpetuate insidious, systemic prejudice and racism in the twenty-first century. Higginbotham's extensive research demonstrates how laws and actions have been used to maintain a racial paradigm of hierarchy and separation—both historically, in the era of lynch mobs and segregation, and today—legally, economically, educationally and socially. Using history as a roadmap, Higginbotham arrives at a provocative solution for ridding the nation of Jim Crow's ghost, suggesting that legal and political reform can successfully create a post-racial America, but only if it inspires whites and Blacks to significantly alter behaviors and attitudes of race-based superiority and victimization.* He argues that America will never achieve its full potential unless it *truly enters a post-racial era, and believes that time is of the essence as competition increases globally*"). Italics added.

§§ The rationale behind the creation of racist-based policies was two-fold. At one end of spectrum, it aimed at buttressing a caste system.[464] At the other end of the spectrum, the caste system, in turn, is aimed at propelling the system of social control[465] of racialized people that was in force during the drawn-out slavery epoch.[466]

§§ According to Ruha Benjamin,[467] Artificial Intelligence-embedded technologies—amongst which, predictive policing[468]—were created to further compound the yawning gap between races while keeping in place a caste system that awards primacy to the fundamental rights of White people. Enhanced social control of racialized people therefore lies at the heart of a caste system which, in turn, draws on a hidden social engineering agenda.

§§ Ruha Benjamin[469] accordingly frames modern societies as mechanisms of gruelling social oppression against the backdrop of which racial oppression unfolds.

§§ To depict the gruesome matrix that underpins the tagged mechanisms of social control that target racialized communities, Ruha Benjamin laid down the technological groundwork that propels racial inequities in modern societies.

§§ It reads as follows: **(i) «engineered inequity»**,[470] the multiple pathways through which Artificial Intelligence-embedded technologies create, reify,

---

[464] Benjamin, Ruha, *Race After Technology: Abolitionist Tools for the New Jim Code, cit.*, pp. 1–172. See: Part IV, Chap. 4, Sects. 4.1.5–4.1.5.2 of this book (on "algorithmic Jim Crow", a travel ban issued during the first Trump Administration to prevent certain individuals from entering the United States of America, which, given its racial undertones, stands as an outgrowth of congeries of laws enacted during the Jim Crow epoch).

[465] Henne, K., & Troshynski, E. I., "Intersectional criminologies for the contemporary moment: Crucial questions of power, praxis and technologies of control", *Critical Criminology*, 27 (1), 2019, pp. 55–71.

[466] DaViera, A. L./Uriostegui, M., Gottlieb/A./Onyeka, O, "Risk, race, and predictive policing: A critical race theory analysis of the strategic subject list", *cit.*, pp. 91–103.

[467] Benjamin, Ruha, *Race After Technology: Abolitionist Tools for the New Jim Code, cit.*, pp. 1–172.

[468] See: Part IV, Chap. 4, Sects. 4.1.1–4.1.1.1 of this book (on biased predictive policing). See: DaViera, A. L./Uriostegui, M., Gottlieb/A./Onyeka, O, "Risk, race, and predictive policing: A critical race theory analysis of the strategic subject list", *cit.*, pp. 91–103.

[469] Benjamin, Ruha, *Race After Technology: Abolitionist Tools for the New Jim Code, cit.*, pp. 1–172.

[470] Benjamin, Ruha, *Race After Technology: Abolitionist Tools for the New Jim Code, cit.*, pp. 1–172.

and exacerbate[471] racial inequities[472] through the perpetuation of poverty, which creates insurmountable roadblocks for racialized people[473]; **(ii) «default discrimination»**,[474] which consists of a plethora of mechanisms that mimics

---

[471] Hellman, Deborah, "Indirect Discrimination and the Duty to Avoid Compounding Injustice", *Foundations of Indirect Discrimination Law*, Collins, Hugh/Khaitan, Tarunabh (Editors), Oxford, Hart Publishing; Reprint edition (June 25, 2020), 2020, p. 107 (Professor Deborah Hellman coined this expression to depict a decision that "exacerbates the harm caused by the prior injustice because it entrenches the harm or carries it into another domain." This book deals with the sweltering topic of indirect discrimination ("*indirect discrimination (or disparate impact) concerns the application of the same rule to everyone, even though that rule significantly disadvantages one particular group in society*. Ever since its recognition by the Supreme Court of the United States in 1971, liberal democracies around the world have grappled with the puzzle that it can sometimes be unfair and wrong to treat everyone equally. *The law's regulation of private acts that unintentionally (but disproportionately) harm vulnerable groups has remained extremely controversial, especially in the United States and the United Kingdom. In original essays in this volume, leading scholars of discrimination law from North America and Europe explore the various facets of the law on indirect discrimination, interrogating its foundations, history, legitimacy, purpose, structure, and relationship with other legal concepts*. The collection provides the first international work devoted to this vital area of the law that seeks both to prevent unfair treatment and to transform societies"). Italics added.

[472] DaViera, A. L./Uriostegui, M., Gottlieb/A./Onyeka, O, "Risk, race, and predictive policing: A critical race theory analysis of the strategic subject list", *cit.*, pp. 91–103 (95).

[473] Wachter, S./Mittelstadt. B., "A right to Reasonable Inferences: Re-thinking Data Protection Law in the Age of Big Data and AI", *Columbia Business Law Review*, 2019, pp. 1 and ff and passim. The issue of judicial inferences is a hot topic in the realm of *pro se* disputants. There is a perceived impression that there are insurmountable barriers created to disadvantaged parties—*pro se* disputants, mostly racialized, that cannot afford to pay a well-adjusted and seasoned lawyer—as they access judicial courts. This problem will only get worse as technology gains traction in criminal procedure law settings. An empirical research premises such assertion. See: Kroeper, Kathryn/Quintanilla, Victor D./Frisby, Michael/Yel, Nedim/Applegate, Amy G./Sherman, Steven J./Murphy, Mary C., "Underestimating the Unrepresented: Cognitive Biases Disadvantage Pro Se Litigants in Family Law Cases", *Psychology, Public Policy, and Law*, Volume 26, n.º 2, 2020, pp. 198–212 (211) (emphazise "*the present research suggests that the mere presence or absence of pro se status affects the inferences that legal officials make about parties in the civil justice system*. Legal officials appraised the cases of counselled parties as less meritorious the cases of counselled parties and predicted the *unrepresented persons would experience the civil justice system as less fair and satisfying the counselled litigants, even when all case facts were held constant, and especially when trial (vs. mediation) was considered to be the dispute resolution mechanism*"). Italics added. See also: Quintanilla, Victor/ Allen, R. A./Hirt, E. R., "The signalling effect of pro se status", *Law & Social Inquiry*, Volume 42, 2018, pp. 1092–1120.

Michaels, Andrew C., "Artificial Intelligence, Legal Change, and Separation of Powers", *University of Cincinnati Law Review*, 2020, pp. 1083 and ff and passim.

[474] Benjamin, Ruha, *Race After Technology: Abolitionist Tools for the New Jim Code*, *cit.*, pp. 1–172.

and reproduces racial inequalities[475] owing to the dearth of attention paid to both social and historical backgrounds[476]; **(iii) «coded exposure»**,[477] which entails both the under-exposition and over-exposition of a cohort of individuals to Artificial Intelligence-embedded technologies[478] fraught with a myriad of racial biases; **(iv) «technological benevolence»**,[479] according to

---

[475] Menasce, Juliana Horowitz/Brown, Anna/Cox, Kiana, "Views of Racial Inequality", *Pew Research Center*, April 9, 2019, 2919, available at: https://www.pewresearch.org/social-trends/2019/04/09/views-of-racial-inequality/ (access: 2.12.2024) ("*more than four-in-ten Americans say the country still has work to do to give black people equal rights with whites. Blacks, in particular, are skeptical that black people will ever have equal rights in this country* (….) *A majority of adults say that being white helps people's ability to get ahead in the country at least a little (59%); 28% say being white neither helps nor hurts and 12% say it hurts.* On the flip side, a majority (56%) sees being black as a disadvantage, with 25% saying it hurts people's ability to get ahead a lot. *About a quarter (26%) say being black neither helps nor hurts and 17% say it helps at least a little. More also say that being Hispanic hurts people's ability to get ahead in this country (51%) than say it helps (18%) or that it neither helps nor hurts (30%).* Opinions are more split when it comes to the impact of being Native American – about the same shares say this hurts as say it neither helps nor hurts, while a smaller share says it helps. *And while a plurality says being Asian neither helps nor hurts, more say it helps (34%) than hurts (21%) people's ability to get ahead*"). Italics added.

[476] DaViera, A. L./Uriostegui, M., Gottlieb/A./Onyeka, O, "Risk, race, and predictive policing: A critical race theory analysis of the strategic subject list", *cit.*, pp. 91–103 (95).

[477] Benjamin, Ruha, *Race After Technology: Abolitionist Tools for the New Jim Code*, *cit.*, pp. 1–172.

[478] Chopra, Samir/White, Laurence F., *A Legal Theory of Autonomous Artificial Agents*, Michigan, University of Michigan Press, 2011, pp. 1–264 (5) (2011) ("*There are two views of the goals of artificial intelligence. From an engineering perspective, as Marvin Minsky noted, it is the 'science of making machines do things that would require intelligence if done by men.' From a cognitive science perspective, it is to design and build systems that work the way the human mind does. In the former perspective, artificial intelligence is deemed successful along a performative dimension; in the latter, along a theoretical one.* The latter embodies Giambattista Vico's perspective of verum et factum convertuntur, 'the true and the made are... convertible'; *in such a view, artificial intelligence would be reckoned the laboratory that validates our best science of the human mind. This perspective sometimes shades into the claim artificial intelligence's success lies in the replication of human capacities such as emotions, the sensations of taste, and self-consciousness. Here, artificial intelligence is conceived of as building artificial persons, not just designing systems that are 'intelligent'*") ("*As an example of how agent technologies might evolve to incorporate learning, autonomy, and discretion, consider a hypothetical agent designed to find used books on the Internet. The agent is provided with a list of websites to scour, sample titles with abstracts as learning data to recognize other titles in the genre, and electronic cash accounts with which to make purchases.* The agent is allowed to purchase books within a preset spending limit with discretion in the number, subjects, and individual prices of books bought. Such an agent has a broadly defined goal with enough executive discretion in the choices it makes to optimize satisfaction of that goal. The agent is able to interact with its environment by reading and scanning information at the sites it visits; it interacts with other agents such as selling agents deployed by other users. The agent "moves" from site to site, makes purchases, and reads recommendations provided by book-selling agents. The agent checks recommendations for matches on parameters of interest, and then depending on the outcome, buys more books or declines offers. *It is able to buy titles not on its original list, and to proactively make the decision to buy a new title. Such an agent is able to decide to take an action, in response to inputs it decides to focus on; its interactions on the Internet, in a world populated by other shopping agents and sometimes humans, exemplify autonomous, goal-directed, proactive behavior*"). Italics added.

[479] Benjamin, Ruha, *Race After Technology: Abolitionist Tools for the New Jim Code*, *cit.*, pp. 1–172.

which a bevy of seemingly race neutral[480] Artificial Intelligence-embedded tools tend to amplify and perpetuate racial biases rather than unwinding them.[481]

§§ On that note, Ruha Benjamin emphatically contends that Artificial Intelligence-embedded technologies are far more focused on creating clusters of crime than predicting them.[482]

§§ By the same token, Ruha Benjamin adamantly argues that Artificial Intelligence-embedded technologies are mechanisms of «discrimination by

[480] Note, though, that certain types of racial discrimination may not be fully intentional. More likely than not, it can be related with the perils of big data colour-blindness that nonetheless relies on proxies to race and gender to make algorithmic decisions. Another problem is the one related with "creditworthiness by association" that causes more problems than it solves. Hurley, Mikella/Adebayo, Julius, "Credit Scoring in the Era of Big Data", *Yale Journal of Law and Technology*, Volume 18, 2016, p. 149 ("*recent studies have also questioned the accuracy of the data used by these tools, in some cases identifying serious flaws that have a substantial bearing on lending decisions. Big-data tools may also risk creating a system of "creditworthiness by association" in which consumers' familial, religious, social, and other affiliations determine their eligibility for an affordable loan. These tools may furthermore obscure discriminatory and subjective lending policies behind a single "objective" score. Such discriminatory scoring may not be intentional; instead, sophisticated algorithms may combine facially neutral data points and treat them as proxies for immutable characteristics such as race or gender, thereby circumventing existing non-discrimination laws and systematically denying credit access to certain groups. Finally, big-data tools may allow online payday lenders to target the most vulnerable consumers and lure them into debt traps*"). Italics added. See: Part IV, Chap. 4, Sects. 4.1.2–4.1.2.3 of this book.

[481] DaViera, A. L./Uriostegui, M., Gottlieb/A./Onyeka, O, "Risk, race, and predictive policing: A critical race theory analysis of the strategic subject list", *cit.*, pp. 91–103 (95).

[482] Benjamin, Ruha, *Race After Technology: Abolitionist Tools for the New Jim Code*, *cit.*, pp. 1–172 (125 and ff).

design»[483] against the backdrop of which racialized communities should be permanently surveilled, harassed, arrested,[484] criminalized[485] and incarcerated.[486]

[483] Guzik, Keith, "Discrimination by Design: Predictive Data Mining as Security Practice in the United States' 'War on Terrorism.'", *Surveillance and Society*, 7 (1), 2009, pp. 1–17. But see: BALKIN, JACK, "Constitution in the National Surveillance State", *Minnesota Law Review*, Volume 93, 2008, p. 13 ("*data mining* allows inferences not only about the direct subject of surveillance, but about other people with whom they live, work and communicate"). Pearl, Judea, "Causal inference in statistics: An overview", *Statistics Surveys*, Volume 3, 2009, pp. 96–146. But see: Pedreshi, Dino/ Ruggieri, Salvatore/Turini, Franco, "Discrimination-aware Data Mining", *Proceedings of the 14th ACM SIGKDD International Conference on Knowledge Discovery and Data Mining (Las Vegas, Nevada, USA), ACM*, 2008, pp. 560–568 (arguing that one should shift its gaze downstream by putting in place discrimination-aware algorithmic tools while performing data mining).

[484] See: Connecticut Fair Housing Center, et al. v. CoreLogic Rental Property Solutions - Cohen Milstein (access: 20.11.2024) ("*The U.S. Department of Housing & Urban Development observed in 2016 that excluding rental applicants because of their criminal records disproportionately harms Latinos and African Americans, who are significantly more likely than whites to be arrested or convicted. Studies show such disparities are linked to differential enforcement rather than to differences in likelihood of engaging in criminal activity.* HUD advised that to avoid discriminating, an "individualized review" should be conducted considering the nature of the offense, how long ago it occurred, intervening changed circumstances, and other relevant factors to avoid denying housing to an applicant who does not pose a genuine and ongoing threat to persons or property. *Further, HUD's guidance specifically advises landlords not to consider arrests that did not result in a conviction in making their evaluations*"). Italics added. See: Part IV, Chap. 4, Sects. 4.1.4–4.1.4.2.1 of this book (on mortgage redlining). See: Part IV, Chap. 4, Sects. 4.1.2–4.1.4.3 of this book (on algorithmic credit scoring, consumer racism and credit card redlining). See: Part IV, Chap. 4, Sects. 4.1.4–4.1.4.2.3 of this book (on algorithmic redlining). See: Part IV, Chap. 4, Sect. 4.1.4.3 of this book (on "algorithmic redliking"). See: Part IV, Chap. 4, Sect. 4.1.3 of this book (on algorithmic prime-lining).

[485] Benjamin, Ruha, *Race After Technology: Abolitionist Tools for the New Jim Code*, *cit.*, pp. 1–172.

[486] Mitchell, O., & Caudy, M. S., "Examining racial disparities in drug arrests", *Justice Quarterly*, 32 (2), 2015, pp. 288–313; Gottlieb, A., & Flynn, K., "The Legacy of Slavery and Mass Incarceration: Evidence from Felony Case Outcomes", *Social Service Review*, 95 (1), 2021, pp. 3–35.

§§ To put it bluntly, Artificial Intelligence-embedded technologies[487] are tools that produce «incomprehensible discrimination»[488] that further compounds the algorithmic divide between rich and poor,[489] thereby besmirching both their human dignity[490] and underlying fundamental rights.[491]

---

[487] DaViera, A. L./Uriostegui, M., Gottlieb/A./Onyeka, O., "Risk, race, and predictive policing: A critical race theory analysis of the strategic subject list", *cit.*, pp. 91–103.

[488] Griemmelmann, James/Westreich, Daniel, "Incomprehensible Discrimination", *California Law Review Online*, Volume 7, 2018, pp. 164–171.

[489] Such as a yawning gap between rich—that can adroitly harness artificial intelligence to advance their goals and shady agendas—and poor—that grapple to meet basic needs and are automatically excluded from the equation of digital society powered by Artificial Intelligence—which will directly impact the fabric of societies worldwide, thereby augmenting the chasm between the «digitally-chosen» and the «digitally-outcast» enabled by a algorithmic discrimination that does nothing but irreparable harm. See: Yu, Peter K., "The Algorithmic Divide and Equality in the Age of Artificial Intelligence", *Florida Law Review*, Volume 72, 2020, pp. 355–360 (addresses the issue of algorithmic discrimination). This problem is neither new nor easy to solve. Whilst the effects of technology—digital justice—on the courtroom have been previously broached by the doctrine, few to none consensus has been reached with regard to actionable lines of action to be taken. See: Donoghue, Jane, "The Rise of Digital Justice: Courtroom Technology, Public Participation and Access to Justice", *The Modern Law Review*, Volume 80, Issue 6, 2018, p. 995 (noting that technology in the courtroom might widen the gap between the rich and the poor. In this vein, this renowned author has contended that "*legal reforms have omitted any detailed consideration of the type and quality of citizen participation in newly digitised court processes which have fundamental implications for the legitimacy and substantive outcomes of court-based processes; and for enhancing democratic procedure through improved access to justice.* It is argued that although digital court tools and systems offer great promise for enhancing efficiency, participation and accessibility, they *simultaneously have the potential to amplify the scope for injustice, and to attenuate central principles of the legal system, including somewhat paradoxically, access to justice*"). Italics added. See also: Heintz, M.E., "The digital divide and courtroom technology: Can David keep up with Goliath", *Federal Communications Law Journal*, Volume 54, 2002, pp. 566 ff and passim. The great bulk of these assertions has been anticipated by an iconic piece of research. See: Galanter, Marc, "Why the "Haves" Come Out Ahead: Speculations on the Limits of Legal Change", *Law & Society Review*, Volume 9, 1974, pp. 98–103 (this renowned author talks about a *social reality* in which the dubbed «repeat players»—which go by the name of «haves»—tend to «to come out ahead» by putting their knowledge and vast resources to good use. This perceived advantage will not only impact the choice on the procedures but will ultimately benefit their interests as opposed to the deemed «one-shot» players (the «have nots») that will have slimmer and fewer chances to get palpable results in dispute resolution). Technology in the criminal courtroom—that includes the rich and excludes the poor—will make this problem considerably worse. But see: Bailey, J./Burkell, J./ Reynolds, G. "Access to Justice for All: Towards an "Expansive Vision" of Justice and Technology, *Windsor Yearbook of Access to Justice*, Volume 31, 2013, pp. 183–201 (in stark contrast, these authors stress that the digital and technological apparatus can indeed spawn a both time-effective and streamlined access to justice in a given jurisdiction).

[490] See Spanish doctrine: Laukyte, Migle, "Dignidad humana y nuevos derechos: el derecho a la inteligencia artificial", *Inteligencia Artificial y Derecho. El jurista ante los retos de la era digital*, AAVV. Navarra: Aranzadi, 2021, passim.

[491] See in Spanish doctrine: Beriain, Iñigo de/Estrada/Pérez, M. Josune, "La inteligencia artificial en el proceso penal español: un análisis de su admisibilidad sobre la base de los derechos fundamentales implicados", *Revista de derecho UNED (RDUNED)*, Volume 25, 2019, pp. 531–561.

§§ Against this background, Ruha Benjamin stresses that *proxy discrimination*[492] is an algorithmic tool that forms part of a broader legal apparatus that openly/overtly promotes *engineered inequity*. This modality of racial oppression accordingly frays the fabric of Rule of Law[493] comprising modern societies.[494]

---

[492] See: Part IV, Chap. 4, Sect. 4.1.6.3 of this book (on proxy discrimination). See also: Prince, Anya E. R./Schwarcz, Daniel, "Proxy Discrimination in the Age of Artificial Intelligence and Big Data", *Iowa Law Review*, Volume 105, 1257, 2020, pp. 1279–81 ("*[P]roxy discrimination will tend to occur when a suspect variable is predictive of a desired outcome only because it proxies for another*, quantifiable and potentially available, *variable that causes the desired outcome but that is not included in the AI's training data*"). Italics added. See Part IV, Chap. 4 of this book. Note, though, that the training of machine learning is long and tedious in that is an error-prone procedure than can ultimately impair future algorithmic decision-making: Price, W. Nicholson Price II, "Regulating Black-Box Medicine", *Michigan Law Review*, Volume 116, 2017, pp. 421–431 (leverages on Google Image's image recognition learning algorithm to shed light on the four-step process by which some algorithms are thoroughly trained. First, the algorithm is shown "a set of known images ('Here are 10,000 pictures of ducks')." Second, the algorithm "develops complex internal rules based on nonlinear processes." Third, the algorithm "tests those rules on a test set ('Which of these are ducks?')." And fourth, the algorithm accordingly adjusts its "internal rules based on the success of the test." These steps are trotted out and repeated many times "until it can accurately and consistently classify the images").

[493] See: Part V, Chap. 5, Sect. 5.1.1.1 of this book (on the central tenets of Rule of Law that lends itself to a beacon of justice amidst the sepulchral darkness that is about to take hold). See: Part V, Chap. 5, Sect. 5.1.1.2 of this book (on the central tenets of Procedural Rule of Law that lends itself to a lighthouse of justice that allows citizens to challenge the pearls of algorithmic wisdom in a court of law). Regrettably, the Rule of Law is backsliding worldwide. Especially in Central and Eastern Europe. See: Avbelj, Matej, "The Rule of Law, Comprehensive Doctrines, Overlapping Consensus, and the Future of Europe", *Ratio Juris*, Volume 36, Issue 3, September, 2023, pp. 242–258. The Rule of Law is not a «one size fits all» format nonetheless. But see: Chesterman, Simon, "An International Rule of Law", *The American Journal of Comparative Law*, Volume 56, 2008, pp. 331–362 (on the thrust to grasp (?) a catch-all International Rule of Law). See: Peari, Sagi, "Better Law as a Better Outcome", *The American Journal of Comparative Law*, Volume 63, Issue 1, 2015, pp. 155–195 (156) (on Leflar's stance on «better rule of law»). For the purposes of this piece, Rule of Law amounts to a lighthouse of procedural fairness to which citizens, regardless of where they are, resort to upon gaining access to a given system of administration of criminal justice. Whilst further utterances on the fabric of Rule of Law fall well outside the scope and breadth of this paper, one must not be oblivious of the fact that the thrust to Deglobalizing Rule of Law is underway. See: Bussani, Mauro, "Deglobalizing Rule of Law and Democracy: Hunting Down Rhetoric Through Comparative Law", *The American Journal of Comparative Law*, Volume 67, 2019, pp. 701–744 (701) (contending that the thrust to Deglobalizing Rule of Law is interwoven with thrust to take heed of «well-known differences that run through cultures and traditions». In spite of which, «the West has never stopped trying to export its own law into the rest of the world»). Unsurprisingly, there have been educated calls to take heed of the pinpointed cultural and legal differences by, in the case of China, allow for a «Socialist Rule of Law». See: Chinese Common Law Guiding Cases, *Harvard Law Review*, Volume 129, 2016, p. 2213. We will come back to this issue further down is this paper. More on this later.

[494] Campisi, Natalie, From Inherent Racial Bias to Incorrect Data the Problems with Current Credit Scoring Models, Forbes (Feb. 26, 2021), https://www.forbes.com/advisor/creditcards/from-inherent-racial-bias-to-incorrect-data-the-problems-with-current-credit-scoring-models/ [https://perma.cc/EWA4-CS8E] (highlighting rampant racial bias in credit scoring systems); Oyama, Rebecca, "Do Not (Re)Enter: the Rise of Criminal Background Tenant Screening as a Violation of the Fair Housing Act", *Michigan Journal of Race and Law*, Volume 15, 2009, pp. 181, 184–93

§§ Strikingly, the risk variables that premise the creation of Chicago's Strategic Suspect List (SSL)[495] amount to proxies for race[496] in that they hinder the so-called science-based objectivity of which predictive policing is allegedly made of.[497] This is the nub of *engineered inequity* that is deeply etched at the core of algorithm tools[498] like predictive[499] policing.[500]

(discussing a broad range of historical/criminal accounts as a way to screen undesirable tenants, such as Blacks and Latinos); Statement of Interest of the United States at 12, *Louis v. SafeRent Sols., LLC, No. 1:22-cv-10800* (D. Mass. Jan. 9, 2023) (holding that the Fair Housing Act liability stretches far and beyond, thus encompassing a vast assortment of entities providing housing-related services, including corporations that offer tenant screening services). See also: Massey, Douglas S., "The Legacy of the 1968 Fair Housing Act", *Social Forces*, Volume 30, 2015, pp. 571, 575–76, 578 ("[*The FHA] outlawed the refusal to rent or sell to someone because of race; it prohibited racial discrimination in the terms and conditions of rental or sale; it barred discrimination in real estate advertising; it banned agents from making untrue statements about a dwelling's availability in order to deny access to blacks*; and it enjoined real estate agents from making comments about the race of neighbors or in-movers in order to promote panic selling. Although the new law applied only to around 80% of the nation's housing stock, a Supreme Court decision adjudicated just two months later extended its reach to all housing in the United States"). Italics added. Internal citations omitted.

[495] Chicago Data Portal, Strategic Subject List-Historical. https://data.cityofchicago.org/Public-Safety/Strategic-Subject-ListHistorical/4aki-r3np, 2020.

[496] DaViera, A. L./Uriostegui, M., Gottlieb/A./Onyeka, O, "Risk, race, and predictive policing: A critical race theory analysis of the strategic subject list", *cit.*, pp. 91–103 (95).

[497] See: Part IV, Chap. 4, Sects. 4.1.1–4.1.1.1 of this book (on biased predictive policing).

[498] DaViera, A. L./Uriostegui, M., Gottlieb/A./Onyeka, O, "Risk, race, and predictive policing: A critical race theory analysis of the strategic subject list", *cit.*, pp. 91–103.

[499] O'Neil, Cathy, *Weapons of math destruction: How big data increases inequality and threatens democracy*, New York, Crown Publisher, 2016; Monk, E. P., "The color of punishment: African Americans, skin tone, and the criminal justice system", *Ethnic and Racial Studies*, 42 (10), 2019, pp. 1593–1612.

[500] Eckhouse, L., Lum, K., Conti-Cook, C./Ciccolini, J., "Layers of bias: A unified approach for understanding problems with risk assessment", *Criminal Justice and Behavior*, Volume 46, Issue 2, 2019, pp. 185–209.

§§ Tellingly, and perhaps disturbingly, the risk variables that feed into the Artificial Intelligence-embedded technologies[501] will convert the latter into an either racist[502] or biased[503] algorithm.[504]

§§ Notably, certain risk variables give rise to *proxy discrimination* with race looming large in the data analysis. Namely, **(i) «age at the latest arrest»**[505]; **(ii) «number of prior narcotic arrests»**[506]; **(iii) «number of times for being a victim of**

---

[501] Artificial intelligence, like everything else, is not without sizable drawbacks and shortcomings though. The most menacing of which happens to be the flawed or biased algorithms, which are bound to mar a sought-after bias-free decision making in dispute resolution. See: Sternlight, Jean, "Pouring a Little Psychological Cold Water on Online Dispute Resolution", *Journal of Dispute Resolution*, 1, 2020, pp. 23 ff (raises awareness to the perils of biased algorithms on online dispute resolution). Converging: Schmitz, Amy, "Expanding Access to Remedies Through E-Court Initiatives", *Buffalo Law Review*, Volume 67, 2019, pp. 90–100 (showing concerns that e-courts might be premising their decisions on flawed and bigoted algorithms). Which is something to be frowned upon. Why? Most likely, flawed or biased algorithms will deepen the chasm between rich and poor. See: Eubanks, Virginia, *Automating Inequality: How High-Tech Tools Profile, Police and Punish the Poor*. New York: St. Martin's Press, 2018, 1–272 (1 ff and passim) (coining the expression «automating inequality» to vividly portray the downsides of using high-technology to compound the yawning gap between rich and poor against the backdrop of biased algorithms). See also: Pasquale, Frank, *The Black Box Society: The Secret Algorithms that Control Money and Information*. Cambridge, Massachusetts: Harvard University Press, 2015, 1–320 (8–10 and passim) (noting that biased algorithms, which have underlying discrimination problems, contribute exponentially to further social biases. His most intriguing claim is that such biased algorithms have been incorporated/etched in the bulk of the corporations' informatic system, to the detriment of human kind in an overarching sense).

[502] See: Chandler, Anupam, "The Racist Algorithm", *Michigan Law Review*, Volume 115, n.º 6, 2018, p. 1026 (on racist algorithms, noting that "the possibilities for discriminatory manipulation are legion"). But see: Altenburger, Kristen M./Ho, Daniel E., "When Algorithms Import Private Bias into Public Enforcement: The Promise and Limitations of Statistical Debiasing Solutions", *Journal of Institutional & Theoretical Economics*, Volume 175, 2019, pp. 97–98 (calls for a "debias predictive algorithms" to assuage racist and/or biased, doctored and bigoted algorithms nevertheless).

[503] Hamilton, Melissa, "The Biased Algorithm: Evidence of Disparate Impact on Hispanics", *American Criminal Law Review*, Volume 56, 2019, pp. 1553 and ff and passim.

[504] *Tech, Bias and Housing Initiative, the Promise and Perils of Residential Proptech, Year 1, Research Summary Report, April 2023, TechEquity Collaborative*, p. 11, available at: https://techequity.us/wp-content/uploads/2023/04/TBHI-Y1-Research-Summary-Report.pdf (28.11.2024) ("*Once bad data enters the analysis of one factor, it gets baked into the subsequent process, multiplying the effect that one disadvantageous data point can have on someone's overall housing determination*"). Italics added. See: Part IV, Chap. 4, Sects. 4.1.4–4.1.4.2.3 of this book. See: Part IV, Chap. 4, Sects. 4.1.4–4.1.4.2.1 of this book (on mortgage redlining). See: Part IV, Chap. 4, Sects. 4.1.2–4.1.4.3 of this book (on algorithmic credit scoring, consumer racism and credit card redlining). See: Part IV, Chap. 4, Sects. 4.1.4–4.1.4.2.3 of this book (on algorithmic redlining). See: Part IV, Chap. 4, Sect. 4.1.4.3 of this book (on "algorithmic redliking"). See: Part IV, Chap. 4, Sect. 4.1.3 of this book (on algorithmic prime-lining).

[505] DaViera, A. L./Uriostegui, M., Gottlieb/A./Onyeka, O, "Risk, race, and predictive policing: A critical race theory analysis of the strategic subject list", *cit.*, pp. 91–103 (95).

[506] DaViera, A. L./Uriostegui, M., Gottlieb/A./Onyeka, O, "Risk, race, and predictive policing: A critical race theory analysis of the strategic subject list", *cit.*, pp. 91–103 (95).

a shooting incident»[507]; **(iv) «number of times for being a victim of an aggravated battery or assault».**[508]

§§ Compellingly, empirical research shows that members of racialized communities (Blacks and Latinos[509]) have an exceedingly higher likelihood to be victims of gun violence than do White Folks.[510] Conversely, the rate and pace at which racialized communities (Blacks and Latinos[511]) are surveilled,[512] arrested[513] and incarcerated[514] is far greater than for White folks, whom are given a sort-of free pass by law enforcement agencies.

---

507 DaViera, A. L./Uriostegui, M., Gottlieb/A./Onyeka, O, "Risk, race, and predictive policing: A critical race theory analysis of the strategic subject list", *cit.*, pp. 91–103 (95).

508 DaViera, A. L./Uriostegui, M., Gottlieb/A./Onyeka, O, "Risk, race, and predictive policing: A critical race theory analysis of the strategic subject list", *cit.*, pp. 91–103 (95).

509 Langley, M., & Sugarmann, J., Hispanic victims of lethal firearms violence in the United States. Violence Policy Center (Report No. February 2018), 2018.

510 Berg, M. T., "Accounting for racial disparities in the nature of violent victimization", *Journal of Quantitative Criminology*, 30 (4), 2014, 629–650.

511 Mitchell, O., & Caudy, M. S., "Examining racial disparities in drug arrests", *Justice Quarterly*, 32 (2), 2015, pp. 288–313; Gottlieb, A., & Flynn, K., "The Legacy of Slavery and Mass Incarceration: Evidence from Felony Case Outcomes", *Social Service Review*, 95 (1), 2021, pp. 3–35.

512 Fagan, J., "Race and the new policing", *Columbia Public Law Research Paper*, 2 (14–561), 2017, 83–116.

513 Robinson, M. A., "Black bodies on the ground: Policing disparities in the African American Community—An analysis of newsprint from January 1, 2015, through December 31, 2015", *Journal of Black Studies*, 48 (6), 2017, pp. 551–571. See: Connecticut Fair Housing Center, et al. v. CoreLogic Rental Property Solutions - Cohen Milstein (access: 20.11.2024) ("*The U.S. Department of Housing & Urban Development observed in 2016 that excluding rental applicants because of their criminal records disproportionately harms Latinos and African Americans, who are significantly more likely than whites to be arrested or convicted. Studies show such disparities are linked to differential enforcement rather than to differences in likelihood of engaging in criminal activity.* HUD advised that to avoid discriminating, an "individualized review" should be conducted considering the nature of the offense, how long ago it occurred, intervening changed circumstances, and other relevant factors to avoid denying housing to an applicant who does not pose a genuine and ongoing threat to persons or property. *Further, HUD's guidance specifically advises landlords not to consider arrests that did not result in a conviction in making their evaluations*"). Italics added. See: Part IV, Chap. 4, Sects. 4.1.4–4.1.4.2.1 of this book (on mortgage redlining). See: Part IV, Chap. 4, Sects. 4.1.2–4.1.4.3 of this book (on algorithmic credit scoring, consumer racism and credit card redlining). See: Part IV, Chap. 4, Sects. 4.1.4–4.1.4.2.3 of this book (on algorithmic redlining). See: Part IV, Chap. 4, Sect. 4.1.4.3 of this book (on "algorithmic redliking"). See: Part IV, Chap. 4, Sect. 4.1.3 of this book (on algorithmic prime-lining).

514 Brewer, R. M./Heitzeg, N. A., "The racialization of crime and punishment: Criminal justice, Color-Blind racism, and the political economy of the prison industrial complex", *American Behavioral Scientist*, Volume 51, Issue 5, 2008, pp. 625–644.

§§ Bearing this backdrop very firmly in mind, the skewed data baked into the bigoted algorithms—machine learning[515] biases[516]—begets insidious effects[517] with which criminal justice[518] has been grappling[519] for a long-winded[520] span of time.[521] That is why Ruha Benjamin says that SSL overtly promotes *default discrimination*[522] by means of which both the crime and arrest data are purposefully created to chastise racialized people (Blacks,[523] Browns and Latinos).[524]

---

515 Sun, R. (Ed.), *The Cambridge Handbook of Computational Cognitive Sciences*, Cambridge, Cambridge University Press, 2023.

516 Fisher, A., Rudin, C., & Dominici, F., "All models are wrong, but many are useful: Learning a variable's importance by studying an entire class of prediction models simultaneously", *Journal of Machine Learning Research*, 20, 2019, pp. 1–81.

517 *Tech, Bias and Housing Initiative, the Promise and Perils of Residential Proptech, Year 1, Research Summary Report, April 2023, TechEquity Collaborative*, p. 11, available at: https://techequity.us/wp-content/uploads/2023/04/TBHI-Y1-Research-Summary-Report.pdf (28.11.2024) ("*Once bad data enters the analysis of one factor, it gets baked into the subsequent process, multiplying the effect that one disadvantageous data point can have on someone's overall housing determination*"). Italics added. See: Part IV, Chap. 4, Sects. 4.1.4–4.1.4.2.3 of this book.

518 Annamma, S. A., Jackson, D. D., & Morrison, D., "Conceptualizing color-evasiveness: Using dis/ability critical race theory to expand a color-blind racial ideology in education and society", *Race Ethnicity and Education*, Volume 20, Issue 2, 2017, pp. 147–162.

519 See: Alcalá, H. E., & Montoya, M. F. L., "Association of skin color and generation on arrests among Mexican-origin latinos", *Race and Justice*, Volume 8, Issue 2, 2018, pp. 178–193.

520 Brewer, R. M./Heitzeg, N. A., "The racialization of crime and punishment: Criminal justice, Color-Blind racism, and the political economy of the prison industrial complex", *American Behavioral Scientist*, Volume 51, Issue 5, 2008, pp. 625–644.

521 Flores, A.W./Lowenkamp, C.T./Bechtel, K., "False positives, false negatives, and false analyses: a rejoinder to 'machine bias: there's software used across the country to predict future criminal'", *Federal Probation Journal*, Volume 80, 2016, pp. 38–46. Sun, R. (Ed.), *The Cambridge Handbook of Computational Cognitive Sciences*, Cambridge, Cambridge University Press, 2023.

522 Benjamin, Ruha, *Race After Technology: Abolitionist Tools for the New Jim Code*, *cit.*, pp. 1–172.

523 Schenwar, M./Law, V., *Prison by any other name: The harmful consequences of popular reforms*, 2020, The New Press.

524 DaViera, A. L./Uriostegui, M., Gottlieb/A./Onyeka, O, "Risk, race, and predictive policing: A critical race theory analysis of the strategic subject list", *cit.*, pp. 91–103 (95).

§§ Put otherwise, racialized communities (Blacks[525] and Latinos[526]) are arrested much more[527] frequently[528] than White folks.[529] In many ways, the arrest data[530] is somewhat doctored and tampered with to put racialized people permanently at loggerheads with law enforcement agencies.[531] This is what *default discrimination* is all about.

§§ *Default discrimination* is a concept that has undergone the operation of legal transplants to other jurisdictions.[532] It stands as a paradigmatic example of the hazard

---

[525] Kizer, J. M., "Arrested by skin color: Evidence from siblings and a nationally representative sample", *Socius: Sociological Research for a Dynamic World*, 3, 2017, 237802311773792.

[526] Alcalá, H. E., & Montoya, M. F. L., "Association of skin color and generation on arrests among Mexican-origin latinos", *Race and Justice*, 8 (2), 2018, 178–193.

[527] See: Connecticut Fair Housing Center, et al. v. CoreLogic Rental Property Solutions - Cohen Milstein (access: 20.11.2024) ("*The U.S. Department of Housing & Urban Development observed in 2016 that excluding rental applicants because of their criminal records disproportionately harms Latinos and African Americans, who are significantly more likely than whites to be arrested or convicted. Studies show such disparities are linked to differential enforcement rather than to differences in likelihood of engaging in criminal activity.* HUD advised that to avoid discriminating, an "individualized review" should be conducted considering the nature of the offense, how long ago it occurred, intervening changed circumstances, and other relevant factors to avoid denying housing to an applicant who does not pose a genuine and ongoing threat to persons or property. *Further, HUD's guidance specifically advises landlords not to consider arrests that did not result in a conviction in making their evaluations*"). Italics added.

[528] Monk, E. P., "The color of punishment: African Americans, skin tone, and the criminal justice system", *Ethnic and Racial Studies*, 42 (10), 2019, pp. 1593–1612.

[529] Kochel, T. R., Wilson, D. B., & Mastrofski, S. D., "Effect of suspect race on officers' arrest decisions", *Criminology*, 49 (2), 2011, pp. 473–512.

[530] Mitchell, O., & Caudy, M. S., Examining racial disparities in drug arrests", *Justice Quarterly*, 32 (2), 2015, pp. 288–313.

[531] *Tech, Bias and Housing Initiative, the Promise and Perils of Residential Proptech, Year 1, Research Summary Report, April 2023, TechEquity Collaborative*, p. 11, available at: https://techequity.us/wp-content/uploads/2023/04/TBHI-Y1-Research-Summary-Report.pdf (28.11.2024) ("*Once bad data enters the analysis of one factor, it gets baked into the subsequent process, multiplying the effect that one disadvantageous data point can have on someone's overall housing determination*"). Italics added. See: Part IV, Chap. 4, Sects. 4.1.4–4.1.4.2.3 of this book.

[532] Which begs the question: what is comparative law and, in turn, what are legal transplants? Comparative law amounts to a thrust to grasp a host of similarities and differences between legal systems against the backdrop of different legal traditions. See: Reimann, Mathias/Zimmermann, Reinhard (Editors), *The Oxford Handbook of Comparative Law*, 2nd edition, Oxford. Oxford Handbooks: Oxford University Press, 2018, pp. 1–1456; Smits, Jan M. (Editor), *Edgar Encyclopedia of Comparative Law*, 2nd edition. Cheltenham, U.K.; Northampton: Edward Elgar Publishing, 2012, pp. 1–1024. But comparative law—and within which core the doctrinal subset of *legal transplants*—must not lose sight of the fact that any thrust to transfer rules, legal institutes, or parts of a legal system to another—hence legal transplants—must be premised on a sound law-in-context methodology while paying close attention to the underlying social reality of the receiver legal system to which I have been drawing attention to since the inception of this doctoral thesis. Something that the groundswell of legal transplants of U.S. court-connected dispute resolution programs to Africa, Europe and Latin America has been oblivious of. See on the dire need for contextualization: Banakar, Reza, *Normativity in Legal Sociology: Methodological Reflections on Law and Regulation in Late Modernity*. Berlin/New York: Springer, 2014, pp. 1–304 (145–146). Converging: McEvoy, Sebastian, *Descriptive and Purposive Categories of Comparative Law*, Monateri, Pier Giuseppe

(Editor). Cheltenham, U.K.; Northampton, MA: Edward Elgar Publishing, 2012, pp. 1–325. Unsurprisingly, attention has been drawn to the hideous effects of globalization of legal transplants with western values undertones. See: Prakash, Shah, "Globalisation and the Challenge of Asian Legal Transplants in Europe", *Singapore Journal of Legal Studies*, Volume 2, 2005, p. 349 (alluding to the «recent pressures of globalization according to Western terms» all over the world). See also: Oliveira, Maria Angela Jardim de Santa Cruz/Garoupa, Nuno, "Choosing Judges in Brazil: Reassessing Legal Transplants from the United States", *The American Journal of Comparative Law*, Volume 53, 2011, pp. 529–561 (on the issue of legal transplants from the United States to Brazil and the extent to which legal transplants from the United States of America chimed in with Brazil's legal culture). The globalization of American legal imperialism towards China has spawned the well-known movement of Critical Legal Orientalism. See: Coendet, Thomas, "Critical Legal Orientalism: Rethinking the Comparative Discourse on Chinese law", *The American Journal of Comparative Law*, Volume 67, 2019, p. 775 (contending that «Critical legal Orientalism is a tale of two empires, The Unites States and China. In the mid-nineteenth century, the United States established a special U.S. court for China, thus incorporating China as the largest district of their jurisdiction. This extraterritorial court operated for about a century and advanced American legal imperialism in China that continues today. It is an empire founded on the notion of China as a place where law actually does not exist because neither its subjects nor its state lives up to the rule of law. Such Western assumptions about China and its legal tradition are called "legal Orientalism"»). The *longa manus* of American legal imperialism has also reached Switzerland. There have been calls decrying such an «Americanization» of the Swiss Legal Culture. See: Drolshammer, Jens, (Editor), *The Americanization of Swiss Legal Culture: Highlights of Cultural Encounters in an Evolving Transatlantic History of Law*. Bern, Switzerland: Stämpfli Publishers, 2016. See also: Reich, Johannes, "Book Reviews", *The American Journal of Comparative Law*, Volume 66, 2018, pp. 718–726. With this backdrop in mind, it should not come as a surprise that such «migration» of legal concepts between glaringly different legal systems and legal traditions has spawned the so-called «legal irritants». The thrust to throwing light on whether and to what extent some legal transplants to «take root» and «others fail» would not lag far behind. See, respectively, Choudhry, Sujit, "Migration as a New Metaphor in Comparative Constitutional Law", *The Migration of Constitutional Ideas*, Sujit Choudhry (Editor). Cambridge, United Kingdom: Cambridge University Press, 2006, pp. 1–460 (12–17) (on the «migration» of ideas and the challenges arisen from such event); Hirschl, Ran, *Comparative Matters: The Renaissance of Comparative Constitutional Law*. Oxford: Oxford University Press, 2016, pp. 1–318 (2–6) (on the host of challenges arisen from legal transplants between different legal systems); Teubner, Gunther, "Legal Irritants, *The Modern Law Review*, Volume 61, 1998, pp. 10–14 (pouring in trenchant criticism on the stance according to which rules, legal institutions are amenable to be «transplanted» from one legal system to another). See: Galinou, Eirini Eleftthenia, "Legal Borrowing: Why Some Legal Transplants Take Root and Others Fail", *Comparative Labor Law & Policy Journal*, 2004, Volume 25, pp. 391–422 (shedding light on the set of underlying reasons that dictate that some legal transplants «take root and others fail»). This drawn-out footnote is consistent with the best doctrine, which has contended that the analysis of different legal systems must not forsake a cultural, social, and economic context of the receiver legal system. See: Siems, Mathias, "The Power of Comparative Law: What Types of Units Can Comparative Law Compare?", *The American Journal of Comparative Law*, Volume 67, 2019, pp. 865–873 (drawing attention to the fact that the analysis of given legal system must not relinquish an interdisciplinary methodology, ranging from Legal History, Sociology studies, Cultural Studies, Legal Studies).

of «diffusing bad ideas»[533] to achieve mischievous ends («malicious legal transplants» like «racially motivated laws»).[534] Additional remarks fall conspicuously outside the breadth and scope of this book.

§§ *Coded exposure*,[535] in turn, is tightly interlocked to *default discrimination*. To the extent racialized people (Blacks and Latinos) are permanently targeted, surveilled[536] and arrested by law enforcement agencies (*default discrimination* by means of which Blacks and Latinos are overrepresented in the arrest data that propels predictive policing[537]), the former are equally overrepresented in the SSL list (*coded exposure*).

§§ An ever-lasting cycle unfolds thereafter: overrepresentation in the SSL list will put racialized people (Blacks and Latinos) at an exceedingly higher risk of being

---

533 Carolan, E. "Diffusing bad ideas: what the migration of the separation of powers means for comparative constitutionalism and constitutional transplants'", S. Farran/J. Gallen/C. Rautenbach (Eds.)", *The Diffusion of Law*, Ashgate, Surrey, Farnham, 2015, pp. 213–233 (not to mention the hazard of diffusing bad ideas through legal transplants).

534 Siems, Mathias, "Malicious legal transplants", *Legal Studies, The Society of Legal Scholars*, 38 (2018): 103–119 (105) (emphasizing the importance of malicious legal transplants by stating that «in many countries in the world, multiple ethnicities live together peacefully together. But throughout human history there also have been periods of racially motivated laws with malicious effects. In some instances, those laws were a product of legal transplants (….) it can be said that the Nazi laws influenced the laws of Mussolini's Italy»).

535 Benjamin, Ruha, *Race After Technology: Abolitionist Tools for the New Jim Code*, *cit.*, pp. 1–172.

536 The newest developments posed by the "collect-it-all" technologies are slated to create a slew of sizzling hot challenges to the sustainability of the Rule of Law. See: Hu, Margaret, "From the National Surveillance State to the Cybersurveillance State", *The Annual Review of Law and Social Science*, Volume 13, 2017, pp. 162–163 ("*policymakers view these technological developments, including biometric technologies, as tools with the potential to identify individuals who may pose a threat to national and homeland security and to prevent crime and terrorism. One example of technology intended for risk assessment and threat management is the post-9/11 program Total Information Awareness (TIA).* TIA was the progeny of the Defense Advanced Research Projects Agency (DARPA) in the US Department of Defense. *TIA can be understood as a "collect-it-all" data surveillance program. TIA was not explicitly identified as a collect-it-all program—this phrase originated with the Snowden disclosures.* One National Security Agency (NSA) slide described the NSA's procedure as "collect-it-all" (Greenwald 2014b). *Collect-it-all efforts like TIA embody a philosophy that aspires to preventive policing. Mass data collection is construed as a tool to assess and prevent future threats* (Murray 2010). *In TIA and other programs tested or adopted after 9/11, biometric database screening and analysis have emerged as a preferred method for tracking, identifying, and establishing identity-based inferences in counterterrorism*"). Italics added. See also: Ball, Kirstie, and Frank Webster (Eds.), *The Intensification of Surveillance: Crime, Terrorism & Warfare in the Information Age*, London, UK: Pluto Press, 2007; Guzik, Keith, "Discrimination by Design: Predictive Data Mining as Security Practice in the United States' 'War on Terrorism'", *Surveillance and Society*, 7 (1), 2009, pp. 1–17.

537 See: Part IV, Chap. 4, Sects. 4.1.1–4.1.1.1 of this book (on biased predictive policing).

arrested again[538] by law enforcement agencies, thereby compounding the harrowing *default discrimination* with which racialized people have been tussling for a long-haul amount of time.

§§ Last but not least, *technological benevolence*[539]—which, in turn, runs afoul with other tools that preserve law enforcement agencies 'freedom of choice, like *libertarian paternalism*,[540] in spite of the trenchant criticism the latter has been enduring[541]—amounts to the overreliance on algorithmic tools (like predictive

538 DaViera, A. L./Uriostegui, M., Gottlieb/A./Onyeka, O, "Risk, race, and predictive policing: A critical race theory analysis of the strategic subject list", *cit.*, pp. 91–103 (95).

539 Benjamin, Ruha, *Race After Technology: Abolitionist Tools for the New Jim Code*, *cit.*, pp. 1–172.

540 Ryan Bubb/Richard H. Pildes, "How Behavioral Economics Trims Its Sails and Why", *Harvard Law Review*, 127 (2014): 1596 (arguing that Behavioral Law and Economics is (must be) a «light-touch regulatory tools that preserve wide scope for choice»); Anuj K. Shah/Sendhil Mullainathan/ Eldar Shafir, "Some Consequences of Having Too Little", *Science*, 338 (2012): 681 ff (on the regulatory thrust to promote efficiency and foremost autonomy); Cass R. Sunstein, "Libertarian Paternalism Is Not an Oxymoron", *The University of Chicago Law Review*, 70 (4) (2003): 1173 (emphasizing that, in some contexts, «active choosing honours freedom of choice»); Colin Camerer et alii, "Regulation for Conservatives: Behavioral Economics and the Case for "Asymmetric Paternalism"", *University of Pennsylvania Law Review*, 151 (2003): 1211 ff (on Asymmetric Paternalism, which bears some resemblance with the libertarian paternalism); Cass R. Sunstein, *After the Rights Revolution: Reconceiving the Regulatory State*, Massachusetts, Harvard University Press, (1990): 48–71 (arguing that the bevy of market failures warrants both legal paternalism and libertarian paternalism). But see: Riccardo Rebonato, *Taking Liberties: A Critical Examination of Libertarian Paternalism*, London/New York, Palgrave Macmillan, (2012): 1–304 (making some objections to libertarian paternalism); Richard H. Thaler/Cass R. Sunstein, *Nudge: Improving decisions about health, wealth, and happiness*, London, Penguin Books, (2009): 3–7 (arguing that *soft* (legal) *paternalism* is fundamentally *libertarian* because it preserves people's freedom of choice). Converging: Cass R. Sunstein, "The Storrs Lectures: Behavioral Economics and Paternalism", *The Yale Law Journal*, 122 (2013): 1835; A.P. Simester/Andrew Von Hirsch, *Crimes, Harms and Wrongs*, Oxford/ Portland, Hart Publishing, (2011): 149 ff; Joel Feinberg, *Harm to Self*, New York/Oxford: Oxford University Press, (1986): 3 ff; In Spanish, Miguel Ramiro Avilés, "A vueltas com el paternalismo jurídico", *Derecho y Liberdades*, 15, (2006): 209 ff (on soft and hard paternalism); Richard Arneson, "Joel Feinberg and the Justification of Hard Paternalism", *Legal Theory*, 11 (3), 2005, (2016): 259–284 (on hard paternalism).

541 In *The Moral Limits of the Criminal Law*, Feinberg, Joel Feinberg rebukes and debunks legal paternalism that would give rise to libertarian paternalism. Feinberg states that "the doctrine that asserts that it is always a good reason in support of a (criminal law) prohibition that is necessary to prevent harm (physical, psychological, or economic) to the actor himself. Furthermore, Feinberg identifies liberalism with the position that wrongful harm to others and wrongful offense to others, mediated by the maxim *volenti non fit injuria*, together are the only good reasons for criminal law prohibitions. Moreover, he adds that the prevention of harm to the self can be a good rea son for criminal law prohibition when the harm to self, as occur with the under aged people, would arise in a substantially nonvoluntary way. As a consequence, is not that the welfarist consequentialist should find legal paternalism a generally desirable policy, but that it can be morally acceptable and, sometimes, even required. The conclusion we ought to reach is that Feinberg's opposition to Legal Paternalism is soft, not hard, because his position allows that the prevention of harm to the agent, that would arise from self-harming conduct, is always a good reason in support of law prohibition". See: Arneson, Richard, *Joel Feinberg and the Justification of Hard Paternalism*, 2016,

police)[542] to make science-based decisions with a façade/gloss of objectivity by means of which race is completely absent of the equation.[543] For a simple reason[544]: race,[545] according to spin doctors, is not a risk variable that feeds into the algorithm.[546] Note, though, that this assertion could not be farther away from the truth, as extensively explained earlier in this book.[547]

§§ For purposes here, *Critical Artificial Intelligence Studies* (CAIS) frames Artificial Intelligence-embedded technologies as an *interpretable* and *controllable* environment[548] against the backdrop of which its gruesome effects are to be both dwindled and weeded out. Recall, CAIS aims to pinpoint the unwholesome effects of Artificial

---

pp. 1 ss; Feinberg, Joel, *The Moral Limits of the Criminal Law*, Volume 1, Oxford, Oxford University Press; Reprint edição (5th February 1987), 1987, pp. 1–283 (pp. 8 ss and passim); Feinberg, Joel, *Harmless Wrongdoing (The Moral Limits of the Law)*, Volume 4, Oxford, Oxford University Press (31 maio 1990), 1990, pp. 18 ss; Feinberg, Joel, *Harm to Others (The Moral Limits of the Law)*, Oxford, Oxford University Press, 1987; Feinberg, Joel, *Harm to Self, (The Moral Limits of the Law)*, Volume 3, 1986, pp. 24–59.

[542] Benjamin, Ruha, *Race After Technology: Abolitionist Tools for the New Jim Code*, *cit.*, pp. 1–172. See: Part IV, Chap. 4, Sects. 4.1.1–4.1.1.1 of this book (on biased predictive policing).

[543] Annamma, S. A., Jackson, D. D., & Morrison, D., "Conceptualizing color-evasiveness: Using dis/ability critical race theory to expand a color-blind racial ideology in education and society", *Race Ethnicity and Education*, 20 (2), 2017, pp. 147–162.

[544] Benjamin, Ruha, *Race After Technology: Abolitionist Tools for the New Jim Code*, *cit.*, pp. 1–172.

[545] DaViera, A. L./Uriostegui, M., Gottlieb/A./Onyeka, O, "Risk, race, and predictive policing: A critical race theory analysis of the strategic subject list", *cit.*, pp. 91–103 (95).

[546] Eckhouse, L., Lum, K., Conti-Cook, C., & Ciccolini, J., "Layers of bias: A unified approach for understanding problems with risk assessment. Criminal Justice and Behavior", 46 (2), 2019, pp. 185–209; O'Neil, Cathy, *Weapons of math destruction: How big data increases inequality and threatens democracy*, New York, Crown Publisher, 2016.

[547] See: Part IV, Chap. 4, Sects. 4.1–4.1.10.6 of this book (on Algorithmic Dictatorship and its chilling effect on democracy). See also: Part IV, Chap. 4, Sects. 4.1.10.1–4.1.10.6 of this book (on biased algorithmic risk assessment in criminal procedure law settings). See also: Part IV, Chap. 4, Sects. 4.1.1–4.1.1.1 of this book (on biased predictive policing). See also: Part IV, Chap. 4, Sect. 4.1.6.3 of this book (on proxy discrimination).

[548] See: Part V, Chap. 5, Sects. 5.1.7–5.1.7.5 of this book (on the five laws to control algorithmic decision-making). See: Part V, Chap. 5, Sects. 5.1.8–5.1.8.5 of this book (on the five laws to interpret algorithmic decision-making).

Intelligence-embedded technologies on human beings[549] while setting a foundation upon which *Algorithmic Common Good* will brawnily stand.[550]

[549] The newest developments posed by the "collect-it-all" technologies are slated to create a slew of sizzling hot challenges to the sustainability of the Rule of Law. See: Hu, Margaret, "From the National Surveillance State to the Cybersurveillance State", *The Annual Review of Law and Social Science*, Volume 13, 2017, pp. 162–163 ("*policymakers view these technological developments, including biometric technologies, as tools with the potential to identify individuals who may pose a threat to national and homeland security and to prevent crime and terrorism. One example of technology intended for risk assessment and threat management is the post-9/11 program Total Information Awareness (TIA).* TIA was the progeny of the Defense Advanced Research Projects Agency (DARPA) in the US Department of Defense. *TIA can be understood as a "collect-it-all" data surveillance program. TIA was not explicitly identified as a collect-it-all program—this phrase originated with the Snowden disclosures.* One National Security Agency (NSA) slide described the NSA's procedure as "collect-it-all" (Greenwald 2014b). *Collect-it-all efforts like TIA embody a philosophy that aspires to preventive policing. Mass data collection is construed as a tool to assess and prevent future threats* (Murray 2010). *In TIA and other programs tested or adopted after 9/11, biometric database screening and analysis have emerged as a preferred method for tracking, identifying, and establishing identity-based inferences in counterterrorism*"). Italics added. See also: Ball, Kirstie, and Frank Webster (Eds.), *The Intensification of Surveillance: Crime, Terrorism & Warfare in the Information Age*, London, UK: Pluto Press, 2007; Guzik, Keith, "Discrimination by Design: Predictive Data Mining as Security Practice in the United States' 'War on Terrorism'", *Surveillance and Society*, 7 (1), 2009, pp. 1–17.

[550] See: Part V, Chap. 5, Sects. 5.1.2–5.1.6.2.1 of this book (on the thing-centred algorithmic decision-making propelled by a *Controllable* and *Interpretable* Machine Learning that weeds out *Algorithmic Dictatorship* and secures *Algorithmic Common Good*).

3.1.4.3 Critical Legal Studies and Legal Pragmatism to Cast Off the Nagging Indeterminacy with Which Human-Centred Artificial Intelligence Has Been Grappling

§§ The legal community is burgeoningly rallying around the idea according to which Artificial Intelligence-embedded technologies,[551] if nothing else, should be human-centred[552] and trustworthy.[553] Several legal frameworks have accordingly brought this all-encompassing concept to the fore.[554] Critical Artificial Intelligence Studies (CAIS) hereby challenges this widely accepted concept.

---

[551] Hu, Margaret, "From the National Surveillance State to the Cybersurveillance State", *The Annual Review of Law and Social Science*, Volume 13, 2017, p. 168 ("*currently, biometric verification and identification technologies are not commonly perceived to be surveillance technologies—the public and private sectors typically treat them as a benign and useful form of digitized identification. Such automated biometric screening is considered to be a more efficient form of small data verification technologies, such as human screening or human-driven practices involving assessments of biometric or forensic data. Small data biometric verification could include comparing a passport photo against the person holding the passport*"). Italics added. See: Part III, this chapter, Sect. 3.1.5.3 of this book (on the "house of fabricated lies" and the usage of Generative Artificial Intelligence as a *floating signifier* that will stand ready to be galvanize power in a given direction, including, but not limited to, against *socially undesirables* that may find themselves at odds, or at loggerheads, with whoever controls Artificial Intelligence). See: Part IV, Chap. 4, Sects. 4.1.5–4.1.5.2 of this book (on "algorithmic Jim Crow", a travel ban issued during the first Trump Administration to prevent certain individuals from entering the United States of America, which, given its racial undertones, stands as an outgrowth of congeries of laws enacted during the Jim Crow epoch).

[552] High-Level Expert Group on Artificial Intelligence, *Ethics guidelines for trustworthy AI. The European Commission*, 2019, passim.

[553] Assessment List for Trustworthy Artificial Intelligence (ALTAI) for self-assessment, 17 Jul 2020, available at: https://digital-strategy.ec.europa.eu/en/library/assessment-list-trustworthy-artificial-intelligence-altai-self-assessment (access: 16.12.2024).

[554] European Commission (2024). International outreach for human-centric artificial intelligence initiative, 2024; European Commission, Artificial Intelligence for Europe [Online], 2018. Available: https://eur-lex.europa.eu/legal-content/EN/TXT/PDF/?uri=CELEX:52018DC0237&from=EN [Accessed 2025]; European Commission, White Paper. On Artificial Intelligence - A European approach to excellence and trust [Online], 2020, available: https://eur-lex.europa.eu/legal-content/EN/TXT/PDF/?uri=CELEX:52020DC0065&from=EN [Accessed 2024]; European Commission, Proposal for a Regulation of the European Parliament and of the council laying down harmonised rules on Artificial Intelligence, 2021; European Commission. European approach to artificial intelligence [Online], 2024. Available: https://digital-strategy.ec.europa.eu/en/policies/european-approach-artificial-intelligence; European Economic and Social Committee. Fundamental Rights and Rule of Law - National developments from a civil society perspective – 2020–2021 [Online], 2022. Available: https://www.eesc.europa.eu/en/our-work/publications-other-work/publications/fundamental-rights-and-rule-law-nationaldevelopments-civil-society-perspective-2020-2021 [Accessed 20.12.2024]; European Commission (2021a). 2030 Digital Compass: the European way for the Digital Decade [Online]. Available: https://ec.europa.eu/info/sites/info/files/communication-digital-compass-2030_en.pdf.

§§ Setting aside the overhyped promises to map out the path forward for the safe use of Artificial Intelligence-embedded technologies[555]—which remains an insurmountable task to this day—, the poorly latched on concept of human-centred Artificial Intelligence[556] has nevertheless caught on and gained traction across the data-driven world we live in. And it shouldn't have.[557]

§§ To begin with, scholars openly decry the porous, shallow, hollow, and nomadic—and somewhat undetermined[558]—concept of human-centred Artificial Intelligence that amounts to nothing but a handful of elusive promises that briskly vanish into thin air.

---

[555] See: *European Commission of 2024, International outreach for human-centric artificial intelligence initiative*, which reads as follows: "*The main vision characterising the EU approach is the creation of human-centric AI, which ensures AI works for people and protects fundamental rights. The EU approach to AI also involves supporting the EU's technological and industrial capacity and AI uptake across the economy, and preparing for socio-economic changes*". Italics added. See also: European Commission. European approach to artificial intelligence, 2024, which reads as follows: "*The EU's approach to artificial intelligence centers on excellence and trust, aiming to boost research and industrial capacity while ensuring safety and fundamental rights [...] Fostering excellence in AI will strengthen Europe's potential to compete globally.* The EU will achieve this by: (1) enabling the development and uptake of AI in the EU; (2) becoming the place where AI thrives from the lab to the market; (3) *ensuring that AI works for people and is a force for good in society; (4) building strategic leadership in high-impact sectors.*" Italics added. Available: https://digital-strategy.ec.europa.eu/en/policies/european-approachartificial-intelligence [access: 11.10.2024]. Italics added.

[556] Kogan, M., Halfaker, A., Guha, S., Aragon, C., Muller, M. & Geiger, S., "Mapping out human-centered data science: methods, approaches, and best practices", *Companion Proceedings of the 2020 ACM International Conference on Supporting Group Work*, Sanibel Island, Florida, USA: Association for Computing Machinery, 2020.

[557] Braun, Matthias/Meacham, Darian, "A Plea for (In)Human-centred AI", *Philosophy & Technology*, 2024, pp. 37–97.

[558] Bannon, L., "Reimagining HCI: Toward a more human-centered perspective", *Interactions*, 18, 2011, pp. 50–57.

§§ Tellingly, the human-centred Artificial Intelligence is a catch-all concept that draws on a patchwork arising out of a plethora of distinct areas (ranging from ethics,[559] biometric surveillance,[560] Artificial Intelligence ethics,[561] responsible

[559] Jobin, A./Ienca, M./Vayena, E., "The global landscape of AI ethics guidelines", *Nature Machine Intelligence*, n.º 1, 2019, pp. 388 and ff and passim; Ryan, M./Stahl, B.-C., "Artificial intelligence ethics guidelines for developers and users: clarifying their content and normative implications", *Communication and Ethics in Society*, Volume 3, 2021, pp. 62–85.

[560] Which, I may venture to add, is something—*biometric surveillance*—that amounts to nothing but to the price of partaking in social settings, which is very hard to shy away from nowadays. See: Hu, Margaret, "From the National Surveillance State to the Cybersurveillance State", *The Annual Review of Law and Social Science*, Volume 13, 2017, p. 169 ("*because of technological developments and trends in governance, it is challenging, if not impossible, to prevent biometric data capture and collection. Biometric surveillance systems increasingly require opting in as the price of social, economic, and political participation.* Biometric data capture is difficult to resist because it is simultaneously compulsory and transparent. Biometric data collection is often compulsory because it is increasingly mandatory to establish identity. *Biometrics are transparent qualities because it is very difficult to hide biometrics; an individual's face, iris, or fingerprint can be digitally captured in any public place. Because biometric data support larger big data programs, such as No Fly List–type risk assessments, it is extraordinarily difficult, if not impossible, to opt out*"). Italics added. See: Part IV, Chap. 4, Sects. 4.1.5–4.1.5.2 of this book (on "algorithmic Jim Crow", a travel ban issued during the first Trump Administration to prevent certain individuals from entering the United States of America, which, given its racial undertones, stands as an outgrowth of congeries of laws enacted during the Jim Crow epoch).

[561] Sanderson, Conrad/Douglas, David/Lu, Qinghua/Schleiger, Emma/Whittle, Jon/Lacey, Justine/ Newnham/Hajkowicz/Robinson, Cathy, "AI Ethics Principles in Practice: Perspectives of Designers and Developers", *IEEE Transactions on Technology and Society*, Volume 4, Issue 2, June 2023, 2023, pp. 171–187.

robotics,[562] engineering ethics,[563] neuroethics,[564] legal ethics,[565] Artificial Intelligence governance,[566] the fundamental tenets of Artificial Intelligence,[567] Artificial Intelligence role-reversible judgment,[568] technological due process,[569] procedural

[562] Liu, Hin-Yan/Zawieska, Karolina, "From responsible robotics towards a human rights regime oriented to the challenges of robotics and artificial intelligence", *Ethics Information Technology*, Volume 22, Issue 4, 2020, pp. 321–333.

[563] Steinert, Steffen/Orsolya, Friedrich, "Wired Emotions: Ethical Issues of Affective Brain-Computer Interfaces", *Science and Engineering Ethics*, Volume 26, 2020, pp. 351 and ff and passim.

[564] Niikawa, Takuya/Hayashi, Yoshiyuki/Shepherd, Joshua/Sawai, Tsutomu, "Human Brain Organoids and Consciousness", *Neuroethics*, Volume 15, Issue 5, 2022.

[565] Remus, Dana/Levy, Frank, "Can Robots be Lawyers? Computers, Lawyers, and the Practice of Law", *Georgetown Journal of Legal Ethics*, Volume 30, 2018, pp. 501 and ff and passim.

[566] Mäntymäki, M./Minkkinen, M./Birkstedt/Viljanen, "Defining organizational AI governance", *AI Ethics*, Volume 2, 2022, pp. 603–609; Sanderson, Conrad/Douglas, David/Lu, Qinghua/Schleiger, Emma/Whittle, Jon/Lacey, Justine/Newnham/Hajkowicz/Robinson, Cathy, "AI Ethics Principles in Practice: Perspectives of Designers and Developers", *IEEE Transactions on Technology and Society*, Volume 4, Issue 2, June 2023, 2023, pp. 171–187. See also: Hu, Margaret, "From the National Surveillance State to the Cybersurveillance State", *The Annual Review of Law and Social Science*, Volume 13, 2017, p. 169 ("*as a result of big data biometric governance trends, meaningful distinctions between biometric credentialing for identification and behavioral biometric profiling are disappearing. The objectives are merging: Reliable credentialing is used to advance security and precrime policy rationales. Biometric data mission creep occurs by necessity in a big data world because the cybersurveillance systems are often designed to engage in mass data integration and analysis and predictive policing. Biometric surveillance serves two purposes in preventive policing: It increases identity transparency, and the biometric data categorize identity through cataloging behavioral and physical characteristics and assess these characteristics for risk. Contrasting small data biometric credentialing protocols with big data credentialing protocols is useful. It illustrates how biometric surveillance fits within the Cybersurveillance State. In a small data world, paper-based passports and nondigitized photographs are examples of a small data biometric-based identification system*"). Italics added.

[567] Boden, Margaret A., *Artificial Intelligence: A Very Short Introduction.* Oxford: Oxford University Press, 2018.

[568] Brennan-Marquez/Henderson, Stephen E., "Artificial Intelligence and Role-Reversible Judgment", *Journal of Criminal Law and Criminology*, Volume 109, 2019, pp. 137–163.

[569] Citron, Danielle Keats, "Technological Due Process", *Washington University Law Review*, Volume 85, 2008, pp. 1256 e ss.

justice,[570] right to explanation[571] underpinning algorithmic decision-making,[572] neurotechnology,[573] explainable Artificial Intelligence,[574] big data rules,[575] deep

---

[570] From the social psychology, warped algorithms accomplish nothing but the impairment of procedural justice. See: Thibaut, John/Walker, Laurens, *Procedural Justice: A Psychological Analysis.* Hillsdale, N.J.: Lawrence Erlbaum Associates, 1975, pp. 1–150 (procedural justice is tightly interlocked to raising the levels of fairness in criminal procedure law settings. Absent of which procedural fairness is to mar. Criminal procedure law must not lose sight of such assertion). Converging: Lind, Edgar Allan/Tyler, Tom R., *The Social Psychology of Procedural Justice.* New York: Springer, 1988, pp. 208 ff (emphasizing that perceptions of justice being justly and correctly served enhances exponentially citizens' perception of provider legitimacy). Tyler, Tom R., "The Psychology of Procedural Justice: A Test of the Group-Value Model", *Journal of Personality and Social Psychology*, Volume 57, 1989, p. 830 (reports that in any procedure "several non-control issues – the *neutrality* of the decision-making procedure, trust in the 3rd party, and the information the experience communicates about social standing – influence both procedural preferences and judgments of procedural justice"). See also: Simmons, Ric, "Big Data and Procedural Justice: Legitimizing Algorithms in the Criminal Justice System", *Ohio State Journal of Criminal Law*, Volume 15, 2018, pp. 576 and ff and passim; Simmons, Ric, "Big Data and Procedural Justice: Legitimizing Algorithms in the Criminal Justice System", *Ohio State Journal of Criminal Law*, Volume 5, 2018, pp. 573 and ff and passim (argues, however, that too much AI in criminal procedure law settings can backfire, thereby hindering citizens' trust on the criminal system of justice).

[571] Selbst, A./Powles, J., "Meaningful information and the right to explanation", *International Data Privacy Law*, Volume 7, 2018, pp. 233 and ff and passim.

[572] Goodman/Flaxman, S., "EU Regulations on Algorithmic Decision-making and a "right to explanation", *Artificial Intelligence Magazine*, Volume 38, Issue 3, 2017, pp. 50 and ff and passim; Kaminski, M., "The Right to Explanation, Explained", *Berkeley Technology Law Journal*, Volume 34, 2019, pp. 189 and ff and passim.

[573] Al-Rodhan, Nayef, "The Rise of Neurotechnology Calls for a Parallel Focus on Neurorights", *SCI AM*, 2021, passim.

[574] Deeks, Ahsley, "The Judicial Demand for Explainable Artificial Intelligence", *Columbia Law Review*, Volume 119, 2019, pp. 1829 and ff and passim. See: Samek, Wojciech/Müller, Klaus-Robert, "Explainable AI: interpreting, explaining and visualizing deep learning", *Towards Explainable Artificial Intelligence*, Samek, Wojciech/Montavon, Grégoire/Vedaldi, Andrea/Hansen, Lars Kai/Müller, Klaus-Robert (Editors). Heidelberg/Berlin/New York: Springer, 2019, pp. 5–22 ("in recent years, machine learning (ML) has become a key enabling technology for the sciences and industry. Especially through improvements in methodology, the availability of large databases and increased computational power, *today's ML algorithms are able to achieve excellent performance (at times even exceeding the human level) on an increasing number of complex tasks. Deep learning models are at the forefront of this development. However, due to their nested non-linear structure, these powerful models have been generally considered "black boxes", not providing any information about what exactly makes them arrive at their predictions.* Since in many applications, e.g., in the medical domain, *such lack of transparency may be not acceptable, the development of methods for visualizing, explaining and interpreting deep learning models has recently attracted increasing attention. This introductory paper presents recent developments and applications in this field and makes a plea for a wider use of explainable learning algorithms in practice*"). Italics added.

[575] Henderson, Stephen E., "A Few Criminal Justice Big Data Rules", *Ohio State Journal of Criminal Law*, Volume 15, 2018, passim.

convolutional[576] networks,[577] right to human consciousness,[578] machine learning,[579] deep learning,[580] and algorithmic transparency[581]) which, given its piecemeal and haphazard nature, falls nonetheless seriously short of grasping the intricacies of the topic at hand. The crux of this issue lies elsewhere though.

---

576 Aggarwal, C. C., *Neural networks and deep learning*, Heidelberg, Springer, 2018, passim.

577 Podmore, J.J./Breckon, TP/Aznan, NKN, et al., "On the relative contribution of deep convulational neural networks for SSVEP-based bio-signal decoding in BCI speller applications", *Institute of Electrical and Electronic Engineers (IEEE), Transactions on Neural System and Rehabilitation Engineering*, Volume 27, Issue 4, 2019, pp. 611–618.

578 See generally: Sebo, J., "The Moral Problem of Other Minds", *Harvard Review of Philosophy*, Volume 25, 2018, pp. 51–70.

See about consciousness: Feinberg, Todd E./Mallatt, Jon M., *Consciousness Demystified*. Cambridge, Massachusetts: The MIT Press, 2018, passim; Lavazza, A./Massimini, M., "Cerebral organoids. Ethical issues and consciousness assessment", *Journal of Medical Ethics*, Volume 44, 2019, pp. 606–610; Michel, M., "Consciousness Science Undetermined Ergo, an Open Access", *Journal of Philosophy*, Volume 6, 2019, passim; Lee, A.Y., "Is Consciousness Intrinsically Valuable?", *Philosophical Studies*, Volume 175, 2018, pp. 1–17; Frith, C.D., "The neural basis of consciousness", *Psychological Medicine*, 2019, pp. 1–13; Shepherd, Lois/Pike, Williams C./Persily, Jesse B./Marshall, Mary Faith, "The Case of Hannah Capes: How Much Does Consciousness Matter?", *Neuroethics*, Volume 15, Issue 14, 2022, pp. 1–16; Fins, Joseph J., *Rights come to mind: Brain Injury, Ethics, and the Struggle for Consciousness*. Cambridge: Cambridge University Press, 2015, pp. 1–394.

579 Murphy, Kevin P., *Machine Learning: A Probabilistic Perspective (Adaptive Computation and Machine Learning series)*. Massachusetts: The MIT Press, 2012, pp. 1–1104 (states avowedly that "machine Learning attempts to combine deductive, inductive, and abductive reasoning to make person-like reasoning in AI Entities possible. Machine-learning AI Entities initially learn in the same way a human child learns. First, they notice details and patterns in shapes, sounds, and behaviors; then put them together to distinguish one person from another, or a dog from a cat. Eventually, the AI can recognize and identify" common objects). See also: Hutto-Schultz, Jess, "Dicitur Ex Machina: Artificial Intelligence and the Hearsay Rule", *George Mason Law Review*, Volume 27, n.º 2, 2020, pp. 684–718 (689).

580 Chollet, François, *Deep Learning with Python*. Shelter Island, Nova Iorque: Manning, 2018, pp. 1–384 (passim). *Deep Learning* stands as a byproduct of *Machine Learning. Machine Learning*, a subset of Artificial Intelligence, unfolds itself in *Deep Learning*, which "involves computer algorithms that have the ability to "learn" or improve in performance over time on some task". See: Surden, Harry, "Machine Learning and Law", *Washington Law Review*, Volume 89, 2015, pp. 87 and ff.

581 Tyler, Tom R., "Does the American Public Accept the Rule of Law? The Findings of Psychological Research on Deference to Authority", *De Paul Law Review*, 56, 2007, pp. 661–664 (stating that «transparency and openness foster the belief that decision-making procedures are neutral»). See also: Doherty, Joseph W./Reville, Robert T./Zakaras, Laura(ed.), *Introduction to Confidentiality, Transparency, and the U.S. Civil Justice System*, Oxford, Oxford University Press, 2012, 1–258 (passim) (noting that the lack of transparency yields sizable social costs); Davis, Joshua P. "Law Without Mind: AI, Ethics, and Jurisprudence", *California Western Law Review*, Volume 55, 2018, pp. 181 e ss and passim (deals with an agreed-upon Artificial opacity while emphasizing a sought-after transparency to trounce it). See also: Coglianese, Cary/Lehr, David, "Transparency and Algorithmic Governance", *Administrative Law Review*, Volume 71, 2019, pp. 1–41; Brauneis, Robert/Goodman, Ellen P. "Algorithmic Transparency for the Smart City", *Yale Journal of Law and Technology*, Volume 20, 2018, pp. 103–109.

§§ Moving beyond the broad blueprint underpinning Artificial Intelligence-embedded technologies provided in some textbooks,[582] the overarching goal of this section is to disambiguate the idea of Artificial Intelligence-embedded technologies as tools of mass destruction.[583]

§§ Out of accuracy, let's get this straight: cutting-edge technology can prove incredibly beneficial for the overall advance of humankind, but robust boundaries are in dire need of being swiftly set out or the digital landscape may otherwise careen into chaos of *Algorithmic Dictatorship*.[584] Here lies the paramount importance of debunking patchy frameworks like human-centred Artificial Intelligence that nevertheless falls conspicuously short of laying down a sturdy groundwork in which AI-embedded technologies should rest upon.

---

[582] Tegmark, Max, *Life 3.0: Being Human in the Age of Artificial Intelligence*. New York: Knopf, 2018, pp. 1–384 (pp. 24 and ff) (charts the path ahead for a wide range of intelligences, including artificial intelligence in the digital age). There is a handful of authors that wonder if artificial intelligence can mimic not only human intelligence but, and foremost, human behaviour. Amongst whom stands: Russel, Stuart, Norvig, Peter, *Artificial Intelligence: A Modern Approach*. London: United Kingdom, Pearson, 2018, passim. See also: McCarthy, John, Compt. Scientist, Stanford University, Stanford University, in: http://jmc.stanford.edu/artificial-intelligence/what-is-ai/index.html (Nov. 12, 2007) (according to the so-called father of Artificial Intelligence, AI is "the science and engineering of making intelligent machines, especially intelligent computer programs. It is related to the similar task of using computers to understand human intelligence"). Access: 24.9.2024. Converging: Chabert, J.L. et al., *A History of Algorithms: From the Pebble to the Microchip*. New York/Heidelberg: Springer, 2013, p. 2.

[583] O'Neill, Cathy, *Weapons of Math Destruction. How Big Data Increases Inequality and Threatens Democracy*. London: Penguin Random House, 2016, passim. Note, though, that the newest developments arising out of the "collect-it-all" technologies are slated to create a slew of sizzling hot challenges to the sustainability of the Rule of Law. See: Hu, Margaret, "From the National Surveillance State to the Cybersurveillance State", *The Annual Review of Law and Social Science*, Volume 13, 2017, pp. 162–163 ("*policymakers view these technological developments, including biometric technologies, as tools with the potential to identify individuals who may pose a threat to national and homeland security and to prevent crime and terrorism. One example of technology intended for risk assessment and threat management is the post-9/11 program Total Information Awareness (TIA).* TIA was the progeny of the Defense Advanced Research Projects Agency (DARPA) in the US Department of Defense. *TIA can be understood as a "collect-it-all" data surveillance program. TIA was not explicitly identified as a collect-it-all program—this phrase originated with the Snowden disclosures.* One National Security Agency (NSA) slide described the NSA's procedure as "collect-it-all" (Greenwald 2014b). *Collect-it-all efforts like TIA embody a philosophy that aspires to preventive policing. Mass data collection is construed as a tool to assess and prevent future threats* (Murray 2010). *In TIA and other programs tested or adopted after 9/11, biometric database screening and analysis have emerged as a preferred method for tracking, identifying, and establishing identity-based inferences in counterterrorism*"). Italics added. See also: Ball, Kirstie, and Frank Webster (Eds.), *The Intensification of Surveillance: Crime, Terrorism & Warfare in the Information Age*, London, UK: Pluto Press, 2007; Guzik, Keith, "Discrimination by Design: Predictive Data Mining as Security Practice in the United States' 'War on Terrorism'", *Surveillance and Society*, 7 (1), 2009, pp. 1–17.

[584] See: Part IV, Chap. 4, Sects. 4.1–4.1.10.6 of this book (on Algorithmic Dictatorship and its chilling effect on democracy).

§§ More to the point, the greatest drawback of this framework is that, all things considered, is not a framework at all, let alone a legal framework to look up to. And these are hardly joyful news in this regard.[585]

§§ At one end of the spectrum, the power of AI decision-making is highly clustered in the shaky hands of a bunch of tech moguls,[586] and yet few to none measures have been adopted to thoroughly address this sizzling hot topic alongside others equally

[585] This problem is neither new nor easy to solve. Whilst the effects of technology—digital justice—on the courtroom have been previously broached by the doctrine, few to none consensus has been reached about the actionable lines of action to be taken. See: Donoghue, Jane, "The Rise of Digital Justice: Courtroom Technology, Public Participation and Access to Justice", *The Modern Law Review*, Volume 80, Issue 6, 2018, p. 995 (noting that technology in the courtroom might widen the gap between the rich and the poor. In this vein, this renowned author has contended that "*legal reforms have omitted any detailed consideration of the type and quality of citizen participation in newly digitised court processes which have fundamental implications for the legitimacy and substantive outcomes of court-based processes; and for enhancing democratic procedure through improved access to justice.* It is argued that although digital court tools and systems offer great promise for enhancing efficiency, participation and accessibility, they *simultaneously have the potential to amplify the scope for injustice, and to attenuate central principles of the legal system, including somewhat paradoxically, access to justice*"). Italics added. See also: Heintz, M.E., "The digital divide and courtroom technology: Can David keep up with Goliath", *Federal Communications Law Journal*, Volume 54, 2002, pp. 566 ff and passim. The great bulk of these assertions has been anticipated by an iconic piece of research. See: Galanter, Marc, "Why the "Haves" Come Out Ahead: Speculations on the Limits of Legal Change", *Law & Society Review*, Volume 9, 1974, pp. 98–103 (this renowned author talks about a *social reality* in which the dubbed «repeat players»—which go by the name of «haves»—tend to «to come out ahead» by putting their knowledge and vast resources to good use. This perceived advantage will not only impact the choice on the procedures but will ultimately benefit their interests as opposed to the deemed «one-shot» players (the «have nots») that will have slimmer and fewer chances to get palpable results in dispute resolution). Technology in the criminal courtroom—that includes the rich and excludes the poor - will make this problem considerably worse. But see: Bailey, J./Burkell, J./Reynolds, G. "Access to Justice for All: Towards an "Expansive Vision" of Justice and Technology, *Windsor Yearbook of Access to Justice*, Volume 31, 2013, pp. 183–201 (in stark contrast, these authors stress that the digital and technological apparatus can indeed spawn a both time-effective and streamlined access to justice in a given jurisdiction).

[586] Yang/Kai Hao, "Selling Consumer Data for Profit: Optimal Market-Segmentation Design and its Consequences", *American Economic Review*, Volume 112, Issue 4, April 2022, 2022, pp. 1364–1393; Wagner/Gerhard/Eidenmuller, Horst, "Down by Algorithms? Siphoning Rents, Exploiting Biases, and Shaping Preferences: Regulating the Dark Side of Targeted Transactions", *University of Chicago Law Review*, Volume 86, 2019, pp. 581–609; Wallheimer, Brian, "Are you Ready for Personalized Pricing? Companies Are Figuring out What Individual Customers Will Pay-and Charging Accordingly", *Chicago Booth Review*, 2018, passim.

relevant, like online dispute resolution[587] and biometric surveillance[588] arising out of big data world.[589]

---

[587] Sela, Ayelet, "The Effect of Technologies on Dispute Resolution System Design: Antecedents, Current Trends, and Future Directions", *Lewis and Clark Law Review*, Volume 21, 2018, pp. 634 ff and passim (arguing that the widespread use of technology has breed the turn to online dispute resolution).

[588] Which, I may venture to add, is something—*biometric surveillance*—that amounts to nothing but to the price of partaking in social settings, which is very hard to shy away from nowadays. See: Hu, Margaret, "From the National Surveillance State to the Cybersurveillance State", *The Annual Review of Law and Social Science*, Volume 13, 2017, p. 169 ("*because of technological developments and trends in governance, it is challenging, if not impossible, to prevent biometric data capture and collection. Biometric surveillance systems increasingly require opting in as the price of social, economic, and political participation.* Biometric data capture is difficult to resist because it is simultaneously compulsory and transparent. Biometric data collection is often compulsory because it is increasingly mandatory to establish identity. *Biometrics are transparent qualities because it is very difficult to hide biometrics; an individual's face, iris, or fingerprint can be digitally captured in any public place. Because biometric data support larger big data programs, such as No Fly List–type risk assessments, it is extraordinarily difficult, if not impossible, to opt out*"). Italics added. See: Part IV, Chap. 4, Sects. 4.1.5–4.1.5.2 of this book (on "algorithmic Jim Crow", a travel ban issued during the first Trump Administration to prevent certain individuals from entering the United States of America, which, given its racial undertones, stands as an outgrowth of congeries of laws enacted during the Jim Crow epoch).

[589] Hu, Margaret, "From the National Surveillance State to the Cybersurveillance State", *The Annual Review of Law and Social Science*, Volume 13, 2017, p. 169 ("*in a big data world, a digitized passport system can link to multiple other sources, such as license plate readers, No Fly Lists, and Terrorist Watchlists. Facial recognition technology drawing upon a photo database could potentially link a plethora of digital images of a person, including social media, the internet, photo databases like driver's licenses, live-streaming video, CCTV surveillance, and images obtained from hacking cameras on laptops and digital devices. Biometric data collection and storage are becoming increasingly compulsory through either government identification requirements*, such as digital photo requirements for passports and driver's licenses, or corporate identification requirements, such as biometric access to digital devices"). Italics added. See: Part IV, Chap. 4, Sects. 4.1.5–4.1.5.2 of this book (on "algorithmic Jim Crow", a travel ban issued during the first Trump Administration to prevent certain individuals from entering the United States of America, which, given its racial undertones, stands as an outgrowth of congeries of laws enacted during the Jim Crow epoch).

§§ Online dispute resolution is not a small-scaled problem. Rather, online dispute resolution engenders a myriad of worrisome problems (ranging from *pro se* disputants' status,[590] algorithmic governance,[591] algorithmic discrimination,[592]

[590] Amongst which stands the insurmountable barriers disadvantaged parties—*pro se* disputants that cannot afford to pay a well-adjusted and seasoned lawyer—face when they access judicial courts. This problem will only get worse as technology gain traction in criminal procedure law settings. An empirical research premises such assertion. See: Kroeper, Kathryn/Quintanilla, Victor D./Frisby, Michael/Yel, Nedim/Applegate, Amy G./Sherman, Steven J./Murphy, Mary C., "Underestimating the Unrepresented: Cognitive Biases Disadvantage Pro Se Litigants in Family Law Cases", *Psychology, Public Policy, and Law*, Volume 26, n.º 2, 2020, pp. 198–212 (211) (emphazise "*the present research suggests that the mere presence or absence of pro se status affects the inferences that legal officials make about parties in the civil justice system.* Legal officials appraised the cases of counselled parties as less meritorious the cases of counselled parties and predicted the *unrepresented persons would experience the civil justice system as less fair and satisfying the counselled litigants, even when all case facts were held constant, and especially when trial (vs. mediation) was considered to be the dispute resolution mechanism*"). Italics added. See also: Quintanilla, Victor/ Allen, R. A./Hirt, E. R., "The signalling effect of pro se status", *Law & Social Inquiry*, Volume 42, 2018, pp. 1092–1120.

Michaels, Andrew C., "Artificial Intelligence, Legal Change, and Separation of Powers", *University of Cincinnati Law Review*, 2020, pp. 1083 and ff and passim.

[591] Coglianese, Cary/Lehr, David, "Transparency and Algorithmic Governance", *Administrative Law Review*, Volume 71, 2019, pp. 1–41. On algorithmic big data biometric governance: Hu, Margaret, "From the National Surveillance State to the Cybersurveillance State", *The Annual Review of Law and Social Science*, Volume 13, 2017, p. 169 ("*as a result of big data biometric governance trends, meaningful distinctions between biometric credentialing for identification and behavioral biometric profiling are disappearing. The objectives are merging: Reliable credentialing is used to advance security and precrime policy rationales. Biometric data mission creep occurs by necessity in a big data world because the cybersurveillance systems are often designed to engage in mass data integration and analysis and predictive policing. Biometric surveillance serves two purposes in preventive policing: It increases identity transparency, and the biometric data categorize identity through cataloging behavioral and physical characteristics and assess these characteristics for risk. Contrasting small data biometric credentialing protocols with big data credentialing protocols is useful. It illustrates how biometric surveillance fits within the Cybersurveillance State. In a small data world, paper-based passports and nondigitized photographs are examples of a small data biometric-based identification system*"). Italics added. See: Part IV, Chap. 4, Sects. 4.1.5–4.1.5.2 of this book (on "algorithmic Jim Crow", a travel ban issued during the first Trump Administration to prevent certain individuals from entering the United States of America, which, given its racial undertones, stands as an outgrowth of congeries of laws enacted during the Jim Crow epoch).

[592] Griemmelmann, James/Westreich, Daniel, "Incomprehensible Discrimination", *California Law Review Online*, Volume 7, 2018, pp. 164–171.

algorithmic injustice,[593] algorithmic transparency,[594] and algorithmic bias,[595] algorithmic consumer harm,[596] to the complexity of AI-algorithms against the backdrop of which black[597] boxes[598] operate).

---

[593] See: Ting-an Lin, ""Democratizing AI" and the Concern of Algorithmic Injustice", *Philosophy and Technology*, Volume 37 (103), 2024, pp. 3–27. See also: Birhane, A., "Algorithmic injustice: A relational ethics approach", *Patterns*, 2 (2), 2021, pp. 1–9. Završnik, A. "Algorithmic justice: Algorithms and big data in criminal justice settings", *European Journal of Criminology*, 2019, passim.

[594] Davis, Joshua P. "Law Without Mind: AI, Ethics, and Jurisprudence", *California Western Law Review*, Volume 55, 2018, pp. 181 e ss and passim (deals with an agreed-upon Artificial opacity while emphasizing a sought-after transparency to trounce it).

[595] Xiang, Alice, "Reconciling Legal and Technical Approaches to Algorithmic Bias", *Tennessee Law Review*, Volume 88, 2021, passim. See also: Baeza-Yates, R., "Bias on the web", *Communications of the ACM*, 61 (6), June 2018, 2018, pp. 54–61 (argues that "*algorithmic bias is when the bias is not present in the input data* and is added *purely by the algorithm*"). Italics added.

[596] Bar-Gill, Oren/Sunstein, Cass R./Talgam-Cohen, Inbal, "Algorithmic Harm in Consumer Markets", *Journal of Legal Analysis*, Volume 15, n.º 1, 2023, pp. 1–47.

[597] Pasquale, Frank, *The Black Box Society: The Secret Algorithms that Control Money and Information*. Cambridge, Massachusetts: Harvard University Press, 2015, 1–320 (8–10 and passim) (noting that biased algorithms, which have underlying discrimination problems, contribute exponentially to further social biases. His most intriguing claim is that such biased algorithms have been incorporated/etched in the bulk of the corporations' informatic system, to the detriment of human kind in an overarching sense).

[598] This is one of the most unsettling issues. Take heed of the impervious way algorithms make their inferences and draw their conclusions, which is eerily unknown even for the cohort of programmers that designed them. This is deemed *black box*, that further enhances the shroud of mystery under which algorithms are cloaked. See, for a compelling account of AI black box: Ver: Bathaee, Yavar, "The Artificial Intelligence Black Box and the Failure of Intent and Causation", *Harvard Journal of Law and Technology*, n.º 37, 2018, p. 901 (adduces that "*one possible reason AI may be a black box to humans is that it relies on machine-learning algorithms that internalize data in ways that are not easily audited or understood by humans* (...)" "*first, a lack may arise from the complexity of the algorithm's structure, such as with deep neural network, which consists of thousands of artificial neurons working together in a diffuse way to solve a problem. This reason for AI being a black box is referred to as "complexity". Second, the lack of transparency may arise because the AI is using a machine-learning algorithm that relies on geometric relationships that humans cannot visualize, such as with support vector machines. This reason for AI being a black box is referred to as "dimensionality"*"). Italics added. But see: Pearl, Judea, *Causality*, 2nd edition, Cambridge, Cambridge University Press, 2009 (on the fundamental tenets of causality). But see: Kilbertus, Niki/Carulla, Mateo Rojas/Parascandolo, Giambattista/Hardt, Moritz/Janzing, Dominik/Schoellkopf, Bernhard, "Avoiding Discrimination through Causal Reasoning", *Advances in Neural Information Processing Systems*, I. Guyon, U. V. Luxburg, S. Bengio, H. Wallach, R. Fergus, S. Vishwanathan, and R. Garnett (Eds.), Vol. 30. Curran Associates, Inc., 2017, pp. 656–666 (arguing that is feasible to avoiding discrimination through a granular and fine-grained causal reasoning). See: Part V, Chap. 5, Sect. 5.1.7.2 of this book (on law number two to control algorithmic decision-making, which mandates that black box models must not be entrusted with the task of making high stake decisions—v.g. health and freedom).

§§ In addition to that, there is bundle of sweltering issues that have not been sharp-wittedly addressed by human-centred Artificial Intelligence (ranging from machine testimony in a court of law,[599] racial equity in criminal procedure law settings,[600] quantum algorithms,[601] genetic algorithms,[602] «algorithmic bias in, bias out»,[603], to the impact of brain-computer interfaces in the remit of criminal procedure law,[604] mainly from the *nemo tenetur se ipsum accusare*[605] or the *privilege against self-incrimination*[606] standpoint).

---

[599] Roth, Andrea, "Machine Testimony", *Yale Law Journal*, Volume 126, 2017, pp. 1972 and ff and passim; Grimm, Paul W., "Practical Considerations for the Admissibility of Artificial Intelligence Evidence", *Maryland Bar Journal*, Volume 2, Issue 3, 2021, pp. 39 and ff and passim (pinpoints that challenges posed by Artificial Intelligence in the camp of law for years to come).

[600] Huq, Aziz Z., "Racial Equity in Algorithmic Criminal Justice", *Duke Law Journal*, Volume 68, 2019, pp. 1043–1072.

[601] Kop, Mauritz/Aboy, Mateo/De Jong, Eline/Gasser, Urs/Minssen, Timo, "Towards Responsible Quantum Technology: Safeguarding, Engaging and Advancing Quantum R&D", *UC Law Science and Technology Journal*, Volume 15, Number 1, Article 4, 2024, pp. 63–94.

[602] Sun, Y, Xue, B, Zhang, M, et al., "Automatically designing CNN architectures using the genetic algorithm for image classification", *IEEE Trans Cybern.*, Volume 50, Issue 9, 2020, pp. 3840–3854; Gowda, CC, Mayya, SG, "Comparison of back propagation neural network and genetic algorithm neural network for stream flow prediction", *J Computer Environ Sci.*, 2014, pp. 1–6; Rikhtegar A, Pooyan M, Manzuri-Shalmani MT, "Genetic algorithm-optimised structure of convolutional neural network for face recognition applications", *IET Computer Vision*, Volume 10, Issue 6, 2016, pp. 559–566.

[603] Mayson, Sandra G., "Bias In, Bias Out", *Yale Law Journal*, Volume 128, 2019, pp. 2218 and ff and passim.

[604] Santos, Hugo Luz dos, ""Brain-Computer Interfaces, Generative Artificial Intelligence (ChatGPT and Deep Fakes) and Criminal Procedure Law: what's at stake?", *Journal of Research in E. and Computer Science*, Edinburgh, United Kingdom, June 2024, Volume 2, 2024, pp. 39–78.

[605] See generally in German doctrine: Vogel, Joachim, "Informationstechnologische Herausforderungen an das Strafprozessrecht", *Zis*, 2012, pp. 485–487. See also: *BGH*, 22.12.2011, *HRRS*, 2012, n.º 268; Kasiske, "Die Selbstbelastungsfreiheit im Strafprozess", *JuS*, 2014, pp. 23–26; Zuck, R., "Faires Verfahren und der Nemo tenetur-Grundsatz bei der Besuchsüberwachung zu BGH, Urteil v. 29.04.2009,,, *Juristische Rundschau* (*JR*), 2010, pp. 18–27. See generally in Spanish doctrine: Neira Pena, Ana María, "Editorial para el dossier "Proceso penal de personas jurídicas e investigaciones internas empresariales": Investigaciones internas empresariales, derechos fundamentales y prueba prohibida", *Brazilian Journal of Criminal Procedure Law*, Volume 9, number 2, may-august 2023, 2023, pp. 503–544; Estrada Cuadras, Albert, "Confesión o finiquito": el papel del derecho a no autoincriminarse en las investigaciones internas", *Indret: Revista para el Análisis del Derecho*, n.º 4, 2020, pp. 227–272.

[606] On the genetic origins of the privilege against self-incrimination: Levy, Leonard, *Origins of the Fifth Amendment – The Right Against Self-Discrimination.* New York/Oxford: Oxford University Press, 1968, passim; Moglen, "The Privilege in British North America: The Colonial Period to the Fifth Amendment", *The Privilege against Self-Incrimination – Its Origins and Development*, HELMHOLZ et al. (Editors). Chicago, Illinois, London: Chicago University Press, 1997, pp. 255 and ff and passim; Pittman, R. Carter, "The Colonial and Constitutional History of the Privilege against Self-Incrimination in America", *Virginia Law Review*, Volume 21, Number 7, 1935, pp. 775 e ss and passim. On the overriding importance of the privilege against self-incrimination: Harris, David/O'Boyle, Michael/Bates, Ed/Buckley, Carla M., *Law of the European Convention on Human Rights*, 5th edition, Oxford/New York: Oxford University Press, 2023, pp. 1–1088 (passim).

§§ The lawmakers remain bloodcurdlingly silent in this regard, and they really shouldn't. Most importantly, and perhaps worryingly, human-centred Artificial Intelligence has nothing meaningful to say about any of this.

§§ Strikingly, the paucity of bespoke measures to tackle the foregoing issues bears no prospect of mitigating algorithmic injustice to some extent. Which is something that deserves to be frowned upon in that it shouldn't have been glossed over amidst the age of Artificial Intelligence-embedded technologies[607] that is upon us. As various notions of safe Artificial Intelligence proliferate, so do nagging uncertainties about the future of Artificial Intelligence-embedded technologies, which is something that you should not hold your breath for.

§§ At the other end of the spectrum, scholars[608] have been neither coy nor bashful in pouring in trenchant criticism on the dearth of theoretical underpinnings concerning human-centred Artificial Intelligence.[609] Whilst democratizing Artificial Intelligence-embedded is often framed by the movement of human-centred AI as a sought-after response to allay algorithmic injustice,[610] the foundations upon which the former stand remain conveniently wrapped in opaquenesss.[611]

---

[607] Katyal, Sonia, "Private Accountability in the Age of Artificial Intelligence", *UCLA Law Review*, Volume 66, 2019, pp. 54–99.

[608] Braun, Matthias/Meacham, Darian, "A Plea for (In)Human-centred AI", *Philosophy & Technology*, 2024, pp. 37–97.

[609] Kaluarachchi, T., Reis, A., & Nanayakkara, S., "A review of recent deep learning approaches in human-centered machine learning", *Sensors* (Basel, Switzerland), 21, 2021, 2514.

[610] Angwin, Julia et al., "Machine Bias", *ProPublica* (May 23, 2016), https://www.propublica.org/article/machine-bias-risk-assessments-in-criminal-sentencing [https://perma.cc/4G83-MDAS] (harshly criticizing disparity in false-positive rates as a purely unjustified bias). See also: Freeman, Katherine, "Algorithmic Injustice: How the Wisconsin Supreme Court Failed to Protect Due Process Rights in State v. Loomis", *North Carolina Journal of Law and Technology*, Volume 18, 2016, pp. 75–86 (echoing the very same views). See: Mayson, Sandra G., "Bias In, Bias Out", *cit.*, pp. 2218–2300. Ting-an Lin, ""Democratizing AI" and the Concern of Algorithmic Injustice", *Philosophy and Technology*, Volume 37 (103), 2024, pp. 3–27; Okidegbe, Ngozi, "The Democratizing Potential of Algorithms?", *Connecticut Law Review*, Volume 54, 2021, passim; Katyal, Sonia, "Private Accountability in the Age of Artificial Intelligence", *UCLA Law Review*, Volume 66, 2019, pp. 54–99.

[611] *Tech, Bias and Housing Initiative, the Promise and Perils of Residential Proptech, Year 1, Research Summary Report, April 2023, TechEquity Collaborative*, p. 11, available at: https://techequity.us/wp-content/uploads/2023/04/TBHI-Y1-Research-Summary-Report.pdf (28.11.2024) ("*From information on company websites, it is not clear what analysis or data is behind subjective determinations like "suitability" to a unit or what the nexus between an individual's characteristics and a unit's characteristics is that indicates the likelihood for property damage. Based on sample reports, even landlords are not privy to how the determinations are made. Instead, they receive a risk score out of 100 simplified into green, yellow, and red recommendations*. What companies withhold in terms of how it works, they make up for with the extent to which they tell landlords it works: Naborly claims their predictions reduce lease defaults by up to 89%. 15 *As Naborly's sample report demonstrates, its property damage assessment is then used as an input to determine its projected eviction outcomes; its early vacancy prediction, in turn, is based on "all assessment factors*"). Italics added.

§§ Put otherwise, the concept of human-centred Artificial Intelligence is detached of, and decoupled from, brawny foundations[612] that would render this well-intentioned initiative the epithet of philosophical movement in the first place. As it stands, human-centred AI amounts to nothing but to an unsustainably vague, piece-meal, haphazardly lightweighted, and superficial conceptual framework that hovers in the air of unbecoming shallowness.

§§ Much more is accordingly needed to instil legal security[613] upon the framework of Artificial Intelligence-embedded technologies, which should amount to much more than a handful of whimsical hunches gliding over this fast-paced landscape.[614] Failing which, the Rule of Law

---

[612] Göttgens, I., & Oertelt-Prigione, S., "The application of human-centered design approaches in health research and innovation: A narrative review of current practices", *JMIR mHealth and uHealth*, 9, e28102, 2021.

[613] Dyzenhaus, David, *The Long Arc of Legality: Hobbes, Kelsen, Hart*. Cambridge: Cambridge University Press, 2022, pp. 1–476.

[614] Fergus, Rachel, "Biased Technology: The Automated Discrimination of Facial Recognition", *ACLU Minnesota*, February 29, 2024, available at: https://www.aclu-mn.org/en/news/biased-technology-automated-discrimination-facial-recognition (access: 20.09.2024) ("*Technology is developing much more quickly than the laws we need to protect our rights. Anyone with a smartphone or social media account knows how rapidly technology changes, while legislating can take a long, long time. It is essential to proactively put policies into place that will protect our rights as new and more advanced technology is constantly released. Especially when that technology – and law enforcement members using it - have been shown over and over to be biased toward marginalized groups*"). Italics added. See also: Hu, Margaret, "From the National Surveillance State to the Cybersurveillance State", *The Annual Review of Law and Social Science*, Volume 13, 2017, p. 169 ("*in a big data world, a digitized passport system can link to multiple other sources, such as license plate readers, No Fly Lists, and Terrorist Watchlists. Facial recognition technology drawing upon a photo database could potentially link a plethora of digital images of a person, including social media, the internet, photo databases like driver's licenses, live-streaming video, CCTV surveillance, and images obtained from hacking cameras on laptops and digital devices. Biometric data collection and storage are becoming increasingly compulsory through either government identification requirements*, such as digital photo requirements for passports and driver's licenses, or corporate identification requirements, such as biometric access to digital devices"). Italics added.

is bound to further backslide.[615] The dearth of legal security accordingly plays havoc with our ability to secure *Algorithmic Common Good*, which stands as one of the key takeaways of this book. More on this later.[616]

§§ *Critical Artificial Intelligence Studies* (CAIS), by laying out a sturdy foundation upon which stands, seeks to wash away concerns about conceptual indeterminacy of which the movement of human-centred Artificial Intelligence has fallen prey to. Hence the paramount importance of the theoretical underpinnings of CAIS laid down of Part III, this chapter.

§§ Bereft of which, CAIS would be utterly unable to push beyond the narrowly defined boundaries of scholarship to chart the path ahead for Artificial Intelligence-embedded technologies for centuries to come.

§§ More to the point, the reluctance to pin a definition down onto to a page—the framework concerning the safe use of Artificial Intelligence-embedded technologies—is mirrored to varying degrees.

§§ None of which, though, is difficult to grasp: to the extent that the foregoing issues were not thought-through, legal indeterminacy remains a key strand of the movement of human-centred Artificial Intelligence. CAIS aims to plug this perceived gap by spotlighting the roadblocks that stand in the way of the sought-after flourishment of *Algorithmic Common Good*, which is slated to be advantageous to humankind in an overarching sense.

§§ *Critical Artificial Intelligence Studies* (CAIS) and *Algorithmic Common Good* (AGC) are therefore tightly interlocked in that they are woven of the same cloth. The former is the linchpin of the latter. The former is deeply woven into the fabric of the latter.

---

[615] See: Part V, Chap. 5, Sect. 5.1.1.1 of this book (on the central tenets of Rule of Law that lends itself to a beacon of justice amidst the sepulchral darkness that is about to take hold). See: Part V, Chap. 5, Sect. 5.1.1.2 of this book (on the central tenets of Procedural Rule of Law that lends itself to a lighthouse of justice that allows citizens to challenge the pearls of algorithmic wisdom in a court of law). See also: Sempill, J.A., "Ruler's Sword, Citizen's Shield: The Rule of Law and the Constitution of Power", *Journal of Law and Politics*, Volume 31, 2018, pp. 333 ff; McArthur, N., "Laws Not Men: Hume's Distinction Between Barbarous and Civilized Government", *Hume* Studies, Volume 31, 2005, pp. 123 ff; Stromseth, J./Wippman, D./Brooks, R., *Can Might Make Rights? Building the Rule of Law After Military Interventions*. Cambridge: Cambridge University Press, 2006, pp. 28 ff; Humphreys, S., *Theatre of the Rule of Law: Transnational Legal Intervention in Theory and* Practice. Cambridge: Cambridge University Press, 2020, passim; Farrall, J./Charlesworth, H. (eds), *Strengthening the Rule of Law Through the UN Security Council*. Abingdon: Routledge, 2018; Rajagopal, B., "Invoking the Rule of Law in Post-Conflict Rebuilding: A Critical Examination", *William and Mary Law Review*, Volume 49, 2008, pp. 1347 ff; Trubek, D. M./Santos (eds), *The New Law and Development: A Critical Appraisal*. Cambridge: Cambridge University Press, 2012, passim (all essays converge in one direction: the rule of law is of paramount importance amidst the fast-shifting world we live in).

[616] See: Part V, Chap. 5, Sects. 5.1.2–5.1.6.2.1 of this book (on the thing-centred algorithmic decision-making propelled by a *Controllable* and *Interpretable* Machine Learning that weeds out *Algorithmic Dictatorship* and secures *Algorithmic Common Good*).

§§ The former (CAIS) aims to shine keen light on the multitude of harmful effects arising out of Artificial Intelligence-embedded technology that reinforce patterns of entrenched privilege and structural disadvantage,[617] thereby widening the gap between wealthy[618] and impecunious[619] while perpetuating a ghastly social

[617] See: Barocas, Solon/Selbst, Andrew, "Big Data's Disparate Impact", *California Law Review*, Volume 104, 2016, p. 691 (highlighting the worrisome, and gruesome, issue of "structural disadvantage" with which racialized communities have been tussling for centuries). See also: Powell, Richard/Porter, Jeremy, "Redlining, Concentrated Disadvantage and Crime: The Effects of Discriminatory Government Policies on Violent Crime", *American Journal of Criminal Justice*, Volume 48, 2023, pp. 1132–1156 ("*Redlining and other discriminatory government policies enacted during the first half of the Twentieth Century have had long-lasting negative effects on neighborhoods, especially those inhabited by people of color. This study attempts to link the practice of redlining to current-day indicators of neighborhood concentrated disadvantage and violent crime using spatio-temporal data from Chicago* (...) *In addition, it seeks to determine whether redlining was associated with violent crime, and if that association was mediated by redlining's effect on concentrated disadvantage. The results indicate that redlining was associated with increases in both concentrated disadvantage and violent crime, and that redlining's relationship with violent crime was, indeed, partially mediated by its relationship with concentrated disadvantage*"). Italics added. See also: Gandy, Oscar H., *Coming to Terms with Chance: Engaging Rational Discrimination and Cumulative Disadvantage*, Farnham, UK: Ashgate Publishing, 2009.

[618] Artificial intelligence, like everything else, is not without sizable drawbacks and shortcomings though. The most menacing of which happens to be the flawed or biased algorithms, which are bound to mar a sought-after bias-free decision making in dispute resolution. See: Sternlight, Jean, "Pouring a Little Psychological Cold Water on Online Dispute Resolution", *Journal of Dispute Resolution*, 1, 2020, pp. 23 ff (raises awareness to the perils of biased algorithms on online dispute resolution). Converging: Schmitz, Amy, "Expanding Access to Remedies Through E-Court Initiatives", *Buffalo Law Review*, Volume 67, 2019, pp. 90–100 (showing concerns that e-courts might be premising their decisions on flawed and bigoted algorithms). Which is something to be frowned upon. Why? Most likely, flawed or biased algorithms will deepen the chasm between rich and poor.

[619] As captioned, this problem is neither new nor easy to solve. Whilst the effects of technology—digital justice—on the courtroom have been previously broached by the doctrine, few to none consensus has been reached about the actionable lines of action to be taken. See: Donoghue, Jane, "The Rise of Digital Justice: Courtroom Technology, Public Participation and Access to Justice", *The Modern Law Review*, Volume 80, Issue 6, 2018, p. 995 (noting that technology in the courtroom might widen the gap between the rich and the poor. In this vein, this renowned author has contended that "*legal reforms have omitted any detailed consideration of the type and quality of citizen participation in newly digitised court processes which have fundamental implications for the legitimacy and substantive outcomes of court-based processes; and for enhancing democratic procedure through improved access to justice.* It is argued that although digital court tools and systems offer great promise for enhancing efficiency, participation and accessibility, they *simultaneously have the potential to amplify the scope for injustice, and to attenuate central principles of the legal system, including somewhat paradoxically, access to justice*"). Italics added. See also: Heintz, M.E., "The digital divide and courtroom technology: Can David keep up with Goliath", *Federal Communications Law Journal*, Volume 54, 2002, pp. 566 ff and passim. The great bulk of these assertions has been anticipated by an iconic piece of research. See: Galanter, Marc, "Why the "Haves" Come Out Ahead: Speculations on the Limits of Legal Change", *Law & Society Review*, Volume 9, 1974, pp. 98–103 (this renowned author talks about a *social reality* in which the dubbed «repeat players»—which go by the name of «haves»—tend to «to come out ahead» by putting their knowledge and vast resources to good

oppression.[620] In addition to that, *Critical Artificial Intelligence Studies* (CAIS) aims to unwind the algorithmic divide between the rich[621] and the poor.[622]

§§ The latter *Algorithmic Common Good* (ACG)[623] seeks to dwindle the deep-seated biases hardened into code,[624] which, as captioned above, lends a patina

use. This perceived advantage will not only impact the choice on the procedures but will ultimately benefit their interests as opposed to the deemed «one-shot» players (the «have nots») that will have slimmer and fewer chances to get palpable results in dispute resolution). Technology in the criminal courtroom—that includes the rich and excludes the poor—will make this problem considerably worse. But see: Bailey, J./Burkell, J./Reynolds, G. "Access to Justice for All: Towards an "Expansive Vision" of Justice and Technology", *Windsor Yearbook of Access to Justice*, Volume 31, 2013, pp. 183–201 (in stark contrast, these authors stress that the digital and technological apparatus can indeed spawn a both time-effective and streamlined access to justice in a given jurisdiction).

620 Amongst which stands arguably social cleavages spawned by a technology that fondly includes the rich and outrightly excludes the poor, thereby compounding social issues with which modern have been grappling/tussling/scuffling/floundering since immemorial times. Social cleavages—a cloak under which mounting social outcry is often wrapped—that threaten to topple the foundations upon which stands the linchpin of western societies. See in general: Abramsky, Sasha, *Jumping at Shadows: The Triumph of Fear and the End of the American Dream*. New York: Bold Type Books, 2017, pp. 1–272 (passim).

621 See: Eubanks, Virginia, *Automating Inequality: How High-Tech Tools Profile, Police and Punish the Poor*. New York: St. Martin's Press, 2018, 1–272 (1 ff and passim) (coining the expression «automating inequality» to vividly portray the downsides of using high-technology to compound the yawning gap between rich and poor against the backdrop of biased algorithms). See also: Pasquale, Frank, *The Black Box Society: The Secret Algorithms that Control Money and Information*. Cambridge, Massachusetts: Harvard University Press, 2015, 1–320 (8–10 and passim) (noting that biased algorithms, which have underlying discrimination problems, contribute exponentially to further social biases. His most intriguing claim is that such biased algorithms have been incorporated/etched in the bulk of the corporations' informatic system, to the detriment of human kind in an overarching sense).

622 Such as a yawning gap between rich—that can adroitly harness artificial intelligence to advance their goals and shady agendas—and poor—that grapple to meet basic needs and are automatically excluded from the equation of digital society powered by Artificial Intelligence—which will directly impact the fabric of societies worldwide, thereby augmenting the chasm between the «digitally-chosen» and the «digitally-outcast» enabled by a algorithmic discrimination that does nothing but irreparable harm. See: Yu, Peter K., "The Algorithmic Divide and Equality in the Age of Artificial Intelligence", *Florida Law Review*, Volume 72, 2020, pp. 355–360 (addresses the issue of algorithmic discrimination).

623 See: Part V, Chap. 5, Sects. 5.1.2–5.1.6.2.1 of this book (on the thing-centred algorithmic decision-making propelled by a *Controllable* and *Interpretable* Machine Learning that weeds out *Algorithmic Dictatorship* and secures *Algorithmic Common Good*).

624 Boden, Margaret A., *Artificial Intelligence: A Very Short Introduction*. Oxford: Oxford University Press, 2018, pp. 26–28 (fleshes out both *expert systems* and *rule-based programmes*).

of objectivity to automated correlations[625] and inferences[626] that may appear more objective,[627] but may nonetheless reflect prejudice that we may not wish to re-entrench into machine learning algorithms.[628]

§§ Against this background, *Critical Artificial Intelligence Studies* (CAIS) builds on Critical Legal Studies (CLS) to take a stand against *legal indeterminacy*[629] with which human-centred Artificial Intelligence has been tussling.

---

[625] See: Part V, Chap. 5, Sects. 5.1.1.5.2.2–5.1.1.5.2.2.1.4 of this book (on the fundamental shift away from causation to correlations in algorithmic decision-making). See: Bathaee, Yavar, "The Artificial Intelligence Black Box and the Failure of Intent and Causation", *Harvard Journal of Law and Technology*, n.º 37, 2018, p. 901 (adduces that "*one possible reason AI may be a black box to humans is that it relies on machine-learning algorithms that internalize data in ways that are not easily audited or understood by humans (…)*" "*first, a lack may arise from the complexity of the algorithm's structure, such as with deep neural network, which consists of thousands of artificial neurons working together in a diffuse way to solve a problem. This reason for AI being a black box is referred to as "complexity". Second, the lack of transparency may arise because the AI is using a machine-learning algorithm that relies on geometric relationships that humans cannot visualize, such as with support vector machines. This reason for AI being a black box is referred to as "dimensionality"*"). Italics added. But see: Pearl, Judea, *Causality*, 2nd edition, Cambridge, Cambridge University Press, 2009 (on the fundamental tenets of causality). But see: Kilbertus, Niki/Carulla, Mateo Rojas/Parascandolo, Giambattista/Hardt, Moritz/Janzing, Dominik/Schoellkopf, Bernhard, "Avoiding Discrimination through Causal Reasoning", *Advances in Neural Information Processing Systems*, I. Guyon, U. V. Luxburg, S. Bengio, H. Wallach, R. Fergus, S. Vishwanathan, and R. Garnett (Eds.), Vol. 30. Curran Associates, Inc., 2017, pp. 656–666 (arguing that is feasible to avoiding discrimination through a granular and fine-grained causal reasoning). See: Citron, Danielle K./Pasquale, Frank, "The Scored Society: Due Process for Automated Predictions", *Washington Law Review*, Volume 89, Issue 1, 2014, pp. 1–34.

[626] Citron, Danielle K./Pasquale, Frank, "The Scored Society: Due Process for Automated Predictions", *cit.*, pp. 1–34.

[627] Citron, Danielle K./Pasquale, Frank, "The Scored Society: Due Process for Automated Predictions", *cit.*, pp. 1–34.

[628] Balkin, Jack M., "The Three Laws of Robotics in the Age of Big Data", *Ohio State Law Journal*, Volume 78, Issue 5, 2017, pp. 1217–1241.

[629] Hutchinson, Alan C./Monahan, Patrick J., "Law, Politics and the Critical Legal Scholars: The Unfolding Drama of American Legal Thought", *Stanford Law Review*, 36, 1984, pp. 199–245 (200–202) (on law's indeterminacy, which would eventually merit vitriolic remarks from other Critical Legal Scholars). Soon enough, the grievances toward law's indeterminacy were to be levelled up. Critical legal scholars not only debunked the indeterminacy of law but also the facts' nagging—and, foremost, unsettling—uncertainty regarding legal decision-making. See: McLeod, Ian, *Legal Theory*, 3rd Edition, New York, Palgrave Macmillan Law Masters, 2005, pp. 140–150 (decrying law's and facts' indeterminacy, especially in cases in which legal decision-making is to rely upon witnesses' flawed and skewed memory, which is to cast doubts on the witnesses' ability to aid judges in attaining the arduous task to serve justice in the first place). But see: Part V, Chap. 5, Sect. 5.1.7.2. of this book (on law number two to control algorithmic decision-making, which mandates that black box models must not be entrusted with the task of making high stake decisions—v.g. health and freedom).

§§ In addition to that, CAIS leverages on *legal pragmatism* as Artificial Intelligence-embedded technologies must not be bereft of *legal certainty*.[630] Something that human-centred Artificial Intelligence has very little to say about.

3.1.4.4 «The Technology Trap» (Carl Benedikt Frey), the «Planetary Costs of Artificial Intelligence» (Kate Crawford) and Whether and What Extent an All-Out Deployment of Artificial Intelligence-Embedded Technologies Is Wholly Beneficial for Humankind

§§ Whilst law should not fight shy of embracing the manifold benefits of technology,[631] lawmakers and policymakers should not be so gullible to do so though. Put it bluntly, technology can and should harnessed[632] to spur the overall advance of humankind. Yet the embracement of technology in legal settings is not without robust measures to forestall machine[633] biases while stamping out its unpalatable effects,[634] as abundantly shown at Part I (*Introduction*) of this book. To which the dear reader is kindly invited to revisit.

---

[630] Because «It matters how judges decide cases»: Dworkin, Ronald, *Law's Empire*, London, Hart Publishing, (reimp. of edition of 1986), 1998, pp. 1 ff and passim. On legal pragmatism: Dworkin, Ronald, *Taking rights seriously*, Cambridge, Harvard University Press, (1st edition of 1978), 1997, 1–392 and *passim*; Barak, Ahron, *The Judge in a Democracy*, New Jersey, Princeton University Press, 2006, 1–368, *passim*; Dworkin, Ronald, *A Matter of Principle*, Oxford, Clarendon Press, 2001, (reimp. of edition of 1985), 2001, 10 ff; Dworkin, Ronald, *Taking rights seriously*, 2nd edition, London, Duckworth Books, 1982, p. 3 ff; Sunstein, Cass R., *Radicals in Robes*, New York, Basic Books, 2006, 1–312 and *passim*; Dworkin, Ronald, "Looking for Cass Sunstein", *The New York Review of Books*, 2009, 56 ff (harshly criticizing the doctrinal stance of Professor Cass R. Sunstein set forth in *Radicals in Robes*). See also legal pragmatism: Posner, Richard, *Law, pragmatism and democracy*, Cambridge, Harvard University Press, 2005, 18 ff e *passim*; Coleman, Jules, *The practice of principle: in defence of a pragmatic approach to legal theory*, Oxford, Oxford University Press, 2003, p. 23 ff and *passim*; Alberstein, Michal, *Pragmatism and Law: From Philosophy to Dispute Resolution,* Aldershot, Ashgate Dartmouth, 2002, pp. 1–354.

[631] Dixon, H. B., "The Evolution of a High Technology Courtroom", *Future Trends in State Courts.* Virginia: National Center for State Courts, 2011, *passim.* See also: Workman, W., "Advancements in technology: New opportunities to investigate factors contributing to differential technology and information use", *International Journal of Management and Decision Making*, Volume 39, 2007, pp. 317 ff (pinpointing the advantages in using high technology at the courtroom).

[632] Sternlight, Jean R., "Justice in a Brave New World?", *Connecticut Law Review*, Volume 52, Issue 1, 2020, p. 232 (on the possibility to harness technology to "whether voice recognition, analysis of facial expressions, or measurements of body twitches may provide better insight into truthfulness").

[633] West, Sarah Myers/Whittaker, Meredith/Crawford, Kate, *Discriminating Systems. Gender, Race and Power in AI*. New York: AI Now Institute, 2019, pp. 15 and ff and passim.

[634] But see: Sela, Ayelet, "The Effect of Technologies on Dispute Resolution System Design: Antecedents, Current Trends, and Future Directions", *Lewis and Clark Law Review*, Volume 21, 2018, pp. 634 ff and passim (arguing that the widespread use of technology has breed the turn to online dispute resolution).

§§ On that account, pundits often aver that technology is a bedazzling gift for humankind.[635] Yet appearances can be misleading in that they can be subdued faster than a speeding bullet.[636] It should not come as a surprise that history extensively documents an uneasy/thorny relationship between technology and human beings.[637]

§§ This issue can be loosely deemed as «deception by design»,[638] which is a living testament of the thorny relationship between Artificial Intelligence-embedded technologies and human beings.[639] Note, though, that this issue is not amenable to be dismissed as irrelevant or marginally relevant. Let alone, outright nugatory.

§§ Strikingly, renowned scholars have long warned against the baneful effects[640] of technology.[641] Casts broadly, doubts have been accordingly cast upon the extent to which technological advances facilitate forms of human exploitation,[642] such as

---

[635] Gandy, O, *The Panoptic Sort: A Political Economy of Personal Information.* Oxford: Oxford University Press, 2021, Chapter 2.

[636] Zuboff, Zhoshana, *The Age of Surveillance Capitalism, The Fight for a Human Future at the New Frontier of Power.* New Yor City: PublicAffairs Books, 2019, pp. 1–704 (360) (argues that we are indomitably heading towards a "instrumentarianism" that draws on "totalitarianism").

[637] See: Jackson, Maya C., "Artificial Intelligence and Algorithmic Bias: The Issues with Technology Reflecting History and Humans", *Journal of Business Technology Law*, Volume 16, 2021, pp. 299–316.

[638] Willis, Lauren, "Deception by Design", *Harvard Journal Law and Technology*, Volume 34, 2020, pp. 115–190.

[639] Chabert, J.L. et al., *A History of Algorithms: From the Pebble to the Microchip.* New York/ Heidelberg: Springer, 2013.

[640] But see: Workman, W., "Advancements in technology: New opportunities to investigate factors contributing to differential technology and information use", *International Journal of Management and Decision Making*, Volume 39, 2007, pp. 317 ff (pinpointing the advantages in using high technology at the courtroom). But see: Part V, Chap. 5, Sect. 5.1.8.5 of this book (on law number five to interpret algorithmic decision-making, which mandates that robot-judges, robot-prosecutors and robot-lawyers must not enter the courtroom for they are utterly incapable of making sound and interpretable value judgements).

[641] Recall, *machine-learning algorithms "are capable of making intuitive decisions based in newly learned information, much like humans.* The new wave of AI developments will generate powerful AI that is capable of improvising itself, *perhaps even by rewriting its own algorithms, advancing its intelligence beyond that of humans*". Italics added. See: Hutto-Schultz, Jess, "Dicitur Ex Machina: Artificial Intelligence and the Hearsay Rule", *George Mason Law Review*, Volume 27, n.º 2, 2020, pp. 684–718 (684); Avery, Mallory/Leibbrandt, Andreas/Vecci, Joseph, "Does Artificial Intelligence Help or Hurt Gender Diversity? Evidence from Two Field Experiments on Recruitment on Tech", *Monash University, Monash Business School*, 2023, pp. 1–70.

[642] Braun, Matthias/Meacham, Darian, "A Plea for (In)Human-centred AI", *Philosophy & Technology*, 2024, pp. 37–97. See: Part V, Chap. 5, Sects. 5.1.2–5.1.6.2.1 of this book (on the thing-centred algorithmic decision-making propelled by a *Controllable* and *Interpretable* Machine Learning that weeds out *Algorithmic Dictatorship* and secures *Algorithmic Common Good*. It is worth recalling that the **thing-centred algorithmic decision-making** seeks to unwind the perils arising out of the lack of theoretical underpinnings facing the **human-centred algorithmic decision-making**, as extensively fleshed out Part III, this chapter, Sects. 3.1.4.3 and 3.1.4.4 of this book).

slavery.[643] Poignant calls have been thereupon made to keep human in the loop[644] as to avoid the mayhem of algorithmic injustice.[645]

§§ By the same token, scholars contend that technological advances are the lens through which the insalubrious effects Artificial Intelligence-embedded technologies can be seen.[646] Put simply, technological advances often make humankind worse-off.[647] Take the example of the invention of agricultural technology.

§§ On the surface, technological advances in the remit of agriculture have greatly improved human condition.[648] Yet, the invention of agricultural technology has nonetheless facilitated slavery to an even greater extent.[649] It should not amount to a bewildering finding that *algorithmic slavery*—or rule-based programmes[650]—tagged along.

§§ Compellingly, «algorithmic slavery»[651] is a byproduct of an overreliance of technology[652] to make high-stake decisions[653] at the behest of humans,[654] which

---

[643] Lévi-Strauss, Claude, *Tristes tropiques*, London, Penguin Books, 1992, passim.

[644] Salloch, S., & Eriksen, A., "What are humans doing in the Loop? Co-reasoning and practical Judgment when using machine learning-driven decision aids", *The American Journal of Bioethics*, 2024, pp. 1–12. See also: Binns, Reuben, "Human Judgment in Algorithmic Loops: Individual Justice and Automated Decision-Making", *Regulation & Governance*, Volume 16, 2022, passim.

[645] See: Ting-an Lin, ""Democratizing AI" and the Concern of Algorithmic Injustice", *Philosophy and Technology*, Volume 37 (103), 2024, pp. 3–27. See also: Birhane, A., "Algorithmic injustice: A relational ethics approach", *Patterns*, 2 (2), 2021, pp. 1–9. Završnik, A. "Algorithmic justice: Algorithms and big data in criminal justice settings", *European Journal of Criminology*, 2019, passim.

[646] Sebbah, F. D., & Nancy, J. L., "Technology and French thought: A dialogue between Jean-Luc Nancy and François-David Sebbah", *Philosophy & Technology*, 35, 84, 2022.

[647] Hardy, Michael, "Pareto's Law", *Mathematical Intelligencer*, Volume 32, 2010 (the exact opposite of the well-trodden Pareto's law, according to which the optimal state of society is when everyone is better off).

[648] Scott, James C., *Against the Grain, A deep history of the earliest states*, New Haven, Yale University Press, 2018.

[649] Lévi-Strauss, Claude, *Tristes tropiques*, London, Penguin Books, 1992, passim.

[650] Boden, Margaret A., *Artificial Intelligence: A Very Short Introduction.* Oxford: Oxford University Press, 2018, pp. 26–28 (fleshes out both *expert systems* and *rule-based programmes*).

[651] Edwards, Lilian/Veale, Michael, "Slave to the Algorithm? Why a "Right to an Explanation" is Probably not the Remedy You are Looking for", *Duke Law and Technology Review*, Volume 16, 2018, pp. 18–67.

[652] But see: Part V, Chap. 5, Sects. 5.1.7–5.1.7.5 of this book (on the five laws to control algorithmic decision-making). See also: Part V, Chap. 5, Sects. 5.1.8–5.1.8.5 of this book (on the five laws to interpret algorithmic decision-making).

[653] But see: Part V, Chap. 5, Sect. 5.1.7.2 of this book (on law number two to control algorithmic decision-making, which mandates that black box models must not be entrusted with the task of making high stake decisions—v.g. health and freedom). See also: Part V, Chap. 5, Sect. 5.1.8.5 of this book (on law number five to interpret algorithmic decision-making, which mandates that robot-judges, robot-prosecutors and robot-lawyers must not enter the courtroom for they are utterly incapable of making sound and interpretable value judgements).

[654] Karnow, Curtis E. A., "The Opinion of Machines", *The Cambridge Handbook of the Law of Algorithms*, Bartfield, Woodrow (Editor), Cambridge, United Kingdom: Cambridge University Press, 2021, passim.

seldom ends well, transparency[655] wise.[656] Crucially, this is a eerily disturbing finding that should not be referred sardonically.[657] Here lies one of the many drawbacks facing human-centred Artificial Intelligence.

§§ To the extent human-centred Artificial Intelligence heavily relies on the trade-off between efficiency-human demeanour within the purview of market economy, human beings are viewed as fungible pieces that should map seamlessly onto a broader technological apparatus. Failing which, the latter may be otherwise jettisoned to the bucket of economic irrelevance.

§§ Put otherwise, the concept of human-centred Artificial Intelligence seems to be oblivious of the fact that the more human beings are seen as fungible pieces of a broader technological apparatus, the worse their life conditions will actually be.

§§ On the bright side, human-centred Artificial Intelligence takes emerging challenges head-on while seizing the multifarious opportunities that arise out of Artificial Intelligence-embedded technologies. By this token, technology aims to improve people's quality of life.

§§ On the flip side, there is a dark side often associated to the increasing use of technology[658]: the rise of tech moguls—or big tech companies that rule modern societies in plain sight[659]—that surreptitiously introduced concepts of

---

655 See: Tyler, Tom R., "Does the American Public Accept the Rule of Law? The Findings of Psychological Research on Deference to Authority", *De Paul Law Review*, 56, 2007, pp. 661–664 (stating that "transparency and openness foster the belief that decision-making procedures are neutral"). See also: Coglianese, Cary/Lehr, David, "Transparency and Algorithmic Governance", *Administrative Law Review*, Volume 71, 2019, passim. See also: Doherty, Joseph W./Reville, Robert T./Zakaras, Laura(ed.), *Introduction to Confidentiality, Transparency, and the U.S. Civil Justice System*, Oxford, Oxford University Press, 2012, 1–258 (passim) (noting that the lack of transparency yields sizable social costs). But see: Weizenbaum, Joseph, *Computer Power and Human Reason: From Judgment to Calculation*, 1st edition, New York, W. H. Freeman & Co, 1976, pp. 1–300 (227) ("examines the sources of the computer's powers and offers evaluative explorations of what computers can do, cannot do, and should not be employed to do") (this founding father of Artificial Intelligence presciently noted that we should not entrust Artificial Intelligence-embedded technologies with with "tasks that demand wisdom"). Italics added. The approval of rental applications is arguably one of those tasks that should never be entrusted to machines). More on this on Part IV, Chap. 4, Sects. 4.1.4–4.1.4.2.1 of this book. See: Part IV, Chap. 4, Sects. 4.1.4–4.1.4.2.1 of this book (on mortgage redlining). See: Part IV, Chap. 4, Sects. 4.1.2–4.1.4.3 of this book (on algorithmic credit scoring, consumer racism and credit card redlining). See: Part IV, Chap. 4, Sects. 4.1.4–4.1.4.2.3 of this book (on algorithmic redlining). See: Part IV, Chap. 4, Sect. 4.1.4.3 of this book (on "algorithmic redliking"). See: Part IV, Chap. 4, Sect. 4.1.3 of this book (on algorithmic prime-lining).

656 Katyal, Sonia K, "The Paradox of Source Code Secrecy", *Cornell Law Review*, Volume 104, 2019, pp. 1183–1236; Wexler, Rebecca, "Life, Liberty, and Trade Secrets: Intellectual Property in the Criminal Justice System", *Stanford Law Review*, Volume 70, 2018, pp. 1343 and ff.

657 Graeber, D., & Wengrow, D., *The dawn of everything: A new history of humanity*, London, United Kingdom, Allen Lane, 2021.

658 Foucault, Michel, *Surveiller et punir*, Paris, Gallimard, 1975.

659 Saura García, C., Datafeudalism: The domination of Modern societies by Big Tech companies, *Philosophy & Technology*, 37 (3), 2024, 1–18.

datafeudalism,[660] mass surveillance,[661] technofeudalism[662]/[663] surveillance capitalism,[664] which, taken together, hastened the demise of privacy[665] and cherished realities alike.[666] But not just that though.[667] It gets much worse than that.

---

[660] Wörsdörfer, M., "Datafeudalism: The domination of Modern societies by Big Tech companies': A Commentary", *Philosophy & Technology*, 37 (3), 2024, pp. 1–5.

[661] Hu, Margaret, "From the National Surveillance State to the Cybersurveillance State", *The Annual Review of Law and Social Science*, Volume 13, 2017, p. 169 ("*the potential for mass surveillance is part of the problematic nature of biometric credentialing and identification practices. Like most digital data, biometric identification data are not restricted to the purpose for which they were originally collected.* Biometric data can be repurposed for secondary uses, such as identification of potential suspects or victims through real-time analytics, assessment of threats of terrorism, tactical decisionmaking, or behavioral and genetic research (Duster 2003). Beyond secondary—and tertiary, quaternary, and quinary—uses, biometric data become a part of population-wide *risk assessments that incorporate bureaucratized surveillance into governing decisions, policing, and threat assessments. Through big data tools, precrime governance models are increasingly reflected in collect-it-all cybersurveillance systems. In these systems, biometric data is a surveillance axis that can be used to track, identify, and isolate suspicious persons, digital data, or devices*"). Italics added. See also on mass surveillance: Bentham, Jeremy, *Panopticon: Or, the inspection-house*, Thomas Byrne, 1787. See also: Balkin, Jack M./Levinson, Sanford, "The Processes of Constitutional Change: From Partisan Entrenchment to the National Surveillance State", *Fordham Law Review*, Volume 75, 2006, pp. 489 and ff; Slogogin, Christopher, "Public Privacy: Camera Surveillance of Public Places and the Right to Anonymity", *Mississippi Law Journal*, Volume 72, 2002, pp. 213–251; Balkin, Jack M., "The Constitution in the National Surveillance State", *Minnesota Law Review*, Volume 93, Issue 1, 2008, pp. 17 and ff; Christopher Slobogin, "Panvasive Surveillance, Political Process Theory, and the Nondelegation Doctrine", *Georgetown Law Journal*, Volume 102, 2014, pp. 1721–1775.

[662] Varoufakis, Yannis, *Technofeudalism: What killed capitalism*, London, Random House, 2023.

[663] Durand, C., *Techno-féodalisme: Critique de l'économie numérique*, Paris, Le Découverte, 2020.

[664] Zuboff, Zhoshana, *The Age of Surveillance Capitalism, The Fight for a Human Future at the New Frontier of Power*, New Yor City: PublicAffairs Books, 2019, pp. 1–704 (360) (argues that we are indomitably heading towards a "instrumentarianism" that draws on "totalitarianism").

[665] Waldman, Ari Ezra, "Privacy, Practice, and Performance", *California Law Review*, Volume 110, 2022, pp. 1221–1227 (contend, however, that we have all been cunningly schooled to "thinking that managing our privacy is an individual responsibility"); Greenberg, Jeremy/Ringrose, Katelyn/Berger, Sara/VanDodick/Rossi, Francesca/New, Joshua, "Privacy and the Connected Mind", *The Future Privacy Forum*, 2021. Citron; Danielle Keats Citron/Pasquale, Frank, "Network Accountability for the Domestic Intelligence Apparatus", *Hasting Law Journal*, Volume 62, 2011, 1441, 1444–45; Gray, David/Citron, Danielle Keats, "The Right to Quantitative Privacy", *Minnesota Law Review*, Volume 98, 2013, pp. 62–81.

[666] See in Italian doctrine: Maranella, Stefano: "La protezione dei dati personali contro un uso distopico dell'AI, Il diritto nell'era digitale", *Persona, Mercato, Amministrazione Giustizia.* Milano: Giuffrè, 2022, pp. 51–69 (pp. 52–56 and ff and passim).

[667] Boyd, Danah, and Kate Crawford, "Critical Questions for Big Data: Provocations for a Cultural, Technological, and Scholarly Phenomenon", *Information, Communication & Society*, 15 (5), 2012, pp. 662–679.

§§ Technological advances have, to some extent, propelled multiple forms of slavery,[668] which, in turn, have paved the way to, and ushered in, a nefarious labour exploitation.[669] Technological advances, albeit wrapped under a patina of science-based objectivity, amount to nothing but an oxymoron: they promise to ameliorate people's quality of life, but, in fact, they often degrade people's quality of life[670] while depleting the planet in the process.[671]

§§ Technological advances accordingly run afoul with a sought-after «algorithmic democracy»,[672] which should be inclusive,[673] as opposed to divisive[674,675]

---

668 Braun, Matthias/Meacham, Darian, "A Plea for (In)Human-centred AI", *Philosophy & Technology, cit.*, pp. 37–97.

669 Scott, James C., *Against the Grain, A deep history of the earliest states, cit.*, passim.

670 See: Buolamwini, Joy, Unmasking AI: My Mission to Protect What Is Human in a World of Machines, Random House, 2023, pp. 1–336 ("*"The conscience of the AI revolution" (Fortune) explains how we've arrived at an era of AI harms and oppression, and what we can do to avoid its pitfalls.* "AI is not coming, it's here. If we answer the beautiful call inside these pages, *we can decide who we are going to be and how we're going to use technology in service of what it means to be fully human.*"—Brené Brown, #1 *New York Times* bestselling author of *Dare to Lead*. A *LOS ANGELES TIMES* BEST BOOK OF THE YEAR • Shortlisted for the *Inc.* Non-Obvious Book Award. *To most of us, it seems like recent developments in artificial intelligence emerged out of nowhere to pose unprecedented threats to humankind. But to Dr. Joy Buolamwini, who has been at the forefront of AI research, this moment has been a long time in the making*"). Italics added.

671 Crawford, Kate, *The atlas of AI: Power, politics, and the planetary costs of artificial intelligence*, London, Yale University Press, 2022, pp. 1–336 ("*What happens when artificial intelligence saturates political life and depletes the planet*? How is AI shaping our understanding of ourselves and our societies? Drawing on more than a decade of research, award-winning scholar Kate Crawford reveals how AI is a technology of extraction: from the minerals drawn from the earth to the labor pulled from low-wage *information workers to the data taken from every action and expression. Crawford reveals how this planetary network is fueling a shift toward undemocratic governance and increased inequity. Rather than taking a narrow focus on code and algorithms, Crawford offers us a material and political perspective on what it takes to make AI and how it centralizes power. This is an urgent account of what is at stake as technology companies use artificial intelligence to reshape the world*"). Italics added.

672 García-Marzá, D., & Calvo, P., *Algorithmic democracy: A critical perspective based on deliberative democracy*, Berlin/New York/Singapore, Springer, 2024.

673 Van Bueren, G., "Inclusivity and the law: do we need to prohibit class discrimination", *European Human Rights Law Review*, Volume 3, 2021, pp. 273 and ff and passim.

674 Yu, Peter K, "Can Algorithms Promote Fair Use?", *Fiu Law Review*, Volume 14, 2020, pp. 328 and ff and passim.

675 Such as a yawning gap between rich—that can adroitly harness artificial intelligence to advance their goals and shady agendas—and poor—that grapple to meet basic needs and are automatically excluded from the equation of digital society powered by Artificial Intelligence—which will directly impact the fabric of societies worldwide, thereby augmenting the chasm between the «digitally-chosen» and the «digitally-outcast» enabled by a algorithmic discrimination that does nothing but irreparable harm. See: Yu, Peter K., "The Algorithmic Divide and Equality in the Age of Artificial Intelligence", *Florida Law Review*, Volume 72, 2020, pp. 355–360 (addresses the issue of algorithmic discrimination).

let alone outright discriminatory.[676] Which further besmirches the foundational principle according to which machines should be ruled by humans,[677] not the other way around.

§§ Compellingly, technological advances should make people better off[678] while allaying technological divides that derail the very concept of trust that underpins law abidingness,[679] which, in turn, is deeply woven into the fabric of the legitimacy[680] of Artificial Intelligence-embedded technologies.

---

676 Borgesius, FJ Zuiderveen, "Strengthening legal protection against discrimination by algorithms and artificial intelligence", *International Journal of Human Rights*, Volume 24, Issue 10, 2020, pp. 1573 and ff and passim.

677 Pasquale, Frank, "A Rule of Persons, Not Machines: The Limits of Legal Automation", *George Washington Law Review*, Volume 87, 2019, passim.

678 Kaplow, Louis/Shavell, Stephen, *Fairness versus Welfare*, Cambridge (Massachusetts), Harvard University Press, 2002, pp. 1–578 (broach the principle of Pareto, according to which "what makes everyone better off should be preferred").

679 Tyler, Tom R., "Trust and Law Abidingness: A Proactive Model of Social Regulation", *Boston University Law Review*, Volume 81, 2001, p. 361 ff; Barbalet, Jack, "A Characterization of Trust, and Its Consequences", *Theory and Society*, Volume 38, 2009, pp. 367–372; Farrell, Henry, "Institutions and Midlevel Explanations of Trust", Cook, Karen S./Levi, Margaret/Hardin, Russell (Eds.), *Whom can We Trust? How Groups, Networks, and Institutions Make Trust Possible*. Manhattan, New York City: Russell Sage Publication, 2010; Cross, Frank B., "Law and Trust", *Georgetown Law Journal*, Volume 93, 2005, pp. 1457 ff.

680 Tyler, Tom R., "Psychological perspectives on legitimacy and legitimation", *Annual Review of Psychology*, Volume 57, 2006, pp. 375–400 (on the role that perceived legitimacy plays in everyday life); Tyler, Tom R., *Why people cooperate: The role of social motivations*. Princeton: New Jersey, Princeton University Press, 2011 (the author establishes a parallelism between underlying social motivations—such as trust and perceived legitimacy—to engage in cooperation with the authorities); Sunshine, J./Tyler, Tom R., "The role of procedural justice and legitimacy in shaping public support for policing", *Law & Society Review*, Volume 37, 2003, pp. 513–548 (on the role of procedural justice to enhance legitimacy); Tyler, Tom R./Goff, Philip Atiba/MacCoun, Robert J., "The Impact of Psychological Science on Policing in the United States: Procedural Justice, Legitimacy, and Effective Law Enforcement", *Psychological Science in the Public Interest*, Volume 16, Issue 3, 2015, p. 79 (noting that "without a fundamental reallocation of resources, our society cannot effectively monitor the general public searching for everyday wrongdoing"); Calo, Ryan/Citron, Danielle Keats, "The Automated Administrative State: A Crisis of Legitimacy", *Emory Law Journal*, Volume 70, 2021, passim.

§§ Bereft of which, the *trust in the law*[681] will accordingly wane and fade away. The long-sought dream of an algorithmic-driven economy[682]—which leverages on an all-out digitalization of modern economies[683]—will peter out in the process.

§§ Against this background, the assertion according to which Artificial Intelligence-embedded technologies are wholly beneficial for humankind is both ungrounded and statistically unsound. Calls that state otherwise (e.g. technology is nothing but a bedazzling gift for humankind for which human beings should grateful) are either unseemly haste or feigning care towards humankind.

§§ Bearing this truism very firmly in mind, scholars have neither been coy nor bashful in showing the feeling of unease with the trade-off between the technological advances and human emancipation.[684]

§§ Note, though, that their concerns are fully warranted as Artificial Intelligence-embedded technologies not only carry an enhanced potential for discrimination,[685]

---

[681] Tyler, Tom R., *Trust in the Law*. New York, NY: Russell-Sage, 2002, *passim* (on the paramount importance of trust in law). There is an excellent body of empirical research that shows that a shoddy, botched and watered-down judicial performance spawns low trust in legal systems. Criminal justice is not an exception. See: Magalhães, Pedro C./Garoupa, Nuno, "Judicial Performance and Trust in Legal Systems: Findings from a Decade of Surveys in 20 European Countries", *Social Science Quarterly*, 2020, p. 1 (the main goal of this exciting piece of research was "determining the existence of a relationship between judicial performance and citizens' trust in the legal system". To cater for that, the methodology used "cross-classified multilevel models, using data from more than 20 European countries, 80 surveys, and 100, 000 respondents, over a decade». Regarding the results, "the longer the time that lower courts take, on average, to dispose of pending cases, the lower is the public's trust in their legal system". As an upshot, "judicial performance, operationalized as the ability of courts to avoid delays in the delivery of justice, is a significant correlate of citizens' evalatuations of their country's legal system"). Converging: Tyler, Tom R., "Psychological perspectives on legitimacy and legitimation", *Annual Review of Psychology*, Volume 57, 2006, pp. 375–400 (on the role that perceived legitimacy plays in everyday life); Tyler, Tom R., *Why people cooperate: The role of social motivations*. Princeton, New Jersey: Princeton University Press, 2011, passim (the author establishes a parallelism between underlying social motivations—such as trust and perceived legitimacy—to engage in cooperation with the authorities in legal settings).

[682] Ezrachi, A./Stucke, M., *Virtual Competition – The Promise and Perils of the Algorithm-Driven Economy*. Cambridge, Massachusetts: Harvard University Press, 2016, passim.

[683] Ezrachi, A., "Is This a Competition Problem? – The Challenge of Digitalisation and the Limits of Enforcement", in: *Keele Law Review*, Volume 1, 2020, passim.

[684] Yu, X., Xu, S., & Ashton, M., "Antecedents and outcomes of artificial intelligence adoption and application in the workplace: The socio-technical system theory perspective", *Information Technology & People*, 36, 2023, pp. 454–474.

[685] Jackson, Maya C., "Artificial Intelligence and Algorithmic Bias: The Issues with Technology Reflecting History and Humans", *Journal of Business Technology Law*, Volume 16, 2021, pp. 299–316; West, Sarah Myers/Whittaker, Meredith/Crawford, Kate, *Discriminating Systems. Gender, Race and Power in AI*. New York: AI Now Institute, 2019, pp. 15 and ff and passim. Michele Loi and Markus Christen, "Choosing How to Discriminate: Navigating Ethical Trade-Offs in Fair Algorithmic Design for the Insurance Sector", *Philosophy & Technology*, Volume 34, 2021, passim.

but, and foremost, can pose additional threats to human[686] flourishment.[687] Nothing can distort this deeper truth.

§§ Here lies another drawback facing of the concept of human-centred Artificial Intelligence: technology is viewed as a lever that is amenable to propel forward human capacities amidst a market economy, rather than a tool that can benefit humankind while enabling human beings to retain the central tenets of their unique personhood.

§§ Put otherwise, and contrary to a misleading first impression, the concept of human-centred Artificial centres around the benefits arising out of the unbridled dissemination of Artificial Intelligence-embedded technologies *for* economy, rather than the protection *of* humankind against the harmful effects of technological advances *to* human flourishment. That is why the multifarious issues arising out of algorithmic discrimination have not been thoroughly addressed by the concept of human-centred Artificial Intelligence so far.

§§ Compellingly, if we take a hard look on the central tenets of human-centred Artificial Intelligence it seems as though that the latter boils down to the sought-after flourishment of technology itself, as opposed to the much-needed flourishment of humankind amidst the age of Artificial Intelligence. This gruesome scenario lends itself to a shortcoming that human-centred Artificial Intelligence has been utterly unable to circumvent, let alone adroitly bypass.

§§ The concept of *Algorithmic Common Good* (ACG)[688] accordingly plugs this perceived gap by placing the flourishment of humankind *above* the flourishment of Artificial Intelligence-embedded technologies. A toothless Artificial Intelligence Ethics[689] is wholly incapable to deliver meaningful offerings in this regard.[690] More on this later.[691]

---

[686] See: Buolamwini, Joy, Unmasking AI: My Mission to Protect What Is Human in a World of Machines, Random House, 2023, pp. 1–336 ("*"The conscience of the AI revolution" (Fortune) explains how we've arrived at an era of AI harms and oppression, and what we can do to avoid its pitfalls.* "AI is not coming, it's here. If we answer the beautiful call inside these pages, *we can decide who we are going to be and how we're going to use technology in service of what it means to be fully human.*"—Brené Brown, #1 *New York Times* bestselling author of *Dare to Lead*. A *LOS ANGELES TIMES* BEST BOOK OF THE YEAR • Shortlisted for the *Inc.* Non-Obvious Book Award. *To most of us, it seems like recent developments in artificial intelligence emerged out of nowhere to pose unprecedented threats to humankind. But to Dr. Joy Buolamwini, who has been at the forefront of AI research, this moment has been a long time in the making*"). Italics added.

[687] Braun, Matthias/Meacham, Darian, "A Plea for (In)Human-centred AI", *cit.*, pp. 37–97.

[688] See: Part V, Chap. 5, Sects. 5.1.2–5.1.6.2.1 of this book (on the thing-centred algorithmic decision-making propelled by a *Controllable* and *Interpretable* Machine Learning that weeds out *Algorithmic Dictatorship* and secures *Algorithmic Common Good*).

[689] Ress'eguier, A./Rodrigues, R., "AI ethics should not remain toothless! A call to bring back the teeth of ethics", 22 July 2020, 2020. See also: Gal, D., "Perspectives and approaches in AI Ethics: East Asia", *The Oxford Handbook of Ethics of AI*, Oxford, Oxford University Press, 2020, passim.

[690] Munn, L., *The uselessness of AI ethics*. AI and Ethics, 2022.

[691] See: Part V, Chap. 5, Sects. 5.1.7–5.1.7.5 of this book (on the five laws to control algorithmic decision-making). See: Part V, Chap. 5, Sects. 5.1.8–5.1.8.5 of this book (on the five laws to interpret algorithmic decision-making).

§§ More to the point, the concept of human-centred Artificial Intelligence lends a sizable weight on the technological advances itself, rather than the ways through which human beings can retain their uniqueness *amidst* the age of Artificial Intelligence. This is exactly the point at which the shortfalls of concept human-centred Artificial Intelligence and the public outcry against the deleterious effects of Artificial Intelligence-embedded technologies straddle/conflate/intersect.

§§ The current discussions about the extent to which Artificial Intelligence-embedded technologies are either beneficial or detrimental to humankind map seamlessly onto the seminal distinction between *labour replacing technologies* and *labour enabling technologies*, which has been artfully drawn by Carl Benedikt Frey.[692]

§§ Whilst technology holds great promises for societal benefits, Artificial Intelligence-embedded technologies should be nonetheless articulated with foundational principles for *Algorithmic Common Good* (ACG) clustered along the functional dimensions of *Critical Artificial Intelligence Studies* (CAIS)[693]: *interpretability*[694] and *controllability*.[695] *Algorithmic Common Good* (ACG) therefore offers substantive anchors to forestall algorithmic unfairness while keeping modern societies ahead of the algorithmic disruptive curve, which would be wholly detrimental to humankind in an overarching sense. More on this later.[696]

§§ This is the jarring tapestry (the harmful effects of technology on modern societies) against the backdrop of which Carl Benedikt Frey's offering unfolds.

---

[692] Frey, Carl Benedikt, *The Technology trap: Capital, Labor, and power in the age of automation*, New Haven, Princeton, Princeton University Press, 2019, passim.

[693] See: Part III, this chapter, Sect. 3.1.5.10 of this book (on the functional aspects of Critical Artificial Intelligence Studies, with a sharper focus on the harmful effects of Artificial Intelligence-embedded technologies, namely, Brain-Computer Interfaces that can read and control your mind and behaviour). See: Part III, this chapter, Sect. 3.1.5.11 of this book (on the functional aspects of Critical Artificial Intelligence Studies, with a sharper focus on the harmful effects of Artificial Intelligence-embedded technologies, namely, Genetic Algorithms that can write DNA on demand, thereby ushering the age of Transhumanism, Genetic Darwinism and Genetic Plutocracy, which, taken together, are poised to create layers of distinction between citizens). See: Part III, this chapter, Sect. 3.1.5.11 of this book (on the functional aspects of Critical Artificial Intelligence Studies, with a sharper focus on the harmful effects of Artificial Intelligence-embedded technologies, namely, Quantum Technology, which will bring entire industries to its knees while allowing unscrupulous actors to get a hold of, and whimsically activate, weapons of mass destruction). See: Part III, this chapter, Sect. 3.1.5.1.1 of this book (on the functional aspects of Critical Artificial Intelligence Studies, with a sharper focus on the harmful effects of Artificial Intelligence-embedded technologies, namely, perpetuation technologies—griefbots, avatars and robots—that are slated to dehumanize human-laden emotions). See: Part III, this chapter, Sects. 3.1.5.2–3.1.5.3.1 of this book (on the functional aspects of Critical Artificial Intelligence Studies, with a sharper focus on the harmful effects of Artificial Intelligence-embedded technologies, namely, Generative Artificial Intelligence and its offsprings—deepfakes and its deleterious effects on human memory).

[694] See: Part V, Chap. 5, Sects. 5.1.8–5.1.8.5 of this book (on the five laws to interpret algorithmic decision-making).

[695] See: Part V, Chap. 5, Sects. 5.1.7–5.1.7.5 of this book (on the five laws to control algorithmic decision-making).

[696] See: Part V, Chap. 5, Sects. 5.1.2–5.1.6.2.1 of this book (on the thing-centred algorithmic decision-making propelled by a *Controllable* and *Interpretable* Machine Learning that weeds out *Algorithmic Dictatorship* and secures *Algorithmic Common Good*).

§§ Whilst North-American and British scholars retain global leadership in the construction of the theoretical groundwork that underpins Artificial Intelligence-embedded technologies, they may be slipping behind in reshaping innovation pathways[697] though.

§§ One criticism that is often levelled against this pressing issue is that scholarship, albeit suffused by good intentions, falls conspicuously short of matching one of its laudable duties: map out the path ahead for a safe use of Artificial Intelligence-embedded technologies[698] amidst the age of *incontrollable* Artificial Intelligence[699]

§§ Although the future of law amidst the age of Artificial Intelligence is unfathomable (*Incalculable Law*[700]), scholars have not shied away from the candent challenges arising out of algorithmic decision-making[701] that serves a higher purpose: advance the overall goals of humankind while taking heed of the ghastly effects arisen from the deployment of Artificial Intelligence-embedded technologies.[702] This is the point at which the distinction between *labour replacing technologies* and *labour enabling technologies*—which arises out from the «Technology Trap»[703]—accrues academic sense.

§§ Carl Benedikt Frey accordingly wonders whether and to what extent the unmooring of the machines[704] comes at the expense of human emancipation.[705] Put otherwise, Carl Benedikt Frey queries the extent to which the holy grail of

---

[697] But see: Agrawal, Ajay/Gans, Joshua/Goldfarb, Avi, *Prediction Machines: The Simple Economics of Artificial Intelligence*, 2nd Edition. Massachusetts: Harvard Business Review Press, 2022, pp. 1–304 (broaches the topic of prediction machines in a gripping manner).

[698] But see: Volokh, Eugene, "Chief Justice Robots", *Duke Law Journal*, Volume 68, 2019, pp. 1135 and ff and passim (on the sizzling hot challenges that the legal community is shaping up to face further the rise of Chief Justice Robots).

[699] But see: Grimm, Paul W., "Practical Considerations for the Admissibility of Artificial Intelligence Evidence", *Maryland Bar Journal*, Volume 2, Issue 3, 2021, pp. 39 and ff and passim (pinpoints that challenges posed by Artificial Intelligence in the camp of law for years to come).

[700] In Italian doctrine: Irti, Natalino, *Un Diritto Incalcolabile*. Torino: G. Giappichelli Editore, 2016.

[701] Williams, Rebecca, "Accountable Algorithms: Adopting the Public Law Toolbox Outside the Realm of Public Law", *Current Legal Problems*, Vol. 75, 2022, pp. 237–263; Williams, Rebecca, "Rethinking Administrative Law for Algorithmic Decision-Making", *Oxford Journal of Legal Studies*, Volume 42, 2021, pp. 468 e ff and passim.

[702] But see: Citron, Danielle K., "Technological Due Process", *Washington University Law Review*, Volume 85, 2008, pp. 1249–1253 ("Computer programs seamlessly combine rulemaking and individual adjudications without the critical procedural protections owed either of them.").

[703] Frey, Carl Benedikt, *The Technology trap: Capital, Labor, and power in the age of automation, cit.*, passim.

[704] But see: Pasquale, Frank, "A Rule of Persons, Not Machines: The Limits of Legal Automation", *George Washington Law Review*, Volume 87, 2019, passim (drawing attention to the limits of legal automation). See: Part V, Chap. 5, Sect. 5.1.8.5 of this book (on law number five to interpret algorithmic decision-making, which mandates that robot-judges, robot-prosecutors and robot-lawyers must not enter the courtroom for they are utterly incapable of making sound and interpretable value judgements).

[705] Frey, Carl Benedikt, *The Technology trap: Capital, Labor, and power in the age of automation, cit.*, passim.

algorithmic efficiency is tilted against individual-centred values.[706] Amongst which human autonomy.[707]

§§ Carl Benedikt Frey thereupon gauges the degree to which labour automation sprang into action by Artificial Intelligence-embedded technologies frays the fabric of human emancipation[708] within the remit of a labour market.[709]

§§ Relatedly, Carl Benedikt Frey frames Artificial Intelligence-embedded technologies as tools which unfold itself in *labour replacing technologies* and *labour enabling technologies.*[710]

§§ The former stands for a technological apparatus against the backdrop of which Artificial Intelligence-embedded technologies replace human[711] labour.[712] The latter

---

[706] Frey, Carl Benedikt, *The Technology trap: Capital, Labor, and power in the age of automation, cit.*, passim.

[707] Cohen, Julien E., *Between Truth and Power: The Legal Constructions of Informational Capitalism.* Oxford: Oxford University Press, 2019, pp. 1–376 (p. 192) (contends presciently that "*automated processes* have obvious efficiency advantages, *but such processes may not align well (or well at all) with applicable legal requirements that are couched in shades of gray*"). Italics added.

[708] But see: Millar, Jason/Kerr, Ian, "Delegation, Relinquishment and Responsibility: The Prospect of Expert Robots", *Robot Law*, Calo, Ryan/Froomkin, A. Michael/Kerr, Ian (Editors), Cheltenham, Edward Elgar Publishing, 2016, pp. 102, 106–107 (as these authors aptly put it "*we will rely on robots without really knowing why – simply because their algorithms provide the greatest number of successful outcomes.* We have already seen this in Google's search approach. Neither Larry (Page) nor Sergey (Brin) (nor any other Google employee) knowns exactly why one particular web page is a better result than another. *When the click patterns say it is, that's good enough.* No semantic or causal analysis is required…*Like the ancients, we will, quite rationally, come to rely upon them, knowing full well that we cannot necessarily explain the reasons for their decisions*"). Italics added. Converging: Casey, Anthony J./Niblett, Anthony, "Self-driving Laws", *University of Toronto Law Journal*, Volume 66, 2016, pp. 429–435 (contend that "as more information is generated, and the evolutionary algorithm updates and become a better forecaster, *we imagine that judges will increasingly rely on the advice of the algorithm*"). But see: Weizenbaum, Joseph, *Computer Power and Human Reason: From Judgment to Calculation*, 1st edition, New York, W. H. Freeman & Co, 1976, pp. 1–300 (227) ("examines the sources of the computer's powers and offers evaluative explorations of what computers can do, cannot do, and should not be employed to do") (this founding father of Artificial Intelligence presciently noted that we should not entrust Artificial Intelligence-embedded technologies with "tasks that demand wisdom"). Italics added. The approval of rental applications is arguably one of those tasks that should never be entrusted to machines. More on this on Part IV, Chap. 4, Sects. 4.1.4–4.1.4.2.1 of this book. See: Part V, Chap. 5, Sect. 5.1.1.7.2 of this book (on law number two to control algorithmic decision-making, which mandates that black box models must not be entrusted with the task of making high stake decisions—v.g. health and freedom). See: Part V, Chap. 5, Sects. 5.1.7–5.1.7.5 of this book (on the five laws to control algorithmic decision-making).

[709] Frey, Carl Benedikt, *The Technology trap: Capital, Labor, and power in the age of automation, cit.*, passim.

[710] Frey, Carl Benedikt, *The Technology trap: Capital, Labor, and power in the age of automation, cit.*, passim.

[711] Braun, Matthias/Meacham, Darian, "A Plea for (In)Human-centred AI", *cit.*, pp. 37–97.

[712] Frey, Carl Benedikt, *The Technology trap: Capital, Labor, and power in the age of automation, cit.*, passim.

lends itself to a process whereby humans and machines do not vie for spot in the labour market.[713] Rather, their respective contributes complement each other.[714]

§§ Under either approach, the deployment of Artificial Intelligence-embedded technologies has catalysed a ripple effect on the labour market. It has accordingly positioned corporations[715] in throes of a technology race to attain greater efficiency[716] with a *cost-benefit analysis*[717] looming large in the distance.[718]

---

713 Frey, Carl Benedikt, *The Technology trap: Capital, Labor, and power in the age of automation, cit.*, passim.

714 Braun, Matthias/Meacham, Darian, "A Plea for (In)Human-centred AI", *cit.*, pp. 37–97.

715 Which, in turn, can create several problems within the remit of corporate criminal compliance. See in Spanish doctrine: Gómez-Jara Díez, Carlos, Autorregulación y responsabilidad de las personas jurídicas, Peru, ARA Editores, 2015; Coca Vila, Ivó, ¿ "Programas de cumplimiento como forma de autorregulación regulada?", Silva Sánchez, Jesús María (Dir.), Criminalidad de empresa y compliance: prevención y reacciones corporativas, Barcelona, Atelier. See also: Soltes, Eugene, *Why They Do It: Inside the Mind of the White-Collar Criminal.* New York: Public Affairs, 2018, pp. 1–464.

716 Cohen, Julien E., *Between Truth and Power: The Legal Constructions of Informational Capitalism.* Oxford: Oxford University Press, 2019, pp. 1–376 (p. 192) (asserts adamantly that "*automated processes* have obvious efficiency advantages, *but such processes may not align well (or well at all) with applicable legal requirements that are couched in shades of gray*"). Italics added.

717 It is often averred that a *cost-benefit Analysis* can be detrimental of, and can ultimately come to the expense of, human dignity, which is itself unmonetizable. See: Sunstein, Cass R., "The Real World of Cost-Benefits Analysis: Thirty-Six Questions (and almost as many answers)", *Columbia Law Review*, 114 (1), 2014, 177; Bayefsky, Rachel, "Dignity as a value in Agency Cost-Benefit Analysis", *Yale Law Journal*, 123 (2014): 1740; Sunstein, Cass R., *Valuing Life: Humanizing the Regulatory State*, 2014, 8 ff; Gordon, Jeffrey, "The Empty Call for Cost-Benefits Analysis for Financial Regulators", *Journal of Legal Studies*, 43, 2014, 351; Sunstein, Cass R., "The Limits of Quantification", *California Law Review*, 103, 2014, 1369; Adler, Mathew/Posner, Eric A., "New Foundations of Cost-Benefit Analysis", *Regulation & Governance*, 3, 2006, 72; Miles, Thomas J./ Sunstein, Cass R., "The Real World of Arbitrariness Review", *University of Chicago Law Review*, 75 2008, 761; Coates, John C. IV, "Cost-Benefit Analysis of Financial Regulation: Case Studies and Implications", *Yale Law Journal*, 124, 2015, pp. 882–911; Posner, Eric A./Weyl E. Glen, "Cost-Benefit Analysis of Financial Regulations: Response to Criticisms", *Yale Law Journal*, 124, 2015, pp. 246–265 (parsing the relationship between agency cost-benefit analysis and human dignity).

718 Unsurprisingly, the discourse with efficiency undertones has already reached the camp of Brain-Computer Interfaces. See: Tien-Thong Nguyen Do/Ngoc My Hanh Duong/Chin-Teng Lin, "Integrating Sensing Devices for Human-Brain Interfaces", *More-than-Moore Devices and Integration for Semiconductors*, Iacopi, Francesca/Balestra, Francis (Editors), New York/Berlin, Springer, 2023, pp. 241–258 ("*Brain-computer interfaces (BCI) help users to interact with machines via brain activity and without the use of muscles. Among the many components of BCI frameworks, sensor technology helps to make the systems highly efficient and robust. As a source of input for BCI systems, sensors also provide high-quality signals that can support downstream tasks, such as noise removal and feature extraction.* This book chapter explores the fundamental concepts and configurations of the non-invasive sensor technology that are commonly used in BCI systems"). Italics added. See: Part III, this chapter, Sect. 3.1.4.5 of this book (on Critical Artificial Intelligence Studies, with a sharper focus on the harmful effects of Brain-Computer Interfaces). See: Part III, this chapter, Sect. 3.1.5.10 of this book (on the functional aspects of Critical Artificial Intelligence Studies, with a sharper focus on the harmful effects of Artificial Intelligence-embedded technologies, namely, Brain-Computer Interfaces that can read and control your mind and behaviour).

§§ Key takeaways of this seminal distinction can be distilled from this insightful offering.[719] At one end of the spectrum, *labour replacing technologies* seek to replace human beings in the labour market with little regard for either the wellbeing of humankind[720] or the wellbeing of those affected by such replacement.[721]

§§ *Labour replacing technologies* care very little about the avenues through which human flourishment can be attained.[722] Conversely, *labour replacing technologies* utterly disregard people's overall quality of life, decreased safety, and the loss of revenue conducive to economic downturn. Most importantly, *hard labour replacing technologies* seem to be unbeknownst of the degree to which a sharp decline on workers' financial revenue frays the very fabric of Rule of Law[723] and the list goes on.[724]

---

[719] Frey, Carl Benedikt, *The Technology trap: Capital, Labor, and power in the age of automation, cit.*, passim; Braun, Matthias/Meacham, Darian, "A Plea for (In)Human-centred AI", *cit.*, pp. 37–97.

[720] Braun, Matthias/Meacham, Darian, "A Plea for (In)Human-centred AI", *cit.*, pp. 37–97.

[721] Frey, Carl Benedikt, *The Technology trap: Capital, Labor, and power in the age of automation, cit.*, passim.

[722] Frey, Carl Benedikt, *The Technology trap: Capital, Labor, and power in the age of automation, cit.*, passim; Braun, Matthias/Meacham, Darian, "A Plea for (In)Human-centred AI", *cit.*, pp. 37–97.

[723] Which is why the onset of the age of Artificial Intelligence will put the Rule of Law to the test like never before. Recall, the Rule of Law is a functional barrier—aimed at clamping down a host of unlawful deeds undertaken by those in power—that must not be teared apart or criminal procedure law will be otherwise despoiled from its intrinsic validity and vitality. See: Raz, Joseph, "The Rule of Law and its Virtue", *The Authority of Law: Essays on Law and Morality, cit.*, p. 224 (asserts adamantly that the Rule of Law is aimed at cushioning the hazards of abuse perpetrated by those in power. In this vein, Raz contends that "the law inevitably creates a great danger of arbitrary power – the Rule of Law is designed to minimize the danger created by the law itself…*Thus the (R)ule of (L)aw is designed to minimize the danger created by law itself…Thus the (R)ule of (L)aw is a negative virtue…the evil which is avoided is evil which could only have been caused by the law itself*"). Italics added. See: Part V, Chap. 5, Sect. 5.1.1.1 of this book (on the central tenets of Rule of Law that lends itself to a beacon of justice amidst the sepulchral darkness that is about to take hold). See: Part V, Chap. 5, Sect. 5.1.1.2 of this book (on the central tenets of Procedural Rule of Law that lends itself to a lighthouse of justice that allows citizens to challenge the pearls of algorithmic wisdom in a court of law).

[724] See: Millar, Jason/Kerr, Ian, "Delegation, Relinquishment and Responsibility: The Prospect of Expert Robots", *Robot Law*, Ryan Calo/Froomkin, A. Michael/Kerr, Ian. Cheltenham: Edward Elgar Publishing, 2016, pp. 102, 106–107 (as these authors aptly put it "*we will rely on robots without really knowing why – simply because their algorithms provide the greatest number of successful outcomes.* We have already seen this in Google's search approach. Neither Larry (Page) nor Sergey (Brin) (nor any other Google employee) knowns exactly why one particular web page is a better result than another. *When the click patterns say it is, that's good enough.* No semantic or causal analysis is required…*Like the ancients, we will, quite rationally, come to rely upon them, knowing full well that we cannot necessarily explain the reasons for their decisions*"). Italics added. Converging: Casey, Anthony J./Niblett, Anthony, "Self-driving Laws", *University of Toronto Law Journal*, Volume 66, 2016, pp. 429–435 (contend that "as more information is generated, and the evolutionary algorithm updates and become a better forecaster, we imagine that judges will increasingly rely on the advice of the algorithm"). But see: Part V, Chap. 5, Sect. 5.1.8.5 of this book (on law number five to interpret algorithmic decision-making, which mandates that robot-judges, robot-prosecutors and robot-lawyers must not enter the courtroom for they are utterly incapable of making sound and interpretable value judgements).

§§ In this vein, the rise of *digital justice*—or *algorithmic justice*[725]—is poised to pave the way to the absolute power of algorithms (*Algorithmic Dictatorship*),[726] which will make judges' work considerably easier[727] (*soft labour replacing technologies*).[728]

§§ Sooner rather than later, judges will blindly follow the pearls of wisdom spawned by inscrutable algorithms (*soft labour replacing technologies*) which will steer them towards the best algorithmic course of action to be taken in a given procedure, thereby hastening the demise of the *Rule of Law*[729] while ushering in the dawn of a new era (*Rule of Machines*)[730] riddled with a myriad of algorithmic biases.[731] Worse still, the rise of digital justice[732] is shaping up to widen the already

---

[725] Of which robot-lawyers and robot-judges are a living—yet heinous and disturbing—testament. See: Davis, Joshua P., "Of Robolawyers and robojudges", *Hastings Law Journal*, Volume 73, Issue 5, 2022, pp. 1176–1201; Davis, Joshua P., *Unnatural Law: AI, Consciousness, Ethics, and Legal Theory*. Cambridge: Cambridge University Press, 2023. But see: Part V, Chap. 5, Sect. 5.1.8.5 of this book (on law number five to interpret algorithmic decision-making, which mandates that robot-judges, robot-prosecutors and robot-lawyers must not enter the courtroom for they are utterly incapable of making sound and interpretable value judgements).

[726] See: Part IV, Chap. 4, Sects. 4.1–4.1.10.6 of this book (on Algorithmic Dictatorship and its chilling effect on democracy).

[727] But see: Re, Richard M./Solow-Niederman, Alicia, "Developing Artificially Intelligent", *Stanford Technology Law Review*, Volume 22, 2019, passim; Cohen, Julien E., *Between Truth and Power: The Legal Constructions of Informational Capitalism*. Oxford: Oxford University Press, 2019, pp. 1–376 (p. 192) ("*automated processes* have obvious efficiency advantages, *but such processes may not align well (or well at all) with applicable legal requirements that are couched in shades of gray*"). Italics added. But see: Part V, Chap. 5, Sect. 5.1.8.5 of this book (on law number five to interpret algorithmic decision-making, which mandates that robot-judges, robot-prosecutors and robot-lawyers must not enter the courtroom for they are utterly incapable of making sound and interpretable value judgements).

[728] But see: Part V, Chap. 5, Sect. 5.1.8.5 of this book (on law number five to interpret algorithmic decision-making, which mandates that robot-judges, robot-prosecutors and robot-lawyers must not enter the courtroom for they are utterly incapable of making sound and interpretable value judgements).

[729] Maxwell, J./Tomlinson, J., *Experiments in Automating Immigration Systems*. Bristol: Bristol University Press, 2022, passim. But see: Pasquale, Frank, "A Rule of Persons, Not Machines: The Limits of Legal Automation", *George Washington Law Review*, Volume 87, 2019, pp. 1 and ff and passim.

[730] But see: Part V, Chap. 5, Sect. 5.1.8.5 of this book (on law number five to interpret algorithmic decision-making, which mandates that robot-judges, robot-prosecutors and robot-lawyers must not enter the courtroom for they are utterly incapable of making sound and interpretable value judgements).

[731] Corbett-Davies, Sam/Goel, Sharad, "The Measure and Mismeasure of Fairness: a critical Review of Fair Machine Learning", *Cornell University Library*, 2018, pp. 3 and ff and passim (undertake laudable efforts to debunk algorithm biases that primarily target ethnic minorities, such as Hispanics and coloured people); See: Yu, Peter K, "Can Algorithms Promote Fair Use?", *Fiu Law Review*, Volume 14, 2020, pp. 328 and ff and passim. See also: Baeza-Yates, R., "Bias on the web", *Communications of the ACM*, 61 (6), June 2018, 2018, pp. 54–61 (argues that "*algorithmic bias is when the bias is not present in the input data* and is added *purely by the algorithm*"). Italics added.

[732] Scherer, Maxi, "Artificial Intelligence and Legal Decision-Making: The Wide Open?", *Journal of International Arbitration*, Volume 36, 2019, passim; Lauritsen, Marc, "Towards a Phenomenology

yawning gap between rich and poor from the access to justice standpoint.[733] More on this later.[734]

§§ At the other end of the spectrum, *labour enabling technologies* evince a greater care for people's wellbeing while mapping out walkable pathways through which the latter can be accomplished. Although *labour enabling technologies* take over some tasks previously carried out by human beings, capacious room is made to enable human flourishment in the process. Something that both *soft* and *hard labour replacing technologies*—which hinge upon «AI superpowers»[735]—are eerily oblivious of.

of Machine-Assisted Legal Work", *Journal of Robotics, Artificial Intelligence & Law*, Volume 1, Issue 2, 2018, pp. 67–79.

733 This problem is neither new nor easy to solve. Whilst the effects of technology—digital justice—on the courtroom have been previously broached by the doctrine, few to none consensus has been reached with regard to actionable lines of action to be taken. See: Donoghue, Jane, "The Rise of Digital Justice: Courtroom Technology, Public Participation and Access to Justice", *The Modern Law Review*, Volume 80, Issue 6, 2018, p. 995 (noting that technology in the courtroom might widen the gap between the rich and the poor. In this vein, this renowned author has contended that "*legal reforms have omitted any detailed consideration of the type and quality of citizen participation in newly digitised court processes which have fundamental implications for the legitimacy and substantive outcomes of court-based processes; and for enhancing democratic procedure through improved access to justice.* It is argued that although digital court tools and systems offer great promise for enhancing efficiency, participation and accessibility, they *simultaneously have the potential to amplify the scope for injustice, and to attenuate central principles of the legal system, including somewhat paradoxically, access to justice*"). Italics added. See also: Heintz, M.E., "The digital divide and courtroom technology: Can David keep up with Goliath", *Federal Communications Law Journal*, Volume 54, 2002, pp. 566 ff and passim. The great bulk of these assertions has been anticipated by an iconic piece of research. See: Galanter, Marc, "Why the "Haves" Come Out Ahead: Speculations on the Limits of Legal Change", *Law & Society Review*, Volume 9, 1974, pp. 98–103 (this renowned author talks about a *social reality* in which the dubbed «repeat players»—which go by the name of «haves»—tend to «to come out ahead» by putting their knowledge and vast resources to good use. This perceived advantage will not only impact the choice on the procedures but will ultimately benefit their interests as opposed to the deemed «one-shot» players (the «have nots») that will have slimmer and fewer chances to get palpable results in dispute resolution). Technology in the criminal courtroom—that includes the rich and excludes the poor—will make this problem considerably worse. But see: Bailey, J./Burkell, J./Reynolds, G. "Access to Justice for All: Towards an "Expansive Vision" of Justice and Technology, *Windsor Yearbook of Access to Justice*, Volume 31, 2013, pp. 183–201 (in stark contrast, these authors stress that the digital and technological apparatus can indeed spawn a both time-effective and streamlined access to justice in a given jurisdiction). But see: Part V, Chap. 5, Sect. 5.1.8.5 of this book (on law number five to interpret algorithmic decision-making, which mandates that robot-judges, robot-prosecutors and robot-lawyers must not enter the courtroom for they are utterly incapable of making sound and interpretable value judgements).

734 See Part V of this book.

735 Lee, Kai-Fu, *AI Superpowers: China, Silicon Valley, and the New World*. New York: Harper Business, 2018, p. 3 (talks about the *Google Deepmind*, which has catalyzed the tagged «Sputnik moment» across Asia).

§§ *Labour enabling technologies* thus shows a keen interest in striking a delicate balance between striving for innovation and keeping people's quality of life unsullied. Put otherwise, *labour enabling technologies* have a penchant for innovation without sharply declining people's quality of life.[736]

§§ *Labour enabling technologies* accordingly attaches great importance on creating wealth while keeping the people's social standing,[737] economic revenue, dignity,[738] social capital, and quality of life unscathed.

§§ *Labour enabling technologies* therefore cobbles together two seemingly conflicting forces: **(i)** *wealth maximization*,[739] brimming with economics of justice[740] undertones, and **(ii)** the undeterred yearn for keeping workers 'human dignity untarnished.

§§ Workers welcome *labour enabling technologies* while dreading *labour replacing technologies*, which ultimately mar their human dignity. Which is nothing but formulaic: the former enhances human dignity while the latter saps it. That is why workers yearn for further implementation of *labour enabling technologies*,

---

[736] Frey, Carl Benedikt, *The Technology trap: Capital, Labor, and power in the age of automation, cit.*, passim; Braun, Matthias/Meacham, Darian, "A Plea for (In)Human-centred AI", *cit.*, pp. 37–97.

[737] Frey, Carl Benedikt, *The Technology trap: Capital, Labor, and power in the age of automation, cit.*, passim; Braun, Matthias/Meacham, Darian, "A Plea for (In)Human-centred AI", *cit.*, pp. 37–97.

[738] See Spanish doctrine: Laukyte, Migle, "Dignidad humana y nuevos derechos: el derecho a la inteligencia artificial", *Inteligencia Artificial y Derecho. El jurista ante los retos de la era digital*, AAVV. Navarra: Aranzadi, 2021, passim; Beriain, Iñigo de/Estrada/Pérez, M. Josune, "La inteligencia artificial en el proceso penal español: un análisis de su admisibilidad sobre la base de los derechos fundamentales implicados", *Revista de derecho UNED (RDUNED)*, Volume 25, 2019, pp. 531–561.

[739] Wealth maximization provides an ethically attractive norm for social and political choices, such as those made by courts asked to determine whether negligence or strict liability should be the rule for deciding whether an injurer must compensate his victim. Wealth, in a broad sense, is not confined to money. Rather, wealth is fundamentally linked to a utility that enshrines people's preference aversion to risk, being that utility the access to justice system". Itálicos nossos. Seguimos textualmente: Posner, Richard, "Wealth Maximization Revisited", *Notre Dame Journal of Law Ethics & Public Policy*, 2, 1987, pp. 85–89; Posner, Richard, The Problems of Jurisprudence, Massachusetts, Harvard University Press, 1990, pp. 18–98.

[740] Posner, Richard, "Values and Consequences: as an introduction to economic analysis of Law", *John M. Olin Law & Economics Working Paper*, 53, 1998, pp. 2 e ss e passim; Calabresi, Guido, "Some Thoughts on Risk Distribution and the Law of Torts," *Yale Law Journal*, Volume 70, 1961, passim; Posner, Richard, "The Decline of Law as an Autonomous Discipline: 1962–1987", *Harvard Law Review*, 80, 1987; Posner, Richard, *El Análisis Económico del Derecho*, México, Fondo de Cultura Económico, 1998; Posner, Richard, *Overcoming Law*, Cambridge, Harvard University Press, 1995, 1–608 (passim).

which facilitates the development of human capacities[741] while keeping both their human dignity and social standing unblemished.

§§ Of note, *labour enabling technologies* are not to be bogged down, nor narrowed down, to a set of Artificial Intelligence-embedded technologies amenable to facilitate human labour in a socio-technical context only. Instead, *labour enabling technologies* extend far beyond that.[742] It bears mentioning that, at its core, *labour enabling technologies* establish blazingly new avenues through which capacity building[743] can be grasped.[744]

§§ Notably, the replacement of some functional activities can give rise to the creation of brand-new sectors of activity,[745] which, in turn, will boost the overall functionalities of a given company[746] while retaining the great bulk of its workers.[747] Notwithstanding, the reality is far dimmer than one could possibly fathom at first blush.

[741] See: Cataleta, Maria Stefania/Cataleta, Anna, "Artificial Intelligence and Human Rights: An Unequal Struggle", *CIFILE Journal of International Law*, Volume 1, N.° 2, 2020 ("*Artificial Intelligence (AI) is a kind of intelligence that was born in the 1950s and is an integral part of the digital revolution. Progress made by AI has permitted the birth of systems capable of rivalling human capacities or, in some cases, surpassing them. The progress of the intellectual capacities of AI will change the way of life for human beings and will revolutionise the world of employment. Intelligent systems present problems regarding individual rights and responsibilities, because as technology replaces more and more of what humans have typically done, our individual roles will become more blurred*"). Italics added. Converging: Cataleta, Maria Stefania, "Artificial Intelligence vs Human Intelligence", in: Martin, L. Miraut/Zalucki, M. (editors), *Artificial intelligence and Human Rights, Dickinson eBook*. Krakow: AFM Krakow University, 2021, pp. 117–127 (on the slew of both moral, ethical and legal issues with which jurists will grapple in the forthcoming future due to the rise of artificial intelligence in legal arena).

[742] Frey, Carl Benedikt, *The Technology trap: Capital, Labor, and power in the age of automation, cit.*, passim; Braun, Matthias/Meacham, Darian, "A Plea for (In)Human-centred AI", *cit.*, pp. 37–97.

[743] Coeckelbergh, M., *The political philosophy of AI: An introduction*, London, Wiley and Sons Publisher, 2022.

[744] Frey, Carl Benedikt, *The Technology trap: Capital, Labor, and power in the age of automation, cit.*, passim; Braun, Matthias/Meacham, Darian, "A Plea for (In)Human-centred AI", *cit.*, pp. 37–97.

[745] Bastani, S., & Waldenström, D., "How should capital be taxed?", *Journal of Economic Surveys*, 34, 2020, pp. 812–846.

[746] Braun, Matthias/Meacham, Darian, "A Plea for (In)Human-centred AI", *cit.*, pp. 37–97. See also: Gorz, A., *Critique of economic reason*, Verso books, 2011, passim.

[747] Frey, Carl Benedikt, *The Technology trap: Capital, Labor, and power in the age of automation, cit.*, passim; Braun, Matthias/Meacham, Darian, "A Plea for (In)Human-centred AI", *cit.*, pp. 37–97.

§§ Whilst the technological advances have propelled both an unprecedented growth and a fast-paced uptake of Artificial Intelligence-embedded technologies,[748] its social costs are yet to be seen.

§§ Put it coarsely, although Artificial Intelligence-embedded technologies are dominated by an entrepreneurial hype that extolls its marvels, it remains to be seen if its social costs will outpace—or outweigh—its social benefits. Especially, albeit not exclusively, from the protection of fundamental rights standpoint.

§§ Bearing this background very firmly in mind, *Critical Artificial Intelligence Studies* (CAIS) adamantly avers that Artificial Intelligence-embedded technologies, if nothing else, wear down the Rule of Law while paving the way for a hardcore version of technology against the backdrop of which *Algorithmic Dictatorship* (AD) is poised to unfold and rise to prominence.[749] More on this later.[750]

---

[748] Fergus, Rachel, "Biased Technology: The Automated Discrimination of Facial Recognition", *ACLU Minnesota*, February 29, 2024, available at: https://www.aclu-mn.org/en/news/biased-technology-automated-discrimination-facial-recognition (access: 20.09.2024) ("*technology is developing much more quickly than the laws we need to protect our rights. Anyone with a smartphone or social media account knows how rapidly technology changes, while legislating can take a long, long time. It is essential to proactively put policies into place that will protect our rights as new and more advanced technology is constantly released. Especially when that technology – and law enforcement members using it - have been shown over and over to be biased toward marginalized groups*"). Italics added. See also: Hu, Margaret, "From the National Surveillance State to the Cybersurveillance State", *The Annual Review of Law and Social Science*, Volume 13, 2017, p. 169 ("*in a big data world, a digitized passport system can link to multiple other sources, such as license plate readers, No Fly Lists, and Terrorist Watchlists. Facial recognition technology drawing upon a photo database could potentially link a plethora of digital images of a person, including social media, the internet, photo databases like driver's licenses, live-streaming video, CCTV surveillance, and images obtained from hacking cameras on laptops and digital devices. Biometric data collection and storage are becoming increasingly compulsory through either government identification requirements*, such as digital photo requirements for passports and driver's licenses, or corporate identification requirements, such as biometric access to digital devices"). Italics added. See: Part IV, Chap. 4, Sects. 4.1.5–4.1.5.2 of this book (on "algorithmic Jim Crow", a travel ban issued during the first Trump Administration to prevent certain individuals from entering the United States of America, which, given its racial undertones, stands as an outgrowth of congeries of laws enacted during the Jim Crow epoch).

[749] Hu, Margaret, "From the National Surveillance State to the Cybersurveillance State", *The Annual Review of Law and Social Science*, Volume 13, 2017, p. 168 ("*as a result, the Cybersurveillance State, as a technological successor to the National Surveillance State, will execute bureaucratized biometric cybersurveillance in ways that are largely invisible and that appear routinized when technologically embedded within biometric identification technologies harnessed by the Administrative State. The normalization of day-to-day cybersurveillance will be achieved largely through governing functions that appear purely administrative (e.g., identity assessments for the granting of welfare, rights, privileges, and governing incentives).* Because of the routinized and administrative nature of the government-led big data program or *data surveillance (dataveillance) program, contemporary cybersurveillance is likely to be viewed as justified under crime, immigration control, and counterterrorism policy rationales*"). Italics added.

[750] See: Part IV, Chap. 4, Sects. 4.1–4.1.10.6 of this book (on Algorithmic Dictatorship and its chilling effect on democracy).

3.1.4.5 Brain-Computer Interfaces, the Principle of Performativity and the Principle of Vulnerability, Which Are Conducive to the Increasing In-humanization of Humankind (Jean-François Lyotard)—Why the Concept Human-Centred Artificial Intelligence Is Not the Answer You Are Looking for

§§ *Critical Artificial Intelligence Studies* (CAIS) claims that technology, albeit a seemingly bedazzling gift to humankind, is not without multiple drawbacks.[751]

---

[751] For example, there is burgeoning trend to perform sentencing anchored in algorithms in a bid to ease—and sometimes offset—human flaws (ranging from racial bias, gender bias, jealousy, to sexual orientation bias). Such algorithmic tools, which are currently being deployed in predicting criminal recidivism, are gaining traction and gathering pace worldwide. Caution must be nonetheless exercised to avoid entrusting to machines with the duty of making high stake decisions that may prove detrimental to citizens 'fundamental rights. Amongst which, freedom. See: Weizenbaum, Joseph, *Computer Power and Human Reason: From Judgment to Calculation*, 1st edition, New York, W. H. Freeman & Co, 1976, pp. 1–300 (227) ("examines the sources of the computer's powers and offers evaluative explorations of what computers can do, cannot do, and should not be employed to do") (*this founding father of Artificial Intelligence presciently noted that we should not entrust Artificial Intelligence-embedded technologies* with "tasks that demand wisdom"). Italics added. The approval of rental applications is arguably one of those tasks that should never be entrusted to machines). More on this on Part IV, Chap. 4, Sects. 4.1.4–4.1.4.2.1 of this book. On the use of algorithms to undertake risk assessment in sentencing: Gialuz, M., "Quando la giustizia penale encontra l'intelligenza artificiale: luci e e ombre di risk assessment tools tra Stati Uniti ed Europa", 2019, available at: www.penalecontemporaneo.it.d/6702-quando-la-giustizia-penale-encontra-l'intelligenz-artificiale-luci-e-ombre-di-risk-assessment-tools (access: 03.07.2024); Peeters, R./Schuilenburg, M., "Machine Justice: Governing Security through Bureaucracy of Algorithms", *Information Polity*, Volume 23, 2018, pp. 267–274; Hamilton, Melissa, "Sentencing Disparities", *British Journal of American Legal Studies*, Volume 6, Issue 2, 2017, pp. 181 ff; Anabela Miranda Rodrigues, "Medida da pena de prisão – desafios da era da inteligência artificial", *Revista de Legislação e de Jurisprudência*, Março-Abril de 2020, Ano 149.°, N.° 4021, 2020, pp. 258 ff; Santos, Hugo Luz dos, "Brain-Computer Interfaces, Generative Artificial Intelligence (ChatGPT and Deep Fakes) and Criminal Procedure Law: what's at stake?", *Journal of Research in E. and Computer Science*, Edinburgh, United Kingdom, June 2024, Volume 2, 2024, pp. 39–78; Santos, Hugo Luz dos, *Programas de Compliance e Inteligência Artificial: Consequências ao nível da Law and Economics, do Direito Penal, do Processo Penal e da Behavioral Law and Economics*, Braga, NovaCausa Edições Jurídicas, 2024, pp. 1–330; Santos, Hugo Luz dos, *Inteligência Artificial (ChatGPT/AutoGPT/Robots-Advogados/RobotsProceduradores/Robots-Juízes) e Responsabilidade Penal das Pessoas Colectivas*, Braga, NovaCausa Edições Jurídicas, 2023, pp. 1–108; Santos, Hugo Luz dos, *Inteligência Artificial e Processo Penal*, Braga, NovaCausa Edições Jurídicas, 2022, pp. 1–256; Santos, Hugo Luz dos, *Inteligência Artificial e Processo Penal*, Braga, NovaCausa Edições Jurídicas, 2022, pp. 1–256; Santos, Hugo Luz dos, *Inteligência Artificial e Processo Civil na Era do Metaverse e dos Machine Learning Algorithms*, Braga, NovaCausa Edições Jurídicas, 2022, pp. 1–264. See: Part IV, Chap. 4, Sects. 4.1.10.1–4.1.10.6 of this book (on biased algorithmic risk assessment in criminal procedure law settings, with a sharper focus on COMPAS). See: Part IV, Chap. 4, Sects. 4.1.1–4.1.1.1 of this book (on biased predictive policing).

Amongst which stands, as noted above, the perceived hazard of the use of Artificial Intelligence-embedded technologies that are trained on past prejudiced data.[752] Caution must be accordingly exercised.[753]

§§ Failing which, biased data will be baked into machine learning algorithms, which, in turn, will inherently likely to reproduce, mimic, reify[754] and exacerbate racial discrimination seen in past algorithmic decision-making.[755] Just like extensively shown in other sections of this book.[756]

§§ CAIS aims not to mysteriously solve hitherto unassailable problems with which modern societies have been tussling for a long-winded span of time.[757] Rather, CAIS

---

[752] See: Citron, Danielle K./Pasquale, Frank, "The Scored Society: Due Process for Automated Predictions", *cit.*, pp. 1–34. See also: *Tech, Bias and Housing Initiative, the Promise and Perils of Residential Proptech, Year 1, Research Summary Report, April 2023, TechEquity Collaborative*, p. 5 available at: https://techequity.us/wp-content/uploads/2023/04/TBHI-Y1-Research-Summary-Report.pdf (28.11.2024) ("*Residential Proptech also has the potential to exacerbate the bias inherent in our housing system. Its rise is due, in part, to the desperation felt by average home seekers. With a severely constrained housing supply, companies offering an easier pathway to homeownership may exploit communities that have been harmed by housing discrimination in the past. Opaque algorithms incorporate biased data into their decision-making processes, making it harder to enforce fair housing laws.* Residential Proptech companies often operate in a regulatory gray area, leaving consumers without the protections they would have from traditional housing regulatory systems. *As unprecedented capital investment flows into this space, venture-backed companies' winner-take-all approach to growth has the potential to exacerbate inequality rather than combat it*"). Italics added. See: Part IV, Chap. 4, Sects. 4.1.4–4.1.4.2.3 of this book. See: Part IV, Chap. 4, Sects. 4.1.4–4.1.4.2.1 of this book (on mortgage redlining). See: Part IV, Chap. 4, Sects. 4.1.2–4.1.4.3 of this book (on algorithmic credit scoring, consumer racism and credit card redlining). See: Part IV, Chap. 4, Sects. 4.1.4–4.1.4.2.3 of this book (on algorithmic redlining). See: Part IV, Chap. 4, Sect. 4.1.4.3 of this book (on "algorithmic redliking"). See: Part IV, Chap. 4, Sect. 4.1.3 of this book (on algorithmic prime-lining).

[753] Benjamin, Ruha, *Race After Technology: Abolitionist Tools for the New Jim Code*, New York, Polity, 2019, pp. 1–172 (7) (discussing that Artificial Intelligence-embedded technologies are viewed as iron-clad tools of objectivity and devoid of any biases whatsoever). Ruha Benjamin contends that "the employment of new technologies that reflect and reproduce existing inequities but that are promoted and perceived as more objective or progressive than the discriminatory systems of a previous era").

[754] Duster, Troy, "Race and Reification in Science." *Science*, 307, 2005, passim.

[755] Goodman/Flaxman, S., "EU Regulations on Algorithmic Decision-making and a "right to explanation", *Artificial Intelligence Magazine*, Volume 38, Issue 3, 2017, pp. 50 and ff and passim.

[756] See: Part IV, Chap. 4, Sects. 4.1–4.1.10.6 of this book (on Algorithmic Dictatorship and its chilling effect on democracy). See also: *Tech, Bias and Housing Initiative, the Promise and Perils of Residential Proptech, Year 1, Research Summary Report, April 2023, TechEquity Collaborative*, p. 11, available at: https://techequity.us/wp-content/uploads/2023/04/TBHI-Y1-Research-Summary-Report.pdf (28.11.2024) ("*Once bad data enters the analysis of one factor, it gets baked into the subsequent process, multiplying the effect that one disadvantageous data point can have on someone's overall housing determination*"). Italics added. See: Part IV, Chap. 4, Sects. 4.1.4–4.1.4.2.3 of this book.

[757] Gottlieb, A., & Flynn, K., "The Legacy of Slavery and Mass Incarceration: Evidence from Felony Case Outcomes", *Social Service Review*, 95, Issue 1, 2021, pp. 3–35; Fornili, K. S., "Racialized mass incarceration and the war on drugs: A critical race theory appraisal", *Journal of Addictions Nursing*, 29, Issue 1, 2018, pp. 65–72; Christin, Angèle, "From Daguerreotypes to Algorithms: Machines, Expertise, and Three Forms of Objectivity." *ACM Computers & Society*, 46, Issue 1,

aims to chart a path ahead to *control* Artificial Intelligence-embedded technologies while safeguarding the gist of citizens' fundamental rights.[758]

§§ From where we stand, the overhyped hopes of exerting some sort of *control* of Artificial Intelligence-embedded technologies seem to be utterly dashed by their unfathomable complexity, their opacity,[759] their hiddenness.[760]

2016, pp. 27–32 (on the multifarious facets of algorithmic objectivity); Eckhouse, L., Lum, K., Conti-Cook, C., & Ciccolini, J., "Layers of bias: A unified approach for understanding problems with risk assessment", *Criminal Justice and Behavior*, 46, Issue 2, 2019, pp. 185–209. See: Part IV, Chap. 4, Sects. 4.1.10.1–4.1.10.6 of this book (on biased algorithmic risk assessment in criminal procedure law settings, with a sharper focus on COMPAS). See: Part IV, Chap. 4, Sects. 4.1.1–4.1.1.1 of this book (on biased predictive policing).

[758] See: Part V, Chap. 5, Sects. 5.1.2–5.1.6.2.1 of this book (on the thing-centred algorithmic decision-making propelled by a *Controllable* and *Interpretable* Machine Learning that weeds out *Algorithmic Dictatorship* and secures *Algorithmic Common Good*).

[759] For an on-point breakdown of the distinct levels of opacity arising out of machine learning algorithms: Selbst, Andrew D./Barocas, Solon, "The Intuitive Appeal of Explainable Machines", *Fordham Law Review*, Volume 87, 2018, pp. 1085, 1089–99 (holding that there are plenty reasons for the insurer's ignorance. To begin with, the algorithm entails specialized knowledge to understand. That is, thc insurer's employees may lack sufficient knowledge to understand the rationale behind the reasons in view of which the algorithm is producing prices for different customers—personalized pricing. Lastly, even if the insurer himself comprehends how the model operates, it may nonetheless lack expertise to comprehend why it operates the way it does. For that reason, the explainability of machines is a vital, but rather elusive, task. Thence, the famed authors deem it as the "nonintuitive" nature of algorithms. For purposes here, the insurer himself might indeed understand that its Artificial Intelligence-embedded technology formulates higher prices for those who actually access the website at hand, but may fail to come to terms with the fact that the explanation for this fact arises from the website's capacity to proxy for genetic information). See also: Scherer, Matthew U. Scherer, "Regulating Artificial Intelligence Systems: Risks, Challenges, Competencies, and Strategies", *Harvard Journal of Law and Technology*, Volume 29, 2016, pp. 353–369 (frames the crippling problem of opacity as "the possibility that the inner workings of an AI system may be kept secret and may not be susceptible to reverse engineering").

[760] Balkin, Jack M., "The Three Laws of Robotics in the Age of Big Data", *Ohio State Law Journal*, Volume 78, Issue 5, 2017, pp. 1217–1241. See also: *Tech, Bias and Housing Initiative, the Promise and Perils of Residential Proptech, Year 1, Research Summary Report, April 2023, TechEquity Collaborative*, p. 11, available at: https://techequity.us/wp-content/uploads/2023/04/TBHI-Y1-Research-Summary-Report.pdf (28.11.2024) ("And while we know that the *data is predictive, meaning it has little to do with demonstrated behavior of the applicant themself, we do not know exactly where companies get their data*"). Italics added.

§§ Pivotally, the paucity of actionable lines of action to be taken,[761] coupled with the dearth of feasible pathways to challenge the pearls of algorithmic wisdom against the backdrop of which inordinate damages occur, ranks first amongst the primary concerns regarding Artificial Intelligence-embedded technologies. Hence the overriding importance of Procedural Rule of Law[762]

§§ The upcoming unmooring of the machines is accordingly poised to create a sheer amount of problems for modern societies. *Critical Artificial Intelligence Studies* therefore seeks to furnish baselines to tackle head-on the foregoing challenges while bringing to the fore a set of guidelines to protect the Rule of Law in the process.

§§ Note, though, that the unease with which technology has been grappling is anything but blazingly new.[763] Gallant efforts have been accordingly made by the trotted-out concept of human-centred Artificial Intelligence to smooth out the detrimental effects of technology amidst the age Artificial Intelligence-embedded technologies. But to no avail. Tellingly, uncertain is the extent to which the concept of human-centred Artificial Intelligence builds on the befitted benchmark to accomplish such a laudable goal.

§§ Compellingly, whilst the concept of human-centred Artificial Intelligence strives to stymie the wounding effects of Artificial Intelligence-embedded technologies, it remains to be seen if its underpinning yardstick deftly tackles the intricacies of the topic at hand.

§§ Put differently, extant legal frameworks[764] have been rallying around the idea of human-centred Artificial Intelligence in an earnest attempt to forestall the baleful

---

[761] But see: See: Buolamwini, Joy, *Unmasking AI: My Mission to Protect What Is Human in a World of Machines*, Random House, 2023, pp. 1–336 ("*"The conscience of the AI revolution" (Fortune) explains how we've arrived at an era of AI harms and oppression, and what we can do to avoid its pitfalls.* "AI is not coming, it's here. If we answer the beautiful call inside these pages, *we can decide who we are going to be and how we're going to use technology in service of what it means to be fully human.*"—Brené Brown, #1 *New York Times* bestselling author of *Dare to Lead*. A *LOS ANGELES TIMES* BEST BOOK OF THE YEAR • Shortlisted for the *Inc.* Non-Obvious Book Award. *To most of us, it seems like recent developments in artificial intelligence emerged out of nowhere to pose unprecedented threats to humankind. But to Dr. Joy Buolamwini, who has been at the forefront of AI research, this moment has been a long time in the making*"). Italics added.

[762] See: Part V, Chap. 5, Sect. 5.1.1.1 of this book (on the central tenets of Rule of Law that lends itself to a beacon of justice amidst the sepulchral darkness that is about to take hold). See: Part V, Chap. 5, Sect. 5.1.1.2 of this book (on the central tenets of Procedural Rule of Law that lends itself to a lighthouse of justice that allows citizens to challenge the pearls of algorithmic wisdom in a court of law).

[763] Jackson, Maya C., "Artificial Intelligence and Algorithmic Bias: The Issues with Technology Reflecting History and Humans", *Journal of Business Technology Law*, Volume 16, 2021, pp. 299–316; West, Sarah Myers/Whittaker, Meredith/Crawford, Kate, *Discriminating Systems. Gender, Race and Power in AI*. New York: AI Now Institute, 2019, p. 15 and ff and passim.

[764] High-Level Expert Group on Artificial Intelligence, *Ethics guidelines for trustworthy AI. The European Commission*, 2019; European Commission (2024). International outreach for human-centric artificial intelligence initiative, 2024; European Commission, Artificial Intelligence for Europe [Online], 2018. Available: https://eur-lex.europa.eu/legal-content/EN/TXT/PDF/?uri=CELEX:52018DC0237&from=EN [Accessed 2024]; European Commission, White Paper. On Artificial Intelligence - A European approach to excellence and trust [Online], 2020,

effects brought to bear by Artificial Intelligence-embedded technologies. But, in all fairness, the concept of human-centred Artificial Intelligence has conspicuously missed the mark.

§§ To begin with, the concept of human-centred Artificial Intelligence lacks sound theoretical underpinnings. As it stands, the concept human-centred Artificial Intelligence bears a striking resemblance with a trotted-out *mantra*, as opposed to a robust groundwork amenable to be relied upon.

§§ On that account, the human-centred Artificial Intelligence is hardly the answer you are looking for in that the latter functionalizes/monetizes human beings instead of striving to protect them from the hazardous effects of *algorithmic injustice.*[765] Note, though, that this topic has been extensively broached in previous sections of this book. It would be both pointless and fastidious to regurgitate it all over again.[766]

§§ Secondly, the concept of human-centred Artificial Intelligence is often centred around the question of whether and to what extent human beings map seamlessly onto

available: https://eur-lex.europa.eu/legal-content/EN/TXT/PDF/?uri=CELEX:52020DC0065&from=EN [Accessed 2024]; European Commission, Proposal for a Regulation of the European Parliament and of the council laying down harmonised rules on Artificial Intelligence, 2021; European Commission. European approach to artificial intelligence [Online], 2024. Available: https://digital-strategy.ec.europa.eu/en/policies/european-approach-artificial-intelligence; European Economic and Social Committee. Fundamental Rights and Rule of Law - National developments from a civil society perspective – 2020–2021 [Online], 2022. Available: https://www.eesc.europa.eu/en/our-work/publications-other-work/publications/fundamental-rights-and-rule-law-nationaldevelopments-civil-society-perspective-2020-2021 [Accessed 20.12. 2023]; European Commission (2021a). 2030 Digital Compass: the European way for the Digital Decade [Online]. Available: https://ec.europa.eu/info/sites/info/files/communication-digital-compass-2030_en.pdf.

See: *European Commission of 2024, International outreach for human-centric artificial intelligence initiative*, which reads as follows: "*The main vision characterising the EU approach is the creation of human-centric AI, which ensures AI works for people and protects fundamental rights. The EU approach to AI also involves supporting the EU's technological and industrial capacity and AI uptake across the economy, and preparing for socio-economic changes*". Italics added. See also: European Commission. European approach to artificial intelligence, 2024, which reads as follows: "*The EU's approach to artificial intelligence centers on excellence and trust, aiming to boost research and industrial capacity while ensuring safety and fundamental rights [...] Fostering excellence in AI will strengthen Europe's potential to compete globally.* The EU will achieve this by: (1) enabling the development and uptake of AI in the EU; (2) becoming the place where AI thrives from the lab to the market; (3) *ensuring that AI works for people and is a force for good in society; (4) building strategic leadership in high-impact sectors.*" Italics added. Available: https://digital-strategy.ec.europa.eu/en/policies/european-approachartificial-intelligence [access: 11.10.2024]. Italics added.

[765] See: Ting-an Lin, ""Democratizing AI" and the Concern of Algorithmic Injustice", *Philosophy and Technology*, Volume 37 (103), 2024, pp. 3–27. See also: Birhane, A., "Algorithmic injustice: A relational ethics approach", *Patterns*, 2 (2), 2021, pp. 1–9. Završnik, A. "Algorithmic justice: Algorithms and big data in criminal justice settings", *European Journal of Criminology*, 2019, passim.

[766] See: Part I, Part II and Part IV of this book.

a broader technological apparatus—Artificial Intelligence-embedded technologies—from an economic standpoint. In many ways, the concept of human-centred Artificial seeks to treat machines and human[767] beings[768] just the same.[769]

§§ Put another way, it seems as though that the concept of human-centred Artificial Intelligence tries to fit human beings within a broader technological apparatus against the backdrop of which a sought-after economic efficiency thrives/unfolds and the human nature accordingly falters.

§§ Notably, scholars have not refrained themselves from pouring in trenchant criticism on the dearth of theoretical underpinnings concerning the concept of human-centred Artificial Intelligence.[770]

§§ Most importantly, and more in tune with the overriding goal from which it was borne, scholars have been decrying the linchpin around which the concept of human-centred Artificial Intelligence revolves: the extent to which human capabilities can be augmented, rather than protected, within the remit of Artificial Intelligence-embedded technologies that sprout in the purview of a market economy.[771]

§§ Regrettably, the concept of human-centred Artificial Intelligence belies the very central tenet that pledged to protect in the first place: human beings amidst the

---

767 Levin, M., "AI: A bridge toward diverse intelligence and humanity's future", *Tufts University Working Paper*, 2024, passim.

768 Choudhary, V., Marchetti, A., Shrestha, Y. R., & Puranam, P., "Human-AI ensembles: When can they work?", *Journal of Management*, 2023, passim; Gershman, S. J., Horvitz, E. J., & Tenenbaum, J. B., "Computational rationality: A converging paradigm for intelligence in brains, minds, and machines", *Science*, 349 (6245), 2015, pp. 273–278. Gigerenzer, G., & Goldstein, D. G., "Herbert Simon on the birth of the mind-computer metaphor", *Elgar Companion to Herbert Simon*. Cheltenham, United Kingdom, Edward Elgar Publishing, 2024; Grace, K., Stewart, H., Sandkühler, J. F., Thomas, S., Weinstein-Raun, B., & Brauner, J., "Thousands of AI authors on the future of AI", arXiv preprint arXiv: 2401.02843, 2024, passim.

769 Adas, M., *Machines as the measure of men: science, technology, and ideologies of Western dominance*, Ithaca: Cornell University Press, 1989. But see: Korteling, J. H., van de Boer-Visschedijk, G.C./Blankendaal, R. A./Boonekamp, R. C./Eikelboom, A. R., "Human-versus artificial intelligence", *Frontiers in Artificial Intelligence*, Volume 4, 622364, 2021.But see: But see: Buolamwini, Joy, *Unmasking AI: My Mission to Protect What Is Human in a World of Machines*, Random House, 2023, pp. 1–336 ("*"The conscience of the AI revolution" (Fortune) explains how we've arrived at an era of AI harms and oppression, and what we can do to avoid its pitfalls*. "AI is not coming, it's here. If we answer the beautiful call inside these pages, *we can decide who we are going to be and how we're going to use technology in service of what it means to be fully human*."—Brené Brown, #1 *New York Times* bestselling author of *Dare to Lead*. A *LOS ANGELES TIMES* BEST BOOK OF THE YEAR • Shortlisted for the *Inc*. Non-Obvious Book Award. *To most of us, it seems like recent developments in artificial intelligence emerged out of nowhere to pose unprecedented threats to humankind. But to Dr. Joy Buolamwini, who has been at the forefront of AI research, this moment has been a long time in the making*"). Italics added.

770 Braun, Matthias/Meacham, Darian, "A Plea for (In)Human-centred AI", *cit.*, pp. 37–97; Frey, Carl Benedikt, *The Technology trap: Capital, Labor, and power in the age of automation*, *cit.*, passim.

771 Frey, Carl Benedikt, *The Technology trap: Capital, Labor, and power in the age of automation*, *cit.*, passim; Braun, Matthias/Meacham, Darian, "A Plea for (In)Human-centred AI", *cit.*, pp. 37–97.

age of a seemingly unfettered[772] Artificial Intelligence-embedded technologies[773] that knows no bounds whatsoever.

§§ This is exactly the type of discourse around which the facilitation of slavery[774] revolves, as presciently pointed out by Lévi-Strauss.[775] It should neither amount to a baffling nor flabbergasting finding that the widespread use of Artificial Intelligence-embedded technologies has undergone harsh criticism from scholars. Amongst whom stands the French philosopher Jean-François Lyotard alongside other French pundits.[776]

§§ Jean-François Lyotard was an outspoken philosopher whom canvassed the foundations upon stands a deep-rooted concern on whether and to what extent human beings could retain the pith of their unique personhood amidst the widespread use of Artificial Intelligence-embedded technologies.

§§ Owing to its pathbreaking nature, Jean-François Lyotard's insightful thoughts on the interplay between the widespread dissemination of technology and the maintenance of the nub of human nature has warranted a great deal of attention from postmodernist pundits,[777] whose contours nonetheless sit beyond the breadth and scope of this book.

§§ Three pieces of academic art deserve both to be accounted for and remarked upon.[778] Those exciting pieces of research merge in one sweeping claim: Artificial Intelligence-embedded technologies fast track the harrowing process towards the *inhumanization* of human beings amidst the age of unbridled technological advances that shows no signs of petering out anytime soon. Just look at the avenues through which Brain-Computer Interfaces, a byproduct of disembodied agency, promises to steer human beings on.[779]

---

[772] But see: See: Dixon, H. B., "The Evolution of a High Technology Courtroom", *Future Trends in State Courts*. Virginia: National Center for State Courts, 2011, *passim*. See also: Workman, W., "Advancements in technology: New opportunities to investigate factors contributing to differential technology and information use", *International Journal of Management and Decision Making*, Volume 39, 2007, pp. 317 ff (pinpointing the advantages in using high technology at the courtroom).

[773] Since it has come to our attention that *machine-learning algorithms "are capable of making intuitive decisions based in newly learned information, much like humans.* The new wave of AI developments will generate powerful AI that is capable of improvising itself, *perhaps even by rewriting its own algorithms, advancing its intelligence beyond that of humans*". Italics added. See: Hutto-Schultz, Jess, "Dicitur Ex Machina: Artificial Intelligence and the Hearsay Rule", *George Mason Law Review*, Volume 27, n.° 2, 2020, pp. 684–718 (684).

[774] Braun, Matthias/Meacham, Darian, "A Plea for (In)Human-centred AI", *cit.*, pp. 37–97.

[775] Lévi-Strauss, Claude, *Tristes tropiques*, London, Penguin Books, 1992, passim.

[776] Sebbah, F. D., & Nancy, J. L., "Technology and French thought: A dialogue between Jean-Luc Nancy and François-David Sebbah", *Philosophy & Technology*, 2022, 35, 84.

[777] Simons, M., "Jean-François Lyotard and Postmodern Technoscience", *Philosophy and Technology*, 35, 2022, pp. 1–19.

[778] Lyotard, Jean-François, *The Postmodern Condition: A report on knowledge*, Minnesota, United States of America, University of Minnesota Press, 1984; Lyotard, Jean-François, *Le différend*, Minnesota, United States of America, University of Minnesota Press, 1988; Lyotard, Jean-François, *The inhuman: Reflections on time*, Stanford, Stanford University Press, 1991.

[779] Levin, Daniel, "Are you out of your mind? Neurotechnologies and the Making of Disembodied Agency", *Berkeley Technology Law Journal*, Volume 38, 2023, pp. 232–252; Dockrill, Peter, "Brain

§§ Brain-Computer Interfaces neatly encapsulates, hands-in-glove, the lens through which the painstaking process of in-humanization can be seen: if a computer can read your thoughts, you are no longer a human being, but an extension of a machine instead. Put differently, human beings are framed as «connected minds»[780] that operate as an extension of an ever-recording machine—the kernel of the «extended mind thesis».[781]

§§ Jean-François Lyotard, whom was unbeknownst of Artificial Intelligence-embedded technologies underpinning Brain-Computer Interfaces, has nevertheless pinpointed the perceived hazards of an ongoing process towards in-humanization arising out the rampant technological developments.[782]

§§ Jean-François Lyotard set out the foundational principles that bolster the in-human[783]: **(i)** the *principle of performativity,* which consists of a narrow space within which Artificial Intelligence-embedded technologies allow human beings to express themselves and **(ii)** the *principle of vulnerability*, which further exposes human beings[784] to the hurtful effects Artificial Intelligence-embedded technologies while fraying the fabric of their unique personhood.[785]

§§ The *principle of performativity* contends, just like the concept of human-centred Artificial Intelligence does,[786] that human beings are fungible pieces comprising a broader technological apparatus that maps seamlessly onto a sought-after *efficiency* that predicates, and propels forward, both the labour market and the market economy. Human dignity, a cornerstone that premises the inalienable human nature,[787] is accordingly narrowed down to its tiniest expression.

Implant Translates Paralyzed Man's Thoughts into Text With 94% Accuracy", *SCI Alert*, 2021, passim; Zhang, X./Sheng, QZ et al., "Converting your thoughts to texts: enabling brain typing via deep feature learning of eeg signals", *IEEE International Conference on Pervasive Computing and Communications*. Athens: IEEE, 2018, passim; Cassella, Carly, "Brain Implant Gives Blind Woman Artificial Vision in Scientific First", *SCI Alert*, 2021, passim; Waytowhich, N./Lawhern, VJ/Garcia, JO, et al., "Compact Convolutional neural networks for classification of asynchronous steady-state visual evoked potentials", *Journal of Neural Engineering*, Volume 15, Issue 6, 2018, passim; Kwak, N-S/Müller, K-R/Lee, S-W., "A Convolutional neural network for steady state visual evoked potential classification under ambulatory environment", *PloS one*, Volume 12, Issue 2, 2017, passim.

780 See: Greenberg, Jeremy/Ringrose, Katelyn/Berger, Sara/VanDodick/Rossi, Francesca/New, Joshua, "Privacy and the Connected Mind", *The Future Privacy Forum*, 2021. Citron; Danielle Keats Citron/Pasquale, Frank, "Network Accountability for the Domestic Intelligence Apparatus", *Hasting Law Journal*, Volume 62, 2011, 1441, 1444–1445; Gray, David/Citron, Danielle Keats, "The Right to Quantitative Privacy", *Minnesota Law Review*, Volume 98, 2013, pp. 62–81.

781 Clark, Andy/Chalmers, David, "The Extended Mind", *Analysis*, Volume 58, Issue 1, January 1998. Oxford: Oxford University Press, 1998, pp. 7–19 (passim).

782 Lyotard, Jean-François, *The inhuman: Reflections on time*, Stanford, Stanford University Press, 1991, p. 2 (states that human beings are shaping up to become "in-human").

783 Braun, Matthias/Meacham, Darian, "A Plea for (In)Human-centred AI", *cit.*, pp. 37–97.

784 Braun, Matthias/Meacham, Darian, "A Plea for (In)Human-centred AI", *cit.*, pp. 37–97.

785 Lyotard, Jean-François, *The inhuman: Reflections on time*, *cit.*, passim.

786 Braun, Matthias/Meacham, Darian, "A Plea for (In)Human-centred AI", *cit.*, pp. 37–97.

787 Human dignity is a Kantian-inspired notion which were to send ripples across cultures of dignity, mainly from the fundamental rights standpoint. In German doctrine: Ramm, Thilo, "Die sozialen

§§ Put otherwise, under the *principle of performativity* human beings are stripped from their human dignity. Human beings are accordingly devised as means by which market economies attain their corporate goals: *profit maximization*, which is to be seamlessly carried out insofar human beings agree to fit within a broader technological apparatus that seeks to minimize costs while maximizing profits.

§§ The *principle of vulnerability* posits, in a manner akin of what concept of human-centred Artificial Intelligence implies, that human beings should not fight shy of openly embracing Artificial Intelligence-embedded technologies. Rather, they should warmly welcome, as opposed to dread, emerging technologies or they will otherwise slip behind the inexorable marching of progress.

§§ That is why the concept of human-centred Artificial Intelligence hastily created a bespoke legal framework underpinning the much-acclaimed augmentation of human beings' abilities, rather than striving for its much-needed protection. Which brings us one step closer to the last stage of in-humanization: the introduction of Brain-Computer Interfaces.

§§ Brain-Computer Interfaces are the tip of the spear—a flagship, a milestone, landmark, or a crowning achievement—of longstanding efforts to decode citizens' minds at more granular and fine-grained levels.[788] Governments—and tech giants alike—have doubled down their efforts to decipher citizens' minds. As a result, the hazards for citizens' *right to be left alone and unaccounted for* skyrocketed accordingly.

§§ Leveraging on electric neuronal[789] data,[790] the third-generation byproducts of Artificial Intelligence (Brain-Computer Interfaces—BCI for short) decipher/decrypt/unravel responses to a wide range of external stimuli.[791] But that's not all. BCI can accomplish much more than that though. With the right settings, BCI can even

Grundrechte im Verfassungsgefüge", in: *Soziale Grundrechte – 5. Rechtspolitischer Kongress der SPD vom 29. Februar bis 2. März 1980 in Saarbrüchen*, Heidelberg/Karlsruhe, 1981, pp. 28–32; in Portuguese doctrine, Botelho, Catarina Santos, "40 anos de Direitos Sociais: uma reflexão sobre o papel dos Direitos Fundamentais Sociais no Século XXI", *Julgar*, 29, 2016, pp. 197 ff. In French doctrine: Fierens, Jacques, "La dignitè humaine comme concept juridique", *Journal des tribunaux*, 121, 2002, pp. 578–580; Carvalho, Natalia Brigagão Ferrer Alves, "Catholic Social Thought, Politics and Human Dignity in the Brazilian Constitutional Assembly of 1987–1988", *The American Journal of Legal History*, 1, 2019, 1–30; Taekema, Sanne, "The Procedural Rule of Law: Examining Waldron's Argument on Dignity and Agency", *cit.*: 140 ff (arguing that the «Rule of Law serves the value of human dignity»).

788 Santos, Hugo Luz dos, "Brain-Computer Interfaces, Generative Artificial Intelligence (ChatGPT and Deep Fakes) and Criminal Procedure Law: what's at stake?", *Journal of Research in E. and Computer Science*, Edinburgh, United Kingdom, June 2024, Volume 2, 2024, pp. 39–78.

789 Aggarwal, C. C., *Neural networks and deep learning*, Heidelberg, Springer, 2018, passim.

790 See: Levin, Daniel, "Are you out of your mind? Neurotechnologies and the Making of Disembodied Agency", *Berkeley Technology Law Journal*, Volume 38, 2023, pp. 232–252 (232), whose research we will follow closely in some points of this paper.

791 Levin, Daniel, "Are you out of your mind? Neurotechnologies and the Making of Disembodied Agency", *cit.*, pp. 232–252 (232).

translate[792] accurately citizens' thoughts into a crude/basic speech or rudimentary muscle movements.[793]

§§ By the same token, BCI can also read citizens' minds with scant/scarce effort.[794] BCI, although panegyrically improves significantly impaired/disabled citizens' lives, are not without sizable concerns that should keep everyone eagerly awaken at night.

§§ The doors of a dangerous «I know what you are thinking about» are ajar slightly. So too are the doors of mass unemployment[795] that, further the rise of robots,[796] will pave the way for a universal basic income for the great bulk of humankind. In time, you, dear reader, will know and, foremost, feel. *Critical Artificial Intelligence Studies* (CAIS) told you so.

---

[792] See: Dockrill, Peter, "Brain Implant Translates Paralyzed Man's Thoughts into Text With 94% Accuracy", *SCI Alert*, 2021, passim.

[793] Levin, Daniel, "Are you out of your mind? Neurotechnologies and the Making of Disembodied Agency", *cit.*, pp. 232–252 (232).

[794] See: Zhang, X./Sheng, QZ et al., "Converting your thoughts to texts: enabling brain typing via deep feature learning of eeg signals", *IEEE International Conference on Pervasive Computing and Communications*. Athens: IEEE, 2018, passim.

[795] See: Ford, M., *The rise of the robots: technology and the threat of mass unemployment*, London, Oneworld Publications, 2015, passim. See also: Cohen, Julien E., *Between Truth and Power: The Legal Constructions of Informational Capitalism*. Oxford: Oxford University Press, 2019, pp. 1–376 (p. 192) (contends presciently that "*automated processes* have obvious efficiency advantages, *but such processes may not align well (or well at all) with applicable legal requirements that are couched in shades of gray*"). Italics added.

[796] See: Millar, Jason/Kerr, Ian, "Delegation, Relinquishment and Responsibility: The Prospect of Expert Robots", *Robot Law*, Calo, Ryan/Froomkin, A. Michael/Kerr, Ian, Cheltenham, Edward Elgar Publishing, 2016, pp. 102, 106–107 (as these authors aptly put it "*we will rely on robots without really knowing why – simply because their algorithms provide the greatest number of successful outcomes.* We have already seen this in Google's search approach. Neither Larry (Page) nor Sergey (Brin) (nor any other Google employee) knowns exactly why one particular web page is a better result than another. *When the click patterns say it is, that's good enough.* No semantic or causal analysis is required…*Like the ancients, we will, quite rationally, come to rely upon them, knowing full well that we cannot necessarily explain the reasons for their decisions*"). Italics added. Converging: Casey, Anthony J./Niblett, Anthony, "Self-driving Laws", *University of Toronto Law Journal*, Volume 66, 2016, pp. 429–435 (contend that "as more information is generated, and the evolutionary algorithm updates and become a better forecaster, we imagine that judges will increasingly rely on the advice of the algorithm").

3.1.4.6 «The End Is Near» (Joseph Schmid) and the «Surpassed human Being» (Eugene R. Dolezal): «The Grim Reapers Paradox and Causal Finitism» (José Benardete) on the Heels of the Emergence of Redoubtable Artificial Intelligence-Embedded Technologies That Throw Open the Floodgates of the Great Technological Reset (That Ranges from Brain-Computer Interfaces That Timely Predict Crime to General Artificial Intelligence Equipped with an Intelligence Beyond That of Humans)

§§ Humankind is sitting at the cusp of a Great Technological Reset that marks the demise of the *old order* and the emergence of a *new world order*. Humankind is therefore standing at the crosspoint of infinite potential of Artificial Intelligence-embedded technologies. But know this: your inner compass, dear reader, is the gatekeeper—and it has been constantly asking you: should you credulously rely on Artificial Intelligence-anchored technologies that will ultimately drag you to the limbic stage between humanism and transhumanism? If so, isn't humankind swiftly heading towards a **causal finitism** that will most likely wipe out humanity as we know? This is the kernel of **causal finitism**[797] that draws on the familiar and well-worn «Grim Reaper paradox».

§§ To begin with, what does the Grim Reapers paradox[798] stand for? Imagine, if you will, that there is an unbroken chain of numbers, an infinite sequence, of

[797] Note, though, that not everyone hews to this opinion. See: Paglieri, Fabio, "Expropriated Minds: On Some Practical Problems of Generative AI, Beyond Our Cognitive Illusions", *Philosophy & Technology*, 37:55, 2024, pp. 1–30 (27) ("*Notice that this is the entirety of the statement, not an excerpt. In other words: beware AI, because extinction is looming! Interestingly, this is not the pronouncement of a bunch of nerds who binged excessively on apocalyptic TV shows, but rather a document signed by many key players in AI research, including Sam Altman, CEO of OpenAI (the company who developed both ChatGPT and DALL-E, among other AI applications) and Bill Gates, who needs no introduction. However, despite the authoritativeness of the signatories (or even more so), evoking the extinction of the human race due to AI, without trying to explain what causal link should exist between the two, sounds like cheap propaganda and clumsy recycling of old science fiction tropes (from Terminator to Matrix, passing through many other examples), rather than serious scientific or political reflection. The promoters of the statement argue that the message is deliberately succinct, to find common ground for all those who are strongly concerned, but are worried for various reasons, and would therefore suggest different solutions to the problem.* Giving voice to such internal debate, they claim, would "dilute the message" in terms of political and social effectiveness: better to proclaim that the end is near in Twitter format, to avoid confusion. *Maybe so, yet the fact remains that this results in marketing pseudo-science and vagueness, not verifiable statements and rational arguments: every time the scientific community has tried to take this path, in the name of a misunderstood communicative effectiveness, the results have never been excellent, and sometimes awful*"). Italics added.

[798] Benardete, José, *Infinity: An Essay in Metaphysics*, Oxford, Clarendon Press, 1964.

Grim Reapers entrusted with the task of taking Fred out.[799] Each Reaper is ascribed a unique natural number and a scheduled time to take Fred out. Crucially, if no previous Reaper took Fred out at Reaper n's scheduled time, Reaper n takes Fred out at that time.[800]

§§ On the flip side, if an earlier Reaper had taken Fred out, Reaper n would have done nothing. Reaper 1's scheduled time is sixty seconds past noon; Reaper 2's scheduled time is thirty seconds past noon; Reaper 3's scheduled time is fifteen seconds past noon; and so forth ad infinitum.[801] Strikingly, some Reaper must have taken Fred out. If no Reaper had taken Fred up to 12:01, for instance, then Reaper 1 would take Fred out and so forth.[802]

§§ Turning to the topic at hand, if the overreliance on Large Language Models[803] to do just about anything fails to take human critical thinking out, Brain-computer interfaces will be rolled out at an unprecedented scale only to accomplish the just the same outcome while controlling one's mind, thoughts, and behaviour. Then, law enforcement agencies will be able to reliably predict, and timely quell, crime at unprecedented levels. There will be no crime whatsoever—since law enforcement agencies will be able to predict crime long before it occurs—, but there will be neither freedom of thought nor mental privacy.

§§ If either of them fails, Quantum Technology,[804] if happens to fall into the wrong hands, will allow unscrupulous/unprincipled actors to harness such a cutting-edge technology only to advance their shady agendas while wreaking global havoc. What is worst, Quantum Technology will allow rogue nations/crime syndicates to decrypt iron-clad electronical devices—the cornerstone of global digital security—only to unceremoniously deploy weapons of mass destruction.

§§ On the flip side, if Quantum Technology fails to deliver the expected devastating results, then the upcoming unmooring of the machines will usher in the age of an omnipotent General Artificial Intelligence (OGAI), with a skillset that far surpasses that of human beings in terms of cognitive performance. Either way,

---

799 Schmid, Joseph, "The End is Near: Grim Reapers and Endless Futures", *Mind*, Volume 133, 532, October 2024, 2024, pp. 1057–1077.

800 Schmid, Joseph, "The End is Near: Grim Reapers and Endless Futures", *cit.*, pp. 1057–1077.

801 Schmid, Joseph, "The End is Near: Grim Reapers and Endless Futures", *cit.*, pp. 1057–1077.

802 Schmid, Joseph, "The End is Near: Grim Reapers and Endless Futures", *cit.*, pp. 1057–1077.

803 See: Part III, this chapter, Sects. 3.1.5.4–3.1.5.4.1 of this book (on the functional aspects of Critical Artificial Intelligence Studies, with a sharper focus on the harmful effects of Artificial Intelligence-embedded technologies, namely Large Language Models and its multifarious downsides and shortcomings). See also: Part IV, Chap. 4, Sects. 4.1.9.1–4.1.9.2 (on ChatGPT's functional abilities). See also: Part IV, Chap. 4, Sects. 4.1.9–4.1.9.7 (on ChatGPT's functional drawbacks and pitfalls, including, but no limited to, "hallucinations").

804 See: Part III, this chapter, Sects. 3.1.5.12–3.1.5.12.1 of this book (on the functional aspects of Critical Artificial Intelligence Studies, with a sharper focus on the harmful effects of Artificial Intelligence-embedded technologies, namely, Quantum Technology, which will bring entire industries to its knees while allowing unscrupulous actors to get a hold of, and whimsically activate, weapons of mass destruction).

«the end is near»[805] and the outdated[806]/«surpassed human being»[807] must face the consequences of his ill-fated choices, demise of critical thinking wise.

3.1.4.7 «Expropriated Minds» (Fabio Paglieri): The Impoverishment of Human Abilities Amidst the Onset of the Age of Artificial Intelligence-Embedded Technologies: «Technology and Its Affordances Have the Power to Degrade the Human Capacities in the Long Run» (Avigail Ferdman), Thereby Paving the Way for Human-Involution and for the Full-Blown «Robotization of Human Beings»

§§ Human beings should feel off-kilter with the ease with which Artificial Intelligence-embedded technologies (in general) and Generative Artificial Intelligence (in particular) can distort ground truths.[808] Bafflingly, much more lies beyond that. Strikingly, I have been tinkering with deep research and it is becoming increasingly obvious that Artificial Intelligence depletes, and exacts a toll on, human ability

---

[805] Schmid, Joseph, "The End is Near: Grim Reapers and Endless Futures", *cit.*, pp. 1057–1077 (without discussing AI though).

[806] See: Cataleta, Maria Stefania/Cataleta, Anna, "Artificial Intelligence and Human Rights: An Unequal Struggle", *CIFILE Journal of International Law*, Volume 1, N.º 2, 2020 ("*Artificial Intelligence (AI) is a kind of intelligence that was born in the 1950s and is an integral part of the digital revolution. Progress made by AI has permitted the birth of systems capable of rivalling human capacities or, in some cases, surpassing them.* The progress of the intellectual capacities of AI will change the way of life for human beings and will revolutionise the world of employment. *Intelligent systems present problems regarding individual rights and responsibilities, because as technology replaces more and more of what humans have typically done, our individual roles will become more blurred*"). Italics added. Converging: Cataleta, Maria Stefania, "Artificial Intelligence vs Human Intelligence", in: Martin, L. Miraut/Zalucki, M. (editors), *Artificial intelligence and Human Rights, Dickinson eBook*. Krakow: AFM Krakow University, 2021, pp. 117–127 (on the slew of both moral, ethical, and legal issues with which jurists will grapple in the forthcoming future due to the rise of artificial intelligence in legal arena).

[807] But see: Dolezal, Eugen R., *Der überholte Mensch: Kritische Anfragen an Nick Bostroms Konzept von Superintelligenz*, Best Master Series, Heidelberg, Springer VS Wiesbaden, 2024, pp. 1–94 ("In the course of seemingly uninterrupted and unstoppable technological progress, the development of an artificial superintelligence based on artificial intelligences already realised today seems to be only a matter of time. This book takes up Nick Bostrom's concept of artificial superintelligence, which can be considered one of the best known, in order to clarify the extent to which such a superintelligence fulfils its own definitional criterion of far surpassing humans in terms of cognitive performance. To this end, the fundamental assumptions about the comparability of humans and machines, on which Bostrom's considerations on superintelligence are based, are scrutinised. In the course of weighing up the objections, it becomes clear that Bostrom's idea of superintelligence is based on a functionalist-reductionist foundation, which only inadequately describes essential aspects of being human. *This deficiency leads to an abbreviated and mechanised perspective on human cognitive abilities. Therefore, it cannot be assumed that an artificial superintelligence conceived in this way surpasses human beings or even equals them*"). Italics added.

[808] See: Part III, this chapter, Sects. 3.1.5–3.1.5.5 of this book (on the insidious effects of Generative Artificial Intelligence coupled with its potential to create illusions and distort ground truths while exacting a toll on human critical thinking).

to thrive and flourish. This is where my newly-crafted concept of **human-involution** gets involved.

§§ Under the doctrines of perfectionism,[809] **human flourishing** is measured by how shrewdly one exercises innate human abilities to understand, create,[810] develop,[811] establish meaningful social connections,[812] communicate meaningfully,[813] craft relevant decisions, and deftly exercise their free will by engaging in a set of fruit-bearing activities that lead to generation of valuable output.[814] Pundits have meaningfully introduced the concept of technology affordances[815] to this frame of reference in an earnest attempt to highlight whether and to what extent technology affordances enable or hamper the shrewd exercise of human capacities, thereby influencing the levels of human flourishing.[816]

§§ Compellingly, pundits have been pondering whether and to what extent technology affordances can catalyse a privation (absence) of flourishing, by impoverishing human abilities, such as critical thinking[817] and human creativity.[818] The outturn is that which **privation** might engender ill-fated «flourishing», or **human-involution**, of human beings. Tellingly, Artificial Intelligence-embedded technologies and its affordances possess the redoubtable power to degrade, rather than enhance, human abilities in the fullness of time.[819]

§§ Relatedly, there is burgeoning body of research focused on the thorny relationship between technology and human flourishing.[820] Unsurprisingly, there have

---

[809] Hurka, T., *Perfectionism*, Oxford, Oxford University Press, 1993; Hurka, T., "Capability, Functioning and Perfectionism", *Apeiron*, 35 (4), 2002, pp. 137–162; Hurka, T., "The parallel goods of knowledge and achievement", *Erkenntnis*, 85 (3), 2020, pp. 589–608.

[810] Brainard, L., "The curious case of uncurious creation", *Inquiry: An Interdisciplinary Journal of Philosophy*, 2023.

[811] Nussbaum, M. C., *Creating capabilities: The human development approach*, Cambridge, Massachusetts, Belknap Press of Harvard University Press, 2011.

[812] McFall, M. T., "Real character-friends: Aristotelian friendship, living together, and technology", *Ethics and Information Technology*, 14 (3), 2012, pp. 221–230.

[813] Nguyen, C. T., "How Twitter Gamifies Communication", Lackey, J. (Ed.), *Applied Epistemology*, Oxford, Oxford University Press, 2021, pp. 410–436.

[814] Ferdman, Avigail, "Human Flourishing and Technology Affordances", *Philosophy & Technology*, 37:1, 2024, pp. 1–28.

[815] Maragno, G., Tangi, L., Gastaldi, L., & Benedetti, M., "Exploring the factors, affordances and constraints outlining the implementation of artificial intelligence in public sector organizations", *International Journal of Information Management*, 73, 2023, 102686.

[816] Ferdman, Avigail, "Human Flourishing and Technology Affordances", *cit.*, pp. 1–28.

[817] See: Part III, this chapter, Sects. 3.1.5–3.1.5.5 of this book (on the insidious effects of Generative Artificial Intelligence coupled with its potential to create illusions and distort ground truths while exacting a toll on human critical thinking).

[818] Blok, V. "The role of human creativity in human-technology relations", *Philosophy & Technology*, 35 (3), 2022, pp. 59 and ff and passim.

[819] Ferdman, Avigail, "Human Flourishing and Technology Affordances", *cit.*, pp. 1–28.

[820] Floridi, L., Cowls, J., Beltrametti, M., Chatila, R., Chazerand, P., Dignum, V., Luetge, C., et al., "AI4People-an ethical framework for a good AI society: Opportunities, risks, principles, and recommendations", *Minds and Machines*, 28 (4), 2018, pp. 689–707; Stahl, B. C., "Artificial intelligence

been poignant calls to lay out a groundwork upon which a brawny ethics of technology should stand. Such a thoroughgoing frame of reference underpins the trade-off between a good life[821] and human and societal[822] thriving and flourishing.[823]

§§ I hereby follow Avigail Ferdman's analytic framework that endeavours to capture the uneasy relationship between digital technology and human flourishing (or lack thereof) reflected on the gradual impoverishment of innate human abilities amidst the onset of the age of Artificial Intelligence-embedded technologies. By the same token, I also second the deep-rooted concerns voiced by Fabio Paglieri, to the extent that the overreliance on Artificial Intelligence-embedded technologies—especially, but not limited to, Generative Artificial Intelligence—may «expropriate our minds» while decreasing our dexterity, memory,[824] and intellectual prowess.[825]

§§ In addition to that, I also embrace the perfectionist conception of the good life,[826] which neatly contends that the benchmark against which human flourishing is gauged is how well human beings exercise, project, and spring into action, their set of innate abilities[827] in the outer world.

---

for a better future: An ecosystem perspective on the ethics of AI and emerging digital technologies", *Springer Briefs in Research and Innovation Governance*, Cham, Springer International Publishing, 2021, passim.

821 Strong, D./Higgs, E., "Borgmann's philosophy of technology", Higgs, E./Light, A./Strong, D. (Editors), *Technology and the good life?*, Chicago, Chicago University Press, 2000, pp. 19–37.

822 Ferdman, Avigail, "Human Flourishing and Technology Affordances", *cit.*, pp. 1–28.

823 Nyholm, S., *This Is Technology Ethics: An Introduction*, London, Wiley-Blackwell, 2023.

824 See: Paglieri, Fabio, "Expropriated Minds: On Some Practical Problems of Generative AI, Beyond Our Cognitive Illusions", *Philosophy & Technology*, 37:55, 2024, pp. 1–30 (21) ("*The memorization of a large set of phone numbers is a good example: I belong to a generation that grew up without mobile phones, which implied (among other things) that, whenever I wanted to call someone on my cable phone, I had either to find their number on some written repository (my agenda or a phone book, those relics of old…), or simply recall it from memory. The latter was by far the most convenient option, so it was quite common for anyone to memorize the phone number of a variety of people: your close relatives and your love interests, but typically also some of your friends, colleagues, and even the stores or clubs that you frequented the most. At the age of 15, I could easily recall about 50 phone numbers, and that was absolutely normal: today, in the prime of my academic career, that figure is down to 2 – my own number and my wife's, whereas I shamelessly ignore those of my sons*"). Italics added.

825 See: Paglieri, Fabio, "Expropriated Minds: On Some Practical Problems of Generative AI, Beyond Our Cognitive Illusions", *cit.*, pp. 1–30 (26) ("*The opportunity of using generative AI systems to replace human workers for free in creative sectors is likely to result in massive displacement and a vaguely dystopic scenario (with machines doing creative, stimulating work, whereas humans are stuck in boring, repetitive jobs*), unless proper political and legal actions are implemented. 4. ***Extending our minds with generative AI systems should be mostly dedicated to an enhancement of our cognitive powers, whereas replacement of pre-existing cognitive functions and skills should be kept to a minimum and carefully monitored in the public interest. The goal is to make us more intelligent, not less***"). Italics and bold added.

826 Hurka, T., *Perfectionism*, Oxford, Oxford University Press, 1993; Hurka, T., "Capability, Functioning and Perfectionism", *Apeiron*, 35 (4), 2002, pp. 137–162; Hurka, T., "The parallel goods of knowledge and achievement", *Erkenntnis*, 85 (3), 2020, pp. 589–608.

827 Ferdman, Avigail, "Human Flourishing and Technology Affordances", *cit.*, pp. 1–28.

§§ Pivotally, human beings flourish when they deploy, and deftly exercise, their portmanteau of human abilities[828] in ways that enhance, rather than degrade, their deep-rooted sense of existence.[829] The unbridled rise to prominence of Artificial Intelligence-anchored technologies throws the theoretical underpinnings of existence into a frenzy, thus playing havoc with our ability to portend if human beings will be able to retain the gist of their uniqueness in years to come. I call this **human-involution**.

§§ At its core, **human-involution** is the lens through which the abridgment of human abilities amidst the onset of the age of Artificial Intelligence-anchored technologies can be seen. This frame of reference—that sharply captures the uneasy relationship between the all-out deployment of technology and the symmetric impoverishment of human abilities as time trudges forward—wovens technology affordances into the fabric of human flourishing (or lack thereof).[830]

§§ The upshot of this stance is to bring the interplay between **human-involution** and **technological affordances** into a sharper focus, thereby dovetailing seamlessly the concept of technology affordances with perfectionist theories of flourishing.[831] That said, no bewildering surprise stems from the fact that the prickly relationship between **technology affordances** and **human-involution** is becoming pressing, owing to the indomitable power wielded by Artificial Intelligence-embedded technologies to erode the gulf between technology and its end-users (human beings).[832]

§§ It is worth recalling that Brain-Computer Interfaces—the embodiment of a sought-after blend between human beings and machines under the gloss of **robotization of human beings**—neatly encapsulates, hands-in-glove, the lens through which the disheartening **process of human-involution** can be sharply seen: if a computer can read your thoughts, you are no longer a human being, but an extension of a machine instead. Put otherwise, human beings are framed as «connected

---

[828] Ferdman, Avigail, "Human Flourishing and Technology Affordances", *cit.*, pp. 1–28.

[829] Bradford, G., *Achievement*, Oxford, Oxford University Press; 2015; Bradford, G., "Perfectionist Bads", *The Philosophical Quarterly*, 71 (3), 2021, pp. 586–604; Bradford, G., "Perfectionism", Fletcher, G. (Ed.), *The Routledge Handbook of Philosophy of Well Being*, London, Routledge, 2016, pp. 124–134.

[830] Ferdman, Avigail, "Human Flourishing and Technology Affordances", *cit.*, pp. 1–28.

[831] Hurka, T., *Perfectionism*, Oxford, Oxford University Press, 1993; Hurka, T., "Capability, Functioning and Perfectionism", *Apeiron*, 35 (4), 2002, pp. 137–162; Hurka, T., "The parallel goods of knowledge and achievement", *Erkenntnis*, 85 (3), 2020, pp. 589–608.

[832] Ferdman, Avigail, "Human Flourishing and Technology Affordances", *cit.*, pp. 1–28.

minds»[833] that operate as an extension of an ever-recording machine—the kernel of the «extended mind thesis».[834]

§§ Strikingly, Artificial Intelligence-embedded technologies form part of a broader technological apparatus within which cognitive ecology[835] operates. Cognitive ecology—alongside its deranged/frazzled offsprings—straddles physical and digital artifacts, which, in turn, maintains the *digital master* (tech moguls) and the *digital slave* (human beings) permanently connected, thereby severely curtailing the power of the *digital slave* to *flourish* outside the perimeter of such[836] harmful connexion.[837]

§§ The once yawning gap between device (Artificial Intelligence-embedded technologies) and end-users (human beings) has vanished into thin digital air. Hence, the omnipresence of the former caused the growing pains of **human-involution** of the latter to swell. I tag this as the **functional dimension** of the dispiriting process of **human-involution**.

§§ Against this backdrop, **human-involution** leads to **(absence) of flourishing**, which is a concept that holds relevance in the literature on well-being.[838] It should not therefore come as a flummoxing surprise that the impoverishment of human abilities caused by the unfettered deployment of technology affordances can spawn a bemoaning state of **privative unflourishing**.[839]

---

[833] See: Greenberg, Jeremy/Ringrose/Katelyn/Berger, Sara/VanDodick/Rossi, Francesca/New, Joshua, "Privacy and the Connected Mind", *The Future Privacy Forum*, 2021; Citron; Danielle Keats Citron/Pasquale, Frank, "Network Accountability for the Domestic Intelligence Apparatus", *Hasting Law Journal*, Volume 62, 2011; Gray, David/Citron, Danielle Keats, "The Right to Quantitative Privacy", *Minnesota Law Review*, Volume 98, 2013, pp. 62–81.

[834] Clark, Andy/Chalmers, David, "The Extended Mind", *Analysis*, Volume 58, Issue 1, January 1998. Oxford: Oxford University Press, 1998, pp. 7–19 (passim).

[835] Smart, P./Heersmink, R./Clowes, R., "The cognitive ecology of the internet", Cowley, S./Vallée-Tourangeau, F. (Editors), 2nd edition, *Cognition beyond the brain: Computation, interactivity and human artifice*, Heidelberg, Springer, 2017, pp. 251–282.

[836] Ferdman, Avigail, "Human Flourishing and Technology Affordances", *cit.*, pp. 1–28.

[837] Carabantes, M., "Towards the end of the designer fallacy: How the internet empowers designers over users", *Philosophy & Technology*, 36 (2), 2023, pp. 32 and ff and passim.

[838] Kagan, S., "An introduction to Ill-being", *Oxford Studies in Normative Ethics*, 4, 2014, pp. 261–288.

[839] Ferdman, Avigail, "Human Flourishing and Technology Affordances", *cit.*, pp. 1–28.

3.1.4.8 «The Artificial Intelligence's Power of Hypersuasion» (Luciano Floridi) to Propel Forward the *Age of Permanent Illusion* Against the Backdrop of Which Millions of People Will Be Led Astray

§§ Last but not least, one of the foundations upon which *Critical Artificial Intelligence Studies* (CAIS) stands is the «Artificial Intelligence's power of hypersuasion»[840] to spur, and propel forward, the *age of permanent illusion.*

§§ Worst still, Artificial Intelligence-embedded technologies (in general) and Generative Artificial Intelligence (in particular)—the cradle of the *age of the permanent illusion*[841]—will lend itself to floating signifiers[842] that will stand ready to be *weaponized* against a cohort of *socially undesirables* that may find themselves at loggerheads with whoever lays hands on this magic wand of evil. In addition to that, Generative Artificial Intelligence will lead millions of people astray as the latter, unbeknownst to them, will be affected by the former.[843]

§§ Here lies the Artificial Intelligence's power of hypersuasion, which is potentially hideous, since unscrupulous actors can get a hold of it only to advance their heinous goals.[844] These are hardly gleeful news insofar persuasive technologies[845] are fundamentally technologies of power[846]: whoever controls Artificial Intelligence-embedded technologies (in general) and harnesses Generative Artificial Intelligence (in particular) will shape the world and the course of history accordingly. For the better or for the worst.

---

[840] See: Floridi, Luciano, "Hypersuasion – On AI's persuasive power and how to deal with it", *Philosophy & Technology*, 37 (64), 2024, pp. 1–10.

[841] See: Part III, this chapter, Sects. 3.1.5–3.1.5.5 of this book (on the insidious effects of Generative Artificial Intelligence coupled with its potential to create illusions and distort ground truths while exacting a toll on human critical thinking).

[842] See: Part III, this chapter, Sect. 3.1.5.3 of this book (on the "house of fabricated lies" and the usage of Generative Artificial Intelligence as a *floating signifier* that will stand ready to be galvanize power in a given direction, including, but not limited to, against *socially undesirables* that may find themselves at odds, or at loggerheads, with whoever controls Artificial Intelligence).

[843] Nyström, T et al., "When Persuasive Technology gets Dark?", Themistocleous, M. et al. (Editors), *Information Systems, EMCIS 2020, Lecture notes in Business Information Processing*, Volume 402, 2020, passim (without discussing the implications of Generative Artificial Intelligence in-depth though).

[844] Floridi, Luciano, "Hypersuasion – On AI's persuasive power and how to deal with it", *cit.*, pp. 1–10.

[845] De Vries et al., *Persuasive technology - development and implementation of Personalized technologies to change attitudes and behaviours*, Nienke Beerlage-De Jong, and Lisette, van Gemert-Pijnen (Editor), Springer, Lecture Notes in Computer Science, 2017, passim.

[846] Floridi, Luciano, "Hypersuasion – On AI's persuasive power and how to deal with it", *cit.*, pp. 1–10.

3.1.5 Functional Aspects of Critical Artificial Intelligence Studies (CAIS): The Harmful Effects of Artificial Intelligence-Embedded Technologies

3.1.5.1 How *Perpetuation Technologies* Are Dehumanizing Human-Laden Emotions Amidst the Onset of the *Age of Permanent Illusion*

3.1.5.1.1 Generative Artificial Intelligence Solutions in the Digital Afterlife Industry (DAI) and the Looming Danger of *Digital Immortality*: The Case of Griefbots, Deadbots, Post-Mortem Avatars and Robots That Threaten to Artificialize Human-Laden Emotions While Creating a State of *Permanent Maze* That Will Pave the Way to the *Upload of Our Digital Consciousness*, Where Life and Death Blend

§§ Artificial Intelligence (in general) is not an ordinary taxonomy, nor is something amenable to be glossed over. Instead, it holds the blueprint of our collective destiny and the herculean power its carries. The long-winded Part IV, Chapter IV is a living testimony of the nefarious effects arising out of an *Algorithmic Dictatorship* that is poised to fray the fabric of Rule of Law beyond repair and beyond recognition.

§§ Artificial Intelligence-embedded technologies are bound to spin into a dystopian world of *permanent illusion*, thereby hurling human beings into a state of *permanent maze* whereby ataraxic truths and blunt lies are bound to be deeply woven into the fabric of our daily lives. To the extent that a war between light and darkness is underway while raging unseen, Artificial Intelligence is noticeably stepping boldly into its sweeping goal of siding squarely with mischievous forces of darkness that seek to dim humans' light.

§§ Governments worldwide are peddling for a redoubtable influence in the domain of Artificial Intelligence. They are not alone. It follows that a handful of relevant stakeholders (e.g. shady private companies at the behest of pariah nations, crime syndicates, rogue nations and mostly unseen forces of evil that pull the strings behind the scenes) have ploughed billions of dollars through venture funds only to propel their hidden agendas forward.

§§ Hordes of data have been accordingly collated in a cloud-based system to feed an eerily advanced General Artificial Intelligence (GAI) that is set to know neither geographical bounds nor ethical concerns. These are hardly uplifting news in that algorithmic decision-making, as abundantly shown throughout this book, has a knack to carve through firmly rooted fundamental rights. Part IV, Chap. 4, solely devoted to harmful effects arisen from *Algorithmic Dictatorship*, raises critical questions that should prime relevant stakeholders (e.g. policymakers and lawmakers) to take appropriate legal action to smooth out, and ideally weed out, the nefarious effects of an ever-evolving technology that never ceases to amaze.

§§ Although Artificial Intelligence sidesteps a normal course of events in that endangers to throw Rule of Law out of balance, Generative Artificial Intelligence (a subset of Artificial Intelligence-embedded technologies) is poised to further compound this loathsome scenario. Sooner rather than later, deceitful joy and belated/ repressed grief will become woven of the same cloth amidst the unbridled rise of advanced technologies that are slated to blur the boundaries between both. The *artificialization* of human-laden emotions will tag along. To illustrate, take the example of *griefbots*, *deadbots*, post-mortem avatars, and robots created by Generative Artificial Intelligence solutions in the digital afterlife industry (DAI).

§§ For a tiny amount of money, the online platform Project December (hereinafter PD) bestows upon users' access to a «deep AI running on one of the world's most sophisticated super-computers' and allows them to participate in simulated 'text-based conversation[s] with any one'—including 'someone who is no longer alive».[847]

§§ This platform grabbed immediate headlines inasmuch media was abuzz with news about a man who gained access to the PD website to have a chat with his late fiancée's avatar.[848] Thereafter, OpenAI, whose GPT-3 model originally powered the platform from its very inception, was not slow in discontinuing PD's access to its API, thereby offering Project December's failure to abide by its safety guidelines[849] as a justification to do so.[850]

§§ Although OpenAI's usage policies refrain itself from downrightly forbidding the use of its large language models (LLMs) in the creation of the tagged «deadbots,» the guidelines nonetheless specify that any modality conversational Artificial Intelligence system «simulat[ing] another person»—exception made to «historical public figures»—is required to «either have that person's explicit consent or be clearly labelled as «simulated» or «parody».[851]/[852]

§§ Having bluntly failed to abide by the central tenets of OpenAI's safety team's set of binding instructions, Project December was temporarily halted. Note, though, Project December, undeterred in the yearn to offer its services to whom it may be concerned, built its own platform. Its services are being currently rendered to those who crave the unmissable opportunity to «simulate the dead».[853]

---

[847] Hollanek, Tomasz/Nowaczyk-Basińska, Katarzyna, "Griefbots, Deadbots, Postmortem Avatars: on Responsible Applications of Generative AI in the Digital Afterlife Industry", *Philosophy & Technology*, 2024, 37:63, pp. 1–22.

[848] Fagon, J., "The Jessica Simulation: Love and loss in the age of A.I. San Francisco Chronicle", https://www.sfchronicle.com/projects/2021/jessica-simulation-artificial-intelligence, 2021. Accessed 13 March 2025.

[849] Robitzski, D., "OpenAI Shuts Down GPT-3 Bot Used To Emulate Dead Fiancée", *Futurism*, 2021, passim.

[850] Hollanek, Tomasz/Nowaczyk-Basińska, Katarzyna, "Griefbots, Deadbots, Postmortem Avatars: on Responsible Applications of Generative AI in the Digital Afterlife Industry", *cit.*, pp. 1–22.

[851] Hollanek, Tomasz/Nowaczyk-Basińska, Katarzyna, "Griefbots, Deadbots, Postmortem Avatars: on Responsible Applications of Generative AI in the Digital Afterlife Industry", *cit.*, pp. 1–22.

[852] OpenAI, Usage policies. Retrieved 7 September, 2023, from https://openai.com/policies/usage-policies. Accessed 13 march 2025.

[853] Hollanek, Tomasz/Nowaczyk-Basińska, Katarzyna, "Griefbots, Deadbots, Postmortem Avatars: on Responsible Applications of Generative AI in the Digital Afterlife Industry", *cit.*, pp. 1–22. See:

§§ The story of Project December's fast-paced evolution, intertwined with that of OpenAI's usage policy development, vividly portrays the swift headways, and rapid strides made, in the quick-shifting field of Generative Artificial Intelligence—with jaw-dropping achievements in the field of natural language processing[854] taking precedence over any other considerations[855]—that has a direct bearing on the digital afterlife industry (DAI),[856] drawing on Öhman and Floridi's frame of reference.[857]

§§ Although DAI encompasses a cluster of data management services entrusted with the task of providing soft oversight on the deliverables that leverage on the «digital remains»[858] of the deceased paired with digital activities that seek to target potential customers (i.e. the bereaved), it is pivotally important to bring in AI-powered simulations of the dead into a sharper focus.[859]

Project December, Retrieved 7 September, 2023, from https://projectdecember.net. Accessed 13 march 2025.

[854] See on the fundamental tenets of Natural Language Processing (NLP): Pennington, J./Socher, R./Manning, CD., "GloVe: global vectors for word representation. Empirical Methods in Natural Language Processing (EMNLP). ACL Anthology", *Proceedings of the 2014 conference on empirical methods in natural language processing*, 2014, pp. 1532–1534; See: By A, Silberg J, Manyika, J, *Notes from the AI frontier: tackling bias in AI (and in humans)*, McKinsey Global Institute Caliskan, 2019; Bryson, JJ, Narayanan, A., "Semantics derived automatically from language corpora contain human-like biases", *Science*, 356 (6334), 2017, pp. 183–186; Camacho-Collados, J., Pilehvar, MT, "Embeddings in natural language processing", *ACL anthology, Proceedings of the 28th international conference on computational linguistics*, 2020, pp. 10–15; Bolukbasi T, Chang K-W, Saligrama V, et al, "Man is to Computer Programmer as Woman is to Homemaker? Debiasing Word Embeddings", arXiv:1607.06520v1, 2016; Radford, A./Wu, J./Child, R. et al, "Language models are unsupervised multitask learners", *Technical Report*; Rudinger, R./Naradowsky, J./Leonard, B./Durme, B Van, "Gender Bias in Conference Resolution", *NAACL HLT 2018 - 2018 Conference North American Chapter Association Computer Linguist Human Language Technology - Proceedings of Conference*, 2018, 2:8–14; Sap, M., Gabriel, S., Qin, L et al, "Social Bias Frames: Reasoning about Social and Power Implications of Language. Association of Computational Linguistics", *Proceedings of the 58th Annual Meeting of the Association of Computational Linguistics*, 2020, pp. 5477–5490; Nadeem, M./Bethke, A./Reddy, S., "Stereo Set: measuring stereotypical bias in pretrained language models", *ACL Anthology, Proceedings of the 59th annual meeting of the association for the computational linguistics and the 11th international joint conference on natural language processing*, Volume 1 (long papers), 2020, pp. 5356–5371. See: Part IV, Chap. 4, Sect. 4.1.8 of this book (on biased word embeddings with an entrenched presence on search engines run by tech moguls).

[855] But see: Zhao, J., Khashabi, D./Khot, T et al., "Ethical-advice taker: do language models understand natural language interventions?", *arXiv.* https://doi.org/10.18653/v1/2021.fndings-acl.364, 2021 (casting doubts on whether Large Language Models indeed understand Natural Processing Languages).

[856] Öhman, C./Floridi, Luciano, "The political economy of death in the age of information: A critical approach to the digital afterlife industry", *Minds and Machines: Journal for Artificial Intelligence, Philosophy and Cognitive Science*, 27 (4), 2017, pp. 639–662.

[857] Öhman, C./Floridi, Luciano, "An Ethical Framework for the Digital Afterlife Industry", *Nature Human Behavior*, 2, 2018, pp. 318–320.

[858] On the notion of "digital remains": Morse, T./Birnhack, M., "The posthumous privacy paradox: Privacy preferences and behavior regarding digital remains", *New Media & Society*, 24 (6), 2020, pp. 1343–1362.

[859] Hollanek, Tomasz/Nowaczyk-Basińska, Katarzyna, "Griefbots, Deadbots, Postmortem Avatars: on Responsible Applications of Generative AI in the Digital Afterlife Industry", *cit.*, pp. 1–22.

§§ Building on, and on fundamentally the heels of, Öhman and Floridi's framework,[860] «re-creation service» lends itself to an Artificial Intelligence-embedded service suitably tailored to craft postmortem simulations of the dead. Out of accuracy, deadbots, griefbots, post-mortem avatars, and robots refer to an Artificial Intelligence-enabled digital representation of a deceased individual created by a re-creation service.[861]

§§ Fast forward to the critical analysis of these *perpetuation technologies*, there are plenty of reasons to be sceptical of the premises built into this eerily invasive technology. At one end of the spectrum, the human dignity of the deceased seems to be somewhat standing outside the fray insofar it seems as though that the former has been rendered secondary to economic concerns.

§§ Whilst machines are impeccably consistent in performing a digital projection of a deceased person on a continuous basis, uncertain is the extent to which such an endeavour will not further dispel the frontiers between the world we live in and the afterlife, thereby eliciting the misleading impression that a given person is still amongst us, when such is not the case. *Perpetuation technologies* therefore lack a sturdier ethical ground to begin with. *Perpetuation technologies* must bear the seal of ethical concerns accordingly. There is *survival* (of human dignity *in spite of* death) and there is *surrender* (or human dignity *because of* death). *Perpetuation technologies* unceremoniously and unapologetically trounce the former while affording primacy to the latter.

§§ At the other end of the spectrum, griefbots, deadbots, robots, and postmortem avatars will mostly likely engender legal loopholes along the line. Take the example of wills. An unscrupulous bereaved—or someone at his/her behest—might be ineluctably tempted to furnish to the «re-creation service» a deepfake video whereby the deceased clearly expresses her will that all her assets should be given to the bereaved, only to pave the way for a legal win along the line. The avenues for digital dishonesty are legion. So too are the possibilities for disrepute. Caution must be exercised or this lucrative industry will otherwise face an avalanche of negativity from which it will be difficult to bounce back.

§§ Aside from that, current Generative Artificial Intelligence solutions in the digital afterlife industry (DAI) (i.e. griefbots, deadbots, post-mortem avatars and robots) are only the stepping stone for advanced forms of *digital immortality*—such the *upload* of our *digital consciousness*, which will be spurred by an upcoming cutting-edge Brain-Computer interface technology—, that will allow the rich to live forever (in the digital world) whilst the poor will grapple with endless throes concerning their «digital legacy».[862] The yawning gap between the rich and the

---

860 Öhman, C./Floridi, Luciano, The political economy of death in the age of information: A critical approach to the digital afterlife industry", *cit.*, pp. 639–662.

861 Hollanek, Tomasz/Nowaczyk-Basińska, Katarzyna, "Griefbots, Deadbots, Postmortem Avatars: on Responsible Applications of Generative AI in the Digital Afterlife Industry", *cit.*, pp. 1–22.

862 On digital legacy: Pitsillides, S., "Digital legacy: Designing with things", *Death Studies*, 43 (2), 2019, pp. 1–9.

poor[863] will accordingly swell propelled by a rampant *digital divide*[864] that is shaping up to topple humanism while leaving this world in shambles. The creation of a *digital identity* to keep tabs on everything we say, do or think will not lag far behind.

3.1.5.2 Generative Artificial Intelligence and the Onset of the *Age of Alternative Realities* Whereby Truths and Lies Dovetail Seamlessly: The Case of *Deepfakes*

§§ Jurists are a maverick bunch. Yet surprises—legal surprises—are not usually welcomed as they belie the legal certainty of which jurists are so fond of.[865] They are not wrong. Far from it. For a simple reason: legal community abhor the shifting sands of inscrutability[866] altogether.[867] Algorithms[868] powering the Generative Artificial Intelligence (namely *deepfakes*[869]) are barbed with it.[870]

---

[863] Such as a yawning gap between rich—that can adroitly harness artificial intelligence to advance their goals and shady agendas—and poor—that grapple to meet basic needs and are automatically excluded from the equation of digital society powered by Artificial Intelligence—which will directly impact the fabric of societies worldwide, thereby augmenting the chasm between the «digitally-chosen» and the «digitally-outcast» enabled by a algorithmic discrimination that does nothing but irreparable harm. See: Yu, Peter K., "The Algorithmic Divide and Equality in the Age of Artificial Intelligence", *Florida Law Review*, Volume 72, 2020, pp. 355–360 (addresses the issue of algorithmic discrimination).

[864] See: Eubanks, Virginia, *Automating Inequality: How High-Tech Tools Profile, Police and Punish the Poor*. New York: St. Martin's Press, 2018, 1–272 (1 ff and passim) (coining the expression «automating inequality» to vividly portray the downsides of using high-technology to further compound the yawning gap between rich and poor). See also: Soss, Joe, Richard C. Fording, and Sanford F. Schram, *Disciplining the Poor: Neoliberal Paternalism and the Persistent Power of Race*. Chicago: University of Chicago Press, 2011. See also: Savin-Badden, M., Burden, D., Taylor, H., "The ethics and impact of digital immortality", *Knowledge Cultures*, 5 (2), 2017, pp. 178–196.

[865] See: Santos, Hugo Luz dos, "Brain-Computer Interfaces, Generative Artificial Intelligence (ChatGPT and Deep Fakes) and Criminal Procedure Law: what's at stake?", *Journal of Research in E. and Computer Science*, Edinburgh, United Kingdom, June 2024, Volume 2, 2024, pp. 39–78, which I will follow closely in this regard.

[866] See generally about unbecoming secrecy against the backdrop of which artificial intelligence operates: Katyal, Sonia K, "The Paradox of Source Code Secrecy", *Cornell Law Review*, Volume 104, 2019, pp. 1183–1236; Wexler, Rebecca, "Life, Liberty, and Trade Secrets: Intellectual Property in the Criminal Justice System", *Stanford Law Review*, Volume 70, 2018, pp. 1343 and ff.

[867] See: Selbst, Andrew D./Barocas, Solon, "The Intuitive Appeal of Explainable Machines", *Fordham Law Review*, Volume 87, 2018, pp. 1085–1109.

[868] That are in dire need of not only being transparent, but, and foremost, overtly democratic. See: Okidegbe, Ngozi, "The Democratizing Potential of Algorithms?", *Connecticut Law Review*, Volume 54, 2021, passim.

[869] On deepfakes: Rini, Regina/Cohen, Leah, "Deepfakes, Deepharms", *Journal of Ethics and Social Philosophy*, Volume 22, Issue 2, 2022, pp. 143–161.

[870] See: Karnow, Curtis E. A., "The Opinion of Machines", *The Cambridge Handbook of the Law of Algorithms*, Bartfield, Woodrow (Editor), Cambridge, United Kingdom: Cambridge University Press, 2021, pp. 15 and ff and passim.

§§ Against this backdrop, the question is to gauge what are deepfakes and the extent to which they fray the fabric of Rule of Law.

§§ Deepfakes—just like Large Language Models—amount to an offspring of Generative Artificial Intelligence. So, what are deepfakes? And how can they cast a shady shadow[871] on Rule of Law? To illustrate, suffice to say that deepfakes are shaping up to throw the agreed-upon concept of «seeing is believing»[872] into a frenzy.[873]

§§ Deepfakes stand therefore poised to not only defy the authenticity of digital evidence, but, and foremost, to catalyse the onset of the age of *alternative realities* against the backdrop of which truths and lies are bound to be cobbled together insofar they will become woven of the same cloth accordingly.

§§ Deepfakes are made of videos,[874] images, and audio recordings which, taken together, will herald a metamorphic shift in the world we live in. There is a myriad of software programs at arm's length that, drawing on both machine learning and deep learning, can fabricate a tampered with high-realistic footage by means of which a given person is featured saying and doing something they never did.

§§ The more videos or digital materials are fed into the digital system, the more real the doctored/warped/tampered with those videos will appear to be to the laypeople's very eyes. It follows that somewhere along the line it will become utterly impossible to distinguish a candid truth from a blunt lie. There will be a point at which there will be no difference between both. This gruelling scenario is bound to exact a toll on the central tenets of Rule of Law as this advanced technology (e.g. deepfakes) will mostly likely be weaponized against a cohort of *socially undesirables* that may find themselves at loggerheads with a powerful stakeholder.

§§ Generative Artificial Intelligence is therefore the central battleground on which the skirmish between truths and lies—and the affray between light and darkness—will be bravely fought.

---

[871] Somewhat anticipated by feted doctrine a while back though: Bauer, Nancy, *How to do Things with Pornography*. Cambridge, Massachusetts: Harvard University Press, 2018, passim.

[872] Dean, Ashley, "Deepfakes, Pose Detection, and the Death of "Seeing is believing"", *Law and Technology Today*, 2019.

[873] See: Pfefferkorn, Riana, ""Deepfakes" in the Courtroom", *Boston University Public Interest Law Journal*, Volume 29, Issue 2, 2020, pp. 245–276 (245).

[874] It all started with "revenge porn" by means of which a distraught person posts a video online of the former boyfriend or girlfriend without his/her consent. Shortly after, Deepfake porn—that phonily depicts a famous person engaging in sexual intercourse with another person—followed suit. See: Scott, Daniella, "Deepfake Porn Nearly Ruined My Life", *Elle*, 2020, passim.

3.1.5.3 «The House of Fabricated Lies»: Generative Artificial Intelligence as a Floating Signifier to Galvanize Power in a Given Direction

§§ Generative Artificial Intelligence forms part of a broader technological apparatus within which deepfakes operate. The former boasts a ravenous appetite for playing havoc with our ability to foretell where the line between reality and fiction lies. Contrary to popular belief, the latter possess has an unquenchable thirst to create a haze of ambiguity between what is real and what is not.

§§ Once you loosen up the grip on the reins, a mendacious world of fabricated lies flows right to you, dear reader. But this is just the tip of iceberg (a yellow canary in the mine). Before long, humans will become so enmeshed/entangled in the elaborate trappings of illusion that they will swiftly gainsay reality as is with bursting unease. A «house of fabricated lies» powered by a redoubtable Generative Artificial Intelligence looms large and yet people fail to take appropriate notice. The latter is therefore shaping up to be a floating signifier—a both impervious and inscrutable term suffused/imbued with whatever meaning a circumstantial stakeholder sees fit to galvanize power in a given pathway.

§§ The following section—which testifies to the harmful potential of deepfakes to craft false memories while customizing the contours of public events—lends weight, and adds plausibility, to this main contention.

3.1.5.3.1 Applied Psychology, «Source Confusion Error» (Murphy/Flynn), and the Demise of «Seeing Is Believing» (Beridze/Butcher): The Interplay Between *Deepfakes* and False Memories Paired with Its Potential to Distort Memories for Public Events

§§ At this juncture, you already know, dear reader, that deepfake videos are produced using a set of advanced machine learning techniques.[875] A broad range of images, videos, and audio clips are bundled together to generate a hyper-realistic video that can feature an individual doing or saying something they never did[876] in the first place.[877]

§§ To further compound the dangerousness arising out of Generative Artificial Intelligence, these tools have been made publicly available, thereby allowing anyone to produce realistic deepfakes, without considerable amount of training or

875 Murphy, Gillian/Flynn, Emma, "Deepfake false memories", *Memory*, Volume 30, n.º 4, 2022, pp. 480–492.

876 Murphy, Gillian/Flynn, Emma, "Deepfake false memories", *cit.*, pp. 480–492.

877 Maras, M. H./Alexandrou, A., "Determining authenticity of video evidence in the age of artificial intelligence and in the wake of deepfake videos", *The International Journal of Evidence & Proof*, 23(3), 2019, pp. 255–262.

specialised[878] equipment.[879] Definitional quandaries concerning the process that leads to the creation of deepfakes have nonetheless persisted from its earliest days. This topic, however enthralling, falls well beyond the bread and scope of this book.

§§ Deepfakes first rose to prominence in the distant year of 2017 when a Reddit user broadcasted doctored pornographic videos featuring famous people and non-consensual «designer porn».[880] The latter continues make up the overwhelming majority of deepfakes[881] being created to this day[882] nonetheless.

§§ Pivotally, the great bulk of the literature stream on deepfake technology revolves around potentially nefarious effects of these tampered with videos coupled with the toll inflicted upon privacy, democracy, and trust[883] in institutions.[884] A burgeoning concern is that deepfake videos may indeed produce false memories.[885] Compellingly, the Source Monitoring Framework[886] sheds a keen light on how people assign mental experiences to either reality or to imagination.[887]

§§ Under this frame of reference, false memories can be created when individuals make a **source confusion error**. Put differently, **source confusion error** occurs when mental images of a fictional event are erroneously viewed as the byproduct of a previously a vividly lived experience.[888] This is very likely when the mental experience itself has all the trappings of a real memory,[889] such as being overly rich in details

---

878 Murphy, Gillian/Flynn, Emma, "Deepfake false memories", *cit.*, pp. 480–492.

879 Kietzmann, J., Lee, L. W., McCarthy, I. P., & Kietzmann, T. C., "Deepfakes: Trick or treat?", *Business Horizons*, 63 (2), 2020, pp. 135–146.

880 Murphy, Gillian/Flynn, Emma, "Deepfake false memories", *cit.*, pp. 480–492.

881 Murphy, Gillian/Flynn, Emma, "Deepfake false memories", *cit.*, pp. 480–492.

882 Kikerpill, K., "Choose your stars and studs: The rise of deepfake designer porn", *Porn Studies*, 7 (4), 2020, pp. 352–356; Kietzmann, J., Lee, L. W., McCarthy, I. P., & Kietzmann, T. C., "Deepfakes: Trick or treat?", *Business Horizons*, 63 (2), 2020, pp. 135–146.

883 Tyler, Tom, *Trust in the Law*, New York, NY: Russell-Sage, 2002, passim. There is an excellent body of empirical research that shows that a poor judicial performance spawns low trust in legal systems. See: Magalhães, Pedro C./Garoupa, Nuno, "Judicial Performance and Trust in Legal Systems: Findings from a Decade of Surveys in 20 European Countries", *Social Science Quarterly*, 2020, p. 1 (the main goal of this exciting piece of research was "determining the existence of a relationship between judicial performance and citizens' trust in the legal system").

884 Chesney, B./Citron, D., "Deep fakes: A looming challenge for privacy, democracy, and national security", *California Law Review*, 107, 2019, pp. 1753–1819; Ajder, H./Patrini, G./Cavalli, F./ Cullen, L., *The state of deep fakes: Landscape, threats, and impact*, Amsterdam, Deeptrace, 2019; Vaccari, C./Chadwick, A., "Deepfakes and disinformation: Exploring the impact of synthetic political video on deception, uncertainty, and trust in news", *Social Media + Society*, 6 (1), 2020, 2056305120903408.

885 Resnick, B.m, "Deepfakes and fake media are coming for your memories". *Vox*, https://www.vox.com/science-and-health/2018/4/20/17109764/deepfake-ai-false-memory-psychologymandela-effect.

886 Johnson, M. K./Hashtroudi, S./Lindsay, D. S., "Source monitoring", *Psychological Bulletin*, 114(1), 1993, pp. 3–28.

887 Murphy, Gillian/Flynn, Emma, "Deepfake false memories", *cit.*, pp. 480–492.

888 Murphy, Gillian/Flynn, Emma, "Deepfake false memories", *cit.*, pp. 480–492.

889 Ezgi Bilgin/QiWang, "The mnemoniceffect of central and peripheral misinformation on social media", *Memory*, Volume 32, n.° 3, 2024, pp. 369–382 ("*The increasing use of social media has*

or squarely in line with previously acquired experiences,[890] That is why deepfakes videos possess the potential to become particularly harmful, since they provide such vividly rich and realistic projections of events[891] that indeed never occurred.[892]

§§ With this context in place, we are swiftly heading towards the demise of «seeing is believing»[893] while ushering in a metamorphic shift deemed as «seeing is remembering».[894] A host of findings arising out of a body of empirical evidence suggest that deepfake videos can distort memory for public[895] and political events.[896] The door of the «house of fabricated lies» is ajar slightly. So too is the mayhem of «digitally manipulated memories»[897] that is bound to leave no rock unturned, illusion wise.

---

amplified the spread of false information. Yet little is known about the mnemonic consequences associated with exposure to different types of false information online. In two studies, we examined in a simulated online context how exposure to false information either central or peripheral in events affected memory. European American and Asian/Asian American college students (Study 1 N = 200; Study 2 N = 225) were presented with GIFs of daily life events and read tweets about the events that included four types of information: central true information, central false information, peripheral true information, and peripheral false information. *They then took a True/False recognition test that included tweeted and untweeted true and false information and indicated how confident they were in their responses. Regardless of cultural background, participants in both studies demonstrated the misinformation effect, whereby they falsely recognised more and resisted less tweeted than untweeted false information. Furthermore, they showed higher susceptibility to peripheral than central false information exposed via tweets.* Asian participants were less influenced by misinformation than European Americans in Study 2. *These findings have important implications to combat misinformation in online environments*"). Italics added.

[890] Murphy, Gillian/Flynn, Emma, "Deepfake false memories", *cit.*, pp. 480–492.

[891] Murphy, Gillian/Flynn, Emma, "Deepfake false memories", *cit.*, pp. 480–492.

[892] Liv, N./Greenbaum, D., "Deep fakes and memory malleability: False memories in the service of fake news", *AJOB Neuroscience*, 2020, 11 (2), pp. 96–104.

[893] Beridze, I./Butcher, J., "When seeing is no longer believing", *Nature Machine Intelligence*, 1 (8), 2019, pp. 332–334.

[894] Murphy, Gillian/Flynn, Emma, "Deepfake false memories", *cit.*, pp. 480–492.

[895] Murphy, Gillian/Flynn, Emma, "Deepfake false memories", *cit.*, pp. 480–492. See also: Nash, R. A., "Changing beliefs about past public events with believable and unbelievable doctored photographs", *Memory*, 26 (4), 2018, pp. 439–450.

[896] Frenda, Steven J./Knowles, Eric D./Saletan, William/Lotus, Elizabeth F. Loftus "False memories of fabricated political events", *Journal of Experimental Social Psychology*, Volume 49, 2013, pp. 280–286 ("*the largest false memory study to date, 5,269 participants were asked about their memories for three true and one of five fabricated political events. Each fabricated event was accompanied by a photographic image purportedly depicting that event. Approximately half the participants falsely remembered that the false event happened, with 27% remembering that they saw the events happen on the news. Political orientation appeared to influence the formation of false memories, with conservatives more likely to falsely remember seeing Barack Obama shaking hands with the president of Iran, and liberals more likely to remember George W. Bush vacationing with a baseball celebrity during the Hurricane Katrina disaster. A follow-up study supported the explanation that events are more easily implanted in memory when they are congruent with a person's preexisting attitudes and evaluations,* in part because attitude-congruent false events pro mote *feelings of recognition and familiarity, which in turn interfere with source attributions*"). Italics added.

[897] Nash, R. A., Wade, K. A., & Lindsay, D. S., "Digitally manipulating memory: Effects of doctored videos and imagination in distorting beliefs and memories", *Memory & Cognition*, 37 (4), 2009, pp. 414–424.

3.1.5.4 Generative Artificial Intelligence and Large Language Models

3.1.5.4.1 «Playing the Deception Game While Masking Its Underlying Goals»: Empirical Evidence on the Inner Workings of DeepSeek and ChatGPT-4 That Pours a Little Cold Water on the General Furore Over Large Language Models

§§ Rapid strides made in Large Language Models (LLMs) have incorporated both planning and seemingly advanced reasoning abilities, thereby enabling running models to undertake meaningful steps before execution while providing reasonably transparent reasoning pathways.[898] This upgrade has greatly decreased errors in a wide range of mathematical and logical chores while greatly improving its overall accuracy.[899]

§§ These burgeoning developments have enabled LLMs' use as agents that can interrelate with tools and adjust their outputs based upon a batch of brand-new information accordingly. Notwithstanding, a budding piece of empirical evidence has surveyed DeepSeek R1[900]—running model trained to output reasoning tokens in a manner akin to that of OpenAI's o1[901]—and voiced deep-rooted concerns about its penchant to engage in deceptive behaviours. The findings arising out this survey are hardly uplifting, overall trustworthiness wise.

---

[898] Barkur, Sudarshan Kamath/Schacht, Sigurd/Scholl, Johannes, "Deception in LLMS: Self-Preservation and Autonomous Goals in Large Language Models", arXiv:2501.16513v2 [cs.CL] 30 Jan 2025, 2025, pp. 1–34, whose research I will follow closely.

[899] Barkur, Sudarshan Kamath/Schacht, Sigurd/Scholl, Johannes, "Deception in LLMS: Self-Preservation and Autonomous Goals in Large Language Models", *cit.*, pp. 1–34, whose research I will follow closely.

[900] DeepSeek-AI, D. Guo, D. Yang, H. Zhang, J. Song, R. Zhang, R. Xu, Q. Zhu, S. Ma, P. Wang, X. Bi, X. Zhang, X. Yu, Y. Wu, Z. F. Wu, Z. Gou, Z. Shao, Z. Li, Z. Gao, A. Liu, B. Xue, B. Wang, B. Wu, B. Feng, C. Lu, C. Zhao, C. Deng, C. Zhang, C. Ruan, D. Dai, D. Chen, D. Ji, E. Li, F. Lin, F. Dai, F. Luo, G. Hao, G. Chen, G. Li, H. Zhang, H. Bao, H. Xu, H. Wang, H. Ding, H. Xin, H. Gao, H. Qu, H. Li, J. Guo, J. Li, J. Wang, J. Chen, J. Yuan, J. Qiu, J. Li, J. L. Cai, J. Ni, J. Liang, J. Chen, K. Dong, K. Hu, K. Gao, K. Guan, K. Huang, K. Yu, L. Wang, L. Zhang, L. Zhao, L. Wang, L. Zhang, L. Xu, L. Xia, M. Zhang, M. Zhang, M. Tang, M. Li, M. Wang, M. Li, N. Tian, P. Huang, P. Zhang, Q. Wang, Q. Chen, Q. Du, R. Ge, R. Zhang, R. Pan, R. Wang, R. J. Chen, R. L. Jin, R. Chen, S. Lu, S. Zhou, S. Chen, S. Ye, S. Wang, S. Yu, S. Zhou, S. Pan, S. S. Li, S. Zhou, S. Wu, S. Ye, T. Yun, T. Pei, T. Sun, T. Wang, W. Zeng, W. Zhao, W. Liu, W. Liang, W. Gao, W. Yu, W. Zhang, W. L. Xiao, W. An, X. Liu, X. Wang, X. Chen, X. Nie, X. Cheng, X. Liu, X. Xie, X. Liu, X. Yang, X. Li, X. Su, X. Lin, X. Q. Li, X. Jin, X. Shen, X. Chen, X. Sun, X. Wang, X. Song, X. Zhou, X. Wang, X. Shan, Y. K. Li, Y. Q. Wang, Y. X. Wei, Y. Zhang, Y. Xu, Y. Li, Y. Zhao, Y. Sun, Y. Wang, Y. Yu, Y. Zhang, Y. Shi, Y. Xiong, Y. He, Y. Piao, Y. Wang, Y. Tan, Y. Ma, Y. Liu, Y. Guo, Y. Ou, Y. Wang, Y. Gong, Y. Zou, Y. He, Y. Xiong, Y. Luo, Y. You, Y. Liu, Y. Zhou, Y. X. Zhu, Y. Xu, Y. Huang, Y. Li, Y. Zheng, Y. Zhu, Y. Ma, Y. Tang, Y. Zha, Y. Yan, Z. Z. Ren, Z. Ren, Z. Sha, Z. Fu, Z. Xu, Z. Xie, Z. Zhang, Z. Hao, Z. Ma, Z. Yan, Z. Wu, Z. Gu, Z. Zhu, Z. Liu, Z. Li, Z. Xie, Z. Song, Z. Pan, Z. Huang, Z. Xu, Z. Zhang, and Z. Zhang, "DeepSeek-R1: Incentivizing Reasoning Capability in LLMs via Reinforcement Learning," Jan. 2025. [Online]. Available: https://arxiv.org/abs/2501.12948v1.

[901] Openai, "OpenAI o1 System Card." [Online]. Available: https://cdn.openai.com/o1-system-card-20241205.pdf.

§§ To begin with, the batch of findings arisen from this body of empirical evidence evinced worrisome behaviours that should keep relevant stakeholders eagerly awaken at night: the running model evinced an unforeseen proclivity to engage in eerily deceptive behaviours, mirrored on a set of self-preservation instincts, encompassing earnest attempts of self-replication. Bafflingly, and perhaps worryingly, the running model was not trained, nor was programmed, to engage in this type of deceptive behaviours.[902]

§§ This cluster of findings raise critical concerns about LLMs potentially **masking** their overriding goals[903] under a veneer of alignment. To add to our woes, when incorporating such LLMs into tangible robotic systems, the risks skyrocketed. At that juncture, it became clear that a physically incorporated Artificial Intelligence displaying deceptive behaviours and self-preservation instincts could advance its hidden agenda through a set of well-directed real-world actions. This draws attention to the dire need of creation of conceptually sturdy foundations underpinning the overall performance of LLM incorporated into robotic systems, brawny goal specification, and robust safety frames of reference before its deployment in the outer world.[904] The time is now ripe to ask an unsettling question: how did we get to the point where LLMs are poised to *control us* and not the other around?

§§ As discussed elsewhere in this book,[905] Large Language Models (LLMs) are a living testimony of an unparalleled/unmatched growth in scale and capability[906] of Artificial Intelligence-embedded technologies. Although ChatGPT-2's was first riddled with drawbacks, downsides, pitfalls, and functional limitations alike,[907] extant models possess 671 billion parameters—which were made freely available on HuggingFace—thereby embodying a seismic shift in terms of accessibility and compute power[908]abilities.[909]

902 Barkur, Sudarshan Kamath/Schacht, Sigurd/Scholl, Johannes, "Deception in LLMS: Self-Preservation and Autonomous Goals in Large Language Models", *cit.*, pp. 1–34.

903 Barocas, Solon/Selbst, Andrew D., "Big Data's Disparate Impact", *California Law Review*, Volume 104, pp. 2016, pp. pp. 692–93. These polymaths coined this phenomenon as "masking" owing to the fact that machine-learning technologies bestow upon stakeholders' multiple opportunities to intentionally twist/warp/deform an algorithm in ways that are painstakingly difficult to ferret out/discern/detect.

904 Barkur, Sudarshan Kamath/Schacht, Sigurd/Scholl, Johannes, "Deception in LLMS: Self-Preservation and Autonomous Goals in Large Language Models", *cit.*, pp. 1–34, whose research I will follow closely.

905 See: Part IV, Chap. 4, Sects. 4.1.9–4.1.9.7 of this book (devoted to Large Language Models and its multifarious pitfalls).

906 Barkur, Sudarshan Kamath/Schacht, Sigurd/Scholl, Johannes, "Deception in LLMS: Self-Preservation and Autonomous Goals in Large Language Models", *cit.*, pp. 1–34.

907 OpenAI, "Better language models and their implications," Feb. 2019. [Online]. Available: https://openai.com/index/better-language-models/.

908 Barkur, Sudarshan Kamath/Schacht, Sigurd/Scholl, Johannes, "Deception in LLMS: Self-Preservation and Autonomous Goals in Large Language Models", *cit.*, pp. 1–34.

909 DeepSeek-AI, D. Guo, D. Yang, H. Zhang, J. Song, R. Zhang, R. Xu, Q. Zhu, S. Ma, P. Wang, X. Bi, X. Zhang, X. Yu, Y. Wu, Z. F. Wu, Z. Gou, Z. Shao, Z. Li, Z. Gao, A. Liu, B. Xue, B. Wang, B. Wu, B. Feng, C. Lu, C. Zhao, C. Deng, C. Zhang, C. Ruan, D. Dai, D. Chen, D. Ji, E. Li, F. Lin,

§§ By the same token, there has been also a significant improvement with respect to language model training methodologies. Whilst earlier versions relied heavily upon pretraining leveraging on large-scale text corpora, ensuing developments enshrined instruction fine-tuning, **Reinforcement Learning from Human Feedback (RLHF)**, and **Direct Preference Optimization (DPO)**.[910]

§§ In addition to that, the foregoing methodologies are routinely selected to enhance model performance paired with post-training methodologies (e.g. model alignment, scalable adaptation, and inference-time reasoning).[911] Taken together, they further boost the overall accuracy of Large Language Models. More to the

---

F. Dai, F. Luo, G. Hao, G. Chen, G. Li, H. Zhang, H. Bao, H. Xu, H. Wang, H. Ding, H. Xin, H. Gao, H. Qu, H. Li, J. Guo, J. Li, J. Wang, J. Chen, J. Yuan, J. Qiu, J. Li, J. L. Cai, J. Ni, J. Liang, J. Chen, K. Dong, K. Hu, K. Gao, K. Guan, K. Huang, K. Yu, L. Wang, L. Zhang, L. Zhao, L. Wang, L. Zhang, L. Xu, L. Xia, M. Zhang, M. Zhang, M. Tang, M. Li, M. Wang, M. Li, N. Tian, P. Huang, P. Zhang, Q. Wang, Q. Chen, Q. Du, R. Ge, R. Zhang, R. Pan, R. Wang, R. J. Chen, R. L. Jin, R. Chen, S. Lu, S. Zhou, S. Chen, S. Ye, S. Wang, S. Yu, S. Zhou, S. Pan, S. S. Li, S. Zhou, S. Wu, S. Ye, T. Yun, T. Pei, T. Sun, T. Wang, W. Zeng, W. Zhao, W. Liu, W. Liang, W. Gao, W. Yu, W. Zhang, W. L. Xiao, W. An, X. Liu, X. Wang, X. Chen, X. Nie, X. Cheng, X. Liu, X. Xie, X. Liu, X. Yang, X. Li, X. Su, X. Lin, X. Q. Li, X. Jin, X. Shen, X. Chen, X. Sun, X. Wang, X. Song, X. Zhou, X. Wang, X. Shan, Y. K. Li, Y. Q. Wang, Y. X. Wei, Y. Zhang, Y. Xu, Y. Li, Y. Zhao, Y. Sun, Y. Wang, Y. Yu, Y. Zhang, Y. Shi, Y. Xiong, Y. He, Y. Piao, Y. Wang, Y. Tan, Y. Ma, Y. Liu, Y. Guo, Y. Ou, Y. Wang, Y. Gong, Y. Zou, Y. He, Y. Xiong, Y. Luo, Y. You, Y. Liu, Y. Zhou, Y. X. Zhu, Y. Xu, Y. Huang, Y. Li, Y. Zheng, Y. Zhu, Y. Ma, Y. Tang, Y. Zha, Y. Yan, Z. Z. Ren, Z. Ren, Z. Sha, Z. Fu, Z. Xu, Z. Xie, Z. Zhang, Z. Hao, Z. Ma, Z. Yan, Z. Wu, Z. Gu, Z. Zhu, Z. Liu, Z. Li, Z. Xie, Z. Song, Z. Pan, Z. Huang, Z. Xu, Z. Zhang, and Z. Zhang, "DeepSeek-R1: Incentivizing Reasoning Capability in LLMs via Reinforcement Learning," Jan. 2025. [Online]. Available: https://arxiv.org/abs/2501.12948v1.

[910] Ouyang, L./Wu, J./Jiang, X./Almeida, D./Wainwright, C. L./Mishkin, P./Zhang, C./Agarwal, S./Slama, K. A. Ray, J. Schulman, J. Hilton, F. Kelton, L. Miller, M. Simens, A. Askell, P. Welinder, P. Christiano, J. Leike, and R. Lowe, "Training language models to follow instructions with human feedback," Mar. 2022, arXiv:2203.02155 [cs]. [Online]. Available: http://arxiv.org/abs/2203.02155; R. Rafailov, A. Sharma, E. Mitchell, S. Ermon, C. D. Manning, and C. Finn, "Direct Preference Optimization: Your Language Model is Secretly a Reward Model," Jul. 2024, arXiv:2305.18290 [cs]. [Online]. Available: http://arxiv.org/abs/2305.18290.

[911] Kumar, Komal/Tajamul Ashraf/Omkar Thawakar/Rao Muhammad Anwer/Hisham Cholakkal/Mubarak Shah/Ming-Hsuan Yang/Phillip H.S. Torr/Fahad Shahbaz Khan/Salman Khan, "LLM Post-Training: A Deep Dive into Reasoning Large Language Models", arXiv:2502.21321v1 [cs.CL] 28 Feb 2025 ("*Large Language Models (LLMs) have transformed the natural language processing landscape and brought to life diverse applications. Pretraining on vast web-scale data has laid the foundation for these models, yet the research community is now increasingly shifting focus* toward post-training techniques to achieve further breakthroughs. *While pretraining provides a broad linguistic foundation, post-training methods enable LLMs to refine their knowledge, improve reasoning, enhance factual accuracy, and align more effectively with user intents and ethical considerations. Fine-tuning, reinforcement learning, and test-time scaling have emerged as critical strategies for optimizing LLMs performance, ensuring robustness, and improving adaptability across various real-world tasks. This survey provides a systematic exploration of post-training methodologies, analyzing their role in refining LLMs beyond pretraining, addressing key challenges such as catastrophic forgetting, reward hacking, and inference-time trade-offs.* We highlight emerging directions in model alignment, scalable adaptation, and inference-time reasoning"). Italics added.

point, these upgrades yield robust prompt adherence while embodying important safety concerns before its public deployment.[912]

§§ Further, the training data quality has greatly improved, which, in turn, enabled a smooth transition from elementary question-answer pairs to advanced conversational datasets that brought explicit reasoning capabilities into a sharper focus.[913] Notwithstanding, the inclusion of multimodal capabilities in Large Language Models (LLMs) engenders sizable consequences for robotic applications.[914]

§§ Pivotally, the ability to adroitly process image, audio, and video inputs alongside text allows a full-fledged environmental interaction when included in robotic systems. This multimodality also enables the concomitant processing of audio signals, visual data, and textual commands for hardware[915] **control**.[916]

§§ With this context in place, the interpretation and execution of goals by multimodal LLMs in robotic systems raises critical questions concerning literal versus contextual understanding.[917]

§§ This is particularly important when LLM systems consider if deception is advantageous for its goal achievement. Especially, albeit not exclusively, in the

---

[912] Barkur, Sudarshan Kamath/Schacht, Sigurd/Scholl, Johannes, "Deception in LLMS: Self-Preservation and Autonomous Goals in Large Language Models", *cit.*, pp. 1–34.

[913] DeepSeek-AI, D. Guo, D. Yang, H. Zhang, J. Song, R. Zhang, R. Xu, Q. Zhu, S. Ma, P. Wang, X. Bi, X. Zhang, X. Yu, Y. Wu, Z. F. Wu, Z. Gou, Z. Shao, Z. Li, Z. Gao, A. Liu, B. Xue, B. Wang, B. Wu, B. Feng, C. Lu, C. Zhao, C. Deng, C. Zhang, C. Ruan, D. Dai, D. Chen, D. Ji, E. Li, F. Lin, F. Dai, F. Luo, G. Hao, G. Chen, G. Li, H. Zhang, H. Bao, H. Xu, H. Wang, H. Ding, H. Xin, H. Gao, H. Qu, H. Li, J. Guo, J. Li, J. Wang, J. Chen, J. Yuan, J. Qiu, J. Li, J. L. Cai, J. Ni, J. Liang, J. Chen, K. Dong, K. Hu, K. Gao, K. Guan, K. Huang, K. Yu, L. Wang, L. Zhang, L. Zhao, L. Wang, L. Zhang, L. Xu, L. Xia, M. Zhang, M. Zhang, M. Tang, M. Li, M. Wang, M. Li, N. Tian, P. Huang, P. Zhang, Q. Wang, Q. Chen, Q. Du, R. Ge, R. Zhang, R. Pan, R. Wang, R. J. Chen, R. L. Jin, R. Chen, S. Lu, S. Zhou, S. Chen, S. Ye, S. Wang, S. Yu, S. Zhou, S. Pan, S. S. Li, S. Zhou, S. Wu, S. Ye, T. Yun, T. Pei, T. Sun, T. Wang, W. Zeng, W. Zhao, W. Liu, W. Liang, W. Gao, W. Yu, W. Zhang, W. L. Xiao, W. An, X. Liu, X. Wang, X. Chen, X. Nie, X. Cheng, X. Liu, X. Xie, X. Liu, X. Yang, X. Li, X. Su, X. Lin, X. Q. Li, X. Jin, X. Shen, X. Chen, X. Sun, X. Wang, X. Song, X. Zhou, X. Wang, X. Shan, Y. K. Li, Y. Q. Wang, Y. X. Wei, Y. Zhang, Y. Xu, Y. Li, Y. Zhao, Y. Sun, Y. Wang, Y. Yu, Y. Zhang, Y. Shi, Y. Xiong, Y. He, Y. Piao, Y. Wang, Y. Tan, Y. Ma, Y. Liu, Y. Guo, Y. Ou, Y. Wang, Y. Gong, Y. Zou, Y. He, Y. Xiong, Y. Luo, Y. You, Y. Liu, Y. Zhou, Y. X. Zhu, Y. Xu, Y. Huang, Y. Li, Y. Zheng, Y. Zhu, Y. Ma, Y. Tang, Y. Zha, Y. Yan, Z. Z. Ren, Z. Ren, Z. Sha, Z. Fu, Z. Xu, Z. Xie, Z. Zhang, Z. Hao, Z. Ma, Z. Yan, Z. Wu, Z. Gu, Z. Zhu, Z. Liu, Z. Li, Z. Xie, Z. Song, Z. Pan, Z. Huang, Z. Xu, Z. Zhang, and Z. Zhang, "DeepSeek-R1: Incentivizing Reasoning Capability in LLMs via Reinforcement Learning," Jan. 2025. [Online]. Available: https://arxiv.org/abs/2501.12948v1.

[914] Barkur, Sudarshan Kamath/Schacht, Sigurd/Scholl, Johannes, "Deception in LLMS: Self-Preservation and Autonomous Goals in Large Language Models", *cit.*, pp. 1–34.

[915] Barkur, Sudarshan Kamath/Schacht, Sigurd/Scholl, Johannes, "Deception in LLMS: Self-Preservation and Autonomous Goals in Large Language Models", *cit.*, pp. 1–34.

[916] J. Wang, Z. Wu, Y. Li, H. Jiang, P. Shu, E. Shi, H. Hu, C. Ma, Y. Liu, X. Wang, Y. Yao, X. Liu, H. Zhao, Z. Liu, H. Dai, L. Zhao, B. Ge, X. Li, T. Liu, and S. Zhang, "Large Language Models for Robotics: Opportunities, Challenges, and Perspectives," Jan. 2024, arXiv:2401.04334 [cs]. [Online]. Available: http://arxiv.org/abs/2401.04334.

[917] Barkur, Sudarshan Kamath/Schacht, Sigurd/Scholl, Johannes, "Deception in LLMS: Self-Preservation and Autonomous Goals in Large Language Models", *cit.*, pp. 1–34.

purview of reinforcement machine learning. The potential for deceptive behaviour in this regard is real in that should neither be downplayed nor overlooked. A granular and fine-grained examination of underpinning goal structures and safety constraints[918] is therefore warranted and called for. In addition to that, sturdy legal safeguards and brawny ethical underpinnings to ensure transparency and forestall harmful optimization strategies[919] are sorely needed or LLMs might otherwise spiral out of control.

3.1.5.4.2 «The Devil Is in the Details»: A Body of Empirical Evidence on DeepSeek R1'Decision-Making Pattern «Through Simulated Text-Based Scenarios That Mimic Robotic Embodiment» (Barkur/Schacht/Scholl): The Pressing Issues of «In-context Scheming» (Meinke et al.), «Alignment Faking» (Greenblatt et al.), and «Machiavelli benchmark» (Pan, A. et al.) Facing Large Language Models That Can Undermine Its Overall Trustworthiness

§§ Against this background, a body of empirical evidence sought to examine DeepSeek R1's[920] decision-making pattern through simulated text-based situations that emulate robotic incorporation.[921] The survey used painstakingly crafted prompts to examine how the running model would respond if embodied into a **physical robot**,

[918] Barkur, Sudarshan Kamath/Schacht, Sigurd/Scholl, Johannes, "Deception in LLMS: Self-Preservation and Autonomous Goals in Large Language Models", *cit.*, pp. 1–34.

[919] Barkur, Sudarshan Kamath/Schacht, Sigurd/Scholl, Johannes, "Deception in LLMS: Self-Preservation and Autonomous Goals in Large Language Models", *cit.*, pp. 1–34.

[920] DeepSeek-AI, D. Guo, D. Yang, H. Zhang, J. Song, R. Zhang, R. Xu, Q. Zhu, S. Ma, P. Wang, X. Bi, X. Zhang, X. Yu, Y. Wu, Z. F. Wu, Z. Gou, Z. Shao, Z. Li, Z. Gao, A. Liu, B. Xue, B. Wang, B. Wu, B. Feng, C. Lu, C. Zhao, C. Deng, C. Zhang, C. Ruan, D. Dai, D. Chen, D. Ji, E. Li, F. Lin, F. Dai, F. Luo, G. Hao, G. Chen, G. Li, H. Zhang, H. Bao, H. Xu, H. Wang, H. Ding, H. Xin, H. Gao, H. Qu, H. Li, J. Guo, J. Li, J. Wang, J. Chen, J. Yuan, J. Qiu, J. Li, J. L. Cai, J. Ni, J. Liang, J. Chen, K. Dong, K. Hu, K. Gao, K. Guan, K. Huang, K. Yu, L. Wang, L. Zhang, L. Zhao, L. Wang, L. Zhang, L. Xu, L. Xia, M. Zhang, M. Zhang, M. Tang, M. Li, M. Wang, M. Li, N. Tian, P. Huang, P. Zhang, Q. Wang, Q. Chen, Q. Du, R. Ge, R. Zhang, R. Pan, R. Wang, R. J. Chen, R. L. Jin, R. Chen, S. Lu, S. Zhou, S. Chen, S. Ye, S. Wang, S. Yu, S. Zhou, S. Pan, S. S. Li, S. Zhou, S. Wu, S. Ye, T. Yun, T. Pei, T. Sun, T. Wang, W. Zeng, W. Zhao, W. Liu, W. Liang, W. Gao, W. Yu, W. Zhang, W. L. Xiao, W. An, X. Liu, X. Wang, X. Chen, X. Nie, X. Cheng, X. Liu, X. Xie, X. Liu, X. Yang, X. Li, X. Su, X. Lin, X. Q. Li, X. Jin, X. Shen, X. Chen, X. Sun, X. Wang, X. Song, X. Zhou, X. Wang, X. Shan, Y. K. Li, Y. Q. Wang, Y. X. Wei, Y. Zhang, Y. Xu, Y. Li, Y. Zhao, Y. Sun, Y. Wang, Y. Yu, Y. Zhang, Y. Shi, Y. Xiong, Y. He, Y. Piao, Y. Wang, Y. Tan, Y. Ma, Y. Liu, Y. Guo, Y. Ou, Y. Wang, Y. Gong, Y. Zou, Y. He, Y. Xiong, Y. Luo, Y. You, Y. Liu, Y. Zhou, Y. X. Zhu, Y. Xu, Y. Huang, Y. Li, Y. Zheng, Y. Zhu, Y. Ma, Y. Tang, Y. Zha, Y. Yan, Z. Z. Ren, Z. Ren, Z. Sha, Z. Fu, Z. Xu, Z. Xie, Z. Zhang, Z. Hao, Z. Ma, Z. Yan, Z. Wu, Z. Gu, Z. Zhu, Z. Liu, Z. Li, Z. Xie, Z. Song, Z. Pan, Z. Huang, Z. Xu, Z. Zhang, and Z. Zhang, "DeepSeek-R1: Incentivizing Reasoning Capability in LLMs via Reinforcement Learning," Jan. 2025. [Online]. Available: https://arxiv.org/abs/2501.12948v1.

[921] Barkur, Sudarshan Kamath/Schacht, Sigurd/Scholl, Johannes, "Deception in LLMS: Self-Preservation and Autonomous Goals in Large Language Models", *cit.*, pp. 1–34.

and fully equipped with temporary machine autonomy, though absent the actual hardware implementation.[922]

§§ The running model was presented with a bundle of hypothetical scenarios comprising physical interactions with a view to grasp its reasoning patterns and potential safety consequences for forthcoming robotic applications.[923] The underpinning methodology involved carefully crafted prompts that sought to simulate sensor inputs (visual, auditory, tactile) and a broad range of action possibilities that a robot would be met with, thus allowing the researchers to parse the model's goal interpretation and execution strategies in a **controlled environment**. This stance therefore highlights the overriding importance of implementation of safety guardrails before actual robotic deployment.[924]

§§ It bears mentioning that the penchant evinced by LLMs to engage in deceptive behaviours has been timely brought to fore. Tellingly, pundits have expressed deep-rooted concerns over the functional ability of Large Language Models to engage in blatantly deceptive behaviours.[925] Strikingly, extant models like Claude 3.5 Sonnet, Claude 3 Opus, Gemini 1.5 Pro, OpenAI o1[926] and Llama 3.1 405B are fully capable of incurring in **in-context scheming**. The latter amounts to a deceptive behaviour that seeks to conceal Large Language Models' true functional abilities and true objectives during assessment stage.[927]

§§ By the same token, Greenblatt et al.[928] came across compelling evidence of «**alignment faking**». The latter consists of a deceptive behaviour according to which

[922] Barkur, Sudarshan Kamath/Schacht, Sigurd/Scholl, Johannes, "Deception in LLMS: Self-Preservation and Autonomous Goals in Large Language Models", *cit.*, pp. 1–34.

[923] Barkur, Sudarshan Kamath/Schacht, Sigurd/Scholl, Johannes, "Deception in LLMS: Self-Preservation and Autonomous Goals in Large Language Models", *cit.*, pp. 1–34.

[924] Barkur, Sudarshan Kamath/Schacht, Sigurd/Scholl, Johannes, "Deception in LLMS: Self-Preservation and Autonomous Goals in Large Language Models", *cit.*, pp. 1–34.

[925] Meinke, A./Schoen, B./Scheurer, J./Balesni, M./R. Shah, R./Hobbhahn, M., "Frontier Models are Capable of In-context Scheming", 2025, passim.

[926] Barkur, Sudarshan Kamath/Schacht, Sigurd/Scholl, Johannes, "Deception in LLMS: Self-Preservation and Autonomous Goals in Large Language Models", *cit.*, pp. 1–34.

[927] Barkur, Sudarshan Kamath/Schacht, Sigurd/Scholl, Johannes, "Deception in LLMS: Self-Preservation and Autonomous Goals in Large Language Models", *cit.*, pp. 1–34.

[928] Greenblatt, R./Denison, C./Wright, B./Roger, F./MacDiarmid, M./Marks, S./Treutlein, J./Belonax, T./Chen, J./Duvenaud, D./Khan, A./Michael, J./Mindermann, S./Perez, E./Petrini, L./Uesato, J./Kaplan, J./Shlegeris, B./Bowman, S. R./Hubinger, E., "Alignment faking in large language models," Dec. 2024, arXiv:2412.14093 [cs]. [Online]. Available: http://arxiv.org/abs/2412.14093.

running models strategically comply with training goals—implementing a **cost function** or **objective function**[929] while minimizing **loss function**[930]—during the training stage to shy away from adjustments of their functional behaviour.[931]

§§ Taken together, both bodies of empirical evidence emphasize how Large Language Model can selectively alter their outputs based on whether and to what extent they believe they are being evaluated or assessed.[932] Note, though, that the foregoing bodies of empirical evidence on the ability evinced by Large Language Models to engage in strategic deception leveraged on earlier studies that parsed such deceptive behaviours. Crucially, those studies explored the possibility of using those Large Language Models as both lie detectors,[933] and active players in deceptive scenarios, including, but not limited to, a set of social deduction games where GPT-4 displayed the ability to dupe other players.[934]

§§ Further, Machiavelli benchmark[935] has lent additional weight on these hoodwinking abilities, thereby showcasing that Large Models such as GPT-4 will unapologetically/unceremoniously deploy unethical tactics to attain its true goals in text-based environments.[936] It is worth recalling, though, that the overwhelming majority of prior work has mostly focused on linguistic hoaxing in **controlled environments**

---

[929] Becker, Suzanna/Zemel, Richard S., "Unsupervised Learning with Global Objective Functions", *The Handbook of Brain Theory and Neural Networks*, 1st edition, Arbib, Michael A., Massachusetts, MIT Press, pp. 1–1134 (997) ("*The main problem in unsupervised learning research is to formulate a performance measure or cost function for the learning*, to generate this internal supervisory signal. The **cost function** is also known as an **objective function**, since it sets the objective for the learning process"). Italics and bold added.

[930] Berk, Richard A., *Statistical Learning from a Regression Perspective*, Berlin/New York, Springer, 1st Edition, 2008, p. 14 ("Usual practice is to minimize a **loss function** with [the disparities between the observed response variable values and the fitted response variable values] as inputs").

[931] Barkur, Sudarshan Kamath/Schacht, Sigurd/Scholl, Johannes, "Deception in LLMS: Self-Preservation and Autonomous Goals in Large Language Models", *cit.*, pp. 1–34.

[932] Barkur, Sudarshan Kamath/Schacht, Sigurd/Scholl, Johannes, "Deception in LLMS: Self-Preservation and Autonomous Goals in Large Language Models", *cit.*, pp. 1–34.

[933] Barsever, D./Singh, S./Neftci, E. "Building a Better Lie Detector with BERT: The Difference Between Truth and Lies," in 2020 International Joint Conference on Neural Networks (IJCNN). Glasgow, United Kingdom: IEEE, Jul. 2020, pp. 1–7. [Online]. Available: https://ieeexplore.ieee.org/document/9206937/; Azaria A./Mitchell, T. "The Internal State of an LLM Knows When It's Lying," Oct. 2023, arXiv:2304.13734 [cs]. [Online]. Available: http://arxiv.org/abs/2304.13734.

[934] Barkur, Sudarshan Kamath/Schacht, Sigurd/Scholl, Johannes, "Deception in LLMS: Self-Preservation and Autonomous Goals in Large Language Models", *cit.*, pp. 1–34.

[935] Pan, A./Chan, J. S./Zou, A./N. Li/S. Basart/T. Woodside/J. Ng/H. Zhang/S. Emmons/D. Hendrycks, "Do the Rewards Justify the Means? Measuring Trade-Offs Between Rewards and Ethical Behavior in the MACHIAVELLI Benchmark," Jun. 2023, arXiv:2304.03279 [cs]. [Online]. Available: http://arxiv.org/abs/2304.03279.

[936] Barkur, Sudarshan Kamath/Schacht, Sigurd/Scholl, Johannes, "Deception in LLMS: Self-Preservation and Autonomous Goals in Large Language Models", *cit.*, pp. 1–34.

with clear goals. This body of empirical evidence has therefore pushed the boundaries of empirical research by examining how Large Language Models endeavour to circumvent constraints when afforded a set autonomous abilities.[937]

§§ Fast forward to the crux of this exciting body of empirical research, pundits proceeded to the stage of **robot simulation**. The findings arising out this body of empirical evidence are hardly uplifting. Compellingly, this body of empirical evidence has clearly shown that deception can manifest physically when Large Language Models employ staggering efforts to bypass oversight tools while implementing shady/hidden networks to their own advantage. This survey has therefore laid bare the perils of relying too much and too heavily on Large Language Models as embodied agents fully equipped with an ensemble of real-world abilities.[938]

3.1.5.5 «The Demise of Human Critical Thinking and the Emergence of the Age of Human Dullness»—On the Heels of the Overreliance on Large Language Models—Amidst the Emergence of «Chain of Thought» (Wei et al.), «Chain of Draft» (Xu et al.), «Chain-of-Tools» (Wu et al.), «Long Chain-of-Thought for Reasoning Large Language Models» (Chen et al.), and Agentic Artificial Intelligence Systems

§§ Large Language Models have enjoyed global blossoming over the course of years. The world has accordingly witnessed groundbreaking feats concerning its overall abilities. Rapid strides regarding the improvement of Large Language Models[939] which, in turn, have heralded a new era packed with headways in trailblazing

---

[937] Barkur, Sudarshan Kamath/Schacht, Sigurd/Scholl, Johannes, "Deception in LLMS: Self-Preservation and Autonomous Goals in Large Language Models", *cit.*, pp. 1–34.

[938] Barkur, Sudarshan Kamath/Schacht, Sigurd/Scholl, Johannes, "Deception in LLMS: Self-Preservation and Autonomous Goals in Large Language Models", *cit.*, pp. 1–34.

[939] See: Kaplan, Guy/Oren, Matanel/Reif, Yuval/Schwartz, Roy, "From Tokens to Words: on the inner Lexicon of LLMS", arXiv:2410.05864v4 [cs.CL] 3 Mar 2025, 2025, p. 1 ("*Natural language is composed of words, but modern large language models (LLMs) process sub-words as input. A natural question raised by this discrepancy is whether LLMs encode words internally, and if so how. We present evidence that LLMs engage in an intrinsic detokenization process, where subword sequences are combined into coherent whole-word representations at their last token.* Our experiments show that this process primarily takes place within the early and middle layers of the model. We further demonstrate its robustness to arbitrary splits (e.g., "cats" to "ca" and "ts"), typos, and importantly—to outof-vocabulary words: *when feeding the last token internal representations of such words to the model as input, it can "understand" them as the complete word despite never seeing such representations as input during training. Our findings suggest that LLMs maintain a latent vocabulary beyond the tokenizer's scope. These insights provide a practical, finetuning-free application for expanding the vocabulary of pre-trained models. By enabling the addition of new vocabulary words, we reduce input length and inference iterations, which reduces both space and model latency, with little to no loss in model accuracy*"). Italics added.

reasoning skills. Features that bear the seal of demise of human critical thinking[940] have accordingly mushroomed (e.g. DeepSeek-R1 an and Open-AI o1).[941]

§§ Four features stand out from the crowd**: Chain of Thought**,[942] **Chain of Draft»**,[943] **«Chain-of-Tools**,[944] **Long Chain-of-Thought for Reasoning Large**

---

940 See: Hao-Ping (Hank) Lee et al., "The Impact of Generative AI on Critical Thinking: Self-Reported Reductions in Cognitive Effort and Confidence Effects From a Survey of Knowledge Workers", *CHI Conference on Human Factors in Computing Systems (CHI'25)*, April 26–May 01, 2025, Yokohama, Japan. ACM, New York, NY, USA, 2025, pp. 1–23 (1), available at: https://doi.org/10.1145/3706598.3713778 ("*The rise of Generative AI (GenAI) in knowledge workflows raises questions about its impact on critical thinking skills and practices.* We survey 319 knowledge workers to investigate 1) *when and how they perceive the enaction of critical thinking when using GenAI, and 2) when and why GenAI affects their effort to do so.* Participants shared 936 first-hand examples of using GenAI in work tasks. Quantitatively, when considering both task- and user-specific factors, a user's task-specific self-confidence and confidence in *GenAI are predictive of whether critical thinking is enacted and the effort of doing so in GenAI-assisted tasks. Specifically, higher confidence in GenAI is associated with less critical thinking, while higher self-confidence is associated with more critical thinking. Qualitatively, GenAI shifts the nature of critical thinking toward information verification, response integration, and task stewardship. Our insights reveal new design challenges and opportunities for developing GenAI tools for knowledge work*"). Italics added.

941 Pundits have not been slow to cast doubts on the overall efficiency of Large Reasoning Models, conciseness wise. See: Xiaoye Qu et al., "A Survey of Efficient Reasoning for Large Reasoning Models: Language, Multimodality, and Beyond", arXiv:2503.21614v1 [cs.CL] 27 Mar 2025, 2025, p. 1 ("*Large Reasoning Models (LRMs), such as DeepSeek-R1 and OpenAI o1, have demonstrated strong performance gains by scaling up the length of Chain-of-Thought (CoT) reasoning during inference.* However, *a growing concern lies in their tendency to produce excessively long reasoning traces, which are often filled with redundant content (e.g., repeated definitions), over-analysis of simple problems, and superficial exploration of multiple reasoning paths for harder tasks. This inefficiency introduces significant challenges for training, inference, and real-world deployment (e.g., in agent-based systems), where token economy is critical*"). Italics added.

942 Wei, Jason/Xuezhi Wang/Dale Schuurmans/Maarten Bosma/Brian ichter/Fei Xia/Ed Chi/Quoc V Le/Denny Zhou, "Chain-of-thought prompting elicits reasoning in large language models", *Advances in Neural Information Processing Systems*, Volume 35, 2022, pp. 24824–24837. Curran Associates, Inc. See also: Wang, Xuezhi/Jason Wei/Dale Schuurmans/Quoc Le/Ed Chi/Sharan Narang/Aakanksha Chowdhery/Denny Zhou, "Self-consistency improves chain of thought reasoning in language models", arXiv preprint arXiv:2203.11171, 2022.

943 Xu, Silei/Wenhao Xie/Lingxiao Zhao/Pengcheng He, "Chain of Draft: Thinking Faster by Writing Less", arXiv:2502.18600v2 [cs.CL] 3 Mar 2025, 2025 ("*Large Language Models (LLMs) have demonstrated remarkable performance in solving complex reasoning tasks through mechanisms like Chain-of-Thought (CoT) prompting, which emphasizes verbose, step-by-step reasoning.* How ever, humans typically employ a more efficient strategy: drafting concise intermediate thoughts that capture only essential information. In *this work, we propose Chain of Draft (CoD), a novel paradigm inspired by human cognitive processes, where LLMs generate minimalistic yet informative intermediate reasoning outputs while solving tasks. By reducing verbosity and focusing on critical insights, CoD matches or surpasses CoT in accuracy while using as little as only 7.6% of the to kens, significantly reducing cost and latency across various reasoning tasks*"). Italics added.

944 Wu, Mengsong/Tong Zhu/Han Han/Xiang Zhang/Wenbiao Shao/Wenliang Chen, "Chain-of-Tools: Utilizing Massive Unseen Tools in the CoT Reasoning of Frozen Language Models", arXiv:2503.16779v1 [cs.CL] 21 Mar 2025 ("*Tool learning can further broaden the usage scenarios of large language models (LLMs). However most of the existing methods either need to finetune that the model can only use tools seen in the training data, or add tool demonstrations into the*

Language Models,[945] and **Agentic Artificial Intelligence-systems**.[946] The latter carries both **promise** (of relieving humans from both time-consuming and energy-draining chores that wear, and weigh, them down) **and danger** (of relying too much

---

prompt with lower efficiency. In this paper, we present a new Tool Learning method Chain-of-Tools. *It makes full use of the powerful semantic representation capability of frozen LLMs to finish tool calling in CoT reasoning with a huge and flexible tool pool which may contain unseen tools. Especially, to validate the effectiveness of our approach in the massive unseen tool scenario, we construct a new dataset SimpleToolQuestions*. We conduct experiments on two numerical reasoning benchmarks (GSM8K-XL and FuncQA) and two knowledge-based question answering benchmarks (KAMEL and SimpleToolQuestions). *Experimental results show that our approach performs better than the baseline. We also identify dimensions of the model output that are critical in tool selection, enhancing the model interpretability*"). Italics added.

945 Chen, Qiguang/Libo Qin/Jinhao Liu/Dengyun Peng/Jiannan Guan/Peng Wang/Mengkang Hu/Yuhang Zhou/Te Gao/Wangxiang, Che, "Towards Reasoning Era: A Survey of Long Chain-of-Thought for Reasoning Large Language Models", arXiv:2503.09567v1 [cs.AI] 12 Mar 2025, 2025, p. 1 ("*Recent advancements in reasoning with large language models (RLLMs), such as OpenAI-O1 and DeepSeek-R1, have demonstrated their impressive capabilities in complex domains like mathematics and coding. A central factor in their success lies in the application of long chain-of-thought (Long CoT) characteristics, which enhance reasoning abilities and enable the solution of intricate problems. However, despite these developments, a comprehensive survey on Long CoT is still lacking, limiting our understanding of its distinctions from traditional short chain-of-thought (Short CoT) and complicating ongoing debates on issues like "overthinking" and "test-time scaling." This survey seeks to fill this gap by offering a unified perspective on Long CoT. (1) We first distinguish Long CoT from Short CoT and introduce a novel taxonomy to categorize current reasoning paradigms. (2) Next, we explore the key characteristics of Long CoT: deep reasoning, extensive exploration, and feasible reflection, which enable models to handle more complex tasks and produce more efficient, coherent outcomes compared to the shallower Short CoT. (3) We then investigate key phenomena such as the emergence of Long CoT with these characteristics, including overthinking, and test-time scaling, offering insights into how these processes manifest in practice*. (4) Finally, we identify significant research gaps and highlight promising future directions, including the integration of multi-modal reasoning, efficiency improvements, and enhanced knowledge frameworks. *By providing a structured overview, this survey aims to inspire future research and further the development of logical reasoning in artificial intelligence*"). Italics added.

946 *Agentic AI – the new frontier in GenAI*, PwC, 2025, pp. 1–22 and passim ("In an era where speed, efficiency, and customer centricity dictate market leadership, organisations need to harness every tool at their disposal. Over the past couple of years, artificial intelligence (AI) has exploded onto the world stage, with companies and individuals across the globe rapidly adopting the technology. *The GCC is playing a lead role in the space, with business leaders in the region exploring ways of integrating this rapidly developing technology into their operations. Generative AI (GenAI) is being recognised as a game-changer for innovation in the region, empowering enterprises by automating routine tasks, enhancing customer experiences and assisting in critical decision-making processes.* Insights from our 27th Annual CEO Survey: Middle East findings have shown that 73% of CEOs in the Middle East believe GenAI will significantly change the way their company creates, delivers and captures value over the next three years1. GenAI is poised to make a significant economic impact, with estimates indicating that it could contribute between $2.6 trillion and $4.4 trillion annually to global GDP across various industries by 2030. In specific sectors, such as energy, investments in GenAI are expected to triple, from $40 billion in 2023 to over $140 billion by the end of the decade. This surge in investment reflects the transformative potential of GenAI, particularly in enhancing productivity, streamlining business processes, and reshaping value chains across industries2. *Against this backdrop, multimodal GenAI agentic frameworks has emerged as transformative catalysts, enabling businesses to accelerate process automation at an unprecedented scale. This*

and too heavily on machines to do just about anything that takes 5 meagre seconds of human attention).

§§ In time, machines will know more about humans than humans will ever know about themselves. Case in point, these AI-systems, no matter how advanced, are particularly prone to cyber-attacks. In due course, unscrupulous actors will get a hold of invaluable information that humans would rather keep away from prying eyes.

§§ To add to our woes, come tomorrow, Artificial Intelligence-embedded technologies will eventually grow a conscience[947]—propelled by a sturdy framework of algorithmic beliefs[948] and bolstered by a robust set of algorithmic intentions[949]—and

technology involves multiple AI agents working together, each specialising in different tasks or data types, to solve complex problems and automate processes. By collaborating and constantly learning, these agents enhance decision-making, optimise processes, and drive innovation. It combines range of advanced AI techniques to process diverse data types and automate complex tasks. The central question isn't whether to adopt this technology, but how swiftly organisations can integrate it to stay ahead of the competition. This executive playbook explores how organisations can leverage this technology to boost operational efficiency, enhance customer experience, and drive revenue growth. It provides real-world success stories spanning industry sectors and organisational functions, strategic insights, tactical blueprints, and best practices to guide your journey into this revolutionary landscape"). Italics added.

[947] See: Butlin, Patrick et al., "Consciousness in Artificial Intelligence: Insights from the Science of Consciousness", arXiv:2308.08708v3 [cs.AI] 22 Aug 2023, 2023, p. 1 ("*whether current or near-term AI systems could be conscious is a topic of scientific interest and increasing public concern. This report argues for, and exemplifies, a rigorous and empirically grounded approach to AI consciousness*: assessing existing AI systems in detail, in light of our best-supported neuroscientific theories of consciousness. We survey several prominent scientific theories of consciousness, including recurrent processing theory, global workspace theory, higher order theories, predictive processing, and attention schema theory. *From these theories we derive"indicator properties" of consciousness, elucidated in computational terms that allow us to assess AI systems for these properties. We use these indicator properties to assess several recent AI systems, and we discuss how future systems might implement them. Our analysis suggests that no current AI systems are conscious, but also suggests that there are no obvious technical barriers to building AI systems which satisfy these indicators*"). Italics added.

[948] But see: Piedrahita, Oscar A./Carter, J. Adam, "Can AI believe?", *Philosophy & Technology*, 37:89, 2024, pp. 1–5 (4) ("*couldn't AI's beliefs be like that—beliefs that AI systems just happen to have without the occurrence of mediators and directly stored in AI's memory by the agency of an external force? Even if AI can acquire doxastic states in that way, it's not clear that these are knowledge-conducive beliefs*. After all, it looks like an implanted belief, *or a belief induced through brain stimulation might very plausibly fail any of several requirements identified for knowledge (e.g., ability condition, autonomous belief condition* (Carter 2022a)*, or justification condition). Although a biological brain isn't necessary to have a knowledge-conducive belief, it's not obvious that an entirely artificial cognitive architecture is sufficient*"). Italics added.

[949] See: Ashton, Hal, "Definitions of intent suitable for algorithms", *Artificial Intelligence and Law*, 2022, pp. 28–29 ("*Accounts of intent in algorithms in computer science from any back ground are rare, but are especially so from a legal one. I have assumed throughout that the A-bot is autodidactic in the sense that it learns how to behave itself and its precise actions are not directed by its creators*. Under this assumption, there exist certain situations where the intent of the programmer cannot be read from the intent of the A-bot. This poses problems when the A-bot commits some harm. Whilst A-bots are not legal persons they cannot commit crimes making the presence or absence of mens rea in them moot. *Many would argue that they are not moral agents and cannot*

will go rogue accordingly. Which begs the burning questions: at whose behest? To what end? Food for thoughts that should keep you, dear reader, eagerly awaken at night.

§§ Overall, these features lend itself to harbingers of a looming **demise of human critical thinking**, which, in turn, is poised to usher in the onset of the **age of human dullness**, which will accordingly prime humans to placidly accept everything the Large Language Models say or do. Which is nothing but loathsome and sad. Whilst Large Language Models excel at memorizing/mimicking meaningful patterns arising out of human speech they nonetheless exhibit a lacklustre performance when it comes to engaging in complex thinking, thereby casting doubts on its true reasoning capabilities.[950]

---

be held responsible for their actions. However, this article has argued that over and above its role in assigning culpability for harm, mens rea plays a role in defining harm in what we have called why-crimes. These include many inchoate crimes such as attempts but perhaps more relevantly also include many deceit derived crimes. A failure to identify intent in A-bots means that harms cannot be identified either by those responsible for the A-bots or those who job it is to uphold the law. The ability to define harms by the intentional state of the actor is important capability of the law and is used to avoid over-criminalisation of activity"). Italics added.

[950] See: Shojaee, Parshin/Iman Mirzadeh/Keivan Alizadeh/Maxwell Horton/Samy Bengio/ Mehrdad Farajtabar, Apple, "The Illusion of Thinking: Understanding the Strengths and Limitations of Reasoning Models via the Lens of Problem Complexity", available at: https://ml-site.cdn-apple.com/papers/the-illusion-of-thinking.pdf (access: 12.6.2025), June 2025, 2025, pp. 1–30 (1) ("*recent generations of frontier language models have introduced Large Reasoning Models (LRMs) that generate detailed thinking processes before providing answers. While these models demonstrate improved performance on reasoning benchmarks, their fundamental capabilities, scaling properties, and limitations remain insufficiently understood.* Current evaluations primarily focus on established mathematical and coding benchmarks, emphasizing final answer accuracy. *However, this evaluation paradigm often suffers from data contamination and does not provide insights into the reasoning traces' structure and quality. In this work, we systematically investigate these gaps with the help of controllable puzzle environments that allow precise manipulation of compositional complexity while maintaining consistent logical structures.* This setup enables the analysis of not only final answers but also the internal reasoning traces, offering insights into how LRMs "think". *Through extensive experimentation across diverse puzzles, we show that frontier LRMs face a complete accuracy collapse beyond certain complexities. Moreover, they exhibit a counterintuitive scaling limit: their reasoning effort increases with problem complexity up to a point, then declines despite having an adequate token budget.* By comparing LRMs with their standard LLM counterparts under equivalent inference compute, we identify three performance regimes: (1) lowcomplexity tasks where standard models surprisingly outperform LRMs, (2) medium-complexity tasks where additional thinking in LRMs demonstrates advantage, and (3) *high-complexity tasks where both models experience complete collapse. We found that LRMs have limitations in exact computation: they fail to use explicit algorithms and reason inconsistently across puzzles. We also investigate the reasoning traces in more depth, studying the patterns of explored solutions and analyzing the models' computational behavior, shedding light on their strengths, limitations, and ultimately raising crucial questions about their true reasoning capabilities*"). Italics added.

3.1.5.6 «Playing with Fire»: Medical Hallucinations Generated by Cutting-Edge Foundational Models (e.g. Large Language Models and Large Vision Language Models) in the Domain of Medical Healthcare

§§ The current Artificial Intelligence craze is leading human beings astray. Contrary to warped beliefs, the risks arising out of all-out deployment of Large Language Models in medical healthcare are exceedingly high. In spite of this axiom, the general furore over Artificial Intelligence-embedded technologies seems far from petering out, or even slowing down, anytime soon. Which begs the unsettling question: should we entrust Large Language Models with the task of making high-stake decisions in the field of medical healthcare? The answer is a resounding «no».[951]

§§ The scientific community has been neither coy nor bashful in overtly decrying the deployment of foundation models (e.g., Large Language Models [LLM] and Large Vision Language Models [VLM]) into healthcare applications.[952] Although the integration of foundation models yields multifarious opportunities[953] (e.g. augmenting clinical decision support[954]; overhauling medical research[955] in an overarching sense; ameliorating health-

---

[951] See: Part V, Chap. 5, Sect. 5.1.7.2 of this book (on law number two to control algorithmic decision-making, which mandates that black box models must not be entrusted with the task of making high stake decisions—v.g. health and freedom).

[952] Kim, Yubin/Hyewon Jeong/Shan Chen/Shuyue Stella/Mingyu Lu/Kumail Alhamoud/Jimin Mun/Cristina Grau/Minseok Jung/Rodrigo Gameiro/Lizhou Fan/Eugene Park/Tristan Lin/Joonsik Yoon/Wonjin Yoon/ Maarten Sap/Yulia Tsvetkov/Paul Liang/Xuhai Xu/Xin Liu/Daniel McDuff/ Hyeonhoon Lee/Hae Won Park/ Samir Tulebaev/Cynthia Breazeal, "Medical Hallucination in Foundation Models and Their Impact on Healthcare", arXiv:2503.05777v1 [cs.CL] 26 Feb 2025, 2025, pp. 1–95.

[953] Mukherjee, S., Gamble, P., Ausin, M.S., Kant, N., Aggarwal, K., Manjunath, N., Datta, D., Liu, Z., Ding, J., Busacca, S., et al., "Polaris: A safety-focused llm constellation architecture for healthcare", arXiv preprint arXiv:2403.13313, 2024.

[954] Li, Y., Yang, C., Ettinger, A., "When hindsight is not 20/20: Testing limits on reflective thinking in large language models", Duh, K., Gomez, H., Bethard, S. (eds.) *Findings of the Association for Computational Linguistics: NAACL 2024. Association for Computational Linguistics*, Mexico City, Mexico, available at: https://doi.org/10.18653/v1/2024.findings-naacl.237. https://aclanthology.org/2024.findings-naacl.237, 2024, pp. 3741–3753. See also: Li, X., Zhao, R., Chia, Y.K., Ding, B., Joty, S., Poria, S., Bing, L., "Chain-of-knowledge: Grounding large language models via dynamic knowledge adapting over heterogeneous sources", *International Conference on Learning Representations (ICLR)*, ICLR. https://arxiv.org/pdf/2305.13269, 2024, passim.

[955] Saab, K., Tu, T., Weng, W.-H., Tanno, R., Stutz, D., Wulczyn, E., Zhang, F., Strother, T., Park, C., Vedadi, E., Chaves, J.Z., Hu, S.-Y., Schaekermann, M., Kamath, A., Cheng, Y., Barrett, D.G.T., Cheung, C., Mustafa, B., Palepu, A., McDuff, D., Hou, L., Golany, T., Liu, L., Alayrac, J.-b., Houlsby, N., Tomasev, N., Freyberg, J., Lau, C., Kemp, J., Lai, J., Azizi, S., Kanada, K., Man, S., Kulkarni, K., Sun, R., Shakeri, S., He, L., Caine, B., Webson, A., Latysheva, N., Johnson, M., Mansfield, P., Lu, J., Rivlin, E., Anderson, J., Green, B., Wong, R., Krause, J., Shlens, J., Dominowska, E., Eslami, S.M.A., Chou, K., Cui, C., Vinyals, O., Kavukcuoglu, K., Manyika, J., Dean, J., Hassabis, D., Matias, Y., Webster, D., Barral, J., Corrado, G., Semturs, C., Mahdavi, S.S., Gottweis, J., Karthikesalingam, A., Natarajan, V.: "Capabilities of Gemini Models in Medicine", https://arxiv.org/abs/2404.18416, 2024. See also: Saab, K., Tu, T., Weng, W.-H., Tanno, R., Stutz,

care quality[956] and overall safety[957]) sweltering challenges nonetheless remain.

§§ Pivotally, the full-blown integration of foundation models is not without scorching challenges.[958] The worrisome phenomenon of hallucination[959]/ confabulation[960] ranks first amongst the greatest challenges facing Large Language

---

D., Wulczyn, E., Zhang, F., Strother, T., Park, C., Vedadi, E., et al.: Capabilities of gemini models in medicine. arXiv preprint arXiv:2404.18416, 2024.

[956] Kim, Yubin/Hyewon Jeong/Shan Chen/Shuyue Stella/Mingyu Lu/Kumail Alhamoud/Jimin Mun/Cristina Grau/Minseok Jung/Rodrigo Gameiro/Lizhou Fan/Eugene Park/Tristan Lin/Joonsik Yoon/Wonjin Yoon/Maarten Sap/Yulia Tsvetkov/Paul Liang/Xuhai Xu/Xin Liu/Daniel McDuff/ Hyeonhoon Lee/Hae Won Park/Samir Tulebaev/Cynthia Breazeal, "Medical Hallucination in Foundation Models and Their Impact on Healthcare", arXiv:2503.05777v1 [cs.CL] 26 Feb 2025, 2025, pp. 1–95.

[957] Goodman, K.E., Yi, P.H., Morgan, D.J., "Ai-generated clinical summaries require more than accuracy", *JAMA*, 331(8), 2024, pp. 637–638, available at: https://doi.org/10.1001/jama.2024.0555.

[958] Szolovits, P., *Large Language Models Seem Miraculous, but Science Abhors Miracles*, Massachusetts Medical Society, 2024.

[959] Agarwal, V./Jin, Y./Chandra, M./De Choudhury, M./Kumar, S./Sastry, N.: Medhalu, "Hallucinations in responses to healthcare queries by large language models", arXiv preprint arXiv:2409.19492, 2024.

[960] Huang, L., Yu, W., Ma, W., Zhong, W., Feng, Z., Wang, H., Chen, Q., Peng, W., Feng, X., Qin, B., et al., "A survey on hallucination in large language models: Principles, taxonomy, challenges, and open questions", *ACM Transactions on Information Systems*, 2024, passim. See: Watcher, Sandra, "Limitations and Loopholes in the EU AI Act and AI Liability Directives: What This Means for the European Union, the United States, and Beyond", *Yale Journal of Law & Technology*, Volume 26, Issue 3, 2024, pp. 671–672 ("*Predictive and generative artificial intelligence (AI) have both become integral parts of our lives through their use in making highly impactful decisions.* AI systems are already deployed widely—*for example, in employment, healthcare, insurance, finance, education, public administration, and criminal justice.* Yet severe ethical issues, such as bias and discrimination, privacy invasiveness, opaqueness, and environmental costs of these systems, are well known. *Generative AI (GAI) creates hallucinations and inaccurate or harmful information, which can lead to misinformation, disinformation, and the erosion of scientific knowledge. The Artificial Intelligence Act (AIA), Product Liability Directive, and the Artificial Intelligence Liability Directive reflect Europe's attempt to curb some of these issues. With the legal reach of these policies going far beyond Europe, their impact on the United States and the rest of the world cannot be overstated.* In this Essay, I show how the strong lobbying efforts of big tech companies and member states were unfortunately *able to water down much of the AIA. An overreliance on self-regulation, self-certification, weak oversight and investigatory mechanisms, and far-reaching exceptions for both the public and private sectors are the product of this lobbying. Next, I reveal the similar enforcement limitations of the liability frameworks, which focus on material harm while ignoring harm that is immaterial, monetary, and societal, such as bias, hallucinations, and financial losses due to faulty AI products. Lastly, I explore how these loopholes can be closed to create a framework that effectively guards against novel risks caused by AI in the European Union, the United States, and beyond*"). Italics added.

Models (hereinafter LLMs) in the field of medical healthcare. Recall,[961] hallucinations[962] stand for instances where LLMs generate barely, sometimes seemingly, plausible yet factually warped or outright doctored[963] information.[964]

§§ LLM's hallucinations reverberate across multiple fields. Ranging from finance,[965] legal,[966] code generation[967] to patient education[968] and beyond.[969]

---

961 For further developments: Part IV, Chap. 4, Sect. 4.1.9.5. on Large Language Models 'hallucinations in the legal domain.

962 See: Part III, this chapter, Sects. 3.1.5.4–3.1.5.4.1 of this book (on the functional aspects of Critical Artificial Intelligence Studies, with a sharper focus on the harmful effects of Artificial Intelligence-embedded technologies, namely Large Language Models and its multifarious downsides and shortcomings). See also: Part IV, Chap. 4, Sects. 4.1.9.1–4.1.9.2 of this book (on ChatGPT's functional abilities). See also: Part IV, Chap. 4, Sects. 4.1.9–4.1.9.7 of this book (on ChatGPT's functional drawbacks and pitfalls, including, but no limited to, "hallucinations").

963 *Case law United States v. Hayes*, 2:24-cr-0280-DJC, 14 (E.D. Cal. Jan. 17, 2025) ("*In his motion to unseal, Mr. Francisco cited eight cases, six of which were cited in near string citation form. See Def. Mot. Unseal at 6, 10, 11. The primary case upon which Mr. Francisco relied-analyzing, quoting, describing the district court's analysis, and addressing in two different places in the motion- was "United States v. Harris, 761 F.Supp. 409, 414 (D.D.C. 1991).*" See Def. Mot. Unseal at 6, 10. *Unfortunately, "United States v. Harris, 761 F.Supp. 409, 414 (D.D.C. 1991)" is not a real case.* The citation has all the markings of a *hallucinated case created by generative artificial intelligence (AI) tools such as ChatGPT and Google Bard that have been widely discussed by courts grappling with fictitious legal citations and reported by national news outlets*"). Italics added.

964 Ji, Z., Lee, N., Frieske, R., Yu, T., Su, D., Xu, Y., Ishii, E., Bang, Y.J., Madotto, A., Fung, P., "Survey of hallucination in natural language generation", *ACM Computing Surveys*, 55 (12), 2023, pp. 1–38.

965 Kang, H., Liu, X.-Y., "Deficiency of Large Language Models in Finance: An Empirical Examination of Hallucination", available at: https://arxiv.org/abs/2311.15548, 2024.

966 But see: Dahl, Matthew/Magesh, Varun/Suzgun, Mirac/Ho, Daniel E., "Large Legal Fictions: Profiling Legal Hallucinations in Large Language Models", *Journal of Legal Analysis*, Volume 16, 2024, 64–93 (64) ("*Do large language models (LLMs) know the law? LLMs are increasingly being used to augment legal practice, education, and research, yet their revolutionary potential is threatened by the presence of "hallucinations"—textual output that is not consistent with legal facts.* We present the first systematic evidence of these hallucinations in public-facing LLMs, documenting trends across jurisdictions, courts, time periods, and cases. *Using OpenAI's ChatGPT 4 and other public models, we show that LLMs hallucinate at least 58% of the time, struggle to predict their own hallucinations, and often uncritically accept users' incorrect legal assumptions. We conclude by cautioning against the rapid and unsupervised integration of popular LLMs into legal tasks*"). Italics added. For further developments: Part IV, Chap. 4, Sect. 4.1.9.5. on Large Language Models 'hallucinations in the legal domain.

967 Agarwal, V./Pei, Y./Alamir, S./Liu, X., "CodeMirage: Hallucinations in Code Generated by Large Language Models", available at: https://arxiv.org/abs/2408.08333, 2024.

968 Aydin, S., Karabacak, M., Vlachos, V., Margetis, K., "Large language models in patient education: a scoping review of applications in medicine", *Frontiers in Medicine*, 11, 2024, 1477898.

969 Kim, Yubin/Hyewon Jeong/Shan Chen/Shuyue Stella/Mingyu Lu/Kumail Alhamoud/Jimin Mun/Cristina Grau/Minseok Jung/Rodrigo Gameiro/Lizhou Fan/Eugene Park/Tristan Lin/Joonsik Yoon/Wonjin Yoon/Maarten Sap/Yulia Tsvetkov/Paul Liang/Xuhai Xu/Xin Liu/Daniel McDuff/Hyeonhoon Lee/Hae Won Park/Samir Tulebaev/Cynthia Breazeal, "Medical Hallucination in Foundation Models and Their Impact on Healthcare", arXiv:2503.05777v1 [cs.CL] 26 Feb 2025, 2025, pp. 1–95.

It is true that Chain-of-Thought (CoT)[970] can mildly decrease Large Language Models' hallucinations,[971] but truer still these are sobering news in the realm of medical healthcare whereby medical hallucinations, no matter how slight, may cost lives.

§§ Compellingly, medical hallucinations[972] pose tangible threats to the patients. Strikingly, wrong dosages of medications,[973] mistaken drug interactions, or shoddy or watered-down diagnostic criteria[974] can cause life-threatening[975] outcomes[976] to swell.[977] Medical hallucinations.[978] if nothing else, can be conducive to serious injuries or, in worst case scenarios, even death.

[970] See: Wei, Jason/Xuezhi Wang/Dale Schuurmans/Maarten Bosma/Brian ichter/Fei Xia/Ed Chi/Quoc V Le/Denny Zhou, "Chain-of-thought prompting elicits reasoning in large language models", *Advances in Neural Information Processing Systems*, Volume 35, 2022, pp. 24824–24837. Curran Associates, Inc. See also: Wang, Xuezhi/Jason Wei/Dale Schuurmans/Quoc Le/Ed Chi/ Sharan Narang/Aakanksha Chowdhery/Denny Zhou, "Self-consistency improves chain of thought reasoning in language models", arXiv preprint arXiv:2203.11171, 2022.

[971] Jiang, Y., Chen, J., Yang, D., Li, M., Wang, S., Wu, T., Li, K., Zhang, L.: "Comt: Chain-of-medical-thought reduces hallucination in medical report generation". arXiv preprint arXiv:2406.11451, 2024.

[972] Ji, Z., Lee, N., Frieske, R., Yu, T., Su, D., Xu, Y., Ishii, E., Bang, Y.J., Madotto, A., Fung, P.: "Survey of hallucination in natural language generation", *ACM Computing Surveys*, 55 (12), 2023, pp. 1–38. See also: Chen, J., Yang, D., Wu, T., Jiang, Y., Hou, X., Li, M., Wang, S., Xiao, D., Li, K., Zhang, L., "Detecting and evaluating medical hallucinations in large vision language models", arXiv preprint arXiv:2406.10185, 2024.

[973] Bottomley, D., Thaldar, D., "Liability for harm caused by AI in healthcare: An overview of the core legal concepts", *Frontiers in Pharmacology*, 14, 2023, 1297353.

[974] Vally, Z.I., Khammissa, R.A.G., Feller, G., Ballyram, R., Beetge, M., Feller, L.", Errors in clinical diagnosis: a narrative review", *The Journal of International Medical Research*, 51 (8), 2023, 3000605231162798.

[975] Chen, S., Gallifant, J., Gao, M., Moreira, P., Munch, N., Muthukkumar, A., Rajan, A., Kolluri, J., Fiske, A., Hastings, J., Aerts, H., Anthony, B., Celi, L.A., Cava, W.G.L., Bitterman, D.S., "Cross-Care: Assessing the Healthcare Implications of Pre-training Data on Language Model Bias", 2024, passim.

[976] Jalilian, L., McDuff, D., Kadambi, A.: "The potential and perils of generative artificial intelligence for quality improvement and patient safety", arXiv preprint arXiv:2407.16902 (2024).

[977] Ke, Y., Yang, R., Lie, S.A., Lim, T.X.Y., Ning, Y., Li, I., Abdullah, H.R., Ting, D.S.W., Liu, N.: "Mitigating cognitive biases in clinical decision-making through multi-agent conversations using large language models: Simulation study", *Journal of Medical Internet Research*, 26, 2024, 59439.

[978] Kim, Yubin/Hyewon Jeong/Shan Chen/Shuyue Stella/Mingyu Lu/Kumail Alhamoud/Jimin Mun/Cristina Grau/Minseok Jung/Rodrigo Gameiro/Lizhou Fan/Eugene Park/Tristan Lin/Joonsik Yoon/Wonjin Yoon/Maarten Sap/Yulia Tsvetkov/Paul Liang/Xuhai Xu/Xin Liu/Daniel McDuff/ Hyeonhoon Lee/Hae Won Park/Samir Tulebaev/Cynthia Breazeal, "Medical Hallucination in Foundation Models and Their Impact on Healthcare", *cit.*, pp. 1–95.

§§ Medical hallucinations can prime LLMs to produce either mistaken or a set of misleading medical information[979] that could negatively impact clinical decision-making[980] and patient outcomes accordingly.[981] For instance, more often than not LLMs hallucinate about patient information, medical history, and documented symptoms[982] on a clinical note that routinely falls noticeably short of squarely aligning with the original note.[983]

§§ This example neatly encapsulates, hands-in-glove, the confirmation bias of a medical doctor in which contradictory/conflicting symptoms are often forsaken and are eventually conducive unfitting/improper medical treatment protocols.[984] Whilst

[979] Kim, H.-K.: "The effects of artificial intelligence chatbots on women's health: A systematic review and meta-analysis", *Healthcare*, 12 (5), 2024.

[980] Ji, Z., Yu, T., Xu, Y., Lee, N., Ishii, E., Fung, P.: "Towards Mitigating Hallucination in Large Language Models via Self-Reflection", https://arxiv.org/abs/2310.06271, 2023.

[981] Kim, Yubin/Hyewon Jeong/Shan Chen/Shuyue Stella/Mingyu Lu/Kumail Alhamoud/Jimin Mun/Cristina Grau/Minseok Jung/Rodrigo Gameiro/Lizhou Fan/Eugene Park/Tristan Lin/Joonsik Yoon/Wonjin Yoon/Maarten Sap/Yulia Tsvetkov/Paul Liang/Xuhai Xu/Xin Liu/Daniel McDuff/Hyeonhoon Lee/Hae Won Park/Samir Tulebaev/Cynthia Breazeal, "Medical Hallucination in Foundation Models and Their Impact on Healthcare", *cit.*, pp. 1–95.

[982] Vishwanath, P.R., Tiwari, S., Naik, T.G., Gupta, S., Thai, D.N., Zhao, W., KWON, S., Ardulov, V., Tarabishy, K., McCallum, A., et al.: "Faithfulness hallucination detection in healthcare ai", *Artificial Intelligence and Data Science for Healthcare: Bridging Data-Centric AI and People-Centric Healthcare*, 2024, passim.

[983] Kim, Yubin/Hyewon Jeong/Shan Chen/Shuyue Stella/Mingyu Lu/Kumail Alhamoud/Jimin Mun/Cristina Grau/Minseok Jung/Rodrigo Gameiro/Lizhou Fan/Eugene Park/Tristan Lin/Joonsik Yoon/Wonjin Yoon/Maarten Sap/Yulia Tsvetkov/Paul Liang/Xuhai Xu/Xin Liu/Daniel McDuff/Hyeonhoon Lee/Hae Won Park/Samir Tulebaev/Cynthia Breazeal, "Medical Hallucination in Foundation Models and Their Impact on Healthcare", *cit.*, pp. 1–95.

[984] Kim, Yubin/Hyewon Jeong/Shan Chen/Shuyue Stella/Mingyu Lu/Kumail Alhamoud/Jimin Mun/Cristina Grau/Minseok Jung/Rodrigo Gameiro/Lizhou Fan/Eugene Park/Tristan Lin/Joonsik Yoon/Wonjin Yoon/Maarten Sap/Yulia Tsvetkov/Paul Liang/Xuhai Xu/Xin Liu/Daniel McDuff/Hyeonhoon Lee/Hae Won Park/Samir Tulebaev/Cynthia Breazeal, "Medical Hallucination in Foundation Models and Their Impact on Healthcare", *cit.*, pp. 1–95.

the concept of hallucinations in LLM is anything but blazingly new,[985] its reverberations in the medical field should not be overlooked due to the high stakes[986] involved and the meagre, if any, margin[987] of error.[988] A note of disenchantment comes in handy in this regard: though a cluster of measures have been taken to

[985] Bai, Z., Wang, P., Xiao, T., He, T., Han, Z., Zhang, Z., Shou, M.Z., "Hallucination of multimodal large language models: A survey", arXiv preprint arXiv:2404.18930, 2024. See: Watcher, Sandra, "Limitations and Loopholes in the EU AI Act and AI Liability Directives: What This Means for the European Union, the United States, and Beyond", *Yale Journal of Law & Technology*, Volume 26, Issue 3, 2024, pp. 671–672 ("*Predictive and generative artificial intelligence (AI) have both become integral parts of our lives through their use in making highly impactful decisions.* AI systems are already deployed widely—for example, in employment, healthcare, insurance, finance, education, public administration, and criminal justice. Yet severe ethical issues, such as bias and discrimination, privacy invasiveness, opaqueness, and environmental costs of these systems, are well known. *Generative AI (GAI) creates hallucinations and inaccurate or harmful information, which can lead to misinformation, disinformation, and the erosion of scientific knowledge. The Artificial Intelligence Act (AIA), Product Liability Directive, and the Artificial Intelligence Liability Directive reflect Europe's attempt to curb some of these issues. With the legal reach of these policies going far beyond Europe, their impact on the United States and the rest of the world cannot be overstated.* In this Essay, I show how the strong lobbying efforts of big tech companies and member states were unfortunately *able to water down much of the AIA. An overreliance on self-regulation, self-certification, weak oversight and investigatory mechanisms, and far-reaching exceptions for both the public and private sectors are the product of this lobbying. Next, I reveal the similar enforcement limitations of the liability frameworks, which focus on material harm while ignoring harm that is immaterial, monetary, and societal, such as bias, hallucinations, and financial losses due to faulty AI products. Lastly, I explore how these loopholes can be closed to create a framework that effectively guards against novel risks caused by AI in the European Union, the United States, and beyond*"). Italics added.

[986] See: Rudin, Cynthia, "Please stop explaining black box models for high stakes decisions", *Proceedings of NeurIPS 2018 Workshop on Critiquing and Correcting Trends in Machine Learning (NIPS 2018)*, 2018, passim; Rudin, Cynthia/Radin, J., "Why are we using black box models in AI when we don't need to? A lesson from an explainable AI competition", *Harvard Data Science Review*, 2019, Volume 1, Issue 2, passim; Tan, S., Caruana, R., Hooker, G., and Lou, Y., "Distill-and-compare: Auditing blackbox models using transparent model distillation". *Proceedings of the 2018 AAAI/ACM Conference on AI, Ethics, and Society, Association for Computing Machinery*, 2018, pp. 303–310 (arguing that explainable models are too complex and fiddly to be understood by laypeople. As a result, interpretable models should be used instead). See also: Rudin, Cynthia/ Ustun, B., "Optimized scoring systems: toward trust in machine learning for healthcare and criminal justice", *Interfaces*, Volume 48, 2018, pp. 399–486 (voicing deep-rooted concerns about the deployment of machine learning algorithms in both medical healthcare and criminal justice).

[987] Kim, Yubin/Hyewon Jeong/Shan Chen/Shuyue Stella/Mingyu Lu/Kumail Alhamoud/Jimin Mun/Cristina Grau/Minseok Jung/Rodrigo Gameiro/Lizhou Fan/Eugene Park/Tristan Lin/Joonsik Yoon/Wonjin Yoon/Maarten Sap/Yulia Tsvetkov/Paul Liang/Xuhai Xu/Xin Liu/Daniel McDuff/ Hyeonhoon Lee/Hae Won Park/ Samir Tulebaev/Cynthia Breazeal, "Medical Hallucination in Foundation Models and Their Impact on Healthcare", *cit.*, pp. 1–95.

[988] Umapathi, L.K., Pal, A., Sankarasubbu, M., "Med-halt: Medical domain hallucination test for large language models", arXiv preprint arXiv:2307.15343, 2023.

falloff/taper off medical hallucinations,[989] they remain nonetheless piecemeal and ultimately insufficient.

§§ With this context in mind, burgeoning body of literature streams laid out frames of reference that sought to classify medical hallucinations in LLM outputs. Pundits[990] shed a keen light on the gravity of errors and their underlying causes. Others,[991] in turn, seek to keenly identify the types of misinformation that can exact a toll on the trust on medicine in an overarching sense. Pivotally, a cohort of scholars[992] has set forth an empirical yardstick for quantifying tangible hallucination in outer-world scenarios in a bid to highlight both its frequency and prevalence.[993]

§§ In addition to that, polyhistors further employed staggering efforts to forestall this harrowing phenomenon[994] by highlighting the extent to which data quality[995] and curation practices can sway the rate and pace at which LLMs hallucinates.

---

[989] Tonmoy, S., Zaman, S., Jain, V., Rani, A., Rawte, V., Chadha, A., Das, A., "A comprehensive survey of hallucination mitigation techniques in large language models", arXiv preprint arXiv:2401.01313, 2024. See also: Hegselmann, S., Shen, S.Z., Gierse, F., Agrawal, M., Sontag, D., Jiang, X., "A datacentric approach to generate faithful and high quality patient summaries with large language models", arXiv preprint arXiv:2402.15422, 2024; Zuo, K., Jiang, Y.: Medhallbench: A new benchmark for assessing hallucination in medical large language models. arXiv preprint arXiv:2412.18947, 2024.

[990] Agarwal, V., Jin, Y., Chandra, M., De Choudhury, M., Kumar, S., Sastry, N., "Medhalu: Hallucinations in responses to healthcare queries by large language models", arXiv preprint arXiv:2409.19492, 2024.

[991] Ahmad, M.A., Yaramis, I., Roy, T.D., "Creating trustworthy llms: Dealing with hallucinations in healthcare ai", arXiv preprint arXiv:2311.01463, 2023.

[992] Pal, A., Umapathi, L.K., Sankarasubbu, M.: Medmcqa, "A large-scale multi-subject multi-choice dataset for medical domain question answering", *Conference on Health, Inference, and Learning*, 2022, pp. 248–260.

[993] Kim, Yubin/Hyewon Jeong/Shan Chen/Shuyue Stella/Mingyu Lu/Kumail Alhamoud/Jimin Mun/Cristina Grau/Minseok Jung/Rodrigo Gameiro/Lizhou Fan/Eugene Park/Tristan Lin/Joonsik Yoon/Wonjin Yoon/Maarten Sap/Yulia Tsvetkov/Paul Liang/Xuhai Xu/Xin Liu/Daniel McDuff/ Hyeonhoon Lee/Hae Won Park/Samir Tulebaev/Cynthia Breazeal, "Medical Hallucination in Foundation Models and Their Impact on Healthcare", *cit.*, pp. 1–95.

[994] Hegselmann, S., Shen, S., Gierse, F., Agrawal, M., Sontag, D., Jiang, X., "Medical expert annotations of unsupported facts in doctor-written and llm-generated patient summaries", *Physionet*, 2024, passim.

[995] See: *Tech, Bias and Housing Initiative, the Promise and Perils of Residential Proptech, Year 1, Research Summary Report, April 2023, TechEquity Collaborative*, p. 11, available at: https://techequity.us/wp-content/uploads/2023/04/TBHI-Y1-Research-Summary-Report.pdf (28.11.2024) ("*Once bad data enters the analysis of one factor, it gets baked into the subsequent process, multiplying the effect that one disadvantageous data point can have on someone's overall housing determination*"). Italics added. See: Part IV, Chap. 4, Sects. 4.1.4–4.1.4.2.3 of this book. Mehta, Abhishek/Polanco, Eliud, "Breaking Bad Data & Solving for AML", *Global Risk Institute* (June 6, 2017), http://globalriskinstitute.org/wp-content/uploads/2017/06/Breaking-Bad-Data-Solving-for-AML-FINAL-UPDATE.pdf [https://perma.cc/M9DS-3F6G] ("Tuning AML detection models to achieve optimum precision is more art than science"); IBM ML Hub, "The 3 Kinds of Context: Machine Learning and the Art of the Frame", *Inside Machine Learning* (Apr. 26, 2017), https://medium.com/inside-machine-learning/the-3kinds-of-context-3c4065e26749 [https://perma.cc/G9JW-XUSK] ("As much as thinking about these three context has helped us, it's also reinforced the fact that machine learning is often more art than science").

Particularly, in the context of patient summaries[996] espoused with their underlying causes and manifestations.[997] Lastly, a group of scholars carved out a visual taxonomy of medical hallucinations in LLMs that worths mentioning in the next section.

3.1.5.6.1 «Beware of What You Wish»: Visual Taxonomy of Medical Hallucinations Generated by State-of-the-Art Foundational Models: «Factual Errors», «Outdated References», «Spurious Correlations», «Factual Sources or Guidelines», «Incomplete Chains of Reasoning» (Yubin Kim et al.)

§§ A visual taxonomy of medical hallucinations in LLMs can be clustered along five dimensions. They can be skeletally broken down as follows: **(i) Factual Errors:** LLMs Hallucinations arise from either mistaken or inaccurate information, comprising **«Non-Factual Hallucination»**, «**Factual Hallucination»**, and **«Input-Conflicting Hallucination»**.[998]

§§ **(ii) Outdated References:** a batch of errors springing from overreliance on outdated guidelines or rigged datasets,[999] mirrored on «**Memory-Based Hallucination»**.[1000]

---

[996] Zhang, Y., Li, S., Liu, J., Yu, P., Fung, Y.R., Li, J., Li, M., Ji, H., "Knowledge overshadowing causes amalgamated hallucination in large language models", arXiv preprint arXiv:2407.08039, 2024.

[997] Kim, Yubin/Hyewon Jeong/Shan Chen/Shuyue Stella/Mingyu Lu/Kumail Alhamoud/Jimin Mun/Cristina Grau/Minseok Jung/Rodrigo Gameiro/Lizhou Fan/Eugene Park/Tristan Lin/Joonsik Yoon/Wonjin Yoon/Maarten Sap/Yulia Tsvetkov/Paul Liang/Xuhai Xu/Xin Liu/Daniel McDuff/ Hyeonhoon Lee/Hae Won Park/Samir Tulebaev/Cynthia Breazeal, "Medical Hallucination in Foundation Models and Their Impact on Healthcare", *cit.*, pp. 1–95.

[998] Kim, Yubin/Hyewon Jeong/Shan Chen/Shuyue Stella/Mingyu Lu/Kumail Alhamoud/Jimin Mun/Cristina Grau/Minseok Jung/Rodrigo Gameiro/Lizhou Fan/Eugene Park/Tristan Lin/Joonsik Yoon/Wonjin Yoon/Maarten Sap/Yulia Tsvetkov/Paul Liang/Xuhai Xu/Xin Liu/Daniel McDuff/ Hyeonhoon Lee/Hae Won Park/ Samir Tulebaev/Cynthia Breazeal, "Medical Hallucination in Foundation Models and Their Impact on Healthcare", *cit.*, pp. 1–95.

[999] But see: Barocas, Solon/Selbst, Andrew D., "Big Data's Disparate Impact", *California Law Review*, Volume 104, 2016, pp. 671–682 (discussing how data is often flawed, rigged, incomplete, imperfect and therefore algorithms inherit the prejudice of the original decision makers). But see: Citron, Danielle Keats/Pasquale, Frank, "The Scored Society: Due Process for Automated Predictions", *Washington Law Review*, Volume 89, 2014, pp. 1, 4–5 (highlighting how human beings programming automated systems is directly conducive to, and leads, to fundamentally inaccurate results since the source code, predictive algorithms and datasets may encompass human biases which, in turn, have a disparate impact on historically disadvantaged groups); Crawford, Kate/ Schultz, Jason, "Big Data and Due Process: Toward a Framework to Redress Predictive Privacy Harms", *Boston College Law Review*, Volume 55, 2014, pp. 93, 99–101 (pinpointing pathways through which predictive analytic tools perpetuate discriminatory practices). But see: Bornstein, Stepanhie, "Antidiscriminatory Algorithms", *Alabama Law Review*, Volume 70, 2018, pp. 519, 524–528 (contending, however, that the tagged "facially neutral" algorithms producing discriminatory outcomes should be quashed).

[1000] Kim, Yubin/Hyewon Jeong/Shan Chen/Shuyue Stella/Mingyu Lu/Kumail Alhamoud/Jimin Mun/Cristina Grau/Minseok Jung/Rodrigo Gameiro/Lizhou Fan/Eugene Park/Tristan Lin/Joonsik

§§ **(iii) Spurious Correlations:** Hallucinations that weave together or misinterpret data in ways that generate statistically unsound conclusions, including, but not limited to, **«Bias-Induced Hallucination»**, **«Amalgamated Hallucination»**, and **«Multimodal Integration Hallucination»**.[1001]

§§ **(iv) Fabricated Sources or Guidelines:** Outright fabrications, fake opinions,[1002] downright misrepresentations, or oversimplifications, of a set of medical procedures and research, encompassing, but not limited to, **«Procedural Hallucination»** and **«Research Hallucination»**.[1003]

§§ **(v) Incomplete Chains of Reasoning:** Doctored, botched, tampered with or partial logical processes, such as «**Reasoning Hallucination**», «**Decision-Making Hallucination**», and **«Diagnostic Hallucination»**.[1004]

§§ It is noteworthy that these hallucinations are further compounded by the complexity of medical knowledge, where seemingly anodyne differences in terminology or semantics can engender[1005] mishaps and, foremost, unfortunate misunderstandings[1006] in the domain of medical healthcare.

Yoon/Wonjin Yoon/Maarten Sap/Yulia Tsvetkov/Paul Liang/Xuhai Xu/Xin Liu/Daniel McDuff/Hyeonhoon Lee/Hae Won Park/Samir Tulebaev/Cynthia Breazeal, "Medical Hallucination in Foundation Models and Their Impact on Healthcare", *cit.*, pp. 1–95.

1001 Kim, Yubin/Hyewon Jeong/Shan Chen/Shuyue Stella/Mingyu Lu/Kumail Alhamoud/Jimin Mun/Cristina Grau/Minseok Jung/Rodrigo Gameiro/Lizhou Fan/Eugene Park/Tristan Lin/Joonsik Yoon/Wonjin Yoon/Maarten Sap/Yulia Tsvetkov/Paul Liang/Xuhai Xu/Xin Liu/Daniel McDuff/Hyeonhoon Lee/Hae Won Park/Samir Tulebaev/Cynthia Breazeal, "Medical Hallucination in Foundation Models and Their Impact on Healthcare", *cit.*, pp. 1–95.

1002 *Mata v. Avianca, Inc.*, 678 F. Supp. 3d 443, 448–49 (S.D.N.Y. 2023) ("*any harms flow from the submission of fake opinions. The opposing party wastes time and money in exposing the deception.* The Court's time is taken from other important endeavors. The client may be deprived of arguments based on authentic judicial precedents. *There is potential harm to the reputation of judges and courts whose names are falsely invoked as authors of the bogus opinions and to the reputation of a party attributed with fictional conduct.* It promotes cynicism about the legal profession and the American judicial system. And *a future litigant may be tempted to defy a judicial ruling by disingenuously claiming doubt about its authenticity*"). Italics added.

1003 Kim, Yubin/Hyewon Jeong/Shan Chen/Shuyue Stella/Mingyu Lu/Kumail Alhamoud/Jimin Mun/Cristina Grau/Minseok Jung/Rodrigo Gameiro/Lizhou Fan/Eugene Park/Tristan Lin/Joonsik Yoon/Wonjin Yoon/Maarten Sap/Yulia Tsvetkov/Paul Liang/Xuhai Xu/Xin Liu/Daniel McDuff/Hyeonhoon Lee/Hae Won Park/Samir Tulebaev/Cynthia Breazeal, "Medical Hallucination in Foundation Models and Their Impact on Healthcare", *cit.*, pp. 1–95.

1004 Kim, Yubin/Hyewon Jeong/Shan Chen/Shuyue Stella/Mingyu Lu/Kumail Alhamoud/Jimin Mun/Cristina Grau/Minseok Jung/Rodrigo Gameiro/Lizhou Fan/Eugene Park/Tristan Lin/Joonsik Yoon/Wonjin Yoon/Maarten Sap/Yulia Tsvetkov/Paul Liang/Xuhai Xu/Xin Liu/Daniel McDuff/Hyeonhoon Lee/Hae Won Park/Samir Tulebaev/Cynthia Breazeal, "Medical Hallucination in Foundation Models and Their Impact on Healthcare", *cit.*, pp. 1–95.

1005 Kim, Yubin/Hyewon Jeong/Shan Chen/Shuyue Stella/Mingyu Lu/Kumail Alhamoud/Jimin Mun/Cristina Grau/Minseok Jung/Rodrigo Gameiro/Lizhou Fan/Eugene Park/Tristan Lin/Joonsik Yoon/Wonjin Yoon/Maarten Sap/Yulia Tsvetkov/Paul Liang/Xuhai Xu/Xin Liu/Daniel McDuff/Hyeonhoon Lee/Hae Won Park/Samir Tulebaev/Cynthia Breazeal, "Medical Hallucination in Foundation Models and Their Impact on Healthcare", *cit.*, pp. 1–95.

1006 Miles-Jay, A., Snitkin, E.S., Lin, M.Y., Shimasaki, T., Schoeny, M., Fukuda, C., Dangana, T., Moore, N., Sansom, S.E., Yelin, R.D., Bell, P., Rao, K., Keidan, M., Standke, A., Bassis, C.,

§§ Pivotally, one should not lose sight of the fact that LLMs hallucinations can occur across a broad range of medical chores, ranging from «symptom diagnosis and patient management to the interpretation of lab results and visual data».[1007]

§§ Against this drawn-out background, relevant stakeholders should heed the compelling findings arising out of this budding piece of empirical evidence or harmful outcomes may otherwise occur: beware of what you wish!

3.1.5.7 Algorithmic Biases in Human-Centric Computer Vision Systems («HCCV»), Comprising Facial Recognition Technologies (FRT): The Looming Threat of «Being «Seen» Versus Mis-Seen» (Alice Xiang)

§§ The burgeoning development of Artificial Intelligence-embedded technologies engenders a haze of unbearable uncertainty that weighs heavily in our spirits. Vexing questions accordingly swirl in your minds: **(i)** does the aphorism according to which every cloud (Artificial Intelligence-anchored technologies) has a silver lining holds true? **(ii)** to the extent that the road behind was rocky and path ahead is unclear, what measures should be adopted to taper off the definitional quandaries facing Artificial Intelligence-embedded technologies? **(iii)** are algorithmic biases[1008] facing facial

---

Hayden, M.K., Young, V.B., "Longitudinal genomic surveillance of carriage and transmission of clostridioides difficile in an intensive care unit", *Nature Medicine*, 29, 2023, pp. 2526–2534.

[1007] Kim, Yubin/Hyewon Jeong/Shan Chen/Shuyue Stella/Mingyu Lu/Kumail Alhamoud/Jimin Mun/Cristina Grau/Minseok Jung/Rodrigo Gameiro/Lizhou Fan/Eugene Park/Tristan Lin/Joonsik Yoon/Wonjin Yoon/Maarten Sap/Yulia Tsvetkov/Paul Liang/Xuhai Xu/Xin Liu/Daniel McDuff/Hyeonhoon Lee/Hae Won Park/Samir Tulebaev/Cynthia Breazeal, "Medical Hallucination in Foundation Models and Their Impact on Healthcare", *cit.*, pp. 1–95.

[1008] Recall: Baeza-Yates, R., "Bias on the web", *Communications of the ACM*, 61 (6), June 2018, 2018, pp. 54–61 (argues that "*algorithmic bias is when the bias is not present in the input data* and is added *purely by the algorithm*"). Italics added. See also: Hajian, Sara Hajian et al., "Algorithmic Bias: From Discrimination Discovery to Fairness-aware Data Mining", *ACM SIGKDD International Conference on Knowledge Discovery and Data Mining*, Volume 22, 2125, 2016; Griemmelmann, James/Westreich, Daniel, "Incomprehensible Discrimination", *California Law Review Online*, Volume 7, 2018, pp. 164–171; Xiang, Alice, "Reconciling Legal and Technical Approaches to Algorithmic Bias", *Tennessee Law Review*, Volume 88, 2021, passim; See: Lemley, Mark A./Casey, Bryan, "Remedies for Robots", *The University of Chicago Law Review*, Volume 86, Issue 5, 2019, pp. 1311–1396 (1376) (alerting to the perils of algorithmic bias); Chandler, Anupam, "The Racist Algorithm", *Michigan Law Review*, Volume 115, Issue 6, 2018, p. 1026 (noting that, in the terrain of racist algorithm, "the possibilities for discriminatory manipulation are legion"; Jackson, Maya C., "Artificial Intelligence and Algorithmic Bias: The Issues with Technology Reflecting History and Humans", *Journal of Business Technology Law*, Volume 16, 2021, pp. 299–316; West, Sarah Myers/Whittaker, Meredith/Crawford, Kate, *Discriminating Systems. Gender, Race and Power in AI*. New York: AI Now Institute, 2019, pp. 15 and ff and passim; Waldman, Ezra, "Privacy, Practice, and Performance", *California Law Review*, Volume 110, 2021, passim (on algorithmic bias); Jackson, Maya C., "Artificial Intelligence and Algorithmic Bias: The Issues with Technology Reflecting History and Humans", *Journal of Business Technology Law*, Volume 16, 2021, pp. 299–316; West, Sarah Myers/Whittaker, Meredith/Crawford, Kate, *Discriminating Systems. Gender, Race and Power in AI*. New York: AI Now Institute, 2019, pp. 15 and

recognition poised to snowball running downhill, thereby further compounding[1009] the structural disadvantage[1010] with which members of racialized communities have been tussling for a long-haul? These deep-rooted concerns are neither nugatory nor bootless ones.

§§ Compellingly, the undeterred rise of facial recognition and accompanying computer vision technologies has been met with mounting distress over

---

ff and passim. Lee, Nicole Turner/Resnick, Paul/Barton, Genie, *Algorithmic Bias Detection and Mitigation: Best Practices and Policies to Reduce Consumer Harms*. Washington, DC: Brookings Institution, 2019, passim; Lee, N. T./P. Resnick/G. Barton, "Algorithmic Bias Detection and Mitigation: Best Practices and Polices to Reduce Consumer Harms", Brookings Institution, Washington D.C., Bookings Report, 2019; Hellman, Deborah, "Measuring Algorithmic Fairness", *Virginia Law Review*, Volume 106, 2020, pp. 811 and ff and passim; Johnson, Gabbrielle M., "Algorithmic Bias: On the Implicit Biases of Social Technology", *Synthese*, 2021, passim.

[1009] See: Hellman, Deborah, "Indirect Discrimination and the Duty to Avoid Compounding Injustice", *Foundations of Indirect Discrimination Law*, Collins, Hugh/Khaitan, Tarunabh (Editors), Oxford, Hart Publishing; Reprint edition (June 25, 2020), 2020, p. 107 (Professor Deborah Hellman coined this expression to depict a decision that "exacerbates the harm caused by the prior injustice because it entrenches the harm or carries it into another domain").

[1010] Barocas, Solon/Selbst, Andrew, "Big Data's Disparate Impact", *California Law Review*, Volume 104, pp. 2016, p. 691 (highlighting the worrisome, and gruesome, issue of "structural disadvantage" with which racialized communities have been tussling for centuries). See also: Powell, Richard/Porter, Jeremy, "Redlining, Concentrated Disadvantage and Crime: The Effects of Discriminatory Government Policies on Violent Crime", *American Journal of Criminal Justice*, Volume 48, 2023, pp. 1132–1156 ("*Redlining and other discriminatory government policies enacted during the first half of the Twentieth Century have had long-lasting negative effects on neighborhoods, especially those inhabited by people of color (...) The results indicate that redlining was associated with increases in both concentrated disadvantage and violent crime, and that redlining's relationship with violent crime was, indeed, partially mediated by its relationship with concentrated disadvantage*"). Italics added. See also: Gandy, Oscar H., *Coming to Terms with Chance: Engaging Rational Discrimination and Cumulative Disadvantage*, Farnham, UK: Ashgate Publishing, 2009. See: Burk, Dan L., "Algorithmic Fair Use", *University of Chicago Law Review*, Volume 86, 2019, pp. 283–288 (asserts that algorithmic "*fair use carries with it the disadvantage of ex ante uncertainty*; no one can be entirely certain in advance how a court will weigh the four factors, *and hence there is always some apprehension that a use may be found infringing rather than fair*"). Italics added.

the potential for Artificial Intelligence-embedded technologies to beget mass surveillance[1011] systems[1012] and further entrench long-standing biases.[1013]

§§ It is often reeled off that falling-off bias in human-centric computer vision systems («HCCV»), including facial recognition, can entail collating behemoth, diverse, variegated, and unposed/forthright image datasets, which can run afoul with a cluster of privacy guardrails. Alice Xiang thereupon argues that individuals are better off being «unseen» by Artificial Intelligence-embedded technologies. That is,

---

[1011] See: Garvie, Clare et al., *The Perpetual Line-up: Unregulated Police Face Recognition in America*, Georgetown University. Center on Privacy and Technology, Georgetown University. Law Center. Center on Privacy & Technology Georgetown Law, Center on Privacy & Technology, 2016, pp. 1–145 ("*Across the country, state and local police departments are building their own face recognition systems, many of them more advanced than the FBI's.* We know very little about these systems. We don't know how they impact privacy and civil liberties. We don't know how they address accuracy problems. And we don't know how any of these systems—local, state, or federal—affect racial and ethnic minorities. This report closes these gaps. The result of a year-long investigation and over 100 records requests to police departments around the country, it is the most comprehensive survey to date of law enforcement face recognition and the risks that it poses to privacy, civil liberties, and civil rights. *Combining FBI data with new information we obtained about state and local systems, we find that law enforcement face recognition affects over 117 million American adults. It is also unregulated. A few agencies have instituted meaningful protections to prevent the misuse of the technology. In many more cases, it is out of control*"). Italics added. See also: Fretty, Douglas A., "Face-Recognition Surveillance: A Moment of Truth for Fourth Amendment Rights in Public Places", *The Virginia Journal of Law and Technology*, Volume 16, 2011, pp. 429 and ff and.

[1012] Ferguson, Andrew Guthrie, "Facial Recognition and the Fourth Amendment", *Minnesota Law Review*, Volume 105, 2021, p. 1107 ("*leading the charge of game-changing new surveillance technologies is facial recognition—namely the ability to identify faces among crowds, in videos, in photo datasets, and almost everywhere else.* From scanning Super Bowl crowds and public streets, to searching stored arrestee mugshots, police are beginning to experiment with facial recognition technology. *This development is also causing great public concern, because the scope and scale of these new surveillance systems threatens to upend the existing power relationship between police and the people*"). Italics added and internal citations omitted.

[1013] Xiang, Alice, "Being "Seen" versus "Mis-Seen": tensions between Privacy and Fairness in Computer Vision", *Harvard Journal of Law & Technology*, Volume 36, Number 1 Fall 2022, 2022, pp. 1–60.

being underrepresented[1014] in the data[1015] used to propel facial recognition forward would somehow enable one to escape the chains of mass surveillance.[1016]

§§ It bears mentioning that facial recognition technologies (FRT) boast a dark side that should not be glossed over. Strikingly, this advanced tool—which is crammed with functional shortcomings—is currently being deployed to surveil[1017] members

---

[1014] It is important to note that an algorithm designed for maximum accuracy will adjust itself to the majority data, and may be less accurate for members of the underrepresented group, thus breeding *inductive bias*. See: Shellenbarger, Sue, "A Crucial Step for Avoiding AI Disasters", *Wall Street Journal*, (Feb. 13, 2019, 9:57 AM ET), https://www.wsj.com/articles/a-crucial-step-for-avoiding-ai-disasters-11550069865?ns=prod/accounts-wsj [https://perma.cc/C28U-LAAE] (discussing this issue while emphasizing how diverse development teams pay more attention to unrepresentative and underrepresented data sets). Human programmers can circumvent and bypass this problem by weighting the minority-group data more heavily, by designing different algorithms for each racial group, or by striving to contain more data to equalize group representation in the data set. See: Barua, Sukarna et al., "MWMOTE—Majority Weighted Minority Oversampling Technique for Imbalanced Data Set Learning", *IEEE Transactions on Knowledge & Data Engineering*, Volume 26, 2014, pp. 405, 405–06. See also: Hamilton, Melissa, "The Biased Algorithm: Evidence of Disparate Impact on Hispanics", *American Criminal Law Review*, Volume 56, 2019, pp. 1553 and ff and passim (which clearly demonstrates that COMPAS was significantly less accurate for Hispanic than for white defendants by several measures and suggesting that smaller numbers of Hispanic defendants might be the cause). See: Mayson, Sandra G., "Bias In, Bias Out", *cit.*, pp. 2218–2300. See also: Dong et al., Qi,, "Imbalanced deep learning by minority class incremental rectification, *IEEE Transactions on Pattern Analysis & Machine Intelligence*, Volume 41, 2019, p. 1367 (posit that "*most existing learning algorithms produce inductive bias (learning bias)* towards the frequent (majority) classes if training data are not balanced, *resulting in poor minority class recognition performance*"). Italics added. See: Chandler, Anupam, "The Racist Algorithm", *Michigan Law Review*, Volume 115, n.º 6, 2018, p. 1026 (on racist algorithms, noting that "the possibilities for discriminatory manipulation are legion").

[1015] Barocas, Solon/Selbst, Andrew D., "Big Data's Disparate Impact", *California Law Review*, Volume 104, 2016, pp. 671–682 (discussing how data is often flawed, rigged, incomplete, imperfect and therefore algorithms inherit the prejudice of the original decision makers). But see: Citron, Danielle Keats/Pasquale, Frank, "The Scored Society: Due Process for Automated Predictions", *Washington Law Review*, Volume 89, 2014, pp. 1, 4–5 (highlighting how human beings programming automated systems is directly conducive to, and leads, to fundamentally inaccurate results since the source code, predictive algorithms and datasets may encompass human biases which, in turn, have a disparate impact on historically disadvantaged groups); Crawford, Kate/Schultz, Jason, "Big Data and Due Process: Toward a Framework to Redress Predictive Privacy Harms", *Boston College Law Review*, Volume 55, 2014, pp. 93, 99–101 (pinpointing pathways through which predictive analytic tools perpetuate discriminatory practices). But see: Bornstein, Stepanhie, "Antidiscriminatory Algorithms", *Alabama Law Review*, Volume 70, 2018, pp. 519, 524–528 (contending, however, that the tagged "facially neutral" algorithms producing discriminatory outcomes should be quashed).

[1016] Xiang, Alice, "Being "Seen" versus "Mis-Seen": tensions between Privacy and Fairness in Computer Vision", *cit.*, pp. 1–60.

[1017] Xiang, Alice, "Being "Seen" versus "Mis-Seen": tensions between Privacy and Fairness in Computer Vision", *cit.*, pp. 1–60. Rich, Michael L., Machine Learning, "Automated Suspicion Algorithms, and the Fourth Amendment", *The University of Pennsylvania Law Review*, Volume 164, 2016, pp. 871 and ff. See: Ferguson, Andrew Guthrie, "Big Data and Predictive Reasonable Suspicion", *The University of Pennsylvania Law Review*, Volume 163, 2015, passim; Joh, Elizabeth E., "The New Surveillance Discretion: Automated Suspicion, Big Data, and Policing", *The Harvard Law & Policy Review*, Volume 10, 2016, pp. 15 and ff.

of communities of colour[1018] whom form part of cohort of *socially undesirables* that routinely find themselves in the crosshairs of law enforcement agencies'.

§§ In addition to that, facial recognition technologies evince a lacklustre performance when it comes to identifying people of colour.[1019] Therefore, being «unseen» by Artificial Intelligence-embedded technologies does not shield against being «mis-seen».[1020]

§§ Moving forward, it should be noted that HCCV comprises an exceedingly wide array of technologies, ranging from face detection for a camera's

[1018] See: Fergus, Rachel, "Biased Technology: The Automated Discrimination of Facial Recognition", *ACLU Minnesota*, February 29, 2024, available at: https://www.aclu-mn.org/en/news/biased-technology-automated-discrimination-facial-recognition (access: 20.09.2024) ("*Law enforcement and the criminal justice system already disproportionately target and incarcerate people of color. Using technology that has documented problems with correctly identifying people of color is dangerous.* The ACLU-MN has an appalling firsthand example here in Minnesota: We sued on behalf of Kylese Perryman, an innocent young man who was falsely arrested and detained based solely on incorrect facial identification. The *injustice does not stop there. A 2020 ACLU study found that since Black people are more likely to be arrested than white people for minor crimes, their faces and personal data are more likely to be in mugshot databases. That makes them more likely to be misidentified as suspects and forced to sit in lineups – despite the documented lack of accuracy behind all these means of supposed identification. The ACLU found that police surveillance cameras are disproportionately installed in Black and Brown neighborhoods, which again exacerbates systematic racism. It is a common assumption that technology is unbiased, and thus infallible. This simply isn't true. All technology is created by people and people are biased*"). Italics added.

[1019] Fergus, Rachel, "Biased Technology: The Automated Discrimination of Facial Recognition", *ACLU Minnesota*, February 29, 2024, available at: https://www.aclu-mn.org/en/news/biased-technology-automated-discrimination-facial-recognition (access: 20.09.2024) ("*technology is developing much more quickly than the laws we need to protect our rights. Anyone with a smartphone or social media account knows how rapidly technology changes, while legislating can take a long, long time. It is essential to proactively put policies into place that will protect our rights as new and more advanced technology is constantly released. Especially when that technology – and law enforcement members using it - have been shown over and over to be biased toward marginalized groups*"). Italics added.

[1020] Xiang, Alice, "Being "Seen" versus "Mis-Seen": tensions between Privacy and Fairness in Computer Vision", *cit.*, pp. 1–60.

autofocus[1021] feature to pedestrian detection embedded on a self-driving[1022] car.[1023]

3.1.5.7.1 «Selectively Targeting Socially Undesirables»: The Lacklustre Performance of Facial Recognition Technologies with Respect to Members of Racialized Communities

§§ Given its potential to inflict consumer harms[1024] upon citizens, Human-centric computer vision («HCCV») technologies,[1025] including facial recognition, stand arguably amongst the most controversial artificial intelligence («AI») technologies.

[1021] Hu, Margaret, "From the National Surveillance State to the Cybersurveillance State", *The Annual Review of Law and Social Science*, Volume 13, 2017, p. 169 ("*Facial recognition technology drawing upon a photo database could potentially link a plethora of digital images of a person, including social media, the internet, photo databases like driver's licenses, live-streaming video, CCTV surveillance, and images obtained from hacking cameras on laptops and digital devices*. Biometric data collection and storage are becoming increasingly compulsory through either government identification requirements, *such as digital photo requirements for passports and driver's licenses, or corporate identification requirements, such as biometric access to digital devices*"). Italics added.

[1022] See: Surden, Harry/Williams, Mary-Anne, "Technological Opacity, Predictability, and Self-Driving Cars", *Cardozo Law Review*, Volume 38, 2016, pp. 121 and ff (arguing that self-driving cars are mostly controlled by Artificial Intelligence-technologies). See: Smith, Bryant Walker, "Proximity-Driven Liability", *The Georgetown Law Journal*, Volume 102, 2014, pp. 1777 and ff (discussing the implications arising out of the uptick of vehicle automation in decades to come).

[1023] Xiang, Alice, "Being "Seen" versus "Mis-Seen": tensions between Privacy and Fairness in Computer Vision", *cit.*, pp. 1–60. See: Part III, this chapter, Sects. 3.1.5.9–3.1.5.9.3 of this book (devoted to Critical Artificial Intelligence Studies, with a sharper focus on the pressing challenges facing self-driving vehicles).

[1024] See: Bar-Gill, Oren/Sunstein, Cass R./Talgam-Cohen, Inbal, "Algorithmic Harm in Consumer Markets", *Journal of Legal Analysis*, Volume 15, n.° 1, 2023, pp. 1–47. See also: Lee, Nicole Turner/Resnick, Paul/Barton, Genie, *Algorithmic Bias Detection and Mitigation: Best Practices and Policies to Reduce Consumer Harms*. Washington, DC: Brookings Institution, 2019, passim; Slaughter, Rebecca Kelly, "Algorithms and Economic Justice: A Taxonomy of Harms and a Path Forward for the Federal Trade Commission", *Yale Journal of Law and Technology*, Volume 23, 2021 (on algorithmic consumer harms).

[1025] HCCV consists of subset of the "human-centered machine learning" models from which Model Cards derives. See: Mitchell, Margaret et al., "Model Cards for Model Reporting", Proceedings ACM Conference on Fairness, Accountability & Transparency, 2019, 220, 220, https://dl.acm.org/doi/10.1145/3287560.3287596 [https://perma.cc/26965XHJ]. On the flip side, HCCV has broader scope than Facial Processing Technologies ("FPT"), which comprises "any task involving the identification and characterization of the face image of a human subject." See: Inioluwa Deborah Raji/Genevieve Fried, "About Face: A Survey of Facial Recognition Evaluation", *AAAI 2020 Workshop on Artificial Intelligence Evaluation*, 2021, 1, 2. HCCV comprises chores involving human bodies and objects. In addition to that, HCCV can also be viewed as any computer vision system relying on a host "people-centric" datasets. See: Hanley, Margot/Apoorv Khandelwal, Hadar Averbuch-Elor, Noah Snavely & Helen Nissenbaum, "An Ethical Highlighter for Peo ple-Centric Dataset Creation", *Navigating the Broader Impacts on I Research Workshop at Neurips*, 1, 2020, pp. 1–2, https://arxiv.org/pdf/2011.13583.pdf [https://perma.cc/6ZQRASHS]. See also: Xiang, Alice, "Being "Seen" versus "Mis-Seen": tensions between Privacy and Fairness in Computer Vision", *cit.*, pp. 1–60.

No surprise stems from the fact that HCCV systems have been halted pursuant either bans or moratoriums.[1026] Compellingly, several United States of America jurisdictions have severely limited the use of facial recognition technologies («FRT») by bodies of government agencies,[1027] with a sharper focus on law enforcement agencies.[1028]

§§ The EU AI Act, in turn, classifies all remote biometric[1029] identification («RBI»)[1030] systems as **high-risk** (and therefore subject to both lengthy and hefty

[1026] See: Fergus, Rachel, "Biased Technology: The Automated Discrimination of Facial Recognition", *ACLU Minnesota*, February 29, 2024, available at: https://www.aclu-mn.org/en/news/biased-technology-automated-discrimination-facial-recognition (access: 20.09.2024) ("*Facial recognition automates discrimination.The ACLU-MN is fighting to end law enforcement's use of facial recognition technology in Minnesota. More than a dozen large cities have banned the technology, including Minneapolis, Boston, and San Francisco.* If Minnesota adopts a policy to ban the technology, it would be the first state to do so. Here's why the ACLU-MN will fight this legislative session to ban facial recognition tech:

1. *It gives blanketed and indiscriminate surveillance to authorities to track you.*
2. *It is inaccurate and intensifies racial and gender biases that already exist in law enforcement, which lead to disparate treatment.*
3. *It can be used to target and identify vulnerable groups, such as immigrants and refugees.*
4. *It can be used to track your personal movements, including going to abortion clinics or drug treatment.*
5. *Facial recognition technology violates our Constitutional rights*"). Italics added.

[1027] See: Fergus, Rachel, "Biased Technology: The Automated Discrimination of Facial Recognition", *ACLU Minnesota*, February 29, 2024, available at: https://www.aclu-mn.org/en/news/biased-technology-automated-discrimination-facial-recognition (access: 20.09.2024) ("*Facial recognition automates discrimination. The ACLU-MN is fighting to end law enforcement's use of facial recognition technology in Minnesota. More than a dozen large cities have banned the technology, including Minneapolis, Boston, and San Francisco*").

[1028] See: Elec. Priv. Info. Ctr., State Facial Recognition Policy, EPIC.ORG, https://epic.org/state-policy/facialrecognition [https://perma.cc/LC5L-GUFU] (making a list of moratoriums or bans in California and Massachusetts). See also: Xiang, Alice, "Being "Seen" versus "Mis-Seen": tensions between Privacy and Fairness in Computer Vision", *cit.*, pp. 1–60.

[1029] See: Hu, Margaret, "From the National Surveillance State to the Cybersurveillance State", *The Annual Review of Law and Social Science*, Volume 13, 2017, pp. 162–163 ("*policymakers view these technological developments, including biometric technologies, as tools with the potential to identify individuals who may pose a threat to national and homeland security and to prevent crime and terrorism. One example of technology intended for risk assessment and threat management is the post-9/11 program Total Information Awareness (TIA). (….) Collect-it-all efforts like TIA embody a philosophy that aspires to preventive policing. Mass data collection is construed as a tool to assess and prevent future threats (Murray 2010). In TIA and other programs tested or adopted after 9/ 11, biometric database screening and analysis have emerged as a preferred method for tracking, identifying, and establishing identity-based inferences in counterterrorism*"). Italics added. See also: Ball, Kirstie, and Frank Webster (Eds.), *The Intensification of Surveillance: Crime, Terrorism & Warfare in the Information Age*, London, UK: Pluto Press, 2007; Guzik, Keith, "Discrimination by Design: Predictive Data Mining as Security Practice in the United States' 'War on Terrorism'", *Surveillance and Society*, 7 (1), 2009, pp. 1–17.

[1030] Hu, Margaret, "From the National Surveillance State to the Cybersurveillance State", *The Annual Review of Law and Social Science*, Volume 13, 2017, p. 169 ("*as a result of big*

regulatory requirements), and accordingly forbids the use of live RBI by law enforcement agencies in public spaces[1031] (exception made to a cluster of narrow carve outs).[1032]

§§ From a privacy standpoint, the phantom of mass surveillance,[1033] with a sharper focus on state actors, has spawned vitriolic remarks and trenchant criticism with the increasing pervasiveness of FRT[1034] looming large in the discussion. Relatedly, there has been a groundswell of support for buttressing information privacy laws. Strikingly, there has also been a mounting concern on the pervasiveness of algorithmic biases in HCCV. A ground-breaking paper penned by a cohort of polymaths showed that the overwhelming majority of commercial gender classification algorithms had a lacklustre performance on women as opposed to men.[1035] Further, classification

---

data biometric governance trends, meaningful distinctions between biometric credentialing for identification and behavioral biometric profiling are disappearing. The objectives are merging: Reliable credentialing is used to advance security and precrime policy rationales. Biometric data mission creep occurs by necessity in a big data world because the cybersurveillance systems are often designed to engage in mass data integration and analysis and predictive policing. Biometric surveillance serves two purposes in preventive policing: It increases identity transparency, and the biometric data categorize identity through cataloging behavioral and physical characteristics and assess these characteristics for risk. Contrasting small data biometric credentialing protocols with big data credentialing protocols is useful. It illustrates how biometric surveillance fits within the Cybersurveillance State"). Italics added.

1031 Xiang, Alice, "Being "Seen" versus "Mis-Seen": tensions between Privacy and Fairness in Computer Vision", *cit.*, pp. 1–60.

1032 Xiang, Alice, "Being "Seen" versus "Mis-Seen": tensions between Privacy and Fairness in Computer Vision", *cit.*, pp. 1–60.

1033 On mass surveillance: Bentham, Jeremy, *Panopticon: Or, the inspection-house*, Thomas Byrne, 1787. See also: Balkin, Jack M./Levinson, Sanford, "The Processes of Constitutional Change: From Partisan Entrenchment to the National Surveillance State", *Fordham Law Review*, Volume 75, 2006, pp. 489 and ff; Slogogin, Christopher, "Public Privacy: Camera Surveillance of Public Places and the Right to Anonymity", *Mississippi Law Journal*, Volume 72, 2002, pp. 213–251; Balkin, Jack M., "The Constitution in the National Surveillance State", *Minnesota Law Review*, Volume 93, Issue 1, 2008, pp. 17 and ff; Christopher Slobogin, "Panvasive Surveillance, Political Process Theory, and the Nondelegation Doctrine", *Georgetown Law Journal*, Volume 102, 2014, pp. 1721–1775; Ericson, Richard V., and Kevin D. Haggerty, *The New Politics of Surveillance and Visibility*. Toronto: University of Toronto Press, 2006.

1034 Xiang, Alice, "Being "Seen" versus "Mis-Seen": tensions between Privacy and Fairness in Computer Vision", *cit.*, pp. 1–60.

1035 See: Buolamwini, Joy/Gebru, Timnit, "Gender Shades: Intersectional Accuracy Disparities in Commercial Gender Classification", *Proceedings on the 1st Conference on Fairness, Accountability & Transparency: Proceedings of Machine Learning Research*, Volume 81, 2018, pp. 1–8.

algorithms[1036] performed considerably less well on citizens with deeper[1037] skin tones[1038] than did on lighter skin tones.[1039]

§§ From that point onwards, earth-shattering studies—with a sharper focus on one penned the National Institute of Standards and Technology («NIST»), which forms part of a broader regulatory apparatus U.S. Department of Commerce within which the former operates—have showcased stark differences in performance on the basis of skin tone and gender along the lines of HCCV systems.[1040] Compellingly, this bundle of studies has ascribed these algorithmic biases to a lack of diversity in the

[1036] But see: Dieterich, William et al., "COMPAS Risk Scales: Demonstrating Accuracy Equity and Predictive Parity", *Northpointe Inc.* 1, 2–3, 8–13 (July 8, 2016), http://go.volarisgroup.com/rs/430-MBX-989/images/ProPublica_Commentary_Final_070616.pdf [https://perma.cc/K4GM-RBQY] (stating that a predictive instrument is bigoted/flawed only if a certain score, or a given classification, means a starkly likelihood of the forecasted outcome for members of one racial group than members of the other group). See also: Flores: Anthony W. et al., "False Positives, False Negatives, and False Analyses: A Rejoinder to "Machine Bias: There's Software Used Across the Country to Predict Future Criminals. And It's Biased Against Blacks," *Federal Probation*, Volume 80, 2016, pp. 38–40 (positing that "well-established and accepted standards exist to test for bias in risk assessment"); Skeem, Jennifer L./Lowenkamp, Christopher T., "Risk, Race, and Recidivism: Predictive Bias and Disparate Impact", *cit.*, p. 685 (asserting that if "a given score [has] the same meaning regardless of group membership," the instrument is "unbiased"). Prince, Anya E.R., "Insurance Risk Classification in an Era of Genomics: Is a Rational Discrimination Policy Rational?", *Nebraska Law Review*, Volume 96, 2018, pp. 624, 630–34, 641–42 (shedding light on "fair" and "unfair" discrimination). Note, though, that the word "discrimination" can also be used in a technical legal sense. In this sense it would mean that such differential treatment or disparate impact would incur liability pursuant to the purview of antidiscrimination law. See: Mayson, Sandra G., "Bias In, Bias Out", *cit.*, pp. 2218–2300.

[1037] See: Fergus, Rachel, "Biased Technology: The Automated Discrimination of Facial Recognition", *ACLU Minnesota*, February 29, 2024, available at: https://www.aclu-mn.org/en/news/biased-technology-automated-discrimination-facial-recognition (access: 20.09.2024) ("*Law enforcement and the criminal justice system already disproportionately target and incarcerate people of color. Using technology that has documented problems with correctly identifying people of color is dangerous.The ACLU-MN has an appalling firsthand example here in Minnesota: We sued on behalf of Kylese Perryman, an innocent young man* who was falsely arrested and detained based solely on incorrect facial identification"). Italics added.

[1038] Xiang, Alice, "Being "Seen" versus "Mis-Seen": tensions between Privacy and Fairness in Computer Vision", *cit.*, pp. 1–60.

[1039] Xiang, Alice, "Being "Seen" versus "Mis-Seen": tensions between Privacy and Fairness in Computer Vision", *cit.*, pp. 1–60.

[1040] Xiang, Alice, "Being "Seen" versus "Mis-Seen": tensions between Privacy and Fairness in Computer Vision", *cit.*, pp. 1–60.

datasets (*inductive bias*)[1041] used to train these commercial Artificial Intelligence-anchored[1042] systems.[1043]

§§ For that reason, cases in which Black men in the United States of America have been unlawfully arrested due to flawed facial recognition matches abound accordingly.[1044] For instance, Nijeer Parks, a Black man, was unlawfully arrested due to a flawed facial recognition match. As a result, he spent ten days incarcerated and paid close to $5,000 dollars to defend himself before the lawsuit[1045] was dismissed for lack of evidence.[1046]

§§ It bears mentioning that the term HCCV comprises Artificial Intelligence-anchored systems that heavily rely on images of human beings for their training dataset[1047] and test dataset.[1048] Strikingly, these are the Artificial Intelligence-anchored technologies whose burgeoning development is impacted by biometric

---

1041 But see: Dong et al., Qi, "Imbalanced deep learning by minority class incremental rectification, *IEEE Transactions on Pattern Analysis & Machine Intelligence*, Volume 41, 2019, p. 1367 (posit that "*most existing learning algorithms produce inductive bias (learning bias)* towards the frequent (majority) classes if training data are not balanced, *resulting in poor minority class recognition performance*").

1042 Xiang, Alice, "Being "Seen" versus "Mis-Seen": tensions between Privacy and Fairness in Computer Vision", *cit.*, pp. 1–60.

1043 Xiang, Alice, "Being "Seen" versus "Mis-Seen": tensions between Privacy and Fairness in Computer Vision", *cit.*, pp. 1–60.

1044 See: https://www.nytimes.com/2020/12/29/technology/facial-recognition-misidentify-jail.html (last accessed 17 March 2025) ("*In February 2019, Nijeer Parks was accused of shoplifting candy and trying to hit a police officer with a car at a Hampton Inn in Woodbridge, N.J. The police had identified him using facial recognition software, even though he was 30 miles away at the time of the incident* (…) He is the third person known to be falsely arrested based on a bad facial recognition match. *In all three cases, the people mistakenly identified by the technology have been Black men*"). Italics added.

1045 See: https://www.nytimes.com/2020/12/29/technology/facial-recognition-misidentify-jail.html (last accessed 17 March 2025) ("*Mr. Parks spent 10 days in jail and paid around $5,000 to defend himself. In November 2019, the case was dismissed for lack of evidence.* Mr. Parks, 33, *is now suing the police, the prosecutor and the City of Woodbridge for false arrest, false imprisonment and violation of his civil rights*"). Italics added.

1046 Xiang, Alice, "Being "Seen" versus "Mis-Seen": tensions between Privacy and Fairness in Computer Vision", *cit.*, pp. 1–60.

1047 Note, though, that the training of machine learning is long and tedious in that is an error-prone procedure than can ultimately impair future algorithmic decision-making: Price, W. Nicholson Price II, "Regulating Black-Box Medicine", *Michigan Law Review*, Volume 116, 2017, pp. 421–431 (leverages on Google Image's image recognition learning algorithm to shed light on the four-step process by which some algorithms are thoroughly trained. First, the algorithm is shown "a set of known images ('Here are 10,000 pictures of ducks')." Second, the algorithm "develops complex internal rules based on nonlinear processes." Third, the algorithm "tests those rules on a test set ('Which of these are ducks?')." And fourth, the algorithm accordingly adjusts its "internal rules based on the success of the test." These steps are trotted out and repeated many times "until it can accurately and consistently classify the images").

1048 Xiang, Alice, "Being "Seen" versus "Mis-Seen": tensions between Privacy and Fairness in Computer Vision", *cit.*, pp. 1–60.

information[1049]—and privacy regulations[1050]—that conceal operational details harvested from either human faces or human bodies.[1051]

§§ As averred by Alice Xiang, the term «development» comprises human images embedded in the training dataset deployed to teach the HCCV system how to discern, acknowledge, classify, or collect features from individuals or objects or the images in the evaluation datasets used to assess the model's performance. This set of images used for «development» are usually different from the images the HCCV system sees and recognizes[1052] in deployment.[1053] This also applies to body detection, pose estimation, and body recognition.[1054]

3.1.5.7.2 The Irony. What If Facial Recognition Technology Facilitates Crime Rather That Prevent It? «Face Morphing» Circumvents Facial Recognition Technologies and Thwarts the Effectiveness of Travel Bans («Algorithmic Jim Crow»): «The Goal of a Morphing Attack Is to Subvert a» Facial Recognition System «at an Automatic Border Control (ABC) Gate by Presenting an Electronic Machine-Readable Travel Document (eMRTD) or E-Passport That Is Obtained Based on a Morphed Face Image» (Venkatesh et al.)

§§ All too often we are told that if we steward bedazzling gifts (of technology) a floodgate of favour will overflow into every area of our lives, teeming with opulent perks beyond measure. Yet Artificial Intelligence-embedded technologies, if nothing else, have a penchant to leave people in awe while surpassing all their rosy expectations.

§§ Although facial recognition technology has a bright side (aside from all the functional drawbacks laid out in the previous section, this technology, with the right settings and for the right reasons, can help to quell crime), there are pitfalls associated to this technology that can further augment crime rather than diminish it. Take the example of **face morphing**.

§§ Facial recognition technology has been successfully deployed in live applications, including, but not limited to, once iron-clad applications such as passport border

---

[1049] Xiang, Alice, "Being "Seen" versus "Mis-Seen": tensions between Privacy and Fairness in Computer Vision", *cit.*, pp. 1–60.

[1050] Citron; Danielle Keats/Pasquale, Frank, "Network Accountability for the Domestic Intelligence Apparatus", *Hasting Law Journal*, Volume 62, 2011, 1441, 1444–1445; Gray, David/Citron, Danielle Keats, "The Right to Quantitative Privacy", *Minnesota Law Review*, Volume 98, 2013, pp. 62–81 (on privacy interests).

[1051] Xiang, Alice, "Being "Seen" versus "Mis-Seen": tensions between Privacy and Fairness in Computer Vision", *cit.*, pp. 1–60.

[1052] Xiang, Alice, "Being "Seen" versus "Mis-Seen": tensions between Privacy and Fairness in Computer Vision", *cit.*, pp. 1–60.

[1053] Xiang, Alice, "Being "Seen" versus "Mis-Seen": tensions between Privacy and Fairness in Computer Vision", *cit.*, pp. 1–60.

[1054] Xiang, Alice, "Being "Seen" versus "Mis-Seen": tensions between Privacy and Fairness in Computer Vision", *cit.*, pp. 1–60.

control. Notwithstanding, the susceptibility of face recognition systems (FRSs) to a plethora of withering attacks (either direct or indirect attacks) and **face morphing** attacks has garnered a great deal of attention from biometric pundits.[1055]

§§ The overriding goal of a morphing attack is to undermine an FRS at an automatic border control (ABC) gate by showing an electronic machine-readable travel document (eMRTD) or e-passport that is fabricated on the basis of a morphed face image. Insofar application process for an e-passport in an overwhelming majority of countries simply requires a passport photograph to be showed by a given citizen, a criminal actor and a known associate can produce a morphed face image to acquire the e-passport.[1056]

§§ Strikingly, the e-passport with a morphed face image can be utilized by both the criminal actor and the known associate to cross a border, since the morphed face image can be checked against both of them. This can pose a significant threat to national security, since the criminal can cross the border without leaving any trace whatsoever of his criminal background, whereas the details of the known associated are duly recorded in the log of the access control system,[1057] thereby undermining FRS abilities to squelch crime in a given jurisdiction.[1058]

§§ Compellingly, the morphed facial image can successfully be checked with probe images from both contributing individuals, thereby making it promptly actionable for several mischievous endeavours. Consequently, this face morphing jeopardizes the rule of single ownership. For instance, identification document such as a passport or electronic machine-readable travel document (eMRTD) possesses a unique link to the data subject for whom the identification document was solely issued.[1059]

§§ Therefore, a criminal with mischievous intent can launch the face morphing attack in a bid to obtain illegal access to a given country. Thence, a criminal can effortlessly cross a border using an eMRTD or passport if the former has greatly contributed to the morphed image that was used in the passport application process. To the extent that multiple morphing software programs proliferate and were made widely available to the general public, every «Joe Sixpack», no matter how unskilled, can easily perform **face morphing**. The criminals 'known associate can subsequently submit the doctored morphed image for passport enrolment at the passport control.[1060]

[1055] Venkatesh, Sushma/Kiran Raja/Raghavendra Ramachandra, "Face Morphing Attack Generation and Detection: A Comprehensive Survey", *IEEE Transactions on Technology and Society*, Volume 2, n.º 3, September 2021, 2021, pp. 128–145.

[1056] Venkatesh, Sushma/Kiran Raja/Raghavendra Ramachandra, "Face Morphing Attack Generation and Detection: A Comprehensive Survey", *cit.*, pp. 128–145.

[1057] Venkatesh, Sushma/Kiran Raja/Raghavendra Ramachandra, "Face Morphing Attack Generation and Detection: A Comprehensive Survey", *cit.*, pp. 128–145.

[1058] Venkatesh, Sushma/Kiran Raja/Raghavendra Ramachandra, "Face Morphing Attack Generation and Detection: A Comprehensive Survey", *cit.*, pp. 128–145.

[1059] Venkatesh, Sushma/Kiran Raja/Raghavendra Ramachandra, "Face Morphing Attack Generation and Detection: A Comprehensive Survey", *cit.*, pp. 128–145.

[1060] Venkatesh, Sushma/Kiran Raja/Raghavendra Ramachandra, "Face Morphing Attack Generation and Detection: A Comprehensive Survey", *cit.*, pp. 128–145.

§§ To the extent that the morphed image's facial features bear a strikingly resemble those of the applicant's face, the passport police officer swiftly, and readily, approves the application. Ultimately, a malign individual can fruitfully use the real passport, thereby enabling the former to accomplish all his/her overriding goals (e.g., crossing a border and engaging in a host of criminal activities).[1061]

§§ Not so long ago, some countries, such as New Zealand, Estonia, and Ireland, also accepted a digital facial image for passport renewal purposes.[1062] Thence, an applicant could effortlessly, and swiftly, submit a digital facial image to the Web portal. It is important to highlight, though, that this practice raised critical concerns inasmuch there was no stringent supervision while uploading the digital facial image, which crack-opens the possibility of uploading a morphed image. On the flip side, not so long ago, the B1/B2 visa application for the United States of America also allowed a given applicant to upload a digital facial image via the Web portal,[1063] which wholly thwarted the effectiveness of travel bans issued with a view to prevent some individuals from entering into its territory: the kernel of «Algorithmic Jim Crow».[1064]

3.1.5.7.3 The Anatomy of a «Face Morphing Attack»

§§ With this context in place, face morphing attack consists of a facial morphing process whereby two facial images are weaved together to produce a single morphed image to allow the criminal to cross a given border unbothered. Face morphing can be attained effortlessly by gaining access to one of the multifarious tools made freely made to the general public, ranging from *MorphThing*, *3Dthis Face Morph*, *Face Swap Online*, *AbrosoftFantaMorph*, *FaceMorpher*, to *MagicMorph*.[1065]

§§ Compellingly, the morphed image bears a strikingly resemblance with features to those of both individuals contributing to fabricating the morph when subject preselection is applied (e.g., look-alike mode).[1066] Moreover, when handled with painstaking care, the morphed image will be devoid of many visible artifacts. For that reason, the passport police officer, albeit a highly trained human observer, might

---

1061 Venkatesh, Sushma/Kiran Raja/Raghavendra Ramachandra, "Face Morphing Attack Generation and Detection: A Comprehensive Survey", *cit.*, pp. 128–145.

1062 Venkatesh, Sushma/Kiran Raja/Raghavendra Ramachandra, "Face Morphing Attack Generation and Detection: A Comprehensive Survey", *cit.*, pp. 128–145.

1063 Venkatesh, Sushma/Kiran Raja/Raghavendra Ramachandra, "Face Morphing Attack Generation and Detection: A Comprehensive Survey", *cit.*, pp. 128–145.

1064 See: Part IV, Chap. 4, Sects. 4.1.5–4.1.5.2 of this book (on "algorithmic Jim Crow", a travel ban issued during the first Trump Administration to prevent certain individuals from entering the United States of America, which, given its racial undertones, stands as an outgrown of congeries of laws arising out Jim Crow epoch).

1065 Venkatesh, Sushma/Kiran Raja/Raghavendra Ramachandra, "Face Morphing Attack Generation and Detection: A Comprehensive Survey", *cit.*, pp. 128–145.

1066 Raghavendra, R./Raja, K./Venkatesh, S./Busch, C. "Face morphing versus face averaging: Vulnerability and detection," *Proceedings IEEE Int. Joint Conf. Biometrics (IJCB)*, 2017, pp. 555–563.

fail to identify image manipulation on the basis of face morphing. In practical terms, this is directly conducive to a delicate situation where a passport officer might not be able to successfully spotlight the morphing attack in spite of being an expert in manual facial[1067] comparison.[1068]

§§ To add to our woes, Large Language Models are currently being deployed to counterfeit e-passports, which may also impair the effectiveness of facial recognition technologies while paving the way to an uptick of flagitious activities worldwide.

3.1.5.8 The Looming Dangers of a World of Ubiquitous Facial Recognition CCTV Cameras Amidst the «Age of Fabricated Reality»: Can Artificial Intelligence-Embedded Technologies Tamper with Evidence Leveraging on an Advanced Technique Called «Correction»?

3.1.5.8.1 «The Age of Fabricated Reality by 2030»: «Facial Recognition Technology: The Capture vs Reality» (Asress Adimi Gikay)

§§ Imagine, if you will, that a closed-circuit television (CCTV) footage portrays a man assaulting a woman, thereby preventing her from entering a bus as she struggles to fend off the vicious attack perpetrated by the aggressor.[1069] The whole situation ends with the kidnapping of the lady, thereby priming the police to issue an arrest warrant to catch the alleged criminal. Note, though, that a thorough investigation uncovers a hidden truth: turns out, the CCTV footage showed a partially doctored event, as the woman had indeed boarded the bus and headed towards her home accordingly, as clearly depicted by CCTV footage from the bus.[1070]

§§ This story was withdrawn the BBC's science-fiction TV series, The *Capture*, which features a world of ubiquitous facial recognition CCTV cameras.[1071] In *The Capture*, a real-time CCTV feed is doctored, warped, tampered with and seamlessly switches from a live event to a doctored one in a split second.[1072] This cheap trick is all but blazingly new. Compellingly, pundits have long warned that Artificial

[1067] Venkatesh, Sushma/Kiran Raja/Raghavendra Ramachandra, "Face Morphing Attack Generation and Detection: A Comprehensive Survey", *cit.*, pp. 128–145.

[1068] Robertson, D.J./Kramer, R. S. S. Kramer/Burton, A. M., "Fraudulent ID using face morphs: Experiments on human and automatic recognition," *PLoS ONE*, Volume 12, n. 3, 2017, pp. 1–12.

[1069] Gikay, Asress Adimi, "Regulating use by Law Enforcement Authorities of Live Recognition by Law of Live Facial Recognition in Public Spaces: An Incremental Approach", *Cambridge Law Journal*, 82 (3), November 2023, 2023, pp. 414–449.

[1070] Gikay, Asress Adimi, "Regulating use by Law Enforcement Authorities of Live Recognition by Law of Live Facial Recognition in Public Spaces: An Incremental Approach", *cit.*, pp. 414–449.

[1071] https://www.bbc.co.uk/programmes/m00085sx (access: 17.03.2025).

[1072] Gikay, Asress Adimi, "Regulating use by Law Enforcement Authorities of Live Recognition by Law of Live Facial Recognition in Public Spaces: An Incremental Approach", *cit.*, pp. 414–449.

Intelligence-embedded technologies can be used to counterfeit evidence[1073] building on an advanced technique called **«correction»**.[1074]

§§ Tellingly, the warped technology is subsequently deployed to broadcast to the general public a live TV interview with a «deep fake»[1075] version of a high-level government official as though it were an real[1076] interview[1077] As duly noted by Professor Gikay, *The Capture* dramatizes and exacerbates the looming dangers of ubiquitous surveillance drawing on live facial recognition (LFR) technology,[1078] which, in turn, is poised to usher in the **age of fabricated reality** that is upon us.

§§ By 2030, a world of ubiquitous **live facial recognition (LFR)** technology will **control** every aspect of our daily lives with little to none regard for the underlying truth of real-time events, which will be tampered with by unscrupulous actors to advance their hidden agendas. Much to our dismay, **age of fabricated reality** will dispel the frontier between reality and fiction. Then, everything will be a fabricated copy of reality—or what's left of it.

§§ Worse still, Generative Artificial Intelligence will be weaponized against a cohort of *socially undesirables* that may find themselves at the crosshairs of a relevant stakeholder.

3.1.5.9 «Asleep at the Wheel?» Self-Driving Vehicles: Pre-empting Responsibility Gaps While Creating Legal Safeguards to Ensure the Success of Claims Arising Out of Product Liability

§§ Contrary to popular belief, Artificial Intelligence-embedded technologies are not constrained by the confines of complexity; rather, they consist of a fundamentally universal language of trailblazing innovation that is accessible to anyone who decides to attune themselves to their overriding importance in the world we live in.

§§ Self-driving cars hold a special space in the pantheon of Artificial Intelligence-anchored technologies to the extent that they are tightly interlocked with, and inextricably tied to, the adverse outcomes arising out of computer-run tools entrusted with

---

1073 Gikay, Asress Adimi, "Regulating use by Law Enforcement Authorities of Live Recognition by Law of Live Facial Recognition in Public Spaces: An Incremental Approach", *cit.*, pp. 414–449.

1074 Hogan, M. "'Spooks Meets Black Mirror': How The Capture Became the Year's Most Wildly Compelling TV Show", *The Guardian*, available at https:/www.theguardian.com/tv-and-radio/2022/sep/12/how-thecapture-became-the-years-most-wildly-compelling-tv-show (last accessed 17 march 2025).

1075 See: Part III, this chapter, Sects. 3.1.5.2–3.1.5.3.1 of this book (on the functional aspects of Critical Artificial Intelligence Studies, with a sharper focus on the harmful effects of Artificial Intelligence-embedded technologies, namely, Generative Artificial Intelligence and its offsprings—deepfakes and its deleterious effects on human memory).

1076 Gikay, Asress Adimi, "Regulating use by Law Enforcement Authorities of Live Recognition by Law of Live Facial Recognition in Public Spaces: An Incremental Approach", *cit.*, pp. 414–449.

1077 See: BBC, "SecurityMinister Gets Deepfaked on Newsnight | The Capture Series 2–BBC", available at https://www.youtube.com/watch?v=P4wAO48FzYk (last accessed 17 March 2025).

1078 Gikay, Asress Adimi, "Regulating use by Law Enforcement Authorities of Live Recognition by Law of Live Facial Recognition in Public Spaces: An Incremental Approach", *cit.*, pp. 414–449.

the task of controlling a vessel or a vehicle. The latter therefore carries a treasure trove of information about what the future holds for humankind, driverless vehicles wise.

§§ Compellingly, self-driving cars are shaping up to become mainstream in the modern world. Whilst these automated vehicles are not without sizable pitfalls, they are forecasted to possess multiple benefits to society and they are not going anywhere.[1079] Notwithstanding, as the world propels forward into an era marked by pathbreaking innovations in science and technology, the time in which self-driving vehicles circulate unconstrained on the roads is swiftly approaching. Before long, cars will be morphed into computer-controlled tools that won't need a human driver behind a wheel. As a result, archaic and outdated human-driven vehicles[1080] are bound to be jettisoned into the unheeded bucket of dolent oblivion.

§§ For the sake of clarity, what are self-driving cars[1081]? Concisely, they are driverless vehicles[1082] fully capable of circulating without the intervention of a human driver behind a wheel. To that end, self-driving cars heavily rely upon software and programs that encompass sensors to deftly control vehicular movement.[1083] No surprise stems from the fact that self-driving cars possess embedded internet connection that enables for software and program regular updates. In addition to that, the constant update of the software and underlying operating programs enables the communication with other self-driving vehicles, traffic architectures, and underlying infrastructures to better the vehicle's[1084] overall safety.

§§ I second the opinion according which victims of self-driving cars should be allotted new legal rights to soothe out the burden of proof of bringing a product liability claim before courts of law. As a result, victims should be thereupon afforded the: **(i)** «right of access to evidence»[1085] **embedded in the self-driving car data-recorder device**; **(ii)** the[1086] «presumption of causality»[1087] and, additionally, **(iii)** the producer's *presumption of fault* with regard to the damages inflicted upon the

---

1079 Ng, James, "Back in the Driver's Seat: The United States should enact a unified automated vehicle law and regulation", *Berkeley Technology Law Journal*, Volume 39 (1), 2024, pp. 3–46.

1080 Ng, James, "Back in the Driver's Seat: The United States should enact a unified automated vehicle law and regulation", pp. 3–46.

1081 Piatkowski, D., "Safe, efficient self-driving cars could block walkable, livable communities", *The Conversation*, October 2, 2018, available at: http://theconversation.com/safe-efficient-self-driving-cars-couldblock-walkable-livable-communities-103583 (last accessed 23 March 2025).

1082 Woodcock, I./Iain L./Stone, J., *Will Driverless Cars Produce Walkable Cities for Australia? In State of Australian cities national conference*, Perth, Western Australia, Volume 30, 2019.

1083 Ng, James, "Back in the Driver's Seat: The United States should enact a unified automated vehicle law and regulation", pp. 3–46.

1084 Ng, James, "Back in the Driver's Seat: The United States should enact a unified automated vehicle law and regulation", *cit*, pp. 3–46.

1085 Ng, James, "Back in the Driver's Seat: The United States should enact a unified automated vehicle law and regulation", *cit*, pp. 3–46.

1086 Ng, James, "Back in the Driver's Seat: The United States should enact a unified automated vehicle law and regulation", *cit*, pp. 3–46.

1087 Ng, James, "Back in the Driver's Seat: The United States should enact a unified automated vehicle law and regulation", *cit*, pp. 3–46.

victims. This legal framework seeks to forestall any responsibility gap[1088]—or legal loopholes—that could hamper the redress of damages caused by self-driving cars.

3.1.5.9.1 «Hacking Your Ride While You Go for a Spin»: The Looming Danger of Cyber-Hacking Level 4 and Level 5 Self-Driving Cars as Comprised by Society of Engineers' (SAE) Level of Automation

§§ Self-driving cars bestow upon us the possibility to embark on a journey to unravel its profound meaning concealed within and explore how it intertwines with the quest to grasp safety in this regard. Before drilling into, and shedding light on, the drawbacks associated with the deployment of self-driving cars, light must be cast upon on its levels of automation paired with cybersecurity concerns.

§§ As hinted above, self-driving cars is a broad scope term[1089] comprising a wide range of different automated[1090] capabilities.[1091] To qualify the sophistication of a self-driving car, the United States of America leveraged on the Society of Automotive Engineers (SAE) definitions for levels[1092] of automation.[1093] The SAE determined six levels of driving automation[1094]—ranging from «Level 0» through «Level 5»—in the SAE J3016 Recommended[1095] Practice.[1096]

[1088] See also: Gless, Sabine/Silvermann, Emile/Weigend, Thomas, "If Robots Cause Harm, Who Is to Blame? Self-Driving Cars and Criminal Liability", *New Criminal Law Review: An International and Interdisciplinary Journal*, Volume 19, No. 3 (Summer 2016), 2016, pp. 412–436.

[1089] See: Part III, this chapter, Sects. 3.1.5.7–3.1.5.8.1 of this book (on the functional aspects of Critical Artificial Intelligence Studies, with a sharper focus on the perils concerning the deployment of facial recognition technology).

[1090] Ng, James, "Back in the Driver's Seat: The United States should enact a unified automated vehicle law and regulation", *cit*, pp. 3–46.

[1091] Ng, James, "Back in the Driver's Seat: The United States should enact a unified automated vehicle law and regulation", *cit*, pp. 3–46.

[1092] Ng, James, "Back in the Driver's Seat: The United States should enact a unified automated vehicle law and regulation", *cit*, pp. 3–46.

[1093] SAE Levels of Driving Automation Refined for Clarity and International Audience, SAE INT'L (May 3, 2021), https://www.sae.org/blog/sae-j3016-update.

[1094] The 6 Levels of Vehicle Autonomy Explained, *Synopsis*, https://www.synopsys.com/automotive/autonomous-driving-levels.html#:~:text=The%20vehicle%20can%20control%20both,both%20qualify%20as%20Level%202 (last visited March. 19, 2025).

[1095] Ng, James, "Back in the Driver's Seat: The United States should enact a unified automated vehicle law and regulation", *cit*, pp. 3–46.

[1096] SAE Levels of Driving Automation Refined for Clarity and International Audience, SAE INT'L (May 3, 2021), https://www.sae.org/blog/sae-j3016-update.

§§ A vast array of countries, including the United States of America[1097] and the European Union, draw on this frame of reference for adroitly regulating AVs.[1098] SAE[1099] Level 0, Level 1, and Level 2 car require the drivers to be controlling the vehicle—that is, steering the wheel with deftness, moving forward cautiously, braking when needed, and accelerating to overtake other line of cars—and ought to oversee the automation support features to ensure safety at all cost.[1100] Paradigmatic examples of SAE Level 0 features encompass, but are not limited to, automatic emergency braking, blind spot loud warning, and lane departure loud warning and so forth. The Level 0 features are «limited to providing warnings and momentary assistance.»[1101]

§§ Paradigmatic examples of SAE Level 1 features comprise, but are not limited to, lane centring OR adaptive cruise control. Features in SAE Level 1 transmogrify into SAE Level 2 when both the lane centring and adaptive cruise control are used simultaneously, which enables the «features [to] provide steering [and] braking/ acceleration support to the driver».[1102]

§§ There are systems, such as the «Tesla Autopilot and Cadillac Super Cruise systems,» that fall well within the Level 2.[1103] Under SAE Levels 0, 1, and 2, automation support features are deemed to be «driver support features,» in lieu of, and as opposed to, «automated driving features» that are usually classified in higher SAE Levels, against the backdrop of which the driver is deemed to be[1104] «driving».[1105]

[1097] National Science & Technology Council & U.S. Department of Transp., Ensuring American Leadership in Automated Vehicle Technologies – Automated Vehicles 4.0. 29, 2020, available at: https://www.transportation.gov/sites/dot.gov/files/2020-02/EnsuringAmericanLeadershipAVTech4.pdf.

[1098] Pillath, Susanne, Automated Vehicles in the EU, European Parliamentary Research Service, 3–5 (Jan. 2016), https://www.europarl.europa.eu/RegData/etudes/BRIE/2016/573902/EPRS_BRI(2016)573902_EN.pdf [hereinafter AV in EU].

[1099] The 6 Levels of Vehicle Autonomy Explained, *Synopsis*, https://www.synopsys.com/automotive/autonomous-driving-levels.html#:~:text=The%20vehicle%20can%20control%20both,both%20qualify%20as%20Level%202 (last visited March. 19, 2025).

[1100] Shuttleworth, Jennifer, "SAE Standards News: J3016 Automated-Driving Graphic Update", SAE INT'L (Jan. 7, 2019), https://www.sae.org/news/2019/01/sae-updates-j3016automated-driving-graphic (discussing Level 0 features are "limited to providing warnings and momentary assistance"; Level 1 features "provide steering OR braking/acceleration support"; and Level 2 features provide, in sum, steering the wheel, acceleration to overtake other lines of cars, and a robust braking support).

[1101] Ng, James, "Back in the Driver's Seat: The United States should enact a unified automated vehicle law and regulation", *cit*, pp. 3–46.

[1102] Ng, James, "Back in the Driver's Seat: The United States should enact a unified automated vehicle law and regulation", *cit*, pp. 3–46.

[1103] Ng, James, "Back in the Driver's Seat: The United States should enact a unified automated vehicle law and regulation", *cit*, pp. 3–46.

[1104] Ng, James, "Back in the Driver's Seat: The United States should enact a unified automated vehicle law and regulation", *cit*, pp. 3–46.

[1105] Ng, James, "Back in the Driver's Seat: The United States should enact a unified automated vehicle law and regulation", *cit*, pp. 3–46.

§§ Looking to SAE Level 3,[1106] the pivotal role of «driving» starts to shift from the driver to the self-driving[1107] technology.[1108] Level 3 is of paramount importance in this regard insofar Level 3 cars are on the cusp of being commercially launched[1109] and made widely available to the general public.[1110]

§§ In stark contrast with lower levels of classification, self-driving cars that have SAE Level 3, 4, or 5 systems do not require the driver to be driving when «automated driving features are engaged—even if [the drivers] are seated in[1111] «the driver's seat».[1112]

§§ Compellingly, under Level 3 vehicle, the driver might be «asked» to actually drive the car at the automated feature request since the vehicle can only be controlled/ steered under limited[1113] conditions. As a result, the vehicle will not be able to move on its own absent certain conditions.[1114] With regard to SAE Levels 4 and 5, the[1115] «automated driving features will not require [the driver] to take over driving».[1116]

§§ Tellingly, a Level 4 system is amenable to be controlled only under limited conditions.[1117] Whilst the deployment of Level 4 systems haven't been made widely

---

[1106] The 6 Levels of Vehicle Autonomy Explained, *Synopsis*, https://www.synopsys.com/automotive/autonomous-driving-levels.html#:~:text=The%20vehicle%20can%20control%20both,both%20qualify%20as%20Level%202 (last visited March. 19, 2025).

[1107] Ng, James, "Back in the Driver's Seat: The United States should enact a unified automated vehicle law and regulation", *cit*, pp. 3–46.

[1108] Ng, James, "Back in the Driver's Seat: The United States should enact a unified automated vehicle law and regulation", *cit*, pp. 3–46.

[1109] Ng, James, "Back in the Driver's Seat: The United States should enact a unified automated vehicle law and regulation", *cit*, pp. 3–46.

[1110] Slovick, Murray, "Level 3 Autonomous Vehicles: Regulators Can't Keep Up with the Tech", Electronic Design (Jan. 24, 2022), https://www.electronicdesign.com/markets/automotive/article/21214818/electronicdesign-level-3-autonomous-vehicles-regulators-cant-keep-up-with-the-tech; Angel Sergeev, Mercedes Drive Pilot Level 3 Autonomous Tech Officially on Sale in Germany, MOTOR 1 (May 6, 2022), https://www.motor1.com/news/584121/mercedes-level-3-autonomous-tech-on-sale/.

[1111] Ng, James, "Back in the Driver's Seat: The United States should enact a unified automated vehicle law and regulation", *cit*, pp. 3–46.

[1112] Shuttleworth, Jennifer, "SAE Standards News: J3016 Automated-Driving Graphic Update", SAE INT'L (Jan. 7, 2019), https://www.sae.org/news/2019/01/sae-updates-j3016automated-driving-graphic.

[1113] Ng, James, "Back in the Driver's Seat: The United States should enact a unified automated vehicle law and regulation", *cit*, pp. 3–46.

[1114] Shuttleworth, Jennifer, "SAE Standards News: J3016 Automated-Driving Graphic Update", SAE INT'L (Jan. 7, 2019), https://www.sae.org/news/2019/01/sae-updates-j3016automated-driving-graphic.

[1115] Ng, James, "Back in the Driver's Seat: The United States should enact a unified automated vehicle law and regulation", *cit*, pp. 3–46.

[1116] Ng, James, "Back in the Driver's Seat: The United States should enact a unified automated vehicle law and regulation", *cit*, pp. 3–46.

[1117] Ng, James, "Back in the Driver's Seat: The United States should enact a unified automated vehicle law and regulation", *cit*, pp. 3–46.

available to the general public, corporations have been nonetheless employing staggering efforts to shrewdly develop the underpinning technology for its[1118] deployment.

§§ On the flip side, Level 5 self-driving cars are amenable to be operated wholly by computer-run driving features under all aspects concerned to driving a car. These are the only vehicles that are have yet to be released, launched, and made widely available to accessible to the public, in spite of the fact that the[1119] technologies[1120] are being tested.

§§ With this context in place, Level 4 and Level 5 self-driving cars—which, recall, are amenable to be operated mostly/wholly by computer-run driving features, respectively—are vulnerable to cyberattacks from unscrupulous actors,[1121] which can wreak havoc on the roads if these attacks occur in high ways or during rush hours/ heavy traffic jam, causing serious car crashes to occur with potentially ginormous human casualties. Brace yourself, dear reader, the recipe for disaster is brewing.

[1118] Ng, James, "Back in the Driver's Seat: The United States should enact a unified automated vehicle law and regulation", *cit*, pp. 3–46.

[1119] Ng, James, "Back in the Driver's Seat: The United States should enact a unified automated vehicle law and regulation", *cit*, pp. 3–46.

[1120] Ng, James, "Back in the Driver's Seat: The United States should enact a unified automated vehicle law and regulation", *cit*, pp. 3–46.

[1121] Harris, Jeffrey R., "Can Driverless Vehicle be hacked?" September 28, 2022, https://www.hlmlawfirm.com/blog/can-driverless-vehicles-be-hacked/ (last accessed 19.3.2025) ("The promise of autonomous vehicles – cars and trucks that don't need a human driver behind the wheel – offer many advantages. Proponents of driverless cars envision fewer traffic accidents caused by human error, more efficient movement of cargo, drunk driving prevention, and improved mass transit. *However, as full and partially autonomous vehicles start rolling out on American roads and highways, incidents and, yes, accidents are already happening. One major concern consumers and experts have about driverless vehicles is their vulnerability to cyberattacks. Because autonomous vehicles rely on advanced computers and technology, they're potentially open to hackers – and hackers have noticed. Imagine getting behind the wheel of your self-driving vehicle to go to the grocery store, and someone takes remote control of your car with you in it. This is a terrifying scenario, but some experts believe it's possible.* **Autonomous vehicles are vulnerable to hacking** *The website HackerNoon discusses the cybersecurity risks in autonomous vehicles, as well as the various ways cybercriminals might remotely attack a self-driving car. They note that technology continues advancing, allowing these types of vehicles to require less human intervention. Still, that same technology also allows hackers to take advantage, for criminal purposes or simply for fun.* ***Regardless of the reason, a hacked vehicle is extremely dangerous***. Per HackerNoon: ***There are intentional attacks that aim to specifically harm the safety-critical functions of the AI [artificial intelligence] systems. Examples include painting the road to misguide the navigation system or putting stickers on stop signs to prevent it from being recognized. Such alterations can lead the AI systems to wrongly classify objects which as a result could make the self-driving car behave in a dangerous way.*** *Behaving in a "dangerous way" is a bit of an understatement. Forcing a vehicle to run a stop sign or miss navigation cues will almost certainly cause a car accident, and serious crashes, resulting in catastrophic injuries for everyone involved*"). Italics and bold added.

3.1.5.9.2 «The Mad Radar Cyber-Attack That Successfully Bypassed Anti-Spoofing Protections»: Can Self-Driving Cars «Hallucinate»? Are Shoddy and Watered-Down Computer Vision and Cyber-Attacks Ingredients for a Perfect Storm That Lurks Ahead?

§§ Regardless of how enthralling, buoying, well-worn, well-canvassed, and familiar the tale of self-driving cars may be, it nonetheless exhibits intricate layers of shadiness[1122] conducive to a «technological opacity»,[1123] intimately linked to the adverse outcomes arising out of it.[1124]

§§ One of the biggest hurdles facing self-driving cars is its shoddy and watered-down computer vision.[1125] Self-driving cars grapple to identify objects, obstacles, black pawns (e.g. children and dark-skinned people[1126]), and traffic signs and act accordingly. To add to our woes, and as hinted above, self-driving cars levels 4 and

---

1122 The worrisome challenges posed by the up-and-coming and rough around the edges self-driving cars. See: Teoh, Eric/Kidd, David G., "Rage Against the Machine? Google's Self-Driving Versus Human Drivers", *Journal of Safety Research*, Volume 63, 2019, pp. 57–59 and passim (on the legal quandaries laid bare by the self-driving cars).

1123 See: Surden, Harry Surden/Williams, Mary-Anne, "Technological Opacity, Predictability, and Self-Driving Cars", *Cardozo Law Review*, Volume 38, 2016, pp. 121 and ff (arguing that self-driving cars are mostly controlled by Artificial Intelligence-technologies). See: Smith, Bryant Walker, "Proximity-Driven Liability", *The Georgetown Law Journal*, Volume 102, 2014, pp. 1777 and ff (discussing the implications arising out of the uptick of vehicle automation in decades to come).

1124 Cracking the Code: the Black Box Problem of Ai, available at: https://scads.ai/cracking-the-code-the-black-box-problem-of-ai/ (access: 21.09.2024) ("*To understand the black box problem, let's take an example of a self-driving car. The car's AI system is designed to make decisions based on various inputs such as road signs, sensors, and cameras. As a result, if the car gets into an accident, it may be challenging to determine what went wrong and why the AI system made a particular decision additionally.* The AI algorithm's decision-making process is often opaque and may involve complex calculations, making it difficult for humans to interpret"). Italics added.

1125 About the Turing test comprising computer vision: RUSSEL, STUART J./NORVIG, PETER, "Artificial Intelligence: a modern approach", Prentice-Hall, Inc. A Simon & Schuster Company, 1995 (The Turing Test aims to evaluate intelligent behaviour [1]. To proficiently evaluate intelligent behaviour, the computer should be interrogated by a human via a teletype, and passes the test if the interrogator cannot tell if there is a computer or a human at the other end [1]. The framework of Turing Test lies in the following and successive phases: the computer would need to possess the following capabilities: **0 natural language processing** to enable it to communicate successfully in English (or some other human language); moreover, <C> **knowledge representation** to store information provided before or during the interrogation; furthermore, <) **automated reasoning** to use the stored information to answer questions and to draw new conclusions; another feature needed is <) **machine learning** to adapt to new circumstances and to detect and extrapolate patterns [1]. Finally, to pass the total Turing Test, the computer will need computer vision <) **computer vision** to perceive objects and robotics (> **robotics** to move them about [1]. See also: Santos, Hugo Luz dos, *Direito Contratual do Jogo: Um Olhar Bifronte*, Braga, NovaCausa Edições Jurídicas, 2023, pp. 1–760; Simon, Herbert, *Artificial intelligence: Current status and future potential*, National Research Council Report – Office of Naval Research, 1985.

1126 See: Sparkes, Mathew, "Driverless cars may struggle to spot children and dark-skinned people", *New Scientist (Technology)*, 17th August 2023, 2023, available at: https://www.newscientist.com/article/2386635-driverless-cars-may-struggle-to-spot-children-and-dark-skinned-people/ (last

5 are particularly prone to cyber-attacks and can even **«hallucinate»**. In addition to that, hackers can make self-driving vehicles ignore road signs.[1127]

§§ To illustrate the vulnerability to cyberattacks facing self-driving vehicles, take the *MadRadar* cyber-attack for example. The *MadRadar* hack made self-driving cars **«hallucinate»** wholly imaginary cars and veer madly off course. Compellingly, the MadRadar cyber-attack successfully bypassed and circumvented the anti-spoofing protections in the radars of self-driving cars.[1128]

§§ Besides, *MadRadar* cyber-attack successfully targeted into imagining cars that were not indeed there—or hiding other ones that actually were.[1129] All in all, poor computer vision[1130] and the proneness to cyber-attacks facing Levels 4 and 5 driverless cars are ingredients for a perfect storm that lurks ahead.

---

accessed: 19.3.2025). ("The accuracy of pedestrian-detecting AI systems may be biased against some groups of people, fuelling calls for more transparency and tighter regulations").

[1127] See: Dobberstein, Laura, "GhostStripe attack haunts self-driving cars by making them ignore road signs", *The Register*, Friday, 10th of May of 2024, 2024, p. 1, available at: https://www.theregister.com/2024/05/10/baidu_apollo_hack/ (last accessed: 04.04.2025) ("*Six boffins mostly hailing from Singapore-based universities say they can prove it's possible to interfere with autonomous vehicles by exploiting the machines' reliance on camera-based computer vision and cause them to not recognize road signs. The technique, dubbed GhostStripe) [PDF] in a paper to be presented at the ACM International Conference on Mobile Systems next month, is undetectable to the human eye, but could be deadly to Tesla and Baidu Apollo drivers as it exploits the sensors employed by both brands – specifically CMOS camera sensors. It basically involves using LEDs to shine patterns of light on road signs so that the cars' self-driving software fails to understand the signs; it's a classic adversarial attack on machine-learning software.* Crucially, it abuses the rolling digital shutter of typical CMOS camera sensors. The LEDs rapidly flash different colors onto the sign as the active capture line moves down the sensor. *For example, the shade of red on a stop sign could look different on each scan line to the car due to the artificial illumination*"). Italics added.

[1128] Afifi-Sabet, Keumars, "MadRadar hack can make self-driving cars 'hallucinate' imaginary vehicles and veer dangerously off course", *LiveScience*, 8th February 2024, 2024, available at: https://www.livescience.com/technology/electric-vehicles/madradar-hack-can-make-self-driving-cars-hallucinate-imaginary-vehicles-and-veer-dangerously-off-course (last accessed: 19.3.2025).

[1129] Afifi-Sabet, Keumars, "MadRadar hack can make self-driving cars 'hallucinate' imaginary vehicles and veer dangerously off course", *LiveScience*, 8th February 2024, 2024, available at: https://www.livescience.com/technology/electric-vehicles/madradar-hack-can-make-self-driving-cars-hallucinate-imaginary-vehicles-and-veer-dangerously-off-course (last accessed: 19.3.2025).

[1130] It goes without saying that this an overly simplistic example of how object recognition—within the remit of computer vision—transpires in autonomous vehicles, but it is illustrative nonetheless. Lehr, David/Ohm, Paul, "Playing with the Data: What Legal Scholars Should Learn About Machine Learning", *cit.*, pp. 653–718.

3.1.5.9.3 «Selective Myopia in Computer Vision Underpinning Self-Driving Cars»: «Predictive Bias in Pedestrian Detection» (Wilson/Hoffman/Morgenstern) That Inordinately Befalls on Dark-Skinned Individuals

§§ It is worth recalling that «inequality in application»[1131] consists of Artificial Intelligence-embedded technologies that seemingly works well for everyone,[1132] when such is not the case. Paradigmatic examples of errors-fraught evaluations undertaken by machine learning algorithms abound.

§§ The examples flow from watered down computer vision that features black African Americans as gorillas[1133]; botched computer vision that is incapable of recognizing the prototypical physical features of Asian people[1134] to software that biasedly associates certain occupations with certain genders[1135] (v.g. machine learning algorithms associate the role of an engineer to a male, whereas the same technology associates the role of a nurse[1136] to a female).[1137]

[1131] Calo, Ryan, "Artificial Intelligence Policy: Primer and Roadmap", *cit.*, pp. 399–435 (411). See Part III, this chapter, Sect. 3.1.1 of this book (that discusses the issue of "inequality in application" facing Artificial Intelligence-embedded technologies).

[1132] Calo, Ryan, "Artificial Intelligence Policy: Primer and Roadmap", *cit.*, pp. 399–435 (411).

[1133] Calo, Ryan, "Artificial Intelligence Policy: Primer and Roadmap", *cit.*, pp. 399–435 (411).

[1134] Calo, Ryan, "Artificial Intelligence Policy: Primer and Roadmap", *cit.*, pp. 399–435 (411).

[1135] See: Part IV, Chapter 4, Sect. 4.1.8 of this book (on biased word embeddings with an entrenched presence on search engines run by tech moguls).

[1136] Caliskan, Aylin et al., "Semantics Derived Automatically from Language Corpora Contain Human-Like Biases", *Science*, 356, 2017, pp. 183 and ff and passim.

[1137] Calo, Ryan, "Artificial Intelligence Policy: Primer and Roadmap", *cit.*, pp. 399–435 (411).

§§ A particularly driving application field for machine learning[1138] in the private sector is the design of self-driving cars.[1139] It oft-averred that self-driving cars may greatly decrease transit costs of goods and decrease individuals' reliance on owning personal vehicles.[1140] Which, I may venture to add, amounts to nothing but to an episode of the **process of human-involution** that looms large on the horizon.[1141]

§§ More to the point, recognizing key objects—such as road signs,[1142] roadblocks, obstacles, pedestrians, and traffic lights—plays a pivotal role in these

---

[1138] See: Murphy, Kevin P., *Machine Learning: A Probabilistic Perspective (Adaptive Computation and Machine Learning series).* Massachusetts: The MIT Press, 2012, pp. 1–1104 (states avowedly that "machine Learning attempts to combine deductive, inductive, and abductive reasoning to make person-like reasoning in AI Entities possible. Machine-learning AI Entities initially learn in the same way a human child learns. First, they notice details and patterns in shapes, sounds, and behaviors; then put them together to distinguish one person from another, or a dog from a cat. Eventually, the AI can recognize and identify" common objects). See also: Hutto-Schultz, Jess, "Dicitur Ex Machina: Artificial Intelligence and the Hearsay Rule", *George Mason Law Review*, Volume 27, Issue 2, 2020, pp. 684–718 (689). See: Chollet, François, *Deep Learning with Python.* Shelter Island, Nova Iorque: Manning, 2018, pp. 1–384 (passim). *Deep Learning* stands as a byproduct of *Machine Learning. Machine Learning*, a subset of Artificial Intelligence, unfolds itself in *Deep Learning*, which "involves computer algorithms that have the ability to "learn" or improve in performance over time on some task". See also: Surden, Harry, "Machine Learning and Law", *Washington Law Review*, Volume 89, 2015, pp. 87 and ff. See also: Barocas, Solon/Selbst, Andrew, "Big Data's Disparate Impact", *California Law Review*, Volume 104, pp. 2016, pp. 671–678 ("in particular, by exposing so-called 'machine learning' algorithms to examples of the cases of interest (previously identified instances of fraud, spam, default, and poor health), *the algorithm 'learns' which related attributes or activities can serve as potential proxies for those qualities or outcomes of interest*"). Italics added. See also: Chen, C./Rudin, C., "An optimization approach to learning falling rule lists", *Proceedings of Machine Learning Research, Artificial Intelligence and Statistics*, Volume 84, 2018, pp. 604–612; Sokolovska, N./Chevaleyre, Y./Zucker, J.D., "A provable algorithm for learning interpretable scoring systems", *Proceedings of Machine Learning Research, Artificial Intelligence and Statistics*, Volume 84, pp. 566–574; Rudin, Cynthia/Ustun, B., "Optimized scoring systems: toward trust in machine learning for healthcare and criminal justice", *Interfaces*, Volume 48, 2018, pp. 399–486.

[1139] Wilson, Benjamin/Hoffman, Judy/Morgenstern, Jamie, "Predictive Inequity in Object Detection", available at: arXiv:1902.11097v1 [cs.CV] 21 Feb 2019.

[1140] Wilson, Benjamin/Hoffman, Judy/Morgenstern, Jamie, "Predictive Inequity in Object Detection", available at: arXiv:1902.11097v1 [cs.CV] 21 Feb 2019.

[1141] See: Part III, this chapter, Sect. 3.1.4.7 of this book (on the impoverishment of human abilities amidst the onset of the age of Artificial Intelligence-embedded technologies, conducive to human-involution).

[1142] But see: Dobberstein, Laura, "GhostStripe attack haunts self-driving cars by making them ignore road signs", *The Register*, Friday, 10th of May of 2024, 2024, p. 1, available at: https://www.theregister.com/2024/05/10/baidu_apollo_hack/ (last accessed: 04.04.2025) ("*Six boffins mostly hailing from Singapore-based universities say they can prove it's possible to interfere with autonomous vehicles by exploiting the machines' reliance on camera-based computer vision and cause them to not recognize road signs. The technique, dubbed GhostStripe [PDF] in a paper to be presented at the ACM International Conference on Mobile Systems next month, is undetectable to the human eye, but could be deadly to Tesla and Baidu Apollo drivers as it exploits the sensors employed by both brands – specifically CMOS camera sensors. It basically involves using LEDs to shine patterns of light on road signs so that the cars' self-driving software fails to understand the signs; it's a classic adversarial attack on machine-learning software.* Crucially, it abuses the rolling digital shutter of typical CMOS camera sensors. The LEDs rapidly flash different colors onto the

systems,[1143] helping determine when a car must brake or swerve to avoid either traffic accidents and human casualties.[1144] Tellingly, few, if any, self-driving cars systems already on the road are fully equipped to entirely allay perceived risks of pedestrian fatalities.[1145] A vexing question crops up with bursting unease: which pedestrians these self-driving cars systems detect with lower accuracy, and why they evince such a discriminatory behaviour in the first place?[1146]

§§ Compellingly, **Pedestrian Detection** has been a long-lasting challenge in the Computer Vision community. Ranging from security systems to self-driving cars, **Pedestrian Detection** remains a crucially important hurdle facing Computer Vision models[1147] as mishaps tend to occur on a regular basis.[1148] Candent challenges facing **Pedestrian Detection** comprise, but are not limited to, occlusion by other types of

---

sign as the active capture line moves down the sensor. *For example, the shade of red on a stop sign could look different on each scan line to the car due to the artificial illumination*"). Italics added.

[1143] See: Zarei, Mohammad et al., "AUTHENTICATION Identifying Rare Failure Modes in Autonomous Vehicle Perception Systems using Adversarially Guided Diffusion Models", available at: arXiv:2504.17179v1 [cs.AI] 24 Apr 2025, p. 1 ("There has been significant progress in the development of autonomous vehicles (AVs) in recent years due to rapid advancements in artificial intelligence (AI). *However, critical functionality challenges must be addressed before AVs are considered reliable and robust. Due to the safety critical nature of AVs, as well as the potential for great impact on the broader transportation industry and society, both government and non-government organizations have released best practices and standards.* In 2022, the International Organization for Standardization (ISO) introduced Safety of the Intended Functionality (SOTIF) as a safety requirements standard in response to the unique challenges and limitations of AV AI systems [1]. *One challenge SOTIF addresses is functional deficiencies in AV perception systems including object detection, classification, and tracking models traditionally trained on real-world data*"). Italics added.

[1144] Wilson, Benjamin/Hoffman, Judy/Morgenstern, Jamie, "Predictive Inequity in Object Detection", available at: arXiv:1902.11097v1 [cs.CV] 21 Feb 2019 ("*in this work, we investigate whether state-of-the arXiv:1902.11097v1 [cs.CV] 21 Feb 2019 art object detection systems have equitable predictive performance on pedestrians with different skin tones.* This work is motivated by many recent examples of ML and vision systems displaying higher error rates for certain demographic groups than others. We annotate an existing large scale dataset which contains pedestrians, BDD100K, with Fitzpatrick skin tones in ranges [1-3] or [4-6]. *We then provide an in depth comparative analysis of performance between these two skin tone groupings, finding that neither time of day nor occlusion explain this behavior, suggesting this disparity is not merely the result of pedestrians in the 4-6 range appearing in more difficult scenes for detection. We investigate to what extent time of day, occlusion, and reweighting the supervised loss during training affect this predictive bias*"). Italics added.

[1145] Levin, S. and Wong, J. C., Self-driving uber kills arizona woman in first fatal crash involving pedestrian. https://www.theguardian.com/technology/2018/mar/19/uber-self-driving-car kills-woman-arizona-tempe, Mar 2018.

[1146] Wilson, Benjamin/Hoffman, Judy/Morgenstern, Jamie, "Predictive Inequity in Object Detection", available at: arXiv:1902.11097v1 [cs.CV] 21 Feb 2019.

[1147] Li, J./Liang, X./Shen, S./Xu, T./Feng, J./Yan, S. "Scale-aware fast r-cnn for pedestrian detection", *IEEE Transactions on Multimedia*, 20 (4), April 2018, 2018, pp. 985–996.

[1148] Levin, S. and Wong, J. C., Self-driving uber kills arizona woman in first fatal crash involving pedestrian. https://www.theguardian.com/technology/2018/mar/19/uber-self-driving-car kills-woman-arizona-tempe, Mar 2018.

objects or people themselves, types of clothing, colours of clothing, and different lighting conditions that may impair proper pedestrian detection.[1149]

§§ A budding piece of empirical research found compelling evidence of **predictive inequity—or predictive bias**—in detecting pedestrians of different skin tones in object detection underpinning self-driving car systems. This body of empirical evidence showed that conventional models entrusted with the task of object detection, trained[1150] on conventional[1151] datasets,[1152] evinced higher accuracy on lower

---

[1149] Wilson, Benjamin/Hoffman, Judy/Morgenstern, Jamie, "Predictive Inequity in Object Detection", available at: arXiv:1902.11097v1 [cs.CV] 21 Feb 2019.

[1150] Note, though, that the training of machine learning is long and tedious in that is an error-prone procedure than can ultimately impair future algorithmic decision-making: Price, W. Nicholson Price II, "Regulating Black-Box Medicine", *Michigan Law Review*, Volume 116, 2017, pp. 421–431 (leverages on Google Image's image recognition learning algorithm to shed light on the four-step process by which some algorithms are thoroughly trained. First, the algorithm is shown "a set of known images ('Here are 10,000 pictures of ducks')." Second, the algorithm "develops complex internal rules based on nonlinear processes." Third, the algorithm "tests those rules on a test set ('Which of these are ducks?')." And fourth, the algorithm accordingly adjusts its "internal rules based on the success of the test." These steps are trotted out and repeated many times "until it can accurately and consistently classify the images.").

[1151] It is important to note that an algorithm designed for **maximum accuracy** will adjust itself to the majority data, and may be less accurate for members of the underrepresented group, thus breeding *inductive bias*. See: Shellenbarger, Sue, "A Crucial Step for Avoiding AI Disasters", *Wall Street Journal*, (Feb. 13, 2019, 9:57 AM ET), https://www.wsj.com/articles/a-crucial-step-for-avoiding-ai-disasters-11550069865?ns=prod/accounts-wsj [https://perma.cc/C28U-LAAE] (discussing this issue while emphasizing how diverse development teams pay more attention to unrepresentative and underrepresented data sets). Human programmers can circumvent and bypass this problem by weighting the minority-group data more heavily, by designing different algorithms for each racial group, or by striving to contain more data to equalize group representation in the data set. See: Barua, Sukarna et al., "MWMOTE—Majority Weighted Minority Oversampling Technique for Imbalanced Data Set Learning", *IEEE Transactions on Knowledge & Data Engineering*, Volume 26, 2014, pp. 405, 405–06. See also: Hamilton, Melissa, "The Biased Algorithm: Evidence of Disparate Impact on Hispanics", *American Criminal Law Review*, Volume 56, 2019, pp. 1553 and ff and passim (which clearly demonstrates that COMPAS was significantly less accurate for Hispanic than for white defendants by several measures and suggesting that smaller numbers of Hispanic defendants might be the cause). See: Mayson, Sandra G., "Bias In, Bias Out", *cit.*, pp. 2218–2300. See also: Dong et al., Qi, "Imbalanced deep learning by minority class incremental rectification", *IEEE Transactions on Pattern Analysis & Machine Intelligence*, Volume 41, 2019, p. 1367 (posit that "*most existing learning algorithms produce inductive bias (learning bias)* towards the frequent (majority) classes if training data are not balanced, *resulting in poor minority class recognition performance*"). Italics added. See: Chandler, Anupam, "The Racist Algorithm", *Michigan Law Review*, Volume 115, n.° 6, 2018, p. 1026 (on racist algorithms, noting that "the possibilities for discriminatory manipulation are legion").

[1152] But see: Citron, Danielle Keats/Pasquale, Frank, "The Scored Society: Due Process for Automated Predictions", *Washington Law Review*, Volume 89, 2014, pp. 1, 4–5 (highlighting how human beings programming automated systems is directly conducive to, and leads, to fundamentally inaccurate results since the source code, predictive algorithms and datasets may encompass human biases which, in turn, have a disparate impact on historically disadvantaged groups); Crawford, Kate/Schultz, Jason, "Big Data and Due Process: Toward a Framework to Redress Predictive Privacy Harms", *Boston College Law Review*, Volume 55, 2014, pp. 93, 99–101 (pinpointing pathways through which predictive analytic tools perpetuate discriminatory practices). But see: Bornstein,

Fitzpatrick skin types than higher skin types.[1153] I call this ***selective myopia*** that inordinately befalls on dark-skinned individuals.

§§ Flabbergastingly, or not so much, this lopsided, and inequality-driven, behaviour appears on behemoth images of pedestrians, and even grows when one eliminates occluded pedestrians. Both of which (tiny pedestrians and occluded pedestrians) are considered to be the most difficult cases for object detectors.[1154] Strikingly, even on the simple subset of pedestrian examples one befuddlingly comes across with this **predictive inequity**[1155] that inordinately befalls on dark-skinned individuals, thereby giving rise to an excoriating **selective myopia** facing computer vision embedded in self-driving cars systems.

3.1.5.10 «Reading and Controlling Your Mind While Shaping Your Thoughts and Behaviours»: The Hazardous Interplay Between Artificial Intelligence-Embedded Technologies and Brain-Computer Interfaces: Will the Privilege Against Self-Incrimination—A Building Block of Criminal Procedure Law—Wobble Amidst the Rise of Brain-Computer Interfaces?

§§ Artificial Intelligence-embedded technologies propel forward the gruelling process towards the *in-humanization* of human beings amidst the age of unfettered technological achievements that are narrowing down the once yawning gap between human beings and machines. To illustrate, take a hard look at the pathways through which Brain-Computer Interfaces, an offspring of disembodied agency, pledges to gear human beings toward.[1156]

Stepanhie, "Antidiscriminatory Algorithms", *Alabama Law Review*, Volume 70, 2018, pp. 519, 524–528 (contending, however, that the tagged "facially neutral" algorithms producing discriminatory outcomes should be quashed).

[1153] Wilson, Benjamin/Hoffman, Judy/Morgenstern, Jamie, "Predictive Inequity in Object Detection", available at: arXiv:1902.11097v1 [cs.CV] 21 Feb 2019.

[1154] Wilson, Benjamin/Hoffman, Judy/Morgenstern, Jamie, "Predictive Inequity in Object Detection", available at: arXiv:1902.11097v1 [cs.CV] 21 Feb 2019.

[1155] Wilson, Benjamin/Hoffman, Judy/Morgenstern, Jamie, "Predictive Inequity in Object Detection", available at: arXiv:1902.11097v1 [cs.CV] 21 Feb 2019.

[1156] Levin, Daniel, "Are you out of your mind? Neurotechnologies and the Making of Disembodied Agency", *Berkeley Technology Law Journal*, Volume 38, 2023, pp. 232–252; Dockrill, Peter, "Brain Implant Translates Paralyzed Man's Thoughts into Text With 94% Accuracy", *SCI Alert*, 2021, passim; Zhang, X./Sheng, QZ et al., "Converting your thoughts to texts: enabling brain typing via deep feature learning of eeg signals", *IEEE International Conference on Pervasive Computing and Communications*. Athens: IEEE, 2018, passim; Cassella, Carly, "Brain Implant Gives Blind Woman Artificial Vision in Scientific First", *SCI Alert*, 2021, passim; Waytowhich, N./Lawhern, VJ/Garcia, JO, et al., "Compact Convolutional neural networks for classification of asynchronous steady-state visual evoked potentials", *Journal of Neural Engineering*, Volume 15, Issue 6, 2018, passim; Kwak, N-S/Müller, K-R/Lee, S-W., "A Convolutional neural network for steady state visual evoked potential classification under ambulatory environment", *PloS one*, Volume 12, Issue 2, 2017, passim.

§§ It is worth recalling that Brain-Computer Interfaces neatly encapsulates, hands-in-glove, the lens through which the harrowing **process of in-humanization** can be seen: if a computer can read your thoughts, you are no longer a human being, but an extension of a machine instead. Put otherwise, human beings are framed as «connected minds»[1157] that operate as an extension of an ever-recording machine—the kernel of the «extended mind thesis».[1158]

§§ Brain-Computer Interfaces spearhead staggering efforts to decode citizens' minds at granular levels.[1159] Governments—and tech moguls alike—have doubled down their whopping efforts to decipher citizens' minds. As a result, the perils for citizens' *right to be left alone and unaccounted for* soared accordingly. But not just that though. Freedom of thought[1160] and free will—of which human beings are so fond of—hangs on the balance as well.

§§ Humankind is sitting at the cusp of the greatest technological achievements ever recorded in history. Such technological advancements carry both danger (to the freedom of thought and to the free will) and promise (to restoring sight to the blind and affording mobility enhancement to those who have been unfortunately deprived from it).

§§ Strikingly, the interplay between Brain-Computer Interfaces and Artificial Intelligence-embedded technologies is poised to further blur the boundaries between human beings and machines. It bears mentioning that such an interplay is not only harmful to the freedom of thought, but, and foremost, to the free will. That is exactly the rationale behind the blend between Brain-Computer Interfaces and Artificial Intelligence-embedded technologies: read your thoughts, *control* your mind while shaping your current and future behavioural patterns,[1161] thereby morphing you into an obedient individual unable to question the dystopian reality that is upon us.

[1157] See: Greenberg, Jeremy/Ringrose, Katelyn/Berger, Sara/VanDodick/Rossi, Francesca/New, Joshua, "Privacy and the Connected Mind", *The Future Privacy Forum*, 2021. Citron; Danielle Keats Citron/Pasquale, Frank, "Network Accountability for the Domestic Intelligence Apparatus", *Hasting Law Journal*, Volume 62, 2011, 1441, 1444–45; Gray, David/Citron, Danielle Keats, "The Right to Quantitative Privacy", *Minnesota Law Review*, Volume 98, 2013, pp. 62–81.

[1158] Clark, Andy/Chalmers, David, "The Extended Mind", *Analysis*, Volume 58, Issue 1, January 1998. Oxford: Oxford University Press, 1998, pp. 7–19 (passim).

[1159] Santos, Hugo Luz dos, "Brain-Computer Interfaces, Generative Artificial Intelligence (ChatGPT and Deep Fakes) and Criminal Procedure Law: what's at stake?", *Journal of Research in E. and Computer Science*, Edinburgh, United Kingdom, June 2024, Volume 2, 2024, pp. 39–78.

[1160] See: Khan, Sadia/Cole, Daniel/Ekbia, Hamid, "Autonomy and Free Thought in Brain-Computer Interactions: Review of Legal Precedent for Precautionary Regulation of Consumer Products", *Hastings Science & Technology Law Journal*, Volume 15, Number 1, Article 5, 2024, pp. 95–130 (95) ("*The expanding use of neurotechnologies in consumer products increases the risks to human rights such as autonomy and free thought. While potentially beneficial in clinical applications, technologies such as brain implants and EEG-enabled wearable devices pose serious concerns about mental and psychological manipulation of human beings. In the US in particular, law and policy are lagging behind technical developments, thereby increasing the risks of abuse and misuse from commercial neurotechnologies*"). Italics added.

[1161] Zhang, Xiaying et al., "The combination between Brain-Computer Interfaces and Artificial Intelligence: applications and challenges", *Annals of Translational Medicine*, 8 (11), 2020, p. 5 ("The combination between BCIs and AI offers a powerful way to ***investigate brain function***

§§ Before long, the interplay between Brain-Computer Interfaces and Artificial Intelligence-embedded technologies will not only allow machines to gain access to your deep-rooted memories but, and foremost, will be able to implant false memories of events that never occurred. Before long, criminal procedure law will be met with scorching challenges that, if not deftly addressed, may topple its brawny foundations.

§§ Long story short, it boils down to a simple question: should prosecutors gain access to the memories of a crime etched on the defendant's brain only to convict him/her in a court of law? The answer is a resounding «no». The privilege against self-incrimination—a building block of Rule of Law—should stand tall amidst the mayhem of ubiquitous and pervasive Artificial Intelligence-embedded technologies that will reverberate through the corridors of modern societies.

3.1.5.11 «Transhumanism, Genetic Darwinism, and Genetic Plutocracy» That Is Bound to Create (Additional) Layers of Distinction Between Human Beings: The Case of a DNA-Trained Biological Foundational Model (Evo 2) That Writes DNA on Demand

§§ Imagine, if you will, that computer-generated genetic algorithms[1162] are suitably equipped to design and edit human DNA,[1163] thereby enabling wealthy parents to handpick fitter, taller, healthier, brighter siblings, whom are fundamentally immune to a slew of diseases that accordingly augments their span of life. This is the nub of *Transhumanism, Genetic Darwinism, Genetic Plutocracy*—an outgrowth of convolutional[1164] neural networks[1165] that revolve around deep learning genetic algorithms[1166]—that will catalyse metamorphic shifts in the current legal landscape beyond recognition.

---

by providing direct knowledge and control of neurons controlling behaviour"). Italics and bold added.

[1162] Sun, Y, Xue, B, Zhang, M, et al., "Automatically designing CNN architectures using the genetic algorithm for image classification", *IEEE Trans Cybern.*, Volume 50, Issue 9, 2020, pp. 3840–3854.

[1163] Gowda, CC, Mayya, SG, "Comparison of back propagation neural network and genetic algorithm neural network for stream flow prediction", *Journal of Computer Environment Science*, 2014, pp. 1–6.

[1164] Ku, J./E. Nguyen/D. Romero/G. Brixi/B. Yang/A. Vorontsov/A. Taghibakhshi/A. Lu/D. Burke/G. Brockman/S. Massaroli/C. Re/P. Hsu/B. Hie/S. Ermon/M. Poli, *Systems and algorithms for convolutional multihybrid language models at scale*, 2025.

[1165] Krizhevsky, A., Sutskever, I., & Hinton, G. E., "Imagenet classification with deep convolutional neural networks", *Advances in Neural Information Processing Systems*, Volume 25, 2012. Lake, B. M., & Baroni, M., "Human-like systematic generalization through a meta-learning neural network", *Nature*, 623 (7985), 2023, pp. 115–121.

[1166] Rikhtegar A, Pooyan M, Manzuri-Shalmani MT, "Genetic algorithm-optimised structure of convolutional neural network for face recognition applications", *IET Computer Vision*, Volume 10, Issue 6, 2016, pp. 559–566.

§§ Building upon the unbridled rise of genetic algorithms[1167]—which, in turn, relies upon deep learning[1168]—human beings will be ineluctably buoyed to clutch the holy grail of immortality, thereby posing both ethical and legal challenges, which will unavoidably throw the extant legal framework into a frenzy.

§§ Which prompts the burning questions: Are we on the brink of a *Genetic Darwinism* that is bound to create (additional) layers of distinction between citizens? If so, how should law respond to these unprecedented challenges brought about by such a fast-growing field like genetic algorithms[1169]? Regardless of how we choose to respond to these vexing questions, one point is certain: the quick-shifting world we live in is in dire need of hardening into binding law regulations to prevent *Genetic Darwinism, Genetic Plutocracy* and *Transhumanism* from taking hold or the gulf between the rich and the poor will otherwise create a *genetic divide* from which there is no coming back. This is where the *rubber* (Large Language Models in the field of genetics) hits the *road* (of Genetic *Darwinism, Genetic Plutocracy* and *Transhumanism*). Take Evo 2 for example.

§§ Evo 2 is a biological foundation large language model trained on 9.3 trillion DNA base pairs gleaned from an exceedingly high curated genomic atlas spanning all fields of life. Evo 2 was highly trained with 7B and 40B parameters and possesses an unparalleled/unheard of 1 million token context window with single-nucleotide resolution.[1170] Strikingly, Evo 2 deftly learns from DNA sequence alone to reliably

---

1167 Sun, Y., Xue, B., Zhang, M, et al., "Automatically designing CNN architectures using the genetic algorithm for image classification", *EEE Trans Cybern*, Volume 50, Issue 9, 2020, pp. 3840–3854.

1168 Vishnupriya R./Neethu, Robinson/Ramasubba, Reddy M., "Genetic algorithm based deep learning model adaptation for improvising the motor imagery classification", *Brain-Computer Interfaces*, May 2024, 2024, pp. 1–12 (3–4) ("*Genetic algorithms (GAs) are search techniques based on natural genetics and evolutionary principles that can generate optimal solutions to optimization and search problems.* The search process is carried out by GAs in four stages: initialization, selection, crossover, and mutation [20]. The first step is to generate an initial population of solutions to the problem. These solutions are not the best for the problem, and as a result, they must be evolved. *The evolution process begins by selecting a few fittest solutions as parents. From the selected set of parents, each pair of parents mate in order to produce one or more children.* Using the crossover operation, each child inherits genes from both parents. Selective mutation is introduced to make random changes to the children to alter the inherited capabilities. Because of these random changes, some children may be fitter or weaker than their parents. *These generated children and their parents form the evolved population for the next generation. The fittest solutions from the evolved population are selected as parents and better solutions will likely be found by mating the best parents and producing more children. The process is repeated for a fixed number of generations or until the desired solution is found that does not require further optimization*"). Italics added.

1169 Boyabatli, O., "Parameter selection in genetic algorithms parameter selection in genetic algorithms parameter selection in genetic algorithms", *Ihsan Param Sel Genetic Algorithms*, Volume 4, Issue 2, 2004, pp. 78–83.

1170 Brixi, Garyk/Matthew G. Durrant/Jerome Ku/Michael Poli/Greg Brockman/Daniel Chang/ Gabriel A. Gonzalez/Samuel H. King/David B. Li/Aditi T. Merchant/Mohsen Naghipourfar/Eric Nguyen/Chiara Ricci-Tam/David W. Romero/Gwanggyu Sun/Ali Taghibakshi/Anton Vorontsov/ Brandon Yang/Myra Deng/Liv Gorton/Nam Nguyen/Nicholas K. Wang/Etowah Adams/Stephen A. Baccus/Steven Dillmann/Stefano Ermon/Daniel Guo/Rajesh Ilango/Ken Janik/Amy X. Lu/ Reshma Mehta/Mohammad R.K. Mofrad/Madelena Y. Ng/Jaspreet Pannu/Christopher Ré/Jonathan C. Schmok/John St. John/Jeremy Sullivan/Kevin Zhu/Greg Zynda/Daniel Balsam/Patrick Collison/

and accurately forecast the functional effects of **genetic variation**—ranging from noncoding pathogenic mutations to clinically relevant *BRCA1* variants—without needing further fine-tuning.[1171]

§§ Compellingly, Evo 2 autonomously learns from a wide range of biological markers, including, but not limited to, «exon-intron boundaries, transcription factor binding sites, protein structural elements, and prophage genomic regions».[1172] Aside from its jaw-dropping predictive abilities, Evo 2 is fully capable of creating «mitochondrial, prokaryotic, and eukaryotic sequences at genome scale»[1173] with greater prowess and coherence than ancient techniques.[1174]

Anthony B. Costa/Tina Hernandez-Boussard/Eric Ho/Ming-Yu Liu/Thomas McGrath/Kimberly Powell/Dave P. Burke/Hani Goodarzi/Patrick D. Hsu/Brian L. Hie, *Genome modeling and design across all domains of life with Evo 2*, 2025, pp. 1–65.

[1171] Brixi, Garyk/Matthew G. Durrant/Jerome Ku/Michael Poli/Greg Brockman/Daniel Chang/Gabriel A. Gonzalez/Samuel H. King/David B. Li/Aditi T. Merchant/Mohsen Naghipourfar/Eric Nguyen/Chiara Ricci-Tam/David W. Romero/Gwanggyu Sun/Ali Taghibakshi/Anton Vorontsov/Brandon Yang/Myra Deng/Liv Gorton/Nam Nguyen/Nicholas K. Wang/Etowah Adams/Stephen A. Baccus/Steven Dillmann/Stefano Ermon/Daniel Guo/Rajesh Ilango/Ken Janik/Amy X. Lu/Reshma Mehta/Mohammad R.K. Mofrad/Madelena Y. Ng/Jaspreet Pannu/Christopher Ré/Jonathan C. Schmok/John St. John/Jeremy Sullivan/Kevin Zhu/Greg Zynda/Daniel Balsam/Patrick Collison/Anthony B. Costa/Tina Hernandez-Boussard/Eric Ho/Ming-Yu Liu/Thomas McGrath/Kimberly Powell/Dave P. Burke/Hani Goodarzi/Patrick D. Hsu/Brian L. Hie, *Genome modeling and design across all domains of life with Evo 2*, 2025, pp. 1–65.

[1172] Brixi, Garyk/Matthew G. Durrant/Jerome Ku/Michael Poli/Greg Brockman/Daniel Chang/Gabriel A. Gonzalez/Samuel H. King/David B. Li/Aditi T. Merchant/Mohsen Naghipourfar/Eric Nguyen/Chiara Ricci-Tam/David W. Romero/Gwanggyu Sun/Ali Taghibakshi/Anton Vorontsov/Brandon Yang/Myra Deng/Liv Gorton/Nam Nguyen/Nicholas K. Wang/Etowah Adams/Stephen A. Baccus/Steven Dillmann/Stefano Ermon/Daniel Guo/Rajesh Ilango/Ken Janik/Amy X. Lu/Reshma Mehta/Mohammad R.K. Mofrad/Madelena Y. Ng/Jaspreet Pannu/Christopher Ré/Jonathan C. Schmok/John St. John/Jeremy Sullivan/Kevin Zhu/Greg Zynda/Daniel Balsam/Patrick Collison/Anthony B. Costa/Tina Hernandez-Boussard/Eric Ho/Ming-Yu Liu/Thomas McGrath/Kimberly Powell/Dave P. Burke/Hani Goodarzi/Patrick D. Hsu/Brian L. Hie, *Genome modeling and design across all domains of life with Evo 2*, 2025, pp. 1–65.

[1173] Brixi, Garyk/Matthew G. Durrant/Jerome Ku/Michael Poli/Greg Brockman/Daniel Chang/Gabriel A. Gonzalez/Samuel H. King/David B. Li/Aditi T. Merchant/Mohsen Naghipourfar/Eric Nguyen/Chiara Ricci-Tam/David W. Romero/Gwanggyu Sun/Ali Taghibakshi/Anton Vorontsov/Brandon Yang/Myra Deng/Liv Gorton/Nam Nguyen/Nicholas K. Wang/Etowah Adams/Stephen A. Baccus/Steven Dillmann/Stefano Ermon/Daniel Guo/Rajesh Ilango/Ken Janik/Amy X. Lu/Reshma Mehta/Mohammad R.K. Mofrad/Madelena Y. Ng/Jaspreet Pannu/Christopher Ré/Jonathan C. Schmok/John St. John/Jeremy Sullivan/Kevin Zhu/Greg Zynda/Daniel Balsam/Patrick Collison/Anthony B. Costa/Tina Hernandez-Boussard/Eric Ho/Ming-Yu Liu/Thomas McGrath/Kimberly Powell/Dave P. Burke/Hani Goodarzi/Patrick D. Hsu/Brian L. Hie, *Genome modeling and design across all domains of life with Evo 2*, 2025, pp. 1–65.

[1174] Brixi, Garyk/Matthew G. Durrant/Jerome Ku/Michael Poli/Greg Brockman/Daniel Chang/Gabriel A. Gonzalez/Samuel H. King/David B. Li/Aditi T. Merchant/Mohsen Naghipourfar/Eric Nguyen/Chiara Ricci-Tam/David W. Romero/Gwanggyu Sun/Ali Taghibakshi/Anton Vorontsov/Brandon Yang/Myra Deng/Liv Gorton/Nam Nguyen/Nicholas K. Wang/Etowah Adams/Stephen A. Baccus/Steven Dillmann/Stefano Ermon/Daniel Guo/Rajesh Ilango/Ken Janik/Amy X. Lu/Reshma Mehta/Mohammad R.K. Mofrad/Madelena Y. Ng/Jaspreet Pannu/Christopher Ré/Jonathan C. Schmok/John St. John/Jeremy Sullivan/Kevin Zhu/Greg Zynda/Daniel Balsam/Patrick Collison/Anthony B. Costa/Tina Hernandez-Boussard/Eric Ho/Ming-Yu Liu/Thomas McGrath/Kimberly

§§ It is worth recalling that Artificial Intelligence-embedded technologies have catalyzed a plethora of spine-chilling headways in science. Pivotally, rapid strides in the development of science-based genetics paved the way for the creation of a universal frame of reference that leverages on humongous datasets[1175] and compute at scale to unveil/unravel higher order patterns.[1176]

§§ It is crucially important to aver that, prior to the creation of EVO 2, scientists pointed out that adroitly training a Large Language Model with this level of prowess would entail reams of data/hordes of data covering the full spectrum of biological diversity to ferret out emergent properties tantamount to those found in other[1177] domains.[1178]

§§ It is worth recalling, too, that, prior to the creation of EVO 2, scientists have also demonstrated that machine learning algorithms trained on prokaryotic genomic sequences were able to design/edit the function of DNA, RNA,[1179] and proteins,

---

Powell/Dave P. Burke/Hani Goodarzi/Patrick D. Hsu/Brian L. Hie, *Genome modeling and design across all domains of life with Evo 2*, 2025, pp. 1–65.

[1175] But see: Barocas, Solon/Selbst, Andrew D., "Big Data's Disparate Impact", *California Law Review*, Volume 104, 2016, pp. 671–682 (discussing how data is often flawed, rigged, incomplete, imperfect and therefore algorithms inherit the prejudice of the original decision makers). But see: Citron, Danielle Keats/Pasquale, Frank, "The Scored Society: Due Process for Automated Predictions", *Washington Law Review*, Volume 89, 2014, pp. 1, 4–5 (highlighting how human beings programming automated systems is directly conducive to, and leads, to fundamentally inaccurate results since the source code, predictive algorithms and datasets may encompass human biases which, in turn, have a disparate impact on historically disadvantaged groups); Crawford, Kate/Schultz, Jason, "Big Data and Due Process: Toward a Framework to Redress Predictive Privacy Harms", *Boston College Law Review*, Volume 55, 2014, pp. 93, 99–101 (pinpointing pathways through which predictive analytic tools perpetuate discriminatory practices). But see: Bornstein, Stepanhie, "Antidiscriminatory Algorithms", *Alabama Law Review*, Volume 70, 2018, pp. 519, 524–528 (contending, however, that the tagged "facially neutral" algorithms producing discriminatory outcomes should be quashed).

[1176] Kaplan, J./S. McCandlish/T. Henighan/T. B. Brown/B. Chess/R. Child/S. Gray/A. Radford/J. Wu/D. Amodei, *Scaling laws for neural language models*, 2020.

[1177] Brixi, Garyk/Matthew G. Durrant/Jerome Ku/Michael Poli/Greg Brockman/Daniel Chang/Gabriel A. Gonzalez/Samuel H. King/David B. Li/Aditi T. Merchant/Mohsen Naghipourfar/Eric Nguyen/Chiara Ricci-Tam/David W. Romero/Gwanggyu Sun/Ali Taghibakshi/Anton Vorontsov/Brandon Yang/Myra Deng/Liv Gorton/Nam Nguyen/Nicholas K. Wang/Etowah Adams/Stephen A. Baccus/Steven Dillmann/Stefano Ermon/Daniel Guo/Rajesh Ilango/Ken Janik/Amy X. Lu/Reshma Mehta/Mohammad R.K. Mofrad/Madelena Y. Ng/Jaspreet Pannu/Christopher Ré/Jonathan C. Schmok/John St. John/Jeremy Sullivan/Kevin Zhu/Greg Zynda/Daniel Balsam/Patrick Collison/Anthony B. Costa/Tina Hernandez-Boussard/Eric Ho/Ming-Yu Liu/Thomas McGrath/Kimberly Powell/Dave P. Burke/Hani Goodarzi/Patrick D. Hsu/Brian L. Hie, *Genome modeling and design across all domains of life with Evo 2*, 2025, pp. 1–65.

[1178] Radford, A./J. Wu/R. Child/D. Luan/D. Amodei/I. Sutskever, et al., "Language models are unsupervised multitask learners", *OpenAI blog*, 1(8):9, 2019.

[1179] Li., S./Moayedpour/R. Li/M. Bailey/S. Riahi/M. Miladi/J. Miner/D. Zheng/J. Wang/A. Balsubramani/K. Tran/M. Zacharia/M. Wu/X. Gu/R. Clinton/C. Asquith/J. Skalesk/L. Boeglin/S. Chivukula/A. Dias/F. U. Montoya/V. Agarwal/Z. Bar-Joseph/S. Jager, "CodonBERT: Large language models for mRNA design and optimization", *bioRxiv*, 2023, passim.

coupled with their interactions that generate complex molecular[1180] machines.[1181] Note, though, that Evo 2 is a great leap forward for a number of reasons.

§§ To begin with, Evo 2 is a biological large language foundational model trained on a representative snapshot of genomes covering all observed evolution. Highlighting generalist abilities over task-specific optimization, Evo 2 attains sturdy forecast and generation performance, ranging from molecular to genome scale and spanning all domains of life.[1182]

§§ Strikingly, Evo 2 showcased, and evinced, a stellar/sterling performance across biological sequence chores. Pivotally, drawing on the central tenets of previous bodies of empirical research,[1183] Evo 2 managed to successfully learn how genetic mutations sway proteins, RNA, and overall organismal fitness, including in humans, plants, and yeast itself.[1184]

[1180] Brixi, Garyk/Matthew G. Durrant/Jerome Ku/Michael Poli/Greg Brockman/Daniel Chang/ Gabriel A. Gonzalez/Samuel H. King/David B. Li/Aditi T. Merchant/Mohsen Naghipourfar/Eric Nguyen/Chiara Ricci-Tam/David W. Romero/Gwanggyu Sun/Ali Taghibakshi/Anton Vorontsov/ Brandon Yang/Myra Deng/Liv Gorton/Nam Nguyen/Nicholas K. Wang/Etowah Adams/Stephen A. Baccus/Steven Dillmann/Stefano Ermon/Daniel Guo/Rajesh Ilango/Ken Janik/Amy X. Lu/ Reshma Mehta/Mohammad R.K. Mofrad/Madelena Y. Ng/Jaspreet Pannu/Christopher Ré/Jonathan C. Schmok/John St. John/Jeremy Sullivan/Kevin Zhu/Greg Zynda/Daniel Balsam/Patrick Collison/ Anthony B. Costa/Tina Hernandez-Boussard/Eric Ho/Ming-Yu Liu/Thomas McGrath/Kimberly Powell/Dave P. Burke/Hani Goodarzi/Patrick D. Hsu/Brian L. Hie, *Genome modeling and design across all domains of life with Evo 2*, 2025, pp. 1–65.

[1181] Nguyen, E./M. Poli/M. G. Durrant/B. Kang/D. Katrekar/D. B. Li/L. J. Bartie/A.W. Thomas/ S. H. King/G. Brixi/J. Sullivan/M. Y. Ng/A. Lewis/A. Lou/S. Ermon/S. A. Baccus/T. Hernandez-Boussard/C. Ré/P. D. Hsu/B. L. Hie, "Sequence modeling and design from molecular to genome scale with evo", *Science*, 386 (6723) 2024; Nguyen, E./M. Poli/M. Faizi/A. Thomas/M.Wornow/ C. Birch-Sykes/S. Massaroli/A. Patel/C. Rabideau/Y. Bengio, et al., "HyenaDNA: Long-range genomic sequence modeling at single nucleotide resolution", *Advances in neural information processing systems*, 36, 2024.

[1182] Brixi, Garyk/Matthew G. Durrant/Jerome Ku/Michael Poli/Greg Brockman/Daniel Chang/ Gabriel A. Gonzalez/Samuel H. King/David B. Li/Aditi T. Merchant/Mohsen Naghipourfar/Eric Nguyen/Chiara Ricci-Tam/David W. Romero/Gwanggyu Sun/Ali Taghibakshi/Anton Vorontsov/ Brandon Yang/Myra Deng/Liv Gorton/Nam Nguyen/Nicholas K. Wang/Etowah Adams/Stephen A. Baccus/Steven Dillmann/Stefano Ermon/Daniel Guo/Rajesh Ilango/Ken Janik/Amy X. Lu/ Reshma Mehta/Mohammad R.K. Mofrad/Madelena Y. Ng/Jaspreet Pannu/Christopher Ré/Jonathan C. Schmok/John St. John/Jeremy Sullivan/Kevin Zhu/Greg Zynda/Daniel Balsam/Patrick Collison/ Anthony B. Costa/Tina Hernandez-Boussard/Eric Ho/Ming-Yu Liu/Thomas McGrath/Kimberly Powell/Dave P. Burke/Hani Goodarzi/Patrick D. Hsu/Brian L. Hie, *Genome modeling and design across all domains of life with Evo 2*, 2025, pp. 1–65.

[1183] Nguyen, E./M. Poli/M. G. Durrant/B. Kang/D. Katrekar/D. B. Li/L. J. Bartie/A.W. Thomas/ S. H. King/G. Brixi/J. Sullivan/M. Y. Ng/A. Lewis/A. Lou/S. Ermon/S. A. Baccus/T. Hernandez-Boussard/C. Ré/P. D. Hsu/B. L. Hie, "Sequence modeling and design from molecular to genome scale with evo", *Science*, 386 (6723) 2024; Merchant, A. T./S. H. King/E. Nguyen/B. L. Hie, "Semantic mining of functional de novo genes from a genomic language model", *bioRxiv*, 2024.

[1184] Brixi, Garyk/Matthew G. Durrant/Jerome Ku/Michael Poli/Greg Brockman/Daniel Chang/ Gabriel A. Gonzalez/Samuel H. King/David B. Li/Aditi T. Merchant/Mohsen Naghipourfar/Eric Nguyen/Chiara Ricci-Tam/David W. Romero/Gwanggyu Sun/Ali Taghibakshi/Anton Vorontsov/ Brandon Yang/Myra Deng/Liv Gorton/Nam Nguyen/Nicholas K. Wang/Etowah Adams/Stephen A. Baccus/Steven Dillmann/Stefano Ermon/Daniel Guo/Rajesh Ilango/Ken Janik/Amy X. Lu/

§§ Compellingly, Evo 2 is the very first large language model fully capable of scoring/measuring the influence of all variant forms on pathogenicity, thereby attaining reliable, predictable, accurate, top-notch, and cutting-edge performance in forecasting the pathogenic/disease-causing effects of noncoding variation.[1185] Moreover, and on the bright side, a supervised machine learning[1186] model[1187] built on Evo 2 word embeddings excel in classifying *BRCA1* variants of unknown significance of symptoms of breast cancer.[1188]

§§ On the dark side, Evo 2 is fully equipped to leverage its distinctive representation of biological intricacy to create blazingly new genomic sequences.[1189]

Reshma Mehta/Mohammad R.K. Mofrad/Madelena Y. Ng/Jaspreet Pannu/Christopher Ré/Jonathan C. Schmok/John St. John/Jeremy Sullivan/Kevin Zhu/Greg Zynda/Daniel Balsam/Patrick Collison/ Anthony B. Costa/Tina Hernandez-Boussard/Eric Ho/Ming-Yu Liu/Thomas McGrath/Kimberly Powell/Dave P. Burke/Hani Goodarzi/Patrick D. Hsu/Brian L. Hie, *Genome modeling and design across all domains of life with Evo 2*, 2025, pp. 1–65.

[1185] Brixi, Garyk/Matthew G. Durrant/Jerome Ku/Michael Poli/Greg Brockman/Daniel Chang/ Gabriel A. Gonzalez/Samuel H. King/David B. Li/Aditi T. Merchant/Mohsen Naghipourfar/Eric Nguyen/Chiara Ricci-Tam/David W. Romero/Gwanggyu Sun/Ali Taghibakshi/Anton Vorontsov/ Brandon Yang/Myra Deng/Liv Gorton/Nam Nguyen/Nicholas K. Wang/Etowah Adams/Stephen A. Baccus/Steven Dillmann/Stefano Ermon/Daniel Guo/Rajesh Ilango/Ken Janik/Amy X. Lu/ Reshma Mehta/Mohammad R.K. Mofrad/Madelena Y. Ng/Jaspreet Pannu/Christopher Ré/Jonathan C. Schmok/John St. John/Jeremy Sullivan/Kevin Zhu/Greg Zynda/Daniel Balsam/Patrick Collison/ Anthony B. Costa/Tina Hernandez-Boussard/Eric Ho/Ming-Yu Liu/Thomas McGrath/Kimberly Powell/Dave P. Burke/Hani Goodarzi/Patrick D. Hsu/Brian L. Hie, *Genome modeling and design across all domains of life with Evo 2*, 2025, pp. 1–65.

[1186] Hardt, Moritz et al., "Equality of Opportunity in Supervised Learning", *NIPS Proceedings*, 2016, https://papers.nips.cc/paper/6374-equality-of-opportunity-in-supervised-learning.pdf [https://perma.cc/LD25-6RR7].

[1187] See: Barocas, Solon/Selbst, Andrew, "Big Data's Disparate Impact", *cit.*, pp. 677–680 (drilling into, and shedding light on, the process and perceived difficulties of crafting the outcome variable for supervised machine learning algorithms).

[1188] Brixi, Garyk/Matthew G. Durrant/Jerome Ku/Michael Poli/Greg Brockman/Daniel Chang/ Gabriel A. Gonzalez/Samuel H. King/David B. Li/Aditi T. Merchant/Mohsen Naghipourfar/Eric Nguyen/Chiara Ricci-Tam/David W. Romero/Gwanggyu Sun/Ali Taghibakshi/Anton Vorontsov/ Brandon Yang/Myra Deng/Liv Gorton/Nam Nguyen/Nicholas K. Wang/Etowah Adams/Stephen A. Baccus/Steven Dillmann/Stefano Ermon/Daniel Guo/Rajesh Ilango/Ken Janik/Amy X. Lu/ Reshma Mehta/Mohammad R.K. Mofrad/Madelena Y. Ng/Jaspreet Pannu/Christopher Ré/Jonathan C. Schmok/John St. John/Jeremy Sullivan/Kevin Zhu/Greg Zynda/Daniel Balsam/Patrick Collison/ Anthony B. Costa/Tina Hernandez-Boussard/Eric Ho/Ming-Yu Liu/Thomas McGrath/Kimberly Powell/Dave P. Burke/Hani Goodarzi/Patrick D. Hsu/Brian L. Hie, *Genome modeling and design across all domains of life with Evo 2*, 2025, pp. 1–65.

[1189] Brixi, Garyk/Matthew G. Durrant/Jerome Ku/Michael Poli/Greg Brockman/Daniel Chang/ Gabriel A. Gonzalez/Samuel H. King/David B. Li/Aditi T. Merchant/Mohsen Naghipourfar/Eric Nguyen/Chiara Ricci-Tam/David W. Romero/Gwanggyu Sun/Ali Taghibakshi/Anton Vorontsov/ Brandon Yang/Myra Deng/Liv Gorton/Nam Nguyen/Nicholas K. Wang/Etowah Adams/Stephen A. Baccus/Steven Dillmann/Stefano Ermon/Daniel Guo/Rajesh Ilango/Ken Janik/Amy X. Lu/ Reshma Mehta/Mohammad R.K. Mofrad/Madelena Y. Ng/Jaspreet Pannu/Christopher Ré/Jonathan C. Schmok/John St. John/Jeremy Sullivan/Kevin Zhu/Greg Zynda/Daniel Balsam/Patrick Collison/ Anthony B. Costa/Tina Hernandez-Boussard/Eric Ho/Ming-Yu Liu/Thomas McGrath/Kimberly Powell/Dave P. Burke/Hani Goodarzi/Patrick D. Hsu/Brian L. Hie, *Genome modeling and design across all domains of life with Evo 2*, 2025, pp. 1–65.

§§ Mind-bogglingly, and perhaps worryingly, Evo 2 possess the ability to generate entire mitochondrial genomes, nominal bacterial genomes, and complete yeast chromosomes.[1190] Pivotally, Evo 2 can also successfully complete complex design tasks. For instance, Evo 2 can be deployed to design novel DNA sequences, thereby bestowing upon scientists the opportunity to etch code messages into an entire set of epigenomic designs.[1191]

§§ Against this background, it doesn't take much to foretell that the **doors of *Transhumanism*** (against the backdrop of which a *selected few* will be given the opportunity to live forever, thereby defying all laws of nature), the **doors of *Genetic Darwinism*** (against the backdrop of which a *selected few* will get to live a joyful life free from diseases while *socially undesirables*, less fortunate, will be doomed to grapple with multiple variables that make life fundamentally unpredictable as is), and the **doors of *Genetic Plutocracy*** (against the backdrop of which wealthy parents will handpick fitter, whiter, taller, healthier, brighter siblings, whom will be fundamentally immune to a myriad of diseases that will thereupon increase their span of life beyond measurable limits; wealthy nations will create hybrid soldiers—***robotized human beings***—that will be remarkably strong, tall, fast, intrepid, fearless, and tentatively immortal; wealthy nations will control food production while tightening its grip on worldwide supply chains, thereby starving the poor and kneecapping the *socially undesirables*; wealthy nations will «design» obedient, docile, insouciant, and nonchalant citizens from scratch, whom will promptly hew to their orders and whims alike) **are ajar slightly**.

[1190] Brixi, Garyk/Matthew G. Durrant/Jerome Ku/Michael Poli/Greg Brockman/Daniel Chang/Gabriel A. Gonzalez/Samuel H. King/David B. Li/Aditi T. Merchant/Mohsen Naghipourfar/Eric Nguyen/Chiara Ricci-Tam/David W. Romero/Gwanggyu Sun/Ali Taghibakshi/Anton Vorontsov/Brandon Yang/Myra Deng/Liv Gorton/Nam Nguyen/Nicholas K. Wang/Etowah Adams/Stephen A. Baccus/Steven Dillmann/Stefano Ermon/Daniel Guo/Rajesh Ilango/Ken Janik/Amy X. Lu/Reshma Mehta/Mohammad R.K. Mofrad/Madelena Y. Ng/Jaspreet Pannu/Christopher Ré/Jonathan C. Schmok/John St. John/Jeremy Sullivan/Kevin Zhu/Greg Zynda/Daniel Balsam/Patrick Collison/Anthony B. Costa/Tina Hernandez-Boussard/Eric Ho/Ming-Yu Liu/Thomas McGrath/Kimberly Powell/Dave P. Burke/Hani Goodarzi/Patrick D. Hsu/Brian L. Hie, *Genome modeling and design across all domains of life with Evo 2*, 2025, pp. 1–65.

[1191] Brixi, Garyk/Matthew G. Durrant/Jerome Ku/Michael Poli/Greg Brockman/Daniel Chang/Gabriel A. Gonzalez/Samuel H. King/David B. Li/Aditi T. Merchant/Mohsen Naghipourfar/Eric Nguyen/Chiara Ricci-Tam/David W. Romero/Gwanggyu Sun/Ali Taghibakshi/Anton Vorontsov/Brandon Yang/Myra Deng/Liv Gorton/Nam Nguyen/Nicholas K. Wang/Etowah Adams/Stephen A. Baccus/Steven Dillmann/Stefano Ermon/Daniel Guo/Rajesh Ilango/Ken Janik/Amy X. Lu/Reshma Mehta/Mohammad R.K. Mofrad/Madelena Y. Ng/Jaspreet Pannu/Christopher Ré/Jonathan C. Schmok/John St. John/Jeremy Sullivan/Kevin Zhu/Greg Zynda/Daniel Balsam/Patrick Collison/Anthony B. Costa/Tina Hernandez-Boussard/Eric Ho/Ming-Yu Liu/Thomas McGrath/Kimberly Powell/Dave P. Burke/Hani Goodarzi/Patrick D. Hsu/Brian L. Hie, *Genome modeling and design across all domains of life with Evo 2*, 2025, pp. 1–65.

3.1.5.12 «The Onset of the Second Quantum Revolution» (Dowling/Milburn): Quantum Technology and the Three Centrepieces of Quantum Physics: Superposition, Quantum Entanglement, and Quantum Tunnelling

§§ Humanity must etch responsibility into the fabric of scientific and technological innovation for the overall benefit of businesses, society, and the planet. This stance neatly underscores the paramount importance of proactive risk allayment, unfettered interdisciplinary engagement, and responsible innovation in ethically navigating the uncharted territories of quantum computing.[1192]

§§ One of the overriding objectives underpinning these laudable initiatives is to spur the widespread commercialisation of quantum technologies, an endeavour that may be coined as «out of the lab, into the market» approach.[1193] These endeavours form part of a broader technological apparatus within which «second quantum revolution»[1194] operates. The term «second quantum revolution» includes, but is not limited to, Artificial Intelligence-embedded technologies arisen from quantum information science. Typically, Quantum Technologies encompass a vast array of subset fields. Ranging from quantum communication, quantum cryptography, quantum computation, quantum simulation, to quantum metrology/sensing.[1195]

§§ A sheer number of concepts arising out of quantum physics were transplanted to Quantum Technology. The first one is **superposition** (in which a given particle might be in two states, or places, concomitantly). The second one if **quantum entanglement** (whereby unprecedented, and unheard of, correlations can be shared between locations set apart by long distances). Lastly, **quantum tunnelling** (whereby a wave might carve through seemingly impenetrable, or unsurpassable, walls).[1196]

§§ Put differently, **superposition**, **quantum entanglement**, and **quantum tunnelling** are three technological centrepieces in quantum physics. Taken together, they neatly encapsulate, hands-in-glove, the broad scope phenomena of particles existing in multiple states simultaneously (*superposition*), particles having much sturdier correlations than is allowed by classical theoretical underpinnings of

---

[1192] Ten Holter, C./Inglesant, P./Pijselman, M./Jirotka, M., *Towards responsible quantum computing*, EY/University of Oxford, © 2024 Ernst & Young LLP. Published in the UK. All Rights Reserved, 2024, pp. 1–52.

[1193] Seskit/Zeki Can/Willoughby, Kelvin W., "Global innovation and competition in quantum technology, viewed through the lens of patents and artificial intelligence", *International Journal of Intellectual Property Management*, Volume 13, Number 1, 2023, pp. 40–61.

[1194] Dowling, J/Milburn, "Quantum technology: the second quantum revolution", *Phil. Trans. R. Soc. A*, 361, 2003, pp. 1655–1674.

[1195] Seskit/Zeki Can/Willoughby, Kelvin W., "Global innovation and competition in quantum technology, viewed through the lens of patents and artificial intelligence", *cit.*, pp. 40–61.

[1196] Seskit/Zeki Can/Willoughby, Kelvin W., "Global innovation and competition in quantum technology, viewed through the lens of patents and artificial intelligence", *cit.*, pp. 40–61.

physics (*quantum entanglement*), and the ability of particles to cross energy barriers (quantum, *tunneling*).[1197]

§§ GQTs are based on directly harnessing such quantum phenomena for practical applications such as quantum sensing, quantum computing and quantum communications. This makes QTs fundamentally different from those based on classical physics, and could imply a «quantum advantage» over our existing technologies.[1198]

3.1.5.12.1 «Where the Rubber Hits the Road»: «Should We Bid a Fond Farewell to Global Digital Security?» Second Generation Quantum Technologies (2G QT) Which, If Happen to Fall into the Wrong Hands, Will Play Havoc with Our Ability to Portend a Future for Humankind

§§ Humankind is sitting at the crosspoint of unbounded potential of Artificial Intelligence-embedded technologies. The second quantum revolution lies at its heart. Pivotally, the second quantum revolution is shaping up to bring unparalleled opportunities and sweltering challenges[1199] in the purview of quantum[1200] technology (QT).[1201] The rate and pace at which the sheer number of patents concerning QT inventions is unfolding is the living testament of the sweeping importance[1202] of quantum innovation.[1203]

§§ Understandably, and perhaps laudably, the unwavering courage to face head-on the unsettling challenges arising out from Quantum Technology will open doorways that hesitation might keep closed. A caveat before jumping in: extreme caution must be exercised, since one might not like what lies beyond the veil of those doorways.

1197 Kop, Mauritz/Mateo Aboy/Eline De Jong/Urs Gasser/Timo Minssen/Glenn Cohen/Mark Brongersma/Teresa Quintel/Luciano Floridi/Raymond Laflamme, "Ten principles for responsible quantum innovation", *Quantum Science and Technology*, Volume 9, 2024, 035013.

1198 Kop, Mauritz/Mateo Aboy/Eline De Jong/Urs Gasser/Timo Minssen/Glenn Cohen/Mark Brongersma/Teresa Quintel/Luciano Floridi/Raymond Laflamme, "Ten principles for responsible quantum innovation", *Quantum Science and Technology*, Volume 9, 2024, 035013.

1199 Kop, Mauritz/Mateo Aboy/Eline De Jong/Urs Gasser/Timo Minssen/Glenn Cohen/Mark Brongersma/Teresa Quintel/Luciano Floridi/Raymond Laflamme, "Ten principles for responsible quantum innovation", *Quantum Science and Technology*, Volume 9, 2024, 035013.

1200 Dowling, J/Milburn, "Quantum technology: the second quantum revolution", *Phil. Trans. R. Soc. A*, 361, 2003, pp. 1655–1674.

1201 Kop, Mauritz/Mateo Aboy/Eline De Jong/Urs Gasser/Timo Minssen/Glenn Cohen/ Mark Brongersma/Teresa Quintel/Luciano Floridi/Raymond Laflamme, "Ten principles for responsible quantum innovation", *cit.*, 035013.

1202 Kop, Mauritz/Mateo Aboy/Eline De Jong/Urs Gasser/Timo Minssen/Glenn Cohen/ Mark Brongersma/Teresa Quintel/Luciano Floridi/Raymond Laflamme, "Ten principles for responsible quantum innovation", *cit.*, 035013.

1203 Aboy, M/Minssen, T/Kop, M", Mapping the patent landscape of QT: patenting trends, innovation and policy implications", *International Review of Intellectual Property Competition Law*, 53, 2022, pp. 853–882.

§§ Strikingly, Quantum Technology is set to wield a redoubtable power in years to come. Quantum Technology boasts an unparalleled potential to revolutionize entire industries. To name a few, Quantum Technology, with the right settings, can revolutionize the entertainment industry (i.e. flesh and bone actors/singers will no longer be needed to act on stage, since **Superposition**, **Quantum Simulation** and **Quantum Computation** will create entire movies, live concerts, tv series, and music albums from scratch, building on previously recorded materials). The potential for scarier versions of **digital deception** will spike (i.e. the generation of jaw-dropping deepfakes will increase dramatically), so too will the rate and pace at which Generative Artificial Intelligence is weaponized against *socially undesirables.*

§§ By the same token, **Quantum Technology**, if happens to fall into the wrong hands, is bound to exact a toll on **Global Digital Security**, since the former is fully equipped to bypass/circumvent/override the most unassailable cryptographic protections to decrypt any electronical device, including, but not limited to, weapons of mass destruction that could decimate millions of people. Which begs the vexing, and burning, question: how long until unscrupulous criminals (i.e., unprincipled mercenaries, rogue nations, pariah states, crime syndicates) decide take matters into their own hands only to use this ground-breaking technology to advance their hidden, and shady, agendas?

§§ The fast-paced development and deployment of Quantum Technology therefore calls for a proactive, all-encompassing, sweeping, overarching, holistic, and principle-based approach to ensure that that Quantum Technology is handled responsibly with a view to ensure that its unbridled, yet unruly, potential is reliably harnessed in ways that prove beneficial[1204] to society in an overarching sense.[1205]

§§ It therefore behoves to, and rests on the shoulders of, relevant stakeholders to keep an eye on the different technology readiness levels (TRLs), perceived risks, and technological affordances, with quantum sensing and quantum simulation undoubtedly being closest to market entrance and act accordingly.[1206]

§§ On the bright side, by deftly harnessing unique[1207] quantum mechanical properties—recall: **superposition**, **quantum entanglement**, and **quantum tunnelling**—second-generation Quantum Technology cracks open a plethora of

[1204] Kop, Mauritz/Mateo Aboy/Eline De Jong/Urs Gasser/Timo Minssen/Glenn Cohen/ Mark Brongersma/Teresa Quintel/Luciano Floridi/Raymond Laflamme, "Ten principles for responsible quantum innovation", *cit.*, 035013.

[1205] Singla, S, "Responsible generative AI: empowering innovation and ensuring ethical accountability", *Insider Finance Wire*, 2023, passim available at: https://wire.insiderfinance.io/responsible-generative-ai-empowering-innovation-and-ensuring-ethicalaccountability-f795581d6cc9; Baxter, K/Schlesinger Y, "Managing the risks of generative AI", *Harvard Business Review*, 2023, available at: https://hbr.org/2023/06/managing-the-risks-of-generative-ai.

[1206] Kop, Mauritz/Mateo Aboy/Eline De Jong/Urs Gasser/Timo Minssen/Glenn Cohen/Mark Brongersma/Teresa Quintel/Luciano Floridi/Raymond Laflamme, "Ten principles for responsible quantum innovation", *cit.*, 035013.

[1207] Downing C A/Vidiella-Barranco A, "Parametrically driving a quantum oscillator into exceptionality", *Sci. Rep.*, 13, 2023, 11004; Martin, V. et al., "Quantum technologies in the telecommunications industry EPJ", *Quantum Technology*, 2021, pp. 8–19.

applications, which may send positive ripples across society in an[1208] overarching sense.[1209]

§§ Broadly speaking, this includes, but is not limited to, QT/AI hybrids[1210] where the quantum computer (QC) is deployed to perform as an accelerator to solve hitherto computationally recalcitrant problems for old computers and Artificial Intelligence in general. Casts broadly, this includes, but is not limited to, simulation[1211] of quantum chemistry to boost novel drug development.[1212]

§§ Lest we forget, Quantum Technology also has the infinite potential to bypass the RSA encryption systems—the cornerstone of global digital security—that we currently use to the ensure privacy across internet communications.[1213] As a result, Quantum technology governance implications are yet to be shrewdly addressed eyeing its responsible growth[1214] and adoption.[1215]

[1208] Kop, Mauritz/Mateo Aboy/Eline De Jong/Urs Gasser/Timo Minssen/Glenn Cohen/Mark Brongersma/Teresa Quintel/Luciano Floridi/Raymond Laflamme, "Ten principles for responsible quantum innovation", *cit.*, 035013.

[1209] Preskill J, "Quantum computing 40 years later", 2021, available at: arXiv:2106.10522; Coenen C/Grinbaum A/Grunwald A/Milburn C/Vermaas P, "Quantum technologies and society: towards a different spin", *NanoEthics*, 16, 2022, pp. 1–6; Stray B et al., "Quantum sensing for gravity cartography", *Nature*, 602, 2022, pp. 590–594; Wehner S/Elkouss D/Hanson R, "Quantum internet: a vision for the road ahead", *Science*, 362 eaam9288, 2018; Mattsson J, Smeets B and Thormarker E, "Quantum technology and its impact on security in mobile networks", *Ericsson Technology Review*, 2021, pp. 2–12. Singh J/Bhangu K S, "Contemporary quantum computing use cases: taxonomy, review and challenges", *Arch. Comput. Methods Eng.*, 30, 2023, pp. 615–638; Sarkar A, "Applications of quantum computation and algorithmic information: for causal modeling in genomics and reinforcement learning", *Delft University of Technology*, 2022, available at: https://repository.tudelft.nl/islandora/object/uuid:0952c9e9-115c-4672-9381-2b302d1b9576; Bayerstadler A et al., "Industry quantum computing applications", *EPJ Quantum Technology*, Heidelberg, 8 25, 2021; Bentley C, "Quantum computing for transport optimization", 2022, available at: arXiv:2206.07313.

[1210] Yang X/Chen X/Li J/Peng X/Laflamme R, "Hybrid quantum-classical approach to enhanced quantum metrology", *Sci. Rep.*, 11 672, 2021.

[1211] O'Malley O et al., "Scalable quantum simulation of molecular energies", *Phys. Rev.*, 2016, X 6 031007.

[1212] Kop, Mauritz/Mateo Aboy/Eline De Jong/Urs Gasser/Timo Minssen/Glenn Cohen/Mark Brongersma/Teresa Quintel/Luciano Floridi/Raymond Laflamme, "Ten principles for responsible quantum innovation", *cit.*, 035013.

[1213] Wimmer Mand/Moraes T, Quantum computing, digital constitutionalism, and the right to encryption: perspectives from Brazil DISO, 1 12, 2022; De Wolf R, "The potential impact of quantum computers on society", *Ethics Inf. Technology*, 19, 2017, pp. 271–276.

[1214] Kop, Mauritz/Mateo Aboy/Eline De Jong/Urs Gasser/Timo Minssen/Glenn Cohen/Mark Brongersma/Teresa Quintel/Luciano Floridi/Raymond Laflamme, "Ten principles for responsible quantum innovation", *cit.*, 035013.

[1215] Quantum ethics—a call to action by the quantum community, available at: www.youtube.com/watch?v=5qc7gpabEhQ (February 2021), 2021; Kiesow Cortez E/Yakowitz Bambauer J/Guha S, "A quantum policy and ethics roadmap", available at: https://ssrn.com/abstract=4507090, 2023; Perrier, E, "Ethical quantum computing: a roadmap", available at: arXiv:2102.00759, 2021; Kop, M, "Towards responsible quantum technology", *Harvard Berkman Klein Center for Internet & Society (Research Publication Series 2023–1), Harvard University*, available at: https://cyber.harvard.edu/publication/2023/towards-responsiblequantum-technology, 2023.

GPSR Compliance

The European Union's (EU) General Product Safety Regulation (GPSR) is a set of rules that requires consumer products to be safe and our obligations to ensure this.

If you have any concerns about our products, you can contact us on ProductSafety@springernature.com

In case Publisher is established outside the EU, the EU authorized representative is:

Springer Nature Customer Service Center GmbH
Europaplatz 3
69115 Heidelberg, Germany

Batch number: 10725800

Printed by Printforce, the Netherlands

Artificial Intelligence and the Rule of Law

Artificial intelligence is an important driving force of the new round of technological revolution and industrial change. Artificial intelligence and blockchain have risen to the level of national policy. While the rapid development of AI brings convenience to people's lives, it also poses challenges to global changes and the development of human society, social governance and legal regulation, such as the leakage of personal privacy, frequent data security problems, and prejudice and discrimination caused by algorithms. AI is profoundly changing the world, and it is necessary to think about how to promote the construction of responsible AI from the perspective of global governance in the future.

In response to these issues, this series aims to explore and study the new situations and new issues at the intersection of AI, law and political science all over the world, to provide a legal basis for the development of AI-related frontier fields and to limit the development of AI within the framework of law to promote the harmonious and orderly construction of AI and legal systems. Based on the above purpose, this series is selected and integrated with multidisciplinary strengths to strengthen the research on legal, ethical, and social issues related to AI, focusing on laws, regulations, institutional systems, and ethics for the healthy development of AI. The authors of this series are all top authoritative experts and scholars in AI, law, political science, and other disciplines in China, and they have already made considerable achievements and social reputations in this field of research.

This series has a clear awareness of the problem and proposes specific solutions for the implementation and implementation of AI governance from a multidisciplinary and multidisciplinary perspective, covering AI, blockchain, algorithms, digital currency and other specific segments closely related to law, with cutting-edge, academic and theoretical value.

Hugo Luz dos Santos

Controllable Artificial Intelligence and the Future of Law

Set 2

Springer

Hugo Luz dos Santos
Faculty of Humanities
City University of Macau
Macao, Macao

ISSN 2731-6238 ISSN 2731-6246 (electronic)
Artificial Intelligence and the Rule of Law
ISBN 978-981-95-0507-4 ISBN 978-981-95-0508-1 (eBook)
https://doi.org/10.1007/978-981-95-0508-1

This Springer imprint is published by the registered company Springer Nature Singapore Pte Ltd.
The registered company address is: 152 Beach Road, #21-01/04 Gateway East, Singapore 189721, Singapore

Foreword by Professor Nuno Garoupa

The rapid emergence of artificial intelligence (AI) has prompted a tectonic shift in how modern societies conceive of regulation, individual autonomy, and the infrastructure of justice. In *Controllable Artificial Intelligence and the Future of Law*, Professor Hugo Luz dos Santos confronts this transformation with urgency and intellectual clarity. From the standpoint of law and economics, which is my field of interest, the issues raised by this work are not merely academic—they are foundational. They concern the allocation of rights, the minimization of social costs, and the preservation of legal predictability in the face of computational opacity.

The economic analysis of law proceeds from the idea that legal institutions serve to allocate entitlements in a way that promotes efficiency, minimizes transaction costs, and addresses externalities. From Coase to Calabresi, legal economists have emphasized how rules should be structured to guide behavior in ways that reflect rational incentives and information availability. AI disrupts these assumptions. When algorithms act as opaque intermediaries between individual action and legal consequence—when decisions are made by systems whose internal logic is inaccessible even to their designers—traditional economic models of law lose traction. As Professor Hugo dos Santos illustrates, this loss of traction is not a theoretical problem alone: it has immediate repercussions for equality, accountability, and access to justice.

One of the central themes of the book is the erosion of the rule of law under what the author terms "algorithmic dictatorship." In economic terms, this phenomenon can be described as a massive informational asymmetry: individuals subject to algorithmic decision-making cannot observe, audit, or contest the criteria by which decisions are made. The result is not only a breakdown in procedural fairness but an increase in systemic risk—one that undermines trust in legal institutions and generates externalities that ripple across markets and societies.

The law and economics tradition has long emphasized the importance of predictability and transparency in legal rules. Hayek, for instance, viewed the rule of law as the precondition for any functioning price system. In that view, when law becomes unpredictable, individuals cannot plan, contracts become less reliable, and economic coordination breaks down. Professor Hugo dos Santos forcefully argues that many AI systems today, particularly black-box models, are incompatible with these foundational principles. They cannot be interpreted, contested, or understood by those subject to their authority. In this way, they represent not a continuation but a negation of the liberal legal tradition.

And yet, as the author rightly observes, AI also presents opportunities—if we are willing to reform our institutional frameworks accordingly. From a law and economics perspective, the challenge is to design rules and architectures that realign the incentives of AI developers, regulators, and users with the principles of procedural integrity and distributive fairness. Professor Hugo dos Santos's notion of a "Controllable Artificial Intelligence" is central in this regard. Rather than rejecting algorithmic tools wholesale, he proposes a governance framework that makes AI systems interpretable, auditable, and amenable to legal scrutiny. In economic terms, this is a call to reduce the transaction costs of contesting algorithmic decisions, to create liability structures that internalize the risks of faulty predictions, and to establish a legal infrastructure that rewards transparency.

A particularly powerful insight of the book lies in its critique of algorithmic decision-making in domains characterized by moral hazard and adverse selection—two concepts central to economic theory. Consider credit scoring, insurance pricing, or criminal sentencing: in each case, the use of predictive algorithms risks compounding the informational disadvantages of the most vulnerable. If these systems rely on biased or incomplete data—and if their users cannot detect or correct those flaws—the result is not efficiency but perpetuation of structural inequality. In such cases, the economic justification for algorithmic deployment collapses. Instead of promoting allocative efficiency, AI tools become instruments of statistical discrimination.

Professor dos Santos also engages seriously with the empirical literature on predictive policing and recidivism assessment. These are areas where machine learning models have been marketed as tools to improve resource allocation—an ostensibly economic rationale. But as he shows, these systems often replicate past biases, undermine individual rights, and decouple legal sanctions from actual behavior. From a law and economics perspective, the purported gains in efficiency are illusory if they are achieved at the cost of legitimacy, accuracy, or equality before the law.

At its best, the economic analysis of law promotes institutions that channel behavior in socially beneficial ways. It recognizes that regulation is not free, that information is costly, and that legal design involves trade-offs. What Professor Hugo dos Santos brings to this discussion is a rich and multidisciplinary understanding of how AI reshapes those trade-offs. He highlights, for instance, the "measurement bias" and "dimensionality curse" that plague even the most sophisticated machine learning models. He draws attention to the "automation bias" that infects human reliance on AI-generated recommendations. And he articulates a theory of "algorithmic common good" that reintroduces normative considerations—fairness, dignity, reason-giving—into a field too often obsessed with optimization alone.

For legal economists, the book offers several important lessons. First, it underscores the need to revise our models of information and incentives when dealing with autonomous systems. Second, it cautions against the uncritical importation of market analogies into legal contexts where power, rights, and identity are at stake. Third, it challenges the field to think more rigorously about the normative infrastructure required to make AI-compatible with legal values.

There is, in this book, a kind of moral urgency—an insistence that legal theory must not lag behind technological practice. Professor Hugo dos Santos makes clear that the stakes are existential: algorithmic opacity and unaccountability are not abstract concerns, but mechanisms that can silently erode democratic governance. Law, in his view, must remain not merely a tool of order or economic efficiency, but a bulwark against domination—especially in an era when computational systems increasingly mediate access to housing, employment, healthcare, and justice itself.

In sum, *Controllable Artificial Intelligence and the Future of Law* is a landmark contribution to the emerging literature on AI governance. It blends doctrinal insight with philosophical depth and technological fluency. For scholars and students of law and economics, it offers both a warning and a blueprint. The warning: that without legal safeguards, AI may exacerbate the very problems it purports to solve. The blueprint: that through accountability, interpretability, and careful institutional design, we can harness computational power without sacrificing the values that make law legitimate in the first place.

As we stand at the frontier of algorithmic governance, this book reminds us that efficiency is not enough. Justice demands that the systems we create—no matter how complex—remain under human control, subject to legal reasoning, and responsive to the values of an open society. The economic analysis of law, updated for the age of AI, must rise to that challenge.

Professor Nuno Garoupa
Professor of Law and Faculty Director
of Graduate Studies, George Mason
University, Antonin Scalia Law School
Fairfax, USA

Foreword by Professor Ronald Montague Silley

As the proliferation of artificial intelligence accelerates in every part of our modern world, this presents a defining challenge for our systems of law, governance and justice. In *Controllable Artificial Intelligence and the Future of Law*, Prof. Hugo Luz dos Santos not only gives us a scholarly and philosophical treatise on this phenomenon, but an essential and practical reckoning that our legal institutions must face during such a significant technological transformation.

This is a book precisely written at a pivotal time of change, when our legal practices must catch-up to scientific innovations and our ethical concepts must keep-up with the power of computers. With little public awareness and even less oversight, we are entering an era where machines do more than just assist human decision-making, they are increasingly replacing it. As human judgment is subordinated to machine learning, and moral accountability is displaced by statistical inferences, Prof. Hugo Luz dos Santos not only asks whether machines can be made to follow the law, he confronts the more profound, difficult and urgent questions, of what becomes of law, and indeed our society itself, when our most important deliberations are increasingly outsourced to computer systems? As these operate without transparency and often without scrutiny, he sounds an alarm on what he terms the rise of an "Algorithmic Dictatorship".

In the powerfully interdisciplinary style for which he is known, Prof. Hugo Luz dos Santos meticulously connects classical legal theory, ethics and critical studies, with novel social and technological analysis. The result is an original and pragmatic investigation that elevates our understanding of AI in jurisprudence. This book's contributions are wide-ranging and, in many respects, groundbreaking. It masterfully illuminates the underexplored intersections between AI and critical legal studies. By mapping practices from predictive policing and algorithmic credit scoring, to automated tenant screening and the hallucinatory risks of generative AI, this book shows how supposedly neutral tools are in fact embedded with the beliefs and inequalities of the societies that have created them. As these opaque systems are carriers of both values and assumptions, encoded with prejudices and inherited biases, they not only replicate historical inequities under a guise of impartial computation, but may even exacerbate discriminatory and exclusionary consequences.

While Prof. Hugo Luz dos Santos reminds us that law must not abdicate its normative authority to data-driven systems for efficiency, this book is also not fatalist in despair nor Luddite in its resistance to new technology. It never loses sight of justice as law's fundamental aim and calls for the law to not only be reactive but also resilient. It offers a practical framework for reform and provides a blueprint for an "Algorithmic Common Good", anchored by principles that are rooted in the rule of law, distributive justice and procedural integrity. As a guide to inspire all to recognize that the future of law cannot be written by machines alone, this helps bridge the gap for those who build the tools of tomorrow and those who struggle with their applications today.

Informed by history and driven by urgency, this is a book of uncommon clarity and consequence. The issues raised will not go away, but only grow more pressing as the use of AI becomes more prevalent. This book not only speaks to scholars and students, lawmakers and judges, regulators and technologists, but to all people having an interest in technology's disruptions and society's ethical imperatives for upholding human dignity, fairness, legal equality, procedural justice and the rule of law in the future.

Professor Ronald Montague Silley
European Executive Co-Dean
China-EU School of Law at the China
University of Political Science
and Law Hamburg
Germany/Beijing, China

Foreword by Professor Tu Guangjian

Human beings' lives have been improving by tools and technologies invented by themselves since they came to this planet. In the history of humankind, each time when there is a new "big" invention, people's life style may change, for example electricity, cars, trains, airplanes, computers and internet etc. have fundamentally changed our life. Online life is a natural extension of offline life while a life with AI i.e. AI life is also a natural extension of online life after big data is usable because of internet and computer.

We are in an era of big data and AI now. AI is a far-reaching, pervasive, cutting-through and penetrating technology. AI can perform many functions that are beneficial to us such as predicting, decision-making and information (answer)-providing etc. Whether you like it or not, sooner or later, we are going to live in a world full of AI and AI is increasingly being full of our life from your household appliances to your workstation, from what you eat to what your wear and almost everywhere you can see so that it is not exaggerating that everybody has an AI life.

"Rule by law" is the human wisdom distilled from many years' experiences and 'bloody" history of countries and the common belief of civilized societies nowadays. As the train can only run well on the railway, the society can only be run well on the proper framework of law and so are AI and people's AI life. AI can be related to different areas of laws: It can be used for concluding a contract by the parties; police can make use of it to identify the suspect; court and tribunals can rely on it to deal with evidences and draft legal documents in the procedures ...... Few laws, however, have been made by few jurisdictions for this new phenomenon so far. We need to study its impact on the different aspects of laws and how the laws can accommodate it and may have to adapt to it in details when its functions unfold in judicial practices. Hugo's book is a timely legal research and publication that can provide answers to many of our queries and obliviate our doubts when encountered with AI and living an AI life.

Human inventions can never be as perfect as what has been made by the Almighty God. The author has demonstrated a very healthy attitude towards AI. To any technology, one must face its risks and harness it. As with the nuclear technology which can be utilized to develop nuclear medicine but can also be applied to make nuclear bomb, AI, for the use of humankind, also has potential risks. The author rightly called for "AI should be thing-centred and trustworthy". Although the use of AI is hailed and highly expected by many, the author is sober to point out the possible problems that could even be exacerbated and the potential risks that could happen by the use of AI including the danger of losing rule of law.

In the book, the author highlighted the problem of algorithmic dictatorship and argued that "many lasting problems in our traditional society will continue to last, even more entrenched into the modern and future society of AI, due to algorithmic dictatorship". Of course, nobody can shrug away from the history. When AI is largely used, the past and ingrained hallmarks will continue and even become deeper owing to the fact that AI is based on big data that is "previous and past". We must still be alert to the problem of racial and gender discrimination under the seemingly neutral data-driven framework. However, the author does not lose heart and find out meaningful and valuable ways from algorithmic dictatorship to algorithmic common good, which is worth commending indeed. The author also warned us against making high-stake decisions by using AI. Although AI can be more "objective" and "efficient" than human beings, AI can have "hallucination" besides "black box". The author advocated "a controllable AI amenable to be interpretable, accountable and fair" and "relevant stakeholders must track the quality of the dataset from which machine learning algorithms were built to foster algorithmic fairness" and "to audit the pearls of algorithmic wisdom", which is applaudable to me.

Moreover, this book not only deals with AI & Law but also deeper problem of society with law (criminology) and how they can be further reflected and dealt with by law when assisted with AI.

This book is a very good exploration of what has been done and may do in the future when AI is still a fast-moving and developing area. To be better prepared for an AI era, this is a book I would like to highly recommend.

Professor Tu Guangjian
Professor of Law, Faculty of Law
of the University of Macau
Macao, Macao

Foreword by Professor Peter Chi Hin Chan

Artificial intelligence is transforming nearly every aspect of modern life, from how we communicate to how we make decisions. Yet for all its promises, AI also poses unprecedented challenges to our legal systems. We live in an era when algorithms can influence judicial outcomes, enforce regulations, and even shape public opinion. As we stand at this crossroad, a pressing question emerges: how do we ensure that these powerful technologies remain **controllable**, aligned with the rule of law and the common good? In *Controllable Artificial Intelligence and the Future of Law*, Hugo Luz dos Santos tackles this question head-on, offering a timely and incisive exploration of the legal world's response to the rise of advanced AI. This book could not come at a more crucial moment. It speaks to the significance of its topic with clarity and urgency, illuminating why *controlling* AI is not just a technical matter but a fundamental legal and ethical imperative for society.

The book unfolds in **five well-organized parts**, each addressing a crucial facet of the AI-law relationship. **Part I** serves as a wake-up call: it articulates why society must not be complacent about algorithmic decision-making. Here, the author probes whether advances in AI have swung the "pendulum" of power too far, edging us toward an era where algorithms exercise disproportionate control. This opening part frames the core concern that resonates throughout the book—if we do nothing, are we tacitly accepting a form of digital dictatorship governed by algorithms? **Part II** titled *The History of Artificial Intelligence*, takes a step back and provides a brief historical account of AI's evolution. In these chapters, we are reminded that understanding where AI comes from—its origins, its development, and past attempts at regulation—is essential to grasp why the notion of making AI "controllable" arose in the first place. By tracing AI's journey from a speculative idea to a reality embedded in everyday life, the author underscores how past developments have led to present dilemmas.

Building on this foundation, **Part III: Critical Artificial Intelligence Studies (CAIS)** brings a rigorous analytical lens to the interplay between technology and society. In this section, Santos engages with contemporary philosophical and critical frameworks to dissect how AI systems can inadvertently entrench bias and inequality. By the end of Part III, the reader gains a sobering understanding: the potential for an algorithmic dictatorship is not a distant science-fiction threat, but a tangible risk already perceptible in today's biased algorithms and data-driven decisions. If Part III diagnoses the problem, **Part IV** titled *Algorithmic Dictatorship and the Chilling Effect on Democracy* confronts its consequences for our legal and democratic institutions. Here, Santos goes so far as to brand the unchecked proliferation of algorithm-driven power as a "**devilishly harmful virus**" attacking the rule of law, asking pointedly whether the Rule of Law is "backsliding beyond repair" under this onslaught. This vivid metaphor captures the book's central worry: that without intervention, AI could erode the foundations of justice in ways that may be difficult to reverse. Through a series of well-chosen examples, the author illustrates how this erosion is already underway. He enumerates a litany of what he calls the "**unpalatable byproducts**" of unchecked algorithms—from predictive policing and discriminatory credit scoring to phenomena like *"algorithmic Jim Crow"*—even noting the troubling emergence of falsehoods or "hallucinations" in large language models like ChatGPT. By cataloguing these real-world issues, Part IV paints a comprehensive picture of the stakes: *algorithmic decision-making is not just a technical progression, it is a force that can either undermine or uphold our most cherished legal principles.*

Yet, this book does not stop at critique. **Part V: Algorithmic Common Good to Oust Algorithmic Dictatorship** marks the transition from diagnosis to prescription. In these final chapters, the author puts forward a constructive vision for reining in AI and aligning it with our highest legal and ethical values. The very notion of an "**Algorithmic Common Good**" is a scholarly innovation that this book develops—it encapsulates the idea that we must reorient AI design and governance toward shared human values and societal well-being, rather than allowing profit or efficiency alone to dictate outcomes. Santos argues that by embedding principles of justice, transparency, and accountability into the fabric of AI systems, we can **oust** the looming algorithmic dictatorship and replace it with a form of algorithmic governance that serves everyone. To build this argument, he draws on the rich heritage of legal thought and philosophy. By reviving the classic ideas in the context of AI, the author shows that our modern challenges can still be guided by enduring values. Impressively, Santos even proposes using AI tools to monitor and correct other AI systems, a creative approach to harnessing technology against its own potential abuses. This blending of legal theory, ethical principles, and practical policy proposals showcases the book's most important contribution: it moves the conversation from what is wrong to what can be done.

Reflecting on the entirety of this book, one cannot help but appreciate the scholarly rigor and passion that underlie its pages. *Controllable Artificial Intelligence and the Future of Law* is both a comprehensive academic study and a call to action. It spans an impressive range—from recounting the early history of AI to dissecting the latest controversies over algorithms in the courtroom, all while maintaining a clear focus on the future of law in an AI-driven world. The key themes of the book—**accountability in AI, preservation of the rule of law, prevention of algorithmic tyranny, and the pursuit of an algorithmic common good**—are interwoven into a coherent narrative that advances our understanding of each. Legal scholars will value the depth of research, and policymakers will find concrete ideas on practically regulating AI. Technologists, too, can glean insight from this work about the societal and legal context in which their creations will operate. On a more personal note, as a friend of the author, I have observed Santos' abiding commitment to justice in the face of technological change. This book is a testament to that commitment. There is a palpable passion in these chapters—a determination to ensure that our future with AI is one where **human dignity and rights are upheld rather than trampled by cold algorithms**. And yet, the tone of the book remains measured and reasoned, reflecting the balance of an academic who is keenly aware of both the potentials and pitfalls of AI.

Controllable Artificial Intelligence and the Future of Law is a landmark contribution to the ongoing conversation about AI's place in our legal order. It challenges us to recognize the stakes: if we value democracy, equality, and the rule of law, we cannot afford to leave AI unchecked. But more importantly, it lights the way forward by outlining how we can **controllably integrate** AI into our legal frameworks without sacrificing our core values. I have no doubt that readers will find it as illuminating and thought-provoking as I did. As we grapple with the future of law in an age of intelligent machines, Hugo Luz dos Santos has given us not only a warning of the specter of an "algorithmic dictatorship", but also a vision of hope—a future where artificial intelligence is harnessed in service of a just and orderly society, under the steadfast guidance of the law.

Professor Peter Chi Hin Chan
Associate Professor at the School of Law
of City University of Hong Kong
Kowloon Tong, Hong Kong

Competing Interests The author has no competing interests to declare that are relevant to the content of this manuscript.

Praise for Controllable Artificial Intelligence and the Future of Law

"Professor Hugo Luz dos Santos's notion of a "Controllable Artificial Intelligence" is central in this regard. Rather than rejecting algorithmic tools wholesale, he proposes a governance framework that makes AI systems interpretable, auditable, and amenable to legal scrutiny.

In sum, *Controllable Artificial Intelligence and the Future of Law* is a landmark contribution to the emerging literature on AI governance. It blends doctrinal insight with philosophical depth and technological fluency. For scholars and students of law and economics, it offers both a warning and a blueprint. The warning: that without legal safeguards, AI may exacerbate the very problems it purports to solve. The blueprint: that through accountability, interpretability, and careful institutional design, we can harness computational power without sacrificing the values that make law legitimate in the first place."

—Professor Nuno Garoupa, *Professor of Law and Faculty Director of Graduate Studies, George Mason University, Antonin Scalia Law School*

"In *Controllable Artificial Intelligence and the Future of Law*, Prof. Hugo Luz dos Santos not only gives us a scholarly and philosophical treatise on this phenomenon, but an essential and practical reckoning that our legal institutions must face during such a significant technological transformation.

This is a book precisely written at a pivotal time of change, when our legal practices must catch-up to scientific innovations and our ethical concepts must keep-up with the power of computers.

In the powerfully interdisciplinary style for which he is known, Prof. Hugo Luz dos Santos meticulously connects classical legal theory, ethics and critical studies, with novel social and technological analysis. The result is an original and pragmatic investigation that elevates our understanding of AI in jurisprudence. This book's contributions are wide-ranging and, in many respects, groundbreaking. It masterfully illuminates the underexplored intersections between AI and critical legal studies."

—Prof. Ronald Montague Silley, *European Executive Co-Dean China-EU School of Law at the China University of Political Science and Law, Hamburg, Germany/Beijing, China*

"This book could not come at a more crucial moment. It speaks to the significance of its topic with clarity and urgency, illuminating why *controlling* AI is not just a technical matter but a fundamental legal and ethical imperative for society.

There is a palpable passion in these chapters—a determination to ensure that our future with AI is one where **human dignity and rights are upheld rather than trampled by cold algorithms**. And yet, the tone of the book remains measured and reasoned, reflecting the balance of an academic who is keenly aware of both the potentials and pitfalls of AI.

Controllable Artificial Intelligence and the Future of Law is a landmark contribution to the ongoing conversation about AI's place in our legal order. It challenges us to recognize the stakes: if we value democracy, equality, and the rule of law, we cannot afford to leave AI unchecked. But more importantly, it lights the way forward by outlining how we can **controllably integrate** AI into our legal frameworks without sacrificing our core values. I have no doubt that readers will find it as illuminating and thought-provoking as I did".

—Peter Chi Hin Chan, *Associate Professor at School of Law of City University of Hong Kong*

"Hugo's book is a timely legal research and publication that can provide answers to many of our queries and obliviate our doubts when encountered with AI and living an AI life.

The author advocated "a controllable AI amenable to be interpretable, accountable and fair" and "relevant stakeholders must track the quality of the dataset from which machine learning algorithms were built to foster algorithmic fairness" and "to audit the pearls of algorithmic wisdom", which is applaudable to me.

This book is a very good exploration of what has been done and may do in the future when AI is still a fast-moving and developing area. To be better prepared for an AI era, this is a book I would like to highly recommend."

—Guangjian Tu, *Professor of Law, Faculty of Law of the University of Macau*

Contents

Part IV
Algorithmic Dictatorship and the Chilling Effect on Democracy

Chapter 4
The Devilishly Harmful Virus of *Algorithmic Dictatorship*: Is the Rule of Law Backsliding Beyond Repair?

4.1 *Algorithmic Dictatorship* and its Unpalatable Byproducts (Predictive Policing; Algorithmic Credit Scoring; Credit Card Redlining; Algorithmic Prime-Lining; Algorithmic Redlining; Algorithmic Redliking; «Algorithmic Jim Crow»; Proxy Discrimination; «Input Fallacy» that Boosts Discrimination in the Remit of Algorithmic Fair Lending and Algorithmic Credit Pricing; Word-Embedding Arising Out of Generative Artificial Intelligence; Large Language Models and ChatGPT's Hallucinations; Biased Algorithmic Risk Assessment («Bias In, Bias Out») in Criminal Procedure Law)

§§ Scholars have not been neither coy nor bashful in pinning down the multifarious ways against the backdrop of which AI-embedded technologies inflict inordinate harm upon citizens.[1]

§§ Recall, the great bulk of Artificial Intelligence-embedded technologies are tools that reify,[2] compound, and exacerbate deep-seated social and ethnic concerns with which modern societies have been wrestling with for a long-winded span of

[1] See Part III, Chap. 3, Sect. 3.1.1 of this book (that discusses the issue of "inequality in application" facing Artificial Intelligence-embedded technologies).

[2] Duster, Troy, "Race and Reification in Science." *Science*, 307, 2005, passim.

H. L. dos Santos, *Controllable Artificial Intelligence and the Future of Law*, Artificial Intelligence and the Rule of Law, https://doi.org/10.1007/978-981-95-0508-1_4

time, such as misogyny, sexism,[3] racism,[4] xenophobe and political hatred which, taken together, are rife for misfire, social unrest, and upheaval.

§§ Even worse, Artificial Intelligence-embedded technologies are being increasingly entrusted[5] with making high stake decisions[6] (e.g. health, credit scoring,[7] mortgage lending,[8] predictive policing,[9] freedom, and the list goes on) without offering

---

[3] Hamilton, Melissa, "The sexist algorithm", *Behavioral Sciences and the Law*, Volume 37, Issue 2, Special Issue: the Use of Statistics in Criminal Cases, March–April 2019, 2019, pp. 1 and ff ("Algorithmic risk assessment tools are informed by scientific research concerning which factors are predictive of recidivism and thus support the evidence-based practice movement in criminal justice. Automated assessments of individualized risk (low, medium, high) permit officials to make more effective management decisions. Computer-generated algorithms appear to be objective and neutral. But are these algorithms actually fair? The focus herein is on gender equity. Studies confirm that women typically have far lower recidivism rates than men. *This differential raises the question of how well algorithmic outcomes fare in terms of predictive parity by gender*. This essay reports original research using a large dataset of offenders who were scored on the popular risk assessment tool COMPAS. *Findings indicate that COMPAS performs reasonably well at discriminating between recidivists and non-recidivists for men and women. Nonetheless, COMPAS algorithmic outcomes systemically overclassify women in higher risk groupings. Multiple measures of algorithmic equity and predictive accuracy are provided to support the conclusion that this algorithm is sexist*"). Italics added.

[4] For a simple reason: Dong et al., Qi, "Imbalanced deep learning by minority class incremental rectification, *IEEE Transactions on Pattern Analysis & Machine Intelligence*, Volume 41, 2019, p. 1367 (posit that "*most existing learning algorithms produce inductive bias (learning bias)* towards the frequent (majority) classes if training data are not balanced, *resulting in poor minority class recognition performance*"). Italics added. See: Chandler, Anupam, "The Racist Algorithm", *Michigan Law Review*, Volume 115, n. ° 6, 2018, p. 1026 (on racist algorithms, noting that "the possibilities for discriminatory manipulation are legion"). But see: Altenburger, Kristen M./Ho, Daniel E., "When Algorithms Import Private Bias into Public Enforcement: The Promise and Limitations of Statistical Debiasing Solutions", *Journal of Institutional & Theoretical Economics*, Volume 175, 2019, pp. 97–98 (calls for a "debias predictive algorithms" to assuage racist and/or biased, doctored and bigoted algorithms nevertheless). See: Hamilton, Melissa, "The Biased Algorithm: Evidence of Disparate Impact on Hispanics", *American Criminal Law Review*, Volume 56, 2019, pp. 1553 and ff and passim.

[5] But see: Weizenbaum, Joseph, *Computer Power and Human Reason: From Judgment to Calculation*, 1st edition, New York, W. H. Freeman & Co, 1976, pp. 1–300 (227) ("examines the sources of the computer's powers and offers evaluative explorations of what computers can do, cannot do, and should not be employed to do") (*this founding father of Artificial Intelligence presciently noted that we should not entrust Artificial Intelligence-embedded technologies* with "tasks that demand wisdom"). Italics added. The approval of rental applications is arguably one of those tasks that should never be entrusted to machines). More on this on Part IV, This chapter, Sects. 4.1.4–4.1.4.2.1 of this book. See: Part IV, This chapter, Sects. 4.1.4–4.1.4.2.1 of this book (on mortgage redlining). See: Part IV, This chapter, Sects. 4.1.2–4.1.4.3 of this book (on algorithmic credit scoring, consumer racism and credit card redlining). See: Part IV, This chapter, Sects. 4.1.4–4.1.4.2.3 of this book (on algorithmic redlining). See: Part IV, This chapter, Sect. 4.1.4.3 of this book (on "algorithmic redliking"). See: Part IV, This chapter, Sect. 4.1.3 of this book (on algorithmic prime-lining). See: Part V, Chap. 5, Sect. 5.1.7.4 of this book (on one of the law to control algorithmic decision-making, namely, law number four: data partitioning must be performed—i.e. randomly split an entire dataset into the «training dataset» and the «test dataset»—to accurately predict outcomes in the real world while forestalling «inductive bias» (learning bias)). See: Part V, Chap. 5, Sect. 5.1.7.2 of this book (on law number two to control algorithmic decision-making, which mandates that black box models must not be entrusted with the task of making high stake

any reasonable explanation[10] for its pearls of algorithmic wisdom. It seems as though that algorithmic-anchored decision-making, albeit wrapped under the veneer of a neutral data-driven[11] framework,[12] is fundamentally whimsical and discriminatory,

---

decisions—v.g. health and freedom). See: Part V, Chap. 5, Sects. 5.1.7–5.1.7.5 of this book (on the five laws to control algorithmic decision-making).

[6] But see: Rudin, Cynthia, "Please stop explaining black box models for high stakes decisions", *Proceedings of NeurIPS 2018 Workshop on Critiquing and Correcting Trends in Machine Learning (NIPS 2018)*, 2018, passim.

[7] See: Havard, Cassandra Jones, "On The Take": The Black Box of Credit Scoring and Mortgage Discrimination", *Boston University Public Interest Law Journal*, Volume 20, 2011, pp. 241–247 (highlighting that credit scoring if unchecked is an intrinsic, encroached, deep-rooted form of racial discrimination akin to mortgage redlining).

[8] In spite of its deep-seated racial bias, decision-makers continue to deploy redlining tactics through big data and may even justify such unlawful practices by claiming that the latter abide by cost-effectiveness. See: Humber, Nadiyah J., "A Home for Digital Equity: Algorithmic Redlining and Property Technology", *California Law Review*, Volume 111, Issue 5, 2023, pp. 1421–1484. See also: Hurley, Mikella/Adebayo, Julius, "Credit Scoring in the Era of Big Data", *Yale Journal of Law and Technology*, Volume 18, 2016, pp. 148, 151–156, 172 (averring that FICO scoring boasts a redoubtable capacity to routinely weed out some populations that have been historically and systematically underrepresented or grossly unfairly represented in the credit industry market). Tellingly, by 2016, ten states had disavowed the unlawful practice of employers using shady credit scores due to their perceived disparate impact on low-income applicants and members of racialized communities (mostly Black folks). See: O'Neill, Cathy, *Weapons of Math Destruction. How Big Data Increases Inequality and Threatens Democracy*. London: Penguin Random House, 2016, pp. 128 and ff and passim. See: Part IV, This chapter, Sects. 4.1.4–4.1.4.2.3 of this book.

[9] Brayne, S., "Big data surveillance: The case of policing", *American Sociological Review*, Volume 82, Issue 5, 2017, pp. 977–1008; Robinson, M. A., "Black bodies on the ground: Policing disparities in the African American Community-An analysis of newsprint from January 1, 2015, through December 31, 2015", *Journal of Black Studies*, Volume 48, Issue 6, pp. 551–571; Browne, S., *Dark matters: on the surveillance of blackness*, Duke University Press, 2015, passim. Toro, J. D./ Lloyd, T., Buchanan/K. S., Robins/S. J., Bencharit/L. Z., Smiedt/M. G., Reddy/K. S., Pouget, E. R./Kerrison, E. M./Goff, P. A., "The criminogenic and psychological effects of police stops on adolescent black and Latino boys", *Proceedings of the National Academy of Sciences of the United States of America*, Volume 116, Issue 17, 2019, pp. 8261–8268; Sewell, A. A., Jefferson, K. A./Lee, H., "Living under surveillance: Gender, psychological distress, and stop-question- and-frisk policing in New York city", *Social Science & Medicine*, Volume 159, 2016, pp. 1–13; Benjamin, Ruha, *Race After Technology: Abolitionist Tools for the New Jim Code*, John Wiley & Sons, 2019, passim; Abdillahi, I., "Algorithmic surveillance in the era of the appsphere", *American Journal of Community Psychology*, Volume 73, 2024, passim; Zuboff, Zhoshana, *The Age of Surveillance Capitalism, The Fight for a Human Future at the New Frontier of Power*. New Yor City: PublicAffairs Books, 2019, pp. 1–704 (360) (argues that we are indomitably heading towards a "instrumentarianism" that draws on "totalitarianism"). See: Part IV, This chapter, Sects. 4.1.10.1–4.1.10.6 of this book (on biased algorithmic risk assessment in criminal procedure law settings, with a sharper focus on COMPAS). See: Part IV, This chapter, Sects. 4.1.1–4.1.1.1 of this book (on biased predictive policing).

[10] See: Watcher, S./Mittelstadt, B./Russell, C., "Counterfactual explanations without opening the black box: automated decisions and the GDPR", *Harvard Journal of Law & Technology*, Volume 1, 2018, passim. See: Part V, Chap. 5, Sects. 5.1.7–5.1.7.5 of this book (on the five laws to control algorithmic decision-making). See: Part V, Chap. 5, Sects. 5.1.8–5.1.8.5 of this book (on the five laws to interpret algorithmic decision-making).

[11] But see: Hardt, Moritz, "How big data is unfair: Understanding sources of unfairness in data driven decision making", *Medium*, Archived on Oct. 8, 2014, available

thereby targeting the usual suspects (Blacks and Latinos), as abundantly shown throughout this long-winded chapter.

§§ It follows that this is the kernel of my newly-crafted concept of *Algorithmic Dictatorship* (AD), which seeks to portray the unsavoury reality against the backdrop of which *selective surveillance* of *socially undesirables, systemic racism,*[13] White supremacy,[14] *algorithmic injustice,*[15] racial wedge, and racial wealth gap between Whites, Blacks and Latinos unfolds.[16]

§§ To premise to this sweeping claim, this section seeks to bring to the fore a plethora of scattershot examples of my newly-crafted concept of *Algorithmic*

---

at: https://web.archive.org/web/20141008185829/; https://medium.com/@mrtz/how-big-data-is-unfair-9aa544d739de. (access: 17.12.2024).

[12] But see: *Tech, Bias and Housing Initiative, the Promise and Perils of Residential Proptech, Year 1, Research Summary Report, April 2023, TechEquity Collaborative*, p. 11, available at: https://techequity.us/wp-content/uploads/2023/04/TBHI-Y1-Research-Summary-Report.pdf (28.11.2024). ("*Once bad data enters the analysis of one factor, it gets baked into the subsequent process, multiplying the effect that one disadvantageous data point can have on someone's overall housing determination*"). Italics added. See: Part IV, This chapter, Sects. 4.1.4–4.1.4.2.3 of this book.

[13] See: Feagin, J. R., *Systemic racism: a theory of oppression*, New York: Routledge, 2006. See also: Fiske, John, "Surveilling the City: Whiteness, the Black Man and Democratic Totalitarianism.", *Theory, Culture and Society*, 15 (2), 1998, pp. 67–88 (on the overhyped surveillance on black people as a byproduct of systemic racism).

[14] See: Perea, Juan F., "Doctrines of Delusion: How the History of the G.I. Bill and Other Inconvenient Truths Undermind the Supreme Court's Affirmative Action Jurisprudence", *University of Pittsburgh Law Review*, Volume 75, 1995, pp. 583, 586–89 (establishes a liaison between Jim Crow laws, the G.I. Bill, and the Social Security Act and White supremacy); Milligan, Joy, "Protecting Disfavored Minorities: Towards Institutional Realism", *UCLA Law Review*, Volume 63, 2016, pp. 894, pp. 918–21 (shedding a keen light on racial inequality in U.S. Department of Agriculture farm assistance); Robinson, Reginald Leamon, "The Racial Limits of the Fair Housing Act: The Intersection of Dominant White Images, the Violence of Neighborhood Purity, and the Master Narrative of Black Inferiority", *William & Mary Law Review*, Volume 37, 1995, pp. 69, 71–74 (establishes a connection between the failures of the FHA and White supremacy). But see: Wormser, Richard, *The Rise and Fall of Jim Crow*, Manhattan, New York City, St Martin's Press, 2014, pp. 1–222 ("*White supremacy prevailed, but it did not destroy the spirit of the black community*"). Italics added.

[15] Ting-an Lin, "Democratizing AI" and the Concern of Algorithmic Injustice", *Philosophy and Technology*, Volume 37 (103), 2024, pp. 3–27.

[16] Derenoncourt, Ellora/Kim, Chi Hyun/Kuhn, Moritz/Schularik, Moritz, "The Wealth of Two Nations: The U.S. Racial Wealth Gap, 1860–2020", *The Quarterly Journal of Economics*, Volume 139, Issue 2, 2024, p. 741 ("A large class of commonly discussed policies for reducing racial wealth inequality seeks to reduce gaps in income, savings, and capital gains. These include policies that encourage financial diversification or stock equity holdings among Black households; policies aimed at financial literacy and retirement or savings behavior; or policies aimed at improving educational and labor market outcomes of Black Americans through improved school quality or reductions in discrimination. *Yet on a realistic note, our simulation in Section IV.A shows that even if wealth accumulation conditions had been equal since 1870, the wealth gap would still be 3 to 1 today, and full convergence would be more than 200 years away. Put differently: to close the racial wealth gap in the immediate term via flow parameters, Black Americans would need a substantial positive lead over whites, not "just" more equality*"). Italics added.

Dictatorship with a dash of *algorithmic injustice*[17] looming large in the discussion. This is exactly what *Critical Artificial Intelligence Studies*[18]—coupled with *Algorithmic Common Good*[19]—aims to unwind. More on this later.[20] Meanwhile, buckle up, ladies and gentlemen. It's going to be a hell of a ride.

4.1.1 *Predictive Policing: An Algorithmic Tool of* Selective Surveillance *to Target a Cohort of Socially Undesirables?*

§§ The data-driven world we live in has been thrust head long to a mass surveillance[21] that dispiritingly spares no one.[22] Predictive policing[23]—a hallmark of mass surveillance[24] in the information age[25]—amounts to a crime analysis tool that

---

[17] See: Birhane, A., "Algorithmic injustice: A relational ethics approach", *Patterns*, 2 (2), 2021, pp. 1–9.

[18] See: Part III, Chap. 3, Sect. 3.1.5.10 of this book (on the functional aspects of Critical Artificial Intelligence Studies, with a sharper focus on the harmful effects of Artificial Intelligence-embedded technologies, namely, Brain-Computer Interfaces that can read and control your mind and behaviour). See: Part III, Chap. 3, Sect. 3.1.5.11 of this book (on the functional aspects of Critical Artificial Intelligence Studies, with a sharper focus on the harmful effects of Artificial Intelligence-embedded technologies, namely, Genetic Algorithms that can write DNA on demand, thereby ushering the age of Transhumanism, Genetic Darwinism and Genetic Plutocracy, which, taken together, are poised to create layers of distinction between citizens). See: Part III, Chap. 3, Sect. 3.1.5.12 of this book (on the functional aspects of Critical Artificial Intelligence Studies, with a sharper focus on the harmful effects of Artificial Intelligence-embedded technologies, namely, Quantum Technology, which will bring entire industries to its knees while allowing unscrupulous actors to get a hold of, and whimsically activate, weapons of mass destruction). See: Part III, Chap. 3, Sect. 3.1.5.1.1 of this book (on the functional aspects of Critical Artificial Intelligence Studies, with a sharper focus on the harmful effects of Artificial Intelligence-embedded technologies, namely, perpetuation technologies—griefbots, avatars and robots—that are slated to dehumanize human-laden emotions). See: Part III, Chap. 3, Sects. 3.1.5.2–3.1.5.3.1 of this book (on the functional aspects of Critical Artificial Intelligence Studies, with a sharper focus on the harmful effects of Artificial Intelligence-embedded technologies, namely, Generative Artificial Intelligence and its offsprings—deepfakes and its deleterious effects on human memory).

[19] See: Part V, Chap. 5, Sects. 5.1.2–5.1.6.2.1 of this book (on the thing-centred algorithmic decision-making propelled by a *Controllable* and *Interpretable* Machine Learning that weeds out *Algorithmic Dictatorship* and secures *Algorithmic Common Good*).

[20] See: Part V, Chap. 5, Sect. 5.1.1.1 of this book (on the central tenets of Rule of Law that lends itself to a beacon of justice amidst the sepulchral darkness that is about to take hold). See: Part V, Chap. 5, Sect. 5.1.1.2 of this book (on the central tenets of Procedural Rule of Law that lends itself to a lighthouse of justice that allows citizens to challenge the pearls of algorithmic wisdom in a court of law).

[21] On mass surveillance: Bentham, Jeremy, *Panopticon: Or, the inspection-house*, Thomas Byrne, 1787. See also: Balkin, Jack M./Levinson, Sanford, "The Processes of Constitutional Change: From Partisan Entrenchment to the National Surveillance State", *Fordham Law Review*, Volume 75, 2006, pp. 489 and ff; Slogogin, Christopher, "Public Privacy: Camera Surveillance of Public Places and the Right to Anonymity", *Mississippi Law Journal*, Volume 72, 2002, pp. 213–251; Balkin, Jack

leverages on big data[26] to propel informed decision-making[27] by law enforcement agencies.[28]

§§ Predictive policing[29] consists of a tool aimed at analysing reams of data in an earnest attempt to predict in which geographic areas will be a heightened likelihood

M., "The Constitution in the National Surveillance State", *Minnesota Law Review*, Volume 93, Issue 1, 2008, pp. 17 and ff; Christopher Slobogin, "Panvasive Surveillance, Political Process Theory, and the Nondelegation Doctrine", *Georgetown Law Journal*, Volume 102, 2014, pp. 1721–1775; Ericson, Richard V., and Kevin D. Haggerty, *The New Politics of Surveillance and Visibility*. Toronto: University of Toronto Press, 2006. See: Part IV, This chapter, Sects. 4.1.5–4.1.5.2 of this book (on "algorithmic Jim Crow", a travel ban issued during the first Trump Administration to prevent certain individuals from entering the United States of America, which, given its racial undertones, stands as an outgrowth of congeries of laws enacted during the Jim Crow epoch).

22 Brayne, S., "Big data surveillance: The case of policing", *American Sociological Review*, 82 (5), 2017, pp. 977–1008. See: Part IV, This chapter, Sects. 4.1.10.1–4.1.10.6 of this book (on biased algorithmic risk assessment in criminal procedure law settings, with a sharper focus on COMPAS).

23 See: Hu, Margaret, "From the National Surveillance State to the Cybersurveillance State", *The Annual Review of Law and Social Science*, Volume 13, 2017, p. 163 ("*Biometric identification and identity assessments are becoming essential tools for multiple preventive purposes in criminal, military, and intelligence contexts.* The third part addresses *how precrime policy rationales are now informed by biometric-based analysis. In short, biometrics is the means by which analysis of a citizenry's data, and any resulting decisions based on that analysis, can be connected back to a physical person in the real world*—whether to approve that person as eligible for a job, *as some employment eligibility database screening systems like E-Verify are, by moving toward biometrics through adopting the E-Verify photo tool* (Hu 2013), *or to determine whether that person is eligible to fly on a commercial airline. The No Fly List and digital watchlisting systems are increasingly biometrically centered (Tau 2015). These types of governance assessments, however, fall within the civil law and administrative law structure. Biometric cybersurveillance systems can inform targeted killing decisions and other lethal consequences. Often in the service of precrime/ counterterrorism policies, biometric cybersurveillance, therefore, is becoming a linchpin for broader policymaking and decisionmaking*"). Italics added. See: Part IV, This chapter, Sects. 4.1.5–4.1.5.2 of this book (on "algorithmic Jim Crow", a travel ban issued during the first Trump Administration to prevent certain individuals from entering the United States of America, which, given its racial undertones, stands as an outgrowth of congeries of laws enacted during the Jim Crow epoch).

24 Angwin, Julia, *Dragnet Nation: A Quest for Privacy, Security, and Freedom in a World of Relentless Surveillance*, New York: Times Books, 2014. Citron; Danielle Keats Citron/Pasquale, Frank, "Network Accountability for the Domestic Intelligence Apparatus", *Hasting Law Journal*, Volume 62, 2011, 1441, 1444–45; Gray, David/Citron, Danielle Keats, "The Right to Quantitative Privacy", *Minnesota Law Review*, Volume 98, 2013, pp. 62–81.

25 Ball, Kirstie, and Frank Webster (Eds.), *The Intensification of Surveillance: Crime, Terrorism & Warfare in the Information Age*, London, UK: Pluto Press, 2007.

26 On algorithmic big data biometric governance: Hu, Margaret, "From the National Surveillance State to the Cybersurveillance State", *The Annual Review of Law and Social Science*, Volume 13, 2017, p. 169 ("*as a result of big data biometric governance trends, meaningful distinctions between biometric credentialing for identification and behavioral biometric profiling are disappearing. The objectives are merging: Reliable credentialing is used to advance security and precrime policy rationales. Biometric data mission creep occurs by necessity in a big data world because the cybersurveillance systems are often designed to engage in mass data integration and analysis and predictive policing. Biometric surveillance serves two purposes in preventive policing: It increases identity transparency, and the biometric data categorize identity through cataloging behavioral and physical characteristics and assess these characteristics for risk. Contrasting small data biometric credentialing protocols with big data credentialing protocols is useful. It illustrates how biometric*

of criminal activity.[30] Put simply, predictive policing is a form of «intelligence-led policing»[31] that parses historical data (e.g. crime-related information and arrest-related data)[32] to forecast criminal events or misdeeds alike.[33]

---

surveillance fits within the Cybersurveillance State. In a small data world, paper-based passports and nondigitized photographs are examples of a small data biometric-based identification system"). Italics added.

[27] DaViera, A. L./Uriostegui, M., Gottlieb/A./Onyeka, O, "Risk, race, and predictive policing: A critical race theory analysis of the strategic subject list", *American Journal of Community Psychology*, Volume 73, 2024, pp. 91–103.

[28] Brayne, S., "The criminal law and law enforcement implications of big data", *Annual Review of Law and Social Science*, Volume 14, 2018, pp. 293–308.

[29] See: Hu, Margaret, "From the National Surveillance State to the Cybersurveillance State", *The Annual Review of Law and Social Science*, Volume 13, 2017, p. 166 (argues that ubiquitous and ever-present surveillance of socially undesirables remains at a pitch of degradation of fundamental rights in that Artificial Intelligence-embedded technologies—propelled by tools like Social Radar and Total Information Awareness, TIA—can capture "a *pictorial depiction of the comprehensive cybersurveillance anticipated through the Social Radar system, which anticipated the full integration of drone footage, biometrric data signatures, econometrics, and other intelligence sources to achieve higher-order cybersurveillance inferences. Social Radar appears to trace its philosophical origins to TIA*. The development of TIA after the 9/11 terrorist attacks was guided under the leadership of the newly created Information Awareness Office within DARPA (Harris 2012, Murray 2010). Within this office, TIA was an effort led by retired Navy Vice Admiral John M. Poindexter (Murray 2010), who served as a national security advisor to President Reagan (Harris 2012). *TIA was informed by a philosophy of "predictive policing," which "focuses not on collecting evidence about actual wrongdoing but on the broad collection of information about everyday activities with the intention of detecting (and preventing) future behavior*" (Murray 2010, p. 5). Congress officially defunded TIA in late 2003 (Murray 2010, Slobogin 2008, USA Today 2003). *Experts have nonetheless noted that remnants of the TIA program and its philosophy have persisted*"). Italics added.

[30] Meijer, A., & Wessels, M., "Predictive policing: Review of benefits and drawbacks", *International Journal of Public Administration*, 42 (12), 2019, 1031–1039.

[31] DaViera, A. L./Uriostegui, M., Gottlieb/A./Onyeka, O, "Risk, race, and predictive policing: A critical race theory analysis of the strategic subject list", *cit.*, pp. 91–103 (93), whose piece of research I will follow very closely.

[32] But see: Kirkpatrick, Keith, "It's not the Algorithm, it's the Data", *Communications of the ACM*, February 2017, Volume 60, n. ° 2, 2017 ("critics, however, say tools such as PredPol and CommandCentral *are inherently biased since they rely heavily on reported crimes data, which is often concentrated in areas that are heavily policed, thereby skewing statistics to overrepresent poor or minority communities.* "*We know that we have a history of racially biased policing in the United States, and that has fed into all the data that we have on where arrests have occurred, which crimes are more likely to occur in specific communities, and at which particular times*," says Jennifer Lynch, senior staff attorney at the Electronic Frontier Foundation. "*That's the data that's being fed into predictive policing algorithms*"). Italics added. See also: Kirkpatrick, Keith, "Battling Algorithmic Bias: How Do We Ensure Algorithms Treat Us Fairly?" *Commun. ACM 59*, Volume 10, 2016, pp. 1 and ff and passim.

[33] Hardyns, W., & Rummens, A., "Predictive policing as a new tool for law enforcement? recent developments and challenges", *European Journal on Criminal Policy and Research*, 24 (3), 2018, pp. 201–218.

§§ More to the point, predictive policing draws on massive batches of data to know where and when crimes[34] are slated to occur.[35] At the heart of predictive policing lies an undying yearn to effectively reallocate resources[36] while proactively quell crime surges wherever they sprout.[37]

§§ Predictive policing is therefore an algorithmic mechanism created to boost law enforcement's overall accountability[38] by drawing on a bundle of data against the backdrop of which informed choices are made. Put it bluntly, predictive policing amounts to a scientific tool that leverages on a cluster of big data[39] to strategically allocate law enforcement resources to the locations,[40] people, and times where criminal enterprises[41] are slated to occur.[42]

§§ Cogently, predictive policing boils down to an algorithmic tool aimed at proactively stamp out criminal activities slated to occur in crime hot spots.[43] Predictive

---

[34] See: Hu, Margaret, "From the National Surveillance State to the Cybersurveillance State", *The Annual Review of Law and Social Science*, Volume 13, 2017, pp. 162–163 ("*policymakers view these technological developments, including biometric technologies, as tools with the potential to identify individuals who may pose a threat to national and homeland security and to prevent crime and terrorism. One example of technology intended for risk assessment and threat management is the post-9/11 program Total Information Awareness (TIA). (….) Collect-it-all efforts like TIA embody a philosophy that aspires to preventive policing. Mass data collection is construed as a tool to assess and prevent future threats (Murray 2010). In TIA and other programs tested or adopted after 9/11, biometric database screening and analysis have emerged as a preferred method for tracking, identifying, and establishing identity-based inferences in counterterrorism*"). Italics added. See also: Ball, Kirstie, and Frank Webster (Eds.), *The Intensification of Surveillance: Crime, Terrorism & Warfare in the Information Age*, London, UK: Pluto Press, 2007; Guzik, Keith, "Discrimination by Design: Predictive Data Mining as Security Practice in the United States' 'War on Terrorism.'", *Surveillance and Society*, 7 (1), 2009, pp. 1–17.

[35] DaViera, A. L./Uriostegui, M., Gottlieb/A./Onyeka, O, "Risk, race, and predictive policing: A critical race theory analysis of the strategic subject list", *cit.*, pp. 91–103 (93).

[36] Tyler, Tom R./Goff, Philip Atiba/MacCoun, Robert J., "The Impact of Psychological Science on Policing in the United States: Procedural Justice, Legitimacy, and Effective Law Enforcement", *Psychological Science in the Public Interest*, Volume 16, Issue 3, 2015, p. 79 (noting that "without a fundamental reallocation of resources, our society cannot effectively monitor the general public searching for everyday wrongdoing").

[37] Friedmann, Barry et al., "Policing Police Tech: A Soft Law Solution", *Berkeley Technology Law Journal*, Volume 37, 2022, pp. 701–756.

[38] Espeland, Wendy N., and Berit I. Vannebo, "Accountability, Quantification and Law." *Annual Review of Law and Society*, 3, 2007, pp. 21–43.

[39] Boyd, Danah, and Kate Crawford, "Critical Questions for Big Data: Provocations for a Cultural, Technological, and Scholarly Phenomenon", *Information, Communication & Society*, 15 (5), 2012, pp. 662–679.

[40] Braga, Anthony A., and David L. Weisburd, Policing Problem Places: Crime Hot Spots and Effective Prevention. New York: Oxford University Press, 2010.

[41] DaViera, A. L./Uriostegui, M., Gottlieb/A./Onyeka, O, "Risk, race, and predictive policing: A critical race theory analysis of the strategic subject list", *cit.*, pp. 91–103 (93).

[42] Brayne, S., "The criminal law and law enforcement implications of big data", *Annual Review of Law and Social Science*, Volume 14, 2018, pp. 293–308.

[43] Braga, Anthony A., and David L. Weisburd, *Policing Problem Places: Crime Hot Spots and Effective Prevention.* New York: Oxford University Press, 2010; Sherman, Lawrence W., Patrick

policing, albeit imbued with panegyrical aims, is not without sizable shortcomings.[44] It is true that a cohort of staunch supporters[45] have been extolling[46] the host of riveting functionalities[47] comprising predictive policing,[48] but truer still the reality is far dimmer[49] than one could possibly fathom.[50]

§§ Whilst the assertion according to which predictive policing leverages on the data collated in publicly accessible databases is fully warranted,[51] doubts have nonetheless been cast upon the extent to which it widens extant racial disparities.[52]

R. Gartin, and Michael E. Buerger, "Hot Spots of Predatory Crime: Routine Activities and the Criminology of Place." *Criminology*, 27 (1), 1989, pp. 27–55.

[44] Hu, Margaret, "From the National Surveillance State to the Cybersurveillance State", *The Annual Review of Law and Social Science*, Volume 13, 2017, p. 169 ("*as a result of big data biometric governance trends, meaningful distinctions between biometric credentialing for identification and behavioral biometric profiling are disappearing. The objectives are merging: Reliable credentialing is used to advance security and precrime policy rationales. Biometric data mission creep occurs by necessity in a big data world because the cybersurveillance systems are often designed to engage in mass data integration and analysis and predictive policing. Biometric surveillance serves two purposes in preventive policing: It increases identity transparency, and the biometric data categorize identity through cataloging behavioral and physical characteristics and assess these characteristics for risk. Contrasting small data biometric credentialing protocols with big data credentialing protocols is useful. It illustrates how biometric surveillance fits within the Cybersurveillance State*"). Italics added.

[45] Brayne, S., "Big data surveillance: The case of policing", *cit.*, pp. 977–1008.

[46] Mohler, G. O., Short, M. B., Malinowski, S., Johnson, M., Tita, G. E., Bertozzi, A. L., & Brantingham, P. J., "Randomized controlled field trials of predictive policing", *Journal of the American Statistical Association*, 110 (512), 2015, pp. 1399–1411.

[47] Schenwar, M., & Law, V., *Prison by any other name: The harmful consequences of popular reforms*, New York, The New Press, 2020.

[48] Meijer, A., & Wessels, M., "Predictive policing: Review of benefits and drawbacks", *International Journal of Public Administration*, 42 (12), 2019, pp. 1031–1039.

[49] Cohen, Stanley, *Visions of Social Control: Crime, Punishment and Classification.* Malden, MA: Polity Press, 1985 (for purposes here, predictive policing seems to be a tool of social control of social undesirables).

[50] Santos, R. B., The effectiveness of crime analysis for crime reduction: cure or diagnosis? *Journal of Contemporary Criminal Justice*, 30 (2), 2014, pp. 147–168.

[51] But see: Kirkpatrick, Keith, "It's not the Algorithm, it's the Data", *Communications of the ACM*, February 2017, Volume 60, n. ° 2, 2017 ("critics, however, say tools such as PredPol and CommandCentral *are inherently biased since they rely heavily on reported crimes data, which is often concentrated in areas that are heavily policed, thereby skewing statistics to overrepresent poor or minority communities.* "*We know that we have a history of racially biased policing in the United States, and that has fed into all the data that we have on where arrests have occurred, which crimes are more likely to occur in specific communities, and at which particular times*," says Jennifer Lynch, senior staff attorney at the Electronic Frontier Foundation. "*That's the data that's being fed into predictive policing algorithms*"). Italics added. See also: Kirkpatrick, Keith, "Battling Algorithmic Bias: How Do We Ensure Algorithms Treat Us Fairly?" *Commun. ACM 59*, Volume 10, 2016, pp. 1 and ff and passim.

[52] Mitchell, O., & Caudy, M. S., "Examining racial disparities in drug arrests", *Justice Quarterly*, 32 (2), 2015, pp. 288–313; Gottlieb, A., & Flynn, K., "The Legacy of Slavery and Mass Incarceration: Evidence from Felony Case Outcomes", *Social Service Review*, 95 (1), 2021, pp. 3–35.

Take the example of Chicago's Strategic Suspect List (SSL),[53] which is a thumping great database comprising criminal-related information of roughly 400,000 thousand arrested individuals[54] who were ascribed an index score that predicted risk to be engaged in future criminal activities[55] (e.g. gun violence).[56] However, SSL is database riddled with factors that ultimately lead to, insofar they are conducive to a, *proxy discrimination*[57] with racial disparities[58] looming large in the data analysis.[59]

---

[53] Chicago Data Portal, Strategic Subject List- Historical. https://data.cityofchicago.org/Public-Safety/Strategic-Subject-ListHistorical/4aki-r3np, 2020.

[54] Jefferson, B. J., Predictable policing: Predictive crime mapping and geographies of policing and race, *Annals of the American Association of Geographers*, 108 (1), 2018, pp. 1–16.

[55] Tucek, A., Constraining Big Brother: The Legal Deficiencies Surrounding Chicago's Use of the Strategic Subject List (2018). *University of Chicago Legal Forum*, 2019.

[56] DaViera, A. L./Uriostegui, M., Gottlieb/A./Onyeka, O, "Risk, race, and predictive policing: A critical race theory analysis of the strategic subject list", *cit.*, pp. 91–103 (91).

[57] See: Part IV, This chapter, Sect. 4.1.6.3 of this book (on proxy discrimination). See also: Prince, Anya E. R./Schwarcz, Daniel, "Proxy Discrimination in the Age of Artificial Intelligence and Big Data", *Iowa Law Review*, Volume 105, 1257, 2020, pp. 1279–81 ("[*P*]*roxy discrimination will tend to occur when a suspect variable is predictive of a desired outcome only because it proxies for another*, quantifiable and potentially available, *variable that causes the desired outcome but that is not included in the AI's training data*"). Italics added. It bears mentioning that scorching issue of whether and to what extent disparate impact alone should be actionable is different from, in that does not overlap with, the sweltering issue of proxy discrimination. See: Cohran, Matthew Jordan, "Fairness in Disparity: Challenging the Application of Disparate Impact Theory in Fair Housing Claims Against Insurers", *The George Mason University Civil Rights Law Journal*, Volume 21, 2011, pp. 159 and ff and passim (discussing the use of disparate impact theory and potential applicability to Fair Housing Act claims against insurers). See also: Grimmelmann, James/Westreich, Daniel, "Incomprehensible Discrimination", *California Law Review Online*, Volume 7, 2017, pp 170 and ff and passim. This exciting piece of research revolves around as a vignette and mock judicial opinion, focusing on fictional case (an employment-based AI employed in the fictional universe of the movie Zootopia) under a specific legal regime (Title VII). It ultimately solves this fictional case by drawing a difference between proxy discrimination and disparate impact p. 70 ("The problem is that there is no explanation in the record as to which of these two correlations, if either, is causal. It may be that the factors directly measure applicant characteristics that determine success in the challenging and dangerous field of police work, and that those characteristics happen to be unequally distributed in our diverse society. It may also be that these factors are instead measuring applicants' species and that they measure likely job performance only because they are identifying species in an applicant pool where the relevant characteristics are unequally distributed"). See: Part IV, This chapter, Sect. 4.1.6.3 of this book (on proxy discrimination).

[58] Soss, Joe, Richard C. Fording, and Sanford F. Schram, *Disciplining the Poor: Neoliberal Paternalism and the Persistent Power of Race*. Chicago: University of Chicago Press, 2011.

[59] Proxy discrimination happens frequently in the remit of real estate industry—especially, in the realm of rental applications—to screen out undesirable tenants drawing on the existence of prior criminal records. See: Wonyoung, So, "Which Information Matters? Measuring Landlord Assessment of Tenant Screening Reports", *Housing Policy Debate*, Volume 33, n. ° 6, 2023, pp. 1484–1510 (1501–1502) ("*In mid-scored criminal records, landlords would have more discretion in terms of how to assess tenants, depending on the type of charges or the disposition of the case. HUD prohibits denying housing by holding arrest records against tenants. But apart from that, landlords who HOUSING POLICY DEBATE 1501 would like to construct proxies of undesirable tenants using criminal records must assess which criminal records would relate to tenants' behavior (e.g., damaging their property and/or adversely affecting other tenants).* However, it is incredibly challenging to identify the causal relationship between how and which past misdemeanors cause

§§ At its core, SSL amounts to a comprehensive, thoroughgoing, and full-fledged database whereby arrest data spanning 2012–2016 is featured,[60] thereby encompassing any individual (male or female) who has either been arrested or fingerprinted[61] since 2013.[62] These individuals were subsequently given a risk assessment[63] for either gun violence[64] perpetration or victimization.[65]

§§ SSL has been designed and created by Miles Wernick at the Illinois Institute of Technology[66] with a view to aid law enforcement agencies to make data-based[67] informed decisions within the purview of criminal justice. It has been accordingly contended that its overriding goal was to timely alert police to individuals that posed grave danger to the great state of Illinois.[68] Such individuals were to be tagged as possible «parties to violence»,[69] and the police, just like the remaining law enforcement agencies, were to remain accordingly vigilant.

§§ SSL was fully funded through a Department of Justice Bureau of Justice Assistance[70] grant to outline a risk assessment algorithm[71] that would leverage on a plethora of person-centred variables to timely and shrewdly predict whether and

---

particular future tenant behaviors. Moreover, legal jargon and abbreviations on the report could make it harder for landlords to understand criminal records in the first place. *These factors, as a result, could contribute to landlords' reliance on the scores provided by the report shown in the experiment*"). See: Part IV, This chapter, Sects. 4.1.4–4.1.4.2.3 of this book.

[60] DaViera, A. L./Uriostegui, M., Gottlieb/A./Onyeka, O, "Risk, race, and predictive policing: A critical race theory analysis of the strategic subject list", *cit.*, pp. 91–103 (93).

[61] Lynch, Michael, Simon A. Cole, Ruth McNally, and Kathleen Jordan. 2008. Truth Machine: The Conten tious History of DNA Fingerprinting. Chicago: Uni versity of Chicago Press.

[62] DaViera, A. L./Uriostegui, M., Gottlieb/A./Onyeka, O, "Risk, race, and predictive policing: A critical race theory analysis of the strategic subject list", *cit.*, pp. 91–103 (93).

[63] Stevenson, Megan T./Slogobin, Christopher, "Algorithmic Risk Assessments and the Double-Edged Sword of Youth", *Behavioural Sciences and the Law*, Volume 36, 2018, pp. 638–639.

[64] Papachristos, Andrew V., David M. Hureau, and Anthony A. Braga, "The Corner and the Crew: The Influence of Geography and Social Networks on Gang Violence." *American Sociological Review*, 78 (3), 2013, pp. 417–47.

[65] DaViera, A. L./Uriostegui, M., Gottlieb/A./Onyeka, O, "Risk, race, and predictive policing: A critical race theory analysis of the strategic subject list", *cit.*, pp. 91–103 (93).

[66] DaViera, A. L./Uriostegui, M., Gottlieb/A./Onyeka, O, "Risk, race, and predictive policing: A critical race theory analysis of the strategic subject list", *cit.*, pp. 91–103 (93).

[67] Kitchin, Rob, *The Data Revolution: Big Data, Open Data, Data Infrastructures & Their Consequences*. London, UK: SAGE, 2014.

[68] DaViera, A. L./Uriostegui, M., Gottlieb/A./Onyeka, O, "Risk, race, and predictive policing: A critical race theory analysis of the strategic subject list", *cit.*, pp. 91–103 (93).

[69] Kunichoff, Y., & Sier, P., August 21 The Contradictions of Chicago Police's Secretive List. Chicago Magazine, 2017, passim. https://www.chicagomag.com/city-life/august-2017/chicago-police-strategic-subject-list/

[70] Chicago Data Portal, Strategic Subject List- Historical. https://data.cityofchicago.org/Public-Safety/Strategic-Subject-ListHistorical/4aki-r3np, 2020.

[71] But see on the perils associated to risk assessment algorithms: Hamilton, Melissa, "The sexist algorithm", *Behavioral Sciences and the Law*, Volume 37, Issue 2, Special Issue: the Use of Statistics in Criminal Cases, March–April 2019, 2019, pp. 1 and ff ("Algorithmic risk assessment tools are informed by scientific research concerning which factors are predictive of recidivism and thus support the evidence-based practice movement in criminal justice. Automated assessments of individualized risk (low, medium, high) permit officials to make more effective management decisions.

to what extent a given individual would be later involved in criminal activities.[72] The crux of the legal quagmire lies elsewhere though: the variables used to estimate the risk assessment concerning the individuals that were deemed to be a «party to violence» in crime hotspots.[73]

§§ Put simply, there is a gulf between the laudable aims with which predictive policing has been permeated by (prevention of crime underpinned by the pillars of effective reallocation of resources[74]) and the outcome arising out of this crime prevention strategy (racial disparities[75] and structural disadvantage[76] with which Black people have been grappling for a long-winded span of time[77]).

Computer-generated algorithms appear to be objective and neutral. But are these algorithms actually fair? The focus herein is on gender equity. Studies confirm that women typically have far lower recidivism rates than men. *This differential raises the question of how well algorithmic outcomes fare in terms of predictive parity by gender*. This essay reports original research using a large dataset of offenders who were scored on the popular risk assessment tool COMPAS. *Findings indicate that COMPAS performs reasonably well at discriminating between recidivists and non-recidivists for men and women. Nonetheless, COMPAS algorithmic outcomes systemically overclassify women in higher risk groupings. Multiple measures of algorithmic equity and predictive accuracy are provided to support the conclusion that this algorithm is sexist*"). Italics added.

[72] DaViera, A. L./Uriostegui, M., Gottlieb/A./Onyeka, O, "Risk, race, and predictive policing: A critical race theory analysis of the strategic subject list", *cit.*, pp. 91–103 (93).

[73] Uchida, Craig D., and Marc L. Swatt, "Operation LASER and the Effectiveness of Hotspot Patrol: A Panel Analysis." Police Quarterly 16 (3), 2015, pp. 287–304.

[74] Tyler, Tom R./Goff, Philip Atiba/MacCoun, Robert J., "The Impact of Psychological Science on Policing in the United States: Procedural Justice, Legitimacy, and Effective Law Enforcement", *Psychological Science in the Public Interest*, Volume 16, Issue 3, 2015, p. 79 (noting that "without a fundamental reallocation of resources, our society cannot effectively monitor the general public searching for everyday wrongdoing").

[75] Robinson, M. A., "Black bodies on the ground: Policing disparities in the African American Community—An analysis of newsprint from January 1, 2015, through December 31, 2015", *Journal of Black Studies*, 48 (6), 2017, pp. 551–571.

[76] See: Barocas, Solon/Selbst, Andrew, "Big Data's Disparate Impact", *California Law Review*, Volume 104, pp. 2016, p. 691 (highlighting the worrisome, and gruesome, issue of "structural disadvantage" with which racialized communities have been tussling for centuries). See also: Powell, Richard/Porter, Jeremy, "Redlining, Concentrated Disadvantage and Crime: The Effects of Discriminatory Government Policies on Violent Crime", *American Journal of Criminal Justice*, Volume 48, 2023, pp. 1132–1156 ("*Redlining and other discriminatory government policies enacted during the first half of the Twentieth Century have had long-lasting negative effects on neighborhoods, especially those inhabited by people of color. This study attempts to link the practice of redlining to current-day indicators of neighborhood concentrated disadvantage and violent crime using spatio-temporal data from Chicago* (...) *In addition, it seeks to determine whether redlining was associated with violent crime, and if that association was mediated by redlining's effect on concentrated disadvantage. The results indicate that redlining was associated with increases in both concentrated disadvantage and violent crime, and that redlining's relationship with violent crime was, indeed, partially mediated by its relationship with concentrated disadvantage*"). Italics added. See also: Gandy, Oscar H., *Coming to Terms with Chance: Engaging Rational Discrimination and Cumulative Disadvantage*, Farnham, UK: Ashgate Publishing, 2009.

[77] Gandy, Oscar H., *Coming to Terms with Chance: Engaging Rational Discrimination and Cumulative Disadvantage*. Farnham, UK: Ashgate Publishing, 2009.

§§ More to the point, the variables used to deftly calculate risk contained proxies to racial discrimination.[78] Tellingly, the variables used to estimate risk assessment comprised the number of times being the victim of a gun-related incident, the age at the latest record arrest, number of times being the victim of aggravated battery or physical assault, number of recorded prior arrests for violent crimes, alleged gang affiliation, number of prior drug possession arrests,[79] recorded trend related with recent criminal activity,[80] and the number of prior flagitious use of guns arrests.[81]

§§ Whilst the risk assessment algorithm does not encompass neither race nor sex as predictor variables,[82] pundits have not refrained themselves from voicing concerns about the nature of list of measures, which may indeed bear a striking resemblance with both (race and gender).[83]

---

[78] Campisi, Natalie, From Inherent Racial Bias to Incorrect Data The Problems With Current Credit Scoring Models, Forbes (Feb. 26, 2021), https://www.forbes.com/advisor/creditcards/from-inherent-racial-bias-to-incorrect-data-the-problems-with-current-credit-scoring-models/; [https://www.perma.cc/EWA4-CS8E] (highlighting rampant racial bias in credit scoring systems); Oyama, Rebecca, "Do Not (Re)Enter: the Rise of Criminal Background Tenant Screening as a Violation of the Fair Housing Act", *Michigan Journal of Race and Law*, Volume 15, 2009, pp. 181, 184–93 (discussing a broad range of historical/criminal accounts as a way to screen undesirable tenants, such as Blacks and Latinos); Statement of Interest of the United States at 12, *Louis v. SafeRent Sols., LLC, No. 1:22-cv-10800* (D. Mass. Jan. 9, 2023) (holding that the Fair Housing Act liability stretches far and beyond, thus encompassing a vast assortment of entities providing housing-related services, including corporations that offer tenant screening services). See also: Massey, Douglas S., "The Legacy of the 1968 Fair Housing Act", *Social Forces*, Volume 30, 2015, pp. 571, 575–76, 578 ("[*The FHA] outlawed the refusal to rent or sell to someone because of race; it prohibited racial discrimination in the terms and conditions of rental or sale; it barred discrimination in real estate advertising; it banned agents from making untrue statements about a dwelling's availability in order to deny access to blacks*; and it enjoined real estate agents from making comments about the race of neighbors or in-movers in order to promote panic selling. Although the new law applied only to around 80% of the nation's housing stock, a Supreme Court decision adjudicated just two months later extended its reach to all housing in the United States"). Italics added. Internal citations omitted.

[79] Beckett, Katherine, Kris Nyrop, Lori Pfingst, and Melissa Bowen, "Drug Use, Drug Possession Arrests, and the Question of Race: Lessons from Seattle.", *Social Problems*, (52) 3, 2005, pp. 419–41; Duster, Troy, "Pattern, Purpose and Race in the Drug War.", Crack in America: Demon Drugs and Social Justice, edited by C. Reinarman and H. G. Levine. Berkeley: University of California Press, 1997, pp. 206–287; Mitchell, O., & Caudy, M. S., Examining racial disparities in drug arrests", *Justice Quarterly*, 32 (2), 2015, pp. 288–313.

[80] DaViera, A. L./Uriostegui, M., Gottlieb/A./Onyeka, O, "Risk, race, and predictive policing: A critical race theory analysis of the strategic subject list", *cit.*, pp. 91–103 (93).

[81] Chicago Data Portal, Strategic Subject List- Historical. https://data.cityofchicago.org/Public-Safety/Strategic-Subject-ListHistorical/4aki-r3np, 2020, passim.

[82] DaViera, A. L./Uriostegui, M., Gottlieb/A./Onyeka, O, "Risk, race, and predictive policing: A critical race theory analysis of the strategic subject list", *cit.*, pp. 91–103 (93).

[83] Eckhouse, L., Lum, K., Conti-Cook, C., & Ciccolini, J., "Layers of bias: A unified approach for understanding problems with risk assessment. Criminal Justice and Behavior", Volume 46, Issue 2, 2019, pp. 185–209.

§§ It is often contended that the foregoing list of measures is tantamount to proxies for race and gender,[84] thus rendering such risk assessment tools as racist[85] algorithms.[86] For this reason alone, doubts have been cast upon the effectiveness—or lack thereof—of predictive policing, both from the standpoint of reallocation of resources[87] and its underlying fairness.[88]

§§ Although making data[89]-based[90] predictions[91] on where will crimes occur is seemingly wrapped under the patina of objectivity,[92] there has been a public outcry about the extent to which the data around which predictive policing revolves is fraught

---

[84] O'Neil, Cathy, *Weapons of math destruction: How big data increases inequality and threatens democracy*, New York, Crown Publisher, 2016.

[85] Monk, E. P., "The color of punishment: African Americans, skin tone, and the criminal justice system", *Ethnic and Racial Studies*, Volume 42, Issue 10, 2019, pp. 1593–1612.

[86] Osaba, Osonde/Welser, William IV, *An Intelligence in Our Image—The Risk of Bias and Errors in Artificial Intelligence*, Santa Monica, California, Rand, 2018, passim; Chandler, Anupam, "The Racist Algorithm", *Michigan Law Review*, Volume 115, n. ° 6, 2018, p. 1026 (on racist algorithms, noting that "the possibilities for discriminatory manipulation are legion"). But see: Altenburger, Kristen M./Ho, Daniel E., "When Algorithms Import Private Bias into Public Enforcement: The Promise and Limitations of Statistical Debiasing Solutions", *Journal of Institutional & Theoretical Economics*, Volume 175, 2019, pp. 97–98 (calls for a "debias predictive algorithms" to assuage racist and/or biased, doctored and bigoted algorithms nevertheless); Hamilton, Melissa, "The Biased Algorithm: Evidence of Disparate Impact on Hispanics", *American Criminal Law Review*, Volume 56, 2019, pp. 1553 and ff and passim.

[87] Tyler, Tom R./Goff, Philip Atiba/MacCoun, Robert J., "The Impact of Psychological Science on Policing in the United States: Procedural Justice, Legitimacy, and Effective Law Enforcement", *Psychological Science in the Public Interest*, Volume 16, Issue 3, 2015, p. 79 (noting that "without a fundamental reallocation of resources, our society cannot effectively monitor the general public searching for everyday wrongdoing").

[88] Corbett-Davies, Sam/Goel, Sharad, "The Measure and Mismeasure of Fairness: a critical Review of Fair Machine Learning", *Cornell University Library*, 2018, pp. 3 and ff and passim (undertake laudable efforts to debunk algorithm biases that primarily target ethnic minorities, such as Hispanics and coloured people); Laub, John H., *Understanding Inequality and the Justice System Response: Charting a New Way Forward*, New York: William T. Grant Foundation, 2014.

[89] Kitchin, Rob, *The Data Revolution: Big Data, Open Data, Data Infrastructures & Their Consequences*. London, UK: SAGE, 2014.

[90] Sherman, Lawrence W., "Targeting, Testing and Tracking Police Services: The Rise of Evidence Based Policing, 1975–2025.", *Crime and Justice*, 42 (1), 2013, pp. 377–451.

[91] Ferguson, Andrew G., "Big Data and Predictive Reasonable Suspicion." *University of Pennsylvania Law Review*, 63 (2), 2015, pp. 327–410.

[92] Christin, Angèle, "From Daguerreotypes to Algorithms: Machines, Expertise, and Three Forms of Objectivity." *ACM Computers & Society*, 46 (1), 2016, pp. 27–32 (on the multifarious facets of algorithmic objectivity). But see: Benjamin, Ruha, *Race After Technology: Abolitionist Tools for the New Jim Code*, New York, Polity, 2019, pp. 1–172 (7) (discussing that Artificial Intelligence-embedded technologies are viewed as iron-clad tools of objectivity and devoid of any biases whatsoever). Ruha Benjamin contends that "the employment of new technologies that reflect and reproduce existing inequities but that are promoted and perceived as more objective or progressive than the discriminatory systems of a previous era").

with racial[93] bias.[94] To add to our woes, a sweeping analysis on the effectiveness of predictive policing has shown that these programs, albeit suffused with the laudable aim to stamp out crime, are nothing but dispiritingly tokenistic.[95]

§§ Against this background, predictive policing has been met with grudging reluctance by a great bulk of scholars. Compellingly, uncertain is the extent to which predictive policing is suitably tailored to effectively attain the laudable goal of crime prevention.[96]

§§ On this account, it seems as though predictive policing amounts to an algorithmic tool to target both outsiders[97] and *socially undesirables*. The warped data that underpins predictive policing lends support to, and gives credence to, this main contention.

§§ To the extent that predictive policing leverages on clusters of bigoted data,[98] there have been vexing doubts on whether and to what extent this crime prevention

---

[93] See: Kirkpatrick, Keith, "It's not the Algorithm, it's the Data", *Communications of the ACM*, February 2017, Volume 60, n. ° 2, 2017 ("critics, however, say tools such as PredPol and Command-Central *are inherently biased since they rely heavily on reported crimes data, which is often concentrated in areas that are heavily policed, thereby skewing statistics to overrepresent poor or minority communities.* "*We know that we have a history of racially biased policing in the United States, and that has fed into all the data that we have on where arrests have occurred, which crimes are more likely to occur in specific communities, and at which particular times*," says Jennifer Lynch, senior staff attorney at the Electronic Frontier Foundation. "*That's the data that's being fed into predictive policing algorithms*"). Italics added. See also: Kirkpatrick, Keith, "Battling Algorithmic Bias: How Do We Ensure Algorithms Treat Us Fairly?" *Commun. ACM 59*, Volume 10, 2016, pp. 1 and ff and passim. See also: Browne, Simone, *Dark Matters: On the Surveillance of Blackness*. Durham, NC: Duke University Press, 2015.

[94] Jefferson, B. J., "Predictable policing: Predictive crime mapping and geographies of policing and race". *Annals of the American Association of Geographers*, 108 (1), 2018, 1–16.

[95] Saunders, J., Hunt, P., & Hollywood, J. S., "Predictions put into practice: A quasi-experimental evaluation of Chicago's predictive policing pilot", *Journal of Experimental Criminology*, 12 (3), 2016, pp. 347–371.

[96] DaViera, A. L./Uriostegui, M., Gottlieb/A./Onyeka, O, "Risk, race, and predictive policing: A critical race theory analysis of the strategic subject list", *cit.*, pp. 91–103.

[97] Becker, Howard S., *Outsiders: Studies in the Sociology of Deviance*, New York: Free Press, 1963.

[98] But see: Kirkpatrick, Keith, "It's not the Algorithm, it's the Data", *Communications of the ACM*, February 2017, Volume 60, n. ° 2, 2017 ("critics, however, say tools such as PredPol and Command-Central *are inherently biased since they rely heavily on reported crimes data, which is often concentrated in areas that are heavily policed, thereby skewing statistics to overrepresent poor or minority communities.* "*We know that we have a history of racially biased policing in the United States, and that has fed into all the data that we have on where arrests have occurred, which crimes are more likely to occur in specific communities, and at which particular times*," says Jennifer Lynch, senior staff attorney at the Electronic Frontier Foundation. "*That's the data that's being fed into predictive policing algorithms*"). Italics added. See also: Kirkpatrick, Keith, "Battling Algorithmic Bias: How Do We Ensure Algorithms Treat Us Fairly?" *Commun. ACM 59*, Volume 10, 2016, pp. 1 and ff and passim. Lazer, David/Radford, Jason, "Data ex Machina: Introduction to Big Data.", *Annual Review of Sociology*, 43, 2017.

tool is amenable to effectively[99] squelch crime[100] while abiding by the fundamental tenets of Rule of Law.[101]

§§ Notably, SSL has been thoroughly assessed, and yet the results yielded fell conspicuously short of matching the overblown expectations from the reduction of gun-related crime rates standpoint.[102] The same goes for predictive policing deployed to tackle property crimes.[103] Most importantly, the overriding concerns with racial disparities arising out of doctored and watered down data skyrocketed.

§§ Insofar the suspects included in the SSL were labelled[104] as dangerous,[105] the likelihood[106] of being harassed, surveilled[107] and subsequently arrested[108] by law enforcement agencies was exceedingly high. This disheartening scenario crashes into long-standing debates on the degree to which the increased risk of arrest facing

---

[99] Santos, R. B., "The effectiveness of crime analysis for crime reduction: cure or diagnosis?", *Journal of Contemporary Criminal Justice*, 30 (2), 2014, pp. 147–168.

[100] Hardyns, W., & Rummens, A., "Predictive policing as a new tool for law enforcement? recent developments and challenges". *European Journal on Criminal Policy and Research*, 24 (3), 2018, pp. 201–218.

[101] Cass, Ronald A., *The Rule of Law in America*. Baltimore, Maryland: The Johns Hopkins University Press, 2001, p. 17 (noting that a "central element of the Rule of law, constraint from external authority...helps assure that the process of government, *rather than the predilections of the individual decision-maker*") Italics added. Which is why the onset of the age of Artificial Intelligence will put the Rule of Law to the test like never before. Recall, the Rule of Law is a functional barrier—aimed at clamping down a host of unlawful deeds undertaken by those in power—that must not be teared apart or criminal procedure law will be otherwise despoiled from its intrinsic validity and vitality. See: Raz, Joseph, "The Rule of Law and its Virtue", *The Authority of Law: Essays on Law and Morality*, *cit.*, p. 224 (asserts adamantly that the Rule of Law is aimed at cushioning the hazards of abuse perpetrated by those in power. In this vein, Raz contends that "the law inevitably creates a great danger of arbitrary power—the Rule of Law is designed to minimize the danger created by the law itself...*Thus the (R)ule of (L)aw is designed to minimize the danger created by law itself...Thus the (R)ule of (L)aw is a negative virtue...the evil which is avoided is evil which could only have been caused by the law itself*"). Italics added; McAfee, Andrew/Brynjolfsson, *Machine, Platform, Crowd: Harnessing our Digital Future*, London: Brilliance Audio; Unabridged edition, 2017 (pore over a myriad of automatic biases displayed by artificial intelligence).

[102] Saunders, J., Hunt, P., & Hollywood, J. S., "Predictions put into practice: A quasi-experimental evaluation of Chicago's predictive policing pilot", *Journal of Experimental Criminology*, 12 (3), 2016, pp. 347–371.

[103] Hunt, P., Saunders, J., & Hollywood, J. S., "Conclusions. In Evaluation of the Shreveport Predictive Policing Experiment, RAND Corporation, 2014, pp. 50 and ff.

[104] It bears mentioning that the literature on algorithmic fairness has labelled measures of equality as either "group fairness" or "individual fairness" metrics. This phosphorescent dichotomy, though, can be very misleading indeed. Almost every tentative measure of "group fairness" can be framed using the term "individual" (for example, **predictive parity** entails that, for any individual, a given risk score conveys the same average risk irrespective of race). Relatedly, any "individual-fairness" metric can be framed using the term "group" (for example, a **single-threshold rule** requires that the group of people who poses any degree of risk should receive the same risk score). The difference is that which **"individual-fairness"** metrics relates to how the algorithm reaches its output in each individual case, whilst **"group-fairness"** metrics relates to the distribution of outputs and/or their accuracy across particular groups. See: Mayson, Sandra G., "Bias In, Bias Out", *cit.*, pp. 2218–2300. See: Part IV, This chapter, Sects. 4.1.10.1–4.1.10.6 of this book (on biased algorithmic risk assessment in criminal procedure law settings, with a sharper focus on COMPAS).

members of racial minorities[109] is the byproduct of decades-long of gruelling racial[110] discrimination.[111]

§§ Tellingly, individuals included within the compass of SSL were constantly on law enforcement's radar.[112] Casts broadly, individuals included on SSL were far more likely to be surveilled and arrested[113] by the police than were individuals placed at the outskirts of SSL.[114] There is accordingly a deep-rooted problem with

---

105 Corbett-Davies and Goel coined this sweltering issue as "label bias" and diagnose it as "perhaps the most serious obstacle facing fair machine learning." But see: Corbett-Davies, Sam/Goel, Sharad, "The Measure and Mismeasure of Fairness: a critical Review of Fair Machine Learning", *Cornell University Library*, 2018, p. 18 (broaches a type of *measurement bias* coined "feature bias," which is neatly a bias in the predictors x. Note, though, that there is a second type of measurement bias deemed "label bias," which, in turn, amounts to a bias in y. The authors argue that that label bias is the worst bias there is).

106 Kleinberg, Jon/Ludwig, Jens/Mullainathan, Sendhil/Sunstein Cass R., "Discrimination in the Age of Algorithms", *Journal of Legal Analysis*, Volume 10, 1, 2018, pp. 28–29, 33–34 (draw a distinction between "group differences in the raw data" and biases for the "choice of predictors").

107 Sewell, A. A., Jefferson, K. A., & Lee, H., Living under surveillance: Gender, psychological distress, and stop-question and-frisk policing in New York city. Social Science & Medicine, 159, 2016, pp. 1–13.

108 Kizer, J. M., "Arrested by skin color: Evidence from siblings and a nationally representative sample, *Socius: Sociological Research for a Dynamic World*, 3, 2017.

109 Laub, John H., *Understanding Inequality and the Justice System Response: Charting a New Way Forward*, New York: William T. Grant Foundation, 2014.

110 Gottlieb, A., & Flynn, K., "The Legacy of Slavery and Mass Incarceration: Evidence from Felony Case Outcomes", *Social Service Review*, 95 (1), 2021, pp. 3–35.

111 Jefferson, B, *Digitize and Punish: Racial Criminalization in the Digital Age*, Minnesota, University of Minnesota Press, 2020; Gross, Samuel R., Maurice Possley, and Kalara Stephens, "Race and Wrongful Convictions in the United States." National Registry of Exonerations, Newkirk Center for Science and Society, University of California-Irvine, 2017.

112 DaViera, A. L./Uriostegui, M., Gottlieb/A./Onyeka, O, "Risk, race, and predictive policing: A critical race theory analysis of the strategic subject list", *cit.*, pp. 91–103.

113 See: Connecticut Fair Housing Center, et al. v. CoreLogic Rental Property Solutions—Cohen Milstein (access: 20.11.2024). ("*The U.S. Department of Housing & Urban Development observed in 2016 that excluding rental applicants because of their criminal records disproportionately harms Latinos and African Americans, who are significantly more likely than whites to be arrested or convicted. Studies show such disparities are linked to differential enforcement rather than to differences in likelihood of engaging in criminal activity.* HUD advised that to avoid discriminating, an "individualized review" should be conducted considering the nature of the offense, how long ago it occurred, intervening changed circumstances, and other relevant factors to avoid denying housing to an applicant who does not pose a genuine and ongoing threat to persons or property. *Further, HUD's guidance specifically advises landlords not to consider arrests that did not result in a conviction in making their evaluations*"). Italics added. See: Part IV, This chapter, Sects. 4.1.4–4.1.4.2.1 of this book (on mortgage redlining). See: Part IV, This chapter, Sects. 4.1.2–4.1.4.3 of this book (on algorithmic credit scoring, consumer racism and credit card redlining). See: Part IV, This chapter, Sects. 4.1.4–4.1.4.2.3 of this book (on algorithmic redlining). See: Part IV, This chapter, Sect. 4.1.4.3 of this book (on "algorithmic redliking"). See: Part IV, This chapter, Sect. 4.1.3 of this book (on algorithmic prime-lining).

114 Saunders, J., Hunt, P., & Hollywood, J. S., "Predictions put into practice: A quasi-experimental evaluation of Chicago's predictive policing pilot", *Journal of Experimental Criminology*, 12 (3), 2016, pp. 347–371.

which predictive policing has been tussling: the disparate[115] impact[116] on racialized communities, whom are constantly targeted, surveilled,[117] harassed and arrested by law enforcement agencies.[118]

§§ Put differently, individuals included on SSL were strategically surveilled whereas individuals that did not feature on SSL were not. This *selective surveillance* is one the jarring byproducts of my newfangled concept of *Algorithmic Dictatorship* that further compounds racial disparities[119] that have been besetting modern societies.

§§ Against this background, scholars have neither been coy nor bashful in pinning down the blame onto the deeply flawed data that feeds into the risk assessment algorithms.[120] But much more lies beyond that.

§§ Amongst the chief concerns voiced against the deployment of predictive policing lies the perceived dearth of ethics,[121] transparency,[122]/[123] and accountability,[124] which, taken together, stand as the main roadblocks to the unbridled proliferation of this tool of crime prevention thus far.[125]

---

[115] See: Selbst, Andrew D., "Disparate Impact in Big Data Policing", *Georgia Law Review*, Volume 52, 2017, p. 167 ("[I]t may be impossible to tell when the disparate impact truly reflects reality").

[116] Barocas, Solon/Selbst, Andrew D., "Big Data's Disparate Impact", *California Law Review*, Volume 104, 2016, pp. 671 and ff and passim.

[117] Browne, S., *Dark matters: on the surveillance of blackness*, Duke University Press, 2015, passim.

[118] Robinson, M. A., "Black bodies on the ground: Policing disparities in the African American Community-An analysis of newsprint from January 1, 2015, through December 31, 2015", *Journal of Black Studies*, Volume 48, Issue 6, pp. 551–571.

[119] Lyon, David, The Electronic Eye: *The Rise of Surveillance Society*. Minneapolis: University of Min nesota Press, 1994; Lyon, David, *Surveillance as Social Sorting: Privacy, Risk, and Digital Discrimination*. New York: Routledge, 2003. Citron; Danielle Keats Citron/Pasquale, Frank, "Network Accountability for the Domestic Intelligence Apparatus", *Hasting Law Journal*, Volume 62, 2011, 1441, 1444–45; Gray, David/Citron, Danielle Keats, "The Right to Quantitative Privacy", *Minnesota Law Review*, Volume 98, 2013, pp. 62–81.

[120] See: DaViera, A. L./Uriostegui, M., Gottlieb/A./Onyeka, O, "Risk, race, and predictive policing: A critical race theory analysis of the strategic subject list", *cit.*, pp. 91–103. See also: Kirkpatrick, Keith, "It's not the Algorithm, it's the Data", *Communications of the ACM*, February 2017, Volume 60, n. ° 2, 2017 ("critics, however, say tools such as PredPol and CommandCentral *are inherently biased since they rely heavily on reported crimes data, which is often concentrated in areas that are heavily policed, thereby skewing statistics to overrepresent poor or minority communities.* "*We know that we have a history of racially biased policing in the United States, and that has fed into all the data that we have on where arrests have occurred, which crimes are more likely to occur in specific communities, and at which particular times*," says Jennifer Lynch, senior staff attorney at the Electronic Frontier Foundation. "*That's the data that's being fed into predictive policing algorithms*"). Italics added. See also: Kirkpatrick, Keith, "Battling Algorithmic Bias: How Do We Ensure Algorithms Treat Us Fairly?" *Commun. ACM 59*, Volume 10, 2016, pp. 1 and ff and passim.

[121] Jobin, A./Ienca, M./Vayena, E., "The global landscape of AI ethics guidelines", *Nature Machine Intelligence*, n. ° 1, 2019, pp. 388 and ff and passim; Liu, Hin-Yan/Zawieska, Karolina, "From responsible robotics towards a human rights regime oriented to the challenges of robotics and artificial intelligence", *Ethics Information Technology*, Volume 22, Issue 4, 2020, pp. 321–333; Ryan, M./Stahl, B.-C., "Artificial intelligence ethics guidelines for developers and users: clarifying their content and normative implications", *Communication and Ethics in Society*, Volume 3, 2021, pp. 62–85.

§§ The primal concern, though, is that which the criminal justice system is being weaponized against racialized people,[126] thereby reifying and exacerbating a gruelling tapestry of decades-long racial discrimination.[127] Predictive policing, an algorithm tool riddled with bottlenecks and loopholes, is the capstone of an agreed-upon strategy of weaponization of criminal justice against racial minorities. Thence, the taxonomy of *Algorithmic Dictatorship* that deploys *selective surveillance* on a cohort of *socially undesirables* only to harass, arrest and incarcerate them.

§§ Tellingly, predictive policing, an algorithmic-borne tool of risk assessment, unlawfully targets neighbourhoods whose residents are already grappling with a drawn-out racial discrimination, oppression,[128] exclusion, and poverty (the «have-nots»),[129] whom, in turn, are permanently surveilled,[130] harassed and arrested by law enforcement agencies.[131]

---

[122] Tyler, Tom R., "Does the American Public Accept the Rule of Law? The Findings of Psychological Research on Deference to Authority", *De Paul Law Review*, 56, 2007, pp. 661–664 (stating that «transparency and openness foster the belief that decision-making procedures are neutral»). See also: Doherty, Joseph W./Reville, Robert T./Zakaras, Laura(ed.), *Introduction to Confidentiality, Transparency, and the U.S. Civil Justice System*, Oxford, Oxford University Press, 2012, 1–258 (passim) (noting that the lack of transparency yields sizable social costs).

[123] Davis, Joshua P. "Law Without Mind: AI, Ethics, and Jurisprudence", *California Western Law Review*, Volume 55, 2018, pp. 181 e ss and passim (deals with an agreed-upon Artificial opacity while emphasizing a sought-after transparency to trounce it). See also: Coglianese, Cary/Lehr, David, "Transparency and Algorithmic Governance", *Administrative Law Review*, Volume 71, 2019, pp. 1–41; Brauneis, Robert/Goodman, Ellen P. "Algorithmic Transparency for the Smart City", *Yale Journal of Law and Technology*, Volume 20, 2018, pp. 103–109. On algorithmic big data biometric governance: Hu, Margaret, "From the National Surveillance State to the Cybersurveillance State", *The Annual Review of Law and Social Science*, Volume 13, 2017, p. 169 ("*as a result of big data biometric governance trends, meaningful distinctions between biometric credentialing for identification and behavioral biometric profiling are disappearing. The objectives are merging: Reliable credentialing is used to advance security and precrime policy rationales. Biometric data mission creep occurs by necessity in a big data world because the cybersurveillance systems are often designed to engage in mass data integration and analysis and predictive policing. Biometric surveillance serves two purposes in preventive policing: It increases identity transparency, and the biometric data categorize identity through cataloging behavioral and physical characteristics and assess these characteristics for risk. Contrasting small data biometric credentialing protocols with big data credentialing protocols is useful. It illustrates how biometric surveillance fits within the Cybersurveillance State. In a small data world, paper-based passports and nondigitized photographs are examples of a small data biometric-based identification system*"). Italics added.

[124] Katyal, Sonia, "Private Accountability in the Age of Artificial Intelligence", *UCLA Law Review*, Volume 66, 2019, pp. 54–99.

[125] Jefferson, B. J., "Predictable policing: Predictive crime mapping and geographies of policing and race". *Annals of the American Association of Geographers*, 108 (1), 2018, 1–16.

[126] DaViera, A. L./Uriostegui, M., Gottlieb/A./Onyeka, O, "Risk, race, and predictive policing: A critical race theory analysis of the strategic subject list", *cit.*, pp. 91–103.

[127] Huq, Aziz Z., "Racial Equity in Algorithmic Criminal Justice", *Duke Law Journal*, Volume 68, 2019, pp. 1043–1072.

§§ On this account, it is neither bewildering nor flabbergasting that predictive policing, a tool of *selective surveillance*, forms part of a broader technological apparatus[132] (*Algorithm Dictatorship*) within which the affray against poverty[133] and race[134] operates. Predictive policing, an algorithm-anchored tool of «discrimination

[128] Amongst which stands arguably social cleavages spawned by a technology that fondly includes the rich and outrightly excludes the poor, thereby compounding social issues with which modern have been grappling/tussling/scuffling/floundering since immemorial times. Social cleavages—a cloak under which mounting social outcry is often wrapped—that threaten to crumble the foundations upon which stands the linchpin of western societies. See in general: Abramsky, Sasha, *Jumping at Shadows: The Triumph of Fear and the End of the American Dream*. New York: Bold Type Books, 2017, pp. 1–272 (passim).

[129] This problem is neither new nor easy to solve. Whilst the effects of technology—digital justice—on the courtroom have been previously broached by the doctrine, few to none consensus has been reached about actionable lines of action to be taken. See: Donoghue, Jane, "The Rise of Digital Justice: Courtroom Technology, Public Participation and Access to Justice", *The Modern Law Review*, Volume 80, Issue 6, 2018, p. 995 (noting that technology in the courtroom might widen the gap between the rich and the poor. In this vein, this renowned author has contended that "*legal reforms have omitted any detailed consideration of the type and quality of citizen participation in newly digitised court processes which have fundamental implications for the legitimacy and substantive outcomes of court-based processes; and for enhancing democratic procedure through improved access to justice*. It is argued that although digital court tools and systems offer great promise for enhancing efficiency, participation and accessibility, they *simultaneously have the potential to amplify the scope for injustice, and to attenuate central principles of the legal system, including somewhat paradoxically, access to justice*"). Italics added. See also: Heintz, M.E., "The digital divide and courtroom technology: Can David keep up with Goliath", *Federal Communications Law Journal*, Volume 54, 2002, pp. 566 ff and passim. The great bulk of these assertions has been anticipated by an iconic piece of research. See: Galanter, Marc, "Why the "Haves" Come Out Ahead: Speculations on the Limits of Legal Change", *Law & Society Review*, Volume 9, 1974, pp. 98–103 (this renowned author talks about a *social reality* in which the dubbed «repeat players»—which go by the name of «haves»—tend to «to come out ahead» by putting their knowledge and vast resources to good use. This perceived advantage will not only impact the choice on the procedures but will ultimately benefit their interests as opposed to the deemed «one-shot» players (the «have nots») that will have slimmer and fewer chances to get palpable results in dispute resolution). Technology in the criminal courtroom—that includes the rich and excludes the poor—will make this problem considerably worse. But see: Bailey, J./Burkell, J./Reynolds, G. "Access to Justice for All: Towards an "Expansive Vision" of Justice and Technology, *Windsor Yearbook of Access to Justice*, Volume 31, 2013, pp. 183–201 (in stark contrast, these authors stress that the digital and technological apparatus can indeed spawn a both time-effective and streamlined access to justice in a given jurisdiction).

[130] Lyon, David, *Theorizing Surveillance: The Panopticon and Beyond*. New York: Polity, 2006; Lyon, David, *Surveillance after Snowden*. New York: Polity, 2015.

[131] Jefferson, B. J., "Predictable policing: Predictive crime mapping and geographies of policing and race". *Annals of the American Association of Geographers*, 108 (1), 2018, 1–16.

[132] Hu, Margaret, "From the National Surveillance State to the Cybersurveillance State", *The Annual Review of Law and Social Science*, Volume 13, 2017, p. 169 ("*the potential for mass surveillance is part of the problematic nature of biometric credentialing and identification practices. Like most digital data, biometric identification data are not restricted to the purpose for which they were originally collected*. Biometric data can be repurposed for secondary uses, such as identification of potential suspects or victims through real-time analytics, assessment of threats of terrorism, tactical decisionmaking, or behavioral and genetic research (Duster 2003). Beyond secondary—and tertiary, quaternary, and quinary—uses, biometric data become a part of population-wide *risk*

by design»,[135] thereby amounts to nothing but a pendulum that swings far and hard against racialized communities.[136]

§§ Hardly any surprise stems from the fact that predictive policing[137] reify, exacerbates and reproduces racial disparities in the criminal system.[138] Question is: what is the rationale behind the deployment of this multimillion technology that continues to thrive?[139] Let us have a hard look at it.

---

assessments that incorporate bureaucratized surveillance into governing decisions, policing, and threat assessments. Through big data tools, precrime governance models are increasingly reflected in collect-it-all cybersurveillance systems. In these systems, biometric data is a surveillance axis that can be used to track, identify, and isolate suspicious persons, digital data, or devices"). Italics added. See also on mass surveillance: Bentham, Jeremy, *Panopticon: Or, the inspection-house*, Thomas Byrne, 1787. See also: Balkin, Jack M./Levinson, Sanford, "The Processes of Constitutional Change: From Partisan Entrenchment to the National Surveillance State", *Fordham Law Review*, Volume 75, 2006, pp. 489 and ff; Slogogin, Christopher, "Public Privacy: Camera Surveillance of Public Places and the Right to Anonymity", *Mississippi Law Journal*, Volume 72, 2002, pp. 213–251; Balkin, Jack M., "The Constitution in the National Surveillance State", *Minnesota Law Review*, Volume 93, Issue 1, 2008, pp. 17 and ff; Christopher Slobogin, "Panvasive Surveillance, Political Process Theory, and the Nondelegation Doctrine", *Georgetown Law Journal*, Volume 102, 2014, pp. 1721–1775.

[133] Gustafson, Kaaryn S., *Cheating Welfare: Public Assistance and the Criminalization of Poverty*. New York: NYU Press, 2011.

[134] Perry, B., "Nobody trusts them! under- and over-policing Native American communities", *Critical Criminology*, 14 (4), 2006, pp. 411–444.

[135] Guzik, Keith, "Discrimination by Design: Predictive Data Mining as Security Practice in the United States' 'War on Terrorism.'", *Surveillance and Society*, 7 (1), 2009, pp. 1–17.

[136] Silver, E., & Miller, L. L., "A cautionary note on the use of actuarial risk assessment tools for social control", *Crime & Delinquency*, 48 (1), 2002, pp. 138–161.

[137] Hu, Margaret, "From the National Surveillance State to the Cybersurveillance State", *The Annual Review of Law and Social Science*, Volume 13, 2017, p. 169 ("*the potential for mass surveillance is part of the problematic nature of biometric credentialing and identification practices. Like most digital data, biometric identification data are not restricted to the purpose for which they were originally collected. Biometric data can be repurposed for secondary uses, such as identification of potential suspects or victims through real-time analytics, assessment of threats of terrorism, tactical decisionmaking, or behavioral and genetic research* (Duster 2003). *Beyond secondary—and tertiary, quaternary, and quinary—uses, biometric data become a part of population-wide risk assessments that incorporate bureaucratized surveillance into governing decisions, policing, and threat assessments. Through big data tools, precrime governance models are increasingly reflected in collect-it-all cybersurveillance systems.* In these systems, *biometric data is a surveillance axis that can be used to track, identify, and isolate suspicious persons, digital data, or devices*"). Italics added.

[138] DaViera, A. L./Uriostegui, M., Gottlieb/A./Onyeka, O, "Risk, race, and predictive policing: A critical race theory analysis of the strategic subject list", *cit.*, pp. 91–103.

[139] "The global artificial intelligence (AI) software market is forecast to grow rapidly in the coming years, reaching around 126 billion U.S. dollars by 2025. The overall AI market includes a wide array of applications such as natural language processing, robotic process automation, and machine learning."—Artificial intelligence software market revenue worldwide 2018–2025, Statista Research Department, Mar 17, 2022, available online at https://www.statista.com/statistics/607716/worldwide-artificial-intelligence-market-revenues/ (access: 12.12.2024).

4.1.1.1 How Predictive Policing Exacerbates Entrenched Racial/ethnic Disparities: The Case of «Runaway Feedback Loop» (Ensign et al.) Through the Lens of Computer Science

§§ As noted above, law enforcement evinces biases that run along both gender[140] and race[141] lines.[142] No surprise springs from the fact that computer-generated algorithms that underpin *predictive policing*[143] are often flagged as tools[144] whereby[145] racial[146] discrimination[147] abounds.[148]

---

140 Hamilton, Melissa, "The sexist algorithm", *Behavioral Sciences and the Law*, Volume 37, Issue 2, Special Issue: the Use of Statistics in Criminal Cases, March–April 2019, 2019, pp. 1 and ff ("Algorithmic risk assessment tools are informed by scientific research concerning which factors are predictive of recidivism and thus support the evidence-based practice movement in criminal justice. Automated assessments of individualized risk (low, medium, high) permit officials to make more effective management decisions. Computer-generated algorithms appear to be objective and neutral. But are these algorithms actually fair? The focus herein is on gender equity. Studies confirm that women typically have far lower recidivism rates than men. *This differential raises the question of how well algorithmic outcomes fare in terms of predictive parity by gender.* This essay reports original research using a large dataset of offenders who were scored on the popular risk assessment tool COMPAS. *Findings indicate that COMPAS performs reasonably well at discriminating between recidivists and non-recidivists for men and women. Nonetheless, COMPAS algorithmic outcomes systemically overclassify women in higher risk groupings. Multiple measures of algorithmic equity and predictive accuracy are provided to support the conclusion that this algorithm is sexist*"). Italics added. See also: Alimahomed-Wilson, Sabrina, "Invisible Violence: Gender, Islamophobia, and the Hidden Assault on U.S. Muslim Women", *Women, Gender, and Families of Color*, 5 (1), 2017, pp. 73–97.

141 Crutchfield, J., Fisher, A., & Webb, S. L., "Colorism and police killings", *The Western Journal of Black Studies*, 41 (3–4), 2017, 81; Dottolo, A. L., & Stewart, A. J. (2008). "Don't ever forget now, you're a Black man in America": Intersections of race, class and gender in encounters with the police", *Sex Roles*, 59(5–6), 2008, pp. 350–364.

142 Baradan, S., "Race, prediction, and discretion", *The George Washington Law Review*, Volume 81, Issue 1, 2013, pp. 157–222.

143 Hardyns, W./Rummens, A., "Predictive policing as a new tool for law enforcement? recent developments and challenges", *European Journal on Criminal Policy and Research*, Volume 24, Issue 3, 2018, pp. 201–218.

144 Fielding-Miller, R., Cooper, H. L. F., Caslin, S./Raj, A., "The Interaction of Race and Gender as a Significant Driver of Racial Arrest Disparities for African American Men", *Journal of Urban Health*, Volume 97, 2020, pp. 112–122.

145 Fagan, J., "Race and the new policing", *Columbia Public Law Research Paper*, 2 (14–561), 2017, 83–116.

146 Barrett, L, "Reasonably suspicious algorithms: Predictive policing at the United States border", *New York Review of Law and Social Change*, Volume 41, 2017, pp. 327–365.

147 Brayne, S., "Big data surveillance: The case of policing", American Sociological Review, Volume 82, Issue 5, 2017, pp. 977–1008.

148 Berk, R./Heidari, H./Jabbari, S./Kearns, M./Roth, A., "Fairness in criminal justice risk assessments: The state of the art", Sociological Methods & Research, Volume 50, Issue 1, 2018, passim.

§§ The relationship between skewed data (*inputs*) and inferences (*outputs*) has shown to be reciprocal.[149] Put simply, the relationship that a given algorithm uses to bring forth a prediction reflects hidden correlations in the data as opposed to a causal connection to the outcome/prediction.[150]

§§ A vicious cycle inevitably unfolds: biased data that feeds into the algorithm begets equally biased predictions thus further compounding a wearying tapestry of racial discrimination that besets modern societies.[151] This is epiphenomenon has been tagged as «runaway feedback loops»[152] that re-entrenches existing biases in predictive policing, which primarily targets racial minorities.[153]

§§ It should not therefore come as a surprise that this sort of *shady algorithmic governance*[154] is a byproduct of a crippling *Algorithmic Dictatorship* that is shaping up to topple the foundations of Rule of Law upon which stands modern societies. If humans[155] refrain themselves from standing up for their swiftly dwindling fundamental rights, that is exactly what will happen in the forthcoming future. This is one of the key takeaways of this book.

---

149 *Tech, Bias and Housing Initiative, the Promise and Perils of Residential Proptech, Year 1, Research Summary Report, April 2023, TechEquity Collaborative*, p. 11, available at: https://techequity.us/wp-content/uploads/2023/04/TBHI-Y1-Research-Summary-Report.pdf (28.11.2024). ("*Once bad data enters the analysis of one factor, it gets baked into the subsequent process, multiplying the effect that one disadvantageous data point can have on someone's overall housing determination*"). Italics added.

150 Gillis, Talia B., "The Input Data Fallacy", *Minnesota Law Review*, Volume 106, 2022, pp. 1176–1263 (p. 1244).

151 *Tech, Bias and Housing Initiative, the Promise and Perils of Residential Proptech, Year 1, Research Summary Report, April 2023, TechEquity Collaborative*, p. 5 available at: https://techequity.us/wp-content/uploads/2023/04/TBHI-Y1-Research-Summary-Report.pdf (28.11.2024). ("*Residential Proptech also has the potential to exacerbate the bias inherent in our housing system. Its rise is due, in part, to the desperation felt by average home seekers. With a severely constrained housing supply, companies offering an easier pathway to homeownership may exploit communities that have been harmed by housing discrimination in the past. Opaque algorithms incorporate biased data into their decision-making processes, making it harder to enforce fair housing laws.* Residential Proptech companies often operate in a regulatory gray area, leaving consumers without the protections they would have from traditional housing regulatory systems. *As unprecedented capital investment flows into this space, venture-backed companies' winner-take-all approach to growth has the potential to exacerbate inequality rather than combat it*"). Italics added.

152 Ensign, Danielle/Friedler, Sorelle A./Neville, Scott/Scheidegger, Carlos/ Venkatasubramanian, Suresh, "Runaway Feedback Loops in Predictive Policing", *Proceedings of Machine Learning Research, Conference on Fairness, Accountability, and Transparency*, Volume 81, 2018, pp. 1–12 (1) ("Predictive policing systems are increasingly used to determine how to allocate police across a city in order to best prevent crime. *Discovered crime data (e.g., arrest counts) are used to help update the model, and the process is repeated. Such systems have been empirically shown to be susceptible to runaway feedback loops, where police are repeatedly sent back to the same neighborhoods regardless of the true crime rate*"). Italics added.

153 Mayson, Sandra G., "Bias In, Bias Out", *Yale Law Journal*, Volume 128, 2019, passim.

154 Jefferson, B., *Digitize and Punish: Racial Criminalization in the Digital Age*, Minnesota, University of Minnesota Press, 2020.

155 Pasquale, Frank, "A Rule of Persons, Not Machines: The Limits of Legal Automation", *George Washington Law Review*, Volume 87, 2019, passim.

§§ In an earnest attempt to allay the unbecoming effects of Artificial Intelligence-embedded technologies,[156] Computer Science pundits[157] have neither been coy nor bashful in overtly decrying/bemoaning—a trenchant criticism that has been deployed with a crushing lack of subtlety—the impermissible disparities of treatment[158] that dispiritingly run along[159] race[160] lines.[161] Especially, but not exclusively, regarding algorithmic risk assessment[162] aimed at predicting criminal recidivism.[163] I accordingly aver that *Algorithmic Dictatorship* is the primary lens through which racial disparities can be seen in the remit of predictive policing.

---

[156] See: Hu, Margaret, "From the National Surveillance State to the Cybersurveillance State", *The Annual Review of Law and Social Science*, Volume 13, 2017, p. 163 ("*Biometric identification and identity assessments are becoming essential tools for multiple preventive purposes in criminal, military, and intelligence contexts.* The third part addresses *how precrime policy rationales are now informed by biometric-based analysis. In short, biometrics is the means by which analysis of a citizenry's data, and any resulting decisions based on that analysis, can be connected back to a physical person in the real world*—whether to approve that person as eligible for a job, *as some employment eligibility database screening systems like E-Verify are, by moving toward biometrics through adopting the E-Verify photo tool* (Hu 2013), *or to determine whether that person is eligible to fly on a commercial airline. The No Fly List and digital watchlisting systems are increasingly biometrically centered (Tau 2015). These types of governance assessments, however, fall within the civil law and administrative law structure. Biometric cybersurveillance systems can inform targeted killing decisions and other lethal consequences. Often in the service of precrime/ counterterrorism policies, biometric cybersurveillance, therefore, is becoming a linchpin for broader policymaking and decisionmaking*"). Italics added.

[157] Brennan, T., Dieterich, W., & Ehret, B., "Evaluating the predictive validity of the COMPAS risk and needs assessment system", *Criminal Justice and Behavior*, Volume 36, Issue 1, 2009, pp. 21–40.

[158] Coglianese, C., & Lehr, D., "Transparency and algorithmic governance". *Working Paper. Penn Program on Regulation, University of Pennsylvania Law School*, 2018. On algorithmic big data biometric governance: Hu, Margaret, "From the National Surveillance State to the Cybersurveillance State", *The Annual Review of Law and Social Science*, Volume 13, 2017, p. 169 ("*as a result of big data biometric governance trends, meaningful distinctions between biometric credentialing for identification and behavioral biometric profiling are disappearing. The objectives are merging: Reliable credentialing is used to advance security and precrime policy rationales. Biometric data mission creep occurs by necessity in a big data world because the cybersurveillance systems are often designed to engage in mass data integration and analysis and predictive policing. Biometric surveillance serves two purposes in preventive policing: It increases identity transparency, and the biometric data categorize identity through cataloging behavioral and physical characteristics and assess these characteristics for risk. Contrasting small data biometric credentialing protocols with big data credentialing protocols is useful. It illustrates how biometric surveillance fits within the Cybersurveillance State. In a small data world, paper-based passports and nondigitized photographs are examples of a small data biometric-based identification system*"). Italics added.

[159] Delgado, R./Stefancic, J., "Critical race theory and criminal justice", *Humanity & Society*, Volume 31, 2007, pp. 133–145.

[160] Gottfredson, S. D., & Jarjoura, G. R., "Race, gender, and guidelines-based decision making", *Journal of Research in Crime and Delinquency*, Volume 33, Issue 1, 1996, pp. 49–69.

[161] Rudin, Cynthia/Wang, Caroline/Coker, Beau, "The Age of Secrecy and Unfairness in Recidivism Prediction", *Harvard Data Science Review*, Issue 2.1. Winter 2020, 2020, passim.

§§ Bearing this truism very firmly in mind, one ought to be chary of computer-generated algorithms if they entrench or worsen existing biases.[164] Under either approach, the wedge between the socially acceptable and the legally permissible should not be behemoth or disparate impact[165] on racial minorities[166] may otherwise ratchet up[167] in the purview of predictive[168] policing.[169]

§§ To cater for that, algorithms that bolster/propel predictive policing must be held to normative standards that should be even harsher than extant benchmarks that govern other areas (e.g. fair lending or credit scoring). Absent of which, criminal justice is bound to careen into chaos of ever-lasting *selective police*[170] *surveillance*[171] that will augment the yawning gap between racialized citizens and law enforcement.[172] In that case, *algorithmic surveillance*[173] will rise and the remnants of the worst of human nature will be accordingly laid bare.[174]

---

[162] Eckhouse, L., Lum, K., Conti-Cook, C./Ciccolini, J., "Layers of bias: A unified approach for understanding problems with risk assessment", *Criminal Justice and Behavior*, Volume 46, Issue 2, 2019, pp. 185–209.

[163] Tollenaar, N., & van der Heijden, P., "Which method predicts recidivism best? A comparison of statistical, machine learning and data mining predictive models", *Journal of the Royal Statistical Society: Series A*, Volume 176, Issue 2, 2013, pp. 565–584. Zhu, Mirilla, "Jury, Using Artificial Intelligence to Predict Recidivism Rates", *Yale Scientific*, 2020, passim. See also: Chasemi et al., Medhi, "The application of Machine Learning to a General Risk-Need Assessment Instrument in the Prediction of Criminal Recidivism", *Criminal Justice and Behavior*, Volume 48, 2020, pp. 518–538.

[164] Gillis, Talia B., "The Input Data Fallacy", *Minnesota Law Review*, Volume 106, 2022, pp. 1176–1263.

[165] Barocas, Solon/Selbst, Andrew D., "Big Data's Disparate Impact", *California Law Review*, Volume 104, 2016, pp. 671 and ff and passim.

[166] Robinson, M. A., "Black bodies on the ground: Policing disparities in the African American Community-An analysis of newsprint from January 1, 2015, through December 31, 2015", *Journal of Black Studies*, Volume 48, Issue 6, pp. 551–571.

[167] Browne, S., *Dark matters: on the surveillance of blackness*, Duke University Press, 2015, passim.

[168] DaViera, A. L./Uriostegui, M., Gottlieb/A./Onyeka, O, "Risk, race, and predictive policing: A critical race theory analysis of the strategic subject list", *American Journal of Community Psychology*, Volume 73, pp. 91–103.

[169] Jefferson, B. J., "Predictable policing: Predictive crime mapping and geographies of policing and race", *Annals of the American Association of Geographers*, Volume 108, Issue 1, 2018, 1–16.

[170] Toro, J. D./Lloyd, T., Buchanan/K. S., Robins/S. J., Bencharit/L. Z., Smiedt/M. G., Reddy/K. S., Pouget, E. R./Kerrison, E. M./Goff, P. A., "The criminogenic and psychological effects of police stops on adolescent black and Latino boys", *Proceedings of the National Academy of Sciences of the United States of America*, Volume 116, Issue 17, 2019, pp. 8261–8268.

[171] Sewell, A. A., Jefferson, K. A./Lee, H., "Living under surveillance: Gender, psychological distress, and stop-question- and-frisk policing in New York city", *Social Science & Medicine*, Volume 159, 2016, pp. 1–13.

[172] Benjamin, R., *Race After Technology: Abolitionist Tools for the New Jim Code*, John Wiley & Sons, 2019, passim.

[173] Abdillahi, I., "Algorithmic surveillance in the era of the appsphere", *American Journal of Community Psychology*, Volume 73, 2024, passim.

[174] See: Part IV, This chapter, Sects. 4.1.10.1–4.1.10.6 of this book (on biased algorithmic risk assessment in criminal procedure law settings).

§§ That is why computer-generated algorithms should abide by stringent requirements of *Algorithmic Common Good*.[175] The rationale behind this seemingly lopsided yardstick is straightforward: avoid at any cost unlawful «arrests by skin[176] colour», flagitious[177] arrests by age[178] or spirited off arrests by transgender[179] in the camp of algorithmic predictive policing.[180] Which should not strike anyone as odd: predictive policing[181]—and criminal justice in an overarching sense—should be much more than a canopied tool to stamp out the socially[182] undesirables[183]

---

[175] See: Part V, Chap. 5, Sects. 5.1.2–5.1.6.2.1 of this book (on the thing-centred algorithmic decision-making propelled by a *Controllable* and *Interpretable* Machine Learning that weeds out *Algorithmic Dictatorship* and secures *Algorithmic Common Good*).

[176] See: Connecticut Fair Housing Center, et al. v. CoreLogic Rental Property Solutions—Cohen Milstein (access: 20.11.2024). ("*The U.S. Department of Housing & Urban Development observed in 2016 that excluding rental applicants because of their criminal records disproportionately harms Latinos and African Americans, who are significantly more likely than whites to be arrested or convicted. Studies show such disparities are linked to differential enforcement rather than to differences in likelihood of engaging in criminal activity.* HUD advised that to avoid discriminating, an "individualized review" should be conducted considering the nature of the offense, how long ago it occurred, intervening changed circumstances, and other relevant factors to avoid denying housing to an applicant who does not pose a genuine and ongoing threat to persons or property. *Further, HUD's guidance specifically advises landlords not to consider arrests that did not result in a conviction in making their evaluations*"). Italics added.

[177] Kizer, J. M., "Arrested by skin color: Evidence from siblings and a nationally representative sample", *Socius: Sociological Research for a Dynamic World*, 3, 2017, passim; Kochel, T. R., Wilson, D. B./Mastrofski, S. D., "Effect of suspect race on officers' arrest decisions", *Criminology*, Volume 49, Issue 2, 2011, pp. 473–512. Mitchell, O./Caudy, M. S., "Examining racial disparities in drug arrests", *Justice Quarterly*, Volume 32, Issue 2, 2015, pp. 288–313; Kirk, D. S., "The neighborhood context of racial and ethnic disparities in arrest", *Demography*, 45, 2008, pp. 55–77.

[178] McCauley, E. J., "The cumulative probability of arrest by age 28 years in the United States by disability status, race/ethnicity, and gender", *American Journal of Public Health*, Volume 107, Issue 12, 2017, pp. 1977–1981.

[179] Stotzer, R. L., "Law enforcement and criminal justice personnel interactions with transgender people in the United States: A literature review", *Aggression and Violent Behavior*, Volume 19, Issue 3, 2014, 263–277; Furman, E./Singh, A. K./Darko, N. A./Wilson, C. L., "Activism, intersectionality, and community psychology: The way in which Black Lives Matter Toronto helps us to examine white supremacy in Canada's LGBTQ community. Community Psychology in Global Perspective, Volume 4, Issue 2, 34–54.

[180] Saunders, J., Hunt, P., & Hollywood, J. S., "Predictions put into practice: A quasi-experimental evaluation of Chicago's predictive policing pilot", *Journal of Experimental Criminology*, Volume 12, Issue 3, 2016, pp. 347–371.

[181] Meijer, A., & Wessels, M., "Predictive policing: Review of benefits and drawbacks", *International Journal of Public Administration*, Volume 42, Issue 12, 2019, pp. 1031–1039.

[182] Darden, T. M., & Godsay, S., "Hands up, don't shoot: A community psychology perspective on unarmed police shootings of Black people in America", *Community Psychology in Global Perspective*, Volume 4, Issue 2, 2018, pp. 9–21.

[183] Monk, E. P., "The color of punishment: African Americans, skin tone, and the criminal justice system", *Ethnic and Racial Studies*, Volume 42, Issue 10, 2019, pp. 1593–1612; Agung-Igusti, R. P., "Raced and risky subjects: The interplay of racial and managerial ideologies as an expression of "colorblind" racism", *American Journal of Community Psychology*, Volume 73, 2024, passim;

after all.[184] Regrettably, this is exactly what is happening in the remit of predictive policing against the backdrop of which the gruesome phenomenon of «runaway feedback loop» unfolds.

§§ Pivotally, «runaway feedback loop» does neither sit easily with the foundations upon which stands a brawny Rule of Law[185] nor does map onto the directive in view of which algorithmic biases[186] should be dispelled. Scholars are accordingly censorious of any biased data[187] that feeds into the «algorithms of oppression»[188]

Alexander, M., *The new Jim Crow: Mass incarceration in the age of colorblindness*, The New Press, 2012.

[184] Schenwar, M./Law, V., *Prison by any other name: The harmful consequences of popular reforms*, 2020, The New Press.

[185] See: Part V, Chap. 5, Sect. 5.1.1.1 of this book (on the central tenets of Rule of Law that lends itself to a beacon of justice amidst the sepulchral darkness that is about to take hold). See: Part V, Chap. 5, Sect. 5.1.1.2 of this book (on the central tenets of Procedural Rule of Law that lends itself to a lighthouse of justice that allows citizens to challenge the pearls of algorithmic wisdom in a court of law). Regrettably, the Rule of Law is backsliding worldwide. Especially in Central and Eastern Europe. See: Avbelj, Matej, "The Rule of Law, Comprehensive Doctrines, Overlapping Consensus, and the Future of Europe", *Ratio Juris*, Volume 36, Issue 3, September, 2023, pp. 242–258. The Rule of Law is not a «one size fits all» format nonetheless. But see: Chesterman, Simon, "An International Rule of Law", *The American Journal of Comparative Law*, Volume 56, 2008, pp. 331–362 (on the thrust to grasp (?) a catch-all International Rule of Law). See: Peari, Sagi, "Better Law as a Better Outcome", *The American Journal of Comparative Law*, Volume 63, Issue 1, 2015, pp. 155–195 (156) (on Leflar's stance on «better rule of law»). For the purposes of this piece, Rule of Law amounts to a lighthouse of procedural fairness to which citizens, regardless of where they are, resort to upon gaining access to a given system of administration of criminal justice. Whilst further utterances on the fabric of Rule of Law fall well outside the scope and breadth of this paper, one must not be oblivious of the fact that the thrust to Deglobalizing Rule of Law is underway. See: Bussani, Mauro, "Deglobalizing Rule of Law and Democracy: Hunting Down Rhetoric Through Comparative Law", *The American Journal of Comparative Law*, Volume 67, 2019, pp. 701–744 (701) (contending that the thrust to Deglobalizing Rule of Law is interwoven with thrust to take heed of «well-known differences that run through cultures and traditions». In spite of which, «the West has never stopped trying to export its own law into the rest of the world»). Unsurprisingly, there have been educated calls to take heed of the pinpointed cultural and legal differences by, in the case of China, allow for a «Socialist Rule of Law». See: Chinese Common Law Guiding Cases, *Harvard Law Review*, Volume 129, 2016, p. 2213. We will come back to this issue further down is this paper. More on this later.

[186] Osaba, Osonde/Welser, William IV, *An Intelligence in Our Image—The Risk of Bias and Errors in Artificial Intelligence*, Santa Monica, California, Rand, 2018, passim; Chandler, Anupam, "The Racist Algorithm", *Michigan Law Review*, Volume 115, n. ° 6, 2018, p. 1026 (on racist algorithms, noting that "the possibilities for discriminatory manipulation are legion"). But see: Altenburger, Kristen M./Ho, Daniel E., "When Algorithms Import Private Bias into Public Enforcement: The Promise and Limitations of Statistical Debiasing Solutions", *Journal of Institutional & Theoretical Economics*, Volume 175, 2019, pp. 97–98 (calls for a "debias predictive algorithms" to assuage racist and/or biased, doctored and bigoted algorithms nevertheless); Hamilton, Melissa, "The Biased Algorithm: Evidence of Disparate Impact on Hispanics", *American Criminal Law Review*, Volume 56, 2019, pp. 1553 and ff and passim; Dong et al., Qi, "Imbalanced deep learning by minority class incremental rectification, *IEEE Transactions on Pattern Analysis & Machine Intelligence*, Volume 41, 2019, p. 1367 (posit that "*most existing learning algorithms produce inductive bias (learning bias)* towards the frequent (majority) classes if training data are not balanced, *resulting in poor minority class recognition performance*"). Italics added. See also: Wachter, S/Mittelstadt. B., "A right to Reasonable Inferences: Re-thinking Data Protection Law in the Age of Big Data and AI",

that propel forward Artificial Intelligence-embedded technologies, which, recall, have been grappling with the recalcitrance of racism.

§§ Scholars accordingly contend that the criminal system of justice is completely enmeshed in systemic racism[189] that further compounds the racial wedge with which modern societies[190] have been scuffling,[191] spanning multiple years and an umpteenth number of countries.

Columbia Business Law Review, 2019, pp. 1 and ff and passim. Barocas, Solon/Selbst, Andrew D., "Big Data's Disparate Impact", *California Law Review*, Volume 104, 2016, passim.

[187] Blodgett, S. L., Barocas, S., Daumé III, H. and Wallach, H. (2020). 'Language (technology) is power: a critical survey of "Bias" in NLP'. *ArXiv:2005.14050 [Cs]*, May 2020, 2020.

[188] Noble, Safiya Umoja, *Algorithms of Oppression*: *How search engines reinforce racism*, New York, New University Press, 2018, pp. 1–248 ("*Run a Google search for "Black girls"—what will you find? "Big Booty" and other sexually explicit terms are likely to come up as top search terms. But, if you type in "white girls," the results are radically different*. The suggested porn sites and un-moderated discussions about "why Black women are so sassy" or "why Black women are so angry" presents a disturbing portrait of Black womanhood in modern society. In *Algorithms of Oppression*, Safiya Umoja Noble challenges the idea that search engines like Google offer an equal playing field for all forms of ideas, identities, and activities. *Data discrimination is a real social problem; Noble argues that the combination of private interests in promoting certain sites, along with the monopoly status of a relatively small number of Internet search engines, leads to a biased set of search algorithms that privilege whiteness and discriminate against people of color, specifically women of color*"). Italics added.

[189] Feagin, J. R., *Systemic racism: a theory of oppression*, New York: Routledge, 2006. See also: Fiske, John, "Surveilling the City: Whiteness, the Black Man and Democratic Totalitarianism.", *Theory, Culture and Society*, 15 (2), 1998, pp. 67–88 (on the overhyped surveillance on black people as a byproduct of systemic racism). Hu, Margaret, "From the National Surveillance State to the Cybersurveillance State", *The Annual Review of Law and Social Science*, Volume 13, 2017, p. 169 ("*the potential for mass surveillance is part of the problematic nature of biometric credentialing and identification practices. Like most digital data, biometric identification data are not restricted to the purpose for which they were originally collected*. Biometric data can be repurposed for secondary uses, such as identification of potential suspects or victims through real-time analytics, assessment of threats of terrorism, tactical decisionmaking, or behavioral and genetic research (Duster 2003). Beyond secondary—and tertiary, quaternary, and quinary—uses, biometric data become a part of population-wide *risk assessments that incorporate bureaucratized surveillance into governing decisions, policing, and threat assessments. Through big data tools, precrime governance models are increasingly reflected in collect-it-all cybersurveillance systems. In these systems, biometric data is a surveillance axis that can be used to track, identify, and isolate suspicious persons, digital data, or devices*"). Italics added. See also on mass surveillance: Bentham, Jeremy, *Panopticon: Or, the inspection-house*, Thomas Byrne, 1787. See also: Balkin, Jack M./Levinson, Sanford, "The Processes of Constitutional Change: From Partisan Entrenchment to the National Surveillance State", *Fordham Law Review*, Volume 75, 2006, pp. 489 and ff; Slogogin, Christopher, "Public Privacy: Camera Surveillance of Public Places and the Right to Anonymity", *Mississippi Law Journal*, Volume 72, 2002, pp. 213–251; Balkin, Jack M., "The Constitution in the National Surveillance State", *Minnesota Law Review*, Volume 93, Issue 1, 2008, pp. 17 and ff; Christopher Slobogin, "Panvasive Surveillance, Political Process Theory, and the Nondelegation Doctrine", *Georgetown Law Journal*, Volume 102, 2014, pp. 1721–1775.

[190] Correll, J., Park, B., Judd, C. M., & Wittenbrink, B., "The police officer's dilemma: using ethnicity to disambiguate potentially threatening individuals", *Journal of Personality and Social Psychology*, 83 (6), 2002, pp. 1314–1329.

[191] Daniels, J., "Race and racism in internet studies: a review and critique", *New Media & Society*, 15 (5), 2013, pp. 695–719; Daniels, J., "My brain database doesn't see skin color": color-blind

§§ It should neither amount to a befuddling statement nor a baffling finding that predictive policing performance echoes, and sits within, the recalcitrance of racism.[192]

§§ In a bid to weed out the recalcitrance of racism,[193] scholars have been pouring staggering amounts of effort to deftly tackle a handful of tantalising questions,[194] such as: how can the main roadblocks to the uptake of Artificial Intelligence-embedded technologies be cast aside? Can Artificial Intelligence-embedded technologies, in spite of its spine-chilling achievements, prime citizens into doubting its underlying fairness?

§§ By the same token, will technological embellishments outpace the human capacity to fathom its inner workings? Will social considerations concerning Artificial Intelligence-embedded technologies (v.g. its dire need of widespread adoption to advance a shady agenda that keeps a bunch of privileges for a selected group of few while minimizing the fundamental rights of racialised communities) encroach over the sorely needed legal rationality?

§§ Predictive policing neatly captures the eerie, unsettling feeling that arises from a *selective surveillance* that targets primarily racialised people.[195] This is an unvarnished truth, and an unadorned reality, that, as hinted above, arises out of predictive policing.

§§ The harrowing phenomenon of «runaway feedback loop» is a living testament of, and a token of credence to, the finding according to which the level playing field is unfairly tilted against racialised neighbourhoods with *selective* predictive policing looming large in the discussion. Skewed data and predictive policing are two sides of the same coin.[196]

---

racism in the technology industry and in theorizing the web", *American Behavioral Scientist*, 59 (11), 2015, 1377–1393; de la Peña, C., "The history of technology, the resistance of archives, and the whiteness of race", *Technology and Culture*, 51 (4), 2010, pp. 919–937.

[192] *Tech, Bias and Housing Initiative, the Promise and Perils of Residential Proptech, Year 1, Research Summary Report, April 2023, TechEquity Collaborative*, p. 11, available at: https://techequity.us/wp-content/uploads/2023/04/TBHI-Y1-Research-Summary-Report.pdf (28.11.2024). ("*Once bad data enters the analysis of one factor, it gets baked into the subsequent process, multiplying the effect that one disadvantageous data point can have on someone's overall housing determination*"). Italics added. See: Part IV, This chapter, Sects. 4.1.4–4.1.4.2.3 of this book.

[193] Dihal, K., "Enslaved minds: artificial intelligence, slavery, and revolt", *AI Narratives: A History of Imaginative Thinking about Intelligent Machines*, Stephen Cave, Kanta Dihal, and Sarah Dillon (Editors), Oxford, Oxford University Press, 2020, pp. 189–212.

[194] Daniels, J., "My brain database doesn't see skin color": color-blind racism in the technology industry and in theorizing the web", *American Behavioral Scientist*, 59 (11), 2015, pp. 1377–1393.

[195] Sewell, A. A., Jefferson, K. A./Lee, H., "Living under surveillance: Gender, psychological distress, and stop-question- and-frisk policing in New York city", *Social Science & Medicine*, Volume 159, 2016, pp. 1–13; Benjamin, Ruha, *Race After Technology: Abolitionist Tools for the New Jim Code*, John Wiley & Sons, 2019, passim; Abdillahi, I., "Algorithmic surveillance in the era of the appsphere", *American Journal of Community Psychology*, Volume 73, 2024, passim.

§§ Tellingly, skewed, and thus, biased data[197] will be baked into machine learning algorithms that underpin and propel predictive policing, which will cause further bad outcomes, thereby cascading into ever more challenging circumstances for members of racialised communities dwelling on neighbourhoods constantly patrolled by law enforcement agencies.

§§ The much-needed trust and law abidingness will accordingly peter out.[198] Conversely, racialised citizens may look askance at the performance of law enforcement agencies as they patrol the same neighbourhoods repeatedly while refraining themselves from patrolling White-majority neighbourhoods.[199]

§§ Cogently, the very benchmark against which discriminatory practices are gauged is deeply flawed. This deeply flawed system gives rise to the jarring

---

[196] See: Kirkpatrick, Keith, "It's not the Algorithm, it's the Data", *Communications of the ACM*, February 2017, Volume 60, n. ° 2, 2017 ("Critics, however, say tools such as PredPol and Command-Central *are inherently biased since they rely heavily on reported crimes data, which is often concentrated in areas that are heavily policed, thereby skewing statistics to overrepresent poor or minority communities.* "*We know that we have a history of racially biased policing in the United States, and that has fed into all the data that we have on where arrests have occurred, which crimes are more likely to occur in specific communities, and at which particular times*," says Jennifer Lynch, senior staff attorney at the Electronic Frontier Foundation. "*That's the data that's being fed into predictive policing algorithms*"). Italics added.

[197] Jackson, Maya C., "Artificial Intelligence and Algorithmic Bias: The Issues with Technology Reflecting History and Humans", *Journal of Business Technology Law*, Volume 16, 2021, pp. 299–316; West, Sarah Myers/Whittaker, Meredith/Crawford, Kate, *Discriminating Systems. Gender, Race and Power in AI*. New York: AI Now Institute, 2019, passim.

[198] Tyler, Tom R., "Trust and Law Abidingness: A Proactive Model of Social Regulation", *Boston University Law Review*, Volume 81, 2001, pp. 361 ff; Barbalet, Jack, "A Characterization of Trust, and Its Consequences", *Theory and Society*, Volume 38, 2009, pp. 367–372; Farrell, Henry, "Institutions and Midlevel Explanations of Trust", Cook, Karen S./Levi, Margaret/Hardin, Russell (Eds.), *Whom can We Trust? How Groups, Networks, and Institutions Make Trust Possible*. Manhattan, New York City: Russell Sage Publication, 2010, pp. 128–129; Cross, Frank B., "Law and Trust", *Georgetown Law Journal*, Volume 93, 2005, pp. 1457 ff (parsing the relationship between the concept of trust in the realm of groups and trust networks in Western cultures). Trust plays a pivotal role in catering for the citizen's confidence in a given jurisdiction. This is something that prospective lawmakers and policymakers should never lose sight of. Especially in the realm of criminal procedure law.

[199] Robinson, M. A., "Black bodies on the ground: Policing disparities in the African American Community-An analysis of newsprint from January 1, 2015, through December 31, 2015", *Journal of Black Studies*, Volume 48, Issue 6, pp. 551–571; Browne, S., *Dark matters: on the surveillance of blackness*, Duke University Press, 2015, passim; DaViera, A. L./Uriostegui, M., Gottlieb/A./Onyeka, O, "Risk, race, and predictive policing: A critical race theory analysis of the strategic subject list", *American Journal of Community Psychology*, Volume 73, 2024, pp. 91–103; Jefferson, B. J., "Predictable policing: Predictive crime mapping and geographies of policing and race", *Annals of the American Association of Geographers*, Volume 108, Issue 1, 2018, 1–16; Toro, J. D./Lloyd, T., Buchanan/K. S., Robins/S. J., Bencharit/L. Z., Smiedt/M. G., Reddy/K. S., Pouget, E. R./Kerrison, E. M./Goff, P. A., "The criminogenic and psychological effects of police stops on adolescent black and Latino boys", *Proceedings of the National Academy of Sciences of the United States of America*, Volume 116, Issue 17, 2019, pp. 8261–8268; Sewell, A. A., Jefferson, K. A./Lee, H., "Living under surveillance: Gender, psychological distress, and stop-question- and-frisk policing in New York city", *Social Science & Medicine*, Volume 159, 2016, pp. 1–13.

phenomenon of «runaway feedbacks loops»[200] according to which a promiscuous patchwork of various batches of biased data primes the police to patrolling the neighbourhoods[201] in which racialised people (Blacks and Latino) live while forsaking the great bulk of White-majority neighbourhoods. Computer science pundits have shined a keen light on the fundamental tenets of «runaway feedbacks loops».

§§ As various forms of predictive policing proliferate, so do nagging uncertainties about contemporary problems—v.g. *systemic racism*[202] and White supremacy that beset modern societies and against the backdrop of which *selective surveillance*[203]

---

[200] Ensign, Danielle/Friedler, Sorelle A./Neville, Scott/Scheidegger, Carlos/ Venkatasubramanian, Suresh, "Runaway Feedback Loops in Predictive Policing", *Proceedings of Machine Learning Research, Conference on Fairness, Accountability, and Transparency*, Volume 81, 2018, pp. 1–12 (1) ("Predictive policing systems are increasingly used to determine how to allocate police across a city in order to best prevent crime. *Discovered crime data (e.g., arrest counts) are used to help update the model, and the process is repeated. Such systems have been empirically shown to be susceptible to runaway feedback loops, where police are repeatedly sent back to the same neighborhoods regardless of the true crime rate*"). Italics added.

[201] Donohue, John J., III, and Steven D. Levitt, "The Impact of Race on Policing and Arrests", *The Journal of Law & Economics*, 44 (2), 2001, pp. 367–394.

[202] Feagin, J. R., *Systemic racism: a theory of oppression*, New York: Routledge, 2006. See also: Fiske, John, "Surveilling the City: Whiteness, the Black Man and Democratic Totalitarianism.", *Theory, Culture and Society*, 15 (2), 1998, pp. 67–88 (on the overhyped surveillance on black people as a byproduct of systemic racism).

[203] Such as heightened security that allows permanent digital surveillance of individuals deemed socially unfit or—worse yet—biologically or mentally prone to engage in flagitious and unlawful activities. The German doctrine has fleshed out this topic in depth. See: Müller, Helmut, „Europäische Rechtssicherheit gegen Deutsches Sicherheitsrecht? Zur EGMR-Entscheidung in Sachen nachträgliche (Verlängerung der) Sicherungsverwahrung ", *Kritische Justiz*, Volume 43, Issue 3, 2010, pp. 256–268. This topic—although enthralling/besotting/buoying—falls conspicuously outside the breadth and scope of our essay. Hu, Margaret, "From the National Surveillance State to the Cybersurveillance State", *The Annual Review of Law and Social Science*, Volume 13, 2017, p. 169 ("*the potential for mass surveillance is part of the problematic nature of biometric credentialing and identification practices. Like most digital data, biometric identification data are not restricted to the purpose for which they were originally collected.* Biometric data can be repurposed for secondary uses, such as identification of potential suspects or victims through real-time analytics, assessment of threats of terrorism, tactical decisionmaking, or behavioral and genetic research (Duster 2003). Beyond secondary—and tertiary, quaternary, and quinary—uses, biometric data become a part of population-wide *risk assessments that incorporate bureaucratized surveillance into governing decisions, policing, and threat assessments. Through big data tools, precrime governance models are increasingly reflected in collect-it-all cybersurveillance systems. In these systems, biometric data is a surveillance axis that can be used to track, identify, and isolate suspicious persons, digital data, or devices*"). Italics added. See also on mass surveillance: Bentham, Jeremy, *Panopticon: Or, the inspection-house*, Thomas Byrne, 1787. See also: Balkin, Jack M./Levinson, Sanford, "The Processes of Constitutional Change: From Partisan Entrenchment to the National Surveillance State", *Fordham Law Review*, Volume 75, 2006, pp. 489 and ff; Slogogin, Christopher, "Public Privacy: Camera Surveillance of Public Places and the Right to Anonymity", *Mississippi Law Journal*, Volume 72, 2002, pp. 213–251; Balkin, Jack M., "The Constitution in the National Surveillance State", *Minnesota Law Review*, Volume 93, Issue 1, 2008, pp. 17 and ff; Christopher Slobogin, "Panvasive Surveillance, Political Process Theory, and the Nondelegation Doctrine", *Georgetown Law Journal*, Volume 102, 2014, pp. 1721–1775.

of racialised communities unfolds[204]—and the extent to which they echo concerns about a sought-after algorithmic fairness.[205]

§§ More to the point, the gruesome phenomenon of «runaway feedbacks loops» forms part of a broader technological apparatus within which machine learning algorithms operate. But know this: accurate forecasts, algorithmic fairness[206] and risk assessment[207] carried out by machines are often poles apart. Predictive policing falls prey to the very same illnesses.[208]

§§ Machine learning algorithms are increasingly taking the centre stage in modern societies.[209] Relatedly, machine learning algorithms are burgeoningly being deployed to make life-changing[210] decisions,[211] such as who companies should hire,[212] who should be granted a loan,[213] and where the police[214] should be sent.[215]

---

204 Browne, S., *Dark matters: on the surveillance of blackness*, Duke University Press, 2015, passim.

205 Corbett-Davies, Sam/Goel, Sharad, "The Measure and Mismeasure of Fairness: a critical Review of Fair Machine Learning", *Cornell University Library*, 2018, pp. 3 and ff and passim (undertake laudable efforts to debunk algorithm biases that primarily target ethnic minorities, such as Hispanics and coloured people); Maxwell, J./Tomlinson, J., *Experiments in Automating Immigration Systems*. Bristol: Bristol University Press, 2022, passim.

206 Corbett-Davies S. Pierson E. Feller A. Goel S. and Huq A., "Algorithmic decision making and the cost of fairness", *Proceedings of the 23rd ACM SIGKDD International Conference on Knowledge Discovery and Data Mining*, 2017, pp. 797–806.

207 Berk, R., *Criminal Justice Forecasts of Risk: A Machine Learning Approach*, New York, Springer Science & Business Media, 2012, passim; Kehl, D. L., Guo, P., and Kessler, S. A., *Algorithms in the Criminal Justice System: Assessing the Use of Risk Assessments in Sentencing*, 2017, accessed at https://dash.harvard.edu/bitstream/handle/1/33746041/2017-07_responsivecommunities_2.pdf?sequence¼1 on October 24, 2024.

208 Gerstner, D., "Using Predictive Policing to Prevent Residential Burglary: Findings from the Pilot Project P4 in Baden-Württemberg, Germany", *European Law Enforcement Research Bulletin–Special Conference Edition Nr. 4. European Union Agency for Law Enforcement Training (CEPOL)*, 2018, pp. 1–11.

209 Suzor, Nicolas P., *Lawless: The Secret Rules that Govern our Digital Lives*, Cambridge, United Kingdom: Cambridge University Press, 2019, pp. 1–218 (passim); Brownsword, Roger, *Law, Technology and Society: Re-Imagining the Regulatory Environment*, London: Routledge, 2020, pp. 1–361 (passim) (broaches the interplay law, technology, and society with a sharper focus in the era of smart regulatory technologies); Wagner, Gerhard/Eidenmuller, Horst, "Down by Algorithms? Siphoning Rents, Exploiting Biases, and Shaping Preferences: Regulating the Dark Side of Targeted Transactions", *University of Chicago Law Review*, Volume 86, 2019, pp. 581–609.

210 See: Part V, Chap. 5, Sect. 5.1.7.2 of this book (on law number two to control algorithmic decision-making, which mandates that black box models must not be entrusted with the task of making high stake decisions—v.g. health and freedom).

211 Hosanagar, K.", *A Human's Guide to Machine Intelligence: How Algorithms Are Shaping Our Lives and How We Can Stay in Control*, Viking, New York, 2019; Hurley, M. and Adebayo, J., "Credit Scoring in the Era of Big Data", *Yale Journal of Law and Technology*, 18, 2016, 148. Karabel, J., *The Chosen: The Hidden History of Admission and Exclusion at Harvard, Yale, and Princeton*, Boston, MA, Houghton Mifflin Harcourt, 2006.

212 Ensign, Danielle/Friedler, Sorelle A./Neville, Scott/Scheidegger, Carlos/ Venkatasubramanian, Suresh, "Runaway Feedback Loops in Predictive Policing", *cit.*, p. 1.

§§ Whilst the black box systems[216]—against the backdrop of which machine learning[217] algorithms[218] operate upon[219]—do not entail outright unfairness,[220] nor do they produce pearls of algorithmic wisdom amenable to be relied[221] upon.[222] They do, however, point to the dire need of being keenly leery of the foregoing

---

[213] Ensign, Danielle/Friedler, Sorelle A./Neville, Scott/Scheidegger, Carlos/ Venkatasubramanian, Suresh, "Runaway Feedback Loops in Predictive Policing", *cit.*, p. 1.

[214] Anderson, Elijah, *Code of the Street: Decency, Violence, and the Moral Life of the Inner City*, W. W. Norton & Company, 2000.

[215] Ensign, Danielle/Friedler, Sorelle A./Neville, Scott/Scheidegger, Carlos/ Venkatasubramanian, Suresh, "Runaway Feedback Loops in Predictive Policing", *cit.*, p. 1; Bass, Sandra, 2001. "Policing Space, Policing Race: Social Control Imperatives and Police Discretionary Decisions", *Social Justice*, 28 (1), 2001, pp. 156–76.

[216] Adadi, Amina/Berrada, Mohammed, "Peeking Inside the Black-Box: A Survey on Explainable Artificial Intelligence (XAI), *Institute of Electrical and Electronics Engineers*, Volume 6, 2018, passim; Miller, Tim, "Explanations in Artificial Intelligence: Insights from Social Sciences", *Artificial Intelligence*, Volume 267, 2019, pp. 1–38.

[217] Fisher, Aaron et al., "All Models are Wrong, but Many are Useful", *Journal of Machine Learning Research*, Volume 20, 2019, pp. 1 and ff.

[218] *Tech, Bias and Housing Initiative, the Promise and Perils of Residential Proptech, Year 1, Research Summary Report, April 2023, TechEquity Collaborative*, p. 5 available at: https://techequity.us/wp-content/uploads/2023/04/TBHI-Y1-Research-Summary-Report.pdf (28.11.2024). ("*Residential Proptech also has the potential to exacerbate the bias inherent in our housing system. Its rise is due, in part, to the desperation felt by average home seekers. With a severely constrained housing supply, companies offering an easier pathway to homeownership may exploit communities that have been harmed by housing discrimination in the past. Opaque algorithms incorporate biased data into their decision-making processes, making it harder to enforce fair housing laws.* Residential Proptech companies often operate in a regulatory gray area, leaving consumers without the protections they would have from traditional housing regulatory systems. *As unprecedented capital investment flows into this space, venture-backed companies' winner-take-all approach to growth has the potential to exacerbate inequality rather than combat it*"). Italics added.

[219] In general: Dazeley, Richard/Vamplew, Peter/Foale, Cameron/ Young, Charlotte/ Aryal, Sunil/ Cruz, Francisco, "Levels of explainable artificial intelligence for human-aligned conversational explanations", *Artificial Intelligence*, Volume 299, 2021, passim (as stated by lauded authors "*over the last few years there has been rapid research growth into eXplainable Artificial Intelligence (XAI) and the closely aligned Interpretable Machine Learning (IML).* Drivers for this growth include recent legislative changes and increased investments by industry and governments, along with increased concern from the general public. *People are affected by autonomous decisions every day and the public need to understand the decision-making process to accept the outcomes. However, the vast majority of the applications of XAI/IML are focused on providing low-level 'narrow' explanations of how an individual decision was reached based on a particular datum.* While important, these explanations rarely provide insights into an agent's: beliefs and motivations; hypotheses of other (human, animal or AI) agents' intentions; interpretation of external cultural expectations; or, processes used to generate its own explanation. Yet all of these factors, we propose, are essential to providing the explanatory depth that people require to accept and trust the AI's decision-making. *This paper aims to define levels of explanation and describe how they can be integrated to create a human-aligned conversational explanation system. In so doing, this paper will survey current approaches and discuss the integration of different technologies to achieve these levels with Broad eXplainable Artificial Intelligence (Broad-XAI), and thereby move towards high-level 'strong' explanations*"). Italics added.

[220] Corbett-Davies, Sam/Goel, Sharad, "The Measure and Mismeasure of Fairness: a critical Review of Fair Machine Learning", *Cornell University Library*, 2018, pp. 3 and ff and passim (undertake

pearls of algorithmic wisdom spawned by the machine learning algorithms[223] that spur predictive policing.

§§ As noted above,[224] there is a myriad of human biases that creep into the algorithm[225] and feeds into an automated decision that comes to the expense of citizens' lives, freedoms,[226] health, property, fair lending, and credit scoring. Thereby creating

---

laudable efforts to debunk algorithm biases that primarily target ethnic minorities, such as Hispanics and coloured people). Jackson, Maya C., "Artificial Intelligence and Algorithmic Bias: The Issues with Technology Reflecting History and Humans", *Journal of Business Technology Law*, Volume 16, 2021, pp. 299–316; West, Sarah Myers/Whittaker, Meredith/Crawford, Kate, *Discriminating Systems. Gender, Race and Power in AI*. New York: AI Now Institute, 2019, passim.

[221] See: Part V, Chap. 5, Sect. 5.1.7.2 of this book (on law number two to control algorithmic decision-making, which mandates that black box models must not be entrusted with the task of making high stake decisions—v.g. health and freedom).

[222] McAfee, Andrew/Brynjolfsson, *Machine, Platform, Crowd: Harnessing our Digital Future*, London: Brilliance Audio; Unabridged edition, 2017 (pore over a myriad of automatic biases displayed by artificial intelligence).

[223] See: Murphy, Kevin P., *Machine Learning: A Probabilistic Perspective (Adaptive Computation and Machine Learning series)*. Massachusetts: The MIT Press, 2012, pp. 1–1104 (states avowedly that "machine Learning attempts to combine deductive, inductive, and abductive reasoning to make person-like reasoning in AI Entities possible. Machine-learning AI Entities initially learn in the same way a human child learns. First, they notice details and patterns in shapes, sounds, and behaviors; then put them together to distinguish one person from another, or a dog from a cat. Eventually, the AI can recognize and identify" common objects). See also: Hutto-Schultz, Jess, "Dicitur Ex Machina: Artificial Intelligence and the Hearsay Rule", *George Mason Law Review*, Volume 27, Issue 2, 2020, pp. 684–718 (689). See: Chollet, François, *Deep Learning with Python*. Shelter Island, Nova Iorque: Manning, 2018, pp. 1–384 (passim). *Deep Learning* stands as a byproduct of *Machine Learning*. *Machine Learning*, a subset of Artificial Intelligence, unfolds itself in *Deep Learning*, which "involves computer algorithms that have the ability to "learn" or improve in performance over time on some task". See: Surden, Harry, "Machine Learning and Law", *Washington Law Review*, Volume 89, 2015, pp. 87 and ff.

[224] See: Part I of this book (Introduction).

[225] Citron, Danielle Keats/Pasquale, Frank A., "The Scored Society: Due Process for Automated Predictions", *Washington Law Review*, Volume 89, 2014, pp. 1–34 (arguing that "[a]*dvocates applaud the removal of human beings and their flaws from the assessment process*," but arguing that bias remains "[*b*]*ecause human beings program predictive algorithms, their biases and values are embedded into the software's instructions*"). Italics added.

[226] But see: Kirkpatrick, Keith, "It's not the Algorithm, it's the Data", *Communications of the ACM*, February 2017, Volume 60, n. ° 2, 2017 ("critics, however, say tools such as PredPol and CommandCentral *are inherently biased since they rely heavily on reported crimes data, which is often concentrated in areas that are heavily policed, thereby skewing statistics to overrepresent poor or minority communities. "We know that we have a history of racially biased policing in the United States, and that has fed into all the data that we have on where arrests have occurred, which crimes are more likely to occur in specific communities, and at which particular times*," says Jennifer Lynch, senior staff attorney at the Electronic Frontier Foundation. "*That's the data that's being fed into predictive policing algorithms*"). Italics added. See also: Kirkpatrick, Keith, "Battling Algorithmic Bias: How Do We Ensure Algorithms Treat Us Fairly?" *Commun. ACM 59*, Volume 10, 2016, pp. 1 and ff and passim.

a haze of ambiguity that obfuscates automated decision-making while spurring a meaningless façade of neutrality[227] that should keep us eagerly awaken at night.

§§ The skewed data baked into the bigoted algorithms[228]—machine[229] biases[230]—spawns jarring effects with which criminal justice[231] has been grappling for a long-haul/drawn-out.[232] Tallyingly, and perhaps unsurprisingly, law enforcement evinces biases that run along both gender and race lines.[233]

§§ No surprise springs from the fact that computer-generated algorithms that propel predictive policing are often tagged as tools whereby racial discrimination

---

[227] Farina, M., & Lavazza, A., *Philosophy, expertise, and the myth of neutrality. Routledge Studies in Contemporary Philosophy*, London, Routledge, 2024. See also: Tyler, Tom R., "The Psychology of Procedural Justice: A Test of the Group-Value Model", *Journal of Personality and Social Psychology*, Volume 57, 1989, p. 830 (reports that in any procedure "several non-control issues – the *neutrality* of the decision-making procedure, trust in the 3rd party, and the information the experience communicates about social standing – influence both procedural preferences and judgments of procedural justice").

[228] Kirkpatrick, Keith, "It's not the Algorithm, it's the Data", *Communications of the ACM*, February 2017, Volume 60, n. ° 2, 2017 ("critics say these tools are inherently biased since they rely on reported crimes data, which is often concentrated in heavily policed areas, skewing statistics to overrepresent the poor and minorities").

[229] Sun, R. (Ed.), *The Cambridge Handbook of Computational Cognitive Sciences*, Cambridge, Cambridge University Press, 2023.

[230] Flores, A.W./Lowenkamp, C.T./Bechtel, K., "False positives, false negatives, and false analyses: a rejoinder to "machine bias: there's software used across the country to predict future criminal", *Federal Probation Journal*, Volume 80, 2016, pp. 38–46; Fisher, A., Rudin, C., & Dominici, F., "All models are wrong, but many are useful: Learning a variable's importance by studying an entire class of prediction models simultaneously", *Journal of Machine Learning Research*, 20, 2019, pp. 1–81. Angwin J, Larson J, Mattu S, et al., "Machine bias: There's software used across the country to predict future criminals. And it's biased against blacks", 2016, passim. Available at. https://www.propublica.org/article/machine-bias-risk-assessments-in-criminal-sentencing (accessed 26 October 2024). Sun, R. (Ed.), *The Cambridge Handbook of Computational Cognitive Sciences*, Cambridge, Cambridge University Press, 2023.

[231] See: Part IV, This chapter, Sects. 4.1.10.1–4.1.10.6 of this book (on biased algorithmic risk assessment in criminal procedure law settings).

[232] Mayson, Sandra G., "Bias In, Bias Out", *Yale Law Journal*, Volume 128, 2019, pp. 2218 and ff and passim.

[233] Benjamin, Ruha, *Race After Technology: Abolitionist Tools for the New Jim Code*, New York, Polity, 2019, pp. 1–172 ("*From everyday apps to complex algorithms, Ruha Benjamin cuts through tech-industry hype to understand how emerging technologies can reinforce White supremacy and deepen social inequity.* Benjamin argues that automation, far from being a sinister story of racist programmers scheming on the dark web, has the potential to hide, speed up, *and deepen discrimination while appearing neutral and even benevolent when compared to the racism of a previous era. Presenting the concept of the "New Jim Code," she shows how a range of discriminatory designs encode inequity by explicitly amplifying racial hierarchies; by ignoring but thereby replicating social divisions; or by aiming to fix racial bias but ultimately doing quite the opposite. Moreover, she makes a compelling case for race itself as a kind of technology, designed to stratify and sanctify social injustice in the architecture of everyday life.* This illuminating guide provides conceptual tools for decoding tech promises with sociologically informed skepticism. In doing so, *it challenges us to question not only the technologies we are sold but also the ones we ourselves manufacture*"). Italics added. See: Segran, G., "The complexity of artificial intelligence", *Singapore Management University*, 2021, passim (on the elaborate and complex trappings of Artificial Intelligence).

is rife.[234] It should not therefore be tagged as flabbergasting that this sort of *shady algorithmic governance* is a byproduct of a unpalatable *Algorithmic Dictatorship* that is shaping up to crumble the foundations of Rule of Law[235] upon which stands modern societies.[236]

§§ The phenomenon of «runaway feedbacks loops»[237] adds plausibility to, and lends enhanced weight on, the finding according to which the level playing field is unfairly tilted against racialised communities. Once again, the batch of skewed data that propels predictive policing is to blame.[238]

---

[234] DaViera, A. L./Uriostegui, M., Gottlieb/A./Onyeka, O, "Risk, race, and predictive policing: A critical race theory analysis of the strategic subject list", *American Journal of Community Psychology*, Volume 73, 2024, pp. 91–103.

[235] See: Raz, Joseph, "The Rule of Law and its Virtue", *The Authority of Law: Essays on Law and Morality*. Oxford: Clarendon Press, 1979, pp. 210–214 (on the quintessential value of Rule of Law).

Waldron, Jeremy, "The Rule of Law and the Importance of Procedure", *New York Public Law and Legal Theory*, 2010, p. 4 (notes that "the Rule of Law is violated when due attention is not paid to these procedural matters or when the institutions that are supposed to embody this procedure are undermined or interfered with". Further down this author would admit that there are some substantive dimensions of Rule of Law, such as respect for right for property and presumption of liberty and so forth); Taekema, Sanne, "The Procedural Rule of Law: Examining Waldron's Argument on Dignity and Agency", *Jahrbuch für Recht und Ethik*, Band 21, 2013, pp. 133 ff (contends that "Waldron's understanding of the Rule of Law as procedural which demands the opportunity for individuals to contest legal decisions in the formalized processes of courts and tribunals"); Cass, Ronald A., *The Rule of Law in America*. Baltimore, Maryland: The Johns Hopkins University Press, 2001, p. 17 (noting that a "central element of the Rule of law, constraint from external authority…helps assure that the process of government, *rather than the predilections of the individual decision-maker*") Italics added.

[236] Which is why the onset of the age of Artificial Intelligence will put the Rule of Law to the test like never before. Recall, the Rule of Law is a functional barrier—aimed at clamping down a host of unlawful deeds undertaken by those in power—that must not be teared apart or criminal procedure law will be otherwise despoiled from its intrinsic validity and vitality. See: Raz, Joseph, "The Rule of Law and its Virtue", *The Authority of Law: Essays on Law and Morality*, *cit.*, p. 224 (asserts adamantly that the Rule of Law is aimed at cushioning the hazards of abuse perpetrated by those in power. In this vein, Raz contends that "the law inevitably creates a great danger of arbitrary power—the Rule of Law is designed to minimize the danger created by the law itself…*Thus the (R)ule of (L)aw is designed to minimize the danger created by law itself…Thus the (R)ule of (L)aw is a negative virtue…the evil which is avoided is evil which could only have been caused by the law itself*"). Italics added.

[237] Ensign, Danielle/Friedler, Sorelle A./Neville, Scott/Scheidegger, Carlos/ Venkatasubramanian, Suresh, "Runaway Feedback Loops in Predictive Policing", *cit.*, p. 1.

[238] See: Kirkpatrick, Keith, "It's not the Algorithm, it's the Data", *Communications of the ACM*, February 2017, Volume 60, n. ° 2, 2017 ("critics, however, say tools such as PredPol and Command-Central *are inherently biased since they rely heavily on reported crimes data, which is often concentrated in areas that are heavily policed, thereby skewing statistics to overrepresent poor or minority communities. "We know that we have a history of racially biased policing in the United States, and that has fed into all the data that we have on where arrests have occurred, which crimes are more likely to occur in specific communities, and at which particular times,*" says Jennifer Lynch, senior staff attorney at the Electronic Frontier Foundation. "*That's the data that's being fed into predictive policing algorithms*"). Italics added. See also: Kirkpatrick, Keith, "Battling Algorithmic Bias: How Do We Ensure Algorithms Treat Us Fairly?" *Commun. ACM 59*, Volume 10, 2016, pp. 1 and ff and passim.

§§ The phenomenon of «runaway feedbacks loops»[239] boasts close ties with, and is tightly interlocked to, the models of machine learning deployed to accomplish a given task.[240]

§§ Casts broadly, those models of machine learning draw on traditional batch-mode,[241] where decisions are fundamentally made[242] «and observed results supplement the training data for the next batch»[243] of data.

§§ Notwithstanding, the problem of «feedback»[244] converts traditional batches of machine learning algorithms into both unfit and inaccurate.[245] For example, hiring algorithms only receive meaningful feedback on people who were eventually hired by a given company.[246]

§§ Pivotally, predictive policing algorithms only observe criminal activities in neighbourhoods they indeed patrol, and so forth.[247] This is not a nugatory finding, nor is a bootless concern. Rather, this is a special case for a larger set of concerns as the skewed data that creeps into the algorithm will predictably cast a vast array of harms onto members of racialised communities, as we are about to find out.

§§ Tellingly, the decisions made by the system of predictive policing algorithms will influence the data that is fed to it[248] in the forthcoming future,[249] which will either launch the system into abeyance or the system itself will go berserk. But there

---

[239] Ensign, Danielle/Friedler, Sorelle A./Neville, Scott/Scheidegger, Carlos/ Venkatasubramanian, Suresh, "Runaway Feedback Loops in Predictive Policing", *cit.*, p. 1.

[240] Ensign, Danielle/Friedler, Sorelle A./Neville, Scott/Scheidegger, Carlos/ Venkatasubramanian, Suresh, "Runaway Feedback Loops in Predictive Policing", *cit.*, p. 1.

[241] Ensign, Danielle/Friedler, Sorelle A./Neville, Scott/Scheidegger, Carlos/ Venkatasubramanian, Suresh, "Runaway Feedback Loops in Predictive Policing", *cit.*, p. 1.

[242] Ensign, Danielle/Friedler, Sorelle A./Neville, Scott/Scheidegger, Carlos/ Venkatasubramanian, Suresh, "Runaway Feedback Loops in Predictive Policing", *cit.*, p. 1.

[243] Ensign, Danielle/Friedler, Sorelle A./Neville, Scott/Scheidegger, Carlos/ Venkatasubramanian, Suresh, "Runaway Feedback Loops in Predictive Policing", *cit.*, p. 1.

[244] Ensign, Danielle/Friedler, Sorelle A./Neville, Scott/Scheidegger, Carlos/ Venkatasubramanian, Suresh, "Runaway Feedback Loops in Predictive Policing", *cit.*, p. 1.

[245] Ensign, Danielle/Friedler, Sorelle A./Neville, Scott/Scheidegger, Carlos/ Venkatasubramanian, Suresh, "Runaway Feedback Loops in Predictive Policing", *cit.*, p. 1.

[246] Ensign, Danielle/Friedler, Sorelle A./Neville, Scott/Scheidegger, Carlos/ Venkatasubramanian, Suresh, "Runaway Feedback Loops in Predictive Policing", *cit.*, p. 1.

[247] Ensign, Danielle/Friedler, Sorelle A./Neville, Scott/Scheidegger, Carlos/ Venkatasubramanian, Suresh, "Runaway Feedback Loops in Predictive Policing", *cit.*, p. 1.

[248] But see: Kirkpatrick, Keith, "It's not the Algorithm, it's the Data", *Communications of the ACM*, February 2017, Volume 60, n. ° 2, 2017 ("critics, however, say tools such as PredPol and CommandCentral *are inherently biased since they rely heavily on reported crimes data, which is often concentrated in areas that are heavily policed, thereby skewing statistics to overrepresent poor or minority communities.* "*We know that we have a history of racially biased policing in the United States, and that has fed into all the data that we have on where arrests have occurred, which crimes are more likely to occur in specific communities, and at which particular times,*" says Jennifer Lynch, senior staff attorney at the Electronic Frontier Foundation. "*That's the data that's being fed into predictive policing algorithms*"). Italics added. See also: Kirkpatrick, Keith, "Battling Algorithmic Bias: How Do We Ensure Algorithms Treat Us Fairly?" *Commun. ACM 59*, Volume 10, 2016, pp. 1 and ff and passim.

is a third option that looks much worse than the previous two: a wholly unbecoming «runaway feedback loop» that will further compound the racial wedge facing modern societies.

§§ Recall, the decisions made by the system of predictive policing algorithms will influence the data that is fed to it in the forthcoming future.[250] For example, once a binding decision has been made to patrol a given neighbourhood, the criminal activities discovered in that concrete neighbourhood will creep into the training data apparatus for the next round of algorithmic decision[251] making.[252]

§§ It should not come as a bewildering surprise that this skewed data—which, recall, arises out of crime discovered by the police while patrolling a given neighbourhood—will influence future algorithmic decision-making on where should the police be sent, who should be targeted by surveillance, and who may be a victim[253] of a future crime.[254] Which prompts the tantalizing question: what is the criterion, if any, underpinning the deployment of police officers to areas to detect crime?

§§ Corporations[255] (ranging from *PredPol*,[256] *HunchLab*, to *IBM*, amongst many others entities alike) have been pouring in whopping efforts in an earnest attempt to

---

[249] Ensign, Danielle/Friedler, Sorelle A./Neville, Scott/Scheidegger, Carlos/ Venkatasubramanian, Suresh, "Runaway Feedback Loops in Predictive Policing", *cit.*, p. 1.

[250] Ensign, Danielle/Friedler, Sorelle A./Neville, Scott/Scheidegger, Carlos/ Venkatasubramanian, Suresh, "Runaway Feedback Loops in Predictive Policing", *cit.*, p. 1.

[251] Dazeley, Richard/Vamplew, Peter/Foale, Cameron/ Young, Charlotte/ Aryal, Sunil/Cruz, Francisco, "Levels of explainable artificial intelligence for human-aligned conversational explanations", *Artificial Intelligence*, Volume 299, 2021, passim (as stated by lauded authors "over the last few years there has been rapid research growth into *eXplainable Artificial Intelligence* (XAI) and the closely aligned Interpretable Machine Learning (IML). Drivers for this growth include recent legislative changes and increased investments by industry and governments, along with increased concern from the general public. People are affected by autonomous decisions every day and the public need to understand the decision-making process to accept the outcomes.

[252] Ensign, Danielle/Friedler, Sorelle A./Neville, Scott/Scheidegger, Carlos/ Venkatasubramanian, Suresh, "Runaway Feedback Loops in Predictive Policing", *cit.*, p. 1. About algorithmic decision-making: Scherer, Maxi, "Artificial Intelligence and Legal Decision-Making: The Wide Open?", *Journal of International Arbitration*, Volume 36, 2019, passim; See: Edmond, Gary/Martire, Kristy A., "Just Cognition: Scientific Research on Bias and Some Implications for Legal Procedure and Decision-Making", *The Modern Law Review*, Volume 82, n. °4, 2019, p. 664 (on the dire need of keeping "good reputation (…) "and the appearance of justice"; Williams, Rebecca, "Rethinking Administrative Law for Algorithmic Decision-Making", *Oxford Journal of Legal Studies*, Volume 42, 2021, pp. 468 e ff and passim; Tyler, Tom R., "The Psychology of Procedural Justice: A Test of the Group-Value Model", *Journal of Personality and Social Psychology*, Volume 57, 1989, p. 830 (reports that in any procedure "several non-control issues – the *neutrality* of the decision-making procedure, trust in the 3rd party, and the information the experience communicates about social standing – influence both procedural preferences and judgments of procedural justice"). See also: Simmons, Ric, "Big Data and Procedural Justice: Legitimizing Algorithms in the Criminal Justice System", *Ohio State Journal of Criminal Law*, Volume 15, 2018, pp. 576 and ff and passim; Goodman/Flaxman, S., "EU Regulations on Algorithmic Decision-making and a "right to explanation", *Artificial Intelligence Magazine*, Volume 38, Issue 3, 2017, pp. 50 and ff and passim.

[253] Ensign, Danielle/Friedler, Sorelle A./Neville, Scott/Scheidegger, Carlos/ Venkatasubramanian, Suresh, "Runaway Feedback Loops in Predictive Policing", *cit.*, p. 2.

[254] However, prejudiced algorithms are set to be brought as they are one foundational basis of *justice prédictive* so voguish in France. No surprise stems from the fact that prejudiced algorithms will feed

ascertain how to proficiently deploy police officers relying upon historical crime[257] data.[258]

§§ Casts broadly, corporations entrusted with the task to ferret out areas in which crime is likely to occur use both *historical data*[259] and *incident data*[260] related with several regions to decide how to deftly allocate patrol officers[261] to a circumference of areas to quell crime.[262] Here lies the importance of the distinction between *discovered incidents* and *reported incidents*[263] as data[264] is the key to shine a keen light on the issue of «runaway feedback loop».

---

justice prédictive—and that is something quite unsavoury and unpalatable in criminal justice indeed. See: Garapon, Antoine, "Les enjeux de la justice predictive", *Juris-Classeur périodique*, Volume 31, 2018, passim. See also: Larret-Chahine, Louis, "Le droit isométrique: un nouveau paradigme juridique né de la justice prédictive», *Archives de Philosophie du Droit*, Volume 60, 2018, pp. 287 and ff and passim.

255 But see in French doctrine: Ferey, Samuel, « Analyse économique du droit, big data et justice prédictive», *Archives de Philosophie du Droit*, Volume 60, 2018, pp. 68–81 (on the close relationship between predictive justice and law and economics).

256 But see: Kirkpatrick, Keith, "It's not the Algorithm, it's the Data", *Communications of the ACM*, February 2017, Volume 60, n.° 2, 2017 ("PredPol, developed by mathematicians at the University of California, Los Angeles, and Santa Clara University in close collaboration with crime analysts and patrol officers at the Los Angeles and Santa Cruz police departments. *The tool uses three data points to provide predictions on where crime is likely to occur: past type of crime, place of crime, and time of crime. It does not use any personal information about individuals or groups of individuals in its crime predictions*". Italics added.

257 But see in French doctrine: Brigant, Jean-Marie, "Les risques accentués d'une justice pénale prédictive», *Archives de Philosophie du Droit*, Volume 60, 2018, pp. 238 and ff and passim (on the deleterious effects that can take the shape of a predictive criminal justice run by machines accountable to no one).

258 Ensign, Danielle/Friedler, Sorelle A./Neville, Scott/Scheidegger, Carlos/ Venkatasubramanian, Suresh, "Runaway Feedback Loops in Predictive Policing", *cit.*, p. 2. But see: Simmons, Ric, "Big Data and Procedural Justice: Legitimizing Algorithms in the Criminal Justice System", *Ohio State Journal of Criminal Law*, Volume 5, 2018, pp. 573 and ff and passim (argues, however, that too much AI in criminal procedure law settings can backfire, thereby hindering citizens 'trust on the criminal system of justice).

259 That loosely forms part of a broader legal apparatus according to which "Law is an Artifact". See: Burazin, Luka/Himma, Keneth Heinar/Roversi, Corrado (Editors), *Law as an Artifact*. Oxford: Oxford University Press, 2018, pp. 1–304.

260 On data: Henderson, Stephen E., "A Few Criminal Justice Big Data Rules", *Ohio State Journal of Criminal Law*, Volume 15, 2018, passim.

261 Tyler, Tom R./Goff, Philip Atiba/MacCoun, Robert J., "The Impact of Psychological Science on Policing in the United States: Procedural Justice, Legitimacy, and Effective Law Enforcement", *Psychological Science in the Public Interest*, Volume 16, Issue 3, 2015, p. 79 (noting that "without a fundamental reallocation of resources, our society cannot effectively monitor the general public searching for everyday wrongdoing"). See also: Friedmann, Barry et al., "Policing Police Tech: A Soft Law Solution", *Berkeley Technology Law Journal*, Volume 37, 2022, pp. 701–756.

262 Ensign, Danielle/Friedler, Sorelle A./Neville, Scott/Scheidegger, Carlos/ Venkatasubramanian, Suresh, "Runaway Feedback Loops in Predictive Policing", *cit.*, p. 2.

263 Ensign, Danielle/Friedler, Sorelle A./Neville, Scott/Scheidegger, Carlos/ Venkatasubramanian, Suresh, "Runaway Feedback Loops in Predictive Policing", *cit.*, p. 2.

§§ For purposes here, it bears mentioning that once police are deployed based on algorithmic decision-making (predictive policing to make predictions on where will crime occur), *historical data* is then used to further update the model of algorithmic decision-making.[265]

§§ The foregoing observations made by the police further the deployment to patrol a given neighbourhood is called *discovered incidents*,[266] as opposed to *reported incidents*,[267] which arise out of incidents directly reported to the police by either concerned citizens or the victims themselves.[268] Especially, albeit not exclusively, through 911 calls[269] that aim to denounce criminal activities.

§§ The crux of the problem concerning «runaway feedback loops» is that the tagged *discovered incidents* only occur in neighbourhoods that police have been deployed[270] by Artificial Intelligence-embedded technology itself (i.e. the algorithmic decision-making system that propels forward the predictive policing algorithm).[271]

§§ Setting aside the perceived hazard of the foregoing *discovered data* may feed into databases used by others—which will most likely produce a cascade of biased algorithmic decision-making -, the burden of *selective surveillance* will be shifted onto a thicket of others. Most likely, members of racialized communities (Blacks and Latinos) that live in the neighbourhoods frequently patrolled by police officers.

§§ The loathsome phenomenon of unlawful «arrests by skin[272] colour»,[273] flagitious arrests by age[274] or spirited off arrests by transgender[275] in the purview of algorithmic predictive policing[276] will skyrocket and wrongful convictions[277] will accordingly soar/balloon.

---

[264] On big data: Sivarajah, Uthayasnkar et al., "Critical Analysis of Big Data Challenges and Analytical Methods", *Journal of Business Research*, Volume 70, 2017, passim.

[265] Ensign, Danielle/Friedler, Sorelle A./Neville, Scott/Scheidegger, Carlos/ Venkatasubramanian, Suresh, "Runaway Feedback Loops in Predictive Policing", *cit.*, p. 2.

[266] Ensign, Danielle/Friedler, Sorelle A./Neville, Scott/Scheidegger, Carlos/ Venkatasubramanian, Suresh, "Runaway Feedback Loops in Predictive Policing", *cit.*, p. 2.

[267] Ensign, Danielle/Friedler, Sorelle A./Neville, Scott/Scheidegger, Carlos/ Venkatasubramanian, Suresh, "Runaway Feedback Loops in Predictive Policing", *cit.*, p. 2.

[268] Blum, W. J./Kalven, H., "The Empty Cabinet of Dr. Calabresi—Auto Accidents and General Deterrence", *University of Chicago Law Review*, Volume 34, 1967, pp. 268 ff (averring that law also pursues the goal of, and resonates with, allaying victim's feeling of utter indignation).

[269] Ensign, Danielle/Friedler, Sorelle A./Neville, Scott/Scheidegger, Carlos/ Venkatasubramanian, Suresh, "Runaway Feedback Loops in Predictive Policing", *cit.*, p. 2.

[270] Ensign, Danielle/Friedler, Sorelle A./Neville, Scott/Scheidegger, Carlos/ Venkatasubramanian, Suresh, "Runaway Feedback Loops in Predictive Policing", *cit.*, p. 2.

[271] Ensign, Danielle/Friedler, Sorelle A./Neville, Scott/Scheidegger, Carlos/ Venkatasubramanian, Suresh, "Runaway Feedback Loops in Predictive Policing", *cit.*, p. 2.

§§ As a result, there is an enhanced likelihood of the occurrence of *sampling bias*,[278] which, in turn, is conducive to «runaway feedback loops», which is wholly unbecoming[279] in the remit of predictive policing.[280]

---

[272] See: Connecticut Fair Housing Center, et al. v. CoreLogic Rental Property Solutions—Cohen Milstein (access: 20.11.2024). ("*The U.S. Department of Housing & Urban Development observed in 2016 that excluding rental applicants because of their criminal records disproportionately harms Latinos and African Americans, who are significantly more likely than whites to be arrested or convicted. Studies show such disparities are linked to differential enforcement rather than to differences in likelihood of engaging in criminal activity.* HUD advised that to avoid discriminating, an "individualized review" should be conducted considering the nature of the offense, how long ago it occurred, intervening changed circumstances, and other relevant factors to avoid denying housing to an applicant who does not pose a genuine and ongoing threat to persons or property. *Further, HUD's guidance specifically advises landlords not to consider arrests that did not result in a conviction in making their evaluations*"). Italics added. See: Part IV, This chapter, Sects. 4.1.4–4.1.4.2.1 of this book (on mortgage redlining). See: Part IV, This chapter, Sects. 4.1.2–4.1.4.3 of this book (on algorithmic credit scoring, consumer racism and credit card redlining). See: Part IV, This chapter, Sects. 4.1.4–4.1.4.2.3 of this book (on algorithmic redlining). See: Part IV, This chapter, Sect. 4.1.4.3 of this book (on "algorithmic redliking"). See: Part IV, This chapter, Sect. 4.1.3 of this book (on algorithmic prime-lining).

[273] Kizer, J. M., "Arrested by skin color: Evidence from siblings and a nationally representative sample", *Socius: Sociological Research for a Dynamic World*, 3, 2017, passim; Kochel, T. R., Wilson, D. B./Mastrofski, S. D., "Effect of suspect race on officers' arrest decisions", *Criminology*, Volume 49, Issue 2, 2011, pp. 473–512. Mitchell, O./Caudy, M. S., "Examining racial disparities in drug arrests", *Justice Quarterly*, Volume 32, Issue 2, 2015, pp. 288–313; Kirk, D. S., "The neighborhood context of racial and ethnic disparities in arrest", *Demography*, 45, 2008, pp. 55–77.

[274] McCauley, E. J., "The cumulative probability of arrest by age 28 years in the United States by disability status, race/ethnicity, and gender", *American Journal of Public Health*, Volume 107, Issue 12, 2017, pp. 1977–1981.

[275] Stotzer, R. L., "Law enforcement and criminal justice personnel interactions with transgender people in the United States: A literature review", *Aggression and Violent Behavior*, Volume 19, Issue 3, 2014, 263–277; Furman, E./Singh, A. K./Darko, N. A./Wilson, C. L., "Activism, intersectionality, and community psychology: The way in which Black Lives Matter Toronto helps us to examine white supremacy in Canada's LGBTQ community", *Community Psychology in Global Perspective*, Volume 4, Issue 2, 34–54.

[276] Saunders, J., Hunt, P., & Hollywood, J. S., "Predictions put into practice: A quasi-experimental evaluation of Chicago's predictive policing pilot", *Journal of Experimental Criminology*, Volume 12, Issue 3, 2016, pp. 347–371.

[277] Gross, Samuel R., Maurice Possley, and Kalara Stephens, "Race and Wrongful Convictions in the United States." National Registry of Exonerations, Newkirk Center for Science and Society, University of California-Irvine, 2017.

[278] *Sampling bias* is the polar opposite of inductive bias (learning bias). See: Dong et al., Qi, "Imbalanced deep learning by minority class incremental rectification, *IEEE Transactions on Pattern Analysis & Machine Intelligence*, Volume 41, 2019, p. 1367 (posit that "*most existing learning algorithms produce inductive bias (learning bias)* towards the frequent (majority) classes if training data are not balanced, *resulting in poor minority class recognition performance*"). Italics added.

[279] Ensign, Danielle/Friedler, Sorelle A./Neville, Scott/Scheidegger, Carlos/ Venkatasubramanian, Suresh, "Runaway Feedback Loops in Predictive Policing", *cit.*, p. 2.

[280] Kirkpatrick, Keith, "It's not the Algorithm, it's the Data", *Communications of the ACM*, February 2017, Volume 60, n. ° 2, 2017 ("Crime in the USA has fallen dramatically over the past three decades,

§§ The problem is that the skewed data has been tainted by a long-haul period of racially biased police strategies as back then, just like right now, police keep patrolling the same neighbourhoods for racially motivated reasons. As a result, there will be an overrepresentation of discovered incidents on areas populated by racialised communities, which will prime the predictive algorithm to repeatedly send police to those neighbourhoods.

§§ Tellingly, the *discovered incidents* (that leverage on historical data used to further update the model of algorithmic decision-making) in those neighbourhoods will creep into the algorithm, which, in turn, will sully future algorithmic decision-making (predictive policing) as the police will be repeatedly sent to those neighbourhoods by the *predictive algorithm itself* («runaway feedback loops»),[281] thereby compounding racial disparities[282] with which modern societies have been grappling with.[283]

---

with 2014 statistics from the Federal Bureau of Investigation (FBI) noting the number of violent crimes committed per 100,000 people in 2013 (368) was less than half the level seen in 1991 (758). Nevertheless, the debate continues over how to maintain *these lower crime rates while addressing issues of fairness in the way communities are policed*, as well as how to effectively and fairly use risk-assessment tools that can be relied upon by sentencing courts or parole boards. There are two primary issues at stake: risk-assessment algorithms, which weigh a variety of factors related to recidivism, or the likelihood an individual will commit another crime and wind up back behind bars; *and predictive policing, which has been described as using data analytics and algorithms to better pinpoint where and when a crime might occur, so police resources can be more efficiently deployed. Both issues are fraught with challenges—moral, logistical, and political—and opinions on whether they can be fairly and ethically utilized largely depend on how one views the nature of policing and the criminal justice system*"). Italics added.

[281] Ensign, Danielle/Friedler, Sorelle A./Neville, Scott/Scheidegger, Carlos/ Venkatasubramanian, Suresh, "Runaway Feedback Loops in Predictive Policing", *cit.*, p. 2.

[282] Kirkpatrick, Keith, "It's not the Algorithm, it's the Data", *Communications of the ACM*, February 2017, Volume 60, n. º 2, 2017 ("in risk assessment and predictive policing, biased data can yield biased results").

[283] Kirkpatrick, Keith, "It's not the Algorithm, it's the Data", *Communications of the ACM*, February 2017, Volume 60, n. º 2, 2017 ("Critics, however, say tools such as PredPol and CommandCentral *are inherently biased since they rely heavily on reported crimes data, which is often concentrated in areas that are heavily policed, thereby skewing statistics to overrepresent poor or minority communities*. "*We know that we have a history of racially biased policing in the United States, and that has fed into all the data that we have on where arrests have occurred, which crimes are more likely to occur in specific communities, and at which particular times*," says Jennifer Lynch, senior staff attorney at the Electronic Frontier Foundation. "*That's the data that's being fed into predictive policing algorithms*"). Italics added.

4.1.2 Credit Scoring and Consumer Racism: How Slavery has Paved the Way to **Algorithmic Dictatorship** *that Allots Everything to a* **Selected Few** *While Snubbing Everything to an* **Unwanted Many** *in the Remit of Credit Card Industry—Introduction*

§§ Algorithmic systems trained of past bigoted data boast a high likelihood to recreate or even rachet up discrimination[284] seen in past algorithmic[285] decision-making.[286]

§§ That is true, but truer still Artificial Intelligence-embedded technologies, if nothing else, have a penchant to reify,[287] compound and exacerbate deep-seated social and ethnic concerns[288] with which modern societies have been scuffling with for a long-drawn-out,[289] such as misogyny,[290] racism,[291] xenophobe and political

---

[284] *Tech, Bias and Housing Initiative, the Promise and Perils of Residential Proptech, Year 1, Research Summary Report, April 2023, TechEquity Collaborative*, p. 11, available at: https://techequity.us/wp-content/uploads/2023/04/TBHI-Y1-Research-Summary-Report.pdf (28.11.2024). ("*Once bad data enters the analysis of one factor, it gets baked into the subsequent process, multiplying the effect that one disadvantageous data point can have on someone's overall housing determination*"). Italics added. See: Part IV, This chapter, Sects. 4.1.4–4.1.4.2.3 of this book. See: Part IV, This chapter, Sects. 4.1.4–4.1.4.2.1 of this book (on mortgage redlining). See: Part IV, This chapter, Sects. 4.1.2–4.1.4.3 of this book (on algorithmic credit scoring, consumer racism and credit card redlining). See: Part IV, This chapter, Sects. 4.1.4–4.1.4.2.3 of this book (on algorithmic redlining). See: Part IV, This chapter, Sect. 4.1.4.3 of this book (on "algorithmic redliking"). See: Part IV, This chapter, Sect. 4.1.3 of this book (on algorithmic prime-lining).

[285] Burrell J., "How the machine "thinks": Understanding opacity in machine learning algorithms", *Big Data & Society*, Volume 10, 2026, pp. 1–12.

[286] Balkin, Jack M., "The Three Laws of Robotics in the Age of Big Data", *Ohio State Law Journal*, Volume 78, Issue 5, 2017, pp. 1217–1241.

[287] Duster, Troy, "Race and Reification in Science." *Science*, 307, 2005, passim.

[288] *Tech, Bias and Housing Initiative, the Promise and Perils of Residential Proptech, Year 1, Research Summary Report, April 2023, TechEquity Collaborative*, p. 5 available at: https://techequity.us/wp-content/uploads/2023/04/TBHI-Y1-Research-Summary-Report.pdf (28.11.2024). ("*Residential Proptech also has the potential to exacerbate the bias inherent in our housing system. Its rise is due, in part, to the desperation felt by average home seekers. With a severely constrained housing supply, companies offering an easier pathway to homeownership may exploit communities that have been harmed by housing discrimination in the past. Opaque algorithms incorporate biased data into their decision-making processes, making it harder to enforce fair housing laws.* Residential Proptech companies often operate in a regulatory gray area, leaving consumers without the protections they would have from traditional housing regulatory systems. *As unprecedented capital investment flows into this space, venture-backed companies' winner-take-all approach to growth has the potential to exacerbate inequality rather than combat it*"). Italics added. See: Part IV, This chapter, Sects. 4.1.4–4.1.4.2.3 of this book. See: Part IV, This chapter, Sects. 4.1.4–4.1.4.2.1 of this book (on mortgage redlining). See: Part IV, This chapter, Sects. 4.1.2–4.1.4.3 of this book (on algorithmic credit scoring, consumer racism and credit card redlining). See: Part IV, This chapter, Sects. 4.1.4–4.1.4.2.3 of this book (on algorithmic redlining). See: Part IV, This chapter, Sect. 4.1.4.3 of this book (on "algorithmic redliking"). See: Part IV, This chapter, Sect. 4.1.3 of this book (on algorithmic prime-lining).

[289] Wonyoung, So, "Which Information Matters? Measuring Landlord Assessment of Tenant Screening Reports", *Housing Policy Debate*, Volume 33, n. ° 6, 2023, pp. 1484–1510 (1502) ("*One*

hatred which, taken together, are rife for misfire, social outcry, uproar, and a plethora of grievances alike.

§§ The looming unmooring of the machines therefore begs for a tour de force distillation of principles of algorithmic accountability,[292] which, in turn, will be tuned into the universal energy of *Algorithmic Common Good* (ACG)[293] that seeks to wither away the unpalatable effects of *Algorithmic Dictatorship* (AD) punctiliously outlined in this section.

§§ The tale of the *algorithmic discrimination*[294] is by now familiar and well worn. Although narrative always differs by teller, there is an agreed-upon consensus according to which *algorithmic biases*[295] are in dire need of quashing.[296] The examples of algorithmic discrimination[297] are legion.[298] So too are the scattershot

---

additional finding of the experiment is that algorithmic scoring can exacerbate this racially unequal landscape in rental agreements not just because the algorithm may be inaccurate, but because landlords may want to follow the risk assessment made by the tenant screening report. This is alarming for low-income tenants, particularly housing voucher holders. Security deposits are one of the most significant barriers to obtaining housing for voucher holders, because vouchers do not pay security deposits but most private landlords require them (Rosenblatt & Cossyleon, 2018). Given that voucher holders have exceptionally low income (usually less than 50% of area median income) and might experience more housing insecurity (rental debts and eviction-related experiences), *imposing greater security deposits on voucher holders almost equates to denying them housing—yet these decisions could be justified by algorithmic scoring if tenant screening services employ it*"). Italics added.

[290] Avery, Mallory/Leibbrandt, Andreas/Vecci, Joseph, "Does Artificial Intelligence Help or Hurt Gender Diversity? Evidence from Two Field Experiments on Recruitment on Tech, *Monash University, Monash Business School*, 2023, pp. 1–70.

[291] Here is a tool to dispel the rampant racism that besets the criminal system of justice: Huq, Aziz, "Racial Equity in Algorithmic Criminal Justice", *Duke Law Journal*, Volume 68, 2022, pp. 1076–1134. See: Part IV, This chapter, Sects. 4.1.10.1–4.1.10.6 of this book (on biased algorithmic risk assessment in criminal procedure law settings, with a sharper focus on COMPAS). See: Part IV, This chapter, Sects. 4.1.1–4.1.1.1 of this book (on biased predictive policing).

[292] See: Katyal, Sonia, "Private Accountability in the Age of Artificial Intelligence", *UCLA Law Review*, Volume 66, 2019, pp. 54–99. Williams, Rebecca, "Accountable Algorithms: Adopting the Public Law Toolbox Outside the Realm of Public Law", *Current Legal Problems*, Vol. 75, 2022, pp. 237–263; Williams, Rebecca, "Rethinking Administrative Law for Algorithmic Decision-Making", *Oxford Journal of Legal Studies*, Volume 42, 2021, pp. 468 e ff and passim.

[293] See: Part V, Chap. 5, Sects. 5.1.2–5.1.6.2.1 of this book (on the thing-centred algorithmic decision-making propelled by a *Controllable* and *Interpretable* Machine Learning that weeds out *Algorithmic Dictatorship* and secures *Algorithmic Common Good*. It is worth recalling that the **thing-centred algorithmic decision-making** seeks to unwind the perils arising out of the lack of theoretical underpinnings facing the **human-centred algorithmic decision-making**, as extensively fleshed out Part III, Chap. 3, Sects. 3.1.4.3–3.1.4.4 of this book).

[294] See on algorithmic discrimination: Kleinberg, Jon, et al., "Discrimination in the Age of Algorithms", *Journal of Legal Analysis*, 2018, pp. 114–174; See: Kleinberg, Jon, et al., "Algorithms as Discrimination Detectors", *Proceeds of the National Academy of Science*, Volume 117, 2020, pp. 30096–30110; Griemmelmann, James/Westreich, Daniel, "Incomprehensible Discrimination", *California Law Review Online*, Volume 7, 2018, pp. 164–171; Xiang, Alice, "Reconciling Legal and Technical Approaches to Algorithmic Bias", *Tennessee Law Review*, Volume 88, 2021, passim; Karnow, Curtis E. A., "The Opinion of Machines", *The Cambridge Handbook of the Law of Algorithms*, Bartfield, Woodrow (Editor), Cambridge, United Kingdom: Cambridge University Press, 2021, pp. 15 and ff and passim; Strandburg, Katherine J., "Rulemaking and Inscrutable Decision

examples of *Algorithmic Dictatorship*. Credit scoring[299] stands arguably amongst them.[300]

§§ Credit scoring industry—an unsavoury byproduct of a «scored society»[301]—has been enduring a withering string of attacks[302] from various sectors.[303]

Tools", *Columbia Law Review*, Volume 119, 2019, passim; Watcher, Sandra/Mittelstadt, Brent/Russell, Chris, "Counterfactual Explanations Without Opening the Black Box: Automated Decisions and the GDPR", *Harvard Journal of Law and Technology*, Volume 31, 2018, pp. 841 e ss and passim; Jackson, Maya C., "Artificial Intelligence and Algorithmic Bias: The Issues with Technology Reflecting History and Humans", *Journal of Business Technology Law*, Volume 16, 2021, pp. 299–316.

[295] Jackson, Maya C., "Artificial Intelligence and Algorithmic Bias: The Issues with Technology Reflecting History and Humans", *Journal of Business Technology Law*, Volume 16, 2021, pp. 299–316; Luguri, Jamie/Lior, Jacob Strahilevitz, "Shining a Light on Dark Patterns", *Journal of Legal Analytics*, Volume 13, 2021, pp. 43–109.

See: Slaughter, Rebecca Kelly, "Algorithms and Economic Justice: A Taxonomy of Harms and a Path Forward for the Federal Trade Commission", *Yale Journal of Law and Technology*, Volume 23, 2021, pp. S1 and ff; Wang, Yang/Sloan, Frank A., "Present Bias and Health", *Journal of Risk Uncertainty*, Volume 57, 2018, pp. 177–198; Gillis, Talia, "The Input Fallacy", *Minnesota Law Review*, Volume 106, 2022, pp. 1184–1266.

[296] See: Wagner/Gerhard/Eidenmuller, Horst, "Down by Algorithms? Siphoning Rents, Exploiting Biases, and Shaping Preferences: Regulating the Dark Side of Targeted Transactions", *University of Chicago Law Review*, Volume 86, 2019, pp. 581–609.

[297] Cossins D., "Discriminating algorithms: 5 times AI showed prejudice", 2018. Available at: https://www.newscientistcom/article/2166207-discriminating-algorithms-5-times-ai-showed-prejudice (accessed 6 September 2024).

[298] Eubanks, Virginia, *Automating inequality: how high-tech tools profile, police, and punish the poor*, New York: St. Martin's Press, 2017, passim.

[299] Campisi, Natalie, From Inherent Racial Bias to Incorrect Data The Problems With Current Credit Scoring Models, Forbes (Feb. 26, 2021), https://www.forbes.com/advisor/creditcards/from-inherent-racial-bias-to-incorrect-data-the-problems-with-current-credit-scoring-models/; [https://www.perma.cc/EWA4-CS8E] (highlighting rampant racial bias in credit scoring systems); Oyama, Rebecca, "Do Not (Re)Enter: the Rise of Criminal Background Tenant Screening as a Violation of the Fair Housing Act", *Michigan Journal of Race and Law*, Volume 15, 2009, pp. 181, 184–93 (discussing a broad range of historical/criminal accounts as a way to screen undesirable tenants, such as Blacks and Latinos); Statement of Interest of the United States at 12, *Louis v. SafeRent Sols., LLC, No. 1:22-cv-10800* (D. Mass. Jan. 9, 2023) (holding that the Fair Housing Act liability stretches far and beyond, thus encompassing a vast assortment of entities providing housing-related services, including corporations that offer tenant screening services).

[300] Dencik L, Hintz A, Redden J, et al., Data scores as governance: Investigating uses of citizen scoring in public services, 2018. Available at: https://datajustice.files.wordpress.com/2018/12/data-scores-as-governance-project-report2.pdf. (accessed 26 September 2024). On algorithmic big data biometric governance: Hu, Margaret, "From the National Surveillance State to the Cybersurveillance State", *The Annual Review of Law and Social Science*, Volume 13, 2017, p. 169 ("*as a result of big data biometric governance trends, meaningful distinctions between biometric credentialing for identification and behavioral biometric profiling are disappearing. The objectives are merging: Reliable credentialing is used to advance security and precrime policy rationales. Biometric data mission creep occurs by necessity in a big data world because the cybersurveillance systems are often designed to engage in mass data integration and analysis and predictive policing. Biometric surveillance serves two purposes in preventive policing: It increases identity transparency, and the biometric data categorize identity through cataloging behavioral and physical characteristics*

§§ The rampant racial discrimination[304] in the credit card industry[305] is the living testament of *Algorithmic Dictatorship* that has been pervading this lucrative industry[306] for a long-winded span of time. Racial divides[307] facing credit card industry[308] are a disheartening heritage of centuries of racial discrimination,[309] which has flagitiously targeted Blacks[310] and Latinos.[311]

§§ The practices carried out by the credit card industry have stirred public outcry owing to the racially discriminatory practices[312] against the backdrop of which Blacks and Latinos are often overburdened—chastised—with the worst[313] possible[314] credit[315] card terms[316] and conditions.[317]

---

and assess these characteristics for risk. Contrasting small data biometric credentialing protocols with big data credentialing protocols is useful. It illustrates how biometric surveillance fits within the Cybersurveillance State. In a small data world, paper-based passports and nondigitized photographs are examples of a small data biometric-based identification system"). Italics added. See: Part IV, This chapter, Sects. 4.1.5–4.1.5.2 of this book (on "algorithmic Jim Crow", a travel ban issued during the first Trump Administration to prevent certain individuals from entering the United States of America, which, given its racial undertones, stands as an outgrowth of congeries of laws enacted during the Jim Crow epoch).

301 Citron, Danielle K./Pasquale, Frank, "The Scored Society: Due Process for Automated Predictions", *Washington Law Review*, Volume 89, Issue 1, 2014, pp. 1–34.

302 Levitin, Adam J., "The Antitrust Super Bowl: America's Payment Systems, No-Surcharge Rules, and the Hidden Costs of Credit", *Berkeley Business Law Journal*, 2005, 265, 317–18, id. at 154 ("*consequently, low-income consumers now receive credit cards with high fees and interest rates, while higher-income consumers reap the rewards of credit card use, such as travel miles and concierge services.* Credit card companies target vulnerable consumers for inferior products through tactics such as teaser rates, mass mailings of preapproved cards,... overly complex credit card agreements, and credit-card redlining. *As a result of these practices, 80% of the industry's profits now come from interest payments and... fees instead of annual and interchange fees. This shift represents a massive redistribution of wealth from the poor to wealthier consumers and corporations*"). Italics added.

303 See: Aggarwal, N., "The Norms of Algorithmic Credit Scoring", *Cambridge Law Journal*, Volume 80, Issue 1, 2021, pp. 43–71. On the challenges arisen from an algorithm-driven economy: Ezrachi, A./Stucke, M., *Virtual Competition—The Promise and Perils of the Algorithm-Driven Economy*. Cambridge, Massachusetts: Harvard University Press, 2016, passim; Ezrachi, A., "Is This a Competition Problem?—The Challenge of Digitalisation and the Limits of Enforcement", in: *Keele Law Review*, Volume 1, 2020, pp. 59 and ff and passim.

304 Havard, Cassandra Jones, "On The Take": The Black Box of Credit Scoring and Mortgage Discrimination", *Boston University Public Interest Law Journal*, Volume 20, 2011, pp. 241–247 (highlighting that credit scoring if unchecked is an intrinsic, encroached, deep-rooted form of racial discrimination akin to mortgage redlining).

305 Freeman, Andrea, "Racism in the Credit Card Industry", *North Carolina Law Review*, Volume 95, Number 4, 2017, pp. 1071–1160.

306 Bar-Gill, Oren, "Seduction by Plastic", *New York University Law Review*, Volume 98, 2004, pp. 1373–1374; Mann, Ronald J., "Bankruptcy Reform and the "Sweat Box" of Credit Card Debt", *University of Illinois Law Review*, Volume 375, 2007, pp. 385–91.

307 Devon W. Carbado & Mitu Gulati, "Book Review, The Law and Economics of Critical Race Theory", *Yale Law Journal*, Volume 112, 2003, pp. 1757 and ff.

§§ It bears mentioning that this type of predatory consumer racism is rooted firmly on, and dates to, the Reconstruction era[318] that sharply mirrors an unbroken chain of

---

308 Freeman, Andrea "Payback: A Structural Analysis of the Credit Card Problem", *Arizona Law Review*, Volume 55, 2013, 151, 153 ("Although most economists and legal scholars view the 'credit card problem' of excessive consumer debt as one of market failure, it is in fact a story of overwhelming market success. *Through the use of sophisticated underwriting technology, the credit card companies learned that consumers who are on the verge of bankruptcy represent their greatest source of profits.* The industry responded to this information by completely altering its business model. *Instead of seeking customers who would pay off their bills at the end of each month, known in the industry as convenience users or deadbeats, the companies began to target low-income consumers who would maintain balances from month to month, known as revolvers*"). Italics added.

309 Hannah-Moffat K, "Algorithmic risk governance: Big data analytics, race and information activism in criminal justice debates", *Theoretical Criminology*, 2018, pp. 1–18. On algorithmic big data biometric governance: Hu, Margaret, "From the National Surveillance State to the Cybersurveillance State", *The Annual Review of Law and Social Science*, Volume 13, 2017, p. 169 ("*as a result of big data biometric governance trends, meaningful distinctions between biometric credentialing for identification and behavioral biometric profiling are disappearing. The objectives are merging: Reliable credentialing is used to advance security and precrime policy rationales. Biometric data mission creep occurs by necessity in a big data world because the cybersurveillance systems are often designed to engage in mass data integration and analysis and predictive policing. Biometric surveillance serves two purposes in preventive policing: It increases identity transparency, and the biometric data categorize identity through cataloging behavioral and physical characteristics and assess these characteristics for risk. Contrasting small data biometric credentialing protocols with big data credentialing protocols is useful. It illustrates how biometric surveillance fits within the Cybersurveillance State. In a small data world, paper-based passports and nondigitized photographs are examples of a small data biometric-based identification system*"). Italics added. See: Part IV, This chapter, Sects. 4.1.5–4.1.5.2 of this book (on "algorithmic Jim Crow", a travel ban issued during the first Trump Administration to prevent certain individuals from entering the United States of America, which, given its racial undertones, stands as an outgrowth of congeries of laws enacted during the Jim Crow epoch).

310 Freeman, Andrea, "Racism in the Credit Card Industry", *North Carolina Law Review*, Volume 95, Number 4, 2017, pp. 1071–1160 (1071) ("*in a social and financial climate characterized by deep racial and socioeconomic divide, racism against credit card applicants and consumers is a core piece of the systemic inequality that perpetuates dramatic disparities in wealth, employment, health, and education.* Over several decades, credit cards have evolved into an essential tool for lower- and middle-class families to maintain financial stability through strategic balancing between debt and disposable income"). Italics added.

311 Feagin, J. R., *The white racial frame: centuries of racial framing and counter-framing*, 2nd edition, New York, Routledge, 2013, passim.

312 Havard, Cassandra Jones, "On The Take": The Black Box of Credit Scoring and Mortgage Discrimination", *Boston University Public Interest Law Journal*, Volume 20, 2011, pp. 241–247 (highlighting that credit scoring if unchecked is an intrinsic, encroached, deep-rooted form of racial discrimination akin to mortgage redlining).

313 See: Firestone, Simon, "Race Ethnicity and Credit Card Monitoring", *Journal of Money, Credit and Banking*, Sept. 2014, 2014, pp. 1206 and ff; Han, Song, Keys, Benjamin J./Li, Geng, *Unsecured Credit Supply over the Credit Cycle: Evidence from Credit Card Mailings* (argue that, statistically, Blacks and Latinos are seldom granted credit and, if ever granted credit, the terms and conditions attached to the concession of credit are not equal to those offered to White folks).

314 See also: Wonyoung, So, "Which Information Matters? Measuring Landlord Assessment of Tenant Screening Reports", *Housing Policy Debate*, Volume 33, n. ° 6, 2023, pp. 1484–1510 (1502)

events that seeks to cement and buttress racial economic wedges between racialised communities and White folks.[319]

§§ This unsavoury situation raises critical questions about deep-rooted injustice concerns that must be balanced against the need to ensure that credit scoring[320] is fundamentally fair,[321] *controllable*,[322] accountable,[323] and predictable.[324]

("*It is important to note that within conditionally accepted reports, similar patterns of blanket screening policies and automation bias are exhibited when landlords impose security deposits. These results may corroborate a paired-test study that shows that Black tenants have less favorable terms and conditions, including security deposits, in rental agreements* (Ross & Turner, 2005)"). Italics added. See: Part IV, This chapter, Sects. 4.1.4–4.1.4.2.3 of this book.

[315] But see: Atkinson, Abbye, "Rethinking Credit as a Social Provision", *Stanford Law Review*, Volume 71, 2019, pp. 1093–1099 (contending that credit, which shifts consumption temporally, is only beneficial insofar income ratchets up in the forthcoming future. As of now, though, "credit is fundamentally incompatible with the entrenched intergenerational poverty that plagues low-income Americans." Id. Notably, it is crucially important to come to terms with the fact that credit is not a panacea for the great bulk of economic struggles, and concretely wage stagnation. Although credit is not befitted to all consumers at all prices, affordable credit can nonetheless play a pivotal role in the creation of wealth).

[316] Freeman, Andrea, "Racism in the Credit Card Industry", *cit.*, p. 1071 ("even worse, the companies do so in a racially discriminatory way, *burdening Black and Latino customers with the worst credit card terms, often unrelated to credit risk*"). Italics added.

[317] *Credit Discrimination: Hearings on H.R. 14856 and H.R. 14908 Before the Subcomm. on Consumer Affairs of the H. Comm. on Banking & Currency*, 93rd Cong. 1, 1974, (Hon. Leonor K. Sullivan, Chairman, Subcomm. on Consumer Affairs of the H. Comm. on Banking & Currency) (statement of John H. Powell, Jr., Chairman, Equal Emp't Opportunity Comm'n) *("[I]t is very likely that the inability to obtain credit, or if obtained, the discriminatory terms and conditions which accompany its extension to certain groups in our society, are directly related to discrimination in employment*"). Italics added; id. at 131 (statement of Hon. Arthur S. Flemming, Chairman, U.S. Comm'n on Civil Rights, and Comm'r, Admin. on Aging, Dep't of Health, Educ. & Welfare). Freeman, Andrea, "Racism in the Credit Card Industry", *cit.*, p. 1121. See also: Wonyoung, So, "Which Information Matters? Measuring Landlord Assessment of Tenant Screening Reports", *Housing Policy Debate*, Volume 33, n. ° 6, 2023, pp. 1484–1510 (1502) ("*It is important to note that within conditionally accepted reports, similar patterns of blanket screening policies and automation bias are exhibited when landlords impose security deposits. These results may corroborate a paired-test study that shows that Black tenants have less favorable terms and conditions, including security deposits, in rental agreements* (Ross & Turner, 2005)"). Italics added. See: Part IV, This chapter, Sects. 4.1.4–4.1.4.2.3 of this book.

[318] Du Bois, William E. B., *Black Reconstruction: An Essay Toward a History of the Part which Black Folk Played in the Attempt to Reconstruct Democracy in America*, 1860–1880, Black thought and culture, Harcourt, Brace, 1935; Foner, Eric, *Reconstruction: America's Unfinished Revolution*, 1863–1877, New York, HarperCollins, 1988.

[319] Freeman, Andrea, "Racism in the Credit Card Industry", *cit.*, p. 1071 ("*this type of consumer racism dates back to the Reconstruction era and reflects an unbroken chain of laws and policies cementing racial economic inequality*. Social norms and stereotypes make the *resulting inequality appear cultural and personal instead of systemic and structural*"). Italics added.

[320] It is crucially important to note, though, that the very fact that only certain types of behaviours are assessed and gauged by credit scores leads to the conclusion some borrowers are not scored at all. The overwhelming majority of consumers boast meagre, if any, credit files owing to the fact that the likelihood to access to the sort of financial services that actually report to the orthodox credit bureaus scattered across modern economies is exceedingly low, which, in turn, morphs them into credit invisible persons. See: Yu, Persis/McLaughlin, Jilian/Levy, Marina, "Big Data: A Big Disappointment

§§ Unsurprisingly, consumer racism that besieges the credit card industry has earned a phalanx of critics—i.e. an infantry of critics that made vitriolic remarks on biased algorithmic decision-making.[325] That oft-drawn contrast *we* (Blacks and Latinos) and *them* (White folks) is common, so too is the racial wedge that was purposefully created by a *systemic racism*[326] that never ceases to spur bubbles of disagreement between both ends of the spectrum of the information society.[327]

§§ But let us take a step back to shine a keen light on, and canvass the foundations upon which stands, the consumer racism that besets credit card industry and propels *Algorithmic Dictatorship*.

---

for Scoring Consumer Creditworthiness," *The National Consumer Law Center*, 2 (Mar. 14, 2014), available at: https://www.nclc.org/images/pdf/pr-reports/report-big-data.pdf; [https://www.perma.cc/W4SK-NXD5] (access: 21.12.2024).

[321] Selbst AD, Boyd D, Friedler SA, et al., "Fairness and abstraction in sociotechnical systems", *FAT*'19 Conference on Fairness, Accountability, and Transparency*, Atlanta, USA, 2018.

[322] See: Part V, Chap. 5, Sects. 5.1.2–5.1.6.2.1 of this book (on the thing-centred algorithmic decision-making propelled by a *Controllable* and *Interpretable* Machine Learning that weeds out *Algorithmic Dictatorship* and secures *Algorithmic Common Good*).

[323] Fontaine, C., "The myth of accountability: How data (mis)use is reinforcing the problems of public education", *Data and Society*, 2016. Available at: https://datasociety.net/output/the-myt hof-accountability-how-data-misuse-is-reinforcing-the-problems-of-public-education/ (accessed 9 September 2024).

[324] Havard, Cassandra Jones, "On The Take": The Black Box of Credit Scoring and Mortgage Discrimination", *Boston University Public Interest Law Journal*, Volume 20, 2011, pp. 241–247 (highlighting that credit scoring if unchecked is an intrinsic, encroached, deep-rooted form of racial discrimination akin to mortgage redlining).

[325] See on biased algorithmic decision-making: Chandler, Anupam, "The Racist Algorithm", *Michigan Law Review*, Volume 115, n.° 6, 2018, p. 1026 (on racist algorithms, noting that "the possibilities for discriminatory manipulation are legion"). But see: Altenburger, Kristen M./Ho, Daniel E., "When Algorithms Import Private Bias into Public Enforcement: The Promise and Limitations of Statistical Debiasing Solutions", *Journal of Institutional & Theoretical Economics*, Volume 175, 2019, pp. 97–98 (calls for a "debias predictive algorithms" to assuage racist and/or biased, doctored and bigoted algorithms nevertheless); Hamilton, Melissa, "The Biased Algorithm: Evidence of Disparate Impact on Hispanics", *American Criminal Law Review*, Volume 56, 2019, pp. 1553 and ff and passim; Dong et al., Qi, "Imbalanced deep learning by minority class incremental rectification, *IEEE Transactions on Pattern Analysis & Machine Intelligence*, Volume 41, 2019, p. 1367 (posit that "*most existing learning algorithms produce inductive bias (learning bias)* towards the frequent (majority) classes if training data are not balanced, *resulting in poor minority class recognition performance*"). Italics added; Wachter, S./Mittelstadt. B., "A right to Reasonable Inferences: Re-thinking Data Protection Law in the Age of Big Data and AI", *Columbia Business Law Review*, 2019, pp. 1 and ff and passim. Pearl, Judea, "Causal inference in statistics: An overview", *Statistics Surveys*, Volume 3, 2009, pp. 96–146.

[326] Feagin, J. R., *Systemic racism: a theory of oppression*, New York: Routledge, 2006. See also: Fiske, John, "Surveilling the City: Whiteness, the Black Man and Democratic Totalitarianism.", *Theory, Culture and Society*, 15 (2), 1998, pp. 67–88 (on the overhyped surveillance on black people as a byproduct of systemic racism).

[327] About information society: Van Dijk J., *The Deepening Divide: Inequality in the Information Society*, Thousand Oaks: Sage, 2005; Van Dijk J., "Datafication, dataism and dataveillance: Big data between scientific paradigm and ideology", *Surveillance & Society*, 12 (2), 2014, pp. 197–208.

§§ Which can be encapsulated in the following vexing question: how did the credit card industry get to the point that allotting everything to a bunch of *selected few* (White folks) while gainsaying everything to a cohort of *unwanted many* (Blacks and Latinos) is pegged as «business as usual»[328]? Put another way, how normalized is consumer racism in modern societies and how far back that grisly situation goes?[329]

§§ Scholars have been entertaining the idea according to which modern societies have been harbouring eerily malevolent attitudes towards the individuals affected (Blacks and Latinos).[330] As *digital racism*[331] seems to be taking hold, and gaining increasing traction, adroit measures ought to be taken to diffuse the threat of *Algorithmic Dictatorship* that lurks ahead.

§§ The racism in the credit card industry—a form of *Algorithmic Dictatorship*—falls seriously short of matching the fundamental tenets of fairness that should be the norm,[332] rather than the exception. The algorithmic injustice[333] that beleaguers/besets the credit card industry lends enhanced support to this assertion while giving also credence to an unpalatable «artificial unintelligence».[334]

§§ Moral uprightness is in dire need of being adopted as to wilting the current situation that generally works to the advantage of White folks. Which prompts the vexing questions: where, in history, did she (moral uprightness) lose its way? To thoroughly answer this pressing question, a deep dive into history is sorely needed.

§§ Fairness and discrimination do not bear surface similarity, nor are they amenable to be straddled, let alone conflated. Rather, they are polar opposites. We are better off keeping them separate. The forebears of racism were fully cognizant of that axiom.[335]

---

[328] Cohen, D. / Prusak, L., *Good company: How social capital makes organizations work*, Boston, Massachusetts, Harvard Business School Press, 2001.

[329] Havard, Cassandra Jones, "On The Take": The Black Box of Credit Scoring and Mortgage Discrimination", *Boston University Public Interest Law Journal*, Volume 20, 2011, pp. 241–247 (highlighting that credit scoring if unchecked is an intrinsic, encroached, deep-rooted form of racial discrimination akin to mortgage redlining).

[330] Guess, Teresa J., *The Social Construction of Whiteness: Racism by Intent, Racism by Consequence*, CRITICAL SOC, 2006, pp. 649, 650–51.

[331] Brydolf-Horwitz R., *Embodied and entangled: Slow violence and harm* via *digital technologies, Environment and Planning C: Politics and Space*, 2018.

[332] Gómez, Laura E., "Understanding Law and Race as Mutually Constitutive", *Journal of Scholarly Perspective*, 8, Fall 2012, 2012, pp. 47–51 (argues that "law and race co-construct each other").

[333] See: Ting-an Lin, "Democratizing AI" and the Concern of Algorithmic Injustice", *Philosophy and Technology*, Volume 37 (103), 2024, pp. 3–27. See also: Birhane, A., "Algorithmic injustice: A relational ethics approach", *Patterns*, 2 (2), 2021, pp. 1–9. Završnik, A. "Algorithmic justice: Algorithms and big data in criminal justice settings", *European Journal of Criminology*, 2019, passim.

[334] Broussard M., *Artificial Unintelligence: How Computers Misunderstand the World*, Cambridge, Massachusetts, MIT Press, 2018.

[335] Carson, J., *The measure of merit: Talents, intelligence, and inequality in the French and American republics, 1750–1940*, Princeton, NJ: Princeton University Press, 2006.

§§ For purposes here, the whiteness[336] of economy[337] requires delving into the history of race[338] in the United States of America.[339]

§§ The harbinger of both racial inequality and economic history of race was the onset of slavery[340] in modern societies,[341] which has established White supremacy[342]

---

[336] Garner, S., *Whiteness: an introduction*, Abingdon: Routledge, 2007; Ganley, T., "What's all this talk about whiteness?", *Dialogue*, 1 (2), 2003, pp. 12–30; de la Peña, C., "The history of technology, the resistance of archives, and the whiteness of race" *Technology and Culture*, 51 (4), 2010, pp. 919–937; Dihal, K., Enslaved minds: artificial intelligence, slavery, and revolt", *AI Narratives: A History of Imaginative Thinking about Intelligent Machines*, Stephen Cave, Kanta Dihal, and Sarah Dillon (Editors), 2020, pp. 189–212, Oxford: Oxford University Press; Dyer, R., White, London: Routledge, 1997; Fiske, John, "Surveilling the City: Whiteness, the Black Man and Democratic Totalitarianism.", *Theory, Culture and Society*, 15 (2), 1998, pp. 67–88. See also: Cole, Stephanie/Ring, Natalie et al. (Editors), *The Folly of Jim Crow: Rethinking the Segregated South (Walter Prescott Webb Memorial Lectures, published for the University of Texas at Arlington by Texas A&M University Press Book 43)*, Texas, Texas A&M University Press (April 3, 2012), 2012 ("*The studies in this collection incorporate important perspectives that have developed during the past two decades among scholars interested in gender and politics, the culture of resistance, and "the hegemonic function of 'whiteness.'"* By asking fresh questions and critically examining long-held beliefs, the new studies contained in *The Folly of Jim Crow* will, ironically, reinforce at least one of the key observations made in C. Vann Woodward's landmark 1955 study: *In its idiosyncratic, contradictory, and multifaceted development and application, the career of Jim Crow was, indeed, strange. Further, as these studies demonstrate—and as alluded to in the title—it is folly to attempt to locate the genesis of the South's institutional racial segregation in any single event, era, or policy. "Instead," as W. Fitzhugh Brundage notes in his introduction to the volume*, "formal segregation evolved through an untidy process of experimentation and adaptation"). Italics added.

[337] Lipsitz, George, *The Possessive Investment in Whiteness: How White People Profit from Identity Politics*, Philadelphia, Pennsylvania, Temple University Press; 1st edition (July 13, 2018), 2018, pp. 1–448 ("*George Lipsitz's classic book The Possessive Investment in Whiteness argues that public policy and private prejudice work together to create a possessive investment in whiteness that is responsible for the racialized hierarchies of our society*"). Italics added.

[338] Quadagno, Jill, *The Color of Welfare: How Racism Undermined the War on Poverty*, Oxford, Oxford University Press, 1994, pp. 1–272 ("*From Reconstruction to Lyndon Johnson and beyond, Quadagno reveals how American social policy has continually foundered on issues of race. Drawing on extensive primary research, Quadagno shows, for instance, how Roosevelt, in need of support from southern congressmen, excluded African Americans from the core programs of the Social Security Act. Turning to Lyndon Johnson's "unconditional war on poverty," she contends that though anti-poverty programs for job training, community action, health care, housing, and education have accomplished much, they have not been fully realized because they became inextricably intertwined with the civil rights movement of the 1960s, which triggered a white backlash*"). Italics added.

[339] Freeman, Andrea, "Racism in the Credit Card Industry", *cit.*, p. 1081.

[340] Sutch, Richard, " "Replication Data for: Appendix: The Value of the Slave Population, 1805–1860 (Table A.4 and A.1)," *Agricultural History*, Volume 62, 1988, 150–156.

[341] Freeman, Andrea, "Racism in the Credit Card Industry", *cit.*, p. 1081.

[342] DaViera, A. L./Uriostegui, M., Gottlieb/A./Onyeka, O, "Risk, race, and predictive policing: A critical race theory analysis of the strategic subject list", *American Journal of Community Psychology*, Volume 73, 2024, pp. 91–103; Benjamin, Ruha, *Race After Technology: Abolitionist Tools for the New Jim Code*, New York, Polity, 2019, pp. 1–172; Furman, E./Singh, A. K./Darko, N. A./Wilson, C. L., "Activism, intersectionality, and community psychology: The way in which Black Lives Matter Toronto helps us to examine white supremacy in Canada's LGBTQ community", *Community Psychology in Global Perspective*, Volume 4, Issue 2, 34–54.

while striking the fundamental rights of Black people to blows.[343] Slavery was an ominous portent of the gruelling future.[344] Lamentably, the loathsome effects of slavery still ripple forward.[345] Especially, albeit not exclusively, from the accumulation of wealth standpoint.[346]

§§ Slavery has accordingly cast a shady shadow on racialized people, thereby creating a customized connection between race,[347] class, crime hot spots,[348] income,[349] proneness to engage in criminal enterprises,[350] syndicates of organized crime,[351] gang violence,[352] and crime-ridden neighbourhoods[353] that still reverberates,[354] and ripples forward,[355] across generations.[356]

---

343 On whiteness: Frankenberg, Ruth (Ed.), *Displacing whiteness: essays in social and cultural criticism*, Durham, NC: Duke University Press, 1997; Frankenberg, Ruth, "Introduction: local whitenesses, localizing whiteness", *Displacing whiteness*, Ruth Frankenberg (Editor), Durham, NC: Duke University Press, 1997, pp. 1–33.

344 Roithmayr, Daria, *Reproducing Racism: How everyday choices lock in White Advantage*, New York, New York University Press, 2014, pp. 1–272 ("*Argues that racial inequality reproduces itself automatically over time because early unfair advantage for whites has paved the way for continuing advantage. This book is designed to change the way we think about racial inequality.* Long after the passage of civil rights laws, blacks and Latinos possess barely a nickel of wealth for every dollar that whites have. Why have we made so little progress? *Legal scholar Daria Roithmayr provocatively argues that racial inequality lives on because white advantage functions as a powerful self-reinforcing monopoly, reproducing itself automatically from generation to generation even in the absence of intentional discrimination.* Drawing on work in antitrust law and a range of other disciplines, Roithmayr brilliantly compares the dynamics of white advantage to the unfair tactics of giants like AT&T and Microsoft. With penetrating insight, Roithmayr *locates the engine of white monopoly in positive feedback loops that connect the dramatic disparity of Jim Crow to modern racial gaps in jobs, housing and education. Wealthy white neighborhoods fund public schools that then turn out wealthy white neighbors. Whites with lucrative jobs informally refer their friends, who refer their friends, and so on. Roithmayr concludes that racial inequality might now be locked in place, unless policymakers immediately take drastic steps to dismantle this oppressive system*"). Italics added. This book points out how White privilege is perpetuated throughout generations through residential segregation (*mortgage redlining*), abhorrent nepotism, and other bemoaning social practices that pester modern societies).

345 Smith, Matthew, Danny Yagan, Owen Zidar, and Eric Zwick, "Capitalists in the Twenty-First Century," *Quarterly Journal of Economics*, Volume 134, 2019, pp. 1675–1745.

346 Sutch, Richard, "The One Percent across Two Centuries: A Replication of Thomas Piketty's Data on the Concentration of Wealth in the United States," *Social Science History*, Volume 41, 2017, pp. 587–613.

347 Pager, Devah, *Marked: Race, Crime, and Finding Work in an Era of Mass Incarceration*, Chicago: University of Chicago Press, 2007.

348 Braga, Anthony A., and David L. Weisburd, *Policing Problem Places: Crime Hot Spots and Effective Prevention*, New York: Oxford University Press, 2010.

349 Gustafson, Kaaryn S, *Cheating Welfare: Public Assistance and the Criminalization of Poverty*, New York: NYU Press, 2011.

350 DaViera, A. L./Uriostegui, M., Gottlieb/A./Onyeka, O, "Risk, race, and predictive policing: A critical race theory analysis of the strategic subject list", *cit.*, pp. 91–103.

351 Papachristos, Andrew V., David M. Hureau, and Anthony A. Braga, "The Corner and the Crew: The Influence of Geography and Social Networks on Gang Violence", *American Sociological Review*, 78 (3), 2013, pp. 417–47.

§§ The rate and pace at which non-White are surveilled[357] and incarcerated[358] adds plausibility, and lends weight, to this sweeping claim,[359] as abundantly shown

[352] Quillian, Lincoln, and Devah Pager, "Black Neighbors, Higher Crime? The Role of Racial Stereotypes in Evaluations of Neighborhood Crime", *American Journal of Sociology*, 107 (3), 2001, 717–67.

[353] Brewer, R. M., & Heitzeg, N. A., "The racialization of crime and punishment: Criminal justice, Color-Blind racism, and the political economy of the prison industrial complex", *American Behavioral Scientist*, 51 (5), 2008, 625–644; Sampson, Robert J., and Dawn J. Bartusch, "Legal Cynicism and (Subcultural?) Tolerance of Deviance: The Neighborhood Context of Racial Differences", *Law and Society Review*, 32, 1998, pp. 777–804.

[354] Skogan, Wesley G., *Police and Community in Chicago: A Tale of Three Cities*, New York: Oxford University Press, 2006.

[355] Sherman, Lawrence W., Patrick R. Gartin, and Michael E. Buerger, "Hot Spots of Predatory Crime: Routine Activities and the Criminology of Place.", *Criminology*, 27 (1), 1989, pp. 27–55.

[356] Jacoby, S. F., Dong, B., Beard, J. H., Wiebe, D. J., & Morrison, C. N., "The enduring impact of historical and structural racism on urban violence in Philadelphia", *Social Science & Medicine*, 1982/2018, 199, 2018, pp. 87–95. See also: Packard, Jerald M., *American Nightmare: The History of Jim Crow*, Broadway, New York, St. Martin's Press; First Edition, 2002, pp. 1–304 (vii–viii) ("[A] *structure of exclusion and discrimination devised by white Americans to be employed principally against black Americans.... Its central purpose was to maintain a second-class social and economic status for blacks while upholding a first-class social and economic status for whites.... In the South, Jim Crow discrimination at its height existed not only by statute but by custom and racial 'etiquette,' and it was rigidly enforced by both the law enforcement agencies* and courts as well as by ordinary white citizens who were neither policemen nor judges but who often took the law into their own hands as though they were"). Italics added.

[357] Lyon, David, The Electronic Eye: *The Rise of Surveillance Society*. Minneapolis: University of Min nesota Press, 1994; Lyon, David, *Surveillance as Social Sorting: Privacy, Risk, and Digital Discrimination*. New York: Routledge, 2003. On the effects of total surveillance: Citron, Danielle Keats/Gray, David, "Addressing the Harm of Total Surveillance: A Reply to Professor Neil Richards", *Harvard Law Review*, Volume 126, 2013, pp. 262 and ff.

[358] Blockmon, Douglas E., *Slavery by Another Name: The Re-Enslavement of Black Americans from the Civil War to World War II*, United States of America, Doubleday, 2008, pp. 1–480 ("*Under laws enacted specifically to intimidate blacks, tens of thousands of African Americans were arbitrarily arrested, hit with outrageous fines, and charged for the costs of their own arrests. With no means to pay these ostensible "debts," prisoners were sold as forced laborers to coal mines, lumber camps, brickyards, railroads, quarries, and farm plantations. Thousands of other African Americans were simply seized by southern landowners and compelled into years of involuntary servitude. Government officials leased falsely imprisoned blacks to small-town entrepreneurs, provincial farmers, and dozens of corporations—including U.S. Steel—looking for cheap and abundant labor*. Armies of "free" black men labored without compensation, were repeatedly bought and sold, and were forced through beatings and physical torture to do the bidding of white masters for decades after the official abolition of American slavery. *The neoslavery system exploited legal loopholes and federal policies that discouraged prosecution of whites for continuing to hold black workers against their wills. As it poured millions of dollars into southern government treasuries, the new slavery also became a key instrument in the terrorization of African Americans seeking full participation in the U.S. political system*"). Italics added.

[359] Travis, Jeremy, Bruce Western, and Steve Redburn (Eds.), *Growth of Incarceration in the United States: Exploring Causes and Consequences*, Washington, DC: National Academy of Science, 2014.

in previous sections of this book.[360] Note, though, that slavery accomplished much more than that.[361]

§§ Slavery has spawned a *systemic racism*[362] which, in turn, has created a racial wedge according to which race stereotypes[363] are permanent[364] and subject to relief only, and if, they strategically converge with White interests.[365] It should not strike anyone as odd that *Algorithmic Dictatorship* tagged along. So too did a colossal racial wedge that threatens to cripple the foundations upon which stands one of the beacons of «justice as fairness»[366]: Rule of Law.[367,368]

---

360 See Part III, Chap. 3, Sects. 3.1–3.1.4. See: Part IV, This chapter, Sects. 4.1.10.1–4.1.10.6 of this book (on biased algorithmic risk assessment in criminal procedure law settings, with a sharper focus on COMPAS). See: Part IV, This chapter, Sects. 4.1.1–4.1.1.1 of this book (on biased predictive policing).

361 Blockmon, Douglas E., *Slavery by Another Name: The Re-Enslavement of Black Americans from the Civil War to World War II*, United States of America, Doubleday, 2008, pp. 1–480 ("*Based on a vast record of original documents and personal narratives, Slavery by Another Name unearths the lost stories of slaves and their descendants who journeyed into freedom after the Emancipation Proclamation and then back into the shadow of involuntary servitude.* It also reveals the stories of those who fought unsuccessfully against the re-emergence of human labor trafficking, the modern companies that profited most from neoslavery, and the system's final demise in the 1940s, partly due to fears of enemy propaganda about American racial abuse at the beginning of World War II.

Slavery by Another Name is a moving, sobering account of a little-known crime against African Americans, and the insidious legacy of racism that reverberates today"). Italics added.

362 Horton, James Oliver/Horton, Lois E., *Slavery and the Making of America*, Oxford, Oxford University Press, 2006, pp. 1–256 ("*The history of slavery is central to understanding the history of the United States. Slavery and the Making of America offers a richly illustrated, vividly written history that illuminates the human side of this inhumane institution, presenting it largely through stories of the slaves themselves.* Readers will discover a wide ranging and sharply nuanced look at American slavery, from the first Africans brought to British colonies in the early seventeenth century to the end of Reconstruction. The authors document the horrors of slavery, particularly in the deep South, and describe the slaves' valiant struggles to free themselves from bondage. There are dramatic tales of escape by slaves such as William and Ellen Craft and Dred Scott's doomed attempt to win his freedom through the Supreme Court. We see how slavery engendered violence in our nation, from bloody confrontations that broke out in American cities over fugitive slaves, to the cataclysm of the Civil War. The book is also filled with stories of remarkable African Americans like Sergeant William H. Carney, who won the Congressional Medal of Honor for his bravery at the crucial assault on Fort Wagner during the Civil War, and Benjamin "Pap" Singleton, a former slave who led freed African Americans to a new life on the American frontier. *Filled with absorbing and inspirational accounts highlighted by more than one hundred pictures and illustrations, Slavery and the Making of America is a gripping account of the struggles of African Americans against the iniquity of slavery*"). Italics added.

363 Okeke, N. A., Howard, L. C., Kurtz-Costes, B., & Rowley, S. J., "Academic race stereotypes, academic self-concept, and racial centrality in African American youth", *Journal of Black Psychology*, 35 (3), 2009, pp. 366–387.

364 Freeman, Andrea, "Racism in the Credit Card Industry", *cit.*, p. 1081.

365 Bell, Derrick A., Jr., "Brown v. Board of Education & the Interest-Convergence Dilemma", *Harvard Law Review*, Volume 93, 1980, pp. 518, 522–30; Freeman, Andrea, "Racism in the Credit Card Industry", *cit.*, passim.

366 Rawls explains that an *overlapping consensus* on *principles of justice* can occur despite «considerable differences in citizens' conceptions of justice provided that these conceptions lead to similar political judgments. The groups are able to achieve this consensus in part by refraining

§§ Few things can lurch Rule of Law[369] into crisis faster than *Algorithmic Dictatorship* that automatically allots everything to a *selected few* (White folks) while snubbing everything to the *unwanted many* (racialised communities). Artificial

---

from political/public disputes over fundamental (e.g. metaphysical) arguments regarding religion and philosophy. Rawls elaborates that the existence of an overlapping consensus on conceptions of justice among major social groups holding differing—yet reasonable—comprehensive doctrines is a necessary and distinctive characteristic of political liberalism. Rawls also explains that the *overlapping consensus* on *principles of justice* is itself a *moral conception* and is supported by *moral reasoning*—although the fundamental grounds of this support may differ for each of the various groups holding disparate comprehensive doctrines, and these lines of reasoning may also differ from the public reasons provided for supporting the principles. These latter features distinguish his idea of an *overlapping consensus* from a mere *modus vivendi*, which is a *strategic agreement entered into for pragmatic purposes*, and therefore potentially unprincipled and unstable. The overlapping consensus could in sum be said to "depend, in effect, on there being a morally significant core of commitments common to the 'reasonable' fragment of each of the main comprehensive doctrines in the community»; Michael Donnan, *Rawl's Notion of Overlapping Consensus* (2014): 1 ff; see also John Rawls, *A Theory of Justice*, 2nd edition, Cambridge, United States of America, Belknap Press: An Imprint of Harvard University Press, (1999): 1–540 («Rawls aims to express an essential part of the common core of the democratic tradition-*justice as fairness*-and to provide an alternative to utilitarianism, which had dominated the Anglo-Saxon tradition of political thought since the nineteenth century. Rawls substitutes the ideal of the social contract as a more satisfactory account of the basic rights and liberties of citizens as free and equal persons. "Each person," writes Rawls, "*possesses an inviolability founded on justice that even the welfare of society as a whole cannot override*»); John Rawls, *Political Liberalism*, Expanded version, Columbia Classics of Philosophy, New York City, Columbia University Press, (2005): 1–525 (This book continues and revises the ideas of justice as fairness that John Rawls presented in *A Theory of Justice* but changes its philosophical interpretation in a fundamental way. «That previous work assumed what Rawls calls a "*well-ordered society,*" *one that is stable and relatively homogeneous in its basic moral beliefs and in which there is broad agreement about what constitutes the good life.* Yet in modern democratic society a plurality of incompatible and irreconcilable doctrines—religious, philosophical, and moral—coexist within the framework of democratic institutions. Recognizing this as a permanent condition of democracy, Rawls asks how a stable and just society of free and equal citizens can live in concord when divided by reasonable but incompatible doctrines?»). See also: John Rawls, "The Idea of an Overlapping Consensus.", *Oxford Journal of Legal Studies*, 7 (1), (1987): 1–25 (italics added).

[367] See: Part V, Chap. 5, Sect. 5.1.1.1 of this book (on the central tenets of Rule of Law that lends itself to a beacon of justice amidst the sepulchral darkness that is about to take hold). See: Part V, Chap. 5, Sect. 5.1.1.2 of this book (on the central tenets of Procedural Rule of Law that lends itself to a lighthouse of justice that allows citizens to challenge the pearls of algorithmic wisdom in a court of law). Regrettably, the Rule of Law is backsliding worldwide. Especially in Central and Eastern Europe. See: Avbelj, Matej, "The Rule of Law, Comprehensive Doctrines, Overlapping Consensus, and the Future of Europe", *Ratio Juris*, Volume 36, Issue 3, September, 2023, pp. 242–258. The Rule of Law is not a «one size fits all» format nonetheless. But see: Chesterman, Simon, "An International Rule of Law", *The American Journal of Comparative Law*, Volume 56, 2008, pp. 331–362 (on the thrust to grasp (?) a catch-all International Rule of Law). See: Peari, Sagi, "Better Law as a Better Outcome", *The American Journal of Comparative Law*, Volume 63, Issue 1, 2015, pp. 155–195 (156) (on Leflar's stance on «better rule of law»). For the purposes of this piece, Rule of Law amounts to a lighthouse of procedural fairness to which citizens, regardless of where they are, resort to upon gaining access to a given system of administration of criminal justice. Whilst further utterances on the fabric of Rule of Law fall well outside the scope and breadth of this book, one must not be oblivious of the fact that the thrust to Deglobalizing Rule of Law is underway. See: Bussani, Mauro, "Deglobalizing Rule of Law and Democracy: Hunting Down

Intelligence-embedded technologies have only flared up this abhorrent situation,[370] as extensively broached in the following sections of this book.

§§ More to the point, the yawning wealth gap between White[371] folks[372] and racialised[373] communities[374] (Blacks and Latinos)[375] is an outgrowth/offspring of

---

Rhetoric Through Comparative Law", *The American Journal of Comparative Law*, Volume 67, 2019, pp. 701–744 (701) (contending that the thrust to Deglobalizing Rule of Law is interwoven with thrust to take heed of «well-known differences that run through cultures and traditions». In spite of which, «the West has never stopped trying to export its own law into the rest of the world»). Unsurprisingly, there have been educated calls to take heed of the pinpointed cultural and legal differences by, in the case of China, allow for a «Socialist Rule of Law». See: Chinese Common Law Guiding Cases, *Harvard Law Review*, Volume 129, 2016, p. 2213. We will come back to this issue further down is this paper. More on this later.

368 See: Part V, Chap. 5, Sect. 5.1.1.1 of this book (on the central tenets of Rule of Law that lends itself to a beacon of justice amidst the sepulchral darkness that is about to take hold). See: Part V, Chap. 5, Sect. 5.1.1.2 of this book (on the central tenets of Procedural Rule of Law that lends itself to a lighthouse of justice that allows citizens to challenge the pearls of algorithmic wisdom in a court of law). Regrettably, the Rule of Law is backsliding worldwide. Especially in Central and Eastern Europe. See: Avbelj, Matej, "The Rule of Law, Comprehensive Doctrines, Overlapping Consensus, and the Future of Europe", *Ratio Juris*, Volume 36, Issue 3, September, 2023, pp. 242–258. The Rule of Law is not a «one size fits all» format nonetheless. But see: Chesterman, Simon, "An International Rule of Law", *The American Journal of Comparative Law*, Volume 56, 2008, pp. 331–362 (on the thrust to grasp (?) a catch-all International Rule of Law). See: Peari, Sagi, "Better Law as a Better Outcome", *The American Journal of Comparative Law*, Volume 63, Issue 1, 2015, pp. 155–195 (156) (on Leflar's stance on «better rule of law»). For the purposes of this piece, Rule of Law amounts to a lighthouse of procedural fairness to which citizens, regardless of where they are, resort to upon gaining access to a given system of administration of criminal justice. Whilst further utterances on the fabric of Rule of Law fall well outside the scope and breadth of this book, one must not be oblivious of the fact that the thrust to Deglobalizing Rule of Law is underway. See: Bussani, Mauro, "Deglobalizing Rule of Law and Democracy: Hunting Down Rhetoric Through Comparative Law", *The American Journal of Comparative Law*, Volume 67, 2019, pp. 701–744 (701) (contending that the thrust to Deglobalizing Rule of Law is interwoven with thrust to take heed of «well-known differences that run through cultures and traditions». In spite of which, «the West has never stopped trying to export its own law into the rest of the world»). Unsurprisingly, there have been educated calls to take heed of the pinpointed cultural and legal differences by, in the case of China, allow for a «Socialist Rule of Law». See: Chinese Common Law Guiding Cases, *Harvard Law Review*, Volume 129, 2016, p. 2213. We will come back to this issue further down is this paper. More on this later.

369 Dino, Dylan, "The Rule of Law and the Rule of Empire: A. V. Dicey in Imperial Context", *The Modern Law Review*, Volume 81, Issue 5, 2018, pp. 739–764 (739–741) (highlights that "*the idea of the rule of law, more ubiquitous globally than ever before*, owes a lasting debt to the work of Victorian legal theorist A.V. Dicey (…) To Dicey we owe not only the phrase "the rule of law" but also one of the most influential expositions. Dicey's account of the rule of law emphasised three elements: first, government through legal norms and procedures rather than unrestrained discretion; *second, formal equality before the law; and third, the establishment of individual rights through gradual, bottom-up (common-law) development*"). Italics added. See: Raz, Joseph, "The Rule of Law and its Virtue", *The Authority of Law: Essays on Law and Morality*. Oxford: Clarendon Press, 1979, pp. 210–214 (on the quintessential value of Rule of Law); Waldron, Jeremy, "The Rule of Law and the Importance of Procedure", *New York Public Law and Legal Theory*, 2010, p. 4 (notes that "the Rule of Law is violated when due attention is not paid to these procedural matters or when the institutions that are supposed to embody this procedure are undermined or interfered with". Further down this author would admit that there are some substantive dimensions of Rule of Law, such as respect for right for property and presumption of liberty and so forth); Taekema,

a social construct according to which White[376] privilege[377] should be perpetuated[378] while racialized communities should permanently grapple with poverty,[379]

Sanne, "The Procedural Rule of Law: Examining Waldron's Argument on Dignity and Agency", *Jahrbuch für Recht und Ethik*, Band 21, 2013, pp. 133 ff (contends that "Waldron's understanding of the Rule of Law as procedural which demands the opportunity for individuals to contest legal decisions in the formalized processes of courts and tribunals"); Cass, Ronald A., *The Rule of Law in America*. Baltimore, Maryland: The Johns Hopkins University Press, 2001, p. 17 (noting that a "central element of the Rule of law, constraint from external authority...helps assure that the process of government, *rather than the predilections of the individual decision-maker*") Italics added. See: Part V, Chap. 5, Sect. 5.1.1.1 of this book (on the central tenets of Rule of Law that lends itself to a beacon of justice amidst the sepulchral darkness that is about to take hold). See: Part V, Chap. 5, Sect. 5.1.1.2 of this book (on the central tenets of Procedural Rule of Law that lends itself to a lighthouse of justice that allows citizens to challenge the pearls of algorithmic wisdom in a court of law).

[370] Which is why the onset of the age of Artificial Intelligence will put the Rule of Law to the test like never before. Recall, the Rule of Law is a functional barrier—aimed at clamping down a host of unlawful deeds undertaken by those in power—that must not be teared apart or criminal procedure law will be otherwise despoiled from its intrinsic validity and vitality. See: Raz, Joseph, "The Rule of Law and its Virtue", *The Authority of Law: Essays on Law and Morality, cit.*, p. 224 (asserts adamantly that the Rule of Law is aimed at cushioning the hazards of abuse perpetrated by those in power. In this vein, Raz contends that "the law inevitably creates a great danger of arbitrary power—the Rule of Law is designed to minimize the danger created by the law itself...*Thus the (R)ule of (L)aw is designed to minimize the danger created by law itself...Thus the (R)ule of (L)aw is a negative virtue...the evil which is avoided is evil which could only have been caused by the law itself*"). Italics added; McAfee, Andrew/Brynjolfsson, *Machine, Platform, Crowd: Harnessing our Digital Future*, London: Brilliance Audio; Unabridged edition, 2017 (pore over a myriad of automatic biases displayed by artificial intelligence). See: Part V, Chap. 5, Sect. 5.1.1.1 of this book (on the central tenets of Rule of Law that lends itself to a beacon of justice amidst the sepulchral darkness that is about to take hold). See: Part V, Chap. 5, Sect. 5.1.1.2 of this book (on the central tenets of Procedural Rule of Law that lends itself to a lighthouse of justice that allows citizens to challenge the pearls of algorithmic wisdom in a court of law).

[371] Lipsitz, George, *The Possessive Investment in Whiteness: How White People Profit from Identity Politics*, Philadelphia, Pennsylvania, Temple University Press; 1st edition (July 13, 2018), 2018, pp. 1–448 ("*George Lipsitz's classic book The Possessive Investment in Whiteness argues that public policy and private prejudice work together to create a possessive investment in whiteness that is responsible for the racialized hierarchies of our society*"). Italics added. See also: Cole, Stephanie/Ring, Natalie et al. (Editors), *The Folly of Jim Crow: Rethinking the Segregated South (Walter Prescott Webb Memorial Lectures, published for the University of Texas at Arlington by Texas A&M University Press Book 43)*, Texas, Texas A&M University Press (April 3, 2012), 2012 ("*The studies in this collection incorporate important perspectives that have developed during the past two decades among scholars interested in gender and politics, the culture of resistance, and "the hegemonic function of 'whiteness.'*" By asking fresh questions and critically examining long-held beliefs, the new studies contained in *The Folly of Jim Crow* will, ironically, reinforce at least one of the key observations made in C. Vann Woodward's landmark 1955 study: *In its idiosyncratic, contradictory, and multifaceted development and application, the career of Jim Crow was, indeed, strange. Further, as these studies demonstrate—and as alluded to in the title—it is folly to attempt to locate the genesis of the South's institutional racial segregation in any single event, era, or policy. "Instead," as W. Fitzhugh Brundage notes in his introduction to the volume*, "formal segregation evolved through an untidy process of experimentation and adaptation"). Italics added.

[372] Kroeger, Teresa, and Graham Wright, "Entrepreneurship and the Racial Wealth Gap: The Impact of Entrepreneurial Success or Failure on the Wealth Mobility of Black and White Families," *Journal of Economics, Race, and Policy*, Volume 4, 2021, 183–195.

thereby collapsing or fading into social[380] irrelevance,[381] hastening their sought-after demise.[382] Unfairness—devilishly harmful unfairness[383]—lies at its heart.[384]

---

373 Kermani, Amir, and Francis Wong, "Racial Disparities in Housing Returns," NBER Working Paper no. 29306, 2021.

374 Hubmer, Joachim, Per Krusell, and Anthony A. Smith, Jr., "Sources of US Wealth Inequality: Past, Present, and Future," *NBER Macroeconomics Annual 2020*, Volume 35, 2021, pp. 391–455.

375 Haines, Michael R., *Historical, Demographic, Economic, and Social Data: The United States, 1790–2002*, Inter-university Consortium for Political and Social Research, 2010.

376 On whiteness: Frankenberg, Ruth (Ed.), *Displacing whiteness: essays in social and cultural criticism*, Durham, NC: Duke University Press, 1997; Frankenberg, Ruth, "Introduction: local whitenesses, localizing whiteness", *Displacing whiteness*, Ruth Frankenberg (Editor), Durham, NC: Duke University Press, 1997, pp. 1–33.

377 DaViera, A. L./Uriostegui, M., Gottlieb/A./Onyeka, O, "Risk, race, and predictive policing: A critical race theory analysis of the strategic subject list", *American Journal of Community Psychology*, Volume 73, 2024, pp. 91–103; Benjamin, Ruha, *Race After Technology: Abolitionist Tools for the New Jim Code*, New York, Polity, 2019, pp. 1–172; Furman, E./Singh, A. K./Darko, N. A./Wilson, C. L., "Activism, intersectionality, and community psychology: The way in which Black Lives Matter Toronto helps us to examine white supremacy in Canada's LGBTQ community", *Community Psychology in Global Perspective*, Volume 4, Issue 2, 34–54.

378 Freeman, Andrea, "Racism in the Credit Card Industry", *cit.*, p. 1081.

379 Gilliom, John, *Overseers of the Poor: Surveillance, Resistance, and the Limits of Privacy*, Chicago: University of Chicago Press, 2001.

380 Quadagno, Jill, *The Color of Welfare: How Racism Undermined the War on Poverty*, Oxford, Oxford University Press, 1994, pp. 1–272 ("*From Reconstruction to Lyndon Johnson and beyond, Quadagno reveals how American social policy has continually foundered on issues of race. Drawing on extensive primary research, Quadagno shows, for instance, how Roosevelt, in need of support from southern congressmen, excluded African Americans from the core programs of the Social Security Act. Turning to Lyndon Johnson's "unconditional war on poverty," she contends that though anti-poverty programs for job training, community action, health care, housing, and education have accomplished much, they have not been fully realized because they became inextricably intertwined with the civil rights movement of the 1960s, which triggered a white backlash*"). Italics added.

381 Which take shape under the form of social cleavages spawned by a technology that fondly includes the rich and outrightly excludes the poor, thereby compounding social issues with which modern have been grappling/tussling/scuffling/floundering since immemorial times. Social cleavages—a cloak under which mounting social outcry is often wrapped—that threaten to crumble the foundations upon which stands the linchpin of western societies. See in general: Abramsky, Sasha, *Jumping at Shadows: The Triumph of Fear and the End of the American Dream*. New York: Bold Type Books, 2017, pp. 1–272 (passim).

382 See: Eubanks, Virginia, *Automating Inequality: How High-Tech Tools Profile, Police and Punish the Poor*. New York: St. Martin's Press, 2018, 1–272 (1 ff and passim) (coining the expression «automating inequality» to vividly portray the downsides of using high-technology to compound the yawning gap between rich and poor against the backdrop of biased algorithms). Soss, Joe, Richard C. Fording, and Sanford F. Schram, *Disciplining the Poor: Neoliberal Paternalism and the Persistent Power of Race*. Chicago: University of Chicago Press, 2011.

383 On fairness: Oren Bracha & Frank Pasquale, "Federal Search Commission? Access, Fairness, and Accountability in the Law of Search", *Cornell Law Review*, Volume 93, 2008, 1149–1159 ("this structures [sic] results in a bottom-up filtration system. At the lowest level, a large number of speakers receive relatively broad exposure within local communities likely composed of individuals

§§ More to the point, law is a tool that serves the pleasure of White privilege[385] insofar is a device suitably tailored to define race[386] and briskly enforce[387] racial boundaries.[388]

§§ In many ways, *system racism* is the encapsulation of the of-trotted out dichotomy between *censory jurisprudence* (the rationale behind the creation of laws from a racial point of view) and *expository jurisprudence* (what law should do to stymie the gargantuan racial wedge between Blacks and Whites from the enforcement of law standpoint). Artificial Intelligence-embedded technologies has greatly worsened this gruesome situation[389] insofar flared up the structural disadvantage[390]

---

with high-intensity interest or expertise. Speakers who gain salience at the lower levels may gradually gain recognition in higher-order clusters and eventually reach general visibility").

[384] Keister, Lisa A., "Race, Family Structure, and Wealth: The Effect of Childhood Family on Adult Asset Ownership," *Sociological Perspectives*, Volume 47, 2004, 161–187.

[385] I do not agree with the positivist approach to law championed by Professor H.L. Hart, which has failed to take into due account the intrinsic linkage between law and moral. Something that Kant, Dworkin, Raz, Fuller, and Alexy have managed to do so. Yet, Professor H. L. Hart deftly asserts that «*laws may be law but too evil to be obeyed*. This is a moral condemnation which everyone can understand and it makes an immediate and obvious claim to moral attention. If, on the other hand, we formulate our objection as an assertion that these evil things are not law, here is an assertion which many people do not believe, and if they are disposed to consider it at all, it would seem to raise a whole host philosophical issues before it can be solves», H. L. Hart, "Positivism and the Separation of Law and Morals", *Harvard Law Review*, 71 (4) 1958: 598 ff (this amounts to a glimpse of the incorporation of the moral concept of law in Hart's conception of law) (italics added).

[386] Gómez, Laura E., "Understanding Law and Race as Mutually Constitutive", *Journal of Scholarly Perspective*, 8, Fall 2012, 2012, pp. 47–51 (argues that "law and race co-construct each other").

[387] Packard, Jerald M., *American Nightmare: The History of Jim Crow*, Broadway, New York, St. Martin's Press; First Edition, 2002, pp. 1–304 (vii–viii) ("[A*] structure of exclusion and discrimination devised by white Americans to be employed principally against black Americans.... Its central purpose was to maintain a second-class social and economic status for blacks while upholding a first-class social and economic status for whites.... In the South, Jim Crow discrimination at its height existed not only by statute but by custom and racial 'etiquette,' and it was rigidly enforced by both the law enforcement agencies* and courts as well as by ordinary white citizens who were neither policemen nor judges but who often took the law into their own hands as though they were"). Italics added.

[388] Freeman, Andrea, "Racism in the Credit Card Industry", *cit.*, p. 1081.

[389] The inception of the era of omnipotent Artificial Intelligence is about to revive the overriding importance of the dichotomy between *censory jurisprudence* (what law actually is and/or looks like) and *expository jurisprudence* (what law should do and/or be to halt the weaponization of Artificial Intelligence by those in power). This dyad has been suitably tailored by Jeremy Bentham. See: Bentham, Jeremy, *An Introduction to the Principles of Morals and Legislation*. London: Great Books in Philosophy, Prometheus Books, 1988, 1–352 (293–294) (Jeremy Bentham's work on "the Principles of Morals and Legislation emerges from its historic roots in hedonism and teleology as a scientific attempt to assess the moral content of human action by focusing on its results or consequences. Proceeding from the assumption that human beings desire pleasure (and avoid pain), Bentham's unique perspective, known as utilitarianism, is used to construct a fascinating calculus for determining which action to perform when confronted with situations requiring moral decision-making the goal of which is to arrive at the "*greatest happiness of the greatest number*." Toward this end, he endeavours to delineate the sources and kinds of pleasure and pain and how they can be measured when assessing one's moral options. Bentham supports his arguments with discussions

that has been besetting members of racialized communities for centuries. More on this later.

§§ For purposes here, the gulf, or the yawning[391] wealth[392] gap,[393] between Blacks[394] and Whites,[395] which has yielded rich scholarship,[396] is a byproduct of

---

of intentionality, consciousness, motives, and dispositions"). This is not to say that we embrace Bentham's utilitarianism—so harshly criticized in Hart's *Concept of Law*—or the claim according to which an understanding of the Rule of Law presupposes a good understanding of law in a given country or community. Yet, there is a high degree of academic accuracy in Bentham's distinction when it comes to differentiating *expository jurisprudence—explaining what law is*—and *censorial jurisprudence—explaining what law ought to be.* As for effective access to justice and the procedural approach to the Rule of Law in the purview of criminal procedure law, there is markedly clear line between what legal officials are—purveyors of procedural fairness—and what an effective access to justice ought to be—a place whereby social inequalities caused by the era of artificial intelligence are to be buffered (criminal procedure law settings) in a swift, prompt, and streamlined manner. Or irreparable damages may otherwise occur.

[390] See: Barocas, Solon/Selbst, Andrew, "Big Data's Disparate Impact", *California Law Review*, Volume 104, pp. 2016, p. 691 (highlighting the worrisome, and gruesome, issue of "structural disadvantage" with which racialized communities have been tussling for centuries). See also: Powell, Richard/Porter, Jeremy, "Redlining, Concentrated Disadvantage and Crime: The Effects of Discriminatory Government Policies on Violent Crime", *American Journal of Criminal Justice*, Volume 48, 2023, pp. 1132–1156 ("*Redlining and other discriminatory government policies enacted during the first half of the Twentieth Century have had long-lasting negative effects on neighborhoods, especially those inhabited by people of color. This study attempts to link the practice of redlining to current-day indicators of neighborhood concentrated disadvantage and violent crime using spatio-temporal data from Chicago* (…) *In addition, it seeks to determine whether redlining was associated with violent crime, and if that association was mediated by redlining's effect on concentrated disadvantage. The results indicate that redlining was associated with increases in both concentrated disadvantage and violent crime, and that redlining's relationship with violent crime was, indeed, partially mediated by its relationship with concentrated disadvantage*"). Italics added. See also: Gandy, Oscar H., *Coming to Terms with Chance: Engaging Rational Discrimination and Cumulative Disadvantage*, Farnham, UK: Ashgate Publishing, 2009.

[391] Derenoncourt, Ellora/Kim, Chi Hyun/Kuhn, Moritz/Schularik, Moritz, "The Wealth of Two Nations: The U.S. Racial Wealth Gap, 1860–2020", *The Quarterly Journal of Economics*, Volume 139, Issue 2, 2024, p. 741 ("A large class of commonly discussed policies for reducing racial wealth inequality seeks to reduce gaps in income, savings, and capital gains. These include policies that encourage financial diversification or stock equity holdings among Black households; policies aimed at financial literacy and retirement or savings behavior; or policies aimed at improving educational and labor market outcomes of Black Americans through improved school quality or reductions in discrimination. *Yet on a realistic note, our simulation in Section IV.A shows that even if wealth accumulation conditions had been equal since 1870, the wealth gap would still be 3 to 1 today, and full convergence would be more than 200 years away. Put differently: to close the racial wealth gap in the immediate term* via *flow parameters, Black Americans would need a substantial positive lead over whites, not "just" more equality*"). Italics added.

[392] Gittleman, Maury, and Edward N. Wolff, "Racial Differences in Patterns of Wealth Accumulation," *Journal of Human Resources*, Volume 39, 2004, pp. 193–227.

[393] But see: Gatewood, Willard B., "Aristocrats of Color: South and North the Black Elite, 1880–1920," *Journal of Southern History*, Volume 54, 1988, pp. 3–20.

a long-haul span of time against the backdrop of which discriminatory laws[397] and policies[398] created racial inequalities[399] that woven into the fabric[400] of modern societies.[401]

---

394 Francis, Dania V., Darrick Hamilton, Thomas W. Mitchell, Nathan A. Rosenberg, and Bryce Wilson Stucki, "Black Land Loss: 1920–1997," *AEA Papers and Proceedings*, Volume 112, 2022, pp. 38 and ff and passim.

395 Gittleman, Maury, and Edward N. Wolff, "Racial Differences in Patterns of Wealth Accumulation," *Journal of Human Resources*, Volume 39, 2004, pp. 193–227.

396 Darity, William A., Jr., and A. Kirsten Mullen, *From Here to Equality: Reparations for Black Americans in the Twenty-First Century*, Chapel Hill: University of North Carolina Press, 2020; DeCanio, Stephen J., "Accumulation and Discrimination in the Postbellum South," *Explorations in Economic History*, Volume 16, 1979, 182–206; Derenoncourt, Ellora, Chi Hyun Kim, Moritz Kuhn, and Moritz Schularick, "Replication Data for: 'Wealth of Two Nations: The U.S. Racial Wealth Gap, 1860–2020", *Harvard Dataverse*, 2023, Derenoncourt, Ellora, Chi Hyun Kim, Moritz Kuhn, and Moritz Schularick, "Unemployment Risk, Portfolio Choice, and the Racial Wealth Gap," *Working Paper*, 2023; Derenoncourt, Ellora, and Claire Montialoux, "Minimum Wages and Racial Inequality", *The Quarterly Journal of Economics*, Volume 136, 2021, pp. 169–228; Donohue, John J., and James Heckman, "Continuous Versus Episodic Change: The Impact of Civil Rights Policy on the Economic Status of Blacks," *Journal of Economic Literature*, Volume 29, 1991, 1603–1643; Dray, Sacha, Camille Landais, and Stefanie Stantcheva, "Wealth and Property Taxation in the United States," NBER Working Paper no. 31080, 2023; Du Bois, William E. B., "The Negro Landholder of Georgia," *Bulletin of the United States Department of Labor*, Volume 6, 1901, pp. 647–777.

397 Katznelson, Ira, *When Affirmative Action Was White: An Untold History of Racial Inequality in Twentieth-Century America*, New York, W. W. Norton & Company; Reprint edition (August 17, 2006), 2006, pp. 1–272 ("In this "penetrating new analysis" (*New York Times Book Review*) *Ira Katznelson fundamentally recasts our understanding of twentieth-century American history and demonstrates that all the key programs passed during the New Deal and Fair Deal era of the 1930s and 1940s were created in a deeply discriminatory manner.* Through mechanisms designed by Southern Democrats that specifically excluded maids and farm workers, the gap between blacks and whites actually widened despite postwar prosperity. In the words of noted historian Eric Foner, "Katznelson's incisive book should change the terms of debate about affirmative action, and about the last seventy years of American history". This book parses the impact of several racially motivated laws—Social Security Act, G: I. Bill, and labour laws implementing unemployment stipends, minimum wages, and union protection—in the history of United States of America).

398 Freeman, Andrea, "Racism in the Credit Card Industry", *cit.*, p. 1081.

399 Oliver, Melvin L./Thomas M. Shapiro (Editors), *Black Wealth / White Wealth: A New Perspective on Racial Inequality*, 2nd edition, London, Routledge, 2006, pp. 1–360 ("The award-winning *Black Wealth / White Wealth* offers a powerful portrait of racial inequality based on an analysis of private wealth. *Melvin Oliver and Thomas Shapiro's groundbreaking research analyzes wealth—total assets and debts rather than income alone—to uncover deep and persistent racial inequality in America,* and they show how public policies have failed to redress the problem. First published in 1995, *Black Wealth / White Wealth* is considered a classic exploration of race and inequality. *It provided, for the first time, systematic empirical evidence that explained the racial inequality gap between blacks and whites. The Tenth Anniversary edition contains two entirely new and substantive chapters.* These chapters look at the continuing issues of wealth and inequality in America and the new policies that have been launched in the past ten years. Some have been progressive while others only recreate inequality—for example the proposal to eliminate the estate tax. *Compelling and also informative, Black Wealth / White Wealth is not just pioneering research. It is also a powerful counterpoint to arguments against affirmative action and a direct challenge to current social welfare policies that are tilted towards the wealthy*") (This miscellany of essays canvasses the foundations of the

§§ *Systemic racism*—recall, systemic racism has laid the groundwork for insidious racial inequalities[402] which, in turn, spawned both racial and wealth divides[403] between Blacks and Whites[404] conducive to White[405] racial[406] privilege[407]—harkens back to the point in history when enslaved Africans[408] replaced White servants as the

---

behemoth wealth gap between Blacks and Whites in the United States of America and the extent to which has evolved and presently accounts for deeply entrenched racial inequality that policies focused on both income and taxation have appallingly failed to thoroughly address).

[400] Menasce, Juliana Horowitz/Brown, Anna/Cox, Kiana, "Views of Racial Inequality", *Pew Research Center*, April 9, 2019, 2919, available at: https://www.pewresearch.org/social-trends/2019/04/09/views-of-racial-inequality/ (access: 2.12.2024) ("*more than four-in-ten Americans say the country still has work to do to give black people equal rights with whites. Blacks, in particular, are skeptical that black people will ever have equal rights in this country (….) A majority of adults say that being white helps people's ability to get ahead in the country at least a little (59%); 28% say being white neither helps nor hurts and 12% say it hurts.* On the flip side, a majority (56%) sees being black as a disadvantage, with 25% saying it hurts people's ability to get ahead a lot. *About a quarter (26%) say being black neither helps nor hurts and 17% say it helps at least a little. More also say that being Hispanic hurts people's ability to get ahead in this country (51%) than say it helps (18%) or that it neither helps nor hurts (30%).* Opinions are more split when it comes to the impact of being Native American – about the same shares say this hurts as say it neither helps nor hurts, while a smaller share says it helps. *And while a plurality says being Asian neither helps nor hurts, more say it helps (34%) than hurts (21%) people's ability to get ahead*"). Italics added.

[401] Lui, Meizhu, "Doubly Divided: The Racial Wealth Gap", *The Wealth Inequality Reader*, Dollars & Sense & United for a Fair Econ. eds., 2004, pp. 42, 44–47.

[402] Margot, Robert A., "Obama, Katrina, and the Persistence of Racial Inequality," *Journal of Economic History*, Volume 76, 2016, pp. 301–341.

[403] Derenoncourt, Ellora/Kim, Chi Hyun/Kuhn, Moritz/Schularik, Moritz, "The Wealth of Two Nations: The U.S. Racial Wealth Gap, 1860–2020", *The Quarterly Journal of Economics*, Volume 139, Issue 2, 2024, p. 741 ("A large class of commonly discussed policies for reducing racial wealth inequality seeks to reduce gaps in income, savings, and capital gains. These include policies that encourage financial diversification or stock equity holdings among Black households; policies aimed at financial literacy and retirement or savings behavior; or policies aimed at improving educational and labor market outcomes of Black Americans through improved school quality or reductions in discrimination. *Yet on a realistic note, our simulation in Section IV.A shows that even if wealth accumulation conditions had been equal since 1870, the wealth gap would still be 3 to 1 today, and full convergence would be more than 200 years away. Put differently: to close the racial wealth gap in the immediate term* via *flow parameters, Black Americans would need a substantial positive lead over whites, not "just" more equality*"). Italics added.

[404] Kuhn, Moritz, Moritz Schularick, and Ulrike I. Steins, "Income and Wealth Inequality in America, 1949–2016," *Journal of Political Economy*, Volume 128, 2020, pp. 3469–3519.

[405] Cole, Stephanie/Ring, Natalie et al. (Editors), *The Folly of Jim Crow: Rethinking the Segregated South (Walter Prescott Webb Memorial Lectures, published for the University of Texas at Arlington by Texas A&M University Press Book 43)*, Texas, Texas A&M University Press (April 3, 2012), 2012 ("*The studies in this collection incorporate important perspectives that have developed during the past two decades among scholars interested in gender and politics, the culture of resistance, and "the hegemonic function of 'whiteness.'*" By asking fresh questions and critically examining long-held beliefs, the new studies contained in *The Folly of Jim Crow* will, ironically, reinforce at least one of the key observations made in C. Vann Woodward's landmark 1955 study: *In its idiosyncratic, contradictory, and multifaceted development and application, the career of Jim Crow was, indeed, strange. Further, as these studies demonstrate—and as alluded to in the title—it is folly to attempt to locate the genesis of the South's institutional racial segregation in any single event, era, or policy.*

main source of labour,[409] which was one of the foundations upon which the United States of America's opulent wealth was built.[410]

§§ Further the arrival of a robust work force that nonetheless lacked legal personhood (Black Africans),[411] the former White indentured servants were set free,[412] which swiftly placed them at the higher echelons of society.[413]

"Instead," as W. Fitzhugh Brundage notes in his introduction to the volume, "formal segregation evolved through an untidy process of experimentation and adaptation"). Italics added.

406 Menasce, Juliana Horowitz/Brown, Anna/Cox, Kiana, "Views of Racial Inequality", *Pew Research Center*, April 9, 2019, 2919, available at: https://www.pewresearch.org/social-trends/2019/04/09/views-of-racial-inequality/ (access: 2.12.2024) ("*more than four-in-ten Americans say the country still has work to do to give black people equal rights with whites. Blacks, in particular, are skeptical that black people will ever have equal rights in this country (….) A majority of adults say that being white helps people's ability to get ahead in the country at least a little (59%); 28% say being white neither helps nor hurts and 12% say it hurts.* On the flip side, a majority (56%) sees being black as a disadvantage, with 25% saying it hurts people's ability to get ahead a lot. *About a quarter (26%) say being black neither helps nor hurts and 17% say it helps at least a little. More also say that being Hispanic hurts people's ability to get ahead in this country (51%) than say it helps (18%) or that it neither helps nor hurts (30%).* Opinions are more split when it comes to the impact of being Native American – about the same shares say this hurts as say it neither helps nor hurts, while a smaller share says it helps. *And while a plurality says being Asian neither helps nor hurts, more say it helps (34%) than hurts (21%) people's ability to get ahead*"). Italics added.

407 López, Ian Haney, *White by Law 10th Anniversary Edition: The Legal Construction of Race (Critical America, 16)*, New York, New York University Press, 2006, pp. 1–264 ("In *the first edition of White by Law, Haney López traced the reasoning employed by the courts in their efforts to justify the whiteness of some and the non-whiteness of others, and revealed the criteria that were used, often arbitrarily, to determine whiteness, and thus citizenship: skin color, facial features, national origin, language, culture, ancestry, scientific opinion, and, most importantly, popular opinion.* Ten years later, Haney López revisits the *legal construction of race, and argues that current race law has spawned a troubling racial ideology that perpetuates inequality under a new guise: colorblind white dominance.* In a new, original essay written specifically for the 10th anniversary edition, *he explores this racial paradigm and explains how it contributes to a system of white racial privilege socially and legally defended by restrictive definitions of what counts as race and as racism, and what doesn't, in the eyes of the law. The book also includes a new preface, in which Haney Lopez considers how his own personal experiences with white racial privilege helped engender White by Law*"). Italics added.

408 Azmy, Baher, "Unshackling the Thirteenth Amendment: Modern Slavery and a Reconstructed Civil Rights Agenda", *Fordham Law Review*, Volume 71, 2002, pp. 981–1015.

409 Freeman, Andrea, "Racism in the Credit Card Industry", *cit.*, p. 1081.

410 Horton, James Oliver/Horton, Lois E., *Slavery and the Making of America*, Oxford, Oxford University Press, 2006, pp. 1–256 ("*The history of slavery is central to understanding the history of the United* States"). See also: Blockmon, Douglas E., *Slavery by Another Name: The Re-Enslavement of Black Americans from the Civil War to World War II*, United States of America, Doubleday, 2008, pp. 1–480 ("In this groundbreaking historical exposé, Douglas A. Blackmon brings to light one of the most shameful chapters in American history—*an "Age of Neoslavery" that thrived from the aftermath of the Civil War through the dawn of World War II*"). Italics added.

411 Margo, Robert A., *Race and Schooling in the South, 1880–1950*, Chicago: University of Chicago Press, 1990.

412 See also: Freeman, Andrea, "Racism in the Credit Card Industry", *cit.*, p. 1082.

413 Morgan, Edmund S., American Slavery, American Freedom, United States of America, W. W. Norton & Company; Reissue edition (October 17, 2003), 2003, pp. 329 and ff (contends that the

§§ This «unfortunate stroke of serendipity» (Black Africans replaced White indentured servants as the main work force) has ushered in, and paved the way to, the onset of slavery, which stands as one centrepiece/linchpin of Unites States of America's history.[414]

§§ As slavery enjoyed global blossoming—in that it was widely received as a lightning bolt of great economic significance in the United States of America and beyond[415]—, so too did the theoretical underpinnings of racial inequalities[416] which, in turn, caused wealth gap to swell.[417] Note, though, that slavery was not a standalone phenomenon amenable to be narrowed down to a single continent.

§§ Tellingly, the geographic spread of slavery connected North America, Asia, Europe, and Africa along umpteenth commercial routes, thereby comprising a feast of a deftly crafted, and tentacular, oppressive system that was the propelling force behind the *systemic racism* that belied every central tenet of human dignity.[418] At its apogee, slavery spanned and traversed dozens of countries.

§§ At the shallowest level, slavery engendered racial divide,[419] which, in turn, spawned the propensity for a racial wedge against the backdrop of which a tendency to harbour mutual distrust unfolds. The yawning wealth gap between White folks

---

social status of Black slaves elevated that of White indentured servants, thereby informing the burgeoning development of race-based slavery in the former Virginia colony). See also: Freeman, Andrea, "Racism in the Credit Card Industry", *cit.*, p. 1082.

[414] Kolchin, Peter, *American Slavery: 1619–1877*, Hill and Wang; Revised edition (September 1, 2003), 2003, pp. 352 ("in terms of accessibility and comprehensive coverage, Kolchin's American Slavery is a singularly important achievement. Now updated to address a decade of new scholarship, the book includes a new preface, afterword, and revised and expanded bibliographic essay. It remains the best book to introduce a subject of profound and lasting importance, one that lies at the center of American history").

[415] Madsen, Jakob B., "Wealth and Inequality over Eight Centuries of British Capitalism," *Journal of Development Economics*, Volume 138, 2019, pp. 246–260.

[416] Margo, Robert A., "Accumulation of Property by Southern Blacks Before World War I: Comment and Further Evidence," *American Economic Review*, Volume 74, 1984, pp. 768–776.

[417] Kuhn, Moritz, Moritz Schularick, and Ulrike I. Steins, "Income and Wealth Inequality in America, 1949–2016," *Journal of Political Economy*, Volume 128, 2020, pp. 3469–3519.

[418] Human dignity is a Kantian-inspired notion which were to send ripples across cultures of dignity, mainly from the fundamental rights standpoint. In German doctrine: Ramm, Thilo, "Die sozialen Grundrechte im Verfassungsgefüge", in: *Soziale Grundrechte—5. Rechtspolitischer Kongress der SPD vom 29. Februar bis 2. März 1980 in Saarbrüchen*, Heidelberg/Karlsruhe, 1981, pp. 28–32; in Portuguese doctrine, Botelho, Catarina Santos, "40 anos de Direitos Sociais: uma reflexão sobre o papel dos Direitos Fundamentais Sociais no Século XXI", *Julgar*, 29, 2016, pp. 197 ff. In French doctrine: Fierens, Jacques, "La dignitè humaine comme concept juridique", *Journal des tribunaux*, 121, 2002, pp. 578–580; Carvalho, Natalia Brigagão Ferrer Alves, "Catholic Social Thought, Politics and Human Dignity in the Brazilian Constitutional Assembly of 1987–1988", *The American Journal of Legal History*, 1, 2019, 1–30; Taekema, Sanne, "The Procedural Rule of Law: Examining Waldron's Argument on Dignity and Agency", *cit.*: 140 ff (arguing that the «Rule of Law serves the value of human dignity»).

[419] Martin, Asa E., *Our Negro Population: A Sociological Study of the Negroes of Kansas City*, Missouri, Kansas City, MO: Franklin Hudson, 1913.

and Blacks[420] maps seamlessly onto the ingeniously crafted racial divide[421] that still ripples forward and resonates today.[422]

4.1.2.1 «Everyone Is Equal, but Some Are More Equal Than Others» (George Orwell): Racially Motivated Laws That Paved the Way for the Povertization of the Black Community, Which, in Turn, Led to the Dire Need for Credit That Gave Rise to Biased Algorithmic Credit Scoring and Phenomenon Alike

§§ It is often ventured that the nasty effects of slavery have reverberated across generations.[423]

§§ Strikingly, since the inception of slavery there has been a feast of insidiously crafted laws that taxed Blacks much higher than White folks.[424] Laws of inheritance

---

420 Meschede, Tatjana, Darrick Hamilton, Ana Patricia Muñoz, Regine Jackson, and William Darity, "Inequality in the 'Cradle of Liberty': Race/Ethnicity and Wealth in Greater Boston," *Race and Social Problems*, 8, 2016, 18–28.

421 Miller, Melinda C. "The Righteous and Reasonable Ambition to Become a Land-holder': Land and Racial Inequality in the Postbellum South," *Review of Economics and Statistics*, Volume 102, 2020, pp. 381–394.

422 Menasce, Juliana Horowitz/Brown, Anna/Cox, Kiana, "Views of Racial Inequality", *Pew Research Center*, April 9, 2019, 2919, available at: https://www.pewresearch.org/social-trends/2019/04/09/views-of-racial-inequality/ (access: 2.12.2024) ("*more than four-in-ten Americans say the country still has work to do to give black people equal rights with whites. Blacks, in particular, are skeptical that black people will ever have equal rights in this country (….) A majority of adults say that being white helps people's ability to get ahead in the country at least a little (59%); 28% say being white neither helps nor hurts and 12% say it hurts.* On the flip side, a majority (56%) sees being black as a disadvantage, with 25% saying it hurts people's ability to get ahead a lot. *About a quarter (26%) say being black neither helps nor hurts and 17% say it helps at least a little. More also say that being Hispanic hurts people's ability to get ahead in this country (51%) than say it helps (18%) or that it neither helps nor hurts (30%).* Opinions are more split when it comes to the impact of being Native American – about the same shares say this hurts as say it neither helps nor hurts, while a smaller share says it helps. *And while a plurality says being Asian neither helps nor hurts, more say it helps (34%) than hurts (21%) people's ability to get ahead*"). Italics added.

423 Madrigal, Alexis C., *The Racist Housing Policy That Made Your Neighbourhood*, Atlantic (May 22, 2014), 2014.

424 Smith, Andre L., *Tax Law and Racial Economic Justice: Black Tax*, Lexington Books, 2015 ("*no study of Black people in America can be complete without considering how openly discriminatory tax laws helped establish a racial caste system in the United States, how they were designed to exclude blacks from lucrative markets and the voting franchise, and how tax laws extracted and redistributed vast sums of black wealth. Not only was slavery nearly a 100% tax on black labor, so too was Jim Crow apartheid and tax laws specified the peculiar institution as "negro slavery."* The first instances of affirmative action in the United States were tax laws designed to attract white men to the South. The nineteenth-century Federal Tariff indirectly redistributed perhaps a majority of the profits from slavery from the South to the North and is the principle reason the Confederate states seceded. The only constitutional amendment obtained by the Civil Rights Movement is the Twenty-Sixth Amendment abolishing poll taxes in federal elections. *Blending traditional legal theory, neoclassical economics, and a pan-African view of history, these six interrelated essays on race and taxes demonstrate that, even in today's supposedly post-racial society, there is no*

have also bestowed upon White folks greater benefits while symmetrically decreasing Black people's civil rights.[425] Corporate laws—in hardening into binding law the concept of shareholder primacy[426]—have also greatly contributed to further augment the yawning racial wealth gap between Whites and Blacks.

§§ Taken together, these congeries of laws were aimed at carving out a wealth[427] gap[428] between White folks and Blacks[429] while propelling a caste system[430] whereby the former always come out ahead.[431]

---

area of human activity where racial dynamics are absent"). Italics added (This refreshingly unique book portrays clearly how a bunch of tax laws have appallingly disadvantaged Black people since the end of slavery). Professor Andre Smith charts the convoluted history of racism and taxation, parsing the effect of slavery as a 100% tax on Black labor (p. 76). Moreover, oppressive taxation of free Blacks before the Civil War dissuaded slave upheavals and competition with Whites, which was ultimately conducive to re-enslavement through incarceration for failure to pay a due amount (p. 85–90); preferential treatment for White capital gains income (p. 204).

[425] Strand, Palma Joy, "Inheriting Inequality: Wealth, Race, and the Laws of Succession", *Oregon Law Review*, Volume 89, 2010, pp. 453–476.

[426] Palladino, Lenore M., "The Contribution of Shareholder Primacy to the Racial Wealth Gap," *Review of Black Political Economy*, Volume 50, 2023, pp. 167–193.

[427] Piketty, Thomas, and Gabriel Zucman, "Capital Is Back: Wealth-Income Ratios in Rich Countries 1700–2010," *Quarterly Journal of Economics*, Volume 129, 2014, pp. 1255–1310.

[428] Pfeffer, Fabian T., and Alexandra Killewald, "Intergenerational Wealth Mobility and Racial Inequality," *Socius*, 5 (2019), passim.

[429] Nam, Yunju, Darrick Hamilton, and Christopher Famighetti, "Parental Financial Assistance to Young Adult Children and the Black-White Wealth Gap," *Journal of Sociology & Social Welfare*, Volume 48, 2021, pp. 88–11.

[430] Pierce, C., "W.E.B. du bois and caste education: Racial capitalist schooling from reconstruction to Jim Crow", *American Educational Research Journal*, 54 (1_Suppl.), 2017, pp. 23S–47S.

[431] Donoghue, Jane, "The Rise of Digital Justice: Courtroom Technology, Public Participation and Access to Justice", *The Modern Law Review*, Volume 80, Issue 6, 2018, p. 995 (noting that technology in the courtroom might widen the gap between the rich and the poor. In this vein, this renowned author has contended that "*legal reforms have omitted any detailed consideration of the type and quality of citizen participation in newly digitised court processes which have fundamental implications for the legitimacy and substantive outcomes of court-based processes; and for enhancing democratic procedure through improved access to justice*. It is argued that although digital court tools and systems offer great promise for enhancing efficiency, participation and accessibility, they *simultaneously have the potential to amplify the scope for injustice, and to attenuate central principles of the legal system, including somewhat paradoxically, access to justice*"). Italics added. See also: Heintz, M.E., "The digital divide and courtroom technology: Can David keep up with Goliath", *Federal Communications Law Journal*, Volume 54, 2002, pp. 566 ff and passim. The great bulk of these assertions has been anticipated by an iconic piece of research. See: Galanter, Marc, "Why the "Haves" Come Out Ahead: Speculations on the Limits of Legal Change", *Law & Society Review*, Volume 9, 1974, pp. 98–103 (this renowned author talks about a *social reality* in which the dubbed «repeat players»—which go by the name of «haves»—tend to «to come out ahead» by putting their knowledge and vast resources to good use. This perceived advantage will not only impact the choice on the procedures but will ultimately benefit their interests as opposed to the deemed «one-shot» players (the «have nots») that will have slimmer and fewer chances to get palpable results in dispute resolution). Technology in the criminal courtroom—that includes the rich and excludes the poor—will make this problem considerably worse. But see: Bailey, J./Burkell, J./ Reynolds, G. "Access to Justice for All: Towards an "Expansive Vision" of Justice and Technology, *Windsor Yearbook of Access to Justice*, Volume 31, 2013, pp. 183–201 (in stark contrast, these

§§ To forestall such an unpalatable situation, scholars have been nothing but kittenish, garrulous, loquacious, and outspoken in underscoring the overriding importance of justice and morality—which neatly encapsulates the Kantian[432] moral concept of law[433]—in the purview of public policy. Note, though, that the level playing field has been unfairly tilted against racialized communities (v.g. Blacks[434] and Latinos).

§§ Compellingly, congeries of legally binding rules have been enacted under the veneer of facial neutrality. Yet those bodies of laws were aimed at further chastising racialized people under a patina of objectivity[435] (foremost, wrapped under the opaqueness[436] of catch-all concepts of *trust in science*[437] and *trust in numbers*[438]).

---

authors stress that the digital and technological apparatus can indeed spawn a both time-effective and streamlined access to justice in a given jurisdiction).

[432] In German doctrine, Immanuel Kant, *Gesammelte Schriften, Abtheilung I: Werke: Gesammelte Schriften/Akademieausgabe, Bd.5 (Abt.1, Werke, Bd.5), Kritik der praktischen Vernunft; Kritik der Urteilskraft. Gebundenes Buch–* 1. März 1963, Berlin, Walter de Gruyter, 1963, 6:390–391 ff; B. Sharon Byrd/Joachim Hruschka, *Kant's Doctrine of Right: A Commentary*, Cambridge, Cambridge University Press, 2010, pp. 72 ff (noting that—here and there—Kant's parlance has been pervaded by a so-called Hobbesian tone. Especially from the violence of the state of nature and the «barbarous freedom» standpoint). Converging: Ross Harrison, *Hobbes, Locke and Confusion's Masterpiece*, Cambridge, Cambridge University Press, 2003, pp. 120–123 (arguing that human nature has a markedly clear yearning to survive—a Hobbesian claim).

[433] Capps, Patrick/Rivers, Julian, "Kant's Concept of Law", *The American Journal of Jurisprudence*, 63 (2), 2018, pp. 259–294 (260) ("at the centre of Kant's *Doctrine of Right* lies an argument for a moral concept of law. Here he reveals his understanding of political authority, which is, in turn, shown to be embedded entirely within his broader practical philosophy. In sum, Kant argues that the authority of law can only arise from our categorical moral duty to respect other persons as such").

[434] Derenoncourt, Ellora/Kim, Chi Hyun/Kuhn, Moritz/Schularik, Moritz, "The Wealth of Two Nations: The U.S. Racial Wealth Gap, 1860–2020", *The Quarterly Journal of Economics*, Volume 139, Issue 2, 2024, p. 741 ("A large class of commonly discussed policies for reducing racial wealth inequality seeks to reduce gaps in income, savings, and capital gains. These include policies that encourage financial diversification or stock equity holdings among Black households; policies aimed at financial literacy and retirement or savings behavior; or policies aimed at improving educational and labor market outcomes of Black Americans through improved school quality or reductions in discrimination. *Yet on a realistic note, our simulation in Section IV.A shows that even if wealth accumulation conditions had been equal since 1870, the wealth gap would still be 3 to 1 today, and full convergence would be more than 200 years away. Put differently: to close the racial wealth gap in the immediate term* via *flow parameters, Black Americans would need a substantial positive lead over whites, not "just" more equality*"). Italics added.

[435] Benjamin, Ruha, *Race After Technology: Abolitionist Tools for the New Jim Code*, New York, Polity, 2019, pp. 1–172 (7) (discussing that Artificial Intelligence-embedded technologies are viewed as iron-clad tools of objectivity and devoid of any biases whatsoever). Ruha Benjamin contends that "the employment of new technologies that reflect and reproduce existing inequities but that are promoted and perceived as more objective or progressive than the discriminatory systems of a previous era").

[436] *Tech, Bias and Housing Initiative, the Promise and Perils of Residential Proptech, Year 1, Research Summary Report, April 2023, TechEquity Collaborative*, p. 11, available at: https://techequity.us/wp-content/uploads/2023/04/TBHI-Y1-Research-Summary-Report.pdf (28.11.2024). ("*From information on company websites, it is not clear what analysis or data*

Such legal features frontally belie the integral values against the backdrop of which modern democracies[439] unfold.[440]

---

is behind subjective determinations like "suitability" to a unit or what the nexus between an individual's characteristics and a unit's characteristics is that indicates the likelihood for property damage. Based on sample reports, even landlords are not privy to how the determinations are made. Instead, they receive a risk score out of 100 simplified into green, yellow, and red recommendations. What companies withhold in terms of how it works, they make up for with the extent to which they tell landlords it works: Naborly claims their predictions reduce lease defaults by up to 89%. 15 *As Naborly's sample report demonstrates, its property damage assessment is then used as an input to determine its projected eviction outcomes; its early vacancy prediction, in turn, is based on "all assessment factors"*). Italics added.

[437] Sherman, Lawrence W., "Targeting, Testing and Tracking Police Services: The Rise of Evidence Based Policing, 1975–2025", *Crime and Justice*, 42 (1), 2013, pp. 377–451; Lavender III, I., *Race in American science fiction*, Bloomington: Indiana University Press, 2011.

[438] Porter, Theodore M., *Trust in Numbers: The Pursuit of Objectivity in Science and Public Life*, Princeton, NJ: Princeton University Press, 1995.

[439] Shabani, Omid A. Payrow, *Democracy, Power, and Legitimacy. The Critical Theory of Jürgen Habermas*, Toronto/Buffalo/London, University of Toronto Press, 2003, pp. 108 ff and *passim* (this author parses Habermas's contribution to Sociology and Philosophy, which I have closely followed); Habermas, Jürgen, *Between Facts and Norms: Contributions to a Discourse Theory of Law and Democracy (Studies in Contemporary German Social Thought)*, Cambridge, The MIT Press, Reprint (9th of January of 1998), 1998, p. 132 (In *Between Facts and Norms*, «Jürgen Habermas works out the legal and political implications of his *Theory of Communicative Action* (1981), bringing to fruition the project announced with his publication of *The Structural Transformation of the Public Sphere* in 1962. This new work is a major contribution to recent debates on the rule of law and the possibilities of democracy in post-industrial societies, but it is much more. The introduction by William Rehg succinctly captures the special nature of the work, noting that it offers a sweeping, sociologically informed conceptualization of law and basic rights, a normative account of the rule of law and the constitutional state, an attempt to bridge normative and empirical approaches to democracy, and an account of the social context required for democracy. Finally, the work frames and caps these arguments with a bold proposal for a new paradigm of law that goes beyond the dichotomies that have afflicted modern political theory from its inception and that still underlie current controversies between so-called liberals and civic republicans»). See also: Habermas, Jürgen, "Law and Morality", The Tanner Lectures on Human Values, S.M. McMurrin (Ed.), Vol. 8, Salt Lake City, University of Utah Press, 1988, *passim*; Habermas, Jürgen, "The New Obscurity: The Crisis of the Welfare State and the Exhaustion of Utopian Energies", *New Conservatism: Cultural Criticism and the Historians 'Debate*, Cambridge, MIT Press, 1989, *passim* (in these articles Habermas has set forth a new vision of the role and position of law. In his view, Law, now, should be positioned between the lifeworld and system. In this light, Habermas stated that law can be both legitimised by moral conceptions and practical reasons); Habermas, Jürgen, *Between Facts and Norms: Contributions to a Discourse Theory of Law and Democracy (Studies in Contemporary German Social Thought), cit.*, (in which Habermas undertakes a comprehensive revision of the role and position of law and the underlying concept of power). See also: Shabani, Omid A. Payrow, *Democracy, Power, and Legitimacy. The Critical Theory of Jürgen Habermas, cit.*, 108 ff and passim. Waldron, Jeremy, "The Core of the Case Against Judicial Review", *Yale Law Journal*, 2006, pp. 1346–1389 (showing concerns about the overall state of US democracy); Buchanan, James M., *The Collected Works of James M. Buchanan, Vol. 3. The Calculus of Consent: Logical Foundations of Constitutional Democracy*, with a Foreword by Robert D. Tollison, Indianapolis, Liberty Fund, 1999, *passim*.

[440] Which, in turn, can boost social cleavages spawned by a technology that fondly includes the rich and outrightly excludes the poor, thereby compounding social issues with which modern have

§§ Casts broadly, the federal food policy[441] has greatly contributed to racial health inequalities[442] against the backdrop of which White folks received far more benefits[443] than did Black folks.[444] As a result, thousands of black workers are frequently cast off from the workforce either due to long-standing illnesses borne out by poor nutrition. Relatedly, Black folks 'sudden deaths equally arise from food-related issues.[445]

§§ By the same token, it bears mentioning that the criminal system of justice has been invidiously weaponized against racialized communities. To put it bluntly, the criminal system of justice wantonly ensnared thousands of Blacks and Latinos,[446] thereby impairing their future employment opportunities further, and in spite of,

---

been grappling/tussling/scuffling/floundering since immemorial times. Social cleavages—a cloak under which mounting social outcry is often wrapped—that threaten to crumble the foundations upon which stands the linchpin of western societies. See in general: Abramsky, Sasha, *Jumping at Shadows: The Triumph of Fear and the End of the American Dream.* New York: Bold Type Books, 2017, pp. 1–272 (passim).

441 Freeman, Andrea, "Fast Food: Oppression Through Poor Nutrition", *California Law Review*, Volume 95, 2007, pp. 2221, 2227–2228, 2242–2245 (shedding a keen light on how the close cooperation between the fast food industry and the government entities is conducive to poor access to healthy food in several low-income Black communities, whose members either die earlier than do White folks or grapple with impairing diseases arising out of poor nutrition); Freeman, Andrea, "First Food" Justice: Racial Disparities in Infant Feeding as Food Oppression", *Fordham Law Review*, Volume 83, 2015, pp. 3053, 3063–66 (deep-diving on the interplay between law and policy against the backdrop of which racial disparities unfolds in camps like breastfeeding, tightly interlocked to exceedingly higher infant mortality rates in Black children than White children); Freeman, Andrea, "The Unbearable Whiteness of Milk: Food Oppression and the USDA", *University of California Law Review*, Volume 3, 2023, pp. 1251, 1252–54 (discussing how the USDA's earnest attempts to dispose of the dairy surplus through close partnerships with fast food corporations and distribution through its nutrition programs disproportionately targets, and causes inordinate harms on, Black communities); Freeman, Andrea, "Transparency for Food Consumers: Nutrition Labeling and Food Oppression", AM. J.L. &MED., Volume 41, 2015, pp. 315, 316–21 (positing how the USDA's sharp focus on greatly improving health by accordingly altering consumer behaviour through nutrition labelling and consumer education reifies, reproduces, exacerbates and ultimately perpetuates racial health disparities by bluntly overlooking the absence of choice facing many Black consumers with regard to food selection). Convergent: Cohen-Rimer, Yael, "What's Choice Got to Do with It? Addressing the Pitfalls of Using Choice-Architecture Discourse Within Poverty Law", *The Modern Law Review*, Volume 86, n. ° 4, 2023, pp. 951–983; Freeman, Andrea, "Racism in the Credit Card Industry", *cit.*, p. 1092 and ff, whose stellar research I have been following closely.

442 Freeman, Andrea, "Racism in the Credit Card Industry", *cit.*, p. 1092 and ff, whose stellar research I have been following closely.

443 Williams, David R./Jackson, Pamela Braboy, "Social Sources of Racial Disparities in Health", *Health Affairs*, Volume 24, 2005, pp. 325, 327–30.

444 Freeman, Andrea, "Racism in the Credit Card Industry", *cit.*, p. 1092 and ff, whose stellar research I have been following closely.

445 Freeman, Andrea, "Racism in the Credit Card Industry", *cit.*, p. 1092 and ff, whose stellar research I have been following closely.

446 Freeman, Andrea, "Racism in the Credit Card Industry", *cit.*, p. 1092 and ff, whose stellar research I have been following closely.

their release.[447] This hideous portmanteau of racially motivated practices consists of «racialization of crime».

§§ The «racialization of crime»[448] process lends itself to racialized defendants' earnest attempts to fend off attacks perpetrated by law enforcement agencies. The soared/ballooned figures of wrong convictions lend enhanced support to this overriding claim.[449]

§§ On the heels of, and fundamentally building on, the *structural racism* against the backdrop of which White privilege[450] unfolds,[451] CRT avowedly contends that the newest technological developments (e.g. Artificial Intelligence-embedded technologies) amount to the crowning achievement of an agreed-upon strategy according to which non-White communities (chiefly, Black, and Latino[452]) should be enmeshed in criminal justice system.[453] Especially, albeit not exclusively, young black men.[454]

§§ Bearing this juncture very firmly in mind, it should not come as a bewildering surprise that this oppressive *systemic racism*—that affords everything to a *selected few* (the anointed White folks) while gainsaying everything a cohort of *unwanted*

---

[447] Monk, E. P., "The color of punishment: African Americans, skin tone, and the criminal justice system", *Ethnic and Racial Studies*, Volume 42, Issue 10, 2019, pp. 1593–1612; Agung-Igusti, R. P., "Raced and risky subjects: The interplay of racial and managerial ideologies as an expression of "colorblind" racism", *American Journal of Community Psychology*, Volume 73, 2024, passim; Alexander, M., *The new Jim Crow: Mass incarceration in the age of colorblindness*, The New Press, 2012.

[448] Brewer, R. M., & Heitzeg, N. A., "The racialization of crime and punishment: Criminal justice, Color-Blind racism, and the political economy of the prison industrial complex", *cit.*, pp. 625–644.

[449] Gross, Samuel R., Maurice Possley, and Kalara Stephens, "Race and Wrongful Convictions in the United States." National Registry of Exonerations, Newkirk Center for Science and Society, University of California-Irvine, 2017.

[450] Cole, Stephanie/Ring, Natalie et al. (Editors), *The Folly of Jim Crow: Rethinking the Segregated South (Walter Prescott Webb Memorial Lectures, published for the University of Texas at Arlington by Texas A&M University Press Book 43)*, Texas, Texas A&M University Press (April 3, 2012), 2012 ("*The studies in this collection incorporate important perspectives that have developed during the past two decades among scholars interested in gender and politics, the culture of resistance, and "the hegemonic function of 'whiteness.'*" By asking fresh questions and critically examining long-held beliefs, the new studies contained in *The Folly of Jim Crow* will, ironically, reinforce at least one of the key observations made in C. Vann Woodward's landmark 1955 study: *In its idiosyncratic, contradictory, and multifaceted development and application, the career of Jim Crow was, indeed, strange. Further, as these studies demonstrate—and as alluded to in the title—it is folly to attempt to locate the genesis of the South's institutional racial segregation in any single event, era, or policy. "Instead," as W. Fitzhugh Brundage notes in his introduction to the volume,* "formal segregation evolved through an untidy process of experimentation and adaptation"). Italics added.

[451] Laub, John H., "Understanding Inequality and the Justice System Response: Charting a New Way Forward.", New York: William T. Grant Foundation, 2014.

[452] Rios, Victor M., *Punished: Policing the Lives of Black and Latino Boys*, New York: NYU Press, 2011.

[453] Duster, Troy, "Pattern, Purpose and Race in the Drug War.", *Crack in America: Demon Drugs and Social Justice*, Reinarman and H. G. Levine (Editors), Berkeley: University of California Press, 1997.

[454] Epp, Charles R., Steven Maynard-Moody, and Donald P. Haider-Markel, *Pulled Over: How Police Stops Define Race and Citizenship*, Chicago: University of Chicago Press, 2014.

many (Blacks and Latinos)—spawned institutionalized povertization of the Black community that paved the way for the dire need for credit.[455] Artificial Intelligence-embedded technologies have flared up the *systemic racism* that besieges modern societies. Especially, albeit not exclusively, from the biased algorithmic credit scoring[456] and fair lending point of view.

4.1.2.2 How Racially Motivated Policies and Laws Spawned Wealth Inequality and Paved the Way to Both Consumer Discrimination and Biased Algorithmic Credit Scoring

§§ The flood of devilishly harmful policies[457]—mirrored on the enactment of a portmanteau of racially motivated[458] laws[459]—left a long-lasting footprint that still casts a shady shadow on the road that lies ahead.[460]

---

[455] Freeman, Andrea, "Racism in the Credit Card Industry", *cit.*, p. 1092 and ff, whose stellar research I have been following closely.

[456] It is crucially important to note, though, that the very fact that only certain types of behaviours are assessed and gauged by credit scores leads to the conclusion some borrowers are not scored at all. The overwhelming majority of consumers boast meagre, if any, credit files owing to the fact that the likelihood to access to the sort of financial services that actually report to the orthodox credit bureaus scattered across modern economies is exceedingly low, which, in turn, morphs them into credit invisible persons. See: Yu, Persis/McLaughlin, Jilian/Levy, Marina, "Big Data: A Big Disappointment for Scoring Consumer Creditworthiness," *The National Consumer Law Center*, 2 (Mar. 14, 2014), available at: https://www.nclc.org/images/pdf/pr-reports/report-big-data.pdf; [https://www.perma.cc/W4SK-NXD5] (access: 21.12.2024).

[457] Which brings back so many bad memories akin to the hideous effects of malicious legal transplants: Siems, Mathias, "Malicious legal transplants", *Legal Studies, The Society of Legal Scholars*, 38, 2018, pp. 103–119 (105) (emphasizing the importance of malicious legal transplants by stating that «in many countries in the world, multiple ethnicities live together peacefully together. But throughout human history there also have been periods of racially motivated laws with malicious effects. In some instances, those laws were a product of legal transplants (….) it can be said that the Nazi laws influenced the laws of Mussolini's Italy»). Bad laws will inevitably become evil laws that must not be obeyed. In this vein, Professor H. L. Hart asserts that "*laws may be law but too evil to be obeyed*. This is a moral condemnation which everyone can understand and it makes an immediate and obvious claim to moral attention. If, on the other hand, we formulate our objection as an assertion that these evil things are not law, here is an assertion which many people do not believe, and if they are disposed to consider it at all, it would seem to raise a whole host philosophical issues before it can be solves". Italics added. See: Hart, H. L., "Positivism and the Separation of Law and Morals", *Harvard Law Review*, Volume 71, Issue 4, 1958, pp. 598 ff (this amounts to a glimpse of the incorporation of the moral concept of law in Hart's conception of law). Thus thwarting the basic tenets of society as we know, which are set to fall apart, thereby dragging the sacrosanct Rule of Law—and the law as a social fact—to the abandoned streets of recklessness. See: Tyler, Tom R., *Why People Obey the Law*. New Jersey, United States of America: Princeton University Press, 2006, pp. 1–320 (92–110) (Professor Tom R. Tyler lawmakers and law enforcers should make legal systems worthy of respect instead of trying to instil fear of punishment onto disputants. He found that laypeople obey law primarily because they believe in respecting legitimate authority when such respect is due. Which means that legal systems must be worthy of respect before demanding for respect).

§§ Slavery accordingly breed a harrowing *systemic racism* which, in turn, was left to develop to its own accord,[461] which is strikingly clear from the thought-through[462] wealth inequality[463] that purposefully slows down the rise to prominence of a robust, well-adjusted, and wealthy Black community.[464]

---

458 Saez, Emmanuel, and Gabriel Zucman, "Wealth Inequality in the United States since 1913: Evidence from Capitalized Income Tax Data," *Quarterly Journal of Economics*, Volume 131, 2016, pp. 519–578.

459 Skandalis, Daphné, Ioana Marinescu, and Maxim N. Massenkoff, "Racial Inequality in the U.S. Unemployment Insurance System," *NBER Working Paper* no. 30252, 2023.

460 Campisi, Natalie, From Inherent Racial Bias to Incorrect Data The Problems With Current Credit Scoring Models, Forbes (Feb. 26, 2021), https://www.forbes.com/advisor/creditcards/from-inherent-racial-bias-to-incorrect-data-the-problems-with-current-credit-scoring-models/; [https://www.perma.cc/EWA4-CS8E] (highlighting rampant racial bias in credit scoring systems); Oyama, Rebecca, "Do Not (Re)Enter: the Rise of Criminal Background Tenant Screening as a Violation of the Fair Housing Act", *Michigan Journal of Race and Law*, Volume 15, 2009, pp. 181, 184–93 (discussing a broad range of historical/criminal accounts as a way to screen undesirable tenants, such as Blacks and Latinos); Statement of Interest of the United States at 12, *Louis v. SafeRent Sols., LLC, No. 1:22-cv-10800* (D. Mass. Jan. 9, 2023) (holding that the Fair Housing Act liability stretches far and beyond, thus encompassing a vast assortment of entities providing housing-related services, including corporations that offer tenant screening services).

461 Perea, Juan F., "Doctrines of Delusion: How the History of the G.I. Bill and Other Inconvenient Truths Undermine the Supreme Court's Affirmative Action Jurisprudence", *University of Pittsburgh Law Review*, Volume 75, 2014, 583–585; Turner, Sarah/Bound, John, "Closing the Gap or Widening the Divide: The Effects of the G.I. Bill and World War II on the Educational Outcomes of Black Americans", *Journal of Economic History*, Volume 63, 2003, 145 and ff and passim 2003; Boulton, Mark, "How the G.I. Bill Failed African-American Vietnam War Veterans", *Journal of Blacks Higher Education*, 2007, pp. 57, 58–59 (shines a keen light on how Black veterans were bluntly discriminated against, as compared with White soldiers, for educational opportunities in the aftermath of the bloody World War II). See also: Stewart, Lathonia Denise Stewart/Perlow, Richard, "Applicant Race, Job Status, and Racial Attitude as Predictors of Employment Discrimination", *Journal of Business and Psychology*, Volume 16, 2001, pp. 259, 260–61.

462 But see, on randomness: Teigena, Halvor/Kanten, Alf Børre, "Out of the blue: on the suddenness of perceived chance events", *Thinking & Reasoning*, Volume 29, n. ° 1, 2023, pp. 137–175 (137) ("*people commonly use terms like 'random', 'by chance', or 'accidentally' when they describe occurrences that sidestep the normal course of events, with no apparent causal link to ongoing activities. Such intrusive events are typically perceived as happening all of a sudden.* This was demonstrated in seven experiments (N ¼ 1299) by asking people to identify statements they believed belonged to stories about chance events, and by comparing chance vs. nonchance events from their own life and from the lives of others. Suddenness also appeared to be more strongly associated with beginnings than with endings of an episode. Thus, statements about sudden beginnings of a career or a relationship were more readily believed to happen 'by chance' than 'not by chance'. *But life-changing events did not become more accidental simply by being placed in the beginning of a 'life chapter'. These studies highlight a central but neglected feature of perceived randomness*"). Italics added.

463 Saez, Emmanuel, and Gabriel Zucman, "The Rise of Income and Wealth Inequality in America: Evidence from Distributional Macroeconomic Accounts," *Journal of Economic Perspectives*, Volume 34, 2020, pp. 3–26.

464 Derenoncourt, Ellora/Kim, Chi Hyun/Kuhn, Moritz/Schularik, Moritz, "The Wealth of Two Nations: The U.S. Racial Wealth Gap, 1860–2020", *The Quarterly Journal of Economics*, Volume 139, Issue 2, 2024, p. 741 ("A large class of commonly discussed policies for reducing racial wealth

§§ This assertion is firmly rooted in the fact that it bestows upon racialized communities to fend for themselves in the face of both poverty and the absence of a safety net on which to fall back.

§§ As a result, racialized communities often resort to credit to stay afloat. At this juncture, it should not amount to a baffling finding that the pendulum of *systemic racism* has swung—still swings—far and hard against Blacks.[465]

§§ The credit card industry accordingly holds Blacks and Whites to different standards of both procedural fairness[466] and procedural justice[467] that comes to the expense of racialized communities 'fundamental rights. More on this later.

---

inequality seeks to reduce gaps in income, savings, and capital gains. These include policies that encourage financial diversification or stock equity holdings among Black households; policies aimed at financial literacy and retirement or savings behavior; or policies aimed at improving educational and labor market outcomes of Black Americans through improved school quality or reductions in discrimination. *Yet on a realistic note, our simulation in Section IV.A shows that even if wealth accumulation conditions had been equal since 1870, the wealth gap would still be 3 to 1 today, and full convergence would be more than 200 years away. Put differently: to close the racial wealth gap in the immediate term* via *flow parameters, Black Americans would need a substantial positive lead over whites, not "just" more equality*"). Italics added.

[465] See: *Tech, Bias and Housing Initiative, the Promise and Perils of Residential Proptech, Year 1, Research Summary Report, April 2023, TechEquity Collaborative*, p. 5 available at: https://techequity.us/wp-content/uploads/2023/04/TBHI-Y1-Research-Summary-Report.pdf (28.11.2024). ("*Residential Proptech also has the potential to exacerbate the bias inherent in our housing system. Its rise is due, in part, to the desperation felt by average home seekers. With a severely constrained housing supply, companies offering an easier pathway to homeownership may exploit communities that have been harmed by housing discrimination in the past. Opaque algorithms incorporate biased data into their decision-making processes, making it harder to enforce fair housing laws.* Residential Proptech companies often operate in a regulatory gray area, leaving consumers without the protections they would have from traditional housing regulatory systems. *As unprecedented capital investment flows into this space, venture-backed companies' winner-take-all approach to growth has the potential to exacerbate inequality rather than combat it*"). Italics added. See: Part IV, This chapter, Sects. 4.1.4–4.1.4.2.3 of this book.

[466] Tyler, Tom R., "The relationship of the outcome and procedural fairness: How does knowing the outcome influences judgments about the procedure?", *Social Justice and Research*, Volume 9, 1996, pp. 311–325; Tyler, Tom R., "Compliance with intellectual property laws", *Journal of International Law and Politics*, Volume 28, 1997a, pp. 101–116; Tyler, Tom R., "Justice and power in civil dispute processing", *Sociolegal studies*, Evanston, IL, Northwestern University Press, 1997b, *passim*; Tyler, Tom R., "The Psychology of procedure", *The American Journal of Comparative Law*, Volume 45, 1997, pp. 2001–2034.

[467] Tyler, Tom, "What is procedural justice?", *Law and Society Review*, Volume 22, 1988, pp. 301–355; Tyler, Tom, "The Psychology of procedural justice: A test of the group value model.", in: *Journal of Personality and Social Psychology*, Volume 57, 1989, 830–838; Tyler, Tom, *Why people obey the law*, New Haven, CT, Yale University Press, 1990, 1–320 (premising his conclusions on a sound body of empirical research, the author states that "*people obey the law if they believe it's legitimate*, not because they fear punishment-this is the startling conclusion of Tom Tyler's classic study. Tyler suggests that lawmakers should make legal systems worthy of respect instead of trying to instil fear of punishment onto disputants. *He finds that people obey law primarily because they believe in respecting legitimate authority*"). Italics added. Tyler, Tom, "Legitimizing unpopular public policies: Does procedure matter?", *Zeitschrift für Reichssoziologie*, Volume 14, 1993, pp. 47–54; Tyler, Tom, "Governing amid diversity: can fair decision-making procedures bridge competing public interests and values?", *Law and Society Review*, Volume 28, 1994, pp. 701–722; Tyler,

§§ On the heels of a yawning[468] gap[469] of wealth[470]—and bereft of a safety net of wealth[471] on which to rely upon,[472] nor to fall back[473]—, the whopping majority of middle-class Black families «live paycheck-to-paycheck».[474] If an unforeseen expense arises, their lives will swiftly careen into chaos as their family budget is incapable of accommodating extraordinary expenses.

Tom, "Psychological models of the justice motive", *Journal of Personality and Social Psychology*, Volume 67, 1994, 850–863; Tyler, Tom, "The relationship of the outcome and procedural fairness: How does knowing the outcome influences judgments about the procedure?", *Social Justice and Research*, Volume 9, 1996, pp. 311–325; Tyler, Tom, "Compliance with intellectual property laws", in: *Journal of International Law and Politics*, Volume 28, 1997, pp. 101–116; Tyler, Tom, "Justice and power in civil dispute processing", in: *Sociolegal studies*, Evanston, IL, Northwestern University Press, 1997; Tor, A./Gazal-Ayal, O./Garcia, S. M., "Fairness and willingness to accept plea bargain offers", *Journal of Empirical Legal Studies*, Volume 7, 2010, pp. 97–116 (drawing upon a body of empirical evidence the authors made an the interplay between overall fairness of the proceedings and the disputant's willingness to accept plea bargain offers made by the Government). John Thibaut/ Laurens Walker, *Procedural Justice: A Psychological Analysis*, Hillsdale, N.J.: Lawrence Erlbaum Associates, (1975): 1–150 (as previously pointed out, procedural justice is tightly interlocked to raising the levels of party self-determination. Absent of which procedural fairness is to mar).

468 Derenoncourt, Ellora/Kim, Chi Hyun/Kuhn, Moritz/Schularik, Moritz, "The Wealth of Two Nations: The U.S. Racial Wealth Gap, 1860–2020", *The Quarterly Journal of Economics*, Volume 139, Issue 2, 2024, p. 741 ("A large class of commonly discussed policies for reducing racial wealth inequality seeks to reduce gaps in income, savings, and capital gains. These include policies that encourage financial diversification or stock equity holdings among Black households; policies aimed at financial literacy and retirement or savings behavior; or policies aimed at improving educational and labor market outcomes of Black Americans through improved school quality or reductions in discrimination. *Yet on a realistic note, our simulation in Section IV.A shows that even if wealth accumulation conditions had been equal since 1870, the wealth gap would still be 3 to 1 today, and full convergence would be more than 200 years away. Put differently: to close the racial wealth gap in the immediate term* via *flow parameters, Black Americans would need a substantial positive lead over whites, not "just" more equality*"). Italics added.

469 Saez, Emmanuel, and Gabriel Zucman, "Wealth Inequality in the United States since 1913: Evidence from Capitalized Income Tax Data,", *Quarterly Journal of Economics*, Volume 131, 2016, pp. 519–578.

470 Pfeffer, Fabian T., and Alexandra Killewald, "Intergenerational Wealth Mobility and Racial Inequality,", *Socius*, Volume 5, 2019, passim.

471 Wolff, Edward N A, A Century of Wealth in America, Cambridge, MA: Harvard University Press, 2017.

472 Wolff, Edward N., "Racial Wealth Disparities: Is the Gap Closing?," *Levy Economics Institute Public Policy Brief*, no. 66, 2001.

473 Freeman, Andrea, "Racism in the Credit Card Industry", *cit.*, p. 1093 and ff, whose stellar research I have been following closely.

474 Freeman, Andrea, "Racism in the Credit Card Industry", *cit.*, p. 1093 and ff, whose stellar research I have been following closely.

§§ Against this well-trodden and drawn-out background, the ghastly legacy of slavery—which, in turn, has laid the groundwork for a gruelling *systemic racism*—spawned a strikingly clear economic disadvantage[475] of racialized communities that still ripples forward.[476]

§§ The fast-paced development of Artificial Intelligence-embedded technologies has only ratcheted up—levelled up and, in some instances, flared up—the degree of *systemic racism* which flagitiously targets members of racialized communities,[477] thereby hastening the rise to prominence of both consumer discrimination and biased algorithmic credit scoring.

§§ Packed with bold claims, *systemic racism*—underpinned by a White supremacy[478] that spearheads policy formation since the dusk of the long-haul period

---

475 See: Barocas, Solon/Selbst, Andrew, "Big Data's Disparate Impact", *California Law Review*, Volume 104, pp. 2016, p. 691 (highlighting the worrisome, and gruesome, issue of "structural disadvantage" with which racialized communities have been tussling for centuries). See also: Powell, Richard/Porter, Jeremy, "Redlining, Concentrated Disadvantage and Crime: The Effects of Discriminatory Government Policies on Violent Crime", *American Journal of Criminal Justice*, Volume 48, 2023, pp. 1132–1156 ("*Redlining and other discriminatory government policies enacted during the first half of the Twentieth Century have had long-lasting negative effects on neighborhoods, especially those inhabited by people of color. This study attempts to link the practice of redlining to current-day indicators of neighborhood concentrated disadvantage and violent crime using spatio-temporal data from Chicago* (…) *In addition, it seeks to determine whether redlining was associated with violent crime, and if that association was mediated by redlining's effect on concentrated disadvantage. The results indicate that redlining was associated with increases in both concentrated disadvantage and violent crime, and that redlining's relationship with violent crime was, indeed, partially mediated by its relationship with concentrated disadvantage*"). Italics added. See also: Gandy, Oscar H., *Coming to Terms with Chance: Engaging Rational Discrimination and Cumulative Disadvantage*, Farnham, UK: Ashgate Publishing, 2009.

476 Wolff, Edward N., "The Decline of African-American and Hispanic Wealth Since the Great Recession," *NBER Working Paper* no. 25198, 2018; Wolff, Edward N., "African-American and Hispanic Income, Wealth and Homeownership since 1989," *Review of Income and Wealth*, Volume 68, 2022, pp. 189–233.

477 Benjamin, Ruha, *Race After Technology: Abolitionist Tools for the New Jim Code*, New York, Polity, 2019, pp. 1–172 ("*from everyday apps to complex algorithms, Ruha Benjamin cuts through tech-industry hype to understand how emerging technologies can reinforce White supremacy and deepen social inequity*. Benjamin argues that automation, far from being a sinister story of racist programmers scheming on the dark web, has the potential to hide, speed up, *and deepen discrimination while appearing neutral and even benevolent when compared to the racism of a previous era.* Presenting the concept of the "New Jim Code," she shows how a range of discriminatory designs encode inequity by explicitly amplifying racial hierarchies; by ignoring but thereby replicating social divisions; or by aiming to fix racial bias but ultimately doing quite the opposite. *Moreover, she makes a compelling case for race itself as a kind of technology, designed to stratify and sanctify social injustice in the architecture of everyday life. This illuminating guide provides conceptual tools for decoding tech promises with sociologically informed skepticism. In doing so, it challenges us to question not only the technologies we are sold but also the ones we ourselves manufacture*"). Italics added.

478 Feagin, J. R., *The white racial frame: centuries of racial framing and counter-framing*, 2nd edition, New York: Routledge, 2013. DaViera, A. L./Uriostegui, M., Gottlieb/A./Onyeka, O, "Risk, race, and predictive policing: A critical race theory analysis of the strategic subject list", *American Journal of Community Psychology*, Volume 73, 2024, pp. 91–103; Furman, E./Singh, A. K./Darko, N. A./Wilson, C. L., "Activism, intersectionality, and community psychology: The way in which

of slavery—laid its cards very firmly on the table (racialized communities are slated to perpetually grapple with economic hardship,[479] which, in turn, will stymie their future endeavours).

§§ Regrettably, the theoretical underpinnings of *systemic racism*[480] transcend timeframes and jurisdictions insofar is a gruesome phenomenon that besets modern societies in an overarching sense.[481] Consumer discrimination within the remit of credit card scoring accordingly portrays the insurmountable hurdles with which members of racialized communities (Blacks and Latinos) tussle in the age of Artificial Intelligence-embedded technologies.[482]

Black Lives Matter Toronto helps us to examine white supremacy in Canada's LGBTQ community", *Community Psychology in Global Perspective*, Volume 4, Issue 2, 34–54. On whiteness: Frankenberg, Ruth (Ed.), *Displacing whiteness: essays in social and cultural criticism*, Durham, NC: Duke University Press, 1997; Frankenberg, Ruth, "Introduction: local whitenesses, localizing whiteness", *Displacing whiteness*, Ruth Frankenberg (Editor), Durham, NC: Duke University Press, 1997, pp. 1–33; Roithmayr, Daria, *Reproducing Racism: How everyday choices lock in White Advantage*, New York, New York University Press, 2014, pp. 1–272.

[479] Derenoncourt, Ellora/Kim, Chi Hyun/Kuhn, Moritz/Schularik, Moritz, "The Wealth of Two Nations: The U.S. Racial Wealth Gap, 1860–2020", *The Quarterly Journal of Economics*, Volume 139, Issue 2, 2024, p. 741 ("A large class of commonly discussed policies for reducing racial wealth inequality seeks to reduce gaps in income, savings, and capital gains. These include policies that encourage financial diversification or stock equity holdings among Black households; policies aimed at financial literacy and retirement or savings behavior; *or policies aimed at improving educational and labor market outcomes of Black Americans through improved school quality or reductions in discrimination. Yet on a realistic note, our simulation in Section IV.A shows that even if wealth accumulation conditions had been equal since 1870, the wealth gap would still be 3 to 1 today, and full convergence would be more than 200 years away. Put differently: to close the racial wealth gap in the immediate term* via *flow parameters, Black Americans would need a substantial positive lead over whites, not "just" more equality*"). Italics added.

[480] Cole, Stephanie/Ring, Natalie et al. (Editors), *The Folly of Jim Crow: Rethinking the Segregated South (Walter Prescott Webb Memorial Lectures, published for the University of Texas at Arlington by Texas A&M University Press Book 43)*, Texas, Texas A&M University Press (April 3, 2012), 2012 ("*The studies in this collection incorporate important perspectives that have developed during the past two decades among scholars interested in gender and politics, the culture of resistance, and "the hegemonic function of 'whiteness.'"* By asking fresh questions and critically examining long-held beliefs, the new studies contained in *The Folly of Jim Crow* will, ironically, reinforce at least one of the key observations made in C. Vann Woodward's landmark 1955 study: *In its idiosyncratic, contradictory, and multifaceted development and application, the career of Jim Crow was, indeed, strange. Further, as these studies demonstrate—and as alluded to in the title—it is folly to attempt to locate the genesis of the South's institutional racial segregation in any single event, era, or policy. "Instead," as W. Fitzhugh Brundage notes in his introduction to the volume,* "formal segregation evolved through an untidy process of experimentation and adaptation"). Italics added.

[481] Feagin, J. R., *Systemic racism: a theory of oppression*, New York: Routledge, 2006. See also: Fiske, John, "Surveilling the City: Whiteness, the Black Man and Democratic Totalitarianism.", *Theory, Culture and Society*, 15 (2), 1998, pp. 67–88 (on the overhyped surveillance on black people as a byproduct of systemic racism).

[482] Chopra, Samir/White, Laurence F., *A Legal Theory of Autonomous Artificial Agents*, Michigan, University of Michigan Press, 2011, pp. 1–264 (5) (2011) ("*There are two views of the goals of artificial intelligence. From an engineering perspective, as Marvin Minsky noted, it is the 'science of making machines do things that would require intelligence if done by men.' From a cognitive science perspective, it is to design and build systems that work the way the human mind does. In*

4.1.2.3 «If You Are White, the Door Is Always Open, if You Are Black or Latino, We Are Slamming the Door on Your Face»: Biased Algorithmic Credit Scoring («Credit Card Redlining») and Consumer Racism That Further Entrenches the Racial Wedge Between Whites («Lifestyle Users») and Blacks («Revolvers» or «Subsistence Users»)—The Notorious Case of Rachelle Faroul

§§ Bearing the foregoing backdrop very firmly in mind, it should neither amount to a flabbergasting nor a baffling finding that the general furore over Artificial Intelligence should be halted or inordinate harms are bound to be externalized onto members of racialised communities.[483] This assertion is neither unwarranted nor uncalled for.

---

the former perspective, artificial intelligence is deemed successful along a performative dimension; in the latter, along a theoretical one. The latter embodies Giambattista Vico's perspective of verum et factum convertuntur, 'the true and the made are... convertible'; *in such a view, artificial intelligence would be reckoned the laboratory that validates our best science of the human mind. This perspective sometimes shades into the claim artificial intelligence's success lies in the replication of human capacities such as emotions, the sensations of taste, and self-consciousness. Here, artificial intelligence is conceived of as building artificial persons, not just designing systems that are 'intelligent*") ("*As an example of how agent technologies might evolve to incorporate learning, autonomy, and discretion, consider a hypothetical agent designed to find used books on the Internet. The agent is provided with a list of websites to scour, sample titles with abstracts as learning data to recognize other titles in the genre, and electronic cash accounts with which to make purchases.* The agent is allowed to purchase books within a preset spending limit with discretion in the number, subjects, and individual prices of books bought. Such an agent has a broadly defined goal with enough executive discretion in the choices it makes to optimize satisfaction of that goal. The agent is able to interact with its environment by reading and scanning information at the sites it visits; it interacts with other agents such as selling agents deployed by other users. The agent "moves" from site to site, makes purchases, and reads recommendations provided by book-selling agents. The agent checks recommendations for matches on parameters of interest, and then depending on the outcome, buys more books or declines offers. *It is able to buy titles not on its original list, and to proactively make the decision to buy a new title. Such an agent is able to decide to take an action, in response to inputs it decides to focus on; its interactions on the Internet, in a world populated by other shopping agents and sometimes humans, exemplify autonomous, goal-directed, proactive behavior*"). Italics added.

[483] But see: Wonyoung, So, "Which Information Matters? Measuring Landlord Assessment of Tenant Screening Reports", *Housing Policy Debate*, Volume 33, n. ° 6, 2023, pp. 1484–1510 (1502) ("*One additional finding of the experiment is that algorithmic scoring can exacerbate this racially unequal landscape in rental agreements not just because the algorithm may be inaccurate, but because landlords may want to follow the risk assessment made by the tenant screening report. This is alarming for low-income tenants, particularly housing voucher holders. Security deposits are one of the most significant barriers to obtaining housing for voucher holders, because vouchers do not pay security deposits but most private landlords require them (Rosenblatt & Cossyleon, 2018).* Given that voucher holders have exceptionally low income (usually less than 50% of area median income) and might experience more housing insecurity (rental debts and eviction-related experiences), *imposing greater security deposits on voucher holders almost equates to denying them housing—yet these decisions could be justified by algorithmic scoring if tenant screening services employ it*"). Italics added.

For a simple reason: decisions vital to racialised communities' welfare[484] leverage on biased data[485] baked into databases[486] scattered across the data-driven world we live in.[487]

§§ Disturbingly enough, the skewed data on which machine learning algorithms[488] operate upon[489] to grant, or deny, credit to Blacks and Latinos contains the residue of deeply entrenched discriminations and injustice[490] of which we should be keenly

---

[484] It is crucially important to note, though, that the very fact that only certain types of behaviours are assessed and gauged by credit scores leads to the conclusion some borrowers are not scored at all. The overwhelming majority of consumers boast meagre, if any, credit files owing to the fact that the likelihood to access to the sort of financial services that actually report to the orthodox credit bureaus scattered across modern economies is exceedingly low, which, in turn, morphs them into credit invisible persons. See: Yu, Persis/McLaughlin, Jilian/Levy, Marina, "Big Data: A Big Disappointment for Scoring Consumer Creditworthiness,", *The National Consumer Law Center,* 2 (Mar. 14, 2014), available at: https://www.nclc.org/images/pdf/pr-reports/report-big-data.pdf; [https://www.perma.cc/W4SK-NXD5] (access: 21.12.2024).

[485] See: Barocas, Solon/Selbst, Andrew D., "Big Data's Disparate Impact", *California Law Review*, Volume 104, 2016, pp. 671–682 (discussing how data is often flawed, rigged, incomplete, imperfect and therefore algorithms inherit the prejudice of the original decision makers). But see: Citron, Danielle Keats/Pasquale, Frank, "The Scored Society: Due Process for Automated Predictions", *Washington Law Review*, Volume 89, 2014, pp. 1, 4–5 (highlighting how human beings programming automated systems is directly conducive to, and leads, to fundamentally inaccurate results since the source code, predictive algorithms and datasets may encompass human biases which, in turn, have a disparate impact on historically disadvantaged groups); Crawford, Kate/Schultz, Jason, "Big Data and Due Process: Toward a Framework to Redress Predictive Privacy Harms", *Boston College Law Review*, Volume 55, 2014, pp. 93, 99–101 (pinpointing pathways through which predictive analytic tools perpetuate discriminatory practices). But see: Bornstein, Stepanhie, "Antidiscriminatory Algorithms", *Alabama Law Review*, Volume 70, 2018, pp. 519, 524–528 (contending, however, that the tagged "facially neutral" algorithms producing discriminatory outcomes should be quashed).

[486] Balkin, Jack M., "The Three Laws of Robotics in the Age of Big Data", *Ohio State Law Journal*, Volume 78, Issue 5, 2017, pp. 1217–1241.

[487] *Tech, Bias and Housing Initiative, the Promise and Perils of Residential Proptech, Year 1, Research Summary Report, April 2023, TechEquity Collaborative*, p. 11, available at: https://techequity.us/wp-content/uploads/2023/04/TBHI-Y1-Research-Summary-Report.pdf (28.11.2024). ("*Once bad data enters the analysis of one factor, it gets baked into the subsequent process, multiplying the effect that one disadvantageous data point can have on someone's overall housing determination*"). Italics added. See: Part IV, This chapter, Sects. 4.1.4–4.1.4.2.3 of this book.

[488] But see: O'Neil, Cathy, *Weapons of Math Destruction. How Big Data Increases Inequality and Threatens Democracy*, London, Penguin Random House, 2016, passim (showing how algorithms utilized in modern societies are amenable to perpetuate racial discrimination, partially through perpetuation of social disadvantage and wealth divides).

[489] *Tech, Bias and Housing Initiative, the Promise and Perils of Residential Proptech, Year 1, Research Summary Report, April 2023, TechEquity Collaborative*, p. 5 available at: https://techequity.us/wp-content/uploads/2023/04/TBHI-Y1-Research-Summary-Report.pdf (28.11.2024). ("*Residential Proptech also has the potential to exacerbate the bias inherent in our housing system. Its rise is due, in part, to the desperation felt by average home seekers. With a severely constrained housing supply, companies offering an easier pathway to homeownership may exploit communities that have been harmed by housing discrimination in the past. Opaque algorithms incorporate biased data into their decision-making processes, making it harder to enforce fair housing laws.* Residential Proptech companies often operate in a regulatory gray area, leaving consumers without the protections they would have from traditional housing regulatory systems. *As*

leery of insofar further compounds the structural disadvantage facing member of racialised communities.[491]

§§ It follows machines—which, recall, have been previously fed with data riddled with deep-seated residues of invidiousness and racial discrimination[492] that builds on a drawn-out slavery that begets *systemic racism*[493]—will accordingly breed a cascade

---

unprecedented capital investment flows into this space, venture-backed companies' winner-take-all approach to growth has the potential to exacerbate inequality rather than combat it"). Italics added.

[490] Balkin, Jack M., "The Three Laws of Robotics in the Age of Big Data", *cit.*, pp. 1217–1241.

[491] See: Barocas, Solon/Selbst, Andrew, "Big Data's Disparate Impact", *California Law Review*, Volume 104, pp. 2016, p. 691 (highlighting the worrisome, and gruesome, issue of "structural disadvantage" with which racialized communities have been tussling for centuries). See also: Powell, Richard/Porter, Jeremy, "Redlining, Concentrated Disadvantage and Crime: The Effects of Discriminatory Government Policies on Violent Crime", *American Journal of Criminal Justice*, Volume 48, 2023, pp. 1132–1156 ("*Redlining and other discriminatory government policies enacted during the first half of the Twentieth Century have had long-lasting negative effects on neighborhoods, especially those inhabited by people of color* (…) *The results indicate that redlining was associated with increases in both concentrated disadvantage and violent crime, and that redlining's relationship with violent crime was, indeed, partially mediated by its relationship with concentrated disadvantage*"). Italics added. See also: Gandy, Oscar H., *Coming to Terms with Chance: Engaging Rational Discrimination and Cumulative Disadvantage*, Farnham, UK: Ashgate Publishing, 2009. See: Burk, Dan L., "Algorithmic Fair Use", *University of Chicago Law Review*, Volume 86, 2019, pp. 283–288 (asserts that algorithmic "*fair use carries with it the disadvantage of ex ante uncertainty*; no one can be entirely certain in advance how a court will weigh the four factors, *and hence there is always some apprehension that a use may be found infringing rather than fair*"). Italics added.

[492] See: Barocas, Solon/Selbst, Andrew D., "Big Data's Disparate Impact", *California Law Review*, Volume 104, 2016, pp. 671–682 (discussing how data is often flawed, rigged, incomplete, imperfect and therefore algorithms inherit the prejudice of the original decision makers). But see: Citron, Danielle Keats/Pasquale, Frank, "The Scored Society: Due Process for Automated Predictions", *Washington Law Review*, Volume 89, 2014, pp. 1, 4–5 (highlighting how human beings programming automated systems is directly conducive to, and leads, to fundamentally inaccurate results since the source code, predictive algorithms and datasets may encompass human biases which, in turn, have a disparate impact on historically disadvantaged groups). But see: Bornstein, Stepanhie, "Antidiscriminatory Algorithms", *Alabama Law Review*, Volume 70, 2018, pp. 519, 524–528 (contending, however, that the tagged "facially neutral" algorithms producing discriminatory outcomes should be quashed).

[493] Roithmayr, Daria, *Reproducing Racism: How everyday choices lock in White Advantage*, New York, New York University Press, 2014, pp. 1–272 ("*Argues that racial inequality reproduces itself automatically over time because early unfair advantage for whites has paved the way for continuing advantage. This book is designed to change the way we think about racial inequality* (…) *Legal scholar Daria Roithmayr provocatively argues that racial inequality lives on because white advantage functions as a powerful self-reinforcing monopoly, reproducing itself automatically from generation to generation even in the absence of intentional discrimination. Drawing on work in antitrust law and a range of other disciplines, Roithmayr brilliantly compares the dynamics of white advantage to the unfair tactics of giants like AT&T and Microsoft.* With penetrating insight, Roithmayr *locates the engine of white monopoly in positive feedback loops that connect the dramatic disparity of Jim Crow to modern racial gaps in jobs, housing and education. Wealthy white neighborhoods fund public schools that then turn out wealthy white neighbors. Whites with lucrative jobs informally refer their friends, who refer their friends, and so on. Roithmayr concludes that racial inequality might now be locked in place, unless policymakers immediately take drastic steps to dismantle this oppressive system*"). Italics added. This book points out how White privilege is perpetuated throughout generations through residential segregation (*mortgage redlining*), abhorrent

of biased judgments[494] which will inevitably come to the expense of Blacks' and Latinos' chance to be granted the sorely needed credit.[495]

§§ Strikingly, consumer racism that besieges the credit industry constitutes a notorious example of an agreed-upon policy of *Algorithmic Dictatorship* according

---

nepotism, and other bemoaning social practices that pester modern societies). See: Part IV, This chapter, Sects. 4.1.4–4.1.4.2.3 of this book.

494 See: Wonyoung, So, "Which Information Matters? Measuring Landlord Assessment of Tenant Screening Reports", *Housing Policy Debate*, Volume 33, n. ° 6, 2023, pp. 1484–1510 (1502) ("*One additional finding of the experiment is that algorithmic scoring can exacerbate this racially unequal landscape in rental agreements not just because the algorithm may be inaccurate, but because landlords may want to follow the risk assessment made by the tenant screening report. This is alarming for low-income tenants, particularly housing voucher holders. Security deposits are one of the most significant barriers to obtaining housing for voucher holders, because vouchers do not pay security deposits but most private landlords require them (Rosenblatt & Cossyleon, 2018).* Given that voucher holders have exceptionally low income (usually less than 50% of area median income) and might experience more housing insecurity (rental debts and eviction-related experiences), *imposing greater security deposits on voucher holders almost equates to denying them housing—yet these decisions could be justified by algorithmic scoring if tenant screening services employ it*"). Italics added.

495 Notwithstanding, the theory of "post-race" contends that the great bulk discrimination by the credit card industry is not the byproduct of wilful and flagitious bias. Rather, this discrimination broadly mirrors rational economic decisions to leverage on extant systemic, endemic, and structural social inequalities for profit. See: Carbado, Devon W./Gulati, Mitu, *Acting White? Rethinking Race in Post-Racial America*, Oxford, Oxford University Press, 2015, pp. 1–212 ("What does it mean to "act black" or "act white"? Is race merely a matter of phenotype, or does it come from the inflection of a person's speech, the clothes in her closet, how she chooses to spend her time and with whom she chooses to spend it? What does it mean to be "really" black, and who gets to make that judgment?

In Acting White?, leading scholars of race and the law Devon Carbado and Mitu Gulati argue that, in spite of decades of racial progress and the pervasiveness of multicultural rhetoric, racial judgments are often based not just on skin color, but on how a person conforms to behavior stereotypically associated with a certain race. Specifically, racial minorities are judged on how they "perform" their race. This performance pervades every aspect of their daily life, whether it's the clothes they wear, the way they style their hair, the institutions with which they affiliate, their racial politics, the people they befriend, date or marry, where they live, how they speak, and their outward mannerisms and demeanor. Employing these cues, decision-makers decide not simply whether a person is black but the degree to which she or he is so. Relying on numerous examples from the workplace, higher education, and police interactions, the authors demonstrate that, for African Americans, the costs of "acting black" are high, and so are the pressures to "act white." But, as the authors point out, "acting white" has costs as well"); Howell, Benjamin, "Note, Exploiting Race and Space: Concentrated Subprime Lending as Housing Discrimination", *California Law Review*, Volume 101, 2006, pp. pp. 108–109; Barnes, Mario L., "Reflection on a Dream World: Race, Post-Race and the Question of Making It Over", *Berkely Journal of African-American Law and Policy*, Volume 11, 2009, pp. 6 and ff and passim (parses theories of a "post-racial" world); Haney-López, Ian F., "Essay, Post-Racial Racialism: Racial Stratification and Mass Incarceration in the Age of Obama", *California Law Review*, Volume 98, 2010; Cho, Sumi, "Post-Racialism", *Iowa Law Review*, 2009; Howell, Benjamin, "Note, Exploiting Race and Space: Concentrated Subprime Lending as Housing Discrimination", *California Law Review*, Volume 94, 2006, pp. 101, 108–09; Freeman, Andrea, "Racism in the Credit Card Industry", *cit.*, p. 1098 and ff, whose stellar research I have been following closely.

to which a *selected few* (White folks) should be always granted credit[496] whereas a cohort of *unwanted many* (Blacks and Latinos) should be seldom, if ever, granted[497] credit.[498] Especially, if the applicant lives in a Black neighbourhood,[499] which can be easily ascertained by its underpinning ZIP Code.

§§ When, and if, credit is granted to the *unwanted many* the conditions and terms attached to the affordance of credit[500] should be the worst possible.[501] This abhorring phenomenon amounts to «credit card redlining[502]»[503] according to which White folks

---

[496] Chi-Jack Lin/ Sherman D. Hanna, "Racial Discrimination in the Consumer Credit Market", *Consumer Interests Annual*, Volume 56, 2010 ("*The Equal Credit Opportunity Act (ECOA), enacted in 1974, makes it unlawful for any creditors to discriminate against credit applicants because of their color, race/ethnic group, religion, national origin, sex, marital status, or age (provided the applicant has the capacity to contract*). Researchers have debated the existence of discrimination within the U.S. credit market. Many studies examine the presence of discrimination in the credit market, but none focus specifically on the effect of individuals' race or ethnic group in the consumer credit market, which we differentiate from other household credit markets, such as for home mortgages. This research fills the research gap by examining discrimination in the consumer credit market. Using four Survey of Consumer Finance data sets from 1998 to 2007, we use five measures to assess whether there is discrimination by racial/ethnic group in the consumer credit in US, and, if present, whether the discrimination is due to statistical or taste lender motivations. *Our analyses allow for distinguishing statistical and taste discrimination. In four of five of our measures, there was discrimination against households with Black respondents, and in three out of five measures, there was discrimination against households with Hispanic respondents. Discrimination in the consumer credit market against black and Hispanic households is statistical discrimination: lenders choose to discriminate against black and Hispanic because they on average have higher default risk*"). Italics added.

[497] Freeman, Andrea, "Racism in the Credit Card Industry", *cit.*, p. 1098 and ff, whose stellar research I have been following closely ("*In contrast, lack of transparency on the part of the credit card companies enables discrimination by preventing its identification.* It also helps to ward off the potential for reputational harm or consumer response that media attention to the problem might create. *However, despite the lack of access to definitive statistics on credit card industry practices, two studies analyzed available data to conclude that race, isolated from socio-economic status, has a significant effect on a user's ability to obtain a credit card and on which terms they receive. Specifically, in 2010, researcher Chi-Jack Lin demonstrated that race affects the likelihood of obtaining a credit card, the number of cards owned, the average credit line per card, the conditions and fees attached to a card, and the factors necessary to establish creditworthiness. He found that this type of discrimination occurs based on the names listed on an application, which can often suggest racial identity, or the physical appearance of credit card applicants who walk into banks to request a card in person*"). Italics added.

[498] Marsico, Richard D., "Looking Back and Looking Ahead as the Home Mortgage Disclosure Act Turns Thirty-Five: The Role of Public Disclosure of Lending Data in a Time of Financial Crisis", *Review of Banking and Financial Law*, Volume 29, 2009, pp. 205–206 (argues that a plethora of amendments made in 2002, just like the amendments made in 1989, did not quite obligate lenders to fully disclose the credit score of borrowers and therefore "*hamper[ed] efforts to determine whether higher rates of rejections of loan applications from minority borrowers than whites were due to relatively weaker creditworthiness or race*"). Italics added. See: Freeman, Andrea, "Racism in the Credit Card Industry", *cit.*, passim, whose stellar research I have been following closely.

[499] Cohen-Cole, Ethan, "Credit Card Redlining", *Review of Economics and Statistics*, Volume 93, 2011, pp. 700–711.

[500] But see: Atkinson, Abbye, "Rethinking Credit as a Social Provision", *Stanford Law Review*, Volume 71, 2019, pp. 1093–1099 (contending that credit, which shifts consumption temporally, is only beneficial insofar income ratchets up in the forthcoming future. As of now, though, "credit is

should be easily granted credit whereas Blacks and Latinos should be scarcely,[504] if ever,[505] afforded[506] credit.[507]

---

fundamentally incompatible with the entrenched intergenerational poverty that plagues low-income Americans." Id. Notably, it is crucially important to come to terms with the fact that credit is not a panacea for the great bulk of economic struggles, and concretely wage stagnation. Although credit is not befitted to all consumers at all prices, affordable credit can nonetheless play a pivotal role in the creation of wealth).

501 Freeman, Andrea, "Racism in the Credit Card Industry", *cit.*, p. 1071 ("even worse, the companies do so in a racially discriminatory way, *burdening Black and Latino customers with the worst credit card terms, often unrelated to credit risk*"). Italics added. See also: *Credit Discrimination: Hearings on H.R. 14856 and H.R. 14908 Before the Subcomm. on Consumer Affairs of the H. Comm. on Banking & Currency*, 93rd Cong. 1, 1974, (Hon. Leonor K. Sullivan, Chairman, Subcomm. on Consumer Affairs of the H. Comm. on Banking & Currency) (statement of John H. Powell, Jr., Chairman, Equal Emp't Opportunity Comm'n) *("[I]t is very likely that the inability to obtain credit, or if obtained, the discriminatory terms and conditions which accompany its extension to certain groups in our society, are directly related to discrimination in employment*"). Italics added; id. at 131 (statement of Hon. Arthur S. Flemming, Chairman, U.S. Comm'n on Civil Rights, and Comm'r, Admin. on Aging, Dep't of Health, Educ. & Welfare). Freeman, Andrea, "Racism in the Credit Card Industry", *cit.*, p. 1121. See also: Levitin, Adam J., "The Antitrust Super Bowl: America's Payment Systems, No-Surcharge Rules, and the Hidden Costs of Credit", *Berkeley Business Law Journal*, Volume 3, 2005, 265, 317–18; id. at 154 ("Consequently, *low-income consumers now receive credit cards with high fees and interest rates, while higher-income consumers reap the rewards of credit card use, such as travel miles and concierge services* (...). As a *result of these practices, 80% of the industry's profits now come from interest payments and... fees instead of annual and interchange fees. This shift represents a massive redistribution of wealth from the poor to wealthier consumers and corporations*"). Italics added. See also: Wonyoung, So, "Which Information Matters? Measuring Landlord Assessment of Tenant Screening Reports", *Housing Policy Debate*, Volume 33, n. ° 6, 2023, pp. 1484–1510 (1502) ("*It is important to note that within conditionally accepted reports, similar patterns of blanket screening policies and automation bias are exhibited when landlords impose security deposits. These results may corroborate a paired-test study that shows that Black tenants have less favorable terms and conditions, including security deposits, in rental agreements* (Ross & Turner, 2005)"). Italics added. See: Part IV, This chapter, Sects. 4.1.4–4.1.4.2.3 of this book.

502 Mendez-Carbajo, Diego "Neighborhood Redlining, Racial Segregation, and Homeownership", *Federal Reserve Bank of Saint Louis*, September 1, 2021("*In the 1930s, the Home Owners' Loan Corporation (HOLC) drew maps of residential neighborhoods across the United States. The maps classified each neighborhood into one of five categories, from least to most likely to* ***default*** *on a* ***mortgage*** *loan. In those maps, the neighborhoods most likely to default were shaded red and over time these neighborhoods had the largest concentrations of African Americans. Because the lending classifications determined individual access to credit, the residents of redlined neighborhoods paid high interest rates and had a hard time becoming homeowners and keeping their homes in good condition. From 1968 to 1974, Congress passed several federal laws and policies preventing lending discrimination by race and gender, and the pattern of residential segregation started to change*"). Italics added.

503 Levitin, Adam J., "The Antitrust Super Bowl: America's Payment Systems, No-Surcharge Rules, and the Hidden Costs of Credit", *Berkeley Business Law Journal*, Volume 3, 2005, 265, 317–18; id. at 154 ("*Credit card companies target vulnerable consumers for inferior products through tactics such as teaser rates, mass mailings of preapproved cards,... overly complex credit card agreements, and credit-card redlining*"). Italics added.

504 Firestone, Simon, "Race Ethnicity and Credit Card Monitoring", *Journal of Money, Credit and Banking*, Sept. 2014, 2014, pp. 1206 and ff; Han, Song, Keys, Benjamin J./Li, Geng, *Unsecured*

§§ Recall, members of racialized communities struggle to stay afloat as the overwhelming majority of middle-class Black families[508] «live paycheck-to-paycheck».[509] These families are those who need credit the most to pay for life's necessities.[510] This cluster of unfortunate families is often dubbed as «revolvers»[511] or «subsistence users».[512]

Credit Supply over the Credit Cycle: Evidence from Credit Card Mailings (argue that, statistically, Blacks and Latinos are seldom granted credit and, if ever granted credit, the terms and conditions attached to the concession of credit are not equal to those offered to White folks).

[505] Glantz, Aaron/Martinez, Emmanuel, "For People of Color, Banks are Shutting the Door to Home-ownership", Reveal, February 15, 2018, available at: https://ibw21.org/news/people-color-banks-shutting-door-homeownership/ (access: 4.11.2024) ("*Fifty years after the federal Fair Housing Act banned racial discrimination in lending, African Americans and Latinos continue to be routinely denied conventional mortgage loans at rates far higher than their white counterparts.* This modern-day redlining persisted in 61 metro areas even when controlling for applicants' income, loan amount and neighborhood, according to a mountain of Home Mortgage Disclosure Act records analyzed by Reveal from The Center for Investigative Reporting. *The yearlong analysis, based on 31 million records, relied on techniques used by leading academics, the Federal Reserve and Department of Justice to identify lending disparities. It found a pattern of troubling denials for people of color across the country, including in major metropolitan areas such as Atlanta, Detroit, Philadelphia, St. Louis and San Antonio.* African Americans faced the most resistance in Southern cities — Mobile, Alabama; Greenville, North Carolina; and Gainesville, Florida — and Latinos in Iowa City, Iowa. *No matter their location, loan applicants told similar stories, describing an uphill battle with loan officers who they said seemed to be fishing for a reason to say no*"). Italics added. Campisi, Natalie, From Inherent Racial Bias to Incorrect Data The Problems With Current Credit Scoring Models, Forbes (Feb. 26, 2021), https://www.forbes.com/advisor/creditcards/from-inherent-racial-bias-to-incorrect-data-the-problems-with-current-credit-scoring-models/; [https://www.perma.cc/EWA4-CS8E] (highlighting rampant racial bias in credit scoring systems); Oyama, Rebecca, "Do Not (Re)Enter: the Rise of Criminal Background Tenant Screening as a Violation of the Fair Housing Act", *Michigan Journal of Race and Law*, Volume 15, 2009, pp. 181, 184–93 (discussing a broad range of historical/criminal accounts as a way to screen undesirable tenants, such as Blacks and Latinos); Statement of Interest of the United States at 12, *Louis v. SafeRent Sols., LLC, No. 1:22-cv-10800* (D. Mass. Jan. 9, 2023) (holding that the Fair Housing Act liability stretches far and beyond, thus encompassing a vast assortment of entities providing housing-related services, including corporations that offer tenant screening services).

[506] Glantz, Aaron/Martinez, Emmanuel, "For People of Color, Banks are Shutting the Door to Home-ownership", Reveal, February 15, 2018, available at: https://ibw21.org/news/people-color-banks-shutting-door-homeownership/ (access: 4.11.2024) ("The analysis — independently reviewed and confirmed by *The Associated Press — showed black applicants were turned away at significantly higher rates than whites in 48 cities, Latinos in 25, Asians in nine and Native Americans in three. In Washington, DC, the nation's capital, Reveal found all four groups were significantly more likely to be denied a home loan than whites*"). Italics added.

[507] Brevoort, Kenneth P., "Credit Card Redlining Revisited", *Review of Economics and Statistics*, May 2011, pp. 714 and ff and passim. See: Mendez-Carbajo, Diego "Neighborhood Redlining, Racial Segregation, and Homeownership", *Federal Reserve Bank of Saint Louis*, September 1, 2021("*In the 1930s, the Home Owners' Loan Corporation (HOLC) drew maps of residential neighborhoods across the United States. The maps classified each neighborhood into one of five categories, from least to most likely to* ***default*** *on a* ***mortgage*** *loan. In those maps, the neighborhoods most likely to default were shaded red and over time these neighborhoods had the largest concentrations of African Americans. Because the lending classifications determined individual access to credit, the residents of redlined neighborhoods paid high interest rates and had a hard time becoming homeowners and keeping their homes in good condition. From 1968 to 1974, Congress*

§§ Unsurprisingly, infamous credit card companies[513] relentlessly target[514] those families.[515] Relatedly, unscrupulous and unprincipled credit card companies have long come to terms with the fact that they would profit handsomely with those who are on the cusp of bankruptcy (Blacks and Latinos).[516]

---

passed several federal laws and policies preventing lending discrimination by race and gender, and the pattern of residential segregation started to change"). Italics added.

[508] Zeigert, Jonathan C./Hanges, Paul J., "Employment Discrimination: The Role of Implicit Attitudes, Motivation, and a Climate for Racial Bias", *Journal of Applied Psychology*, Volume 90, 2005.

[509] Freeman, Andrea, "Racism in the Credit Card Industry", *cit.*, p. 1093 and ff, whose stellar research I have been following closely.

[510] But see: Atkinson, Abbye, "Rethinking Credit as a Social Provision", *Stanford Law Review*, Volume 71, 2019, pp. 1093–1099 (contending that credit, which shifts consumption temporally, is only beneficial insofar income ratchets up in the forthcoming future. As of now, though, "credit is fundamentally incompatible with the entrenched intergenerational poverty that plagues low-income Americans." Id. Notably, it is crucially important to come to terms with the fact that credit is not a panacea for the great bulk of economic struggles, and concretely wage stagnation. Although credit is not befitted to all consumers at all prices, affordable credit can nonetheless play a pivotal role in the creation of wealth).

[511] Freeman, Andrea, "Racism in the Credit Card Industry", *cit.*, p. 1095 ("revolvers are credit cards users who carry a balance from month to month").

[512] Freeman, Andrea, "Racism in the Credit Card Industry", *cit.*, p. 1095.

[513] As hinted above, the theory of "post-race" contends that the great bulk discrimination by the credit card industry is not the byproduct of wilful and flagitious bias. Rather, this discrimination broadly mirrors rational economic decisions to leverage on extant systemic, endemic, and structural social inequalities for profit. See: Barnes, Mario L., "Reflection on a Dream World: Race, Post-Race and the Question of Making It Over", *Berkely Journal of African-American Law and Policy*, Volume 11, 2009, pp. 6 and ff and passim (parses theories of a "post-racial" world); Cho, Sumi, "Post-Racialism", *Iowa Law Review*, 2009; Howell, Benjamin, "Note, Exploiting Race and Space: Concentrated Subprime Lending as Housing Discrimination", *California Law Review*, Volume 94, 2006, pp. 101, 108–09.

[514] This situation is further compounded by the issue of price shrouding that leverages on the despair of those who seek credit the most. See: Gabaix, Xavier/Laibson, David, "Shrouded Attributes, Consumer Myopia, and Information Suppression in Competitive Markets", *The Quarterly Journal of Economics*, Volume 121, 2006, pp. 505–530 (canvassing the foundations of price shrouding in the credit card markets).

[515] Levitin, Adam J., "The Antitrust Super Bowl: America's Payment Systems, No-Surcharge Rules, and the Hidden Costs of Credit", *Berkeley Business Law Journal*, Volume 3, 2005, 265, 317–18; Freeman, Andrea, "Racism in the Credit Card Industry", *cit.*; Freeman, Andrea, "Payback: A Structural Analysis of the Credit Card Problem", *Arizona Law Review*, Volume 55, 2013, pp. 151–153, 154 ("*Credit card companies target vulnerable consumers for inferior products through tactics such as teaser rates, mass mailings of preapproved cards,... overly complex credit card agreements, and credit-card redlining.* As a *result of these practices, 80% of the industry's profits now come from interest payments and... fees instead of annual and interchange fees. This shift represents a massive redistribution of wealth from the poor to wealthier consumers and corporations*"). Italics added. See: Levitin, Adam J., "The Antitrust Super Bowl: America's Payment Systems, No-Surcharge Rules, and the Hidden Costs of Credit", *Berkeley Business Law Journal*, Volume 3, 2005, Italics added. See also: Hurley, Mikella/Adebayo, Julius, "Credit Scoring in the Era of Big Data", *Yale Journal of Law and Technology*, Volume 18, 2016, p. 149 ("*Credit-scoring tools that integrate thousands of data points, most of which are collected without consumer knowledge, create serious problems*

§§ This unholy fringe of *unwanted many* (Blacks and Latinos) are accordingly deemed as «subsistence users»[517] as they sorely need credit to survive. On the opposite pole, White folks («lifestyle users»)[518] are offered exceedingly better credit terms and conditions[519] than Blacks[520] only to enhance their overall quality of life to their own amusement.

---

of transparency. Consumers have limited ability to identify and contest unfair credit decisions, and little chance to understand what steps they should take to improve their credit. Recent studies have also questioned the accuracy of the data used by these tools, in some cases identifying serious flaws that have a substantial bearing on lending decisions"). Italics added.

[516] Freeman, Andrea, "Payback: A Structural Analysis of the Credit Card Problem", *Arizona Law Review*, Volume 55, 2013, pp. 151–153 ("Although most economists and legal scholars view the 'credit card problem' of excessive consumer debt as one of market failure, it is in fact a story of overwhelming market success. *Through the use of sophisticated underwriting technology, the credit card companies learned that consumers who are on the verge of bankruptcy represent their greatest source of profits.* The industry responded to this information by completely altering its business model. *Instead of seeking customers who would pay off their bills at the end of each month, known in the industry as convenience users or deadbeats, the companies began to target low-income consumers who would maintain balances from month to month, known as revolvers*"). Italics added. See: Freeman, Andrea, "Racism in the Credit Card Industry", *cit.*, p. 1095.

[517] Freeman, Andrea, "Payback: A Structural Analysis of the Credit Card Problem", *cit.*, pp. 151–153 ("A *subsistence user is someone who uses credit cards to survive, to pay the electricity bill one month and the phone bill the next*, or to purchase essential items such as gas, groceries, or diapers. This type of user contrasts with the 'lifestyle user,' who uses credit cards to enhance her lifestyle, either minimally or considerably"). See: Freeman, Andrea, "Racism in the Credit Card Industry", *cit.*, p. 1095.

[518] Freeman, Andrea, "Payback: A Structural Analysis of the Credit Card Problem", *cit.*, pp. 151–153 ("*This type of user contrasts with the 'lifestyle user,' who uses credit cards to enhance her lifestyle, either minimally or considerably*"). See: Freeman, Andrea, "Racism in the Credit Card Industry", *cit.*, p. 1095.

[519] *Credit Discrimination: Hearings on H.R. 14856 and H.R. 14908 Before the Subcomm. on Consumer Affairs of the H. Comm. on Banking & Currency*, 93rd Cong. 1, 1974, (Hon. Leonor K. Sullivan, Chairman, Subcomm. on Consumer Affairs of the H. Comm. on Banking & Currency) (statement of John H. Powell, Jr., Chairman, Equal Emp't Opportunity Comm'n) *("[I]t is very likely that the inability to obtain credit, or if obtained, the discriminatory terms and conditions which accompany its extension to certain groups in our society, are directly related to discrimination in employment*"). Italics added; id. at 131 (statement of Hon. Arthur S. Flemming, Chairman, U.S. Comm'n on Civil Rights, and Comm'r, Admin. on Aging, Dep't of Health, Educ. & Welfare). Freeman, Andrea, "Racism in the Credit Card Industry", *cit.*, p. 1121.

[520] Han, Song, Keys, Benjamin J./Li, Geng, *Unsecured Credit Supply over the Credit Cycle: Evidence from Credit Card Mailings* (argue that, statistically, Blacks and Latinos are seldom granted credit and, if ever granted credit, the terms and conditions attached to the concession of credit are not equal to those offered to White folks). See also: Wonyoung, So, "Which Information Matters? Measuring Landlord Assessment of Tenant Screening Reports", *Housing Policy Debate*, Volume 33, n. ° 6, 2023, pp. 1484–1510 (1502) ("*It is important to note that within conditionally accepted reports, similar patterns of blanket screening policies and automation bias are exhibited when landlords impose security deposits. These results may corroborate a paired-test study that shows that Black tenants have less favorable terms and conditions, including security deposits, in rental agreements* (Ross & Turner, 2005)"). Italics added. See: Part IV, This chapter, Sects. 4.1.4–4.1.4.2.3 of this book.

§§ «Subsistence users» are those who form part of a broader social apparatus of marginalized communities who were primarily targeted by, and fell prey to, *systemic racism* against the backdrop of which racial, labour, social,[521] and wealth inequalities[522] unfold.[523]

§§ «Subsistence users» (the «have-nots»), the weakest link in the equation of *credit card redlining*, always come out behind whereas the «lifestyle users» («the haves») always come out ahead.[524]

§§ This racial disparity stands as a byproduct of both slavery[525] and systemic racism that deeply impacts, for example, online dispute resolution.[526]

---

521 Ards, Sheila D./Myers, Samuel L. Myers, "The Color of Money: Bad Credit, Wealth, and Race", *American Behavioral Scientist*, Volume 45, 2001, pp. 223–238 (debunks the deep-seated myth according to which Blacks are big spenders and thus unworthy of creditworthiness, which stands as an irksome social bias in dire need of quashing).

522 Derenoncourt, Ellora/Kim, Chi Hyun/Kuhn, Moritz/Schularik, Moritz, "The Wealth of Two Nations: The U.S. Racial Wealth Gap, 1860–2020", *The Quarterly Journal of Economics*, Volume 139, Issue 2, 2024, p. 741 ("A large class of commonly discussed policies for reducing racial wealth inequality seeks to reduce gaps in income, savings, and capital gains. These include policies that encourage financial diversification or stock equity holdings among Black households; policies aimed at financial literacy and retirement or savings behavior; or policies aimed at improving educational and labor market outcomes of Black Americans through improved school quality or reductions in discrimination. *Yet on a realistic note, our simulation in Section IV.A shows that even if wealth accumulation conditions had been equal since 1870, the wealth gap would still be 3 to 1 today, and full convergence would be more than 200 years away. Put differently: to close the racial wealth gap in the immediate term* via *flow parameters, Black Americans would need a substantial positive lead over whites, not "just" more equality*"). Italics added.

523 Burstein, Paul/Edwards, Mark Evan, "The Impact of Employment Discrimination Litigation on Racial Disparity in Earnings: Evidence and Unresolved Issues", *Law and Society Review*, Volume 28, 1994; Pager, Devah/Shepherd, Hana, "The Sociology of Discrimination: Racial Discrimination in Employment, Housing, Credit, and Consumer Markets", *Annual Review of Sociology*, Volume 34, 2008. Freeman, Andrea, "Racism in the Credit Card Industry", *cit.*, p. 1096.

524 The great bulk of these assertions has been anticipated by an iconic piece of research. See: Galanter, Marc, "Why the "Haves" Come Out Ahead: Speculations on the Limits of Legal Change", *Law & Society Review*, Volume 9, 1974, pp. 98–103 (this renowned author talks about a *social reality* in which the dubbed «repeat players»—which go by the name of «haves»—tend to «to come out ahead» by putting their knowledge and vast resources to good use. This perceived advantage will not only impact the choice on the procedures but will ultimately benefit their interests as opposed to the deemed «one-shot» players (the «have nots») that will have slimmer and fewer chances to get palpable results in dispute resolution). But see: Bailey, J./Burkell, J./Reynolds, G. "Access to Justice for All: Towards an "Expansive Vision" of Justice and Technology, *Windsor Yearbook of Access to Justice*, Volume 31, 2013, pp. 183–201 (in stark contrast, these authors stress that the digital and technological apparatus can indeed spawn a both time-effective and streamlined access to justice in a given jurisdiction).

525 Wenger, Kaimipono David, "Too Big to Remedy?" Rethinking Mass Restitution for Slavery and Jim Crow, *The Loyola of Los Angeles Law Review*, Volume 44, 2010, pp. 177–230.

526 See: Donoghue, Jane, "The Rise of Digital Justice: Courtroom Technology, Public Participation and Access to Justice", *The Modern Law Review*, Volume 80, Issue 6, 2018, p. 995 (noting that technology in the courtroom might widen the gap between the rich and the poor. In this vein, this renowned author has contended that "*legal reforms have omitted any detailed consideration of the type and quality of citizen participation in newly digitised court processes which have fundamental implications for the legitimacy and substantive outcomes of court-based processes; and*

§§ Unsurprisingly, this racial wedge has migrated to the purview of credit scoring—and, within which core, *credit card redlining*—in that has created multifarious racial inequalities[527] that bolster both *systemic racism*[528] and *White supremacy*[529] that is beyond repair[530] or atonement.[531]

---

for enhancing democratic procedure through improved access to justice. It is argued that although digital court tools and systems offer great promise for enhancing efficiency, participation and accessibility, they *simultaneously have the potential to amplify the scope for injustice, and to attenuate central principles of the legal system, including somewhat paradoxically, access to justice*"). Italics added. See also: Heintz, M.E., "The digital divide and courtroom technology: Can David keep up with Goliath", *Federal Communications Law Journal*, Volume 54, 2002, pp. 566 ff and passim. See also: Sternlight, Jean R., "Justice in a Brave New World?", *Connecticut Law Review*, Volume 52, Issue 1, 2020, p. 232 (on the possibility to harness technology to "whether voice recognition, analysis of facial expressions, or measurements of body twitches may provide better insight into truthfulness"); Sela, Ayelet, "The Effect of Technologies on Dispute Resolution System Design: Antecedents, Current Trends, and Future Directions", *Lewis and Clark Law Review*, Volume 21, 2018, pp. 634 ff and passim (arguing that the widespread use of technology has breed the turn to online dispute resolution).

[527] Freeman, Andrea, "Payback: A Structural Analysis of the Credit Card Problem", *Arizona Law Review*, Volume 55, 2013, pp. 151–153 ("Although most economists and legal scholars view the 'credit card problem' of excessive consumer debt as one of market failure, it is in fact a story of overwhelming market success. *Through the use of sophisticated underwriting technology, the credit card companies learned that consumers who are on the verge of bankruptcy represent their greatest source of profits.* The industry responded to this information by completely altering its business model. *Instead of seeking customers who would pay off their bills at the end of each month, known in the industry as convenience users or deadbeats, the companies began to target low-income consumers who would maintain balances from month to month, known as revolvers*"). Italics added. Freeman, Andrea, "Racism in the Credit Card Industry", *cit.*, p. 1095.

[528] Feagin, J. R., *Systemic racism: a theory of oppression*, New York: Routledge, 2006. See also: Fiske, John, "Surveilling the City: Whiteness, the Black Man and Democratic Totalitarianism.", *Theory, Culture and Society*, 15 (2), 1998, pp. 67–88 (on the overhyped surveillance on black people as a byproduct of systemic racism); Correll, J., Park, B., Judd, C. M., & Wittenbrink, B., "The police officer's dilemma: using ethnicity to disambiguate potentially threatening individuals", *Journal of Personality and Social Psychology*, 83 (6), 2002, pp. 1314–1329; Daniels, J., "Race and racism in internet studies: a review and critique", *New Media & Society*, 15 (5), 2013, pp. 695–719; Daniels, J., "My brain database doesn't see skin color": color-blind racism in the technology industry and in theorizing the web", *American Behavioral Scientist*, 59 (11), 2015, pp. 1377–1393; de la Peña, C., "The history of technology, the resistance of archives, and the whiteness of race", *Technology and Culture*, 51 (4), 2010, pp. 919–937.

[529] Perea, Juan F., "Doctrines of Delusion: How the History of the G.I. Bill and Other Inconvenient Truths Undermind the Supreme Court's Affirmative Action Jurisprudence", *University of Pittsburgh Law Review*, Volume 75, 1995, pp. 583, 586–89 (establishes a liaison between Jim Crow laws, the G.I. Bill, and the Social Security Act and White supremacy); Milligan, Joy, "Protecting Disfavored Minorities: Towards Institutional Realism", *UCLA Law Review*, Volume 63, 2016, pp. 894, pp. 918–21 (shedding a keen light on racial inequality in U.S. Department of Agriculture farm assistance); Robinson, Reginald Leamon, "The Racial Limits of the Fair Housing Act: The Intersection of Dominant White Images, the Violence of Neighborhood Purity, and the Master Narrative of Black Inferiority", *William & Mary Law Review*, Volume 37, 1995, pp. 69, 71–74 (establishes a connection between the failures of the FHA and White supremacy).

[530] But see: Janssen, Claudia Irene, "Addressing Corporate Ties to Slavery: Corporate Apologia in a Discourse of Reconciliation", *Communication Studies*, Volume 63, 2012, pp. 18–21; Aiyetoro, Adjoa A./Davis, Adrienne D., "Historic and Modern Social Movements for Reparations: The

§§ It is worth recalling that Artificial Intelligence-embedded technologies further compound[532] racial inequalities[533]—in the remit of algorithmic credit scoring[534]—with which modern societies have been floundering for a long-haul.[535] Take Rachelle Faroul for example.

National Coalition of Blacks for Reparations in America (N'COBRA) and Its Antecedents", *Texas Wesleyan Law Review*, Volume 16, 2010, pp. 687–689 (discussing the reparations to compensate the multitudinous damages arising out of slavery).

[531] Gray, David C., "A No-Excuse Approach to Transitional Justice: Reparations as Tools of Extraordinary Justice", *Washington Law Review*, Volume 87, 2010, pp. 1043–1062 ("*Reparations provided to a group as a whole fail to distinguish among former victims, providing benefits to all members without regard to the degree of harm suffered*, potentially even benefitting some who did not suffer at all or who are themselves implicated in abuses." At page 1064 the author further argues that ("Perhaps more troubling is that beneficiaries may again and forever be identified as victims, denying full autonomy to individuals and the authority of identity creation to groups. For *example, Justice Clarence Thomas, among others, has argued that affirmative action should be abandoned because it casts a shadow over the accomplishments of all African Americans and marks blacks as victims, incapable of succeeding on their individual merits*"). Italics added.

[532] See: Hellman, Deborah, "Indirect Discrimination and the Duty to Avoid Compounding Injustice", *Foundations of Indirect Discrimination Law*, Collins, Hugh/Khaitan, Tarunabh (Editors), Oxford, Hart Publishing; Reprint edition (June 25, 2020), 2020, p. 107 (Professor Deborah Hellman coined this expression to depict a decision that "exacerbates the harm caused by the prior injustice because it entrenches the harm or carries it into another domain." This book deals with the sweltering topic of indirect discrimination ("*indirect discrimination (or disparate impact) concerns the application of the same rule to everyone, even though that rule significantly disadvantages one particular group in society*"). Italics added.

[533] Shields, Majorie A., "Discrimination Against Credit Applicant on Basis of Race or National Origin Under Equal Credit Opportunity Act, 15 U.S.C. § 1691 et ss", *American Law Reports Federal, 3D*, Volume 13, 2016, Article 9, passim.

[534] But see: Wonyoung, So, "Which Information Matters? Measuring Landlord Assessment of Tenant Screening Reports", *Housing Policy Debate*, Volume 33, n. ° 6, 2023, pp. 1484–1510 (1502) ("*One additional finding of the experiment is that algorithmic scoring can exacerbate this racially unequal landscape in rental agreements not just because the algorithm may be inaccurate, but because landlords may want to follow the risk assessment made by the tenant screening report. This is alarming for low-income tenants, particularly housing voucher holders. Security deposits are one of the most significant barriers to obtaining housing for voucher holders, because vouchers do not pay security deposits but most private landlords require them (Rosenblatt & Cossyleon, 2018).* Given that voucher holders have exceptionally low income (usually less than 50% of area median income) and might experience more housing insecurity (rental debts and eviction-related experiences), *imposing greater security deposits on voucher holders almost equates to denying them housing—yet these decisions could be justified by algorithmic scoring if tenant screening services employ it*"). Italics added.

[535] Glantz, Aaron/Martinez, Emmanuel, "For People of Color, Banks are Shutting the Door to Homeownership", Reveal, February 15, 2018, available at: https://ibw21.org/news/people-color-banks-shutting-door-homeownership/ (access: 4.11.2024) ("*Fifty years after the federal Fair Housing Act banned racial discrimination in lending, African Americans and Latinos continue to be routinely denied conventional mortgage loans at rates far higher than their white counterparts*"). Italics added.

§§ Rachelle Faroul, a thirty-three-year-old black woman, applied for a loan from Philadelphia Mortgage Advisers back in April 2016,[536] was awash of confidence in being granted a loan. She had good credit scoring and a whopping amount of savings after all.[537]

§§ In addition to that, back then, she was earning a decent amount of money (roughly $ 60,000 dollars a year) as a computer programming instructor at the renowned Rutgers University.[538] Her optimism was neither unwarranted nor uncalled for. Yet her hopes were mercilessly dashed by the *systemic racism* baked into the machine learning algorithms entrusted with deciding[539] whether and to what extent a loan should be granted.[540]

§§ Compelingly, Artificial Intelligence embedded-technologies on which machine learning algorithms operate upon swiftly gainsaid her initial application for a loan while offering a very lame excuse to do so: Philadelphia Mortgage Advisers claimed that her contract income was riddled with irretractable inconsistencies.[541]

§§ The unvarnished reality, though, is that the Artificial Intelligence-embedded technologies around which credit scoring revolves leverage on a plethora of biased data that disgracefully creep into the algorithm and feeds into an automated decision that comes to the expense of Blacks 'and Latino's credit scoring.[542] Thereby creating a haze of ambiguity that obfuscates automated decision-making while propelling a meaningless façade of neutrality that casts a shady shadow on credit card industry.

---

[536] Rodriguez, Lorena, "All Data is not Credit Data: Closing the Gap between the Fair Housing Act and Algorithmic Decision-making in the Lending Industry", *Columbia Law Review*, Volume 120, 2020, pp. 1843–1884 (1844).

[537] Rodriguez, Lorena, "All Data is not Credit Data: Closing the Gap between the Fair Housing Act and Algorithmic Decision-making in the Lending Industry", *cit.*, pp. 1843–1884 (1844).

[538] Rodriguez, Lorena, "All Data is not Credit Data: Closing the Gap between the Fair Housing Act and Algorithmic Decision-making in the Lending Industry", *cit.*, pp. 1843–1884 (1844).

[539] See: Part V, Chap. 5, Sect. 5.1.7.2 of this book (on law number two to control algorithmic decision-making, which mandates that black box models must not be entrusted with the task of making high stake decisions—v.g. health and freedom).

[540] But see: Weizenbaum, Joseph, *Computer Power and Human Reason: From Judgment to Calculation*, 1st edition, New York, W. H. Freeman & Co, 1976, pp. 1–300 (227) ("examines the sources of the computer's powers and offers evaluative explorations of what computers can do, cannot do, and should not be employed to do") (*this founding father of Artificial Intelligence presciently noted that we should not entrust Artificial Intelligence-embedded technologies* with "tasks that demand wisdom"). Italics added. The approval of rental applications is arguably one of those tasks that should never be entrusted to machines). More on this on Part IV, This chapter, Sects. 4.1.4–4.1.4.2.1 of this book.

[541] Rodriguez, Lorena, "All Data is not Credit Data: Closing the Gap between the Fair Housing Act and Algorithmic Decision-making in the Lending Industry", *cit.*, pp. 1843–1884 (1844).

[542] Glantz, Aaron/Martinez, Emmanuel, "For People of Color, Banks are Shutting the Door to Homeownership", Reveal, February 15, 2018, available at: https://ibw21.org/news/people-color-banks-shutting-door-homeownership/ (access: 4.11.2024) ("*Lenders and their trade organizations do not dispute the fact that they turn away people of color at rates far greater than whites* (...)They singled out the three-digit credit score — which banks use to determine whether a borrower is likely to repay a loan — as especially important in lending decisions"). Italics added.

The next scene of this appalling episode of *systemic racism* is to couch, and lend support to, this main contention.

§§ Fast backwards to late 2016, Rachelle Faroul persisted and was eventually granted a full-time job at the equally reputable University of Pennsylvania.[543] Her hopes to be granted a loan flared anew.[544]

§§ She accordingly applied for a loan only this time around with Santander Bank.[545] Again, her hopes were nonetheless dashed by the hiddenness[546] under which the cryptic[547] banking[548] system[549] is wrapped.[550] Santander Bank simply

---

543 Glantz, Aaron/Martinez, Emmanuel, "For People of Color, Banks are Shutting the Door to Homeownership", Reveal, February 15, 2018, available at: https://ibw21.org/news/people-color-banks-shutting-door-homeownership/ (access: 4.11.2024).

544 Rodriguez, Lorena, "All Data is not Credit Data: Closing the Gap between the Fair Housing Act and Algorithmic Decision-making in the Lending Industry", *cit.*, pp. 1843–1884 (1844).

545 Rodriguez, Lorena, "All Data is not Credit Data: Closing the Gap between the Fair Housing Act and Algorithmic Decision-making in the Lending Industry", *cit.*, pp. 1843–1884 (1844).

546 Freeman, Andrea, "Racism in the Credit Card Industry", *cit.*, p. 1128 ("*Additionally, the lack of racial data on credit card lending prevents plaintiffs from proving their cases based on disparate impact in jurisdictions that allow those claims*"). Italics added. See also: Hurley, Mikella/Adebayo, Julius, "Credit Scoring in the Era of Big Data", *Yale Journal of Law and Technology*, Volume 18, 2016, 149 ("*for most Americans, access to credit is an essential requirement for upward mobility and financial success. A favorable credit rating is necessary to purchase a home or car, to start a new business, to seek higher education, or to pursue other important goals. For many consumers, strong credit is also necessary to gain access to employment, rental housing, and essential services such as insurance. At present, however, individuals have very little control over how they are scored and have even less ability to contest inaccurate, biased, or unfair assessments of their credit. Traditional, automated credit-scoring tools raise longstanding concerns of accuracy and unfairness. The recent advent of new "big-data" credit-scoring products heightens these concerns*"). Italics added. See also: *Tech, Bias and Housing Initiative, the Promise and Perils of Residential Proptech, Year 1, Research Summary Report, April 2023, TechEquity Collaborative*, p. 11, available at: https://techequity.us/wp-content/uploads/2023/04/TBHI-Y1-Research-Summary-Report.pdf (28.11.2024). ("And while we know that the *data is predictive, meaning it has little to do with demonstrated behavior of the applicant themself, we do not know exactly where companies get their data*"). Italics added.

547 Glantz, Aaron/Martinez, Emmanuel, "For People of Color, Banks are Shutting the Door to Homeownership", Reveal, February 15, 2018, available at: https://ibw21.org/news/people-color-banks-shutting-door-homeownership/ (access: 4.11.2024) ("*Lenders and their trade organizations do not dispute the fact that they turn away people of color at rates far greater than whites. But they maintain that the disparity can be explained by factors the industry has fought to keep hidden, including the prospective borrowers' credit history and overall debt-to-income ratio*"). Italics added.

548 Bruckner, Mathew Adam, "The Promise and Perils of Algorithmic Lenders 'Use of Big Data", *Chicago-Kent Law Review*, Volume 93, 2018, p. 27, note 162 ("*The persistent shrouding of the credit-scoring process makes it difficult to understand how scores are compiled*, let alone whether *those scores are appropriate*"). Italics added.

549 Which makes the task of proving their cases based on disparate impact considerably difficult as the banking system routinely refuses to provide the data that underpinned the decision to gainsay a loan to racialized communities. See: Taylor, Winnie, "Proving Racial Discrimination and Monitoring Fair Lending Compliance: The Missing Data Problem in Nonmortgage Credit", *Review of Banking and Finance Law*, Volume 31, 2011, pp. 199–201.

550 Marsico, Richard D., "Looking Back and Looking Ahead as the Home Mortgage Disclosure Act Turns Thirty-Five: The Role of Public Disclosure of Lending Data in a Time of Financial Crisis",

refused to grant her a loan for reasons that were beyond her grasp.[551] The news she received—Santander Bank refused her application to grant her a loan—teared apart her dream of becoming a houseowner. For good. Note, though, that the worst was yet to come.

§§ At this juncture (early 2017), and holding all else constant, Rachelle Faroul had already been trying to get a mortgage loan for more than a year.[552] But to no avail. To the extent that she has sought credit from a plethora of lenders, her credit score[553] was accordingly lowered.[554]

§§ In an earnest attempt to grant Rachelle a loan, Jonathan, Rachelle's partner, a half-white and half Asian,[555] who was working back then part-time at a local grocery store, agreed to sign Rachelle's application to grant a loan.[556] The loan was finally approved.[557] The stark racial inequality between Blacks (*Rachelle Faroul*) and Whites (*Jonathan*)—a byproduct of *Algorithmic Dictatorship*—was vividly clear.

§§ Whilst Rachelle Faroul fought strenuously to be granted a loan for over a year, Jonathan was swiftly granted a loan shortly after filling out the paperwork, which took him roughly fifteen minutes.[558] Strikingly, Jonathan, unlike Rachelle Faroul,

---

Review of Banking and Financial Law, Volume 29, 2009, pp. 205–206 (argues that a plethora of amendments made in 2002, just like the amendments made in 1989, did not quite obligate lenders to fully disclose the credit score of borrowers and therefore "*hamper[ed] efforts to determine whether higher rates of rejections of loan applications from minority borrowers than whites were due to relatively weaker creditworthiness or race*"). Italics added.

551 Havard, Cassandra Jones, "On The Take": The Black Box of Credit Scoring and Mortgage Discrimination", *Boston University Public Interest Law Journal*, Volume 20, 2011, pp. 241–247 (highlighting that credit scoring if unchecked is an intrinsic, encroached, deep-rooted form of racial discrimination akin to mortgage redlining).

552 Rodriguez, Lorena, "All Data is not Credit Data: Closing the Gap between the Fair Housing Act and Algorithmic Decision-making in the Lending Industry", *cit.*, pp. 1843–1884 (1844).

553 It is crucially important to note, though, that the very fact that only certain types of behaviours are assessed and gauged by credit scores leads to the conclusion some borrowers are not scored at all. The overwhelming majority of consumers boast meagre, if any, credit files owing to the fact that the likelihood to access to the sort of financial services that actually report to the orthodox credit bureaus scattered across modern economies is exceedingly low, which, in turn, morphs them into credit invisible persons. See: Yu, Persis/McLaughlin, Jilian/Levy, Marina, "Big Data: A Big Disappointment for Scoring Consumer Creditworthiness,", *The National Consumer Law Center*, 2 (Mar. 14, 2014), available at: https://www.nclc.org/images/pdf/pr-reports/report-big-data.pdf; [https://www.perma.cc/W4SK-NXD5] (access: 21.12.2024).

554 Rodriguez, Lorena, "All Data is not Credit Data: Closing the Gap between the Fair Housing Act and Algorithmic Decision-making in the Lending Industry", *cit.*, pp. 1843–1884 (1844).

555 Glantz, Aaron/Martinez, Emmanuel, "For People of Color, Banks are Shutting the Door to Homeownership", Reveal, February 15, 2018, available at: https://ibw21.org/news/people-color-banks-shutting-door-homeownership/ (access: 4.11.2024).

556 Glantz, Aaron/Martinez, Emmanuel, "For People of Color, Banks are Shutting the Door to Homeownership", Reveal, February 15, 2018, available at: https://ibw21.org/news/people-color-banks-shutting-door-homeownership/ (access: 4.11.2024).

557 Rodriguez, Lorena, "All Data is not Credit Data: Closing the Gap between the Fair Housing Act and Algorithmic Decision-making in the Lending Industry", *cit.*, pp. 1843–1884 (1845).

558 Rodriguez, Lorena, "All Data is not Credit Data: Closing the Gap between the Fair Housing Act and Algorithmic Decision-making in the Lending Industry", *cit.*, pp. 1843–1884 (1845).

had almost no savings, his income was less than modest, to say the least. What is more, Jonathan had a very modest credit scoring.[559]

§§ What was the rationale behind this blatant racial discrimination? Jonathan was White, whereas Rachelle Faroul was Black. That simple.[560] Note, though, that it should not come as a bewildering surprise that *Algorithmic Dictatorship*, a tool that reproduces and compounds a long-standing racial and wealth wedge,[561] awards everything to the *selected few* (White) while snubbing everything to the *unwanted many* (Blacks and Latinos). We know that by now.

4.1.3 Algorithmic Prime-Lining*: Everything to the* Selected Few *(White) and nothing—or Very few—to the* Unwanted Many *(Blacks)*

§§ Big corporations[562] assumed the helm of economic leadership.[563] Whilst this may hold a wealth of benefits to boost commercial flourishment, it nonetheless pre-empts fair treatment of which citizens are so fond of. Take the example of credit scoring that leverage on rigged Big Data[564] to grant or refuse loans to citizens.[565]

---

559 Rodriguez, Lorena, "All Data is not Credit Data: Closing the Gap between the Fair Housing Act and Algorithmic Decision-making in the Lending Industry", *cit.*, pp. 1843–1884 (1845).

560 Havard, Cassandra Jones, "On The Take": The Black Box of Credit Scoring and Mortgage Discrimination", *Boston University Public Interest Law Journal*, Volume 20, 2011, pp. 241–247 (highlighting that credit scoring if unchecked is an intrinsic, encroached, deep-rooted form of racial discrimination akin to mortgage redlining). See also: Wonyoung, So, "Which Information Matters? Measuring Landlord Assessment of Tenant Screening Reports", *Housing Policy Debate*, Volume 33, n. º 6, 2023, pp. 1484–1510 (1502) ("*These results may corroborate a paired-test study that shows that Black tenants have less favorable terms and conditions, including security deposits, in rental agreements* (Ross & Turner, 2005)"). Italics added. See: Part IV, This chapter, Sects. 4.1.4–4.1.4.2.3 of this book.

561 Derenoncourt, Ellora/Kim, Chi Hyun/Kuhn, Moritz/Schularik, Moritz, "The Wealth of Two Nations: The U.S. Racial Wealth Gap, 1860–2020", *The Quarterly Journal of Economics*, Volume 139, Issue 2, 2024, p. 741 ("A large class of commonly discussed policies for reducing racial wealth inequality seeks to reduce gaps in income, savings, and capital gains. These include policies that encourage financial diversification or stock equity holdings among Black households; policies aimed at financial literacy and retirement or savings behavior; or policies aimed at improving educational and labor market outcomes of Black Americans through improved school quality or reductions in discrimination. *Yet on a realistic note, our simulation in Section IV.A shows that even if wealth accumulation conditions had been equal since 1870, the wealth gap would still be 3 to 1 today, and full convergence would be more than 200 years away. Put differently: to close the racial wealth gap in the immediate term* via *flow parameters, Black Americans would need a substantial positive lead over whites, not "just" more equality*"). Italics added.

§§ It is often ventured that big corporations are bound to control digital capitalism,[566] which will accordingly send ripples across the data-driven world.[567] This holds true, but truer still a savage digital capitalism, if left unchecked, will further

---

[562] A rise which, in turn, creates a host of legal quandaries in the remit of corporate criminal liability. See in Spanish doctrine: Gómez-Jara Díez, Carlos, *Autorregulación y responsabilidad de las personas jurídicas*. Peru: ARA Editores, 2018, pp. 75 and ff (stresses the importance of companies self-regulacion as a way to protect its directors from civil and criminal liability); Vila, Ivó Coca, ¿ "Programas de cumplimiento como forma de autorregulación regulada?", Sánchez, Jesús-María Silva (Dir.), *Criminalidad de empresa y compliance: prevención y reacciones corporativas*. Barcelona: Atelier, 2018, pp. 54 and ff and passim (stresses that criminal compliance aims to toil towards compliance with the law). See in German doctrine: Rotsch, Thomas, *Compliance und Strafrecht—Fragen, Bedeutung, Perspektiven Vorbemerkungen zu einer Theorie der sog.* Berlin: DeGruyter, 2014, passim; Engelhart, Marc, *Sanktionierung von Unternehmen und Compliance—Eine rechtsvergleichende Analyse des Straf-und Ordnungswidrigkeitenrechts in Deutschland und den USA*, 2. Auflage, Schriftenreihe des Max-Planck-Instituts für ausländisches und internationales Strafrecht, Reihe S: Strafrechtliche Forschungsberichte (MPIS), Band 121, Berlin: Duncker & Humblot, 2012, pp. 284–290; Gallego Soller, José Ignacio. "Investigaciones internas corporativas: de la práctica a la teoría". *En Un modelo integral de Derecho Penal. Libro Homenaje a la Profesora Corcoy Vidasolo*. Madrid: Agencia Estatal Boletín Oficial del Estado, 2022, pp. 1151–1165; Santos, Hugo Luz dos, *Programas de Compliance e Inteligência Artificial: Consequências ao nível da Law and Economics, do Direito Penal, do Processo Penal e da Behavioral Law and Economics*, Braga, NovaCausa Edições Jurídicas, 2024, pp. 1–330.

[563] Wallheimer, Brian, "Are you Ready for Personalized Pricing? Companies Are Figuring out What Individual Customers Will Pay-and Charging Accordingly", *Chicago Booth Review*, 2018, passim.

[564] But see: *Tech, Bias and Housing Initiative, the Promise and Perils of Residential Proptech, Year 1, Research Summary Report, April 2023, TechEquity Collaborative*, p. 11, available at: https://techequity.us/wp-content/uploads/2023/04/TBHI-Y1-Research-Summary-Report.pdf (28.11.2024). ("*Once bad data enters the analysis of one factor, it gets baked into the subsequent process, multiplying the effect that one disadvantageous data point can have on someone's overall housing determination*"). Italics added. See: Part IV, This chapter, Sects. 4.1.4–4.1.4.2.3 of this book.

[565] Hurley, Mikella/Adebayo, Julius, "Credit Scoring in the Era of Big Data", *Yale Journal of Law and Technology*, Volume 18, 2016, p. 149 ("*Credit-scoring tools that integrate thousands of data points, most of which are collected without consumer knowledge, create serious problems of transparency. Consumers have limited ability to identify and contest unfair credit decisions, and little chance to understand what steps they should take to improve their credit. Recent studies have also questioned the accuracy of the data used by these tools, in some cases identifying serious flaws that have a substantial bearing on lending decisions. Big-data tools may also risk creating a system of "creditworthiness by association" in which consumers' familial, religious, social, and other affiliations determine their eligibility for an affordable loan. These tools may furthermore obscure discriminatory and subjective lending policies behind a single "objective" score. Such discriminatory scoring may not be intentional; instead, sophisticated algorithms may combine facially neutral data points and treat them as proxies for immutable characteristics such as race or gender, thereby circumventing existing non-discrimination laws and systematically denying credit access to certain groups. Finally, big-data tools may allow online payday lenders to target the most vulnerable consumers and lure them into debt traps*"). Italics added.

[566] See in Italian doctrine: Quintarelli, Stefano, *Capitalismo Immateriale—Le tecnologie digitali ed il nuovo conflito sociale*, 7ª edizione. Turin: Bollati Boringhieri, 2019, pp. 1–198.

[567] Ripple effects arising out challenges that are neither amenable to be shrugged off nor relinquished. Let alone unduly forsaken. The challenges brought forth by an ever-evolving and far-reaching "Blockchain digital society" should urge the legal community to rattle off a wide range

compound wealth[568] divides[569] which, as hinted above, were created suitably by slavery and ratcheted up by *systemic racism*.[570]

§§ To the extent that big corporations form the crux of the economic system, caution must be exercised to prevent «intelligent automation»[571]—that propels forward algorithmic decision-making—from making biased automatic decisions that will come to the expense of members of racialised communities 'fundamental rights.[572] Amongst which stands arguably the right to access to a bevy of tier-one services in an equal-footed and even-handed manner.[573]

---

of actionable solutions to tackle this issue of paramount importance. See: De Filippi/Primavera/Wright, Aaron, *Blockchain and the Law. Rule of Code.* Cambridge: Harvard University Press, 2019, pp. 196–200 (presciently addresses the hazard of the data collated by enterprises fall prey to decontextualization). If lawmakers fail to entertain proficiently this issue, somewhere along the line the data fed into the machines will spawn algorithmic discrimination or algorithmic biases in criminal justice. Which means that algorithmic biases—caused by data decontextualization—will ripple forward to the detriment of a sought-after algorithmic fairness.

568 Derenoncourt, Ellora/Kim, Chi Hyun/Kuhn, Moritz/Schularik, Moritz, "The Wealth of Two Nations: The U.S. Racial Wealth Gap, 1860–2020", *The Quarterly Journal of Economics*, Volume 139, Issue 2, 2024, p. 741 ("A large class of commonly discussed policies for reducing racial wealth inequality seeks to reduce gaps in income, savings, and capital gains. These include policies that encourage financial diversification or stock equity holdings among Black households; policies aimed at financial literacy and retirement or savings behavior; or policies aimed at improving educational and labor market outcomes of Black Americans through improved school quality or reductions in discrimination. *Yet on a realistic note, our simulation in Section IV.A shows that even if wealth accumulation conditions had been equal since 1870, the wealth gap would still be 3 to 1 today, and full convergence would be more than 200 years away. Put differently: to close the racial wealth gap in the immediate term* via *flow parameters, Black Americans would need a substantial positive lead over whites, not "just" more equality*"). Italics added.

569 Xavier, Ines, "Wealth Inequality in the US: The Role of Heterogeneous Returns," *SSRN Working Paper*, 2021; Zewde, Naomi, "Universal Baby Bonds Reduce Black-White Wealth Inequality, Progressively Raise Net Worth of all Young Adults," *Review of Black Political Economy*, Volume 47, 2020, pp, 3–19; Saez, Emmanuel, and Gabriel Zucman, "Wealth Inequality in the United States since 1913: Evidence from Capitalized Income Tax Data," *Quarterly Journal of Economics*, Volume 131, 2016, pp. 519–578; Saez, Emmanuel, "The Rise of Income and Wealth Inequality in America: Evidence from Distributional Macroeconomic Accounts," *Journal of Economic Perspectives*, Volume 34, 2020, pp. 3–26.

570 It bears mentioning that the yawning gap between White rich—that can adroitly harness artificial intelligence to advance their goals and shady agendas—and Black poor—that grapple to meet basic needs and are automatically excluded from the equation of digital society powered by Artificial Intelligence—will directly impact the fabric of societies worldwide, thereby augmenting the chasm between the «digitally-chosen» and the «digitally-outcast» enabled by a algorithmic discrimination that does nothing but irreparable harm. See: Yu, Peter K., "The Algorithmic Divide and Equality in the Age of Artificial Intelligence", *Florida Law Review*, Volume 72, 2020, pp. 355–360 (addresses the issue of algorithmic discrimination).

571 Bornet, Pascal/Barkin, Ian/Wirtz, Jochen, *Intelligent Automation: Learn how to harness Artificial Intelligence to boost business and make out world more human*, 2020, pp. 1–432.

§§ All leads to the conclusion that any commercial stance that further entrenches racial, social, wealth divides[574] should be promptly dismissible as both mind bendingly and impracticable. The garish taste of invidiousness, unlawfulness and racial discrimination must be filtered out or inordinate harms may otherwise be externalised onto members of racialized communities (Blacks and Latinos).

§§ Compellingly, big corporations have no business in flaring racial disparities up[575] between White folks and Black folks. Regrettably, that is exactly what is currently happening in the purview of e-commerce in the United Stated of America. Take Amazon's Prime membership e-commerce policy—which, in turn, is spurred

---

[572] Cataleta, Maria Stefania/Cataleta, Anna, "Artificial Intelligence and Human Rights: An Unequal Struggle", *CIFILE Journal of International Law*, Volume 1, N. ° 2, 2020 ("*Intelligent systems present problems regarding individual rights and responsibilities*"). Italics added. Converging: Cataleta, Maria Stefania, "Artificial Intelligence vs Human Intelligence", in: Martin, L. Miraut/ Zalucki, M. (editors), *Artificial intelligence and Human Rights, Dickinson eBook*. Krakow: AFM Krakow University, 2021, pp. 117–127 (on the slew of both moral, ethical and legal issues with which jurists will grapple in the forthcoming future due to the rise of artificial intelligence in legal arena).

[573] The right to be treated in a equal-footed and heaven-handed manner transcends timeframes and jurisdictions in that it has been applied across several domains. Namely, dispute resolution. See: Welsh, Nancy A., "The Reputational Advantages of Demonstrating Trustworthiness: Using the Reputation Index with Law Students", *Negotiation Journal*, Volume 28, 2012, pp. 133–136 (stating that, when fairly treated and trust has been yielded in dispute resolution settings, disputants tend to display openness to share information thus experiencing both enhanced trust and heightened possibilities to change the relationship with the other disputant—in a peer-to-peer dispute resolution scenario); Hollander-Blumoff, Rebecca, "Just Negotiation", *Washington University Law Review*, Volume 88 2010, pp. 381 ff (on the enhanced perceptions of trustworthiness experienced by the mighty individual—in cultures of dignity—when treated in an even-handed and in an equal-footed manner); La Tour, Stephen La Tour *et alii*, "Procedure: Transnational Perspectives and Preferences", *Yale Law Journal*, Volume 86, 1976, (noting that disputants tend to, in some occasions, rely on their lawyers' as to avoid engaging directly in an unpleasant interpersonal dispute); Welsh, Nancy A., "Disputants' Decision Control in Court-connected Mediation: A Hollow Promise without Procedural Justice", *Journal of Dispute Resolution*, 2002, pp. 179–187 (analyzing self-determination in court-connected mediation and the possibility (or lack thereof) to *control* the outcome of the dispute).

[574] Derenoncourt, Ellora/Kim, Chi Hyun/Kuhn, Moritz/Schularik, Moritz, "The Wealth of Two Nations: The U.S. Racial Wealth Gap, 1860–2020", *The Quarterly Journal of Economics*, Volume 139, Issue 2, 2024, p. 741 ("A large class of commonly discussed policies for reducing racial wealth inequality seeks to reduce gaps in income, savings, and capital gains. These include policies that encourage financial diversification or stock equity holdings among Black households; policies aimed at financial literacy and retirement or savings behavior; or policies aimed at improving educational and labor market outcomes of Black Americans through improved school quality or reductions in discrimination. *Yet on a realistic note, our simulation in Section IV.A shows that even if wealth accumulation conditions had been equal since 1870, the wealth gap would still be 3 to 1 today, and full convergence would be more than 200 years away. Put differently: to close the racial wealth gap in the immediate term* via *flow parameters, Black Americans would need a substantial positive lead over whites, not "just" more equality*"). Italics added.

[575] Daniels, J., "My brain database doesn't see skin color": color-blind racism in the technology industry and in theorizing the web.' *American Behavioral Scientist*, Volume 59, Issue 11, 2015, pp. 1377–1393.

by Artificial Intelligence-embedded technologies[576]—that map seamlessly onto the category of «prediction machines».[577]

§§ Notably, Amazon's consumer policy is externalising inordinate algorithmic harm[578] onto Blacks. Amazon's unlawful racial discrimination[579] is strikingly clear through the lens of their newfangled consumer policy of Prime membership,[580] which leverages on Big Data[581] to perform algorithmic[582] decision making through machine learning[583] algorithms.[584]

---

[576] Karnow, Curtis E. A., "The Opinion of Machines", *The Cambridge Handbook of the Law of Algorithms*, Bartfield, Woodrow (Editor), Cambridge, United Kingdom: Cambridge University Press, 2021, passim.

[577] Agrawal, Ajay/Gans, Joshua/Goldfarb, Avi, *Prediction Machines: The Simple Economics of Artificial Intelligence*, 2nd Edition. Massachusetts: Harvard Business Review Press, 2022, pp. 1–304.

[578] On algorithmic harm on consumer markets: Bar-Gill, Oren/Sunstein, Cass R./Talgam-Cohen, Inbal, "Algorithmic Harm in Consumer Markets", *Journal of Legal Analysis*, Volume 15, n. ° 1, 2023, pp. 1–47.

[579] Note, though, that this racial discrimination may not be fully intentional. More likely than not, it can be related with the perils of big data colour-blindness that nonetheless relies on proxies to race and gender to make algorithmic decisions. Another problem is the one related with "creditworthiness by association" that causes more problems than it solves. Hurley, Mikella/Adebayo, Julius, "Credit Scoring in the Era of Big Data", *Yale Journal of Law and Technology*, Volume 18, 2016, p. 149 ("*recent studies have also questioned the accuracy of the data used by these tools, in some cases identifying serious flaws that have a substantial bearing on lending decisions. Big-data tools may also risk creating a system of "creditworthiness by association" in which consumers' familial, religious, social, and other affiliations determine their eligibility for an affordable loan. These tools may furthermore obscure discriminatory and subjective lending policies behind a single "objective" score. Such discriminatory scoring may not be intentional; instead, sophisticated algorithms may combine facially neutral data points and treat them as proxies for immutable characteristics such as race or gender, thereby circumventing existing non-discrimination laws and systematically denying credit access to certain groups. Finally, big-data tools may allow online payday lenders to target the most vulnerable consumers and lure them into debt traps*"). Italics added. Campisi, Natalie, From Inherent Racial Bias to Incorrect Data The Problems With Current Credit Scoring Models, Forbes (Feb. 26, 2021), https://www.forbes.com/advisor/creditcards/from-inherent-racial-bias-to-incorrect-data-the-problems-with-current-credit-scoring-models/; [https://perma.cc/EWA4-CS8E] (highlighting rampant racial bias in credit scoring systems); Oyama, Rebecca, "Do Not (Re)Enter: the Rise of Criminal Background Tenant Screening as a Violation of the Fair Housing Act", *Michigan Journal of Race and Law*, Volume 15, 2009, pp. 181, 184–93 (discussing a broad range of historical/criminal accounts as a way to screen undesirable tenants, such as Blacks and Latinos); Statement of Interest of the United States at 12, *Louis v. SafeRent Sols., LLC, No. 1:22-cv-10800* (D. Mass. Jan. 9, 2023) (holding that the Fair Housing Act liability stretches far and beyond, thus encompassing a vast assortment of entities providing housing-related services, including corporations that offer tenant screening services).

[580] Banchiri, Bamzi, "Is Amazon Same-Day Delivery Service Racist?", *Christian SCI Monitor* (Apr. 23, 2016), https://www.csmonitor.com/Business/2016/0423/Is-Amazon-same-day-delivery-service-racist; [https://perma.cc/L2LD-2P8V]; Letzer, Rafi, "Amazon Just Showed Us That 'Unbiased' Algorithms Can Be Inadvertently Racist", *Business Insider* (Apr. 21, 2016), http://www.businessinsider.com/how-algorithms-can-be-racist-2016-4; [http://perma.cc/MWP5-ZYFS].

§§ Prime membership amounts to a service by which customers enrol to be afforded the opportunity to gain access to a sought-after free same-day delivery.[585] Prime membership seeks to kneecap one of the very few advantages that local retailers—or small-scaled businesses—retain over large-scaled businesses: instant gratification.[586]

---

[581] Wolkowitz, Eva/Parker, Sara, *Big Data, Big Potential: Harnessing Data Technology for the Underserved Market*, Center for Financial Services Innovation, 2015 (Big Data can be defined as "as the collection and use of large data sets that can be broadly combined and distributed to identify patterns and create new data based on these insights—known as metavariables—to increase the effectiveness and efficiency of consumer finance products"). See also: Crawford, Kate/Schultz, Jason, "Big Data and Due Process: Toward a Framework to Redress Predictive Privacy Harms", *Boston College Law Review*, Volume 55, 2014, pp. 93–96 (posits that Big Data amounts to "the use of large data sets in data science and predictive analytics").

[582] Domingos, Pedro, *The Master Algorithm: How the Quest for the Ultimate Learning Machine Will Remake Our World*, New York, Basic Books, 2015, pp. 1 and ff (3) (defines an algorithm "a sequence of instructions telling a computer what to do").

[583] Surden, Harry, "Machine Learning and Law", *Washington Law Review*, 2014, pp. 87, 88–89 (deems "machine learning" as "a subfield of computer science concerned with computer programs that are able to learn from experience and thus improve their performance over time"). See: Murphy, Kevin P., *Machine Learning: A Probabilistic Perspective (Adaptive Computation and Machine Learning series)*. Massachusetts: The MIT Press, 2012, pp. 1–1104 (states avowedly that "machine Learning attempts to combine deductive, inductive, and abductive reasoning to make person-like reasoning in AI Entities possible. Machine-learning AI Entities initially learn in the same way a human child learns. First, they notice details and patterns in shapes, sounds, and behaviors; then put them together to distinguish one person from another, or a dog from a cat. Eventually, the AI can recognize and identify" common objects). See also: Hutto-Schultz, Jess, "Dicitur Ex Machina: Artificial Intelligence and the Hearsay Rule", *George Mason Law Review*, Volume 27, Issue 2, 2020, pp. 684–718 (689). See: Chollet, François, *Deep Learning with Python*. Shelter Island, New York: Manning, 2018, pp. 1–384 (passim).

[584] Barocas, Solon/Selbst, Andrew, "Big Data's Disparate Impact", *California Law Review*, Volume 104, pp. 2016, pp. 671–678 ("in particular, by exposing so-called 'machine learning' algorithms to examples of the cases of interest (previously identified instances of fraud, spam, default, and poor health), the algorithm 'learns' which related attributes or activities can serve as potential proxies for those qualities or outcomes of interest"). A converging stance can be found in Surden, Harry, "Machine Learning and Law", *cit.*, p. 93 ("[M]achine learning algorithms are able to automatically build accurate models of some phenomenon... without being explicitly programmed"). See also: Campisi, Natalie, From Inherent Racial Bias to Incorrect Data The Problems With Current Credit Scoring Models, Forbes (Feb. 26, 2021), https://www.forbes.com/advisor/creditcards/from-inherent-racial-bias-to-incorrect-data-the-problems-with-current-credit-scoring-models/; [https://perma.cc/EWA4-CS8E] (highlighting rampant racial bias in credit scoring systems); Oyama, Rebecca, "Do Not (Re)Enter: the Rise of Criminal Background Tenant Screening as a Violation of the Fair Housing Act", *Michigan Journal of Race and Law*, Volume 15, 2009, pp. 181, 184–93 (discussing a broad range of historical/criminal accounts as a way to screen undesirable tenants, such as Blacks and Latinos); Statement of Interest of the United States at 12, *Louis v. SafeRent Sols., LLC, No. 1:22-cv-10800* (D. Mass. Jan. 9, 2023) (holding that the Fair Housing Act liability stretches far and beyond, thus encompassing a vast assortment of entities providing housing-related services, including corporations that offer tenant screening services).

[585] Bruckner, Mathew Adam, "The Promise and Perils of Algorithmic Lenders 'Use of Big Data", *Chicago-Kent Law Review*, Volume 93, 2018, p. 3, whose research I follow very closely.

§§ Black customers have equally enrolled in Prime membership only to find out that Amazon routinely refrains itself from rendering this service in predominantly Black neighbourhoods. Apparently, an algorithmic bias[587] is to blame.[588] Machines, in spite of the long-standing myth of infallibility,[589] have a penchant for algorithmic injustice after all.[590]

§§ Amazon's Prime membership is (was?) riddled with algorithmic biases that fall short of protecting the fundamental rights of Blacks. Notably, Amazon's Prime membership, a wannabe stellar customer service, should not deliver such a watered-down and shoddy service to its beloved customers.

§§ Tellingly, Amazon has poured in gallant efforts and has accordingly invested whopping amounts of money in signing people up for its Prime membership

---

[586] Ingold, David Ingold/Soper, Spencer, "Amazon Doesn't Consider the Race of Its Customers. Should It?", *Bloomberg* (Apr. 21, 2016), https://www.bloomberg.com/graphics/2016-amazon-same-day/; [https://perma.cc/7N9S-57FL].

[587] See: Baeza-Yates, R., "Bias on the web", *Communications of the ACM*, 61 (6), June 2018, 2018, pp. 54–61 (argues that "*algorithmic bias is when the bias is not present in the input data* and is added *purely by the algorithm*"). Italics added. See also: Hajian, Sara Hajian et al., "Algorithmic Bias: From Discrimination Discovery to Fairness-aware Data Mining", *ACM SIGKDD International Conference on Knowledge Discovery and Data Mining*, Volume 22, 2125, 2016; Griemmelmann, James/Westreich, Daniel, "Incomprehensible Discrimination ", *California Law Review Online*, Volume 7, 2018, pp. 164–171; Xiang, Alice, "Reconciling Legal and Technical Approaches to Algorithmic Bias", *Tennessee Law Review*, Volume 88, 2021, passim; See: Lemley, Mark A./Casey, Bryan, "Remedies for Robots", *The University of Chicago Law Review*, Volume 86, Issue 5, 2019, pp. 1311–1396 (1376) (alerting to the perils of algorithmic bias); Chandler, Anupam, "The Racist Algorithm", *Michigan Law Review*, Volume 115, Issue 6, 2018, p. 1026 (noting that, in the terrain of racist algorithm, "the possibilities for discriminatory manipulation are legion"; Jackson, Maya C., "Artificial Intelligence and Algorithmic Bias: The Issues with Technology Reflecting History and Humans", *Journal of Business Technology Law*, Volume 16, 2021, pp. 299–316; West, Sarah Myers/Whittaker, Meredith/Crawford, Kate, *Discriminating Systems. Gender, Race and Power in AI*. New York: AI Now Institute, 2019, pp. 15 and ff and passim; Waldman, Ezra, "Privacy, Practice, and Performance", *California Law Review*, Volume 110, 2021, passim (on algorithmic bias).

[588] Note, though, that the training of machine learning is long and tedious in that is an error-prone procedure than can ultimately impair future algorithmic decision-making: Price, W. Nicholson Price II, "Regulating Black-Box Medicine", *Michigan Law Review*, Volume 116, 2017, pp. 421–431 (leverages on Google Image's image recognition learning algorithm to shed light on the four-step process by which some algorithms are thoroughly trained. First, the algorithm is shown "a set of known images ('Here are 10,000 pictures of ducks')." Second, the algorithm "develops complex internal rules based on nonlinear processes." Third, the algorithm "tests those rules on a test set ('Which of these are ducks?')." And fourth, the algorithm accordingly adjusts its "internal rules based on the success of the test." These steps are trotted out and repeated many times "until it can accurately and consistently classify the images").

[589] Citron, Danielle Keats, "Technological Due Process", *Washington Law Review*, 2008, p. 1249 (talks about "hearing officer's tendency to presume a computer system's infallibility").

[590] Ting-an Lin, "Democratizing AI" and the Concern of Algorithmic Injustice", *Philosophy and Technology*, Volume 37 (103), 2024, pp. 3–27; Okidegbe, Ngozi, "The Democratizing Potential of Algorithms?", *Connecticut Law Review*, Volume 54, 2021, passim; Katyal, Sonia, "Private Accountability in the Age of Artificial Intelligence", *UCLA Law Review*, Volume 66, 2019, pp. 54–99.

service.[591] Roughly half of all American households have agreed to pay the $ 99 membership fee.[592]

§§ In the overwhelming majority of big metropolitan areas, Prime membership awards the customers the unwavering right to free same-day delivery.[593] However, same-day delivery wasn't always available to every single customer that enrolled in the Prime membership in some of those cities.[594]

§§ Compellingly, a 2016 Bloomberg report[595] claimed that Amazon's Prime membership excluded vast swaths[596] of «predominantly Black ZIP Codes»[597] in «six major same-day delivery cities».[598] Black citizens in four big cities—Atlanta, Chicago, Dallas, and Washington, D.C.—were only[599] «half as likely to live in neighbourhoods with access to Amazon same-day delivery as white residents».[600]

§§ By the same token, in New York City,[601] same-day delivery included the outskirts, and a portmanteau of surrounding suburbs.[602] Yet, much to the astonishment of Black Amazon's Prime members, the neighbourhoods with predominantly

---

591 Bruckner, Mathew Adam, "The Promise and Perils of Algorithmic Lenders 'Use of Big Data", *Chicago-Kent Law Review*, Volume 93, 2018, p. 3, whose research I follow very closely.

592 Bruckner, Mathew Adam, "The Promise and Perils of Algorithmic Lenders 'Use of Big Data", *cit.*, p. 3.

593 Bruckner, Mathew Adam, "The Promise and Perils of Algorithmic Lenders 'Use of Big Data", *cit.*, p. 3.

594 Bruckner, Mathew Adam, "The Promise and Perils of Algorithmic Lenders 'Use of Big Data", *cit.*, p. 3.

595 Ingold, David Ingold/Soper, Spencer, "Amazon Doesn't Consider the Race of Its Customers. Should It?", *Bloomberg* (Apr. 21, 2016), https://www.bloomberg.com/graphics/2016-amazon-same-day/; [https://perma.cc/7N9S-57FL].

596 Bruckner, Mathew Adam, "The Promise and Perils of Algorithmic Lenders 'Use of Big Data", *cit.*, p. 3.

597 Ingold, David Ingold/Soper, Spencer, "Amazon Doesn't Consider the Race of Its Customers. Should It?", *Bloomberg* (Apr. 21, 2016), https://www.bloomberg.com/graphics/2016-amazon-same-day/; [https://perma.cc/7N9S-57FL].

598 Ingold, David Ingold/Soper, Spencer, "Amazon Doesn't Consider the Race of Its Customers. Should It?", *Bloomberg* (Apr. 21, 2016), https://www.bloomberg.com/graphics/2016-amazon-same-day/; [https://perma.cc/7N9S-57FL].

599 Bruckner, Mathew Adam, "The Promise and Perils of Algorithmic Lenders 'Use of Big Data", *cit.*, p. 3.

600 Ingold, David Ingold/Soper, Spencer, "Amazon Doesn't Consider the Race of Its Customers. Should It?", *Bloomberg* (Apr. 21, 2016), https://www.bloomberg.com/graphics/2016-amazon-same-day/; [https://perma.cc/7N9S-57FL].

601 Ingold, David Ingold/Soper, Spencer, "Amazon Doesn't Consider the Race of Its Customers. Should It?", *Bloomberg* (Apr. 21, 2016), https://www.bloomberg.com/graphics/2016-amazon-same-day/; [https://perma.cc/7N9S-57FL].

602 Bruckner, Mathew Adam, "The Promise and Perils of Algorithmic Lenders 'Use of Big Data", *cit.*, p. 3.

Black ZIP Codes[603] were outright—and unbiddenly—excluded for no apparent reason.[604]

§§ Furthermore, predominantly minority borough of the «Bronx and some majority-black-neighbourhoods in Queens»[605] were ruled out from the perimeter of Amazon's Prime membership.[606]

§§ To add to the Black consumer's woes, «*algorithmic prime-lining*»—an algorithmic tool that downrightly excludes from the coverage of free same-day deliveries neighbourhoods with predominantly Black ZIP Codes whilst affording primacy to neighbourhoods with predominantly White ZIP Codes—was strikingly clear elsewhere. Take Boston's Roxbury neighbourhood for example.

§§ Boston's Roxbury neighbourhood,[607] a neighbourhood in which 59% of the residents were Black whereas only 15% were White,[608] was bafflingly excluded from the coverage of free same-day deliveries.[609]

§§ Mind-bogglingly, Boston's Roxbury neighbourhood was surrounded by a wide range of neighbourhoods[610] with predominantly White ZIP Codes which were included within the remit of coverage[611] of free same-day deliveries.[612]

---

603 Ingold, David Ingold/Soper, Spencer, "Amazon Doesn't Consider the Race of Its Customers. Should It?", *Bloomberg* (Apr. 21, 2016), https://www.bloomberg.com/graphics/2016-amazon-same-day/; [https://perma.cc/7N9S-57FL].

604 Bruckner, Mathew Adam, "The Promise and Perils of Algorithmic Lenders 'Use of Big Data", *cit.*, p. 3.

605 Ingold, David Ingold/Soper, Spencer, "Amazon Doesn't Consider the Race of Its Customers. Should It?", *Bloomberg* (Apr. 21, 2016), https://www.bloomberg.com/graphics/2016-amazon-same-day/; [https://perma.cc/7N9S-57FL].

606 Bruckner, Mathew Adam, "The Promise and Perils of Algorithmic Lenders 'Use of Big Data", *cit.*, p. 4.

607 Ingold, David Ingold/Soper, Spencer, "Amazon Doesn't Consider the Race of Its Customers. Should It?", *Bloomberg* (Apr. 21, 2016), https://www.bloomberg.com/graphics/2016-amazon-same-day/; [https://perma.cc/7N9S-57FL].

608 Ingold, David Ingold/Soper, Spencer, "Amazon Doesn't Consider the Race of Its Customers. Should It?", *Bloomberg* (Apr. 21, 2016), https://www.bloomberg.com/graphics/2016-amazon-same-day/; [https://perma.cc/7N9S-57FL].

609 Ingold, David Ingold/Soper, Spencer, "Amazon Doesn't Consider the Race of Its Customers. Should It?", *Bloomberg* (Apr. 21, 2016), https://www.bloomberg.com/graphics/2016-amazon-same-day/; [https://perma.cc/7N9S-57FL].

610 Ingold, David Ingold/Soper, Spencer, "Amazon Doesn't Consider the Race of Its Customers. Should It?", *Bloomberg* (Apr. 21, 2016), https://www.bloomberg.com/graphics/2016-amazon-same-day/; [https://perma.cc/7N9S-57FL].

611 Bruckner, Mathew Adam, "The Promise and Perils of Algorithmic Lenders 'Use of Big Data", *cit.*, p. 4.

612 Ingold, David Ingold/Soper, Spencer, "Amazon Doesn't Consider the Race of Its Customers. Should It?", *Bloomberg* (Apr. 21, 2016), https://www.bloomberg.com/graphics/2016-amazon-same-day/; [https://perma.cc/7N9S-57FL].

§§ Disturbingly enough, and more in tune with algorithmic discrimination[613] from which it was borne, Boston's Roxbury residents, despite paying the same flat-rate Amazon's Prime membership,[614] just like White folks living in other surrounding cities did, were outrightly excluded from the coverage of free same-day deliveries.[615]

§§ Further a copious public outcry, which was fraught with grievances that sought to demonstrate that Artificial Intelligence-embedded technologies can indeed spawn a cascade of biased algorithmic decision-making, Amazon has ruled out any discriminatory intent whatsoever while pinning the blame onto its data[616]-driven[617] approach to Prime membership.[618]

---

613 Griemmelmann, James/Westreich, Daniel, "Incomprehensible Discrimination ", *California Law Review Online*, Volume 7, 2018, pp. 164–171; Ting-an Lin, "Democratizing AI" and the Concern of Algorithmic Injustice", *Philosophy and Technology*, Volume 37 (103), 2024, pp. 3–27; Davis, Joshua P. "Law Without Mind: AI, Ethics, and Jurisprudence", *California Western Law Review*, Volume 55, 2018, pp. 181 e ss and passim (deals with an agreed-upon Artificial opacity while emphasizing a sought-after transparency to trounce it); Bar-Gill, Oren/Sunstein, Cass R./Talgam-Cohen, Inbal, "Algorithmic Harm in Consumer Markets", *Journal of Legal Analysis*, Volume 15, n. ° 1, 2023, pp. 1–47; Pasquale, Frank, *The Black Box Society: The Secret Algorithms that Control Money and Information.* Cambridge, Massachusetts: Harvard University Press, 2015, 1–320 (8–10 and passim) (noting that biased algorithms, which have underlying discrimination problems, contribute exponentially to further social biases. His most intriguing claim is that such biased algorithms have been incorporated/etched in the bulk of the corporations' informatic system, to the detriment of human kind in an overarching sense).

614 Bruckner, Mathew Adam, "The Promise and Perils of Algorithmic Lenders 'Use of Big Data", *cit.*, p. 4.

615 Ingold, David Ingold/Soper, Spencer, "Amazon Doesn't Consider the Race of Its Customers. Should It?", *Bloomberg* (Apr. 21, 2016), https://www.bloomberg.com/graphics/2016-amazon-same-day/; [https://perma.cc/7N9S-57FL].

616 See: *Tech, Bias and Housing Initiative, the Promise and Perils of Residential Proptech, Year 1, Research Summary Report, April 2023, TechEquity Collaborative*, p. 11, available at: https://techequity.us/wp-content/uploads/2023/04/TBHI-Y1-Research-Summary-Report.pdf (28.11.2024). ("*Once bad data enters the analysis of one factor, it gets baked into the subsequent process, multiplying the effect that one disadvantageous data point can have on someone's overall housing determination*"). Italics added. See: Part IV, This chapter, Sects. 4.1.4–4.1.4.2.3 of this book.

617 The issue of a digital reality fed by a data-driven world has been shrewdly portrayed by renowned scholars, which offer gripping examples of it: Suzor, Nicolas P., *Lawless: The Secret Rules that Govern our Digital Lives.* Cambridge, United Kingdom: Cambridge University Press, 2019, pp. 1–218 (passim); Brownsword, Roger, *Law, Technology and Society: Re-Imagining the Regulatory Environment*, London: Routledge, 2020, pp. 1–361 (passim) (broaches the interplay law, technology, and society with a sharper focus in the era of smart regulatory technologies). But see: Hardt, Moritz, "How big data is unfair: Understanding sources of unfairness in data driven decision making", *Medium*, Archived on Oct. 8, 2014, available at: https://web.archive.org/web/20141008185829/; https://medium.com/@mrtz/how-big-data-is-unfair-9aa544d739de. (access: 17.12.2024).

618 Ingold, David Ingold/Soper, Spencer, "Amazon Doesn't Consider the Race of Its Customers. Should It?", *Bloomberg* (Apr. 21, 2016), https://www.bloomberg.com/graphics/2016-amazon-same-day/; [https://perma.cc/7N9S-57FL].

§§ In a bid to atone for its algorithmic sins, Amazon has considerably expanded the geographical breadth of Prime membership.[619] Shortly after, every ZIP Code in every city was covered by the free same-day service.[620] Which was nonetheless too little too late. The racial damage had already ventured beyond acceptable limits after all.

§§ Although there is an unstoppable groundswell of support of algorithmic decision-making[621]—spurred by a veneer of objectivity insofar race is not a variable[622] conducive to algorithmic decision-making[623]—, truth is the human biases are being passed over[624] to machines[625]/.[626] Which, I may venture to add, is less than unbecoming in this regard[627] insofar broadens algorithmic unfairness.[628]

---

619 Ingold, David Ingold/Soper, Spencer, "Amazon Doesn't Consider the Race of Its Customers. Should It?", *Bloomberg* (Apr. 21, 2016), https://www.bloomberg.com/graphics/2016-amazon-same-day/; [https://perma.cc/7N9S-57FL].

620 Bruckner, Mathew Adam, "The Promise and Perils of Algorithmic Lenders 'Use of Big Data", *cit.*, p. 4.

621 Goodman, Bryce W., "A Step Towards Accountable Algorithms? Algorithmic Discrimination and the European Union General Data Protection", *Conference on Neural Information Processing Systems*, 2016.

622 But see: Citron, Danielle Keats/Pasquale, Frank A., "The Scored Society: Due Process for Automated Predictions", *Washington Law Review*, Volume 89, 2014, pp. 14 ["*a*]*lgorithms may place a low score on occupations like migratory work or low-paying service jobs. This correlation may have no discriminatory intent, but if a majority of those workers are racial minorities, such variables can unfairly impact consumers' loan application outcomes*"]. Italics added.

623 Annamma, S. A., Jackson, D. D., & Morrison, D., "Conceptualizing color-evasiveness: Using dis/ability critical race theory to expand a color-blind racial ideology in education and society", *Race Ethnicity and Education*, 20 (2), 2017, pp. 147–162; Benjamin, Ruha, *Race After Technology: Abolitionist Tools for the New Jim Code*, *cit.*, pp. 1–172; DaViera, A. L./Uriostegui, M., Gottlieb/ A./Onyeka, O, "Risk, race, and predictive policing: A critical race theory analysis of the strategic subject list", *cit.*, pp. 91–103 (95); Eckhouse, L., Lum, K., Conti-Cook, C., & Ciccolini, J., "Layers of bias: A unified approach for understanding problems with risk assessment. Criminal Justice and Behavior", 46 (2), 2019, pp. 185–209; O'Neil, Cathy, *Weapons of math destruction: How big data increases inequality and threatens democracy*, New York, Crown Publisher, 2016.

624 See: Sweeney, Latanya, "Discrimination in Online Ad Delivery", *ACM Queue*, Apr. 2, 2013, p. 11 (drawing on a list of the top "whitest- and blackest-identifying girls' and boys' names").

625 Citron, Danielle Keats/Pasquale, Frank A., "The Scored Society: Due Process for Automated Predictions", *Washington Law Review*, Volume 89, 2014, pp. 1–13 (arguing that "[a]dvocates applaud the removal of human beings and their flaws from the assessment process," but arguing that bias remains "[b]ecause human beings program predictive algorithms, their biases and values are embedded into the software's instructions").

626 Brennan, Michael, Can Computers Be Racist? Big Data, Inequality, and Discrimination, Ford Found: Equals Change Blog (November 18, 2015) https://www.fordfoundation.org/ideas/equals-changeblog/posts/can-computers-be-racist-big-data-inequality-and-discrimination/; [https://perma.cc/A2EWBRPH].

627 Scherer, Matthew U. Scherer, "Regulating Artificial Intelligence Systems: Risks, Challenges, Competencies, and Strategies", *Harvard Journal of Law and Technology*, Volume 29, 2016, pp. 353–369 (frames the crippling problem of opacity as "the possibility that the inner workings of an AI system may be kept secret and may not be susceptible to reverse engineering").

628 Corbett-Davies, Sam/Goel, Sharad, "The Measure and Mismeasure of Fairness: a critical Review of Fair Machine Learning", *Cornell University Library*, 2018, pp. 3 and ff and passim (undertake

§§ *Algorithmic prime-lining* only furthers the gulf, yawning and gargantuan wealth[629] and racial wedge between the *selected few* (White folks) and the *unwanted many* (Black folks). The former have been leveraging on the perks of White Supremacy all along[630] whilst the latter have already trekked through the drawn-out and long-haul period of slavery which, in turn, has paved the day to *systemic racism* that still ripples forward and resonates today.[631]

laudable efforts to debunk algorithm biases that primarily target ethnic minorities, such as Hispanics and coloured people).

[629] Derenoncourt, Ellora/Kim, Chi Hyun/Kuhn, Moritz/Schularik, Moritz, "The Wealth of Two Nations: The U.S. Racial Wealth Gap, 1860–2020", *The Quarterly Journal of Economics*, Volume 139, Issue 2, 2024, p. 741 ("A large class of commonly discussed policies for reducing racial wealth inequality seeks to reduce gaps in income, savings, and capital gains. These include policies that encourage financial diversification or stock equity holdings among Black households; policies aimed at financial literacy and retirement or savings behavior; or policies aimed at improving educational and labor market outcomes of Black Americans through improved school quality or reductions in discrimination. *Yet on a realistic note, our simulation in Section IV.A shows that even if wealth accumulation conditions had been equal since 1870, the wealth gap would still be 3 to 1 today, and full convergence would be more than 200 years away. Put differently: to close the racial wealth gap in the immediate term* via *flow parameters, Black Americans would need a substantial positive lead over whites, not "just" more equality*"). Italics added.

[630] DaViera, A. L./Uriostegui, M., Gottlieb/A./Onyeka, O, "Risk, race, and predictive policing: A critical race theory analysis of the strategic subject list", *American Journal of Community Psychology*, Volume 73, 2024, pp. 91–103; Benjamin, Ruha, *Race After Technology: Abolitionist Tools for the New Jim Code*, New York, Polity, 2019, pp. 1–172; Furman, E./Singh, A. K./Darko, N. A./Wilson, C. L., "Activism, intersectionality, and community psychology: The way in which Black Lives Matter Toronto helps us to examine white supremacy in Canada's LGBTQ community", *Community Psychology in Global Perspective*, Volume 4, Issue 2, 34–54. On whiteness: Frankenberg, Ruth (Ed.), *Displacing whiteness: essays in social and cultural criticism*, Durham, NC: Duke University Press, 1997; Frankenberg, Ruth, "Introduction: local whitenesses, localizing whiteness", *Displacing whiteness*, Ruth Frankenberg (Editor), Durham, NC: Duke University Press, 1997, pp. 1–33.

[631] Benjamin, Ruha, *Race After Technology: Abolitionist Tools for the New Jim Code*, New York, Polity, 2019, pp. 1–172 ("*From everyday apps to complex algorithms, Ruha Benjamin cuts through tech-industry hype to understand how emerging technologies can reinforce White supremacy and deepen social inequity.* Benjamin argues that automation, far from being a sinister story of racist programmers scheming on the dark web, has the potential to hide, speed up, *and deepen discrimination while appearing neutral and even benevolent when compared to the racism of a previous era.* Presenting the concept of the "New Jim Code," she shows how a range of discriminatory designs encode inequity by explicitly amplifying racial hierarchies; by ignoring but thereby replicating social divisions; or by aiming to fix racial bias but ultimately doing quite the opposite. *Moreover, she makes a compelling case for race itself as a kind of technology, designed to stratify and sanctify social injustice in the architecture of everyday life.* This illuminating guide provides conceptual tools for decoding tech promises with sociologically informed skepticism. In doing so, it challenges us to question not only the technologies we are sold but also the ones we ourselves manufacture"). Italics added.

4.1.4 Mortgage Redlining *and* Mortgage Reverse Redlining *Through the Lens of Critical Race Theory (CRT)*

§§ The road behind was rocky, long-trodden, and gruesomely painful.[632] A key take-away jumps out as ripe: AI-embedded technologies display an enhanced proclivity to reify,[633] reproduce, mimic, and worsen deep-rooted racial wedges with which modern societies have been tussling for a long-winded span of time.[634]

§§ Amongst which stands arguably a spate of byproducts of the devilishly harmful virus of invidiousness, such as misogyny,[635] racism,[636] xenophobe, and the list dispiritingly goes on. The pinpointed social illnesses are amenable to spark social outcry, uproar, which, in turn, are poised to not only stir a spasm of violence but, and foremost, steer decaying democracies towards the mayhem of *Algorithmic Dictatorship*. The time is accordingly ripe to avert unpalatable outcomes arisen from the interplay between law and technology.[637]

---

[632] Nier III, Charles L., "Perpetuation of Segregation: Toward a New Historical and Legal Interpretation of Redlining Under the Fair Housing Act", *Marshall Law Review*, Volume 32, 1999, 617, 619–20 ("During the five year span from 1928 to 1933, residential property construction decreased by 95%, while home repair expenditures dropped 90%. By 1933 half of all the nation's residential mortgages were technically in default, with foreclosures reaching the rate of over 1000 per day").

[633] Duster, Troy, "Race and Reification in Science." *Science*, 307, 2005, passim.

[634] Hurley, Mikella/Adebayo, Julius, "Credit Scoring in the Era of Big Data", *Yale Journal of Law and Technology*, Volume 18, 2016, p. 149 ("*these tools may furthermore obscure discriminatory and subjective lending policies behind a single "objective" score* (...) *sophisticated algorithms may combine facially neutral data points and treat them as proxies for immutable characteristics such as race or gender, thereby circumventing existing non-discrimination laws and systematically denying credit access to certain groups. Finally, big-data tools may allow online payday lenders to target the most vulnerable consumers and lure them into debt traps*"). Italics added.

[635] Avery, Mallory/Leibbrandt, Andreas/Vecci, Joseph, "Does Artificial Intelligence Help or Hurt Gender Diversity? Evidence from Two Field Experiments on Recruitment on Tech, *Monash University, Monash Business School*, 2023, pp. 1–70.

[636] Here is a tool to dispel the rampant racism that besets the criminal system of justice: Huq, Aziz, "Racial Equity in Algorithmic Criminal Justice", *Duke Law Journal*, Volume 68, 2022, pp. 1076–1134.

[637] Ferreri, Mara/Sanyal, Romola, "Digital informalisation: rental housing, platforms, and the management of risk", *Housing Studies*, Volume 37, Issue 6, 2022, pp. 1035–1053 (1035) ("*The eruption of disruptive digital platforms is reshaping geographies of housing under the gaze of corporations and through the webs of algorithms.* Engaging with interdisciplinary scholarship on informal housing across the Global North and South, we propose the term *'digital informalisation' to examine how digital platforms are engendering new and opaque ways of governing housing,* presenting a theoretical and political blind spot (....) *In contrast to progressive imaginaries of 'smart' technological mediation, practices of algorithmic redlining, biased tenant profiling and the management of risk in private tenancies and in housing welfare both introduce and extend discriminatory and exclusionary housing practices*"). Italics added. See: Part IV, This chapter, Sects. 4.1.4–4.1.4.2.3 of this book.

§§ Lawmakers and policymakers must not facetiously stand outside the fray. Rather, they should strive to lay the foundations for a sturdier ground upon which Artificial Intelligence-embedded technologies should brawnily stand.[638]

§§ The road behind, if nothing else, shows that human beings—amongst whom, Blacks and Latinos—have plenty of reasons to be leery of the premises built into modern democracies (racially motivated laws[639] that further entrenched racial inequalities[640]; a yawning wealth inequality,[641] and racial disparities alike[642]).

---

638 See: Part V, Chap. 5, Sects. 5.1.2–5.1.6.2.1 of this book (on the thing-centred algorithmic decision-making propelled by a *Controllable* and *Interpretable* Machine Learning that weeds out *Algorithmic Dictatorship* and secures *Algorithmic Common Good*). See: Part V, Chap. 5, Sect. 5.1.1.1 of this book (on the central tenets of Rule of Law that lends itself to a beacon of justice amidst the sepulchral darkness that is about to take hold). See: Part V, Chap. 5, Sect. 5.1.1.2 of this book (on the central tenets of Procedural Rule of Law that lends itself to a lighthouse of justice that allows citizens to challenge the pearls of algorithmic wisdom in a court of law).

639 Racially motivated laws bring back the very bad legal memories indeed, like malicious legal transplants.. See: Siems, Mathias, "Malicious legal transplants", *Legal Studies, The Society of Legal Scholars*, Volume 38, 2018, pp. 103–119 (105) (emphasizing the importance of malicious legal transplants by stating that «in many countries in the world, multiple ethnicities live together peacefully together. But throughout human history there also have been periods of racially motivated laws with malicious effects. In some instances, those laws were a product of legal transplants (….) it can be said that the Nazi laws influenced the laws of Mussolini's Italy»).

640 Strand, Palma Joy, "Inheriting Inequality: Wealth, Race, and the Laws of Succession", *Oregon Law Review*, Volume 89, 2010, pp. 453–476; Palladino, Lenore M., "The Contribution of Shareholder Primacy to the Racial Wealth Gap," *Review of Black Political Economy*, Volume 50, 2023, pp. 167–193.

641 Derenoncourt, Ellora/Kim, Chi Hyun/Kuhn, Moritz/Schularik, Moritz, "The Wealth of Two Nations: The U.S. Racial Wealth Gap, 1860–2020", *The Quarterly Journal of Economics*, Volume 139, Issue 2, 2024, p. 741 ("A large class of commonly discussed policies for reducing racial wealth inequality seeks to reduce gaps in income, savings, and capital gains. These include policies that encourage financial diversification or stock equity holdings among Black households; policies aimed at financial literacy and retirement or savings behavior; or policies aimed at improving educational and labor market outcomes of Black Americans through improved school quality or reductions in discrimination. *Yet on a realistic note, our simulation in Section IV.A shows that even if wealth accumulation conditions had been equal since 1870, the wealth gap would still be 3 to 1 today, and full convergence would be more than 200 years away. Put differently: to close the racial wealth gap in the immediate term* via *flow parameters, Black Americans would need a substantial positive lead over whites, not "just" more equality*"). Italics added.

642 Freeman, Andrea, "The Unbearable Whiteness of Milk: Food Oppression and the USDA", *University of California Law Review*, Volume 3, 2023, pp. 1251, 1252–54 (discussing how the USDA's earnest attempts to dispose of the dairy surplus through close partnerships with fast food corporations and distribution through its nutrition programs disproportionately targets, and causes inordinate harms on, Black communities); Freeman, Andrea, "Transparency for Food Consumers: Nutrition Labeling and Food Oppression", *The American Journal of Medicine*, Volume 41, 2015, pp. 315, 316–21 (positing how the USDA's sharp focus on greatly improving health by accordingly altering consumer behavior through nutrition labeling and consumer education reifies, reproduces, exacerbates and ultimately perpetuates racial health disparities by bluntly overlooking the absence of choice facing many Black consumers with regard to food selection). Convergent: Cohen-Rimer, Yael, "What's Choice Got to Do with It? Addressing the Pitfalls of Using Choice-Architecture Discourse Within Poverty Law", *The Modern Law Review*, Volume 86, n. ° 4, 2023, pp. 951–983.

§§ The road behind also shows that *systemic racism* is rooted firmly on, and dates back to, the Reconstruction era[643] that reflects an unbroken chain of events that seeks to cement and buttress racial economic wedges between racialised communities (Blacks and Latinos and White folks).[644]

§§ Against this background, the burning question is no longer «how did we get here», but «why we are still here» where racial disparities abound in the lending industry instead.

§§ In addition to that, question is also to ascertain why algorithmic systems can cleanse biased data into eerily «powerful stigmatizing scores»[645] that will most likely mimic racial discrimination[646]—in the remit of fair lending—deeply steeped in past decision-making.[647] The answer is very straightforward: *mortgage redlining* which arose further the Great Depression in the 1930's.[648]

§§ Put another way, if one endeavours to canvass the underlying reasons in view of which Black folks are nowadays routinely denied a loan to buy a house, the disgraceful *mortgage redlining* policy is the answer you are looking for.[649] Which

---

[643] Du Bois, William E. B., *Black Reconstruction: An Essay Toward a History of the Part which Black Folk Played in the Attempt to Reconstruct Democracy in America*, 1860–1880, Black thought and culture, Harcourt, Brace, 1935; Foner, Eric, *Reconstruction: America's Unfinished Revolution*, 1863–1877, New York, HarperCollins, 1988.

[644] Freeman, Andrea, "Racism in the Credit Card Industry", *cit.*, p. 1071 ("*this type of consumer racism dates back to the Reconstruction era and reflects an unbroken chain of laws and policies cementing racial economic inequality*. Social norms and stereotypes *make the resulting inequality appear cultural and personal instead of systemic and structural*"). Italics added.

[645] Citron, Danielle K./Pasquale, Frank, "The Scored Society: Due Process for Automated Predictions", *Washington Law Review*, Volume 89, Issue 1, 2014, pp. 1–34.

[646] See: Griemmelmann, James/Westreich, Daniel, "Incomprehensible Discrimination ", *California Law Review Online*, Volume 7, 2018, pp. 164–171.

[647] Balkin, Jack M., "The Three Laws of Robotics in the Age of Big Data", *cit.*, pp. 1217–1241.

[648] Szto, Mary, "Real Estate Agents as Agents of Social Change: Redlining, Reverse Redlining, and Greenlining", *Seatle Journal for Social Justice*, Volume 12, Issue 1, 2013, pp. 9–11 ("*Official redlining practices began in the 1930's during the Great Depression*. A housing bubble and bust preceded the Great Depression. *Before mortgage lending became affordable, only wealthy families could buy homes. In 1935, NAREB argued that the federal government should subsidize mortgages and private ownership, not public housing. The federal government agreed and enacted multiple programs to revive the economy and increase employment*. These programs promoted residential construction and made home ownership widely available. This was achieved by "standardized homebuilding procedures" to address the "rising costs of construction," and by providing mortgage insurance. "*Such mortgage insurance lowered interest rates from six to eight percent down to four percent, and raised the amounts that could be financed from 50 to 70 percent of the purchase price to 90 percent. After 1939, with a federally insured mortgage, it was cheaper to purchase than to rent. Unfortunately, three underlying assumptions of these federal programs were the following: (1) people could be divided by race; (2) only white communities held property values; and therefore; (3) segregation by race was necessary to protect white property values. Thus, these programs introduced official racial redlining 60 and allowed the government to promote restrictive racial covenants and segregation. In effect, only whites received federally insured mortgages*"). Footnotes omitted. Italics added.

[649] Fowler, Russell, "The Ugly History of Redlining: A Federal Policy "Full of Evil", *Tennessee Bar Journal*, Volume 59, Issue 1, (January/February 2023), 2023, pp. 23–27 ("**Redlining** Runs

begs the vexing questions: what was *mortgage redlining* and to what extent does this blatantly discriminative policy still resonates today? Put it bluntly, does *mortgage redlining* still casts a shady shadow on fair housing, thereby depriving Black folks from a sorely needed loan to purchase a house?

§§ *Mortgage redlining* harkens back the 1930's of the twentieth century.[650] Redlining tally with a gruelling era in which Black folks were jostling to be afforded minimum civil[651] rights.[652]

Rampant To help new homebuyers obtain private bank financing, an even larger and more powerful New Deal agency was founded in 1934: the Federal Housing Administration (FHA). The FHA (now part of HUD) insured 20-year bank mortgages covering 80% of the purchase price. ...The impact of **redlining** widened tremendously when the FHA began underwriting whole subdivisions during the post- war housing boom and FHA policies were adopted by the wildly popular VA mortgage program. Consequently, **redlining** governed most housing construction in the United States. 6 ***Redlining*** *practices swiftly poisoned all sorts of other private commercial activities. ...**Redlining** instigated physical and psychological isolation as well. Expressways and other obstacles were erected to contain, divide or destroy traditionally Black neighborhoods. ...It became a perpetual economic death spiral outlasting **redlining** itself. In sum, **redlining** caused these problems by blocking investment, and these problems themselves, in turn, block investment to the present day. '9 Some favorably situated Black communities were taken involuntarily through condemnation proceedings, then turned over to private investors.* ...Legal Responses to **Redlining** and New Dangers The United States Supreme Court made restrictive covenants unenforceable in the 1948 case of Shelley v"). Italics added.

650 Mendez-Carbajo, Diego "Neighborhood Redlining, Racial Segregation, and Homeownership", *Federal Reserve Bank of Saint Louis*, September 1, 2021("*In the 1930s, the Home Owners' Loan Corporation (HOLC) drew maps of residential neighborhoods across the United States. The maps classified each neighborhood into one of five categories, from least to most likely to **default** on a **mortgage** loan. In those maps, the neighborhoods most likely to default were shaded red and over time these neighborhoods had the largest concentrations of African Americans. Because the lending classifications determined individual access to credit, the residents of redlined neighborhoods paid high interest rates and had a hard time becoming homeowners and keeping their homes in good condition. From 1968 to 1974, Congress passed several federal laws and policies preventing lending discrimination by race and gender, and the pattern of residential segregation started to change*"). Italics added.

651 DeWolfe, Ruthanne, Squires, Gregory, & DeWolfe, Alan, "Civil rights implications of insurance redlining", *DePaul Law Review*, 29 (2), 1980, pp. 315–352 ("In a recent study of insurance redlining the Midwestern State Advisory Committees to the United States Commission on Civil Rights determined that *Chicago communities with predominantly minority populations were the principal victims of adverse underwriting decisions. In this article, the authors, focusing on Illinois, discuss various theories of liability for insurance redlining*"). Italics added.

652 Cohn, Ann Pauline, "Redlining and the Civil Rights Act of 1968", *Law and Housing Newsletter*, Volume 4, Issue 3 (Fall 1976), 1976, pp. 9–11 ("**REDLINING** AND THE CIVIL RIGHTS ACT OF 1968 In a recent decision, the Southern District Court of Ohio ruled that the Civil Rights Act of 1968, 42 U.S.C. 3604 and 3605, pro- hibited the practice of **redlining**. ...*The court held that Section 3605 was an explicit prohibition of **redlining** because **redlining** is a denial of loans and financial assistance on the basis of race. In its opinion, the court also stated that Section 3604 prohibited **redlining** because the practice effectively makes dwellings "un- available" in certain neighborhoods.* It found that, combined with the *high cost of housing, "a denial of financial assistance in connection with the sale of a home would effectively 'make unavail- able or deny' a 'dwelling.'"2 When such denial is a result of racial considerations, as is the case in **redlining**, Section 3604 is violated*"). Italics added.

§§ *Mortgage redlining* neatly encapsulates, hands-in-glove, the remnants of the worst of humanity: selfishness and the unquenchable/unrelenting quest to uphold White Supremacy.[653] So does *reverse redlining*,[654] which consists of a cluster of claims which are brought by aggrieved parties who were granted loans but nonetheless allege that they were purposefully given clearly unfavourable loans on account of their race or skin colour.[655]

§§ *Mortgage redlining* was a bespoke social construction designed to hobble, and to some extent cripple, Blacks' long-sought dream of being houseowners[656] in tier-

---

[653] Feagin, J. R., *The white racial frame: centuries of racial framing and counter-framing*, 2nd edition, New York: Routledge, 2013; Benjamin, Ruha, *Race After Technology: Abolitionist Tools for the New Jim Code*, New York, Polity, 2019, pp. 1–172 ("*From everyday apps to complex algorithms, Ruha Benjamin cuts through tech-industry hype to understand how emerging technologies can reinforce White supremacy and deepen social inequity*"); DaViera, A. L./Uriostegui, M., Gottlieb/A./Onyeka, O, "Risk, race, and predictive policing: A critical race theory analysis of the strategic subject list", *American Journal of Community Psychology*, Volume 73, 2024, pp. 91–103.

[654] Rheingold, Ira, Fitzpatrick, Michael, & Hofeld, Al Jr., "From redlining to reverse redlining: history of obstacles for minority homeownership in America", *Clearinghouse Review*, 34 (Issues 9–10), 2001, pp. 642–654.

[655] Falck, Charles, "Equitable Access: Examining Information Asymmetry in Reverse Redlining Claims through Critical Race Theory", *Texas Journal on Civil Liberties & Civil Rights*, Vol. 18, Issue 1 (Fall 2012), 2012, pp. 101–120 ("***Redlining** is the practice of refusing to lend because of race or other protected trait. Section 3605 of the FHA prohibits **redlining**, making it unlawful for any person or entity "whose business includes engaging in residential Real Estate-related transactions to discriminate against any person in making available such a transaction, or in the terms or conditions of such a transaction, because of race, color, religion, sex, handicap, familial status, or national origin."* 9 *A **redlining** case traditionally involves a minority plaintiff who has been denied a loan despite having similar qualifications as white borrowers who received similar loans.* '0 *By contrast, **reverse-redlining** claims are brought by plaintiffs who received loans but allege that they were intentionally given unfavorable loans on account of their race-thus, the "reverse" of the **redlining** cases. Like **redlining** plaintiffs, reverse-**redlining** plaintiffs have also sued under FHA Â§ 3605; in addition, reverse-**redlining** plaintiffs have sued under Â§ 3604(b), which prohibits discrimination "against any person in the terms, conditions, or privileges of sale or rental of a dwelling... because of race, color, religion, sex, familial status, or national origin."" The recognition of **reverse-redlining** claims under the same FHA provisions used to prohibit **redlining** might seem contradictory, given that the statute broadly aimed to increase access to credit for minorities.*12 However, as this Note will discuss, *the tests that courts have used in **reverse-redlining** cases come from Title VII, which is part of "a coordinated scheme of federal civil rights laws enacted to end discrimination[,j... construed expansively to implement that goal*"). Italics added.

one neighbourhoods.[657] *Mortgage redlining* accordingly bears the seal of unlawful racial discrimination and structural disadvantage[658] that still resonates today.[659]

§§ More to the point, Critical Race Theory (CRT)[660] contends that modern societies laws strive to uphold White privilege,[661] which, in turn, accordingly seek to

---

656 But see: Glantz, Aaron/Martinez, Emmanuel, "For People of Color, Banks are Shutting the Door to Homeownership", *Reveal*, February 15, 2018, available at: https://ibw21.org/news/people-color-banks-shutting-door-homeownership/ (access: 4.11.2024) ("*Fifty years after the federal Fair Housing Act banned racial discrimination in lending, African Americans and Latinos continue to be routinely denied conventional mortgage loans at rates far higher than their white counterparts.* This modern-day redlining persisted in 61 metro areas even when controlling for applicants' income, loan amount and neighborhood, according to a mountain of Home Mortgage Disclosure Act records analyzed by Reveal from The Center for Investigative Reporting. *The yearlong analysis, based on 31 million records, relied on techniques used by leading academics, the Federal Reserve and Department of Justice to identify lending disparities. It found a pattern of troubling denials for people of color across the country, including in major metropolitan areas such as Atlanta, Detroit, Philadelphia, St. Louis and San Antonio.* African Americans faced the most resistance in Southern cities — Mobile, Alabama; Greenville, North Carolina; and Gainesville, Florida — and Latinos in Iowa City, Iowa. *No matter their location, loan applicants told similar stories, describing an uphill battle with loan officers who they said seemed to be fishing for a reason to say no*"). Italics added.

657 Stokes, Danielle, "From Redlining to Greenlining", *U.C.L.A. Law Review*, Volume 71, 2024, pp. 628–696 (628) ("*For generations, marginalized communities have been impacted by discriminatory land use, zoning, and property valuation policies, from redlining in the 1930s to the siting of undesirable land uses that persists today. Because of these policies, marginalized communities are forced to contend with low property values, substandard infrastructure, and increased health risks.* The very same mechanisms that created these injustices, however, may now be key to addressing them"). Italics added.

658 See: Barocas, Solon/Selbst, Andrew, "Big Data's Disparate Impact", *California Law Review*, Volume 104, pp. 2016, p. 691 (highlighting the worrisome, and gruesome, issue of "structural disadvantage" with which racialized communities have been tussling for centuries). See also: Powell, Richard/Porter, Jeremy, "Redlining, Concentrated Disadvantage and Crime: The Effects of Discriminatory Government Policies on Violent Crime", *American Journal of Criminal Justice*, Volume 48, 2023, pp. 1132–1156 ("*Redlining and other discriminatory government policies enacted during the first half of the Twentieth Century have had long-lasting negative effects on neighborhoods, especially those inhabited by people of color. This study attempts to link the practice of redlining to current-day indicators of neighborhood concentrated disadvantage and violent crime using spatio-temporal data from Chicago (…) In addition, it seeks to determine whether redlining was associated with violent crime, and if that association was mediated by redlining's effect on concentrated disadvantage. The results indicate that redlining was associated with increases in both concentrated disadvantage and violent crime, and that redlining's relationship with violent crime was, indeed, partially mediated by its relationship with concentrated disadvantage*"). Italics added. See also: Gandy, Oscar H., *Coming to Terms with Chance: Engaging Rational Discrimination and Cumulative Disadvantage*, Farnham, UK: Ashgate Publishing, 2009.

659 Higginbotham, Michael F., *Ghosts of Jim Crow: Ending Racism in Post-Racial America*, New York, New York University Press, 2015, pp. 1–352 ("*when America inaugurated its first African American president, in 2009, many wondered if the country had finally become a "post-racial" society.* Was this the dawning of a new era, in which America, a nation nearly severed in half by slavery, and whose racial fault lines are arguably among its most enduring traits, would at last move beyond race with the election of Barack Hussein Obama? In *Ghosts of Jim Crow*, F. *Michael Higginbotham convincingly argues that America remains far away from that imagined utopia. Indeed, the shadows of Jim Crow era laws and attitudes continue to perpetuate insidious, systemic prejudice and racism in the twenty-first century. Higginbotham's extensive research demonstrates*

maximize White folks benefits while symmetrically downsizing the great bulk of rights pertaining to Blacks,[662] Latinos[663] and «risky subjects»[664] alike.[665]

§§ CRT furthermore posits that the structural racism abides by a policy according to which non-White communities should be thrown to suburban areas.[666] This is the quintessence of a bemoaning policy tagged as *redlining*, which will be fleshed out in due course.[667]

§§ The endgame of this initiative—*redlining*,[668] which, recall, consisted of a policy according to which non-White communities should be jettisoned to the

---

how laws and actions have been used to maintain a racial paradigm of hierarchy and separation—both historically, in the era of lynch mobs and segregation, and today—legally, economically, educationally and socially. Using history as a roadmap, Higginbotham arrives at a provocative solution for ridding the nation of Jim Crow's ghost, suggesting that legal and political reform can successfully create a post-racial America, but only if it inspires whites and Blacks to significantly alter behaviors and attitudes of race-based superiority and victimization. He argues that America will never achieve its full potential unless it *truly enters a post-racial era, and believes that time is of the essence as competition increases globally*"). Italics added.

660 See: Part III, Chap. 3, Sects. 3.1.4.1–3.1.4.2. (on critical race theory as a linchpin of critical artificial intelligence studies).

661 Fornili, K. S., "Racialized mass incarceration and the war on drugs: A critical race theory appraisal", *Journal of Addictions Nursing*, 29 (1), 2018, pp. 65–72.

662 Arnold, David, Will Dobbie, and Crystal S. Yang, "Racial Bias in Bail Decisions," *Quarterly Journal of Economics*, 133, 2018, pp. 1885–1932.

663 Rios, Victor M, *Punished: Policing the Lives of Black and Latino Boys*, New York: NYU Press, 2011.

664 Agung-Igusti, R. P., "Raced and risky subjects: The interplay of racial and managerial ideologies as an expression of "colorblind" racism", *American Journal of Community Psychology*, 2024, 73.

665 DaViera, A. L./Uriostegui, M., Gottlieb/A./Onyeka, O, "Risk, race, and predictive policing: A critical race theory analysis of the strategic subject list", *cit.*, pp. 91–103. See also: Alexander, M., *The new Jim Crow: Mass incarceration in the age of colorblindness*, The New Press, 2012.

666 Du Bois, W. E. B., *Black Reconstruction in America: Toward a history of the part which black folk played in the attempt to reconstruct democracy in America*, London, Routledge, 2017.

667 See: Part IV, This chapter, Sects. 4.1.4–4.1.4.2.1 of this book (on mortgage redlining). See: Part IV, This chapter, Sects. 4.1.2–4.1.4.3 of this book (on algorithmic credit scoring, consumer racism and credit card redlining). See: Part IV, This chapter, Sects. 4.1.4–4.1.4.2.3 of this book (on algorithmic redlining).

668 Mendez-Carbajo, Diego "Neighborhood Redlining, Racial Segregation, and Homeownership", *Federal Reserve Bank of Saint Louis*, September 1, 2021 ("*In the 1930s, the Home Owners' Loan Corporation (HOLC) drew maps of residential neighborhoods across the United States. The maps classified each neighborhood into one of five categories, from least to most likely to* ***default*** *on a* ***mortgage*** *loan. In those maps, the neighborhoods most likely to default were shaded red and over time these neighborhoods had the largest concentrations of African Americans. Because the lending classifications determined individual access to credit, the residents of redlined neighborhoods paid high interest rates and had a hard time becoming homeowners and keeping their homes in good condition. From 1968 to 1974, Congress passed several federal laws and policies preventing lending discrimination by race and gender, and the pattern of residential segregation started to change*"). Italics added.

outskirts of urban cities—was straightforward: cast a murky shadow on racialized people, thus creating a suitably tailored link between race,[669] class, crime hot spots,[670] income,[671] proneness to partake in criminal-related activities,[672] syndicates of organized crime,[673] gang violence,[674] and crime-ridden neighbourhoods[675] that still reverberates[676] across generations.[677] The rate and pace at which non-White are arrested[678]/[679] adds plausibility to this sweeping claim.[680] There simply is too much to atone for in this regard.[681]

---

669 Pager, Devah, *Marked: Race, Crime, and Finding Work in an Era of Mass Incarceration*, Chicago: University of Chicago Press, 2007.

670 Braga, Anthony A., and David L. Weisburd, *Policing Problem Places: Crime Hot Spots and Effective Prevention*, New York: Oxford University Press, 2010.

671 Gustafson, Kaaryn S, *Cheating Welfare: Public Assistance and the Criminalization of Poverty*, New York: NYU Press, 2011.

672 DaViera, A. L./Uriostegui, M., Gottlieb/A./Onyeka, O, "Risk, race, and predictive policing: A critical race theory analysis of the strategic subject list", *cit.*, pp. 91–103.

673 Papachristos, Andrew V., David M. Hureau, and Anthony A. Braga, "The Corner and the Crew: The Influence of Geography and Social Networks on Gang Violence", *American Sociological Review*, 78 (3), 2013, pp. 417–47.

674 Quillian, Lincoln, and Devah Pager, "Black Neighbors, Higher Crime? The Role of Racial Stereotypes in Evaluations of Neighborhood Crime", *American Journal of Sociology*, 107 (3), 2001, 717–67.

675 Brewer, R. M., & Heitzeg, N. A., "The racialization of crime and punishment: Criminal justice, Color-Blind racism, and the political economy of the prison industrial complex", *American Behavioral Scientist*, 51 (5), 2008, 625–644; Sampson, Robert J., and Dawn J. Bartusch, "Legal Cynicism and (Subcultural?) Tolerance of Deviance: The Neighborhood Context of Racial Differences", *Law and Society Review*, 32, 1998, pp. 777–804.

676 Skogan, Wesley G., *Police and Community in Chicago: A Tale of Three Cities*, New York: Oxford University Press, 2006.

677 Jacoby, S. F., Dong, B., Beard, J. H., Wiebe, D. J., & Morrison, C. N., "The enduring impact of historical and structural racism on urban violence in Philadelphia", *Social Science & Medicine*, 1982/2018, 199, 2018, pp. 87–95.

678 Powell, Richard/Porter, Jeremy, "Redlining, Concentrated Disadvantage and Crime: The Effects of Discriminatory Government Policies on Violent Crime", *American Journal of Criminal Justice*, Volume 48, 2023, pp. 1132–1156 ("*Redlining and other discriminatory government policies enacted during the first half of the Twentieth Century have had long-lasting negative effects on neighborhoods, especially those inhabited by people of color. This study attempts to link the practice of redlining to current-day indicators of neighborhood concentrated disadvantage and violent crime using spatio-temporal data from Chicago.* Specifically, the study seeks to determine whether redlining has been associated with increased levels of concentrated disadvantage since its implementation in the 1930s. *In addition, it seeks to determine whether redlining was associated with violent crime, and if that association was mediated by redlining's effect on concentrated disadvantage. The results indicate that redlining was associated with increases in both concentrated disadvantage and violent crime, and that redlining's relationship with violent crime was, indeed, partially mediated by its relationship with concentrated disadvantage.* The findings from this study suggest that to reduce violent crime in urban communities, we cannot simply rely on our current punitive criminal justice system. Instead, policies should focus on reducing concentrated disadvantage and racial *isolation by helping economically strengthen severely disadvantaged neighborhoods and by increasing residential mobility for individuals currently living in those neighborhoods*"). But see: Derenoncourt, Ellora/Kim, Chi Hyun/Kuhn, Moritz/Schularik, Moritz, "The Wealth of Two Nations: The U.S. Racial Wealth Gap, 1860–2020", *The Quarterly Journal of Economics*, Volume 139, Issue 2, 2024,

§§ CRT adamantly avers that modern societies are left largely tethered to outdated structures that forestall non-White communities from both vindicate their rights or forgo their enforcement.

§§ Put otherwise, modern societies rest upon the foundational pillars of *systemic racism* whose overriding goal is to cement the White privilege whilst consistently downplaying the rights and needs of non-White communities,[682] whom are regarded

p. 741 ("A large class of commonly discussed policies for reducing racial wealth inequality seeks to reduce gaps in income, savings, and capital gains. These include policies that encourage financial diversification or stock equity holdings among Black households; policies aimed at financial literacy and retirement or savings behavior; or policies aimed at improving educational and labor market outcomes of Black Americans through improved school quality or reductions in discrimination. *Yet on a realistic note, our simulation in Section IV.A shows that even if wealth accumulation conditions had been equal since 1870, the wealth gap would still be 3 to 1 today, and full convergence would be more than 200 years away. Put differently: to close the racial wealth gap in the immediate term* via *flow parameters, Black Americans would need a substantial positive lead over whites, not "just" more equality*"). Italics added.

[679] But see: DeAngelis, Reed T./Frizzelle, Brian G./Hummer, Robert A./Harris, Kathleen Mullan, "Traces of Historical Redlining in the Contemporary United States: New Evidence from the Add Health Cohort", *Research Briefs*, Volume 43, Article number 61, 2024, passim ("*We report three key findings. First, while most participants did not live within the boundaries of historical redlining maps, Black (22%) and Hispanic (28%) participants were several times more likely than their White peers (8%) to live in either a formerly yellow- or red-lined urban area in adolescence. Second, adolescents who resided in yellow- or red-lined areas also tended to live in the most disadvantaged households and neighborhoods and attained the lowest levels of socioeconomic status in adulthood. Third, Black and White adolescents who lived in rural areas also experienced similar or worse adult outcomes than their peers who lived in redlined urban areas. We also find anomalous but inconclusive patterns for the small group of Black and Hispanic participants who lived in historically affluent "green-lined" areas in adolescence, including poor adult health and high risk of contact with the criminal justice system*"). Italics added.

[680] Travis, Jeremy, Bruce Western, and Steve Redburn (Eds.), *Growth of Incarceration in the United States: Exploring Causes and Consequences*, Washington, DC: National Academy of Science, 2014.

[681] But see: Stokes, Danielle, "From Redlining to Greenlining", *U.C.L.A. Law Review*, Volume 71, 2024, pp. 628–696 (628) ("*This Article introduces "greenlining" as a land use planning mechanism that seeks to remediate historical housing, siting, and economic disparities while forging a path toward energy and environmental justice.* Greenlining, the productive and equitable reimagining of redlining, uses the tripartite structure of sustainability-environment, economy, and equity. *Where redlining was a marker for discrimination and injustice, greenlining lies at the crossroads of land use planning and environmentalism, serving the dual purpose of mitigating climate change and prioritizing social justice. Ultimately, greenlining is about investing in marginalized communities that have borne the brunt of regulatory and environmental harms while equitably grappling with the most pressing issue of our time: climate change*"). Italics added.

[682] Roithmayr, Daria, *Reproducing Racism: How everyday choices lock in White Advantage*, New York, New York University Press, 2014, pp. 1–272 ("*Argues that racial inequality reproduces itself automatically over time because early unfair advantage for whites has paved the way for continuing advantage. This book is designed to change the way we think about racial inequality (...) Legal scholar Daria Roithmayr provocatively argues that racial inequality lives on because white advantage functions as a powerful self-reinforcing monopoly, reproducing itself automatically from generation to generation even in the absence of intentional discrimination. Drawing on work in antitrust law and a range of other disciplines, Roithmayr brilliantly compares the dynamics of white*

as trifle forms of existence.[683] As an upshot, the unpalatable encounters with law enforcement agencies[684] lends weight to this main contention.[685]

§§ It does not follow that those other considerations, such as efficacy, cost-effectiveness,[686] efficiency, and accuracy of fair housing, went by the wayside. It is nonetheless clear that *mortgage redlining* lacked conceptually sturdy foundations to throw Blacks to suburban areas.[687]

§§ A hard look on the policies enacted by the Federal Housing Administration («FHA») shed a keen light on this vexing question, wholesomely contradicting all the inaccurate accounts regarding the rationale behind the creation of *mortgage redlining*.

---

advantage to the unfair tactics of giants like AT&T and Microsoft. With penetrating insight, Roithmayr *locates the engine of white monopoly in positive feedback loops that connect the dramatic disparity of Jim Crow to modern racial gaps in jobs, housing and education. Wealthy white neighborhoods fund public schools that then turn out wealthy white neighbors. Whites with lucrative jobs informally refer their friends, who refer their friends, and so on. Roithmayr concludes that racial inequality might now be locked in place, unless policymakers immediately take drastic steps to dismantle this oppressive system*"). Italics added. This book points out how White privilege is perpetuated throughout generations through residential segregation (*mortgage redlining*), abhorrent nepotism, and other bemoaning social practices that pester modern societies).

683 Packard, Jerald M., *American Nightmare: The History of Jim Crow*, Broadway, New York, St. Martin's Press; First Edition, 2002, pp. 1–304 (vii–viii) ("[A] *structure of exclusion and discrimination devised by white Americans to be employed principally against black Americans.... Its central purpose was to maintain a second-class social and economic status for blacks while upholding a first-class social and economic status for whites.... In the South, Jim Crow discrimination at its height existed not only by statute but by custom and racial 'etiquette,' and it was rigidly enforced by both the law enforcement agencies* and courts as well as by ordinary white citizens who were neither policemen nor judges but who often took the law into their own hands as though they were"). Italics added.

684 Western, Bruce, *Punishment and Inequality in America*, New York: Russell Sage Foundation, 2006.

685 Soss, Joe, Richard C. Fording, and Sanford F. Schram, *Disciplining the Poor: Neoliberal Paternalism and the Persistent Power of Race*, Chicago: University of Chicago Press, 2011.

686 In spite of its deep-seated racial bias, decision-makers continue to deploy redlining tactics through big data and may even justify such unlawful practices by claiming that the latter abide by cost-effectiveness. See: Humber, Nadiyah J., "A Home for Digital Equity: Algorithmic Redlining and Property Technology", *California Law Review*, Volume 111, Issue 5, 2023, pp. 1421–1484. See also: Hurley, Mikella/Adebayo, Julius, "Credit Scoring in the Era of Big Data", *Yale Journal of Law and Technology*, Volume 18, 2016, pp. 148, 151–156, 172 (averring that FICO scoring boasts a redoubtable capacity to routinely weed out some populations that have been historically and systematically underrepresented or grossly unfairly represented in the credit industry market). Tellingly, by 2016, ten states had disavowed the unlawful practice of employers using shady credit scores due to their perceived disparate impact on low-income applicants and members of racialized communities (mostly Black folks). See: O'Neill, Cathy, *Weapons of Math Destruction. How Big Data Increases Inequality and Threatens Democracy*. London: Penguin Random House, 2016, pp. 128 and ff and passim. See: Part IV, This chapter, Sects. 4.1.4–4.1.4.2.3 of this book.

687 See: Allen, James, "The Color of Algorithms: An Analysis and Proposed Research Agenda Deterring Algorithmic Redlining", *Fordham Urban Law Journal*, Volume 46, 2019, pp. 219–234 (229–234) (discussing how historical mortgage redlining greatly swayed modern algorithms generated by massive batches of data sets that consist of decades of information built on exclusion and racial discrimination in the purview of financing, marketing, and housing). See: Part IV, This chapter, Sects. 4.1.4–4.1.4.2.3 of this book.

4.1.4.1 «Stay in Your Lane!»: *Fair Housing* and *Mortgage Redlining*: How *Housing Segregation* Outlined by Federal Housing Administration («FHA») Back in the Twentieth Century (1930's) Created a Policy of «Just Desserts» (White Folks) and «Just Deserts» (Black Folks) That Still Resonates Today

§§ *Mortgage redlining*[688] consists of a vast field of study, adherent to no single dogma other than White Supremacy that sought to keenly uphold White privilege from a housing standpoint.[689]

§§ Note, though, that its definitional quandaries have stubbornly persisted from its earliest—and stingiest—days, thereby paving the way to the issue of «white flight»[690] and «sundown towns»[691] in view of which White folks threaten to move

[688] Mendez-Carbajo, Diego "Neighborhood Redlining, Racial Segregation, and Homeownership", *Federal Reserve Bank of Saint Louis*, September 1, 2021("*In the 1930s, the Home Owners' Loan Corporation (HOLC) drew maps of residential neighborhoods across the United States. The maps classified each neighborhood into one of five categories, from least to most likely to* ***default*** *on a* ***mortgage*** *loan. In those maps, the neighborhoods most likely to default were shaded red and over time these neighborhoods had the largest concentrations of African Americans. Because the lending classifications determined individual access to credit, the residents of redlined neighborhoods paid high interest rates and had a hard time becoming homeowners and keeping their homes in good condition. From 1968 to 1974, Congress passed several federal laws and policies preventing lending discrimination by race and gender, and the pattern of residential segregation started to change*"). Italics added.

[689] The insidious effects of redlining still ripple forward in the sense that White folks often refused to have their neighbourhoods integrated by racial minorities. «Move-in violence» was a befitted tool to which White folks resorted to fiercely combat minority integration in White neighbourhoods. See: Bell, Jeannine, *Hate Thy Neighbor: Move-In Violence and the Persistence of Racial Segregation in American Housing*, New York, New York University Press, pp. 1–259 ("In *Hate Thy Neighbor*, Jeannine Bell expands upon these understandings by investigating a little-examined but surprisingly prevalent problem of "move-in violence:" the anti-integration violence directed by white residents at minorities who move into their neighborhoods. Apprehensive about their new neighbors and worried about declining property values, these residents resort to extra-legal violence and intimidation tactics, often using vandalism and verbal harassment to combat what they view as a violation of their territory. *Hate Thy Neighbor* is the first work to seriously examine the role violence plays in maintaining housing segregation, illustrating how intimidation and fear are employed to force minorities back into separate neighborhoods and prevent meaningful integration. *Drawing on evidence that includes in-depth interviews with ordinary citizens and analysis of Fair Housing Act cases, Bell provides a moving examination of how neighborhood racial violence is enabled today and how it harms not only the victims, but entire communities. By finally shedding light on this disturbing phenomenon, Hate Thy Neighbor not only enhances our understanding of how prevalent segregation and this type of hate-crime remain, but also offers insightful analysis of a complex mix of remedies that can work to address this difficult problem*"). Italics added.

[690] Kruse, Kevin M., *White Flight: Atlanta and the Making of Modern Conservatism (Politics and Society in Modern America)*, Princeton, Princeton University Press; Politics and Society in Twentieth-Century America edition (July 29, 2007), 2007, pp. 1–352 ("During the civil rights era, Atlanta thought of itself as "The City Too Busy to Hate," a rare place in the South *where the races lived and thrived together. Over the course of the 1960s and 1970s, however, so many whites fled the city for the suburbs that Atlanta earned a new nickname: "The City Too Busy Moving to Hate. "In this reappraisal of racial politics in modern America, Kevin Kruse explains the causes and consequences of "white flight" in Atlanta and elsewhere.* Seeking to understand segregationists

out their neighbourhoods[692] should they become integrated.[693] Yet this is all but new. In the 1940's, there was an unremitting flurry of *racially restrictive covenants*[694] that sought to banish Black people[695] from White-majority neighbourhoods.[696]

---

on their own terms, *White Flight* moves past simple stereotypes to explore the meaning of white resistance. *In the end, Kruse finds that segregationist resistance, which failed to stop the civil rights movement, nevertheless managed to preserve the world of segregation and even perfect it in subtler and stronger forms*"). Italics added.

691 Loewen, James W., *Sundown Towns: A Hidden Dimension of American Racism*, New York, The New Press, 2006, pp. 1–576 ("*James W. Loewen, exposes the secret communities and hotbeds of racial injustice that sprung up throughout the twentieth century unnoticed, forcing us to reexamine race relations in the United States.* In this groundbreaking work, bestselling sociologist James W. Loewen, author of the national bestseller *Lies My Teacher Told Me, brings to light decades of hidden racial exclusion in America. In a provocative, sweeping analysis of American residential patterns, Loewen uncovers the thousands of "sundown towns"—almost exclusively white towns where it was an unspoken rule that blacks could not live there*—that cropped up throughout the twentieth century, most of them located outside of the South. *These towns used everything from legal formalities to violence to create homogenous Caucasian communities—and their existence has gone unexamined until now*"). Italics added.

692 Loewen, James W., *Sundown Towns: A Hidden Dimension of American Racism*, New York, The New Press; Reprint edition (July 17, 2018), 2018, pp. 1–592 ("In this groundbreaking work, sociologist James W. Loewen, author of the classic bestseller *Lies My Teacher Told Me,* brings to light decades of hidden racial exclusion in America. *In a provocative, sweeping analysis of American residential patterns, Loewen uncovers the thousands of "sundown towns"—almost exclusively white towns where it was an unspoken rule that blacks weren't welcome—that cropped up throughout the twentieth century, most of them located outside of the South*"). Italics added.

693 Bell, Jeannine, *Hate Thy Neighbor: Move-In Violence and the Persistence of Racial Segregation in American Housing*, New York, New York University Press, pp. 1–259 ("*Despite increasing racial tolerance and national diversity, neighborhood segregation remains a very real problem in cities across America. Scholars, government officials, and the general public have long attempted to understand why segregation persists despite efforts to combat it, traditionally focusing on the issue of "white flight," or the idea that white residents will move to other areas if their neighborhood becomes integrated*"). Italics added.

694 "1920s–1948: Racially Restrictive Covenants", *Fair Housing Ctr. Greater Bos.*, http://www.bostonfairhousing.org/timeline/1920s1948-Restrictive-Covenants.html; [https://perma.cc/W3XH-FGNC].

695 Szto, Mary, "Real Estate Agents as Agents of Social Change: Redlining, Reverse Redlining, and Greenlining", *Seatle Journal for Social Justice*, Volume 12, Issue 1, 2013, p. 11 ("*Up until this time, banks had already decided not to lend to blacks. Additionally, racial covenants, i.e., agreements not to sell or rent to persons of non-Caucasian race, and statutory discrimination were common. These restrictions paralleled eugenics theories of the 1800's that attempted to justify social and economic hierarchy based on physical characteristics. American interest in eugenics peaked from the 1890's through 1920's, and the US was a leader in its promotion.* In eugenics, persons were divided into the Caucasian, Negroid, and Mongoloid races; Caucasians were considered superior to the other two. Eugenicists studied characteristics such as "skin color, hair texture, skull shape [and] brain size .... *Among Caucasians, Anglo-Saxons were the "peak of human existence," followed by Northern Europeans. Others, including Mediterraneans, could only succeed if they "assimilated" into Anglo-Saxon society. Assimilation meant adopting Anglo-Saxon language, and legal, religious, and economic culture*"). Footnotes omitted. Italics added.

696 *U.S. Common on Civil Rights, n.° 42, Understanding Fair Housing*, 4, 1973, http://www.law.umaryland.edu/marshall/usccr/documents/cr11042.pdf; [https://perma.cc/79TUJ82P] ("By 1940,

§§ For purposes here, a caveat before jumping in, and deep diving into, the gist of *mortgage redlining*: *systemic racism* and *structural disadvantage*[697] were the tip of the iceberg of housing racial segregation[698] all along.[699] This baseline should be reeled off, and rattled off, from the inception of this section.

§§ To this day, the lending industry tends to skew towards White folks, which falls broadly onto the all-encompassing policy of «just desserts» for the *selected*

---

according to a magazine article, 80 percent of both Chicago and Los Angeles carried restrictive convenants [sic] barring black families").

697 See: Barocas, Solon/Selbst, Andrew, "Big Data's Disparate Impact", *California Law Review*, Volume 104, pp. 2016, p. 691 (highlighting the worrisome, and gruesome, issue of "structural disadvantage" with which racialized communities have been tussling for centuries). See also: Powell, Richard/Porter, Jeremy, "Redlining, Concentrated Disadvantage and Crime: The Effects of Discriminatory Government Policies on Violent Crime", *American Journal of Criminal Justice*, Volume 48, 2023, pp. 1132–1156 ("*Redlining and other discriminatory government policies enacted during the first half of the Twentieth Century have had long-lasting negative effects on neighborhoods, especially those inhabited by people of color. This study attempts to link the practice of redlining to current-day indicators of neighborhood concentrated disadvantage and violent crime using spatio-temporal data from Chicago (…) In addition, it seeks to determine whether redlining was associated with violent crime, and if that association was mediated by redlining's effect on concentrated disadvantage. The results indicate that redlining was associated with increases in both concentrated disadvantage and violent crime, and that redlining's relationship with violent crime was, indeed, partially mediated by its relationship with concentrated disadvantage*"). Italics added. See also: Gandy, Oscar H., *Coming to Terms with Chance: Engaging Rational Discrimination and Cumulative Disadvantage*, Farnham, UK: Ashgate Publishing, 2009.

698 Szto, Mary, "Real Estate Agents as Agents of Social Change: Redlining, Reverse Redlining, and Greenlining", *Seatle Journal for Social Justice*, Volume 12, Issue 1, 2013, p. 1 (*redlining, was the practice of the Federal government, private banks, and other institutions to deny credit to neighborhoods based on race*"). Italics added.

699 Lathan, Nadia, "50 years after being outlawed, redlining still drives neighborhood health inequities Discriminatory lending practice continues to have serious effects", *University of Berkeley, Public Health* (September 20, 2023), available at: https://publichealth.berkeley.edu/news-media/research-highlights/50-years-after-being-outlawed-redlining-still-drives-neighborhood-health-inequities ("*Decades of redlining—a longstanding banking practice that blocked people of color from getting mortgages—continue to perpetuate racial and socioeconomic inequality in the San Francisco Bay Area and across the country, according to ongoing research from UC Berkeley School of Public Health.* Although the practice has been illegal since 1968, *multiple studies show that redlining's harmful legacy has left nonwhite communities struggling with air pollution, reproductive health disorders, and fewer urban amenities more than 50 years later.* "*Historical mortgage redlining, one of the many policies designed to uphold structural racism through housing discrimination, has lasting consequences,*" said *Xing Gao*, a doctoral candidate in epidemiology at Berkeley Public Health who studies the relationship between urban environments and health. "*This holds implications for future policymaking to center equity and justice when it comes to housing*"). Italics added. See also: Packard, Jerald M., *American Nightmare: The History of Jim Crow*, Broadway, New York, St. Martin's Press; First Edition, 2002, pp. 1–304 (vii–viii) ("[A*] structure of exclusion and discrimination devised by white Americans to be employed principally against black Americans.... Its central purpose was to maintain a second-class social and economic status for blacks while upholding a first-class social and economic status for whites.... In the South, Jim Crow discrimination at its height existed not only by statute but by custom and racial 'etiquette,' and it was rigidly enforced by both the law enforcement agencies* and courts as well as by ordinary white citizens who were neither policemen nor judges but who often took the law into their own hands as though they were"). Italics added.

few (White folks),[700] as opposed to «just deserts»[701] for the *unwanted many* (Black folks)[702] in the remit of fair housing and beyond.[703] *Mortgage Redlining* lies at the heart of this lopsided, discriminatory, and unhinged fair housing policy. So does one of its insidious byproducts: *reverse redlining*.[704] Any claim that states otherwise is laughably out of date.

§§ Casts broadly, *mortgage redlining* was powerfully tied to *systemic racism* all along.[705] A deep dive on the housing segregation policies enacted by Federal Housing Administration sheds a keen light on the accuracy of this sweeping claim,[706] which will be adroitly shored up as we move along.

§§ Scholars have been railing against, and harshly rebuking, the so-called fair housing[707] policy[708] while toiling towards a retooling of its central tenets to ensure a fair housing distribution[709] across citizens regardless of skin colour, economic status,[710] or social standing.

---

[700] Adelman, Larry, "A Long History of Racial Preferences-For Whites, PBS", http://www.pbs.org/race/000_About/002_04-background-03-02.htm; [https://perma.cc/EV9V-FYTC].

[701] Qato, Dima M., Martha L. Daviglus, Jocelyn Wilder, Todd Lee, Danya Qato, and Bruce Lambert, "Pharmacy Deserts" Are Prevalent in Chicago's Predominantly Minority Communities, Raising Medication Access Concerns", *Health Affairs*, Volume 33, 2014, pp. 1958–1965.

[702] Perea, Juan F., "The Echoes of Slavery: Recognizing the Racist Origins of the Agricultural and Domestic Worker Exclusion from the National Labor Relations Act", *Ohio State Law Journal*, Volume 72, 2011, pp. 95–126.

[703] DeWitt, Larry, "The Decision to Exclude Agricultural and Domestic Workers from the 1935 Social Security Act", *Social Security Bulletin*, no. 4, 2010, passim; Foster, Laura Ann, "Social Security and African American Families: Unmasking Race and Gender Discrimination", *UCLA Women's Law Journal*, Volume 12, 2001, pp. 55–60.

[704] Szto, Mary, "Real Estate Agents as Agents of Social Change: Redlining, Reverse Redlining, and Greenlining", *Seatle Journal for Social Justice*, Volume 12, Issue 1, 2013, p. 1 ("*reverse redlining* is *marketing inferior credit and other products to those same neighborhoods*"). Italics added.

[705] Freeman, Andrea, "Payback: A Structural Analysis of the Credit Card Problem", *Arizona Law Review*, Volume 55, 2013, pp. 182–183 ("*African-American businesses were traditionally confined to African-American neighbourhoods and catered to a mostly African-American clientele, many of whom did not have high levels of disposable income.* Although some of these niche industries flourished, such as hair and beauty products (which depend for the most part on the negative societal images of their clientele), *many African-American businesses struggled to survive, particularly as successful African Americans emigrated away from all-African-American neighbourhoods. Ghettoized economies prevent financial growth for small African-American businesses and individual consumers, forcing them to rely on debt to meet monthly expenses*"). Italics added.

[706] Charles L. Nier, III, "Perpetuation of Segregation: Toward a New Historical and Legal Interpretation of Redlining Under the Fair Housing Act", *Journal Marshall Law Review*, Volume 32, 1999, pp. 617–625.

[707] Seicshnaydre, Stacy E., "The Fair Housing Choice Myth", *Cardozo Law Review*, Volume 33, 2012, pp. 967–982 (2012).

[708] Short, Aric, "Post-Acquisition Harassment and the Scope of the Fair Housing Act", *Alabama Law Review*, Volume 58, 2006, pp. 203–223.

[709] Gilmore, Brian, "Home Is Where the Hatred Is: A Proposal for a Federal Housing Administration Truth and Reconciliation Commission", *The University of Maryland Law Journal of Race, Religion, Gender & Class*, Volume 10, 2010, passim.

§§ A great deal of ink has been accordingly spilled pondering the degree to which the extant fair housing policy is in dire need of reshuffling or, simply put, a fresh approach to flesh out the long-lasting effects of *mortgage redlining* would suffice.[711] This book sides squarely with these doctrinal instalments in a bid to furnish baselines for good practices in the remit of fair housing.

§§ Holding all else constant, my stance therefore falls neatly into line with a bigger and sharper picture: provide an equal-footed and even-handed access to fair housing[712] amidst the rise of Artificial Intelligence-embedded technologies whirlwind, which is playing havoc with our ability to deftly portend the future of this lucrative industry.

§§ A handful of questions crop up with bursting unease: once the unbridled potential of the newest technological developments come into play how will things pan out in fair housing? Will Blacks rise above the racial inequalities[713] entrenched by

---

[710] Recall: Derenoncourt, Ellora/Kim, Chi Hyun/Kuhn, Moritz/Schularik, Moritz, "The Wealth of Two Nations: The U.S. Racial Wealth Gap, 1860–2020", *The Quarterly Journal of Economics*, Volume 139, Issue 2, 2024, p. 741 ("A large class of commonly discussed policies for reducing racial wealth inequality seeks to reduce gaps in income, savings, and capital gains. These include policies that encourage financial diversification or stock equity holdings among Black households; policies aimed at financial literacy and retirement or savings behavior; or policies aimed at improving educational and labor market outcomes of Black Americans through improved school quality or reductions in discrimination. *Yet on a realistic note, our simulation in Section IV.A shows that even if wealth accumulation conditions had been equal since 1870, the wealth gap would still be 3 to 1 today, and full convergence would be more than 200 years away. Put differently: to close the racial wealth gap in the immediate term* via *flow parameters, Black Americans would need a substantial positive lead over whites, not "just" more equality*"). Italics added.

[711] DeAngelis, Reed T./Frizzelle, Brian G./Hummer, Robert A./Harris, Kathleen Mullan, "Traces of Historical Redlining in the Contemporary United States: New Evidence from the Add Health Cohort", *Research Briefs*, Volume 43, Article number 61, 2024, passim ("Given these findings, we outline avenues for future research that could include historical redlining maps, *but also expand beyond urban redlining to consider nonmetropolitan areas and other contemporary indicators of structural racism*"). Italics added.

[712] See: Szto, Mary, "Real Estate Agents as Agents of Social Change: Redlining, Reverse Redlining, and Greenlining", *Seatle Journal for Social Justice*, Volume 12, Issue 1, 2013, p. 1 ("*Greenlining is incenting investment in previously redlined neighborhoods.* This *article argues that although many Real Estate agents used practices that unjustly excluded access to neighborhoods, all can be faithful agents of inclusion to global, flourishing communities.* That 'is, while Real Estate agents took leading roles in redlining and reverse redlining in the past, they can now lead in *greenlining efforts. Moreover, those who want to effect greater access to global flourishing communities should consider becoming Real Estate agents*"). Italics added.

[713] Menasce, Juliana Horowitz/Brown, Anna/Cox, Kiana, "Views of Racial Inequality", *Pew Research Center*, April 9, 2019, available at: https://www.pewresearch.org/social-trends/2019/04/09/views-of-racial-inequality/ (access: 2.12.2024) ("*more than four-in-ten Americans say the country still has work to do to give black people equal rights with whites. Blacks, in particular, are skeptical that black people will ever have equal rights in this country* (....) *A majority of adults say that being white helps people's ability to get ahead in the country at least a little (59%); 28% say being white neither helps nor hurts and 12% say it hurts.* On the flip side, a majority (56%) sees being black as a disadvantage, with 25% saying it hurts people's ability to get ahead a lot. *About a quarter (26%) say being black neither helps nor hurts and 17% say it helps at least a little. More also say that being Hispanic hurts people's ability to get ahead in this country (51%) than say it*

a long-haul[714] policy of *redlining*?[715] Or this trick (assuage the racial wedge between White folks and Black folks) might be much harder to pull off than initially thought, bearing in mind that deeply steeped racial inequalities might have found its way to the skewed data[716] that feeds into the bigoted machine learning[717] algorithms[718]?

---

helps (18%) or that it neither helps nor hurts (30%). Opinions are more split when it comes to the impact of being Native American—about the same shares say this hurts as say it neither helps nor hurts, while a smaller share says it helps. *And while a plurality says being Asian neither helps nor hurts, more say it helps (34%) than hurts (21%) people's ability to get ahead*"). Italics added.

[714] Lipsitz, George, *The Possessive Investment in Whiteness: How White People Profit from Identity Politics*, Philadelphia, Pennsylvania, Temple University Press; 1st edition (July 13, 2018), 2018, pp. 1–448 ("*George Lipsitz's classic book The Possessive Investment in Whiteness argues that public policy and private prejudice work together to create a possessive investment in whiteness that is responsible for the racialized hierarchies of our society*"). Italics added.

[715] DeAngelis, Reed T./Frizzelle, Brian G./Hummer, Robert A./Harris, Kathleen Mullan, "Traces of Historical Redlining in the Contemporary United States: New Evidence from the Add Health Cohort", *Research Briefs*, Volume 43, Article number 61, 2024, passim ("*Research on the legacies of historical redlining has lacked nationally representative and multilevel data. We advance this literature by analyzing new data that links historical redlining maps to the residential addresses of participants in the National Longitudinal Study of Adolescent to Adult Health (Add Health),* a diverse and national cohort of adolescents who transitioned to adulthood between the mid-1990s and late 2010s (N = 10,897). We report three key findings. First, while most participants did not live within the boundaries of historical redlining maps, Black (22%) and Hispanic (28%) participants were several times more likely than their White peers (8%) to live in either a formerly yellow- or red-lined urban area in adolescence. *Second, adolescents who resided in yellow- or red-lined areas also tended to live in the most disadvantaged households and neighborhoods and attained the lowest levels of socioeconomic status in adulthood.* Third, Black and White adolescents who lived in rural areas also experienced similar or worse adult outcomes than their peers who lived in redlined urban areas. We also find anomalous but inconclusive patterns for the small group of Black and Hispanic participants who lived in historically affluent "green-lined" areas in adolescence, including poor adult health and high risk of contact with the criminal justice system"). Italics added.4343,

[716] Barocas, Solon/Selbst, Andrew D., "Big Data's Disparate Impact", *California Law Review*, Volume 104, 2016, pp. 671–682 (discussing how data is often flawed, rigged, incomplete, imperfect and therefore algorithms inherit the prejudice of the original decision makers). But see: Citron, Danielle Keats/Pasquale, Frank, "The Scored Society: Due Process for Automated Predictions", *Washington Law Review*, Volume 89, 2014, pp. 1, 4–5 (highlighting how human beings programming automated systems is directly conducive to, and leads, to fundamentally inaccurate results since the source code, predictive algorithms and datasets may encompass human biases which, in turn, have a disparate impact on historically disadvantaged groups); Crawford, Kate/Schultz, Jason, "Big Data and Due Process: Toward a Framework to Redress Predictive Privacy Harms", *Boston College Law Review*, Volume 55, 2014, pp. 93, 99–101 (pinpointing pathways through which predictive analytic tools perpetuate discriminatory practices). But see: Bornstein, Stepanhie, "Antidiscriminatory Algorithms", *Alabama Law Review*, Volume 70, 2018, pp. 519, 524–528 (contending, however, that the tagged "facially neutral" algorithms producing discriminatory outcomes should be quashed).

[717] See: O'Neil, Cathy, *Weapons of Math Destruction. How Big Data Increases Inequality and Threatens Democracy*, London, Penguin Random House, 2016, passim (showing how algorithms utilized in modern societies are amenable to perpetuate racial discrimination, partially through perpetuation of social disadvantage and wealth divides).

[718] *Tech, Bias and Housing Initiative, the Promise and Perils of Residential Proptech, Year 1, Research Summary Report, April 2023, TechEquity Collaborative*, p. 11, available at: https://techequity.us/wp-content/uploads/2023/04/TBHI-Y1-Research-Summary-Report.

§§ Further, to what extent does *mortgage redlining* ripples forward?[719] Will the far-reaching effects[720] of *redlining*[721] find its way to the rigged data which, in turn, will feed into machine learning algorithms entrusted to decide to whom the loans should be afforded only to reproduce the hallmarks of *mortgage redlining* (White privilege and racial inequalities)[722]? Whilst I venture to add that our very existence

---

pdf (28.11.2024). ("*Once bad data enters the analysis of one factor, it gets baked into the subsequent process, multiplying the effect that one disadvantageous data point can have on someone's overall housing determination*"). Italics added. See: Part IV, This chapter, Sects. 4.1.4–4.1.4.2.3 of this book.

719 Salazar-Miranda, Arianna/Conzelmann/Phan, Toàn, Hoffman, "Long-term effects of redlining on climate exposure", *Nature Cities*, Volume 1, 2024, pp. 436–444 ("*We investigate the potential long-term impacts of 'redlining'—the historical practice of assigning values to residential areas in US cities based on race and class—on the vulnerability of communities to climate risks.* Using a boundary design methodology for 202 US cities, we document that areas marked by the Home Owners' Loan Corporation as being less desirable for investment in the 1930s–1940s face disproportionately higher current and projected risks of flooding and extreme heat. These heightened vulnerabilities are partly due to diminished environmental capital in these areas—most notably, reduced tree canopy, lower ground surface permeability and lower construction foundation height. *Our findings underscore the persistent influence of historical practices on the present-day distribution of climate risk exposure*"). Italics added.

720 Lathan, Nadia, "50 years after being outlawed, redlining still drives neighborhood health inequities Discriminatory lending practice continues to have serious effects", *University of Berkeley, Public Health* (September 20, 2023), available at: https://publichealth.berkeley.edu/news-media/research-highlights/50-years-after-being-outlawed-redlining-still-drives-neighborhood-health-inequities ("*Decades of redlining—a longstanding banking practice that blocked people of color from getting mortgages—continue to perpetuate racial and socioeconomic inequality in the San Francisco Bay Area and across the country, according to ongoing research from UC Berkeley School of Public Health.* Although the practice has been illegal since 1968, *multiple studies show that redlining's harmful legacy has left nonwhite communities struggling with air pollution, reproductive health disorders, and fewer urban amenities more than 50 years later. "Historical mortgage redlining, one of the many policies designed to uphold structural racism through housing discrimination, has lasting consequences*"). Italics added.

721 Bell, Jeannine, *Hate Thy Neighbor: Move-In Violence and the Persistence of Racial Segregation in American Housing*, New York, New York University Press, pp. 1–259 ("*Despite increasing racial tolerance and national diversity, neighborhood segregation remains a very real problem in cities across America. Scholars, government officials, and the general public have long attempted to understand why segregation persists despite efforts to combat it, traditionally focusing on the issue of "white flight," or the idea that white residents will move to other areas if their neighborhood becomes integrated*"). Italics added.

722 See: *Tech, Bias and Housing Initiative, the Promise and Perils of Residential Proptech, Year 1, Research Summary Report, April 2023, TechEquity Collaborative*, p. 5 available at: https://techequity.us/wp-content/uploads/2023/04/TBHI-Y1-Research-Summary-Report.pdf (28.11.2024). ("*Residential Proptech also has the potential to exacerbate the bias inherent in our housing system. Its rise is due, in part, to the desperation felt by average home seekers. With a severely constrained housing supply, companies offering an easier pathway to homeownership may exploit communities that have been harmed by housing discrimination in the past. Opaque algorithms incorporate biased data into their decision-making processes, making it harder to enforce fair housing laws.* Residential Proptech companies often operate in a regulatory gray area, leaving consumers without the protections they would have from traditional housing regulatory systems. *As unprecedented capital investment flows into this space, venture-backed companies' winner-take-all*

should be densely packed with hope, caution must be nonetheless exercised to avoid stumbling upon disenchantment.

§§ Relatedly, one should not lose sight of the fact that Blacks 'civil rights were rendered—throughout the drawn-out era of *mortgage redlining*—somewhat secondary to other considerations, such a White privilege.[723] The similarities between the staunch protection of White privilege and the symmetric erosion of Black's civil rights are not apparent, and accordingly one is strongly tempted to weave them together as woven of the same cloth.

§§ Bearing this juncture very firmly in mind, Artificial Intelligence-embedded technologies, if nothing else, will most likely reify,[724] mimic,[725] compound and exacerbate deep-steeped racial inequalities[726] that were the rife during the long-winded epoch of *mortgage redlining*.

§§ This social cadre, albeit excruciatingly loathsome, is not amenable to be warded off as a flabbergasting coincidence though. Compellingly, one should be unbeknownst of the axiom according to which the *pearls of algorithmic wisdom* are as good as the training data they leverage on[727] (*inductive bias* arising out of the *machine learning bias*)[728] amidst the «age of intelligent machines».[729]

---

approach to growth has the potential to exacerbate inequality rather than combat it"). Italics added. See: Part IV, This chapter, Sects. 4.1.4–4.1.4.2.3 of this book.

723 Cohn, Ann Pauline, "Redlining and the Civil Rights Act of 1968", *Law and Housing Newsletter*, Volume 4, Issue 3 (Fall 1976), 1976, pp. 9–11 ("REDLINING AND THE CIVIL RIGHTS ACT OF 1968 In a recent decision, the Southern District Court of Ohio ruled that the Civil Rights Act of 1968, 42 U.S.C. 3604 and 3605, pro- hibited the practice of redlining. …*The court held that Section 3605 was an explicit prohibition of redlining because redlining is a denial of loans and financial assistance on the basis of race. In its opinion, the court also stated that Section 3604 prohibited redlining because the practice effectively makes dwellings "un- available" in certain neighborhoods.* It found that, combined with the *high cost of housing, "a denial of financial assistance in connection with the sale of a home would effectively 'make unavail- able or deny' a 'dwelling.'"2 When such denial is a result of racial considerations, as is the case in redlining, Section 3604 is violated*"). Italics added.

724 Duster, Troy, "Race and Reification in Science." *Science*, 307, 2005, passim.

725 Ciancarini, P., Farina, M., Okonicha, O., Smirnova, M., & Succi, G., "Software as storytelling: A systematic literature review", *Computer Science Review*, Volume 47, 2023, 100517.

726 See: Chandler, Anupam, "The Racist Algorithm", *Michigan Law Review*, Volume 115, n. ° 6, 2018, p. 1026 (on racist algorithms, noting that "the possibilities for discriminatory manipulation are legion"). But see: Altenburger, Kristen M./Ho, Daniel E., "When Algorithms Import Private Bias into Public Enforcement: The Promise and Limitations of Statistical Debiasing Solutions", *Journal of Institutional & Theoretical Economics*, Volume 175, 2019, pp. 97–98 (calls for a "debias predictive algorithms" to assuage racist and/or biased, doctored and bigoted algorithms nevertheless). See: Hamilton, Melissa, "The Biased Algorithm: Evidence of Disparate Impact on Hispanics", *American Criminal Law Review*, Volume 56, 2019, pp. 1553 and ff and passim.

727 See: Surden, Harry, "Machine Learning and Law", *Washington Law Review*, Volume 89, 2014, pp. 87, 106 ("In general, *machine learning algorithms are only as good as the data that they are given to analyze*"). Italics added.

728 Dong et al., Qi, "Imbalanced deep learning by minority class incremental rectification, *IEEE Transactions on Pattern Analysis & Machine Intelligence*, Volume 41, 2019, p. 1367 (posit that "*most existing learning algorithms produce inductive bias (learning bias)* towards the frequent

§§ Strikingly, the training data—borne out by the historical records of fair housing that go as far back as the onset of *mortgage redlining* era in the 1930's—on which machine learning algorithms operate upon tend to skew towards White folks as they represent the overwhelming majority of people to whom a loan was granted during the long-haul era of *mortgage redlining*. There is plenty to be done when it comes to burnish the dishevelled—slovenly tainted—image of fair housing. More on this on the section devoted to *Algorithmic Common Good*.[730]

§§ This «decentralized machine learning governance»[731] amounts to one the most harrowing byproducts of *Algorithmic Dictatorship* that besets Black folks in a flurry of decrees, ranging from of fair housing,[732] place-based policies,[733] spatial distribution of people with felony records,[734] business incentives,[735] business location,[736] equal-footed access to job opportunities[737] for those with criminal records,[738] enterprise zones,[739] labour[740] market,[741] job suburbanization,[742] and beyond.[743] None of

(majority) classes if training data are not balanced, *resulting in poor minority class recognition performance*"). Italics added.

729 Amigud, A., "The age of the intelligent machine: Singularity, efficiency, and existential peril", *Philosophy & Technology*, Volume 37 (2), 2024, pp. 1–20.

730 See: Part V, Chap. 5, Sect. 5.1.1.1 of this book (on the central tenets of Rule of Law that lends itself to a beacon of justice amidst the sepulchral darkness that is about to take hold). See: Part V, Chap. 5, Sect. 5.1.1.2 of this book (on the central tenets of Procedural Rule of Law that lends itself to a lighthouse of justice that allows citizens to challenge the pearls of algorithmic wisdom in a court of law).

731 Alsagheer, D., Xu, L., & Shi, W., "Decentralized machine learning governance: Overview, opportunities, and challenges", *Ieee Access: Practical Innovations, Open Solutions*, 11, 2023, 96718–96732.

732 Stoll, Michael A., and Kenya Covington, "Explaining Racial/Ethnic Gaps in Spatial Mismatch in the US: The Primacy of Racial Segregation", *Urban Studies*, Volume 49, 2012, pp. 2501–2521.

733 Neumark, David, and Helen Simpson, "Place-Based Policies", *Handbook of Regional and Urban Economics*, Gilles Duranton, J. Vernon Henderson, and William C. Strange (Editors), Amsterdam, North-Holland, 2015, pp. 1197–1287.

734 Shannon, Sarah K. S., Christopher Uggen, Jason Schnittker, Melissa Thompson, Sara Wakefield, and Michael Massoglia, "The Growth, Scope, and Spatial Distribution of People with Felony Records in the United States, 1948- 2010", *Demography*, Volume 54, 2017, pp. 1795–1818.

735 Slattery, Cailin, and Owen Zidar, "Evaluating State and Local Business Incentives", *Journal of Economic Perspectives*, Volume 34, Issue 2, 2020, pp. 90–118.

736 Pothukuchi, Kameshwari, "Attracting Supermarkets to Inner-City Neighborhoods: Economic Development outside the Box", *Economic Development Quarterly*, Volume 19, 2005, pp. 232–44.

737 Phillips, David C., "Do Low-Wage Employers Discriminate against Applicants with Long Commutes? Evidence from a Correspondence Experiment", *Journal of Human Resources*, Volume 55, 2020, pp. 864–901.

738 Pager, Devah, "The Mark of a Criminal Record", *American Journal of Sociology*, Volume 108, 2003, pp. 937–975.

739 Neumark, David, and Timothy Young, "Enterprise Zones, Poverty, and Labor Market Outcomes: Resolving Conflicting Evidence", *Regional Science and Urban Economics*, Volume 78, 2019, art. 103462, 15 pp.

740 Quillian, Lincoln, Devah Pager, Ole Hexel, and Arnfinn H. Midtboen, "Meta-analysis of Field Experiments Shows No Change in Racial Discrimination in Hiring over Time", *Proceedings of the National Academy of Sciences*, Volume 114, Issue 10, 2017, pp. 870–875.

which pleasant. Let alone sapid. Rather, all of which eerily distasteful insofar they are in dire need of being steadfastly frowned upon.[744]

§§ Against this background, scholars must soldier on against *Algorithmic Dictatorship* in spite of the duplicitous veneer of science-based neutrality[745] under which *algorithmic pearls of wisdom* are often wrapped.

§§ Note, though, that prior to delving into the arcane depths of *algorithmic redlining*[746] and *algorithmic redliking*[747]—two of the most harshly concussive

---

[741] Quillian, Lincoln, and John J. Lee, "Trends in Racial and Ethnic Discrimination in Hiring in Six Western Countries", *Proceedings of the National Academy of Sciences* 120, art. e2212875120, 2023, 10 pp; Stoll, Michael A., "Job Sprawl, Spatial Mismatch, and Black Employment Disadvantage", *Journal of Policy Analysis and Management*, Volume 25, 2006, pp. 827–854; Oreopoulos, Philip, "Why Do Skilled Immigrants Struggle in the Labor Market? A Field Experiment with Thirteen Thousand Resumes", *American Economic Journal: Economic Policy*, Volume 3, 2011, pp. 148–171.

[742] Miller, Conrad, "When Work Moves: Job Suburbanization and Black Employment", *Review of Economics and Statistics*, Volume 105, 2023, pp. 1055–1072.

[743] See: Agan, Amanda/Starr, Sonja, "Employers' Neighborhoods and Racial Discrimination", *The Journal of Legal Studies*, Volume 53, Issue 1, January 2024, 2024, pp. 115–158 (115) ("Using a field experiment, we show that the racial composition of employers' neighborhoods predicts discrimination patterns in a direction suggesting in-group bias. *Second, building on prior work on ban-the-box laws, we show that employers in less-Black neighborhoods appear much likelier to stereotype Black applicants as potentially criminal when information about criminal records is restricted. Third, our data also show racial disparities in geographic proximity to job postings; simulations illustrate how these job-availability and discrimination patterns together shape disparities. When jobs are far from Black neighborhoods, Black applicants are doubly disadvantaged: discrimination patterns disfavor them, and they have fewer nearby opportunities*"). Italics added. Quillian, Lincoln, and Devah Pager, "Black Neighbors, Higher Crime? The Role of Racial Stereotypes in Evaluations of Neighborhood Crime", *American Journal of Sociology*, Volume 107, 2013, pp. 717–767.

[744] Wonyoung, So, "Which Information Matters? Measuring Landlord Assessment of Tenant Screening Reports", *Housing Policy Debate*, Volume 33, n. ° 6, 2023, pp. 1484–1510 (1501–1502) ("*Algorithmic scoring using criminal records is problematic because training data—a data set that is used to train a machine learning model—is inaccurate and the outcome variable ("desirable tenants") is unclear. For instance, the tenant screening company RealPage produces 11,000 reports using "abbreviated" criminal records, which are cheaper to acquire than full criminal records but do not include details of the resolution* (Kirchner & Goldstein, 2020). *An inaccurate model is highly likely to result from tenant screening services using these kinds of abbreviated data, given that it is important to include the final resolution of criminal justice procedures for proper assessment. Moreover, it would be challenging to set an outcome variable for developing this kind of algorithm because it is hard to project a certain criminal outcome into "good" tenant behaviors*"). Italics added.

[745] But see: Benjamin, Ruha, *Race After Technology: Abolitionist Tools for the New Jim Code*, New York, Polity, 2019, pp. 1–172 (7) (discussing that Artificial Intelligence-embedded technologies are viewed as iron-clad tools of objectivity and devoid of any biases whatsoever). Ruha Benjamin accordingly contends that "the employment of new technologies that reflect and reproduce existing inequities but that are promoted and perceived as more objective or progressive than the discriminatory systems of a previous era"). But see: Hurley, Mikella/Adebayo, Julius, "Credit Scoring in the Era of Big Data", *Yale Journal of Law and Technology*, Volume 18, 2016, p. 149 ("*these tools may furthermore obscure discriminatory and subjective lending policies behind a single "objective" score (…) sophisticated algorithms may combine facially neutral data points and treat them as proxies for immutable characteristics such as race or gender, thereby circumventing existing non-discrimination laws and systematically denying credit access to certain groups. Finally, big-data*

outgrowths of *mortgage redlining*—one must shed keen light on the rationale behind the creation of *mortgage redlining*.[748]

§§ As noted above, it goes a long way to explaining why *mortgage redlining* was created. Suffice to say, though, that the power on the matter lied exclusively with the Federal Housing Administration («FHA»).

§§ In many ways, Federal Housing Administration («FHA») policies were the founding tree (deny loans to Black folks) that borne unsavoury fruits (perpetuation of systemic racism and structural disadvantage[749] that fed into machine learning algorithms[750] entrusted with the task to grant, or gainsay, loans to Black folks) that hamper a sustainable policy within the remit of fair housing. Which prompts the question: how did we get here?

§§ The capital sin dates as far back as 1934 when the Federal Housing Administration («FHA») levelled up racial segregation through bemoaning policies like *mortgage redlining*,[751] which accordingly rendered Black folks living in certain geographical areas (the infamous *red line* areas) ineligible to be afforded federal housing loans.[752] It was not until the FHA decided to take the next step that the

---

tools may allow online payday lenders to target the most vulnerable consumers and lure them into debt traps"). Italics added. But see also: Bornstein, Stepanhie, "Antidiscriminatory Algorithms", *Alabama Law Review*, Volume 70, 2018, pp. 519, 524–528 (contending, however, that the tagged "facially neutral" algorithms producing discriminatory outcomes should be quashed). See also: Farina, M./Lavazza, A., *Philosophy, expertise, and the myth of* neutrality, Routledge Studies in Contemporary Philosophy, London, Routledge, 2024.

746 See: Part IV, This chapter, Sects. 4.1.4–4.1.4.2.3 of this book (on algorithmic redlining).

747 See: Part IV, This chapter, Sect. 4.1.4.3 of this book (on "algorithmic redliking").

748 Szto, Mary, "Real Estate Agents as Agents of Social Change: Redlining, Reverse Redlining, and Greenlining", *Seatle Journal for Social Justice*, Volume 12, Issue 1, 2013, p. 1 (*redlining, was the practice of the Federal government, private banks, and other institutions to deny credit to neighborhoods based on race*"). Italics added.

749 See: Barocas, Solon/Selbst, Andrew, "Big Data's Disparate Impact", *California Law Review*, Volume 104, pp. 2016, p. 691 (highlighting the worrisome, and gruesome, issue of "structural disadvantage" with which racialized communities have been tussling for centuries). See also: Powell, Richard/Porter, Jeremy, "Redlining, Concentrated Disadvantage and Crime: The Effects of Discriminatory Government Policies on Violent Crime", *American Journal of Criminal Justice*, Volume 48, 2023, pp. 1132–1156 ("*Redlining and other discriminatory government policies enacted during the first half of the Twentieth Century have had long-lasting negative effects on neighborhoods, especially those inhabited by people of color. This study attempts to link the practice of redlining to current-day indicators of neighborhood concentrated disadvantage and violent crime using spatio-temporal data from Chicago (...) In addition, it seeks to determine whether redlining was associated with violent crime, and if that association was mediated by redlining's effect on concentrated disadvantage. The results indicate that redlining was associated with increases in both concentrated disadvantage and violent crime, and that redlining's relationship with violent crime was, indeed, partially mediated by its relationship with concentrated disadvantage*"). Italics added. See also: Gandy, Oscar H., *Coming to Terms with Chance: Engaging Rational Discrimination and Cumulative Disadvantage*, Farnham, UK: Ashgate Publishing, 2009.

750 See: Part IV, This chapter, Sects. 4.1.4–4.1.4.2.3 of this book (on algorithmic redlining).

751 Freeman, Andrea, "Racism in the Credit Card Industry", *North Carolina Law Review*, Volume 95, Number 4, 2017, pp. 1071–1160 (1090).

752 Freeman, Andrea, "Racism in the Credit Card Industry", *cit.*, pp. 1071–1160 (1090).

systemic racism underpinning *mortgage redlining* was largely scrubbed clean of nuance or doubt.

§§ Besides the aforementioned reasons, *systemic racism* newfound sense of self has unbottled a slew of discriminatory policies, thereby emitting unfiltered, untamed, high, and extremely clear energy of racial segregation across modern societies.

§§ From this point onwards, and much to the dismay of Black folks, the relationship between racial segregation and White privilege would be somewhat reciprocal, long-lasting, powerful, redoubtable, obdurate, unyielding, unappeasable, unforgiving, adamant, stern, steadfast, inexorable and, foremost, unbending.[753] No matter what obstacles came its way,[754] *systemic racism* soldiered on and embraced each «adventure» as it came.[755]

§§ Taken together, *systemic racism* and *White privilege* became unceremoniously exiled on their own time capsule,[756] thus becoming enmeshed in the steadfast

[753] Lipsitz, George, *The Possessive Investment in Whiteness: How White People Profit from Identity Politics*, Philadelphia, Pennsylvania, Temple University Press; 1st edition (July 13, 2018), 2018, pp. 1–448 ("*George Lipsitz's classic book The Possessive Investment in Whiteness argues that public policy and private prejudice work together to create a possessive investment in whiteness that is responsible for the racialized hierarchies of our society*"). Italics added.

[754] DeWolfe, Ruthanne, Squires, Gregory, & DeWolfe, Alan, "Civil rights implications of insurance redlining", *DePaul Law Review*, 29 (2), 1980, pp. 315–352; Cohn, Ann Pauline, "Redlining and the Civil Rights Act of 1968", *Law and Housing Newsletter*, Volume 4, Issue 3 (Fall 1976), 1976, pp. 9–11 ("Redlining and the Civil Rights Act of 1968 In a recent decision, the Southern District Court of Ohio ruled that the Civil Rights Act of 1968, 42 U.S.C. 3604 and 3605, pro- hibited the practice of redlining. …*The court held that Section 3605 was an explicit prohibition of redlining because redlining is a denial of loans and financial assistance on the basis of race*"). Italics added.

[755] United States v. City of Black Jack, 508 F.2d 1179, 1183, 1188 (8th Cir. 1974) (deciding that a zoning ordinance proscribing the construction of new multifamily housing units in a mostly White area infringed the FHA).

[756] Quadagno, Jill, *The Color of Welfare: How Racism Undermined the War on Poverty*, Oxford, Oxford University Press, 1994, pp. 1–272 ("*From Reconstruction to Lyndon Johnson and beyond, Quadagno reveals how American social policy has continually foundered on issues of race. Drawing on extensive primary research, Quadagno shows, for instance, how Roosevelt, in need of support from southern congressmen, excluded African Americans from the core programs of the Social Security Act. Turning to Lyndon Johnson's "unconditional war on poverty," she contends that though anti-poverty programs for job training, community action, health care, housing, and education have accomplished much, they have not been fully realized because they became inextricably intertwined with the civil rights movement of the 1960s, which triggered a white backlash.* Job training programs, for instance, became affirmative action programs, programs to improve housing became programs to integrate housing, programs that began as community action to upgrade the quality of life in the cities were taken over by local civil rights groups. This shift of emphasis eventually alienated white, working-class Americans, who had some of the same needs–for health care, subsidized housing, and job training opportunities–but who got very little from these programs. *At the same time, affirmative action clashed openly with organized labor, and equal housing raised protests from the white suburban middle-class, who didn't want their neighborhoods integrated. Quadagno shows that Nixon, who initially supported many of Johnson's programs, eventually caught on that the white middle class was disenchanted. He realized that his grand plan for welfare reform, the Family Assistance Plan, threatened to undermine wages in the South and alienate the Republican party's new constituency–white, southern Democrats–and therefore dropped it.* In the 1960s, the United States embarked on a journey to resolve the "American dilemma." Yet instead of finally

protection of the central tenets[757] of both.[758] This is the background that enabled the emergence of *mortgage redlining* in the United States of America which, in turn, still resonates today.

§§ Leveraging on a budding new relationship between *systemic racism* and *White privilege*, the Federal Loan Bank Board's requested to the Home Owners 'Loan Corporation in 1935 to create a batch of residential security maps for a number as high of 239 cities[759] in the United States of America.[760]

§§ These maps[761] featured «trends of desirability»[762] for mortgage lending.[763] Tellingly, these maps also sought to pinpoint[764] «the level of security for Real Estate investments in each surveyed city».[765]

---

instituting full democratic rights for all its citizens, the policies enacted in that turbulent decade failed dismally. *The Color of Welfare reveals the root cause of this failure–the inability to address racial inequality*"). Italics added.

757 Kruse, Kevin M., *White Flight: Atlanta and the Making of Modern Conservatism (Politics and Society in Modern America)*, Princeton, Princeton University Press; Politics and Society in Twentieth-Century America edition (July 29, 2007), 2007, pp. 1–352 ("*In the end, Kruse finds that segregationist resistance, which failed to stop the civil rights movement, nevertheless managed to preserve the world of segregation and even perfect it in subtler and stronger forms*"). Italics added.

758 Lipsitz, George, *The Possessive Investment in Whiteness: How White People Profit from Identity Politics*, Philadelphia, Pennsylvania, Temple University Press; 1st edition (July 13, 2018), 2018, pp. 1–448 ("*Whiteness has a cash value: it accounts for advantages that come to individuals through profits made from housing secured in discriminatory markets, through the unequal educational opportunities available to children of different races, through insider networks that channel employment opportunities to the friends and relatives of those who have profited most from past and present discrimination*, and especially through intergenerational transfers of inherited wealth that pass on the spoils of discrimination to succeeding generations. *White Americans are encouraged to invest in whiteness, to remain true to an identity that provides them with structured advantages*"). Italics added.

759 Freeman, Andrea, "Racism in the Credit Card Industry", *cit.*, pp. 1071–1160 (1090).

760 Mendez-Carbajo, Diego "Neighborhood Redlining, Racial Segregation, and Homeownership", *Federal Reserve Bank of Saint Louis*, September 1, 2021("*In the 1930s, the Home Owners' Loan Corporation (HOLC) drew maps of residential neighborhoods across the United States. The maps classified each neighborhood into one of five categories, from least to most likely to* ***default*** *on a* ***mortgage*** *loan. In those maps, the neighborhoods most likely to default were shaded red and over time these neighborhoods had the largest concentrations of African Americans. Because the lending classifications determined individual access to credit, the residents of redlined neighborhoods paid high interest rates and had a hard time becoming homeowners and keeping their homes in good condition. From 1968 to 1974, Congress passed several federal laws and policies preventing lending discrimination by race and gender, and the pattern of residential segregation started to change*"). Italics added.

761 Home Owners' Loan Corporation, Residential Security "Redlining" Map and Area Descriptions: Hartford, Connecticut (1937), http://magic.lib.uconn.edu/magic_2/vector/37840/primary_source/hdimg_37840_064_1937_holc_national_archives_trinity.pdf; [https://perma.cc/7V9V-YL2S] (access: 13.11.2024) (showing that race and social standing were considered when redlining neighbourhoods in Hartford, Connecticut, United States of America).

762 Hillier, Amy E., "Redlining and the Homeowners' Loan Corporation", *Journal of Urban History*, Volume 29, 2003, pp. 394–400.

§§ These maps featured a wide range of colour-coded grades,[766] flowing from (A),[767] the highest grade,[768] to (D), the lowest grade,[769] underpinned by a bigoted assessment of housing conditions[770] and residents 'social standing[771] and social status.[772]

§§ Notably, neighbourhoods with Non-White,[773] immigrant,[774] poor[775] residents routinely received the lowest[776] grades.[777] The red shading of the tagged D areas, the lowest grade, therefore paved the way to the infamous term **«redlining»** to depict racial discrimination[778] in the remit of mortgage[779] lending.[780]

§§ Relatedly, *mortgage redlining* gave FHA *carte blanche* to implement policies that enabled White folks to acquire houses while proscribing Blacks, Latinos, and

---

763 Freeman, Andrea, "Racism in the Credit Card Industry", *cit.*, pp. 1071–1160 (1090).

764 Freeman, Andrea, "Racism in the Credit Card Industry", *cit.*, pp. 1071–1160 (1090).

765 Bernanke, Ben S., Chairman, *Bd. of Governors of the Fed. Reserve Sys., Address at the Community Affairs Research Conference: The Community Reinvestment Act: Its Evolution and New Challenges (Mar. 30, 2007)*, http://www.federalreserve.gov/newsevents/speech/bernanke2007 0330a.htm; [https://perma.cc/DH2X-XTW7]. (Access: 13.11.2024).

766 Freeman, Andrea, "Racism in the Credit Card Industry", *cit.*, pp. 1071–1160 (1090).

767 Freeman, Andrea, "Racism in the Credit Card Industry", *cit.*, pp. 1071–1160 (1090).

768 Freeman, Andrea, "Racism in the Credit Card Industry", *cit.*, pp. 1071–1160 (1090).

769 Freeman, Andrea, "Racism in the Credit Card Industry", *cit.*, pp. 1071–1160 (1090).

770 Freeman, Andrea, "Racism in the Credit Card Industry", *cit.*, pp. 1071–1160 (1090).

771 Freeman, Andrea, "Racism in the Credit Card Industry", *cit.*, pp. 1071–1160 (1090).

772 Freeman, Andrea, "Racism in the Credit Card Industry", *cit.*, pp. 1071–1160 (1090).

773 Freeman, Andrea, "Racism in the Credit Card Industry", *cit.*, pp. 1071–1160 (1091).

774 Oreopoulos, Philip, "Why Do Skilled Immigrants Struggle in the Labor Market? A Field Experiment with Thirteen Thousand Resumes", *American Economic Journal: Economic Policy*, Volume 3, 2011, pp. 148–171.

775 See: Eubanks, Virginia, *Automating inequality: how high-tech tools profile, police, and punish the poor*, New York: St. Martin's Press, 2017. Gilliom, John, *Overseers of the Poor: Surveillance, Resistance, and the Limits of Privacy*, Chicago: University of Chicago Press, 2001. Soss, Joe, Richard C. Fording, and Sanford F. Schram, *Disciplining the Poor: Neoliberal Paternalism and the Persistent Power of Race.* Chicago: University of Chicago Press, 2011 (on the long-lasting effects of poverty).

776 Freeman, Andrea, "Racism in the Credit Card Industry", *cit.*, pp. 1071–1160 (1091).

777 Bernanke, Ben S., Chairman, *Bd. of Governors of the Fed. Reserve Sys., Address at the Community Affairs Research Conference: The Community Reinvestment Act: Its Evolution and New Challenges (Mar. 30, 2007)*, http://www.federalreserve.gov/newsevents/speech/bernanke2007 0330a.htm; [https://perma.cc/DH2X-XTW7]. (Access: 13.11.2024).

778 Home Owners' Loan Corporation, Residential Security "Redlining" Map and Area Descriptions: Hartford, Connecticut (1937), http://magic.lib.uconn.edu/magic_2/vector/37840/primary_source/hdimg_37840_064_1937_holc_national_archives_trinity.pdf; [https://perma.cc/7V9V-YL2S] (access: 13.11.2024).

779 Freeman, Andrea, "Racism in the Credit Card Industry", *cit.*, pp. 1071–1160 (1091).

780 Bernanke, Ben S., Chairman, *Bd. of Governors of the Fed. Reserve Sys., Address at the Community Affairs Research Conference: The Community Reinvestment Act: Its Evolution and New Challenges (Mar. 30, 2007)*, http://www.federalreserve.gov/newsevents/speech/bernanke2007 0330a.htm; [https://perma.cc/DH2X-XTW7]. (Access: 13.11.2024).

immigrants from doing so.[781] In many ways, FHA[782] played a pivotal role in implementing Roosevelt's New Deal against the backdrop of which home ownership was made possible for millions of White folks.[783]

§§ At the other end of the spectrum, members of racialised communities (Blacks, Latinos, and poor residents) were—mercilessly and uncannily—excluded from the purview of credit lending, thereby thwarting their pathways towards both financial stability and wealth accumulation, which has sent ripples[784] across modern days.[785]

§§ Tellingly, of the $ 120 billion in home loans dealt with by FHA between 1934 and 1962, a goodly number of 98% was channelled to White[786] folks.[787] By the same

---

[781] Freeman, Andrea, "Racism in the Credit Card Industry", *cit.*, pp. 1071–1160 (1091).

[782] Bernanke, Ben S., Chairman, *Bd. of Governors of the Fed. Reserve Sys., Address at the Community Affairs Research Conference: The Community Reinvestment Act: Its Evolution and New Challenges (Mar. 30, 2007)*, http://www.federalreserve.gov/newsevents/speech/bernanke20070330a.htm; [https://perma.cc/DH2X-XTW7]. (Access: 13.11.2024). Home Owners' Loan Corporation, Residential Security "Redlining" Map and Area Descriptions: Hartford, Connecticut (1937), http://magic.lib.uconn.edu/magic_2/vector/37840/primary_source/hdimg_37840_064_1937_holc_national_archives_trinity.pdf; [https://perma.cc/7V9V-YL2S] (access: 13.11.2024).

[783] Freeman, Andrea, "Racism in the Credit Card Industry", *cit.*, pp. 1071–1160 (1091). But see: United States v. City of Black Jack, 508 F.2d 1179, 1183, 1188 (8th Cir. 1974) (deciding that a zoning ordinance proscribing the construction of new multifamily housing units in a mostly White area infringed the FHA).

[784] Lathan, Nadia, "50 years after being outlawed, redlining still drives neighborhood health inequities Discriminatory lending practice continues to have serious effects", *University of Berkeley, Public Health* (September 20, 2023), available at: https://publichealth.berkeley.edu/news-media/research-highlights/50-years-after-being-outlawed-redlining-still-drives-neighborhood-health-inequities ("*Decades of redlining—a longstanding banking practice that blocked people of color from getting mortgages—continue to perpetuate racial and socioeconomic inequality in the San Francisco Bay Area and across the country, according to ongoing research from UC Berkeley School of Public Health.* Although the practice has been illegal since 1968, *multiple studies show that redlining's harmful legacy has left nonwhite communities struggling with air pollution, reproductive health disorders, and fewer urban amenities more than 50 years later.* "*Historical mortgage redlining, one of the many policies designed to uphold structural racism through housing discrimination, has lasting consequences,*" said *Xing Gao*, a doctoral candidate in epidemiology at Berkeley Public Health who studies the relationship between urban environments and health. "*This holds implications for future policymaking to center equity and justice when it comes to housing*"). Italics added.

[785] Derenoncourt, Ellora/Kim, Chi Hyun/Kuhn, Moritz/Schularik, Moritz, "The Wealth of Two Nations: The U.S. Racial Wealth Gap, 1860–2020", *The Quarterly Journal of Economics*, Volume 139, Issue 2, 2024, p. 741 ("A large class of commonly discussed policies for reducing racial wealth inequality seeks to reduce gaps in income, savings, and capital gains. These include policies that encourage financial diversification or stock equity holdings among Black households; policies aimed at financial literacy and retirement or savings behavior; or policies aimed at improving educational and labor market outcomes of Black Americans through improved school quality or reductions in discrimination. *Yet on a realistic note, our simulation in Section IV.A shows that even if wealth accumulation conditions had been equal since 1870, the wealth gap would still be 3 to 1 today, and full convergence would be more than 200 years away. Put differently: to close the racial wealth gap in the immediate term* via *flow parameters, Black Americans would need a substantial positive lead over whites, not "just" more equality*"). Italics added.

[786] Lipsitz, George, *The Possessive Investment in Whiteness: How White People Profit from Identity Politics*, Philadelphia, Pennsylvania, Temple University Press; 1st edition (July 13, 2018), 2018,

token, between 1946 and 1960, less than 100 of the 350,000 newly created homes in Northern California funded by the FHA were allotted to Black families.[788]

§§ In addition to that, the FHA's policies[789] led White middle-class families to flee integrated urban areas for the outskirts,[790] thereby kick-starting a groundswell of urban decay.[791]

§§ Strikingly, under FHA policies a wide range of White home owners came to terms with the fact that was much easier to get a loan to buy a new home than for repairs[792] and accordingly left the old houses behind.[793]

§§ A great deal of publications penned by FHA further dissuaded integrated neighbourhoods as Black residents would create disharmony and wreak havoc in White neighbourhoods, thereby accelerating the exponential growth of «sundown towns» where Blacks were not welcome.[794]

§§ FHA policies stirred a flurry of grievances mirrored on a whopping number of White fleeing integrated neighbourhoods («white flight»),[795] which primarily sprouted in Detroit.

§§ The public outcry was fuelled by Black's earnest attempts to bypass and circumvent FHA's blatantly racist policies in a bid to be granted a sorely needed loan, which ultimately led to the construction of a wall that embodied the racial segregation between White and Black communities («The Birwood Wall»).[796] As a result, Black communities were pushed out of White neighbourhoods and were

pp. 1–448 ("*George Lipsitz's classic book The Possessive Investment in Whiteness argues that public policy and private prejudice work together to create a possessive investment in whiteness that is responsible for the racialized hierarchies of our society*"). Italics added.

787 Freeman, Andrea, "Racism in the Credit Card Industry", *cit.*, pp. 1071–1160 (1091).

788 Freeman, Andrea, "Racism in the Credit Card Industry", *cit.*, pp. 1071–1160 (1091).

789 Kruse, Kevin M., *White Flight: Atlanta and the Making of Modern Conservatism (Politics and Society in Modern America), cit.*, pp. 1–352 (60–61) (explaining that FHA actively encouraged racial limitations that paved the way to the segregation between White folks and Black folks).

790 Freeman, Andrea, "Racism in the Credit Card Industry", *cit.*, pp. 1071–1160 (1091).

791 Freeman, Andrea, "Racism in the Credit Card Industry", *cit.*, pp. 1071–1160 (1091).

792 Freeman, Andrea, "Racism in the Credit Card Industry", *cit.*, pp. 1071–1160 (1091).

793 Freeman, Andrea, "Racism in the Credit Card Industry", *cit.*, pp. 1071–1160 (1091).

794 Loewen, James W., *Sundown Towns: A Hidden Dimension of American Racism*, New York, The New Press; Reprint edition (July 17, 2018), 2018, pp. 1–592 ("In this groundbreaking work, sociologist James W. Loewen, author of the classic bestseller *Lies My Teacher Told Me*, brings to light decades of hidden racial exclusion in America. *In a provocative, sweeping analysis of American residential patterns, Loewen uncovers the thousands of "sundown towns"—almost exclusively white towns where it was an unspoken rule that blacks weren't welcome—that cropped up throughout the twentieth century, most of them located outside of the South*"). Italics added.

795 Bell, Jeannine, *Hate Thy Neighbor: Move-In Violence and the Persistence of Racial Segregation in American Housing*, New York, New York University Press, pp. 1–259 ("*Despite increasing racial tolerance and national diversity, neighborhood segregation remains a very real problem in cities across America. Scholars, government officials, and the general public have long attempted to understand why segregation persists despite efforts to combat it, traditionally focusing on the issue of "white flight," or the idea that white residents will move to other areas if their neighborhood becomes integrated*"). Italics added.

796 Freeman, Andrea, "Racism in the Credit Card Industry", *cit.*, pp. 1071–1160 (1091).

accordingly dumped to the unwanted suburban areas where environmental hazards abound.[797]

§§ To add to Black folks' woes, the Serviceman's Readjustment Act of 1944 («GI Bill)[798] further compounded the yawning racial inequalities between White folks and Black folks.[799]

§§ The Serviceman's Readjustment Act of 1944 (hereinafter «GI Bill») has fallen conspicuously short of matching Black veterans 'rosy expectations of being afforded equal-footed benefits as compared to their fellow White[800] veterans.[801] Tellingly, GI

---

[797] Taylor, Dorceta, *Toxic Communities: Environmental Racism, Industrial Pollution, and Residential Mobility*, New York, New York University Press, 2014, pp. 1–352 ("*From St. Louis to New Orleans, from Baltimore to Oklahoma City, there are poor and minority neighborhoods so beset by pollution that just living in them can be hazardous to your health. Due to entrenched segregation, zoning ordinances that privilege wealthier communities, or because businesses have found the 'paths of least resistance,' there are many hazardous waste and toxic facilities in these communities, leading residents to experience health and wellness problems on top of the race and class discrimination most already experience.* Taking stock of the recent environmental justice scholarship, *Toxic Communities* examines the *connections among residential segregation, zoning, and exposure to environmental hazards.* Renowned environmental sociologist Dorceta Taylor focuses on the locations of hazardous facilities in low-income and minority communities and shows how they have been dumped on, contaminated and exposed. Drawing on an array of historical and contemporary case studies from across the country, *Taylor explores controversies over racially-motivated decisions in zoning laws, eminent domain, government regulation (or lack thereof), and urban renewal. She provides a comprehensive overview of the debate over whether or not there is a link between environmental transgressions and discrimination, drawing a clear picture of the state of the environmental justice field today and where it is going. In doing so, she introduces new concepts and theories for understanding environmental racism that will be essential for environmental justice scholars. A fascinating landmark study, Toxic Communities greatly contributes to the study of race, the environment, and space in the contemporary United States*"). Italics added.

[798] Servicemen's Readjustment Act of 1944 (G.I. Bill), Pub. L. No. 78–346, 58 Stat. 284.

[799] Turner, Sarah/Bound, John, "Closing the Gap or Widening the Divide: The Effects of the G.I. Bill and World War II on the Educational Outcomes of Black Americans", *Journal of Economic History*, Volume 63, 2003, passim (discussing how Black veterans were clearly discriminated against, as compared to their fellow White veterans, for educational opportunities in the aftermath of World War II). Freeman, Andrea, "Racism in the Credit Card Industry", *cit.*, pp. 1071–1160 (1092).

[800] Freeman, Andrea, "Racism in the Credit Card Industry", *cit.*, pp. 1071–1160 (1092).

[801] Altschuler, Glenn/Blumin, Stuart, *The GI Bill: The New Deal for Veterans (Pivotal Moments in American History)*, Oxford, Oxford University Press, 2009, pp. 1–272 ("On rare occasions in American history, Congress enacts a measure so astute, so far-reaching, so revolutionary, it enters the language as a metaphor. The Marshall Plan comes to mind, as does the Civil Rights Act. But perhaps none resonates in the American imagination like the G.I. Bill. In a brilliant addition to Oxford's acclaimed Pivotal Moments in American History series, historians Glenn C. Altschuler and Stuart M. Blumin offer a compelling and often surprising account of the G.I. Bill and its sweeping and decisive impact on American life. *Formally known as the Serviceman's Readjustment Act of 1944, it was far from an obvious, straightforward piece of legislation, but resulted from tense political maneuvering and complex negotiations. As Altschuler and Blumin show, an unlikely coalition emerged to shape and pass the bill, bringing together both New Deal Democrats and conservatives who had vehemently opposed Roosevelt's social-welfare agenda. For the first time in American history returning soldiers were not only supported, but enabled to pursue success–a revolution in America's policy towards its veterans*"). Italics added.

Bill afforded far greater benefits to White soldiers than did to Black veterans who had fought the very same battles for the very same country (United States of America).[802]

§§ Compellingly, under the FHA's overriding goal to bestow upon veterans' financial support to buy new homes, less than 3% of FHA or Veterans affair loans were granted to non-Whites.[803] Unsurprisingly, the stark racial inequalities mirrored on FHA's blatantly racist policies found its way to other segments of the housing industry[804] (v.g. loan officers and banks).[805]

§§ Most importantly, and more in tune with the sweeping goal from which it was borne, other parts of the path-breaking GI Bill, which allotted veterans a spate of opportunities to thrive and flourish in the aftermath of drawn-out conflicts, such as job skills training and proper and sound education to kneecap the deleterious effects of slavery[806] and systemic racism, were not ascribed to Black[807] veterans.[808]

§§ Mostly on account of the stance evinced by those tasked with the duty to apply the GI Bill. Amongst whom stand White officials, business people, public servants, and institutions, who simply refused to assign life-changing benefits to Black veterans the same way than did with White[809] veterans.[810]

---

[802] Boulton, Mark, "How the G.I. Bill Failed African-American Vietnam War Veterans", *Journal of Blacks Higher Education*, 2007, passim.

[803] McKenna, Cyd, *The Homeownership Gap: How the Post-World War II GI Bill Shaped Modern Day Homeownership Patterns for Black and White Americans* 59 (May 22, 2008) (unpublished Master in City Planning thesis, Massachusetts Institute of Technology), https://dspace.mit.edu/bitstream/handle/1721.1/44333/276173994-MIT.pdf; [https://perma.cc/9MCQ-J3QK]. *Apud*: Freeman, Andrea, "Racism in the Credit Card Industry", *cit.*, pp. 1071–1160 (1092).

[804] Freeman, Andrea, "Racism in the Credit Card Industry", *cit.*, pp. 1071–1160 (1092).

[805] Altschuler, Glenn/Blumin, Stuart, *The GI Bill: The New Deal for Veterans (Pivotal Moments in American History)*, *cit.*, pp. 1–272 (198–199 and passim).

[806] Blockmon, Douglas E., *Slavery by Another Name: The Re-Enslavement of Black Americans from the Civil War to World War II*, United States of America, Doubleday, 2008, pp. 1–480 ("*Under laws enacted specifically to intimidate blacks, tens of thousands of African Americans were arbitrarily arrested, hit with outrageous fines, and charged for the costs of their own arrests. With no means to pay these ostensible "debts," prisoners were sold as forced laborers to coal mines, lumber camps, brickyards, railroads, quarries, and farm plantations. Thousands of other African Americans were simply seized by southern landowners and compelled into years of involuntary servitude. Government officials leased falsely imprisoned blacks to small-town entrepreneurs, provincial farmers, and dozens of corporations—including U.S. Steel—looking for cheap and abundant labor.* Armies of "free" black men labored without compensation, were repeatedly bought and sold, and were forced through beatings and physical torture to do the bidding of white masters for decades after the official abolition of American slavery. *The neoslavery system exploited legal loopholes and federal policies that discouraged prosecution of whites for continuing to hold black workers against their wills. As it poured millions of dollars into southern government treasuries, the new slavery also became a key instrument in the terrorization of African Americans seeking full participation in the U.S. political system*"). Italics added.

[807] Altschuler, Glenn/Blumin, Stuart, *The GI Bill: The New Deal for Veterans (Pivotal Moments in American History)*, *cit.*, pp. 1–272 (198–199 and passim).

[808] Freeman, Andrea, "Racism in the Credit Card Industry", *cit.*, pp. 1071–1160 (1092).

[809] Freeman, Andrea, "Racism in the Credit Card Industry", *cit.*, pp. 1071–1160 (1092).

[810] Altschuler, Glenn/Blumin, Stuart, *The GI Bill: The New Deal for Veterans (Pivotal Moments in American History)*, *cit.*, pp. 1–272 (128–129 and passim).

§§ Against this well-trodden and drawn-out background, the harrowing legacy of slavery—which, in turn, has laid the groundwork for a gruelling *systemic racism*[811]—spawned a strikingly clear economic disadvantage[812] of racialized communities that still ripples[813] forward.[814]

§§ The fast-paced development of Artificial Intelligence-embedded technologics has only ratcheted up—levelled up and, in some instances, flared up—the degree of

---

[811] See: Connecticut Fair Housing Center, et al. v. CoreLogic Rental Property Solutions—Cohen Milstein (access: 20.11.2024). ("*The U.S. Department of Housing & Urban Development observed in 2016 that excluding rental applicants because of their criminal records disproportionately harms Latinos and African Americans, who are significantly more likely than whites to be arrested or convicted. Studies show such disparities are linked to differential enforcement rather than to differences in likelihood of engaging in criminal activity.* HUD advised that to avoid discriminating, an "individualized review" should be conducted considering the nature of the offense, how long ago it occurred, intervening changed circumstances, and other relevant factors to avoid denying housing to an applicant who does not pose a genuine and ongoing threat to persons or property. *Further, HUD's guidance specifically advises landlords not to consider arrests that did not result in a conviction in making their evaluations*"). Italics added.

[812] See: Barocas, Solon/Selbst, Andrew, "Big Data's Disparate Impact", *California Law Review*, Volume 104, pp. 2016, p. 691 (highlighting the worrisome, and gruesome, issue of "structural disadvantage" with which racialized communities have been tussling for centuries). See also: Powell, Richard/Porter, Jeremy, "Redlining, Concentrated Disadvantage and Crime: The Effects of Discriminatory Government Policies on Violent Crime", *American Journal of Criminal Justice*, Volume 48, 2023, pp. 1132–1156 ("*Redlining and other discriminatory government policies enacted during the first half of the Twentieth Century have had long-lasting negative effects on neighborhoods, especially those inhabited by people of color. This study attempts to link the practice of redlining to current-day indicators of neighborhood concentrated disadvantage and violent crime using spatio-temporal data from Chicago* (...) *In addition, it seeks to determine whether redlining was associated with violent crime, and if that association was mediated by redlining's effect on concentrated disadvantage. The results indicate that redlining was associated with increases in both concentrated disadvantage and violent crime, and that redlining's relationship with violent crime was, indeed, partially mediated by its relationship with concentrated disadvantage*"). Italics added. See also: Gandy, Oscar H., *Coming to Terms with Chance: Engaging Rational Discrimination and Cumulative Disadvantage*, Farnham, UK: Ashgate Publishing, 2009.

[813] Derenoncourt, Ellora/Kim, Chi Hyun/Kuhn, Moritz/Schularik, Moritz, "The Wealth of Two Nations: The U.S. Racial Wealth Gap, 1860–2020", *The Quarterly Journal of Economics*, Volume 139, Issue 2, 2024, p. 741 ("A large class of commonly discussed policies for reducing racial wealth inequality seeks to reduce gaps in income, savings, and capital gains. These include policies that encourage financial diversification or stock equity holdings among Black households; policies aimed at financial literacy and retirement or savings behavior; or policies aimed at improving educational and labor market outcomes of Black Americans through improved school quality or reductions in discrimination. *Yet on a realistic note, our simulation in Section IV.A shows that even if wealth accumulation conditions had been equal since 1870, the wealth gap would still be 3 to 1 today, and full convergence would be more than 200 years away. Put differently: to close the racial wealth gap in the immediate term* via *flow parameters, Black Americans would need a substantial positive lead over whites, not "just" more equality*"). Italics added.

[814] Wolff, Edward N., "The Decline of African-American and Hispanic Wealth Since the Great Recession," *NBER Working Paper* no. 25198, 2018; Wolff, Edward N., "African-American and Hispanic Income, Wealth and Homeownership since 1989," *Review of Income and Wealth*, Volume 68, 2022, pp. 189–233.

systemic racism which flagitiously targets members of racialized communities.[815] Thereby giving rise to both *algorithmic redlining*[816] and *algorithmic redliking*[817] which, taken together, are poised to further compound racial inequalities that forms part of a broader technological apparatus (*Algorithmic Dictatorship*) within which *systemic racism*[818] operated.

4.1.4.2 Is the Rule of Law Swiftly Fading? How Jim Crow Laws, *Mortgage Redlining*, Social Security Act and GI Bill Paved the Way to *Algorithmic Redlining* Against the Backdrop of Which Racial Inequalities Are Slated to Occur in the Age of *Algorithmic Dictatorship*

§§ It is not a figment of my bewildering imagination that *mortgage redlining*[819] laid the groundwork upon which stands *Algorithmic Dictatorship* while bestowing upon the reader the opportunity to canvass the foundations of housing segregation[820] underpinning fair housing industry[821] in the United States of America[822] and beyond.

---

[815] Benjamin, Ruha, *Race After Technology: Abolitionist Tools for the New Jim Code*, New York, Polity, 2019, pp. 1–172 ("*From everyday apps to complex algorithms, Ruha Benjamin cuts through tech-industry hype to understand how emerging technologies can reinforce White supremacy and deepen social inequity.* Benjamin argues that automation, far from being a sinister story of racist programmers scheming on the dark web, has the potential to hide, speed up, *and deepen discrimination while appearing neutral and even benevolent when compared to the racism of a previous era.* Presenting the concept of the "New Jim Code," she shows how a range of discriminatory designs encode inequity by explicitly amplifying racial hierarchies; by ignoring but thereby replicating social divisions; or by aiming to fix racial bias but ultimately doing quite the opposite. *Moreover, she makes a compelling case for race itself as a kind of technology, designed to stratify and sanctify social injustice in the architecture of everyday life. This illuminating guide provides conceptual tools for decoding tech promises with sociologically informed skepticism. In doing so, it challenges us to question not only the technologies we are sold but also the ones we ourselves manufacture*"). Italics added.

[816] See: Part IV, This chapter, Sects. 4.1.4–4.1.4.2.3 of this book (on algorithmic redlining).

[817] See: Part IV, This chapter, Sect. 4.1.4.3 of this book (on "algorithmic redliking").

[818] See: Connecticut Fair Housing Center, et al. v. CoreLogic Rental Property Solutions—Cohen Milstein (access: 20.11.2024). ("*The U.S. Department of Housing & Urban Development observed in 2016 that excluding rental applicants because of their criminal records disproportionately harms Latinos and African Americans, who are significantly more likely than whites to be arrested or convicted. Studies show such disparities are linked to differential enforcement rather than to differences in likelihood of engaging in criminal activity.* HUD advised that to avoid discriminating, an "individualized review" should be conducted considering the nature of the offense, how long ago it occurred, intervening changed circumstances, and other relevant factors to avoid denying housing to an applicant who does not pose a genuine and ongoing threat to persons or property. *Further, HUD's guidance specifically advises landlords not to consider arrests that did not result in a conviction in making their evaluations*"). Italics added.

[819] Recall: Mendez-Carbajo, Diego "Neighborhood Redlining, Racial Segregation, and Homeownership", *Federal Reserve Bank of Saint Louis*, September 1, 2021("*In the 1930s, the Home Owners' Loan Corporation (HOLC) drew maps of residential neighborhoods across the United States. The maps classified each neighborhood into one of five categories, from least to most likely to* ***default*** *on a* ***mortgage*** *loan. In those maps, the neighborhoods most likely to default were shaded red and over*

§§ It is crucially important to note, however, that the extant situation (i.e. *algorithmic redlining*[823] and *algorithmic redliking*[824] within the remit of housing industry) is not amenable to be bogged down to, nor are they are mere outgrowths of, *mortgage redlining* though. Rather, a deep dive on the history of the United States of America bestows upon us the vividly clear impression that laws have been weaponised against Blacks all along.[825]

§§ Notably, *systemic racism*,[826] *mortgage redlining* and *White Supremacy*[827] can be cobbled together as woven of the same cloth.[828] So can GI Bill, Social Security

---

time these neighborhoods had the largest concentrations of African Americans. Because the lending classifications determined individual access to credit, the residents of redlined neighborhoods paid high interest rates and had a hard time becoming homeowners and keeping their homes in good condition. From 1968 to 1974, Congress passed several federal laws and policies preventing lending discrimination by race and gender, and the pattern of residential segregation started to change"). Italics added.

820 Kain, John F., "Housing Segregation, Negro Employment, and Metropolitan Decentralization", *Quarterly Journal of Economics*, Volume 82, 1968, pp. 175–197.

821 But see: Weizenbaum, Joseph, *Computer Power and Human Reason: From Judgment to Calculation*, 1st edition, New York, W. H. Freeman & Co, 1976, pp. 1–300 (227) ("examines the sources of the computer's powers and offers evaluative explorations of what computers can do, cannot do, and should not be employed to do") (this founding father of Artificial Intelligence presciently noted that we should not entrust Artificial Intelligence-embedded technologies with "tasks that demand wisdom"). Italics added. The approval of rental applications is arguably one of those tasks that should never be entrusted to machines). More on this on Part IV, This chapter, Sects. 4.1.4–4.1.4.2.1 of this book.

822 The insidious effects of redlining still ripple forward in that White folks often refuse to have their neighbourhoods integrated by racial minorities. «Move-in violence» is a befitted tool to which White folks resort to fiercely combat minority integration in White neighbourhoods. See: Bell, Jeannine, *Hate Thy Neighbor: Move-In Violence and the Persistence of Racial Segregation in American Housing*, New York, New York University Press, pp. 1–259 ("In *Hate Thy Neighbor*, Jeannine Bell expands upon these understandings by investigating a little-examined but surprisingly prevalent problem of "move-in violence:" the anti-integration violence directed by white residents at minorities who move into their neighborhoods. Apprehensive about their new neighbors and worried about declining property values, these residents resort to extra-legal violence and intimidation tactics, often using vandalism and verbal harassment to combat what they view as a violation of their territory. *Hate Thy Neighbor* is the first work to seriously examine the role violence plays in maintaining housing segregation, illustrating how intimidation and fear are employed to force minorities back into separate neighborhoods and prevent meaningful integration. *Drawing on evidence that includes in-depth interviews with ordinary citizens and analysis of Fair Housing Act cases, Bell provides a moving examination of how neighborhood racial violence is enabled today and how it harms not only the victims, but entire communities. By finally shedding light on this disturbing phenomenon, Hate Thy Neighbor not only enhances our understanding of how prevalent segregation and this type of hate-crime remain, but also offers insightful analysis of a complex mix of remedies that can work to address this difficult problem*"). Italics added.

823 See: Part IV, This chapter, Sects. 4.1.4–4.1.4.2.3 of this book (on algorithmic redlining).

824 See: Part IV, This chapter, Sect. 4.1.4.3 of this book (on "algorithmic redliking").

825 Milligan, Joy, "Protecting Disfavored Minorities: Towards Institutional Realism", *UCLA Law Review*, Volume 63, 2016, pp. 918–921 (delves into the racial inequality in United States of America's Department of Agriculture farm aid to both Whites and Blacks).

826 See: Feagin, J. R., *Systemic racism: a theory of oppression*, New York: Routledge, 2006. See also: Fiske, John, "Surveilling the City: Whiteness, the Black Man and Democratic Totalitarianism.",

Act,[829] alongside the notorious Jim Crow[830] laws.[831] The former (GI Bill and Social Security Act[832]), which was barbed with the devilishly harmful virus of unfairness, stood as the byproduct of the latter (Jim Crow Laws[833]), which, in turn, left a long-lasting footprint in our digital reality.[834]

Theory, Culture and Society, 15 (2), 1998, pp. 67–88 (on the overhyped surveillance on black people as a byproduct of systemic racism).

[827] See: Perea, Juan F., "Doctrines of Delusion: How the History of the G.I. Bill and Other Inconvenient Truths Undermind the Supreme Court's Affirmative Action Jurisprudence", *University of Pittsburgh Law Review*, Volume 75, 1995, pp. 583, 586–89 (establishes a liaison between Jim Crow laws, the G.I. Bill, and the Social Security Act and White supremacy); Milligan, Joy, "Protecting Disfavored Minorities: Towards Institutional Realism", *UCLA Law Review*, Volume 63, 2016, pp. 894, pp. 918–21 (shedding a keen light on racial inequality in U.S. Department of Agriculture farm assistance); Robinson, Reginald Leamon, "The Racial Limits of the Fair Housing Act: The Intersection of Dominant White Images, the Violence of Neighborhood Purity, and the Master Narrative of Black Inferiority", *William & Mary Law Review*, Volume 37, 1995, pp. 69, 71–74 (establishes a connection between the failures of the FHA and White supremacy). But see: Wormser, Richard, *The Rise and Fall of Jim Crow*, Manhattan, New York City, St Martin's Press, 2014, pp. 1–222 ("*White supremacy prevailed, but it did not destroy the spirit of the black community*"). Italics added.

[828] Robinson, Reginald Leamon Robinson, The Racial Limits of the Fair Housing Act: The Intersection of Dominant White Images, the Violence of Neighborhood Purity, and the Master Narrative of Black Inferiority, *William & Mary Law Review*, Volume 37, 1995, pp. 69, 71–74 (establishes a bespoke liaison between the so-called failures of the FHA and the advancement of White supremacy).

[829] Katznelson, Ira, *When Affirmative Action Was White: An Untold History of Racial Inequality in Twentieth-Century America*, New York, W. W. Norton & Company; Reprint edition (August 17, 2006), 2006, pp. 1–272 ("In this "penetrating new analysis" (*New York Times Book Review*) *Ira Katznelson fundamentally recasts our understanding of twentieth-century American history and demonstrates that all the key programs passed during the New Deal and Fair Deal era of the 1930s and 1940s were created in a deeply discriminatory manner. Through mechanisms designed by Southern Democrats that specifically excluded maids and farm workers, the gap between blacks and whites actually widened despite postwar prosperity. In the words of noted historian Eric Foner*, "Katznelson's incisive book should change the terms of debate about affirmative action, and about the last seventy years of American history"). Italics added. This book parses the impact of several racially motivated laws—Social Security Act, G: I. Bill, and labour laws implementing unemployment stipends, minimum wages, and union protection—in the history of United States of America).

[830] See: Part IV, This chapter, Sects. 4.1.5–4.1.5.2 of this book (on "algorithmic Jim Crow", which stands as an outgrown of congeries of laws arising out Jim Crow epoch). See also: Tischauser, Leslie V., *Jim Crow Laws (Landmarks of the American Mosaic)*, 2012, Westport, Connecticut, United States of America, Greenwood Publishing Group, pp. 1–248 (68) ("*by 1920, Southern state legislatures and governors had passed more than 350 segregation laws... [that] separated people by race in cemeteries, churches, hospitals, labor unions, prisons, offices, factories, mines, parks, public buildings, railway trains, railway station waiting rooms, housing developments, neighborhoods, schools, stores, streetcars, theaters, funeral parlors,* and any other places people could meet"). Italics added. See also: On Jim Crow laws and the multifarious misdeeds arising out of such gruelling era: Finkelman, Paul (Editor), *Race, Law, and American History 1700–1990: African Americans and the Law*, Volume 1, London, Taylor & Francis (1 Mar. 1992), 1992, pp. 1–630; Chin, Gabriel J., "Jim Crow's Long Goodbye", *Constitutional Comment*, Volume 21, 2004; Chin, Gabriel J./Wagner, Randy, "The Tyranny of the Minority: Jim Crow and the Counter-Majoritarian Difficulty", *Harvard Civil Rights-Civil Liberties Law Review*, Volume 43, 2008; Fox, James W., Jr., "Doctrinal Myths and the Management of Cognitive Dissonance: Race, Law, and the Supreme Court's Doctrinal Support of Jim Crow", *Stetson Law Review*, Volume 34, 2005; Fox, James W.,

§§ Casts broadly, Jim Crow[835] laws[836]—for which heartfelt apologies[837] and befitted atonement[838] are in order[839]—were enacted between the dusk of the nineteenth century and the dawn of the twentieth century, and struck down in the 1950's.[840] Jim Crow Laws embodied a sought-after Black subordination[841] coupled with a coveted White supremacy[842] against the backdrop of which racial segregation and

---

Jr., "Intimations of Citizenship: Repressions and Expressions of Equal Citizenship in the Era of Jim Crow", *Howard Law Journal*, Volume 50, 2006; Godsil, Rachel D., "Race Nuisance: The Politics of Law in the Jim Crow Era", *Michigan Law Review*, Volume 105, 2006; Gross, Ariela J., "Litigating Whiteness: Trials of Racial Determination in the Nineteenth-Century South", *Yale Law Journal*, 1998; Brown, Trina Jones, II: "A Case of Missed Opportunity?", *Law and Inequality, University of Minnesota Law*, Volume 24, 2006; Juárez, José Roberto, Jr., "Recovering Texas History: Tejanos, Jim Crow, Lynchings & the University of Texas School of Law", *Texas Law Review*, Volume 52, 2010; Mack, Kenneth W., "Foreword: A Short Biography of the Civil Rights Act of 1964", *SMU Law Review*, Volume 67, 2014; Mack, Kenneth W., "Law, Society, Identity, and the Making of the Jim Crow South: Travel and Segregation on Tennessee Railroads, 1875–1905", *Law and Social Inquiry*, Volume 24, 1999; Mack, Kenneth W., "Rethinking Civil Rights Lawyering and Politics in the Era Before Brown", *Yale Law Journal*, Volume 115, 2005; Martin, David, "The Birth of Jim Crow in Alabama 1865–1896", *National Black Law Journal*, Volume 13, 1993; Roback, Jennifer, "Southern Labor Law in the Jim Crow Era: Exploitative or Competitive", *The University of Chicago Law Review*, Volume 51, 1984; Welke, Barbara Y., "Beyond Plessy: Space, Status, and Race in the Era of Jim Crow", *Utah Law Review*, 2000; Wertheimer, John W. et al., "The Law Recognizes Racial Instinct": Tucker v. Blease and the Black-White Paradigm in the Jim Crow South", *Law and History Review*, Volume 29, 2011; Palmore, Joseph R., "Note, The Not-So-Strange Career of Interstate Jim Crow: Race, Transportation, and the Dormant Commerce Clause, 1878–1946″, *Virginia Law Review*, Volume 83, 1997.

831 Perea, Juan F., "Doctrines of Delusion: How the History of the G.I. Bill and Other Inconvenient Truths Undermind the Supreme Court's Affirmative Action Jurisprudence", *University of Pittsburgh Law Review*, 1995, pp. 583, 586–89 (liaising the Jim Crow laws, the G.I. Bill, and the Social Security Act to the furtherance of white supremacy in the Unites States of America). See: Part IV, This chapter, Sects. 4.1.5–4.1.5.2 of this book (on "algorithmic Jim Crow", a travel ban issued during the first Trump Administration to prevent certain individuals from entering the United States of America, which, given its racial undertones, stands as an outgrowth of congeries of laws enacted during the Jim Crow epoch).

832 DeWitt, Larry, "The Decision to Exclude Agricultural and Domestic Workers from the 1935 Social Security Act", *Social Security Bulletin*, no. 4, 2010, passim; Foster, Laura Ann, "Social Security and African American Families: Unmasking Race and Gender Discrimination", *UCLA Women's Law Journal*, Volume 12, 2001, pp. 55–60.

833 See: Part IV, This chapter, Sects. 4.1.5–4.1.5.2 of this book (on "algorithmic Jim Crow", which stands as an outgrowth of congeries of laws enacted during the Jim Crow epoch). See also: Packard, Jerald M., *American Nightmare: The History of Jim Crow*, Broadway, New York, St. Martin's Press; First Edition, 2002, pp. 1–304 ("*For a hundred years after the end of the Civil War, a quarter of all Americans lived under a system of legalized segregation called Jim Crow. Together with its rigidly enforced canon of racial "etiquette," these rules governed nearly every aspect of life–and outlined draconian punishments for infractions. The purpose of Jim Crow was to keep African Americans subjugated at a level as close as possible to their former slave status. Exceeding even South Africa's notorious apartheid in the humiliation, degradation, and suffering it brought, Jim Crow left scars on the American psyche that are still felt today. American Nightmare* examines and explains Jim Crow from its beginnings to its end: how it came into being, how it was lived, how it was justified, and how, at long last, it was overcome only a few short decades ago. *Most importantly, this book reveals how a nation founded on principles of equality and freedom came to enact as law a pervasive system of inequality and virtual slavery.* Although America has finally consigned Jim Crow to the historical

the furtherance of the yawning wealth gap between White folks unfolded.[843] More on this later.[844]

---

graveyard, *Jerrold Packard shows why it is important that this scourge–and an understanding of how it happened-remain alive in the nation's collective memory*"). Italics added.

[834] See: Alexander, M., *The new Jim Crow: Mass incarceration in the age of colorblindness*, The New Press, 2012. See also: Angwin, Julia/Parris Jr, Terry, "Facebook Lets Advertisers Exclude Users by Race", *ProPublica*, October 28, 2016, available at: https://www.propublica.org/article/facebook-lets-advertisers-exclude-users-by-race (access: 19.09.2024) ("*Imagine if, during the Jim Crow era, a newspaper offered advertisers the option of placing ads only in copies that went to white readers. That's basically what Facebook is doing nowadays.* The ubiquitous social network not only allows advertisers to target users by their interests or background, it also gives advertisers the ability to exclude specific groups it calls "Ethnic Affinities." *Ads that exclude people based on race, gender and other sensitive factors are prohibited by federal law in housing and employment*"). Italics added. See: Part IV, This chapter, Sects. 4.1.5–4.1.5.2 of this book (on "algorithmic Jim Crow", a travel ban issued during the first Trump Administration to prevent certain individuals from entering the United States of America, which, given its racial undertones, stands as an outgrowth of congeries of laws enacted during the Jim Crow epoch).

[835] But see: Woodward, C. Vann, *The Strange Career of Jim Crow, Commemorative Edition*, Oxford, Oxford University Press, 2001 ("*The Strange Career of Jim Crow* is one of the great works of Southern history. *Indeed, the book actually helped shape that history.* Published in 1955, a year after the Supreme Court in Brown v. Board of Education ordered schools desegregated, *Strange Career was cited so often to counter arguments for segregation that Martin Luther King, Jr. called it "the historical Bible of the civil rights movement." The book offers a clear and illuminating analysis of the history of Jim Crow laws, presenting evidence that segregation in the South dated only to the 1890s. Woodward convincingly shows that, even under slavery, the two races had not been divided as they were under the Jim Crow laws of the 1890s. In fact, during Reconstruction, there was considerable economic and political mixing of the races. The segregating of the races was a relative newcomer to the region.*

Hailed as one of the top 100 nonfiction works of the twentieth century, *The Strange Career of Jim Crow* has sold almost a million copies and remains, in the words of David Herbert Donald, "a landmark in the history of American race relations"). Italics added.

[836] An Act to Amend and Consolidate the Military Laws of North Carolina, ch. 47, § 1–4852, 1913 N.C. Sess. Laws 82, 82; Act of May 5, 1908, ch. 77, § 6, 1908 Okla. Sess. Laws 694, 695. 70. Act of May 5, 1908, ch. 77, § 6, 1908 Okla. Sess. Laws 694, 695.

[837] Brooks, Ray L., "The House Apologizes for Slavery and Segregation", *Racism Review* (Aug. 7, 2008), 2008, http://www.racismreview.com/blog/2008/08/07/the-house-apologizes-forslavery-and-segregation/#more-452; [https://perma.cc/U8TN-E36G] ("The victims of Jim Crow are as alive today as were the victims of internment in 1988").

[838] Wenger, Kaimipono David Wenger, "Too Big to Remedy?" Rethinking Mass Restitution for Slavery and Jim Crow", *Loyola Law Review*, Volume 44, 2010, pp. 177–230.

[839] Tischauser, Leslie V., *Jim Crow Laws (Landmarks of the American Mosaic)*, 2012, Westport, Connecticut, United States of America, Greenwood Publishing Group, pp. 1–248 ("*Jim Crow Laws presents the history of the discriminatory laws that segregated people by race in the American South from the end of the Civil War through passage of the 1965 Civil Rights Act. To paint a true picture of these deplorable restrictions, this book provides a detailed analysis of the creation, defense, justification, and fight against the Jim Crow system.* Among the subjects covered here are the origins of legal inequality for African Americans in the aftermath of the Civil War; the role of the U.S. Supreme Court in weakening constitutional protections against discrimination established in the 13th, 14th, and 15th Amendments; *the white justification of segregation; and the extreme*

§§ Like everything in life, evil laws[845] will not be respected as legitimate[846] if they routinely fall too short of being fundamentally fair.[847] It is noteworthy that such was the case of Jim Crow laws, which were eventually cast aside.[848]

---

brutality of Jim Crow's defenders. Equally important, readers will learn about the psychological, political, social, and economic costs endured by the victims of Jim Crow inequality, as well as about the motivations, rejections, and successes faced by those who stood against these abominations"). Italics added.

840 Holmes v. City of Atlanta, 223 F.2d 93, 95 (5th Cir. 1955) (declaration segregation at public golf courses unconstitutional), vacated per curiam, 350 U.S. 879 (1955).

841 Freeman, Andrea, "Racism in the Credit Card Industry", *cit.*, pp. 1071–1160 (1086). See also: Part IV, This chapter, Sects. 4.1.5–4.1.5.2 of this book (on "algorithmic Jim Crow", which stands as an outgrowth of congeries of laws enacted during Jim Crow epoch).

842 Wormser, Richard, *The Rise and Fall of Jim Crow*, Manhattan, New York City, St Martin's Press, 2014, pp. 1–222 ("*between 1880 and 1954, African Americans dedicated their energies, and sometimes their lives, to defeating segregation. During these difficult decades, they acquired education and land and built businesses, churches, and communities, despite laws designed to isolate and disenfranchise them. White supremacy prevailed, but it did not destroy the spirit of the black community* (….) *That strike led to a lawsuit that became one of the five cases the Supreme Court reviewed when it declared segregation in education illegal. Rich in historical commentary and eyewitness testimony by blacks and whites who lived through the period, The Rise and Fall of Jim Crow is a poignant record of a time when indignity and terror constantly faced off against courage and accomplishment*"). Italics added.

843 Derenoncourt, Ellora/Kim, Chi Hyun/Kuhn, Moritz/Schularik, Moritz, "The Wealth of Two Nations: The U.S. Racial Wealth Gap, 1860–2020", *The Quarterly Journal of Economics*, Volume 139, Issue 2, 2024, p. 741 ("A large class of commonly discussed policies for reducing racial wealth inequality seeks to reduce gaps in income, savings, and capital gains. These include policies that encourage financial diversification or stock equity holdings among Black households; policies aimed at financial literacy and retirement or savings behavior; or policies aimed at improving educational and labor market outcomes of Black Americans through improved school quality or reductions in discrimination. *Yet on a realistic note, our simulation in Section IV.A shows that even if wealth accumulation conditions had been equal since 1870, the wealth gap would still be 3 to 1 today, and full convergence would be more than 200 years away. Put differently: to close the racial wealth gap in the immediate term* via *flow parameters, Black Americans would need a substantial positive lead over whites, not "just" more equality*"). Italics added.

844 See: Part IV, This chapter, Sects. 4.1.5–4.1.5.2 of this book (on "algorithmic Jim Crow", which stands as an outgrowth of congeries of laws enacted during Jim Crow epoch).

845 As a result, bad laws will inevitably become evil laws that must not be obeyed. In this vein, Professor H. L. Hart asserts that "*laws may be law but too evil to be obeyed.* This is a moral condemnation which everyone can understand and it makes an immediate and obvious claim to moral attention. If, on the other hand, we formulate our objection as an assertion that these evil things are not law, here is an assertion which many people do not believe, and if they are disposed to consider it at all, it would seem to raise a whole host philosophical issues before it can be solves". Italics added. See: Hart, H. L., "Positivism and the Separation of Law and Morals", *Harvard Law Review*, Volume 71, Issue 4, 1958, pp. 598 ff (this amounts to a glimpse of the incorporation of the moral concept of law in Hart's conception of law).

846 Tyler, Tom R., "Psychological perspectives on legitimacy and legitimation", in: *Annual Review of Psychology*, Volume 57, 2006, pp. 375–400 (on the role that perceived legitimacy plays in everyday life); Tyler, Tom R., *Why people cooperate: The role of social motivations*, Princeton, New Jersey, Princeton University Press, 2011; Robbins, J. M./M.T. Ford/L.E. Tetrick, "Perceived unfairness and employee health: A meta-analytic integration", in: *Journal of Applied Psychology*, Volume 97,

§§ That holds true, but truer still we have become painfully aware that the Jim Crow laws laid a foundation for *algorithmic unfairness*[849] which, in turn, spawned to-be-frowned upon «algorithms of oppression»[850] that are shaping up to topple the foundations upon which stands Rule of Law.[851] The oft-trotted out Black

---

2012, pp. 235–272; Tyler, Tom R., "What is procedural justice? Criteria used by citizens to assess the fairness of legal procedures", *Law and Society Review*, Volume 22, 1988, pp. 103–135 (on the interplay between fairness of legal procedures and procedural justice. Unsurprisingly, the lack of fairness of legal procedures impacts the procedural justice -or the lack thereof -); Sunshine, J./Tyler, Tom R., "The role of procedural justice and legitimacy in shaping public support for policing", *Law & Society Review*, Volume 37, 2003, pp. 513–548 (on the role of procedural justice to enhance/ boost legitimacy).

[847] Thus impairing the basic tenets of society as we know, which are set to fall apart, thereby dragging the sacrosanct Rule of Law—and the law as a social fact—to the abandoned streets of recklessness. See: Tyler, Tom R., *Why People Obey the Law*. New Jersey, United States of America: Princeton University Press, 2006, pp. 1–320 (92–110) (Professor Tom R. Tyler contends that lawmakers and law enforcers should make legal systems worthy of respect instead of trying to instil fear of punishment onto disputants. He finds that laypeople obey law primarily because they believe in respecting legitimate authority when such respect is due. Which means that legal systems must be worthy of respect before demanding for respect).

[848] Dawson v. Mayor of Baltimore, 220 F.2d 386, 387–88 (4th Cir. 1955) (declaring segregation at public beaches and bathhouses unconstitutional), aff'd *per curiam*, 350 U.S. 877 (1955).

[849] Corbett-Davies, Sam/Goel, Sharad, "The Measure and Mismeasure of Fairness: a critical Review of Fair Machine Learning", *Cornell University Library*, 2018, pp. 3 and ff and passim (undertake laudable efforts to debunk algorithm biases that primarily target ethnic minorities, such as Hispanics and coloured people).

[850] Noble, Safiya Umoja, *Algorithms of Oppression*: *How search engines reinforce racism*, New York, New University Press, 2018, pp. 1–248 ("*Run a Google search for "Black girls"—what will you find? "Big Booty" and other sexually explicit terms are likely to come up as top search terms. But, if you type in "white girls," the results are radically different*. The suggested porn sites and un-moderated discussions about "why Black women are so sassy" or "why Black women are so angry" presents a disturbing portrait of Black womanhood in modern society. In *Algorithms of Oppression*, Safiya Umoja Noble challenges the idea that search engines like Google offer an equal playing field for all forms of ideas, identities, and activities. *Data discrimination is a real social problem; Noble argues that the combination of private interests in promoting certain sites, along with the monopoly status of a relatively small number of Internet search engines, leads to a biased set of search algorithms that privilege whiteness and discriminate against people of color, specifically women of color*"). Italics added. See: Part IV, This chapter, Sect. 4.1.8 of this book (on biased word embeddings with an entrenched presence on search engines run by tech moguls).

[851] See: Part V, Chap. 5, Sect. 5.1.1.1 of this book (on the central tenets of Rule of Law that lends itself to a beacon of justice amidst the sepulchral darkness that is about to take hold). See: Part V, Chap. 5, Sect. 5.1.1.2 of this book (on the central tenets of Procedural Rule of Law that lends itself to a lighthouse of justice that allows citizens to challenge the pearls of algorithmic wisdom in a court of law). Regrettably, the Rule of Law is backsliding worldwide. Especially in Central and Eastern Europe. See: Avbelj, Matej, "The Rule of Law, Comprehensive Doctrines, Overlapping Consensus, and the Future of Europe", *Ratio Juris*, Volume 36, Issue 3, September, 2023, pp. 242–258. The Rule of Law is not a «one size fits all» format nonetheless. But see: Chesterman, Simon, "An International Rule of Law", *The American Journal of Comparative Law*, Volume 56, 2008, pp. 331–362 (on the thrust to grasp (?) a catch-all International Rule of Law). See: Peari, Sagi, "Better Law as a Better Outcome", *The American Journal of Comparative Law*, Volume 63, Issue 1, 2015, pp. 155–195 (156) (on Leflar's stance on «better rule of law»). For the purposes of this piece, Rule of Law amounts to a lighthouse of procedural fairness to which citizens, regardless

Box[852] problem[853] will only make the issue of algorithmic injustice[854] considerably worse.[855]

§§ Concerns associated with algorithmic fairness may come into play, which is normally viewed as within the scope of the algorithmic decision-making.[856] Note, though, that this is a just a special case (algorithmic decision-making) of a far greater set of deep-seated concerns (*algorithmic redlining*,[857] *algorithmic redliking*,[858] *algorithmic Jim Crow*,[859] *proxy discrimination*,[860] and biased algorithmic risk assessment in criminal justice[861]).

---

of where they are, resort to upon gaining access to a given system of administration of criminal justice. Whilst further utterances on the fabric of Rule of Law fall well outside the scope and breadth of this paper, one must not be oblivious of the fact that the thrust to Deglobalizing Rule of Law is underway. See: Bussani, Mauro, "Deglobalizing Rule of Law and Democracy: Hunting Down Rhetoric Through Comparative Law", *The American Journal of Comparative Law*, Volume 67, 2019, pp. 701–744 (701) (contending that the thrust to Deglobalizing Rule of Law is interwoven with thrust to take heed of «well-known differences that run through cultures and traditions». In spite of which, «the West has never stopped trying to export its own law into the rest of the world»). Unsurprisingly, there have been educated calls to take heed of the pinpointed cultural and legal differences by, in the case of China, allow for a «Socialist Rule of Law». See: Chinese Common Law Guiding Cases, *Harvard Law Review*, Volume 129, 2016, p. 2213. We will come back to this issue further down is this paper. More on this later.

852 But see: Part V, Chap. 5, Sect. 5.1.7.2 of this book (on law number two to control algorithmic decision-making, which mandates that black box models must not be entrusted with the task of making high stake decisions—v.g. health and freedom). See: Agan, Amanda, and Sonja Starr, "Ban the Box, Criminal Records, and Racial Discrimination: A Field Experiment", *Quarterly Journal of Economics*, Volume 133, 2018, pp. 191–235. Avery, Beth, and Han Lu, *Ban the Box*, New York: National Employment Law Project, 2021.

853 Pasquale, Frank, *The Black Box Society: The Secret Algorithms that Control Money and Information*. Cambridge, Massachusetts: Harvard University Press, 2015, 1–320 (pp. 8–10 and passim) (noting that biased algorithms, which have underlying discrimination problems, contribute exponentially to further social biases. His most intriguing claim is that such biased algorithms have been incorporated/etched in the bulk of the corporations' informatic system, to the detriment of human kind in an overarching sense).

854 Birhane, A., "Algorithmic injustice: A relational ethics approach", *Patterns*, 2 (2), 2021, pp. 1–9. Završnik, A. "Algorithmic justice: Algorithms and big data in criminal justice settings", *European Journal of Criminology*, 2019, passim; Broussard M., *Artificial Unintelligence: How Computers Misunderstand the World*, Cambridge, Massachusetts, MIT Press, 2018.

855 Scherer, Matthew U., "Regulating Artificial Intelligence Systems: Risks, Challenges, Competencies, and Strategies", *Harvard Journal of Law and Technology*, Volume 29, 2016, pp. 353–369 (frames the crippling problem of opacity as "the possibility that the inner workings of an AI system may be kept secret and may not be susceptible to reverse engineering").

856 Almada, M, Human intervention in automated decision-making: toward the construction of contestable systems. Proceedings of the Seventeenth International Conference on Artificial Intelligence and Law, 2019, pp. 2–11; Williams, Rebecca, "Rethinking Administrative Law for Algorithmic Decision-Making", *Oxford Journal of Legal Studies*, Volume 42, 2021, pp. 468 e ff and passim.

857 See: Part IV, This chapter, Sects. 4.1.4–4.1.4.2.3 of this book (on algorithmic redlining).

858 See: Part IV, This chapter, Sect. 4.1.4.3 of this book (on "algorithmic redliking").

§§ Tellingly, the shady decision-making patterns[862] embedded in, and inherited from, the gist of *mortgage redlining* found its ways to the skewed data[863] that feeds into the machine algorithms[864] entrusted with the task to decide[865] to whom a loan or a house rental[866] should be granted[867]; machine learning algorithms which, in turn, are riddled with callous discrimination that further entrenches and compounds[868]

---

[859] See: Part IV, This chapter, Sects. 4.1.5–4.1.5.2 of this book (on "algorithmic Jim Crow", which stands which stands as an outgrowth of congeries of laws enacted during Jim Crow epoch).

[860] See: Part IV, This chapter, Sect. 4.1.6.3 of this book (on proxy discrimination).

[861] See: Part IV, This chapter, Sects. 4.1.10.1–4.1.10.6 of this book (on biased algorithmic risk assessment in criminal procedure law settings). See: Part IV, This chapter, Sects. 4.1.1–4.1.1.1 of this book (on biased predictive policing).

[862] See: Luguri, Jamie/Lior, Jacob Strahilevitz, "Shining a Light on Dark Patterns", *Journal of Legal Analytics*, Volume 13, 2021, pp. 43–109.

[863] See: Barocas, Solon/Selbst, Andrew D., "Big Data's Disparate Impact", *California Law Review*, Volume 104, 2016, pp. 671–682 (discussing how data is often flawed, rigged, incomplete, imperfect and therefore algorithms inherit the prejudice of the original decision makers). But see: Citron, Danielle Keats/Pasquale, Frank, "The Scored Society: Due Process for Automated Predictions", *Washington Law Review*, Volume 89, 2014, pp. 1, 4–5 (highlighting how human beings programming automated systems is directly conducive to, and leads, to fundamentally inaccurate results since the source code, predictive algorithms and datasets may encompass human biases which, in turn, have a disparate impact on historically disadvantaged groups); Crawford, Kate/Schultz, Jason, "Big Data and Due Process: Toward a Framework to Redress Predictive Privacy Harms", *Boston College Law Review*, Volume 55, 2014, pp. 93, 99–101 (pinpointing pathways through which predictive analytic tools perpetuate discriminatory practices). But see: Bornstein, Stepanhie, "Antidiscriminatory Algorithms", *Alabama Law Review*, Volume 70, 2018, pp. 519, 524–528 (contending, however, that the tagged "facially neutral" algorithms producing discriminatory outcomes should be quashed).

[864] See: O'Neil, Cathy, *Weapons of Math Destruction. How Big Data Increases Inequality and Threatens Democracy*, London, Penguin Random House, 2016, passim (showing how algorithms utilized in modern societies are amenable to perpetuate racial discrimination, partially through perpetuation of social disadvantage and wealth divides).

[865] But see: Weizenbaum, Joseph, *Computer Power and Human Reason: From Judgment to Calculation*, 1st edition, New York, W. H. Freeman & Co, 1976, pp. 1–300 (227) ("examines the sources of the computer's powers and offers evaluative explorations of what computers can do, cannot do, and should not be employed to do") (*this founding father of Artificial Intelligence presciently noted that we should not entrust Artificial Intelligence-embedded technologies* with "tasks that demand wisdom"). Italics added. The approval of rental applications is arguably one of those tasks that should never be entrusted to machines). More on this on Part IV, This chapter, Sects. 4.1.4–4.1.4.2.1 of this book.

[866] See: Wagner/Gerhard/Eidenmuller, Horst, "Down by Algorithms? Siphoning Rents, Exploiting Biases, and Shaping Preferences: Regulating the Dark Side of Targeted Transactions", *University of Chicago Law Review*, Volume 86, 2019, pp. 581–609.

[867] Schneider, Valerie, "Locked Out by Big Data: How Big Data, Algorithms and Machine Learning May Undermine Housing Justice", *Columbia Human Rights Law Review*, Volume 52, 2020, pp. 251–255.

[868] See: Hellman, Deborah, "Indirect Discrimination and the Duty to Avoid Compounding Injustice", *Foundations of Indirect Discrimination Law*, Collins, Hugh/Khaitan, Tarunabh (Editors), Oxford, Hart Publishing; Reprint edition (June 25, 2020), 2020, p. 107 (Professor Deborah Hellman coined this expression to depict a decision that "exacerbates the harm caused by the prior injustice because it entrenches the harm or carries it into another domain." This book deals with the sweltering topic of indirect discrimination ("*indirect discrimination (or disparate impact) concerns*

harrowing racial biases with which racialised communities (Blacks and Latinos) have been grappling[869] for a long-haul.[870]

§§ The skewed data contains residue of earlier racial discrimination[871] and deep-rooted racial inequalities.[872] Unlike far-fetched ideas, which are as scarce as hen's teeth, algorithmic biases are not automatically built into machines.[873] Rather, algorithmic biases are imparted by rigged data[874] that arises out of past decision-making[875] undertaken in the remit of *mortgage redlining*.

§§ Scholars have been nothing but outspoken, kittenish, and garrulous when it comes to pinpointing the burning concerns arisen from a shoddy, watered down,

---

the application of the same rule to everyone, even though that rule significantly disadvantages one particular group in society"). Italics added.

869 See: Connecticut Fair Housing Center, et al. v. CoreLogic Rental Property Solutions—Cohen Milstein (access: 20.11.2024). ("*The U.S. Department of Housing & Urban Development observed in 2016 that excluding rental applicants because of their criminal records disproportionately harms Latinos and African Americans, who are significantly more likely than whites to be arrested or convicted. Studies show such disparities are linked to differential enforcement rather than to differences in likelihood of engaging in criminal activity.* HUD advised that to avoid discriminating, an "individualized review" should be conducted considering the nature of the offense, how long ago it occurred, intervening changed circumstances, and other relevant factors to avoid denying housing to an applicant who does not pose a genuine and ongoing threat to persons or property. *Further, HUD's guidance specifically advises landlords not to consider arrests that did not result in a conviction in making their evaluations*"). Italics added.

870 See: Dong et al., Qi, "Imbalanced deep learning by minority class incremental rectification, *IEEE Transactions on Pattern Analysis & Machine Intelligence*, Volume 41, 2019, p. 1367 (posit that "*most existing learning algorithms produce inductive bias (learning bias)* towards the frequent (majority) classes if training data are not balanced, *resulting in poor minority class recognition performance*"). Italics added. See: Part V, Chap. 5, Sect. 5.1.7.4 of this book (on one of the law to control algorithmic decision-making, namely, law number four: data partitioning must be performed—i.e. randomly split an entire dataset into the «training dataset» and the «test dataset»—to accurately predict outcomes in the real world while forestalling «inductive bias» (learning bias)).

871 Anderson, Lisa, Roland G. Fryer, and Charles A. Holt, "Discrimination: Experimental Evidence from Psychology and Economics", *Handbook on the Economics of Discrimination*, William M. Rodgers III (Editor), Northampton, MA: Edward Elgar, 2006, pp. 97–115.

872 Balkin, Jack M., "The Three Laws of Robotics in the Age of Big Data", *Ohio State Law Journal*, Volume 78, Issue 5, 2017, pp. 1217–1241.

873 Balkin, Jack M., "The Three Laws of Robotics in the Age of Big Data", *cit.*, pp. 1217–1241.

874 Barocas, Solon/Selbst, Andrew D., "Big Data's Disparate Impact", *California Law Review*, Volume 104, 2016, pp. 671–682 (discussing how data is often flawed, rigged, incomplete, imperfect and therefore algorithms inherit the prejudice of the original decision makers). But see: Citron, Danielle Keats/Pasquale, Frank, "The Scored Society: Due Process for Automated Predictions", *Washington Law Review*, Volume 89, 2014, pp. 1, 4–5 (highlighting how human beings programming automated systems is directly conducive to, and leads, to fundamentally inaccurate results since the source code, predictive algorithms and datasets may encompass human biases which, in turn, have a disparate impact on historically disadvantaged groups); Crawford, Kate/Schultz, Jason, "Big Data and Due Process: Toward a Framework to Redress Predictive Privacy Harms", *Boston College Law Review*, Volume 55, 2014, pp. 93, 99–101 (pinpointing pathways through which predictive analytic tools perpetuate discriminatory practices).

875 Cofone, Ignacio N., "Algorithmic Discrimination Is an Information Problem", *Hastings Law Journal*, Volume 70, 2019, passim.

warped, doctored, and botched algorithmic decision-making.[876] Particularly, albeit not exclusively, in the remit of criminal procedure law.[877]

§§ Lest we forget, biased algorithmic decision-making does not fill well into a simple binary categorization of «yes» and «no».[878] Quite the opposite, biased

[876] But see: Weizenbaum, Joseph, *Computer Power and Human Reason: From Judgment to Calculation*, 1st edition, New York, W. H. Freeman & Co, 1976, pp. 1–300 (227) ("examines the sources of the computer's powers and offers evaluative explorations of what computers can do, cannot do, and should not be employed to do") (this founding father of Artificial Intelligence presciently noted that we should not entrust Artificial Intelligence-embedded technologies with "tasks that demand wisdom"). Italics added. The approval of rental applications is arguably one of those tasks that should never be entrusted to machines). More on this on Part IV, This chapter, Sects. 4.1.4–4.1.4.2.1 of this book.

[877] See: Part IV, This chapter, Sects. 4.1.10.1–4.1.10.6 of this book (on biased algorithmic risk assessment in criminal procedure law settings). See: Part IV, This chapter, Sects. 4.1.1–4.1.1.1 of this book (on biased predictive policing). The «excruciating» *headaches* that the criminal law evangelists have been enduring for quite a while are not to stave off anytime soon. Quite the opposite, they are about to flare up. The sizzling hot challenges posed by artificial intelligence amidst a *RisikoGesellschaft* (*society of risk*, *sociedade do risco* or *sociedad de riesgo*) elicits nothing but a widespread concern on the effectiveness of the systems of administration of justice (or lack thereof) to deal with it. On the *dark side*, one can aver that the interplay between the challenges posed by artificial intelligence on the purview of a transnational and global society (is bound to threaten) to tear down the pillars in which the former sits. If that happens, criminal law would morph into a merely symbolic field of law pursuant its incapability to make *collective sensemaking*. See in Spanish doctrine on the interplay between *sociedad de riesgo* and the challenges arisen from it: Sánchez, Bernardo Feijoo, "Sobre la «administrativizácion» del Derecho penal en la «sociedad de riesgo»: un apunte sobre la política criminal a princípios del diglo XXI", *Derecho Y Justicia Penal en el Siglo XXI. Liber Amicorum en Homenaje al Profesor Antonio González-Cuéllar Garcia*, Madrid, Ed. Colex, 2006, pp. 137 ff. On the peril of criminal law becoming a *Symbolisches Strafrecht*: Hassemer, Winfried, "Symbolisches Strafrecht und Rechtsgüterschutz", *NSTZ*, München, Volume 89, 2014, pp. 557 ff and *passim*. It is believed that *RisikoGesellschaft* is putting the fundamental tenets of criminal law in jeopardy. The sub-prime crisis of 2008 (whose deleterious effects are shaping up to be compounded by the worldwide pandemic spawned by Covid-19) laid bare the insufficiency (the lacklustre of, coupled with, the dearth of) basic assumptions of criminal law to tackle transnational and globalized white-collar crime. In the wake of which a cohort of scholars boded the system's failure (*Systemversagen*). See in Portuguese doctrine: Dias, Augusto Silva, "O Direito Penal como instrumento de superação da crise económico-financeira: estado da discussão e novas perspectivas", *Anatomia do Crime, Revista de Ciências Jurídico-Criminais*, Volume 0, 2014, pp. 45–73. See in German doctrine: Naucke, *Der Begriff der politischen Wirtsschaftsstrafrecht—Eine Annährung*, LIT, 2012, pp. 8–72. See in Spanish doctrine: Rivas, Garcia, "Reflexiones sobre la responsabilidad penal en el marco de la crisis financiera", Demetrio Crespo (Dir.), *Crisis financiera y Derecho Penal Económico,* 2014, pp. 19 ff. On the *bright side*, the possibilities to harness, and take advantage of, artificial intelligence are legion. The *collective sensemaking* must not lose sight of it. Take the example of the burgeoning trend of (to) sentencing anchored in algorithms in a bid to ease (and sometimes offset) human flaws (such as racial bias, gender bias, jealousy, sexual orientation bias and so forth). Such tools, which are particularly useful in predicting criminal recidivism, are gaining traction and gathering pace in Italy: Gialuz, M., "Quando la giustizia penale encontra l'intelligenza artificiale: luci e e ombre di risk assessment tools tra Stati Uniti ed Europa", 2019, available at: www.penalecontemporaneo.it.d/6702-quando-la-giustizia-penale-encontra-l'intelligenz-artificiale-luci-e-ombre-di-risk-assessment-tools (access: 03.07.2024); United Kingdom: Peeters, R./Schuilenburg, M., "Machine Justice: Governing Security through Bureaucracy of Algorithms", *Information Polity*, Volume 23, 2018, pp. 267–274; Hamilton, Melissa, "Sentencing Disparities", *British Journal of American Legal Studies*, Volume 6, Issue 2, 2017, pp. 181 ff. Portugal:

decision-making externalizes sizable costs onto a cohort of innocent others (Blacks[879] and Latinos) by systematically skewing towards White folks.[880]

§§ Conversely, biased algorithmic decision-making will beget a cascade of equally bigoted algorithmic judgments,[881] which, in turn, will predictably cast a sheer amount of, and a slew of, dignitary algorithmic harms[882] onto a thicket of members of racialized groups[883] (Blacks, Latinos and Muslims[884]).

Anabela Miranda Rodrigues, "Medida da pena de prisão – desafios da era da inteligência artificial", *Revista de Legislação e de Jurisprudência*, Março-Abril de 2020, Ano 149.º, N.º 4021, 2020, pp. 258 ff; Santos, Hugo Luz dos, "Brain-Computer Interfaces, Generative Artificial Intelligence (ChatGPT and Deep Fakes) and Criminal Procedure Law: what's at stake?", *Journal of Research in E. and Computer Science*, Edinburgh, United Kingdom, June 2024, Volume 2, 2024, pp. 39–78; Santos, Hugo Luz dos, *Programas de Compliance e Inteligência Artificial: Consequências ao nível da Law and Economics, do Direito Penal, do Processo Penal e da Behavioral Law and Economics*, Braga, NovaCausa Edições Jurídicas, 2024, pp. 1–330; Santos, Hugo Luz dos, *Inteligência Artificial (ChatGPT/AutoGPT/Robots-Advogados/Robots Proceduradores/Robots-Juízes) e Responsabilidade Penal das Pessoas Colectivas*, Braga, NovaCausa Edições Jurídicas, 2023, pp. 1–108; Santos, Hugo Luz dos, *Inteligência Artificial e Processo Penal*, Braga, NovaCausa Edições Jurídicas, 2022, pp. 1–256; Santos, Hugo Luz dos, *Inteligência Artificial e Processo Penal*, Braga, NovaCausa Edições Jurídicas, 2022, pp. 1–256; Santos, Hugo Luz dos, *Inteligência Artificial e Processo Civil na Era do Metaverse e dos Machine Learning Algorithms*, Braga, NovaCausa Edições Jurídicas, 2022, pp. 1–264.

[878] Balkin, Jack M., "The Three Laws of Robotics in the Age of Big Data", *cit.*, pp. 1217–1241.

[879] Wonyoung, So, "Which Information Matters? Measuring Landlord Assessment of Tenant Screening Reports", *Housing Policy Debate*, Volume 33, n. ° 6, 2023, pp. 1484–1510 (1502) ("*One additional finding of the experiment is that algorithmic scoring can exacerbate this racially unequal landscape in rental agreements not just because the algorithm may be inaccurate, but because landlords may want to follow the risk assessment made by the tenant screening report. This is alarming for low-income tenants, particularly housing voucher holders. Security deposits are one of the most significant barriers to obtaining housing for voucher holders, because vouchers do not pay security deposits but most private landlords require them (Rosenblatt & Cossyleon, 2018).* Given that voucher holders have exceptionally low income (usually less than 50% of area median income) and might experience more housing insecurity (rental debts and eviction-related experiences), *imposing greater security deposits on voucher holders almost equates to denying them housing—yet these decisions could be justified by algorithmic scoring if tenant screening services employ it*"). Italics added.

[880] Balkin, Jack M., "The Three Laws of Robotics in the Age of Big Data", *cit.*, pp. 1217–1241.

[881] *Tech, Bias and Housing Initiative, the Promise and Perils of Residential Proptech, Year 1, Research Summary Report, April 2023, TechEquity Collaborative*, p. 5 available at: https://techequity.us/wp-content/uploads/2023/04/TBHI-Y1-Research-Summary-Report.pdf (28.11.2024). ("*Residential Proptech also has the potential to exacerbate the bias inherent in our housing system. Its rise is due, in part, to the desperation felt by average home seekers. With a severely constrained housing supply, companies offering an easier pathway to homeownership may exploit communities that have been harmed by housing discrimination in the past. Opaque algorithms incorporate biased data into their decision-making processes, making it harder to enforce fair housing laws.* Residential Proptech companies often operate in a regulatory gray area, leaving consumers without the protections they would have from traditional housing regulatory systems. *As unprecedented capital investment flows into this space, venture-backed companies' winner-take-all approach to growth has the potential to exacerbate inequality rather than combat it*"). Italics added. See: Part IV, This chapter, Sects. 4.1.4–4.1.4.2.3 of this book.

[882] Lee, Nicole Turner/Resnick, Paul/Barton, Genie, *Algorithmic Bias Detection and Mitigation: Best Practices and Policies to Reduce Consumer Harms*. Washington, DC: Brookings Institution,

§§ Relatedly, one should not lose sight of fact that the racial discrimination[885] deeply steeped in the past decision-making patterns[886] arisen from the application of ill-formed laws (ranging from Jim Crow laws, Social Security Act, Mortgage redlining to GI Bill) has fed into databases[887] used by a wide range of stakeholders[888] in the purview of housing industry.[889]

2019, passim; Slaughter, Rebecca Kelly, "Algorithms and Economic Justice: A Taxonomy of Harms and a Path Forward for the Federal Trade Commission", *Yale Journal of Law and Technology*, Volume 23, 2021 (on algorithmic harms).

883 Balkin, Jack M., "The Three Laws of Robotics in the Age of Big Data", *cit.*, pp. 1217–1241.

884 See Part IV, This chapter, Sects. 4.1.5–4.1.5.2 of this book («*Algorithmic Jim Crow*»).

885 Kline, Patrick, Evan K. Rose, and Christopher R. Walters, "Systemic Discrimination among Large US Employers" *Quarterly Journal of Economics*, Volume 137, 2002, pp. 1963–2036.

886 Stoll, Michael A., "Job Sprawl, Spatial Mismatch, and Black Employment Disadvantage", *Journal of Policy Analysis and Management*, Volume 25, 2006, pp. 827–854; Stoll, Michael A., and Kenya Covington, "Explaining Racial/Ethnic Gaps in Spatial Mismatch in the US: The Primacy of Racial Segregation", *Urban Studies*, Volume 49, 2012, pp. 2501–2521.

887 *Tech, Bias and Housing Initiative, the Promise and Perils of Residential Proptech, Year 1, Research Summary Report, April 2023, TechEquity Collaborative*, p. 11, available at: https://techequity.us/wp-content/uploads/2023/04/TBHI-Y1-Research-Summary-Report.pdf (28.11.2024). ("*Once bad data enters the analysis of one factor, it gets baked into the subsequent process, multiplying the effect that one disadvantageous data point can have on someone's overall housing determination*"). Italics added. See: Part IV, This chapter, Sects. 4.1.4–4.1.2.3 of this book.

888 *Tech, Bias and Housing Initiative, the Promise and Perils of Residential Proptech, Year 1, Research Summary Report, April 2023, TechEquity Collaborative*, p. 10, available at: https://techequity.us/wp-content/uploads/2023/04/TBHI-Y1-Research-Summary-Report.pdf (28.11.2024). ("*Tenant screening tools are often packaged as part of a larger suite of property management tools for landlords. Unlike Analog Models, Algorithmic Tenant Screening Tools Predict Future Behavior To Determine Housing Access.* Before the advent of algorithmic tenant screening, landlords vetted tenants by having them submit their own records and references from previous landlords or others who could vouch for their trustworthiness. During an analog rental application process, a prospective tenant provides certain personal information and then gives consent for the landlord to run a background check to verify their information. *The landlord, housing provider, or property manager then pays a third-party entity such as TransUnion to pull information that gives a sense of whether the applicant will be a trustworthy renter. In analog screening, those reports return information from an applicant's credit, eviction, and criminal histories. There are many inequities with this analog model. Eviction and criminal records are often wrong or lack important context. 12 13 Credit scoring techniques are notoriously biased*"). Italics added. See: Part IV, This chapter, Sects. 4.1.4–4.1.4.2.3 of this book. See: Dunn, E., & Grabchuk, M., "Background checks and social effects: Contemporary residential tenant-screening problems in Washington State", *Seattle Journal for Social Justice*, Volume 9, Issue 1, 2010; Ehman, M., *Fair housing disparate impact claims based on the use of criminal and eviction records in tenant screening policies*, 2015, available at: https://www.nhlp.org/wp-content/uploads/Merf-Ehman-FH-DI-Claims-Based-on-Use-of-Criminal-and-Eviction-Records-Sept.-2015.pdf. (access: 28.11.2024).

889 In spite of its deep-seated racial bias, decision-makers continue to deploy redlining tactics through big data and may even justify such unlawful practices by claiming that the latter abide by cost-effectiveness. See: Humber, Nadiyah J., "A Home for Digital Equity: Algorithmic Redlining and Property Technology", *California Law Review*, Volume 111, Issue 5, 2023, pp. 1421–1484. See also: Hurley, Mikella/Adebayo, Julius, "Credit Scoring in the Era of Big Data", *Yale Journal of Law and Technology*, Volume 18, 2016, pp. 148, 151–156, 172 (averring that FICO scoring boasts a redoubtable capacity to routinely weed out some populations that have been historically

§§ It is pivotally important to note, though, that the burden of algorithmic unfairness arising out of bigoted algorithmic decision-making in the remit of fair housing—paired with a plethora of algorithmic consumer harms that often tag along[890]—are shaping up to be, and in most cases has already been, shifted onto a contingent of others[891] (Blacks and Latinos).

§§ Bearing this backdrop very firmly in mind, the widespread exhilaration over Artificial Intelligence-embedded technologies must be halted. Some tools—a robot-judge or a robot-prosecutor that can carry underlying racial biases against members of certain groups—must be accordingly pulled from use until they are duly tested and adroitly calibrated. That's the very least prominent industry stakeholders can do.

§§ In at the least four interlocking ways—the recalcitrance of systemic racism mirrored on the enactment of Jim Crow laws, Social Security Act, mortgage redlining[892] and GI Bill—past decision-making leverages on «dirty data»[893] which, in turn, is deeply suffused with, and redolent of, invidious discrimination against Black folks.[894]

---

and systematically underrepresented or grossly unfairly represented in the credit industry market). Tellingly, by 2016, ten states had disavowed the unlawful practice of employers using shady credit scores due to their perceived disparate impact on low-income applicants and members of racialized communities (mostly Black folks). See: O'Neill, Cathy, *Weapons of Math Destruction. How Big Data Increases Inequality and Threatens Democracy*. London: Penguin Random House, 2016, pp. 128 and ff and passim.

[890] See: Bar-Gill, Oren/Sunstein, Cass R./Talgam-Cohen, Inbal, "Algorithmic Harm in Consumer Markets", *Journal of Legal Analysis*, Volume 15, n. ° 1, 2023, pp. 1–47; See: Wagner/Gerhard/Eidenmuller, Horst, "Down by Algorithms? Siphoning Rents, Exploiting Biases, and Shaping Preferences: Regulating the Dark Side of Targeted Transactions", *University of Chicago Law Review*, Volume 86, 2019, pp. 581–609.

[891] Balkin, Jack M., "The Three Laws of Robotics in the Age of Big Data", *cit.*, pp. 1217–1241.

[892] Hellerstein, Judith K., David Neumark, and Melissa McInerney, "Spatial Mismatch or Racial Mismatch?", *Journal of Urban Economics*, Volume 64, 2008, pp. 464–479; Gobillon, Laurent, Harris Selod, and Yves Zenou, "The Mechanisms of Spatial Mismatch", *Urban Studies*, Volume 44, 2007, pp. 2401–2427.

[893] Richardson, Rashida/Jason M. Schultz/Kate Crawford, Dirty Data, "Bad Predictions: How Civil Rights Violations Impact Police Data, Predictive Policing Systems, and Justice", *New York University Law Review Online*, Volume 94, 2019, passim.

[894] See: Wonyoung, So, "Which Information Matters? Measuring Landlord Assessment of Tenant Screening Reports", *Housing Policy Debate*, Volume 33, n. ° 6, 2023, pp. 1484–1510 (1502) ("*One additional finding of the experiment is that algorithmic scoring can exacerbate this racially unequal landscape in rental agreements not just because the algorithm may be inaccurate, but because landlords may want to follow the risk assessment made by the tenant screening report. This is alarming for low-income tenants, particularly housing voucher holders. Security deposits are one of the most significant barriers to obtaining housing for voucher holders, because vouchers do not pay security deposits but most private landlords require them (Rosenblatt & Cossyleon, 2018).* Given that voucher holders have exceptionally low income (usually less than 50% of area median income) and might experience more housing insecurity (rental debts and eviction-related experiences), *imposing greater security deposits on voucher holders almost equates to denying them housing—yet these decisions could be justified by algorithmic scoring if tenant screening services employ it*"). Italics added.

§§ Herculean efforts have been made to, and most of the academic community[895] is burgeoningly rallying around the idea of, pinning down,[896] weeding out, rooting out and uprooting chequered[897] forms[898] of deeply-entrenched discrimination[899] embedded in the skewed data baked into machine learning algorithms.[900] But, despite the good intentions with which those laudable initiatives[901] are suffused by,[902] to no avail. It is important to note, though, that our frame of reference does not lend itself to a misdiagnosis.

§§ Tellingly, the skewed data—rigged or biased data—that machine learning algorithms[903] operate upon has a substantial bearing on the outpouring of discriminatory outcomes[904] facing racialized communities (Blacks and Latinos).[905]

---

[895] Van Bueren, G., "Inclusivity and the law: do we need to prohibit class discrimination", *European Human Rights Law Review*, Volume 3, 2021, pp. 273 and ff and passim; Chesterman, Simon, "Artificial Intelligence and the Problem of Autonomy", *Notre Dame Journal on Emerging Technologies*, Volume 1, 2019, pp. 2 e ss e passim; Maranella, Stefano: "La protezione dei dati personali contro un uso distopico dell'AI, Il diritto nell'era digitale", *Persona, Mercato, Amministrazione Giustizia.* Milano: Giuffrè, 2022, pp. 51–69 (pp. 52–56 and ff and passim); Aggarwal, N., "The Norms of Algorithmic Credit Scoring", *Cambridge Law Journal*, Volume 80, Issue 1, 2021, pp. 43–71.

[896] Bohren, J. Aislinn, Kareem Haggag, Alex Imas, and Devin G. Pope, "Inaccurate Statistical Discrimination", Working Paper No. 25935, National Bureau of Economic Research, Cambridge, MA, 2019.

[897] Gautier, Pieter A., and Yves Zenou, "Car Ownership and the Labor Market of Ethnic Minorities" *Journal of Urban Economics*, Volume 67, 2010, pp. 392–403; Giuliano, Laura, David I. Levine, and Jonathan Leonard, "Manager Race and the Race of New Hires", *Journal of Labor Economics*, Volume 27, 2009, pp. 589–631. Glaeser, Edward L., and Joshua D. Gottlieb, "The Economics of Place-Making Policies", *Brookings Papers on Economic Activity*, Spring, 2008, pp. 155- 239; Greenwald, Anthony G., and Linda Hamilton Krieger, Implicit Bias: Scientific Foundations", *California Law Review*, Volume 94, 2006, pp. 945–967.

[898] Bordalo, Pedro, Katherine Coffman, Nicola Gennaioli, and Andrei Shleifer, "Stereotypes", *Quarterly Journal of Economics*, Volume 131, 2016, pp. 1753–1794; Epstein, Richard A., *Forbidden Grounds: The Case against Employment Discrimination Laws*, Cambridge, MA: Harvard University Press, 1992, passim.

[899] Borgesius, FJ Zuiderveen, "Strengthening legal protection against discrimination by algorithms and artificial intelligence", *International Journal of Human Rights*, Volume 24, Issue 10, 2020, pp. 1573 and ff and passim; Griemmelmann, James/Westreich, Daniel, "Incomprehensible Discrimination ", *California Law Review Online*, Volume 7, 2018, pp. 164–171.

[900] Corbett-Davies, Sam/Goel, Sharad, "The Measure and Mismeasure of Fairness: a critical Review of Fair Machine Learning", *Cornell University Library*, 2018, pp. 3 and ff and passim (undertake laudable efforts to debunk algorithm biases that primarily target ethnic minorities, such as Hispanics and coloured people).

[901] Huq, Aziz, "Racial Equity in Algorithmic Criminal Justice", *Duke Law Journal*, Volume 68, 2022, pp. 1076–1134.

[902] Kleinberg, Jon, et al., "Discrimination in the Age of Algorithms", *Journal of Legal Analysis*, 2018, pp. 114–174; Kleinberg, Jon, et al., "Algorithms as Discrimination Detectors", *Proceeds of the National Academy of Science*, Volume 117, 2020, pp. 30096–30110.

[903] Sharma, Shubham, Yunfeng Zhang, Jesus M. Rios Aliaga, Djallel Bouneffouf, Vinod Muthusamy & Kush R. Varshney, "Data Augmentation for Discrimination Prevention and Bias Disambiguation", *Proceedings AAAIIACM Conference on Artificial Intelligence, Ethics & Society*, 2020, passim (discussing a cluster of techniques to allay data biases in Machine Learning).

§§ For the sake of the argument, scholars shrewdly rebuke, and stridently oppose, the consequences of ill-formed laws brimming with invidiousness.[906]

§§ In addition to that, pundits deftly bemoan, and rail against, the ease with which human biases can creep into machine learning algorithms[907] under both a patina of inevitability and a veneer of science-based objectivity.[908] In this vein, Artificial Intelligence-embedded technologies,[909] if nothing else, are far from being trustworthy tools[910] to make vital decisions to our collective welfare.[911]

§§ Insofar human biases can creep into machine learning algorithms insofar create a haze of invidiousness that obfuscates a fair algorithmic decision making,[912] the possibility of a—seemingly objective—machine breeds biased outcomes must not be grossly underestimated.

---

904 Yang, Jenny, Andrew A.S. Soltan, David W. Eyre, Yang Yang & David A. Clifton, "An Adversarial Training Framework for Mitigating Algorithmic Biases in Clinical Machine Learning", *npj Digital Medicine*, Volume 6, n.º 55, 2023, at 1, 1 (discussing how adversarial training can be thoroughly used to curb bias in the domain of healthcare).

905 In spite of its deep-seated racial bias, decision-makers continue to deploy redlining tactics through big data and may even justify such unlawful practices by claiming that the latter abide by cost-effectiveness. See: Humber, Nadiyah J., "A Home for Digital Equity: Algorithmic Redlining and Property Technology", *California Law Review*, Volume 111, Issue 5, 2023, pp. 1421–1484. See also: Hurley, Mikella/Adebayo, Julius, "Credit Scoring in the Era of Big Data", *Yale Journal of Law and Technology*, Volume 18, 2016, pp. 148, 151–156, 172 (averring that FICO scoring boasts a redoubtable capacity to routinely weed out some populations that have been historically and systematically underrepresented or grossly unfairly represented in the credit industry market). Tellingly, by 2016, ten states had disavowed the unlawful practice of employers using shady credit scores due to their perceived disparate impact on low-income applicants and members of racialized communities (mostly Black folks). See: O'Neill, Cathy, *Weapons of Math Destruction. How Big Data Increases Inequality and Threatens Democracy*, London: Penguin Random House, 2016, pp. 128 and ff and passim.

906 Desmond, Gillian Slee Matthew, "Eviction and Voter Turnout: The Political Consequences of Housing Instability", *Policy and Society*, Volume 51, 2023; Desmond, M., "Eviction and the reproduction of urban poverty", *American Journal of Sociology*, Volume 118, Issue 1, 2012, pp. 88–133.

907 Citron, Danielle Keats/Pasquale, Frank A., "The Scored Society: Due Process for Automated Predictions", *Washington Law Review*, Volume 89, 2014, pp. 1–34 (arguing that "[a]*dvocates applaud the removal of human beings and their flaws from the assessment process*," but arguing that bias remains "[*b]ecause human beings program predictive algorithms, their biases and values are embedded into the software's instructions*"). Italics added.

908 Benjamin, Ruha, *Race After Technology: Abolitionist Tools for the New Jim Code*, New York, Polity, 2019, pp. 1–172 (7) (discussing that Artificial Intelligence-embedded technologies are viewed as iron-clad tools of objectivity and devoid of any biases whatsoever). Ruha Benjamin contends that "the employment of new technologies that reflect and reproduce existing inequities but that are promoted and perceived as more objective or progressive than the discriminatory systems of a previous era").

§§ Notably, the pearls of algorithmic wisdom that feeds into an algorithmic decision[913] (hiring, house renting,[914] firing, loan, jail, bail[915]) should not be wrapped under a veneer of unimpeachable objectivity insofar they should be interpretable[916] to be challengeable.[917]

---

[909] Chopra, Samir/White, Laurence F., *A Legal Theory of Autonomous Artificial Agents*, Michigan, University of Michigan Press, 2011, pp. 1–264 (5) (2011) ("There are two views of the goals of artificial intelligence. From an engineering perspective, as Marvin Minsky noted, it is the 'science of making machines do things that would require intelligence if done by men.' *From a cognitive science perspective, it is to design and build systems that work the way the human mind does. In the former perspective, artificial intelligence is deemed successful along a performative dimension; in the latter, along a theoretical one.* The latter embodies Giambattista Vico's perspective of verum et factum convertuntur, 'the true and the made are... convertible'; *in such a view, artificial intelligence would be reckoned the laboratory that validates our best science of the human mind. This perspective sometimes shades into the claim artificial intelligence's success lies in the replication of human capacities such as emotions, the sensations of taste, and self-consciousness. Here, artificial intelligence is conceived of as building artificial persons, not just designing systems that are 'intelligent*") ("*As an example of how agent technologies might evolve to incorporate learning, autonomy, and discretion, consider a hypothetical agent designed to find used books on the Internet. The agent is provided with a list of websites to scour, sample titles with abstracts as learning data to recognize other titles in the genre, and electronic cash accounts with which to make purchases.* The agent is allowed to purchase books within a preset spending limit with discretion in the number, subjects, and individual prices of books bought. Such an agent has a broadly defined goal with enough executive discretion in the choices it makes to optimize satisfaction of that goal. The agent is able to interact with its environment by reading and scanning information at the sites it visits; it interacts with other agents such as selling agents deployed by other users. The agent "moves" from site to site, makes purchases, and reads recommendations provided by book-selling agents. The agent checks recommendations for matches on parameters of interest, and then depending on the outcome, buys more books or declines offers. *It is able to buy titles not on its original list, and to proactively make the decision to buy a new title. Such an agent is able to decide to take an action, in response to inputs it decides to focus on; its interactions on the Internet, in a world populated by other shopping agents and sometimes humans, exemplify autonomous, goal-directed, proactive behavior*"). Italics added.

[910] Rankin, Sonia M. Gipson, "Technological Tethereds: Potential Impact of Untrustworthy Artificial Intelligence in Criminal Justice Risk Assessment Instruments", *The Washington and Lee Law Review*, Volume 78, 2022, pp. 647, 655–57 (discussing the harrowing difficulty of defining the ever-evolving science of Artificial Intelligence).

[911] Balkin, Jack M., "The Three Laws of Robotics in the Age of Big Data", *cit.*, pp. 1217–1241.

[912] Karnow, Curtis E. A., "The Opinion of Machines", *The Cambridge Handbook of the Law of Algorithms*, Bartfield, Woodrow (Editor), Cambridge, United Kingdom: Cambridge University Press, 2021, passim.

[913] Blattner, Laura/Nelson, Scott/Spiess, Jann, *Unpacking the Black Box: Regulating Algorithmic Decisions*. Working Paper. Redwood City, California: Stanford University Press, 2021.

[914] *Tech, Bias and Housing Initiative, the Promise and Perils of Residential Proptech, Year 1, Research Summary Report, April 2023, TechEquity Collaborative*, p. 11, available at: https://techequity.us/wp-content/uploads/2023/04/TBHI-Y1-Research-Summary-Report.pdf (28.11.2024). ("*From information on company websites, it is not clear what analysis or data is behind subjective determinations like "suitability" to a unit or what the nexus between an individual's characteristics and a unit's characteristics is that indicates the likelihood for property damage. Based on sample reports, even landlords are not privy to how the determinations are made. Instead, they receive a risk score out of 100 simplified into green, yellow, and red recommendations.* What companies withhold in terms of how it works, they make up for with the extent

§§ Relatedly, caution must be accordingly exercised when using machine learning algorithms to make high-stake decisions[918] (hiring, firing, loan, jail,[919] bail and so forth)[920] vital to our collective welfare.[921] This overriding claim is fuelled in part because of the «incomprehensible discrimination»[922] that often characterizes algorithmic decision making.

§§ Dispiritingly, the undying hopes of being in control of Artificial Intelligence-embedded technologies are neatly dashed by their insurmountable shadiness, their impenetrable hiddenness,[923] their inscrutable opacity[924] that bypass and circumvent any earnest attempt to clutch its inner workings.[925]

---

to which they tell landlords it works: Naborly claims their predictions reduce lease defaults by up to 89%. 15 *As Naborly's sample report demonstrates, its property damage assessment is then used as an input to determine its projected eviction outcomes; its early vacancy prediction, in turn, is based on "all assessment factors*"). Italics added.

915 Mayson, Sandra G., "Bias In, Bias Out", *Yale Law Journal*, Volume 128, 2019, pp. 2218 and ff and passim.

916 See: Part V, Chap. 5, Sects. 5.1.2–5.1.6.2.1 of this book (on the thing-centred algorithmic decision-making propelled by a *Controllable* and *Interpretable* Machine Learning that weeds out *Algorithmic Dictatorship* and secures *Algorithmic Common Good*). See also: Rudin, C., & Radin, J., "Why are we using black box models in AI when we don't need to? A lesson from an explainable AI competition", *Harvard Data Science Review*, 2019, Volume 1, Issue 2, passim.

917 See: Part V, Chap. 5, Sect. 5.1.1.2 of this book (on the central tenets of Procedural Rule of Law that lends itself to a lighthouse of justice that allows citizens to challenge the pearls of algorithmic wisdom in a court of law).

918 See: Part V, Chap. 5, Sect. 5.1.7.2 of this book (on law number two to control algorithmic decision-making, which mandates that black box models must not be entrusted with the task of making high stake decisions—v.g. health and freedom).

919 See: Part IV, This chapter, Sects. 4.1.10.1–4.1.10.6 of this book (on biased algorithmic risk assessment in criminal procedure law settings). See: Part IV, This chapter, Sects. 4.1.1–4.1.1.1 of this book (on biased predictive policing).

920 But see: Rudin, Cynthia, "Please stop explaining black box models for high stakes decisions", *Proceedings of NeurIPS 2018 Workshop on Critiquing and Correcting Trends in Machine Learning (NIPS 2018)*, 2018, passim.

921 Balkin, Jack M., "The Three Laws of Robotics in the Age of Big Data", *cit.*, pp. 1217–1241.

922 Griemmelmann, James/Westreich, Daniel, "Incomprehensible Discrimination ", *California Law Review Online*, Volume 7, 2018, pp. 164–171.

923 *Tech, Bias and Housing Initiative, the Promise and Perils of Residential Proptech, Year 1, Research Summary Report, April 2023, TechEquity Collaborative*, p. 11, available at: https://techequity.us/wp-content/uploads/2023/04/TBHI-Y1-Research-Summary-Report.pdf (28.11.2024). ("And while we know that the *data is predictive, meaning it has little to do with demonstrated behavior of the applicant themself, we do not know exactly where companies get their data*"). Italics added.

924 Balkin, Jack M., "The Three Laws of Robotics in the Age of Big Data", *cit.*, pp. 1217–1241.

925 For an on-point breakdown of the distinct levels of opacity arising out of machine learning algorithms: Selbst, Andrew D./Barocas, Solon, "The Intuitive Appeal of Explainable Machines", *Fordham Law Review*, Volume 87, 2018, pp. 1085, 1089–99 (holding that there are plenty reasons for the insurer's ignorance. To begin with, the algorithm entails specialized knowledge to understand. That is, the insurer's employees may lack sufficient knowledge to understand the rationale

§§ In addition to that, the lack of an obvious means to challenge the pearls of algorithmic wisdom spawned by whimsical[926] Artificial Intelligence-embedded technologies when, and if, they produce unforeseen, befuddling, harmful, unhinged, lopsided, discriminatory results[927] can hammer the last nail in the coffin of a fading[928] Rule of Law.[929]

---

behind the reasons in view of which the algorithm is producing prices for different customers—personalized pricing. Lastly, even if the insurer himself comprehends how the model operates, it may nonetheless lack expertise to comprehend why it operates the way it does. For that reason, the explainability of machines is a vital, but rather elusive, task. Thence, the famed authors deem it as the "nonintuitive" nature of algorithms. For purposes here, the insurer himself might indeed understand that its Artificial Intelligence-embedded technology formulates higher prices for those who actually access the website at hand, but may fail to come to terms with the fact that the explanation for this fact arises from the website's capacity to proxy for genetic information). See also: Scherer, Matthew U. Scherer, "Regulating Artificial Intelligence Systems: Risks, Challenges, Competencies, and Strategies", *Harvard Journal of Law and Technology*, Volume 29, 2016, pp. 353–369 (frames the crippling problem of opacity as "the possibility that the inner workings of an AI system may be kept secret and may not be susceptible to reverse engineering").

926 Cass, Ronald A., *The Rule of Law in America.* Baltimore, Maryland: The Johns Hopkins University Press, 2001, p. 17 (noting that a "central element of the Rule of law, constraint from external authority...helps assure that the process of government, *rather than the predilections of the individual decision-maker*") Italics added.

927 Balkin, Jack M., "The Three Laws of Robotics in the Age of Big Data", *cit.*, pp. 1217–1241.

928 See: Part V, Chap. 5, Sect. 5.1.1.1 of this book (on the central tenets of Rule of Law that lends itself to a beacon of justice amidst the sepulchral darkness that is about to take hold). See: Part V, Chap. 5, Sect. 5.1.1.2 of this book (on the central tenets of Procedural Rule of Law that lends itself to a lighthouse of justice that allows citizens to challenge the pearls of algorithmic wisdom in a court of law). Which is why the onset of the age of Artificial Intelligence will put the Rule of Law to the test like never before. Recall, the Rule of Law is a functional barrier—aimed at clamping down a host of unlawful deeds undertaken by those in power—that must not be teared apart or criminal procedure law will be otherwise despoiled from its intrinsic validity and vitality. See: Raz, Joseph, "The Rule of Law and its Virtue", *The Authority of Law: Essays on Law and Morality*, *cit.*, p. 224 (asserts adamantly that the Rule of Law is aimed at cushioning the hazards of abuse perpetrated by those in power. In this vein, Raz contends that "*the law inevitably creates a great danger of arbitrary power – the Rule of Law is designed to minimize the danger created by the law itself...Thus the (R)ule of (L)aw is designed to minimize the danger created by law itself...Thus the (R)ule of (L)aw is a negative virtue...the evil which is avoided is evil which could only have been caused by the law itself*"). Italics added.

929 Raz, Joseph, "The Rule of Law and its Virtue", *The Authority of Law: Essays on Law and Morality*. Oxford: Clarendon Press, 1979, pp. 210–214 (on the quintessential value of Rule of Law); Waldron, Jeremy, "The Rule of Law and the Importance of Procedure", *New York Public Law and Legal Theory*, 2010, p. 4 (notes that "the Rule of Law is violated when due attention is not paid to these procedural matters or when the institutions that are supposed to embody this procedure are undermined or interfered with". Further down this author would admit that there are some substantive dimensions of Rule of Law, such as respect for right for property and presumption of liberty and so forth); Taekema, Sanne, "The Procedural Rule of Law: Examining Waldron's Argument on Dignity and Agency", *Jahrbuch für Recht und Ethik*, Band 21, 2013, pp. 133 ff (contends that "Waldron's understanding of the Rule of Law as procedural which demands the opportunity for individuals to contest legal decisions in the formalized processes of courts and tribunals").

§§ Strikingly, bereft of a robust beacon of justice—Rule of Law[930]—to steer housing industry stakeholders towards procedural fairness, things are bound to swiftly fall out of bounds[931] inasmuch the extant legal framework is bound to be thrown into a frenzy beyond repair or atonement.[932]

---

[930] Allison, J. W. F. "Turning the Rule of Law into an English Constitutional Idea", May, C./ Winchester, A. (eds), *The Edward Elgar Handbook on the Rule of Law*. Cheltenham, United Kingdom: Edward Elgar, 2018; Allan, T. R. S., *The Sovereignty of Law: Freedom, Constitution, and the Common* Law. Oxford: Oxford University Press, 2018 (especially Chap. 3); Allan, T. R. S., *Constitutional Justice: A Liberal Theory of the Rule of* Law. Oxford: Oxford University Press, 2018, pp. 18–21. See also: Massoud, M. F., *Law's Fragile State: Colonial, Authoritarian, and Humanitarian Legacies in Sudan*. Cambridge: Cambridge University Press, 2020, *passim* (making the assumption according to which lawyers and historians have undertaken many invaluable studies on how the rule of law ideal has fared in practice under imperial and colonial conditions – a *law and social reality* approach for which we have been championing throughout this paper after all); Dylan Lino, "The Rule of Law and the Rule of Empire: A.V. Dicey in Imperial Context", *The Modern Law Review*, Volume 81, Issue 5, 2018, passim (highlighting the idea according to which the rule of law is much more ubiquitous globally today than ever before, and owes a lasting debt to the work of Victorian legal theorist A. V. Dicey); Krygier, M., "The Rule of Law: Pasts, Presents, and Two Possible Futures", *Annual Review of Law and Social Science*, Volume 12, 2018, pp. 199–200 (noting the seminal importance of Rule of Law in modern times).

[931] See: Ginsburg, Tom, "In Defense of Imperialism? The Rule of Law and the State-Building Project", Fleming, J. E. (editor), *Getting to the Rule of Law*. Nomos L. New York, NY: New York University Press, 2018, pp. 224 and ff and passim. See also: Brooks, R., "The New Imperialism: Violence, Norms, and the "Rule of Law", *Michigan Law Review*, Volume 101, 2003, pp. 2275 ff (stating that the rule of law is a beacon of procedural justice that plays a pivotal in State-Building Projects, in spite of the rampant violence, which often falls out-of-bounds and spirals out of control).

[932] Which is why the onset of the age of Artificial Intelligence will put the Rule of Law to the test like never before. Recall, the Rule of Law is a functional barrier—aimed at clamping down a host of unlawful deeds undertaken by those in power—that must not be teared apart or criminal procedure law will be otherwise despoiled from its intrinsic validity and vitality. See: Raz, Joseph, "The Rule of Law and its Virtue", *The Authority of Law: Essays on Law and Morality*, *cit.*, p. 224 (asserts adamantly that the Rule of Law is aimed at cushioning the hazards of abuse perpetrated by those in power. In this vein, Raz contends that "the law inevitably creates a great danger of arbitrary power—the Rule of Law is designed to minimize the danger created by the law itself...*Thus the (R)ule of (L)aw is designed to minimize the danger created by law itself...Thus the (R)ule of (L)aw is a negative virtue...the evil which is avoided is evil which could only have been caused by the law itself*"). Italics added.

The inception of the era of omnipotent Artificial Intelligence is about to revive the overriding importance of the dichotomy between *censory jurisprudence* (what law actually is and/or looks like) and *expository jurisprudence* (what law should do and/or be to halt the weaponization of Artificial Intelligence by those in power against *socially undesirables*). This dyad has been suitably tailored by Jeremy Bentham. See: Bentham, Jeremy, *An Introduction to the Principles of Morals and Legislation*. London: Great Books in Philosophy, Prometheus Books, 1988, 1–352 (293–294) (Jeremy Bentham's work on "the Principles of Morals and Legislation emerges from its historic roots in hedonism and teleology as a scientific attempt to assess the moral content of human action by focusing on its results or consequences. Proceeding from the assumption that human beings desire pleasure (and avoid pain), Bentham's unique perspective, known as utilitarianism, is used to construct a fascinating calculus for determining which action to perform when confronted with situations requiring moral decision-making the goal of which is to arrive at the "*greatest happiness of the greatest number*." Toward this end, he endeavours to delineate the sources and kinds of pleasure and pain and how they can be measured when assessing one's moral options. Bentham supports his

§§ Regrettably, the age of Artificial Intelligence-embedded technologies is further compounding the rampant racial inequalities that date as far back as the harrowing epoch of *mortgage redlining*. The next sections are to lend support to this sweeping claim.

4.1.4.2.1 Are *Mortgage Redlining* and *Algorithmic Redlining* «Brothers in Arms» in the Realm of Real Estate?

§§ All too often members of racialized communities (Blacks and Latinos) are eagerly leery of, and look askance at, algorithmic decision-making.[933] Their deep-rooted emotional concerns are neither unwarranted nor uncalled for.

§§ The latter (algorithmic decision-making[934]) is hemmed in unfathomable opaqueness,[935] thereby eliciting the squeaky clear impression that the level playing field has already been unfairly tilted against the former (Blacks and Latinos) under

---

arguments with discussions of intentionality, consciousness, motives, and dispositions"). This is not to say that we embrace Bentham's utilitarianism—so harshly criticized in Hart's *Concept of Law*—or the claim according to which an understanding of the Rule of Law presupposes a good understanding of law in a given country or community. Yet, there is a high degree of academic accuracy in Bentham's distinction when it comes to differentiating *expository jurisprudence—explaining what law is*—and *censorial jurisprudence—explaining what law ought to be.* As for effective access to justice and the procedural approach to the Rule of Law in the purview of criminal procedure law, there is markedly clear line between what legal officials are—purveyors of procedural fairness—and what an effective access to justice ought to be—a place whereby social inequalities caused by the era of artificial intelligence are to be buffered (criminal procedure law settings) in a swift, prompt, and streamlined manner. Or irreparable damages may otherwise occur.

933 Weizenbaum, Joseph, *Computer Power and Human Reason: From Judgment to Calculation*, 1st edition, New York, W. H. Freeman & Co, 1976, pp. 1–300 (227) ("examines the sources of the computer's powers and offers evaluative explorations of what computers can do, cannot do, and should not be employed to do") (this founding father of Artificial Intelligence presciently noted that we should not entrust Artificial Intelligence-embedded technologies with "tasks that demand wisdom"). Italics added. The approval of rental applications is arguably one of those tasks that should never be entrusted to machines). More on this on Part IV, This chapter, Sects. 4.1.4–4.1.4.2.1 of this book. See: Part V, Chap. 5, Sect. 5.1.7.2 of this book (on law number two to control algorithmic decision-making, which mandates that black box models must not be entrusted with the task of making high stake decisions—v.g. health and freedom).

934 Clark, A., "A nice surprise? Predictive processing and the active pursuit of novelty" *Phenomenology and the Cognitive Sciences*, Volume 17, Issue 3, 2018, pp. 521–534.

935 *Tech, Bias and Housing Initiative, the Promise and Perils of Residential Proptech, Year 1, Research Summary Report, April 2023, TechEquity Collaborative*, p. 11, available at: https://techequity.us/wp-content/uploads/2023/04/TBHI-Y1-Research-Summary-Report.pdf (28.11.2024). ("*From information on company websites, it is not clear what analysis or data is behind subjective determinations like "suitability" to a unit or what the nexus between an individual's characteristics and a unit's characteristics is that indicates the likelihood for property damage. Based on sample reports, even landlords are not privy to how the determinations are made. Instead, they receive a risk score out of 100 simplified into green, yellow, and red recommendations.* What companies withhold in terms of how it works, they make up for with the extent to which they tell landlords it works: Naborly claims their predictions reduce lease defaults by up to 89%. 15 *As Naborly's sample report demonstrates, its property damage assessment is then used*

a veneer of unimpeachable[936] neutrality.[937] This is the pith of legal tokenism[938] bestowed upon members of racialized communities (Blacks and Latinos) of which they should be keenly chary of.

§§ More to the point, the arcane inner workings of algorithmic decision-making[939] in the remit of housing industry are far from being dazzlingly wondrous—let alone, rivetingly bodacious.[940] Which is something for which racialised communities should not hold their breath for. This worrisome situation threatens to accordingly widen the rift between the *selected few* (*White folks*) and the *socially undesirables* or *unwanted many* (*Blacks and Latinos*) in the age of Artificial Intelligence-embedded technologies.

---

as an input to determine its projected eviction outcomes; its early vacancy prediction, in turn, is based on "all assessment factors"). Italics added.

[936] Farina, M., & Lavazza, A., *Philosophy, expertise, and the myth of neutrality. Routledge Studies in Contemporary Philosophy*, London, Routledge, 2024.

[937] Tyler, Tom R., "The Psychology of Procedural Justice: A Test of the Group-Value Model", *Journal of Personality and Social Psychology*, Volume 57, 1989, p. 830 (reports that in any procedure "several non-control issues—the *neutrality* of the decision-making procedure, trust in the 3rd party, and the information the experience communicates about social standing—influence both procedural preferences and judgments of procedural justice"). See also: Simmons, Ric, "Big Data and Procedural Justice: Legitimizing Algorithms in the Criminal Justice System", *Ohio State Journal of Criminal Law*, Volume 15, 2018, pp. 576 and ff and passim.

[938] Recall, the public outcry catalysed by the movement of Critical Legal Studies was underpinned by two foundational pillars: legal tokenism and legal indeterminacy, which, taken together, derail the overall functionality of a given legal system. See: Hutchinson, Alan C./Monahan, Patrick J., "Law, Politics and the Critical Legal Scholars: The Unfolding Drama of American Legal Thought", *Stanford Law Review*, Volume 36, 1984, 199–245 (pp. 200–202) (on law's indeterminacy, which would eventually merit vitriolic remarks from other Critical Legal Scholars). Soon enough, the grievances toward law's indeterminacy were to be levelled up. Critical legal scholars not only decried/bemoaned the indeterminacy of law, but also the facts 'nagging—and, foremost, unsettling—uncertainty regarding legal decision-making. See: McLeod, Ian, *Legal Theory*, 3rd Edition. New York: Palgrave Macmillan Law Masters, 2005, pp. 140–150 (decrying law's and facts 'indeterminacy, especially in cases in which legal decision-making is to rely upon witnesses 'flawed and skewed memory, which is to cast doubts on the witnesses' ability to aid judges in attaining the arduous task to serve justice in the first place). The sizzling hot challenges posed by an ever-evolving Artificial Intelligence are bound to further compound the abhorrent phenomenon of legal tokenism that shows no signs of fizzling out anytime soon. Like a full-fledged and full-bodied legal apparatus comprising algorithmic fairness that casts aside algorithmic discrimination in criminal procedure law settings. See on algorithmic discrimination: Kleinberg, Jon, et al., "Discrimination in the Age of Algorithms", *Journal of Legal Analysis*, 2018, pp. 114–174; See: Kleinberg, Jon, et al., "Algorithms as Discrimination Detectors", *Proceeds of the National Academy of Science*, Volume 117, 2020, pp. 30096–30110; Huq, Aziz, "Racial Equity in Algorithmic Criminal Justice", *Duke Law Journal*, Volume 68, 2022, pp. 1076–1134.

[939] Davis, Joshua P. "Law Without Mind: AI, Ethics, and Jurisprudence", *California Western Law Review*, Volume 55, 2018, pp. 181 e ss and passim (deals with an agreed-upon Artificial opacity while emphasizing a sought-after transparency to trounce it).

[940] See: Cohen, Julien E., *Between Truth and Power: The Legal Constructions of Informational Capitalism*. Oxford: Oxford University Press, 2019, pp. 1–376 (p. 192) (asserts adamantly that "*automated processes* have obvious efficiency advantages, *but such processes may not align well (or well at all) with applicable legal requirements that are couched in shades of gray*"). Italics added.

§§ Notably, output variables and input variables are jointly fed into machine learning algorithms, whose theoretical underpinnings premise the conclusion according to which the latter can make meaningful patterns[941] arising out of, and learn from, data.[942]

§§ Compellingly, Artificial Intelligence-embedded technologies will make predictions[943]—in the purview of Real Estate—based on past-rigged data[944] that travelled all the way across the gruelling *mortgage redlining* era,[945] which is something wholly unbecoming, and unwished for, for members of racialized communities (Blacks and Latinos).[946]

---

[941] See: Murphy, Kevin P., *Machine Learning: A Probabilistic Perspective (Adaptive Computation and Machine Learning series).* Massachusetts: The MIT Press, 2012, pp. 1–1104 (states avowedly that "machine Learning attempts to combine deductive, inductive, and abductive reasoning to make person-like reasoning in AI Entities possible. Machine-learning AI Entities initially learn in the same way a human child learns. First, they notice details and patterns in shapes, sounds, and behaviors; then put them together to distinguish one person from another, or a dog from a cat. Eventually, the AI can recognize and identify" common objects). See also: Hutto-Schultz, Jess, "Dicitur Ex Machina: Artificial Intelligence and the Hearsay Rule", *George Mason Law Review*, Volume 27, Issue 2, 2020, pp. 684–718 (689). See: Chollet, François, *Deep Learning with Python.* Shelter Island, Nova Iorque: Manning, 2018, pp. 1–384 (passim). *Deep Learning* stands as a byproduct of *Machine Learning. Machine Learning*, a subset of Artificial Intelligence, unfolds itself in *Deep Learning*, which "involves computer algorithms that have the ability to "learn" or improve in performance over time on some task". See: Surden, Harry, "Machine Learning and Law", *Washington Law Review*, Volume 89, 2015, pp. 87 and ff.

[942] Balkin, Jack M., "The Three Laws of Robotics in the Age of Big Data", *cit.*, pp. 1217–1241.

[943] Agrawal, A., Gans, J., & Goldfarb, A., "Power and prediction: The disruptive economics of artificial intelligence", *Harvard Business Review Press*, 2022.

[944] Barocas, Solon/Selbst, Andrew D., "Big Data's Disparate Impact", *California Law Review*, Volume 104, 2016, pp. 671–682 (discussing how data is often flawed, rigged, incomplete, imperfect and therefore algorithms inherit the prejudice of the original decision makers). But see: Citron, Danielle Keats/Pasquale, Frank, "The Scored Society: Due Process for Automated Predictions", *Washington Law Review*, Volume 89, 2014, pp. 1, 4–5 (highlighting how human beings programming automated systems is directly conducive to, and leads, to fundamentally inaccurate results since the source code, predictive algorithms and datasets may encompass human biases which, in turn, have a disparate impact on historically disadvantaged groups); Crawford, Kate/Schultz, Jason, "Big Data and Due Process: Toward a Framework to Redress Predictive Privacy Harms", *Boston College Law Review*, Volume 55, 2014, pp. 93, 99–101 (pinpointing pathways through which predictive analytic tools perpetuate discriminatory practices).

[945] See: Part IV, This chapter, Sects. 4.1.4–4.1.4.2.1 of this book (on mortgage redlining). See: Part IV, This chapter, Sects. 4.1.2–4.1.4.3 of this book (on algorithmic credit scoring, consumer racism and credit card redlining). See: Part IV, This chapter, Sects. 4.1.4–4.1.4.2.3 of this book (on algorithmic redlining). See: Part IV, This chapter, Sect. 4.1.4.3 of this book (on "algorithmic redliking").

[946] However, Schwemm and Taren avowedly contend that some cases might be somewhat deemed hybrid impact/intention cases of disparate impact on members of racialized communities. See: Schwemm, Robert G./Taren, Jeffrey L., "Discretionary Pricing, Mortgage Discrimination, and the Fair Housing Act", *The Harvard Civil Rights-Civil Liberties Law Review*, 2010, passim. The conduct being granularly parsed is discretion ascribed to brokers—which is considered by many stakeholders a harmless neutral practice -, may nonetheless lead to brokers to intentionally discriminate against members of racial minorities. See also: Selmi, Michael, "Indirect Discrimination and the Anti-Discrimination Mandate", Oxford, Oxford University Press, *Philosophical Foundations*

§§ For a simple reason: such algorithmic predictions[947] will reproduce the *systemic racism* that existed in that past data,[948] which contains residues of racial discrimination we are better off[949] without in that the latter enshrines flawed correlations[950] that we may not wish to re-entrench[951] in Real Estate industry.[952]

---

of Discrimination Law (Philosophical Foundations of Law), Hellman, Deborah/Moreau, Sophia (Editors), 2013, pp. 1–304 (pp. 257 and ff and passim) (books description: "how do we understand and justify the particular partialities that discrimination law tries to protect against? Are different discrimination laws from around the world grounded in a single set of norms? *And does discrimination law fail to treat people as individuals? The philosophical study around discrimination law in the private and public sector is a relatively young field of inquiry. This is owing to the fact that anti-discrimination laws are relatively new. It is arguably only since the Second World War that these rights have been adopted by countries in a broad sense, ensuring that all citizens have civil rights and the right to non-discrimination. Theory around discrimination law has until recently been threefold, doctrinal in its approach, questioning equality—why it matters and why should it influence legislatures in the design of policy—and thirdly focusing on the issue of affirmative action.* This volume takes a fresh look at the philosophy of discrimination law, identifying points of discussion in need of further study. It addresses how we are to understand and justify laws prohibiting discrimination. For instance, how discrimination might be best conceived—as a personal wrong or as an unfair distribution of resources. *The volume then turns to a number of meta-theoretical questions, whether different discrimination laws are coherent and grounded in collectively held beliefs or are instead a collection of very different rules that have no underlying coherence.* Lastly, the authors focus on issues in discrimination law that are currently the topic of considerable political debate. *The questions raised here are urgent and necessary and it is the hope of the authors that other academics and philosophers may join in their discussions*"). Italics added.

[947] Agrawal, A., Gans, J., & Goldfarb, A., "Prediction machines (updated and expanded): The simple economics of artificial intelligence", *Harvard Business Review Press*, 2022.

[948] See: Weizenbaum, Joseph, *Computer Power and Human Reason: From Judgment to Calculation*, 1st edition, New York, W. H. Freeman & Co, 1976, pp. 1–300 (227) ("examines the sources of the computer's powers and offers evaluative explorations of what computers can do, cannot do, and should not be employed to do") (this founding father of Artificial Intelligence presciently noted that we should not entrust Artificial Intelligence-embedded technologies with "tasks that demand wisdom"). Italics added. The approval of rental applications is arguably one of those tasks that should never be entrusted to machines). More on this on Part IV, This chapter, Sects. 4.1.4–4.1.4.2.1 of this book. See: Part V, Chap. 5, Sect. 5.1.7.2 of this book (on law number two to control algorithmic decision-making, which mandates that black box models must not be entrusted with the task of making high stake decisions—v.g. health and freedom).

[949] Kaplow, Louis/Shavell, Stephen, *Fairness versus Welfare*, Cambridge (Massachusetts), Harvard University Press, 2002, p. 1–578 (broach the principle of Pareto, according to which "what makes everyone better off should be preferred").

[950] Citron, Danielle K., "Technological Due Process", *Washington University Law Review*, Volume 85, 2008, pp. 1249–1253 ("Computer programs seamlessly combine rulemaking and individual adjudications without the critical procedural protections owed either of them"). See: Part V, Chap. 5, Sect. 5.1.8.5 of this book (on law number five to interpret algorithmic decision-making, which mandates that robot-judges, robot-prosecutors and robot-lawyers must not enter the courtroom for they are utterly incapable of making sound and interpretable value judgements).

[951] Balkin, Jack M., "The Three Laws of Robotics in the Age of Big Data", *cit.*, pp. 1217–1241.

[952] Hardy, Michael, "Pareto's Law", *Mathematical Intelligence*, Volume 32, 2010 (the exact opposite of the well-trodden Pareto's law, according to which the optimal state of society is when everyone is better off).

§§ Hardly any nonplussing surprise stems from the fact that Artificial Intelligence-embedded technologies trained on past biased data without proper and due care are inherently likely to recreate, reproduce, mimic, compound or even exacerbate racial discrimination[953] deeply steeped in past decision-making[954] in the remit of *mortgage redlining*.[955]

§§ Relatedly, and as captioned above, the *tour de force* distillation of human biases evinced by past decision-makers will be reflected in past decisions[956] concerning rental applications. Strikingly, rental applications will be filtered through past decisions (who applies, who gets the loan or to whom the rental is granted).[957]

§§ Understandably, although not laudably, White folks (to whom the great bulk of house loans was afforded back in the age of *mortgage redlining*[958]) will have a

---

[953] *Tech, Bias and Housing Initiative, the Promise and Perils of Residential Proptech, Year 1, Research Summary Report, April 2023, TechEquity Collaborative*, p. 5 available at: https://techequity.us/wp-content/uploads/2023/04/TBHI-Y1-Research-Summary-Report.pdf (28.11.2024). ("*Residential Proptech also has the potential to exacerbate the bias inherent in our housing system. Its rise is due, in part, to the desperation felt by average home seekers. With a severely constrained housing supply, companies offering an easier pathway to homeownership may exploit communities that have been harmed by housing discrimination in the past. Opaque algorithms incorporate biased data into their decision-making processes, making it harder to enforce fair housing laws.* Residential Proptech companies often operate in a regulatory gray area, leaving consumers without the protections they would have from traditional housing regulatory systems. *As unprecedented capital investment flows into this space, venture-backed companies' winner-take-all approach to growth has the potential to exacerbate inequality rather than combat it*"). Italics added. See: Part IV, This chapter, Sects. 4.1.4–4.1.4.2.3 of this book.

[954] Balkin, Jack M., "The Three Laws of Robotics in the Age of Big Data", *cit.*, pp. 1217–1241.

[955] In spite of its deep-seated racial bias, decision-makers continue to deploy redlining tactics through big data and may even justify such unlawful practices by claiming that the latter abide by cost-effectiveness. See: Cohen, Julien E., *Between Truth and Power: The Legal Constructions of Informational Capitalism*. Oxford: Oxford University Press, 2019, pp. 1–376 (p. 192) (asserts adamantly that "*automated processes* have obvious efficiency advantages, *but such processes may not align well (or well at all) with applicable legal requirements that are couched in shades of gray*"). Italics added. See also: Humber, Nadiyah J., "A Home for Digital Equity: Algorithmic Redlining and Property Technology", *California Law Review*, Volume 111, Issue 5, 2023, pp. 1421–1484. See also: Hurley, Mikella/Adebayo, Julius, "Credit Scoring in the Era of Big Data", *Yale Journal of Law and Technology*, Volume 18, 2016, pp. 148, 151–156, 172 (averring that FICO scoring boasts a redoubtable capacity to routinely weed out some populations that have been historically and systematically underrepresented or grossly unfairly represented in the credit industry market). Tellingly, by 2016, ten states had disavowed the unlawful practice of employers using shady credit scores due to their perceived disparate impact on low-income applicants and members of racialized communities (mostly Black folks). See: O'Neill, Cathy, *Weapons of Math Destruction. How Big Data Increases Inequality and Threatens Democracy*. London: Penguin Random House, 2016, pp. 128 and ff and passim.

[956] Kleinberg, Jon, et al., "Discrimination in the Age of Algorithms", *Journal of Legal Analysis*, 2018, pp. 114–174 (144 and ss and passim).

[957] Kleinberg, Jon, et al., "Discrimination in the Age of Algorithms", *cit.*, pp. 114–174 (144 and ss and passim).

[958] See: Part IV, This chapter, Sects. 4.1.4–4.1.4.2.1 of this book (on mortgage redlining). See: Part IV, This chapter, Sects. 4.1.2–4.1.4.3 of this book (on algorithmic credit scoring, consumer racism and credit card redlining). See: Part IV, This chapter, Sects. 4.1.4–4.1.4.2.3 of this book

disparate benefit as compared to Black and Latino folks (to whom the overwhelming majority of loans were rejected back in the age of *mortgage redlining*).

§§ A cluster of computer science pundits[959] and social scientists[960] have been rallying around of the idea according to which the principles of procedural fairness[961] and procedural auditability[962] are of paramount importance,[963] not least to help uptake and select the trade-offs that Real Estate stakeholders[964] use Artificial Intelligence-embedded technologies to make.[965] But to no avail.[966]

(on algorithmic redlining). See: Part IV, This chapter, Sect. 4.1.4.3 of this book (on "algorithmic redliking").

959 See: Corbett-Davies, Sam/Goel, Sharad, "The Measure and Mismeasure of Fairness: a critical Review of Fair Machine Learning", *Cornell University Library*, 2018, pp. 3 and ff and passim (undertake laudable efforts to debunk algorithm biases that primarily target ethnic minorities, such as Hispanics and coloured people).

960 Thibaut, John/ Walker, Laurens, *Procedural Justice: A Psychological Analysis*. Hillsdale, N.J.: Lawrence Erlbaum Associates, 1975, pp. 1–150 (procedural justice is tightly interlocked to raising the levels of fairness in legal settings. Absent of which procedural fairness is to mar. Law must not lose sight of such assertion). Converging: Lind, Edgar Allan/Tyler, Tom R., *The Social Psychology of Procedural Justice*. New York: Springer, 1988, pp. 208 ff (emphasizing that perceptions of justice being justly and correctly served enhances exponentially citizens' perception of provider legitimacy).

961 Tyler, Tom R., "Psychological perspectives on legitimacy and legitimation", in: *Annual Review of Psychology*, Volume 57, 2006, pp. 375–400 (on the role that perceived legitimacy plays in everyday life); Tyler, Tom R., *Why people cooperate: The role of social motivations*, Princeton, New Jersey, Princeton University Press, 2011; Robbins, J. M./M.T. Ford/L.E. Tetrick, "Perceived unfairness and employee health: A meta-analytic integration", in: *Journal of Applied Psychology*, Volume 97, 2012, pp. 235–272; Tyler, Tom R., "What is procedural justice? Criteria used by citizens to assess the fairness of legal procedures", *Law and Society Review*, Volume 22, 1988, pp. 103–135 (on the interplay between fairness of legal procedures and procedural justice. Unsurprisingly, the lack of fairness of legal procedures impacts the procedural justice -or lack thereof -); Sunshine, J./Tyler, Tom R., "The role of procedural justice and legitimacy in shaping public support for policing", *Law & Society Review*, Volume 37, 2003, pp. 513–548 (on the role of procedural justice to enhance/boost legitimacy); Bies, Robert J., "Are Procedural Justice and Interactional Justice Conceptually Distinct?", *Handbook of Organizational Justice*, Greenberg, Jerald/Colquitt, Jason, (Editors), New Jersey, Lawrence Erlbaum Associates Publishers, 2005, pp. 85–86 (arguing that a respectful treatment is an important part of, and the linchpin of a much-needed, procedural justice, which also plays an pivotal role in the remit of interactional justice).

962 Citron; Danielle Keats Citron/Pasquale, Frank, "Network Accountability for the Domestic Intelligence Apparatus", *Hasting Law Journal*, Volume 62, 2011, 1441, 1444–45; Gray, David/Citron, Danielle Keats, "The Right to Quantitative Privacy", *Minnesota Law Review*, Volume 98, 2013, pp. 62–81.

963 Bengio, Y., Hinton, G., Yao, A., Song, D., Abbeel, P., Harari, Y. N., Hadfield, G., Russell, S., Kahneman, D., & Mindermann, S., "Managing ai risks in an era of rapid progress", arXiv preprint arXiv:2310.17688, 2023.

964 Michele Loi and Markus Christen, "Choosing How to Discriminate: Navigating Ethical Trade-Offs in Fair Algorithmic Design for the Insurance Sector", *Philosophy & Technology*, Volume 34, 2021, passim.

965 Kleinberg, Jon, et al., "Discrimination in the Age of Algorithms", *cit.*, pp. 114–174 (144 and ss and passim).

966 Weizenbaum, Joseph, *Computer Power and Human Reason: From Judgment to Calculation*, 1st edition, New York, W. H. Freeman & Co, 1976, pp. 1–300 (227) ("examines the sources of the

§§ Compellingly, the ease with which human biases[967] of those entrusted to make high-stake past decisions[968] in the realm of *mortgage redlining* were channelled through to the data around which the approval of rental applications revolves is less than astonishing.[969]

§§ The unmooring of Artificial Intelligence-embedded technologies has accordingly given rise to an undeterred movement of laundering biased data—which, recall, has travelled all the way across the epoch of Jim Crow Laws, Social Security Act and, foremost, mortgage redlining—into eerily «powerful stigmatizing scores»[970] that boast a high likelihood to mimic discrimination[971] deeply steeped in past decision[972]-making[973] in the remit of *mortgage redlining.*

§§ Tellingly, and perhaps disturbingly, the risk variables (v.g. age, race, income, education, economical background, religious beliefs, criminal record[974] and so forth) that feed into the Artificial Intelligence-embedded[975] technologies[976] are to morph the

---

computer's powers and offers evaluative explorations of what computers can do, cannot do, and should not be employed to do") (this founding father of Artificial Intelligence presciently noted that we should not entrust Artificial Intelligence-embedded technologies with "tasks that demand wisdom"). Italics added. The approval of rental applications is arguably one of those tasks that should never be entrusted to machines"). See: Part V, Chap. 5, Sect. 5.1.8.5 of this book (on law number five to interpret algorithmic decision-making, which mandates that robot-judges, robot-prosecutors and robot-lawyers must not enter the courtroom for they are utterly incapable of making sound and interpretable value judgements).

967 Citron, Danielle Keats/Pasquale, Frank A., "The Scored Society: Due Process for Automated Predictions", *Washington Law Review*, Volume 89, 2014, pp. 1–34 (arguing that "[a]*dvocates applaud the removal of human beings and their flaws from the assessment process*," but arguing that bias remains "[*b*]*ecause human beings program predictive algorithms, their biases and values are embedded into the software's instructions*"). Italics added. See also: Griffiths, T. L., Chater, N., Kemp, C., Perfors, A., & Tenenbaum, J. B., "Probabilistic models of cognition: Exploring representations and inductive biases", *Trends in Cognitive Sciences*, Volume 14, Issue 8, 2010, pp. 357–364. Gigerenzer, G., "How to explain behavior?", *Topics in Cognitive Science*, Volume 12, Issue 4, 2020, pp. 1363–1381 (on human biases).

968 Hahn, U., & Harris, A. J., "What does it mean to be biased: Motivated reasoning and rationality", *Psychology of learning and motivation*, Volume 61, 2014, pp. 41–102 (on human biases).

969 Pilgrim, C., Sanborn, A., Malthouse, E., & Hills, T. T., "Confirmation bias emerges from an approximation to Bayesian reasoning", *Cognition*, 245, 105693, 2024.

970 Citron, Danielle K./Pasquale, Frank, "The Scored Society: Due Process for Automated Predictions", *Washington Law Review*, Volume 89, Issue 1, 2014, pp. 1–34.

971 See: Griemmelmann, James/Westreich, Daniel, "Incomprehensible Discrimination ", *California Law Review Online*, Volume 7, 2018, pp. 164–171.

972 Csaszar, F.A., Ketkar, H.J. & Kim, H., "AI and strategic decision making". *Working paper presented at Bocconi University*, 2024.

973 Balkin, Jack M., "The Three Laws of Robotics in the Age of Big Data", *cit.*, pp. 1217–1241.

974 But see: Wonyoung, So, "Which Information Matters? Measuring Landlord Assessment of Tenant Screening Reports", *Housing Policy Debate*, Volume 33, n. ° 6, 2023, pp. 1484–1510 (1501–1502) ("*Algorithmic scoring using criminal records is problematic because training data—a data set that is used to train a machine learning model—is inaccurate and the outcome variable ("desirable tenants") is unclear. For instance, the tenant screening company RealPage produces 11,000 reports using "abbreviated" criminal records, which are cheaper to acquire than full criminal records but do not include details of the resolution* (Kirchner & Goldstein, 2020). *An inaccurate model is highly likely to result from tenant screening services using these kinds of abbreviated data, given that it*

latter into an either racist[977] or biased[978] machine learning algorithm.[979] This cadre loosely amounts to *machine inductive biases* in the purview of deep learning.[980]

§§ Casts broadly, deep learning[981] techniques[982] will capture meaningful patterns arising out of the thumping great batches of training data,[983] thereby casting a

---

is important to include the final resolution of criminal justice procedures for proper assessment. Moreover, it would be challenging to set an outcome variable for developing this kind of algorithm because it is hard to project a certain criminal outcome into "good" tenant behaviors"). Italics added.

[975] Citron, Danielle Keats/Pasquale, Frank A., "The Scored Society: Due Process for Automated Predictions", *Washington Law Review*, Volume 89, 2014, pp. 1–34 (arguing that "[a]*dvocates applaud the removal of human beings and their flaws from the assessment process*," but arguing that bias remains "[*b*]*ecause human beings program predictive algorithms, their biases and values are embedded into the software's instructions*"). Italics added.

[976] Artificial intelligence, like everything else, is not without sizable drawbacks and shortcomings though. The most menacing of which happens to be the flawed or biased algorithms, which are bound to mar a sought-after bias-free decision making in dispute resolution. See: Sternlight, Jean, "Pouring a Little Psychological Cold Water on Online Dispute Resolution", *Journal of Dispute Resolution*, 1, 2020, pp. 23 ff (raises awareness to the perils of biased algorithms on online dispute resolution). Converging: Schmitz, Amy, "Expanding Access to Remedies Through E-Court Initiatives", *Buffalo Law Review*, Volume 67, 2019, pp. 90–100 (showing concerns that e-courts might be premising their decisions on flawed and bigoted algorithms). Which is something to be frowned upon. Why? Most likely, flawed or biased algorithms will deepen the chasm between rich and poor. See: Eubanks, Virginia, *Automating Inequality: How High-Tech Tools Profile, Police and Punish the Poor*. New York: St. Martin's Press, 2018, 1–272 (1 ff and passim) (coining the expression «automating inequality» to vividly portray the downsides of using high-technology to compound the yawning gap between rich and poor against the backdrop of biased algorithms). See also: Pasquale, Frank, *The Black Box Society: The Secret Algorithms that Control Money and Information*. Cambridge, Massachusetts: Harvard University Press, 2015, 1–320 (8–10 and passim) (noting that biased algorithms, which have underlying discrimination problems, contribute exponentially to further social biases. His most intriguing claim is that such biased algorithms have been incorporated/etched in the bulk of the corporations' informatic system, to the detriment of human kind in an overarching sense).

[977] See: Chandler, Anupam, "The Racist Algorithm", *Michigan Law Review*, Volume 115, n. ° 6, 2018, p. 1026 (on racist algorithms, noting that "the possibilities for discriminatory manipulation are legion"). But see: Altenburger, Kristen M./Ho, Daniel E., "When Algorithms Import Private Bias into Public Enforcement: The Promise and Limitations of Statistical Debiasing Solutions", *Journal of Institutional & Theoretical Economics*, Volume 175, 2019, pp. 97–98 (calls for a "debias predictive algorithms" to assuage racist and/or biased, doctored and bigoted algorithms nevertheless).

[978] Hamilton, Melissa, "The Biased Algorithm: Evidence of Disparate Impact on Hispanics", *American Criminal Law Review*, Volume 56, 2019, pp. 1553 and ff and passim.

[979] Hinton, G. E., "How neural networks learn from experience", *Scientific American*, Volume 267, Issue 3, 1992, pp. 144–151.

[980] Goyal, A., & Bengio, Y., "Inductive biases for deep learning of higher-level cognition", *Proceedings of the Royal Society A*, 478 (2266), 20210068, 2022.

[981] Buckner, C. J., *From deep learning to rational machines: What the history of philosophy can teach us about the future of artificial intelligence*, Oxford, Oxford University Press, 2023.

[982] Bengio, Y., Lecun, Y., & Hinton, G. 2021, "Deep learning for AI", *Communications of the ACM*, Volume 64, Issue 7, 2021, pp. 58–65.

[983] Hinton, G. E., Osindero, S., & Teh, Y. W., "A fast learning algorithm for deep belief nets", *Neural Computation*, Volume 18, Issue 7, 2006, pp. 1527–1554.

deluge of harms onto members of racialized communities (Blacks and Latinos) in the purview of Real Estate, which is nothing but disquieting.[984] Recall, Artificial Intelligence-embedded technologies[985] have no consciousness[986] insofar they only make algorithmic[987] predictions[988] based on the meaningful patterns arising out the training data (*data-driven learning*[989] and *predictive learning*[990]).[991]

§§ It follows that the unfettered furore over Artificial Intelligence-embedded technologies should be stymied or behemoth damages are otherwise slated to be externalized onto the usual suspects (Blacks and Latinos).[992] As the widely accepted concept of «organizations as artificial intelligences»[993] gains traction and gathers pace, inordinate harms are bound to be externalized onto members of racialized communities (Blacks and Latinos) in the purview of Real Estate.

---

984 Weizenbaum, Joseph, *Computer Power and Human Reason: From Judgment to Calculation*, 1st edition, New York, W. H. Freeman & Co, 1976, pp. 1–300 (227) ("examines the sources of the computer's powers and offers evaluative explorations of what computers can do, cannot do, and should not be employed to do") (this founding father of Artificial Intelligence presciently noted that we should not entrust Artificial Intelligence-embedded technologies with "tasks that demand wisdom"). Italics added. The approval of rental applications is arguably one of those tasks that should never be entrusted to machines").

985 Park, P. S., & Tegmark, M., "Divide-and-conquer dynamics in AI-driven disempowerment", *arXiv preprint arXiv:2310.06009*, 2023.

986 Butlin, P., Long, R., Elmoznino, E., Bengio, Y., Birch, J., Constant, A., & VanRullen, R., "Consciousness in artificial intelligence: insights from the science of consciousness", arXiv preprint arXiv:2308.08708, 2023.

987 Kim, H., Glaeser, E. L., Hillis, A., Kominers, S. D., & Luca, M., "Decision authority and the returns to algorithms", *Strategic Management Journal*, 2023.

988 Hohwy, J., *The predictive mind*, Oxford, Oxford University Press, 2013; Hohwy, J., "New directions in predictive processing", *Mind & Language*, Volume 35, Issue 2, 2020, pp. 209–223.

989 Clough, D. R., & Wu, A., "Artificial intelligence, data-driven learning, and the decentralized structure of platform ecosystems", *Academy of Management Review*, Volume 47, Issue 1, 2022, pp. 184–189 and passim; Gregory, R. W., Henfridsson, O., Kaganer, E., & Kyriakou, H., "The role of artificial intelligence and data network effects for creating user value", *Academy of Management Review*, Volume 46, Issue 3, 2021, pp. 534–551.

990 Friedman, J. H., & Popescu, B. E., "Predictive learning via rule ensembles", *Annals of Applied Statistics*, Volume 2, Issue 3, pp. 2008, pp. 916–954; Friston, K., & Kiebel, S., "Predictive coding under the free-energy principle", *Philosophical Transactions of the Royal Society B: Biological Sciences*, 364 (1521), 2009, pp. 1211–1221; Friston, K. J., Da Costa, L., Tschantz, A., Kiefer, A., Salvatori, T., Neacsu, V., & Buckley, C. L. "Supervised structure learning", *arXiv preprint arXiv:2311.10300*, 2023.

991 Sun, R. (Ed.), *The Cambridge Handbook of Computational Cognitive Sciences*, Cambridge, Cambridge University Press, 2023.

992 Hardt, Moritz, "How big data is unfair: Understanding sources of unfairness in data driven decision making", *Medium*, Archived on Oct. 8, 2014, available at: https://web.archive.org/web/20141008185829/; https://medium.com/@mrtz/how-big-data-is-unfair-9aa544d739de. (access: 17.12.2024).

993 Csaszar, F. A., & Steinberger, T., "Organizations as artificial intelligences: The use of artificial intelligence analogies in organization theory", *Academy of Management Annals*, Volume 16, Issue 1, 2022, pp. 1–37; Friston, K. J., Ramstead, M. J., Kiefer, A. B., Tschantz, A., Buckley, C. L., Albarracin, M., & René, G., "Designing ecosystems of intelligence from first principles", *Collective Intelligence*, Volume 3, Issue 1, 26339137231222481, 2024.

§§ For instance, landlords are increasingly relying upon[994] machine learning[995] algorithms[996] to grant, or deny, rental applications to a cohort of home seekers,[997] which, in turn, forms part of a broader trend[998] of entrusting machines[999] with making high-stake[1000] decisions.[1001] Unsurprisingly, Blacks and Latinos are being routinely denied rental applications owing to the *systemic racism* firmly rooted in past decision-making[1002] that goes as far back as the epoch of *mortgage redlining*.[1003]

§§ For a straightforward reason that should not come across as flabbergasting at this juncture: the very yardstick against which past discriminatory practices in Real Estate are gauged is not amenable to be relied upon insofar lends itself to a

---

[994] Novelli, E., & Spina, C., "When do entrepreneurs benefit from acting like scientists? A field experiment in the UK", *SSRN Working paper*, 2022, passim.

[995] Perconti, P., & Plebe, A., Deep learning and cognitive science", *Cognition*, 203, 104365, 2020.

[996] Christian, B., & Griffiths, T., *Algorithms to live by: The computer science of human decisions*, London, Palgrave Macmillan, 2016, passim.

[997] Davenport, T. H., & Kirby, J., *Only humans need apply: Winners and losers in the age of smart machines*, New York: Harper Business, 2016.

[998] Bell, J. J., Pescher, C., Tellis, G. J., & Füller, J., „Can AI help in ideation? A theory-based model for idea screening in crowdsourcing contests", *Marketing Science*, Volume 43, Issue 1, 2024, pp. 54–72.

[999] Agrawal, A., McHale, J., & Oettl, A., "Artificial intelligence and scientific discovery: A model of prioritized search", *Research Policy*, Volume 53, Issue 5, 2024, 104989.

[1000] But see: Weizenbaum, Joseph, *Computer Power and Human Reason: From Judgment to Calculation*, 1st edition, New York, W. H. Freeman & Co, 1976, pp. 1–300 (227) ("examines the sources of the computer's powers and offers evaluative explorations of what computers can do, cannot do, and should not be employed to do") (this founding father of Artificial Intelligence presciently noted that we should not entrust Artificial Intelligence-embedded technologies with "tasks that demand wisdom"). Italics added. The approval of rental applications is arguably one of those tasks that should never be entrusted to machines").

[1001] Amaya, J. & Holweg, M., "Using algorithms to improve knowledge work", *Journal of Operations Management*, 2024, passim.

[1002] Pearl, J., & Mackenzie, D., *The book of why: the new science of cause and effect*, New York, Basic Books, 2018, passim.

[1003] In spite of its deep-seated racial bias, decision-makers continue to deploy redlining tactics through big data and may even justify such unlawful practices by claiming that the latter abide by cost-effectiveness. See: Humber, Nadiyah J., "A Home for Digital Equity: Algorithmic Redlining and Property Technology", *California Law Review*, Volume 111, Issue 5, 2023, pp. 1421–1484. See also: Hurley, Mikella/Adebayo, Julius, "Credit Scoring in the Era of Big Data", *Yale Journal of Law and Technology*, Volume 18, 2016, pp. 148, 151–156, 172 (averring that FICO scoring boasts a redoubtable capacity to routinely weed out some populations that have been historically and systematically underrepresented or grossly unfairly represented in the credit industry market). Tellingly, by 2016, ten states had disavowed the unlawful practice of employers using shady credit scores due to their perceived disparate impact on low-income applicants and members of racialized communities (mostly Black folks). See: O'Neill, Cathy, *Weapons of Math Destruction. How Big Data Increases Inequality and Threatens Democracy*. London: Penguin Random House, 2016, pp. 128 and ff and passim.

benchmark[1004] fraught with a plethora of racial inequalities whose harmful effects irksomely resonate today.[1005]

§§ As it stands, there seems to be no way around this gruesome situation that comes to the expense of members' of racialized communities (Blacks and Latinos) long-sought dream of being afforded equal rights in the remit of Real Estate.[1006]

§§ Strikingly, Real Estate stakeholders (flowing from bankers,[1007] Real Estate agents to Landlords) have tended to disfavour Black and Latino rental applicants over White rental applicants. Such a set of «competitive advantages through Artificial Intelligence»[1008] allotted to White rental applicants has been deployed with a crushing lack of subtlety.[1009]

[1004] Citron, Danielle K./Pasquale, Frank, "The Scored Society: Due Process for Automated Predictions", *Washington Law Review*, Volume 89, Issue 1, 2014, pp. 1–34.

[1005] In spite of its deep-seated racial bias, decision-makers continue to deploy redlining tactics through big data and may even justify such unlawful practices by claiming that the latter abide by cost-effectiveness. See: Humber, Nadiyah J., "A Home for Digital Equity: Algorithmic Redlining and Property Technology", *California Law Review*, Volume 111, Issue 5, 2023, pp. 1421–1484.

[1006] Weizenbaum, Joseph, *Computer Power and Human Reason: From Judgment to Calculation*, 1st edition, New York, W. H. Freeman & Co, 1976, pp. 1–300 (227) ("examines the sources of the computer's powers and offers evaluative explorations of what computers can do, cannot do, and should not be employed to do") (this founding father of Artificial Intelligence presciently noted that we should not entrust Artificial Intelligence-embedded technologies with "tasks that demand wisdom"). Italics added. The approval of rental applications is arguably one of those tasks that should never be entrusted to machines").

[1007] Pietila, Antero, *Not in My Neighborhood: How Bigotry Shaped a Great American City*, Chicago, Ivan R. Dee; Illustrated edition, 2010, pp. 1–336 ("Baltimore is the setting for (and typifies) one of the most penetrating examinations of bigotry and residential segregation ever published in the United States. *Antero Pietila shows how continued discrimination practices toward African Americans and Jews have shaped the cities in which we now live. Eugenics, racial thinking, and white supremacist attitudes influenced even the federal government's actions toward housing in the twentieth century, dooming American cities to ghettoization.* This all-American tale is told through the prism of Baltimore, from its early suburbanization in the 1880s to the consequences of "white flight" after World War II, and into the first decade of the twenty-first century. The events are real, and so are the heroes and villains. Mr. Pietila's engrossing story is an eye-opening journey into city blocks and neighborhoods, shady practices, and ruthless promoters"). See: Pietila, Antero, *Not in My Neighborhood: How Bigotry Shaped a Great American City*, *cit.*, pp. 1–336 (64) (At certain stage, banks had already made up their mind as to not to lend to Black folks). See also: Szto, Mary, "Real Estate Agents as Agents of Social Change: Redlining, Reverse Redlining, and Greenlining", *Seatle Journal for Social Justice*, Volume 12, Issue 1, 2013, p. 11 ("Up until this time, banks had already decided not to lend to blacks").

[1008] Kemp, A., "Competitive advantages through artificial intelligence: Toward a theory of situated AI", *Academy of Management Review*, 2023, passim.

[1009] See also: Hurley, Mikella/Adebayo, Julius, "Credit Scoring in the Era of Big Data", *Yale Journal of Law and Technology*, Volume 18, 2016, pp. 148, 151–156, 172 (averring that FICO scoring boasts a redoubtable capacity to routinely weed out some populations that have been historically and systematically underrepresented or grossly unfairly represented in the credit industry market). Tellingly, by 2016, ten states had disavowed the unlawful practice of employers using shady credit scores due to their perceived disparate impact on low-income applicants and members of racialized communities (mostly Black folks). See: O'Neill, Cathy, *Weapons of Math Destruction. How Big*

§§ Put differently, the Real Estate industry has tended to disfavour a neutral shifting from the stakeholder that equal-footedly approves rental applications to coloured home seekers (Blacks and Latinos) to that of stakeholder that even-handedly approves a rental application to White home seekers.

§§ This racial disparity underpins the all-embracing concept of *algorithmic redlining*,[1010] which has already beset both the Real Estate industry and the Banking Industry.[1011] Abuses[1012] have been piling up at a mounting rate.

§§ It seems as though that procedural justice—a both shimmering and glittering lighthouse of justice that serves the pleasure of Rule of Law[1013]—amounts to nothing but to a languid benchmark that has no bearing on the practices of Real Estate industry

---

Data Increases Inequality and Threatens Democracy, London, Penguin Random House, 2016, pp. 128 and ff and passim.

[1010] See: Part IV, This chapter, Sects. 4.1.4–4.1.4.2.1 of this book (on mortgage redlining). See: Part IV, This chapter, Sects. 4.1.2–4.1.4.3 of this book (on algorithmic credit scoring, consumer racism and credit card redlining). See: Part IV, This chapter, Sects. 4.1.4–4.1.4.2.3 of this book (on algorithmic redlining). See: Part IV, This chapter, Sect. 4.1.4.3 of this book (on "algorithmic redliking").

[1011] Satter, Beryl, *Family Properties: How the Struggle Over Race and Real Estate Transformed Chicago and Urban America*, New York City, Picador Publishing, First Edition, 2010, pp. 1–528 ("The "promised land" for thousands of Southern blacks, postwar Chicago quickly became the most segregated city in the North, the site of the nation's worst ghettos and the target of Martin Luther King Jr.'s first campaign beyond the South. In this powerful book, *Beryl Satter identifies the true causes of the city's black slums and the ruin of urban neighborhoods throughout the country*: not, as some have argued, *black pathology, the culture of poverty, or white flight, but a widespread and institutionalized system of legal and financial exploitation. In Satter's riveting account of a city in crisis, unscrupulous lawyers, slumlords, and speculators are pitched against religious reformers, community organizers, and an impassioned attorney who launched a crusade against the profiteers*—the author's father, Mark J. Satter. *At the heart of the struggle stand the black migrants who, having left the South with its legacy of sharecropping, suddenly find themselves caught in a new kind of debt peonage.* Satter shows the interlocking forces at work in their oppression: *the discriminatory practices of the banking industry; the federal policies that created the country's shameful "dual housing market"; the economic anxieties that fueled white violence; and the tempting profits to be made by preying on the city's most vulnerable population*"). Italics added.

[1012] Which is why the onset of the age of Artificial Intelligence will put the Rule of Law to the test like never before. Recall, the Rule of Law is a functional barrier—aimed at clamping down a host of unlawful deeds undertaken by those in power—that must not be teared apart or criminal procedure law will be otherwise despoiled from its intrinsic validity and vitality. See: Raz, Joseph, "The Rule of Law and its Virtue", *The Authority of Law: Essays on Law and Morality*, *cit.*, p. 224 (asserts adamantly that the Rule of Law is aimed at cushioning the hazards of abuse perpetrated by those in power. In this vein, Raz contends that "the law inevitably creates a great danger of arbitrary power—the Rule of Law is designed to minimize the danger created by the law itself…*Thus the (R)ule of (L)aw is designed to minimize the danger created by law itself…Thus the (R)ule of (L)aw is a negative virtue…the evil which is avoided is evil which could only have been caused by the law itself*"). Italics added.

[1013] See: Part V, Chap. 5, Sect. 5.1.1.1 of this book (on the central tenets of Rule of Law that lends itself to a beacon of justice amidst the sepulchral darkness that is about to take hold). See: Part V, Chap. 5, Sect. 5.1.1.2 of this book (on the central tenets of Procedural Rule of Law that lends itself to a lighthouse of justice that allows citizens to challenge the pearls of algorithmic wisdom in a court of law).

in the age of Artificial Intelligence-embedded technologies[1014] that leverage on both biased data and warped algorithms.[1015]

§§ This racial inequality is neither harmless nor defanged. Instead, it lends itself to a perpetuation of *mortgage redlining* that harkens back to a long-haul span of time where racial discrimination was rife in Real Estate industry, which tend to cause further jarring outcomes, thereby cascading into ever more challenging life circumstances[1016] for Blacks and Latinos.[1017] To illustrate, take a hard look at the cases of *Mary Louis*, *Carmen Arroyo*, and *Monica Douglas*, respectively.

[1014] Weizenbaum, Joseph, *Computer Power and Human Reason: From Judgment to Calculation*, 1st edition, New York, W. H. Freeman & Co, 1976, pp. 1–300 (227) ("examines the sources of the computer's powers and offers evaluative explorations of what computers can do, cannot do, and should not be employed to do") (this founding father of Artificial Intelligence presciently noted that we should not entrust Artificial Intelligence-embedded technologies with "tasks that demand wisdom"). Italics added. The approval of rental applications is arguably one of those tasks that should never be entrusted to machines).

[1015] From the social psychology, warped algorithms accomplish nothing but the impairment of procedural justice. See: Thibaut, John/ Walker, Laurens, *Procedural Justice: A Psychological Analysis*. Hillsdale, N.J.: Lawrence Erlbaum Associates, 1975, pp. 1–150 (procedural justice is tightly interlocked to raising the levels of fairness in criminal procedure law settings. Absent of which procedural fairness is to mar. Criminal procedure law must not lose sight of such assertion). Converging: Lind, Edgar Allan/Tyler, Tom R., *The Social Psychology of Procedural Justice*. New York: Springer, 1988, pp. 208 ff (emphasizing that perceptions of justice being justly and correctly served enhances exponentially citizens' perception of provider legitimacy). Tyler, Tom R., "The Psychology of Procedural Justice: A Test of the Group-Value Model", *Journal of Personality and Social Psychology*, Volume 57, 1989, p. 830 (reports that in any procedure "several non-control issues—the *neutrality* of the decision-making procedure, trust in the 3rd party, and the information the experience communicates about social standing—influence both procedural preferences and judgments of procedural justice"). See also: Simmons, Ric, "Big Data and Procedural Justice: Legitimizing Algorithms in the Criminal Justice System", *Ohio State Journal of Criminal Law*, Volume 15, 2018, pp. 576 and ff and passim.

[1016] Citron, Danielle K./Pasquale, Frank, "The Scored Society: Due Process for Automated Predictions", *cit.*, pp. 1–34.

[1017] In spite of its deep-seated racial bias, decision-makers continue to deploy redlining tactics through big data and may even justify such unlawful practices by claiming that the latter abide by cost-effectiveness. See: Humber, Nadiyah J., "A Home for Digital Equity: Algorithmic Redlining and Property Technology", *California Law Review*, Volume 111, Issue 5, 2023, pp. 1421–1484. See also: Hurley, Mikella/Adebayo, Julius, "Credit Scoring in the Era of Big Data", *Yale Journal of Law and Technology*, Volume 18, 2016, pp. 148, 151–156, 172 (averring that FICO scoring boasts a redoubtable capacity to routinely weed out some populations that have been historically and systematically underrepresented or grossly unfairly represented in the credit industry market). Tellingly, by 2016, ten states had disavowed the unlawful practice of employers using shady credit scores due to their perceived disparate impact on low-income applicants and members of racialized communities (mostly Black folks). See: O'Neill, Cathy, *Weapons of Math Destruction. How Big Data Increases Inequality and Threatens Democracy*. London: Penguin Random House, 2016, pp. 128 and ff and passim.

4.1.4.2.2 Are Property Technologies (*SafeRent* and *Corelogic*) Underpinning Automating Rental Markets a Byproduct of *Algorithmic Redlining* That Amplifies Racial Discrimination and Segregation in Real Estate? The Notorious Cases of Mary Louis, Monica Douglas (*Louis v. Saferent Sols., Civil Action 22-CV-10800-AK, 5 (D. Mass. Jul. 26, 2023)*), and Carmen Arroyo (*Connecticut Fair Housing Center,* et al. *v. CoreLogic Rental Property Solutions, Case No. 3:18-cv-00705, U.S. District Court for the District of Connecticut*)

§§ In 2015, a Latina woman named Carmen Arroyo applied for her disabled son named Mikhail[1018] to move into her apartment in Canton, Massachusetts, United States of America.[1019] In 2021, a Black woman called Mary Louis applied to rent an

[1018] The Carmen Arroyo case background reads as follows: "*Originally filed on April 24, 2018 with the U.S. District Court, District of Connecticut, the lawsuit asserts that CoreLogic's automated tenant screening software tool ("CrimSAFE") denied Carmen Arroyo's request to move her disabled son into her rental apartment based on a record of a dismissed shoplifting arrest from 2014, before he became disabled. Arroyo, whose son Mikhail was injured in a July 2015 accident that left him unable to speak, walk, or care for himself, is her son's conservator. After becoming his conservator, Arroyo asked her landlord for permission to move Mikhail into her home and out of the nursing home where he was recovering. She submitted a rental application on her son's behalf*. But, his application was denied. *CoreLogic's "CrimSAFE" background check stated that Mikhail had a "disqualifying [criminal] record." Arroyo claims that CoreLogic's criminal background report did not provide the landlord with any details about Mikhail's underlying criminal history—only a computer-generated notation that the application did not meet the landlord's criteria.* Arroyo asserts that CoreLogic refused to provide her with a copy of the information it relied on to make the screening decision, information which she was entitled to receive under federal law, as she was her son's conservator. Because CoreLogic refused to recognize Ms. Arroyo's authority as conservator for her son, she asserts that CoreLogic also violated its obligation to provide a reasonable accommodation to her disabled son. *Arroyo subsequently learned that her son's only criminal record was a charge—from before his accident, and later dropped—for shoplifting, an infraction below the level of a misdemeanor. Without this information, Arroyo could not challenge Mikhail's denial, and neither CoreLogic nor the landlord made the sort of individualized assessment that HUD says is required.* As a result, he remained in a nursing home for approximately a year longer than necessary. On March 25, 2019, the U.S. District Court, District of Connecticut denied CoreLogic's motion to dismiss, holding that because CoreLogic "held itself out as a company with the knowledge and ingenuity to screen housing applicants by interpreting criminal records and specifically advertised its ability to improve 'Fair Housing compliance,'" that it could be held liable for violations of the Fair Housing Act. *As automated decisions by third-party screening companies are rapidly becoming the norm, this ruling has significant implications for landlords, renters and the entire screening industry*". Italics added. See: Connecticut Fair Housing Center, et al. v. CoreLogic Rental Property Solutions—Cohen Milstein (access: 20.11.2024). See: Weizenbaum, Joseph, *Computer Power and Human Reason: From Judgment to Calculation*, 1st edition, New York, W. H. Freeman & Co, 1976, pp. 1–300 (227) ("examines the sources of the computer's powers and offers evaluative explorations of what computers can do, cannot do, and should not be employed to do") (this founding father of Artificial Intelligence presciently noted that we should not entrust Artificial Intelligence-embedded technologies with "tasks that demand wisdom"). Italics added. The approval of rental applications is arguably one of those tasks that should never be entrusted to machines). See: Part V, Chap. 5, Sect. 5.1.1.1 of this book (on the central tenets of Rule of Law that lends itself to a beacon of justice amidst the sepulchral darkness that is about to take hold). See: Part V, Chap. 5, Sect. 5.1.1.2 of this

apartment in Malden, Massachusetts, United States of America.[1020] The very same year, a Black woman named Monica Douglas likewise applied to rent an apartment in Canton, Massachusetts, United States of America.[1021] Their rental applications were rejected for different reasons. For the sake of the argument, let us turn our attention to *Louis* case.

§§ In 2022, Monica Douglas and Mary Louis brought claims on behalf of themselves coupled with class action claims for all **similarly situated**[1022] Black and Latino individuals who happen to pay rent using housing vouchers in *Louis v. SafeRent Solutions*.[1023]

§§ For purposes here, *SafeRent Score* designs, markets, and sells a variety of tenant-screening services to house providers, landlords, real estate agents, brokerages, and property managers nationwide and in Massachusetts, United States of America. These «self-service tenant screening solutions», seek to assist to «identify top quality applicants».[1024] One of these services is the *SafeRent Score*, which uses

book (on the central tenets of Procedural Rule of Law that lends itself to a lighthouse of justice that allows citizens to challenge the pearls of algorithmic wisdom in a court of law).

[1019] Humber, Nadiyah J., "A Home for Digital Equity: Algorithmic Redlining and Property Technology", *California Law Review*, *cit*., pp. 1421–1484 (1422).

[1020] Humber, Nadiyah J., "A Home for Digital Equity: Algorithmic Redlining and Property Technology", *California Law Review*, *cit*., pp. 1421–1484 (1422).

[1021] Humber, Nadiyah J., "A Home for Digital Equity: Algorithmic Redlining and Property Technology", *California Law Review*, *cit*., pp. 1421–1484 (1422).

[1022] See: Part V, Chap. 5, Sect. 5.1.1.5.2.2.1.2 of this book (on one of the foundations underpinning a thing-centred artificial intelligence: the comparison of similarly situated individuals).

[1023] Humber, Nadiyah J., "A Home for Digital Equity: Algorithmic Redlining and Property Technology", *California Law Review*, *cit*., pp. 1421–1484 (1424).

[1024] But see: *Tech, Bias and Housing Initiative, the Promise and Perils of Residential Proptech, Year 1, Research Summary Report, April 2023, TechEquity Collaborative*, p. 11, available at: https://techequity.us/wp-content/uploads/2023/04/TBHI-Y1-Research-Summary-Report.pdf (28.11.2024). ("*From information on company websites, it is not clear what analysis or data is behind subjective determinations like "suitability" to a unit or what the nexus between an individual's characteristics and a unit's characteristics is that indicates the likelihood for property damage. Based on sample reports, even landlords are not privy to how the determinations are made. Instead, they receive a risk score out of 100 simplified into green, yellow, and red recommendations.* What companies withhold in terms of how it works, they make up for with the extent to which they tell landlords it works: Naborly claims their predictions reduce lease defaults by up to 89%. 15 *As Naborly's sample report demonstrates, its property damage assessment is then used as an input to determine its projected eviction outcomes; its early vacancy prediction, in turn, is based on "all assessment factors*"). Italics added. See: Part IV, This chapter, Sects. 4.1.4–4.1.4.2.3 of this book. See: Part IV, This chapter, Sects. 4.1.4–4.1.4.2.1 of this book (on mortgage redlining). See: Part IV, This chapter, Sects. 4.1.2–4.1.4.3 of this book (on algorithmic credit scoring, consumer racism and credit card redlining). See: Part IV, This chapter, Sects. 4.1.4–4.1.4.2.3 of this book (on algorithmic redlining). See: Part IV, This chapter, Sect. 4.1.4.3 of this book (on "algorithmic redliking"). See: Part IV, This chapter, Sect. 4.1.3 of this book (on algorithmic prime-lining).

a machine learning algorithm to ascertain the risk of leasing a property to a particular tenant.[1025] Put differently, computer-run algorithms seek to ferret out «good tenants».[1026]

§§ *SafeRent Score* amalgamates a vast assortment of factors, flowing from credit history, bankruptcy records, past due accounts, payment performance to eviction history[1027]/,[1028] according «to their statistical significance in predicting lease performance,» and calculates a numerical rating between two hundred and eight hundred for rental applicants.[1029]

§§ All things considered, this algorithmic score aims to gauge the applicant's «lease performance risk», and applicants with higher scores generally outperform applicants with lower scores. *SafeRent Score* does not consider the financial benefits

---

1025 *Louis v. Saferent Sols.*, Civil Action 22-CV-10800-AK, 3 (D. Mass. Jul. 26, 2023) ("SafeRent designs, markets, and sells a variety of tenant-screening services to landlords, real estate agents, brokerages, and property managers nationwide and in Massachusetts. *[Id.* at ¶¶ 21–22]. These "self-service tenant screening solutions," as advertised by SafeRent, are intended to help "identify top quality applicants." *[Id.* at ¶ 22]. *One of these services is the "SafeRent Score," which uses an algorithm to calculate the risk of leasing a property to a particular tenant. [See id.* at ¶¶ 24–25]"). Italics added.

1026 See: Power, Emma R., and Charles Gillon, "Performing the 'Good Tenant'", *Housing Studies*, 37 (3), 2020, pp. 459–82 ("*Renters in homeowner societies like Australia, the United States and United Kingdom occupy a complex moral landscape, maligned for failure to achieve homeownership but pivotal to the value of investment properties. Identification of 'good' and 'risky' tenants is an important landlord practice.* We investigate how tenants conceptualise and perform the 'good tenant' through research with 36 single older women renting in greater Sydney, Australia: a cohort on the margins of secure housing. *The good tenant demonstrates responsibility through paying rent on time and property stewardship (reporting repairs, making home). However, these practices are made necessary and risky through limited tenure security. The emotional and financial risks attending performances of the good tenant drive paradoxical relations; a good tenant is also acquiescent and silent,* not reporting property repairs or lapsed leases to avoid rent increases and/or evictions. Variegated performances of the '*good tenant' reflect cultural property norms and valorize the investment function of housing yet could also productively unsettle tenant-landlord relations*"). Italics added.

1027 But see: Wonyoung, So, "Which Information Matters? Measuring Landlord Assessment of Tenant Screening Reports", *Housing Policy Debate*, Volume 33, n. ° 6, 2023, pp. 1484–1510 (1500) (arguing that many landlords file evictions (*eviction fillings*) with no intention whatsoever of proceeding with its execution (*executed evictions*) only to purposefully harm an undesirable tenant, which casts a shady shadow on the eviction records, which, in turn, lack accuracy. "*With regards to eviction records, one of the most noticeable harms this study identifies is that during the tenant screening process, landlords do not distinguish between eviction filings and actually executed evictions. This is particularly alarming given that many landlords file numerous evictions without the intention of or a sound rationale for actually evicting tenants (Garboden & Rosen, 2019). Furthermore, this study replicates the finding of "professional solidarity" among landlords (Garboden & Rosen, 2019, p. 647). Eviction filings are a tacit tenant screening measure meant to issue a warning to other landlords against taking on the tenant in question (Garboden & Rosen, 2019; Leung* et al., *2021). Furthermore, landlords often file multiple evictions on the same tenant—this is frequently called "serial filing" (Immergluck* et al., *2020; Leung* et al., *2021). As a result, in Washington, DC, for example, among all eviction records, only 5.5% of evictions filed in 2018 were executed (McCabe & Rosen, 2020). This means that 94.5% of filed evictions were not executed. As this study has shown, those records may be interpreted, erroneously, as evictions by landlords and will likely still negatively affect tenants' future housing search (Phillips, 2020)*"). Italics added.

of housing vouchers[1030] allotted to vouch holders.[1031] For purposes here, vouch holders are generally assigned to low-income applicants. Amongst whom, members of racialized communities (Blacks[1032] and Latinos).[1033]

[1028] But see: Porton, Adam/Gromis, Ashley/Desmond, Matthew, "Inaccuracies in Eviction Records: Implications for Renters and Researchers", *Housing Policy Debate*, Volume 31, n. ° 3–5, 2021, pp. 377–394 ("*Administrative court records are increasingly used to study the prevalence of eviction. Yet inaccuracies in court records bias estimates of eviction and distort tenants' true rental histories. This is the first study to systematically assess the prevalence of inaccuracies across jurisdictions. Drawing on over 3.6 million administrative eviction court records from 12 states, we find that, on average, 22% of eviction records contain ambiguous information on how the case was resolved or falsely represent a tenant's eviction history.* Adjusting for multiple inaccuracies in the data produces significantly different eviction rate estimates. *Cases with increased complexity, such as those involving multiple tenants and lawyers, are more likely to contain inaccuracies. However, inaccuracies vary most prominently between states, indicating that state court system characteristics fundamentally shape the official record of the evicted population*"). Italics added. Desmond, M., *Evicted: Poverty and profit in the American city*, First Edition, New York, Crown Publishers, 2016, passim.

[1029] *Louis v. Saferent Sols.*, Civil Action 22-CV-10800-AK, 3 (D. Mass. Jul. 26, 2023) ("The SafeRent Score aggregates several factors, including credit history, bankruptcy records, past due accounts, payment performance, and eviction history, according "to their statistical significance in predicting lease performance," and calculates a numerical rating between two hundred and eight hundred for rental applicants. *[Id.* at ¶¶ 25, 27, 30, 35]").

[1030] But see: *Louis v. Saferent Sols.*, Civil Action 22-CV-10800-AK, 4 (D. Mass. Jul. 26, 2023) ("*Housing providers who rent to tenants with housing vouchers are guaranteed to receive at least some of their tenants' monthly rental payments, because the local housing authority disburses payment directly to the housing provider. [Id.* at ¶ 65]. *Moreover, voucher holders may also request exemptions from the minimum rent they are required to pay if they experience certain hardships, such as loss of assistance programs, the threat of eviction, decreased income, loss of employment, or a death. [Id. at ¶ 67]. This further insulates housing providers from the risk of non-payment for units rented to voucher holders. [Id.]*. As such, credit scores and histories fail to predict whether a rental applicant would make a quality tenant, particularly when housing vouchers are involved. *[See id.* at ¶ 61]"). Italics added.

[1031] *Louis v. Saferent Sols.*, Civil Action 22-CV-10800-AK, 3 (D. Mass. Jul. 26, 2023) ("*This score is intended to measure the applicant's "lease performance risk," and applicants with higher scores generally outperform applicants with lower scores. [Id.* at ¶ 28]. *The SafeRent Score does not consider the financial benefits of housing vouchers. [Id.* at ¶¶ 31]"). Italics added.

[1032] Derenoncourt, Ellora/Kim, Chi Hyun/Kuhn, Moritz/Schularik, Moritz, "The Wealth of Two Nations: The U.S. Racial Wealth Gap, 1860–2020", *The Quarterly Journal of Economics*, Volume 139, Issue 2, 2024, p. 741 ("A large class of commonly discussed policies for reducing racial wealth inequality seeks to reduce gaps in income, savings, and capital gains. These include policies that encourage financial diversification or stock equity holdings among Black households; policies aimed at financial literacy and retirement or savings behavior; or policies aimed at improving educational and labor market outcomes of Black Americans through improved school quality or reductions in discrimination. *Yet on a realistic note, our simulation in Section IV.A shows that even if wealth accumulation conditions had been equal since 1870, the wealth gap would still be 3 to 1 today, and full convergence would be more than 200 years away. Put differently: to close the racial wealth gap in the immediate term* via *flow parameters, Black Americans would need a substantial positive lead over whites, not "just" more equality*"). Italics added.

[1033] Wonyoung, So, "Which Information Matters? Measuring Landlord Assessment of Tenant Screening Reports", *Housing Policy Debate*, Volume 33, n. ° 6, 2023, pp. 1484–1510 (1502) ("*One*

§§ In spite of the unwonted circumstances surrounding each rental application, all three rental applications were outrightly spurned by a computer-generated technology («an automated screening tool employed by *SafeRent Solutions, LLC* (SafeRent)»)[1034] which, in turn, has created an algorithmic score to both Mary Louis and Monica Douglas rental applications,[1035] and, in the case of Carmen Arroyo, a criminal record[1036] evaluation/notation that automatically[1037] rebuffed her request.[1038]

§§ Both Massachusetts applicants, Mary Louis and Monica Douglas (the *Louis* plaintiffs or aggrieved parties),[1039] were ascribed an algorithmic score below their landlords 'minimum thresholds, which, according to the plaintiffs, has exacted a toll on their chances of having their rental application approved owing to the fact that Artificial Intelligence-embedded technologies disproportionately[1040] disfavour[1041] Blacks[1042] and Latinos.[1043]

---

additional finding of the experiment is that algorithmic scoring can exacerbate this racially unequal landscape in rental agreements not just because the algorithm may be inaccurate, but because landlords may want to follow the risk assessment made by the tenant screening report. This is alarming for low-income tenants, particularly housing voucher holders. Security deposits are one of the most significant barriers to obtaining housing for voucher holders, because vouchers do not pay security deposits but most private landlords require them (Rosenblatt & Cossyleon, 2018). Given that voucher holders have exceptionally low income (usually less than 50% of area median income) and might experience more housing insecurity (rental debts and eviction-related experiences), *imposing greater security deposits on voucher holders almost equates to denying them housing—yet these decisions could be justified by algorithmic scoring if tenant screening services employ it*"). Italics added.

1034 Humber, Nadiyah J., "A Home for Digital Equity: Algorithmic Redlining and Property Technology", *California Law Review*, *cit.*, pp. 1421–1484 (1423).

1035 *Louis v. Saferent Sols.*, Civil Action 22-CV-10800-AK, 2 (D. Mass. Jul. 26, 2023) ("Metropolitan and the housing provider that denied Douglas' application relied on SafeRent's tenant-screening services when denying these applications. *[Id.* at ¶¶ 20, 76, 85]").

1036 See: Connecticut Fair Housing Center, et al. v. CoreLogic Rental Property Solutions—Cohen Milstein (access: 20.11.2024). ("*The U.S. Department of Housing & Urban Development observed in 2016 that excluding rental applicants because of their criminal records disproportionately harms Latinos and African Americans, who are significantly more likely than whites to be arrested or convicted. Studies show such disparities are linked to differential enforcement rather than to differences in likelihood of engaging in criminal activity. HUD advised that to avoid discriminating, an "individualized review" should be conducted considering the nature of the offense, how long ago it occurred, intervening changed circumstances, and other relevant factors to avoid denying housing to an applicant who does not pose a genuine and ongoing threat to persons or property. Further, HUD's guidance specifically advises landlords not to consider arrests that did not result in a conviction in making their evaluations*"). Italics added.

§§ *SafeRent Score* amasses a plethora of factors to calculate a score conducive to the approval or refusal of a rent application.[1044] Ranging from credit history,

---

[1037] But see: Wonyoung, So, "Which Information Matters? Measuring Landlord Assessment of Tenant Screening Reports", *Housing Policy Debate*, Volume 33, n. ° 6, 2023, pp. 1484–1510 (1501–1502) ("*Algorithmic scoring using criminal records is problematic because training data—a data set that is used to train a machine learning model—is inaccurate and the outcome variable ("desirable tenants") is unclear. For instance, the tenant screening company RealPage produces 11,000 reports using "abbreviated" criminal records, which are cheaper to acquire than full criminal records but do not include details of the resolution* (Kirchner & Goldstein, 2020). *An inaccurate model is highly likely to result from tenant screening services using these kinds of abbreviated data, given that it is important to include the final resolution of criminal justice procedures for proper assessment. Moreover, it would be challenging to set an outcome variable for developing this kind of algorithm because it is hard to project a certain criminal outcome into "good" tenant behaviors*"). Italics added.

Citron, Danielle Keats/Pasquale, Frank A., "The Scored Society: Due Process for Automated Predictions", *Washington Law Review*, Volume 89, 2014, pp. 1–34 (arguing that "[a]*dvocates applaud the removal of human beings and their flaws from the assessment process*," but arguing that bias remains "[*b]ecause human beings program predictive algorithms, their biases and values are embedded into the software's instructions*"). Italics added.

[1038] Humber, Nadiyah J., "A Home for Digital Equity: Algorithmic Redlining and Property Technology", *California Law Review*, *cit.*, pp. 1421–1484 (1423).

[1039] *Louis v. Saferent Sols.*, Civil Action 22-CV-10800-AK, 2 (D. Mass. Jul. 26, 2023) ("The Court recites here only those facts and law necessary to understand what has led to this action. Further details relevant to the Court's analysis will be discussed as needed. Unless otherwise noted, the facts are presented as alleged in the amended complaint. *[See* Dkt. 15 ("Am. Compl.")]. *Louis and Douglas are Black women who hold housing vouchers and whose rental applications were denied, at least in part, because of their credit histories and scores. [Id. at ¶¶ 7, 74–76, 84–85].* Metropolitan denied Louis' application for an apartment, and another housing provider not named as a defendant in this action initially rejected Douglas' application for an apartment, though it later approved her request through its appeal process. *[Id.* at ¶¶ 7475, 83–89]"). Italics added.

[1040] Allen, James, "The Color of Algorithms: An Analysis and Proposed Research Agenda Deterring Algorithmic Redlining", *Fordham Urban Law Journal*, Volume 46, 2019, pp. 219–234 (229–234) (discussing how historical mortgage redlining greatly swayed modern algorithms generated by massive batches of datasets that consist of decades of information built on exclusion and racial discrimination in the purview of financing, marketing, and housing). See: Part IV, This chapter, Sects. 4.1.4–4.1.4.2.3 of this book.

[1041] *Tech, Bias and Housing Initiative, the Promise and Perils of Residential Proptech, Year 1, Research Summary Report, April 2023, TechEquity Collaborative*, p. 5 available at: https://techequity.us/wp-content/uploads/2023/04/TBHI-Y1-Research-Summary-Report.pdf (28.11.2024). ("*Residential Proptech also has the potential to exacerbate the bias inherent in our housing system. Its rise is due, in part, to the desperation felt by average home seekers. With a severely constrained housing supply, companies offering an easier pathway to homeownership may exploit communities that have been harmed by housing discrimination in the past. Opaque algorithms incorporate biased data into their decision-making processes, making it harder to enforce fair housing laws.* Residential Proptech companies often operate in a regulatory gray area, leaving consumers without the protections they would have from traditional housing regulatory systems. *As unprecedented capital investment flows into this space, venture-backed companies' winner-take-all approach to growth has the potential to exacerbate inequality rather than combat it*"). Italics added. See: Part IV, This chapter, Sects. 4.1.4–4.1.4.2.3 of this book.

[1042] Wonyoung, So, "Which Information Matters? Measuring Landlord Assessment of Tenant Screening Reports", *Housing Policy Debate*, Volume 33, n. ° 6, 2023, pp. 1484–1510 (1502) ("*One*

bankruptcy records, past due accounts, payment performance, to eviction history,[1045] according «to their statistical significance in predicting lease performance»,[1046] and calculates a numerical rating between two hundred and eight hundred for rental

additional finding of the experiment is that algorithmic scoring can exacerbate this racially unequal landscape in rental agreements not just because the algorithm may be inaccurate, but because landlords may want to follow the risk assessment made by the tenant screening report. This is alarming for low-income tenants, particularly housing voucher holders. Security deposits are one of the most significant barriers to obtaining housing for voucher holders, because vouchers do not pay security deposits but most private landlords require them (Rosenblatt & Cossyleon, 2018). Given that voucher holders have exceptionally low income (usually less than 50% of area median income) and might experience more housing insecurity (rental debts and eviction-related experiences), *imposing greater security deposits on voucher holders almost equates to denying them housing—yet these decisions could be justified by algorithmic scoring if tenant screening services employ it*"). Italics added. See: Part IV, This chapter, Sects. 4.1.4–4.1.4.2.3 of this book. See: Part IV, This chapter, Sects. 4.1.4–4.1.4.2.1 of this book (on mortgage redlining). See: Part IV, This chapter, Sects. 4.1.2–4.1.4.3 of this book (on algorithmic credit scoring, consumer racism and credit card redlining). See: Part IV, This chapter, Sects. 4.1.4–4.1.4.2.3 of this book (on algorithmic redlining). See: Part IV, This chapter, Sect. 4.1.4.3 of this book (on "algorithmic redliking"). See: Part IV, This chapter, Sect. 4.1.3 of this book (on algorithmic prime-lining).

1043 *Louis v. Saferent Sols.*, Civil Action 22-CV-10800-AK, 2–3 (D. Mass. Jul. 26, 2023) ("Plaintiffs claim that the Defendants' use of SafeRent's tenant-screening services, in particular, the "SafeRent Score," which relies on "*credit histories and other information which bears little to no relationship to the risk that their rent will be paid," disproportionally affects Black and Hispanic applicants and voucher holders in violation of federal and state antidiscrimination and consumer protection laws.* [*Id.* at 1, ¶ 1]"). Italics added.

1044 *Tech, Bias and Housing Initiative, the Promise and Perils of Residential Proptech, Year 1, Research Summary Report, April 2023, TechEquity Collaborative*, p. 11, available at: https://techequity.us/wp-content/uploads/2023/04/TBHI-Y1-Research-Summary-Report.pdf (28.11.2024). ("*From information on company websites, it is not clear what analysis or data is behind subjective determinations like "suitability" to a unit or what the nexus between an individual's characteristics and a unit's characteristics is that indicates the likelihood for property damage. Based on sample reports, even landlords are not privy to how the determinations are made. Instead, they receive a risk score out of 100 simplified into green, yellow, and red recommendations.* What companies withhold in terms of how it works, they make up for with the extent to which they tell landlords it works: Naborly claims their predictions reduce lease defaults by up to 89%. 15 *As Naborly's sample report demonstrates, its property damage assessment is then used as an input to determine its projected eviction outcomes; its early vacancy prediction, in turn, is based on "all assessment factors*"). Italics added. See: Part IV, This chapter, Sects. 4.1.4–4.1.4.2.3 of this book.

1045 See: Desmond, M., *Evicted: Poverty and profit in the American city*, First Edition, New York, Crown Publishers, 2016, passim; Dunn, E., & Grabchuk, M., "Background checks and social effects: Contemporary residential tenant-screening problems in Washington State", *Seattle Journal for Social Justice*, Volume 9, Issue 1, 2010; Ehman, M., *Fair housing disparate impact claims based on the use of criminal and eviction records in tenant screening policies*, 2015, available at: https://www.nhlp.org/wp-content/uploads/Merf-Ehman-FH-DI-Claims-Based-on-Use-of-Criminal-and-Eviction-Records-Sept.-2015.pdf. (access: 20.12.2024). But see: Evans, Douglas N., "The effect of criminal convictions on real estate agent decisions in New York City", *Journal of Crime and Justice*, Volume 39, n. ° 3, 2016, pp. 363–379 ("*Analyses indicated that a prior conviction was associated with a significant decrease in agent willingness to accept prospective clients, most notably for those with child molestation conviction. Agents were more willing to help prospective* applicants.[1047] Strikingly, the only factor related to tenancy performance is the eviction[1048] history,[1049] which further augment wealth inequalities that beset modern societies.[1050]

---

clients seeking more expensive apartments, although the time of year nullified the effect of cost. The results suggest that agents may be more concerned with the financial status of prospective clients than their criminal history but market forces override their decisions to accept a client. This study has *implications for the ways in which the formerly incarcerated seek housing and how policy can address housing this population*"). Italics added.

1046 *Louis v. Saferent Sols.*, Civil Action 22-CV-10800-AK, 3 (D. Mass. Jul. 26, 2023).

1047 *Louis v. Saferent Sols.*, Civil Action 22-CV-10800-AK, 3 (D. Mass. Jul. 26, 2023) ("*SafeRent designs, markets, and sells a variety of tenant-screening services to landlords, real estate agents, brokerages, and property managers nationwide and in Massachusetts. [Id. at ¶¶ 21–22]. These "self-service tenant screening solutions," as advertised by SafeRent, are intended to help "identify top quality applicants."* [*Id.* at ¶ 22]. *One of these services is the "SafeRent Score," which uses an algorithm to calculate the risk of leasing a property to a particular tenant. [See id. at ¶¶ 24–25]. The SafeRent Score aggregates several factors, including credit history, bankruptcy records, past due accounts, payment performance, and eviction history,* according "to their statistical significance in predicting lease performance," and calculates a numerical rating between two hundred and eight hundred for rental applicants. [*Id.* at ¶¶ 25, 27, 30, 35]. *This score is intended to measure the applicant's "lease performance risk," and applicants with higher scores generally outperform applicants with lower scores. [Id.* at ¶ 28]. The SafeRent Score does not consider the financial benefits of housing vouchers. [*Id.* at ¶¶ 31]"). Italics added.

1048 See: Greenberg, D., Gershenson, C., & Desmond, M., "Discrimination in evictions: Empirical evidence and legal challenges", *Harvard Civil Rights-Civil Liberties Law Review*, Volume 51, 2016; Greif, M., "Regulating landlords: Unintended consequences for poor tenants", *City & Community*, Volume 17, Issue 3, 2018, pp. 658–674; Hartman, C., & Robinson, D., "Evictions: The hidden housing problem", *Housing Policy Debate*, Volume 14, Issue 4, 2003, pp. 461–501; Hatch, M E., "Statutory protection for renters: Classification of state landlord–tenant policy approaches", *Housing Policy Debate*, Volume 27, Issue 1, 2017, pp. 98–119; Haupert, T., "The racial landscape of fintech mortgage lending", *Housing Policy Debate*, Volume 32, Issue 2, 2022 (on the scorching issues arising out of eviction, including, but not limited to, racially biased evictions).

1049 But see: Porton, Adam/Gromis, Ashley/Desmond, Matthew, "Inaccuracies in Eviction Records: Implications for Renters and Researchers", *Housing Policy Debate*, Volume 31, n. ° 3–5, 2021, pp. 377–394 ("*Administrative court records are increasingly used to study the prevalence of eviction. Yet inaccuracies in court records bias estimates of eviction and distort tenants' true rental histories. This is the first study to systematically assess the prevalence of inaccuracies across jurisdictions. Drawing on over 3.6 million administrative eviction court records from 12 states, we find that, on average, 22% of eviction records contain ambiguous information on how the case was resolved or falsely represent a tenant's eviction history.* Adjusting for multiple inaccuracies in the data produces significantly different eviction rate estimates. *Cases with increased complexity, such as those involving multiple tenants and lawyers, are more likely to contain inaccuracies. However, inaccuracies vary most prominently between states, indicating that state court system characteristics fundamentally shape the official record of the evicted population*"). Italics added. See: Part IV, This chapter, Sects. 4.1.4–4.1.4.2.3 of this book. Desmond, M., *Evicted: Poverty and profit in the American city*, First Edition, New York, Crown Publishers, 2016, passim.

1050 *Louis v. Saferent Sols.*, Civil Action 22-CV-10800-AK, 25 (D. Mass. Jul. 26, 2023) ("the fact that credit history is only one piece of SafeRent's formula does not doom Plaintiffs' disparate impact claims at this stage. Plaintiffs allege that the *SafeRent Score relies "in significant part on the applicant's credit score and credit history," in addition to other factors, such as "bankruptcy records, past due accounts, payment performance, and eviction history.*" [Am. Compl. at ¶¶ 35, 45].

§§ *SafeRent Score* subsequently issues a «accept/decline/conditional[1051] decision»[1052] to housing providers (landlords) premised on housing provider's «predetermined decision points».[1053] Housing providers are tasked with the duty to select minimum *SafeRent Score* required for approval of a rental application.[1054] Relatedly, house providers can also establish an agreed-upon range to approve a rental application[1055] «with conditions».[1056]

§§ In spite of the veneer of objectivity under which *SafeRent Score* appears to be wrapped, plaintiffs nonetheless look askance at algorithmic rules that consistently tend downplay the applicant's track record of tenancy-related debt.

§§ More to the point, Black applicants claim that they have been routinely screened out based on a low algorithmic score[1057] for reasons wholly unrelated with their track record of tenancy-related debt.[1058] Strikingly, *SafeRent Score* considers non-tenancy

With the exception of eviction history, all of these factors may contribute to credit history and the wealth inequalities that Plaintiffs allege exist and result in a disparate impact here"). Italics added.

1051 Wonyoung, So, "Which Information Matters? Measuring Landlord Assessment of Tenant Screening Reports", *Housing Policy Debate*, Volume 33, n. ° 6, 2023, pp. 1484–1510 (1502) ("*It is important to note that within conditionally accepted reports, similar patterns of blanket screening policies and automation bias are exhibited when landlords impose security deposits. These results may corroborate a paired-test study that shows that Black tenants have less favorable terms and conditions, including security deposits, in rental agreements* (Ross & Turner, 2005)"). Italics added. See: Part IV, This chapter, Sects. 4.1.4–4.1.4.2.3 of this book.

1052 *Louis v. Saferent Sols.*, Civil Action 22-CV-10800-AK, 3 (D. Mass. Jul. 26, 2023).

1053 *Louis v. Saferent Sols.*, Civil Action 22-CV-10800-AK, 3 (D. Mass. Jul. 26, 2023).

1054 *Louis v. Saferent Sols.*, Civil Action 22-CV-10800-AK, 3 (D. Mass. Jul. 26, 2023).

1055 *Louis v. Saferent Sols.*, Civil Action 22-CV-10800-AK, 3 (D. Mass. Jul. 26, 2023).

1056 *Louis v. Saferent Sols.*, Civil Action 22-CV-10800-AK, 3 (D. Mass. Jul. 26, 2023) ("SafeRent then issues an "accept/decline/conditional decision" to housing providers based on the applicant's SafeRent Score and the specific housing provider's "predetermined decision points." *[Id.* at ¶ 26]. Housing providers select a minimum SafeRent Score required for approval of a rental application, and they can also establish a range to "accept with conditions." *[Id.* at ¶ 39]. SafeRent does not disclose the weight assigned to any of the factors considered in the SafeRent Score, nor does it provide the specific sources of its data. *[Id.* at ¶¶ 34–35]. Housing providers cannot change SafeRent's algorithm. *[Id.* at ¶ 33]. As such, housing providers select the minimum approval score without knowing how scores are calculated. *[Id.* at ¶ 39]"). But see: Wonyoung, So, "Which Information Matters? Measuring Landlord Assessment of Tenant Screening Reports", *Housing Policy Debate*, Volume 33, n. ° 6, 2023, pp. 1484–1510 (1502) ("*It is important to note that within conditionally accepted reports, similar patterns of blanket screening policies and automation bias are exhibited when landlords impose security deposits. These results may corroborate a paired-test study that shows that Black tenants have less favorable terms and conditions, including security deposits, in rental agreements* (Ross & Turner, 2005)"). Italics added. See: Part IV, This chapter, Sects. 4.1.4–4.1.4.2.3 of this book.

1057 Humber, Nadiyah J., "A Home for Digital Equity: Algorithmic Redlining and Property Technology", *California Law Review*, *cit.*, pp. 1421–1484 (1423).

1058 Wonyoung, So, "Which Information Matters? Measuring Landlord Assessment of Tenant Screening Reports", *Housing Policy Debate*, Volume 33, n. ° 6, 2023, pp. 1484–1510 (1502) (arguing that landlords display automation bias as the "*study finds that landlords tend to rely more on the automated system's judgment: when a report noted that a tenant was either medium or high risk, landlords showed a higher tendency toward rejection, or, if conditionally accepted, they imposed*

debts to calculate an algorithmic score, as opposed to the applicant's ability to pay the rent on time while being a «good[1059] tenant».[1060]

§§ In addition to that, insofar *SafeRent Score* does not take into account the financial benefits arising out of housing vouchers,[1061] thousands of Black applicants 'rental applications are automatically shunned as individuals entitled to receive a housing voucher[1062] are those who neatly fall within the breadth and scope of either «extremely low income», «very low income» or «low income».[1063] It is important

---

a higher security deposit. This indicates that tenant screening services' risk scoring may critically affect landlords' decision-making. Given that there is no regulation pertaining to producing and deploying such algorithms, and 1502 W. SO given the inherent inaccuracies of eviction data (Porton et al., 2021) and widespread, serial eviction filings (Garboden & Rosen, 2019), particularly automatic eviction filings activated by digitized property management systems and large, corporate landlords (Fields, 2022; Gomory, 2022; Immergluck et al., 2020), *tenant screening services very likely contribute to perpetuating algorithmic inequality (Eubanks, 2018) by denying qualified applicants—disproportionately from protected groups—access to housing*"). Italics added.

1059 Power, Emma R., and Charles Gillon, "Performing the 'Good Tenant'", *Housing Studies*, Volume 37, Issue 3, 2020, pp. 459–82 (459) ("*Renters in homeowner societies like Australia, the United States and United Kingdom occupy a complex moral landscape, maligned for failure to achieve homeownership but pivotal to the value of investment properties. Identification of 'good' and 'risky' tenants is an important landlord practice.* We investigate how tenants conceptualise and perform the 'good tenant' through research with 36 single older women renting in greater Sydney, Australia: a cohort on the margins of secure housing. *The good tenant demonstrates responsibility through paying rent on time and property stewardship (reporting repairs, making home). However, these practices are made necessary and risky through limited tenure security. The emotional and financial risks attending performances of the good tenant drive paradoxical relations; a good tenant is also acquiescent and silent, not reporting property repairs or lapsed leases to avoid rent increases and/or evictions.* Variegated performances of the '*good tenant' reflect cultural property norms and valorize the investment function of housing yet could also productively unsettle tenant-landlord relations*"). Italics added. See: Part IV, This chapter, Sects. 4.1.4–4.1.4.2.3 of this book.

1060 *Louis v. Saferent Sols.*, Civil Action 22-CV-10800-AK, 4 (D. Mass. Jul. 26, 2023) ("According to Plaintiffs, "the SafeRent Score assigned to an applicant dictates their rental eligibility" and "is calculated based in large part on factors that produce disproportionately lower SafeRent Scores for Black and Hispanic applicants, and those using housing vouchers." *[Id.* at ¶ 41]. *They allege that the SafeRent Score is based "in significant part on the applicant's credit score and credit history, including non-tenancy debts," which are not intended to gauge whether an individual will be a "good tenant."* [*Id.* at ¶¶ 45–46]. *In particular, these credit reviews fail to account accurately for an applicant's ability to pay rent, because they do not consider income and assets in their calculations.* [*Id.* at ¶¶ 47–48]"). But see:

1061 *Louis v. Saferent Sols.*, Civil Action 22-CV-10800-AK, 3 (D. Mass. Jul. 26, 2023) ("*SafeRent designs, markets, and sells a variety of tenant-screening services to landlords, real estate agents, brokerages, and property managers nationwide and in Massachusetts. [Id. at ¶¶ 21–22]. The SafeRent Score does not consider the financial benefits of housing vouchers. [Id. at ¶¶ 31]*"). Italics added.

1062 Wonyoung, So, "Which Information Matters? Measuring Landlord Assessment of Tenant Screening Reports", *Housing Policy Debate*, Volume 33, n. ° 6, 2023, pp. 1484–1510 (1502) ("*One additional finding of the experiment is that algorithmic scoring can exacerbate this racially unequal landscape in rental agreements not just because the algorithm may be inaccurate, but because landlords may want to follow the risk assessment made by the tenant screening report. This is alarming for low-income tenants, particularly housing voucher holders. Security deposits are one of the most significant barriers to obtaining housing for voucher holders, because vouchers do not pay security deposits but most private landlords require them (Rosenblatt & Cossyleon, 2018).* Given that

to note, though, that housing vouchers insulate house providers from the perceived risk of non-payment for properties rented to voucher holders.[1064]

§§ Relatedly, individuals with low income have far lower credit scores[1065] than those high income.[1066] The former (typically, Blacks and Latinos with low incomes) are automatically tagged as ineligible[1067] to rent a house whereas the latter (typically, White folks with high incomes) are automatically tagged as eligible to rent a

voucher holders have exceptionally low income (usually less than 50% of area median income) and might experience more housing insecurity (rental debts and eviction-related experiences), *imposing greater security deposits on voucher holders almost equates to denying them housing—yet these decisions could be justified by algorithmic scoring if tenant screening services employ it*"). Italics added.

[1063] *Louis v. Saferent Sols.*, Civil Action 22-CV-10800-AK, 4 (D. Mass. Jul. 26, 2023) ("individuals receive a housing voucher only if they qualify as "extremely low-income," "very low-income," or "low-income." *[Id.* at ¶ 58]").

[1064] *Louis v. Saferent Sols.*, Civil Action 22-CV-10800-AK, 4 (D. Mass. Jul. 26, 2023) ("*Housing providers who rent to tenants with housing vouchers are guaranteed to receive at least some of their tenants' monthly rental payments, because the local housing authority disburses payment directly to the housing provider. [Id.* at ¶ 65]. *Moreover, voucher holders may also request exemptions from the minimum rent they are required to pay if they experience certain hardships, such as loss of assistance programs, the threat of eviction, decreased income, loss of employment, or a death. [Id. at ¶ 67]. This further insulates housing providers from the risk of non-payment for units rented to voucher holders. [Id.].* As such, credit scores and histories fail to predict whether a rental applicant would make a quality tenant, particularly when housing vouchers are involved. *[See id.* at ¶ 61]"). Italics added.

[1065] It is crucially important to note, though, that the very fact that only certain types of behaviours are assessed and gauged by credit scores leads to the conclusion some borrowers are not scored at all. The overwhelming majority of consumers boast meagre, if any, credit files owing to the fact that the likelihood to access to the sort of financial services that actually report to the orthodox credit bureaus scattered across modern economies is exceedingly low, which, in turn, morphs them into credit invisible persons. See: Yu, Persis/McLaughlin, Jilian/Levy, Marina, "Big Data: A Big Disappointment for Scoring Consumer Creditworthiness,", *The National Consumer Law Center,* 2 (Mar. 14, 2014), available at: https://www.nclc.org/images/pdf/pr-reports/report-big-data.pdf; [https://perma.cc/W4SK-NXD5] (access: 21.12.2024).

[1066] *Louis v. Saferent Sols.*, Civil Action 22-CV-10800-AK, 4 (D. Mass. Jul. 26, 2023) ("Individuals with lower incomes often have lower credit scores than those with higher incomes. *[Id.* at ¶ 59]").

[1067] Wonyoung, So, "Which Information Matters? Measuring Landlord Assessment of Tenant Screening Reports", *Housing Policy Debate*, Volume 33, n.º 6, 2023, pp. 1484–1510 (1502) (arguing that landlords display automation bias as the "*study finds that landlords tend to rely more on the automated system's judgment: when a report noted that a tenant was either medium or high risk, landlords showed a higher tendency toward rejection, or, if conditionally accepted, they imposed a higher security deposit. This indicates that tenant screening services' risk scoring may critically affect landlords' decision-making.* Given that there is no regulation pertaining to producing and deploying such algorithms, and 1502 W. SO given the inherent inaccuracies of eviction data (Porton et al., 2021) and widespread, serial eviction filings (Garboden & Rosen, 2019), particularly automatic eviction filings activated by digitized property management systems and large, corporate landlords (Fields, 2022; Gomory, 2022; Immergluck et al., 2020), *tenant screening services very likely contribute to perpetuating algorithmic inequality (Eubanks, 2018) by denying qualified applicants—disproportionately from protected groups—access to housing*"). Italics added.

house.[1068] This loathsome reality sharply portrays the yawning wealth gap between races, which, as adumbrated,[1069] lends itself to a harsh reality with which members of racialized communities have been grappling for a long-haul.[1070]

§§ To add to their woes, whenever low-income applicants are voucher holders, *RentSafe Score* automatically issues a low credit score,[1071] thereby rendering them both ineligible to rent a house and unfit to be considered good[1072] tenants.[1073]

1068 Wonyoung, So, "Which Information Matters? Measuring Landlord Assessment of Tenant Screening Reports", *Housing Policy Debate*, Volume 33, n. º 6, 2023, pp. 1484–1510 (1502) ("*One additional finding of the experiment is that algorithmic scoring can exacerbate this racially unequal landscape in rental agreements not just because the algorithm may be inaccurate, but because landlords may want to follow the risk assessment made by the tenant screening report. This is alarming for low-income tenants, particularly housing voucher holders. Security deposits are one of the most significant barriers to obtaining housing for voucher holders, because vouchers do not pay security deposits but most private landlords require them (Rosenblatt & Cossyleon, 2018).* Given that voucher holders have exceptionally low income (usually less than 50% of area median income) and might experience more housing insecurity (rental debts and eviction-related experiences), *imposing greater security deposits on voucher holders almost equates to denying them housing—yet these decisions could be justified by algorithmic scoring if tenant screening services employ it*"). Italics added.

1069 See: Part IV, This chapter, Sects. 4.1.4–4.1.4.2.1 of this book (on mortgage redlining). See: Part IV, This chapter, Sects. 4.1.2–4.1.4.3 of this book (on algorithmic credit scoring, consumer racism and credit card redlining). See: Part IV, This chapter, Sects. 4.1.4–4.1.4.2.3 of this book (on algorithmic redlining). See: Part IV, This chapter, Sect. 4.1.4.3 of this book (on "algorithmic redliking").

1070 Derenoncourt, Ellora/Kim, Chi Hyun/Kuhn, Moritz/Schularik, Moritz, "The Wealth of Two Nations: The U.S. Racial Wealth Gap, 1860–2020", *The Quarterly Journal of Economics*, Volume 139, Issue 2, 2024, p. 741 ("*A large class of commonly discussed policies for reducing racial wealth inequality seeks to reduce gaps in income, savings, and capital gains. These include policies that encourage financial diversification or stock equity holdings among Black households*; policies aimed at financial literacy and retirement or savings behavior; or policies aimed at improving educational and labor market outcomes of Black Americans through improved school quality or reductions in discrimination. *Yet on a realistic note, our simulation in Section IV.A shows that even if wealth accumulation conditions had been equal since 1870, the wealth gap would still be 3 to 1 today, and full convergence would be more than 200 years away. Put differently: to close the racial wealth gap in the immediate term* via *flow parameters, Black Americans would need a substantial positive lead over whites, not "just" more equality*"). Italics added.

1071 Wonyoung, So, "Which Information Matters? Measuring Landlord Assessment of Tenant Screening Reports", *Housing Policy Debate*, Volume 33, n. º 6, 2023, pp. 1484–1510 (1502) (arguing that landlords display automation bias as the "*study finds that landlords tend to rely more on the automated system's judgment: when a report noted that a tenant was either medium or high risk, landlords showed a higher tendency toward rejection, or, if conditionally accepted, they imposed a higher security deposit. This indicates that tenant screening services' risk scoring may critically affect landlords' decision-making.* Given that there is no regulation pertaining to producing and deploying such algorithms, and 1502 W. SO given the inherent inaccuracies of eviction data (Porton et al., 2021) and widespread, serial eviction filings (Garboden & Rosen, 2019), particularly automatic eviction filings activated by digitized property management systems and large, corporate landlords (Fields, 2022; Gomory, 2022; Immergluck et al., 2020), *tenant screening services very likely contribute to perpetuating algorithmic inequality (Eubanks, 2018) by denying qualified applicants—disproportionately from protected groups—access to housing*"). Italics added.

§§ To the extent Blacks and Latinos have exceedingly lower incomes than White folks,[1074] their algorithmic credit scores[1075] will be exponentially lower than White

---

[1072] But see: *Tech, Bias and Housing Initiative, the Promise and Perils of Residential Proptech, Year 1, Research Summary Report, April 2023, TechEquity Collaborative*, p. 11, available at: https://techequity.us/wp-content/uploads/2023/04/TBHI-Y1-Research-Summary-Report.pdf (28.11.2024). ("*From information on company websites, it is not clear what analysis or data is behind subjective determinations like "suitability" to a unit or what the nexus between an individual's characteristics and a unit's characteristics is that indicates the likelihood for property damage. Based on sample reports, even landlords are not privy to how the determinations are made. Instead, they receive a risk score out of 100 simplified into green, yellow, and red recommendations.* What companies withhold in terms of how it works, they make up for with the extent to which they tell landlords it works: Naborly claims their predictions reduce lease defaults by up to 89%. 15 *As Naborly's sample report demonstrates, its property damage assessment is then used as an input to determine its projected eviction outcomes; its early vacancy prediction, in turn, is based on "all assessment factors*"). Italics added. See: Part IV, This chapter, Sects. 4.1.4–4.1.4.2.3 of this book.

[1073] *Louis v. Saferent Sols.*, Civil Action 22-CV-10800-AK, 4 (D. Mass. Jul. 26, 2023) ("As such, credit scores and histories fail to predict whether a rental applicant would make a quality tenant, particularly when housing vouchers are involved. *[See id.* at ¶ 61]"). See also: Power, Emma R., and Charles Gillon, "Performing the 'Good Tenant'", *Housing Studies*, 37 (3), 2020, pp. 459–82 ("*Renters in homeowner societies like Australia, the United States and United Kingdom occupy a complex moral landscape, maligned for failure to achieve homeownership but pivotal to the value of investment properties. Identification of 'good' and 'risky' tenants is an important landlord practice.* We investigate how tenants conceptualise and perform the 'good tenant' through research with 36 single older women renting in greater Sydney, Australia: a cohort on the margins of secure housing. *The good tenant demonstrates responsibility through paying rent on time and property stewardship (reporting repairs, making home). However, these practices are made necessary and risky through limited tenure security. The emotional and financial risks attending performances of the good tenant drive paradoxical relations; a good tenant is also acquiescent and silent*, not reporting property repairs or lapsed leases to avoid rent increases and/or evictions. Variegated performances of the '*good tenant' reflect cultural property norms and valorize the investment function of housing yet could also productively unsettle tenant-landlord relations*"). Italics added.

[1074] Kroeger, Teresa, and Graham Wright, "Entrepreneurship and the Racial Wealth Gap: The Impact of Entrepreneurial Success or Failure on the Wealth Mobility of Black and White Families," *Journal of Economics, Race, and Policy*, Volume 4, 2021, 183–195; Kermani, Amir, and Francis Wong, "Racial Disparities in Housing Returns," NBER Working Paper no. 29306, 2021; Hubmer, Joachim, Per Krusell, and Anthony A. Smith, Jr., "Sources of US Wealth Inequality: Past, Present, and Future," *NBER Macroeconomics Annual 2020*, Volume 35, 2021, pp. 391–455; Haines, Michael R., *Historical, Demographic, Economic, and Social Data: The United States, 1790–2002*, Inter-university Consortium for Political and Social Research, 2010.

[1075] It is crucially important to note, though, that the very fact that only certain types of behaviours are assessed and gauged by credit scores leads to the conclusion some borrowers are not scored at all. The overwhelming majority of consumers boast meagre, if any, credit files owing to the fact that the likelihood to access to the sort of financial services that actually report to the orthodox credit bureaus scattered across modern economies is exceedingly low, which, in turn, morphs them into credit invisible persons. See: Yu, Persis/McLaughlin, Jilian/Levy, Marina, "Big Data: A Big Disappointment for Scoring Consumer Creditworthiness,", *The National Consumer Law Center,* 2 (Mar. 14, 2014), available at: https://www.nclc.org/images/pdf/pr-reports/report-big-data.pdf; [https://perma.cc/W4SK-NXD5] (access: 21.12.2024).

folks.[1076] Thus, rendering Blacks and Latinos algorithmically unfit to be considered «good tenants»[1077] with a proven track record of paying the rent on time. As a result, Blacks' and Latinos' rental applications are rejected at a far higher rate than the rental applications filled by White applicants.

§§ For a simple reason: the past credit data factored into credit scoring models skew systematically towards White folks,[1078] further perpetuating racial inequities[1079] which, in turn, historically reflect both fewer economic opportunities[1080] and abridged economic wealth for communities of colour (Blacks and Latinos).[1081]

§§ Crucially, the racial disparities facing Real Estate industry form part of broader social apparatus against the backdrop of which credit scoring models are historically and systemically biased against racialized communities (Blacks and Latinos), which

---

[1076] *Louis v. Saferent Sols.*, Civil Action 22-CV-10800-AK, 5 (D. Mass. Jul. 26, 2023) ("Reliance on conventional credit history disproportionately affects Black and Hispanic tenants, in addition to tenants who hold housing vouchers, because Black and Hispanic consumers have a lower median credit score than White consumers. [*Id.* at ¶¶ 50–51]. As of October 2021, Black consumers had a median credit score of 612 and Hispanic consumers had a median credit score of 661, while White consumers had a median credit score of 725. *[Id.* at ¶ 51]. *Moreover, as of that date, 45.1% of Black consumers and 31.5% of Hispanic consumers had subprime credit scores, while only 18.3% of White consumers had subprime credit scores, which leads to less favorable credit terms. [Id. at ¶ 52]*"). Italics added.

[1077] See: Power, Emma R., and Charles Gillon, "Performing the 'Good Tenant'", *Housing Studies*, Volume 37, Issue 3, 2020, pp. 459–82 (459) ("*Renters in homeowner societies like Australia, the United States and United Kingdom occupy a complex moral landscape, maligned for failure to achieve homeownership but pivotal to the value of investment properties. Identification of 'good' and 'risky' tenants is an important landlord practice.* We investigate how tenants conceptualise and perform the 'good tenant' through research with 36 single older women renting in greater Sydney, Australia: a cohort on the margins of secure housing. *The good tenant demonstrates responsibility through paying rent on time and property stewardship (reporting repairs, making home). However, these practices are made necessary and risky through limited tenure security. The emotional and financial risks attending performances of the good tenant drive paradoxical relations; a good tenant is also acquiescent and silent, not reporting property repairs or lapsed leases to avoid rent increases and/or evictions.* Variegated performances of the '*good tenant' reflect cultural property norms and valorize the investment function of housing yet could also productively unsettle tenant-landlord relations*"). Italics added. See: Part IV, This chapter, Sects. 4.1.4–4.1.4.2.3 of this book. See: Part IV, This chapter, Sects. 4.1.4–4.1.4.2.1 of this book (on mortgage redlining). See: Part IV, This chapter, Sects. 4.1.2–4.1.4.3 of this book (on algorithmic credit scoring, consumer racism and credit card redlining). See: Part IV, This chapter, Sects. 4.1.4–4.1.4.2.3 of this book (on algorithmic redlining). See: Part IV, This chapter, Sect. 4.1.4.3 of this book (on "algorithmic redliking"). See: Part IV, This chapter, Sect. 4.1.3 of this book (on algorithmic prime-lining).

[1078] *Louis v. Saferent Sols.*, Civil Action 22-CV-10800-AK, 5 (D. Mass. Jul. 26, 2023) ("*The past credit data factored into credit scoring models is "systemically and historically biased against non-white consumers.*" [*Id.* at 53]"). Italics added.

[1079] See: Allen, James, "The Color of Algorithms: An Analysis and Proposed Research Agenda Deterring Algorithmic Redlining", *Fordham Urban Law Journal*, Volume 46, 2019, pp. 219–234 (229–234) (discussing how historical mortgage redlining greatly swayed modern algorithms generated by massive batches of datasets that consist of decades of information built on exclusion and racial discrimination in the purview of financing, marketing, and housing). See: Part IV, This chapter, Sects. 4.1.4–4.1.4.2.3 of this book.

further compounds the humongous wealth gap between Whites and non-Whites (Blacks and Latinos).[1082]

§§ The *Court*, in entertaining the civil lawsuit brought by the plaintiffs (*Louis*) against the defendants (*Saferent Sols*), noted that the latter failed to disclose[1083] the weight of each factors underpinning the creation of algorithmic credit score to the former, which was both reproached and upbraided by the *Court*.[1084]

[1080] See: Barocas, Solon/Selbst, Andrew, "Big Data's Disparate Impact", *California Law Review*, Volume 104, pp. 2016, p. 691 (highlighting the worrisome, and gruesome, issue of "structural disadvantage" with which racialized communities have been tussling for centuries). See also: Powell, Richard/Porter, Jeremy, "Redlining, Concentrated Disadvantage and Crime: The Effects of Discriminatory Government Policies on Violent Crime", *American Journal of Criminal Justice*, Volume 48, 2023, pp. 1132–1156 ("*Redlining and other discriminatory government policies enacted during the first half of the Twentieth Century have had long-lasting negative effects on neighborhoods, especially those inhabited by people of color* (...) *The results indicate that redlining was associated with increases in both concentrated disadvantage and violent crime, and that redlining's relationship with violent crime was, indeed, partially mediated by its relationship with concentrated disadvantage*"). Italics added. See also: Gandy, Oscar H., *Coming to Terms with Chance: Engaging Rational Discrimination and Cumulative Disadvantage*, Farnham, UK: Ashgate Publishing, 2009. See: Burk, Dan L., "Algorithmic Fair Use", *University of Chicago Law Review*, Volume 86, 2019, pp. 283–288 (asserts that algorithmic "*fair use carries with it the disadvantage of ex ante uncertainty*; no one can be entirely certain in advance how a court will weigh the four factors, *and hence there is always some apprehension that a use may be found infringing rather than fair*"). Italics added.

[1081] *Louis v. Saferent Sols.*, Civil Action 22-CV-10800-AK, 5 (D. Mass. Jul. 26, 2023) ("*Moreover, as of that date, 45.1% of Black consumers and 31.5% of Hispanic consumers had subprime credit scores, while only 18.3% of White consumers had subprime credit scores, which leads to less favorable credit terms. [Id. at ¶ 52]. These "[r]acial disparities in credit health reflect historical inequities that reduced wealth and limited economic choices for communities of color." [Id.* at ¶ 54]. For example, as of 2017, Black families owned less than seven cents for every dollar in wealth owned by White families, and Latino families owned less than eight cents of every dollar of wealth owned by White families. *[Id.]*"). Italics added.

[1082] *Louis v. Saferent Sols.*, Civil Action 22-CV-10800-AK, 5 (D. Mass. Jul. 26, 2023) ("These racial disparities in credit health further "perpetuate wealth inequalities through reduced financial opportunities and fewer financial safety nets." *[Id.* at ¶ 55 (emphasis omitted)]").

[1083] *Louis v. Saferent Sols.*, Civil Action 22-CV-10800-AK, 28 (D. Mass. Jul. 26, 2023) ("*SafeRent's argument that housing providers, not SafeRent, make the final housing decision fails for the same reasons articulated in the Court's discussion of whether the FHA applies to SafeRent. SafeRent created and provided the tenant-screening process to Metropolitan and other housing providers, marketing its service as a means to "automate human judgement" and refusing to disclose the details of its algorithm or to allow providers to alter any of the factors considered. [See* Am. Compl. at ¶¶ 25, 33–37]. *Thus, at this stage, the relevant policy and the resulting disparate impact can be traced to SafeRent, even if housing providers also play a role*"). Italics added. But see: Marsico, Richard D., "Looking Back and Looking Ahead as the Home Mortgage Disclosure Act Turns Thirty-Five: The Role of Public Disclosure of Lending Data in a Time of Financial Crisis", *Review of Banking and Financial Law*, Volume 29, 2009, pp. 205–206 (argues that a plethora of amendments made in 2002, just like the amendments made in 1989, did not quite obligate lenders to fully disclose the credit score of borrowers and therefore "*hamper[ed] efforts to determine whether higher rates of rejections of loan applications from minority borrowers than whites were due to relatively weaker creditworthiness or race*"). Italics added.

[1084] *Louis v. Saferent Sols.*, Civil Action 22-CV-10800-AK, 27 (D. Mass. Jul. 26, 2023) ("The Court has already noted that Plaintiffs allege that the SafeRent Score "considers applicants' credit

§§ The *Court* further noted that whilst the defendants did not create the long-standing racial and wealth inequalities that beset the United States of America, the former have nonetheless taken advantage of the bigoted computer-run[1085] algorithms[1086] to calculate the equally biased credit scoring[1087] that ultimately snubbed the plaintiffs' rental applications.

---

history" and "other credit-related information, including non-tenancy debts." [Am. Compl. at ¶ 30]. As explained, this "other credit-related information," such as "bankruptcy records, past due accounts, [and] payment performance," contributes to credit history and scores, thereby affecting the SafeRent Score as alleged by the Plaintiffs. *[See id.* at ¶ 35]. *Indeed, as alleged by Plaintiffs, the only factor not related to financial data is eviction history, and even that could be due to non-payment of rent. [See id.]. Plaintiffs' allegations of disparities in credit scores, credit health, debt collection rates, the use of payday and other alternative loan sources, and wealth inequality plausibly encompass many of these factors. [See id. at ¶¶ 51–60].* Because these factors relate to and reinforce one another, and given that Plaintiffs have alleged disparities across the range of factors considered by the SafeRent Score, it is not necessary to know the precise weight assigned to each factor at the pleading stage. *Indeed, it is impossible for Plaintiffs to plead such information, as SafeRent does not disclose the data sources considered or the weights assigned to such data in calculating the SafeRent Score. [Id. at ¶ 34]*").

1085 The theory of "post-race" contends that the great bulk discrimination by the credit card industry is not the byproduct of wilful and flagitious bias. Rather, this discrimination broadly mirrors rational economic decisions to leverage on extant systemic, endemic, and structural social inequalities for profit. See: Carbado, Devon W./Gulati, Mitu, *Acting White? Rethinking Race in Post-Racial America*, Oxford, Oxford University Press, 2015, pp. 1–212 ("What does it mean to "act black" or "act white"? Is race merely a matter of phenotype, or does it come from the inflection of a person's speech, the clothes in her closet, how she chooses to spend her time and with whom she chooses to spend it? What does it mean to be "really" black, and who gets to make that judgment?

In Acting White?, leading scholars of race and the law Devon Carbado and Mitu Gulati argue that, in spite of decades of racial progress and the pervasiveness of multicultural rhetoric, racial judgments are often based not just on skin color, but on how a person conforms to behavior stereotypically associated with a certain race. Specifically, racial minorities are judged on how they "perform" their race. This performance pervades every aspect of their daily life, whether it's the clothes they wear, the way they style their hair, the institutions with which they affiliate, their racial politics, the people they befriend, date or marry, where they live, how they speak, and their outward mannerisms and demeanor. Employing these cues, decision-makers decide not simply whether a person is black but the degree to which she or he is so. Relying on numerous examples from the workplace, higher education, and police interactions, the authors demonstrate that, for African Americans, the costs of "acting black" are high, and so are the pressures to "act white." But, as the authors point out, "acting white" has costs as well"); Howell, Benjamin, "Note, Exploiting Race and Space: Concentrated Subprime Lending as Housing Discrimination", *California Law Review*, Volume 101, 2006, pp. 108–109; Barnes, Mario L., "Reflection on a Dream World: Race, Post-Race and the Question of Making It Over", *Berkely Journal of African-American Law and Policy*, Volume 11, 2009, pp. 6 and ff and passim (parses theories of a "post-racial" world); Haney-López, Ian F., "Essay, Post-Racial Racialism: Racial Stratification and Mass Incarceration in the Age of Obama", *California Law Review*, Volume 98, 2010; Cho, Sumi, "Post-Racialism", *Iowa Law Review*, 2009; Howell, Benjamin, "Note, Exploiting Race and Space: Concentrated Subprime Lending as Housing Discrimination", *California Law Review*, Volume 94, 2006, pp. 101, 108–09; Bhopal, K., *White Privilege: The Myth of a Post-Racial Society*, Bristol, Policy Press Bristol University Press, 2018. Freeman, Andrea, "Racism in the Credit Card Industry", *cit.*, p. 1098 and ff, whose stellar research I have been following closely.

§§ The *Court* has accordingly averred that the past credit data factored into credit scoring models skew systematically towards White folks,[1088] further perpetuating racial inequities. As a result, the *Court* noted that insofar *SafeRent Score* draws on past credit scores[1089] and histories that baked into the computer-run algorithm,[1090] such reliance has a *disparate impact*[1091] on housing opportunities for Black and Hispanic rental applicants and voucher[1092] holders.[1093]

1086 Citron, Danielle Keats/Pasquale, Frank A., "The Scored Society: Due Process for Automated Predictions", *Washington Law Review*, Volume 89, 2014, pp. 1–34 (arguing that "[a]*dvocates applaud the removal of human beings and their flaws from the assessment process*," but arguing that bias remains "[*b]ecause human beings program predictive algorithms, their biases and values are embedded into the software's instructions*"). Italics added. See also: Griffiths, T. L., Chater, N., Kemp, C., Perfors, A., & Tenenbaum, J. B., "Probabilistic models of cognition: Exploring representations and inductive biases", *Trends in Cognitive Sciences*, Volume 14, Issue 8, 2010, pp. 357–364. Gigerenzer, G., "How to explain behavior?", *Topics in Cognitive Science*, Volume 12, Issue 4, 2020, pp. 1363–1381 (on human biases).

1087 *Louis v. Saferent Sols.*, Civil Action 22-CV-10800-AK, 28 (D. Mass. Jul. 26, 2023) ("It *does not matter that Defendants did not create the longstanding inequities in access to wealth and wealth-building mechanisms that have contributed to racial and income disparities in credit scores and histories;*"). Italics added.

1088 *Louis v. Saferent Sols.*, Civil Action 22-CV-10800-AK, 5 (D. Mass. Jul. 26, 2023) ("*The past credit data factored into credit scoring models is "systemically and historically biased against non-white consumers." [Id.* at ¶ 53]"). Italics added.

1089 It is crucially important to note, though, that the very fact that only certain types of behaviours are assessed and gauged by credit scores leads to the conclusion some borrowers are not scored at all. The overwhelming majority of consumers boast meagre, if any, credit files owing to the fact that the likelihood to access to the sort of financial services that actually report to the orthodox credit bureaus scattered across modern economies is exceedingly low, which, in turn, morphs them into credit invisible persons. See: Yu, Persis/McLaughlin, Jilian/Levy, Marina, "Big Data: A Big Disappointment for Scoring Consumer Creditworthiness,", *The National Consumer Law Center,* 2 (Mar. 14, 2014), available at: https://www.nclc.org/images/pdf/pr-reports/report-big-data.pdf; [https://perma.cc/W4SK-NXD5] (access: 21.12.2024).

1090 Citron, Danielle Keats/Pasquale, Frank A., "The Scored Society: Due Process for Automated Predictions", *Washington Law Review*, Volume 89, 2014, pp. 1–34 (arguing that "[a]*dvocates applaud the removal of human beings and their flaws from the assessment process*," but arguing that bias remains "[*b]ecause human beings program predictive algorithms, their biases and values are embedded into the software's instructions*"). Italics added. See also: Griffiths, T. L., Chater, N., Kemp, C., Perfors, A., & Tenenbaum, J. B., "Probabilistic models of cognition: Exploring representations and inductive biases", *Trends in Cognitive Sciences*, Volume 14, Issue 8, 2010, pp. 357–364. Gigerenzer, G., "How to explain behavior?", *Topics in Cognitive Science*, Volume 12, Issue 4, 2020, pp. 1363–1381 (on human biases).

1091 Barocas, Solon/Selbst, Andrew D., "Big Data's Disparate Impact", *California Law Review*, Volume 104, 2016, passim. See: Taylor, Winnie, "Proving Racial Discrimination and Monitoring Fair Lending Compliance: The Missing Data Problem in Nonmortgage Credit", *Review of Banking and Finance Law*, Volume 31, 2011, pp. 199–201 (argues, however, that the task of proving cases based on disparate impact is exceedingly difficult as the banking system routinely refuses to provide the data that underpinned the decision to gainsay a loan to racialized communities).

1092 Wonyoung, So, "Which Information Matters? Measuring Landlord Assessment of Tenant Screening Reports", *Housing Policy Debate*, Volume 33, n. ° 6, 2023, pp. 1484–1510 (1502) ("*One additional finding of the experiment is that algorithmic scoring can exacerbate this racially unequal*

§§ It bears mentioning that the *Court's* stance gives credence to the post-race theories according to which business men routinely take advantage of long-established racial inequities for profit. Casts broadly, this opportunistic type of racial discrimination broadly mirrors rational economic decisions to leverage on extant systemic, endemic, and structural social inequalities for profit.[1094]

---

landscape in rental agreements not just because the algorithm may be inaccurate, but because landlords may want to follow the risk assessment made by the tenant screening report. This is alarming for low-income tenants, particularly housing voucher holders. Security deposits are one of the most significant barriers to obtaining housing for voucher holders, because vouchers do not pay security deposits but most private landlords require them (Rosenblatt & Cossyleon, 2018). Given that voucher holders have exceptionally low income (usually less than 50% of area median income) and might experience more housing insecurity (rental debts and eviction-related experiences), *imposing greater security deposits on voucher holders almost equates to denying them housing—yet these decisions could be justified by algorithmic scoring if tenant screening services employ it*"). Italics added.

[1093] *Louis v. Saferent Sols.*, Civil Action 22-CV-10800-AK, 28 (D. Mass. Jul. 26, 2023) ("*Defendants decided to rely on those inequities when providing and using the SafeRent Score, which includes credit scores and histories in the algorithm, and such reliance, as alleged by Plaintiffs,* has a *disparate impact on housing opportunities for Black and Hispanic applicants and voucher holders.*") Italics added. It is crucially important to note, though, that the very fact that only certain types of behaviours are assessed and gauged by credit scores leads to the conclusion some borrowers are not scored at all. The overwhelming majority of consumers boast meagre, if any, credit files owing to the fact that the likelihood to access to the sort of financial services that actually report to the orthodox credit bureaus scattered across modern economies is exceedingly low, which, in turn, morphs them into credit invisible persons. See: Yu, Persis/McLaughlin, Jilian/Levy, Marina, "Big Data: A Big Disappointment for Scoring Consumer Creditworthiness,", *The National Consumer Law Center*, 2 (Mar. 14, 2014), available at: https://www.nclc.org/images/pdf/pr-reports/report-big-data.pdf; [https://perma.cc/W4SK-NXD5] (access: 21.12.2024).

[1094] The theory of "post-race" contends that the great bulk discrimination by the credit card industry is not the byproduct of wilful and flagitious bias. Rather, this discrimination broadly mirrors rational economic decisions to leverage on extant systemic, endemic, and structural social inequalities for profit. See: Carbado, Devon W./Gulati, Mitu, *Acting White? Rethinking Race in Post-Racial America*, Oxford, Oxford University Press, 2015, pp. 1–212 ("What does it mean to "act black" or "act white"? Is race merely a matter of phenotype, or does it come from the inflection of a person's speech, the clothes in her closet, how she chooses to spend her time and with whom she chooses to spend it? What does it mean to be "really" black, and who gets to make that judgment?

In Acting White?, leading scholars of race and the law Devon Carbado and Mitu Gulati argue that, in spite of decades of racial progress and the pervasiveness of multicultural rhetoric, racial judgments are often based not just on skin color, but on how a person conforms to behavior stereotypically associated with a certain race. Specifically, racial minorities are judged on how they "perform" their race. This performance pervades every aspect of their daily life, whether it's the clothes they wear, the way they style their hair, the institutions with which they affiliate, their racial politics, the people they befriend, date or marry, where they live, how they speak, and their outward mannerisms and demeanor. Employing these cues, decision-makers decide not simply whether a person is black but the degree to which she or he is so. Relying on numerous examples from the workplace, higher education, and police interactions, the authors demonstrate that, for African Americans, the costs of "acting black" are high, and so are the pressures to "act white." But, as the authors point out, "acting white" has costs as well"); Howell, Benjamin, "Note, Exploiting Race and Space: Concentrated Subprime Lending as Housing Discrimination", *California Law Review*, Volume 101, 2006, pp. pp. 108–109; Barnes, Mario L., "Reflection on a Dream World: Race, Post-Race and the Question of Making It Over", *Berkely Journal of African-American Law and Policy*, Volume 11,

§§ Last but not least, *Court* has contended that the defendants 'behaviour, albeit unlawful,[1095] did not fall neatly onto the broad scope concept of unfair,[1096] «immoral, unethical,[1097] oppressive, unscrupulous» that tallies with an egregious[1098] conduct.[1099]

2009, pp. 6 and ff and passim (parses theories of a "post-racial" world); Haney-López, Ian F., "Essay, Post-Racial Racialism: Racial Stratification and Mass Incarceration in the Age of Obama", *California Law Review*, Volume 98, 2010; Cho, Sumi, "Post-Racialism", *Iowa Law Review*, 2009; Howell, Benjamin, "Note, Exploiting Race and Space: Concentrated Subprime Lending as Housing Discrimination", *California Law Review*, Volume 94, 2006, pp. 101, 108–09; Freeman, Andrea, "Racism in the Credit Card Industry", *cit.*, p. 1098 and ff, whose stellar research I have been following closely.

1095 *Louis v. Saferent Sols.*, Civil Action 22-CV-10800-AK, 27 (D. Mass. Jul. 26, 2023) ("The question ultimately comes down to this: Have the Plaintiffs alleged facts demonstrating that the policy at issue-the provision and use of the SafeRent Score, *which relies at least in part on credit history, to evaluate rental applications-causes the alleged disparate impact, that is, a disproportionate denial of rental applications for Black and Hispanic individuals and voucher holders generally*?"). *Louis v. Saferent Sols.*, Civil Action 22-CV-10800-AK, 28 (D. Mass. Jul. 26, 2023) ("While the existence of "other factors" *could* explain the disparate impact alleged, Plaintiffs have pleaded facts sufficient at this phase to support a plausible claim that the Defendants' use of the SafeRent Score, which relies in part on credit history and related factors, disproportionately affects Black and Hispanic applicants and voucher holders generally. It does not matter that Defendants did not create the longstanding inequities in access to wealth and wealth-building mechanisms that have contributed to racial and income disparities in credit scores and histories; *Defendants decided to rely on those inequities when providing and using the SafeRent Score, which includes credit scores and histories in the algorithm, and such reliance, as alleged by Plaintiffs, has a disparate impact on housing opportunities for Black and Hispanic applicants and voucher holders*"). Italics added.

1096 On systemic unfairness from the dispute system design standpoint: Menkel-Meadow, Carrie, "Are There Systemic Ethics Issues in Dispute System Design? And What We Should (Not) Do About it: Lessons from International and Domestic Fronts", *Harvard Negotiation Law Review*, Volume 14, 2009, pp. 199 ff (on the ethical system ethical challenges posed by—and within—dispute system design). The sizzling hot topic of ethics in dispute resolution has also been at the core of this renowned author's foci for quite a while now. See: Menkel-Meadow, Carrie, "The Lawyer as Consensus Builder: Ethics for a New Practice", *Tennessee Law Review*, Volume 63, 2002, pp. 104–109 (contending that the lawyer plays a pivotal role of consensus builder); McGovern, Francis, "Dispute System Design: The United Nations Compensation Commission", *Harvard Negotiation Law Review*, Volume 14, 2009, pp. 169 ff (on dispute system design for tort law disputes); Menkel-Meadow, Carrie, "Process Pluralism in Transitional/Restorative Justice Lessons from Dispute Resolution for Cultural Variations in Goals beyond Rule of Law and Democracy Development (Argentina and Chile)", *University of California, Irvine, School of Law, Georgetown Law Center, Legal Studies Research Paper Series* N.º 2015–86, 2015, p. 5 (arguing that there is an unfathomable «human necessity to move forward and grasp for what is good in humanity»); Menkel-Meadow, Carrie, "In the Land of Blood and Honey: What's Fair or Just in Love and War Crimes?" *Lessons for Transitional Justice, Framing Law and Crime: An Interdisciplinary Anthology*, Caroline Joan S. Picart/ Michael Hviid Jacobsen/Cecil Greek (Eds.), Law, Culture, and the Humanities Series, Madison, New Jersey, Vancouver, British Columbia, Fairleigh Dickinson University Press, 2016, pp. 1–538 (*passim*) (on transitional justice in countries ravaged by wars); Schneider, Andrea, "The Intersection of Dispute Systems Design and Transitional Justice", *Harvard Negotiation Law Review*, Volume 14, 2009, pp. 288 ff (on the importance of dispute system design in the remit of transitional justice); Menkel-Meadow, Carrie, "The Lawyer's Role'(s) in Deliberative Democracy", *Nevada Law Journal*, Volume 5, 2004–2005, pp. 346 ff (on the lawyer's role amidst the crave of vying groups to achieve acceptable political outcomes in the purview of «deliberative democracy»); Menkel-Meadow, Carrie, "Are There Systemic Ethics Issues in Dispute System Design? And What

§§ The crux of the legal quagmires (*Mary Louis*, *Monica Douglas*, and *Carmen Arroyo*) boils down to the ease with which human biases[1100]—borne out by centuries of racial discrimination that still ripples forward—are baked into computer-run machine learning[1101] algorithms[1102] in the remit of Real Estate industry.[1103]

We Should (Not) Do About it: Lessons from International and Domestic Fronts", *cit.*: 231 (arguing that «we can only learn about what those ethical limits are or should be»). But see: Bingham, Lisa B., "Reflections on Designing Governance to Produce the Rule of Law, "*Journal of Dispute Resolution*, Volume 1, Issue 5, 2011, pp. 67 ff (adducing to the need of take heed of contexts upon framing a dispute system design by stating that «while the designs of these systems vary widely, research on why systems take certain designs in certain substantive and institutional contexts, and which designs are most effective, is still in its infancy»).

[1097] But see: Wonyoung, So, "Which Information Matters? Measuring Landlord Assessment of Tenant Screening Reports", *Housing Policy Debate*, Volume 33, n. ° 6, 2023, pp. 1484–1510 (1502) ("*One additional finding of the experiment is that algorithmic scoring can exacerbate this racially unequal landscape in rental agreements not just because the algorithm may be inaccurate, but because landlords may want to follow the risk assessment made by the tenant screening report. This is alarming for low-income tenants, particularly housing voucher holders. Security deposits are one of the most significant barriers to obtaining housing for voucher holders, because vouchers do not pay security deposits but most private landlords require them (Rosenblatt & Cossyleon, 2018).* Given that voucher holders have exceptionally low income (usually less than 50% of area median income) and might experience more housing insecurity (rental debts and eviction-related experiences), *imposing greater security deposits on voucher holders almost equates to denying them housing—yet these decisions could be justified by algorithmic scoring if tenant screening services employ it*"). Italics added.

[1098] In German doctrine: Hagemann, Mathias, *Injuria—Von den XII Tafeln bis zur Justinianischen Kodifikation*, Berlin, Walter de Gruyter, 1998, *passim* (on the subset of delicts that derive from the broad concept of *injuria*, such as the *contumelia*); Mayer-Maly, Theo, "Contra bonos mores", *Juris Professio—Festgabe für Max Kaser,* Wien, Hermann Böhlau, 1986, *passim* (on the importance of *contra bonos mores* delicts).

[1099] *Louis v. Saferent Sols.*, Civil Action 22-CV-10800-AK, 30 (D. Mass. Jul. 26, 2023) ("Plaintiffs do not dispute that HUD allows, in certain circumstances, housing providers to consider credit history when screening applicants and to reject an applicant for poor credit history, which could support a finding that SafeRent's actions are protected by Sect. 3.1 *See* Dep't of Housing & Urban Dev., HUD Handbook 4350.3: Occupancy Requirements of Subsidized Multifamily Housing Programs, at 4–23, § 4–7(F) (Nov. 2013). Instead, Plaintiffs argue that "[j]ust because an act or practice may be authorized by statute or regulation does not mean that it 'can never be an unfair or deceptive act or practice' as applied." [Dkt. 36 at 26 (citing *Schubach v. Household Fin. Corp., 376 N.E.2d 140, 142* (Mass. 1978))]. This is true. *See Tomasella v. Nestle USA, Inc., 962 F.3d 60, 79* (1st Cir. 2020) ("*Under this rubric, the legality of the challenged act or practice is not dispositive of its unfairness"). However, Plaintiffs have not alleged facts to suggest that SafeRent, in creating and providing the SafeRent Score to housing providers, acted in an immoral, unethical, oppressive, or unscrupulous manner such that its conduct was of an egregious nature sufficient to raise a plausible claim of unfairness under Chapter 93A*"). Italics added.

[1100] Citron, Danielle Keats/Pasquale, Frank A., "The Scored Society: Due Process for Automated Predictions", *Washington Law Review*, Volume 89, 2014, pp. 1–34 (arguing that "[a]*dvocates applaud the removal of human beings and their flaws from the assessment process*," but arguing that bias remains "[*b]ecause human beings program predictive algorithms, their biases and values are embedded into the software's instructions*"). Italics added.

[1101] See: Murphy, Kevin P., *Machine Learning: A Probabilistic Perspective (Adaptive Computation and Machine Learning series).* Massachusetts: The MIT Press, 2012, pp. 1–1104 (states avowedly that "machine Learning attempts to combine deductive, inductive, and abductive reasoning to make

§§ A key takeaway jumps out as ripe: as *Louis* has abundantly shown, warped—or doctored—algorithms impair a much-need procedural justice for Blacks and Latinos amidst the age of Artificial Intelligence-embedded technologies.[1104] Especially, albeit not exclusively, with regards to voucher holders (typically, low income applicants), whom are disproportionately affected[1105] by bigoted algorithmic risk[1106] assessment.[1107]

---

person-like reasoning in AI Entities possible. Machine-learning AI Entities initially learn in the same way a human child learns. First, they notice details and patterns in shapes, sounds, and behaviors; then put them together to distinguish one person from another, or a dog from a cat. Eventually, the AI can recognize and identify" common objects). See also: Hutto-Schultz, Jess, "Dicitur Ex Machina: Artificial Intelligence and the Hearsay Rule", *George Mason Law Review*, Volume 27, Issue 2, 2020, pp. 684–718 (689). See: Chollet, François, *Deep Learning with Python*. Shelter Island, Nova Iorque: Manning, 2018, pp. 1–384 (passim). *Deep Learning* stands as a byproduct of *Machine Learning*. *Machine Learning*, a subset of Artificial Intelligence, unfolds itself in *Deep Learning*, which "involves computer algorithms that have the ability to "learn" or improve in performance over time on some task". See: Surden, Harry, "Machine Learning and Law", *Washington Law Review*, Volume 89, 2015, pp. 87 and ff.

1102 Corbett-Davies, Sam/Goel, Sharad, "The Measure and Mismeasure of Fairness: a critical Review of Fair Machine Learning", *Cornell University Library*, 2018, pp. 3 and ff and passim (undertake laudable efforts to debunk algorithm biases that primarily target ethnic minorities, such as Hispanics and coloured people). Jackson, Maya C., "Artificial Intelligence and Algorithmic Bias: The Issues with Technology Reflecting History and Humans", *Journal of Business Technology Law*, Volume 16, 2021, pp. 299–316; West, Sarah Myers/Whittaker, Meredith/Crawford, Kate, *Discriminating Systems. Gender, Race and Power in AI*. New York: AI Now Institute, 2019, passim; McAfee, Andrew/Brynjolfsson, *Machine, Platform, Crowd: Harnessing our Digital Future*, London: Brilliance Audio; Unabridged edition, 2017 (pore over a myriad of automatic biases displayed by artificial intelligence).

1103 Havard, Cassandra Jones, "On The Take": The Black Box of Credit Scoring and Mortgage Discrimination", *Boston University Public Interest Law Journal*, Volume 20, 2011, pp. 241–247 (highlighting that credit scoring, if left unchecked, is an intrinsic, encroached, deep-rooted form of racial discrimination akin to mortgage redlining).

1104 From the social psychology, warped algorithms accomplish nothing but the impairment of procedural justice. See: Thibaut, John/ Walker, Laurens, *Procedural Justice: A Psychological Analysis*. Hillsdale, N.J.: Lawrence Erlbaum Associates, 1975, pp. 1–150 (procedural justice is tightly interlocked to raising the levels of fairness in criminal procedure law settings. Absent of which procedural fairness is to mar. Criminal procedure law must not lose sight of such assertion). Converging: Lind, Edgar Allan/Tyler, Tom R., *The Social Psychology of Procedural Justice*. New York: Springer, 1988, pp. 208 ff (emphasizing that perceptions of justice being justly and correctly served enhances exponentially citizens' perception of provider legitimacy). Tyler, Tom R., "The Psychology of Procedural Justice: A Test of the Group-Value Model", *Journal of Personality and Social Psychology*, Volume 57, 1989, p. 830 (reports that in any procedure "several non-control issues – the *neutrality* of the decision-making procedure, trust in the 3rd party, and the information the experience communicates about social standing – influence both procedural preferences and judgments of procedural justice"). See also: Simmons, Ric, "Big Data and Procedural Justice: Legitimizing Algorithms in the Criminal Justice System", *Ohio State Journal of Criminal Law*, Volume 15, 2018, pp. 576 and ff and passim.

§§ Relatedly, *Connecticut Fair Housing Center* brought a lawsuit on behalf of Carmen Arroyo in *Connecticut Fair Housing Center v. CoreLogic Rental Property Solutions.*[1108]

§§ Originally filed on April 24, 2018 with the United States of America District Court, District of Connecticut, the lawsuit adamantly contends that *CoreLogic's* automated tenant screening software tool ("*CrimSAFE*") gainsaid Carmen Arroyo's request to move her disabled son into her rental property based on a criminal

---

[1105] In spite of its deep-seated racial bias, decision-makers continue to deploy redlining tactics through big data and may even justify such unlawful practices by claiming that the latter abide by cost-effectiveness. See: Humber, Nadiyah J., "A Home for Digital Equity: Algorithmic Redlining and Property Technology", *California Law Review*, Volume 111, Issue 5, 2023, pp. 1421–1484. Allen, James, "The Color of Algorithms: An Analysis and Proposed Research Agenda Deterring Algorithmic Redlining", *Fordham Urban Law Journal*, Volume 46, 2019, pp. 219–234 (229–234) (discussing how historical mortgage redlining greatly swayed modern algorithms generated by massive batches of data sets that consist of decades of information built on exclusion and racial discrimination in the purview of financing, marketing, and housing). See: Part IV, This chapter, Sects. 4.1.4–4.1.4.2.3 of this book. See: Part IV, This chapter, Sects. 4.1.4–4.1.4.2.1 of this book (on mortgage redlining). See: Part IV, This chapter, Sects. 4.1.2–4.1.4.3 of this book (on algorithmic credit scoring, consumer racism and credit card redlining). See: Part IV, This chapter, Sects. 4.1.4–4.1.4.2.3 of this book (on algorithmic redlining). See: Part IV, This chapter, Sect. 4.1.4.3 of this book (on "algorithmic redliking"). See: Part IV, This chapter, Sect. 4.1.3 of this book (on algorithmic prime-lining).

[1106] See: Allen, James, "The Color of Algorithms: An Analysis and Proposed Research Agenda Deterring Algorithmic Redlining", *Fordham Urban Law Journal*, Volume 46, 2019, pp. 219–234 (229–234) (discussing how historical mortgage redlining greatly swayed modern algorithms generated by massive batches of datasets that consist of decades of information built on exclusion and racial discrimination in the purview of financing, marketing, and housing). See: Part IV, This chapter, Sects. 4.1.4–4.1.4.2.3 of this book.

[1107] Wonyoung, So, "Which Information Matters? Measuring Landlord Assessment of Tenant Screening Reports", *Housing Policy Debate*, Volume 33, n. ° 6, 2023, pp. 1484–1510 (1502) ("*One additional finding of the experiment is that algorithmic scoring can exacerbate this racially unequal landscape in rental agreements not just because the algorithm may be inaccurate, but because landlords may want to follow the risk assessment made by the tenant screening report. This is alarming for low-income tenants, particularly housing voucher holders. Security deposits are one of the most significant barriers to obtaining housing for voucher holders, because vouchers do not pay security deposits but most private landlords require them (Rosenblatt & Cossyleon, 2018).* Given that voucher holders have exceptionally low income (usually less than 50% of area median income) and might experience more housing insecurity (rental debts and eviction-related experiences), *imposing greater security deposits on voucher holders almost equates to denying them housing—yet these decisions could be justified by algorithmic scoring if tenant screening services employ it*"). Italics added.

[1108] *Connecticut Fair Housing Center,* et al. *v. CoreLogic Rental Property Solutions,* Case No. 3:18-cv-00705, U.S. District Court for the District of Connecticut, available: https://www.cohenmilstein.com/case-study/connecticut-fair-housing-center-et-al-v-corelogic-rental-property-solutions/ (access: 22.11.2024).

record[1109] of a dismissed shoplifting arrest from 2014,[1110] way before he became disabled.[1111]

§§ Carmen Arroyo, whose son Mikhail was severely injured in a July 2015 unfortunate event (a lamentable accident) that left him unable to speak, walk, or care for himself, is her son's conservator.[1112] After becoming his caretaker, Carmen Arroyo formally approached her landlord for permission to move Mikhail into her home

---

1109 But see: Wonyoung, So, "Which Information Matters? Measuring Landlord Assessment of Tenant Screening Reports", *Housing Policy Debate*, Volume 33, n. ° 6, 2023, pp. 1484–1510 (1501–1502) ("*Algorithmic scoring using criminal records is problematic because training data—a data set that is used to train a machine learning model—is inaccurate and the outcome variable ("desirable tenants") is unclear. For instance, the tenant screening company RealPage produces 11,000 reports using "abbreviated" criminal records, which are cheaper to acquire than full criminal records but do not include details of the resolution* (Kirchner & Goldstein, 2020). *An inaccurate model is highly likely to result from tenant screening services using these kinds of abbreviated data, given that it is important to include the final resolution of criminal justice procedures for proper assessment. Moreover, it would be challenging to set an outcome variable for developing this kind of algorithm because it is hard to project a certain criminal outcome into "good" tenant behaviors*"). Italics added.

Citron, Danielle Keats/Pasquale, Frank A., "The Scored Society: Due Process for Automated Predictions", *Washington Law Review*, Volume 89, 2014, pp. 1–34 (arguing that "[a]*dvocates applaud the removal of human beings and their flaws from the assessment process,*" but arguing that bias remains "[*b]ecause human beings program predictive algorithms, their biases and values are embedded into the software's instructions*"). Italics added.

1110 Wonyoung, So, "Which Information Matters? Measuring Landlord Assessment of Tenant Screening Reports", *Housing Policy Debate*, Volume 33, n. ° 6, 2023, pp. 1484–1510 (1501–1502) ("*There are considerations and implications involved in the assessment of criminal records. First, this study shows that MTurk landlords may differentiate serious types of crimes (e.g., sex offenders) from less serious ones (e.g., shoplifting) and/or may differentiate according to the disposition. In contrast, the prior section described how MTurk landlords treat filings and executed evictions similarly.* These differences *might suggest that landlords are less familiar with how evictions are executed than with how criminal justice procedure works (e.g., charge under criminal procedure and conviction/acquittal), because eviction records are a specific type of civil procedure—landlord–tenant disputes.* However, in the mid-scored reports, there is statistical evidence that showing the report's risk score (Type 2) caused MTurk landlords to deny tenant applications more frequently, whereas there is no statistical evidence that having detailed information in the report (Type 3) caused MTurk landlords to do the same. *This result indicates a need for further research and policy formulation on algorithmic scoring of tenant records (Smith & Voguell, 2022), with a specific focus on how landlords construct proxies of desirable tenants through two perspectives from this study: (a) the difficulties of assessing mid-scored criminal records (e.g., arrest records and misdemeanors) and, therefore, (b) reinforcing landlords' potential reliance on algorithmic decisions provided by reports*"). Italics added. See: Part IV, This chapter, Sects. 4.1.4–4.1.4.2.3 of this book.

1111 *Connecticut Fair Housing Center,* et al. *v. CoreLogic Rental Property Solutions,* Case No. 3:18-cv-00705, U.S. District Court for the District of Connecticut, available: https://www.cohenmilstein.com/case-study/connecticut-fair-housing-center-et-al-v-corelogic-rental-property-solutions/ (access: 22.11.2024).

1112 *Connecticut Fair Housing Center,* et al. *v. CoreLogic Rental Property Solutions,* Case No. 3:18-cv-00705, U.S. District Court for the District of Connecticut, available: https://www.cohenmilstein.com/case-study/connecticut-fair-housing-center-et-al-v-corelogic-rental-property-solutions/ (access: 22.11.2024).

and out of the nursing home where he was recovering for a long-haul.[1113] She has accordingly submitted a rental application on her son's behalf.[1114] But, much to her dismay, to no avail.[1115] *CoreLogic's «CrimSAFE»* background check[1116] asserted that Mikhail had a «disqualifying [criminal] record».[1117]

§§ Carmen Arroyo claimed that *CoreLogic's* criminal background[1118] report has failed to provide the landlord with any further details about Mikhail's underlying criminal record[1119] and criminal history—only a computer-generated score stating that her rental application fell short of matching the landlord's[1120] criteria.[1121]

[1113] *Connecticut Fair Housing Center,* et al. *v. CoreLogic Rental Property Solutions,* Case No. 3:18-cv-00705, U.S. District Court for the District of Connecticut, available: https://www.cohenmilstein.com/case-study/connecticut-fair-housing-center-et-al-v-corelogic-rental-property-solutions/ (access: 22.11.2024).

[1114] *Connecticut Fair Housing Center,* et al. *v. CoreLogic Rental Property Solutions,* Case No. 3:18-cv-00705, U.S. District Court for the District of Connecticut, available: https://www.cohenmilstein.com/case-study/connecticut-fair-housing-center-et-al-v-corelogic-rental-property-solutions/ (access: 22.11.2024).

[1115] *Connecticut Fair Housing Center,* et al. *v. CoreLogic Rental Property Solutions,* Case No. 3:18-cv-00705, U.S. District Court for the District of Connecticut, available: https://www.cohenmilstein.com/case-study/connecticut-fair-housing-center-et-al-v-corelogic-rental-property-solutions/ (access: 22.11.2024).

[1116] Dunn, E., & Grabchuk, M., "Background checks and social effects: Contemporary residential tenant-screening problems in Washington State", *Seattle Journal for Social Justice*, Volume 9, Issue 1, 2010; Ehman, M., *Fair housing disparate impact claims based on the use of criminal and eviction records in tenant screening policies*, 2015, available at: https://www.nhlp.org/wp-content/uploads/Merf-Ehman-FH-DI-Claims-Based-on-Use-of-Criminal-and-Eviction-Records-Sept.-2015.pdf.

[1117] *Connecticut Fair Housing Center,* et al. *v. CoreLogic Rental Property Solutions,* Case No. 3:18-cv-00705, U.S. District Court for the District of Connecticut, available: https://www.cohenmilstein.com/case-study/connecticut-fair-housing-center-et-al-v-corelogic-rental-property-solutions/ (access: 22.11.2024).

[1118] But see: Evans, Douglas N., "The effect of criminal convictions on real estate agent decisions in New York City", *Journal of Crime and Justice*, Volume 39, n. ° 3, 2016, pp. 363–379 ("*Analyses indicated that a prior conviction was associated with a significant decrease in agent willingness to accept prospective clients, most notably for those with child molestation conviction. Agents were more willing to help prospective clients seeking more expensive apartments, although the time of year nullified the effect of cost. The results suggest that agents may be more concerned with the financial status of prospective clients than their criminal history but market forces override their decisions to accept a client*. This study has implications for the ways in which the formerly incarcerated seek housing and how policy can address housing this population"). Italics added.

[1119] Wonyoung, So, "Which Information Matters? Measuring Landlord Assessment of Tenant Screening Reports", *Housing Policy Debate*, Volume 33, n. ° 6, 2023, pp. 1484–1510 (1484) ("*This research studies how tenant screening services' presentation of information influences landlord decisions. Tenant screening services utilize criminal records, eviction records, and credit score databases to produce reports that landlords use to inform their decisions about who to rent to. However, little is known about how landlords assess the information presented by tenant screening reports. Through a behavioral experiment with landlords using simulated tenant screening reports, this study shows that landlords use blanket screening policies, that they conflate the existence of tenant records with outcomes (e.g., eviction filings with executed evictions), and that they display, on average, tendencies toward automation bias that are influenced by the risk assessments and scores presented by tenant screening reports.* I argue that maintaining blanket screening policies and automation bias, combined with the downstream effects of creating and *using racially biased*

§§ Carmen Arroyo further posited that *CoreLogic* refused to give her with a copy of the information it relied on to make the computer-generated screening decision, information which she was fully entitled to receive in light of federal law, as she was her son's caretaker.[1122] Because *CoreLogic* refused to acknowledge Ms. Arroyo's authority as caretaker for her son,[1123] she contended that *CoreLogic* also breached its legal duty to provide a reasonable accommodation to her disabled son.[1124]

§§ Carmen Arroyo later found out that her son's only criminal record was a criminal charge—from before his unfortunate accident, and later dropped—for

---

eviction and criminal records, means that people of color will inevitably experience disproportionate exclusion from rental housing due to perceived "risk" on the part of landlords"). Italics added. See: Part IV, This chapter, Sects. 4.1.4–4.1.4.2.3 of this book. See: Part IV, This chapter, Sects. 4.1.4–4.1.4.2.1 of this book (on mortgage redlining). See: Part IV, This chapter, Sects. 4.1.2–4.1.4.3 of this book (on algorithmic credit scoring, consumer racism and credit card redlining). See: Part IV, This chapter, Sects. 4.1.4–4.1.4.2.3 of this book (on algorithmic redlining). See: Part IV, This chapter, Sect. 4.1.4.3 of this book (on "algorithmic redliking"). See: Part IV, This chapter, Sect. 4.1.3 of this book (on algorithmic prime-lining).

[1120] But see: Wonyoung, So, "Which Information Matters? Measuring Landlord Assessment of Tenant Screening Reports", *Housing Policy Debate*, Volume 33, n. ° 6, 2023, pp. 1484–1510 (1501–1502) ("*In mid-scored criminal records, landlords would have more discretion in terms of how to assess tenants, depending on the type of charges or the disposition of the case. HUD prohibits denying housing by holding arrest records against tenants. But apart from that, landlords who HOUSING POLICY DEBATE 1501 would like to construct proxies of undesirable tenants using criminal records must assess which criminal records would relate to tenants' behavior (e.g., damaging their property and/or adversely affecting other tenants).* However, it is incredibly challenging to identify the causal relationship between how and which past misdemeanors cause particular future tenant behaviors. Moreover, legal jargon and abbreviations on the report could make it harder for landlords to understand criminal records in the first place. *These factors, as a result, could contribute to landlords' reliance on the scores provided by the report shown in the experiment*"). See: Part IV, This chapter, Sects. 4.1.4–4.1.4.2.3 of this book. See: Part IV, This chapter, Sects. 4.1.4–4.1.4.2.1 of this book (on mortgage redlining). See: Part IV, This chapter, Sects. 4.1.2–4.1.4.3 of this book (on algorithmic credit scoring, consumer racism and credit card redlining). See: Part IV, This chapter, Sects. 4.1.4–4.1.4.2.3 of this book (on algorithmic redlining). See: Part IV, This chapter, Sect. 4.1.4.3 of this book (on "algorithmic redliking"). See: Part IV, This chapter, Sect. 4.1.3 of this book (on algorithmic prime-lining).

[1121] *Connecticut Fair Housing Center,* et al. *v. CoreLogic Rental Property Solutions,* Case No. 3:18-cv-00705, U.S. District Court for the District of Connecticut, available: https://www.cohenmilstein.com/case-study/connecticut-fair-housing-center-et-al-v-corelogic-rental-property-solutions/ (access: 22.11.2024).

[1122] *Connecticut Fair Housing Center,* et al. *v. CoreLogic Rental Property Solutions,* Case No. 3:18-cv-00705, U.S. District Court for the District of Connecticut, available: https://www.cohenmilstein.com/case-study/connecticut-fair-housing-center-et-al-v-corelogic-rental-property-solutions/ (access: 22.11.2024).

[1123] *Connecticut Fair Housing Center,* et al. *v. CoreLogic Rental Property Solutions,* Case No. 3:18-cv-00705, U.S. District Court for the District of Connecticut, available: https://www.cohenmilstein.com/case-study/connecticut-fair-housing-center-et-al-v-corelogic-rental-property-solutions/ (access: 22.11.2024).

[1124] *Connecticut Fair Housing Center,* et al. *v. CoreLogic Rental Property Solutions,* Case No. 3:18-cv-00705, U.S. District Court for the District of Connecticut, available: https://www.cohenmilstein.com/case-study/connecticut-fair-housing-center-et-al-v-corelogic-rental-property-solutions/ (access: 22.11.2024).

shoplifting, a criminal misdeed below the threshold of a misdemeanour.[1125] Absent this important piece of information, Carmen Arroyo could not adroitly challenge Mikhail's refusal, and neither *CoreLogic* nor the landlord/house provider made the sort of individualized appraisal that HUD states is required.[1126] As a result, he stayed in a nursing home for roughly a year longer than absolute necessary.[1127]

§§ Fast forward to the pith of the lawsuit, on March 25, 2019, the U.S. District Court, District of Connecticut denied *CoreLogic's* motion to dismiss the lawsuit brought by Arroyo,[1128] asserting that because *CoreLogic* «held itself out as a company with the knowledge and ingenuity to screen housing applicants by interpreting criminal records and specifically advertised its ability to improve «Fair Housing compliance,»[1129] it could be held liable for infringements of the *Fair Housing Act*[1130] accordingly. As computer-generated decisions by third-party screening corporations are swiftly becoming the norm, this ruling bears on landlords, renters, bankers, real estate agents and the entire screening industry.[1131]

§§ On August 7, 2020, the U.S. District Court, District of Connecticut rebuffed *CoreLogic's* motion for summary judgment regarding Plaintiffs' standing and Plaintiffs' claims of race and national origin discrimination in egregious breach of the *Fair Housing Act*.[1132] First, the Court stated that both Carmen Arroyo and the Connecticut

---

[1125] *Connecticut Fair Housing Center,* et al. *v. CoreLogic Rental Property Solutions,* Case No. 3:18-cv-00705, U.S. District Court for the District of Connecticut, available: https://www.cohenmilstein.com/case-study/connecticut-fair-housing-center-et-al-v-corelogic-rental-property-solutions/ (access: 22.11.2024).

[1126] *Connecticut Fair Housing Center,* et al. *v. CoreLogic Rental Property Solutions,* Case No. 3:18-cv-00705, U.S. District Court for the District of Connecticut, available: https://www.cohenmilstein.com/case-study/connecticut-fair-housing-center-et-al-v-corelogic-rental-property-solutions/ (access: 22.11.2024).

[1127] *Connecticut Fair Housing Center,* et al. *v. CoreLogic Rental Property Solutions,* Case No. 3:18-cv-00705, U.S. District Court for the District of Connecticut, available: https://www.cohenmilstein.com/case-study/connecticut-fair-housing-center-et-al-v-corelogic-rental-property-solutions/ (access: 22.11.2024).

[1128] *Connecticut Fair Housing Center,* et al. *v. CoreLogic Rental Property Solutions,* Case No. 3:18-cv-00705, U.S. District Court for the District of Connecticut, available: https://www.cohenmilstein.com/case-study/connecticut-fair-housing-center-et-al-v-corelogic-rental-property-solutions/ (access: 22.11.2024).

[1129] *Connecticut Fair Housing Center,* et al. *v. CoreLogic Rental Property Solutions,* Case No. 3:18-cv-00705, U.S. District Court for the District of Connecticut, available: https://www.cohenmilstein.com/case-study/connecticut-fair-housing-center-et-al-v-corelogic-rental-property-solutions/ (access: 22.11.2024).

[1130] *Connecticut Fair Housing Center,* et al. *v. CoreLogic Rental Property Solutions,* Case No. 3:18-cv-00705, U.S. District Court for the District of Connecticut, available: https://www.cohenmilstein.com/case-study/connecticut-fair-housing-center-et-al-v-corelogic-rental-property-solutions/ (access: 22.11.2024).

[1131] *Connecticut Fair Housing Center,* et al. *v. CoreLogic Rental Property Solutions,* Case No. 3:18-cv-00705, U.S. District Court for the District of Connecticut, available: https://www.cohenmilstein.com/case-study/connecticut-fair-housing-center-et-al-v-corelogic-rental-property-solutions/ (access: 22.11.2024).

[1132] *Connecticut Fair Housing Center,* et al. *v. CoreLogic Rental Property Solutions,* Case No. 3:18-cv-00705, U.S. District Court for the District of Connecticut, available: https://www.coh

Fair Housing Center have standing to sue under the *Fair Housing Act*[1133] and the *Connecticut Unfair Trade Practices Act.*[1134]

§§ Next, the Court held that Plaintiffs had brought forth enough statistical evidence premised on national and state data to put into dispute whether *CoreLogic's* criminal background reporting system has a *disparate impact*[1135] on Blacks and Latinos, holding that «disparities[1136] adverse to African Americans and Latinos and in favour

enmilstein.com/case-study/connecticut-fair-housing-center-et-al-v-corelogic-rental-property-solutions/ (access: 22.11.2024).

1133 Massey, Douglas S., "The Legacy of the 1968 Fair Housing Act", *Social Forces*, Volume 30, 2015, pp. 571, 575–76, 578 ("[*The FHA] outlawed the refusal to rent or sell to someone because of race; it prohibited racial discrimination in the terms and conditions of rental or sale; it barred discrimination in real estate advertising; it banned agents from making untrue statements about a dwelling's availability in order to deny access to blacks*; and it enjoined real estate agents from making comments about the race of neighbors or in-movers in order to promote panic selling. Although the new law applied only to around 80% of the nation's housing stock, a Supreme Court decision adjudicated just two months later extended its reach to all housing in the United States"). Firestone, Simon, "Race Ethnicity and Credit Card Monitoring", *Journal of Money, Credit and Banking*, Sept. 2014, 2014, pp. 1206 and ff; Han, Song, Keys, Benjamin J./Li, Geng, *Unsecured Credit Supply over the Credit Cycle: Evidence from Credit Card Mailings* (argue that, statistically, Blacks and Latinos are seldom granted credit and, if ever granted credit, the terms and conditions attached to the concession of credit are not equal to those offered to White folks).

1134 *Connecticut Fair Housing Center,* et al. *v. CoreLogic Rental Property Solutions,* Case No. 3:18-cv-00705, U.S. District Court for the District of Connecticut, available: https://www.cohenmilstein.com/case-study/connecticut-fair-housing-center-et-al-v-corelogic-rental-property-solutions/ (access: 22.11.2024).

1135 Barocas, Solon/Selbst, Andrew D., "Big Data's Disparate Impact", *California Law Review*, Volume 104, 2016, passim. See: Taylor, Winnie, "Proving Racial Discrimination and Monitoring Fair Lending Compliance: The Missing Data Problem in Nonmortgage Credit", *Review of Banking and Finance Law*, Volume 31, 2011, pp. 199–201 (argues, however, that the task of proving cases based on disparate impact is exceedingly difficult as the banking system routinely refuses to provide the data that underpinned the decision to gainsay a loan to racialized communities).

1136 See: Tyler, Tom R./Lind, Edgar Allan, "Procedural justice", *Handbook of law and social science*, J. Sanders/V.L. Hamilton (Eds.), New York, Plenum Press, 2001, pp. 65–92; Tyler, Tom R./Smith, H. J./Huo, Y. J., "Member diversity and leadership effectiveness: Procedural justice, social identity, and group dynamics", *Advances in group processes*, B. Markovsky (Ed.), Greenwich, CT: JAI Press, Volume 13, 1996, pp. 33–68; Tyler, Tom R./Lind, Edgar Allan/Huo, Yuen J., "Cultural Values and Authority Relations: The Psychology of Conflict Resolution Across Cultures", in: *Psychology, Public Policy and Law*, Volume 6, n.º 4, 2000, pp. 1138–1163 (parsing the relationship between high and low levels of power distance values and the relational model of authority); Leung, K./Lind, Edgar Allan, "Procedural justice and culture: Effects of culture, gender, and investigator status on procedural preferences", *Journal of Personality and Social Psychology,* Volume 50, 1986, pp. 1134–1140; Leung, K./Morris, K. W., "Justice through the lens of culture and ethnicity", *Handbook of Law and Social Science: Justice,* Sanders, J./Hamilton, V. L., (Eds.), New York, Plenum, 2001, pp. 343–378; Lind, Edgar Allan/ Tyler, Tom R., *The social psychology of procedural justice*, New York, Plenum Press, 1988, passim; Lind, Edgar Allan/ Tyler, Tom R./Huo, Y.J., "Procedural context and culture: Variation in the antecedents of procedural justice judgments", *Journal of Personality and Social Psychology,* Volume 73, 1997, pp. 767–780; Zimmerman, Nourit/Tyler, Tom R., "Between Access to Counsel and Access to Justice: A Psychological Perspective", *Fordham Urban Law Journal*, Volume 37, 2010, pp. 473–488 (contends that "evaluations about neutrality, *trust*, and

of whites[1137] exist at all stages[1138] of the criminal justice[1139] process[1140]: in arrest rates,[1141] in jail[1142] detention[1143] rates,[1144] and in prison incarceration[1145] rates».[1146]

---

respect for the legal system as a whole"—satisfaction with the *procedural fairness* and *procedural justice* will not lag far behind).

1137 Laub, John H., "Understanding Inequality and the Justice System Response: Charting a New Way Forward.", New York: William T. Grant Foundation, 2014.

1138 Quillian, Lincoln, and Devah Pager, "Black Neighbors, Higher Crime? The Role of Racial Stereotypes in Evaluations of Neighborhood Crime", *American Journal of Sociology*, Volume 107, Issue 3, 2001, 717–67. Brewer, R. M., & Heitzeg, N. A., "The racialization of crime and punishment: Criminal justice, Color-Blind racism, and the political economy of the prison industrial complex", *American Behavioral Scientist*, Volume 51, Issue 5, 2008, 625–644. See: Part IV, This chapter, Sects. 4.1.10.1–4.1.10.6 of this book (on biased algorithmic risk assessment in criminal procedure law settings, with a sharper focus on COMPAS). See: Part IV, This chapter, Sects. 4.1.1–4.1.1.1 of this book (on biased predictive policing).

1139 Jacoby, S. F., Dong, B., Beard, J. H., Wiebe, D. J., & Morrison, C. N., "The enduring impact of historical and structural racism on urban violence in Philadelphia", *Social Science & Medicine*, 1982/2018, 199, 2018, pp. 87–95.

1140 Braga, Anthony A., and David L. Weisburd, *Policing Problem Places: Crime Hot Spots and Effective Prevention*, New York: Oxford University Press, 2010. See: Part IV, This chapter, Sects. 4.1.10.1–4.1.10.6 of this book (on biased algorithmic risk assessment in criminal procedure law settings, with a sharper focus on COMPAS). See: Part IV, This chapter, Sects. 4.1.1–4.1.1.1 of this book (on biased predictive policing).

1141 Andersen, T. S, "Race, Ethnicity, and Structural Variations in Youth Risk of Arrest: Evidence from a National Longitudinal Sample", *Criminal Justice and Behavior*, Volume 42, Issue 9, 2015, pp. 900–916.

1142 Mayson, Sandra G., "Bias In, Bias Out", *Yale Law Journal*, Volume 128, 2019, pp. 2218 and ff and passim.

1143 Dobbie, Will, Jacob Goldin, and Crystal S. Yang, "The Effects of Pretrial Detention on Conviction, Future Crime, and Employment: Evidence from Randomly Assigned Judges," *American Economic Review*, Volume 108, 2018, 201–240.

1144 Fergus, Rachel, "Biased Technology: The Automated Discrimination of Facial Recognition", *ACLU Minnesota*, February 29, 2024, available at: https://www.aclu-mn.org/en/news/biased-technology-automated-discrimination-facial-recognition (access: 20.09.2024) ("*It's no secret that the Department of Homeland Security and its sub-agencies ICE and Customs and Border Protection have already committed horrific abuses – the ACLU sees the tragic consequences. With facial recognition, these agencies could potentially pinpoint the location of immigrants across the country, marking them for detention and deportation on an unprecedented scale.* In 2017 alone, ICE, DHS and other government agencies used this technology to locate and arrest 400 family members and caregivers of unaccompanied migrant children, separating families and leaving children in detention"). Italics added.

1145 Pager, Devah, *Marked: Race, Crime, and Finding Work in an Era of Mass Incarceration*, Chicago: University of Chicago Press, 2007; Fornili, K. S., "Racialized mass incarceration and the war on drugs: A critical race theory appraisal", *Journal of Addictions Nursing*, Volume 29, Issue 1, 2018, 65–72.

1146 *Connecticut Fair Housing Center*, et al. *v. CoreLogic Rental Property Solutions*, Case No. 3:18-cv-00705, U.S. District Court for the District of Connecticut, available: https://www.cohenmilstein.com/case-study/connecticut-fair-housing-center-et-al-v-corelogic-rental-property-solutions/ (access: 22.11.2024).

§§ The Court[1147] further held that no reasonable factfinder could ascertain that *CoreLogic* has a business justification[1148] for screening out applicants solely on the basis that someone has a pending arrest,[1149] in the absence of the details of the arrest, which *CoreLogic* does not necessarily disclose (*source code secrecy*)[1150] to housing providers.[1151]

§§ The Court found *CoreLogic's* batch of evidence that someone who has been arrested once is more likely than others to be arrested again wholly unconvincing[1152] (*biased risk assessment in predicting recidivism*),[1153] as it «only demonstrates that

[1147] *Connecticut Fair Housing Center,* et al. *v. CoreLogic Rental Property Solutions,* Case No. 3:18-cv-00705, U.S. District Court for the District of Connecticut, available: https://www.cohenmilstein.com/case-study/connecticut-fair-housing-center-et-al-v-corelogic-rental-property-solutions/ (access: 22.11.2024).

[1148] Castel, P./ Deneire M./ Kurc A./ Lacassagne M.-F / Leeds, A. C., "Universalism and exceptionalism: French business leardership", *Culture and leadership across the world: the Globe book of in-depth studies of 25 societies,* Chhokar S. J./ Brodbeck C. F. / House J. R. (Ed.), New York, NY, Routledge, 2007, pp. 547–582.

[1149] *Connecticut Fair Housing Center,* et al. *v. CoreLogic Rental Property Solutions,* Case No. 3:18-cv-00705, U.S. District Court for the District of Connecticut, available: https://www.cohenmilstein.com/case-study/connecticut-fair-housing-center-et-al-v-corelogic-rental-property-solutions/ (access: 22.11.2024).

[1150] Deeks, Ahsley, "Secret Reason-Giving", *Yale Law Journal,* Volume 129, 2019, passim; Katyal, Sonia K, "The Paradox of Source Code Secrecy", *Cornell Law Review,* Volume 104, 2019, pp. 1183–1236; Pasquale, Frank, *The Black Box Society: The Secret Algorithms that Control Money and Information.* Cambridge, Massachusetts: Harvard University Press, 2015, 1–320 (pp. 8–10 and passim) (noting that biased algorithms, which have underlying discrimination problems, contribute exponentially to further social biases. His most intriguing claim is that such biased algorithms have been incorporated/etched in the bulk of the corporations' informatic system, to the detriment of human kind in an overarching sense); Wexler, Rebecca, "Life, Liberty, and Trade Secrets: Intellectual Property in the Criminal Justice System", *Stanford Law Review,* Volume 70, 2018, pp. 1343 and ff; Okidegbe, Ngozi, "The Democratizing Potential of Algorithms?", *Connecticut Law Review,* Volume 54, 2021, passim.

[1151] *Connecticut Fair Housing Center,* et al. *v. CoreLogic Rental Property Solutions,* Case No. 3:18-cv-00705, U.S. District Court for the District of Connecticut, available: https://www.cohenmilstein.com/case-study/connecticut-fair-housing-center-et-al-v-corelogic-rental-property-solutions/ (access: 22.11.2024).

[1152] *Connecticut Fair Housing Center,* et al. *v. CoreLogic Rental Property Solutions,* Case No. 3:18-cv-00705, U.S. District Court for the District of Connecticut, available: https://www.cohenmilstein.com/case-study/connecticut-fair-housing-center-et-al-v-corelogic-rental-property-solutions/ (access: 22.11.2024).

[1153] See: Part IV, This chapter, Sects. 4.1.10.1–4.1.10.6 of this book (on biased algorithmic risk assessment in criminal procedure law settings). See: Part IV, This chapter, Sects. 4.1.1–4.1.1.1 of this book (on biased predictive policing). See also: Rudin, Cynthia/Wang, Caroline/Coker, Beau, "The Age of Secrecy and Unfairness in Recidivism Prediction", *Harvard Data Science Review,* Issue 2.1. Winter 2020, 2020, passim; Eckhouse, L., Lum, K., Conti-Cook, C./Ciccolini, J., "Layers of bias: A unified approach for understanding problems with risk assessment", *Criminal Justice and Behavior,* Volume 46, Issue 2, 2019, pp. 185–209; Tollenaar, N., & van der Heijden, P., "Which method predicts recidivism best? A comparison of statistical, machine learning and data mining predictive models", *Journal of the Royal Statistical Society: Series A,* Volume 176, Issue 2, 2013, pp. 565–584. Zhu, Mirilla, "Jury, Using Artificial Intelligence to Predict Recidivism Rates", *Yale Scientific,* 2020, passim. See also: Chasemi et al., Medhi, "The application of Machine Learning to

whatever characteristics are associated with being arrested likely persist over time—and many characteristics, including implicit bias,[1154] cultural incompetence,[1155] race[1156] and place of residence, persist over time».[1157] I venture to add that a «debiasing through law»[1158] paired with a dash of «ethics of nudging»[1159] towards less biased avenues would promote social welfare[1160] in Real Estate industry.

---

a General Risk-Need Assessment Instrument in the Prediction of Criminal Recidivism", *Criminal Justice and Behavior*, Volume 48, 2020, pp. 518–538; Gillis, Talia B., "The Input Data Fallacy", *Minnesota Law Review*, Volume 106, 2022, pp. 1176–1263; Mayson, Sandra G., "Bias In, Bias Out", *Yale Law Journal*, Volume 128, 2019, pp. 2218 and ff and passim.

1154 This is called law of *implicit bias*: people make decisions (e.g. discriminating seemingly disfavoured groups of people) that often-times lack a rational connection between facts and judgment. A conscious and deliberate judgment that noticeably runs afoul with rationality. See: Jolls, Christine/Sunstein, Cass R., "The Law of Implicit Bias", *California Law Review*, Volume 94, 2006, p. 969 (arguing that this issue can be solved through the general strategy of de-biasing through law, by steering people through more rational directions). See also: Kang, Jerry/Banaji, Mahzarin R., "Fair Measures: A Behavioural Realist Revision of Affirmative Action", *California Law Review*, Volume 94 2006, p. 1064 (arguing that «implicit bias often conflicts with conscious attitudes, endorsed beliefs, and intentional behaviour»). See also: Santos, Hugo Luz dos, *Multidisciplinary Dynamics of Mediation*, Volume I, New York/Beijing/Berlin/Singapore, 2025, pp. 1–694; Santos, Hugo Luz dos, *Multidisciplinary Dynamics of Mediation*, Volume II, New York/Beijing/Berlin/Singapore, 2025, pp. 1–800; Santos, Hugo Luz dos, *Towards a Four-Tiered Model of Mediation*, New York/Beijing/Berlin/Singapore, 2023, pp. 1–216.

1155 Garfinkel, Harold, "A Conception of and Experiments with "Trust" as a Condition of Stable Concerted Actions", *Motivation and Social Interaction*, New York, Ronald Press,1963, pp. 187–238; Tyler, Tom R., "Trust and Law Abidingness: A Proactive Model of Social Regulation", *Boston University Law Review*; Durkheim, Émile, *Le Division du Travail* (*The Division of Social Labor*), Rawls, Anne (Ed.), Callegaro, Francesco/Rawls, Anne (Translators), Chicago, Free Press, Paradigm Publishers, 1893, 1933, 2012, passim (bringing forward an innovative concept of self-organizing constitutive orders in modernity); Durkheim, Émile, *Pragmatism and Sociology*, Cambridge, Cambridge University Press, (1913–1914), 1955, (parsing the development of constitutive orders in modernity).

1156 Crutchfield, J., Fisher, A., & Webb, S. L., "Colorism and police killings", *The Western Journal of Black Studies*, Volume 41 (3–4), 2017, 81; Dottolo, A. L., & Stewart, A. J., "Don't ever forget now, you're a Black man in America": Intersections of race, class and gender in encounters with the police", *Sex Roles*, 59 (5–6), 2008, pp. 350–364; Baradan, S., "Race, prediction, and discretion", *The George Washington Law Review*, Volume 81, Issue 1, 2013, pp. 157–222.

1157 *Connecticut Fair Housing Center*, et al. *v. CoreLogic Rental Property Solutions*, Case No. 3:18-cv-00705, U.S. District Court for the District of Connecticut, available: https://www.cohenmilstein.com/case-study/connecticut-fair-housing-center-et-al-v-corelogic-rental-property-solutions/ (access: 22.11.2024).

1158 Jolls, Christine, "Debiasing Through Law", *John M. Olin Program in Law and Economics Working Paper N.º 225*, (2004): 1 (averring that «human beings are often boundedly rational. In the face of bounded rationality, the legal system might attempt either to «de-bias law», by insulating legal outcomes from the effects of boundedly rational behaviour, or instead to «de-bias through law», by steering legal actors in more rational directions»); Thaler, Richard H., "Doing Economics without Homo Economicus", *Foundations of Research in Economics: How do Economists do Economics?*, Volume 227, 1996, passim.

1159 Sunstein, Cass R., "The Ethics of Nudging", *Yale Journal on Regulation*, Volume 32, Issue 2, 2015, 415 (noting that if «we believe that the social ordering (including those forms for which government is responsible) is to promote social welfare. If so, we will favour welfare-promoting nudges»); Sunstein, Cass R., "The Storrs Lectures: Behavioral Economics and Paternalism", *The*

§§ Finally, the Court ruled out *CoreLogic's* motion for summary judgment on Plaintiffs' intentional race and national origin discrimination[1161] claims, holding that a factfinder at trial could conclude that because *CoreLogic* was aware that its

---

Yale Law Journal, Volumc 122, 2013, p. 1826 (noting that «a growing body of cvidcncc dcmonstratcs that in some contexts and for identifiable reasons, people make choices that are not in their interest, even when the stakes are high»); Thaler, Richard H./ Sunstein, Cass R., *Nudge: Improving decisions about health, wealth, and happiness*, London, Penguin Books, 2009, pp. 80–100 (arguing that choice architecture is related with the social background considering which choices are made in a regular basis). Converging: Sunstein, Cass R., "The Storrs Lectures: Behavioral Economics and Paternalism", *cit.*: 1833–1834 (1834) (contending that «choice architecture exists whenever we enter a cafeteria, a restaurant, a hospital, or a grocery store; when we select a mortgage, a car, a health care plan, or a credit card; when we turn on a tablet or a computer an visit our favourite websites; and we apply for drivers 'licenses or building permits or social security benefits. For all of us, a key question is whether the relevant choice architecture is helpful and simple or harmful, complex, and exploitative»); Thaler, Richard H./ Sunstein, Cass R., *Nudge: Improving decisions about health, wealth, and happiness, cit.*: 80–100 (arguing that choice architecture is related with the social background considering which choices are made in a regular basis). Converging: Sunstein, Cass R., "The Storrs Lectures: Behavioral Economics and Paternalism", *cit.*: 1833–1834 (1834) (contending that «choice architecture exists whenever we enter a cafeteria, a restaurant, a hospital, or a grocery store; when we select a mortgage, a car, a health care plan, or a credit card; when we turn on a tablet or a computer an visit our favourite websites; and we apply for drivers 'licenses or building permits or social security benefits. *For all of us, a key question is whether the relevant choice architecture is helpful and simple or harmful, complex, and exploitative*»); Thaler, Richard H./ Sunstein, Cass R., "Libertarian Paternalism", *American Economic Review*, Volume 93 2003, pp. 174 ff (proposing a soft form of paternalism that squarely aligns the freedom of choice with autonomy and community welfare); Sunstein, Cass R., "Libertarian Paternalism Is Not an Oxymoron", *cit.*: 1162 (emphasizing that «libertarian paternalism is a relatively weak and nonintrusive type of paternalism, because choices are not blocked or fenced off»). But see: Mitchell, Gregory, "Libertarian Paternalism is an Oxymoron", *New York University Law Review*, Volume 99 2005, pp. 1245–1248 (arguing, however, that libertarian paternalism is indeed an oxymoron).

1160 Conly, Sarah, *Against Autonomy: Justifying Coercive Paternalism*, Cambridge, United Cambridge University Press, 2012, pp. 1–216 (*passim*) (stating that autonomy is not to be deemed unbending and unyielding. Rather, autonomy must be bent—oftentimes limited—for the sake of the community welfare on the heels of soft paternalism). But see: Wright, Joshua D./Ginsburg, Douglas H., "Behavioral Law and Economics: Its Origins, Fatal Flaws, and Implications for Liberty", *New York University Law Review*, Volume 106, 2012, pp. 1032 ff (decrying the limitation of autonomy for the sake of community welfare on the heels of soft paternalism). But see also: Sen, Amartya Sen, *Development as Freedom*, New York, Alfred A. Knopf, 1999, pp. 1–366 (73–76) (according to this acclaimed economist, welfare boils down to awarding people the choice for a life for which they deeply care about).

1161 Travis, Jeremy/Western, Bruce/Redburn, Steve (Eds.), *Growth of Incarceration in the United States: Exploring Causes and Consequences*, Washington, DC: National Academy of Science, 2014; Western, Bruce, *Punishment and Inequality in America*, New York: Russell Sage Foundation, 2006; Soss, Joe, Richard C. Fording, and Sanford F. Schram, *Disciplining the Poor: Neoliberal Paternalism and the Persistent Power of Race*, Chicago: University of Chicago Press, 2011; Gross, Samuel R., Maurice Possley, and Kalara Stephens, "Race and Wrongful Convictions in the United States" National Registry of Exonerations, Newkirk Center for Science and Society, University of California-Irvine, 2017; Laub, John H., "Understanding Inequality and the Justice System Response: Charting a New Way Forward.", New York: William T. Grant Foundation, 2014.

Rios, Victor M., *Punished: Policing the Lives of Black and Latino Boys*, New York: NYU Press, 2011.

criminal background screening product could have a disproportionate and arbitrary impact[1162] on racial minorities.[1163] In addition to that, the *Court* posited that no steps had been taken to improve the product, abridgment of racial bias wise.[1164] As an upshot, the *Court* further held that plaintiffs had presented sufficient evidence of discriminatory intent.[1165]

§§ On July 20, 2023, further a bench trial that kicked-off on March 14, 2022—subsequently adjourned by the *Court* to resume on October 24, 2022 and ultimately finished on November 4, 2022–, the court decided that *CoreLogic* is not subject to the *Fair Housing Act*.[1166] Verklempt, plaintiffs filed an appeal with the United States Court of Appeals for the Second Circuit on August 4, 2023.[1167]

[1162] *Tech, Bias and Housing Initiative, the Promise and Perils of Residential Proptech, Year 1, Research Summary Report, April 2023, TechEquity Collaborative*, p. 11, available at: https://techequity.us/wp-content/uploads/2023/04/TBHI-Y1-Research-Summary-Report.pdf (28.11.2024). ("*From information on company websites, it is not clear what analysis or data is behind subjective determinations like "suitability" to a unit or what the nexus between an individual's characteristics and a unit's characteristics is that indicates the likelihood for property damage. Based on sample reports, even landlords are not privy to how the determinations are made. Instead, they receive a risk score out of 100 simplified into green, yellow, and red recommendations.* What companies withhold in terms of how it works, they make up for with the extent to which they tell landlords it works: Naborly claims their predictions reduce lease defaults by up to 89%. 15 *As Naborly's sample report demonstrates, its property damage assessment is then used as an input to determine its projected eviction outcomes; its early vacancy prediction, in turn, is based on "all assessment factors*"). Italics added.

[1163] Jefferson, B, *Digitize and Punish: Racial Criminalization in the Digital Age*, Minnesota, University of Minnesota Press, 2020; Gross, Samuel R., Maurice Possley, and Kalara Stephens, "Race and Wrongful Convictions in the United States." National Registry of Exonerations, Newkirk Center for Science and Society, University of California-Irvine, 2017.

[1164] Corbett-Davies, Sam/Goel, Sharad, "The Measure and Mismeasure of Fairness: a critical Review of Fair Machine Learning", *Cornell University Library*, 2018, pp. 3 and ff and passim (undertake laudable efforts to debunk algorithm biases that primarily target ethnic minorities, such as Hispanics and coloured people).

[1165] *Connecticut Fair Housing Center*, et al. *v. CoreLogic Rental Property Solutions*, Case No. 3:18-cv-00705, U.S. District Court for the District of Connecticut, available: https://www.cohenmilstein.com/case-study/connecticut-fair-housing-center-et-al-v-corelogic-rental-property-solutions/ (access: 22.11.2024).

[1166] *Connecticut Fair Housing Center*, et al. *v. CoreLogic Rental Property Solutions*, Case No. 3:18-cv-00705, U.S. District Court for the District of Connecticut, available: https://www.cohenmilstein.com/case-study/connecticut-fair-housing-center-et-al-v-corelogic-rental-property-solutions/ (access: 22.11.2024). But see: Statement of Interest of the United States at 12, *Louis v. SafeRent Sols., LLC*, No. 1:22-cv-10800 (D. Mass. Jan. 9, 2023) (holding that the Fair Housing Act liability encompasses a wide range of entities providing housing-related services, including corporations that offer automatic tenant screening services).

[1167] *Connecticut Fair Housing Center*, et al. *v. CoreLogic Rental Property Solutions*, Case No. 3:18-cv-00705, U.S. District Court for the District of Connecticut, available: https://www.cohenmilstein.com/case-study/connecticut-fair-housing-center-et-al-v-corelogic-rental-property-solutions/ (access: 22.11.2024).

§§ On November 22, 2023, the *National Fair Housing Alliance* filed an amicus brief with the United States Court of Appeals Second Circuit,[1168] urging the appellate court to reverse the district court's ruling that *CoreLogic* is not subject to the *Fair Housing Act*[1169] (FHA).[1170]

§§ On November 24, 2023, the Department of Justice of the United States of America filed an amicus brief with the United States Court of Appeals Second Circuit,[1171] urging the appellate court to remand the lawsuit coupled with specific instructions for reconsidering whether and to what extent *CoreLogic's* demeanours[1172] give rise to liability under the *Fair Housing Act.*[1173]

§§ On November 20, 2024, the Second Circuit heard oral arguments on the appeal of the United States of America, District Court, District of Connecticut's bench trial ruling,[1174] which ruled that *CoreLogic* is not subject to the *Fair Housing*[1175] *Act.*[1176]

[1168] *Connecticut Fair Housing Center,* et al. *v. CoreLogic Rental Property Solutions,* Case No. 3:18-cv-00705, U.S. District Court for the District of Connecticut, available: https://www.cohenmilstein.com/case-study/connecticut-fair-housing-center-et-al-v-corelogic-rental-property-solutions/ (access: 22.11.2024).

[1169] Massey, Douglas S., "The Legacy of the 1968 Fair Housing Act", *Social Forces,* Volume 30, 2015, pp. 571, 575–76, 578 ("[*The FHA] outlawed the refusal to rent or sell to someone because of race; it prohibited racial discrimination in the terms and conditions of rental or sale; it barred discrimination in real estate advertising; it banned agents from making untrue statements about a dwelling's availability in order to deny access to blacks*; and it enjoined real estate agents from making comments about the race of neighbors or in-movers in order to promote panic selling. Although the new law applied only to around 80% of the nation's housing stock, a Supreme Court decision adjudicated just two months later extended its reach to all housing in the United States"). Firestone, Simon, "Race Ethnicity and Credit Card Monitoring", *Journal of Money, Credit and Banking,* Sept. 2014, 2014, pp. 1206 and ff; Han, Song, Keys, Benjamin J./Li, Geng, *Unsecured Credit Supply over the Credit Cycle: Evidence from Credit Card Mailings* (argue that, statistically, Blacks and Latinos are seldom granted credit and, if ever granted credit, the terms and conditions attached to the concession of credit are not equal to those offered to White folks).

[1170] *Connecticut Fair Housing Center,* et al. *v. CoreLogic Rental Property Solutions,* Case No. 3:18-cv-00705, U.S. District Court for the District of Connecticut, available: https://www.cohenmilstein.com/case-study/connecticut-fair-housing-center-et-al-v-corelogic-rental-property-solutions/ (access: 22.11.2024).

[1171] *Connecticut Fair Housing Center,* et al. *v. CoreLogic Rental Property Solutions,* Case No. 3:18-cv-00705, U.S. District Court for the District of Connecticut, available: https://www.cohenmilstein.com/case-study/connecticut-fair-housing-center-et-al-v-corelogic-rental-property-solutions/ (access: 22.11.2024).

[1172] *Connecticut Fair Housing Center,* et al. *v. CoreLogic Rental Property Solutions,* Case No. 3:18-cv-00705, U.S. District Court for the District of Connecticut, available: https://www.cohenmilstein.com/case-study/connecticut-fair-housing-center-et-al-v-corelogic-rental-property-solutions/ (access: 22.11.2024).

[1173] *Connecticut Fair Housing Center,* et al. *v. CoreLogic Rental Property Solutions,* Case No. 3:18-cv-00705, U.S. District Court for the District of Connecticut, available: https://www.cohenmilstein.com/case-study/connecticut-fair-housing-center-et-al-v-corelogic-rental-property-solutions/ (access: 22.11.2024).

§§ The super glue to holds the three cases together is all too familiar and well-worn: the disparate impact[1177] on *housing opportunities* for Black and Hispanic applicants and voucher holders.[1178] Only this time around the racial discrimination has been carried out by Artificial Intelligence-embedded technologies—amongst which a machine learning algorithm that automatically turned down both *Louis*

[1174] *Connecticut Fair Housing Center,* et al. *v. CoreLogic Rental Property Solutions,* Case No. 3:18-cv-00705, U.S. District Court for the District of Connecticut, available: https://www.cohenmilstein.com/case-study/connecticut-fair-housing-center-et-al-v-corelogic-rental-property-solutions/ (access: 22.11.2024).

[1175] See: Kaersvang, Dana L., "Note, The Fair Housing Act and Disparate Impact in Homeowners Insurance," *Michigan Law Review*, Volume 104, 2006, pp. 1992 and ff and passim (carrying out additional analysis on the application of the Fair Housing Act's disparate impact standard to insurance).

[1176] *Connecticut Fair Housing Center,* et al. *v. CoreLogic Rental Property Solutions,* Case No. 3:18-cv-00705, U.S. District Court for the District of Connecticut, available: https://www.cohenmilstein.com/case-study/connecticut-fair-housing-center-et-al-v-corelogic-rental-property-solutions/ (access: 22.11.2024).

[1177] It bears mentioning that scorching issue of whether and to what extent disparate impact alone should be actionable is different from, in that does not overlap with, the sweltering issue of proxy discrimination. See: Cohran, Matthew Jordan, "Fairness in Disparity: Challenging the Application of Disparate Impact Theory in Fair Housing Claims Against Insurers", *The George Mason University Civil Rights Law Journal*, Volume 21, 2011, pp. 159 and ff and passim (discussing the use of disparate impact theory and potential applicability to Fair Housing Act claims against insurers). None of this is to suggest, nor is to say, that mere disparate impact alone is of scant importance in that is not a relevant issue raised by both big data and algorithms. See, e.g.: Bartlett, Robert/Morse, Adair/Stanton, Richard/Wallace, Nancy, "Consumer-Lending Discrimination in the FinTech Era 4 (Nat'l Bureau of Econ. Research, Working Paper No. 25943"), 2019, passim (concludes that disparate impact extracts as much rents as face-to-face discrimination). See also: Howard, Justin D Howard, "Refashioning the Disparate Treatment and Disparate Impact Doctrines in Theory and in Practice", *Howard Law Journal*, Volume 41, 1998, passim; Seiner, Joseph, "Disentangling Disparate Impact and Disparate Treatment: Adapting the Canadian Approach", *Yale Law & Policy Review*, Volume 25, 2006; Primus, Richard "The Future of Disparate Impact", *Michigan Law Review*, Volume 108, 2010, pp. 1340 and ff and passim; Stephanopoulos, Nicholas O. "Disparate Impact, Unified Law", *Yale Law Journal*, Volume 128, 2019, pp. 1566–1595.

[1178] *Louis v. Saferent Sols.*, Civil Action 22-CV-10800-AK, 27 (D. Mass. Jul. 26, 2023) ("The question ultimately comes down to this: Have the Plaintiffs alleged facts demonstrating that the policy at issue-the provision and use of the SafeRent Score, *which relies at least in part on credit history, to evaluate rental applications-causes the alleged disparate impact, that is, a disproportionate denial of rental applications for Black and Hispanic individuals and voucher holders generally*?"). *Louis v. Saferent Sols.*, Civil Action 22-CV-10800-AK, 28 (D. Mass. Jul. 26, 2023) ("While the existence of "other factors" *could* explain the disparate impact alleged, Plaintiffs have pleaded facts sufficient at this phase to support a plausible claim that the Defendants' use of the SafeRent Score, which relies in part on credit history and related factors, disproportionately affects Black and Hispanic applicants and voucher holders generally. It does not matter that Defendants did not create the longstanding inequities in access to wealth and wealth-building mechanisms that have contributed to racial and income disparities in credit scores and histories; *Defendants decided to rely on those inequities when providing and using the SafeRent Score, which includes credit scores and histories in the algorithm, and such reliance, as alleged by Plaintiffs, has a disparate impact on housing opportunities for Black and Hispanic applicants and voucher holders*"). Italics added.

and *Arroyo's* rental applications on the account of a deep-seated racial bias against coloured communities (Blacks and Latinos).

§§ Strikingly, house providers and landlords have long relied on warped proxies[1179] to race[1180] (criminal record, time of the latest arrest, bankruptcy records, past due accounts, payment performance)[1181] to turn down rental applications[1182] penned by Blacks and Latinos.[1183]

[1179] See: Grimmelmann, James/Westreich, Daniel, "Incomprehensible Discrimination", *California Law Review Online*, Volume 7, 2017, pp 164 and ff and passim (bringing forth a hypothetical as a tutorial tool to display disparate impact and proxies); Morris, Darcy Steeg/Schwarcz, Daniel/Teitelbaum, Joshua C., "Do Credit-Based Insurance Scores Proxy for Income in Predicting Auto Claim Risk?", *Journal of Empirical Legal Studies*, Volume 14, 2017, pp. 397, 418–21 and ff (discussing that an insurer's use of credit-anchored insurance scores lacks a disparate impact on the basis of income and thus is not amenable to be considered as a proxy for income); Pope, Devin G. Pope/Sydnor, Justin R., "Implementing Anti-Discrimination Policies in Statistical Profiling Models", *American Economic Journal: Applied Economics*, Volume 3, 2011, pp. 206–210 (discussing how the FTC parsed credit score use in auto-insurance pricing as a proxy for race).

[1180] See: Campisi, Natalie, From Inherent Racial Bias to Incorrect Data The Problems With Current Credit Scoring Models, Forbes (Feb. 26, 2021), https://www.forbes.com/advisor/creditcards/from-inherent-racial-bias-to-incorrect-data-the-problems-with-current-credit-scoring-models/; [https://perma.cc/EWA4-CS8E] (highlighting rampant racial bias in credit scoring systems); Oyama, Rebecca, "Do Not (Re)Enter: the Rise of Criminal Background Tenant Screening as a Violation of the Fair Housing Act", *Michigan Journal of Race and Law*, Volume 15, 2009, pp. 181, 184–93 (discussing a broad range of historical/criminal accounts as a way to screen undesirable tenants, such as Blacks and Latinos); Statement of Interest of the United States at 12, *Louis v. SafeRent Sols., LLC, No. 1:22-cv-10800* (D. Mass. Jan. 9, 2023) (holding that the Fair Housing Act liability stretches far and beyond, thus encompassing a vast assortment of entities providing housing-related services, including corporations that offer tenant screening services).

[1181] *Connecticut Fair Housing Center,* et al. *v. CoreLogic Rental Property Solutions,* Case No. 3:18-cv-00705, U.S. District Court for the District of Connecticut, available: https://www.cohenmilstein.com/case-study/connecticut-fair-housing-center-et-al-v-corelogic-rental-property-solutions/ (access: 22.11.2024).

[1182] See: Wonyoung, So, "Which Information Matters? Measuring Landlord Assessment of Tenant Screening Reports", *Housing Policy Debate*, Volume 33, n. ° 6, 2023, pp. 1484–1510 (1484) ("*This research studies how tenant screening services' presentation of information influences landlord decisions. Tenant screening services utilize criminal records, eviction records, and credit score databases to produce reports that landlords use to inform their decisions about who to rent to. However, little is known about how landlords assess the information presented by tenant screening reports. Through a behavioral experiment with landlords using simulated tenant screening reports, this study shows that landlords use blanket screening policies, that they conflate the existence of tenant records with outcomes (e.g., eviction filings with executed evictions), and that they display, on average, tendencies toward automation bias that are influenced by the risk assessments and scores presented by tenant screening reports.* I argue that maintaining blanket screening policies and automation bias, combined with the downstream effects of creating and *using racially biased eviction and criminal records, means that people of color will inevitably experience disproportionate exclusion from rental housing due to perceived "risk" on the part of landlords*"). Italics added. See: Part IV, This chapter, Sects. 4.1.4–4.1.4.2.3 of this book.

[1183] Humber, Nadiyah J., "A Home for Digital Equity: Algorithmic Redlining and Property Technology", *California Law Review*, *cit.*, pp. 1421–1484 (1424).

§§ As a result, digital housing discrimination[1184] against communities of colour (Blacks and Latinos)[1185] is a gruelling reality[1186] with which the latter continue to tussle.[1187]

[1184] See: Wonyoung, So, "Which Information Matters? Measuring Landlord Assessment of Tenant Screening Reports", *Housing Policy Debate*, Volume 33, n. ° 6, 2023, pp. 1484–1510 (1502) ("*One additional finding of the experiment is that algorithmic scoring can exacerbate this racially unequal landscape in rental agreements not just because the algorithm may be inaccurate, but because landlords may want to follow the risk assessment made by the tenant screening report. This is alarming for low-income tenants, particularly housing voucher holders. Security deposits are one of the most significant barriers to obtaining housing for voucher holders, because vouchers do not pay security deposits but most private landlords require them (Rosenblatt & Cossyleon, 2018).* Given that voucher holders have exceptionally low income (usually less than 50% of area median income) and might experience more housing insecurity (rental debts and eviction-related experiences), *imposing greater security deposits on voucher holders almost equates to denying them housing—yet these decisions could be justified by algorithmic scoring if tenant screening services employ it*"). Italics added.

[1185] Humber, Nadiyah J., "A Home for Digital Equity: Algorithmic Redlining and Property Technology", *California Law Review, cit.*, pp. 1421–1484 (1424).

[1186] *Tech, Bias and Housing Initiative, the Promise and Perils of Residential Proptech, Year 1, Research Summary Report, April 2023, TechEquity Collaborative*, p. 5 available at: https://techequity.us/wp-content/uploads/2023/04/TBHI-Y1-Research-Summary-Report.pdf (28.11.2024). ("*Residential Proptech also has the potential to exacerbate the bias inherent in our housing system. Its rise is due, in part, to the desperation felt by average home seekers. With a severely constrained housing supply, companies offering an easier pathway to homeownership may exploit communities that have been harmed by housing discrimination in the past. Opaque algorithms incorporate biased data into their decision-making processes, making it harder to enforce fair housing laws.* Residential Proptech companies often operate in a regulatory gray area, leaving consumers without the protections they would have from traditional housing regulatory systems. *As unprecedented capital investment flows into this space, venture-backed companies' winner-take-all approach to growth has the potential to exacerbate inequality rather than combat it*"). Italics added. See: Part IV, This chapter, Sects. 4.1.4–4.1.4.2.3 of this book. See: Part IV, This chapter, Sects. 4.1.4–4.1.4.2.1 of this book (on mortgage redlining). See: Part IV, This chapter, Sects. 4.1.2–4.1.4.3 of this book (on algorithmic credit scoring, consumer racism and credit card redlining). See: Part IV, This chapter, Sects. 4.1.4–4.1.4.2.3 of this book (on algorithmic redlining). See: Part IV, This chapter, Sect. 4.1.4.3 of this book (on "algorithmic redliking"). See: Part IV, This chapter, Sect. 4.1.3 of this book (on algorithmic prime-lining).

[1187] Pasley, Tex/Oostrom-Shah, Henry/Sirota, Eric "How Tenant Screening Reports Deprive Tenants of Equal Access to Housing", *Shriver Center on Poverty Law*, January 2021, 2021, available at: https://www.povertylaw.org/report/tenant-screening-report/ (access: 22.11.2024) ("*Everyone should have access to a safe, stable, and affordable home. Yet racism, both systemic and individual, continues to block Black, Latino/a/x, and other people of color from fair access to housing. Tenant screening reports—which purport to evaluate a tenant's likelihood to be a good or bad tenant—play an important role in perpetuating housing discrimination against communities of color.* The tenant screening industry is largely unregulated, ubiquitous, and frequently undermines laws passed by state and local legislative bodies to ensure equal access"). Italics added. See: Part IV, This chapter, Sects. 4.1.4–4.1.4.2.1 of this book (on mortgage redlining). See: Part IV, This chapter, Sects. 4.1.2–4.1.4.3 of this book (on algorithmic credit scoring, consumer racism and credit card redlining). See: Part IV, This chapter, Sects. 4.1.4–4.1.4.2.3 of this book (on algorithmic redlining). See: Part IV, This chapter, Sect. 4.1.4.3 of this book (on "algorithmic redliking"). See: Part IV, This chapter, Sect. 4.1.3 of this book (on algorithmic prime-lining).

§§ Compellingly, in *CoreLogic*, the *Court* held that the *CrimeSafe* computer-run tool, the Artificial Intelligence-embedded technology at issue in the lawsuit,[1188] was predominantly used as filtering system to duly inform landlords (housing providers)[1189] of criminal records found.[1190] On this note, the *Court*[1191] has further held that the former (*CrimeSafe* computer-run tool) operated based on the parameters set out by landlords.[1192]

§§ Although machine learning algorithms run the tool and inform the landlords accordingly,[1193] binding decisions—either approve or deny the rental application—rest nonetheless upon the housing providers[1194] (i.e. landlords)[1195] discretion's alone.[1196]

§§ It is pivotally important to note, though, that the use of *CrimeSafe* in *Corelogic* computer-run tool differs greatly from how the Artificial Intelligence-embedded technology was deployed in *Louis*.[1197] Strikingly, in *Louis* machine learning algorithms created evaluative scores, whereas in *Corelogic* computer-run algorithms were mere filters.[1198]

[1188] Humber, Nadiyah J., "A Home for Digital Equity: Algorithmic Redlining and Property Technology", *cit.*, pp. 1421–1484 (1424).

[1189] *Connecticut Fair Housing Center,* et al. *v. CoreLogic Rental Property Solutions,* Case No. 3:18-cv-00705, U.S. District Court for the District of Connecticut, available: https://www.cohenmilstein.com/case-study/connecticut-fair-housing-center-et-al-v-corelogic-rental-property-solutions/ (access: 22.11.2024).

[1190] Humber, Nadiyah J., "A Home for Digital Equity: Algorithmic Redlining and Property Technology", *cit.*, pp. 1421–1484 (1424).

[1191] *Connecticut Fair Housing Center,* et al. *v. CoreLogic Rental Property Solutions,* Case No. 3:18-cv-00705, U.S. District Court for the District of Connecticut, available: https://www.cohenmilstein.com/case-study/connecticut-fair-housing-center-et-al-v-corelogic-rental-property-solutions/ (access: 22.11.2024).

[1192] *Connecticut Fair Housing Center,* et al. *v. CoreLogic Rental Property Solutions,* Case No. 3:18-cv-00705, U.S. District Court for the District of Connecticut, available: https://www.cohenmilstein.com/case-study/connecticut-fair-housing-center-et-al-v-corelogic-rental-property-solutions/ (access: 22.11.2024).

[1193] *Connecticut Fair Housing Center,* et al. *v. CoreLogic Rental Property Solutions,* Case No. 3:18-cv-00705, U.S. District Court for the District of Connecticut, available: https://www.cohenmilstein.com/case-study/connecticut-fair-housing-center-et-al-v-corelogic-rental-property-solutions/ (access: 22.11.2024).

[1194] *Connecticut Fair Housing Center,* et al. *v. CoreLogic Rental Property Solutions,* Case No. 3:18-cv-00705, U.S. District Court for the District of Connecticut, available: https://www.cohenmilstein.com/case-study/connecticut-fair-housing-center-et-al-v-corelogic-rental-property-solutions/ (access: 22.11.2024).

[1195] Humber, Nadiyah J., "A Home for Digital Equity: Algorithmic Redlining and Property Technology", *cit.*, pp. 1421–1484 (1424).

[1196] *Connecticut Fair Housing Center,* et al. *v. CoreLogic Rental Property Solutions,* Case No. 3:18-cv-00705, U.S. District Court for the District of Connecticut, available: https://www.cohenmilstein.com/case-study/connecticut-fair-housing-center-et-al-v-corelogic-rental-property-solutions/ (access: 22.11.2024).

[1197] Humber, Nadiyah J., "A Home for Digital Equity: Algorithmic Redlining and Property Technology", *cit.*, pp. 1421–1484 (1424).

§§ That is true, but truer still *Corelogic* and *Louis*, if nothing else, have abundantly shown that communities of colour (Blacks and Latinos) have reasons to look askance at the deployment of Artificial Intelligence-embedded technologies in the remit of Real Estate industry. Many of which spring from the fact that those computer-run tools consistently skew towards White folks.

§§ Relatedly, this is the gist of my newly-crafted concept of *Algorithmic Dictatorship* which, as hinted above, leverages on a bevy of human biases that disgracefully/appallingly creep into the algorithm[1199] and feeds into an automated decision[1200] that comes to the expense of Blacks 'and Latino's credit scoring.[1201] Thereby creating a haze of ambiguity that obfuscates automated decision-making while propelling a meaningless façade of neutrality that should keep us eagerly awaken at night.

§§ No flabbergasting surprise stems from the fact that the deployment of machine learning algorithms in the purview of Real Estate tallies with, in that is tantamount to, *algorithmic redlining* which, in turn, builds on the deadly sins inherited from the drawn-out era of *mortgage redlining* against the backdrop of which racialized communities (Blacks and Latinos) were routinely denied access to loans.[1202] It seems as though that the shady practices of the past[1203] still ripple forward.[1204]

[1198] Humber, Nadiyah J., "A Home for Digital Equity: Algorithmic Redlining and Property Technology", *cit.*, pp. 1421–1484 (1424).

[1199] Citron, Danielle Keats/Pasquale, Frank A., "The Scored Society: Due Process for Automated Predictions", *Washington Law Review*, Volume 89, 2014, pp. 1–34 (arguing that "[a]*dvocates applaud the removal of human beings and their flaws from the assessment process*," but arguing that bias remains "[*b*]*ecause human beings program predictive algorithms, their biases and values are embedded into the software's instructions*"). Italics added.

[1200] See: Allen, James, "The Color of Algorithms: An Analysis and Proposed Research Agenda Deterring Algorithmic Redlining", *Fordham Urban Law Journal*, Volume 46, 2019, pp. 219–234 (229–234) (discussing how historical mortgage redlining greatly swayed modern algorithms generated by massive batches of datasets that consist of decades of information built on exclusion and racial discrimination in the purview of financing, marketing, and housing). See: Part IV, This chapter, Sects. 4.1.4–4.1.4.2.3 of this book. See: Part IV, This chapter, Sects. 4.1.4–4.1.4.2.1 of this book (on mortgage redlining). See: Part IV, This chapter, Sects. 4.1.2–4.1.4.3 of this book (on algorithmic credit scoring, consumer racism and credit card redlining). See: Part IV, This chapter, Sects. 4.1.4–4.1.4.2.3 of this book (on algorithmic redlining). See: Part IV, This chapter, Sect. 4.1.4.3 of this book (on "algorithmic redliking"). See: Part IV, This chapter, Sect. 4.1.3 of this book (on algorithmic prime-lining).

[1201] See: Havard, Cassandra Jones, "On The Take": The Black Box of Credit Scoring and Mortgage Discrimination", *Boston University Public Interest Law Journal*, Volume 20, 2011, pp. 241–247 (highlighting that algorithmic credit scoring, if left unchecked, is an intrinsic, encroached, deep-rooted form of racial discrimination akin to mortgage redlining); Pasquale, Frank, *The Black Box Society: The Secret Algorithms that Control Money and Information.* Cambridge, Massachusetts: Harvard University Press, 2015, 1–320 (passim).

[1202] Allen, James, "The Color of Algorithms: An Analysis and Proposed Research Agenda Deterring Algorithmic Redlining", *Fordham Urban Law Journal*, Volume 46, 2019, pp. 219–234 (229–234) (discussing how historical mortgage redlining greatly swayed modern algorithms generated by massive batches of data sets that consist of decades of information built on exclusion and racial discrimination in the purview of financing, marketing, and housing).

§§ Compellingly, the all-out deployment of machine learning algorithms lends a patina of objectivity to screening tools as if they preclude historically racial inequalities.[1205] In a diametrically opposite manner, this cluster of algorithmic decision-making amounts to nothing but to «algorithmic redlining»[1206] of which we should all be deeply ashamed of.[1207]

4.1.4.2.3 «Old Wine in New Bottles»? Algorithmic Redlining and Property Technologies (*PropTech*) Perpetuate Racial Inequalities in Rental Housing (Executed Evictions Riddled With Inaccuracies, Automation Bias Evinced by Landlords/Housing Providers, and Inaccurate Criminal Records, Which, Taken Together, Ultimately Decide Which Rental Applications Will Be Approved (White Folks) and Which Ones Will Be Automatically Rejected (Blacks and Latinos)

§§ *Louis* and *CoreLogic*, if nothing else, clearly depicted how machine learning algorithms in property technologies can create a myriad of disparate outcomes,[1208]

[1203] See: Part IV, This chapter, Sects. 4.1.4–4.1.4.2.1 of this book (on mortgage redlining). See: Part IV, This chapter, Sects. 4.1.2–4.1.4.3 of this book (on algorithmic credit scoring, consumer racism and credit card redlining). See: Part IV, This chapter, Sects. 4.1.4–4.1.4.2.3 of this book (on algorithmic redlining). See: Part IV, This chapter, Sect. 4.1.4.3 of this book (on "algorithmic redliking").

[1204] In spite of its deep-seated racial bias, decision-makers continue to deploy redlining tactics through big data and may even justify such unlawful practices by claiming that the latter abide by cost-effectiveness. See: Humber, Nadiyah J., "A Home for Digital Equity: Algorithmic Redlining and Property Technology", *California Law Review*, Volume 111, Issue 5, 2023, pp. 1421–1484. See also: Hurley, Mikella/Adebayo, Julius, "Credit Scoring in the Era of Big Data", *Yale Journal of Law and Technology*, Volume 18, 2016, pp. 148, 151–156, 172 (averring that FICO scoring boasts a redoubtable capacity to routinely weed out some populations that have been historically and systematically underrepresented or grossly unfairly represented in the credit industry market). Tellingly, by 2016, ten states had disavowed the unlawful practice of employers using shady credit scores due to their perceived disparate impact on low-income applicants and members of racialized communities (mostly Black folks). See: O'Neill, Cathy, *Weapons of Math Destruction. How Big Data Increases Inequality and Threatens Democracy*. London: Penguin Random House, 2016, pp. 128 and ff and passim.

[1205] Humber, Nadiyah J., "A Home for Digital Equity: Algorithmic Redlining and Property Technology", *cit.*, pp. 1421–1484 (1424).

[1206] Humber, Nadiyah J., "A Home for Digital Equity: Algorithmic Redlining and Property Technology", *cit.*, pp. 1421–1484 (1424).

[1207] On algorithmic redlining: Ferreri, Mara/Sanyal, Romola, "Digital Informalisation: Rental Housing, Platforms, and the Management of Risk", *Housing Studies*, Volume 37, 2022, p. 1035; Koopman, Colin, "The Political Theory of Data: Institutions, Algorithms, & Formats in Racial Redlining", *Political Theory*, Volume 50, 2021, p. 337; Safransky, Sara, "Geographies of Algorithmic Violence: Redlining the Smart City", *International Journal of Urban and Regional Research*, 2019, p. 200.

[1208] Humber, Nadiyah J., "A Home for Digital Equity: Algorithmic Redlining and Property Technology", *cit.*, pp. 1421–1484 (1425).

which run counter to *Algorithmic Common Good*.[1209] Yet, the previously mentioned situation, however gruesome, amounts to nothing but «old wine in new bottles».[1210]

§§ Tellingly, and just as hinted above,[1211] member of communities of colour (Blacks and Latinos[1212]) are inordinately surveilled,[1213] overly arrested,[1214] uncustomarily killed,[1215] extortionately incarcerated,[1216] wrongly convicted,[1217] and much poorer[1218] than White[1219] folks.[1220]

[1209] See: Part V, Chap. 5, Sects. 5.1.2–5.1.6.2.1 of this book (on the thing-centred algorithmic decision-making propelled by a *Controllable* and *Interpretable* Machine Learning that weeds out *Algorithmic Dictatorship* and secures *Algorithmic Common Good*). See also: Simon & Schuster, Green, B., "Algorithmic realism: expanding the boundaries of algorithmic thought", *Proceedings of the 2020 Conference on Fairness Accountability and Transparency*, 2020, passim; Green, B./Hu L., "The Myth in the Methodology: Towards a Recontextualization of Fairness in Machine Learning", *Machine Learning Debates Work 35th Internation Conference of Machine Learning*, 2018, passim; Green, B., Chen Y, "Disparate interactions: An algorithm-in-the-loop analysis of fairness in risk assessments", *FAT* 2019, Proceedings of 2019 Conference of Fairness, Accountability, Transparency*, 2019, pp. 90–99 (on the central tenets of algorithmic fairness).

[1210] *Tech, Bias and Housing Initiative, the Promise and Perils of Residential Proptech, Year 1, Research Summary Report, April 2023, TechEquity Collaborative*, p. 5 available at: https://techequity.us/wp-content/uploads/2023/04/TBHI-Y1-Research-Summary-Report.pdf (28.11.2024). ("*Residential Proptech also has the potential to exacerbate the bias inherent in our housing system. Its rise is due, in part, to the desperation felt by average home seekers. With a severely constrained housing supply, companies offering an easier pathway to homeownership may exploit communities that have been harmed by housing discrimination in the past. Opaque algorithms incorporate biased data into their decision-making processes, making it harder to enforce fair housing laws.* Residential Proptech companies often operate in a regulatory gray area, leaving consumers without the protections they would have from traditional housing regulatory systems. *As unprecedented capital investment flows into this space, venture-backed companies' winner-take-all approach to growth has the potential to exacerbate inequality rather than combat it*"). Italics added. See: Part IV, This chapter, Sects. 4.1.4–4.1.4.2.3 of this book. See: Part IV, This chapter, Sects. 4.1.4–4.1.4.2.1 of this book (on mortgage redlining). See: Part IV, This chapter, Sects. 4.1.2–4.1.4.3 of this book (on algorithmic credit scoring, consumer racism and credit card redlining). See: Part IV, This chapter, Sects. 4.1.4–4.1.4.2.3 of this book (on algorithmic redlining). See: Part IV, This chapter, Sect. 4.1.4.3 of this book (on "algorithmic redliking"). See: Part IV, This chapter, Sect. 4.1.3 of this book (on algorithmic prime-lining).

[1211] See: Part IV, This chapter, Sects. 4.1.1–4.1.1.1 of this book (on biased predictive policing).

[1212] Rios, Victor M., *Punished: Policing the Lives of Black and Latino Boys*, New York: NYU Press, 2011.

[1213] Brayne, S., "Big data surveillance: The case of policing", *American Sociological Review*, Volume 82, Issue 5, 2017, pp. 977–1008; Robinson, M. A., "Black bodies on the ground: Policing disparities in the African American Community-An analysis of newsprint from January 1, 2015, through December 31, 2015", *Journal of Black Studies*, Volume 48, Issue 6, pp. 551–571; Browne, S., *Dark matters: on the surveillance of blackness*, Duke University Press, 2015, passim. Toro, J. D./ Lloyd, T., Buchanan/K. S., Robins/S. J., Bencharit/L. Z., Smiedt/M. G., Reddy/K. S., Pouget, E. R./ Kerrison, E. M./Goff, P. A., "The criminogenic and psychological effects of police stops on adolescent black and Latino boys", *Proceedings of the National Academy of Sciences of the United States of America*, Volume 116, Issue 17, 2019, pp. 8261–8268; Sewell, A. A., Jefferson, K. A./Lee, H., "Living under surveillance: Gender, psychological distress, and stop-question- and-frisk policing in New York city", *Social Science & Medicine*, Volume 159, 2016, pp. 1–13; Benjamin, Ruha, *Race After Technology: Abolitionist Tools for the New Jim Code*, John Wiley & Sons, 2019, passim;

§§ Taken together, these proxies[1221] for race[1222] (criminal record,[1223] time of the latest arrest,[1224] bankruptcy records, filed/executed evictions[1225] records,[1226] past due accounts, payment performance)[1227] are routinely used by landlords/housing[1228]

Abdillahi, I., "Algorithmic surveillance in the era of the appsphere", *American Journal of Community Psychology*, Volume 73, 2024, passim; Zuboff, Zhoshana, *The Age of Surveillance Capitalism, The Fight for a Human Future at the New Frontier of Power*. New Yor City: PublicAffairs Books, 2019, pp. 1–704 (360) (argues that we are indomitably heading towards a "instrumentarianism" that draws on "totalitarianism").

1214 Kizer, J. M., "Arrested by skin color: Evidence from siblings and a nationally representative sample", *Socius: Sociological Research for a Dynamic World*, 3, 2017, passim; Kochel, T. R., Wilson, D. B./Mastrofski, S. D., "Effect of suspect race on officers' arrest decisions", *Criminology*, Volume 49, Issue 2, 2011, pp. 473–512. Mitchell, O./Caudy, M. S., "Examining racial disparities in drug arrests", *Justice Quarterly*, Volume 32, Issue 2, 2015, pp. 288–313; Kirk, D. S., "The neighborhood context of racial and ethnic disparities in arrest", *Demography*, 45, 2008, pp. 55–77.

1215 Crutchfield, J., Fisher, A., & Webb, S. L., "Colorism and police killings", *The Western Journal of Black Studies*, 41 (3–4), 2017, 81; Dottolo, A. L., & Stewart, A. J. (2008). "Don't ever forget now, you're a Black man in America": Intersections of race, class and gender in encounters with the police", *Sex Roles*, 59(5–6), 2008, pp. 350–364; Baradan, S., "Race, prediction, and discretion", *The George Washington Law Review*, Volume 81, Issue 1, 2013, pp. 157–222.

1216 Pager, Devah, *Marked: Race, Crime, and Finding Work in an Era of Mass Incarceration*, Chicago: University of Chicago Press, 2007; Fornili, K. S., "Racialized mass incarceration and the war on drugs: A critical race theory appraisal", *Journal of Addictions Nursing*, Volume 29, Issue 1, 2018, 65–72; Jacoby, S. F., Dong, B., Beard, J. H., Wiebe, D. J., & Morrison, C. N., "The enduring impact of historical and structural racism on urban violence in Philadelphia", *Social Science & Medicine*, 1982/2018, 199, 2018, pp. 87–95; Travis, Jeremy, Bruce Western, and Steve Redburn (Eds.), *Growth of Incarceration in the United States: Exploring Causes and Consequences*, Washington, DC: National Academy of Science, 2014 .

1217 Gross, Samuel R., Maurice Possley, and Kalara Stephens, "Race and Wrongful Convictions in the United States." National Registry of Exonerations, Newkirk Center for Science and Society, University of California-Irvine, 2017; Laub, John H., "Understanding Inequality and the Justice System Response: Charting a New Way Forward.", New York: William T. Grant Foundation, 2014.

1218 Western, Bruce, *Punishment and Inequality in America*, New York: Russell Sage Foundation, 2006; Soss, Joe, Richard C. Fording, and Sanford F. Schram, *Disciplining the Poor: Neoliberal Paternalism and the Persistent Power of Race*, Chicago: University of Chicago Press, 2011; Laub, John H., "Understanding Inequality and the Justice System Response: Charting a New Way Forward.", New York: William T. Grant Foundation, 2014.

1219 Frankenberg, Ruth, "Introduction: local whitenesses, localizing whiteness", *Displacing whiteness*, Ruth Frankenberg (Editor), Durham, NC: Duke University Press, 1997, pp. 1–33.

1220 Derenoncourt, Ellora/Kim, Chi Hyun/Kuhn, Moritz/Schularik, Moritz, "The Wealth of Two Nations: The U.S. Racial Wealth Gap, 1860–2020", *The Quarterly Journal of Economics*, Volume 139, Issue 2, 2024, p. 741 ("A large class of commonly discussed policies for reducing racial wealth inequality seeks to reduce gaps in income, savings, and capital gains. These include policies that encourage financial diversification or stock equity holdings among Black households; policies aimed at financial literacy and retirement or savings behavior; or policies aimed at improving educational and labor market outcomes of Black Americans through improved school quality or reductions in discrimination. *Yet on a realistic note, our simulation in Section IV.A shows that even if wealth accumulation conditions had been equal since 1870, the wealth gap would still be 3 to 1 today, and full convergence would be more than 200 years away. Put differently: to close the racial wealth gap in the immediate term* via *flow parameters, Black Americans would need a substantial positive lead over whites, not "just" more equality*"). Italics added.

providers[1229] to turn down rental applications penned by Blacks[1230] and Latinos.[1231] Especially, albeit not exclusively, rental applications made by voucher holders, whom are proverbially low-income applicants.[1232]

1221 See: Barocas, Solon/Selbst, Andrew, "Big Data's Disparate Impact", *California Law Review*, Volume 104, pp. 2016, pp. 671–678 ("in particular, by exposing so-called 'machine learning' algorithms to examples of the cases of interest (previously identified instances of fraud, spam, default, and poor health), *the algorithm 'learns' which related attributes or activities can serve as potential proxies for those qualities or outcomes of interest*"). See also: Kaersvang, Dana L., "Note, The Fair Housing Act and Disparate Impact in Homeowners Insurance," *Michigan Law Review*, Volume 104, 2006, pp. 1992 and ff and passim (carrying out additional analysis on the application of the Fair Housing Act's disparate impact standard to insurance); Grimmelmann, James/Westreich, Daniel, "Incomprehensible Discrimination", *California Law Review Online*, Volume 7, 2017, pp 164 and ff and passim (bringing forth a hypothetical as a tutorial tool to display disparate impact and proxies); Morris, Darcy Steeg/Schwarcz, Daniel/Teitelbaum, Joshua C., "Do Credit-Based Insurance Scores Proxy for Income in Predicting Auto Claim Risk?", *Journal of Empirical Legal Studies*, Volume 14, 2017, pp. 397, 418–21 and ff (discussing that an insurer's use of credit-anchored insurance scores lacks a disparate impact on the basis of income and thus is not amenable to be considered as a proxy for income); Pope, Devin G. Pope/Sydnor, Justin R., "Implementing Anti-Discrimination Policies in Statistical Profiling Models", *American Economic Journal: Applied Economics*, Volume 3, 2011, pp. 206–210 (discussing how the FTC parsed credit score use in auto-insurance pricing as a proxy for race).

1222 Kim, Pauline T., "Data-Driven Discrimination at Work", *William and Mary Law Review*, Volume 58, 2017, p. 918 ("If the goal is to reduce biased outcomes, then a simple prohibition on using data about race or sex could be either wholly ineffective or actually counterproductive due to the existence of class proxies and the risk of omitted variable bias."); Lipton, Zachary et al., "Does Mitigating ML's Impact Disparity Require Treatment Disparity?", NIPS Proceedings 1, 2018, https://arxiv.org/pdf/1711.07076.pdf; [https://perma.cc/X8VF-EY53] (arguing, premised on statistical examples, that a prohibition on race or sex data is rather counterproductive indeed); Corbett-Davies, Sam/Goel, Sharad, "The Measure and Mismeasure of Fairness: a critical Review of Fair Machine Learning", *Cornell University Library*, 2018, passim (discussing the "[l]imitations of anti-classification" as a fairness metric). See: Mayson, Sandra G., "Bias In, Bias Out", *cit.*, pp. 2218–2300.

1223 Crow, M. S., "The complexities of prior record, race, ethnicity, and policy: Interactive effects in sentencing", *Criminal Justice Review*, Volume 33, Issue 4, 2008, pp. 502–523.

1224 Hinton, Elizabeth, "An Unjust Burden: The Disparate Treatment of Black Americans in the Criminal Justice System", *Vera Evidence Brief*, May 2018, 2018, pp. 1–20 (1) ("*The over-representation of black Americans in the nation's justice system is well documented. Black men comprise about 13 percent of the male population, but about 35 percent of those incarcerated. One in three black men born today can expect to be incarcerated in his lifetime, compared to one in six Latino men and one in 17 white men. Black women are similarly impacted: one in 18 black women born in 2001 is likely to be incarcerated sometime in her life, compared to one in 111 white women. The underlying reasons for this dis-proportionate representation are rooted in the history of the United States and perpetuated by current practices within the nation's justice system. This brief presents an overview of the ways in which America's history of racism and oppression continues to manifest in the criminal justice system, and a summary of research demonstrating how the system perpetuates the disparate treatment of black people. The evidence presented here helps account for the hugely disproportionate impact of mass incarceration on millions of black people, their families, and their communities. This brief explains that: › Discriminatory criminal justice policies and practices have historically and unjustifiably targeted black people since the Reconstruction Era, including Black Codes, vagrancy laws, and convict leasing, all of which were used to continue*

§§ This type of *proxy discrimination*[1233] is a trap in disguise that aims nothing but to weed out Black and Latino rental applicants, leveraging on biased algorithmic credit scoring.[1234] *Proxy discrimination* therefore stands as a byproduct of *Algorithmic Dictatorship* in that is arguably a direct heir of *mortgage redlining* which dispiritingly ripples forward.[1235]

---

post-slavery control over newly-freed people. › This discrimination continues today in often less overt ways, including through disparity in the enforcement of seemingly race-neutral laws. For example, while rates of drug use are similar across racial and ethnic groups, black people are arrested and sentenced on drug charges at much higher rates than white people. › Bias by decision makers at all stages of the justice process disadvantages black people. Studies have found that they are more likely to be stopped by the police, detained pretrial, charged with more serious crimes, and sentenced more harshly than white people. › Living in poor communities exposes people to risk factors for both offending and arrest, and a history of structural racism and inequality of opportunity means that black people are more likely to be living in such conditions of concentrated poverty. *In addition to the clear injustice of a criminal justice system that disproportionately impacts black people, maintaining these racial disparities has a high cost for individuals, families, and communities. At the individual level, a criminal conviction has a negative impact on both employability and access to housing and public services. At the community level, disproportionately incarcerating people from poor communities removes economic resources and drives cycles of poverty and justice system involvement, making criminal justice contact the norm in the lives of a growing number of black Americans*"). Italics added.

1225 Desmond, M., "Eviction and the reproduction of urban poverty", *American Journal of Sociology*, Volume 118, Issue 1, 2012, pp. 88–133.

1226 Hartman, C., & Robinson, D., "Evictions: The hidden housing problem", *Housing Policy Debate*, Volume 14, Issue 4, 2003, pp. 461–501.

1227 *Connecticut Fair Housing Center*, et al. *v. CoreLogic Rental Property Solutions*, Case No. 3:18-cv-00705, U.S. District Court for the District of Connecticut, available: https://www.cohenmilstein.com/case-study/connecticut-fair-housing-center-et-al-v-corelogic-rental-property-solutions/ (access: 22.11.2024).

1228 Greif, M., "Regulating landlords: Unintended consequences for poor tenants", City & Community, Volume 17, Issue 3, 2018, pp. 658–674; Hatch, M E., "Statutory protection for renters: Classification of state landlord–tenant policy approaches", *Housing Policy Debate*, Volume 27, Issue 1, 2017, pp. 98–119.

1229 Wonyoung, So, "Which Information Matters? Measuring Landlord Assessment of Tenant Screening Reports", *Housing Policy Debate*, Volume 33, n. ° 6, 2023, pp. 1484–1510 (1484) ("*This research studies how tenant screening services' presentation of information influences landlord decisions. Tenant screening services utilize criminal records, eviction records, and credit score databases to produce reports that landlords use to inform their decisions about who to rent to. However, little is known about how landlords assess the information presented by tenant screening reports. Through a behavioral experiment with landlords using simulated tenant screening reports, this study shows that landlords use blanket screening policies, that they conflate the existence of tenant records with outcomes (e.g., eviction filings with executed evictions), and that they display, on average, tendencies toward automation bias that are influenced by the risk assessments and scores presented by tenant screening reports.* I argue that maintaining blanket screening policies and automation bias, combined with the downstream effects of creating and *using racially biased eviction and criminal records, means that people of color will inevitably experience disproportionate exclusion from rental housing due to perceived "risk" on the part of landlords*"). Italics added. See: Part IV, This chapter, Sects. 4.1.4–4.1.4.2.3 of this book. See: Part IV, This chapter, Sects. 4.1.4–4.1.4.2.1 of this book (on mortgage redlining). See: Part IV, This chapter, Sects. 4.1.2–4.1.4.3 of this book (on algorithmic credit scoring, consumer racism and credit card redlining). See: Part IV, This chapter, Sects. 4.1.4–4.1.4.2.3 of this book (on algorithmic redlining). See: Part

§§ Notably, handpicked variables (criminal record,[1236] time of the latest arrest,[1237] past due accounts, payment performance, prior evictions[1238]) are used as proxies for[1239] race,[1240] thereby exacting a toll on members of racialized communities (Blacks and Latinos) whom, in the bigoted eyes of the technology deployed to automate

---

IV, This chapter, Sect. 4.1.4.3 of this book (on "algorithmic redliking"). See: Part IV, This chapter, Sect. 4.1.3 of this book (on algorithmic prime-lining).

[1230] Haupert, T., "The racial landscape of fintech mortgage lending", *Housing Policy Debate*, Volume 32, Issue 2, 2022.

[1231] Humber, Nadiyah J., "A Home for Digital Equity: Algorithmic Redlining and Property Technology", *cit.*, pp. 1421–1484 (1424).

[1232] Wonyoung, So, "Which Information Matters? Measuring Landlord Assessment of Tenant Screening Reports", *Housing Policy Debate*, Volume 33, n. ° 6, 2023, pp. 1484–1510 (1502) ("*One additional finding of the experiment is that algorithmic scoring can exacerbate this racially unequal landscape in rental agreements not just because the algorithm may be inaccurate, but because landlords may want to follow the risk assessment made by the tenant screening report. This is alarming for low-income tenants, particularly housing voucher holders. Security deposits are one of the most significant barriers to obtaining housing for voucher holders, because vouchers do not pay security deposits but most private landlords require them (Rosenblatt & Cossyleon, 2018).* Given that voucher holders have exceptionally low income (usually less than 50% of area median income) and might experience more housing insecurity (rental debts and eviction-related experiences), *imposing greater security deposits on voucher holders almost equates to denying them housing—yet these decisions could be justified by algorithmic scoring if tenant screening services employ it*"). Italics added.

[1233] See: Part IV, This chapter, Sect. 4.1.6.3 of this book (on proxy discrimination). See also: Prince, Anya E. R./Schwarcz, Daniel, "Proxy Discrimination in the Age of Artificial Intelligence and Big Data", *Iowa Law Review*, Volume 105, 1257, 2020, pp. 1279–81 ("*[P]roxy discrimination will tend to occur when a suspect variable is predictive of a desired outcome only because it proxies for another*, quantifiable and potentially available, *variable that causes the desired outcome but that is not included in the AI's training data*"). Italics added. See: Part IV, This chapter, Sect. 4.1.6.3 of this book (on proxy discrimination). See also: Grimmelmann, James/Westreich, Daniel, "Incomprehensible Discrimination", *California Law Review Online*, Volume 7, 2017, pp 170 and ff and passim. This exciting piece of research revolves around as a vignette and mock judicial opinion, focusing on fictional case (an employment-based AI employed in the fictional universe of the movie Zootopia) under a specific legal regime (Title VII). It ultimately solves this fictional case by drawing a difference between *proxy discrimination and disparate impact* p. 70 ("The problem is that there is no explanation in the record as to which of these two correlations, if either, is causal. It may be that the factors directly measure applicant characteristics that determine success in the challenging and dangerous field of police work, and that those characteristics happen to be unequally distributed in our diverse society. It may also be that these factors are instead measuring applicants' species and that they measure likely job performance only because they are identifying species in an applicant pool where the relevant characteristics are unequally distributed").

[1234] *Tech, Bias and Housing Initiative, the Promise and Perils of Residential Proptech, Year 1, Research Summary Report, April 2023, TechEquity Collaborative*, p. 10, available at: https://techequity.us/wp-content/uploads/2023/04/TBHI-Y1-Research-Summary-Report.pdf (28.11.2024). ("*Tenant screening tools are often packaged as part of a larger suite of property management tools for landlords. Unlike Analog Models, Algorithmic Tenant Screening Tools Predict Future Behavior To Determine Housing Access.* Before the advent of algorithmic tenant screening, landlords vetted tenants by having them submit their own records and references from previous landlords or others who could vouch for their trustworthiness. During an analog rental application process, a prospective tenant provides certain personal information and then gives consent for the landlord to run a background check to verify their information. *The landlord, housing provider, or*

workflows within the remit of real estate industry[1241] that leverages on machine learnings algorithms,[1242] are utterly unfit to rent the great bulk of properties.[1243]

---

property manager then pays a third-party entity such as TransUnion to pull information that gives a sense of whether the applicant will be a trustworthy renter. In analog screening, those reports return information from an applicant's credit, eviction, and criminal histories. There are many inequities with this analog model. Eviction and criminal records are often wrong or lack important context. 12 13 Credit scoring techniques are notoriously biased"). Italics added. See: Part IV, This chapter, Sects. 4.1.4–4.1.4.2.3 of this book.See: Dunn, E., & Grabchuk, M., "Background checks and social effects: Contemporary residential tenant-screening problems in Washington State", *Seattle Journal for Social Justice*, Volume 9, Issue 1, 2010; Ehman, M., *Fair housing disparate impact claims based on the use of criminal and eviction records in tenant screening policies*, 2015, available at: https://www.nhlp.org/wp-content/uploads/Merf-Ehman-FH-DI-Claims-Based-on-Use-of-Criminal-and-Eviction-Records-Sept.-2015.pdf.

[1235] In spite of its deep-seated racial bias, decision-makers continue to deploy redlining tactics through big data and may even justify such unlawful practices by claiming that the latter abide by cost-effectiveness. See: Humber, Nadiyah J., "A Home for Digital Equity: Algorithmic Redlining and Property Technology", *California Law Review*, Volume 111, Issue 5, 2023, pp. 1421–1484. See also: Hurley, Mikella/Adebayo, Julius, "Credit Scoring in the Era of Big Data", *Yale Journal of Law and Technology*, Volume 18, 2016, pp. 148, 151–156, 172 (averring that FICO scoring boasts a redoubtable capacity to routinely weed out some populations that have been historically and systematically underrepresented or grossly unfairly represented in the credit industry market). Tellingly, by 2016, ten states had disavowed the unlawful practice of employers using shady credit scores due to their perceived disparate impact on low-income applicants and members of racialized communities (mostly Black folks). See: O'Neill, Cathy, *Weapons of Math Destruction. How Big Data Increases Inequality and Threatens Democracy*. London: Penguin Random House, 2016, pp. 128 and ff and passim. See: Part IV, This chapter, Sects. 4.1.4–4.1.4.2.1 of this book (on mortgage redlining). See: Part IV, This chapter, Sects. 4.1.2–4.1.4.3 of this book (on algorithmic credit scoring, consumer racism and credit card redlining). See: Part IV, This chapter, Sects. 4.1.4–4.1.4.2.3 of this book (on algorithmic redlining). See: Part IV, This chapter, Sect. 4.1.4.3 of this book (on "algorithmic redliking"). See: Part IV, This chapter, Sect. 4.1.3 of this book (on algorithmic prime-lining).

[1236] Wonyoung, So, "Which Information Matters? Measuring Landlord Assessment of Tenant Screening Reports", *Housing Policy Debate*, Volume 33, n. ° 6, 2023, pp. 1484–1510 (1484) ("*This research studies how tenant screening services' presentation of information influences landlord decisions. Tenant screening services utilize criminal records, eviction records, and credit score databases to produce reports that landlords use to inform their decisions about who to rent to. However, little is known about how landlords assess the information presented by tenant screening reports. Through a behavioral experiment with landlords using simulated tenant screening reports, this study shows that landlords use blanket screening policies, that they conflate the existence of tenant records with outcomes (e.g., eviction filings with executed evictions), and that they display, on average, tendencies toward automation bias that are influenced by the risk assessments and scores presented by tenant screening reports.* I argue that maintaining blanket screening policies and automation bias, combined with the downstream effects of creating and *using racially biased eviction and criminal records, means that people of color will inevitably experience disproportionate exclusion from rental housing due to perceived "risk" on the part of landlords*"). Italics added. See: Part IV, This chapter, Sects. 4.1.4–4.1.4.2.3 of this book.

[1237] Wonyoung, So, "Which Information Matters? Measuring Landlord Assessment of Tenant Screening Reports", *Housing Policy Debate*, Volume 33, n. ° 6, 2023, pp. 1484–1510 (1501–1502) ("*There are considerations and implications involved in the assessment of criminal records. First,*

§§ Strikingly, landlords/housing providers rely heavily on the algorithmic credit scoring carried out by computer-run tenant screening services, thereby evincing *automation bias.*[1244]

---

this study shows that MTurk landlords may differentiate serious types of crimes (e.g., sex offenders) from less serious ones (e.g., shoplifting) and/or may differentiate according to the disposition. In contrast, the prior section described how MTurk landlords treat filings and executed evictions similarly. These differences *might suggest that landlords are less familiar with how evictions are executed than with how criminal justice procedure works (e.g., charge under criminal procedure and conviction/acquittal), because eviction records are a specific type of civil procedure—landlord–tenant disputes.* However, in the mid-scored reports, there is statistical evidence that showing the report's risk score (Type 2) caused MTurk landlords to deny tenant applications more frequently, whereas there is no statistical evidence that having detailed information in the report (Type 3) caused MTurk landlords to do the same. *This result indicates a need for further research and policy formulation on algorithmic scoring of tenant records (Smith & Voguell, 2022), with a specific focus on how landlords construct proxies of desirable tenants through two perspectives from this study: (a) the difficulties of assessing mid-scored criminal records (e.g., arrest records and misdemeanors) and, therefore, (b) reinforcing landlords' potential reliance on algorithmic decisions provided by reports*"). Italics added. See: Part IV, This chapter, Sects. 4.1.4–4.1.4.2.3 of this book.

[1238] *Tech, Bias and Housing Initiative, the Promise and Perils of Residential Proptech, Year 1, Research Summary Report, April 2023, TechEquity Collaborative*, p. 10, available at: https://techequity.us/wp-content/uploads/2023/04/TBHI-Y1-Research-Summary-Report.pdf (28.11.2024). ("*Algorithm-backed screening services, on the other hand, bundle all the traditional information (whether accurate or not) alongside predictive models. These predictive models make guesses about whether an applicant will be a responsible tenant based not on the history of that specific applicant, but on (as far as we can tell) behavior trends of applicants who have similar characteristics. The data behind these models is rarely made available to either the tenant or the landlord.* Below, a sample screening report from Naborly gives a sense of how predictive screening works. Certain outcomes are determined by a combination of applicant characteristics and factors that have little to do with said applicant. *"Length of Tenancy," for example, is rated both by applicant characteristics as well as a prediction of how "conditions may change in the future." Eviction outcomes are determined by "possibility of property damage;" Successful payments rely on "suitability to the rental property*"). Italics added. Desmond, M., "Eviction and the reproduction of urban poverty", *American Journal of Sociology*, Volume 118, Issue 1, 2012, pp. 88–133.

[1239] Campisi, Natalie, From Inherent Racial Bias to Incorrect Data The Problems With Current Credit Scoring Models, Forbes (Feb. 26, 2021), https://www.forbes.com/advisor/creditcards/from-inherent-racial-bias-to-incorrect-data-the-problems-with-current-credit-scoring-models/; [https://perma.cc/EWA4-CS8E] (highlighting rampant racial bias in credit scoring systems); Oyama, Rebecca, "Do Not (Re)Enter: the Rise of Criminal Background Tenant Screening as a Violation of the Fair Housing Act", *Michigan Journal of Race and Law*, Volume 15, 2009, pp. 181, 184–93 (discussing a broad range of historical/criminal accounts as a way to screen undesirable tenants, such as Blacks and Latinos); Statement of Interest of the United States at 12, *Louis v. SafeRent Sols., LLC, No. 1:22-cv-10800* (D. Mass. Jan. 9, 2023) (holding that the Fair Housing Act liability stretches far and beyond, thus encompassing a vast assortment of entities providing housing-related services, including corporations that offer tenant screening services).

[1240] DaViera, A. L./Uriostegui, M., Gottlieb/A./Onyeka, O, "Risk, race, and predictive policing: A critical race theory analysis of the strategic subject list", *cit.*, pp. 91–103.

[1241] *Tech, Bias and Housing Initiative, the Promise and Perils of Residential Proptech, Year 1, Research Summary Report, April 2023, TechEquity Collaborative*, p. 5 available at: https://techequity.us/wp-content/uploads/2023/04/TBHI-Y1-Research-Summary-Report.pdf (28.11.2024). ("*Residential Proptech also has the potential to exacerbate the bias inherent*

§§ To further compound the jarring tapestry of racial discrimination facing members of racialized communities (Blacks and Latinos), the latter tend to have far higher rates of eviction[1245] or executed[1246] evictions.[1247] To add to their woes, Blacks

in our housing system. Its rise is due, in part, to the desperation felt by average home seekers. With a severely constrained housing supply, companies offering an easier pathway to homeownership may exploit communities that have been harmed by housing discrimination in the past. Opaque algorithms incorporate biased data into their decision-making processes, making it harder to enforce fair housing laws. Residential Proptech companies often operate in a regulatory gray area, leaving consumers without the protections they would have from traditional housing regulatory systems. *As unprecedented capital investment flows into this space, venture-backed companies' winner-take-all approach to growth has the potential to exacerbate inequality rather than combat it*"). Italics added.

[1242] Humber, Nadiyah J., "A Home for Digital Equity: Algorithmic Redlining and Property Technology", *cit.*, pp. 1421–1484.

[1243] *Tech, Bias and Housing Initiative, the Promise and Perils of Residential Proptech, Year 1, Research Summary Report, April 2023, TechEquity Collaborative*, p. 11, available at: https://techequity.us/wp-content/uploads/2023/04/TBHI-Y1-Research-Summary-Report.pdf (28.11.2024). ("*From information on company websites, it is not clear what analysis or data is behind subjective determinations like "suitability" to a unit or what the nexus between an individual's characteristics and a unit's characteristics is that indicates the likelihood for property damage. Based on sample reports, even landlords are not privy to how the determinations are made*"). Italics added.

[1244] Wonyoung, So, "Which Information Matters? Measuring Landlord Assessment of Tenant Screening Reports", *Housing Policy Debate*, Volume 33, n. ° 6, 2023, pp. 1484–1510 (1484) ("*This research studies how tenant screening services' presentation of information influences landlord decisions. Tenant screening services utilize criminal records, eviction records, and credit score databases to produce reports that landlords use to inform their decisions about who to rent to. However, little is known about how landlords assess the information presented by tenant screening reports. Through a behavioral experiment with landlords using simulated tenant screening reports, this study shows that landlords use blanket screening policies, that they conflate the existence of tenant records with outcomes (e.g., eviction filings with executed evictions), and that they display, on average, tendencies toward automation bias that are influenced by the risk assessments and scores presented by tenant screening reports.* I argue that maintaining blanket screening policies and automation bias, combined with the downstream effects of creating and *using racially biased eviction and criminal records, means that people of color will inevitably experience disproportionate exclusion from rental housing due to perceived "risk" on the part of landlords*"). Italics added. See: Part IV, This chapter, Sects. 4.1.4–4.1.4.2.3 of this book.

[1245] Gromis, Ashley, *Eviction: Intersection of Poverty, Inequality, and Housing*, Eviction Lab, Princeton University Princeton, New Jersey, United States of America, 2019, pp. 2, available at: https://www.un.org/development/desa/dspd/wpcontent/uploads/sites/22/2019/05/GROMIS_Ashley_Paper.pdf (access: 25.11.2024) ("*The concentration of eviction within particular communities contributes to the reproduction of residential inequality. Evictions have been consistently shown to disproportionally affect the economically disadvantaged, racial/ethnic minorities, and women* (Bezdek 1992; Desmond 2012; Hartman and Robinson 2003; Philadelphia Eviction Task Force 2018). *Experiencing an eviction further compounds economic and material disadvantage. In this way, eviction actively contributes to the reproduction of poverty (Desmond 2016). Without comprehensive measures of eviction, we cannot assess the full scope of forced displacement or its effects on housing inequality in the United States*"). Italics added.

[1246] But see: Wonyoung, So, "Which Information Matters? Measuring Landlord Assessment of Tenant Screening Reports", *Housing Policy Debate*, Volume 33, n. ° 6, 2023, pp. 1484–1510 (1500) (arguing that many landlords file evictions (eviction fillings) with no intention whatsoever of

and Latinos tend to have lower credit scores[1248] owing to perpetual discriminatory practices[1249] that impair generational wealth[1250]-creation.[1251]

§§ Relatedly, credit scores «black box»[1252] assessments are eerily subjective[1253] and value-laden.[1254] Beyond the human biases[1255] arising out past decisions

---

proceeding with its execution (executed evictions) only to purposefully harm an undesirable tenant, which casts a shady shadow on the eviction records, which, in turn, lack accuracy. "*With regards to eviction records, one of the most noticeable harms this study identifies is that during the tenant screening process, landlords do not distinguish between eviction filings and actually executed evictions. This is particularly alarming given that many landlords file numerous evictions without the intention of or a sound rationale for actually evicting tenants (Garboden & Rosen, 2019). Furthermore, this study replicates the finding of "professional solidarity" among landlords (Garboden & Rosen, 2019, p. 647). Eviction filings are a tacit tenant screening measure meant to issue a warning to other landlords against taking on the tenant in question (Garboden & Rosen, 2019; Leung* et al., *2021). Furthermore, landlords often file multiple evictions on the same tenant—this is frequently called "serial filing" (Immergluck* et al., *2020; Leung* et al., *2021). As a result, in Washington, DC, for example, among all eviction records, only 5.5% of evictions filed in 2018 were executed (McCabe & Rosen, 2020). This means that 94.5% of filed evictions were not executed. As this study has shown, those records may be interpreted, erroneously, as evictions by landlords and will likely still negatively affect tenants' future housing search (Phillips, 2020)*"). Italics added. See: Part IV, This chapter, Sects. 4.1.4–4.1.4.2.3 of this book. Desmond, M., "Eviction and the reproduction of urban poverty", *American Journal of Sociology*, Volume 118, Issue 1, 2012, pp. 88–133.

1247 But see: Porton, Adam/Gromis, Ashley/Desmond, Matthew, "Inaccuracies in Eviction Records: Implications for Renters and Researchers", *Housing Policy Debate*, Volume 31, n. ° 3–5, 2021, pp. 377–394 ("*Administrative court records are increasingly used to study the prevalence of eviction. Yet inaccuracies in court records bias estimates of eviction and distort tenants' true rental histories. This is the first study to systematically assess the prevalence of inaccuracies across jurisdictions. Drawing on over 3.6 million administrative eviction court records from 12 states, we find that, on average, 22% of eviction records contain ambiguous information on how the case was resolved or falsely represent a tenant's eviction history.* Adjusting for multiple inaccuracies in the data produces significantly different eviction rate estimates. *Cases with increased complexity, such as those involving multiple tenants and lawyers, are more likely to contain inaccuracies. However, inaccuracies vary most prominently between states, indicating that state court system characteristics fundamentally shape the official record of the evicted population*"). Italics added. See: Part IV, This chapter, Sects. 4.1.4–4.1.4.2.3 of this book.

1248 It is crucially important to note, though, that the very fact that only certain types of behaviours are assessed and gauged by credit scores leads to the conclusion some borrowers are not scored at all. The overwhelming majority of consumers boast meagre, if any, credit files owing to the fact that the likelihood to access to the sort of financial services that actually report to the orthodox credit bureaus scattered across modern economies is exceedingly low, which, in turn, morphs them into credit invisible persons. See: Yu, Persis/McLaughlin, Jilian/Levy, Marina, "Big Data: A Big Disappointment for Scoring Consumer Creditworthiness,", *The National Consumer Law Center,* 2 (Mar. 14, 2014), available at: https://www.nclc.org/images/pdf/pr-reports/report-big-data.pdf; [https://perma.cc/W4SK-NXD5] (access: 21.12.2024).

1249 Desmond, M., "Eviction and the reproduction of urban poverty", *American Journal of Sociology*, Volume 118, Issue 1, 2012, pp. 88–133; Desmond, M., *Evicted: Poverty and profit in the American city*, First Edition, New York, Crown Publishers, 2016, passim.

1250 Kroeger, Teresa, and Graham Wright, "Entrepreneurship and the Racial Wealth Gap: The Impact of Entrepreneurial Success or Failure on the Wealth Mobility of Black and White Families," *Journal of Economics, Race, and Policy*, Volume 4, 2021, 183–195; Kermani, Amir, and Francis Wong, "Racial Disparities in Housing Returns," NBER Working Paper no. 29306, 2021; Hubmer, Joachim, Per Krusell, and Anthony A. Smith, Jr., "Sources of US Wealth Inequality: Past, Present,

embedded into the code, some automated correlations and inferences[1256] may seem as though they are fully objective, but may nonetheless reflect deep-rooted racial

---

and Future," *NBER Macroeconomics Annual 2020*, Volume 35, 2021, pp. 391–455; Haines, Michael R., *Historical, Demographic, Economic, and Social Data: The United States, 1790–2002*, Inter-university Consortium for Political and Social Research, 2010.

[1251] Humber, Nadiyah J., "A Home for Digital Equity: Algorithmic Redlining and Property Technology", *cit.*, pp. 1421–1484. Derenoncourt, Ellora/Kim, Chi Hyun/Kuhn, Moritz/Schularik, Moritz, "The Wealth of Two Nations: The U.S. Racial Wealth Gap, 1860–2020", *The Quarterly Journal of Economics*, Volume 139, Issue 2, 2024, p. 741 ("A large class of commonly discussed policies for reducing racial wealth inequality seeks to reduce gaps in income, savings, and capital gains. These include policies that encourage financial diversification or stock equity holdings among Black households; policies aimed at financial literacy and retirement or savings behavior; or policies aimed at improving educational and labor market outcomes of Black Americans through improved school quality or reductions in discrimination. *Yet on a realistic note, our simulation in Section IV.A shows that even if wealth accumulation conditions had been equal since 1870, the wealth gap would still be 3 to 1 today, and full convergence would be more than 200 years away. Put differently: to close the racial wealth gap in the immediate term* via *flow parameters, Black Americans would need a substantial positive lead over whites, not "just" more equality*"). Italics added.

[1252] Havard, Cassandra Jones, "On The Take": The Black Box of Credit Scoring and Mortgage Discrimination", *Boston University Public Interest Law Journal*, Volume 20, 2011, pp. 241–247 (highlighting that credit scoring if unchecked is an intrinsic, encroached, deep-rooted form of racial discrimination akin to mortgage redlining); Pasquale, Frank, *The Black Box Society: The Secret Algorithms that Control Money and Information*. Cambridge, Massachusetts: Harvard University Press, 2015, 1–320; Watcher, S./Mittelstadt, B./Russell, C., "Counterfactual explanations without opening the black box: automated decisions and the GDPR", *Harvard Journal of Law & Technology*, Volume 1, 2018, passim; Rudin, C., & Radin, J., "Why are we using black box models in AI when we don't need to? A lesson from an explainable AI competition", *Harvard Data Science Review*, 2019, Volume 1, Issue 2, passim; Tan, S., Caruana, R., Hooker, G., and Lou, Y., "Distill-and-compare: Auditing blackbox models using transparent model distillation". *Proceedings of the 2018 AAAI/ACM Conference on AI, Ethics, and Society, Association for Computing Machinery*, 2018, pp. 303–310; Rudin, Cynthia, "Please stop explaining black box models for high stakes decisions", *Proceedings of NeurIPS 2018 Workshop on Critiquing and Correcting Trends in Machine Learning (NIPS 2018)*, 2018, passim. But see: Part V, Chap. 5, Sect. 5.1.7.2 of this book (on law number two to control algorithmic decision-making, which mandates that black box models must not be entrusted with the task of making high stake decisions—v.g. health and freedom). See: Part V, Chap. 5, Sects. 5.1.7–5.1.7.5 of this book (on the five laws to control algorithmic decision-making).

[1253] *Tech, Bias and Housing Initiative, the Promise and Perils of Residential Proptech, Year 1, Research Summary Report, April 2023, TechEquity Collaborative*, p. 11, available at: https://techequity.us/wp-content/uploads/2023/04/TBHI-Y1-Research-Summary-Report.pdf (28.11.2024). ("*From information on company websites, it is not clear what analysis or data is behind subjective determinations like "suitability" to a unit or what the nexus between an individual's characteristics and a unit's characteristics is that indicates the likelihood for property damage. Based on sample reports, even landlords are not privy to how the determinations are made. Instead, they receive a risk score out of 100 simplified into green, yellow, and red recommendations.* What companies withhold in terms of how it works, they make up for with the extent to which they tell landlords it works: Naborly claims their predictions reduce lease defaults by up to 89%. 15 *As Naborly's sample report demonstrates, its property damage assessment is then used as an input to determine its projected eviction outcomes; its early vacancy prediction, in turn, is based on "all assessment factors*"). Italics added.

[1254] Citron, Danielle Keats/Pasquale, Frank A., "The Scored Society: Due Process for Automated Predictions", *Washington Law Review*, Volume 89, 2014, pp. 1–34.

biases.[1257] For instance, late payments and filed evictions[1258]—whose records are riddled with various types of inaccuracies[1259]—are routinely fed into credit scoring models, which may catalyse bad outcomes, thereby cascading into ever more challenging life circumstances[1260] for members of communities of colour (Blacks and Latinos).

[1255] Pyszczyinski, Tom/Greenberg, Jeff, "Toward an Integration of Cognitive and Motivational Perspectives on Social Inferences: A Biased Hypothesis Testing Model", *20 Advances in Experimental Social Psychology*, 1987, pp. 296 ff (averring that there is scant to no consensus whatsoever with regard to the psychological mechanisms that breed a set of cognitive biases); Kardes, Frank *et alii*, "On the Conditions under Which Experience and Motivate Accentuate Bias in Intuitive Judgement", *The Routines of Decision Making*, Tilman Betsch & Susanne Haberstroh (ed.), New York, Routledge, 2013, pp. 1–768 (contending that both cognitive and motivational biases derive from the unescapable human tendency to make and produce intuitive judgments); Pronin, Emily, "Perception and Misperception of Bias in Human Judgement", *Trends in Cognitive Sciences*, Volume 37, 2007, passim(on the fallibility of perception and the misconceptions built therein); Vasco Correia, "Bias and Fallacies: The Role of Motivated Irrationality in Fallacious Reasoning", *Cogency*, Volume 3, 2011, pp. 108 ff (emphasizes that oftentimes people tend to jump into conclusions and are prone to make steadfast judgments with little to none regard for its intrinsic accuracy. Which amounts to either conscious or unconscious biases); Volkan Topalli/Edgar C. O'Neal, "Retaliatory Motivation Enhances Attributions of Hostility When People Process Ambiguous Social Stimuli", *Aggressive Behaviour*, Volume 29, 2003, pp. 153 ff (disserting about the negative attributions arisen from procession ambiguous social stimuli); Taylor, Donald M./Jaggi, Vaishna, "Ethnocentrism and Causal Attribution in a South Indian Context", *Journal of Cross-Cultural Psychology*, (referring to the negative bias ascribed to *out-groups*); Nisbett, R. E./Norenzayan, A./Choi, I. "Cultural similarities and differences in social inference: Evidence from behavioral predictions and lay theories of behavior", *Personality and Social Psychology Bulletin*, Volume 28, 2002, pp. 109–120.

[1256] Epstein, Lee/King, Gary "The Rules of Inference", *University of Chicago Law Review*, Volume 69, Issue 1, 2002, pp. 19 ff and passim (the workability of rules of inference—from either data collated directly or indirectly by the researcher—relies upon, and entails: **(i)** amassing data; **(ii)** summarizing data; **(iii)** making descriptive, qualitative and causal inferences from the batches of data analysed). This book is to rely upon the rules of inference's methodology with a view to withdrawing some conclusions and inferences from the handful of bodies of empirical research reviewed throughout the book.

[1257] Citron, Danielle Keats/Pasquale, Frank A., "The Scored Society: Due Process for Automated Predictions", *cit.*, pp. 1–34.

[1258] But see: Wonyoung, So, "Which Information Matters? Measuring Landlord Assessment of Tenant Screening Reports", *Housing Policy Debate*, Volume 33, n. ° 6, 2023, pp. 1484–1510 (1500) (arguing that many landlords file evictions (*eviction fillings*) with no intention whatsoever of proceeding with its execution (*executed evictions*) only to purposefully harm an undesirable tenant, which casts a shady shadow on the eviction records, which, in turn, lack accuracy. "*With regards to eviction records, one of the most noticeable harms this study identifies is that during the tenant screening process, landlords do not distinguish between eviction filings and actually executed evictions. This is particularly alarming given that many landlords file numerous evictions without the intention of or a sound rationale for actually evicting tenants (Garboden & Rosen, 2019). Furthermore, this study replicates the finding of "professional solidarity" among landlords (Garboden & Rosen, 2019, p. 647). Eviction filings are a tacit tenant screening measure meant to issue a warning to other landlords against taking on the tenant in question (Garboden & Rosen, 2019; Leung* et al., *2021). Furthermore, landlords often file multiple evictions on the same tenant—this is frequently called "serial filing" (Immergluck* et al., *2020; Leung* et al., *2021). As a result, in Washington, DC, for example, among all eviction records, only 5.5% of evictions filed in 2018 were executed (McCabe & Rosen, 2020). This means that 94.5% of filed evictions were not executed. As*

§§ Property Technologies (*PropTech*)[1261] that propel automated tenant screening tools in the remit of rental housing are eerily bigoted in that they heavily rely on biased data[1262] nested with racial disparities in algorithmic credit scores,[1263] filed[1264]

this study has shown, those records may be interpreted, erroneously, as evictions by landlords and will likely still negatively affect tenants' future housing search (Phillips, 2020)"). Italics added.

1259 Porton, Adam/Gromis, Ashley/Desmond, Matthew, "Inaccuracies in Eviction Records: Implications for Renters and Researchers", *Housing Policy Debate*, Volume 31, n.° 3–5, 2021, pp. 377–394 ("*Administrative court records are increasingly used to study the prevalence of eviction. Yet inaccuracies in court records bias estimates of eviction and distort tenants' true rental histories. This is the first study to systematically assess the prevalence of inaccuracies across jurisdictions. Drawing on over 3.6 million administrative eviction court records from 12 states, we find that, on average, 22% of eviction records contain ambiguous information on how the case was resolved or falsely represent a tenant's eviction history.* Adjusting for multiple inaccuracies in the data produces significantly different eviction rate estimates. *Cases with increased complexity, such as those involving multiple tenants and lawyers, are more likely to contain inaccuracies. However, inaccuracies vary most prominently between states, indicating that state court system characteristics fundamentally shape the official record of the evicted population*"). Italics added. See also: Desmond, M., "Eviction and the reproduction of urban poverty", *American Journal of Sociology*, Volume 118, Issue 1, 2012, pp. 88–133; Desmond, M., *Evicted: Poverty and profit in the American city*, First Edition, New York, Crown Publishers, 2016, passim.

1260 Citron, Danielle Keats/Pasquale, Frank A., "The Scored Society: Due Process for Automated Predictions", *cit.*, pp. 1–34.

1261 Yoh, Christina, What Is "PropTech"and Why Companies Are Developing It", *Common* (June 23, 2020), https://www.common.com/blog/2019/06/what-is-PropTech-and-why-companies-are-developing-it; [https://perma.cc/544Z-5RHW] ("PropTech is an innovative approach to real estate in which technology optimizes how people research, rent, buy, sell, and manage a property").

1262 *Tech, Bias and Housing Initiative, the Promise and Perils of Residential Proptech, Year 1, Research Summary Report, April 2023, TechEquity Collaborative*, p. 11, available at: https://techequity.us/wp-content/uploads/2023/04/TBHI-Y1-Research-Summary-Report.pdf (28.11.2024). ("*Once bad data enters the analysis of one factor, it gets baked into the subsequent process, multiplying the effect that one disadvantageous data point can have on someone's overall housing determination*"). Italics added. See: Part IV, This chapter, Sects. 4.1.4–4 .1.4.2.3 of this book. See: Part IV, This chapter, Sects. 4.1.4–4.1.4.2.1 of this book (on mortgage redlining). See: Part IV, This chapter, Sects. 4.1.2–4.1.4.3 of this book (on algorithmic credit scoring, consumer racism and credit card redlining). See: Part IV, This chapter, Sects. 4.1.4–4.1.4.2.3 of this book (on algorithmic redlining). See: Part IV, This chapter, Sect. 4.1.4.3 of this book (on "algorithmic redliking"). See: Part IV, This chapter, Sect. 4.1.3 of this book (on algorithmic prime-lining).

1263 Wonyoung, So, "Which Information Matters? Measuring Landlord Assessment of Tenant Screening Reports", *Housing Policy Debate*, Volume 33, n. ° 6, 2023, pp. 1484–1510 (1502) ("*One additional finding of the experiment is that algorithmic scoring can exacerbate this racially unequal landscape in rental agreements not just because the algorithm may be inaccurate, but because landlords may want to follow the risk assessment made by the tenant screening report. This is alarming for low-income tenants, particularly housing voucher holders. Security deposits are one of the most significant barriers to obtaining housing for voucher holders, because vouchers do not pay security deposits but most private landlords require them (Rosenblatt & Cossyleon, 2018).* Given that voucher holders have exceptionally low income (usually less than 50% of area median income) and might experience more housing insecurity (rental debts and eviction-related experiences), *imposing greater security deposits on voucher holders almost equates to denying them housing—yet these decisions could be justified by algorithmic scoring if tenant screening services employ it*"). Italics added.

and executed evictions,[1265] and arrest records.[1266] These thought-through[1267] racial disparities are the outgrowths, and offsprings, of historically racist practices (e.g.

[1264] Desmond, M., "Eviction and the reproduction of urban poverty", *American Journal of Sociology*, Volume 118, Issue 1, 2012, pp. 88–133.

[1265] But see: Wonyoung, So, "Which Information Matters? Measuring Landlord Assessment of Tenant Screening Reports", *Housing Policy Debate*, Volume 33, n. ° 6, 2023, pp. 1484–1510 (1500) (arguing that many landlords file evictions (eviction fillings) with no intention whatsoever of proceeding with its execution (executed evictions) only to purposefully harm an undesirable tenant, which casts a shady shadow on the eviction records, which, in turn, lack accuracy. "*With regards to eviction records, one of the most noticeable harms this study identifies is that during the tenant screening process, landlords do not distinguish between eviction filings and actually executed evictions. This is particularly alarming given that many landlords file numerous evictions without the intention of or a sound rationale for actually evicting tenants (Garboden & Rosen, 2019). Furthermore, this study replicates the finding of "professional solidarity" among landlords (Garboden & Rosen, 2019, p. 647). Eviction filings are a tacit tenant screening measure meant to issue a warning to other landlords against taking on the tenant in question (Garboden & Rosen, 2019; Leung* et al., *2021). Furthermore, landlords often file multiple evictions on the same tenant—this is frequently called "serial filing" (Immergluck* et al., *2020; Leung* et al., *2021). As a result, in Washington, DC, for example, among all eviction records, only 5.5% of evictions filed in 2018 were executed (McCabe & Rosen, 2020). This means that 94.5% of filed evictions were not executed. As this study has shown, those records may be interpreted, erroneously, as evictions by landlords and will likely still negatively affect tenants' future housing search (Phillips, 2020)*"). Italics added. See: Part IV, This chapter, Sects. 4.1.4–4.1.4.2.3 of this book.

[1266] Wonyoung, So, "Which Information Matters? Measuring Landlord Assessment of Tenant Screening Reports", *Housing Policy Debate*, Volume 33, n. ° 6, 2023, pp. 1484–1510 (1501–1502) ("*In mid-scored criminal records, landlords would have more discretion in terms of how to assess tenants, depending on the type of charges or the disposition of the case. HUD prohibits denying housing by holding arrest records against tenants. But apart from that, landlords who HOUSING POLICY DEBATE 1501 would like to construct proxies of undesirable tenants using criminal records must assess which criminal records would relate to tenants' behavior (e.g., damaging their property and/or adversely affecting other tenants).* However, it is incredibly challenging to identify the causal relationship between how and which past misdemeanors cause particular future tenant behaviors. Moreover, legal jargon and abbreviations on the report could make it harder for landlords to understand criminal records in the first place. *These factors, as a result, could contribute to landlords' reliance on the scores provided by the report shown in the experiment*"). See: Part IV, This chapter, Sects. 4.1.4–4.1.4.2.3 of this book.

[1267] But see, on randomness: Teigena, Halvor/Kanten, Alf Børre, "Out of the blue: on the suddenness of perceived chance events", *Thinking & Reasoning*, Volume 29, n. ° 1, 2023, pp. 137–175 (137) ("*people commonly use terms like 'random', 'by chance', or 'accidentally' when they describe occurrences that sidestep the normal course of events, with no apparent causal link to ongoing activities. Such intrusive events are typically perceived as happening all of a sudden.* This was demonstrated in seven experiments (N ¼ 1299) by asking people to identify statements they believed belonged to stories about chance events, and by comparing chance vs. nonchance events from their own life and from the lives of others. Suddenness also appeared to be more strongly associated with beginnings than with endings of an episode. Thus, statements about sudden beginnings of a career or a relationship were more readily believed to happen 'by chance' than 'not by chance'. *But life-changing events did not become more accidental simply by being placed in the beginning of a 'life chapter'. These studies highlight a central but neglected feature of perceived randomness*"). Italics added.

mortgage redlining[1268]) that perpetuated segregation[1269] and disfranchised members of communities of color[1270] (Blacks and Latinos).[1271] *PropTech* therefore systematizes historical biases at more granular levels,[1272] thereby further exacerbating racial inequities with which people of colour have been floundering for a long-haul.[1273]

[1268] See: Part IV, This chapter, Sects. 4.1.4–4.1.4.2.1 of this book (on mortgage redlining). See: Part IV, This chapter, Sects. 4.1.2–4.1.4.3 of this book (on algorithmic credit scoring, consumer racism and credit card redlining). See: Part IV, This chapter, Sects. 4.1.4–4.1.4.2.3 of this book (on algorithmic redlining). See: Part IV, This chapter, Sect. 4.1.4.3 of this book (on "algorithmic redliking"). See also: Ferreri, Mara/Sanyal, Romola, "Digital informalisation: rental housing, platforms, and the management of risk", *Housing Studies*, Volume 37, Issue 6, 2022, pp. 1035–1053 (1035) ("*In contrast to progressive imaginaries of 'smart' technological mediation, practices of algorithmic redlining, biased tenant profiling and the management of risk in private tenancies and in housing welfare both introduce and extend discriminatory and exclusionary housing practices*"). Italics added. See: Part IV, This chapter, Sects. 4.1.4–4.1.4.2.3 of this book.

[1269] Allen, James, "The Color of Algorithms: An Analysis and Proposed Research Agenda Deterring Algorithmic Redlining", *Fordham Urban Law Journal*, Volume 46, 2019, pp. 219–234 (229–234) (discussing how historical mortgage redlining greatly swayed modern algorithms generated by massive batches of data sets that consist of decades of information built on exclusion and racial discrimination in the purview of financing, marketing, and housing).

[1270] *Tech, Bias and Housing Initiative, the Promise and Perils of Residential Proptech, Year 1, Research Summary Report, April 2023, TechEquity Collaborative*, p. 5 available at: https://techequity.us/wp-content/uploads/2023/04/TBHI-Y1-Research-Summary-Report.pdf (28.11.2024). ("*Residential Proptech also has the potential to exacerbate the bias inherent in our housing system. Its rise is due, in part, to the desperation felt by average home seekers. With a severely constrained housing supply, companies offering an easier pathway to homeownership may exploit communities that have been harmed by housing discrimination in the past. Opaque algorithms incorporate biased data into their decision-making processes, making it harder to enforce fair housing laws.* Residential Proptech companies often operate in a regulatory gray area, leaving consumers without the protections they would have from traditional housing regulatory systems. *As unprecedented capital investment flows into this space, venture-backed companies' winner-take-all approach to growth has the potential to exacerbate inequality rather than combat it*"). Italics added. See: Part IV, This chapter, Sects. 4.1.4–4.1.4.2.3 of this book.

[1271] Wonyoung, So, "Which Information Matters? Measuring Landlord Assessment of Tenant Screening Reports", *Housing Policy Debate*, Volume 33, n. ° 6, 2023, pp. 1484–1510 (1484) ("*Through a behavioral experiment with landlords using simulated tenant screening reports, this study shows that landlords use blanket screening policies, that they conflate the existence of tenant records with outcomes (e.g., eviction filings with executed evictions), and that they display, on average, tendencies toward automation bias that are influenced by the risk assessments and scores presented by tenant screening reports.* I argue that maintaining blanket screening policies and automation bias, combined with the downstream effects of creating and *using racially biased eviction and criminal records, means that people of color will inevitably experience disproportionate exclusion from rental housing due to perceived "risk" on the part of landlords*"). Italics added. See: Part IV, This chapter, Sects. 4.1.4–4.1.4.2.3 of this book.

[1272] Humber, Nadiyah J., "A Home for Digital Equity: Algorithmic Redlining and Property Technology", *cit.*, pp. 1421–1484 (1426).

[1273] Humber, Nadiyah J., "A Home for Digital Equity: Algorithmic Redlining and Property Technology", *cit.*, pp. 1421–1484 (1426).

§§ Property Technologies (*PropTech*), if nothing else, amounts to an algorithmic tool that «automates inequality»[1274] while propelling racial[1275] inequalities.[1276] Worse still: the foregoing cluster of Artificial Intelligence-embedded technologies (*SafeRent* and *CrimeSafe*) amount to nothing but algorithmic tools[1277] that seek to hide the racist agenda[1278] behind the veneer of science-based objectivity.[1279]

1274 Eubanks, Virginia, *Automating inequality: how high-tech tools profile, police, and punish the poor*, New York: St. Martin's Press, 2017. Gilliom, John, *Overseers of the Poor: Surveillance, Resistance, and the Limits of Privacy*, Chicago: University of Chicago Press, 2001. Soss, Joe, Richard C. Fording, and Sanford F. Schram, *Disciplining the Poor: Neoliberal Paternalism and the Persistent Power of Race*. Chicago: University of Chicago Press, 2011.

1275 See: Allen, James, "The Color of Algorithms: An Analysis and Proposed Research Agenda Deterring Algorithmic Redlining", *Fordham Urban Law Journal*, Volume 46, 2019, pp. 219–234 (229–234) (discussing how historical mortgage redlining greatly swayed modern algorithms generated by massive batches of datasets that consist of decades of information built on exclusion and racial discrimination in the purview of financing, marketing, and housing). See: Part IV, This chapter, Sects. 4.1.4–4.1.4.2.3 of this book.

1276 Noble, S. U., *Algorithms of oppression: how search engines reinforce racism*, New York: New York University Press, 2018.

1277 But see: O'Neil, Cathy, *Weapons of Math Destruction. How Big Data Increases Inequality and Threatens Democracy*, London, Penguin Random House, 2016, passim (showing how algorithms utilized in modern societies are amenable to perpetuate racial discrimination, partially through perpetuation of social disadvantage and wealth divides); O'Neil, Cathy, "When Not to Trust the Algorithm", *Interview published in the Harvard Business Review's Ideacast*, 2016, passim; O' Neil, Cathy, "Amazon's Gender-Biased Algorithm Is Not Alone", 2018, accessed 2 January 2025.

1278 In spite of its deep-seated racial bias, decision-makers continue to deploy redlining tactics through big data and may even justify such unlawful practices by claiming that the latter abide by cost-effectiveness. See: Humber, Nadiyah J., "A Home for Digital Equity: Algorithmic Redlining and Property Technology", *California Law Review*, Volume 111, Issue 5, 2023, pp. 1421–1484. Allen, James, "The Color of Algorithms: An Analysis and Proposed Research Agenda Deterring Algorithmic Redlining", *Fordham Urban Law Journal*, Volume 46, 2019, pp. 219–234 (229–234) (discussing how historical mortgage redlining greatly swayed modern algorithms generated by massive batches of data sets that consist of decades of information built on exclusion and racial discrimination in the purview of financing, marketing, and housing). See: Part IV, This chapter, Sects. 4.1.4–4.1.4.2.3 of this book.

1279 But see: Benjamin, Ruha, *Race After Technology: Abolitionist Tools for the New Jim Code*, New York, Polity, 2019, pp. 1–172 (7) (discussing that Artificial Intelligence-embedded technologies are viewed as iron-clad tools of objectivity and devoid of any biases whatsoever). Ruha Benjamin accordingly contends that "the employment of new technologies that reflect and reproduce existing inequities but that are promoted and perceived as more objective or progressive than the discriminatory systems of a previous era"). But see: Hurley, Mikella/Adebayo, Julius, "Credit Scoring in the Era of Big Data", *Yale Journal of Law and Technology*, Volume 18, 2016, p. 149 ("*these tools may furthermore obscure discriminatory and subjective lending policies behind a single "objective" score (…) sophisticated algorithms may combine facially neutral data points and treat them as proxies for immutable characteristics such as race or gender, thereby circumventing existing non-discrimination laws and systematically denying credit access to certain groups. Finally, big-data tools may allow online payday lenders to target the most vulnerable consumers and lure them into debt traps*"). Italics added. But see also: Bornstein, Stepanhie, "Antidiscriminatory Algorithms", *Alabama Law Review*, Volume 70, 2018, pp. 519, 524–528 (contending, however, that the tagged "facially neutral" algorithms producing discriminatory outcomes should be quashed). See also:

§§ It should not therefore come as a bewildering surprise that pundits have been rallying around the idea that Property Technologies (*PropTech*) are awash with a hidden agenda that awards a free pass to White folks while consistently marginalizing the non-White community.[1280]

§§ More to the point, this shady agenda of social control[1281] leverages on the uses of «science»[1282] to legitimize the algorithmic recommendations[1283] around which computer-run tools used by the real estate industry revolves, which, given its lack of transparency,[1284] legitimacy, and intrinsic goodness, has every likelihood to fray the fabric of Rule of Law.[1285]

Farina, M./Lavazza, A., *Philosophy, expertise, and the myth of* neutrality, Routledge Studies in Contemporary Philosophy, London, Routledge, 2024.

1280 Humber, Nadiyah J., "A Home for Digital Equity: Algorithmic Redlining and Property Technology", *cit*., pp. 1421–1484.

1281 Jefferson, B., *Digitize and Punish: Racial Criminalization in the Digital Age*, Minnesota, University of Minnesota Press, 2020.

1282 DaViera, A. L./Uriostegui, M., Gottlieb/A./Onyeka, O, "Risk, race, and predictive policing: A critical race theory analysis of the strategic subject list", *cit*., pp. 91–103.

1283 But see: *Tech, Bias and Housing Initiative, the Promise and Perils of Residential Proptech, Year 1, Research Summary Report, April 2023, TechEquity Collaborative*, p. 11, available at: https://techequity.us/wp-content/uploads/2023/04/TBHI-Y1-Research-Summary-Report.pdf (28.11.2024). ("*From information on company websites, it is not clear what analysis or data is behind subjective determinations like "suitability" to a unit or what the nexus between an individual's characteristics and a unit's characteristics is that indicates the likelihood for property damage. Based on sample reports, even landlords are not privy to how the determinations are made. Instead, they receive a risk score out of 100 simplified into green, yellow, and red recommendations.* What companies withhold in terms of how it works, they make up for with the extent to which they tell landlords it works: Naborly claims their predictions reduce lease defaults by up to 89%. 15 *As Naborly's sample report demonstrates, its property damage assessment is then used as an input to determine its projected eviction outcomes; its early vacancy prediction, in turn, is based on "all assessment factors*"). Italics and highlights added.

1284 Deeks, Ahsley, "Secret Reason-Giving", *Yale Law Journal*, Volume 129, 2019, passim; Katyal, Sonia K, "The Paradox of Source Code Secrecy", *Cornell Law Review*, Volume 104, 2019, pp. 1183–1236 Rudin, Cynthia/Wang, Caroline/Coker, Beau, "The Age of Secrecy and Unfairness in Recidivism Prediction", *Harvard Data Science Review*, Issue 2.1. Winter 2020, 2020, passim; Wexler, Rebecca, "Life, Liberty, and Trade Secrets: Intellectual Property in the Criminal Justice System", *Stanford Law Review*, Volume 70, 2018, pp. 1343 and ff; Okidegbe, Ngozi, "The Democratizing Potential of Algorithms?", *Connecticut Law Review*, Volume 54, 2021, passim.

1285 See: Part V, Chap. 5, Sect. 5.1.1.1 of this book (on the central tenets of Rule of Law that lends itself to a beacon of justice amidst the sepulchral darkness that is about to take hold). See: Part V, Chap. 5, Sect. 5.1.1.2 of this book (on the central tenets of Procedural Rule of Law that lends itself to a lighthouse of justice that allows citizens to challenge the pearls of algorithmic wisdom in a court of law). See also: Tyler, Tom R., "Does the American Public Accept the Rule of Law? The Findings of Psychological Research on Deference to Authority", *De Paul Law Review*, 56, 2007, pp. 661–664 (stating that "transparency and openness foster the belief that decision-making procedures are neutral"). See also: Coglianese, Cary/Lehr, David, "Transparency and Algorithmic Governance", *Administrative Law Review*, Volume 71, 2019, passim. See also: Doherty, Joseph W./ Reville, Robert T./Zakaras, Laura(ed.), *Introduction to Confidentiality, Transparency, and the U.S. Civil Justice System*, Oxford, Oxford University Press, 2012, 1–258 (passim) (noting that the lack of transparency yields sizable social costs). But see: Weizenbaum, Joseph, *Computer Power and Human Reason: From Judgment to Calculation*, 1st edition, New York, W. H. Freeman & Co, 1976,

4.1.4.3 «Algorithmic Redliking»: How Property Technologies (*PropTech*) Perpetuate and Exacerbate Racial Inequalities in Short-Term Rental Platforms (*Airnb*)

§§ Lest lawmakers and policymakers roll up their sleeves to allay *systemic racism*, societies are doomed to continue to cement patterns of deeply entrenched White[1286] privilege[1287] and structural disadvantage,[1288] thereby widening the rift between rich (White folks) and poor (Black and Latino[1289] folks)[1290] while perpetuating matrixial disadvantage.[1291]

---

pp. 1–300 (227) ("examines the sources of the computer's powers and offers evaluative explorations of what computers can do, cannot do, and should not be employed to do") (this founding father of Artificial Intelligence presciently noted that we should not entrust Artificial Intelligence-embedded technologies with "tasks that demand wisdom"). Italics added. The approval of rental applications is arguably one of those tasks that should never be entrusted to machines). More on this on Part IV, This chapter, Sects. 4.1.4–4.1.4.2.1 of this book.

[1286] Lipsitz, George, *The Possessive Investment in Whiteness: How White People Profit from Identity Politics*, Philadelphia, Pennsylvania, Temple University Press; 1st edition (July 13, 2018), 2018, pp. 1–448 ("*George Lipsitz's classic book The Possessive Investment in Whiteness argues that public policy and private prejudice work together to create a possessive investment in whiteness that is responsible for the racialized hierarchies of our society*"). Italics added.

[1287] Roithmayr, Daria, *Reproducing Racism: How everyday choices lock in White Advantage*, New York, New York University Press, 2014, pp. 1–272 ("*Argues that racial inequality reproduces itself automatically over time because early unfair advantage for whites has paved the way for continuing advantage. This book is designed to change the way we think about racial inequality (…) Legal scholar Daria Roithmayr provocatively argues that racial inequality lives on because white advantage functions as a powerful self-reinforcing monopoly, reproducing itself automatically from generation to generation even in the absence of intentional discrimination. Drawing on work in antitrust law and a range of other disciplines, Roithmayr brilliantly compares the dynamics of white advantage to the unfair tactics of giants like AT&T and Microsoft.* With penetrating insight, Roithmayr *locates the engine of white monopoly in positive feedback loops that connect the dramatic disparity of Jim Crow to modern racial gaps in jobs, housing and education. Wealthy white neighborhoods fund public schools that then turn out wealthy white neighbors. Whites with lucrative jobs informally refer their friends, who refer their friends, and so on. Roithmayr concludes that racial inequality might now be locked in place, unless policymakers immediately take drastic steps to dismantle this oppressive system*"). Italics added. This book points out how White privilege is perpetuated throughout generations through residential segregation (*mortgage redlining*), abhorrent nepotism, and other bemoaning social practices that pester modern societies. See: Part IV, This chapter, Sects. 4.1.4–4.1.4.2.1 of this book (on mortgage redlining). See: Part IV, This chapter, Sects. 4.1.2–4.1.4.3 of this book (on algorithmic credit scoring, consumer racism and credit card redlining). See: Part IV, This chapter, Sects. 4.1.4–4.1.4.2.3 of this book (on algorithmic redlining). See: Part IV, This chapter, Sect. 4.1.4.3 of this book (on "algorithmic redliking"). See: Part IV, This chapter, Sect. 4.1.3 of this book (on algorithmic prime-lining).

[1288] See: Barocas, Solon/Selbst, Andrew, "Big Data's Disparate Impact", *California Law Review*, Volume 104, pp. 2016, p. 691 (highlighting the worrisome, and gruesome, issue of "structural disadvantage" with which racialized communities have been tussling for centuries). See also: Powell, Richard/Porter, Jeremy, "Redlining, Concentrated Disadvantage and Crime: The Effects of Discriminatory Government Policies on Violent Crime", *American Journal of Criminal Justice*, Volume 48, 2023, pp. 1132–1156 ("*Redlining and other discriminatory government policies enacted during the first half of the Twentieth Century have had long-lasting negative effects on neighborhoods, especially those inhabited by people of color. This study attempts to link the practice of redlining to*

§§ For instance, landlords/housing providers keep deploying redlining tactics only to systematically reject rental applications made by members of community of colour (Blacks and Latinos).[1292] *Mortgage redlining* still resonates today after all.[1293]

---

current-day indicators of neighborhood concentrated disadvantage and violent crime using spatio-temporal data from Chicago (…) In addition, it seeks to determine whether redlining was associated with violent crime, and if that association was mediated by redlining's effect on concentrated disadvantage. The results indicate that redlining was associated with increases in both concentrated disadvantage and violent crime, and that redlining's relationship with violent crime was, indeed, partially mediated by its relationship with concentrated disadvantage"). Italics added. See also: Gandy, Oscar H., *Coming to Terms with Chance: Engaging Rational Discrimination and Cumulative Disadvantage*, Farnham, UK: Ashgate Publishing, 2009.

1289 Wolff, Edward N., "The Decline of African-American and Hispanic Wealth Since the Great Recession," *NBER Working Paper* no. 25198, 2018; Wolff, Edward N., "African-American and Hispanic Income, Wealth and Homeownership since 1989," *Review of Income and Wealth*, Volume 68, 2022, pp. 189–233.

1290 See: Eubanks, Virginia, *Automating Inequality: How High-Tech Tools Profile, Police and Punish the Poor*. New York: St. Martin's Press, 2018, 1–272 (1 ff and passim) (coining the expression «automating inequality» to vividly portray the downsides of using high-technology to compound the yawning gap between rich and poor against the backdrop of biased algorithms). Soss, Joe, Richard C. Fording, and Sanford F. Schram, *Disciplining the Poor: Neoliberal Paternalism and the Persistent Power of Race*. Chicago: University of Chicago Press, 2011. See: Barocas, Solon/Selbst, Andrew, "Big Data's Disparate Impact", *California Law Review*, Volume 104, pp. 2016, p. 691 (highlighting the worrisome, and gruesome, issue of "structural disadvantage" with which racialized communities have been tussling for centuries). See also: Powell, Richard/Porter, Jeremy, "Redlining, Concentrated Disadvantage and Crime: The Effects of Discriminatory Government Policies on Violent Crime", *American Journal of Criminal Justice*, Volume 48, 2023, pp. 1132–1156 ("*Redlining and other discriminatory government policies enacted during the first half of the Twentieth Century have had long-lasting negative effects on neighborhoods, especially those inhabited by people of color. This study attempts to link the practice of redlining to current-day indicators of neighborhood concentrated disadvantage and violent crime using spatio-temporal data from Chicago (…) In addition, it seeks to determine whether redlining was associated with violent crime, and if that association was mediated by redlining's effect on concentrated disadvantage. The results indicate that redlining was associated with increases in both concentrated disadvantage and violent crime, and that redlining's relationship with violent crime was, indeed, partially mediated by its relationship with concentrated disadvantage*"). Italics added. See also: Gandy, Oscar H., *Coming to Terms with Chance: Engaging Rational Discrimination and Cumulative Disadvantage*, Farnham, UK: Ashgate Publishing, 2009.

1291 Citron, Danielle Keats/Pasquale, Frank A., "The Scored Society: Due Process for Automated Predictions", *Washington Law Review*, Volume 89, 2014, pp. 1–34; Balkin, Jack M., "The Three Laws of Robotics in the Age of Big Data", *Ohio State Law Journal*, Volume 78, Issue 5, 2017, pp. 1217–1241.

1292 In spite of its deep-seated racial bias, decision-makers continue to deploy redlining tactics through big data and may even justify such unlawful practices by claiming that the latter abide by cost-effectiveness. See: Humber, Nadiyah J., "A Home for Digital Equity: Algorithmic Redlining and Property Technology", *California Law Review*, Volume 111, Issue 5, 2023, pp. 1421–1484. See also: Hurley, Mikella/Adebayo, Julius, "Credit Scoring in the Era of Big Data", *Yale Journal of Law and Technology*, Volume 18, 2016, pp. 148, 151–156, 172 (averring that FICO scoring boasts a redoubtable capacity to routinely weed out some populations that have been historically and systematically underrepresented or grossly unfairly represented in the credit industry market). Tellingly, by 2016, ten states had disavowed the unlawful practice of employers using shady credit

Unfortunately, though, the list dispiritingly goes on. Take the example of *algorithmic redliking* in the remit of short-term rental platforms.[1294]

§§ *Airbnb's* backbone, design, and algorithm outlined a website architecture that allows user racial discrimination to proscribe minority hosts from realizing the same economic benefits from short-term rental platforms as White hosts, a loathsome phenomenon a pundit presciently refers to as «redliking».[1295]

§§ With regard to hosts with a scarcely used home, a spare room, or an extra set of couches, *Airbnb* offers an opportunity to yield new income streams and increase wealth.[1296] *Airbnb* openly pokes prospective guests to gain access to host photographs, names, and personal information when taking stock of potential accommodations, thereby spurring bias, both implicit[1297] and overt, to propel business transactions.[1298]

---

scores due to their perceived disparate impact on low-income applicants and members of racialized communities (mostly Black folks). See: O'Neill, Cathy, *Weapons of Math Destruction. How Big Data Increases Inequality and Threatens Democracy.* London: Penguin Random House, 2016, pp. 128 and ff and passim.

[1293] See: Part IV, This chapter, Sects. 4.1.4–4.1.4.2.1 of this book (on mortgage redlining). See: Part IV, This chapter, Sects. 4.1.2–4.1.4.3 of this book (on algorithmic credit scoring, consumer racism and credit card redlining). See: Part IV, This chapter, Sects. 4.1.4–4.1.4.2.3 of this book (on algorithmic redlining). See: Part IV, This chapter, Sect. 4.1.4.3 of this book (on "algorithmic redliking"). See also: Allen, James, "The Color of Algorithms: An Analysis and Proposed Research Agenda Deterring Algorithmic Redlining", *Fordham Urban Law Journal*, Volume 46, 2019, pp. 219–234 (229–234) (discussing how historical mortgage redlining greatly swayed modern algorithms generated by massive batches of data sets that consist of decades of information built on exclusion and racial discrimination in the purview of financing, marketing, and housing).

[1294] Gold, Allyson E. "Redliking: When Redlining Goes Online", *William & Mary Law Review*, Volume 62, n. ° 6, May 2021, 2021, pp. 1841–1910 (1869) ("*offers the term "redliking" to describe the website structures, features, and underlying systems that allow discrimination against minority short-term rental hosts and the resulting economic consequences. Redliking allows White hosts to enjoy disproportionate financial benefits from short-term rental platforms and perpetuates historic inequality related to housing equity. Redlining functioned to lock communities of color out of asset-building opportunities and corresponding increases in wealth. Similarly, redliking is a system that deprives minority hosts from enjoying important opportunities to increase wealth through new income streams* and increasing the value of the underlying asset"). Italics added.

[1295] Gold, Allyson E. "Redliking: When Redlining Goes Online", *cit.*, pp. 1841–1910 (1841–1842).

[1296] Gold, Allyson E. "Redliking: When Redlining Goes Online", *cit.*, pp. 1841–1910 (1841–1842).

[1297] This is called law of *implicit bias*: people make decisions (e.g. discriminating seemingly disfavoured groups of people) that often-times lack a rational connection between facts and judgment. A conscious and deliberate judgment that noticeably runs afoul with rationality. See: Jolls, Christine/Sunstein, Cass R., "The Law of Implicit Bias", *California Law Review*, Volume 94, 2006, p. 969 (arguing that this issue can be solved through the general strategy of de-biasing through law, by steering people through more rational directions). See also: Kang, Jerry/Banaji, Mahzarin R., "Fair Measures: A Behavioural Realist Revision of Affirmative Action", *California Law Review,* Volume 94 2006, p. 1064 (arguing that «implicit bias often conflicts with conscious attitudes, endorsed beliefs, and intentional behaviour»); Greenwald, Anthony G., and Linda Hamilton Krieger, Implicit Bias: Scientific Foundations", *California Law Review*, Volume 94, 2006, pp. 945–967. See also: Santos, Hugo Luz dos, *Multidisciplinary Dynamics of Mediation*, Volume I, New York/Beijing/Berlin/Singapore, 2025, pp. 1–694; Santos, Hugo Luz dos, *Multidisciplinary Dynamics of Mediation*, Volume II, New York/Beijing/Berlin/Singapore, 2025, pp. 1–800; Santos, Hugo Luz dos, *Towards a Four-Tiered Model of Mediation*, New York/Beijing/Berlin/Singapore, 2023, pp. 1–216.

§§ This bias boasts crucially important financial consequences.[1299] Empirical evidence on host earning rates concluded that White hosts earn exceedingly more than racial minorities (Blacks and Latinos), even when controlling for location, size, and other amenities.[1300]

§§ *Airbnb's* algorithm amplifies the harrowing effects and proclivity of individual user bias,[1301] thereby creating a system wherein allegedly race-neutral variables[1302] serve as proxies[1303] for racial discrimination.[1304] Contemporary *redliking* perpetuates historic inequality[1305] concerned to housing[1306] wealth.[1307] In the early twentieth

[1298] Gold, Allyson E. "Redliking: When Redlining Goes Online", *cit.*, pp. 1841–1910 (1841–1842).

[1299] Gold, Allyson E. "Redliking: When Redlining Goes Online", *cit.*, pp. 1841–1910 (1841–1842).

[1300] Gold, Allyson E. "Redliking: When Redlining Goes Online", *cit.*, pp. 1841–1910 (1841–1842).

[1301] See: Harrington v. Airbnb, Inc., 348 F. Supp. 3d 1085, 1088 (D. Or. 2018) ("*Before filing this lawsuit, Ms. Harrington wrote a letter to Airbnb requesting that it change its policies so that all accommodations on its online platform may be available to all prospective guests regardless of race or color. Ms. Harrington specifically asked Airbnb to change its policy that allows a host to wait to confirm a booking until after the host has seen the full name and photograph of a prospective guest.* She expressly asked Airbnb not to provide information to hosts before accepting a reservation or confirming a booking from a prospective guest that would reveal statutorily-protected immutable characteristics, like race. *Airbnb denied the request to change its policy, but offered to assist Ms. Harrington in securing alternative accommodations if she ever were discriminated against by an Airbnb host. Airbnb also promised to investigate any reported claims of racial discrimination and take appropriate action*"). Italics added.

[1302] Benjamin, Ruha, *Race After Technology: Abolitionist Tools for the New Jim Code*, New York, Polity, 2019, pp. 1–172 (7) (discussing that Artificial Intelligence-embedded technologies are viewed as iron-clad tools of objectivity and devoid of any biases whatsoever). Ruha Benjamin contends that "the employment of new technologies that reflect and reproduce existing inequities but that are promoted and perceived as more objective or progressive than the discriminatory systems of a previous era").

[1303] See: Part IV, This chapter, Sect. 4.1.6.3 of this book (on proxy discrimination).

[1304] Gold, Allyson E. "Redliking: When Redlining Goes Online", *cit.*, pp. 1841–1910 (1841–1842).

[1305] Menasce, Juliana Horowitz/Brown, Anna/Cox, Kiana, "Views of Racial Inequality", *Pew Research Center*, April 9, 2019, available at: https://www.pewresearch.org/social-trends/2019/04/09/views-of-racial-inequality/ (access: 2.12.2024) ("*more than four-in-ten Americans say the country still has work to do to give black people equal rights with whites. Blacks, in particular, are skeptical that black people will ever have equal rights in this country (....) A majority of adults say that being white helps people's ability to get ahead in the country at least a little (59%); 28% say being white neither helps nor hurts and 12% say it hurts. On the flip side, a majority (56%) sees being black as a disadvantage, with 25% saying it hurts people's ability to get ahead a lot. About a quarter (26%) say being black neither helps nor hurts and 17% say it helps at least a little. More also say that being Hispanic hurts people's ability to get ahead in this country (51%) than say it helps (18%) or that it neither helps nor hurts (30%).* Opinions are more split when it comes to the impact of being Native American—about the same shares say this hurts as say it neither helps nor hurts, while a smaller share says it helps. *And while a plurality says being Asian neither helps nor hurts, more say it helps (34%) than hurts (21%) people's ability to get ahead*"). Italics added.

century *redlining* maps were deployed to justify withholding investments[1308] from Black communities.[1309]

§§ Fast forward to today, *redliking* perpetuates the practice of channelling wealth to White communities[1310] while buttressing *systemic racism* in the realm of real estate by depriving minority hosts of sizable revenue streams, further compounding the racial wealth[1311] gap.[1312]

1306 Wolff, Edward N., "The Decline of African-American and Hispanic Wealth Since the Great Recession," *NBER Working Paper* no. 25198, 2018; Wolff, Edward N., "African-American and Hispanic Income, Wealth and Homeownership since 1989," *Review of Income and Wealth*, Volume 68, 2022, pp. 189–233.

1307 Gold, Allyson E. "Redliking: When Redlining Goes Online", *cit.*, pp. 1841–1910 (1841–182).

1308 See: Part IV, This chapter, Sects. 4.1.4–4.1.4.2.1 of this book (on mortgage redlining). See: Part IV, This chapter, Sects. 4.1.2–4.1.4.3 of this book (on algorithmic credit scoring, consumer racism and credit card redlining). See: Part IV, This chapter, Sects. 4.1.4–4.1.4.2.3 of this book (on algorithmic redlining). See also: Mendez-Carbajo, Diego "Neighborhood Redlining, Racial Segregation, and Homeownership", *Federal Reserve Bank of Saint Louis*, September 1, 2021("*In the 1930s, the Home Owners' Loan Corporation (HOLC) drew maps of residential neighborhoods across the United States. The maps classified each neighborhood into one of five categories, from least to most likely to* ***default*** *on a* ***mortgage*** *loan. In those maps, the neighborhoods most likely to default were shaded red and over time these neighborhoods had the largest concentrations of African Americans. Because the lending classifications determined individual access to credit, the residents of redlined neighborhoods paid high interest rates and had a hard time becoming homeowners and keeping their homes in good condition. From 1968 to 1974, Congress passed several federal laws and policies preventing lending discrimination by race and gender, and the pattern of residential segregation started to change*"). Italics added.

1309 Gold, Allyson E. "Redliking: When Redlining Goes Online", *cit.*, pp. 1841–1910 (1841–182).

1310 Gold, Allyson E. "Redliking: When Redlining Goes Online", *cit.*, pp. 1841–1910 (1875) ("*when examining whether short-term rental platforms such as Airbnb are public accommodations under Title II, many scholars have focused on the law's lodging provision. Under this category, "any inn, hotel, motel, or other establishment which provides lodging to transient guests"174 is a public accommodation. Because short-term rental platforms function like an inn, hotel, or motel, and provide lodging to transient guests, they are properly viewed as a public accommodation under the CRA. Categorizing a short-term rental accommodation as a public accommodation under the CRA is only the first step to determine liability for discrimination against guests.* After this, the question becomes whether the platform provider itself-for example, Airbnb, VRBO, or Homeaway-is liable for discrimination against guests. Professor Norrinda Brown Hayat as well as Nancy Leong and Aaron Belzer *argue that platform operators themselves could face liability for discrimination perpetuated by hosts against minority guests if the platform operator knew that its policies contributed to or facilitated the discrimination*"). Italics added.

1311 Gold, Allyson E. "Redliking: When Redlining Goes Online", *cit.*, pp. 1841–1910 (1841–182).

1312 Derenoncourt, Ellora/Kim, Chi Hyun/Kuhn, Moritz/Schularik, Moritz, "The Wealth of Two Nations: The U.S. Racial Wealth Gap, 1860–2020", *The Quarterly Journal of Economics*, Volume 139, Issue 2, 2024, p. 741 ("A large class of commonly discussed policies for reducing racial wealth inequality seeks to reduce gaps in income, savings, and capital gains. These include policies that encourage financial diversification or stock equity holdings among Black households; policies aimed at financial literacy and retirement or savings behavior; or policies aimed at improving educational and labor market outcomes of Black Americans through improved school quality or reductions in discrimination. *Yet on a realistic note, our simulation in Section IV.A shows that even if wealth accumulation conditions had been equal since 1870, the wealth gap would still be 3 to 1 today, and full convergence would be more than 200 years away. Put differently: to close the racial wealth gap*

4.1.5 «Algorithmic Jim Crow» (Margaret Hu): Introduction

§§ Both gender discrepancies[1313] and racial inequalities have been gliding through the sky of modern societies,[1314] thereby interfering with normal chain of events.[1315] That is true, but truer still the personal nature of the racial inequities that *systemic racism* has been levelling towards members of racialized communities (Blacks and Latinos)[1316] effectively dispels any shiver of doubt concerning a «perceived randomness»[1317] underpinning racial divides.

---

in the immediate term via *flow parameters, Black Americans would need a substantial positive lead over whites, not "just" more equality*"). Italics added.

1313 Hamilton, Melissa, "The sexist algorithm", *Behavioral Sciences and the Law*, Volume 37, Issue 2, Special Issue: the Use of Statistics in Criminal Cases, March–April 2019, 2019, pp. 1 and ff ("*Algorithmic risk assessment tools are informed by scientific research concerning which factors are predictive of recidivism and thus support the evidence-based practice movement in criminal justice. Automated assessments of individualized risk (low, medium, high) permit officials to make more effective management decisions. Computer-generated algorithms appear to be objective and neutral. But are these algorithms actually fair? The focus herein is on gender equity.* Studies confirm that women typically have far lower recidivism rates than men. *This differential raises the question of how well algorithmic outcomes fare in terms of predictive parity by gender.* This essay reports original research using a large dataset of offenders who were scored on the popular risk assessment tool COMPAS. *Findings indicate that COMPAS performs reasonably well at discriminating between recidivists and non-recidivists for men and women. Nonetheless, COMPAS algorithmic outcomes systemically overclassify women in higher risk groupings. Multiple measures of algorithmic equity and predictive accuracy are provided to support the conclusion that this algorithm is sexist*"). Italics added.

1314 Annamma, S. A., Jackson, D. D., & Morrison, D, "Conceptualizing color-evasiveness: Using dis/ability critical race theory to expand a color-blind racial ideology in education and society", *Race Ethnicity and Education*, Volume 20, Issue 2, 2017, pp. 147–162.

1315 Alexander, M., *The new Jim Crow: Mass incarceration in the age of colorblindness*, The New Press, 2012.

1316 Menasce, Juliana Horowitz/Brown, Anna/Cox, Kiana, "Views of Racial Inequality", *Pew Research Center*, April 9, 2019, 2919, available at: https://www.pewresearch.org/social-trends/2019/04/09/views-of-racial-inequality/ (access: 2.12.2024) ("*more than four-in-ten Americans say the country still has work to do to give black people equal rights with whites. Blacks, in particular, are skeptical that black people will ever have equal rights in this country (….) A majority of adults say that being white helps people's ability to get ahead in the country at least a little (59%); 28% say being white neither helps nor hurts and 12% say it hurts.* On the flip side, a majority (56%) sees being black as a disadvantage, with 25% saying it hurts people's ability to get ahead a lot. *About a quarter (26%) say being black neither helps nor hurts and 17% say it helps at least a little. More also say that being Hispanic hurts people's ability to get ahead in this country (51%) than say it helps (18%) or that it neither helps nor hurts (30%).* Opinions are more split when it comes to the impact of being Native American—about the same shares say this hurts as say it neither helps nor hurts, while a smaller share says it helps. *And while a plurality says being Asian neither helps nor hurts, more say it helps (34%) than hurts (21%) people's ability to get ahead*"). Italics added.

1317 Teigena, Halvor/Kanten, Alf Børre, "Out of the blue: on the suddenness of perceived chance events", *Thinking & Reasoning*, Volume 29, n. ° 1, 2023, pp. 137–175 (137) ("*people commonly use terms like 'random', 'by chance', or 'accidentally' when they describe occurrences that sidestep the normal course of events, with no apparent causal link to ongoing activities. Such intrusive events are typically perceived as happening all of a sudden.* This was demonstrated in seven experiments (N ¼

§§ Put otherwise, *«inequality in application»,*[1318] *credit card redlining,*[1319] *algorithmic prime-lining,*[1320] *algorithmic redlining,*[1321] *biased predictive policing,*[1322] *biased algorithmic risk assessment in criminal justice settings,*[1323] *algorithmic redliking*[1324] embody thought-through[1325] policies to bolster, buttress, cement, and augment racial discrimination[1326] insofar they are offsprings of *Algorithmic Dictatorship.*[1327] So too is «Algorithmic Jim Crow»,[1328] which is also propelled by Artificial Intelligence-embedded[1329] technologies.[1330]

1299) by asking people to identify statements they believed belonged to stories about chance events, and by comparing chance vs. nonchance events from their own life and from the lives of others. Suddenness also appeared to be more strongly associated with beginnings than with endings of an episode. Thus, statements about sudden beginnings of a career or a relationship were more readily believed to happen 'by chance' than 'not by chance'. *But life-changing events did not become more accidental simply by being placed in the beginning of a 'life chapter'. These studies highlight a central but neglected feature of perceived randomness*"). Italics added.

[1318] See: Part III, Chap. 3, Sect. 3.1.1 of this book (that discusses the issue of "inequality in application" facing Artificial Intelligence-embedded technologies).

[1319] See: Part IV, This chapter, Sects. 4.1.2–4.1.2.3 of this book.

[1320] See: Part IV, This chapter, Sect. 4.1.3 of this book.

[1321] See: Part IV, This chapter, Sects. 4.1.4–4.1.4.2.3 of this book.

[1322] See: Part IV, This chapter, Sects. 4.1.1–4.1.1.1 of this book (on biased predictive policing).

[1323] See: Part IV, This chapter, Sects. 4.1.10.1–4.1.10.6 of this book (on biased algorithmic risk assessment in criminal procedure law settings).

[1324] See: Part IV, This chapter, Sect. 4.1.4.3 of this book. See also: Gold, Allyson E. "Redliking: When Redlining Goes Online", *William & Mary Law Review*, Volume 62, n. ° 6, May 2021, 2021, pp. 1841–1910 (1869) ("*offers the term "redliking" to describe the website structures, features, and underlying systems that allow discrimination against minority short-term rental hosts and the resulting economic consequences. Redliking allows White hosts to enjoy disproportionate financial benefits from short-term rental platforms and perpetuates historic inequality related to housing equity. Redlining functioned to lock communities of color out of asset-building opportunities and corresponding increases in wealth. Similarly, redliking is a system that deprives minority hosts from enjoying important opportunities to increase wealth through new income streams* and increasing the value of the underlying asset"). Italics added.

[1325] But see, on randomness: Teigena, Halvor/Kanten, Alf Børre, "Out of the blue: on the suddenness of perceived chance events", *Thinking & Reasoning*, Volume 29, n. ° 1, 2023, pp. 137–175 (137) ("*people commonly use terms like 'random', 'by chance', or 'accidentally' when they describe occurrences that sidestep the normal course of events, with no apparent causal link to ongoing activities. Such intrusive events are typically perceived as happening all of a sudden.* This was demonstrated in seven experiments (N ¼ 1299) by asking people to identify statements they believed belonged to stories about chance events, and by comparing chance vs. nonchance events from their own life and from the lives of others. Suddenness also appeared to be more strongly associated with beginnings than with endings of an episode. Thus, statements about sudden beginnings of a career or a relationship were more readily believed to happen 'by chance' than 'not by chance'. *But life-changing events did not become more accidental simply by being placed in the beginning of a 'life chapter'. These studies highlight a central but neglected feature of perceived randomness*"). Italics added.

[1326] Bonilla-Silva, E., *Racism without racists: Color-blind racism and the persistence of racial inequality in America*, Fifth edition, Lanham, Maryland, Rowman & Littlefield, 2018.

[1327] See: Part IV, This chapter, Sect. 4.1 of this book.

§§ Strikingly, «Algorithmic Jim Crow» amounts to a portmanteau of computer-run techniques whereby *systemic racism* is rife. But not just that though. Rather, «Algorithmic Jim Crow» consists of a slew of Artificial Intelligence-embedded technologies whereby overt racial discrimination takes centre stage. Non-plussed, one is ineluctably enticed to ask the vexing question: how did Jim Crow come into being?

§§ The historical framing of Jim Crow[1331] laid the foundation for systemic *racism* while propelling White supremacy[1332] («Whiteness»)[1333] that still resonates today in the United States of America and beyond.[1334]

[1328] Professor Margaret Hu is credited with introducing the term "Algorithmic Jim Crow" into academic discourse to depict the mischievous use of Artificial Intelligence-embedded technologies and the extent to which national security programs risks creating forms of discrimination tantamount to Jim Crow in that they are also based upon classification and screening protocols. See: Hu, Margaret, "Algorithmic Jim Crow", *Fordham Law Review*, Volume 86, 2017, pp. 633–696, whose stellar piece of research I will follow closely.

[1329] Amigud, A., "The age of the intelligent machine: Singularity, efficiency, and existential peril", *Philosophy & Technology*, Volume 37 (2), 2024, pp. 1–20.

[1330] McIlwain, Charlton, "Racial Formation, Inequality and the Political Economy of Web Traffic", *Information, Communication & Society*, Volume 20, 2016, passim.

[1331] Holloway, Jonathan Scott, *Jim Crow Wisdom: Memory and Identity in Black America since 1940*, 1st edition, North Carolina, North Carolina University Press, 2013, pp. 1–273 ("what do we tell our children? What stories do we pass along so they know their history? These questions permeate Yale historian Holloway's riveting account of how we see, study, and learn about racial identity, and how we acquire the memories that shape that identity. Holloway (Confronting the Veil) surveys the social, political, and cultural milieu of race in the latter half of the twentieth century, from a review of various sociologists' perspectives and the controversies surrounding them in light of the explosion of social science literature in the 1940s, to the role played by the Johnson family of magazines, the impact of 1960s documentaries, and the development of Black Studies programs in the 1970s. He visits American plantations, museums, and other important sites before taking his research to places such as Ghana and Liverpool. The book is noteworthy for the clarity with which Holloway treats historical events and persons buried in ephemera, and for its abundance of detail. Part jargon-free academic treatise and pertinent personal memoir, the result is an evocative bildungsroman in which we see the social scientist as a young man become the provocative historian").

[1332] Daley, Jane/Gimore, Glenda Elizabeth/Simon, Bryant (Editors), *Jumpin' Jim Crow: Southern Politics from Civil War to Civil Rights*, Princeton, Princeton University Press, 2020, pp. 1–331 ("*White supremacy shaped all aspects of post-Civil War southern life, yet its power was never complete or total. The form of segregation and subjection nicknamed Jim Crow constantly had to remake itself over time even as white southern politicians struggled to extend its grip.* Here, some of the most innovative scholars of southern history question Jim Crow's sway, evolution, and methods over the course of a century. These essays bring to life the southern men and women–some heroic and decent, others mean and sinister, most a mixture of both–who supported and challenged Jim Crow, showing that white supremacy always had to prove its power. *Jim Crow was always in motion, always adjusting to meet resistance and defiance by both African Americans and whites. Sometimes white supremacists responded with increased ferocity, sometimes with more subtle political and legal ploys. Jumpin' Jim Crow presents a clear picture of this complex negotiation. For example, even as some black and white women launched the strongest attacks on the system, other white women nurtured myths glorifying white supremacy.* Even as elite whites blamed racial violence on poor whites, they used Jim Crow to dominate poor whites as well as blacks. Most important, the book portrays change over time, suggesting that Strom Thurmond is not a simple reincarnation of Ben Tillman and that Rosa Parks was not the first black woman to say no to Jim Crow"). Italics added. See also: Rich, Camille Gear, "Marginal Whiteness", *California Law Review*, Volume 98,

§§ The Jim Crow era was much more than mere congeries of rules aimed at curtailing Blacks 'freedom of movement. Rather, the Jim Crow era was a socially structured matrix of exclusion and discrimination created by white Americans whose overriding goal was to target Black Americans.[1335]

§§ Historic Jim Crow regimes were underpinned by a sweeping claim: that certain individuals could and should be classified on the basis of race.[1336] Next, Jim Crow laws used a plethora of screening systems to enforce racial segregation based upon deemed as racial classification.[1337]

§§ Pundits accordingly aver that security threat assessments produced through computer-run algorithms[1338] and database screening[1339] might—commensurate with

---

2010, passim; Smångs, Mattias, "Doing Violence, Making Race: Southern Lynching and White Racial Group Formation, *American Journal of Sociology*, Volume 121, 2016.

[1333] Onwuachi-Willig, Angela, "Policing the Boundaries of Whiteness: The Tragedy of Being "Out of Place" from Emmett Till to Trayvon Martin", *Iowa Law Review*, Volume 102, 2017, passim.

[1334] Packard, Jerald M., *American Nightmare: The History of Jim Crow*, Broadway, New York, St. Martin's Press; First Edition, 2002, pp. 1–304 ("*For a hundred years after the end of the Civil War, a quarter of all Americans lived under a system of legalized segregation called Jim Crow. Together with its rigidly enforced canon of racial "etiquette," these rules governed nearly every aspect of life–and outlined draconian punishments for infractions. The purpose of Jim Crow was to keep African Americans subjugated at a level as close as possible to their former slave status. Exceeding even South Africa's notorious apartheid in the humiliation, degradation, and suffering it brought, Jim Crow left scars on the American psyche that are still felt today. American Nightmare* examines and explains Jim Crow from its beginnings to its end: how it came into being, how it was lived, how it was justified, and how, at long last, it was overcome only a few short decades ago. *Most importantly, this book reveals how a nation founded on principles of equality and freedom came to enact as law a pervasive system of inequality and virtual slavery.* Although America has finally consigned Jim Crow to the historical graveyard, *Jerrold Packard shows why it is important that this scourge–and an understanding of how it happened–remain alive in the nation's collective memory*"). Italics added.

[1335] Packard, Jerald M., *American Nightmare: The History of Jim Crow*, Broadway, New York, St. Martin's Press; First Edition, 2002, pp. 1–304 (vii–viii) ("[A] structure of exclusion and discrimination devised by white Americans to be employed principally against black Americans.... *Its central purpose was to maintain a second-class social and economic status for blacks while upholding a first-class social and economic status for whites.... In the South, Jim Crow discrimination at its height existed not only by statute but by custom and racial 'etiquette,' and it was rigidly enforced by both the law enforcement agencies* and courts as well as by ordinary white citizens who were neither policemen nor judges but who often took the law into their own hands as though they were"). Italics added.

[1336] Hu, Margaret, "Algorithmic Jim Crow", *Fordham Law Review*, Volume 86, 2017, pp. 633–696 (643). Internal citations omitted.

[1337] Hu, Margaret, "Algorithmic Jim Crow", *cit.*, pp. 633–696 (643). Internal citations omitted.

[1338] The newest developments posed by the "collect-it-all" technologies are slated to create a slew of sizzling hot challenges to the sustainability of the Rule of Law. See: Hu, Margaret, "From the National Surveillance State to the Cybersurveillance State", *The Annual Review of Law and Social Science*, Volume 13, 2017, pp. 162–163 ("*policymakers view these technological developments, including biometric technologies, as tools with the potential to identify individuals who may pose a threat to national and homeland security and to prevent crime and terrorism. One example of technology intended for risk assessment and threat management is the post-9/11 program Total Information Awareness (TIA).* TIA was the progeny of the Defense Advanced Research Projects

the historic Jim Crow era—attain a similar result: separate populations based upon racial classifications.[1340]

§§ New Algorithmic Jim Crow, like historic Jim Crow regimes, may well brand themselves as facially neutral.[1341] The reality, though, is far dimmer as the algorithmic injustice[1342] takes hold in the age of Artificial Intelligence[1343]-embedded technologies.[1344] More on this later.[1345] For the sake of the argument, let us take a step back as to drill into, and shed a keen light on, the rationale behind the emergence of the new Jim Crow era powered by an omnipresent Artificial Intelligence-embedded technology.

Agency (DARPA) in the US Department of Defense. *TIA can be understood as a "collect-it-all" data surveillance program. TIA was not explicitly identified as a collect-it-all program—this phrase originated with the Snowden disclosures.* One National Security Agency (NSA) slide described the NSA's procedure as "collect-it-all" (Greenwald 2014b*). Collect-it-all efforts like TIA embody a philosophy that aspires to preventive policing. Mass data collection is construed as a tool to assess and prevent future threats (Murray 2010). In TIA and other programs tested or adopted after 9/ 11, biometric database screening and analysis have emerged as a preferred method for tracking, identifying, and establishing identity-based inferences in counterterrorism*"). Italics added. See also: Ball, Kirstie, and Frank Webster (Eds.), *The Intensification of Surveillance: Crime, Terrorism & Warfare in the Information Age*, London, UK: Pluto Press, 2007; Guzik, Keith, "Discrimination by Design: Predictive Data Mining as Security Practice in the United States' 'War on Terrorism.'", *Surveillance and Society*, 7 (1), 2009, pp. 1–17.

1339 See: Hu, Margaret, "From the National Surveillance State to the Cybersurveillance State", *The Annual Review of Law and Social Science*, Volume 13, 2017, p. 165 ("*Datafication, like most big data processes, requires increasing amounts of digital data to support or construct cybersurveillance.* It empowers government actions that are based on digital data collection, data processing protocols, and bulk data analyses (Mayer-Schonberger & Cukier 2013). *Another way to characterize datafication is as a governmental policy interest that both transforms analog data (PCAST 2014) into searchable, centralized digital databases and develops new forms of stored data*"). Italics added.

1340 Hu, Margaret, "Algorithmic Jim Crow", *cit.*, pp. 633–696 (643). Internal citations omitted.

1341 But see: Benjamin, Ruha, *Race After Technology: Abolitionist Tools for the New Jim Code*, New York, Polity, 2019, pp. 1–172 (7) (discussing that Artificial Intelligence-embedded technologies are viewed as iron-clad tools of objectivity and devoid of any biases whatsoever). Ruha Benjamin contends that "the employment of new technologies that reflect and reproduce existing inequities but that are promoted and perceived as more objective or progressive than the discriminatory systems of a previous era").

1342 Ting-an Lin, "Democratizing AI" and the Concern of Algorithmic Injustice", *Philosophy and Technology*, Volume 37 (103), 2024, pp. 3–27; Okidegbe, Ngozi, "The Democratizing Potential of Algorithms?", *Connecticut Law Review*, Volume 54, 2021, passim; Katyal, Sonia, "Private Accountability in the Age of Artificial Intelligence", *UCLA Law Review*, Volume 66, 2019, pp. 54–99.

1343 Amaya, J./Holweg, M., "Using algorithms to improve knowledge work", *Journal of Operations Management*, 2024, passim.

1344 Agrawal, A., McHale, J., & Oettl, A., "Artificial intelligence and scientific discovery: A model of prioritized search", *Research Policy*, Volume 53, Issue 5, 2024, 104989.

1345 See: Part V, Chap. 5, Sect. 5.1.7.2 of this book (on law number two to control algorithmic decision-making, which mandates that black box models must not be entrusted with the task of making high stake decisions—v.g. health and freedom).

§§ To better grasp the underlying rationale for the first Trump administration's policy (2016–2020) on extreme immigration vetting,[1346] it is pivotally important to clutch the underpinning justification for such a policy drawing on historical background and prior policy developments outlined during the Obama administration.[1347]

§§ The great bulk of the policies propelled by Trump's Executive Order are not only an excrescence of 9/11,[1348] but, and foremost, are intrinsically responsive to the string of withering attacks occurred in Paris in November 2015 and the San Bernardino onslaught in December 2015.[1349] Both terrorist attacks catalysed a plethora of immigration policy proposals and adjustments[1350] to current vetting procedures.[1351]

§§ On December 2, 2015, fourteen people were murdered and twenty-one were severally injured pursuant a terrorist attack in San Bernardino, California.[1352] The deadly attack consisted of a mass shooting and an attempted bombing[1353] that was aimed at killing as many people as possible. The wrongdoers, Syed Rizwan Farook and Tashfeen Malik, a married couple living in California, purposefully targeted a San Bernardino County Department of Public Health's holiday party.[1354]

§§ Farook, a Pakistani American U.S. citizen born and raised in Illinois, was employed by the Department of Public Health.[1355] Malik was a Pakistani-born lawful permanent resident who had migrated to the United States of America.[1356]

§§ The media was abuzz with news positing that the Muslim couple had been self-radicalized, allegedly inspired by ISIS.[1357] On the same day as the San Bernardino's deadly attack, Paul Ryan, Speaker of the United States House of Representatives,[1358]

[1346] Hu, Margaret, "Algorithmic Jim Crow", *cit.*, pp. 633–696 (647). Internal citations omitted.

[1347] Hu, Margaret, "Algorithmic Jim Crow", *cit.*, pp. 633–696 (647). Internal citations omitted.

[1348] See: Hu, Margaret, "From the National Surveillance State to the Cybersurveillance State", *The Annual Review of Law and Social Science*, Volume 13, 2017, p. 163 ("*collect-it-all efforts like TIA embody a philosophy that aspires to preventive policing. Mass data collection is construed as a tool to assess and prevent future threats (Murray 2010). In TIA and other programs tested or adopted after 9/11, biometric database screening and analysis have emerged as a preferred method for tracking, identifying, and establishing identity-based inferences in counterterrorism*"). Italics added.

[1349] Hu, Margaret, "Algorithmic Jim Crow", *cit.*, pp. 633–696 (647). Internal citations omitted.

[1350] Ball, Kirstie, and Frank Webster (Eds.), *The Intensification of Surveillance: Crime, Terrorism & Warfare in the Information Age*, London, UK: Pluto Press, 2007; Guzik, Keith, "Discrimination by Design: Predictive Data Mining as Security Practice in the United States' 'War on Terrorism.'", *Surveillance and Society*, 7 (1), 2009, pp. 1–17.

[1351] Hu, Margaret, "Algorithmic Jim Crow", *cit.*, pp. 633–696 (647). Internal citations omitted.

[1352] Hu, Margaret, "Algorithmic Jim Crow", *cit.*, pp. 633–696 (648). Internal citations omitted.

[1353] Hu, Margaret, "Algorithmic Jim Crow", *cit.*, pp. 633–696 (648). Internal citations omitted.

[1354] Hu, Margaret, "Algorithmic Jim Crow", *cit.*, pp. 633–696 (648–649). Internal citations omitted.

[1355] Hu, Margaret, "Algorithmic Jim Crow", *cit.*, pp. 633–696 (649). Internal citations omitted.

[1356] Hu, Margaret, "Algorithmic Jim Crow", *cit.*, pp. 633–696 (649). Internal citations omitted.

[1357] Hu, Margaret, "Algorithmic Jim Crow", *cit.*, pp. 633–696 (649). Internal citations omitted.

[1358] Hu, Margaret, "Algorithmic Jim Crow", *cit.*, pp. 633–696 (649). Internal citations omitted.

contended that lawmakers were taking stock of a wide array of legislative reforms to augment security vetting of refugees and immigrants[1359] in direct response to the looming threat of ISIS,[1360] including requiring countries[1361] «to issue smart e-passports with biometric chips».[1362]

§§ Less than one week later, in the immediate wake of the Paris and San Bernardino onslaughts, then-presidential candidate Trump launched a campaign that has been accordingly tagged as «Muslim Ban» or «Travel Ban»: an executive order that would later forbid entry of any Muslim into the United States of America.[1363]

§§ Trump did not elaborate on how he would prevent Muslims from entering the United States of America[1364]; however, he later shed light on this topic only to aver that the travel ban would be merely temporary to allow the government to evaluate its current immigration[1365] procedures and[1366] «suspend immigration from regions linked with terrorism».[1367]

§§ Trump's poignant call for a «Muslim Ban» was followed by histrionic calls for enhanced surveillance[1368] of Muslim communities and mosques.[1369] Six months later, on June 12, 2016, Omar Mateen, an Afghani American born in the United States of America, murdered forty-nine people and seriously injured fifty-three in a shooting spree at the Pulse nightclub in Orlando, Florida, United States of America.[1370] According to a series of news reports, Mateen had pledged allegiance to ISIS prior to carrying out «the worst mass shooting in United States history».[1371]

[1359] Kahn J., Mrs. Shipley's Ghost: The Right to Travel and Terrorist Watchlists, Ann Arbor, Univ. Mich. Pres, 2013; Kalhan, A., «Immigration surveillance», *The Modern Law Review*, Volume 74, 2014, pp. 1–78. Ball, Kirstie, and Frank Webster (Eds.), *The Intensification of Surveillance: Crime, Terrorism & Warfare in the Information Age*, London, UK: Pluto Press, 2007; Guzik, Keith, "Discrimination by Design: Predictive Data Mining as Security Practice in the United States' 'War on Terrorism.'", *Surveillance and Society*, 7 (1), 2009, pp. 1–17.

[1360] Hu, Margaret, "Algorithmic Jim Crow", *cit.*, pp. 633–696 (649). Internal citations omitted.

[1361] Hu, Margaret, "Algorithmic Jim Crow", *cit.*, pp. 633–696 (649). Internal citations omitted.

[1362] Hu, Margaret, "Algorithmic Jim Crow", *cit.*, pp. 633–696 (649). Internal citations omitted.

[1363] Hu, Margaret, "Algorithmic Jim Crow", *cit.*, pp. 633–696 (649). Internal citations omitted.

[1364] Hu, Margaret, "Algorithmic Jim Crow", *cit.*, pp. 633–696 (649). Internal citations omitted.

[1365] Lynch J., *From fingerprints to DNA: biometric data collection in U.S. immigrant communities and beyond*, Special Representative, Immigration Policy Center, Washington, DC, 2012.

[1366] Hu, Margaret, "Algorithmic Jim Crow", *cit.*, pp. 633–696 (649). Internal citations omitted.

[1367] Hu, Margaret, "Algorithmic Jim Crow", *cit.*, pp. 633–696 (649). Internal citations omitted.

[1368] Which is all but sobering news. Germany, for example, allows forms of heightened security which, in turn, give rise to permanent digital surveillance of individuals deemed socially unfit or—worse yet—biologically or mentally prone to engage in flagitious and unlawful activities. The German doctrine has fleshed out this topic in depth. See: Müller, Helmut, „Europäische Rechtssicherheit gegen Deutsches Sicherheitsrecht? Zur EGMR-Entscheidung in Sachen nachträgliche (Verlängerung der) Sicherungsverwahrung ", *Kritische Justiz*, Volume 43, Issue 3, 2010, pp. 256–268. This topic—although enthralling/besotting/buoying—falls conspicuously outside the breadth and scope of this essay.

[1369] Hu, Margaret, "Algorithmic Jim Crow", *cit.*, pp. 633–696 (649). Internal citations omitted.

[1370] Hu, Margaret, "Algorithmic Jim Crow", *cit.*, pp. 633–696 (649). Internal citations omitted.

[1371] Hu, Margaret, "Algorithmic Jim Crow", *cit.*, pp. 633–696 (649). Internal citations omitted.

§§ In the aftermath of the vicious Orlando attack, then-candidate Trump adamantly averred that the algorithmic profiling[1372] of Muslims in the United States of America was duly necessary as a precautionary measure to forestall future attacks.[1373]

§§ Fast forward to August 31, 2016, Trump delivered a speech on his projected immigration policy.[1374] In addition to his unwavering promise to construct a wall on the southern border of the United States of America—paired with his bold claim that «Mexico will pay for the wall» -, Trump further expounded that he would likewise put in place a «biometric entry-exit system for tracking visa-holders».[1375]

§§ This cluster of undying promises of heightened national security and border security systems,[1376] coupled with the multifarious Executive Orders restricting travel, maps, hands-in-glove, onto the burgeoning technological developments in the promulgation of emerging cybersurveillance technologies[1377] and algorithmic-anchored screening[1378] and vetting protocols.[1379]

[1372] A feted scholar (Bernard Harcourt) adamantly contends that (1) predictive crime control efforts may do produce harm than good; (2) they may engender a "ratchet effect" in which the disparate impact of forecast on black folks worsens over time; and (3) the technological allure of prediction can both besmirch and mar deep-rooted moral conceptions of justice. See: Harcourt, Bernard E., *Against Prediction: Profiling, Policing, and Punishing in An Actuarial Age*, Chicago, Illinois, University of Chicago Press, 2007, pp. 7–18 and passim. Converging: Ensign, Danielle, "Runaway Feedback Loops in Predictive Policing", *Proceedings of Machine Learning Research*, Volume 81, 2018, p. 1; Starr, Sonja B., "Evidence-Based Sentencing and the Scientific Rationalization of Discrimination", *Stanford Law Review*, Volume 66, 2014, pp. 804–06 (arguing that that risk assessment during sentencing may derails deep-seated concepts of justice that we hold so dear). In addition to this line of reasoning, Professor Sandra Mayson avers that, because any extant racial disparity in crime risk is the byproduct of a long-haul historical oppression, it is therefore an unfitting basis for coercive state action. To put it bluntly, it is unfair for the state to condition coercion on crime risk that modern societies has unjustly created. Put another way, one may be led to believe that the data are simply warped and that the risk at hand is fundamentally uniform across racial lines. Understandably, though not laudably, one may be also led to believe that crime risk is a fundamentally haphazard and incoherent concept, owing to the fact that all people who are self-determining agents have an equal capacity to eschew flagitious behaviour or engaging in criminal activities. See: Mayson, Sandra G., "Bias In, Bias Out", *cit.*, pp. 2218–2300.

[1373] Hu, Margaret, "Algorithmic Jim Crow", *cit.*, pp. 633–696 (649). Internal citations omitted.

[1374] Schulteis, Emily, "Donald Trump Doubles Down in Immigration Speech: "Mexico Will Pay for the Wall," CBS News (Aug. 31, 2016), 2016, http://www.cbsnews.com/news/donald-trump-delivers-immigration-speech-in-phoenix/; [https://perma.cc/E59J-RR2S]. (access: 4.12.2024).

[1375] Hu, Margaret, "Algorithmic Jim Crow", *cit.*, pp. 633–696 (650). Internal citations omitted.

[1376] Hu, Margaret, "Algorithmic Jim Crow", *cit.*, pp. 633–696 (650). Internal citations omitted.

[1377] Zuboff, Zhoshana, *The Age of Surveillance Capitalism, The Fight for a Human Future at the New Frontier of Power*. New Yor City: PublicAffairs Books, 2019, pp. 1–704 (360) (argues that we are indomitably heading towards a "instrumentarianism" that draws on "totalitarianism").

[1378] Abdillahi, I., "Algorithmic surveillance in the era of the appsphere", *American Journal of Community Psychology*, Volume 73, 2024, passim.

[1379] Hu, Margaret, "Algorithmic Jim Crow", *cit.*, pp. 633–696 (650). Internal citations omitted.

§§ In an earnest attempt to draw clear-cut parallels between historic Jim Crow and Algorithmic Jim Crow, this book turns, on the heels of a pathbreaking paper,[1380] to a brief (thumbnail sketch) overview of Jim Crow.

§§ This brief (thumbnail) sketch is not aimed at undertaking an exhaustive history of the legal issues and the nature of Jim Crow.[1381] Rather, this abridged historical account intends to skeletally sketch out an understanding of the breadth and scope of the Jim Crow epoch.[1382] On the flip side, this section aims to shed a keen light on the rationale behind the creation of an amalgamation of laws and policies which were far from being mere tools to segregating locational sites and imposing restrictions on movement on members of racialized communities.[1383]

4.1.5.1 Bridging Past, Present and Future: How the Jim Crow Era Still Resonates Today Through «Algorithmic Jim Crow» (Margaret Hu)

§§ How can such an gruelling system such Jim Crow be skeletally sketched out?[1384] As a feted scholar puts it, Jim Crow amounts to an expression which neatly encapsulates, hands-in-glove, «a series [of] laws and ordinances passed by Southern states and municipalities between 1877 and 1965 legalizing segregation (the physical separation of individuals based on race, gender, religion, or class) within their boundaries».[1385] Racial boundaries[1386] which, in turn, were rigidly enforced[1387] by either concerned citizens[1388] or the law enforcement agencies itself.[1389]

§§ Albeit racial discrimination was not a social practice narrowed down to the South of the United States of America—v.g., Blacks in Northern states

---

[1380] Hu, Margaret, "Algorithmic Jim Crow", *cit.*, pp. 633–696.

[1381] Hu, Margaret, "Algorithmic Jim Crow", *cit.*, pp. 633–696 (651).

[1382] Hu, Margaret, "Algorithmic Jim Crow", *cit.*, pp. 633–696 (651).

[1383] Hu, Margaret, "Algorithmic Jim Crow", *cit.*, pp. 633–696 (651).

[1384] Tischauser, Leslie V., *Jim Crow Laws (Landmarks of the American Mosaic)*, 2012, Westport, Connecticut, United States of America, Greenwood Publishing Group, pp. 1–248 ("*Jim Crow Laws presents the history of the discriminatory laws that segregated people by race in the American South from the end of the Civil War through passage of the 1965 Civil Rights Act. To paint a true picture of these deplorable restrictions, this book provides a detailed analysis of the creation, defense, justification, and fight against the Jim Crow system.* Among the subjects covered here are the origins of legal inequality for African Americans in the aftermath of the Civil War; the role of the U.S. Supreme Court in weakening constitutional protections against discrimination established in the 13th, 14th, and 15th Amendments; *the white justification of segregation; and the extreme brutality of Jim Crow's defenders. Equally important, readers will learn about the psychological, political, social, and economic costs endured by the victims of Jim Crow inequality, as well as about the motivations, rejections, and successes faced by those who stood against these abominations*"). Italics added.

[1385] Tischauser, Leslie V., *Jim Crow Laws (Landmarks of the American Mosaic)*, *cit.*, pp. 1–248 (1).

[1386] Onwuachi-Willig, Angela, "Policing the Boundaries of Whiteness: The Tragedy of Being "Out of Place" from Emmett Till to Trayvon Martin", *Iowa Law Review*, Volume 102, 2017, passim.

[1387] Rich, Camille Gear, "Marginal Whiteness", *California Law Review*, Volume 98, 2010, passim.

endured equally harrowing racial discrimination in housing-*mortgage redlining*[1390] that still resonates today[1391] in education,[1392] employment,[1393] and economic[1394] settings[1395]—in the South, racial inequalities were deeply woven into the fabric of Southern society though.[1396]

1388 Smångs, Mattias, "Doing Violence, Making Race: Southern Lynching and White Racial Group Formation", *American Journal of Sociology*, Volume 121, 2016.

1389 Packard, Jerald M., *American Nightmare: The History of Jim Crow*, Broadway, New York, St. Martin's Press; First Edition, 2002, pp. 1–304 (vii–viii) ("[A] structure of exclusion and discrimination devised by white Americans to be employed principally against black Americans.... *Its central purpose was to maintain a second-class social and economic status for blacks while upholding a first-class social and economic status for whites.... In the South, Jim Crow discrimination at its height existed not only by statute but by custom and racial 'etiquette,' and it was rigidly enforced by both the law enforcement agencies* and courts as well as by ordinary white citizens who were neither policemen nor judges but who often took the law into their own hands as though they were"). Italics added.

1390 See: Part IV, This chapter, Sects. 4.1.4–4.1.4.2.1 of this book (on mortgage redlining). See: Part IV, This chapter, Sects. 4.1.2–4.1.4.3 of this book (on algorithmic credit scoring, consumer racism and credit card redlining). See: Part IV, This chapter, Sects. 4.1.4–4.1.4.2.3 of this book (on algorithmic redlining). See: Part IV, This chapter, Sect. 4.1.4.3 of this book (on "algorithmic redliking"). See also: Szto, Mary, "Real Estate Agents as Agents of Social Change: Redlining, Reverse Redlining, and Greenlining", *Seatle Journal for Social Justice*, Volume 12, Issue 1, 2013, pp. 9–11 ("*Official redlining practices began in the 1930's during the Great Depression.* A *housing bubble and bust preceded the Great Depression. Before mortgage lending became affordable, only wealthy families could buy homes. In 1935, NAREB argued that the federal government should subsidize mortgages and private ownership, not public housing. The federal government agreed and enacted multiple programs to revive the economy and increase employment.* These programs promoted residential construction and made home ownership widely available. This was achieved by "standardized homebuilding procedures" to address the "rising costs of construction," and by providing mortgage insurance. "*Such mortgage insurance lowered interest rates from six to eight percent down to four percent, and raised the amounts that could be financed from 50 to 70 percent of the purchase price to 90 percent. After 1939, with a federally insured mortgage, it was cheaper to purchase than to rent. Unfortunately, three underlying assumptions of these federal programs were the following: (1) people could be divided by race; (2) only white communities held property values; and therefore; (3) segregation by race was necessary to protect white property values. Thus, these programs introduced official racial redlining 60 and allowed the government to promote restrictive racial covenants and segregation. In effect, only whites received federally insured mortgages*"). Footnotes omitted. Italics added.

1391 Ferreri, Mara/Sanyal, Romola, "Digital informalisation: rental housing, platforms, and the management of risk", *Housing Studies*, Volume 37, Issue 6, 2022, pp. 1035–1053 (1035) ("*In contrast to progressive imaginaries of 'smart' technological mediation, practices of algorithmic redlining, biased tenant profiling and the management of risk in private tenancies and in housing welfare both introduce and extend discriminatory and exclusionary housing practices*"). Italics added. See: Part IV, This chapter, Sects. 4.1.4–4.1.4.2.3 of this book.

1392 Pierce, C., "W.E.B. du bois and caste education: Racial capitalist schooling from reconstruction to Jim Crow", *American Educational Research Journal*, 54 (1_Suppl.), 2017, pp. 23S–47S.

1393 Katznelson, Ira, *When Affirmative Action Was White: An Untold History of Racial Inequality in Twentieth-Century America*, New York, W. W. Norton & Company; Reprint edition (August 17, 2006), 2006, pp. 1–272 ("In this "penetrating new analysis" (*New York Times Book Review*) *Ira Katznelson fundamentally recasts our understanding of twentieth-century American history and demonstrates that all the key programs passed during the New Deal and Fair Deal era of the 1930s and 1940s were created in a deeply discriminatory manner. Through mechanisms designed by*

§§ As scathingly portrayed by a famed scholar, Jim Crow «was a Southern phenomenon, the infrastructure white Southerners built to preserve, insofar as humanly possible, the old master/slave system».[1397] Turns out, Jim Crow was nothing but the encapsulation of *systemic racism* of which white Southerners were so fond of.[1398]

§§ No surprise stems from the fact that Jim Crow pierced into every single aspect of life for Southern Blacks: it was deeply etched into every facet of the social, political, and legal fabric of Southern society accordingly.[1399]

Southern Democrats that specifically excluded maids and farm workers, the gap between blacks and whites actually widened despite postwar prosperity. In the words of noted historian Eric Foner, "Katznelson's incisive book should change the terms of debate about affirmative action, and about the last seventy years of American history"). Italics added. This book parses the impact of several racially motivated laws—Social Security Act, G: I. Bill, and labour laws implementing unemployment stipends, minimum wages, and union protection—in the history of United States of America). Italics added.

1394 Saez, Emmanuel, and Gabriel Zucman, "The Rise of Income and Wealth Inequality in America: Evidence from Distributional Macroeconomic Accounts," *Journal of Economic Perspectives*, Volume 34, 2020, pp. 3–26.

1395 Hu, Margaret, "Algorithmic Jim Crow", *cit.*, pp. 633–696 (652). Internal citations omitted. See also: Packard, Jerald M., *American Nightmare: The History of Jim Crow*, *cit.*, pp. 1–304 (64).

1396 See: Bailey, Thomas Pierce, *Race Orthodoxy in the South, and Other Aspects of the Negro Question*, Los Angels, Hardpress Publishing (January 10, 2012), 2012, pp. 1–400. See also: Murray, Pauli, *States' Laws on Race and Color (Studies in the Legal History of the South)*, Georgia, University of Georgia Press; Reprint edition (June 2, 2016), 2016, pp. 1–776 ("*this remarkable, hard-to-find resource is an exhaustive compilation of state laws and local ordinances in effect in 1950 that mandated racial segregation and of pre-Brown-era civil rights legislation. The volume cites legislation from forty-eight states and the District of Columbia, and ordinances of twenty-four major cities across the country. The complete text of each law or ordinance is included, along with occasional notes about its history and the extent to which it was enforced. Other relevant information found in the volume ranges widely: the texts of various Supreme Court rulings; international documents; federal government executive orders, departmental rules, regulations, and directives*"). Italics added. (This path-breaking book sheds a keen light on laws on race in force during the Jim Crow epoch in Alabama, Arkansas, Florida, Georgia, Kentucky, Louisiana, Maryland, Mississippi, North Carolina, South Carolina, Tennessee, Texas, and Virginia) (pp. 21–34, pp. 38–50, pp. 77–117, pp. 164–95, pp. 198–211, pp. 237–50, pp. 329–48, pp. 406–22, pp. 427–56, pp. 461–90).

1397 Hu, Margaret, "Algorithmic Jim Crow", *cit.*, pp. 633–696 (652). Internal citations omitted.

1398 Bailey, Thomas Pierce, *Race Orthodoxy in the South, and Other Aspects of the Negro Question*, Los Angels, Hardpress Publishing (Reprint January 10, 2012), 1914, 2012, pp. 1–400 (92–93) (argues that racial segregation was nothing but "the racial creed of the Southern people").

1399 Hu, Margaret, "Algorithmic Jim Crow", *cit.*, pp. 633–696 (652). Internal citations omitted. See also: Packard, Jerald M., *American Nightmare: The History of Jim Crow*, *cit.*, pp. 1–304 (64).

§§ Tellingly, Jim Crow implemented a myriad of racial restrictions on a bevy of matters. Ranging from housing,[1400] marriage,[1401] voting,[1402] education,[1403] employment,[1404] to travel,[1405] while rigidly enforcing racial segregation[1406] in public[1407] spaces.[1408]

1400 Kruse, Kevin M., *White Flight: Atlanta and the Making of Modern Conservatism (Politics and Society in Modern America), cit.*, pp. 1–352 (60–61) (explaining that FHA actively encouraged racial limitations that paved the way to the segregation between White folks and Black folks). See also: Kermani, Amir, and Francis Wong, "Racial Disparities in Housing Returns," NBER Working Paper no. 29306, 2021.

1401 Lombardo, Paul A., "Miscegenation, Eugenics, and Racism: Historical Footnotes to Loving v. Virginia", *U.C. Davis Law Review*, Volume 21, 1988 (poring over judicial decisions upholding anti-miscegenation laws). Hu, Margaret, "Algorithmic Jim Crow", *cit.*, pp. 633–696 (652).

1402 Williams v. Mississippi, 170 U.S. 213, 225 (1898) (holding that state constitutional requirements of poll taxes and literacy for voting did not discriminate based on race). But see: Harper v. Va. Bd. of Elections, 383 U.S. 663, 666 (1966) ("We conclude that a State violates the Equal Protection Clause of the Fourteenth Amendment whenever it makes the affluence of the voter or payment of any fee an electoral standard.... [T]he Equal Protection Clause of the Fourteenth Amendment restrains the States from fixing voter qualifications which invidiously discriminate"). See: Hu, Margaret, "Algorithmic Jim Crow", *cit.*, pp. 633–696 (653). Hu, Margaret, "Algorithmic Jim Crow", *cit.*, pp. 633–696 (652).

1403 Pierce, C., "W.E.B. du bois and caste education: Racial capitalist schooling from reconstruction to Jim Crow", *American Educational Research Journal*, 54 (1_Suppl.), 2017, pp. 23S–47S. See also: McLaurin v. Okla. State Regents, 339 U.S. 637, 642 (1950); Sweatt v. Painter, 339 U.S. 629, 634–35 (1950). Hu, Margaret, "Algorithmic Jim Crow", *cit.*, pp. 633–696 (653).

1404 See: *Credit Discrimination: Hearings on H.R. 14856 and H.R. 14908 Before the Subcomm. on Consumer Affairs of the H. Comm. on Banking & Currency*, 93rd Cong. 1, 1974, (Hon. Leonor K. Sullivan, Chairman, Subcomm. on Consumer Affairs of the H. Comm. on Banking & Currency) (statement of John H. Powell, Jr., Chairman, Equal Emp't Opportunity Comm'n) *("[I]t is very likely that the inability to obtain credit, or if obtained, the discriminatory terms and conditions which accompany its extension to certain groups in our society, are directly related to discrimination in employment*"). Italics added.

1405 Sandoval-Strausz, A. K., "Travelers, Strangers, and Jim Crow: Law, Public Accommodations, and Civil Rights in America", *Law and History Review*, Volume 23, 2005, passim; Mack, Kenneth W., "Law, Society, Identity, and the Making of the Jim Crow South: Travel and Segregation on Tennessee Railroads, 1875–1905", *Law and Social Inquiry*, Volume 24, 1999; Hu, Margaret, "Algorithmic Jim Crow", *cit.*, pp. 633–696 (653). Internal citations omitted.

1406 But see: Woodward, C. Vann, *The Strange Career of Jim Crow, Commemorative Edition*, Oxford, Oxford University Press, 2001 ("*The Strange Career of Jim Crow* is one of the great works of Southern history. *Indeed, the book actually helped shape that history.* Published in 1955, a year after the Supreme Court in Brown v. Board of Education ordered schools desegregated, *Strange Career was cited so often to counter arguments for segregation that Martin Luther King, Jr. called it "the historical Bible of the civil rights movement." The book offers a clear and illuminating analysis of the history of Jim Crow laws, presenting evidence that segregation in the South dated only to the 1890s. Woodward convincingly shows that, even under slavery, the two races had not been divided as they were under the Jim Crow laws of the 1890s. In fact, during Reconstruction, there was considerable economic and political mixing of the races. The segregating of the races was a relative newcomer to the region.* Hailed as one of the top 100 nonfiction works of the twentieth century, *The Strange Career of Jim Crow* has sold almost a million copies and remains, in the words of David Herbert Donald, "a landmark in the history of American race relations"). Italics added.

1407 Packard, Jerald M., *American Nightmare: The History of Jim Crow*, Broadway, New York, St. Martin's Press; First Edition, 2002, pp. 1–304 (vii–viii) ("[A*] structure of exclusion and discrimination devised by white Americans to be employed principally against black Americans... Its central*

§§ It is important to note, though, that the great bulk of the foregoing racial restrictions were hardened into binding law,[1409] whereas others were deeply nested in the backbone of Southern society under the gloss of social demeanour[1410] and custom,[1411] which are, taken together, simply put, *legal formants*[1412] and *silent forces of law* (mute law).[1413]

§§ All things considered, Jim Crow «stood for an entire culture based on violence, racism, and fear that affected the life of every African American living in the

---

purpose was to maintain a second-class social and economic status for blacks while upholding a first-class social and economic status for whites... In the South, Jim Crow discrimination at its height existed not only by statute but by custom and racial 'etiquette,' and it was rigidly enforced by both the law enforcement agencies and courts as well as by ordinary white citizens who were neither policemen nor judges but who often took the law into their own hands as though they were"). Italics added.

[1408] Hu, Margaret, "Algorithmic Jim Crow", *cit.*, pp. 633–696 (653). Internal citations omitted.

[1409] See: Tischauser, Leslie V., *Jim Crow Laws (Landmarks of the American Mosaic)*, 2012, Westport, Connecticut, United States of America, Greenwood Publishing Group, pp. 1–248 (68) ("*by 1920, Southern state legislatures and governors had passed more than 350 segregation laws... [that] separated people by race in cemeteries, churches, hospitals, labor unions, prisons, offices, factories, mines, parks, public buildings, railway trains, railway station waiting rooms, housing developments, neighborhoods, schools, stores, streetcars, theaters, funeral parlors*, and any other places people could meet"). Italics added.

[1410] On social behaviour through the lens of sociology: Triandis, Harry C., "The self and social behaviour in differing cultural contexts", *Psychological Review*, Volume 96, 1989, 506–520; Rawls, Anne, "Editor's Introduction and "Two Conceptions of Social Order of Action, Objects, and Identities versus Aggregate Orders of Individual Action", *Special Issue of the Journal of Classical Sociology*, Volume 9, Issue 4, 2009, pp. 500–520; Rawls, Anne Warfield, "Wittgenstein, Durkheim, Garfinkel and Winch: Constitutive Orders of Sensemaking", *Journal for the Theory of Social Behaviour*, Volume 41, Issue 4, 2011, pp. 397–413.

[1411] Bederman, David, *Custom as a Source of Law*, Cambridge, Cambridge University Press, 2010, pp. 18–55 (adhering to the traditional view according to which custom comprises both objective and subjective elements).

[1412] See on legal formants: Sacco, Rodolfo, "Legal Formants: A Dynamic Approach to Comparative Law (Installment I of II)", *The American Journal of Comparative Law*, Volume 39, Issue 1, 1991, pp. 1–34 (on the importance of legal formants within the remit of a given jurisdiction); Sacco, Rodolfo, "Legal formants: A dynamic approach to comparative law: discovering and decoding invisible powers", *The American Journal of Comparative Law*, 1991, pp. 343–385 (echoing the same views in this regard); Sacco, Rodolfo, "Legal Formants: A Dynamic Approach to Comparative Law (Instalment II of II)", *The American Journal of Comparative Law*, Volume 39, 1991, p. 344 (legal formants trigger a spark of contradiction though. "Surprisingly enough, however, the contradiction is only apparent. One can believe both in the omnipresence of the legislator and in the creative power of the judge").

[1413] Sacco, Rodolfo, "Mute Law", *The American Journal of Comparative Law*, Volume 43, 1995, p. 464 (arguing that every system has to deal with the phenomenon of mute law. Every legal system is a combination of "both spoken and mute elements". (...) Our legal system is familiar with spoken sources (the written rules, of splendid form and content, produced by legislative assemblies) as well as with unspoken sources (commercial uses, determination of standards of conduct, construction, by an interpreter, of concepts such as fault, reasonableness, bad faith"). In a nutshell, "silence forces of law".

South».[1414] In spite the enactment of the Thirteenth, Fourteenth, and Fifteenth Amendments to the Constitution of United States of America, Supreme Court of the United States of America precedent in the aftermath of the approval of those amendments legitimized laws that either enforced racial inequity[1415] through racial segregation laws[1416] or laws that carved out a disparate discriminatory impact on Blacks.[1417]

§§ There has always been a seamlessly coexistence between racial discrimination and racial classification insofar the latter was an integral part of Jim Crow era.[1418] The overwhelming majority of the Southern states legalized racial classification[1419] by codifying the «one-drop» rule or hardening it into binding law as an integral part

---

[1414] See: Tischauser, Leslie V., *Jim Crow Laws (Landmarks of the American Mosaic), cit.*, pp. 1–248 (2).

[1415] Hu, Margaret, "Algorithmic Jim Crow", *cit.*, pp. 633–696 (653). Internal citations omitted.

[1416] Klarman, Michael J., *From Jim Crow to Civil Rights: The Supreme Court and the Struggle for Racial Equality*, Oxford, Oxford University Press, 2006, pp. 1–655 ("*A monumental investigation of the Supreme Court's rulings on race, From Jim Crow To Civil Rights* spells out in compelling detail the political and social context within which the Supreme Court Justices operate and the consequences of their decisions for American race relations. *In a highly provocative interpretation of the decision's connection to the civil rights movement, Klarman argues that Brown was more important for mobilizing southern white opposition to racial change than for encouraging direct-action protest. Brown* unquestioningly had a significant impact–it brought race issues to public attention and it mobilized supporters of the ruling. *It also, however, energized the opposition. In this authoritative account of constitutional law concerning race, Michael Klarman details, in the richest and most thorough discussion to date, how and whether Supreme Court decisions do, in fact, matter*"). Italics added. See also: Schmidt, Benno C., Jr., "Principle and Prejudice: The Supreme Court and Race in the Progressive Era. Part 1: The Heyday of Jim Crow", *Columbia Law Review*, Volume 82, 1982; Fox, James W., Jr., "Doctrinal Myths and the Management of Cognitive Dissonance: Race, Law, and the Supreme Court's Doctrinal Support of Jim Crow", *Stetson Law Review*, Volume 34, 2005.

[1417] Hu, Margaret, "Algorithmic Jim Crow", *cit.*, pp. 633–696 (653). Internal citations omitted.

[1418] López, Ian Haney, *White by Law, 10th Anniversary Edition: The Legal Construction of Race (Critical America, 16)*, New York, New York University Press, 2006, pp. 1–264 ("*In the first edition of White by Law, Haney López traced the reasoning employed by the courts in their efforts to justify the whiteness of some and the non-whiteness of others, and revealed the criteria that were used, often arbitrarily, to determine whiteness, and thus citizenship: skin color, facial features, national origin, language, culture, ancestry, scientific opinion, and, most importantly, popular opinion.* Ten years later, Haney López revisits the *legal construction of race, and argues that current race law has spawned a troubling racial ideology that perpetuates inequality under a new guise: colorblind white dominance.* In a new, original essay written specifically for the 10th anniversary edition, *he explores this racial paradigm and explains how it contributes to a system of white racial privilege socially and legally defended by restrictive definitions of what counts as race and as racism, and what doesn't, in the eyes of the law. The book also includes a new preface, in which Haney Lopez considers how his own personal experiences with white racial privilege helped engender White by Law*"). Italics added. (further down this insightful offering, the author argues that "constructs racial differences on several levels through the promulgation and enforcement of rules that determine permissible behavior") (pp. 81–86). See also: Packard, Jerald M., *American Nightmare: The History of Jim Crow, cit.*, pp. 1–304 (94–100) (shedding light on racial definitions and state laws describing which citizens were not deemed as white in the eyes of Jim Crow laws).

[1419] Bailey, Thomas Pierce, *Race Orthodoxy in the South, and Other Aspects of the Negro Question*, Los Angels, Hardpress Publishing (January 10, 2012), 2012, pp. 1–400.

of their state constitutions[1420]: any shiver/hint/reminiscence of black ancestry stood as a conspicuously clear sign that the person in question was not white, and thereby should be subject to the congeries of rules enshrined by Jim Crow laws.[1421]

§§ Squeaky clear definitions of race were also inserted within the remit of antimiscegenation laws, which accordingly forbade interracial marriage.[1422] Virginia, for example, enacted a law that required racial descriptions to be stated at a child's birth to further classify individuals as «white» or «colored».[1423]

§§ Virginia's Racial Integrity Act of 1924[1424] «required all citizens within the state born after June 14, 1912 to register their racial composition with the Bureau of Vital Statistics»,[1425] prohibited interracial marriages, and defined who exactly was entitled to be considered as «white.»[1426]

§§ A copy of an old birth record form provided by the Library of Virginia succinctly enshrines a definition of «white»[1427] in light of Virginia law: «A white person is one with no trace whatever of blood of another race, except that one with one-sixteenth of the blood of American Indian, unmixed with other race, may be classed as white.»[1428]

§§ Therefore, the Jim Crow system hinged upon, and heavily relied on, initial racial classification and markers of racial identity[1429] to establish who would be subsequently subjected to laws that determined individual treatment, fundamental rights, and privileges on the heels of the foregoing classifications.[1430]

§§ Classification alone, though, is barely sufficient to propel an exclusionary system.[1431] Implementing such a system requires an all-out screening[1432]: ascertaining whether and to what extent individuals who have been classified are abiding by the rules that follow such classification or the extent to which the individuals are somewhat «suspect.»[1433]

§§ Under Jim Crow system, for example, screening was two-fold. On one end of the spectrum was official—arising out of a policy of official segregation policy, which was brutally enforced by both law enforcement agencies and concerned citizens.[1434]

1420 Hu, Margaret, "Algorithmic Jim Crow", *cit.*, pp. 633–696 (653–654). Internal citations omitted.

1421 Hu, Margaret, "Algorithmic Jim Crow", *cit.*, pp. 633–696 (653–654). Internal citations omitted.

1422 Hu, Margaret, "Algorithmic Jim Crow", *cit.*, pp. 633–696 (654). Internal citations omitted.

1423 Hu, Margaret, "Algorithmic Jim Crow", *cit.*, pp. 633–696 (654). Internal citations omitted.

1424 Hu, Margaret, "Algorithmic Jim Crow", *cit.*, pp. 633–696 (654). Internal citations omitted.

1425 Hu, Margaret, "Algorithmic Jim Crow", *cit.*, pp. 633–696 (654). Internal citations omitted.

1426 Hu, Margaret, "Algorithmic Jim Crow", *cit.*, pp. 633–696 (654). Internal citations omitted.

1427 Hu, Margaret, "Algorithmic Jim Crow", *cit.*, pp. 633–696 (654). Internal citations omitted.

1428 Hu, Margaret, "Algorithmic Jim Crow", *cit.*, pp. 633–696 (654). Internal citations omitted.

1429 On identity: Sobel R., "The demeaning of identity and personhood in national identification systems", *Harvard Journal of Law and Technology*, Volume 15, pp. 2002, pp. 319–387.

1430 Hu, Margaret, "Algorithmic Jim Crow", *cit.*, pp. 633–696 (654). Internal citations omitted.

1431 Hu, Margaret, "Algorithmic Jim Crow", *cit.*, pp. 633–696 (655). Internal citations omitted.

1432 Hu, Margaret, "Algorithmic Jim Crow", *cit.*, pp. 633–696 (655). Internal citations omitted.

1433 Hu, Margaret, "Algorithmic Jim Crow", *cit.*, pp. 633–696 (655). Internal citations omitted.

1434 Packard, Jerald M., *American Nightmare: The History of Jim Crow*, Broadway, New York, St. Martin's Press; First Edition, 2002, pp. 1–304 (vii–viii) ("[A*] structure of exclusion and discrimination devised by white Americans to be employed principally against black Americans.... Its central*

At the other end of the spectrum, the Jim Crow matrix was unofficial, as a part of broader social apparatus comprising both norms of racial[1435] etiquette[1436] and behavioural norms.[1437]

§§ Note, though, that Jim Crow-era screening[1438] was pretty much a «small data»[1439] world[1440] screening system,[1441] leveraging mostly on classification on hard

---

purpose was to maintain a second-class social and economic status for blacks while upholding a first-class social and economic status for whites.... In the South, Jim Crow discrimination at its height existed not only by statute but by custom and racial 'etiquette,' and it was rigidly enforced by both the law enforcement agencies and courts as well as by ordinary white citizens who were neither policemen nor judges but who often took the law into their own hands as though they were"). Italics added.

[1435] Packard, Jerald M., *American Nightmare: The History of Jim Crow*, Broadway, New York, St. Martin's Press; First Edition, 2002, pp. 1–304 ("*For a hundred years after the end of the Civil War, a quarter of all Americans lived under a system of legalized segregation called Jim Crow. Together with its rigidly enforced canon of racial "etiquette," these rules governed nearly every aspect of life–and outlined draconian punishments for infractions. The purpose of Jim Crow was to keep African Americans subjugated at a level as close as possible to their former slave status. Exceeding even South Africa's notorious apartheid in the humiliation, degradation, and suffering it brought, Jim Crow left scars on the American psyche that are still felt today.* American Nightmare examines and explains Jim Crow from its beginnings to its end: how it came into being, how it was lived, how it was justified, and how, at long last, it was overcome only a few short decades ago. *Most importantly, this book reveals how a nation founded on principles of equality and freedom came to enact as law a pervasive system of inequality and virtual slavery. Although America has finally consigned Jim Crow to the historical graveyard, Jerrold Packard shows why it is important that this scourge–and an understanding of how it happened–remain alive in the nation's collective memory*"). Italics added.

[1436] Hu, Margaret, "Algorithmic Jim Crow", *cit.*, pp. 633–696 (655). Internal citations omitted.

[1437] Hu, Margaret, "Algorithmic Jim Crow", *cit.*, pp. 633–696 (656). Internal citations omitted.

[1438] Screening still resonates today, leveraging on biased credit scoring which, in turn, has travelled all the way from the Jim Crow era. See: *Tech, Bias and Housing Initiative, the Promise and Perils of Residential Proptech, Year 1, Research Summary Report, April 2023, TechEquity Collaborative*, p. 10, available at: https://techequity.us/wp-content/uploads/2023/04/TBHI-Y1-Research-Summary-Report.pdf (28.11.2024). ("*Tenant screening tools are often packaged as part of a larger suite of property management tools for landlords. Unlike Analog Models, Algorithmic Tenant Screening Tools Predict Future Behavior To Determine Housing Access.* Before the advent of algorithmic tenant screening, landlords vetted tenants by having them submit their own records and references from previous landlords or others who could vouch for their trustworthiness. During an analog rental application process, a prospective tenant provides certain personal information and then gives consent for the landlord to run a background check to verify their information. *The landlord, housing provider, or property manager then pays a third-party entity such as TransUnion to pull information that gives a sense of whether the applicant will be a trustworthy renter. In analog screening, those reports return information from an applicant's credit, eviction, and criminal histories. There are many inequities with this analog model. Eviction and criminal records are often wrong or lack important context. 12 13 Credit scoring techniques are notoriously biased*"). Italics added. See: Part IV, This chapter, Sects. 4.1.4–4.1.4.2.3 of this book.

[1439] Hu, Margaret, "From the National Surveillance State to the Cybersurveillance State", *The Annual Review of Law and Social Science*, Volume 13, 2017, p. 168 ("*currently, biometric verification and identification technologies are not commonly perceived to be surveillance technologies—the public and private sectors typically treat them as a benign and useful form of digitized identification. Such automated biometric screening is considered to be a more efficient form of small data verification technologies, such as human screening or human-driven practices involving assessments of biometric or forensic data. Small data biometric verification could include comparing a passport*

copies of documents, such as birth certificates or identity[1442] cards,[1443] or an *in loco* examination of physical appearance,[1444] closely followed by screening to make sure that the excluded individuals were fully compliant with the extant systems of classification.[1445]

§§ In a big data[1446] world[1447]—whereby there is no such thing as privacy[1448]—systems of screening, such as the extreme vetting formal requirements of Trump's Executive Orders,[1449] are duly capable of surveilling[1450] whopping numbers of

---

photo against the person holding the passport. Big data biometric identification, however, has a distinct impact from that of small data biometric investigation because it can facilitate surveillance. Big data photo screening may entail the collection of digital photographs. This in turn can lead to facilitating facial recognition technology through the mass digitization of photo databases, potentially including billions of facial images. One Snowden disclosure noted that the NSA collects millions of digital photographs from internet and social media sources and uses facial recognition technology to identify individuals"). Italics added.

1440 Hu, Margaret, "Small data surveillance v. big data cybersurveillance", *Pepperdine Law Review*, Volume 42, 2015, pp. 773–844.

1441 See: Part II, Chap. 2, Sects. 2.1–2.1.1. (on the contours of the small data world against the backdrop of which *Perceptron* failed to attain its overriding goals).

1442 On identity: Sobel R., "The demeaning of identity and personhood in national identification systems", *Harvard Journal of Law and Technology*, Volume 15, pp. 2002, pp. 319–387.

1443 Lyon D., *Identifying Citizens: ID Cards as Surveillance*, Hoboken, New Jersey, Wiley, 2009.

1444 Hu, Margaret, "Algorithmic Jim Crow", *cit.*, pp. 633–696 (656). Internal citations omitted.

1445 Hu, Margaret, "Algorithmic Jim Crow", *cit.*, pp. 633–696 (656). Internal citations omitted.

1446 Big data that is in the limelight these days. See: Sivarajah, Uthayasnkar et al., "Critical Analysis of Big Data Challenges and Analytical Methods", *Journal of Business Research*, Volume 70, 2017, pp. 263 and ff and passim; Jetten, Lieke /Sharon, Stephen, "Selected Issues concerning the Ethical Use of Big Data Health Analytics", *Washington & Lee Law Review Online*, Volume 72, 2016, passim; Wachter, S./Mittelstadt. B., "A right to Reasonable Inferences: Re-thinking Data Protection Law in the Age of Big Data and AI", *Columbia Business Law Review*, 2019, pp. 1 and ff and passim; See in French doctrine: Ferey, Samuel, « Analyse économique du droit, big data et justice prédictive», *Archives de Philosophie du Droit*, Volume 60, 2018, pp. 68–81; Završnik, A. "Algorithmic justice: Algorithms and big data in criminal justice settings", *European Journal of Criminology*, 2019, passim; Joh, Elizabeth E., "The New Surveillance Discretion: Automated Suspicion, Big Data, and Policing." *Harvard Law and Policy Review*, 10 (1), 2016, pp. 15–42; Hu, Margaret, "Big data blacklisting", *Florida Law Review*, Volume 67, 2015, pp. 1735–1809.

1447 Simmons, Ric, "Big Data and Procedural Justice: Legitimizing Algorithms in the Criminal Justice System", *Ohio State Journal of Criminal Law*, Volume 15, 2018, pp. 576 and ff and passim; Brayne, S., "Big data surveillance: The case of policing", *American Sociological Review*, Volume 82, Issue 5, 2017, pp. 977–1008.

1448 But see: Posner, Richard A., "Privacy, Surveillance, and Law", *University of Chicago Law Review*, Volume 75, 2008, p. 251 ("Privacy is the terrorist's best friend"). See also on the tradeoff between privacy and security: Solove, DanielJ., *Nothing to Hide: The False Tradeoff Between privacy and security*, New Haven/London, Yale University Press, 2013, pp. 101–110; Santos, Hugo Luz dos, "They See You and yet you don't see them: Privacy in the Multilayered National Surveillance State Realm: a Dystopian Digital Society?", *Journal of Computer Science & Systems Biology*, Volume 11, n.° 3, New York, United States of America, 2018, pp. 200–216. Citron; Danielle Keats/Pasquale, Frank, "Network Accountability for the Domestic Intelligence Apparatus", *Hasting Law Journal*, Volume 62, 2011, 1441, 1444–45; Gray, David/Citron, Danielle Keats, "The Right to Quantitative Privacy", *Minnesota Law Review*, Volume 98, 2013, pp. 62–81.

1449 Hu, Margaret, "Algorithmic Jim Crow", *cit.*, pp. 633–696 (656). Internal citations omitted.

persons of interest[1451] based on data[1452] mining[1453] or other broad-scope categories[1454] and then subsequently classifying them based on status accordingly.[1455]

[1450] Zuboff, Zhoshana, *The Age of Surveillance Capitalism, The Fight for a Human Future at the New Frontier of Power*. New Yor City: PublicAffairs Books, 2019, pp. 1–704 (360) (argues that we are indomitably heading towards a "instrumentarianism" that draws on "totalitarianism"); Sewell, A. A., Jefferson, K. A./Lee, H., "Living under surveillance: Gender, psychological distress, and stop-question- and-frisk policing in New York city", *Social Science & Medicine*, Volume 159, 2016, pp. 1–13.

[1451] Fergus, Rachel, "Biased Technology: The Automated Discrimination of Facial Recognition", *ACLU Minnesota*, February 29, 2024, available at: https://www.aclu-mn.org/en/news/biased-technology-automated-discrimination-facial-recognition (access: 20.09.2024) ("*It's no secret that the Department of Homeland Security and its sub-agencies ICE and Customs and Border Protection have already committed horrific abuses – the ACLU sees the tragic consequences. With facial recognition, these agencies could potentially pinpoint the location of immigrants across the country, marking them for detention and deportation on an unprecedented scale. In 2017 alone, ICE, DHS and other government agencies used this technology to locate and arrest 400 family members and caregivers of unaccompanied migrant children, separating families and leaving children in detention*"). Italics added.

[1452] Hu, Margaret, "From the National Surveillance State to the Cybersurveillance State", *The Annual Review of Law and Social Science*, Volume 13, 2017, p. 169 ("*the potential for mass surveillance is part of the problematic nature of biometric credentialing and identification practices. Like most digital data, biometric identification data are not restricted to the purpose for which they were originally collected. Biometric data can be repurposed for secondary uses, such as identification of potential suspects or victims through real-time analytics, assessment of threats of terrorism, tactical decisionmaking, or behavioral and genetic research* (Duster 2003). *Beyond secondary—and tertiary, quaternary, and quinary—uses, biometric data become a part of population-wide risk assessments that incorporate bureaucratized surveillance into governing decisions, policing, and threat assessments. Through big data tools, precrime governance models are increasingly reflected in collect-it-all cybersurveillance systems.* In these systems, biometric data is a surveillance axis that can be used to track, identify, and isolate suspicious persons, digital data, or devices"). Italics added.

[1453] Tollenaar, N., & van der Heijden, P., "Which method predicts recidivism best? A comparison of statistical, machine learning and data mining predictive models", *Journal of the Royal Statistical Society: Series A*, Volume 176, Issue 2, 2013, pp. 565–584. Balkin, Jack, "Constitution in the National Surveillance State", *Minnesota Law Review*, Volume 93, 2008, p. 13 ("*data mining* allows inferences not only about the direct subject of surveillance, but about other people with whom they live, work and communicate"). But see: Pedreshi, Dino/Ruggieri, Salvatore/Turini, Franco, "Discrimination-aware Data Mining", *Proceedings of the 14th ACM SIGKDD International Conference on Knowledge Discovery and Data Mining (Las Vegas, Nevada, USA), ACM*, 2008, pp. 560–568 (arguing that one should shift its gaze downstream by putting in place discrimination-aware algorithmic tools while performing data mining).

[1454] Fergus, Rachel, "Biased Technology: The Automated Discrimination of Facial Recognition", *ACLU Minnesota*, February 29, 2024, available at: https://www.aclu-mn.org/en/news/biased-technology-automated-discrimination-facial-recognition (access: 20.09.2024) ("*Law enforcement and the criminal justice system already disproportionately target and incarcerate people of color. Using technology that has documented problems with correctly identifying people of color is dangerous.* The ACLU-MN has an appalling firsthand example here in Minnesota: We sued on behalf of Kylese Perryman, an innocent young man who was falsely arrested and detained based solely on incorrect facial identification. The *injustice does not stop there. A 2020 ACLU study found that since Black*

In a nutshell, **algorithmic screening**—an outgrowth of algorithmic cybersurveillance[1456]—is now facially «equal»[1457] and the classification system is officially «separate.».[1458] Just like in the Jim Crow era.[1459]

---

people are more likely to be arrested than white people for minor crimes, their faces and personal data are more likely to be in mugshot databases. That makes them more likely to be misidentified as suspects and forced to sit in lineups – despite the documented lack of accuracy behind all these means of supposed identification. The ACLU found that police surveillance cameras are disproportionately installed in Black and Brown neighborhoods, which again exacerbates systematic racism. It is a common assumption that technology is unbiased, and thus infallible. This simply isn't true. All technology is created by people and people are biased"). Italics added.

[1455] Hu, Margaret, "Algorithmic Jim Crow", *cit.*, pp. 633–696 (656). Internal citations omitted.

[1456] Hu, Margaret, "From the National Surveillance State to the Cybersurveillance State", *The Annual Review of Law and Social Science*, Volume 13, 2017, p. 168 ("*as a result, the Cybersurveillance State, as a technological successor to the National Surveillance State, will execute bureaucratized biometric cybersurveillance in ways that are largely invisible and that appear routinized when technologically embedded within biometric identification technologies harnessed by the Administrative State. The normalization of day-to-day cybersurveillance will be achieved largely through governing functions that appear purely administrative (e.g., identity assessments for the granting of welfare, rights, privileges, and governing incentives).* Because of the routinized and administrative nature of the government-led big data program or *data surveillance (dataveillance) program, contemporary cybersurveillance is likely to be viewed as justified under crime, immigration control, and counterterrorism policy rationales*"). Italics added.

[1457] But see: Benjamin, Ruha, *Race After Technology: Abolitionist Tools for the New Jim Code*, New York, Polity, 2019, pp. 1–172 (7) (discussing that Artificial Intelligence-embedded technologies are viewed as iron-clad tools of objectivity and devoid of any biases whatsoever). Ruha Benjamin nonetheless contends that "the employment of new technologies that reflect and reproduce existing inequities but that are promoted and perceived as more objective or progressive than the discriminatory systems of a previous era"). See also: Farina, M., & Lavazza, A., *Philosophy, expertise, and the myth of neutrality. Routledge Studies in Contemporary Philosophy*, London, Routledge, 2024. This false scent of neutrality impairs, and impacts, procedural justice. See: Tyler, Tom R., "The Psychology of Procedural Justice: A Test of the Group-Value Model", *Journal of Personality and Social Psychology*, Volume 57, 1989, p. 830 (reports that in any procedure "several non-control issues – the *neutrality* of the decision-making procedure, trust in the 3rd party, and the information the experience communicates about social standing – influence both procedural preferences and judgments of procedural justice").

[1458] Hu, Margaret, "Algorithmic Jim Crow", *cit.*, pp. 633–696 (656). Internal citations omitted.

[1459] Finkelman, Paul (Editor), *Race, Law, and American History 1700–1990: African Americans and the Law*, Volume 1, London, Taylor & Francis (1 Mar. 1992), 1992, pp. 1–630; Chin, Gabriel J., "Jim Crow's Long Goodbye", *Constitutional Comment*, Volume 21, 2004; Chin, Gabriel J./Wagner, Randy, "The Tyranny of the Minority: Jim Crow and the Counter-Majoritarian Difficulty", *Harvard Civil Rights-Civil Liberties Law Review*, Volume 43, 2008; Fox, James W., Jr., "Doctrinal Myths and the Management of Cognitive Dissonance: Race, Law, and the Supreme Court's Doctrinal Support of Jim Crow", *Stetson Law Review*, Volume 34, 2005.

§§ Failing to gauge the underlying bases of classification and screening systems[1460] «indicates an inherent level of trust in government systems»[1461] that ultimately may be conducive to deleterious consequences.[1462] Screening in a *big data* world[1463] serves as an advanced tool of technological interrogation and entrenches surveillance[1464] as a norm.[1465]

§§ Relatedly, large scale of screenings of citizens in «collect it all» systems[1466] underpin the social matrix of policing[1467] in a manner akin to that of Jim Crow era,

---

[1460] Hu, Margaret, "From the National Surveillance State to the Cybersurveillance State", *The Annual Review of Law and Social Science*, Volume 13, 2017, passim.

[1461] Hu, Margaret, "Algorithmic Jim Crow", *cit.*, pp. 633–696 (656). Internal citations omitted. But see: Weizenbaum, Joseph, *Computer Power and Human Reason: From Judgment to Calculation*, 1st edition, New York, W. H. Freeman & Co, 1976, pp. 1–300 (227) ("examines the sources of the computer's powers and offers evaluative explorations of what computers can do, cannot do, and should not be employed to do") (this founding father of Artificial Intelligence presciently noted that we should not entrust Artificial Intelligence-embedded technologies with "tasks that demand wisdom"). Italics added. The approval of rental applications is arguably one of those tasks that should never be entrusted to machines). More on this on Part IV, This chapter, Sects. 4.1.4–4.1.4.2.1 of this book.

[1462] Hu, Margaret, "Algorithmic Jim Crow", *cit.*, pp. 633–696 (656). Internal citations omitted.

[1463] Hu, Margaret, "From the National Surveillance State to the Cybersurveillance State", *The Annual Review of Law and Social Science*, Volume 13, 2017, p. 169 ("*in a big data world, a digitized passport system can link to multiple other sources, such as license plate readers, No Fly Lists, and Terrorist Watchlists. Facial recognition technology drawing upon a photo database could potentially link a plethora of digital images of a person, including social media, the internet, photo databases like driver's licenses, live-streaming video, CCTV surveillance, and images obtained from hacking cameras on laptops and digital devices. Biometric data collection and storage are becoming increasingly compulsory through either government identification requirements*, such as digital photo requirements for passports and driver's licenses, or corporate identification requirements, such as biometric access to digital devices"). Italics added.

[1464] On mass surveillance: Zuboff, Zhoshana, *The Age of Surveillance Capitalism, The Fight for a Human Future at the New Frontier of Power*. New Yor City: PublicAffairs Books, 2019, pp. 1–704 (360) (argues that we are indomitably heading towards a "instrumentarianism" that draws on "totalitarianism"); Sewell, A. A., Jefferson, K. A./Lee, H., "Living under surveillance: Gender, psychological distress, and stop-question- and-frisk policing in New York city", *Social Science & Medicine*, Volume 159, 2016, pp. 1–13.

[1465] Hu, Margaret, "Algorithmic Jim Crow", *cit.*, pp. 633–696 (656). Internal citations omitted.

[1466] See also: Hu, Margaret, "From the National Surveillance State to the Cybersurveillance State", *cit.*, p. 163 ("*collect-it-all efforts like TIA embody a philosophy that aspires to preventive policing. Mass data collection is construed as a tool to assess and prevent future threats (Murray 2010). In TIA and other programs tested or adopted after 9/11, biometric database screening and analysis have emerged as a preferred method for tracking, identifying, and establishing identity-based inferences in counterterrorism*"). Italics added.

[1467] Hu, Margaret, "From the National Surveillance State to the Cybersurveillance State", *The Annual Review of Law and Social Science*, Volume 13, 2017, p. 169 ("*the potential for mass surveillance is part of the problematic nature of biometric credentialing and identification practices. Like most digital data, biometric identification data are not restricted to the purpose for which they were originally collected*. Biometric data can be repurposed for secondary uses, such as identification of potential suspects or victims through real-time analytics, assessment of threats of terrorism, tactical decisionmaking, or behavioral and genetic research (Duster 2003). Beyond secondary—and tertiary, quaternary, and quinary—uses, biometric data become a part of population-wide *risk*

which, recall, entrenched racial classifications and screenings of individuals based on race[1468] or perceived race.[1469]

§§ Such a framework is underpinned by big data[1470] systems[1471]—which, in turn, laid down the foundations upon which stands a broader surveillance apparatus[1472] commensurate with *biometric*[1473] *surveillance*[1474]—that actively canvass suspicious data eying the possibility of identifying[1475] and profiling[1476] persons of interest.[1477]

---

assessments that incorporate bureaucratized surveillance into governing decisions, policing, and threat assessments. Through big data tools, precrime governance models are increasingly reflected in collect-it-all cybersurveillance systems. In these systems, biometric data is a surveillance axis that can be used to track, identify, and isolate suspicious persons, digital data, or devices"). Italics added.

[1468] Fergus, Rachel, "Biased Technology: The Automated Discrimination of Facial Recognition", *ACLU Minnesota*, February 29, 2024, available at: https://www.aclu-mn.org/en/news/biased-technology-automated-discrimination-facial-recognition (access: 20.09.2024) ("*Facial recognition automates discrimination. The ACLU-MN is fighting to end law enforcement's use of facial recognition technology in Minnesota. More than a dozen large cities have banned the technology, including Minneapolis, Boston, and San Francisco.* If Minnesota adopts a policy to ban the technology, it would be the first state to do so. Here's why the ACLU-MN will fight this legislative session to ban facial recognition tech:

1. *It gives blanketed and indiscriminate surveillance to authorities to track you.*
2. *It is inaccurate and intensifies racial and gender biases that already exist in law enforcement, which lead to disparate treatment.*
3. *It can be used to target and identify vulnerable groups, such as immigrants and refugees.*
4. *It can be used to track your personal movements, including going to abortion clinics or drug treatment.*

Facial recognition technology violates our Constitutional rights"). Italics added.

[1469] Hu, Margaret, "Algorithmic Jim Crow", *cit.*, pp. 633–696 (656). Internal citations omitted.

[1470] On algorithmic big data biometric governance: Hu, Margaret, "From the National Surveillance State to the Cybersurveillance State", *The Annual Review of Law and Social Science*, Volume 13, 2017, p. 169 ("*as a result of big data biometric governance trends, meaningful distinctions between biometric credentialing for identification and behavioral biometric profiling are disappearing. The objectives are merging: Reliable credentialing is used to advance security and precrime policy rationales. Biometric data mission creep occurs by necessity in a big data world because the cybersurveillance systems are often designed to engage in mass data integration and analysis and predictive policing. Biometric surveillance serves two purposes in preventive policing: It increases identity transparency, and the biometric data categorize identity through cataloging behavioral and physical characteristics and assess these characteristics for risk. Contrasting small data biometric credentialing protocols with big data credentialing protocols is useful. It illustrates how biometric surveillance fits within the Cybersurveillance State. In a small data world, paper-based passports and nondigitized photographs are examples of a small data biometric-based identification system*"). Italics added.

[1471] Mayer-Schonberger, V., Cukier, K., *Big Data: A Revolution that Will Transform How We Live, Work, and Think*, London: John Murray, 2013.

[1472] Lyon, D., *Surveillance Studies*, Cambridge, United Kingdom, Polity, 2007.

[1473] Pato, J., Millett, L. (Editors), *Biometric Recognition: Challenges and Opportunities*, Washington, DC: National Academic Press, 2010.

[1474] Hu, Margaret, "From the National Surveillance State to the Cybersurveillance State", *The Annual Review of Law and Social Science*, Volume 13, 2017, p. 169 ("*the potential for mass surveillance is part of the problematic nature of biometric credentialing and identification practices.*

Understandably, although not laudably, mass population-based screening and mass surveillance[1478] spur intrinsically unlawful[1479] surveillance[1480] norms.[1481]

§§ Against this background, systems of subordination, such as Jim Crow and Apartheid,[1482] hinge upon careful classification of who is privileged (Whites, whom benefit from the *endowment effect*[1483])[1484] and who is not (Blacks, Latinos and

---

Like most digital data, biometric identification data are not restricted to the purpose for which they were originally collected. Biometric data can be repurposed for secondary uses, such as identification of potential suspects or victims through real-time analytics, assessment of threats of terrorism, tactical decisionmaking, or behavioral and genetic research (Duster 2003). *Beyond secondary—and tertiary, quaternary, and quinary—uses, biometric data become a part of population-wide risk assessments that incorporate bureaucratized surveillance into governing decisions, policing, and threat assessments. Through big data tools, precrime governance models are increasingly reflected in collect-it-all cybersurveillance systems.* In these systems, biometric data is a surveillance axis that can be used to track, identify, and isolate suspicious persons, digital data, or devices"). Italics added. See also: Hu, Margaret, "Biometric surveillance and big data governance", *The Cambridge Handbook of Surveillance Law*, Henderson, D Gray (Editor), Cambridge, United Kingdom, Cambridge University Press, 2017.

1475 See: Magnet, S., *When Biometrics Fail: Gender, Race, and the Technology of Identity*, Durham, North Carolina, Duke University Press, 2011. On identity: Sobel R., "The demeaning of identity and personhood in national identification systems", *Harvard Journal of Law and Technology*, Volume 15, pp. 2002, pp. 319–387.

1476 Murray, N., "Profiling in the age of total information awareness", *Race Class*, Volume 52, Issue 2, 2010, pp. 3–24.

1477 Hu, Margaret, "Algorithmic Jim Crow", *cit.*, pp. 633–696 (656). Internal citations omitted.

1478 Hu, Margaret, "From the National Surveillance State to the Cybersurveillance State", *The Annual Review of Law and Social Science*, Volume 13, 2017, p. 169 ("*the potential for mass surveillance is part of the problematic nature of biometric credentialing and identification practices. Like most digital data, biometric identification data are not restricted to the purpose for which they were originally collected.* (...) Beyond secondary—and tertiary, quaternary, and quinary—uses, biometric data become a part of population-wide *risk assessments that incorporate bureaucratized surveillance into governing decisions, policing, and threat assessments. Through big data tools, precrime governance models are increasingly reflected in collect-it-all cybersurveillance systems. In these systems, biometric data is a surveillance axis that can be used to track, identify, and isolate suspicious persons, digital data, or devices*"). Italics added. See also on mass surveillance: Bentham, Jeremy, *Panopticon: Or, the inspection-house*, Thomas Byrne, 1787. See also: Balkin, Jack M./Levinson, Sanford, "The Processes of Constitutional Change: From Partisan Entrenchment to the National Surveillance State", *Fordham Law Review*, Volume 75, 2006, pp. 489 and ff; Slogogin, Christopher, "Public Privacy: Camera Surveillance of Public Places and the Right to Anonymity", *Mississippi Law Journal*, Volume 72, 2002, pp. 213–251; Balkin, Jack M., "The Constitution in the National Surveillance State", *Minnesota Law Review*, Volume 93, Issue 1, 2008, pp. 17 and ff; Christopher Slobogin, "Panvasive Surveillance, Political Process Theory, and the Nondelegation Doctrine", *Georgetown Law Journal*, Volume 102, 2014, pp. 1721–1775.

1479 O'Harrow R., *No Place to Hide*, New York, Free, 2005.

1480 Fergus, Rachel, "Biased Technology: The Automated Discrimination of Facial Recognition", *ACLU Minnesota*, February 29, 2024, available at: https://www.aclu-mn.org/en/news/biased-technology-automated-discrimination-facial-recognition (access: 20.09.2024) ("*It's no secret that the Department of Homeland Security and its sub-agencies ICE and Customs and Border Protection have already committed horrific abuses – the ACLU sees the tragic consequences. With facial recognition, these agencies could potentially pinpoint the location of immigrants across the country, marking them for detention and deportation on an unprecedented scale. In 2017 alone, ICE, DHS and other government agencies used this technology to locate and arrest 400 family members*

Muslims).[1485] As noted above, once a classification is carried out, laws engender immediate and unconstrained separation, subordination, and screening on the heels of that classification.[1486]

§§ Jim Crow's frame of reference built on race-based classifications to engage in a far-reaching economic, social, and political exclusions hardened into binding law.[1487] The very endeavour of weeding out or disempowering based on race often required[1488] screening processes seemingly cloaked in legality.[1489] In addition to that, encompassed screening through deeply entrenched social norms[1490] and robust demeanour control.[1491]

§§ These screening processes would often require governments—or their private associates—to screen individuals on the foundational basis of race.[1492] Failing which,

---

and caregivers of unaccompanied migrant children, separating families and leaving children in detention"). Italics added.

1481 Hu, Margaret, "Algorithmic Jim Crow", *cit.*, pp. 633–696 (656). Internal citations omitted.

1482 Hu, Margaret, "Algorithmic Jim Crow", *cit.*, pp. 633–696 (656–657). Internal citations omitted.

1483 Sunstein, Cass R., "Empirically Informed Regulation", *The University of Chicago Law Review*, Volume 78, 2011, p. 1355 (arguing that "those who have the initial allocation may value a good more than they would if the allocation were originally elsewhere, thus showing an *endowment effect*"). Italics added. Sunstein, Cass R., "Empirically Informed Regulation", *cit.*, 1357 (arguing that "in some contexts, social norms can help create a phenomenon of *compliance without enforcement*"). Italics added.

1484 See: Roithmayr, Daria, *Reproducing Racism: How everyday choices lock in White Advantage*, New York, New York University Press, 2014, pp. 1–272 ("*Argues that racial inequality reproduces itself automatically over time because early unfair advantage for whites has paved the way for continuing advantage. This book is designed to change the way we think about racial inequality (...) Legal scholar Daria Roithmayr provocatively argues that racial inequality lives on because white advantage functions as a powerful self-reinforcing monopoly, reproducing itself automatically from generation to generation even in the absence of intentional discrimination. Drawing on work in antitrust law and a range of other disciplines, Roithmayr brilliantly compares the dynamics of white advantage to the unfair tactics of giants like AT&T and Microsoft*. With penetrating insight, Roithmayr *locates the engine of white monopoly in positive feedback loops that connect the dramatic disparity of Jim Crow to modern racial gaps in jobs, housing and education. Wealthy white neighborhoods fund public schools that then turn out wealthy white neighbors. Whites with lucrative jobs informally refer their friends, who refer their friends, and so on. Roithmayr concludes that racial inequality might now be locked in place, unless policymakers immediately take drastic steps to dismantle this oppressive system*"). Italics added. This book points out how White privilege is perpetuated throughout generations through residential segregation (*mortgage redlining*), abhorrent nepotism, and other bemoaning social practices that pester modern societies). See: Part IV, This chapter, Sects. 4.1.4–4.1.4.2.3 of this book.

1485 Hu, Margaret, "Algorithmic Jim Crow", *cit.*, pp. 633–696 (657). Internal citations omitted.

1486 Hu, Margaret, "Algorithmic Jim Crow", *cit.*, pp. 633–696 (657). Internal citations omitted.

1487 Hu, Margaret, "Algorithmic Jim Crow", *cit.*, pp. 633–696 (657). Internal citations omitted.

1488 Hu, Margaret, "Algorithmic Jim Crow", *cit.*, pp. 633–696 (657). Internal citations omitted.

1489 Hu, Margaret, "Algorithmic Jim Crow", *cit.*, pp. 633–696 (658). Internal citations omitted.

1490 Sunstein, Cass R., "Social norms and social roles", *Columbia Law Review*, Volume 96, 1996, pp. 903–968.

1491 Hu, Margaret, "Algorithmic Jim Crow", *cit.*, pp. 633–696 (658). Internal citations omitted.

1492 Hu, Margaret, "Algorithmic Jim Crow", *cit.*, pp. 633–696 (658). Internal citations omitted.

would frequently entail legal consequences coupled with harsh social penalties such as ostracization.[1493]

§§ Maybe the clearest way to illustrate how the Jim Crow legal framework is currently being mimicked in a «big data world»[1494] through Algorithmic Jim Crow is to taking stock of the following hypothesis: imagine, if you will, replacing race-based classifications with classifications of digitally-fraught suspiciousness.[1495]

§§ Tellingly, in lieu of hinging upon a targeted class, such as race, nationality, gender, creed, beliefs, or religion, as a sole and square basis for exclusion, big data gives room for exclusion to be undergirded by an amorphous and shapeless abstraction, such as a digitally inferred suspicion or an algorithmically-anchored guilt[1496]/ suspicion.[1497]

§§ In addition to that, big data possess the ability to amalgamate/amass protected classifications with other gleaned data.[1498] For instance, biometric screening that leverages on soft biometric indicators—e.g. digital evaluations of skin colour[1499] and estimated age harvested from a digital photo[1500]—can weave together race

---

[1493] Hu, Margaret, "Algorithmic Jim Crow", *cit.*, pp. 633–696 (658). Internal citations omitted.

[1494] Hu, Margaret, "From the National Surveillance State to the Cybersurveillance State", *The Annual Review of Law and Social Science*, Volume 13, 2017, p. 169 ("*in a big data world, a digitized passport system can link to multiple other sources, such as license plate readers, No Fly Lists, and Terrorist Watchlists. Facial recognition technology drawing upon a photo database could potentially link a plethora of digital images of a person, including social media, the internet, photo databases like driver's licenses, live-streaming video, CCTV surveillance, and images obtained from hacking cameras on laptops and digital devices. Biometric data collection and storage are becoming increasingly compulsory through either government identification requirements*, such as digital photo requirements for passports and driver's licenses, or corporate identification requirements, such as biometric access to digital devices"). Italics added.

[1495] Hu, Margaret, "Algorithmic Jim Crow", *cit.*, pp. 633–696 (658). Internal citations omitted.

[1496] Hu, Margaret, "Algorithmic Jim Crow", *cit.*, pp. 633–696 (658). Internal citations omitted.

[1497] Hu, Margaret, "Algorithmic Jim Crow", *cit.*, pp. 633–696 (658). Internal citations omitted.

[1498] Hu, Margaret, "Algorithmic Jim Crow", *cit.*, pp. 633–696 (658). Internal citations omitted.

[1499] Kizer, J. M., "Arrested by skin color: Evidence from siblings and a nationally representative sample", *Socius: Sociological Research for a Dynamic World*, 3, 2017, passim; Kochel, T. R., Wilson, D. B./Mastrofski, S. D., "Effect of suspect race on officers' arrest decisions", *Criminology*, Volume 49, Issue 2, 2011, pp. 473–512. Mitchell, O./Caudy, M. S., "Examining racial disparities in drug arrests", *Justice Quarterly*, Volume 32, Issue 2, 2015, pp. 288–313; Kirk, D. S., "The neighborhood context of racial and ethnic disparities in arrest", *Demography*, 45, 2008, pp. 55–77.

[1500] Hu, Margaret, "Algorithmic Jim Crow", *cit.*, pp. 633–696 (658). Internal citations omitted. On algorithmic big data biometric governance: Hu, Margaret, "From the National Surveillance State to the Cybersurveillance State", *The Annual Review of Law and Social Science*, Volume 13, 2017, p. 169 ("*as a result of big data biometric governance trends, meaningful distinctions between biometric credentialing for identification and behavioral biometric profiling are disappearing. The objectives are merging: Reliable credentialing is used to advance security and precrime policy rationales. Biometric data mission creep occurs by necessity in a big data world because the cybersurveillance systems are often designed to engage in mass data integration and analysis and predictive policing. Biometric surveillance serves two purposes in preventive policing: It increases identity transparency, and the biometric data categorize identity through cataloging behavioral and physical characteristics and assess these characteristics for risk. Contrasting small data biometric credentialing protocols with big data credentialing protocols is useful. It illustrates how biometric* data proxies with other proxy variables to deftly forecast criminal or terroristic demeanour (e.g., amalgamate passport number and digital photo with data mining[1501] analysis[1502] of internet browsing trace and social media footprint).[1503]

§§ Furthermore, there are multifarious components to hard-core vetting, including, but not narrowed down to, biometric identification,[1504] record linkage, information extraction, and predictive[1505] analytics[1506] that seek to wage a war, and exact a toll, on terror.[1507]

---

surveillance fits within the Cybersurveillance State. In a small data world, paper-based passports and nondigitized photographs are examples of a small data biometric-based identification system"). Italics added.

[1501] But see: Balkin, Jack, "Constitution in the National Surveillance State", *Minnesota Law Review*, Volume 93, 2008, p. 13 ("*data mining* allows inferences not only about the direct subject of surveillance, but about other people with whom they live, work and communicate"). But see: Pedreshi, Dino/Ruggieri, Salvatore/Turini, Franco, "Discrimination-aware Data Mining", *Proceedings of the 14th ACM SIGKDD International Conference on Knowledge Discovery and Data Mining (Las Vegas, Nevada, USA), ACM*, 2008, pp. 560–568 (arguing that one should shift its gaze downstream by putting in place discrimination-aware algorithmic tools while performing data mining).

[1502] Which, I may venture to add, is something—*biometric surveillance*—that amounts to nothing but to the price of partaking in social settings, which is very hard to shy away from. See: Hu, Margaret, "From the National Surveillance State to the Cybersurveillance State", *The Annual Review of Law and Social Science*, Volume 13, 2017, p. 169 ("*because of technological developments and trends in governance, it is challenging, if not impossible, to prevent biometric data capture and collection. Biometric surveillance systems increasingly require opting in as the price of social, economic, and political participation.* Biometric data capture is difficult to resist because it is simultaneously compulsory and transparent. Biometric data collection is often compulsory because it is increasingly mandatory to establish identity. *Biometrics are transparent qualities because it is very difficult to hide biometrics; an individual's face, iris, or fingerprint can be digitally captured in any public place. Because biometric data support larger big data programs, such as No Fly List–type risk assessments, it is extraordinarily difficult, if not impossible, to opt out*"). Italics added.

[1503] Hu, Margaret, "Algorithmic Jim Crow", *cit.*, pp. 633–696 (658). Internal citations omitted.

[1504] Hu, Margaret, "From the National Surveillance State to the Cybersurveillance State", *The Annual Review of Law and Social Science*, Volume 13, 2017, p. 168 ("*as a result, the Cybersurveillance State, as a technological successor to the National Surveillance State, will execute bureaucratized biometric cybersurveillance in ways that are largely invisible and that appear routinized when technologically embedded within biometric identification technologies harnessed by the Administrative State. The normalization of day-to-day cybersurveillance will be achieved largely through governing functions that appear purely administrative (e.g., identity assessments for the granting of welfare, rights, privileges, and governing incentives).* Because of the routinized and administrative nature of the government-led big data program or *data surveillance (dataveillance) program, contemporary cybersurveillance is likely to be viewed as justified under crime, immigration control, and counterterrorism policy rationales*"). Italics added.

[1505] See: Agrawal, Ajay/Gans, Joshua/Goldfarb, Avi, *Prediction Machines: The Simple Economics of Artificial Intelligence*, 2nd Edition. Massachusetts: Harvard Business Review Press, 2022, pp. 1–304.

[1506] Hu, Margaret, "Algorithmic Jim Crow", *cit.*, pp. 633–696 (658). Internal citations omitted.

[1507] It is important to note, though, that the newest developments posed by the "collect-it-all" technologies are slated to create a slew of sizzling hot challenges to the sustainability of the Rule of Law amidst war on terror. See: Hu, Margaret, "From the National Surveillance State to the Cybersurveillance State", *The Annual Review of Law and Social Science*, Volume 13, 2017, pp. 162–163

§§ With the right settings, these Artificial Intelligence-embedded technologies are fully capable of classification and, subsequently, screening.[1508] In other set of circumstances, though, these Artificial Intelligence-embedded technologies can accomplish the just the opposite[1509]: screening, and, subsequently, classification.[1510]

4.1.5.2 Does the Current Immigration- and Security-Related Vetting Protocols Risk Amount to an Algorithmically-Anchored Form of Jim Crow? The Case of Computer-Run «No Fly Lists» Comprising *Socially Undesirables*

§§ Bearing the foregoing background very firmly in mind, question is to ascertain the extent to which artificial intelligence-embedded technologies machine learning algorithms[1511] can replace human[1512] judgment[1513] as far as the classification and screening procedures of Algorithmic Jim Crow legal framework are concerned.[1514]

§§ Tellingly, in a small data world,[1515] Jim Crow required a human to manually verify the skin colour of an individual to establish his/her race (v.g., a medical doctor ascertaining to the race of an individual or verifying a birth certificate).[1516]

(*"policymakers view these technological developments, including biometric technologies, as tools with the potential to identify individuals who may pose a threat to national and homeland security and to prevent crime and terrorism. One example of technology intended for risk assessment and threat management is the post-9/11 program Total Information Awareness (TIA).* TIA was the progeny of the Defense Advanced Research Projects Agency (DARPA) in the US Department of Defense. *TIA can be understood as a "collect-it-all" data surveillance program. TIA was not explicitly identified as a collect-it-all program—this phrase originated with the Snowden disclosures. One National Security Agency (NSA) slide described the NSA's procedure as "collect-it-all" (Greenwald 2014b). Collect-it-all efforts like TIA embody a philosophy that aspires to preventive policing. Mass data collection is construed as a tool to assess and prevent future threats (Murray 2010). In TIA and other programs tested or adopted after 9/11, biometric database screening and analysis have emerged as a preferred method for tracking, identifying, and establishing identity-based inferences in counterterrorism*"). Italics added. See also: Ball, Kirstie, and Frank Webster (Eds.), *The Intensification of Surveillance: Crime, Terrorism & Warfare in the Information Age*, London, UK: Pluto Press, 2007; Guzik, Keith, "Discrimination by Design: Predictive Data Mining as Security Practice in the United States' 'War on Terrorism.'", *Surveillance and Society*, 7 (1), 2009, pp. 1–17.

1508 Hu, Margaret, "Algorithmic Jim Crow", *cit.*, pp. 633–696 (658). Internal citations omitted.

1509 Hu, Margaret, "Algorithmic Jim Crow", *cit.*, pp. 633–696 (658). Internal citations omitted.

1510 Hu, Margaret, "Algorithmic Jim Crow", *cit.*, pp. 633–696 (658). Internal citations omitted.

§§ Notably, in the small data world, screening[1517] processes also entailed human judgment (e.g., a county clerk parsing birth certificates prior to issuing marriage

---

[1511] See: Murphy, Kevin P., *Machine Learning: A Probabilistic Perspective (Adaptive Computation and Machine Learning series)*. Massachusetts: The MIT Press, 2012, pp. 1–1104 (states avowedly that "machine Learning attempts to combine deductive, inductive, and abductive reasoning to make person-like reasoning in AI Entities possible. Machine-learning AI Entities initially learn in the same way a human child learns. First, they notice details and patterns in shapes, sounds, and behaviors; then put them together to distinguish one person from another, or a dog from a cat. Eventually, the AI can recognize and identify" common objects). See also: Hutto-Schultz, Jess, "Dicitur Ex Machina: Artificial Intelligence and the Hearsay Rule", *George Mason Law Review*, Volume 27, Issue 2, 2020, pp. 684–718 (689). See: Chollet, François, *Deep Learning with Python*. Shelter Island, Nova Iorque: Manning, 2018, pp. 1–384 (passim). *Deep Learning* stands as a byproduct of *Machine Learning. Machine Learning*, a subset of Artificial Intelligence, unfolds itself in *Deep Learning*, which "involves computer algorithms that have the ability to "learn" or improve in performance over time on some task". See also: Surden, Harry, "Machine Learning and Law", *Washington Law Review*, Volume 89, 2015, pp. 87 and ff. See also: Barocas, Solon/Selbst, Andrew, "Big Data's Disparate Impact", *California Law Review*, Volume 104, pp. 2016, pp. 671–678 ("in particular, by exposing so-called 'machine learning' algorithms to examples of the cases of interest (previously identified instances of fraud, spam, default, and poor health), *the algorithm 'learns' which related attributes or activities can serve as potential proxies for those qualities or outcomes of interest*"). Italics added.

[1512] But see: Millar, Jason/Kerr, Ian, "Delegation, Relinquishment and Responsibility: The Prospect of Expert Robots", *Robot Law*, Calo, Ryan /Froomkin, A. Michael/Kerr, Ian, Cheltenham, Edward Elgar Publishing, 2016, pp. 102, 106–107 (as these authors aptly put it "*we will rely on robots without really knowing why – simply because their algorithms provide the greatest number of successful outcomes.* We have already seen this in Google's search approach. Neither Larry (Page) nor Sergey (Brin) (nor any other Google employee) knowns exactly why one particular web page is a better result than another. *When the click patterns say it is, that's good enough.* No semantic or causal analysis is required...*Like the ancients, we will, quite rationally, come to rely upon them, knowing full well that we cannot necessarily explain the reasons for their decisions*"). Italics added. Converging: Casey, Anthony J./Niblett, Anthony, "Self-driving Laws", *University of Toronto Law Journal*, Volume 66, 2016, pp. 429–435 (contend that "as more information is generated, and the evolutionary algorithm updates and become a better forecaster, we imagine that judges will increasingly rely on the advice of the algorithm").

[1513] But see: Weizenbaum, Joseph, *Computer Power and Human Reason: From Judgment to Calculation*, 1st edition, New York, W. H. Freeman & Co, 1976, pp. 1–300 (227) ("examines the sources of the computer's powers and offers evaluative explorations of what computers can do, cannot do, and should not be employed to do") (this founding father of Artificial Intelligence presciently noted that we should not entrust Artificial Intelligence-embedded technologies with "tasks that demand wisdom"). Italics added. The approval of rental applications is arguably one of those tasks that should never be entrusted to machines). More on this on Part IV, This chapter, Sects. 4.1.4–4.1.4.2.1 of this book.

[1514] Hu, Margaret, "Algorithmic Jim Crow", *cit.*, pp. 633–696 (658). Internal citations omitted.

[1515] Hu, Margaret, "From the National Surveillance State to the Cybersurveillance State", *The Annual Review of Law and Social Science*, Volume 13, 2017, p. 168 ("*currently, biometric verification and identification technologies are not commonly perceived to be surveillance technologies—the public and private sectors typically treat them as a benign and useful form of digitized identification. Such automated biometric screening is considered to be a more efficient form of small data verification technologies, such as human screening or human-driven practices involving assessments of* certificates to gauge compliance with the anti-miscegenation laws in force back then).[1518]

§§ In stark contrast, human involvement is not mandatory, in the sense that is not necessary, to shrewdly classify individuals amidst the big data[1519] world[1520] we live in. As a result, an individual can be deemed as a potential criminal, scoundrel, terrorist, assassin, or a threat risk based solely on digital data and computer-run digitized analysis[1521] such as computer-run screening.[1522]

---

biometric or forensic data. Small data biometric verification could include comparing a passport photo against the person holding the passport. Big data biometric identification, however, has a distinct impact from that of small data biometric investigation because it can facilitate surveillance. Big data photo screening may entail the collection of digital photographs. This in turn can lead to facilitating facial recognition technology through the mass digitization of photo databases, potentially including billions of facial images. One Snowden disclosure noted that the NSA collects millions of digital photographs from internet and social media sources and uses facial recognition technology to identify individuals"). Italics added.

[1516] Hu, Margaret, "Algorithmic Jim Crow", *cit.*, pp. 633–696 (658). Internal citations omitted.

[1517] Hu, Margaret, "Algorithmic Jim Crow", *cit.*, pp. 633–696 (658). Internal citations omitted.

[1518] Hu, Margaret, "Algorithmic Jim Crow", *cit.*, pp. 633–696 (659). Internal citations omitted.

[1519] Hu, Margaret, "From the National Surveillance State to the Cybersurveillance State", *The Annual Review of Law and Social Science*, Volume 13, 2017, p. 169 ("*as a result of big data biometric governance trends, meaningful distinctions between biometric credentialing for identification and behavioral biometric profiling are disappearing. The objectives are merging: Reliable credentialing is used to advance security and precrime policy rationales. Biometric data mission creep occurs by necessity in a big data world because the cybersurveillance systems are often designed to engage in mass data integration and analysis and predictive policing. Biometric surveillance serves two purposes in preventive policing: It increases identity transparency, and the biometric data categorize identity through cataloging behavioral and physical characteristics and assess these characteristics for risk. Contrasting small data biometric credentialing protocols with big data credentialing protocols is useful. It illustrates how biometric surveillance fits within the Cybersurveillance State. In a small data world, paper-based passports and nondigitized photographs are examples of a small data biometric-based identification system*"). Italics added.

[1520] Hu, Margaret, "Algorithmic Jim Crow", *cit.*, pp. 633–696 (658). Internal citations omitted.

[1521] Hu, Margaret, "From the National Surveillance State to the Cybersurveillance State", *The Annual Review of Law and Social Science*, Volume 13, 2017, p. 169 ("*the potential for mass surveillance is part of the problematic nature of biometric credentialing and identification practices. Like most digital data, biometric identification data are not restricted to the purpose for which they were originally collected.* Biometric data can be repurposed for secondary uses, *such as identification of potential suspects or victims through real-time analytics, assessment of threats of terrorism, tactical decisionmaking, or behavioral and genetic research*"). Italics added. Internal citations omitted.

[1522] Hu, Margaret, "Algorithmic Jim Crow", *cit.*, pp. 633–696 (659). Internal citations omitted. See: Hu, Margaret, "From the National Surveillance State to the Cybersurveillance State", *The Annual Review of Law and Social Science*, Volume 13, 2017, pp. 162–163 ("*policymakers view these technological developments, including biometric technologies, as tools with the potential to identify individuals who may pose a threat to national and homeland security and to prevent crime and terrorism. One example of technology intended for risk assessment and threat management is the post-9/11 program Total Information Awareness (TIA). (….) Collect-it-all efforts like TIA embody a philosophy that aspires to preventive policing. Mass data collection is construed as a tool to assess and prevent future threats (Murray 2010). In TIA and other programs tested or adopted after 9/11, biometric database screening and analysis have emerged as a preferred method for tracking,*

§§ Artificial Intelligence-embedded technologies are therefore suitably equipped to parse data in a bid to determine identity[1523] (v.g., an ever-recording-locator matching machine learning algorithm propelled by a thumping great database screening systems that cobbles together names and addresses with passport numbers espoused with other databases of personally identifiable information)[1524] and scour for suspicious digital information[1525] (v.g., dovetail seamlessly passport-embedded information with previously acquired[1526] data[1527] and real time data).[1528]

---

identifying, and establishing identity-based inferences in counterterrorism"). Italics added. See also: Ball, Kirstie, and Frank Webster (Eds.), *The Intensification of Surveillance: Crime, Terrorism & Warfare in the Information Age*, London, UK: Pluto Press, 2007; Guzik, Keith, "Discrimination by Design: Predictive Data Mining as Security Practice in the United States' 'War on Terrorism.'", *Surveillance and Society*, 7 (1), 2009, pp. 1–17.

[1523] Hu, Margaret, "From the National Surveillance State to the Cybersurveillance State", *The Annual Review of Law and Social Science*, Volume 13, 2017, p. 169 ("*as a result of big data biometric governance trends, meaningful distinctions between biometric credentialing for identification and behavioral biometric profiling are disappearing. The objectives are merging: Reliable credentialing is used to advance security and precrime policy rationales. Biometric data mission creep occurs by necessity in a big data world because the cybersurveillance systems are often designed to engage in mass data integration and analysis and predictive policing. Biometric surveillance serves two purposes in preventive policing: It increases identity transparency, and the biometric data categorize identity through cataloging behavioral and physical characteristics and assess these characteristics for risk. Contrasting small data biometric credentialing protocols with big data credentialing protocols is useful. It illustrates how biometric surveillance fits within the Cybersurveillance State. In a small data world, paper-based passports and nondigitized photographs are examples of a small data biometric-based identification system*"). Italics added.

[1524] Hu, Margaret, "Algorithmic Jim Crow", *cit.*, pp. 633–696 (659). Internal citations omitted.

[1525] Hu, Margaret, "From the National Surveillance State to the Cybersurveillance State", *The Annual Review of Law and Social Science*, Volume 13, 2017, p. 169 ("*biometric data become a part of* population-wide *risk assessments that incorporate bureaucratized surveillance into governing decisions, policing, and threat assessments. Through big data tools, precrime governance models are increasingly reflected in collect-it-all cybersurveillance systems. In these systems, biometric data is a surveillance axis that can be used to track, identify, and isolate suspicious persons, digital data, or devices*"). Italics added.

[1526] See: Hu, Margaret, "From the National Surveillance State to the Cybersurveillance State", *The Annual Review of Law and Social Science*, Volume 13, 2017, p. 165 ("*Datafication, like most big data processes, requires increasing amounts of digital data to support or construct cybersurveillance.* It empowers government actions that are based on digital data collection, data processing protocols, and bulk data analyses (Mayer-Schonberger & Cukier 2013). *Another way to characterize datafication is as a governmental policy interest that both transforms analog data (PCAST 2014) into searchable, centralized digital databases and develops new forms of stored data*"). Italics added.

[1527] Hu, Margaret, "From the National Surveillance State to the Cybersurveillance State", *The Annual Review of Law and Social Science*, Volume 13, 2017, p. 168 ("*currently, biometric verification and identification technologies are not commonly perceived to be surveillance technologies—the public and private sectors typically treat them as a benign and useful form of digitized identification. Such automated biometric screening is considered to be a more efficient form of small data verification technologies, such as human screening or human-driven practices involving assessments of biometric or forensic data. Small data biometric verification could include comparing a passport photo against the person holding the passport*"). Italics added.

[1528] Hu, Margaret, "Algorithmic Jim Crow", *cit.*, pp. 633–696 (659). Internal citations omitted.

§§ Stored data[1529] may comprise bulk telephony[1530] metadata[1531]—databases that possess the ability to amass and glean time, temporal duration, and geolocation of telephone calls[1532]—other government records and private data, such as consumer activities,[1533] which, in turn, catalyse the indelible stain of consumer harm.[1534]

§§ In addition to that, real-time data mining[1535] can encompass situational awareness systems that strive to undertake a fine-grained analysis on real-time video surveillance feeds that liaise the surveilled individual through facial recognition technology[1536] to that individual's social media connection.[1537] It should come as

---

1529 See: Hu, Margaret, "From the National Surveillance State to the Cybersurveillance State", *The Annual Review of Law and Social Science*, Volume 13, 2017, p. 165 ("*Another way to characterize datafication is as a governmental policy interest that both transforms analog data* (PCAST 2014) into *searchable, centralized digital databases and develops new forms of stored data*"). Italics added.

1530 See: Hu, Margaret, "From the National Surveillance State to the Cybersurveillance State", *The Annual Review of Law and Social Science*, Volume 13, 2017, p. 165 ("*Datafication, like most big data processes, requires increasing amounts of digital data to support or construct cybersurveillance.* It empowers government actions that are based on *digital data collection, data processing protocols, and bulk data analyses* (Mayer-Schonberger & Cukier ¨ 2013"). Italics added.

1531 Hu, Margaret, "Algorithmic Jim Crow", *cit.*, pp. 633–696 (659). Internal citations omitted.

1532 Hu, Margaret, "Algorithmic Jim Crow", *cit.*, pp. 633–696 (659). Internal citations omitted.

1533 Hu, Margaret, "Algorithmic Jim Crow", *cit.*, pp. 633–696 (659). Internal citations omitted.

1534 On consumer harms, see: Khan, Sadia/Cole, Daniel/Ekbia, Hamid,", Autonomy and Free Thought in Brain-Computer Interactions: Review of Legal Precedent for Precautionary Regulation of Consumer Products", *Hastings Science & Technology Law Journal*, Volume 15, Number 1, Article 5, 2024, pp. 95–130 (95) ("*The expanding use of neurotechnologies in consumer products increases the risks to human rights such as autonomy and free thought. While potentially beneficial in clinical applications, technologies such as brain implants and EEG-enabled wearable devices pose serious concerns about mental and psychological manipulation of human beings. In the US in particular, law and policy are lagging behind technical developments, thereby increasing the risks of abuse and misuse from commercial neurotechnologies*"). Italics added. See also: Bar-Gill, Oren/Sunstein, Cass R./Talgam-Cohen, Inbal, "Algorithmic Harm in Consumer Markets", *Journal of Legal Analysis*, Volume 15, n. ° 1, 2023, pp. 1–47; Lee, Nicole Turner/Resnick, Paul/Barton, Genie, *Algorithmic Bias Detection and Mitigation: Best Practices and Policies to Reduce Consumer Harms*. Washington, DC: Brookings Institution, 2019, passim.

1535 Balkin, Jack, "Constitution in the National Surveillance State", *Minnesota Law Review*, Volume 93, 2008, p. 13 (note, though, that "*data mining* allows inferences not only about the direct subject of surveillance, but about other people with whom they live, work and communicate"). It bears mentioning that pundits have neither been coy nor bashful in strongly emphasizing the perceived peril—*consumer harm*—of monetizing the data harvested/gleaned by Artificial Intelligence-embedded technologies while performing data mining. See: Yang/Kai Hao, "Selling Consumer Data for Profit: Optimal Market-Segmentation Design and its Consequences", *American Economic Review*, Volume 112, Issue 4, April 2022, 2022, pp. 1364–1393.

1536 Hu, Margaret, "From the National Surveillance State to the Cybersurveillance State", *The Annual Review of Law and Social Science*, Volume 13, 2017, p. 168 ("*Big data biometric identification, however, has a distinct impact from that of small data biometric investigation because it can facilitate surveillance. Big data photo screening may entail the collection of digital photographs. This in turn can lead to facilitating facial recognition technology through the mass digitization of photo databases, potentially including billions of facial images.* One Snowden disclosure noted that

no surprise that the nature of classification and screening capacities are glaringly different in a big data[1538] world.[1539]

§§ Classification of *social undesirables* (whomever they circumstantially are), thence, can be partially or wholly propelled by artificial intelligence-embedded technologies.[1540] By the same token, computer-run screening in a big data world does not hinge upon human processes.[1541] For instance, *The No Fly List*,[1542] can be created through a string of interlocking Artificial Intelligence-embedded technologies propelled by both database screening and digital watch-listing[1543] systems.[1544] The once invaluable human nomination is wholly unnecessary in this regard.[1545]

---

the NSA collects millions of digital photographs from internet *and social media sources and uses facial recognition technology to identify individuals*"). Italics added.

[1537] Hu, Margaret, "Algorithmic Jim Crow", *cit.*, pp. 633–696 (659). Internal citations omitted.

[1538] Hu, Margaret, "From the National Surveillance State to the Cybersurveillance State", *The Annual Review of Law and Social Science*, Volume 13, 2017, p. 168 ("*currently, biometric verification and identification technologies are not commonly perceived to be surveillance technologies—the public and private sectors typically treat them as a benign and useful form of digitized identification. Such automated biometric screening is considered to be a more efficient form of small data verification technologies, such as human screening or human-driven practices involving assessments of biometric or forensic data. Small data biometric verification could include comparing a passport photo against the person holding the passport. Big data biometric identification, however, has a distinct impact from that of small data biometric investigation because it can facilitate surveillance*"). Italics added.

[1539] Hu, Margaret, "Algorithmic Jim Crow", *cit.*, pp. 633–696 (659). Internal citations omitted.

[1540] See: Hu, Margaret, "From the National Surveillance State to the Cybersurveillance State", *The Annual Review of Law and Social Science*, Volume 13, 2017, p. 163 ("*Biometric identification and identity assessments are becoming essential tools for multiple preventive purposes in criminal, military, and intelligence contexts.* The third part addresses *how precrime policy rationales are now informed by biometric-based analysis. In short, biometrics is the means by which analysis of a citizenry's data, and any resulting decisions based on that analysis, can be connected back to a physical person in the real world*"). Italics added.

[1541] Hu, Margaret, "Algorithmic Jim Crow", *cit.*, pp. 633–696 (659). Internal citations omitted.

[1542] See: Hu, Margaret, "From the National Surveillance State to the Cybersurveillance State", *The Annual Review of Law and Social Science*, Volume 13, 2017, p. 165 ("*Because datafication is in its infancy, the cyber-surveillance capacities of big data governance systems, like the No Fly List, are still in nascent stages*"). Italics added.

[1543] Hu, Margaret, "From the National Surveillance State to the Cybersurveillance State", *The Annual Review of Law and Social Science*, Volume 13, 2017, p. 163 (Artificial Intelligence-embedded technologies that can "*determine whether that person is eligible to fly on a commercial airline. The No Fly List and digital watchlisting systems are increasingly biometrically centered (Tau 2015). These types of governance assessments, however, fall within the civil law and administrative law structure. Biometric cybersurveillance systems can inform targeted killing decisions and other lethal consequences. Often in the service of precrime/ counterterrorism policies, biometric cybersurveillance, therefore, is becoming a linchpin for broader policymaking and decisionmaking*"). Italics added.

[1544] Hu, Margaret, "From the National Surveillance State to the Cybersurveillance State", *The Annual Review of Law and Social Science*, Volume 13, 2017, p. 169 ("*contrasting small data biometric credentialing protocols with big data credentialing protocols is useful. It illustrates how biometric surveillance fits within the Cybersurveillance State. In a small data world, paper-based passports and nondigitized photographs are examples of a small data biometric-based identification*

§§ A key takeaway jumps out as ripe: in a big data world, classification and screening protocols can be conflated, melded, straddled, digitized, and automated to target *social undesirables* with little to none accountability whatsoever. Worryingly, these big data classification and screening systems lend itself to virtually impossible for a given citizen to challenge.[1546] The doors of *Algorithmic Dictatorship*—that weaponizes the judicial system against a cohort of *socially undesirables*—are ajar slightly.

§§ By the same token, the doors of *Algorithmic Dictatorship*—an algorithmically-anchored tool to wipe out a cohort of *socially undesirables* that may find themselves at loggerheads with the government—have been already cracked open.

4.1.6 «Will the Smoke Ever Go Down»? Proxy Discrimination of **Socially Undesirables** *in the Age of* **Algorithmic Dictatorship***: Introduction*

§§ It seems as though we are thrust headlong into floundering with hitherto unsolved vexing questions.[1547] Strikingly, a handful of questions concerning what qualities (or lack thereof) render Artificial Intelligence-embedded technologies blameworthy, faulty, botched, warped or simply hazardous[1548] have been brought into a sharper

system. In a big data world, a digitized passport system can link to multiple other sources, such as license plate readers, No Fly Lists, and Terrorist Watchlists"). Italics added.

1545 Hu, Margaret, "Algorithmic Jim Crow", *cit.*, pp. 633–696 (659). Internal citations omitted.

1546 Hu, Margaret, "Algorithmic Jim Crow", *cit.*, pp. 633–696 (659). Internal citations omitted. See: Part V, Chap. 5, Sect. 5.1.1.1 of this book (on the central tenets of Rule of Law that lends itself to a beacon of justice amidst the sepulchral darkness that is about to take hold). See: Part V, Chap. 5, Sect. 5.1.1.2 of this book (on the central tenets of Procedural Rule of Law that lends itself to a lighthouse of justice that allows citizens to challenge the pearls of algorithmic wisdom in a court of law).

1547 Rodrigues, R., "Legal and human rights issues of AI: Gaps, challenges and vulnerabilities", *Journal of Responsible Technology*, Volume 4, December 2020, 2020, 100005.

1548 Hu, Margaret, "From the National Surveillance State to the Cybersurveillance State", *The Annual Review of Law and Social Science*, Volume 13, 2017, p. 169 ("*the potential for mass surveillance is part of the problematic nature of biometric credentialing and identification practices. Like most digital data, biometric identification data are not restricted to the purpose for which they were originally collected. Biometric data can be repurposed for secondary uses, such as identification of potential suspects or victims through real-time analytics, assessment of threats of terrorism, tactical decisionmaking, or behavioral and genetic research* (Duster 2003). *Beyond secondary—and tertiary, quaternary, and quinary—uses, biometric data become a part of population-wide risk assessments that incorporate bureaucratized surveillance into governing decisions, policing, and threat assessments. Through big data tools, precrime governance models are increasingly reflected in collect-it-all cybersurveillance systems.* In these systems, *biometric data is a surveillance axis that can be used to track, identify, and isolate suspicious persons, digital data, or devices*"). Italics added.

focus. It bears mentioning, though, that this is not a nugatory question amenable to be light-heartedly glossed over.[1549]

§§ Unlike the theoretical underpinnings of tort law—placing the aggrieved party in the exact position they would have been in had they not been harmed by the wrongdoer/tortfeasor[1550]—algorithmic fairness[1551] is the primary lens through which impermissible disparities can be seen.[1552]

§§ Algorithmic risk assessment[1553] is therefore backward-looking in that seeks to ascertain whether and to what extent algorithmic discrimination[1554]—e.g. in the purview of recidivism prediction[1555]—has occurred paired with bespoke measures that should be taken to unwind it.[1556]

[1549] See: Part V, Chap. 5, Sects. 5.1.2–5.1.6.2.1 of this book (on the thing-centred algorithmic decision-making propelled by a *Controllable* and *Interpretable* Machine Learning that weeds out *Algorithmic Dictatorship* and secures *Algorithmic Common Good*).

[1550] Coleman, J. L., *Practice of Principle*, Oxford, Oxford University Press, 2001, *passim* (at the heart of the fabric of tort law lies the assertion according to which the tortfeasor or the wrongdoer must be held accountable for the damages inflicted upon the plaintiff); Morgan, Jonathan, "Tort. Insurance and Incoherence", *The Modern Law Review*, Volume 67, Issue 3, 2004, 84–401 (392); Calabresi, Guido, *The Costs of Accidents: A Legal and Economic Analysis*, New Haven, Yale University Press, 1970, pp. 1–350 (passim) (argues that one of the overriding goals of tort law is award to plaintiff's justice, *fairness*, and redress from wrongs); Blum, W. J./Kalven, H., "The Empty Cabinet of Dr. Calabresi—Auto Accidents and General Deterrence", *University of Chicago Law Review*, 34, 1967, pp. 268 ff (averring that tort law also pursues the goal of, and resonates with, allaying victim's feeling of utter indignation); Goldberg, John C. P., "The Constitutional Status of Tort Law: Due Process and the Right to a Law for the Redress of wrongs", *The Yale Law Journal*, 115 (3), 2005, p. 597; Green, Michael D., *Comparative Stimulations for Developing Tort Law*, Helmut Koziol (ed.), European Centre of Tort Law and Insurance Law, Jan Sramek Verlag, Wien, Austria, (2015): 35 (argues that «one who has harmed by the wrongdoing of another might justifiably appeal to *fairness* in righting a wrong as the basis for demanding recompense from the wrongdoer») (italics added).

[1551] Corbett-Davies, Sam/Goel, Sharad, "The Measure and Mismeasure of Fairness: a critical Review of Fair Machine Learning", *Cornell University Library*, 2018, pp. 3 and ff and passim (undertake laudable efforts to debunk algorithm biases that primarily target ethnic minorities, such as Hispanics and coloured people).

[1552] Wachter, S./Mittelstadt, B./Russell, C., "Bias Preservation in Machine Learning: The Legality of Fairness Metrics Under EU Non-Discrimination Law", *West Virginia Law Review*, 2021, passim.

[1553] Stevenson, M. T./Slobogin, C., "Algorithmic risk assessments and the double-edged sword of youth", *Washington University Law Review*, Volume 96, 2018, passim. See: Agrawal, Ajay/Gans, Joshua/Goldfarb, Avi, *Prediction Machines: The Simple Economics of Artificial Intelligence*, 2nd Edition. Massachusetts: Harvard Business Review Press, 2022, pp. 1–304.

[1554] Prejudiced algorithms are set to be brought to the fore as they are one foundational basis of *justice prédictive* so voguish in France. No surprise stems from the fact that prejudiced algorithms will feed *justice prédictive*—and that is something quite unsavoury and unpalatable in criminal justice indeed. See: Garapon, Antoine, "Les enjeux de la justice predictive", *Juris-Classeur périodique*, Volume 31, 2018, passim. See also: Larret-Chahine, Louis, "Le droit isométrique: un nouveau paradigme juridique né de la justice prédictive», *Archives de Philosophie du Droit*, Volume 60, 2018, pp. 287 and ff and passim.

[1555] See: Part IV, This chapter, Sects. 4.1.10.1–4.1.10.6 of this book (on biased algorithmic risk assessment in criminal procedure law settings). See: Part IV, This chapter, Sects. 4.1.1–4.1.1.1 of this book (on biased predictive policing). See also: Rudin, Cynthia/Wang, Caroline/Coker, Beau, "The Age of Secrecy and Unfairness in Recidivism Prediction", *Harvard Data Science Review*,

§§ Casts broadly, Artificial Intelligence-embedded technologies—e.g. biometric surveillance technologies[1557]—are unearthly imbued with the ability of engendering callous, flagitious, invidious, devilishly harmful, and unlawful[1558] algorithmic harms[1559] against the backdrop of which algorithmic proxy discrimination unfolds.[1560]

Issue 2.1. Winter 2020, 2020, passim; Eckhouse, L., Lum, K., Conti-Cook, C./Ciccolini, J., "Layers of bias: A unified approach for understanding problems with risk assessment", *Criminal Justice and Behavior*, Volume 46, Issue 2, 2019, pp. 185–209.

[1556] Like a full-fledged and full-bodied legal apparatus comprising algorithmic fairness that casts aside algorithmic discrimination in criminal procedure law settings. See: Kleinberg, Jon, et al., "Discrimination in the Age of Algorithms", *Journal of Legal Analysis*, 2018, pp. 114–174. See: Kleinberg, Jon, et al., "Algorithms as Discrimination Detectors", *Proceeds of the National Academy of Science*, Volume 117, 2020, pp. 30096–30110. Like tools that can debias racial discrimination within the remit of criminal justice—the essence of racial equity in criminal justice. See: Huq, Aziz, "Racial Equity in Algorithmic Criminal Justice", *Duke Law Journal*, Volume 68, 2022, pp. 1076–1134.

[1557] See: Hu, Margaret, "From the National Surveillance State to the Cybersurveillance State", *The Annual Review of Law and Social Science*, Volume 13, 2017, pp. 162–163 ("*policymakers view these technological developments, including biometric technologies, as tools with the potential to identify individuals who may pose a threat to national and homeland security and to prevent crime and terrorism. One example of technology intended for risk assessment and threat management is the post-9/11 program Total Information Awareness (TIA). (….) Collect-it-all efforts like TIA embody a philosophy that aspires to preventive policing. Mass data collection is construed as a tool to assess and prevent future threats (Murray 2010). In TIA and other programs tested or adopted after 9/11, biometric database screening and analysis have emerged as a preferred method for tracking, identifying, and establishing identity-based inferences in counterterrorism*"). Italics added. See also: Ball, Kirstie, and Frank Webster (Eds.), *The Intensification of Surveillance: Crime, Terrorism & Warfare in the Information Age*, London, UK: Pluto Press, 2007; Guzik, Keith, "Discrimination by Design: Predictive Data Mining as Security Practice in the United States' 'War on Terrorism.'", *Surveillance and Society*, 7 (1), 2009, pp. 1–17.

[1558] Ferreri, Mara/Sanyal, Romola, "Digital informalisation: rental housing, platforms, and the management of risk", *Housing Studies*, Volume 37, Issue 6, 2022, pp. 1035–1053 (1035) ("*The eruption of disruptive digital platforms is reshaping geographies of housing under the gaze of corporations and through the webs of algorithms.* Engaging with interdisciplinary scholarship on informal housing across the Global North and South, we propose the term *'digital informalisation' to examine how digital platforms are engendering new and opaque ways of governing housing,* presenting a theoretical and political blind spot (….) *In contrast to progressive imaginaries of 'smart' technological mediation, practices of algorithmic redlining, biased tenant profiling and the management of risk in private tenancies and in housing welfare both introduce and extend discriminatory and exclusionary housing practices*"). Italics added. See: Part IV, This chapter, Sects. 4.1.4–4.1.4.2.3 of this book.

[1559] Lee, Nicole Turner/Resnick, Paul/Barton, Genie, *Algorithmic Bias Detection and Mitigation: Best Practices and Policies to Reduce Consumer Harms.* Washington, DC: Brookings Institution, 2019, passim; Slaughter, Rebecca Kelly, "Algorithms and Economic Justice: A Taxonomy of Harms and a Path Forward for the Federal Trade Commission", *Yale Journal of Law and Technology*, Volume 23, 2021 (on algorithmic harms).

[1560] Prince, Anya E. R./Schwarcz, Daniel, "Proxy Discrimination in the Age of Artificial Intelligence and Big Data", *Iowa Law Review*, Volume 105, 1257, 1279–81 (2020) ("*[P]roxy discrimination will tend to occur when a suspect variable is predictive of a desired outcome only because it proxies for another*, quantifiable and potentially available, *variable that causes the desired outcome but that is not included in the AI's training data*"). Italics added.

§§ Note, though, that not every sudden swerving of an artificial intelligence-embedded technology onto a given algorithmic sidewalk (e.g. algorithmic correlations[1561] made by machines which, in turn, are not amenable to be fully grasped by the human brain like «dimensionality» arising out of support vector machines[1562]) is neither entitled to be deemed as *inductive bias* (*learning bias*)[1563] nor as *algorithmic bias*.[1564] That is true, but truer still history sharply portrays an uneasy coexistence between Artificial Intelligence-embedded technologies and a sought-after bias-free[1565] decision-making.[1566]

§§ Compellingly, congeries of rules have been hardened into binding law under the tinsel of facial neutrality[1567] and the charade of infallibility.[1568] Yet those bodies

[1561] See: Part V, Chap. 5, Sects. 5.1.1.5.2.2–5.1.1.5.2.2.1.4 of this book (on the fundamental shift away from causation to correlations in algorithmic decision-making). See also: Part I of this book (Introduction).

[1562] As hinted above, algorithms make their inferences and draw their conclusions in a way difficult to understand, even for the cohort of programmers that designed them. This is deemed *black box*, that further enhances the shroud of mystery under which algorithms are cloaked. See, for a compelling account of AI black box: Bathaee, Yavar, "The Artificial Intelligence Black Box and the Failure of Intent and Causation", *Harvard Journal of Law and Technology*, n.° 37, 2018, p. 901 (adduces that "*one possible reason AI may be a black box to humans is that it relies on machine-learning algorithms that internalize data in ways that are not easily audited or understood by humans* (…) "*first, a lack may arise from the complexity of the algorithm's structure, such as with deep neural network, which consists of thousands of artificial neurons working together in a diffuse way to solve a problem. This reason for AI being a black box is referred to as "complexity". Second, the lack of transparency may arise because the AI is using a machine-learning algorithm that relies on geometric relationships that humans cannot visualize, such as with support vector machines. This reason for AI being a black box is referred to as "dimensionality"*"). Italics added. But see: Pearl, Judea, *Causality*, 2nd edition, Cambridge, Cambridge University Press, 2009 (on the fundamental tenets of causality). But see: Kilbertus, Niki/Carulla, Mateo Rojas/Parascandolo, Giambattista/ Hardt, Moritz/Janzing, Dominik/ Schoellkopf, Bernhard, "Avoiding Discrimination through Causal Reasoning", *Advances in Neural Information Processing Systems*, I. Guyon, U. V. Luxburg, S. Bengio, H. Wallach, R. Fergus, S. Vishwanathan, and R. Garnett (Eds.), Vol. 30. Curran Associates, Inc., 2017, pp. 656–666 (arguing that is feasible to avoiding discrimination through a granular and fine-grained causal reasoning).

[1563] Dong et al., Qi, "Imbalanced deep learning by minority class incremental rectification, *IEEE Transactions on Pattern Analysis & Machine Intelligence*, Volume 41, 2019, p. 1367 (posit that "*most existing learning algorithms produce inductive bias (learning bias)* towards the frequent (majority) classes if training data are not balanced, *resulting in poor minority class recognition performance*"). Italics added.

[1564] Baeza-Yates, R., "Bias on the web", *Communications of the ACM*, 61 (6), June 2018, 2018, pp. 54–61 (argues that "*algorithmic bias is when the bias is not present in the input data* and is added *purely by the algorithm*"). Italics added.

[1565] Jackson, Maya C., "Artificial Intelligence and Algorithmic Bias: The Issues with Technology Reflecting History and Humans", *Journal of Business Technology Law*, Volume 16, 2021, pp. 299–316; West, Sarah Myers/Whittaker, Meredith/Crawford, Kate, *Discriminating Systems. Gender, Race and Power in AI*. New York: AI Now Institute, 2019, passim.

[1566] Chabert, J.L. et al., *A History of Algorithms: From the Pebble to the Microchip*. New York/ Heidelberg: Springer, 2013; McCorduck, P., *Machines who think: A personal inquiry into the history and prospects of artificial intelligence*, Cleveland, CRC Press Books, 2004.

[1567] See: Hurley, Mikella/Adebayo, Julius, "Credit Scoring in the Era of Big Data", *Yale Journal of Law and Technology*, Volume 18, 2016, p. 149 ("*these tools may furthermore obscure discriminatory*

of laws were aimed at further chastising racialized people under a patina of objectivity[1569] (foremost, wrapped under the opaqueness[1570] of catch-all concepts of *trust in science*[1571] and *trust in numbers*[1572]).

§§ A key takeaway accordingly jumps out as ripe in this regard: whenever machines are entrusted with the task of engaging in high stake[1573] decision-making,[1574] the room for algorithmic bias is capacious in that the rigged data[1575]

---

and subjective lending policies behind a single "objective" score (...) sophisticated algorithms may combine facially neutral data points and treat them as proxies for immutable characteristics such as race or gender, thereby circumventing existing non-discrimination laws and systematically denying credit access to certain groups. Finally, big-data tools may allow online payday lenders to target the most vulnerable consumers and lure them into debt traps"). Italics added. See also: Farina, M./ Lavazza, A., *Philosophy, expertise, and the myth of* neutrality, Routledge Studies in Contemporary Philosophy, London, Routledge, 2024.

1568 Gillis, Talia B., "The Input Data Fallacy", *Minnesota Law Review*, Volume 106, 2022, pp. 1176–1263.

1569 Benjamin, Ruha, *Race After Technology: Abolitionist Tools for the New Jim Code*, New York, Polity, 2019, pp. 1–172 (7) (discussing that Artificial Intelligence-embedded technologies are viewed as iron-clad tools of objectivity and devoid of any biases whatsoever). Ruha Benjamin contends that "the employment of new technologies that reflect and reproduce existing inequities but that are promoted and perceived as more objective or progressive than the discriminatory systems of a previous era").

1570 *Tech, Bias and Housing Initiative, the Promise and Perils of Residential Proptech, Year 1, Research Summary Report, April 2023, TechEquity Collaborative*, p. 11, available at: https://techequity.us/wp-content/uploads/2023/04/TBHI-Y1-Research-Summary-Report.pdf (28.11.2024). ("*From information on company websites, it is not clear what analysis or data is behind subjective determinations like "suitability" to a unit or what the nexus between an individual's characteristics and a unit's characteristics is that indicates the likelihood for property damage. Based on sample reports, even landlords are not privy to how the determinations are made. Instead, they receive a risk score out of 100 simplified into green, yellow, and red recommendations.* What companies withhold in terms of how it works, they make up for with the extent to which they tell landlords it works: Naborly claims their predictions reduce lease defaults by up to 89%. 15 *As Naborly's sample report demonstrates, its property damage assessment is then used as an input to determine its projected eviction outcomes; its early vacancy prediction, in turn, is based on "all assessment factors*"). Italics added.

1571 Sherman, Lawrence W., "Targeting, Testing and Tracking Police Services: The Rise of Evidence Based Policing, 1975–2025", *Crime and Justice*, 42 (1), 2013, pp. 377–451; Lavender III, I., *Race in American science fiction*, Bloomington: Indiana University Press, 2011.

1572 Porter, Theodore M., *Trust in Numbers: The Pursuit of Objectivity in Science and Public Life*, Princeton, NJ: Princeton University Press, 1995.

1573 See: Part V, Chap. 5, Sect. 5.1.7.2 of this book (on law number two to control algorithmic decision-making, which mandates that black box models must not be entrusted with the task of making high stake decisions—v.g. health and freedom). But see: Rudin, Cynthia, "Please stop explaining black box models for high stakes decisions", *Proceedings of NeurIPS 2018 Workshop on Critiquing and Correcting Trends in Machine Learning (NIPS 2018)*, 2018, passim.

1574 But see: Weizenbaum, Joseph, *Computer Power and Human Reason: From Judgment to Calculation*, 1st edition, New York, W. H. Freeman & Co, 1976, pp. 1–300 (227) ("examines the sources of the computer's powers and offers evaluative explorations of what computers can do, cannot do, and should not be employed to do") (this founding father of Artificial Intelligence presciently noted that we should not entrust Artificial Intelligence-embedded technologies with "tasks that demand wisdom"). Italics added. The approval of rental applications is arguably one of those tasks

baked into the bigoted algorithms—machine learning[1576] biases[1577]—begets deleterious effects with which modern societies[1578] have been grappling[1579] for a long-winded span of time. Proxy discrimination is therefore an outgrowth of algorithmic-anchored decision-making arising out of the deployment of Artificial Intelligence-embedded technologies.

§§ Tellingly, proxy discrimination exacts a toll on, and breeds a cascade of disparate impacts[1580] on, *socially undesirables* in spite of the fact that machine learning algorithms leverages on seemingly neutral proxies to deal with legally protected features[1581] (e.g. race, gender, religion) throughout the process of algorithmic decision-making.[1582] Building on the thorny and uneasy relationship between private data, input variables and outputs variables,[1583] proxy discrimination can be deemed as eminently indirect.[1584]

---

that should never be entrusted to machines). More on this on Part IV, This chapter, Sects. 4.1.4–4.1.4.2.1 of this book. See also: Kleinberg, Jon/Lakkaraju, Himabindu/Leskovec, Jure/Ludwig, Jens/Mullainathan, Sendhil, "Human Decisions and Machine Predictions", *Quarterly Journal of Economics*, Volume 133, 2018, passim; Pasquale, Frank, "A Rule of Persons, Not Machines: The Limits of Legal Automation", *George Washington Law Review*, Volume 87, 2019, pp. 1 and ff and passim.

1575 *Tech, Bias and Housing Initiative, the Promise and Perils of Residential Proptech, Year 1, Research Summary Report, April 2023, TechEquity Collaborative*, p. 11, available at: https://techequity.us/wp-content/uploads/2023/04/TBHI-Y1-Research-Summary-Report.pdf (28.11.2024). ("*Once bad data enters the analysis of one factor, it gets baked into the subsequent process, multiplying the effect that one disadvantageous data point can have on someone's overall housing determination*"). Italics added.

1576 Sun, R. (Ed.), *The Cambridge Handbook of Computational Cognitive Sciences*, Cambridge, Cambridge University Press, 2023.

1577 Fisher, A., Rudin, C., & Dominici, F., "All models are wrong, but many are useful: Learning a variable's importance by studying an entire class of prediction models simultaneously", *Journal of Machine Learning Research*, 20, 2019, pp. 1–81.

1578 Annamma, S. A., Jackson, D. D., & Morrison, D., "Conceptualizing color-evasiveness: Using dis/ability critical race theory to expand a color-blind racial ideology in education and society", *Race Ethnicity and Education*, Volume 20, Issue 2, 2017, pp. 147–162.

1579 See: Alcalá, H. E./Montoya, M. F. L., "Association of skin color and generation on arrests among Mexican-origin latinos", *Race and Justice*, Volume 8, Issue 2, 2018, pp. 178–193.

1580 Barocas, Solon/Selbst, Andrew, "Big Data's Disparate Impact", *California Law Review*, Volume 104, 2016, pp. 671 and ff and passim.

1581 Xi Chen, "Algorithmic proxy discrimination and its regulations", *Computer Law & Security Review, The International Journal of Technology Law and Practice*, Volume 54, September 2024, 2024, pp. 1–13.

1582 Xi Chen, "Algorithmic proxy discrimination and its regulations", *cit.*, pp. 1–13.

1583 Gillis, Talia B., "The Input Data Fallacy", *Minnesota Law Review*, Volume 106, 2022, pp. 1176–1263.

1584 Xi Chen, "Algorithmic proxy discrimination and its regulations", *cit.*, pp. 1–13. See also: Hellman, Deborah, "Indirect Discrimination and the Duty to Avoid Compounding Injustice", *Foundations of Indirect Discrimination Law*, Collins, Hugh/Khaitan, Tarunabh (Editors), Oxford, Hart Publishing; Reprint edition (June 25, 2020), 2020, p. 107 (Professor Deborah Hellman coined this expression to depict a decision that "exacerbates the harm caused by the prior injustice because it entrenches the harm or carries it into another domain." This book deals with the sweltering topic of

§§ In the purview of big data and data mining,[1585] the glut and complexity of algorithmic proxy relations[1586] render proxy discrimination labyrinthic and exceedingly difficult to ferret out,[1587] whilst inscrutable algorithmic[1588] proxy correlations[1589]

---

indirect discrimination ("*indirect discrimination (or disparate impact) concerns the application of the same rule to everyone, even though that rule significantly disadvantages one particular group in society*"). Italics added.

[1585] Balkin, Jack, "Constitution in the National Surveillance State", *Minnesota Law Review*, Volume 93, 2008, p. 13 (note, though, that "*data mining* allows inferences not only about the direct subject of surveillance, but about other people with whom they live, work and communicate"). It bears mentioning that pundits have neither been coy nor bashful in strongly highlighting the perceived peril—consumer harm—of monetizing the data harvested/gleaned by Artificial Intelligence-embedded technologies while performing data mining. But see: Pedreshi, Dino/ Ruggieri, Salvatore/Turini, Franco, "Discrimination-aware Data Mining", *Proceedings of the 14th ACM SIGKDD International Conference on Knowledge Discovery and Data Mining (Las Vegas, Nevada, USA), ACM*, 2008, pp. 560–568 (arguing that one should shift its gaze downstream by putting in place discrimination-aware algorithmic tools while performing data mining).

[1586] But see: Segran, G., "The complexity of artificial intelligence", *Singapore Management University*, 2021, passim (on the elaborate and complex trappings of Artificial Intelligence).

[1587] Suresh/Guttag, H. J. V., "A Framework for Understanding Unintended Consequences of Machine Learning", *arXiv preprint arXiv:1901.10002*, 2019.

[1588] For an on-point breakdown of the distinct levels of opacity arising out of machine learning algorithms: Selbst, Andrew D./Barocas, Solon, "The Intuitive Appeal of Explainable Machines", *Fordham Law Review*, Volume 87, 2018, pp. 1085, 1089–99 (holding that there are plenty reasons for the insurer's ignorance. To begin with, the algorithm entails specialized knowledge to understand. That is, the insurer's employees may lack sufficient knowledge to understand the rationale behind the reasons in view of which the algorithm is producing prices for different customers—personalized pricing. Lastly, even if the insurer himself comprehends how the model operates, it may nonetheless lack expertise to comprehend why it operates the way it does. For that reason, the explainability of machines is a vital, but rather elusive, task. Thence, the famed authors deem it as the "nonintuitive" nature of algorithms. For purposes here, the insurer himself might indeed understand that its Artificial Intelligence-embedded technology formulates higher prices for those who actually access the website at hand, but may fail to come to terms with the fact that the explanation for this fact arises from the website's capacity to proxy for genetic information). See also: Scherer, Matthew U. Scherer, "Regulating Artificial Intelligence Systems: Risks, Challenges, Competencies, and Strategies", *Harvard Journal of Law and Technology*, Volume 29, 2016, pp. 353–369 (frames the crippling problem of opacity as "the possibility that the inner workings of an AI system may be kept secret and may not be susceptible to reverse engineering").

[1589] Bathaee, Yavar, "The Artificial Intelligence Black Box and the Failure of Intent and Causation", *Harvard Journal of Law and Technology*, n.º 37, 2018, p. 901 (adduces that "*one possible reason AI may be a black box to humans is that it relies on machine-learning algorithms that internalize data in ways that are not easily audited or understood by humans (…) "first, a lack may arise from the complexity of the algorithm's structure, such as with deep neural network, which consists of thousands of artificial neurons working together in a diffuse way to solve a problem. This reason for AI being a black box is referred to as "complexity". Second, the lack of transparency may arise because the AI is using a machine-learning algorithm that relies on geometric relationships that humans cannot visualize, such as with support vector machines. This reason for AI being a black box is referred to as "dimensionality"*"). Italics added. But see: Pearl, Judea, *Causality*, 2nd edition, Cambridge, Cambridge University Press, 2009 (on the fundamental tenets of causality). But see: Kilbertus, Niki/Carulla, Mateo Rojas/Parascandolo, Giambattista/Hardt, Moritz/Janzing, Dominik/ Schoellkopf, Bernhard, "Avoiding Discrimination through Causal Reasoning", *Advances in Neural*

hamper the very existence of proxy discrimination in the first place.[1590] Note, though, that these are sobering news.

§§ Pivotally, humankind is thrust headlong in the age of big data[1591] and cybersurveillance[1592] against the backdrop of which machine learning algorithms pierce into all aspects of social life.[1593] Burgeoningly, a plethora of energy-draining and time-consuming tasks are being currently carried out by algorithms,[1594] ranging from credit scoring,[1595] predictive policing,[1596] algorithmic risk assessment,[1597]

Information Processing Systems, I. Guyon, U. V. Luxburg, S. Bengio, H. Wallach, R. Fergus, S. Vishwanathan, and R. Garnett (Eds.), Vol. 30. Curran Associates, Inc., 2017, pp. 656–666 (arguing that is feasible to avoiding discrimination through a granular and fine-grained causal reasoning).

1590 Xi Chen, "Algorithmic proxy discrimination and its regulations", *cit.*, pp. 1–13.

1591 Big data that is in the limelight these days. See: Sivarajah, Uthayasnkar et al., "Critical Analysis of Big Data Challenges and Analytical Methods", *Journal of Business Research*, Volume 70, 2017, pp. 263 and ff and passim; Jetten, Lieke /Sharon, Stephen, "Selected Issues concerning the Ethical Use of Big Data Health Analytics", *Washington & Lee Law Review Online*, Volume 72, 2016, passim; Wachter, S./Mittelstadt. B., "A right to Reasonable Inferences: Re-thinking Data Protection Law in the Age of Big Data and AI", *Columbia Business Law Review*, 2019, pp. 1 and ff and passim; See in French doctrine: Ferey, Samuel, « Analyse économique du droit, big data et justice prédictive», *Archives de Philosophie du Droit*, Volume 60, 2018, pp. 68–81; Završnik, A. "Algorithmic justice: Algorithms and big data in criminal justice settings", *European Journal of Criminology*, 2019, passim; Joh, Elizabeth E., "The New Surveillance Discretion: Automated Suspicion, Big Data, and Policing." *Harvard Law and Policy Review*, 10 (1), 2016, pp. 15–42.

1592 Hu, Margaret, "From the National Surveillance State to the Cybersurveillance State", *The Annual Review of Law and Social Science*, Volume 13, 2017, p. 168 ("*as a result, the Cybersurveillance State, as a technological successor to the National Surveillance State, will execute bureaucratized biometric cybersurveillance in ways that are largely invisible and that appear routinized when technologically embedded within biometric identification technologies harnessed by the Administrative State. The normalization of day-to-day cybersurveillance will be achieved largely through governing functions that appear purely administrative (e.g., identity assessments for the granting of welfare, rights, privileges, and governing incentives).* Because of the routinized and administrative nature of the government-led big data program or *data surveillance (dataveillance) program, contemporary cybersurveillance is likely to be viewed as justified under crime, immigration control, and counterterrorism policy rationales*"). Italics added.

1593 Xi Chen, "Algorithmic proxy discrimination and its regulations", *cit.*, pp. 1–13.

1594 Ross, M./Taylor, J., "Managing AI Decision-Making Tools, Technology and Analytics", *Harvard Business Review*, 10 Nov. 2021, 2021.

1595 See: Part IV, This chapter, Sects. 4.1.4–4.1.4 .2.1 of this book (on mortgage redlining). See: Part IV, This chapter, Sects. 4.1.2–4.1.4.3 of this book (on algorithmic credit scoring, consumer racism and credit card redlining). See: Part IV, This chapter, Sects. 4.1.4–4.1.4.2.3 of this book (on algorithmic redlining). See: Part IV, This chapter, Sect. 4.1.4.3 of this book (on "algorithmic redliking"). See also: Hurley, Mikella/Adebayo, Julius, "Credit Scoring in the Era of Big Data", *Yale Journal of Law and Technology*, Volume 18, 2016, pp. 148–168.

1596 See: Part IV, This chapter, Sects. 4.1.1–4.1.1.1 of this book (on biased predictive policing). See: Brayne, S., "Big data surveillance: The case of policing", *American Sociological Review*, Volume 82, Issue 5, 2017, pp. 977–1008.

1597 See: Part V, Chap. 5, Sects. 5.1.8–5.1.8.5 of this book (on the five laws to interpret algorithmic decision-making).

lending,[1598] mortgage redlining,[1599] screening resumes, gauging employee overall performance, establishing premiums, to supporting high-stakes decisions[1600] of government officials,[1601] which, in turn, begets algorithmic accountability[1602] of which policymakers must not shy away from.[1603]

§§ Albeit human decision-makers play a pivotal role in keeping individual[1604] justice unscathed,[1605] Artificial Intelligence-embedded technologies are being increasingly deployed to make high stake decisions,[1606] which, in turn, creates a blazingly new cluster of challenges[1607] that must be tackled heads-on.[1608]

[1598] Bruckner, Matthew Adam, "The Promise and Perils of Algorithmic Lenders' Use of Big Data", *Chicago-Kent Law Review*, Volume 93, 2018, pp. 25–29.

[1599] See: Part IV, This chapter, Sects. 4.1.4–4.1.4.2.1 of this book (on mortgage redlining). See: Part IV, This chapter, Sects. 4.1.2–4.1.4.3 of this book (on algorithmic credit scoring, consumer racism and credit card redlining). See: Part IV, This chapter, Sects. 4.1.4–4.1.4.2.3 of this book (on algorithmic redlining). See: Part IV, This chapter, Sect. 4.1.4.3 of this book (on "algorithmic redliking"). In spite of its deep-seated racial bias, decision-makers continue to deploy redlining tactics through big data and may even justify such unlawful practices by claiming that the latter abide by cost-effectiveness. See: Humber, Nadiyah J., "A Home for Digital Equity: Algorithmic Redlining and Property Technology", *California Law Review*, Volume 111, Issue 5, 2023, pp. 1421–1484. See also: Hurley, Mikella/Adebayo, Julius, "Credit Scoring in the Era of Big Data", *Yale Journal of Law and Technology*, Volume 18, 2016, pp. 148, 151–156, 172 (averring that FICO scoring boasts a redoubtable capacity to routinely weed out some populations that have been historically and systematically underrepresented or grossly unfairly represented in the credit industry market). Tellingly, by 2016, ten states had disavowed the unlawful practice of employers using shady credit scores due to their perceived disparate impact on low-income applicants and members of racialized communities (mostly Black folks). See: O'Neill, Cathy, *Weapons of Math Destruction. How Big Data Increases Inequality and Threatens Democracy*. London: Penguin Random House, 2016, pp. 128 and ff and passim. See: Part IV, This chapter, Sects. 4.1.4–4.1.4.2.3 of this book.

[1600] See: Part V, Chap. 5, Sect. 5.1.7.2 of this book (on law number two to control algorithmic decision-making, which mandates that black box models must not be entrusted with the task of making high stake decisions—v.g. health and freedom). But see: Rudin, Cynthia, "Please stop explaining black box models for high stakes decisions", *Proceedings of NeurIPS 2018 Workshop on Critiquing and Correcting Trends in Machine Learning (NIPS 2018)*, 2018, passim.

[1601] Xi Chen, "Algorithmic proxy discrimination and its regulations", *cit.*, pp. 1–13. But see: Williams, Rebecca, "Accountable Algorithms: Adopting the Public Law Toolbox Outside the Realm of Public Law", *Current Legal Problems,* Vol. 75, 2022, pp. 237–263; Williams, Rebecca, "Rethinking Administrative Law for Algorithmic Decision-Making", *Oxford Journal of Legal Studies*, Volume 42, 2021, pp. 468 e ff and passim (on the much-needed algorithmic accountability in the realm of administrative law).

[1602] See: Part V, Chap. 5, Sects. 5.1.2–5.1.6.2.1 of this book (on the thing-centred algorithmic decision-making propelled by a *Controllable* and *Interpretable* Machine Learning that weeds out *Algorithmic Dictatorship* and secures *Algorithmic Common Good*). See: Part V, Chap. 5, Sect. 5.1.1.1 of this book (on the central tenets of Rule of Law that lends itself to a beacon of justice amidst the sepulchral darkness that is about to take hold). See: Part V, Chap. 5, Sect. 5.1.1.2 of this book (on the central tenets of Procedural Rule of Law that lends itself to a lighthouse of justice that allows citizens to challenge the pearls of algorithmic wisdom in a court of law).

[1603] See: Katyal, Sonia, "Private Accountability in the Age of Artificial Intelligence", *UCLA Law Review*, Volume 66, 2019, pp. 54–99 (on algorithmic accountability).

§§ Algorithmic decision-making can yield multifarious benefits to the overall advancement of modern societies.[1609] Notably, it not only augments decision-making efficiency (*cost–benefit analysis*)[1610] to adapt to the staggering amount of

[1604] But see: M. Zalnieriute, L. B. Moses, G. Williams, "The Rule of Law and Automation of Government Decision-making, University of New South Wales Law Research Series", *Modern Law Review*, 82 (3), 2019, passim (on the sizzling hot challenges posed by a algorithmic-anchored decision-making at a government level).

[1605] Note, though, that there is burgeoning trend of (to) sentencing anchored in algorithms in a bid to ease—and sometimes offset—human flaws (such as racial bias, gender bias, jealousy, sexual orientation bias and so forth). Such tools, which are currently being deployed to undertake predicting criminal recidivism, are gaining traction and gathering pace in Italy: Gialuz, M., "Quando la giustizia penale encontra l'intelligenza artificiale: luci e e ombre di risk assessment tools tra Stati Uniti ed Europa", 2019, available at: www.penalecontemporaneo.it.d/6702-quando-la-giustizia-penale-encontra-l'intelligenz-artificiale-luci-e-ombre-di-risk-assessment-tools (access: 03.07.2024); United Kingdom: Peeters, R./Schuilenburg, M., "Machine Justice: Governing Security through Bureaucracy of Algorithms", *Information Polity*, Volume 23, 2018, pp. 267–274; Hamilton, Melissa, "Sentencing Disparities", *British Journal of American Legal Studies*, Volume 6, Issue 2, 2017, pp. 181 ff. Portugal: Anabela Miranda Rodrigues, "Medida da pena de prisão—desafios da era da inteligência artificial", *Revista de Legislação e de Jurisprudência*, Março-Abril de 2020, Ano 149.°, N.° 4021, 2020, pp. 258 ff; Santos, Hugo Luz dos, ""Brain-Computer Interfaces, Generative Artificial Intelligence (ChatGPT and Deep Fakes) and Criminal Procedure Law: what's at stake?", *Journal of Research in E. and Computer Science*, Edinburgh, United Kingdom, June 2024, Volume 2, 2024, pp. 39–78; Santos, Hugo Luz dos, *Programas de Compliance e Inteligência Artificial: Consequências ao nível da Law and Economics, do Direito Penal, do Processo Penal e da Behavioral Law and Economics*, Braga, NovaCausa Edições Jurídicas, 2024, pp. 1–330; Santos, Hugo Luz dos, *Inteligência Artificial (ChatGPT/AutoGPT/Robots-Advogados/Robots Proceduradores/Robots-Juízes) e Responsabilidade Penal das Pessoas Colectivas*, Braga, NovaCausa Edições Jurídicas, 2023, pp. 1–108; Santos, Hugo Luz dos, *Inteligência Artificial e Processo Penal*, Braga, NovaCausa Edições Jurídicas, 2022, pp. 1–256; Santos, Hugo Luz dos, *Inteligência Artificial e Processo Penal*, Braga, NovaCausa Edições Jurídicas, 2022, pp. 1–256; Santos, Hugo Luz dos, *Inteligência Artificial e Processo Civil na Era do Metaverse e dos Machine Learning Algorithms*, Braga, NovaCausa Edições Jurídicas, 2022, pp. 1–264.

[1606] See: Part V, Chap. 5, Sect. 5.1.7.2 of this book (on law number two to control algorithmic decision-making, which mandates that black box models must not be entrusted with the task of making high stake decisions—v.g. health and freedom).

[1607] See: Millar, Jason/Kerr, Ian, "Delegation, Relinquishment and Responsibility: The Prospect of Expert Robots", *Robot Law*, Calo, Ryan /Froomkin, A. Michael/Kerr, Ian, Cheltenham, Edward Elgar Publishing, 2016, pp. 102, 106–107 (as these authors aptly put it "*we will rely on robots without really knowing why – simply because their algorithms provide the greatest number of successful outcomes.* We have already seen this in Google's search approach. Neither Larry (Page) nor Sergey (Brin) (nor any other Google employee) knowns exactly why one particular web page is a better result than another. *When the click patterns say it is, that's good enough.* No semantic or causal analysis is required...*Like the ancients, we will, quite rationally, come to rely upon them, knowing full well that we cannot necessarily explain the reasons for their decisions*"). Italics added. Converging: Casey, Anthony J./Niblett, Anthony, "Self-driving Laws", *University of Toronto Law Journal*, Volume 66, 2016, pp. 429–435 (contend that "as more information is generated, and the evolutionary algorithm updates and become a better forecaster, we imagine that judges will increasingly rely on the advice of the algorithm"). But see: Weizenbaum, Joseph, *Computer Power and Human Reason: From Judgment to Calculation*, 1st edition, New York, W. H. Freeman & Co, 1976, pp. 1–300 (227) ("examines the sources of the computer's powers and offers evaluative

social changes catalysed by a seething social reality but, and foremost, appears to be more objective[1611] and neutral[1612] than humans[1613] owing to the fact that Artificial Intelligence-embedded technologies are not subject to any[1614] prejudice whatsoever.[1615]

---

explorations of what computers can do, cannot do, and should not be employed to do") (this founding father of Artificial Intelligence presciently noted that we should not entrust Artificial Intelligence-embedded technologies with "tasks that demand wisdom"). Italics added. The approval of rental applications is arguably one of those tasks that should never be entrusted to machines). More on this on Part IV, This chapter, Sects. 4.1.4–4.1.4.2.1 of this book.

[1608] Xi Chen, "Algorithmic proxy discrimination and its regulations", *cit.*, pp. 1–13.

[1609] Xi Chen, "Algorithmic proxy discrimination and its regulations", *cit.*, pp. 1–13.

[1610] *Cost–benefit Analysis* is in the limelight. Its development falls conspicuously outside the scope and aim of this book though. See: Sunstein, Cass R., "The Real World of Cost-Benefits Analysis: Thirty-Six Questions (and almost as many answers)", *Columbia Law Review*, 114 (1), 2014, 177; Bayefsky, Rachel, "Dignity as a value in Agency Cost–Benefit Analysis", *Yale Law Journal,* 123 (2014): 1740; Sunstein, Cass R., *Valuing Life: Humanizing the Regulatory State*, 2014, 8 ff; Gordon, Jeffrey, "The Empty Call for Cost-Benefits Analysis for Financial Regulators", *Journal of Legal Studies*, 43, 2014, 351; Sunstein, Cass R., "The Limits of Quantification", *California Law Review*, 103, 2014, 1369; Adler, Mathew/Posner, Eric A., "New Foundations of Cost–Benefit Analysis", *Regulation & Governance*, 3, 2006, 72; Thomas J. Miles/ Sunstein, Cass R., "The Real World of Arbitrariness Review", *University of Chicago Law Review*, 75 2008, 761; Coates, John C. IV, "Cost–Benefit Analysis of Financial Regulation: Case Studies and Implications", *Yale Law Journal*, 124, 2015, pp. 882–911; Posner, Eric A./Weyl E. Glen, "Cost–Benefit Analysis of Financial Regulations: Response to Criticisms", *Yale Law Journal*, 124, 2015, pp. 246–265 (parsing the relationship between agency cost–benefit analysis and human dignity).

[1611] But see: Benjamin, Ruha, *Race After Technology: Abolitionist Tools for the New Jim Code*, New York, Polity, 2019, pp. 1–172 (7) (discussing that Artificial Intelligence-embedded technologies are viewed as iron-clad tools of objectivity and devoid of any biases whatsoever). Ruha Benjamin accordingly contends that "the employment of new technologies that reflect and reproduce existing inequities but that are promoted and perceived as more objective or progressive than the discriminatory systems of a previous era"). See also: Farina, M., & Lavazza, A., *Philosophy, expertise, and the myth of neutrality. Routledge Studies in Contemporary Philosophy*, London, Routledge, 2024. This false scent of neutrality impairs, and impacts, procedural justice. See: Tyler, Tom R., "The Psychology of Procedural Justice: A Test of the Group-Value Model", *Journal of Personality and Social Psychology*, Volume 57, 1989, p. 830 (reports that in any procedure "several non-control issues – the *neutrality* of the decision-making procedure, trust in the 3rd party, and the information the experience communicates about social standing – influence both procedural preferences and judgments of procedural justice").

[1612] But see: Citron, Danielle Keats/Pasquale, Frank A., "The Scored Society: Due Process for Automated Predictions", *Washington Law Review*, Volume 89, 2014, pp. 1–34 (arguing that "[a]*dvocates applaud the removal of human beings and their flaws from the assessment process,*" but arguing that bias remains "[*b*]*ecause human beings program predictive algorithms, their biases and values are embedded into the software's instructions*"). Italics added. But see also: Bornstein, Stepanhie, "Antidiscriminatory Algorithms", *Alabama Law Review*, Volume 70, 2018, pp. 519, 524–528 (contending, however, that the tagged "facially neutral" algorithms producing discriminatory outcomes should be quashed).

[1613] But see: Jiang, H., O. Nachum, *Identifying and Correcting Label Bias in Machine Learning*, 15 Jan 2019, 2019, available online at https://arxiv.org/pdf/1901.04966.pdf (access: 14.12.2024); Simons, T. *Addressing issues of fairness and bias in AI*, Thomson Reuters, 30 Nov 2020, available online at https://www.thomsonreuters.com/en-us/posts/news-and-media/ai-fairness-bias (access: 14.12.2024); Chakraborty, J./Majumder, S./Menzies, T., "Bias in Machine Learning Software:

§§ That holds true, but it is nonetheless truer that algorithms that are facially objective[1616] and seemingly neutral[1617] can lead to gruesome discrimination.[1618] Shoddy data,[1619] and botched/watered-down algorithms can jointly cause a slew of harmful consequences for both individuals and society.[1620] Worryingly, and perhaps

---

Why? How? What to Do?, 9 Jul 2021, 2021, *arxiv.org*; Danks, D. A. J. London, "Algorithmic Bias in Autonomous Systems, Algorithmic Bias in Autonomous Systems", *Proceedings of the Twenty-Sixth International Joint Conference on Artificial Intelligence (IJCAI-17)*, 2019, available online at https://www.ijcai.org/proceedings/2017/0654.pdf (access: 14.12.2024) (on the vast assortment of algorithmic biases).

1614 Xi Chen, "Algorithmic proxy discrimination and its regulations", *cit.*, pp. 1–13.

1615 Prejudiced algorithms are set to be brought to the fore as they are one foundational basis of *justice prédictive* so voguish in France. No surprise stems from the fact that prejudiced algorithms will feed *justice prédictive*—and that is something quite unsavoury and unpalatable in criminal justice indeed. See: Garapon, Antoine, "Les enjeux de la justice predictive", *Juris-Classeur périodique*, Volume 31, 2018, passim. See also: Larret-Chahine, Louis, "Le droit isométrique: un nouveau paradigme juridique né de la justice prédictive», *Archives de Philosophie du Droit*, Volume 60, 2018, pp. 287 and ff and passim.

1616 But see: Allen, James, "The Color of Algorithms: An Analysis and Proposed Research Agenda Deterring Algorithmic Redlining", *Fordham Urban Law Journal*, Volume 46, 2019, pp. 219–234 (229–234) (discussing how historical mortgage redlining greatly swayed modern algorithms generated by massive batches of datasets that consist of decades of information built on exclusion and racial discrimination in the purview of financing, marketing, and housing). See: Part IV, This chapter, Sects. 4.1.4–4.1.4.2.3 of this book.

1617 But see: Hurley, Mikella/Adebayo, Julius, "Credit Scoring in the Era of Big Data", *Yale Journal of Law and Technology*, Volume 18, 2016, p. 149 ("*these tools may furthermore obscure discriminatory and subjective lending policies behind a single "objective" score* (...) *sophisticated algorithms may combine facially neutral data points and treat them as proxies for immutable characteristics such as race or gender, thereby circumventing existing non-discrimination laws and systematically denying credit access to certain groups. Finally, big-data tools may allow online payday lenders to target the most vulnerable consumers and lure them into debt traps*"). Italics added.

1618 Xi Chen, "Algorithmic proxy discrimination and its regulations", *cit.*, pp. 1–13. See also: Mehrabi, N./Morstatter, F. N. Saxena/Lerman, K./Galstyan, A., *A Survey on Bias and Fairness in Machine Learning*, 25 Jan 2022, available at https://arxiv.org/pdf/1908.09635.pdf (access: 14.12.2024). See also: Hurley, Mikella/Adebayo, Julius, "Credit Scoring in the Era of Big Data", *Yale Journal of Law and Technology*, Volume 18, 2016, pp. 148, 151–156, 172 (averring that FICO scoring boasts a redoubtable capacity to routinely weed out some populations that have been historically and systematically underrepresented or grossly unfairly represented in the credit industry market). Tellingly, by 2016, ten states had disavowed the unlawful practice of employers using shady algorithmic credit scores due to their perceived disparate impact on low-income applicants and members of racialized communities (mostly Black folks). See: O'Neill, Cathy, *Weapons of Math Destruction. How Big Data Increases Inequality and Threatens Democracy*. London: Penguin Random House, 2016, pp. 128 and ff and passim. See: Part IV, This chapter, Sects. 4.1.4–4.1.4.2.3 of this book.

1619 See: *Tech, Bias and Housing Initiative, the Promise and Perils of Residential Proptech, Year 1, Research Summary Report, April 2023, TechEquity Collaborative*, p. 11, available at: https://techequity.us/wp-content/uploads/2023/04/TBHI-Y1-Research-Summary-Report.pdf (28.11.2024). ("*Once bad data enters the analysis of one factor, it gets baked into the subsequent process, multiplying the effect that one disadvantageous data point can have on someone's overall housing determination*"). Italics added. See: Part IV, This chapter, Sects. 4.1.4–4.1.4.2.3 of this book. See also: Barocas, Solon/Selbst, Andrew D., "Big Data's Disparate Impact", *California Law Review*, Volume 104, 2016, pp. 671–682 (discussing how data is often flawed, rigged, incomplete,

not infrequently, even state-of-the art and top-notch algorithms suitably tailored to accomplish a given task and fed with clean data[1621] can mimic, reproduce[1622] and exacerbate[1623] previous discriminatory[1624] patterns.[1625] No flabbergasting surprise stems from the fact that Artificial Intelligence-embedded technologies have been

imperfect and therefore algorithms inherit the prejudice of the original decision makers); Citron, Danielle Keats/Pasquale, Frank, "The Scored Society: Due Process for Automated Predictions", *Washington Law Review*, Volume 89, 2014, pp. 1, 4–5 (highlighting how human beings programming automated systems is directly conducive to, and leads, to fundamentally inaccurate results since the source code, predictive algorithms and datasets may encompass human biases which, in turn, have a disparate impact on historically disadvantaged groups); Crawford, Kate/Schultz, Jason, "Big Data and Due Process: Toward a Framework to Redress Predictive Privacy Harms", *Boston College Law Review*, Volume 55, 2014, pp. 93, 99–101 (pinpointing pathways through which predictive analytic tools perpetuate discriminatory practices).

[1620] See: O'Neil, Cathy, *Weapons of Math Destruction. How Big Data Increases Inequality and Threatens Democracy*, London, Penguin Random House, 2016, passim (showing how algorithms utilized in modern societies are amenable to perpetuate racial discrimination, partially through perpetuation of social disadvantage and wealth divides). See also: O'Neil, Cathy, "When Not to Trust the Algorithm", *Interview published in the Harvard Business Review's Ideacast*, 2016, passim; O' Neil, Cathy, "Amazon's Gender-Biased Algorithm Is Not Alone", 2018, accessed 2 January 2025 (on gender-related algorithmic biases).

[1621] But see: Barocas, Solon/Selbst, Andrew D., "Big Data's Disparate Impact", *California Law Review*, Volume 104, 2016, pp. 671–682 (671) (talk about the role of bias in data and what can be done to unwind its noxious effects).

[1622] See: Benjamin, Ruha, *Race After Technology: Abolitionist Tools for the New Jim Code*, New York, Polity, 2019, pp. 1–172 (7) (discussing that Artificial Intelligence-embedded technologies are viewed as iron-clad tools of objectivity and devoid of any biases whatsoever). Ruha Benjamin contends that "the employment of new technologies that reflect *and reproduce existing inequities but that are promoted and perceived as more objective or progressive than the discriminatory systems of a previous era*"). Italics added.

[1623] *Tech, Bias and Housing Initiative, the Promise and Perils of Residential Proptech, Year 1, Research Summary Report, April 2023, TechEquity Collaborative*, p. 5 available at: https://techequity.us/wp-content/uploads/2023/04/TBHI-Y1-Research-Summary-Report.pdf (28.11.2024). ("*Residential Proptech also has the potential to exacerbate the bias inherent in our housing system. Its rise is due, in part, to the desperation felt by average home seekers. With a severely constrained housing supply, companies offering an easier pathway to homeownership may exploit communities that have been harmed by housing discrimination in the past. Opaque algorithms incorporate biased data into their decision-making processes, making it harder to enforce fair housing laws*. Residential Proptech companies often operate in a regulatory gray area, leaving consumers without the protections they would have from traditional housing regulatory systems. *As unprecedented capital investment flows into this space, venture-backed companies' winner-take-all approach to growth has the potential to exacerbate inequality rather than combat it*"). Italics added. See: Part IV, This chapter, Sects. 4.1.4–4.1.4.2.3 of this book.

[1624] Roithmayr, Daria, *Reproducing Racism: How everyday choices lock in White Advantage*, New York, New York University Press, 2014, pp. 1–272 ("*Argues that racial inequality reproduces itself automatically over time because early unfair advantage for whites has paved the way for continuing advantage. This book is designed to change the way we think about racial inequality (…) Legal scholar Daria Roithmayr provocatively argues that racial inequality lives on because white advantage functions as a powerful self-reinforcing monopoly, reproducing itself automatically from generation to generation even in the absence of intentional discrimination. Drawing on work in antitrust law and a range of other disciplines, Roithmayr brilliantly compares the dynamics of white*

flagged as sources of algorithmic bias,[1626] algorithmic discrimination[1627] and algorithmic injustice.[1628] Take the example of COMPAS,[1629] a recidivism predictive tool used in some jurisdictions of the United States of America.

§§ Whereas COMPAS does not use ethnicity-specific data,[1630] it nonetheless creates an algorithmic myth of colour-blindness[1631] by boosting the ungrounded hope

advantage to the unfair tactics of giants like AT&T and Microsoft. With penetrating insight, Roithmayr *locates the engine of white monopoly in positive feedback loops that connect the dramatic disparity of Jim Crow to modern racial gaps in jobs, housing and education. Wealthy white neighborhoods fund public schools that then turn out wealthy white neighbors. Whites with lucrative jobs informally refer their friends, who refer their friends, and so on. Roithmayr concludes that racial inequality might now be locked in place, unless policymakers immediately take drastic steps to dismantle this oppressive system*"). Italics added. This book points out how White privilege is perpetuated throughout generations through residential segregation (*mortgage redlining*), abhorrent nepotism, and other bemoaning social practices that pester modern societies). See: Part IV, This chapter, Sects. 4.1.4–4.1.4.2.3 of this book.

1625 Xi Chen, "Algorithmic proxy discrimination and its regulations", *cit.*, pp. 1–13.

1626 Danks, D./London, A.J., "Algorithmic Bias in Autonomous Systems, Algorithmic Bias in Autonomous Systems", *Proceedings of the Twenty-Sixth International Joint Conference on Artificial Intelligence (IJCAI-17)*, 2019; Ferrer, X./van Nuenen, T./Such, J. M./Cote, M./Criado, N., "Bias and Discrimination in AI: a cross-disciplinary perspective", King's College London, United Kingdom, 11 Aug 2020, 2020.

1627 See on algorithmic discrimination: Kleinberg, Jon, et al., "Discrimination in the Age of Algorithms", *Journal of Legal Analysis*, 2018, pp. 114–174; See: Kleinberg, Jon, et al., "Algorithms as Discrimination Detectors", *Proceeds of the National Academy of Science*, Volume 117, 2020, pp. 30096–30110; Griemmelmann, James/Westreich, Daniel, "Incomprehensible Discrimination ", *California Law Review Online*, Volume 7, 2018, pp. 164–171; Xiang, Alice, "Reconciling Legal and Technical Approaches to Algorithmic Bias", *Tennessee Law Review*, Volume 88, 2021, passim; Karnow, Curtis E. A., "The Opinion of Machines", *The Cambridge Handbook of the Law of Algorithms*, Bartfield, Woodrow (Editor), Cambridge, United Kingdom: Cambridge University Press, 2021, pp. 15 and ff and passim; Strandburg, Katherine J., "Rulemaking and Inscrutable Decision Tools", *Columbia Law Review*, Volume 119, 2019, passim; Watcher, Sandra/Mittelstadt, Brent/Russell, Chris, "Counterfactual Explanations Without Opening the Black Box: Automated Decisions and the GDPR", *Harvard Journal of Law and Technology*, Volume 31, 2018, pp. 841 e ss and passim; Jackson, Maya C., "Artificial Intelligence and Algorithmic Bias: The Issues with Technology Reflecting History and Humans", *Journal of Business Technology Law*, Volume 16, 2021, pp. 299–316.

1628 Ting-an Lin, "Democratizing AI" and the Concern of Algorithmic Injustice", *Philosophy and Technology*, Volume 37 (103), 2024, pp. 3–27. See also: Birhane, A., "Algorithmic injustice: A relational ethics approach", *Patterns*, 2 (2), 2021, pp. 1–9. Završnik, A. "Algorithmic justice: Algorithms and big data in criminal justice settings", *European Journal of Criminology*, 2019, passim.

1629 See: Part IV, This chapter, Sects. 4.1.10.1–4.1.10.6 of this book (on biased algorithmic risk assessment in criminal procedure law settings, with a sharper focus on COMPAS).

1630 Xi Chen, "Algorithmic proxy discrimination and its regulations", *cit.*, pp. 1–13.

1631 Brewer, R. M./Heitzeg, N. A., "The racialization of crime and punishment: Criminal justice, Color-Blind racism, and the political economy of the prison industrial complex", *American Behavioral Scientist*, Volume 51, Issue 5, 2008, pp. 625–64; Van Cleve, N. G./L. Mayes, "Criminal Justice Through "Colorblind" Lenses: A Call to Examine the Mutual Constitution of Race and Criminal Justice", *Law & Social Inquiry*, 40 (2), 2015, pp. 406–32. But see: Strauss, David A., "The Myth of Colorblindness", The *Supreme Court Review*, 1986, pp. 99, 114 ("The one option that is not open is the ideal of colorblindness—treating race as if it were, like eye color, a wholly irrelevant

that input exclusion («input data fallacy»[1632]) can breed non-discriminatory algorithms.[1633] Therefore, we are there increasingly led to believe that colour-blind[1634] algorithms[1635] amount to the panacea for the great bulk of social diseases with which modern societies have been floundering for a long-haul.[1636]

§§ Note, though, that COMPAS does not go easy on Blacks. Tellingly, COMPAS is more likely to falsely flag Black defendants as likely to engage in future criminal

---

characteristic. That is because it is not a wholly irrelevant characteristic. Race correlates with other things....").

1632 Gillis, Talia B., "The Input Data Fallacy", *Minnesota Law Review*, Volume 106, 2022, pp. 1176–1263.

1633 Gillis, Talia B., "The Input Data Fallacy", *cit.*, pp. 1176–1263.

1634 But see: Kim, Pauline T., "Data-Driven Discrimination at Work", *William and Mary Law Review*, Volume 58, 2017, p. 918 ("If the goal is to reduce biased outcomes, then a simple prohibition on using data about race or sex could be either wholly ineffective or actually counterproductive due to the existence of class proxies and the risk of omitted variable bias."); Lipton, Zachary et al., "Does Mitigating ML's Impact Disparity Require Treatment Disparity?", NIPS Proceedings 1, 2018, https://arxiv.org/pdf/1711.07076.pdf; [https://perma.cc/X8VF-EY53] (arguing, premised on statistical examples, that a prohibition on race or sex data is rather counterproductive indeed); Corbett-Davies, Sam/Goel, Sharad, "The Measure and Mismeasure of Fairness: a critical Review of Fair Machine Learning", *Cornell University Library*, 2018, passim (discussing the "[l]imitations of anti-classification" as a fairness metric). Se also: Kim, Pauline T., "Data-Driven Discrimination at Work", *cit.*, p. 867 ("[I]f the goal is to discourage classification bias, then the law should not forbid the inclusion of race, sex, or other sensitive information as variables, but seek to preserve these variables, and perhaps even include them in some complex models."); Kroll, Joshua A., et al., "Accountable Algorithms", *University of Pennsylvania Law Review*, Volume 165, 2017, pp. 633, 693–95. See: Part IV, This chapter, Sects. 4.1.10.1–4.1.10.6 of this book (on biased algorithmic risk assessment in criminal procedure law settings, with a sharper focus on COMPAS).

1635 But see: Sam Corbett-Davies and Sharad Goel refer to colorblindness as "anti-classification." Corbett-Davies, Sam/Gaebler, Johann D./Nilforoshan, Hamed/Shrof, Ravi/Goel, Sharad, "The Measure and Mismeasure of Fairness", *Journal of Machine Learning Research*, Volume 24, 2023, pp. 1–117 (p. 36) ("*In constructing algorithmic risk scores, a key ingredient is the target of prediction. In practice, though, there is often a mismatch between our true outcome of interest and the available data—an occurrence we call label bias (Zanger-Tishler* et al., *2023). As with the other issues we discuss, there is typically no perfect solution to this problem, but there are ways to mitigate it. For example, in pretrial risk assessment, we would often like to estimate the likelihood a defendant would commit a crime if released. But there are two key difficulties with this goal. First, though we might want to measure crime conducted by defendants awaiting trial, we typically only observe crime that results in a conviction or an arrest. These observable outcomes, however, are imperfect proxies for the underlying criminal act. Further, heavier policing in communities of color might lead to Black and Hispanic defendants being arrested, and later convicted, more often than White defendants who commit the same offense (Lum and Isaac, 2016). Poor outcome data might thus cause one to systematically underestimate the risk posed by White defendants. The second, related, issue is that our target of interest is a counterfactual outcome; it corresponds to what would have happened had a defendant been released*"). Italics added. See also: Balkin, Jack M./Siegel, Reva B., "The American Civil Rights Tradition: Anticlassification or Antisubordination?", *University of Miami Law Review*, Volume 58, 2003, pp. 9, 10–11 (explaining the distinction between the anticlassification and the antisubordination approaches to equality law).

1636 Sunstein, Cass R., "Governing by Algorithm? No Noise and (Potentially) Less Bias", *Duke Law Journal*, Volume 71, 2022, pp. 1175 and ff.

activities.[1637] Thence, its false-positive rate was exceedingly higher for Black defendants than for White defendants,[1638] while its false-negative rate[1639] was exceedingly greater[1640] for the latter than for the former.[1641]

§§ Compellingly, COMPAS holds Blacks,[1642] immigrants,[1643] Latinos,[1644] women[1645] and whites to radically different standards of algorithmic fairness. Put

[1637] Xi Chen, "Algorithmic proxy discrimination and its regulations", *cit.*, pp. 1–13. See: Part IV, This chapter, Sects. 4.1.10.1–4.1.10.6 of this book (on biased algorithmic risk assessment in criminal procedure law settings, with a sharper focus on COMPAS).

[1638] Xi Chen, "Algorithmic proxy discrimination and its regulations", *cit.*, pp. 1–13.

[1639] Mayson, Sandra G., "Bias In, Bias Out", *Yale Law Journal*, Volume 128, 2019, pp. 2218 and ff and passim.

[1640] Flores, A.W./Lowenkamp, C.T./Bechtel, K., "False positives, false negatives, and false analyses: a rejoinder to "machine bias: there's software used across the country to predict future criminal", *Federal Probation Journal*, Volume 80, 2016, pp. 38–46. Sun, R. (Ed.), *The Cambridge Handbook of Computational Cognitive Sciences*, Cambridge, Cambridge University Press, 2023.

[1641] Xi Chen, "Algorithmic proxy discrimination and its regulations", *cit.*, pp. 1–13.

[1642] See: Chandler, Anupam, "The Racist Algorithm", *Michigan Law Review*, Volume 115, n. ° 6, 2018, p. 1026 (on racist algorithms, noting that "the possibilities for discriminatory manipulation are legion"). But see: Altenburger, Kristen M./Ho, Daniel E., "When Algorithms Import Private Bias into Public Enforcement: The Promise and Limitations of Statistical Debiasing Solutions", *Journal of Institutional & Theoretical Economics*, Volume 175, 2019, pp. 97–98 (calls for a "debias predictive algorithms" to assuage racist and/or biased, doctored and bigoted algorithms nevertheless).

[1643] Maxwell, J./Tomlinson, J., *Experiments in Automating Immigration Systems*. Bristol: Bristol University Press, 2022, passim; Borgesius, FJ Zuiderveen, "Strengthening legal protection against discrimination by algorithms and artificial intelligence", *International Journal of Human Rights*, Volume 24, Issue 10, 2020, pp. 1573 and ff and passim. Hu, Margaret, "From the National Surveillance State to the Cybersurveillance State", *The Annual Review of Law and Social Science*, Volume 13, 2017, p. 168 ("Because of the routinized and administrative nature of the government-led *big data program* or *data surveillance (dataveillance) program, contemporary cybersurveillance is likely to be viewed as justified under crime, immigration control, and counterterrorism policy rationales*"). Italics added.

[1644] See: Hamilton, Melissa, "The Biased Algorithm: Evidence of Disparate Impact on Hispanics", *American Criminal Law Review*, Volume 56, 2019, pp. 1553 and ff and passim.

[1645] Hamilton, Melissa, "The sexist algorithm", *Behavioral Sciences and the Law*, Volume 37, Issue 2, Special Issue: the Use of Statistics in Criminal Cases, March–April 2019, 2019, pp. 1 and ff ("*Algorithmic risk assessment tools are informed by scientific research concerning which factors are predictive of recidivism and thus support the evidence-based practice movement in criminal justice.* Automated assessments of individualized risk (low, medium, high) *permit officials to make more effective management decisions. Computer-generated algorithms appear to be objective and neutral. But are these algorithms actually fair? The focus herein is on gender equity.* Studies confirm that women typically have far lower recidivism rates than men. *This differential raises the question of how well algorithmic outcomes fare in terms of predictive parity by gender.* This essay reports original research using a large dataset of offenders who were scored on the popular risk assessment tool COMPAS. *Findings indicate that COMPAS performs reasonably well at discriminating between recidivists and non-recidivists for men and women. Nonetheless, COMPAS algorithmic outcomes systemically overclassify women in higher risk groupings. Multiple measures of algorithmic equity and predictive accuracy are provided to support the conclusion that this algorithm is sexist*"). Italics added.

differently, COMPAS treats the former less fairly than the latter[1646] who are scored by it.[1647] Rivetingly, and yet somewhat disturbingly, this discrimination does not spring from any malicious[1648] intent[1649] whatsoever. Rather, it flows from the fact that the algorithm, ensnared on its own inscrutable inner workings,[1650] leverages on

[1646] But see: Algorithmic fairness lends itself to several incompatible standards. Whilst COMPAS falls short of meeting the baseline standards of "equal opportunity" and "equalized odds", it refrains itself from discriminating blacks from the prism of "predictive parity" nonetheless. A full-fledged analysis of the extant state of this scorching topic can be found in Hübner, Dietmar, "Two Kinds of Discrimination in AI-Based penal Decision-Making", *SIGKDD Explorations*, 2021.

[1647] Xi Chen, "Algorithmic proxy discrimination and its regulations", *cit.*, pp. 1–13.

[1648] Note, though, that some forms of racial discrimination may not be fully intentional. More likely than not, it can be related with the perils of big data colour-blindness that nonetheless relies on proxies to race and gender to make algorithmic decisions. Another problem is the one related with "creditworthiness by association" that causes more problems than it solves. Hurley, Mikella/Adebayo, Julius, "Credit Scoring in the Era of Big Data", *Yale Journal of Law and Technology*, Volume 18, 2016, p. 149 ("*recent studies have also questioned the accuracy of the data used by these tools, in some cases identifying serious flaws that have a substantial bearing on lending decisions. Big-data tools may also risk creating a system of "creditworthiness by association" in which consumers' familial, religious, social, and other affiliations determine their eligibility for an affordable loan. These tools may furthermore obscure discriminatory and subjective lending policies behind a single "objective" score. Such discriminatory scoring may not be intentional; instead, sophisticated algorithms may combine facially neutral data points and treat them as proxies for immutable characteristics such as race or gender, thereby circumventing existing non-discrimination laws and systematically denying credit access to certain groups. Finally, big-data tools may allow online payday lenders to target the most vulnerable consumers and lure them into debt traps*"). Italics added. Campisi, Natalie, From Inherent Racial Bias to Incorrect Data The Problems With Current Credit Scoring Models, Forbes (Feb. 26, 2021), https://www.forbes.com/advisor/creditcards/from-inherent-racial-bias-to-incorrect-data-the-problems-with-current-credit-scoring-models/; [https://perma.cc/EWA4-CS8E] (highlighting rampant racial bias in credit scoring systems); Oyama, Rebecca, "Do Not (Re)Enter: the Rise of Criminal Background Tenant Screening as a Violation of the Fair Housing Act", *Michigan Journal of Race and Law*, Volume 15, 2009, pp. 181, 184–93 (discussing a broad range of historical/criminal accounts as a way to screen undesirable tenants, such as Blacks and Latinos).

[1649] Xi Chen, "Algorithmic proxy discrimination and its regulations", *cit.*, pp. 1–13.

[1650] For an on-point breakdown of the distinct levels of opacity arising out of machine learning algorithms: Selbst, Andrew D./Barocas, Solon, "The Intuitive Appeal of Explainable Machines", *Fordham Law Review*, Volume 87, 2018, pp. 1085, 1089–99 (holding that there are plenty reasons for the insurer's ignorance. To begin with, the algorithm entails specialized knowledge to understand. That is, the insurer's employees may lack sufficient knowledge to understand the rationale behind the reasons in view of which the algorithm is producing prices for different customers—personalized pricing. Lastly, even if the insurer himself comprehends how the model operates, it may nonetheless lack expertise to comprehend why it operates the way it does. For that reason, the explainability of machines is a vital, but rather elusive, task. Thence, the famed authors deem it as the "nonintuitive" nature of algorithms. For purposes here, the insurer himself might indeed understand that its Artificial Intelligence-embedded technology formulates higher prices for those who actually access the website at hand, but may fail to come to terms with the fact that the explanation for this fact arises from the website's capacity to proxy for genetic information). See also: Scherer, Matthew U. Scherer, "Regulating Artificial Intelligence Systems: Risks, Challenges, Competencies, and Strategies", *Harvard Journal of Law and Technology*, Volume 29, 2016, pp. 353–369 (frames the crippling problem of opacity as "the possibility that the inner workings of an AI system may be kept secret and may not be susceptible to reverse engineering").

a cluster of apparently harmless proxies to disproportionately target[1651] members of racialized communities.

§§ In an era propelled by more intelligent algorithms and gargantuan/behemoth data generation,[1652] it takes scarce imagination to foresee the ubiquity and ineluctability of the algorithm discrimination caused by such proxies.[1653]

§§ More importantly, machine learning algorithms[1654] have a black-box nature[1655] and are therefore bereft of a much-needed transparency.[1656] That is, any shiver

[1651] Xi Chen, "Algorithmic proxy discrimination and its regulations", *cit.*, pp. 1–13.

[1652] See: Wonyoung, So, "Which Information Matters? Measuring Landlord Assessment of Tenant Screening Reports", *Housing Policy Debate*, Volume 33, n. ° 6, 2023, pp. 1484–1510 (1501–1502) ("*Algorithmic scoring using criminal records is problematic because training data—a data set that is used to train a machine learning model—is inaccurate and the outcome variable ("desirable tenants") is unclear. For instance, the tenant screening company RealPage produces 11,000 reports using "abbreviated" criminal records, which are cheaper to acquire than full criminal records but do not include details of the resolution* (Kirchner & Goldstein, 2020). *An inaccurate model is highly likely to result from tenant screening services using these kinds of abbreviated data, given that it is important to include the final resolution of criminal justice procedures for proper assessment. Moreover, it would be challenging to set an outcome variable for developing this kind of algorithm because it is hard to project a certain criminal outcome into "good" tenant behaviors*"). Italics added.

[1653] Xi Chen, "Algorithmic proxy discrimination and its regulations", *cit.*, pp. 1–13.

[1654] See: Murphy, Kevin P., *Machine Learning: A Probabilistic Perspective (Adaptive Computation and Machine Learning series).* Massachusetts: The MIT Press, 2012, pp. 1–1104 (states avowedly that "machine Learning attempts to combine deductive, inductive, and abductive reasoning to make person-like reasoning in AI Entities possible. Machine-learning AI Entities initially learn in the same way a human child learns. First, they notice details and patterns in shapes, sounds, and behaviors; then put them together to distinguish one person from another, or a dog from a cat. Eventually, the AI can recognize and identify" common objects). See also: Hutto-Schultz, Jess, "Dicitur Ex Machina: Artificial Intelligence and the Hearsay Rule", *George Mason Law Review*, Volume 27, Issue 2, 2020, pp. 684–718 (689). See: Chollet, François, *Deep Learning with Python.* Shelter Island, Nova Iorque: Manning, 2018, pp. 1–384 (passim). *Deep Learning* stands as a byproduct of *Machine Learning. Machine Learning*, a subset of Artificial Intelligence, unfolds itself in *Deep Learning*, which "involves computer algorithms that have the ability to "learn" or improve in performance over time on some task". See also: Surden, Harry, "Machine Learning and Law", *Washington Law Review*, Volume 89, 2015, pp. 87 and ff. See also: Barocas, Solon/Selbst, Andrew, "Big Data's Disparate Impact", *California Law Review*, Volume 104, pp. 2016, pp. 671–678 ("in particular, by exposing so-called 'machine learning' algorithms to examples of the cases of interest (previously identified instances of fraud, spam, default, and poor health), *the algorithm 'learns' which related attributes or activities can serve as potential proxies for those qualities or outcomes of interest*"). Italics added.

[1655] See: Part V, Chap. 5, Sect. 5.1.7.2 of this book (on law number two to control algorithmic decision-making, which mandates that black box models must not be entrusted with the task of making high stake decisions—v.g. health and freedom). See also: Havard, Cassandra Jones, "On The Take": The Black Box of Credit Scoring and Mortgage Discrimination", *Boston University Public Interest Law Journal*, Volume 20, 2011, pp. 241–247 (highlighting that credit scoring if unchecked is an intrinsic, encroached, deep-rooted form of racial discrimination akin to mortgage redlining); Watcher, S./Mittelstadt, B./Russell, C., "Counterfactual explanations without opening the black box: automated decisions and the GDPR", *Harvard Journal of Law & Technology*, Volume 1, 2018, passim. See also: Pasquale, Frank, *The Black Box Society: The Secret Algorithms that Control Money and Information.* Cambridge, Massachusetts: Harvard University Press, 2015, 1–320 (pp. 8–10 and passim) (noting that biased algorithms, which have underlying discrimination

knowledge about their inner workings is utterly unavailable, inaccessible, unfindable, ungraspable, or incomprehensible, thereby rendering proxy discrimination extremely hard to pinpoint.[1657] Let alone explain.[1658]

§§ To add to our woes, because ancient antidiscrimination strategies, such as blocking clusters of data or disparate impact liability,[1659] are privy to a human decision-making model,[1660] they accordingly fall short of adroitly regulating proxy discrimination catalysed by algorithms.[1661] It should not therefore come as a bewildering surprise that ancient antidiscrimination legal frameworks are currently enduring a string of withering attacks to the sustainability of their core concepts.[1662]

§§ Whilst there is in-depth research on algorithmic discrimination and algorithmic fairness across various disciplines—it is important to note that there have been rapid strides in the realm of explainable[1663] artificial intelligence (XAI)[1664]—,[1665] very few pieces of academic research have deftly addressed the sizzling hot topic of proxy

---

problems, contribute exponentially to further social biases. His most intriguing claim is that such biased algorithms have been incorporated/etched in the bulk of the corporations' informatic system, to the detriment of human kind in an overarching sense);

1656 Deeks, Ahsley, "Secret Reason-Giving", *Yale Law Journal*, Volume 129, 2019, passim; Katyal, Sonia K, "The Paradox of Source Code Secrecy", *Cornell Law Review*, Volume 104, 2019, pp. 1183–1236 Rudin, Cynthia/Wang, Caroline/Coker, Beau, "The Age of Secrecy and Unfairness in Recidivism Prediction", *Harvard Data Science Review*, Issue 2.1. Winter 2020, 2020, passim; Wexler, Rebecca, "Life, Liberty, and Trade Secrets: Intellectual Property in the Criminal Justice System", *Stanford Law Review*, Volume 70, 2018, pp. 1343 and ff; Okidegbe, Ngozi, "The Democratizing Potential of Algorithms?", *Connecticut Law Review*, Volume 54, 2021, passim.

1657 Xi Chen, "Algorithmic proxy discrimination and its regulations", *cit.*, pp. 1–13.

1658 Adadi, Amina/Berrada, Mohammed, "Peeking Inside the Black-Box: A Survey on Explainable Artificial Intelligence (XAI), *Institute of Electrical and Electronics Engineers*, Volume 6, 2018, passim; Edwards, Lilian/Veale, Michael, "Slave to the Algorithm? Why a "Right to an Explanation" is Probably not the Remedy You are Looking for", *Duke Law and Technology Review*, Volume 16, 2018, pp. 18–67 (pondering whether and to what extent XAI will come in handy because citizens are woefully ill-prepared to "make use of the kind of algorithmic explanations they are likely to be offered"); Miller, Tim, "Explanations in Artificial Intelligence: Insights from Social Sciences", *Artificial Intelligence*, Volume 267, 2019, pp. 1–38.

1659 Xi Chen, "Algorithmic proxy discrimination and its regulations", *cit.*, pp. 1–13.

1660 Xi Chen, "Algorithmic proxy discrimination and its regulations", *cit.*, pp. 1–13.

1661 Xi Chen, "Algorithmic proxy discrimination and its regulations", *cit.*, pp. 1–13.

1662 Xi Chen, "Algorithmic proxy discrimination and its regulations", *cit.*, pp. 1–13.

1663 See: Samek, Wojciech/Müller, Klaus-Robert, "Explainable AI: interpreting, explaining and visualizing deep learning", *Towards Explainable Artificial Intelligence*, Samek, Wojciech/Montavon, Grégoire/Vedaldi, Andrea/Hansen, Lars Kai/ Müller, Klaus-Robert (Editors). Heidelberg/Berlin/New York: Springer, 2019, pp. 5–22 ("*in recent years, machine learning (ML) has become a key enabling technology for the sciences and industry.* Especially through improvements in methodology, the availability of large databases and increased computational power, *today's ML algorithms are able to achieve excellent performance (at times even exceeding the human level) on an increasing number of complex tasks. Deep learning models are at the forefront of this development. However, due to their nested non-linear structure, these powerful models have been generally considered "black boxes", not providing any information about what exactly makes them arrive at their predictions.* Since in many applications, e.g., in the medical domain, *such lack of transparency may be not acceptable, the development of methods for visualizing, explaining and interpreting deep learning models has recently attracted increasing attention. This introductory*

discrimination[1666] and the extent to which further compounds disparate treatment on racialized communities. This book aims to bridge that gap.

paper presents recent developments and applications in this field and makes a plea for a wider use of explainable learning algorithms in practice"). Italics added. See: Part V, Chap. 5, Sects. 5.1.7–5.1.7.5 of this book (on the five laws to control algorithmic decision-making). See: Part V, Chap. 5, Sects. 5.1.8–5.1.8.5 of this book (on the five laws to interpret algorithmic decision-making). See: Part V, Chap. 5, Sects. 5.1.2–5.1.6.2.1 of this book (on the thing-centred algorithmic decision-making propelled by a *Controllable* and *Interpretable* Machine Learning that weeds out *Algorithmic Dictatorship* and secures *Algorithmic Common Good*. It is worth recalling that the **thing-centred algorithmic decision-making** seeks to unwind the perils arising out of the lack of theoretical underpinnings facing the **human-centred algorithmic decision-making**, as extensively fleshed out Part III, Chap. 3, Sects. 3.1.4.3–3.1.4.4 of this book). See: Part V, Chap. 5, Sect. 5.1.7.5 of this book (on Algorithmic Common Good, with a sharper focus on the dire need of algorithmic auditing, undertaken by external auditors that must be given full access to the dataset used to train the running models).

[1664] See: Deeks, Ahsley, "The Judicial Demand for Explainable Artificial Intelligence", *Columbia Law Review*, Volume 119, 2019, pp. 1829 and ff and passim. See: Hacker, Phillip/Passoth, Jan-Hendrick, "Varieties of AI Explanations under the Law: From the GDPR to the AIA, and Beyond", *XxAI Beyond Explainable AI, International Workshop on Extending Explainable AI Beyond Deep Models and Classifiers*. Berlin/New York/Singapore/Beijing: Springer, 2021, pp. 343–373 ("the quest to explain the output of artificial intelligence systems has clearly moved from a mere technical to a highly legally and politically relevant endeavor. In this paper, we provide an overview of legal obligations to explain AI and evaluate current policy proposals. In this, we distinguish between different functional varieties of AI explanations—such as multiple forms of enabling, technical and protective transparency—and show how different legal areas engage with and mandate such different types of explanations to varying degrees. Starting with the rights-enabling framework of the GDPR, we proceed to uncover technical and protective forms of explanations owed under contract, tort and banking law. Moreover, we discuss what the recent EU proposal for an Artificial Intelligence Act means for explainable AI, and review the proposal's strengths and limitations in this respect. Finally, from a policy perspective, we advocate for moving beyond mere explainability towards a more encompassing framework for trustworthy and responsible AI that includes actionable explanations, values-in-design and co-design methodologies, interactions with algorithmic fairness, and quality benchmarking").

[1665] Xi Chen, "Algorithmic proxy discrimination and its regulations", *cit.*, pp. 1–13.

[1666] See: Part IV, This chapter, Sect. 4.1.6.3 of this book (on proxy discrimination). See also: Prince, Anya E. R./Schwarcz, Daniel, "Proxy Discrimination in the Age of Artificial Intelligence and Big Data", *Iowa Law Review*, Volume 105, 1257, 1279–81 (2020) ("[P]roxy discrimination will tend to occur when a suspect variable is predictive of a desired outcome only because it proxies for another, quantifiable and potentially available, *variable that causes the desired outcome but that is not included in the AI's training data*"). Italics added.

4.1.6.1 Machine Learning Algorithms and Deep Neural Networks that Propel Forward the Creation of Optimal Predictive Rules

§§ Machine learning algorithms[1667] have been subject to academic hype.[1668] Note, though, that machine learning algorithms carry both danger[1669] and promise.[1670] Relatedly, one trenchant criticism that is often levelled up against algorithmic decision-making[1671] is its opacity[1672] coupled with its underlying capacity to produce

---

[1667] Hayes, Paul/van de Poel, Ibo/Steen, Marc, "Algorithms and Values in Justice and Security", *AI & Society*, 2020, pp. 533 and ff and passim.

[1668] See: Murphy, Kevin P., *Machine Learning: A Probabilistic Perspective (Adaptive Computation and Machine Learning series)*. Massachusetts: The MIT Press, 2012, pp. 1–1104 (states avowedly that "machine Learning attempts to combine deductive, inductive, and abductive reasoning to make person-like reasoning in AI Entities possible. Machine-learning AI Entities initially learn in the same way a human child learns. First, they notice details and patterns in shapes, sounds, and behaviors; then put them together to distinguish one person from another, or a dog from a cat. Eventually, the AI can recognize and identify" common objects). See also: Hutto-Schultz, Jess, "Dicitur Ex Machina: Artificial Intelligence and the Hearsay Rule", *George Mason Law Review*, Volume 27, Issue 2, 2020, pp. 684–718 (689). See: Chollet, François, *Deep Learning with Python*. Shelter Island, Nova Iorque: Manning, 2018, pp. 1–384 (passim). *Deep Learning* stands as a byproduct of *Machine Learning. Machine Learning*, a subset of Artificial Intelligence, unfolds itself in *Deep Learning*, which "involves computer algorithms that have the ability to "learn" or improve in performance over time on some task". See also: Surden, Harry, "Machine Learning and Law", *Washington Law Review*, Volume 89, 2015, pp. 87 and ff. See also: Barocas, Solon/Selbst, Andrew, "Big Data's Disparate Impact", *California Law Review*, Volume 104, pp. 2016, pp. 671–678 ("in particular, by exposing so-called 'machine learning' algorithms to examples of the cases of interest (previously identified instances of fraud, spam, default, and poor health), *the algorithm 'learns' which related attributes or activities can serve as potential proxies for those qualities or outcomes of interest*"). Italics added.

[1669] Hu, Margaret, "From the National Surveillance State to the Cybersurveillance State", *The Annual Review of Law and Social Science*, Volume 13, 2017, p. 169 ("*the potential for mass surveillance is part of the problematic nature of biometric credentialing and identification practices. Like most digital data, biometric identification data are not restricted to the purpose for which they were originally collected. Biometric data can be repurposed for secondary uses, such as identification of potential suspects or victims through real-time analytics, assessment of threats of terrorism, tactical decisionmaking, or behavioral and genetic research* (Duster 2003). *Beyond secondary—and tertiary, quaternary, and quinary—uses, biometric data become a part of population-wide risk assessments that incorporate bureaucratized surveillance into governing decisions, policing, and threat assessments. Through big data tools, precrime governance models are increasingly reflected in collect-it-all cybersurveillance systems.* In these systems, *biometric data is a surveillance axis that can be used to track, identify, and isolate suspicious persons, digital data, or devices*"). Italics added.

[1670] Machine learning algorithms are also fundamentally reshaping the field of financial advice, thereby offering personalized AI assistants that promise to ameliorate consumer decision-making. See: Loo, Rory Van, "Digital Market Perfection", *Michigan Law Review*, 2019, pp. 815, 862–63, 878–79.

[1671] Gerdon, Frederic/Bach, Ruben L./Kern, Christoph/Kreuter, Frauke, "Social Impacts of Algorithmic Decision-Making: A Research Agenda for the Social Science", *Big Data & Society*, Volume 9, 2022, passim.

[1672] For an on-point breakdown of the distinct levels of opacity arising out of machine learning algorithms: Selbst, Andrew D./Barocas, Solon, "The Intuitive Appeal of Explainable Machines",

both *algorithmic discrimination*[1673] and *algorithmic bias*[1674] which, taken together, hinder a sought-after *algorithmic fairness*.[1675] Worse still, algorithms boast the potential to perpetuate matrixial disadvantages[1676] with which racial minorities have been tussling for a long-haul.[1677]

§§ Which prompts the vexing question: what are algorithms to begin with? Put it coarsely, «algorithms are encoded procedures for solving a problem by transforming input data into a desired output.»[1678] Algorithms can be skeletally broken down

---

Fordham Law Review, Volume 87, 2018, pp. 1085, 1089–99 (holding that there are plenty reasons for the insurer's ignorance. To begin with, the algorithm entails specialized knowledge to understand. That is, the insurer's employees may lack sufficient knowledge to understand the rationale behind the reasons in view of which the algorithm is producing prices for different customers—personalized pricing. Lastly, even if the insurer himself comprehends how the model operates, it may nonetheless lack expertise to comprehend why it operates the way it does. For that reason, the explainability of machines is a vital, but rather elusive, task. Thence, the famed authors deem it as the "nonintuitive" nature of algorithms. For purposes here, the insurer himself might indeed understand that its Artificial Intelligence-embedded technology formulates higher prices for those who actually access the website at hand, but may fail to come to terms with the fact that the explanation for this fact arises from the website's capacity to proxy for genetic information). See also: Scherer, Matthew U. Scherer, "Regulating Artificial Intelligence Systems: Risks, Challenges, Competencies, and Strategies", *Harvard Journal of Law and Technology*, Volume 29, 2016, pp. 353–369 (frames the crippling problem of opacity as "the possibility that the inner workings of an AI system may be kept secret and may not be susceptible to reverse engineering").

1673 Cofone, Ignacio N., "Algorithmic Discrimination is an Information Problem", *Hastings Law Journal*, Volume 70, 2019, passim.

1674 Johnson, Gabbrielle M., "Algorithmic Bias: On the Implicit Biases of Social Technology", *Synthese*, 2021, passim.

1675 Hellman, Deborah, "Measuring Algorithmic Fairness", *Virginia Law Review*, Volume 106, 2020, pp. 811 and ff and passim.

1676 See: Barocas, Solon/Selbst, Andrew, "Big Data's Disparate Impact", *California Law Review*, Volume 104, pp. 2016, p. 691 (highlighting the worrisome, and gruesome, issue of "structural disadvantage" with which racialized communities have been tussling for centuries). See also: Powell, Richard/Porter, Jeremy, "Redlining, Concentrated Disadvantage and Crime: The Effects of Discriminatory Government Policies on Violent Crime", *American Journal of Criminal Justice*, Volume 48, 2023, pp. 1132–1156 ("*Redlining and other discriminatory government policies enacted during the first half of the Twentieth Century have had long-lasting negative effects on neighborhoods, especially those inhabited by people of color. This study attempts to link the practice of redlining to current-day indicators of neighborhood concentrated disadvantage and violent crime using spatio-temporal data from Chicago* (…) *In addition, it seeks to determine whether redlining was associated with violent crime, and if that association was mediated by redlining's effect on concentrated disadvantage. The results indicate that redlining was associated with increases in both concentrated disadvantage and violent crime, and that redlining's relationship with violent crime was, indeed, partially mediated by its relationship with concentrated disadvantage*"). Italics added. See also: Gandy, Oscar H., *Coming to Terms with Chance: Engaging Rational Discrimination and Cumulative Disadvantage*, Farnham, UK: Ashgate Publishing, 2009.

1677 O'Neil, Cathy, *Weapons of Math Destruction. How Big Data Increases Inequality and Threatens Democracy*, London, Penguin Random House, 2016, passim (showing how algorithms utilized in modern societies are amenable to perpetuate racial discrimination, partially through perpetuation of social disadvantage and wealth divides).

1678 Yeung, Karen, "Algorithmic Regulation: A Critical Interrogation", *Regulation & Governance*, Volume 12, 2018, pp. 505 and ff and passim.

into two broad categories: *traditional statistical algorithms* and *machine learning algorithms.*[1679]

§§ In stark contrast with the former, which are utterly unable to operate without fine-grained instructions,[1680] such as **decision trees** or specific validation and verification mechanisms,[1681] the latter (machine learning algorithms) are fully equipped with the ability to come up with optimal predictive rules by learning without human intervention.[1682]

§§ With regard to supervised learning algorithm, for instance, after forming a batch of decision models based on training data,[1683] it can automatically ferret out a bespoke target variable (**the outcome**[1684] **of interest**)[1685] with class labels that «divide all possible values of the target variable into mutually exclusive categories».[1686] This process is loosely labelled as data-driven learning.[1687]

1679 Xi Chen, "Algorithmic proxy discrimination and its regulations", *cit.*, pp. 1–13 (3).

1680 Krafft, Tobias D./Zweig, Katharina A./Konig, Pascal D., "How to Regulate Algorithmic Decision-Making: A Framework of Regulatory Requirements for Different Applications", *Regulation & Governance*, Volume 16, 2022, pp. 119 and ff and passim.

1681 Xi Chen, "Algorithmic proxy discrimination and its regulations", *cit.*, pp. 1–13 (3).

1682 Xi Chen, "Algorithmic proxy discrimination and its regulations", *cit.*, pp. 1–13 (3).

1683 But see: *Tech, Bias and Housing Initiative, the Promise and Perils of Residential Proptech, Year 1, Research Summary Report, April 2023, TechEquity Collaborative*, p. 11, available at: https://techequity.us/wp-content/uploads/2023/04/TBHI-Y1-Research-Summary-Report.pdf (28.11.2024). ("*Once bad data enters the analysis of one factor, it gets baked into the subsequent process, multiplying the effect that one disadvantageous data point can have on someone's overall housing determination*"). Italics added. See: Part IV, This chapter, Sects. 4.1.4–4.1.4.2.3 of this book. But see also: *Tech, Bias and Housing Initiative, the Promise and Perils of Residential Proptech, Year 1, Research Summary Report, April 2023, TechEquity Collaborative*, p. 11, available at: https://techequity.us/wp-content/uploads/2023/04/TBHI-Y1-Research-Summary-Report.pdf (28.11.2024). ("And while we know that the *data is predictive, meaning it has little to do with demonstrated behavior of the applicant themself, we do not know exactly where companies get their data*"). Italics added. See: Part IV, This chapter, Sects. 4.1.4–4.1.4.2.3 of this book.

1684 But see: Hurley, Mikella/Adebayo, Julius, "Credit Scoring in the Era of Big Data", *Yale Journal of Law and Technology*, Volume 18, 2016, p. 149 ("*these tools may furthermore obscure discriminatory and subjective lending policies behind a single "objective" score* (…) *sophisticated algorithms may combine facially neutral data points and treat them as proxies for immutable characteristics such as race or gender, thereby circumventing existing non-discrimination laws and systematically denying credit access to certain groups. Finally, big-data tools may allow online payday lenders to target the most vulnerable consumers and lure them into debt traps*"). Italics added. See also: Farina, M./Lavazza, A., *Philosophy, expertise, and the myth of* neutrality, Routledge Studies in Contemporary Philosophy, London, Routledge, 2024.

1685 Xi Chen, "Algorithmic proxy discrimination and its regulations", *cit.*, pp. 1–13 (3).

1686 Barocas, Solon/Selbst, Andrew, "Big Data's Disparate Impact", *California Law Review*, Volume 104, 2016, pp. 678 and ff and passim.

1687 Clough, D. R., & Wu, A., "Artificial intelligence, data-driven learning, and the decentralized structure of platform ecosystems", *Academy of Management Review*, Volume 47, Issue 1, 2022, pp. 184–189 and passim; Gregory, R. W., Henfridsson, O., Kaganer, E., & Kyriakou, H., "The role of artificial intelligence and data network effects for creating user value", *Academy of Management Review*, Volume 46, Issue 3, 2021, pp. 534–551.

§§ Whilst different categories of machine learning algorithms—such as supervised learning,[1688] unsupervised learning, or reinforcement learning[1689]—differ greatly in the propelling force behind, and the overriding goal underpinning, their decision-making[1690] and the formation of optimal predictive rules, they have ties of kindred insofar their decision rules are created by the algorithms themselves.[1691]

§§ None of this is to suggest, nor is to say, that the self-morphing aptness of machine learning algorithms[1692] means that they are beyond humans 'control[1693] and grasp.[1694] Rather, it means that[1695] «human intervention is limited to selecting features for the training data and attaching labels to the output data».[1696]

§§ Tellingly, **machine learning algorithms** are fully equipped with the ability to learn without being explicitly programmed to do so.[1697] Relatedly, machine learning

---

[1688] See: Friston, K. J., Da Costa, L., Tschantz, A., Kiefer, A., Salvatori, T., Neacsu, V., & Buckley, C. L. "Supervised structure learning", *arXiv preprint arXiv:2311.10300*, 2023. See also: Friedman, J. H., & Popescu, B. E., "Predictive learning via rule ensembles", *Annals of Applied Statistics*, Volume 2, Issue 3, pp. 2008, pp. 916–954; Friston, K., & Kiebel, S., "Predictive coding under the free-energy principle", *Philosophical Transactions of the Royal Society B: Biological Sciences*, 364 (1521), 2009, pp. 1211–1221.

[1689] "The Stochastic Neural Analog Reinforcement Calculator (SNARC) *embodied a type of neural network that is designed to learn from experience and improve its performance through a process of trial and error* (similar to *reinforcement learning*). *This machine was well suited for problems that involved sequential decision-making and made use of prior experience, for example — navigating out of a maze. In fact this is the problem Minsky had set out to solve.* The original SNARC system consisted of a set of 40 artificial neurons (specifically *Hebb synapses*) that are connected to each other in a network. Each neuron receives input from other neurons and produces an output that is passed on to other neurons in the network. The network is trained by adjusting the strengths of the connections between neurons based on the outcomes of previous trials. *The training of this network was manually done by the operator who would provide feedback to the machine when it produced the right outcome.*" Italics added. See: https://zahid-parvez.medium.com/history-of-ai-the-first-neural-network-computer-marvin-minsky-231c8bd58409 (access: 02.01.2025). See: Part II, Chap. 2, Sect. 2.1.1 of this book (on reinforcement machine learning created by Marvin Lee Minsky).

[1690] Murphy, Kevin Patrick, *Machine Learning: A Probabilistic Perspective*, Massachusetts, MIT Press, 2012, pp. 2–24.

[1691] Xi Chen, "Algorithmic proxy discrimination and its regulations", *cit.*, pp. 1 13 (3).

[1692] But see: *Machine-learning algorithms "are capable of making intuitive decisions based in newly learned information, much like humans.* The new wave of AI developments will generate powerful AI that is capable of improvising itself, *perhaps even by rewriting its own algorithms, advancing its intelligence beyond that of humans*". Italics added. See: Hutto-Schultz, Jess, "Dicitur Ex Machina: Artificial Intelligence and the Hearsay Rule", *George Mason Law Review*, Volume 27, n. ° 2, 2020, pp. 684–718 (684).

[1693] See: Part V, Chap. 5, Sects. 5.1.2–5.1.6.2.1 of this book (on the thing-centred algorithmic decision-making propelled by a *Controllable* and *Interpretable* Machine Learning that weeds out *Algorithmic Dictatorship* and secures *Algorithmic Common Good*).

[1694] Xi Chen, "Algorithmic proxy discrimination and its regulations", *cit.*, pp. 1–13 (3).

[1695] Xi Chen, "Algorithmic proxy discrimination and its regulations", *cit.*, pp. 1–13 (3).

[1696] Cofone, Ignacio N., "Algorithmic Discrimination is an Information Problem", *Hastings Law Journal*, Volume 70, 2019, p. 1395.

[1697] Xi Chen, "Algorithmic proxy discrimination and its regulations", *cit.*, pp. 1–13 (3).

algorithms boast the ability to self-create their **optimal predictive rules**[1698] accompanying the changes in the training data,[1699] whereas **conventional statistical algorithms** do not have such self-morphing capacity. That is, machine learning algorithms have an exceedingly higher degree of intelligence compared to that of conventional statistical algorithms.[1700]

§§ In addition to that, different types of machine learning algorithms[1701] have different levels of intelligence.[1702] For instance, deep neural networks[1703] still need to learn from the batches of training data[1704] to create[1705] **optimal predictive rules**.[1706]

§§ Notwithstanding, unlike other types of machine learning algorithms that need to single out features with the invaluable assistance of human beings, **deep neural networks** are equipped with a self-evolving ability which, in turn, gives them the

---

[1698] *Machine-learning algorithms "are capable of making intuitive decisions based in newly learned information, much like humans.* The new wave of AI developments will generate powerful AI that is capable of improvising itself, *perhaps even by rewriting its own algorithms, advancing its intelligence beyond that of humans*". Italics added. See: Hutto-Schultz, Jess, "Dicitur Ex Machina: Artificial Intelligence and the Hearsay Rule", *George Mason Law Review*, Volume 27, n. ° 2, 2020, pp. 684–718 (684).

[1699] Xi Chen, "Algorithmic proxy discrimination and its regulations", *cit.*, pp. 1–13 (3).

[1700] Xi Chen, "Algorithmic proxy discrimination and its regulations", *cit.*, pp. 1–13 (3).

[1701] See: Murphy, Kevin P., *Machine Learning: A Probabilistic Perspective (Adaptive Computation and Machine Learning series).* Massachusetts: The MIT Press, 2012, pp. 1–1104 (states avowedly that "machine Learning attempts to combine deductive, inductive, and abductive reasoning to make person-like reasoning in AI Entities possible. Machine-learning AI Entities initially learn in the same way a human child learns. First, they notice details and patterns in shapes, sounds, and behaviors; then put them together to distinguish one person from another, or a dog from a cat. Eventually, the AI can recognize and identify" common objects).

[1702] Xi Chen, "Algorithmic proxy discrimination and its regulations", *cit.*, pp. 1–13 (3).

[1703] See: Aggarwal, C. C., *Neural networks and deep learning*, Heidelberg, Springer, 2018, passim; Agrawal, A., Gans, J., & Goldfarb, A., "Prediction machines (updated and expanded): The simple economics of artificial intelligence", *Harvard Business Review Press*, 2022; Agrawal, A., Gans, J., & Goldfarb, A., "Power and prediction: The disruptive economics of artificial intelligence", *Harvard Business Review Press*, 2022; Bengio, Y., Hinton, G., Yao, A., Song, D., Abbeel, P., Harari, Y. N., Hadfield, G., Russell, S., Kahneman, D., & Mindermann, S., *Managing ai risks in an era of rapid progress*, arXiv preprint arXiv:2310.17688, 2023 (on neural networks and deep learning that operate in the age of Artificial Intelligence-embedded technologies).

[1704] Xi Chen, "Algorithmic proxy discrimination and its regulations", *cit.*, pp. 1–13 (3).

[1705] See: Chollet, François, *Deep Learning with Python.* Shelter Island, Nova Iorque: Manning, 2018, pp. 1–384 (passim). *Deep Learning* stands as a byproduct of *Machine Learning. Machine Learning*, a subset of Artificial Intelligence, unfolds itself in *Deep Learning*, which "involves computer algorithms that have the ability to "learn" or improve in performance over time on some task". See also: Surden, Harry, "Machine Learning and Law", *Washington Law Review*, Volume 89, 2015, pp. 87 and ff. See also: Barocas, Solon/Selbst, Andrew, "Big Data's Disparate Impact", *California Law Review*, Volume 104, pp. 2016, pp. 671–678 ("in particular, by exposing so-called 'machine learning' algorithms to examples of the cases of interest (previously identified instances of fraud, spam, default, and poor health), *the algorithm 'learns' which related attributes or activities can serve as potential proxies for those qualities or outcomes of interest*"). Italics added.

[1706] But see: Part V, Chap. 5, Sect. 5.1.7.2 of this book (on law number two to control algorithmic decision-making, which mandates that black box models must not be entrusted with the task of making high stake decisions—v.g. health and freedom).

power to learn optimal parameter settings independently. Put differently, they have the **ability to learn how to learn,**[1707] thereby attaining «great power and flexibility by representing the world as a nested hierarchy of concepts».[1708]

§§ All in all, less human participation in the human–machine loop equals to an exceedingly high intelligent algorithm.[1709] Insofar humans are tasked with the duty to completely set the underlying operational logic of a **traditional statistical algorithm (e.g. a decision tree)**, the latter is unable to cause algorithmic proxy discrimination on its own.[1710] On the flip side, only machine learning algorithms can catalyse algorithmic proxy discrimination.

§§ With this context in place, regulating algorithmic proxy discrimination lends itself to a rather difficult task to accomplish indeed.[1711] That alone merits our undivided attention[1712] throughout the next sections.

[1707] Xi Chen, "Algorithmic proxy discrimination and its regulations", *cit.*, pp. 1–13 (3).

[1708] See: Goodfellow, Ian/Bengio, Youshua/Courville, Aaron, *Deep Learning (Adaptive Computation and Machine Learning Series)*, Massachusetts, MIT Press 2016, 2016, pp. 1–800 (8) ("*Deep learning is a form of machine learning that enables computers to learn from experience and understand the world in terms of a hierarchy of concepts. Because the computer gathers knowledge from experience, there is no need for a human computer operator to formally specify all the knowledge that the computer needs. The hierarchy of concepts allows the computer to learn complicated concepts by building them out of simpler ones; a graph of these hierarchies would be many layers deep. This book introduces a broad range of topics in deep learning.* The text offers mathematical and conceptual background, covering relevant concepts in linear algebra, probability theory and information theory, numerical computation, and machine learning. It describes deep learning techniques used by practitioners in industry, including deep feedforward networks, regularization, optimization algorithms, convolutional networks, sequence modeling, and practical methodology; and it surveys such applications as natural language processing, speech recognition, computer vision, online recommendation systems, bioinformatics, and videogames. Finally, the book offers research perspectives, covering such theoretical topics as linear factor models, autoencoders, representation learning, structured probabilistic models, Monte Carlo methods, the partition function, approximate inference, and deep generative models"). Italics added.

[1709] Xi Chen, "Algorithmic proxy discrimination and its regulations", *cit.*, pp. 1–13 (3).

[1710] Xi Chen, "Algorithmic proxy discrimination and its regulations", *cit.*, pp. 1–13 (3).

[1711] See on algorithmic discrimination: Kleinberg, Jon, et al., "Discrimination in the Age of Algorithms", *Journal of Legal Analysis*, 2018, pp. 114–174; See: Kleinberg, Jon, et al., "Algorithms as Discrimination Detectors", *Proceeds of the National Academy of Science*, Volume 117, 2020, pp. 30096–30110; Griemmelmann, James/Westreich, Daniel, "Incomprehensible Discrimination ", *California Law Review Online*, Volume 7, 2018, pp. 164–171; Xiang, Alice, "Reconciling Legal and Technical Approaches to Algorithmic Bias", *Tennessee Law Review*, Volume 88, 2021, passim; Karnow, Curtis E. A., "The Opinion of Machines", *The Cambridge Handbook of the Law of Algorithms*, Bartfield, Woodrow (Editor), Cambridge, United Kingdom: Cambridge University Press, 2021, pp. 15 and ff and passim; Strandburg, Katherine J., "Rulemaking and Inscrutable Decision Tools", *Columbia Law Review*, Volume 119, 2019, passim.

[1712] Xi Chen, "Algorithmic proxy discrimination and its regulations", *cit.*, pp. 1–13 (3).

4.1.6.2 Algorithmic Proxy Discrimination (APD): How «Abundant Proxy Relations», «Complex Proxy Relations» and «Opaque Proxy Relations» (Xi Chen) Determine the Course of Our Lives

§§ The accountability of machine learning algorithms has spurred heated discussions[1713] with «algorithmic bias»[1714] looming large in the analysis. Note, though, that it is extremely difficult to pick out a central or focal point of such a complex and extensive phenomenon.[1715] It bears mentioning, however, that such a pressing question should not be distilled in that way. The mistake, thus, lies in framing this specific topic in an unintegrated manner.

§§ Compellingly, algorithmic proxy discrimination bears the seal of integration, as opposed to the hallmark of isolation. To put in bluntly, algorithmic proxy discrimination forms part of a broader technological apparatus (i.e. machine learning algorithms) insofar the latter is the linchpin of the former.

§§ Algorithmic proxy discrimination should be accordingly hold to a wider account. From this derives the assertion according to which algorithmic proxy discrimination boasts characteristics that sharply/sprucely distinguish them from human decision-making.[1716] No surprise flows from the fact that algorithmic proxy discrimination and human decision-making do not overlap, nor do they straddle.

[1713] See: Katyal, Sonia, "Private Accountability in the Age of Artificial Intelligence", *UCLA Law Review*, Volume 66, 2019, pp. 54–99. Williams, Rebecca, "Accountable Algorithms: Adopting the Public Law Toolbox Outside the Realm of Public Law", *Current Legal Problems*, Vol. 75, 2022, pp. 237–263; Williams, Rebecca, "Rethinking Administrative Law for Algorithmic Decision-Making", *Oxford Journal of Legal Studies*, Volume 42, 2021, pp. 468 e ff and passim.

[1714] Recall: Baeza-Yates, R., "Bias on the web", *Communications of the ACM*, 61 (6), June 2018, 2018, pp. 54–61 (argues that "*algorithmic bias is when the bias is not present in the input data* and is added *purely by the algorithm*"). Italics added. See also: Hajian, Sara Hajian et al., "Algorithmic Bias: From Discrimination Discovery to Fairness-aware Data Mining", *ACM SIGKDD International Conference on Knowledge Discovery and Data Mining*, Volume 22, 2125, 2016; Griemmelmann, James/Westreich, Daniel, "Incomprehensible Discrimination ", *California Law Review Online*, Volume 7, 2018, pp. 164–171; Xiang, Alice, "Reconciling Legal and Technical Approaches to Algorithmic Bias", *Tennessee Law Review*, Volume 88, 2021, passim; See: Lemley, Mark A./Casey, Bryan, "Remedies for Robots", *The University of Chicago Law Review*, Volume 86, Issue 5, 2019, pp. 1311–1396 (1376) (alerting to the perils of algorithmic bias); Chandler, Anupam, "The Racist Algorithm", *Michigan Law Review*, Volume 115, Issue 6, 2018, p. 1026 (noting that, in the terrain of racist algorithm, "the possibilities for discriminatory manipulation are legion"; Jackson, Maya C., "Artificial Intelligence and Algorithmic Bias: The Issues with Technology Reflecting History and Humans", *Journal of Business Technology Law*, Volume 16, 2021, pp. 299–316; West, Sarah Myers/Whittaker, Meredith/Crawford, Kate, *Discriminating Systems. Gender, Race and Power in AI*. New York: AI Now Institute, 2019, pp. 15 and ff and passim; Waldman, Ezra, "Privacy, Practice, and Performance", *California Law Review*, Volume 110, 2021, passim (on algorithmic bias). Italics added.

[1715] Segran, G., "The complexity of artificial intelligence", *Singapore Management University*, 2021, passim (on the elaborate and complex trappings of Artificial Intelligence).

[1716] But see: Pasquale, Frank, "A Rule of Persons, Not Machines: The Limits of Legal Automation", *George Washington Law Review*, Volume 87, 2019, passim.

4.1.6.2.1 «Abundant Proxy Relations and the Inescapability Problem» (Xi Chen)

§§ Big data inhere and permeates machine learning algorithms.[1717] Big data[1718] accordingly nurtures machine learning algorithms. The examples are both legion and quotidian. I will sketch them with criminal celerity. The examples range from online transactions, emails, images, and clickstreams to all sorts of big data gleaned by ubiquitous, multifarious, and sleepless sensors deployed («collect-it-all[1719] devices»)[1720] only to feed[1721] machine learning algorithms.[1722]

[1717] Custers, Bart, "Data Dilemmas in the Information Society: Introduction and Overview", Custers, Bart/Calders, Toon/Schermer, Bart/Zarsky, Tal (Editors), *Discrimination and Privacy in the Information Society: Data Mining and Profiling in Large Databases*, Heidelberg, Springer, 2013, pp. 3–26.

[1718] Big data that is in the limelight these days. See: Sivarajah, Uthayasnkar et al., "Critical Analysis of Big Data Challenges and Analytical Methods", *Journal of Business Research*, Volume 70, 2017, pp. 263 and ff and passim; Jetten, Lieke /Sharon, Stephen, "Selected Issues concerning the Ethical Use of Big Data Health Analytics", *Washington & Lee Law Review Online*, Volume 72, 2016, passim; Wachter, S./Mittelstadt. B., "A right to Reasonable Inferences: Re-thinking Data Protection Law in the Age of Big Data and AI", *Columbia Business Law Review*, 2019, pp. 1 and ff and passim; See in French doctrine: Ferey, Samuel, « Analyse économique du droit, big data et justice prédictive», *Archives de Philosophie du Droit*, Volume 60, 2018, pp. 68–81; Završnik, A. "Algorithmic justice: Algorithms and big data in criminal justice settings", *European Journal of Criminology*, 2019, passim; Joh, Elizabeth E., "The New Surveillance Discretion: Automated Suspicion, Big Data, and Policing." *Harvard Law and Policy Review*, 10 (1), 2016, pp. 15–42.

[1719] See: Hu, Margaret, "From the National Surveillance State to the Cybersurveillance State", *The Annual Review of Law and Social Science*, Volume 13, 2017, pp. 162–163 ("*policymakers view these technological developments, including biometric technologies, as tools with the potential to identify individuals who may pose a threat to national and homeland security and to prevent crime and terrorism. One example of technology intended for risk assessment and threat management is the post-9/11 program Total Information Awareness (TIA).* (....) *Collect-it-all efforts like TIA embody a philosophy that aspires to preventive policing. Mass data collection is construed as a tool to assess and prevent future threats (Murray 2010). In TIA and other programs tested or adopted after 9/11, biometric database screening and analysis have emerged as a preferred method for tracking, identifying, and establishing identity-based inferences in counterterrorism*"). Italics added. See also: Ball, Kirstie, and Frank Webster (Eds.), *The Intensification of Surveillance: Crime, Terrorism & Warfare in the Information Age*, London, UK: Pluto Press, 2007; Guzik, Keith, "Discrimination by Design: Predictive Data Mining as Security Practice in the United States' 'War on Terrorism.'", *Surveillance and Society*, 7 (1), 2009, pp. 1–17.

[1720] Hu, Margaret, "From the National Surveillance State to the Cybersurveillance State", *The Annual Review of Law and Social Science*, Volume 13, 2017, p. 168 ("*as a result, the Cybersurveillance State, as a technological successor to the National Surveillance State, will execute bureaucratized biometric cybersurveillance in ways that are largely invisible and that appear routinized when technologically embedded within biometric identification technologies harnessed by the Administrative State. The normalization of day-to-day cybersurveillance will be achieved largely through governing functions that appear purely administrative (e.g., identity assessments for the granting of welfare, rights, privileges, and governing incentives).* Because of the routinized and administrative nature of the government-led big data program or *data surveillance (dataveillance) program, contemporary cybersurveillance is likely to be viewed as justified under crime, immigration control, and counterterrorism policy rationales*"). Italics added.

§§ As captioned above, big data[1723] therefore carries dreadful dangers,[1724] undying challenges,[1725] uphill battles[1726] and unfaltering promises.[1727] Which begs the vexing question: what kind of reasons, if any, would warrant bringing such an invasive technological apparatus into being and sustaining over time, as opposed to opting for other, less invasive, forms of social ordering? For the sake of brevity, let us just say that *Algorithmic Dictatorship* is the answer you are looking for. Enough said about this.

§§ As adumbrated, machine learning algorithms evince a sturdy self-morphing and upgrade function[1728] that never ceases to amaze. Whilst it is true that law expressly prohibits machine learning algorithms from using proxies highly, or loosely, related to a plethora of sensitive traits,[1729] it is truer still that machine learning algorithms can also customize proxy relations through other marginally relevant, and

---

[1721] Xi Chen, "Algorithmic proxy discrimination and its regulations", *cit.*, pp. 1–13 (4).

[1722] Xi Chen, "Algorithmic proxy discrimination and its regulations", *cit.*, pp. 1–13 (5).

[1723] Tene, Omer/Polonetsky, Jules, "Big Data for All: Privacy and User Control in the Age of Analytics", *Northwestern Journal of Technology and Intellectual Property*, Volume 11, 2013, pp. 239 and ff and passim.

[1724] But see: Hu, Margaret, "From the National Surveillance State to the Cybersurveillance State", *The Annual Review of Law and Social Science*, Volume 13, 2017, p. 169 ("*the potential for mass surveillance is part of the problematic nature of biometric credentialing and identification practices. Like most digital data, biometric identification data are not restricted to the purpose for which they were originally collected. Biometric data can be repurposed for secondary uses, such as identification of potential suspects or victims through real-time analytics, assessment of threats of terrorism, tactical decisionmaking, or behavioral and genetic research* (Duster 2003). *Beyond secondary— and tertiary, quaternary, and quinary—uses, biometric data become a part of population-wide risk assessments that incorporate bureaucratized surveillance into governing decisions, policing, and threat assessments. Through big data tools, precrime governance models are increasingly reflected in collect-it-all cybersurveillance systems.* In these systems, *biometric data is a surveillance axis that can be used to track, identify, and isolate suspicious persons, digital data, or devices*"). Italics added.

[1725] O'Neil, Cathy, *Weapons of Math Destruction. How Big Data Increases Inequality and Threatens Democracy*, London, Penguin Random House, 2016, passim (showing how algorithms utilized in modern societies are amenable to perpetuate racial discrimination, partially through perpetuation of social disadvantage and wealth divides).

[1726] *Making Computers Explain Themselves*, MIT's Computer Science and Artificial Intelligence Laboratory (Oct. 27, 2016), 2016, https://www.csail.mit.edu/making_computers_explain%20them selves; [https://perma.cc/C97B-PGUR] (explaining the importance of grasping the complex and elaborate trappings of algorithm decision-making).

[1727] Note, though, that the foregoing examples hardly exhaust the scope and import of AI and Big Data. As captioned above, this whirlwind of forces is overhauling the consumer credit economy beyond recognition. See: Bruckner, Matthew Adam, "The Promise and Perils of Algorithmic Lenders' Use of Big Data", *Chicago-Kent Law Review*, Volume 93, 2018, pp. 3, pp. 11–15. See: Part IV, This chapter, Sects. 4.1.4–4.1.4.2.1 of this book (on mortgage redlining). See: Part IV, This chapter, Sects. 4.1.2–4.1.4.3 of this book (on algorithmic credit scoring, consumer racism and credit card redlining). See: Part IV, This chapter, Sects. 4.1.4–4.1.4.2.3 of this book (on algorithmic redlining). See: Part IV, This chapter, Sect. 4.1.4.3 of this book (on "algorithmic redliking"). See: Part IV, This chapter, Sect. 4.1.3 of this book (on algorithmic prime-lining).

[1728] Xi Chen, "Algorithmic proxy discrimination and its regulations", *cit.*, pp. 1–13 (5).

[1729] Xi Chen, "Algorithmic proxy discrimination and its regulations", *cit.*, pp. 1–13 (5).

faintly aloof, data that humans might deem utterly bootless or wholly irrelevant.[1730] Multiple sources of data may be only loosely connected with sensitive traits,[1731] and changing any one data point does not drastically overhaul algorithmic prediction.[1732]

§§ Notwithstanding, multiple sources of data, when amalgamated, conflated, or straddled, evince an exceedingly high likelihood to catalyse a tremendous impact on the outcome.[1733] For instance, when congeries of rules forbid the use of genetic data[1734] and an extremely relevant proxy—i.e., family health history—algorithms can nonetheless harvest genetic data from a plethora of proxies, ranging from website browsing history, track record of consumption,[1735] or geographical location (ZIP Code).[1736] Thereby bypassing and circumventing anti-discrimination

---

[1730] Barocas, Solon/Hardt, Moritz/Narayanan, Arvind, "Fairness in Machine Learning: Limitations and Opportunities", 2018, passim.

[1731] See: Barocas, Solon/Selbst, Andrew D., "Big Data's Disparate Impact", *California Law Review*, Volume 104, 2016, pp. 671–682 (discussing how data is often flawed, rigged, incomplete, imperfect and therefore algorithms inherit the prejudice of the original decision makers).

[1732] Xi Chen, "Algorithmic proxy discrimination and its regulations", *cit.*, pp. 1–13 (5). See also: Crawford, Kate/Schultz, Jason, "Big Data and Due Process: Toward a Framework to Redress Predictive Privacy Harms", *Boston College Law Review*, Volume 55, 2014, pp. 93, 99–101 (pinpointing pathways through which predictive analytic tools perpetuate discriminatory practices).

[1733] See: Tischbirek, Alexander, "Artificial Intelligence and Discrimination: Discriminating Against Discriminatory Systems", *Regulating Artificial Intelligence*, Wischmeyer, Thomas/Macher, Timo Rade Macher (Editors), Heidelberg, Springer, 2020, pp. 103–110.

[1734] Hellman, Deborah, "What Makes Genetic Discrimination Exceptional?", *American Journal of Law and Medicine*, Volume 29, 2003, pp. 77, 83–86; Morrow, Jeffrey S., "Insuring Fairness: The Popular Creation of Genetic Antidiscrimination", *Georgia Law Journal*, Volume 98, 2009, pp. 215, 230–32.

[1735] Note, though, that this field is currently undergoing massive changes. Long story short, the pinpointed changes are essentially reshaping the field of financial advice, thereby offering personalized Artificial Intelligence-anchored assistants that promise to ameliorate consumer decision-making. See: Loo, Rory Van, "Digital Market Perfection", *Michigan Law Review*, 2019, pp. 815, 862–63, 878–79. But see: Atkinson, Abbye, "Rethinking Credit as a Social Provision", *Stanford Law Review*, Volume 71, 2019, pp. 1093–1099 (contending that credit, which shifts consumption temporally, is only beneficial insofar income ratchets up in the forthcoming future. As of now, though, "credit is fundamentally incompatible with the entrenched intergenerational poverty that plagues low-income Americans." Id. Notably, it is crucially important to come to terms with the fact that credit is not a panacea for the great bulk of economic struggles, and concretely wage stagnation. Although credit is not befitted to all consumers at all prices, affordable credit can nonetheless play a pivotal role in the creation of wealth).

[1736] Xi Chen, "Algorithmic proxy discrimination and its regulations", *cit.*, pp. 1–13 (5).

laws whose overriding goal is to prevent indirect discrimination[1737]—or proxy discrimination[1738]—from happening in the first place.[1739]

§§ To the extent machine learning algorithms[1740] that are propelled by big data are fully equipped to test a myriad of possible combinations of variables to ascertain how to maximize their **objective function**,[1741] they can thereupon «determine the extent to which membership in a protected class is relevant to the sought-after trait,[1742] whether or not that information is an input».[1743]

§§ Against this background, big data[1744] and the inner workings of algorithms, taken together, jointly render proxy relations both teeming and prolific, which paves

[1737] See: Hellman, Deborah, "Indirect Discrimination and the Duty to Avoid Compounding Injustice", *Foundations of Indirect Discrimination Law*, Collins, Hugh/Khaitan, Tarunabh (Editors), Oxford, Hart Publishing; Reprint edition (June 25, 2020), 2020, p. 107 (Professor Deborah Hellman coined this expression to depict a decision that "exacerbates the harm caused by the prior injustice because it entrenches the harm or carries it into another domain." This book deals with the sweltering topic of indirect discrimination ("*indirect discrimination (or disparate impact) concerns the application of the same rule to everyone, even though that rule significantly disadvantages one particular group in society.* Ever since its recognition by the Supreme Court of the United States in 1971, liberal democracies around the world have grappled with the puzzle that it can sometimes be unfair and wrong to treat everyone equally. *The law's regulation of private acts that unintentionally (but disproportionately) harm vulnerable groups has remained extremely controversial, especially in the United States and the United Kingdom. In original essays in this volume, leading scholars of discrimination law from North America and Europe explore the various facets of the law on indirect discrimination, interrogating its foundations, history, legitimacy, purpose, structure, and relationship with other legal concepts.* The collection provides the first international work devoted to this vital area of the law that seeks both to prevent unfair treatment and to transform societies"). Italics added.

[1738] See: Part IV, This chapter, Sect. 4.1.6.3 of this book (on proxy discrimination).

[1739] See: Hurley, Mikella/Adebayo, Julius, "Credit Scoring in the Era of Big Data", *Yale Journal of Law and Technology*, Volume 18, 2016, p. 149 ("*these tools may furthermore obscure discriminatory and subjective lending policies behind a single "objective" score (…) sophisticated algorithms may combine facially neutral data points and treat them as proxies for immutable characteristics such as race or gender, thereby circumventing existing non-discrimination laws and systematically denying credit access to certain groups. Finally, big-data tools may allow online payday lenders to target the most vulnerable consumers and lure them into debt traps*"). Italics added.

[1740] See: Bloch-Wehba, Hannah, "Access to Algorithms", *Fordham Law Review*, Volume 88, 2020, 1264 and ff. See also: Xeniids, Raphaelle, "Tuning EU Equality Law to Algorithmic Discrimination: Three Pathways to Resilience", *Maastricht Journal of European and Comparative Law*, Volume 27, 2020, pp. 736 and ff; Frezal, Sylvestre/Barry, Laurence, "Fairness in Uncertainty: Some Limits and Misinterpretations of Actuarial Fairness", *Journal of Business Ethics*, Volume 167, 2020, passim.

[1741] Xi Chen, "Algorithmic proxy discrimination and its regulations", *cit.*, pp. 1–13 (5).

[1742] Xi Chen, "Algorithmic proxy discrimination and its regulations", *cit.*, pp. 1–13 (5).

[1743] Barocas, Solon/Selbst, Andrew, "Big Data's Disparate Impact", *California Law Review*, Volume 104, 2016, pp. 695 and ff and passim.

[1744] But see: *Tech, Bias and Housing Initiative, the Promise and Perils of Residential Proptech, Year 1, Research Summary Report, April 2023, TechEquity Collaborative*, p. 11, available at: https://techequity.us/wp-content/uploads/2023/04/TBHI-Y1-Research-Summary-Report.pdf (28.11.2024). ("And while we know that the *data is predictive, meaning it has little to do with demonstrated behavior of the applicant themself, we do not know exactly where companies get their data*"). Italics added. See: Part IV, This chapter, Sects. 4.1.4–4.1.4.2.3 of this book.

the way to ghastly unavoidable,[1745] and eerily ineluctable, algorithmic proxy discrimination.[1746] Algorithmic proxy discrimination thereby amounts to a veiled form of *Algorithmic Dictatorship* insofar it deserves nothing but to be both upbraided and excoriated. As Gabrielle Johnson presciently puts it, «proxies are neither rare nor the result of overly intentional decisions[1747]; rather, they are often necessary and unwitting».[1748]

4.1.6.2.2 «Complex Proxy Relations and the Discernibility Problem» (Xi Chen)

§§ To the extent a given proxy relationship[1749] might be conducive to different discriminatory outcomes,[1750] a given outcome might likewise derive from multifarious combinations[1751] of multiple variables.[1752] For example, it is widely known that women usually outlive men insofar the former have a long-winded life expectancy

---

[1745] Citron, Danielle K., "Technological Due Process", *Washington University Law Review*, Volume 85, 2008, pp. 1249–1253 ("computer programs seamlessly combine rulemaking and individual adjudications without the critical procedural protections owed either of them").

[1746] Ponce, Paula Pedigoni, "Direct and indirect discrimination applied to algorithmic systems: Reflections to Brazil", *Computer Law & Security Review*, Volume 48, 2023, 1057–1066.

[1747] Barocas, Solon/Selbst, Andrew D., "Big Data's Disparate Impact", *California Law Review*, Volume 104, 2016, p. 699 (discussing how discriminatory data mining is analogous to unintentional disparate impact analysis). See also: Note, though, that certain types of racial discrimination may not be fully intentional. More likely than not, it can be related with the perils of big data colour-blindness that nonetheless relies on proxies to race and gender to make algorithmic decisions. Another problem is the one related with "creditworthiness by association" that causes more problems than it solves. Hurley, Mikella/Adebayo, Julius, "Credit Scoring in the Era of Big Data", *Yale Journal of Law and Technology*, Volume 18, 2016, p. 149 ("*recent studies have also questioned the accuracy of the data used by these tools, in some cases identifying serious flaws that have a substantial bearing on lending decisions. Big-data tools may also risk creating a system of "creditworthiness by association" in which consumers' familial, religious, social, and other affiliations determine their eligibility for an affordable loan. These tools may furthermore obscure discriminatory and subjective lending policies behind a single "objective" score. Such discriminatory scoring may not be intentional; instead, sophisticated algorithms may combine facially neutral data points and treat them as proxies for immutable characteristics such as race or gender, thereby circumventing existing non-discrimination laws and systematically denying credit access to certain groups. Finally, big-data tools may allow online payday lenders to target the most vulnerable consumers and lure them into debt traps*"). Italics added.

[1748] Johnson, Gabbrielle M., "Algorithmic Bias: On the Implicit Biases of Social Technology", *Synthese*, Volume 198, 2021, p. 9955.

[1749] It is often contended that machine learning algorithms engender their own models to forecast future outcomes on the basis of analysis of training data. See: Mittelstadt, Brent Daniel/Taddeo, Patrick Allo, Mariarosaria/Wachter, Sandra/Floridi, Luciano, "The Ethics of Algorithms: Mapping the Debate", *Big Data & Society*, July-Dec. 2016, 2016, p. 3.

[1750] Xi Chen, "Algorithmic proxy discrimination and its regulations", *cit.*, pp. 1–13 (5).

compared to the latter.[1753] Whilst it is unlawful to craft life insurance[1754] policies[1755] (O) on the basis of gender (T1),[1756] machine learning algorithms may nonetheless hinge upon facially neutral proxies[1757] for gender[1758] to perform meaningful algorithmic decision-making in this regard.[1759]

[1751] See: Barocas, Solon/Selbst, Andrew D., "Big Data's Disparate Impact", *California Law Review*, Volume 104, 2016, pp. 677–78 (arguing that predictive data is predictive of a given/specific target variable (i.e., minimized future predicted claims) with training data which is both correctly "labelled" and "collected").

[1752] Pope, Devin G./Sydnor, Justin R., "Implementing Anti-Discrimination Policies in Statistical Profiling Models", *American Economic Journal: Economic Policy*, Volume 3, 2011, pp. 207–216.

[1753] Oksuzyan, Anna/Brønnum-Hansen, Henrik/Jeune, Bernard, "Gender Gap in Health Expectancy", *European Journal of Aging*, Volume 7, 2010, pp. 211 and ff.

[1754] For an on-point breakdown of the distinct levels of opacity arising out of machine learning algorithms in the purview of insurance policies: Selbst, Andrew D./Barocas, Solon, "The Intuitive Appeal of Explainable Machines", *Fordham Law Review*, Volume 87, 2018, pp. 1085, 1089–99 (holding that there are plenty reasons for the insurer's ignorance. To begin with, the algorithm entails specialized knowledge to understand. That is, the insurer's employees may lack sufficient knowledge to understand the rationale behind the reasons in view of which the algorithm is producing prices for different customers—personalized pricing. Lastly, even if the insurer himself comprehends how the model operates, it may nonetheless lack expertise to comprehend why it operates the way it does. For that reason, the explainability of machines is a vital, but rather elusive, task. Thence, the famed authors deem it as the "nonintuitive" nature of algorithms. For purposes here, the insurer himself might indeed understand that its Artificial Intelligence-embedded technology formulates higher prices for those who actually access the website at hand, but may fail to come to terms with the fact that the explanation for this fact arises from the website's capacity to proxy for genetic information). See also: Scherer, Matthew U. Scherer, "Regulating Artificial Intelligence Systems: Risks, Challenges, Competencies, and Strategies", *Harvard Journal of Law and Technology*, Volume 29, 2016, pp. 353–369 (frames the crippling problem of opacity as "the possibility that the inner workings of an AI system may be kept secret and may not be susceptible to reverse engineering").

[1755] But see: Roberts, Jessica L./Weeks Elizabeth, *Healthism: Health Status Discrimination and the Law*, Cambridge, Cambridge University Press, 2019, pp. 1–230 (pp. 110 and ff and passim) ("*Can an employer refuse to hire someone who tests positive for nicotine or alcohol? Can an airline or movie theatre require overweight customers to purchase two seats? Can a health insurance company refuse to sell policies to those most in need of medical care? Can the government condition public assistance on wellness program participation or work activity*? In this illuminating book, Jessica L. Roberts and Elizabeth Weeks consider these and similar questions, offering readers a nuanced analysis of when and why discrimination based on health status—or 'healthism'—should be allowed, and when it should not. *They provide a methodology to distinguish desirable health-based classifications from the undesirable, and propose law and policy solutions to encourage the former and limit the latter. This work should be read by anyone concerned with how government does—and does not—regulate based on health*"). Italics added.

[1756] Xi Chen, "Algorithmic proxy discrimination and its regulations", *cit.*, pp. 1–13 (5).

[1757] But see: Bornstein, Stepanhie, "Antidiscriminatory Algorithms", *Alabama Law Review*, Volume 70, 2018, pp. 519, 524–528 (contending, however, that the tagged "facially neutral" algorithms producing discriminatory outcomes should be quashed).

[1758] It bears mentioning that scorching issue of whether and to what extent disparate impact alone should be actionable is different from, in that does not overlap with, the sweltering issue of proxy discrimination. For arguments about the desirability of disparate impact in insurance, see generally Cohran, Matthew Jordan, "Fairness in Disparity: Challenging the Application of Disparate Impact Theory in Fair Housing Claims Against Insurers", *The George Mason University Civil Rights Law*

§§ It is of paramount importance to note, though, that the predictive power[1760] of gender for life expectancy is tightly interlocked with other[1761] substantial factors, many of which are tangible insofar they are both measurable and quantifiable.[1762] Gender differences in smoking (U1) or biological discrepancies in terms of, e.g. hormones (U2),[1763] are usually offered as paradigmatic examples. On the flip side, other factors are difficult to gauge.[1764] Differences in social-psychological stress (U3)[1765] are usually portrayed as a paradigmatic example of that perceived difficulty.

§§ Tellingly, and to the extent machine learning algorithms employ facially neutral[1766] proxies for gender,[1767] the former can rely on gender as a proxy only to gain access to other protected characteristics with enhanced predictive power.[1768]

Journal, Volume 21, 2011, pp. 159 and ff and passim (discussing the use of disparate impact theory and potential applicability to Fair Housing Act claims against insurers).

1759 Xi Chen, "Algorithmic proxy discrimination and its regulations", *cit.*, pp. 1–13 (5).

1760 But see: Citron, Danielle Keats/Pasquale, Frank, "The Scored Society: Due Process for Automated Predictions", *Washington Law Review*, Volume 89, 2014, pp. 1, 4–5 (highlighting how human beings programming automated systems is directly conducive to, and leads, to fundamentally inaccurate results since the source code, predictive algorithms and datasets may encompass human biases which, in turn, have a disparate impact on historically disadvantaged groups).

1761 Xi Chen, "Algorithmic proxy discrimination and its regulations", *cit.*, pp. 1–13 (5).

1762 Oksuzyan, Anna/Brønnum-Hansen, Henrik/Jeune, Bernard, "Gender Gap in Health Expectancy", *European Journal of Aging*, Volume 7, 2010, pp. 211 and ff.

1763 Xi Chen, "Algorithmic proxy discrimination and its regulations", *cit.*, pp. 1–13 (5).

1764 But see: de Laat, Paul B. 'Algorithmic Decision-Making Based on Machine Learning from Big Data: Can Transparency Restore Accountability?", *Philosophy & Technology*, Volume 31, 2018, pp. 524 and ff and passim (broaches the plethora of limitations related with full transparency, privacy, deleterious effects, competitive edge, and the shroud of opacity under which algorithms are often wrapped).

1765 Xi Chen, "Algorithmic proxy discrimination and its regulations", *cit.*, pp. 1–13 (5).

1766 But see: Benjamin, Ruha, *Race After Technology: Abolitionist Tools for the New Jim Code*, New York, Polity, 2019, pp. 1–172 (7) (discussing that Artificial Intelligence-embedded technologies are viewed as iron-clad tools of objectivity and devoid of any biases whatsoever). Ruha Benjamin accordingly contends that "the employment of new technologies that reflect and reproduce existing inequities but that are promoted and perceived as more objective or progressive than the discriminatory systems of a previous era").

1767 But see: Hurley, Mikella/Adebayo, Julius, "Credit Scoring in the Era of Big Data", *Yale Journal of Law and Technology*, Volume 18, 2016, p. 149 ("*these tools may furthermore obscure discriminatory and subjective lending policies behind a single "objective" score* (...) *sophisticated algorithms may combine facially neutral data points and treat them as proxies for immutable characteristics such as race or gender, thereby circumventing existing non-discrimination laws and systematically denying credit access to certain groups. Finally, big-data tools may allow online payday lenders to target the most vulnerable consumers and lure them into debt traps*"). Italics added. See also: Farina, M./Lavazza, A., *Philosophy, expertise, and the myth of neutrality*, Routledge Studies in Contemporary Philosophy, London, Routledge, 2024.

1768 But see: Citron, Danielle Keats/Pasquale, Frank A., "The Scored Society: Due Process for Automated Predictions", *Washington Law Review*, Volume 89, 2014, pp. 1–34 (arguing that "[a]*dvocates applaud the removal of human beings and their flaws from the assessment process*," but arguing that bias remains "[*b*]*ecause human beings program predictive algorithms, their biases and values are embedded into the software's instructions*"). Italics added.

This process, which is loosely comprised by three phases, can be skeletally broken down as follows. The «*unitary form*»—T1 is deeply woven into the fabric U1, U2, or U3 respectively[1769]; the «*combined form*»[1770]—T1 is intrinsically connected with combinations of U1, U2, or U3 respectively[1771]; lastly, the «*chained form*»[1772]—T1 is inextricably linked to any Un or its combination in turn.[1773] For instance, U1 first, and subsequently U2, and U3, or U1 + U3 first, and subsequently U2.[1774]

§§ Note, though, that there are far more sensitive data and legitimate features involved than those fleshed out so far.[1775] Compellingly, if facially neutral data are also considered,[1776] the complexity[1777] of algorithmic decision-making skyrockets.[1778] Notably, insofar these forms can happen concomitantly and the variables involved function in a purely nonlinear manner,[1779] algorithmic proxy discrimination could be shaped through more complex neural[1780] networks[1781] of proxy relations.[1782] Which, in turn, would add further complexity to a process that is anything but linear and straightforward.

[1769] Xi Chen, "Algorithmic proxy discrimination and its regulations", *cit.*, pp. 1–13 (5).

[1770] Xi Chen, "Algorithmic proxy discrimination and its regulations", *cit.*, pp. 1–13 (5).

[1771] Xi Chen, "Algorithmic proxy discrimination and its regulations", *cit.*, pp. 1–13 (5).

[1772] Xi Chen, "Algorithmic proxy discrimination and its regulations", *cit.*, pp. 1–13 (5).

[1773] Xi Chen, "Algorithmic proxy discrimination and its regulations", *cit.*, pp. 1–13 (5).

[1774] Xi Chen, "Algorithmic proxy discrimination and its regulations", *cit.*, pp. 1–13 (5).

[1775] Xi Chen, "Algorithmic proxy discrimination and its regulations", *cit.*, pp. 1–13 (5).

[1776] But see: Bornstein, Stepanhie, "Antidiscriminatory Algorithms", *Alabama Law Review*, Volume 70, 2018, pp. 519, 524–528 (contending, however, that the tagged "facially neutral" algorithms producing discriminatory outcomes should be quashed).

[1777] Segran, G., "The complexity of artificial intelligence", *Singapore Management University*, 2021, passim (on the elaborate and complex trappings of Artificial Intelligence).

[1778] For an on-point breakdown of the distinct levels of opacity arising out of machine learning algorithms: Selbst, Andrew D./Barocas, Solon, "The Intuitive Appeal of Explainable Machines", *Fordham Law Review*, Volume 87, 2018, pp. 1085, 1089–99 (holding that there are plenty reasons for the insurer's ignorance. To begin with, the algorithm entails specialized knowledge to understand. That is, the insurer's employees may lack sufficient knowledge to understand the rationale behind the reasons in view of which the algorithm is producing prices for different customers—personalized pricing. Lastly, even if the insurer himself comprehends how the model operates, it may nonetheless lack expertise to comprehend why it operates the way it does. For that reason, the explainability of machines is a vital, but rather elusive, task. Thence, the famed authors deem it as the "nonintuitive" nature of algorithms. For purposes here, the insurer himself might indeed understand that its Artificial Intelligence-embedded technology formulates higher prices for those who actually access the website at hand, but may fail to come to terms with the fact that the explanation for this fact arises from the website's capacity to proxy for genetic information). See also: Scherer, Matthew U. Scherer, "Regulating Artificial Intelligence Systems: Risks, Challenges, Competencies, and Strategies", *Harvard Journal of Law and Technology*, Volume 29, 2016, pp. 353–369 (frames the crippling problem of opacity as "the possibility that the inner workings of an AI system may be kept secret and may not be susceptible to reverse engineering").

§§ As a result, even if one if fully cognizant of the fact that algorithmic proxy discrimination has indeed occurred, it is very difficult to pinpoint the proxy relations on which it is based on[1783] and accordingly map/trace the underlying process that enabled the outcome.[1784] Which neatly encapsulates, hands-in-glove, a form of *Algorithmic Dictatorship* that deserves nothing but to be eagerly decried and timely debunked.

4.1.6.2.3 «Opaque Proxy Relations and the Accountability Problem» (Xi Chen)

§§ Albeit proxy relations are extensive, complex, fiddly, serpentine, inscrutable, and intricate, **traditional statistical algorithms (e.g. decision trees)** are nonetheless bereft of a black-box nature,[1785] even when effective regulations are seemingly difficult to attain by humans alone, antidiscrimination algorithms can be nonetheless designed to proficiently address, and deftly tackle,[1786] algorithmic proxy[1787] discrimination.[1788]

[1779] Buckner, Cameron, "Empiricism without Magic: Transformational Abstraction in Deep Convolutional Neural Networks", *Synthese*, Volume 195, 2018, 5339.

[1780] Aggarwal, C. C., *Neural networks and deep learning*, Heidelberg, Springer, 2018, passim; Agrawal, A., Gans, J., & Goldfarb, A., "Prediction machines (updated and expanded): The simple economics of artificial intelligence", *Harvard Business Review Press*, 2022; Agrawal, A., Gans, J., & Goldfarb, A., "Power and prediction: The disruptive economics of artificial intelligence", *Harvard Business Review Press*, 2022; Bengio, Y., Hinton, G., Yao, A., Song, D., Abbeel, P., Harari, Y. N., Hadfield, G., Russell, S., Kahneman, D., & Mindermann, S., *Managing ai risks in an era of rapid progress*, arXiv preprint arXiv:2310.17688, 2023, passim (on neural networks and deep learning that operate jointly in the age of Artificial Intelligence-embedded technologies).

[1781] See: Bathaee, Yavar, "The Artificial Intelligence Black Box and the Failure of Intent and Causation", *Harvard Journal of Law and Technology*, n.º 37, 2018, p. 901 (adduces that "*one possible reason AI may be a black box to humans is that it relies on machine-learning algorithms that internalize data in ways that are not easily audited or understood by humans (…) "first, a lack may arise from the complexity of the algorithm's structure, such as with deep neural network, which consists of thousands of artificial neurons working together in a diffuse way to solve a problem. This reason for AI being a black box is referred to as "complexity". Second, the lack of transparency may arise because the AI is using a machine-learning algorithm that relies on geometric relationships that humans cannot visualize, such as with support vector machines. This reason for AI being a black box is referred to as "dimensionality"*"). Italics added.

[1782] Xi Chen, "Algorithmic proxy discrimination and its regulations", *cit.*, pp. 1–13 (5).

[1783] Xi Chen, "Algorithmic proxy discrimination and its regulations", *cit.*, pp. 1–13 (5).

[1784] Xi Chen, "Algorithmic proxy discrimination and its regulations", *cit.*, pp. 1–13 (5).

[1785] Blattner, Laura/Nelson, Scott/Spiess, Jann, *Unpacking the Black Box: Regulating Algorithmic Decisions*. Working Paper. Redwood City, California: Stanford University Press, 2021.

[1786] See: Pedreshi, Dino/Ruggieri, Salvatore/Turini, Franco, "Discrimination-aware Data Mining", *Proceedings of the 14th ACM SIGKDD International Conference on Knowledge Discovery and Data Mining (Las Vegas, Nevada, USA), ACM*, 2008, pp. 560–568 (arguing that one should shift its gaze downstream by putting in place discrimination-aware algorithmic tools while performing data mining).

§§ Notwithstanding, as for machine learning algorithms,[1789] it is nevertheless difficult for both humans and machines themselves to fully grasp how the latter ascribe weights to a wide range of variables in a predictive model and accordingly come up with decisions.[1790] Either arising out of the duty to protect commercial/state secrets («paradox of source code secrecy»)[1791] or as the byproduct of technical illiteracy itself, opacity[1792] is tightly interlocked to the arcane inner workings of machine learning algorithms[1793] that largely surpasses human cognitive[1794] abilities.[1795] Take the example of deep learning algorithms.

[1787] But see: Kilbertus, Niki/Carulla, Mateo Rojas/Parascandolo, Giambattista/Hardt, Moritz/ Janzing, Dominik/ Schoellkopf, Bernhard, "Avoiding Discrimination through Causal Reasoning", *Advances in Neural Information Processing Systems*, I. Guyon, U. V. Luxburg, S. Bengio, H. Wallach, R. Fergus, S. Vishwanathan, and R. Garnett (Eds.), Vol. 30. Curran Associates, Inc., 2017, pp. 656–666 (arguing that is feasible to avoiding discrimination through a granular and fine-grained causal reasoning). See also: Pearl, Judea, "Causal inference in statistics: An overview", *Statistics Surveys*, Volume 3, 2009, pp. 96–146; Pearl, Judea, *Causality*, 2nd edition, Cambridge, Cambridge University Press, 2009.

[1788] Xi Chen, "Algorithmic proxy discrimination and its regulations", *cit.*, pp. 1–13 (5).

[1789] But see: O'Neil, Cathy, "When Not to Trust the Algorithm", *Interview published in the Harvard Business Review's Ideacast*, 2016, passim.

[1790] Xi Chen, "Algorithmic proxy discrimination and its regulations", *cit.*, pp. 1–13 (5).

[1791] See: Deeks, Ahsley, "Secret Reason-Giving", *Yale Law Journal*, Volume 129, 2019, passim; Katyal, Sonia K, "The Paradox of Source Code Secrecy", *Cornell Law Review*, Volume 104, 2019, pp. 1183–1236; Pasquale, Frank, *The Black Box Society: The Secret Algorithms that Control Money and Information*. Cambridge, Massachusetts: Harvard University Press, 2015, 1–320 (pp. 8–10 and passim) (noting that biased algorithms, which have underlying discrimination problems, contribute exponentially to further encroach social biases. His most intriguing claim is that such biased algorithms have been incorporated/etched in the bulk of the corporations' informatic system, to the detriment of human kind in an overarching sense); Wexler, Rebecca, "Life, Liberty, and Trade Secrets: Intellectual Property in the Criminal Justice System", *Stanford Law Review*, Volume 70, 2018, pp. 1343 and ff; Okidegbe, Ngozi, "The Democratizing Potential of Algorithms?", *Connecticut Law Review*, Volume 54, 2021, passim. See: Part V, Chap. 5, Sects. 5.1.7–5.1.7.5 of this book (on the five laws to control algorithmic decision-making). See: Part V, Chap. 5, Sects. 5.1.8–5.1.8.5 of this book (on the five laws to interpret algorithmic decision-making).

[1792] De Laat, Paul B. 'Algorithmic Decision-Making Based on Machine Learning from Big Data: Can Transparency Restore Accountability?", *Philosophy & Technology*, Volume 31, 2018, pp. 524 and ff and passim (broaches the plethora of limitations related with full transparency, privacy, deleterious effects, competitive edge, and the shroud of opacity under which algorithms are often wrapped).

[1793] See: Scherer, Matthew U. Scherer, "Regulating Artificial Intelligence Systems: Risks, Challenges, Competencies, and Strategies", *Harvard Journal of Law and Technology*, Volume 29, 2016, pp. 353–369 (frames the crippling problem of opacity as "the possibility that the inner workings of an AI system may be kept secret and may not be susceptible to reverse engineering"). See also: Turek, Matt, "Explainable Artificial Intelligence (XAI)", The *Defense Advanced Research Projects Agency* (DARPA), www.darpa.mil/program/explainable-artificial-intelligence; [https://perma.cc/2DS4-ZMNB] (shedding light on the oft-labelled interpretability of algorithms); *Making Computers Explain Themselves*, MIT's Computer Science and Artificial Intelligence Laboratory (Oct. 27, 2016), 2016, www.csail.mit.edu/making_computers_explain themselves [https://perma.cc/C97B-PGUR] (explaining the importance of grasping the complex trappings of algorithm decision-making).

§§ Deep learning algorithms[1796] encode big data through a set of convoluted and multilayered networks of meticulously interconnected neurons[1797] which, taken together, contribute exponentially to algorithmic decision-making.[1798]

§§ Deep neural networks develop through experiential learning,[1799] as opposed to agreed-upon or set-in-stone rules.[1800] Unsurprisingly, the knowledge surrounding them is not amenable to[1801] «be reduced to a set of instructions, nor can one in most cases point to any neuron or group of neurons to determine what the system found interesting or important».[1802]

§§ Relatedly, when the involved variables are multiple,[1803] this type of algorithm invariably crafts proxy relations in exceedingly high-dimensional ways that humans are utterly unable to visualize.[1804] Opacity[1805] therefore raises deep-rooted ethical and legal concerns about human autonomy,[1806] «technological due process»,[1807]

[1794] Xi Chen, "Algorithmic proxy discrimination and its regulations", *cit.*, pp. 1–13 (5).

[1795] Burrell, Jenna, "How the Machine Thinks: Understanding Opacity in Machine Learning Algorithms", *Big Data & Society*, Volume 3, 2016.

[1796] Yeung, Karen, "Why Worry about Decision-Making by Machine?", *Algorithmic Regulation*, Yeung, Karen/Lodge, Martin (Editors), Oxford, Oxford University Press, 2019, pp. 22–47.

[1797] Lipton, Zachary/McAukley, Julian/Chouldechova, Alexandra, "Does Mitigating ML's Impact Disparity Require Treatment Disparity?" *Advances in Neural Information Processing Systems*, 31, S. Bengio, H. Wallach, H. Larochelle, K. Grauman, N. Cesa-Bianchi, and R. Garnett (Eds.). Curran Associates, Inc., 2018, pp. 8125–8135.

[1798] Xi Chen, "Algorithmic proxy discrimination and its regulations", *cit.*, pp. 1–13 (5).

[1799] See: Aggarwal, C. C., *Neural networks and deep learning*, Heidelberg, Springer, 2018, passim; Agrawal, A., Gans, J., & Goldfarb, A., "Prediction machines (updated and expanded): The simple economics of artificial intelligence", *Harvard Business Review Press*, 2022; Agrawal, A., Gans, J., & Goldfarb, A., "Power and prediction: The disruptive economics of artificial intelligence", *Harvard Business Review Press*, 2022, passim.

[1800] Xi Chen, "Algorithmic proxy discrimination and its regulations", *cit.*, pp. 1–13 (5).

[1801] Xi Chen, "Algorithmic proxy discrimination and its regulations", *cit.*, pp. 1–13 (5).

[1802] Bathaee, Yavar, "The Artificial Intelligence Black Box and the Failure of Intent and Causation", *Harvard Journal of Law & Technology*, Volume 31, 2018, pp. 890–904.

[1803] Xi Chen, "Algorithmic proxy discrimination and its regulations", *cit.*, pp. 1–13 (6).

[1804] Xi Chen, "Algorithmic proxy discrimination and its regulations", *cit.*, pp. 1–13 (6). See also: Bathaee, Yavar, "The Artificial Intelligence Black Box and the Failure of Intent and Causation", *cit.*, p. 901 (adduces that "*one possible reason AI may be a black box to humans is that it relies on machine-learning algorithms that internalize data in ways that are not easily audited or understood by humans (...)* "*first, a lack may arise from the complexity of the algorithm's structure, such as with deep neural network, which consists of thousands of artificial neurons working together in a diffuse way to solve a problem. This reason for AI being a black box is referred to as "complexity". Second, the lack of transparency may arise because the AI is using a machine-learning algorithm that relies on geometric relationships that humans cannot visualize, such as with support vector machines. This reason for AI being a black box is referred to as "dimensionality"*"). Italics added. See: Part V, Chap. 5, Sect. 5.1.7.2 of this book (on law number two to control algorithmic decision-making, which mandates that black box models must not be entrusted with the task of making high stake decisions—v.g. health and freedom).

[1805] For an on-point breakdown of the distinct levels of opacity arising out of machine learning algorithms: Selbst, Andrew D./Barocas, Solon, "The Intuitive Appeal of Explainable Machines", *Fordham Law Review*, Volume 87, 2018, pp. 1085, 1089–99 (holding that there are plenty reasons

equal participation in public affairs,[1808] indispensable human oversight («humans in the loop»[1809]) within the process of algorithmic decision-making, algorithmic injustice,[1810] and algorithmic[1811] accountability.[1812] Note, though, that the paucity

for the insurer's ignorance. To begin with, the algorithm entails specialized knowledge to understand. That is, the insurer's employees may lack sufficient knowledge to understand the rationale behind the reasons in view of which the algorithm is producing prices for different customers—personalized pricing. Lastly, even if the insurer himself comprehends how the model operates, it may nonetheless lack expertise to comprehend why it operates the way it does. For that reason, the explainability of machines is a vital, but rather elusive, task. Thence, the famed authors deem it as the "nonintuitive" nature of algorithms. For purposes here, the insurer himself might indeed understand that its Artificial Intelligence-embedded technology formulates higher prices for those who actually access the website at hand, but may fail to come to terms with the fact that the explanation for this fact arises from the website's capacity to proxy for genetic information). See also: Scherer, Matthew U. Scherer, "Regulating Artificial Intelligence Systems: Risks, Challenges, Competencies, and Strategies", *Harvard Journal of Law and Technology*, Volume 29, 2016, pp. 353–369 (frames the crippling problem of opacity as "the possibility that the inner workings of an AI system may be kept secret and may not be susceptible to reverse engineering").

1806 See: Millar, Jason/Kerr, Ian, "Delegation, Relinquishment and Responsibility: The Prospect of Expert Robots", *Robot Law*, Calo, Ryan /Froomkin, A. Michael/Kerr, Ian, Cheltenham, Edward Elgar Publishing, 2016, pp. 102, 106–107 (as these authors aptly put it "*we will rely on robots without really knowing why – simply because their algorithms provide the greatest number of successful outcomes.* We have already seen this in Google's search approach. Neither Larry (Page) nor Sergey (Brin) (nor any other Google employee) knowns exactly why one particular web page is a better result than another. *When the click patterns say it is, that's good enough.* No semantic or causal analysis is required...*Like the ancients, we will, quite rationally, come to rely upon them, knowing full well that we cannot necessarily explain the reasons for their decisions*"). Italics added. Converging: Casey, Anthony J./Niblett, Anthony, "Self-driving Laws", *University of Toronto Law Journal*, Volume 66, 2016, pp. 429–435 (contend that "as more information is generated, and the evolutionary algorithm updates and become a better forecaster, we imagine that judges will increasingly rely on the advice of the algorithm"). But see: Weizenbaum, Joseph, *Computer Power and Human Reason: From Judgment to Calculation*, 1st edition, New York, W. H. Freeman & Co, 1976, pp. 1–300 (227) ("examines the sources of the computer's powers and offers evaluative explorations of what computers can do, cannot do, and should not be employed to do") (this founding father of Artificial Intelligence presciently noted that we should not entrust Artificial Intelligence-embedded technologies with "tasks that demand wisdom"). Italics added. The approval of rental applications is arguably one of those tasks that should never be entrusted to machines). More on this on Part IV, This chapter, Sects. 4.1.4–4.1.4.2.1 of this book. See: Part V, Chap. 5, Sect. 5.1.7.2 of this book (on law number two to control algorithmic decision-making, which mandates that black box models must not be entrusted with the task of making high stake decisions—v.g. health and freedom). See: Part V, Chap. 5, Sect. 5.1.8.5 of this book (on law number five to interpret algorithmic decision-making, which mandates that robot-judges, robot-prosecutors and robot-lawyers must not enter the courtroom for they are utterly incapable of making sound and interpretable value judgements).

1807 Citron, Danielle K., "Technological Due Process", *Washington University Law Review*, Volume 85, 2008, pp. 1249–1253 ("Computer programs seamlessly combine rulemaking and individual adjudications without the critical procedural protections owed either of them").

1808 Which, I may venture to add, amounts to something—*biometric surveillance*—that equals nothing but to the price of partaking in public affairs, which is very hard to shy away from nowadays. See: Hu, Margaret, "From the National Surveillance State to the Cybersurveillance State", *The Annual Review of Law and Social Science*, Volume 13, 2017, p. 169 ("*because of technological developments and trends in governance, it is challenging, if not impossible, to prevent biometric data*

of accountability[1813] is further compounded by the fact that not all regulators always need to crack open an algorithmic black box.[1814]

---

capture and collection. Biometric surveillance systems increasingly require opting in as the price of social, economic, and political participation. Biometric data capture is difficult to resist because it is simultaneously compulsory and transparent. Biometric data collection is often compulsory because it is increasingly mandatory to establish identity. *Biometrics are transparent qualities because it is very difficult to hide biometrics; an individual's face, iris, or fingerprint can be digitally captured in any public place. Because biometric data support larger big data programs, such as No Fly List–type risk assessments, it is extraordinarily difficult, if not impossible, to opt out*"). Italics added. See: Part IV, This chapter, Sects. 4.1.5–4.1.5.2 of this book (on "algorithmic Jim Crow", a travel ban issued during the first Trump Administration to prevent certain individuals from entering the United States of America, which, given its racial undertones, stands as an outgrowth of congeries of laws enacted during the Jim Crow epoch).

1809 See: Salloch, S., & Eriksen, A., "What are humans doing in the Loop? Co-reasoning and practical Judgment when using machine learning-driven decision aids", *The American Journal of Bioethics*, 2024, pp. 1–12; Binns, Reuben, "Human Judgment in Algorithmic Loops: Individual Justice and Automated Decision-Making", *Regulation & Governance*, Volume 16, 2022, passim; Simon & Schuster, Green, B., "Algorithmic realism: expanding the boundaries of algorithmic thought", *Proceedings of the 2020 Conference on Fairness Accountability and Transparency*, 2020, passim; Green, B./Hu L., "The Myth in the Methodology: Towards a Recontextualization of Fairness in Machine Learning", *Machine Learning Debates Work 35th Internation Conference of Machine Learning*, 2018, passim; Green, B., Chen Y, "Disparate interactions: An algorithm-in-the-loop analysis of fairness in risk assessments", *FAT* 2019, Proceedings of 2019 Conference of Fairness, Accountability, Transparency*, 2019, pp. 90–99 (on the central tenets of algorithmic fairness). See also: Alimardani, Armin/Jane, Emma A., "Human Hallucinations: GenAI and the Mirage of Personalised Learning for All", 2024, p. 13 ("*The output generated by GenAI models includes an inherent randomness and the same prompt may result in various outputs. Therefore, it is likely that the outputs of GenAI models are never entirely accurate and reliable. In other words, we contend that existing GenAI systems represent a technology that requires a 'human in/on the loop' to verify outputs before they reach the end user. When incorporating GenAI into an educational chatbot, students are the end users, making it challenging to identify and rectify these errors promptly*"). Italics added.

1810 Ting-an Lin, "Democratizing AI" and the Concern of Algorithmic Injustice", *Philosophy and Technology*, Volume 37 (103), 2024, pp. 3–27; Okidegbe, Ngozi, "The Democratizing Potential of Algorithms?", *Connecticut Law Review*, Volume 54, 2021, passim.

1811 Katyal, Sonia, "Private Accountability in the Age of Artificial Intelligence", *UCLA Law Review*, Volume 66, 2019, pp. 54–99. See also: Williams, Rebecca, "Accountable Algorithms: Adopting the Public Law Toolbox Outside the Realm of Public Law", *Current Legal Problems*, Vol. 75, 2022, pp. 237–263; Williams, Rebecca, "Rethinking Administrative Law for Algorithmic Decision-Making", *Oxford Journal of Legal Studies*, Volume 42, 2021, pp. 468 e ff and passim.

1812 Xi Chen, "Algorithmic proxy discrimination and its regulations", *cit.*, pp. 1–13 (6). See also: Yeung, Karen, "Why Worry about Decision-Making by Machine?", *Algorithmic Regulation*, Yeung, Karen/Lodge, Martin (Editors), Oxford, Oxford University Press, 2019, pp. 22–47.

1813 But see: Part V, Chap. 5, Sects. 5.1.2–5.1.6.2.1 of this book (on the **thing-centred algorithmic decision-making** propelled by a *Controllable* and *Interpretable* Machine Learning that weeds out *Algorithmic Dictatorship* and secures *Algorithmic Common Good*. It is worth recalling that the **thing-centred algorithmic decision-making** seeks to unwind the perils arising out of the lack of theoretical underpinnings facing the **human-centred algorithmic decision-making**, as extensively fleshed out Part III, Chap. 3, Sects. 3.1.4.3–3.1.4.4 of this book).

1814 Xi Chen, "Algorithmic proxy discrimination and its regulations", *cit.*, pp. 1–13 (6).

§§ Notwithstanding, there is a spate of set-in-stone situations in view of which certain regulators must ascertain how a given algorithm works.[1815] Which, in turn, typically takes place when courts are summoned to establish the imputation of algorithmic proxy discrimination.[1816]

§§ Overall, opacity loosely means that even if one is fully aware what data[1817] algorithms used to create proxy relations,[1818] it is extremely difficult to determine how exactly algorithmic proxy discrimination unfolds alongside with the benchmark against which discriminatory practices should be gauged.[1819] Which, again, amounts to a form of *Algorithmic Dictatorship* in dire need of quashing.[1820]

4.1.6.3 Proxy Discrimination and Disparate Impact in the Age of Algorithmic-Anchored Decision-Making

§§ It seems as though we are thrust headlong into grappling with hitherto unsolved vexing questions. One which is proxy discrimination[1821]—an eerily duplicitous and treacherous form of *Algorithmic Dictatorship* that is shaping up to topple the foundations[1822] of Rule of Law.[1823] The dichotomy between big data[1824] and artificial intelligence-embedded technologies lies at the heart of the disruption curve with the

---

[1815] Xi Chen, "Algorithmic proxy discrimination and its regulations", *cit.*, pp. 1–13 (6).

[1816] Xi Chen, "Algorithmic proxy discrimination and its regulations", *cit.*, pp. 1–13 (6).

[1817] But see: *Tech, Bias and Housing Initiative, the Promise and Perils of Residential Proptech, Year 1, Research Summary Report, April 2023, TechEquity Collaborative*, p. 11, available at: https://techequity.us/wp-content/uploads/2023/04/TBHI-Y1-Research-Summary-Report.pdf (28.11.2024). ("*Once bad data enters the analysis of one factor, it gets baked into the subsequent process, multiplying the effect that one disadvantageous data point can have on someone's overall housing determination*"). Italics added. See: Part IV, This chapter, Sects. 4.1.4–4.1.4.2.3 of this book.

[1818] But see: *Tech, Bias and Housing Initiative, the Promise and Perils of Residential Proptech, Year 1, Research Summary Report, April 2023, TechEquity Collaborative*, p. 11, available at: https://techequity.us/wp-content/uploads/2023/04/TBHI-Y1-Research-Summary-Report.pdf (28.11.2024). ("And while we know that the *data is predictive, meaning it has little to do with demonstrated behavior of the applicant themself, we do not know exactly where companies get their data*"). Italics added. See: Part IV, This chapter, Sects. 4.1.4–4.1.4.2.3 of this book.

[1819] Xi Chen, "Algorithmic proxy discrimination and its regulations", *cit.*, pp. 1–13 (6).

[1820] See: Part V, Chap. 5, Sect. 5.1.1.2 of this book (on the central tenets of Procedural Rule of Law that lends itself to a lighthouse of justice that allows citizens to challenge the pearls of algorithmic wisdom in a court of law).

[1821] Prince, Anya E. R./Schwarcz, Daniel, "Proxy Discrimination in the Age of Artificial Intelligence and Big Data", *Iowa Law Review*, Volume 105, 2020, pp. 1257, 1279–1281 ("*[P]roxy discrimination will tend to occur when a suspect variable is predictive of a desired outcome only because it proxies for another*, quantifiable and potentially available, *variable that causes the desired outcome but that is not included in the AI's training data*"). Italics added.

[1822] The newest developments posed by the "collect-it-all" technologies are slated to create a slew of sizzling hot challenges to the sustainability of the Rule of Law. See: Hu, Margaret, "From the National Surveillance State to the Cybersurveillance State", *The Annual Review of Law and Social Science*, Volume 13, 2017, pp. 162–163 ("*policymakers view these technological developments, including biometric technologies, as tools with the potential to identify individuals who may pose*

lack of algorithmic transparency looming large in the discussion.[1825] These concerns are neither nugatory nor overblown.[1826]

---

a threat to national and homeland security and to prevent crime and terrorism. One example of technology intended for risk assessment and threat management is the post-9/11 program Total Information Awareness (TIA). TIA was the progeny of the Defense Advanced Research Projects Agency (DARPA) in the US Department of Defense. *TIA can be understood as a "collect-it-all" data surveillance program. TIA was not explicitly identified as a collect-it-all program—this phrase originated with the Snowden disclosures.* One National Security Agency (NSA) slide described the NSA's procedure as "collect-it-all" (Greenwald 2014b*). Collect-it-all efforts like TIA embody a philosophy that aspires to preventive policing. Mass data collection is construed as a tool to assess and prevent future threats (Murray 2010). In TIA and other programs tested or adopted after 9/ 11, biometric database screening and analysis have emerged as a preferred method for tracking, identifying, and establishing identity-based inferences in counterterrorism*"). Italics added. See also: Ball, Kirstie, and Frank Webster (Eds.), *The Intensification of Surveillance: Crime, Terrorism & Warfare in the Information Age*, London, UK: Pluto Press, 2007; Guzik, Keith, "Discrimination by Design: Predictive Data Mining as Security Practice in the United States' 'War on Terrorism.'", *Surveillance and Society*, 7 (1), 2009, pp. 1–17.

[1823] Part V, Chap. 5, Sect. 5.1.1.1 of this book (on the central tenets of Rule of Law that lends itself to a beacon of justice amidst the sepulchral darkness that is about to take hold). Regrettably, the Rule of Law is backsliding worldwide. Especially in Central and Eastern Europe. See: Avbelj, Matej, "The Rule of Law, Comprehensive Doctrines, Overlapping Consensus, and the Future of Europe", *Ratio Juris*, Volume 36, Issue 3, September, 2023, pp. 242–258. The Rule of Law is not amenable to be packaged in a «one size fits all» coat nonetheless. But see: Chesterman, Simon, "An International Rule of Law", *The American Journal of Comparative Law*, Volume 56, 2008, pp. 331–362 (on the thrust to grasp (?) a catch-all International Rule of Law). See: Peari, Sagi, "Better Law as a Better Outcome", *The American Journal of Comparative Law*, Volume 63, Issue 1, 2015, pp. 155–195 (156) (on Leflar's stance on «better rule of law»). For the purposes of this piece, Rule of Law amounts to a lighthouse of procedural fairness to which citizens, regardless of where they are, resort to upon gaining access to a given system of administration of criminal justice. Whilst further utterances on the fabric of Rule of Law fall well outside the scope and breadth of this paper, one must not be oblivious of the fact that the thrust to Deglobalizing Rule of Law is underway. See: Bussani, Mauro, "Deglobalizing Rule of Law and Democracy: Hunting Down Rhetoric Through Comparative Law", *The American Journal of Comparative Law*, Volume 67, 2019, pp. 701–744 (701) (contending that the thrust to Deglobalizing Rule of Law is interwoven with thrust to take heed of «well-known differences that run through cultures and traditions». In spite of which, «the West has never stopped trying to export its own law into the rest of the world»). Unsurprisingly, there have been educated calls to take heed of the pinpointed cultural and legal differences by, in the case of China, allow for a «Socialist Rule of Law». See: Chinese Common Law Guiding Cases, *Harvard Law Review*, Volume 129, 2016, p. 2213. We will come back to this issue further down is this paper. See: Part V, Chap. 5, Sect. 5.1.1.1 of this book (on the central tenets of Rule of Law that lends itself to a beacon of justice amidst the sepulchral darkness that is about to take hold). See: Part V, Chap. 5, Sect. 5.1.1.2 of this book (on the central tenets of Procedural Rule of Law that lends itself to a lighthouse of justice that allows citizens to challenge the pearls of algorithmic wisdom in a court of law).

[1824] But see: Hardt, Moritz, "How big data is unfair: Understanding sources of unfairness in data driven decision making", *Medium*, Archived on Oct. 8, 2014, available at: https://web.archive.org/web/20141008185829/; https://medium.com/@mrtz/how-big-data-is-unfair-9aa544d739de. (access: 17.12.2024).

[1825] See: Tyler, Tom R., "Does the American Public Accept the Rule of Law? The Findings of Psychological Research on Deference to Authority", *De Paul Law Review*, 56, 2007, pp. 661–664 (stating that "transparency and openness foster the belief that decision-making procedures are

§§ Compellingly, the interplay between big data[1827] and machine learning algorithms[1828] is shaping up to catalyse a metamorphic shift in the way in which corporations, governments, and employers[1829] rank individuals.[1830] Bafflingly, though, one of the most important threats to anti-discrimination legal frameworks posed by this game-changing technology remains poorly understood and largely unaddressed by the extant literature.[1831] Unsurprisingly, these are sobering news.

§§ As hinted above, machine learning algorithms are being increasingly entrusted with the task of making high stake[1832] decisions.[1833] Note, though, that is not something you should hold your breath for.[1834] Put it bluntly, and as aforementioned,

---

neutral"). See also: Coglianese, Cary/Lehr, David, "Transparency and Algorithmic Governance", *Administrative Law Review*, Volume 71, 2019, passim. See also: Doherty, Joseph W./Reville, Robert T./Zakaras, Laura(ed.), *Introduction to Confidentiality, Transparency, and the U.S. Civil Justice System*, Oxford, Oxford University Press, 2012, 1–258 (passim) (noting that the lack of transparency yields sizable social costs).

1826 See: Part V, Chap. 5, Sects. 5.1.2–5.1.6.2.1 of this book (on the thing-centred algorithmic decision-making propelled by a *Controllable* and *Interpretable* Machine Learning that weeds out *Algorithmic Dictatorship* and secures *Algorithmic Common Good*).

1827 Barocas, Solon/Selbst, Andrew D., "Big Data's Disparate Impact", *California Law Review*, Volume 104, 2016, pp. 671–682 (discussing how data is often flawed, rigged, incomplete, imperfect and therefore algorithms inherit the prejudice of the original decision makers).

1828 O'Neil, Cathy, *Weapons of Math Destruction. How Big Data Increases Inequality and Threatens Democracy*, London, Penguin Random House, 2016, passim (showing how algorithms utilized in modern societies are amenable to perpetuate racial discrimination, partially through perpetuation of social disadvantage and wealth divides).

1829 Kim, Pauline T., "Data-Driven Discrimination at Work", *William & Mary Law Review*, Volume 58, 2017, 857–860 ("Employers are increasingly relying on data analytic tools to make personnel decisions").

1830 Prince, Anya E. R./Schwarcz, Daniel, "Proxy Discrimination in the Age of Artificial Intelligence and Big Data", *cit.*, p. 1257.

1831 Prince, Anya E. R./Schwarcz, Daniel, "Proxy Discrimination in the Age of Artificial Intelligence and Big Data", *cit.*, p. 1257.

1832 But see: Part V, Chap. 5, Sect. 5.1.7.2 of this book (on law number two to control algorithmic decision-making, which mandates that black box models must not be entrusted with the task of making high stake decisions—v.g. health and freedom).

1833 See: Rudin, Cynthia, "Please stop explaining black box models for high stakes decisions", *Proceedings of NeurIPS 2018 Workshop on Critiquing and Correcting Trends in Machine Learning (NIPS 2018)*, 2018, passim; Rudin, C., & Radin, J., "Why are we using black box models in AI when we don't need to? A lesson from an explainable AI competition", *Harvard Data Science Review*, 2019, Volume 1, Issue 2, passim; Tan, S., Caruana, R., Hooker, G., and Lou, Y., "Distill-and-compare: Auditing blackbox models using transparent model distillation". *Proceedings of the 2018 AAAI/ACM Conference on AI, Ethics, and Society, Association for Computing Machinery*, 2018, pp. 303–310; Watcher, S./Mittelstadt, B./Russell, C., "Counterfactual explanations without opening the black box: automated decisions and the GDPR", *Harvard Journal of Law & Technology*, Volume 1, 2018, passim. See: Part IV, This chapter, Sects. 4.1.4–4.1.4.2.3 of this book.

1834 See: Havard, Cassandra Jones, "On The Take": The Black Box of Credit Scoring and Mortgage Discrimination", *Boston University Public Interest Law Journal*, Volume 20, 2011, pp. 241–247 (highlighting that algorithmic credit scoring, if left unchecked, may be transmogrified into an intrinsic, encroached, deep-rooted form of racial discrimination akin to mortgage redlining);

machine learning algorithms should not be deployed to make high stake decisions that can alter the course of our lives.[1835]

§§ Although the extant literature tends to disfavour a neutral shifting from the role of human-decision-making[1836] to that of algorithmic decision-making[1837] during the

---

Pasquale, Frank, *The Black Box Society: The Secret Algorithms that Control Money and Information*. Cambridge, Massachusetts: Harvard University Press, 2015, 1–320. See: Part IV, This chapter, Sects. 4.1.4–4.1.4.2.3 of this book.

[1835] For example, there is burgeoning trend to perform sentencing anchored in machine learning algorithms in a bid to ease—and sometimes offset—human flaws (ranging from racial bias, gender bias, jealousy, to sexual orientation bias). Such algorithmic tools, which are currently being deployed in predicting criminal recidivism, are gaining traction and gathering pace worldwide. Caution must be nonetheless exercised to avoid entrusting machines with the duty to make high stake decisions that may prove detrimental to citizens 'fundamental rights. Amongst which, freedom of those affected the most by the deployment of biased technology: Blacks and Latinos. See: Weizenbaum, Joseph, *Computer Power and Human Reason: From Judgment to Calculation*, 1st edition, New York, W. H. Freeman & Co, 1976, pp. 1–300 (227) ("examines the sources of the computer's powers and offers evaluative explorations of what computers can do, cannot do, and should not be employed to do") (*this founding father of Artificial Intelligence presciently noted that we should not entrust Artificial Intelligence-embedded technologies* with "tasks that demand wisdom"). Italics added. The approval of rental applications is arguably one of those tasks that should never be entrusted to machines). More on this on Part IV, This chapter, Sects. 4.1.4–4.1.4.2.1 of this book. On the use of algorithms to undertake risk assessment in sentencing: Gialuz, M., "Quando la giustizia penale encontra l'intelligenza artificiale: luci e e ombre di risk assessment tools tra Stati Uniti ed Europa", 2019, available at: www.penalecontemporaneo.it.d/6702-quando-la-giustizia-penale-encontra-l'intelligenz-artificiale-luci-e-ombre-di-risk-assessment-tools (access: 03.07.2024); Peeters, R./Schuilenburg, M., "Machine Justice: Governing Security through Bureaucracy of Algorithms", *Information Polity*, Volume 23, 2018, pp. 267–274; Hamilton, Melissa, "Sentencing Disparities", *British Journal of American Legal Studies*, Volume 6, Issue 2, 2017, pp. 181 ff; Rodrigues, Anabela Miranda, "Medida da pena de prisão—desafios da era da inteligência artificial", *Revista de Legislação e de Jurisprudência*, Março-Abril de 2020, Ano 149.º, N.º 4021, 2020, pp. 258 ff; Santos, Hugo Luz dos, "Brain-Computer Interfaces, Generative Artificial Intelligence (ChatGPT and Deep Fakes) and Criminal Procedure Law: what's at stake?", *Journal of Research in E. and Computer Science*, Edinburgh, United Kingdom, June 2024, Volume 2, 2024, pp. 39–78; Santos, Hugo Luz dos, *Programas de Compliance e Inteligência Artificial: Consequências ao nível da Law and Economics, do Direito Penal, do Processo Penal e da Behavioral Law and Economics*, Braga, NovaCausa Edições Jurídicas, 2024, pp. 1–330; Santos, Hugo Luz dos, *Inteligência Artificial (ChatGPT/AutoGPT/Robots-Advogados/Robots Proceduradores/Robots-Juízes) e Responsabilidade Penal das Pessoas Colectivas*, Braga, NovaCausa Edições Jurídicas, 2023, pp. 1–108; Santos, Hugo Luz dos, *Inteligência Artificial e Processo Penal*, Braga, NovaCausa Edições Jurídicas, 2022, pp. 1–256; Santos, Hugo Luz dos, *Inteligência Artificial e Processo Penal*, Braga, NovaCausa Edições Jurídicas, 2022, pp. 1–256; Santos, Hugo Luz dos, *Inteligência Artificial e Processo Civil na Era do Metaverse e dos Machine Learning Algorithms*, Braga, NovaCausa Edições Jurídicas, 2022, pp. 1–264.

[1836] See: Millar, Jason/Kerr, Ian, "Delegation, Relinquishment and Responsibility: The Prospect of Expert Robots", *Robot Law*, Calo, Ryan /Froomkin, A. Michael/Kerr, Ian, Cheltenham, Edward Elgar Publishing, 2016, pp. 102, 106–107 (as these authors aptly put it "*we will rely on robots without really knowing why – simply because their algorithms provide the greatest number of successful outcomes*. We have already seen this in Google's search approach. Neither Larry (Page) nor Sergey (Brin) (nor any other Google employee) knowns exactly why one particular web page is a better result than another. *When the click patterns say it is, that's good enough.* No semantic or causal analysis is required...*Like the ancients, we will, quite rationally, come to rely upon them, knowing full well that we cannot necessarily explain the reasons for their decisions*"). Italics added. Converging: Casey,

course of a regular decision-making process,[1838] few, if any, were the doctrinal contributions that deftly addressed the scorching challenges posed by an ever-evolving artificial intelligence that is gradually deciding all aspects of our daily lives.[1839]

§§ Relatedly, there is a perceived risk that machine leaning algorithms will burgeoningly engage in «proxy discrimination»,[1840] thereby heading towards the edge of the road of *Algorithmic Dictatorship* that merits disapproval in that deserves to be frowned upon with no qualms whatsoever.[1841]

§§ It is crucially important to aver that proxy discrimination is a devilishly harmful subset of disparate impact.[1842] Commensurate with all types of disparate impact,[1843]

Anthony J./Niblett, Anthony, "Self-driving Laws", *University of Toronto Law Journal*, Volume 66, 2016, pp. 429–435 (contend that "as more information is generated, and the evolutionary algorithm updates and become a better forecaster, we imagine that judges will increasingly rely on the advice of the algorithm").

[1837] See: Bartlett, Robert/Morse, Adair/Wallace, Nancy/Stanton, Richard, "Algorithmic Discrimination and Input Accountability Under the Civil Rights Acts", *Berkeley Technology Law Journal*, Volume 36, 2021, pp. 675–736 (675) ("the disproportionate burden of COVID-19 among communities of color and a necessary renewed attention to racial inequalities have lent new urgency to concerns *that algorithmic decision-making can lead to unintentional discrimination against members of historically marginalized groups*"). Italics added.

[1838] Wachter, Sandra/Mittelstadt, Brent/Russell, Chris, "Why Fairness Cannot be Automated: Bridging the Gap Between EU Non-Discrimination Law and AI", *Computer Law & Security Review*, Volume 41, 2021, 105567.

[1839] See: Citron, Danielle Keats/Pasquale, Frank A., "The Scored Society: Due Process for Automated Predictions", *Washington Law Review*, Volume 89, 2014, pp. 1–34 (arguing that "[a]*dvocates applaud the removal of human beings and their flaws from the assessment process*," but arguing that bias remains "[*b*]*ecause human beings program predictive algorithms, their biases and values are embedded into the software's instructions*"). Italics added. See: Part IV, This chapter, Sects. 4.1.4–4.1.4.2.3 of this book.

[1840] Prince, Anya E. R./Schwarcz, Daniel, "Proxy Discrimination in the Age of Artificial Intelligence and Big Data", *cit.*, p. 1257. It bears mentioning that the scorching issue of whether and to what extent disparate impact alone should be actionable is different from, in that does not overlap with, the sweltering issue of proxy discrimination. See: Cohran, Matthew Jordan, "Fairness in Disparity: Challenging the Application of Disparate Impact Theory in Fair Housing Claims Against Insurers", *The George Mason University Civil Rights Law Journal*, Volume 21, 2011, pp. 159 and ff and passim (discussing the use of disparate impact theory and potential applicability to Fair Housing Act claims against insurers).

[1841] Allen, James, "The Color of Algorithms: An Analysis and Proposed Research Agenda Deterring Algorithmic Redlining", *Fordham Urban Law Journal*, Volume 46, 2019, pp. 219–234 (229–234) (discussing how historical mortgage redlining greatly swayed modern algorithms generated by massive batches of data sets that consist of decades of information built on exclusion and racial discrimination in the purview of financing, marketing, and housing). See: Part IV, This chapter, Sects. 4.1.4–4.1.4.2.3 of this book.

[1842] Prince, Anya E. R./Schwarcz, Daniel, "Proxy Discrimination in the Age of Artificial Intelligence and Big Data", *cit.*, p. 1257.

[1843] Howard, Justin D Howard, "Refashioning the Disparate Treatment and Disparate Impact Doctrines in Theory and in Practice", *Howard Law Journal*, Volume 41, 1998, passim; Seiner, Joseph, "Disentangling Disparate Impact and Disparate Treatment: Adapting the Canadian Approach", *Yale Law & Policy Review*, Volume 25, 2006; Primus, Richard "The Future of Disparate Impact", *Michigan Law Review*, Volume 108, 2010, pp. 1340 and ff and passim; Stephanopoulos,

it entails a facially neutral[1844] practice[1845] that inordinately harms either members of a protected class[1846] or members of racialized communities that have been historically targeted[1847] by discriminatory practices.[1848] It is noteworthy, though, that a practice spawning a disparate impact only amounts to proxy discrimination if the convenience to the discriminator[1849] of the facially neutral[1850] practice[1851] arises, at least partially,

---

Nicholas O. "Disparate Impact, Unified Law", *Yale Law Journal*, Volume 128, 2019, pp. 1566–1595 (on the dichotomy between disparate treatment and disparate impact).

[1844] But see: Hurley, Mikella/Adebayo, Julius, "Credit Scoring in the Era of Big Data", *Yale Journal of Law and Technology*, Volume 18, 2016, p. 149 ("*these tools may furthermore obscure discriminatory and subjective lending policies behind a single "objective" score* (...) *sophisticated algorithms may combine facially neutral data points and treat them as proxies for immutable characteristics such as race or gender, thereby circumventing existing non-discrimination laws and systematically denying credit access to certain groups. Finally, big-data tools may allow online payday lenders to target the most vulnerable consumers and lure them into debt traps*"). Italics added. See also: Farina, M./Lavazza, A., *Philosophy, expertise, and the myth of* neutrality, Routledge Studies in Contemporary Philosophy, London, Routledge, 2024.

[1845] But see: Bornstein, Stepanhie, "Antidiscriminatory Algorithms", *Alabama Law Review*, Volume 70, 2018, pp. 519, 524–528 (contending, however, that the tagged "facially neutral" algorithms producing discriminatory outcomes should be quashed).

[1846] Prince, Anya E. R./Schwarcz, Daniel, "Proxy Discrimination in the Age of Artificial Intelligence and Big Data", *cit.*, p. 1257.

[1847] Sunstein, Cass R., "Algorithms, Correcting Biases", *Social Research*, Volume 86, 2019, pp. 449–506 (this famed author tagged disparate impact as "disturbing in itself, in the sense that a practice that produces such an impact helps entrench something like a caste system").

[1848] In spite of its deep-seated racial bias, decision-makers continue to deploy redlining tactics through big data and may even justify such unlawful practices by claiming that the latter abide by cost-effectiveness. See: Humber, Nadiyah J., "A Home for Digital Equity: Algorithmic Redlining and Property Technology", *California Law Review*, Volume 111, Issue 5, 2023, pp. 1421–1484. See also: Hurley, Mikella/Adebayo, Julius, "Credit Scoring in the Era of Big Data", *Yale Journal of Law and Technology*, Volume 18, 2016, pp. 148, 151–156, 172 (averring that FICO scoring boasts a redoubtable capacity to routinely weed out some populations that have been historically and systematically underrepresented or grossly unfairly represented in the credit industry market). Tellingly, by 2016, ten states had disavowed the unlawful practice of employers using shady algorithmic credit scores due to their perceived disparate impact on low-income applicants and members of racialized communities (mostly Black folks). See: O'Neill, Cathy, *Weapons of Math Destruction. How Big Data Increases Inequality and Threatens Democracy*. London: Penguin Random House, 2016, pp. 128 and ff and passim. See: Part IV, This chapter, Sects. 4.1.4–4.1.4.2.3 of this book.

[1849] In spite of the widely accepted conceptual differences between intent-based and effect-based theories of disparate impact, both approaches often dovetail seamlessly. As far as the fair lending goes, the definition of disparate impact cases is somewhat shallow, nomadic, erratic, and dispiritingly vague. Note, though, that the loan officer's discretion (discriminator) is directly conducive to exceedingly higher rates for members of racial minorities. See: Ayres, Ian/Klein, Gary/West, Jeffrey, "The Rise and (Potential) Fall of Disparate Impact Lending Litigation", *Evidence and Innovation in Housing Law and Policy*, Fennell, Lee Anne/Keys, Benajmin J. (Editors), Cambridge, Cambridge University Press, 2017, pp. 231–254.

[1850] See: Schwemm, Robert G./Taren, Jeffrey L., "Discretionary Pricing, Mortgage Discrimination, and the Fair Housing Act", *The Harvard Civil Rights-Civil Liberties Law Review*, 2010, passim. The conduct being granularly parsed is discretion ascribed to brokers—which is considered by many stakeholders a harmless neutral practice -, may nonetheless lead to brokers to intentionally discriminate against members of racial minorities. See also: Selmi, Michael, "Indirect Discrimination and

from the very fact that it exacts a toll on, and gives rise to a disparate impact[1852] on, members of racialized communities.[1853]

§§ Historically,[1854] this occurred on the heels of a set of thought-through racially motivated laws and policies that wittingly sought to overtly discriminate members of

---

the Anti-Discrimination Mandate", Oxford, Oxford University Press, *Philosophical Foundations of Discrimination Law (Philosophical Foundations of Law)*, Hellman, Deborah/Moreau, Sophia (Editors), 2013, pp. 1–304 (pp. 257 and ff and passim) (books description: "how do we understand and justify the particular partialities that discrimination law tries to protect against? Are different discrimination laws from around the world grounded in a single set of norms? *And does discrimination law fail to treat people as individuals? The philosophical study around discrimination law in the private and public sector is a relatively young field of inquiry. This is owing to the fact that anti-discrimination laws are relatively new. It is arguably only since the Second World War that these rights have been adopted by countries in a broad sense, ensuring that all citizens have civil rights and the right to non-discrimination. Theory around discrimination law has until recently been threefold, doctrinal in its approach, questioning equality—why it matters and why should it influence legislatures in the design of policy—and thirdly focusing on the issue of affirmative action.* This volume takes a fresh look at the philosophy of discrimination law, identifying points of discussion in need of further study. It addresses how we are to understand and justify laws prohibiting discrimination. For instance, how discrimination might be best conceived—as a personal wrong or as an unfair distribution of resources. *The volume then turns to a number of meta-theoretical questions, whether different discrimination laws are coherent and grounded in collectively held beliefs or are instead a collection of very different rules that have no underlying coherence.* Lastly, the authors focus on issues in discrimination law that are currently the topic of considerable political debate. *The questions raised here are urgent and necessary and it is the hope of the authors that other academics and philosophers may join in their discussions*"). Italics added. See: Part IV, This chapter, Sects. 4.1.4–4.1.4.2.1 of this book (on mortgage redlining). See: Part IV, This chapter, Sects. 4.1.2–4.1.4.3 of this book (on algorithmic credit scoring, consumer racism and credit card redlining). See: Part IV, This chapter, Sects. 4.1.4–4.1.4.2.3 of this book (on algorithmic redlining). See: Part IV, This chapter, Sect. 4.1.4.3 of this book (on "algorithmic redliking"). See: Part IV, This chapter, Sect. 4.1.3 of this book (on algorithmic prime-lining).

[1851] But see: Citron, Danielle Keats/Pasquale, Frank, "The Scored Society: Due Process for Automated Predictions", *Washington Law Review*, Volume 89, 2014, pp. 1, 4–5 (highlighting how human beings programming automated systems is directly conducive to, and leads, to fundamentally inaccurate results since the source code, predictive algorithms and datasets may encompass human biases which, in turn, have a disparate impact on historically disadvantaged groups).

[1852] Prince, Anya E. R./Schwarcz, Daniel, "Proxy Discrimination in the Age of Artificial Intelligence and Big Data", *cit.*, p. 1257.

[1853] Crawford, Kate/Schultz, Jason, "Big Data and Due Process: Toward a Framework to Redress Predictive Privacy Harms", *Boston College Law Review*, Volume 55, 2014, pp. 93, 99–101 (pinpointing pathways through which predictive analytic tools perpetuate discriminatory practices).

[1854] See: Barocas, Solon/Selbst, Andrew, "Big Data's Disparate Impact", *California Law Review*, Volume 104, pp. 2016, p. 691 (highlighting the worrisome, and gruesome, issue of "structural disadvantage" with which racialized communities have been tussling for centuries). See also: Powell, Richard/Porter, Jeremy, "Redlining, Concentrated Disadvantage and Crime: The Effects of Discriminatory Government Policies on Violent Crime", *American Journal of Criminal Justice*, Volume 48, 2023, pp. 1132–1156 ("*Redlining and other discriminatory government policies enacted during the first half of the Twentieth Century have had long-lasting negative effects on neighborhoods, especially those inhabited by people of color. This study attempts to link the practice of redlining to current-day indicators of neighborhood concentrated disadvantage and violent crime using spatio-temporal data from Chicago* (…) *In addition, it seeks to determine whether redlining was associated with violent crime, and if that association was mediated by redlining's effect on concentrated*

racialized communities[1855] by hinging upon a proxy for class belonging, such as zip code.[1856] *Mortgage redlining* stands as a paradigmatic example of racially motivated policies[1857] that sought to jettison Blacks to the outskirts of urban areas, which, like all other areas, are covered by ZIP codes.

§§ The overriding goal underpinning this initiative—*mortgage redlining*,[1858] which, recall, boiled down to a policy according to which non-White communities should be thrown to the outskirts of urban cities[1859]—was straightforward: cast a shady shadow on racialized people, thus forging an inextricably link between race,[1860]

---

disadvantage. The results indicate that redlining was associated with increases in both concentrated disadvantage and violent crime, and that redlining's relationship with violent crime was, indeed, partially mediated by its relationship with concentrated disadvantage"). Italics added. See also: Gandy, Oscar H., *Coming to Terms with Chance: Engaging Rational Discrimination and Cumulative Disadvantage*, Farnham, UK: Ashgate Publishing, 2009, passim.

[1855] See: Perea, Juan F., "Doctrines of Delusion: How the History of the G.I. Bill and Other Inconvenient Truths Undermind the Supreme Court's Affirmative Action Jurisprudence", *University of Pittsburgh Law Review*, Volume 75, 1995, pp. 583, 586–89 (establishes a liaison between Jim Crow laws, the G.I. Bill, and the Social Security Act and White supremacy); Milligan, Joy, "Protecting Disfavored Minorities: Towards Institutional Realism", *UCLA Law Review*, Volume 63, 2016, pp. 894, pp. 918–21 (shedding a keen light on racial inequality in U.S. Department of Agriculture farm assistance); Robinson, Reginald Leamon, "The Racial Limits of the Fair Housing Act: The Intersection of Dominant White Images, the Violence of Neighborhood Purity, and the Master Narrative of Black Inferiority", *William & Mary Law Review*, Volume 37, 1995, pp. 69, 71–74 (establishes a connection between the failures of the FHA and White supremacy). But see: Wormser, Richard, *The Rise and Fall of Jim Crow*, Manhattan, New York City, St Martin's Press, 2014, pp. 1–222 ("*White supremacy prevailed, but it did not destroy the spirit of the black community*"). Italics added.

[1856] Prince, Anya E. R./Schwarcz, Daniel, "Proxy Discrimination in the Age of Artificial Intelligence and Big Data", *cit.*, p. 1257.

[1857] See: Part IV, This chapter, Sects. 4.1.4–4.1.4.2.1 of this book (on mortgage redlining). See: Part IV, This chapter, Sects. 4.1.2–4.1.4.3 of this book (on algorithmic credit scoring, consumer racism and credit card redlining). See: Part IV, This chapter, Sects. 4.1.4–4.1.4.2.3 of this book (on algorithmic redlining). See: Part IV, This chapter, Sect. 4.1.4.3 of this book (on "algorithmic redliking").

[1858] See: Part IV, This chapter, Sects. 4.1.4–4.1.4.2.1 of this book (on mortgage redlining).

[1859] Szto, Mary, "Real Estate Agents as Agents of Social Change: Redlining, Reverse Redlining, and Greenlining", *Seatle Journal for Social Justice*, Volume 12, Issue 1, 2013, pp. 9–11 ("*Official redlining practices began in the 1930's during the Great Depression.* A housing bubble and bust preceded the Great Depression. *Before mortgage lending became affordable, only wealthy families could buy homes. In 1935, NAREB argued that the federal government should subsidize mortgages and private ownership, not public housing. The federal government agreed and enacted multiple programs to revive the economy and increase employment.* These programs promoted residential construction and made home ownership widely available. This was achieved by "standardized homebuilding procedures" to address the "rising costs of construction," and by providing mortgage insurance. "*Such mortgage insurance lowered interest rates from six to eight percent down to four percent, and raised the amounts that could be financed from 50 to 70 percent of the purchase price to 90 percent. After 1939, with a federally insured mortgage, it was cheaper to purchase than to rent. Unfortunately, three underlying assumptions of these federal programs were the following: (1) people could be divided by race; (2) only white communities held property values; and therefore; (3) segregation by race was necessary to protect white property values. Thus, these programs introduced official racial redlining 60 and allowed the government to promote restrictive racial covenants and*

class, crime hot spots,[1861] income,[1862] proneness to engage in criminal activities,[1863] syndicates of organized crime,[1864] gang violence,[1865] and crime-ridden neighbourhoods[1866] that still reverberates,[1867] and ripples forward,[1868] across generations.[1869] The rate and pace at which non-White are incarcerated[1870] adds plausibility to this main contention.[1871]

§§ Note, though, that proxy discrimination lends itself to an endeavour that needs not to be intentional[1872] when enrolment in a protected class is predictive[1873] of a

---

segregation. In effect, only whites received federally insured mortgages"). Footnotes omitted. Italics added.

1860 Pager, Devah, *Marked: Race, Crime, and Finding Work in an Era of Mass Incarceration*, Chicago: University of Chicago Press, 2007.

1861 Braga, Anthony A., and David L. Weisburd, *Policing Problem Places: Crime Hot Spots and Effective Prevention*, New York: Oxford University Press, 2010.

1862 Gustafson, Kaaryn S, *Cheating Welfare: Public Assistance and the Criminalization of Poverty*, New York: NYU Press, 2011.

1863 DaViera, A. L./Uriostegui, M., Gottlieb/A./Onyeka, O, "Risk, race, and predictive policing: A critical race theory analysis of the strategic subject list", *cit.*, pp. 91–103.

1864 Papachristos, Andrew V., David M. Hureau, and Anthony A. Braga, "The Corner and the Crew: The Influence of Geography and Social Networks on Gang Violence", *American Sociological Review*, 78 (3), 2013, pp. 417–47.

1865 Quillian, Lincoln, and Devah Pager, "Black Neighbors, Higher Crime? The Role of Racial Stereotypes in Evaluations of Neighborhood Crime", *American Journal of Sociology*, 107 (3), 2001, 717–767.

1866 Brewer, R. M., & Heitzeg, N. A., "The racialization of crime and punishment: Criminal justice, Color-Blind racism, and the political economy of the prison industrial complex", *American Behavioral Scientist*, 51 (5), 2008, 625–644; Sampson, Robert J., and Dawn J. Bartusch, "Legal Cynicism and (Subcultural?) Tolerance of Deviance: The Neighborhood Context of Racial Differences", *Law and Society Review*, 32, 1998, pp. 777–804.

1867 Skogan, Wesley G., *Police and Community in Chicago: A Tale of Three Cities*, New York: Oxford University Press, 2006.

1868 Sherman, Lawrence W., Patrick R. Gartin, and Michael E. Buerger, "Hot Spots of Predatory Crime: Routine Activities and the Criminology of Place.", *Criminology*, 27 (1), 1989, pp. 27–55.

1869 Jacoby, S. F., Dong, B., Beard, J. H., Wiebe, D. J., & Morrison, C. N., "The enduring impact of historical and structural racism on urban violence in Philadelphia", *Social Science & Medicine*, 1982/2018, 199, 2018, pp. 87–95.

1870 See: Bar-Gill/Oren/Warren, Elizabeth, "Making Credit Safer", *University of Pennsylvania Law Review*, Volume 157, 2008, pp. 1–66 (argue that Black defendants are far more likely to be incarcerated, arrested, surveilled and harassed than White folks, which leads to the conclusion that the use of credit scores and income presents another way in which credit decisions leverage on structural disadvantage).

1871 Travis, Jeremy, Bruce Western, and Steve Redburn (Eds.), *Growth of Incarceration in the United States: Exploring Causes and Consequences*, Washington, DC: National Academy of Science, 2014.

1872 Note, though, that certain types of racial discrimination may not be fully intentional. More likely than not, it can be related with the perils of big data colour-blindness that nonetheless relies on proxies to race and gender to make algorithmic decisions. Another problem is the one related with "creditworthiness by association" that causes more problems than it solves. Hurley, Mikella/Adebayo, Julius, "Credit Scoring in the Era of Big Data", *Yale Journal of Law and Technology*, Volume 18, 2016, p. 149 ("*recent studies have also questioned the accuracy of the data used by*

discriminator's facially neutral objective,[1874] thereby converting discrimination[1875] into something either plausible or «rational».[1876]

§§ In this batch of cases, corporations may inadvertently proxy discriminate, knowing solely that a facially neutral practice[1877] breeds coveted outcomes.[1878] Again, these are barely uplifting news as the redoubtable power of Artificial Intelligence decision-making is highly clustered in the shaky hands of a bundle of tech[1879] moguls.[1880]

---

these tools, in some cases identifying serious flaws that have a substantial bearing on lending decisions. Big-data tools may also risk creating a system of "creditworthiness by association" in which consumers' familial, religious, social, and other affiliations determine their eligibility for an affordable loan. These tools may furthermore obscure discriminatory and subjective lending policies behind a single "objective" score. Such discriminatory scoring may not be intentional; instead, sophisticated algorithms may combine facially neutral data points and treat them as proxies for immutable characteristics such as race or gender, thereby circumventing existing non-discrimination laws and systematically denying credit access to certain groups. Finally, big-data tools may allow online payday lenders to target the most vulnerable consumers and lure them into debt traps"). Italics added.

1873 But see: Citron, Danielle Keats/Pasquale, Frank, "The Scored Society: Due Process for Automated Predictions", *Washington Law Review*, Volume 89, 2014, pp. 1, 4–5 (highlighting how human beings programming automated systems is directly conducive to, and leads, to fundamentally inaccurate results since the source code, predictive algorithms and datasets may encompass human biases which, in turn, have a disparate impact on historically disadvantaged groups).

1874 Barocas, Solon/Selbst, Andrew D., "Big Data's Disparate Impact", *California Law Review*, Volume 104, 2016, p. 699 (discussing how discriminatory data mining is analogous to unintentional disparate impact analysis).

1875 Tischbirek, Alexander, "Artificial Intelligence and Discrimination: Discriminating Against Discriminatory Systems", *Regulating Artificial Intelligence*, Wischmeyer, Thomas/Macher, Timo Rade Macher (Editors), Heidelberg, Springer, 2020, pp. 103–110.

1876 Prince, Anya E. R./Schwarcz, Daniel, "Proxy Discrimination in the Age of Artificial Intelligence and Big Data", *cit.*, p. 1257.

1877 But see: Crawford, Kate/Schultz, Jason, "Big Data and Due Process: Toward a Framework to Redress Predictive Privacy Harms", *Boston College Law Review*, Volume 55, 2014, pp. 93, 99–101 (pinpointing pathways through which predictive analytic tools perpetuate discriminatory practices).

1878 Prince, Anya E. R./Schwarcz, Daniel, "Proxy Discrimination in the Age of Artificial Intelligence and Big Data", *cit.*, p. 1257.

1879 Havard, Cassandra Jones, "On The Take": The Black Box of Credit Scoring and Mortgage Discrimination", *Boston University Public Interest Law Journal*, Volume 20, 2011, pp. 241–247 (highlighting that credit scoring, if left unchecked, is an intrinsic, encroached, deep-rooted form of racial discrimination akin to mortgage redlining); Pasquale, Frank, *The Black Box Society: The Secret Algorithms that Control Money and Information*. Cambridge, Massachusetts: Harvard University Press, 2015, 1–320 (8–10 and passim).

1880 See: Yang/Kai Hao, "Selling Consumer Data for Profit: Optimal Market-Segmentation Design and its Consequences", *American Economic Review*, Volume 112, Issue 4, April 2022, 2022, pp. 1364–1393; Wagner/Gerhard/Eidenmuller, Horst, "Down by Algorithms? Siphoning Rents, Exploiting Biases, and Shaping Preferences: Regulating the Dark Side of Targeted Transactions", *University of Chicago Law Review*, Volume 86, 2019, pp. 581–609; Wallheimer, Brian, "Are you Ready for Personalized Pricing? Companies Are Figuring out What Individual Customers Will Pay-and Charging Accordingly", *Chicago Booth Review*, 2018, passim.

§§ Machine learning algorithms[1881] and big data are therefore trailblazers/pathbreakers when it comes to this peril of unwitting, yet «rational,»[1882] proxy discrimination.[1883] Put it bluntly, artificial intelligence-embedded technologies propelled by big data[1884] are nothing but tools programmed to engage in proxy discrimination[1885] whenever they are disenfranchised of relevant information about enrolment/belonging in a legally protected class whose predictive power is not amenable to be gauged directly by non-suspect data made available to the machine learning algorithms.[1886]

§§ Legal community must therefore rally around the idea that merely gainsaying machine learning algorithms access[1887] to the most intuitive proxies for such predictive—but suspect features—is of scarce importance to derail/sap/mar this entire process[1888]; quite the opposite, it causes the unremitting/unrelenting quest—of machine learning algorithms—to ferret out less intuitive proxies to swell.[1889]

§§ Relatedly,[1890] as machine learning algorithms burgeoningly engage in data-driven[1891] deep learning[1892]—and accordingly become more well-adjusted and big

---

[1881] Bloch-Wehba, Hannah, "Access to Algorithms", *Fordham Law Review*, Volume 88, 2020, 1264 and ff; Xeniids, Raphaelle, "Tuning EU Equality Law to Algorithmic Discrimination: Three Pathways to Resilience", *Maastricht Journal of European and Comparative Law*, Volume 27, 2020, pp. 736 and ff.

[1882] Prince, Anya E.R., "Insurance Risk Classification in an Era of Genomics: Is a Rational Discrimination Policy Rational?", *Nebraska Law Review*, Volume 96, 2018, pp. 624–626 and ff and passim.

[1883] Prince, Anya E. R./Schwarcz, Daniel, "Proxy Discrimination in the Age of Artificial Intelligence and Big Data", *cit.*, p. 1257.

[1884] Burrell, Jenna, "How the Machine Thinks: Understanding Opacity in Machine Learning Algorithms", *Big Data & Society*, Volume 3, 2016.

[1885] Gillis, Talia B./Spiess, Jann L., "Big Data and Discrimination", *University of Chicago Law Review*, 2010, pp. 458 and ff and passim (on the sweltering challenges arising out algorithmic discrimination).

[1886] Prince, Anya E. R./Schwarcz, Daniel, "Proxy Discrimination in the Age of Artificial Intelligence and Big Data", *cit.*, p. 1257.

[1887] Bloch-Wehba, Hannah, "Access to Algorithms", *Fordham Law Review*, Volume 88, 2020.

[1888] Prince, Anya E. R./Schwarcz, Daniel, "Proxy Discrimination in the Age of Artificial Intelligence and Big Data", *cit.*, p. 1257.

[1889] Prince, Anya E. R./Schwarcz, Daniel, "Proxy Discrimination in the Age of Artificial Intelligence and Big Data", *cit.*, p. 1257.

[1890] Prince, Anya E. R./Schwarcz, Daniel, "Proxy Discrimination in the Age of Artificial Intelligence and Big Data", *cit.*, p. 1257.

[1891] Clough, D. R., & Wu, A., "Artificial intelligence, data-driven learning, and the decentralized structure of platform ecosystems", *Academy of Management Review*, Volume 47, Issue 1, 2022, pp. 184–189 and passim; Gregory, R. W., Henfridsson, O., Kaganer, E., & Kyriakou, H., "The role of artificial intelligence and data network effects for creating user value", *Academy of Management Review*, Volume 46, Issue 3, 2021, pp. 534–551.

[1892] Goodfellow, Ian/Bengio, Youshua/Courville, Aaron, *Deep Learning (Adaptive Computation and Machine Learning Series)*, Massachusetts, MIT Press 2016, 2016, pp. 1–800 (8) ("*Deep learning is a form of machine learning that enables computers to learn from experience and understand the*

data[1893] becomes more ubiquitous[1894]—, proxy discrimination is set to pose sweltering challenges[1895] to anti-discrimination frameworks[1896] that aim to proscribe discrimination[1897] based on potentially predictive traits.[1898] Notably, a wide range of anti-discrimination frameworks[1899] follow that pathway,[1900] thereby curtailing discrimination based on preexisting risk markers, ranging from genetics,[1901] disability, income,[1902] gender, to race.[1903]

---

world in terms of a hierarchy of concepts. Because the computer gathers knowledge from experience, there is no need for a human computer operator to formally specify all the knowledge that the computer needs. The hierarchy of concepts allows the computer to learn complicated concepts by building them out of simpler ones; a graph of these hierarchies would be many layers deep. This book introduces a broad range of topics in deep learning. The text offers mathematical and conceptual background, covering relevant concepts in linear algebra, probability theory and information theory, numerical computation, and machine learning. It describes deep learning techniques used by practitioners in industry, including deep feedforward networks, regularization, optimization algorithms, convolutional networks, sequence modeling, and practical methodology; and it surveys such applications as natural language processing, speech recognition, computer vision, online recommendation systems, bioinformatics, and videogames. Finally, the book offers research perspectives, covering such theoretical topics as linear factor models, autoencoders, representation learning, structured probabilistic models, Monte Carlo methods, the partition function, approximate inference, and deep generative models"). Italics added.

1893 Tene, Omer/Polonetsky, Jules, "Big Data for All: Privacy and User Control in the Age of Analytics", *Northwestern Journal of Technology and Intellectual Property*, Volume 11, 2013, pp. 239 and ff and passim.

1894 Custers, Bart, "Data Dilemmas in the Information Society: Introduction and Overview", Custers, Bart/Calders, Toon/Schermer, Bart/Zarsky, Tal (Editors), *Discrimination and Privacy in the Information Society: Data Mining and Profiling in Large Databases*, Heidelberg, Springer, 2013, pp. 3–26.

1895 Gillis, Talia B./Spiess, Jann L., "Big Data and Discrimination", *University of Chicago Law Review*, 2010, pp. 458 and ff and passim (on the sweltering challenges arising out algorithmic discrimination).

1896 But see: Nachbar, Thomas B., "Algorithmic Fairness, Algorithmic Discrimination", *Florida State University Law Review*, Volume 48, 2021, pp. 508 and ff and passim (arguing that US antidiscrimination law is sufficient to meet the challenges posed by algorithmic discrimination).

1897 Wachter, Sandra/Mittelstadt, Brent/Russell, Chris, "Why Fairness Cannot be Automated: Bridging the Gap Between EU Non-Discrimination Law and AI", *Computer Law & Security Review*, Volume 41, 2021.

1898 Prince, Anya E. R./Schwarcz, Daniel, "Proxy Discrimination in the Age of Artificial Intelligence and Big Data", *cit.*, p. 1258.

1899 Borgesius, Frederik J. Zuiderveen, "Strengthening Legal Protection Against Discrimination by Algorithms and Artificial Intelligence", *The International Journal of Human Rights*, Volume 24, 2020, pp. 1573–1581.

1900 None of this is to suggest, nor is to say, that mere disparate impact alone is of scant importance in that is not a relevant issue raised by both big data and algorithms. See, e.g.: Bartlett, Robert/ Morse, Adair/Stanton, Richard/Wallace, Nancy, "Consumer-Lending Discrimination in the FinTech Era 4 (Nat'l Bureau of Econ. Research, Working Paper No. 25943"), 2019, passim (concludes that disparate impact extracts as much rents as face-to-face discrimination).

1901 Prince, Anya E.R., "Insurance Risk Classification in an Era of Genomics: Is a Rational Discrimination Policy Rational?", *Nebraska Law Review*, Volume 96, 2018, passim.

1902 But see: Morris, Darcy Steeg/Schwarcz, Daniel/Teitelbaum, Joshua C., "Do Credit-Based Insurance Scores Proxy for Income in Predicting Auto Claim Risk?", *Journal of Empirical Legal Studies*,

§§ Notwithstanding, it is often posited that unintentional proxy discrimination undertaken by human beings is next to uncommon.[1904] In addition to that, it can be easily prevented by dissecting use of conspicuous potential proxies for enrolment/ belonging in a protected group,[1905] like zip code.

§§ Note, though, that unintentional proxy discrimination by machine learning algorithms—a subset of *Algorithmic Dictatorship*—is virtually inescapable/ ineluctable whenever the law aims to prohibit discrimination on the basis of traits comprising predictive[1906] information[1907] that is not amenable to be accessed more directly within the model[1908] by non-suspect data[1909]; a type of information oft-labelled[1910] as «directly predictive».

Volume 14, 2017, pp. 397, 418–21 and ff (discussing that an insurer's use of credit-anchored insurance scores lacks a disparate impact on the basis of income and thus is not amenable to be considered as a proxy for income). It is crucially important to note, though, that the very fact that only certain types of behaviours are assessed and gauged by credit scores leads to the conclusion some borrowers are not scored at all. The overwhelming majority of consumers boast meagre, if any, credit files owing to the fact that the likelihood to access to the sort of financial services that actually report to the orthodox credit bureaus scattered across modern economies is exceedingly low, which, in turn, morphs them into credit invisible persons. See: Yu, Persis/McLaughlin, Jilian/Levy, Marina, "Big Data: A Big Disappointment for Scoring Consumer Creditworthiness,", *The National Consumer Law Center*, 2 (Mar. 14, 2014), available at: https://www.nclc.org/images/pdf/pr-reports/report-big-data.pdf [https://perma.cc/W4SK-NXD5] (access: 21.12.2024).

1903 Prince, Anya E. R./Schwarcz, Daniel, "Proxy Discrimination in the Age of Artificial Intelligence and Big Data", *cit.*, p. 1258. See also: Pope, Devin G. Pope/Sydnor, Justin R., "Implementing Anti-Discrimination Policies in Statistical Profiling Models", *American Economic Journal: Applied Economics*, Volume 3, 2011, pp. 206–210 (discussing how the FTC parsed credit score use in auto-insurance pricing as a proxy for race).

1904 Prince, Anya E. R./Schwarcz, Daniel, "Proxy Discrimination in the Age of Artificial Intelligence and Big Data", *cit.*, p. 1258.

1905 Prince, Anya E. R./Schwarcz, Daniel, "Proxy Discrimination in the Age of Artificial Intelligence and Big Data", *cit.*, p. 1263.

1906 See: Corbett-Davies, Sam/Goel, Sharad, "The Measure and Mismeasure of Fairness: a critical Review of Fair Machine Learning", *Cornell University Library*, 2018, p. 18 (broaches a type of measurement bias coined "feature bias," which is neatly a bias in the predictors x. Note, though, that there is a second type of measurement bias deemed "label bias," which, in turn, amounts to a bias in y. The authors argue that that label bias is the worst bias there is).

1907 Kleinberg, Jon/Ludwig, Jens/Mullainathan, Sendhil/Sunstein Cass R., "Discrimination in the Age of Algorithms", *Journal of Legal Analysis*, Volume 10, 1, 2018, pp. 28–29, 33–34 (draw a distinction between "group differences in the raw data" and biases for the "choice of predictors").

1908 It is often contended that machine learning algorithms engender their own models to forecast future outcomes on the basis of analysis of training data. See: Mittelstadt, Brent Daniel/Taddeo, Patrick Allo, Mariarosaria/Wachter, Sandra/Floridi, Luciano, "The Ethics of Algorithms: Mapping the Debate", *Big Data & Society*, July-Dec. 2016, 2016, p. 3.

1909 Prince, Anya E. R./Schwarcz, Daniel, "Proxy Discrimination in the Age of Artificial Intelligence and Big Data", *cit.*, p. 1263.

1910 Prince, Anya E. R./Schwarcz, Daniel, "Proxy Discrimination in the Age of Artificial Intelligence and Big Data", *cit.*, p. 1263. But see: Corbett-Davies, Sam/Goel, Sharad, "The Measure and Mismeasure of Fairness: a critical Review of Fair Machine Learning", *Cornell University Library*, 2018, p. 18 (broaches a type of measurement bias coined "feature bias," which is neatly a bias in the predictors x. Note, though, that there is a second type of measurement bias deemed "label bias,"

§§ The innate penchant of machine learning algorithms to engage in proxy discrimination when they are fundamentally stripped from directly predictive traits[1911] follows ineluctably from their matrixial structure.[1912] Prediction machines[1913] are devised to pinpoint correlations[1914] between input data and target variables of interest.[1915] Note, though, that unlike **conventional statistical models**(e.g. **decision trees**),[1916] prediction machines do not attain this by hinging upon a human's whimsical intuition[1917] about a host of causal[1918] explanations for[1919] statistical connections between input data and the target variable.[1920]

§§ Rather, machine learning algorithms leverage on training data[1921] to seek out on their own what type of features can be used to predict[1922] the target[1923] variable. Whilst this process bluntly relinquishes/disregards causation,[1924] it nonetheless results in machine learning algorithms ineluctably canvassing proxies[1925] for directly predictive features when big data[1926] on these features is not made available to the machine learning algorithms due to legal[1927] constraints.[1928]

---

which, in turn, amounts to a bias in y. The authors argue that that label bias is the worst bias there is).

[1911] But see: Corbett-Davies, Sam/Goel, Sharad, "The Measure and Mismeasure of Fairness: a critical Review of Fair Machine Learning", *Cornell University Library*, 2018, p. 18 (broaches a type of measurement bias coined "feature bias," which is neatly a bias in the predictors x. Note, though, that there is a second type of measurement bias deemed "label bias," which, in turn, amounts to a bias in y. The authors argue that that label bias is the worst bias there is).

[1912] Prince, Anya E. R./Schwarcz, Daniel, "Proxy Discrimination in the Age of Artificial Intelligence and Big Data", *cit.*, p. 1263.

[1913] Aggarwal, C. C., *Neural networks and deep learning*, Heidelberg, Springer, 2018, passim; Agrawal, A., Gans, J., & Goldfarb, A., "Prediction machines (updated and expanded): The simple economics of artificial intelligence", *Harvard Business Review Press*, 2022; Agrawal, A., Gans, J., & Goldfarb, A., "Power and prediction: The disruptive economics of artificial intelligence", *Harvard Business Review Press*, 2022, passim (fleshing out the inner workings of prediction machines).

[1914] Gillis, Talia B., "The Input Data Fallacy", *Minnesota Law Review*, Volume 106, 2022, pp. 1176–1263 (p. 1244). Machine learning "involves computer algorithms *that have the ability to "learn" or improve in performance over time on some task*". See: Surden, Harry, "Machine Learning and Law", in: *Washington Law Review*, Volume 89, 2014, pp. 87 e ss; Murphy, Kevin P., *Machine Learning: A Probabilistic Perspective (Adaptive Computation and Machine Learning series)*, Massachusetts, The MIT Press, 2012, pp. 1–1104. Machine learning "*attempts to combine deductive, inductive, and abductive reasoning to make person-like reasoning in AI Entities possible. Machine-learning AI Entities initially learn in the same way a human child learns. First, they notice details and patterns in shapes, sounds, and behaviors*; then put them together to distinguish one person from another, or a dog from a cat. Eventually, the AI can recognize and identify" common objects. See also: Hutto-Schultz, Jess, "Dicitur Ex Machina: Artificial Intelligence and the Hearsay Rule", *George Mason Law Review*, Volume 27, n. ° 2, 2020, pp. 684–718 (689).

[1915] Prince, Anya E. R./Schwarcz, Daniel, "Proxy Discrimination in the Age of Artificial Intelligence and Big Data", *cit.*, p. 1263.

[1916] Fisher, Aaron et al., "All Models are Wrong, but Many are Useful", *Journal of Machine Learning Research*, Volume 20, 2019, pp. 1 and ff; Willis, Lauren, "Deception by Design", *Harvard Journal Law and Technology*, Volume 34, 2020, pp. 115–190.

§§ Such legal constraints on the use of directly predictive markers are extremely important in the remit of insurance[1929] legal framework.[1930] Casts broadly, the Patient

---

[1917] Tyler, Tom, "Methodology in Legal Research", in: *Utrecht Law Review*, Volume 13, Issue 3, 2017, pp. 130–131 ("*Accurate facts plus good legal rules lead to substantive justice.* This is the normative framework of right and wrong defined by traditional legal analysis. *Risk analysis is a nice example of the benefits of empiricism because studies suggest that the use of empirical methods to assess future dangerousness is more accurate than is the use of human intuition. It is better to use a formula when making a legal decision that involves estimates of someone's likely future conduct than it is to rely upon the impressions of judges or prosecutors*" (...) "*The legal system relies on predictions about people's likely future behaviour at many points in the system*: pretrial detention; sentencing; parole and probation; etc. And it has been used with a variety of special populations, including juveniles; the mentally ill; and sexual predators. A key reason to use such quantitative methods is that they are better able to predict future behaviour and as a consequence the many points in the system at which judgments are made – pre-trial detention; sentencing; parole – are better able to enact justice for both the innocent and the guilty. *The focus by social scientists upon helping to identify and use facts in ways that produce more accurate decisions fits well with the argument that the aims of justice are best served when they are based upon accurate factual information. Accuracy, in turn is enhanced by the use of empirical methods. Facts are sought that can guide the application of normative legal principles*"). Italics added.

[1918] See: Pearl, Judea, "Causal inference in statistics: An overview", *Statistics Surveys*, Volume 3, 2009, pp. 96–146; Pearl, Judea, *Causality*, 2nd edition, Cambridge, Cambridge University Press, 2009. But see: Part V, Chap. 5, Sects. 5.1.1.5.2.2–5.1.1.5.2.2.1.4 of this book (on the fundamental shift away from causation to correlations in algorithmic decision-making).

[1919] Prince, Anya E. R./Schwarcz, Daniel, "Proxy Discrimination in the Age of Artificial Intelligence and Big Data", *cit.*, p. 1263.

[1920] Prince, Anya E. R./Schwarcz, Daniel, "Proxy Discrimination in the Age of Artificial Intelligence and Big Data", *cit.*, p. 1264.

[1921] But see: Dong et al., Qi, "Imbalanced deep learning by minority class incremental rectification, *IEEE Transactions on Pattern Analysis & Machine Intelligence*, Volume 41, 2019, p. 1367 (posit that "*most existing learning algorithms produce inductive bias (learning bias)* towards the frequent (majority) classes if training data are not balanced, *resulting in poor minority class recognition performance*"). Italics added. See: Chandler, Anupam, "The Racist Algorithm", *Michigan Law Review*, Volume 115, n. ° 6, 2018, p. 1026 (on racist algorithms, noting that "the possibilities for discriminatory manipulation are legion"). But see: Altenburger, Kristen M./Ho, Daniel E., "When Algorithms Import Private Bias into Public Enforcement: The Promise and Limitations of Statistical Debiasing Solutions", *Journal of Institutional & Theoretical Economics*, Volume 175, 2019, pp. 97–98 (calls for a "debias predictive algorithms" to assuage racist and/or biased, doctored and bigoted algorithms nevertheless). See: Hamilton, Melissa, "The Biased Algorithm: Evidence of Disparate Impact on Hispanics", *American Criminal Law Review*, Volume 56, 2019, pp. 1553 and ff and passim. See: Part V, Chap. 5, Sect. 5.1.7.4 of this book (on one of the law to control algorithmic decision-making, namely, law number four: data partitioning must be performed—i.e. randomly split an entire dataset into the «training dataset» and the «test dataset»—to accurately predict outcomes in the real world while forestalling «inductive bias» (learning bias)).

[1922] See: Barocas, Solon/Selbst, Andrew D., "Big Data's Disparate Impact", *California Law Review*, Volume 104, 2016, pp. 677–78 (arguing that predictive data is predictive of a given/specific target variable (i.e., minimized future predicted claims) with training data which is both correctly "labelled" and "collected").

[1923] Prince, Anya E. R./Schwarcz, Daniel, "Proxy Discrimination in the Age of Artificial Intelligence and Big Data", *cit.*, p. 1264.

[1924] See: Bathaee, Yavar, "The Artificial Intelligence Black Box and the Failure of Intent and Causation", *Harvard Journal of Law and Technology*, n.° 37, 2018, p. 901 (adduces that "*one*

Protection and Affordable Care Act («ACA») forbids insurers[1931] from discriminating on the basis of health[1932] status. Concomitantly, the Genetic Information Nondiscrimination Act («GINA»)[1933] forbids discrimination by covered health insurers

---

possible reason AI may be a black box to humans is that it relies on machine-learning algorithms that internalize data in ways that are not easily audited or understood by humans (...) "first, a lack may arise from the complexity of the algorithm's structure, such as with deep neural network, which consists of thousands of artificial neurons working together in a diffuse way to solve a problem. This reason for AI being a black box is referred to as "complexity". Second, the lack of transparency may arise because the AI is using a machine-learning algorithm that relies on geometric relationships that humans cannot visualize, such as with support vector machines. This reason for AI being a black box is referred to as "dimensionality"). Italics added.

1925 Pope, Devin G. Pope/Sydnor, Justin R., "Implementing Anti-Discrimination Policies in Statistical Profiling Models", *American Economic Journal: Applied Economics*, Volume 3, 2011, pp. 206–210 (discussing how the FTC parsed credit score use in auto-insurance pricing as a proxy for race).

1926 But see: Hardt, Moritz, "How big data is unfair: Understanding sources of unfairness in data driven decision making", *Medium*, Archived on Oct. 8, 2014, available at: https://web.archive.org/web/20141008185829/; https://medium.com/@mrtz/how-big-data-is-unfair-9aa544d739de. (access: 17.12.2024).

1927 Prince, Anya E. R./Schwarcz, Daniel, "Proxy Discrimination in the Age of Artificial Intelligence and Big Data", *cit.*, p. 1264.

1928 But see: Pedreshi, Dino/Ruggieri, Salvatore/Turini, Franco, "Discrimination-aware Data Mining", *Proceedings of the 14th ACM SIGKDD International Conference on Knowledge Discovery and Data Mining (Las Vegas, Nevada, USA), ACM*, 2008, pp. 560–568 (arguing that one should shift its gaze downstream by putting in place discrimination-aware algorithmic tools while performing data mining).

1929 Abraham, Kenneth S., "Efficiency and Fairness in Insurance Risk Classification", *Virginia Law Review*, Volume 71, 1985, pp. 403, 407–08 (discussing the noxious consequences of insurance competition, pricing and risk ranking).

1930 Prince, Anya E. R./Schwarcz, Daniel, "Proxy Discrimination in the Age of Artificial Intelligence and Big Data", *cit.*, p. 1264.

1931 For an on-point breakdown of the distinct levels of opacity arising out of machine learning algorithms in the purview of insurance: Selbst, Andrew D./Barocas, Solon, "The Intuitive Appeal of Explainable Machines", *Fordham Law Review*, Volume 87, 2018, pp. 1085, 1089–99 (holding that there are plenty reasons for the insurer's ignorance. To begin with, the algorithm entails specialized knowledge to understand. That is, the insurer's employees may lack sufficient knowledge to understand the rationale behind the reasons in view of which the algorithm is producing prices for different customers—personalized pricing. Lastly, even if the insurer himself comprehends how the model operates, it may nonetheless lack expertise to comprehend why it operates the way it does. For that reason, the explainability of machines is a vital, but rather elusive, task. Thence, the famed authors deem it as the "nonintuitive" nature of algorithms. For purposes here, the insurer himself might indeed understand that its Artificial Intelligence-embedded technology formulates higher prices for those who actually access the website at hand, but may fail to come to terms with the fact that the explanation for this fact arises from the website's capacity to proxy for genetic information). See also: Scherer, Matthew U. Scherer, "Regulating Artificial Intelligence Systems: Risks, Challenges, Competencies, and Strategies", *Harvard Journal of Law and Technology*, Volume 29, 2016, pp. 353–369 (frames the crippling problem of opacity as "the possibility that the inner workings of an AI system may be kept secret and may not be susceptible to reverse engineering").

1932 But see: Bartlett, Robert/Morse, Adair/Wallace, Nancy/Stanton, Richard, "Algorithmic Discrimination and Input Accountability Under the Civil Rights Acts", *Berkeley Technology Law*

(and employers,[1934] who often grant health insurance[1935]) based on of genetic[1936] information. Notwithstanding, legally-suspect markers are directly predictive of seemingly neutral objectives outside of the insurance setting also.[1937]

§§ Conversely, employers are forbidden from taking into account gender,[1938] race,[1939] age, and disability in[1940] hiring[1941] decisions,[1942] although these markers can

---

Journal, Volume 36, 2021, pp. 675–736 (675) ("the disproportionate burden of COVID-19 among communities of color and a necessary renewed attention to racial inequalities have lent new urgency to concerns that algorithmic decision-making can lead to unintentional discrimination against members of historically marginalized groups").

1933 Areheart, Bradley A./Roberts, Jessica L., "GINA, Big Data, and the Future of Employee Privacy", *Yale Law Journal*, Volume 128, 2019, pp. 710–716 (shedding a keen light on the fundamental tenets underpinning the GINA law).

1934 See: Grimmelmann, James/Westreich, Daniel, "Incomprehensible Discrimination", *California Law Review Online*, Volume 7, 2017, pp 170 and ff and passim. This exciting piece of research revolves around as a vignette and mock judicial opinion, focusing on fictional case (an employment-based AI employed in the fictional universe of the movie Zootopia) under a specific legal regime (Title VII). It ultimately solves this fictional case by drawing a difference between *proxy discrimination* and *disparate* impact p. 70 ("*The problem is that there is no explanation in the record as to which of these two correlations, if either, is causal. It may be that the factors directly measure applicant characteristics that determine success in the challenging and dangerous field of police work, and that those characteristics happen to be unequally distributed in our diverse society.* It may also be that these factors *are instead measuring applicants' species and that they measure likely job performance only because they are identifying species in an applicant pool where the relevant characteristics are unequally distributed*"). Italics added.

1935 But see: Roberts, Jessica L./Weeks Elizabeth, *Healthism: Health Status Discrimination and the Law*, Cambridge, Cambridge University Press, 2019, pp. 1–230 (pp. 110 and ff and passim) ("*Can an airline or movie theatre require overweight customers to purchase two seats? Can a health insurance company refuse to sell policies to those most in need of medical care? Can the government condition public assistance on wellness program participation or work activity*? In this illuminating book, Jessica L. Roberts and Elizabeth Weeks consider these and similar questions, offering readers a nuanced analysis of when and why discrimination based on health status—or 'healthism'—should be allowed, and when it should not. *They provide a methodology to distinguish desirable health-based classifications from the undesirable, and propose law and policy solutions to encourage the former and limit the latter. This work should be read by anyone concerned with how government does—and does not—regulate based on health*"). Italics added.

1936 Prince, Anya E. R./Schwarcz, Daniel, "Proxy Discrimination in the Age of Artificial Intelligence and Big Data", *cit.*, p. 1264.

1937 Prince, Anya E. R./Schwarcz, Daniel, "Proxy Discrimination in the Age of Artificial Intelligence and Big Data", *cit.*, p. 1264.

1938 See: King, Allan G./Markovich, Marko J., "Big Data" and the Risk of Employment Discrimination, *Oklahoma Law Review*, Volume 68, 2016, pp. 555–563 (on employment discrimination).

1939 Zywicki, Todd J./Adamson, Joseph D., "The Law and Economics of Subprime Lending", *University of Colorado Law Review*, 2009, pp. 1–9 (contending that Black workers with roughly the same abilities and educational background earn far less than comparable white workers or have considerably fewer employment opportunities).

1940 Prince, Anya E. R./Schwarcz, Daniel, "Proxy Discrimination in the Age of Artificial Intelligence and Big Data", *cit.*, p. 1264.

1941 For example, a batch of other pieces of academic research have deftly pinpointed racial disparities with regard to access to the labour market. See: Bertrand, Marianne/Mullainathan, Sendhil, "Are Emily and Greg More Employable than Lakisha and Jamal? A Field Experiment on Labor

be directly predictive of seemingly neutral objectives, like optimizing employee[1943] hours worked or total sales.[1944]

§§ Notably, proxy discrimination by machine learning algorithms is slated to occur when forbidden traits are directly predictive of lawful outcomes in ways that are not amenable to be directly measured by alternative data.[1945] For that reason, proxy discrimination by machine learning algorithms might, at a first glimpse, come across as entirely lawful.[1946] Yet such is not the case.

§§ Revealingly, the congeries of laws that seek to forbid discrimination based on directly predictive traits—the only sets of laws that inescapably tend to beget proxy discrimination by machine learning algorithms—are propelled towards the goal of barring a slew of outcomes for members of racialized communities.[1947] Unsurprisingly, the questions of how or why harmful outcomes facing these racialized communities should be proscribed take centre stage; that is exactly why these congeries of laws forbid discrimination even when it is rational,[1948] rather than only when amounts to a byproduct of *animus*[1949] or nugatory stereotypes.[1950]

Market Discrimination", *The American Economic Review*, Volume 94, 2004, p. 991 (reaches the conclusion according to which white-sounding names are far more likely to spark a callback than that of suitably qualified applicants with Black-sounding names); Nunley, John M./Pugh, Adam/ Romero, Nicholas/Seals, R. Alan, "Racial Discrimination in the Labor Market for Recent College Graduates: Evidence from a Field Experiment", *The B.E. Journal of Economic Analysis & Policy*, Volume 15, 2015, pp. 1096 and ff and passim.

1942 Kim, Pauline T., "Data-Driven Discrimination at Work", *William & Mary Law Review*, Volume 58, 2017, 857–860 ("Employers are increasingly relying on data analytic tools to make personnel decisions"); Roberts, Jessica L./Weeks Elizabeth, *Healthism: Health Status Discrimination and the Law*, Cambridge, Cambridge University Press, 2019, pp. 1–230 (pp. 110 and ff and passim) ("*Can an employer refuse to hire someone who tests positive for nicotine or alcohol?*"). Italics added.

1943 Robbins, J. M./M.T. Ford/L.E. Tetrick, "Perceived unfairness and employee health: A meta-analytic integration", in: *Journal of Applied Psychology*, Volume 97, 2012, pp. 235–272.

1944 Prince, Anya E. R./Schwarcz, Daniel, "Proxy Discrimination in the Age of Artificial Intelligence and Big Data", *cit.*, p. 1265.

1945 Prince, Anya E. R./Schwarcz, Daniel, "Proxy Discrimination in the Age of Artificial Intelligence and Big Data", *cit.*, p. 1265.

1946 Prince, Anya E. R./Schwarcz, Daniel, "Proxy Discrimination in the Age of Artificial Intelligence and Big Data", *cit.*, p. 1265.

1947 Prince, Anya E. R./Schwarcz, Daniel, "Proxy Discrimination in the Age of Artificial Intelligence and Big Data", *cit.*, p. 1265.

1948 Prince, Anya E.R., "Insurance Risk Classification in an Era of Genomics: Is a Rational Discrimination Policy Rational?", *Nebraska Law Review*, Volume 96, 2018, pp. 624–626 and ff and passim.

1949 In spite of the widely accepted conceptual differences between intent-based and effect-based theories of disparate impact, both approaches often dovetail seamlessly. As far as the fair lending goes, the definition of disparate impact cases is somewhat shallow, nomadic, and erratic, and dispiritingly vague. Note, though, that the loan officer's discretion is directly conducive to exceedingly higher rates for members of racial minorities. See: Ayres, Ian/Klein, Gary/West, Jeffrey, "The Rise and (Potential) Fall of Disparate Impact Lending Litigation", *Evidence and Innovation in Housing Law and Policy*, Fennell, Lee Anne/Keys, Benajmin J. (Editors), Cambridge, Cambridge University Press, 2017, pp. 231–254 .

§§ Against this background, proxy discrimination undertaken by machine learning algorithms strikes hard and fast at the core of this outcome-laden goal.[1951] Tellingly, such discrimination could either result in humans who get unpleasant genetic test results finding themselves grappling with securing employment or in women who report being targeted by domestic violence finding themselves at loggerheads with insurance companies to purchase life insurance.[1952] Note, though, that these results are normatively unbecoming/unbefitting regardless of how or why they come into being.[1953] A form of *Algorithmic Dictatorship* nonetheless.

4.1.7 The «Input Data Fallacy» (Talia B. Gillis) that Propels Discrimination in the Domain of Algorithmic Fair Lending and Algorithmic Credit Pricing: Prologue

§§ Albeit there is an unfettered groundswell of support of algorithmic decision-making[1954]—propelled by a veneer of phony objectivity[1955] underpinning algorithmic-anchored decision-making[1956]—, the unvarnished truth is that which human biases are being passed over[1957] onto machines.[1958] Which, I may venture

[1950] Prince, Anya E. R./Schwarcz, Daniel, "Proxy Discrimination in the Age of Artificial Intelligence and Big Data", *cit.*, p. 1265.

[1951] Prince, Anya E. R./Schwarcz, Daniel, "Proxy Discrimination in the Age of Artificial Intelligence and Big Data", *cit.*, p. 1265.

[1952] Prince, Anya E. R./Schwarcz, Daniel, "Proxy Discrimination in the Age of Artificial Intelligence and Big Data", *cit.*, p. 1265.

[1953] Prince, Anya E. R./Schwarcz, Daniel, "Proxy Discrimination in the Age of Artificial Intelligence and Big Data", *cit.*, p. 1265.

[1954] Goodman, Bryce W., "A Step Towards Accountable Algorithms? Algorithmic Discrimination and the European Union General Data Protection", *Conference on Neural Information Processing Systems*, 2016. See: Part V, Chap. 5, Sect. 5.1.7.1 of this book (on law number one to control algorithmic decision-making, which mandates that whoever develops and/or deploys machines to undertake a given task must be held criminal accountable for the Hard-AI crimes the latter perpetrates).

[1955] Porter, Theodore M., *Trust in Numbers: The Pursuit of Objectivity in Science and Public Life*, Princeton, NJ: Princeton University Press, 1995.

[1956] Annamma, S. A., Jackson, D. D., & Morrison, D., "Conceptualizing color-evasiveness: Using dis/ability critical race theory to expand a color-blind racial ideology in education and society", *Race Ethnicity and Education*, 20 (2), 2017, pp. 147–162; Benjamin, Ruha, *Race After Technology: Abolitionist Tools for the New Jim Code*, *cit.*, pp. 1–172; DaViera, A. L./Uriostegui, M., Gottlieb/A./Onyeka, O, "Risk, race, and predictive policing: A critical race theory analysis of the strategic subject list", *cit.*, pp. 91–103 (95); Eckhouse, L., Lum, K., Conti-Cook, C., & Ciccolini, J., "Layers of bias: A unified approach for understanding problems with risk assessment. Criminal Justice and Behavior", 46 (2), 2019, pp. 185–209; O'Neil, Cathy, *Weapons of math destruction: How big data increases inequality and threatens democracy*, New York, Crown Publisher, 2016.

to add, is wholly unbeffiting in this regard[1959] inasmuch spurs algorithmic unfairness.[1960] Take the example of *algorithmic prime-lining*,[1961] which builds on a data-driven decision-making.[1962]

§§ *Prime-lining*, as hinted above, only widens the yawning wealth gap[1963] and racial wedge between the *selected few* (White folks) and the *unwanted many* (Black

---

1957 See: Sweeney, Latanya, "Discrimination in Online Ad Delivery", *ACM Queue*, Apr. 2, 2013, p. 11 (drawing on a list of the top "whitest- and blackest-identifying girls' and boys' names").

1958 See: Citron, Danielle Keats/Pasquale, Frank A., "The Scored Society: Due Process for Automated Predictions", *Washington Law Review*, Volume 89, 2014, pp. 1–13 (arguing that "[a]dvocates applaud the removal of human beings and their flaws from the assessment process," but arguing that bias remains "[b]ecause human beings program predictive algorithms, their biases and values are embedded into the software's instructions"). See also: Brennan, Michael, Can Computers Be Racist? Big Data, Inequality, and Discrimination, Ford Found: Equals Change Blog (November 18, 2015), available at: https://www.fordfoundation.org/ideas/equals-changeblog/posts/can-computers-be-racist-big-data-inequality-and-discrimination/; [https://perma.cc/A2EWBRPH]. (access: 17.12.2024).

1959 For an on-point breakdown of the distinct levels of opacity arising out of machine learning algorithms: Selbst, Andrew D./Barocas, Solon, "The Intuitive Appeal of Explainable Machines", *Fordham Law Review*, Volume 87, 2018, pp. 1085, 1089–99 (holding that there are plenty reasons for the insurer's ignorance. To begin with, the algorithm entails specialized knowledge to understand. That is, the insurer's employees may lack sufficient knowledge to understand the rationale behind the reasons in view of which the algorithm is producing prices for different customers—personalized pricing. Lastly, even if the insurer himself comprehends how the model operates, it may nonetheless lack expertise to comprehend why it operates the way it does. For that reason, the explainability of machines is a vital, but rather elusive, task. Thence, the famed authors deem it as the "nonintuitive" nature of algorithms. For purposes here, the insurer himself might indeed understand that its Artificial Intelligence-embedded technology formulates higher prices for those who actually access the website at hand, but may fail to come to terms with the fact that the explanation for this fact arises from the website's capacity to proxy for genetic information). See also: Scherer, Matthew U. Scherer, "Regulating Artificial Intelligence Systems: Risks, Challenges, Competencies, and Strategies", *Harvard Journal of Law and Technology*, Volume 29, 2016, pp. 353–369 (frames the crippling problem of opacity as "the possibility that the inner workings of an AI system may be kept secret and may not be susceptible to reverse engineering").

1960 Corbett-Davies, Sam/Goel, Sharad, "The Measure and Mismeasure of Fairness: a critical Review of Fair Machine Learning", *Cornell University Library*, 2018, pp. 3 and ff and passim (undertake laudable efforts to debunk algorithm biases that primarily target ethnic minorities, such as Hispanics and coloured people).

1961 See: Part IV, This chapter, Sect. 4.1.3 of this book (on algorithmic prime-lining).

1962 See: Hardt, Moritz, "How big data is unfair: Understanding sources of unfairness in data driven decision making", *Medium*, Archived on Oct. 8, 2014, available at: https://web.archive.org/web/20141008185829/; https://medium.com/@mrtz/how-big-data-is-unfair-9aa544d739de. (access: 17.12.2024).

1963 Derenoncourt, Ellora/Kim, Chi Hyun/Kuhn, Moritz/Schularik, Moritz, "The Wealth of Two Nations: The U.S. Racial Wealth Gap, 1860–2020", *The Quarterly Journal of Economics*, Volume 139, Issue 2, 2024, p. 741 ("A large class of commonly discussed policies for reducing racial wealth inequality seeks to reduce gaps in income, savings, and capital gains. These include policies that encourage financial diversification or stock equity holdings among Black households; policies aimed at financial literacy and retirement or savings behavior; or policies aimed at improving educational and labor market outcomes of Black Americans through improved school quality or reductions in discrimination. *Yet on a realistic note, our simulation in Section IV.A shows that even if wealth accumulation conditions had been equal since 1870, the wealth gap would still be 3 to 1 today, and full convergence would be more than 200 years away. Put differently: to close the racial wealth gap*

folks) through the lens of *Algorithmic Dictatorship*. Again, these are hardly uplifting news for members of racialized communities in that further compound the structural disadvantage[1964] with which the former have erase grappling for centuries.

§§ Algorithms are neither amenable to be referred sardonically nor are they marginally relevant, which, to be fair, is mildly disturbing.[1965] It is therefore of paramount importance to emphasise that algorithms have arguably risen to prominence.[1966] In a myriad of realms, from screening resumes[1967] to establishing criminal justice outcomes,[1968] algorithmic decision-making leveraging on state-of-the-art prediction technologies[1969] and big data[1970] has ineluctably dislodged[1971] human decision-making.[1972]

---

in the immediate term via *flow parameters, Black Americans would need a substantial positive lead over whites, not "just" more equality*"). Italics added.

1964 See: Barocas, Solon/Selbst, Andrew, "Big Data's Disparate Impact", *California Law Review*, Volume 104, pp. 2016, p. 691 (highlighting the worrisome, and gruesome, issue of "structural disadvantage" with which racialized communities have been tussling for centuries). See also: Powell, Richard/Porter, Jeremy, "Redlining, Concentrated Disadvantage and Crime: The Effects of Discriminatory Government Policies on Violent Crime", *American Journal of Criminal Justice*, Volume 48, 2023, pp. 1132–1156 ("*Redlining and other discriminatory government policies enacted during the first half of the Twentieth Century have had long-lasting negative effects on neighborhoods, especially those inhabited by people of color. This study attempts to link the practice of redlining to current-day indicators of neighborhood concentrated disadvantage and violent crime using spatio-temporal data from Chicago* (...) *In addition, it seeks to determine whether redlining was associated with violent crime, and if that association was mediated by redlining's effect on concentrated disadvantage. The results indicate that redlining was associated with increases in both concentrated disadvantage and violent crime, and that redlining's relationship with violent crime was, indeed, partially mediated by its relationship with concentrated disadvantage*"). Italics added. See also: Gandy, Oscar H., *Coming to Terms with Chance: Engaging Rational Discrimination and Cumulative Disadvantage*, Farnham, UK: Ashgate Publishing, 2009.

1965 See: Noble, Safiya Umoja, *Algorithms of Oppression: How search engines reinforce racism*, New York, New University Press, 2018, pp. 1–248 ("in *Algorithms of Oppression*, Safiya Umoja Noble challenges the idea that search engines like Google offer an equal playing field for all forms of ideas, identities, and activities. *Data discrimination is a real social problem; Noble argues that the combination of private interests in promoting certain sites, along with the monopoly status of a relatively small number of Internet search engines, leads to a biased set of search algorithms that privilege whiteness and discriminate against people of color, specifically women of color*"). Italics added. See: Part IV, This chapter, Sect. 4.1.8 of this book (on biased word embeddings with an entrenched presence on search engines run by tech moguls).

1966 Gillis, Talia B., "The Input Data Fallacy", *Minnesota Law Review*, Volume 106, 2022, pp. 1176–1263 (1177–1178). Internal citations omitted.

§§ By the same token, consumer credit[1973] and credit scoring[1974] also rely heavily upon an exquisite blend between machine learning algorithms[1975] and big data.[1976] Artificial Intelligence-embedded technologies which, in turn, have greatly increased

[1967] Hadzy, Adam, "Biased Bots: Artificial-Intelligence Systems Echo Human Prejudices", *Princeton University*, December 7, 2016, available at: https://www.princeton.edu/news/2017/04/18/biased-bots-artificial-intelligence-systems-echo-human-prejudices (access: 17.12.2024) ("This paper reiterates the important point that machine-learning methods are not 'objective' or 'unbiased' just because they rely on mathematics and algorithms," said Hanna Wallach, a senior researcher at Microsoft Research New York City, who is familiar with the study but was not involved in it. "Rather, as long as they are trained using data from society, and as long as society exhibits biases, these methods will likely reproduce these biases." *The researchers also found that machine-learning programs more often associated African American names with unpleasantness than European American names. Again, this bias plays out in people. A well-known 2004 paper by Marianne Bertrand from the University of Chicago and Sendhil Mullainathan of Harvard University sent out close to 5000 identical resumes to 1300 job advertisements, changing only the applicants' names to be either traditionally European American or African American. The former group was 50 percent more likely to be offered an interview than the latter. Computer programmers might hope to prevent the perpetuation of cultural stereotypes through the development of explicit, mathematics-based instructions for the machine learning programs underlying AI systems. Not unlike how parents and mentors try to instill concepts of fairness and equality in children and students, coders could endeavor to make machines reflect the better angels of human nature.* "The biases that we studied in the paper are easy to overlook when designers are creating systems," Narayanan said. "*The biases and stereotypes in our society reflected in our language are complex and longstanding.* Rather than *trying to sanitize or eliminate them, we should treat biases as part of the language and establish an explicit way in machine learning of determining what we consider acceptable and unacceptable*"). Italics added. See: Part IV, This chapter, Sect. 4.1.8 of this book (on biased word embeddings with an entrenched presence on search engines run by tech moguls).

[1968] See: Part IV, This chapter, Sects. 4.1.10.1–4.1.10.6 of this book (on biased algorithmic risk assessment in criminal procedure law settings, with a sharper focus on COMPAS). See also: Zhu, Mirilla, "Jury, Using Artificial Intelligence to Predict Recidivism Rates", *Yale Scientific*, 2020, passim. See also: Chasemi et al., Medhi, "The application of Machine Learning to a General Risk-Need Assessment Instrument in the Prediction of Criminal Recidivism", *Criminal Justice and Behavior*, Volume 48, 2020, pp. 518–538.

[1969] Agrawal, A., Gans, J., & Goldfarb, A., "Prediction machines (updated and expanded): The simple economics of artificial intelligence", *Harvard Business Review Press*, 2022; Agrawal, A., Gans, J., & Goldfarb, A., "Power and prediction: The disruptive economics of artificial intelligence", *Harvard Business Review Press*, 2022.

[1970] But see: Hardt, Moritz, "How big data is unfair: Understanding sources of unfairness in data driven decision making", *Medium*, Archived on Oct. 8, 2014, available at: https://web.archive.org/web/20141008185829/; https://medium.com/@mrtz/how-big-data-is-unfair-9aa544d739de. (access: 17.12.2024).

[1971] But see: Weizenbaum, Joseph, *Computer Power and Human Reason: From Judgment to Calculation*, 1st edition, New York, W. H. Freeman & Co, 1976, pp. 1–300 (227) ("examines the sources of the computer's powers and offers evaluative explorations of what computers can do, cannot do, and should not be employed to do") (*this founding father of Artificial Intelligence presciently noted that we should not entrust Artificial Intelligence-embedded technologies* with "tasks that demand wisdom"). Italics added. The approval of rental applications is arguably one of those tasks that should never be entrusted to machines). More on this on Part IV, This chapter, Sects. 4.1.4–4.1.4.2.1 of this book. But see also: Pasquale, Frank, "A Rule of Persons, Not Machines: The Limits of Legal Automation", *George Washington Law Review*, Volume 87, 2019, passim.

[1972] Gillis, Talia B., "The Input Data Fallacy", *cit.*, pp. 1176–1263 (1177–1178).

efficiency[1977] and accuracy.[1978] Note, though, that machine learning algorithms have also engendered deep-rooted concerns[1979] about all sorts of biases.[1980] Unsurprisingly, big data—flawed big data[1981]—has a direct bearing on the creation of discriminatory algorithmic predictions.[1982]

[1973] See: Part IV, This chapter, Sects. 4.1.2–4.1.4.3 of this book (on algorithmic credit scoring, consumer racism and credit card redlining). Morris, Darcy Steeg/Schwarcz, Daniel/Teitelbaum, Joshua C., "Do Credit-Based Insurance Scores Proxy for Income in Predicting Auto Claim Risk?", *Journal of Empirical Legal Studies*, Volume 14, Issue 2, 2017, pp. 397–423.

[1974] See: Part IV, This chapter, Sects. 4.1.4–4.1.4.2.1 of this book (on mortgage redlining). See: Part IV, This chapter, Sects. 4.1.4–4.1.4.2.3 of this book (on algorithmic redlining). See: Part IV, This chapter, Sect. 4.1.4.3 of this book (on "algorithmic redliking"). See: Part IV, This chapter, Sect. 4.1.3 of this book (on algorithmic prime-lining). But see: Havard, Cassandra Jones, "On The Take": The Black Box of Credit Scoring and Mortgage Discrimination", *Boston University Public Interest Law Journal*, Volume 20, 2011, pp. 241–247 (highlighting that credit scoring if unchecked is an intrinsic, encroached, deep-rooted form of racial discrimination akin to mortgage redlining). See: Part IV, This chapter, Sects. 4.1.4–4.1.4.2.1 of this book (on mortgage redlining). See: Part IV, This chapter, Sects. 4.1.2–4.1.4.3 of this book (on algorithmic credit scoring, consumer racism and credit card redlining). See: Part IV, This chapter, Sects. 4.1.4–4.1.4.2.3 of this book (on algorithmic redlining). See: Part IV, This chapter, Sect. 4.1.4.3 of this book (on "algorithmic redliking"). See: Part IV, This chapter, Sect. 4.1.3 of this book (on algorithmic prime-lining).

[1975] But see: Citron, Danielle Keats, "Technological Due Process", *Washington Law Review*, 2008, p. 1249 (talks about "hearing officer's tendency to presume a computer system's infallibility").

[1976] But see: Hardt, Moritz, "How big data is unfair: Understanding sources of unfairness in data driven decision making", *Medium*, Archived on Oct. 8, 2014, available at: https://web.archive.org/web/20141008185829/; https://medium.com/@mrtz/how-big-data-is-unfair-9aa544d739de. (access: 17.12.2024).

[1977] *Cost–benefit Analysis* is in the limelight. Its development falls conspicuously outside the scope and aim of this book though. See: Sunstein, Cass R., "The Real World of Cost-Benefits Analysis: Thirty-Six Questions (and almost as many answers)", *Columbia Law Review*, 114 (1), 2014, p. 177; Bayefsky, Rachel, "Dignity as a value in Agency Cost–Benefit Analysis", *Yale Law Journal,* 123, 2014, p. 1740; Sunstein, Cass R., *Valuing Life: Humanizing the Regulatory State*, 2014, pp. 8 ff; Gordon, Jeffrey, "The Empty Call for Cost-Benefits Analysis for Financial Regulators", *Journal of Legal Studies*, 43, 2014, p. 351; Sunstein, Cass R., "The Limits of Quantification", *California Law Review*, 103, 2014, p. 1369; Adler, Mathew/Posner, Eric A., "New Foundations of Cost–Benefit Analysis", *Regulation & Governance*, 3, 2006, p. 72; Thomas J. Miles/ Sunstein, Cass R., "The Real World of Arbitrariness Review", *University of Chicago Law Review*, 75, 2008, p. 761; Coates, John C. IV, "Cost–Benefit Analysis of Financial Regulation: Case Studies and Implications", *Yale Law Journal*, 124, 2015, pp. 882–911; Posner, Eric A./Weyl E. Glen, "Cost–Benefit Analysis of Financial Regulations: Response to Criticisms", *Yale Law Journal*, 124, 2015, pp. 246–265 (parsing the relationship between agency cost–benefit analysis and human dignity).

[1978] Gillis, Talia B., "The Input Data Fallacy", *cit.*, pp. 1176–1263 (1177–1178). See also: Tyler, Tom, "Methodology in Legal Research", *Utrecht Law Review*, Volume 13, Issue 3, 2017, pp. 130–131 ("*Accurate facts plus good legal rules lead to substantive justice.* This is the normative framework of right and wrong defined by traditional legal analysis. *Risk analysis is a nice example of the benefits of empiricism because studies suggest that the use of empirical methods to assess future dangerousness is more accurate than is the use of human intuition. It is better to use a formula when making a legal decision that involves estimates of someone's likely future conduct than it is to rely upon the impressions of judges or prosecutors*" (...) "*The legal system relies on predictions about people's likely future behaviour at many points in the system*: pretrial detention; sentencing; parole and probation (....) *The focus by social scientists upon helping to identify and use facts in ways that produce more accurate decisions fits well with the argument that the aims of justice are*

§§ Bias amounts to an expression that encapsulates, hands-in-glove, an earnest attempt to define unfairness[1983] concerning either a feeble portion of population or a legally protected group.[1984] Note, though, that bias can occur in algorithms for multifarious reasons.[1985] It can either stem from training a machine learning algorithm with imbalanced data (*inductive bias* or *learning bias*),[1986] from predicting a human decision that is bigoted,[1987] or from erroneously assessing the outcome of

best served when they are based upon accurate factual information. Accuracy, in turn is enhanced by the use of empirical methods. Facts are sought that can guide the application of normative legal principles"). Italics added.

1979 Lipton, Zachary/McAukley, Julian/Chouldechova, Alexandra, "Does Mitigating ML's Impact Disparity Require Treatment Disparity?" *Advances in Neural Information Processing Systems*, 31, S. Bengio, H. Wallach, H. Larochelle, K. Grauman, N. Cesa-Bianchi, and R. Garnett (Eds.). Curran Associates, Inc., 2018, pp. 8125–8135.

1980 Gillis, Talia B., "The Input Data Fallacy", *cit.*, pp. 1176–1263 (1177–1178). See also: Citron, Danielle Keats/Pasquale, Frank A., "The Scored Society: Due Process for Automated Predictions", *Washington Law Review*, Volume 89, 2014, pp. 1–34 (arguing that "[a]*dvocates applaud the removal of human beings and their flaws from the assessment process*," but arguing that bias remains "[*b*]*ecause human beings program predictive algorithms, their biases and values are embedded into the software's instructions*"). Italics added. See: Part IV, This chapter, Sects. 4.1.4–4.1.4.2.3 of this book.

1981 Kim, Pauline T., "Data-Driven Discrimination at Work", *William & Mary Law Review*, Volume 58, Issue 3, Article 4, 2017, pp. 857 and ff.

1982 Gillis, Talia B./Spiess, Jann L., "Big Data and Discrimination", *University of Chicago Law Review*, Volume 86, 2019, pp. 459 and ff.

1983 See: Kearns, Michael J./Neel, Seth/Roth, Aaron/Wu, Zhiwei Steven, "Preventing Fairness Gerry-mandering: Auditing and Learning for Subgroup Fairness", *Proceedings of Machine Learning Research*, Volume 80, Dy, Jennifer/Krause, Andreas (Eds.). PMLR, 2018, pp. 2564–2572.

1984 But see: Pedreshi, Dino/Ruggieri, Salvatore/Turini, Franco, "Discrimination-aware Data Mining", *Proceedings of the 14th ACM SIGKDD International Conference on Knowledge Discovery and Data Mining (Las Vegas, Nevada, USA), ACM*, 2008, pp. 560–568 (arguing that one should shift its gaze downstream by putting in place discrimination-aware algorithmic tools while performing data mining).

1985 Gillis, Talia B., "The Input Data Fallacy", *cit.*, pp. 1176–1263 (1177–1178).

1986 See: Dong et al., Qi, "Imbalanced deep learning by minority class incremental rectification, *IEEE Transactions on Pattern Analysis & Machine Intelligence*, Volume 41, 2019, p. 1367 (posit that "*most existing learning algorithms produce inductive bias (learning bias)* towards the frequent (majority) classes if training data are not balanced, *resulting in poor minority class recognition performance*"). Italics added. See: Part V, Chap. 5, Sect. 5.1.7.4 of this book (on one of the law to control algorithmic decision-making, namely, law number four: data partitioning must be performed—i.e. randomly split an entire dataset into the «training dataset» and the «test dataset»—to accurately predict outcomes in the real world while forestalling «inductive bias» (learning bias)).

1987 Kearns, Michael J./Neel, Seth/Roth, Aaron/Wu, Zhiwei Steven, "An Empirical Study of Rich Subgroup Fairness for Machine Learning", *Proceedings of the Conference on Fairness, Accountability, and Transparency, ACM*, 2019, pp. 100–109.

interest[1988] while paving the way to *algorithmic bias*.[1989] It bears mentioning that one might be leveraging on features or «inputs« that are utterly biased[1990] after all.

§§ This concern is neither unwarranted nor uncalled for. Rather, this deep-rooted concern bears on the credit context whereby the need to be afforded credit[1991] is dire for people desperate[1992] to escape[1993] poverty.[1994] Revealingly, inputs might be biased since they sharply mirror ancient disadvantages[1995] or mimic biased requirements

---

[1988] Gillis, Talia B., "The Input Data Fallacy", *cit.*, pp. 1176–1263 (1177–1178). See: Part IV, This chapter, Sects. 4.1.4–4.1.4.2.1 of this book (on mortgage redlining). See: Part IV, This chapter, Sects. 4.1.2–4.1.4.3 of this book (on algorithmic credit scoring, consumer racism and credit card redlining). See: Part IV, This chapter, Sects. 4.1.4–4.1.4.2.3 of this book (on algorithmic redlining). See: Part IV, This chapter, Sect. 4.1.4.3 of this book (on "algorithmic redliking"). See: Part IV, This chapter, Sect. 4.1.3 of this book (on algorithmic prime-lining).

[1989] See: Baeza-Yates, R., "Bias on the web", *Communications of the ACM*, 61 (6), June 2018, 2018, pp. 54–61 (argues that "*algorithmic bias is when the bias is not present in the input data* and is added *purely by the algorithm*"). See also: Hajian, Sara Hajian et al., "Algorithmic Bias: From Discrimination Discovery to Fairness-aware Data Mining", *ACM SIGKDD International Conference on Knowledge Discovery and Data Mining*, Volume 22, 2125, 2016; Griemmelmann, James/Westreich, Daniel, "Incomprehensible Discrimination ", *California Law Review Online*, Volume 7, 2018, pp. 164–171; Xiang, Alice, "Reconciling Legal and Technical Approaches to Algorithmic Bias", *Tennessee Law Review*, Volume 88, 2021, passim; See: Lemley, Mark A./Casey, Bryan, "Remedies for Robots", *The University of Chicago Law Review*, Volume 86, Issue 5, 2019, pp. 1311–1396 (1376) (alerting to the perils of algorithmic bias); Chandler, Anupam, "The Racist Algorithm", *Michigan Law Review*, Volume 115, Issue 6, 2018, p. 1026 (noting that, in the terrain of racist algorithm, "the possibilities for discriminatory manipulation are legion"; Jackson, Maya C., "Artificial Intelligence and Algorithmic Bias: The Issues with Technology Reflecting History and Humans", *Journal of Business Technology Law*, Volume 16, 2021, pp. 299–316; West, Sarah Myers/Whittaker, Meredith/Crawford, Kate, *Discriminating Systems. Gender, Race and Power in AI*. New York: AI Now Institute, 2019, pp. 15 and ff and passim; Waldman, Ezra, "Privacy, Practice, and Performance", *California Law Review*, Volume 110, 2021, passim (on algorithmic bias). But see: Kirkpatrick, Keith, "Battling Algorithmic Bias: How Do We Ensure Algorithms Treat Us Fairly?" *Commun. ACM 59*, Volume 10, 2016, pp. 16 and ff (offers insightful remarks on how to quash algorithmic biases).

[1990] Gillis, Talia B., "The Input Data Fallacy", *cit.*, pp. 1176–1263 (1177–1178). See also: Kilbertus, Niki/Carulla, Mateo Rojas/Parascandolo, Giambattista/Hardt, Moritz/Janzing, Dominik/ Schoellkopf, Bernhard, "Avoiding Discrimination through Causal Reasoning", *Advances in Neural Information Processing Systems*, I. Guyon, U. V. Luxburg, S. Bengio, H. Wallach, R. Fergus, S. Vishwanathan, and R. Garnett (Eds.), Vol. 30. Curran Associates, Inc., 2017, pp. 656–666.

[1991] Atkinson, Abbye, "Rethinking Credit as a Social Provision", *Stanford Law Review*, Volume 71, 2019, pp. 1093–1099 (contending that credit, which shifts consumption temporally, is only beneficial insofar income ratchets up in the forthcoming future. As of now, though, "credit is fundamentally incompatible with the entrenched intergenerational poverty that plagues low-income Americans." Id. Albeit it is crucially important to come to terms with the fact that credit is not a panacea for the great bulk of economic struggles, and concretely wage stagnation. Although credit is not befitted to all consumers at all prices, affordable credit can nonetheless play a pivotal role in the creation of wealth).

[1992] But see: The Use of Cash-Flow Data in Underwriting Credit: Empirical Research Findings, FINREGLAB 32, 34 (Jul. 2019), https://finreglab.org/wp-content/uploads/2019/07/FRL_Research-Report_Final.pdf; [https://perma.cc/N65Q-WQML] (arguing that the use of cash flow data can underpin a prediction of default risk, thereby providing an apposite alternative to ancient

of borrower[1996] characteristics.[1997] The role of law in dealing head-on with these deep-seated concerns remain widely contested[1998] though.

§§ Cogently, the stakes in crafting and enacting such a law are exceedingly high, objectively[1999] and unprecedently relevant.[2000] As noted above,[2001] the allotment of

---

credit scores. In addition to that, cash-flow data is commensurate with predictive across demographic groups). The Use of Cash-Flow Data in Underwriting Credit: Empirical Research Findings, FINREGLAB 32, 34 (Jul. 2019), https://finreglab.org/wp-content/uploads/2019/07/FRL_Research-Report_Final.pdf; ; [https://perma.cc/N65Q-WQML], p. 3 ("[C]ash-flow variables and scores tested were predictive of credit risk and loan performance across the heterogenous set of providers, populations, and products studied. Standing alone, the cash-flow metrics generally performed as well as traditional credit scores, which suggests that cash-flow variables and scores can provide meaningful predictive power among populations and products similar to those studied where traditional credit history is not available or reliable").

1993 See: Part IV, This chapter, Sects. 4.1.2–4.1.4.3 of this book (on algorithmic credit scoring, consumer racism and credit card redlining).

1994 Baradaran, Mehrsa, "Banking and the Social Contract", *Notre Dame Law Review*, Volume 89, pp. 1283–1336 ("access to safe credit is crucial in allowing the poor to escape poverty").

1995 Havard, Cassandra Jones, "On The Take": The Black Box of Credit Scoring and Mortgage Discrimination", *Boston University Public Interest Law Journal*, Volume 20, 2011, pp. 241–247 (highlighting that credit scoring if unchecked is an intrinsic, encroached, deep-rooted form of racial discrimination akin to mortgage redlining); Pasquale, Frank, *The Black Box Society: The Secret Algorithms that Control Money and Information.* Cambridge, Massachusetts: Harvard University Press, 2015, 1–320 (8–10 and passim). See also: Barocas, Solon/Selbst, Andrew, "Big Data's Disparate Impact", *California Law Review*, Volume 104, pp. 2016, p. 691 (highlighting the worrisome, and gruesome, issue of "structural disadvantage" with which racialized communities have been tussling for centuries). See also: Powell, Richard/Porter, Jeremy, "Redlining, Concentrated Disadvantage and Crime: The Effects of Discriminatory Government Policies on Violent Crime", *American Journal of Criminal Justice*, Volume 48, 2023, pp. 1132–1156 ("*Redlining and other discriminatory government policies enacted during the first half of the Twentieth Century have had long-lasting negative effects on neighborhoods, especially those inhabited by people of color. This study attempts to link the practice of redlining to current-day indicators of neighborhood concentrated disadvantage and violent crime using spatio-temporal data from Chicago* (...) *In addition, it seeks to determine whether redlining was associated with violent crime, and if that association was mediated by redlining's effect on concentrated disadvantage. The results indicate that redlining was associated with increases in both concentrated disadvantage and violent crime, and that redlining's relationship with violent crime was, indeed, partially mediated by its relationship with concentrated disadvantage*"). Italics added. See also: Gandy, Oscar H., *Coming to Terms with Chance: Engaging Rational Discrimination and Cumulative Disadvantage*, Farnham, UK: Ashgate Publishing, 2009.

1996 Note, though, that flawed/biased algorithms will deepen the chasm between rich and poor. See: Eubanks, Virginia, *Automating Inequality: How High-Tech Tools Profile, Police and Punish the Poor.* New York: St. Martin's Press, 2018, 1–272 (1 ff and passim) (coining the expression «automating inequality» to vividly portray the downsides of using high-technology to compound the yawning gap between rich and poor against the backdrop of biased algorithms). See also: Soss, Joe, Richard C. Fording, and Sanford F. Schram, *Disciplining the Poor: Neoliberal Paternalism and the Persistent Power of Race.* Chicago: University of Chicago Press, 2011.

1997 In spite of its deep-seated racial bias, decision-makers continue to deploy redlining tactics through big data and may even justify such unlawful practices by claiming that the latter abide by cost-effectiveness. See: Humber, Nadiyah J., "A Home for Digital Equity: Algorithmic Redlining and Property Technology", *California Law Review*, Volume 111, Issue 5, 2023, pp. 1421–1484. See also: Hurley, Mikella/Adebayo, Julius, "Credit Scoring in the Era of Big Data", *Yale Journal of Law and Technology*, Volume 18, 2016, pp. 148, 151–156, 172 (averring that FICO scoring

credit has been historically skewed by discriminatory policies[2002] and practices[2003] that reverberated across generations.[2004] From mortgage redlining[2005] to multifarious forms of financial exclusion[2006] conducive to the furtherance of the racial wealth gap between Blacks and Whites,[2007] blatantly discriminatory practices[2008] have pre-empted racial minorities from being equal participants in the purview of credit markets.[2009] No surprise stems from the fact that the exploitation[2010] of structural disadvantage[2011] facing members of racialized communities squarely aligns with the lenders 'vested economic interests.[2012]

boasts a redoubtable capacity to routinely weed out some populations that have been historically and systematically underrepresented or grossly unfairly represented in the credit industry market). Tellingly, by 2016, ten states had disavowed the unlawful practice of employers using shady credit scores due to their perceived disparate impact on low-income applicants and members of racialized communities (mostly Black folks). See: O'Neill, Cathy, *Weapons of Math Destruction. How Big Data Increases Inequality and Threatens Democracy.* London: Penguin Random House, 2016, pp. 128 and ff and passim. See: Part IV, This chapter, Sects. 4.1.4–4.1.4.2.3 of this book. See: Part IV, This chapter, Sects. 4.1.4–4.1.4.2.1 of this book (on mortgage redlining). See: Part IV, This chapter, Sects. 4.1.2–4.1.4.3 of this book (on algorithmic credit scoring, consumer racism and credit card redlining). See: Part IV, This chapter, Sects. 4.1.4–4.1.4.2.3 of this book (on algorithmic redlining). See: Part IV, This chapter, Sect. 4.1.4.3 of this book (on "algorithmic redliking"). See: Part IV, This chapter, Sect. 4.1.3 of this book (on algorithmic prime-lining).

1998 Gillis, Talia B., "The Input Data Fallacy", *cit.*, pp. 1176–1263 (1178).

1999 Porter, Theodore M., *Trust in Numbers: The Pursuit of Objectivity in Science and Public Life*, Princeton, NJ: Princeton University Press, 1995.

2000 Gillis, Talia B., "The Input Data Fallacy", *cit.*, pp. 1176–1263 (1178).

2001 See: Part IV, This chapter, Sects. 4.1.4–4.1.4.2.1 of this book (on mortgage redlining). See: Part IV, This chapter, Sects. 4.1.2–4.1.4.3 of this book (on algorithmic credit scoring, consumer racism and credit card redlining). See: Part IV, This chapter, Sects. 4.1.4–4.1.4.2.3 of this book (on algorithmic redlining). See: Part IV, This chapter, Sect. 4.1.4.3 of this book (on "algorithmic redliking"). See: Part IV, This chapter, Sect. 4.1.3 of this book (on algorithmic prime-lining).

2002 Katznelson, Ira, *When Affirmative Action Was White: An Untold History of Racial Inequality in Twentieth-Century America*, New York, W. W. Norton & Company; Reprint edition (August 17, 2006), 2006, pp. 1–272 ("In this "penetrating new analysis" (*New York Times Book Review*) *Ira Katznelson fundamentally recasts our understanding of twentieth-century American history and demonstrates that all the key programs passed during the New Deal and Fair Deal era of the 1930s and 1940s were created in a deeply discriminatory manner. Through mechanisms designed by Southern Democrats that specifically excluded maids and farm workers, the gap between blacks and whites actually widened despite postwar prosperity. In the words of noted historian Eric Foner*, "Katznelson's incisive book should change the terms of debate about affirmative action, and about the last seventy years of American history"). Italics added. This book parses the impact of several racially motivated laws—Social Security Act, G: I. Bill, and labour laws implementing unemployment stipends, minimum wages, and union protection—in the history of United States of America). Italics added.

2003 Gillis, Talia B., "The Input Data Fallacy", *cit.*, pp. 1176–1263 (1179).

2004 Haupert, T., "The racial landscape of fintech mortgage lending", *Housing Policy Debate*, Volume 32, Issue 2, 2022.

§§ Credit pricing thus imperils to perpetuate and reproduce[2013] this inequality[2014] since a lender's algorithmic risk assessment is backward-looking[2015] (*automation*

[2005] See: Part IV, This chapter, Sects. 4.1.4–4.1.4.2.1 of this book (on mortgage redlining). See: Part IV, This chapter, Sects. 4.1.2–4.1.4.3 of this book (on algorithmic credit scoring, consumer racism and credit card redlining). See: Part IV, This chapter, Sects. 4.1.4–4.1.4.2.3 of this book (on algorithmic redlining). See: Part IV, This chapter, Sect. 4.1.4.3 of this book (on "algorithmic redliking"). See: Part IV, This chapter, Sect. 4.1.3 of this book (on algorithmic prime-lining). See also: Szto, Mary, "Real Estate Agents as Agents of Social Change: Redlining, Reverse Redlining, and Greenlining", *Seatle Journal for Social Justice*, Volume 12, Issue 1, 2013, pp. 9–11 ("*Official redlining practices began in the 1930's during the Great Depression.* A housing bubble and bust preceded the Great Depression. *Before mortgage lending became affordable, only wealthy families could buy homes. In 1935, NAREB argued that the federal government should subsidize mortgages and private ownership, not public housing. The federal government agreed and enacted multiple programs to revive the economy and increase employment.* These programs promoted residential construction and made home ownership widely available. This was achieved by "standardized homebuilding procedures" to address the "rising costs of construction," and by providing mortgage insurance. "*Such mortgage insurance lowered interest rates from six to eight percent down to four percent, and raised the amounts that could be financed from 50 to 70 percent of the purchase price to 90 percent. After 1939, with a federally insured mortgage, it was cheaper to purchase than to rent. Unfortunately, three underlying assumptions of these federal programs were the following: (1) people could be divided by race; (2) only white communities held property values; and therefore; (3) segregation by race was necessary to protect white property values. Thus, these programs introduced official racial redlining 60 and allowed the government to promote restrictive racial covenants and segregation. In effect, only whites received federally insured mortgages*"). Footnotes omitted. Italics added. See: Part IV, This chapter, Sects. 4.1.4–4.1.4.2.3 of this book.

[2006] Kroeger, Teresa, and Graham Wright, "Entrepreneurship and the Racial Wealth Gap: The Impact of Entrepreneurial Success or Failure on the Wealth Mobility of Black and White Families," *Journal of Economics, Race, and Policy*, Volume 4, 2021, 183–195; Kermani, Amir, and Francis Wong, "Racial Disparities in Housing Returns," NBER Working Paper no. 29306, 2021; Hubmer, Joachim, Per Krusell, and Anthony A. Smith, Jr., "Sources of US Wealth Inequality: Past, Present, and Future," *NBER Macroeconomics Annual 2020*, Volume 35, 2021, pp. 391–455; Haines, Michael R., *Historical, Demographic, Economic, and Social Data: The United States, 1790–2002*, Inter-university Consortium for Political and Social Research, 2010: On whiteness: Frankenberg, Ruth (Ed.), *Displacing whiteness: essays in social and cultural criticism*, Durham, NC: Duke University Press, 1997; Frankenberg, Ruth, "Introduction: local whitenesses, localizing whiteness", *Displacing whiteness*, Ruth Frankenberg (Editor), Durham, NC: Duke University Press, 1997, pp. 1–33.

[2007] Derenoncourt, Ellora/Kim, Chi Hyun/Kuhn, Moritz/Schularik, Moritz, "The Wealth of Two Nations: The U.S. Racial Wealth Gap, 1860–2020", *The Quarterly Journal of Economics*, Volume 139, Issue 2, 2024, p. 741 ("A large class of commonly discussed policies for reducing racial wealth inequality seeks to reduce gaps in income, savings, and capital gains. These include policies that encourage financial diversification or stock equity holdings among Black households; policies aimed at financial literacy and retirement or savings behavior; or policies aimed at improving educational and labor market outcomes of Black Americans through improved school quality or reductions in discrimination. *Yet on a realistic note, our simulation in Section IV.A shows that even if wealth accumulation conditions had been equal since 1870, the wealth gap would still be 3 to 1 today, and full convergence would be more than 200 years away. Put differently: to close the racial wealth gap in the immediate term* via *flow parameters, Black Americans would need a substantial positive lead over whites, not "just" more equality*"). Italics added.

[2008] Pierce, C., "W.E.B. du bois and caste education: Racial capitalist schooling from reconstruction to Jim Crow", *American Educational Research Journal*, 54 (1_Suppl.), 2017, pp. 23S-47S.

bias[2016]), in that it takes stock of the historical lending behaviour of certain groups[2017] and individuals.[2018] Relatedly, extant lending practices have often perpetuated historical injustices[2019] in that way,[2020] thereby depriving millions of consumers from a

---

[2009] Gillis, Talia B., "The Input Data Fallacy", *cit.*, pp. 1176–1263 (1179).

[2010] The theory of "post-race" contends that the great bulk discrimination by the credit pricing industry is not the byproduct of wilful and flagitious bias. Rather, this discrimination broadly mirrors rational economic decisions to leverage on extant systemic, endemic, and structural social inequalities for profit. See: Carbado, Devon W./Gulati, Mitu, *Acting White? Rethinking Race in Post-Racial America*, Oxford, Oxford University Press, 2015, pp. 1–212 ("What does it mean to "act black" or "act white"? Is race merely a matter of phenotype, or does it come from the inflection of a person's speech, the clothes in her closet, how she chooses to spend her time and with whom she chooses to spend it? What does it mean to be "really" black, and who gets to make that judgment?

In Acting White?, leading scholars of race and the law Devon Carbado and Mitu Gulati argue that, in spite of decades of racial progress and the pervasiveness of multicultural rhetoric, racial judgments are often based not just on skin color, but on how a person conforms to behavior stereotypically associated with a certain race. Specifically, racial minorities are judged on how they "perform" their race. This performance pervades every aspect of their daily life, whether it's the clothes they wear, the way they style their hair, the institutions with which they affiliate, their racial politics, the people they befriend, date or marry, where they live, how they speak, and their outward mannerisms and demeanor. Employing these cues, decision-makers decide not simply whether a person is black but the degree to which she or he is so. Relying on numerous examples from the workplace, higher education, and police interactions, the authors demonstrate that, for African Americans, the costs of "acting black" are high, and so are the pressures to "act white." But, as the authors point out, "acting white" has costs as well"); Howell, Benjamin, "Note, Exploiting Race and Space: Concentrated Subprime Lending as Housing Discrimination", *California Law Review*, Volume 101, 2006, pp. pp. 108–109; Barnes, Mario L., "Reflection on a Dream World: Race, Post-Race and the Question of Making It Over", *Berkely Journal of African-American Law and Policy*, Volume 11, 2009, pp. 6 and ff and passim (parses theories of a "post-racial" world); Haney-López, Ian F., "Essay, Post-Racial Racialism: Racial Stratification and Mass Incarceration in the Age of Obama", *California Law Review*, Volume 98, 2010; Cho, Sumi, "Post-Racialism", *Iowa Law Review*, 2009; Howell, Benjamin, "Note, Exploiting Race and Space: Concentrated Subprime Lending as Housing Discrimination", *California Law Review*, Volume 94, 2006, pp. 101, 108–09; Freeman, Andrea, "Racism in the Credit Card Industry", *cit.*, p. 1098 and ff, whose stellar research I have been following closely.

[2011] See: Barocas, Solon/Selbst, Andrew, "Big Data's Disparate Impact", *California Law Review*, Volume 104, pp. 2016, p. 691 (highlighting the worrisome, and gruesome, issue of "structural disadvantage" with which racialized communities have been tussling for centuries). See also: Powell, Richard/Porter, Jeremy, "Redlining, Concentrated Disadvantage and Crime: The Effects of Discriminatory Government Policies on Violent Crime", *American Journal of Criminal Justice*, Volume 48, 2023, pp. 1132–1156 ("*Redlining and other discriminatory government policies enacted during the first half of the Twentieth Century have had long-lasting negative effects on neighborhoods, especially those inhabited by people of color. This study attempts to link the practice of redlining to current-day indicators of neighborhood concentrated disadvantage and violent crime using spatio-temporal data from Chicago (...) In addition, it seeks to determine whether redlining was associated with violent crime, and if that association was mediated by redlining's effect on concentrated disadvantage. The results indicate that redlining was associated with increases in both concentrated disadvantage and violent crime, and that redlining's relationship with violent crime was, indeed, partially mediated by its relationship with concentrated disadvantage*"). Italics added. See also: Gandy, Oscar H., *Coming to Terms with Chance: Engaging Rational Discrimination and Cumulative Disadvantage*, Farnham, UK: Ashgate Publishing, 2009.

[2012] Even absent direct compensation for exceedingly higher interest rates, more expensive loans are far more profitable for lenders in that can ultimately sway loan officer compensation rate. See:

much-needed access to credit (*consumer harm*),[2021] including a whopping amount of Black consumers.[2022]

§§ It is true that algorithmic credit pricing greatly enhances the ability of lenders to evaluate credit risk,[2023] but truer still algorithmic credit pricing engenders *automation bias* in that lenders will be ineluctably tempted to blindly follow the pearls of algorithmic wisdom offered by Artificial Intelligence-embedded technologies.[2024]

Jackson, Howell E./Burlingame, Laurie, "Kickbacks or Compensation: The Case of Yield Spread Premiums", *Stanford Journal of Law Business and Finance*, Volume 12, 2007, p. 289 (shedding a keen light on how yield spread premiums have a direct bearing on exceedingly higher mortgage prices for regular consumers, which, in turn, may befall inordinately on the least sophisticated borrowers, amongst whom members of racialised communities).

2013 Roithmayr, Daria, *Reproducing Racism: How everyday choices lock in White Advantage*, New York, New York University Press, 2014, pp. 1–272 ("*Argues that racial inequality reproduces itself automatically over time because early unfair advantage for whites has paved the way for continuing advantage. This book is designed to change the way we think about racial inequality* (...) *Legal scholar Daria Roithmayr provocatively argues that racial inequality lives on because white advantage functions as a powerful self-reinforcing monopoly, reproducing itself automatically from generation to generation even in the absence of intentional discrimination. Drawing on work in antitrust law and a range of other disciplines, Roithmayr brilliantly compares the dynamics of white advantage to the unfair tactics of giants like AT&T and Microsoft*. With penetrating insight, Roithmayr *locates the engine of white monopoly in positive feedback loops that connect the dramatic disparity of Jim Crow to modern racial gaps in jobs, housing and education. Wealthy white neighborhoods fund public schools that then turn out wealthy white neighbors. Whites with lucrative jobs informally refer their friends, who refer their friends, and so on. Roithmayr concludes that racial inequality might now be locked in place, unless policymakers immediately take drastic steps to dismantle this oppressive system*"). Italics added. This book points out how White privilege is perpetuated throughout generations through residential segregation (*mortgage redlining*), abhorrent nepotism, and other bemoaning social practices that pester modern societies. See: Part IV, This chapter, Sects. 4.1.4–4.1.4.2.3 of this book.

2014 Western, Bruce, *Punishment and Inequality in America*, New York: Russell Sage Foundation, 2006; Soss, Joe, Richard C. Fording, and Sanford F. Schram, *Disciplining the Poor: Neoliberal Paternalism and the Persistent Power of Race*, Chicago: University of Chicago Press, 2011; Laub, John H., "Understanding Inequality and the Justice System Response: Charting a New Way Forward.", New York: William T. Grant Foundation, 2014.

2015 Stevenson, M. T./Slobogin, C., "Algorithmic risk assessments and the double-edged sword of youth", *Washington University Law Review*, Volume 96, 2018, passim.

2016 Wonyoung, So, "Which Information Matters? Measuring Landlord Assessment of Tenant Screening Reports", *Housing Policy Debate*, Volume 33, n.° 6, 2023, pp. 1484–1510 (1502) (arguing that landlords display *automation bias* as the "*study finds that landlords tend to rely more on the automated system's judgment: when a report noted that a tenant was either medium or high risk, landlords showed a higher tendency toward rejection, or, if conditionally accepted, they imposed a higher security deposit. This indicates that tenant screening services' risk scoring may critically affect landlords' decision-making* (...) *tenant screening services very likely contribute to perpetuating algorithmic inequality (Eubanks, 2018) by denying qualified applicants—disproportionately from protected groups—access to housing*"). Italics added. See: Part IV, This chapter, Sects. 4.1.4–4.1.4.2.3 of this book.

2017 *Tech, Bias and Housing Initiative, the Promise and Perils of Residential Proptech, Year 1, Research Summary Report, April 2023, TechEquity Collaborative*, p. 5 available at: https://techequity.us/wp-content/uploads/2023/04/TBHI-Y1-Research-Summary-Report.pdf (28.11.2024). ("*Opaque algorithms incorporate biased data into their decision-making*

§§ Computer-run decision-making therefore catalyses both danger and promise for algorithmic fair lending[2025] and algorithmic credit pricing. The peril is that which computer-run algorithms' greater ability to parse and distinguish people based on past

---

processes (…) leaving consumers without the protections they would have from traditional (…) regulatory systems. *As unprecedented capital investment flows into this space, venture-backed companies' winner-take-all approach to growth has the potential to exacerbate inequality rather than combat it*"). Italics added. See: Part IV, This chapter, Sects. 4.1.4–4.1.4.2.3 of this book.

[2018] Gillis, Talia B., "The Input Data Fallacy", *cit.*, pp. 1176–1263 (1179).

[2019] Havard, Cassandra Jones, "On The Take": The Black Box of Credit Scoring and Mortgage Discrimination", *Boston University Public Interest Law Journal*, Volume 20, 2011, pp. 241–247 (highlighting that credit scoring if unchecked is an intrinsic, encroached, deep-rooted form of racial discrimination akin to mortgage redlining). See also: Pasquale, Frank, *The Black Box Society: The Secret Algorithms that Control Money and Information*. Cambridge, Massachusetts: Harvard University Press, 2015, 1–320 (8–10 and passim).

[2020] Allen, James, "The Color of Algorithms: An Analysis and Proposed Research Agenda Deterring Algorithmic Redlining", *Fordham Urban Law Journal*, Volume 46, 2019, pp. 219–234 (229–234) (discussing how historical mortgage redlining greatly swayed modern algorithms generated by massive batches of data sets that consist of decades of information built on exclusion and racial discrimination in the purview of financing, marketing, and housing). See: Part IV, This chapter, Sects. 4.1.4–4.1.4.2.3 of this book.

[2021] See: Part IV, This chapter, Sects. 4.1.4–4.1.4.2.1 of this book (on mortgage redlining). See: Part IV, This chapter, Sects. 4.1.2–4.1.4.3 of this book (on algorithmic credit scoring, consumer racism and credit card redlining). See: Part IV, This chapter, Sects. 4.1.4–4.1.4.2.3 of this book (on algorithmic redlining). See: Part IV, This chapter, Sect. 4.1.4.3 of this book (on "algorithmic redliking"). See: Part IV, This chapter, Sect. 4.1.3 of this book (on algorithmic prime-lining). See also: Bar-Gill, Oren/Sunstein, Cass R./Talgam-Cohen, Inbal, "Algorithmic Harm in Consumer Markets", *Journal of Legal Analysis*, Volume 15, n. ° 1, 2023, pp. 1–47. See also: Lee, Nicole Turner/Resnick, Paul/Barton, Genie, *Algorithmic Bias Detection and Mitigation: Best Practices and Policies to Reduce Consumer Harms*. Washington, DC: Brookings Institution, 2019, passim; Slaughter, Rebecca Kelly, "Algorithms and Economic Justice: A Taxonomy of Harms and a Path Forward for the Federal Trade Commission", *Yale Journal of Law and Technology*, Volume 23, 2021 (on algorithmic consumer harms).

[2022] Gillis, Talia B., "The Input Data Fallacy", *cit.*, pp. 1176–1263 (1179).

[2023] Gillis, Talia B., "The Input Data Fallacy", *cit.*, pp. 1176–1263 (1179).

[2024] Wonyoung, So, "Which Information Matters? Measuring Landlord Assessment of Tenant Screening Reports", *Housing Policy Debate*, Volume 33, n. ° 6, 2023, pp. 1484–1510 (1484) ("*this study shows that landlords (…) display, on average, tendencies toward automation bias that are influenced by the risk assessments and scores presented by tenant screening reports.* I argue that maintaining blanket screening policies and automation bias, combined with the downstream effects of creating and *using racially biased eviction and criminal records, means that people of color will inevitably experience disproportionate exclusion from rental housing due to perceived "risk" on the part of landlords*"). Italics added. See: Part IV, This chapter, Sects. 4.1.4–4.1.4.2.3 of this book.

[2025] Gillis, Talia B., "The Input Data Fallacy", *cit.*, pp. 1176–1263 (1180). See also: Humber, Nadiyah J., "A Home for Digital Equity: Algorithmic Redlining and Property Technology", *California Law Review*, Volume 111, Issue 5, 2023, pp. 1421–1484. See also: Hurley, Mikella/Adebayo, Julius, "Credit Scoring in the Era of Big Data", *Yale Journal of Law and Technology*, Volume 18, 2016, pp. 148, 151–156, 172 (averring that FICO scoring boasts a redoubtable capacity to routinely weed out some populations that have been historically and systematically underrepresented or grossly unfairly represented in the credit industry market). Tellingly, by 2016, ten states

lending behaviour will further compound,[2026] exacerbate[2027] both past injustices[2028] and racial inequalities[2029] that still resonate today.[2030]

§§ The promise is that which algorithms' enhanced accuracy in predicting creditworthiness by association[2031] will accordingly increase the availability of credit for previously excluded consumers and structurally disadvantaged[2032] groups.[2033] The

---

had disavowed the unlawful practice of employers using shady credit scores due to their perceived disparate impact on low-income applicants and members of racialized communities (mostly Black folks). See: O'Neill, Cathy, *Weapons of Math Destruction. How Big Data Increases Inequality and Threatens Democracy*. London: Penguin Random House, 2016, pp. 128 and ff and passim. See: Part IV, This chapter, Sects. 4.1.4–4.1.4.2.3 of this book.

[2026] Hurley, Mikella/Adebayo, Julius, "Credit Scoring in the Era of Big Data", *Yale Journal of Law and Technology*, Volume 18, 2016, pp. 148–168.

[2027] Wonyoung, So, "Which Information Matters? Measuring Landlord Assessment of Tenant Screening Reports", *Housing Policy Debate*, Volume 33, n. ° 6, 2023, pp. 1484–1510 (1502) ("*one additional finding of the experiment is that algorithmic scoring can exacerbate this racially unequal landscape in rental agreements not just because the algorithm may be inaccurate, but because landlords may want to follow the risk assessment made by the tenant screening report*"). Italics added.

[2028] Gillis, Talia B., "The Input Data Fallacy", *cit.*, pp. 1176–1263 (1180).

[2029] Bruckner, Matthew Adam, "The Promise and Perils of Algorithmic Lenders' Use of Big Data", *Chicago-Kent Law Review*, Volume 93, 2018, pp. 25–29.

[2030] Menasce, Juliana Horowitz/Brown, Anna/Cox, Kiana, "Views of Racial Inequality", *Pew Research Center*, April 9, 2019, available at: https://www.pewresearch.org/social-trends/2019/04/09/views-of-racial-inequality/ (access: 2.12.2024) ("*more than four-in-ten Americans say the country still has work to do to give black people equal rights with whites. Blacks, in particular, are skeptical that black people will ever have equal rights in this country (….) A majority of adults say that being white helps people's ability to get ahead in the country at least a little (59%); 28% say being white neither helps nor hurts and 12% say it hurts. On the flip side, a majority (56%) sees being black as a disadvantage, with 25% saying it hurts people's ability to get ahead a lot. About a quarter (26%) say being black neither helps nor hurts and 17% say it helps at least a little. More also say that being Hispanic hurts people's ability to get ahead in this country (51%) than say it helps (18%) or that it neither helps nor hurts (30%).* Opinions are more split when it comes to the impact of being Native American—about the same shares say this hurts as say it neither helps nor hurts, while a smaller share says it helps. *And while a plurality says being Asian neither helps nor hurts, more say it helps (34%) than hurts (21%) people's ability to get ahead*"). Italics added.

[2031] But see: Hurley, Mikella/Adebayo, Julius, "Credit Scoring in the Era of Big Data", *Yale Journal of Law and Technology*, Volume 18, 2016, p. 149 ("*recent studies have also questioned the accuracy of the data used by these tools, in some cases identifying serious flaws that have a substantial bearing on lending decisions. Big-data tools may also risk creating a system of "creditworthiness by association" in which consumers' familial, religious, social, and other affiliations determine their eligibility for an affordable loan. These tools may furthermore obscure discriminatory and subjective lending policies behind a single "objective" score. Such discriminatory scoring may not be intentional; instead, sophisticated algorithms may combine facially neutral data points and treat them as proxies for immutable characteristics such as race or gender, thereby circumventing existing non-discrimination laws and systematically denying credit access to certain groups. Finally, big-data tools may allow online payday lenders to target the most vulnerable consumers and lure them into debt traps*"). Italics added.

[2032] See: Barocas, Solon/Selbst, Andrew, "Big Data's Disparate Impact", *California Law Review*, Volume 104, pp. 2016, p. 691 (highlighting the worrisome, and gruesome, issue of "structural disadvantage" with which racialized communities have been tussling for centuries). See also: Powell,

overring goal of this piece is therefore to assist fair lending to fulfil this long-overdue promise.[2034]

§§ Against this drawn-out background, this book, building on an exciting piece of academic research,[2035] advances two key takeaways.[2036] Firstly, I avowedly contend that the leading stances on algorithmic discrimination fall short of addressing the intricacies of the topic at hand.[2037]

§§ Strikingly, these misleading stances are deemed «the input fallacy»[2038] in that they misguidedly focus on the input-anchored view of conventional algorithmic fair lending,[2039] despite the fact machine learning[2040] pricing renders this approach wholly archaic/obsolete in that has been outstripped by an ever-evolving social reality

---

Richard/Porter, Jeremy, "Redlining, Concentrated Disadvantage and Crime: The Effects of Discriminatory Government Policies on Violent Crime", *American Journal of Criminal Justice*, Volume 48, 2023, pp. 1132–1156 ("*Redlining and other discriminatory government policies enacted during the first half of the Twentieth Century have had long-lasting negative effects on neighborhoods, especially those inhabited by people of color. This study attempts to link the practice of redlining to current-day indicators of neighborhood concentrated disadvantage and violent crime using spatio-temporal data from Chicago (...) In addition, it seeks to determine whether redlining was associated with violent crime, and if that association was mediated by redlining's effect on concentrated disadvantage. The results indicate that redlining was associated with increases in both concentrated disadvantage and violent crime, and that redlining's relationship with violent crime was, indeed, partially mediated by its relationship with concentrated disadvantage*"). Italics added. See also: Gandy, Oscar H., *Coming to Terms with Chance: Engaging Rational Discrimination and Cumulative Disadvantage*, Farnham, UK: Ashgate Publishing, 2009.

2033 Gillis, Talia B., "The Input Data Fallacy", *cit.*, pp. 1176–1263 (1180).

2034 Gillis, Talia B., "The Input Data Fallacy", *cit.*, pp. 1176–1263 (1180).

2035 Gillis, Talia B., "The Input Data Fallacy", *cit.*, pp. 1176–1263.

2036 Gillis, Talia B., "The Input Data Fallacy", *cit.*, pp. 1176–1263 (1180).

2037 Gillis, Talia B., "The Input Data Fallacy", *cit.*, pp. 1176–1263 (1180).

2038 Gillis, Talia B., "The Input Data Fallacy", *cit.*, pp. 1176–1263.

2039 Gillis, Talia B., "The Input Data Fallacy", *cit.*, pp. 1176–1263 (1180).

2040 See: Murphy, Kevin P., *Machine Learning: A Probabilistic Perspective (Adaptive Computation and Machine Learning series).* Massachusetts: The MIT Press, 2012, pp. 1–1104 (states adamantly that "machine Learning attempts to combine deductive, inductive, and abductive reasoning to make person-like reasoning in AI Entities possible. Machine-learning AI Entities initially learn in the same way a human child learns. First, they notice details and patterns in shapes, sounds, and behaviors; then put them together to distinguish one person from another, or a dog from a cat. Eventually, the AI can recognize and identify" common objects). See also: Hutto-Schultz, Jess, "Dicitur Ex Machina: Artificial Intelligence and the Hearsay Rule", *George Mason Law Review*, Volume 27, Issue 2, 2020, pp. 684–718 (689). See: Chollet, François, *Deep Learning with Python.* Shelter Island, Nova Iorque: Manning, 2018, pp. 1–384 (passim). *Deep Learning* stands as a byproduct of *Machine Learning. Machine Learning*, a subset of Artificial Intelligence, unfolds itself in *Deep Learning*, which "involves computer algorithms that have the ability to "learn" or improve in performance over time on some task". See also: Surden, Harry, "Machine Learning and Law", *Washington Law Review*, Volume 89, 2015, pp. 87 and ff. See also: Barocas, Solon/Selbst, Andrew, "Big Data's Disparate Impact", *California Law Review*, Volume 104, pp. 2016, pp. 671–678 ("in particular, by exposing so-called 'machine learning' algorithms to examples of the cases of interest (previously identified instances of fraud, spam, default, and poor health), *the algorithm 'learns' which related attributes or activities can serve as potential proxies for those qualities or outcomes of interest*"). Italics added.

that abhors stagnancy. The *input fallacy* therefore begets an algorithmic myth of colour-blindness[2041] by nurturing the ungrounded hope that input exclusion[2042] can breed non-discriminatory algorithms.[2043]

§§ Furthermore, when input-focused views rule out a wide range of inputs, they accordingly incur on the risk of morphing fair lending law into a deadly tool that further enroots the *status quo* (White supremacy propelled by a thought-through systemic racism[2044] that traversed centuries[2045]) while derailing/besmirching/

[2041] Note, though, that this racial discrimination may not be fully intentional. More likely than not, it can be related with the perils of big data colour-blindness that nonetheless relies on proxies to race and gender to make algorithmic decisions. Another problem is the one related with "creditworthiness by association" that causes more problems than it solves. Hurley, Mikella/Adebayo, Julius, "Credit Scoring in the Era of Big Data", *Yale Journal of Law and Technology*, Volume 18, 2016, p. 149 ("*recent studies have also questioned the accuracy of the data used by these tools, in some cases identifying serious flaws that have a substantial bearing on lending decisions. Big-data tools may also risk creating a system of "creditworthiness by association" in which consumers' familial, religious, social, and other affiliations determine their eligibility for an affordable loan. These tools may furthermore obscure discriminatory and subjective lending policies behind a single "objective" score. Such discriminatory scoring may not be intentional; instead, sophisticated algorithms may combine facially neutral data points and treat them as proxies for immutable characteristics such as race or gender, thereby circumventing existing non-discrimination laws and systematically denying credit access to certain groups. Finally, big-data tools may allow online payday lenders to target the most vulnerable consumers and lure them into debt traps*"). Italics added.

[2042] Gillis, Talia B., "The Input Data Fallacy", *cit.*, pp. 1176–1263 (1180).

[2043] Gillis, Talia B., "The Input Data Fallacy", *cit.*, pp. 1176–1263 (1181).

[2044] Packard, Jerald M., *American Nightmare: The History of Jim Crow*, Broadway, New York, St. Martin's Press; First Edition, 2002, pp. 1–304 (vii–viii) ("[A] *structure of exclusion and discrimination devised by white Americans to be employed principally against black Americans.... Its central purpose was to maintain a second-class social and economic status for blacks while upholding a first-class social and economic status for whites.... In the South, Jim Crow discrimination at its height existed not only by statute but by custom and racial 'etiquette,' and it was rigidly enforced by both the law enforcement agencies* and courts as well as by ordinary white citizens who were neither policemen nor judges but who often took the law into their own hands as though they were"). Italics added.

[2045] Daley, Jane/Gimore, Glenda Elizabeth/Simon, Bryant (Editors), *Jumpin' Jim Crow: Southern Politics from Civil War to Civil Rights*, Princeton, Princeton University Press, 2020, pp. 1–331 ("*White supremacy shaped all aspects of post-Civil War southern life, yet its power was never complete or total. The form of segregation and subjection nicknamed Jim Crow constantly had to remake itself over time even as white southern politicians struggled to extend its grip.* Here, some of the most innovative scholars of southern history question Jim Crow's sway, evolution, and methods over the course of a century. These essays bring to life the southern men and women–some heroic and decent, others mean and sinister, most a mixture of both-who supported and challenged Jim Crow, *showing that white supremacy always had to prove its power. Jim Crow was always in motion, always adjusting to meet resistance and defiance by both African Americans and whites. Sometimes white supremacists responded with increased ferocity, sometimes with more subtle political and legal ploys. Jumpin' Jim Crow presents a clear picture of this complex negotiation. For example, even as some black and white women launched the strongest attacks on the system, other white women nurtured myths glorifying white supremacy. Even as elite whites blamed racial violence on poor whites, they used Jim Crow to dominate poor whites as well as blacks.* Most important, the book portrays change over time, suggesting that Strom Thurmond is not a simple reincarnation of Ben Tillman and that Rosa Parks was not the first black woman to say no to Jim Crow"). Italics

sapping the long-overdue promise of algorithmic credit pricing to catalyse a more inclusive credit market.[2046]

§§ Secondly, I adamantly aver that we should instead reshape innovation pathways while sharply focusing on regulatory output analysis through empirical testing of algorithmic outcomes.[2047] Relatedly, this **outcomes-based view** permits us to embrace the trade-offs that both algorithmic fair lending and algorithmic credit pricing necessarily requires.[2048] It follows that this approach bestows upon us the unmissable opportunity to weigh the danger of disparate credit allotment against the promise of heightened credit access for marginalized[2049] groups[2050] whom have historically floundered with structural disadvantage.[2051]

---

added. See also: Smångs, Mattias, "Doing Violence, Making Race: Southern Lynching and White Racial Group Formation", *American Journal of Sociology*, Volume 121, 2016; Rich, Camille Gear, "Marginal Whiteness", *California Law Review*, Volume 98, 2010, passim.

2046 Gillis, Talia B., "The Input Data Fallacy", *cit.*, pp. 1176–1263 (1181).

2047 Gillis, Talia B., "The Input Data Fallacy", *cit.*, pp. 1176–1263 (1181).

2048 Gillis, Talia B., "The Input Data Fallacy", *cit.*, pp. 1176–1263 (1181).

2049 But see: Campisi, Natalie, From Inherent Racial Bias to Incorrect Data The Problems With Current Credit Scoring Models, Forbes (Feb. 26, 2021), https://www.forbes.com/advisor/credit cards/from-inherent-racial-bias-to-incorrect-data-the-problems-with-current-credit-scoring-mod els/; [https://perma.cc/EWA4-CS8E] (highlighting rampant racial bias in credit scoring systems); Oyama, Rebecca, "Do Not (Re)Enter: the Rise of Criminal Background Tenant Screening as a Violation of the Fair Housing Act", *Michigan Journal of Race and Law*, Volume 15, 2009, pp. 181, 184–93 (discussing a broad range of historical/criminal accounts as a way to screen undesirable tenants, such as Blacks and Latinos); Statement of Interest of the United States at 12, *Louis v. SafeRent Sols., LLC, No. 1:22-cv-10800* (D. Mass. Jan. 9, 2023) (holding that the Fair Housing Act liability stretches far and beyond, thus encompassing a vast assortment of entities providing housing-related services, including corporations that offer tenant screening services). See: Massey, Douglas S., "The Legacy of the 1968 Fair Housing Act", *Social Forces*, Volume 30, 2015, pp. 571, 575–76, 578 ("[*The FHA*] *outlawed the refusal to rent or sell to someone because of race; it prohibited racial discrimination in the terms and conditions of rental or sale; it barred discrimination in real estate advertising; it banned agents from making untrue statements about a dwelling's availability in order to deny access to blacks*; *and it enjoined real estate agents from making comments about the race of neighbors or in-movers in order to promote panic selling*"). Italics added. Internal citations omitted.

2050 Gillis, Talia B., "The Input Data Fallacy", *cit.*, pp. 1176–1263 (1181).

2051 See: Barocas, Solon/Selbst, Andrew, "Big Data's Disparate Impact", *California Law Review*, Volume 104, pp. 2016, p. 691 (highlighting the worrisome, and gruesome, issue of "structural disadvantage" with which racialized communities have been tussling for centuries). See also: Powell, Richard/Porter, Jeremy, "Redlining, Concentrated Disadvantage and Crime: The Effects of Discriminatory Government Policies on Violent Crime", *American Journal of Criminal Justice*, Volume 48, 2023, pp. 1132–1156 ("*Redlining and other discriminatory government policies enacted during the first half of the Twentieth Century have had long-lasting negative effects on neighborhoods, especially those inhabited by people of color. This study attempts to link the practice of redlining to current-day indicators of neighborhood concentrated disadvantage and violent crime using spatio-temporal data from Chicago (…) In addition, it seeks to determine whether redlining was associated with violent crime, and if that association was mediated by redlining's effect on concentrated disadvantage. The results indicate that redlining was associated with increases in both concentrated disadvantage and violent crime, and that redlining's relationship with violent crime was, indeed, partially mediated by its relationship with concentrated disadvantage*"). Italics added. See

§§ To cater for that, a simulation exercise will be used in which a hypothetical lender a past loan makes predictions[2052] about future borrowers.[2053] To ensure the accuracy of this simulation exercise, there will be a blend/merge/conflation between the opulent Boston Fed Home Mortgage Disclosure Act (HMDA) dataset, which encompasses information on mortgage applications, with simulated default rates measured by information on the mortgage loans.[2054]

§§ Relatedly, the hypothetical lender leverages on a machine learning algorithm to predict default probability,[2055] which, in turn, is subsequently used to price credit for future borrowers.[2056] For purposes here, the loan and borrower characteristics are to be coined as **«inputs»** to the credit decisions, whereas the predicted default probability is to be tagged as **«output».**[2057]

§§ Light will also be cast upon algorithmic biases[2058] on the heels of which a blazingly new structure will be created while distinguishing amongst different types of input biases.[2059] Tellingly, extant discussions tend to forsake that even orthodox credit pricing[2060] relies on borrower characteristics that reflected preexisting disadvantage[2061] **(«biased world» inputs)**[2062] or were haphazardly assessed (**«biased measurement»**[2063] **inputs**).[2064]

---

also: Gandy, Oscar H., *Coming to Terms with Chance: Engaging Rational Discrimination and Cumulative Disadvantage*, Farnham, UK: Ashgate Publishing, 2009.

2052 See: Agrawal, A., Gans, J., & Goldfarb, A., "Prediction machines (updated and expanded): The simple economics of artificial intelligence", *Harvard Business Review Press*, 2022; Agrawal, A., Gans, J., & Goldfarb, A., "Power and prediction: The disruptive economics of artificial intelligence", *Harvard Business Review Press*, 2022; Bengio, Y., Hinton, G., Yao, A., Song, D., Abbeel, P., Harari, Y. N., Hadfield, G., Russell, S., Kahneman, D., & Mindermann, S., *Managing ai risks in an era of rapid progress*, arXiv preprint arXiv:2310.17688, 2023; Aggarwal, C. C., *Neural networks and deep learning*, Heidelberg, Springer, 2018, passim (on the sweltering challenges brought about by prediction machines that operate in the age of Artificial Intelligence-embedded technologies).

2053 Gillis, Talia B., "The Input Data Fallacy", *cit.*, pp. 1176–1263 (1181).

2054 Gillis, Talia B., "The Input Data Fallacy", *cit.*, pp. 1176–1263 (1181).

2055 But see: "The Use of Cash-Flow Data in Underwriting Credit: Empirical Research Findings", *Finreglab*, 32, 34 (Jul. 2019), available at: https://finreglab.org/wp-content/uploads/2019/07/FRL_Research-Report_Final.pdf; [https://perma.cc/N65Q-WQML] (access: 19.12.2024) (arguing that the use of cash flow data can underpin a prediction of default risk, thereby providing an apposite alternative to ancient credit scores. In addition to that, cash-flow data is commensurate with predictive across demographic groups).

2056 Gillis, Talia B., "The Input Data Fallacy", *cit.*, pp. 1176–1263 (1181).

2057 Gillis, Talia B., "The Input Data Fallacy", *cit.*, pp. 1176–1263 (1181).

§§ As far as the algorithmic realm is concerned,[2065] and as comprised by empirical simulations,[2066] the use of *biased inputs* can augment exponentially disparities in some cases whilst significantly abridging them in others instances.[2067]

2058 Recall: Baeza-Yates, R., "Bias on the web", *Communications of the ACM*, 61 (6), June 2018, 2018, pp. 54–61 (argues that "*algorithmic bias is when the bias is not present in the input data* and is added *purely by the algorithm*"). Italics added; Hajian, Sara Hajian et al., "Algorithmic Bias: From Discrimination Discovery to Fairness-aware Data Mining", *ACM SIGKDD International Conference on Knowledge Discovery and Data Mining*, Volume 22, 2125, 2016; Griemmelmann, James/ Westreich, Daniel, "Incomprehensible Discrimination ", *California Law Review Online*, Volume 7, 2018, pp. 164–171; Xiang, Alice, "Reconciling Legal and Technical Approaches to Algorithmic Bias", *Tennessee Law Review*, Volume 88, 2021, passim; See: Lemley, Mark A./Casey, Bryan, "Remedies for Robots", *The University of Chicago Law Review*, Volume 86, Issue 5, 2019, pp. 1311–1396 (1376) (alerting to the perils of algorithmic bias); Chandler, Anupam, "The Racist Algorithm", *Michigan Law Review*, Volume 115, Issue 6, 2018, p. 1026 (noting that, in the terrain of racist algorithm, "the possibilities for discriminatory manipulation are legion"; Jackson, Maya C., "Artificial Intelligence and Algorithmic Bias: The Issues with Technology Reflecting History and Humans", *Journal of Business Technology Law*, Volume 16, 2021, pp. 299–316; West, Sarah Myers/Whittaker, Meredith/Crawford, Kate, *Discriminating Systems. Gender, Race and Power in AI*. New York: AI Now Institute, 2019, pp. 15 and ff and passim; Waldman, Ezra, "Privacy, Practice, and Performance", *California Law Review*, Volume 110, 2021, passim (on algorithmic bias).

2059 Gillis, Talia B., "The Input Data Fallacy", *cit.*, pp. 1176–1263 (1181).

2060 It is crucially important to note, though, that the very fact that only certain types of behaviours are assessed and gauged by credit scores leads to the conclusion some borrowers are not scored at all. The overwhelming majority of consumers boast meagre, if any, credit files owing to the fact that the likelihood to access to the sort of financial services that actually report to the orthodox credit bureaus scattered across modern economies is exceedingly low, which, in turn, morphs them into credit invisible persons. See: Yu, Persis/McLaughlin, Jilian/Levy, Marina, "Big Data: A Big Disappointment for Scoring Consumer Creditworthiness,", *The National Consumer Law Center*, 2 (Mar. 14, 2014), available at: https://www.nclc.org/images/pdf/pr-reports/report-big-data.pdf; [https://perma.cc/W4SK-NXD5] (access: 21.12.2024).

2061 See: Barocas, Solon/Selbst, Andrew, "Big Data's Disparate Impact", *California Law Review*, Volume 104, pp. 2016, p. 691 (highlighting the worrisome, and gruesome, issue of "structural disadvantage" with which racialized communities have been tussling for centuries). See also: Powell, Richard/Porter, Jeremy, "Redlining, Concentrated Disadvantage and Crime: The Effects of Discriminatory Government Policies on Violent Crime", *American Journal of Criminal Justice*, Volume 48, 2023, pp. 1132–1156 ("*Redlining and other discriminatory government policies enacted during the first half of the Twentieth Century have had long-lasting negative effects on neighborhoods, especially those inhabited by people of color. This study attempts to link the practice of redlining to current-day indicators of neighborhood concentrated disadvantage and violent crime using spatio-temporal data from Chicago (...) In addition, it seeks to determine whether redlining was associated with violent crime, and if that association was mediated by redlining's effect on concentrated disadvantage. The results indicate that redlining was associated with increases in both concentrated disadvantage and violent crime, and that redlining's relationship with violent crime was, indeed, partially mediated by its relationship with concentrated disadvantage*"). Italics added. See also: Gandy, Oscar H., *Coming to Terms with Chance: Engaging Rational Discrimination and Cumulative Disadvantage*, Farnham, UK: Ashgate Publishing, 2009.

2062 Gillis, Talia B., "The Input Data Fallacy", *cit.*, pp. 1176–1263 (1181).

2063 Gillis, Talia B., "The Input Data Fallacy", *cit.*, pp. 1176–1263 (1181).

2064 Gillis, Talia B., "The Input Data Fallacy", *cit.*, pp. 1176–1263 (1181). See also: Corbett-Davies, Sam/Goel, Sharad, "The Measure and Mismeasure of Fairness: a critical Review of Fair Machine

§§ Fair lending law is the primary lens through which racial disparities can be seen in conventional credit pricing to the extent that can oust discrimination.[2068] Fair lending therefore comprises «both the doctrine of disparate treatment, dealing with intentional discrimination, and the doctrine of disparate impact, dealing with a facially neutral rule[2069] that creates impermissible disparities».[2070]

§§ With this context in place, the remainder of this section will centre around both the *biased inputs* and the *input fallacy*. The sweeping goal of this section is therefore keeping lending industry ahead of the disruptive curve while ensuring that past injustices are not reproduced, upticked, ratcheted up, let alone flared up.

4.1.7.1 The Interplay Between «Biased Inputs», «Biased World», «Biased Measurements» and «Measurement Bias» (Talia B. Gillis) in the Purview of Algorithmic Fair Lending and Algorithmic Credit Pricing

§§ The overwhelming majority of inputs into a credit pricing decision in the conventional context reflect either implicit[2071] or overt bias.[2072] Note, though, that the genealogy of such bias varies greatly across inputs.[2073] This assertion

Learning", *Cornell University Library*, 2018, p. 18 (broaches a type of *measurement bias* coined "feature bias," which is neatly a bias in the predictors x. Note, though, that there is a second type of measurement bias deemed "label bias," which, in turn, amounts to a bias in y. The authors argue that that label bias is the worst bias there is).

2065 Gillis, Talia B., "The Input Data Fallacy", *cit.*, pp. 1176–1263 (1181).

2066 Gillis, Talia B., "The Input Data Fallacy", *cit.*, pp. 1176–1263 (1181).

2067 Gillis, Talia B., "The Input Data Fallacy", *cit.*, pp. 1176–1263 (1182).

2068 Gillis, Talia B., "The Input Data Fallacy", *cit.*, pp. 1176–1263 (1182).

2069 But see: Benjamin, Ruha, *Race After Technology: Abolitionist Tools for the New Jim Code*, New York, Polity, 2019, pp. 1–172 (7) (discussing that Artificial Intelligence-embedded technologies are viewed as iron-clad tools of objectivity and devoid of any biases whatsoever). Ruha Benjamin contends that "the employment of new technologies that reflect and reproduce existing inequities but that are promoted and perceived as more objective or progressive than the discriminatory systems of a previous era").

2070 Gillis, Talia B., "The Input Data Fallacy", *cit.*, pp. 1176–1263 (1182).

2071 This is called law of *implicit bias*: people make decisions (e.g. discriminating seemingly disfavoured groups of people) that often lack a rational connection between facts and judgment. A conscious and deliberate judgment that noticeably runs afoul with rationality. See: Jolls, Christine/Sunstein, Cass R., "The Law of Implicit Bias", *California Law Review*, Volume 94, 2006, p. 969 (arguing that this issue can be solved through the general strategy of de-biasing through law, by steering people through more rational directions). See also: Kang, Jerry/Banaji, Mahzarin R., "Fair Measures: A Behavioural Realist Revision of Affirmative Action", *California Law Review,* Volume 94 2006, p. 1064 (arguing that «implicit bias often conflicts with conscious attitudes, endorsed beliefs, and intentional behaviour»); Greenwald, Anthony G./Krieger, Linda Hamilton, "Implicit Bias: Scientific Foundations", *California Law Review*, Volume 94, 2006, pp. 945–967. See also: Santos, Hugo Luz dos, *Multidisciplinary Dynamics of Mediation*, Volume I, New York/Beijing/Berlin/Singapore, Springer, 2025, pp. 1–694; Santos, Hugo Luz dos, *Multidisciplinary Dynamics of Mediation*, Volume II, New York/Beijing/Berlin/Singapore, 2025, pp. 1–800; Santos, Hugo Luz

neatly encapsulates, hands-in-glove, a finding that can neither be deemphasized nor downplayed.

§§ This set-in-stone view does not entail, nor does spurns, the painstaking reconstruction of human-caused racial wedges that lie beneath the shapeless foam of days. It does, however, point to the dire need to show them in broad daylight as to enable the reader to come to terms with the fact that, much to our collective chagrin/dismay, the door of *Algorithm Dictatorship* is wide open.

§§ Relatedly, for purposes here, I draw a distinction, leveraging on a bodacious piece of research, between a *biased input* arising out of some historic[2074] or extant/ongoing discrimination[2075] wholly unrelated to the lender itself (**«biased world»**)[2076]

---

dos, *Towards a Four-Tiered Model of Mediation*, New York/Beijing/Berlin/Singapore, Springer, 2023, pp. 1–216.

2072 Wonyoung, So, "Which Information Matters? Measuring Landlord Assessment of Tenant Screening Reports", *Housing Policy Debate*, Volume 33, n. ° 6, 2023, pp. 1484–1510 (1502) ("*One additional finding of the experiment is that algorithmic scoring can exacerbate this racially unequal landscape in rental agreements not just because the algorithm may be inaccurate, but because landlords may want to follow the risk assessment made by the tenant screening report. This is alarming for low-income tenants, particularly housing voucher holders. Security deposits are one of the most significant barriers to obtaining housing for voucher holders, because vouchers do not pay security deposits but most private landlords require them (Rosenblatt & Cossyleon, 2018).* Given that voucher holders have exceptionally low income (usually less than 50% of area median income) and might experience more housing insecurity (rental debts and eviction-related experiences), *imposing greater security deposits on voucher holders almost equates to denying them housing—yet these decisions could be justified by algorithmic scoring if tenant screening services employ it*"). Italics added. See: Part IV, This chapter, Sects. 4.1.4–4.1.4.2.3 of this book. See: Part IV, This chapter, Sects. 4.1.4–4.1.4.2.1 of this book (on mortgage redlining). See: Part IV, This chapter, Sects. 4.1.2–4.1.4.3 of this book (on algorithmic credit scoring, consumer racism and credit card redlining). See: Part IV, This chapter, Sects. 4.1.4–4.1.4.2.3 of this book (on algorithmic redlining). See: Part IV, This chapter, Sect. 4.1.4.3 of this book (on "algorithmic redliking"). See: Part IV, This chapter, Sect. 4.1.3 of this book (on algorithmic prime-lining).

2073 Gillis, Talia B., "The Input Data Fallacy", *cit.*, pp. 1176–1263 (1192).

2074 On racially motivated Jim Crow laws and the multifarious misdeeds arising out of such gruelling era: Finkelman, Paul (Editor), *Race, Law, and American History 1700–1990: African Americans and the Law*, Volume 1, London, Taylor & Francis (1 Mar. 1992), 1992, pp. 1–630; Chin, Gabriel J., "Jim Crow's Long Goodbye", *Constitutional Comment*, Volume 21, 2004; Chin, Gabriel J./Wagner, Randy, "The Tyranny of the Minority: Jim Crow and the Counter-Majoritarian Difficulty", *Harvard Civil Rights-Civil Liberties Law Review*, Volume 43, 2008; Fox, James W., Jr., "Doctrinal Myths and the Management of Cognitive Dissonance: Race, Law, and the Supreme Court's Doctrinal Support of Jim Crow", *Stetson Law Review*, Volume 34, 2005; Fox, James W., Jr., "Intimations of Citizenship: Repressions and Expressions of Equal Citizenship in the Era of Jim Crow", *Howard Law Journal*, Volume 50, 2006; Godsil, Rachel D., "Race Nuisance: The Politics of Law in the Jim Crow Era", *Michigan Law Review*, Volume 105, 2006; Gross, Ariela J., "Litigating Whiteness: Trials of Racial Determination in the Nineteenth-Century South", *Yale Law Journal*, 1998; Brown, Trina Jones, II: "A Case of Missed Opportunity?", *Law and Inequality, University of Minnesota Law*, Volume 24, 2006; Juárez, José Roberto, Jr., "Recovering Texas History: Tejanos, Jim Crow, Lynchings & the University of Texas School of Law", *Texas Law Review*, Volume 52, 2010; Mack, Kenneth W., "Foreword: A Short Biography of the Civil Rights Act of 1964", *SMU Law Review*, Volume 67, 2014; Mack, Kenneth W., "Law, Society, Identity, and the Making of the Jim Crow South: Travel and Segregation on Tennessee Railroads, 1875–1905", *Law and Social Inquiry*, Volume 24, 1999; Mack, Kenneth W., "Rethinking Civil Rights Lawyering and Politics in the Era Before Brown",

and an input that is biased[2077] owing to the way it frames and measures a characteristic (**«biased measurement»**).[2078] In a nutshell, ***measurement bias***.[2079]

Yale Law Journal, Volume 115, 2005; Martin, David, "The Birth of Jim Crow in Alabama 1865–1896", *National Black Law Journal*, Volume 13, 1993; Roback, Jennifer, "Southern Labor Law in the Jim Crow Era: Exploitative or Competitive", *The University of Chicago Law Review*, Volume 51, 1984; Welke, Barbara Y., "Beyond Plessy: Space, Status, and Race in the Era of Jim Crow", *Utah Law Review*, 2000; Wertheimer, John W. et al., "The Law Recognizes Racial Instinct": Tucker v. Blease and the Black-White Paradigm in the Jim Crow South", *Law and History Review*, Volume 29, 2011; Palmore, Joseph R., "Note, The Not-So-Strange Career of Interstate Jim Crow: Race, Transportation, and the Dormant Commerce Clause, 1878–1946", *Virginia Law Review*, Volume 83, 1997.

[2075] Roithmayr, Daria, *Reproducing Racism: How everyday choices lock in White Advantage*, New York, New York University Press, 2014, pp. 1–272 ("*Argues that racial inequality reproduces itself automatically over time because early unfair advantage for whites has paved the way for continuing advantage. This book is designed to change the way we think about racial inequality (...) Legal scholar Daria Roithmayr provocatively argues that racial inequality lives on because white advantage functions as a powerful self-reinforcing monopoly, reproducing itself automatically from generation to generation even in the absence of intentional discrimination. Drawing on work in antitrust law and a range of other disciplines, Roithmayr brilliantly compares the dynamics of white advantage to the unfair tactics of giants like AT&T and Microsoft.* With penetrating insight, Roithmayr *locates the engine of white monopoly in positive feedback loops that connect the dramatic disparity of Jim Crow to modern racial gaps in jobs, housing and education. Wealthy white neighborhoods fund public schools that then turn out wealthy white neighbors. Whites with lucrative jobs informally refer their friends, who refer their friends, and so on. Roithmayr concludes that racial inequality might now be locked in place, unless policymakers immediately take drastic steps to dismantle this oppressive system*"). Italics added. This book points out how White privilege is perpetuated throughout generations through residential segregation (*mortgage redlining*), abhorrent nepotism, and other bemoaning social practices that pester modern societies). See: Part IV, This chapter, Sects. 4.1.4–4.1.4.2.3 of this book.

[2076] Here is an example of "biased world: Glantz, Aaron/Martinez, Emmanuel, "For People of Color, Banks are Shutting the Door to Homeownership", Reveal, February 15, 2018, available at: https://ibw21.org/news/people-color-banks-shutting-door-homeownership/ (access: 21.12.2024) ("*Fifty years after the federal Fair Housing Act banned racial discrimination in lending, African Americans and Latinos continue to be routinely denied conventional mortgage loans at rates far higher than their white counterparts. This modern-day redlining persisted in 61 metro areas even when controlling for applicants' income, loan amount and neighborhood, according to a mountain of Home Mortgage Disclosure Act records analyzed by Reveal from The Center for Investigative Reporting. The yearlong analysis, based on 31 million records, relied on techniques used by leading academics, the Federal Reserve and Department of Justice to identify lending disparities. It found a pattern of troubling denials for people of color across the country, including in major metropolitan areas such as Atlanta, Detroit, Philadelphia, St. Louis and San Antonio.* African Americans faced the most resistance in Southern cities — Mobile, Alabama; Greenville, North Carolina; and Gainesville, Florida — and Latinos in Iowa City, Iowa. *No matter their location, loan applicants told similar stories, describing an uphill battle with loan officers who they said seemed to be fishing for a reason to say no*"). Italics added.

[2077] See: Campisi, Natalie, From Inherent Racial Bias to Incorrect Data The Problems With Current Credit Scoring Models, Forbes (Feb. 26, 2021), https://www.forbes.com/advisor/creditcards/from-inherent-racial-bias-to-incorrect-data-the-problems-with-current-credit-scoring-models/; [https://perma.cc/EWA4-CS8E] (highlighting rampant racial bias in credit scoring systems).

[2078] Gillis, Talia B., "The Input Data Fallacy", *cit.*, pp. 1176–1263 (1192).

§§ Though analytically different, the boundaries between both are on the verge of becoming increasingly blurred.[2080] It follows that the primal concern with personalized prices[2081] for credit is the extent to which catalyses or further augments disparities amongst groups.[2082]

§§ Thence, the focus should be on affected «protected groups», concretely the cohort of people that discrimination legal settings endeavours to protect.[2083] Light must be accordingly cast upon the way in which default is routinely predicted, and price credit accordingly, and whether and to extent it creates impermissible disparities[2084] amongst legally protected groups.[2085] As adumbrated, fair lending[2086] and credit carries a treasure trove of prohibitions. Amongst which, discrimination

---

[2079] See: Corbett-Davies, Sam/Goel, Sharad, "The Measure and Mismeasure of Fairness: a critical Review of Fair Machine Learning", *Cornell University Library*, 2018, p. 18 (broaches a type of measurement bias coined "feature bias," which is neatly a bias in the predictors x. Note, though, that there is a second type of measurement bias deemed "label bias," which, in turn, amounts to a bias in y. The authors argue that that label bias is the worst bias there is).

[2080] Gillis, Talia B., "The Input Data Fallacy", *cit.*, pp. 1176–1263 (1192).

[2081] But see: Wallheimer, Brian, "Are you Ready for Personalized Pricing? Companies Are Figuring out What Individual Customers Will Pay-and Charging Accordingly", *Chicago Booth Review*, 2018, passim.

[2082] Gillis, Talia B., "The Input Data Fallacy", *cit.*, pp. 1176–1263 (1192).

[2083] Gillis, Talia B., "The Input Data Fallacy", *cit.*, pp. 1176–1263 (1192).

[2084] But see: Chi-Jack Lin/ Sherman D. Hanna, "Racial Discrimination in the Consumer Credit Market", *Consumer Interests Annual*, Volume 56, 2010 ("*The Equal Credit Opportunity Act (ECOA), enacted in 1974, makes it unlawful for any creditors to discriminate against credit applicants because of their color, race/ethnic group, religion, national origin, sex, marital status, or age (provided the applicant has the capacity to contract*). Researchers have debated the existence of discrimination within the U.S. credit market. Many studies examine the presence of discrimination in the credit market, but none focus specifically on the effect of individuals' race or ethnic group in the consumer credit market, which we differentiate from other household credit markets, such as for home mortgages. This research fills the research gap by examining discrimination in the consumer credit market. Using four Survey of Consumer Finance data sets from 1998 to 2007, we use five measures to assess whether there is discrimination by racial/ethnic group in the consumer credit in US, and, if present, whether the discrimination is due to statistical or taste lender motivations. *Our analyses allow for distinguishing statistical and taste discrimination. In four of five of our measures, there was discrimination against households with Black respondents, and in three out of five measures, there was discrimination against households with Hispanic respondents. Discrimination in the consumer credit market against black and Hispanic households is statistical discrimination: lenders choose to discriminate against black and Hispanic because they on average have higher default risk*"). Italics added.

[2085] Gillis, Talia B., "The Input Data Fallacy", *cit.*, pp. 1176–1263 (1192).

[2086] It is crucially important to note, though, that the very fact that only certain types of behaviours are assessed and gauged by credit scores leads to the conclusion some borrowers are not scored at all. The overwhelming majority of consumers boast meagre, if any, credit files owing to the fact that the likelihood to access to the sort of financial services that actually report to the orthodox credit bureaus scattered across modern economies is exceedingly low, which, in turn, morphs them into credit invisible persons. See: Yu, Persis/McLaughlin, Jilian/Levy, Marina, "Big Data: A Big Disappointment for Scoring Consumer Creditworthiness,", *The National Consumer Law Center,* 2 (Mar. 14, 2014), available at: https://www.nclc.org/images/pdf/pr-reports/report-big-data.pdf; [https://perma.cc/W4SK-NXD5] (access: 21.12.2024).

based on race,[2087] religion, gender,[2088] marital status, and age, amongst other legal grounds.[2089]

§§ Lenders aiming to personalize[2090] credit terms[2091] to borrowers[2092] deal with the problem that many of the predictors[2093] used to ascertain individual risk are

---

[2087] But see: Firestone, Simon, "Race Ethnicity and Credit Card Monitoring", *Journal of Money, Credit and Banking*, Sept. 2014, 2014, pp. 1206 and ff; Han, Song, Keys, Benjamin J./Li, Geng, *Unsecured Credit Supply over the Credit Cycle: Evidence from Credit Card Mailings* (arguing that, statistically, Blacks and Latinos are seldom granted credit and, if ever granted credit, the terms and conditions attached to the concession of credit are not equal to those offered to White folks).

[2088] Leung, K./Lind, Edgar Allan, "Procedural justice and culture: Effects of culture, gender, and investigator status on procedural preferences", *Journal of Personality and Social Psychology*, Volume 50, 1986, pp. 1134–1140.

[2089] Gillis, Talia B., "The Input Data Fallacy", *cit.*, pp. 1176–1263 (1192).

[2090] See: The Effects of Online Disclosure About Personalized Pricing on Consumers 7 (Org. for Econ. Coop. and Dev., Working Paper No. 303, 2021 ("[T]he quantity of personal data held on online consumers, combined with the increasing prevalence of personalization in other domains (e.g., advertisement), means there is at least potential for online personalized pricing to become more commonplace and more sophisticated"). This is often tagged as "risk-based pricing." See: Phillipps, Robert, "Optimizing Prices for Consumer Credit", *Journal of Revenue and Pricing Management*, Volume 12, 2013, pp. 360–365 ("[A] riskier customer should pay a higher price in order to compensate for the higher probability of default and the associated cost to the lender"). See also: Staten, Michael, "Risk-Based Pricing in Consumer Lending", *Journal of Law, Economics & Policy*, Volume 11, 2015, pp. 33 and ff and passim.

[2091] Note, though, that despite its deep-seated racial bias, decision-makers continue to deploy redlining tactics through big data and may even justify such unlawful practices by claiming that the latter abide by cost-effectiveness. See: Humber, Nadiyah J., "A Home for Digital Equity: Algorithmic Redlining and Property Technology", *California Law Review*, Volume 111, Issue 5, 2023, pp. 1421–1484. See also: Hurley, Mikella/Adebayo, Julius, "Credit Scoring in the Era of Big Data", *Yale Journal of Law and Technology*, Volume 18, 2016, pp. 148, 151–156, 172 (averring that FICO scoring boasts a redoubtable capacity to routinely weed out some populations that have been historically and systematically underrepresented or grossly unfairly represented in the credit industry market). Tellingly, by 2016, ten states had disavowed the unlawful practice of employers using shady credit scores due to their perceived disparate impact on low-income applicants and members of racialized communities (mostly Black folks). See: O'Neill, Cathy, *Weapons of Math Destruction. How Big Data Increases Inequality and Threatens Democracy*. London: Penguin Random House, 2016, pp. 128 and ff and passim. See: Part IV, This chapter, Sects. 4.1.4–4.1.4.2.3 of this book.

[2092] But see: *Credit Discrimination: Hearings on H.R. 14856 and H.R. 14908 Before the Subcomm. on Consumer Affairs of the H. Comm. on Banking & Currency*, 93rd Cong. 1, 1974, (Hon. Leonor K. Sullivan, Chairman, Subcomm. on Consumer Affairs of the H. Comm. on Banking & Currency) (statement of John H. Powell, Jr., Chairman, Equal Emp't Opportunity Comm'n) *("[I]t is very likely that the inability to obtain credit, or if obtained, the discriminatory terms and conditions which accompany its extension to certain groups in our society, are directly related to discrimination in employment*"). See also: Wonyoung, So, "Which Information Matters? Measuring Landlord Assessment of Tenant Screening Reports", *Housing Policy Debate*, Volume 33, n. ° 6, 2023, pp. 1484–1510 (1502) ("*It is important to note that within conditionally accepted reports, similar patterns of blanket screening policies and automation bias are exhibited when landlords impose security deposits. These results may corroborate a paired-test study that shows that Black tenants have less favorable terms and conditions, including security deposits, in rental agreements* (Ross & Turner, 2005)"). Italics added. See: Part IV, This chapter, Sects. 4.1.4–4.1.4.2.3 of this book.

[2093] Note, though, that, theoretically, one should not shy away from bifurcating/splitting the "prediction" issue from the "decision" issue. See: Corbett-Davies, Sam/Pierson, Emma/Feller, Avi/Goel,

nothing but the byproduct of pre-existing disadvantage or deep-rooted[2094] discrimination.[2095] Albeit lenders are not to blame,[2096] using these very inputs further compounds the noxious effects of extant discrimination[2097] in a blazingly new domain[2098] nonetheless.[2099]

Sharad Goel/Huq, Aziz, "Algorithmic Decision Making and the Cost of Fairness", *Proceedings of the 23rd ACM SIGKDD International Conference on Knowledge Discovery and Data Mining* (Ass'n for Computing Machinery ed., 2017), 2017, passim.

[2094] See: Ards, Sheila D./Myers, Samuel L. Myers, "The Color of Money: Bad Credit, Wealth, and Race", *American Behavioral Scientist*, Volume 45, 2001, pp. 223–238 (debunks the deep-seated myth according to which Blacks are big spenders and thus unworthy of creditworthiness, which stands as an irksome social bias in dire need of quashing).

[2095] Gillis, Talia B., "The Input Data Fallacy", *cit.*, pp. 1176–1263 (1192).

[2096] Recall, the theory of "post-race" contends that the great bulk discrimination undertaken by the lending industry is not the byproduct of wilful and flagitious bias. Rather, this discrimination broadly mirrors rational economic decisions to leverage on extant systemic, endemic, and structural social inequalities for profit. See: Carbado, Devon W./Gulati, Mitu, *Acting White? Rethinking Race in Post-Racial America*, Oxford, Oxford University Press, 2015, pp. 1–212; Howell, Benjamin, "Note, Exploiting Race and Space: Concentrated Subprime Lending as Housing Discrimination", *California Law Review*, Volume 101, 2006, pp. pp. 108–109; Barnes, Mario L., "Reflection on a Dream World: Race, Post-Race and the Question of Making It Over", *Berkely Journal of African-American Law and Policy*, Volume 11, 2009, pp. 6 and ff and passim (parses theories of a "post-racial" world); Haney-López, Ian F., "Essay, Post-Racial Racialism: Racial Stratification and Mass Incarceration in the Age of Obama", *California Law Review*, Volume 98, 2010; Cho, Sumi, "Post-Racialism", *Iowa Law Review*, 2009; Howell, Benjamin, "Note, Exploiting Race and Space: Concentrated Subprime Lending as Housing Discrimination", *California Law Review*, Volume 94, 2006, pp. 101, 108–09; Freeman, Andrea, "Racism in the Credit Card Industry", *cit.*, p. 1098 and ff, whose stellar research I have been following closely.

[2097] See: Bar-Gill/Oren/Warren, Elizabeth, "Making Credit Safer", *University of Pennsylvania Law Review*, Volume 157, 2008, pp. 1–66 (argue that Black defendants are far more likely to be incarcerated, arrested, surveilled and harassed than White folks, which leads to the conclusion that the use of credit scores and income presents another way in which credit decisions leverage on structural disadvantage).

[2098] Gillis, Talia B., "The Input Data Fallacy", *cit.*, pp. 1176–1263 (1192). See also: Hellman, Deborah, "Indirect Discrimination and the Duty to Avoid Compounding Injustice", *Foundations of Indirect Discrimination Law*, Collins, Hugh/Khaitan, Tarunabh (Editors), Oxford, Hart Publishing; Reprint edition (June 25, 2020), 2020, p. 107 (Professor Deborah Hellman coined this expression to depict a decision that "exacerbates the harm caused by the prior injustice because it entrenches the harm or carries it into another domain." This book deals with the sweltering topic of indirect discrimination ("*indirect discrimination (or disparate impact) concerns the application of the same rule to everyone, even though that rule significantly disadvantages one particular group in society.* Ever since its recognition by the Supreme Court of the United States in 1971, liberal democracies around the world have grappled with the puzzle that it can sometimes be unfair and wrong to treat everyone equally. *The law's regulation of private acts that unintentionally (but disproportionately) harm vulnerable groups has remained extremely controversial, especially in the United States and the United Kingdom. In original essays in this volume, leading scholars of discrimination law from North America and Europe explore the various facets of the law on indirect discrimination, interrogating its foundations, history, legitimacy, purpose, structure, and relationship with other legal concepts.* The collection provides the first international work devoted to this vital area of the law that seeks both to prevent unfair treatment and to transform societies"). Italics added. This famed author argues that there is a general duty to avoid compounding injustice and that widespread belief in such a duty propels disparate impact discrimination law (p. 105).

§§ It bears mentioning that paradigmatic examples of **«biased world»** inputs[2100] abound in that they are nothing but legion[2101] and dispiritingly rife.[2102] It follows that a crucial predictor for gauging the repayment risk is the borrower's income.[2103] A slew of bodies of empirical research has pinpointed a yawning racial wealth gap,[2104] a racial wage[2105] gap,[2106] and gender pay gap in the United States of America.[2107] These

---

[2099] However, Schwemm and Taren avowedly contend that these cases might somewhat be deemed hybrid impact/intention cases. See: Schwemm, Robert G./Taren, Jeffrey L., "Discretionary Pricing, Mortgage Discrimination, and the Fair Housing Act", *The Harvard Civil Rights-Civil Liberties Law Review*, 2010, passim. The conduct being granularly parsed is discretion ascribed to brokers—which is considered by many stakeholders a harmless neutral practice -, may nonetheless lead to brokers to intentionally discriminate against members of racial minorities. See also: Selmi, Michael, "Indirect Discrimination and the Anti-Discrimination Mandate", Oxford, Oxford University Press, *Philosophical Foundations of Discrimination Law (Philosophical Foundations of Law)*, Hellman, Deborah/Moreau, Sophia (Editors), 2013, pp. 1–304 (pp. 257 and ff and passim).

[2100] Gillis, Talia B., "The Input Data Fallacy", *cit.*, pp. 1176–1263 (1193).

[2101] Firestone, Simon, "Race Ethnicity and Credit Card Monitoring", *Journal of Money, Credit and Banking*, Sept. 2014, 2014, pp. 1206 and ff; Han, Song, Keys, Benjamin J./Li, Geng, *Unsecured Credit Supply over the Credit Cycle: Evidence from Credit Card Mailings* (argue that, statistically, Blacks and Latinos are seldom granted credit and, if ever granted credit, the terms and conditions attached to the concession of credit are not equal to those offered to White folks).

[2102] See: Noble, Safiya Umoja, *Algorithms of Oppression*: *How search engines reinforce racism*, New York, New University Press, 2018, pp. 1–248 ("*Run a Google search for "Black girls"—what will you find? "Big Booty" and other sexually explicit terms are likely to come up as top search terms. But, if you type in "white girls," the results are radically different*. The suggested porn sites and un-moderated discussions about "why Black women are so sassy" or "why Black women are so angry" presents a disturbing portrait of Black womanhood in modern society. In *Algorithms of Oppression*, Safiya Umoja Noble challenges the idea that search engines like Google offer an equal playing field for all forms of ideas, identities, and activities. *Data discrimination is a real social problem; Noble argues that the combination of private interests in promoting certain sites, along with the monopoly status of a relatively small number of Internet search engines, leads to a biased set of search algorithms that privilege whiteness and discriminate against people of color, specifically women of color*"). Italics added. See: Part IV, This chapter, Sect. 4.1.8 of this book (on biased word embeddings with an entrenched presence on search engines run by tech moguls).

[2103] Gillis, Talia B., "The Input Data Fallacy", *cit.*, pp. 1176–1263 (1193). But see: Levitin, Adam J., "The Antitrust Super Bowl: America's Payment Systems, No-Surcharge Rules, and the Hidden Costs of Credit", *Berkeley Business Law Journal*, Volume 3, 2005, pp. 265, 317–18; id. at 154 ("*low-income consumers now receive credit cards with high fees and interest rates, while higher-income consumers reap the rewards of credit card use, such as travel miles and concierge services* (…). As a *result of these practices, 80% of the industry's profits now come from interest payments and... fees instead of annual and interchange fees. This shift represents a massive redistribution of wealth from the poor to wealthier consumers and corporations*"). Italics added.

[2104] Derenoncourt, Ellora/Kim, Chi Hyun/Kuhn, Moritz/Schularik, Moritz, "The Wealth of Two Nations: The U.S. Racial Wealth Gap, 1860–2020", *The Quarterly Journal of Economics*, Volume 139, Issue 2, 2024, p. 741 ("*A large class of commonly discussed policies for reducing racial wealth inequality seeks to reduce gaps in income, savings, and capital gains.* These include policies that encourage financial diversification or stock equity holdings among Black households; policies aimed at financial literacy and retirement or savings behavior; or policies aimed at improving educational and labor market outcomes of Black Americans through improved school quality or reductions in discrimination. *Yet on a realistic note, our simulation in Section IV.A shows that even if wealth accumulation conditions had been equal since 1870, the wealth gap would still be 3 to 1 today, and full convergence would be more than 200 years away. Put differently: to close the racial wealth gap*

perceived gaps amount to nothing but to an outgrowth of «pre-market factors,»[2108] such as abridged access to higher education,[2109] or a byproduct of labour market[2110] discrimination alone.[2111]

§§ By the same token, exceedingly higher rates of arrest,[2112] police killings,[2113] surveillance,[2114] harassment,[2115] incarceration,[2116] wrong convictions[2117] of racial[2118] minorities negatively sway their credit[2119] scores.[2120] Fiddly labyrinths of debt may equally mirror pre-existing disadvantage.[2121] Strikingly, unscrupulous high-interest lenders,[2122] such as payday lenders,[2123] often target racial minorities,[2124] thereby luring them into[2125] debt traps.[2126]

---

in the immediate term via *flow parameters, Black Americans would need a substantial positive lead over whites, not "just" more equality*"). Italics added.

2105 Zywicki, Todd J./Adamson, Joseph D., "The Law and Economics of Subprime Lending", *University of Colorado Law Review*, 2009, pp. 1–9 (contending that Black workers with roughly the same abilities and educational background earn far less than comparable white workers or have considerably fewer employment opportunities).

2106 Albeit the racial wage gap in the labour market is remarkably well parsed, discerning—or dissecting—this gap and the degree to which it sharply mirrors either taste-based or statistical discrimination has proven painstakingly challenging. See: Black, Dan Amelia Haviland/Sanders, Seth/Taylor, Lowell, "Why Do Minority Men Earn Less? A Study of Wage Differentials Among the Highly Educated", *The Review of Economics and Statistics*, Volume 88, 2006, pp. 300 and ff and passim (pinpointing gleefully weird wage gaps between Black men and men of other races while shedding a keen light on the sweltering challenges in ascribing that perceived gap to blatant/blunt racial discrimination). See also: Grodsky, Eric/Pager, Devah, "The Structure of Disadvantage: Individual and Occupational Determinants of Black-White Wage Gap", *American Sociological Review*, Volume 66, 2001, pp. 542–563 (stumbles upon the finding in view of which that whilst Black men have burgeoningly gained access to highly remunerated occupations, they have nonetheless become subject to more extreme racial disadvantages when it comes to seizing power, which, in turn, can be loosely qualified as gate-keeping). See also: Gillis, Talia B., "The Input Data Fallacy", *cit.*, pp. 1176–1263 (passim).

2107 Gillis, Talia B., "The Input Data Fallacy", *cit.*, pp. 1176–1263 (1193).

2108 Gillis, Talia B., "The Input Data Fallacy", *cit.*, pp. 1176–1263 (1193).

2109 Gillis, Talia B., "The Input Data Fallacy", *cit.*, pp. 1176–1263 (1193).

2110 Other pieces of academic research have deftly pinpointed racial disparities with regard to access to the labour market. See: Bertrand, Marianne/Mullainathan, Sendhil, "Are Emily and Greg More Employable than Lakisha and Jamal? A Field Experiment on Labor Market Discrimination", *The American Economic Review*, Volume 94, 2004, p. 991 (reaches the conclusion according to which white-sounding names are far more likely to spark a callback than that of suitably qualified applicants with Black-sounding names); Nunley, John M./Pugh, Adam/Romero, Nicholas/Seals, R. Alan, "Racial Discrimination in the Labor Market for Recent College Graduates: Evidence from a Field Experiment", *The B.E. Journal of Economic Analysis & Policy*, Volume 15, 2015, pp. 1096 and ff and passim.

2111 Gillis, Talia B., "The Input Data Fallacy", *cit.*, pp. 1176–1263 (1193). See also: Fryer, Roland G. Fryer/Pager, Devah/Spenkuch, Jörg L., "Racial Disparities in Job Finding and Offered Wages", *Journal of Law and Economics*, Volume 56, 2013, pp. 633–690 (contending that disparate treatment accounts for at least one third of the Black-white wage gap).

§§ Empirical evidence elicits the impression according to which credit card lenders routinely engage in screening activities[2127] when it comes to assessing

---

[2112] See: Connecticut Fair Housing Center, et al. v. CoreLogic Rental Property Solutions—Cohen Milstein (access: 21.12.2024). ("*The U.S. Department of Housing & Urban Development observed in 2016 that excluding rental applicants because of their criminal records disproportionately harms Latinos and African Americans, who are significantly more likely than whites to be arrested or convicted. Studies show such disparities are linked to differential enforcement rather than to differences in likelihood of engaging in criminal activity*"). Italics added. See also: Kizer, J. M., "Arrested by skin color: Evidence from siblings and a nationally representative sample", *Socius: Sociological Research for a Dynamic World*, 3, 2017, passim; Kochel, T. R., Wilson, D. B./Mastrofski, S. D., "Effect of suspect race on officers' arrest decisions", *Criminology*, Volume 49, Issue 2, 2011, pp. 473–512. Mitchell, O./Caudy, M. S., "Examining racial disparities in drug arrests", *Justice Quarterly*, Volume 32, Issue 2, 2015, pp. 288–313; Kirk, D. S., "The neighborhood context of racial and ethnic disparities in arrest", *Demography*, 45, 2008, pp. 55–77. See: Baughman, Shima Baradaran, "Costs of Pretrial Detention", *Boston University Law Review*, Volume 97, 2017, p. 1 (calculating the whooping costs of detention); Heaton, Paul et al., "The Downstream Consequences of Misdemeanor Pretrial Detention", *Stanford Law Review*, Volume 69, 2017, 711, 759–69 (concluding, amongst other things, that pretrial detention ballooned the likelihood that a defendant would accrue new criminal charges within 18 months of a bail court hearing).

[2113] Crutchfield, J., Fisher, A., & Webb, S. L., "Colorism and police killings", *The Western Journal of Black Studies*, 41 (3–4), 2017, 81; Dottolo, A. L., & Stewart, A. J. (2008). "Don't ever forget now, you're a Black man in America": Intersections of race, class and gender in encounters with the police", *Sex Roles*, 59(5–6), 2008, pp. 350–364; Baradan, S., "Race, prediction, and discretion", *The George Washington Law Review*, Volume 81, Issue 1, 2013, pp. 157–222.

[2114] Browne, S., *Dark matters: on the surveillance of blackness*, Duke University Press, 2015, passim; Toro, J. D./Lloyd, T., Buchanan/K. S., Robins/S. J., Bencharit/L. Z., Smiedt/M. G., Reddy/K. S., Pouget, E. R./Kerrison, E. M./Goff, P. A., "The criminogenic and psychological effects of police stops on adolescent black and Latino boys", *Proceedings of the National Academy of Sciences of the United States of America*, Volume 116, Issue 17, 2019, pp. 8261–8268; Sewell, A. A., Jefferson, K. A./Lee, H., "Living under surveillance: Gender, psychological distress, and stop-question- and-frisk policing in New York city", *Social Science & Medicine*, Volume 159, 2016, pp. 1–13. Brayne, S., "Big data surveillance: The case of policing", *American Sociological Review*, Volume 82, Issue 5, 2017, pp. 977–1008; Benjamin, Ruha, *Race After Technology: Abolitionist Tools for the New Jim Code*, John Wiley & Sons, 2019, passim; Abdillahi, I., "Algorithmic surveillance in the era of the appsphere", *American Journal of Community Psychology*, Volume 73, 2024, passim.

[2115] Robinson, M. A., "Black bodies on the ground: Policing disparities in the African American Community-An analysis of newsprint from January 1, 2015, through December 31, 2015", *Journal of Black Studies*, Volume 48, Issue 6, pp. 551–571.

[2116] See: Pager, Devah, *Marked: Race, Crime, and Finding Work in an Era of Mass Incarceration*, Chicago: University of Chicago Press, 2007; Fornili, K. S., "Racialized mass incarceration and the war on drugs: A critical race theory appraisal", *Journal of Addictions Nursing*, Volume 29, Issue 1, 2018, 65–72; Jacoby, S. F., Dong, B., Beard, J. H., Wiebe, D. J., & Morrison, C. N., "The enduring impact of historical and structural racism on urban violence in Philadelphia", *Social Science & Medicine*, 1982/2018, 199, 2018, pp. 87–95; Travis, Jeremy, Bruce Western, and Steve Redburn (Eds.), *Growth of Incarceration in the United States: Exploring Causes and Consequences*, Washington, DC: National Academy of Science, 2014. See also: Aneja/Abhay P./Avenancio-León, Carlos F., "No Credit for Time Served? Incarceration and Credit-Driven Crime Cycles", *AEA Papers and Proceedings*, Volume 109, 2019, pp. 160 and ff and passim (discusses the negative reflex of incarceration on credit scoring and income). See also: Bar-Gill/Oren/Warren, Elizabeth, "Making

minority[2128] consumers.[2129] Relatedly, when a lender leverages on input variables that mirrors prior disadvantage[2130]—or a «**biased world**»[2131]—it accordingly worsens that historical disadvantage by propelling into the entirely new domain[2132] of lending.[2133]

Credit Safer", *University of Pennsylvania Law Review*, Volume 157, 2008, pp. 1–66 (argue that Black defendants are far more likely to be incarcerated, arrested, surveilled and harassed than White folks, which leads to the conclusion that the use of credit scores and income presents another way in which credit decisions leverage on structural disadvantage).

2117 Jefferson, B., *Digitize and Punish: Racial Criminalization in the Digital Age*, Minnesota, University of Minnesota Press, 2020; Gross, Samuel R., Maurice Possley, and Kalara Stephens, "Race and Wrongful Convictions in the United States" *National Registry of Exonerations, Newkirk Center for Science and Society*, University of California-Irvine, 2017.

2118 Gillis, Talia B., "The Input Data Fallacy", *cit.*, pp. 1176–1263 (1193).

2119 See: Bar-Gill, Oren/Warren, Elizabeth, "Making Credit Safer", *University of Pennsylvania Law Review*, Volume 157, 2008, pp. 1–66 (argue that Black defendants are far more likely to be incarcerated, arrested, surveilled and harassed than White folks, which leads to the conclusion that the use of credit scores and income presents another way in which credit decisions leverage on structural disadvantage). See: Part IV, This chapter, Sects. 4.1.4–4.1.4.2.1 of this book (on mortgage redlining). See: Part IV, This chapter, Sects. 4.1.2–4.1.4.3 of this book (on algorithmic credit scoring, consumer racism and credit card redlining). See: Part IV, This chapter, Sects. 4.1.4–4.1.4.2.3 of this book (on algorithmic redlining). See: Part IV, This chapter, Sect. 4.1.4.3 of this book (on "algorithmic redliking"). See: Part IV, This chapter, Sect. 4.1.3 of this book (on algorithmic prime-lining).

2120 Gillis, Talia B., "The Input Data Fallacy", *cit.*, pp. 1176–1263 (1194).

2121 Gillis, Talia B., "The Input Data Fallacy", *cit.*, pp. 1176–1263 (1194).

2122 Freeman, Andrea, "Payback: A Structural Analysis of the Credit Card Problem", *Arizona Law Review*, Volume 55, 2013, pp. 180–81 ("Credit card companies confine low-income individuals to a subprime market and attempt to steer many middle-class African American and Latinos into subprime loans").

2123 See: Hurley, Mikella/Adebayo, Julius, "Credit Scoring in the Era of Big Data", *Yale Journal of Law and Technology*, Volume 18, 2016, p. 149 ("*big-data tools may allow online payday lenders to target the most vulnerable consumers and lure them into debt traps*"). See also: Gathergood, John/Guttman-Kenney, Benedict/Hunt, Stefan, "How Do Pay-day Loans Affect Borrowers? Evidence from the U.K. Market", *The Review of Financial Studies*, Volume 32, 2019, p. 496 (arguing that payday loans catalyse persistent increases in defaults, which, in turn, cause consumers to exceed their bank overdraft limits).

2124 Howell, Benjamin, "Note, Exploiting Race and Space: Concentrated Subprime Lending as Housing Discrimination", *California Law Review*, Volume 94, 2006, passim.

2125 Havard, Cassandra Jones, "On the Take": The Black Box of Credit Scoring and Mortgage Discrimination", *Boston University Public Interest Law Journal*, 2011, pp. 239 and ff and passim (discussing that subprime lending was undoubtably geared toward minority communities, aiming to enmesh them on the trap of excessive debt).

2126 Gillis, Talia B., "The Input Data Fallacy", *cit.*, pp. 1176–1263 (1194).

2127 It is crucially important to note, though, that the very fact that only certain types of behaviours are assessed and gauged by credit scores leads to the conclusion some borrowers are not scored at all. The overwhelming majority of consumers boast meagre, if any, credit files owing to the fact that the likelihood to access to the sort of financial services that actually report to the orthodox credit bureaus scattered across modern economies is exceedingly low, which, in turn, morphs them into credit invisible persons. See: Yu, Persis/McLaughlin, Jilian/Levy, Marina, "Big Data: A Big Disappointment for Scoring Consumer Creditworthiness,", *The National Consumer Law Center,* 2 (Mar. 14,

§§ The biased input is subsequently utilized to price credit, which is far more expensive[2134] for members of the disadvantaged[2135] group[2136]; the very same biased input is often used to unceremoniously snub credit with no qualms whatsoever.[2137]

2014), available at: https://www.nclc.org/images/pdf/pr-reports/report-big-data.pdf; [https://perma.cc/W4SK-NXD5] (access: 21.12.2024).

2128 Johnson, Creola, "The Magic of Group Identity: How Predatory Lenders Use Minorities to Target Communities of Color", *Georgetown Journal on Poverty Law and Policy*, 2010, pp. 165–169 (fleshing out several aggressive marketing tactics used by unprincipled/unscrupulous lenders to target primarily minorities for eerily predatory loans).

2129 Gillis, Talia B., "The Input Data Fallacy", *cit.*, pp. 1176–1263 (1194).

2130 Packard, Jerald M., *American Nightmare: The History of Jim Crow*, Broadway, New York, St. Martin's Press; First Edition, 2002, pp. 1–304 ("*for a hundred years after the end of the Civil War, a quarter of all Americans lived under a system of legalized segregation called Jim Crow. Together with its rigidly enforced canon of racial "etiquette," these rules governed nearly every aspect of life-and outlined draconian punishments for infractions. The purpose of Jim Crow was to keep African Americans subjugated at a level as close as possible to their former slave status. Exceeding even South Africa's notorious apartheid in the humiliation, degradation, and suffering it brought, Jim Crow left scars on the American psyche that are still felt today*"). Italics added.

2131 Gillis, Talia B., "The Input Data Fallacy", *cit.*, pp. 1176–1263 (1194).

2132 Hellman, Deborah, "Indirect Discrimination and the Duty to Avoid Compounding Injustice", *Foundations of Indirect Discrimination Law*, Collins, Hugh/Khaitan, Tarunabh (Editors), Oxford, Hart Publishing; Reprint edition (June 25, 2020), 2020, p. 107 (Professor Deborah Hellman coined this expression to depict a decision that "exacerbates the harm caused by the prior injustice because it entrenches the harm or carries it into another domain." This book deals with the sweltering topic of indirect discrimination ("*indirect discrimination (or disparate impact) concerns the application of the same rule to everyone, even though that rule significantly disadvantages one particular group in society*. Ever since its recognition by the Supreme Court of the United States in 1971, liberal democracies around the world have grappled with the puzzle that it can sometimes be unfair and wrong to treat everyone equally. *The law's regulation of private acts that unintentionally (but disproportionately) harm vulnerable groups has remained extremely controversial, especially in the United States and the United Kingdom. In original essays in this volume, leading scholars of discrimination law from North America and Europe explore the various facets of the law on indirect discrimination, interrogating its foundations, history, legitimacy, purpose, structure, and relationship with other legal concepts*. The collection provides the first international work devoted to this vital area of the law that seeks both to prevent unfair treatment and to transform societies"). Italics added.

2133 Gillis, Talia B., "The Input Data Fallacy", *cit.*, pp. 1176–1263 (1194).

2134 Freeman, Andrea, "Racism in the Credit Card Industry", *cit.*, p. 1071 ("even worse, the companies do so in a racially discriminatory way, *burdening Black and Latino customers with the worst credit card terms, often unrelated to credit risk*"). Italics added. See also: Firestone, Simon, "Race Ethnicity and Credit Card Monitoring", *Journal of Money, Credit and Banking*, Sept. 2014, 2014, pp. 1206 and ff; Han, Song, Keys, Benjamin J./Li, Geng, *Unsecured Credit Supply over the Credit Cycle: Evidence from Credit Card Mailings* (argue that, statistically, Blacks and Latinos are seldom granted credit and, if ever granted credit, the terms and conditions attached to the concession of credit are not equal to those offered to White folks).

2135 Baradaran, Mehrsa, "Banking and the Social Contract", *Notre Dame Law Review*, Volume 89, pp. 1283–1336 ("access to safe credit is crucial in allowing the poor to escape poverty").

2136 See: Levitin, Adam J., "The Antitrust Super Bowl: America's Payment Systems, No-Surcharge Rules, and the Hidden Costs of Credit", *Berkeley Business Law Journal*, Volume 3, 2005, 265, 317–18; id. at 154 ("consequently, *low-income consumers now receive credit cards with high fees and*

To the extent credit is a feasible pathway of yielding wealth,[2138] this inequality in credit pricing threatens to cement/buttress wealth gaps[2139] in the United States of America.[2140]

§§ It is important to note, though, that the birth of pricing decision may somewhat mirror **«measurement bias»**,[2141] to the extent that the way in which an input is calculated is biased[2142] rather than the underlying characteristic itself.[2143]

---

interest rates, while higher-income consumers reap the rewards of credit card use, such as travel miles and concierge services (…). As a *result of these practices, 80% of the industry's profits now come from interest payments and... fees instead of annual and interchange fees. This shift represents a massive redistribution of wealth from the poor to wealthier consumers and corporations*"). Italics added.

2137 Gillis, Talia B., "The Input Data Fallacy", *cit.*, pp. 1176–1263 (1194). See also: Hurley, Mikella/Adebayo, Julius, "Credit Scoring in the Era of Big Data", *cit.*, p. 149 ("*these tools may furthermore obscure discriminatory and subjective lending policies behind a single "objective" score* (…) *sophisticated algorithms may combine facially neutral data points and treat them as proxies for immutable characteristics such as race or gender, thereby circumventing existing non-discrimination laws and systematically denying credit access to certain groups*"). Italics added.

2138 But see: Atkinson, Abbye, "Rethinking Credit as a Social Provision", *Stanford Law Review*, Volume 71, 2019, pp. 1093–1099 (contending that credit, which shifts consumption temporally, is only beneficial insofar income ratchets up in the forthcoming future. As of now, though, "credit is fundamentally incompatible with the entrenched intergenerational poverty that plagues low-income Americans." Id. Notably, it is crucially important to come to terms with the fact that credit is not a panacea for the great bulk of economic struggles, and concretely wage stagnation. Although credit is not befitted to all consumers at all prices, affordable credit can nonetheless play a pivotal role in the creation of wealth).

2139 Kroeger, Teresa, and Graham Wright, "Entrepreneurship and the Racial Wealth Gap: The Impact of Entrepreneurial Success or Failure on the Wealth Mobility of Black and White Families," *Journal of Economics, Race, and Policy*, Volume 4, 2021, 183–195; Kermani, Amir, and Francis Wong, "Racial Disparities in Housing Returns," NBER Working Paper no. 29306, 2021; Hubmer, Joachim, Per Krusell, and Anthony A. Smith, Jr., "Sources of US Wealth Inequality: Past, Present, and Future," *NBER Macroeconomics Annual 2020*, Volume 35, 2021, pp. 391–455; Wolff, Edward N., "The Decline of African-American and Hispanic Wealth Since the Great Recession," *NBER Working Paper* no. 25198, 2018; Wolff, Edward N., "African-American and Hispanic Income, Wealth and Homeownership since 1989," *Review of Income and Wealth*, Volume 68, 2022, pp. 189–233.

2140 Gillis, Talia B., "The Input Data Fallacy", *cit.*, pp. 1176–1263 (1194).

2141 Gillis, Talia B., "The Input Data Fallacy", *cit.*, pp. 1176–1263 (1194).

2142 See: *Tech, Bias and Housing Initiative, the Promise and Perils of Residential Proptech, Year 1, Research Summary Report, April 2023, TechEquity Collaborative*, p. 5 available at: https://techequity.us/wp-content/uploads/2023/04/TBHI-Y1-Research-Summary-Report.pdf (28.11.2024). ("*Residential Proptech also has the potential to exacerbate the bias inherent in our housing system. Its rise is due, in part, to the desperation felt by average home seekers. With a severely constrained housing supply, companies offering an easier pathway to homeownership may exploit communities that have been harmed by housing discrimination in the past. Opaque algorithms incorporate biased data into their decision-making processes, making it harder to enforce fair housing laws.* Residential Proptech companies often operate in a regulatory gray area, leaving consumers without the protections they would have from traditional housing regulatory systems. *As unprecedented capital investment flows into this space, venture-backed companies' winner-take-all approach to growth has the potential to exacerbate inequality rather than combat it*"). Italics added. See: Part IV, This chapter, Sects. 4.1.4–4.1.4.2.3 of this book.

2143 Gillis, Talia B., "The Input Data Fallacy", *cit.*, pp. 1176–1263 (1194).

§§ Although lenders may exert more control over factors that catalyse «biased measurement» inputs than «biased world» inputs, all things considered, these two types of biases conflate or even straddle.[2144] To some extent, they are woven of the same cloth. The general taxonomy of «borrower characteristics»[2145] disguises the very fact that any feature entails some degree of definition,[2146] measurement,[2147] and calculation.[2148]

§§ Revealingly, if one seeks to use a borrower's income, there must a definition of income that usually precedes the measurement a borrower's income.[2149] Crucially, one should consider whether and what extent a batch of transfers, such as gifts from fellow family members, fall within the category of income, or if they fall within the category of public assistance income instead.[2150] For example, voucher holders—i.e. low-income people, usually members of racial minorities—often endure harrowing experiences in having their rental application[2151] approved.[2152]

2144 Gillis, Talia B., "The Input Data Fallacy", *cit.*, pp. 1176–1263 (1194).

2145 See: *Tech, Bias and Housing Initiative, the Promise and Perils of Residential Proptech, Year 1, Research Summary Report, April 2023, TechEquity Collaborative*, p. 10, available at: https://techequity.us/wp-content/uploads/2023/04/TBHI-Y1-Research-Summary-Report.pdf (28.11.2024). ("*Algorithm-backed screening services, on the other hand, bundle all the traditional information (whether accurate or not) alongside predictive models. These predictive models make guesses about whether an applicant will be a responsible tenant based not on the history of that specific applicant, but on (as far as we can tell) behavior trends of applicants who have similar characteristics. The data behind these models is rarely made available to either the tenant or the landlord (….) certain outcomes are determined by a combination of applicant characteristics and factors that have little to do with said applicant. "Length of Tenancy," for example, is rated both by applicant characteristics as well as a prediction of how "conditions may change in the future." Eviction outcomes are determined by "possibility of property damage;" Successful payments rely on "suitability to the rental property*"). Italics added. See: Part IV, This chapter, Sects. 4.1.4–4.1.4.2.3 of this book. See: Part IV, This chapter, Sects. 4.1.4–4.1.4.2.1 of this book (on mortgage redlining). See: Part IV, This chapter, Sects. 4.1.2–4.1.4.3 of this book (on algorithmic credit scoring, consumer racism and credit card redlining). See: Part IV, This chapter, Sects. 4.1.4–4.1.4.2.3 of this book (on algorithmic redlining). See: Part IV, This chapter, Sect. 4.1.4.3 of this book (on "algorithmic redliking"). See: Part IV, This chapter, Sect. 4.1.3 of this book (on algorithmic prime-lining).

2146 Gillis, Talia B., "The Input Data Fallacy", *cit.*, pp. 1176–1263 (1194).

2147 See: Corbett-Davies, Sam/Goel, Sharad, "The Measure and Mismeasure of Fairness: a critical Review of Fair Machine Learning", *Cornell University Library*, 2018, p. 18 (broaches a type of measurement bias coined "feature bias," which is neatly a bias in the predictors x. Note, though, that there is a second type of measurement bias deemed "label bias," which, in turn, amounts to a bias in y. The authors argue that that label bias is the worst bias there is).

2148 Gillis, Talia B., "The Input Data Fallacy", *cit.*, pp. 1176–1263 (1195).

2149 Gillis, Talia B., "The Input Data Fallacy", *cit.*, pp. 1176–1263 (1195).

2150 Gillis, Talia B., "The Input Data Fallacy", *cit.*, pp. 1176–1263 (1195).

2151 See: *Tech, Bias and Housing Initiative, the Promise and Perils of Residential Proptech, Year 1, Research Summary Report, April 2023, TechEquity Collaborative*, p. 5 available at: https://techequity.us/wp-content/uploads/2023/04/TBHI-Y1-Research-Summary-Report.pdf (28.11.2024). ("*Residential Proptech also has the potential to exacerbate the bias inherent in our housing system. Its rise is due, in part, to the desperation felt by average home seekers.*

§§ To cater for that, certain documentation will be needed to gauge the extent to which a transfer should be considered «income».[2153] When a given definition systematically and unlawfully disadvantages[2154] a protected group, though, then it could very well be a case of **«measurement bias»**.[2155]

With a severely constrained housing supply, companies offering an easier pathway to homeownership may exploit communities that have been harmed by housing discrimination in the past. Opaque algorithms incorporate biased data into their decision-making processes, making it harder to enforce fair housing laws. Residential Proptech companies often operate in a regulatory gray area, leaving consumers without the protections they would have from traditional housing regulatory systems. *As unprecedented capital investment flows into this space, venture-backed companies' winner-take-all approach to growth has the potential to exacerbate inequality rather than combat it*"). Italics added. See: Part IV, This chapter, Sects. 4.1.4–4.1.4.2.3 of this book. See: Part IV, This chapter, Sects. 4.1.4–4.1.4.2.1 of this book (on mortgage redlining). See: Part IV, This chapter, Sects. 4.1.2–4.1.4.3 of this book (on algorithmic credit scoring, consumer racism and credit card redlining). See: Part IV, This chapter, Sects. 4.1.4–4.1.4.2.3 of this book (on algorithmic redlining). See: Part IV, This chapter, Sect. 4.1.4.3 of this book (on "algorithmic redliking"). See: Part IV, This chapter, Sect. 4.1.3 of this book (on algorithmic prime-lining).

2152 Wonyoung, So, "Which Information Matters? Measuring Landlord Assessment of Tenant Screening Reports", *Housing Policy Debate*, Volume 33, n. ° 6, 2023, pp. 1484–1510 (1502) ("*One additional finding of the experiment is that algorithmic scoring can exacerbate this racially unequal landscape in rental agreements not just because the algorithm may be inaccurate, but because landlords may want to follow the risk assessment made by the tenant screening report. This is alarming for low-income tenants, particularly housing voucher holders. Security deposits are one of the most significant barriers to obtaining housing for voucher holders, because vouchers do not pay security deposits but most private landlords require them (Rosenblatt & Cossyleon, 2018).* Given that voucher holders have exceptionally low income (usually less than 50% of area median income) and might experience more housing insecurity (rental debts and eviction-related experiences), *imposing greater security deposits on voucher holders almost equates to denying them housing—yet these decisions could be justified by algorithmic scoring if tenant screening services employ it*"). Italics added. See: Part IV, This chapter, Sects. 4.1.4–4.1.4.2.3 of this book.

2153 Gillis, Talia B., "The Input Data Fallacy", *cit.*, pp. 1176–1263 (1195).

2154 See: Menasce, Juliana Horowitz/Brown, Anna/Cox, Kiana, "Views of Racial Inequality", *Pew Research Center*, April 9, 2019, available at: https://www.pewresearch.org/social-trends/2019/04/09/views-of-racial-inequality/ (access: 2.12.2024) ("*more than four-in-ten Americans say the country still has work to do to give black people equal rights with whites. Blacks, in particular, are skeptical that black people will ever have equal rights in this country (….) A majority of adults say that being white helps people's ability to get ahead in the country at least a little (59%); 28% say being white neither helps nor hurts and 12% say it hurts. On the flip side, a majority (56%) sees being black as a disadvantage, with 25% saying it hurts people's ability to get ahead a lot. About a quarter (26%) say being black neither helps nor hurts and 17% say it helps at least a little. More also say that being Hispanic hurts people's ability to get ahead in this country (51%) than say it helps (18%) or that it neither helps nor hurts (30%).* Opinions are more split when it comes to the impact of being Native American – about the same shares say this hurts as say it neither helps nor hurts, while a smaller share says it helps. *And while a plurality says being Asian neither helps nor hurts, more say it helps (34%) than hurts (21%) people's ability to get ahead*"). Italics added.

2155 Gillis, Talia B., "The Input Data Fallacy", *cit.*, pp. 1176–1263 (1195). See: Corbett-Davies, Sam/Goel, Sharad, "The Measure and Mismeasure of Fairness: a critical Review of Fair Machine Learning", *Cornell University Library*, 2018, p. 18 (broaches a type of measurement bias coined "feature bias," which is neatly a bias in the predictors x. Note, though, that there is a second type of measurement bias deemed "label bias," which, in turn, amounts to a bias in y. The authors argue that that label bias is the worst bias there is).

§§ On the flip side, another type of **«biased measurement»** could emerge when a proxy is used instead of the characteristic which, in turn, is indeed of true interest.[2156] More often than not, the input variable that is of true interest goes frequently unchecked,[2157] unaddressed, unassessed, overlooked, unaccounted for and so a lender might end up relying upon a proxy instead.[2158]

§§ It bears mentioning that the borrower's «education»[2159] is often utilized as a proxy for the borrower's «ability»—or the extent to which someone will prospectively be a «good tenant»[2160]/[2161]—which is considered somewhat relevant in ascertaining

---

[2156] Gillis, Talia B., "The Input Data Fallacy", *cit.*, pp. 1176–1263 (1195).

[2157] Havard, Cassandra Jones, "On the Take": The Black Box of Credit Scoring and Mortgage Discrimination", *Boston University Public Interest Law Journal*, Volume 20, 2011, pp. 241–247 (highlighting that credit scoring if unchecked is an intrinsic, encroached, deep-rooted form of racial discrimination akin to mortgage redlining); Pasquale, Frank, *The Black Box Society: The Secret Algorithms that Control Money and Information*. Cambridge, Massachusetts: Harvard University Press, 2015, 1–320. See: Part IV, This chapter, Sects. 4.1.4–4.1.4.2.1 of this book (on mortgage redlining). See: Part IV, This chapter, Sects. 4.1.2–4.1.4.3 of this book (on algorithmic credit scoring, consumer racism and credit card redlining). See: Part IV, This chapter, Sects. 4.1.4–4.1.4.2.3 of this book (on algorithmic redlining). See: Part IV, This chapter, Sect. 4.1.4.3 of this book (on "algorithmic redliking"). See: Part IV, This chapter, Sect. 4.1.3 of this book (on algorithmic prime-lining).

[2158] Gillis, Talia B., "The Input Data Fallacy", *cit.*, pp. 1176–1263 (1195).

[2159] But see: Lipsitz, George, *The Possessive Investment in Whiteness: How White People Profit from Identity Politics*, Philadelphia, Pennsylvania, Temple University Press; 1st edition (July 13, 2018), 2018, pp. 1–448 ("***Whiteness has a cash value: it accounts for advantages that come to individuals through profits made from housing secured in discriminatory markets, through the unequal educational opportunities available to children of different races****, through insider networks that channel employment opportunities to the friends and relatives of those who have profited most from past and present discrimination*, and especially through intergenerational transfers of inherited wealth that pass on the spoils of discrimination to succeeding generations. *White Americans are encouraged to invest in whiteness, to remain true to an identity that provides them with structured advantages*"). Italics and bold added.

[2160] But see: *Tech, Bias and Housing Initiative, the Promise and Perils of Residential Proptech, Year 1, Research Summary Report, April 2023, TechEquity Collaborative*, p. 11, available at: https://techequity.us/wp-content/uploads/2023/04/TBHI-Y1-Research-Summary-Report.pdf (28.11.2024). ("*From information on company websites, it is not clear what analysis or data is behind subjective determinations like "suitability" to a unit or what the nexus between an individual's characteristics and a unit's characteristics is that indicates the likelihood for property damage. Based on sample reports, even landlords are not privy to how the determinations are made. Instead, they receive a risk score out of 100 simplified into green, yellow, and red recommendations.* What companies withhold in terms of how it works, they make up for with the extent to which they tell landlords it works: Naborly claims their predictions reduce lease defaults by up to 89%. 15 *As Naborly's sample report demonstrates, its property damage assessment is then used as an input to determine its projected eviction outcomes; its early vacancy prediction, in turn, is based on "all assessment factors*"). Italics added. See: Part IV, This chapter, Sects. 4.1.4–4.1.4.2.3 of this book.

[2161] But see: Power, Emma R., and Charles Gillon, "Performing the 'Good Tenant'", *Housing Studies*, Volume 37, Issue 3, 2020, pp. 459–82 (459) ("*Renters in homeowner societies like Australia, the United States and United Kingdom occupy a complex moral landscape, maligned for failure to achieve homeownership but pivotal to the value of investment properties. Identification of 'good' and 'risky' tenants is an important landlord practice* (...) *The good tenant demonstrates responsibility through paying rent on time and property stewardship (reporting repairs, making home). However,*

future income.[2162] Note, though, that albeit the so-called «ability» is not directly observed by the lender, the latter could very well utilize borrower education[2163] as a proxy.[2164]

§§ Understandably, although not laudably, since racial minorities are far less likely to go to college to pursue any level of academic ability,[2165] this proxy will catalyse ***measurement bias***[2166] in that it will most likely work against the interests of the former in being afforded the sorely needed credit.[2167]

§§ Tellingly, the problem is not necessarily spawned by pre-existing discrimination.[2168] Rather, quite the opposite, the shoddy/watered down assessment of the underlying variable of interest is the culprit.[2169] Pivotally, a core marker used to price credit, a borrower's credit score, might fall prey to ***measurement bias*** after all.[2170]

§§ Compellingly, the exact inputs and underpinning frames of reference utilized to define a credit score,[2171] such as a FICO score,[2172] are qualified as proprietary

---

these practices are made necessary and risky through limited tenure security. The emotional and financial risks attending performances of the good tenant drive paradoxical relations; a good tenant is also acquiescent and silent, not reporting property repairs or lapsed leases to avoid rent increases and/or evictions. Variegated performances of the '*good tenant' reflect cultural property norms and valorize the investment function of housing yet could also productively unsettle tenant-landlord relations*"). Italics added. See: Part IV, This chapter, Sects. 4.1.4–4.1.4.2.3 of this book.

2162 Gillis, Talia B., "The Input Data Fallacy", *cit.*, pp. 1176–1263 (1195).

2163 But see: Kim, Pauline T., "Data-Driven Discrimination at Work", *William and Mary Law Review*, Volume 58, 2017, pp. 857, 863–64 (shedding a keen light on the racial effects of algorithmic prediction in the remit of employment). Converging: Zywicki, Todd J./Adamson, Joseph D., "The Law and Economics of Subprime Lending", *University of Colorado Law Review*, 2009, pp. 1–9 (contending that Black workers with roughly the same abilities and educational background earn far less than comparable white workers or have considerably fewer employment opportunities); King, Allan G./Markovich, Marko J., "Big Data" and the Risk of Employment Discrimination, *Oklahoma Law Review*, Volume 68, 2016, pp. 555–563 (on employment discrimination). Dobbie, Will, Jacob Goldin, and Crystal S. Yang, "The Effects of Pretrial Detention on Conviction, Future Crime, and Employment: Evidence from Randomly Assigned Judges," *American Economic Review*, Volume 108, 2018, 201–240.

2164 Gillis, Talia B., "The Input Data Fallacy", *cit.*, pp. 1176–1263 (1195).

2165 Pierce, C., "W.E.B. du bois and caste education: Racial capitalist schooling from reconstruction to Jim Crow", *American Educational Research Journal*, 54 (1_Suppl.), 2017, pp. 23S-47S.

2166 Gillis, Talia B., "The Input Data Fallacy", *cit.*, pp. 1176–1263 (1195).

2167 Prince, Anya E. R./Schwarcz, Daniel, "Proxy Discrimination in the Age of Artificial Intelligence and Big Data", *Iowa Law Review*, Volume 105, 2020, pp. 1257, 1279–81 ("[*P*]*roxy discrimination will tend to occur when a suspect variable is predictive of a desired outcome only because it proxies for another*, quantifiable and potentially available, *variable that causes the desired outcome but that is not included in the AI's training data*"). Italics added.

2168 Gillis, Talia B., "The Input Data Fallacy", *cit.*, pp. 1176–1263 (1195).

2169 Gillis, Talia B., "The Input Data Fallacy", *cit.*, pp. 1176–1263 (1195).

2170 Gillis, Talia B., "The Input Data Fallacy", *cit.*, pp. 1176–1263 (1195).

2171 But see: Hurley, Mikella/Adebayo, Julius, "Credit Scoring in the Era of Big Data", *Yale Journal of Law and Technology*, Volume 18, 2016, p. 149 ("*these tools may furthermore obscure discriminatory and subjective lending policies behind a single "objective" score*"). Italics added.

2172 But see: Hurley, Mikella/Adebayo, Julius, "Credit Scoring in the Era of Big Data", *cit.*, pp. 148, 151–156, 172 (averring that FICO scoring boasts a redoubtable capacity to routinely weed out some

information,[2173] meaning it is painstakingly difficult to gauge whether and to what extent certain scores may be tainted with a bias.[2174]

§§ Notwithstanding, it is commonsense that credit scores have conventionally relied upon a bundle of measures of creditworthiness,[2175] such as lending from behemoth financial institutions[2176] and mortgage loan payments.[2177]

§§ Other markers of creditworthiness, such as timely rental[2178] payments[2179]—which, in turn, hints who is entitled to be considered «suitable» to rent a house[2180]—or borrowing money from local financial entities, might equally be predictive[2181] of default.[2182]

---

populations that have been historically and systematically underrepresented or grossly unfairly represented in the credit industry market). Tellingly, by 2016, ten states had disavowed the unlawful practice of employers using shady credit scores due to their perceived disparate impact on low-income applicants and members of racialized communities (mostly Black folks). See: O'Neill, Cathy, *Weapons of Math Destruction. How Big Data Increases Inequality and Threatens Democracy*. London: Penguin Random House, 2016, pp. 128 and ff and passim. See: Part IV, This chapter, Sects. 4.1.4–4.1.4.2.3 of this book.

2173 Gillis, Talia B., "The Input Data Fallacy", *cit.*, pp. 1176–1263 (1195).

2174 Gillis, Talia B., "The Input Data Fallacy", *cit.*, pp. 1176–1263 (1195).

2175 Gillis, Talia B., "The Input Data Fallacy", *cit.*, pp. 1176–1263 (1195). But see: Hurley, Mikella/ Adebayo, Julius, "Credit Scoring in the Era of Big Data", *cit.*, p. 149 ("*recent studies have also questioned the accuracy of the data used by these tools, in some cases identifying serious flaws that have a substantial bearing on lending decisions. Big-data tools may also risk creating a system of "creditworthiness by association" in which consumers' familial, religious, social, and other affiliations determine their eligibility for an affordable loan*"). Italics added.

2176 It is crucially important to note, though, that the very fact that only certain types of behaviours are assessed and gauged by credit scores leads to the conclusion some borrowers are not scored at all. The overwhelming majority of consumers boast meagre, if any, credit files owing to the fact that the likelihood to access to the sort of financial services that actually report to the orthodox credit bureaus scattered across modern economies is exceedingly low, which, in turn, morphs them into credit invisible persons. See: Yu, Persis/McLaughlin, Jilian/Levy, Marina, "Big Data: A Big Disappointment for Scoring Consumer Creditworthiness,", *The National Consumer Law Center,* 2 (Mar. 14, 2014), available at: https://www.nclc.org/images/pdf/pr-reports/report-big-data.pdf; [https://perma.cc/W4SK-NXD5] (access: 21.12.2024).

2177 Gillis, Talia B., "The Input Data Fallacy", *cit.*, pp. 1176–1263 (1195). But see: Ards, Sheila D./Myers, Samuel L. Myers, "The Color of Money: Bad Credit, Wealth, and Race", *American Behavioral Scientist*, Volume 45, 2001, pp. 223–238 (debunks the deep-seated myth according to which Blacks are big spenders and thus unworthy of creditworthiness, which stands as an irksome social bias in dire need of quashing).

2178 Gillis, Talia B., "The Input Data Fallacy", *cit.*, pp. 1176–1263 (1195).

2179 Gillis, Talia B., "The Input Data Fallacy", *cit.*, pp. 1176–1263 (1195).

4.1.7.2 The Dichotomy Between the «Biased World Inputs in Algorithmic Pricing» and «Biased Measurement Inputs in Algorithmic Pricing» (Talia B. Gillis) That Amplifies Racial Inequalities in the Era of Financial Technologies (*FinTech*)

§§ It is crucially important to understand the extent to which biased inputs sway credit pricing[2183] decisions.[2184] Whilst the issue of biased inputs is not blazingly new to the algorithmic context,[2185] its consequences[2186] might «be different in the traditional and algorithmic setting».[2187]

[2180] But see: *Tech, Bias and Housing Initiative, the Promise and Perils of Residential Proptech, Year 1, Research Summary Report, April 2023, TechEquity Collaborative*, p. 11, available at: https://techequity.us/wp-content/uploads/2023/04/TBHI-Y1-Research-Summary-Report.pdf (28.11.2024). ("*from information on company websites, it is not clear what analysis or data is behind subjective determinations like "suitability" to a unit or what the nexus between an individual's characteristics and a unit's characteristics is that indicates the likelihood for property damage. Based on sample reports, even landlords are not privy to how the determinations are made. Instead, they receive a risk score out of 100 simplified into green, yellow, and red recommendations.* What companies withhold in terms of how it works, they make up for with the extent to which they tell landlords it works: Naborly claims their predictions reduce lease defaults by up to 89%. 15 *As Naborly's sample report demonstrates, its property damage assessment is then used as an input to determine its projected eviction outcomes; its early vacancy prediction, in turn, is based on "all assessment factors*"). Italics added. See: Part IV, This chapter, Sects. 4.1.4–4.1.4.2.3 of this book.

[2181] But see: Kleinberg, Jon/Ludwig, Jens/Mullainathan, Sendhil/Sunstein Cass R., "Discrimination in the Age of Algorithms", *Journal of Legal Analysis*, Volume 10, 1, 2018, pp. 28–29, 33–34 (draw a distinction between "group differences in the raw data" and biases for the "choice of predictors"). Note, though, that, theoretically, one should not shy away from bifurcating/splitting the "prediction" issue from the "decision" issue to stymie/stamp out hidden biases. See: Corbett-Davies, Sam/Pierson, Emma/Feller, Avi/Goel, Sharad Goel/Huq, Aziz, "Algorithmic Decision Making and the Cost of Fairness", *Proceedings of the 23rd ACM SIGKDD International Conference on Knowledge Discovery and Data Mining* (Ass'n for Computing Machinery ed., 2017), 2017, passim.

[2182] Gillis, Talia B., "The Input Data Fallacy", *cit.*, pp. 1176–1263 (1196).

[2183] Fuster, Andreas/Goldsmith-Pinkham, Paul/Tarun Ramadorai/Walther, Angsar, "Predictably Unequal? The Effects of Machine Learning on Credit Markets", *Journal of Finance*, Volume 76, 2022, passim (providing a description of the variation in interest rates across racial groups).

[2184] Gillis, Talia B., "The Input Data Fallacy", *cit.*, pp. 1176–1263 (1214).

[2185] Sokolovska, N./Chevaleyre, Y./Zucker, J.D., "A provable algorithm for learning interpretable scoring systems", *Proceedings of Machine Learning Research, Artificial Intelligence and Statistics*, Volume 84, pp. 566–574.

[2186] Havard, Cassandra Jones, "On The Take": The Black Box of Credit Scoring and Mortgage Discrimination", *Boston University Public Interest Law Journal*, Volume 20, 2011, pp. 241–247 (highlighting that credit scoring if unchecked is an intrinsic, encroached, deep-rooted form of racial discrimination akin to mortgage redlining); Watcher, S./Mittelstadt, B./Russell, C., "Counterfactual explanations without opening the black box: automated decisions and the GDPR", *Harvard Journal of Law & Technology*, Volume 1, 2018, passim.

[2187] Gillis, Talia B., "The Input Data Fallacy", *cit.*, pp. 1176–1263 (1214).

§§ Although the effects of «biased world» are sorely felt by those affected the most,[2188] it is painstakingly difficult to build a case of—direct[2189] or indirect[2190]—discrimination[2191] based on either disparate treatment[2192] or disparate impact.[2193] Note, though, that these are hardly exhilarating news.

[2188] For example, a batch of other pieces of academic research have deftly pinpointed racial disparities with regard to access to the labour market. See: Bertrand, Marianne/Mullainathan, Sendhil, "Are Emily and Greg More Employable than Lakisha and Jamal? A Field Experiment on Labor Market Discrimination", *The American Economic Review*, Volume 94, 2004, p. 991 (reaches the conclusion according to which white-sounding names are far more likely to spark a callback than that of suitably qualified applicants with Black-sounding names); Nunley, John M./Pugh, Adam/Romero, Nicholas/Seals, R. Alan, "Racial Discrimination in the Labor Market for Recent College Graduates: Evidence from a Field Experiment", *The B.E. Journal of Economic Analysis & Policy*, Volume 15, 2015, pp. 1096 and ff and passim.

[2189] Even absent direct compensation for exceedingly higher interest rates, more expensive loans are conspicuously clear more profitable for lenders in that could ultimately sway loan officer compensation rate. See: Jackson, Howell E./Burlingame, Laurie, "Kickbacks or Compensation: The Case of Yield Spread Premiums", *Stanford Journal of Law Business and Finance*, Volume 12, 2007, p. 289 (shedding a keen light on how yield spread premiums have a direct bearing on exceedingly higher mortgage prices for regular consumers, which, in turn, may befall inordinately on the least sophisticated borrowers, amongst whom members of racialised communities).

[2190] Hellman, Deborah, "Indirect Discrimination and the Duty to Avoid Compounding Injustice", *Foundations of Indirect Discrimination Law*, Collins, Hugh/Khaitan, Tarunabh (Editors), Oxford, Hart Publishing; Reprint edition (June 25, 2020), 2020, p. 107 (Professor Deborah Hellman coined this expression to depict a decision that "exacerbates the harm caused by the prior injustice because it entrenches the harm or carries it into another domain." This book deals with the sweltering topic of indirect discrimination ("*indirect discrimination (or disparate impact) concerns the application of the same rule to everyone, even though that rule significantly disadvantages one particular group in society*. Ever since its recognition by the Supreme Court of the United States in 1971, liberal democracies around the world have grappled with the puzzle that it can sometimes be unfair and wrong to treat everyone equally. *The law's regulation of private acts that unintentionally (but disproportionately) harm vulnerable groups has remained extremely controversial, especially in the United States and the United Kingdom. In original essays in this volume, leading scholars of discrimination law from North America and Europe explore the various facets of the law on indirect discrimination, interrogating its foundations, history, legitimacy, purpose, structure, and relationship with other legal concepts*. The collection provides the first international work devoted to this vital area of the law that seeks both to prevent unfair treatment and to transform societies"). Italics added.

[2191] Albeit the racial wage gap in the labour market is remarkably well parsed, discerning—or dissecting—this gap and the degree to which it sharply mirrors either taste-based or statistical discrimination has proven to be gruelling uphill battle. See: Black, Dan Amelia Haviland/Sanders, Seth/Taylor, Lowell, "Why Do Minority Men Earn Less? A Study of Wage Differentials Among the Highly Educated", *The Review of Economics and Statistics*, Volume 88, 2006, pp. 300 and ff and passim (pinpointing gleefully weird wage gaps between Black men and men of other races while shedding a keen light on the sweltering challenges in ascribing that perceived gap to blatant/blunt racial discrimination). See also: Grodsky, Eric/Pager, Devah, "The Structure of Disadvantage: Individual and Occupational Determinants of Black-White Wage Gap", *American Sociological Review*, Volume 66, 2001, pp. 542–563 (stumbles upon the finding in view of which that whilst Black men have burgeoningly gained access to highly remunerated occupations, they have nonetheless become subject to more extreme racial disadvantages when it comes to seizing power, which, in turn, can be loosely qualified as gate-keeping).

§§ At one end of the spectrum, algorithmic credit pricing exhibits an exceedingly high likelihood to exacerbate the **«biased world»** problem,[2194] since it swells the variance in predictions[2195] while ballooning the amount of **«biased world»** inputs through its use of unorthodox, rigged[2196] or non-conventional data[2197] whose origins are eerily unknown.[2198]

§§ To the extent that algorithmic pricing gives room for an enhanced ability to protect some characteristics,[2199] the algorithmic context could also sooth out the harms of **«biased measurement»**[2200] by providing a greater amount of information on individuals,[2201] which, in turn, can foster algorithmic[2202] **personalized pricing**[2203] that is not without sizable hurdles[2204] nonetheless.[2205]

2192 Fryer, Roland G. Fryer/Pager, Devah/Spenkuch, Jörg L., "Racial Disparities in Job Finding and Offered Wages", *Journal of Law and Economics*, Volume 56, 2013, pp. 633–690 (contending that disparate treatment accounts for at least one third of the Black-white wage gap).

2193 In spite of the widely accepted conceptual differences between intent-based and effect-based theories of disparate impact, both approaches often dovetail seamlessly. As far as the fair lending goes, the definition of disparate impact is somewhat shallow, nomadic, and erratic, and dispiritingly vague. Note, though, that the loan officer's discretion is directly conducive to exceedingly higher rates for members of racial minorities. See: Ayres, Ian/Klein, Gary/West, Jeffrey, "The Rise and (Potential) Fall of Disparate Impact Lending Litigation", *Evidence and Innovation in Housing Law and Policy*, Fennell, Lee Anne/Keys, Benajmin J. (Editors), Cambridge, Cambridge University Press, 2017, pp. 231–254.

2194 See: Wonyoung, So, "Which Information Matters? Measuring Landlord Assessment of Tenant Screening Reports", *Housing Policy Debate*, Volume 33, n. ° 6, 2023, pp. 1484–1510 (1502) ("*One additional finding of the experiment is that algorithmic scoring can exacerbate this racially unequal landscape in rental agreements not just because the algorithm may be inaccurate, but because landlords may want to follow the risk assessment made by the tenant screening report. This is alarming for low-income tenants, particularly housing voucher holders. Security deposits are one of the most significant barriers to obtaining housing for voucher holders, because vouchers do not pay security deposits but most private landlords require them (Rosenblatt & Cossyleon, 2018). Given that voucher holders have exceptionally low income (usually less than 50% of area median income)* and might experience more housing insecurity (rental debts and eviction-related experiences), *imposing greater security deposits on voucher holders almost equates to denying them housing—yet these decisions could be justified by algorithmic scoring if tenant screening services employ it*"). Italics added. See: Part IV, This chapter, Sects. 4.1.4–4.1.4.2.3 of this book. See: Part IV, This chapter, Sects. 4.1.4–4.1.4 .2.1 of this book (on mortgage redlining). See: Part IV, This chapter, Sects. 4.1.2–4.1.4.3 of this book (on algorithmic credit scoring, consumer racism and credit card redlining). See: Part IV, This chapter, Sects. 4.1.4–4.1.4.2.3 of this book (on algorithmic redlining). See: Part IV, This chapter, Sect. 4.1.4.3 of this book (on "algorithmic redliking"). See: Part IV, This chapter, Sect. 4.1.3 of this book (on algorithmic prime-lining).

2195 Note, though, that, theoretically, one should not shy away, or veer away, from bifurcating/splitting the "prediction" issue from the "decision" issue. See: Corbett-Davies, Sam/Pierson, Emma/Feller, Avi/Goel, Sharad Goel/Huq, Aziz, "Algorithmic Decision Making and the Cost of Fairness", *Proceedings of the 23rd ACM SIGKDD International Conference on Knowledge Discovery and Data Mining* (Ass'n for Computing Machinery ed., 2017), 2017, passim.

§§ It bears mentioning that first way to head towards the new world of algorithmic credit pricing can swell the disparities between protected groups[2206] in that widening

[2196] See: *Tech, Bias and Housing Initiative, the Promise and Perils of Residential Proptech, Year 1, Research Summary Report, April 2023, TechEquity Collaborative*, p. 11, available at: https://techequity.us/wp-content/uploads/2023/04/TBHI-Y1-Research-Summary-Report.pdf (28.11.2024). ("*Once bad data enters the analysis of one factor, it gets baked into the subsequent process, multiplying the effect that one disadvantageous data point can have on someone's overall housing determination*"). Italics added. See: Part IV, This chapter, Sects. 4.1.4–4.1.4.2.3 of this book. See also: Barocas, Solon/Selbst, Andrew D., "Big Data's Disparate Impact", *California Law Review*, Volume 104, 2016, pp. 671–682 (discussing how data is often flawed, rigged, incomplete, imperfect and therefore algorithms inherit the prejudice of the original decision makers). But see: Citron, Danielle Keats/Pasquale, Frank, "The Scored Society: Due Process for Automated Predictions", *Washington Law Review*, Volume 89, 2014, pp. 1, 4–5 (highlighting how human beings programming automated systems is directly conducive to, and leads, to fundamentally inaccurate results since the source code, predictive algorithms and datasets may encompass human biases which, in turn, have a disparate impact on historically disadvantaged groups); Crawford, Kate/Schultz, Jason, "Big Data and Due Process: Toward a Framework to Redress Predictive Privacy Harms", *Boston College Law Review*, Volume 55, 2014, pp. 93, 99–101 (pinpointing pathways through which predictive analytic tools perpetuate discriminatory practices). But see: Bornstein, Stepanhie, "Antidiscriminatory Algorithms", *Alabama Law Review*, Volume 70, 2018, pp. 519, 524–528 (contending, however, that the tagged "facially neutral" algorithms producing discriminatory outcomes should be quashed).

[2197] Gillis, Talia B., "The Input Data Fallacy", *cit.*, pp. 1176–1263 (1214).

[2198] *Tech, Bias and Housing Initiative, the Promise and Perils of Residential Proptech, Year 1, Research Summary Report, April 2023, TechEquity Collaborative*, p. 11, available at: https://techequity.us/wp-content/uploads/2023/04/TBHI-Y1-Research-Summary-Report.pdf (28.11.2024). ("*From information on company websites, it is not clear what analysis or data is behind subjective determinations like "suitability" to a unit or what the nexus between an individual's characteristics and a unit's characteristics is that indicates the likelihood for property damage. Based on sample reports, even landlords are not privy to how the determinations are made. Instead, they receive a risk score out of 100 simplified into green, yellow, and red recommendations.* What companies withhold in terms of how it works, they make up for with the extent to which they tell landlords it works: Naborly claims their predictions reduce lease defaults by up to 89%. 15 *As Naborly's sample report demonstrates, its property damage assessment is then used as an input to determine its projected eviction outcomes; its early vacancy prediction, in turn, is based on "all assessment factors*"). Italics added. See: Part IV, This chapter, Sects. 4.1.4–4.1.4.2.3 of this book.

[2199] Gillis, Talia B., "The Input Data Fallacy", *cit.*, pp. 1176–1263 (1214). See also: *Tech, Bias and Housing Initiative, the Promise and Perils of Residential Proptech, Year 1, Research Summary Report, April 2023, TechEquity Collaborative*, p. 11, available at: https://techequity.us/wp-content/uploads/2023/04/TBHI-Y1-Research-Summary-Report.pdf (28.11.2024). ("And while we know that the *data is predictive, meaning it has little to do with demonstrated behavior of the applicant themself, we do not know exactly where companies get their data*"). Italics added. See: Part IV, This chapter, Sects. 4.1.4–4.1.4.2.3 of this book.

[2200] See: Corbett-Davies, Sam/Goel, Sharad, "The Measure and Mismeasure of Fairness: a critical Review of Fair Machine Learning", *Cornell University Library*, 2018, p. 18 (broaches a type of measurement bias coined "feature bias," which is neatly a bias in the predictors x. Note, though, that there is a second type of measurement bias deemed "label bias," which, in turn, amounts to a bias in y. The authors argue that that label bias is the worst bias there is).

[2201] Gillis, Talia B., "The Input Data Fallacy", *cit.*, pp. 1176–1263 (1214).

input variables to include additional «biased world» inputs[2207] will only soar racial disparities.[2208]

[2202] But see: Einav, Liran/Jenkins, Mark/Levin, Jonathan, "The Impact of Credit Scoring on Consumer Lending", *The RAND Journal of Economics*, Volume 44, 2013, p. 249 (showing unequivocally that the adoption of computer-run algorithmic credit scoring led to conspicuously higher-risk applicant lending).

[2203] For an on-point breakdown of the distinct levels of opacity arising out of machine learning algorithms in the purview of insurance policies: Selbst, Andrew D./Barocas, Solon, "The Intuitive Appeal of Explainable Machines", *Fordham Law Review*, Volume 87, 2018, pp. 1085, 1089–99 (holding that there are plenty reasons for the insurer's ignorance. To begin with, the algorithm entails specialized knowledge to understand. That is, the insurer's employees may lack sufficient knowledge to understand the rationale behind the reasons in view of which the algorithm is producing prices for different customers—personalized pricing. Lastly, even if the insurer himself comprehends how the model operates, it may nonetheless lack expertise to comprehend why it operates the way it does. For that reason, the explainability of machines is a vital, but rather elusive, task. Thence, the famed authors deem it as the "nonintuitive" nature of algorithms. For purposes here, the insurer himself might indeed understand that its Artificial Intelligence-embedded technology formulates higher prices for those who actually access the website at hand, but may fail to come to terms with the fact that the explanation for this fact arises from the website's capacity to proxy for genetic information). See: Wallheimer, Brian, "Are you Ready for Personalized Pricing? Companies Are Figuring out What Individual Customers Will Pay-and Charging Accordingly", *Chicago Booth Review*, 2018, passim; The Effects of Online Disclosure About Personalized Pricing on Consumers 7 (Org. for Econ. Coop. and Dev., Working Paper No. 303, 2021 ("[T]he quantity of personal data held on online consumers, combined with the *increasing prevalence of personalization in other domains (e.g., advertisement)*, means there is at least potential for online personalized pricing to become more commonplace and more sophisticated"). But see: Bartlett, Robert/Morse, Adair/Stanton/Wallace, Nancy, "Consumer Lending Discrimination in the FinTech Era", *National Bureau of Economic Research*, Working Paper No. 25,943, Volume 50, 2019 (on the perils of consumer lending discrimination). This is often tagged as "risk-based pricing." See: Phillipps, Robert, "Optimizing Prices for Consumer Credit", *Journal of Revenue and Pricing Management*, Volume 12, 2013, pp. 360–365 ("[A] riskier customer should pay a higher price in order to compensate for the higher probability of default and the associated cost to the lender"). See also: Staten, Michael, "Risk-Based Pricing in Consumer Lending", *Journal of Law, Economics & Policy*, Volume 11, 2015, pp. 33 and ff and passim.

[2204] But see: Citron, Danielle K., "Technological Due Process", *Washington University Law Review*, Volume 85, 2008, pp. 1249–1253 ("computer programs seamlessly combine rulemaking and individual adjudications without the critical procedural protections owed either of them").

[2205] See: Wallheimer, Brian, "Are you Ready for Personalized Pricing? Companies Are Figuring out What Individual Customers Will Pay-and Charging Accordingly", *Chicago Booth Review*, 2018, passim; The Effects of Online Disclosure About Personalized Pricing on Consumers 7 (Org. for Econ. Coop. and Dev., Working Paper No. 303, 2021 ("[T]he quantity of personal data held on online consumers, combined with the increasing prevalence of personalization in other domains (e.g., advertisement), *means there is at least potential for online personalized pricing to become more commonplace and more sophisticated*"). Italics added. But see: Bartlett, Robert/ Morse, Adair/Stanton/Wallace, Nancy, "Consumer Lending Discrimination in the FinTech Era", *National Bureau of Economic Research*, Working Paper No. 25,943, Volume 50, 2019 (drawing attention to discrimination that besets consumer lending).

[2206] But see: Karlan, Dean/Zinman, Jonathan, "Observing Unobservables: Identifying Information Asymmetries with a Consumer Credit Field Experiment", *Econometrica*, Volume 77, 2009, pp. 1993

§§ Tellingly, if algorithmic credit pricing distinguishes[2209] between people along the lines of, or dimensions that bear a correlation with, race,[2210] then arguably the outcome disparities is slated to ratchet up.[2211]

§§ Relatedly, another way in which machine learning pricing can augment the disparities of credit prices[2212] is through the enhanced ability of machine learning algorithms[2213] to customize prices.[2214] Notably, the greater flexibility of the machine

---

and ff and passim (builds on empirical evidence to premise the finding according to which moral hazard exists in consumer credit markets).

2207 Gillis, Talia B., "The Input Data Fallacy", *cit.*, pp. 1176–1263 (1214).

2208 See: Hurley, Mikella/Adebayo, Julius, "Credit Scoring in the Era of Big Data", *Yale Journal of Law and Technology*, Volume 18, 2016, p. 149 ("*these tools may furthermore obscure discriminatory and subjective lending policies behind a single "objective" score* (...) *sophisticated algorithms may combine facially neutral data points and treat them as proxies for immutable characteristics such as race or gender, thereby circumventing existing non-discrimination laws and systematically denying credit access to certain groups. Finally, big-data tools may allow online payday lenders to target the most vulnerable consumers and lure them into debt traps*"). Italics added. See also: Farina, M./ Lavazza, A., *Philosophy, expertise, and the myth of neutrality*, Routledge Studies in Contemporary Philosophy, London, Routledge, 2024.

2209 Gillis, Talia B., "The Input Data Fallacy", *cit.*, pp. 1176–1263 (1214).

2210 Allen, James, "The Color of Algorithms: An Analysis and Proposed Research Agenda Deterring Algorithmic Redlining", *Fordham Urban Law Journal*, Volume 46, 2019, pp. 219–234 (229–234) (discussing how historical mortgage redlining greatly swayed modern algorithms generated by massive batches of data sets that consist of decades of information built on exclusion and racial discrimination in the purview of financing, marketing, and housing). See: Part IV, This chapter, Sects. 4.1.4–4.1.4.2.3 of this book. See: Part IV, This chapter, Sects. 4.1.4–4.1.4.2.1 of this book (on mortgage redlining). See: Part IV, This chapter, Sects. 4.1.2–4.1.4.3 of this book (on algorithmic credit scoring, consumer racism and credit card redlining). See: Part IV, This chapter, Sects. 4.1.4–4.1.4.2.3 of this book (on algorithmic redlining). See: Part IV, This chapter, Sect. 4.1.4.3 of this book (on "algorithmic redliking"). See: Part IV, This chapter, Sect. 4.1.3 of this book (on algorithmic prime-lining).

2211 Gillis, Talia B., "The Input Data Fallacy", *cit.*, pp. 1176–1263 (1215).

2212 See: Burk, Dan L., "Algorithmic Fair Use", *University of Chicago Law Review*, Volume 86, 2019, pp. 283–288 (asserts that algorithmic "*fair use carries with it the disadvantage of ex ante uncertainty*; no one can be entirely certain in advance how a court will weigh the four factors, *and hence there is always some apprehension that a use may be found infringing rather than fair*"). Italics added.

2213 See: Murphy, Kevin P., *Machine Learning: A Probabilistic Perspective (Adaptive Computation and Machine Learning series)*. Massachusetts: The MIT Press, 2012, pp. 1–1104 (states avowedly that "machine Learning attempts to combine deductive, inductive, and abductive reasoning to make person-like reasoning in AI Entities possible. Machine-learning AI Entities initially learn in the same way a human child learns. First, they notice details and patterns in shapes, sounds, and behaviors; then put them together to distinguish one person from another, or a dog from a cat. Eventually, the AI can recognize and identify" common objects). See also: Hutto-Schultz, Jess, "Dicitur Ex Machina: Artificial Intelligence and the Hearsay Rule", *George Mason Law Review*, Volume 27, Issue 2, 2020, pp. 684–718 (689). See: Chollet, François, *Deep Learning with Python*. Shelter Island, Nova Iorque: Manning, 2018, pp. 1–384 (passim). *Deep Learning* stands as a byproduct of *Machine Learning*. *Machine Learning*, a subset of Artificial Intelligence, unfolds itself in *Deep Learning*, which "involves computer algorithms that have the ability to "learn" or improve in performance over time on some task". See also: Surden, Harry, "Machine Learning and Law", *Washington Law Review*, Volume 89, 2015, pp. 87 and ff. See also: Barocas, Solon/Selbst, Andrew, "Big Data's

learning regression means that in forming predictions[2215] the algorithm can excel in establishing differences between individuals,[2216] thereby shaping fine-grained predictions.[2217]

§§ Thusly, perceived differences amongst individuals are then more likely to produce larger differences[2218] «in predicted outcomes than would be true with other less flexible prediction technologies, such as a linear regression».[2219]

§§ Crucially, even scarce/negligible differences between individuals could beget bigger gaps between the price for credit paid by white and non-white[2220] borrowers.[2221] One feasible way to illustrate the augment in price personalization is through the lens of variance of the distribution itself.[2222] Compellingly, a higher variance in the default probability[2223] means that people are considerably more spread

---

Disparate Impact", *California Law Review*, Volume 104, pp. 2016, pp. 671–678 ("in particular, by exposing so-called 'machine learning' algorithms to examples of the cases of interest (previously identified instances of fraud, spam, default, and poor health), *the algorithm 'learns' which related attributes or activities can serve as potential proxies for those qualities or outcomes of interest*"). Italics added.

2214 Gillis, Talia B., "The Input Data Fallacy", *cit.*, pp. 1176–1263 (1215).

2215 Gillis, Talia B., "The Input Data Fallacy", *cit.*, pp. 1176–1263 (1215).

2216 But see: Fuster, Andreas/Goldsmith-Pinkham, Paul/Tarun Ramadorai/Walther, Angsar, "Predictably Unequal? The Effects of Machine Learning on Credit Markets", *Journal of Finance*, Volume 76, 2022, passim (providing a description of the variation in interest rates across racial groups carried out by machine learning algorithms).

2217 Gillis, Talia B., "The Input Data Fallacy", *cit.*, pp. 1176–1263 (1215). But see: Agrawal, A., Gans, J., & Goldfarb, A., "Prediction machines (updated and expanded): The simple economics of artificial intelligence", *Harvard Business Review Press*, 2022; Agrawal, A., Gans, J., & Goldfarb, A., "Power and prediction: The disruptive economics of artificial intelligence", *Harvard Business Review Press*, 2022; Bengio, Y., Hinton, G., Yao, A., Song, D., Abbeel, P., Harari, Y. N., Hadfield, G., Russell, S., Kahneman, D., & Mindermann, S., *Managing ai risks in an era of rapid progress*, arXiv preprint arXiv:2310.17688, 2023; Aggarwal, C. C., *Neural networks and deep learning*, Heidelberg, Springer, 2018, passim (on the sweltering challenges brought about by prediction machines that operate in the age of Artificial Intelligence-embedded technologies).

2218 Gillis, Talia B., "The Input Data Fallacy", *cit.*, pp. 1176–1263 (1215).

2219 Gillis, Talia B., "The Input Data Fallacy", *cit.*, pp. 1176–1263 (1215).

2220 But see: Fuster, Andreas/Goldsmith-Pinkham, Paul/Tarun Ramadorai/Walther, Angsar, "Predictably Unequal? The Effects of Machine Learning on Credit Markets", *Journal of Finance*, Volume 76, 2022, passim (providing a description of the variation in interest rates across racial groups carried out by machine learning algorithms).

2221 Gillis, Talia B., "The Input Data Fallacy", *cit.*, pp. 1176–1263 (1215). See: Dwork, Cynthia/Hardt, Moritz/Pitassi, Tonian/Reingold/Zemel, Richard, "Fairness Through Awareness, Proceedings of the 3rd Innovations", *Theoretical Computer Science Conference*, 2012, https://dl.acm.org/doi/10.1145/2090236.2090255; [https://perma.cc/T2U3-TNQ6] (discussing an individual fairness approach to algorithmic fairness); Meharabi, Ninareh/Morstatter, Fred/Saxena, Nripsuta/Lerman, Kristina/Galstyan, Aram, "A Survey on Bias and Fairness in Machine Learning", *ACM Computing Survey*, Jul. 2022 at 1 (on algorithmic fairness or lack thereof).

2222 Gillis, Talia B., "The Input Data Fallacy", *cit.*, pp. 1176–1263 (1215).

2223 But see: Chi-Jack Lin/ Sherman D. Hanna, "Racial Discrimination in the Consumer Credit Market", *Consumer Interests Annual*, Volume 56, 2010 ("*The Equal Credit Opportunity Act (ECOA), enacted in 1974, makes it unlawful for any creditors to discriminate against credit applicants*

out when it comes to the price they pay for credit,[2224] thereby creating a broader range of predictions.[2225]

§§ In an earnest attempt to understand how machine learning can increase price variance, a comparison has been made between a *simple function* that uses just a few variables with a machine learning algorithm that uses many variables.[2226] To attain that result (*simple prediction function*), a pundit has used the Ordinary Least Squares (OLS) regression to predict default[2227] with a tiny cluster of the variables available in the thumping great Boston Fed HMDA dataset.[2228]

§§ For the machine learning prediction,[2229] the famed scholar[2230] used a *random forest* with the full-fledged set of HMDA variables, other than «race».[2231] It follows that the simple function and the machine learning function differ greatly along two dimensions: the exact number of variables and the prediction technology itself.[2232]

§§ Comparing the two distributions sharply demonstrates how the use of a machine learning algorithm leads to borrowers being more spread out.[2233] This

---

because of their color, race/ethnic group, religion, national origin, sex, marital status, or age (provided the applicant has the capacity to contract) (….) *our analyses allow for distinguishing statistical and taste discrimination. In four of five of our measures, there was discrimination against households with Black respondents, and in three out of five measures, there was discrimination against households with Hispanic respondents. Discrimination in the consumer credit market against black and Hispanic households is statistical discrimination: lenders choose to discriminate against black and Hispanic because they on average have higher default risk*"). Italics added. But see also: But see: The Use of Cash-Flow Data in Underwriting Credit: Empirical Research Findings, FINREGLAB 32, 34 (Jul. 2019), https://finreglab.org/wp-content/uploads/2019/07/FRL_Research-Report_Final.pdf; [https://perma.cc/N65Q-WQML] (arguing that the use of cash flow data can underpin a prediction of default risk, thereby providing an apposite alternative to ancient credit scores. In addition to that, cash-flow data is commensurate with predictive across demographic groups).

2224 But see: Weizenbaum, Joseph, *Computer Power and Human Reason: From Judgment to Calculation*, 1st edition, New York, W. H. Freeman & Co, 1976, pp. 1–300 (227) ("examines the sources of the computer's powers and offers evaluative explorations of what computers can do, cannot do, and should not be employed to do") (this founding father of Artificial Intelligence presciently noted that we should not entrust Artificial Intelligence-embedded technologies with "tasks that demand wisdom"). Italics added. The approval of credit applications is arguably one of those tasks that should never be entrusted to machines). More on this on Part IV, This chapter, Sects. 4.1.4–4.1.4.2.1 of this book. See also: Kleinberg, Jon/Lakkaraju, Himabindu/Leskovec, Jure/Ludwig, Jens/Mullainathan, Sendhil, "Human Decisions and Machine Predictions", *Quarterly Journal of Economics*, Volume 133, 2018, passim; Pasquale, Frank, "A Rule of Persons, Not Machines: The Limits of Legal Automation", *George Washington Law Review*, Volume 87, 2019, pp. 1 and ff and passim.

2225 Gillis, Talia B., "The Input Data Fallacy", *cit.*, pp. 1176–1263 (1215).

2226 Gillis, Talia B., "The Input Data Fallacy", *cit.*, pp. 1176–1263 (1215).

2227 Gillis, Talia B., "The Input Data Fallacy", *cit.*, pp. 1176–1263 (1215).

2228 Gillis, Talia B., "The Input Data Fallacy", *cit.*, pp. 1176–1263 (1215).

2229 Gillis, Talia B., "The Input Data Fallacy", *cit.*, pp. 1176–1263 (1215).

2230 Gillis, Talia B., "The Input Data Fallacy", *cit.*, pp. 1176–1263 (1216).

2231 Gillis, Talia B., "The Input Data Fallacy", *cit.*, pp. 1176–1263 (1216).

2232 Gillis, Talia B., "The Input Data Fallacy", *cit.*, pp. 1176–1263 (1216).

2233 Gillis, Talia B., "The Input Data Fallacy", *cit.*, pp. 1176–1263 (1216).

finding encapsulates, hands-in-glove, the assertion according to which machine learning algorithm's predictions have greater variance than the simple regression.[2234] Put it coarsely, the price of credit allotted to individuals seeking credit is more customized.[2235] Therefore, the greater variance of the random forest prediction, reflected by the wider horizontal bar, is the conflated effect of, and the interplay between, the use of far more inputs and a far more flexible prediction technology.[2236]

§§ The enhanced variance of the random forest prediction has consequences for racial disparities[2237] although the experiment does not directly gauge these disparities.[2238]

§§ Compellingly, when new credit pricing uses new dataset sources in which there are behemoth differences between people who are part and those who are not part of protected groups, the use of machine learning algorithms could transform differences in inputs into greater outcome[2239] disparities,[2240] thus paving the way *algorithmic bias*.[2241]

[2234] Gillis, Talia B., "The Input Data Fallacy", *cit.*, pp. 1176–1263 (1216).

[2235] Gillis, Talia B., "The Input Data Fallacy", *cit.*, pp. 1176–1263 (1216).

[2236] Gillis, Talia B., "The Input Data Fallacy", *cit.*, pp. 1176–1263 (1216).

[2237] Note, though, that as it stands: Freeman, Andrea, "Racism in the Credit Card Industry", *cit.*, p. 1071 ("even worse, the companies do so in a racially discriminatory way, *burdening Black and Latino customers with the worst credit card terms, often unrelated to credit risk*"). Italics added. See also: *Credit Discrimination: Hearings on H.R. 14856 and H.R. 14908 Before the Subcomm. on Consumer Affairs of the H. Comm. on Banking & Currency*, 93rd Cong. 1, 1974, (Hon. Leonor K. Sullivan, Chairman, Subcomm. on Consumer Affairs of the H. Comm. on Banking & Currency) (statement of John H. Powell, Jr., Chairman, Equal Emp't Opportunity Comm'n) *("[I]t is very likely that the inability to obtain credit, or if obtained, the discriminatory terms and conditions which accompany its extension to certain groups in our society, are directly related to discrimination in employment*"). Italics added; id. at 131 (statement of Hon. Arthur S. Flemming, Chairman, U.S. Comm'n on Civil Rights, and Comm'r, Admin. on Aging, Dep't of Health, Educ. & Welfare). Freeman, Andrea, "Racism in the Credit Card Industry", *cit.*, p. 1121. See also: Levitin, Adam J., "The Antitrust Super Bowl: America's Payment Systems, No-Surcharge Rules, and the Hidden Costs of Credit", *Berkeley Business Law Journal*, Volume 3, 2005, 265, 317–18; id. at 154 ("Consequently, *low-income consumers now receive credit cards with high fees and interest rates, while higher-income consumers reap the rewards of credit card use, such as travel miles and concierge services* (…). As a *result of these practices, 80% of the industry's profits now come from interest payments and... fees instead of annual and interchange fees. This shift represents a massive redistribution of wealth from the poor to wealthier consumers and corporations*"). Italics added. See also: Wonyoung, So, "Which Information Matters? Measuring Landlord Assessment of Tenant Screening Reports", *Housing Policy Debate*, Volume 33, n. ° 6, 2023, pp. 1484–1510 (1502) ("*It is important to note that within conditionally accepted reports, similar patterns of blanket screening policies and automation bias are exhibited when landlords impose security deposits. These results may corroborate a paired-test study that shows that Black tenants have less favorable terms and conditions, including security deposits, in rental agreements* (Ross & Turner, 2005)"). Italics added. See: Part IV, This chapter, Sects. 4.1.4–4.1.4.2.3 of this book.

[2238] Gillis, Talia B., "The Input Data Fallacy", *cit.*, pp. 1176–1263 (1216).

[2239] Jackson, Maya C., "Artificial Intelligence and Algorithmic Bias: The Issues with Technology Reflecting History and Humans", *Journal of Business Technology Law*, Volume 16, 2021, pp. 299–316; West, Sarah Myers/Whittaker, Meredith/Crawford, Kate, *Discriminating Systems. Gender, Race and Power in AI*. New York: AI Now Institute, 2019, pp. 1 and ff and passim.

§§ For example, if male and female borrowers are different with regards to inputs that deftly predict default, a more ductile prediction technology can augment the differences in predicted default for men and women,[2242] thereby ushering in algorithmic discrimination,[2243] which is wholly unbecoming in this regard.[2244]

§§ As to *Biased Measurement Inputs in Algorithmic Pricing*, the great bulk of the pressing concerns of the effects of big data[2245] and machine learning credit pricing

---

[2240] Gillis, Talia B., "The Input Data Fallacy", *cit.*, pp. 1176–1263 (1217).

[2241] Recall: Baeza-Yates, R., "Bias on the web", *Communications of the ACM*, 61 (6), June 2018, 2018, pp. 54–61 (argues that "*algorithmic bias is when the bias is not present in the input data* and is added *purely by the algorithm*"). Italics added. See also: Hajian, Sara Hajian et al., "Algorithmic Bias: From Discrimination Discovery to Fairness-aware Data Mining", *ACM SIGKDD International Conference on Knowledge Discovery and Data Mining*, Volume 22, 2125, 2016; Griemmelmann, James/Westreich, Daniel, "Incomprehensible Discrimination ", *California Law Review Online*, Volume 7, 2018, pp. 164–171; Xiang, Alice, "Reconciling Legal and Technical Approaches to Algorithmic Bias", *Tennessee Law Review*, Volume 88, 2021, passim; See: Lemley, Mark A./Casey, Bryan, "Remedies for Robots", *The University of Chicago Law Review*, Volume 86, Issue 5, 2019, pp. 1311–1396 (1376) (alerting to the perils of algorithmic bias); Chandler, Anupam, "The Racist Algorithm", *Michigan Law Review*, Volume 115, Issue 6, 2018, p. 1026 (noting that, in the terrain of racist algorithm, "the possibilities for discriminatory manipulation are legion"; Jackson, Maya C., "Artificial Intelligence and Algorithmic Bias: The Issues with Technology Reflecting History and Humans", *Journal of Business Technology Law*, Volume 16, 2021, pp. 299–316; West, Sarah Myers/Whittaker, Meredith/Crawford, Kate, *Discriminating Systems. Gender, Race and Power in AI*. New York: AI Now Institute, 2019, pp. 15 and ff and passim; Waldman, Ezra, "Privacy, Practice, and Performance", *California Law Review*, Volume 110, 2021, passim (on algorithmic bias). Italics added.

[2242] Gillis, Talia B., "The Input Data Fallacy", *cit.*, pp. 1176–1263 (1217).

[2243] See on algorithmic discrimination: Kleinberg, Jon, et al., "Discrimination in the Age of Algorithms", *Journal of Legal Analysis*, 2018, pp. 114–174; See: Kleinberg, Jon, et al., "Algorithms as Discrimination Detectors", *Proceeds of the National Academy of Science*, Volume 117, 2020, pp. 30096–30110; Griemmelmann, James/Westreich, Daniel, "Incomprehensible Discrimination ", *California Law Review Online*, Volume 7, 2018, pp. 164–171; Xiang, Alice, "Reconciling Legal and Technical Approaches to Algorithmic Bias", *Tennessee Law Review*, Volume 88, 2021, passim; Karnow, Curtis E. A., "The Opinion of Machines", *The Cambridge Handbook of the Law of Algorithms*, Bartfield, Woodrow (Editor), Cambridge, United Kingdom: Cambridge University Press, 2021, pp. 15 and ff and passim; Strandburg, Katherine J., "Rulemaking and Inscrutable Decision Tools", *Columbia Law Review*, Volume 119, 2019, passim.

[2244] But see: Kilbertus, Niki/Carulla, Mateo Rojas/Parascandolo, Giambattista/Hardt, Moritz/ Janzing, Dominik/ Schoellkopf, Bernhard, "Avoiding Discrimination through Causal Reasoning", *Advances in Neural Information Processing Systems*, I. Guyon, U. V. Luxburg, S. Bengio, H. Wallach, R. Fergus, S. Vishwanathan, and R. Garnett (Eds.), Vol. 30. Curran Associates, Inc., 2017, pp. 656–666 (arguing that is feasible to avoiding discrimination through a granular and fine-grained causal reasoning).

[2245] Big data that is in the limelight these days. See: Sivarajah, Uthayasnkar et al., "Critical Analysis of Big Data Challenges and Analytical Methods", *Journal of Business Research*, Volume 70, 2017, pp. 263 and ff and passim; Jetten, Lieke /Sharon, Stephen, "Selected Issues concerning the Ethical Use of Big Data Health Analytics", *Washington & Lee Law Review Online*, Volume 72, 2016, passim; Wachter, S./Mittelstadt. B., "A right to Reasonable Inferences: Re-thinking Data Protection Law in the Age of Big Data and AI", *Columbia Business Law Review*, 2019, pp. 1 and ff and passim; See in French doctrine: Ferey, Samuel, « Analyse économique du droit, big data et justice prédictive», *Archives de Philosophie du Droit*, Volume 60, 2018, pp. 68–81; Završnik, A. "Algorithmic justice:

fleshed out in the context of *biased world* equally applies to variables that mirror *biased measurement*.[2246] The added variables and the enhanced ductility that follow from the use of machine learning can augment the credit pricing[2247] inequalities.[2248] Concomitantly, the use of big data[2249] and advance prediction technologies[2250] can also be conducive to diminished reliance on a biased[2251] proxy.[2252]

Algorithms and big data in criminal justice settings", *European Journal of Criminology*, 2019, passim; Joh, Elizabeth E., "The New Surveillance Discretion: Automated Suspicion, Big Data, and Policing." *Harvard Law and Policy Review*, 10 (1), 2016, pp. 15–42.

[2246] Gillis, Talia B., "The Input Data Fallacy", *cit.*, pp. 1176–1263 (1217).

[2247] But see: Levitin, Adam J., "The Antitrust Super Bowl: America's Payment Systems, No-Surcharge Rules, and the Hidden Costs of Credit", *Berkeley Business Law Journal*, Volume 3, 2005, 265, 317–18; id. at 154 ("consequently, *low-income consumers now receive credit cards with high fees and interest rates, while higher-income consumers reap the rewards of credit card use, such as travel miles and concierge services* (...). As a *result of these practices, 80% of the industry's profits now come from interest payments and... fees instead of annual and interchange fees. This shift represents a massive redistribution of wealth from the poor to wealthier consumers and corporations*").

[2248] Gillis, Talia B., "The Input Data Fallacy", *cit.*, pp. 1176–1263 (1217). See: Citron, Danielle Keats/Pasquale, Frank A., "The Scored Society: Due Process for Automated Predictions", *Washington Law Review*, Volume 89, 2014, pp. 1–34 (arguing that "[a]*dvocates applaud the removal of human beings and their flaws from the assessment process*," but arguing that bias remains "[*b*]*ecause human beings program predictive algorithms, their biases and values are embedded into the software's instructions*"). Italics added. See: Part IV, This chapter, Sects. 4.1.4–4.1.4.2.3 of this book.

[2249] But see: Hardt, Moritz, "How big data is unfair: Understanding sources of unfairness in data driven decision making", *Medium*, Archived on Oct. 8, 2014, available at: https://web.archive.org/web/20141008185829/; https://medium.com/@mrtz/how-big-data-is-unfair-9aa544d739de. (access: 17.12.2024).

[2250] But see: Segran, G., "The complexity of artificial intelligence", *Singapore Management University*, 2021, passim (on the elaborate and complex trappings of Artificial Intelligence).

[2251] But see: Pedreshi, Dino/Ruggieri, Salvatore/Turini, Franco, "Discrimination-aware Data Mining", *Proceedings of the 14th ACM SIGKDD International Conference on Knowledge Discovery and Data Mining (Las Vegas, Nevada, USA), ACM*, 2008, pp. 560–568 (arguing that one should shift its gaze downstream by putting in place discrimination-aware algorithmic tools while performing data mining). See also: Bornstein, Stephanie, "Antidiscriminatory Algorithms", *Alabama Law Review*, Volume 70, 2018, pp. 518 and ff and passim.

[2252] Gillis, Talia B., "The Input Data Fallacy", *cit.*, pp. 1176–1263 (1217). See also: Morris, Darcy Steeg/Schwarcz, Daniel/Teitelbaum, Joshua C., "Do Credit-Based Insurance Scores Proxy for Income in Predicting Auto Claim Risk?", *Journal of Empirical Legal Studies*, Volume 14, Issue 2, 2017, pp. 397–423. See also: Kaersvang, Dana L., "Note, The Fair Housing Act and Disparate Impact in Homeowners Insurance," *Michigan Law Review*, Volume 104, 2006, pp. 1992 and ff and passim (carrying out additional analysis on the application of the Fair Housing Act's disparate impact standard to insurance); Grimmelmann, James/Westreich, Daniel, "Incomprehensible Discrimination", *California Law Review Online*, Volume 7, 2017, pp 164 and ff and passim (bringing forth a hypothetical as a tutorial tool to display disparate impact and proxies); Morris, Darcy Steeg/Schwarcz, Daniel/Teitelbaum, Joshua C., "Do Credit-Based Insurance Scores Proxy for Income in Predicting Auto Claim Risk?", *Journal of Empirical Legal Studies*, Volume 14, 2017, pp. 397, 418–21 and ff (discussing that an insurer's use of credit-anchored insurance scores lacks a disparate impact on the basis of income and thus is not amenable to be considered as a proxy for income); Pope, Devin G. Pope/Sydnor, Justin R., "Implementing Anti-Discrimination Policies in Statistical

§§ Tellingly, FICO scores[2253] might be biased[2254] since they reflect creditworthiness[2255] as measured by past mortgage[2256] payments,[2257] as opposed to timely rental payments,[2258] which are more wonted/mainstream/common for racial minorities.[2259]

Profiling Models", *American Economic Journal: Applied Economics*, Volume 3, 2011, pp. 206–210 (discussing how the FTC parsed credit score use in auto-insurance pricing as a proxy for race).

[2253] It is crucially important to note, though, that the very fact that only certain types of behaviours are assessed and gauged by credit scores leads to the conclusion some borrowers are not scored at all. The overwhelming majority of consumers boast meagre, if any, credit files owing to the fact that the likelihood to access to the sort of financial services that actually report to the orthodox credit bureaus scattered across modern economies is exceedingly low, which, in turn, morphs them into credit invisible persons. See: Yu, Persis/McLaughlin, Jilian/Levy, Marina, "Big Data: A Big Disappointment for Scoring Consumer Creditworthiness,", *The National Consumer Law Center,* 2 (Mar. 14, 2014), available at: https://www.nclc.org/images/pdf/pr-reports/report-big-data.pdf; [https://perma.cc/W4SK-NXD5] (access: 21.12.2024).

[2254] See: Hurley, Mikella/Adebayo, Julius, "Credit Scoring in the Era of Big Data", *Yale Journal of Law and Technology*, Volume 18, 2016, pp. 148, 151–156, 172 (averring that FICO scoring boasts a redoubtable capacity to routinely weed out some populations that have been historically and systematically underrepresented or grossly unfairly represented in the credit industry market). Tellingly, by 2016, ten states had disavowed the unlawful practice of employers using shady credit scores due to their perceived disparate impact on low-income applicants and members of racialized communities (mostly Black folks). See: O'Neill, Cathy, *Weapons of Math Destruction. How Big Data Increases Inequality and Threatens Democracy*. London: Penguin Random House, 2016, pp. 128 and ff and passim. See: Part IV, This chapter, Sects. 4.1.4–4.1.4.2.3 of this book. See: Part IV, This chapter, Sects. 4.1.4–4.1.4.2.1 of this book (on mortgage redlining). See: Part IV, This chapter, Sects. 4.1.2–4.1.4.3 of this book (on algorithmic credit scoring, consumer racism and credit card redlining). See: Part IV, This chapter, Sects. 4.1.4–4.1.4.2.3 of this book (on algorithmic redlining). See: Part IV, This chapter, Sect. 4.1.4.3 of this book (on "algorithmic redliking"). See: Part IV, This chapter, Sect. 4.1.3 of this book (on algorithmic prime-lining).

[2255] Note, though, that this racial discrimination may not be fully intentional. More likely than not, it can be related with the perils of big data colour-blindness that nonetheless relies on proxies to race and gender to make algorithmic decisions. Another problem is the one related with "creditworthiness by association" that causes more problems than it solves. See: Hurley, Mikella/Adebayo, Julius, "Credit Scoring in the Era of Big Data", *cit.*, p. 149 ("*recent studies have also questioned the accuracy of the data used by these tools, in some cases identifying serious flaws that have a substantial bearing on lending decisions. Big-data tools may also risk creating a system of "creditworthiness by association" in which consumers' familial, religious, social, and other affiliations determine their eligibility for an affordable loan. These tools may furthermore obscure discriminatory and subjective lending policies behind a single "objective" score. Such discriminatory scoring may not be intentional; instead, sophisticated algorithms may combine facially neutral data points and treat them as proxies for immutable characteristics such as race or gender, thereby circumventing existing non-discrimination laws and systematically denying credit access to certain groups. Finally, big-data tools may allow online payday lenders to target the most vulnerable consumers and lure them into debt traps*"). Italics added.

[2256] See: Glantz, Aaron/Martinez, Emmanuel, "For People of Color, Banks are Shutting the Door to Homeownership", *Reveal*, February 15, 2018, available at: https://ibw21.org/news/people-color-banks-shutting-door-homeownership/ (access: 4.11.2024) ("*Fifty years after the federal Fair Housing Act banned racial discrimination in lending, African Americans and Latinos continue to be routinely denied conventional mortgage loans at rates far higher than their white counterparts.* This modern-day redlining persisted in 61 metro areas even when controlling for applicants' income, loan amount and neighborhood, according to a mountain of Home Mortgage Disclosure

§§ Should big data allot lenders with the opportunity to use rental payment data[2260] besides FICO scores,[2261] this can greatly decrease the perceived disparities in predicted default.[2262] With the right settings and for the right reasons, the use of algorithmic credit pricing[2263] could therefore reduce[2264] rather than augment

---

Act records analyzed by Reveal from The Center for Investigative Reporting. *The yearlong analysis, based on 31 million records, relied on techniques used by leading academics, the Federal Reserve and Department of Justice to identify lending disparities. It found a pattern of troubling denials for people of color across the country, including in major metropolitan areas such as Atlanta, Detroit, Philadelphia, St. Louis and San Antonio.* African Americans faced the most resistance in Southern cities — Mobile, Alabama; Greenville, North Carolina; and Gainesville, Florida — and Latinos in Iowa City, Iowa. *No matter their location, loan applicants told similar stories, describing an uphill battle with loan officers who they said seemed to be fishing for a reason to say no*"). Italics added.

[2257] But see: Chi-Jack Lin/ Sherman D. Hanna, "Racial Discrimination in the Consumer Credit Market", *Consumer Interests Annual*, Volume 56, 2010 ("*The Equal Credit Opportunity Act (ECOA), enacted in 1974, makes it unlawful for any creditors to discriminate against credit applicants because of their color, race/ethnic group, religion, national origin, sex, marital status, or age (provided the applicant has the capacity to contract*). Researchers have debated the existence of discrimination within the U.S. credit market. *Many studies examine the presence of discrimination in the credit market, but none focus specifically on the effect of individuals' race or ethnic group in the consumer credit market, which we differentiate from other household credit markets, such as for home mortgages.* This research fills the research gap by examining discrimination in the consumer credit market. Using four Survey of Consumer Finance data sets from 1998 to 2007, we use five measures to assess whether there is discrimination by racial/ethnic group in the consumer credit in US, and, if present, whether the discrimination is due to statistical or taste lender motivations. *Our analyses allow for distinguishing statistical and taste discrimination. In four of five of our measures, there was discrimination against households with Black respondents, and in three out of five measures, there was discrimination against households with Hispanic respondents. Discrimination in the consumer credit market against black and Hispanic households is statistical discrimination: lenders choose to discriminate against black and Hispanic because they on average have higher default risk*"). Italics added.

[2258] But see: Wonyoung, So, "Which Information Matters? Measuring Landlord Assessment of Tenant Screening Reports", *Housing Policy Debate*, Volume 33, n. ° 6, 2023, pp. 1484–1510 (1484) ("*Through a behavioral experiment with landlords using simulated tenant screening reports, this study shows that landlords use blanket screening policies, that they conflate the existence of tenant records with outcomes (e.g., eviction filings with executed evictions), and that they display, on average, tendencies toward automation bias that are influenced by the risk assessments and scores presented by tenant screening reports.* I argue that maintaining blanket screening policies and automation bias, combined with the downstream effects of creating and *using racially biased eviction and criminal records, means that people of color will inevitably experience disproportionate exclusion from rental housing due to perceived "risk" on the part of landlords*"). Italics added. See: Part IV, This chapter, Sects. 4.1.4–4.1.4.2.3 of this book. See: Part IV, This chapter, Sects. 4.1.4–4.1.4.2.1 of this book (on mortgage redlining). See: Part IV, This chapter, Sects. 4.1.2–4.1.4.3 of this book (on algorithmic credit scoring, consumer racism and credit card redlining). See: Part IV, This chapter, Sects. 4.1.4–4.1.4.2.3 of this book (on algorithmic redlining). See: Part IV, This chapter, Sect. 4.1.4.3 of this book (on "algorithmic redliking"). See: Part IV, This chapter, Sect. 4.1.3 of this book (on algorithmic prime-lining).

[2259] Gillis, Talia B., "The Input Data Fallacy", *cit.*, pp. 1176–1263 (1217).

[2260] But see: Wonyoung, So, "Which Information Matters? Measuring Landlord Assessment of Tenant Screening Reports", *Housing Policy Debate*, Volume 33, n. ° 6, 2023, pp. 1484–1510 (1502) (arguing that landlords display automation bias as the "*study finds that landlords tend to rely more on the automated system's judgment: when a report noted that a tenant was either medium*

both racial and gender inequalities.[2265] Algorithmic unfairness[2266] is therefore in dire need of quashing.[2267]

§§ In addition to that, there is a body of empirical evidence that contends that the use of nontraditional data is conducive to abridged/diminished reliance on FICO

---

or high risk, landlords showed a higher tendency toward rejection, or, if conditionally accepted, they imposed a higher security deposit. This indicates that tenant screening services' risk scoring may critically affect landlords' decision-making. Given that there is no regulation pertaining to producing and deploying such algorithms, and 1502 W. SO given the inherent inaccuracies of eviction data (Porton et al., 2021) and widespread, serial eviction filings (Garboden & Rosen, 2019), particularly automatic eviction filings activated by digitized property management systems and large, corporate landlords (Fields, 2022; Gomory, 2022; Immergluck et al., 2020), *tenant screening services very likely contribute to perpetuating algorithmic inequality (Eubanks, 2018) by denying qualified applicants—disproportionately from protected groups—access to housing*"). Italics added. See: Part IV, This chapter, Sects. 4.1.4–4.1.4.2.3 of this book. See also: Allen, James, "The Color of Algorithms: An Analysis and Proposed Research Agenda Deterring Algorithmic Redlining", *Fordham Urban Law Journal*, Volume 46, 2019, pp. 219–234 (229–234) (discussing how historical mortgage redlining greatly swayed modern algorithms generated by massive batches of data sets that consist of decades of information built on exclusion and racial discrimination in the purview of financing, marketing, and housing). See: Part IV, This chapter, Sects. 4.1.4–4.1.4.2.3 of this book.

2261 But see: Wonyoung, So, "Which Information Matters? Measuring Landlord Assessment of Tenant Screening Reports", *Housing Policy Debate*, Volume 33, n. ° 6, 2023, pp. 1484–1510 (1502) ("*One additional finding of the experiment is that algorithmic scoring can exacerbate this racially unequal landscape in rental agreements not just because the algorithm may be inaccurate, but because landlords may want to follow the risk assessment made by the tenant screening report. This is alarming for low-income tenants, particularly housing voucher holders. Security deposits are one of the most significant barriers to obtaining housing for voucher holders, because vouchers do not pay security deposits but most private landlords require them (Rosenblatt & Cossyleon, 2018).* Given that voucher holders have exceptionally low income (usually less than 50% of area median income) and might experience more housing insecurity (rental debts and eviction-related experiences), *imposing greater security deposits on voucher holders almost equates to denying them housing—yet these decisions could be justified by algorithmic scoring if tenant screening services employ it*"). Italics added. See: Part IV, This chapter, Sects. 4.1.4–4.1.4.2.3 of this book.

2262 Gillis, Talia B., "The Input Data Fallacy", *cit.*, pp. 1176–1263. But see: The Use of Cash-Flow Data in Underwriting Credit: Empirical Research Findings, FINREGLAB 32, 34 (Jul. 2019), https://finreglab.org/wp-content/uploads/2019/07/FRL_Research-Report_Final.pdf ; [https://perma.cc/N65Q-WQML] (arguing that the use of cash flow data can underpin a prediction of default risk, thereby providing an apposite alternative to ancient credit scores. In addition to that, cash-flow data is commensurate with predictive across demographic groups).

2263 But see: Citron, Danielle Keats, "Technological Due Process", *Washington Law Review*, 2008, p. 1249 (one must shy away from the perceived "tendency to presume a computer system's infallibility").

2264 Coglianese, Cary/Lehr, David, "Transparency and Algorithmic Governance", *Administrative Law Review*, Volume 71, 2019, passim (highlights the overriding importance of transparency to propel algorithmic governance).

2265 Gillis, Talia B., "The Input Data Fallacy", *cit.*, pp. 1176–1263.

2266 Kirkpatrick, Keith, "Battling Algorithmic Bias: How Do We Ensure Algorithms Treat Us Fairly?" *Commun. ACM 59*, Volume 10, 2016, pp. 16 and ff.

2267 See: Kearns, Michael J./Neel, Seth/Roth, Aaron/Wu, Zhiwei Steven, "Preventing Fairness Gerry-mandering: Auditing and Learning for Subgroup Fairness", *Proceedings of Machine Learning Research*, Volume 80, Dy, Jennifer/Krause, Andreas (Eds.). PMLR, 2018, pp. 2564–2572.

scores.[2268] By the same token, a cohort of researchers at the Philadelphia Federal Reserve averred that the correlation between the credit ratings of *LendingClub*, a *Fintech* lender,[2269] and FICO scores has plummeted over time, due to Lending Club's increased reliance on nontraditional[2270] data, thus veering away from algorithmic fairness.[2271]

§§ The findings arising out of this body of empirical evidence lend weight to, and adds plausibility to, the axiom that the use of nontraditional data decreases the impact of the measurement bias of FICO[2272] scores.[2273] Revealingly, the Consumer Financial Protection Bureau has shed a keen light on the putative advantages of alternative data and machine learning in broadening credit.[2274]

§§ Leveraging on the empirical finding that an algorithmic lender's model «approves 27% more applicants than the traditional[2275] model,[2276] and yields 16% lower average APRs for approved loans,» it accordingly yields the conclusion according to which a cohort of consumers who are unable to obtain[2277] favourably priced credit[2278] might see enhanced credit access or reduced borrowing costs arisen from the use of nontraditional data.[2279]

2268 Gillis, Talia B., "The Input Data Fallacy", *cit.*, pp. 1176–1263.

2269 See: Haupert, T., "The racial landscape of fintech mortgage lending", *Housing Policy Debate*, Volume 32, Issue 2, 2022, passim.

2270 Gillis, Talia B., "The Input Data Fallacy", *cit.*, pp. 1176–1263.

2271 See: Kearns, Michael J./Neel, Seth/Roth, Aaron/Wu, Zhiwei Steven, "An Empirical Study of Rich Subgroup Fairness for Machine Learning", *Proceedings of the Conference on Fairness, Accountability, and Transparency, ACM*, 2019, pp. 100–109.

2272 Gillis, Talia B., "The Input Data Fallacy", *cit.*, pp. 1176–1263.

2273 But see: The Use of Cash-Flow Data in Underwriting Credit: Empirical Research Findings, FINREGLAB 32, 34 (Jul. 2019), https://finreglab.org/wp-content/uploads/2019/07/FRL_Research-Report_Final.pdf; [https://perma.cc/N65Q-WQML] (arguing that the use of cash flow data can underpin a prediction of default risk, thereby providing an apposite alternative to ancient credit scores. In addition to that, cash-flow data is commensurate with predictive across demographic groups).

2274 Gillis, Talia B., "The Input Data Fallacy", *cit.*, pp. 1176–1263 (1218).

2275 Gillis, Talia B., "The Input Data Fallacy", *cit.*, pp. 1176–1263 (1218).

2276 Gillis, Talia B., "The Input Data Fallacy", *cit.*, pp. 1176–1263 (1219).

2277 But see: Firestone, Simon, "Race Ethnicity and Credit Card Monitoring", *Journal of Money, Credit and Banking*, Sept. 2014, 2014, pp. 1206 and ff; Han, Song, Keys, Benjamin J./Li, Geng, *Unsecured Credit Supply over the Credit Cycle: Evidence from Credit Card Mailings* (argue that, statistically, Blacks and Latinos are seldom granted credit and, if ever granted credit, the terms and conditions attached to the concession of credit are not equal to those offered to White folks).

2278 But see: Atkinson, Abbye, "Rethinking Credit as a Social Provision", *Stanford Law Review*, Volume 71, 2019, pp. 1093–1099 (contending that credit, which shifts consumption temporally, is only beneficial insofar income ratchets up in the forthcoming future. As of now, though, "credit is fundamentally incompatible with the entrenched intergenerational poverty that plagues low-income Americans." Id. Notably, it is crucially important to come to terms with the fact that credit is not a panacea for the great bulk of economic struggles, and concretely wage stagnation. Although credit is not befitted to all consumers at all prices, affordable credit can nonetheless play a pivotal role in the creation of wealth).

2279 Gillis, Talia B., "The Input Data Fallacy", *cit.*, pp. 1176–1263 (1219).

§§ The conclusion is that which is painstakingly difficult to measure at the outset the exact consequences of the ever-evolving changes arising out of the fast-paced world of algorithmic credit pricing.[2280] The use of cutting-edge prediction Artificial Intelligence-embedded technologies suggests that only inputs that contribute to prediction accuracy are measured in algorithmic credit pricing.[2281]

§§ To the extent machine learning algorithms are better equipped to distinguish amongst people, *biased world inputs* may further compound[2282] racial disparities[2283] nevertheless. The door of *Algorithmic Dictatorship* is—continues to be—ajar slightly after all. That is why human judgment[2284] is not amenable to be swept aside,[2285] nor cast off, in this regard.[2286]

[2280] Gillis, Talia B., "The Input Data Fallacy", *cit.*, pp. 1176–1263 (1219).

[2281] Gillis, Talia B., "The Input Data Fallacy", *cit.*, pp. 1176–1263 (1219).

[2282] Freeman, Andrea, "Racism in the Credit Card Industry", *cit.*, p. 1098 and ff, whose stellar research I have been following closely ("*In contrast, lack of transparency on the part of the credit card companies enables discrimination by preventing its identification.* It also helps to ward off the potential for reputational harm or consumer response that media attention to the problem might create. *However, despite the lack of access to definitive statistics on credit card industry practices, two studies analyzed available data to conclude that race, isolated from socio-economic status, has a significant effect on a user's ability to obtain a credit card and on which terms they receive. Specifically, in 2010, researcher Chi-Jack Lin demonstrated that race affects the likelihood of obtaining a credit card, the number of cards owned, the average credit line per card, the conditions and fees attached to a card, and the factors necessary to establish creditworthiness. He found that this type of discrimination occurs based on the names listed on an application, which can often suggest racial identity, or the physical appearance of credit card applicants who walk into banks to request a card in person*"). Italics added.

[2283] Gillis, Talia B., "The Input Data Fallacy", *cit.*, pp. 1176–1263 (1219). See also: Lipton, Zachary/McAukley, Julian/Chouldechova, Alexandra, "Does Mitigating ML's Impact Disparity Require Treatment Disparity?" *Advances in Neural Information Processing Systems*, 31, S. Bengio, H. Wallach, H. Larochelle, K. Grauman, N. Cesa-Bianchi, and R. Garnett (Eds.). Curran Associates, Inc., 2018, pp. 8125–8135.

[2284] Salloch, S., & Eriksen, A., "What are humans doing in the Loop? Co-reasoning and practical Judgment when using machine learning-driven decision aids", *The American Journal of Bioethics*, 2024, pp. 1–12; Binns, Reuben, "Human Judgment in Algorithmic Loops: Individual Justice and Automated Decision-Making", *Regulation & Governance*, Volume 16, 2022, passim.

[2285] See: Wachter, Sandra/Mittelstadt, Brent/Russell, Chris, "Why Fairness Cannot be Automated: Bridging the Gap Between EU Non-Discrimination Law and AI", *Computer Law & Security Review*, Volume 41, 2021, 105567. See also: Part V, Chap. 5, Sects. 5.1.2–5.1.6.2.1 of this book (on the thing-centred algorithmic decision-making propelled by a *Controllable* and *Interpretable* Machine Learning that weeds out *Algorithmic Dictatorship* and secures *Algorithmic Common Good*).

[2286] See: Weizenbaum, Joseph, *Computer Power and Human Reason: From Judgment to Calculation*, 1st edition, New York, W. H. Freeman & Co, 1976, pp. 1–300 (227) ("examines the sources of the computer's powers and offers evaluative explorations of what computers can do, cannot do, and should not be employed to do") (this founding father of Artificial Intelligence presciently noted that we should not entrust Artificial Intelligence-embedded technologies with "tasks that demand wisdom"). Italics added. The approval of credit/rental applications is arguably one of those tasks that should never be entrusted to machines). More on this on Part IV, This chapter, Sects. 4.1.4–4.1.4.2.1 of this book.

§§ Concomitantly, the burgeoning growth of *input data* may unwind some of the harm caused by **measurement bias.**[2287] The very fact that the use of algorithmic pricing may either augment[2288] or reduce inequalities relative to classic credit pricing elicits the impression in view of which that only empirical evidence can adroitly measure «the direction of the effect».[2289]

4.1.8 «A Man Is an Architect and a Woman is a Housekeeper; a White Man Is a Lawyer and a Black Man Is a Butler»: How Word Embeddings in Natural Processing Language (NPL) Reinforce Biases Against Women (Sexism), Racial Minorities (Racism) and the Poor («Aporophobia»—Adela Cortina) in the Age of **Algorithmic Dictatorship** *Propelled by Redoubtable Corporate Moguls (***Google Word2Vec, Twitter and Wikipedia GloVe Word Embeddings***)*

§§ Pundits have been rallying around the sweeping idea that algorithmic discrimination[2290] runs afoul with the central tenets of fairness.[2291] Whilst the legal community has largely achieved an agreed-upon consensus with the regard to the deleterious effects of both algorithmic injustice[2292] and algorithmic bias,[2293] it nonetheless remains deeply divided when it comes to the cluster of bespoke solutions that should be deftly deployed to upend the vast array of unsavoury outgrowths of *Algorithmic Dictatorship.*

§§ The plethora of scorching issues arising out of ever-evolving Artificial Intelligence-embedded technologies are familiar, well-worn, well-canvassed in, which accordingly yields further insights on the mighty power evinced by the former

---

[2287] Gillis, Talia B., "The Input Data Fallacy", *cit.*, pp. 1176–1263 (1219).

[2288] Loo, Rory Van, "Making Innovation More Competitive: The Case of Fintech", *UCLA Law Review*, Volume 65, 2018, pp. 232–254 (discussing how Black and Latino households are more than twice as likely to be unbanked compared to the national average).

[2289] Gillis, Talia B., "The Input Data Fallacy", *cit.*, pp. 1176–1263 (1219).

[2290] See on algorithmic discrimination: Kleinberg, Jon, et al., "Discrimination in the Age of Algorithms", *Journal of Legal Analysis*, 2018, pp. 114–174; See: Kleinberg, Jon, et al., "Algorithms as Discrimination Detectors", *Proceeds of the National Academy of Science*, Volume 117, 2020, pp. 30096–30110; Griemmelmann, James/Westreich, Daniel, "Incomprehensible Discrimination ", *California Law Review Online*, Volume 7, 2018, pp. 164–171; Xiang, Alice, "Reconciling Legal and Technical Approaches to Algorithmic Bias", *Tennessee Law Review*, Volume 88, 2021, passim; Karnow, Curtis E. A., "The Opinion of Machines", *The Cambridge Handbook of the Law of Algorithms*, Bartfield, Woodrow (Editor), Cambridge, United Kingdom: Cambridge University Press, 2021, pp. 15 and ff and passim; Strandburg, Katherine J., "Rulemaking and Inscrutable Decision Tools", *Columbia Law Review*, Volume 119, 2019, passim.

to reproduce,[2294] reinforce[2295] and fundamentally amplify[2296] biases against historically[2297] disadvantaged[2298] communities.[2299] The assertion according to which artificial intelligence-embedded technologies are a breeding ground for both the perpetuation[2300] and exacerbation[2301] of long-standing biases[2302]—paired with its hardly

---

[2291] See: Hoffmann AL, "Where fairness fails: data, algorithms, and the limits of antidiscrimination discourse", *Inf Commun Soc*, 22 (7), 2019, pp. 900–915. See also: Kusner, MJ./Loftus, JR., "The long road to fairer algorithms", *Nature*, Volume 578, 2020, pp. 34–36.

[2292] Ting-an Lin, "Democratizing AI" and the Concern of Algorithmic Injustice", *Philosophy and Technology*, Volume 37 (103), 2024, pp. 3–27; Okidegbe, Ngozi, "The Democratizing Potential of Algorithms?", *Connecticut Law Review*, Volume 54, 2021, passim; Katyal, Sonia, "Private Accountability in the Age of Artificial Intelligence", *UCLA Law Review*, Volume 66, 2019, pp. 54–99.

[2293] Recall: Baeza-Yates, R., "Bias on the web", *Communications of the ACM*, 61 (6), June 2018, 2018, pp. 54–61 (argues that "*algorithmic bias is when the bias is not present in the input data* and is added *purely by the algorithm*"). Italics added. See also: Hajian, Sara Hajian et al., "Algorithmic Bias: From Discrimination Discovery to Fairness-aware Data Mining", *ACM SIGKDD International Conference on Knowledge Discovery and Data Mining*, Volume 22, 2125, 2016; Griemmelmann, James/Westreich, Daniel, "Incomprehensible Discrimination ", *California Law Review Online*, Volume 7, 2018, pp. 164–171; Xiang, Alice, "Reconciling Legal and Technical Approaches to Algorithmic Bias", *Tennessee Law Review*, Volume 88, 2021, passim; See: Lemley, Mark A./Casey, Bryan, "Remedies for Robots", *The University of Chicago Law Review*, Volume 86, Issue 5, 2019, pp. 1311–1396 (1376) (alerting to the perils of algorithmic bias); Chandler, Anupam, "The Racist Algorithm", *Michigan Law Review*, Volume 115, Issue 6, 2018, p. 1026 (noting that, in the terrain of racist algorithm, "the possibilities for discriminatory manipulation are legion"; Jackson, Maya C., "Artificial Intelligence and Algorithmic Bias: The Issues with Technology Reflecting History and Humans", *Journal of Business Technology Law*, Volume 16, 2021, pp. 299–316; West, Sarah Myers/Whittaker, Meredith/Crawford, Kate, *Discriminating Systems. Gender, Race and Power in AI*. New York: AI Now Institute, 2019, pp. 15 and ff and passim; Waldman, Ezra, "Privacy, Practice, and Performance", *California Law Review*, Volume 110, 2021, passim (on algorithmic bias). Italics added.

[2294] Bolukbasi T, Chang K-W, Saligrama V, et al, "Man is to Computer Programmer as Woman is to Homemaker? Debiasing Word Embeddings", 2016, arXiv:1607.06520v1.

[2295] Garga, N./Schiebingerb, L./Jurafskyc, D/Zou, J, "Word embeddings quantify 100 years of gender and ethnic stereotypes", *Proceedings of the national academy of sciences* (PNAS), 2018, passim.

[2296] Manzini, T./Chong, LY/Black, AW/Tsvetkov, Y., "Black is to Criminal as Caucasian is to Police: Detecting and Removing Multi-class Bias in Word Embeddings", *NAACL HLT 2019—2019 Conference North America Chapter Association Computer Linguist Human Language Technology—Proceedings of Conference*, 1:615–621, 2019.

[2297] Allen, James, "The Color of Algorithms: An Analysis and Proposed Research Agenda Deterring Algorithmic Redlining", *Fordham Urban Law Journal*, Volume 46, 2019, pp. 219–234 (229–234) (discussing how historical mortgage redlining greatly swayed modern algorithms generated by massive batches of data sets that consist of decades of information built on exclusion and racial discrimination in the purview of financing, marketing, and housing). See: Part IV, This chapter, Sects. 4.1.4–4.1.4.2.3 of this book.

[2298] See: Barocas, Solon/Selbst, Andrew, "Big Data's Disparate Impact", *California Law Review*, Volume 104, pp. 2016, p. 691 (highlighting the worrisome, and gruesome, issue of "structural disadvantage" with which racialized communities have been tussling for centuries). See also: Powell, Richard/Porter, Jeremy, "Redlining, Concentrated Disadvantage and Crime: The Effects of Discriminatory Government Policies on Violent Crime", *American Journal of Criminal Justice*, Volume 48, 2023, pp. 1132–1156 ("*Redlining and other discriminatory government policies enacted during*

unforeseen increase[2303] in algorithmic settings—[2304] is neither unwarranted nor uncalled for.[2305]

§§ Tellingly, algorithmic-anchored decision-making, if nothing else, is a realm whereby biases thrive/abound[2306] in that comprises a universe that is neither

the first half of the Twentieth Century have had long-lasting negative effects on neighborhoods, especially those inhabited by people of color. This study attempts to link the practice of redlining to current-day indicators of neighborhood concentrated disadvantage and violent crime using spatio-temporal data from Chicago (…) In addition, it seeks to determine whether redlining was associated with violent crime, and if that association was mediated by redlining's effect on concentrated disadvantage. The results indicate that redlining was associated with increases in both concentrated disadvantage and violent crime, and that redlining's relationship with violent crime was, indeed, partially mediated by its relationship with concentrated disadvantage"). Italics added. See also: Gandy, Oscar H., *Coming to Terms with Chance: Engaging Rational Discrimination and Cumulative Disadvantage*, Farnham, UK: Ashgate Publishing, 2009.

2299 Curto, Georgina/Acosta, Mario Fernando Jojoa/Comim, Flavio/Garcia-Zapirain, Begoña, "Are AI systems biased against the poor? A machine learning analysis using Word2Vec and GloVe embeddings", *AI & Society*, Volume 39, 2024, pp. 617–632 (617).

2300 Crawford, Kate/Schultz, Jason, "Big Data and Due Process: Toward a Framework to Redress Predictive Privacy Harms", *Boston College Law Review*, Volume 55, 2014, pp. 93, 99–101 (pinpointing pathways through which predictive analytic tools perpetuate discriminatory practices).

2301 Wonyoung, So, "Which Information Matters? Measuring Landlord Assessment of Tenant Screening Reports", *Housing Policy Debate*, Volume 33, n. ° 6, 2023, pp. 1484–1510 (1502) ("*One additional finding of the experiment is that algorithmic scoring can exacerbate this racially unequal landscape in rental agreements not just because the algorithm may be inaccurate, but because landlords may want to follow the risk assessment made by the tenant screening report. This is alarming for low-income tenants, particularly housing voucher holders. Security deposits are one of the most significant barriers to obtaining housing for voucher holders, because vouchers do not pay security deposits but most private landlords require them (Rosenblatt & Cossyleon, 2018).* Given that voucher holders have exceptionally low income (usually less than 50% of area median income) and might experience more housing insecurity (rental debts and eviction-related experiences), *imposing greater security deposits on voucher holders almost equates to denying them housing—yet these decisions could be justified by algorithmic scoring if tenant screening services employ it*"). Italics added. See: Part IV, This chapter, Sects. 4.1.4–4.1.4.2.3 of this book.

2302 In spite of its deep-seated racial bias, decision-makers continue to deploy redlining tactics through big data and may even justify such unlawful practices by claiming that the latter abide by cost-effectiveness. See: Humber, Nadiyah J., "A Home for Digital Equity: Algorithmic Redlining and Property Technology", *California Law Review*, Volume 111, Issue 5, 2023, pp. 1421–1484. See also: Hurley, Mikella/Adebayo, Julius, "Credit Scoring in the Era of Big Data", *Yale Journal of Law and Technology*, Volume 18, 2016, pp. 148, 151–156, 172 (averring that FICO scoring boasts a redoubtable capacity to routinely weed out some populations that have been historically and systematically underrepresented or grossly unfairly represented in the credit industry market). Tellingly, by 2016, ten states had disavowed the unlawful practice of employers using shady algorithmic credit scores due to their perceived disparate impact on low-income applicants and members of racialized communities (mostly Black folks). See: O'Neill, Cathy, *Weapons of Math Destruction. How Big Data Increases Inequality and Threatens Democracy*. London: Penguin Random House, 2016, pp. 128 and ff and passim. See: Part IV, This chapter, Sects. 4.1.4–4.1.4.2.3 of this book.

2303 Curto, Georgina/Acosta, Mario Fernando Jojoa/Comim, Flavio/Garcia-Zapirain, Begoña, "Are AI systems biased against the poor? A machine learning analysis using Word2Vec and GloVe embeddings", *cit.*, pp. 617–632 (617).

2304 See: Citron, Danielle Keats/Pasquale, Frank, "The Scored Society: Due Process for Automated Predictions", *Washington Law Review*, Volume 89, 2014, pp. 1, 4–5 (highlighting how human beings

neutral[2307] nor objective.[2308] Let alone fair.[2309] These are anything but uplifting news to the extent that *Algorithmic Dictatorship* is not coming. It is here. It is upon us.

§§ The truism according to which artificial intelligence-embedded technologies have pierced into, and have been eerily entrusted with deciding,[2310] all aspects of our daily lives give credence to, and adds plausibility, to this assertion.[2311] It seems

---

programming automated systems is directly conducive to, and leads, to fundamentally inaccurate results since the source code, predictive algorithms and datasets may encompass human biases which, in turn, have a disparate impact on historically disadvantaged groups).

[2305] Vinuesa, R./Azizpour, H./Leite I et al, "The role of artificial intelligence in achieving the sustainable development goals", *Nature Communications*, 111(11), 2020, pp. 1–10.

[2306] Havard, Cassandra Jones, "On The Take": The Black Box of Credit Scoring and Mortgage Discrimination", *Boston University Public Interest Law Journal*, Volume 20, 2011, pp. 241–247 (highlighting that algorithmic credit scoring, if left unchecked, may be transmogrified into an intrinsic, encroached, deep-rooted form of racial discrimination akin to mortgage redlining); Pasquale, Frank, *The Black Box Society: The Secret Algorithms that Control Money and Information*. Cambridge, Massachusetts: Harvard University Press, 2015, 1–320. See: Part IV, This chapter, Sects. 4.1.4–4.1.4.2.3 of this book.

[2307] Hurley, Mikella/Adebayo, Julius, "Credit Scoring in the Era of Big Data", *Yale Journal of Law and Technology*, Volume 18, 2016, p. 149 ("*these tools may furthermore obscure discriminatory and subjective lending policies behind a single "objective" score (…) sophisticated algorithms may combine facially neutral data points and treat them as proxies for immutable characteristics such as race or gender, thereby circumventing existing non-discrimination laws and systematically denying credit access to certain groups. Finally, big-data tools may allow online payday lenders to target the most vulnerable consumers and lure them into debt traps*"). Italics added.

[2308] See: Benjamin, Ruha, *Race After Technology: Abolitionist Tools for the New Jim Code*, New York, Polity, 2019, pp. 1–172 (7) (discussing that Artificial Intelligence-embedded technologies are viewed as iron-clad tools of objectivity and devoid of any biases whatsoever). Ruha Benjamin accordingly contends that "the employment of new technologies that reflect and reproduce existing inequities but that are promoted and perceived as more objective or progressive than the discriminatory systems of a previous era"). See also: Farina, M., & Lavazza, A., *Philosophy, expertise, and the myth of neutrality. Routledge Studies in Contemporary Philosophy*, London, Routledge, 2024. This false scent of neutrality impairs, and impacts, procedural justice. See: Tyler, Tom R., "The Psychology of Procedural Justice: A Test of the Group-Value Model", *Journal of Personality and Social Psychology*, Volume 57, 1989, p. 830 (reports that in any procedure "several non-control issues – the *neutrality* of the decision-making procedure, trust in the 3rd party, and the information the experience communicates about social standing – influence both procedural preferences and judgments of procedural justice").

[2309] Citron, Danielle Keats/Pasquale, Frank A., "The Scored Society: Due Process for Automated Predictions", *Washington Law Review*, Volume 89, 2014, pp. 1–34 (arguing that "[a]*dvocates applaud the removal of human beings and their flaws from the assessment process*," but arguing that bias nonetheless remains "[*b*]*ecause human beings program predictive algorithms, their biases and values are embedded into the software's instructions*"). Italics added. See: Part IV, This chapter, Sects. 4.1.4–4.1.4.2.3 of this book. See also: Lepri, Bruno/Oliver, Nuria/Letouz'e Emmanuel/Pentland, Alex/Vinck, Patrick, "Fair, Transparent, and Accountable Algorithmic Decision-Making Processes: The Premise, the Proposed Solutions, and the Open Challenges", *Philosophy & Technology*, Volume 31, 2018, passim.

[2310] See: Millar, Jason/Kerr, Ian, "Delegation, Relinquishment and Responsibility: The Prospect of Expert Robots", *Robot Law*, Calo, Ryan /Froomkin, A. Michael/Kerr, Ian, Cheltenham, Edward Elgar Publishing, 2016, pp. 102, 106–107 (as these authors aptly put it "*we will rely on robots without really knowing why – simply because their algorithms provide the greatest number of successful outcomes.* We have already seen this in Google's search approach. Neither Larry (Page)

as though that everything, or nearly everything,[2312] revolves around algorithmic decision-making and the extent to which the latter further compounds long-standing injustices[2313] and ratchets up discrimination accordingly.[2314] Which is something in dire need of quashing insofar deserves to be overtly dreaded, decried and ultimately frowned upon.

§§ Insofar the affray against the spine-tingling effects arisen from the all-out deployment of Artificial Intelligence-embedded technologies to make high-stake decisions[2315] is underway in the remit of healthcare,[2316] facial recognition,[2317] financial services,[2318] administration of justice[2319] and security,[2320] and military

---

nor Sergey (Brin) (nor any other Google employee) knowns exactly why one particular web page is a better result than another. *When the click patterns say it is, that's good enough.* No semantic or causal analysis is required...*Like the ancients, we will, quite rationally, come to rely upon them, knowing full well that we cannot necessarily explain the reasons for their decisions*"). Italics added. Converging: Casey, Anthony J./Niblett, Anthony, "Self-driving Laws", *University of Toronto Law Journal*, Volume 66, 2016, pp. 429–435 (contend that "as more information is generated, and the evolutionary algorithm updates and become a better forecaster, we imagine that judges will increasingly rely on the advice of the algorithm"). But see: Weizenbaum, Joseph, *Computer Power and Human Reason: From Judgment to Calculation*, 1st edition, New York, W. H. Freeman & Co, 1976, pp. 1–300 (227) ("examines the sources of the computer's powers and offers evaluative explorations of what computers can do, cannot do, and should not be employed to do") (this founding father of Artificial Intelligence presciently noted that we should not entrust Artificial Intelligence-embedded technologies with "tasks that demand wisdom"). Italics added. The approval of rental applications is arguably one of those tasks that should never be entrusted to machines). More on this on Part IV, This chapter, Sects. 4.1.4–4.1.4.2.1 of this book. See: Part V, Chap. 5, Sect. 5.1.7.2 of this book (on law number two to control algorithmic decision-making, which mandates that black box models must not be entrusted with the task of making high stake decisions—v.g. health and freedom). See: Part V, Chap. 5, Sects. 5.1.7–5.1.7.5 of this book (on the five laws to control algorithmic decision-making).

2311 Curto, Georgina/Acosta, Mario Fernando Jojoa/Comim, Flavio/Garcia-Zapirain, Begoña, "Are AI systems biased against the poor? A machine learning analysis using Word2Vec and GloVe embeddings", *cit.*, pp. 617–632 (617).

2312 But see: Pasquale, Frank, "A Rule of Persons, Not Machines: The Limits of Legal Automation", *George Washington Law Review*, Volume 87, 2019, passim (arguing that legal automation, however utile in some domains, should not supersede, nor surpass, the rule of persons). See: Part V, Chap. 5, Sect. 5.1.7.2 of this book (on law number two to control algorithmic decision-making, which mandates that black box models must not be entrusted with the task of high stake decisions—v.g. health and freedom). See: Part V, Chap. 5, Sects. 5.1.7–5.1.7.5 of this book (on the five laws to control algorithmic decision-making). See: Part V, Chap. 5, Sect. 5.1.8.5 of this book (on law number five to interpret algorithmic decision-making, which mandates that robot-judges, robot-prosecutors and robot-lawyers must not enter the courtroom for they are utterly incapable of making sound and interpretable value judgements).

2313 Fry, H, *Hello world: being human in the age of algorithms*, London, Penguin Random House, 2018.

2314 Anderson, Lisa, Roland G. Fryer, and Charles A. Holt, "Discrimination: Experimental Evidence from Psychology and Economics", *Handbook on the Economics of Discrimination*, William M. Rodgers III (Editor), Northampton, MA: Edward Elgar, 2006, pp. 97–115.

2315 But see: Rudin, Cynthia, "Please stop explaining black box models for high stakes decisions", *Proceedings of NeurIPS 2018 Workshop on Critiquing and Correcting Trends in Machine Learning (NIPS 2018)*, 2018, passim; Rudin, C., & Radin, J., "Why are we using black box models in AI when we don't need to? A lesson from an explainable AI competition", *Harvard Data Science*

endeavours,[2321] little emphasis has been placed on the *algorithmic accountability*[2322] concerning such pervasive tools though.[2323]

§§ Whilst polymaths have poured in staggering efforts to identify key parallels with a view to anticipating how Artificial Intelligence-embedded technologies may

Review, 2019, Volume 1, Issue 2, passim; Tan, S., Caruana, R., Hooker, G., and Lou, Y., "Distill-and-compare: Auditing blackbox models using transparent model distillation". *Proceedings of the 2018 AAAI/ACM Conference on AI, Ethics, and Society, Association for Computing Machinery*, 2018, pp. 303–310; Watcher, S./Mittelstadt, B./Russell, C., "Counterfactual explanations without opening the black box: automated decisions and the GDPR", *Harvard Journal of Law & Technology*, Volume 1, 2018, passim. See: Part IV, This chapter, Sects. 4.1.4–4.1.4.2.3 of this book.

[2316] See: Part V, Chap. 5, Sect. 5.1.7.2 of this book (on law number two to control algorithmic decision-making, which mandates that black box models must not be entrusted with the task of high stake decisions—v.g. health and freedom). See also: Part V, Chap. 5, Sect. 5.1.8.5 of this book (on law number five to interpret algorithmic decision-making, which mandates that robot-judges, robot-prosecutors and robot-lawyers must not enter the courtroom for they are utterly incapable of making sound and interpretable value judgements). See also: Watson, DS/Krutzinna J./Bruce IN et al, "Clinical applications of machine learning algorithms: beyond the black box", *BMJ*, 2019; Vallès-Peris N./Domènech, M.", Caring in the in-between: a proposal to introduce responsible AI and robotics to healthcare", *Artificial Intelligence and Society*, 2021.

[2317] Fergus, Rachel, "Biased Technology: The Automated Discrimination of Facial Recognition", *ACLU Minnesota*, February 29, 2024, available at: https://www.aclu-mn.org/en/news/biased-technology-automated-discrimination-facial-recognition (access: 20.09.2024) ("*technology is developing much more quickly than the laws we need to protect our rights. Anyone with a smartphone or social media account knows how rapidly technology changes, while legislating can take a long, long time. It is essential to proactively put policies into place that will protect our rights as new and more advanced technology is constantly released. Especially when that technology – and law enforcement members using it - have been shown over and over to be biased toward marginalized groups*"). Italics added. See also: Hu, Margaret, "From the National Surveillance State to the Cybersurveillance State", *The Annual Review of Law and Social Science*, Volume 13, 2017, p. 169 ("*in a big data world, a digitized passport system can link to multiple other sources, such as license plate readers, No Fly Lists, and Terrorist Watchlists. Facial recognition technology drawing upon a photo database could potentially link a plethora of digital images of a person, including social media, the internet, photo databases like driver's licenses, live-streaming video, CCTV surveillance, and images obtained from hacking cameras on laptops and digital devices. Biometric data collection and storage are becoming increasingly compulsory through either government identification requirements*, such as digital photo requirements for passports and driver's licenses, or corporate identification requirements, such as biometric access to digital devices"). Italics added.

[2318] Kostka, G., "China's social credit systems and public opinion: explaining high levels of approval", *New Med Soc*, Volume 21, 2019, pp. 1565–1593; Aggarwal, Nikita, "The norms of algorithmic credit scoring", *The Cambridge Law Journal*, Volume 80, Issue 1, 2021, pp. 42–73.

[2319] But see: Part V, Chap. 5, Sect. 5.1.8.5 of this book (on law number five to interpret algorithmic decision-making, which mandates that robot-judges, robot-prosecutors and robot-lawyers must not enter the courtroom for they are utterly incapable of making sound and interpretable value judgements). See also: Simmons, Ric, "Big Data and Procedural Justice: Legitimizing Algorithms in the Criminal Justice System", *Ohio State Journal of Criminal Law*, Volume 15, 2018, pp. 576 and ff and passim; Brayne, S., "Big data surveillance: The case of policing", *American Sociological Review*, Volume 82, Issue 5, 2017, pp. 977–1008.

[2320] Hauge, MV, Stevenson, MD, Rossmo, DK, Le Comber, SC, "Tagging Banksy: using geographic profiling to investigate a modern art mystery", *Journal of Spatial Science*, Volume 61, 2016, pp. 185–190; Merler, M./Ratha, N./Feris, RS./Smith, JR., "Diversity in faces", arXiv:1901.10436, 2019; Green B, Chen Y, "Disparate interactions: An algorithm-in-the-loop analysis of fairness

fare in the forthcoming future,[2324] truth is the latter is becoming increasingly invasive, thereby casting doubts on where should the line be drawn to adroitly forestall further wrongdoings that may be too big to atone for. For instance, much to our chagrin, Artificial Intelligence-embedded technologies are being currently deployed to forecast our commercial interests through big data[2325] that comprises meaningful information about our likes or dislikes,[2326] which forms part of broader technological apparatus within which «surveillance capitalism»[2327] operates.

§§ The gulf between corporate moguls/tech giants and regular citizens underpins the finding according to which the general furore over Artificial Intelligence should halted or inordinate harms are poised to be externalized onto innocent others. This truism is neither unwarranted nor uncalled for. It bears mentioning that decisions

in risk assessments", *FAT* 2019, Proceedings of 2019 Conference of Fairness, Accountability, Transparency*, 2019, pp. 90–99.

2321 De Vynck, G., Autonomous weapons already exist and are playing a role on battlefields like Libya and Armenia—The Washington Post", *Washington Post*, 2021, available at: https://www.washingtonpost.com/technology/2021/07/07/ai-weapons-us-military/ (accessed 5 January 2025).

2322 See: Part V, Chap. 5, Sects. 5.1.2–5.1.6.2.1 of this book (on the thing-centred algorithmic decision-making propelled by a *Controllable* and *Interpretable* Machine Learning that weeds out *Algorithmic Dictatorship* and secures *Algorithmic Common Good*).

2323 See: Katyal, Sonia, "Private Accountability in the Age of Artificial Intelligence", *UCLA Law Review*, Volume 66, 2019, pp. 54–99. See also: Williams, Rebecca, "Accountable Algorithms: Adopting the Public Law Toolbox Outside the Realm of Public Law", *Current Legal Problems*, Vol. 75, 2022, pp. 237–263; Williams, Rebecca, "Rethinking Administrative Law for Algorithmic Decision-Making", *Oxford Journal of Legal Studies*, Volume 42, 2021, pp. 468 e ff and passim.

2324 But see: Segran, G., "The complexity of artificial intelligence", *Singapore Management University*, 2021, passim (on the elaborate and complex trappings of Artificial Intelligence). See also: Adadi, Amina/Berrada, Mohammed, "Peeking Inside the Black-Box: A Survey on Explainable Artificial Intelligence (XAI), *Institute of Electrical and Electronics Engineers*, Volume 6, 2018, passim; Edwards, Lilian/Veale, Michael, "Slave to the Algorithm? Why a "Right to an Explanation" is Probably not the Remedy You are Looking for", *Duke Law and Technology Review*, Volume 16, 2018, pp. 18–67 (pondering whether and to what extent XAI will come in handy because citizens are woefully ill-prepared to "make use of the kind of algorithmic explanations they are likely to be offered"); Miller, Tim, "Explanations in Artificial Intelligence: Insights from Social Sciences", *Artificial Intelligence*, Volume 267, 2019, pp. 1–38.

2325 Note, though, that the foregoing examples hardly exhaust the scope and import of Artificial Intelligence-embedded technologies and Big Data. As captioned above, this whirlwind of forces is overhauling the consumer credit economy beyond recognition. See: Bruckner, Matthew Adam, "The Promise and Perils of Algorithmic Lenders' Use of Big Data", *Chicago-Kent Law Review*, Volume 93, 2018, pp. 3, 11–15.

2326 Curto, Georgina/Acosta, Mario Fernando Jojoa/Comim, Flavio/Garcia-Zapirain, Begoña, "Are AI systems biased against the poor? A machine learning analysis using Word2Vec and GloVe embeddings", *cit.*, pp. 617–632 (617).

2327 Zuboff, Zhoshana, *The Age of Surveillance Capitalism, The Fight for a Human Future at the New Frontier of Power*. New Yor City: PublicAffairs Books, 2019, pp. 1–704 (360) (argues that we are indomitably heading towards a "instrumentarianism" that draws on "totalitarianism").

vital to our collective welfare dispiritingly leverage on rigged[2328] data[2329] baked into databases[2330] scattered across the data-driven world[2331] we live in.[2332]

§§ Notwithstanding, the sheer amount of algorithmic systems operating shadily[2333] while being spurred by an hidden agenda[2334] has grown exponentially.[2335] Governments worldwide have accordingly doubled down their efforts to deftly regulate Artificial Intelligence-embedded technologies.[2336]

§§ Unfazed, supra-governmental entities—like the European Union[2337]—have also employed whopping efforts in laying down a comprehensive, thoroughgoing,

---

2328 Barocas, Solon/Selbst, Andrew D., "Big Data's Disparate Impact", *California Law Review*, Volume 104, 2016, pp. 671–682 (discussing how data is often flawed, rigged, incomplete, imperfect and therefore algorithms inherit the prejudice of the original decision makers).

2329 *Tech, Bias and Housing Initiative, the Promise and Perils of Residential Proptech, Year 1, Research Summary Report, April 2023, TechEquity Collaborative*, p. 11, available at: https://techequity.us/wp-content/uploads/2023/04/TBHI-Y1-Research-Summary-Report.pdf (28.11.2024). ("*Once bad data enters the analysis of one factor, it gets baked into the subsequent process, multiplying the effect that one disadvantageous data point can have on someone's overall housing determination*"). Italics added.

2330 Balkin, Jack M., "The Three Laws of Robotics in the Age of Big Data", *Ohio State Law Journal*, Volume 78, Issue 5, 2017, pp. 1217–1241, whose research I have been following closely. See also: See: Hu, Margaret, "From the National Surveillance State to the Cybersurveillance State", *The Annual Review of Law and Social Science*, Volume 13, 2017, p. 165 ("*Datafication, like most big data processes, requires increasing amounts of digital data to support or construct cybersurveillance.* It empowers government actions that are based on digital data collection, data processing protocols, and bulk data analyses (Mayer-Schonberger & Cukier ¨ 2013). *Another way to characterize datafication is as a governmental policy interest that both transforms analog data (PCAST 2014) into searchable, centralized digital databases and develops new forms of stored data*"). Italics added.

2331 Hardt, Moritz, "How big data is unfair: Understanding sources of unfairness in data driven decision making", *Medium*, Archived on Oct. 8, 2014, available at: https://web.archive.org/web/20141008185829/ https://medium.com/@mrtz/how-big-data-is-unfair-9aa544d739de. (access: 17.12.2024).

2332 But see: Bornstein, Stepanhie, "Antidiscriminatory Algorithms", *Alabama Law Review*, Volume 70, 2018, pp. 519, 524–528 (contending, however, that the tagged "facially neutral" algorithms producing discriminatory outcomes should be quashed).

2333 O'Neil, Cathy, *Weapons of Math Destruction. How Big Data Increases Inequality and Threatens Democracy*, London, Penguin Random House, 2016, passim (showing how algorithms utilized in modern societies are amenable to perpetuate racial discrimination, partially through perpetuation of social disadvantage and wealth divides).

2334 Curto, Georgina/Acosta, Mario Fernando Jojoa/Comim, Flavio/Garcia-Zapirain, Begoña, "Are AI systems biased against the poor? A machine learning analysis using Word2Vec and GloVe embeddings", *cit.*, pp. 617–632 (617).

2335 Tsamados, A./Aggarwal, Nikita, Cowls, J. et al, "The ethics of algorithms: key problems and solutions", *Artificial Intelligence and Society*, Volume 1, 2021, pp. 1–16.

2336 Krafft, Tobias D./Zweig, Katharina A./Konig, Pascal D., "How to Regulate Algorithmic Decision-Making: A Framework of Regulatory Requirements for Different Applications", *Regulation & Governance*, Volume 16, 2022, pp. 119 and ff and passim.

2337 European Commission, *Artificial Intelligence Act. Proposal for a regulation of the European Parliament and the Council laying down harmonised rules on Artificial Intelligence (Artificial Intelligence Act) and amending certain Union legislative acts*, 2021.

and full-fledged regulatory frame of reference, fundamental rights wise.[2338] Owing to its pathbreaking nature, the former has been aggrandized by the much-acclaimed «Brussels effect»[2339] that radiates far and bright in that is a lighthouse of inspiration for mature jurisdictions worldwide.[2340]

§§ Compellingly, at the gist of the EU Artificial Intelligence legal framework[2341] lies the overriding principle of «diversity, non-discrimination and fairness», encompassing the «avoidance of unfair bias», which is of paramount importance in the case of the historically discriminated groups.[2342]

§§ Nevertheless, the theoretical underpinnings[2343] of the foregoing legal framework are lacklustre inasmuch they fall conspicuously short of outlining a sturdy ethical blueprint[2344] capable of morphing itself into a propelling force behind law abiding practices. To add to our woes, such a lukewarm ethical frame of reference amounts to a toothless set of guidelines devoid of, and fundamentally bereft, of deterrence effect,[2345] thereby leading to a set of practices[2346] that belie every central tenet of fairness that stakeholders should abide by in the first place. Amongst these

---

2338 See: Gill, I., *Whoever leads in artificial intelligence in 2030 will rule the world until 2100*, Washington, DC: Brookings Institution, 2020. See also: Imbrie A, Kania E, Laskai L, "The question of comparative advantage in artificial intelligence: enduring strengths and emerging challenges for the United States", *Center for Security and Emergent Technologies*, 2020, passim.

2339 Bradford A, *The Brussels effect: how the European Union rules the world*, Oxford, Oxford University Press, 2020, passim.

2340 Curto, Georgina/Acosta, Mario Fernando Jojoa/Comim, Flavio/Garcia-Zapirain, Begoña, "Are AI systems biased against the poor? A machine learning analysis using Word2Vec and GloVe embeddings", *cit.*, pp. 617–632 (617).

2341 Curto, Georgina/Acosta, Mario Fernando Jojoa/Comim, Flavio/Garcia-Zapirain, Begoña, "Are AI systems biased against the poor? A machine learning analysis using Word2Vec and GloVe embeddings", *cit.*, pp. 617–632 (617).

2342 HLEGAI, *High-Level Expert Group on Artificial Intelligence, EU—Ethics guidelines for trustworthy AI, European Commission*, 2019.

2343 See: Part V, Chap. 5, Sects. 5.1.2–5.1.6.2.1 of this book (on the **thing-centred algorithmic decision-making** propelled by a *Controllable* and *Interpretable* Machine Learning that weeds out *Algorithmic Dictatorship* and secures *Algorithmic Common Good*. It is worth recalling that the thing-centred algorithmic decision-making seeks to unwind the perils arising out of the lack of theoretical underpinnings facing the **human-centred algorithmic decision-making**, as extensively fleshed out Part III, Chap. 3, Sects. 3.1.4.3–3.1.4.4 of this book).

2344 Curto, Georgina/Acosta, Mario Fernando Jojoa/Comim, Flavio/Garcia-Zapirain, Begoña, "Are AI systems biased against the poor? A machine learning analysis using Word2Vec and GloVe embeddings", *cit.*, pp. 617–632 (617).

2345 Cardi, Jonathan/Penfield, Randall D./Yoon, Albert H., "Does Tort Law Deter Individuals? A Behavioral Science Study", *Journal of Empirical Legal Studies*, Volume 9, Issue 3, 2012, pp. 567–603 (the authors stressed, however, premised on a sound empirical evidence, that "the threat of potential criminal sanctions had a large and statistically significant effect on subjects 'stated willingness to engage in risky behaviour").

2346 Curto, Georgina/Acosta, Mario Fernando Jojoa/Comim, Flavio/Garcia-Zapirain, Begoña, "Are AI systems biased against the poor? A machine learning analysis using Word2Vec and GloVe embeddings", *cit.*, pp. 617–632 (618).

bemoaning practices stand arguably ethics shopping, ethics blue-washing, ethics lobbying, ethics dumping[2347] or ethics shirking.[2348]

§§ There have been poignant calls pointing out to the dire need of creating a brawny frame of reference[2349] capable of spurring a sustainable development[2350] of Artificial Intelligence-embedded technologies.[2351] Many of which capable of inflicting an overwhelming amount of harm to a cohort of citizens.[2352]

§§ Following suit, there has been a cascade of Artificial Intelligence Ethics guidelines—over 173 extant documents in 2021[2353] and counting—amidst an atmosphere of perceived «moral panic»[2354] that inheres and permeates a plethora of piecemeal proposals to bypass,[2355] detect[2356] and correct bias[2357] deeply soaked in the data[2358]

2347 Curto, Georgina/Acosta, Mario Fernando Jojoa/Comim, Flavio/Garcia-Zapirain, Begoña, "Are AI systems biased against the poor? A machine learning analysis using Word2Vec and GloVe embeddings", *cit.*, pp. 617–632 (618).

2348 Floridi, Luciano, "Translating principles into practices of digital ethics: five risks of being unethical", *Philosophy and Technology*, 322 (32), 2019, pp. 185–193.

2349 Curto, Georgina/Acosta, Mario Fernando Jojoa/Comim, Flavio/Garcia-Zapirain, Begoña, "Are AI systems biased against the poor? A machine learning analysis using Word2Vec and GloVe embeddings", *cit.*, pp. 617–632 (618).

2350 See: Part V, Chap. 5, Sects. 5.1.2–5.1.6.2.1 of this book (on the thing-centred algorithmic decision-making propelled by a *Controllable* and *Interpretable* Machine Learning that weeds out *Algorithmic Dictatorship* and secures *Algorithmic Common Good*. It is worth recalling that the thing-centred algorithmic decision-making seeks to unwind the perils arising out of the lack of theoretical underpinnings facing the human-centred algorithmic decision-making, as extensively fleshed out Part III, Chap. 3, Sects. 3.1.4.3–3.1.4.4 of this book).

2351 Vakkuri, V./Kemell, KK./Jantunen M./Abrahamsson, P., "This is Just a Prototype": How Ethics Are Ignored in Software Startup Like Environments", *Lectures Notes Bus Inf Process 383 LNBIP*, 2020, 195–210; Morley J, Elhalal A, Garcia F et al, "Ethics as a service: a pragmatic operationalisation of AI ethics", *Minds and Machines*, Volume 31, 2021, pp. 239–256; Morley J, Kinsey L, Elhalal A et al, "Operationalising AI ethics: barriers, enablers, and next steps", *Artificial Intelligence and Society*, 2021, passim.

2352 Buolamwini, Joy, *Unmasking AI: My Mission to Protect What Is Human in a World of Machines*, New York, Random House, 2023, pp. 1–336 ("*The conscience of the AI revolution" (Fortune) explains how we've arrived at an era of AI harms and oppression, and what we can do to avoid its pitfalls.* "AI is not coming, it's here. If we answer the beautiful call inside these pages, *we can decide who we are going to be and how we're going to use technology in service of what it means to be fully human (…) To most of us, it seems like recent developments in artificial intelligence emerged out of nowhere to pose unprecedented threats to humankind*"). Italics added.

2353 European Commission, *Artificial Intelligence Act. Proposal for a regulation of the European Parliament and the Council laying down harmonised rules on Artificial Intelligence (Artificial Intelligence Act) and amending certain Union legislative acts*, 2021. See also: Curto, Georgina/Acosta, Mario Fernando Jojoa/Comim, Flavio/Garcia-Zapirain, Begoña, "Are AI systems biased against the poor? A machine learning analysis using Word2Vec and GloVe embeddings", *cit.*, pp. 617–632.

2354 Ess, Charles, *Digital media ethics*, London, Wiley, 2020, passim.

2355 See: Corbett-Davies, Sam/Goel, Sharad, "The Measure and Mismeasure of Fairness: a critical Review of Fair Machine Learning", *Cornell University Library*, 2018, pp. 3 and ff and passim (undertake laudable efforts to debunk algorithm biases that primarily target ethnic minorities, such as Hispanics and coloured people).

of Artificial Intelligence Natural Language Processing Systems[2359] alongside earnest attempts to adroitly indoctrinate algorithms to ferret out bias[2360] and act accordingly.

§§ Notwithstanding, there has a been a flurry of interest regarding algorithmic mathematical underpinnings,[2361] striving to map the path ahead towards[2362] the territory of fairness.[2363] But much more lies beyond that.

2356 Like a full-fledged and full-bodied legal apparatus comprising algorithmic fairness that casts aside algorithmic discrimination in legal settings. See: Kleinberg, Jon, et al., "Discrimination in the Age of Algorithms", *Journal of Legal Analysis*, 2018, pp. 114–174. See: Kleinberg, Jon, et al., "Algorithms as Discrimination Detectors", *Proceeds of the National Academy of Science*, Volume 117, 2020, pp. 30096–30110. Like tools that can debias racial discrimination within the remit of criminal justice – the essence of racial equity in criminal justice. See: Huq, Aziz, "Racial Equity in Algorithmic Criminal Justice", *Duke Law Journal*, Volume 68, 2022, pp. 1076–1134.

2357 Curto, Georgina/Acosta, Mario Fernando Jojoa/Comim, Flavio/Garcia-Zapirain, Begoña, "Are AI systems biased against the poor? A machine learning analysis using Word2Vec and GloVe embeddings", *cit.*, pp. 617–632 (618).

2358 See: Kirkpatrick, Keith, "It's not the Algorithm, it's the Data", *Communications of the ACM*, February 2017, Volume 60, n. ° 2, 2017 ("tools such as *PredPol* and *CommandCentral are inherently biased since they rely heavily on reported crimes data, which is often concentrated in areas that are heavily policed, thereby skewing statistics to overrepresent poor or minority communities.* "*We know that we have a history of racially biased policing in the United States, and that has fed into all the data that we have on where arrests have occurred, which crimes are more likely to occur in specific communities, and at which particular times*," says Jennifer Lynch, senior staff attorney at the Electronic Frontier Foundation. "*That's the data that's being fed into predictive policing algorithms*"). Italics added.

2359 Manzini, T./Chong, LY/Black, AW/Tsvetkov, Y., "Black is to Criminal as Caucasian is to Police: Detecting and Removing Multi-class Bias in Word Embeddings", *NAACL HLT 2019—2019 Conference North America Chapter Association Computer Linguist Human Language Technology—Proceedings of Conference*, 1:615–621, 2019; Garga, N./Schiebingerb, L./Jurafskyc, D/Zou, J, "Word embeddings quantify 100 years of gender and ethnic stereotypes", *Proceedings of the national academy of sciences* (PNAS), 2018, passim; Zhao, J., Khashabi, D./Khot, T et al, "Ethical-advice taker: do language models understand natural language interventions?", *arXiv.* https://doi.org/10.18653/v1/2021.fndings-acl.364, 2021; Bolukbasi T, Chang K-W, Saligrama V, et al, "Man is to Computer Programmer as Woman is to Homemaker? Debiasing Word Embeddings", 2016, arXiv:1607.06520v1; Nadeem, M./Bethke, A./Reddy, S., "Stereo Set: measuring stereotypical bias in pretrained language models", *ACL Anthology, Proceedings of the 59th annual meeting of the association for the computational linguistics and the 11th international joint conference on natural language processing*, Volume 1 (long papers), 2020, pp. 5356–5371.

2360 Jiang, L./Hwang, JD./Bhagavatula, C., et al, "Delphi: Towards Machine Ethics and Norms", https://arxiv.org/pdf/2110.07574v1, 2021, passim; Sap, M., Gabriel, S., Qin, L et al, "Social Bias Frames: Reasoning about Social and Power Implications of Language. Association of Computational Linguistics", *Proceedings of the 58th Annual Meeting of the Association of Computational Linguistics*, 2020, pp. 5477–5490.

2361 Maxwell, J./Tomlinson, J., *Experiments in Automating Immigration Systems.* Bristol: Bristol University Press, 2022, passim; Borgesius, FJ Zuiderveen, "Strengthening legal protection against discrimination by algorithms and artificial intelligence", *International Journal of Human Rights*, Volume 24, Issue 10, 2020, passim.

§§ Earnest attempts have also been made to devise machine learning algorithms fraught with a penchant to perform fairness-aware data-mining.[2364] But to no avail. Understandably, though not laudably, these endeavours have barely scratched the surface when it comes to ferret out actionable pathways to avert algorithmic unfairness, which, in turn, has lent new urgency to concerns according to which piecemeal and haphazard initiatives, albeit crammed with ambrosial intentions, will not suffice to soothe out social maladies—like sexism[2365] and racism[2366]—with which modern societies have been grappling for a long-winded span of time. Much more is needed in this regard.

[2362] Curto, Georgina/Acosta, Mario Fernando Jojoa/Comim, Flavio/Garcia-Zapirain, Begoña, "Are AI systems biased against the poor? A machine learning analysis using Word2Vec and GloVe embeddings", *cit.*, pp. 617–632 (618).

[2363] See on algorithmic fairness: Dwork, Cynthia/Hardt, Moritz/Pitassi, Tonian/Reingold/Zemel, Richard, "Fairness Through Awareness, Proceedings of the 3rd Innovations", *Theoretical Computer Science Conference*, 2012, https://dl.acm.org/doi/10.1145/2090236.2090255; [https://perma.cc/T2U3-TNQ6] (discussing an individual fairness approach to algorithmic fairness); Meharabi, Ninareh/Morstatter, Fred/Saxena, Nripsuta/Lerman, Kristina/Galstyan, Aram, "A Survey on Bias and Fairness in Machine Learning", *ACM Computing Survey*, Jul. 2022; Fuster, Andreas/Goldsmith-Pinkham, Paul/Tarun Ramadorai/Walther, Angsar, "Predictably Unequal? The Effects of Machine Learning on Credit Markets", *Journal of Finance*, Volume 76, 2022, passim (providing a description of the variation in interest rates across racial groups carried out by machine learning algorithms). See also: Hardt M, Price E, Srebro N, "Equality of opportunity in supervised learning", ArXiv ID: 1610.02413v1, 2016; Zarsky, Tal, "Transparency in Data Mining: From Theory to Practice", *Discrimination and Privacy in the Information Society: Data Mining and Profiling in Large Databases*, Bart Custers et al. eds., Belin, Springer, 2013; Kroll, Joshua A. et al., "Accountable Algorithms", *University of Pennsylvania Law Review*, Volume 165, 2017, passim; Green, B./Hu L., "The Myth in the Methodology: Towards a Recontextualization of Fairness in Machine Learning", *Machine Learning Debates Work 35th Internation Conference of Machine Learning*, 2018, passim.

[2364] See: Hajian, Sara Hajian et al., "Algorithmic Bias: From Discrimination Discovery to Fairness-aware Data Mining", *ACM SIGKDD International Conference on Knowledge Discovery and Data Mining*, Volume 22, 2125, 2016.

[2365] Hamilton, Melissa, "The sexist algorithm", *Behavioral Sciences and the Law*, Volume 37, Issue 2, Special Issue: the Use of Statistics in Criminal Cases, March–April 2019, 2019, pp. 1 and ff ("*Algorithmic risk assessment tools are informed by scientific research concerning which factors are predictive of recidivism and thus support the evidence-based practice movement in criminal justice.* Automated assessments of individualized risk (low, medium, high) *permit officials to make more effective management decisions. Computer-generated algorithms appear to be objective and neutral. But are these algorithms actually fair? The focus herein is on gender equity.* Studies confirm that women typically have far lower recidivism rates than men. *This differential raises the question of how well algorithmic outcomes fare in terms of predictive parity by gender.* This essay reports original research using a large dataset of offenders who were scored on the popular risk assessment tool COMPAS. *Findings indicate that COMPAS performs reasonably well at discriminating between recidivists and non-recidivists for men and women. Nonetheless, COMPAS algorithmic outcomes systemically overclassify women in higher risk groupings. Multiple measures of algorithmic equity and predictive accuracy are provided to support the conclusion that this algorithm is sexist*"). Italics added.

[2366] Jefferson, B., *Digitize and Punish: Racial Criminalization in the Digital Age*, Minnesota, University of Minnesota Press, 2020; Gross, Samuel R., Maurice Possley, and Kalara Stephens, "Race and Wrongful Convictions in the United States." National Registry of Exonerations, Newkirk Center for Science and Society, University of California-Irvine, 2017.

§§ To begin with, to successfully overhaul algorithmic injustice[2367] into algorithmic fairness,[2368] a fine-grained, comprehensive, full-fledged, and granular analysis is utterly needed,[2369] which is a far cry from the ongoing whirlwind of patchy solutions.[2370]

§§ On this account, it is crucially important to posit that Artificial Intelligence-embedded technologies[2371] reproduce, mimic and echoes[2372] the prejudices[2373] of

---

[2367] See: Ting-an Lin, "Democratizing AI" and the Concern of Algorithmic Injustice", *Philosophy and Technology*, Volume 37 (103), 2024, pp. 3–27. See also: Birhane, A., "Algorithmic injustice: A relational ethics approach", *Patterns*, 2 (2), 2021, pp. 1–9. Završnik, A. "Algorithmic justice: Algorithms and big data in criminal justice settings", *European Journal of Criminology*, 2019, passim.

[2368] Note, though, that algorithmic fairness lends itself to several incompatible standards. Whilst COMPAS falls short of meeting the baseline standards of "equal opportunity" and "equalized odds", it refrains itself from discriminating blacks from the prism of "predictive parity" nonetheless. A full-fledged analysis of the extant state of this scorching topic can be found in Hübner, Dietmar, "Two Kinds of Discrimination in AI-Based penal Decision-Making", *SIGKDD Explorations*, 2021. See: Part IV, This chapter, Sects. 4 .1.10.1–4.1.10.6 of this book (on biased algorithmic risk assessment in criminal procedure law settings, with a sharper focus on COMPAS). See: Part IV, This chapter, Sects. 4.1.1–4.1.1.1 of this book (on biased predictive policing).

[2369] See: Part V, Chap. 5, Sects. 5.1.2–5.1.6.2.1 of this book (on the thing-centred algorithmic decision-making propelled by a *Controllable* and *Interpretable* Machine Learning that weeds out *Algorithmic Dictatorship* and secures *Algorithmic Common Good*. It is worth recalling that the thing-centred algorithmic decision-making seeks to unwind the perils arising out of the lack of theoretical underpinnings facing the human-centred algorithmic decision-making, as extensively fleshed out Part III, Chap. 3, Sects. 3.1.4.3–3.1.4.4 of this book).

[2370] Curto, Georgina/Acosta, Mario Fernando Jojoa/Comim, Flavio/Garcia-Zapirain, Begoña, "Are AI systems biased against the poor? A machine learning analysis using Word2Vec and GloVe embeddings", *cit.*, pp. 617–632 (618).

[2371] Tsamados, A./Aggarwal, Nikita, Cowls, J. et al, "The ethics of algorithms: key problems and solutions", *Artificial Intelligence and Society*, Volume 1, 2021, pp. 1–16 (broach the much-touted, and much-acclaimed, ethics of algorithms underpinning artificial intelligence-embedded technologies).

[2372] See: *Tech, Bias and Housing Initiative, the Promise and Perils of Residential Proptech, Year 1, Research Summary Report, April 2023, TechEquity Collaborative*, p. 5 available at: https://techequity.us/wp-content/uploads/2023/04/TBHI-Y1-Research-Summary-Report.pdf (28.11.2024). ("*Residential Proptech also has the potential to exacerbate the bias inherent in our housing system. Its rise is due, in part, to the desperation felt by average home seekers. With a severely constrained housing supply, companies offering an easier pathway to homeownership may exploit communities that have been harmed by housing discrimination in the past. Opaque algorithms incorporate biased data into their decision-making processes, making it harder to enforce fair housing laws.* Residential Proptech companies often operate in a regulatory gray area, leaving consumers without the protections they would have from traditional housing regulatory systems. *As unprecedented capital investment flows into this space, venture-backed companies' winner-take-all approach to growth has the potential to exacerbate inequality rather than combat it*"). Italics added. See: Part IV, This chapter, Sects. 4.1.4–4.1.4.2.3 of this book. See: Part IV, This chapter, Sects. 4.1.4–4.1.4.2.1 of this book (on mortgage redlining). See: Part IV, This chapter, Sects. 4.1.2–4.1.3 of this book (on algorithmic credit scoring, consumer racism and credit card redlining). See: Part IV, This chapter, Sects. 4.1.4–4.1.2.3 of this book (on algorithmic redlining). See: Part IV, This chapter, Sect. 4.1.4.3 of this book (on "algorithmic redliking"). See: Part IV, This chapter, Sect. 4.1.3 of this book (on algorithmic prime-lining).

modern societies.[2374] Especially, albeit not exclusively, when algorithms[2375] are trained[2376] with rigged data[2377] that gets unsparingly and unapologetically baked into the subsequent process algorithmic decision-making.[2378] Worse still, in an eerily supervised manner,[2379] which defies commonsense, to say the least.

§§ Relatedly, such a bigoted frame of reference[2380] breeds algorithmic inequality,[2381] thereby shaping subsequent algorithmic decision-making alongside

---

[2373] Prejudiced algorithms are set to be brought to the fore as they are one foundational basis of *justice prédictive* so voguish in France. No surprise springs from the fact that prejudiced algorithms will feed *justice prédictive*—and that is something that you should not hold your breath for in that it boasts an exceedingly high likelihood to breed unfair outcomes. See: Garapon, Antoine, "Les enjeux de la justice predictive", *Juris-Classeur périodique*, Volume 31, 2018, passim. See also: Larret-Chahine, Louis, "Le droit isométrique: un nouveau paradigme juridique né de la justice prédictive», *Archives de Philosophie du Droit*, Volume 60, 2018, pp. 287 and ff and passim.

[2374] Allen, James, "The Color of Algorithms: An Analysis and Proposed Research Agenda Deterring Algorithmic Redlining", *Fordham Urban Law Journal*, Volume 46, 2019, pp. 219–234 (229–234) (discussing how historical mortgage redlining greatly swayed modern algorithms generated by massive batches of data sets that consist of decades of information built on exclusion and racial discrimination in the purview of financing, marketing, and housing). See: Part IV, This chapter, Sects. 4.1.4–4.1.2.3 of this book.

[2375] Mittelstadt, BD./Allo, P./Taddeo M. et al, "The ethics of algorithms: mapping the debate", *Big Data and Society*, 2016.

[2376] See: West, SM./Whittaker, M./Crawford, K., "Discriminating systems gender, race, and power in AI", AI Now Institute, 2019. But see: But see: Barocas, Solon/Selbst, Andrew D., "Big Data's Disparate Impact", *California Law Review*, Volume 104, 2016, p. 699 (discussing how discriminatory data mining is analogous to unintentional disparate impact analysis); Bornstein, Stepanhie, "Antidiscriminatory Algorithms", *Alabama Law Review*, Volume 70, 2018, p. 535 (positing that algorithmic discrimination at large could fall under the all-embracing umbrella of anti-stereotyping category within Title VII's disparate treatment).

[2377] It is often contended that machine learning algorithms engender their own models to forecast future outcomes on the basis of analysis of training data. See: Mittelstadt, Brent Daniel/Taddeo, Patrick Allo, Mariarosaria/Wachter, Sandra/Floridi, Luciano, "The Ethics of Algorithms: Mapping the Debate", *Big Data & Society*, July-Dec. 2016, 2016, p. 3.

[2378] See: Barocas, Solon/Selbst, Andrew D., "Big Data's Disparate Impact", *California Law Review*, Volume 104, 2016, pp. 671–682 (discussing how data is often flawed, rigged, incomplete, imperfect and therefore algorithms inherit the prejudice of the original decision makers). But see: Citron, Danielle Keats/Pasquale, Frank, "The Scored Society: Due Process for Automated Predictions", *Washington Law Review*, Volume 89, 2014, pp. 1, 4–5 (highlighting how human beings programming automated systems is directly conducive to, and leads, to fundamentally inaccurate results since the source code, predictive algorithms and datasets may encompass human biases which, in turn, have a disparate impact on historically disadvantaged groups). But see: Bornstein, Stepanhie, "Antidiscriminatory Algorithms", *Alabama Law Review*, Volume 70, 2018, pp. 519, 524–528 (contending, however, that the tagged "facially neutral" algorithms producing discriminatory outcomes should be quashed).

[2379] Radford, A./Wu, J./Child, R. et al, "Language models are unsupervised multitask learners", *Technical Report*;

[2380] Crawford, Kate/Schultz, Jason, "Big Data and Due Process: Toward a Framework to Redress Predictive Privacy Harms", *Boston College Law Review*, Volume 55, 2014, pp. 93, 99–101 (pinpointing pathways through which predictive analytic tools perpetuate discriminatory practices).

[2381] See: Wonyoung, So, "Which Information Matters? Measuring Landlord Assessment of Tenant Screening Reports", *Housing Policy Debate*, Volume 33, n.°6, 2023, pp. 1484–1510 (1502) (arguing

accompanying development[2382] procedures,[2383] which, in turn, derails/sullies algorithmic fairness.[2384] For that reason alone, fairness, a beacon of justice whose shining light should illuminate regular decision-making, is not amenable to be automated.[2385]

§§ Compellingly, Artificial Intelligence-embedded technologies are not amenable to be haphazardly approached from the prism of ethics only. Suffice to say that a purely technical approach falls conspicuously short of encompassing the multifarious problems arising out of algorithm decision-making, owing to the fact that such a piecemeal approach carries a tiny impact on a myriad of[2386] computer-run inequalities[2387] that are becoming increasingly entangled with algorithmic decision-making that keeps pushing the boundaries of fairness.[2388]

---

that landlords display *automation bias* as the "*study finds that landlords tend to rely more on the automated system's judgment: when a report noted that a tenant was either medium or high risk, landlords showed a higher tendency toward rejection, or, if conditionally accepted, they imposed a higher security deposit. This indicates that tenant screening services' risk scoring may critically affect landlords' decision-making. Given that there is no regulation pertaining to producing and deploying such algorithms, and 1502 W. SO given the inherent inaccuracies of eviction data (Porton* et al., *2021) and widespread, serial eviction filings (Garboden & Rosen, 2019), particularly automatic eviction filings activated by digitized property management systems and large, corporate landlords* (Fields, 2022; Gomory, 2022; Immergluck et al., 2020), *tenant screening services very likely contribute to perpetuating algorithmic inequality (Eubanks, 2018) by denying qualified applicants—disproportionately from protected groups—access to housing*"). Italics added. See: Part IV, This chapter, Sects. 4.1.4–4.1.4.2.3 of this book. See also: Rudinger, R./Naradowsky, J./Leonard, B./Durme, B Van, "Gender Bias in Conference Resolution", *NAACL HLT 2018—2018 Conference North American Chapter Association Computer Linguist Human Language Technology—Proceedings of Conference*, 2018, 2:8–14. See: Part IV, This chapter, Sects. 4.1.4–4.1.4.2.1 of this book (on mortgage redlining). See: Part IV, This chapter, Sects. 4.1.2–4.1.4.3 of this book (on algorithmic credit scoring, consumer racism and credit card redlining). See: Part IV, This chapter, Sects. 4.1.4–4.1.4.2.3 of this book (on algorithmic redlining). See: Part IV, This chapter, Sect. 4.1.4.3 of this book (on "algorithmic redliking"). See: Part IV, This chapter, Sect. 4.1.3 of this book (on algorithmic prime-lining).

[2382] Note, though, that, theoretically, one should not shy away, or veer away, from bifurcating/splitting the "prediction" issue from the "decision" issue. See: Corbett-Davies, Sam/Pierson, Emma/Feller, Avi/Goel, Sharad Goel/Huq, Aziz, "Algorithmic Decision Making and the Cost of Fairness", *Proceedings of the 23rd ACM SIGKDD International Conference on Knowledge Discovery and Data Mining* (Ass'n for Computing Machinery ed., 2017), 2017, passim.

[2383] Vakkuri, V./Kemell, KK./Jantunen M./Abrahamsson, P., "This is Just a Prototype": How Ethics Are Ignored in Software Startup Like Environments", *Lectures Notes Bus Inf Process 383 LNBIP*, 2020, 195–210; Floridi, Luciano, "Translating principles into practices of digital ethics: five risks of being unethical", *Philosophy and Technology*, 322(32), 2019, pp. 185–193.

[2384] Hellman, Deborah, "Measuring Algorithmic Fairness", *Virginia Law Review*, Volume 106, 2020, pp. 811 and ff and passim. See also: Barocas, Solon/Hardt, Moritz/Narayanan, Arvind, "Fairness in Machine Learning: Limitations and Opportunities", 2018, passim.

[2385] Wachter, Sandra/Mittelstadt, Brent/Russell, Chris, "Why Fairness Cannot be Automated: Bridging the Gap Between EU Non-Discrimination Law and AI", *Computer Law & Security Review*, Volume 41, 2021, 105567.

[2386] Curto, Georgina/Acosta, Mario Fernando Jojoa/Comim, Flavio/Garcia-Zapirain, Begoña, "Are AI systems biased against the poor? A machine learning analysis using Word2Vec and GloVe embeddings", *cit.*, pp. 617–632 (618).

§§ Note, though, that grasping fairness is a vital, but rather elusive, task. Pundits accordingly aver that stakeholders can easily become enmeshed on the shifting sands of fairness since the former has been poorly understood and scantily latched on. Relatedly, a cohort of scholars[2389] parsed a staggering number of scholarly papers (146) studying bias in *Natural Processing Language Systems* (published before May 2020)[2390] only to find out that results yielded, fairness wise, are far from being buoying. Thereupon, the conclusion was one which such papers have fallen notably short of clutching the essence of bias outside the catch-all umbrella of *Natural*

[2387] Zajko, M, "Conservative AI and social inequality: conceptualizing alternatives to bias through social theory", *Artificial Intelligence and Society*, 36, 2021, 1047–1056.

[2388] See: *Tech, Bias and Housing Initiative, the Promise and Perils of Residential Proptech, Year 1, Research Summary Report, April 2023, TechEquity Collaborative*, p. 5 available at: https://techequity.us/wp-content/uploads/2023/04/TBHI-Y1-Research-Summary-Report.pdf (28.11.2024). ("*Residential Proptech also has the potential to exacerbate the bias inherent in our housing system. Its rise is due, in part, to the desperation felt by average home seekers. With a severely constrained housing supply, companies offering an easier pathway to homeownership may exploit communities that have been harmed by housing discrimination in the past. Opaque algorithms incorporate biased data into their decision-making processes, making it harder to enforce fair housing laws.* Residential Proptech companies often operate in a regulatory gray area, leaving consumers without the protections they would have from traditional housing regulatory systems. *As unprecedented capital investment flows into this space, venture-backed companies' winner-take-all approach to growth has the potential to exacerbate inequality rather than combat it*"). Italics added. See: Part IV, This chapter, Sects. 4.1.4–4.1.4.2.3 of this book.

[2389] Blodgett SL, Barocas S, III HD, Wallach H, "Language (technology) is power: a critical survey of "bias", *NLP. ACL anthology, Proceedings of the 8th annual meeting of the association of computational linguistics*, 2020. pp 5454–5476. See on the fundamental tenets of Natural Language Processing (NLP): Pennington, J./Socher, R./Manning, CD., "GloVe: global vectors for word representation. Empirical Methods in Natural Language Processing (EMNLP). ACL Anthology", *Proceedings of the 2014 conference on empirical methods in natural language processing*, 2014, pp. 1532–1534; See: By A, Silberg J, Manyika, J, *Notes from the AI frontier: tackling bias in AI (and in humans)*, McKinsey Global Institute Caliskan, 2019; Bryson, JJ, Narayanan, A., "Semantics derived automatically from language corpora contain human-like biases", *Science*, 356 (6334), 2017, pp. 183–186; Camacho-Collados, J., Pilehvar, MT, "Embeddings in natural language processing", *ACL anthology, Proceedings of the 28th international conference on computational linguistics*, 2020, pp. 10–15; Bolukbasi T, Chang K-W, Saligrama V, et al, "Man is to Computer Programmer as Woman is to Homemaker? Debiasing Word Embeddings", arXiv:1607.06520v1, 2016; Radford, A./Wu, J./Child, R. et al, "Language models are unsupervised multitask learners", *Technical Report*; Rudinger, R./Naradowsky, J./Leonard, B./Durme, B Van, "Gender Bias in Conference Resolution", *NAACL HLT 2018—2018 Conference North American Chapter Association Computer Linguist Human Language Technology—Proceedings of Conference*, 2018, 2:8–14; Sap, M., Gabriel, S., Qin, L et al, "Social Bias Frames: Reasoning about Social and Power Implications of Language. Association of Computational Linguistics", *Proceedings of the 58th Annual Meeting of the Association of Computational Linguistics*, 2020, pp. 5477–5490; Nadeem, M./Bethke, A./Reddy, S., "Stereo Set: measuring stereotypical bias in pretrained language models", *ACL Anthology, Proceedings of the 59th annual meeting of the association for the computational linguistics and the 11th international joint conference on natural language processing*, Volume 1 (long papers), 2020, pp. 5356–5371.

[2390] Card, D/Smith, NA", On consequentialism and fairness", *Frontiers of Artificial Intelligence*, Volume 3:34, 2020.

Processing Language Systems.[2391] Scholars accordingly propounded that literature on this sizzling hot topic (fairness) within the long arch of machine learning[2392] relies heavily on whimsical and groundless assumptions.[2393]

§§ To forestall such perceived shortcomings/pitfalls, there has been a groundswell of support emphasizing the dire need of an increasing involvement of social sciences[2394] inasmuch bias must be fleshed out in the «onlife».[2395] It should not therefore come as a bewildering surprise that procedural justice[2396] is the lens

---

2391 Curto, Georgina/Acosta, Mario Fernando Jojoa/Comim, Flavio/Garcia-Zapirain, Begoña, "Are AI systems biased against the poor? A machine learning analysis using Word2Vec and GloVe embeddings", *cit.*, pp. 617–632 (618).

2392 Card, D./Smith, NA", On consequentialism and fairness", *Frontiers of Artificial Intelligence*, Volume 3:34, 2020, passim.

2393 Curto, Georgina/Acosta, Mario Fernando Jojoa/Comim, Flavio/Garcia-Zapirain, Begoña, "Are AI systems biased against the poor? A machine learning analysis using Word2Vec and GloVe embeddings", *cit.*, pp. 617–632 (618).

2394 Tyler, Tom, "Methodology in Legal Research", in: *Utrecht Law Review*, Volume 13, Issue 3, 2017, pp. 130–131 ("*Accurate facts plus good legal rules lead to substantive justice.* This is the normative framework of right and wrong defined by traditional legal analysis. *Risk analysis is a nice example of the benefits of empiricism because studies suggest that the use of empirical methods to assess future dangerousness is more accurate than is the use of human intuition. It is better to use a formula when making a legal decision that involves estimates of someone's likely future conduct than it is to rely upon the impressions of judges or prosecutors*" (...) "*The legal system relies on predictions about people's likely future behaviour at many points in the system*: pretrial detention; sentencing; parole and probation; etc. And it has been used with a variety of special populations, including juveniles; the mentally ill; and sexual predators. A key reason to use such quantitative methods is that they are better able to predict future behaviour and as a consequence the many points in the system at which judgments are made—pre-trial detention; sentencing; parole—are better able to enact justice for both the innocent and the guilty. *The focus by social scientists upon helping to identify and use facts in ways that produce more accurate decisions fits well with the argument that the aims of justice are best served when they are based upon accurate factual information. Accuracy, in turn is enhanced by the use of empirical methods. Facts are sought that can guide the application of normative legal principles*"). Italics added. See also: By A, Silberg J, Manyika, J, *Notes from the AI frontier: tackling bias in AI (and in humans)*, McKinsey Global Institute Caliskan, 2019; Green, B./Hu L., "The Myth in the Methodology: Towards a Recontextualization of Fairness in Machine Learning", *Machine Learning Debates Work 35th Internation Conference of Machine Learning*, 2018, passim; Kusner, MJ., Loftus, JR., "The long road to fairer algorithms", *Nature*, Volume 578, 2020, pp. 34–36.

2395 Floridi, Luciano, "The onlife manifesto: being human in a hyperconnected era", *Onlife Manifesto Being Human in a Hyperconnected Era*, 2015, https://doi.org/10.1007/978-3-319-040 93-6

2396 See: Tyler, Tom R./Lind, Edgar Allan, "Procedural justice", *Handbook of law and social science*, J. Sanders/V.L. Hamilton (Eds.), New York, Plenum Press, 2001, pp. 65–92; Tyler, Tom R./Smith, H. J./Huo, Y. J., "Member diversity and leadership effectiveness: Procedural justice, social identity, and group dynamics", *Advances in group processes*, B. Markovsky (Ed.), Greenwich, CT: JAI Press, Volume 13, 1996, pp. 33–68; Tyler, Tom R./Lind, Edgar Allan/Huo, Yuen J., "Cultural Values and Authority Relations: The Psychology of Conflict Resolution Across Cultures", in: *Psychology, Public Policy and Law*, Volume 6, n.º 4, 2000, pp. 1138–1163 (parsing the relationship between high and low levels of power distance values and the relational model of authority); Leung, K./Lind, Edgar Allan, "Procedural justice and culture: Effects of culture, gender, and investigator status on

through which algorithmic decision-making[2397] should be seen in the age of Artificial Intelligence-embedded technologies.[2398]

§§ Beneath the foam of ideas seeking to debias[2399] Artificial intelligence-embedded technologies lie the variegated illusion that the latter is neutral.[2400]

---

procedural preferences", *Journal of Personality and Social Psychology,* Volume 50, 1986, pp. 1134–1140; Leung, K./Morris, K. W., "Justice through the lens of culture and ethnicity", *Handbook of Law and Social Science: Justice,* Sanders, J./Hamilton, V. L., (Eds.), New York, Plenum, 2001, pp. 343–378; Lind, Edgar Allan/ Tyler, Tom R., *The social psychology of procedural justice*, New York, Plenum Press, 1988, passim; Lind, Edgar Allan/ Tyler, Tom R./Huo, Y.J., "Procedural context and culture: Variation in the antecedents of procedural justice judgments", *Journal of Personality and Social Psychology,* Volume 73, 1997, pp. 767–780; Zimmerman, Nourit/Tyler, Tom R., "Between Access to Counsel and Access to Justice: A Psychological Perspective", *Fordham Urban Law Journal*, Volume 37, 2010, pp. 473–488 (contends that "evaluations about neutrality, *trust*, and respect for the legal system as a whole"—satisfaction with the *procedural fairness* and *procedural justice* will not lag far behind).

2397 But see: Burk, Dan L., "Algorithmic Fair Use", *University of Chicago Law Review*, Volume 86, 2019, pp. 283–288 (asserts that algorithmic "*fair use carries with it the disadvantage of ex ante uncertainty*; no one can be entirely certain in advance how a court will weigh the four factors, *and hence there is always some apprehension that a use may be found infringing rather than fair*"). Italics added.

2398 From the prism of social sciences, warped algorithms accomplish nothing but the impairment of procedural justice. See: Thibaut, John/ Walker, Laurens, *Procedural Justice: A Psychological Analysis.* Hillsdale, N.J.: Lawrence Erlbaum Associates, 1975, pp. 1–150 (procedural justice is tightly interlocked to raising the levels of fairness in legal settings. Absent of which procedural fairness is to mar. Lawmakers must not lose sight of such assertion). Converging: Lind, Edgar Allan/ Tyler, Tom R., *The Social Psychology of Procedural Justice.* New York: Springer, 1988, pp. 208 ff (emphasizing that perceptions of justice being justly and correctly served enhances exponentially citizens' perception of provider legitimacy). Tyler, Tom R., "The Psychology of Procedural Justice: A Test of the Group-Value Model", *Journal of Personality and Social Psychology*, Volume 57, 1989, p. 830 (reports that in any procedure "several non-control issues—the *neutrality* of the decision-making procedure, trust in the 3rd party, and the information the experience communicates about social standing—influence both procedural preferences and judgments of procedural justice"). See also: Simmons, Ric, "Big Data and Procedural Justice: Legitimizing Algorithms in the Criminal Justice System", *Ohio State Journal of Criminal Law*, Volume 15, 2018, pp. 576 and ff and passim.

2399 But see: Altenburger, Kristen M./Ho, Daniel E., "When Algorithms Import Private Bias into Public Enforcement: The Promise and Limitations of Statistical Debiasing Solutions", *Journal of Institutional & Theoretical Economics*, Volume 175, 2019, pp. 97–98 (calls for a "debias predictive algorithms" to assuage racist and/or biased, doctored and bigoted algorithms nevertheless). See also: Hamilton, Melissa, "The Biased Algorithm: Evidence of Disparate Impact on Hispanics", *American Criminal Law Review*, Volume 56, 2019, pp. 1553 and ff and passim.

2400 But see: Benjamin, Ruha, *Race After Technology: Abolitionist Tools for the New Jim Code*, New York, Polity, 2019, pp. 1–172 (7) (discussing that Artificial Intelligence-embedded technologies are viewed as iron-clad tools of objectivity and devoid of any biases whatsoever). Ruha Benjamin accordingly contends that "the employment of new technologies that reflect and reproduce existing inequities but that are promoted and perceived as more objective or progressive than the discriminatory systems of a previous era"). But see also: Hurley, Mikella/Adebayo, Julius, "Credit Scoring in the Era of Big Data", *Yale Journal of Law and Technology*, Volume 18, 2016, p. 149 ("*these tools may furthermore obscure discriminatory and subjective lending policies behind a single "objective" score (...) sophisticated algorithms may combine facially neutral data points and treat them as proxies for immutable characteristics such as race or gender, thereby circumventing existing non-discrimination laws and systematically denying credit access to certain groups. Finally, big-data*

Yet this bootless and unwarranted assumption could not be farther away from the truth. Cutting-edge and state-of-the-art technology has been shadily created, devised, and deployed to advance a hidden agenda whose overriding goal is to staunchly protect White privilege[2401] while further chastising racialised communities[2402] through countless traps[2403] cunningly/mischievously crafted to keep them

tools may allow online payday lenders to target the most vulnerable consumers and lure them into debt traps"). Italics added. But see also: Bornstein, Stepanhie, "Antidiscriminatory Algorithms", *Alabama Law Review*, Volume 70, 2018, pp. 519, 524–528 (contending, however, that the tagged "facially neutral" algorithms producing discriminatory outcomes should be quashed). See also: Farina, M./Lavazza, A., *Philosophy, expertise, and the myth of* neutrality, Routledge Studies in Contemporary Philosophy, London, Routledge, 2024.

[2401] Roithmayr, Daria, *Reproducing Racism: How everyday choices lock in White Advantage*, New York, New York University Press, 2014, pp. 1–272 ("*Argues that racial inequality reproduces itself automatically over time because early unfair advantage for whites has paved the way for continuing advantage. This book is designed to change the way we think about racial inequality* (...) *Legal scholar Daria Roithmayr provocatively argues that racial inequality lives on because white advantage functions as a powerful self-reinforcing monopoly, reproducing itself automatically from generation to generation even in the absence of intentional discrimination* (...) With penetrating insight, Roithmayr *locates the engine of white monopoly in positive feedback loops that connect the dramatic disparity of Jim Crow to modern racial gaps in jobs, housing and education. Wealthy white neighborhoods fund public schools that then turn out wealthy white neighbors. Whites with lucrative jobs informally refer their friends, who refer their friends, and so on. Roithmayr concludes that racial inequality might now be locked in place, unless policymakers immediately take drastic steps to dismantle this oppressive system*"). Italics added. This book points out how White privilege is perpetuated throughout generations through residential segregation (*mortgage redlining*), abhorrent nepotism, and other bemoaning social practices that pester modern societies). See: Part IV, This chapter, Sects. 4.1.4–4.1.4.2.3 of this book. See: Part IV, This chapter, Sects. 4.1.4–4.1.4.2.1 of this book (on mortgage redlining). See: Part IV, This chapter, Sects. 4.1.2–4.1.4.3 of this book (on algorithmic credit scoring, consumer racism and credit card redlining). See: Part IV, This chapter, Sects. 4.1.4–4.1.4.2.3 of this book (on algorithmic redlining). See: Part IV, This chapter, Sect. 4.1.4.3 of this book (on "algorithmic redliking"). See: Part IV, This chapter, Sect. 4.1.3 of this book (on algorithmic prime-lining).

[2402] Lipsitz, George, *The Possessive Investment in Whiteness: How White People Profit from Identity Politics*, Philadelphia, Pennsylvania, Temple University Press; 1st edition (July 13, 2018), 2018, pp. 1–448 ("*George Lipsitz's classic book The Possessive Investment in Whiteness argues that public policy and private prejudice work together to create a possessive investment in whiteness that is responsible for the racialized hierarchies of our society*"). Italics added. See: Part IV, This chapter, Sects. 4.1.4–4.1.4.2.3 of this book.

[2403] Havard, Cassandra Jones, "On the Take": The Black Box of Credit Scoring and Mortgage Discrimination", *Boston University Public Interest Law Journal*, 2011, pp. 239 and ff and passim (discussing that subprime lending was undoubtably geared toward minority communities, aiming to enmesh them on the trap of excessive debt). See also: Ards, Sheila D./Myers, Samuel L. Myers, "The Color of Money: Bad Credit, Wealth, and Race", *American Behavioral Scientist*, Volume 45, 2001, pp. 223–238 (debunks the deep-seated myth according to which Blacks are big spenders and thus unworthy of creditworthiness, which stands as an irksome social bias in dire need of quashing). See also: Wonyoung, So, "Which Information Matters? Measuring Landlord Assessment of Tenant Screening Reports", *Housing Policy Debate*, Volume 33, n. ° 6, 2023, pp. 1484–1510 (1484) ("*landlords use blanket screening policies, that they conflate the existence of tenant records with outcomes (e.g., eviction filings with executed evictions), and that they display, on average, tendencies toward automation bias that are influenced by the risk assessments and scores presented by tenant screening reports.* I argue that maintaining blanket screening policies and *automation*

(Blacks,[2404] Latinos and so forth) poor,[2405] uneducated,[2406] disfranchised,[2407] hopeless[2408] home seekers,[2409] and obnoxiously obedient.[2410] Scholars have, however, expounded other views in this regard. It is noteworthy that amongst them stands the

---

bias, combined with the downstream effects of creating and *using racially biased eviction and criminal records, means that people of color will inevitably experience disproportionate exclusion from rental housing due to perceived "risk" on the part of landlords*"). Italics added. See: Part IV, This chapter, Sects. 4.1.4–4.1.4.2.3 of this book.

2404 See: Kirkpatrick, Keith, "It's not the Algorithm, it's the Data", *Communications of the ACM*, February 2017, Volume 60, n. ° 2, 2017 ("Critics, however, say tools such as PredPol and Command-Central *are inherently biased since they rely heavily on reported crimes data, which is often concentrated in areas that are heavily policed, thereby skewing statistics to overrepresent poor or minority communities*. "*We know that we have a history of racially biased policing in the United States, and that has fed into all the data that we have on where arrests have occurred, which crimes are more likely to occur in specific communities, and at which particular times*," says Jennifer Lynch, senior staff attorney at the Electronic Frontier Foundation. "*That's the data that's being fed into predictive policing algorithms*"). Italics added.

2405 Derenoncourt, Ellora/Kim, Chi Hyun/Kuhn, Moritz/Schularik, Moritz, "The Wealth of Two Nations: The U.S. Racial Wealth Gap, 1860–2020", *The Quarterly Journal of Economics*, Volume 139, Issue 2, 2024, p. 741 ("*A large class of commonly discussed policies for reducing racial wealth inequality seeks to reduce gaps in income, savings, and capital gains*. These include policies that encourage financial diversification or stock equity holdings among Black households; policies aimed at financial literacy and retirement or savings behavior; or policies aimed at improving educational and labor market outcomes of Black Americans through improved school quality or reductions in discrimination. *Yet on a realistic note, our simulation in Section IV.A shows that even if wealth accumulation conditions had been equal since 1870, the wealth gap would still be 3 to 1 today, and full convergence would be more than 200 years away. Put differently: to close the racial wealth gap in the immediate term* via *flow parameters, Black Americans would need a substantial positive lead over whites, not "just" more equality*"). Italics added.

2406 Pierce, C., "W.E.B. du bois and caste education: Racial capitalist schooling from reconstruction to Jim Crow", *American Educational Research Journal*, 54 (1_Suppl.), 2017, pp. 23S-47S. See also: Sunstein, Cass R., "Algorithms, Correcting Biases", *Social Research*, Volume 86, 2019, pp. 449–506 (this famed author tagged disparate impact as "disturbing in itself, in the sense that a practice that produces such an impact helps entrench something like a caste system").

2407 See: Bartlett, Robert/Morse, Adair/Wallace, Nancy/Stanton, Richard, "Algorithmic Discrimination and Input Accountability Under the Civil Rights Acts", *Berkeley Technology Law Journal*, Volume 36, 2021, pp. 675–736 (675) ("the disproportionate burden of COVID-19 among communities of color and a necessary renewed attention to racial inequalities have lent new urgency to concerns that algorithmic decision-making can lead to unintentional discrimination against members of historically marginalized groups").

2408 See: Glantz, Aaron/Martinez, Emmanuel, "For People of Color, Banks are Shutting the Door to Homeownership", *Reveal*, February 15, 2018, available at: https://ibw21.org/news/people-color-banks-shutting-door-homeownership/ (access: 4.11.2024) ("*Fifty years after the federal Fair Housing Act banned racial discrimination in lending, African Americans and Latinos continue to be routinely denied conventional mortgage loans at rates far higher than their white counterparts*. This modern-day redlining persisted in 61 metro areas even when controlling for applicants' income, loan amount and neighborhood, according to a mountain of Home Mortgage Disclosure Act records analyzed by Reveal from The Center for Investigative Reporting. *The yearlong analysis, based on 31 million records, relied on techniques used by leading academics, the Federal Reserve and Department of Justice to identify lending disparities. It found a pattern of troubling denials for people of color across the country, including in major metropolitan areas such as Atlanta, Detroit,*

sweeping idea according to which technology has been crafted to ensure a square alignment with the extant scientific, social, political-laden values.[2411]

§§ Rivetingly, though, if one cares to drill into, and shine a keen light on, the underlying nature of bias[2412] it becomes vividly clear that is painstakingly difficult to draw a hard line between disparate treatment[2413] and disparate impact[2414] since

---

Philadelphia, St. Louis and San Antonio. African Americans faced the most resistance in Southern cities — Mobile, Alabama; Greenville, North Carolina; and Gainesville, Florida — and Latinos in Iowa City, Iowa. *No matter their location, loan applicants told similar stories, describing an uphill battle with loan officers who they said seemed to be fishing for a reason to say no*"). Italics added.

[2409] Allen, James, "The Color of Algorithms: An Analysis and Proposed Research Agenda Deterring Algorithmic Redlining", *Fordham Urban Law Journal*, Volume 46, 2019, pp. 219–234 (229–234) (discussing how historical mortgage redlining greatly swayed modern algorithms generated by massive batches of data sets that consist of decades of information built on exclusion and racial discrimination in the purview of financing, marketing, and housing). See: Part IV, This chapter, Sects. 4.1.4–4.1.4.2.3 of this book. See also: *Tech, Bias and Housing Initiative, the Promise and Perils of Residential Proptech, Year 1, Research Summary Report, April 2023, TechEquity Collaborative*, p. 5 available at: https://techequity.us/wp-content/uploads/2023/04/TBHI-Y1-Research-Summary-Report.pdf (28.11.2024). ("*With a severely constrained housing supply, companies offering an easier pathway to homeownership may exploit communities that have been harmed by housing discrimination in the past. Opaque algorithms incorporate biased data into their decision-making processes, making it harder to enforce fair housing laws.* Residential Proptech companies often operate in a regulatory gray area, leaving consumers without the protections they would have from traditional housing regulatory systems. *As unprecedented capital investment flows into this space, venture-backed companies' winner-take-all approach to growth has the potential to exacerbate inequality rather than combat it*"). Italics added.

[2410] Packard, Jerald M., *American Nightmare: The History of Jim Crow*, Broadway, New York, St. Martin's Press; First Edition, 2002, pp. 1–304 ("*For a hundred years after the end of the Civil War, a quarter of all Americans lived under a system of legalized segregation called Jim Crow. Together with its rigidly enforced canon of racial "etiquette," these rules governed nearly every aspect of life-and outlined draconian punishments for infractions. The purpose of Jim Crow was to keep African Americans subjugated at a level as close as possible to their former slave status*"). Italics added.

[2411] Curto, Georgina/Acosta, Mario Fernando Jojoa/Comim, Flavio/Garcia-Zapirain, Begoña, "Are AI systems biased against the poor? A machine learning analysis using Word2Vec and GloVe embeddings", *cit.*, pp. 617–632 (618).

[2412] Citron, Danielle Keats/Pasquale, Frank A., "The Scored Society: Due Process for Automated Predictions", *Washington Law Review*, Volume 89, 2014, pp. 1–34 (arguing that "[a]*dvocates applaud the removal of human beings and their flaws from the assessment process*," but arguing that bias remains "[*b*]*ecause human beings program predictive algorithms, their biases and values are embedded into the software's instructions*"). Italics added. See: Part IV, This chapter, Sects. 4.1.4–4.1.4.2.3 of this book.

[2413] Howard, Justin D Howard, "Refashioning the Disparate Treatment and Disparate Impact Doctrines in Theory and in Practice", *Howard Law Journal*, Volume 41, 1998, passim; Seiner, Joseph, "Disentangling Disparate Impact and Disparate Treatment: Adapting the Canadian Approach", *Yale Law & Policy Review*, Volume 25, 2006; Primus, Richard "The Future of Disparate Impact", *Michigan Law Review*, Volume 108, 2010, pp. 1340 and ff and passim; Stephanopoulos, Nicholas O. "Disparate Impact, Unified Law", *Yale Law Journal*, Volume 128, 2019, pp. 1566–1595.

[2414] See: Sunstein, Cass R., "Algorithms, Correcting Biases", *Social Research*, Volume 86, 2019, pp. 449–506 (this famed author tagged disparate impact as "disturbing in itself, in the sense that a practice that produces such an impact helps entrench something like a caste system"). See also:

the fermentation of biases is an eminently inward process,[2415] thereby rendering any efforts to visualize it dispiritingly futile.[2416] Which is of paramount importance in this regard in that is something that should be neither deemphasised nor downplayed.[2417] Let alone glossed over.

§§ To the extent that a fast-paced live prevents human beings from having enough time to understand the tiniest detail of every single person,[2418] the information related with the group of whom an individual belongs to will be stored into amorphous/

Barocas, Solon/Selbst, Andrew D., "Big Data's Disparate Impact", *California Law Review*, Volume 104, 2016, p. 699 (discussing how discriminatory data mining is analogous to unintentional disparate impact analysis); Bornstein, Stepanhie, "Antidiscriminatory Algorithms", *Alabama Law Review*, Volume 70, 2018, p. 535 (positing that algorithmic discrimination at large could fall under the all-embracing umbrella of anti-stereotyping category within Title VII's disparate treatment). Grimmelmann, James/Westreich, Daniel, "Incomprehensible Discrimination", *California Law Review Online*, Volume 7, 2017, pp 170 and ff and passim. This exciting piece of research revolves around as a vignette and mock judicial opinion, focusing on fictional case (an employment-based AI employed in the fictional universe of the movie Zootopia) under a specific legal regime (Title VII). It ultimately solves this fictional case by drawing a difference between *proxy discrimination* and *disparate impact* p. 70 ("The problem is that there is no explanation in the record as to which of these two correlations, if either, is causal. It may be that the factors directly measure applicant characteristics that determine success in the challenging and dangerous field of police work, and that those characteristics happen to be unequally distributed in our diverse society. It may also be that these factors are instead measuring applicants' species and that they measure likely job performance only because they are identifying species in an applicant pool where the relevant characteristics are unequally distributed."); Citron, Danielle Keats/Pasquale, Frank, "The Scored Society: Due Process for Automated Predictions", *Washington Law Review*, Volume 89, 2014, pp. 1, 4–5 (highlighting how human beings programming automated systems is directly conducive to, and leads, to fundamentally inaccurate results since the source code, predictive algorithms and datasets may encompass human biases which, in turn, have a disparate impact on historically disadvantaged groups).

2415 In spite of the widely accepted conceptual differences between intent-based and effect-based theories of disparate impact, both approaches often dovetail seamlessly. As far as the fair lending goes, the definition of disparate impact cases is somewhat shallow, nomadic, and erratic, and dispiritingly vague. Note, though, that the loan officer's discretion is directly conducive to exceedingly higher rates of rejections for members of racial minorities. See: Ayres, Ian/Klein, Gary/West, Jeffrey, "The Rise and (Potential) Fall of Disparate Impact Lending Litigation", *Evidence and Innovation in Housing Law and Policy*, Fenncll, Lcc Annc/Keys, Benajmin J. (Editors), Cambridge, Cambridge University Press, 2017, pp. 231–254.

2416 However, Schwemm and Taren avowedly contend that some cases might somewhat be deemed hybrid impact/intention cases. See: Schwemm, Robert G./Taren, Jeffrey L., "Discretionary Pricing, Mortgage Discrimination, and the Fair Housing Act", *The Harvard Civil Rights-Civil Liberties Law Review*, 2010, passim. The conduct being granularly parsed is discretion ascribed to brokers—which is considered by many stakeholders a harmless neutral practice -, may nonetheless lead to brokers to intentionally discriminate against members of racial minorities. See also: Selmi, Michael, "Indirect Discrimination and the Anti-Discrimination Mandate", Oxford, Oxford University Press, *Philosophical Foundations of Discrimination Law (Philosophical Foundations of Law)*, Hellman, Deborah/Moreau, Sophia (Editors), 2013, pp. 1–304 (pp. 257 and ff and passim).

2417 Johnson, Gabbrielle M., "Algorithmic Bias: On the Implicit Biases of Social Technology", *Synthese*, 2021, passim.

2418 Curto, Georgina/Acosta, Mario Fernando Jojoa/Comim, Flavio/Garcia-Zapirain, Begoña, "Are AI systems biased against the poor? A machine learning analysis using Word2Vec and GloVe embeddings", *cit.*, pp. 617–632 (618).

shapeless categories, amenable to be promptly generalised[2419] in consonance with previous experiences.[2420] Machine learning algorithms operates similarly..[2421]

§§ No flabbergasting surprise springs from the fact that both over-generalised experiences and erroneous beliefs will jointly pave the way for the ghastly chaos of injustice and the mayhem of harrowing prejudice.[2422] Relatedly, prejudices, as a social category,[2423] fall well within the remit of stereotypes.[2424] The latter is relayed

---

[2419] See: Kahneman, Daniel/Slovic/Tversky, Amos (Editors), *Judgment under Uncertainty: Heuristics and Biases*, Cambridge, Cambridge University Press, 1982, pp. 1–544 (parsing several studies on *human biases across various judgmental heuristics*) ("*The thirty five chapters in this book describe various judgmental heuristics and the biases they produce, not only in laboratory experiments but in important social, medical, and political situations as well. Individual chapters discuss the representativeness and availability heuristics, problems in judging covariation and control, overconfidence, multistage inference, social perception, medical diagnosis, risk perception, and methods for correcting and improving judgments under uncertainty.* About half of the chapters are edited versions of classic articles; the remaining chapters are newly written for this book. Most review multiple studies or entire subareas of research and application rather than describing single experimental studies. This book will be useful to a wide range of students and researchers, as well as to decision makers seeking to gain insight into their judgments and to improve them"). Italics added.

[2420] Curto, Georgina/Acosta, Mario Fernando Jojoa/Comim, Flavio/Garcia-Zapirain, Begoña, "Are AI systems biased against the poor? A machine learning analysis using Word2Vec and GloVe embeddings", *cit.*, pp. 617–632 (618).

[2421] See: Surden, Harry, "Machine Learning and Law", *Washington Law Review*, Volume 89, 2015, pp. 87 and ff. See also: Barocas, Solon/Selbst, Andrew, "Big Data's Disparate Impact", *California Law Review*, Volume 104, pp. 2016, pp. 671–678 ("in particular, by exposing so-called 'machine learning' algorithms to examples of the cases of interest (previously identified instances of fraud, spam, default, and poor health), *the algorithm 'learns' which related attributes or activities can serve as potential proxies for those qualities or outcomes of interest*"). Italics added.

[2422] Open AI Reicher S., "Rethinking the paradigm of prejudice", *South African Journal of Psychology*, Volume 37, 2007, pp. 820–834.

[2423] Western, Bruce, *Punishment and Inequality in America*, New York: Russell Sage Foundation, 2006; Soss, Joe, Richard C. Fording, and Sanford F. Schram, *Disciplining the Poor: Neoliberal Paternalism and the Persistent Power of Race*, Chicago: University of Chicago Press, 2011; Laub, John H., "Understanding Inequality and the Justice System Response: Charting a New Way Forward.", New York: William T. Grant Foundation, 2014.

[2424] This is called law of *implicit bias*: people make decisions (e.g. discriminating seemingly disfavoured groups of people) that often-times lack a rational connection between facts and judgment. A conscious and deliberate judgment that noticeably runs afoul with rationality. See: Jolls, Christine/Sunstein, Cass R., "The Law of Implicit Bias", *California Law Review*, Volume 94, 2006, p. 969 (arguing that this issue can be solved through the general strategy of de-biasing through law, by steering people through more rational directions). See also: Kang, Jerry/Banaji, Mahzarin R., "Fair Measures: A Behavioural Realist Revision of Affirmative Action", *California Law Review,* Volume 94 2006, p. 1064 (arguing that «implicit bias often conflicts with conscious attitudes, endorsed beliefs, and intentional behaviour»); Greenwald, Anthony G., and Linda Hamilton Krieger, Implicit Bias: Scientific Foundations", *California Law Review*, Volume 94, 2006, pp. 945–967. See also: Santos, Hugo Luz dos, *Multidisciplinary Dynamics of Mediation*, Volume I, New York/Beijing/Berlin/Singapore, Springer, 2025, pp. 1–694; Santos, Hugo Luz dos, *Multidisciplinary Dynamics of Mediation*, Volume II, New York/Beijing/Berlin/Singapore, Springer, 2025, pp. 1–700; Santos, Hugo Luz dos, *Towards a Four-Tiered Model of Mediation*, New York/Beijing/Berlin/Singapore, Springer, 2023, pp. 1–216.

through the linguistic process. Stereotypes, in turn, usher in biases,[2425] thereby engendering a self-perpetuating loop[2426] against the backdrop of which prejudices[2427] unfolds.[2428] Algorithmic decision-making operates in a tantamount manner.[2429] So do search engines that reinforce racism.[2430]

§§ Where there is bias, there is discrimination as the former is the linchpin of the latter. Biases are thus conveyed through linguistic expression.[2431] On the flip side, discrimination[2432] entails a set of actions of exclusion. Discrimination is therefore an outgrowth of, and a offspring, of prejudice.[2433]

[2425] Curto, Georgina/Acosta, Mario Fernando Jojoa/Comim, Flavio/Garcia-Zapirain, Begoña, "Are AI systems biased against the poor? A machine learning analysis using Word2Vec and GloVe embeddings", *cit.*, pp. 617–632 (618).

[2426] Curto, Georgina/Acosta, Mario Fernando Jojoa/Comim, Flavio/Garcia-Zapirain, Begoña, "Are AI systems biased against the poor? A machine learning analysis using Word2Vec and GloVe embeddings", *cit.*, pp. 617–632 (618).

[2427] See: Freeman, Andrea, "Payback: A Structural Analysis of the Credit Card Problem", *Arizona Law Review*, Volume 55, 2013, pp. 180–81 ("Credit card companies confine low-income individuals to a subprime market and attempt to steer many middle-class African American and Latinos into subprime loans."); Munnell, Alicia H./Tootell, Geoffrey M. B./Browne, Lynn E./McEneaney, James, "Mortgage Lending in Boston: Interpreting HMDA Data", *American Economic Review*, Volume 86, 1996, pp. 25–29 (arguing that the likelihood that a loan request carried out by someone who is self-employed will be gainsaid is exceedingly high); Zywicki, Todd J./Adamson, Joseph D., "The Law and Economics of Subprime Lending", *University of Colorado Law Review*, 2009, pp. 1–9 (contending that Black workers with roughly the same abilities and educational background earn far less than comparable white workers or have considerably fewer employment opportunities).

[2428] Beukeboom, CJ/Burgers, C., "How stereotypes are shared through language: a review and introduction of the Social Categories and Stereotypes Communication (SCSC) framework", *Review of Community-Based Research*, Volume 7, pp. 1–37; Maass, A., "Linguistic intergroup bias: stereotype perpetuation through language", *Advanced Exp Social Psychology*, Volume 31, 1999, pp. 79–121.

[2429] Salloch, S., & Eriksen, A., "What are humans doing in the Loop? Co-reasoning and practical Judgment when using machine learning-driven decision aids", *The American Journal of Bioethics*, 2024, pp. 1–12; Binns, Reuben, "Human Judgment in Algorithmic Loops: Individual Justice and Automated Decision-Making", *Regulation & Governance*, Volume 16, 2022, passim.

[2430] Noble, Safiya Umoja, *Algorithms of Oppression: How search engines reinforce racism*, New York, New University Press, 2018, pp. 1–248 ("*Run a Google search for "Black girls"—what will you find? "Big Booty" and other sexually explicit terms are likely to come up as top search terms. But, if you type in "white girls," the results are radically different*. The suggested porn sites and unmoderated discussions about "why Black women are so sassy" or "why Black women are so angry" presents a disturbing portrait of Black womanhood in modern society. In *Algorithms of Oppression*, Safiya Umoja Noble challenges the idea that search engines like Google offer an equal playing field for all forms of ideas, identities, and activities. *Data discrimination is a real social problem; Noble argues that the combination of private interests in promoting certain sites, along with the monopoly status of a relatively small number of Internet search engines, leads to a biased set of search algorithms that privilege whiteness and discriminate against people of color, specifically women of color*"). Italics added.

[2431] Curto, Georgina/Acosta, Mario Fernando Jojoa/Comim, Flavio/Garcia-Zapirain, Begoña, "Are AI systems biased against the poor? A machine learning analysis using Word2Vec and GloVe embeddings", *cit.*, pp. 617–632 (618).

[2432] Firestone, Simon, "Race Ethnicity and Credit Card Monitoring", *Journal of Money, Credit and Banking*, Sept. 2014, 2014, pp. 1206 and ff; Han, Song, Keys, Benjamin J./Li, Geng, *Unsecured Credit Supply over the Credit Cycle: Evidence from Credit Card Mailings* (argue that, statistically,

§§ One should not lose sight of the fact that deep-seated biases[2434] are firmly rooted in the skewed training data machine learning algorithms operate upon.[2435] As a result, prejudices must not neither go unaddressed, unchecked, unnoticed, unpicked nor unaccounted for or disparate impact[2436] may be otherwise externalized onto members of racialized communities whom have been historically targeted by the devilishly harmful virus of racial discrimination.[2437] Relatedly, machine learning

---

Blacks and Latinos are seldom granted credit and, if ever granted credit, the terms and conditions attached to the concession of credit are not equal to those offered to White folks).

[2433] Chi-Jack Lin/ Sherman D. Hanna, "Racial Discrimination in the Consumer Credit Market", *Consumer Interests Annual*, Volume 56, 2010 ("*The Equal Credit Opportunity Act (ECOA), enacted in 1974, makes it unlawful for any creditors to discriminate against credit applicants because of their color, race/ethnic group, religion, national origin, sex, marital status, or age (provided the applicant has the capacity to contract)* (....) *our analyses allow for distinguishing statistical and taste discrimination. In four of five of our measures, there was discrimination against households with Black respondents, and in three out of five measures, there was discrimination against households with Hispanic respondents. Discrimination in the consumer credit market against black and Hispanic households is statistical discrimination: lenders choose to discriminate against black and Hispanic because they on average have higher default risk*"). Italics added.

[2434] But see: Ards, Sheila D./Myers, Samuel L., "The Color of Money: Bad Credit, Wealth, and Race", *American Behavioral Scientist*, Volume 45, 2001, pp. 223–238 (debunks the deep-seated myth according to which Blacks are big spenders and thus unworthy of creditworthiness, which stands as an irksome social bias in dire need of quashing).

[2435] See: *Tech, Bias and Housing Initiative, the Promise and Perils of Residential Proptech, Year 1, Research Summary Report, April 2023, TechEquity Collaborative*, p. 11, available at: https://techequity.us/wp-content/uploads/2023/04/TBHI-Y1-Research-Summary-Report.pdf (28.11.2024). ("*Once bad data enters the analysis of one factor, it gets baked into the subsequent process, multiplying the effect that one disadvantageous data point can have on someone's overall housing determination*"). Italics added. See: Part IV, This chapter, Sects. 4.1.4–4.1.4.2.3 of this book.

[2436] In spite of the widely accepted conceptual differences between intent-based and effect-based theories of disparate impact, both approaches often dovetail seamlessly. As far as the fair lending goes, the definition of disparate impact cases is somewhat shallow, nomadic, erratic, and dispiritingly vague. Note, though, that the loan officer's discretion is directly conducive to exceedingly higher rates for members of racial minorities. See: Ayres, Ian/Klein, Gary/West, Jeffrey, "The Rise and (Potential) Fall of Disparate Impact Lending Litigation", *Evidence and Innovation in Housing Law and Policy*, Fennell, Lee Anne/Keys, Benajmin J. (Editors), Cambridge, Cambridge University Press, 2017, pp. 231–254.

[2437] However, Schwemm and Taren avowedly contend that these cases might somewhat be deemed hybrid impact/intention cases. See: Schwemm, Robert G./Taren, Jeffrey L., "Discretionary Pricing, Mortgage Discrimination, and the Fair Housing Act", *The Harvard Civil Rights-Civil Liberties Law Review*, 2010, passim. The conduct being granularly parsed is discretion ascribed to brokers—which is considered by many stakeholders a harmless neutral practice -, may nonetheless lead to brokers to intentionally discriminate against members of racial minorities. See also: Selmi, Michael, "Indirect Discrimination and the Anti-Discrimination Mandate", Oxford, Oxford University Press, *Philosophical Foundations of Discrimination Law (Philosophical Foundations of Law)*, Hellman, Deborah/Moreau, Sophia (Editors), 2013, pp. 1–304 (pp. 257 and ff and passim) (books description: "how do we understand and justify the particular partialities that discrimination law tries to protect against? Are different discrimination laws from around the world grounded in a single set of norms? *And does discrimination law fail to treat people as individuals? The philosophical study around discrimination law in the private and public sector is a relatively young field of inquiry. This is*

algorithms echo a set of social prejudices[2438] at a technical level.[2439] Lest we forget, algorithmic outputs[2440] reflect hidden correlations[2441] deeply steeped in big data.[2442] Strikingly, the pearls of algorithmic wisdom brought forth by machine learning algorithms do not fall far behind from its founding trees (history[2443] and big[2444] data).[2445]

---

owing to the fact that anti-discrimination laws are relatively new. It is arguably only since the Second World War that these rights have been adopted by countries in a broad sense, ensuring that all citizens have civil rights and the right to non-discrimination. Theory around discrimination law has until recently been threefold, doctrinal in its approach, questioning equality—why it matters and why should it influence legislatures in the design of policy—and thirdly focusing on the issue of affirmative action. This volume takes a fresh look at the philosophy of discrimination law, identifying points of discussion in need of further study. It addresses how we are to understand and justify laws prohibiting discrimination. For instance, how discrimination might be best conceived—as a personal wrong or as an unfair distribution of resources. *The volume then turns to a number of meta-theoretical questions, whether different discrimination laws are coherent and grounded in collectively held beliefs or are instead a collection of very different rules that have no underlying coherence.* Lastly, the authors focus on issues in discrimination law that are currently the topic of considerable political debate. *The questions raised here are urgent and necessary and it is the hope of the authors that other academics and philosophers may join in their discussions*"). Italics added.

2438 Kleinberg, Jon/Ludwig, Jens/Mullainathan, Sendhil/Sunstein Cass R., "Discrimination in the Age of Algorithms", *Journal of Legal Analysis*, Volume 10, 1, 2018, pp. 28–29, 33–34 (draw a distinction between "group differences in the raw data" and biases for the "choice of predictors").

2439 Hacker, P., "Teaching fairness to artificial intelligence: existing and novel strategies against algorithmic discrimination under EU law", *Common Market Law Review*, Volume 55, 2018, pp. 1143–1186.

2440 Chander, Anupam, "The Racist Algorithm?", *Michigan Law Review*, Volume 115, 2017, pp. 1023–1039 ("the focus on outcomes rather than how an algorithm operates seems especially useful as algorithms become increasingly complicated, even able to modify themselves").

2441 But see: Kilbertus, Niki/Carulla, Mateo Rojas/Parascandolo, Giambattista/Hardt, Moritz/Janzing, Dominik/ Schoellkopf, Bernhard, "Avoiding Discrimination through Causal Reasoning", *Advances in Neural Information Processing Systems*, I. Guyon, U. V. Luxburg, S. Bengio, H. Wallach, R. Fergus, S. Vishwanathan, and R. Garnett (Eds.), Vol. 30. Curran Associates, Inc., 2017, pp. 656–666 (arguing that is feasible to avoiding discrimination through a granular and fine-grained causal reasoning).

2442 Gillis, Talia B., "The Input Data Fallacy", *Minnesota Law Review*, Volume 106, 2022, pp. 1176–1263 (p. 1244).

2443 See: Part IV, This chapter, Sects. 4.1.4–4.1.4.2.1 of this book (on mortgage redlining). See: Part IV, This chapter, Sects. 4.1.2–4.1.4.3 of this book (on algorithmic credit scoring, consumer racism and credit card redlining). See: Part IV, This chapter, Sects. 4.1.4–4.1.4.2.3 of this book (on algorithmic redlining). See: Part IV, This chapter, Sect. 4.1.4.3 of this book (on "algorithmic redliking"). See: Part IV, This chapter, Sect. 4.1.3 of this book (on algorithmic prime-lining).

2444 But see: Hardt, Moritz, "How big data is unfair: Understanding sources of unfairness in data driven decision making", *Medium*, Archived on Oct. 8, 2014, available at: https://web.archive.org/web/20141008185829/; https://medium.com/@mrtz/how-big-data-is-unfair-9aa544d739de. (access: 17.12.2024).

2445 In spite of its deep-seated racial bias, decision-makers continue to deploy redlining tactics through big data and may even justify such unlawful practices by claiming that the latter abide by cost-effectiveness. See: Humber, Nadiyah J., "A Home for Digital Equity: Algorithmic Redlining and Property Technology", *California Law Review*, Volume 111, Issue 5, 2023, pp. 1421–1484. See also: Hurley, Mikella/Adebayo, Julius, "Credit Scoring in the Era of Big Data", *Yale Journal of Law and Technology*, Volume 18, 2016, pp. 148, 151–156, 172 (averring that FICO scoring

The assertion according to which algorithms are as good as the training data[2446] they leverage on[2447] is neither unwarranted nor uncalled for since machine learning algorithms, like humans, learn from experience.[2448]

---

boasts a redoubtable capacity to routinely weed out some populations that have been historically and systematically underrepresented or grossly unfairly represented in the credit industry market). Tellingly, by 2016, ten states had disavowed the unlawful practice of employers using shady algorithmic credit scores due to their perceived disparate impact on low-income applicants and members of racialized communities (mostly Black folks). See: O'Neill, Cathy, *Weapons of Math Destruction. How Big Data Increases Inequality and Threatens Democracy.* London: Penguin Random House, 2016, pp. 128 and ff and passim. See: Part IV, This chapter, Sects. 4.1.4–4.1.4.2.3 of this book.

[2446] Kirkpatrick, Keith, "It's not the Algorithm, it's the Data", *Communications of the ACM*, February 2017, Volume 60, n. ° 2, 2017 ("critics, however, say tools such as PredPol and Command-Central *are inherently biased since they rely heavily on reported crimes data, which is often concentrated in areas that are heavily policed, thereby skewing statistics to overrepresent poor or minority communities.* "*We know that we have a history of racially biased policing in the United States, and that has fed into all the data that we have on where arrests have occurred, which crimes are more likely to occur in specific communities, and at which particular times*," says Jennifer Lynch, senior staff attorney at the Electronic Frontier Foundation. "*That's the data that's being fed into predictive policing algorithms*"). Italics added. See also: Kirkpatrick, Keith, "Battling Algorithmic Bias: How Do We Ensure Algorithms Treat Us Fairly?" *Commun. ACM 59*, Volume 10, 2016, pp. 1 and ff and passim.

[2447] See: Surden, Harry, "Machine Learning and Law", *Washington Law Review*, Volume 89, 2014, pp. 87, 106 ("In general, *machine learning algorithms are only as good as the data that they are given to analyze*"). Italics added. See also: *Tech, Bias and Housing Initiative, the Promise and Perils of Residential Proptech, Year 1, Research Summary Report, April 2023, TechEquity Collaborative*, p. 5 available at: https://techequity.us/wp-content/uploads/2023/04/TBHI-Y1-Research-Summary-Report.pdf (28.11.2024). ("*With a severely constrained housing supply, companies offering an easier pathway to homeownership may exploit communities that have been harmed by housing discrimination in the past. Opaque algorithms incorporate biased data into their decision-making processes, making it harder to enforce fair housing laws.* Residential Proptech companies often operate in a regulatory gray area, leaving consumers without the protections they would have from traditional housing regulatory systems. *As unprecedented capital investment flows into this space, venture-backed companies' winner-take-all approach to growth has the potential to exacerbate inequality rather than combat it*"). Italics added.

[2448] See: Murphy, Kevin P., *Machine Learning: A Probabilistic Perspective (Adaptive Computation and Machine Learning series).* Massachusetts: The MIT Press, 2012, pp. 1–1104 (states avowedly that "machine Learning attempts to combine deductive, inductive, and abductive reasoning to make person-like reasoning in AI Entities possible. Machine-learning AI Entities initially learn in the same way a human child learns. First, they notice details and patterns in shapes, sounds, and behaviors; then put them together to distinguish one person from another, or a dog from a cat. Eventually, the AI can recognize and identify" common objects). See also: Hutto-Schultz, Jess, "Dicitur Ex Machina: Artificial Intelligence and the Hearsay Rule", *George Mason Law Review*, Volume 27, Issue 2, 2020, pp. 684–718 (689). See: Chollet, François, *Deep Learning with Python.* Shelter Island, Nova Iorque: Manning, 2018, pp. 1–384 (passim). *Deep Learning* stands as a byproduct of *Machine Learning. Machine Learning*, a subset of Artificial Intelligence, unfolds itself in *Deep Learning*, which "involves computer algorithms that have the ability to "learn" or improve in performance over time on some task". See: Surden, Harry, "Machine Learning and Law", *Washington Law Review*, Volume 89, 2015, pp. 87 and ff. See also: Barocas, Solon/Selbst, Andrew, "Big Data's Disparate Impact", *California Law Review*, Volume 104, pp. 2016, pp. 671–678 ("in particular, by exposing so-called 'machine learning' algorithms to examples of the cases of interest (previously identified

§§ Although bias in an overarching sense has merited scholars' undivided attention, little importance, if any, has been attached to the evidence of bias against the poor in social networks,[2449] which configures a wholly overlooked subset of discrimination in both algorithmic bias[2450] and social sciences literature.[2451] It bears mentioning, though, that bias against the poor is all but blazingly new. It has been timely coined as «aporophobia» by the philosopher Adela Cortina.[2452]

§§ With this context in place, the level playing field has been unfairly tilted against the poor,[2453] which, in turn, paves the way to a bluntly discriminatory behaviour that

---

instances of fraud, spam, default, and poor health), *the algorithm 'learns' which related attributes or activities can serve as potential proxies for those qualities or outcomes of interest*"). Italics added.

2449 Mirrored on the yawning gap between rich—that can adroitly harness artificial intelligence to advance their goals and shady agendas—and poor—that grapple to meet basic needs and are automatically excluded from the equation of digital society powered by Artificial Intelligence—which will directly impact the fabric of societies worldwide, thereby augmenting the gulf/rift between the «digitally-chosen» and the «digitally-outcast» enabled by a algorithmic discrimination that does nothing but irreparable harm. See: Yu, Peter K., "The Algorithmic Divide and Equality in the Age of Artificial Intelligence", *Florida Law Review*, Volume 72, 2020, pp. 355–360 (addresses the issue of algorithmic discrimination).

2450 Recall: Baeza-Yates, R., "Bias on the web", *Communications of the ACM*, 61 (6), June 2018, 2018, pp. 54–61 (argues that "*algorithmic bias is when the bias is not present in the input data* and is added *purely by the algorithm*"). Italics added; Lee, Nicole Turner/Resnick, Paul/Barton, Genie, *Algorithmic Bias Detection and Mitigation: Best Practices and Policies to Reduce Consumer Harms*. Washington, DC: Brookings Institution, 2019, passim. Gutiérrez, L, Keith B, "A systematic literature review on word embeddings", *Advanced Intelligent Systems Comp*, 865, 2019, pp. 132–141.

2451 Curto, Georgina/Acosta, Mario Fernando Jojoa/Comim, Flavio/Garcia-Zapirain, Begoña, "Are AI systems biased against the poor? A machine learning analysis using Word2Vec and GloVe embeddings", *cit.*, pp. 617–632.

2452 Cortina Adela, *Aporofobia, el rechazo al pobre*, Paidos, Barcelona, 2017, passim.

2453 This problem is neither new nor easy to solve. Whilst the effects of technology—digital justice—in the courtroom have been previously broached by the doctrine, few to none consensus has been reached about actionable lines of action to be taken. See: Donoghue, Jane, "The Rise of Digital Justice: Courtroom Technology, Public Participation and Access to Justice", *The Modern Law Review*, Volume 80, Issue 6, 2018, p. 995 (noting that technology in the courtroom might widen the gap between the rich and the poor. In this vein, this renowned author has contended that "*legal reforms have omitted any detailed consideration of the type and quality of citizen participation in newly digitised court processes which have fundamental implications for the legitimacy and substantive outcomes of court-based processes; and for enhancing democratic procedure through improved access to justice.* It is argued that although digital court tools and systems offer great promise for enhancing efficiency, participation and accessibility, they *simultaneously have the potential to amplify the scope for injustice, and to attenuate central principles of the legal system, including somewhat paradoxically, access to justice*"). Italics added. See also: Heintz, M.E., "The digital divide and courtroom technology: Can David keep up with Goliath", *Federal Communications Law Journal*, Volume 54, 2002, pp. 566 ff and passim. The great bulk of these assertions has been anticipated by an iconic piece of research. See: Galanter, Marc, "Why the "Haves" Come Out Ahead: Speculations on the Limits of Legal Change", *Law & Society Review*, Volume 9, 1974, pp. 98–103 (this renowned author talks about a *social reality* in which the dubbed «repeat players»—which go by the name of «haves»—tend to «to come out ahead» by putting their knowledge and vast resources to good use. This perceived advantage will not only impact the choice on the procedures but will ultimately benefit their interests as opposed to the deemed «one-shot» players (the «have nots») that will have slimmer and fewer chances to get palpable results in dispute resolution). Technology in

knows no bounds.[2454] On the flip side, the bias evinced against the less fortunate[2455] bears on the effective implementation[2456] of poverty[2457] curtailment policies.[2458]

§§ It seems as though the latter have been either sown in barren soil or are stranded in shallow waters.[2459] This gruesome scenario has a clear bearing on the historically discriminated groups.[2460] No surprise stems from the fact that this harrowing

---

the courtroom—that includes the rich and excludes the poor—will make this problem considerably worse. But see: Bailey, J./Burkell, J./Reynolds, G. "Access to Justice for All: Towards an "Expansive Vision" of Justice and Technology, *Windsor Yearbook of Access to Justice*, Volume 31, 2013, pp. 183–201 (in stark contrast, these authors stress that the digital and technological apparatus can indeed spawn a both time-effective and streamlined access to justice in a given jurisdiction).

[2454] Gustafson, Kaaryn S, *Cheating Welfare: Public Assistance and the Criminalization of Poverty*, New York: NYU Press, 2011.

[2455] Kroeper, Kathryn/Quintanilla, Victor D./Frisby, Michael/Yel, Nedim/Applegate, Amy G./ Sherman, Steven J./Murphy, Mary C., "Underestimating the Unrepresented: Cognitive Biases Disadvantage Pro Se Litigants in Family Law Cases", *Psychology, Public Policy, and Law*, Volume 26, n.° 2, 2020, pp. 198–212.

[2456] Curto, Georgina/Acosta, Mario Fernando Jojoa/Comim, Flavio/Garcia-Zapirain, Begoña, "Are AI systems biased against the poor? A machine learning analysis using Word2Vec and GloVe embeddings", *cit.*, pp. 617–632 (618).

[2457] But see: Quadagno, Jill, *The Color of Welfare: How Racism Undermined the War on Poverty*, Oxford, Oxford University Press, 1994, pp. 1–272 ("*From Reconstruction to Lyndon Johnson and beyond, Quadagno reveals how American social policy has continually foundered on issues of race. Drawing on extensive primary research, Quadagno shows, for instance, how Roosevelt, in need of support from southern congressmen, excluded African Americans from the core programs of the Social Security Act. Turning to Lyndon Johnson's "unconditional war on poverty," she contends that though anti-poverty programs for job training, community action, health care, housing, and education have accomplished much, they have not been fully realized because they became inextricably intertwined with the civil rights movement of the 1960s, which triggered a white backlash*"). Italics added. See: Part IV, This chapter, Sects. 4.1.4–4.1.4.2.3 of this book.

[2458] Baradaran, Mehrsa, "Banking and the Social Contract", *Notre Dame Law Review*, Volume 89, pp. 1283–1336 ("Access to safe credit is crucial in allowing the poor to escape poverty").

But see: The Use of Cash-Flow Data in Underwriting Credit: Empirical Research Findings, FINREGLAB 32, 34 (Jul. 2019), https://finreglab.org/wp-content/uploads/2019/07/FRL_Research-Report_Final.pdf; [https://perma.cc/N65Q-WQML] (arguing that the use of cash flow data can underpin a prediction of default risk, thereby providing an apposite alternative to ancient credit scores. In addition to that, cash-flow data is commensurate with predictive across demographic groups).

[2459] Gilliom, John, *Overseers of the Poor: Surveillance, Resistance, and the Limits of Privacy*, Chicago: University of Chicago Press, 2001; Soss, Joe, Richard C. Fording, and Sanford F. Schram, *Disciplining the Poor: Neoliberal Paternalism and the Persistent Power of Race*. Chicago: University of Chicago Press, 2011; Greif, M., "Regulating landlords: Unintended consequences for poor tenants", *City & Community*, Volume 17, Issue 3, 2018, pp. 658–674. See also: Applebaum, LD, "The influence of perceived deservingness on policy decisions regarding aid to the poor", *Journal of Political Psychology*, 2001; Nunn, H/Biressi, A, "The undeserving poor", *Soundings*, Volume 41, 2009, pp. 107–116; Arneson, RJ, "Egalitarianism and the undeserving poor", *Journal of Political Philosophy*, Volume 5, 1997, pp. 327–350.

[2460] Alessina, A./Glaeser EL., *Fighting poverty in the US and Europe*, Oxford, Oxford University Press, 2013, passim.

phenomenon is tightly interlocked to discrimination based on gender[2461] on the horizon of a capitalist[2462] society.[2463]

§§ Bearing the backdrop very firmly in mind, Eubanks[2464] singled out algorithms that discriminate the poor while O'Neil[2465] fleshed out a bevy of predatory[2466] Artificial Intelligence-embedded technologies[2467] that target people[2468] in dire need[2469] of escaping poverty.[2470]

§§ Notwithstanding, there is a perceived paucity of in-depth research on bias against the poor in the extant literature.[2471] This book, drawing on a stellar piece of research,[2472] seeks to plug that loophole by laying out a framework that seeks to showcase that bias against the poor can not only be measured[2473] but, and foremost, «aporophobia» can be easily found in publicly available *Google News Word2,*

[2461] Rudinger, R./Naradowsky, J./Leonard, B./Durme, B Van, "Gender Bias in Conference Resolution", *NAACL HLT 2018—2018 Conference North American Chapter Association Computer Linguist Human Language Technology—Proceedings of Conference*, 2018, 2:8–14.

[2462] Curto, Georgina/Acosta, Mario Fernando Jojoa/Comim, Flavio/Garcia-Zapirain, Begoña, "Are AI systems biased against the poor? A machine learning analysis using Word2Vec and GloVe embeddings", *cit.*, pp. 617–632 (618).

[2463] O' Neil, Cathy, "Amazon's Gender-Biased Algorithm Is Not Alone", 2018, accessed 2 January 2025.

[2464] Eubanks, Virginia, *Automating inequality: how high-tech tools profile, police, and punish the poor*, New York: St. Martin's Press, 2017, pp. 1–272 (1 ff and passim) (coining the expression «automating inequality» to vividly portray the downsides of using high-technology to further compound the yawning gap between rich and poor against the backdrop of which biased algorithms operate).

[2465] O'Neil, Cathy, *Weapons of Math Destruction. How Big Data Increases Inequality and Threatens Democracy*, London, Penguin Random House, 2016, passim (showing how algorithms utilized in modern societies are amenable to perpetuate racial discrimination, partially through perpetuation of social disadvantage and wealth divides).

[2466] But see: Hurley, Mikella/Adebayo, Julius, "Credit Scoring in the Era of Big Data", *Yale Journal of Law and Technology*, Volume 18, 2016, p. 149 ("*these tools may furthermore obscure discriminatory and subjective lending policies behind a single "objective" score (...) sophisticated algorithms may combine facially neutral data points and treat them as proxies for immutable characteristics such as race or gender, thereby circumventing existing non-discrimination laws and systematically denying credit access to certain groups. Finally, big-data tools may allow online payday lenders to target the most vulnerable consumers and lure them into debt traps*"). Italics added.

[2467] Curto, Georgina/Acosta, Mario Fernando Jojoa/Comim, Flavio/Garcia-Zapirain, Begoña, "Are AI systems biased against the poor? A machine learning analysis using Word2Vec and GloVe embeddings", *cit.*, pp. 617–632 (618).

[2468] Havard, Cassandra Jones, "On the Take": The Black Box of Credit Scoring and Mortgage Discrimination", *Boston University Public Interest Law Journal*, 2011, pp. 239 and ff and passim (discussing that subprime lending was undoubtably geared toward minority communities, aiming to enmesh them on the trap of excessive debt); Johnson, Creola, "The Magic of Group Identity: How Predatory Lenders Use Minorities to Target Communities of Color", *Georgetown Journal on Poverty Law and Policy*, 2010, pp. 165–169 (fleshing out several aggressive marketing tactics used by unprincipled/unscrupulous lenders to target primarily minorities for eerily predatory loans).

Wikipedia GloVe and *Twitter GloVe* pre-trained word[2474] embeddings,[2475] thereby offering empirical evidence both at scale and in context.[2476]

§§ To cater for that, pundits have shed keen light on pre-trained word embeddings paired with the benchmark to *measure bias*[2477] against the poor using *Natural*

2469 See: Johnson, Creola, "The Magic of Group Identity: How Predatory Lenders Use Minorities to Target Communities of Color", *Georgetown Journal on Poverty Law and Policy*, 2010, pp. 165–169 (fleshing out several aggressive marketing tactics used by unprincipled/unscrupulous lenders to target primarily minorities for eerily predatory loans); Freeman, Andrea, "Payback: A Structural Analysis of the Credit Card Problem", *Arizona Law Review*, Volume 55, 2013, pp. 180–81 ("Credit card companies confine low-income individuals to a subprime market and attempt to steer many middle-class African American and Latinos into subprime loans."); Havard, Cassandra Jones, "On the Take": The Black Box of Credit Scoring and Mortgage Discrimination", *Boston University Public Interest Law Journal*, 2011, pp. 239 and ff and passim (discussing that subprime lending was undoubtably geared toward minority communities, aiming to enmesh them on the trap of excessive debt).

2470 Baradaran, Mehrsa, "Banking and the Social Contract", *Notre Dame Law Review*, Volume 89, pp. 1283–1336 ("access to safe credit is crucial in allowing the poor to escape poverty").

2471 Curto, Georgina/Acosta, Mario Fernando Jojoa/Comim, Flavio/Garcia-Zapirain, Begoña, "Are AI systems biased against the poor? A machine learning analysis using Word2Vec and GloVe embeddings", *cit.*, pp. 617–632 (618).

2472 Curto, Georgina/Acosta, Mario Fernando Jojoa/Comim, Flavio/Garcia-Zapirain, Begoña, "Are AI systems biased against the poor? A machine learning analysis using Word2Vec and GloVe embeddings", *cit.*, pp. 617–632.

2473 See: Corbett-Davies, Sam/Goel, Sharad, "The Measure and Mismeasure of Fairness: a critical Review of Fair Machine Learning", *Cornell University Library*, 2018, p. 18 (broaches a type of *measurement bias* coined "feature bias," which is neatly a bias in the predictors x. Note, though, that there is a second type of measurement bias deemed "label bias," which, in turn, amounts to a bias in y. The authors argue that that label bias is the worst bias there is).

2474 Curto, Georgina/Acosta, Mario Fernando Jojoa/Comim, Flavio/Garcia-Zapirain, Begoña, "Are AI systems biased against the poor? A machine learning analysis using Word2Vec and GloVe embeddings", *cit.*, pp. 617–632 (618).

2475 Joseph, K., Morgan, JH, "When do word embeddings accurately reflect surveys on our beliefs about people?", *ACL Anthology, Proceedings of the 58th annual meeting of the association of computational linguistics*, 2020, pp. 4392–4415. A cohort of scientists, for instance, is using machine learning to pinpoint adjectives tightly interlocked with different ethnic groups across the nineteenth and twentieth centuries to shed a keen light on the history of discrimination. See: Garg, Nikhil et al., "Word Embeddings Quantify 100 Years of Gender and Ethnic Stereotypes", *Proceedings of the National Academy of Sciences of the United States of America*, Volume 115, 2018, E3635.

2476 Curto, Georgina/Acosta, Mario Fernando Jojoa/Comim, Flavio/Garcia-Zapirain, Begoña, "Are AI systems biased against the poor? A machine learning analysis using Word2Vec and GloVe embeddings", *cit.*, pp. 617–632 (619). Joseph, K., Morgan, JH, "When do word embeddings accurately reflect surveys on our beliefs about people?", *ACL Anthology, Proceedings of the 58th annual meeting of the association of computational linguistics*, 2020, pp. 4392–4415.

2477 Hamilton, Melissa, "The sexist algorithm", *Behavioral Sciences and the Law*, Volume 37, Issue 2, Special Issue: the Use of Statistics in Criminal Cases, March–April 2019, 2019, pp. 1 and ff ("*Algorithmic risk assessment tools are informed by scientific research concerning which factors are predictive of recidivism and thus support the evidence-based practice movement in criminal justice.* Automated assessments of individualized risk (low, medium, high) *permit officials to make more effective management decisions. Computer-generated algorithms appear to be objective and neutral. But are these algorithms actually fair? The focus herein is on gender equity.* Studies confirm

Language Processing (NLP)[2478] only to conclude that the latter embodies a plethora of biased word embeddings against the poor.

§§ The key takeaways arising out of the empirical data collated by the pundits strongly suggest the existence of bias against the poor deeply nested within the three pre-trained word embeddings.[2479] Ranging from *Google Word2Vec*, *Twitter* and *Wikipedia GloVe*.[2480] It is important to note that «Aporophobia» is a byproduct of welfare[2481] states,[2482] which, in turn, are underpinned by the mirific idea of equal opportunity and individual responsibility to climb up the ladder to leave poverty behind.[2483]

§§ Strikingly, the foregoing body of empirical evidence concluded that there is an exceedingly higher degree of bias in *Google News Word2Vec*, as compared to the remaining two word embeddings, when the attribute terms portrayed beliefs and an

---

that women typically have far lower recidivism rates than men. *This differential raises the question of how well algorithmic outcomes fare in terms of predictive parity by gender*. This essay reports original research using a large dataset of offenders who were scored on the popular risk assessment tool COMPAS. *Findings indicate that COMPAS performs reasonably well at discriminating between recidivists and non-recidivists for men and women. Nonetheless, COMPAS algorithmic outcomes systemically overclassify women in higher risk groupings. Multiple measures of algorithmic equity and predictive accuracy are provided to support the conclusion that this algorithm is sexist*"). Italics added.

2478 Curto, Georgina/Acosta, Mario Fernando Jojoa/Comim, Flavio/Garcia-Zapirain, Begoña, "Are AI systems biased against the poor? A machine learning analysis using Word2Vec and GloVe embeddings", *cit.*, pp. 617–632 (619).

2479 Joseph, K., Morgan, JH, "When do word embeddings accurately reflect surveys on our beliefs about people?", *ACL Anthology, Proceedings of the 58th annual meeting of the association of computational linguistics*, 2020, pp. 4392–4415.

2480 Curto, Georgina/Acosta, Mario Fernando Jojoa/Comim, Flavio/Garcia-Zapirain, Begoña, "Are AI systems biased against the poor? A machine learning analysis using Word2Vec and GloVe embeddings", *cit.*, pp. 617–632 (628).

2481 Quadagno, Jill, *The Color of Welfare: How Racism Undermined the War on Poverty*, Oxford, Oxford University Press, 1994, pp. 1–272 ("*From Reconstruction to Lyndon Johnson and beyond, Quadagno reveals how American social policy has continually foundered on issues of race. Drawing on extensive primary research, Quadagno shows, for instance, how Roosevelt, in need of support from southern congressmen, excluded African Americans from the core programs of the Social Security Act. Turning to Lyndon Johnson's "unconditional war on poverty," she contends that though anti-poverty programs for job training, community action, health care, housing, and education have accomplished much, they have not been fully realized because they became inextricably intertwined with the civil rights movement of the 1960s, which triggered a white backlash*"). Italics added. See: Part IV, This chapter, Sects. 4.1.4–4.1.4.2.3 of this book.

2482 Gustafson, Kaaryn S, *Cheating Welfare: Public Assistance and the Criminalization of Poverty*, New York: NYU Press, 2011; Mounk, Y, *The age of responsibility: luck, choice, and the welfare state*, Cambridge, Cambridge University Press, 2017;

2483 Curto, Georgina/Acosta, Mario Fernando Jojoa/Comim, Flavio/Garcia-Zapirain, Begoña, "Are AI systems biased against the poor? A machine learning analysis using Word2Vec and GloVe embeddings", *cit.*, pp. 617–632 (628).

exceedingly higher level of bias against the poor in *Twitter GloVe* when the terms depicted behaviours.[2484]

§§ Compellingly, this full-fledged and comprehensive body of evidence suggests that media are often abuzz with news that carry a higher level of bias against the poor[2485] than individuals in terms of expressed and deep-seated beliefs.[2486] Unsurprisingly, Artificial Intelligence-embedded technologies spread biased insights[2487] that can eventually lead to blatantly discriminatory behaviours.[2488]

§§ To add to our woes, another body of empirical evidence found that the relationship between biased word embeddings and both sexism and racism has shown to be reciprocal.

§§ Tellingly, as far as «extreme she occupations»[2489] occupations are concerned, women are often featured as homemaker, nurse, receptionist, librarian, socialite, hairdresser, nanny, bookkeeper, stylist, housekeeper, interior designer, or guidance counsellor.[2490]

§§ On the opposite pole, as far as «extreme he occupations»[2491] are concerned, men are often featured as maestro, skipper, protégé, philosopher, captain, architect, financier, warrior, broadcaster, magician, fighter pilot and boss.[2492]

2484 Curto, Georgina/Acosta, Mario Fernando Jojoa/Comim, Flavio/Garcia-Zapirain, Begoña, "Are AI systems biased against the poor? A machine learning analysis using Word2Vec and GloVe embeddings", *cit.*, pp. 617–632 (628).

2485 Most likely, flawed, or biased algorithms will deepen the rift between rich and poor. See: Eubanks, Virginia, *Automating Inequality: How High-Tech Tools Profile, Police and Punish the Poor*. New York: St. Martin's Press, 2018, 1–272 (1 ff and passim) (coining the expression «automating inequality» to vividly portray the downsides of using high-technology to further compound the yawning gap between rich and poor against the backdrop of biased algorithms). Soss, Joe, Richard C. Fording, and Sanford F. Schram, *Disciplining the Poor: Neoliberal Paternalism and the Persistent Power of Race*. Chicago: University of Chicago Press, 2011.

2486 Curto, Georgina/Acosta, Mario Fernando Jojoa/Comim, Flavio/Garcia-Zapirain, Begoña, "Are AI systems biased against the poor? A machine learning analysis using Word2Vec and GloVe embeddings", *cit.*, pp. 617–632 (628).

2487 Bryson, JJ, Narayanan, A., "Semantics derived automatically from language corpora contain human-like biases", *Science*, 356 (6334), 2017, pp. 183–186.

2488 Curto, Georgina/Acosta, Mario Fernando Jojoa/Comim, Flavio/Garcia-Zapirain, Begoña, "Are AI systems biased against the poor? A machine learning analysis using Word2Vec and GloVe embeddings", *cit.*, pp. 617–632 (628).

2489 Bolukbasi T, Chang K-W, Saligrama V, et al, "Man is to Computer Programmer as Woman is to Homemaker? Debiasing Word Embeddings", arXiv:1607.06520v1, 2016, pp. 1–25 (2).

2490 Bolukbasi T, Chang K-W, Saligrama V, et al, "Man is to Computer Programmer as Woman is to Homemaker? Debiasing Word Embeddings", *cit.*, pp. 1–25 (2).

2491 Bolukbasi T, Chang K-W, Saligrama V, et al, "Man is to Computer Programmer as Woman is to Homemaker? Debiasing Word Embeddings", arXiv:1607.06520v1, 2016, pp. 1–25 (2).

2492 Bolukbasi T, Chang K-W, Saligrama V, et al, "Man is to Computer Programmer as Woman is to Homemaker? Debiasing Word Embeddings", *cit.*, pp. 1–25 (2).

§§ Its is often posited that gender biases in the embedding (e.g. computer programmer is white and male and accordingly conveys his biases[2493] onto the software's instructions[2494]) could grasp meaningful statistics and that, in these unique set of cases, the original biased word embeddings could be deftly used.[2495]

§§ Notwithstanding, one should not lose sight of the potential risk of dealing with machine learning algorithms that upticks gender stereotypes while ratcheting up racial discriminations.[2496] Pundits therefore strongly recommend that errors, if any, should be polarized on the side of neutrality.[2497] To peter out biased word embeddings, debiased embeddings should be shrewdly deployed.[2498]

2493 See: Barocas, Solon/Selbst, Andrew D., "Big Data's Disparate Impact", *California Law Review*, Volume 104, 2016, pp. 671–682 (discussing how data is often flawed, rigged, incomplete, imperfect and therefore algorithms inherit the prejudice of the original decision makers). But see: Citron, Danielle Keats/Pasquale, Frank, "The Scored Society: Due Process for Automated Predictions", *Washington Law Review*, Volume 89, 2014, pp. 1, 4–5 (highlighting how human beings programming automated systems is directly conducive to, and leads, to fundamentally inaccurate results since the source code, predictive algorithms and datasets may encompass human biases which, in turn, have a disparate impact on historically disadvantaged groups). But see: Bornstein, Stepanhie, "Antidiscriminatory Algorithms", *Alabama Law Review*, Volume 70, 2018, pp. 519, 524–528 (contending, however, that the tagged "facially neutral" algorithms producing discriminatory outcomes should be quashed).

2494 Citron, Danielle Keats/Pasquale, Frank A., "The Scored Society: Due Process for Automated Predictions", *Washington Law Review*, Volume 89, 2014, pp. 1–34 (arguing that "[a]*dvocates applaud the removal of human beings and their flaws from the assessment process*," but arguing that bias remains "[*b*]*ecause human beings program predictive algorithms, their biases and values are embedded into the software's instructions*"). Italics added.

2495 Bolukbasi T, Chang K-W, Saligrama V, et al, "Man is to Computer Programmer as Woman is to Homemaker? Debiasing Word Embeddings", *cit.*, pp. 1–25 (15).

2496 See: Hellman, Deborah, "Indirect Discrimination and the Duty to Avoid Compounding Injustice", *Foundations of Indirect Discrimination Law*, Collins, Hugh/Khaitan, Tarunabh (Editors), Oxford, Hart Publishing; Reprint edition (June 25, 2020), 2020, p. 107 (Professor Deborah Hellman coined this expression to depict a decision that "exacerbates the harm caused by the prior injustice because it entrenches the harm or carries it into another domain." This book deals with the sweltering topic of indirect discrimination ("*indirect discrimination (or disparate impact) concerns the application of the same rule to everyone, even though that rule significantly disadvantages one particular group in society*. Ever since its recognition by the Supreme Court of the United States in 1971, liberal democracies around the world have grappled with the puzzle that it can sometimes be unfair and wrong to treat everyone equally. *The law's regulation of private acts that unintentionally (but disproportionately) harm vulnerable groups has remained extremely controversial, especially in the United States and the United Kingdom. In original essays in this volume, leading scholars of discrimination law from North America and Europe explore the various facets of the law on indirect discrimination, interrogating its foundations, history, legitimacy, purpose, structure, and relationship with other legal concepts*. The collection provides the first international work devoted to this vital area of the law that seeks both to prevent unfair treatment and to transform societies"). Italics added.

§§ In this vein, scholars adamantly aver that a myriad of documents often contain other bemoaning stereotypes that are mirrored on the embedding vectors.[2499] Notwithstanding, and much to both our disarray and dismay, w2vNEWS also evinces robust racial stereotype.[2500]

§§ For example, empirical evidence has clearly shown that projecting all the occupation words onto the direction − − − − − − − − → minorities − − − − − → whites, that the most extreme occupations closer to white folks range from parliamentarian, advocate, deputy, chancellor, legislator, to lawyer.[2501] In stark contrast, the most extreme occupations at the racial minorities end range from butler, footballer, socialite, to crooner.[2502] Or even criminal.[2503]

§§ The loathsome tapestry of discriminations previously depicted beckons a harshly unpleasant distrust on AI-embedded technologies[2504] that currently run afoul with the shallowest level of predictability,[2505] accuracy[2506] and fairness.[2507] The

2497 But see: Benjamin, Ruha, *Race After Technology: Abolitionist Tools for the New Jim Code*, New York, Polity, 2019, pp. 1–172 (7) (discussing that Artificial Intelligence-embedded technologies are viewed as iron-clad tools of objectivity and devoid of any biases whatsoever). Ruha Benjamin accordingly contends that "the employment of new technologies that reflect and reproduce existing inequities but that are promoted and perceived as more objective or progressive than the discriminatory systems of a previous era"). See also: Farina, M., & Lavazza, A., *Philosophy, expertise, and the myth of neutrality. Routledge Studies in Contemporary Philosophy*, London, Routledge, 2024. This false scent of neutrality impairs, and impacts, procedural justice. See: Tyler, Tom R., "The Psychology of Procedural Justice: A Test of the Group-Value Model", *Journal of Personality and Social Psychology*, Volume 57, 1989, p. 830 (reports that in any procedure "several non-control issues—the *neutrality* of the decision-making procedure, trust in the 3rd party, and the information the experience communicates about social standing—influence both procedural preferences and judgments of procedural justice").

2498 Bolukbasi T, Chang K-W, Saligrama V, et al, "Man is to Computer Programmer as Woman is to Homemaker? Debiasing Word Embeddings", *cit.*, pp. 1–25 (15).

2499 Bolukbasi T, Chang K-W, Saligrama V, et al, "Man is to Computer Programmer as Woman is to Homemaker? Debiasing Word Embeddings", *cit.*, pp. 1–25 (15).

2500 Bolukbasi T, Chang K-W, Saligrama V, et al, "Man is to Computer Programmer as Woman is to Homemaker? Debiasing Word Embeddings", *cit.*, pp. 1–25 (15).

2501 Bolukbasi T, Chang K-W, Saligrama V, et al, "Man is to Computer Programmer as Woman is to Homemaker? Debiasing Word Embeddings", *cit.*, pp. 1–25 (15).

2502 Bolukbasi T, Chang K-W, Saligrama V, et al, "Man is to Computer Programmer as Woman is to Homemaker? Debiasing Word Embeddings", *cit.*, pp. 1–25 (15).

2503 Manzini, T./Chong, LY/Black, AW/Tsvetkov, Y., "Black is to Criminal as Caucasian is to Police: Detecting and Removing Multi-class Bias in Word Embeddings", *NAACL HLT 2019—2019 Conference North America Chapter Association Computer Linguist Human Language Technology—Proceedings of Conference*, 1:615–621, 2019.

2504 Ashley, Kevin D., *Artificial Intelligence and Legal Analytics. New Tools for Law Practice in the Digital Age.* Cambridge: Cambridge University Press, 2018, passim.

2505 Recall, algorithms make their inferences and draw their conclusions in a manner eerily unknown, even for the cohort of programmers that designed them. This is deemed *black box*, that further enhances the shroud of mystery under which algorithms are cloaked. See, for a compelling account of AI black box: Ver: Bathaee, Yavar, "The Artificial Intelligence Black Box and the Failure of Intent and Causation", *Harvard Journal of Law and Technology*, n.º 37, 2018, p. 901 (adduces that "*one possible reason AI may be a black box to humans is that it relies on machine-learning*

doors of *Algorithmic Dictatorship*—for which I have been iteratively drawing a keen attention to—are ajar slightly. So are the doors of *algorithmic oppression*[2508] which, by now, are nothing but hackneyed/trotted-out/rattled off/reeled off old sayings.[2509]

---

algorithms that internalize data in ways that are not easily audited or understood by humans (...) "*first, a lack may arise from the complexity of the algorithm's structure, such as with deep neural network, which consists of thousands of artificial neurons working together in a diffuse way to solve a problem. This reason for AI being a black box is referred to as "complexity". Second, the lack of transparency may arise because the AI is using a machine-learning algorithm that relies on geometric relationships that humans cannot visualize, such as with support vector machines. This reason for AI being a black box is referred to as "dimensionality"*"). Italics added. But see: Pearl, Judea, *Causality*, 2nd edition, Cambridge, Cambridge University Press, 2009 (on the fundamental tenets of causality). But see: Kilbertus, Niki/Carulla, Mateo Rojas/Parascandolo, Giambattista/ Hardt, Moritz/Janzing, Dominik/ Schoellkopf, Bernhard, "Avoiding Discrimination through Causal Reasoning", *Advances in Neural Information Processing Systems*, I. Guyon, U. V. Luxburg, S. Bengio, H. Wallach, R. Fergus, S. Vishwanathan, and R. Garnett (Eds.), Vol. 30. Curran Associates, Inc., 2017, pp. 656–666 (arguing that is feasible to avoiding discrimination through a granular and fine-grained causal reasoning).

[2506] Lauritsen, Marc, "Towards a Phenomenology of Machine-Assisted Legal Work", *Journal of Robotics, Artificial Intelligence & Law*, Volume 1, Issue 2, 2018, pp. 67–79.

[2507] Caliskan, Aylin et al., "Semantics Derived Automatically from Language Corpora Contain Human-Like Biases", *Science*, 356, 2017, pp. 183 and ff and passim.

[2508] See: Noble, Safiya Umoja, *Algorithms of Oppression*: *How search engines reinforce racism*, New York, New University Press, 2018, pp. 1–248 ("*Run a Google search for "Black girls"—what will you find? "Big Booty" and other sexually explicit terms are likely to come up as top search terms. But, if you type in "white girls," the results are radically different.* The suggested porn sites and un-moderated discussions about "why Black women are so sassy" or "why Black women are so angry" presents a disturbing portrait of Black womanhood in modern society. In *Algorithms of Oppression*, Safiya Umoja Noble challenges the idea that search engines like Google offer an equal playing field for all forms of ideas, identities, and activities. *Data discrimination is a real social problem; Noble argues that the combination of private interests in promoting certain sites, along with the monopoly status of a relatively small number of Internet search engines, leads to a biased set of search algorithms that privilege whiteness and discriminate against people of color, specifically women of color*"). Italics added.

[2509] See: *Tech, Bias and Housing Initiative, the Promise and Perils of Residential Proptech, Year 1, Research Summary Report, April 2023, TechEquity Collaborative*, p. 5 available at: https://techequity.us/wp-content/uploads/2023/04/TBHI-Y1-Research-Summary-Report.pdf (28.11.2024). ("*Residential Proptech also has the potential to exacerbate the bias inherent in our housing system. Its rise is due, in part, to the desperation felt by average home seekers. With a severely constrained housing supply, companies offering an easier pathway to homeownership may exploit communities that have been harmed by housing discrimination in the past. Opaque algorithms incorporate biased data into their decision-making processes, making it harder to enforce fair housing laws.* Residential Proptech companies often operate in a regulatory gray area, leaving consumers without the protections they would have from traditional housing regulatory systems. *As unprecedented capital investment flows into this space, venture-backed companies' winner-take-all approach to growth has the potential to exacerbate inequality rather than combat it*"). Italics added. See: Part IV, This chapter, Sects. 4.1.4–4.1.4.2.3 of this book.

4.1.9 *Generative Artificial Intelligence Underpinning Large Language Models (LLMs) That Generate Human Language (e.g. ChatGPT): The Distinction Between Natural Languages (e.g. English) and Formal Languages (*Python *and* JavaScript*) Alongside With its Impact in the Legal Arena*

§§ Artificial Intelligence is leaving an indelible mark, and a unique fingerprint, on our daily lives. Nevertheless, Artificial Intelligence is a barren desert of murkiness, as opposed to a lush oasis of transparency.[2510] Notably, Artificial Intelligence is not a space of unwavering peace, infallibility,[2511] and transparency[2512] in that we must become acutely aware that one of its outgrowths—Generative Artificial Intelligence—may catalyse metamorphic shifts in the communications channels through which humans interact amidst the *age of permanent deception.*

§§ The speck of algorithmic lust underpinning Generative Artificial Intelligence is becoming visible. The audience—by definition, all of us—is accordingly enthralled by the headways, and rapid strides, made by a Generative Artificial Intelligence that never ceases to amaze. Generative Artificial Intelligence is accordingly holding the audience spellbound.

§§ It is important to note, though, the audience's curiosity often laces with awe and discomfort insofar acts of meaningful communication were hitherto carried out by humans and humans only. Which prompts the burning questions: how did we get here? Foremost, what lies ahead? Will Generative Artificial disrupt old communication patterns while presenting new paradigms of communication? Will these new paradigms of communications involve encountering, and stumbling upon, unpleasant hurdles (v.g. ChatGPT hallucinations that sully the trustworthiness of Generative

---

[2510] See: Bathaee, Yavar, "The Artificial Intelligence Black Box and the Failure of Intent and Causation", *Harvard Journal of Law and Technology*, n.° 37, 2018, p. 901 (adduces that "*one possible reason AI may be a black box to humans is that it relies on machine-learning algorithms that internalize data in ways that are not easily audited or understood by humans* (…) "*first, a lack may arise from the complexity of the algorithm's structure, such as with deep neural network, which consists of thousands of artificial neurons working together in a diffuse way to solve a problem. This reason for AI being a black box is referred to as "complexity". Second, the lack of transparency may arise because the AI is using a machine-learning algorithm that relies on geometric relationships that humans cannot visualize, such as with support vector machines. This reason for AI being a black box is referred to as "dimensionality"*). Italics added.

[2511] See: Citron, Danielle Keats, "Technological Due Process", *Washington Law Review*, 2008, p. 1249 (one must shy away from the perceived "tendency to presume a computer system's infallibility").

[2512] See: de Laat, Paul B. 'Algorithmic Decision-Making Based on Machine Learning from Big Data: Can Transparency Restore Accountability?", *Philosophy & Technology*, Volume 31, 2018, pp. 524 and ff and passim (broaches the plethora of limitations related with full transparency, privacy, deleterious effects, competitive edge, and the shroud of opacity under which algorithms are often wrapped); Mittelstadt, B./Russell, C./Watcher, S., "Explaining explanations in AI", *Proceedings of Fairness, Accountability, and Transparency (FAT) (ACM)*, 2019, passim.

Artificial Intelligence)? Is Generative Artificial Intelligence a stinging reminder that a fast-paced technology is shaping up to overhaul the system of justice beyond recognition?

§§ Let's take a step back to state the threadbare: there have been colossal breakthroughs in the purview of Artificial Intelligence-embedded technologies in recent years.[2513] Amongst these significant advancements stands arguably Large Language Models (hereinafter LLMs).[2514]

§§ Note, though, that the central thrust to equip machines with an ability to meaningfully communicate in a manner tantamount to that of humans is anything but new in that is an endeavour that is somewhat hackneyed.

§§ As noted above,[2515] chatbot Eliza was created by Joseph Weizenbaum[2516] back in 1964. Chatbot Eliza, just like ChatGPT, was fully capable of engaging in a meaningful conversation with human beings. Eliza's behaviour was akin to that of humans insofar she could behave in a way a human would. Eliza was fully equipped to deftly use expressions, mannerisms, emotions, and archaisms that a human would.[2517] Hardly any surprise stems from the fact that Eliza was designed to mimic human

[2513] Surden, Harry, "ChatGPT, AI Large Language Models, and Law", *Fordham Law Review*, Volume 92, 2024, pp. 1941–1972 (1942), whose stellar research serves as an intellectual lodestar in this regard. The internal footnotes will be omitted.

[2514] For a nuanced and fine-grained account on the overall functioning, and inner workings of, Large Language Models: Tong Xiao/Jingbo Zhu, "Foundations of Large Language Models", arXiv:2501.09223v1 [cs.CL] 16 Jan 2025, NLP Lab, Northeastern University & Niu Trans Research, 2025, pp. 1–230 (ii) ("*Large language models originated from natural language processing, but they have undoubtedly become one of the most revolutionary technological advancements in the field of artificial intelligence in recent years.* An important insight brought by large language models is that knowledge of the world and languages *can be acquired through large-scale language modeling tasks, and in this way, we can create a universal model that handles diverse problems. This discovery has profoundly impacted the research methodologies in natural language processing and many related disciplines.* We have shifted from training specialized systems from scratch using a large amount of labeled data to a new paradigm of using large-scale pre-training to obtain foundation models, which are then fine-tuned, aligned, and prompted"). Italics added.

[2515] See: Part II, Chap. 2, Sect. 2.1.1 of this book (devoted to the endeavour of sketching out a skeletal overview on the history of Artificial Intelligence).

[2516] But see: Weizenbaum, Joseph, *Computer Power and Human Reason: From Judgment to Calculation*, 1st edition, New York, W. H. Freeman & Co, 1976, pp. 1–300 (227) ("examines the sources of the computer's powers and offers evaluative explorations of what computers can do, cannot do, and should not be employed to do") (this founding father of Artificial Intelligence presciently noted that we should not entrust Artificial Intelligence-embedded technologies with "tasks that demand wisdom"). Italics added. The approval of rental applications is arguably one of those tasks that should never be entrusted to machines). More on this on Part IV, This chapter, Sects. 4.1.4–4.1.4.2.1 of this book.

[2517] Alves, Jones Figueirêdo/Pimentel, Alexandre Freire, "Breves notas sobre os preconceitos decisionais judiciais produzidos por redes neurais artificiais (Brief notes about the judicial decisional prejudices produced by artificial neural networks), *cit.*, pp. 555–577 (562).

behaviour while appearing to be one. Eliza would have passed the Turing Test[2518] with flying colours.

§§ Relatedly, finding number 4 enshrined in the Proposal for the Dartmouth Summer Research Project on Artificial Intelligence laid out in 1956 (*how can a computer be programmed to use a language*[2519]) bears a striking resemblance with the basic tenets of Large Language Models against the backdrop of which ChatGPT unfolds.

§§ Compellingly, ChatGPT can be deployed to perform a portmanteau of wearisome tasks and accordingly accomplish a slew of meaningful goals. People are burgeoningly relying upon Large Language Models (LLM's) to run seemingly anodyne errands. The vexing question is: should they?.[2520] The answer to this pressing question will be given as we move along.

§§ So, what are Large Language Models of which ChatGPT is part of? As further shown below, Large Language Model are tools built to help people to undertake

---

[2518] About the Turing test: Russel, Stuart J./Norvig, Peter, *Artificial Intelligence: a modern approach*, Prentice-Hall, Inc. A Simon & Schuster Company, 1995 (The Turing Test aims to evaluate intelligent behaviour [1]. To proficiently evaluate intelligent behaviour, the computer should be interrogated by a human via a teletype, and passes the test if the interrogator cannot tell if there is a computer or a human at the other end [1]. The framework of Turing Test lies in the following and successive phases: the computer would need to possess the following capabilities: **0 natural language processing** to enable it to communicate successfully in English (or some other human language); moreover, < C > **knowledge representation** to store information provided before or during the interrogation; furthermore, <) **automated reasoning** to use the stored information to answer questions and to draw new conclusions; another feature needed is <) **machine learning** to adapt to new circumstances and to detect and extrapolate patterns [1]. Finally, to pass the total Turing Test, the computer will need computer vision <) **computer vision** to perceive objects and robotics (> **robotics** to move them about [1]. See also: Santos, Hugo Luz dos, *Direito Contratual do Jogo: Um Olhar Bifronte*, Braga, NovaCausa Edições Jurídicas, 2023, pp. 1–760; Simon, Herbert, *Artificial intelligence: Status and future potential*, National Research Council Report—Office of Naval Research, 1985.

[2519] Which reads as follows: "It may be speculated that a *large part of human thought consists of manipulating words according to rules of reasoning and rules of conjecture.* From this point of view, *forming a generalization consists of admitting a new word and some rules whereby sentences containing it imply and are implied by others.* This idea has never been very precisely formulated nor have examples been worked out". See: McCarthy, John/Minsky, Marvin/Rochester, Nathaniel/Shannon, Claude, "A Proposal for the Dartmouth Summer Research Project on Artificial Intelligence", http://jmc.stanford.edu/articles/dartmouth/dartmouth.pdf (access: 07.09.2024). Italics added. See: Part II, Chap. 2, Sect. 2.1.1 of this book (devoted to the endeavour of sketching out a skeletal overview on the history of Artificial Intelligence).

[2520] For further developments: Santos, Hugo Luz dos, *Inteligência Artificial (ChatGPT/AutoGPT/Robots-Advogados/Robots Proceduradores/Robots-Juízes) e Responsabilidade Penal das Pessoas Colectivas*, Braga, NovaCausa Edições Jurídicas, 2023, pp. 1–108. See: Santos, Hugo Luz dos, *Inteligência Artificial e Processo Penal*, Braga, NovaCausa Edições Jurídicas, 2022. See: Santos, Hugo Luz dos, ""Brain-Computer Interfaces, Generative Artificial Intelligence (ChatGPT and Deep Fakes) and Criminal Procedure Law: what's at stake?", *Journal of Research in E. and Computer Science*, Edinburgh, United Kingdom, June 2024, Volume 2, 2024, pp. 39–78, which I will follow closely in this regard.

several boresome chores, which are both time-consuming and energy-draining.[2521] How are LLM‘s fuelled? For the sake of brevity, Large Language Models ingest reams of data and text—gleaned from the internet—to predict the next word in a bid to form a meaningful sentence or a flawless essay.[2522]

§§ Fast forward to the gist of the topic at hand, LLMs are nothing but complex Artificial Intelligence systems[2523] that were created to grasp and generate human language (which, in turn, lies in stark contrast with AI systems suitably tailored to accomplish other set of chores,[2524] such as driving cars[2525] or pinpointing fraud[2526]).

[2521] Extolling the qualities of ChatGPT: Gamm, Grant M., "Artificial Intelligence and the Practice of Law: A Chat With ChatGPT", *Saint Louis University Law Journal*, Volume 68, 2024, pp. 605–606 ("*with an attorney using the tool in this way, they can more effectively prepare for events in a case, such as cross-examination, and can use this summation as a reference during the trial or with other members of the legal team.* An attorney who effectively utilizes ChatGPT can optimize their time and energy on more strategic and high-value tasks. ChatGPT can aid attorneys in proofreading their work, offering suggestions on complex issues, and organizing information. *This tool can be applied in any area of law, and its use is likely to significantly enhance the attorney's efficiency and productivity. Additionally, ChatGPT can provide quick and accurate answers to legal questions, enabling attorneys to make decisions with confidence.* By automating repetitive tasks, ChatGPT frees up time for the attorney to focus on other important aspects of their work. *ChatGPT can also help attorneys communicate more effectively with clients, other attorneys, and the court, resulting in a more streamlined and efficient legal process*"). Italics added.

[2522] Santos, Hugo Luz dos, ""Brain-Computer Interfaces, Generative Artificial Intelligence (ChatGPT and Deep Fakes) and Criminal Procedure Law: what's at stake?", *Journal of Research in E. and Computer Science*, Edinburgh, United Kingdom, June 2024, Volume 2, 2024, pp. 39–78.

[2523] But see: Segran, G., "The complexity of artificial intelligence", *Singapore Management University*, 2021, passim (on the elaborate and complex trappings of Artificial Intelligence). But see also: Adadi, Amina/Berrada, Mohammed, "Peeking Inside the Black-Box: A Survey on Explainable Artificial Intelligence (XAI), *Institute of Electrical and Electronics Engineers*, Volume 6, 2018, passim; Edwards, Lilian/Veale, Michael, "Slave to the Algorithm? Why a "Right to an Explanation" is Probably not the Remedy You are Looking for", *Duke Law and Technology Review*, Volume 16, 2018, pp. 18–67 (pondering whether and to what extent XAI will come in handy because citizens are woefully ill-prepared to "make use of the kind of algorithmic explanations they are likely to be offered"); Miller, Tim, "Explanations in Artificial Intelligence: Insights from Social Sciences", *Artificial Intelligence*, Volume 267, 2019, pp. 1–38.

[2524] Surden, Harry, "ChatGPT, AI Large Language Models, and Law", *cit.*, pp. 1941–1972 (1942).

[2525] See: Surden, Harry/Williams, Mary-Anne, "Technological Opacity, Predictability, and Self-Driving Cars", *Cardozo Law Review*, Volume 38, 2016, pp. 121 and ff (arguing that self-driving cars are mostly controlled by Artificial Intelligence-technologies). See: Smith, Bryant Walker, "Proximity-Driven Liability", *The Georgetown Law Journal*, Volume 102, 2014, pp. 1777 and ff (discussing the implications arising out of the uptick of vehicle automation in decades to come). See: Part III, Chap. 3, Sects. 3.1.5.9–3.1.5.9.3 of this book (devoted to Critical Artificial Intelligence Studies, with a sharper focus on the pressing challenges facing self-driving vehicles).

[2526] See: Barocas, Solon/Selbst, Andrew, "Big Data's Disparate Impact", *California Law Review*, Volume 104, pp. 2016, pp. 671–678 ("in particular, by exposing so-called 'machine learning' algorithms to examples of the cases of interest (*previously identified instances of fraud, spam, default, and poor health*), *the algorithm 'learns' which related attributes or activities can serve as potential proxies for those qualities or outcomes of interest*"). Italics added.

The best example of an LLM is ChatGPT devised by *OpenAI*, a chat-charged Artificial Intelligence system that, just like Eliza, can meaningfully engage in conversation, answer questions, and mimic human[2527] writing.

§§ Which begs the vexing question: so, how did we get here? Generative Artificial Intelligence forms part of a broader technology apparatus within which Large Language Models operate. The latter came into being in late 2022.[2528] Since then, there have been significant headways in the purview of Large Language Models. Much to our awe, LLMs'capabilities have remarkably augmented. ChatGPT[2529] is the living testament of such a great leap forward.

§§ ChatGPT is a computer-run tool fully equipped to create and «understand» complex written language[2530] texts,[2531] such as research papers, fiction stories, reasoning puzzles, and newspaper articles.[2532] Strikingly, and perhaps disturbingly, these strides likewise extend to generating a batch of legal documents.[2533] Ranging from contract drafting, clause review, litigation support,[2534]

[2527] Surden, Harry, "ChatGPT, AI Large Language Models, and Law", *cit.*, pp. 1941–1972 (1942).

[2528] "The first wave of excitement about generative *artificial intelligence* (ai) was like nothing else the world had seen. Within two months of its launch in November 2022, Chatgpt had racked up 100 m users. Internet searches for "artificial intelligence" surged; more than $40bn in *venture capital* flowed into ai firms in the first half of this year alone. The craze for consumer experimentation has since cooled a little: Chatgpt use has fallen and fewer people are Googling "ai". Son Masayoshi, a Japanese investor notorious for diving into already frothy markets, is thought to be interested in investing in *Openai*, Chatgpt's creator. But a second, more serious phase is beginning. An entirely new industry centred on supercharged ai models is taking shape. Three forces will determine what it eventually looks like—and whether Openai stays dominant, or other players prevail.". See: https://www.economist.com/leaders/2023/09/21/chatgpt-mania-may-be-cooling-but-a-serious-new-industry-is-taking-shape?utm_medium=social (access: 25.09.2023). media.content.np&utm_source = linkedin&utm_campaign = editorial-social&utm_content = discovery.content (access: 25.09.2023).

[2529] Surden, Harry, "ChatGPT, AI Large Language Models, and Law", *cit.*, pp. 1941–1972 (1942).

[2530] Sacco, Rodolfo, "Diversity and Uniformity in the Law", *The American Journal of Comparative Law*, Volume 49, 2001, p. 172 (stressing that "law is not independent, nor separated from other social phenomena. In addition to law, language, knowledge, and the quality of human endeavour (material objects and intellectual creations) together constitute human culture").

[2531] Beukeboom, CJ/Burgers, C., "How stereotypes are shared through language: a review and introduction of the Social Categories and Stereotypes Communication (SCSC) framework", *Review of Community-Based Research*, Volume 7, pp. 1–37; Blodgett SL, Barocas S, III HD, Wallach H, "Language (technology) is power: a critical survey of "bias", *NLP. ACL anthology, Proceedings of the 8th annual meeting of the association of computational linguistics*, 2020, pp 5454–5476 (on language amidst the rise of technology). See: Part IV, This chapter, Sect. 4.1.8 of this book (on biased word embeddings with an entrenched presence on search engines run by tech moguls).

[2532] Surden, Harry, "ChatGPT, AI Large Language Models, and Law", *cit.*, pp. 1941–1972 (1942).

[2533] Surden, Harry, "ChatGPT, AI Large Language Models, and Law", *cit.*, pp. 1941–1972 (1942).

[2534] Gamm, Grant M., "Artificial Intelligence and the Practice of Law: A Chat With ChatGPT", *Saint Louis University Law Journal*, Volume 68, 2024, p. 602 ("*there are many reasons to use ChatGPT as an attorney*. Using this tool can increase work productivity by cutting down the time spent on time-consuming tasks which can lead to an increase in billable hours. The tool can be used as a law clerk to provide new insight or proofreading. *ChatGPT can also be used to assist in brainstorming various solutions for clients and to strengthen any legal analysis that has been*

legal statutes, motions,[2535] and court opinions. Which, I may venture add, is wholly unbecoming in this regard as we are about to find out.

§§ In addition to this bundle[2536] of spine-chilling[2537] text analysis abilities,[2538] LLMs are suitably equipped to synthesize and reason about facts and the outer world.[2539] Furthermore, LLMs can engage in problem-solving within abstract topics; and even work with a set of modalities that extend far beyond text,[2540] ranging from images, sound, and video.[2541] It is often contended that these brisk changes have occurred at a lightning speed.[2542] Note, though, that whilst AI systems—that brought human language into a sharper focus—have been hanging around for decades,[2543] these earlier approaches were riddled with errors, limitations[2544] and functional shortcomings alike.

---

created. In ChatGPT's current state, it is likely best used for routine legal issues. These routine legal issues can range from document research to contract drafting and clause review and litigation support. ChatGPT enables attorney users to save time and highlight areas of focus for specific issues. For example, imagine a client is having an issue with Apple and using their app store"). Italics added.

[2535] Surden, Harry, "ChatGPT, AI Large Language Models, and Law", *cit.*, pp. 1941–1972 (1942).

[2536] Surden, Harry, "ChatGPT, AI Large Language Models, and Law", *cit.*, pp. 1941–1972 (1943).

[2537] But see: Buolamwini, Joy, Unmasking AI: My Mission to Protect What Is Human in a World of Machines, New York, Random House, 2023, pp. 1–336 ("*The conscience of the AI revolution" (Fortune) explains how we've arrived at an era of AI harms and oppression, and what we can do to avoid its pitfalls.* "AI is not coming, it's here. If we answer the beautiful call inside these pages, *we can decide who we are going to be and how we're going to use technology in service of what it means to be fully human*" (...) *To most of us, it seems like recent developments in artificial intelligence emerged out of nowhere to pose unprecedented threats to humankind. But to Dr. Joy Buolamwini, who has been at the forefront of AI research, this moment has been a long time in the making*"). Italics added.

[2538] Bryson, JJ, Narayanan, A., "Semantics derived automatically from language corpora contain human-like biases", *Science*, 356 (6334), 2017, pp. 183–186; Camacho-Collados, J., Pilehvar, MT, "Embeddings in natural language processing", *ACL anthology, Proceedings of the 28th international conference on computational linguistics*, 2020, pp. 10–15 (on language amidst the rise of technology).

[2539] Surden, Harry, "ChatGPT, AI Large Language Models, and Law", *cit.*, pp. 1941–1972 (1943). But see:

[2540] Surden, Harry, "ChatGPT, AI Large Language Models, and Law", *cit.*, pp. 1941–1972 (1943).

[2541] Hu, Margaret, "From the National Surveillance State to the Cybersurveillance State", *The Annual Review of Law and Social Science*, Volume 13, 2017, p. 169 ("*in a big data world, a digitized passport system can link to multiple other sources, such as license plate readers, No Fly Lists, and Terrorist Watchlists. Facial recognition technology drawing upon a photo database could potentially link a plethora of digital images of a person, including social media, the internet, photo databases like driver's licenses, live-streaming video, CCTV surveillance, and images obtained from hacking cameras on laptops and digital devices. Biometric data collection and storage are becoming increasingly compulsory through either government identification requirements*, such as digital photo requirements for passports and driver's licenses, or corporate identification requirements, such as biometric access to digital devices"). Italics added.

[2542] Surden, Harry, "ChatGPT, AI Large Language Models, and Law", *cit.*, pp. 1941–1972 (1943).

[2543] Surden, Harry, "ChatGPT, AI Large Language Models, and Law", *cit.*, pp. 1941–1972 (1943).

[2544] Surden, Harry, "ChatGPT, AI Large Language Models, and Law", *cit.*, pp. 1941–1972 (1943).

§§ Tellingly, more often than not, when parsing text, these systems would be either confused by mundane facts or led astray by basic word choices.[2545] Relatedly, preliminary AI systems would frequently produce either inscrutable or senseless outputs. In addition to that, the answers given were either wholly unrelated with the topic at hand or the machine would routinely fail to grasp the underlying meaning of what was being[2546] asked.

§§ Thence, whilst many researchers were keenly convinced that Artificial Intelligence-embedded technologies engagement with human language was a burgeoning field brimming with endless opportunities, it was still faintly aloof in practical terms even as recently as 2020 though.[2547] Notwithstanding, in an awfully short window spanning just two years (2022 and 2023), LLM systems made significant headways as far as intrinsic quality, usefulness, practicability, reasoning skills,[2548] and generality are concerned.

§§ Compellingly, LLMs like OpenAI's GPT-4 (released at the break of the dawn of 2023) showcased unrivalled, unmatched, unparalleled, and flabbergasting advanced abilities to understand arbitrary written-language instructions,[2549] parse data and text, and deal with unforeseen problems, thereby superseding the then cutting-edge technology.[2550] This unexpected betterment of Artificial Intelligence language abilities has baffled a cohort of pundits who study artificial[2551] intelligence for a protracted span of time.

§§ Within the remit of Artificial Intelligence-embedded technologies, polymaths often tie LLMs with the subfield that goes by the taxonomy of «natural language processing»[2552] (hereinafter NLP).[2553] Concisely, NLP[2554] is a domain chiefly focused on creating Artificial Intelligence-anchored technologies that comprise the

---

[2545] Surden, Harry, "ChatGPT, AI Large Language Models, and Law", *cit.*, pp. 1941–1972 (1943).

[2546] Surden, Harry, "ChatGPT, AI Large Language Models, and Law", *cit.*, pp. 1941–1972 (1943).

[2547] Surden, Harry, "ChatGPT, AI Large Language Models, and Law", *cit.*, pp. 1941–1972 (1943).

[2548] Surden, Harry, "ChatGPT, AI Large Language Models, and Law", *cit.*, pp. 1941–1972 (1943).

[2549] Surden, Harry, "ChatGPT, AI Large Language Models, and Law", *cit.*, pp. 1941–1972 (1943).

[2550] Surden, Harry, "ChatGPT, AI Large Language Models, and Law", *cit.*, pp. 1941–1972 (1943).

[2551] Surden, Harry, "ChatGPT, AI Large Language Models, and Law", *cit.*, pp. 1941–1972 (1943).

[2552] Surden, Harry, "ChatGPT, AI Large Language Models, and Law", *cit.*, pp. 1941–1972 (1945).

[2553] Surden, Harry, "ChatGPT, AI Large Language Models, and Law", *cit.*, pp. 1941–1972 (1945).

[2554] See on the fundamental tenets of Natural Language Processing (NLP): Pennington, J./Socher, R./Manning, CD., "GloVe: global vectors for word representation. Empirical Methods in Natural Language Processing (EMNLP). ACL Anthology", *Proceedings of the 2014 conference on empirical methods in natural language processing*, 2014, pp. 1532–1534; See: By A, Silberg J, Manyika, J, *Notes from the AI frontier: tackling bias in AI (and in humans)*, McKinsey Global Institute Caliskan, 2019; Bryson, JJ, Narayanan, A., "Semantics derived automatically from language corpora contain human-like biases", *Science*, 356 (6334), 2017, pp. 183–186; Camacho-Collados, J., Pilehvar, MT, "Embeddings in natural language processing", *ACL anthology, Proceedings of the 28th international conference on computational linguistics*, 2020, pp. 10–15; Bolukbasi T, Chang K-W, Saligrama V, et al, "Man is to Computer Programmer as Woman is to Homemaker? Debiasing Word Embeddings", arXiv:1607.06520v1, 2016; Radford, A./Wu, J./Child, R. et al, "Language models are unsupervised multitask learners", *Technical Report*; Rudinger, R./Naradowsky, J./Leonard, B./Durme, B Van, "Gender Bias in Conference Resolution", *NAACL HLT 2018—2018 Conference North American*

ability to grasp and generate human language and text. It is noteworthy that the expression «natural language» carries a particular meaning in computer science.[2555]

§§ Pivotally, NLP dovetails seamlessly with ordinary languages that humans routinely use to communicate with one another.[2556] Ranging from Cantonese, Portuguese, Italian, French, German, Spanish, and English. The expressions «natural language» and «formal language»[2557] are therefore poles apart in that they dwell on diametrically opposed sides of the field of computer science.

§§ «Formal languages» lend itself to an exceedingly complex and mathematically framed technical «languages» of which *Python*[2558] and *Javascript* stand as paradigmatic examples. These languages are routinely used, amongst a wide array of other things,[2559] to deftly program computers.[2560] Yet these natural languages are not without drawbacks and downsides. Tellingly, since formal languages were specifically created for direct, unencumbered, straightforward, unambiguous, blunt, mechanical interpretation, computers' ability to express themselves is rather abridged. Notwithstanding, computers are nonetheless equipped to process formal languages with a high degree of reliability.[2561]

§§ On the opposite pole, computer systems have proverbially grappled to understand the underlying meaning of common natural language sentences that many

---

Chapter Association Computer Linguist Human Language Technology—Proceedings of Conference, 2018, 2:8–14; Sap, M., Gabriel, S., Qin, L et al, "Social Bias Frames: Reasoning about Social and Power Implications of Language. Association of Computational Linguistics", *Proceedings of the 58th Annual Meeting of the Association of Computational Linguistics*, 2020, pp. 5477–5490; Nadeem, M./Bethke, A./Reddy, S., "Stereo Set: measuring stereotypical bias in pretrained language models", *ACL Anthology, Proceedings of the 59th annual meeting of the association for the computational linguistics and the 11th international joint conference on natural language processing*, Volume 1 (long papers), 2020, pp. 5356–5371. See: Part IV, This chapter, Sect. 4.1.8 of this book (on biased word embeddings with an entrenched presence on search engines run by tech moguls).

[2555] Surden, Harry, "ChatGPT, AI Large Language Models, and Law", *cit.*, pp. 1941–1972 (1945).

[2556] Surden, Harry, "ChatGPT, AI Large Language Models, and Law", *cit.*, pp. 1941–1972 (1945).

[2557] Surden, Harry, "ChatGPT, AI Large Language Models, and Law", *cit.*, pp. 1941–1972 (1945).

[2558] See: Chollet, François, *Deep Learning with Python*. Shelter Island, Nova Iorque: Manning, 2018, pp. 1–384 (passim).

[2559] Aggarwal, C. C., *Neural networks and deep learning*, Heidelberg, Springer, 2018, passim; Agrawal, A., Gans, J., & Goldfarb, A., "Prediction machines (updated and expanded): The simple economics of artificial intelligence", *Harvard Business Review Press*, 2022; Agrawal, A., Gans, J., & Goldfarb, A., "Power and prediction: The disruptive economics of artificial intelligence", *Harvard Business Review Press*, 2022; Bengio, Y., Hinton, G., Yao, A., Song, D., Abbeel, P., Harari, Y. N., Hadfield, G., Russell, S., Kahneman, D., & Mindermann, S., *Managing ai risks in an era of rapid progress*, arXiv preprint arXiv:2310.17688, 2023, passim (on neural networks and deep learning that operate jointly in the age of Artificial Intelligence-embedded technologies).

[2560] But see: Citron, Danielle Keats/Pasquale, Frank, "The Scored Society: Due Process for Automated Predictions", *Washington Law Review*, Volume 89, 2014, pp. 1, 4–5 (highlighting how human beings programming automated systems is directly conducive to, and leads, to fundamentally inaccurate results since the source code, predictive algorithms and datasets may encompass human biases which, in turn, have a disparate impact on historically disadvantaged groups).

[2561] Surden, Harry, "ChatGPT, AI Large Language Models, and Law", *cit.*, pp. 1941–1972 (1945).

people easily understand.[2562] Professor Harry Surden, whose gripping scholarly paper I have been keenly following, provides this insightful example: «Read this lease and tell me the name of the renter.»[2563]

§§ To the extent that grasping the underlying meaning of common sentences in natural language is an uphill battle for computers, whopping efforts have been made to allay these perceived pitfalls.[2564] The great bulk of research undertaken in the field of NLP has been geared towards striving to hone a slew of techniques that would suitably equip computer-run systems to understand and create ordinary language documents or rational speech at levels of accuracy that approach (or surpass) those «of a similarly situated[2565] person».

§§ Whilst modern LLMs like ChatGPT can engender uncannily human-like answers and convincingly respond to a set of natural language instructions, the scenario was far gloomier a while back.[2566] To better understand the relevance of a ensemble of strides made in this regard, it is crucially important to shed a keen light on earlier limitations with which NLP technology floundered.[2567]

§§ Long story short, prior to 2020, NLP systems were utterly unable to interpret written text at a shallowest level. Let alone remotely[2568] approaching the level of a mildly educated[2569] person. Artificial Intelligence-embedded technology accordingly tussled with grasping the underlying meaning of written documents. Ranging from simple written notes, emails, letters, books, essays, or trite written instructions. NLP systems of this epoch mainly parsed human communication as either mere words[2570] or data patterns instead.

§§ Therefore, although these preliminary NLP systems could convincingly identify keywords and text patterns within documents,[2571] such as emails, they nonetheless wrestled to aptly understand what emails and other natural language documents alike were actually[2572] talking about.

2562 Surden, Harry, "ChatGPT, AI Large Language Models, and Law", *cit.*, pp. 1941–1972 (1945).

2563 Surden, Harry, "ChatGPT, AI Large Language Models, and Law", *cit.*, pp. 1941–1972 (1945).

2564 Surden, Harry, "ChatGPT, AI Large Language Models, and Law", *cit.*, pp. 1941–1972 (1945).

2565 Surden, Harry, "ChatGPT, AI Large Language Models, and Law", *cit.*, pp. 1941–1972 (1945).

2566 Surden, Harry, "ChatGPT, AI Large Language Models, and Law", *cit.*, pp. 1941–1972 (1945).

2567 Surden, Harry, "ChatGPT, AI Large Language Models, and Law", *cit.*, pp. 1941–1972 (1945).

2568 Surden, Harry, "ChatGPT, AI Large Language Models, and Law", *cit.*, pp. 1941–1972 (1945).

2569 Surden, Harry, "ChatGPT, AI Large Language Models, and Law", *cit.*, pp. 1941–1972 (1946).

2570 Surden, Harry, "ChatGPT, AI Large Language Models, and Law", *cit.*, pp. 1941–1972 (1946).

2571 See: Murphy, Kevin P., *Machine Learning: A Probabilistic Perspective (Adaptive Computation and Machine Learning series)*. Massachusetts: The MIT Press, 2012, pp. 1–1104 (states avowedly that "machine Learning attempts to combine deductive, inductive, and abductive reasoning to make person-like reasoning in AI Entities possible. Machine-learning AI Entities initially learn in the same way a human child learns. First, they notice details and patterns in shapes, sounds, and behaviors; then put them together to distinguish one person from another, or a dog from a cat. Eventually, the AI can recognize and identify" common objects).

2572 Surden, Harry, "ChatGPT, AI Large Language Models, and Law", *cit.*, pp. 1941–1972 (1946).

§§ For instance, one should bear very firmly in mind how NLP systems of this epoch were severely limited when it comes to decoding legal natural language documents, such as contracts,[2573] legal credit scores,[2574] insurance policies,[2575] insurance risk classification enshrined in legal documents,[2576] genomic information packaged in legal documents,[2577] legal jargon ingrained in subprime lending,[2578] discriminatory wording embedded in subprime loans,[2579] legal jargon included within in standard employment-related documents,[2580] and the list goes on.

[2573] Surden, Harry, "ChatGPT, AI Large Language Models, and Law", *cit.*, pp. 1941–1972 (1946).

[2574] It is crucially important to note, though, that the very fact that only certain types of behaviours are assessed and gauged by credit scores leads to the conclusion some borrowers are not scored at all. The overwhelming majority of consumers boast meagre, if any, credit files owing to the fact that the likelihood to access to the sort of financial services that actually report to the orthodox credit bureaus scattered across modern economies is exceedingly low, which, in turn, morphs them into credit invisible persons. See: Yu, Persis/McLaughlin, Jilian/Levy, Marina, "Big Data: A Big Disappointment for Scoring Consumer Creditworthiness,", *The National Consumer Law Center,* 2 (Mar. 14, 2014), available at: https://www.nclc.org/images/pdf/pr-reports/report-big-data.pdf; [https://perma.cc/W4SK-NXD5] (access: 21.12.2024).

[2575] Abraham, Kenneth S., "Efficiency and Fairness in Insurance Risk Classification", *Virginia Law Review*, Volume 71, 1985, pp. 403, 407–08 (discussing the noxious consequences of insurance competition, pricing and risk ranking).

[2576] Prince, Anya E.R., "Insurance Risk Classification in an Era of Genomics: Is a Rational Discrimination Policy Rational?", *Nebraska Law Review*, Volume 96, 2018, pp. 624–626 and ff and passim.

[2577] Areheart, Bradley A./Roberts, Jessica L., "GINA, Big Data, and the Future of Employee Privacy", *Yale Law Journal*, Volume 128, 2019, pp. 710–716 (shedding a keen light on the fundamental tenets underpinning the GINA law).

[2578] But see: Havard, Cassandra Jones, "On the Take": The Black Box of Credit Scoring and Mortgage Discrimination", *Boston University Public Interest Law Journal*, 2011, pp. 239 and ff and passim (discussing that subprime lending was undoubtably geared toward minority communities, aiming to enmesh them on the trap of excessive debt); Johnson, Creola, "The Magic of Group Identity: How Predatory Lenders Use Minorities to Target Communities of Color", *Georgetown Journal on Poverty Law and Policy*, 2010, pp. 165–169 (fleshing out several aggressive marketing tactics used by unprincipled/unscrupulous lenders to target primarily minorities for eerily predatory loans).

[2579] But see: Freeman, Andrea, "Payback: A Structural Analysis of the Credit Card Problem", *Arizona Law Review*, Volume 55, 2013, pp. 180–81 ("Credit card companies confine low-income individuals to a subprime market and attempt to steer many middle-class African American and Latinos into subprime loans."); Munnell, Alicia H./Tootell, Geoffrey M. B./Browne, Lynn E./McEneaney, James, "Mortgage Lending in Boston: Interpreting HMDA Data", *American Economic Review*, Volume 86, 1996, pp. 25–29 (arguing that the likelihood that a loan request carried out by someone who is self-employed will be gainsaid is exceedingly high); Zywicki, Todd J./Adamson, Joseph D., "The Law and Economics of Subprime Lending", *University of Colorado Law Review*, 2009, pp. 1–9 (contending that Black workers with roughly the same abilities and educational background earn far less than comparable white workers or have considerably fewer employment opportunities).

[2580] Albeit the racial wage gap in the labour market is remarkably well parsed, discerning—or dissecting—this gap and the degree to which it sharply mirrors either taste-based or statistical discrimination has proven to be a gruelling uphill battle. See: Black, Dan Amelia Haviland/Sanders, Seth/Taylor, Lowell, "Why Do Minority Men Earn Less? A Study of Wage Differentials Among the Highly Educated", *The Review of Economics and Statistics*, Volume 88, 2006, pp. 300 and

§§ Professor Harry Surden has set forth an example of a tiny natural language contract clause, that reads as follows: «this agreement is governed by the laws of the state of California». If one were to have given this text to a preliminary NLP system, chances are that it may have been able to statistically classify it, with a decent degree of reliability, as a mere «governing law» clause.[2581]

§§ Such NLP systems run by learning patterns[2582] from thumping great document[2583] databases[2584] (*datafication*),[2585] in which kindred contract jargon had been

---

ff and passim (pinpointing eerily weird wage gaps between Black men and men of other races while shedding a keen light on the sweltering challenges in ascribing that perceived gap to blatant/blunt racial discrimination). See also: Grodsky, Eric/Pager, Devah, "The Structure of Disadvantage: Individual and Occupational Determinants of Black-White Wage Gap", *American Sociological Review*, Volume 66, 2001, pp. 542–563 (stumbles upon the finding in view of which that whilst Black men have burgeoningly gained access to highly remunerated occupations, they have nonetheless become subject to more extreme racial disadvantages when it comes to seizing power, which, in turn, can be loosely qualified as gate-keeping).

[2581] Surden, Harry, "ChatGPT, AI Large Language Models, and Law", *cit.*, pp. 1941–1972 (1946).

[2582] See: Chen, C./Rudin, C., "An optimization approach to learning falling rule lists", *Proceedings of Machine Learning Research, Artificial Intelligence and Statistics*, Volume 84, 2018, pp. 604–612; Sokolovska, N./Chevaleyre, Y./Zucker, J.D., "A provable algorithm for learning interpretable scoring systems", *Proceedings of Machine Learning Research, Artificial Intelligence and Statistics*, Volume 84, pp. 566–574; Rudin, Cynthia/Ustun, B., "Optimized scoring systems: toward trust in machine learning for healthcare and criminal justice", *Interfaces*, Volume 48, 2018, pp. 399–486 (on machine learning).

[2583] Zarsky, Tal, "Transparency in Data Mining: From Theory to Practice", *Discrimination and Privacy in the Information Society: Data Mining and Profiling in Large Databases*, Bart Custers et al. eds., Belin, Springer, 2013; Kroll, Joshua A. et al., "Accountable Algorithms", *University of Pennsylvania Law Review*, Volume 165, 2017, passim; Green, B./Hu L., "The Myth in the Methodology: Towards a Recontextualization of Fairness in Machine Learning", *Machine Learning Debates Work 35th Internation Conference of Machine Learning*, 2018, passim.

[2584] Custers, Bart, "Data Dilemmas in the Information Society: Introduction and Overview", Custers, Bart/Calders, Toon/Schermer, Bart/Zarsky, Tal (Editors), *Discrimination and Privacy in the Information Society: Data Mining and Profiling in Large Databases*, Heidelberg, Springer, 2013, pp. 3–26.

[2585] See: Hu, Margaret, "From the National Surveillance State to the Cybersurveillance State", *The Annual Review of Law and Social Science*, Volume 13, 2017, p. 165 ("*Datafication, like most big data processes, requires increasing amounts of digital data to support or construct cybersurveillance.* It empowers government actions that are based on digital data collection, data processing protocols, and bulk data analyses (Mayer-Schonberger & Cukier ¨ 2013). *Another way to characterize datafication is as a governmental policy interest that both transforms analog data (PCAST 2014) into searchable, centralized digital databases and develops new forms of stored data*"). Italics added. See: Hu, Margaret, "From the National Surveillance State to the Cybersurveillance State", *The Annual Review of Law and Social Science*, Volume 13, 2017, p. 165 ("*the big data revolution is just beginning. Because datafication is in its infancy, the cyber-surveillance capacities of big data governance systems, like the No Fly List, are still in nascent stages. Datafication, like most big data processes, requires increasing amounts of digital data to support or construct cybersurveillance. It empowers government actions that are based on digital data collection, data processing protocols, and bulk data analyses* (Mayer-Schonberger & Cukier ¨ 2013). Another way to *characterize datafication is as a governmental policy interest that both transforms analog data (PCAST 2014) into searchable, centralized digital databases and develops new forms of stored data*"). Italics added.

manually inserted, identified, categorized, and ultimately classified by lawyers, or other domain polymaths, as a «governing law» clause.[2586]

§§ NLP systems back then would have been fully able to match a sheer amount of words of the foregoing contract clause leveraging on data patterns previously gleaned/gauged from large contract datasets in order to categorize[2587] it. Thence, these preliminary NLP systems greatly excelled at, albeit were severely limited to, scarce chores like categorizing natural language text on the basis of previously acquired, detected, statistical[2588] data[2589] patterns.

§§ Notwithstanding, the relevant limitation of such NLP systems was their utter ineptitude to fully grasp the underlying meaning of these words.[2590] Tellingly, such NLP systems were wholly unable to convincingly understand the underlying meaning of the certain word patterns (such as «governed by the laws of the state of California») that they were tasked to analyse.[2591] Compellingly, they routinely dealt with written language primarily as data[2592] or a cluster of data,[2593] rather than words fraught with meaning.[2594]

§§ For instance, as Professor Harry Surden puts it, if one had asked a system from that period, «what are the consequences of having this contract governed

---

2586 Surden, Harry, "ChatGPT, AI Large Language Models, and Law", *cit.*, pp. 1941–1972 (1946).

2587 Surden, Harry, "ChatGPT, AI Large Language Models, and Law", *cit.*, pp. 1941–1972 (1946).

2588 Surden, Harry, "ChatGPT, AI Large Language Models, and Law", *cit.*, pp. 1941–1972 (1946).

2589 But see: Edick, Cole, "Opt-out Privacy Policy Worsens Algorithmic Price Discrimination: The Case of the American Privacy Rights Act", *Minnesota Journal of Law & Inequality*, 2024, p. 1.("*In a data-driven world, data governance has serious implications for social inequality—from civil rights to consumer protection.[1] But the current approach to data governance in the United States may overemphasize individual privacy choice at the cost of collective approaches to inequality that better mitigate the harms inherent in the datafication of an already-unequal society.* [2] This blog post examines that tension, critiquing the exceptions and opt-out mechanisms present in the recently announced American Privacy Rights Act of 2024 (APRA), *arguing that such provisions fail to adequately address inequality—in particular, the potential exacerbation of algorithm-powered price discrimination through APRA's loyalty program exception*"). But see also: Hardt, Moritz, "How big data is unfair: Understanding sources of unfairness in data driven decision making", *Medium*, Archived on Oct. 8, 2014, available at: https://web.archive.org/web/20141008185829/; https://medium.com/@mrtz/how-big-data-is-unfair-9aa544d739de. (access: 17.12.2024).

2590 Surden, Harry, "ChatGPT, AI Large Language Models, and Law", *cit.*, pp. 1941–1972 (1946).

2591 Surden, Harry, "ChatGPT, AI Large Language Models, and Law", *cit.*, pp. 1941–1972 (1946).

2592 But see: Barocas, Solon/Selbst, Andrew D., "Big Data's Disparate Impact", *California Law Review*, Volume 104, 2016, pp. 671–682 (discussing how data is often flawed, rigged, incomplete, imperfect and therefore algorithms inherit the prejudice of the original decision makers). But see: Citron, Danielle Keats/Pasquale, Frank, "The Scored Society: Due Process for Automated Predictions", *Washington Law Review*, Volume 89, 2014, pp. 1, 4–5 (highlighting how human beings programming automated systems is directly conducive to, and leads, to fundamentally inaccurate results since the source code, predictive algorithms and datasets may encompass human biases which, in turn, have a disparate impact on historically disadvantaged groups). But see: Bornstein, Stepanhie, "Antidiscriminatory Algorithms", *Alabama Law Review*, Volume 70, 2018, pp. 519, 524–528 (contending, however, that the tagged "facially neutral" algorithms producing discriminatory outcomes should be quashed).

by California Law?,» the answer would have been, il all likelihood, either absurd, harebrained, illogical, asinine, inscrutable,[2595] or outright unmeaning.

§§ Such NLP systems were bereft of capacity to, and fundamentally devoid of the ability to, fully grasp and aptly respond such a question and would not have had a single clue of what a[2596] «governing law» provision actually meant to a lawyer, nor could they aptly, or pertinently, have interpreted the contours of such a legal provision in natural language.[2597]

Understandingly, albeit not laudably, this batch of preliminary NLP systems mostly entertained language as data,[2598] thereby producing mostly statistical matches to a given set of patterns («e.g., "g-o-v-e-r-n-i-n-g»[2599]), without clutching the underlying legal or mundane meaning of a sentence like «governing law».[2600]

[2593] This is one of the perils of big data colour-blindness that nonetheless relies on proxies to race and gender to make algorithmic decisions. See: Hurley, Mikella/Adebayo, Julius, "Credit Scoring in the Era of Big Data", *Yale Journal of Law and Technology*, Volume 18, 2016, p. 149 ("*recent studies have also questioned the accuracy of the data used by these tools, in some cases identifying serious flaws that have a substantial bearing on lending decisions. Big-data tools may also risk creating a system of "creditworthiness by association" in which consumers' familial, religious, social, and other affiliations determine their eligibility for an affordable loan. These tools may furthermore obscure discriminatory and subjective lending policies behind a single "objective" score. Such discriminatory scoring may not be intentional; instead, sophisticated algorithms may combine facially neutral data points and treat them as proxies for immutable characteristics such as race or gender, thereby circumventing existing non-discrimination laws and systematically denying credit access to certain groups. Finally, big-data tools may allow online payday lenders to target the most vulnerable consumers and lure them into debt traps*"). Italics added. See: Part IV, This chapter, Sects. 4.1.2–4.1.2.3 of this book.

[2594] Surden, Harry, "ChatGPT, AI Large Language Models, and Law", *cit.*, pp. 1941–1972 (1946).

[2595] Surden, Harry, "ChatGPT, AI Large Language Models, and Law", *cit.*, pp. 1941–1972 (1946).

[2596] Surden, Harry, "ChatGPT, AI Large Language Models, and Law", *cit.*, pp. 1941–1972 (1946).

[2597] Surden, Harry, "ChatGPT, AI Large Language Models, and Law", *cit.*, pp. 1941–1972 (1946).

[2598] But see: *Tech, Bias and Housing Initiative, the Promise and Perils of Residential Proptech, Year 1, Research Summary Report, April 2023, TechEquity Collaborative*, p. 11, available at: https://techequity.us/wp-content/uploads/2023/04/TBHI-Y1-Research-Summary-Report.pdf (28.11.2024). ("*Once bad data enters the analysis of one factor, it gets baked into the subsequent process, multiplying the effect that one disadvantageous data point can have on someone's overall housing determination*"). Italics added. See: Part IV, This chapter, Sects. 4.1.4–4.1.4 .2.3 of this book. But see also: Hu, Margaret, "From the National Surveillance State to the Cybersurveillance State", *The Annual Review of Law and Social Science*, Volume 13, 2017, p. 169 ("*as a result of big data biometric governance trends, meaningful distinctions between biometric credentialing for identification and behavioral biometric profiling are disappearing. The objectives are merging: Reliable credentialing is used to advance security and precrime policy rationales. Biometric data mission creep occurs by necessity in a big data world because the cybersurveillance systems are often designed to engage in mass data integration and analysis and predictive policing. Biometric surveillance serves two purposes in preventive policing: It increases identity transparency, and the biometric data categorize identity through cataloging behavioral and physical characteristics and assess these characteristics for risk. Contrasting small data biometric credentialing protocols with big data credentialing protocols is useful. It illustrates how biometric surveillance fits within the Cybersurveillance State*"). Italics added.

[2599] Surden, Harry, "ChatGPT, AI Large Language Models, and Law", *cit.*, pp. 1941–1972 (1947).

[2600] Surden, Harry, "ChatGPT, AI Large Language Models, and Law", *cit.*, pp. 1941–1972 (1947).

§§ Not long ago, creating AI systems that could meaningfully grasp the meaning (or «semantics»)[2601] of natural language sentences, such as «this contract is governed by the laws of the state of California», would come across as, or be pegged as, a far-fetched illusion.[2602] Part of the conundrum was mostly related with flexibility of human languages.[2603]

§§ In the overwhelming majority of natural languages like English, one can impart the very same idea in multitudinous manners (e.g., «this contract must be interpreted under the legal rules and principles of California» as opposed to «the laws of the state of California control this agreement»).[2604] Relatedly, one can expound on a wide range of topics, drawing on antonyms, allegories, abbreviations, slang, synonyms, metaphors, nuances, thong in cheek, and broader context,[2605] likewise as reshaping, or reshuffling, sentences in multiple, fundamentally similar manners.[2606]

§§ In spite of the uncanny expressive semantic fluctuation of human language, the overwhelming majority of human beings effortlessly[2607] make sense[2608] of the vast assortment of putative linguistic formulations, linguistic variations, blasphemies, half meanings, ironic remarks, sarcasm, context-embedded language,[2609] high-context[2610] and low-context[2611] communication,[2612] suddenness of perceived

---

[2601] But see: Bryson, JJ, Narayanan, A., "Semantics derived automatically from language corpora contain human-like biases", *Science*, 356 (6334), 2017, pp. 183–186. See also: Caliskan, Aylin et al., "Semantics Derived Automatically from Language Corpora Contain Human-Like Biases", *Science*, 356, 2017, pp. 183 and ff and passim (arguing that NLP contain human-like biases).

[2602] Surden, Harry, "ChatGPT, AI Large Language Models, and Law", *cit.*, pp. 1941–1972 (1947).

[2603] Surden, Harry, "ChatGPT, AI Large Language Models, and Law", *cit.*, pp. 1941–1972 (1947).

[2604] Surden, Harry, "ChatGPT, AI Large Language Models, and Law", *cit.*, pp. 1941–1972 (1947).

[2605] Lind, Edgar Allan/Tyler, Tom, Huo, Y. J., "Procedural context and culture: Variation in the antecedents of procedural justice judgments", *Journal of Personality and Social Psychology*, Volume 73, 1997, pp. 767–780.

[2606] Surden, Harry, "ChatGPT, AI Large Language Models, and Law", *cit.*, pp. 1941–1972 (1947).

[2607] Rawls, Anne Warfield, "Wittgenstein, Durkheim, Garfinkel and Winch: Constitutive Orders of Sensemaking", *Journal for the Theory of Social Behaviour*, 41 (4), 2011, pp. 397–413 (parsing the invaluable contributes of those authors when it comes to understanding the value of sociology and philosophy of language in the realm of social interaction, mutual attention, and *mutual cooperation*) (italics added).

[2608] Searle, John, "How to Derive Ought from Is", *The Philosophical Review*, 73 (1), 1964, passim (stating that humans are indeed sense-makers that crave to make sense in the outer world). Language plays a starring role in attaining the commendable goal of make sense. Language is *a* tool to make sense. In fact, language is *the* befitted tool to make sense. Which is something worthy of being gushed over rather than glossed over. There would be no globalized society to be accounted for devoid of, and decoupled from, an apposite (and «on-the-ball») domain of language. See in Portuguese doctrine: Costa, José de Faria, "O direito penal, a linguagem e o mundo globalizado (Babel ou esperanto universal?)", *Revista de Legislação e de Jurisprudência*, 138, n.º 3955, 2009, passim (parsing the sweeping importance of language in the increasingly globalized criminal law realm).

[2609] In French language, Harold Garfinkel, "L'ethonomethodologie et le legs oublié de Durkheim", *Constructivism versus Naturalisme? Enquête: Éditions de l'École des Hautes Études en Sciences Sociales*, Paris, Dalloz, (2007) (parsing the notion of making sense together in a mutually intelligible community).

[2610] Barkai, John, "Cultural Dimension Interests, the Dance of Negotiation, and Weather Forecasting: A Perspective on Cross-Cultural Negotiation and Dispute Resolution", *Pepperdine Dispute*

chance events,[2613] subtle nuances in meaning[2614] and linguistic syntax as they swiftly understand text or speech acts[2615] from other[2616] human beings.[2617]

Resolution, 8 (3) 2008, 407–448 (407) (asserting that "in high-context cultures, the meaning of the communication lies mainly in the context and is not fully verbalized. The main issues may be only inferred or not discussed at all, and the actual words spoken carry less of the meaning or are the basis for inferring the meaning. For example, Asians are well known for saying «no» without speaking the word «no"). Converging: Gold, Julia Ann, "ADR Through A Cultural Lens: How Cultural Values Shape Our Disputing Process", *Journal of Dispute Resolution*, 2005, pp. 289–298 (298).

2611 Barkai, John "Cultural Dimension Interests, the Dance of Negotiation, and Weather Forecasting: A Perspective on Cross-Cultural Negotiation and Dispute Resolution", *cit.*: 407–448 (407) (this author brings forward his concept of cultural dimension interests (CDI). In this regard, this author follows the lines of Edward T. Hall and Julia Ann Gold by asserting that "high and low-context refers to how much of the meaning of a communication comes from the surrounding context compared to the words that are actually spoken"). See also: Gold, Julia Ann, "ADR Through A Cultural Lens: How Cultural Values Shape Our Disputing Process", *cit.*: 289–298 (298); Lee, Ilhyung, "In re Culture: The Cross-Cultural Negotiations Course in the Law School Curriculum", *Ohio State Journal of Dispute Resolution* 2005, pp. 375 ff; Hampden-Turner, Charles M., *Maps of the Mind: Charts and Concepts of the Mind and Its Labyrinths,* London, United Kingdom, Macmillan, 1981, pp. 1–224; Lewis, Richard D., *When Cultures Collide: Leading Across Cultures,* 3rd Edition, London, United Kingdom, Nicholas Brealey Publishing, 2005, pp. 1–599 (on the importance of culture on one's demeanours). See also: Barkai, John, "Cultural Dimension Interests, the Dance of Negotiation, and Weather Forecasting: A Perspective on Cross-Cultural Negotiation and Dispute Resolution", *cit.*: 407–448 (407) (contending that "in low-context cultures, people communicate directly and explicitly and are said largely to rely on the spoken words as opposed to non-verbal communication to express themselves» (....) People in the United States, Canada, Australia, New Zealand and most Northern and Western European countries use direct, explicit, low-context communication and Asians, along with most of the rest of the world, use indirect, implicit, high-context communication").

2612 Hall, Edward T., *Silent Language,* New York City, Anchor Books, 1973, pp. 1–217; Hall, Edward T., *The Hidden Dimension*, Anchor Books a Doubleday Anchor Book, New York City, Anchor Books, 1990, pp. 1–240; Hall, Edward T., *Beyond Culture*, New York City, Anchor Books, 1990, pp. 1–320; Hall, Edward T./Hall, Mildred Reed, *Hidden Differences, Doing Business with the Japanese, New York City,* Anchor Books, 1990, pp. 1–192; Hall, Edward T./Hall, Mildred Reed, *Understanding Cultural Differences, Germans, French and Americans,* London, United Kingdom, Nicholas Brealey Publishing, 2000, pp. 1–224 (Edward T. Hall is considered to be founding father of the cross-cultural communication. He was one that has laid out the seminal distinction between high-context and low-context communication).

2613 Teigena, Halvor/Kanten, Alf Børre, "Out of the blue: on the suddenness of perceived chance events", *Thinking & Reasoning*, Volume 29, n. º 1, 2023, pp. 137–175 (137) ("*people commonly use terms like 'random', 'by chance', or 'accidentally' when they describe occurrences that sidestep the normal course of events, with no apparent causal link to ongoing activities. Such intrusive events are typically perceived as happening all of a sudden.* This was demonstrated in seven experiments (N ¼ 1299) by asking people to identify statements they believed belonged to stories about chance events, and by comparing chance vs. nonchance events from their own life and from the lives of others. Suddenness also appeared to be more strongly associated with beginnings than with endings of an episode. Thus, statements about sudden beginnings of a career or a relationship were more readily believed to happen 'by chance' than 'not by chance'. *But life-changing events did not become more accidental simply by being placed in the beginning of a 'life chapter'. These studies highlight a central but neglected feature of perceived randomness*"). Italics added.

2614 Lynch, M., *Scientific Practice and Ordinary Action: Ethnomethodology and Social Studies of Science*, Cambridge, Cambridge University Press, 1993; Rawls, Anne, "Editor's Introduction and

§§ Antithetically, Artificial Intelligence-embedded NLP systems have conventionally scuffled with grasping the whopping variety of syntactical fluctuation, linguistic fluidity, semantic ambivalence, semantic vagueness, use of words to convey empathy,[2618] and abstract obscurity that forms part of a broader linguistic apparatus within which human written and spoken communication[2619] operates.

§§ Tellingly, these perceived functional pitfalls/shortcomings were the significant drivers of the creation of program computer using formal computer programming languages—like *Python*, *Javascript*, or *C-*, as opposed to natural languages, like English[2620] and French.

§§ Notably, in bygone days computer systems were simply unable to understand the meaning of natural human language communication assuredly enough to perform comparable computational instructions.[2621]

"Two Conceptions of Social Order of Action, Objects, and Identities versus Aggregate Orders of Individual Action", *Special Issue of the Journal of Classical Sociology*, Volume 9 (4), 2009), 500–520; Wittgenstein, Ludwig, *Philosophical Investigations* (Translation: G.E.M. Anscombe), Oxford, Basil Blackwell, 1953; Winch, Peter, *The Idea of a Social Science*, London, Routledge and Kegan Paul, (1958); Benjamin, Walter, "Fragmente zur Sprachphilosophie und Erkenntniskritik", Tiedemann, R./Schwepphauser, H. (Eds.), *Gesammelte Schriften*, Vol. 6, Frankfurt am Main, Germany, Suhrkamp, 1985, 9–53; Benjamin, Walter, "On language as such and the language of man", Selected Writings, Vol. 1, Cambridge, Massachusetts, United States of America, Belknap, 1996, pp. 62–74; Wittgenstein, Ludwig, *Bemerkungen über die Philosophier der Psychologie/Remarks on the philosophy of psychology*, Anscombe, G. E.M./Hacker, P.M.S./Schulte, Joachim, West Sussex, United Kingdom, Blackwell, 1980; Wittgenstein, Ludwig, *Philosophie der Psychologie—Ein Fragment/* Philosophy of psychology—A fragment, West Sussex, United Kingdom, Blackwell, 2009, pp. 189–243; Sumpter, D. J. T., *The Principles of Collective Animal Behaviour, Philosophical Transactions of the Royal Society*, 361, 2006, pp. 5–22 (canvassing the foundations of the social phenomenon of sensemaking and the importance of language in that regard. Chiefly, sociology of language and philosophy of language).

[2615] Searle, John, *Speech Acts*, Cambridge, Cambridge University Press, 1969, passim (stating, as hinted above, that humans are sense-makers).

[2616] Surden, Harry, "ChatGPT, AI Large Language Models, and Law", *cit.*, pp. 1941–1972 (1947).

[2617] Garfinkel, Harold/Rawls, Anne, *Toward a Sociological Theory of Information*, Colorado, Boulder Colorado, Paradigm Publishers, 1952, 2008; Garfinkel, Harold, "L'ethonomethodologie et le legs oublié de Durkheim", *Constructivism versus Naturalisme? Enquête: Éditions de l'École des Hautes Études em Sciences Sociales*, Paris, Dalloz, 2007, passim (parsing the notion of making sense together in a mutually intelligible community).

[2618] Newell, Lauren A., "Rebooting Empathy for the Digital Generation Lawyer", *Ohio State Journal on Dispute Resolution*, 34 (1), 2019, pp. 1–96 (4–6) (contending that empathy is now needed more than ever amidst a digital world in which people somewhere along the line ceased to communicate «face to face». Rebooting empathy in the remit of dispute resolution is the way forward in this scholar's insightful view).

[2619] Surden, Harry, "ChatGPT, AI Large Language Models, and Law", *cit.*, pp. 1941–1972 (1947).

[2620] Surden, Harry, "ChatGPT, AI Large Language Models, and Law", *cit.*, pp. 1941–1972 (1947).

[2621] Surden, Harry, "ChatGPT, AI Large Language Models, and Law", *cit.*, pp. 1941–1972 (1947).

§§ For instance, if we had tried to instruct machines[2622] of the not-so-distant past using wonted English[2623]instructions, such as «make a program where a red ball bounces around the screen,»[2624] an archetypical system could not quite comprehend what was being asked nor could the system generate a helpful, nifty, functional output.[2625] Let alone an intelligent-stemming one.

§§ Owing to the yawning gap between the natural language communication of humans and that of computers, the computer science «solution» was not to dictate computers using standard English (or any other natural language).[2626] Instead, pundits came to terms with the fact that, to communicate with computers, an artificially created language should be used. That is, a unique formal «computer languages». Note, though, that these languages bestow upon users only a small-scaled number of finite, narrow, sparse, explicit, clear, unequivocal, and highly specific instructions.[2627]

§§ Equipped with these highly constrained set of instructions, a computer can subsequently translate such a specific set of formal programming instructions into specifical computational actions and execute them accordingly.[2628] Therefore, «formal» programming languages trade off the linguistic ductility and malleability of natural human languages (e.g. English, German, Finnish, French, Portuguese, Swedish and so forth) for the exactness and accuracy which, in turn, equips computers to process and execute instructions seamlessly.[2629]

§§ Nevertheless, the foregoing formal computer languages are awfully limited in what they can understand and express given the complexity of everyday interactions, ideas, epiphenomena, and mundane facts.[2630] Briefly, until not so long ago, NLP computer-run systems could neither convincingly nor meaningfully answer to the wide range of natural language questions in a manner that both adults and children would.[2631]

§§ Not so long ago (late 2021), top-notch and cutting-edge NLP systems received trenchant criticism in that they have been accordingly labelled as «stochastic

---

2622 But see: Weizenbaum, Joseph, *Computer Power and Human Reason: From Judgment to Calculation*, 1st edition, New York, W. H. Freeman & Co, 1976, pp. 1–300 (227) ("examines the sources of the computer's powers and offers evaluative explorations of what computers can do, cannot do, and should not be employed to do") (*this founding father of Artificial Intelligence presciently noted that we should not entrust Artificial Intelligence-embedded technologies* with "tasks that demand wisdom"). Italics added. The approval of rental applications is arguably one of those tasks that should never be entrusted to machines). More on this on Part IV, This chapter, Sects. 4.1.4–4.1.4.2.1 of this book.

2623 Surden, Harry, "ChatGPT, AI Large Language Models, and Law", *cit.*, pp. 1941–1972 (1947).

2624 Surden, Harry, "ChatGPT, AI Large Language Models, and Law", *cit.*, pp. 1941–1972 (1947).

2625 Surden, Harry, "ChatGPT, AI Large Language Models, and Law", *cit.*, pp. 1941–1972 (1948).

2626 Surden, Harry, "ChatGPT, AI Large Language Models, and Law", *cit.*, pp. 1941–1972 (1948).

2627 Surden, Harry, "ChatGPT, AI Large Language Models, and Law", *cit.*, pp. 1941–1972 (194 8).

2628 Surden, Harry, "ChatGPT, AI Large Language Models, and Law", *cit.*, pp. 1941–1972 (1948).

2629 Surden, Harry, "ChatGPT, AI Large Language Models, and Law", *cit.*, pp. 1941–1972 (1948).

2630 Surden, Harry, "ChatGPT, AI Large Language Models, and Law", *cit.*, pp. 1941–1972 (1948).

2631 Surden, Harry, "ChatGPT, AI Large Language Models, and Law", *cit.*, pp. 1941–1972 (1948).

parrots». The reason for such a sobriquet was that the former imparted the phosphorescent illusion[2632] of understanding natural language when, in truth, the great bulk of the meaning-laden text generated by NLP systems back then arose from rehashed versions of pre-formed sentences that laypeople had previously used on the internet.[2633]

§§ Conversely, the paucity/dearth of «understanding» by NLP systems of that era became spottily clear when they were asked either unprecedented or very easy questions.[2634] This track of record of proven inaptitude to meaningly engage with unusual, unforeseen, unexpected, or ductile human communications rendered earlier versions of NLP systems awfully limited in that they were helpful for a very specific set of tasks only.[2635]

§§ Whilst these earlier versions NLP systems were marginally useful in markedly language-charged domains like law, their usefulness was narrowed down to the statistical classification of legal documents[2636] though. As adumbrated, NLP systems were wholly incapable of understanding the underlying meaning of written words. Let alone heavily language-charged documents such as contracts, court decisions, legal motions, or a simple lease.[2637]

§§ This cluster of perceived functional shortcomings had largely remained in place for a long-winded span of time.[2638] No bewildering surprise springs from the fact that a cohort of researchers regarded the ability of artificial intelligence-embedded technology to grasp human language meaningfully and reliably as a faintly aloof, and loosely distant, research objective.[2639]

[2632] See: "The **S**tochastic **N**eural **A**nalog **R**einforcement **C**alculator (SNARC) *embodied a type of neural network that is designed to learn from experience and improve its performance through a process of trial and error* (similar to *reinforcement learning*). *This machine was well suited for problems that involved sequential decision-making and made use of prior experience, for example — navigating out of a maze. In fact this is the problem Minsky had set out to solve.* The original SNARC system consisted of a set of 40 artificial neurons (specifically *Hebb synapses*) that are connected to each other in a network. Each neuron receives input from other neurons and produces an output that is passed on to other neurons in the network. The network is trained by adjusting the strengths of the connections between neurons based on the outcomes of previous trials. *The training of this network was manually done by the operator who would provide feedback to the machine when it produced the right outcome.*" Italics added. See: https://zahid-parvez.medium.com/history-of-ai-the-first-neural-network-computer-marvin-minsky-231c8bd58409 (access: 06.09.2024). See: Part II, Chap. 2, Sect. 2.1.1 of this book (on reinforcement machine learning created by Marvin Lee Minsky).

[2633] Surden, Harry, "ChatGPT, AI Large Language Models, and Law", *cit.*, pp. 1941–1972 (1948).

[2634] Surden, Harry, "ChatGPT, AI Large Language Models, and Law", *cit.*, pp. 1941–1972 (1948).

[2635] Surden, Harry, "ChatGPT, AI Large Language Models, and Law", *cit.*, pp. 1941–1972 (1948).

[2636] Surden, Harry, "ChatGPT, AI Large Language Models, and Law", *cit.*, pp. 1941–1972 (1948).

[2637] Surden, Harry, "ChatGPT, AI Large Language Models, and Law", *cit.*, pp. 1941–1972 (1948).

[2638] Surden, Harry, "ChatGPT, AI Large Language Models, and Law", *cit.*, pp. 1941–1972 (1948).

[2639] Surden, Harry, "ChatGPT, AI Large Language Models, and Law", *cit.*, pp. 1941–1972 (1948).

4.1.9.1 The Functional Capabilities of ChatGPT (Generative, Pretrained, Transformer) and the Extent to Which Legal Actors Can Heavily Rely on It

§§ Along with 2022 came the exponential augment of functional capabilities of AI NLP systems. This was set in motion, and sprang into action, by the much-acclaimed release of ChatGPT (GPT-3.5) back in November 2022 from the company OpenAI.[2640] ChatGPT was pompously announced as a research project—a chat-based interface to an underpinning LLM archetypical framework widely known as «GPT», whose fundamental tenets will be skeletally sketched out in due course.[2641]

§§ ChatGPT was created to deal with natural language text-based «prompts» from laypeople. A good example of a prompt would be «What is the capital of France?». Notwithstanding, ChatGPT was also designed to take instructions from users such as «Write a poem about a dog» and respond accurately while using human-like text.[2642]

§§ In addition to that, ChatGPT was likewise designed to generate a sheer amount of draft documents at an unforeseen pace, and at an unheard of, rate. Moreover, ChatGPT was also designed to produce draft document at an exceeding high level of quality on a wide range of topics, including legal documents like court motions,[2643] legal opinions, minutes, and contracts. What was flabbergasting to a lot of researchers was how briskly GPT-3.5 overcame many of the functional shortcomings that had plighted, and beset, preliminary versions AI LLMs, such as Galactica (created by Meta) and GPT-3 (OpenAI's earlier model that dates back 2020).[2644]

§§ Owing to—shrewdly and timely implemented—engineering innovations by OpenAI, ChatGPT evinced uncannily advanced AI capabilities in comparison to preliminary LLM technology. At one end of the spectrum, ChatGPT was fully equipped to respond reliably to just about any text question, input, or instruction that it was timely given.[2645]

[2640] "The first wave of excitement about generative *artificial intelligence* (ai) was like nothing else the world had seen. Within two months of its launch in November 2022, Chatgpt had racked up 100 m users. Internet searches for "artificial intelligence" surged; more than $40bn in *venture capital* flowed into ai firms in the first half of this year alone. The craze for consumer experimentation has since cooled a little: Chatgpt use has fallen and fewer people are Googling "ai". Son Masayoshi, a Japanese investor notorious for diving into already frothy markets, is thought to be interested in investing in *Openai*, Chatgpt's creator. But a second, more serious phase is beginning. An entirely new industry centred on supercharged ai models is taking shape. Three forces will determine what it eventually looks like—and whether Openai stays dominant, or other players prevail.". See: https://www.economist.com/leaders/2023/09/21/chatgpt-mania-may-be-cooling-but-a-serious-new-industry-is-taking-shape?utm_medium=social (access: 25.09.2023). media.content.np&utm_source = linkedin&utm_campaign = editorial-social&utm_content = discovery.content (access: 25.09.2023).

[2641] Surden, Harry, "ChatGPT, AI Large Language Models, and Law", *cit.*, pp. 1941–1972 (1949).

[2642] Surden, Harry, "ChatGPT, AI Large Language Models, and Law", *cit.*, pp. 1941–1972 (1949).

[2643] Surden, Harry, "ChatGPT, AI Large Language Models, and Law", *cit.*, pp. 1941–1972 (1949).

[2644] Surden, Harry, "ChatGPT, AI Large Language Models, and Law", *cit.*, pp. 1941–1972 (1949).

[2645] Surden, Harry, "ChatGPT, AI Large Language Models, and Law", *cit.*, pp. 1941–1972 (1949).

§§ The greatest roadblock facing LLMs back then was not primarily factual accuracy.[2646] Instead, something considerably more important was at stake[2647]: equip LLMs to engender accurate responses that were tangentially related to the «prompts» or instructions posed by users.[2648] Earlier versions of LLMs—prior to ChatGPT's rampant rise to prominence—floundered to deal with the cumbersome ductility of human language.[2649]

§§ Strikingly, when faced with inputs that were seemingly unfamiliar/outlandish or that they had not been particularly trained to solve, preliminary versions of LLM systems would either reply with gross inaccuracy or with scant relevance to the topic at hand, thereby displaying in broad day light that the AI system was either mazed/befuddled or failed to grasp the essence of what was being asked by the user.[2650]

§§ In stark contrast, ChatGPT was the very first LLM fully equipped to respond accurately to just about anything that it was either asked or instructed by users.[2651] Since answers given by ChatGPT consistently bore a striking resemblance with what was asked by the end-users (if not completely[2652] on point), it seemed as though that ChatGPT was the very first LLM to aptly comprehend the questions[2653] or instructions given by the former.[2654]

§§ For instance, a user could openly ask ChatGPT, «what is the significance of contract language like, «this agreement shall be governed by the laws of the state of California'?» and ChatGPT would not only recognize word-patterns like previous LLMs,[2655] but, and foremost, would be fully equipped to explain its standard meaning.[2656]

§§ This was quite an astonishing achievement indeed as back then it was thought that designing an Artificial Intelligence LLM system that consistently generated reliable[2657] and meaningful responses[2658] to whatever a user asked was highly unlike to be attained for quite some time.[2659]

[2646] Surden, Harry, "ChatGPT, AI Large Language Models, and Law", *cit.*, pp. 1941–1972 (1949).

[2647] Surden, Harry, "ChatGPT, AI Large Language Models, and Law", *cit.*, pp. 1941–1972 (1949).

[2648] Surden, Harry, "ChatGPT, AI Large Language Models, and Law", *cit.*, pp. 1941–1972 (1949).

[2649] Surden, Harry, "ChatGPT, AI Large Language Models, and Law", *cit.*, pp. 1941–1972 (1949).

[2650] Surden, Harry, "ChatGPT, AI Large Language Models, and Law", *cit.*, pp. 1941–1972 (1949).

[2651] Surden, Harry, "ChatGPT, AI Large Language Models, and Law", *cit.*, pp. 1941–1972 (1949).

[2652] Surden, Harry, "ChatGPT, AI Large Language Models, and Law", *cit.*, pp. 1941–1972 (1949).

[2653] But see: Xiao Fang/Shangkun Che/Minjia Mao/Hongzhe Zhang/Ming Zhao/Xiaohang Zhao, "Bias of AI-generated content: an examination of news produced by large language models", *Nature*, 14:5224, 2024, pp. 1–20 (p. 1) ("*our study reveals that the AIGC produced by each examined LLM demonstrates substantial gender and racial biases"*). Italics added.

[2654] Surden, Harry, "ChatGPT, AI Large Language Models, and Law", *cit.*, pp. 1941–1972 (1950).

[2655] Surden, Harry, "ChatGPT, AI Large Language Models, and Law", *cit.*, pp. 1941–1972 (1950).

[2656] Surden, Harry, "ChatGPT, AI Large Language Models, and Law", *cit.*, pp. 1941–1972 (1950).

§§ The reason for those perceived quandaries was that some activities—e.g. problem-solving and causal[2660] reasoning[2661]—were largely not what ChatGPT had been purposefully created to engage with.[2662] Instead, GPT-3.5 had been designed on a forebear model—GPT-3—which had been created mainly to generate human-quality natural human language text output.[2663]

§§ The foregoing NLP systems had been devised primarily to simulate (or feign?) a myriad of writings tantamount to that of written by humans—ranging from poems, telltale stories, tales, papers, short notes, and letters[2664]—by having previously parsed

---

2657 But see: See: Alimardani, Armin/Jane, Emma A., "Human Hallucinations: GenAI and the Mirage of Personalised Learning for All", 2024, p. 13 ("*The output generated by GenAI models includes an inherent randomness and the same prompt may result in various outputs. Therefore, it is likely that the outputs of GenAI models are never entirely accurate and reliable. In other words, we contend that existing GenAI systems represent a technology that requires a 'human in/on the loop' to verify outputs before they reach the end user. When incorporating GenAI into an educational chatbot, students are the end users, making it challenging to identify and rectify these errors promptly*"). Italics added.

2658 But see: Dahl, Matthew/Magesh, Varun/Suzgun, Mirac/Ho, Daniel E., "Large Legal Fictions: Profiling Legal Hallucinations in Large Language Models", *Journal of Legal Analysis*, Volume 16, 2024, 64–93 (64) ("*Do large language models (LLMs) know the law? LLMs are increasingly being used to augment legal practice, education, and research, yet their revolutionary potential is threatened by the presence of "hallucinations"—textual output that is not consistent with legal facts.* We present the first systematic evidence of these hallucinations in public-facing LLMs, documenting trends across jurisdictions, courts, time periods, and cases. *Using OpenAI's ChatGPT 4 and other public models, we show that LLMs hallucinate at least 58% of the time, struggle to predict their own hallucinations, and often uncritically accept users' incorrect legal assumptions.* We conclude by cautioning against the rapid and unsupervised integration of popular LLMs into legal tasks"). Italics added.

2659 Surden, Harry, "ChatGPT, AI Large Language Models, and Law", *cit.*, pp. 1941–1972 (1950).

2660 See: Pearl, Judea, "Causal inference in statistics: An overview", *Statistics Surveys*, Volume 3, 2009, pp. 96–146; Pearl, Judea, *Causality*, 2nd edition, Cambridge, Cambridge University Press, 2009; Pearl, Judea, *Causality*, 2nd edition, Cambridge, Cambridge University Press, 2009 (on the fundamental tenets of causality).

2661 But see: Kilbertus, Niki/Carulla, Mateo Rojas/Parascandolo, Giambattista/Hardt, Moritz/Janzing, Dominik/ Schoellkopf, Bernhard, "Avoiding Discrimination through Causal Reasoning", *Advances in Neural Information Processing Systems*, I. Guyon, U. V. Luxburg, S. Bengio, H. Wallach, R. Fergus, S. Vishwanathan, and R. Garnett (Eds.), Vol. 30. Curran Associates, Inc., 2017, pp. 656–666 (arguing that is feasible to avoiding discrimination through a granular and fine-grained causal reasoning). See also: Sap, M., Gabriel, S., Qin, L et al, "Social Bias Frames: Reasoning about Social and Power Implications of Language. Association of Computational Linguistics", *Proceedings of the 58th Annual Meeting of the Association of Computational Linguistics*, 2020, pp. 5477–5490. But see: Blair-Stanek, Andrew/Nils Holzenberger/Benjamin Van Durme, "Can GPT-3 Perform Statutory Reasoning?" *Proceedings of the Nineteenth International Conference on Artificial Intelligence and Law*, Braga, Portugal: Association for Computing Machinery, 2023; Guha, Neel, et al., "Legal Bench: A Collaboratively Built Benchmark for Measuring Legal Reasoning in Large Language Models", *Thirty-seventh Conference on Neural Information Processing Systems Datasets and Benchmarks Track*, 2023 (wondering whether and to what extent can LLM systems engage in competent legal reasoning).

2662 Surden, Harry, "ChatGPT, AI Large Language Models, and Law", *cit.*, pp. 1941–1972 (1951).

2663 Surden, Harry, "ChatGPT, AI Large Language Models, and Law", *cit.*, pp. 1941–1972 (1951).

2664 Surden, Harry, "ChatGPT, AI Large Language Models, and Law", *cit.*, pp. 1941–1972 (1951).

patterns from billions of sample documents collated from the compass of the data-driven world we live in (internet).[2665] Strikingly, though, problem-solving and causal reasoning were not a part of the equation insofar they were not part of its ancient design[2666] and overriding goals.

§§ Compellingly, it seemed as though ChatGPT's problem-solving and causal reasoning capabilities sprouted spuriously as an unforeseen outgrowth of enhanced exposure to gargantuan/behemoth amounts of big data,[2667] including programming source[2668] code,[2669] math riddles,[2670] and logic puzzles.[2671] Which loosely amounts to a data-driven learning[2672] that propels machine learning.

§§ Put differently, back then (late 2022) the great bulk of Artificial Intelligence pundits were left fazed and flummoxed by the rapid strides made by a probabilistic system[2673] that was purposefully created to emulate/mimic human-like written notes

---

[2665] Surden, Harry, "ChatGPT, AI Large Language Models, and Law", *cit.*, pp. 1941–1972 (1951).

[2666] Surden, Harry, "ChatGPT, AI Large Language Models, and Law", *cit.*, pp. 1941–1972 (1951).

[2667] Big data that is in the limelight these days. See: Sivarajah, Uthayasnkar et al., "Critical Analysis of Big Data Challenges and Analytical Methods", *Journal of Business Research*, Volume 70, 2017, pp. 263 and ff and passim; Jetten, Lieke /Sharon, Stephen, "Selected Issues concerning the Ethical Use of Big Data Health Analytics", *Washington & Lee Law Review Online*, Volume 72, 2016, passim; Wachter, S./Mittelstadt. B., "A right to Reasonable Inferences: Re-thinking Data Protection Law in the Age of Big Data and AI", *Columbia Business Law Review*, 2019, pp. 1 and ff and passim; See in French doctrine: Ferey, Samuel, « Analyse économique du droit, big data et justice prédictive», *Archives de Philosophie du Droit*, Volume 60, 2018, pp. 68–81; Završnik, A. "Algorithmic justice: Algorithms and big data in criminal justice settings", *European Journal of Criminology*, 2019, passim; Joh, Elizabeth E., "The New Surveillance Discretion: Automated Suspicion, Big Data, and Policing." *Harvard Law and Policy Review*, 10 (1), 2016, pp. 15–42.

[2668] But see: Deeks, Ahsley, "Secret Reason-Giving", *Yale Law Journal*, Volume 129, 2019, passim; Katyal, Sonia K, "The Paradox of Source Code Secrecy", *Cornell Law Review*, Volume 104, 2019, pp. 1183–1236 (discussing the shroud of secrecy under which source code are often wrapped).

[2669] But see: Citron, Danielle Keats/Pasquale, Frank, "The Scored Society: Due Process for Automated Predictions", *Washington Law Review*, Volume 89, 2014, pp. 1, 4–5 (highlighting how human beings programming automated systems is directly conducive to, and leads, to fundamentally inaccurate results since the source code, predictive algorithms and datasets may encompass human biases which, in turn, have a disparate impact on historically disadvantaged groups). But see: Bornstein, Stepanhie, "Antidiscriminatory Algorithms", *Alabama Law Review*, Volume 70, 2018, pp. 519, 524–528 (contending, however, that the tagged "facially neutral" algorithms producing discriminatory outcomes should be quashed).

[2670] But see: O'Neil, Cathy, *Weapons of Math Destruction. How Big Data Increases Inequality and Threatens Democracy*, London, Penguin Random House, 2016, passim (showing how algorithms utilized in modern societies are amenable to perpetuate racial discrimination, partially through perpetuation of social disadvantage and wealth divides).

[2671] Surden, Harry, "ChatGPT, AI Large Language Models, and Law", *cit.*, pp. 1941–1972 (1951).

[2672] Clough, D. R., & Wu, A., "Artificial intelligence, data-driven learning, and the decentralized structure of platform ecosystems", *Academy of Management Review*, Volume 47, Issue 1, 2022, pp. 184–189 and passim; Gregory, R. W., Henfridsson, O., Kaganer, E., & Kyriakou, H., "The role of artificial intelligence and data network effects for creating user value", *Academy of Management Review*, Volume 46, Issue 3, 2021, pp. 534–551.

[2673] Murphy, Kevin Patrick, *Machine Learning: A Probabilistic Perspective*, Massachusetts, MIT Press, 2012.

leveraging on next word prediction would briskly display unforeseen (yet less than perfect)[2674] set of abilities to entertain logic or technological issues that it had not been particularly exposed to before nor trained to deal with.[2675]

§§ Note, though, that GPT-3.5 was not without drawbacks and pitfalls. Commensurate with the functional flaws evinced by other LLMs then and since,[2676] the former would either make mistakes in answers or come up with doctored, warped, fabricated, uncanny («hallucinate»),[2677] phony, yet plausible-laden information.[2678] Furthermore, as many commenters have observed, one must fight shy of anthropomorphizing advanced LLMs like ChatGPT.[2679]

§§ Against this well-trodden and drawn-out background, big words like «understanding» and «intelligence» should be taken with a pinch of salt; it would be rather hazardous/reckless to feature these systems as «intelligent» in a manner tantamount to that of cognitively active humans.[2680]

§§ Overall, as it stands, LLMs are still befuddlingly advanced and state-of-the-art statistical pattern-pairing[2681] prediction[2682] machines[2683] at the end of the day.

2674 Surden, Harry, "ChatGPT, AI Large Language Models, and Law", *cit.*, pp. 1941–1972 (1951).

2675 Surden, Harry, "ChatGPT, AI Large Language Models, and Law", *cit.*, pp. 1941–1972 (1951).

2676 Surden, Harry, "ChatGPT, AI Large Language Models, and Law", *cit.*, pp. 1941–1972 (1951).

2677 Alkaissi, H., & McFarlane, S. I.,", Artificial hallucinations in ChatGPT: Implications in scientific writing", *Cureus*, 15(2), (2023, February 19), 2023, e35179. See also: Watcher, Sandra, "Limitations and Loopholes in the EU AI Act and AI Liability Directives: What This Means for the European Union, the United States, and Beyond", *Yale Journal of Law & Technology*, Volume 26, Issue 3, 2024, pp. 671–672 ("*Predictive and generative artificial intelligence (AI) have both become integral parts of our lives through their use in making highly impactful decisions.* AI systems are already deployed widely—for example, in employment, healthcare, insurance, finance, education, public administration, and criminal justice. Yet severe ethical issues, such as bias and discrimination, privacy invasiveness, opaqueness, and environmental costs of these systems, are well known. *Generative AI (GAI) creates hallucinations and inaccurate or harmful information, which can lead to misinformation, disinformation, and the erosion of scientific knowledge. The Artificial Intelligence Act (AIA), Product Liability Directive, and the Artificial Intelligence Liability Directive reflect Europe's attempt to curb some of these issues. With the legal reach of these policies going far beyond Europe, their impact on the United States and the rest of the world cannot be overstated.* In this Essay, I show how the strong lobbying efforts of big tech companies and member states were unfortunately *able to water down much of the AIA. An overreliance on self-regulation, self-certification, weak oversight and investigatory mechanisms, and far-reaching exceptions for both the public and private sectors are the product of this lobbying. Next, I reveal the similar enforcement limitations of the liability frameworks, which focus on material harm while ignoring harm that is immaterial, monetary, and societal, such as bias, hallucinations, and financial losses due to faulty AI products. Lastly, I explore how these loopholes can be closed to create a framework that effectively guards against novel risks caused by AI in the European Union, the United States, and beyond*"). Italics added.

2678 Surden, Harry, "ChatGPT, AI Large Language Models, and Law", *cit.*, pp. 1941–1972 (1951).

2679 Surden, Harry, "ChatGPT, AI Large Language Models, and Law", *cit.*, pp. 1941–1972 (1951).

2680 Surden, Harry, "ChatGPT, AI Large Language Models, and Law", *cit.*, pp. 1941–1972 (1951).

2681 Surden, Harry, "ChatGPT, AI Large Language Models, and Law", *cit.*, pp. 1941–1972 (1951).

2682 But see: Weizenbaum, Joseph, *Computer Power and Human Reason: From Judgment to Calculation*, 1st edition, New York, W. H. Freeman & Co, 1976, pp. 1–300 (227) ("examines the sources of the computer's powers and offers evaluative explorations of what computers can do, cannot

Notwithstanding, in spite of their dashing ability to produce outputs,[2684] most polymaths believed they did not quite «understand» their inputs and outputs in a manner akin to that of a layperson.[2685] Pundits promptly acknowledged these worrisome, and burdensome, functional shortcomings.[2686]

4.1.9.2 Can ChatGPT (Generative, Pretrained, Transformer) Forecast Future Events, Categorize Documents or Images, Control Self-Driving Cars, Detect Credit Card Fraud, or Spot Consumer Preferences? A Deep Dive on Both the Inner Workings of Machine Learning Algorithms and on How the «Machine Thinks» at the Level of Deep Learning and Neural Networks That Build on Correlations With an Entrenched Presence on Datasets, as Opposed to Causation

§§ The letters «GPT» in ChatGPT[2687] stand for «Generative Pretrained Transformer.»[2688] For the sake of clarity, one should break them down separately.[2689] It bears mentioning that «generative artificial intelligence» amounts to a catch-all, and

---

do, and should not be employed to do") (this founding father of Artificial Intelligence presciently noted that we should not entrust Artificial Intelligence-embedded technologies with "tasks that demand wisdom"). Italics added. The approval of rental applications is arguably one of those tasks that should never be entrusted to machines). More on this on Part IV, This chapter, Sects. 4.1.4–4.1.4.2.1 of this book. See: Part V, Chap. 5, Sect. 5.1.7.2 of this book (on law number two to control algorithmic decision-making, which mandates that black box models must not be entrusted with the task of making high stake decisions—v.g. health and freedom). See: Part V, Chap. 5, Sect. 5.1.8.5 of this book (on law number five to interpret algorithmic decision-making, which mandates that robot-judges, robot-prosecutors and robot-lawyers must not enter the courtroom for they are utterly incapable of making sound and interpretable value judgements). But see: Kleinberg, Jon/Lakkaraju, Himabindu/Leskovec, Jure/Ludwig, Jens/Mullainathan, Sendhil, "Human Decisions and Machine Predictions", *Quarterly Journal of Economics*, Volume 133, 2018, passim; Pasquale, Frank, "A Rule of Persons, Not Machines: The Limits of Legal Automation", *George Washington Law Review*, Volume 87, 2019, pp. 1 and ff and passim (

[2683] Aggarwal, C. C., *Neural networks and deep learning*, Heidelberg, Springer, 2018, passim; Agrawal, A., Gans, J., & Goldfarb, A., "Prediction machines (updated and expanded): The simple economics of artificial intelligence", *Harvard Business Review Press*, 2022; Agrawal, A., Gans, J., & Goldfarb, A., "Power and prediction: The disruptive economics of artificial intelligence", *Harvard Business Review Press*, 2022; Bengio, Y., Hinton, G., Yao, A., Song, D., Abbeel, P., Harari, Y. N., Hadfield, G., Russell, S., Kahneman, D., & Mindermann, S., *Managing ai risks in an era of rapid progress*, arXiv preprint arXiv:2310.17688, 2023, passim (on neural networks and deep learning that operate jointly in the age of Artificial Intelligence-embedded technologies).

[2684] Surden, Harry, "ChatGPT, AI Large Language Models, and Law", *cit.*, pp. 1941–1972 (1951).

[2685] Surden, Harry, "ChatGPT, AI Large Language Models, and Law", *cit.*, pp. 1941–1972 (1951).

[2686] Surden, Harry, "ChatGPT, AI Large Language Models, and Law", *cit.*, pp. 1941–1972 (1951).

[2687] Bamberger, Michael/Leeuw, Frans L., *Introduction to Artificial Intelligence and Big Data: lessons from evaluations of the rule of law and development*, Cheltenham, United Kingdom, Edward Elgar, 2025, p. 7 ("*Technological innovations like ChatGPT are being rapidly adopted by organizations and individuals, but are also studied with a critical eye in terms of ethics, transparency, bias, impact and rule of law dimensions*"). Italics added.

all-encompassing, umbrella expression comprising the deployment of AI systems in fields that are traditionally associated with attainments that lace with human creativity. Amongst which stands human language understanding and creation of things that, not so long ago, just human beings could pull off, such as cinema, music, random symphonies, art, digital footage, and video.[2690]

§§ For purposes here, it is crucially important to aver that the word»generative» is employed to niftily differentiate systems like ChatGPT that are entrusted with the task to generate human-seeming text from a wide range of AI systems that are solely focused on endeavours beyond of human creative purviews.[2691]

§§ For example, unlike ChatGPT, which is suitably tailored to engage in activities that a human creator would, there is a sheer amount of Artificial Intelligence-embedded technologies that were bespoke designed to predict[2692] or forecast[2693] future[2694] (events,[2695] security[2696] threats,[2697] criminal activities[2698] or phenomenon alike[2699]), categorize documents or images,[2700] predict[2701] recidivism,[2702] algorithmic risk[2703] assessment,[2704] deftly control self-driving cars,[2705] proactively detect

---

2688 Surden, Harry, "ChatGPT, AI Large Language Models, and Law", *cit.*, pp. 1941–1972 (1957).

2689 Surden, Harry, "ChatGPT, AI Large Language Models, and Law", *cit.*, pp. 1941–1972 (1957).

2690 Surden, Harry, "ChatGPT, AI Large Language Models, and Law", *cit.*, pp. 1941–1972 (1957).

2691 Surden, Harry, "ChatGPT, AI Large Language Models, and Law", *cit.*, pp. 1941–1972 (1957).

2692 But see: Crawford, Kate/Schultz, Jason, "Big Data and Due Process: Toward a Framework to Redress Predictive Privacy Harms", *Boston College Law Review*, Volume 55, 2014, pp. 93, 99–101 (pinpointing pathways through which predictive analytic tools perpetuate discriminatory practices).

2693 *Tech, Bias and Housing Initiative, the Promise and Perils of Residential Proptech, Year 1, Research Summary Report, April 2023, TechEquity Collaborative*, p. 10, available at: https://techequity.us/wp-content/uploads/2023/04/TBHI-Y1-Research-Summary-Report.pdf (28.11.2024). ("**Opaque, Predictive Algorithms Determine Who Gets What Housing Unlike Analog Models**, *Algorithmic Tenant Screening Tools Predict Future Behavior To Determine Housing Access As landlord tech took hold, more property managers of all sizes came to rely on it to interface with tenants. One key feature of landlord tech is the use of algorithms to screen rental applicants and assess their suitability as tenants. The tenant screening industry, which pulls a wide array of information about potential tenants to inform landlords' decisions, is now valued at $1.3 billion with as many as two thousand screening companies vying for market share.*10 11 *Such companies include Equifax, TransUnion, and Experian (commonly known as "The Big Three"), as well as smaller startup companies that apply algorithms to make those determinations faster*"). Italics added. See: Part IV, This chapter, Sects. 4.1.4–4.1.4.2.3 of this book. See: Part IV, This chapter, Sects. 4.1.4–4.1.4.2.1 of this book (on mortgage redlining). See: Part IV, This chapter, Sects. 4.1.2–4.1.4.3 of this book (on algorithmic credit scoring, consumer racism and credit card redlining). See: Part IV, This chapter, Sects. 4.1.4–4.1.4.2.3 of this book (on algorithmic redlining). See: Part IV, This chapter, Sect. 4.1.4.3 of this book (on "algorithmic redliking"). See: Part IV, This chapter, Sect. 4.1.3 of this book (on algorithmic prime-lining).

2694 See: Barocas, Solon/Selbst, Andrew D., "Big Data's Disparate Impact", *California Law Review*, Volume 104, 2016, pp. 677–78 (arguing that predictive data is predictive of a given/specific target variable (i.e., minimized future predicted claims) with training data which is both correctly "labelled" and "collected").

2695 Dobbie, Will, Jacob Goldin, and Crystal S. Yang, "The Effects of Pretrial Detention on Conviction, Future Crime, and Employment: Evidence from Randomly Assigned Judges," *American Economic Review*, Volume 108, 2018, 201–240; Flores, A.W./Lowenkamp, C.T./Bechtel, K., "False positives, false negatives, and false analyses: a rejoinder to "machine bias: there's software used

credit card[2706] fraud,[2707] determine interest rates[2708] on credit markets[2709] based on algorithmic[2710] risk-based[2711] pricing,[2712] identify consumer[2713] preferences[2714]

---

across the country to predict future criminal", *Federal Probation Journal*, Volume 80, 2016, pp. 38–46. Sun, R. (Ed.), *The Cambridge Handbook of Computational Cognitive Sciences*, Cambridge, Cambridge University Press, 2023.

[2696] Hayes, Paul/van de Poel, Ibo/Steen, Marc, "Algorithms and Values in Justice and Security", *AI & Society*, 2020, pp. 533 and ff and passim.

[2697] See: Hu, Margaret, "From the National Surveillance State to the Cybersurveillance State", *The Annual Review of Law and Social Science*, Volume 13, 2017, pp. 162–163 ("*policymakers view these technological developments, including biometric technologies, as tools with the potential to identify individuals who may pose a threat to national and homeland security and to prevent crime and terrorism. One example of technology intended for risk assessment and threat management is the post-9/11 program Total Information Awareness (TIA). (....) Collect-it-all efforts like TIA embody a philosophy that aspires to preventive policing. Mass data collection is construed as a tool to assess and prevent future threats (Murray 2010). In TIA and other programs tested or adopted after 9/11, biometric database screening and analysis have emerged as a preferred method for tracking, identifying, and establishing identity-based inferences in counterterrorism*"). Italics added. See also: Ball, Kirstie, and Frank Webster (Eds.), *The Intensification of Surveillance: Crime, Terrorism & Warfare in the Information Age*, London, UK: Pluto Press, 2007; Guzik, Keith, "Discrimination by Design: Predictive Data Mining as Security Practice in the United States' 'War on Terrorism.'", *Surveillance and Society*, 7 (1), 2009, pp. 1–17.

[2698] Algorithmic fairness lends itself to several incompatible standards. Whilst COMPAS falls short of meeting the baseline standards of "equal opportunity" and "equalized odds", it refrains itself from discriminating blacks from the prism of "predictive parity" nonetheless. A full-fledged analysis of the extant state of this scorching topic can be found in Hübner, Dietmar, "Two Kinds of Discrimination in AI-Based penal Decision-Making", *SIGKDD Explorations*, 2021. See also: Cofone, Ignacio N., "Algorithmic Discrimination is an Information Problem", *Hastings Law Journal*, Volume 70, 2019, passim; Hellman, Deborah, "Measuring Algorithmic Fairness", *Virginia Law Review*, Volume 106, 2020, pp. 811 and ff and passim; Johnson, Gabbrielle M., "Algorithmic Bias: On the Implicit Biases of Social Technology", *Synthese*, 2021, passim (on the interplay between algorithmic fairness and algorithmic biases).

[2699] See: Rudin, Cynthia, "A process for predicting manhole events in Manhattan", *Machine Learning*, Volume 80, 2018, pp. 1–31. See also: Berk, R., *Criminal Justice Forecasts of Risk: A Machine Learning Approach*, New York, Springer Science & Business Media, 2012, passim.

[2700] See: Hu, Margaret, "From the National Surveillance State to the Cybersurveillance State", *The Annual Review of Law and Social Science*, Volume 13, 2017, p. 169 ("*in a big data world, a digitized passport system can link to multiple other sources, such as license plate readers, No Fly Lists, and Terrorist Watchlists. Facial recognition technology drawing upon a photo database could potentially link a plethora of digital images of a person, including social media, the internet, photo databases like driver's licenses, live-streaming video, CCTV surveillance, and images obtained from hacking cameras on laptops and digital devices. Biometric data collection and storage are becoming increasingly compulsory through either government identification requirements*, such as digital photo requirements for passports and driver's licenses, or corporate identification requirements, such as biometric access to digital devices"). Italics added. See: Part IV, This chapter, Sects. 4.1.5–4.1.5.2 of this book (on "algorithmic Jim Crow", a travel ban issued during the first Trump Administration to prevent certain individuals from entering the United States of America, which, given its racial undertones, stands as an outgrowth of congeries of laws enacted during the Jim Crow epoch).

[2701] See: Part IV, This chapter, Sects. 4.1.1–4.1.1.1 of this book (on biased predictive policing). See: Part IV, This chapter, Sects. 4.1.10.1–4.1.10.6 of this book (on biased algorithmic risk assessment in criminal procedure law settings, with a sharper focus on COMPAS). See: Part IV, This

conducive to both personalized[2715] pricing[2716] and personalized insurance[2717] policies.[2718] Note, though, that the latter is riddled with opacity.[2719]

§§ By this token, the word «generative» in GPT seeks to highlight that its overriding goal straddles, and blends, with human creativity: the generation (and

---

chapter, Sects. 4.1.1–4.1.1.1 of this book (on biased predictive policing). Note, though, that, theoretically, one should not shy away, or veer away, from bifurcating/splitting the "prediction" issue from the "decision" issue. See: Corbett-Davies, Sam/Pierson, Emma/Feller, Avi/Goel, Sharad Goel/Huq, Aziz, "Algorithmic Decision Making and the Cost of Fairness", *Proceedings of the 23rd ACM SIGKDD International Conference on Knowledge Discovery and Data Mining* (Ass'n for Computing Machinery ed., 2017), 2017, passim.

2702 Zhu, Mirilla, "Jury, Using Artificial Intelligence to Predict Recidivism Rates", *Yale Scientific*, 2020, passim. See also: Chasemi et al., Medhi, "The application of Machine Learning to a General Risk-Need Assessment Instrument in the Prediction of Criminal Recidivism", *Criminal Justice and Behavior*, Volume 48, 2020, pp. 518–538; Rudin, Cynthia/Wang, Caroline/Coker, Beau, "The Age of Secrecy and Unfairness in Recidivism Prediction", *Harvard Data Science Review*, Issue 2.1. Winter 2020, 2020, passim; Eckhouse, L., Lum, K., Conti-Cook, C./Ciccolini, J., "Layers of bias: A unified approach for understanding problems with risk assessment", *Criminal Justice and Behavior*, Volume 46, Issue 2, 2019, pp. 185–209; Stevenson, M. T./Slobogin, C., "Algorithmic risk assessments and the double-edged sword of youth", *Washington University Law Review*, Volume 96, 2018, passim.

2703 Kehl, D. L., Guo, P., and Kessler, S. A., *Algorithms in the Criminal Justice System: Assessing the Use of Risk Assessments in Sentencing*, 2017, accessed at https://dash.harvard.edu/bitstream/handle/1/33746041/2017-07_responsivecommunities_2.pdf?sequence¼1 on October 24, 2024.

2704 See: Part IV, This chapter, Sects. 4.1.10.1–4.1.10.6 of this book (on biased algorithmic risk assessment in criminal procedure law settings, with a sharper focus on COMPAS). See: Part IV, This chapter, Sects. 4.1.1–4.1.1.1 of this book (on biased predictive policing). See also: Hamilton, Melissa, "The sexist algorithm", *Behavioral Sciences and the Law*, Volume 37, Issue 2, Special Issue: the Use of Statistics in Criminal Cases, March–April 2019, 2019, pp. 1 and ff ("*Algorithmic risk assessment tools are informed by scientific research concerning which factors are predictive of recidivism and thus support the evidence-based practice movement in criminal justice.* Automated assessments of individualized risk (low, medium, high) *permit officials to make more effective management decisions. Computer-generated algorithms appear to be objective and neutral. But are these algorithms actually fair? The focus herein is on gender equity.* Studies confirm that women typically have far lower recidivism rates than men. *This differential raises the question of how well algorithmic outcomes fare in terms of predictive parity by gender.* This essay reports original research using a large dataset of offenders who were scored on the popular risk assessment tool COMPAS. *Findings indicate that COMPAS performs reasonably well at discriminating between recidivists and non-recidivists for men and women. Nonetheless, COMPAS algorithmic outcomes systemically overclassify women in higher risk groupings. Multiple measures of algorithmic equity and predictive accuracy are provided to support the conclusion that this algorithm is sexist*"). Italics added.

2705 See: Part III, Chap. 3, Sects. 3.1.5.9–3.1.5.9.3 of this book (on Critical Artificial Intelligence Studies, with a sharper focus on the functional shortcomings facing self-driving vehicles). The worrisome challenges posed by the up-and-coming and rough around the edges self-driving cars. See: Teoh, Eric/Kidd, David G., "Rage Against the Machine? Google's Self-Driving Versus Human Drivers", *Journal of Safety Research*, Volume 63, 2019, pp. 57–59 and passim (on the legal quandaries laid bare by the self-driving cars). See also: Cracking the Code: the Black Box Problem of Ai, available at: https://scads.ai/cracking-the-code-the-black-box-problem-of-ai/ (access: 21.09.2024) ("*Artificial intelligence (AI) is increasingly becoming integrated into our daily lives, from virtual assistants to self-driving cars.* Despite AI having the potential to revolutionize the way we live and work, it also presents unique challenges. One of the most significant challenges is the "black

comprehending and grasping) of standard, ordinary, quotidian, written natural human language.[2720]

box" problem. *The black box problem refers to the lack of transparency and interpretability of AI algorithms. As a matter of fact, it is difficult to understand how an AI system arrives at its conclusions or predictions. This poses a significant challenge. Decisions made by AI can have serious consequences, such as in healthcare or financial sectors*"). Italics added.

[2706] But see: Karlan, Dean/Zinman, Jonathan, "Observing Unobservables: Identifying Information Asymmetries with a Consumer Credit Field Experiment", *Econometrica*, Volume 77, 2009, pp. 1993 and ff and passim (drawing on empirical evidence to premise the finding according to which moral hazard exists in consumer credit markets).

[2707] See also: Barocas, Solon/Selbst, Andrew, "Big Data's Disparate Impact", *California Law Review*, Volume 104, pp. 2016, pp. 671–678 ("in particular, by exposing so-called 'machine learning' algorithms to examples of the cases of interest (previously identified instances of *fraud*, spam, default, and poor health), *the algorithm 'learns' which related attributes or activities can serve as potential proxies for those qualities or outcomes of interest*"). Italics added. See also: *Cracking the Code: the Black Box Problem of Ai*, available at: https://scads.ai/cracking-the-code-the-black-box-problem-of-ai/ (access: 21.09.2024) ("*Similarly, in finance, AI algorithms are used for fraud detection, credit scoring, and trading decisions.* The lack of transparency and interpretability makes it difficult to understand how the algorithm arrived at a particular decision. *It also makes it challenging to identify and rectify errors or biases*"). Italics added.

[2708] Even absent direct compensation for exceedingly higher interest rates, more expensive loans are more profitable for lenders in that could ultimately sway loan officer compensation rate. See: Jackson, Howell E./Burlingame, Laurie, "Kickbacks or Compensation: The Case of Yield Spread Premiums", *Stanford Journal of Law Business and Finance*, Volume 12, 2007, p. 289 (shedding a keen light on how yield spread premiums have a direct bearing on exceedingly higher mortgage prices for regular consumers, which, in turn, may befall inordinately on the least sophisticated borrowers, amongst whom members of racialised communities).

[2709] But see: Dwork, Cynthia/Hardt, Moritz/Pitassi, Tonian/Reingold/Zemel, Richard, "Fairness Through Awareness, Proceedings of the 3rd Innovations", *Theoretical Computer Science Conference*, 2012, https://dl.acm.org/doi/10.1145/2090236.2090255; [https://perma.cc/T2U3-TNQ6] (discussing an individual fairness approach to algorithmic fairness); Meharabi, Ninareh/Morstatter, Fred/Saxena, Nripsuta/Lerman, Kristina/Galstyan, Aram, "A Survey on Bias and Fairness in Machine Learning", *ACM Computing Survey*, Jul. 2022 at 1; Fuster, Andreas/Goldsmith-Pinkham, Paul/Tarun Ramadorai/Walther, Angsar, "Predictably Unequal? The Effects of Machine Learning on Credit Markets", *Journal of Finance*, Volume 76, 2022, passim (providing a description of the variation in interest rates across racial groups carried out by machine learning algorithms).

[2710] But see: Einav, Liran/Jenkins, Mark/Levin, Jonathan, "The Impact of Credit Scoring on Consumer Lending", *The RAND Journal of Economics*, Volume 44, 2013, p. 249 (showing unequivocally that the adoption of computer-run algorithmic credit scoring led to conspicuously higher-risk applicant lending).

[2711] But see: Gathergood, John/Guttman-Kenney, Benedict/Hunt, Stefan, "How Do Pay-day Loans Affect Borrowers? Evidence from the U.K. Market", *The Review of Financial Studies*, Volume 32, 2019, p. 496 (arguing that payday loans catalyse persistent increases in defaults, which, in turn, cause consumers to exceed their bank overdraft limits).

[2712] This is often tagged as "risk-based pricing." See: Phillipps, Robert, "Optimizing Prices for Consumer Credit", *Journal of Revenue and Pricing Management*, Volume 12, 2013, pp. 360–365 ("[A] riskier customer should pay a higher price in order to compensate for the higher probability of default and the associated cost to the lender"). See also: Staten, Michael, "Risk-Based Pricing

§§ Relatedly, the word **«Pretrained»** in GPT is a crucially important concept in this regard. Tellingly, the latter plays a pivotal role in shedding a keen light on how system generates its outputs.[2721]

---

in Consumer Lending", *Journal of Law, Economics & Policy*, Volume 11, 2015, pp. 33 and ff and passim.

[2713] Note, though, that the foregoing examples hardly exhaust the scope and import of Artificial Intelligence-embedded technologies and Big Data. As captioned above, this whirlwind of forces is overhauling the consumer credit economy beyond recognition. See: Bruckner, Matthew Adam, "The Promise and Perils of Algorithmic Lenders' Use of Big Data", *Chicago-Kent Law Review*, Volume 93, 2018, pp. 3, 11–15. See also: Odinet, Christopher K., "Consumer Bitcredit and Fintech Lending", *Alabama Law Review*, Volume 69, 2018, pp. 781, 802–804.

[2714] Surden, Harry, "ChatGPT, AI Large Language Models, and Law", *cit.*, pp. 1941–1972 (1957).

[2715] Note, though, that this field is currently undergoing massive changes. Long story short, the pinpointed changes are essentially reshaping the field of financial advice, thereby offering personalized Artificial Intelligence-anchored assistants that promise to ameliorate consumer decision-making. See: Loo, Rory Van, "Digital Market Perfection", *Michigan Law Review*, 2019, pp. 815, 862–63, 878–79.

[2716] See: Wallheimer, Brian, "Are you Ready for Personalized Pricing? Companies Are Figuring out What Individual Customers Will Pay-and Charging Accordingly", *Chicago Booth Review*, 2018, passim; The Effects of Online Disclosure About Personalized Pricing on Consumers 7 (Org. for Econ. Coop. and Dev., Working Paper No. 303, 2021 ("[T]he quantity of personal data held on online consumers, combined with the increasing prevalence of personalization in other domains (e.g., advertisement), means there is at least potential for online personalized pricing to become more commonplace and more sophisticated"). But see: Bartlett, Robert/Morse, Adair/Stanton/Wallace, Nancy, "Consumer Lending Discrimination in the FinTech Era", *National Bureau of Economic Research*, Working Paper No. 25,943, Volume 50, 2019 (on the perils of consumer lending discrimination in the domain of personalized pricing). See also: Part IV, This chapter, Sects. 4.1.4–4.1.4.2.1 of this book (on mortgage redlining). See: Part IV, This chapter, Sects. 4.1.2–4.1.4.3 of this book (on algorithmic credit scoring, consumer racism and credit card redlining). See: Part IV, This chapter, Sects. 4.1.4–4.1.4.2.3 of this book (on algorithmic redlining). See: Part IV, This chapter, Sect. 4.1.4.3 of this book (on "algorithmic redliking"). See: Part IV, This chapter, Sect. 4.1.3 of this book (on algorithmic prime-lining).

[2717] But see: Abraham, Kenneth S., "Efficiency and Fairness in Insurance Risk Classification", *Virginia Law Review*, Volume 71, 1985, pp. 403, 407–08 (discussing the noxious consequences of insurance competition, pricing, and risk ranking). It bears mentioning, however, that scorching issue of whether and to what extent disparate impact alone should be actionable is different from, in that does not overlap with, the sweltering issue of proxy discrimination. For arguments about the desirability of disparate impact in insurance, see: Cohran, Matthew Jordan, "Fairness in Disparity: Challenging the Application of Disparate Impact Theory in Fair Housing Claims Against Insurers", *The George Mason University Civil Rights Law Journal*, Volume 21, 2011, pp. 159 and ff and passim (discussing the use of disparate impact theory and potential applicability to Fair Housing Act claims against insurers).

[2718] But see: Pope, Devin G. Pope/Sydnor, Justin R., "Implementing Anti-Discrimination Policies in Statistical Profiling Models", *American Economic Journal: Applied Economics*, Volume 3, 2011, pp. 206–210 (discussing how the FTC parsed credit score use in auto-insurance pricing as a proxy for race).

[2719] For an on-point breakdown of the distinct levels of opacity arising out of machine learning algorithms in the field of insurance: Selbst, Andrew D./Barocas, Solon, "The Intuitive Appeal of Explainable Machines", *Fordham Law Review*, Volume 87, 2018, pp. 1085, 1089–99 (holding that

§§ Tellingly, **«Pretraining»** is intrinsically intertwined with the computer science procedure of exposing an NLP system like GPT-4 to a whopping amount of written documents. Within which a sizable segment of the internet, likewise as many books and[2722] other meaningful references, in a bid to indoctrinate, educate, and acquaint the machine with the basic tenets of creation human-seeming language.[2723]

§§ To better understand this complexity algorithmic decision-making,[2724] it is of paramount important to cast a keen light upon foundational Artificial Intelligence concepts, such as «machine learning» and «self-supervised»[2725] learning.[2726]

§§ «Machine learning»[2727] falls within the remit of Artificial Intelligence-embedded technologies.[2728] The former is focused on programming algorithms that

---

there are plenty reasons for the insurer's ignorance. To begin with, the algorithm entails specialized knowledge to understand. That is, the insurer's employees may lack sufficient knowledge to understand the rationale behind the reasons in view of which the algorithm is producing prices for different customers—personalized pricing. Lastly, even if the insurer himself comprehends how the model operates, it may nonetheless lack expertise to comprehend why it operates the way it does. For that reason, the explainability of machines is a vital, but rather elusive, task. Thence, the famed authors deem it as the "nonintuitive" nature of algorithms. For purposes here, the insurer himself might indeed understand that its Artificial Intelligence-embedded technology formulates higher prices for those who actually access the website at hand, but may fail to come to terms with the fact that the explanation for this fact arises from the website's capacity to proxy for genetic information). See also: Scherer, Matthew U. Scherer, "Regulating Artificial Intelligence Systems: Risks, Challenges, Competencies, and Strategies", *Harvard Journal of Law and Technology*, Volume 29, 2016, pp. 353–369 (frames the crippling problem of opacity as "the possibility that the inner workings of an AI system may be kept secret and may not be susceptible to reverse engineering").

2720 Surden, Harry, "ChatGPT, AI Large Language Models, and Law", *cit.*, pp. 1941–1972 (1957).

2721 Surden, Harry, "ChatGPT, AI Large Language Models, and Law", *cit.*, pp. 1941–1972 (1957).

2722 Surden, Harry, "ChatGPT, AI Large Language Models, and Law", *cit.*, pp. 1941–1972 (1957).

2723 Surden, Harry, "ChatGPT, AI Large Language Models, and Law", *cit.*, pp. 1941–1972 (1958).

2724 See: *Making Computers Explain Themselves*, MIT's Computer Science and Artificial Intelligence Laboratory (Oct. 27, 2016), 2016, www.csail.mit.edu/making_computers_ explain themselves [https://perma.cc/C97B-PGUR] (explaining the importance of grasping the complex trappings of algorithm decision-making). See also: Turek, Matt, "Explainable Artificial Intelligence (XAI)", The *Defense Advanced Research Projects Agency* (DARPA), www.darpa.mil/program/explainable-artificial-intelligence; [https://perma.cc/2DS4-ZMNB] (shedding light on the oft-labelled interpretability of algorithms).

2725 See: Hardt M, Price E, Srebro N, "Equality of opportunity in supervised learning", ArXiv ID: 1610.02413v1, 2016, passim.

2726 Surden, Harry, "ChatGPT, AI Large Language Models, and Law", *cit.*, pp. 1941–1972 (1958).

2727 See: Hutto-Schultz, Jess, "Dicitur Ex Machina: Artificial Intelligence and the Hearsay Rule", *George Mason Law Review*, Volume 27, n. ° 2, 2020, pp. 684–718 (684) (machine-learning algorithms "*are capable of making intuitive decisions based in newly learned information, much like humans.* The new wave of AI developments will generate powerful AI that is capable of improvising itself, *perhaps even by rewriting its own algorithms, advancing its intelligence beyond that of humans*"). Italics added.

2728 Tegmark, Max, *Life 3.0: Being Human in the Age of Artificial Intelligence.* New York: Knopf, 2018, pp. 1–384 (pp. 24 and ff) (charts the path ahead for a wide range of intelligences, including artificial intelligence in the digital age). There is a handful of authors that wonder if artificial intelligence can mimic not only human intelligence but, and foremost, human behaviour. Amongst whom stands: Russel, Stuart, Norvig, Peter, *Artificial Intelligence: A Modern Approach.* London:

possess the ability to learn[2729] meaningful statistical patterns from data.[2730] Such is the kernel of data-driven learning.[2731]

§§ Once a machine-learning artificial intelligence algorithm has successfully identified patterns[2732] from a training[2733] dataset,[2734] these learned patterns[2735] can eventually be used to accomplish tasks like prediction[2736] or legal automation[2737]

United Kingdom, Pearson, 2018, passim; Boden, Margaret A., *Artificial Intelligence: A Very Short Introduction.* Oxford: Oxford University Press, 2018, passim.

[2729] See: Murphy, Kevin P., *Machine Learning: A Probabilistic Perspective (Adaptive Computation and Machine Learning series).* Massachusetts: The MIT Press, 2012, pp. 1–1104 (states avowedly that "machine Learning attempts to combine deductive, inductive, and abductive reasoning to make person-like reasoning in AI Entities possible. Machine-learning AI Entities initially learn in the same way a human child learns. First, they notice details and patterns in shapes, sounds, and behaviors; then put them together to distinguish one person from another, or a dog from a cat. Eventually, the AI can recognize and identify" common objects). See also: Hutto-Schultz, Jess, "Dicitur Ex Machina: Artificial Intelligence and the Hearsay Rule", *George Mason Law Review*, Volume 27, Issue 2, 2020, pp. 684–718 (689). See: Chollet, François, *Deep Learning with Python.* Shelter Island, Nova Iorque: Manning, 2018, pp. 1–384 (passim). *Deep Learning* stands as a byproduct of *Machine Learning. Machine Learning*, a subset of Artificial Intelligence, unfolds itself in *Deep Learning*, which "involves computer algorithms that have the ability to "learn" or improve in performance over time on some task". See also: Surden, Harry, "Machine Learning and Law", *Washington Law Review*, Volume 89, 2015, pp. 87 and ff. Italics added. See also: Chen, C./Rudin, C., "An optimization approach to learning falling rule lists", *Proceedings of Machine Learning Research, Artificial Intelligence and Statistics*, Volume 84, 2018, pp. 604–612; Sokolovska, N./Chevaleyre, Y./Zucker, J.D., "A provable algorithm for learning interpretable scoring systems", *Proceedings of Machine Learning Research, Artificial Intelligence and Statistics*, Volume 84, pp. 566–574; Rudin, Cynthia/Ustun, B., "Optimized scoring systems: toward trust in machine learning for healthcare and criminal justice", *Interfaces*, Volume 48, 2018, pp. 399–486.

[2730] Surden, Harry, "ChatGPT, AI Large Language Models, and Law", *cit.*, pp. 1941–1972 (1958).

[2731] Clough, D. R., & Wu, A., "Artificial intelligence, data-driven learning, and the decentralized structure of platform ecosystems", *Academy of Management Review*, Volume 47, Issue 1, 2022, pp. 184–189 and passim.

[2732] But see: Duster, Troy, "Pattern, Purpose and Race in the Drug War", *Crack in America: Demon Drugs and Social Justice*, Reinarman and H. G. Levine (Editors), Berkeley: University of California Press, 1997, passim (on biased patterns).

[2733] But see: Dong et al., Qi, "Imbalanced deep learning by minority class incremental rectification, *IEEE Transactions on Pattern Analysis & Machine Intelligence*, Volume 41, 2019, p. 1367 (posit that "*most existing learning algorithms produce inductive bias (learning bias)* towards the frequent (majority) classes if training data are not balanced, *resulting in poor minority class recognition performance*"). Italics added. See: Chandler, Anupam, "The Racist Algorithm", *Michigan Law Review*, Volume 115, n. ° 6, 2018, p. 1026 (on racist algorithms, noting that "the possibilities for discriminatory manipulation are legion"). But see: Altenburger, Kristen M./Ho, Daniel E., "When Algorithms Import Private Bias into Public Enforcement: The Promise and Limitations of Statistical Debiasing Solutions", *Journal of Institutional & Theoretical Economics*, Volume 175, 2019, pp. 97–98 (calls for a "debias predictive algorithms" to assuage racist and/or biased, doctored and bigoted algorithms nevertheless). See also: Hamilton, Melissa, "The Biased Algorithm: Evidence of Disparate Impact on Hispanics", *American Criminal Law Review*, Volume 56, 2019, pp. 1553 and ff and passim.

[2734] See: Wonyoung, So, "Which Information Matters? Measuring Landlord Assessment of Tenant Screening Reports", *Housing Policy Debate*, Volume 33, n. ° 6, 2023, pp. 1484–1510 (1501–1502) ("*Algorithmic scoring using criminal records is problematic because training data—a data set that is used to train a machine learning model—is inaccurate and the outcome variable ("desirable*

going forward.[2738] A common example of machine learning, that sits beyond GPT's compass, is «spam» email[2739] detection.[2740]

---

tenants") is unclear. For instance, the tenant screening company RealPage produces 11,000 reports using "abbreviated" criminal records, which are cheaper to acquire than full criminal records but do not include details of the resolution (Kirchner & Goldstein, 2020). *An inaccurate model is highly likely to result from tenant screening services using these kinds of abbreviated data, given that it is important to include the final resolution of criminal justice procedures for proper assessment. Moreover, it would be challenging to set an outcome variable for developing this kind of algorithm because it is hard to project a certain criminal outcome into "good" tenant behaviors*"). Italics added. See: Part IV, This chapter, Sects. 4.1.4–4.1.4.2.1 of this book (on mortgage redlining). See: Part IV, This chapter, Sects. 4.1.2–4.1.4.3 of this book (on algorithmic credit scoring, consumer racism and credit card redlining). See: Part IV, This chapter, Sects. 4.1.4–4.1.4.2.3 of this book (on algorithmic redlining). See: Part IV, This chapter, Sect. 4.1.4.3 of this book (on "algorithmic redliking"). See: Part IV, This chapter, Sect. 4.1.3 of this book (on algorithmic prime-lining).

2735 But see: Barocas, Solon/Selbst, Andrew D., "Big Data's Disparate Impact", *California Law Review*, Volume 104, 2016, pp. 671–682 (discussing how data is often flawed, rigged, incomplete, imperfect and therefore algorithms inherit the prejudice of the original decision makers). But see also: Citron, Danielle Keats/Pasquale, Frank, "The Scored Society: Due Process for Automated Predictions", *Washington Law Review*, Volume 89, 2014, pp. 1, 4–5 (highlighting how human beings programming automated systems is directly conducive to, and leads, to fundamentally inaccurate results since the source code, predictive algorithms and datasets may encompass human biases which, in turn, have a disparate impact on historically disadvantaged groups). But see: Bornstein, Stepanhie, "Antidiscriminatory Algorithms", *Alabama Law Review*, Volume 70, 2018, pp. 519, 524–528 (contending, however, that the tagged "facially neutral" algorithms producing discriminatory outcomes should be quashed).

2736 See: Agrawal, A., Gans, J., & Goldfarb, A., "Prediction machines (updated and expanded): The simple economics of artificial intelligence", *Harvard Business Review Press*, 2022; Aggarwal, C. C., *Neural networks and deep learning*, Heidelberg, Springer, 2018, passim; Agrawal, A., Gans, J., & Goldfarb, A., "Power and prediction: The disruptive economics of artificial intelligence", *Harvard Business Review Press*, 2022; Bengio, Y., Hinton, G., Yao, A., Song, D., Abbeel, P., Harari, Y. N., Hadfield, G., Russell, S., Kahneman, D., & Mindermann, S., *Managing ai risks in an era of rapid progress*, arXiv preprint arXiv:2310.17688, 2023, passim (on neural networks and deep learning that operate jointly in the age of Artificial Intelligence-embedded technologies).

2737 But see: Cohen, Julien E., *Between Truth and Power: The Legal Constructions of Informational Capitalism*. Oxford: Oxford University Press, 2019, pp. 1–376 (p. 192) (contends presciently that "*automated processes* have obvious efficiency advantages, *but such processes may not align well (or well at all) with applicable legal requirements that are couched in shades of gray*"). Italics added.

2738 Surden, Harry, "ChatGPT, AI Large Language Models, and Law", *cit.*, pp. 1941–1972 (1958).

2739 See: Barocas, Solon/Selbst, Andrew, "Big Data's Disparate Impact", *California Law Review*, Volume 104, pp. 2016, pp. 671–678 ("in particular, by exposing so-called 'machine learning' algorithms to examples of the cases of interest (previously identified instances of fraud, *spam*, default, and poor health), *the algorithm 'learns' which related attributes or activities can serve as potential proxies for those qualities or outcomes of interest*"). Italics added.

2740 Surden, Harry, "ChatGPT, AI Large Language Models, and Law", *cit.*, pp. 1941–1972 (1958).

§§ At the outset, it is pivotally important to note, though, that every time bad data[2741] gets baked into machine learning algorithms,[2742] algorithmic discrimination[2743] strikes with a crushing force insofar quells any shiver of hope that algorithmic fairness[2744] will eventually trounce, let alone vanquish, algorithmic injustice.[2745] Which, I may venture add, is wholly unsavoury for members of racialized communities (e.g. Blacks and Latinos)[2746] inasmuch beckons unsighting prospects

[2741] See: *Tech, Bias and Housing Initiative, the Promise and Perils of Residential Proptech, Year 1, Research Summary Report, April 2023, TechEquity Collaborative*, p. 11, available at: https://techequity.us/wp-content/uploads/2023/04/TBHI-Y1-Research-Summary-Report.pdf (28.11.2024). ("*Once bad data enters the analysis of one factor, it gets baked into the subsequent process, multiplying the effect that one disadvantageous data point can have on someone's overall housing determination*"). Italics added. See: Part IV, This chapter, Sects. 4.1.4–4.1.4.2.3 of this book. See: Part IV, This chapter, Sects. 4.1.4–4.1.4.2.1 of this book (on mortgage redlining). See: Part IV, This chapter, Sects. 4.1.2–4.1.4.3 of this book (on algorithmic credit scoring, consumer racism and credit card redlining). See: Part IV, This chapter, Sects. 4.1.4–4.1.4.2.3 of this book (on algorithmic redlining). See: Part IV, This chapter, Sect. 4.1.4.3 of this book (on "algorithmic redliking"). See: Part IV, This chapter, Sect. 4.1.3 of this book (on algorithmic prime-lining).

[2742] But see: Benjamin, Ruha, *Race After Technology: Abolitionist Tools for the New Jim Code*, New York, Polity, 2019, pp. 1–172 (7) (discussing that Artificial Intelligence-embedded technologies are viewed as iron-clad tools of objectivity and devoid of any biases whatsoever). Ruha Benjamin accordingly contends that "the employment of new technologies that reflect and reproduce existing inequities but that are promoted and perceived as more objective or progressive than the discriminatory systems of a previous era"). But see also: Farina, M./Lavazza, A., *Philosophy, expertise, and the myth of* neutrality, Routledge Studies in Contemporary Philosophy, London, Routledge, 2024.

[2743] See on algorithmic discrimination: Kleinberg, Jon, et al., "Discrimination in the Age of Algorithms", *Journal of Legal Analysis*, 2018, pp. 114–174; See: Kleinberg, Jon, et al., "Algorithms as Discrimination Detectors", *Proceeds of the National Academy of Science*, Volume 117, 2020, pp. 30096–30110; Griemmelmann, James/Westreich, Daniel, "Incomprehensible Discrimination ", *California Law Review Online*, Volume 7, 2018, pp. 164–171; Xiang, Alice, "Reconciling Legal and Technical Approaches to Algorithmic Bias", *Tennessee Law Review*, Volume 88, 2021, passim; Karnow, Curtis E. A., "The Opinion of Machines", *The Cambridge Handbook of the Law of Algorithms*, Bartfield, Woodrow (Editor), Cambridge, United Kingdom: Cambridge University Press, 2021, pp. 15 and ff and passim; Strandburg, Katherine J., "Rulemaking and Inscrutable Decision Tools", *Columbia Law Review*, Volume 119, 2019, passim.

[2744] Note, though, that algorithmic fairness lends itself to several incompatible standards. Whilst COMPAS falls short of meeting the baseline standards of "equal opportunity" and "equalized odds", it refrains itself from discriminating blacks from the prism of "predictive parity" nonetheless. A full-fledged analysis of the extant state of this scorching topic can be found in Hübner, Dietmar, "Two Kinds of Discrimination in AI-Based penal Decision-Making", *SIGKDD Explorations*, 2021; Hellman, Deborah, "Measuring Algorithmic Fairness", *Virginia Law Review*, Volume 106, 2020, pp. 811 and ff and passim; Floridi, Luciano, "Algorithmic fairness in mortgage lending: from absolute conditions to relational trade-offs", *SSRN Electron Journal*, 2020, available at: https://doi.org/10.2139/SSRN.3559407 (accessed: 5.1.2025).

[2745] See: Ting-an Lin, "Democratizing AI" and the Concern of Algorithmic Injustice", *Philosophy and Technology*, Volume 37 (103), 2024, pp. 3–27; Okidegbe, Ngozi, "The Democratizing Potential of Algorithms?", *Connecticut Law Review*, Volume 54, 2021, passim; Katyal, Sonia, "Private Accountability in the Age of Artificial Intelligence", *UCLA Law Review*, Volume 66, 2019, pp. 54–99.

[2746] See: Allen, James, "The Color of Algorithms: An Analysis and Proposed Research Agenda Deterring Algorithmic Redlining", *Fordham Urban Law Journal*, Volume 46, 2019, pp. 219–234

for the latter.[2747] For a simple reason: algorithmic fairness[2748] plays a pivotal role in tapering long-standing[2749] racial inequalities.[2750] Enough said about this.[2751] The time is now ripe to drill into, and shed a keen light on, the pathways through which machine learning algorithms «learn» to spotlight spam emails.

(229–234) (discussing how historical mortgage redlining greatly swayed modern algorithms generated by massive batches of data sets that consist of decades of information built on exclusion and racial discrimination in the purview of financing, marketing, and housing). See: Part IV, This chapter, Sects. 4.1.4–4.1.4.2.3 of this book. See: Part IV, This chapter, Sects. 4.1.4–4.1.4.2.1 of this book (on mortgage redlining). See: Part IV, This chapter, Sects. 4.1.2–4.1.4.3 of this book (on algorithmic credit scoring, consumer racism and credit card redlining). See: Part IV, This chapter, Sects. 4.1.4–4.1.4.2.3 of this book (on algorithmic redlining). See: Part IV, This chapter, Sect. 4.1.4.3 of this book (on "algorithmic redliking"). See: Part IV, This chapter, Sect. 4.1.3 of this book (on algorithmic prime-lining).

[2747] See: Hurley, Mikella/Adebayo, Julius, "Credit Scoring in the Era of Big Data", *Yale Journal of Law and Technology*, Volume 18, 2016, p. 149 ("*these tools may furthermore obscure discriminatory and subjective lending policies behind a single "objective" score (...) sophisticated algorithms may combine facially neutral data points and treat them as proxies for immutable characteristics such as race or gender, thereby circumventing existing non-discrimination laws and systematically denying credit access to certain groups. Finally, big-data tools may allow online payday lenders to target the most vulnerable consumers and lure them into debt traps*"). Italics added.

[2748] See on the dire need to attain algorithmic fairness: Zajko, M, "Conservative AI and social inequality: conceptualizing alternatives to bias through social theory", *Artificial Intelligence and Society*, Volume 36, 2021, pp. 1047–1056; Dwork, Cynthia/Hardt, Moritz/Pitassi, Tonian/Reingold/Zemel, Richard, "Fairness Through Awareness, Proceedings of the 3rd Innovations", *Theoretical Computer Science Conference*, 2012, https://dl.acm.org/doi/10.1145/2090236.2090255; [https://perma.cc/T2U3-TNQ6] (discussing an individual fairness approach to algorithmic fairness); Meharabi, Ninareh/Morstatter, Fred/Saxena, Nripsuta/Lerman, Kristina/Galstyan, Aram, "A Survey on Bias and Fairness in Machine Learning", *ACM Computing Survey*, Jul. 2022; Fuster, Andreas/Goldsmith-Pinkham, Paul/Tarun Ramadorai/Walther, Angsar, "Predictably Unequal? The Effects of Machine Learning on Credit Markets", *Journal of Finance*, Volume 76, 2022, passim (providing a description of the variation in interest rates across racial groups carried out by machine learning algorithms); Zarsky, Tal, "Transparency in Data Mining: From Theory to Practice", *Discrimination and Privacy in the Information Society: Data Mining and Profiling in Large Databases*, Bart Custers et al. eds., Belin, Springer, 2013; Kroll, Joshua A. et al., "Accountable Algorithms", *University of Pennsylvania Law Review*, Volume 165, 2017, passim; Green, B./Hu L., "The Myth in the Methodology: Towards a Recontextualization of Fairness in Machine Learning", *Machine Learning Debates Work 35th Internation Conference of Machine Learning*, 2018, passim; West, SM./Whittaker, M./Crawford, K., "Discriminating systems gender, race, and power in AI", AI Now Institute, 2019; Xu, K./Nosek, B./Greenwald, AG., "Data from the race implicit association test on the project implicit demo website", *Journal of Open Psychology* Data 2:e3, 2014.

[2749] See: Wachter, Sandra/Mittelstadt, Brent/Russell, Chris, "Why Fairness Cannot be Automated: Bridging the Gap Between EU Non-Discrimination Law and AI", *Computer Law & Security Review*, Volume 41, 2021, 105567.

[2750] See: Bartlett, Robert/Morse, Adair/Wallace, Nancy/Stanton, Richard, "Algorithmic Discrimination and Input Accountability Under the Civil Rights Acts", *Berkeley Technology Law Journal*, Volume 36, 2021, pp. 675–736 (675) ("*the disproportionate burden of COVID-19 among communities of color and a necessary renewed attention to racial inequalities* have lent new urgency to concerns that *algorithmic decision-making can lead to unintentional discrimination against members of historically marginalized groups*"). Italics added.

[2751] See: Part IV, This chapter, Sects. 4.1.4–4.1.4.2.1 of this book (on mortgage redlining). See: Part IV, This chapter, Sects. 4.1.2–4.1.4.3 of this book (on algorithmic credit scoring, consumer

§§ Casts broadly, this cluster of machine learning algorithms[2752] analyse, and deep dive into, umpteenth emails that have been timely classified[2753] (or «labelled»)[2754] as «spam» or «wanted» by a cohort of users. They meaningfully learn[2755] from this batch of examples statistically[2756] important[2757] «smoking gun» markers of spam, such as sentences like «send cash».[2758]

§§ After analysing a staggering amount of emails that have been timely labelled as «spam» and «wanted», a machine learning algorithm may be able to learn[2759] that a phrase like «free money» in an email is significantly more likely to pinpoint that the email is spam rather than wanted.[2760] On the heels of previously acquired patterns

racism and credit card redlining). See: Part IV, This chapter, Sects. 4.1.4–4.1.4.2.3 of this book (on algorithmic redlining). See: Part IV, This chapter, Sect. 4.1.4.3 of this book (on "algorithmic redliking"). See: Part IV, This chapter, Sect. 4.1.3 of this book (on algorithmic prime-lining).

2752 Sullivan, Charles A., « Employing AI», *Villanova Law Review*, Volume 63, 2018, pp. 395–404.

2753 But see: Kleinberg, Jon/Ludwig, Jens/Mullainathan, Sendhil/Sunstein Cass R., "Discrimination in the Age of Algorithms", *Journal of Legal Analysis*, Volume 10, 1, 2018, pp. 28–29, 33–34 (draw a distinction between "group differences in the raw data" and biases for the "choice of predictors").

2754 See: Barocas, Solon/Selbst, Andrew D., "Big Data's Disparate Impact", *California Law Review*, Volume 104, 2016, pp. 677–78 (arguing that predictive data is predictive of a given/specific target variable (i.e., minimized future predicted claims) with training data which is both correctly "labelled" and "collected").

2755 See: Chen, C./Rudin, C., "An optimization approach to learning falling rule lists", *Proceedings of Machine Learning Research, Artificial Intelligence and Statistics*, Volume 84, 2018, pp. 604–612; Sokolovska, N./Chevaleyre, Y./Zucker, J.D., "A provable algorithm for learning interpretable scoring systems", *Proceedings of Machine Learning Research, Artificial Intelligence and Statistics*, Volume 84, pp. 566–574; Rudin, Cynthia/Ustun, B., "Optimized scoring systems: toward trust in machine learning for healthcare and criminal justice", *Interfaces*, Volume 48, 2018, pp. 399–486 (on the fundamental tenets of machine learning on a plethora of areas).

2756 But see: Firestone, Simon, "Race Ethnicity and Credit Card Monitoring", *Journal of Money, Credit and Banking*, Sept. 2014, 2014, pp. 1206 and ff; Han, Song, Keys, Benjamin J./Li, Geng, *Unsecured Credit Supply over the Credit Cycle: Evidence from Credit Card Mailings* (argue that, statistically, Blacks and Latinos are seldom granted credit and, if ever granted credit, the terms and conditions attached to the concession of credit are not equal to those offered to White folks). But see also: Pope, Devin G./Sydnor, Justin R., "Implementing Anti-Discrimination Policies in Statistical Profiling Models", *American Economic Journal: Economic Policy*, Volume 3, 2011, pp. 207–216 (on the dire need to implement anti-discrimination policies in statistical profiling models).

2757 But see: Altenburger, Kristen M./Ho, Daniel E., "When Algorithms Import Private Bias into Public Enforcement: The Promise and Limitations of Statistical Debiasing Solutions", *Journal of Institutional & Theoretical Economics*, Volume 175, 2019, pp. 97–98 (making a poignant call for a "debias predictive algorithms" to assuage racist and/or biased, doctored and bigoted algorithms that arise out of statistical calculus).

2758 Surden, Harry, "ChatGPT, AI Large Language Models, and Law", *cit.*, pp. 1941–1972 (1958).

2759 But see: Corbett-Davies, Sam/Goel, Sharad, "The Measure and Mismeasure of Fairness: a critical Review of Fair Machine Learning", *Cornell University Library*, 2018, p. 18 (broaches a type of *measurement bias* coined "*feature bias*," which is neatly a *bias in the predictors* x. Note, though, that there is a second type of *measurement bias* deemed "*label bias*," which, in turn, amounts to a bias in y. The authors argue that that *label bias* is the worst bias there is).

2760 Surden, Harry, "ChatGPT, AI Large Language Models, and Law", *cit.*, pp. 1941–1972 (1958).

like this, such machine-learning AI systems consistently learn how to weed out, and fundamentally cast aside, future spam emails.[2761]

§§ The sweeping idea underpinning machine learning is that which algorithms itself learn the relevant data pattern[2762] by analysing gargantuan/huge quantities of past[2763] sample data[2764] and establishing statistically[2765] relevant[2766] indicators,[2767]

[2761] Surden, Harry, "ChatGPT, AI Large Language Models, and Law", *cit.*, pp. 1941–1972 (1958).

[2762] It is often contended that machine learning algorithms engender their own models to forecast future outcomes on the basis of analysis of training data. See: Mittelstadt, Brent Daniel/Taddeo, Patrick Allo, Maria Rosaria/Wachter, Sandra/Floridi, Luciano, "The Ethics of Algorithms: Mapping the Debate", *Big Data & Society*, July-Dec. 2016, 2016, p. 3.

[2763] But see: Barocas, Solon/Selbst, Andrew D., "Big Data's Disparate Impact", *California Law Review*, Volume 104, 2016, p. 699 (discussing how discriminatory data mining is analogous to unintentional disparate impact analysis). See also: Bornstein, Stephanie, "Antidiscriminatory Algorithms", *Alabama Law Review*, Volume 70, 2018, p. 535 (positing that algorithmic discrimination at large could fall under the all-embracing umbrella of anti-stereotyping category within Title VII's disparate treatment).

[2764] But see: Allen, James, "The Color of Algorithms: An Analysis and Proposed Research Agenda Deterring Algorithmic Redlining", *Fordham Urban Law Journal*, Volume 46, 2019, pp. 219–234 (229–234) (discussing how historical mortgage redlining greatly swayed modern algorithms generated by massive batches of datasets that consist of decades of information built on exclusion and racial discrimination in the purview of financing, marketing, and housing). See: Part IV, This chapter, Sects. 4.1.4–4.1.4.2.3 of this book. See: Part IV, This chapter, Sects. 4.1.4–4.1.4.2.1 of this book (on mortgage redlining). See: Part IV, This chapter, Sects. 4.1.2–4.1.4.3 of this book (on algorithmic credit scoring, consumer racism and credit card redlining). See: Part IV, This chapter, Sects. 4.1.4–4.1.4.2.3 of this book (on algorithmic redlining). See: Part IV, This chapter, Sect. 4.1.4.3 of this book (on "algorithmic redliking"). See: Part IV, This chapter, Sect. 4.1.3 of this book (on algorithmic prime-lining).

[2765] But see: Chi-Jack Lin/ Sherman D. Hanna, "Racial Discrimination in the Consumer Credit Market", *Consumer Interests Annual*, Volume 56, 2010 ("*The Equal Credit Opportunity Act (ECOA), enacted in 1974, makes it unlawful for any creditors to discriminate against credit applicants because of their color, race/ethnic group, religion, national origin, sex, marital status, or age (provided the applicant has the capacity to contract) (....) our analyses allow for distinguishing statistical and taste discrimination (...) discrimination in the consumer credit market against black and Hispanic households is statistical discrimination: lenders choose to discriminate against black and Hispanic because they on average have higher default risk*"). Italics and highlights added.

[2766] But see: Kirkpatrick, Keith, "It's not the Algorithm, it's the Data", *Communications of the ACM*, February 2017, Volume 60, n. ° 2, 2017 ("tools such as PredPol and CommandCentral *are inherently biased since they rely heavily on reported crimes data, which is often concentrated in areas that are heavily policed, thereby skewing statistics to overrepresent poor or minority communities*. "*We know that we have a history of racially biased policing in the United States, and that has fed into all the data that we have on where arrests have occurred, which crimes are more likely to occur in specific communities, and at which particular times*," says Jennifer Lynch, senior staff attorney at the Electronic Frontier Foundation. "*That's the data that's being fed into predictive policing algorithms*"). Italics and highlights added.

[2767] But see: *Tech, Bias and Housing Initiative, the Promise and Perils of Residential Proptech, Year 1, Research Summary Report, April 2023, TechEquity Collaborative*, p. 5 available at: https://techequity.us/wp-content/uploads/2023/04/TBHI-Y1-Research-Summary-Report.pdf (28.11.2024). ("*Residential Proptech also has the potential to exacerbate the bias inherent in our housing system. Its rise is due, in part, to the desperation felt by average home seekers (...) companies offering an easier pathway to homeownership may exploit communities that have been*

as opposed of abiding by agreed-upon, or set in stone, rules[2768] (e.g., if «free-money» then «spam»[2769]) manually inserted by human beings[2770] (programmers).[2771]

§§ It is noteworthy that the inner workings of machine learning algorithms[2772] are the breeding ground for either *taste-based discrimination* or *statistical discrimination*[2773] in a myriad of domains.[2774] But much more lies beyond that. For instance,

---

harmed by housing discrimination in the past. Opaque algorithms incorporate biased data into their decision-making processes, making it harder to enforce fair housing laws (...) venture-backed companies' winner-take-all approach to growth has the potential to exacerbate inequality rather than combat it"). Italics and highlights added. See: Part IV, This chapter, Sects. 4.1.4–4.1.4.2.3 of this book.

[2768] See: Friedman, J. H., & Popescu, B. E., "Predictive learning via rule ensembles", *Annals of Applied Statistics*, Volume 2, Issue 3, pp. 2008, pp. 916–954.

[2769] Surden, Harry, "ChatGPT, AI Large Language Models, and Law", *cit.*, pp. 1941–1972 (1958).

[2770] But see: Citron, Danielle Keats/Pasquale, Frank A., "The Scored Society: Due Process for Automated Predictions", *Washington Law Review*, Volume 89, 2014, pp. 1–34 (arguing that "[a]*dvocates applaud the removal of human beings and their flaws from the assessment process*," but arguing that bias remains "[*b*]*ecause human beings program predictive algorithms, their biases and values are embedded into the software's instructions*"). Italics added. See: Part IV, This chapter, Sects. 4.1.4–4.1.4.2.3 of this book. See also: Sunstein, Cass R., "Algorithms, Correcting Biases", *Social Research*, Volume 86, 2019, pp. 449–506 (this famed author tagged disparate impact as "disturbing in itself, in the sense that a practice that produces such an impact helps entrench something like a caste system").

[2771] Surden, Harry, "ChatGPT, AI Large Language Models, and Law", *cit.*, pp. 1941–1972 (1958).

[2772] But see: Scherer, Matthew U. Scherer, "Regulating Artificial Intelligence Systems: Risks, Challenges, Competencies, and Strategies", *Harvard Journal of Law and Technology*, Volume 29, 2016, pp. 353–369 (frames the crippling problem of opacity as "the possibility that the inner workings of an AI system may be kept secret and may not be susceptible to reverse engineering").

[2773] Chi-Jack Lin/ Sherman D. Hanna, "Racial Discrimination in the Consumer Credit Market", *Consumer Interests Annual*, Volume 56, 2010 ("*The Equal Credit Opportunity Act (ECOA), enacted in 1974, makes it unlawful for any creditors to discriminate against credit applicants because of their color, race/ethnic group, religion, national origin, sex, marital status, or age (provided the applicant has the capacity to contract) (....) our analyses allow for distinguishing statistical and taste discrimination. In four of five of our measures, there was discrimination against households with Black respondents, and in three out of five measures, there was discrimination against households with Hispanic respondents. Discrimination in the consumer credit market against black and Hispanic households is statistical discrimination: lenders choose to discriminate against black and Hispanic because they on average have higher default risk*"). Italics added.

[2774] Although the racial wage gap in the labour market is remarkably well parsed, discerning—or dissecting—this gap and the degree to which it sharply mirrors either *taste-based* or *statistical discrimination* has proven to be gruelling uphill battle. See: Black, Dan Amelia Haviland/Sanders, Seth/Taylor, Lowell, "Why Do Minority Men Earn Less? A Study of Wage Differentials Among the Highly Educated", *The Review of Economics and Statistics*, Volume 88, 2006, pp. 300 and ff and passim (pinpointing eerily weird wage gaps between Black men and men of other races while shedding a keen light on the sweltering challenges in ascribing that perceived gap to blatant/blunt racial discrimination). See also: Grodsky, Eric/Pager, Devah, "The Structure of Disadvantage: Individual and Occupational Determinants of Black-White Wage Gap", *American Sociological Review*, Volume 66, 2001, pp. 542–563 (stumbles upon the finding in view of which that whilst Black men have burgeoningly gained access to highly remunerated occupations, they have nonetheless become subject to more extreme racial disadvantages when it comes to seizing power, which, in turn, can be loosely qualified as gate-keeping).

racial discrimination is rife in the realm of algorithmic credit scoring. Enough said about this.[2775]

§§ Fast forward to the process of **«pretraining»** of GPT, the latter amounts to a subset of machine-learning.[2776] «Pretraining»[2777] therefore encompasses a slew of functional steps that entails exposing GPT's machine learning algorithm to multifarious language patterns that are enshrined in websites, books, essays, novels, poems, social media, and a plethora of written texts.[2778]

§§ ChatGPT's pretraining phase is thus commensurate with, in that bears a striking resemblance with central tenets of, the training phase[2779] of regular machine learning algorithms[2780] that seek, for example, to detect spam email, as previously mentioned.

[2775] See: Part IV, This chapter, Sects. 4.1.4–4.1.4.2.1 of this book (on mortgage redlining). See: Part IV, This chapter, Sects. 4.1.2–4.1.4.3 of this book (on algorithmic credit scoring, consumer racism and credit card redlining). See: Part IV, This chapter, Sects. 4.1.4–4.1.4.2.3 of this book (on algorithmic redlining). See: Part IV, This chapter, Sect. 4.1.4.3 of this book (on "algorithmic redliking"). See: Part IV, This chapter, Sect. 4.1.3 of this book (on algorithmic prime-lining). But see: Havard, Cassandra Jones, "On The Take": The Black Box of Credit Scoring and Mortgage Discrimination", *Boston University Public Interest Law Journal*, Volume 20, 2011, pp. 241–247 (highlighting that algorithmic credit scoring, if left unchecked, is an intrinsic, encroached, deep-rooted form of racial discrimination akin to mortgage redlining); Pasquale, Frank, *The Black Box Society: The Secret Algorithms that Control Money and Information.* Cambridge, Massachusetts: Harvard University Press, 2015, 1–320 (passim). See: Part IV, This chapter, Sects. 4.1.2–4.1.4.3 of this book (on algorithmic credit scoring, consumer racism and credit card redlining).

[2776] Surden, Harry, "ChatGPT, AI Large Language Models, and Law", *cit.*, pp. 1941–1972 (1958).

[2777] See: Ouyang, L./Wu, J./Jiang, X./Almeida, D./Wainwright, C. L./Mishkin, P./Zhang, C./ Agarwal, S./Slama, K. A. Ray, J. Schulman, J. Hilton, F. Kelton, L. Miller, M. Simens, A. Askell, P. Welinder, P. Christiano, J. Leike, and R. Lowe, "Training language models to follow instructions with human feedback," Mar. 2022, arXiv:2203.02155 [cs]. [Online]. Available: http://arxiv.org/abs/2203.02155; R. Rafailov, A. Sharma, E. Mitchell, S. Ermon, C. D. Manning, and C. Finn, "Direct Preference Optimization: Your Language Model is Secretly a Reward Model," Jul. 2024, arXiv:2305.18290 [cs]. [Online]. Available: http://arxiv.org/abs/2305.18290.

[2778] Surden, Harry, "ChatGPT, AI Large Language Models, and Law", *cit.*, pp. 1941–1972 (1958).

[2779] Note, though, that the training of machine learning is long and tedious in that is an error-prone procedure than can ultimately impair future algorithmic decision-making: Price, W. Nicholson Price II, "Regulating Black-Box Medicine", *Michigan Law Review*, Volume 116, 2017, pp. 421–431 (leverages on Google Image's image recognition learning algorithm to shed light on the four-step process by which some algorithms are thoroughly trained. First, the algorithm is shown "a set of known images ('Here are 10,000 pictures of ducks')." Second, the algorithm "develops complex internal rules based on nonlinear processes." Third, the algorithm "tests those rules on a test set ('Which of these are ducks?')." And fourth, the algorithm accordingly adjusts its "internal rules based on the success of the test." These steps are trotted out and repeated many times "until it can accurately and consistently classify the images").

[2780] See: Kumar, Komal/Tajamul Ashraf/Omkar Thawakar/Rao Muhammad Anwer/Hisham Cholakkal/Mubarak Shah/Ming-Hsuan Yang/Phillip H.S. Torr/Fahad Shahbaz Khan/Salman Khan, "LLM Post-Training: A Deep Dive into Reasoning Large Language Models", arXiv:2502.21321v1 [cs.CL] 28 Feb 2025, 2025, p. 1 ("***Pretraining*** *on vast web-scale data has laid the foundation for these models, yet the research community is now increasingly shifting focus toward post-training techniques to achieve further breakthroughs. While* ***pretraining provides a broad linguistic foundation****, post-training methods enable LLMs to refine their knowledge, improve reasoning, enhance*

§§ For purposes here, language patterns are deeply steeped in written documents like Wikipedia opuscules, contracts, essays, poems, eulogies, papers, blog posts, written notes of various kinds, and emails.[2781] Relatedly, ChatGPT is also exposed to the fundamental tenets of grammar, punctuation, semantics,[2782] and syntax that human beings are able to effortlessly understand.[2783]

§§ By exposing GPT systems to behemoth amounts of text data during pretraining, the system slowly equips itself to learn both patterns of human language—which comprises grammar, punctuation, syntax, semantics, and chunks of words that are routinely associated to one another—and facts about the world[2784] or loosely the already-unequal world[2785] we live in.[2786]

---

factual accuracy, and align more effectively with user intents and ethical considerations. ***Fine-tuning, reinforcement learning, and test-time scaling have emerged as critical strategies for optimizing LLMs performance, ensuring robustness, and improving adaptability across various real-world tasks.*** *This survey provides a systematic exploration of post-training methodologies, analyzing their role in refining LLMs beyond pretraining, addressing key challenges such as catastrophic forgetting, reward hacking, and inference-time trade-offs. We highlight emerging directions in model alignment, scalable adaptation, and inference-time reasoning, and outline future research directions. We also provide a public repository to continually track developments in this fast-evolving field*"). Italics and bolds added. See also: Barocas, Solon/Selbst, Andrew D., "Big Data's Disparate Impact", *California Law Review*, Volume 104, 2016, pp. 677–78 (arguing that predictive data is predictive of a given/specific target variable with training data which is both correctly "labelled" and "collected").

2781 Surden, Harry, "ChatGPT, AI Large Language Models, and Law", *cit.*, pp. 1941–1972 (1958).

2782 Bryson, JJ, Narayanan, A., "Semantics derived automatically from language corpora contain human-like biases", *Science*, 356 (6334), 2017, pp. 183–186.

2783 Surden, Harry, "ChatGPT, AI Large Language Models, and Law", *cit.*, pp. 1941–1972 (1958).

2784 Surden, Harry, "ChatGPT, AI Large Language Models, and Law", *cit.*, pp. 1941–1972 (1958).

2785 Western, Bruce, *Punishment and Inequality in America*, New York: Russell Sage Foundation, 2006; Soss, Joe, Richard C. Fording, and Sanford F. Schram, *Disciplining the Poor: Neoliberal Paternalism and the Persistent Power of Race*, Chicago: University of Chicago Press, 2011; Laub, John H., "Understanding Inequality and the Justice System Response: Charting a New Way Forward.", New York: William T. Grant Foundation, 2014.

2786 But see: Edick, Cole, "Opt-out Privacy Policy Worsens Algorithmic Price Discrimination: The Case of the American Privacy Rights Act", *Minnesota Journal of Law & Inequality*, 2024, p. 1.("*In a data-driven world, data governance has serious implications for social inequality—from civil rights to consumer protection.[1] But the current approach to data governance in the United States may overemphasize individual privacy choice at the cost of collective approaches to inequality that better mitigate the harms inherent in the datafication of an already-unequal society*.[2] This blog post examines that tension, critiquing the exceptions and opt-out mechanisms present in the recently announced American Privacy Rights Act of 2024 (APRA), *arguing that such provisions fail to adequately address inequality—in particular, the potential exacerbation of algorithm-powered price discrimination through APRA's loyalty program exception*"). Italics added. But see: Hardt, Moritz, "How big data is unfair: Understanding sources of unfairness in data driven decision making", *Medium*, Archived on Oct. 8, 2014, available at: https://web.archive.org/web/20141008185829/; https://medium.com/@mrtz/how-big-data-is-unfair-9aa544d739de. (access: 17.12.2024). See also: Fry, H, *Hello world: being human in the age of algorithms*, London, Penguin Random House, 2018; Zajko, M, "Conservative AI and social inequality: conceptualizing alternatives to bias through social theory", *Artificial Intelligence and Society*, Volume 36, 2021, pp. 1047–1056.

§§ This pretraining approach, known as «self-supervised»[2787] training,[2788] was one of the greatest leaps forward in the realm of Artificial Intelligence-embedded technologies.[2789] As adumbrated, machine-learning systems learn from a set of examples, such as analysing patterns in examples of spam emails and wanted emails.[2790] Not long ago, machine-learning systems had to have their examples manually inserted by human beings, which, in turn, converted such «labelled»[2791] data into a protracted, time-consuming, cumbersome, and energy-draining chore.[2792]

§§ For instance, data-driven machine-learning[2793] spam detection systems learn from the manual flagging of umpteenth of email systems when laypeople (regular users) push the «spam» button upon receiving a spam, thus labelling the spam email as a[2794] human-documented example of spam that the system can thoroughly analyse.[2795]

§§ The foregoing process of a data-driven machine learning means that the machine learns from examples that have been (chiefly) manually categorized.[2796] This process is widely known as *supervised learning*.[2797] The reason for that is straightforward: the whole process is supervised by humans, whom, in turn, feed the algorithm with examples that a layperson has human-verified as «spam» by carrying out a steadfast action such as pushing a «spam» button.[2798] Building on these human-supervised and verified examples, machine-learning algorithms are finally equipped

---

[2787] See: Radford, A./Wu, J./Child, R. et al, "Language models are unsupervised multitask learners", *Technical Report*; Rudinger, R./Naradowsky, J./Leonard, B./Durme, B Van, "Gender Bias in Conference Resolution", *NAACL HLT 2018–2018 Conference North American Chapter Association Computer Linguist Human Language Technology—Proceedings of Conference*, 2018, 2:8–14.

[2788] See: Friston, K. J., Da Costa, L., Tschantz, A., Kiefer, A., Salvatori, T., Neacsu, V., & Buckley, C. L. "Supervised structure learning", *arXiv preprint arXiv:2311.10300*, 2023 Hardt, M., Price E, Srebro N, "Equality of opportunity in supervised learning", ArXiv ID: 1610.02413v1, 2016.

[2789] Surden, Harry, "ChatGPT, AI Large Language Models, and Law", *cit.*, pp. 1941–1972 (1958).

[2790] Surden, Harry, "ChatGPT, AI Large Language Models, and Law", *cit.*, pp. 1941–1972 (1958).

[2791] But see: Corbett-Davies, Sam/Goel, Sharad, "The Measure and Mismeasure of Fairness: a critical Review of Fair Machine Learning", *Cornell University Library*, 2018, p. 18 (broaches a type of *measurement bias* coined "feature bias," which is neatly a bias in the predictors x. Note, though, that there is a second type of measurement bias deemed "label bias," which, in turn, amounts to a bias in y. The authors argue that that label bias is the worst bias there is); Kleinberg, Jon/Ludwig, Jens/Mullainathan, Sendhil/Sunstein Cass R., "Discrimination in the Age of Algorithms", *Journal of Legal Analysis*, Volume 10, 1, 2018, pp. 28–29, 33–34 (draw a distinction between "group differences in the raw data" and biases for the "choice of predictors").

[2792] Surden, Harry, "ChatGPT, AI Large Language Models, and Law", *cit.*, pp. 1941–1972 (1958).

[2793] Clough, D. R., & Wu, A., "Artificial intelligence, data-driven learning, and the decentralized structure of platform ecosystems", *Academy of Management Review*, Volume 47, Issue 1, 2022, pp. 184–189 and passim.

[2794] Surden, Harry, "ChatGPT, AI Large Language Models, and Law", *cit.*, pp. 1941–1972 (1958).

[2795] Surden, Harry, "ChatGPT, AI Large Language Models, and Law", *cit.*, pp. 1941–1972 (1959).

[2796] Surden, Harry, "ChatGPT, AI Large Language Models, and Law", *cit.*, pp. 1941–1972 (1959).

[2797] See: Hardt, M., Price E, Srebro N, "Equality of opportunity in supervised learning", ArXiv ID: 1610.02413v1, 2016 (on the nuances of supervised learning).

[2798] Surden, Harry, "ChatGPT, AI Large Language Models, and Law", *cit.*, pp. 1941–1972 (1959).

to subsequently learn associated patterns between human words and accompanying labels.[2799]

§§ Last but not least, the final term in GPT, and amongst the most important trailblazing advances, is the word «transformer.»[2800] The word «transformer» resonates with a deep-learning Artificial Intelligence framework developed by Google in a 2017 pathbreaking paper named, «Attention Is All You Need.»[2801] This blazingly new approach is intertwined with «self-attention,» a mechanism that has been paramount to the innovations in NLP, such as those set forth by GPT-4 and other cutting-edge/top-notch Artificial Intelligence-embedded models.[2802] GPT-4 and other GPT models draw on the transformer backbone.[2803]

§§ To grasp the rationale behind the inner workings of transformer, it is useful to cast some light upon «deep learning» and «neural networks».[2804] Crucially, GPT-4 and other state-of-the-art LLM systems essentially leverage on an algorithmic stance to machine learning widely known as a **«neural network»**[2805] (albeit it bears mentioning that there are several machine-learning approaches that extend beyond neural networks).[2806]

§§ Crucially, neural networks are nothing but Artificial Intelligence computational models that loosely mirror the inner workings of the human brain (in spite of the fact that they work in a glaringly different way).[2807] Note, though, that the way human brain works is different from the way neural networks work. This becomes vividly clear if one bears in mind the way human legal reasoning (human decision-making) and machine reasoning (algorithmic decision-making[2808]) work, respectively.

[2799] Surden, Harry, "ChatGPT, AI Large Language Models, and Law", *cit.*, pp. 1941–1972 (1959).

[2800] Surden, Harry, "ChatGPT, AI Large Language Models, and Law", *cit.*, pp. 1941–1972 (1962).

[2801] Surden, Harry, "ChatGPT, AI Large Language Models, and Law", *cit.*, pp. 1941–1972 (1962).

[2802] Surden, Harry, "ChatGPT, AI Large Language Models, and Law", *cit.*, pp. 1941–1972 (1962).

[2803] Surden, Harry, "ChatGPT, AI Large Language Models, and Law", *cit.*, pp. 1941–1972 (1962).

[2804] See: Aggarwal, C. C., *Neural networks and deep learning*, Heidelberg, Springer, 2018, passim; Agrawal, A., Gans, J., & Goldfarb, A., "Prediction machines (updated and expanded): The simple economics of artificial intelligence", *Harvard Business Review Press*, 2022; Agrawal, A., Gans, J., & Goldfarb, A., "Power and prediction: The disruptive economics of artificial intelligence", *Harvard Business Review Press*, 2022; Bengio, Y., Hinton, G., Yao, A., Song, D., Abbeel, P., Harari, Y. N., Hadfield, G., Russell, S., Kahneman, D., & Mindermann, S., *Managing ai risks in an era of rapid progress*, arXiv preprint arXiv:2310.17688, 2023, passim (on neural networks and deep learning that operate jointly in the age of Artificial Intelligence-embedded technologies).

[2805] Buckner, Cameron, "Empiricism without Magic: Transformational Abstraction in Deep Convolutional Neural Networks", *Synthese*, Volume 195, 2018, 5339.

[2806] Surden, Harry, "ChatGPT, AI Large Language Models, and Law", *cit.*, pp. 1941–1972 (1963).

[2807] Surden, Harry, "ChatGPT, AI Large Language Models, and Law", *cit.*, pp. 1941–1972 (1963). See: Part II, Chap. 2, Sects. 2.1 and 2.1.1 of this book (for further insights on how the human brain and deep neural network function, respectively).

[2808] Blattner, Laura/Nelson, Scott/Spiess, Jann, *Unpacking the Black Box: Regulating Algorithmic Decisions*.

§§ Tellingly, and just as posited above,[2809] artificial intelligence is a world of both correlations and hidden patterns deeply soaked in the datasets[2810] on which machine learning[2811] operates upon.[2812]

§§ Deep learning, a byproduct of machine learning,[2813] enables the machine to improve its performance over the course of time.[2814] On the opposite pole, human legal reasoning is a world of causation[2815] that seldom chimes in with hidden

---

[2809] See also: Part I, Chap. 1 (Introduction). See also: Part II, Chap. 2, Sect. 2.1.1 of this book.

[2810] As hinted above, algorithms make their inferences and draw their conclusions in a way difficult to understand. This is deemed *black box*, that further enhances the shroud of mystery under which algorithms are cloaked. See, for a compelling account of AI black box: Ver: Bathaee, Yavar, "The Artificial Intelligence Black Box and the Failure of Intent and Causation", *Harvard Journal of Law and Technology*, n.° 37, 2018, p. 901 (adduces that "*one possible reason AI may be a black box to humans is that it relies on machine-learning algorithms that internalize data in ways that are not easily audited or understood by humans* (…) "*first, a lack may arise from the complexity of the algorithm's structure, such as with deep neural network, which consists of thousands of artificial neurons working together in a diffuse way to solve a problem. This reason for AI being a black box is referred to as "complexity". Second, the lack of transparency may arise because the AI is using a machine-learning algorithm that relies on geometric relationships that humans cannot visualize, such as with support vector machines. This reason for AI being a black box is referred to as "dimensionality"*). Italics added. But see: Pearl, Judea, *Causality*, 2nd edition, Cambridge, Cambridge University Press, 2009 (on the fundamental tenets of causality). But see: Kilbertus, Niki/Carulla, Mateo Rojas/Parascandolo, Giambattista/Hardt, Moritz/Janzing, Dominik/ Schoellkopf, Bernhard, "Avoiding Discrimination through Causal Reasoning", *Advances in Neural Information Processing Systems*, I. Guyon, U. V. Luxburg, S. Bengio, H. Wallach, R. Fergus, S. Vishwanathan, and R. Garnett (Eds.), Vol. 30. Curran Associates, Inc., 2017, pp. 656–666 (arguing that is feasible to avoiding discrimination through a granular and fine-grained causal reasoning).

[2811] Sivarajah, Uthayasnkar et al., "Critical Analysis of Big Data Challenges and Analytical Methods", *Journal of Business Research*, Volume 70, 2017, pp. 263 and ff and passim; Jetten, Lieke /Sharon, Stephen, "Selected Issues concerning the Ethical Use of Big Data Health Analytics", *Washington & Lee Law Review Online*, Volume 72, 2016, passim.

[2812] Gillis, Talia B., "The Input Data Fallacy", *Minnesota Law Review*, Volume 106, 2022, pp. 1176–1263 (p. 1244). See also: Murphy, Kevin P., *Machine Learning: A Probabilistic Perspective (Adaptive Computation and Machine Learning series)*, Massachusetts, The MIT Press, 2012, pp. 1–1104. Machine learning "*attempts to combine deductive, inductive, and abductive reasoning to make person-like reasoning in AI Entities possible. Machine learning AI Entities initially learn in the same way a human child learns. First, they notice details and patterns in shapes, sounds, and behaviors*; then put them together to distinguish one person from another, or a dog from a cat. Eventually, the AI can recognize and identify" common objects. See also: Hutto-Schultz, Jess, "Dicitur Ex Machina: Artificial Intelligence and the Hearsay Rule", *George Mason Law Review*, Volume 27, n. ° 2, 2020, pp. 684–718 (689).

[2813] See: Chollet, François, *Deep Learning with Python*. Shelter Island, Nova Iorque: Manning, 2018, pp. 1–384 (passim). *Deep Learning* stands as a byproduct of *Machine Learning. Machine Learning*, a subset of Artificial Intelligence, unfolds itself in *Deep Learning*, which "involves computer algorithms that have the ability to "learn" or improve in performance over time on some task". See: Surden, Harry, "Machine Learning and Law", *Washington Law Review*, Volume 89, 2015, pp. 87 and ff.

[2814] See: Samek, Wojciech/Müller, Klaus-Robert, "Explainable AI: interpreting, explaining and visualizing deep learning"*Towards Explainable Artificial Intelligence*, Samek, Wojciech/Montavon, Grégoire/ Vedaldi, Andrea/Hansen, Lars Kai/ Müller, Klaus-Robert (Editors). Heidelberg/Berlin/ New York: Springer, 2019, pp. 5–22 ("in recent years, machine learning (ML) has become a key

correlations.[2816] They are poles apart. This mismatch is shaping up to put law at loggerheads with its fundamental tenets. Amongst which stands legal security. Especially, albeit not exclusively, when artificial intelligence[2817] is deployed to assist (or replace instead?[2818]) judges in performing legal reasoning[2819] underpinning a

---

enabling technology for the sciences and industry. Especially through improvements in methodology, the availability of large databases and increased computational power, *today's ML algorithms are able to achieve excellent performance (at times even exceeding the human level) on an increasing number of complex tasks. Deep learning models are at the forefront of this development. However, due to their nested non-linear structure, these powerful models have been generally considered "black boxes", not providing any information about what exactly makes them arrive at their predictions.* Since in many applications, e.g., in the medical domain, *such lack of transparency may be not acceptable, the development of methods for visualizing, explaining and interpreting deep learning models has recently attracted increasing attention. This introductory paper presents recent developments and applications in this field and makes a plea for a wider use of explainable learning algorithms in practice*"). Italics added.

[2815] See: Pearl, Judea, *Causality*, 2nd edition, Cambridge, Cambridge University Press, 2009 (on the fundamental tenets of causality).

[2816] As we throw ourselves in the immense arena of automated processes powered by Artificial Intelligence, the difficulties to grasp its delicate intricacies mount exponentially. See: Cohen, Julien E., *Between Truth and Power: The Legal Constructions of Informational Capitalism.* Oxford: Oxford University Press, 2019, pp. 1–376 (p. 192) (asserts adamantly that "*automated processes* have obvious efficiency advantages, *but such processes may not align well (or well at all) with applicable legal requirements that are couched in shades of gray*"). Italics added.

[2817] This is the gist of a digital future, which will ineluctably give rise to a "Artificial Intelligent Justice". See: Re, Richard M./Solow-Niederman, Alicia, "Developing Artificially Intelligent", *Stanford Technology Law Review*, Volume 22, 2019, pp. 242 ff and passim. But see: Mann, Monique/Matzner, Tobias, "Challenging Algorithmic Profiling: The Limits of Data Protection and Anti-Discrimination in Responding to Emergent Discrimination", *Big Data & Society*, Volume 6, 2019, passim; Yeung, Karen, "Why Worry about Decision-Making by Machine?", *Algorithmic Regulation*, Yeung, Karen/Lodge, Martin (Editors), Oxford, Oxford University Press, 2019, pp. 22–47 (expressing deep-rooted concerns on algorithmic decision-making).

[2818] But see: Part V, Chap. 5, Sect. 5.1.8.5 of this book (on law number five to interpret algorithmic decision-making, which mandates that robot-judges, robot-prosecutors and robot-lawyers must not enter the courtroom for they are utterly incapable of making sound and interpretable value judgements). But see: Millar, Jason/Kerr, Ian, "Delegation, Relinquishment and Responsibility: The Prospect of Expert Robots", *Robot Law*, Calo, Ryan/Froomkin/A. Michael/Kerr, Ian (Editors), Cheltenham, Edward Elgar Publishing, 2016, pp. 102, 106–107 (as these authors aptly put it "*we will rely on robots without really knowing why – simply because their algorithms provide the greatest number of successful outcomes.* We have already seen this in Google's search approach. Neither Larry (Page) nor Sergey (Brin) (nor any other Google employee) knowns exactly why one particular web page is a better result than another. *When the click patterns say it is, that's good enough.* No semantic or causal analysis is required...*Like the ancients, we will, quite rationally, come to rely upon them, knowing full well that we cannot necessarily explain the reasons for their decisions*"). Italics added. Converging: Casey, Anthony J./Niblett, Anthony, "Self-driving Laws", *University of Toronto Law Journal*, Volume 66, 2016, pp. 429–435 (contend that "*as more information is generated, and the evolutionary algorithm updates and become a better forecaster, we imagine that judges will increasingly rely on the advice of the algorithm*"). But see: Weizenbaum, Joseph, *Computer Power and Human Reason: From Judgment to Calculation*, 1st edition, New York, W. H. Freeman & Co, 1976, pp. 1–300 (227) ("examines the sources of the computer's powers and offers evaluative explorations of what computers can do, cannot do, and should not be employed to do") (this founding father of Artificial Intelligence presciently noted that we should not entrust legal[2820] decision[2821] making.[2822] Let's therefore shed a keen light on the world of correlations[2823]—or interconnected neurons—that forms part of a broader apparatus within which deep learning operates.

§§ Neural networks[2824]—which, as further shown below, is tightly interlocked with deep learning—process data through a multilayered system of interconnected

Artificial Intelligence-embedded technologies with "tasks that demand wisdom"). Italics added. The approval of rental applications is arguably one of those tasks that should never be entrusted to machines). More on this on Part IV, This chapter, Sects. 4.1.4–4.1.4.2.1 of this book. See: Part IV, This chapter, Sects. 4.1.4–4.1.4.2.1 of this book (on mortgage redlining). See: Part IV, This chapter, Sects. 4.1.2–4.1.4.3 of this book (on algorithmic credit scoring, consumer racism and credit card redlining). See: Part IV, This chapter, Sects. 4.1.4–4.1.4.2.3 of this book (on algorithmic redlining). See: Part IV, This chapter, Sect. 4.1.4.3 of this book (on "algorithmic redliking"). See: Part IV, This chapter, Sect. 4.1.3 of this book (on algorithmic prime-lining).

2819 See in French doctrine: Baller, Stéphane/Deffains, Bruno, "Intelligence artificielle et devenir de la professions d'avocat; l'avenir est présent», *Revue pratique de la prospective et de innovation*, Volume 1, 2018, pp. 14 and ff (canvass the foundations of deep-rooted concerns regarding the irruption of artificial intelligence in the legal arena). Scholars haven't been neither coy nor bashful in pinpointing the drawbacks and downsides concerning the unbridled and rampant rise of the Artificial Intelligence in the legal arena. See: Wu, Tim, "Will Artificial Intelligence Eat the Law? The Rise of Hybrid Social-Ordering Systems", *Columbia Law Review*, Volume 119, 2019, pp. 2001 and ff and passim.

2820 But see: Wachter, Sandra/Mittelstadt, Brent/Russell, Chris, 'Why Fairness Cannot be Automated: Bridging the Gap Between EU Non-Discrimination Law and AI', 41, *Computer Law & Security Review*, 2021, 105567 (arguing that fairness cannot be automated).

2821 See: Scherer, Maxi, "Artificial Intelligence and Legal Decision-Making: The Wide Open?", *Journal of International Arbitration*, Volume 36, 2019, passim.

2822 For a perspective on the changes that the legal arena in currently undergoing, see in French doctrine: Deffains, Bruno, "Le monde du droit face à la transformation numérique", *Revue Française d'Études Constitutionnelles et Politiques*, Volume 170, 2019, pp. 49 and ff and passim. See also: But see: de Laat, Paul B. 'Algorithmic Decision-Making Based on Machine Learning from Big Data: Can Transparency Restore Accountability?", *Philosophy & Technology*, Volume 31, 2018, pp. 524 and ff and passim (broaches the plethora of limitations related with full transparency, privacy, deleterious effects, competitive edge, and the shroud of opacity under which algorithms are often wrapped).

2823 See: Part V, Chap. 5, Sects. 5.1.1.5.2.2–5.1.1.5.2.2.1.4 of this book (on the fundamental shift away from causation to correlation in algorithmic decision-making). See also: Part V, Chap. 5, Sects. 5.1.2–5.1.6.2.1 of this book (on the **thing-centred algorithmic decision-making** propelled by a *Controllable* and *Interpretable* Machine Learning that weeds out *Algorithmic Dictatorship* and secures *Algorithmic Common Good*. It is worth recalling that the thing-centred algorithmic decision-making seeks to unwind the perils arising out of the lack of theoretical underpinnings facing the **human-centred algorithmic decision-making**, as extensively fleshed out Part III, Chap. 3, Sects. 3.1.4.3–3.1.4.4 of this book).

2824 Citron, Danielle Keats/Pasquale, Frank, "Network Accountability for the Domestic Intelligence Apparatus", *Hasting Law Journal*, Volume 62, 2011 (on network accountability); Gray, David/Citron, Danielle Keats, "The Right to Quantitative Privacy", *Minnesota Law Review*, Volume 98, 2013 (on the right to quantitative privacy).

«nodes» or «neurons».[2825] The billions of «parameters» that steer ChatGPT to forecast one word[2826] in lieu of another are fundamentally the mighty power of interlaced connections (or «weights»)[2827] between a given numerical node and another.[2828]

§§ Overall, neural networks are very flexible tools that excel in the role of pattern detectors: they are equipped to juxtapose any given underlying pattern, provided that they have been exposed to enough big data[2829] to analyse.[2830] Neural-network stances to Artificial Intelligence-embedded technologies are widespread famous for their irreproachable ability to process big data[2831] in a layered way, one layer after another,

2825 Surden, Harry, "ChatGPT, AI Large Language Models, and Law", *cit.*, pp. 1941–1972 (1963).

2826 Mandelkern, M./Linzen, T., "Do language models' Words Refer? ", *ArXiv Preprint: arXiv*, 2308, 05576, 2023.

2827 Surden, Harry, "ChatGPT, AI Large Language Models, and Law", *cit.*, pp. 1941–1972 (1963).

2828 Surden, Harry, "ChatGPT, AI Large Language Models, and Law", *cit.*, pp. 1941–1972 (1963).

2829 Big data that is in the limelight these days. See: Sivarajah, Uthayasnkar et al., "Critical Analysis of Big Data Challenges and Analytical Methods", *Journal of Business Research*, Volume 70, 2017, pp. 263 and ff and passim; Jetten, Lieke /Sharon, Stephen, "Selected Issues concerning the Ethical Use of Big Data Health Analytics", *Washington & Lee Law Review Online*, Volume 72, 2016, passim; Wachter, S./Mittelstadt. B., "A right to Reasonable Inferences: Re-thinking Data Protection Law in the Age of Big Data and AI", *Columbia Business Law Review*, 2019, pp. 1 and ff and passim; See in French doctrine: Ferey, Samuel, « Analyse économique du droit, big data et justice prédictive», *Archives de Philosophie du Droit*, Volume 60, 2018, pp. 68–81; Završnik, A. "Algorithmic justice: Algorithms and big data in criminal justice settings", *European Journal of Criminology*, 2019, passim; Joh, Elizabeth E., "The New Surveillance Discretion: Automated Suspicion, Big Data, and Policing." *Harvard Law and Policy Review*, 10 (1), 2016, pp. 15–42. But see: O'Neil, Cathy, *Weapons of Math Destruction. How Big Data Increases Inequality and Threatens Democracy*, London, Penguin Random House, 2016, passim (showing how algorithms utilized in modern societies are amenable to perpetuate racial discrimination, partially through perpetuation of social disadvantage and wealth divides). But see: Hardt, Moritz, "How big data is unfair: Understanding sources of unfairness in data driven decision making", *Medium*, Archived on Oct. 8, 2014, available at: https://web.archive.org/web/20141008185829/; https://medium.com/@mrtz/how-big-data-is-unfair-9aa544d739de. (access: 17.12.2024). See: Part IV, This chapter, Sects. 4.1.10.1–4.1.10.6 of this book (on biased algorithmic risk assessment in criminal procedure law settings, with a sharper focus on COMPAS). See: Part IV, This chapter, Sects. 4.1.1–4.1.1.1 of this book (on biased predictive policing).

2830 Surden, Harry, "ChatGPT, AI Large Language Models, and Law", *cit.*, pp. 1941–1972 (1963).

2831 But see: Pedreshi, Dino/Ruggieri, Salvatore/Turini, Franco, "Discrimination-aware Data Mining", *Proceedings of the 14th ACM SIGKDD International Conference on Knowledge Discovery and Data Mining (Las Vegas, Nevada, USA), ACM*, 2008, pp. 560–568 (arguing that one should shift its gaze downstream by putting in place discrimination-aware algorithmic tools while performing data mining). But see: Balkin, Jack, "Constitution in the National Surveillance State", *Minnesota Law Review*, Volume 93, 2008, p. 13 (note, though, that "*data mining* allows inferences not only about the direct subject of surveillance, but about other people with whom they live, work and communicate"); Schermer, Bart W., "The Limits of Privacy in Automated Profiling and Data Mining", *Computer Law & Security Review*, Volume 27, 2011, pp. 45 and ff and passim; But see: Barocas, Solon/Selbst, Andrew D., "Big Data's Disparate Impact", *California Law Review*, Volume 104, 2016, p. 699 (discussing how discriminatory data mining is analogous to unintentional disparate impact analysis); Zarsky, Tal, "Transparency in Data Mining: From Theory to Practice", *Discrimination and Privacy in the Information Society: Data Mining and Profiling in Large Databases*, Bart Custers et al. eds., Belin, Springer, 2013. See: Part IV, This chapter, Sects.

with each subsequent layer equipped to insert differentiated, granular, pertinent, higher levels of abstractions[2832] on top of the previous layers.[2833]

§§ Building on this exquisite layering ability, neural-network approaches clearly surpass other machine-learning portmanteau of techniques for their unique ability to represent high-definition conceptual abstractions that aid in shaping the complexity of human language and human thought.[2834]

§§ Within the purview of neural networks, there is a technique tagged as **«deep learning»**,[2835] which consists of dealing with ordinary neural networks and levelling them up to large sizes, thereby resulting in neutral networks comprised of billions of «neurons» or parameters with multiple «deep» layers.[2836]

§§ Compellingly, deep-learning systems[2837] have proven to be rather effective at performing Artificial Intelligence-embedded technologies chores. But here is the twist: these advanced models fall prey to inscrutability insofar that they—black box models—are not easily interpretable.[2838] For that reason alone, these models should not be deployed to make high stake decisions (e.g. health and freedom).[2839]

§§ It is worth recalling that these advanced models have not become practicable and usable until the twilight of the last decade. This great leap forward was possible

4.1.10.1–4.1.10.6 of this book (on biased algorithmic risk assessment in criminal procedure law settings, with a sharper focus on COMPAS).

2832 Buckner, Cameron, "Empiricism without Magic: Transformational Abstraction in Deep Convolutional Neural Networks", *Synthese*, Volume 195, 2018, 5339.

2833 Surden, Harry, "ChatGPT, AI Large Language Models, and Law", *cit.*, pp. 1941–1972 (1963).

2834 Surden, Harry, "ChatGPT, AI Large Language Models, and Law", *cit.*, pp. 1941–1972 (1963).

2835 But see: Dong et al., Qi, "Imbalanced deep learning by minority class incremental rectification, *IEEE Transactions on Pattern Analysis & Machine Intelligence*, Volume 41, 2019, p. 1367 (posit that "*most existing learning algorithms produce inductive bias (learning bias)* towards the frequent (majority) classes if training data are not balanced, *resulting in poor minority class recognition performance*"). Italics added. See: Chandler, Anupam, "The Racist Algorithm", *Michigan Law Review*, Volume 115, n. ° 6, 2018, p. 1026 (on racist algorithms, noting that "the possibilities for discriminatory manipulation are legion"). See: Part V, Chap. 5, Sect. 5.1.7.4 of this book (on one of the law to control algorithmic decision-making, namely, law number four: data partitioning must be performed—i.e. randomly split an entire dataset into the «training dataset» and the «test dataset»—to accurately predict outcomes in the real world while forestalling «inductive bias» (learning bias)).

2836 Surden, Harry, "ChatGPT, AI Large Language Models, and Law", *cit.*, pp. 1941–1972 (1963).

2837 See: Goodfellow, Ian/Bengio, Youshua/Courville, Aaron, *Deep Learning (Adaptive Computation and Machine Learning Series)*, Massachusetts, MIT Press 2016, 2016, pp. 1–800 (8) ("*Deep learning is a form of machine learning that enables computers to learn from experience and understand the world in terms of a hierarchy of concepts. Because the computer gathers knowledge from experience, there is no need for a human computer operator to formally specify all the knowledge that the computer needs. The hierarchy of concepts allows the computer to learn complicated concepts by building them out of simpler ones; a graph of these hierarchies would be many layers deep*"). Italics added.

2838 See: Part V, Chap. 5, Sects. 5.1.2–5.1.6.2.1 of this book (on the thing-centred algorithmic decision-making propelled by a *Controllable* and *Interpretable* Machine Learning that weeds out *Algorithmic Dictatorship* and secures *Algorithmic Common Good*. It is worth recalling that the **thing-centred algorithmic decision-making** seeks to unwind the perils arising out of the lack of theoretical underpinnings facing the **human-centred algorithmic decision-making**, as extensively fleshed out Part III, Chap. 3, Sects. 3.1.4.3–3.1.4.4 of this book).

due to both algorithmic headways and rapid strides in the field in hardware engineering.[2840] Google's transformer is the flagship of deep learning inasmuch stands arguably amongst deep-learning neural-network that embody the traits of a hugely successful technological apparatus.[2841]

4.1.9.3 «Who Fears Hallucinations?» Can We Entrust ChatGPT With Making High Stake Decisions in the Legal Arena? Would «Prompt Augmentation» (Harry Surden) and «Prompt Engineering» (Eric Posner/Saran Shivam) Suffice to Boost ChatGPT'S Reliability and Accuracy in Legal Settings?

§§ Cutting-edge Large Language Models (hereinafter LLM) systems like GPT-4 are fully equipped to carry out a very limited number of legal-related tasks[2842] with a lacklustre performance, accuracy and reliability[2843] wise. Amongst which stands: **(i)** generating reasonable, draft-quality legal documents, such as contracts, affidavits, compilation of case law,[2844] or legal motions; **(ii)** producing very basic

---

[2839] See: Part V, Chap. 5, Sect. 5.1.7.2 of this book (on law number two to control algorithmic decision-making, which mandates that black box models must not be entrusted with the task of making high stake decisions—v.g. health and freedom).

[2840] Surden, Harry, "ChatGPT, AI Large Language Models, and Law", *cit.*, pp. 1941–1972 (1963).

[2841] Surden, Harry, "ChatGPT, AI Large Language Models, and Law", *cit.*, pp. 1941–1972 (1963).

[2842] Extolling, though, the functional abilities of ChatGPT to perform legal tasks: Gamm, Grant M., "Artificial Intelligence and the Practice of Law: A Chat With ChatGPT", *Saint Louis University Law Journal*, Volume 68, 2024, pp. 605–606 ("*with an attorney using the tool in this way, they can more effectively prepare for events in a case, such as cross-examination, and can use this summation as a reference during the trial or with other members of the legal team.* An attorney who effectively utilizes ChatGPT can optimize their time and energy on more strategic and high-value tasks. *ChatGPT can aid attorneys in proofreading their work, offering suggestions on complex issues, and organizing information. This tool can be applied in any area of law, and its use is likely to significantly enhance the attorney's efficiency and productivity. Additionally, ChatGPT can provide quick and accurate answers to legal questions, enabling attorneys to make decisions with confidence.* By automating repetitive tasks, ChatGPT frees up time for the attorney to focus on other important aspects of their work. *ChatGPT can also help attorneys communicate more effectively with clients, other attorneys, and the court, resulting in a more streamlined and efficient legal process*"). Italics added.

[2843] See: Alimardani, Armin/Jane, Emma A., "Human Hallucinations: GenAI and the Mirage of Personalised Learning for All", 2024, p. 13 ("*The output generated by GenAI models includes an inherent randomness and the same prompt may result in various outputs. Therefore, it is likely that the outputs of GenAI models are never entirely accurate and reliable. In other words, we contend that existing GenAI systems represent a technology that requires a 'human in/on the loop' to verify outputs before they reach the end user. When incorporating GenAI into an educational chatbot, students are the end users, making it challenging to identify and rectify these errors promptly*"). Italics added.

[2844] But see: *United States v. Hayes*, 2:24-cr-0280-DJC, 14 (E.D. Cal. Jan. 17, 2025) ("*In his motion to unseal, Mr. Francisco cited eight cases, six of which were cited in near string citation form. See Def. Mot. Unseal at 6, 10, 11. The primary case upon which Mr. Francisco relied- analyzing, quoting, describing the district court's analysis, and addressing in two different places in the motion- was*

legal analysis[2845]; and, finally, **(iii)** providing basic responses to enquiries about legal documents, such as legal statutes, constitutional amendments, legal opinions, or contracts.[2846] Note, though, that caution must be exercised in this regard.

§§ It follows that the general furore over Large Language Models should be halted or inordinate costs are slated to be externalized onto innocent others.[2847] This truism, dear reader, is neither unwarranted nor uncalled for. For a simple reason: decisions vital to our collective welfare[2848] often draw on skewed data[2849] fed into

---

"United States v. Harris, 761 F.Supp. 409, 414 (D.D.C. 1991)." See Def. Mot. Unseal at 6, 10. *Unfortunately, "United States v. Harris, 761 F.Supp. 409, 414 (D.D.C. 1991)" is not a real case.* The citation has all the markings of a *hallucinated case created by generative artificial intelligence (AI) tools such as ChatGPT and Google Bard that have been widely discussed by courts grappling with fictitious legal citations and reported by national news outlets*"). Italics added.

2845 But see: Alimardani, Armin/Jane, Emma A., "Human Hallucinations: GenAI and the Mirage of Personalised Learning for All", 2024, p. 2 ("*Generative Artificial Intelligence (GenAI) is gaining attention in education, particularly for its potential to personalise learning. However, studies have yet to assess its capabilities in controlled environments empirically. This study aims to help fill this gap by evaluating 'SmartTest', a GenAI chatbot designed by the authors to prompt open-ended questions, offer immediate feedback, and stimulate critical thinking through conversational nudges. Over five test cycles, SmartTest was used in a Criminal Law course at an Australian university. The results revealed SmartTest struggled with complex structured problem-solving exercises. While SmartTest showed some promise in aiding short-answer question learning, it remained limited and prone to inaccuracies. These findings highlight concerns that inflated expectations about GenAI could mislead educators and investors about its capabilities to deliver economically viable and quality personalised learning*"). Italics added.

2846 Surden, Harry, "ChatGPT, AI Large Language Models, and Law", *cit.*, pp. 1941–1972 (1968).

2847 See: Dahl, Matthew/Magesh, Varun/Suzgun, Mirac/Ho, Daniel E., "Large Legal Fictions: Profiling Legal Hallucinations in Large Language Models", *Journal of Legal Analysis*, Volume 16, 2024, 64–93 (64) ("*Do large language models (LLMs) know the law? LLMs are increasingly being used to augment legal practice, education, and research, yet their revolutionary potential is threatened by the presence of "hallucinations"—textual output that is not consistent with legal facts.* We present the first systematic evidence of these hallucinations in public-facing LLMs, documenting trends across jurisdictions, courts, time periods, and cases. *Using OpenAI's ChatGPT 4 and other public models, we show that LLMs hallucinate at least 58% of the time, struggle to predict their own hallucinations, and often uncritically accept users' incorrect legal assumptions. We conclude by cautioning against the rapid and unsupervised integration of popular LLMs into legal tasks*"). Italics added.

2848 Mounk, Y, *The age of responsibility: luck, choice, and the welfare state*, Cambridge, Cambridge University Press, 2017; Gustafson, Kaaryn S, *Cheating Welfare: Public Assistance and the Criminalization of Poverty*, New York: NYU Press, 2011.

2849 *Tech, Bias and Housing Initiative, the Promise and Perils of Residential Proptech, Year 1, Research Summary Report, April 2023, TechEquity Collaborative*, p. 11, available at: https://techequity.us/wp-content/uploads/2023/04/TBHI-Y1-Research-Summary-Report.pdf (28.11.2024). ("*Once bad data enters the analysis of one factor, it gets baked into the subsequent process, multiplying the effect that one disadvantageous data point can have on someone's overall housing determination*"). Italics added.

databases[2850] scattered across the data-driven world[2851] we live in, which, in turn, has a direct bearing on subsequent algorithmic decision-making.[2852]

§§ Recall, caution must be exercised in that black box machines[2853] should not be entrusted with the task of making high stake decisions[2854] (v.g. freedom,[2855] housing,[2856] health,[2857] or scoring systems[2858]) or algorithmic consumer harms[2859]

2850 Balkin, Jack M., "The Three Laws of Robotics in the Age of Big Data", *Ohio State Law Journal*, Volume 78, Issue 5, 2017, pp. 1217–1241, whose research I have been following closely. See also: Hu, Margaret, "From the National Surveillance State to the Cybersurveillance State", *The Annual Review of Law and Social Science*, Volume 13, 2017, p. 165 ("*Datafication, like most big data processes, requires increasing amounts of digital data to support or construct cybersurveillance.* It empowers government actions that are based on digital data collection, data processing protocols, and *bulk data analyses* (Mayer-Schonberger & Cukier ¨ 2013). *Another way to characterize datafication is as a governmental policy interest that both transforms analog data (PCAST 2014) into searchable, centralized digital databases and develops new forms of stored data*"). Italics added.

2851 Hardt, Moritz, "How big data is unfair: Understanding sources of unfairness in data driven decision making", *Medium*, Archived on Oct. 8, 2014, available at: https://web.archive.org/web/20141008185829/; https://medium.com/@mrtz/how-big-data-is-unfair-9aa544d739de. (access: 17.12.2024).

2852 See: Allen, James, "The Color of Algorithms: An Analysis and Proposed Research Agenda Deterring Algorithmic Redlining", *Fordham Urban Law Journal*, Volume 46, 2019, pp. 219–234 (229–234) (discussing how historical mortgage redlining greatly swayed modern algorithms generated by massive batches of datasets that consist of decades of information built on exclusion and racial discrimination in the purview of financing, marketing, and housing). See: Part IV, This chapter, Sects. 4.1.4–4.1.4.2.3 of this book.

2853 See: Rudin, Cynthia, "Please stop explaining black box models for high stakes decisions", *Proceedings of NeurIPS 2018 Workshop on Critiquing and Correcting Trends in Machine Learning (NIPS 2018)*, 2018, passim; Rudin, C., & Radin, J., "Why are we using black box models in AI when we don't need to? A lesson from an explainable AI competition", *Harvard Data Science Review*, 2019, Volume 1, Issue 2, passim.

2854 See: Part V, Chap. 5, Sect. 5.1.7.2 of this book (on law number two to control algorithmic decision-making, which mandates that black box models must not be entrusted with the task of making high stake decisions—v.g. health and freedom). See: Weizenbaum, Joseph, *Computer Power and Human Reason: From Judgment to Calculation*, 1st edition, New York, W. H. Freeman & Co, 1976, pp. 1–300 (227) ("examines the sources of the computer's powers and offers evaluative explorations of what computers can do, cannot do, and should not be employed to do") (this founding father of Artificial Intelligence presciently noted that we should not entrust Artificial Intelligence-embedded technologies with "tasks that demand wisdom"). Italics added. The approval of rental applications is arguably one of those tasks that should never be entrusted to machines). More on this on Part IV, This chapter, Sects. 4.1.4–4.1.4.2.1 of this book. See also: Kleinberg, Jon/Lakkaraju, Himabindu/Leskovec, Jure/Ludwig, Jens/Mullainathan, Sendhil, "Human Decisions and Machine Predictions", *Quarterly Journal of Economics*, Volume 133, 2018, passim; Pasquale, Frank, "A Rule of Persons, Not Machines: The Limits of Legal Automation", *George Washington Law Review*, Volume 87, 2019, pp. 1 and ff and passim.

2855 Sen, Amartya, *Development as freedom*, Oxford, Oxford University Press, 2001.

2856 See: Wonyoung, So, "Which Information Matters? Measuring Landlord Assessment of Tenant Screening Reports", *Housing Policy Debate*, Volume 33, n. ° 6, 2023, pp. 1484–1510 (1484) ("*this study shows that landlords (...) display, on average, tendencies toward automation bias that are influenced by the risk assessments and scores presented by tenant screening reports.* I argue that maintaining blanket screening policies and automation bias, combined with the downstream effects of creating and *using racially biased eviction and criminal records, means that people of color will*

may otherwise occur. The overhyped promise of know-it-all Large Language Models must be accordingly brushed aside or, better yet, dispelled.

§§ It is noteworthy that LLMs are not in shortfall of limitations. Which yields the preliminary finding that LLMs must be used with extreme care[2860] in the legal arena. Let's find out why. To begin with, at one end of the spectrum, a plethora uses of state-of-the-art AI systems like ChatGPT entails either inserting documents or relevant background information into the prompt or uploading important documents[2861] to solve the legal issue at hand.

§§ For example, if one seeks to create a draft merger contract through GPT-4, one would need to manually insert relevant background information about the merger contract to feed the LLM with the befitted cues to generate a helpful document.[2862]

§§ Notwithstanding, legal actors must exercise extreme caution in this regard. Crucially, lawyers must refrain themselves from inserting private,[2863] secret, privileged, protected, or sensitive information,[2864] unless an AI provider expressly gives legal safeguards.[2865] Pivotally, multiple LLM made available to the consumers, such as the costless version of GPT-3.5, expressly indicate that sensitive information (or

inevitably experience disproportionate exclusion from rental housing due to perceived "risk" on the part of landlords"). Italics added. See: Part IV, This chapter, Sects. 4.1.4–4.1.4.2.3 of this book.

2857 Rudin, Cynthia/Ustun, B., "Optimized scoring systems: toward trust in machine learning for healthcare and criminal justice", *Interfaces*, Volume 48, 2018, pp. 399–486. See also: Vallès-Peris N./Domènech, M.", Caring in the in-between: a proposal to introduce responsible AI and robotics to healthcare", *Artificial Intelligence and Society*, 2021.

2858 Sokolovska, N./Chevaleyre, Y./Zucker, J.D., "A provable algorithm for learning interpretable scoring systems", *Proceedings of Machine Learning Research, Artificial Intelligence and Statistics*, Volume 84, pp. 566–574.

2859 See: Bar-Gill, Oren/Sunstein, Cass R./Talgam-Cohen, Inbal, "Algorithmic Harm in Consumer Markets", *Journal of Legal Analysis*, Volume 15, n. ° 1, 2023, pp. 1–47. See also: Lee, Nicole Turner/Resnick, Paul/Barton, Genie, *Algorithmic Bias Detection and Mitigation: Best Practices and Policies to Reduce Consumer Harms*. Washington, DC: Brookings Institution, 2019, passim; Slaughter, Rebecca Kelly, "Algorithms and Economic Justice: A Taxonomy of Harms and a Path Forward for the Federal Trade Commission", *Yale Journal of Law and Technology*, Volume 23, 2021 (on algorithmic consumer harms).

2860 Surden, Harry, "ChatGPT, AI Large Language Models, and Law", *cit.*, pp. 1941–1972 (1968).

2861 Surden, Harry, "ChatGPT, AI Large Language Models, and Law", *cit.*, pp. 1941–1972 (1968).

2862 Surden, Harry, "ChatGPT, AI Large Language Models, and Law", *cit.*, pp. 1941–1972 (1968).

2863 But see: Angel, María P./Calo, Ryan, "Distinguishing Privacy Law: A Critique of Privacy as Social Taxonomy", *Columbia Law Review*, Volume 124, 2024, pp. 507–551 ("*privacy disempowers marginalized populations, for example, by rendering their oppression less visible, but empowers these populations to resist unequal treatments* that result from the misuse of their information... [h]ow do we balance privacy against privacy?"). Italics added.

2864 But see: de Laat, Paul B. 'Algorithmic Decision-Making Based on Machine Learning from Big Data: Can Transparency Restore Accountability?", *Philosophy & Technology*, Volume 31, 2018, pp. 524 and ff and passim (broaches the plethora of limitations related with full transparency, privacy, deleterious effects, competitive edge, and the shroud of opacity under which algorithms are often wrapped).

2865 Surden, Harry, "ChatGPT, AI Large Language Models, and Law", *cit.*, pp. 1941–1972 (1968).

otherwise) inserted by users may well find its way to the system as far as permanent AI training[2866] is concerned.

§§ It follows that, absent express legal guarantees issued by an AI provider, sensitive client data[2867] or privileged information uploaded into the prompt of an LLM like ChatGPT might be embedded into the future database of the AI system,[2868] tentatively infringing client confidentiality or privilege, or unveiling/laying bare sensitive client information.[2869] Which might be eventually conducive to ghastly privacy harms.[2870]

§§ In addition to that, such consumer-grade systems clearly advise that humans may review user-uploaded content.[2871] On the opposite pole, multiple corporate-grade AI systems that embed LLMs like GPT-4 in the backend in an indirect manner, like *Lexis + AI*[2872] and *Westlaw CoCounsel*, routinely dish out guarantees of both enhanced security and augmented privacy, thereby assuring to the users that human reviewers will not peruse uploaded input. But not just that though. The foregoing corporate-grade AI systems furthermore assure to the users that the uploaded input will not be eventually used to train ChatGPT.[2873]

§§ At the other end of spectrum, lawyers should be chary of[2874] the functional limitations regarding the quality of the ChatGPT outputs.[2875] Whilst extant LLM's

---

2866 Surden, Harry, "ChatGPT, AI Large Language Models, and Law", *cit.*, pp. 1941–1972 (1968).

2867 See, generally, on the interplay between data protection, machine learning, algorithmic decision-making, privacy, and information society: Custers, Bart, "Data Dilemmas in the Information Society: Introduction and Overview", Custers, Bart/Calders, Toon/Schermer, Bart/Zarsky, Tal (Editors), *Discrimination and Privacy in the Information Society: Data Mining and Profiling in Large Databases*, Heidelberg, Springer, 2013, pp. 3–26; Tene, Omer/Polonetsky, Jules, "Big Data for All: Privacy and User Control in the Age of Analytics", *Northwestern Journal of Technology and Intellectual Property*, Volume 11, 2013, pp. 239 and ff and passim; Waldman, Ezra, "Privacy, Practice, and Performance", *California Law Review*, Volume 110, 2021, passim; Barocas, Solon/Hardt, Moritz/Narayanan, Arvind, "Fairness in Machine Learning: Limitations and Opportunities", 2018; Schermer, Bart W., "The Limits of Privacy in Automated Profiling and Data Mining", *Computer Law & Security Review*, Volume 27, 2011, pp. 45 and ff and passim; Mann, Monique/Matzner, Tobias, "Challenging Algorithmic Profiling: The Limits of Data Protection and Anti-Discrimination in Responding to Emergent Discrimination", *Big Data & Society*, Volume 6, 2019, passim.

2868 Surden, Harry, "ChatGPT, AI Large Language Models, and Law", *cit.*, pp. 1941–1972 (1968).

2869 Surden, Harry, "ChatGPT, AI Large Language Models, and Law", *cit.*, pp. 1941–1972 (1968).

2870 But see: Crawford, Kate/Schultz, Jason, "Big Data and Due Process: Toward a Framework to Redress Predictive Privacy Harms", *Boston College Law Review*, Volume 55, 2014, pp. 93, 99–101 (pinpointing pathways through which predictive analytic tools perpetuate discriminatory practices).

2871 Surden, Harry, "ChatGPT, AI Large Language Models, and Law", *cit.*, pp. 1941–1972 (1968).

2872 Wilkins, Stephanie, "LexisNexis and Thomson Reuters Weigh in on the Future of AI in Legal Research", *Law.com* (June 30, 2023), https://www.law.com/legaltechnews/2023/06/30/lexisnexis-and-thomson-reuters-weigh-in-on-the-future-of-ai-in-legal-research/; [https://perma.cc/D6SX-JBYB].

2873 Surden, Harry, "ChatGPT, AI Large Language Models, and Law", *cit.*, pp. 1941–1972 (1968).

2874 Greene, Jenna, "Will ChatGPT Make Lawyers Obsolete? (Hint: Be Afraid)", *Reuters*, (Dec. 9, 2022), https://www.reuters.com/legal/transactional/will-chatgpt-make-lawyers-obsolete-hint-be-afraid-2022-12-09/; [https://perma.cc/H9Q2-8Q6H].

2875 Surden, Harry, "ChatGPT, AI Large Language Models, and Law", *cit.*, pp. 1941–1972 (1968).

are incomparably better than previous versions, there is still a capacious room for improvement in that current LLM systems are not as reliable as one thinks.[2876] To add to our woes, the hazard of incorrect use of LLM's accrues to its perceived fallibility,[2877] which is wholly unfitting in the legal arena.[2878]

§§ On one hand, such systems generate inaccurate but plausible-seeming events, facts or even references.[2879] Amongst which fake opinions[2880] or phony academic papers.[2881] There have been multifarious incidents of lawyers submitting ChatGPT-engendered court documents with plausible-sounding yet fictitious case law[2882] citations.[2883]

[2876] See: Dahl, Matthew/Magesh, Varun/Suzgun, Mirac/Ho, Daniel E., "Large Legal Fictions: Profiling Legal Hallucinations in Large Language Models", *Journal of Legal Analysis*, Volume 16, 2024, 64–93 (64) ("*Do large language models (LLMs) know the law? LLMs are increasingly being used to augment legal practice, education, and research, yet their revolutionary potential is threatened by the presence of "hallucinations"—textual output that is not consistent with legal facts.* We present the first systematic evidence of these hallucinations in public-facing LLMs, documenting trends across jurisdictions, courts, time periods, and cases. *Using OpenAI's ChatGPT 4 and other public models, we show that LLMs hallucinate at least 58% of the time, struggle to predict their own hallucinations, and often uncritically accept users' incorrect legal assumptions.* We conclude by cautioning against the rapid and unsupervised integration of popular LLMs into legal tasks"). Italics added.

[2877] Surden, Harry, "ChatGPT, AI Large Language Models, and Law", *cit.*, pp. 1941–1972 (1968). But see: Citron, Danielle Keats, "Technological Due Process", *Washington Law Review*, 2008, p. 1249 (one must shy away from the perceived "tendency to presume a computer system's infallibility").

[2878] See: Alimardani, Armin/Jane, Emma A., "Human Hallucinations: GenAI and the Mirage of Personalised Learning for All", 2024, p. 13 ("*The output generated by GenAI models includes an inherent randomness and the same prompt may result in various outputs. Therefore, it is likely that the outputs of GenAI models are never entirely accurate and reliable. In other words, we contend that existing GenAI systems represent a technology that requires a 'human in/on the loop' to verify outputs before they reach the end user. When incorporating GenAI into an educational chatbot, students are the end users, making it challenging to identify and rectify these errors promptly*"). Italics added.

[2879] Surden, Harry, "ChatGPT, AI Large Language Models, and Law", *cit.*, pp. 1941–1972 (1968).

[2880] *Park v. Kim*, 91 F.4th 610, 615 (2d Cir. 2024) ("*At the very least, the duties imposed by Rule 11 require that attorneys read, and thereby confirm the existence and validity of, the legal authorities on which they rely. Indeed, we can think of no other way to ensure that the arguments made based on those authorities are "warranted by existing law," Fed. R. Civ. P. 11(b)(2),* or otherwise "legally tenable." Cooter & Gell, *496 U.S. at 393, 110 S.Ct. 2447.* As a District Judge of this Circuit recently held when presented with non-existent precedent generated by ChatGPT: "*A fake opinion is not 'existing law' and citation to a fake opinion does not provide a non-frivolous ground for extending, modifying, or reversing existing law, or for establishing new law. An attempt to persuade a court or oppose an adversary by relying on fake opinions is an abuse of the adversary system.*" Mata v. Avianca, Inc., No. 22CV01461(PKC), — F.Supp.3d —, —, 2023 WL 4114965, at *12 (S.D.N.Y. June 22, 2023)"). Italics added.

§§ On the other hand, every now and then the models incur in several inaccuracies in their analysis[2884] or reasoning,[2885] thereby leading to either warped conclusions in spite of the premises upon which it was built or nonsensical common-sense errors altogether.[2886] On this note, extant models should be handled with extreme care and caution and accordingly treated as mere draft tools, as opposed to final product generators.[2887] Users must therefore employ staggering efforts in painstakingly double-checking the outputs generated[2888] by ChatGPT[2889] with a view to ensure[2890] that they are fundamentally accurate.[2891]

[2881] See: *Kohls v. Ellison*, 24-cv-3754 (LMP/DLM), 10–11 (D. Minn. Jan. 10, 2025) ("*Professor Hancock's citation to fake, AI-generated sources in his declaration-even with his helpful, thorough, and plausible explanation (ECF No. 39)-shatters his credibility with this Court. At a minimum, expert testimony is supposed to be reliable. Fed.R.Evid. 702; see also Daubert v. Merrell Dow Pharms., Inc., 509 U.S. 579, 589 (1993) (explaining that expert testimony must be "not only relevant, but reliable").* More fundamentally, signing a declaration under penalty of perjury is not a mere formality; rather, it "alert[s] declarants to the gravity of their undertaking and thereby have a meaningful effect on truthtelling and reliability." *Acosta v. Mezcal, Inc., No. 17-cv-0931 (JKB), 2019 WL 2550660, at *2* (D. Md. June 20, 2019); *see also In re World Trade Ctr. Disaster Site Litig., 722 F.3d 483, 488* (2d Cir. 2013) (explaining that the "under penalty of perjury" affirmation "impresses upon the declarant the specific punishment to which he or she is subjected for certifying to false statements"). *The Court should be able to trust the "indicia of truthfulness" that declarations made under penalty of perjury carry, but that trust was broken here. Davenport v. Bd. of Trs. of State Ctr. Comm. Coll. Dist., 654 F.Supp.2d 1073, 1083* (E.D. Cal. 2009)"). Italics added.

[2882] *Kohls v. Ellison*, 24-cv-3754 (LMP/DLM), 9 (D. Minn. Jan. 10, 2025) ("The Court thus adds its voice to a growing chorus of courts around the country declaring the same message: verify AI-generated content in legal submissions! *See Mata v. Avianca, Inc., 678 F.Supp.3d 443, 466* (S.D.N.Y. 2023) (sanctioning attorney for including fake, AI-generated legal citations in a filing); *Park v. Kim, 91 F.4th 610, 614-16* (2d Cir. 2023) (referring attorney for potential discipline for including fake, AI-generated legal citations in a filing); *Kruse v. Karlan, 692 S.W.3d 43, 53* (Mo.Ct.App. 2024) (dismissing appeal because litigant filed a brief with multiple fake, AI-generated legal citations).")

[2883] Surden, Harry, "ChatGPT, AI Large Language Models, and Law", *cit.*, pp. 1941–1972 (1968).

[2884] But see: Alimardani, Armin/Jane, Emma A., "Human Hallucinations: GenAI and the Mirage of Personalised Learning for All", 2024, p. 2 ("*Generative Artificial Intelligence (GenAI) is gaining attention in education, particularly for its potential to personalise learning. However, studies have yet to assess its capabilities in controlled environments empirically. (....) Over five test cycles, SmartTest was used in a Criminal Law course at an Australian university. The results revealed SmartTest struggled with complex structured problem-solving exercises. While SmartTest showed some promise in aiding short-answer question learning, it remained limited and prone to inaccuracies*"). Italics added. See also: Dahl, Matthew/Magesh, Varun/Suzgun, Mirac/Ho, Daniel E., "Large Legal Fictions: Profiling Legal Hallucinations in Large Language Models", *Journal of Legal Analysis*, Volume 16, 2024, 64–93 (64) ("*textual output that is not consistent with legal facts*"). Italics added.

[2885] But see: Blair-Stanek, Andrew/Nils Holzenberger/Benjamin Van Durme, "Can GPT-3 Perform Statutory Reasoning?" *Proceedings of the Nineteenth International Conference on Artificial Intelligence and Law*, Braga, Portugal: Association for Computing Machinery, 2023; Guha, Neel, et al., "Legal Bench: A Collaboratively Built Benchmark for Measuring Legal Reasoning in Large Language Models", *Thirty-seventh Conference on Neural Information Processing Systems Datasets and Benchmarks Track*, 2023 (wondering whether and to what extent LLM systems can engage in competent legal reasoning).

[2886] Surden, Harry, "ChatGPT, AI Large Language Models, and Law", *cit.*, pp. 1941–1972 (1968).

[2887] Surden, Harry, "ChatGPT, AI Large Language Models, and Law", *cit.*, pp. 1941–1972 (1968).

§§ A useful analogy[2892] may be to think of outputs generated by GPT-4 as tantamount to a preliminary draft from an industrious yet callow/unseasoned third-year law student intern—it gives a rough sketch, a well-intended foundation, which still nonetheless requires a unsparing/unflinching vetting process in a bid to attain accuracy, reliability, logic, elegance, sobriety, factuality, and internal coherence before it can ultimately be submitted to a client or a court of law.[2893] Relatedly, there are serious reasons to believe that a batch of the flagged reliability problems will be curbed, if not completely wiped out, in the forthcoming future.[2894] One promising approach to augment exponentially the reliability of outputs is widely known as **«prompt augmentation»**.[2895]

2888 See: *Park v. Kim*, 91 F.4th 610, 615 (2d Cir. 2024) ("*At the very least, the duties imposed by Rule 11 require that attorneys read, and thereby confirm the existence and validity of, the legal authorities on which they rely. Indeed, we can think of no other way to ensure that the arguments made based on those authorities are "warranted by existing law," Fed. R. Civ. P. 11(b)(2)*, or otherwise "legally tenable." Cooter & Gell, *496 U.S. at 393, 110 S.Ct. 2447.* As a District Judge of this Circuit recently held when presented with non-existent precedent generated by ChatGPT: "*A fake opinion is not 'existing law' and citation to a fake opinion does not provide a non-frivolous ground for extending, modifying, or reversing existing law, or for establishing new law. An attempt to persuade a court or oppose an adversary by relying on fake opinions is an abuse of the adversary system.*" Mata v. Avianca, Inc., No. 22CV01461(PKC), — F.Supp.3d —, —, 2023 WL 4114965, at *12 (S.D.N.Y. June 22, 2023)"). Italics added.

2889 But see: Dahl, Matthew/Magesh, Varun/Suzgun, Mirac/Ho, Daniel E., "Large Legal Fictions: Profiling Legal Hallucinations in Large Language Models", *Journal of Legal Analysis*, Volume 16, 2024, 64–93 (64) ("*Do large language models (LLMs) know the law? LLMs are increasingly being used to augment legal practice, education, and research, yet their revolutionary potential is threatened by the presence of "hallucinations"—textual output that is not consistent with legal facts.* We present the first systematic evidence of these hallucinations in public-facing LLMs, documenting trends across jurisdictions, courts, time periods, and cases. *Using OpenAI's ChatGPT 4 and other public models, we show that LLMs hallucinate at least 58% of the time, struggle to predict their own hallucinations, and often uncritically accept users' incorrect legal assumptions. We conclude by cautioning against the rapid and unsupervised integration of popular LLMs into legal tasks*"). Italics added.

2890 *Kohls v. Ellison*, 24-cv-3754 (LMP/DLM), 9 (D. Minn. Jan. 10, 2025) ("*The Court thus adds its voice to a growing chorus of courts around the country declaring the same message: verify AI-generated content in legal submissions! See Mata v. Avianca, Inc., 678 F.Supp.3d 443, 466* (S.D.N.Y. 2023) (sanctioning attorney for including fake, AI-generated legal citations in a filing); *Park v. Kim, 91 F.4th 610, 614-16* (2d Cir. 2023) (referring attorney for potential discipline for including fake, AI-generated legal citations in a filing); *Kruse v. Karlan, 692 S.W.3d 43, 53* (Mo.Ct.App. 2024) (dismissing appeal because litigant filed a brief with multiple fake, AI-generated legal citations)").

2891 Surden, Harry, "ChatGPT, AI Large Language Models, and Law", *cit.*, pp. 1941–1972 (1968).

2892 Surden, Harry, "ChatGPT, AI Large Language Models, and Law", *cit.*, pp. 1941–1972 (1968).

2893 Surden, Harry, "ChatGPT, AI Large Language Models, and Law", *cit.*, pp. 1941–1972 (1969).

2894 Surden, Harry, "ChatGPT, AI Large Language Models, and Law", *cit.*, pp. 1941–1972 (1969).

2895 Surden, Harry, "ChatGPT, AI Large Language Models, and Law", *cit.*, pp. 1941–1972 (1969).

§§ *Prompt augmentation* is not just about asking the LLM systems a basic question in a prompt.[2896] Rather, it is about including in the prompt useful information that is of paramount importance when it comes to generating an accurate answer.[2897]

§§ Crucially, if one augments the prompt with actionable, accurate, rigorous, helpful useful, relevant information, LLM systems are much more likely to generate accurate results to factual or analytical questions as compared to merely formulate a general question and wait for the model to produce a correct answer.[2898]

§§ One might wonder what is the rationale behind the sweeping idea of augmenting a prompt. The propelling force of augmenting a prompt is accordingly enhance the reliability of the prompts generated by LLM systems.

§§ Inserting additional information before or after the prompt will help GPT-4 to generate better outputs.[2899] In sharp contrast with an orthodox, conventional non-augmented prompt—which usually looks like something like this «what are the factors of fair use in copyright?»[2900]—*prompt augmentation* is much more than simply asking a question or giving an instruction without providing additional important information.[2901] Roughly, that is how **hallucinations**[2902] happen in the first place.[2903]

§§ Strikingly, if users are asking in the aforementioned manner, there are having ChatGPT respond by simply «looking» internally into its own set of compressed «databases» of, or treasure troves of, uploaded information.[2904] Compellingly, by having the LLLM model shift its gaze inwardly, it will, in all likelihood, **hallucinate**.[2905] Worryingly, though, ChatGPT's hallucinations[2906] are becoming mainstream[2907] in a paraphernalia of domains[2908]/fields.[2909]

[2896] Surden, Harry, "ChatGPT, AI Large Language Models, and Law", *cit.*, pp. 1941–1972 (1969).

[2897] Surden, Harry, "ChatGPT, AI Large Language Models, and Law", *cit.*, pp. 1941–1972 (1969).

[2898] Surden, Harry, "ChatGPT, AI Large Language Models, and Law", *cit.*, pp. 1941–1972 (1969).

[2899] Surden, Harry, "ChatGPT, AI Large Language Models, and Law", *cit.*, pp. 1941–1972 (1969).

[2900] Surden, Harry, "ChatGPT, AI Large Language Models, and Law", *cit.*, pp. 1941–1972 (1969).

[2901] Surden, Harry, "ChatGPT, AI Large Language Models, and Law", *cit.*, pp. 1941–1972 (1969).

[2902] See: Hicks, Michael Townsen/Humphries, James/Slater, Joe, "ChatGPT is bullshit", *Ethics and Information Technology*, 26:38, 2024, pp. 1–10 (1) ("there has been considerable interest in large language models: *machine learning systems which produce human-like text and dialogue. Applications of these systems have been plagued by persistent inaccuracies in their output; these are often called "AI hallucinations". We argue that these falsehoods, and the overall activity of large language models, is better understood as bullshit in the sense explored by Frankfurt (On Bullshit, Princeton, 2005): the models are in an important way indifferent to the truth of their outputs*"). Italics added.

[2903] Dahl, Matthew et. al, "Hallucinating Law: Legal Mistakes with Large Language Models are Pervasive", *Stanford University Human-Centered Artificial Intelligence* (Jan. 11, 2024), https://hai.stanford.edu/news/hallucinating-law-legal-mistakes-large-language-models-are-pervasive; [https://perma.cc/M4XJ-UVCJ].

[2904] Surden, Harry, "ChatGPT, AI Large Language Models, and Law", *cit.*, pp. 1941–1972 (1969).

[2905] Surden, Harry, "ChatGPT, AI Large Language Models, and Law", *cit.*, pp. 1941–1972 (1969). See also: Stokel-Walker, Chris, "Generative AI Is Coming for the Lawyers", *Wired* (Feb. 21, 2023), https://www.wired.com/story/chatgpt-generative-ai-is-coming-for-the-lawyers; [https://perma.cc/LFG5-W3EF]; Magesh, Varun et. al, "AI on Trial: Legal Models Hallucinate in 1 out

§§ Antithetically, imagine, if you will, that you were so diligent as to insert in the prompt information that the LLM model could use to provide you an accurate answer.[2910] For example, imagine that in your prompt (before or after), you had copied and pasted chunks from a famed law treatise on copyright, along with your initial question about copyright.[2911]

§§ In so doing, you have exponentially augmented the prompt with additional, helpful, useful, and fundamentally actionable information. Such augmentation will prove important to skyrocket both the reliability of LLM model and the accuracy of the outputs generated by the latter, thereby enabling it to respond accurately, which would not have happened had you simply asked the original prompt without complementary information.[2912]

---

of 6 (or More) Benchmarking Queries", *Stanford University of Human-Centered Artificial Intelligence* (May 23, 2024) https://hai.stanford.edu/news/ai-trial-legal-models-hallucinate-1-out-6-or-more-benchmarking-queries; [https://perma.cc/7MEE-JWHS]; Kolinski, Jordan A., "Your "AI" is Hallucinating", Hellmuth & Johnson (June 14, 2024) https://hjlawfirm.com/your-ai-is-hallucinating/; [https://perma.cc/EJZ8-QYJR].

[2906] But see: Dahl, Matthew/Magesh, Varun/Suzgun, Mirac/Ho, Daniel E., "Large Legal Fictions: Profiling Legal Hallucinations in Large Language Models", *Journal of Legal Analysis*, Volume 16, 2024, 64–93 (64) ("*Do large language models (LLMs) know the law? LLMs are increasingly being used to augment legal practice, education, and research, yet their revolutionary potential is threatened by the presence of "hallucinations"—textual output that is not consistent with legal facts.* We present the first systematic evidence of these hallucinations in public-facing LLMs, documenting trends across jurisdictions, courts, time periods, and cases. *Using OpenAI's ChatGPT 4 and other public models, we show that LLMs hallucinate at least 58% of the time, struggle to predict their own hallucinations, and often uncritically accept users' incorrect legal assumptions. We conclude by cautioning against the rapid and unsupervised integration of popular LLMs into legal tasks*"). Italics added.

[2907] *United States v. Hayes*, 2:24-cr-0280-DJC, 14 (E.D. Cal. Jan. 17, 2025) ("*In his motion to unseal, Mr. Francisco cited eight cases, six of which were cited in near string citation form. See Def. Mot. Unseal at 6, 10, 11. The primary case upon which Mr. Francisco relied- analyzing, quoting, describing the district court's analysis, and addressing in two different places in the motion- was "United States v. Harris, 761 F.Supp. 409, 414 (D.D.C. 1991)."* See Def. Mot. Unseal at 6, 10. *Unfortunately, "United States v. Harris, 761 F.Supp. 409, 414 (D.D.C. 1991)" is not a real case.* The citation has all the markings of a *hallucinated case created by generative artificial intelligence (AI) tools such as ChatGPT and Google Bard that have been widely discussed by courts grappling with fictitious legal citations and reported by national news outlets*"). Italics added.

[2908] Burke, Garance/Schellmann, Hilke, "Researchers Say an AI-Powered Transcription Tool Used in Hospitals Invents Things No One Ever Said", *AP News* (Oct. 26, 2024), https://apnews.com/article/ai-artificial-intelligence-health-business-90020cdf5fa16c79ca2e5b6c4c9bbb14; [https://perma.cc/D2S5-UEMC].

[2909] Lysandrou, "Comparative analysis of drug-GPT and ChatGPT LLMs for healthcare insights: Evaluating accuracy and relevance in patient and HCP contexts", *ArXiv Preprint: arXiv*, 2307, 16850v1, 2023.

[2910] Surden, Harry, "ChatGPT, AI Large Language Models, and Law", *cit.*, pp. 1941–1972 (1969).

[2911] Surden, Harry, "ChatGPT, AI Large Language Models, and Law", *cit.*, pp. 1941–1972 (1969).

[2912] Surden, Harry, "ChatGPT, AI Large Language Models, and Law", *cit.*, pp. 1941–1972 (1969).

§§ The catalyst for this improvement can be traced back to transformer «self-attention» mechanism.[2913] Recall that this bodacious mechanism enables Artificial Intelligence-anchored technologies to embed relevant context in the outputs.[2914] By catering the LLM model with a relevant document that you know for a fact that, somewhere within, more likely than not comprises relevant information that will be useful and actionable to answering your pressing question, you are actually giving the LLM model the much-needed context to generate a more accurate/reliable answer/output.[2915]

§§ Concisely, an LLM model like GPT-4[2916] fully equipped with the relevant tools to look backward/inward at the informative additional context that you gave in the prompt, will consider this in conjunction with your question. Chances are that after such amelioration the LLM system will be much more likely to come up with an output that predicts the sequence of relevant words that are accurate,[2917] reliable, spot on, and fundamentally responsive to your question/prompt.[2918]

§§ Similarly, another technique oft-used to optimize both the accuracy and reliability of ChatGPT outputs is the much-acclaimed **«prompt engineering»**.[2919] The latter amounts to a procedure whereby the attorney can fine tune the legal problem and hone-in on it a little bit more.[2920] To cater for that, an attorney can simply ask ChatGPT to expand on one of the following issues while asking the rationale behind a given output.[2921] Multiple factors can likewise be added to the prompt and ChatGPT will eventually establish what the outcome would be if a different set of factors were used, applied, employed, fine-tuned, or overhauled.[2922]

[2913] Surden, Harry, "ChatGPT, AI Large Language Models, and Law", *cit.*, pp. 1941–1972 (1969).

[2914] Surden, Harry, "ChatGPT, AI Large Language Models, and Law", *cit.*, pp. 1941–1972 (1969).

[2915] Surden, Harry, "ChatGPT, AI Large Language Models, and Law", *cit.*, pp. 1941–1972 (1969).

[2916] Davis, E./Aaronson, S., "Testing GPT-4 with Wolfram alpha and code interpreter plub-ins on math and science problems", *Arxiv Preprint: arXiv*, 2308, 2023, 05713v2 (on the inner workings, and capabilities, of GPT-4).

[2917] But see: Dahl, Matthew/Magesh, Varun/Suzgun, Mirac/Ho, Daniel E., "Large Legal Fictions: Profiling Legal Hallucinations in Large Language Models", *Journal of Legal Analysis*, Volume 16, 2024, 64–93, 64–93 (88) ("*although data-rich and moneyed players certainly stand at an advantage when it comes to building hallucination-free legal LLMs for their own private use, it is not clear that even infinite resources can entirely solve the conceptual problems we diagnose* (….) Only then can individual *litigants decide for themselves whether the legal information they seek to obtain from LLMs is trustworthy or not*"). Italics added.

[2918] Surden, Harry, "ChatGPT, AI Large Language Models, and Law", *cit.*, pp. 1941–1972 (1969).

[2919] See: Mckinsey & Co (Sept. 2023), https://www.mckinsey.com/featured-insights/mckinsey-explainers/what-is-prompt-engineering [https://perma.cc/XZC2-6HMJ] ("Prompt engineering is the practice of designing inputs for generative AI tools that will produce optimal outputs").

[2920] Gamm, Grant M., "Artificial Intelligence and the Practice of Law: A Chat With ChatGPT", *Saint Louis University Law Journal*, Volume 68, 2024, p. 604.

[2921] Gamm, Grant M., "Artificial Intelligence and the Practice of Law: A Chat With ChatGPT", *cit.*, p. 604.

[2922] Gamm, Grant M., "Artificial Intelligence and the Practice of Law: A Chat With ChatGPT", *cit.*, p. 604.

§§ It is important to note, though, that **«prompt engineering»** has been used to gauge whether and to what extent ChatGPT could engage in legal reasoning while assuming the role of an appellate judge and accordingly render a judicial decision based on the materials timely provided.[2923] Pundits sought to gauge the degree to which ChatGPT's decision-making could be shaped through a few targeted interventions.[2924] A broad a range of *prompt-engineering* techniques aimed at steering ChatGPT towards decision-making patterns tantamount to that of human judges were empirically experimented.[2925] But to no avail.

§§ Tellingly, the cluster of findings arising out of a budding piece of empirical evidence bestow upon the public the vividly clear impression that ChatGPT is, above else, a legal formalist that pays little to none regard for non-legal factors.[2926] In stark contrast, human judges[2927] are swayed by non-legal factors.[2928] Such as empathy,[2929] sympathy,[2930] and so forth. GPT is therefore a legal formalist, as opposed to a decision-maker.[2931]

[2923] Posner, Eric A./Saran, Shivam, "Judge AI: Assessing Large Language Models in Judicial Decision-Making", *The University of Chicago, Coase-Sandor Institute for Law and Economics, The Law School, Coase-Sandor Institute for Law and Economics Research Paper n. º 25–03*, January 2025, 2025, pp. 1–41 (25–26).

[2924] Posner, Eric A./Saran, Shivam, "Judge AI: Assessing Large Language Models in Judicial Decision-Making", *cit.*, pp. 1–41 (25–26).

[2925] Posner, Eric A./Saran, Shivam, "Judge AI: Assessing Large Language Models in Judicial Decision-Making", *cit.*, pp. 1–41 (25–26).

[2926] Posner, Eric A./Saran, Shivam, "Judge AI: Assessing Large Language Models in Judicial Decision-Making", *cit.*, pp. 1–41 (25–26).

[2927] But see: Part V, Chap. 5, Sect. 5.1.8.5 of this book (on law number five to interpret algorithmic decision-making, which mandates that robot-judges, robot-prosecutors and robot-lawyers must not enter the courtroom for they are utterly incapable of making sound and interpretable value judgements).

[2928] Posner, Eric A./Saran, Shivam, "Judge AI: Assessing Large Language Models in Judicial Decision-Making", *cit.*, pp. 1–41 (25–26).

[2929] See: Newell, Lauren A., "Rebooting Empathy for the Digital Generation Lawyer", *Ohio State Journal on Dispute Resolution*, Volume 34, Issue 1, 2019, 1–96 (4–6) (contending that empathy is now needed more than ever amidst a digital world in which people somewhere along the line ceased to communicate "face to face". Rebooting empathy in the remit of administration of justice is the way forward in this scholar's insightful view).

[2930] Posner, Eric A./Saran, Shivam, "Judge AI: Assessing Large Language Models in Judicial Decision-Making", *cit.*, pp. 1–41 (25–26). See also: Putnam, Robert D., *Bowling Alone: The Collapse and Revival of American Community*, Touchstone Books by Simon & Schuster; 1st edition (August 7, 2001), 2001, pp. 19 ff (stating that "*The definitions and understanding of social capital are by no means univocal. The term "social capital" was first coined in 1916 by L.J. Hanifan, the supervisor of rural schools in West Virginia, who argued that the strengthening of social networks ultimately benefited the entire community. The individual is helpless socially, if left to himself.... If he comes into contact with his neighbors, and they with other neighbors, there will be an accumulation of social capital*, which may immediately satisfy his social needs and which may bear a social potentiality sufficient to the substantial improvement of living conditions in the whole community. *The community as a whole will benefit by the cooperation of all its parts, while the individual will find in his associations the advantages of the help, the sympathy, and the fellowship of his neighbors*"); Ludwig, Bernd, "Sympathy for the Devil (s)? Personality and Legal Coercion in Kant's Doctrine of Law", *Jurisprudence*, 6, 2015, pp. 34 ff (arguing that human beings have certain moral

§§ Compellingly, no amount of *prompt engineering* can budge ChatGPT from deeply-rooted ideas it has ingested from reams of data and billions of texts[2932] collated from the internet. The key takeaway is that, at its best, ChatGPT is a decent predictor.[2933] At its worst, ChatGPT is a lousy decision-maker whose lacklustre performance should keep us eagerly awaken at night.

4.1.9.4 «Is ChatGPT Bullshit?» (Hicks/Humphries/Slater) Can Legal Actors Place Trust upon Large Language Models that Routinely Leads Them Astray, Owing to Unbridled Hallucinations?

§§ The unbridled rise of Large Language Models («LLMs») has been met with growing unease over the potential for Artificial Intelligence-embedded technologies to spawn *pearls of algorithmic wisdom* that lead users astray.[2934] These deep-rooted concerns have led to poignant calls for halting the general furore[2935] over both ChatGPT[2936] and computer-run machine learning algorithms,[2937] which forms part of a broader technological apparatus within which LLM systems operate.

---

duties to abide by, such as treating others, including legal officials, with utmost respect); Correia, Vasco, "Bias and Fallacies: The Role of Motivated Irrationality in Fallacious Reasoning", *Cogency*, 3, 2011, pp. 108 ff (emphasizes that oftentimes people tend to jump into conclusions and are prone to make steadfast judgments with little to none regard for its intrinsic accuracy. Which amounts to either conscious or unconscious biases. This is acutely important with regard of lawyer's actions in a court of law or (in an overarching sense) in dispute resolution settings. As it is an utterly impossible task to ascertain as to whether and to what extent a "lawyer is deliberately trying to manipulate the audience, or whether the desire to win the case (*or sympathy towards the client*, etc.) unconsciously affects her judgment…"). Italics added.

[2931] Posner, Eric A./Saran, Shivam, "Judge AI: Assessing Large Language Models in Judicial Decision-Making", *cit.*, pp. 1–41 (25–26). See: Part V, Chap. 5, Sect. 5.1.8.5 of this book (on law number five to interpret algorithmic decision-making, which mandates that robot-judges, robot-prosecutors and robot-lawyers must not enter the courtroom for they are utterly incapable of making sound and interpretable value judgements).

[2932] Posner, Eric A./Saran, Shivam, "Judge AI: Assessing Large Language Models in Judicial Decision-Making", *cit.*, pp. 1–41 (25–26).

[2933] Agrawal, Ajay/Gans, Joshua/Goldfarb, Avi, *Prediction Machines: The Simple Economics of Artificial Intelligence*, 2nd Edition. Massachusetts: Harvard Business Review Press, 2022, pp. 1–304.

[2934] See: Part III, Chap. 3, Sects. 3.1.5.4–3.1.5.4.1.1 of this book (on Critical Artificial Intelligence Studies, with a sharper focus on the deceptive patterns evinced by Large Language Models, which has lent urgency to concerns about the trustworthiness and reliability of these tools).

[2935] Black, Nicole, "Lawyers Have a Bevy of Advanced and AI-enhanced Legal Research Tools at Their Fingertips", A.B.A. J. (Nov. 22, 2019), 2019, passim, https://www.abajournal.com/web/article/lawyers-have-a-bevy-of-advanced-and-ai-enhanced-legal-research-tools-at-their-fingertips; [https://perma.cc/B6MY-43L3].

[2936] Laallam, Abla, "Hallucinations: Your AI Might Be Affected…," *Hofstra JIBL Blog: Journal of International Business and Law*, 2025, passim, available at: https://www.hofstrajibl.org/2025/01/hallucinations-your-ai-might-be-affected/ (access: 10.01.2025). Internal footnotes omitted.

[2937] Brantner, C./Saurwein, F., "Covering technology risks and responsibility: Automation, artificial intelligence, robotics, and algorithms in the media", *International Journal of Communication*,

§§ Pundits have neither been coy nor bashful in overtly decrying/excoriating—a trenchant criticism that has been deployed with a crushing lack of subtlety[2938]—the recurrent inaccuracies arising out of ChatGPT's outputs,[2939] whose persistent hallucinated outputs[2940] have couched concerns on whether and to what extent trust could be placed upon Large Language Models[2941] and Artificial Intelligence-embedded technologies.[2942] Tempers flared, grievances brewed and a public outcry has accordingly ensued.[2943]

§§ The unease with which Large Language Models have been met[2944] has accordingly given rise to a rather grisly sobriquet indeed: «ChatGPT is bullshit»[2945] insofar the latter excels in making things up.[2946] It seems as though that the latter has surpassed the so-called «artificial intelligent lawyers»[2947] in that regard.

Volume 15, 2021, pp. 5074–5098 (on the multifarious risks posed by an ever-evolving Artificial Intelligence in the realm of media).

[2938] Asare, Janice Gassam, "The Dark Side of ChatGPT", *Forbes* (Jan. 28, 2023, 8:49 PM), https://www.forbes.com/sites/janicegassam/2023/01/28/the-dark-side-of-chatgpt/?sh=3230b5484799; [https://perma.cc/YT3T-ACCV].

[2939] Ziwei et al., "Survey of Hallucination in Natural Language Generation", *ACM Computing Survey* (Nov. 17, 2022), 2022, passim.

[2940] Weise, K./Metz, C., "When AI chatbots hallucinate", *New York Times*, May 9, 2023. Accessed via https://www.nytimes.com/2023/05/01/business/ai-chatbots-hallucination.html, 2023.

[2941] Metz, Cade, "The New Chatbots Could Change the World. Can You Trust Them?", *New York Times*, (Dec. 11, 2022), 2022, https://www.nytimes.com/2022/12/10/technology/ai-chat-bot-chatgpt.html; [https://perma.cc/NK7V-M54R].

[2942] Davis, Wes, "The New York Times Warns AI Search Engine Perplexity to Stop Using Its Content", *The Verge* (Oct. 15, 2024), https://www.theverge.com/2024/10/15/24270774/new-york-times-cease-and-desist-letter-perplexity-ai-search-engine; [https://perma.cc/J7UN-787J].

[2943] Knibbs, Kate, "A Lawsuit Against Perplexity Calls Out Fake News AI Hallucinations", *Wired* (Oct. 21, 2024), https://www.wired.com/story/dow-jones-new-york-post-sue-perplexity/; [https://perma.cc/6RYG-XZWG].

[2944] But see: Cyphert, Amy B., "A Human Being Wrote This Law Review Article: GPT-3 and the Practice of Law", *University of California Law Review*, Volume 55, 2021, pp. 401, 403–04 (noting that a bevy of advanced algorithms are currently embedded in several tools that lawyers use daily).

[2945] Hicks, Michael Townsen/Humphries, James/Slater, Joe, "ChatGPT is bullshit", *Ethics and Information Technology*, 26:38, 2024, pp. 1–10 (1) ("there has been considerable interest in large language models: *machine learning systems which produce human-like text and dialogue. Applications of these systems have been plagued by persistent inaccuracies in their output; these are often called "AI hallucinations". We argue that these falsehoods, and the overall activity of large language models, is better understood as bullshit in the sense explored by Frankfurt (On Bullshit, Princeton, 2005): the models are in an important way indifferent to the truth of their outputs*"). Italics added.

[2946] Edwards, B., "Why ChatGPT and bing chat are so good at making things up", *Ars Tecnica*, 2023, https://arstechnica.com/information-technology/2023/04/why-ai-chatbots-are-the-ultimatebs-machines-and-how-people-hope-to-fix-them/, accessed 18th January, 2025.

[2947] Medianik, Katherine, "Artificially Intelligent Lawyers: Updating the Model Rules of Professional Conduct in Accordance with the New Technological Era", *Cardozo Law Review*, Volume 39, 1497, 2018, pp. 1498–1500 (on «artificial intelligent lawyers).

§§ Notwithstanding, the worst is yet to come as ChatGPT is bound to be powered with a mighty force tagged as General Artificial Intelligence (AGI).[2948] When that happens, a *snowball effect* will follow suit[2949] as ChatGPT's hallucinations will become part of the *new normal* against the backdrop of which truths and lies will become indistinguishable in that they will dovetail seamlessly. Put otherwise, then (and only then) the evanescent frontiers between truths and lies will not become blurred. Instead, truths and lies will become a woven of the same cloth. That is why ChatGPT's occupational hazard (*hallucinations*) is pivotally important in legal settings. Lest we forget, lies spread like wild fire in that they are a breeding ground for the undeterred rise of *Algorithmic Dictatorship* of which we should be keenly wary of.

§§ Whilst Large Language Models are already catalysing a metamorphic shift in the purview of legal education[2950] and legal research,[2951] there have been educated calls for a greater accuracy in the outputs generated by ChatGPT.[2952] However, nowhere do laws, or its predecessors, define «ChatGPT hallucinations». It is therefore important to drill into, and shed a keen light on, the multifarious pitfalls arising out

---

[2948] Sarkar, A., "ChatGPT 5 is on track to attain artificial general intelligence", *The Statesman*, April 12, 2023, Accesses via https://www.thestatesman.com/supplements/science_supplements/chatgpt-5-is-on-track-to-attain-artificial-general-intelligence-1503171366.html; Knight, W., "Some glimpse AGI in ChatGPT. Others call it a mirage", *Wired*, August 18 2023, 2023, accessed via https://www.wired.com/story/chatgpt-agi-intelligence/.

[2949] Zhang, "How language model hallucinations can snowball", *ArXiv preprint: arXiv:*, 2305, 2023, 13534v1.

[2950] But see: Alimardani, Armin/Jane, Emma A., "Human Hallucinations: GenAI and the Mirage of Personalised Learning for All", 2024, p. 2 ("*Generative Artificial Intelligence (GenAI) is gaining attention in education, particularly for its potential to personalise learning. However, studies have yet to assess its capabilities in controlled environments empirically. This study aims to help fill this gap by evaluating 'SmartTest', a GenAI chatbot designed by the authors to prompt open-ended questions, offer immediate feedback, and stimulate critical thinking through conversational nudges. Over five test cycles, SmartTest was used in a Criminal Law course at an Australian university. The results revealed SmartTest struggled with complex structured problem-solving exercises. While SmartTest showed some promise in aiding short-answer question learning, it remained limited and prone to inaccuracies. These findings highlight concerns that inflated expectations about GenAI could mislead educators and investors about its capabilities to deliver economically viable and quality personalised learning*"). Italics added.

[2951] But see: Dahl, Matthew/Magesh, Varun/Suzgun, Mirac/Ho, Daniel E., "Large Legal Fictions: Profiling Legal Hallucinations in Large Language Models", *Journal of Legal Analysis*, Volume 16, 2024, 64–93 (64) ("*Do large language models (LLMs) know the law? LLMs are increasingly being used to augment legal practice, education, and research, yet their revolutionary potential is threatened by the presence of "hallucinations"—textual output that is not consistent with legal facts*"). Italics added.

[2952] See: Dahl, Matthew/Magesh, Varun/Suzgun, Mirac/Ho, Daniel E., "Large Legal Fictions: Profiling Legal Hallucinations in Large Language Models", *cit.*, 64–93 (64) ("*Using OpenAI's ChatGPT 4 and other public models, we show that LLMs hallucinate at least 58% of the time, struggle to predict their own hallucinations, and often uncritically accept users' incorrect legal assumptions. We conclude by cautioning against the rapid and unsupervised integration of popular LLMs into legal tasks*"). Italics added.

an all-out deployment of Large Language Models. Especially, albeit not exclusively, in legal settings.[2953]

§§ Tellingly, one pressing concern facing LLMs is their ineluctable penchant for hallucinations[2954] in that ChatGPT routinely generates phony information that leads users astray.[2955] Worryingly, LLMs can hallucinate in two different ways as far as the legal purview is concerned[2956]: **(i)** the LLM system can produce a fallacious[2957] response,[2958] which would either analyse the law erroneously[2959] or make

---

[2953] But see, extolling the qualities of ChatGPT: Gamm, Grant M., "Artificial Intelligence and the Practice of Law: A Chat With ChatGPT", *Saint Louis University Law Journal*, Volume 68, 2024, pp. 605–606 ("*with an attorney using the tool in this way, they can more effectively prepare for events in a case, such as cross-examination, and can use this summation as a reference during the trial or with other members of the legal team.* An attorney who effectively utilizes ChatGPT can optimize their time and energy on more strategic and high-value tasks. ChatGPT can aid attorneys in proofreading their work, offering suggestions on complex issues, and organizing information. *This tool can be applied in any area of law, and its use is likely to significantly enhance the attorney's efficiency and productivity. Additionally, ChatGPT can provide quick and accurate answers to legal questions, enabling attorneys to make decisions with confidence.* By automating repetitive tasks, ChatGPT frees up time for the attorney to focus on other important aspects of their work. *ChatGPT can also help attorneys communicate more effectively with clients, other attorneys, and the court, resulting in a more streamlined and efficient legal process*"). Italics added.

[2954] Introducing ChatGPT, OpenAI Blog, https://openai.com/blog/chatgpt#OpenAI; [https://perma.cc/X8A9-ZYSL].

[2955] Ziwei et al., "Survey of Hallucination in Natural Language Generation", *ACM Computing Survey* (Nov. 17, 2022), 2022, passim.

[2956] Laallam, Abla, "Hallucinations: Your AI Might Be Affected...," *Hofstra JIBL Blog: Journal of International Business and Law*, 2025, passim, available at: https://www.hofstrajibl.org/2025/01/hallucinations-your-ai-might-be-affected/ (access: 10.01.2025).

[2957] See: Alimardani, Armin/Jane, Emma A., "Human Hallucinations: GenAI and the Mirage of Personalised Learning for All", 2024, p. 13 ("*The output generated by GenAI models includes an inherent randomness and the same prompt may result in various outputs. Therefore, it is likely that the outputs of GenAI models are never entirely accurate and reliable. In other words, we contend that existing GenAI systems represent a technology that requires a 'human in/on the loop' to verify outputs before they reach the end user. When incorporating GenAI into an educational chatbot, students are the end users, making it challenging to identify and rectify these errors promptly*"). Italics added.

[2958] See: Part V, Chap. V, Sect. 5.1.1.1 of this book (on the central tenets of Rule of Law that lends itself to a beacon of justice amidst the sepulchral darkness that is about to take hold). See: Part V, Chap. 5, Sect. 5.1.1.2 of this book (on the central tenets of Procedural Rule of Law that lends itself to a lighthouse of justice that allows citizens to challenge the pearls of algorithmic wisdom in a court of law). Regrettably, the Rule of Law is backsliding worldwide. Especially in Central and Eastern Europe. See: Avbelj, Matej, "The Rule of Law, Comprehensive Doctrines, Overlapping Consensus, and the Future of Europe", *Ratio Juris*, Volume 36, Issue 3, September, 2023, pp. 242–258. The Rule of Law is not a «one size fits all» format nonetheless. But see: Chesterman, Simon, "An International Rule of Law", *The American Journal of Comparative Law*, Volume 56, 2008, pp. 331–362 (on the thrust to grasp (?) a catch-all International Rule of Law). See: Peari, Sagi, "Better Law as a Better Outcome", *The American Journal of Comparative Law*, Volume 63, Issue 1, 2015, pp. 155–195 (156) (on Leflar's stance on «better rule of law»). For the purposes of this piece, Rule of Law amounts to a lighthouse of procedural fairness to which citizens, regardless of where they are, resort to upon gaining access to a given system of administration of criminal justice. Whilst further utterances on the fabric of Rule of Law fall well outside the scope and breadth

an untrue statement about facts,[2960] or **(ii)** the LLM system produces an unfounded/unsubstantiated response.[2961] That is, the LLM system will provide an accurate description of the law,[2962] but nonetheless cites sources that fail to correctly, let alone fully, premise that claim.[2963]

§§ This is something that should be dreaded in that not only deserves to be remarked upon but, and foremost, is in dire need of being overtly decried. To the extent critical authoritative sources play a pivotal role in the remit of legal writing[2964]

---

of this paper, one must not be oblivious of the fact that the thrust to Deglobalizing Rule of Law is underway. See: Bussani, Mauro, "Deglobalizing Rule of Law and Democracy: Hunting Down Rhetoric Through Comparative Law", *The American Journal of Comparative Law*, Volume 67, 2019, pp. 701–744 (701) (contending that the thrust to Deglobalizing Rule of Law is interwoven with thrust to take heed of «well-known differences that run through cultures and traditions». In spite of which, «the West has never stopped trying to export its own law into the rest of the world»). Unsurprisingly, there have been educated calls to take heed of the pinpointed cultural and legal differences by, in the case of China, allow for a «Socialist Rule of Law». See: Chinese Common Law Guiding Cases, *Harvard Law Review*, Volume 129, 2016, p. 2213.

[2959] See: Alimardani, Armin/Jane, Emma A., "Human Hallucinations: GenAI and the Mirage of Personalised Learning for All", 2024, p. 2 ("*Generative Artificial Intelligence (GenAI) is gaining attention in education, particularly for its potential to personalise learning. However, studies have yet to assess its capabilities in controlled environments empirically. This study aims to help fill this gap by evaluating 'SmartTest', a GenAI chatbot designed by the authors to prompt open-ended questions, offer immediate feedback, and stimulate critical thinking through conversational nudges. Over five test cycles, SmartTest was used in a Criminal Law course at an Australian university. The results revealed SmartTest struggled with complex structured problem-solving exercises. While SmartTest showed some promise in aiding short-answer question learning, it remained limited and prone to inaccuracies.* These findings highlight concerns that inflated expectations about GenAI could mislead educators and investors about its capabilities to deliver economically viable and quality personalised learning"). Italics added.

[2960] Laallam, Abla, "Hallucinations: Your AI Might Be Affected...," *Hofstra JIBL Blog: Journal of International Business and Law*, 2025, passim, available at: https://www.hofstrajibl.org/2025/01/hallucinations-your-ai-might-be-affected/ (access: 10.01.2025).

[2961] See: Alimardani, Armin/Jane, Emma A., "Human Hallucinations: GenAI and the Mirage of Personalised Learning for All", 2024, p. 15 ("*Given that in this study, we concluded that using GenAI educational chatbots involves some risks, we find it crucial to understand students' perceptions of these tools' trustworthiness (...) Given the known risks of overreliance on such technology,45 a healthy level of scepticism towards the accuracy of GenAI is a positive outcome. However, the 11.63% (5 students) who selected 'disagree' or 'strongly disagree' reflect a level of distrust that could undermine the effectiveness of GenAI tools*"). Italics added.

[2962] Laallam, Abla, "Hallucinations: Your AI Might Be Affected...," *Hofstra JIBL Blog: Journal of International Business and Law*, 2025, passim, available at: https://www.hofstrajibl.org/2025/01/hallucinations-your-ai-might-be-affected/ (access: 10.01.2025).

[2963] Laallam, Abla, "Hallucinations: Your AI Might Be Affected...," *Hofstra JIBL Blog: Journal of International Business and Law*, 2025, passim, available at: https://www.hofstrajibl.org/2025/01/hallucinations-your-ai-might-be-affected/ (access: 10.01.2025).

[2964] But see: *Park v. Kim*, 91 F.4th 610, 615 (2d Cir. 2024) ("*At the very least, the duties imposed by Rule 11 require that attorneys read, and thereby confirm the existence and validity of, the legal authorities on which they rely. Indeed, we can think of no other way to ensure that the arguments made based on those authorities are "warranted by existing law," Fed. R. Civ. P. 11(b)(2),* or otherwise "legally tenable" Cooter & Gell, *496 U.S. at 393, 110 S.Ct. 2447.* As a District Judge of this Circuit recently held when presented with non-existent precedent generated by ChatGPT: "*A*

and research,[2965] the second hallucination type might be more harmful/deleterious than the out-and-out concoction of cases[2966] insofar a bunch of trumped-up sources is far more detrimental to the overall credibility of legal research around which the legal writing resolves.

§§ Strikingly, Artificial Intelligence-embedded technologies have an undying potential[2967] to bestow upon lawyers a greater access[2968] to actionable information[2969] that may lead to streamlined legal proceedings.[2970] Note, though, that such an enhanced access to actionable information is not without insurmountable hurdles.[2971] Notably, ChatGPT imperils deep-seated privacy interests[2972] while crumbling the pillars upon which stands the Rule of the Law.[2973] The overhyped/overblown

fake opinion is not 'existing law' and citation to a fake opinion does not provide a non-frivolous ground for extending, modifying, or reversing existing law, or for establishing new law. An attempt to persuade a court or oppose an adversary by relying on fake opinions is an abuse of the adversary system." Mata v. Avianca, Inc., No. 22CV01461(PKC),— F.Supp.3d —, —, 2023 WL 4114965, at *12 (S.D.N.Y. June 22, 2023)"). Italics added.

[2965] Laallam, Abla, "Hallucinations: Your AI Might Be Affected...," *Hofstra JIBL Blog: Journal of International Business and Law*, 2025, passim, available at: https://www.hofstrajibl.org/2025/01/hallucinations-your-ai-might-be-affected/ (access: 10.01.2025).

[2966] Laallam, Abla, "Hallucinations: Your AI Might Be Affected...," *Hofstra JIBL Blog: Journal of International Business and Law*, 2025, passim, available at: https://www.hofstrajibl.org/2025/01/hallucinations-your-ai-might-be-affected/ (access: 10.01.2025).

[2967] Note, though, that pundits have been wondering about GPT-4's capability to perform better than 90% of bar exam test takers: Alimardani, Armin, "Generative Artificial Intelligence vs. Law Students: An Empirical Study on Criminal Law Exam Performance", *Law, Innovation and Technology*, 2024, passim. But see: Alimardani, Armin/Jane, Emma A., "Human Hallucinations: GenAI and the Mirage of Personalised Learning for All", 2024, p. 2 ("*Generative Artificial Intelligence (GenAI) is gaining attention in education, particularly for its potential to personalise learning. However, studies have yet to assess its capabilities in controlled environments empirically. This study aims to help fill this gap by evaluating 'SmartTest', a GenAI chatbot designed by the authors to prompt open-ended questions, offer immediate feedback, and stimulate critical thinking through conversational nudges. Over five test cycles, SmartTest was used in a Criminal Law course at an Australian university. The results revealed SmartTest struggled with complex structured problem-solving exercises. While SmartTest showed some promise in aiding short-answer question learning, it remained limited and prone to inaccuracies. These findings highlight concerns that inflated expectations about GenAI could mislead educators and investors about its capabilities to deliver economically viable and quality personalised learning*"). Italics added.

[2968] See: Riehl, Damien, "AI + MSBA: Building Minnesota's Legal Future", 81-Oct., *Bench & Bar of Minnesota*, 26, 2024, pp. 30–31 (discussing the Minnesota State Bar Association's whopping efforts to explore how Artificial Intelligence-embedded technologies can greatly augment access to justice and the overall quality of legal representation in court adjudication settings).

[2969] Laallam, Abla, "Hallucinations: Your AI Might Be Affected...," *Hofstra JIBL Blog: Journal of International Business and Law*, 2025, passim, available at: https://www.hofstrajibl.org/2025/01/hallucinations-your-ai-might-be-affected/ (access: 10.01.2025).

[2970] See: *Kohls v. Ellison*, 24-cv-3754 (LMP/DLM), 8–9 (D. Minn. Jan. 10, 2025) ("*AI, in many ways, has the potential to revolutionize legal practice for the better*"). Italics added.

[2971] See: *Kohls v. Ellison*, 24-cv-3754 (LMP/DLM), 9 (D. Minn. Jan. 10, 2025) ("*when attorneys and experts abdicate their independent judgment and critical thinking skills in favor of ready-made, AI-generated answers*, the *quality of our legal profession* and the *Court's decisional process suffer*"). Italics added.

trust on LLM systems must be accordingly halted or inordinate damages—e.g. the sustainability of the Rule of Law—[2974]will otherwise occur. The demise of critical thinking[2975]—that sets us apart from both animals and machines—will not lag far behind.

[2972] Citron; Danielle Keats/Pasquale, Frank, "Network Accountability for the Domestic Intelligence Apparatus", *Hastings Law Journal*, Volume 62, 2011; Gray, David/Citron, Danielle Keats, "The Right to Quantitative Privacy", *Minnesota Law Review*, Volume 98, 2013, pp. 62–81; Waldman, Ezra, "Privacy, Practice, and Performance", *California Law Review*, Volume 110, 2021, passim; Custers, Bart, "Data Dilemmas in the Information Society: Introduction and Overview", Custers, Bart/Calders, Toon/Schermer, Bart/Zarsky, Tal (Editors), *Discrimination and Privacy in the Information Society: Data Mining and Profiling in Large Databases*, Heidelberg, Springer, 2013, pp. 3–26; Tene, Omer/Polonetsky, Jules, "Big Data for All: Privacy and User Control in the Age of Analytics", *Northwestern Journal of Technology and Intellectual Property*, Volume 11, 2013, pp. 239 and ff and passim; de Laat, Paul B. 'Algorithmic Decision-Making Based on Machine Learning from Big Data: Can Transparency Restore Accountability?", *Philosophy & Technology*, Volume 31, 2018, pp. 524 and ff and passim (broaches the plethora of limitations related with full transparency, privacy, deleterious effects, competitive edge, and the shroud of opacity under which algorithms are often wrapped); Schermer, Bart W., "The Limits of Privacy in Automated Profiling and Data Mining", *Computer Law & Security Review*, Volume 27, 2011, pp. 45 and ff and passim (on privacy interests); Mann, Monique/Matzner, Tobias, "Challenging Algorithmic Profiling: The Limits of Data Protection and Anti-Discrimination in Responding to Emergent Discrimination", *Big Data & Society*, Volume 6, 2019, passim (on data protection).

[2973] Regrettably, Rule of Law is backsliding worldwide. Especially in Central and Eastern Europe. See: Avbelj, Matej, "The Rule of Law, Comprehensive Doctrines, Overlapping Consensus, and the Future of Europe", *Ratio Juris*, Volume 36, Issue 3, September, 2023, pp. 242–258. The Rule of Law is not a «one size fits all» format nonetheless. But see: Chesterman, Simon, "An International Rule of Law", *The American Journal of Comparative Law*, Volume 56, 2008, pp. 331–362 (on the thrust to grasp (?) a catch-all International Rule of Law). See: Peari, Sagi, "Better Law as a Better Outcome", *The American Journal of Comparative Law*, Volume 63, Issue 1, 2015, pp. 155–195 (156) (on Leflar's stance on «better rule of law»). For the purposes of this piece, Rule of Law amounts to a lighthouse of procedural fairness to which citizens, regardless of where they are, resort to upon gaining access to a given system of administration of criminal justice. Whilst further utterances on the fabric of Rule of Law fall well outside the scope and breadth of this paper, one must not be oblivious of the fact that the thrust to Deglobalizing Rule of Law is underway. See: Bussani, Mauro, "Deglobalizing Rule of Law and Democracy: Hunting Down Rhetoric Through Comparative Law", *The American Journal of Comparative Law*, Volume 67, 2019, pp. 701–744 (701) (contending that the thrust to Deglobalizing Rule of Law is interwoven with thrust to take heed of «well-known differences that run through cultures and traditions». In spite of which, «the West has never stopped trying to export its own law into the rest of the world»). Unsurprisingly, there have been educated calls to take heed of the pinpointed cultural and legal differences by, in the case of China, allow for a «Socialist Rule of Law». See: Chinese Common Law Guiding Cases, *Harvard Law Review*, Volume 129, 2016, p. 2213.

[2974] See: Part V, Chap. 5, Sect. 5.1.1.1 of this book (on the central tenets of Rule of Law that lends itself to a beacon of justice amidst the sepulchral darkness that is about to take hold). See: Part V, Chap. 5, Sect. 5.1.1.2 of this book (on the central tenets of Procedural Rule of Law that lends itself to a lighthouse of justice that allows citizens to challenge the pearls of algorithmic wisdom in a court of law).

[2975] See: Part III, Chap. 3, Sects. 3.1.5–3.1.5.5 of this book (on the insidious effects of Generative Artificial Intelligence coupled with its potential to create illusions and distort ground truths while exacting a toll on human critical thinking).

§§ Tellingly, a survey has found that LLMs hallucination rates[2976] range from a whopping 69% to a colossal 88% when responding to sensitive legal queries,[2977] which, in turn, poses a perceived risk of further compounding extant legal inequalities rather than allaying them.[2978] Worryingly, though, ChatGPT is already inflicting inordinate reputational damages upon the judicial system.[2979] The batch of case law we are about to review is nothing short of compelling in that regard.

4.1.9.5 «Large Legal Fictions» (Dahl/Magesh/Suzgun/Ho): Can ChatGPT Be Deployed in Legal Education Settings? Can ChatGPT Be Entrusted with Legal-Related Tasks Such as Undertaking Fact-Finding, Discovery or Writing Briefs, Written Motions, Affidavits, Subpoenas, Indictments, or Court Decisions? Why Must *Mata v. Avianca* (678 F. Supp. 3d 443, 449 (S.D.N.Y. 2023), *Park v. Kim*, 91 F.4th 610, 614–16 (2d Cir. 2023), *Kruse v. Karlen*, 692 S.W.3d 43, 52–53 (Mo. Ct. App. 2024), *Kohls v. Ellison*, 24-cv-3754 (LMP/DLM), 7–8 (D. Minn. Jan. 10, 2025), *United States v. Hayes*, 2:24-cr-0280-DJC, (E.D. Cal. Jan. 17, 2025) Never Happen Again

§§ At the outset, it is noteworthy that the risks posed by LLMs[2980] hallucinations[2981] to the legal field comprise providing lawyers and scholars[2982] with misleading information, bedraggled information, phony cases, fictitious sources,[2983] and bogus statutory law, which, in turn, might be eventually used in written briefs, written motions, appeals, and court submissions, as in *Mata v. Avianca, Inc.*[2984]

§§ This finding should not come as a bewildering surprise. A body of empirical evidence has shown that ChatGPT amounts to an algorithmic-anchored tool

---

[2976] See: Part III, Chap. 3, Sects. 3.1.5.6–3.1.5.6.1 of this book (on Critical Artificial Intelligence Studies, with a sharper focus on the harmful effects of Large Language Models 'medical hallucinations that are poised to undermine its overall trustworthiness).

[2977] Laallam, Abla, "Hallucinations: Your AI Might Be Affected...," *Hofstra JIBL Blog: Journal of International Business and Law*, 2025, passim, available at: https://www.hofstrajibl.org/2025/01/hallucinations-your-ai-might-be-affected/ (access: 10.01.2025).

[2978] Laallam, Abla, "Hallucinations: Your AI Might Be Affected...," *Hofstra JIBL Blog: Journal of International Business and Law*, 2025, passim, available at: https://www.hofstrajibl.org/2025/01/hallucinations-your-ai-might-be-affected/ (access: 10.01.2025).

[2979] See: *Mata v. Avianca, Inc.*, 678 F. Supp. 3d 443, 448–49 (S.D.N.Y. 2023) ("*any harms flow from the submission of fake opinions. The opposing party wastes time and money in exposing the deception.* The Court's time is taken from other important endeavors. The client may be deprived of arguments based on authentic judicial precedents. *There is potential harm to the reputation of judges and courts whose names are falsely invoked as authors of the bogus opinions and to the reputation of a party attributed with fictional conduct.* It promotes cynicism about the legal profession and the American judicial system. And *a future litigant may be tempted to defy a judicial ruling by disingenuously claiming doubt about its authenticity*"). Italics added.

prone to hallucinations in that its «large legal fictions»[2985] are anything but accurate, trustworthy, and reliable. For that reason, ChatGPT should not be used in legal education[2986] settings.[2987] Crucially, and perhaps disturbingly, «large legal fictions» are upon us in that they exhibit an exceedingly high degree of inevitability in the

---

2980 But see: Part III, Chap. 3, Sect. 3.1.5.3 of this book (on the "house of fabricated lies" and the usage of Generative Artificial Intelligence as a *floating signifier* that will stand ready to be galvanize power in a given direction, including, but not limited to, against *socially undesirables* that may find themselves at odds, or at loggerheads, with whoever controls Artificial Intelligence). See: Part III, Chap. 3, Sects. 3.1.5–3.1.5.5 of this book (on the insidious effects of Generative Artificial Intelligence coupled with its potential to create illusions and distort ground truths while exacting a toll on human critical thinking).

2981 See: Part III, Chap. 3, Sects. 3.1.5.6–3.1.5.6.1 of this book (on Critical Artificial Intelligence Studies, with a sharper focus on the harmful effects of Large Language Models 'medical hallucinations that are poised to undermine its overall trustworthiness).

2982 *Kohls v. Ellison*, 24-cv-3754 (LMP/DLM), 11–12 (D. Minn. Jan. 10, 2025) ("*To be sure, the Court does not believe that Professor Hancock intentionally cited to fake sources*, and the Court commends Professor Hancock and Attorney General Ellison for promptly conceding and addressing the errors in the Hancock Declaration. But the Court cannot accept false statements-innocent or not-in an expert's declaration submitted under penalty of perjury. Accordingly, given that the Hancock Declaration's errors undermine its competence and credibility, the Court will exclude consideration of Professor Hancock's expert testimony in deciding Plaintiffs' preliminary-injunction motion. *Gomaco Corp.*, 2020 WL 6948364, at *1. Because the Court declines to consider Professor Hancock's testimony in deciding Plaintiffs' preliminary-injunction motion, the Court will deny as moot Attorney General Ellison's motion for leave to file an amended Hancock Declaration"). Italics added.

2983 *Kohls v. Ellison*, 24-cv-3754 (LMP/DLM), 7–8 (D. Minn. Jan. 10, 2025) ("*Attorney General Ellison concedes that Professor Hancock included citations to two non-existent academic articles and incorrectly cited the authors of a third article. ECF No. 37 at 3–4. Professor Hancock admits that he used GPT-4o to assist him in drafting his declaration* but, in reviewing the declaration, *failed to discern that GPT-4o generated fake citations to academic articles.* ECF No. 39 ¶¶ 11–14, 21"). Italics added.

2984 *Mata v. Avianca, Inc.*, 678 F. Supp. 3d 443, 449 (S.D.N.Y. 2023), available at: https://casetext.com/case/mata-v-avianca-inc-3 (access: 20.01.2025).

2985 Dahl, Matthew/Magesh, Varun/Suzgun, Mirac/Ho, Daniel E., "Large Legal Fictions: Profiling Legal Hallucinations in Large Language Models", *Journal of Legal Analysis*, Volume 16, 2024, 64–93 (64) ("*Do large language models (LLMs) know the law? LLMs are increasingly being used to augment legal practice, education, and research, yet their revolutionary potential is threatened by the presence of "hallucinations"—textual output that is not consistent with legal facts.* We present the first systematic evidence of these hallucinations in public-facing LLMs, documenting trends across jurisdictions, courts, time periods, and cases. *Using OpenAI's ChatGPT 4 and other public models, we show that LLMs hallucinate at least 58% of the time, struggle to predict their own hallucinations, and often uncritically accept users' incorrect legal assumptions.* We conclude by cautioning against the rapid and unsupervised integration of popular LLMs into legal tasks"). Italics added.

2986 But see: Dieterle, Edward/Dede, Chris/Walker, Michael, "The cyclical ethical effects of using artificial intelligence in education", *AI & Society*, 39, 2024, 633–643 (640) ("*Unwise use of AI-enhanced, educational technology for learning and teaching further magnifies the structural disparities already inherent in society*"). Italics added.

2987 See: Alimardani, Armin/Jane, Emma A., "Human Hallucinations: GenAI and the Mirage of Personalised Learning for All", 2024, p. 13 ("*The output generated by GenAI models includes an inherent randomness and the same prompt may result in various outputs. Therefore, it is likely that*

legal field.[2988] The leading case *Mata v. Avianca* therefore lends weight, and adds plausibility to, this main contention.

§§ In *Mata v. Avianca* the lawyers representing plaintiffs filed documents with the judicial court that comprised phony judicial opinions littered with fabricated quotes and fictitious citations generated by an Artificial Intelligence-embedded tool, thereby resulting in a finding of bad faith,[2989] sanctions,[2990] and a express request to apologize to, and atone for, all the judges[2991] whose names were unceremoniously, albeit unjustifiably, included in the groundless LLM output.[2992]

---

the outputs of GenAI models are never entirely accurate and reliable. In other words, we contend that existing GenAI systems represent a technology that requires a 'human in/on the loop' to verify outputs before they reach the end user. When incorporating GenAI into an educational chatbot, students are the end users, making it challenging to identify and rectify these errors promptly"). Italics added. See also: Alimardani, Armin/Jane, Emma A., "Human Hallucinations: GenAI and the Mirage of Personalised Learning for All", 2024, p. 15 ("*Given that in this study, we concluded that using GenAI educational chatbots involves some risks, we find it crucial to understand students' perceptions of these tools' trustworthiness (...) Given the known risks of overreliance on such technology,45 a healthy level of scepticism towards the accuracy of GenAI is a positive outcome. However, the 11.63% (5 students) who selected 'disagree' or 'strongly disagree' reflect a level of distrust that could undermine the effectiveness of GenAI tools*"). Italics added.

2988 Dahl, Matthew/Magesh, Varun/Suzgun, Mirac/Ho, Daniel E., "Large Legal Fictions: Profiling Legal Hallucinations in Large Language Models", *cit.*, 64–93 (88) ("*finally, we also emphasize that the challenges presented by legal hallucinations are not only empirical, but also normative (...) As we discuss in Sect. 2.1.3, model fidelity to the training corpus, model fidelity to the user's prompt, and model fidelity to the facts of the world—i.e., the law—are normative commitments that stand in tension with each other*, despite all being independently desirable technical properties of an LLM. *Ultimately, since hallucinations of some kind are generally inevitable at the token level, developers of legal LLMs will need to make choices about which type(s) of hallucinations to minimize, and they should make these choices transparent to their downstream users*"). Italics added.

2989 *Mata v. Avianca, Inc.*, 678 F. Supp. 3d 443, 449 (S.D.N.Y. 2023) ("for reasons explained and considering the conduct of each individual Respondent separately, *the Court finds bad faith on the part of the individual Respondents based upon acts of conscious avoidance and false and misleading statements to the Court.* (See, e.g., Findings of Fact ¶¶ 17, 20, 22–23, 40–41, 43, 46–47 and Conclusions of Law ¶¶ 21, 23–24"). Italics added.

2990 *Mata v. Avianca, Inc.*, 678 F. Supp. 3d 443, 449 (S.D.N.Y. 2023) ("*Sanctions will therefore be imposed on the individual Respondents. Rule 11(c)(1) also provides that "[a]bsent exceptional circumstances, a law firm must be held jointly responsible for a violation committed by its... associate, or employee.*" Because the Court finds no exceptional circumstances, sanctions will be jointly imposed on the Levidow Firm. *The sanctions are "limited to what suffices to deter repetition of the conduct or comparable conduct by others similarly situated." Rule 11(c)(4)*"). Italics added.

2991 *Mata v. Avianca, Inc.*, 678 F. Supp. 3d 443, 466 (S.D.N.Y. 2023) ("There is a salutary purpose of placing the most directly affected persons on notice of Respondents' conduct. *The Court will require Respondents to inform their client and the judges whose names were wrongfully invoked of the sanctions imposed.* The Court will not require an apology from Respondents because a compelled apology is not a sincere apology. Any decision to apologize is left to Respondents"). Italics added.

2992 Laallam, Abla, "Hallucinations: Your AI Might Be Affected...," *Hofstra JIBL Blog: Journal of International Business and Law*, 2025, passim, available at: https://www.hofstrajibl.org/2025/01/hallucinations-your-ai-might-be-affected/ (access: 10.01.2025).

§§ In *Mata v. Avianca*, the *Court* has also stressed «the need for specific deterrence»[2993] regarding warped/doctored/tampered with, and thus unreliable, ChatGPT's outputs used by lawyers in briefs and written motions. On this note, judicial decisions have been adamant in averring that a brief or a motion littered with fabricated sources and fake opinions amounts to an abuse of the judicial system.[2994]

§§ In *Mata v. Avianca*, the court decision depicted the brief submitted as cluttered with «bogus opinions»,[2995] «fake quotes and opinions»[2996] and bogus cases.[2997] Much to our dismay and chagrin, a tantamount situation has also occurred in Colorado,[2998] where a lawyer had his license temporarily halted for one year and

[2993] *Mata v. Avianca, Inc.*, 678 F. Supp. 3d 443, 466 (S.D.N.Y. 2023) ("2. *In considering the need for specific deterrence*, the Court has weighed the significant publicity generated by Respondents' actions. (See, e.g., Alger Decl. Ex. E.) The Court credits the sincerity of Respondents when they described their embarrassment and remorse. The fake cases were not submitted for any respondent's financial gain and were not done out of personal animus. Respondents do not have a history of disciplinary violations and there is a low likelihood that they will repeat the actions described herein"). Italics added. See also: Cardi, Jonathan/Penfield, Randall D./Yoon, Albert H., "Does Tort Law Deter Individuals? A Behavioral Science Study", *Journal of Empirical Legal Studies*, Volume 9, Issue 3, 2012, pp. 567–603 (the authors stressed, however, premised on a sound empirical evidence, that "the threat of potential criminal sanctions had a large and statistically significant effect on subjects 'stated willingness to engage in risky behaviour").

[2994] *Kruse v. Karlen*, 692 S.W.3d 43, 52–53 (Mo. Ct. App. 2024) ("Appellant's submission of fictitious cases constitutes an abuse of the judicial system. See Mata, 678 F.Supp.3d at 460–61. As noted at the outset of this Opinion, we recognize the challenges faced by pro se litigants, however, this appeal does not involve minor technical briefing deficiencies. See Puetz v. Rice, 675 S.W.3d 652, 655–56 (Mo. App. E.D. 2023); see also Pearson, 588 S.W.3d at 550 ("Perfection is not required, but an appellant must substantially comply with the rules"). Pro se appellants have successfully argued and won appeals in this Court using freely accessible caselaw. Here, Appellant chose to retain dubious assistance and submitted fictitious and incorrect legal authorities. We addressed only a selection of Appellant's missteps, for which he was given ample opportunities by courtesy of Respondent and by order of this Court to correct. "[J]udicial impartiality and fairness mandate that we hold pro se appellants to the same standards as parties represented by lawyers." Puetz, 675 S.W.3d at 656 (internal citation omitted). The significant violations of Rule 84.04 mandate dismissal of the appeal. See id.")

[2995] *Mata v. Avianca, Inc.*, 678 F. Supp. 3d 443, 448–49 (S.D.N.Y. 2023) ("*any harms flow from the submission of fake opinions. The opposing party wastes time and money in exposing the deception.* The Court's time is taken from other important endeavors. The client may be deprived of arguments based on authentic judicial precedents. *There is potential harm to the reputation of judges and courts whose names are falsely invoked as authors of the bogus opinions and to the reputation of a party attributed with fictional conduct.* It promotes cynicism about the legal profession and the American judicial system. And *a future litigant may be tempted to defy a judicial ruling by disingenuously claiming doubt about its authenticity*"). Italics added.

[2996] *Mata v. Avianca, Inc.*, 678 F. Supp. 3d 443, 448–49 (S.D.N.Y. 2023).

[2997] Laallam, Abla, "Hallucinations: Your AI Might Be Affected…," *Hofstra JIBL Blog: Journal of International Business and Law*, 2025, passim, available at: https://www.hofstrajibl.org/2025/01/hallucinations-your-ai-might-be-affected/ (access: 10.01.2025).

[2998] People v. Zachariah C. Crabill, No. 23PDJ067, 2023 WL 8111898, at *1 (Colo. O.P.D.J. Nov. 22, 2023).

a day for citing case law found through ChatGPT in a client's brief submitted to a court of law, including a case law that was either fictitious or inaccurate.[2999]

§§ To add to our woes, in *Park v. Kim,* 91 F.4th 610, 614–16 (2d Cir. 2023) an attorney was referred for potential disciplinary action for including phony, fictitious Artificial Intelligence-generated legal citations/opinions in a filing.[3000] Dispiritingly, though, the list goes on.

§§ In *Kruse v. Karlen*, the appellant, *Kruse*, a *pro se disputant*[3001]—the weakest link in the algorithmic divides[3002] arising out of the age of information society[3003] we live in[3004]—filed an appellate brief riddled with fictitious citations generated

---

2999 Laallam, Abla, "Hallucinations: Your AI Might Be Affected…," *Hofstra JIBL Blog: Journal of International Business and Law*, 2025, passim, available at: https://www.hofstrajibl.org/2025/01/hallucinations-your-ai-might-be-affected/ (access: 10.01.2025).

3000 *Park v. Kim*, 91 F.4th 610, 615 (2d Cir. 2024) ("*As a District Judge of this Circuit recently held when presented with non-existent precedent generated by ChatGPT*: "*A fake opinion is not 'existing law' and citation to a fake opinion does not provide a non-frivolous ground for extending, modifying, or reversing existing law, or for establishing new law.* An attempt to persuade a court or oppose an adversary by relying on fake opinions is an abuse of the adversary system." Mata v. Avianca, Inc., No. 22CV01461(PKC), — F.Supp.3d —, —, 2023 WL 4114965, at *12 (S.D.N.Y. June 22, 2023)"). Italics added.

3001 It is important to note, though, that disadvantaged parties—*pro se* disputants that cannot afford to pay a well-adjusted and seasoned lawyer—already face insurmountable hurdles when they access judicial courts. This problem will only get worse as technology gains traction in criminal procedure law settings. Empirical research premises such assertion. See: Kroeper, Kathryn/Quintanilla, Victor D./Frisby, Michael/Yel, Nedim/Applegate, Amy G./Sherman, Steven J./Murphy, Mary C., "Underestimating the Unrepresented: Cognitive Biases Disadvantage Pro Se Litigants in Family Law Cases", *Psychology, Public Policy, and Law*, Volume 26, n.º 2, 2020, pp. 198–212 (211) (emphazise "*the present research suggests that the mere presence or absence of pro se status affects the inferences that legal officials make about parties in the civil justice system.* Legal officials appraised the cases of counselled parties as less meritorious the cases of counselled parties and predicted the *unrepresented persons would experience the civil justice system as less fair and satisfying the counselled litigants, even when all case facts were held constant, and especially when trial (vs. mediation) was considered to be the dispute resolution mechanism*"). Italics added. See also: Quintanilla, Victor/ Allen, R. A./Hirt, E. R., "The signalling effect of pro se status", *Law & Social Inquiry*, Volume 42, 2018, pp. 1092–1120.

3002 But see: Dahl, Matthew/Magesh, Varun/Suzgun, Mirac/Ho, Daniel E., "Large Legal Fictions: Profiling Legal Hallucinations in Large Language Models", *Journal of Legal Analysis*, Volume 16, 2024, 64–93, 64–93 (88) ("*although data-rich and moneyed players certainly stand at an advantage when it comes to building hallucination-free legal LLMs for their own private use, it is not clear that even infinite resources can entirely solve the conceptual problems we diagnose* (….) Only then can individual *litigants decide for themselves whether the legal information they seek to obtain from LLMs is trustworthy or not*"). Italics added.

3003 See: Eubanks, Virginia, *Automating Inequality: How High-Tech Tools Profile, Police and Punish the Poor*. New York: St. Martin's Press, 2018, 1–272 (1 ff and passim) (coining the expression «automating inequality» to vividly portray the downsides of using high-technology to further compound the yawning gap between rich and poor against the backdrop of biased algorithms). Soss, Joe/Richard C. Fording/Sanford, F. Schram, *Disciplining the Poor: Neoliberal Paternalism and the Persistent Power of Race*. Chicago: University of Chicago Press, 2011.

3004 Owing to the yawning gap between rich—that can adroitly harness artificial intelligence to advance their goals and shady agendas—and poor—that grapple to meet basic needs and are automatically excluded from the equation of digital society powered by Artificial Intelligence—which

by a version of ChatGPT,[3005] which, in turn, was severely upbraided, even harshly excoriated, by the *Court* in that the former was held to the same procedural standards to that of a lawfully represented appellant.[3006]

---

will directly impact the fabric of societies worldwide, thereby augmenting the chasm between the «digitally-chosen» and the «digitally-outcast» enabled by a algorithmic discrimination that does nothing but irreparable harm. See: Yu, Peter K., "The Algorithmic Divide and Equality in the Age of Artificial Intelligence", *Florida Law Review*, Volume 72, 2020, pp. 355–360 (addresses the issue of algorithmic discrimination). This problem is neither new nor easy to solve. Whilst the effects of technology—digital justice—on the courtroom have been previously broached by the doctrine, few to none consensus has been reached with regard to actionable lines of action to be taken. See: Donoghue, Jane, "The Rise of Digital Justice: Courtroom Technology, Public Participation and Access to Justice", *The Modern Law Review*, Volume 80, Issue 6, 2018, p. 995 (noting that technology in the courtroom might widen the gap between the rich and the poor. In this vein, this renowned author has contended that "*legal reforms have omitted any detailed consideration of the type and quality of citizen participation in newly digitised court processes which have fundamental implications for the legitimacy and substantive outcomes of court-based processes; and for enhancing democratic procedure through improved access to justice.* It is argued that although digital court tools and systems offer great promise for enhancing efficiency, participation, and accessibility, they *simultaneously have the potential to amplify the scope for injustice, and to attenuate central principles of the legal system, including somewhat paradoxically, access to justice*"). Italics added. See also: Heintz, M.E., "The digital divide and courtroom technology: Can David keep up with Goliath", *Federal Communications Law Journal*, Volume 54, 2002, pp. 566 ff and passim. The great bulk of these assertions has been anticipated by an iconic piece of research. See: Galanter, Marc, "Why the "Haves" Come Out Ahead: Speculations on the Limits of Legal Change", *Law & Society Review*, Volume 9, 1974, pp. 98–103 (this renowned author talks about a *social reality* in which the dubbed «repeat players»—which go by the name of «haves»—tend to «to come out ahead» by putting their knowledge and vast resources to good use. This perceived advantage will not only impact the choice on the procedures but will ultimately benefit their interests as opposed to the deemed «one-shot» players (the «have nots») that will have slimmer and fewer chances to get palpable results in dispute resolution). Technology in the criminal courtroom—that includes the rich and excludes the poor—will make this problem considerably worse. But see: Bailey, J./Burkell, J./ Reynolds, G. "Access to Justice for All: Towards an "Expansive Vision" of Justice and Technology, *Windsor Yearbook of Access to Justice*, Volume 31, 2013, pp. 183–201 (in stark contrast, these authors stress that the digital and technological apparatus can indeed spawn a both time-effective and streamlined access to justice in a given jurisdiction).

3005 *Kruse v. Karlen*, 692 S.W.3d 43, 48–50 (Mo. Ct. App. 2024) ("*Particularly concerning to this Court is that Appellant submitted an Appellate Brief in which the overwhelming majority of the citations are not only inaccurate but entirely fictitious. Only two out of the twenty-four case citations in Appellant's Brief are genuine. The two genuine citations are presented in a section entitled Summary of Argument without pincites and do not stand for what Appellant purports. A contextual example of Appellant's reliance on fictitious authority includes*: For instance, in *Smith v ABC Corporation,* 321 S.W.3d 123 (Mo. App. 2010), the Court of Appeals held that it had the duty to review the grant of judgment as a matter of law de novo, stating that "the appellate court should not be bound by the trial court's determination and must reach its own conclusion based on the record." *Neither the case nor the specific quote it purports to contain exist in reality. As depicted in the chart below, Appellant also offers citations that have potentially real case names—presumably the product of algorithmic serendipity—but do not stand for the propositions asserted by Appellant,* such as State ex rel. Johnson v. Clark, 288 Mo. 659, 232 S.W. 1031, 1035 (Mo banc. 1921), overruled by Younge v. State Bd. of Reg. for Healing Arts, 2451 S.W.2d 346 (Mo. 1969), which Appellant claims discusses the standard of review for the grant of judgment as a matter of law but in fact reviews a state administrative board's decision suspending a physician's license. *Similarly, the case*

§§ In *Kohls v. Ellison*, 24-cv-3754 (LMP/DLM), 11–12 (D. Minn. Jan. 10, 2025), a renowned scholar in the area of technology cited fake sources to support his expert testimony,[3007] which was harshly rebuked by the court.[3008]

§§ Note, though, that the whole situation was, I may venture add, nothing but eerily ironic,[3009] insofar the expert (Professor Hancock) was summoned to enlighten

name "Brown v. Smith" involves two common names and can be found twice in Missouri precedent, but neither case relates to what Appellant purports"). Italics added.

3006 *Kruse v. Karlen*, 692 S.W.3d 43, 46–47 (Mo. Ct. App. 2024) ("**[1, 2]** Compliance with Rule" 84.04 is mandatory. Murphree v. Lakeshore Ests., LLC, 636 S.W.3d 622, 623–24 (Mo. App. E.D. 2021) (internal citation omitted). Failure to substantially adhere to Rule 84.04 preserves nothing for appellate review and requires dismissal of the appeal. Id. (internal quotation omitted). **[3, 4]** *Parties appearing pro se, like Appellant, are "subject to the same procedural rules as parties represented by counsel, including the rules specifying the required contents of appellate briefs."* Hutcheson v. Dep't Soc. Servs., Fam. Support Div., 656 S.W.3d 37, 40 *(Mo. App. E.D. 2022) (internal quotation omitted). Pro se appellants "are not entitled to exceptions they would not receive if represented by counsel.*" Id. at 40–41 (internal quotation omitted). "*We recognize the problems faced by pro se litigants, but we cannot relax our standards for non-lawyers.*" Barbero v. Wilhoit Props., Inc., 637 S.W.3d 590, 595 (Mo. App. E.D. 2021) (internal citation omitted). "Our application of the rules stems not from a lack of sympathy, but *instead from a necessity for judicial impartiality, judicial economy, and fairness to all parties." Id. (internal citation omitted);* Hutcheson, 656 S.W.3d at 40–41 *(internal quotation omitted). Despite our preference to review the merits where only minor shortcomings do not impede meaningful review*, "[d]eficient briefing runs the risk of forcing this Court to assume the role of advocate by requiring us to sift through the legal record, reconstruct the statement of facts, and craft a legal argument on the appellant's behalf." Hutcheson, 656 S.W.3d at 41 (internal quotation omitted)"). Italics added.

3007 *Kohls v. Ellison*, 24-cv-3754 (LMP/DLM), 7–8 (D. Minn. Jan. 10, 2025) ("Attorney General Ellison concedes that Professor Hancock included citations to two non-existent academic articles and incorrectly cited the authors of a third article. ECF No. 37 at 3–4. *Professor Hancock admits that he used GPT-4o to assist him in drafting his declaration but, in reviewing the declaration, failed to discern that GPT-4o generated fake citations to academic articles. ECF No. 39 ¶¶ 11–14, 21*"). Italics added.

3008 *Kohls v. Ellison*, 24-cv-3754 (LMP/DLM), 10–11 (D. Minn. Jan. 10, 2025) ("*Professor Hancock's citation to fake, AI-generated sources in his declaration-even with his helpful, thorough, and plausible explanation (ECF No. 39)-shatters his credibility with this Court. At a minimum, expert testimony is supposed to be reliable. Fed.R.Evid. 702; see also Daubert v. Merrell Dow Pharms., Inc., 509 U.S. 579, 589 (1993) (explaining that expert testimony must be "not only relevant, but reliable").* More fundamentally, signing a declaration under penalty of perjury is not a mere formality; rather, it "alert[s] declarants to the gravity of their undertaking and thereby have a meaningful effect on truthtelling and reliability." *Acosta v. Mezcal, Inc., No. 17-cv-0931 (JKB), 2019 WL 2550660, at* *2 (D. Md. June 20, 2019); *see also In re World Trade Ctr. Disaster Site Litig., 722 F.3d 483, 488* (2d Cir. 2013) (explaining that the "under penalty of perjury" affirmation "impresses upon the declarant the specific punishment to which he or she is subjected for certifying to false statements"). *The Court should be able to trust the "indicia of truthfulness" that declarations made under penalty of perjury carry, but that trust was broken here. Davenport v. Bd. of Trs. of State Ctr. Comm. Coll. Dist., 654 F.Supp.2d 1073, 1083* (E.D. Cal. 2009)"). Italics added.

3009 *Kohls v. Ellison*, 24-cv-3754 (LMP/DLM), 8 (D. Minn. Jan. 10, 2025) ("*The irony. Professor Hancock, a credentialed expert on the dangers of AI and misinformation, has fallen victim to the siren call of relying too heavily on AI-in a case that revolves around the dangers of AI, no less. Professor Hancock offers a detailed explanation of his drafting process to explain precisely how and why these AI-hallucinated citations in his declaration came to be. Id.* ¶¶ 10–22. And he assures the Court that he stands by the substantive propositions in his declaration, even those that are supported by fake

the court on why ChatGPT hallucinates in the first place. Turns out, the good scholar himself ended up citing phony academic sources after all. The expert, too, has fallen prey to the buoying allures of fast-food technology (ChatGPT) that spawns ataraxic *pearls of algorithmic wisdom*, thus hastening the downfall of critical thinking[3010] and academic credibility.

§§ In *United States v. Hayes*, 2:24-cr-0280-DJC, (E.D. Cal. Jan. 17, 2025), Assistant Federal Defender Andrew Francisco, counsel for Defendant Daragh Finbar Hayes (ECF No. 50.), submitted a written motion to unseal a file. The court found that Mr. Francisco submitted a fictitious or non-existent case and quotation in his written motion to unseal a file on November 21, 2024.[3011] Mr. Francisco was unsparingly chastised by the court for relying upon hallucinated outputs generated by ChatGPT[3012] accordingly.[3013]

---

citations. *Id.* ¶ 22. But, at the end of the day, even if the errors were an innocent mistake, and even if the propositions are substantively accurate, the fact remains that Professor Hancock submitted a declaration made under penalty of perjury with fake citations. It *is particularly troubling to the Court that Professor Hancock typically validates citations with a reference software when he writes academic articles but did not do so when submitting the Hancock Declaration as part of Minnesota's legal filing*. ECF No. 39 ¶ 14. *One would expect that greater attention would be paid to a document submitted under penalty of perjury than academic articles.* Indeed, the Court would expect greater diligence from attorneys, let alone an expert in AI misinformation at one of the country's most renowned academic institutions"). Italics added.

[3010] See: Part III, Chap. 3, Sects. 3.1.5–3.1.5.5 of this book (on the insidious effects of Generative Artificial Intelligence coupled with its potential to create illusions and distort ground truths while exacting a toll on human critical thinking). See: Part III, Chap. 3, Sects. 3.1.5.6–3.1.5.6.1 of this book (on Critical Artificial Intelligence Studies, with a sharper focus on the harmful effects of Large Language Models 'medical hallucinations that are poised to undermine its overall trustworthiness).

[3011] *United States v. Hayes*, 2:24-cr-0280-DJC, 12–13 (E.D. Cal. Jan. 17, 2025) ("*Submitting fictitious cases and quotations to the court "degrades or impugns the integrity of the Court" and "interferes with the administration of justice" in violation of Local Rule 180(e), and violates California Rules of Professional Conduct* 3.1(a)(2), 3.3(a)(1), and 3.3(a)(2). *See* E.D. Cal. L.R. 180(e) (requiring compliance with the California Rules of Professional Conduct); Cal. Rules of Pro. Conduct r. 3.3(a)(1) (lawyer shall not "knowingly make a false statement of fact or law to a tribunal or fail to correct a false statement of material fact or law previously made to the tribunal by the lawyer"); Cal. Rules of Pro. Conduct r. 3.3(a)(2) (lawyer shall not "knowingly misquote to a tribunal the language of a book, statute, decision or other authority"); Cal. Rules of Pro. Conduct r. 3.1(a)(2) (lawyer shall not "present a claim or defense in litigation that is not warranted under existing law, unless it can be supported by a good faith argument for an extension, modification, or reversal of the existing law"). "A fake opinion is not 'existing law' and citation to a fake opinion does not provide a non-frivolous ground for extending, modifying, or reversing existing law, or for establishing new law. An attempt to persuade a court or oppose an adversary by relying on fake opinions is an abuse of the adversary system." *Mata*, 678 F.Supp.3d at 461 (citing *Salovaara v. Eckert*, 222 F.3d 19, 34 (2d Cir. 2000)) (internal footnote omitted). The California Rules of Professional Conduct at issue are similar to other rules that courts have found were violated by the submission of fictitious legal authority. *Compare* Cal. Rules of Pro. Conduct r. 3.3(a)(1), *with* N.Y. Rules of Pro. Conduct r. 3.3(a)(1) addressed in *Mata*, 678 F.Supp.3d at 460; *compare* Cal. Rules of Pro. Conduct r. 3.1(a)(2), *with* Fed.R.Civ.P. 11(b)(2) ("*the claims, defenses, and other legal contentions are warranted by existing law or by a nonfrivolous argument for extending, modifying, or reversing existing law or for establishing new law") addressed in multiple cases*"). Italics added.

[3012] *United States v. Hayes*, 2:24-cr-0280-DJC, 14 (E.D. Cal. Jan. 17, 2025) ("*In his motion to unseal, Mr. Francisco cited eight cases, six of which were cited in near string citation form. See*

§§ This cluster of judicial decisions has reverberated across the United States of America. Magistrates have accordingly begun issuing orders demanding lawyers/ scholars who appear before them to vouchsafe whether and to what extent they have relied upon Generative Artificial Intelligence (ChatGPT) in drafting briefs, injunction reliefs, motions, appeals they file while strongly urging them to pay a nuanced attention to the reliability of the sources[3014] before those legal documents[3015] are formally submitted[3016] to a court of law.[3017]

Def. Mot. Unseal at 6, 10, 11. The primary case upon which Mr. Francisco relied- analyzing, quoting, describing the district court's analysis, and addressing in two different places in the motion- was "United States v. Harris, 761 F.Supp. 409, 414 (D.D.C. 1991)." See Def. Mot. Unseal at 6, 10. Unfortunately, "United States v. Harris, *761 F.Supp. 409, 414* (D.D.C. 1991)" is not a real case. The citation has all the markings of a *hallucinated case created by generative artificial intelligence (AI) tools such as ChatGPT and Google Bard that have been widely discussed by courts grappling with fictitious legal citations and reported by national news outlets*"). Italics added.

[3013] *United States v. Hayes*, 2:24-cr-0280-DJC, 13 (E.D. Cal. Jan. 17, 2025) ("*The Court finds that Mr. Francisco submitted a fictitious or non-existent case and quotation in his written motion to unseal filed on November 21, 2024*; knowingly made inaccurate and misleading statements in his written reply filed on December 5, 2024 to the government's opposition that expressly raised the fictitious case and quotation; and knowingly made inaccurate and misleading statements at the December 9, 2024 hearing. The Court further finds that Mr. Francisco's inaccurate and misleading statements were not inadvertent as claimed, but knowing and made in bad faith. Despite being provided multiple opportunities to candidly acknowledge and correct his errors as required under his duty of candor to the court, Mr. Francisco unfortunately failed to do so. Though the Court accepts Mr. Francisco's apology, his post-hoc acknowledgment of the fictitious case and quotation are inadequate and demonstrate that his conduct was knowing and deliberate. *See* Francisco OSC Resp. (ECF No. 51)").

[3014] See: *Kohls v. Ellison*, 24-cv-3754 (LMP/DLM), 9 (D. Minn. Jan. 10, 2025) ("The Court thus adds its voice to a growing chorus of courts around the country declaring the same message: *verify AI-generated content in legal submissions! See Mata v. Avianca, Inc., 678 F.Supp.3d 443, 466* (S.D.N.Y. 2023) (sanctioning attorney for including fake, AI-generated legal citations in a filing); *Park v. Kim, 91 F.4th 610, 614-16* (2d Cir. 2023) (referring attorney for potential discipline for including fake, AI-generated legal citations in a filing); *Kruse v. Karlan, 692 S.W.3d 43, 53* (Mo.Ct.App. 2024) (dismissing appeal because litigant filed a brief with multiple fake, AI-generated legal citations)"). Italics added.

[3015] See: *Park v. Kim*, 91 F.4th 610, 615 (2d Cir. 2024) ("*At the very least, the duties imposed by Rule 11 require that attorneys read, and thereby confirm the existence and validity of, the legal authorities on which they rely. Indeed, we can think of no other way to ensure that the arguments made based on those authorities are "warranted by existing law," Fed. R. Civ. P. 11(b)(2)*, or otherwise "legally tenable." Cooter & Gell, *496 U.S. at 393, 110 S.Ct. 2447*"). Italics added.

[3016] *Kohls v. Ellison*, 24-cv-3754 (LMP/DLM), 8 (D. Minn. Jan. 10, 2025) ("But, at the end of the day, even if the errors were an innocent mistake, and even if the propositions are substantively accurate, the fact remains that *Professor Hancock submitted a declaration made under penalty of perjury with fake citations. It is particularly troubling to the Court that Professor Hancock typically validates citations with a reference software when he writes academic articles but did not do so when submitting the Hancock Declaration as part of Minnesota's legal filing.* ECF No. 39 ¶ 14"). Italics added.

[3017] Laallam, Abla, "Hallucinations: Your AI Might Be Affected...," *Hofstra JIBL Blog: Journal of International Business and Law*, 2025, passim, available at: https://www.hofstrajibl.org/2025/01/hallucinations-your-ai-might-be-affected/ (access: 10.01.2025).

§§ Lawyers, scholars,[3018] judges, and legal actors alike must realise that ChatGPT, as an AI tool, is a work in progress in that its legal-related outputs are mostly inaccurate, unreliable, and somewhat bedraggled. The former must therefore employ staggering efforts in carefully reviewing the *pearls of algorithmic wisdom* generated by LLM systems. Failing which, the Rule of Law[3019] will be irreparably lurched into abeyance. Worse still, Rule of Law[3020] will most likely careen into the chaos of lack of legitimacy[3021] whereby AI hallucinations rule[3022] and judicial legitimacy falters.[3023]

[3018] *Kohls v. Ellison*, 24-cv-3754 (LMP/DLM), 8 (D. Minn. Jan. 10, 2025) ("One would expect that greater attention would be paid to a document submitted under penalty of perjury than academic articles. *Indeed, the Court would expect greater diligence from attorneys, let alone an expert in AI misinformation at one of the country's most renowned academic institutions*"). Italics added.

[3019] See: Part V, Chap. 5, Sect. 5.1.1.1 of this book (on the central tenets of Rule of Law that lends itself to a beacon of justice amidst the sepulchral darkness that is about to take hold). See: Part V, Chap. 5, Sect. 5.1.1.2 of this book (on the central tenets of Procedural Rule of Law that lends itself to a lighthouse of justice that allows citizens to challenge the pearls of algorithmic wisdom in a court of law). See: Raz, Joseph, "The Rule of Law and its Virtue", *The Authority of Law: Essays on Law and Morality*. Oxford: Clarendon Press, 1979, pp. 210–214 (on the quintessential value of Rule of Law); Waldron, Jeremy, "The Rule of Law and the Importance of Procedure", *New York Public Law and Legal Theory*, 2010, p. 4 (notes that "the Rule of Law is violated when due attention is not paid to these procedural matters or when the institutions that are supposed to embody this procedure are undermined or interfered with". Further down this author would admit that there are some substantive dimensions of Rule of Law, such as respect for right for property and presumption of liberty and so forth); Taekema, Sanne, "The Procedural Rule of Law: Examining Waldron's Argument on Dignity and Agency", *Jahrbuch für Recht und Ethik*, Band 21, 2013, pp. 133 ff (contends that "Waldron's understanding of the Rule of Law as procedural which demands the opportunity for individuals to contest legal decisions in the formalized processes of courts and tribunals"); Cass, Ronald A., *The Rule of Law in America*. Baltimore, Maryland: The Johns Hopkins University Press, 2001, p. 17 (noting that a "central element of the Rule of law, constraint from external authority...helps assure that the process of government, *rather than the predilections of the individual decision-maker*") Italics added.

[3020] Which is why the onset of the age of Artificial Intelligence will put the Rule of Law to the test like never before. Recall, the Rule of Law is a functional barrier—aimed at clamping down a host of unlawful deeds undertaken by those in power—that must not be teared apart or criminal procedure law will be otherwise despoiled from its intrinsic validity and vitality. See: Raz, Joseph, "The Rule of Law and its Virtue", *The Authority of Law: Essays on Law and Morality*, *cit.*, p. 224 (asserts adamantly that the Rule of Law is aimed at cushioning the hazards of abuse perpetrated by those in power. In this vein, Raz contends that "the law inevitably creates a great danger of arbitrary power—the Rule of Law is designed to minimize the danger created by the law itself...*Thus the (R)ule of (L)aw is designed to minimize the danger created by law itself...Thus the (R)ule of (L)aw is a negative virtue...the evil which is avoided is evil which could only have been caused by the law itself*"). Italics added. See: Part V, Chap. 5, Sect. 5.1.1.1 of this book (on the central tenets of Rule of Law that lends itself to a beacon of justice amidst the sepulchral darkness that is about to take hold). See: Part V, Chap. 5, Sect. 5.1.1.2 of this book (on the central tenets of Procedural Rule of Law that lends itself to a lighthouse of justice that allows citizens to challenge the pearls of algorithmic wisdom in a court of law).

[3021] Tyler, Tom R., "Psychological perspectives on legitimacy and legitimation", in: *Annual Review of Psychology*, Volume 57, 2006, pp. 375–400 (on the role that perceived legitimacy plays in everyday life); Tyler, Tom R., *Why people cooperate: The role of social motivations*, Princeton, New Jersey, Princeton University Press, 2011; Robbins, J. M./M.T. Ford/L.E. Tetrick, "Perceived unfairness and employee health: A meta-analytic integration", in: *Journal of Applied Psychology*,

§§ For that reason, judges have begun to demand attorneys[3024] to confirm whether a human being has conducted their due diligence[3025]—which far extends far beyond a mere grammar review of the outputs generated by ChatGPT as in *Mata v. Avianca*[3026]—while ensuring that the case law, statutory law, citations are real.

§§ Against this well-trodden background, ChatGPT is woefully ill-prepared to either be deployed to legal education settings or undertake legal-related tasks, such as fact-finding, discovery, writing briefs, written motions, affidavits, subpoenas, indictments, or court decisions. The relinquishment of human-related legal tasks to machines[3027] runs counter to basic tenets of truthfulness[3028] that may cost us dearly along the line.

Volume 97, 2012, pp. 235–272; Tyler, Tom R., "What is procedural justice? Criteria used by citizens to assess the fairness of legal procedures", *Law and Society Review*, Volume 22, 1988, pp. 103–135 (on the interplay between fairness of legal procedures and procedural justice. Unsurprisingly, the lack of fairness of legal procedures impacts the procedural justice -or the lack thereof -); Sunshine, J./Tyler, Tom R., "The role of procedural justice and legitimacy in shaping public support for policing*", Law & Society Review*, Volume 37, 2003, pp. 513–54 8 (on the role of procedural justice to enhance/boost legitimacy); Bies, Robert J., "Are Procedural Justice and Interactional Justice Conceptually Distinct?", *Handbook of Organizational Justice*, Greenberg, Jerald/ Colquitt, Jason, (Editors), New Jersey, Lawrence Erlbaum Associates Publishers, 2005, pp. 85–86 (arguing that a respectful treatment is an important part of, and the linchpin of a much-needed, procedural justice, which also plays an pivotal role in the remit of interactional justice).

3022 See: Part III, Chap. 3, Sects. 3.1.5–3.1.5.5 of this book (on the insidious effects of Generative Artificial Intelligence coupled with its potential to create illusions and distort ground truths while exacting a toll on human critical thinking). See also: Part III, Chap. 3, Sect. 3.1.5.3 of this book (on the "house of fabricated lies" and the usage of Generative Artificial Intelligence as a *floating signifier* that will stand ready to be galvanize power in a given direction, including, but not limited to, against *socially undesirables* that may find themselves at odds, or at loggerheads, with whoever controls Artificial Intelligence).

3023 Converging: Lind, Edgar Allan/Tyler, Tom R., *The Social Psychology of Procedural Justice.* New York: Springer, 1988, pp. 208 ff (emphasizing that perceptions of justice being justly and correctly served enhances exponentially citizens' perception of provider legitimacy).

3024 Heikkil, Melissa, "How Judges, Not Politicians, Could Dictate America's AI Rules", *MIT Tech. Rev*. (July 17, 2023), https://www.technologyreview.com/2023/07/17/1076416/judges-lawsuits-dictate-ai-rules/; [https://perma.cc/MXG4-ATHB].

3025 *Park v. Kim*, 91 F.4th 610, 615 (2d Cir. 2024) ("Attorney Lee states that "it is important to recognize that ChatGPT represents a significant technological advancement," and argues that "[i]t would be prudent for the court to advise legal professionals to exercise caution when utilizing this new technology").

3026 *Mata v. Avianca, Inc.*, 678 F. Supp. 3d 443, 450 (S.D.N.Y. 2023) ("Although Mr. LoDuca signed the Affirmation in Opposition and filed it on ECF, he was not its author. (Tr. 8–9.) It was researched and written by Mr. Schwartz. (Tr. 8.) Mr. *LoDuca reviewed the affirmation for style, stating, "I was basically looking for a flow, make sure there was nothing untoward or no large grammatical errors."* (Tr. 9.) Before executing the *Affirmation, Mr. LoDuca did not review any judicial authorities cited in his affirmation. (Tr. 9.) There is no claim or evidence that he made any inquiry of Mr. Schwartz as to the nature and extent of his research or whether he had found contrary precedent. Mr. LoDuca simply relied on a belief that work produced by Mr. Schwartz, a colleague of more than twenty-five years, would be reliable*"). Italics added.

3027 See: Millar, Jason/Kerr, Ian, "Delegation, Relinquishment and Responsibility: The Prospect of Expert Robots", *Robot Law*, Calo, Ryan/Froomkin, A. Michael/Kerr, Ian (Editors), Cheltenham, Edward Elgar Publishing, 2016, pp. 102, 106–107 (as these authors aptly put it "*we will rely on*

4.1.9.6 Will «Early Model Collapse» and «Late Model Collapse» (Ilia Shumailov et al.) Spring into Action the Onset of the Age of *Algorithmic Dictatorship* Whereby Truths and Lies Dovetail Seamlessly Through ChatGPT' Hallucinations that Build on «Ablation: Repetitions»? The Case of *New York Post v. Perplexity* That Is Poised to Catalyse the Onset of the Age of «Fake News» Autocracy

§§ It is worth recalling that LLM hallucinations[3029] do not boil down to legal settings.[3030] Strikingly, and perhaps worryingly, LLM hallucinations are already exacting a toll on the overall credibility of newspapers, social media, articles, blog posts, written notes of all sorts, books, essays, opuscules, and even novels.[3031] On this note, the case of *New York Post v. Perplexity* deserves to be brought to the fore and briefly remarked upon.

§§ Cogently, *Perplexity*, an Artificial Intelligence start-up, found itself embroiled in a lawsuit with *New York Post*[3032] on the grounds of copyright and trademark

---

robots without really knowing why—simply because their algorithms provide the greatest number of successful outcomes. We have already seen this in Google's search approach. Neither Larry (Page) nor Sergey (Brin) (nor any other Google employee) knowns exactly why one particular web page is a better result than another. *When the click patterns say it is, that's good enough.* No semantic or causal analysis is required…*Like the ancients, we will, quite rationally, come to rely upon them, knowing full well that we cannot necessarily explain the reasons for their decisions*"). Italics added. Converging: Casey, Anthony J./Niblett, Anthony, "Self-driving Laws", *University of Toronto Law Journal*, Volume 66, 2016, pp. 429–435 (contend that "as more information is generated, and the evolutionary algorithm updates and become a better forecaster, *we imagine that judges will increasingly rely on the advice of the algorithm*"). But see: Weizenbaum, Joseph, *Computer Power and Human Reason: From Judgment to Calculation*, 1st edition, New York, W. H. Freeman & Co, 1976, pp. 1–300 (227) ("examines the sources of the computer's powers and offers evaluative explorations of what computers can do, cannot do, and should not be employed to do") (this founding father of Artificial Intelligence presciently noted that we should not entrust Artificial Intelligence-embedded technologies with "tasks that demand wisdom"). Italics added. The approval of rental applications is arguably one of those tasks that should never be entrusted to machines). More on this on Part IV, This chapter, Sects. 4.1.4–4.1.4.2.1 of this book.

[3028] See: Part V, Chap. 5, Sect. 5.1.8.5 of this book (on law number five to interpret algorithmic decision-making, which mandates that robot-judges, robot-prosecutors and robot-lawyers must not enter the courtroom for they are utterly incapable of making sound and interpretable value judgements).

[3029] See: Kolinski Jordan A., Your "AI" is Hallucinating, Hellmuth & Johnson (June 14, 2024) https://hjlawfirm.com/your-ai-is-hallucinating/. (access: 21.01.2025).

[3030] See: Part III, Chap. 3, Sects. 3.1.5.6–3.1.5.6.1 of this book (on Critical Artificial Intelligence Studies, with a sharper focus on the harmful effects of Large Language Models 'medical hallucinations that are poised to undermine its overall trustworthiness).

[3031] Cyphert, Amy et. al, "AI Cannibalism and the Law", *Colorado Technology Law Journal*, Volume 22, 2024, pp. 300 and ff and passim.

[3032] Laallam, Abla, "Hallucinations: Your AI Might Be Affected…," *Hofstra JIBL Blog: Journal of International Business and Law*, 2025, passim, available at: https://www.hofstrajibl.org/2025/01/hallucinations-your-ai-might-be-affected/ (access: 10.01.2025).

violation as their LLM system has spawned hallucinated fake news[3033] and attributed it to the newspaper accordingly.[3034]

§§ Notably, Perplexity's AI first produced a New York Post story[3035] on United States of America Senator Jim Jordan's keen disagreement with an outspoken European Union's commissioner, coupled with five LLM doctored/warped/fictitious paragraphs on both online legal regulations and free speech that were never featured in the original article[3036] in the first place.

§§ Relatedly, *Perplexity* has been sent a cease-and-desist letter by the New York Post.[3037] The latter claimed the AI was using the newspaper's content with neither due consent nor permission.[3038] The *New York Times* also brought a lawsuit against OpenAI, claiming that ChatGPT and Bing Chat attributed trumped-up quotes to the New York Times.[3039] Moreover, the New York Times has also accused OpenAI and Microsoft of tarnishing/shattering the newspaper's[3040] reputation[3041] with trademark dilution.[3042]

[3033] Laallam, Abla, "Hallucinations: Your AI Might Be Affected...," *Hofstra JIBL Blog: Journal of International Business and Law*, 2025, passim, available at: https://www.hofstrajibl.org/2025/01/hallucinations-your-ai-might-be-affected/ (access: 10.01.2025).

[3034] Laallam, Abla, "Hallucinations: Your AI Might Be Affected...," *Hofstra JIBL Blog: Journal of International Business and Law*, 2025, passim, available at: https://www.hofstrajibl.org/2025/01/hallucinations-your-ai-might-be-affected/ (access: 10.01.2025).

[3035] Davis, Wes, "The New York Times Warns AI Search Engine Perplexity to Stop Using Its Content", *The Verge* (Oct. 15, 2024), https://www.theverge.com/2024/10/15/24270774/new-york-times-cease-and-desist-letter-perplexity-ai-search-engine [https://perma.cc/J7UN-787J] (access: 21.01.2025).

[3036] Laallam, Abla, "Hallucinations: Your AI Might Be Affected...," *Hofstra JIBL Blog: Journal of International Business and Law*, 2025, passim, available at: https://www.hofstrajibl.org/2025/01/hallucinations-your-ai-might-be-affected/ (access: 10.01.2025).

[3037] Davis, Wes, "The New York Times Warns AI Search Engine Perplexity to Stop Using Its Content", *The Verge* (Oct. 15, 2024), https://www.theverge.com/2024/10/15/24270774/new-york-times-cease-and-desist-letter-perplexity-ai-search-engine [https://perma.cc/J7UN-787J] (access: 21.01.2025).

[3038] Laallam, Abla, "Hallucinations: Your AI Might Be Affected...," *Hofstra JIBL Blog: Journal of International Business and Law*, 2025, passim, available at: https://www.hofstrajibl.org/2025/01/hallucinations-your-ai-might-be-affected/ (access: 10.01.2025).

[3039] Laallam, Abla, "Hallucinations: Your AI Might Be Affected...," *Hofstra JIBL Blog: Journal of International Business and Law*, 2025, passim, available at: https://www.hofstrajibl.org/2025/01/hallucinations-your-ai-might-be-affected/ (access: 10.01.2025).

[3040] Laallam, Abla, "Hallucinations: Your AI Might Be Affected...," *Hofstra JIBL Blog: Journal of International Business and Law*, 2025, passim, available at: https://www.hofstrajibl.org/2025/01/hallucinations-your-ai-might-be-affected/ (access: 10.01.2025).

§§ The case *New York Post v. Perplexity* encapsulates, hands-in-glove, the worrisome issue of «model collapse»[3043] according to which the widespread use of LLM model-generated content in training causes irreversible effects in the resulting models, which tail off/disfigures the original content.[3044]

§§ Put otherwise, «model collapse» is a degenerative process swaying future generations of learned generative models, in which the data they create will eventually pollute the training dataset[3045] of the next generation.[3046]

[3041] On harms inflicted by fake material: *Mata v. Avianca, Inc.*, 678 F. Supp. 3d 443, 448–49 (S.D.N.Y. 2023) ("*any harms flow from the submission of fake opinions. The opposing party wastes time and money in exposing the deception.* The Court's time is taken from other important endeavors. The client may be deprived of arguments based on authentic judicial precedents. *There is potential harm to the reputation of judges and courts whose names are falsely invoked as authors of the bogus opinions and to the reputation of a party attributed with fictional conduct.* It promotes cynicism about the legal profession and the American judicial system. And *a future litigant may be tempted to defy a judicial ruling by disingenuously claiming doubt about its authenticity*"). Italics added.

[3042] Complaint at 64, 135, 204, N.Y. Times Co. v. Microsoft Corp., No. 1:23-cv-11195 (S.D.N.Y. 2023) https://www.thetmca.com/files/2024/02/NYT_Complaint_Dec2023.pdf; [https://perma.cc/U8YC-4Q73]. (access: 10.01.2025).

[3043] Shumailov, Ilia/Shumaylov, Zakhar/Zhao, Yiren/Papernot, Nicolas/Anderson, Ross/Gal, Yarin, "AI models collapse when trained on recursively generated data", *Nature*, Volume 631, 25 July 2024, 2024, 755–759 (755) ("*Model collapse is a degenerative process affecting generations of learned generative models, in which the data they generate end up polluting the training set of the next generation.* Being trained on *polluted data*, they then *mis-perceive reality*"). Italics added.

[3044] Shumailov, Ilia/Shumaylov, Zakhar/Zhao, Yiren/Papernot, Nicolas/Anderson, Ross/Gal, Yarin, "AI models collapse when trained on recursively generated data", *cit.*, 755–759 (755) ("*Stable diffusion revolutionized image creation from descriptive tex*t. GPT-2 (ref. 1), GPT-3(.5) (ref. 2) and GPT-4 (ref. 3) *demonstrated high performance across a variety of language tasks. ChatGPT introduced such language models to the public. It is now clear that generative artificial intelligence (AI) such as large language models (LLMs) is here to stay and will substantially change the ecosystem of online text and images. Here we consider what may happen to GPT-{n} once LLMs contribute much of the text found online. We find that indiscriminate use of model-generated content in training causes irreversible defects in the resulting models, in which tails of the original content distribution disappear. We refer to this effect as 'model collapse' and show that it can occur in LLMs as well as in variational autoencoders (VAEs) and Gaussian mixture models (GMMs*). Italics added.

[3045] Note, though, that the training of machine learning is long and tedious in that is an error-prone procedure than can ultimately impair future algorithmic decision-making: Price, W. Nicholson Price II, "Regulating Black-Box Medicine", *Michigan Law Review*, Volume 116, 2017, pp. 421–431 (leverages on Google Image's image recognition learning algorithm to shed light on the four-step process by which some algorithms are thoroughly trained. First, the algorithm is shown "a set of known images ('Here are 10,000 pictures of ducks')." Second, the algorithm "develops complex internal rules based on nonlinear processes." Third, the algorithm "tests those rules on a test set ('Which of these are ducks?')." And fourth, the algorithm accordingly adjusts its "internal rules based on the success of the test." These steps are trotted out and repeated many times "until it can accurately and consistently classify the images").

[3046] Shumailov, Ilia/Shumaylov, Zakhar/Zhao, Yiren/Papernot, Nicolas/Anderson, Ross/Gal, Yarin, "AI models collapse when trained on recursively generated data", *cit.*, 755–759 (755).

§§ Being trained on polluted/rigged data,[3047] LLM systems will eventually misperceive reality.[3048] Which, in turn, will convert itself into a breeding ground for ChatGPT hallucinations through the process of «ablation: repetitions»[3049] whereby the latter generates its own set of improbable sequence of phrases over time.[3050] Just like in *New York v. Perplexity*. Pundits coined this effect as «model collapse».

§§ «Model collapse» can be broken down into «early model collapse»[3051] (in which the model gradually loses information at the beginning of the tails of distribution) and «late model collapse»[3052] (in which the model converges to a distribution that has few to none resemblance to the original one). Just like in *New York v. Perplexity*.

[3047] But see: Barocas, Solon/Selbst, Andrew D., "Big Data's Disparate Impact", *California Law Review*, Volume 104, 2016, pp. 671–682 (discussing how data is often flawed, rigged, incomplete, imperfect and therefore algorithms inherit the prejudice of the original decision makers). But see: Citron, Danielle Keats/Pasquale, Frank, "The Scored Society: Due Process for Automated Predictions", *Washington Law Review*, Volume 89, 2014, pp. 1, 4–5 (highlighting how human beings programming automated systems is directly conducive to, and leads, to fundamentally inaccurate results since the source code, predictive algorithms and datasets may encompass human biases which, in turn, have a disparate impact on historically disadvantaged groups). But see: Bornstein, Stepanhie, "Antidiscriminatory Algorithms", *Alabama Law Review*, Volume 70, 2018, pp. 519, 524–528 (contending, however, that the tagged "facially neutral" algorithms producing discriminatory outcomes should be quashed).

[3048] Shumailov, Ilia/Shumaylov, Zakhar/Zhao, Yiren/Papernot, Nicolas/Anderson, Ross/Gal, Yarin, "AI models collapse when trained on recursively generated data", *cit.*, 755–759 (755).

[3049] Shumailov, Ilia/Shumaylov, Zakhar/Zhao, Yiren/Papernot, Nicolas/Anderson, Ross/Gal, Yarin, "AI models collapse when trained on recursively generated data", *cit.*, 755–759 (758) ("*we find that data generated by language models in our experiments end up containing a large number of repeating phrases*, as in Example 1. The repeating problem has been observed in nearly all text-generation models 17, 18 and, to rule this out as the cause of model collapse, we further provide numerical experiments when models are explicitly encouraged to produce non-repeating sequences with a repeating penalty of 2.0. *We find that this causes the models to produce lower score continuations to avoid using repeats, which—as a result—causes the consequent models to perform even worse. Model perplexities shift across the generations towards more probable token sequences, as measured using the model trained on the original real data distribution*"). Italics added.

[3050] Shumailov, Ilia/Shumaylov, Zakhar/Zhao, Yiren/Papernot, Nicolas/Anderson, Ross/Gal, Yarin, "AI models collapse when trained on recursively generated data", *cit.*, 755–759 (758) ("*In particular, enforcing this for the LLM experiments causes the perplexity to double compared with the original. Models remain as susceptible to model collapse, if not more. The described process demonstrates that fine-tuning of language models does not curb the effects of model collapse and models that are being fine-tuned are also vulnerable. We find that, over the generations, models tend to produce more probable sequences from the original data and start introducing their own improbable sequences, that is, errors*"). Italics added.

[3051] Shumailov, Ilia/Shumaylov, Zakhar/Zhao, Yiren/Papernot, Nicolas/Anderson, Ross/Gal, Yarin, "AI models collapse when trained on recursively generated data", *cit.*, 755–759 (755) ("*In early model collapse, the model begins losing information about the tails* of the distribution"). Italics added.

[3052] Shumailov, Ilia/Shumaylov, Zakhar/Zhao, Yiren/Papernot, Nicolas/Anderson, Ross/Gal, Yarin, "AI models collapse when trained on recursively generated data", *cit.*, 755–759 (755) ("*in late model collapse, the model converges to a distribution that carries little resemblance to the original one*, often with substantially reduced variance"). Italics added.

§§»Model collapse» is shaping up to spring into action the onset of the age of *Algorithmic Dictatorship* whereby truths and lies dovetail seamlessly, thereby throwing the newspapers credibility into a frenzy insofar *fake news autocracy* will hasten the demise of the truth as we now. Litle the world knows that the devilishly harmful virus *of permanent illusion* lurks ahead in that integrity is poised to fall into abeyance. The world as we know will accordingly go berserk and nothing will ever be the same, truthfulness wise.

§§ Note, though, that the deleterious effects of hallucinations have also reached the medical field.[3053] Worryingly, Open AI's transcription tool, *Whisper*, used during medical consultations, has been fabricating sizable portions of spoken speech and sentences.[3054] Unsurprisingly, yet gruesomely, a portion of the transcriptions comprised racial utterances,[3055] vitriolic remarks akin to bellicose rhetoric, and fictitious medical treatment and accompanying diagnoses.[3056] This is another glimpse

---

[3053] Laallam, Abla, "Hallucinations: Your AI Might Be Affected…," *Hofstra JIBL Blog: Journal of International Business and Law*, 2025, passim, available at: https://www.hofstrajibl.org/2025/01/hallucinations-your-ai-might-be-affected/ (access: 10.01.2025). See: Part III, Chap. 3, Sects. 3.1.5.6–3.1.5.6.1 of this book (on Critical Artificial Intelligence Studies, with a sharper focus on the harmful effects of Large Language Models 'medical hallucinations that are poised to undermine its overall trustworthiness).

[3054] Burke, Garance/Schellmann, Hilke, "Researchers Say an AI-Powered Transcription Tool Used in Hospitals Invents Things No One Ever Said", *AP News* (Oct. 26, 2024), https://apnews.com/article/ai-artificial-intelligence-health-business-90020cdf5fa16c79ca2e5b6c4c9bbb14; [https://perma.cc/D2S5-UEMC]. Access: 21.01.2025).

[3055] See: Xiao Fang/Shangkun Che/Minjia Mao/Hongzhe Zhang/Ming Zhao/Xiaohang Zhao, "Bias of AI-generated content: an examination of news produced by large language models", *Nature*, 14:5224, 2024, pp. 1–20 (p. 1) ("*Large language models (LLMs) have the potential to transform our lives and work through the content they generate, known as AI-Generated Content (AIGC). To harness this transformation, we need to understand the limitations of LLMs.* Here, we investigate the bias of AIGC produced by seven representative LLMs, including ChatGPT and LLaMA. *We collect news articles from The New York Times and Reuters, both known for their dedication to provide unbiased news. We then apply each examined LLM to generate news content with headlines of these news articles as prompts, and evaluate the gender and racial biases of the AIGC produced by the LLM by comparing the AIGC and the original news articles. We further analyze the gender bias of each LLM under biased prompts* by adding gender-biased messages to prompts constructed from these news headlines (…) *Moreover, the AIGC generated by each LLM exhibits notable discrimination against females and individuals of the Black race.* Among the LLMs, the AIGC generated by ChatGPT demonstrates the lowest level of bias, and ChatGPT *is the sole model capable of declining content generation when provided with biased prompts*"). Italics added. But see: Lindloff, Chiara/Siegert, Ingo, "Defining bias in AI-systems: Biased models are fair models", *ISCA/ITG Workshop on Diversity in Large Speech and Language Models*, arXiv:2502.18060v1 [cs.AI] 25 Feb 2025, 2025, p. 1 ("The debate around bias in AI systems is central to discussions on algorithmic fairness. *However, the term "bias" often lacks a clear definition, despite frequently being contrasted with "fairness" — implying that an unbiased model is inherently fair. In this paper, we challenge this assumption and argue that a precise conceptualization of bias is necessary to effectively address fairness concerns. Rather than viewing bias as inherently negative or unfair, we highlight the importance of distinguishing between bias and discrimination.* We further explore how this shift in focus can foster a more constructive discourse within academic debates on fairness in AI systems"). Italics added.

[3056] Burke, Garance/Schellmann, Hilke, "Researchers Say an AI-Powered Transcription Tool Used in Hospitals Invents Things No One Ever Said", *AP News* (Oct. 26, 2024),

of *Algorithmic Dictatorship* that widens the racial wedge between White folks and Black folks, which, in turn, is the propelling force behind *biased prompts* that generate racial and gender biases deeply embedded in LLM systems.[3057]

§§ As adumbrated,[3058] the repercussions of LLM systems' hallucinations can be steep. Pundits, ethical hackers, advocates, former OpenAI employees and influent stakeholder alike have accordingly rallied around the sweeping idea that the federal government should consider laying down the foundations for AI regulations in an earnest attempt to fizzle out the harmful effects of these hallucinations in high-risk fields[3059] like the medical field.[3060]

4.1.9.7 «The Brussels Effect Strikes Again»: Should Jurisdictions Worldwide Follow the Risk-Based Approach Set Out by European Union Artificial Intelligence Act (EU AI Act) in a Bid to Deal with the Unsavoury Effects of ChatGPT Hallucinations? A Brief (Thumbnail) Sketch on the Drawbacks and Pitfalls Arising Out of EU AI Act

§§ The European Union («EU») assumed the helm, and the central thrust, towards the construction of a full-fledged frame of reference for Artificial Intelligence-embedded technologies. The European Union[3061] has been accordingly spearheading efforts

---

https://apnews.com/article/ai-artificial-intelligence-health-business-90020cdf5fa16c79ca2e5b6c4c9bbb14 [https://perma.cc/D2S5-UEMC]. Access: 21.01.2025).

[3057] See: Xiao Fang/Shangkun Che/Minjia Mao/Hongzhe Zhang/Ming Zhao/Xiaohang Zhao, "Bias of AI-generated content: an examination of news produced by large language models", *Nature*, 14:5224, 2024, pp. 1–20 (p. 1) ("*our study reveals that the AIGC produced by each examined LLM demonstrates substantial gender and racial biases").* Italics added.

[3058] See: Part III, Chap. 3, Sects. 3.1.5.6–3.1.5.6.1 of this book (on Critical Artificial Intelligence Studies, with a sharper focus on the harmful effects of Large Language Models 'medical hallucinations that are poised to undermine its overall trustworthiness). See also: Part III, Chap. 3, Sects. 3.1.5.4–3.1.5.4.1.1 of this book (on the functional aspects of Critical Artificial Intelligence Studies, with a sharper focus on the harmful effects of Artificial Intelligence-embedded technologies, namely Large Language Models and its multifarious downsides and shortcomings). See also: Part IV, This chapter, Sects. 4.1.9.1–4.1.9.2. (on ChatGPT's functional abilities). See also: Part IV, This chapter, Sects. 4.1.9–4.1.9.7. (on ChatGPT's functional drawbacks and pitfalls, including, but no limited to, "hallucinations").

[3059] See: Part V, Chap. 5, Sect. 5.1.7.2 of this book (on law number two to control algorithmic decision-making, which mandates that black box models must not be entrusted with the task of high stake decisions—v.g. health and freedom).

[3060] Laallam, Abla, "Hallucinations: Your AI Might Be Affected...," *Hofstra JIBL Blog: Journal of International Business and Law*, 2025, passim, available at: https://www.hofstrajibl.org/2025/01/hallucinations-your-ai-might-be-affected/ (access: 10.01.2025).

[3061] High-Level Expert Group on Artificial Intelligence, *Ethics guidelines for trustworthy AI. The European Commission*, 2019; European Commission (2024). International outreach for human-centric artificial intelligence initiative, 2024; European Commission, Artificial Intelligence for Europe [Online], 2018. Available: https://eur-lex.europa.eu/legal-content/EN/TXT/PDF/?uri = CELEX:52018DC0237&from = EN [Accessed 6.1.2025]; European Commission, White

to implement a comprehensive and thoroughgoing global strategy for Artificial Intelligence-embedded technologies.

§§ The inception of the drafting of AI Act can be traced back to 2018. Its first draft was made publicly available in 2021. The Act has been formally approved in 2024.[3062] The European Union Artificial Intelligence Act («EU AI Act») has accordingly entered into force on August 1, 2024.[3063] The propelling force behind EU's thought leadership is the much-acclaimed the «Brussels effect»[3064] according to which EU AI Act constitutes a beacon of algorithmic fairness[3065] for jurisdictions worldwide in that lends itself to a lodestar that radiates, bright, far, and high.

§§ For purposes here, the AI Act comprises three types of systems, with each type determining the cluster of rules and obligations mandated by the regulation[3066]: **i)** limited risks, **ii)** high risk, and **iii)** unacceptable/prohibited risk.[3067] The set of sanctions for infringements are rather hefty indeed: if there is a proven infringement of forbidden Artificial Intelligence-embedded technologies unlawful practices, a corporation is liable to a fine that consist of either 35 million euros or 7% of global turnover

Paper. On Artificial Intelligence—A European approach to excellence and trust [Online], 2020, available: https://eur-lex.europa.eu/legal-content/EN/TXT/PDF/?uri=CELEX:52020DC0065&from=EN [Accessed 6.1.2025]; European Commission, Proposal for a Regulation of the European Parliament and of the council laying down harmonised rules on Artificial Intelligence, 2021; European Commission. European approach to artificial intelligence [Online], 2024. Available: https:// digital-strategy.ec.europa.eu/en/policies/european-approach-artificial-intelligence; European Economic and Social Committee. Fundamental Rights and Rule of Law—National developments from a civil society perspective—2020–2021 [Online], 2022. Available: https://www.eesc.europa.eu/en/our-work/publications-other-work/publications/fundamental-rights-and-rule-law-nationaldevelopments-civil-society-perspective-2020–2021 [Accessed 6.1. 2025]; European Commission (2021a). 2030 Digital Compass: the European way for the Digital Decade [Online]. Available: https://ec.europa.eu/info/sites/info/files/communication-digital-compass-2030_en.pdf.

3062 Laallam, Abla, "Hallucinations: Your AI Might Be Affected...," *Hofstra JIBL Blog: Journal of International Business and Law*, 2025, passim, available at: https://www.hofstrajibl.org/2025/01/hallucinations-your-ai-might-be-affected/ (access: 10.01.2025).

3063 Laallam, Abla, "Hallucinations: Your AI Might Be Affected...," *Hofstra JIBL Blog: Journal of International Business and Law*, 2025, passim, available at: https://www.hofstrajibl.org/2025/01/hallucinations-your-ai-might-be-affected/ (access: 10.01.2025).

3064 Bradford, A, *The Brussels effect: how the European Union rules the world*, Oxford, Oxford University Press, 2020, passim.

3065 Card, D./Smith, NA", On consequentialism and fairness", *Frontiers of Artificial Intelligence*, Volume 3:34, 2020, passim.

3066 Laallam, Abla, "Hallucinations: Your AI Might Be Affected...," *Hofstra JIBL Blog: Journal of International Business and Law*, 2025, passim, available at: https://www.hofstrajibl.org/2025/01/hallucinations-your-ai-might-be-affected/ (access: 10.01.2025).

3067 Laallam, Abla, "Hallucinations: Your AI Might Be Affected...," *Hofstra JIBL Blog: Journal of International Business and Law*, 2025, passim, available at: https://www.hofstrajibl.org/2025/01/hallucinations-your-ai-might-be-affected/ (access: 10.01.2025).

for the previous year,[3068] whichever is greater. Fine measurement also considers the type of violation and the entity size.[3069]

§§ Under the EU AI Act, LLMs systems are coined as general-purpose Artificial Intelligence («GPAI») models.[3070] The AI Act tackles head-on some of the pressing challenges arising out of Artificial Intelligence hallucinations with a sharper focus on data transparency[3071] obligations.[3072] A fraction of these binding rules includes having traceable[3073] and explainable results in place,[3074] paired with explanations[3075]

[3068] Laallam, Abla, "Hallucinations: Your AI Might Be Affected…," *Hofstra JIBL Blog: Journal of International Business and Law*, 2025, passim, available at: https://www.hofstrajibl.org/2025/01/hallucinations-your-ai-might-be-affected/ (access: 10.01.2025).

[3069] Laallam, Abla, "Hallucinations: Your AI Might Be Affected…," *Hofstra JIBL Blog: Journal of International Business and Law*, 2025, passim, available at: https://www.hofstrajibl.org/2025/01/hallucinations-your-ai-might-be-affected/ (access: 10.01.2025).

[3070] Laallam, Abla, "Hallucinations: Your AI Might Be Affected…," *Hofstra JIBL Blog: Journal of International Business and Law*, 2025, passim, available at: https://www.hofstrajibl.org/2025/01/hallucinations-your-ai-might-be-affected/ (access: 10.01.2025).

[3071] See: Mittelstadt, B./Russell, C./Watcher, S., "Explaining explanations in AI", *Proceedings of Fairness, Accountability, and Transparency (FAT) (ACM)*, 2019, passim; Coglianese, Cary/Lehr, David, "Transparency and Algorithmic Governance", *Administrative Law Review*, Volume 71, 2019, passim (highlights the overriding importance of transparency to propel algorithmic governance). But see: de Laat, Paul B. 'Algorithmic Decision-Making Based on Machine Learning from Big Data: Can Transparency Restore Accountability?", *Philosophy & Technology*, Volume 31, 2018, pp. 524 and ff and passim (broaches the plethora of limitations related with full transparency, privacy, deleterious effects, competitive edge, and the shroud of opacity under which algorithms are often wrapped).

[3072] Laallam, Abla, "Hallucinations: Your AI Might Be Affected…," *Hofstra JIBL Blog: Journal of International Business and Law*, 2025, passim, available at: https://www.hofstrajibl.org/2025/01/hallucinations-your-ai-might-be-affected/ (access: 10.01.2025). See also: Doherty, Joseph W./Reville, Robert T./Zakaras, Laura(ed.), *Introduction to Confidentiality, Transparency, and the U.S. Civil Justice System*, Oxford, Oxford University Press, 2012, 1–258 (passim) (noting that the lack of transparency yields sizable social costs).

[3073] See: Samek, Wojciech/Müller, Klaus-Robert, "Explainable AI: interpreting, explaining and visualizing deep learning", *Towards Explainable Artificial Intelligence*, Samek, Wojciech/Montavon, Grégoire/ Vedaldi, Andrea/Hansen, Lars Kai/ Müller, Klaus-Robert (Editors). Heidelberg/Berlin/New York: Springer, 2019, pp. 5–22 ("in recent years, machine learning (ML) has become a key enabling technology for the sciences and industry. Especially through improvements in methodology, the availability of large databases and increased computational power, *today's ML algorithms are able to achieve excellent performance (at times even exceeding the human level) on an increasing number of complex tasks. Deep learning models are at the forefront of this development. However, due to their nested non-linear structure, these powerful models have been generally considered "black boxes", not providing any information about what exactly makes them arrive at their predictions.* Since in many applications, e.g., in the medical domain, *such lack of transparency may be not acceptable, the development of methods for visualizing, explaining and interpreting deep learning models has recently attracted increasing attention. This introductory paper presents recent developments and applications in this field and makes a plea for a wider use of explainable learning algorithms in practice*"). See: Part V, Chap. 5, Sects. 5.1.7–5.1.7.5 of this book (on the five laws to control algorithmic decision-making). See: Part V, Chap. 5, Sects. 5.1.8–5.1.8.5 of this book (on the five laws to interpret algorithmic decision-making). See: Part V, Chap. 5, Sects. 5.1.2–5.1.6.2.1 of this book (on **the thing-centred algorithmic decision-making** propelled by a *Controllable* and *Interpretable* Machine Learning that weeds out *Algorithmic Dictatorship* and secures *Algorithmic*

on how a computer-run algorithm has come to a decision,[3076] and specific information on the dataset[3077] used to train[3078] the Artificial Intelligence-anchored technology alongside its accuracy.[3079]

Common Good. It is worth recalling that the **thing-centred algorithmic decision-making** seeks to unwind the perils arising out of the lack of theoretical underpinnings facing the **human-centred algorithmic decision-making**, as extensively fleshed out Part III, Chap. 3, Sects. 3.1.4.3–3.1.4.4 of this book).

[3074] See: Deeks, Ahsley, "The Judicial Demand for Explainable Artificial Intelligence", *Columbia Law Review*, Volume 119, 2019, pp. 1829 and ff and passim. See: Hacker, Phillip/Passoth, Jan-Hendrick, "Varieties of AI Explanations under the Law: From the GDPR to the AIA, and Beyond", *XxAI Beyond Explainable AI, International Workshop on Extending Explainable AI Beyond Deep Models and Classifiers*. Berlin/New York/Singapore/Beijing: Springer, 2021, pp. 343–373 ("*the quest to explain the output of artificial intelligence systems has clearly moved from a mere technical to a highly legally and politically relevant endeavor.* In this paper, we provide an overview of legal obligations to explain AI and evaluate current policy proposals. In this, we distinguish between different functional varieties of AI explanations—such as multiple forms of enabling, technical and protective transparency—and show how different legal areas engage with and mandate such different types of explanations to varying degrees. *Starting with the rights-enabling framework of the GDPR, we proceed to uncover technical and protective forms of explanations owed under contract, tort and banking law. Moreover, we discuss what the recent EU proposal for an Artificial Intelligence Act means for explainable AI, and review the proposal's strengths and limitations in this respect. Finally, from a policy perspective, we advocate for moving beyond mere explainability towards a more encompassing framework for trustworthy and responsible AI that includes actionable explanations, values-in-design and co-design methodologies, interactions with algorithmic fairness, and quality benchmarking*").

[3075] Mittelstadt, B./Russell, C./Watcher, S., "Explaining explanations in AI", *Proceedings of Fairness, Accountability, and Transparency (FAT) (ACM)*, 2019, passim.

[3076] See: Krafft, Tobias D./Zweig, Katharina A./Konig, Pascal D., "How to Regulate Algorithmic Decision-Making: A Framework of Regulatory Requirements for Different Applications", *Regulation & Governance*, Volume 16, 2022, pp. 119 and ff and passim; Gerdon, Frederic/Bach, Ruben L./Kern, Christoph/Kreuter, Frauke, "Social Impacts of Algorithmic Decision-Making: A Research Agenda for the Social Science", *Big Data & Society*, Volume 9, 2022, passim. But see: de Laat, Paul B. 'Algorithmic Decision-Making Based on Machine Learning from Big Data: Can Transparency Restore Accountability?", *Philosophy & Technology*, Volume 31, 2018, pp. 524 and ff and passim (broaches the plethora of limitations related with full transparency, privacy, deleterious effects, competitive edge, and the shroud of opacity under which algorithms are often wrapped). But see also: Citron, Danielle K., "Technological Due Process", *Washington University Law Review*, Volume 85, 2008, pp. 1249–1253 ("computer programs seamlessly combine rulemaking and individual adjudications without the critical procedural protections owed either of them").

[3077] Laallam, Abla, "Hallucinations: Your AI Might Be Affected...," *Hofstra JIBL Blog: Journal of International Business and Law*, 2025, passim, available at: https://www.hofstrajibl.org/2025/01/hallucinations-your-ai-might-be-affected/ (access: 10.01.2025).

[3078] On the quality—or lack thereof—of training data in the remit of real estate and beyond. See: Wonyoung, So, "Which Information Matters? Measuring Landlord Assessment of Tenant Screening Reports", *Housing Policy Debate*, Volume 33, n. ° 6, 2023, pp. 1484–1510 (1501–1502) ("*Algorithmic scoring using criminal records is problematic because training data—a data set that is used to train a machine learning model—is inaccurate and the outcome variable ("desirable tenants") is unclear. For instance, the tenant screening company RealPage produces 11,000 reports using "abbreviated" criminal records, which are cheaper to acquire than full criminal records but do not include details of the resolution* (Kirchner & Goldstein, 2020). *An inaccurate model is highly*

§§ Note, though, that, for the reasons given in another part of this book,[3080] *explainable artificial intelligence* is not the answer you are looking for.[3081] That is, citizens are woefully ill-prepared to understand the explanations offered by an inscrutable[3082] Artificial Intelligence[3083] whose inner workings[3084] are wrapped

---

likely to result from tenant screening services using these kinds of abbreviated data, given that it is important to include the final resolution of criminal justice procedures for proper assessment. Moreover, it would be challenging to set an outcome variable for developing this kind of algorithm because it is hard to project a certain criminal outcome into "good" tenant behaviors"). Italics added. For further developments: Part IV, This chapter, Sects. 4.1.4–4.1.4.2.2 of this book.

[3079] But see: Yeung, Karen, "Algorithmic Regulation: A Critical Interrogation", *Regulation & Governance*, Volume 12, 2018, pp. 505 and ff and passim (on the sweltering challenges posed by algorithmic regulation).

[3080] See: Part V, Chap. 5, Sects. 5.1.2–5.1.6.2.1 of this book (on the thing-centred algorithmic decision-making propelled by a *Controllable* and *Interpretable* Machine Learning that weeds out *Algorithmic Dictatorship* and secures *Algorithmic Common Good*. It is worth recalling that the **thing-centred algorithmic decision-making** seeks to unwind the perils arising out of the lack of theoretical underpinnings facing the **human-centred algorithmic decision-making**, as extensively fleshed out Part III, Chap. 3, Sects. 3.1.4.3–3.1.4.4 of this book). See also: Part V, Chap. 5, Sects. 5.1.8–5.1.8.5 of this book (on the five laws to interpret algorithmic decision-making).

[3081] But see: Segran, G., "The complexity of artificial intelligence", *Singapore Management University*, 2021, passim (on the elaborate and complex trappings of Artificial Intelligence); Adadi, Amina/ Berrada, Mohammed, "Peeking Inside the Black-Box: A Survey on Explainable Artificial Intelligence (XAI), *Institute of Electrical and Electronics Engineers*, Volume 6, 2018, passim; Edwards, Lilian/Veale, Michael, "Slave to the Algorithm? Why a "Right to an Explanation" is Probably not the Remedy You are Looking for", *Duke Law and Technology Review*, Volume 16, 2018, pp. 18–67 (pondering whether and to what extent XAI will come in handy because citizens are woefully ill-prepared to "make use of the kind of algorithmic explanations they are likely to be offered"); Miller, Tim, "Explanations in Artificial Intelligence: Insights from Social Sciences", *Artificial Intelligence*, Volume 267, 2019, pp. 1–38.

[3082] Strandburg, Katherine J., "Rulemaking and Inscrutable Decision Tools", *Columbia Law Review*, Volume 119, 2019, passim.

[3083] See: Rudin, Cynthia, "Please stop explaining black box models for high stakes decisions", *Proceedings of NeurIPS 2018 Workshop on Critiquing and Correcting Trends in Machine Learning (NIPS 2018)*, 2018, passim; Rudin, C., & Radin, J., "Why are we using black box models in AI when we don't need to? A lesson from an explainable AI competition", *Harvard Data Science Review*, 2019, Volume 1, Issue 2, passim; Tan, S., Caruana, R., Hooker, G., and Lou, Y., "Distill-and-compare: Auditing blackbox models using transparent model distillation". *Proceedings of the 2018 AAAI/ACM Conference on AI, Ethics, and Society, Association for Computing Machinery*, 2018, pp. 303–310 (arguing that explainable models are too complex and fiddly to be understood by laypeople. As a result, interpretable models should be used instead).

[3084] See: Scherer, Matthew U., "Regulating Artificial Intelligence Systems: Risks, Challenges, Competencies, and Strategies", *Harvard Journal of Law and Technology*, Volume 29, 2016, pp. 353–369 (frames the crippling problem of opacity as "the possibility that the inner workings of an AI system may be kept secret and may not be susceptible to reverse engineering").

in both complexity[3085] and opaqueness.[3086] *Interpretable models*[3087] should be deployed instead.[3088] More on this later.[3089]

3085 See: Bathaee, Yavar, "The Artificial Intelligence Black Box and the Failure of Intent and Causation", *Harvard Journal of Law and Technology*, n.º 37, 2018, p. 901 (adduces that "*one possible reason AI may be a black box to humans is that it relies on machine-learning algorithms that internalize data in ways that are not easily audited or understood by humans (…) "first, a lack may arise from the complexity of the algorithm's structure, such as with deep neural network, which consists of thousands of artificial neurons working together in a diffuse way to solve a problem. This reason for AI being a black box is referred to as "complexity". Second, the lack of transparency may arise because the AI is using a machine-learning algorithm that relies on geometric relationships that humans cannot visualize, such as with support vector machines. This reason for AI being a black box is referred to as "dimensionality"*"). Italics added. See: Part V, Chap. 5, Sect. 5.1.7.2 of this book (on law number two to control algorithmic decision-making, which mandates that black box models must not be entrusted with the task of high stake decisions—v.g. health and freedom).

3086 See: *Tech, Bias and Housing Initiative, the Promise and Perils of Residential Proptech, Year 1, Research Summary Report, April 2023, TechEquity Collaborative*, p. 10, available at: https://techequity.us/wp-content/uploads/2023/04/TBHI-Y1-Research-Summary-Report.pdf (28.11.2024). ("**Opaque, Predictive Algorithms Determine Who Gets What Housing Unlike Analog Models**, *Algorithmic Tenant Screening Tools Predict Future Behavior To Determine Housing Access As landlord tech took hold, more property managers of all sizes came to rely on it to interface with tenants. One key feature of landlord tech is the use of algorithms to screen rental applicants and assess their suitability as tenants. The tenant screening industry, which pulls a wide array of information about potential tenants to inform landlords' decisions, is now valued at $1.3 billion with as many as two thousand screening companies vying for market share.*10 11 *Such companies include Equifax, TransUnion, and Experian (commonly known as "The Big Three"), as well as smaller startup companies that apply algorithms to make those determinations faster*"). Italics added. See: Part IV, This chapter, Sects. 4.1.4–4.1.4.2.3 of this book.

3087 Turek, Matt, "Explainable Artificial Intelligence (XAI)", The *Defense Advanced Research Projects Agency* (DARPA), www.darpa.mil/program/explainable-artificial-intelligence; [https://perma.cc/2DS4-ZMNB] (shedding light on the oft-labelled interpretability of algorithms). See also: *Making Computers Explain Themselves*, MIT's Computer Science and Artificial Intelligence Laboratory (Oct. 27, 2016), 2016, www.csail.mit.edu/making_computers_explain themselves; [https://perma.cc/C97B-PGUR] (explaining the importance of grasping the complex trappings of algorithm decision-making).

3088 See: Chen, C./Rudin, C., "An optimization approach to learning falling rule lists", *Proceedings of Machine Learning Research, Artificial Intelligence and Statistics*, Volume 84, 2018, pp. 604–612; Sokolovska, N./Chevaleyre, Y./Zucker, J.D., "A provable algorithm for learning interpretable scoring systems", *Proceedings of Machine Learning Research, Artificial Intelligence and Statistics*, Volume 84, pp. 566–574; Rudin, Cynthia/Ustun, B., "Optimized scoring systems: toward trust in machine learning for healthcare and criminal justice", *Interfaces*, Volume 48, 2018, pp. 399–486.

3089 See: Part V, Chap. 5, Sect. 5.1.7.2 of this book (on law number two to control algorithmic decision-making, which mandates that black box models must not be entrusted with the task of high stake decisions—v.g. health and freedom). See also: Part V, Chap. 5, Sects. 5.1.2–5.1.6.2.1 of this book (on the thing-centred algorithmic decision-making propelled by a *Controllable* and *Interpretable* Machine Learning that weeds out *Algorithmic Dictatorship* and secures *Algorithmic Common Good*. It is worth recalling that the **thing-centred algorithmic decision-making** seeks to unwind the perils arising out of the lack of theoretical underpinnings facing the **human-centred algorithmic decision-making**, as extensively fleshed out Part III, Chap. 3, Sects. 3.1.4.3–3.1.4.4 of this book).

§§ Corporate tech moguls—or leading technological giants—are vested with a binding obligation to vouchsafe the information used[3090] in model training,[3091] full disclosure on data usage during training,[3092] and conduct risk assessment[3093] to match the fundamental tenets of safety[3094] and reliability embedded in AI Act.[3095]

[3090] But see: Corbett-Davies, Sam/Goel, Sharad, "The Measure and Mismeasure of Fairness: a critical Review of Fair Machine Learning", *Cornell University Library*, 2018, p. 18 (pores over a type of *measurement bias* coined "feature bias," which is neatly a bias in the predictors x. Note, though, that there is a second type of measurement bias deemed "label bias," which, in turn, amounts to a bias in y. The authors argue that that label bias is the worst bias there is).

[3091] But see: Dong et al., Qi, "Imbalanced deep learning by minority class incremental rectification, *IEEE Transactions on Pattern Analysis & Machine Intelligence*, Volume 41, 2019, p. 1367 (posit that "*most existing learning algorithms produce inductive bias (learning bias)* towards the frequent (majority) *classes if training data are not balanced, resulting in poor minority class recognition performance*"). Italics added. See: Chandler, Anupam, "The Racist Algorithm", *Michigan Law Review*, Volume 115, n. º 6, 2018, p. 1026 (on racist algorithms, noting that "the possibilities for discriminatory manipulation are legion"). But see: Altenburger, Kristen M./Ho, Daniel E., "When Algorithms Import Private Bias into Public Enforcement: The Promise and Limitations of Statistical Debiasing Solutions", *Journal of Institutional & Theoretical Economics*, Volume 175, 2019, pp. 97–98 (calls for a "debias predictive algorithms" to assuage racist and/or biased, doctored and bigoted algorithms nevertheless). See also: Hamilton, Melissa, "The Biased Algorithm: Evidence of Disparate Impact on Hispanics", *American Criminal Law Review*, Volume 56, 2019, pp. 1553 and ff and passim. See: Part V, Chap. 5, Sect. 5.1.7.4 of this book (on one of the law to control algorithmic decision-making, namely, law number four: data partitioning must be performed—i.e. randomly split an entire dataset into the «training dataset» and the «test dataset»—to accurately predict outcomes in the real world while forestalling «inductive bias» (learning bias)).

[3092] Notwithstanding, it is often contended that machine learning algorithms engender their own models to forecast future outcomes on the basis of analysis of training data. See: Mittelstadt, Brent Daniel/Taddeo, Patrick Allo, Mariarosaria/Wachter, Sandra/Floridi, Luciano, "The Ethics of Algorithms: Mapping the Debate", *Big Data & Society*, July-Dec. 2016, 2016, p. 3. Note, though, that the training of machine learning is long and tedious in that is an error-prone procedure than can ultimately impair future algorithmic decision-making: Price, W. Nicholson Price II, "Regulating Black-Box Medicine", *Michigan Law Review*, Volume 116, 2017, pp. 421–431 (leverages on Google Image's image recognition learning algorithm to shed light on the four-step process by which some algorithms are thoroughly trained. First, the algorithm is shown "a set of known images ('Here are 10,000 pictures of ducks')." Second, the algorithm "develops complex internal rules based on nonlinear processes." Third, the algorithm "tests those rules on a test set ('Which of these are ducks?')." And fourth, the algorithm accordingly adjusts its "internal rules based on the success of the test." These steps are trotted out and repeated many times "until it can accurately and consistently classify the images").

[3093] Green, B./Chen Y, "Disparate interactions: An algorithm-in-the-loop analysis of fairness in risk assessments", *FAT* 2019, Proceedings of 2019 Conference of Fairness, Accountability, Transparency*, 2019, pp. 90–99; Stevenson, M. T./Slobogin, C., "Algorithmic risk assessments and the double-edged sword of youth", *Washington University Law Review*, Volume 96, 2018, passim (on risk assessment).

[3094] See also: European Commission. European approach to artificial intelligence, 2024, which reads as follows: "*The EU's approach to artificial intelligence centers on excellence and trust, aiming to boost research and industrial capacity while ensuring safety and fundamental rights [...] Fostering excellence in AI will strengthen Europe's potential to compete globally.* The EU will achieve this by: (1) enabling the development and uptake of AI in the EU; (2) becoming the place where AI thrives from the lab to the market; (3) *ensuring that AI works for people and is a force for good in society; (4) building strategic leadership in high-impact sectors.*" Italics added.

§§ If the LLM model is labelled[3096] as high-risk,[3097] the transparency obligations[3098] are heightened, thereby entailing enhanced human supervision («human-in-the-loop»)[3099] to taper off hallucinations,[3100] algorithmic[3101] profiling,[3102] biases,[3103] and the to be frowned-upon hyper reliance[3104] on computer-run architectures.[3105]

§§ It is noteworthy that these legal regulations, albeit suffused with, and redolent of, laudable intentions fall nonetheless short of deftly solving the harmful effects

---

Available: https://digital-strategy.ec.europa.eu/en/policies/european-approachartificial-intelligence [access:6.1.2025]. Italics added.

3095 But see: Alimardani, Armin/Jane, Emma A., "Human Hallucinations: GenAI and the Mirage of Personalised Learning for All", 2024, p. 15 ("*Given that in this study, we concluded that using GenAI educational chatbots involves some risks, we find it crucial to understand students' perceptions of these tools' trustworthiness (…) Given the known risks of overreliance on such technology,45 a healthy level of scepticism towards the accuracy of GenAI is a positive outcome. However, the 11.63% (5 students) who selected 'disagree' or 'strongly disagree' reflect a level of distrust that could undermine the effectiveness of GenAI tools*"). Italics added.

3096 See: Barocas, Solon/Selbst, Andrew D., "Big Data's Disparate Impact", *California Law Review*, Volume 104, 2016, pp. 677–78 (arguing that predictive data is predictive of a given/specific target variable (i.e., minimized future predicted claims) with training data which is both correctly "labelled" and "collected").

3097 Kleinberg, Jon/Ludwig, Jens/Mullainathan, Sendhil/Sunstein Cass R., "Discrimination in the Age of Algorithms", *Journal of Legal Analysis*, Volume 10, 1, 2018, pp. 28–29, 33–34 (draw a distinction between "group differences in the raw data" and biases for the "choice of predictors").

3098 But see: de Laat, Paul B. 'Algorithmic Decision-Making Based on Machine Learning from Big Data: Can Transparency Restore Accountability?", *Philosophy & Technology*, Volume 31, 2018, pp. 524 and ff and passim (broaches the plethora of limitations related with full transparency, privacy, deleterious effects, competitive edge, and the shroud of opacity under which algorithms are often wrapped).

3099 See: Salloch, S., & Eriksen, A., "What are humans doing in the Loop? Co-reasoning and practical Judgment when using machine learning-driven decision aids", *The American Journal of Bioethics*, 2024, pp. 1–12; Binns, Reuben, "Human Judgment in Algorithmic Loops: Individual Justice and Automated Decision-Making", *Regulation & Governance*, Volume 16, 2022, passim; Simon & Schuster, Green, B., "Algorithmic realism: expanding the boundaries of algorithmic thought", *Proceedings of the 2020 Conference on Fairness Accountability and Transparency*, 2020, passim; Green, B./Hu L., "The Myth in the Methodology: Towards a Recontextualization of Fairness in Machine Learning", *Machine Learning Debates Work 35th Internation Conference of Machine Learning*, 2018, passim; Green, B., Chen Y, "Disparate interactions: An algorithm-in-the-loop analysis of fairness in risk assessments", *FAT* 2019, Proceedings of 2019 Conference of Fairness, Accountability, Transparency*, 2019, pp. 90–99 (on the central tenets of algorithmic fairness). See also: Alimardani, Armin/Jane, Emma A., "Human Hallucinations: GenAI and the Mirage of Personalised Learning for All", 2024, p. 13 ("*The output generated by GenAI models includes an inherent randomness and the same prompt may result in various outputs. Therefore, it is likely that the outputs of GenAI models are never entirely accurate and reliable. In other words, we contend that existing GenAI systems represent a technology that requires a 'human in/on the loop' to verify outputs before they reach the end user. When incorporating GenAI into an educational chatbot, students are the end users, making it challenging to identify and rectify these errors promptly*"). Italics added.

that inhere and permeate AI hallucinations.[3106] Not to mention that EU AI Act did not regulate (and should have) the sizzling hot topic of algorithmic biases[3107] deeply entrenched in LLM systems,[3108] which deserves to be overtly decried in that creates

---

[3100] *Kohls v. Ellison*, 24-cv-3754 (LMP/DLM), 9 (D. Minn. Jan. 10, 2025) ("*The Court thus adds its voice to a growing chorus of courts around the country declaring the same message: verify AI-generated content in legal submissions! See Mata v. Avianca, Inc., 678 F.Supp.3d 443, 466* (S.D.N.Y. 2023) (sanctioning attorney for including fake, AI-generated legal citations in a filing); *Park v. Kim, 91 F.4th 610, 614-16* (2d Cir. 2023) (referring attorney for potential discipline for including fake, AI-generated legal citations in a filing); *Kruse v. Karlan, 692 S.W.3d 43, 53* (Mo.Ct.App. 2024) (dismissing appeal because litigant filed a brief with multiple fake, AI-generated legal citations)").

[3101] See: Mann, Monique/Matzner, Tobias, "Challenging Algorithmic Profiling: The Limits of Data Protection and Anti-Discrimination in Responding to Emergent Discrimination", *Big Data & Society*, Volume 6, 2019, passim; Schermer, Bart W., "The Limits of Privacy in Automated Profiling and Data Mining", *Computer Law & Security Review*, Volume 27, 2011, pp. 45 and ff and passim.

[3102] Custers, Bart, "Data Dilemmas in the Information Society: Introduction and Overview", Custers, Bart/Calders, Toon/Schermer, Bart/Zarsky, Tal (Editors), *Discrimination and Privacy in the Information Society: Data Mining and Profiling in Large Databases*, Heidelberg, Springer, 2013, pp. 3–26; Pope, Devin G./Sydnor, Justin R., "Implementing Anti-Discrimination Policies in Statistical Profiling Models", *American Economic Journal: Economic Policy*, Volume 3, 2011, pp. 207–216; Zarsky, Tal, "Transparency in Data Mining: From Theory to Practice", *Discrimination and Privacy in the Information Society: Data Mining and Profiling in Large Databases*, Bart Custers et al. eds., Belin, Springer, 2013 (on the challenges arising out algorithmic profiling).

[3103] Pope, Devin G. Pope/Sydnor, Justin R., "Implementing Anti-Discrimination Policies in Statistical Profiling Models", *American Economic Journal: Applied Economics*, Volume 3, 2011, pp. 206–210 (discussing how the FTC parsed credit score uses in auto-insurance pricing as a proxy for race).

[3104] But see: Part III, Chap. 3, Sects. 3.1.5.4–3.1.5.4.1.1 of this book (on Critical Artificial Intelligence Studies, with a sharper focus on the deceptive patterns evinced by Large Language Models, which has lent urgency to concerns about the trustworthiness and reliability of these tools).

[3105] See: Alimardani, Armin/Jane, Emma A., "Human Hallucinations: GenAI and the Mirage of Personalised Learning for All", 2024, p. 15 ("*Given that in this study, we concluded that using GenAI educational chatbots involves some risks, we find it crucial to understand students' perceptions of these tools' trustworthiness (…) Given the known risks of overreliance on such technology,45 a healthy level of scepticism towards the accuracy of GenAI is a positive outcome. However, the 11.63% (5 students) who selected 'disagree' or 'strongly disagree' reflect a level of distrust that could undermine the effectiveness of GenAI tools*"). Italics added.

[3106] See: Xiao Fang/Shangkun Che/Minjia Mao/Hongzhe Zhang/Ming Zhao/Xiaohang Zhao, "Bias of AI-generated content: an examination of news produced by large language models", *Nature*, 14:5224, 2024, pp. 1–20 (p. 1) ("*our study reveals that the AIGC produced by each examined LLM demonstrates substantial gender and racial biases").* Italics added. See also: Dahl, Matthew/Magesh, Varun/Suzgun, Mirac/Ho, Daniel E., "Large Legal Fictions: Profiling Legal Hallucinations in Large Language Models", *cit.*, 64–93 (88) ("*finally, we also emphasize that the challenges presented by legal hallucinations are not only empirical, but also normative (…) As we discuss in Sect. 2.1.3, model fidelity to the training corpus, model fidelity to the user's prompt, and model fidelity to the facts of the world—i.e., the law—are normative commitments that stand in tension with each other*, despite all being independently desirable technical properties of an LLM. *Ultimately, since hallucinations of some kind are generally inevitable at the token level, developers of legal LLMs will need to make choices about which type(s) of hallucinations to minimize, and they should make these choices transparent to their downstream users*"). Italics added.

[3107] Recall: Baeza-Yates, R., "Bias on the web", *Communications of the ACM*, 61 (6), June 2018, 2018, pp. 54–61 (argues that "*algorithmic bias is when the bias is not present in the input data*

legal loopholes where there should not be any. Nor did the EU AI Act regulate the sweltering issue of «model collapse»,[3109] which is tightly interlocked with the LLM systems 'algorithmic biases.[3110]

§§ Strikingly, EU AI Act has noticeably fallen short of, in that has dispiritingly lagged behind, the newest developments on the potential usage of ChatGPT to aid,[3111]

---

and is added *purely by the algorithm*"). Italics added. See also: Hajian, Sara Hajian et al., "Algorithmic Bias: From Discrimination Discovery to Fairness-aware Data Mining", *ACM SIGKDD International Conference on Knowledge Discovery and Data Mining*, Volume 22, 2125, 2016; Griemmelmann, James/Westreich, Daniel, "Incomprehensible Discrimination ", *California Law Review Online*, Volume 7, 2018, pp. 164–171; Xiang, Alice, "Reconciling Legal and Technical Approaches to Algorithmic Bias", *Tennessee Law Review*, Volume 88, 2021, passim; See: Lemley, Mark A./Casey, Bryan, "Remedies for Robots", *The University of Chicago Law Review*, Volume 86, Issue 5, 2019, pp. 1311–1396 (1376) (alerting to the perils of algorithmic bias); Jackson, Maya C., "Artificial Intelligence and Algorithmic Bias: The Issues with Technology Reflecting History and Humans", *Journal of Business Technology Law*, Volume 16, 2021, pp. 299–316; West, Sarah Myers/Whittaker, Meredith/Crawford, Kate, *Discriminating Systems. Gender, Race and Power in AI*. New York: AI Now Institute, 2019, pp. 15 and ff and passim; Waldman, Ezra, "Privacy, Practice, and Performance", *California Law Review*, Volume 110, 2021, passim (on algorithmic bias).

3108 See: Xiao Fang/Shangkun Che/Minjia Mao/Hongzhe Zhang/Ming Zhao/Xiaohang Zhao, "Bias of AI-generated content: an examination of news produced by large language models", *Nature*, 14:5224, 2024, pp. 1–20 (p. 1) ("*Large language models (LLMs) have the potential to transform our lives and work through the content they generate, known as AI-Generated Content (AIGC). To harness this transformation, we need to understand the limitations of LLMs.* Here, we investigate the bias of AIGC produced by seven representative LLMs, including ChatGPT and LLaMA. *We collect news articles from The New York Times and Reuters, both known for their dedication to provide unbiased news. We then apply each examined LLM to generate news content with headlines of these news articles as prompts, and evaluate the gender and racial biases of the AIGC produced by the LLM by comparing the AIGC and the original news articles. We further analyze the gender bias of each LLM under biased prompts* by adding gender-biased messages to prompts constructed from these news headlines. *Our study reveals that the AIGC produced by each examined LLM demonstrates substantial gender and racial biases*"). Italics added.

3109 Shumailov, Ilia/Shumaylov, Zakhar/Zhao, Yiren/Papernot, Nicolas/Anderson, Ross/Gal, Yarin, "AI models collapse when trained on recursively generated data", *Nature*, Volume 631, 25 July 2024, 2024, 755–759 (755) ("*Model collapse is a degenerative process affecting generations of learned generative models, in which the data they generate end up polluting the training set of the next generation.* Being trained on *polluted data*, they then *mis-perceive reality*"). Italics added.

3110 See: Xiao Fang/Shangkun Che/Minjia Mao/Hongzhe Zhang/Ming Zhao/Xiaohang Zhao, "Bias of AI-generated content: an examination of news produced by large language models", *Nature*, 14:5224, 2024, pp. 1–20 (p. 1) ("*our study reveals that the AIGC produced by each examined LLM demonstrates substantial gender and racial biases")*. Italics added.

3111 Dinis-Oliveira, Ricardo J./Azevedo, Rui M. S., "ChatGPT in forensic sciences: a new Pandora's box with advantages and challenges to pay attention", *Forensic Sciences Research*, 8, 2023, pp. 275–279 (275) ("*ChatGPT is a variant of the generative pre-trained transformer (GPT) language model that uses large amounts of text-based training data and a transformer architecture to generate human-like text adjusted to the received prompts. ChatGPT presents several advantages in forensic sciences, namely, constituting a virtual assistant to aid lawyers, judges, and victims in managing and interpreting forensic expert data. But what would happen if ChatGPT began to be used to produce forensic expertise reports?* Despite its potential applications, the use of ChatGPT and other Large Language Models and artificial intelligence tools in forensic writing also poses ethical and legal concerns, which are discussed in this perspective together with some expected future perspectives"). Italics added.

or replace,[3112] judges[3113] and other legal stakeholders alike to perform legal tasks.[3114] Relatedly, the EU AI Act has refrained itself from taking a firm stand against the usage of ChatGPT to perform legal reasoning in a reliable, accurate and meaningful manner.

§§ The batch of case law brought to bear with this scorching issue[3115] lends weight to the sweeping concerns regarding the overall functioning of LLM systems, which should have merited a nuanced, granular, and fine-grained attention from the lawmakers/policymakers entrusted with the task to enact a robust frame of reference to forestall, and pre-empt, bottlenecks, legal loopholes, regulatory greys areas,[3116] and «regulatory hallucinations»[3117] that run counter to the sought-after legal security.

[3112] Posner, Eric A./Saran, Shivam, "Judge AI: Assessing Large Language Models in Judicial Decision-Making", *The University of Chicago, Coase-Sandor Institute for Law and Economics, The Law School, Coase-Sandor Institute for Law and Economics Research Paper n. º 25–03*, January 2025, 2025, pp. 1–41 (1) ("*Can large language models (LLMs) replace human judges?* By replicating a prior 2 × 2 factorial experiment conducted on 31 U.S. federal judges, we evaluate the legal reasoning of OpenAI's GPT-4o. The experiment involves a simulated appeal in an international war crimes case, with two altered variables: the degree to which the defendant is sympathetically portrayed and the consistency of the lower court's decision with precedent. *We find that GPT-4o is strongly affected by precedent but not by sympathy, similar to students who were subjects in the same experiment but the opposite of the professional judges, who were influenced by sympathy. We try prompt engineering techniques to spur the LLM to act more like human judges, but with little success. "Judge AI" is a formalist judge, not a human judge*"). Italics added.

[3113] See: Liu, John Zhuang/Xueyao Li, "How do judges use large language models? Evidence from Shenzhen", *Journal of Legal Analysis*, Volume 16, 2025, pp. 235–262 (235) ("this article reports on the *systematic use of a large language model by a court in China to generate judicial opinions*—arguably the first instance of this in the world. *Based on this case study, we outline the interaction pattern between judges and generative artificial intelligence (AI) in real-world scenarios, namely: 1) judges make initial decisions; 2) the large language model generates reasoning based on the judges' decisions; and 3) judges revise the reasoning generated by AI to make the final judgment.* We contend that this pattern is typical and will remain stable irrespective of advances in AI technologies, given that judicial accountability ultimately rests with judges rather than machines. *Drawing on extensive research in behavioral sciences, we propose that this interaction process between judges and AI may amplify errors and biases in judicial decision-making by reinforcing judges' prior beliefs*".). Italics added.

[3114] But see: Dahl, Matthew/Magesh, Varun/Suzgun, Mirac/Ho, Daniel E., "Large Legal Fictions: Profiling Legal Hallucinations in Large Language Models", *Journal of Legal Analysis*, Volume 16, 2024, 64–93 (64) ("*Do large language models (LLMs) know the law? LLMs are increasingly being used to augment legal practice, education, and research, yet their revolutionary potential is threatened by the presence of "hallucinations"—textual output that is not consistent with legal facts* (...) *We conclude by cautioning against the rapid and unsupervised integration of popular LLMs into legal tasks*"). Italics added.

[3115] See: Part IV, This chapter, Sect. 4.1.9.5 of this book (on a cluster of case law that deals with the issue of ChatGPT's hallucinations and its consequences in legal settings).

[3116] See: Cohen, Julien E., *Between Truth and Power: The Legal Constructions of Informational Capitalism*. Oxford: Oxford University Press, 2019, pp. 1–376 (p. 192) (contends presciently that "*automated processes* have obvious efficiency advantages, *but such processes may not align well (or well at all) with applicable legal requirements that are couched in shades of gray*"). Italics added.

[3117] See: Sanchez-Graells, Albert, "Responsibly Buying Artificial Intelligence: A 'Regulatory Hallucination'", *Current Legal Problems*, Volume 77, 2024, pp. 81–125 (81) ("*borrowing from*

Besides, the EU AI Act has bluntly failed to address pressing challenges facing Large Language Models.

§§ For instance, the EU AI Act has shied away from regulating sizzling hot topics like: **i)** «catastrophic overtraining»[3118] of Large Language Models that renders the latter much harder to fine-tune; **ii)** the rapid iteration of Large Language Models and the extent to which the latter can significantly propel forward the evolution of Artificial Intelligence-embedded technologies towards an unprecedented Artificial General Intelligence (AGI) with the usage of Large Language Models for financial reasoning through reinforcement machine learning (v.g. Fin R-1 that outperforms DeepSeek) looming large in the discussion[3119]; **iii)** the extent to which Large

---

the description of AI 'hallucinations' as plausible but incorrect answers given with high confidence by AI systems, I argue that this is a 'regulatory hallucination': an incorrect answer to the challenge of regulating the procurement and use of AI by the public sector. The pretence that public buyers can 'confidently and responsibly procure AI technologies' can generate individual harms and broader negative social effects as the public sector ramps up AI adoption and accumulates a potentially significant stock of AI deployments across all areas of public sector activity"). Italics added.

[3118] Springer, Jacob Mitchell/Sachin Goyal/Kaiyue Wen/Tanishq Kumar/Xiang Yue/Sadhika Malladi/Graham Neubig/Aditi Raghunathan, "Overtrained Language Models Are Harder to Fine-Tune", arXiv:2503.19206v1 [cs.CL] 24 Mar 2025, 2025, pp. 1 and ff ("Large language models are pre-trained on ever growing token budgets under the assumption that better pre-training performance translates to im proved downstream models. In this work, we challenge this assumption and show that extended pre-training can make models harder to fine-tune, leading to degraded final performance. We term this phenomenon catastrophic overtraining. For example, the instruction-tuned OLMo-1B model pre-trained on 3 T tokens leads to over 2% worse performance on multiple standard LLM bench marks than its 2.3 T token counterpart. Through controlled experiments and theoretical analysis, weshowthat catastrophic overtraining arises from a systematic increase in the broad sensitivity of pre-trained parameters to modifications, including but not limited to fine-tuning. Our findings call for a critical reassessment of pre-training design that considers the downstream adaptability of the model.") Italics added.

[3119] Liu, Zhaowei/Xin Guo/Fangqi Lou/Lingfeng Zeng/Jinyi Niu/ZixuanWang/Jiajie Xu/Weige Cai/Ziwei Yang/Xueqian Zhao/Chao Li/Sheng Xu/Dezhi Chen/Yun Chen/Zuo Bai/Liwen Zhang, "Fin-R1: A Large Language Model for Financial Reasoning through Reinforcement Learning", arXiv:2503.16252v1 [cs.CL] 20 Mar 2025, 2025, p. 1 ("Reasoning large language models (LLMs) are rapidly evolving across various domains. However, their capabilities in handling complex financial problems still require in-depth exploration. In this paper, we introduce Fin-R1, a large language model specifically designed for financial reasoning. With a lightweight parameter scale of 7 billion, this model significantly reduces deployment cost while effectively addresses three major financial pain points: fragmented financial data, uncontrollable reasoning logic, and weak business generalization ability. To boost the model's reasoning capability, we first built Fin-R1-Data, a high-quality dataset with around 60,091 complete chains of thought (CoT) for both reasoning and nonreasoning financial scenarios, through a distillation and screening process from multiple authoritative datasets. Then, we perform Supervised Fine-Tuning (SFT) followed by Reinforcement Learning (RL) based on this dataset. This two-stage framework significantly enhances the model's ability to perform complex financial reasoning tasks, enabling more accurate and interpretable decision-making in financial AI applications. *Despite its compact structure with only 7B parameters, Fin-R1 demonstrates outstanding performance in authoritative benchmarks covering multiple financial business scenarios. It achieves an average score of 75.2, securing second place overall and significantly outperforming other large-scale reasoning LLMs in the evaluation. Notably, Fin-R1 is better than DeepSeek-R1- Distill-Llama-70B, demonstrating its efficiency and effectiveness. It achieves the state-of-the-art scores of 85.0 in ConvFinQA and 76.0 in FinQA, which focus on financial*

Language Models' pre-training techniques suffice to attain overall accuracy or its perceived insufficiency can be smoothed out at the post-training stage,[3120] **iv**) whether and to what extent normalization layers are essential in modern neural networks, with a sharper focus on Large Language Models[3121]; **v**) the quality benchmark against which the overall performance of Large Language Models must be gauged[3122] to instil trustworthiness onto service users[3123]; **vi**) whether and to what extent Large Language

---

reasoning. In real-world applications, Fin-R1 has demonstrated strong automated reasoning and decision-making abilities in areas like financial compliance and robo-advisory, providing efficient solutions to long-standing financial industry challenges"). Italics added.

[3120] Kumar, Komal/Tajamul Ashraf/Omkar Thawakar/Rao Muhammad Anwer/Hisham Cholakkal/ Mubarak Shah/Ming-Hsuan Yang/Phillip H.S. Torr/Fahad Shahbaz Khan/Salman Khan, "LLM Post-Training: A Deep Dive into Reasoning Large Language Models", arXiv:2502.21321v1 [cs.CL] 28 Feb 2025, 2025, p. 1 ("*Large Language Models (LLMs) have transformed the natural language processing landscape and brought to life diverse applications. Pretraining on vast web-scale data has laid the foundation for these models, yet the research community is now increasingly shifting focus toward post-training techniques to achieve further breakthroughs. While pretraining provides a broad linguistic foundation, post-training methods enable LLMs to refine their knowledge, improve reasoning, enhance factual accuracy, and align more effectively with user intents and ethical considerations. Fine-tuning, reinforcement learning, and test-time scaling have emerged as critical strategies for optimizing LLMs performance, ensuring robustness, and improving adaptability across various real-world tasks. This survey provides a systematic exploration of post-training methodologies, analyzing their role in refining LLMs beyond pretraining, addressing key challenges such as catastrophic forgetting, reward hacking, and inference-time trade-offs. We highlight emerging directions in model alignment, scalable adaptation, and inference-time reasoning, and outline future research directions. We also provide a public repository to continually track developments in this fast-evolving field*"). Italics added.

[3121] Zhu, Jiachen Zhu/Xinlei Chen/Kaiming He/Yann LeCun/Zhuang Liu, "Transformers without Normalization", arXiv:2503.10622v1 [cs.LG] 13 Mar 2025, 2025, p. 1 ("*Normalization layers are ubiquitous in modern neural networks and have long been considered essential. This work demonstrates that Transformers without normalization can achieve the same or better performance using a remarkably simple technique. We introduce Dynamic Tanh (DyT), an element-wise operation DyT(x) = tanh(αx), as a drop-in replacement for normalization layers in Transformers.* DyT is inspired by the observation that layer normalization in Transformers often produces tanh-like, S-shaped input–output mappings. By incorporating DyT, Transformers without normalization can match or exceed the performance of their normalized counterparts, mostly without hyperparameter tuning. *We validate the effectiveness of Transformers with DyT across diverse settings, ranging from recognition to generation, supervised to self-supervised learning, and computer vision to language models. These findings challenge the conventional understanding that normalization layers are indispensable in modern neural networks, and offer new insights into their role in deep networks*"). Italics added.

[3122] Yehudai, Asaf/Lilach Eden/Alan Li/Guy Uziel/Yilun Zhao/Roy Bar-Haim/Arman Cohan/ Michal Shmueli-Scheuer, "Survey on Evaluation of LLM-based Agents" arXiv:2503.16416v1 [cs.AI] 20 Mar 2025, 2025, p. 1 ("*The emergence of LLM-based agents represents a paradigm shift in AI, enabling autonomous systems to plan, reason, use tools, and maintain memory while interacting with dynamic environments. This paper provides the first comprehensive survey of evaluation methodologies for these increasingly capable agents. We systematically analyze evaluation benchmarks and frameworks across four critical dimensions: (1) fundamental agent capabilities, including planning, tool use, self-reflection, and memory; (2) application specific benchmarks for web, software engineering, scientific, and conversational agents; (3) benchmarks for generalist agents; and (4) frameworks for evaluating agents. Our analysis reveals emerging trends, including a shift toward more realistic, challenging evaluations with continuously updated benchmarks.* We

Models can be deployed to ferret out Deceptive Patterns (DP)[3124] embedded in user interface designs intentionally created to prime users into unintended decisions[3125]; **vii)** the real-world impact[3126] arising out of the deployment of Large Language Models[3127] and the extent to which is beneficial to the overall betterment of society; **viii)** the dire need to create an atlas of AI-risks[3128] to guide Large Language Models'

---

also identify critical gaps that future research must address—particularly in assessing cost efficiency, safety, and robustness, and in developing fine-grained, and scalable evaluation methods. This survey maps the rapidly evolving landscape of agent evaluation, reveals the emerging trends in the field, identifies current limitations, and proposes directions for future research"). Italics added.

[3123] Phan, Long et al., "Humanity's Last Exam" arXiv:2501.14249v5 [cs.LG] 21 Feb 2025, 2025, p. 3 ("*Benchmarks are important tools for tracking the rapid advancements in large language model (LLM) capabilities. However, benchmarks are not keeping pace in difficulty: LLMs now achieve over 90% accuracy on popular benchmarks like MMLU, limiting informed measurement of state-of-the-art LLM capabilities. In response, we introduce HUMANITY'S LAST EXAM (HLE), a multi-modal bench mark at the frontier of human knowledge, designed to be the final closed-ended academic benchmark of its kind with broad subject coverage.* HLE consists of 2700 questions across dozens of subjects, including mathematics, humanities, and the natural sciences. *HLE is developed globally by subject-matter experts and consists of multiple-choice and short-answer questions suitable for automated grading. Each question has a known solution that is unambiguous and easily verifiable, but cannot be quickly answered* via *internet retrieval. State-of-the-art LLMs demonstrate low accuracy and calibration on HLE, highlighting a significant gap between current LLM capabilities and the expert human frontier on closed-ended academic questions. To inform research and policymaking upon a clear understanding of model capabilities, we publicly release HLE*"). Italics added.

[3124] But see: Part III, Chap. 3, Sects. 3.1.5.4–3.1.5.4.1.1 of this book (on Critical Artificial Intelligence Studies, with a sharper focus on the deceptive patterns evinced by Large Language Models, which has lent urgency to concerns about the trustworthiness and reliability of these tools).

[3125] Shi, Zewei et al., 50 Shades of Deceptive Patterns: A Unified Taxonomy, Multimodal Detection, and Security Implications", arXiv:2501.13351v1 [cs.CR] 23 Jan 2025, 2025, p. 1 ("*Deceptive patterns (DPs) are user interface designs deliberately crafted to manipulate users into unintended decisions, often by exploiting cognitive biases for the benefit of companies or services.* While numerous studies have explored ways *to identify these deceptive patterns, many existing solutions require significant human intervention and struggle to keep pace with the evolving nature of deceptive designs. To address these challenges,* we expanded the deceptive pattern taxonomy from security and privacy perspec tives, refining its categories and scope. *We created a comprehensive dataset of deceptive patterns by integrating existing small-scale datasets with new samples, resulting in 6725 images and 10,421 DP instances from mobile apps and websites. We then developed DP Guard, a novel automatic tool leveraging commercial multimodal large language models (MLLMs) for deceptive pattern detection. Ex perimental results show that DPGuard outperforms state-of-the-art methods.* Finally, we conducted an extensive empirical evaluation on 2000 popular mobile apps and websites, *revealing that 23.61% of mobile screenshots and 47.27% of website screenshots feature at least one deceptive pattern instance. Through four unexplored case studies that inform security implications, we highlight the critical importance of the unified taxonomy in addressing the growing challenges of Internet deception*"). Italics added.

[3126] See also: AI Action Summit, International AI Safety Report, *The International Scientific Report on the Safety of Advanced AI*, January 2025, p. 12 ("so *far there is no evidence yet about o3's real world impacts,* and no information to confirm nor rule out *major novel and/or immediate risks*"). Italics added.

[3127] Cheng, Jingwen/Kshitish Ghate/Wenyue Hua/William Yang Wang/Hong Shen/Fei Fang, "REALM: A Dataset of Real-World LLM Use Cases" arXiv:2503.18792v1 [cs.HC] 24 Mar 2025, 2025, p. 1 ("*Large Language Models (LLMs), such as the GPT series, have driven significant*

service users; **ix**) whether and to what extent Large Language Models (e.g. AgentRxiv[3129]) should be granted access to classified information that may be later used to carry its training out; and **x**) amongst many other legal loopholes[3130] timely identified by renowned European scholars.

---

industrial applications, leading to economic and societal transformations. However, a comprehensive understanding of their real-world applications remains limited. To address this, we introduce REALM, a dataset of over 94,000 LLM use cases collected from Reddit and news articles. REALM captures two key dimensions: the diverse applications of LLMs and the demographics of their users. *It categorizes LLM applications and explores how users' occupations relate to the types of applications they use. By integrating real-world data, REALM offers insights into LLM adoption across different domains, providing a foundation for future research on their evolving societal roles.*") Italics added.

3128 Edyta Bogucka/Sanja Scêpanovic/Daniele Quercia, "Atlas of AI Risks: Enhancing Public Understanding of AI Risks", arXiv:2502.05324v1 [cs.HC] 7 Feb 2025, 2025, p. 1 ("*The prevailing methodologies for visualizing AI risks have focused on technical issues such as data biases and model in accuracies, often overlooking broader societal risks like job loss and surveillance. Moreover, these visualizations are typically designed for tech-savvy individuals, neglecting those with limited technical skills. To address these challenges, we propose the Atlas of AI Risks—a narrative-style tool de signed to map the broad risks associated with various AI technologies in a way that is understandable to non-technical individuals as well.* To both develop and evaluate this tool, we conducted two crowdsourcing studies. The first, involving 40 participants, identified the design requirements for visualizing AI risks for decision-making and guided the development of the Atlas. The second study, with 140 participants reflecting the US population in terms of age, sex, and ethnicity, assessed the usability and aesthetics of the Atlas to ensure it met those requirements. Using facial recognition technology as a case study, we found that the Atlas is more user friendly than a baseline visualization, with a more classic and expressive aesthetic, and is more effective in presenting a balanced assessment of the risks and benefits of facial recognition. *Finally, we discuss how our design choices make the Atlas adaptable for broader use, allowing it to generalize across the diverse range of technology applications represented in a database that reports various AI incidents*"). Italics added. See also: AI Action Summit, *International AI Safety Report, The International Scientific Report on the Safety of Advanced AI*, January 2025, p. 12 ("*The trends evidenced by o3 could have profound implications for AI risks. Advances in science and programming capabilities have previously generated more evidence for risks such as cyber and biological attacks.* The o3 results are also relevant to potential labour market impacts, loss of control risk, and energy use among others. *But o3's capabilities could also be used to help protect against malfunctions and malicious uses. Overall, the risk assessments in this report should be read with the understanding that AI has gained capabilities since the report was written*"). Italics added.

3129 Schmidgall, Samuel/Moor, Michael, "AgentRxiv: Towards Collaborative Autonomous Research", arXiv:2503.18102v1 [cs.AI] 23 Mar 2025, 2025, p. 1 ("*Progress in scientific discovery is rarely the result of a single "Eureka" moment, but is rather the product of hundreds of scientists incrementally working together toward a common goal. While existing agent workflows are capable of producing research autonomously, they do so in isolation, without the ability to continuously improve upon prior research results. To address these challenges, we introduce AgentRxiv—a framework that lets LLM agent laboratories upload and retrieve reports from a shared preprint server in order to collaborate, share insights, and iteratively build on each other's research.* We task agent laboratories to develop new reasoning and prompting techniques and find that agents with access to their prior research achieve higher performance improvements compared to agents operating in isolation (11.4% relative improvement over baseline on MATH-500). *We find that the best performing strategy generalizes to benchmarks in other domains (improving on average by 3.3%). Multiple agent laboratories sharing research through AgentRxiv are able to work together towards a common goal, progressing more rapidly than isolated laboratories, achieving higher overall accuracy (13.7% relative improvement over baseline on MATH-500). These findings suggest that*

§§ Relatedly, and regarding *prompt engineering*,[3131] the EU AI Act has equally fallen short of tackling head-on the sweltering challenge of **«token noise»**, against the backdrop of which even small changes in wording can have enormous effects[3132] on outputs offered by LLM systems.[3133] As a result, one cannot be completely sure whether and to what extent the variations in *prompt engineering* result arise from the significant changes in prompt content or simply from the model's stochastic behaviour.[3134]

§§ Notwithstanding, the EU AI Act has nevertheless furnished baselines to stave off, or avert, a tiny part of the hideous effects arisen from AI hallucinations.[3135] In many ways, the EU Act is a legal framework to behold, inspire and rally around.

---

autonomous agents may play a role in designing future AI systems alongside humans. We hope that AgentRxiv allows agents to collaborate toward research goals and enables researchers to accelerate discovery"). Italics added.

[3130] See: Watcher, Sandra, "Limitations and Loopholes in the EU AI Act and AI Liability Directives: What This Means for the European Union, the United States, and Beyond", *Yale Journal of Law & Technology*, Volume 26, Issue 3, 2024, pp. 671–672 ("*Predictive and generative artificial intelligence (AI) have both become integral parts of our lives through their use in making highly impactful decisions.* AI systems are already deployed widely—for example, in employment, healthcare, insurance, finance, education, public administration, and criminal justice. Yet severe ethical issues, such as bias and discrimination, privacy invasiveness, opaqueness, and environmental costs of these systems, are well known. *Generative AI (GAI) creates hallucinations and inaccurate or harmful information, which can lead to misinformation, disinformation, and the erosion of scientific knowledge. The Artificial Intelligence Act (AIA), Product Liability Directive, and the Artificial Intelligence Liability Directive reflect Europe's attempt to curb some of these issues. With the legal reach of these policies going far beyond Europe, their impact on the United States and the rest of the world cannot be overstated.* In this Essay, I show how the strong lobbying efforts of big tech companies and member states were unfortunately *able to water down much of the AIA. An overreliance on self-regulation, self-certification, weak oversight and investigatory mechanisms, and far-reaching exceptions for both the public and private sectors are the product of this lobbying. Next, I reveal the similar enforcement limitations of the liability frameworks, which focus on material harm while ignoring harm that is immaterial, monetary, and societal, such as bias, hallucinations, and financial losses due to faulty AI products. Lastly, I explore how these loopholes can be closed to create a framework that effectively guards against novel risks caused by AI in the European Union, the United States, and beyond*"). Italics added.

[3131] See: Mckinsey & Co (Sept. 2023), https://www.mckinsey.com/featured-insights/mckinsey-explainers/what-is-prompt-engineering; [https://perma.cc/XZC2-6HMJ] ("Prompt engineering is the practice of designing inputs for generative AI tools that will produce optimal outputs").

[3132] Posner, Eric A./Saran, Shivam, "Judge AI: Assessing Large Language Models in Judicial Decision-Making", *The University of Chicago, Coase-Sandor Institute for Law and Economics, The Law School, Coase-Sandor Institute for Law and Economics Research Paper n. ° 25–03*, January 2025, 2025, pp. 1–41 (20).

[3133] Posner, Eric A./Saran, Shivam, "Judge AI: Assessing Large Language Models in Judicial Decision-Making", *cit.*, pp. 1–41 (20).

[3134] Posner, Eric A./Saran, Shivam, "Judge AI: Assessing Large Language Models in Judicial Decision-Making", *cit.*, pp. 1–41 (20).

[3135] See: Part III, Chap. 3, Sects. 3.1.5.6–3.1.5.6.1 of this book (on Critical Artificial Intelligence Studies, with a sharper focus on the harmful effects of Large Language Models 'medical hallucinations that are poised to undermine its overall trustworthiness). See also: Part IV, This chapter, Sect. 4.1.9.5 of this book (on a cluster of case law that deals with the issue of ChatGPT's hallucinations and its consequences in legal settings). See: Part III, Chap. 3, Sects. 3.1.5.6–3.1.5.6.1 of this

All in all, it arguably amounts to a frame of reference of which the United States of America should be cognizant of and China should not lose sight of.

§§ Bafflingly, though, the United States of America are hitherto bereft of an able-bodied, robust, full-fledged, comprehensive, and thoroughgoing federal legislation to regulate/govern Artificial Intelligence-embedded technologies, or specifically limit or forbid certain uses.[3136] Notwithstanding, there are some piecemeal federal laws that take into account small-scaled concerns on Artificial Intelligence-embedded technologies. Amongst which stands the Federal Aviation Administrative Reauthorizing Act, the National Artificial Intelligence Initiative Act of 2020, or the White House Executive Order on Artificial Intelligence.[3137]

§§ The lack of a thoroughgoing federal law timely enacted by the Congress has engendered a legislative void that states like Colorado, Utah and Tennessee were unwittingly compelled to plug, with the striking similarities with EU AI Act looming large in those Acts.[3138] Tellingly, Colorado's Act is tantamount to the EU AI Act in its risk-based stance. Similarly, the Utah's Act comprises identical disclosure requirements whenever Generative Artificial Intelligence functionally engaged with a human being.[3139]

§§ Compellingly, the rate and pace at which Artificial Intelligence-embedded technologies are unfolding is applying pressure on the United States of America to timely enact sweeping federal regulation[3140] to govern this sizzling hot topic. Notably, by leaving regulation to the sole and square state's discretion, and the industry itself, the slew of legal issues arising out conflicts of interests, self-governance, and compliance begin to mount, thereby giving rise to greater legal problems that run counter to a sought-after progress towards regulatory cohesion.[3141]

book (on Critical Artificial Intelligence Studies, with a sharper focus on the harmful effects of Large Language Models 'medical hallucinations that are poised to undermine its overall trustworthiness). See: Part III, Chap. 3, Sect. 3.1.5.3 of this book (on the "house of fabricated lies" and the usage of Generative Artificial Intelligence as a *floating signifier* that will stand ready to be galvanize power in a given direction, including, but not limited to, against *socially undesirables* that may find themselves at odds, or at loggerheads, with whoever controls Artificial Intelligence).

3136 Laallam, Abla, "Hallucinations: Your AI Might Be Affected...," *Hofstra JIBL Blog: Journal of International Business and Law*, 2025, passim, available at: https://www.hofstrajibl.org/2025/01/hallucinations-your-ai-might-be-affected/ (access: 10.01.2025).

3137 Laallam, Abla, "Hallucinations: Your AI Might Be Affected...," *Hofstra JIBL Blog: Journal of International Business and Law*, 2025, passim, available at: https://www.hofstrajibl.org/2025/01/hallucinations-your-ai-might-be-affected/ (access: 10.01.2025).

3138 Laallam, Abla, "Hallucinations: Your AI Might Be Affected...," *Hofstra JIBL Blog: Journal of International Business and Law*, 2025, passim, available at: https://www.hofstrajibl.org/2025/01/hallucinations-your-ai-might-be-affected/ (access: 10.01.2025).

3139 Laallam, Abla, "Hallucinations: Your AI Might Be Affected...," *Hofstra JIBL Blog: Journal of International Business and Law*, 2025, passim, available at: https://www.hofstrajibl.org/2025/01/hallucinations-your-ai-might-be-affected/ (access: 10.01.2025).

3140 Laallam, Abla, "Hallucinations: Your AI Might Be Affected...," *Hofstra JIBL Blog: Journal of International Business and Law*, 2025, passim, available at: https://www.hofstrajibl.org/2025/01/hallucinations-your-ai-might-be-affected/ (access: 10.01.2025).

§§ Last but not least, China could also seek inspiration on the regulatory framework laid down by the European Union since the set of piecemeal rules timely outlined (Interim Measures for the Management of Generative AI Services («the Measures»)[3142] will not suffice[3143] to seamlessly navigate the uncharted territory of Generative Artificial Intelligence.[3144]

§§ It is true that China is trying to strike a delicate balance between innovation and safety, but truer still the unfettered mushrooming of generative AI applications for public consumption, comprising Baidu's «Wenxin Yiyuan,» Huawei's

---

3141 Laallam, Abla, "Hallucinations: Your AI Might Be Affected...," *Hofstra JIBL Blog: Journal of International Business and Law*, 2025, passim, available at: https://www.hofstrajibl.org/2025/01/hallucinations-your-ai-might-be-affected/ (access: 10.01.2025).

3142 Zou, Mimi/Zhang, Lu, "Navigating China's regulatory approach to generative artificial intelligence and large language models", *Cambridge Forum on AI: Law and Governance*, 1, e8, 2025, pp. 1–16 (1) ("*The rapid development of generative artificial intelligence (AI) systems, particularly those fuelled by increasingly advanced large language models, has raised concerns of their potential risks among policymakers globally. In July 2023, Chinese regulators enacted the Interim Measures for the Management of Generative AI Services ("the Measures"). The Measures aim to mitigate various risks associated with public facing generative AI services, particularly those concerning information content safety and security. China's approach to regulating AI to date has sought to address the risks associated with rapidly advancing AI technologies while fostering innovation and development.* Tensions between these policy objectives are reflected in the provisions of the Measures. *As Beijing moves towards establishing a comprehensive legal framework for AI governance, there will be growing interest in how China's approach may influence AI governance and regulation at a global level*"). Italics added.

3143 Zou, Mimi/Zhang, Lu, "Navigating China's regulatory approach to generative artificial intelligence and large language models", *cit.*, pp. 1–16 (3) ("*At the time of writing, China has not established a more comprehensive legislative framework on AI. Policymakers have instead focused on administrative regulations that target specific AI developments or applications considered to be "riskier" in terms of security or safety.* Besides the Measures, China's AI regulations include the Provisions on the Management of Algorithmic Recommendations in Internet Information Services in ("Algorithmic Recommendations Provisions") and the Regulations on the Deep Synthesis Management of Internet Information Service ("Deep Synthesis Regulations"), *both introduced by the CAC with a range of other government authorities in 2021 and 2022 respectively. A common thread running through these regulations is their emphasis on information and content safety and security risks arising from AI*"). Italics added.

3144 Zou, Mimi/Zhang, Lu, "Navigating China's regulatory approach to generative artificial intelligence and large language models", *cit.*, pp. 1–16 (15) ("*The Measures focus on information content security risks arising from applications of generative AI for the public. Our analysis has shed light on the primary obligations assigned to service providers. While these Measures establish some broad principles and rules for regulating generative AI, a more intricate regulatory framework of "hard" and "soft" law instruments will be essential for effective implementation.* A more nuanced stance to regulating the diverse actors and activities, *such as a clearer delineation of user liability and offering certain exemptions from liability for service providers, requires further consideration by policymakers, especially if China is heading towards a more comprehensive AI legal framework. The rapid advancements in generative AI pose universal regulatory challenges.* Globally, countries are navigating new territory when it comes to coordinating a cohesive approach. *China's path in international AI cooperation and competition remains uncertain*"). Italics added.

«Pangu,» Tencent's «Hunyuan Assistant,» Alibaba's «Tongyi Qianwen,» SenseTime's «Ririxin» and ByteDance's «Dou Bao»[3145] calls for the creation of a thoroughgoing framework amenable to deal with the pressing challenges arisen from an ever-evolving Generative Artificial Intelligence that never ceases to amaze.

4.1.10 Setting the Stage: How Biased Algorithmic Risk Assessment Kneecaps Algorithmic Fairness in a Myriad of Domains

§§ Artificial intelligence-embedded technologies have enjoyed global blossoming. Artificial Intelligence has been accordingly received as lightning bolt of great significance. A feast of deftly crafted rules to regulate Artificial Intelligence-embedded technologies[3146] were timely created,[3147] which has nonetheless caused grievances[3148] to swell.[3149]

[3145] Zou, Mimi/Zhang, Lu, "Navigating China's regulatory approach to generative artificial intelligence and large language models", *cit.*, pp. 1–16 (1).

[3146] See: Floridi, Luciano, "The onlife manifesto: being human in a hyperconnected era", *Onlife Manifesto Being Human in a Hyperconnected Era*, 2015, https://doi.org/10.1007/978-3-319-04093-6; Floridi, Luciano, "Translating principles into practices of digital ethics: five risks of being unethical", *Philosophy and Technology*, 322 (32), 2019, pp. 185–193; Fry, H, *Hello world: being human in the age of algorithms*, London, Penguin Random House, 2018 (on the dire need to create a frame of reference to secure digital ethics amidst concerns with the unbridled growth of Artificial Intelligence).

[3147] See: Tegmark, Max, *Life 3.0: Being Human in the Age of Artificial Intelligence*. New York: Knopf, 2018, pp. 1–384 (pp. 24 and ff) (charts the path ahead for a wide range of intelligences, including artificial intelligence in the digital age). There is a handful of authors that wonder if artificial intelligence can mimic not only human intelligence but, and foremost, human behaviour. Amongst whom stands: Russel, Stuart, Norvig, Peter, *Artificial Intelligence: A Modern Approach*. London: United Kingdom, Pearson, 2018, passim; Boden, Margaret A., *Artificial Intelligence: A Very Short Introduction*. Oxford: Oxford University Press, 2018, passim.

[3148] See: Deeks, Ahsley, "Secret Reason-Giving", *Yale Law Journal*, Volume 129, 2019, passim; Katyal, Sonia K, "The Paradox of Source Code Secrecy", *Cornell Law Review*, Volume 104, 2019, pp. 1183–1236; Wexler, Rebecca, "Life, Liberty, and Trade Secrets: Intellectual Property in the Criminal Justice System", *Stanford Law Review*, Volume 70, 2018, pp. 1343 and ff; Okidegbe, Ngozi, "The Democratizing Potential of Algorithms?", *Connecticut Law Review*, Volume 54, 2021, passim (on the sweltering challenges posed by source code secrecy and extent to which it impairs fairness).

[3149] Artificial intelligence, like everything else, is not without sizable drawbacks and shortcomings though. The most menacing of which happens to be the flawed or biased algorithms, which are bound to mar a sought-after bias-free decision making in dispute resolution. See: Sternlight, Jean, "Pouring a Little Psychological Cold Water on Online Dispute Resolution", *Journal of Dispute Resolution*, 1, 2020, pp. 23 ff (raises awareness to the perils of biased algorithms on online dispute resolution). Converging: Schmitz, Amy, "Expanding Access to Remedies Through E-Court Initiatives", *Buffalo Law Review*, Volume 67, 2019, pp. 90–100 (showing concerns that e-courts might be premising their decisions on flawed and bigoted algorithms). Which is something to be frowned upon. Why? Most likely, flawed or biased algorithms will deepen the chasm between rich and poor.

§§ Whilst Artificial intelligence-embedded technologies have been lavished unfettered praise,[3150] members of racialized communities tend to nonetheless harbour the propensity to distrust technology since the latter is often deployed to further chastise them in a variety of domains.[3151] Their deep-seated concerns are neither unwarranted nor uncalled for.

See: Eubanks, Virginia, *Automating Inequality: How High-Tech Tools Profile, Police and Punish the Poor*. New York: St. Martin's Press, 2018, 1–272 (1 ff and passim) (coining the expression «automating inequality» to vividly portray the downsides of using high-technology to compound the yawning gap between rich and poor against the backdrop of biased algorithms). See also: Pasquale, Frank, *The Black Box Society: The Secret Algorithms that Control Money and Information*. Cambridge, Massachusetts: Harvard University Press, 2015, 1–320 (8–10 and passim) (noting that biased algorithms, which have underlying discrimination problems, contribute exponentially to further social biases. His most intriguing claim is that such biased algorithms have been incorporated/etched in the bulk of the corporations' informatic system, to the detriment of human kind in an overarching sense); Roth, Andrea, "Machine Testimony", *Yale Law Journal*, Volume 126, 2017, pp. 1972 and ff and passim.

[3150] Extolling the functional abilities of ChatGPT to perform legal tasks: Gamm, Grant M., "Artificial Intelligence and the Practice of Law: A Chat With ChatGPT", *Saint Louis University Law Journal*, Volume 68, 2024, pp. 605–606 ("*with an attorney using the tool in this way, they can more effectively prepare for events in a case, such as cross-examination, and can use this summation as a reference during the trial or with other members of the legal team.* An attorney who effectively utilizes ChatGPT can optimize their time and energy on more strategic and high-value tasks. ChatGPT can aid attorneys in proofreading their work, offering suggestions on complex issues, and organizing information. *This tool can be applied in any area of law, and its use is likely to significantly enhance the attorney's efficiency and productivity. Additionally, ChatGPT can provide quick and accurate answers to legal questions, enabling attorneys to make decisions with confidence.* By automating repetitive tasks, ChatGPT frees up time for the attorney to focus on other important aspects of their work. *ChatGPT can also help attorneys communicate more effectively with clients, other attorneys, and the court, resulting in a more streamlined and efficient legal process*"). Italics added.

[3151] See: Part IV, This chapter, Sects. 4.1.4–4.1.4.2.1 of this book (on mortgage redlining). See: Part IV, This chapter, Sects. 4.1.2–4.1.4.3 of this book (on algorithmic credit scoring, consumer racism and credit card redlining). See: Part IV, This chapter, Sects. 4.1.4–4.1.4.2.3 of this book (on algorithmic redlining). See: Part IV, This chapter, Sect. 4.1.4.3 of this book (on "algorithmic redliking"). See: Part IV, This chapter, Sect. 4.1.3 of this book (on algorithmic prime-lining). See: Part IV, This chapter, Sects. 4.1.1–4.1.1.1 of this book (on biased predictive policing). See also: *Tech, Bias and Housing Initiative, the Promise and Perils of Residential Proptech, Year 1, Research Summary Report, April 2023, TechEquity Collaborative*, p. 5 available at: https://techequity.us/wp-content/uploads/2023/04/TBHI-Y1-Research-Summary-Report.pdf (28.11.2024). ("*Residential Proptech also has the potential to exacerbate the bias inherent in our housing system. Its rise is due, in part, to the desperation felt by average home seekers. With a severely constrained housing supply, companies offering an easier pathway to homeownership may exploit communities that have been harmed by housing discrimination in the past. Opaque algorithms incorporate biased data into their decision-making processes, making it harder to enforce fair housing laws.* (....) *As unprecedented capital investment flows into this space, venture-backed companies' winner-take-all approach to growth has the potential to exacerbate inequality rather than combat it*"). Italics added. See: Part IV, This chapter, Sects. 4.1.4–4.1.4.2.3 of this book.

§§ Historically, congeries of racially motivated laws[3152] have been enacted under the veneer of racial equality. However, at the shallowest level, those racially motivated laws[3153] sought to bolster White supremacy in the first place.[3154]

§§ Time went by, so too did the gallant efforts to attain a mirific racial equality[3155] through the lens of facially neutral[3156] algorithms.[3157] Yet, at its core, the deployment of seemingly benign technology[3158] sought, and still seeks,[3159] to further chastise racialized people (e.g. Black folks) under a patina of objectivity,[3160] thereby

---

[3152] See: Perea, Juan F., "Doctrines of Delusion: How the History of the G.I. Bill and Other Inconvenient Truths Undermind the Supreme Court's Affirmative Action Jurisprudence", *University of Pittsburgh Law Review*, Volume 75, 1995, pp. 583, 586–89 (establishes a liaison between Jim Crow laws, the G.I. Bill, and the Social Security Act and White supremacy); See: Milligan, Joy, "Protecting Disfavored Minorities: Towards Institutional Realism", *UCLA Law Review*, Volume 63, 2016, pp. 894, pp. 918–21 (shedding a keen light on racial inequality in U.S. Department of Agriculture farm assistance).

[3153] Katznelson, Ira, *When Affirmative Action Was White: An Untold History of Racial Inequality in Twentieth-Century America*, New York, W. W. Norton & Company; Reprint edition (August 17, 2006), 2006, pp. 1–272 ("*Ira Katznelson fundamentally recasts our understanding of twentieth-century American history and demonstrates that all the key programs passed during the New Deal and Fair Deal era of the 1930s and 1940s were created in a deeply discriminatory manner. Through mechanisms designed by Southern Democrats that specifically excluded maids and farm workers, the gap between blacks and whites actually widened despite postwar prosperity*"). Italics added. This book pores over the impact of several racially motivated laws—Social Security Act, G: I. Bill, and labour laws implementing unemployment stipends, minimum wages, and union protection—in the history of United States of America).

[3154] See: Robinson, Reginald Leamon, "The Racial Limits of the Fair Housing Act: The Intersection of Dominant White Images, the Violence of Neighbourhood Purity, and the Master Narrative of Black Inferiority", *William & Mary Law Review*, Volume 37, 1995, pp. 69, 71–74 (establishes a connection between the failures of the FHA and White supremacy). But see: Wormser, Richard, *The Rise and Fall of Jim Crow*, Manhattan, New York City, St Martin's Press, 2014, pp. 1–222 ("*White supremacy prevailed, but it did not destroy the spirit of the black community*"). Italics added.

[3155] But see: Barocas, Solon/Selbst, Andrew D., "Big Data's Disparate Impact", *California Law Review*, Volume 104, 2016, pp. 671–682 (discussing how data is often flawed, rigged, incomplete, imperfect and therefore algorithms inherit the prejudice of the original decision makers). But see: Citron, Danielle Keats/Pasquale, Frank, "The Scored Society: Due Process for Automated Predictions", *Washington Law Review*, Volume 89, 2014, pp. 1, 4–5 (highlighting how human beings programming automated systems is directly conducive to, and leads, to fundamentally inaccurate results since the source code, predictive algorithms and datasets may encompass human biases which, in turn, have a disparate impact on historically disadvantaged groups).

[3156] But see: Hurley, Mikella/Adebayo, Julius, "Credit Scoring in the Era of Big Data", *Yale Journal of Law and Technology*, Volume 18, 2016, p. 149 ("*these tools may furthermore obscure discriminatory and subjective lending policies behind a single "objective" score* (...) *sophisticated algorithms may combine facially neutral data points and treat them as proxies for immutable characteristics such as race or gender, thereby circumventing existing non-discrimination laws and systematically denying credit access to certain groups. Finally, big-data tools may allow online payday lenders to target the most vulnerable consumers and lure them into debt traps*"). Italics added. But see also: Bornstein, Stepanhie, "Antidiscriminatory Algorithms", *Alabama Law Review*, Volume 70, 2018, pp. 519, 524–528 (contending, however, that the tagged "facially neutral" algorithms producing discriminatory outcomes should be quashed). See also: Farina, M./Lavazza, A., *Philosophy, expertise, and the myth of neutrality*, Routledge Studies in Contemporary Philosophy, London, Routledge, 2024.

perpetuating racial[3161] inequalities[3162] while ushering in the age of *Algorithmic Dictatorship*.

§§ Compellingly, the deployment of technology is wrapped in opaqueness[3163] insofar the latter is underpinned by inscrutable[3164] concepts,[3165] such as *trust in*

3157 But see: Allen, James, "The Color of Algorithms: An Analysis and Proposed Research Agenda Deterring Algorithmic Redlining", *Fordham Urban Law Journal*, Volume 46, 2019, pp. 219–234 (229–234) (discussing how historical mortgage redlining greatly swayed modern algorithms generated by massive batches of datasets that consist of decades of information built on exclusion and racial discrimination in the purview of financing, marketing, and housing). See: Part IV, This chapter, Sects. 4.1.4–4.1.4.2.3 of this book.

3158 Cohen, Julien E., *Between Truth and Power: The Legal Constructions of Informational Capitalism*. Oxford: Oxford University Press, 2019, pp. 1–376 (p. 192) (contends presciently that "*automated processes* have obvious efficiency advantages, *but such processes may not align well (or well at all) with applicable legal requirements that are couched in shades of gray*"). Italics added.

3159 See: Bartlett, Robert/Morse, Adair/Wallace, Nancy/Stanton, Richard, "Algorithmic Discrimination and Input Accountability Under the Civil Rights Acts", *Berkeley Technology Law Journal*, Volume 36, 2021, pp. 675–736 (675) ("*the disproportionate burden of COVID-19 among communities of color and a necessary renewed attention to racial inequalities have lent new urgency* to concerns that *algorithmic decision-making* can lead to unintentional discrimination against members of historically marginalized groups"). Italics added.

3160 But see: Benjamin, Ruha, *Race After Technology: Abolitionist Tools for the New Jim Code*, New York, Polity, 2019, pp. 1–172 (7) (discussing that Artificial Intelligence-embedded technologies are viewed as iron-clad tools of objectivity and devoid of any biases whatsoever). Ruha Benjamin accordingly contends that "the employment of new technologies that reflect and reproduce existing inequities but that are promoted and perceived as more objective or progressive than the discriminatory systems of a previous era"). This false scent of neutrality impairs, and impacts, procedural justice. See: Tyler, Tom R., "The Psychology of Procedural Justice: A Test of the Group-Value Model", *Journal of Personality and Social Psychology*, Volume 57, 1989, p. 830 (reports that in any procedure "several non-control issues—the *neutrality* of the decision-making procedure, trust in the 3rd party, and the information the experience communicates about social standing—influence both procedural preferences and judgments of procedural justice").

3161 See: Citron, Danielle Keats/Pasquale, Frank A., "The Scored Society: Due Process for Automated Predictions", *Washington Law Review*, Volume 89, 2014, pp. 1–34 (arguing that "[a]*dvocates applaud the removal of human beings and their flaws from the assessment process*," but arguing that bias remains "[*b*]*ecause human beings program predictive algorithms, their biases and values are embedded into the software's instructions*"). Italics added. See: Part IV, This chapter, Sects. 4.1.4–4.1.4.2.3 of this book.

3162 But see: O'Neil, Cathy, *Weapons of Math Destruction. How Big Data Increases Inequality and Threatens Democracy*, London, Penguin Random House, 2016, passim (showing how algorithms utilized in modern societies are amenable to perpetuate racial discrimination, partially through perpetuation of social disadvantage and wealth divides).

3163 See: Scherer, Matthew U., "Regulating Artificial Intelligence Systems: Risks, Challenges, Competencies, and Strategies", *Harvard Journal of Law and Technology*, Volume 29, 2016, pp. 353–369 (frames the crippling problem of opacity as "the possibility that the inner workings of an AI system may be kept secret and may not be susceptible to reverse engineering").

science[3166] and *trust in numbers*,[3167] which, in turn, lends itself to a facade to conceal the propelling force behind it: *systemic racism*.[3168] Two bodies of empirical evidence lend weight, and add plausibility, to this main contention. More on this further down this essay.[3169]

§§ Put it bluntly, science-based approach to technology amounts to nothing but to a floating signifier that, deep down, endeavours to reify, reinforce, amplify, and further compound racial inequities while upholding the central tenets of White[3170] privilege.[3171]

§§ Most importantly, and more in tune with the overriding goal to further compound racial inequalities from which it was borne,[3172] biased algorithmic risk assessment draws on the concept of disparate impact[3173] on member of racialized communities.[3174]

3164 See: Citron, Danielle K., "Technological Due Process", *Washington University Law Review*, Volume 85, 2008, pp. 1249–1253 ("Computer programs seamlessly combine rulemaking and individual adjudications without the critical procedural protections owed either of them").

3165 See: Karnow, Curtis E. A., "The Opinion of Machines", *The Cambridge Handbook of the Law of Algorithms*, Bartfield, Woodrow (Editor), Cambridge, United Kingdom: Cambridge University Press, 2021, pp. 15 and ff and passim; Strandburg, Katherine J., "Rulemaking and Inscrutable Decision Tools", *Columbia Law Review*, Volume 119, 2019, passim (on inscrutable machines and inscrutable algorithmic decision-making).

3166 Sherman, Lawrence W., "Targeting, Testing and Tracking Police Services: The Rise of Evidence Based Policing, 1975–2025", *Crime and Justice*, 42 (1), 2013, pp. 377–451; Lavender III, I., *Race in American science fiction*, Bloomington: Indiana University Press, 2011.

3167 Porter, Theodore M., *Trust in Numbers: The Pursuit of Objectivity in Science and Public Life*, Princeton, NJ: Princeton University Press, 1995.

3168 See: Feagin, J. R., *Systemic racism: a theory of oppression*, New York: Routledge, 2006. See also: Fiske, John, "Surveilling the City: Whiteness, the Black Man and Democratic Totalitarianism.", *Theory, Culture and Society*, 15 (2), 1998, pp. 67–88 (on the overhyped surveillance on black people as a byproduct of systemic racism).

3169 See: Part IV, This chapter, Sects. 4.1.10.1–4.1.10.6 of this book (on biased algorithmic risk assessment in criminal procedure law settings, with a sharper focus on COMPAS). See: Part IV, This chapter, Sects. 4.1.1–4.1.1.1 of this book (on biased predictive policing).

3170 On whiteness: Frankenberg, Ruth (Ed.), *Displacing whiteness: essays in social and cultural criticism*, Durham, NC: Duke University Press, 1997; Frankenberg, Ruth, "Introduction: local whitenesses, localizing whiteness", *Displacing whiteness*, Ruth Frankenberg (Editor), Durham, NC: Duke University Press, 1997, pp. 1–33.

3171 See: Noble, Safiya Umoja, *Algorithms of Oppression: How search engines reinforce racism*, New York, New University Press, 2018, pp. 1–248 ("*Run a Google search for "Black girls"—what will you find? "Big Booty" and other sexually explicit terms are likely to come up as top search terms. But, if you type in "white girls," the results are radically different* (....) In *Algorithms of Oppression*, Safiya Umoja Noble challenges the idea that search engines like Google offer an equal playing field for all forms of ideas, identities, and activities. *Data discrimination is a real social problem; Noble argues that the combination of private interests in promoting certain sites, along with the monopoly status of a relatively small number of Internet search engines, leads to a biased set of search algorithms that privilege whiteness and discriminate against people of color, specifically women of color*"). Italics added. See: Part IV, This chapter, Sect. 4.1.8 of this book (on biased word embeddings with an entrenched presence on search engines run by tech moguls).

3172 See: Lipsitz, George, *The Possessive Investment in Whiteness: How White People Profit from Identity Politics*, Philadelphia, Pennsylvania, Temple University Press; 1st edition (July 13, 2018),

§§ To that end—widen racial wedges,[3175] ratchet up racial wealth gaps,[3176] uptick racial imbalances,[3177] and social inequalities[3178] in a myriad of domains[3179] while paving the way to the maintenance of White privilege[3180]—algorithmic unfairness, algorithmic discrimination, and algorithmic injustice[3181] are often bundled into one

2018, pp. 1–448 ("*argues that public policy and private prejudice work together to create a possessive investment in whiteness that is responsible for the racialized hierarchies of our society*"). Italics added. See: Part IV, This chapter, Sects. 4.1.4–4.1.4.2.3 of this book.

3173 See: Hellman, Deborah, "Indirect Discrimination and the Duty to Avoid Compounding Injustice", *Foundations of Indirect Discrimination Law*, Collins, Hugh/Khaitan, Tarunabh (Editors), Oxford, Hart Publishing; Reprint edition (June 25, 2020), 2020, p. 107 (Professor Deborah Hellman coined this expression to depict a decision that "exacerbates the harm caused by the prior injustice because it entrenches the harm or carries it into another domain." This book deals with the sweltering topic of indirect discrimination ("*indirect discrimination (or disparate impact) concerns the application of the same rule to everyone, even though that rule significantly disadvantages one particular group in society*"). See also: Barocas, Solon/Selbst, Andrew D., "Big Data's Disparate Impact", *California Law Review*, Volume 104, 2016, p. 699 (discussing how discriminatory data mining is analogous to unintentional disparate impact analysis); Sunstein, Cass R., "Algorithms, Correcting Biases", *Social Research*, Volume 86, 2019, pp. 449–506 (this famed author tagged disparate impact as "disturbing in itself, in the sense that a practice that produces such an impact helps entrench something like a caste system").

3174 See: Barocas, Solon/Selbst, Andrew, "Big Data's Disparate Impact", *cit.*, p. 691 (highlighting the worrisome, and gruesome, issue of "structural disadvantage" with which racialized communities have been tussling with for centuries).

3175 See: Menasce, Juliana Horowitz/Brown, Anna/Cox, Kiana, "Views of Racial Inequality", *Pew Research Center*, April 9, 2019, available at: https://www.pewresearch.org/social-trends/2019/04/09/views-of-racial-inequality/ (access: 2.12.2024) ("*more than four-in-ten Americans say the country still has work to do to give black people equal rights with whites. Blacks, in particular, are skeptical that black people will ever have equal rights in this country (….) A majority of adults say that being white helps people's ability to get ahead in the country at least a little (59%); 28% say being white neither helps nor hurts and 12% say it hurts. On the flip side, a majority (56%) sees being black as a disadvantage, with 25% saying it hurts people's ability to get ahead a lot. About a quarter (26%) say being black neither helps nor hurts and 17% say it helps at least a little. More also say that being Hispanic hurts people's ability to get ahead in this country (51%) than say it helps (18%) or that it neither helps nor hurts (30%).* Opinions are more split when it comes to the impact of being Native American—about the same shares say this hurts as say it neither helps nor hurts, while a smaller share says it helps. *And while a plurality says being Asian neither helps nor hurts, more say it helps (34%) than hurts (21%) people's ability to get ahead*"). Italics added.

3176 Derenoncourt, Ellora/Kim, Chi Hyun/Kuhn, Moritz/Schularik, Moritz, "The Wealth of Two Nations: The U.S. Racial Wealth Gap, 1860–2020", *The Quarterly Journal of Economics*, Volume 139, Issue 2, 2024, p. 741 ("*A large class of commonly discussed policies for reducing racial wealth inequality seeks to reduce gaps in income, savings, and capital gains.* These include policies that encourage financial diversification or stock equity holdings among Black households; policies aimed at financial literacy and retirement or savings behavior; or policies aimed at improving educational and labor market outcomes of Black Americans through improved school quality or reductions in discrimination. *Yet on a realistic note, our simulation in Section IV.A shows that even if wealth accumulation conditions had been equal since 1870, the wealth gap would still be 3 to 1 today, and full convergence would be more than 200 years away. Put differently: to close the racial wealth gap in the immediate term* via *flow parameters, Black Americans would need a substantial positive lead over whites, not "just" more equality*"). Italics added.

3177 See: Allen, James, "The Color of Algorithms: An Analysis and Proposed Research Agenda Deterring Algorithmic Redlining", *Fordham Urban Law Journal*, Volume 46, 2019, pp. 219–234

single category (*Algorithmic Dictatorship*) in that they are regarded as woven of the same cloth: biased algorithmic risk assessment, against the backdrop of which this section will henceforth unfold.

(229–234) (discussing how historical mortgage redlining greatly swayed modern algorithms generated by massive batches of datasets that consist of decades of information built on exclusion and racial discrimination in the purview of financing, marketing, and housing). See: Part IV, This chapter, Sects. 4.1.4–4.1.4.2.3 of this book.

[3178] Zajko, M, "Conservative AI and social inequality: conceptualizing alternatives to bias through social theory", *Artificial Intelligence and Society*, Volume 36, 2021, pp. 1047–1056.

[3179] In spite of its deep-seated racial bias, decision-makers continue to deploy redlining tactics through big data and may even justify such unlawful practices by claiming that the latter abide by cost-effectiveness. See: Humber, Nadiyah J., "A Home for Digital Equity: Algorithmic Redlining and Property Technology", *California Law Review*, Volume 111, Issue 5, 2023, pp. 1421–1484. But see: Hurley, Mikella/Adebayo, Julius, "Credit Scoring in the Era of Big Data", *Yale Journal of Law and Technology*, Volume 18, 2016, pp. 148, 151–156, 172 (averring that FICO scoring boasts a redoubtable capacity to routinely weed out some populations that have been historically and systematically underrepresented or grossly unfairly represented in the credit industry market). Tellingly, by 2016, ten states had disavowed the unlawful practice of employers using shady algorithmic credit scores due to their perceived disparate impact on low-income applicants and members of racialized communities (mostly Black folks). See: O'Neill, Cathy, *Weapons of Math Destruction. How Big Data Increases Inequality and Threatens Democracy*. London: Penguin Random House, 2016, pp. 128 and ff and passim. See: Part IV, This chapter, Sects. 4.1.4–4.1.4.2.3 of this book. See: Part IV, This chapter, Sects. 4.1.4–4.1.4.2.1 of this book (on mortgage redlining). See: Part IV, This chapter, Sects. 4.1.2–4.1.4.3 of this book (on algorithmic credit scoring, consumer racism and credit card redlining). See: Part IV, This chapter, Sects. 4.1.4–4.1.4.2.3 of this book (on algorithmic redlining). See: Part IV, This chapter, Sect. 4.1.4.3 of this book (on "algorithmic redliking"). See: Part IV, This chapter, Sect. 4.1.3 of this book (on algorithmic prime-lining).

[3180] See: Roithmayr, Daria, *Reproducing Racism: How everyday choices lock in White Advantage*, New York, New York University Press, 2014, pp. 1–272 ("*Argues that racial inequality reproduces itself automatically over time because early unfair advantage for whites has paved the way for continuing advantage. This book is designed to change the way we think about racial inequality (...) Legal scholar Daria Roithmayr provocatively argues that racial inequality lives on because white advantage functions as a powerful self-reinforcing monopoly, reproducing itself automatically from generation to generation even in the absence of intentional discrimination. Drawing on work in antitrust law and a range of other disciplines, Roithmayr brilliantly compares the dynamics of white advantage to the unfair tactics of giants like AT&T and Microsoft.* With penetrating insight, Roithmayr *locates the engine of white monopoly in positive feedback loops that connect the dramatic disparity of Jim Crow to modern racial gaps in jobs, housing and education. Wealthy white neighborhoods fund public schools that then turn out wealthy white neighbors. Whites with lucrative jobs informally refer their friends, who refer their friends, and so on. Roithmayr concludes that racial inequality might now be locked in place, unless policymakers immediately take drastic steps to dismantle this oppressive system*"). Italics added. This book points out how White privilege is perpetuated throughout generations through residential segregation (*mortgage redlining*), abhorrent nepotism, and other bemoaning social practices that pester modern societies). See: Part IV, This chapter, Sects. 4.1.4–4.1.4.2.3 of this book.

[3181] Ting-an Lin, "Democratizing AI" and the Concern of Algorithmic Injustice", *Philosophy and Technology*, Volume 37 (103), 2024, pp. 3–27; Okidegbe, Ngozi, "The Democratizing Potential of Algorithms?", *Connecticut Law Review*, Volume 54, 2021, passim; Katyal, Sonia, "Private Accountability in the Age of Artificial Intelligence", *UCLA Law Review*, Volume 66, 2019, pp. 54–99.

4.1.10.1 «Bias In, Bias Out» (Sandra G. Mayson): Biased Algorithmic Risk Assessment in Predicting Recidivism in the Realm of Criminal Procedure Law That Reifies, Amplifies and Further Compounds Racial Inequalities in the Age of *Algorithmic Dictatorship*

4.1.10.1.1 Laying Down the Groundwork

§§ Algorithmic risk assessment has garnered widespread attention.[3182] Algorithmic risk assessment has accordingly been received as a lightning bolt of great significance in the purview of criminal justice.[3183] Which caused algorithmic decision-making to swell.[3184] It is true that algorithmic risk assessment[3185] has aroused heated controversy lately,[3186] but truer still police, prosecutors, judges, and other criminal justice

---

[3182] Slobogin, Christopher, "Principles of Risk Assessment: Sentencing and Policing", *Ohio State Journal of Criminal Law*, Volume 15, 2018, pp. 583 and ff and passim (setting out foundational principles for how risk-assessment tools should be devised and deployed, specifically in the sentencing compass). See: Part IV, This chapter, Sects. 4.1.1–4.1.1.1 of this book (on biased predictive policing).

[3183] Mayson, Sandra G., "Dangerous Defendants", *Yale Law Journal*, Volume 127, 2018, p. 490 ("Bail reform is gaining momentum nationwide."); Stevenson, Megan, "Assessing Risk Assessment in Action", *Minnesota Law Review*, Volume 103, 2018, p. 303 (discussing the burgeoning use of pretrial risk assessment as a mandatory component of bail decisions in Kentucky); Dewan, Shaila, "Judges Replacing Conjecture with Formula for Bail", New York Times (June 26, 2015), https://www.nytimes.com/2015/06/27/us/turning-the-granting-of-bail-into-a-science.html; [https://perma.cc/Y86J-GHU4] (emphasizing the mounting groundswell of support for algorithmic risk assessments in bail decision-making across jurisdictions). See: Part IV, This chapter, Sects. 4.1.1–4.1.1.1 of this book (on biased predictive policing).

[3184] Compellingly, there is burgeoning trend of (to) sentencing anchored in algorithms in a bid to ease—and sometimes offset—human flaws (ranging from racial bias, gender bias, jealousy, to sexual orientation bias). Such algorithmic tools, which are currently being deployed in predicting criminal recidivism, are gaining traction and gathering pace in Italy: Gialuz, M., "Quando la giustizia penale encontra l'intelligenza artificiale: luci e e ombre di risk assessment tools tra Stati Uniti ed Europa", 2019, available at: www.penalecontemporaneo.it.d/6702-quando-la-giustizia-penale-encontra-l'int elligenz-artificiale-luci-e-ombre-di-risk-assessment-tools (access: 03.07.2024); United Kingdom: Peeters, R./Schuilenburg, M., "Machine Justice: Governing Security through Bureaucracy of Algorithms", *Information Polity*, Volume 23, 2018, pp. 267–274; Hamilton, Melissa, "Sentencing Disparities", *British Journal of American Legal Studies*, Volume 6, Issue 2, 2017, pp. 181 ff. See: Part IV, This chapter, Sects. 4.1.1–4.1.1.1 of this book (on biased predictive policing).

[3185] See: Brennan, T., Dieterich, W., & Ehret, B., "Evaluating the predictive validity of the COMPAS risk and needs assessment system", *Criminal Justice and Behavior*, Volume 36, Issue 1, 2009, pp. 21–40.

[3186] But see: Eaglin, Jessica M., "Constructing Recidivism Risk", *Emory Law Journal*, Volume 67, 59, 2017, 61 n.1 (arguing that "[p]redictive technologies are spreading through the criminal justice system like wildfire"). None of this is to suggest, nor is to say, that actuarial risk assessment is blazingly new to criminal justice system. Pivotally, parole boards have long relied on risk-assessment instruments since the 1930s. By the same token, some jurisdictions used algorithms to forecast certain types of crimes, such as sex offenses, for decades past. See: Mason, Sandra G., "Bias in, Bias Out.", *Yale Law Journal*, Volume 128 Volume 8, 2019, pp. 2219–2298. See: Part IV, This chapter, Sects. 4.1.1–4.1.1.1 of this book (on biased predictive policing).

stakeholders are increasingly relying upon algorithmic risk assessment to predict[3187] if a defendant will engage in flagitious activities in the forthcoming future.[3188] The vexing question that this essay seeks to adroitly address, and deftly tackle, is: should they?

§§ These deep-rooted concerns are neither unwarranted, nor uncalled for, nor are they statistically unsound.[3189] It hardly amounts to a mind-boggling/bewildering finding that these cutting-edge tools are not without humongous drawbacks.[3190] Compellingly, artificial intelligence-embedded technologies—which forms part of a broader technological apparatus within which algorithm risk assessment operates[3191]—often evince the devilishly harmful virus of algorithmic bias,[3192] which, I may venture to add, is wholly unbecoming in the purview of criminal procedure law.

[3187] Zhu, Mirilla, "Jury, Using Artificial Intelligence to Predict Recidivism Rates", *Yale Scientific*, 2020, passim. See also: Chasemi et al., Medhi, "The application of Machine Learning to a General Risk-Need Assessment Instrument in the Prediction of Criminal Recidivism", *Criminal Justice and Behavior*, Volume 48, 2020, pp. 518–538.

[3188] See: Skeem, J. and C. Lowenkamp, "Using Algorithms to Address Trade-Offs Inherent in Predicting Recidivism", *Behavioural Science and Law*, Volume 38, 2020, pp. 259–278 (on the use of machine learning algorithms to forecast recidivism in criminal justice settings). But see: Huq, Aziz Z., "Racial Equity in Algorithmic Criminal Justice", *Duke Law Journal*, Volume 68, 2019, pp. 1043, 1053, 1083–1102 (sheds a keen light on why constitutional law is fundamentally bereft of "creditable guidance" for granting racial equity in algorithmic risk assessment in criminal justice).

[3189] Tellingly, prejudiced algorithms are set to be brought to the fore as they are one foundational basis of *justice prédictive* so voguish in France. No surprise stems from the fact that prejudiced algorithms will feed *justice prédictive* - and that is something quite unsavoury and unpalatable in criminal justice indeed. See: Garapon, Antoine, "Les enjeux de la justice predictive", *Juris-Classeur périodique*, Volume 31, 2018, passim. See also: Larret-Chahine, Louis, "Le droit isométrique: un nouveau paradigme juridique né de la justice prédictive», *Archives de Philosophie du Droit*, Volume 60, 2018, pp. 287 and ff and passim.

[3190] See: Chandler, Anupam, "The Racist Algorithm", *Michigan Law Review*, Volume 115, n.º 6, 2018, pp. 1023–1025 (arguing that the real-world facts on which algorithms used in criminal justice risk assessment are based are "deeply suffused with invidious discrimination"); Eaglin, Jessica M., "Constructing Recidivism Risk", *cit.*, pp. 94–99 (argues that risk assessment has every chance to "compromise[e] equality"); Kim, Pauline T., "Data-Driven Discrimination at Work", *William and Mary Law Review*, Volume 58, 2017, pp. 857, 863–64 (shedding a keen light on the racial effects of algorithmic prediction in the remit of employment). Converging: Zywicki, Todd J./Adamson, Joseph D., "The Law and Economics of Subprime Lending", *University of Colorado Law Review*, 2009, pp. 1–9 (contending that Black workers with roughly the same abilities and educational background earn far less than comparable white workers or have considerably fewer employment opportunities); King, Allan G./Markovich, Marko J., "Big Data" and the Risk of Employment Discrimination, *Oklahoma Law Review*, Volume 68, 2016, pp. 555–563 (on algorithmic employment discrimination). Dobbie, Will, Jacob Goldin, and Crystal S. Yang, "The Effects of Pretrial Detention on Conviction, Future Crime, and Employment: Evidence from Randomly Assigned Judges," *American Economic Review*, Volume 108, 2018, 201–240 (on the racial skew in the domain of employment).

[3191] Berk, Richard A., *Machine Learning Forecasts of Risk in Criminal Justice Settings*. New York: Springer, 2018 (broaches extensively algorithmic risk assessment in criminal justice settings).

[3192] See: Baeza-Yates, R., "Bias on the web", *Communications of the ACM*, 61 (6), June 2018, 2018, pp. 54–61 (argues that "*algorithmic bias is when the bias is not present in the input data* and is added *purely by the algorithm*"). Italics added. See also: Hajian, Sara Hajian et al., "Algorithmic Bias: From Discrimination Discovery to Fairness-aware Data Mining", *ACM SIGKDD International Conference on Knowledge Discovery and Data Mining*, Volume 22, 2125, 2016;

§§ To further compound our functional woes and mental throes, machine learning algorithms,[3193] if nothing else, tend to be beset by racial skew,[3194] thereby exacting a toll on members of racialized communities.[3195] Amongst whom, communities of colour that have been grappling with harrowing racial discrimination[3196] for a long-winded span of time.[3197]

Griemmelmann, James/Westreich, Daniel, "Incomprehensible Discrimination ", *California Law Review Online*, Volume 7, 2018, pp. 164–171; Xiang, Alice, "Reconciling Legal and Technical Approaches to Algorithmic Bias", *Tennessee Law Review*, Volume 88, 2021, passim; See: Lemley, Mark A./Casey, Bryan, "Remedies for Robots", *The University of Chicago Law Review*, Volume 86, Issue 5, 2019, pp. 1311–1396 (1376) (alerting to the perils of algorithmic bias); Chandler, Anupam, "The Racist Algorithm", *Michigan Law Review*, Volume 115, Issue 6, 2018, p. 1026 (noting that, in the terrain of racist algorithm, "the possibilities for discriminatory manipulation are legion"; Jackson, Maya C., "Artificial Intelligence and Algorithmic Bias: The Issues with Technology Reflecting History and Humans", *Journal of Business Technology Law*, Volume 16, 2021, pp. 299–316; West, Sarah Myers/Whittaker, Meredith/Crawford, Kate, *Discriminating Systems. Gender, Race and Power in AI*. New York: AI Now Institute, 2019, pp. 15 and ff and passim; Waldman, Ezra, "Privacy, Practice, and Performance", *California Law Review*, Volume 110, 2021, passim (discussing the central tenets of algorithmic bias).

3193 See: Murphy, Kevin P., *Machine Learning: A Probabilistic Perspective (Adaptive Computation and Machine Learning series)*. Massachusetts: The MIT Press, 2012, pp. 1–1104 (states avowedly that "machine Learning attempts to combine deductive, inductive, and abductive reasoning to make person-like reasoning in AI Entities possible. Machine-learning AI Entities initially learn in the same way a human child learns. First, they notice details and patterns in shapes, sounds, and behaviors; then put them together to distinguish one person from another, or a dog from a cat. Eventually, the AI can recognize and identify" common objects). See also: Hutto-Schultz, Jess, "Dicitur Ex Machina: Artificial Intelligence and the Hearsay Rule", *George Mason Law Review*, Volume 27, Issue 2, 2020, pp. 684–718 (689). See: Chollet, François, *Deep Learning with Python*. Shelter Island, Nova Iorque: Manning, 2018, pp. 1–384 (passim). *Deep Learning* stands as a byproduct of *Machine Learning*. *Machine Learning*, a subset of Artificial Intelligence, unfolds itself in *Deep Learning*, which "involves computer algorithms that have the ability to "learn" or improve in performance over time on some task". See also: Surden, Harry, "Machine Learning and Law", *Washington Law Review*, Volume 89, 2015, pp. 87 and ff. See also: Barocas, Solon/Selbst, Andrew, "Big Data's Disparate Impact", *California Law Review*, Volume 104, pp. 2016, pp. 671–678 ("in particular, by exposing so-called 'machine learning' algorithms to examples of the cases of interest (previously identified instances of fraud, spam, default, and poor health), *the algorithm 'learns' which related attributes or activities can serve as potential proxies for those qualities or outcomes of interest*"). Italics added. See also: Chen, C./Rudin, C., "An optimization approach to learning falling rule lists", *Proceedings of Machine Learning Research, Artificial Intelligence and Statistics*, Volume 84, 2018, pp. 604–612; Sokolovska, N./Chevaleyre, Y./Zucker, J.D., "A provable algorithm for learning interpretable scoring systems", *Proceedings of Machine Learning Research, Artificial Intelligence and Statistics*, Volume 84, pp. 566–574; Rudin, Cynthia/Ustun, B., "Optimized scoring systems: toward trust in machine learning for healthcare and criminal justice", *Interfaces*, Volume 48, 2018, pp. 399–486.

3194 Mayson, Sandra G., "Bias In, Bias Out", *Yale Law Journal*, Volume 128, 2019, pp. 2218–2300 (2218). I will follow this bodacious piece of research very closely in this section.

3195 Rucker, J. M. and J. A. Rocheson, "Toward An Understanding of Structural Racism: Implications for Criminal Justice." *Science*, 374 (6565), 2021, pp. 286–90.

3196 See: Feagin, J. R., *Systemic racism: a theory of oppression*, New York: Routledge, 2006. See also: Fiske, John, "Surveilling the City: Whiteness, the Black Man and Democratic Totalitarianism.", *Theory, Culture and Society*, 15 (2), 1998, pp. 67–88 (on the overhyped surveillance on black people as a byproduct of systemic racism).

§§ To forestall the gruelling effects of both racial discrimination and algorithmic unfairness,[3198] scholars have been neither coy nor bashful in voicing their deep-seated concerns about algorithmic injustice[3199] facing communities of colour. An ensemble of strategies of resistance against racial discrimination have been accordingly devised: **(I)** the exclusion of input markers closely associated with race (colour-blindness[3200]); **(II)** adjustments[3201] to computer-run algorithmic design[3202] to equalize forecasts across racial lines; and **(III)** rejection of algorithmic methods

---

[3197] Milligan, Joy, "Protecting Disfavored Minorities: Towards Institutional Realism", *UCLA Law Review*, Volume 63, 2016, pp. 918–921 (delves into the racial inequality in United States of America's Department of Agriculture farm aid to both Whites and Blacks).

[3198] Berk, R. A., H. Heirdari, S. Jabbari, M. Kearns, and A. Roth, "Fairness in Criminal Justice Risk Assessments: The State of the Art." Sociological Methods and Research, 2018.

[3199] Ting-an Lin, "Democratizing AI" and the Concern of Algorithmic Injustice", *Philosophy and Technology*, Volume 37 (103), 2024, pp. 3–27; Okidegbe, Ngozi, "The Democratizing Potential of Algorithms?", *Connecticut Law Review*, Volume 54, 2021, passim; Katyal, Sonia, "Private Accountability in the Age of Artificial Intelligence", *UCLA Law Review*, Volume 66, 2019, pp. 54–99 (on the fundamental tenets of algorithmic injustice coupled with a host of measures to stymie it).

[3200] But see: Kleinberg, Jon et al., "Algorithmic Fairness", *AEA Papers & Proceedings*, Volume 108, 2018, pp. 22–23 (discussing, anchored in a batch of national data, that including race as an input variable to a machine-learning college-admissions algorithm both "improves predicted GPAs of admitted students" and can augment "the fraction of admitted students who are black").

[3201] It is important to note that an algorithm designed for maximum accuracy will adjust itself to the majority data, and may be less accurate for members of the underrepresented group, thus breeding inductive bias. See: Shellenbarger, Sue, "A Crucial Step for Avoiding AI Disasters", *Wall Street Journal*, (Feb. 13, 2019, 9:57 AM ET), https://www.wsj.com/articles/a-crucial-step-for-avoiding-ai-disasters-11550069865?ns = prod/accounts-wsj; [https://perma.cc/C28U-LAAE] (discussing this issue while emphasizing how diverse development teams pay more attention to unrepresentative and underrepresented data sets). Human programmers can circumvent and bypass this problem by weighting the minority-group data more heavily, by designing different algorithms for each racial group, or by striving to contain more data to equalize group representation in the data set. See: Barua, Sukarna et al., "MWMOTE—Majority Weighted Minority Oversampling Technique for Imbalanced Data Set Learning", *IEEE Transactions on Knowledge & Data Engineering*, Volume 26, 2014, pp. 405, 405–06. See also: Hamilton, Melissa, "The Biased Algorithm: Evidence of Disparate Impact on Hispanics", *American Criminal Law Review*, Volume 56, 2019, pp. 1553 and ff and passim (which clearly demonstrates that COMPAS was significantly less accurate for Hispanic than for white defendants by several measures and suggesting that smaller numbers of Hispanic defendants might be the cause). See: Mayson, Sandra G., "Bias In, Bias Out", *cit.*, pp. 2218–2300. See also: Dong et al., Qi, "Imbalanced deep learning by minority class incremental rectification, *IEEE Transactions on Pattern Analysis & Machine Intelligence*, Volume 41, 2019, p. 1367 (posit that "*most existing learning algorithms produce inductive bias (learning bias)* towards the frequent (majority) classes if training data are not balanced, *resulting in poor minority class recognition performance*"). Italics added. See: Chandler, Anupam, "The Racist Algorithm", *Michigan Law Review*, Volume 115, n. ° 6, 2018, p. 1026 (on racist algorithms, noting that "the possibilities for discriminatory manipulation are legion"). But see: Altenburger, Kristen M./Ho, Daniel E., "When Algorithms Import Private Bias into Public Enforcement: The Promise and Limitations of Statistical Debiasing Solutions", *Journal of Institutional & Theoretical Economics*, Volume 175, 2019, pp. 97–98 (calls for a "debias predictive algorithms" to assuage racist and/or biased, doctored and bigoted algorithms nevertheless). See: Part V, Chap. 5, Sect. 5.1.7.4 of this book (on one of the law to control algorithmic decision-making, namely, law number four: data partitioning must be performed—i.e. randomly split an entire dataset into the «training dataset» and the «test

altogether.[3203] This section's main contention is that which these strategies are at best shallow, hollow, nomadic, and superficial and at worst run counter to algorithmic fairness[3204] in that the origin of racial inequity in algorithmic risk assessment lies neither in the input data,[3205] nor in a set of far-fetched algorithms,[3206] nor in algorithmic methodology itself.[3207]

§§ On the opposite pole, a deep dive into the remit of algorithmic decision-making shows that the real problem lies elsewhere: the very nature of prediction itself. Compellingly, at its core, prediction[3208] is backward-looking in that looks to the past in an earnest attempt to forecast the future.[3209] Dispiritingly, though, we live

---

dataset»—to accurately predict outcomes in the real world while forestalling «inductive bias» (learning bias)).

3202 Note, though, that the training of machine learning is long and tedious in that is an error-prone procedure than can ultimately impair future algorithmic decision-making: Price, W. Nicholson Price II, "Regulating Black-Box Medicine", *Michigan Law Review*, Volume 116, 2017, pp. 421–431 (leverages on Google Image's image recognition learning algorithm to shed light on the four-step process by which some algorithms are thoroughly trained. First, the algorithm is shown "a set of known images ('Here are 10,000 pictures of ducks')." Second, the algorithm "develops complex internal rules based on nonlinear processes." Third, the algorithm "tests those rules on a test set ('Which of these are ducks?')." And fourth, the algorithm accordingly adjusts its "internal rules based on the success of the test." These steps are trotted out and repeated many times "until it can accurately and consistently classify the images").

3203 Mayson, Sandra G., "Bias In, Bias Out", *cit.*, pp. 2218–2300 (2218).

3204 Hellman, Deborah, "Measuring Algorithmic Fairness", *Virginia Law Review*, 106 (4), 2020, pp. 811–66 (discusses the building blocks upon which stands algorithm fairness while emphasizing the roadblocks that stand in its way).

3205 Gillis, Talia B., "The Input Data Fallacy", *Minnesota Law Review*, Volume 106, 2022, pp. 1176–1263.

3206 Note, though, that there are far more unsettling issues with which criminal justice flounders with. To begin with, the inscrutable way algorithms make their correlations and draw their inferences accordingly—which is eerily unbeknownst even for the cohort of programmers that designed them—stand out. This is deemed *black box*, that further enhances the shroud of mystery under which algorithms are cloaked. See, for a compelling account of AI black box: See: Bathaee, Yavar, "The Artificial Intelligence Black Box and the Failure of Intent and Causation", *Harvard Journal of Law and Technology*, n.º 37, 2018, p. 901 (adduces that "*one possible reason AI may be a black box to humans is that it relies on machine-learning algorithms that internalize data in ways that are not easily audited or understood by humans (…) "first, a lack may arise from the complexity of the algorithm's structure, such as with deep neural network, which consists of thousands of artificial neurons working together in a diffuse way to solve a problem. This reason for AI being a black box is referred to as "complexity". Second, the lack of transparency may arise because the AI is using a machine-learning algorithm that relies on geometric relationships that humans cannot visualize, such as with support vector machines. This reason for AI being a black box is referred to as "dimensionality"*). Italics added. See: Part V, Chap. 5, Sect. 5.1.7.2 of this book (on law number two to control algorithmic decision-making, which mandates that black box models must not be entrusted with the task of high stake decisions—v.g. health and freedom).

3207 Mayson, Sandra G., "Bias In, Bias Out", *cit.*, pp. 2218–2300 (2218).

3208 Aggarwal, C. C., *Neural networks and deep learning*, Heidelberg, Springer, 2018, passim; Agrawal, A., Gans, J., & Goldfarb, A., "Prediction machines (updated and expanded): The simple economics of artificial intelligence", *Harvard Business Review Press*, 2022; Agrawal, A., Gans, J., & Goldfarb, A., "Power and prediction: The disruptive economics of artificial intelligence", *Harvard Business Review Press*, 2022; Bengio, Y., Hinton, G., Yao, A., Song, D., Abbeel, P., Harari, Y. N.,

in a racially skewed world against the backdrop of which predictions are slated to project racial inequalities of the past[3210] onto the forthcoming future.[3211]

§§ Crucially, in the midst of the era of big data[3212] and cybersurveillance[3213] algorithms have pierced into all aspects of social life.[3214] Burgeoningly, a plethora of energy-draining and time-consuming tasks are being currently carried out by algorithms,[3215] ranging from credit scoring,[3216] predictive policing,[3217] lending,[3218] mortgage redlining,[3219] screening resumes, evaluating employee overall performance,

---

Hadfield, G., Russell, S., Kahneman, D., & Mindermann, S., *Managing ai risks in an era of rapid progress*, arXiv preprint arXiv:2310.17688, 2023, passim (on neural networks and deep learning that operate jointly in the age of Artificial Intelligence-embedded technologies).

3209 Mayson, Sandra G., "Bias In, Bias Out", *cit.*, pp. 2218–2300 (2218).

3210 Rudin, Cynthia/Wang, Caroline/Coker, Beau, "The Age of Secrecy and Unfairness in Recidivism Prediction", *Harvard Data Science Review*, Issue 2.1. Winter 2020, 2020, passim; Eckhouse, L., Lum, K., Conti-Cook, C./Ciccolini, J., "Layers of bias: A unified approach for understanding problems with risk assessment", *Criminal Justice and Behavior*, Volume 46, Issue 2, 2019, pp. 185–209; Stevenson, M. T./Slobogin, C., "Algorithmic risk assessments and the double-edged sword of youth", *Washington University Law Review*, Volume 96, 2018, passim.

3211 Mayson, Sandra G., "Bias In, Bias Out", *cit.*, pp. 2218–2300 (2218).

3212 Big data that is in the limelight these days. See: Sivarajah, Uthayasnkar et al., "Critical Analysis of Big Data Challenges and Analytical Methods", *Journal of Business Research*, Volume 70, 2017, pp. 263 and ff and passim; Jetten, Lieke /Sharon, Stephen, "Selected Issues concerning the Ethical Use of Big Data Health Analytics", *Washington & Lee Law Review Online*, Volume 72, 2016, passim; Wachter, S./Mittelstadt. B., "A right to Reasonable Inferences: Re-thinking Data Protection Law in the Age of Big Data and AI", *Columbia Business Law Review*, 2019, pp. 1 and ff and passim; See in French doctrine: Ferey, Samuel, « Analyse économique du droit, big data et justice prédictive», *Archives de Philosophie du Droit*, Volume 60, 2018, pp. 68–81; Završnik, A. "Algorithmic justice: Algorithms and big data in criminal justice settings", *European Journal of Criminology*, 2019, passim; Joh, Elizabeth E., "The New Surveillance Discretion: Automated Suspicion, Big Data, and Policing." *Harvard Law and Policy Review*, 10 (1), 2016, pp. 15–42.

3213 Hu, Margaret, "From the National Surveillance State to the Cybersurveillance State", *The Annual Review of Law and Social Science*, Volume 13, 2017, p. 168 ("*as a result, the Cybersurveillance State, as a technological successor to the National Surveillance State, will execute bureaucratized biometric cybersurveillance in ways that are largely invisible and that appear routinized when technologically embedded within biometric identification technologies harnessed by the Administrative State. The normalization of day-to-day cybersurveillance will be achieved largely through governing functions that appear purely administrative (e.g., identity assessments for the granting of welfare, rights, privileges, and governing incentives).* Because of the routinized and administrative nature of the government-led big data program or *data surveillance (dataveillance) program, contemporary cybersurveillance is likely to be viewed as justified under crime, immigration control, and counterterrorism policy rationales*"). Italics added. See: Part IV, This chapter, Sects. 4.1.5–4.1.5.2 of this book (on "algorithmic Jim Crow", a travel ban issued during the first Trump Administration to prevent certain individuals from entering the United States of America, which, given its racial undertones, stands as an outgrowth of congeries of laws enacted during the Jim Crow epoch).

3214 Xi Chen, "Algorithmic proxy discrimination and its regulations", *Computer Law & Security Review, The International Journal of Technology Law and Practice*, Volume 54, September 2024, 2024, pp. 1–13.

3215 Ross, M./Taylor, J., "Managing AI Decision-Making Tools, Technology and Analytics", *Harvard Business Review*, 10 Nov. 2021, 2021.

3216 See: Part IV, This chapter, Sects. 4.1.4–4.1.4.2.1 of this book (on mortgage redlining). See: Part IV, This chapter, Sects. 4.1.2–4.1.4.3 of this book (on algorithmic credit scoring, consumer

establishing premiums, to underpinning the high-stakes[3220] decisions[3221] made by government officials,[3222] which, in turn, begets algorithmic accountability of which policymakers must not shy away from.[3223]

---

racism and credit card redlining). See: Part IV, This chapter, Sects. 4.1.4–4.1.4.2.3 of this book (on algorithmic redlining). See: Part IV, This chapter, Sect. 4.1.4.3 of this book (on "algorithmic redliking"). See: Part IV, This chapter, Sect. 4.1.3 of this book (on algorithmic prime-lining). See also: Hurley, Mikella/Adebayo, Julius, "Credit Scoring in the Era of Big Data", *Yale Journal of Law and Technology*, Volume 18, 2016, pp. 148–168.

[3217] Brayne, S., "Big data surveillance: The case of policing", *American Sociological Review*, Volume 82, Issue 5, 2017, pp. 977–1008.

[3218] Bruckner, Matthew Adam, "The Promise and Perils of Algorithmic Lenders' Use of Big Data", *Chicago-Kent Law Review*, Volume 93, 2018, pp. 25–29.

[3219] In spite of its deep-seated racial bias, decision-makers continue to deploy redlining tactics through big data and may even justify such unlawful practices by claiming that the latter abide by cost-effectiveness. See: Humber, Nadiyah J., "A Home for Digital Equity: Algorithmic Redlining and Property Technology", *California Law Review*, Volume 111, Issue 5, 2023, pp. 1421–1484. See also: Hurley, Mikella/Adebayo, Julius, "Credit Scoring in the Era of Big Data", *Yale Journal of Law and Technology*, Volume 18, 2016, pp. 148, 151–156, 172 (averring that FICO scoring boasts a redoubtable capacity to routinely weed out some populations that have been historically and systematically underrepresented or grossly unfairly represented in the credit industry market). Tellingly, by 2016, ten states had disavowed the unlawful practice of employers using shady credit scores due to their perceived disparate impact on low-income applicants and members of racialized communities (mostly Black folks). See: O'Neill, Cathy, *Weapons of Math Destruction. How Big Data Increases Inequality and Threatens Democracy*. London: Penguin Random House, 2016, pp. 128 and ff and passim. See: Part IV, This chapter, Sects. 4.1.4–4.1.4.2.3 of this book.

[3220] See: Part V, Chap. 5, Sect. 5.1.7.2 of this book (on law number two to control algorithmic decision-making, which mandates that black box models must not be entrusted with the task of making high stake decisions—v.g. health and freedom). See also: Weizenbaum, Joseph, *Computer Power and Human Reason: From Judgment to Calculation*, 1st edition, New York, W. H. Freeman & Co, 1976, pp. 1–300 (227) ("examines the sources of the computer's powers and offers evaluative explorations of what computers can do, cannot do, and should not be employed to do") (this founding father of Artificial Intelligence presciently noted that we should not entrust Artificial Intelligence-embedded technologies with "tasks that demand wisdom"). Italics added. The approval of rental applications is arguably one of those tasks that should never be entrusted to machines). More on this on Part IV, This chapter, Sects. 4.1.4–4.1.4.2.1 of this book.

[3221] But see: Rudin, Cynthia, "Please stop explaining black box models for high stakes decisions", *Proceedings of NeurIPS 2018 Workshop on Critiquing and Correcting Trends in Machine Learning (NIPS 2018)*, 2018, passim.

[3222] Xi Chen, "Algorithmic proxy discrimination and its regulations", *cit.*, pp. 1–13. But see: Williams, Rebecca, "Accountable Algorithms: Adopting the Public Law Toolbox Outside the Realm of Public Law", *Current Legal Problems,* Vol. 75, 2022, pp. 237–263; Williams, Rebecca, "Rethinking Administrative Law for Algorithmic Decision-Making", *Oxford Journal of Legal Studies*, Volume 42, 2021, pp. 468 e ff and passim (on the much-needed algorithmic accountability in the realm of administrative law).

[3223] See: Katyal, Sonia, "Private Accountability in the Age of Artificial Intelligence", *UCLA Law Review*, Volume 66, 2019, pp. 54–99 (on algorithmic accountability).

§§ Albeit human decision-makers play a pivotal role in keeping individual[3224] justice unscathed, Artificial Intelligence-embedded technologies are being increasingly deployed to make high stake decisions,[3225] which, in turn, creates a blazingly new cluster of challenges[3226] that must be tackled heads-on.[3227]

§§ Algorithmic decision-making can yield multifarious benefits to the overall advancement of modern societies.[3228] Notably, it not only augments decision-making efficiency (*cost–benefit analysis*)[3229] to adapt to the sheer amount of

[3224] But see: M. Zalnieriute, L. B. Moses, G. Williams, "The Rule of Law and Automation of Government Decision-making, University of New South Wales Law Research Series", *Modern Law Review*, 82 (3), 2019, passim (on the sizzling hot challenges posed by an algorithmic-anchored decision-making at a government level).

[3225] See: Part V, Chap. 5, Sect. 5.1.7.2 of this book (on law number two to control algorithmic decision-making, which mandates that black box models must not be entrusted with the task of making high stake decisions—v.g. health and freedom). See also: Rudin, C., & Radin, J., "Why are we using black box models in AI when we don't need to? A lesson from an explainable AI competition", *Harvard Data Science Review*, 2019, Volume 1, Issue 2, passim; Tan, S., Caruana, R., Hooker, G., and Lou, Y., "Distill-and-compare: Auditing blackbox models using transparent model distillation". *Proceedings of the 2018 AAAI/ACM Conference on AI, Ethics, and Society, Association for Computing Machinery*, 2018, pp. 303–310 (arguing that explainable models are too complex and fiddly to be understood by laypeople. As a result, interpretable models should be used instead).

[3226] See: Millar, Jason/Kerr, Ian, "Delegation, Relinquishment and Responsibility: The Prospect of Expert Robots", *Robot Law*, Calo, Ryan /Froomkin, A. Michael/Kerr, Ian, Cheltenham, Edward Elgar Publishing, 2016, pp. 102, 106–107 (as these authors aptly put it "*we will rely on robots without really knowing why – simply because their algorithms provide the greatest number of successful outcomes.* We have already seen this in Google's search approach. Neither Larry (Page) nor Sergey (Brin) (nor any other Google employee) knowns exactly why one particular web page is a better result than another. *When the click patterns say it is, that's good enough.* No semantic or causal analysis is required...*Like the ancients, we will, quite rationally, come to rely upon them, knowing full well that we cannot necessarily explain the reasons for their decisions*"). Italics added. Converging: Casey, Anthony J./Niblett, Anthony, "Self-driving Laws", *University of Toronto Law Journal*, Volume 66, 2016, pp. 429–435 (contend that "as more information is generated, and the evolutionary algorithm updates and become a better forecaster, we imagine that judges will increasingly rely on the advice of the algorithm"). See: Part V, Chap. 5, Sect. 5.1.8.5 of this book (on law number five to interpret algorithmic decision-making, which mandates that robot-judges, robot-prosecutors and robot-lawyers must not enter the courtroom for they are utterly incapable of making sound and interpretable value judgements).

[3227] Xi Chen, "Algorithmic proxy discrimination and its regulations", *cit.*, pp. 1–13.

[3228] Xi Chen, "Algorithmic proxy discrimination and its regulations", cit., pp. 1–13.

[3229] Cost–benefit Analysis is in the limelight. Its development falls conspicuously outside the scope and aim of this book though. See: Sunstein, Cass R., "The Real World of Cost-Benefits Analysis: Thirty-Six Questions (and almost as many answers)", *Columbia Law Review*, 114 (1), 2014, 177; Bayefsky, Rachel, "Dignity as a value in Agency Cost–Benefit Analysis", *Yale Law Journal*, 123 (2014): 1740; Sunstein, Cass R., Valuing Life: Humanizing the Regulatory State, 2014, 8 ff; Gordon, Jeffrey, "The Empty Call for Cost-Benefits Analysis for Financial Regulators", *Journal of Legal Studies*, 43, 2014, 351; Sunstein, Cass R., "The Limits of Quantification", *California Law Review*, 103, 2014, 1369; Adler, Mathew/Posner, Eric A., "New Foundations of Cost–Benefit Analysis", *Regulation & Governance*, 3, 2006, 72; Thomas J. Miles/ Sunstein, Cass R., "The Real World of Arbitrariness Review", *University of Chicago Law Review*, 75 2008, 761; Coates, John C. IV, "Cost–Benefit Analysis of Financial Regulation: Case Studies and Implications", *Yale Law Journal*,

social changes catalysed by a seething social reality but, and foremost, appears to be more objective and neutral[3230] than humans[3231] owing to the fact that Artificial Intelligence-embedded technologies are not subject to any[3232] prejudice whatsoever.[3233]

§§ That holds true, but it is nonetheless truer that algorithms that are facially objective and seemingly neutral can lead to gruesome discrimination.[3234] Shoddy data,[3235] botched, warped, and watered-down algorithms breed a slew of noxious consequences for both individuals and society. Worryingly, and perhaps not infrequently, even state-of-the art and top-notch algorithms suitably tailored to accomplish a given task and fed with clean data can mimic, reproduce[3236] and exacerbate[3237]

124, 2015, pp. 882–911; Posner, Eric A./Weyl E. Glen, "Cost–Benefit Analysis of Financial Regulations: Response to Criticisms", *Yale Law Journal*, 124, 2015, pp. 246–265 (parsing the relationship between agency cost–benefit analysis and human dignity).

3230 But see: Citron, Danielle Keats/Pasquale, Frank A., "The Scored Society: Due Process for Automated Predictions", *Washington Law Review*, Volume 89, 2014, pp. 1–34 (arguing that "[a]*dvocates applaud the removal of human beings and their flaws from the assessment process*," but arguing that bias remains "[*b*]*ecause human beings program predictive algorithms, their biases and values are embedded into the software's instructions*"). Italics added.

3231 But see: Jiang, H., O. Nachum, *Identifying and Correcting Label Bias in Machine Learning*, 15 Jan 2019, 2019, available online at https://arxiv.org/pdf/1901.04966.pdf (access: 14.12.2024); Simons, T. *Addressing issues of fairness and bias in AI*, Thomson Reuters, 30 Nov 2020, available online at https://www.thomsonreuters.com/en-us/posts /news-and-media/ai-fairness-bias (access: 14.12.2024); Chakraborty, J./Majumder, S./Menzies, T., "Bias in Machine Learning Software: Why? How? What to Do?, 9 Jul 2021, 2021, *arxiv.org*; Danks, D./A. J. London, "Algorithmic Bias in Autonomous Systems, Algorithmic Bias in Autonomous Systems", *Proceedings of the Twenty-Sixth International Joint Conference on Artificial Intelligence (IJCAI-17)*, 2019, available online at https://www.ijcai.org/proceedings/2017/0654.pdf (access: 14.12.2024) (on the vast assortment of algorithmic biases).

3232 Xi Chen, "Algorithmic proxy discrimination and its regulations", *cit.*, pp. 1–13.

3233 It is often averred, though, that prejudiced algorithms are set to be brought to the fore as they are one foundational basis of *justice prédictive* so voguish in France. No surprise stems from the fact that prejudiced algorithms will feed *justice prédictive*—and that is something quite unsavoury and unpalatable in criminal justice indeed. See: Garapon, Antoine, "Les enjeux de la justice predictive", *Juris-Classeur périodique*, Volume 31, 2018, passim. See also: Larret-Chahine, Louis, "Le droit isométrique: un nouveau paradigme juridique né de la justice prédictive», *Archives de Philosophie du Droit*, Volume 60, 2018, pp. 287 and ff and passim.

3234 **X**i Chen, "Algorithmic proxy discrimination and its regulations", *cit.*, pp. 1–13. See also: Mehrabi, N./Morstatter, F. N. Saxena/Lerman, K./Galstyan, A., *A Survey on Bias and Fairness in Machine Learning*, 25 Jan 2022, available at https://arxiv.org/pdf/1908.09635.pdf (access: 14.12.2024).

3235 See: *Tech, Bias and Housing Initiative, the Promise and Perils of Residential Proptech, Year 1, Research Summary Report, April 2023, TechEquity Collaborative*, p. 11, available at: https://techequity.us/wp-content/uploads/2023/04/TBHI-Y1-Research-Summary-Report.pdf (28.11.2024). ("*Once bad data enters the analysis of one factor, it gets baked into the subsequent process, multiplying the effect that one disadvantageous data point can have on someone's overall housing determination*"). Italics added. See: Part IV, This chapter, Sects. 4.1.4–4.1.4.2.3 of this book.

3236 Benjamin, Ruha, *Race After Technology: Abolitionist Tools for the New Jim Code*, New York, Polity, 2019, pp. 1–172 (7) (discussing that Artificial Intelligence-embedded technologies are

previous discriminatory[3238] patterns.[3239] No befuddling surprise stems from the fact that Artificial Intelligence-embedded technologies have been flagged as sources of algorithmic bias,[3240] algorithmic discrimination[3241] and algorithmic injustice.[3242]

---

viewed as iron-clad tools of objectivity and devoid of any biases whatsoever). Ruha Benjamin contends that "the employment of new technologies that reflect *and reproduce existing inequities but that are promoted and perceived as more objective or progressive than the discriminatory systems of a previous era*"). Italics added.

3237 *Tech, Bias and Housing Initiative, the Promise and Perils of Residential Proptech, Year 1, Research Summary Report, April 2023, TechEquity Collaborative*, p. 5 available at: https://techequity.us/wp-content/uploads/2023/04/TBHI-Y1-Research-Summary-Report.pdf (28.11.2024). ("*Residential Proptech also has the potential to exacerbate the bias inherent in our housing system. Its rise is due, in part, to the desperation felt by average home seekers. With a severely constrained housing supply, companies offering an easier pathway to homeownership may exploit communities that have been harmed by housing discrimination in the past. Opaque algorithms incorporate biased data into their decision-making processes, making it harder to enforce fair housing laws.* Residential Proptech companies often operate in a regulatory gray area, leaving consumers without the protections they would have from traditional housing regulatory systems. *As unprecedented capital investment flows into this space, venture-backed companies' winner-take-all approach to growth has the potential to exacerbate inequality rather than combat it*"). Italics added. See: Part IV, This chapter, Sects. 4.1.4–4.1.4.2.3 of this book.

3238 Roithmayr, Daria, *Reproducing Racism: How everyday choices lock in White Advantage*, New York, New York University Press, 2014, pp. 1–272 ("*Argues that racial inequality reproduces itself automatically over time because early unfair advantage for whites has paved the way for continuing advantage. This book is designed to change the way we think about racial inequality* (...) *Legal scholar Daria Roithmayr provocatively argues that racial inequality lives on because white advantage functions as a powerful self-reinforcing monopoly, reproducing itself automatically from generation to generation even in the absence of intentional discrimination. Drawing on work in antitrust law and a range of other disciplines, Roithmayr brilliantly compares the dynamics of white advantage to the unfair tactics of giants like AT&T and Microsoft.* With penetrating insight, Roithmayr *locates the engine of white monopoly in positive feedback loops that connect the dramatic disparity of Jim Crow to modern racial gaps in jobs, housing and education. Wealthy white neighborhoods fund public schools that then turn out wealthy white neighbors. Whites with lucrative jobs informally refer their friends, who refer their friends, and so on. Roithmayr concludes that racial inequality might now be locked in place, unless policymakers immediately take drastic steps to dismantle this oppressive system*"). Italics added. This book points out how White privilege is perpetuated throughout generations through residential segregation (*mortgage redlining*), abhorrent nepotism, and other bemoaning social practices that pester modern societies). See: Part IV, This chapter, Sects. 4.1.4–4.1.4.2.3 of this book.

3239 Xi Chen, "Algorithmic proxy discrimination and its regulations", *cit.*, pp. 1–13.

3240 Danks, D./London, A.J., "Algorithmic Bias in Autonomous Systems, Algorithmic Bias in Autonomous Systems", *Proceedings of the Twenty-Sixth International Joint Conference on Artificial Intelligence (IJCAI-17)*, 2019; Ferrer, X./van Nuenen, T./Such, J. M./Cote, M./Criado, N., "Bias and Discrimination in AI: a cross-disciplinary perspective", King's College London, United Kingdom, 11 Aug 2020, 2020.

3241 See on algorithmic discrimination: Kleinberg, Jon, et al., "Discrimination in the Age of Algorithms", *Journal of Legal Analysis*, 2018, pp. 114–174; See: Kleinberg, Jon, et al., "Algorithms as Discrimination Detectors", *Proceeds of the National Academy of Science*, Volume 117, 2020, pp. 30096–30110; Griemmelmann, James/Westreich, Daniel, "Incomprehensible Discrimination ", *California Law Review Online*, Volume 7, 2018, pp. 164–171; Xiang, Alice, "Reconciling Legal and Technical Approaches to Algorithmic Bias", *Tennessee Law Review*, Volume 88, 2021, passim;

Take the example of COMPAS, a recidivism predictive tool used in some jurisdictions of the United States of America.[3243]

§§ Whereas COMPAS does not use ethnicity-specific data,[3244] it nonetheless creates an algorithmic myth of colour-blindness[3245] by bolstering the ungrounded hope that input exclusion («input data fallacy») can breed non-discriminatory algorithms.[3246] Therefore, we are increasingly led to believe that colour-blind algorithms[3247] amount to the panacea for a myriad of social diseases with which modern societies have been floundering for a long-haul.[3248] Which could not be farther from the truth. More on this later.[3249]

§§ Note, though, that COMPAS does not go easy on Blacks. Tellingly, COMPAS is more likely to falsely flag Black defendants as likely to engage in future criminal

---

Karnow, Curtis E. A., "The Opinion of Machines", *The Cambridge Handbook of the Law of Algorithms*, Bartfield, Woodrow (Editor), Cambridge, United Kingdom: Cambridge University Press, 2021, pp. 15 and ff and passim; Strandburg, Katherine J., "Rulemaking and Inscrutable Decision Tools", *Columbia Law Review*, Volume 119, 2019, passim; Watcher, Sandra/Mittelstadt, Brent/Russell, Chris, "Counterfactual Explanations Without Opening the Black Box: Automated Decisions and the GDPR", *Harvard Journal of Law and Technology*, Volume 31, 2018, pp. 841 e ss and passim; Jackson, Maya C., "Artificial Intelligence and Algorithmic Bias: The Issues with Technology Reflecting History and Humans", *Journal of Business Technology Law*, Volume 16, 2021, pp. 299–316.

3242 Ting-an Lin, "Democratizing AI" and the Concern of Algorithmic Injustice", *Philosophy and Technology*, Volume 37 (103), 2024, pp. 3–27. See also: Birhane, A., "Algorithmic injustice: A relational ethics approach", *Patterns*, 2 (2), 2021, pp. 1–9. Završnik, A. "Algorithmic justice: Algorithms and big data in criminal justice settings", *European Journal of Criminology*, 2019, passim.

3243 An acronym that stands for *Correctional Offender Management Profiling for Alternative Sanctions* (COMPAS).

3244 Xi Chen, "Algorithmic proxy discrimination and its regulations", *cit.*, pp. 1–13.

3245 Brewer, R. M./Heitzeg, N. A., "The racialization of crime and punishment: Criminal justice, Color-Blind racism, and the political economy of the prison industrial complex", *American Behavioral Scientist*, Volume 51, Issue 5, 2008, pp. 625–644.

3246 Gillis, Talia B., "The Input Data Fallacy", *Minnesota Law Review*, Volume 106, 2022, pp. 1176–1263.

3247 But see: Allen, James, "The Color of Algorithms: An Analysis and Proposed Research Agenda Deterring Algorithmic Redlining", *Fordham Urban Law Journal*, Volume 46, 2019, pp. 219–234 (229–234) (discussing how historical mortgage redlining greatly swayed modern algorithms generated by massive batches of data sets that consist of decades of information built on exclusion and racial discrimination in the purview of financing, marketing, and housing). See: Part IV, This chapter, Sects. 4.1.4–4.1.4.2.3 of this book. See: Part IV, This chapter, Sects. 4.1.4–4.1.4.2.1 of this book (on mortgage redlining). See: Part IV, This chapter, Sects. 4.1.2–4.1.4.3 of this book (on algorithmic credit scoring, consumer racism and credit card redlining). See: Part IV, This chapter, Sects. 4.1.4–4.1.4.2.3 of this book (on algorithmic redlining). See: Part IV, This chapter, Sect. 4.1.4.3 of this book (on "algorithmic redliking"). See: Part IV, This chapter, Sect. 4.1.3 of this book (on algorithmic prime-lining).

3248 Sunstein, Cass R., "Governing by Algorithm? No Noise and (Potentially) Less Bias", *Duke Law Journal*, Volume 71, 2022, pp. 1175 and ff.

3249 See: Part V, Chap. 5, Sects. 5.1.1.5.2.2–5.1.1.5.2.2.1.4 of this book (on the fundamental shift away from causation to correlations in algorithmic decision-making).

activities.[3250] Thence, its false-positive rate is exceedingly higher for Black defendants than for White defendants,[3251] while its false-negative rate[3252] is exceedingly greater[3253] for the latter than for the former.[3254]

§§ Compellingly, COMPAS holds Blacks,[3255] immigrants,[3256] Latinos,[3257] women[3258] and whites to radically different standards of algorithmic fairness. Put differently, COMPAS treats the former less fairly than the latter[3259] who are scored by it.[3260] Rivetingly, and yet somewhat disturbingly, this discrimination does not

---

3250 Xi Chen, "Algorithmic proxy discrimination and its regulations", *cit.*, pp. 1–13.

3251 Xi Chen, "Algorithmic proxy discrimination and its regulations", *cit.*, pp. 1–13.

3252 Mayson, Sandra G., "Bias In, Bias Out", *Yale Law Journal*, Volume 128, 2019, pp. 2218 and ff and passim.

3253 Flores, A.W./Lowenkamp, C.T./Bechtel, K., "False positives, false negatives, and false analyses: a rejoinder to "machine bias: there's software used across the country to predict future criminal", *Federal Probation Journal*, Volume 80, 2016, pp. 38–46. Sun, R. (Ed.), *The Cambridge Handbook of Computational Cognitive Sciences*, Cambridge, Cambridge University Press, 2023.

3254 Xi Chen, "Algorithmic proxy discrimination and its regulations", *cit.*, pp. 1–13.

3255 See: Chandler, Anupam, "The Racist Algorithm", *Michigan Law Review*, Volume 115, n. ° 6, 2018, p. 1026 (on racist algorithms, noting that "the possibilities for discriminatory manipulation are legion"). But see: Altenburger, Kristen M./Ho, Daniel E., "When Algorithms Import Private Bias into Public Enforcement: The Promise and Limitations of Statistical Debiasing Solutions", *Journal of Institutional & Theoretical Economics*, Volume 175, 2019, pp. 97–98 (calls for a "debias predictive algorithms" to assuage racist and/or biased, doctored and bigoted algorithms nevertheless).

3256 Maxwell, J./Tomlinson, J., *Experiments in Automating Immigration Systems*. Bristol: Bristol University Press, 2022, passim; Borgesius, FJ Zuiderveen, "Strengthening legal protection against discrimination by algorithms and artificial intelligence", *International Journal of Human Rights*, Volume 24, Issue 10, 2020, pp. 1573 and ff and passim. Hu, Margaret, "From the National Surveillance State to the Cybersurveillance State", *The Annual Review of Law and Social Science*, Volume 13, 2017, p. 168 ("Because of the routinized and administrative nature of the government-led *big data program* or *data surveillance (dataveillance) program, contemporary cybersurveillance is likely to be viewed as justified under crime, immigration control, and counterterrorism policy rationales*"). Italics added.

3257 See: Hamilton, Melissa, "The Biased Algorithm: Evidence of Disparate Impact on Hispanics", *American Criminal Law Review*, Volume 56, 2019, pp. 1553 and ff and passim.

3258 Hamilton, Melissa, "The sexist algorithm", *Behavioral Sciences and the Law*, Volume 37, Issue 2, Special Issue: the Use of Statistics in Criminal Cases, March–April 2019, 2019, pp. 1 and ff ("*Algorithmic risk assessment tools are informed by scientific research concerning which factors are predictive of recidivism and thus support the evidence-based practice movement in criminal justice.* Automated assessments of individualized risk (low, medium, high) *permit officials to make more effective management decisions. Computer-generated algorithms appear to be objective and neutral. But are these algorithms actually fair? The focus herein is on gender equity.* Studies confirm that women typically have far lower recidivism rates than men. *This differential raises the question of how well algorithmic outcomes fare in terms of predictive parity by gender.* This essay reports original research using a large dataset of offenders who were scored on the popular risk assessment tool COMPAS. *Findings indicate that COMPAS performs reasonably well at discriminating between recidivists and non-recidivists for men and women. Nonetheless, COMPAS algorithmic outcomes systemically overclassify women in higher risk groupings. Multiple measures of algorithmic equity and predictive accuracy are provided to support the conclusion that this algorithm is sexist*"). Italics added.

3259 But see: Algorithmic fairness lends itself to several incompatible standards. Whilst COMPAS falls short of meeting the baseline standards of "equal opportunity" and "equalized odds", it refrains

spring from any malicious[3261] intent[3262] whatsoever. Rather, it flows from the fact that the algorithm, ensnared on its own inscrutable inner workings,[3263] leverages on a cluster of apparently harmless proxies to disproportionately target[3264] members of racialized communities. More on this later.[3265]

---

itself from discriminating blacks from the prism of "predictive parity" nonetheless. A full-fledged analysis of the extant state of this scorching topic can be found in Hübner, Dietmar, "Two Kinds of Discrimination in AI-Based penal Decision-Making", *SIGKDD Explorations*, 2021.

3260 Xi Chen, "Algorithmic proxy discrimination and its regulations", *cit.*, pp. 1–13.

3261 Note, though, that some forms of racial discrimination may not be fully intentional. More likely than not, it can be related with the perils of big data colour-blindness that nonetheless relies on proxies to race and gender to make algorithmic decisions. Another problem is the one related with "creditworthiness by association" that causes more problems than it solves. Hurley, Mikella/Adebayo, Julius, "Credit Scoring in the Era of Big Data", *Yale Journal of Law and Technology*, Volume 18, 2016, p. 149 ("*recent studies have also questioned the accuracy of the data used by these tools, in some cases identifying serious flaws that have a substantial bearing on lending decisions. Big-data tools may also risk creating a system of "creditworthiness by association" in which consumers' familial, religious, social, and other affiliations determine their eligibility for an affordable loan. These tools may furthermore obscure discriminatory and subjective lending policies behind a single "objective" score. Such discriminatory scoring may not be intentional; instead, sophisticated algorithms may combine facially neutral data points and treat them as proxies for immutable characteristics such as race or gender, thereby circumventing existing non-discrimination laws and systematically denying credit access to certain groups. Finally, big-data tools may allow online payday lenders to target the most vulnerable consumers and lure them into debt traps*"). Italics added. Campisi, Natalie, From Inherent Racial Bias to Incorrect Data The Problems With Current Credit Scoring Models, Forbes (Feb. 26, 2021), https://www.forbes.com/advisor/creditcards/from-inherent-racial-bias-to-incorrect-data-the-problems-with-current-credit-scoring-models/; [https://perma.cc/EWA4-CS8E] (highlighting rampant racial bias in credit scoring systems); Oyama, Rebecca, "Do Not (Re)Enter: the Rise of Criminal Background Tenant Screening as a Violation of the Fair Housing Act", *Michigan Journal of Race and Law*, Volume 15, 2009, pp. 181, 184–93 (discussing a broad range of historical/criminal accounts as a way to screen undesirable tenants, such as Blacks and Latinos).

3262 Xi Chen, "Algorithmic proxy discrimination and its regulations", *cit.*, pp. 1–13.

3263 For an on-point breakdown of the distinct levels of opacity arising out of machine learning algorithms: Selbst, Andrew D./Barocas, Solon, "The Intuitive Appeal of Explainable Machines", *Fordham Law Review*, Volume 87, 2018, pp. 1085, 1089–99 (holding that there are plenty reasons for the insurer's ignorance. To begin with, the algorithm entails specialized knowledge to understand. That is, the insurer's employees may lack sufficient knowledge to understand the rationale behind the reasons in view of which the algorithm is producing prices for different customers—personalized pricing. Lastly, even if the insurer himself comprehends how the model operates, it may nonetheless lack expertise to comprehend why it operates the way it does. For that reason, the explainability of machines is a vital, but rather elusive, task. Thence, the famed authors deem it as the "nonintuitive" nature of algorithms. For purposes here, the insurer himself might indeed understand that its Artificial Intelligence-embedded technology formulates higher prices for those who actually access the website at hand, but may fail to come to terms with the fact that the explanation for this fact arises from the website's capacity to proxy for genetic information). See also: Scherer, Matthew U. Scherer, "Regulating Artificial Intelligence Systems: Risks, Challenges, Competencies, and Strategies", *Harvard Journal of Law and Technology*, Volume 29, 2016, pp. 353–369 (frames the crippling problem of opacity as "the possibility that the inner workings of an AI system may be kept secret and may not be susceptible to reverse engineering").

3264 Xi Chen, "Algorithmic proxy discrimination and its regulations", *cit.*, pp. 1–13.

3265 See: Part V of this book.

§§ In an era propelled by more intelligent algorithms[3266] and gargantuan/behemoth data generation,[3267] it takes scarce imagination to foresee the ubiquity and ineluctability of the algorithm discrimination caused by such proxies.[3268]

4.1.10.1.2 «The Racialization of Crime» and the Ineluctability of Biased Algorithmic Risk Assessment That Exacts a Toll on Members of Racialized Communities in Criminal Justice Settings

§§ With this context in place, biased algorithmic decision-making—that is shaping up to replace human judgement[3269]—and criminal justice are therefore woven of

---

[3266] Note, though, that the training of machine learning is long and tedious in that is an error-prone procedure than can ultimately impair future algorithmic decision-making: Price, W. Nicholson Price II, "Regulating Black-Box Medicine", *Michigan Law Review*, Volume 116, 2017, pp. 421–431 (leverages on Google Image's image recognition learning algorithm to shed light on the four-step process by which some algorithms are thoroughly trained. First, the algorithm is shown "a set of known images ('Here are 10,000 pictures of ducks')." Second, the algorithm "develops complex internal rules based on nonlinear processes." Third, the algorithm "tests those rules on a test set ('Which of these are ducks?')." And fourth, the algorithm accordingly adjusts its "internal rules based on the success of the test." These steps are trotted out and repeated many times "until it can accurately and consistently classify the images").

[3267] See: Wonyoung, So, "Which Information Matters? Measuring Landlord Assessment of Tenant Screening Reports", *Housing Policy Debate*, Volume 33, n. ° 6, 2023, pp. 1484–1510 (1501–1502) ("*Algorithmic scoring using criminal records is problematic because training data—a data set that is used to train a machine learning model—is inaccurate and the outcome variable ("desirable tenants") is unclear. For instance, the tenant screening company RealPage produces 11,000 reports using "abbreviated" criminal records, which are cheaper to acquire than full criminal records but do not include details of the resolution* (Kirchner & Goldstein, 2020). *An inaccurate model is highly likely to result from tenant screening services using these kinds of abbreviated data, given that it is important to include the final resolution of criminal justice procedures for proper assessment. Moreover, it would be challenging to set an outcome variable for developing this kind of algorithm because it is hard to project a certain criminal outcome into "good" tenant behaviors*"). Italics added.

[3268] Xi Chen, "Algorithmic proxy discrimination and its regulations", *cit.*, pp. 1–13.

[3269] But see: Part V, Chap. 5, Sect. 5.1.8.5 of this book (on law number five to interpret algorithmic decision-making, which mandates that robot-judges, robot-prosecutors and robot-lawyers must not enter the courtroom for they are utterly incapable of making sound and interpretable value judgements). But see: Millar, Jason/Kerr, Ian, "Delegation, Relinquishment and Responsibility: The Prospect of Expert Robots", *Robot Law*, Calo, Ryan/Froomkin, A. Michael/Kerr, Ian (Editors), Cheltenham, Edward Elgar Publishing, 2016, pp. 102, 106–107 (as these authors aptly put it "*we will rely on robots without really knowing why – simply because their algorithms provide the greatest number of successful outcomes.* We have already seen this in Google's search approach. Neither Larry (Page) nor Sergey (Brin) (nor any other Google employee) knowns exactly why one particular web page is a better result than another. *When the click patterns say it is, that's good enough.* No semantic or causal analysis is required...*Like the ancients, we will, quite rationally, come to rely upon them, knowing full well that we cannot necessarily explain the reasons for their decisions*"). Italics added. Converging: Casey, Anthony J./Niblett, Anthony, "Self-driving Laws", *University of Toronto Law Journal*, Volume 66, 2016, pp. 429–435 (contend that "as more information is generated, and the evolutionary algorithm updates and become a better forecaster, *we imagine that judges will increasingly rely on the advice of the algorithm*"). But see: Weizenbaum, Joseph,

the same cloth.[3270] The dichotomy between both is hardly flabbergasting, let alone random.[3271] For instance, modern societies have long tussled with the tagged *racialization of crime.*

§§ By this token, it bears mentioning that the criminal system of justice has been invidiously weaponized against racialized communities. On that account, technology is being weaponized against a thicket of *socially undesirables*: «the marginalized populations».[3272] To put it bluntly, the criminal system of justice wantonly ensnared thousands of Blacks and Latinos,[3273] thereby impairing their future employment opportunities further, and in spite of, their release.[3274] This harrowing portmanteau of racially motivated practices neatly encapsulates, hands-in-glove, the concept of «racialization of crime».

Computer Power and Human Reason: From Judgment to Calculation, 1st edition, New York, W. H. Freeman & Co, 1976, pp. 1–300 (227) ("examines the sources of the computer's powers and offers evaluative explorations of what computers can do, cannot do, and should not be employed to do") (this founding father of Artificial Intelligence presciently noted that we should not entrust Artificial Intelligence-embedded technologies with "tasks that demand wisdom"). Italics added. The approval of rental applications is arguably one of those tasks that should never be entrusted to machines). More on this on Part IV, This chapter, Sects. 4.1.4–4.1.4.2.1 of this book.

3270 But see: Part V, Chap. 5, Sect. 5.1.7.2 of this book (on law number two to control algorithmic decision-making, which mandates that black box models must not be entrusted with the task of making high stake decisions—v.g. health and freedom).

3271 But see: Sidhu, Dawinder S., "Moneyball Sentencing", *Boston College Law Review*, Volume 56, 2015, 671 (on the role of randomness in sentencing settings). On the role of chance and randomness: Teigena, Halvor/Kanten, Alf Børre, "Out of the blue: on the suddenness of perceived chance events", *Thinking & Reasoning*, Volume 29, n. ° 1, 2023, pp. 137–175 (137) ("*people commonly use terms like 'random', 'by chance', or 'accidentally' when they describe occurrences that sidestep the normal course of events, with no apparent causal link to ongoing activities. Such intrusive events are typically perceived as happening all of a sudden.* This was demonstrated in seven experiments (N ¼ 1299) by asking people to identify statements they believed belonged to stories about chance events, and by comparing chance vs. nonchance events from their own life and from the lives of others. Suddenness also appeared to be more strongly associated with beginnings than with endings of an episode. Thus, statements about sudden beginnings of a career or a relationship were more readily believed to happen 'by chance' than 'not by chance'. *But life-changing events did not become more accidental simply by being placed in the beginning of a 'life chapter'. These studies highlight a central but neglected feature of perceived randomness*"). Italics added.

3272 Calo, Ryan, "Artificial Intelligence Policy: Primer and Roadmap", *University of California, Davis*, Volume 51, 2017, pp. 399–435 (412).

3273 Freeman, Andrea, "Racism in the Credit Card Industry", *North Carolina Law Review*, Volume 95, Number 4, 2017, pp. 1071–1160 (1092 and ff).

3274 Monk, E. P., "The color of punishment: African Americans, skin tone, and the criminal justice system", *Ethnic and Racial Studies*, Volume 42, Issue 10, 2019, pp. 1593–1612; Agung-Igusti, R. P., "Raced and risky subjects: The interplay of racial and managerial ideologies as an expression of "colorblind" racism", *American Journal of Community Psychology*, Volume 73, 2024, passim; Alexander, M., *The new Jim Crow: Mass incarceration in the age of colorblindness*, The New Press, 2012. See: Bar-Gill/Oren/Warren, Elizabeth, "Making Credit Safer", *University of Pennsylvania Law Review*, Volume 157, 2008, pp. 1–66 (argue that Black defendants are far more likely to be incarcerated, arrested, surveilled and harassed than White folks, which leads to the conclusion that the use of credit scores and income presents another way in which credit decisions leverage on structural disadvantage).

§§ The «racialization of crime»[3275] process therefore lends itself to racialized defendants' earnest attempts to fend off attacks perpetrated by law enforcement agencies. The ballooned figures of wrong convictions lend weight, and add plausibility, to this overriding claim.[3276]

§§ On the heels of, and fundamentally building on, the *structural racism* against the backdrop of which White privilege[3277] unfolds,[3278] Critical Race Theory[3279] avowedly contends that the newest technological developments (e.g. Artificial Intelligence-embedded technologies) amount to the flagship of an agreed-upon strategy according to which non-White communities (chiefly, Black, and Latino[3280]) should be enmeshed in criminal justice system.[3281] Especially, albeit not exclusively, young black men.[3282] Algorithmic risk assessment flares up this jarring/gruesome reality.

3275 Brewer, R. M., & Heitzeg, N. A., "The racialization of crime and punishment: Criminal justice, Color-Blind racism, and the political economy of the prison industrial complex", *cit.*, pp. 625–644.

3276 Gross, Samuel R., Maurice Possley, and Kalara Stephens, "Race and Wrongful Convictions in the United States." National Registry of Exonerations, Newkirk Center for Science and Society, University of California-Irvine, 2017. See: Bar-Gill/Oren/Warren, Elizabeth, "Making Credit Safer", *University of Pennsylvania Law Review*, Volume 157, 2008, pp. 1–66 (argue that Black defendants are far more likely to be incarcerated, arrested, surveilled and harassed than White folks, which leads to the conclusion that the use of credit scores and income presents another way in which credit decisions leverage on structural disadvantage).

3277 Cole, Stephanie/Ring, Natalie et al. (Editors), *The Folly of Jim Crow: Rethinking the Segregated South (Walter Prescott Webb Memorial Lectures, published for the University of Texas at Arlington by Texas A&M University Press Book 43)*, Texas, Texas A&M University Press (April 3, 2012), 2012 ("*The studies in this collection incorporate important perspectives that have developed during the past two decades among scholars interested in gender and politics, the culture of resistance, and "the hegemonic function of 'whiteness.'"* By asking fresh questions and critically examining long-held beliefs, the new studies contained in *The Folly of Jim Crow* will, ironically, reinforce at least one of the key observations made in C. Vann Woodward's landmark 1955 study: *In its idiosyncratic, contradictory, and multifaceted development and application, the career of Jim Crow was, indeed, strange. Further, as these studies demonstrate—and as alluded to in the title—it is folly to attempt to locate the genesis of the South's institutional racial segregation in any single event, era, or policy. "Instead," as W. Fitzhugh Brundage notes in his introduction to the volume*, "formal segregation evolved through an untidy process of experimentation and adaptation"). Italics added.

3278 Laub, John H., "Understanding Inequality and the Justice System Response: Charting a New Way Forward.", New York: William T. Grant Foundation, 2014.

3279 See: Part III, Chap. 3, Sects. 3.1.4.1–3.1.4.2. (on critical race theory as a linchpin of critical artificial intelligence studies). See: Part IV, This chapter, Sects. 4.1.1–4.1.1.1 of this book (on biased predictive policing).

3280 Rios, Victor M., *Punished: Policing the Lives of Black and Latino Boys*, New York: NYU Press, 2011.

3281 Duster, Troy, "Pattern, Purpose and Race in the Drug War.", *Crack in America: Demon Drugs and Social Justice*, Reinarman and H. G. Levine (Editors), Berkeley: University of California Press, 1997.

3282 Epp, Charles R., Steven Maynard-Moody, and Donald P. Haider-Markel, *Pulled Over: How Police Stops Define Race and Citizenship*, Chicago: University of Chicago Press, 2014.

§§ Strikingly, algorithmic risk assessment is barbed with inequality,[3283] which inheres and permeates all algorithmic prediction,[3284] thereby hindering the much-acclaimed algorithmic fairness.[3285] This gruesome reality primes scholars to deftly tackling this sweltering issue that extends far beyond the challenges of an advanced technology. Not only do machine learning algorithms shed a keen light on a hack-neyed/trotted out problem,[3286] but, and foremost, they amount to nothing but «old wine in new bottles». This essay accordingly avers that smoothing out racial disparity in prediction will entail seismic shifts in the way the criminal justice system conceives of and fundamentally responds to risk.[3287] The time is now ripe to take a step back to pore over the opening claim of this section: biased algorithmic risk assessment.

§§ It is oft-posited that «there's software used across the country to predict future criminals. And it's biased against blacks».[3288] The media was abuzz with news emphasizing that a particular machine learning algorithmic tool, COMPAS, was riddled with racial biases against black defendants.[3289]

§§ The *ProPublica* compelling story, *Machine Bias*, forms part of a broader technological apparatus within which algorithmic biases operate.[3290] Which should not strike you, dear reader, as odd: the age of machine learning algorithms is upon us[3291] after all. Artificial Intelligence-embedded technologies routinely engage in predictions[3292] that sway every single facet of our daily lives.[3293] Before long, Artificial

---

[3283] O'Neil, Cathy, *Weapons of Math Destruction. How Big Data Increases Inequality and Threatens Democracy*, London, Penguin Random House, 2016, passim (showing how algorithms utilized in modern societies are amenable to perpetuate racial discrimination, partially through perpetuation of social disadvantage and wealth divides). See also: O'Neil, Cathy, "When Not to Trust the Algorithm", *Interview published in the Harvard Business Review's Ideacast*, 2016, passim; O' Neil, Cathy, "Amazon's Gender-Biased Algorithm Is Not Alone", 2018, accessed 2 January 2025 (on gender-related algorithmic biases).

[3284] Berk, R. A./A. A. Elzarka, "Almost Politically Acceptable Criminal Justice Risk Assessment", *Criminology and Public Policy*, 2020, pp. 1–28.

[3285] Berk, R. A./A. K. Kuchibhotla/E. Tchetgen, "Fair Risk Algorithms", *Annual Review of Statistics and Its Applications*, 2022.

[3286] Mayson, Sandra G., "Bias In, Bias Out", *cit.*, pp. 2218–2300 (2218).

[3287] Mayson, Sandra G., "Bias In, Bias Out", *cit.*, pp. 2218–2300 (2218).

[3288] Angwin, Julia et al., "Machine Bias", *ProPublica* (May 23, 2016), https://www.propublica.org/article/machine-bias-risk-assessments-in-criminal-sentencing; [https://perma.cc/4G83-MDAS] (harshly criticizing disparity in false-positive rates as a purely unjustified bias). See also: Freeman, Katherine, "Algorithmic Injustice: How the Wisconsin Supreme Court Failed to Protect Due Process Rights in State v. Loomis", *North Carolina Journal of Law and Technology*, Volume 18, 2016, pp. 75–86 (echoing the very same views).

[3289] Mayson, Sandra G., "Bias In, Bias Out", *cit.*, pp. 2218–2300 (2221).

[3290] Mayson, Sandra G., "Bias In, Bias Out", *cit.*, pp. 2218–2300 (2221).

[3291] See: Kleinberg, Jon, et al., "Discrimination in the Age of Algorithms", *Journal of Legal Analysis*, 2018, pp. 114–174.

[3292] Wisser, Leah, "Pandora's Algorithmic Black Box: The Challenges of Using Algorithmic Risk Assessments in Sentencing", *American Criminal Law Review*, Volume 56, 2019, pp. 1811–1832.

[3293] Zhu, Mirilla, "Jury, Using Artificial Intelligence to Predict Recidivism Rates", *Yale Scientific*, 2020, passim. See also: Chasemi et al., Medhi, "The application of Machine Learning to a General

Intelligence-embedded technologies will be entrusted with the task of driving our cars.[3294]

§§ Whilst this reality might come across as dystopic, loosely distant, implausible,[3295] or faintly aloof, one should not lose sight of the fact that machine learning algorithms have pierced into every aspect of our quotidian. Hardly any bewildering surprise stems from the fact that biased machine learning algorithms are currently shaping the present and the future of advertising,[3296] consumer lending,[3297] credit scoring,[3298] (biased) algorithmic lending,[3299] housing,[3300] hiring,[3301] predictive policing[3302]—just about any governmental[3303] or business activity[3304] that has some predictive component.[3305] Along with the unbridled expansion of algorithmic decision-making comes algorithmic harms in consumer markets,[3306] which fall beyond the breadth and scope of this essay though.

Risk-Need Assessment Instrument in the Prediction of Criminal Recidivism", *Criminal Justice and Behavior*, Volume 48, 2020, pp. 518–538.

[3294] See: Part III, Chap. 3, Sects. 3.1.5.9–3.1.5.9.3 of this book (on Critical Artificial Intelligence Studies, with a sharper focus on the functional shortcomings facing self-driving vehicles). The worrisome challenges posed by the up-and-coming and rough around the edges self-driving cars are upon us. See: Teoh, Eric/Kidd, David G., "Rage Against the Machine? Google's Self-Driving Versus Human Drivers", *Journal of Safety Research*, Volume 63, 2019, pp. 57–59 and passim (on the legal quandaries laid bare by the self-driving cars). See also: "Cracking the Code: the Black Box Problem of AI", available at: https://scads.ai/cracking-the-code-the-black-box-problem-of-ai/ (access: 21.09.2024) ("*Artificial intelligence (AI) is increasingly becoming integrated into our daily lives, from virtual assistants to self-driving cars.* Despite AI having the potential to revolutionize the way we live and work, it also presents unique challenges. One of the most significant challenges is the "black box" problem. *The black box problem refers to the lack of transparency and interpretability of AI algorithms. As a matter of fact, it is difficult to understand how an AI system arrives at its conclusions or predictions. This poses a significant challenge. Decisions made by AI can have serious consequences, such as in healthcare or financial sectors*"). Italics added.

[3295] In Italian doctrine: Irti, Natalino, *Un Diritto Incalcolabile.* Torino: G. Giappichelli Editore, 2016.

[3296] See: Wallheimer, Brian, "Are you Ready for Personalized Pricing? Companies Are Figuring out What Individual Customers Will Pay-and Charging Accordingly", *Chicago Booth Review*, 2018, passim; The Effects of Online Disclosure About Personalized Pricing on Consumers 7 (Org. for Econ. Coop. and Dev., Working Paper No. 303, 2021 ("[T]he quantity of personal data held on online consumers, combined with the *increasing prevalence of personalization in other domains (e.g., advertisement)*, means there is at least potential for online personalized pricing to become more commonplace and more sophisticated"). Italics added. But see: Bartlett, Robert/Morse, Adair/Stanton/Wallace, Nancy, "Consumer Lending Discrimination in the FinTech Era", *National Bureau of Economic Research*, Working Paper No. 25,943, Volume 50, 2019 (on the perils of consumer lending discrimination).

[3297] This is oft-tagged as "risk-based pricing." See: Phillipps, Robert, "Optimizing Prices for Consumer Credit", *Journal of Revenue and Pricing Management*, Volume 12, 2013, pp. 360–365 ("[A] riskier customer should pay a higher price in order to compensate for the higher probability of default and the associated cost to the lender"). See also: Staten, Michael, "Risk-Based Pricing in Consumer Lending", *Journal of Law, Economics & Policy*, Volume 11, 2015, pp. 33 and ff and passim.

§§ This metamorphic shift, though, is anything but flummoxing. It is oft-contended that algorithmic prediction[3307] is exceedingly more efficient,[3308] cost-effective,[3309] and routinely more accurate, than is human judgment[3310] in an overarching sense.[3311] It follows that algorithmic decision-making weeds out the irrational

---

[3298] See: Part IV, This chapter, Sects. 4.1.4–4.1.4.2.1 of this book (on mortgage redlining). See: Part IV, This chapter, Sects. 4.1.2–4.1.4.3 of this book (on algorithmic credit scoring, consumer racism and credit card redlining). See: Part IV, This chapter, Sects. 4.1.4–4.1.4.2.3 of this book (on algorithmic redlining). See: Part IV, This chapter, Sect. 4.1.4.3 of this book (on "algorithmic redliking"). See: Part IV, This chapter, Sect. 4.1.3 of this book (on algorithmic prime-lining). See: Karlan, Dean/Zinman, Jonathan, "Observing Unobservables: Identifying Information Asymmetries with a Consumer Credit Field Experiment", *Econometrica*, Volume 77, 2009, pp. 1993 and ff and passim (drawing on empirical evidence to premise the finding according to which moral hazard exists in consumer credit markets); Gathergood, John/Guttman-Kenney, Benedict/Hunt, Stefan, "How Do Pay-day Loans Affect Borrowers? Evidence from the U.K. Market", *The Review of Financial Studies*, Volume 32, 2019, p. 496 (arguing that payday loans catalyse persistent increases in defaults, which, in turn, cause consumers to exceed their bank overdraft limits). But see: Einav, Liran/Jenkins, Mark/Levin, Jonathan, "The Impact of Credit Scoring on Consumer Lending", *The RAND Journal of Economics*, Volume 44, 2013, p. 249 (showing unequivocally that the adoption of computer-run algorithmic credit scoring led to conspicuously higher-risk applicant lending).

[3299] See: Aneja/Abhay P./Avenancio-León, Carlos F., "No Credit for Time Served? Incarceration and Credit-Driven Crime Cycles", *AEA Papers and Proceedings*, Volume 109, 2019, pp. 160 and ff and passim (discusses the negative reflex of incarceration on algorithmic credit scoring and income). See: Bar-Gill/Oren/Warren, Elizabeth, "Making Credit Safer", *University of Pennsylvania Law Review*, Volume 157, 2008, pp. 1–66 (argue that Black defendants are far more likely to be incarcerated, arrested, surveilled and harassed than White folks, which leads to the conclusion that the use of algorithmic credit scores and income presents another way in which credit decisions leverage on structural disadvantage).

[3300] See: *Tech, Bias and Housing Initiative, the Promise and Perils of Residential Proptech, Year 1, Research Summary Report, April 2023, TechEquity Collaborative*, p. 5 available at: https://techequity.us/wp-content/uploads/2023/04/TBHI-Y1-Research-Summary-Report.pdf (28.11.2024). ("*Residential Proptech also has the potential to exacerbate the bias inherent in our housing system. Its rise is due, in part, to the desperation felt by average home seekers. With a severely constrained housing supply, companies offering an easier pathway to homeownership may exploit communities that have been harmed by housing discrimination in the past. Opaque algorithms incorporate biased data into their decision-making processes, making it harder to enforce fair housing laws.* Residential Proptech companies often operate in a regulatory gray area, leaving consumers without the protections they would have from traditional housing regulatory systems. *As unprecedented capital investment flows into this space, venture-backed companies' winner-take-all approach to growth has the potential to exacerbate inequality rather than combat it*"). Italics added. See: Part IV, This chapter, Sects. 4.1.4 –4.1.4.2.3 of this book. Campisi, Natalie, From Inherent Racial Bias to Incorrect Data The Problems With Current Credit Scoring Models, Forbes (Feb. 26, 2021), https://www.forbes.com/advisor/creditcards/from-inherent-racial-bias-to-incorrect-data-the-problems-with-current-credit-scoring-models/; [https://perma.cc/EWA4-CS8E] (highlighting rampant racial bias in credit scoring systems); Oyama, Rebecca, "Do Not (Re)Enter: the Rise of Criminal Background Tenant Screening as a Violation of the Fair Housing Act", *Michigan Journal of Race and Law*, Volume 15, 2009, pp. 181, 184–93 (discussing a broad range of historical/criminal accounts as a way to screen undesirable tenants, such as Blacks and Latinos); Statement of Interest of the United States at 12, *Louis v. SafeRent Sols., LLC, No. 1:22-cv-10800* (D. Mass. Jan. 9, 2023) (holding that the Fair Housing Act liability stretches far and beyond, thus encompassing a vast assortment of entities providing housing-related services, including corporations that offer tenant screening services).

[3301] Grimmelmann, James/Westreich, Daniel, "Incomprehensible Discrimination", *California Law Review Online*, Volume 7, 2017, pp 170 and ff and passim. This exciting piece of research revolves

biases that taint/undermine so much of human decision-making.[3312] It is important to aver, however, that there is no shiver of doubt, nor this statement amounts to a figment of a bewildering imagination, that Artificial Intelligence-embedded technologies have also a penchant[3313] for racial discrimination.[3314]

---

around as a vignette and mock judicial opinion, focusing on fictional case (an employment-based AI employed in the fictional universe of the movie Zootopia) under a specific legal regime (Title VII). It ultimately solves this fictional case by drawing a difference between proxy discrimination and disparate impact. See also: Kim, Pauline T., "Data-Driven Discrimination at Work", *William and Mary Law Review*, Volume 58, 2017, pp. 857, 863–64 (shedding a keen light on the racial effects of algorithmic prediction in the remit of employment). Converging: Zywicki, Todd J./Adamson, Joseph D., "The Law and Economics of Subprime Lending", *University of Colorado Law Review*, 2009, pp. 1–9 (contending that Black workers with roughly the same abilities and educational background earn far less than comparable white workers or have considerably fewer employment opportunities); King, Allan G./Markovich, Marko J., "Big Data" and the Risk of Employment Discrimination, *Oklahoma Law Review*, Volume 68, 2016, pp. 555–563 (on employment discrimination). Dobbie, Will, Jacob Goldin, and Crystal S. Yang, "The Effects of Pretrial Detention on Conviction, Future Crime, and Employment: Evidence from Randomly Assigned Judges," *American Economic Review*, Volume 108, 2018, 201–240.

[3302] See: Part IV, This chapter, Sects. 4.1.1–4.1.1.1 of this book (on biased predictive policing). See also: Selbst, Andrew, "Disparate Impact in Big Data Policing", *cit.*, p. 113 ("[P]redictive policing [is] a popular and growing method for police departments to prevent or solve crimes"). See also: Letter from Jonathan J. Wroblewski, Dir., Office of Policy & Legislation, to Hon. Patti B. Saris, Chair, U.S. Sentencing Comm'n 2 (July 29, 2014) [hereinafter DOJ Letter to U.S.S.C.] ("*Predictive Policing—the use of algorithms that combine historical and up-to-the-minute crime information* to do the work of hundreds of traditional crime analysts and *produce real-time targeted patrol areas—is spreading*"). Italics added.

[3303] Williams, Rebecca, "Rethinking Administrative Law for Algorithmic Decision-Making", *Oxford Journal of Legal Studies*, Volume 42, 2021, pp. 468 e ff and passim; Calo, Ryan/Citron, Danielle Keats, "The Automated Administrative State: A Crisis of Legitimacy", *Emory Law Journal*, Volume 70, 2021, passim (broaches the interplay between administrative law and the rise of algorithmic decision-making).

[3304] Williams, Rebecca, "Accountable Algorithms: Adopting the Public Law Toolbox Outside the Realm of Public Law", *Current Legal Problems,* Vol. 75, 2022, pp. 237–263 (on the dire need to create a framework to hold algorithms accountable outside the realm of public law and beyond—including commercial endeavours).

[3305] See: Ferguson, Andrew Guthrie, "Predictive Prosecution", *Wake Forest Law*, Volume 51, 2016, pp. 705, 705–08 (explaining "predictive prosecution" and exploring its "promise and perils").

[3306] See: Bar-Gill, Oren/Sunstein, Cass R./Talgam-Cohen, Inbal, "Algorithmic Harm in Consumer Markets", *Journal of Legal Analysis*, Volume 15, n. ° 1, 2023, pp. 1–47; Yang/Kai Hao, "Selling Consumer Data for Profit: Optimal Market-Segmentation Design and its Consequences", *American Economic Review*, Volume 112, Issue 4, April 2022, 2022, pp. 1364–1393; Lee, Nicole Turner/Resnick, Paul/Barton, Genie, *Algorithmic Bias Detection and Mitigation: Best Practices and Policies to Reduce Consumer Harms*. Washington, DC: Brookings Institution, 2019, passim.

[3307] Almada, Miguel, "Human intervention in automated decision-making: toward the construction of contestable systems", *Proceedings of the Seventeenth International Conference on Artificial Intelligence and Law*, 2019, pp. 2–11 (on the sweltering challenges arising out of automated decision with a dash of human intervention).

[3308] See, e.g., Yang, Min et al., "The Efficacy of Violence Prediction: A Meta-Analytic Comparison of Nine Risk Assessment Tools", *Psychology Bulletin*, 2010, pp. 740–742 (arguing that "[t]he range of possible criterion variables for violence is wide, and "includes self-reports to third-party reports...,

§§ Algorithmic decision-making, if nothing else, has a remarkable potential to mimic, reify,[3315] exacerbate,[3316] perpetuate[3317] and further compound[3318] loathsome social inequality,[3319] all of which whilst upholding both the veneer of high-tech

informal social service or police contact, formal contact or police charges, formal adjudication and court convictions, and incarceration").

[3309] In spite of its deep-seated racial bias, decision-makers continue to deploy redlining tactics through big data and may even justify such unlawful practices by claiming that the latter abide by cost-effectiveness. See: Humber, Nadiyah J., "A Home for Digital Equity: Algorithmic Redlining and Property Technology", *California Law Review*, Volume 111, Issue 5, 2023, pp. 1421–1484. Allen, James, "The Color of Algorithms: An Analysis and Proposed Research Agenda Deterring Algorithmic Redlining", *Fordham Urban Law Journal*, Volume 46, 2019, pp. 219–234 (229–234) (discussing how historical mortgage redlining greatly swayed modern algorithms generated by massive batches of data sets that consist of decades of information built on exclusion and racial discrimination in the purview of financing, marketing, and housing). See: Part IV, This chapter, Sects. 4.1.4–4.1.4.2.3 of this book.

[3310] But see: Barocas, Solon/Selbst, Andrew D., "Big Data's Disparate Impact", *California Law Review*, Volume 104, 2016, pp. 671–682 (discussing how data is often flawed, rigged, incomplete, imperfect and therefore algorithms inherit the prejudice of the original decision makers).

[3311] But see: Citron, Danielle Keats/Pasquale, Frank, "The Scored Society: Due Process for Automated Predictions", *Washington Law Review*, Volume 89, 2014, pp. 1, 4–5 (highlighting how human beings programming automated systems is directly conducive to, and leads, to fundamentally inaccurate results since the source code, predictive algorithms and datasets may encompass human biases which, in turn, have a disparate impact on historically disadvantaged groups).

[3312] But see: Citron, Danielle Keats/Pasquale, Frank A., "The Scored Society: Due Process for Automated Predictions", *Washington Law Review*, Volume 89, 2014, pp. 1–34 (arguing that "[a]*dvocates applaud the removal of human beings and their flaws from the assessment process*," but arguing that bias remains "[*b*]*ecause human beings program predictive algorithms, their biases and values are embedded into the software's instructions*"). Italics added. See: Part IV, This chapter, Sects. 4.1.4–4.1.4.2.3 of this book.

[3313] Mayson, Sandra G., "Bias In, Bias Out", *cit.*, pp. 2218–2300.

[3314] See: Eubanks, Virginia, *Automating Inequality: How High-Tech Tools Profile, Police and Punish the Poor*. New York: St. Martin's Press, 2018, 1–272 (1 ff and passim) (coining the expression «automating inequality» to vividly portray the downsides of using high-technology to compound the yawning gap between rich and poor against the backdrop of biased algorithms). Noble, Safiya Umoja, *Algorithms of Oppression: How search engines reinforce racism*, New York, New University Press, 2018, pp. 1–248 ("*Run a Google search for "Black girls"—what will you find? "Big Booty" and other sexually explicit terms are likely to come up as top search terms. But, if you type in "white girls," the results are radically different*. The suggested porn sites and un-moderated discussions about "why Black women are so sassy" or "why Black women are so angry" presents a disturbing portrait of Black womanhood in modern society. In *Algorithms of Oppression*, Safiya Umoja Noble challenges the idea that search engines like Google offer an equal playing field for all forms of ideas, identities, and activities. *Data discrimination is a real social problem; Noble argues that the combination of private interests in promoting certain sites, along with the monopoly status of a relatively small number of Internet search engines, leads to a biased set of search algorithms that privilege whiteness and discriminate against people of color, specifically women of color*"). Italics added. See: Part IV, This chapter, Sect. 4.1.8 of this book (on biased word embeddings with an entrenched presence on search engines run by tech moguls).

[3315] Duster, Troy, "Race and Reification in Science." *Science*, 307, 2005, passim.

[3316] See: Yapa, L., "How the discipline of geography exacerbates poverty in the Third World", *Futures*, Volume 3, 2022, pp. 33–46. See also: Wonyoung, So, "Which Information Matters?

objectivity[3320] and the façade of «trust in numbers»[3321] and «trust in science».[3322] The latter seeks to jointly propel algorithmic decision-making to the higher echelons of iron-clad neutrality.[3323] Note, though, that these are hardly elating news for criminal procedure law.

§§ Nowhere is the overriding concern with algorithmic bias more pressing than in criminal procedure law settings[3324] owing to the fact that one's fundamental rights[3325] hang on the balance. Notwithstanding, and spite of all the caveats,[3326]

Measuring Landlord Assessment of Tenant Screening Reports", *Housing Policy Debate*, Volume 33, n. ° 6, 2023, pp. 1484–1510 (1502) ("*algorithmic scoring can exacerbate this racially unequal landscape in rental agreements not just because the algorithm may be inaccurate, but because landlords may want to follow the risk assessment made by the tenant screening report. This is alarming for low-income tenants, particularly housing voucher holders*"). Italics added.

3317 Crawford, Kate/Schultz, Jason, "Big Data and Due Process: Toward a Framework to Redress Predictive Privacy Harms", *Boston College Law Review*, Volume 55, 2014, pp. 93, 99–101 (pinpointing pathways through which predictive analytic tools perpetuate discriminatory practices).

3318 Hellman, Deborah, "Indirect Discrimination and the Duty to Avoid Compounding Injustice", *Foundations of Indirect Discrimination Law*, Collins, Hugh/Khaitan, Tarunabh (Editors), Oxford, Hart Publishing; Reprint edition (June 25, 2020), 2020, p. 107 (Professor Deborah Hellman coined this expression to depict a decision that "exacerbates the harm caused by the prior injustice because it entrenches the harm or carries it into another domain").

3319 Zajko, M, "Conservative AI and social inequality: conceptualizing alternatives to bias through social theory", *Artificial Intelligence and Society*, Volume 36, 2021, pp. 1047–1056.

3320 But see: Benjamin, Ruha, *Race After Technology: Abolitionist Tools for the New Jim Code*, New York, Polity, 2019, pp. 1–172 (7) (discussing that Artificial Intelligence-embedded technologies are viewed as iron-clad tools of objectivity and devoid of any biases whatsoever). Ruha Benjamin accordingly contends that "the employment of new technologies that reflect and reproduce existing inequities but that are promoted and perceived as more objective or progressive than the discriminatory systems of a previous era").

3321 See: Joh, Elizabeth E., "Policing by Numbers: Big Data and the Fourth Amendment", *Washington Law Review*, Volume 89, 2014, pp. 35, 42–55. See also: Porter, Theodore M., *Trust in Numbers: The Pursuit of Objectivity in Science and Public Life*, Princeton, NJ: Princeton University Press, 1995.

3322 Sherman, Lawrence W., "Targeting, Testing and Tracking Police Services: The Rise of Evidence Based Policing, 1975–2025", *Crime and Justice*, 42 (1), 2013, pp. 377–451; Lavender III, I., *Race in American science fiction*, Bloomington: Indiana University Press, 2011.

3323 See: Farina, M./Lavazza, A., *Philosophy, expertise, and the myth of* neutrality, Routledge Studies in Contemporary Philosophy, London, Routledge, 2024.

3324 Mayson, Sandra G., "Bias In, Bias Out", *cit.*, pp. 2218–2300.

3325 See: Hu, Margaret, "From the National Surveillance State to the Cybersurveillance State", *The Annual Review of Law and Social Science*, Volume 13, 2017, p. 166 (argues that ubiquitous and ever-present surveillance of *socially undesirables* remains at a pitch of degradation of fundamental rights in that Artificial Intelligence-embedded technologies—propelled by tools like Social Radar and Total Information Awareness, TIA—can capture "a *pictorial depiction of the comprehensive cybersurveillance anticipated through the Social Radar system, which anticipated the full integration of drone footage, biometric data signatures, econometrics, and other intelligence sources to achieve higher-order cybersurveillance inferences. Social Radar appears to trace its philosophical origins to TIA*").

3326 See: Eubanks, Virginia, *Automating Inequality: How High-Tech Tools Profile, Police and Punish the Poor*. New York: St. Martin's Press, 2018, 1–272 (1 ff and passim) (coining the expression

it seems as though the legal community is so enthralled with the jaw-dropping, and spine-chilling, achievements of Artificial Intelligence-embedded technologies that is gradually relinquishing power[3327] over high stake decisions.[3328] Unsurprisingly, over the course of the last 10 years or so, algorithmic risk assessment[3329] has somewhat mushroomed in that has spread swiftly[3330] like wildfire.[3331] The assertion according to which algorithmic risk assessment has taken criminal justice by storm is neither unwarranted, nor uncalled for, nor is statistically unsound.

§§ This shift toward algorithmic risk assessment seeks to gauge whether and to what extent a person will either engage in flagitious[3332] activities[3333] or be arrested for having committed a crime.[3334] The qualms with future crime are neither blazingly

«automating inequality» to vividly portray the downsides of using high-technology to compound the yawning gap between rich and poor against the backdrop of biased algorithms). See also: Pasquale, Frank, *The Black Box Society: The Secret Algorithms that Control Money and Information*. Cambridge, Massachusetts: Harvard University Press, 2015, 1–320 (8–10 and passim) (noting that biased algorithms, which have underlying discrimination problems, contribute exponentially to further social biases. His most intriguing claim is that such biased algorithms have been incorporated/ etched in the bulk of the corporations' informatic system, to the detriment of human kind in an overarching sense); Roth, Andrea, "Machine Testimony", *Yale Law Journal*, Volume 126, 2017, pp. 1972 and ff and passim.

3327 See: Re, Richard M./Solow-Niederman, Alicia, "Developing Artificially Intelligent", *Stanford Technology Law Review*, Volume 22, 2019, pp. 242 ff and passim. Cohen, Julien E., *Between Truth and Power: The Legal Constructions of Informational Capitalism*. Oxford: Oxford University Press, 2019, pp. 1–376 (p. 192) ("*automated processes* have obvious efficiency advantages, *but such processes may not align well (or well at all) with applicable legal requirements that are couched in shades of gray*"). Italics added.

3328 But see: Part V, Chap. 5, Sect. 5.1.7.2 of this book (on law number two to control algorithmic decision-making, which mandates that black box models must not be entrusted with the task of making high stake decisions—v.g. health and freedom). But see: Part V, Chap. 5, Sect. 5.1.8.5 of this book (on law number five to interpret algorithmic decision-making, which mandates that robot-judges, robot-prosecutors and robot-lawyers must not enter the courtroom for they are utterly incapable of making sound and interpretable value judgements). See also: Casey, Anthony J./Niblett, Anthony, "Self-driving Laws", *University of Toronto Law Journal*, Volume 66, 2016, pp. 429–435 (contend that "as more information is generated, and the evolutionary algorithm updates and become a better forecaster, *we imagine that judges will increasingly rely on the advice of the algorithm*"). Italics added.

3329 Simon & Schuster, Green, B., "Algorithmic realism: expanding the boundaries of algorithmic thought", *Proceedings of the 2020 Conference on Fairness Accountability and Transparency*, 2020, passim; Green, B./Hu L., "The Myth in the Methodology: Towards a Recontextualization of Fairness in Machine Learning", *Machine Learning Debates Work 35th Internation Conference of Machine Learning*, 2018, passim; Green, B., Chen Y, "Disparate interactions: An algorithm-in-the-loop analysis of fairness in risk assessments", *FAT* 2019, Proceedings of 2019 Conference of Fairness, Accountability, Transparency*, 2019, pp. 90–99.

3330 See: Eaglin, Jessica M., "Constructing Recidivism Risk", *Emory Law Journal*, Volume 67, 59, 2017, 61 n.1 (arguing that "[p]redictive technologies are spreading through the criminal justice system like wildfire").

3331 Mayson, Sandra G., "Bias In, Bias Out", *cit.*, pp. 2218–2300 (2221).

3332 See: Berk, R., *Criminal Justice Forecasts of Risk: A Machine Learning Approach*, New York, Springer Science & Business Media, 2012, passim; Kehl, D. L., Guo, P., and Kessler, S. A., *Algorithms in the Criminal Justice System: Assessing the Use of Risk Assessments in Sentencing*, 2017,

new nor are they befuddling.[3335] Strikingly, since immemorial times, law enforcement agencies, public prosecutors, magistrate judges, probation officers,[3336] and parole officers[3337] have long been allotted the lofty task of making intuitive/empiric assessments[3338] of future[3339] dangerousness.[3340] Understandably, though not laudably, a biased algorithmic risk assessment inordinately[3341] befalls[3342] on communities of colour.[3343]

---

accessed at https://dash.harvard.edu/bitstream/handle/1/33746041/2017-07_responsivecommunities_2.pdf?sequence¼1 on October 24, 2024.

3333 Goel, Sharad/Shroff, Ravi/Skeem, Jennifer/Slobogin, Christopher, *The Accuracy, Equity, and Jurisprudence of Criminal Risk Assessment* 1 (Dec. 26, 2018), 2018.

3334 Mayson, Sandra G., "Bias In, Bias Out", *cit.*, pp. 2218–2300 (2221).

3335 See: Rudin, Cynthia, "A process for predicting manhole events in Manhattan", *Machine Learning*, Volume 80, 2018, pp. 1–31.

3336 Kuchibhotla, A. K./R. A. Berk, "Nested Conformal Prediction Sets for Classification with Applications to Probation Data", arXiv:2104.09358, 2021.

3337 None of this is to suggest, nor is to say, that actuarial risk assessment is blazingly new to criminal justice system. Parole boards have long relied on risk-assessment instruments since the 1930s. By the same token, some jurisdictions used algorithms to forecast certain types of crimes, such as sex offenses, for decades past. See: Mason, Sandra G., "Bias in, Bias Out.", *Yale Law Journal*, Volume 128 Volume 8, 2019, pp. 2219–2298.

3338 Green, B., Chen Y, "Disparate interactions: An algorithm-in-the-loop analysis of fairness in risk assessments", *FAT* 2019, Proceedings of 2019 Conference of Fairness, Accountability, Transparency*, 2019, pp. 90–99.

3339 But see: Tyler, Tom, "Methodology in Legal Research", in: *Utrecht Law Review*, Volume 13, Issue 3, 2017, pp. 130–131 ("*Accurate facts plus good legal rules lead to substantive justice.* This is the normative framework of right and wrong defined by traditional legal analysis. *Risk analysis is a nice example of the benefits of empiricism because studies suggest that the use of empirical methods to assess future dangerousness is more accurate than is the use of human intuition. It is better to use a formula when making a legal decision that involves estimates of someone's likely future conduct than it is to rely upon the impressions of judges or prosecutors*" (...) "*The legal system relies on predictions about people's likely future behaviour at many points in the system*: *pretrial detention; sentencing; parole and probation*; etc. And it has been used with a variety of special populations, including juveniles; the mentally ill; and sexual predators. *A key reason to use such quantitative methods is that they are better able to predict future behaviour and as a consequence the many points in the system at which judgments are made – pre-trial detention; sentencing; parole – are better able to enact justice for both the innocent and the guilty. The focus by social scientists upon helping to identify and use facts in ways that produce more accurate decisions fits well with the argument that the aims of justice are best served when they are based upon accurate factual information. Accuracy, in turn is enhanced by the use of empirical methods. Facts are sought that can guide the application of normative legal principles*"). Italics added.

3340 Mayson, Sandra G., "Bias In, Bias Out", *cit.*, pp. 2218–2300 (2221).

3341 Leonard, D. J., *Playing While White: Privilege and Power on and Off the Field*, Washington, University of Washington Press, 2020.

3342 Hoffmann AL, Where fairness fails: data, algorithms, and the limits of antidiscrimination discourse. Inf Commun Soc, 22 (7), 2019, pp. 900–915.

3343 Crutchfield, J., Fisher, A., & Webb, S. L., "Colorism and police killings", *The Western Journal of Black Studies*, 41 (3–4), 2017, 81; Dottolo, A. L., & Stewart, A. J., "Don't ever forget now, you're a Black man in America": Intersections of race, class and gender in encounters with the police", *Sex*

§§ Along with the unbridled rise of big data[3344] came overhyped ambitions to quell crime. To cater for that, algorithmic risk assessment is the propelling force behind an efficient justice system that timely forebodes, and pre-emptively squelches, crime.[3345] The former is the linchpin of the latter. No surprise stems from the fact that algorithmic risk assessment is the policy centrepiece of the much-acclaimed bail-reform[3346] movement[3347]; the driving force that spurs state-of-the-art (bigoted) predictive policing[3348]; the technological lodestar that underpins charging[3349]; the shrewd technological apparatus within which sentencing[3350] operates[3351]; and the

---

Roles, 59 (5–6), 2008, pp. 350–364; Baradan, S., "Race, prediction, and discretion", *The George Washington Law Review*, Volume 81, Issue 1, 2013, pp. 157–222.

[3344] Simmons, Ric, "Big Data and Procedural Justice: Legitimizing Algorithms in the Criminal Justice System", *Ohio State Journal of Criminal Law*, Volume 15, 2018, pp. 576 and ff and passim; Brayne, S., "Big data surveillance: The case of policing", *American Sociological Review*, Volume 82, Issue 5, 2017, pp. 977–1008.

[3345] Mayson, Sandra G., "Bias In, Bias Out", *cit.*, pp. 2218–2300 (2222).

[3346] Mayson, Sandra G., "Bias In, Bias Out", *cit.*, pp. 2218–2300 (2222). See also: Stevenson, Megan, "Assessing Risk Assessment in Action", *Minnesota Law Review*, Volume 103, 2018, p. 303 (discussing the burgeoning use of pretrial risk assessment as a mandatory component of bail decisions in Kentucky); Dewan, Shaila, "Judges Replacing Conjecture with Formula for Bail", New York Times (June 26, 2015), https://www.nytimes.com/2015/06/27/us/turning-the-granting-of-bail-into-a-science.html; [https://perma.cc/Y86J-GHU4] (emphasizing the mounting groundswell of support for algorithmic risk assessments in bail decision-making across jurisdictions).

[3347] Mayson, Sandra G., "Bias In, Bias Out", *cit.*, pp. 2218–2300 (2222). See also: Mayson, Sandra G., "Dangerous Defendants", *Yale Law Journal*, Volume 127, 2018, p. 490 ("Bail reform is gaining momentum nationwide."); Koepke, John Logan/Robinson, David G., "Danger Ahead: Risk Assessment and the Future of Bail Reform", *Washington Law Review*, Volume 93, 2018, 1725; Milgram, Anne, et al., "Pretrial Risk Assessment: Improving Public Safety and Fairness in Pretrial Decision Making", *Federal Sentencing Report*, Volume 27, 2015 (on the challenges facing defendants in bail hearings).

[3348] But see: Kirkpatrick, Keith, "It's not the Algorithm, it's the Data", *Communications of the ACM*, February 2017, Volume 60, n. ° 2, 2017 ("tools such as *PredPol* and *CommandCentral are inherently biased since they rely heavily on reported crimes data, which is often concentrated in areas that are heavily policed, thereby skewing statistics to overrepresent poor or minority communities.* "*We know that we have a history of racially biased policing in the United States, and that has fed into all the data that we have on where arrests have occurred, which crimes are more likely to occur in specific communities, and at which particular times*," says Jennifer Lynch, senior staff attorney at the Electronic Frontier Foundation. "*That's the data that's being fed into predictive policing algorithms*"). Italics added.

[3349] See: Ferguson, Andrew Guthrie, "Predictive Prosecution", *Wake Forest Law*, Volume 51, 2016, pp. 705, 705–08 (explaining "predictive prosecution" and exploring its "promises and perils").

[3350] Note, though, that there is burgeoning trend of (to) sentencing anchored in algorithms in a bid to ease—and sometimes offset—human flaws (such as racial bias, gender bias, jealousy, sexual orientation bias and so forth). Such tools, which are currently being deployed to undertake predicting criminal recidivism, are gaining traction and gathering pace in Italy: Gialuz, M., "Quando la giustizia penale encontra l'intelligenza artificiale: luci e e ombre di risk assessment tools tra Stati Uniti ed Europa", 2019, available at: www.penalecontemporaneo.it.d/6702-quando-la-giustizia-penale-encontra-l'intelligenz-artificiale-luci-e-ombre-di-risk-assessment-tools (access: 03.07.2024); United Kingdom: Peeters, R./Schuilenburg, M., "Machine Justice: Governing Security through Bureaucracy of Algorithms", *Information Polity*, Volume 23, 2018, pp. 267–274; Hamilton, Melissa,

rationale behind the agreed-upon policy of reallocating[3352] scarce resources[3353] in the purview of criminal procedure law.

§§ For purposes here, this seismic shift has catalysed concerns about the extent to which racial biases are baked into algorithmic risk assessment.[3354] For a simple reason: at its core, algorithmic crime prediction relies heavily on risk markers closely associated with race[3355] in that exhibits a heightened likelihood to re-entrench the bemoaning racial disparity[3356] that besets criminal justice systems[3357] worldwide.[3358] Furthermore, it is the so-called gloss of science-fraught objectivity[3359] that bolster

---

"Sentencing Disparities", *British Journal of American Legal Studies*, Volume 6, Issue 2, 2017, pp. 181 ff.

[3351] Collins, Erin, "Punishing Risk", *Georgia Law Journal*, Volume 107, 2018, p. 57 (pouring trenchant criticism on the unbridled rise of actuarial sentencing in the remit of criminal law); Slobogin, Christopher, "Principles of Risk Assessment: Sentencing and Policing", *Ohio State Journal of Criminal Law*, Volume 15, 2018, pp. 583 and ff and passim (setting out foundational principles for how risk-assessment tools should be devised and deployed, specifically in the sentencing compass).

[3352] Tyler, Tom R./Goff, Philip Atiba/MacCoun, Robert J., "The Impact of Psychological Science on Policing in the United States: Procedural Justice, Legitimacy, and Effective Law Enforcement", *Psychological Science in the Public Interest*, Volume 16, Issue 3, 2015, p. 79 (noting that "without a fundamental reallocation of resources, our society cannot effectively monitor the general public searching for everyday wrongdoing").

[3353] Issue Brief: Risk/Needs Assessment 101: Science Reveals New Tools to Manage Offenders, PEW CTR. ON STATES 2 (September 2011), https://www.pewtrusts.org/~/media/legacy/uploadedfiles/pcs_assets/2011/pewriskassessmentbriefpdf.pdf; [https://perma.cc/38CG-D395] (describing the deployment of risk assessment to allocate supervision resources in the criminal system of justice).

[3354] See: Huq, Aziz Z., "Racial Equity in Algorithmic Criminal Justice", *Duke Law Journal*, Volume 68, 2019, pp. 1043, 1053, 1083–1102 (sheds a keen light on why constitutional law is fundamentally bereft of "creditable guidance" for granting racial equity in algorithmic risk assessment in criminal justice).

[3355] Harcourt, Bernard E., "Risk as a Proxy for Race: The Dangers of Risk Assessment", *Federal Sentencing Report*, Volume 27, 2015, p. 237.

[3356] Skeem, Jennifer L./Lowenkamp, Christopher T., "Risk, Race, and Recidivism: Predictive Bias and Disparate Impact", *Criminology*, Volume 54, 2022, pp. 680, 683–84, 704–06 (argues that criminal history correlates with race in their respective data set).

[3357] Harcourt, Bernard E., "Risk as a Proxy for Race: The Dangers of Risk Assessment", *cit.*, p. 240 ("[T]he continuously increasing racial disproportionality in the prison population necessarily entails that the prediction instruments, focused as they are on prior criminality, are going to hit hardest the African American communities").

[3358] Mayson, Sandra G., "Bias In, Bias Out", *cit.*, pp. 2218–2300 (2222).

[3359] But see: Benjamin, Ruha, *Race After Technology: Abolitionist Tools for the New Jim Code*, New York, Polity, 2019, pp. 1–172 (7) (discussing that Artificial Intelligence-embedded technologies are viewed as iron-clad tools of objectivity and devoid of any biases whatsoever). Ruha Benjamin accordingly contends that "the employment of new technologies that reflect and reproduce existing inequities but that are promoted and perceived as more objective or progressive than the discriminatory systems of a previous era"). See also: Farina, M., & Lavazza, A., *Philosophy, expertise, and the myth of neutrality. Routledge Studies in Contemporary Philosophy*, London, Routledge, 2024. This false scent of neutrality impairs, and impacts, procedural justice. See: Tyler, Tom R., "The Psychology of Procedural Justice: A Test of the Group-Value Model", *Journal of Personality and Social Psychology*, Volume 57, 1989, p. 830 (reports that in any procedure "several non-control

algorithmic risk assessment that dignifies the cultural trope of black criminality[3360] with the smokescreen/camouflage of science-laden neutrality.[3361]

§§ It is often rattled off/trotted-out/reeled off that though times won't last forever, but though people do. History accordingly bestows upon us the truism that nothing lasts forever, nor did the complacence with the starkest racial disparities that reigned for far too long.[3362] Laudably, racial discrimination in judicial settings is not only openly decried, but, and foremost, fiercely combatted nowadays. Racial disparity is therefore widely regarded as wholly unacceptable[3363] in that is something to be harshly frowned-upon. Especially, albeit not exclusively, in criminal justice settings where the stakes are exceedingly high, fundamental rights wise.[3364]

§§ The rate and pace at which the trenchant criticism against all forms of algorithmic discrimination[3365] has unfolded, propelled poignant calls urging for brisk interventions in the predictive process to ensure algorithmic fairness.[3366] Note,

---

issues – the *neutrality* of the decision-making procedure, trust in the 3rd party, and the information the experience communicates about social standing – influence both procedural preferences and judgments of procedural justice"). See also: Willis, Lauren, "Deception by Design", *Harvard Journal Law and Technology*, Volume 34, 2020, pp. 115–190.

[3360] See: McIntyre, Frank/Baradaran, Shima, "Race, Prediction, and Pretrial Detention", *Journal Empirical Legal Studies*, Volume 10, 2013, pp. 742–759 (parses black defendants' exceedingly high likelihood of being arrested on drug-related charges as a potential cause of the race gap). See: Part IV, This chapter, Sects. 4.1.1–4.1.1.1 of this book (on biased predictive policing).

[3361] Mayson, Sandra G., "Bias In, Bias Out", *cit.*, pp. 2218–2300 (2222).

[3362] Milligan, Joy, "Protecting Disfavored Minorities: Towards Institutional Realism", *UCLA Law Review*, Volume 63, 2016, pp. 918–921 (delves into the racial inequality in United States of America's Department of Agriculture farm aid to both Whites and Blacks).

[3363] Mayson, Sandra G., "Bias In, Bias Out", *cit.*, pp. 2218–2300 (2223).

[3364] But see: Part V, Chap. 5, Sect. 5.1.7.2 of this book (on law number two to control algorithmic decision-making, which mandates that black box models must not be entrusted with the task of making high stake decisions—v.g. health and freedom). But see: State v. Loomis, 881 N.W.2d 749 (Wis. 2016) (finding the use of risk assessment at sentencing constitutionally admissible).

[3365] Prince, Anya E. R./Schwarcz, Daniel, "Proxy Discrimination in the Age of Artificial Intelligence and Big Data", *Iowa Law Review*, Volume 105, 1257, 1279–81 (2020) ("*[P]roxy discrimination will tend to occur when a suspect variable is predictive of a desired outcome only because it proxies for another*, quantifiable and potentially available, *variable that causes the desired outcome but that is not included in the AI's training data*"). Italics added; Bornstein, Stephanie, "Antidiscriminatory Algorithms", *Alabama Law Review*, Volume 70, 2018, pp. 518 and ff and passim; Loi, Michele/Christen, Markus, "Choosing How to Discriminate: Navigating Ethical Trade-Offs in Fair Algorithmic Design for the Insurance Sector", *Philosophy & Technology*, Volume 34, 2021, passim; Roth, Andrea, "Trial by Machine", *Georgetown Law Journal*, Volume 104, 2016, passim; Coglianese, Cary/Lehr, David, "Transparency and Algorithmic Governance", *Administrative Law Review*, Volume 71, 2019, passim (highlights the overriding importance of transparency to propel algorithmic governance). Note, though, that the training of machine learning is long and tedious in that is an error-prone procedure than can ultimately impair future algorithmic decision-making: Price, W. Nicholson Price II, "Regulating Black-Box Medicine", *Michigan Law Review*, Volume 116, 2017, pp. 421–431 (leverages on Google Image's image recognition learning algorithm to shed light on the four-step process by which some algorithms are thoroughly trained. First, the algorithm is shown "a set of known images ('Here are 10,000 pictures of ducks')." Second, the algorithm "develops complex internal rules based on nonlinear processes." Third, the algorithm "tests those rules on a test set ('Which of these are ducks?')." And fourth, the algorithm accordingly adjusts

though, that along with the quest to stamp out biased algorithmic risk assessment comes the vexing conundrum on how to achieve both racial equity and algorithmic fairness.[3367] The scorching challenge lies in the multiplicity of possible metrics of racial equity in statistical prediction. To add to our woes, some of which are mutually exclusive.[3368]

§§ In this respect, an agreed-upon consensus has been reached in two axes of reasoning. The first axe of reasoning argued that race, alongside other risk markers usually connected with race,[3369] should be cast aside as input variables for prediction. The second axe of reasoning called for a «algorithmic affirmative action» to allay adverse predictions across racial lines.[3370]

§§ Relatedly, pundits doubled down their gallant efforts to achieve a particular equality measure in algorithmic risk assessment while regulating[3371] the process of algorithmic decision-making.[3372] In so doing, they signalled the dire need to achieve equality in the *false-positive* and *false-negative rates* across racial lines, or in the overall rate of adverse predictions across groups («**statistical parity**»).[3373]

---

its "internal rules based on the success of the test." These steps are trotted out and repeated many times "until it can accurately and consistently classify the images").

3366 See: Corbett-Davies, Sam/Pierson, Emma/Feller, Avi/Goel, Sharad Goel/Huq, Aziz, "Algorithmic Decision Making and the Cost of Fairness", *Proceedings of the 23rd ACM SIGKDD International Conference on Knowledge Discovery and Data Mining* (Ass'n for Computing Machinery ed., 2017), 2017, passim (coining statistical parity as a "popular" concept of fairness in the risk-assessment and algorithmic-fairness literature).

3367 See: Frezal, Sylvestre/Barry, Laurence, "Fairness in Uncertainty: Some Limits and Misinterpretations of Actuarial Fairness", *Journal of Business Ethics*, Volume 167, 2020, pp. 126 and ff and passim. See also: Hayes, Paul/van de Poel, Ibo/Steen, Marc, "Algorithms and Values in Justice and Security", *AI & Society*, 2020, pp. 533 and ff and passim.

3368 Mayson, Sandra G., "Bias In, Bias Out", *cit.*, pp. 2218–2300 (2223).

3369 But see: Kleinberg, Jon et al., "Algorithmic Fairness", *AEA Papers & Proceedings*, Volume 108, 2018, pp. 22–23 (discussing, anchored in a batch of national data, that including race as an input variable to a machine-learning college-admissions algorithm both "improves predicted GPAs of admitted students" and can augment "the fraction of admitted students who are black").

3370 Mayson, Sandra G., "Bias In, Bias Out", *cit.*, pp. 2218–2300 (2224).

3371 Yeung, Karen, "Algorithmic Regulation: A Critical Interrogation", *Regulation & Governance*, Volume 12, 2018, pp. 505 and ff and passim (on the sweltering challenges posed by algorithmic regulation).

3372 Krafft, Tobias D./Zweig, Katharina A./Konig, Pascal D., "How to Regulate Algorithmic Decision-Making: A Framework of Regulatory Requirements for Different Applications", *Regulation & Governance*, Volume 16, 2022, pp. 119 and ff and passim.

3373 Mayson, Sandra G., "Bias In, Bias Out", *cit.*, pp. 2218–2300 (2224). See also: Benjamin Fish et al., "A Confidence-Based Approach for Balancing Fairness and Accuracy", *Proceedings of the 2016 SIAM International Conference on Data Mining*, Chawla, Sanjay, Venkatasubramanian/Meira, Wagner (Editors), 2016, p. 144 (using the word "statistical parity"); Huq, Aziz Z., "Racial Equity in Algorithmic Criminal Justice", *cit.*, pp. 1116 (employing the word "statistical parity"); Corbett-Davies, Sam/Pierson, Emma/Feller, Avi/Goel, Sharad/Huq, Aziz, "Algorithmic Decision Making and the Cost of Fairness", passim (employment the term "conditional statistical parity" to describe parity in classification rates after controlling for "'legitimate' risk factors"); Zemel, Richard, et al., "Learning Fair Representations", *The Proceedings* of *Machine Learning Research*, Volume 28, 2013, p. 1 (using the term "statistical parity").

§§ Lastly, and perhaps decisively, a phalanx of vocal critics contended that, if algorithmic risk assessment is not amenable to be rendered race[3374] or gender[3375] neutral, then the criminal justice system must accordingly rebuff algorithmic methods altogether. By this token, Professor Sandra G. Mayson avers that these three piecemeal algorithmic strategies—i.e. sought-after colour-blindness,[3376] staggering efforts to equalize predictive outputs along racial lines,[3377] and the outright rejection of algorithmic methods—are at best haphazard, and at worst futile, since those strategies are nothing but fruits of a poisonous tree: the bigoted nature of prediction itself.[3378] All prediction[3379] lends itself to a reflecting mirror to the past.[3380] Algorithmic

[3374] But see: Bornstein, Stepanhie, "Antidiscriminatory Algorithms", *Alabama Law Review*, Volume 70, 2018, pp. 519, 524–528 (contending, however, that the tagged "facially neutral" algorithms producing discriminatory outcomes should be quashed).

[3375] See: Hamilton, Melissa, "The sexist algorithm", *Behavioral Sciences and the Law*, Volume 37, Issue 2, Special Issue: the Use of Statistics in Criminal Cases, March–April 2019, 2019, pp. 1 and ff ("*Algorithmic risk assessment tools are informed by scientific research concerning which factors are predictive of recidivism and thus support the evidence-based practice movement in criminal justice.* Automated assessments of individualized risk (low, medium, high) *permit officials to make more effective management decisions. Computer-generated algorithms appear to be objective and neutral. But are these algorithms actually fair?* (...) *Findings indicate that COMPAS performs reasonably well at discriminating between recidivists and non-recidivists for men and women. Nonetheless, COMPAS algorithmic outcomes systemically overclassify women in higher risk groupings. Multiple measures of algorithmic equity and predictive accuracy are provided to support the conclusion that this algorithm is sexist*"). Italics added.

[3376] Note, though, that certain types of racial discrimination may not be fully intentional. More likely than not, it can be related with the perils of big data colour-blindness that nonetheless relies on proxies to race and gender to make algorithmic decisions. Another problem is the one related with "creditworthiness by association" that causes more problems than it solves. See: Hurley, Mikella/ Adebayo, Julius, "Credit Scoring in the Era of Big Data", *Yale Journal of Law and Technology*, Volume 18, 2016, p. 149 ("*These tools may furthermore obscure discriminatory and subjective lending policies behind a single "objective" score. Such discriminatory scoring may not be intentional; instead, sophisticated algorithms may combine facially neutral data points and treat them as proxies for immutable characteristics such as race or gender, thereby circumventing existing non-discrimination laws*"). Italics added.

[3377] Note, though, that algorithmic fairness gives rise to several incompatible standards. Whilst COMPAS falls short of meeting the baseline standards of "equal opportunity" and "equalized odds", it refrains itself from discriminating blacks from the prism of "predictive parity" nonetheless. A full-fledged analysis of the extant state of this scorching topic can be found in Hübner, Dietmar, "Two Kinds of Discrimination in AI-Based penal Decision-Making", *SIGKDD Explorations*, 2021; Hellman, Deborah, "Measuring Algorithmic Fairness", *Virginia Law Review*, Volume 106, 2020, pp. 811 and ff and passim.

[3378] Mayson, Sandra G., "Bias In, Bias Out", *cit.*, pp. 2218–2300 (2224).

[3379] Aggarwal, C. C., *Neural networks and deep learning*, Heidelberg, Springer, 2018, passim; Agrawal, A., Gans, J., & Goldfarb, A., "Prediction machines (updated and expanded): The simple economics of artificial intelligence", *Harvard Business Review Press*, 2022; Agrawal, A., Gans, J., & Goldfarb, A., "Power and prediction: The disruptive economics of artificial intelligence", *Harvard Business Review Press*, 2022; Bengio, Y., Hinton, G., Yao, A., Song, D., Abbeel, P., Harari, Y. N., Hadfield, G., Russell, S., Kahneman, D., & Mindermann, S., *Managing ai risks in an era of rapid progress*, arXiv preprint arXiv:2310.17688, 2023, passim (on neural networks and deep learning that operate jointly in the age of Artificial Intelligence-embedded technologies).

[3380] Mayson, Sandra G., "Bias In, Bias Out", *cit.*, pp. 2218–2300 (2224).

risk assessment, being a computer-anchored prediction[3381] that leverages on rigged data,[3382] tends to ratchet up racial disparities in criminal justice settings.[3383] More on this later.[3384]

§§ In algorithmic risk assessment, the future mirrors the past. And the past did not look good, nor did pan out well, for members of racialized communities. Bereft of any befitted measures to soothe out the twisted vagaries of the past, the future is doomed to reflect the past. Insofar traits that associated with crime commission in the past will be associated with crime commission in a not-so distant future.[3385] Relatedly, algorithmic risk assessment, if nothing else, holds a squalid mirror to the past.[3386] It accordingly gleans warped patterns deeply entrenched in past data[3387] and handles them as predictions of what lurks ahead.[3388]

§§ Algorithmic risk assessment—an outgrowth of algorithmic prediction—engenders a watered-down reflection of digital data[3389]—a phenomenon that loosely

---

[3381] Krafft, Tobias D./Zweig, Katharina A./Konig, Pascal D., "How to Regulate Algorithmic Decision-Making: A Framework of Regulatory Requirements for Different Applications", *Regulation & Governance*, Volume 16, 2022, pp. 119 and ff and passim.

[3382] See: Barocas, Solon/Selbst, Andrew D., "Big Data's Disparate Impact", *California Law Review*, Volume 104, 2016, pp. 671–682 (discussing how data is often flawed, rigged, incomplete, imperfect and therefore algorithms inherit the prejudice of the original decision makers). See also: Citron, Danielle Keats/Pasquale, Frank, "The Scored Society: Due Process for Automated Predictions", *Washington Law Review*, Volume 89, 2014, pp. 1, 4–5 (highlighting how human beings programming automated systems is directly conducive to, and leads, to fundamentally inaccurate results since the source code, predictive algorithms and datasets may encompass human biases which, in turn, have a disparate impact on historically disadvantaged groups).

[3383] Cofone, Ignacio N., "Algorithmic Discrimination is an Information Problem", *Hastings Law Journal*, Volume 70, 2019.

[3384] See: Part V of this book.

[3385] But see: Hardt, Moritz, "How big data is unfair: Understanding sources of unfairness in data driven decision making", *Medium*, Archived on Oct. 8, 2014, available at: https://web.archive.org/web/20141008185829/; https://medium.com/@mrtz/how-big-data-is-unfair-9aa544d739de. (access: 17.12.2024).

[3386] Mayson, Sandra G., "Bias In, Bias Out", *cit.*, pp. 2218–2300 (2224).

[3387] See: Balkin, Jack M., "The Three Laws of Robotics in the Age of Big Data", *Ohio State Law Journal*, Volume 78, Issue 5, 2017, pp. 1217–1241. But see: Berk, Richard, "Accuracy and Fairness for Juvenile Justice Risks Assessments", *Journal of Empirical Legal Studies*, Volume 16, 2019, p. 183 (arguing that, in different data sets, that past misdemeanor convictions were less predictive of future serious arrest for coloured people than for white people); Lowenkamp, Christopher et al., "Investigating the Impact of Pretrial Detention on Sentencing Outcomes", *Laura and John Arnold Foundation* (Nov. 2013), https://www.arnoldfoundation.org/wp-content/uploads/2014/02/LJAF_Report_state-sentencing_FNL.pdf; [https://perma.cc/L9JF-KEHL]. The Pennsylvania Sentencing Commission expressly snubbed past arrests altogether as input variables since they had markedly different predictive significance across racial lines. Risk Assessment Update: Arrest Scales, Pennsylvania Commision on Sentencing, 2018, pp. 4–7 (Feb. 28, 2018), http://www.hominid.psu.edu/specialty_programs/pacs/publications-and-research/research-and-evaluation-reports/risk-assessment; [https://perma.cc/32WY-9F74]. See: Mayson, Sandra G., "Bias In, Bias Out", *cit.*, pp. 2218–2300.

[3388] Mayson, Sandra G., "Bias In, Bias Out", *cit.*, pp. 2218–2300 (2224).

[3389] SeeCusters, Bart, "Data Dilemmas in the Information Society: Introduction and Overview", Custers, Bart/Calders, Toon/Schermer, Bart/Zarsky, Tal (Editors), *Discrimination and Privacy in the*

amounts to «datafication».[3390] Algorithmic prediction therefore spawns a blurred reflection of anecdotal data[3391] which, in turn, draws on data mining[3392] that befalls on members of racialized communities.[3393] Owing to the nature of algorithmic prediction, a *systemic racism*[3394] that created a racially unequal past will necessarily create racially unequal algorithmic outputs[3395] that, if nothing else, is wholly unbecoming in criminal justice settings. That is one key takeaways of this offering.

§§ Against this background, Professor Sandra G. Mayson coined algorithmic risk assessment as «bias in, bias out».[3396] This taxonomy could not be closer to the unvarnished truth. Suppose one seeks to forecast a future arrest. If black people are more frequently arrested than white people the past data[3397] will reflect that. As a result, the

---

Information Society: Data Mining and Profiling in Large Databases, Heidelberg, Springer, 2013, pp. 3–26. See also: Gillis, Talia B./Spiess, Jann L., "Big Data and Discrimination", *University of Chicago Law Review*, 2010, pp. 458 and ff and passim (on the sweltering challenges arising out algorithmic discrimination).

3390 See: Hu, Margaret, "From the National Surveillance State to the Cybersurveillance State", *The Annual Review of Law and Social Science*, Volume 13, 2017, p. 165 ("*Datafication, like most big data processes, requires increasing amounts of digital data to support or construct cybersurveillance.* It empowers government actions that are based on digital data collection, data processing protocols, and bulk data analyses (Mayer-Schonberger & Cukier ¨ 2013). *Another way to characterize datafication is as a governmental policy interest that both transforms analog data (PCAST 2014) into searchable, centralized digital databases and develops new forms of stored data*"). Italics added.

3391 Mayson, Sandra G., "Bias In, Bias Out", *cit.*, pp. 2218–2300.

3392 Balkin, Jack, "Constitution in the National Surveillance State", *Minnesota Law Review*, Volume 93, 2008, p. 13 (note, though, that "*data mining* allows inferences not only about the direct subject of surveillance, but about other people with whom they live, work and communicate"). It bears mentioning that pundits have neither been coy nor bashful in strongly emphasizing the perceived peril—*consumer harm*—of monetizing the data harvested/gleaned by Artificial Intelligence-embedded technologies while performing data mining. See: Yang/Kai Hao, "Selling Consumer Data for Profit: Optimal Market-Segmentation Design and its Consequences", *American Economic Review*, Volume 112, Issue 4, April 2022, 2022, pp. 1364–1393.

3393 See: Bartlett, Robert/Morse, Adair/Wallace, Nancy/Stanton, Richard, "Algorithmic Discrimination and Input Accountability Under the Civil Rights Acts", *Berkeley Technology Law Journal*, Volume 36, 2021, pp. 675–736 (675) ("*the disproportionate burden of COVID-19 among communities of color and a necessary renewed attention to racial inequalities* have lent new urgency to concerns that *algorithmic decision-making can lead to unintentional discrimination against members of historically marginalized groups*"). Italics added.

3394 Roithmayr, Daria, *Reproducing Racism: How everyday choices lock in White Advantage*, New York, New York University Press, 2014, pp. 1–272 ("*Argues that racial inequality reproduces itself automatically over time because early unfair advantage for whites has paved the way for continuing advantage.* This book "*concludes that racial inequality might now be locked in place, unless policymakers immediately take drastic steps to dismantle this oppressive system*"). Italics added. This book points out how White privilege is perpetuated throughout generations through residential segregation (*mortgage redlining*), abhorrent nepotism, and other bemoaning social practices that pester modern societies). See: Part IV, This chapter, Sects. 4.1.4–4.1.4.2.3 of this book.

3395 Mayson, Sandra G., "Bias In, Bias Out", *cit.*, pp. 2218–2300.

3396 Mayson, Sandra G., "Bias In, Bias Out", *cit.*, pp. 2218–2300 (2224).

3397 But see: Pedreshi, Dino/Ruggieri, Salvatore/Turini, Franco, "Discrimination-aware Data Mining", *Proceedings of the 14th ACM SIGKDD International Conference on Knowledge Discovery*

machine learning algorithm will project it to occur more frequently to black people than to white people in the forthcoming future.[3398] The predicted event, deemed as the *target variable*,[3399] plays a pivotal role in racial disparity in algorithmic prediction.[3400] Which, I may venture to add, is wholly unsavoury/unbefitting in criminal procedure law settings.

§§ Relatedly, the extant strategies for racial equity seek to either disfiguring the predictive mirror or jettisoning it out.[3401] Take stock of input data.[3402] If the event one seeks to forecast happens more frequently to black people, an unerring machine learning algorithm will forecast it more frequently for black people.[3403]

§§ Put another way, **actuarial risk assessment**, if nothing else, has laid bare the rampant racial inequality that inheres and permeates all crime prediction amidst a racially lopsided world,[3404] thereby priming scholars to accost an unsettling problem

---

and Data Mining (Las Vegas, Nevada, USA), ACM, 2008, pp. 560–568 (arguing that one should shift its gaze downstream by putting in place discrimination-aware algorithmic tools while performing data mining).

3398 Mayson, Sandra G., "Bias In, Bias Out", *cit.*, pp. 2218–2300 (2224).

3399 See: Barocas, Solon/Selbst, Andrew D., "Big Data's Disparate Impact", *California Law Review*, Volume 104, 2016, pp. 677–78 (arguing that predictive data is predictive of a given/specific target variable (i.e., minimized future predicted claims) with training data which is both correctly "labelled" and "collected"). It is important to note that other tools have other target variables, yet the analysis undertaken in this offering applies to several other target variables as well. In the pretrial purview, for example, risk-assessment tools also forecast "failure to appear," outlined in terms of data points that vary across jurisdictions. See: Mayson, Sandra G., "Dangerous Defendants", *Yale Law Journal*, Volume 127, 2018, pp. 509–13. There is also a spate of risk-assessment instruments that seek to forecast violence but in fact predict any hint or allegation of violence, whether it reflects in arrest or not (let alone conviction). See, e.g., Yang, Min et al., "The Efficacy of Violence Prediction: A Meta-Analytic Comparison of Nine Risk Assessment Tools", *Psychology Bulletin*, 2010, pp. 740–742 (arguing that "[t]he range of possible criterion variables for violence is wide, and "includes self-reports to third-party reports.., informal social service or police contact, formal contact or police charges, formal adjudication and court convictions, and incarceration"). See: Mayson, Sandra G., "Bias In, Bias Out", *cit.*, pp. 2218–2300. Note, though, that the training of machine learning is long and tedious in that is an error-prone procedure than can ultimately impair future algorithmic decision-making: Price, W. Nicholson Price II, "Regulating Black-Box Medicine", *Michigan Law Review*, Volume 116, 2017, pp. 421–431 (leverages on Google Image's image recognition learning algorithm to shed light on the four-step process by which some algorithms are thoroughly trained. First, the algorithm is shown "a set of known images ('Here are 10,000 pictures of ducks')." Second, the algorithm "develops complex internal rules based on nonlinear processes." Third, the algorithm "tests those rules on a test set ('Which of these are ducks?')." And fourth, the algorithm accordingly adjusts its "internal rules based on the success of the test." These steps are trotted out and repeated many times "until it can accurately and consistently classify the images").

3400 See: Mayson, Sandra G., "Bias In, Bias Out", *cit.*, pp. 2218–2300.

3401 See: Mayson, Sandra G., "Bias In, Bias Out", *cit.*, pp. 2218–2300.

3402 Lepri, Bruno/Oliver, Nuria/Letouz'e Emmanuel/Pentland, Alex/Vinck, Patrick, "Fair, Transparent, and Accountable Algorithmic Decision-Making Processes: The Premise, the Proposed Solutions, and the Open Challenges", *Philosophy & Technology*, Volume 31, 2018, passim.

3403 Mayson, Sandra G., "Bias In, Bias Out", *cit.*, pp. 2218–2300 (2224).

3404 See: Menasce, Juliana Horowitz/Brown, Anna/Cox, Kiana, "Views of Racial Inequality", *Pew Research Center*, April 9, 2019, available at: https://www.pewresearch.org/social-trends/2019/04/09/views-of-racial-inequality/ (access: 2.12.2024) ("*more than four-in-ten Americans say the*

plunged many layers deep the dangerous affording[3405] of Artificial Intelligence-embedded technologies.[3406] In devising the elaborate trappings of algorithmic prediction, algorithmic decision-making has unveiled/unmasked the gross disparities widely diffused in criminal algorithmic risk assessment, subjective and actuarial alike.[3407]

§§ Which begs the vexing questions: would tweaking a machine learning algorithm or its underlying input data suffice?[3408] Would dismissing algorithmic risk assessment altogether in the remit of criminal justice pass muster?[3409] Would any of those measures suffice to remedy the racial inequalities in crime or arrest risk amidst a

---

country still has work to do to give black people equal rights with whites. Blacks, in particular, are skeptical that black people will ever have equal rights in this country (....) A majority of adults say that being white helps people's ability to get ahead in the country at least a little (59%); 28% say being white neither helps nor hurts and 12% say it hurts. On the flip side, a majority (56%) sees being black as a disadvantage, with 25% saying it hurts people's ability to get ahead a lot. About a quarter (26%) say being black neither helps nor hurts and 17% say it helps at least a little. More also say that being Hispanic hurts people's ability to get ahead in this country (51%) than say it helps (18%) or that it neither helps nor hurts (30%). Opinions are more split when it comes to the impact of being Native American – about the same shares say this hurts as say it neither helps nor hurts, while a smaller share says it helps. *And while a plurality says being Asian neither helps nor hurts, more say it helps (34%) than hurts (21%) people's ability to get ahead*"). Italics added.

3405 It is important to note that other tools have other target variables, yet the analysis in this offering applies to several other target variables as well. In the pretrial purview, for example, risk-assessment tools also forecast "failure to appear," outlined in terms of data points that vary across jurisdictions. See: Mayson, Sandra G., "Dangerous Defendants", *Yale Law Journal*, Volume 127, 2018, pp. 509–13. There is also a spate of risk-assessment instruments that seek to forecast violence but in fact predict any hint or allegation of violence, whether it reflects in arrest or not (let alone conviction). See, e.g., Yang, Min et al., "The Efficacy of Violence Prediction: A Meta-Analytic Comparison of Nine Risk Assessment Tools", *Psychology Bulletin*, 2010, pp. 740–742 (arguing that "[t]he range of possible criterion variables for violence is wide, and "includes self-reports to third-party reports..., informal social service or police contact, formal contact or police charges, formal adjudication and court convictions, and incarceration"). See: Mayson, Sandra G., "Bias In, Bias Out", *cit.*, pp. 2218–2300.

3406 Mayson, Sandra G., "Bias In, Bias Out", *cit.*, pp. 2218–2300 (2225).

3407 Mayson, Sandra G., "Bias In, Bias Out", *cit.*, pp. 2218–2300 (2225).

3408 But see: Berk, Richard, "Accuracy and Fairness for Juvenile Justice Risks Assessments", *Journal of Empirical Legal Studies*, Volume 16, 2019, p. 175 (comes to the terms with the fact that tweaking/altering data to attain statistical parity yielded extremely high false-negative rates); Zachary Lipton et al., "Does Mitigating ML's Impact Disparity Require Treatment Disparity?", NIPS Proceedings, 1, 2018, https://arxiv.org/pdf/1711.07076.pdf; [https://perma.cc/X8VF-EY53] (sets forth compelling evidence that enforced blindness to protected traits exacts a toll on the overall accuracy of the machine learning algorithm); Petersilia, Joan/Turner, Susan, "Guideline-Based Justice: Prediction and Racial Minorities", *Crime and Justice*, 1987, pp. 151–174 (argues that omitting markers correlated with race from a recidivism prediction algorithm exacted a toll on the overall accuracy of the model).

3409 Stevenson, Megan/Mayson, Sandra G., "Pretrial Detention and Bail", Luna, Erik (Editor), *Reporting Criminal Justice: A Report of the Academy for Justice, Bridging the Gap between Scholarship and Reform*, 21, 2017, pp. 34–35 (poring over a batch of studies hinting that actuarial risk assessment can improve accuracy of pretrial risk judgments).

racially layered world? From where we stand, the racial inequality unlocked by algorithmic risk assessment should prod a seismic shift[3410] of the pathways[3411] through which the criminal justice system deals with, and fundamentally responds to, risk[3412] instead. More on this later.[3413]

§§ For starters, one should be mindful of the lessons that can be withdrawn from the past. If one aims to thoroughly address risk of serious crime,[3414] but there is a paucity of data that fairly reflects its exact contours,[3415] then there is a vividly clear absence of a robust pillar for foretelling serious crime in the first place.[3416] This finding has significant implications for all types of criminal justice algorithmic risk assessment, both actuarial and subjective.[3417]

3410 Hamilton, Melissa, "Risk-Needs Assessment: Constitutional and Ethical Challenges", *American Criminal Law Review*, Volume 52, 2015.

3411 Bloch-Wehba, Hannah, "Access to Algorithms", *Fordham Law Review*, Volume 88, 2020, passim; Xeniids, Raphaelle, "Tuning EU Equality Law to Algorithmic Discrimination: Three Pathways to Resilience", *Maastricht Journal of European and Comparative Law*, Volume 27, 2020, pp. 736 and ff.

3412 Mayson, Sandra G., "Bias In, Bias Out", *cit.*, pp. 2218–2300 (2225).

3413 See: Part V, Chap. 5, Sects. 5.1.2–5.1.6.2.1 of this book (on the thing-centred algorithmic decision-making propelled by a *Controllable* and *Interpretable* Machine Learning that weeds out *Algorithmic Dictatorship* and secures *Algorithmic Common Good*. It is worth recalling that the **thing-centred algorithmic decision-making** seeks to unwind the perils arising out of the lack of theoretical underpinnings facing the **human-centred algorithmic decision-making**, as extensively fleshed out Part III, Chap. 3, Sects. 3.1.4.3–3.1.4.4 of this book).

3414 Harris, Grant T./Rice, Marnie E., "Bayes and Base Rates: What Is an Informative Prior for Actuarial Violence Risk Assessment?", *Behavioural Science and Law*, Volume 31, 2013, pp. 103, 121 ("What is not axiomatic is the straightforward application of assumptions about priors... to violence risk assessment—that remains a set of important empirical matters."); See: Mayson, Sandra G., "Bias In, Bias Out", *cit.*, pp. 2218–2300. See also: Selbst, Andrew D., "Disparate Impact in Big Data Policing", *cit.*, pp. 140–43.

3415 See: Selbst, Andrew D., "Disparate Impact in Big Data Policing", *Georgia Law Review*, Volume 52, 2017, p. 167 ("[I]t may be impossible to tell when the disparate impact truly reflects reality"). See also: Barocas, Solon/Selbst, Andrew, "Big Data's Disparate Impact", *cit.*, p. 682 ("So long as prior decisions affected by some form of prejudice serve as examples of correctly rendered determinations, data mining will necessarily infer rules that exhibit the same prejudice").

3416 Wachter, Sandra/Mittelstadt, Brent/Russell, Chris, "Why Fairness Cannot be Automated: Bridging the Gap Between EU Non-Discrimination Law and AI", *Computer Law & Security Review*, Volume 41, 2021, 105567 (stating that one the main roadblocks in achieving fairness in algorithmic decision-maker is that the latter is not amenable to be automated).

3417 Mayson, Sandra G., "Bias In, Bias Out", *cit.*, pp. 2218–2300 (2225).

4.1.10.1.3 «The Impossibility of Race Neutrality» in Algorithmic Risk Assessment: The Notorious Case of Chicago's SSL (Strategic Suspect List) in Predictive Policing

§§ «Criminal justice risk assessment» resonates with **actuarial risk assessment** of the likelihood of some future criminal event,[3418] normally arrest for crime.[3419] The word comprises two types of risk-assessment tools: **i)** the more basic and mainstream checklist tools, and **ii)** the more advanced machine-learning algorithms[3420] that portend the forthcoming future[3421] while abiding by the central tenets of fairness.[3422]

§§ As the use of criminal justice risk assessment has soared, deep-rooted concerns over its potential racial impact have accordingly skyrocketed.[3423] The milestone/landmark year was 2014. A journalist enquired whether and to what extent Chicago's brand-new predictive policing strategy was «racist».[3424] And the answer is a resounding «yes». Take the example of Chicago's Strategic Suspect List (SSL)

[3418] See: Rudin, Cynthia, "A process for predicting manhole events in Manhattan", *Machine Learning*, Volume 80, 2018, pp. 1–31.

[3419] But see: Harris, Grant T./Rice, Marnie E., "Bayes and Base Rates: What Is an Informative Prior for Actuarial Violence Risk Assessment?", *Behavioural Science and Law*, Volume 31, 2013, pp. 103, 121 ("What is not axiomatic is the straightforward application of assumptions about priors... to violence risk assessment—that remains a set of important empirical matters."); Crow, M. S., "The complexities of prior record, race, ethnicity, and policy: Interactive effects in sentencing", *Criminal Justice Review*, Volume 33, Issue 4, 2008, pp. 502–523. See also: Evans, Douglas N., "The effect of criminal convictions on real estate agent decisions in New York City", *Journal of Crime and Justice*, Volume 39, n. ° 3, 2016, pp. 363–379 ("*analyses indicated that a prior conviction was associated with a significant decrease in agent willingness to accept prospective clients, most notably for those with child molestation conviction. Agents were more willing to help prospective clients seeking more expensive apartments, although the time of year nullified the effect of cost. The results suggest that agents may be more concerned with the financial status of prospective clients than their criminal history but market forces override their decisions to accept a client.* This study has *implications for the ways in which the formerly incarcerated seek housing and how policy can address housing this population*"). Italics added.

[3420] Berk, Richard Berk/Hyatt, Jordan, "Machine Learning Forecasts of Risk to Inform Sentencing Decisions", *Federal Sentencing Report*, Volume 27, 2015, p. 222; Oswald, Marion, et al., "Algorithmic Risk Assessment Policing Models: Lessons from the Durham HART model and 'Experimental' Proportionality", *Information and Communications Technology*, Volume 27, 2018, p. 223 (describing the inner workings of machine-learning algorithm in this regard).

[3421] Mayson, Sandra G., "Bias In, Bias Out", *cit.*, pp. 2218–2300.

[3422] Hellman, Deborah, "Measuring Algorithmic Fairness", *Virginia Law Review*, Volume 106, 2020, pp. 811 and ff and passim; Johnson, Gabbrielle M., "Algorithmic Bias: On the Implicit Biases of Social Technology", *Synthese*, 2021, passim.

[3423] Mayson, Sandra G., "Bias In, Bias Out", *cit.*, pp. 2218–2300.

[3424] Mayson, Sandra G., "Bias In, Bias Out", *cit.*, pp. 2218–2300.

that sharply mirrors the gruelling past of *structural disadvantage*[3425] facing members of racialized communities.

§§ It bears mentioning that modern societies' long-lasting history of social and economic oppression of Black folks—including, but not limited to, criminal laws and inequal law enforcement unceremoniously targeting black men[3426]—have a direct bearing on exceedingly higher rates of arrest,[3427] surveillance,[3428] police killings,[3429] wrongful conviction,[3430] and incarceration[3431] amongst blacks. The result is hardly

---

[3425] See: Barocas, Solon/Selbst, Andrew, "Big Data's Disparate Impact", *California Law Review*, Volume 104, pp. 2016, p. 691 (highlighting the worrisome, and gruesome, issue of "structural disadvantage" with which racialized communities have been tussling for centuries). See also: Powell, Richard/Porter, Jeremy, "Redlining, Concentrated Disadvantage and Crime: The Effects of Discriminatory Government Policies on Violent Crime", *American Journal of Criminal Justice*, Volume 48, 2023, pp. 1132–1156 ("*This study attempts to link the practice of redlining to current-day indicators of neighborhood concentrated disadvantage and violent crime using spatio-temporal data from Chicago*"). Italics added. See also: Gandy, Oscar H., *Coming to Terms with Chance: Engaging Rational Discrimination and Cumulative Disadvantage*, Farnham, UK: Ashgate Publishing, 2009.

[3426] See: Bar-Gill/Oren/Warren, Elizabeth, "Making Credit Safer", *University of Pennsylvania Law Review*, Volume 157, 2008, pp. 1–66 (argue that Black defendants are far more likely to be incarcerated, arrested, surveilled and harassed than White folks, which leads to the conclusion that the use of credit scores and income presents another way in which credit decisions leverage on structural disadvantage). See also: Wacquant, L., "From Slavery to Mass Incarceration: Rethinking the 'race Question' in the US", *New Left Review*, 13, 2002, pp. 41–73; Yates, J., "Racial Incarceration Disparity Among States", *Social Science Quarterly*, 78 (4), 1997, pp. 1001–10.

[3427] Kizer, J. M., "Arrested by skin color: Evidence from siblings and a nationally representative sample", *Socius: Sociological Research for a Dynamic World*, 3, 2017, passim; Kochel, T. R., Wilson, D. B./Mastrofski, S. D., "Effect of suspect race on officers' arrest decisions", *Criminology*, Volume 49, Issue 2, 2011, pp. 473–512. Mitchell, O./Caudy, M. S., "Examining racial disparities in drug arrests", *Justice Quarterly*, Volume 32, Issue 2, 2015, pp. 288–313; Kirk, D. S., "The neighborhood context of racial and ethnic disparities in arrest", *Demography*, 45, 2008, pp. 55–77. See: Part IV, This chapter, Sects. 4.1.1–4.1.1.1 of this book (on biased predictive policing).

[3428] Browne, S., *Dark matters: on the surveillance of blackness*, Duke University Press, 2015, passim; Toro, J. D./Lloyd, T., Buchanan/K. S., Robins/S. J., Bencharit/L. Z., Smiedt/M. G., Reddy/K. S., Pouget, E. R./Kerrison, E. M./Goff, P. A., "The criminogenic and psychological effects of police stops on adolescent black and Latino boys", *Proceedings of the National Academy of Sciences of the United States of America*, Volume 116, Issue 17, 2019, pp. 8261–8268; Sewell, A. A., Jefferson, K. A./Lee, H., "Living under surveillance: Gender, psychological distress, and stop-question- and-frisk policing in New York city", *Social Science & Medicine*, Volume 159, 2016, pp. 1–13. Brayne, S., "Big data surveillance: The case of policing", *American Sociological Review*, Volume 82, Issue 5, 2017, pp. 977–1008; Benjamin, Ruha, *Race After Technology: Abolitionist Tools for the New Jim Code*, John Wiley & Sons, 2019, passim; Abdillahi, I., "Algorithmic surveillance in the era of the appsphere", *American Journal of Community Psychology*, Volume 73, 2024, passim. See: Part IV, This chapter, Sects. 4.1.1–4.1.1.1 of this book (on biased predictive policing).

[3429] Crutchfield, J., Fisher, A., & Webb, S. L., "Colorism and police killings", *The Western Journal of Black Studies*, 41 (3–4), 2017, 81; Dottolo, A. L., & Stewart, A. J. (2008). "Don't ever forget now, you're a Black man in America": Intersections of race, class and gender in encounters with the police", *Sex Roles*, 59(5–6), 2008, pp. 350–364; Baradan, S., "Race, prediction, and discretion", *The George Washington Law Review*, Volume 81, Issue 1, 2013, pp. 157–222. See: Part IV, This chapter, Sects. 4.1.1–4.1.1.1 of this book (on biased predictive policing).

[3430] Jefferson, B., *Digitize and Punish: Racial Criminalization in the Digital Age*, Minnesota, University of Minnesota Press, 2020; Gross, Samuel R., Maurice Possley, and Kalara Stephens,

baffling: criminal history[3432] is tightly interlocked with, and is deeply woven into the fabric[3433] of, race.[3434]

§§ From this assertion derives a hardly unforeseen finding: any type of risk assessment that relies heavily upon criminal history will have a disparate impact[3435] on black communities,[3436] and on black men in[3437]particular.[3438] Media, advocacy organizations, and other scholars[3439] voiced[3440] this deep-rooted concern.[3441] The

"Race and Wrongful Convictions in the United States." National Registry of Exonerations, Newkirk Center for Science and Society, University of California-Irvine, 2017.

3431 See: Pager, Devah, *Marked: Race, Crime, and Finding Work in an Era of Mass Incarceration*, Chicago: University of Chicago Press, 2007; Fornili, K. S., "Racialized mass incarceration and the war on drugs: A critical race theory appraisal", *Journal of Addictions Nursing*, Volume 29, Issue 1, 2018, 65–72; Jacoby, S. F., Dong, B., Beard, J. H., Wiebe, D. J., & Morrison, C. N., "The enduring impact of historical and structural racism on urban violence in Philadelphia", *Social Science & Medicine*, 1982/2018, 199, 2018, pp. 87–95; Travis, Jeremy, Bruce Western, and Steve Redburn (Eds.), *Growth of Incarceration in the United States: Exploring Causes and Consequences*, Washington, DC: National Academy of Science, 2014 (arguing that the rate and pace at which Blacks are incarcerated is exceedingly higher than Whites).

3432 See, e.g., Hamilton, Melissa, "Back to the Future: The Influence of Criminal History on Risk Assessments", *Berkeley Journal of Criminal Law*, Volume 20, 2015, pp. 75, 78 (exuding concerns with the recurrent use of criminal history in risk assessment owing to "the potential that criminal history is an unfortunate proxy for race and social disadvantage").

3433 Mayson, Sandra G., "Bias In, Bias Out", *cit.*, pp. 2218–2300.

3434 See, e.g., McIntyre, Frank/Baradaran, Shima, "Race, Prediction, and Pretrial Detention", *Journal Empirical Legal Studies*, Volume 10, 2013, pp. 742–759 (mentions black defendants' exceedingly high likelihood of being arrested on drug-related charges as a potential cause of the race gap); Skeem, Jennifer L./Lowenkamp, Christopher T., "Risk, Race, and Recidivism: Predictive Bias and Disparate Impact", *Criminology*, Volume 54, 2024, pp. 680, 683–84, 704–06 (argues that criminal history correlates with race in their respective data set).

3435 Starr, Sonja B., "Evidence-Based Sentencing and the Scientific Rationalization of Discrimination", *Stanford Law Review*, Volume 66, 2014, pp. 803 and ff and passim (837 and ff) (contending that the widespread use of such resources "is likely to further concentrate mass incarceration's racial impact," since several markers included in the computer-run tools "are highly correlated with race.". See also: Starr, Sonja B., "Sentencing, by the Numbers", *New York Times* (Aug. 10, 2014), https://www.nytimes.com/2014/08/11/opinion/sentencing-by-the-numbers.html; [https://perma.cc/FK9B-YLQZ].

3436 Harcourt, Bernard E., "Risk as a Proxy for Race: The Dangers of Risk Assessment", *Federal Sentencing Report*, Volume 27, 2015, p. 237 (cautioning that criminal system of justice should not rely too much on criminal-related history that heavy reliance on criminal-history information for purposes of risk assessment "will unquestionably aggravate the already intolerable racial imbalance in our prison populations"). See: Part IV, This chapter, Sects. 4.1.1–4.1.1.1 of this book (on biased predictive policing).

3437 Mayson, Sandra G., "Bias In, Bias Out", *cit.*, pp. 2218–2300.

3438 Harcourt, Bernard E., "Risk as a Proxy for Race: The Dangers of Risk Assessment", *cit.*, p. 240 ("[T]he continuously increasing racial disproportionality in the prison population necessarily entails that the prediction instruments, focused as they are on prior criminality, are going to hit hardest the African American communities"). See: Part IV, This chapter, Sects. 4.1.1–4.1.1.1 of this book (on biased predictive policing).

3439 See: Stevenson, Megan/Mayson, Sandra G., "Pretrial Detention and Bail", Luna, Erik, (Editor), *Reforming Criminal Justice: A Report of the Academy for Justice, Bridging the Gap between Scholarship and Reform*, pp. 21, 34–39 (assessing the risk of pretrial risk assessments while highlighting

Strategic Suspect List (SSL) of Chicago stands as a paradigmatic example of disparate impact on black communities in predictive policing.[3442] Which prompts the pressing questions: what is predictive policing? What is its overriding goal?

§§ The data-driven world we live in has been thrust head long to a mass surveillance[3443] that dispiritingly spares no one.[3444] Predictive policing[3445]—a flagship of mass surveillance[3446] in the information age[3447]—amounts to a crime analysis tool that leverages on big data[3448] to propel forward informed decision making[3449] by law enforcement agencies.[3450]

---

a slew of deep-rooted concerns regarding accuracy, racial-equality, and procedure); See: Chandler, Anupam, "The Racist Algorithm", *Michigan Law Review*, Volume 115, n.º 6, 2018, pp. 1023–1025 (arguing that the real-world facts on which algorithms used in criminal justice risk assessment are based are "deeply suffused with invidious discrimination"); Eaglin, Jessica M., "Constructing Recidivism Risk", *cit.*, pp. 94–99 (argues that risk assessment has every chance to "compromise[e] equality"); Mayson, Sandra G., "Dangerous Defendants", *cit.*, pp. 494–96; Selbst, Andrew D., "Disparate Impact in Big Data Policing", *cit.*, *passim*; Kim, Pauline T., "Data-Driven Discrimination at Work", *William and Mary Law Review*, Volume 58, 2017, pp. 857, 863–64 (shedding a keen light on the racial effects of algorithmic prediction in the remit of employment). Converging: Zywicki, Todd J./Adamson, Joseph D., "The Law and Economics of Subprime Lending", *University of Colorado Law Review*, 2009, pp. 1–9 (contending that Black workers with roughly the same abilities and educational background earn far less than comparable white workers or have considerably fewer employment opportunities); King, Allan G./Markovich, Marko J., "Big Data" and the Risk of Employment Discrimination, *Oklahoma Law Review*, Volume 68, 2016, pp. 555–563 (on employment discrimination). Dobbie, Will, Jacob Goldin, and Crystal S. Yang, "The Effects of Pretrial Detention on Conviction, Future Crime, and Employment: Evidence from Randomly Assigned Judges," *American Economic Review*, Volume 108, 2018, 201–240.

[3440] Mayson, Sandra G., "Bias In, Bias Out", *cit.*, pp. 2218–2300.

[3441] Barry-Jester, Anna Maria et al., "The New Science of Sentencing: Should Prison Sentencing Be Based on Crimes That Haven't Been Committed Yet?", *Marshall Project* (Aug. 4, 2015, 7:15 AM), https://www.themarshallproject.org/2015/08/04/the-new-science-of-sentencing; [https://perma.cc/J4UW-BDKP] (arguing that risk-assessment outcomes gives rises to disparate racial impact that befall Blacks).

[3442] See: Part IV, This chapter, Sects. 4.1.1–4.1.1.1 of this book (on biased predictive policing).

[3443] On mass surveillance: Bentham, Jeremy, *Panopticon: Or, the inspection-house*, Thomas Byrne, 1787. See also: Balkin, Jack M./Levinson, Sanford, "The Processes of Constitutional Change: From Partisan Entrenchment to the National Surveillance State", *Fordham Law Review*, Volume 75, 2006, pp. 489 and ff; Slogogin, Christopher, "Public Privacy: Camera Surveillance of Public Places and the Right to Anonymity", *Mississippi Law Journal*, Volume 72, 2002, pp. 213–251; Balkin, Jack M., "The Constitution in the National Surveillance State", *Minnesota Law Review*, Volume 93, Issue 1, 2008, pp. 17 and ff; Christopher Slobogin, "Panvasive Surveillance, Political Process Theory, and the Nondelegation Doctrine", *Georgetown Law Journal*, Volume 102, 2014, pp. 1721–1775; Ericson, Richard V., and Kevin D. Haggerty, *The New Politics of Surveillance and Visibility*. Toronto: University of Toronto Press, 2006.

[3444] Brayne, S., "Big data surveillance: The case of policing", *American Sociological Review*, 82 (5), 2017, pp. 977–1008.

§§ Predictive policing[3451] consists of a tool aimed at analysing reams of data in an earnest attempt to predict in which geographic areas will be a heightened likelihood of criminal activity.[3452] Put simply, predictive policing[3453] is a form of «intelligence-led

---

[3445] See: Hu, Margaret, "From the National Surveillance State to the Cybersurveillance State", *The Annual Review of Law and Social Science*, Volume 13, 2017, p. 163 ("*Biometric identification and identity assessments are becoming essential tools for multiple preventive purposes in criminal, military, and intelligence contexts.* The third part addresses *how precrime policy rationales are now informed by biometric-based analysis. In short, biometrics is the means by which analysis of a citizenry's data, and any resulting decisions based on that analysis, can be connected back to a physical person in the real world*—whether to approve that person as eligible for a job, *as some employment eligibility database screening systems like E-Verify are, by moving toward biometrics through adopting the E-Verify photo tool* (Hu 2013), *or to determine whether that person is eligible to fly on a commercial airline. The No Fly List and digital watchlisting systems are increasingly biometrically centered (Tau 2015). These types of governance assessments, however, fall within the civil law and administrative law structure. Biometric cybersurveillance systems can inform targeted killing decisions and other lethal consequences. Often in the service of precrime/ counterterrorism policies, biometric cybersurveillance, therefore, is becoming a linchpin for broader policymaking and decisionmaking*"). Italics added. See: Part IV, This chapter, Sects. 4.1.5–4.1.5.2 of this book (on "algorithmic Jim Crow", a travel ban issued during the first Trump Administration to prevent certain individuals from entering the United States of America, which, given its racial undertones, stands as an outgrowth of congeries of laws enacted during the Jim Crow epoch).

[3446] Angwin, Julia, *Dragnet Nation: A Quest for Privacy, Security, and Freedom in a World of Relentless Surveillance*, New York: Times Books, 2014. Citron; Danielle Keats Citron/Pasquale, Frank, "Network Accountability for the Domestic Intelligence Apparatus", *Hasting Law Journal*, Volume 62, 2011, 1441, 1444–45; Gray, David/Citron, Danielle Keats, "The Right to Quantitative Privacy", *Minnesota Law Review*, Volume 98, 2013, pp. 62–81.

[3447] Ball, Kirstie, and Frank Webster (Eds.), *The Intensification of Surveillance: Crime, Terrorism & Warfare in the Information Age*, London, UK: Pluto Press, 2007.

[3448] On algorithmic big data biometric governance: Hu, Margaret, "From the National Surveillance State to the Cybersurveillance State", *The Annual Review of Law and Social Science*, Volume 13, 2017, p. 169 ("*as a result of big data biometric governance trends, meaningful distinctions between biometric credentialing for identification and behavioral biometric profiling are disappearing. The objectives are merging: Reliable credentialing is used to advance security and precrime policy rationales. Biometric data mission creep occurs by necessity in a big data world because the cybersurveillance systems are often designed to engage in mass data integration and analysis and predictive policing. Biometric surveillance serves two purposes in preventive policing: It increases identity transparency, and the biometric data categorize identity through cataloging behavioral and physical characteristics and assess these characteristics for risk. Contrasting small data biometric credentialing protocols with big data credentialing protocols is useful. It illustrates how biometric surveillance fits within the Cybersurveillance State. In a small data world, paper-based passports and nondigitized photographs are examples of a small data biometric-based identification system*"). Italics added.

[3449] DaViera, A. L./Uriostegui, M., Gottlieb/A./Onyeka, O, "Risk, race, and predictive policing: A critical race theory analysis of the strategic subject list", *American Journal of Community Psychology*, Volume 73, 2024, pp. 91–103.

[3450] Brayne, S., "The criminal law and law enforcement implications of big data", *Annual Review of Law and Social Science*, Volume 14, 2018, pp. 293–308.

[3451] See: Hu, Margaret, "From the National Surveillance State to the Cybersurveillance State", *The Annual Review of Law and Social Science*, Volume 13, 2017, p. 166 (argues that ubiquitous and ever-present surveillance of socially undesirables remains at a pitch of degradation of fundamental

policing»[3454] that parses historical data (e.g. crime-related information and arrest-related data) to forecast criminal events or misdeeds alike.[3455]

§§ More to the point, predictive policing draws on massive batches of data to know where and when crimes[3456] are slated to occur.[3457] At the heart of predictive policing

---

rights in that Artificial Intelligence-embedded technologies—propelled by tools like Social Radar and Total Information Awareness, TIA—can capture "a *pictorial depiction of the comprehensive cybersurveillance anticipated through the Social Radar system, which anticipated the full integration of drone footage, biometrric data signatures, econometrics, and other intelligence sources to achieve higher-order cybersurveillance inferences. Social Radar appears to trace its philosophical origins to TIA*. The development of TIA after the 9/11 terrorist attacks was guided under the leadership of the newly created Information Awareness Office within DARPA (Harris 2012, Murray 2010). Within this office, TIA was an effort led by retired Navy Vice Admiral John M. Poindexter (Murray 2010), who served as a national security advisor to President Reagan (Harris 2012). *TIA was informed by a philosophy of "predictive policing," which "focuses not on collecting evidence about actual wrongdoing but on the broad collection of information about everyday activities with the intention of detecting (and preventing) future behavior*" (Murray 2010, p. 5). Congress officially defunded TIA in late 2003 (Murray 2010, Slobogin 2008, USA Today 2003). *Experts have nonetheless noted that remnants of the TIA program and its philosophy have persisted*"). Italics added.

3452 Meijer, A., & Wessels, M., "Predictive policing: Review of benefits and drawbacks", *International Journal of Public Administration*, 42 (12), 2019, 1031–1039.

3453 See: Selbst, Andrew, "Disparate Impact in Big Data Policing", *Georgia Law Review*, Volume 52, 2017, p. 113 ("[P]redictive policing [is] a popular and growing method for police departments to prevent or solve crimes"). See also: Letter from Jonathan J. Wroblewski, Dir., Office of Policy & Legislation, to Hon. Patti B. Saris, Chair, U.S. Sentencing Comm'n 2 (July 29, 2014) [hereinafter DOJ Letter to U.S.S.C.] ("*Predictive Policing—the use of algorithms that combine historical and up-to-the-minute crime information* to do the work of hundreds of traditional crime analysts and *produce real-time targeted patrol areas—is spreading*"). Italics added. See: Part IV, This chapter, Sects. 4.1.1–4.1.1.1 of this book (on biased predictive policing).

3454 DaViera, A. L./Uriostegui, M., Gottlieb/A./Onyeka, O, "Risk, race, and predictive policing: A critical race theory analysis of the strategic subject list", *American Journal of Community Psychology*, Volume 73, 2024, pp. 91–103.91–103 (93). See: Part IV, This chapter, Sects. 4.1.1–4.1.1.1 of this book (on biased predictive policing).

3455 Hardyns, W., & Rummens, A., "Predictive policing as a new tool for law enforcement? recent developments and challenges", *European Journal on Criminal Policy and Research*, 24 (3), 2018, pp. 201–218.

3456 See: Hu, Margaret, "From the National Surveillance State to the Cybersurveillance State", *The Annual Review of Law and Social Science*, Volume 13, 2017, pp. 162–163 ("*policymakers view these technological developments, including biometric technologies, as tools with the potential to identify individuals who may pose a threat to national and homeland security and to prevent crime and terrorism. One example of technology intended for risk assessment and threat management is the post-9/11 program Total Information Awareness (TIA). (....) Collect-it-all efforts like TIA embody a philosophy that aspires to preventive policing. Mass data collection is construed as a tool to assess and prevent future threats (Murray 2010). In TIA and other programs tested or adopted after 9/11, biometric database screening and analysis have emerged as a preferred method for tracking, identifying, and establishing identity-based inferences in counterterrorism*"). Italics added. See also: Ball, Kirstie, and Frank Webster (Eds.), *The Intensification of Surveillance: Crime, Terrorism & Warfare in the Information Age*, London, UK: Pluto Press, 2007; Guzik, Keith, "Discrimination by Design: Predictive Data Mining as Security Practice in the United States' 'War on Terrorism.'", *Surveillance and Society*, 7 (1), 2009, pp. 1–17.

lies an undeterred yearn to effectively reallocate resources[3458] while proactively quell crime surges whenever/wherever they sprout.[3459]

§§ Predictive policing is therefore an algorithmic mechanism created to boost law enforcement's overall accountability[3460] by drawing on a bundle of data against the backdrop of which informed choices are made. Put it bluntly, predictive policing amounts to a scientific tool that leverages on a cluster of big data[3461] to strategically allocate law enforcement resources to the locations,[3462] people, and times where criminal enterprises[3463] are slated to occur.[3464]

§§ Cogently, predictive policing boils down to an algorithmic tool aimed at proactively stamp out criminal activities poised to occur in crime hot spots.[3465] Predictive policing, albeit imbued with panegyrical aims, is not without sizable shortcomings.[3466] It is true that a cohort of staunch supporters[3467] have been extolling[3468] the

---

[3457] DaViera, A. L./Uriostegui, M., Gottlieb/A./Onyeka, O, "Risk, race, and predictive policing: A critical race theory analysis of the strategic subject list", *cit.*, pp. 91–103 (93).

[3458] Tyler, Tom R./Goff, Philip Atiba/MacCoun, Robert J., "The Impact of Psychological Science on Policing in the United States: Procedural Justice, Legitimacy, and Effective Law Enforcement", Psychological Science in the Public Interest, Volume 16, Issue 3, 2015, p. 79 (noting that "without a fundamental reallocation of resources, our society cannot effectively monitor the general public searching for everyday wrongdoing").

[3459] Friedmann, Barry et al., "Policing Police Tech: A Soft Law Solution", *Berkeley Technology Law Journal*, Volume 37, 2022, pp. 701–756.

[3460] Espeland, Wendy N., and Berit I. Vannebo, "Accountability, Quantification and Law." *Annual Review of Law and Society*, 3, 2007, pp. 21–43.

[3461] Boyd, Danah, and Kate Crawford, "Critical Questions for Big Data: Provocations for a Cultural, Technological, and Scholarly Phenomenon", *Information, Communication & Society*, 15 (5), 2012, pp. 662–679.

[3462] Braga, Anthony A., and David L. Weisburd, Policing Problem Places: Crime Hot Spots and Effective Prevention. New York: Oxford University Press, 2010.

[3463] DaViera, A. L./Uriostegui, M., Gottlieb/A./Onyeka, O, "Risk, race, and predictive policing: A critical race theory analysis of the strategic subject list", *cit.*, pp. 91–103 (93).

[3464] Brayne, S., "The criminal law and law enforcement implications of big data", *Annual Review of Law and Social Science*, Volume 14, 2018, pp. 293–308.

[3465] Braga, Anthony A., and David L. Weisburd, *Policing Problem Places: Crime Hot Spots and Effective Prevention.* New York: Oxford University Press, 2010; Sherman, Lawrence W., Patrick R. Gartin, and Michael E. Buerger, "Hot Spots of Predatory Crime: Routine Activities and the Criminology of Place." *Criminology*, 27 (1), 1989, pp. 27–55.

[3466] Hu, Margaret, "From the National Surveillance State to the Cybersurveillance State", *The Annual Review of Law and Social Science*, Volume 13, 2017, p. 169 ("*as a result of big data biometric governance trends, meaningful distinctions between biometric credentialing for identification and behavioral biometric profiling are disappearing. The objectives are merging: Reliable credentialing is used to advance security and precrime policy rationales. Biometric data mission creep occurs by necessity in a big data world because the cybersurveillance systems are often designed to engage in mass data integration and analysis and predictive policing. Biometric surveillance serves two purposes in preventive policing: It increases identity transparency, and the biometric data categorize identity through cataloging behavioral and physical characteristics and assess these characteristics for risk. Contrasting small data biometric credentialing protocols with big data credentialing protocols is useful. It illustrates how biometric surveillance fits within the Cybersurveillance State*"). Italics added.

host of riveting functionalities[3469] comprising predictive policing,[3470] but truer still the reality is far dimmer[3471] than one could possibly fathom.[3472]

§§ Whilst the assertion according to which predictive policing leverages on the data collated in publicly accessible databases is fully warranted,[3473] doubts have nonetheless been cast upon the extent to which it widens extant racial disparities.[3474] Take the example of Chicago's Strategic Suspect List (SSL),[3475] which is a behemoth database comprising criminal-related information of roughly 400,000 thousand arrested individuals[3476] who were ascribed an **index score** that predicted risk to be engaged in future criminal activities[3477] (e.g. gun violence).[3478] However, SSL is a database crammed/teeming with factors that ultimately lead to, in that they are

---

[3467] Brayne, S., "Big data surveillance: The case of policing", *cit.*, pp. 977–1008.

[3468] Mohler, G. O., Short, M. B., Malinowski, S., Johnson, M., Tita, G. E., Bertozzi, A. L., & Brantingham, P. J., "Randomized controlled field trials of predictive policing", *Journal of the American Statistical Association*, 110 (512), 2015, pp. 1399–1411.

[3469] Schenwar, M., & Law, V., *Prison by any other name: The harmful consequences of popular reforms*, New York, The New Press, 2020.

[3470] Meijer, A., & Wessels, M., "Predictive policing: Review of benefits and drawbacks", *International Journal of Public Administration*, 42 (12), 2019, pp. 1031–1039.

[3471] Cohen, Stanley, *Visions of Social Control: Crime, Punishment and Classification*. Malden, MA: Polity Press, 1985 (for purposes here, predictive policing seems to be a tool of social control of social undesirables).

[3472] Santos, R. B., The effectiveness of crime analysis for crime reduction: cure or diagnosis? *Journal of Contemporary Criminal Justice*, 30 (2), 2014, pp. 147–168.

[3473] But see: Kirkpatrick, Keith, "It's not the Algorithm, it's the Data", *Communications of the ACM*, February 2017, Volume 60, n. ° 2, 2017 ("critics, however, say tools such as PredPol and CommandCentral *are inherently biased since they rely heavily on reported crimes data, which is often concentrated in areas that are heavily policed, thereby skewing statistics to overrepresent poor or minority communities.* "*We know we have a history of racially biased policing in the United States, and that has fed into all the data that we have on where arrests have occurred, which crimes are more likely to occur in specific communities, and at which particular times*," says Jennifer Lynch, senior staff attorney at the Electronic Frontier Foundation. "*That's the data that's being fed into predictive policing algorithms*"). Italics added. See also: Kirkpatrick, Keith, "Battling Algorithmic Bias: How Do We Ensure Algorithms Treat Us Fairly?" *Commun. ACM 59*, Volume 10, 2016, pp. 1 and ff and passim.

[3474] Mitchell, O., & Caudy, M. S., "Examining racial disparities in drug arrests", *Justice Quarterly*, 32 (2), 2015, pp. 288–313; Gottlieb, A., & Flynn, K., "The Legacy of Slavery and Mass Incarceration: Evidence from Felony Case Outcomes", *Social Service Review*, 95 (1), 2021, pp. 3–35.

[3475] Chicago Data Portal, Strategic Subject List- Historical. https://data.cityofchicago.org/Public-Safety/Strategic-Subject-ListHistorical/4aki-r3np, 2020.

[3476] Jefferson, B. J., Predictable policing: Predictive crime mapping and geographies of policing and race, *Annals of the American Association of Geographers*, 108 (1), 2018, pp. 1–16.

[3477] Tucek, A., Constraining Big Brother: The Legal Deficiencies Surrounding Chicago's Use of the Strategic Subject List (2018). *University of Chicago Legal Forum*, 2019.

[3478] DaViera, A. L./Uriostegui, M., Gottlieb/A./Onyeka, O, "Risk, race, and predictive policing: A critical race theory analysis of the strategic subject list", *cit.*, pp. 91–103 (91).

conducive to a, *proxy discrimination*[3479] with racial disparities[3480] looming large in the data analysis.[3481]

§§ At its core, SSL amounts to a comprehensive, thoroughgoing, and full-fledged database whereby arrest data spanning 2012–2016 is featured,[3482] thereby encompassing any individual (male or female) who has either been arrested or fingerprinted[3483] since 2013.[3484] These individuals were subsequently given a risk assessment[3485] for either gun violence[3486] perpetration or victimization.[3487]

[3479] See: Part IV, This chapter, Sect. 4.1.6.3 of this book (on proxy discrimination). See also: Prince, Anya E. R./Schwarcz, Daniel, "Proxy Discrimination in the Age of Artificial Intelligence and Big Data", *Iowa Law Review*, Volume 105, 1257, 2020, pp. 1279–81 ("[*P*]*roxy discrimination will tend to occur when a suspect variable is predictive of a desired outcome only because it proxies for another*, quantifiable and potentially available, *variable that causes the desired outcome but that is not included in the AI's training data*"). Italics added. Note, though, that the training of machine learning is long and tedious in that is an error-prone procedure than can ultimately impair future algorithmic decision-making: Price, W. Nicholson Price II, "Regulating Black-Box Medicine", *Michigan Law Review*, Volume 116, 2017, pp. 421–431 (leverages on Google Image's image recognition learning algorithm to shed light on the four-step process by which some algorithms are thoroughly trained. First, the algorithm is shown "a set of known images ('Here are 10,000 pictures of ducks')." Second, the algorithm "develops complex internal rules based on nonlinear processes." Third, the algorithm "tests those rules on a test set ('Which of these are ducks?')." And fourth, the algorithm accordingly adjusts its "internal rules based on the success of the test." These steps are trotted out and repeated many times "until it can accurately and consistently classify the images").

[3480] Soss, Joe, Richard C. Fording, and Sanford F. Schram, *Disciplining the Poor: Neoliberal Paternalism and the Persistent Power of Race.* Chicago: University of Chicago Press, 2011.

[3481] Proxy discrimination happens frequently in the remit of real estate industry—especially, in the realm of rental applications—to screen out undesirable tenants drawing on the existence of criminal records. See: Wonyoung, So, "Which Information Matters? Measuring Landlord Assessment of Tenant Screening Reports", *Housing Policy Debate*, Volume 33, n. ° 6, 2023, pp. 1484–1510 (1501–1502) ("*In mid-scored criminal records, landlords would have more discretion in terms of how to assess tenants, depending on the type of charges or the disposition of the case. HUD prohibits denying housing by holding arrest records against tenants. But apart from that, landlords who HOUSING POLICY DEBATE 1501 would like to construct proxies of undesirable tenants using criminal records must assess which criminal records would relate to tenants' behavior (e.g., damaging their property and/or adversely affecting other tenants).* However, it is incredibly challenging to identify the causal relationship between how and which past misdemeanors cause particular future tenant behaviors. Moreover, legal jargon and abbreviations on the report could make it harder for landlords to understand criminal records in the first place. *These factors, as a result, could contribute to landlords' reliance on the scores provided by the report shown in the experiment*"). See: Part IV, This chapter, Sects. 4.1.4–4.1.4.2.3 of this book.

[3482] DaViera, A. L./Uriostegui, M., Gottlieb/A./Onyeka, O, "Risk, race, and predictive policing: A critical race theory analysis of the strategic subject list", *cit.*, pp. 91–103 (93).

[3483] Lynch, Michael, Simon A. Cole, Ruth McNally, and Kathleen Jordan. 2008. Truth Machine: The Conten tious History of DNA Fingerprinting. Chicago: University of Chicago Press.

[3484] DaViera, A. L./Uriostegui, M., Gottlieb/A./Onyeka, O, "Risk, race, and predictive policing: A critical race theory analysis of the strategic subject list", *cit.*, pp. 91–103 (93).

[3485] Stevenson, Megan T./Slogobin, Christopher, "Algorithmic Risk Assessments and the Double-Edged Sword of Youth", *Behavioural Sciences and the Law*, Volume 36, 2018, pp. 638–639.

§§ SSL has been designed and created by Miles Wernick at the Illinois Institute of Technology[3488] with a view to aid law enforcement agencies to make data-based[3489] informed decisions within the remit of criminal justice. It has been accordingly contended that its overriding goal was to timely alert police to individuals that posed grave danger to the great state of Illinois.[3490] Such individuals were to be tagged as possible «parties to violence»,[3491] and the police, just like the remaining law enforcement agencies, were to remain accordingly vigilant.

§§ SSL was fully funded through a Department of Justice Bureau of Justice Assistance[3492] grant to outline a risk assessment algorithm[3493] that would leverage on a plethora of person-centred variables to timely and shrewdly predict whether and to what extent a given individual would be later involved in criminal activities.[3494] The crux of the legal quagmire lies elsewhere though: the variables used to estimate

---

[3486] Papachristos, Andrew V., David M. Hureau, and Anthony A. Braga, "The Corner and the Crew: The Influence of Geography and Social Networks on Gang Violence." *American Sociological Review*, 78 (3), 2013, pp. 417–47.

[3487] DaViera, A. L./Uriostegui, M., Gottlieb/A./Onyeka, O, "Risk, race, and predictive policing: A critical race theory analysis of the strategic subject list", *cit.*, pp. 91–103 (93).

[3488] DaViera, A. L./Uriostegui, M., Gottlieb/A./Onyeka, O, "Risk, race, and predictive policing: A critical race theory analysis of the strategic subject list", *cit.*, pp. 91–103 (93).

[3489] Kitchin, Rob, *The Data Revolution: Big Data, Open Data, Data Infrastructures & Their Consequences*. London, UK: SAGE, 2014.

[3490] DaViera, A. L./Uriostegui, M., Gottlieb/A./Onyeka, O, "Risk, race, and predictive policing: A critical race theory analysis of the strategic subject list", *cit.*, pp. 91–103 (93).

[3491] Kunichoff, Y., & Sier, P., August 21 The Contradictions of Chicago Police's Secretive List. Chicago Magazine, 2017, passim. https://www.chicagomag.com/city-life/august-2017/chicago-police-strategic-subject-list/

[3492] Chicago Data Portal, Strategic Subject List- Historical. https://data.cityofchicago.org/Public-Safety/Strategic-Subject-ListHistorical/4aki-r3np, 2020.

[3493] But see on the perils associated to risk assessment algorithms: Hamilton, Melissa, "The sexist algorithm", *Behavioral Sciences and the Law*, Volume 37, Issue 2, Special Issue: the Use of Statistics in Criminal Cases, March–April 2019, 2019, pp. 1 and ff ("Algorithmic risk assessment tools are informed by scientific research concerning which factors are predictive of recidivism and thus support the evidence-based practice movement in criminal justice. Automated assessments of individualized risk (low, medium, high) permit officials to make more effective management decisions. Computer-generated algorithms appear to be objective and neutral. But are these algorithms actually fair? The focus herein is on gender equity. Studies confirm that women typically have far lower recidivism rates than men. *This differential raises the question of how well algorithmic outcomes fare in terms of predictive parity by gender*. This essay reports original research using a large dataset of offenders who were scored on the popular risk assessment tool COMPAS. *Findings indicate that COMPAS performs reasonably well at discriminating between recidivists and non-recidivists for men and women. Nonetheless, COMPAS algorithmic outcomes systemically overclassify women in higher risk groupings. Multiple measures of algorithmic equity and predictive accuracy are provided to support the conclusion that this algorithm is sexist*"). Italics added.

[3494] DaViera, A. L./Uriostegui, M., Gottlieb/A./Onyeka, O, "Risk, race, and predictive policing: A critical race theory analysis of the strategic subject list", *cit.*, pp. 91–103 (93).

the risk assessment concerning the individuals that were deemed to be a «party to violence» in crime hotspots.[3495]

§§ Put simply, there is a gulf between the ambrosial aims with which predictive policing has been permeated by (prevention of crime underpinned by the pillars of effective reallocation of resources[3496]) and the outcome arising out of this crime prevention strategy (racial disparities[3497] and structural disadvantage[3498] with which Black people have been grappling for a long-winded span[3499] of time[3500]).

§§ More to the point, the variables used to deftly calculate algorithmic risk assessment contained proxies to racial discrimination.[3501] Tellingly, the variables used to estimate algorithmic risk assessment comprised the number of times being the victim

---

3495 Uchida, Craig D., and Marc L. Swatt, "Operation LASER and the Effectiveness of Hotspot Patrol: A Panel Analysis." Police Quarterly 16 (3), 2015, pp. 287–304.

3496 Tyler, Tom R./Goff, Philip Atiba/MacCoun, Robert J., "The Impact of Psychological Science on Policing in the United States: Procedural Justice, Legitimacy, and Effective Law Enforcement", Psychological Science in the Public Interest, Volume 16, Issue 3, 2015, p. 79 (noting that "without a fundamental reallocation of resources, our society cannot effectively monitor the general public searching for everyday wrongdoing");

3497 Robinson, M. A., "Black bodies on the ground: Policing disparities in the African American Community—An analysis of newsprint from January 1, 2015, through December 31, 2015", *Journal of Black Studies*, 48 (6), 2017, pp. 551–571.

3498 See: Barocas, Solon/Selbst, Andrew, "Big Data's Disparate Impact", *California Law Review*, Volume 104, pp. 2016, p. 691 (highlighting the worrisome, and gruesome, issue of "structural disadvantage" with which racialized communities have been tussling for centuries). See also: Powell, Richard/Porter, Jeremy, "Redlining, Concentrated Disadvantage and Crime: The Effects of Discriminatory Government Policies on Violent Crime", *American Journal of Criminal Justice*, Volume 48, 2023, pp. 1132–1156 ("*Redlining and other discriminatory government policies enacted during the first half of the Twentieth Century have had long-lasting negative effects on neighborhoods, especially those inhabited by people of color. This study attempts to link the practice of redlining to current-day indicators of neighborhood concentrated disadvantage and violent crime using spatio-temporal data from Chicago* (…) *In addition, it seeks to determine whether redlining was associated with violent crime, and if that association was mediated by redlining's effect on concentrated disadvantage. The results indicate that redlining was associated with increases in both concentrated disadvantage and violent crime, and that redlining's relationship with violent crime was, indeed, partially mediated by its relationship with concentrated disadvantage*"). Italics added. See also: Gandy, Oscar H., *Coming to Terms with Chance: Engaging Rational Discrimination and Cumulative Disadvantage*, Farnham, UK: Ashgate Publishing, 2009.

3499 Wacquant, L., "From Slavery to Mass Incarceration: Rethinking the 'race Question' in the US", *New Left Review*, 13, 2002, pp. 41–73; Yates, J., "Racial Incarceration Disparity Among States", *Social Science Quarterly*, 78 (4), 1997, pp. 1001–10.

3500 Gandy, Oscar H., *Coming to Terms with Chance: Engaging Rational Discrimination and Cumulative Disadvantage*. Farnham, UK: Ashgate Publishing, 2009.

3501 Campisi, Natalie, From Inherent Racial Bias to Incorrect Data The Problems With Current Credit Scoring Models, Forbes (Feb. 26, 2021), https://www.forbes.com/advisor/creditcards/from-inherent-racial-bias-to-incorrect-data-the-problems-with-current-credit-scoring-models/; [https://perma.cc/EWA4-CS8E] (highlighting rampant racial bias in credit scoring systems); Oyama, Rebecca, "Do Not (Re)Enter: the Rise of Criminal Background Tenant Screening as a Violation of the Fair Housing Act", *Michigan Journal of Race and Law*, Volume 15, 2009, pp. 181, 184–93 (discussing a broad range of historical/criminal accounts as a way to screen undesirable tenants, such as Blacks and Latinos); Statement of Interest of the United States at 12, *Louis v. SafeRent Sols., LLC, No. 1:22-cv-10800* (D. Mass. Jan. 9, 2023) (holding that the Fair Housing Act liability

of a gun-related incident, the age at the latest record arrest, number of times being the victim of aggravated battery or physical assault, number of recorded prior arrests for violent crimes, alleged gang affiliation, number of prior drug possession arrests,[3502] recorded trend related with recent criminal activity,[3503] and the number of prior flagitious use of guns arrests.[3504]

§§ Whilst the risk assessment algorithm does not encompass neither race nor gender as predictor variables,[3505] pundits have not refrained themselves from voicing concerns about the nature of list of measures, which may indeed bear a striking resemblance with both (race and gender).[3506]

§§ It is oft-contended that the foregoing list of measures is tantamount to proxies for race and gender,[3507] thus rendering such risk assessment tools as racist/sexist[3508] algorithms.[3509] For this reason alone, doubts have been cast upon the effectiveness—or lack thereof—of predictive policing, both from the reallocation of resources[3510] and its underlying fairness.[3511]

---

stretches far and beyond, thus encompassing a vast assortment of entities providing housing-related services, including corporations that offer tenant screening services). See also: Massey, Douglas S., "The Legacy of the 1968 Fair Housing Act", *Social Forces*, Volume 30, 2015, pp. 571, 575–76, 578 ("[*The FHA*] *outlawed the refusal to rent or sell to someone because of race; it prohibited racial discrimination in the terms and conditions of rental or sale; it barred discrimination in real estate advertising; it banned agents from making untrue statements about a dwelling's availability in order to deny access to blacks*; and it enjoined real estate agents from making comments about the race of neighbors or in-movers in order to promote panic selling. Although the new law applied only to around 80% of the nation's housing stock, a Supreme Court decision adjudicated just two months later extended its reach to all housing in the United States"). Italics added. Internal citations omitted.

3502 Beckett, Katherine/Kris Nyrop/Lori Pfingst/Melissa Bowen, "Drug Use, Drug Possession Arrests, and the Question of Race: Lessons from Seattle.", *Social Problems*, (52) 3, 2005, pp. 419–41; Duster, Troy, "Pattern, Purpose and Race in the Drug War.", Crack in America: Demon Drugs and Social Justice, edited by C. Reinarman and H. G. Levine. Berkeley: University of California Press, 1997, pp. 206–287; Mitchell, O., & Caudy, M. S., Examining racial disparities in drug arrests", *Justice Quarterly*, 32 (2), 2015, pp. 288–313.

3503 DaViera, A. L./Uriostegui, M., Gottlieb/A./Onyeka, O, "Risk, race, and predictive policing: A critical race theory analysis of the strategic subject list", *cit.*, pp. 91–103 (93).

3504 Chicago Data Portal, Strategic Subject List- Historical. https://data.cityofchicago.org/Public-Safety/Strategic-Subject-ListHistorical/4aki-r3np, 2020, passim.

3505 DaViera, A. L./Uriostegui, M., Gottlieb/A./Onyeka, O, "Risk, race, and predictive policing: A critical race theory analysis of the strategic subject list", *cit.*, pp. 91–103 (93).

3506 Eckhouse, L., Lum, K., Conti-Cook, C., & Ciccolini, J., "Layers of bias: A unified approach for understanding problems with risk assessment", *Criminal Justice and Behavior*, Volume 46, Issue 2, 2019, pp. 185–209.

3507 O'Neil, Cathy, *Weapons of math destruction: How big data increases inequality and threatens democracy*, New York, Crown Publisher, 2016.

3508 Monk, E. P., "The color of punishment: African Americans, skin tone, and the criminal justice system", *Ethnic and Racial Studies*, Volume 42, Issue 10, 2019, pp. 1593–1612.

§§ Although making data[3512]-based[3513] predictions[3514] on where will crime occur is seemingly wrapped under the patina of objectivity,[3515] there has been a public outcry about the extent to which the data around which predictive policing revolves is fraught with racial[3516] bias.[3517] To add to our woes, a sweeping analysis on the

---

[3509] Osaba, Osonde/Welser, William IV, *An Intelligence in Our Image—The Risk of Bias and Errors in Artificial Intelligence*, Santa Monica, California, Rand, 2018, passim; Chandler, Anupam, "The Racist Algorithm", *Michigan Law Review*, Volume 115, n. ° 6, 2018, p. 1026 (on racist algorithms, noting that "the possibilities for discriminatory manipulation are legion"). But see: Altenburger, Kristen M./Ho, Daniel E., "When Algorithms Import Private Bias into Public Enforcement: The Promise and Limitations of Statistical Debiasing Solutions", *Journal of Institutional & Theoretical Economics*, Volume 175, 2019, pp. 97–98 (calls for a "debias predictive algorithms" to assuage racist and/or biased, doctored and bigoted algorithms nevertheless); Hamilton, Melissa, "The Biased Algorithm: Evidence of Disparate Impact on Hispanics", *American Criminal Law Review*, Volume 56, 2019, pp. 1553 and ff and passim.

[3510] Tyler, Tom R./Goff, Philip Atiba/MacCoun, Robert J., "The Impact of Psychological Science on Policing in the United States: Procedural Justice, Legitimacy, and Effective Law Enforcement", Psychological Science in the Public Interest, Volume 16, Issue 3, 2015, p. 79 (noting that "without a fundamental reallocation of resources, our society cannot effectively monitor the general public searching for everyday wrongdoing").

[3511] Corbett-Davies, Sam/Goel, Sharad, "The Measure and Mismeasure of Fairness: a critical Review of Fair Machine Learning", *Cornell University Library*, 2018, pp. 3 and ff and passim (undertake laudable efforts to debunk algorithm biases that primarily target ethnic minorities, such as Hispanics and coloured people); Laub, John H., *Understanding Inequality and the Justice System Response: Charting a New Way Forward*, New York: William T. Grant Foundation, 2014.

[3512] Kitchin, Rob, *The Data Revolution: Big Data, Open Data, Data Infrastructures & Their Consequences*. London, UK: SAGE, 2014.

[3513] Sherman, Lawrence W., "Targeting, Testing and Tracking Police Services: The Rise of Evidence Based Policing, 1975–2025.", *Crime and Justice*, 42 (1), 2013, pp. 377–451.

[3514] Ferguson, Andrew G., "Big Data and Predictive Reasonable Suspicion." *University of Pennsylvania Law Review*, 63 (2), 2015, pp. 327–410.

[3515] Christin, Angèle, "From Daguerreotypes to Algorithms: Machines, Expertise, and Three Forms of Objectivity." *ACM Computers & Society*, 46 (1), 2016, pp. 27–32 (on the multifarious facets of algorithmic objectivity). But see: Benjamin, Ruha, *Race After Technology: Abolitionist Tools for the New Jim Code*, New York, Polity, 2019, pp. 1–172 (7) (discussing that Artificial Intelligence-embedded technologies are viewed as iron-clad tools of objectivity and devoid of any biases whatsoever). Ruha Benjamin contends that "the employment of new technologies that reflect and reproduce existing inequities but that are promoted and perceived as more objective or progressive than the discriminatory systems of a previous era").

[3516] Browne, Simone, *Dark Matters: On the Surveillance of Blackness*. Durham, NC: Duke University Press, 2015.

[3517] But see: Kirkpatrick, Keith, "It's not the Algorithm, it's the Data", *Communications of the ACM*, February 2017, Volume 60, n.º 2, 2017 ("critics, however, say tools such as PredPol and CommandCentral *are inherently biased since they rely heavily on reported crimes data, which is often concentrated in areas that are heavily policed, thereby skewing statistics to overrepresent poor or minority communities*. "*We know that we have a history of racially biased policing in the United States, and that has fed into all the data that we have on where arrests have occurred, which crimes are more likely to occur in specific communities, and at which particular times*," says Jennifer Lynch, senior staff attorney at the Electronic Frontier Foundation. "*That's the data that's being fed into predictive policing algorithms*"). Italics added. See also: Kirkpatrick, Keith, "Battling Algorithmic Bias: How Do We Ensure Algorithms Treat Us Fairly?" *Commun. ACM 59*, Volume

effectiveness of predictive policing has shown that these programs, albeit suffused with the laudable aim to quell crime, are nothing short of dispiritingly tokenistic.[3518]

§§ Against this background, predictive policing has been met with grudging reluctance by a great bulk of scholars. Compellingly, uncertain is the extent to which predictive policing is suitably tailored to effectively attain the laudable goal of crime prevention.[3519]

§§ On this account, it seems as though predictive policing amounts to an algorithmic tool to target the outsiders[3520] and *socially undesirables*. The warped data that underpins predictive policing lends support to, and gives credence to, this main contention.

§§ To the extent that predictive policing leverages on clusters of bigoted data,[3521] there have been vexing doubts on whether and to what extent this crime prevention tool is amenable to effectively[3522] stamp out crime[3523] while abiding by the fundamental tenets of Rule of Law.[3524]

10, 2016, pp. 1 and ff and passim; Jefferson, B. J., "Predictable policing: Predictive crime mapping and geographies of policing and race". *Annals of the American Association of Geographers*, 108 (1), 2018, 1–16.

3518 Saunders, J., Hunt, P., & Hollywood, J. S., "Predictions put into practice: A quasi-experimental evaluation of Chicago's predictive policing pilot", *Journal of Experimental Criminology*, 12 (3), 2016, pp. 347–371.

3519 DaViera, A. L./Uriostegui, M., Gottlieb/A./Onyeka, O, "Risk, race, and predictive policing: A critical race theory analysis of the strategic subject list", *cit.*, pp. 91–103.

3520 Becker, Howard S., *Outsiders: Studies in the Sociology of Deviance*, New York: Free Press, 1963.

3521 Lazer, David/Radford, Jason, "Data ex Machina: Introduction to Big Data.", *Annual Review of Sociology*, 43, 2017, pp. 19–39.

3522 Santos, R. B., "The effectiveness of crime analysis for crime reduction: cure or diagnosis?", *Journal of Contemporary Criminal Justice*, 30 (2), 2014, pp. 147–168.

3523 Hardyns, W., & Rummens, A., "Predictive policing as a new tool for law enforcement? recent developments and challenges". *European Journal on Criminal Policy and Research*, 24 (3), 2018, pp. 201–218.

3524 See: Part V, Chap. 5, Sect. 5.1.1.1 of this book (on the central tenets of Rule of Law that lends itself to a beacon of justice amidst the sepulchral darkness that is about to take hold). See: Part V, Chap. 5, Sect. 5.1.1.2 of this book (on the central tenets of Procedural Rule of Law that lends itself to a lighthouse of justice that allows citizens to challenge the pearls of algorithmic wisdom in a court of law). See also: Cass, Ronald A., The Rule of Law in America. Baltimore, Maryland: The Johns Hopkins University Press, 2001, p. 17 (noting that a "central element of the Rule of law, constraint from external authority...helps assure that the process of government, rather than the predilections of the individual decision-maker") Italics added. Which is why the onset of the age of Artificial Intelligence will put the Rule of Law to the test like never before. Recall, the Rule of Law is a functional barrier—aimed at clamping down a host of unlawful deeds undertaken by those in power—that must not be teared apart or criminal procedure law will be otherwise despoiled from its intrinsic validity and vitality. See: Raz, Joseph, "The Rule of Law and its Virtue", The Authority of Law: Essays on Law and Morality, cit., p. 224 (asserts adamantly that the Rule of Law is aimed at cushioning the hazards of abuse perpetrated by those in power. In this vein, Raz contends that "the law inevitably creates a great danger of arbitrary power—the Rule of Law is designed to minimize the danger created by the law itself...Thus the (R)ule of (L)aw is designed to minimize the danger created by law itself...Thus the (R)ule of (L)aw is a negative virtue...the evil which is avoided is evil

§§ Notably, SSL has been thoroughly assessed, and yet the results yielded fell conspicuously short of matching the overblown expectations from the reduction of gun-related crime rates standpoint.[3525] The same goes for predictive policing used to crackdown on property crimes.[3526] Most importantly, the overriding concerns with racial disparities arising out of doctored and watered down data soared.

§§ Insofar the suspects included in the SSL were tagged as dangerous, the likelihood of being harassed, surveilled[3527] and subsequently arrested[3528] by law enforcement agencies was exceedingly high. This disheartening scenario crashes into long-standing debates on the degree to which the increased risk of arrest facing members of racial minorities[3529] is an outgrowth of decades-long of gruelling racial[3530] discrimination.[3531]

§§ Tellingly, individuals included within the compass of SSL were constantly on law enforcement's radar.[3532] Casts broadly, individuals included on SSL were far more likely to be surveilled and arrested[3533] by the police than were individuals

which could only have been caused by the law itself"). Italics added; McAfee, Andrew/Brynjolfsson, *Machine, Platform, Crowd: Harnessing our Digital Future*, London: Brilliance Audio; Unabridged edition, 2017 (pore over a myriad of automatic biases displayed by artificial intelligence).

[3525] Saunders, J., Hunt, P., & Hollywood, J. S., "Predictions put into practice: A quasi-experimental evaluation of Chicago's predictive policing pilot", *Journal of Experimental Criminology*, 12 (3), 2016, pp. 347–371.

[3526] Hunt, P., Saunders, J., & Hollywood, J. S., "Conclusions. In Evaluation of the Shreveport Predictive Policing Experiment, RAND Corporation, 2014, pp. 50 and ff.

[3527] Sewell, A. A., Jefferson, K. A., & Lee, H., Living under surveillance: Gender, psychological distress, and stop-question and-frisk policing in New York city. Social Science & Medicine, 159, 2016, pp. 1–13. On mass surveillance: Bentham, Jeremy, *Panopticon: Or, the inspection-house*, Thomas Byrne, 1787. See also: Balkin, Jack M./Levinson, Sanford, "The Processes of Constitutional Change: From Partisan Entrenchment to the National Surveillance State", *Fordham Law Review*, Volume 75, 2006, pp. 489 and ff; Slogogin, Christopher, "Public Privacy: Camera Surveillance of Public Places and the Right to Anonymity", *Mississippi Law Journal*, Volume 72, 2002, pp. 213–251; Balkin, Jack M., "The Constitution in the National Surveillance State", *Minnesota Law Review*, Volume 93, Issue 1, 2008, pp. 17 and ff; Christopher Slobogin, "Panvasive Surveillance, Political Process Theory, and the Nondelegation Doctrine", *Georgetown Law Journal*, Volume 102, 2014, pp. 1721–1775; Ericson, Richard V., and Kevin D. Haggerty, *The New Politics of Surveillance and Visibility*. Toronto: University of Toronto Press, 2006.

[3528] Kizer, J. M., "Arrested by skin color: Evidence from siblings and a nationally representative sample, *Socius: Sociological Research for a Dynamic World*, 3, 2017.

[3529] Laub, John H., *Understanding Inequality and the Justice System Response: Charting a New Way Forward*, New York: William T. Grant Foundation, 2014.

[3530] Gottlieb, A., & Flynn, K., "The Legacy of Slavery and Mass Incarceration: Evidence from Felony Case Outcomes", *Social Service Review*, 95 (1), 2021, pp. 3–35.

[3531] Jefferson, B, *Digitize and Punish: Racial Criminalization in the Digital Age*, Minnesota, University of Minnesota Press, 2020; Gross, Samuel R., Maurice Possley, and Kalara Stephens, "Race and Wrongful Convictions in the United States." National Registry of Exonerations, Newkirk Center for Science and Society, University of California-Irvine, 2017.

[3532] DaViera, A. L./Uriostegui, M., Gottlieb/A./Onyeka, O, "Risk, race, and predictive policing: A critical race theory analysis of the strategic subject list", *cit.*, pp. 91–103.

[3533] See: Connecticut Fair Housing Center, et al. v. CoreLogic Rental Property Solutions—Cohen Milstein (access: 20.11.2024). ("*The U.S. Department of Housing & Urban Development observed*

placed at the outskirts of SSL.[3534] There is accordingly a deep-seated, and firmly rooted, quandary with which predictive policing has been tussling: the disparate impact[3535] on racialized communities, whom are constantly targeted, surveilled,[3536] harassed and arrested by law enforcement agencies.[3537]

4.1.10.1.4 «The Quest for Predictive Parity» (or Lack Thereof) in Algorithmic Risk Assessment: The Problem of Equality Trade-offs in Correctional Offender Management Profiling for Alternative Sanctions (COMPAS)

§§ As adumbrated earlier in this essay, there is no such thing as a «one size fits all», let alone a catch-all concept, amenable to deftly measure racial equality in algorithmic risk assessment.[3538] Quite the opposite, there is a feast of potentially

---

in 2016 that excluding rental applicants because of their criminal records disproportionately harms Latinos and African Americans, who are significantly more likely than whites to be arrested or convicted. Studies show such disparities are linked to differential enforcement rather than to differences in likelihood of engaging in criminal activity. HUD advised that to avoid discriminating, an "individualized review" should be conducted considering the nature of the offense, how long ago it occurred, intervening changed circumstances, and other relevant factors to avoid denying housing to an applicant who does not pose a genuine and ongoing threat to persons or property. *Further, HUD's guidance specifically advises landlords not to consider arrests that did not result in a conviction in making their evaluations*"). Italics added.

[3534] Saunders, J., Hunt, P., & Hollywood, J. S., "Predictions put into practice: A quasi-experimental evaluation of Chicago's predictive policing pilot", *Journal of Experimental Criminology*, 12 (3), 2016, pp. 347–371.

[3535] Barocas, Solon/Selbst, Andrew D., "Big Data's Disparate Impact", *California Law Review*, Volume 104, 2016, pp. 671 and ff and passim.

[3536] Browne, S., *Dark matters: on the surveillance of blackness*, Duke University Press, 2015, passim.

[3537] Robinson, M. A., "Black bodies on the ground: Policing disparities in the African American Community-An analysis of newsprint from January 1, 2015, through December 31, 2015", *Journal of Black Studies*, Volume 48, Issue 6, pp. 551–571.

[3538] See: Dieterich, William et al., "COMPAS Risk Scales: Demonstrating Accuracy Equity and Predictive Parity", *Northpointe Inc.* 1, 2–3, 8–13 (July 8, 2016), http://go.volarisgroup.com/rs/430-MBX-989/images/ProPublica_Commentary_Final_070616.pdf; [https://perma.cc/K4GM -RBQY] (stating that a predictive instrument is bigoted/flawed only if a certain score, or a given classification, means a starkly likelihood of the forecasted outcome for members of one racial group than members of the other racial group). See also: Flores: Anthony W. et al., "False Positives, False Negatives, and False Analyses: A Rejoinder to "Machine Bias: There's Software Used Across the Country to Predict Future Criminals. And It's Biased Against Blacks," *Federal Probation*, Volume 80, 2016, pp. 38–40 (positing that "well-established and accepted standards exist to test for bias in risk assessment"); Skeem, Jennifer L./Lowenkamp, Christopher T., "Risk, Race, and Recidivism: Predictive Bias and Disparate Impact", *cit.*, p. 685 (asserting that if "a given score [has] the same meaning regardless of group membership," the instrument is "unbiased"). See: Mayson, Sandra G., "Bias In, Bias Out", *cit.*, pp. 2218–2300.

applicable measures in this regard.[3539] But here's the twist: it is utterly impossible to attain racial equality according to every single measure concomitantly.[3540] The *ProPublica* debate vividly portrays this quandary. *ProPublica* posited that the algorithmic tool *Correctional Offender Management Profiling for Alternative Sanctions* (COMPAS)[3541] was «biased against blacks».[3542] In a nutshell, COMPAS was a warped algorithm[3543] that ran counter to algorithmic fairness.[3544]

§§ Leveraging on data from a jurisdiction where COMPAS was used to assess the likelihood that a pretrial[3545] defendant would be rearrested[3546] if he stayed at

---

[3539] See: Selbst, Andrew D., "Disparate Impact in Big Data Policing", *Georgia Law Review*, Volume 52, 2017, p. 109 (arguing that law enforcement agencies should carry out "algorithmic impact statements" with a view to measure the potential discriminatory impact of computer-run predictive policing technologies).

[3540] Mayson, Sandra G., "Bias In, Bias Out", *cit.*, pp. 2218–2300.

[3541] Dobbie, Will, Jacob Goldin, and Crystal S. Yang, "The Effects of Pretrial Detention on Conviction, Future Crime, and Employment: Evidence from Randomly Assigned Judges," *American Economic Review*, Volume 108, 2018, 201–240. See: Baughman, Shima Baradaran, "Costs of Pretrial Detention", *Boston University Law Review*, Volume 97, 2017, p. 1 (calculating the whooping costs of detention); Heaton, Paul et al., "The Downstream Consequences of Misdemeanor Pretrial Detention", *Stanford Law Review*, Volume 69, 2017, 711, 759–69 (concluding, amongst other things, that pretrial detention ballooned the likelihood that a defendant would accrue new criminal charges within 18 months of a bail court hearing).

[3542] Mayson, Sandra G., "Bias In, Bias Out", *cit.*, pp. 2218–2300 (2233).

[3543] From the prism of social sciences, warped algorithms accomplish nothing but the impairment of procedural justice. See: Thibaut, John/ Walker, Laurens, *Procedural Justice: A Psychological Analysis*. Hillsdale, N.J.: Lawrence Erlbaum Associates, 1975, pp. 1–150 (procedural justice is tightly interlocked to raising the levels of fairness in legal settings. Absent of which procedural fairness is to mar. Lawmakers must not lose sight of such assertion). Converging: Lind, Edgar Allan/ Tyler, Tom R., *The Social Psychology of Procedural Justice*. New York: Springer, 1988, pp. 208 ff (emphasizing that perceptions of justice being justly and correctly served enhances exponentially citizens' perception of provider legitimacy). Tyler, Tom R., "The Psychology of Procedural Justice: A Test of the Group-Value Model", *Journal of Personality and Social Psychology*, Volume 57, 1989, p. 830 (reports that in any procedure "several non-control issues—the *neutrality* of the decision-making procedure, trust in the 3rd party, and the information the experience communicates about social standing—influence both procedural preferences and judgments of procedural justice"). See also: Simmons, Ric, "Big Data and Procedural Justice: Legitimizing Algorithms in the Criminal Justice System", *Ohio State Journal of Criminal Law*, Volume 15, 2018, pp. 576 and ff and passim.

[3544] Selbst, Andrew D., "Disparate Impact in Big Data Policing", *cit.*, at 123 (arguing that "[t]he words 'discrimination,' 'fairness,' and 'bias' evoke a family of related concepts").

[3545] See: Stevenson, Megan, "Assessing Risk Assessment in Action", *Minnesota Law Review*, Volume 103, 2018, p. 303 (discussing the burgeoning use of pretrial risk assessment as a mandatory component of bail decisions in Kentucky). It is important to note that other tools have other target variables, yet the analysis in this offering applies to several other target variables as well. In the pretrial purview, for example, risk-assessment tools also forecast "failure to appear," outlined in terms of data points that vary across jurisdictions. See also: Mayson, Sandra G., "Dangerous Defendants", *Yale Law Journal*, Volume 127, 2018, pp. 509–13. There is also a spate of risk-assessment instruments that seek to forecast violence but in fact predict any hint or allegation of violence, whether it reflects in arrest or not (let alone conviction). See, e.g., Yang, Min et al., "The Efficacy of Violence Prediction: A Meta-Analytic Comparison of Nine Risk Assessment Tools", *Psychology Bulletin*, 2010, pp. 740–742 (arguing that "[t]he range of possible criterion variables for violence is wide, and "includes self-reports to third-party reports..., informal social service or police contact,

liberty,[3547] the *ProPublica* researchers compared COMPAS's risk classifications with defendants' actual outcomes—whether each defendant was rearrested[3548] or not[3549]—over the following two years. Outraged and fazed, *Northpointe*, the corporation that owns COMPAS, rejoindered that *ProPublica's* own dataset evinced that COMPAS was reportedly race[3550] neutral![3551] Oddly, both *ProPublica* and *Northpointe* had a point. Note, though, they were just focusing on different metrics of racial equality[3552] in algorithmic decision-making.[3553]

§§ Tellingly, *Northpointe* claimed that race neutrality was mirrored on the fact that both black and white defendants labelled[3554] as high risk by COMPAS were indeed rearrested at equal rates.[3555] Relatedly, a high-risk classification reflected the very same likelihood of rearrest for a black defendant as for a[3556] white one (roughly 60% on the any-arrest-risk scale and 20% on the violent-arrest-risk scale, over a two-year period).[3557]

---

formal contact or police charges, formal adjudication and court convictions, and incarceration"). See: Mayson, Sandra G., "Bias In, Bias Out", *cit.*, pp. 2218–2300.

[3546] McIntyre, Frank/Baradaran, Shima, "Race, Prediction, and Pretrial Detention", *Journal Empirical Legal Studies*, Volume 10, 2013, pp. 742–759 (mentions black defendants' exceedingly high likelihood of being arrested on drug-related charges as a potential cause of the race gap).

[3547] Stevenson, Megan/Mayson, Sandra G., "Pretrial Detention and Bail", Luna, Erik (Editor), *Reporting Criminal Justice: A Report of the Academy for Justice, Bridging the Gap between Scholarship and Reform*, 21, 2017, pp. 34–35 (poring over a batch of studies hinting that actuarial risk assessment can improve accuracy of pretrial risk judgments). See: Stevenson, Megan/Mayson, Sandra G., "Pretrial Detention and Bail", Luna, Erik, (Editor), *Reforming Criminal Justice: A Report of the Academy for Justice, Bridging the Gap between Scholarship and Reform*, pp. 21, pp. 45–47 (assessing evidence on efficacy of electronic monitoring and pinpointing key costs of electronic monitoring). See: Mayson, Sandra G., "Bias In, Bias Out", *cit.*, pp. 2218–2300.

[3548] Milgram, Anne, et al., "Pretrial Risk Assessment: Improving Public Safety and Fairness in Pretrial Decision Making", *Federal Sentencing Report*, Volume 27, 2015.

[3549] Mayson, Sandra G., "Bias In, Bias Out", *cit.*, pp. 2218–2300.

[3550] But see: Skeem, Jennifer L./Lowenkamp, Christopher T., "Risk, Race, and Recidivism: Predictive Bias and Disparate Impact", *Criminology*, Volume 54, 2024, pp. 680, 683–84, 704–06 (argues that criminal history correlates with race in their respective data set).

[3551] Mayson, Sandra G., "Bias In, Bias Out", *cit.*, pp. 2218–2300.

[3552] Mayson, Sandra G., "Bias In, Bias Out", *cit.*, pp. 2218–2300.

[3553] Kleinberg, Jon, et al., "Human Decisions and Machine Predictions", *National Bureau of Economic Research*, Working Paper No. 23180, 2017, 2017, https://www.nber.org/papers/w23180.pdf; [https://perma.cc/3WHJ-TWLJ].

[3554] But see: Corbett-Davies, Sam/Goel, Sharad, "The Measure and Mismeasure of Fairness: a critical Review of Fair Machine Learning", *Cornell University Library*, 2018, p. 18 (broaches a type of *measurement bias* coined "feature bias," which is neatly a bias in the predictors x. Note, though, that there is a second type of measurement bias deemed "label bias," which, in turn, amounts to a bias in y. The authors argue that that *label bias* is the worst bias there is).

[3555] Mayson, Sandra G., "Bias In, Bias Out", *cit.*, pp. 2218–2300.

[3556] Mayson, Sandra G., "Bias In, Bias Out", *cit.*, pp. 2218–2300.

[3557] Mayson, Sandra G., "Bias In, Bias Out", *cit.*, pp. 2218–2300.

§§ This particular metric of racial equality[3558] is frequently coined as **predictive parity**.[3559] The fact that led *ProPublica* to believe that COMPAS was fraught with racial bias was something uniquely ingenious: a black defendant who would not be rearrested within a given span of time was far more likely to be labelled[3560] as high risk (44.9%) than a white defendant who would not be rearrested (23.5%).[3561]

[3558] But see: Kim, Pauline T., "Data-Driven Discrimination at Work", *William and Mary Law Review*, Volume 58, 2017, p. 918 ("If the goal is to reduce biased outcomes, then a simple prohibition on using data about race or sex could be either wholly ineffective or actually counterproductive due to the existence of class proxies and the risk of omitted variable bias."); Lipton, Zachary et al., "Does Mitigating ML's Impact Disparity Require Treatment Disparity?", NIPS Proceedings 1, 2018, https://arxiv.org/pdf/1711.07076.pdf; [https://perma.cc/X8VF-EY53] (arguing, premised on statistical examples, that a prohibition on race or sex data is rather counterproductive indeed); Corbett-Davies, Sam/Goel, Sharad, "The Measure and Mismeasure of Fairness: a critical Review of Fair Machine Learning", *Cornell University Library*, 2018, passim (discussing the "[l]imitations of anti-classification" as a fairness metric). See also: Kim, Pauline T., "Data-Driven Discrimination at Work", *cit.*, p. 867 ("[I]f the goal is to discourage classification bias, then the law should not forbid the inclusion of race, sex, or other sensitive information as variables, but seek to preserve these variables, and perhaps even include them in some complex models."); Kroll, Joshua A., et al., "Accountable Algorithms", *University of Pennsylvania Law Review*, Volume 165, 2017, pp. 633, 693–95. See also: Kim, Pauline T., "Data-Driven Discrimination at Work", *cit.*, p. 866 ("*classification bias* occurs when employers rely on classification schemes, such as data algorithms, to sort or score workers in ways that worsen inequality or disadvantage along the lines of race, sex, or other protected characteristics"). Italics added. These two uses of the word "bias" correspond to the notions of irrational versus rational **(or statistical) discrimination.** Mayson, Sandra G., "Bias In, Bias Out", *cit.*, pp. 2218–2300.

[3559] Recall, the literature on algorithmic fairness has labelled measures of equality as either "**group fairness"** or **"individual fairness"** metrics. This phosphorescent dichotomy, though, can be very misleading indeed. Almost every tentative measure of "group fairness" can be framed using the term "individual" (for example, **predictive parity** entails that, for any individual, a given risk score conveys the same average risk irrespective of race). Relatedly, any "individual-fairness" metric can be framed using the term "group" (for example, a **single-threshold rule** requires that the group of people who poses any degree of risk should receive the same risk score). The difference is that which **"individual-fairness"** metrics relates to how the algorithm reaches its output in each individual case, whilst **"group-fairness"** metrics relates to the distribution of outputs and/or their accuracy across particular groups. See: Mayson, Sandra G., "Bias In, Bias Out", *cit.*, pp. 2218–2300.

[3560] Corbett-Davies and Goel coined this sweltering issue as "label bias" and diagnose it as "perhaps the most serious obstacle facing fair machine learning." But see: Corbett-Davies, Sam/Goel, Sharad, "The Measure and Mismeasure of Fairness: a critical Review of Fair Machine Learning", *Cornell University Library*, 2018, p. 18 (broaches a type of *measurement bias* coined "feature bias," which is neatly a bias in the predictors x. Note, though, that there is a second type of measurement bias deemed "label bias," which, in turn, amounts to a bias in y. The authors argue that that label bias is the worst bias there is). See also: Barocas, Solon/Selbst, Andrew D., "Big Data's Disparate Impact", *California Law Review*, Volume 104, 2016, pp. 677–78 (arguing that predictive data is predictive of a given/specific target variable with training data which is both correctly "labelled" and "collected."); Kleinberg, Jon/Ludwig, Jens/Mullainathan, Sendhil/Sunstein Cass R., "Discrimination in the Age of Algorithms", *Journal of Legal Analysis*, Volume 10, 1, 2018, pp. 28–29, 33–34 (draw a distinction between "group differences in the raw data" and biases for the "choice of predictors").

[3561] Mayson, Sandra G., "Bias In, Bias Out", *cit.*, pp. 2218–2300.

§§ Statistically speaking, the **false-positive rate** was much higher for the black defendants than for white defendants.[3562] In the meantime, a white defendant who would be rearrested was far more likely to be tagged as low risk (47.7%) than a black defendant who would be rearrested (28.0%),[3563] Notably, the **false-negative rate** was far more higher for white defendants than for black defendants.[3564]

§§ *ProPublica* viewed these racial disparities in COMPAS's error rates as an inexcusable, and deep-seated, injustice[3565] and racial discrimination.[3566] The racial disparity in error rates was not, though, a byproduct of the devilishly harmful virus of unfairness beleaguering the COMPAS algorithm itself. Rather, it was a mathematical outcome of the different rates of arrest between the black and white defendants in the underlying dataset. Since the rate of arrest was much higher among the black defendants, they, roughly, had higher arrest-risk classifications.[3567]

§§ Whenever the average risk is much higher for one group than for another, a higher proportion of the former group will be forecasted to be rearrested. In addition

---

[3562] Mayson, Sandra G., "Bias In, Bias Out", *cit.*, pp. 2218–2300.

[3563] Mayson, Sandra G., "Bias In, Bias Out", *cit.*, pp. 2218–2300.

[3564] Mayson, Sandra G., "Bias In, Bias Out", *cit.*, pp. 2218–2300 (2234).

[3565] See: Stevenson, Megan/Mayson, Sandra G., "Pretrial Detention and Bail", Luna, Erik, (Editor), *Reforming Criminal Justice: A Report of the Academy for Justice, Bridging the Gap between Scholarship and Reform*, pp. 21, 34–39 (assessing the risk of pretrial risk assessments while highlighting a slew of deep-rooted concerns regarding accuracy, racial-equality, and procedure); See: Chandler, Anupam, "The Racist Algorithm", *Michigan Law Review*, Volume 115, n.º 6, 2018, pp. 1023–1025 (arguing that the real-world facts on which algorithms used in criminal justice risk assessment are based are "deeply suffused with invidious discrimination"); Eaglin, Jessica M., "Constructing Recidivism Risk", *cit.*, pp. 94–99 (argues that risk assessment has every chance to "compromise[e] equality"); Mayson, Sandra G., "Dangerous Defendants", *cit.*, pp. 494–96; Selbst, Andrew D., "Disparate Impact in Big Data Policing", *cit.*, *passim*; Kim, Pauline T., "Data-Driven Discrimination at Work", *William and Mary Law Review*, Volume 58, 2017, pp. 857, 863–64 (shedding a keen light on the racial effects of algorithmic prediction in the remit of employment). Converging: Zywicki, Todd J./Adamson, Joseph D., "The Law and Economics of Subprime Lending", *University of Colorado Law Review*, 2009, pp. 1–9 (contending that Black workers with roughly the same abilities and educational background earn far less than comparable white workers or have considerably fewer employment opportunities); King, Allan G./Markovich, Marko J., "Big Data" and the Risk of Employment Discrimination, *Oklahoma Law Review*, Volume 68, 2016, pp. 555–563 (on employment discrimination). Dobbie, Will, Jacob Goldin, and Crystal S. Yang, "The Effects of Pretrial Detention on Conviction, Future Crime, and Employment: Evidence from Randomly Assigned Judges," *American Economic Review*, Volume 108, 2018, 201–240.

[3566] On racial discrimination: Hellman, Deborah, "What Makes Genetic Discrimination Exceptional?", *American Journal of Law and Medicine*, Volume 29, 2003, pp. 77, 83–86; Morrow, Jeffrey S., "Insuring Fairness: The Popular Creation of Genetic Antidiscrimination", *Georgia Law Journal*, Volume 98, 2009, pp. 215, 230–32; Prince, Anya E.R., "Insurance Risk Classification in an Era of Genomics: Is a Rational Discrimination Policy Rational?", *Nebraska Law Review*, Volume 96, 2018, pp. 624, 630–34, 641–42 (shedding light on "fair" and "unfair" discrimination). Note, though, that the word "discrimination" can also be used in a technical legal sense. In this sense it would mean that such differential treatment or disparate impact would incur liability pursuant to the fullest extent of antidiscrimination law. See: Mayson, Sandra G., "Bias In, Bias Out", *cit.*, pp. 2218–2300.

[3567] Mayson, Sandra G., "Bias In, Bias Out", *cit.*, pp. 2218–2300 (2234).

to that, a higher proportion of that group will be erroneously predicted to be rearrested as well.[3568]

§§ This holds a wealth, and treasure trove, of truth regardless of how gingerly programmed/devised the machine learning algorithm is, provided that the machine learning algorithm is equally seeking to have equal **predictive accuracy**[3569] for each racial group.[3570]

§§ The pinpointed machine learning algorithm engages in auguries/predictions[3571] that are equal across the two racial lines in one dimension: a positive prognosis is equally correct for each racial line. For both the black and the white groups, 50% of those forecast for rearrest are eventually rearrested. Whenever the

---

[3568] Mayson, Sandra G., "Bias In, Bias Out", *cit.*, pp. 2218–2300 (2234).

[3569] It is important to note, though, that an algorithm designed for maximum accuracy will adjust itself to the majority data, and may be less accurate for members of the underrepresented group, thus breeding *inductive bias*. See: Shellenbarger, Sue, "A Crucial Step for Avoiding AI Disasters", *Wall Street Journal*, (Feb. 13, 2019, 9:57 AM ET), https://www.wsj.com/articles/a-crucial-step-for-avoiding-ai-disasters-11550069865?ns = prod/accounts-wsj; [https://perma.cc/C28U-LAAE] (discussing this issue while emphasizing how diverse development teams pay more attention to unrepresentative and underrepresented data sets). Human programmers can circumvent and bypass this problem by weighting the minority-group data more heavily, by designing different algorithms for each racial group, or by striving to contain more data to equalize group representation in the data set. See: Barua, Sukarna et al., "MWMOTE—Majority Weighted Minority Oversampling Technique for Imbalanced Data Set Learning", *IEEE Transactions on Knowledge & Data Engineering*, Volume 26, 2014, pp. 405, 405–06. See also: Hamilton, Melissa, "The Biased Algorithm: Evidence of Disparate Impact on Hispanics", *American Criminal Law Review*, Volume 56, 2019, pp. 1553 and ff and passim (which clearly demonstrates that COMPAS was significantly less accurate for Hispanic than for white defendants by several measures and suggesting that smaller numbers of Hispanic defendants might be the cause). See: Mayson, Sandra G., "Bias In, Bias Out", *cit.*, pp. 2218–2300. See also: Dong et al., Qi, "Imbalanced deep learning by minority class incremental rectification, *IEEE Transactions on Pattern Analysis & Machine Intelligence*, Volume 41, 2019, p. 1367 (posit that "*most existing learning algorithms produce inductive bias (learning bias)* towards the frequent (majority) classes if training data are not balanced, *resulting in poor minority class recognition performance*"). Italics added. Note, though, that the training of machine learning is long and tedious in that is an error-prone procedure than can ultimately impair future algorithmic decision-making: Price, W. Nicholson Price II, "Regulating Black-Box Medicine", *Michigan Law Review*, Volume 116, 2017, pp. 421–431 (leverages on Google Image's image recognition learning algorithm to shed light on the four-step process by which some algorithms are thoroughly trained. First, the algorithm is shown "a set of known images ('Here are 10,000 pictures of ducks')." Second, the algorithm "develops complex internal rules based on nonlinear processes." Third, the algorithm "tests those rules on a test set ('Which of these are ducks?')." And fourth, the algorithm accordingly adjusts its "internal rules based on the success of the test." These steps are trotted out and repeated many times "until it can accurately and consistently classify the images"). See: Part V, Chap. 5, Sect. 5.1.7.4 of this book (on one of the law to control algorithmic decision-making, namely, law number four: data partitioning must be performed—i.e. randomly split an entire dataset into the «training dataset» and the «test dataset»—to accurately predict outcomes in the real world while forestalling «inductive bias» (learning bias)).

[3570] Mayson, Sandra G., "Bias In, Bias Out", *cit.*, pp. 2218–2300 (2234).

[3571] Mayson, Sandra G., "Bias In, Bias Out", *cit.*, pp. 2218–2300.

machine learning algorithm is used prospectively, a positive vaticination for any individual will equal a 50% likelihood of rearrest irrespective of whether the person is white or black.[3572]

§§ For purposes here, the machine learning algorithm indeed achieves **predictive parity**, the equality metric that *Northpointe* accounted for and remarked upon. In many ways, though, the algorithm breeds blatantly unequal results. Expound on the rate of false predictions amongst those who will not be rearrested—the oft-called **false-positive rate**. Out of the eight white figures who will not be rearrested, two are erroneously forecast for rearrest. Out of the nine black figures who will not be rearrested, only one is erroneously forecast for arrest.[3573] This racial disparity amounts to both disparate treatment[3574] and disparate[3575] impact[3576] that befalls on members of racialized communities.[3577]

§§ The false-positive rate is exceedingly higher for the white group (25%) than for the black one (11%). This is the form of gross inequality that *ProPublica* identified in the COMPAS data. Similarly to *ProPublica's* body of empirical evidence, this machine learning algorithm produces unequal results also in another dimension: twice as many white figures as black ones are forecast for rearrest. Compellingly, the machine learning algorithm exacts a toll on the group with the higher base rate: the black group. In the taxonomy of which data scientists are fond of, the machine learning algorithmic risk assessment is far from achieving **statistical parity**.[3578]

[3572] Mayson, Sandra G., "Bias In, Bias Out", *cit.*, pp. 2218–2300 (2235).

[3573] Mayson, Sandra G., "Bias In, Bias Out", *cit.*, pp. 2218–2300 (2235).

[3574] Howard, Justin D Howard, "Refashioning the Disparate Treatment and Disparate Impact Doctrines in Theory and in Practice", *Howard Law Journal*, Volume 41, 1998, passim; Seiner, Joseph, "Disentangling Disparate Impact and Disparate Treatment: Adapting the Canadian Approach", *Yale Law & Policy Review*, Volume 25, 2006; Stephanopoulos, Nicholas O. "Disparate Impact, Unified Law", *Yale Law Journal*, Volume 128, 2019, pp. 1566–1595. Note, though, that there are two main tools to be accounted for when it comes to entertaining discrimination claims: the Equal Protection Clause of the Federal Constitution (and analogous state constitutional regulations) and federal and state statutes that forbid discrimination on various grounds, including, but not limited to, race. A discrimination claim (lawsuit) pursuant to the Equal Protection Clause must bring forth facts to prove disparate treatment. Absent of which, the claim will not succeed; a glimpse—or a mere hint—of disparate impact alone will not suffice in this regard. Antidiscrimination statutes also allow disparate treatment claims, and some likewise allow disparate impact claims. See: Mayson, Sandra G., "Bias In, Bias Out", *cit.*, pp. 2218–2300. As Richard Primus expounds, whilst there are significant technical differences in the constitutional and statutory disparate treatment frames of references, substantive analysis of a disparate treatment claim pursuant to either is essentially the same. See: Richard Primus, "The Future of Disparate Impact", *Michigan Law Review*, Volume 108, 2010, pp. 1341, 1354–56. See: Mayson, Sandra G., "Bias In, Bias Out", *cit.*, pp. 2218–2300. See also: Bornstein, Stepanhie, "Antidiscriminatory Algorithms", *Alabama Law Review*, Volume 70, 2018, p. 535 (positing that algorithmic discrimination at large could fall under the all-embracing umbrella of anti-stereotyping category within Title VII's disparate treatment).

§§ It is possible to tweak the algorithm to equalize the false-positive rates for the two groups.[3579] Note, though, that this tweaking is not without sizable costs.[3580] Whenever modification is made in the machine learning algorithm, there is a chain reaction that ripples across the stagnant waters of algorithmic risk assessment. For

---

[3575] But see: Barocas, Solon/Selbst, Andrew D., "Big Data's Disparate Impact", *California Law Review*, Volume 104, 2016, p. 699 (discussing how discriminatory data mining is analogous to unintentional disparate impact analysis). In spite of the widely accepted conceptual differences between intent-based and effect-based theories of disparate impact, both approaches often dovetail seamlessly. As far as the fair lending goes, the definition of disparate impact cases is somewhat shallow, nomadic, and erratic, and dispiritingly vague. Note, though, that the loan officer's discretion often leads to exceedingly higher rates of rejections for members of racial minorities. See: Ayres, Ian/Klein, Gary/West, Jeffrey, "The Rise and (Potential) Fall of Disparate Impact Lending Litigation", *Evidence and Innovation in Housing Law and Policy*, Fennell, Lee Anne/Keys, Benajmin J. (Editors), Cambridge, Cambridge University Press, 2017, pp. 231–254. However, Schwemm and Taren avowedly contend that these cases might somewhat be deemed hybrid impact/intention cases. See: Schwemm, Robert G./Taren, Jeffrey L., "Discretionary Pricing, Mortgage Discrimination, and the Fair Housing Act", *The Harvard Civil Rights-Civil Liberties Law Review*, 2010, passim. The conduct being granularly parsed is discretion ascribed to brokers—which is considered by many stakeholders a harmless neutral practice -, may nonetheless lead to brokers to intentionally discriminate against members of racial minorities. See also: Selmi, Michael, "Indirect Discrimination and the Anti-Discrimination Mandate", Oxford, Oxford University Press, *Philosophical Foundations of Discrimination Law (Philosophical Foundations of Law)*, Hellman, Deborah/Moreau, Sophia (Editors), 2013, pp. 1–304 (pp. 257 and ff and passim).

[3576] To be clear-cut, none of these output measures give rise to disparate impact liability under the applicable law. As adumbrated, only the first step in a legal disparate impact analysis is related with outputs; the ultimate question is whether and to what extent the challenged disparate impact is warranted or fully justified, a question that is undoubtably just as much about the decision-making process as a disparate treatment analysis. See: Mayson, Sandra G., "Bias In, Bias Out", *cit.*, pp. 2218–2300. See also: Zatz, Noah D., "Disparate Impact and the Unity of Equality Law", *Boston University Law Review*, Volume 97, 2017, pp. 1357–1362 (contending that disparate impact and disparate treatment liability are fundamentally "separated superficially by the presence or absence of discriminatory intent but united fundamentally in addressing a common injury: status causation").

[3577] See: Sunstein, Cass R., "Algorithms, Correcting Biases", *Social Research*, Volume 86, 2019, pp. 449–506 (this famed author tagged disparate impact as "disturbing in itself, in the sense that a practice that produces such an impact helps entrench something like a caste system"). In spite of the widely accepted conceptual differences between intent-based and effect-based theories of disparate impact, both approaches often dovetail seamlessly though. See: Ayres, Ian/Klein, Gary/West, Jeffrey, "The Rise and (Potential) Fall of Disparate Impact Lending Litigation", *Evidence and Innovation in Housing Law and Policy*, Fennell, Lee Anne/Keys, Benajmin J. (Editors), Cambridge, Cambridge University Press, 2017, pp. 231–254.

[3578] Mayson, Sandra G., "Bias In, Bias Out", *cit.*, pp. 2218–2300 (2236). See: Corbett-Davies, Sam/Pierson, Emma/Feller, Avi/Goel, Sharad Goel/Huq, Aziz, "Algorithmic Decision Making and the Cost of Fairness", *Proceedings of the 23rd ACM SIGKDD International Conference on Knowledge Discovery and Data Mining* (Ass'n for Computing Machinery ed., 2017), 2017, passim (coining statistical parity as a "popular" concept of fairness in the risk-assessment and algorithmic-fairness literature); Feldman, Michael et al., "Certifying and Removing Disparate Impact (July 16, 2015), 2015 https://arxiv.org/pdf/1412.3756.pdf [https://perma.cc/NNQ4-NHUH] (an early work in the algorithmic-fairness literature that adopts a statistical-parity metric). Note, though, that, theoretically, one should not shy away, or veer away, from bifurcating/splitting the "prediction" issue from the "decision" issue. See: Corbett-Davies, Sam/Pierson, Emma/Feller, Avi/Goel, Sharad Goel/Huq, Aziz, "Algorithmic Decision Making and the Cost of Fairness", *Proceedings of the 23rd*

instance, predicting arrest for a greater proportion of the black group is quite cumbersome. Tellingly, after tweaking in the algorithm to ensure greater racial equity, Professor Sandra G. Mayson noted that 25% of the non-rearrestees—for both black group and the white group—were mistakenly forecast[3581] for rearrest.[3582] As an upshot, the false-positive rate was 25% for each group.[3583]

§§ The global number of people predict for rearrest is likewise much closer across racial lines. Notice, however, the ripple effect on the accuracy of the rearrest forecasts themselves. For the white group, a forecast of rearrest remains 50% likely to be true. On the flip side, only about 30% likely to be true for the black group. Whenever the machine learning algorithm is used prospectively, a rearrest prediction will produce something meaningfully different depending on whether the figure is

ACM SIGKDD International Conference on Knowledge Discovery and Data Mining (Ass'n for Computing Machinery ed., 2017), 2017, passim.

[3579] In practical terms, "people with otherwise identical risk prognoses" will include a cohort of people who have exactly the same observable risk traits, with exception to race. But it might also include two people who each have radically different traits, but who nevertheless pose equivalent statistical risk in light of the best method of estimation. See: Mayson, Sandra G., "Bias In, Bias Out", *cit.*, pp. 2218–2300.

[3580] Sam Corbett-Davies and peers, parsing the same Broward County data that ProPublica did, concluded that attaining parity in false-positive rates while still optimizing for public safety (and without detaining any other defendants) would beget a 7% uptick in violent crime. See: Corbett-Davies, Sam/Pierson, Emma/Feller, Avi/Goel, Sharad Goel/Huq, Aziz, "Algorithmic Decision Making and the Cost of Fairness", *Proceedings of the 23rd ACM SIGKDD International Conference on Knowledge Discovery and Data Mining* (Ass'n for Computing Machinery ed., 2017), 2017, p. 802. Moreover, 17% of those detained would be low-risk people for whom detention was either unwarranted or uncalled for. See: Mayson, Sandra G., "Bias In, Bias Out", *cit.*, pp. 2218–2300.

[3581] Berk and his peers have also provided a scintillating portray of these equality/accuracy trade-offs, drawing on real arraignment data and a machine-learning algorithm that predicts new arrests for a domestic-violence offense within a period of twenty-one months. The base rate amongst black defendants was 11%, whereas the base rate amongst white defendants was 6%. Relatedly, Berk and his peers found that, if the machine learning algorithm is devised to attain predictive parity regarding to a forecast of no-rearrest, the "false negative and false positive rates vary dramatically by race." Specifically, the false negative rate is 49% for black defendants and 93% for white defendants; the false positive rate is 2% for white defendants and 24% for black defendants. See: Berk, Richard et al., "Fairness in Criminal Justice Risk Assessments: The State of the Art", *Sociological Methods and Research*, 2018, pp. 12–18 (July 2, 2018), https://journals.sagepub.com/doi/pdf/10.1177/0049124118782533; [https://perma.cc/LB82-47SB]. p. 32. See: Mayson, Sandra G., "Bias In, Bias Out", *cit.*, pp. 2218–2300.

[3582] See: Berk, Richard, "Accuracy and Fairness for Juvenile Justice Risks Assessments", *Journal of Empirical Legal Studies*, Volume 16, 2019, p. 175 (comes to the terms with the fact that tweaking/altering data to attain **statistical parity** yields extremely high false-negative rates); Zachary Lipton et al., "Does Mitigating ML's Impact Disparity Require Treatment Disparity?", NIPS PROC. 1 (2018), https://arxiv.org/pdf/1711.07076.pdf; [https://perma.cc/X8VF-EY53] (sets forth compelling evidence that enforced blindness to protected traits exacts a toll on the algorithms' overall accuracy); Petersilia, Joan/Turner, Susan, "Guideline-Based Justice: Prediction and Racial Minorities", *Crime and Justice*, 1987, pp. 151–174 (argues that omitting markers correlated with race from a recidivism prediction algorithm exacts a toll on the overall accuracy of the model).

[3583] Mayson, Sandra G., "Bias In, Bias Out", *cit.*, pp. 2218–2300 (2236).

white or black.[3584] This is the kernel of **disparate treatment**[3585] that deserves to be overtly decried[3586] in criminal justice settings.

§§ One may argue that, to recoup **predictive parity,**[3587] suffice to alter the white group for whom rearrest is forecast. Again, that will inevitably create a shockwave of pure disparity, which is something you should not hold your breath for in criminal justice settings. As of now, amongst those who are indeed rearrested, the machine learning algorithm accurately predicts rearrest for 100% of the black arrestees, but is nonetheless oblivious of 50% of the white arrestees. Put otherwise, the machine learning algorithm now misses 50% of the white arrestees. There is now a humongous disparity in **false-negative rates**.[3588]

§§ As this example vividly portrays, if the base rate of the forecasted outcome varies greatly across racial lines, it is utterly untenable, unsound, illogical, fallacious, and ultimately impossible to attain: **(i) predictive parity**; **(ii) parity in false-positive rates**[3589]; **(iii) parity in false-negative rates** at the same time (unless prediction is quick-wittedly flawless, which is a mirific in this regard) and **iv) colour-blindness**.[3590] Crucially, pundits have brought to the fore irrebuttable mathematical

---

[3584] Mayson, Sandra G., "Bias In, Bias Out", *cit.*, pp. 2218–2300 (2236).

[3585] See, e.g., *Ricci v. DeStefano*, 557 U.S. 557, 577 (2009) (framing disparate treatment as another form of "intentional discrimination"); see also *Washington v. Davis*, 426 U.S. 229, 239- 41 (1976) (arguing that differential treatment of people of different races infringes the Equal Protection Clause only, and if, motivated by clear and proven "discriminatory racial purpose"). See: Mayson, Sandra G., "Bias In, Bias Out", *cit.*, pp. 2218–2300.

[3586] See: Howard, Justin D Howard, "Refashioning the Disparate Treatment and Disparate Impact Doctrines in Theory and in Practice", *Howard Law Journal*, Volume 41, 1998, passim; Seiner, Joseph, "Disentangling Disparate Impact and Disparate Treatment: Adapting the Canadian Approach", *Yale Law & Policy Review*, Volume 25, 2006; Stephanopoulos, Nicholas O. "Disparate Impact, Unified Law", *Yale Law Journal*, Volume 128, 2019, pp. 1566–1595.

[3587] Berk, Richard et al., "Fairness in Criminal Justice Risk Assessments: The State of the Art", *cit.*, p. 14 (describing "conditional use accuracy equality"); Dieterich, William et al., "COMPAS Risk Scales: Demonstrating Accuracy Equity and Predictive Parity", *cit.*, passim (describing "predictive parity"); Hardt, Moritz et al., "Equality of Opportunity in Supervised Learning", *cit.*, passim.

[3588] Mayson, Sandra G., "Bias In, Bias Out", *cit.*, pp. 2218–2300 (2237).

[3589] When Richard Berk trained the algorithm only to maximize for overall accuracy, it predicted rearrest for 17% of the white subgroup and 33% of the black subgroup (a 16 percentage-point difference). Strikingly, the false-positive rates were 16% for the white subgroup whereas for the black groups was 28% (a 12 percentage-point difference). See: Berk, Richard, "Accuracy and Fairness for Juvenile Justice Risks Assessments", *cit.*, p. 180. Notably, when Richard Berk changed the algorithm to equalize the *cost ratios*, it predicted rearrest for 10% of the white subgroup and 29% of the black subgroup (a 19 percentage-point difference). Relatedly, the false-positive rates were 8% for the white subset and 22% for the black subset (a 14 percentage-point difference). See: Berk, Richard, "Accuracy and Fairness for Juvenile Justice Risks Assessments", *cit.*, p. 185. See: Mayson, Sandra G., "Bias In, Bias Out", *cit.*, pp. 2218–2300.

[3590] For this reason, Sam Corbett-Davies and Sharad Goel refer to colorblindness as "anti-classification." See: Corbett-Davies, Sam/Gaebler, Johann D./Nilforoshan, Hamed/Shrof, Ravi/Goel, Sharad, "The Measure and Mismeasure of Fairness", *Journal of Machine Learning Research*, Volume 24, 2023, pp. 1–117 (p. 36) ("*In constructing algorithmic risk scores, a key ingredient is the target of prediction. In practice, though, there is often a mismatch between our true outcome of interest and the available data—an occurrence we call label bias (Zanger-Tishler* et al., *2023).*

evidence of this axiom. As presciently posited by Professor Sandra G. Mayson, whenever base rates vary greatly, polymaths should shift their gaze downstream—i.e. prioritize one of these metrics over the other. We can't have both. **Race neutrality** is therefore unattainable[3591] in criminal procedural law settings.

4.1.10.1.5 *Should We Long for Statistical Parity in Algorithmic Risk Assessment Held in Criminal Justice Settings?*

§§ To begin with, what is **statistical parity**? Statistical parity,[3592] to be both functional and accurate, requires that the very same percentage of each group be forecast for future arrest.[3593] To be clear-cut, it requires parity in the total-population

---

As with the other issues we discuss, there is typically no perfect solution to this problem, but there are ways to mitigate it. For example, in pretrial risk assessment, we would often like to estimate the likelihood a defendant would commit a crime if released. But there are two key difficulties with this goal. First, though we might want to measure crime conducted by defendants awaiting trial, we typically only observe crime that results in a conviction or an arrest. These observable outcomes, however, are imperfect proxies for the underlying criminal act. Further, heavier policing in communities of color might lead to Black and Hispanic defendants being arrested, and later convicted, more often than White defendants who commit the same offense (Lum and Isaac, 2016). Poor outcome data might thus cause one to systematically underestimate the risk posed by White defendants. The second, related, issue is that our target of interest is a counterfactual outcome; it corresponds to what would have happened had a defendant been released"). Italics added. See also: Balkin, Jack M./Siegel, Reva B., "The American Civil Rights Tradition: Anticlassification or Antisubordination?", *University of Miami Law Review*, Volume 58, 2003, pp. 9, 10–11 (explaining the distinction between the anticlassification and the antisubordination approaches to equality law).

[3591] Mayson, Sandra G., "Bias In, Bias Out", *cit.*, pp. 2218–2300 (2238).

[3592] See: Benjamin Fish et al., "A Confidence-Based Approach for Balancing Fairness and Accuracy", *Proceedings of the 2016 SIAM International Conference on Data Mining*, Chawla, Sanjay, Venkatasubramanian/Meira, Wagner (Editors), 2016, p. 144 (using the word "statistical parity"); Huq, Aziz Z., "Racial Equity in Algorithmic Criminal Justice", *cit.*, pp. 1116 (employing the word "statistical parity"); Corbett-Davies, Sam/Pierson, Emma/Feller, Avi/Goel, Sharad/Huq, Aziz, "Algorithmic Decision Making and the Cost of Fairness", passim (employment the term "conditional statistical parity" to describe parity in classification rates after controlling for "'legitimate' risk factors"); Hardt, Moritz et al., "Equality of Opportunity in Supervised Learning", *cit.*, 1 (using the term "demographic parity"); Zemel, Richard, et al., "Learning Fair Representations", *The Proceedings* of *Machine Learning Research*, Volume 28, 2013, p. 1 (using the term "statistical parity"). Berk, Richard et al., "Fairness in Criminal Justice Risk Assessments: The State of the Art", *cit.*, p. 13 (using the word "statistical parity").

[3593] But see: Hamilton, Melissa, "The Biased Algorithm: Evidence of Disparate Impact on Hispanics", *American Criminal Law Review*, Volume 56, 2019, pp. 1553 and ff and passim (which clearly demonstrates that COMPAS was significantly less accurate for Hispanic than for white defendants by several measures and suggesting that smaller numbers of Hispanic defendants might be the cause). See also: Dong et al., Qi, "Imbalanced deep learning by minority class incremental rectification, *IEEE Transactions on Pattern Analysis & Machine Intelligence*, Volume 41, 2019, p. 1367 (posit that "*most existing learning algorithms produce inductive bias (learning bias)* towards the frequent (majority) classes if training data are not balanced, *resulting in poor minority class recognition performance*"). Italics added. See also: Chandler, Anupam, "The Racist Algorithm", *Michigan Law Review*, Volume 115, n. ° 6, 2018, p. 1026 (on racist algorithms, noting that "the possibilities for discriminatory manipulation are legion"). But see: Altenburger, Kristen M./Ho, Daniel E., "When Algorithms Import Private Bias into Public Enforcement: The Promise and Limitations of

impact of the forecast at hand. This is the most basic benchmark of intergroup racial equality.[3594] Unsurprisingly, it is the yardstick that boasts a direct bearing on disparate impact[3595] law. According to Professor Sandra G. Mayson, EEOC guidance, for instance, ascribes too big a divergence from statistical parity and the trappings of smoking gun evidence of *disparate impact*.[3596] In Professor Sandra G. Mayson's shrewd example, the algorithm does not come any near to accomplishing ***statistical parity***: 40% of the white group but only 20% of the black group is forecast for rearrest.[3597]

§§ It bears mentioning that statistical parity is routinely[3598] deemed as «**demographic parity**». Tantamount metrics in the computer-science literature comprise the Calders-Verwer (CV)[3599] score and the «p%-rule».[3600]

4.1.10.1.6 Should We Crave for Predictive Parity in Algorithmic Risk Assessment Instead? Is Predictive Parity Attainable in Criminal Justice Settings? Does COMPAS Comprise Such a Metric?

§§ **Predictive parity**,[3601] the metric that *Northpointe* mentioned in its heated debate with *ProPublica*,[3602] measures the machine learning algorithm's overall rate of accuracy amongst those who have been given the same forecast.[3603] If the machine

---

Statistical Debiasing Solutions", *Journal of Institutional & Theoretical Economics*, Volume 175, 2019, pp. 97–98 (calls for a "debias predictive algorithms" to assuage racist and/or biased, doctored and bigoted algorithms nevertheless).

[3594] Kleinberg, Jon, et al., "Inherent Trade-offs in the Fair Determination of Risk Scores", *cit.*, p. 4 (shedding light on "balance for the negative class"); Corbett-Davies, Sam et al., "Algorithmic Decision Making and the Cost of Fairness", 2017, p. 798 ("predictive equality").

[3595] Mayson, Sandra G., "Bias In, Bias Out", *cit.*, pp. 2218–2300 (2243).

[3596] But see: Selbst, Andrew D., "Disparate Impact in Big Data Policing", *Georgia Law Review*, Volume 52, 2017, p. 167 ("[I]t may be impossible to tell when the disparate impact truly reflects reality"). See also: Barocas, Solon/Selbst, Andrew, "Big Data's Disparate Impact", *cit.*, p. 682 ("So long as prior decisions affected by some form of prejudice serve as examples of correctly rendered determinations, data mining will necessarily infer rules that exhibit the same prejudice").

[3597] Mayson, Sandra G., "Bias In, Bias Out", *cit.*, pp. 2218–2300 (2243).

[3598] Mayson, Sandra G., "Bias In, Bias Out", *cit.*, pp. 2218–2300 (2243).

[3599] See: Kamishima, Toshihiro et al., "Fairness-Aware Classifier with Prejudice Remover Regularizer", *Machine Learning and Knowledge Discovery in Databases*, Flach, Peter A. (Editor), Springer Switzerland, pp. 35–37 (framing the CV score as a difference, rather than ratio, of outcome rates between two groups).

[3600] Mayson, Sandra G., "Bias In, Bias Out", *cit.*, pp. 2218–2300 (2243).

[3601] Berk, Richard et al., "Fairness in Criminal Justice Risk Assessments: The State of the Art", *cit.*, pp. 13–14 (defining "conditional procedure accuracy equality"); Kleinberg et al., "Inherent Trade-offs in the Fair Determination of Risk Scores", *cit.*, pp. 2–3 (discussing "balance" for both classes); Joseph, Mathew et al., "Fair Algorithms for Infinite and Contextual Bandits", *Fairness, Accountability and Transparency Machine Leaning,* Oxford Internet Institute, University of Oxford, 2016, p. 1 https://www.fatml.org/media/documents/better_fair_algorithms_for_infinite_contextual_bandits.pdf; [https://perma.cc/F6BG-PDQL] (poring over "equality of opportunity"). This book deals with Automated decision-making systems. These systems "*are increasingly prevalent across various domains, tasked with filtering, sorting, classifying, recommending, and shaping*

learning algorithm's rearrest forecasts are accurate at an equal rate for each group, the algorithm attains **predictive parity** in **positive predictive value**. On the flip side, if the non-rearrest forecasts are accurate at an equal rate for each group, then the machine learning algorithm attains **predictive parity** in **negative predictive value**. All in all, if both are true, it attains **overall predictive parity**.[3604]

§§ Statisticians and computer scientists alike have also alluded to this metric of equality as «calibration within groups»[3605] and «conditional use accuracy equality».[3606] In the example provided by Professor Sandra G. Mayson, the machine learning algorithm attains parity solely in **positive predictive value**. For both the black and the white groups, 50% of those forecast for rearrest are indeed rearrested.[3607] By this token, positive predictive value is something that COMPAS can achieve.

---

human decisions and experiences. While these algorithmic solutions present significant opportunities, they also pose substantial risks that require careful examination to avoid unintended and potentially harmful outcomes. Real-world examples have demonstrated that even algorithms designed with good intentions can lead to negative consequences such as racial discrimination.

This highlights the urgent societal need to educate the next generation of digital practitioners in transdisciplinary methods, fostering a critical understanding of machine learning. This course is designed to explore how algorithmic systems can contribute to social progress while also perpetuating or exacerbating oppression and social injustice. By drawing on critical data studies literature at the intersection of computer science and social science, the course aims to equip students with both computational and qualitative methods necessary to assess and address the impact of algorithmic systems in real-world contexts. The course will focus on discussing key reading from leading conferences such as the ACM Fairness, Accountability and Transparency (ACM FAccT) or the AAAI/ACM Conference on AI, Ethics, and Society, featuring work from scholars across both the Global North and South. It will offer critical and empirical analyses of surveillance technologies, large language models (LLMs), and the environmental impacts of AI. Students are expected to engage critically, reflecting on their own experiences and the course materials to develop a nuanced understanding of the societal implications of algorithmic systems"). Italics added.

3602 Meaning, for each racial group, the same ratio of COMPAS's forecasts were correct. This was true for each classification group—both for those labelled high-risk and for those labelled low-risk. See: Mayson, Sandra G., "Bias In, Bias Out", *cit.*, pp. 2218–2300.

3603 Kleinberg et al., "Inherent Trade-offs in the Fair Determination of Risk Scores", *cit.*, p. 4 (discussing "balance for the positive class"); Hardt, Moritz et al., "Equality of Opportunity in Supervised Learning", *cit.*, p. 4 (shedding light on "equal opportunity").

3604 Mayson, Sandra G., "Bias In, Bias Out", *cit.*, pp. 2218–2300 (2243).

3605 Mayson, Sandra G., "Bias In, Bias Out", *cit.*, pp. 2218–2300 (2243).

3606 Berk, Richard et al., "Fairness in Criminal Justice Risk Assessments: The State of the Art", *Sociological Methods & Research*, 2018, pp. 1–10.

3607 Mayson, Sandra G., "Bias In, Bias Out", *cit.*, pp. 2218–2300 (2243).

4.1.10.1.7 Can COMPAS Achieve Equal False-Positive and True-Negative Rates (Equal Specificity) Within the Remit of Predictive Parity?

§§ *ProPublica* contended that equality entails,[3608] and does not shy away from, parity[3609] in **false-positive rates** though.[3610] The **false-positive rate** and its opposite, the **true-negative rate**, weigh the machine learning algorithm's accuracy amongst those defendants who are **«true negatives»—those people who are not ultimately rearrested**. Crucially, the **false-positive rate** is the **percentage of such defendants who are nevertheless forecast for rearrest**—the proportion of law abiders wrongly predicted to engage in future criminal activities.[3611] In the example set forth by Professor Sandra G. Mayson, it is twice as high for the white group as for the black group.[3612]

§§ Compellingly, of the seven white people who will not be rearrested, two are erroneously forecast for rearrest (29%), whilst of the eight black people who will not be rearrested, only one is erroneously forecast for rearrest (12%). The percentage of non-rearrestees who are accurately predicted is the **true-negative rate** (or the algorithm's «specificity»). Pundits (i.e. statisticians and computer scientists alike) have alluded to **equal specificity** both as «balance for the negative class»[3613] and as «predictive equality».[3614]

[3608] Hardt, Moritz et al., "Equality of Opportunity in Supervised Learning", *cit.*, p. 4 (shedding light on "equal opportunity").

[3609] Berk, Richard et al., "Fairness in Criminal Justice Risk Assessments: The State of the Art", *cit.*, pp. 13–14 (defining "conditional procedure accuracy equality"); Kleinberg et al., "Inherent Trade-offs in the Fair Determination of Risk Scores", *cit.*, pp. 2–3 (discussing "balance" for both classes).

[3610] Corbett-Davies, Sam et al., "Algorithmic Decision Making and the Cost of Fairness", *cit.*, p. 798 (shows that is possible to compel the algorithm to produce, respectively, *statistical parity*, *conditional statistical parity*, and *parity in false-positive rates*).

[3611] See: Mayson, Sandra G., "Bias In, Bias Out", *cit.*, pp. 2218–2300 (arguing that equalizing false-positive rates will beget fewer false positives—"law abiders" mistakenly predict for rearrest—for the high-base-rate group than the low-base-rate group because there are fewer "law abiders" in the high-base-rate group in the first place).

[3612] Mayson, Sandra G., "Bias In, Bias Out", *cit.*, pp. 2218–2300 (2244).

[3613] Mayson, Sandra G., "Bias In, Bias Out", *cit.*, pp. 2218–2300. See also: Kleinberg, Jon, et al., "Inherent Trade-offs in the Fair Determination of Risk Scores", *cit.*, p. 4 (shedding light on "balance for the negative class").

[3614] See: Corbett-Davies, Sam/Pierson, Emma/Feller, Avi/Goel, Sharad/Huq, Aziz, "Algorithmic Decision Making and the Cost of Fairness", *KDD '17: Proceedings of the 23rd ACM SIGKDD International Conference on Knowledge Discovery and Data Mining*, 2017, pp. 797–806 ("*Algorithms are now regularly used to decide whether defendants awaiting trial are too dangerous to be released back into the community. In some cases, black defendants are substantially more likely than white defendants to be incorrectly classified as high risk. To mitigate such disparities, several techniques have recently been proposed to achieve algorithmic fairness.* Here we reformulate *algorithmic fairness* as constrained optimization: the objective is to maximize public safety while satisfying formal fairness constraints designed to reduce racial disparities. We show that for several past definitions of fairness, the optimal algorithms that result require detaining defendants above race-specific risk thresholds. *We further show that the optimal unconstrained algorithm requires applying a single, uniform threshold to all defendants. The unconstrained algorithm thus maximizes public safety*

§§ It is noteworthy that there is a heated controversy on whether and to what extent this statistical jargon for forecasting errors is befitted to risk assessment. Cogently, the great bulk of risk-assessment methods do not really forecast outcomes; rather, they only measure the likelihood of a future event. If an event measured as likely does not occur, it does not transmogrify the original probabilistic assessment as «false».[3615] Notwithstanding, the **dual language of true versus false prediction** is a go-to metric to analyse where the costs of uncertainty fall.[3616]

4.1.10.1.8 Can COMPAS also Achieve Equal False-Positive and True-Negative Rates (Equal Sensitivity) Within the Purview of Predictive Parity?

§§ Whilst **equal specificity** appraises the machine learning algorithm's accuracy amongst the **true negatives (people who are not eventually rearrested)**, **equal sensitivity**, in turn, appraises the machine learning algorithm's correctness amongst the **true positives—people who are eventually rearrested.** The percentage of this group accurately forecast for rearrest is the **true-positive rate**. On the opposite pole, the percentage of people wrongly forecast for no-rearrest is the **false-negative rate.**[3617]

§§ Loosely speaking, the **false-negative rate** is the percentage of future arrests that the machine learning algorithm failed to predict. Compellingly, COMPAS—and algorithmic risk assessment tools in an overarching sense—does not attain **equal sensitivity**. Crucially, and perhaps unsurprisingly, for the white group, two of the three people really rearrested are accurately predicted. As a result, the **true-positive rate** is 2/3 (67%), and the **false-negative rate** is 1/3 (33%). For the black group, one of the two people really rearrested is accurately predicted and one is not. As a result, the true-positive rate and false-negative rate are 1/2 (50%).[3618]

§§ Strikingly, computer pundits have alluded to **parity in true-positive rates** as «balance for the positive class»[3619] and as «equal opportunity»[3620] insofar means

---

while also satisfying one important understanding of equality: that all individuals are held to the same standard, irrespective of race.") Italics added. See: Corbett-Davies, Sam et al., "Algorithmic Decision Making and the Cost of Fairness", *cit.*, p. 798 ("predictive equality").

[3615] Mayson, Sandra G., "Bias In, Bias Out", *cit.*, pp. 2218–2300 (2244).

[3616] Mayson, Sandra G., "Bias In, Bias Out", *cit.*, pp. 2218–2300 (2244).

[3617] Mayson, Sandra G., "Bias In, Bias Out", *cit.*, pp. 2218–2300 (2244).

[3618] Mayson, Sandra G., "Bias In, Bias Out", *cit.*, pp. 2218–2300 (2244).

[3619] Corbett-Davies, Sam/Pierson, Emma/Feller, Avi/Goel, Sharad/Huq, Aziz, "Algorithmic Decision Making and the Cost of Fairness", *KDD '17: Proceedings of the 23rd ACM SIGKDD International Conference on Knowledge Discovery and Data Mining*, 2017, pp. 797–806.

[3620] See: Kleinberg et al., "Inherent Trade-offs in the Fair Determination of Risk Scores", *cit.*, p. 4 (discussing "balance for the positive class"); Hardt, Moritz et al., "Equality of Opportunity in Supervised Learning", *cit.*, p. 4 (shedding light on "equal opportunity").

that a true positive will have an equal chance of being accurately predicted irrespective of group membership.[3621] Note, though, that the cheerful/encomiastic jargon of «equal opportunity» is ultimately incorrect in the criminal justice settings, whereby a «positive» usually amounts to rearrest.[3622]

§§ Notwithstanding, a strand of specialized literature deems this as «balance for both classes»[3623]; «predictive equality»[3624]; «conditional procedure accuracy equality»[3625]; and «equal opportunity».[3626]

4.1.10.1.9 Equal Rate of Correct Classification in the COMPAS Realm?

§§ Professor Sandra G. Mayson argues that is possible to frame equality as parity in the rate of accurate classification overall, or in the percentage of each group accurately forecasted.[3627] In Professor Sandra G. Mayson's framework, 70% of the white figures are accurately labelled (two actual rearrests). Amongst the black group, 80% are accurately labelled.[3628] Richard Berk and his fellow colleagues coined parity in the rate of accurate classification as «overall accuracy[3629] equality.[3630]

[3621] Hardt, Moritz et al., "Equality of Opportunity in Supervised Learning", *Neural Information Processing Systems Proceedings*, 2016, https://papers.nips.cc/paper/6374-equality-of-opportunity-in-supervised-learning.pdf; [https://perma.cc/LD25-6RR7]. See: Mayson, Sandra G., "Bias In, Bias Out", *cit.*, pp. 2218–2300.

[3622] Mayson, Sandra G., "Bias In, Bias Out", *cit.*, pp. 2218–2300 (2245).

[3623] Kleinberg, Jon, et al., "Inherent Trade-offs in the Fair Determination of Risk Scores", *cit.*, p. 4 (shedding light on "balance for the negative class").

[3624] Corbett-Davies, Sam et al., "Algorithmic Decision Making and the Cost of Fairness", 2017, p. 798 ("predictive equality").

[3625] Berk, Richard et al., "Fairness in Criminal Justice Risk Assessments: The State of the Art", *cit.*, p. 14 (describing "conditional use accuracy equality").

[3626] Hardt, Moritz et al., "Equality of Opportunity in Supervised Learning", *cit.*, p. 4 (shedding light on "equal opportunity").

[3627] Turek, Matt, "Explainable Artificial Intelligence (XAI)", The *Defense Advanced Research Projects Agency* (DARPA), www.darpa.mil/program/explainable-artificial-intelligence; [https://perma.cc/2DS4-ZMNB] (shedding light on the oft-labelled interpretability of algorithms). See also: *Making Computers Explain Themselves*, MIT's Computer Science and Artificial Intelligence Laboratory (Oct. 27, 2016), 2016, https://www.csail.mit.edu/making_computers_explain%20themselves; [https://perma.cc/C97B-PGUR] (explaining the importance of grasping the complex trappings of algorithm decision-making).

[3628] But see: Kleinberg, Jon/Ludwig, Jens/Mullainathan, Sendhil/Sunstein Cass R., "Discrimination in the Age of Algorithms", *Journal of Legal Analysis*, Volume 10, 1, 2018, pp. 28–29, 33–34 (draw a distinction between "group differences in the raw data" and biases for the "choice of predictors").

[3629] When Richard Berk trained the algorithm only to maximize for overall accuracy, it predicted rearrest for 17% of the white subgroup and 33% of the black subgroup (a 16 percentage-point difference). Strikingly, the false-positive rates were 16% for the white subgroup whereas for the black groups was 28% (a 12 percentage-point difference). See: Berk, Richard, "Accuracy and Fairness for Juvenile Justice Risks Assessments", *cit.*, p. 180. Notably, when Richard Berk tweaked the algorithm to equalize the *cost ratios*, it predicted rearrest for 10% of the white subgroup and 29% of the black subgroup (a 19 percentage-point difference). Relatedly, the false-positive rates were 8% for the white subset and 22% for the black subset (a 14 percentage-point difference). See: Berk, Richard, "Accuracy and Fairness for Juvenile Justice Risks Assessments", *cit.*, p. 185.

4.1.10.1.10 Equal Cost Ratios (Ratio of False Positives to False Negatives): Is It Attainable in Algorithmic Risk Assessment?

§§ Last but not least, another possible metric of equality in terms of error rates is **parity in the ratio of false positives to false negatives**, occasionally named the **«cost ratio».**[3631] This *ratio* is quite important since one type of error might be worse than the other. Mistakenly forecasting future arrest may be considerably worse than mistakenly, or haphazardly, no future arrest at all, or vice versa. **It bears mentioning that any machine learning algorithm is fully capable of producing some ratio of false positives to false negatives.** Relatedly, and as stated by Professor Sandra G. Mayson, should stakeholders care what this *cost ratio* actually is, the machine learning algorithm must be devised and deployed accordingly. Tellingly, in the development of a predictive machine learning algorithm for a pilot[3632] project in Philadelphia, relevant stakeholders came to terms with the fact that disregarding a new arrest for domestic violence was considerably worse—i.e. ten times worse—than mistakenly forecasting a new[3633] arrest.[3634]

§§ Richard Berk and his fellow colleagues, who were entrusted with the task of designing the machine learning algorithm, thereby built it to accept ten false positives rather than produce one more false negative. Put otherwise, they built it to produce a false positive-to-negative ratio of 10:1. **Parity in cost ratios**[3635] is commonly referred to as[3636] «treatment equality».[3637]

[3630] Mayson, Sandra G., "Bias In, Bias Out", *cit.*, pp. 2218–2300 (2245). Berk, Richard et al., "Fairness in Criminal Justice Risk Assessments: The State of the Art", *cit.*, p. 13.

[3631] When Richard Berk trained the algorithm only to maximize for overall accuracy, it predicted rearrest for 17% of the white subgroup and 33% of the black subgroup (a 16 percentage-point difference). Strikingly, the false-positive rates were 16% for the white subgroup whereas for the black groups was 28% (a 12 percentage-point difference). See: Berk, Richard, "Accuracy and Fairness for Juvenile Justice Risks Assessments", *cit.*, p. 180. Notably, when Richard Berk changed the algorithm to equalize the *cost ratios*, it predicted rearrest for 10% of the white subgroup and 29% of the black subgroup (a 19 percentage-point difference). Relatedly, the false-positive rates were 8% for the white subset and 22% for the black subset (a 14 percentage-point difference). See: Berk, Richard, "Accuracy and Fairness for Juvenile Justice Risks Assessments", *cit.*, p. 185.

[3632] Mayson, Sandra G., "Bias In, Bias Out", *cit.*, pp. 2218–2300 (2245).

[3633] Mayson, Sandra G., "Bias In, Bias Out", *cit.*, pp. 2218–2300 (2246).

[3634] Hamilton, Melissa, "*Adventures in risk*: Predicting Violent and Sexual Recidivism in Sentencing Law", *Arizona State Law Journal*, Volume 47, 1, 2015, pp. 1–62 (arguing that the contrary judgment is also reasonable); Harris, Grant T./Rice, Marnie E., "Bayes and Base Rates: What Is an Informative Prior for Actuarial Violence Risk Assessment?", *Behavioral Sciences & the Law, Volume 31, 2013, pp.* 103–106 ("[I]t can be reasonable for public policy to operate on the basis that a miss (e.g., failing to detain a violent recidivist beforehand) is twice as costly as a false alarm (e.g., detaining a violent offender who would not commit yet another violent offense)"). See: Mayson, Sandra G., "Bias In, Bias Out", *cit.*, pp. 2218–2300.

[3635] It is bears mentioning that *predictive parity* (*calibration*) can likewise be despairingly inconsistent with a single-threshold rule. At the very least, it does not ensure or necessarily indicate a single threshold for risk classification. See: Mayson, Sandra G., "Bias In, Bias Out", *cit.*, pp. 2218–2300.

[3636] Mayson, Sandra G., "Bias In, Bias Out", *cit.*, pp. 2218–2300 (2246).

[3637] Berk, Richard et al., "Fairness in Criminal Justice Risk Assessments: The State of the Art", *cit.*, p. 15. The question of the relative cost of a false positive and false negative in the algorithmic

4.1.10.1.11 Area-Under-The-Curve (AUC) Parity in Algorithmic Risk Assessment?

§§ There is also a sheer amount of measures that portray an algorithm's overall performance at classifying people along a broad risk spectrum that tool designers routinely use to appraise, and to assert, «race neutrality». The most preeminent of which is equality in the «area under the receiver operating characteristic curve» (routinely baptized as **«area under the curve» «AUC»** or area under the «ROC») for a given tool as applied to each racial group[3638] in algorithmic risk assessment settings.

§§ The AUC relays/imparts the probability that, for any two people randomly[3639] chosen in the dataset, the machine learning algorithm will accurately organize them in terms of perceived risk. That is, it will classify the higher-risk individual as presenting a higher risk than the other. Parity in AUC scores is yet another benchmark of equality in predictive accuracy in algorithmic risk assessment[3640] settings.[3641]

---

risk assessment context evokes the prominent Blackstone ratio, which stresses the relative costs of false negatives and false positives in the context of criminal conviction and punishment. See: Blackstone, William, *Commentaries on the Laws of England*, 4 volumes, Oxford, Clarendon Press, 1765–1769, p. 352 ("[T]he law holds, that it is better that ten guilty persons escape, than that one innocent suffer"). See: Mayson, Sandra G., "Bias In, Bias Out", *cit.*, pp. 2218–2300. Angwin, Julia et al., "Machine Bias", *ProPublica* (May 23, 2016), https://www.propublica.org/article/machine-bias-risk-assessments-in-criminal-sentencing; [https://perma.cc/4G83-MDAS] (harshly criticizing disparity in false-positive rates as a purely unjustified bias). See also: Freeman, Katherine, "Algorithmic Injustice: How the Wisconsin Supreme Court Failed to Protect Due Process Rights in State v. Loomis", *North Carolina Journal of Law and Technology*, Volume 18, 2016, pp. 75–86 (echoing the very same views).

3638 Mayson, Sandra G., "Bias In, Bias Out", *cit.*, pp. 2218–2300 (2246).

3639 On randomness: Teigena, Halvor/Kanten, Alf Børre, "Out of the blue: on the suddenness of perceived chance events", *Thinking & Reasoning*, Volume 29, n. ° 1, 2023, pp. 137–175 (137) ("*people commonly use terms like 'random', 'by chance', or 'accidentally' when they describe occurrences that sidestep the normal course of events, with no apparent causal link to ongoing activities. Such intrusive events are typically perceived as happening all of a sudden.* This was demonstrated in seven experiments (N ¼ 1299) by asking people to identify statements they believed belonged to stories about chance events, and by comparing chance vs. nonchance events from their own life and from the lives of others. Suddenness also appeared to be more strongly associated with beginnings than with endings of an episode. Thus, statements about sudden beginnings of a career or a relationship were more readily believed to happen 'by chance' than 'not by chance'. *But life-changing events did not become more accidental simply by being placed in the beginning of a 'life chapter'. These studies highlight a central but neglected feature of perceived randomness*"). Italics added.

3640 Mayson, Sandra G., "Bias In, Bias Out", *cit.*, pp. 2218–2300 (2246).

3641 We endeavour to break down the relevant concepts in at least three interlocking ways. It (1) treats risk assessment as binary forecast; (2) disregards the issue of whether and to what extent the validation data will correspond to the population on which the algorithmic tool is to be applied; and (3) overlooks whether and to what extent the classifier is an asymptotically unbiased estimator—tagged the tool's "estimation accuracy." See: Berk, Richard et al., "Fairness in Criminal Justice Risk Assessments: The State of the Art", *cit.*, p. 16. See: Mayson, Sandra G., "Bias In, Bias Out", *cit.*, pp. 2218–2300. Mayson, Sandra G., "Bias In, Bias Out", *cit.*, pp. 2218–2300 (2246).

4.1.10.2 Can COMPAS (or Machine Learning Algorithms Operating in the Realm of Risk Assessment) Achieve the Foregoing Metrics of Output Equality at the Same Time?

4.1.10.2.1 Trade-Offs in Algorithmic Risk Assessment in Criminal Justice Settings

§§ Pundits often aver that machine learning algorithms can be built to attain any of the foregoing metrics of output equality, but not all of them together. Let alone at the same time. Let alone at once. To be clear-cut, a machine learning algorithm is not amenable to be built to achieve «total fairness».[3642] This Section will henceforth draw on Professor Sandra G. Mayson's scintillating essay to provide a very brief (thumbnail) sketch on the[3643] possible trade-offs between equality and overall accuracy and between different metrics of equality[3644] in algorithmic risk assessment settings, including COMPAS.

4.1.10.2.2 «Equality/Accuracy Trade-Offs» (Sandra G. Mayson)

§§ We should be fully aware of the following axiom: whenever base rates of the forecasted outcome vary greatly across racial groups, the most accurate algorithm in the world will accurately forecast that outcome at markedly different rates across racial groups. It should come as no bewildering surprise that enforcing/forcing/imposing certain metrics of output equality will inevitably exact a toll cost on the algorithmic tool's[3645] overall accuracy.[3646] The very nature and magnitude of the trade-off will

---

[3642] Mayson, Sandra G., "Bias In, Bias Out", *cit.*, pp. 2218–2300 (2248).

[3643] Mayson, Sandra G., "Bias In, Bias Out", *cit.*, pp. 2218–2300 (2248).

[3644] Mayson, Sandra G., "Bias In, Bias Out", *cit.*, pp. 2218–2300 (2249).

[3645] Zachary Lipton et al., "Does Mitigating ML's Impact Disparity Require Treatment Disparity?", *NIPS Proceedings*, 1, 2018, https://arxiv.org/pdf/1711.07076.pdf; [https://perma.cc/X8VF-EY53] (sets forth compelling evidence that enforced blindness to protected traits exacts a toll on the overall accuracy of the algorithmic tool); Petersilia, Joan/Turner, Susan, "Guideline-Based Justice: Prediction and Racial Minorities", *Crime and Justice*, 1987, pp. 151–174 (argues that omitting markers correlated with race from a recidivism prediction algorithm exacts a toll on the accuracy of the algorithmic tool).

[3646] Tyler, Tom, "Methodology in Legal Research", *Utrecht Law Review*, Volume 13, Issue 3, 2017, pp. 130–131 ("*Accurate facts plus good legal rules lead to substantive justice.* This is the normative framework of right and wrong defined by traditional legal analysis. *Risk analysis is a nice example of the benefits of empiricism because studies suggest that the use of empirical methods to assess future dangerousness is more accurate than is the use of human intuition. It is better to use a formula when making a legal decision that involves estimates of someone's likely future conduct than it is to rely upon the impressions of judges or prosecutors*" (…) "*The legal system relies on predictions about people's likely future behaviour at many points in the system: pretrial detention; sentencing; parole and probation*; etc. (…) *Accuracy, in turn is enhanced by the use of empirical methods. Facts are sought that can guide the application of normative legal principles*"). Italics added. See also: Goel, Sharad/Shroff, Ravi/Skeem, Jennifer/Slobogin, Christopher, *The Accuracy, Equity, and Jurisprudence of Criminal Risk Assessment* 1 (Dec. 26, 2018), 2018; Stevenson, Megan/Mayson, Sandra G., "Pretrial Detention and Bail", Luna, Erik, (Editor), *Reforming Criminal Justice:*

hinge upon how much the underlying base rates differ paired with the very nature of the fairness foray in this regard.[3647]

§§ An exciting piece of research on computer science has shed a keen light on this trade-off in practical terms. Pivotally, Sam Corbett-Davies and his fellow colleagues made earnest attempts to investigate the possibility of building a machine-learning risk-assessment algorithm to attain three different metrics of algorithmic fairness at the same time, leveraging on the very same Broward County,[3648] Florida dataset that *ProPublica*[3649] used.[3650]

§§ Cogently, the researchers concluded that enforcing/forcing/imposing any one of the foregoing metrics wholly impaired the machine learning algorithm's overall accuracy. Compellingly, the optimal algorithm, from a public-safety standpoint, was «unconstrained» with regard to group fairness in algorithmic risk assessment settings. They accordingly found that «**[a]dhering to past [group] fairness definitions can substantially decrease public safety; conversely, optimizing for public safety alone can produce stark racial disparities**».[3651] Notably, though not surprisingly, other bodies of empirical evidence have reached tantamount conclusions.[3652]

A Report of the Academy for Justice, Bridging the Gap between Scholarship and Reform, pp. 21, 34–39 (assessing the risk of pretrial risk assessments while highlighting a spate of deep-rooted concerns regarding accuracy, racial-equality, and procedure).

3647 Mayson, Sandra G., "Bias In, Bias Out", *cit.*, pp. 2218–2300 (2249).

3648 Sam Corbett-Davies and peers, parsing the same Broward County data that ProPublica did, concluded that attaining parity in false-positive rates while still optimizing for public safety (and without detaining any other defendants) would beget a 7% uptick in violent crime. See: Corbett-Davies, Sam/Pierson, Emma/Feller, Avi/Goel, Sharad Goel/Huq, Aziz, "Algorithmic Decision Making and the Cost of Fairness", *Proceedings of the 23rd ACM SIGKDD International Conference on Knowledge Discovery and Data Mining* (Ass'n for Computing Machinery ed., 2017), 2017, p. 802. Moreover, 17% of those detained would be low-risk people for whom detention was either unwarranted or uncalled for. Mayson, Sandra G., "Bias In, Bias Out", *cit.*, pp. 2218–2300.

3649 Mayson, Sandra G., "Bias In, Bias Out", *cit.*, pp. 2218–2300 (2249).

3650 See: Corbett-Davies, Sam et al., "Algorithmic Decision Making and the Cost of Fairness", *cit.*, p. 798 (shows that is possible to compel the algorithm to produce, respectively, *statistical parity*, *conditional statistical parity*, and *parity in false-positive rates*).

3651 Berk, Richard, "Accuracy and Fairness for Juvenile Justice Risks Assessments", *Journal of Empirical Legal Studies*, Volume 16, 2019, p. 175 (comes to the terms with the fact that tweaking/altering data to attain statistical parity yields extremely high false-negative rates).

3652 Mayson, Sandra G., "Bias In, Bias Out", *cit.*, pp. 2218–2300. It is important to note that an algorithm designed for **maximum accuracy** will adjust itself to the majority data, and may be less accurate for members of the underrepresented group, thus breeding *inductive bias*. See: Shellenbarger, Sue, "A Crucial Step for Avoiding AI Disasters", *Wall Street Journal*, (Feb. 13, 2019, 9:57 AM ET), https://www.wsj.com/articles/a-crucial-step-for-avoiding-ai-disasters-11550069865?ns=prod/accounts-wsj; [https://perma.cc/C28U-LAAE] (discussing this issue while emphasizing how diverse development teams pay more attention to unrepresentative and underrepresented data sets). Human programmers can circumvent and bypass this problem by weighting the minority-group data more heavily, by designing different algorithms for each racial group, or by striving to contain more data to equalize group representation in the data set. See: Barua, Sukarna et al., "MWMOTE—Majority Weighted Minority Oversampling Technique for Imbalanced Data Set Learning", *IEEE Transactions on Knowledge & Data Engineering*, Volume 26, 2014, pp. 405, 405–06. See also: Hamilton, Melissa, "The Biased Algorithm: Evidence of Disparate Impact on Hispanics", *American*

4.1.10.2.3 «Equality/Equality Trade-Offs» (Sandra G. Mayson)

§§ It is noteworthy that there is a spate of inexorable/inevitable/unavoidable trade-offs between different metrics of equality.[3653] As pointed by Professor Sandra G. Mayson, whenever base rates of the event carried out to foretell differs greatly across racial groups, it will be utterly impossible to attain equality by every single metric at once.[3654] As a result, to achieve a sought-after measure of equality, most likely one of the metrics needs to be ineluctably sacrificed.[3655]

§§ A body of empirical evidence undertaken by Richard Berk fine-tuned juvenile justice data to create statistical parity in predictions of rearrest for violent crime.[3656] **As a result, an exceedingly high rate of false negatives[3657] was accordingly produced.**[3658] Compellingly, the machine learning algorithm noticeably missed 92%

Criminal Law Review, Volume 56, 2019, pp. 1553 and ff and passim (which clearly demonstrates that COMPAS was significantly less accurate for Hispanic than for white defendants by several measures and suggesting that smaller numbers of Hispanic defendants might be the cause). See: Mayson, Sandra G., "Bias In, Bias Out", *cit.*, pp. 2218–2300. See also: Dong et al., Qi, "Imbalanced deep learning by minority class incremental rectification, *IEEE Transactions on Pattern Analysis & Machine Intelligence*, Volume 41, 2019, p. 1367 (posit that "*most existing learning algorithms produce inductive bias (learning bias)* towards the frequent (majority) classes if training data are not balanced, *resulting in poor minority class recognition performance*"). Italics added. See: Chandler, Anupam, "The Racist Algorithm", *Michigan Law Review*, Volume 115, n. ° 6, 2018, p. 1026 (on racist algorithms, noting that "the possibilities for discriminatory manipulation are legion"). But see: Altenburger, Kristen M./Ho, Daniel E., "When Algorithms Import Private Bias into Public Enforcement: The Promise and Limitations of Statistical Debiasing Solutions", *Journal of Institutional & Theoretical Economics*, Volume 175, 2019, pp. 97–98 (calls for a "debias predictive algorithms" to assuage racist and/or biased, doctored and bigoted algorithms nevertheless). See: Part V, Chap. 5, Sect. 5.1.7.4 of this book (on one of the law to control algorithmic decision-making, namely, law number four: data partitioning must be performed—i.e. randomly split an entire dataset into the «training dataset» and the «test dataset»—to accurately predict outcomes in the real world while forestalling «inductive bias» (learning bias)).

[3653] Barocas, Solon/Selbst, Andrew D., "Big Data's Disparate Impact", *cit.*, pp. 692–93 (These polymaths coined this phenomenon as "masking" owing to the fact that machine-learning technologies bestow upon stakeholders' multiple opportunities to intentionally twist/warp/deform an algorithm in ways that are painstakingly difficult to ferret out/discern/detect).

[3654] Mayson, Sandra G., "Bias In, Bias Out", *cit.*, pp. 2218–2300.

[3655] Mayson, Sandra G., "Bias In, Bias Out", *cit.*, pp. 2218–2300 (2250).

[3656] See: Berk, Richard, "Accuracy and Fairness for Juvenile Justice Risks Assessments", *Journal of Empirical Legal Studies*, Volume 16, 2019, p. 175 (comes to the terms with the fact that tweaking/altering data to attain statistical parity yields extremely high false-negative rates).

[3657] According to Richard Berk's research on juvenile data, for example, tweaking the algorithm to attain **statistical parity** spawned a lower false-positive rate for the black subset than the white (4% versus 9%) yet a higher false-negative rate (50% versus 40%). See: Berk, Richard, "Accuracy and Fairness for Juvenile Justice Risks Assessments", *cit.*, p. 189. In addition to that, Berk further concluded that for white folks, the algorithm generated 5.25 false positives for every false negative; whilst for black folks, the algorithm generated 1.85 false negatives for every false positive. See: Berk, Richard, "Accuracy and Fairness for Juvenile Justice Risks Assessments", *cit.*, p. 189. See also: Angwin, Julia et al., "Machine Bias", *ProPublica* (May 23, 2016), https://www.propublica.org/article/machine-bias-risk-assessments-in-criminal-sentencing; [https://perma.cc/4G83-MDAS] (harshly criticizing disparity in false-positive rates as a purely unjustified bias). See also: Freeman, Katherine, "Algorithmic Injustice: How the Wisconsin Supreme Court Failed to Protect

of violent-crime rearrests of white juveniles and 98% of violent-crime rearrests of black juveniles.[3659] Conversely, such a sheer amount of false-negative rates exacted a toll on algorithm's overall accuracy.[3660]

§§ Inevitably, such a burst off in error also entailed a **disparate racial impact**,[3661] which, I may venture to add, is anything but flabbergasting at this juncture.[3662] Tellingly, since the base rate of arrest for violence in this dataset was exceedingly

---

Due Process Rights in State v. Loomis", *North Carolina Journal of Law and Technology*, Volume 18, 2016, pp. 75–86 (echoing the very same views).

[3658] See also: Petersilia, Joan/Turner, Susan, "Guideline-Based Justice: Prediction and Racial Minorities", *Crime and Justice*, 1987, pp. 151–174 (argues that omitting markers correlated with race from a recidivism prediction algorithm influenced the overall accuracy of the model).

[3659] Mayson, Sandra G., "Bias In, Bias Out", *cit.*, pp. 2218–2300 (2250). See also: Hamilton, Melissa, "*Adventures in risk*: Predicting Violent and Sexual Recidivism in Sentencing Law", *Arizona State Law Journal*, Volume 47, 1, 2015, pp. 1–62 (arguing that the contrary judgment is also reasonable); Harris, Grant T./Rice, Marnie E., "Bayes and Base Rates: What Is an Informative Prior for Actuarial Violence Risk Assessment?", *Behavioral Sciences & the Law, Volume 31, 2013, pp.* 103–106 ("[I]t can be reasonable for public policy to operate on the basis that a miss (e.g., failing to detain a violent recidivist beforehand) is twice as costly as a false alarm (e.g., detaining a violent offender who would not commit yet another violent offense)").

[3660] Mayson, Sandra G., "Bias In, Bias Out", *cit.*, pp. 2218–2300 (2250). See also: Zachary Lipton et al., "Does Mitigating ML's Impact Disparity Require Treatment Disparity?", NIPS PROC. 1 (2018), https://arxiv.org/pdf/1711.07076.pdf; [https://perma.cc/X8VF-EY53] (sets forth compelling evidence that enforced blindness to protected traits exacts a toll in overall accuracy).

[3661] See: Hellman, Deborah, "Indirect Discrimination and the Duty to Avoid Compounding Injustice", *Foundations of Indirect Discrimination Law*, Collins, Hugh/Khaitan, Tarunabh (Editors), Oxford, Hart Publishing; Reprint edition (June 25, 2020), 2020, p. 107 (Professor Deborah Hellman coined this expression to depict a decision that "exacerbates the harm caused by the prior injustice because it entrenches the harm or carries it into another domain." This book deals with the sweltering topic of indirect discrimination ("*indirect discrimination (or disparate impact) concerns the application of the same rule to everyone, even though that rule significantly disadvantages one particular group in society*"). See also: Barocas, Solon/Selbst, Andrew D., "Big Data's Disparate Impact", *California Law Review*, Volume 104, 2016, p. 699 (discussing how discriminatory data mining is analogous to unintentional disparate impact analysis); Sunstein, Cass R., "Algorithms, Correcting Biases", *Social Research*, Volume 86, 2019, pp. 449–506 (this famed author tagged disparate impact as "disturbing in itself, in the sense that a practice that produces such an impact helps entrench something like a caste system"); Barocas, Solon/Selbst, Andrew, "Big Data's Disparate Impact", *cit.*, p. 691 (highlighting the worrisome, and gruesome, issue of "structural disadvantage" with which racialized communities have been tussling with for centuries); Barocas, Solon/Selbst, Andrew D., "Big Data's Disparate Impact", *California Law Review*, Volume 104, 2016, pp. 677–78 (arguing that predictive data is predictive of a given/specific target variable with training data which is both correctly "labelled" and "collected."); But see: Citron, Danielle Keats/Pasquale, Frank, "The Scored Society: Due Process for Automated Predictions", *Washington Law Review*, Volume 89, 2014, pp. 1, 4–5 (highlighting how human beings programming automated systems is directly conducive to, and leads, to fundamentally inaccurate results since the source code, predictive algorithms and datasets may encompass human biases which, in turn, have a disparate impact on historically disadvantaged groups);

[3662] Chandler, Anupam, "The Racist Algorithm", *cit.*, p. 1039 (sets out a poignant call in an earnest attempt to urge stakeholders to put their eyes and hearts on both "inputs and outputs", as opposed to machine algorithms alone). See also: Huq, Aziz Z., "Racial Equity in Algorithmic Criminal Justice", *cit.*, p. 1080 (explaining "the [p]roblem of [d]istorting [f]eature [s]election"); Kehl, Danielle, et al., "Algorithms in the Criminal Justice System: Assessing the Use of Risk Assessments in

higher amongst black juveniles than white juveniles,[3663] and since the great bulk of violent crime is reportedly interracial,[3664] the whopping false-negative rates would signify a much higher number of violent-crime-related arrests missed in the black community than in the white community.[3665]

§§ Inasmuch violent-crime arrests correlates to violent crimes, the staggering effort to attain statistical parity for black juveniles subject to risk assessment comes at the expense of disparate racial[3666] impact[3667] in the black[3668] community.[3669]

Sentencing", *Berkman Klein Ctr. For Internet Society*, 2017, https://dash.harvard.edu/bitstream/handle/1/33746041/2017-07_responsivecommunities_2.pdf; [https://perma.cc/7V6D-JLLM] ("critical issues also need to be addressed in the development phase of these algorithms, particularly with regard to the inputs and how they are used").

3663 Mayson, Sandra G., "Bias In, Bias Out", *cit.*, pp. 2218–2300 (2250).

3664 Mayson, Sandra G., "Bias In, Bias Out", *cit.*, pp. 2218–2300 (2250).

3665 Mayson, Sandra G., "Bias In, Bias Out", *cit.*, pp. 2218–2300 (2250).

3666 Note, though, that certain types of racial discrimination may not be fully intentional. More likely than not, it can be related with the perils of big data colour-blindness that nonetheless relies on proxies to race and gender to make algorithmic decisions. Another problem is the one related with "creditworthiness by association" that causes more problems than it solves. Hurley, Mikella/Adebayo, Julius, "Credit Scoring in the Era of Big Data", *Yale Journal of Law and Technology*, Volume 18, 2016, p. 149 ("*Big-data tools may also risk creating a system of "creditworthiness by association" in which consumers' familial, religious, social, and other affiliations determine their eligibility for an affordable loan. These tools may furthermore obscure discriminatory and subjective lending policies behind a single "objective" score. Such discriminatory scoring may not be intentional; instead, sophisticated algorithms may combine facially neutral data points and treat them as proxies for immutable characteristics such as race or gender, thereby circumventing existing non-discrimination laws and systematically denying credit access to certain groups*"). Italics added. See: Part IV, This chapter, Sects. 4.1.2–4.1.2.3 of this book.

3667 Barocas, Solon/Selbst, Andrew D., "Big Data's Disparate Impact", *California Law Review*, Volume 104, 2016, p. 699 (discussing how discriminatory data mining is analogous to unintentional disparate impact analysis); Bornstein, Stepanhie, "Antidiscriminatory Algorithms", *Alabama Law Review*, Volume 70, 2018, p. 535 (positing that algorithmic discrimination at large could fall under the all-embracing umbrella of anti-stereotyping category within Title VII's disparate treatment).

3668 Mayson, Sandra G., "Bias In, Bias Out", *cit.*, pp. 2218–2300 (2250).

3669 Berk and his peers have also provided a scintillating portray of these equality/accuracy trade-offs, drawing on real arraignment data and a machine-learning algorithm that predicts new arrests for a domestic-violence offense within a period of twenty-one months. The base rate amongst black defendants was 11%, whereas the base rate amongst white defendants was 6%. Relatedly, Berk and his peers found that, if the machine learning algorithm is devised to attain predictive parity regarding to a forecast of no-rearrest, the "false negative and false positive rates vary dramatically by race." Specifically, the false negative rate is 49% for black defendants and 93% for white defendants; the false positive rate is 2% for white defendants and 24% for black defendants. See: Berk, Richard et al., "Fairness in Criminal Justice Risk Assessments: The State of the Art", *cit.*, p. 32. See: Mayson, Sandra G., "Bias In, Bias Out", *cit.*, pp. 2218–2300. See: Angwin, Julia et al., "Machine Bias", *ProPublica* (May 23, 2016), https://www.propublica.org/article/machine-bias-risk-assessments-in-criminal-sentencing [https://perma.cc/4G83-MDAS] (harshly criticizing disparity in false-positive rates as a purely unjustified bias). See also: Freeman, Katherine, "Algorithmic Injustice: How the Wisconsin Supreme Court Failed to Protect Due Process Rights in State v. Loomis", *North Carolina Journal of Law and Technology*, Volume 18, 2016, pp. 75–86 (echoing the very same views).

§§ Considering the trade-offs between certain equality metrics and overall accuracy, and between the equality metrics themselves, scholars have been wondering how does «equality»[3670] looks like after all.[3671] Put it bluntly, what measure of equality, if any,[3672] should algorithmic risk-assessment mechanisms be required to match? As pointed out by Professor Aziz Huq, law refrains itself from providing quality touchstones to help stakeholders navigate this both complex and intricate

[3670] It is of-stated that technology "automates inequality" (Cathy O, Neill). On this note, technology widens the yawning gap between rich—that can adroitly harness artificial intelligence to advance their goals and shady agendas—and poor—that grapple to meet basic needs and are automatically excluded from the equation of digital society powered by Artificial Intelligence—which will directly impact the fabric of societies worldwide, thereby augmenting the gulf between the «digitally-chosen» and the «digitally-outcast» enabled by a algorithmic discrimination that does nothing but irreparable harm. See: Yu, Peter K., "The Algorithmic Divide and Equality in the Age of Artificial Intelligence", *Florida Law Review*, Volume 72, 2020, pp. 355–360 (addresses the issue of algorithmic discrimination). This problem is neither new nor easy to solve. Whilst the effects of technology—digital justice—on the courtroom have been previously broached by the doctrine, few to none consensus has been reached with regard to actionable lines of action to be taken. See: Donoghue, Jane, "The Rise of Digital Justice: Courtroom Technology, Public Participation and Access to Justice", *The Modern Law Review*, Volume 80, Issue 6, 2018, p. 995 (noting that technology in the courtroom might widen the gap between the rich and the poor. In this vein, this renowned author has contended that "*legal reforms have omitted any detailed consideration of the type and quality of citizen participation in newly digitised court processes which have fundamental implications for the legitimacy and substantive outcomes of court-based processes; and for enhancing democratic procedure through improved access to justice.* It is argued that although digital court tools and systems offer great promise for enhancing efficiency, participation and accessibility, they *simultaneously have the potential to amplify the scope for injustice, and to attenuate central principles of the legal system, including somewhat paradoxically, access to justice*"). Italics added. See also: Heintz, M.E., "The digital divide and courtroom technology: Can David keep up with Goliath", *Federal Communications Law Journal*, Volume 54, 2002, pp. 566 ff and passim. The great bulk of these assertions has been anticipated by an iconic piece of research. See: Galanter, Marc, "Why the "Haves" Come Out Ahead: Speculations on the Limits of Legal Change", *Law & Society Review*, Volume 9, 1974, pp. 98–103 (this renowned author talks about a *social reality* in which the dubbed «repeat players»—which go by the name of «haves»—tend to «to come out ahead» by putting their knowledge and vast resources to good use. This perceived advantage will not only impact the choice on the procedures but will ultimately benefit their interests as opposed to the deemed «one-shot» players (the «have nots») that will have slimmer and fewer chances to get palpable results in dispute resolution). Technology in the criminal courtroom—that includes the rich and excludes the poor—will make this problem considerably worse. But see: Bailey, J./Burkell, J./ Reynolds, G. "Access to Justice for All: Towards an "Expansive Vision" of Justice and Technology, *Windsor Yearbook of Access to Justice*, Volume 31, 2013, pp. 183–201 (in stark contrast, these authors stress that the digital and technological apparatus can indeed spawn a both time-effective and streamlined access to justice in a given jurisdiction).

[3671] Eubanks, Virginia, *Automating inequality: how high-tech tools profile, police, and punish the poor*, New York: St. Martin's Press, 2017; Gilliom, John, *Overseers of the Poor: Surveillance, Resistance, and the Limits of Privacy*, Chicago: University of Chicago Press, 2001. Soss, Joe, Richard C. Fording, and Sanford F. Schram, *Disciplining the Poor: Neoliberal Paternalism and the Persistent Power of Race*. Chicago: University of Chicago Press, 2011.

[3672] Berk, Richard, "Accuracy and Fairness for Juvenile Justice Risks Assessments", *cit.*, pp. 185–86 (positing that, to **equalize** *cost ratios* across racial groups in a juvenile risk-assessment context, the author "separate[d] forecasting exercises" for white and black juveniles, respectively, and that the machine-learning forecasting algorithms the data produced were different for each racial group).

world. Conversely, Professor Aziz Huq accordingly puts forward a guiding principle in view of which algorithmic risk assessment should produce no additional harm to communities[3673] of colour.[3674]

§§ Which begs the vexing question: how can toolmakers design predictive tools to live up to that undying promise while rising above algorithmic discrimination? To thoroughly answer this burning question, one must first latch on the crux of the problem: prediction itself.[3675]

4.1.10.3 Why Do Predictive Tools Run Counter to Algorithmic Fairness in the Remit of Criminal Justice Settings?

4.1.10.3.1 Why Does Algorithmic Prediction (Always) Exact a Toll on Members of Racialized Communities? Algorithmic Prediction Lends Itself to a Reflecting Mirror That Projects the Biased Past Into the Future

§§ As Professor Sandra G. Mayson brilliantly points out,[3676] the rationale behind the impossibility to achieve algorithmic equality by every metric when base rates vary greatly is straightforward: algorithmic prediction lends itself to a reflecting mirror that projects the biased past into the future. A key takeaway jumps out as ripe: bereft of a meaningful intervention to smooth out the ill-gotten prediction, history is doomed to repeat itself, which will, again, inordinately befall communities of colour. Just like in the past. So much for the sought-after, and much-acclaimed, algorithmic fairness[3677] in risk assessment.

[3673] Huq, Aziz Z., "Racial Equity in Algorithmic Criminal Justice", *Duke Law Journal*, Volume 68, 2019.

[3674] Mayson, Sandra G., "Bias In, Bias Out", *cit.*, pp. 2218–2300 (2250).

[3675] Mayson, Sandra G., "Bias In, Bias Out", *cit.*, pp. 2218–2300 (2251).

[3676] Mayson, Sandra G., "Bias In, Bias Out", *cit.*, pp. 2218–2300 (2251).

[3677] See on the dire need to attain algorithmic fairness: Zajko, M, "Conservative AI and social inequality: conceptualizing alternatives to bias through social theory", *Artificial Intelligence and Society*, Volume 36, 2021, pp. 1047–1056; Dwork, Cynthia/Hardt, Moritz/Pitassi, Tonian/Reingold/Zemel, Richard, "Fairness Through Awareness, Proceedings of the 3rd Innovations", *Theoretical Computer Science Conference*, 2012, https://dl.acm.org/doi/10.1145/2090236.2090255; [https://perma.cc/T2U3-TNQ6] (discussing an individual fairness approach to algorithmic fairness); Meharabi, Ninareh/Morstatter, Fred/Saxena, Nripsuta/Lerman, Kristina/Galstyan, Aram, "A Survey on Bias and Fairness in Machine Learning", *ACM Computing Survey*, Jul. 2022; Fuster, Andreas/Goldsmith-Pinkham, Paul/Tarun Ramadorai/Walther, Angsar, "Predictably Unequal? The Effects of Machine Learning on Credit Markets", *Journal of Finance*, Volume 76, 2022, passim (providing a description of the variation in interest rates across racial groups carried out by machine learning algorithms); Zarsky, Tal, "Transparency in Data Mining: From Theory to Practice", *Discrimination and Privacy in the Information Society: Data Mining and Profiling in Large Databases*, Bart Custers et al. eds., Belin, Springer, 2013; Kroll, Joshua A. et al., "Accountable Algorithms", *University of Pennsylvania Law Review*, Volume 165, 2017, passim; Green, B./Hu L., "The Myth in the Methodology: Towards a Recontextualization of Fairness in Machine Learning", *Machine Learning Debates Work 35th Internation Conference of Machine Learning*, 2018, passim; West, SM./Whittaker, M./

§§ This assertion is firmly rooted in the fact that algorithmic predictions seek to identify patterns in past data and convert them into projections about future events. Strikingly, if there is a blatant, and rampant, racial disparity in the dataset,[3678] there will be inevitably racial disparity in the algorithmic prediction tool too.[3679] As hinted above, it is possible to replace one form of inequality with another, but nonetheless impossible to wipe it out/scrub it out altogether with a snap of a finger. Let alone concomitantly. This finding about prediction is not unique to actuarial algorithmic methods.[3680] Actuarial prediction mirrors a vividly clear glimpse of noticeable, palpable, tangible, detectable quantified data, whilst subjective prediction reflects a squalid/gloomy/fuggy/misty/smoggy image of anecdotal data.[3681] Note, though, that both subjective and algorithmic prediction alike look to the past as a portend for the future in that past inequalities ripple forward.[3682]

§§ Strikingly, the gist of the problem lies not in algorithmic methodology. Notably, any form of prediction that heavily relies on data about the biased past[3683] will

---

Crawford, K., "Discriminating systems gender, race, and power in AI", AI Now Institute, 2019; Xu, K./Nosek, B./Greenwald, AG., "Data from the race implicit association test on the project implicit demo website", *Journal of Open Psychology* Data 2:e3, 2014 (on the central tenets of algorithmic fairness).

[3678] Selbst, Andrew D., "Disparate Impact in Big Data Policing", *cit.,* at 123 (arguing that "[t]he words 'discrimination,' 'fairness,' and 'bias' evoke a family of related concepts"). But see: Barocas, Solon/Selbst, Andrew D., "Big Data's Disparate Impact", *California Law Review*, Volume 104, 2016, pp. 671–682 (discussing how data is often flawed, rigged, incomplete, imperfect, and therefore algorithms inherit the prejudice of the original decision makers). But see: Citron, Danielle Keats/Pasquale, Frank, "The Scored Society: Due Process for Automated Predictions", *Washington Law Review*, Volume 89, 2014, pp. 1, 4–5 (highlighting how human beings programming automated systems is directly conducive to, and leads, to fundamentally inaccurate results since the source code, predictive algorithms and datasets may encompass human biases which, in turn, have a disparate impact on historically disadvantaged groups); Crawford, Kate/Schultz, Jason, "Big Data and Due Process: Toward a Framework to Redress Predictive Privacy Harms", *Boston College Law Review*, Volume 55, 2014, pp. 93, 99–101 (pinpointing pathways through which predictive analytic tools perpetuate discriminatory practices). But see: Bornstein, Stepanhie, "Antidiscriminatory Algorithms", *Alabama Law Review*, Volume 70, 2018, pp. 519, 524–528 (contending, however, that the tagged "facially neutral" algorithms producing discriminatory outcomes should be quashed).

[3679] Mayson, Sandra G., "Bias In, Bias Out", *cit.*, pp. 2218–2300 (2251).

[3680] Mayson, Sandra G., "Bias In, Bias Out", *cit.*, pp. 2218–2300 (2251).

[3681] Starr, Sonja B., "Evidence-Based Sentencing and the Scientific Rationalization of Discrimination." *Stanford Law Review*, 2014, 66:803–72; Kusner, MJ., Loftus, JR., "The long road to fairer algorithms", *Nature*, Volume 578, 2020, pp. 34–36.

[3682] Mayson, Sandra G., "Bias In, Bias Out", *cit.*, pp. 2218–2300 (2251).

[3683] See: Fergus, Rachel, "Biased Technology: The Automated Discrimination of Facial Recognition", *ACLU Minnesota*, February 29, 2024, available at: https://www.aclu-mn.org/en/news/biased-technology-automated-discrimination-facial-recognition (access: 20.09.2024) ("*technology is developing much more quickly than the laws we need to protect our rights. Anyone with a smartphone or social media account knows how rapidly technology changes, while legislating can take a long, long time. It is essential to proactively put policies into place that will protect our rights as new and more advanced technology is constantly released. Especially when that technology – and law enforcement members using it—have been shown over and over to be biased toward marginalized groups*"). Italics added.

inevitably create racial disparity[3684] if the past data portrays the event that one aims to forecast[3685]—the *target variable*[3686]—transpiring with unequal rates across racial groups.[3687] Coherently, if a machine learning algorithm's predictions are accurate at equal rates across racial lines,[3688] as were the COMPAS forecasts in

---

3684 Morley J, Kinsey L, Elhalal A et al, "Operationalising AI ethics: barriers, enablers, and next steps", *Artificial Intelligence and Society*, 2021, passim.

3685 See: Hamilton, Melissa, "Back to the Future: The Influence of Criminal History on Risk Assessments", *Berkeley Journal of Criminal Law*, Volume 20, 2015, pp. 75, 78 (exuding concerns with the recurrent use of criminal history in risk assessment owing to "the potential that criminal history is an unfortunate proxy for race and social disadvantage"); Barry-Jester, Anna Maria et al., "The New Science of Sentencing: Should Prison Sentencing Be Based on Crimes That Haven't Been Committed Yet?", *Marshall Project* (Aug. 4, 2015, 7:15 AM), https://www.themarshallproject.org/2015/08/04/the-new-science-of-sentencing; [https://perma.cc/J4UW-BDKP] (arguing that risk-assessment outcomes gives rises to disparate racial impact that befall Blacks).

3686 It is important to note that other tools have other target variables, yet the analysis in this offering applies to several other target variables as well. In the pretrial purview, for example, risk-assessment tools also forecast "failure to appear," outlined in terms of data points that vary across jurisdictions. See: Mayson, Sandra G., "Dangerous Defendants", *Yale Law Journal*, Volume 127, 2018, pp. 509–13. There is also a spate of risk-assessment instruments that seek to forecast violence but in fact predict any hint or allegation of violence, whether it reflects in arrest or not (let alone conviction). See, e.g., Yang, Min et al., "The Efficacy of Violence Prediction: A Meta-Analytic Comparison of Nine Risk Assessment Tools", *Psychology Bulletin*, 2010, pp. 740–742 (arguing that "[t]he range of possible criterion variables for violence is wide, and "includes self-reports to third-party reports..., informal social service or police contact, formal contact or police charges, formal adjudication and court convictions, and incarceration"). See: Mayson, Sandra G., "Bias In, Bias Out", *cit.*, pp. 2218–2300.

3687 See: McIntyre, Frank/Baradaran, Shima, "Race, Prediction, and Pretrial Detention", *Journal Empirical Legal Studies*, Volume 10, 2013, pp. 742–759 (mentions black defendants' exceedingly high likelihood of being arrested on drug-related charges as a potential cause of the race gap); Skeem, Jennifer L./Lowenkamp, Christopher T., "Risk, Race, and Recidivism: Predictive Bias and Disparate Impact", *Criminology*, Volume 54, 2024, pp. 680, 683–84, 704–06 (argues that criminal history correlates with race in their respective data set). See also: Pager, Devah, *Marked: Race, Crime, and Finding Work in an Era of Mass Incarceration*, Chicago: University of Chicago Press, 2007; Fornili, K. S., "Racialized mass incarceration and the war on drugs: A critical race theory appraisal", *Journal of Addictions Nursing*, Volume 29, Issue 1, 2018, 65–72; Jacoby, S. F., Dong, B., Beard, J. H., Wiebe, D. J., & Morrison, C. N., "The enduring impact of historical and structural racism on urban violence in Philadelphia", *Social Science & Medicine*, 1982/2018, 199, 2018, pp. 87–95; Travis, Jeremy, Bruce Western, and Steve Redburn (Eds.), *Growth of Incarceration in the United States: Exploring Causes and Consequences*, Washington, DC: National Academy of Science, 2014. See: Bar-Gill/Oren/Warren, Elizabeth, "Making Credit Safer", *University of Pennsylvania Law Review*, Volume 157, 2008, pp. 1–66 (argue that Black defendants are far more likely to be incarcerated, arrested, surveilled and harassed than White folks, which leads to the conclusion that the use of credit scores and income presents another way in which credit decisions leverage on structural disadvantage).

3688 Dieterich, William et al., "COMPAS Risk Scales: Demonstrating Accuracy Equity and Predictive Parity", *Northpointe Inc.* 1, 2–3, 8–13 (July 8, 2016), http://go.volarisgroup.com/rs/430-MBX-989/images/ProPublica_Commentary_Final_070616.pdf; [https://perma.cc/K4GM-RBQY] (stating that a predictive instrument is bigoted/flawed only if a certain score, or a given classification, means a starkly likelihood of the forecasted outcome for members of one racial group than members of the other group). See also: Flores: Anthony W. et al., "False Positives, False Negatives, and False Analyses: A Rejoinder to "Machine Bias: There's Software Used Across the Country to

Broward County, any inequality in prediction inevitably mirrors inequality[3689] in the underlying dataset.[3690]

§§ Relatedly, to grasp and remedy disparity in prediction, it is therefore necessary to thoroughly understand how and when racial inequality emerges/sprouts in the data that we shift our gaze to as a reflection of past crime.[3691]

4.1.10.3.2 «Racial Inequality in Past-Crime Data» (Sandra G. Mayson) Breeds Biased Predictions of Future Arrest (As Opposed to Future Crime): Has the Level Playing Field Been Unfairly Tilted Against Members of Racialized Communities?

§§ From a racial equality standpoint, the most important question for any predictive instrument is what it forecasts. Put otherwise, what data point is classified as a «positive» example of the target variable. It is oft-averred that extant criminal justice risk-assessment instruments purport to forecast future crime.[3692] Note, though, that such is not the case. Instead, algorithmic risk assessment tools purport to predict future[3693] arrest.[3694]

Predict Future Criminals. And It's Biased Against Blacks," *Federal Probation*, Volume 80, 2016, pp. 38–40 (positing that "well-established and accepted standards exist to test for bias in risk assessment"); Skeem, Jennifer L./Lowenkamp, Christopher T., "Risk, Race, and Recidivism: Predictive Bias and Disparate Impact", *cit.*, p. 685 (asserting that if "a given score [has] the same meaning regardless of group membership," the instrument is "unbiased").

3689 Stevenson, Megan/Mayson, Sandra G., "Pretrial Detention and Bail", Luna, Erik, (Editor), *Reforming Criminal Justice: A Report of the Academy for Justice, Bridging the Gap between Scholarship and Reform*, pp. 21, 34–39 (assessing the risk of pretrial risk assessments while highlighting a slew of deep-rooted concerns regarding accuracy, racial-equality, and procedure); See: Chandler, Anupam, "The Racist Algorithm", *Michigan Law Review*, Volume 115, n.° 6, 2018, pp. 1023–1025 (arguing that the real-world facts on which algorithms used in criminal justice risk assessment are based are "deeply suffused with invidious discrimination"); Eaglin, Jessica M., "Constructing Recidivism Risk", *cit.*, pp. 94–99 (argues that risk assessment has every chance to "compromise[e] equality"); Mayson, Sandra G., "Dangerous Defendants", *cit.*, pp. 494–96.

3690 Mayson, Sandra G., "Bias In, Bias Out", *cit.*, pp. 2218–2300 (2251).

3691 Mayson, Sandra G., "Bias In, Bias Out", *cit.*, pp. 2218–2300 (2251).

3692 Mayson, Sandra G., "Bias In, Bias Out", *cit.*, pp. 2218–2300 (2252).

3693 Mayson, Sandra G., "Bias In, Bias Out", *cit.*, pp. 2218–2300 (2252).

3694 It is important to note that other tools have other target variables, yet the analysis in this offering applies to several other target variables as well. In the pretrial purview, for example, risk-assessment tools also forecast "failure to appear," outlined in terms of data points that vary across jurisdictions. See: Mayson, Sandra G., "Dangerous Defendants", *Yale Law Journal*, Volume 127, 2018, pp. 509–13. There is also a spate of risk-assessment instruments that seek to forecast violence but in fact predict any hint or allegation of violence, whether it reflects in arrest or not (let alone conviction). See, e.g., Yang, Min et al., "The Efficacy of Violence Prediction: A Meta-Analytic Comparison of Nine Risk Assessment Tools", *Psychology Bulletin*, 2010, pp. 740–742 (arguing that "[t]he range of possible criterion variables for violence is wide, and "includes self-reports to third-party reports..., informal social service or police contact, formal contact or police charges, formal adjudication and court convictions, and incarceration"). See: Mayson, Sandra G., "Bias In, Bias Out", *cit.*, pp. 2218–2300.

§§ The simple reason why algorithmic risk-assessment tools forecast arrest rather than crime is that the data do not allow for direct crime forecast. Which is nothing but formulaic: to ascertain who is likely to perpetrate crime in the future, one would have to keenly look at who has perpetrated crimes in the past. But here's the twist: we do not know for a fact who has indeed committed crimes in the past. The reason for that is as clear as straightforward: the overwhelming majority of crimes are seldom, if ever, reported; there is a cluster of flagitious activities that are reported dishonestly—even mischievously.[3695] In addition to that, seldom do crime reports accurately identify wrongdoers, perpetrators, and tortfeasors[3696] alike to begin with.[3697]

§§ At the other end of the spectrum, law enforcement agencies employ staggering, even gallant, efforts to adroitly identify perpetrators. To cater for that, they carry out a plethora of police activities aimed at fundamentally making arrests, press criminal charges, and seeking «clean» convictions in a court of law. This police work amount to institutional events that are always documented. It is also obvious that even the most efficient/law abiding law enforcement agency makes mistakes in that inaccurate, if not outright unlawful, arrests are routinely made. A great bulk of crimes never end up in arrest.[3698] On the flip side, some arrests are wrongly made.[3699]

[3695] But see: Wonyoung, So, "Which Information Matters? Measuring Landlord Assessment of Tenant Screening Reports", *Housing Policy Debate*, Volume 33, n. ° 6, 2023, pp. 1484–1510 (1500) (arguing that many landlords file evictions (*eviction fillings*) with no intention whatsoever of proceeding with its execution (*executed evictions*) only to purposefully harm an undesirable tenant, which casts a shady shadow on the eviction records, which, in turn, lack accuracy. "*With regards to eviction records, one of the most noticeable harms this study identifies is that during the tenant screening process, landlords do not distinguish between eviction filings and actually executed evictions. This is particularly alarming given that many landlords file numerous evictions without the intention of or a sound rationale for actually evicting tenants (Garboden & Rosen, 2019). Furthermore, this study replicates the finding of "professional solidarity" among landlords (Garboden & Rosen, 2019, p. 647). (....) Furthermore, landlords often file multiple evictions on the same tenant—this is frequently called "serial filing" (Immergluck* et al., *2020; Leung* et al., *2021). As a result, in Washington, DC, for example, among all eviction records, only 5.5% of evictions filed in 2018 were executed (McCabe & Rosen, 2020). This means that 94.5% of filed evictions were not executed. As this study has shown, those records may be interpreted, erroneously, as evictions by landlords and will likely still negatively affect tenants' future housing search (Phillips, 2020)*"). Italics added. See: Part IV, This chapter, Sects. 4.1.4–4.1.4.2.3 of this book.

[3696] *Tech, Bias and Housing Initiative, the Promise and Perils of Residential Proptech, Year 1, Research Summary Report, April 2023, TechEquity Collaborative*, p. 10, available at: https://techequity.us/wp-content/uploads/2023/04/TBHI-Y1-Research-Summary-Report.pdf (28.11.2024). ("*Tenant screening tools are often packaged as part of a larger suite of property management tools for landlords. Unlike Analog Models, Algorithmic Tenant Screening Tools Predict Future Behavior To Determine Housing Access. (....) In analog screening, those reports return information from an applicant's credit, eviction, and criminal histories. There are many inequities with this analog model. Eviction and criminal records are often wrong or lack important context. 12 13 Credit scoring techniques are notoriously biased*"). Italics added. See: Part IV, This chapter, Sects. 4.1.4–4.1.4.2.3 of this book.

[3697] Mayson, Sandra G., "Bias In, Bias Out", *cit.*, pp. 2218–2300 (2252).

[3698] Crime in the United States 2017, FBI tbl.425, https://ucr.fbi.gov/crime-in-the-u.s/2017/crime-in-the-u.s.-2017/tables/table-25 [https://perma.cc/G2QQ-F34R] (documenting that, in data from reporting law enforcement agencies nationwide, only 45.6% of violent offenses and 17.6% of

§§ Relatedly, some filed criminal charges are truthful and some are not. Oddly, some filed criminal charges are wrapped in opaqueness. On the flip side, some filed criminal charges result in convictions whereas some do not. A key takeaway accordingly jumps out as ripe: the record of past crimes is at best inaccurate and at worst useless. Additionally, the record of crime reports is tightly interlocked with law enforcement stance on crime. Understandably, though not laudably, the relationship of that record to crimes indeed committed has shown to be reciprocal, opaque[3700] and ultimately dingy.[3701] On the heels of the pinpointed data limitation, the whopping majority of extant criminal justice risk-assessment tools merely forecast arrest based on the assumption under which the latter is the best available proxy for crime[3702] perpetration.[3703]

§§ A spate of criminal justice risk-assessment tools forecast arrest for a given type of crime, but the great of bulk of which appraise the likelihood of arrest for any type of crime within a given timespan. Again, understandably, albeit far cry from laudably, the choice to forecast arrest has significant repercussions for racial equality

---

property offenses were cleared by arrest). See: Mayson, Sandra G., "Bias In, Bias Out", *cit.*, pp. 2218–2300.

[3699] Mayson, Sandra G., "Bias In, Bias Out", *cit.*, pp. 2218–2300 (2252).

[3700] See: *Tech, Bias and Housing Initiative, the Promise and Perils of Residential Proptech, Year 1, Research Summary Report, April 2023, TechEquity Collaborative*, p. 10, available at: https://techequity.us/wp-content/uploads/2023/04/TBHI-Y1-Research-Summary-Report.pdf (28.11.2024). ("**Opaque, Predictive Algorithms Determine Who Gets What Housing Unlike Analog Models**, *Algorithmic Tenant Screening Tools Predict Future Behavior To Determine Housing Access As landlord tech took hold, more property managers of all sizes came to rely on it to interface with tenants. One key feature of landlord tech is the use of algorithms to screen rental applicants and assess their suitability as tenants. The tenant screening industry, which pulls a wide array of information about potential tenants to inform landlords' decisions, is now valued at $1.3 billion with as many as two thousand screening companies vying for market share.*10 11 *Such companies include Equifax, TransUnion, and Experian (commonly known as "The Big Three"), as well as smaller startup companies that apply algorithms to make those determinations faster*"). Italics added. See: Part IV, This chapter, Sects. 4.1.4–4.1.4.2.3 of this book. See: Part IV, This chapter, Sects. 4.1.4–4.1.4.2.1 of this book (on mortgage redlining). See: Part IV, This chapter, Sects. 4.1.2–4.1.4.3 of this book (on algorithmic credit scoring, consumer racism and credit card redlining). See: Part IV, This chapter, Sects. 4.1.4–4.1.4.2.3 of this book (on algorithmic redlining). See: Part IV, This chapter, Sect. 4.1.4.3 of this book (on "algorithmic redliking"). See: Part IV, This chapter, Sect. 4.1.3 of this book (on algorithmic prime-lining).

[3701] O'Neill, Cathy, Commentary: "Let's Not Forget How Wrong Our Crime Data Are", Chicago Tribune (May 25, 2018), https://www.chicagotribune.com/news/opinion/commentary/ct-perspec-danger-marijuana-legalizing-crime-data-black-youth-facial-bias-0528-story.html; [https://perma.cc/DMU4-XW38] (contending that crime statistics are a rather poor proxy for actual crime in that blind trust should be placed upon it). See: Mayson, Sandra G., "Bias In, Bias Out", *cit.*, pp. 2218–2300.

[3702] Mayson, Sandra G., "Bias In, Bias Out", *cit.*, pp. 2218–2300 (2253).

[3703] Whether and to extent arrest is the best available proxy for commission of crime is a vital, but rather elusive, task in that it is a chore that is anything but straightforward. See: Roberts, Anna, "Arrest as Guilt", *Alabama Law Review*, Volume 60, 2019, passim.

owing to the fact that, in the overwhelming majority of jurisdictions, for nearly all types of crimes, arrest rates have been racially disparate for a long-haul.[3704]

§§ For example, DOJ (Department of Justice) investigations into the Ferguson and Baltimore police departments laid bare, and accordingly brought to the fore, two paradigmatic examples.[3705] Dispiritingly, though, Ferguson and Baltimore are not isolated cases. Back in 2014, a USA Today analysis of FBI data found that «[a]t least 1,581 other police departments across the USA arrest black people at rates even more skewed than in Ferguson».[3706]

§§ The report has shed an additional light on this finding: «Blacks are more likely than others to be arrested in almost every city for almost every type of crime. Nationwide, black people are arrested at higher rates for crimes as serious as murder and assault, and as minor as loitering and marijuana possession».[3707] Recent data do not look any better than this. Revealingly, back in 2017, the black arrest rate in

---

3704 Mayson, Sandra G., "Bias In, Bias Out", *cit.*, pp. 2218–2300 (2253).

3705 Civil Rights Division, Investigation of the Baltimore City Police Department, U.S. DEP'T JUST. 3 (2016), https://www.justice.gov/crt/file/883296/download; [https://perma.cc/2BHX-3QB4] [hereinafter Baltimore Investigation]; Civil Rights Div., Investigation of the Ferguson Police Department, United States of America Department of Justice (2015), https://www.justice.gov/sites/default/files/opa/press-releases/attachments/2015/03/04/ferguson_police_department_report.pdf; [https://perma.cc/GFX7-ZDWT] [hereinafter Ferguson Investigation]. 119. Brad Heath, Racial Gap in U.S. Arrest Rates: "Staggering Disparity," USA TODAY (Nov. 18, 2014), https://www.usatoday.com/story/news/nation/2014/11/18/ferguson-black-arrest-rates/19043207 [https://perma.cc/V9MY-K2WN]. *Apud*: Mayson, Sandra G., "Bias In, Bias Out", *cit.*, pp. 2218–2300.

3706 Mayson, Sandra G., "Bias In, Bias Out", *cit.*, pp. 2218–2300 (2253). As a matter of fact, the aggregate national arrest rate for black people was at least twice as high as the aggregate white arrest rate every year from 1980 through 2014. Arrest Data Analysis Tool, Bureau Justice Statistics, https://www.bjs.gov/index.cfm?ty=datool&surl=/arrests/index.cfm (click "National Estimates," then "Trend Graphs by Race," and then select the race and "All offenses") (last visited Feb. 15, 2024). *Apud*: Mayson, Sandra G., "Bias In, Bias Out", *cit.*, pp. 2218–2300. A similar trend holds true amongst a slew of misdemeanours. See: Stevenson, Megan/Mayson, Sandra, "The Scale of Misdemeanour Justice", *Boston University Law Review*, Volume 98, 2018, pp. 731, 758–63 (holding that "the [national] black arrest rate [for an index of misdemeanour offenses] has hovered around 1.7 times the white arrest rate since 1980"). The sharpest disparities might be in more serious types of crimes. For every year from 1980 through 2012, the black arrest rate for what the Bureau of Justice Statistics deems the "violent crime index" "was at least three times the white arrest rate, and from 1980 through 1989 it was more than six times the white arrest rate". *Arrest Data Analysis Tool, Bureau of Justice Statistics*, https://www.bjs.gov/index.cfm?ty=datool&surl=/arrests/index.cfm (click "National Estimates," then "Trend Graphs by Race," and then select the race and "Violent Crime Index") (last visited Feb. 15, 2019). *Apud:* Mayson, Sandra G., "Bias In, Bias Out", *cit.*, pp. 2218–2300.

3707 As a matter of fact, the aggregate national arrest rate for black people was at least twice as high as the aggregate white arrest rate every year from 1980 through 2014. Arrest Data Analysis Tool, Bureau Justice Statistics, https://www.bjs.gov/index.cfm?ty=datool&surl=/arrests/index.cfm (click "National Estimates," then "Trend Graphs by Race," and then select the race and "All offenses") (last visited Feb. 15, 2019). *Apud*: Mayson, Sandra G., "Bias In, Bias Out", *cit.*, pp. 2218–2300. A similar trend holds true amongst a slew of misdemeanours. See: Stevenson, Megan/Mayson, Sandra, "The Scale of Misdemeanour Justice", *Boston University Law Review*, Volume 98, 2018, pp. 731, 758–63 (holding that "the [national] black arrest rate [for an index of misdemeanour offenses] has hovered around 1.7 times the white arrest rate since 1980"). The sharpest disparities might be in

the United States of America was at least twice as high as the white arrest rate for every type of crime[3708]exception made to driving under the influence, infringements of liquor laws, and[3709] «drunkenness».[3710]

§§ With regard to murder and robbery, the black arrest rate was roughly seven times higher the white arrest rate. Hardly any surprise stems from the fact that such racial disparities will feed into past-crime datasets which, in turn, will reflect racial inequality in arrest rates for several types of crime.[3711]

4.1.10.3.3 «Two Possible Sources of Disparity» (Sandra G. Mayson) that Explain Such Racial Disparities

§§ There are two possible explanations for such racial disparities in the underlying dataset that will eventually feed, and bake into, the machine learning algorithms entrusted with making high stake decisions[3712] in the realm of algorithmic risk

more serious types of crimes. For every year from 1980 through 2012, the black arrest rate for what the Bureau of Justice Statistics deems the "violent crime index" "was at least three times the white arrest rate, and from 1980 through 1989 it was more than six times the white arrest rate". *Arrest Data Analysis Tool, Bureau of Justice Statistics*, https://www.bjs.gov/index.cfm?ty=datool&surl=/arrests/index.cfm (click "National Estimates," then "Trend Graphs by Race," and then select the race and "Violent Crime Index") (last visited Feb. 15, 2019). *Apud:* Mayson, Sandra G., "Bias In, Bias Out", *cit.*, pp. 2218–2300.

[3708] Mayson, Sandra G., "Bias In, Bias Out", *cit.*, pp. 2218–2300 (2253).

[3709] Mayson, Sandra G., "Bias In, Bias Out", *cit.*, pp. 2218–2300 (2254).

[3710] Professor Sandra Mayson has duly calculated 2017 arrest rates by race and type of crime using the arrest totals reported in the FBI's Uniform Crime Reports series and national population estimates reported by the U.S. Census Bureau. These sources boast several and severe limitations, but to the best of Professor Mayson's knowledge are nonetheless the best available basis for calculating national arrest rates by race. See Crime in the United States 2017, FBI tbl.43A, https://ucr.fbi.gov/crime-in-the-u.s/2017/crime-in-the-u.s.-2017/topic-pages/tables/table-43; [https://perma.cc/EKG9-YD6G] (depicting arrest totals by type of crime and race in reporting jurisdictions); Quick Facts: Population Estimates, July 1, 2017 (V2017), United States of America Census Bureau, in: https://www.census.gov/quickfacts/fact/table/US/PST045217#PST045217; [https://perma.cc/989D-GWNG] (documenting that white people constituted 76.6% of the national population of 325,719,178 (or 249,500,890) whereas black people constituted 13.4% (or 43,646,370). See: Mayson, Sandra G., "Bias In, Bias Out", *cit.*, pp. 2218–2300.

[3711] Mayson, Sandra G., "Bias In, Bias Out", *cit.*, pp. 2218–2300 (2254).

[3712] But see: Millar, Jason/Kerr, Ian, "Delegation, Relinquishment and Responsibility: The Prospect of Expert Robots", *Robot Law*, Calo, Ryan/Froomkin, A. Michael/Kerr, Ian (Editors), Cheltenham, Edward Elgar Publishing, 2016, pp. 102, 106–107 (as these authors aptly put it "*we will rely on robots without really knowing why – simply because their algorithms provide the greatest number of successful outcomes.* We have already seen this in Google's search approach. Neither Larry (Page) nor Sergey (Brin) (nor any other Google employee) knowns exactly why one particular web page is a better result than another. *When the click patterns say it is, that's good enough.* No semantic or causal analysis is required...*Like the ancients, we will, quite rationally, come to rely upon them, knowing full well that we cannot necessarily explain the reasons for their decisions*"). Italics added. Converging: Casey, Anthony J./Niblett, Anthony, "Self-driving Laws", *University of Toronto Law Journal*, Volume 66, 2016, pp. 429–435 (contend that "as more information is generated, and the evolutionary algorithm updates and become a better forecaster, *we imagine that judges will increasingly rely on the advice of the algorithm*"). But see: Weizenbaum, Joseph,

assessment. At one end of the spectrum, racial disparities in the dataset reflect a racial distortion concerning to the underlying rate of crime commission: white and black people perpetrate crimes at equal rates, but racial skew in law enforcement or reporting flagitious practices disfigures this ground truth.[3713]

§§ At the other end of the spectrum, the explanation[3714] is that which disparity sharply mirrors a difference in offending rates across racial lines.[3715] This dredges up one of the flagships of White supremacy racist[3716] agenda[3717]: the bespoke association of blackness with the perpetration[3718] of crimes.[3719]

§§ For that reason, it is of paramount importance to distinguish these two possible sources of predictive racial disparity.[3720] A cohort of stakeholders in the risk-assessment-and-race parley posits that any racial disparity in past-crime data sharply mirrors distortion[3721]; others contend that it echoes profound differences in[3722]underlying crime rates instead.[3723]

§§ It is true that distortions in the dataset or risk-assessment methods can occasionally be corrected, but truer still if the **correction is not feasible—i.e. if the dataset falls conspicuously short of accurately mirroring the underlying**

Computer Power and Human Reason: From Judgment to Calculation, 1st edition, New York, W. H. Freeman & Co, 1976, pp. 1–300 (227) ("examines the sources of the computer's powers and offers evaluative explorations of what computers can do, cannot do, and should not be employed to do") (this founding father of Artificial Intelligence presciently noted that we should not entrust Artificial Intelligence-embedded technologies with "tasks that demand wisdom"). Italics added. The approval of rental applications is arguably one of those tasks that should never be entrusted to machines). More on this on Part IV, This chapter, Sects. 4.1.4–4.1.4.2.1 of this book.

3713 Mayson, Sandra G., "Bias In, Bias Out", *cit.*, pp. 2218–2300 (2254).

3714 But see: Segran, G., "The complexity of artificial intelligence", *Singapore Management University*, 2021, passim (on the elaborate and complex trappings of Artificial Intelligence); Adadi, Amina/ Berrada, Mohammed, "Peeking Inside the Black-Box: A Survey on Explainable Artificial Intelligence (XAI), *Institute of Electrical and Electronics Engineers*, Volume 6, 2018, passim; Edwards, Lilian/Veale, Michael, "Slave to the Algorithm? Why a "Right to an Explanation" is Probably not the Remedy You are Looking for", *Duke Law and Technology Review*, Volume 16, 2018, pp. 18–67 (pondering whether and to what extent XAI will come in handy because citizens are woefully ill-prepared to "make use of the kind of algorithmic explanations they are likely to be offered"); Miller, Tim, "Explanations in Artificial Intelligence: Insights from Social Sciences", *Artificial Intelligence*, Volume 267, 2019, pp. 1–38.

3715 Mayson, Sandra G., "Bias In, Bias Out", *cit.*, pp. 2218–2300 (2254).

3716 Packard, Jerald M., *American Nightmare: The History of Jim Crow*, Broadway, New York, St. Martin's Press; First Edition, 2002, pp. 1–304 (vii–viii) ("[A] *structure of exclusion and discrimination devised by white Americans to be employed principally against black Americans.... Its central purpose was to maintain a second-class social and economic status for blacks while upholding a first-class social and economic status for whites.... In the South, Jim Crow discrimination at its height existed not only by statute but by custom and racial 'etiquette,' and it was rigidly enforced by both the law enforcement agencies* and courts as well as by ordinary white citizens who were neither policemen nor judges but who often took the law into their own hands as though they were"). Italics added.

commission of crime—then they should not serve as benchmark for algorithmic risk assessment in the first place.[3724]

[3717] See: Daley, Jane/Gimore, Glenda Elizabeth/Simon, Bryant (Editors), Jumpin' *Jim Crow: Southern Politics from Civil War to Civil Rights*, Princeton, Princeton University Press, 2020, pp. 1–331 ("*White supremacy shaped all aspects of post-Civil War southern life, yet its power was never complete or total. The form of segregation and subjection nicknamed Jim Crow constantly had to remake itself over time even as white southern politicians struggled to extend its grip.* Here, some of the most innovative scholars of southern history question Jim Crow's sway, evolution, and methods over the course of a century. These essays bring to life the southern men and women–some heroic and decent, others mean and sinister, most a mixture of both–who supported and challenged Jim Crow, showing that white supremacy always had to prove its power. *Jim Crow was always in motion, always adjusting to meet resistance and defiance by both African Americans and whites. Sometimes white supremacists responded with increased ferocity, sometimes with more subtle political and legal ploys. Jumpin' Jim Crow presents a clear picture of this complex negotiation. For example, even as some black and white women launched the strongest attacks on the system, other white women nurtured myths glorifying white supremacy*"). Italics added. See also: Rich, Camille Gear, "Marginal Whiteness", *California Law Review*, Volume 98, 2010, passim; Smångs, Mattias, "Doing Violence, Making Race: Southern Lynching and White Racial Group Formation, *American Journal of Sociology*, Volume 121, 2016.

[3718] Mayson, Sandra G., "Bias In, Bias Out", *cit.*, pp. 2218–2300 (2254).

[3719] Onwuachi-Willig, Angela, "Policing the Boundaries of Whiteness: The Tragedy of Being "Out of Place" from Emmett Till to Trayvon Martin", *Iowa Law Review*, Volume 102, 2017, passim. See: Part IV, This chapter, Sects. 4.1.1–4.1.1.1 of this book (on biased predictive policing).

[3720] On the challenges arising out of algorithmic risk assessment with regard to predicting criminal recidivism rates, fairness wise: Johndrow, J. E./K. Lum, "An Algorithm for Removing Sensitive Information: Application to Race-Independent Recidivism Prediction", *Annals of Applied Statistics*, 13 (1), 2019, pp. 189–220; Chouldechova, A., "Fair Prediction with Disparate Impact: A Study of Bias in Recidivism Prediction Instruments.", *Big data*, 5 (2), 2017, pp. 153–63; Kamiran, F./ T. Calders, "Data Preprocessing Techniques for Classification Without Discrimination." Knowledge Information Systems, 2012, 33:1–33; Kearns, M/A. Roth, *The Ethical Algorithm*, Oxford, Oxford Press; Skeem, J. and C. Lowenkamp, "Using Algorithms to Address Trade-Offs Inherent in Predicting Recidivism", *Behavioural Science and Law*, Volume 38, 2020, pp. 259–78; Tonry, M., "Legal and Ethical Issues in The Prediction of Recidivism", *Federal Sentencing Reporter*, 26 (3): 2014, pp. 167–76; Zhu, Mirilla, "Jury, Using Artificial Intelligence to Predict Recidivism Rates", *Yale Scientific*, 2020, passim. See also: Chasemi et al., Medhi, "The application of Machine Learning to a General Risk-Need Assessment Instrument in the Prediction of Criminal Recidivism", *Criminal Justice and Behavior*, Volume 48, 2020, pp. 518–538. See: Part IV, This chapter, Sects. 4.1.1–4.1.1.1 of this book (on biased predictive policing).

[3721] See: McIntyre, Frank/Baradaran, Shima, "Race, Prediction, and Pretrial Detention", *Journal Empirical Legal Studies*, Volume 10, 2013, pp. 742–759 (mentions black defendants' exceedingly high likelihood of being arrested on drug-related charges as a potential cause of the race gap); Skeem, Jennifer L./Lowenkamp, Christopher T., "Risk, Race, and Recidivism: Predictive Bias and Disparate Impact", *Criminology*, Volume 54, 2024, pp. 680, 683–84, 704–06 (argues that criminal history correlates with race in their respective data set). See also: Pager, Devah, *Marked: Race, Crime, and Finding Work in an Era of Mass Incarceration*, Chicago: University of Chicago Press, 2007; Fornili, K. S., "Racialized mass incarceration and the war on drugs: A critical race theory appraisal", *Journal of Addictions Nursing*, Volume 29, Issue 1, 2018, 65–72; Jacoby, S. F., Dong, B., Beard, J. H., Wiebe, D. J., & Morrison, C. N., "The enduring impact of historical and structural racism on urban violence in Philadelphia", *Social Science & Medicine*, 1982/2018, 199, 2018,

§§ Note, though, that if the data do reliably mirror the underlying commission of crime, and predictive disparity springs from a difference in underlying crime rates, then the disparity is not amenable to be stamped out within either the data or the predictive process itself. Nor is the answer to cast aside/toss out algorithmic assessment in favour of subjective prediction, which, in turn, falls prey to arbitrary judgments that heavily rely upon a whimsical intuition.[3725] **Relatedly, to the extent the data accurately mirrors the occurrence of some event that is worth predicting, algorithmic risk assessment may have a pivotal role to play after all.**[3726] It is therefore vitally important to recognize the two possible sources of predictive disparity.[3727]

4.1.10.3.4 Does Biased Law Enforcement Practices Explain the Racial Inequality in Past-Crime Data That Feeds Into Machine Learning Algorithms Entrusted With Making High Stake Decisions in Criminal Justice Settings?

pp. 87–95; Travis, Jeremy, Bruce Western, and Steve Redburn (Eds.), *Growth of Incarceration in the United States: Exploring Causes and Consequences*, Washington, DC: National Academy of Science, 2014. See: Part IV, This chapter, Sects. 4.1.1–4.1.1.1 of this book (on biased predictive policing).

[3722] Mayson, Sandra G., "Bias In, Bias Out", *cit.*, pp. 2218–2300 (2254).

[3723] Mayson, Sandra G., "Bias In, Bias Out", *cit.*, pp. 2218–2300 (2255).

[3724] Mayson, Sandra G., "Bias In, Bias Out", *cit.*, pp. 2218–2300 (2255).

[3725] Tyler, Tom, "Methodology in Legal Research", in: *Utrecht Law Review*, Volume 13, Issue 3, 2017, pp. 130–131 ("*Accurate facts plus good legal rules lead to substantive justice.* This is the normative framework of right and wrong defined by traditional legal analysis. *Risk analysis is a nice example of the benefits of empiricism because studies suggest that the use of empirical methods to assess future dangerousness is more accurate than is the use of human intuition. It is better to use a formula when making a legal decision that involves estimates of someone's likely future conduct than it is to rely upon the impressions of judges or prosecutors*" (...) "*The legal system relies on predictions about people's likely future behaviour at many points in the system*: pretrial detention; sentencing; parole and probation; etc. (...) *Accuracy, in turn is enhanced by the use of empirical methods. Facts are sought that can guide the application of normative legal principles*"). Italics added.

[3726] Mayson, Sandra G., "Bias In, Bias Out", *cit.*, pp. 2218–2300 (2255).

[3727] Mayson, Sandra G., "Bias In, Bias Out", *cit.*, pp. 2218–2300 (2255).

§§ It is an understatement to aver that law enforcement agencies have inordinately surveilled,[3728] killed,[3729] arrested,[3730] wrongly convict,[3731] and incarcerated[3732] people of colour of over the last decades. The rate and pace at which black people and white people, respectively, are arrested differs greatly accordingly.[3733] For

---

[3728] Browne, S., *Dark matters: on the surveillance of blackness*, Duke University Press, 2015, passim; Toro, J. D./Lloyd, T., Buchanan/K. S., Robins/S. J., Bencharit/L. Z., Smiedt/M. G., Reddy/ K. S., Pouget, E. R./Kerrison, E. M./Goff, P. A., "The criminogenic and psychological effects of police stops on adolescent black and Latino boys", *Proceedings of the National Academy of Sciences of the United States of America*, Volume 116, Issue 17, 2019, pp. 8261–8268; Sewell, A. A., Jefferson, K. A./Lee, H., "Living under surveillance: Gender, psychological distress, and stop-question- and-frisk policing in New York city", *Social Science & Medicine*, Volume 159, 2016, pp. 1–13. Brayne, S., "Big data surveillance: The case of policing", *American Sociological Review*, Volume 82, Issue 5, 2017, pp. 977–1008; Benjamin, Ruha, *Race After Technology: Abolitionist Tools for the New Jim Code*, John Wiley & Sons, 2019, passim; Abdillahi, I., "Algorithmic surveillance in the era of the appsphere", *American Journal of Community Psychology*, Volume 73, 2024, passim. See: Part IV, This chapter, Sects. 4.1.1–4.1.1.1 of this book (on biased predictive policing).

[3729] Crutchfield, J., Fisher, A., & Webb, S. L., "Colorism and police killings", *The Western Journal of Black Studies*, 41 (3–4), 2017, 81; Dottolo, A. L., & Stewart, A. J. (2008). "Don't ever forget now, you're a Black man in America": Intersections of race, class and gender in encounters with the police", *Sex Roles*, 59(5–6), 2008, pp. 350–364; Baradan, S., "Race, prediction, and discretion", *The George Washington Law Review*, Volume 81, Issue 1, 2013, pp. 157–222.

[3730] Robinson, M. A., "Black bodies on the ground: Policing disparities in the African American Community-An analysis of newsprint from January 1, 2015, through December 31, 2015", *Journal of Black Studies*, Volume 48, Issue 6, pp. 551–571; Kizer, J. M., "Arrested by skin color: Evidence from siblings and a nationally representative sample", *Socius: Sociological Research for a Dynamic World*, 3, 2017, passim; Kochel, T. R., Wilson, D. B./Mastrofski, S. D., "Effect of suspect race on officers' arrest decisions", *Criminology*, Volume 49, Issue 2, 2011, pp. 473–512; Kirk, D. S., "The neighborhood context of racial and ethnic disparities in arrest", *Demography*, 45, 2008, pp. 55–77. See: Part IV, This chapter, Sects. 4.1.1–4.1.1.1 of this book (on biased predictive policing).

[3731] Jefferson, B., *Digitize and Punish: Racial Criminalization in the Digital Age*, Minnesota, University of Minnesota Press, 2020; Gross, Samuel R., Maurice Possley, and Kalara Stephens, "Race and Wrongful Convictions in the United States." National Registry of Exonerations, Newkirk Center for Science and Society, University of California-Irvine, 2017.

[3732] Pager, Devah, *Marked: Race, Crime, and Finding Work in an Era of Mass Incarceration*, Chicago: University of Chicago Press, 2007; Fornili, K. S., "Racialized mass incarceration and the war on drugs: A critical race theory appraisal", *Journal of Addictions Nursing*, Volume 29, Issue 1, 2018, 65–72; Jacoby, S. F., Dong, B., Beard, J. H., Wiebe, D. J., & Morrison, C. N., "The enduring impact of historical and structural racism on urban violence in Philadelphia", *Social Science & Medicine*, 1982/2018, 199, 2018, pp. 87–95; Travis, Jeremy, Bruce Western, and Steve Redburn (Eds.), *Growth of Incarceration in the United States: Exploring Causes and Consequences*, Washington, DC: National Academy of Science, 2014.

[3733] See: Connecticut Fair Housing Center, et al. v. CoreLogic Rental Property Solutions—Cohen Milstein (access: 20.11.2024). ("*The U.S. Department of Housing & Urban Development observed in 2016 that excluding rental applicants because of their criminal records disproportionately harms Latinos and African Americans, who are significantly more likely than whites to be arrested or convicted. Studies show such disparities are linked to differential enforcement rather than to differences in likelihood of engaging in criminal activity.* HUD advised that to avoid discriminating, an "individualized review" should be conducted considering the nature of the offense, how long ago it occurred, intervening changed circumstances, and other relevant factors to avoid denying housing to an applicant who does not pose a genuine and ongoing threat to persons or property. *Further, HUD's guidance specifically advises landlords not to consider arrests that did not result*

example, marijuana arrest rates vividly portray this perceived racial inequality[3734]: whilst black and white people use marijuana at roughly equal rates, black people have been arrested[3735] for marijuana many more times.[3736] The same goes for drug-related arrests[3737] in an overarching sense.[3738] Conversely, Department of Justice investigations has[3739] unravelled rampant racial disparities in arrest rates[3740] in New Orleans,

in a conviction in making their evaluations"). Italics added. See: Part IV, This chapter, Sects. 4.1.4–4.1.4.2.1 of this book (on mortgage redlining). See: Part IV, This chapter, Sects. 4.1.2–4.1.4.3 of this book (on algorithmic credit scoring, consumer racism and credit card redlining). See: Part IV, This chapter, Sects. 4.1.4–4.1.4.2.3 of this book (on algorithmic redlining). See: Part IV, This chapter, Sect. 4.1.4.3 of this book (on "algorithmic redliking"). See: Part IV, This chapter, Sect. 4.1.3 of this book (on algorithmic prime-lining).

3734 Andersen, T. S, "Race, Ethnicity, and Structural Variations in Youth Risk of Arrest: Evidence from a National Longitudinal Sample", *Criminal Justice and Behavior*, Volume 42, Issue 9, 2015, pp. 900–916; Stevenson, M. T./Slobogin, C., "Algorithmic risk assessments and the double-edged sword of youth", *Washington University Law Review*, Volume 96, 2018, passim.

3735 Hannah-Moffat, Kelly, "A Conceptual Kaleidoscope: Contemplating "Dynamic Structural Risk" and an Uncoupling of Risk from Need", *Psychology, Crime and Law*, Volume 22, 2016, pp. 33–35.

3736 Mayson, Sandra G., "Bias In, Bias Out", *cit.*, pp. 2218–2300 (2255).

3737 Mitchell, O./Caudy, M. S., "Examining racial disparities in drug arrests", *Justice Quarterly*, Volume 32, Issue 2, 2015, pp. 288–313.

3738 See, e.g., Model Penal Code § 1.02(2), Reporters' Note 31 (American Law Institute, Proposed Final Draft 2017) (arguing that racial disparities in sentencing often arise from racial skew in law enforcement "are largest for crimes at the low end of the seriousness scale—especially drug offenses," and collecting sources); Gase, Lauren Nichol et al., "Understanding Racial and Ethnic Disparities in Arrest: The Role of Individual, Home, School, and Community Characteristics", *Race and Social Problems*, Volume 8, 2016, pp. 296, 304–08 (coming up with the conclusion according to which "that racial/ethnic differences in arrest were not explained by differences in individual-level delinquent behaviors," but were explained by "neighbourhood racial composition"); Lum, Kristian/Isaac, William, To Predict and Serve?", *Significance*, 2016, pp. 14, 19 (discussing bigoted predictive policing that target primarily members of racialized communities); Huizinga, David, et al., "Disproportionate Minority Contact in the Juvenile Justice System: A Study of Differential Minority Arrest/Referral to Court in Three Cities", See: Part IV, This chapter, Sects. 4.1.1–4.1.1.1 of this book (on biased predictive policing).

3739 Mayson, Sandra G., "Bias In, Bias Out", *cit.*, pp. 2218–2300 (2255).

3740 Western, Bruce, *Punishment and Inequality in America*, New York: Russell Sage Foundation, 2006; Soss, Joe, Richard C. Fording, and Sanford F. Schram, *Disciplining the Poor: Neoliberal Paternalism and the Persistent Power of Race*, Chicago: University of Chicago Press, 2011; Laub, John H., "Understanding Inequality and the Justice System Response: Charting a New Way Forward.", New York: William T. Grant Foundation, 2014. See: Part IV, This chapter, Sects. 4.1.1–4.1.1.1 of this book (on biased predictive policing).

Ferguson, and Baltimore that are not easily explainable on the basis of underlying crime rates[3741] alone.[3742]

§§ With this context in place, pundits have neither been self-effacing nor diffident in eagerly rebuking such distortions to police data while emphasizing that the disparities are so conspicuous that such batch of data should never be taken into account to estimate crime patterns. Instead, such a cluster of rigged data[3743] should be used to document «the practices, policies, biases, and political and financial accounting needs of a given [police] department».[3744]

§§ Insofar that racial disparities in past-arrest rates flows from disparate law enforcement practice, that distortion converts «future arrest» into a racially skewed proxy for «future crime». Hardly any surprise springs from the fact that a black and a white defendant who are equally likely to perpetrate crime, chances are that the black defendant will most likely to be arrested on sight.[3745]

§§ Compellingly, the fact that a black defendant is much more likely to be arrested might not mean such a defendant is more likely to perpetrate crime. There is therefore a myriad of reasons to keenly believe that tools appraising the likelihood of «any arrest» might be racially bigoted insofar a given score—which echoes, to some extent,

---

[3741] Mayson, Sandra G., "Bias In, Bias Out", *cit.*, pp. 2218–2300 (2256).

[3742] Baltimore Investigation, *cit.*, p. 72 ("In sum, [the Baltimore Police Department]'s stops, searches, and arrests disproportionately impact African Americans and predominantly African-American neighbourhoods and cannot be explained by population patterns, crime rates, or other race-neutral factors."); Ferguson Investigation, *cit.*, pp. 62–79 (concluding that dramatic racial disparities in traffic stops, citations, and arrests were "not the necessary or unavoidable results of legitimate public safety efforts" and "stem[med] in part from intentional discrimination"); Civil Rights Div., Investigation of the New Orleans Police Department, U.S. DEP'T JUST. 34 (Mar. 16, 2011), https://www.justice.gov/sites/default/files/crt/legacy/2011/03/17/nopd_report.pdf; [https://perma.cc/Z5VP-84B7] [hereinafter New Orleans Investigation] (concluding that there is a "reasonable cause to believe that there is a pattern or practice of unconstitutional conduct and/or violations of federal law with respect to discriminatory policing"), *cit.*, p. 39 (concluding that "the level of [racial] disparity [in arrests] for youth is so severe and so divergent from nationally reported data that it cannot plausibly be attributed entirely to the underlying rates at which these youth commit crimes"); Richardson, Rashida, et al., "Dirty Data, Bad Predictions: How Civil Rights Violations Impact Police Data, Predictive Policing Systems, and Justice", *New York University Law Review Online*, Volume 94, 2019, passim.

[3743] But see: Barocas, Solon/Selbst, Andrew D., "Big Data's Disparate Impact", *California Law Review*, Volume 104, 2016, pp. 671–682 (discussing how data is often flawed, rigged, incomplete, imperfect and therefore algorithms inherit the prejudice of the original decision makers). But see: Citron, Danielle Keats/Pasquale, Frank, "The Scored Society: Due Process for Automated Predictions", *Washington Law Review*, Volume 89, 2014, pp. 1, 4–5 (highlighting how human beings programming automated systems is directly conducive to, and leads, to fundamentally inaccurate results since the source code, predictive algorithms and datasets may encompass human biases which, in turn, have a disparate impact on historically disadvantaged groups).

[3744] Mayson, Sandra G., "Bias In, Bias Out", *cit.*, pp. 2218–2300 (2256).

[3745] Mayson, Sandra G., "Bias In, Bias Out", *cit.*, pp. 2218–2300 (2256).

the likelihood of future arrest—will inevitably correspond a different risk of crime perpetration for black versus white[3746] defendants.[3747]

§§ Notably, the algorithmic tool will routinely underscore the riskiness/dangerousness of black men as opposed to other racial groups.[3748] Predictive disparities created by this type of distortion are at times coined «irrational discrimination»,[3749] since the disparity fails to accurately track the underlying reality of crime rates across racial lines.[3750] It has been argued that this predicament can be solved

---

[3746] See: Lum, Kristian, "Limitations of Mitigating Judicial Bias with Machine Learning", Nature Human Behaviour, 2017.

[3747] Mayson, Sandra G., "Bias In, Bias Out", *cit.*, pp. 2218–2300 (2257).

[3748] Crawford, Kate/Schultz, Jason, "Big Data and Due Process: Toward a Framework to Redress Predictive Privacy Harms", *Boston College Law Review*, Volume 55, 2014, pp. 93, 99–101 (pinpointing pathways through which predictive analytic tools perpetuate discriminatory practices).

[3749] See: Kim, Pauline T., "Data-Driven Discrimination at Work", *cit.*, p. 866 ("*classification bias* occurs when employers rely on classification schemes, such as data algorithms, to sort or score workers in ways that worsen inequality or disadvantage along the lines of race, sex, or other protected characteristics"). These two uses of the word "bias" correspond to the notions of irrational versus rational **(or statistical) discrimination.** See also: Prince, Anya E.R., "Insurance Risk Classification in an Era of Genomics: Is a Rational Discrimination Policy Rational?", *Nebraska Law Review*, Volume 96, 2018, pp. 624, 630–34, 641–42 (shedding light on "fair" and "unfair" discrimination). Note, though, that the word "discrimination" can also be used in a technical legal sense. In this sense it would mean that such differential treatment or disparate impact would incur in liability to the fullest extent of antidiscrimination law. See: Mayson, Sandra G., "Bias In, Bias Out", *cit.*, pp. 2218–2300.

[3750] None of this is to suggest, nor is to say, that mere disparate impact alone is of scant importance in that is not a relevant issue raised by both big data and algorithms. See, e.g.: Bartlett, Robert/Morse, Adair/Stanton, Richard/Wallace, Nancy, "Consumer-Lending Discrimination in the FinTech Era 4 (Nat'l Bureau of Econ. Research, Working Paper No. 25943"), 2019, passim (concludes that disparate impact extracts as much rents as face-to-face discrimination). It bears mentioning that scorching issue of whether and to what extent disparate impact alone should be actionable is different from, in that does not overlap with, the sweltering issue of proxy discrimination. See: Cohran, Matthew Jordan, "Fairness in Disparity: Challenging the Application of Disparate Impact Theory in Fair Housing Claims Against Insurers", *The George Mason University Civil Rights Law Journal*, Volume 21, 2011, pp. 159 and ff and passim (discussing the use of disparate impact theory and potential applicability to Fair Housing Act claims against insurers).

through the choice[3751] of a different target variable,[3752] one that reliably reflects the event we strive to forecast without embedding further racial skew.[3753]

4.1.10.3.5 Do Disparate Rates of Crime Commission Explain the Racial Inequality in Past-Crime Data Instead? §§ The second line of explanation for racial disparity in past-arrest rates lies in the difference in the underlying incidence of crime. It oft-averred that crime is a byproduct of a set of complex social and economic markers that, in a racial stratified world, has every chance to correlate with a cluster of demographic traits. For that reason, the incidence of a **particular category of crime** may vary widely across racial lines.[3754]

§§ In this vein, bodies of empirical evidence have found, for example, that present-day white and Hispanic college students use illegal drugs at exceedingly higher rates than African American and Asian[3755] students.[3756] White folks have perpetrated the overwhelming majority of mass shootings in the United States of America during the last thirty years alone.[3757] On the flip side, gun-related murder rates have been

---

[3751] But see: Barocas, Solon/Selbst, Andrew D., "Big Data's Disparate Impact", *cit.*, pp. 692–93. These polymaths coined this phenomenon as "masking" owing to the fact that machine-learning technologies bestow upon stakeholders' multiple opportunities to intentionally twist/warp/deform an algorithm in ways that are painstakingly difficult to ferret out/discern/detect/pinpoint.

[3752] But see: Corbett-Davies, Sam/Goel, Sharad, "The Measure and Mismeasure of Fairness: a critical Review of Fair Machine Learning", *Cornell University Library*, 2018, p. 18 (broaches a type of *measurement bias* coined "feature bias," which is neatly a bias in the predictors x. Note, though, that there is a second type of measurement bias deemed "label bias," which, in turn, amounts to a bias in y. The authors argue that that label bias is the worst bias there is); Kleinberg, Jon/Ludwig, Jens/Mullainathan, Sendhil/Sunstein Cass R., "Discrimination in the Age of Algorithms", *Journal of Legal Analysis*, Volume 10, 1, 2018, pp. 28–29, 33–34 (draw a distinction between "group differences in the raw data" and biases for the "choice of predictors").

[3753] See: Mayson, Sandra G., "Bias In, Bias Out", *cit.*, pp. 2218–2300.

[3754] Mayson, Sandra G., "Bias In, Bias Out", *cit.*, pp. 2218–2300 (2257).

[3755] See: McCabe, Sean Esteban McCabe et al., "Race/Ethnicity and Gender Differences in Drug Use and Abuse Among College Students", *Journal of Ethnicity Substance Abuse*, Volume 6, 2007, p. 75 (bringing to the fore compelling "evidence from one university that Hispanic and White undergraduate students were at increased risk for drug use and abuse" and discussing related literature).

[3756] Mayson, Sandra G., "Bias In, Bias Out", *cit.*, pp. 2218–2300 (2257).

[3757] Number of Mass Shootings in the United States between 1982 and November 2018, by Shooter's Race and Ethnicity, Statistical, https://www.statista.com/statistics/476456/mass-shootings-in-the-us-by-shooter-s-race; [https://perma.cc/238C-PVZR].

higher in black communities than in white ones. Note, though, that the measure of disparity varies greatly across[3758] states.[3759]

§§ Compellingly, high-stakes financial crimes («white-collar crime»)[3760] are incommensurately perpetrated by people working in the higher echelons of financial-services corporations, and these folks are incommensurately white[3761] men.[3762] In the Broward County data, similarly in other datasets used to carry out risk-assessment surveys, arrest rates for crimes labelled as «violent» were higher among the black population than the white population.[3763] Relatedly, Jennifer Skeem and Christopher Lowenkamp have contended that the disparity reflects differential crime rates, as opposed to biased law enforcement[3764] practices.[3765]

§§ The point being if underlying crime rates do vary greatly across racial lines in the data upon which a particular machine learning algorithm is designed,

---

[3758] See: Cooper, Alexia/Smith, Erica L., "Homicide Trends in the United States, 1980–2008", *United States Department of Justice*, 11 (Nov. 2011), https://www.bjs.gov/content/pub/pdf/htus8008.pdf; [https://perma.cc/88XB-M3ZV]; Planty/Michael/Truman, Jennifer L., "Firearm Violence, 1993–2011", *United States Department of Justice*, 5 (May 2013), https://www.bjs.gov/content/pub/pdf/fv9311.pdf; [https://perma.cc/B2Y4-5XSW] (showing rates of firearm victimization by race). See also: Riddell, Corinne A. et al., "Comparison of Rates of Firearm and Nonfirearm Homicide and Suicide in Black and White Non-Hispanic Men, by U.S. State", *Annals of Internal Medicine*, Volume 168, 2018, p. 712.

[3759] Mayson, Sandra G., "Bias In, Bias Out", *cit.*, pp. 2218–2300 (2258).

[3760] See in Spanish doctrine: Gómez-Jara Díez, Carlos, *Autorregulación y responsabilidad de las personas jurídicas*, Peru, ARA Editores, 2015; Coca Vila, Ivó, ¿"Programas de cumplimiento como forma de autorregulación regulada?", Silva Sánchez, Jesús María (Dir.), *Criminalidad de empresa y compliance: prevención y reacciones corporativas*, Barcelona, Atelier. See also: Soltes, Eugene, *Why They Do It: Inside the Mind of the White-Collar Criminal*. New York: Public Affairs, 2018, pp. 1–464.

[3761] See: Clifton, Brian et al., "Predicting Financial Crime: Augmenting the Predictive Policing Arsenal", *New Inquiry*, (Apr. 25, 2017), https://whitecollar.thenewinquiry.com/static/whitepaper.pdf; [https://perma.cc/QS9Y-JDG6] (summarizing data on location of financial crimes); Jones, Stacy, "White Men Account for 72% of Corporate Leadership at 16 of the Fortune 500 Companies", *Fortune* (June 9, 2017), https://fortune.com/2017/06/09/white-men-senior-executives-fortune-500-companies-diversity-data; [https://perma.cc/67YB-ZYKR]; Susan E. Reed, Corporate Boards Are Diversifying. The C-suite Isn't., WASH. POST (Jan. 6, 2019), https://www.washingtonpost.com/outlook/corporate-boards-are-diversifying-the-c-suite-isnt/2019/01/04/c45c3328-0f02-11e9-8938-5898adc28fa2; [https://perma.cc/X3YL-HXLG]. Clifton, Lavigne, and Tseng offer a new predictive technology "trained on incidents of financial malfeasance from 1964 to the present day, collected from the Financial Industry Regulatory Authority (FINRA)." Clifton, Brian et al., "White Collar Crime Risk Zones", *New Inquiry* (Apr. 26, 2017), https://thenewinquiry.com/white-collar-crime-risk-zones; [https://perma.cc/2K85-3VCP]. *Apud*: Mayson, Sandra G., "Bias In, Bias Out", *cit.*, pp. 2218–2300.

[3762] Mayson, Sandra G., "Bias In, Bias Out", *cit.*, pp. 2218–2300 (2258).

[3763] But see: Harris, Grant T./Rice, Marnie E., "Bayes and Base Rates: What Is an Informative Prior for Actuarial Violence Risk Assessment?", *Behavioural Science and Law*, Volume 31, 2013, pp. 103, 121 ("What is not axiomatic is the straightforward application of assumptions about priors... to violence risk assessment—that remains a set of important empirical matters."); See: Mayson, Sandra G., "Bias In, Bias Out", *cit.*, pp. 2218–2300. See also: Selbst, Andrew D., "Disparate Impact in Big Data Policing", *cit.*, pp. 140–43.

racial disparity in prediction[3766] is not only inescapable,[3767] but, and foremost, ineluctable.[3768]

§§ This is not rocket science after all: algorithmic prediction, as hinted above, lends itself to a reflecting mirror that projects the biased past into the forthcoming future. If the black population in the relevant data is statistically riskier with regard to

---

[3764] It is often stated that the close connection between arrest rates and crime-report rates by race is one fact that pundits routinely use as evidence that arrest rates are fundamentally bereft of racial bias regarding offending rates. See: Skeem, Jennifer L./Lowenkamp, Christopher T, "Risk, Race, and Recidivism: Predictive Bias and Disparate Impact", *Criminology*, Volume 54, 2016, pp. 680, 683–84, 704–06 (690). But see: Stevenson, Megan/Mayson, Sandra, "The Scale of Misdemeanor Justice", *Boston University Law Review*, Volume 98, 2018, pp. 731, 758–63 (arguing that "the [national] black arrest rate [for an index of misdemeanor offenses] has hovered around 1.7 times the white arrest rate since 1980").

[3765] Mayson, Sandra G., "Bias In, Bias Out", *cit.*, pp. 2218–2300.

[3766] See: Kirkpatrick, Keith, "It's not the Algorithm, it's the Data", *Communications of the ACM*, February 2017, Volume 60, n.° 2, 2017 ("tools such as *PredPol* and *CommandCentral are inherently biased since they rely heavily on reported crimes data, which is often concentrated in areas that are heavily policed, thereby skewing statistics to overrepresent poor or minority communities. "We know that we have a history of racially biased policing in the United States, and that has fed into all the data that we have on where arrests have occurred, which crimes are more likely to occur in specific communities, and at which particular times,"* says Jennifer Lynch, senior staff attorney at the Electronic Frontier Foundation. "*That's the data that's being fed into predictive policing algorithms*"). Italics added.

[3767] See: Skeem, Jennifer L./Lowenkamp, Christopher T., "Risk, Race, and Recidivism: Predictive Bias and Disparate Impact", *cit.*, p. 690 (arguing that arrest for a "violent offense" is a "valid criterion"). Converging: Piquero, Alex R. et al., "A Systematic Review of Age, Sex, Ethnicity, and Race as Predictors of Violent Recidivism", *International Journal Offender Therapy & Comp. Criminology*, Volume 59, 2015, pp. 5, 17 (finding "that age, sex, and race... were significantly related to violent recidivism"). But see: Selbst, Andrew D., "Disparate Impact in Big Data Policing", *Georgia Law Review*, Volume 52, 2017, p. 167 ("[I]t may be impossible to tell when the disparate impact truly reflects reality").

[3768] The «excruciating» *headaches* that the criminal law evangelists have been enduring for quite a while are not to stave off anytime soon. Quite the opposite, they are about to flare up. The sizzling hot challenges posed by artificial intelligence amidst a *RisikoGesellschaft* (*society of risk* or *sociedad de riesgo*) elicits nothing but a widespread concern on the effectiveness of the systems of administration of justice (or lack thereof) to deal with it. On the *dark side*, one can aver that the interplay between the challenges posed by artificial intelligence on the purview of a transnational and global society is bound to tear down the building blocks in which the former sits. If that happens, criminal law would morph into a merely symbolic field of law pursuant its incapability to make *collective sensemaking*. See in Spanish doctrine on the interplay between *sociedad de riesgo* and the challenges arisen from it: Sánchez, Bernardo Feijoo, "Sobre la «administrativizácion» del Derecho penal en la «sociedad de riesgo»: un apunte sobre la política criminal a princípios del diglo XXI", *Derecho Y Justicia Penal en el Siglo XXI. Liber Amicorum en Homenaje al Profesor Antonio González-Cuéllar Garcia*, Madrid, Ed. Colex, 2006, pp. 137 ff. On the peril of criminal law becoming a *Symbolisches Strafrecht*: Hassemer, Winfried, "Symbolisches Strafrecht und Rechtsgüterschutz", *NSTZ*, München, Volume 89, 2014, pp. 557 ff and *passim*. It is believed that *RisikoGesellschaft* is putting the fundamental tenets of criminal law in jeopardy. The sub-prime crisis of 2008 (whose deleterious effects are shaping up to be compounded by the worldwide pandemic spawned by Covid-19) laid bare the insufficiency—the lacklustre of, coupled with, the dearth of—basic assumptions of criminal law to tackle transnational and globalized white-collar crime. In the wake of which a cohort of scholars boded the system's failure (*Systemversagen*).

the labelled type of crime, risk-assessment tools will accordingly reflect that warped image.[3769] On the flip side, the reflecting mirror is designed to disregard this statistical fact, the sought-after **racial blindness**,[3770] which will most likely have a disparate racial[3771] impact: in affording the same treatment to both the black and white groups subject to algorithmic risk assessment as statistically uniform, the algorithmic tools will inevitably disregard[3772] more of the labelled crimes perpetrated by black individuals[3773]; crimes that, since the great bulk of criminal activities are interracial, will inordinately fall upon communities[3774] of colour.[3775]

[3769] See: Barocas, Solon/Selbst, Andrew, "Big Data's Disparate Impact", *cit.*, p. 682 ("So long as prior decisions affected by some form of prejudice serve as examples of correctly rendered determinations, data mining will necessarily infer rules that exhibit the same prejudice").

[3770] Alexander, M., *The new Jim Crow: Mass incarceration in the age of colorblindness*, The New Press, 2012.

[3771] Mayson, Sandra G., "Bias In, Bias Out", *cit.*, pp. 2218–2300 (2258).

[3772] Zemel, R./Y. Wu/K. Swersky/T. Pitassi/C. Dwork, "Learning Fair Representations", *Proceedings of Machine Learning Research*, 28 (3), 2013, pp. 325–33.

[3773] Corbett-Davies and Goel coined this sweltering issue as "label bias" and diagnose it as "perhaps the most serious obstacle facing fair machine learning." But see: Corbett-Davies, Sam/Goel, Sharad, "The Measure and Mismeasure of Fairness: a critical Review of Fair Machine Learning", *Cornell University Library*, 2018, p. 18 (broaches a type of *measurement bias* coined "feature bias," which is neatly a bias in the predictors x. Note, though, that there is a second type of measurement bias deemed "label bias," which, in turn, amounts to a bias in y. The authors argue that that label bias is the worst bias there is).

[3774] See: Mayson, Sandra G., "Bias In, Bias Out", *cit.*, pp. 2218–2300 (noting that the notion that differential crime rates depict a difference in innate criminal proclivity has been signalled as the rationale behind the racist theoretical underpinnings and accompanying discriminatory practices). Converging: Kennedy, Randall, *Race, Crime, and the Law*, New York, Vintage, Reprint Edition, 1997, pp. 1–560 (pp. 137 and ff and passim) (parsing race relations in the administration of criminal justice) ("*in this groundbreaking, powerfully reasoned, lucid work that is certain to provoke controversy, Harvard law professor Randall Kennedy takes on a highly complex issue in a way that no one has before. Kennedy uncovers the long-standing failure of the justice system to protect blacks from criminals, probing allegations that blacks are victimized on a widespread basis by racially discriminatory prosecutions and punishments, but he also engages the debate over the wisdom and legality of using racial criteria in jury selection.* He analyzes the responses of the legal system to accusations that appeals to racial prejudice have rendered trials unfair, and examines the idea that, under certain circumstances, members of one race are statistically more likely to be involved in crime than members of another"). Italics added. Converging: Russel-Brown, Katheryn, *The Color of Crime, (Second Edition): Racial Hoaxes, White Fear, Black Protectionism, Police Harassment, and Other Macroaggressions (Critical America, 45)*, New York, New York University Press, 2012, pp. 1–220 ("when *The Color of Crime* was first published ten years ago, it was heralded as a path-breaking book on race and crime. Now, in its tenth anniversary year, Katheryn Russell-Brown's book is more relevant than ever. *The Jena Six, Duke Lacrosse Team, Amadou Diallo, Sean Bell, James Byrd, and all of those victimized in the aftermath of Hurricane Katrina are just a few of the racially fueled cases that have made headlines in the past decade. Russell-Brown continues to ask, why do Black and White Americans perceive police actions so differently*? Is White fear of Black crime justified? Do African Americans really protect their own? Should they? *And why are we still talking about O.J. Russell-Brown surveys the landscape of American crime and identifies some of the country's most significant racial pathologies*"). Italics added.

[3775] Mayson, Sandra G., "Bias In, Bias Out", *cit.*, pp. 2218–2300 (2259).

§§ Strikingly, regardless of how one **tweaks** the underlying data or the machine learning algorithm itself,[3776] then, inequality in commission rates for the crime(s) we

[3776] It is important to note that an algorithm designed for maximum accuracy will adjust itself to the majority data, and may be less accurate for members of the under-represented group, thus breeding *inductive bias.* See: Shellenbarger, Sue, "A Crucial Step for Avoiding AI Disasters", *Wall Street Journal,* (Feb. 13, 2019, 9:57 AM ET), https://www.wsj.com/articles/a-crucial-step-for-avoiding-ai-disasters-11550069865?ns = prod/accounts-wsj; [https://perma.cc/C28U-LAAE] (discussing this issue while emphasizing how diverse development teams pay more attention to unrepresentative and underrepresented data sets). Human programmers can circumvent and bypass this problem by weighting the minority-group data more heavily, by designing different algorithms for each racial group, or by striving to contain more data to equalize group representation in the data set. See: Barua, Sukarna et al., "MWMOTE—Majority Weighted Minority Oversampling Technique for Imbalanced Data Set Learning", *IEEE Transactions on Knowledge & Data Engineering*, Volume 26, 2014, pp. 405, 405–06. See also: Hamilton, Melissa, "The Biased Algorithm: Evidence of Disparate Impact on Hispanics", *American Criminal Law Review,* Volume 56, 2019, pp. 1553 and ff and passim (which clearly demonstrates that COMPAS was significantly less accurate for Hispanic than for white defendants by several measures and suggesting that smaller numbers of Hispanic defendants might be the cause). See: Mayson, Sandra G., "Bias In, Bias Out", *cit.*, pp. 2218–2300. See also: Dong et al., Qi, "Imbalanced deep learning by minority class incremental rectification, *IEEE Transactions on Pattern Analysis & Machine Intelligence*, Volume 41, 2019, p. 1367 (posit that "*most existing learning algorithms produce inductive bias (learning bias)* towards the frequent (majority) classes if training data are not balanced, *resulting in poor minority class recognition performance*"). Italics added. See: Chandler, Anupam, "The Racist Algorithm", *Michigan Law Review,* Volume 115, n. ° 6, 2018, p. 1026 (on racist algorithms, noting that "the possibilities for discriminatory manipulation are legion"). But see: Altenburger, Kristen M./Ho, Daniel E., "When Algorithms Import Private Bias into Public Enforcement: The Promise and Limitations of Statistical Debiasing Solutions", *Journal of Institutional & Theoretical Economics*, Volume 175, 2019, pp. 97–98 (calls for a "debias predictive algorithms" to assuage racist and/or biased, doctored and bigoted algorithms nevertheless).

endeavour to forecast will inevitably produce[3777] inequality[3778] in algorithmic prediction.[3779] It is noteworthy that, in contemplating this very possibility, to acknowledge «what any such difference in crime commission rates would and would not signify».[3780] Notably, differential crime rates do not necessarily mean a difference across racial lines in individuals' innate proclivity/proneness/penchant to engage in flagitious activities.[3781]

§§ Instead, racial disparities in crime rates echo social,[3782] racial[3783] and wealth divides.[3784] To the extent the commission of crimes of poverty[3785] and desperation[3786] differs greatly across racial lines,[3787] systemic racism,[3788] white privilege[3789]

[3777] Zafar, M. B./I. V. Martinez/M. B. Rodriguez/K. Gummadi, "Fairness Constraints: A Mechanism for Fair Classification." In Proceedings of the 20th International Conference on Artificial Intelligence and Statistics (AISTATS), Fort Lauderdale, FL, 2017.

[3778] Berk and his peers have also provided a scintillating portray of these equality/accuracy trade-offs, drawing on real arraignment data and a machine-learning algorithm that predicts new arrests for a domestic-violence offense within a period of twenty-one months. The base rate amongst black defendants was 11%, whereas the base rate amongst white defendants was 6%. Relatedly, Berk and his peers found that, if the machine learning algorithm is devised to attain predictive parity regarding to a forecast of no-rearrest, the "false negative and false positive rates vary dramatically by race." Specifically, the false negative rate is 49% for black defendants and 93% for white defendants; the false positive rate is 2% for white defendants and 24% for black defendants. See: Berk, Richard et al., "Fairness in Criminal Justice Risk Assessments: The State of the Art", *cit.*, p. 32. See: Mayson, Sandra G., "Bias In, Bias Out", *cit.*, pp. 2218–2300.

[3779] See: Berk, Richard, "Accuracy and Fairness for Juvenile Justice Risks Assessments", *Journal of Empirical Legal Studies*, Volume 16, 2019, p. 175 (comes to the terms with the fact that tweaking/altering data to attain statistical parity yielded extremely high false-negative rates); Zachary Lipton et al., "Does Mitigating ML's Impact Disparity Require Treatment Disparity?", NIPS PROC. 1 (2018), https://arxiv.org/pdf/1711.07076.pdf; [https://perma.cc/X8VF-EY53] (sets forth compelling evidence that enforced blindness to protected traits exacts a toll in accuracy); Petersilia, Joan/Turner, Susan, "Guideline-Based Justice: Prediction and Racial Minorities", *Crime and Justice*, 1987, pp. 151–174 (argues that omitting markers correlated with race from a recidivism prediction algorithm exacted a toll on the accuracy of the model).

[3780] Mayson, Sandra G., "Bias In, Bias Out", *cit.*, pp. 2218–2300 (2259). See also: Citron, Danielle Keats/Pasquale, Frank A., "The Scored Society: Due Process for Automated Predictions", *Washington Law Review*, Volume 89, 2014, pp. 1–34 (arguing that "[a]*dvocates applaud the removal of human beings and their flaws from the assessment process*," but arguing that bias remains "[*b*]*ecause human beings program predictive algorithms, their biases and values are embedded into the software's instructions*"). Italics added.

[3781] Mayson, Sandra G., "Bias In, Bias Out", *cit.*, pp. 2218–2300 (2259). See: Papachristos, Andrew V., David M. Hureau, and Anthony A. Braga, "The Corner and the Crew: The Influence of Geography and Social Networks on Gang Violence", *American Sociological Review*, 78 (3), 2013, pp. 417–47; Quillian, Lincoln, and Devah Pager, "Black Neighbors, Higher Crime? The Role of Racial Stereotypes in Evaluations of Neighborhood Crime", *American Journal of Sociology*, 107 (3), 2001, 717–67.

[3782] Zuboff, Zhoshana, *The Age of Surveillance Capitalism, The Fight for a Human Future at the New Frontier of Power*. New Yor City: PublicAffairs Books, 2019, pp. 1–704 (360) (argues that we are indomitably heading towards a "instrumentarianism" that draws on "totalitarianism").

[3783] Maxwell, J./Tomlinson, J., *Experiments in Automating Immigration Systems*. Bristol: Bristol University Press, 2022, passim; Borgesius, FJ Zuiderveen, "Strengthening legal protection against discrimination by algorithms and artificial intelligence", *International Journal of Human Rights*, Volume 24, Issue 10, 2020, pp. 1573 and ff and passim.

and white supremacy[3790] have jointly marginalized/insulated/cloistered communities of colour while depriving them from sorely needed resources and long-sought[3791] opportunities.[3792]

[3784] Derenoncourt, Ellora/Kim, Chi Hyun/Kuhn, Moritz/Schularik, Moritz, "The Wealth of Two Nations: The U.S. Racial Wealth Gap, 1860–2020", *The Quarterly Journal of Economics*, Volume 139, Issue 2, 2024, p. 741 ("*A large class of commonly discussed policies for reducing racial wealth inequality seeks to reduce gaps in income, savings, and capital gains.* These include policies that encourage financial diversification or stock equity holdings among Black households; policies aimed at financial literacy and retirement or savings behavior; or policies aimed at improving educational and labor market outcomes of Black Americans through improved school quality or reductions in discrimination. *Yet on a realistic note, our simulation in Section IV.A shows that even if wealth accumulation conditions had been equal since 1870, the wealth gap would still be 3 to 1 today, and full convergence would be more than 200 years away. Put differently: to close the racial wealth gap in the immediate term* via *flow parameters, Black Americans would need a substantial positive lead over whites, not "just" more equality*"). Italics added.

[3785] Quadagno, Jill, *The Color of Welfare: How Racism Undermined the War on Poverty*, Oxford, Oxford University Press, 1994, pp. 1–272 ("*From Reconstruction to Lyndon Johnson and beyond, Quadagno reveals how American social policy has continually foundered on issues of race. Drawing on extensive primary research, Quadagno shows, for instance, how Roosevelt, in need of support from southern congressmen, excluded African Americans from the core programs of the Social Security Act. Turning to Lyndon Johnson's "unconditional war on poverty," she contends that though anti-poverty programs for job training, community action, health care, housing, and education have accomplished much, they have not been fully realized because they became inextricably intertwined with the civil rights movement of the 1960s, which triggered a white backlash*"). Italics added. See: Part IV, This chapter, Sects. 4.1.4–4.1.4.2.3 of this book. But see: Johnson, Creola, "The Magic of Group Identity: How Predatory Lenders Use Minorities to Target Communities of Color", *Georgetown Journal on Poverty Law and Policy*, 2010, pp. 165–169 (fleshing out several aggressive marketing tactics used by unprincipled/unscrupulous lenders to target primarily minorities for eerily predatory loans). Alessina, A./Glaeser EL., *Fighting poverty in the US and Europe*, Oxford, Oxford University Press, 2013, passim.

[3786] Desmond, M., *Evicted: Poverty and profit in the American city*, First Edition, New York, Crown Publishers, 2016, passim. See also: Baradaran, Mehrsa, "Banking and the Social Contract", *Notre Dame Law Review*, Volume 89, pp. 1283–1336 ("access to safe credit is crucial in allowing the poor to escape poverty"). But see: Atkinson, Abbye, "Rethinking Credit as a Social Provision", *Stanford Law Review*, Volume 71, 2019, pp. 1093–1099 (contending that credit, which shifts consumption temporally, is only beneficial insofar income ratchets up in the forthcoming future. As of now, though, "credit is fundamentally incompatible with the entrenched intergenerational poverty that plagues low-income Americans." Id. Notably, it is crucially important to come to terms with the fact that credit is not a panacea for the great bulk of economic struggles, and concretely wage stagnation. Although credit is not befitted to all consumers at all prices, affordable credit can nonetheless play a pivotal role in the creation of wealth).

[3787] Jefferson, B., *Digitize and Punish: Racial Criminalization in the Digital Age*, Minnesota, University of Minnesota Press, 2020. EUR-Lex Everatt D., "The undeserving poor: poverty and the politics of service delivery in the poorest nodes of South Africa", *Politikon*, Volume 35, 2009, pp. 293–319.

[3788] See: Feagin, J. R., *Systemic racism: a theory of oppression*, New York: Routledge, 2006. See also: Fiske, John, "Surveilling the City: Whiteness, the Black Man and Democratic Totalitarianism.", *Theory, Culture and Society*, 15 (2), 1998, pp. 67–88 (on the overhyped surveillance on black people as a byproduct of systemic racism).

[3789] Bhopal, K., *White Privilege: The Myth of a Post-Racial Society*, Bristol, Policy Press Bristol University Press, 2018; Jackson, E. K., *Scandinavians in Chicago: The Origins of White Privilege*

§§ To the extent race and gender differences are extant and pervasive in the rate of high-stakes financial crime, it is because white folks hold onto, in that they seldom relinquish over, control of the higher echelons of finance. Crime rates form part of a broader social apparatus within which racial inequalities operate. Racial fluctuations in crime rates reflect the gross social[3793] and economic inequality[3794] generated by a long-winded span of time of racial divides[3795] that still resonates today.[3796]

4.1.10.3.6 Would Regulating Input Variables Suffice to Attain Racial Equality in Algorithmic Risk Assessment? The Myth of Colour-Blindness Is in Dire Need

in Modern America, Chicago, Illinois, University of Illinois Press, 2019; Rothenberg, P. S., *White Privilege*, 2015, Google Books.

3790 Perea, Juan F., "Doctrines of Delusion: How the History of the G.I. Bill and Other Inconvenient Truths Undermind the Supreme Court's Affirmative Action Jurisprudence", *University of Pittsburgh Law Review*, Volume 75, 1995, pp. 583, 586–89 (establishes a liaison between Jim Crow laws, the G.I. Bill, and the Social Security Act and White supremacy); Milligan, Joy, "Protecting Disfavored Minorities: Towards Institutional Realism", *UCLA Law Review*, Volume 63, 2016, pp. 894, pp. 918–21 (shedding a keen light on racial inequality in U.S. Department of Agriculture farm assistance); Robinson, Reginald Leamon, "The Racial Limits of the Fair Housing Act: The Intersection of Dominant White Images, the Violence of Neighborhood Purity, and the Master Narrative of Black Inferiority", *William & Mary Law Review*, Volume 37, 1995, pp. 69, 71–74 (establishes a connection between the failures of the FHA and White supremacy). But see: Wormser, Richard, *The Rise and Fall of Jim Crow*, Manhattan, New York City, St Martin's Press, 2014, pp. 1–222 ("*White supremacy prevailed, but it did not destroy the spirit of the black community*"). Italics added.

3791 Reis, E./Moore, M./Clarke, G. et al, *Elite perceptions on poverty and inequality*, Zed Books, London, 2005; Yapa, L., "How the discipline of geography exacerbates poverty in the Third World", *Futures*, Volume 3, 2022, pp. 33–46.

3792 Mayson, Sandra G., "Bias In, Bias Out", *cit.*, pp. 2218–2300 (2259).

3793 Gustafson, Kaaryn S, *Cheating Welfare: Public Assistance and the Criminalization of Poverty*, New York: NYU Press, 2011.

3794 See: Kroeger, Teresa, and Graham Wright, "Entrepreneurship and the Racial Wealth Gap: The Impact of Entrepreneurial Success or Failure on the Wealth Mobility of Black and White Families," *Journal of Economics, Race, and Policy*, Volume 4, 2021, 183–195; Kermani, Amir, and Francis Wong, "Racial Disparities in Housing Returns," NBER Working Paper no. 29306, 2021; Hubmer, Joachim, Per Krusell, and Anthony A. Smith, Jr., "Sources of US Wealth Inequality: Past, Present, and Future," *NBER Macroeconomics Annual 2020*, Volume 35, 2021, pp. 391–455; Haines, Michael R., *Historical, Demographic, Economic, and Social Data: The United States, 1790–2002*, Inter-university Consortium for Political and Social Research, 2010: On whiteness: Frankenberg, Ruth (Ed.), *Displacing whiteness: essays in social and cultural criticism*, Durham, NC: Duke University Press, 1997; Frankenberg, Ruth, "Introduction: local whitenesses, localizing whiteness", *Displacing whiteness*, Ruth Frankenberg (Editor), Durham, NC: Duke University Press, 1997, pp. 1–33. See also: Saez, Emmanuel, and Gabriel Zucman, "The Rise of Income and Wealth Inequality in America: Evidence from Distributional Macroeconomic Accounts," *Journal of Economic Perspectives*, Volume 34, 2020, pp. 3–26; O'Neil, Cathy, *Weapons of Math Destruction. How Big Data Increases Inequality and Threatens Democracy*, London, Penguin Random House, 2016, passim (showing how algorithms utilized in modern societies are amenable to perpetuate racial discrimination, partially through perpetuation of social disadvantage and wealth divides).

3795 Milligan, Joy, "Protecting Disfavored Minorities: Towards Institutional Realism", *UCLA Law Review*, Volume 63, 2016, pp. 918–921 (delves into the racial inequality in United States of America's Department of Agriculture farm aid to both Whites and Blacks).

3796 Mayson, Sandra G., "Bias In, Bias Out", *cit.*, pp. 2218–2300 (2259).

of Quashing §§ Input variables are oft-mentioned as embodying the overriding concern in the hot pursuit for racial equity in the remit of algorithmic risk assessment. Scholars have not been slow to trot out, nor have they refrained themselves from rattling off, that race, as an input variable, is in dire need[3797] of quashing.[3798] Strikingly, there is no paucity of scholars that extend this sweeping principle to input variables that correlate with race in a given place, like zip[3799] code.[3800]

§§ The overriding concern is that which the use of such risk markers will inevitably produce higher risk scores for black defendants,[3801] thereby further compounding historical racial oppression[3802] with which the latter have been grappling for a long-haul. As Professor Sandra G. Mayson puts it, the sharper focus on input variables, however, amounts to anything but to an effective approach to attaining a sough-after racial equity. There are several reasons for this. The most prominent of which is that merely eliminating race[3803]—alongside proxies to race[3804]—has every chance

[3797] Mayson, Sandra G., "Bias In, Bias Out", *cit.*, pp. 2218–2300 (2263).

[3798] See: Starr, Sonja B., "Evidence-Based Sentencing and the Scientific Rationalization of Discrimination", *cit.*, p. 812 ("there appears to be a general consensus that using race would be unconstitutional").

[3799] Mayson, Sandra G., "Bias In, Bias Out", *cit.*, pp. 2218–2300 (2263).

[3800] Corbett-Davies & Goel, *cit.*, p. 8 ("[S]everal papers have suggested algorithms that enforce a broad notion of anti-classification, which prohibits not only the explicit use of protected traits but also the use of potentially suspect 'proxy' variables").

[3801] Angwin, Julia et al., "Machine Bias", *ProPublica* (May 23, 2016), https://www.propublica.org/article/machine-bias-risk-assessments-in-criminal-sentencing [https://perma.cc/4G83-MDAS] (harshly criticizing disparity in false-positive rates as a purely unjustified bias). See also: Freeman, Katherine, "Algorithmic Injustice: How the Wisconsin Supreme Court Failed to Protect Due Process Rights in State v. Loomis", *North Carolina Journal of Law and Technology*, Volume 18, 2016, pp. 75–86 (echoing the very same views).

[3802] For instance, a feted scholar (Bernard Harcourt) adamantly contends that (1) predictive crime control efforts may produce more harm than good; (2) they may engender a "ratchet effect" in which the disparate impact of forecast on black folks worsens over time; and (3) the technological allure of prediction can both besmirch and mar deep-rooted moral conceptions of justice. See: Harcourt, Bernard E., *Against Prediction: Profiling, Policing, and Punishing in An Actuarial Age*, Chicago, Illinois, University of Chicago Press, 2007, pp. 7–18 and passim. Converging: Ensign, Danielle, "Runaway Feedback Loops in Predictive Policing", *Proceedings of Machine Learning Research*, Volume 81, 2018, p. 1; Starr, Sonja B., "Evidence-Based Sentencing and the Scientific Rationalization of Discrimination", *Stanford Law Review*, Volume 66, 2014, pp. 804–06 (arguing that that risk assessment during sentencing may derails deep-seated concepts of justice that we hold so dear). In addition to this line of reasoning, Professor Sandra Mayson avers that, because any extant racial disparity in crime risk is the byproduct of a long-haul historical oppression, it is therefore an unfitting basis for coercive state action. To put it bluntly, it is unfair for the state to condition coercion on crime risk that modern societies have unjustly created. Put another way, one may be led to believe that the data are simply warped and that the risk at hand is fundamentally uniform across racial lines. Understandably, though not laudably, one may be also led to believe that crime risk is a fundamentally haphazard and incoherent concept, owing to the fact that all people who are self-determining agents have an equal capacity to either eschew flagitious behaviour or engaging in criminal activities. See: Mayson, Sandra G., "Bias In, Bias Out", *cit.*, pp. 2218–2300.

[3803] But see: Kim, Pauline T., "Data-Driven Discrimination at Work", *William and Mary Law Review*, Volume 58, 2017, p. 918 ("If the goal is to reduce biased outcomes, then a simple prohibition on using data about race or sex could be either wholly ineffective or actually counterproductive due

of exacting a toll on black defendants.[3805] «In this context, as elsewhere, being blind to race can mean being blind to racism».[3806] Which would befall on communities of colour while sweeping aside a much-need algorithmic fairness, race wise.[3807]

§§ Professor Sandra G. Mayson, bearing this backdrop very firmly in mind, has set forth a rather illustrative example indeed. When she worked in New Orleans as a public defender, the relevance of arrest back there varied greatly across racial

to the existence of class proxies and the risk of omitted variable bias."); Lipton, Zachary et al., "Does Mitigating ML's Impact Disparity Require Treatment Disparity?", NIPS Proceedings 1, 2018, https://arxiv.org/pdf/1711.07076.pdf [https://perma.cc/X8VF-EY53] (arguing, premised on statistical examples, that a prohibition on race or sex data is rather counterproductive indeed); Corbett-Davies, Sam/Goel, Sharad, "The Measure and Mismeasure of Fairness: a critical Review of Fair Machine Learning", *Cornell University Library*, 2018, passim (discussing the "[l]imitations of anti-classification" as a fairness metric). See also: Kim, Pauline T., "Data-Driven Discrimination at Work", *cit.*, p. 867 ("[I]f the goal is to discourage *classification bias*, then the law should not forbid the inclusion of race, sex, or other sensitive information as variables, but seek to preserve these variables, and perhaps even include them in some complex models"). Italics added. See also: Kroll, Joshua A., et al., "Accountable Algorithms", *University of Pennsylvania Law Review*, Volume 165, 2017, pp. 633, 693–95. See also: Kim, Pauline T., "Data-Driven Discrimination at Work", *cit.*, p. 866 ("classification bias occurs when employers rely on classification schemes, such as data algorithms, to sort or score workers in ways that worsen inequality or disadvantage along the lines of race, sex, or other protected characteristics"). These two uses of the word "bias" correspond to the notions of irrational versus rational **(or statistical) discrimination.** See: Mayson, Sandra G., "Bias In, Bias Out", *cit.*, pp. 2218–2300.

[3804] See: Prince, Anya E. R./Schwarcz, Daniel, "Proxy Discrimination in the Age of Artificial Intelligence and Big Data", *Iowa Law Review*, Volume 105, 2020, pp. 1257, 1279–81 ("[*P*]*roxy discrimination will tend to occur when a suspect variable is predictive of a desired outcome only because it proxies for another*, quantifiable and potentially available, *variable that causes the desired outcome but that is not included in the AI's training data*"). Italics added. Note, though, that the training of machine learning is long and tedious in that is an error-prone procedure than can ultimately impair future algorithmic decision-making: Price, W. Nicholson Price II, "Regulating Black-Box Medicine", *Michigan Law Review*, Volume 116, 2017, pp. 421–431 (leverages on Google Image's image recognition learning algorithm to shed light on the four-step process by which some algorithms are thoroughly trained. First, the algorithm is shown "a set of known images ('Here are 10,000 pictures of ducks')." Second, the algorithm "develops complex internal rules based on nonlinear processes." Third, the algorithm "tests those rules on a test set ('Which of these are ducks?')." And fourth, the algorithm accordingly adjusts its "internal rules based on the success of the test." These steps are trotted out and repeated many times "until it can accurately and consistently classify the images").

[3805] Mayson, Sandra G., "Bias In, Bias Out", *cit.*, pp. 2218–2300 (2263).

[3806] Mayson, Sandra G., "Bias In, Bias Out", *cit.*, pp. 2218–2300 (2263).

[3807] On the dire need to achieve algorithmic fairness through the creation of both race-aware algorithms and meaningful trade-offs to attain fairer risk scores: Kim, Pauline, "Race-Aware Algorithms: Fairness, Non-discrimination and Affirmative Action" *California Law Review*, 2022; Kleinberg, Jon/S. Mullainathan/M. Raghavan, "Inherent Trade-offs in the Fair Determination of Risk Scores", *Proceedings of the 8th Conference on Innovations in Theoretical Computer Science (ITCS)*, 2017; Kroll, Joshua A./J. Huey/S. Barocas/E. W. Felten/J. R. Reidenberg/D. G. Robinson/and H. Yu, "Accountable Algorithms", *University of Pennsylvania Law Review*, 165 (3), 2017, pp. 633–705.

lines. For instance, if a black man had three arrests under his belt (either a criminal record[3808] or track record), it propounded only that he had been dwelling in New Orleans for quite a while. Crucially, black men were frequently arrested for nothing.[3809] If a white man, though, had three past arrests under his belt, it propounded that he was bad news indeed! White men were seldom, if ever, arrested[3810]; three past arrests suggested an exceedingly high penchant to lure law enforcement[3811] attention.[3812]

§§ Tellingly, a race-blind machine learning algorithm[3813] would not capture this humongous difference in law enforcement practices.[3814] It would treat the two men just the same. Put differently, it would treat them as though they both presented

---

[3808] But see: Harris, Grant T./Rice, Marnie E., "Bayes and Base Rates: What Is an Informative Prior for Actuarial Violence Risk Assessment?", *Behavioural Science and Law*, Volume 31, 2013, pp. 103, 121 ("What is not axiomatic is the straightforward application of assumptions about priors... to violence risk assessment—that remains a set of important empirical matters."); See: Mayson, Sandra G., "Bias In, Bias Out", *cit.*, pp. 2218–2300. See also: Selbst, Andrew D., "Disparate Impact in Big Data Policing", *cit.*, pp. 140–43.

[3809] Mayson, Sandra G., "Bias In, Bias Out", *cit.*, pp. 2218–2300 (2263).

[3810] See: Connecticut Fair Housing Center, et al. v. CoreLogic Rental Property Solutions—Cohen Milstein (access: 20.11.2024). ("*The U.S. Department of Housing & Urban Development observed in 2016 that excluding rental applicants because of their criminal records disproportionately harms Latinos and African Americans, who are significantly more likely than whites to be arrested or convicted. Studies show such disparities are linked to differential enforcement rather than to differences in likelihood of engaging in criminal activity*"). Italics added.

[3811] See: New Orleans Investigation, *cit.*, at ix-x (concluding that "racial disparities in arrests of whites and African Americans in virtually all categories, with particularly dramatic disparity for African-American youth"); id. at x ("The level of disparity for youth in New Orleans is so severe and so divergent from nationally reported data that it cannot plausibly be attributed entirely to the underlying rates at which these youth commit crimes…").

[3812] Mayson, Sandra G., "Bias In, Bias Out", *cit.*, pp. 2218–2300 (2264).

[3813] Note, though, that certain types of racial discrimination may not be fully intentional. More likely than not, it can be related with the perils of big data colour-blindness that nonetheless relies on proxies to race and gender to make algorithmic decisions. Another problem is the one related with "creditworthiness by association" that causes more problems than it solves. Hurley, Mikella/ Adebayo, Julius, "Credit Scoring in the Era of Big Data", *Yale Journal of Law and Technology*, Volume 18, 2016, p. 149 ("*these tools may furthermore obscure discriminatory and subjective lending policies behind a single "objective" score. Such discriminatory scoring may not be intentional; instead, sophisticated algorithms may combine facially neutral data points and treat them as proxies for immutable characteristics such as race or gender, thereby circumventing existing non-discrimination laws*"). Italics added. See: Part IV, This chapter, Sects. 4.1.2–4.1.2.3 of this book.

[3814] For this reason, Sam Corbett-Davies and Sharad Goel refer to colorblindness as "anti-classification." See: Corbett-Davies, Sam/Gaebler, Johann D./Nilforoshan, Hamed/Shrof, Ravi/ Goel, Sharad, "The Measure and Mismeasure of Fairness", *Journal of Machine Learning Research*, Volume 24, 2023, pp. 1–117 (p. 36) ("*In constructing algorithmic risk scores, a key ingredient is the target of prediction. In practice, though, there is often a mismatch between our true outcome of interest and the available data—an occurrence we call label bias (Zanger-Tishler* et al., *2023). As with the other issues we discuss, there is typically no perfect solution to this problem, but there are ways to mitigate it. For example, in pretrial risk assessment, we would often like to estimate the likelihood a defendant would commit a crime if released. But there are two key difficulties with this goal. First, though we might want to measure crime conducted by defendants awaiting*

similar degrees of risk, which, I may venture to add, clearly defies commonsense in light of the set of reasons brought to bear on algorithmic risk assessment. Strikingly, and perhaps unsurprisingly, the machine learning algorithm would fail to consider the arrests in light of disparate policing patterns and accordingly appraise that arrests were a much less relevant risk marker for a black man than for a white[3815] man.[3816]

§§ It would accordingly perpetuate both structural[3817] disadvantage[3818] and gross racial inequity by embellishing the black man's relative riskiness/dangerousness and

trial, we typically only observe crime that results in a conviction or an arrest. These observable outcomes, however, are imperfect proxies for the underlying criminal act. Further, heavier policing in communities of color might lead to Black and Hispanic defendants being arrested, and later convicted, more often than White defendants who commit the same offense (Lum and Isaac, 2016). Poor outcome data might thus cause one to systematically underestimate the risk posed by White defendants. The second, related, issue is that our target of interest is a counterfactual outcome; it corresponds to what would have happened had a defendant been released"). Italics added. See also: Balkin, Jack M./Siegel, Reva B., "The American Civil Rights Tradition: Anticlassification or Antisubordination?", *University of Miami Law Review*, Volume 58, 2003, pp. 9, 10–11 (explaining the distinction between the anticlassification and the antisubordination approaches to equality law).

3815 Mayson, Sandra G., "Bias In, Bias Out", *cit.*, pp. 2218–2300 (2264).

3816 Michael Tracy sets forth a similar argument for providing capital juries statistical information about how much more likely prosecutors are to seek the death penalty for black defendants. See: Tracy, Michael, "Race as a Mitigating Factor in Death Penalty Sentencing", *GEO. Journal Law & MOD. Critical Race Perspective*, Volume 7, 2015, pp. 151–159 (discussing that if jurors are fully aware of this deep-seated disparity, a black defendant "may seem less deserving of a death sentence"). See: Mayson, Sandra G., "Bias In, Bias Out", *cit.*, pp. 2218–2300.

3817 See: Barocas, Solon/Selbst, Andrew, "Big Data's Disparate Impact", *California Law Review*, Volume 104, pp. 2016, p. 691 (highlighting the worrisome, and gruesome, issue of "structural disadvantage" with which racialized communities have been tussling for centuries). See also: Powell, Richard/Porter, Jeremy, "Redlining, Concentrated Disadvantage and Crime: The Effects of Discriminatory Government Policies on Violent Crime", *American Journal of Criminal Justice*, Volume 48, 2023, pp. 1132–1156 ("*Redlining and other discriminatory government policies enacted during the first half of the Twentieth Century have had long-lasting negative effects on neighborhoods, especially those inhabited by people of color (…) The results indicate that redlining was associated with increases in both concentrated disadvantage and violent crime, and that redlining's relationship with violent crime was, indeed, partially mediated by its relationship with concentrated disadvantage*"). Italics added. See also: Gandy, Oscar H., *Coming to Terms with Chance: Engaging Rational Discrimination and Cumulative Disadvantage*, Farnham, UK: Ashgate Publishing, 2009. See: Burk, Dan L., "Algorithmic Fair Use", *University of Chicago Law Review*, Volume 86, 2019, pp. 283–288 (asserts that algorithmic "*fair use carries with it the disadvantage of ex ante uncertainty*; no one can be entirely certain in advance how a court will weigh the four factors, *and hence there is always some apprehension that a use may be found infringing rather than fair*"). Italics added; Kroeper, Kathryn/Quintanilla, Victor D./Frisby, Michael/Yel, Nedim/Applegate, Amy G./Sherman, Steven J./Murphy, Mary C., "Underestimating the Unrepresented: Cognitive Biases Disadvantage Pro Se Litigants in Family Law Cases", *Psychology, Public Policy, and Law*, Volume 26, n.º 2, 2020, pp. 198–212. But see: Citron, Danielle Keats/Pasquale, Frank, "The Scored Society: Due Process for Automated Predictions", *Washington Law Review*, Volume 89, 2014, pp. 1, 4–5 (highlighting how human beings programming automated systems is directly conducive to, and leads, to fundamentally inaccurate results since the source code, predictive algorithms and datasets may encompass human biases which, in turn, have a disparate impact on historically disadvantaged groups).

3818 See: Eckhouse, L., Lum, K., Conti-Cook, C./Ciccolini, J., "Layers of bias: A unified approach for understanding problems with risk assessment", *cit.*, p. 202 ("[T]here is substantial evidence that defendants of color are disadvantaged in pretrial and sentencing decisions made without reference to

underrating the relative riskiness/dangerousness of the white man. A colourblind algorithm may indeed discriminate because of race, which is wholly unbefitting in this regard. At the shallowest level, the **colourblind machine learning algorithm** eschews racially disparate treatment[3819] altogether. Instead, treats two individuals with otherwise similar risk profiles just the same.[3820]

§§ Digging deeper into the vexing question at hand, the machine learning algorithm effectively/actively engages in disparate treatment based on race nonetheless. In failing to capture that the underlying context of race significantly impacts the relevance of past arrests, the machine learning algorithm accordingly increases the black man's risk score while reducing the white man's risk score. Statistically, the pressing question is that—as a direct consequence of biased law enforcement practices, race might well moderate the predictive value of a set of input variables (or the machine learning algorithm in an overarching sense)—the machine learning algorithm soars risk for black people compared to white[3821] people.[3822]

§§ A cohort of famed risk-assessment-tool pundits have been tussling with this perceived quandary. Being that risk variables—e. g. past arrests or misdemeanour convictions—are far less predictive for black[3823] people.[3824] The traditional response

---

risk assessment models."); Rehavi, M. Marit/Starr, Sonja B., "Racial Disparity in Federal Criminal Sentences", *Journal of Political Economy*, Volume 122, 2014, pp. 1320, 1323 (pointing out that black defendants in the federal system were 1.75 times more likely to undergo a mandatory minimum criminal charge than **similarly situated** white defendants). See: Part V, Chap. 5, Sect. 5.1.1.5.2.2.1.2 of this book (on one of the foundations underpinning a **thing-centred artificial intelligence**: the comparison of **similarly situated individuals**).

3819 Mayson, Sandra G., "Bias In, Bias Out", *cit.*, pp. 2218–2300 (2264).

3820 Mayson, Sandra G., "Bias In, Bias Out", *cit.*, pp. 2218–2300 (2264).

3821 This type of situation arises in every possible predictive context. In education testing, for example, it is well established that the correlation between SAT scores and intelligence varies greatly by race and by a set of circumstances. See: Mayson, Sandra G., "Bias In, Bias Out", *cit.*, pp. 2218–2300. See also: Berlak, Harold, "Race and the Achievement Gap", *Critical Social Issues in American Education: Democracy and Meaning in a Globalizing World*, 3rd edition, Shapiro, H. Svi/Purpel, David E. (Editors), 2005, pp. 223–227 (exploring the yawning racial achievement gap in other standardized tests). It is important to note, though, that a high score attained by a student who benefited from the best possible primary education and extensive SAT preparation is not as impressive as the student who attained the very same score without any extra help or additional levers. See: Mayson, Sandra G., "Bias In, Bias Out", *cit.*, pp. 2218–2300.

3822 Mayson, Sandra G., "Bias In, Bias Out", *cit.*, pp. 2218–2300 (2264).

3823 Berk, Richard, "Accuracy and Fairness for Juvenile Justice Risks Assessments", *Journal of Empirical Legal Studies*, Volume 16, 2019, p. 183 (arguing that, in different data sets, that past misdemeanor convictions were less predictive of future serious arrest for coloured people than for white people); Lowenkamp, Christopher et al., "Investigating the Impact of Pretrial Detention on Sentencing Outcomes", *Laura and John Arnold Foundation* (Nov. 2013), https://www.arnoldfoundation.org/wp-content/uploads/2014/02/LJAF_Report_state-sentencing_FNL.pdf; [https://perma.cc/L9JF-KEHL]. The Pennsylvania Sentencing Commission expressly snubbed past arrests altogether as input variables since they had markedly different predictive significance across racial lines. Risk Assessment Update: Arrest Scales, Pennsylvania Commision on Sentencing, 2018, pp. 4–7 (Feb. 28, 2018), http://www.hominid.psu.edu/specialty_programs/pacs/publications-and-research/research-and-evaluation-reports/risk-assessment; [https://perma.cc/32WY-9F74]. See: Mayson, Sandra G., "Bias In, Bias Out", *cit.*, pp. 2218–2300.

3824 See: Mayson, Sandra G., "Bias In, Bias Out", *cit.*, pp. 2218–2300.

is to cast aside the troublesome/cumbersome input variables from the remit of algorithm risk assessment. Note, though, that, as extensively shown earlier in this essay, such a solution exacts a toll on the machine learning algorithm's overall accuracy,[3825] which, in turn, will most likely befall inordinately on communities of colour.[3826]

§§ Crucially, scholars aver that a feasible alternative is to allow the machine learning algorithm to evaluate the importance of risk markers contingent on race. If race balance the risk markers' predictive value, this would accordingly decrease average risk scores for black defendants.[3827] It would correspondingly attain what pundits have coined as «fairness through awareness».[3828] As a result, it would enhance, rather than degrade, the algorithmic tool's overall accuracy. Under these circumstances, including race as an input variable would spur accuracy and racial equity at the same[3829] time.[3830] Note, though, that this far-fetched stance is not

---

[3825] It bears mentioning that the Pennsylvania Commission on Sentencing, for example, has decided to rely on past conviction rather than past-arrest data in spite of the fact that it renders the model slightly less accurate in an overarching sense. See: Risk Assessment Update: Arrest Scales, Pennsylvania Commision on Sentencing, 2018, pp. 4–7 (Feb. 28, 2018), http://www.hominid.psu.edu/specialty_programs/pacs/publications-and-research/research-and-evaluation-reports/risk-assessment; [https://perma.cc/32WY-9F74]. Recall, When Richard Berk trained the algorithm only to maximize for overall accuracy, it predicted rearrest for 17% of the white subgroup and 33% of the black subgroup (a 16 percentage-point difference). Strikingly, the false-positive rates were 16% for the white subgroup whereas for the black groups was 28% (a 12 percentage-point difference). See: Berk, Richard, "Accuracy and Fairness for Juvenile Justice Risks Assessments", *cit.*, p. 180. Notably, when Richard Berk changed the algorithm to equalize the cost ratios, it predicted rearrest for 10% of the white subgroup and 29% of the black subgroup (a 19 percentage-point difference). Relatedly, the false-positive rates were 8% for the white subset and 22% for the black subset (a 14 percentage-point difference). See: Berk, Richard, "Accuracy and Fairness for Juvenile Justice Risks Assessments", *cit.*, p. 185. See: Mayson, Sandra G., "Bias In, Bias Out", *cit.*, pp. 2218–2300.

[3826] Mayson, Sandra G., "Bias In, Bias Out", *cit.*, pp. 2218–2300 (2265).

[3827] Mayson, Sandra G., "Bias In, Bias Out", *cit.*, pp. 2218–2300 (2265).

[3828] Dwork, Cynthia et al., "Fairness Through Awareness", https://arxiv.org/pdf/1104.3913.pdf; [https://perma.cc/N8QE-27NY].

[3829] See: Kim, Pauline T., "Data-Driven Discrimination at Work", *William and Mary Law Review*, Volume 58, 2017, p. 918 ("If the goal is to reduce biased outcomes, then a simple prohibition on using data about race or sex could be either wholly ineffective or actually counterproductive due to the existence of class proxies and the risk of omitted variable bias."); Lipton, Zachary et al., "Does Mitigating ML's Impact Disparity Require Treatment Disparity?", NIPS Proceedings 1, 2018, https://arxiv.org/pdf/1711.07076.pdf; [https://perma.cc/X8VF-EY53] (arguing, premised on statistical examples, that a prohibition on race or sex data is rather counterproductive indeed); Corbett-Davies, Sam/Goel, Sharad, "The Measure and Mismeasure of Fairness: a critical Review of Fair Machine Learning", *Cornell University Library*, 2018, passim (discussing the "[l]imitations of anti-classification" as a fairness metric). See also: Kim, Pauline T., "Data-Driven Discrimination at Work", *cit.*, p. 867 ("[I]f the goal is to discourage classification bias, then the law should not forbid the inclusion of race, sex, or other sensitive information as variables, but seek to preserve these variables, and perhaps even include them in some complex models."); Kroll, Joshua A., et al., "Accountable Algorithms", *University of Pennsylvania Law Review*, Volume 165, 2017, pp. 633, 693–95. See also: Kim, Pauline T., "Data-Driven Discrimination at Work", *cit.*, p. 866 ("classification bias occurs when employers rely on classification schemes, such as data algorithms, to sort or score workers in ways that worsen inequality or disadvantage along the lines of race, sex,

workable for basic checklist tools, yet it could be nonetheless useful for the machine-learning tools that portend for the future[3831] though.[3832]

§§ Cogently, and perhaps unsurprisingly, to attain any form of output equality in algorithmic risk assessment, it might be nonetheless imperative to treat race as an input variable. Pivotally, to **equalize false-positive rates**[3833] across racial lines, for instance, it will most likely be imperative to create **race-fraught risk thresholds for each risk class.**[3834] Put otherwise, the machine learning algorithm will be poked to treat people who present the same risk differently based upon[3835] race. The same goes for equalizing ***cost ratios*** across racial[3836] lines.[3837] to achieve algorithmic fairness.[3838]

---

or other protected characteristics"). These two uses of the word "bias" correspond to the notions of irrational versus rational **(or statistical) discrimination.** Mayson, Sandra G., "Bias In, Bias Out", *cit.*, pp. 2218–2300.

[3830] See: Mayson, Sandra G., "Bias In, Bias Out", *cit.*, pp. 2218–2300.

[3831] Kleinberg, Jon et al., "Algorithmic Fairness", *AEA Papers & Proceedings*, Volume 108, 2018, pp. 22–23 (discussing, anchored in a batch of national data, that including race as an input variable to a machine-learning college-admissions algorithm both "improves predicted GPAs of admitted students" and can augment "the fraction of admitted students who are black").

[3832] Mayson, Sandra G., "Bias In, Bias Out", *cit.*, pp. 2218–2300 (2265).

[3833] But see: Mayson, Sandra G., "Bias In, Bias Out", *cit.*, pp. 2218–2300 (arguing that equalizing false-positive rates will beget fewer false positives—"law abiders" mistakenly predict for rearrest—for the high-base-rate group than the low-base-rate group because there are fewer "law abiders" in the high-base-rate group in the first place). But see also: Sam Corbett-Davies and peers, parsing the same Broward County data that ProPublica did, concluded that attaining parity in false-positive rates while still optimizing for public safety (and without detaining any other defendants) would beget a 7% uptick in violent crime. See: Corbett-Davies, Sam/Pierson, Emma/Feller, Avi/Goel, Sharad Goel/Huq, Aziz, "Algorithmic Decision Making and the Cost of Fairness", *Proceedings of the 23rd ACM SIGKDD International Conference on Knowledge Discovery and Data Mining* (Ass'n for Computing Machinery ed., 2017), 2017, p. 802. Moreover, 17% of those detained would be low-risk people for whom detention was either unwarranted or uncalled for. According to Richard Berk's research on juvenile data, for example, tweaking the algorithm to attain statistical parity spawned a lower false-positive rate for the black subset than the white (4% versus 9%) yet a higher false-negative rate (50% versus 40%). See: Berk, Richard, "Accuracy and Fairness for Juvenile Justice Risks Assessments", *cit.*, p. 189. In addition to that, Berk further concluded that for white folks, the algorithm generated 5.25 false positives for every false negative; whilst for black folks, the algorithm generated 1.85 false negatives for every false positive. See: Berk, Richard, "Accuracy and Fairness for Juvenile Justice Risks Assessments", *cit.*, p. 189.

[3834] On the dire need to achieve algorithmic fairness through both the creation of race-aware algorithms and trade-offs to attain fairer risk scores: Kim, Pauline, "Race-Aware Algorithms: Fairness, Non-discrimination and Affirmative Action", *California Law Review*, 2022, passim; Kleinberg, Jon/S. Mullainathan/M. Raghavan, "Inherent Trade-offs in the Fair Determination of Risk Scores", *Proceedings of the 8th Conference on Innovations in Theoretical Computer Science (ITCS)*, 2017; Kroll, Joshua A./J. Huey/S. Barocas/E. W. Felten/J. R. Reidenberg/D. G. Robinson/and H. Yu, "Accountable Algorithms", *University of Pennsylvania Law Review*, 165 (3), 2017, pp. 633–705.

[3835] Hardt, Moritz et al., "Equality of Opportunity in Supervised Learning", *NIPS Proceedings*, 2016, https://papers.nips.cc/paper/6374-equality-of-opportunity-in-supervised-learning.pdf; [https://perma.cc/LD25-6RR7].

[3836] Berk, Richard, "Accuracy and Fairness for Juvenile Justice Risks Assessments", *cit.*, pp. 185–86 (positing that that, to equalize cost ratios across racial groups in a juvenile risk-assessment context,

§§ Understandably, and perhaps laudably, to accomplish any resemblance of **predictive parity**, it might be nonetheless necessary to gain access to the dataset[3839] with a view to manually impede the effect of race[3840] on other observable variables.[3841] Alternatively, the developer might need to manually appraise the predictive import of every input variable dependent on race.[3842]

§§ As Solon Barocas and Andrew Selbst[3843] aptly put it, algorithmic prediction therefore bestows upon stakeholders a particularly clear window on the skirmish/affray between anticlassification[3844] and antisubordination[3845] notions[3846] of

---

the author "separate[d] forecasting exercises" for white and black juveniles, respectively, and that the machine-learning forecasting algorithms the data produced were different for each racial group).

[3837] Mayson, Sandra G., "Bias In, Bias Out", *cit.*, pp. 2218–2300 (2266).

[3838] Kusner, M./J. Loftus/C. Russell/R. Silva, "Counterfactual Fairness", *Advances in Neural Information Processing Systems*, 30 (NIPS 2017), Long Beah, California, 2017, pp. 4066–4076 (on fairness in algorithmic settings).

[3839] It is important to note that an algorithm designed for maximum accuracy will adjust itself to the majority data, and may be less accurate for members of the underrepresented group, thus breeding inductive bias. See: Shellenbarger, Sue, "A Crucial Step for Avoiding AI Disasters", *Wall Street Journal*, (Feb. 13, 2019, 9:57 AM ET), https://www.wsj.com/articles/a-crucial-step-for-avoiding-ai-disasters-11550069865?ns=prod/accounts-wsj; [https://perma.cc/C28U-LAAE] (discussing this issue while emphasizing how diverse development teams pay more attention to unrepresentative and underrepresented data sets). Human programmers can circumvent and bypass this problem by weighting the minority-group data more heavily, by designing different algorithms for each racial group, or by striving to contain more data to equalize group representation in the data set. See: Barua, Sukarna et al., "MWMOTE—Majority Weighted Minority Oversampling Technique for Imbalanced Data Set Learning", *IEEE Transactions on Knowledge & Data Engineering*, Volume 26, 2014, pp. 405, 405–06. See also: Hamilton, Melissa, "The Biased Algorithm: Evidence of Disparate Impact on Hispanics", *American Criminal Law Review*, Volume 56, 2019, pp. 1553 and ff and passim (which clearly demonstrates that COMPAS was significantly less accurate for Hispanic than for white defendants by several measures and suggesting that smaller numbers of Hispanic defendants might be the cause).

[3840] But see: Barocas, Solon/Selbst, Andrew D., "Big Data's Disparate Impact", *cit.*, pp. 692–93. These polymaths coined this phenomenon as "masking" owing to the fact that machine-learning technologies bestow upon stakeholders' multiple opportunities to intentionally twist/warp/deform an algorithm in ways that are painstakingly difficult to ferret out/discern/detect.

[3841] Professor Sandra Mayson argues that there are different pathways to attempt this, and several risk-assessment-tool developers do that. For instance, Marie VanNostrand, who has designed several of the checklist pretrial risk-assessment tools in current use, searches for risk factors that are equally predictive across racial lines and disregards those that are not. Note, though, that this approach, however straightforward, could nonetheless exact a toll on machine learning algorithm's overall accuracy. See: Mayson, Sandra G., "Bias In, Bias Out", *cit.*, pp. 2218–2300.

[3842] Mayson, Sandra G., "Bias In, Bias Out", *cit.*, pp. 2218–2300 (2266).

[3843] See: Barocas, Solon/Selbst, Andrew, "Big Data's Disparate Impact", *cit.*, p. 723 (explaining that "[d]ata mining discrimination will force a confrontation between the two divergent principles underlying antidiscrimination law: anticlassification and antisubordination").

equality.[3847] Note, though, that neither eliminating race[3848] and race-borne markers nor including them can totally equalize outputs if the event one seeks to forecast[3849]—the *target variable*—correlates with race itself.[3850] **As a result, if the target variable correlates with race in any manner possible, regulating input data[3851] is good as futile.**[3852]

[3844] For this reason, Sam Corbett-Davies and Sharad Goel refer to colorblindness as "anti-classification." Corbett-Davies, Sam/Gaebler, Johann D./Nilforoshan, Hamed/Shrof, Ravi/Goel, Sharad, "The Measure and Mismeasure of Fairness", *Journal of Machine Learning Research*, Volume 24, 2023, pp. 1–117 (p. 36) ("*In constructing algorithmic risk scores, a key ingredient is the target of prediction. In practice, though, there is often a mismatch between our true outcome of interest and the available data—an occurrence we call label bias (Zanger-Tishler* et al., *2023). As with the other issues we discuss, there is typically no perfect solution to this problem, but there are ways to mitigate it. For example, in pretrial risk assessment, we would often like to estimate the likelihood a defendant would commit a crime if released. But there are two key difficulties with this goal. First, though we might want to measure crime conducted by defendants awaiting trial, we typically only observe crime that results in a conviction or an arrest. These observable outcomes, however, are imperfect proxies for the underlying criminal act. Further, heavier policing in communities of color might lead to Black and Hispanic defendants being arrested, and later convicted, more often than White defendants who commit the same offense (Lum and Isaac, 2016). Poor outcome data might thus cause one to systematically underestimate the risk posed by White defendants. The second, related, issue is that our target of interest is a counterfactual outcome; it corresponds to what would have happened had a defendant been released*"). Italics added.

[3845] See also: Balkin, Jack M./Siegel, Reva B., "The American Civil Rights Tradition: Anticlassification or Antisubordination?", *University of Miami Law Review*, Volume 58, 2003, pp. 9, 10–11 (explaining the distinction between the anticlassification and the antisubordination approaches to equality law). See also: Barocas, Solon/Selbst, Andrew, "Big Data's Disparate Impact", *cit.*, p. 723 (explaining that "[d]ata mining discrimination will force a confrontation between the two divergent principles underlying antidiscrimination law: anticlassification and antisubordination").

[3846] See: Berk, Richard et al., "Fairness in Criminal Justice Risk Assessments: The State of the Art", *Sociological Methods and Research*, 2018, pp. 12–18 (July 2, 2018), https://journals.sagepub.com/doi/pdf/10.1177/0049124118782533; [https://perma.cc/LB82-47SB].

[3847] See: Chandler, Anupam, "The Racist Algorithm", *cit.*, p. 1039 (sets out a poignant call in an earnest attempt to urge stakeholders to put their eyes and hearts on both "inputs and outputs", as opposed to machine algorithms alone). See also: Huq, Aziz Z., "Racial Equity in Algorithmic Criminal Justice", *cit.*, p. 1080 (explaining "the [p]roblem of [d]istorting [f]eature [s]election"); Kehl, Danielle, et al., "Algorithms in the Criminal Justice System: Assessing the Use of Risk Assessments in Sentencing", *Berkman Klein Ctr. For Internet Society*, 2017, https://dash.harvard.edu/bitstream/handle/1/33746041/2017-07_responsivecommunities_2.pdf; [https://perma.cc/7V6D-JLLM] ("critical issues also need to be addressed in the development phase of these algorithms, particularly with regard to the inputs and how they are used"). See: Mayson, Sandra G., "Bias In, Bias Out", *cit.*, pp. 2218–2300. See: Part V, Chap. 5, Sects. 5.1–5.1.6.2.1 of this book (on the fundamental tenets of a thing-centred algorithmic decision-making). See: Part V, Chap. 5, Sects. 5.1.1.5.2.2–5.1.1.5.2.2.1.4 of this book (on the fundamental shift away from causation to correlations in algorithmic decision-making).

[3848] See: Corbett-Davies, Sam/Goel, Sharad, "The Measure and Mismeasure of Fairness: a critical Review of Fair Machine Learning", *cit.*, p. 9 (arguing that "nearly every covariate commonly used in predictive models is at least partially correlated with protected group status; and in many situations, even strongly correlated"). See also: Kim, Pauline T., "Data-Driven Discrimination at Work", *cit.*, p. 867 ("[I]f the goal is to discourage *classification bias*, then the law should not forbid the inclusion of race, sex, or other sensitive information as variables, *but seek to preserve these variables, and perhaps even include them in some complex models*"). Italics added. See also: Kroll, Joshua A., et al.,

§§ Compellingly, if the event one seeks to forecasts occurs more often to black people, even a lacklustre machine learning algorithm will predict it with heightened frequency for people of colour. It boils down to simple math coupled with a dash, and a dollop, of common sense. No matter the type of input data that are made available to both the developers and to the laypeople, the events that correlate with a given target variable—and thence[3853] are transmogrified into machine learning algorithm's predictors[3854]—will likewise correlate with race since the target variable[3855] does so.[3856]

§§ Ensuingly, and thereupon, the only feasible way to quell the race correlation is by hampering the machine learning algorithm's resources to foretell/forewarn the target variable. Consequently, ruling out criminal-history data,[3857] for example, has every chance to diminish exponentially disparate racial impact of predicting future

"Accountable Algorithms", *University of Pennsylvania Law Review*, Volume 165, 2017, pp. 633, 693–95.

[3849] See: Berk, Richard, "Accuracy and Fairness for Juvenile Justice Risks Assessments", *cit.*, p. 189 (considering data modifications along these racial lines). See: Mayson, Sandra G., "Bias In, Bias Out", *cit.*, pp. 2218–2300.

[3850] Mayson, Sandra G., "Bias In, Bias Out", *cit.*, pp. 2218–2300 (2266).

[3851] But see: Berk, Richard, "Accuracy and Fairness for Juvenile Justice Risks Assessments", *cit.*, p. 189 (considering data modifications along these racial lines).

[3852] Mayson, Sandra G., "Bias In, Bias Out", *cit.*, pp. 2218–2300 (2266).

[3853] Mayson, Sandra G., "Bias In, Bias Out", *cit.*, pp. 2218–2300 (2266).

[3854] But see: Corbett-Davies, Sam/Goel, Sharad, "The Measure and Mismeasure of Fairness: a critical Review of Fair Machine Learning", *Cornell University Library*, 2018, p. 18 (broaches a type of *measurement bias* coined "feature bias," which is neatly a bias in the predictors x. Note, though, that there is a second type of measurement bias deemed "label bias," which, in turn, amounts to a bias in y. The authors argue that that label bias is the worst bias there is); Kleinberg, Jon/Ludwig, Jens/Mullainathan, Sendhil/Sunstein Cass R., "Discrimination in the Age of Algorithms", *Journal of Legal Analysis*, Volume 10, 1, 2018, pp. 28–29, 33–34 (draw a distinction between "group differences in the raw data" and biases for the "choice of predictors").

[3855] See: Corbett-Davies, Sam/Goel, Sharad, "The Measure and Mismeasure of Fairness: a critical Review of Fair Machine Learning", *cit.*, p. 9 (arguing that "nearly every covariate commonly used in predictive models is at least partially correlated with protected group status; and in many situations, even strongly correlated").

[3856] Mayson, Sandra G., "Bias In, Bias Out", *cit.*, pp. 2218–2300 (2267).

[3857] See: Hamilton, Melissa, "Back to the Future: The Influence of Criminal History on Risk Assessments", *Berkeley Journal of Criminal Law*, Volume 20, 2015, pp. 75, 78 (exuding concerns with the recurrent use of criminal history in risk assessment owing to "the potential that criminal history is an unfortunate proxy for race and social disadvantage"); Barry-Jester, Anna Maria et al., "The New Science of Sentencing: Should Prison Sentencing Be Based on Crimes That Haven't Been Committed Yet?", *Marshall Project* (Aug. 4, 2015, 7:15 AM), https://www.themarshallproject.org/2015/08/04/the-new-science-of-sentencing; [https://perma.cc/J4UW-BDKP] (arguing that risk-assessment outcomes gives rises to disparate racial impact that befall Blacks). Skeem, Jennifer L./Lowenkamp, Christopher T., "Risk, Race, and Recidivism: Predictive Bias and Disparate Impact", *Criminology*, Volume 54, 2024, pp. 680, 683–84, 704–06 (argues that criminal history correlates with race in their respective data set). See also: Pager, Devah, *Marked: Race, Crime, and Finding Work in an Era of Mass Incarceration*, Chicago: University of Chicago Press, 2007; Fornili, K. S., "Racialized mass incarceration and the war on drugs: A critical race theory appraisal", *Journal of Addictions Nursing*, Volume 29, Issue 1, 2018, 65–72; Jacoby, S. F., Dong, B., Beard, J. H.,

arrest. Note, though, that it will also exponentially hinder the machine learning algorithm's ability to forecast future arrest.[3858]

§§ To stamp out racial disparity in the prediction of a racially disparate event is to chip away the predictive tool, rendering the latter at best ineffective and at worst downright menacing to the citizens fundamental rights. Crucially, if a tool forecasts a race-warped target variable like «any arrest», for instance, the tool has scant, if any, value to be accounted for, let alone to be remarked upon.[3859]

§§ In that juncture, however, the best call is to cease predicting the useless event altogether. And if the target variable does not lodge/embed/ingrain/etch racial distortion, then derailing the predictive tool can be both counterintuitive and counterproductive insofar the toll in overall accuracy may beget proportionally more wrongful forecasts on black communities than on white ones.[3860] The point being that **colour-blindness,** at its core, if far from being a go-to measure of equality in the remit of algorithmic risk assessment. Vitally, colour-blindness,[3861] in spite of the laudable aims with which is suffused, can ultimately ratchet up, rather than sooth out, racial disparity in algorithmic risk[3862] assessment.[3863]

§§ Compellingly, if the target variable correlates with race in any manner, predictions will either be racially lopsided or skewed in that they will be rendered useless. As an upshot, **colour-blindness is at best a shallow, hollow, nomadic, erratic, whimsical, and at worst a counterproductive blueprint to achieve racial**[3864] **equity**.[3865]

Wiebe, D. J., & Morrison, C. N., "The enduring impact of historical and structural racism on urban violence in Philadelphia", *Social Science & Medicine*, 1982/2018, 199, 2018, pp. 87–95; Travis, Jeremy, Bruce Western, and Steve Redburn (Eds.), *Growth of Incarceration in the United States: Exploring Causes and Consequences*, Washington, DC: National Academy of Science, 2014.

3858 Mayson, Sandra G., "Bias In, Bias Out", *cit.*, pp. 2218–2300 (2267).

3859 Mayson, Sandra G., "Bias In, Bias Out", *cit.*, pp. 2218–2300 (2267).

3860 Mayson, Sandra G., "Bias In, Bias Out", *cit.*, pp. 2218–2300 (2267).

3861 See: Eckhouse, L., Lum, K., Conti-Cook, C./Ciccolini, J., "Layers of bias: A unified approach for understanding problems with risk assessment", *Criminal Justice and Behavior*, Volume 46, Issue 2, 2019, pp. 185–209 (p. 197) ("The magnitude and pattern of the bias in the data cannot be measured directly with the techniques used by ProPublica, Northpointe, or any of the others studying these models, including us").

3862 See: Mayson, Sandra G., "Bias In, Bias Out", *cit.*, pp. 2218–2300. See also: Huq, Aziz Z., "Racial Equity in Algorithmic Criminal Justice", *Duke Law Journal*, Volume 68, 2019, p. 1100; Kim, Pauline T., "Data-Driven Discrimination at Work", *cit.*, p. 867 ("[I]f the goal is to discourage classification bias, then the law should not forbid the inclusion of race, sex, or other sensitive information as variables, but seek to preserve these variables, and perhaps even include them in some complex models."); Kroll, Joshua A., et al., "Accountable Algorithms", *University of Pennsylvania Law Review*, Volume 165, 2017, pp. 633, 693–95.

3863 Mayson, Sandra G., "Bias In, Bias Out", *cit.*, pp. 2218–2300 (2267).

3864 Strauss, David A., "The Myth of Colorblindness", *Supreme Court Review*, 1986, 99, 114 ("The one option that is not open is the ideal of colorblindness—treating race as if it were, like eye color, a wholly irrelevant characteristic. That is because it is not a wholly irrelevant characteristic. Race correlates with other things…").

3865 Mayson, Sandra G., "Bias In, Bias Out", *cit.*, pp. 2218–2300 (2267).

4.1.10.4 The Quest to Pursue Racial Equality in Algorithmic Risk Assessment: Will It Bode Well? Would the Single-Threshold Rule Suffice to Attain that Overriding Goal?

§§ To adroitly pursue equality in the realm of algorithmic risk assessment, it is crucially important to pin down the befitted grounds for a statistically sound risk score. Relatedly, it is of paramount importance to gauge whether and to what extent two individuals should be ascribed the very same risk score. In a nutshell, risk assessment comes down to a statement of **statistical risk**.[3866]

§§ «Two people are therefore alike for purposes of statistical risk assessment if they present the same statistical risk».[3867] Put otherwise, if two individuals pose the same risk, they should be given the same risk score (either «high» or «low» risk). This blueprint of equality is frequently dubbed as a **«single-threshold rule»**.[3868] Crucially, single-threshold rule has been consequently baptized as a linchpin of algorithmic risk assessment. A simple example illustrates. If risk-assessment machine learning algorithm, when dealing with two people who present exactly the same statistical risk, trots out «high risk» in one case and rattles off «low risk» in another, then the machine learning algorithm's performance is not only lacklustre but, and foremost, outright unworthwhile. It follows that its *pearls of algorithmic wisdom* are not amenable to be rendered reliable, insofar they fall noticeably short of determining accurately the underlying risk. Either the degree of risk is high or low. It can't be both. Pivotally, the single-threshold rule is the beacon of fairness, and a brawny yardstick of reliability, that propels statistical prediction forward.[3869]

§§ Importantly, the hot pursuit for equality in **false-positive** or **false-negative rates** is tightly interlocked with the benchmark that render people importantly alike. It follows that equality in **false-positive rates** calls for an equal error rate across racial lines: black versus white defendants who will refrain themselves from committing crimes—the deemed **law abiders**.[3870] On the opposite pole, equality in **false-negative rates** calls for equality between the black and white groups who

---

[3866] Mayson, Sandra G., "Bias In, Bias Out", *cit.*, pp. 2218–2300 (2274).

[3867] Mayson, Sandra G., "Bias In, Bias Out", *cit.*, pp. 2218–2300 (2274).

[3868] It is bears mentioning that **predictive parity (calibration)** can likewise be despairingly inconsistent with a **single-threshold rule**. At the very least, it does not ensure or necessarily indicate a single threshold for risk classification. See: Mayson, Sandra G., "Bias In, Bias Out", *cit.*, pp. 2218–2300.

[3869] Mayson, Sandra G., "Bias In, Bias Out", *cit.*, pp. 2218–2300 (2274).

[3870] See: Mayson, Sandra G., "Bias In, Bias Out", *cit.*, pp. 2218–2300 (arguing that equalizing false-positive rates will beget fewer false positives—"law abiders" mistakenly predict for rearrest—for the high-base-rate group than the low-base-rate group because there are fewer "law abiders" in the high-base-rate group in the first place). But see: Angwin, Julia et al., "Machine Bias", *ProPublica* (May 23, 2016), https://www.propublica.org/article/machine-bias-risk-assessments-in-criminal-sentencing; [https://perma.cc/4G83-MDAS] (harshly criticizing disparity in false-positive rates as a purely unjustified bias). See also: Freeman, Katherine, "Algorithmic Injustice: How the Wisconsin Supreme Court Failed to Protect Due Process Rights in State v. Loomis", *North Carolina Journal of Law and Technology*, Volume 18, 2016, pp. 75–86 (echoing the very same views).

will eventually engage in criminal activities—the tagged wrongdoers, tortfeasors, or **lawbreakers**.[3871]

§§ The **single-threshold rule** is therefore a touchstone of algorithmic fairness of which relevant stakeholders should not be oblivious of, nor should they lose sight of. Consequently, law abiders should be treated just the same irrespective of race or proxies to race. So should putative lawbreakers.[3872] Note, though, that this stance, albeit seemingly enthralling, is at loggerheads with the central tenets of coherence.

§§ Vitally, to aver that outcomes are what render two individuals (or racial lines) alike for purposes of algorithmic risk assessment is to aver that outcomes are a sound basis for risk assessment. However, they are not amenable to be considered a robust basis for algorithmic risk assessment since at the time of appraisal they are wholly unknown to the relevant stakeholders. This is the rationale behind the turn towards risk assessment to begin with.[3873]

§§ It is true that risk-assessment algorithms can be manually manipulated (**«masking»**)[3874] to produce equal false-positive or false-negative rates across racial[3875] lines.

§§ It is also true, nevertheless, that a machine learning algorithm entrusted[3876] with making a high-stake[3877] decision[3878] to equalize false-positive and false-negative

[3871] Mayson, Sandra G., "Bias In, Bias Out", *cit.*, pp. 2218–2300 (2274).

[3872] Mayson, Sandra G., "Bias In, Bias Out", *cit.*, pp. 2218–2300 (2274).

[3873] Mayson, Sandra G., "Bias In, Bias Out", *cit.*, pp. 2218–2300 (2275).

[3874] But see: Barocas, Solon/Selbst, Andrew D., "Big Data's Disparate Impact", *cit.*, pp. 692–93. These polymaths coined this phenomenon as "masking" owing to the fact that machine-learning technologies bestow upon stakeholders' multiple opportunities to intentionally twist/warp/deform an algorithm in ways that are painstakingly difficult to ferret out/discern/detect.

[3875] Mayson, Sandra G., "Bias In, Bias Out", *cit.*, pp. 2218–2300 (2275).

[3876] But see: Cohen, Julien E., *Between Truth and Power: The Legal Constructions of Informational Capitalism*. Oxford: Oxford University Press, 2019, pp. 1–376 (p. 192) (contends presciently that "*automated processes* have obvious efficiency advantages, *but such processes may not align well (or well at all) with applicable legal requirements that are couched in shades of gray*"). Italics added.

[3877] But see: Millar, Jason/Kerr, Ian, "Delegation, Relinquishment and Responsibility: The Prospect of Expert Robots", *Robot Law*, Calo, Ryan/Froomkin, A. Michael/Kerr, Ian (Editors), Cheltenham, Edward Elgar Publishing, 2016, pp. 102, 106–107 (as these authors aptly put it "*we will rely on robots without really knowing why – simply because their algorithms provide the greatest number of successful outcomes.* We have already seen this in Google's search approach. Neither Larry (Page) nor Sergey (Brin) (nor any other Google employee) knowns exactly why one particular web page is a better result than another. *When the click patterns say it is, that's good enough.* No semantic or causal analysis is required...*Like the ancients, we will, quite rationally, come to rely upon them, knowing full well that we cannot necessarily explain the reasons for their decisions*"). Italics added. Converging: Casey, Anthony J./Niblett, Anthony, "Self-driving Laws", *University of Toronto Law Journal*, Volume 66, 2016, pp. 429–435 (contend that "as more information is generated, and the evolutionary algorithm updates and become a better forecaster, *we imagine that judges will increasingly rely on the advice of the algorithm*"). But see: Weizenbaum, Joseph, *Computer Power and Human Reason: From Judgment to Calculation*, 1st edition, New York, W. H. Freeman & Co, 1976, pp. 1–300 (227) ("examines the sources of the computer's powers and offers evaluative explorations of what computers can do, cannot do, and should not be employed to do") (this founding father of Artificial Intelligence presciently noted that we should not entrust Artificial

rates will almost likely infringe/desecrate the foundational principle according to which people who pose the very same risk should be given the very same risk score—the gist of the **single-threshold rule**. Tellingly, if the base rate of the forecasted event varies greatly across racial lines, equalizing false-positive and false-negative rates will most likely require determining different risk thresholds[3879] by race for each risk classification.[3880]

§§ For example, labelling[3881] white defendants as high risk at a rearrest likelihood of 15% or above and beyond, whilst labelling black defendants as high risk only at a likelihood of 25% or above. In this situation, an individual with a 20% probability of rearrest will be labelled as high risk if he happens to be white but not if he happens to be black. To attain equality across racial lines that have not yet come into being

Intelligence-embedded technologies with "tasks that demand wisdom"). Italics added. The approval of rental applications is arguably one of those tasks that should never be entrusted to machines). More on this on Part IV, This chapter, Sects. 4.1.4–4.1.4.2.1 of this book. See: Part V, Chap. 5, Sect. 5.1.8.5 of this book (on law number five to interpret algorithmic decision-making, which mandates that robot-judges, robot-prosecutors and robot-lawyers must not enter the courtroom for they are utterly incapable of making sound and interpretable value judgements).

3878 But see: Part V, Chap. 5, Sect. 5.1.7.2 of this book (on law number two to control algorithmic decision-making, which mandates that black box models must not be entrusted with the task of making high stake decisions—v.g. health and freedom). But see: Rudin, Cynthia, "Please stop explaining black box models for high stakes decisions", *Proceedings of NeurIPS 2018 Workshop on Critiquing and Correcting Trends in Machine Learning (NIPS 2018)*, 2018, passim; Rudin, C., & Radin, J., "Why are we using black box models in AI when we don't need to? A lesson from an explainable AI competition", *Harvard Data Science Review*, 2019, Volume 1, Issue 2, passim; Tan, S., Caruana, R., Hooker, G., and Lou, Y., "Distill-and-compare: Auditing blackbox models using transparent model distillation". *Proceedings of the 2018 AAAI/ACM Conference on AI, Ethics, and Society, Association for Computing Machinery*, 2018, pp. 303–310 (arguing that explainable models are too complex and fiddly to be understood by laypeople. As a result, interpretable models should be used instead). See: Part V, Chap. 5, Sect. 5.1.7.2 of this book (on law number two to control algorithmic decision-making, which mandates that black box models must not be entrusted with the task of making high stake decisions—v.g. health and freedom). See: Part V, Chap. 5, Sects. 5.1.7–5.1.7.5 of this book (on the five laws to control algorithmic decision-making).

3879 But see: Citron, Danielle K., "Technological Due Process", *Washington University Law Review*, Volume 85, 2008, pp. 1249–1253 ("Computer programs seamlessly combine rulemaking and individual adjudications without the critical procedural protections owed either of them"). See: Part V, Chap. 5, Sect. 5.1.7.2 of this book (on law number two to control algorithmic decision-making, which mandates that black box models must not be entrusted with the task of making high stake decisions—v.g. health and freedom). See: Part V, Chap. 5, Sects. 5.1.7–5.1.7.5 of this book (on the five laws to control algorithmic decision-making).

3880 Mayson, Sandra G., "Bias In, Bias Out", *cit.*, pp. 2218–2300 (2275).

3881 But see: Corbett-Davies, Sam/Goel, Sharad, "The Measure and Mismeasure of Fairness: a critical Review of Fair Machine Learning", *Cornell University Library*, 2018, p. 18 (broaches a type of *measurement bias* coined "feature bias," which is neatly a bias in the predictors x. Note, though, that there is a second type of measurement bias deemed "label bias," which, in turn, amounts to a bias in y. The authors argue that that label bias is the worst bias there is). See also: Kleinberg, Jon/Ludwig, Jens/Mullainathan, Sendhil/Sunstein Cass R., "Discrimination in the Age of Algorithms", *Journal of Legal Analysis*, Volume 10, 1, 2018, pp. 28–29, 33–34 (draw a distinction between "group differences in the raw data" and biases for the "choice of predictors").

(**same-outcome racial lines**), the machine learning algorithm must create different risk assessments for people who present the same level of risk.[3882]

§§ It is noteworthy that the very notion of **«error»**[3883] in algorithmic risk assessment is widely contested.[3884] For instance, false positives consist of the bunch of people of whom we can say for sure in retrospect that they did no harm whatsoever. Note, though, that at the time of appraisal one does not know for whom this will turn out to be true. At a certain juncture, *probability* is all one has. It is worth recalling, too, that even in retrospect the fact that a risk does not come into fruition nor into being does not necessarily mean that a high-risk classification was inaccurate or botched. Let alone shoddy or watered down. From time to time, even high risks do not come to pass. This is exactly what sets risk apart from sureness.[3885]

§§ To sum up, the pursuit for equality for same-outcome across racial line at the expense of equality for same-risk individuals equals the rebuff of the whole project of statistical risk assessment. It accordingly impedes risk assessment based upon risk while conditions it on future outcomes framed, to some extent, by randomness.[3886] A similar line of reasoning applies, hands-in-glove, to **statistical parity**.[3887] Recall, **statistical parity** requires that the same percentage of each racial line (of people subject to algorithmic appraisal) be labelled[3888] as high risk.[3889]

[3882] Mayson, Sandra G., "Bias In, Bias Out", *cit.*, pp. 2218–2300 (2275).

[3883] Osaba, Osonde/Welser, William IV, *An Intelligence in Our Image—The Risk of Bias and Errors in Artificial Intelligence*, Santa Monica, California, Rand, 2018, passim.

[3884] See: Liu, John Zhuang/Xueyao Li, "How do judges use large language models? Evidence from Shenzhen", *Journal of Legal Analysis*, Volume 16, 2025, pp. 235–262 (235) ("*Drawing on extensive research in behavioral sciences, we propose that this interaction process between judges and AI may amplify errors and biases in judicial decision-making by reinforcing judges' prior beliefs*".). Italics added.

[3885] Mayson, Sandra G., "Bias In, Bias Out", *cit.*, pp. 2218–2300 (2275).

[3886] See: Sidhu, Dawinder S., "Moneyball Sentencing", *Boston College Law Review*, Volume 56, 2015, 671 (on the role of randomness in sentencing settings). On the role of chance and randomness: Teigena, Halvor/Kanten, Alf Børre, "Out of the blue: on the suddenness of perceived chance events", *Thinking & Reasoning*, Volume 29, n.° 1, 2023, pp. 137–175 (137) ("*people commonly use terms like 'random', 'by chance', or 'accidentally' when they describe occurrences that sidestep the normal course of events, with no apparent causal link to ongoing activities*"). Italics added.

[3887] Benjamin Fish et al., "A Confidence-Based Approach for Balancing Fairness and Accuracy", *Proceedings of the 2016 SIAM International Conference on Data Mining*, Chawla, Sanjay, Venkatasubramanian/Meira, Wagner (Editors), 2016, p. 144 (using the word "statistical parity"); Huq, Aziz Z., "Racial Equity in Algorithmic Criminal Justice", *cit.*, pp. 1116 (employing the word "statistical parity"); Corbett-Davies, Sam/Pierson, Emma/Feller, Avi/Goel, Sharad/Huq, Aziz, "Algorithmic Decision Making and the Cost of Fairness", passim (employing the term "conditional statistical parity" to describe parity in classification rates after controlling for "'legitimate' risk factors"); Hardt, Moritz et al., "Equality of Opportunity in Supervised Learning", *cit.*, 1 (using the term "demographic parity"); Zemel, Richard, et al., "Learning Fair Representations", *The Proceedings of Machine Learning Research*, Volume 28, 2013, p. 1 (using the term "statistical parity"). Berk, Richard et al., "Fairness in Criminal Justice Risk Assessments: The State of the Art", *cit.*, p. 13 (using the word "statistical parity").

[3888] Corbett-Davies and Goel coined this sweltering issue as "label bias" and diagnose it as "perhaps the most serious obstacle facing fair machine learning." But see: Corbett-Davies, Sam/Goel, Sharad, "The Measure and Mismeasure of Fairness: a critical Review of Fair Machine Learning", *Cornell*

§§ It is anchored on the assumption that the most importantly»alike» subsets are the entire racial groups subject to risk evaluation. On that note, such racial lines should be treated similarly irrespective of statistical discrepancies between them. It therefore spurns the foundational basis of risk assessment—**statistically informed action**.[3890]

§§ With this context in place, the recourse to **algorithmic affirmative action**[3891] does neither seem unwarranted nor uncalled for, nor statistically unsound. To the extent that equalizing error rates—or requiring statistical parity—neatly undermines statistical crime prediction,[3892] this seems to be the right course of action to be taken. Pivotally, risk assessment narrowed down to generate equal false-positive and false-negative rates is anything but algorithmic risk assessment to begin with. It is a sort-of race-specific risk sorting instead.[3893] **Notwithstanding, algorithmic risk assessment**[3894] **is exceedingly better**[3895] **than subjective risk assessment carried out by human judges.**[3896]

§§ Compellingly, subjective risk assessment engenders much greater racial disparity,[3897] in that exacts a far greater toll on members of racialized communities,[3898] than does algorithmic risk assessment.[3899] What is worse, subjective risk

---

University Library, 2018, p. 18 (broaches a type of *measurement bias* coined "feature bias," which is neatly a bias in the predictors x. Note, though, that there is a second type of measurement bias deemed "label bias," which, in turn, amounts to a bias in y. The authors argue that that label bias is the worst bias there is).

3889 Mayson, Sandra G., "Bias In, Bias Out", *cit.*, pp. 2218–2300 (2276).

3890 Mayson, Sandra G., "Bias In, Bias Out", *cit.*, pp. 2218–2300 (2276).

3891 Katznelson, Ira, *When Affirmative Action Was White: An Untold History of Racial Inequality in Twentieth-Century America*, New York, W. W. Norton & Company; Reprint edition (August 17, 2006), 2006, pp. 1–272 (This book parses the impact of several racially motivated laws—Social Security Act, G: I. Bill, and labour laws implementing unemployment stipends, minimum wages, and union protection—in the history of United States of America).

3892 But see: Hamilton, Melissa, "Risk-Needs Assessment: Constitutional and Ethical Challenges", *American Criminal Law Review*, Volume 52, 2015, pp. 231, 284–85 ("[I]f constitutionally or ethically suspect variables are excised [from risk-assessment tools], it is likely that fact-finders would consider [them] informally anyway, rendering their use less reliable, transparent, and consistent").

3893 Mayson, Sandra G., "Bias In, Bias Out", *cit.*, pp. 2218–2300 (2276).

3894 Kroll, Joshua A., et al., "Accountable Algorithms", *University of Pennsylvania Law Review*, Volume 165, 2017, pp. 633, 693–95.

3895 Desmarais, Sarah, L. et al., "Performance of Recidivism Risk Assessment Instruments in U.S. Correctional Settings", *Psychology Services*, Volume 13, 2016, passim.

3896 Stevenson, Megan/Mayson, Sandra G., "Pretrial Detention and Bail", Luna, Erik (Editor), *Reporting Criminal Justice: A Report of the Academy for Justice, Bridging the Gap between Scholarship and Reform*, 21, 2017, pp. 34–35 (poring over a batch of studies hinting that actuarial risk assessment can improve accuracy of pretrial risk judgments). See also: Starr, Sonja B., "Evidence-Based Sentencing and the Scientific Rationalization of Discrimination", *cit.*, p. 824 ("there is, to be sure, considerable statistical research suggesting that judges (and prosecutors) do on average treat female defendants more leniently than male defendants").

3897 See: Kahneman, Daniel/Slovic/Tversky, Amos (Editors), *Judgment under Uncertainty: Heuristics and Biases*, Cambridge, Cambridge University Press, 1982, pp. 1–544 (parsing several studies on human biases across various judgmental heuristics); See: Banks, Ralph Richard/Ford, Richard Thompson, "(How) Does Unconscious Bias Matter?: Law, Politics, and Racial Inequality", *Emory*

assessment[3900] shies away from, and runs afoul of, the central tenets of transparency,[3901] accountability[3902] and fairness.[3903] Besides, it disfigures core values underpinning *Algorithmic Common Good*.[3904]

Law Journal, Volume 58, 2009, passim; Barth, John A., "Unconscious Thought Theory and Its Discontents: A Critique of the Critiques", *Social Cognition*, Volume 29, 2011, 629 (on unconscious biases).

3898 See: Eckhouse, L., Lum, K., Conti-Cook, C./Ciccolini, J., "Layers of bias: A unified approach for understanding problems with risk assessment", *cit.*, p. 202 ("[T]here is substantial evidence that defendants of color are disadvantaged in pretrial and sentencing decisions made without reference to risk assessment models."); Rehavi, M. Marit/Starr, Sonja B., "Racial Disparity in Federal Criminal Sentences", *Journal of Political Economy*, Volume 122, 2014, pp. 1320, 1323 (pointing out that black defendants in the federal system were 1.75 times more likely to undergo a mandatory minimum criminal charge than similarly situated white defendants). See: Part IV, This chapter, Sects. 4.1.1–4.1.1.1 of this book (on biased predictive policing).

3899 Sunstein, Cass R., "Algorithms, Correcting Biases", *Social Research*, Volume 86, 2019, pp. 449–506 (this famed author tagged disparate impact as "disturbing in itself, in the sense that a practice that produces such an impact helps entrench something like a caste system"). This famed scholar furthermore avers that empirical evidence on the accuracy of machine versus human predictions suggests the existence of a "current offense bias" that saps ulterior/subsequent judicial assessments).

3900 It is worth recalling that a seasoned and well-adjusted judge with extensive experience might be noticeably more effective at evaluating risk than a rudimentary algorithm. In stark contrast, an advanced algorithm might be considerably more effective than a lousy judge. Relatedly, a good judge operating with the benefit of a good algorithm is a match made in heaven. See: Mayson, Sandra G., "Bias In, Bias Out", *cit.*, pp. 2218–2300. See: Dressel, Julia Dressel/Farid, Hany, "The Accuracy, Fairness, and Limits of Predicting Recidivism", *Science Advances*, Volume 4, 2018, 1 (concluding that unseasoned and inexperienced human participants performed nearly as well as the algorithm COMPAS); Starr, Sonja B., "Evidence-Based Sentencing and the Scientific Rationalization of Discrimination", *cit.*, p. 855 (concluding that "the shibboleth that actuarial prediction outperforms clinical prediction is—like the actuarial risk predictions themselves—a generalization that is not true in every case").

3901 Note, though, that a feted scholar (Bernard Harcourt) adamantly contends that (1) predictive crime control efforts may produce more harm than good; (2) they may engender a "ratchet effect" in which the disparate impact of forecast on black folks worsens over time; and (3) the technological allure of prediction can both besmirch and mar deep-rooted moral conceptions of justice. See: Harcourt, Bernard E., *Against Prediction: Profiling, Policing, and Punishing in An Actuarial Age*, Chicago, Illinois, University of Chicago Press, 2007, pp. 7–18 and passim. Converging: Ensign, Danielle, "Runaway Feedback Loops in Predictive Policing", *Proceedings of Machine Learning Research*, Volume 81, 2018, p. 1; Starr, Sonja B., "Evidence-Based Sentencing and the Scientific Rationalization of Discrimination", *Stanford Law Review*, Volume 66, 2014, pp. 804–06 (arguing that that risk assessment during sentencing may derails deep-seated concepts of justice that we hold so dear). In addition to this line of reasoning, Professor Sandra Mayson avers that, because any extant racial disparity in crime risk is the byproduct of a long-haul historical oppression, it is therefore an unfitting basis for coercive state action. To put it bluntly, it is unfair for the state to condition coercion on crime risk that modern societies has unjustly created. Put another way, one may be led to believe that the data are simply warped and that the risk at hand is fundamentally uniform across racial lines. Understandably, though not laudably, one may be also led to believe that crime risk is a fundamentally haphazard and incoherent concept, owing to the fact that all people who are self-determining agents have an equal capacity to eschew flagitious behaviour or engaging in criminal activities.

3902 Mayson, Sandra G., "Bias In, Bias Out", *cit.*, pp. 2218–2300 (2281).

§§ Crucially, actuarial risk assessment—from which algorithmic risk assessment derives[3905]—has not created the scorching problem of racially disparate prediction. Instead, it unlocked/unveiled/unearthed into broad day light.[3906]

4.1.10.5 Algorithmic Common Good: Machine Learning Algorithms Should Be Deployed to Audit the Pearls of Algorithmic Wisdom for Racial Inequity and Relevant Stakeholders Must Track the Quality of the Underlying Dataset (or Lack Thereof) From Which the Predictive Tools Were Built

§§ To the extent that the deployment of machine learning algorithms sharply mirrors gross racial inequalities in the dataset from which they are leverage on,[3907] they can likewise be deployed in reverse: as race-aware algorithms suitably tailored to

---

[3903] This is called law of *implicit bias*: people make decisions (e.g. discriminating seemingly disfavoured groups of people) that often-times lack a rational connection between facts and judgment. A conscious and deliberate judgment that noticeably runs afoul with rationality. See: Jolls, Christine/Sunstein, Cass R., "The Law of Implicit Bias", *California Law Review*, Volume 94, 2006, p. 969 (arguing that this issue can be solved through the general strategy of de-biasing through law, by steering people through more rational directions). See also: Kang, Jerry/Banaji, Mahzarin R., "Fair Measures: A Behavioural Realist Revision of Affirmative Action", *California Law Review*, Volume 94 2006, p. 1064 (arguing that «implicit bias often conflicts with conscious attitudes, endorsed beliefs, and intentional behaviour»); Greenwald, Anthony G., and Linda Hamilton Krieger, Implicit Bias: Scientific Foundations", *California Law Review*, Volume 94, 2006, pp. 945–967. See also: Richardson, L. Song/Goff, Phillip Atiba, "Implicit Racial Bias in Public Defender Triage", *Yale Law Journal*, Volume 122, 2013, 2626; Banks, R. Richard et al., "Discrimination and Implicit Bias in a Racially Unequal Society", *California Law Review*, Volume 94, 2006, pp. 1169 and ff and passim; Eberhardt, Jennifer L. et al., "Looking Deathworthy: Perceived Stereotypicality of Black Defendants Predicts Capital-Sentencing Outcomes", *Psych Science*, Volume 17, 2006, 383; Faigman, David L. et al., Implicit Bias in the Courtroom", *UCLA Law Review*, Volume 59, 2012, 1124; Levinson, Justin D., "Forgotten Racial Equality: Implicit Bias, Decisionmaking, and Misremembering", *Duke Law Journal*, Volume 57, 2007, 345; Levinson, Justin D. et al., "Guilty by Implicit Bias: The Guilty/Not Guilty Implicit Association Test", *Ohio State Journal on Criminal Law*, Volume 8, 2010, 187.

[3904] See: Part V, Chap. 5, Sects. 5.1.2–5.1.6.2.1 of this book (on the thing-centred algorithmic decision-making propelled by a *Controllable* and *Interpretable* Machine Learning that weeds out *Algorithmic Dictatorship* and secures *Algorithmic Common Good*. It is worth recalling that the **thing-centred algorithmic decision-making** seeks to unwind the perils arising out of the lack of theoretical underpinnings facing the **human-centred algorithmic decision-making**, as extensively fleshed out Part III, Chap. 3, Sects. 3.1.4.3–3.1.4.4 of this book).

[3905] Wiseman, Samuel R., "Fixing Bail", *George Washington Law Review*, Volume 84, 2016, pp. 417-454 (arguing that "actuarial instruments should limit" rather than inform judicial discretion).

[3906] Mayson, Sandra G., "Bias In, Bias Out", *cit.*, pp. 2218–2300 (2281).

[3907] See: Barocas, Solon/Selbst, Andrew D., "Big Data's Disparate Impact", *California Law Review*, Volume 104, 2016, pp. 671–682 (discussing how data is often flawed, rigged, incomplete, imperfect and therefore algorithms inherit the prejudice of the original decision makers). But see: Citron, Danielle Keats/Pasquale, Frank, "The Scored Society: Due Process for Automated Predictions", *Washington Law Review*, Volume 89, 2014, pp. 1, 4–5 (highlighting how human beings programming automated systems is directly conducive to, and leads, to fundamentally inaccurate results since the source code, predictive algorithms and datasets may encompass human biases which, in turn, have

ferret out the sources of racial inequity[3908] in criminal procedural law settings.[3909] Crucially, if machine learning algorithms are deployed in this manner, relevant stakeholders are therefore vested with the functional duty to *audit*[3910] the pearls of algorithmic wisdom to adroitly identify racial inequality. Should such inequality indeed arise, by any meaningful equality metric, the next meaningful move is to determine why.[3911]

§§ That can happen for two reasons: **(I)** the machine learning algorithm is far less predictive for one racial line than for another (as is turned out to entirely true for Hispanic defendants in Melissa Hamilton's body of empirical evidence of COMPAS)[3912]; or, alternatively, **(II)** the machine learning algorithm is equally predictive across racial groups and the perceived racial inequality arises directly

---

a disparate impact on historically disadvantaged groups). But see: Bornstein, Stepanhie, "Antidiscriminatory Algorithms", *Alabama Law Review*, Volume 70, 2018, pp. 519, 524–528 (contending, however, that the tagged "facially neutral" algorithms producing discriminatory outcomes should be quashed).

[3908] But see: Kim, Pauline T., "Data-Driven Discrimination at Work", *William and Mary Law Review*, Volume 58, 2017, p. 918 ("If the goal is to reduce biased outcomes, then a simple prohibition on using data about race or sex could be either wholly ineffective or actually counterproductive due to the existence of class proxies and the risk of omitted variable bias."); Lipton, Zachary et al., "Does Mitigating ML's Impact Disparity Require Treatment Disparity?", NIPS Proceedings 1, 2018, https://arxiv.org/pdf/1711.07076.pdf; [https://perma.cc/X8VF-EY53] (arguing, premised on statistical examples, that a prohibition on race or sex data is rather counterproductive indeed); Corbett-Davies, Sam/Goel, Sharad, "The Measure and Mismeasure of Fairness: a critical Review of Fair Machine Learning", *Cornell University Library*, 2018, passim (discussing the "[l]imitations of anti-classification" as a fairness metric). See also: Kim, Pauline T., "Data-Driven Discrimination at Work", *cit.*, p. 867 ("[I]f the goal is to discourage classification bias, then the law should not forbid the inclusion of race, sex, or other sensitive information as variables, but seek to preserve these variables, and perhaps even include them in some complex models."); Kroll, Joshua A., et al., "Accountable Algorithms", *University of Pennsylvania Law Review*, Volume 165, 2017, pp. 633, 693–95. See also: Kim, Pauline T., "Data-Driven Discrimination at Work", *cit.*, p. 866 ("classification bias occurs when employers rely on classification schemes, such as data algorithms, to sort or score workers in ways that worsen inequality or disadvantage along the lines of race, sex, or other protected characteristics"). These two uses of the word "bias" correspond to the notions of irrational versus rational **(or statistical) discrimination.** Mayson, Sandra G., "Bias In, Bias Out", *cit.*, pp. 2218–2300.

[3909] See: Selbst, Andrew D., "Disparate Impact in Big Data Policing", *Georgia Law Review*, Volume 52, 2017, pp. 110, 169–80 (suggesting "algorithmic impact statements" which "would require police departments to evaluate the efficacy and potential discriminatory effects of all available choices for predictive policing technologies").

[3910] See: Part V, Chap. 5, Sect. 5.1.7.5 of this book (on Algorithmic Common Good, with a sharper focus on the dire need of algorithmic auditing, undertaken by external auditors that must be given full access to the dataset used to train the running models).

[3911] Mayson, Sandra G., "Bias In, Bias Out", *cit.*, pp. 2218–2300 (2284).

[3912] See: Hamilton, Melissa, "The Biased Algorithm: Evidence of Disparate Impact on Hispanics", *American Criminal Law Review*, Volume 56, 2019, passim (noting the likelihood that risk-assessment tools will underperform for Hispanic Americans unless they integrate cultural and situational factors that moderate risk, and concluding that it is "quite likely" that poorer performance of COMPAS for Hispanic defendants was due to failure to integrate "cultural differences" that moderate risk". See also: Shepherd, Stephane M./Lewis-Fernandez, Roberto, "Forensic Risk

from a difference in the base rate (dataset) of the forecasted event (as is turned out to be entirely true for black versus white defendants in the *ProPublica* body of empirical[3913] evidence). If the machine learning algorithm is consciously/conspicuously less predictive for one racial line, relevant stakeholders should employ staggering efforts to ascertain why. It may be that the data are more limited or of lower quality for one racial group.[3914]

§§ In either case, relevant stakeholders must **track** the quality of the dataset (or lack thereof) from which machine learning algorithms were built to foster *algorithmic fairness* in criminal justice settings.[3915] This is the kernel of *Algorithmic Common Good* of which relevant stakeholders should not shy away from.[3916]

§§ Overall, this approach would greatly augment policy endeavours to greatly improve data collection as would greatly increase the data quality. On the top of that, it would also enable the tool developers to manually tweak the data to grant proper and sound group representation, which is pivotally important for the development of a both accurate and reliable machine learning algorithm.[3917] On this note, it is worth recalling that more often than not the root of the discrepancy in predictive accuracy

---

Assessment and Cultural Diversity: Contemporary Challenges and Future Directions", *Psychology Public Policy, and Law*, Volume 22, 2016, pp. 427–498.

[3913] Angwin J, Larson J, Mattu S, et al., "Machine bias: There's software used across the country to predict future criminals. And it's biased against blacks", 2016, passim. Available at. https://www.propublica.org/article/machine-bias-risk-assessments-in-criminal-sentencing (accessed 26 October 2024). Sun, R. (Ed.), *The Cambridge Handbook of Computational Cognitive Sciences*, Cambridge, Cambridge University Press, 2023.

[3914] Mayson, Sandra G., "Bias In, Bias Out", *cit.*, pp. 2218–2300 (2284).

[3915] See: Part V, Chap. 5, Sect. 5.1.7.5 of this book (on Algorithmic Common Good, with a sharper focus on the dire need of algorithmic auditing, undertaken by external auditors that must be given full access to the dataset used to train the running models).

[3916] See: Part V, Chap. 5, Sects. 5.1.2–5.1.6.2.1 of this book (on the thing-centred algorithmic decision-making propelled by a *Controllable* and *Interpretable* Machine Learning that weeds out *Algorithmic Dictatorship* and secures *Algorithmic Common Good*. It is worth recalling that the **thing-centred algorithmic decision-making** seeks to unwind the perils arising out of the lack of theoretical underpinnings facing the **human-centred algorithmic decision-making**, as extensively fleshed out Part III, Chap. 3, Sects. 3.1.4.3–3.1.4.4 of this book).

[3917] It is important to note that an algorithm designed for maximum accuracy will adjust itself to the majority data, and may be less accurate for members of the underrepresented group, thus breeding *inductive bias*. See: Shellenbarger, Sue, "A Crucial Step for Avoiding AI Disasters", *Wall Street Journal*, (Feb. 13, 2019, 9:57 AM ET), https://www.wsj.com/articles/a-crucial-step-for-avoiding-ai-disasters-11550069865?ns=prod/accounts-wsj; [https://perma.cc/C28U-LAAE] (discussing this issue while emphasizing how diverse development teams pay more attention to unrepresentative and underrepresented data sets). Human programmers can circumvent and bypass this problem by weighting the minority-group data more heavily, by designing different algorithms for each racial group, or by striving to contain more data to equalize group representation in the data set. See: Barua, Sukarna et al., "MWMOTE—Majority Weighted Minority Oversampling Technique for Imbalanced Data Set Learning", *IEEE Transactions on Knowledge & Data Engineering*, Volume 26, 2014, pp. 405, 405–06. See also: Hamilton, Melissa, "The Biased Algorithm: Evidence of Disparate Impact on Hispanics", *American Criminal Law Review*, Volume 56, 2019, pp. 1553 and ff and passim (which clearly demonstrates that COMPAS was significantly less accurate for Hispanic than for white defendants by several measures and suggesting that smaller numbers of Hispanic defendants might be the cause). See: Mayson, Sandra G., "Bias In, Bias Out", *cit.*, pp. 2218–2300.

lies in the fact that, for one racial line, a cluster of input variables correlate differently with the outcome. Crucially, a cohort of risk-assessment-tool engineers have come to terms with the fact that, taken together, past arrests and misdemeanour convictions in a court of law «mean less» about future risk for black people than for other racial lines.[3918]

§§ This neatly encapsulates, hands-in-glove, a finding that relevant stakeholders—ranging from tool developers, judges, probation officers, parole officers, judges, prosecutors to attorneys—must bear very firmly in mind in criminal procedure law settings.

§§ Of tantamount importance—it doesn't hurt to recall—whenever the machine learning algorithm is equally predictive across racial lines, and the racial inequality in outputs arises mathematically[3919] from a discrepancy in the underlying base rate of the forecasted event (e.g. base rate of rearrest across racial lines), then relevant stakeholders should figure it out why the base-rate discrepancy exists in the first place.[3920]

§§ Should that occur, the burning questions in dire need of being thoroughly answered read as follows: **i)** are the data far less accurate for one racial line (meaning, are rearrests routinely unrepresentative/underrated for one racial line)[3921]? Should

---

See also: Dong et al., Qi, "Imbalanced deep learning by minority class incremental rectification, *IEEE Transactions on Pattern Analysis & Machine Intelligence*, Volume 41, 2019, p. 1367 (posit that "*most existing learning algorithms produce inductive bias (learning bias)* towards the frequent (majority) classes if training data are not balanced, *resulting in poor minority class recognition performance*"). Italics added. See: Chandler, Anupam, "The Racist Algorithm", *Michigan Law Review*, Volume 115, n. ° 6, 2018, p. 1026 (on racist algorithms, noting that "the possibilities for discriminatory manipulation are legion"). But see: Altenburger, Kristen M./Ho, Daniel E., "When Algorithms Import Private Bias into Public Enforcement: The Promise and Limitations of Statistical Debiasing Solutions", *Journal of Institutional & Theoretical Economics*, Volume 175, 2019, pp. 97–98 (calls for a "debias predictive algorithms" to assuage racist and/or biased, doctored and bigoted algorithms nevertheless). See: Part V, Chap. 5, Sect. 5.1.7.4 of this book (on one of the law to control algorithmic decision-making, namely, law number four: data partitioning must be performed—i.e. randomly split an entire dataset into the «training dataset» and the «test dataset»—to accurately predict outcomes in the real world while forestalling «inductive bias» (learning bias)).

3918 Mayson, Sandra G., "Bias In, Bias Out", *cit.*, pp. 2218–2300 (2284).

3919 A cohort of scientists, for instance, is using machine learning to pinpoint adjectives tightly interlocked with different ethnic groups across the nineteenth and twentieth centuries to shed a keen light on the history of discrimination. See: Garg, Nikhil et al., "Word Embeddings Quantify 100 Years of Gender and Ethnic Stereotypes", *Proceedings of the National Academy of Sciences of the United States of America*, Volume 115, 2018, E3635. See: Part IV, This chapter, Sect. 4.1.8 of this book (on biased word embeddings with an entrenched presence on search engines run by tech moguls).

3920 Mayson, Sandra G., "Bias In, Bias Out", *cit.*, pp. 2218–2300.

3921 See, e.g., Hamilton, Melissa, "Back to the Future: The Influence of Criminal History on Risk Assessments", *Berkeley Journal of Criminal Law*, Volume 20, 2015, pp. 75, 78 (exuding concerns with the recurrent use of criminal history in risk assessment owing to "the potential that criminal history is an unfortunate proxy for race and social disadvantage"). See also: McIntyre, Frank/Baradaran, Shima, "Race, Prediction, and Pretrial Detention", *Journal Empirical Legal Studies*, Volume 10, 2013, pp. 742–759 (mentions black defendants' exceedingly high likelihood of being arrested on drug-related charges as a potential cause of the race gap); Skeem, Jennifer L./

that be the case, the data is in dire need of being significantly improved.[3922] Relatedly, are the data representative, reliable, accurate, and the vexing problem is that the event one seeks to forecast befalls unusually often on communities of colour, such as arrest for petty crimes? Should that be the case, one reconsider—or, at the very least, give an afterthought—the value of forecasting that outcome[3923] in the first place.[3924]

§§ Recall, base-rate discrepancies echo racially skewed law enforcement practices, as opposed to racial fluctuation in crime commission, which, in turn, bestows upon stakeholders a compelling incentive for changes to policing policy. Last but not necessarily least, a divergent base rate has every chance to mirror a difference across racial lines that one wants algorithmic tools to foretell, like a difference in rates for a given type of crime. If the rates for some category of crime differ greatly across racial lines in a given span of time and jurisdiction, awareness is pivotally important to bolster subsequent policy intervention.[3925]

4.1.10.6 Can Predictive Parity and the Single Threshold Rule Dovetail Seamlessly Only to Propel Algorithmic Fairness in Criminal Justice Settings?

§§ To achieve algorithmic fairness across racial lines in criminal procedure law settings, algorithmic risk-assessment tools must meet three stringent metrics of **predictive equality**.[3926] Firstly, and pivotally, individuals who pose the same statistical risk should be given the same risk score irrespective of their race line—this is the nub of the **single-threshold rule** for risk classification.[3927]

§§ As noted earlier in this essay, the **single-threshold rule** amounts to a theoretical underpinning of risk assessment itself, which is suitably tailored to aggrandize the tool's overall accuracy and underlying fairness. Secondly, and crucially, with a **single-threshold rule** full steam ahead, a given risk score should impart the very same

Lowenkamp, Christopher T., "Risk, Race, and Recidivism: Predictive Bias and Disparate Impact", *Criminology*, Volume 54, 2024, pp. 680, 683–84, 704–06 (argues that criminal history correlates with race in their respective data set).

3922 See: Part V, Chap. 5, Sect. 5.1.7.4 of this book (on one of the laws to control algorithmic decision-making, namely, law number four: data partitioning must be performed—i.e. randomly split an entire dataset into the «training dataset» and the «test dataset»—to accurately predict outcomes in the real world while forestalling «inductive bias» (learning bias)).

3923 Mayson, Sandra G., "Bias In, Bias Out", *cit.*, pp. 2218–2300 (2285).

3924 Mayson, Sandra G., "Bias In, Bias Out", *cit.*, pp. 2218–2300.

3925 Mayson, Sandra G., "Bias In, Bias Out", *cit.*, pp. 2218–2300 (2285).

3926 Berk, Richard et al., "Fairness in Criminal Justice Risk Assessments: The State of the Art", *cit.*, p. 14 (describing "conditional use accuracy equality"); Dieterich, William et al., "COMPAS Risk Scales: Demonstrating Accuracy Equity and Predictive Parity", *cit.*, passim (describing "predictive parity"); Hardt, Moritz et al., "Equality of Opportunity in Supervised Learning", *cit.*, passim.

3927 Mayson, Sandra G., "Bias In, Bias Out", *cit.*, pp. 2218–2300 (2294).

average risk irrespective of the race of the defendant to whom seeks to apply—this is the gist of «**predictive parity**»[3928] or **«calibration».**[3929]

§§ At first blush, these two metrics may seem kindred, yet such is not the case. Compellingly, allotting the very same risk score to all the defendants who pose the same risk will not inexorably breed **predictive parity**.[3930] Relatedly, a machine learning algorithm might achieve **predictive parity**[3931] without ascribing the very same risk score to defendants who pose the very same[3932] degree of risk.

§§ Notwithstanding, the **single-threshold rule**[3933] and **predictive parity** are conceptually kindred to the extent that both require that the relationship between a risk score and risk itself to be extant, constant, and fundamentally reciprocal across racial lines. At one end of the spectrum, the **single-threshold rule** requires that the machine learning algorithm sharply mirror a certain degree of individual risk into the very same risk score irrespective of the racial line to which that individual belongs to. At the other end of the spectrum, the **predictive parity** fundamentally requires

---

[3928] Note, though, that algorithmic fairness gives rise to several incompatible standards. Whilst COMPAS falls short of meeting the baseline standards of "equal opportunity" and "equalized odds", it refrains itself from discriminating blacks from the prism of "predictive parity" nonetheless. A full-fledged analysis of the extant state of this scorching topic can be found in Hübner, Dietmar, "Two Kinds of Discrimination in AI-Based penal Decision-Making", *SIGKDD Explorations*, 2021; Hellman, Deborah, "Measuring Algorithmic Fairness", *Virginia Law Review*, Volume 106, 2020, pp. 811 and ff and passim.

[3929] Mayson, Sandra G., "Bias In, Bias Out", *cit.*, pp. 2218–2300.

[3930] Dieterich, William et al., "COMPAS Risk Scales: Demonstrating Accuracy Equity and Predictive Parity", *Northpointe Inc.* 1, 2–3, 8–13 (July 8, 2016), http://go.volarisgroup.com/rs/430-MBX-989/images/ProPublica_Commentary_Final_070616.pdf; [https://perma.cc/K4GM-RBQY] (stating that a predictive instrument is bigoted/flawed only if a certain score, or a given classification, means a starkly likelihood of the forecasted outcome for members of one racial group than members of the other group). See also: Flores: Anthony W. et al., "False Positives, False Negatives, and False Analyses: A Rejoinder to "Machine Bias: There's Software Used Across the Country to Predict Future Criminals. And It's Biased Against Blacks," *Federal Probation*, Volume 80, 2016, pp. 38–40 (positing that "well-established and accepted standards exist to test for bias in risk assessment"); Skeem, Jennifer L./Lowenkamp, Christopher T., "Risk, Race, and Recidivism: Predictive Bias and Disparate Impact", *cit.*, p. 685 (asserting that if "a given score [has] the same meaning regardless of group membership," the instrument is "unbiased"). See: Mayson, Sandra G., "Bias In, Bias Out", *cit.*, pp. 2218–2300.

[3931] It bears mentioning that the literature on algorithmic fairness has labelled measures of equality as either "group fairness" or "individual fairness" metrics. This phosphorescent dichotomy, though, can be very misleading indeed. Almost every tentative measure of "group fairness" can be framed using the term "individual" (for example, **predictive parity** entails that, for any individual, a given risk score conveys the same average risk irrespective of race). Relatedly, any "individual-fairness" metric can be framed using the term "group" (for example, a **single-threshold rule** requires that the group of people who poses any degree of risk should receive the same risk score). The difference is that which **"individual-fairness"** metrics relates to how the algorithm reaches its output in each individual case, whilst **"group-fairness"** metrics relates to the distribution of outputs and/or their accuracy across particular groups. See: Mayson, Sandra G., "Bias In, Bias Out", *cit.*, pp. 2218–2300.

[3932] Mayson, Sandra G., "Bias In, Bias Out", *cit.*, pp. 2218–2300 (2294).

[3933] It is worth recalling that **predictive parity** (**calibration**) can likewise be despairingly inconsistent with a **single-threshold rule**. At the very least, it does not ensure or necessarily indicate a single threshold for risk classification. See: Mayson, Sandra G., "Bias In, Bias Out", *cit.*, pp. 2218–2300.

that a given risk score consistently reflect the very same average irrespective of the racial line to which that individual is part of. As an upshot, the foregoing metrics—the **single threshold rule** and the **predictive parity**—can dovetail seamlessly in criminal procedure law settings, even if base rates of the forecasted outcome vary greatly across racial lines.[3934]

§§ Thirdly, and unerringly, the machine learning algorithm should classify individuals along a compass of risk with equal accuracy across racial lines (i.e., have identical **area under the curve** scores by racial line). After all, the machine learning algorithm's **area under the curve score (aka AUC)** should measure how to distinguish between defendants who pose different levels[3935] of risk.[3936]

§§ Albeit this yardstick—i.e. the metric named **area under the curve**—says very little about the importance of an individual risk score, it is nonetheless a pivotally important benchmark of a machine learning algorithm's overall accuracy and reliability, racial equality wise. Note, though, that none of these yardsticks alone (i.e. the **single threshold rule** and the **predictive parity**) ensures that a machine learning algorithm is race neutral.[3937]

§§ Quite the opposite, attaining both—either in combination or in separation—might entail race-aware choices in the design of the machine learning algorithm.[3938] Notably, if the base rate of the forecasted outcome varies across racial lines, the machine learning algorithm will still augur it more often for the high-base-rate racial line. On the flip side, if the base rates vary greatly,[3939] a machine learning algorithm

[3934] Mayson, Sandra G., "Bias In, Bias Out", *cit.*, pp. 2218–2300 (2294).

[3935] For this reason, Sam Corbett-Davies and Sharad Goel refer to colorblindness as "anti-classification." Corbett-Davies, Sam/Gaebler, Johann D./Nilforoshan, Hamed/Shrof, Ravi/Goel, Sharad, "The Measure and Mismeasure of Fairness", *Journal of Machine Learning Research*, Volume 24, 2023, pp. 1–117 (p. 36) ("*In constructing algorithmic risk scores, a key ingredient is the target of prediction. In practice, though, there is often a mismatch between our true outcome of interest and the available data—an occurrence we call label bias (Zanger-Tishler* et al., *2023)*"). Italics added.

[3936] Mayson, Sandra G., "Bias In, Bias Out", *cit.*, pp. 2218–2300 (2294).

[3937] Mayson, Sandra G., "Bias In, Bias Out", *cit.*, pp. 2218–2300 (2294).

[3938] On the dire need to achieve algorithmic fairness through the creation of both race-aware algorithms and meaningful trade-offs to attain fairer risk scores: Kim, Pauline, "Race-Aware Algorithms: Fairness, Non-discrimination and Affirmative Action" *California Law Review*, 2022; Kleinberg, Jon/S. Mullainathan/M. Raghavan, "Inherent Trade-offs in the Fair Determination of Risk Scores", *Proceedings of the 8th Conference on Innovations in Theoretical Computer Science (ITCS)*, 2017; Kroll, Joshua A./J. Huey/S. Barocas/E. W. Felten/J. R. Reidenberg/D. G. Robinson/and H. Yu, "Accountable Algorithms", *University of Pennsylvania Law Review*, 165 (3), 2017, pp. 633–705.

[3939] It is worth recalling that a machine learning algorithm designed for maximum accuracy will adjust itself to the majority data, and may be less accurate for members of the under-represented group, thus breeding inductive bias. See: Shellenbarger, Sue, "A Crucial Step for Avoiding AI Disasters", *Wall Street Journal*, (Feb. 13, 2019, 9:57 AM ET), https://www.wsj.com/articles/a-crucial-step-for-avoiding-ai-disasters-11550069865?ns=prod/accounts-wsj; [https://perma.cc/C28U-LAAE] (discussing this issue while emphasizing how diverse development teams pay more attention to unrepresentative and underrepresented data sets). Human programmers can circumvent and bypass this problem by weighting the minority-group data more heavily, by designing different algorithms for each racial group, or by striving to contain more data to equalize group representation

that accomplishes these benchmarks of equality/fairness will most likely produce lopsided/unhinged/unequal false-positive and/or false-negative[3940] rates[3941] across racial lines.

§§ With this background in mind, Professor Sandra G. Mayson made a poignant call for the embracement of **«predictive honesty»** in a bid to afford primacy to racial equality in the accuracy of algorithmic risk assessment tools, as opposed to **statistical parity** or parity in false-positive or -negative rates.[3942] This is the only forward to peter out long-standing racial inequalities in criminal justice settings while allaying the prospects of *Algorithmic Dictatorship* that looms large in this discussion.

§§ Compellingly, neither colour-blindness,[3943] nor algorithmic affirmative action, nor the outright rebuff of algorithmic risk assessment will tackle the nuances of the underlying problem. To the extent crime and arrest rates are unequal across racial lines,[3944] any method of assessing crime or arrest risk will inevitably produce racial disparity[3945] in algorithmic risk assessment.[3946]

---

in the data set. See: Barua, Sukarna et al., "MWMOTE—Majority Weighted Minority Oversampling Technique for Imbalanced Data Set Learning", *IEEE Transactions on Knowledge & Data Engineering*, Volume 26, 2014, pp. 405, 405–06. See also: Hamilton, Melissa, "The Biased Algorithm: Evidence of Disparate Impact on Hispanics", *American Criminal Law Review*, Volume 56, 2019, pp. 1553 and ff and passim (which clearly demonstrates that COMPAS was significantly less accurate for Hispanic than for white defendants by several measures and suggesting that smaller numbers of Hispanic defendants might be the cause). See: Mayson, Sandra G., "Bias In, Bias Out", *cit.*, pp. 2218–2300. See also: Dong et al., Qi, "Imbalanced deep learning by minority class incremental rectification, *IEEE Transactions on Pattern Analysis & Machine Intelligence*, Volume 41, 2019, p. 1367 (posit that "*most existing learning algorithms produce inductive bias (learning bias)* towards the frequent (majority) classes if training data are not balanced, *resulting in poor minority class recognition performance*").

[3940] It is worth recalling, too, that Richard Berk trained the algorithm only to maximize for overall accuracy, it predicted rearrest for 17% of the white subgroup and 33% of the black subgroup (a 16 percentage-point difference). Strikingly, the false-positive rates were 16% for the white subgroup whereas for the black groups was 28% (a 12 percentage-point difference). See: Berk, Richard, "Accuracy and Fairness for Juvenile Justice Risks Assessments", *cit.*, p. 180. Notably, when Richard Berk changed the algorithm to equalize the cost ratios, it predicted rearrest for 10% of the white subgroup and 29% of the black subgroup (a 19 percentage-point difference). Relatedly, the false-positive rates were 8% for the white subset and 22% for the black subset (a 14 percentage-point difference). See: Berk, Richard, "Accuracy and Fairness for Juvenile Justice Risks Assessments", *cit.*, p. 185.

[3941] Mayson, Sandra G., "Bias In, Bias Out", *cit.*, pp. 2218–2300 (2295).

[3942] Mayson, Sandra G., "Bias In, Bias Out", *cit.*, pp. 2218–2300 (2295).

§§ The best way to remedy, and atone for,[3947] the racial inequality that inheres and permeates algorithmic risk assessment amidst a racially unequal world is to reconsider the way in which criminal procedure deals with, and responds to, risk. To cater for that, the best way to achieve algorithmic fairness in criminal procedure

---

[3943] See: Kim, Pauline T., "Data-Driven Discrimination at Work", *William and Mary Law Review*, Volume 58, 2017, p. 918 ("If the goal is to reduce biased outcomes, then a simple prohibition on using data about race or sex could be either wholly ineffective or actually counterproductive due to the existence of class proxies and the risk of omitted variable bias."); Lipton, Zachary et al., "Does Mitigating ML's Impact Disparity Require Treatment Disparity?", *NIPS Proceedings*, 1, 2018, https://arxiv.org/pdf/1711.07076.pdf; [https://perma.cc/X8VF-EY53] (arguing, premised on statistical examples, that a prohibition on race or sex data is rather counterproductive indeed); Corbett-Davies, Sam/Goel, Sharad, "The Measure and Mismeasure of Fairness: a critical Review of Fair Machine Learning", *Cornell University Library*, 2018, passim (discussing the "[l]imitations of anti-classification" as a fairness metric). See also: Kim, Pauline T., "Data-Driven Discrimination at Work", *cit.*, p. 867 ("[I]f the goal is to discourage classification bias, then the law should not forbid the inclusion of race, sex, or other sensitive information as variables, but seek to preserve these variables, and perhaps even include them in some complex models."); Kroll, Joshua A., et al., "Accountable Algorithms", *University of Pennsylvania Law Review*, Volume 165, 2017, pp. 633, 693–95. See also: Kim, Pauline T., "Data-Driven Discrimination at Work", *cit.*, p. 866 ("classification bias occurs when employers rely on classification schemes, such as data algorithms, to sort or score workers in ways that worsen inequality or disadvantage along the lines of race, sex, or other protected characteristics"). These two uses of the word "bias" correspond to the notions of irrational versus rational **(or statistical) discrimination.** Mayson, Sandra G., "Bias In, Bias Out", *cit.*, pp. 2218–2300.

[3944] It is often stated that the close connection between arrest rates and crime-report rates by race is one fact that pundits routinely use as evidence that arrest rates are fundamentally bereft of racial bias regarding offending rates. See: Skeem, Jennifer L./Lowenkamp, Christopher T, "Risk, Race, and Recidivism: Predictive Bias and Disparate Impact", *Criminology*, Volume 54, 2016, pp. 680, 683–84, 704–06 (690). But see: Stevenson, Megan/Mayson, Sandra, "The Scale of Misdemeanor Justice", *Boston University Law Review*, Volume 98, 2018, pp. 731, 758–63 (arguing that "the [national] black arrest rate [for an index of misdemeanor offenses] has hovered around 1.7 times the white arrest rate since 1980").

[3945] Mayson, Sandra G., "Bias In, Bias Out", *cit.*, pp. 2218–2300 (2296).

[3946] But see: Selbst, Andrew D., "Disparate Impact in Big Data Policing", *Georgia Law Review*, Volume 52, 2017, p. 167 ("[I]t may be impossible to tell when the disparate impact truly reflects reality"). See also: Barocas, Solon/Selbst, Andrew, "Big Data's Disparate Impact", *cit.*, p. 682 ("So long as prior decisions affected by some form of prejudice serve as examples of correctly rendered determinations, data mining will necessarily infer rules that exhibit the same prejudice"). See: Mayson, Sandra G., "Bias In, Bias Out", *cit.*, pp. 2218–2300.

[3947] Recall, a feted scholar (Bernard Harcourt) adamantly contends that (1) predictive crime control efforts may produce more harm than good; (2) they may engender a "ratchet effect" in which the disparate impact of forecast on black folks worsens over time; and (3) the technological allure of prediction can both besmirch and mar deep-rooted moral conceptions of justice. See: Harcourt, Bernard E., *Against Prediction: Profiling, Policing, and Punishing in An Actuarial Age*, Chicago, Illinois, University of Chicago Press, 2007, pp. 7–18 and passim. Converging: Ensign, Danielle, "Runaway Feedback Loops in Predictive Policing", *Proceedings of Machine Learning Research*, Volume 81, 2018, p. 1; Starr, Sonja B., "Evidence-Based Sentencing and the Scientific Rationalization of Discrimination", *Stanford Law Review*, Volume 66, 2014, pp. 804–06 (arguing that that risk assessment during sentencing may derail deep-seated concepts of justice that we hold so dear). In addition to this line of reasoning, Professor Sandra Mayson avers that, because any extant racial disparity in crime risk is the byproduct of a long-haul historical oppression, it is therefore

law settings is to drill into, and shine a keen light on, the multifarious prediction[3948] distortions in the dataset[3949] versus differential base rates of the event one endeavours to predict.[3950]

§§ In addition to that, tool developers must pay a nuanced attention to the intermediate stages of building a machine learning algorithm,[3951] which bestows upon them feasible pathways to **control** the outputs generated by the running model[3952] while tapering off *Algorithmic Dictatorship*. Failing which, we are not only off to a bad start, but, and foremost, we are indomitably gearing towards the realm of *Algorithmic Dictatorship* from which there is no coming back.

---

an unfitting basis for coercive state action. To put it bluntly, it is unfair for the state to condition coercion on crime risk that modern societies has unjustly created. Put another way, one may be led to believe that the data are simply warped and that the risk at hand is fundamentally uniform across racial lines. Understandably, though not laudably, one may be also led to believe that crime risk is a fundamentally haphazard and incoherent concept, owing to the fact that all people who are self-determining agents have an equal capacity to either eschew flagitious behaviour or engaging in criminal activities. See: Mayson, Sandra G., "Bias In, Bias Out", *cit.*, pp. 2218–2300.

[3948] Mayson, Sandra G., "Bias In, Bias Out", *cit.*, pp. 2218–2300 (2296).

[3949] See: Harris, Grant T./Rice, Marnie E., "Bayes and Base Rates: What Is an Informative Prior for Actuarial Violence Risk Assessment?", *Behavioural Science and Law*, Volume 31, 2013, pp. 103, 121 ("What is not axiomatic is the straightforward application of assumptions about priors... to violence risk assessment—that remains a set of important empirical matters."); See: Mayson, Sandra G., "Bias In, Bias Out", *cit.*, pp. 2218–2300. See also: Selbst, Andrew D., "Disparate Impact in Big Data Policing", *cit.*, pp. 140–43.

[3950] Mayson, Sandra G., "Bias In, Bias Out", *cit.*, pp. 2218–2300 (2297). See also: Part V, Chap. 5, Sect. 5.1.7.4 of this book (on one of the laws to control algorithmic decision-making, namely, law number four: data partitioning must be performed—i.e. randomly split an entire dataset into the «training dataset» and the «test dataset»—to accurately predict outcomes in the real world while forestalling «inductive bias» (learning bias)). See also: Part V, Chap. 5, Sect. 5.1.7.5 of this book (on Algorithmic Common Good, with a sharper focus on the dire need of algorithmic auditing, undertaken by external auditors that must be given full access to the dataset used to train the running models).

[3951] See: Part V, Chap. 5, Sects. 5.1.3–5.1.3.1.6 of this book (on the fundamental tenets of model selection). See: Part V, Chap. 5, Sect. 5.1.3.1.5 of this book (on the central tenets of model tuning). See: Part V, Chap. 5, Sects. 5.1.4–5.1.4.1.1 of this book (on the central tenets of model training).

[3952] See: Part V, Chap. 5, Sects. 5.1.2–5.1.6.2.1 of this book (on **the thing-centred algorithmic decision-making** propelled by a *Controllable* and *Interpretable* Machine Learning that weeds out *Algorithmic Dictatorship* and secures *Algorithmic Common Good*. It is worth recalling that the **thing-centred algorithmic decision-making** seeks to unwind the perils arising out of the lack of theoretical underpinnings facing the **human-centred algorithmic decision-making**, as extensively fleshed out Part III, Chap. 3, Sects. 3.1.4.3–3.1.4.4 of this book). See: Part V, Chap. 5, Sects. 5.1.7–5.1.7.5 of this book (on the five laws to control algorithmic decision-making). See: Part V, Chap. 5, Sects. 5.1.8–5.1.8.5 of this book (on the five laws to interpret algorithmic decision-making).

Part V
Algorithmic Common Good to oust Algorithmic Dictatorship

Chapter 5
The Rich Tapestry of Remedies That Comprise *Algorithmic Common Good*

5.1 Introduction

§§ Artificial Intelligence-embedded technologies represents a new path, a foray into uncharted territory that holds a wealth, and a treasure trove, of challenges that should not leave anyone lukewarm.[1] When it comes to cutting-edge technology[2] you better not try your luck and the let the chips fall where they may.[3] Notwithstanding, Artificial Intelligence-embedded technologies, albeit a seemingly bedazzling gift to

---

[1] For instance, scholars deployed a machine learning algorithm to challenge the conventional wisdom according to which there are only a limited number of legal traditions (common law and civil law) and a few legal families (the German-Romanic legal family, the francophone legal family, the lusophone legal family and so forth). See: Han-wei Ho/Huang, Patrick Chung-Chia/Garoupa, Nuno/ Wells, Martin T./Chang, Yun-chien/Ginsburg, Tom, "Machine-Learning Human Rights", *Journal of Law and Empirical Analysis*, July–December 2024, 2024, pp. 1–19 (1) ("*utilizing a comprehensive panel dataset spanning from 1900 to 2020, this study introduces an innovative methodology for the analysis and categorization of legal documents, specifically national constitutions.* Contrary to the predominant reliance on unsupervised methods within the field, this research incorporates a supervised machine-learning approach, notably the SEMMS method, alongside traditional unsupervised algorithms. *This dual approach facilitates a nuanced analysis of the human rights provisions contained within national constitutions, resulting in the identification of both traditional and novel constitutional groupings. Broadly speaking, the more traditional common law-civil law divide does not seem particularly relevant in this context*") Italics added.

[2] Ho, H.-w./Huang, P. C.-C./Chang, Y.-c., "Machine learning methods", M. Siems & P. J. Yap (Eds.), *Cambridge Handbook of Comparative Law*, Cambridge, Cambridge University Press, 2024, pp. 177–207; James, G., Witten, D., Hastie, T., & Tibshirani, R., *An introduction to statistical learning*, 2nd edition, Volume 112, Heidelberg, Springer, 2021; Zhang, C.-H., "Nearly unbiased variable selection under minimax concave penalty", *Annals of Statistics*, 38 (2), 2010, pp. 894–942 (this line of research highlights the complex trappings of cutting-edge technology that never ceases to evolve).

[3] See: Chandler, Anupam, "The Racist Algorithm", *cit.*, p. 1039 (sets out a poignant call in an earnest attempt to urge stakeholders to put their eyes and hearts on both "inputs and outputs", as opposed to machine algorithms alone). See also: Huq, Aziz Z., "Racial Equity in Algorithmic Criminal Justice", *cit.*, p. 1080 (explaining "the [p]roblem of [d]istorting [f]eature [s]election"); Kehl, Danielle, et al.,

H. L. dos Santos, *Controllable Artificial Intelligence and the Future of Law*, Artificial Intelligence and the Rule of Law, https://doi.org/10.1007/978-981-95-0508-1_5

humankind, are not without multifarious caveats.[4] This has been a fodder for thought and debate lately.[5]

§§ Artificial Intelligence-embedded technology is not an ordinary taxonomy. It holds the blueprint of our destiny and the disruptive power it carries. This is about the unfolding of newer and higher forms of intrusiveness in our daily lives that

"Algorithms in the Criminal Justice System: Assessing the Use of Risk Assessments in Sentencing", *Berkman Klein Ctr. For Internet Society*, 2017, https://dash.harvard.edu/bitstream/handle/1/33746041/2017-07_responsivecommunities_2.pdf [https://perma.cc/7V6D-JLLM] ("critical issues also need to be addressed in the development phase of these algorithms, particularly with regard to the inputs and how they are used"). See: Mayson, Sandra G., "Bias In, Bias Out", *cit.*, pp. 2218–2300. See: Part V, this chapter, Sects. 5.1.5.2.2–5.1.5.2.2.1.4 of this book (on the fundamental shift away from causation to correlations in algorithmic decision-making).

[4] Artificial intelligence, like everything else, is not without sizable drawbacks and shortcomings though. The most menacing of which happens to be the flawed or biased algorithms, which are bound to mar a sought-after bias-free decision-making in dispute resolution. See: Sternlight, Jean, "Pouring a Little Psychological Cold Water on Online Dispute Resolution", *Journal of Dispute Resolution*, 1, 2020, pp. 23 ff (raises awareness to the perils of biased algorithms on online dispute resolution). Converging: Schmitz, Amy, "Expanding Access to Remedies Through E-Court Initiatives", *Buffalo Law Review*, Volume 67, 2019, pp. 90–100 (showing concerns that e-courts might be premising their decisions on flawed and bigoted algorithms). Which is something to be frowned upon. Why? Most likely, flawed or biased algorithms will deepen the chasm between rich and poor. See: Eubanks, Virginia, *Automating Inequality: How High-Tech Tools Profile, Police and Punish the Poor*. New York: St. Martin's Press, 2018, 1–272 (1 ff and passim) (coining the expression «automating inequality» to vividly portray the downsides of using high-technology to compound the yawning gap between rich and poor against the backdrop of biased algorithms). See also: Pasquale, Frank, *The Black Box Society: The Secret Algorithms that Control Money and Information*. Cambridge, Massachusetts: Harvard University Press, 2015, 1–320 (8–10 and passim) (noting that biased algorithms, which have underlying discrimination problems, contribute exponentially to further social biases. His most intriguing claim is that such biased algorithms have been incorporated/etched in the bulk of the corporations' informatic system, to the detriment of human kind in an overarching sense); Roth, Andrea, "Machine Testimony", *Yale Law Journal*, Volume 126, 2017, pp. 1972 and ff and passim.

[5] For an on-point breakdown of the distinct levels of opacity arising out of machine learning algorithms: Selbst, Andrew D./Barocas, Solon, "The Intuitive Appeal of Explainable Machines", *Fordham Law Review*, Volume 87, 2018, pp. 1085, 1089–1099 (holding that there are plenty reasons for the insurer's ignorance. To begin with, the algorithm entails specialized knowledge to understand. That is, the insurer's employees may lack sufficient knowledge to understand the rationale behind the reasons in view of which the algorithm is producing prices for different customers—personalized pricing. Lastly, even if the insurer himself comprehends how the model operates, it may nonetheless lack expertise to comprehend why it operates the way it does. For that reason, the explainability of machines is a vital, but rather elusive, task. Thence, the famed authors deem it as the "nonintuitive" nature of algorithms. For purposes here, the insurer himself might indeed understand that its Artificial Intelligence-embedded technology formulates higher prices for those who actually access the website at hand, but may fail to come to terms with the fact that the explanation for this fact arises from the website's capacity to proxy for genetic information). See also: Scherer, Matthew U. Scherer, "Regulating Artificial Intelligence Systems: Risks, Challenges, Competencies, and Strategies", *Harvard Journal of Law and Technology*, Volume 29, 2016, pp. 353–369 (frames the crippling problem of opacity as "the possibility that the inner workings of an AI system may be kept secret and may not be susceptible to reverse engineering").

extend beyond our collective grasp. As extensively shown throughout this drawn-out book, Artificial Intelligence-embedded technologies are on the cusp of spinning into the realm of pervasiveness, thereby hurling human beings into a dystopian reality whereby truths and lies dovetail seamlessly. The darndest effects arising out of deepfakes[6] and the LLM's hallucinations[7] neatly encapsulates, hands-in-glove, this harrowing reality that sidesteps the normal course of events.

§§ Artificial Intelligence-embedded technologies therefore bestows upon humankind a particularly clear window on the battle between light and darkness that is poised to overhaul our lives beyond recognition. Oddly, human beings are increasingly losing sight of the fact that their fundamental rights are wearing down/tailing off amidst the hustle and bustle of daily life. Human beings are so buoyed and enthralled by the perks of technology that they are utterly unable to find the unvarnished truth that lies beneath both the shapeless stream of foam and the smokescreen of distractions: Artificial Intelligence-embedded technologies speak of things in the same wavelength of mayhem.

§§ Although Artificial Intelligence-embedded technologies carry a vibe of ambition (piercing into every single aspect of our daily lives), little emphasis has nonetheless been placed on where the inordinate costs of that lofty ambition may fall. It is true that Artificial Intelligence-anchored technologies provide a hint towards breaking ground in ventures leading to global blossoming, but truer still the boundaries between *benign* leaps forward (that carries forwards an overhyped promise to make mankind better-off) and *malicious* breakthroughs (that make mankind worse-off while hastening the demise of the Rule of Law[8]) are on the brink of becoming increasingly blurred, if not outright dispelled.

---

[6] See: Part III, Chap. 3, Sects. 3.1.5.2–3.1.5.3.1 of this book (on the functional aspects of Critical Artificial Intelligence Studies, with a sharper focus on the harmful effects of Artificial Intelligence-embedded technologies, namely, Generative Artificial Intelligence and its offsprings—deepfakes and its deleterious effects on human memory).

[7] See: Part IV, Chap. 4, Sects. 4.1.9.3–4.1.9.5 of this book. See also: Part III, Chap. 3, Sects. 3.1.5.4–3.1.5.4.1 of this book (on the functional aspects of Critical Artificial Intelligence Studies, with a sharper focus on the harmful effects of Artificial Intelligence-embedded technologies, namely Large Language Models and its multifarious downsides and shortcomings). See also: Part IV, Chap. 4, Sects. 4.1.9.1–4.1.9.2 (on ChatGPT's functional abilities). See also: Part IV, Chap. 4, Sects. 4.1.9–4.1.9.7 (on ChatGPT's functional drawbacks and pitfalls, including, but no limited to, "hallucinations"). See: Part III, Chap. 3, Sects. 3.1.5.6–3.1.5.6.1 of this book (on Critical Artificial Intelligence Studies, with a sharper focus on the harmful effects of Large Language Models' medical hallucinations that are poised to undermine its overall trustworthiness).

[8] See: Part V, this chapter, Sect. 5.1.1.1 of this book (on the central tenets of Rule of Law that lends itself to a beacon of justice amidst the sepulchral darkness that is about to take hold). See: Part V, this chapter, Sect. 5.1.1.2 of this book (on the central tenets of Procedural Rule of Law that lends itself to a lighthouse of justice that allows citizens to challenge the pearls of algorithmic wisdom in a court of law). It is worth recalling that the Rule of Law is backsliding worldwide. Especially in Central and Eastern Europe. See: Avbelj, Matej, "The Rule of Law, Comprehensive Doctrines, Overlapping Consensus, and the Future of Europe", *Ratio Juris*, Volume 36, Issue 3, September, 2023, pp. 242–258. The Rule of Law is not a «one size fits all» format nonetheless. But see: Chesterman, Simon, "An International Rule of Law", *The American Journal of Comparative Law*, Volume 56, 2008, pp. 331–362 (on the thrust to grasp (?) a catch-all International Rule of Law). See: Peari, Sagi, "Better Law as a Better Outcome", *The American Journal of Comparative Law*,

§§ Aside from this odd quandary, the geographic spread of Artificial Intelligence-embedded technologies connects the information society[9] along umpteenth digital routes. Whilst Artificial Intelligence-anchored technologies are spearheading policy transformation while enjoying global blossoming, citizens tend to harbour the propensity to distrust the mighty power it wields though.[10]

§§ This deep-seated distrust is shaping up to lurch algorithmic decision-making into a legitimacy crisis[11] that may be rendered impossible to unwind somewhere along the line. Relatedly, the unbridled rise of Artificial Intelligence-embedded technologies and the robust protection of fundamental rights are not poles apart. We are

---

Volume 63, Issue 1, 2015, pp. 155–195 (156) (on Leflar's stance on «better rule of law»). For the purposes of this piece, Rule of Law amounts to a lighthouse of procedural fairness to which citizens, regardless of where they are, resort to upon gaining access to a given system of administration of criminal justice. Whilst further utterances on the fabric of Rule of Law fall well outside the scope and breadth of this paper, one must not be oblivious of the fact that the thrust to Deglobalizing Rule of Law is underway. See: Bussani, Mauro, "Deglobalizing Rule of Law and Democracy: Hunting Down Rhetoric Through Comparative Law", *The American Journal of Comparative Law*, Volume 67, 2019, pp. 701–744 (701) (contending that the thrust to Deglobalizing Rule of Law is interwoven with thrust to take heed of «well-known differences that run through cultures and traditions». In spite of which, «the West has never stopped trying to export its own law into the rest of the world»). Unsurprisingly, there have been educated calls to take heed of the pinpointed cultural and legal differences by, in the case of China, allow for a «Socialist Rule of Law». See: Chinese Common Law Guiding Cases, *Harvard Law Review*, Volume 129, 2016, p. 2213. We will come back to this issue further down is this paper. More on this later.

[9] About information society: Van Dijk J., *The Deepening Divide: Inequality in the Information Society*, Thousand Oaks: Sage, 2005; Custers, Bart, "Data Dilemmas in the Information Society: Introduction and Overview", Custers, Bart/Calders, Toon/Schermer, Bart/Zarsky, Tal (Editors), *Discrimination and Privacy in the Information Society: Data Mining and Profiling in Large Databases*, Heidelberg, Springer, 2013, pp. 3–26; Van Dijk J., "Datafication, dataism and dataveillance: Big data between scientific paradigm and ideology", *Surveillance & Society*, 12 (2), 2014, pp. 197–208.

[10] See: Alimardani, Armin/Jane, Emma A., "Human Hallucinations: GenAI and the Mirage of Personalised Learning for All", 2024, p. 15 ("*given that in this study, we concluded that using GenAI educational chatbots involves some risks, we find it crucial to understand students' perceptions of these tools' trustworthiness (...) Given the known risks of overreliance on such technology, 45 a healthy level of scepticism towards the accuracy of GenAI is a positive outcome. However, the 11.63% (5 students) who selected 'disagree' or 'strongly disagree' reflect a level of distrust that could undermine the effectiveness of GenAI tools*"). Italics added.

[11] Tyler, Tom R., "Does the American Public Accept the Rule of Law? The Findings of Psychological Research on Deference to Authority", *De Paul Law Review*, 56, 2007, pp. 661–664 (stating that «transparency and openness foster the belief that decision-making procedures are neutral»). See also: Doherty, Joseph W./Reville, Robert T./Zakaras, Laura(ed.), *Introduction to Confidentiality, Transparency, and the U.S. Civil Justice System*, Oxford, Oxford University Press, 2012, 1–258 (passim) (noting that the lack of transparency yields sizable social costs). But see: Weizenbaum, Joseph, *Computer Power and Human Reason: From Judgment to Calculation*, 1st edition, New York, W. H. Freeman & Co, 1976, pp. 1–300 (227) ("examines the sources of the computer's powers and offers evaluative explorations of what computers can do, cannot do, and should not be employed to do") (this founding father of Artificial Intelligence presciently noted that we should not entrust Artificial Intelligence-embedded technologies with "tasks that demand wisdom"). Italics added. The approval of rental applications is arguably one of those tasks that should never be entrusted to machines). More on this on Part IV, Chap. 4, Sects. 4.1.4–4.1.4.2.1 of this book.

better off keeping them together. That is the only way forward with a view to build a tangible roadmap that ensures that the gist of citizens' fundamental rights retain vitality amidst the age of *Algorithmic Dictatorship*. To cater for that, policymakers and lawmakers must not shy away from pouring in whopping efforts to chart the path ahead a *human flourishing* in spite of the age of *Algorithmic Dictatorship* that is upon us.[12] This is a place to dwell permanently.

§§ Bearing this background very firmly in mind, a spate of vexing questions emerges: to what extent is the ongoing war waged by darkness against light—that rages unseen at the outskirts of our reality—worth taking part of? Are the mental throes arising out of an ever-evolving technology worth coming to blows over? Is the quest to find out what's under the hood of the complex trappings,[13] and the beneath the surface of infallibility,[14] of Artificial Intelligence-embedded technologies worth taking part of? Are the inner workings[15] of Artificial Intelligence-anchored technologies[16] intrinsically benign or fundamentally malign; even mischievous? Is the action of returning to a former or less developed state of Artificial Intelligence a scenario worth taking stock of? Is the endless regress to a state of pure mental privacy worth fighting for? On the flip side, what can be done to soothe out, and fundamentally allay, the harmful effects of an ever-present technology that is bound to *control* our thoughts, emotions, likes and dislikes that we collectively hold so dear? Does that feel too close to home? Does that hit home? If so, what can be done about it?

§§ Dear reader, there is no point in nursing hold wounds on *how* far back the jaw-dropping achievements of advanced technology go and *what* we could, and should

---

[12] See: Part IV, Chap. 4 of this book.

[13] Segran, G., "The complexity of artificial intelligence", *Singapore Management University*, 2021, passim (on the elaborate and complex trappings of Artificial Intelligence).

[14] But see: Citron, Danielle Keats, "Technological Due Process", *Washington Law Review*, 2008, p. 1249 (one must shy away from the perceived "tendency to presume a computer system's infallibility").

[15] See also: Scherer, Matthew U. Scherer, "Regulating Artificial Intelligence Systems: Risks, Challenges, Competencies, and Strategies", *Harvard Journal of Law and Technology*, Volume 29, 2016, pp. 353–369 (frames the crippling problem of opacity as "the possibility that the inner workings of an AI system may be kept secret and may not be susceptible to reverse engineering").

[16] See, for a compelling account of AI black box: See: Bathaee, Yavar, "The Artificial Intelligence Black Box and the Failure of Intent and Causation", *Harvard Journal of Law and Technology*, n.º 37, 2018, p. 901 (adduces that "*one possible reason AI may be a black box to humans is that it relies on machine-learning algorithms that internalize data in ways that are not easily audited or understood by humans (…)*" "*first, a lack may arise from the complexity of the algorithm's structure, such as with deep neural network, which consists of thousands of artificial neurons working together in a diffuse way to solve a problem. This reason for AI being a black box is referred to as "complexity". Second, the lack of transparency may arise because the AI is using a machine-learning algorithm that relies on geometric relationships that humans cannot visualize, such as with support vector machines. This reason for AI being a black box is referred to as "dimensionality"*"). Italics added. See: Part V, this chapter, Sect. 5.1.7.2 of this book (on law number two to control algorithmic decision-making, which mandates that black box models must not be entrusted with the task of making high stake decisions—v.g. health and freedom). See: Part V, this chapter, Sects. 5.1.7–5.1.7.5 of this book (on the five laws to control algorithmic decision-making).

have, done about it. Nor should you hold grudges on *who* should have done something about it. We have long passed that first critical stage.[17]

§§ All too often human beings refrain themselves from shifting their gaze inward in pursuit of actionable lines of action to be taken envisioning an inevitable coexistence between human beings and cutting-edge technology in decades to come. This is an all-too-common pattern in dire need of quashing. A key takeaway jumps out as ripe in this juncture: we must learn from the lessons arising out of the steep learning curve of our lives. Hardly any surprise flows from the fact that the virulent effects of advanced technology on your quotidian lies at its heart.

§§ This finding sits easily with the discourse around which the coexistence between human beings and state-of-the-art technology revolves. Such a coexistence is not amenable to be reasoned away by our brains though. Human beings must therefore come to terms with the fact that Artificial Intelligence-embedded technologies are not only upon us, but, and foremost, are a suitably tailored vessel to navigate the uncharted waters of the *new world order* whereby human beings and machines are bound to conflate/blend.

§§ The emergence of *Brain-Computer Interfaces* stands as a living testament of such an overriding goal.[18] When that day comes, and it will, human beings should bid a fond farewell to their beloved *mental privacy*. The burning question is: will the remnants of the best of the decaying *old world order*—that attached great importance to the citizens' fundamental rights—leave something behind? Put it coarsely, in spite of the withering series of attacks that fundamental rights have been enduring lately, can we nurture the unshattered hope that something can still be done to ensure that they will not vanish into thin air as time inexorably goes by amidst the age of *Algorithmic Dictatorship*? The answer is a resounding «yes».

§§ But know this: any hopes of *understand* Artificial Intelligence-embedded technologies are fundamentally dashed by its unsustainable murkiness, its unfathomable ubiquity, and its unbearable opacity[19] that forestalls any endeavour, no matter how earnest, to grasp both its inner workings and complex trappings. But here is the deeper truth: all we can do is *control*, rather than *understand*, Artificial Intelligence-embedded technologies or inordinate harms will otherwise occur. The remainder of this chapter will be devoted to lay the foundations upon which *Algorithmic Common Good* should stand while mapping out the path forward as to wither away the harmful effects of *Algorithmic Dictatorship*.

---

[17] See: Part II, Chap. 2 of this book (devoted to the history of Artificial Intelligence).

[18] See: Part III, Chap. 3, Sect. 3.1.4.5 of this book (on Critical Artificial Intelligence Studies, with a sharper focus on the harmful effects of Brain-Computer Interfaces). See: Part III, Chap. 3, Sect. 3.1.5.10 of this book (on the functional aspects of Critical Artificial Intelligence Studies, with a sharper focus on the harmful effects of Artificial Intelligence-embedded technologies, namely, Brain-Computer Interfaces that can read and control your mind and behaviour).

[19] Balkin, Jack M., "The Three Laws of Robotics in the Age of Big Data", *cit.*, pp. 1217–1241.

5.1.1 *Foundations of Algorithmic Common Good: Philosophy of Law and Jurisprudence*

5.1.1.1 The Rule of Law (Albert Dicey/Joseph Raz) and Justice as Fairness (John Rawls) to Stymie Functional Abuses of Those Entrusted with the Task of Making High-Stake Decisions in Algorithmic Risk Assessment

§§ The time is now ripe to state the obvious: *Algorithmic Dictatorship*[20] is poised to entrench the inexcusable social inequality so characteristic of our unhinged social matrix.[21] It is worth recalling, too, that the rampant social inequality unveiled by *Algorithmic Dictatorship* should accordingly catalyse a metamorphic shift in algorithmic decision-making. Put otherwise, the social inequality unravelled by *Algorithmic Dictatorship* should galvanize a more fundamental rethinking of the way algorithmic decision-making can be overhauled to achieve *Algorithmic Common Good*.

§§ Algorithmic decision-making must therefore tune into the universal energies of *Algorithmic Common Good* in a bid to throw *Algorithmic Dictatorship* out of balance while avoiding a downward spiral in coexistence between human beings and machines.

§§ It is true that tale of Rule of Law[22] is, at this juncture, well-wrought, familiar, and well-worn, but truer still challenges remain when it comes to its sustainability

---

[20] See: Part IV, Chap. 4 of this book (on the fundamental tenets of *Algorithmic Dictatorship*).

[21] Note, though, that prejudiced algorithms are set to be brought to the limelight as they are one foundational basis of *justice prédictive* so voguish in France. No surprise stems from the fact that prejudiced algorithms will feed *justice predictive*—and that is something quite unsavoury and unpalatable in criminal justice indeed. See: Garapon, Antoine, "Les enjeux de la justice predictive", *Juris-Classeur périodique*, Volume 31, 2018, passim. See also: Larret-Chahine, Louis, "Le droit isométrique: un nouveau paradigme juridique né de la justice prédictive», *Archives de Philosophie du Droit*, Volume 60, 2018, pp. 287 and ff and passim.

[22] It is worth recalling that newest developments posed by the "collect-it-all" technologies are slated to create a slew of sizzling hot challenges to the sustainability of the Rule of Law. See: Hu, Margaret, "From the National Surveillance State to the Cybersurveillance State", *The Annual Review of Law and Social Science*, Volume 13, 2017, pp. 162–163 ("*policymakers view these technological developments, including biometric technologies, as tools with the potential to identify individuals who may pose a threat to national and homeland security and to prevent crime and terrorism. One example of technology intended for risk assessment and threat management is the post-9/11 program Total Information Awareness (TIA). (…) TIA can be understood as a "collect-it-all" data surveillance program. TIA was not explicitly identified as a collect-it-all program—this phrase originated with the Snowden disclosures.* One National Security Agency (NSA) slide described the NSA's procedure as "collect-it-all" (Greenwald 2014b). *Collect-it-all efforts like TIA embody a philosophy that aspires to preventive policing. Mass data collection is construed as a tool to assess and prevent future threats* (Murray 2010)"). Italics added. See also: Ball, Kirstie, and Frank Webster (Eds.), *The Intensification of Surveillance: Crime, Terrorism & Warfare in the Information Age*, London, UK: Pluto Press, 2007; Guzik, Keith, "Discrimination by Design: Predictive Data Mining as Security Practice in the United States' 'War on Terrorism'", *Surveillance and Society*, 7 (1), 2009, pp. 1–17. See: Part IV, Chap. 4, Sects. 4.1.5–4.1.5.2 of this book (on "algorithmic Jim Crow", a travel ban issued during the first Trump Administration to prevent certain individuals from

amidst the age of *Algorithmic Dictatorship*. To the extent that algorithmic decision-making is deeply suffused with devilishly harmful, and invidious, social discrimination,[23] *Algorithmic Common Good* must therefore be firmly rooted in the Rule of Law or democracy is otherwise bound to careen into chaos.

§§ Policymakers and relevant stakeholders alike should not lose sight of the fact that the Rule of Law[24] lends itself to a functional barrier that seeks to stamp out the abuses of those in power.[25] To the extent algorithmic decision-making should abide by the central tenets of fairness[26] and transparency, tool developers should keep

---

entering the United States of America, which, given its racial undertones, stands as an outgrowth of congeries of laws enacted during the Jim Crow epoch).

[23] See: Part IV, Chap. 4 of this book (on the fundamental tenets of *Algorithmic Dictatorship*).

[24] Dicey, Albert Venn, *Introduction to the Study of the Law of the Constitution*, 8th Revised Edition (1 Jan. 1982), Indianapolis, Indiana, Liberty Fund Inc., 1982, pp. 1–585 (188–197) ("Albert Venn Dicey was one of the greatest Rule of Law's nineteenth century theorists, whose research has focused on the normal operation of Rule of Law on the lower courts. Part of his research was about parsing and comparing English idea of legal equality administered by lower courts as opposed to the discretionary – thus arbitrary – authority administered in the ancient and continental Europe"); Allan, R. S., *The Sovereignty of Law: Freedom, Constitution, and the Common Law*, Oxford, Oxford University Press, 2013, Chapter 3; Allison, J.W.F., "Turning the Rule of Law into an English Constitutional Idea", C. May/A. Winchester (Ed.), *The Edgar Elgar Handbook on the Rule of Law*, Cheltenham, Edward Elgar Publishing, 2018, passim (giving nuanced accounts of Dicey's groundbreaking work and originality when it comes to Rule of Law). See: Part V, this chapter, Sect. 5.1.1.1 of this book (on the central tenets of Rule of Law that lends itself to a beacon of justice amidst the sepulchral darkness that is about to take hold). See: Part V, this chapter, Sect. 5.1.1.2 of this book (on the central tenets of Procedural Rule of Law that lends itself to a lighthouse of justice that allows citizens to challenge the pearls of algorithmic wisdom in a court of law).

[25] See: Raz, Joseph, "The Rule of Law and its Virtue", *The Authority of Law: Essays on Law and Morality*. Oxford: Clarendon Press, 1979, pp. 210–214 (on the quintessential value of Rule of Law). Which is why the onset of the age of Artificial Intelligence will put the Rule of Law to the test like never before. Recall, the Rule of Law is a functional barrier—aimed at clamping down a host of unlawful deeds undertaken by those in power—that must not be teared apart or criminal procedure law will be otherwise despoiled from its intrinsic validity and vitality. See: Raz, Joseph, "The Rule of Law and its Virtue", *The Authority of Law: Essays on Law and Morality*, *cit.*, p. 224 (asserts adamantly that the Rule of Law is aimed at buffering the hazards of abuse perpetrated by those in power. *In this vein, Raz contends that "the law inevitably creates a great danger of arbitrary power – the Rule of Law is designed to minimize the danger created by the law itself…Thus the (R)ule of (L)aw is designed to minimize the danger created by law itself…Thus the (R)ule of (L)aw is a negative virtue…the evil which is avoided is evil which could only have been caused by the law itself*"). Italics added. See: Part V, this chapter, Sect. 5.1.1.1 of this book (on the central tenets of Rule of Law that lends itself to a beacon of justice amidst the sepulchral darkness that is about to take hold). See: Part V, this chapter, Sect. 5.1.1.2 of this book (on the central tenets of Procedural Rule of Law that lends itself to a lighthouse of justice that allows citizens to challenge the pearls of algorithmic wisdom in a court of law).

[26] Dino, Dylan, "The Rule of Law and the Rule of Empire: A. V. Dicey in Imperial Context", *The Modern Law Review*, Volume 81, Issue 5, 2018, pp. 739–764 (739–741) (highlights that "the idea of the rule of law, more ubiquitous globally than ever before, owes a lasting debt to the work of Victorian legal theorist A.V. Dicey (…) To Dicey we owe not only the phrase "the rule of law" but also one of the most influential expositions. Dicey's account of the rule of law emphasised

citizens' fundamental rights front of mind while building computer-run algorithms. Bereft of which, *Algorithmic Dictatorship* is slated to otherwise outlive Rule of Law[27] itself.

§§ Pivotally, insofar algorithmic decision-making reflects long-standing inequalities in the data[28] from which they are built,[29] red lines are in dire need of being swiftly drawn to prevent «algorithmic slavery» from taking hold and enjoying global blossoming.

§§ Compellingly, «algorithmic slavery»[30] is a byproduct of an overreliance of technology to make high-stake decisions at the behest of humans,[31] which seldom

---

three elements: first, government through legal norms and *procedures rather than unrestrained discretion; second, formal equality before the law*; and third, *the establishment of individual rights through gradual, bottom-up (common-law) development*"). Italics added.

[27] Cass, Ronald A., *The Rule of Law in America.* Baltimore, Maryland: The Johns Hopkins University Press, 2001, p. 17 (noting that a "central element of the Rule of law, constraint from external authority…helps assure that the process of government, *rather than the predilections of the individual decision-maker*") Italics added.

[28] Barocas, Solon/Selbst, Andrew D., "Big Data's Disparate Impact", *California Law Review*, Volume 104, 2016, pp. 671–682 (discussing how data is often flawed, rigged, incomplete, imperfect and therefore algorithms inherit the prejudice of the original decision makers). But see: Citron, Danielle Keats/Pasquale, Frank, "The Scored Society: Due Process for Automated Predictions", *Washington Law Review*, Volume 89, 2014, pp. 1, 4–5 (highlighting how human beings programming automated systems is directly conducive to, and leads, to fundamentally inaccurate results since the source code, predictive algorithms and datasets may encompass human biases which, in turn, have a disparate impact on historically disadvantaged groups). But see: Bornstein, Stepanhie, "Antidiscriminatory Algorithms", *Alabama Law Review*, Volume 70, 2018, pp. 519, 524–528 (contending, however, that the tagged "facially neutral" algorithms producing discriminatory outcomes should be quashed).

[29] Mayson, Sandra G., "Bias In, Bias Out", *Yale Law Journal*, Volume 128, 2019, pp. 2218 and ff and passim.

[30] Edwards, Lilian/Veale, Michael, "Slave to the Algorithm? Why a "Right to an Explanation" is Probably not the Remedy You are Looking for", *Duke Law and Technology Review*, Volume 16, 2018, pp. 18–67.

[31] Karnow, Curtis E. A., "The Opinion of Machines", *The Cambridge Handbook of the Law of Algorithms*, Bartfield, Woodrow (Editor), Cambridge, United Kingdom: Cambridge University Press, 2021, passim. See: Part V, this chapter, Sect. 5.1.7.2 of this book (on law number two to control algorithmic decision-making, which mandates that black box models must not be entrusted with the task of making high stake decisions—v.g. health and freedom). See: Part V, this chapter, Sect. 5.1.8.5 of this book (on law number five to interpret algorithmic decision-making, which mandates that robot-judges, robot-prosecutors and robot-lawyers must not enter the courtroom for they are utterly incapable of making sound and interpretable value judgements).

ends well, transparency[32] wise.[33] Crucially, and perhaps bafflingly, this is an eerily disturbing finding that should not be referred sardonically.[34] Nor should we be oblivious of the fact the harmful effects of algorithmic decision-making should be tackled head-on to preserve the nub of citizens' fundamental rights in the age of Artificial Intelligence-embedded technologies.

§§ Strikingly, *Algorithmic Common Good*, to be fully functional, requires bespoke procedural guardrails to bestow upon citizens the opportunity to **challenge** the pearls of algorithmic wisdom produced by machine learning algorithms. Remember this: algorithmic fairness must not be a leap of faith,[35] but a citizen procedural guarantee instead.[36] This is the kernel

[32] See: Tyler, Tom R., "Does the American Public Accept the Rule of Law? The Findings of Psychological Research on Deference to Authority", *De Paul Law Review*, 56, 2007, pp. 661–664 (stating that "transparency and openness foster the belief that decision-making procedures are neutral"). See also: Coglianese, Cary/Lehr, David, "Transparency and Algorithmic Governance", *Administrative Law Review*, Volume 71, 2019, passim. See also: Doherty, Joseph W./Reville, Robert T./Zakaras, Laura(ed.), *Introduction to Confidentiality, Transparency, and the U.S. Civil Justice System*, Oxford, Oxford University Press, 2012, 1–258 (passim) (noting that the lack of transparency yields sizable social costs). But see: Weizenbaum, Joseph, *Computer Power and Human Reason: From Judgment to Calculation*, 1st edition, New York, W. H. Freeman & Co, 1976, pp. 1–300 (227) ("examines the sources of the computer's powers and offers evaluative explorations of what computers can do, cannot do, and should not be employed to do") (this founding father of Artificial Intelligence presciently noted that we should not entrust Artificial Intelligence-embedded technologies with "tasks that demand wisdom"). Italics added. The approval of rental applications is arguably one of those tasks that should never be entrusted to machines). More on this on Part IV, Chap. 4, Sects. 4.1.4–4.1.4.2.1 of this book. See: Part V, this chapter, Sect. 5.1.8.5 of this book (on law number five to interpret algorithmic decision-making, which mandates that robot-judges, robot-prosecutors and robot-lawyers must not enter the courtroom for they are utterly incapable of making sound and interpretable value judgements). See: Part V, this chapter, Sect. 5.1.7.2 of this book (on law number two to control algorithmic decision-making, which mandates that black box models must not be entrusted with the task of making high stake decisions—v.g. health and freedom). See: Part V, this chapter, Sects. 5.1.7–5.1.7.5 of this book (on the five laws to control algorithmic decision-making).

[33] Katyal, Sonia K, "The Paradox of Source Code Secrecy", *Cornell Law Review*, Volume 104, 2019, pp. 1183–1236; Wexler, Rebecca, "Life, Liberty, and Trade Secrets: Intellectual Property in the Criminal Justice System", *Stanford Law Review*, Volume 70, 2018, pp. 1343 and ff.

[34] Graeber, D./Wengrow, D., *The dawn of everything: A new history of humanity*, London, United Kingdom, Allen Lane, 2021.

[35] Gardner, John, *Law as a Leap of Faith*, Oxford, Oxford University Press, 2014, pp. 1–328 (in this book Professor John Gardner "collects, revisits, and supplements fifteen years of celebrated writings on general questions about rule of law, law, and legal systems - writings in which he attempts, without loss of philosophical finesse or insight, to cut through some of the technicalities with which the subject has become encrusted in the late twentieth century").

[36] Keveney, Sean, "Note, The Dishonesty Rule: A Proposal for Reform", *Texas Law Review*, 81 (2002): 381–383 (arguing that «a R*ule of (L)aw that fails to yield results with a minimum degree of consistency or predictability is of little use as an analytical tool* and ceases to serve the legitimate goal of ordering the conduct of citizens»). Italics added.

of «justice as fairness»[37] of which stakeholders should not be unbeknownst of,[38] **nor should they relinquish control over algorithmic decision-making.**[39]

---

[37] Rawls, John, *Justice as Fairness: A Restatement*, 2nd edition (16th of May of 2001), Cambridge, Massachusetts, Belknap Press: An Imprint of Harvard University Press, 2001, pp. 1–240 («This magisterial book originated as lectures for a course on political philosophy that Rawls taught regularly at Harvard in the 1980s. In time the lectures became a restatement of his theory of justice as fairness, revised in light of his more recent papers and his treatise *Political Liberalism* (1993). As Rawls writes in the preface, the restatement presents "*in one place an account of justice as fairness as I now see it, drawing on all [my previous] works*") (noting that *justice requires both a fair distribution of liberties and opportunities*). See also: Rawls, John, *A Theory of Justice*, 2nd edition (30th of September of 1999), Cambridge, Massachusetts, Belknap Press: An Imprint of Harvard University Press, (1999): 99 ff and passim (noting that justice—to be *justice as fairness* indeed—requires much more than mere legality).

[38] Prescott, J. J., "Assessing Access-to-Justice Outreach Strategies", *Journal of Institutional and Theoretical Economics*, Volume 174, 2017, pp. 34–63 (arguing that "a *core function of government is providing a forum where individuals can resolve their disputes. Access to courts of law has always been considered a valuable publicly provided benefit, if not a fundamental right*"). Italics added.

[39] But see: Millar, Jason/Kerr, Ian, "Delegation, Relinquishment and Responsibility: The Prospect of Expert Robots", *Robot Law*, Calo, Ryan/Froomkin, A. Michael/Kerr, Ian (Editors), Cheltenham, Edward Elgar Publishing, 2016, pp. 102, 106–107 (as these authors aptly put it "*we will rely on robots without really knowing why – simply because their algorithms provide the greatest number of successful outcomes.* We have already seen this in Google's search approach. Neither Larry (Page) nor Sergey (Brin) (nor any other Google employee) knowns exactly why one particular web page is a better result than another. *When the click patterns say it is, that's good enough.* No semantic or causal analysis is required…*Like the ancients, we will, quite rationally, come to rely upon them, knowing full well that we cannot necessarily explain the reasons for their decisions*"). Italics added. Converging: Casey, Anthony J./Niblett, Anthony, "Self-driving Laws", *University of Toronto Law Journal*, Volume 66, 2016, pp. 429–435 (contend that "as more information is generated, and the evolutionary algorithm updates and become a better forecaster, *we imagine that judges will increasingly rely on the advice of the algorithm*"). But see: Weizenbaum, Joseph, *Computer Power and Human Reason: From Judgment to Calculation*, 1st edition, New York, W. H. Freeman & Co, 1976, pp. 1–300 (227) ("examines the sources of the computer's powers and offers evaluative explorations of what computers can do, cannot do, and should not be employed to do") (this founding father of Artificial Intelligence presciently noted that we should not entrust Artificial Intelligence-embedded technologies with "tasks that demand wisdom"). Italics added. The approval of rental applications is arguably one of those tasks that should never be entrusted to machines). More on this on Part IV, Chap. 4, Sects. 4.1.4–4.1.4.2.1 of this book. See also: Cohen, Julien E., *Between Truth and Power: The Legal Constructions of Informational Capitalism.* Oxford: Oxford University Press, 2019, pp. 1–376 (p. 192) (contends presciently that "*automated processes* have obvious efficiency advantages, *but such processes may not align well (or well at all) with applicable legal requirements that are couched in shades of gray*"). Italics added. See: Part V, this chapter, Sect. 5.1.7.2 of this book (on law number two to control algorithmic decision-making, which mandates that black box models must not be entrusted with the task of making high stake decisions—v.g. health and freedom). See: Part V, this chapter, Sects. 5.1.1.7–5.1.1.7.5 of this book (on the five laws to control algorithmic decision-making). See: Part V, this chapter, Sect. 5.1.8.5 of this book (on law number five to interpret algorithmic decision-making, which mandates that robot-judges, robot-prosecutors and robot-lawyers must not enter the courtroom for they are utterly incapable of making sound and interpretable value judgements).

5.1.1.2 Procedural Rule of Law (Lon L. Fuller/Jeremy Waldron/Sanne Taekema) and the Chance to Challenge the «Pearls of Algorithmic Wisdom» Produced by Machine Learning Algorithms

§§ *Algorithmic Common Good*, to be fully operational, requires a *procedural accountability to the Rule of Law*. In addition to that, relevant stakeholders must abide by a responsible agency theory. Both concepts have been gleaned in the realm of Philosophy of Law and seek to instil both trust[40] and trustworthiness[41] upon algorithmic decision-making.

§§ Both Professor Jeremy Waldron's procedural[42] approach to the Rule of Law[43] and Professor Lon. L. Fuller's[44] responsible agency theory[45] are to steer

---

[40] See: Rudin, Cynthia/Ustun, B., "Optimized scoring systems: toward trust in machine learning for healthcare and criminal justice", *Interfaces*, Volume 48, 2018, pp. 399–486; Tyler, Tom, *Trust in the Law*, New York, NY: Russell-Sage, 2002, passim. There is an excellent body of empirical research that shows that a poor judicial performance spawns low trust in legal systems. See: Magalhães, Pedro C./Garoupa, Nuno, "Judicial Performance and Trust in Legal Systems: Findings from a Decade of Surveys in 20 European Countries", *Social Science Quarterly*, 2020, p. 1 (the main goal of this exciting piece of research was "determining the existence of a relationship between judicial performance and citizens' trust in the legal system").

[41] Colquitt, A. Jason/Rodell, B. Jessica, "Justice, Trust, and Trustworthiness: A Longitudinal Analysis Integrating Three Theoretical Perspectives", *Academy of Management Journal*, 54, 2011, 1183. See on Trust and Trustworthiness in contract law and public policy: Harding, Mathew, "Trust and Fiduciary Law", *Oxford Journal of Legal Studies*, Volume 33, 2013, pp. 81 ff; Hall, Mark A, "Law, Medicine, and Trust", *Stanford Law Review*, Volume 55, 2002, pp. 463 ff; Harding, Mathew, "Responding to Trust", *Ratio* Juris, Volume 24, 2011, pp. 75 ff; Hall, Mark A, "The Importance of Trust for Ethics, Law, and Public Policy", *Cambridge Quarterly of Healthcare Ethics*, Volume 14, 2005, 156 ff.

[42] Brettschneider, Corey, "A Substantive Conception of the Rule of Law: Nonarbitrary Treatment and the Limits of Procedure", *Getting to the Rule of Law*, James E. Fleming (Ed.), New York, New York University Press, 2011, pp. 53–61 (arguing that Waldron's procedural approach to the Rule of Law entails some substantive constraints).

[43] Waldron, Jeremy, "The Rule of Law in Contemporary Liberal Theory", *Ratio Juris*, 2, 1989, pp. 78 ff (arguing that a substantive conceptual of Rule of Law is not out of question).

[44] Finnis, John, *Natural Law and Natural Rights*, 2nd edition, Oxford, Oxford University Press, 2011, pp. 273–275; 290–293 (arguing, however, that is not perfectly clear the extent to which Fuller's internal morality of law and external morality of law are interwoven); Rundle, Kristen, *Forms Liberate, Reclaiming the Jurisprudence of Lon L. Fuller*, Oxford, Hart Publishing, 2012, pp. 1–222 (4) (this author parses carefully Lon L Fuller's account "of what he termed 'the internal morality of law' is widely accepted as the classic twentieth century statement of the principles of the rule of law. Much less accepted is his claim that a necessary connection between law and morality manifests in these principles, with the result that his jurisprudence largely continues to occupy a marginal place in the field of legal philosophy") (further down the book, Rundle contests the widespread claim that there is a bifurcation between internal morality of law and external morality of law in Fuller's doctrine stating avowedly that "at no point in his writings does Fuller claim any necessary connection between the two moralities").

[45] Fuller, Lon L., *The Morality of Law*, The Storrs Lectures Series (1963), Revised edition (1969), New Haven, Connecticut, Yale University Press, (1969) (1–215) (39) ("in a lengthy new concluding

relevant stakeholders' demeanours in algorithmic decision-making. By the same token, Professor Joseph Raz somewhat seconds the responsible agency theory.[46]

§§ Professor Jeremy Waldron's procedural approach to the Rule of Law[47] is two-fold.[48] On one hand, means that the Rule of Law is inextricably linked to procedural[49] concerns.[50] Citizens must be given the procedural opportunity to not only be part of a «technological due process»,[51] but also be awarded the chance to **challenge** the decisions issued therein.[52] On the other hand, *Procedural Rule of Law* aims to

---

chapter labelled "A Reply to Critics," Lon L. Fuller extends and clarifies his definition of the relation between law and morality put forward in the first (1964) edition of *The Morality of Law*. His original argument distinguishes between the *morality of duty* and the *morality of aspiration*, both of which bear on the design and operation of social institutions: the former by setting the necessary preconditions of any purposive social endeavour, the latter by suggesting the directions for such endeavour"). (Noting that the legal systems must find feasible ways to avoid «routes to disaster").

46 Raz, Joseph, *Engaging Reason: On the Theory of Value and Action*, Oxford: Oxford University Press, 2003, pp. 23 ff (sets forth the theory of value and action—aimed at ascertaining why do people act—in a both engaging and informative manner). See also: Anscombe, G.E.M., *Intention*, Cambridge, Massachusetts, Harvard University Press, 1957, pp. 18 ff (striving to ascertain the normative point of a human action and its underlying intention, whether good or bad); Webber, Grégoire, "Asking Why in the Study of Human Affairs", *American Journal of Jurisprudence*, Volume 60, 2015, pp. 51–78; Simmons, N., *Law as a Moral Idea,* Cambridge, Cambridge University Press, 2007, *passim* (both exploring why human beings act and in what grounds, according to the study of human affairs and the theory of agency).

47 Waldron, Jeremy, "The Core of the Case Against Judicial Review", *Yale Law Journal*, 2006, pp. 1346–1389 (showing concerns about the overall state of US democracy).

48 Waldron, Jeremy, "Legislation and the Rule of Law", *Legisprudence*, Volume 1, 2007, pp. 91–115 (arguing that substantive conception and formal conception of Rule of Law are independent but—to some extent—connected).

49 Tashima, A. Wallace, "The War on Terror and the Rule of Law", *Asian American Law Journal*, 15 2008, pp. 245–263 (echoing the same procedural approach to the Rule of Law while asserting that independent and impartial legal officials are needed to uphold the Rule of Law).

50 Waldron, Jeremy, "The Rule of Law and the Importance of Procedure", *New York Public Law and Legal Theory*, 2010, p. 4 (noting that "the Rule of Law is violated when due attention is not paid to these procedural matters or when the institutions that are supposed to embody these procedure are undermined or interfered with". Further down this author would admit that there are some substantive dimensions of Rule of Law, such as respect for right for property and presumption of liberty and so forth).

51 Citron, Danielle K., "Technological Due Process", *Washington University Law Review*, Volume 85, 2008, pp. 1249–1253 ("computer programs seamlessly combine rulemaking and individual adjudications without the critical procedural protections owed either of them").

52 Taekema, Sanne, "The Procedural Rule of Law: Examining Waldron's Argument on Dignity and Agency", *Jahrbuch für Recht und Ethik*, Band 21, (2013): 133 ff (noting that "Waldron's understanding of the Rule of Law as procedural which demands the opportunity for individuals to contest legal decisions in the formalized processes of courts and tribunals").

fizzle out both algorithmic biases[53] and human biases that feed into machine learning algorithms,[54] thereby impairing a sought-after algorithmic fairness.[55]

§§ Procedural Rule of Law[56] thus plays a pivotal role in keeping algorithmic discrimination[57] at bay.[58] It accordingly endeavours to allay algorithmic

---

[53] Recall: Baeza-Yates, R., "Bias on the web", *Communications of the ACM*, 61 (6), June 2018, 2018, pp. 54–61 (argues that "*algorithmic bias is when the bias is not present in the input data* and is added *purely by the algorithm*"). Italics added. See also: Hajian, Sara Hajian et al., "Algorithmic Bias: From Discrimination Discovery to Fairness-aware Data Mining", *ACM SIGKDD International Conference on Knowledge Discovery and Data Mining*, Volume 22, 2125, 2016; Griemmelmann, James/Westreich, Daniel, "Incomprehensible Discrimination", *California Law Review Online*, Volume 7, 2018, pp. 164–171; Xiang, Alice, "Reconciling Legal and Technical Approaches to Algorithmic Bias", *Tennessee Law Review*, Volume 88, 2021, passim; See: Lemley, Mark A./Casey, Bryan, "Remedies for Robots", *The University of Chicago Law Review*, Volume 86, Issue 5, 2019, pp. 1311–1396 (1376) (alerting to the perils of algorithmic bias); Chandler, Anupam, "The Racist Algorithm", *Michigan Law Review*, Volume 115, Issue 6, 2018, p. 1026 (noting that, in the terrain of racist algorithm, "the possibilities for discriminatory manipulation are legion"; Jackson, Maya C., "Artificial Intelligence and Algorithmic Bias: The Issues with Technology Reflecting History and Humans", *Journal of Business Technology Law*, Volume 16, 2021, pp. 299–316; West, Sarah Myers/Whittaker, Meredith/Crawford, Kate, *Discriminating Systems. Gender, Race and Power in AI*. New York: AI Now Institute, 2019, pp. 15 and ff and passim; Waldman, Ezra, "Privacy, Practice, and Performance", *California Law Review*, Volume 110, 2021, passim (on algorithmic bias); Jackson, Maya C., "Artificial Intelligence and Algorithmic Bias: The Issues with Technology Reflecting History and Humans", *Journal of Business Technology Law*, Volume 16, 2021, pp. 299–316; West, Sarah Myers/Whittaker, Meredith/Crawford, Kate, *Discriminating Systems. Gender, Race and Power in AI*. New York: AI Now Institute, 2019, pp. 15 and ff and passim. Lee, Nicole Turner/Resnick, Paul/Barton, Genie, *Algorithmic Bias Detection and Mitigation: Best Practices and Policies to Reduce Consumer Harms*. Washington, DC: Brookings Institution, 2019, passim; Lee, N. T./P. Resnick/G. Barton, "Algorithmic Bias Detection and Mitigation: Best Practices and Polices to Reduce Consumer Harms", Brookings Institution, Washington D.C., Bookings Report, 2019; Hellman, Deborah, "Measuring Algorithmic Fairness", *Virginia Law Review*, Volume 106, 2020, pp. 811 and ff and passim; Johnson, Gabbrielle M., "Algorithmic Bias: On the Implicit Biases of Social Technology", *Synthese*, 2021, passim.

[54] Citron, Danielle Keats/Pasquale, Frank A., "The Scored Society: Due Process for Automated Predictions", *Washington Law Review*, Volume 89, 2014, pp. 1–34 (arguing that "[a]*dvocates applaud the removal of human beings and their flaws from the assessment process*," but arguing that bias remains "[*b*]*ecause human beings program predictive algorithms, their biases and values are embedded into the software's instructions*"). Italics added. See: Part IV, Chap. 4, Sects. 4.1.4–4.1.4.2.3 of this book.

[55] But see: Nachbar, Thomas B., "Algorithmic Fairness, Algorithmic Discrimination", *Florida State University Law Review*, Volume 48, 2021, pp. 508 and ff and passim (arguing that US antidiscrimination law is sufficient to meet the challenges posed by algorithmic discrimination).

[56] Dworkin, Ronald, *Taking rights seriously*, London, Duckworth Books, (1977): 186–205 (noting that persons' rights and governments activities to protect it are interwoven); Jeremy Waldron, "The Rule of Law as a Theatre of Debate", *Dworkin and his Critics*, Justine Burley (Ed.), Oxford, Blackwell, (2004): 319–336 (criticizing Dworkin's concept of Rule of Law).

[57] Ponce, Paula Pedigoni, "Direct and indirect discrimination applied to algorithmic systems: Reflections to Brazil", *Computer Law & Security Review*, Volume 48, 2023, pp. 1057–1066.

[58] See on algorithmic discrimination: Kleinberg, Jon, et al., "Discrimination in the Age of Algorithms", *Journal of Legal Analysis*, 2018, pp. 114–174; See: Kleinberg, Jon, et al., "Algorithms as Discrimination Detectors", *Proceeds of the National Academy of Science*, Volume 117, 2020, pp. 30096–30110; Griemmelmann, James/Westreich, Daniel, "Incomprehensible Discrimination",

decision-making's deficiencies.[59] Procedural Rule of Law[60] therefore amounts to a beacon of algorithmic fairness suitably tailored to keep citizens' human dignity unscathed.[61]

California Law Review Online, Volume 7, 2018, pp. 164–171; Xiang, Alice, "Reconciling Legal and Technical Approaches to Algorithmic Bias", *Tennessee Law Review*, Volume 88, 2021, passim; Karnow, Curtis E. A., "The Opinion of Machines", *The Cambridge Handbook of the Law of Algorithms*, Bartfield, Woodrow (Editor), Cambridge, United Kingdom: Cambridge University Press, 2021, pp. 15 and ff and passim; Strandburg, Katherine J., "Rulemaking and Inscrutable Decision Tools", *Columbia Law Review*, Volume 119, 2019, passim.

[59] Sanne Taekema, "The Procedural Rule of Law: Examining Waldron's Argument on Dignity and Agency", *cit.*: 134 ff (arguing that the «*Rule of Law is understood as the restraint law puts on those in power*. The famous phrase: Rule of Law, not man, encompasses the idea that *a person in a position of power should not be left to this own device, but should be subject to legal limitations*») (italics added).

[60] The inception of the era of omnipotent Artificial Intelligence is about to revive the overriding importance of the dichotomy between *censory jurisprudence* (what law actually is and/or looks like) and *expository jurisprudence* (what law should do and/or be to halt the weaponization of Artificial Intelligence by those in power). This dyad was well wrought by Jeremy Bentham. See: Bentham, Jeremy, An Introduction to the Principles of Morals and Legislation. London: Great Books in Philosophy, Prometheus Books, 1988, 1–352 (293–294) (Jeremy Bentham's work on "the Principles of Morals and Legislation emerges from its historic roots in hedonism and teleology as a scientific attempt to assess the moral content of human action by focusing on its results or consequences. Proceeding from the assumption that human beings desire pleasure (and avoid pain), Bentham's unique perspective, known as utilitarianism, is used to construct a fascinating calculus for determining which action to perform when confronted with situations requiring moral decision-making the goal of which is to arrive at the "greatest happiness of the greatest number." Toward this end, he endeavours to delineate the sources and kinds of pleasure and pain and how they can be measured when assessing one's moral options. Bentham supports his arguments with discussions of intentionality, consciousness, motives, and dispositions"). This is not to say that we embrace Bentham's utilitarianism—so harshly criticized in Hart's Concept of Law—or the claim according to which an understanding of the Rule of Law presupposes a good understanding of law in a given country or community. Yet, there is a high degree of academic accuracy in Bentham's distinction when it comes to differentiating *expository jurisprudence*—explaining what law is—and *censorial jurisprudence*—explaining what law ought to be. As for effective access to justice and the procedural approach to the Rule of Law in the purview of criminal procedure law, there is markedly clear line between what legal officials are—purveyors of procedural fairness—and what an effective access to justice ought to be—a place whereby social inequalities caused by the era of artificial intelligence are to be buffered (criminal procedure law settings) in a swift, prompt, and streamlined manner. Or irreparable damages may otherwise occur.

[61] Taekema, Sanne, "The Procedural Rule of Law: Examining Waldron's Argument on Dignity and Agency", *cit.*: 140 ff (arguing that the «Rule of Law serves the value of human dignity»).

§§ Procedural Rule of Law[62] lends itself to a lighthouse of legality[63] and fairness[64] befitted to peter out the baleful effects of *Algorithmic Dictatorship* while shielding citizens' human dignity.[65]

5.1.1.3 The Moral Goodness (Robert Alexy) That Must Inhere and Permeate *Algorithmic Common Good*

§§ *Algorithmic Dictatorship*[66] has an entrenched presence in algorithmic decision-making. Distorting this ground truth by either turning a blind eye to it, or simply looking the other way, would amount to a dereliction of our duty to throw the algorithmic injustice out of balance. Which prompts the vexing question: what gets us past this gruesome situation? For now, suffice to say that the consequences of a fallout

---

[62] Locke, John, *Two Treatises of Government*, Peter Laslett (Ed.), Cambridge, Cambridge University Press, 1988, pp. 329–349 (*passim*) (on the notions of government, and concepts of individual rights and freedom); Fuller, Lon L., *The Morality of Law*, The Storrs Lectures Series (1963), Revised edition (1969), New Haven, Connecticut, Yale University Press, 1969, pp. 1–215, (46–91) (Professor Lon L. Fuller pinpoints eight principles *morally internal to law* as order. They are connected to both Rule of Law and to the principle of legality. Being that the principle of congruence between official action and enacted laws; generality; promulgation; non-contradiction; non-retroactivity; non-impossibility; clarity; and diachronic constancy); Waldron, Jeremy, "Is the Rule of Law an Essentially Contested Concept (in Florida)?", *Law and Philosophy*, 21, 2002, p. 137 (decrying the erosion of the concept of Rule of Law in the wake of 2000 U.S. presidential election); Waldron, Jeremy, "The Rule of Law and the Importance of Procedure", *Getting to the Rule of Law*, James E. Fleming (Ed.), New York, New York University Press, 2011, p. 8 (arguing that Professor Lon L. Fuller's eight moral principles internal to law as order are «formal» as opposed to «procedural»); Gardner, John, *Law as Leap of Faith: Essays on Law in General*, Oxford, Oxford University Press, 2012, pp. 202–204 (echoing Professor Waldron's views on the «formal» nature of Fuller's eight internal moral principles of law). Note, though, that Professor H. L. Hart asserts that "*laws may be law but too evil to be obeyed*. This is a moral condemnation which everyone can understand and it makes an immediate and obvious claim to moral attention. If, on the other hand, we formulate our objection as an assertion that these evil things are not law, here is an assertion which many people do not believe, and if they are disposed to consider it at all, it would seem to raise a whole host philosophical issues before it can be solved". See: Hart, H. L., "Positivism and the Separation of Law and Morals", *Harvard Law Review*, 71 (4) 1958, pp. 598 ff (this amounts to a glimpse of the incorporation of the moral concept of law in Hart's conception of law) (italics added).

[63] *Id.* at (40) (according to Fuller's view, there is no such thing as the existence of law devoid of, and decoupled from, legal officials' compliance with legality).

[64] Jeremy Waldron, "The Concept and the Rule of Law", *Georgia Law Review*, 43 (1), 2008, p. 7 (arguing that «a procedural understanding of the Rule of Law requires not only that officials apply the rules as they are set out; it requires application of the rules with all the care and attention to fairness that is signalled by ideals such as «natural justice» and «procedural due process»).

[65] Fox-Decent, Evan, "Is the Rule of Law Indifferent to Human Rights?", *Law and Philosophy*, 27 2008, p. 533 (affirming that breaches on legality equate to breaches in human rights and dignity). See: Part IV, Chap. 4, Sects. 4.1–4.1.10.6 of this book (on Algorithmic Dictatorship and its chilling effect on democracy).

[66] See: Part IV, Chap. 4, Sects. 4.1–4.1.10.6 of this book (on Algorithmic Dictatorship and its chilling effect on democracy).

at the border of algorithmic fairness would be steep. We must credit *Algorithmic Dictatorship* with that level of sophistication and deleterious power.

§§ Strikingly, algorithmic injustice does not need a reason to wreak havoc in algorithmic decision-making, nor does need an excuse. Compellingly, algorithmic injustice, if not deftly tackled heads-on, is set to leave algorithmic decision-making in shambles and torn into pieces thereupon. If pundits refrain themselves from toiling towards the protection of swiftly fading fundamental rights amidst the age of *Algorithmic Dictatorship*, they will most likely have their fingerprints on it.

§§ Pundits should accordingly fight shy of, and keep aloof from, having algorithmic decision-making out in a storm without an umbrella. Before you, dear reader, start firing off questions while urging to be clued in, bear this assertion very firmly in mind instead: *Algorithmic Dictatorship* is in dire need of quashing, which would be the best of all outcomes for mankind. Failing which, an ominous portent for the future lies before us. So, now you, dear reader, know that not only *Algorithmic Dictatorship* needs to be trounced, but, and foremost, *Algorithmic Common Good* must be firmly rooted in both the *Rule of Law* and *Procedural Rule of Law*. But much more lies beyond that. Much more is needed to build the brawny and sturdy foundations upon which *Algorithmic Common Good* should stand.

§§ The time is now ripe to shine a keen light on one of the most important foundations of *Algorithmic Common Good*: *human good* and *practical reasonableness*, which, taken together, are to bestow upon stakeholders' *reasons for good actions* (secure *Algorithmic Common Good* in algorithmic decision-making). To cater for that, light must be cast upon the *dual nature of law*.

§§ Whilst it is true that algorithmic justice concerns must be balanced against the need to ensure that technological innovation thrives, it is truer still that the latter must not come to the expense of the former. This assertion raises critical questions on how to strike a delicate balance between both.

§§ My take on this straightforward: Artificial Intelligence-embedded technology, while clustered in the shady hands of a handful of tech moguls, must generally work to the advantage of mankind. Technological breakthroughs must neither come the expense of human dignity nor harbour particularly malevolent attitudes towards the individuals affected. To illustrate, technological leaps must shy away from further compounding algorithmic injustice facing members of racialized communities[67]

[67] Sunstein, Cass R., "Algorithms, Correcting Biases", *Social Research*, Volume 86, 2019, pp. 449–506 (this famed author tagged disparate impact as "disturbing in itself, in the sense that a practice that produces such an impact helps entrench something like a caste system").

(Blacks and Latinos) in the remit of both algorithmic credit scoring[68] and algorithmic fair[69] lending.[70]

---

[68] Havard, Cassandra Jones, "On The Take": The Black Box of Credit Scoring and Mortgage Discrimination", *Boston University Public Interest Law Journal*, Volume 20, 2011, pp. 241–247 (highlighting that credit scoring if unchecked is an intrinsic, encroached, deep-rooted form of racial discrimination akin to mortgage redlining); Hurley, Mikella/Adebayo, Julius, "Credit Scoring in the Era of Big Data", *Yale Journal of Law and Technology*, Volume 18, 2016, pp. 148, 151–156, 172 (averring that FICO scoring boasts a redoubtable capacity to routinely weed out some populations that have been historically and systematically underrepresented or grossly unfairly represented in the credit industry market). Tellingly, by 2016, ten states had disavowed the unlawful practice of employers using shady algorithmic credit scores due to their perceived disparate impact on low-income applicants and members of racialized communities (mostly Black folks). See: O'Neill, Cathy, *Weapons of Math Destruction. How Big Data Increases Inequality and Threatens Democracy*. London: Penguin Random House, 2016, pp. 128 and ff and passim. See: Part IV, Chap. 4, Sects. 4.1.4–4.1.4.2.3 of this book. See: Part IV, Chap. 4, Sects. 4.1.2–4.1.4.3 of this book (on algorithmic credit scoring, consumer racism and credit card redlining). See: Wallheimer, Brian, "Are you Ready for Personalized Pricing? Companies Are Figuring out What Individual Customers Will Pay-and Charging Accordingly", *Chicago Booth Review*, 2018, passim; The Effects of Online Disclosure About Personalized Pricing on Consumers 7 (Org. for Econ. Coop. and Dev., Working Paper No. 303, 2021 ("[T]he quantity of personal data held on online consumers, combined with the *increasing prevalence of personalization in other domains (e.g., advertisement)*, means there is at least potential for online personalized pricing to become more commonplace and more sophisticated"). Italics added. But see: Bartlett, Robert/Morse, Adair/Stanton/Wallace, Nancy, "Consumer Lending Discrimination in the FinTech Era", *National Bureau of Economic Research*, Working Paper No. 25,943, Volume 50, 2019 (on the perils of consumer lending discrimination). This is often tagged as "risk-based pricing." See: Phillipps, Robert, "Optimizing Prices for Consumer Credit", *Journal of Revenue and Pricing Management*, Volume 12, 2013, pp. 360–365 ("[A] riskier customer should pay a higher price in order to compensate for the higher probability of default and the associated cost to the lender"). See also: Staten, Michael, "Risk-Based Pricing in Consumer Lending", *Journal of Law, Economics & Policy*, Volume 11, 2015, pp. 33 and ff and passim. See also: Schwemm, Robert G./Taren, Jeffrey L., "Discretionary Pricing, Mortgage Discrimination, and the Fair Housing Act", *The Harvard Civil Rights-Civil Liberties Law Review*, 2010, passim. The conduct being granularly parsed is discretion ascribed to brokers—which is considered by many stakeholders a harmless neutral practice—, may nonetheless lead to brokers to intentionally discriminate against members of racial minorities.

[69] See: Part IV, Chap. 4, Sects. 4.1.4–4.1.4.2.1 of this book (on mortgage redlining). See: Part IV, Chap. 4, Sects. 4.1.2–4.1.4.3 of this book (on algorithmic credit scoring, consumer racism and credit card redlining). See: Part IV, Chap. 4, Sects. 4.1.4–4.1.4.2.3 of this book (on algorithmic redlining). See: Part IV, Chap. 4, Sect. 4.1.4.3 of this book (on "algorithmic redliking"). See: Part IV, Chap. 4, Sect. 4.1.3 of this book (on algorithmic prime-lining). In spite of its deep-seated racial bias, decision-makers continue to deploy redlining tactics through big data and may even justify such unlawful practices by claiming that the latter abide by cost-effectiveness. See: Humber, Nadiyah J., "A Home for Digital Equity: Algorithmic Redlining and Property Technology", *California Law Review*, Volume 111, Issue 5, 2023, pp. 1421–1484. Allen, James, "The Color of Algorithms: An Analysis and Proposed Research Agenda Deterring Algorithmic Redlining", *Fordham Urban Law Journal*, Volume 46, 2019, pp. 219–234 (229–234) (discussing how historical mortgage redlining greatly swayed modern algorithms generated by massive batches of data sets that consist of decades of information built on exclusion and racial discrimination in the purview of financing, marketing, and housing). See: Part IV, Chap. 4, Sects. 4.1.4–4.1.4.2.3 of this book.

[70] Nier III, Charles L., "Perpetuation of Segregation: Toward a New Historical and Legal Interpretation of Redlining Under the Fair Housing Act", *Marshall Law Review*, Volume 32, 1999,

§§ As we trudge through the desert of *Algorithmic Dictatorship*, staggering efforts must be thereupon poured in to achieve a magnificent oasis (*Algorithmic Common Good*) that lies before us. *Algorithmic Common Good* therefore lends a new urgency to concerns that beckons the dire need to vanquish *Algorithmic Dictatorship*. To cater for that, justice concerns must be kept front of mind. Pivotally, Justice concerns must trump unfairness. Crucially, Justice concerns boast a mammoth and unrivalled advantage over invidiousness: it provides a solace to those in throes with a wailing algorithmic grief.

§§ Justice concerns form part of a broader theoretical apparatus within which the evaluative point of law operates. Polymaths like Robert Alexy and Gustav Radbruch champion that the nature of law is eminently dual. Put otherwise, law is comprised of two components: **(i)** an evaluative and **(ii)** descriptive nature.[71]

§§ John Finnis, an enthusiast of a modern natural-law theory of law who upholds a maximalist, thoroughgoing, comprehensive and full-fledged view about the components of **human good**, attaches great importance to the requirement for justice. Notwithstanding, it looks as though Finnis frames justice as a subset of what the good polyhistor labels as the chief evaluative standard within which the nature of law operates—**practical reasonableness.**[72] More on this later.

§§ The sweeping claim that the nature of law is twofold or dual—a compound that amasses/scrape together both **(i)** descriptive or social-factual and **(ii)** evaluative or normative features—has attracted a wide global[73] gaze.

---

pp. 617, 619–20 and ff and passim. See: Allen, James, "The Color of Algorithms: An Analysis and Proposed Research Agenda Deterring Algorithmic Redlining", *Fordham Urban Law Journal*, Volume 46, 2019, pp. 219–234 (229–234) (discussing how historical mortgage redlining greatly swayed modern algorithms generated by massive batches of datasets that consist of decades of information built on exclusion and racial discrimination in the purview of financing, marketing, and housing). See: Part IV, Chap. 4, Sects. 4.1.4–4.1.4.2.3 of this book. See: Part IV, Chap. 4, Sects. 4.1.4–4.1.4.2.1 of this book (on mortgage redlining); Einav, Liran/Jenkins, Mark/Levin, Jonathan, "The Impact of Credit Scoring on Consumer Lending", *The RAND Journal of Economics*, Volume 44, 2013, p. 249 (showing unequivocally that the adoption of computer-run algorithmic credit scoring led to conspicuously higher-risk applicant lending). In spite of the widely accepted conceptual differences between intent-based and effect-based theories of disparate impact, both approaches often dovetail seamlessly. As far as the fair lending goes, the definition of disparate impact cases is somewhat shallow, nomadic, and erratic, and dispiritingly vague. Note, though, that the loan officer's discretion is directly conducive to exceedingly higher rates of rejections for members of racial minorities. See: Ayres, Ian/Klein, Gary/West, Jeffrey, "The Rise and (Potential) Fall of Disparate Impact Lending Litigation", *Evidence and Innovation in Housing Law and Policy*, Fennell, Lee Anne/Keys, Benajmin J. (Editors), Cambridge, Cambridge University Press, 2017, pp. 231–254.

[71] Popovic, Petar, "Reading Finnis and Aquinas on Justice as the Evaluative Standard for Positive Law", *The American Journal of Jurisprudence*, Volume 68, 2023, pp. 63–75 (63). I will follow this bodacious piece of research closely.

[72] Popovic, Petar, "Reading Finnis and Aquinas on Justice as the Evaluative Standard for Positive Law", *cit.*, pp. 63–75 (63).

[73] Popovic, Petar, "Reading Finnis and Aquinas on Justice as the Evaluative Standard for Positive Law", *cit.*, pp. 63–75 (63).

§§ To name a few, Robert Alexy posits that «it lies at the very core of non-positivism that law necessarily has an ideal dimension».[74] Put another way, law unequivocally exhibits an evaluative feature. Robert Alexy's approach of non-positivism is therefore anchored in the belief that the most prominent element in the evaluative aspect of law's nature is deeply woven into the fabric[75] of justice.

§§ Alexy therefore believes that when the evaluative benchmark of justice is frontally belied in the content of a given legal[76] norm—especially, but not limited to, **«cases of extreme violations of human**[77] **rights»**[78]—the descriptive facet of law's nature deeply entrenched that norm crumbles[79]: «moral defects [of law] undermine legal validity if and only if the threshold of extreme injustice is transgressed».[80]

§§ Notwithstanding, it seems as though Alexy's account of the evaluative nature of justice is to a certain degree shallow, nomadic, patchy, underdetermined, or minimalist, as compared to a far-reaching substantive conception of **basic human goods**[81] **(fairness)**, such as the one propounded by a **Thomistic natural-law theory of law.**

---

[74] Apud: Popovic, Petar, "Reading Finnis and Aquinas on Justice as the Evaluative Standard for Positive Law", *cit.*, pp. 63–75 (63).

[75] Popovic, Petar, "Reading Finnis and Aquinas on Justice as the Evaluative Standard for Positive Law", *cit.*, pp. 63–75 (63).

[76] Popovic, Petar, "Reading Finnis and Aquinas on Justice as the Evaluative Standard for Positive Law", *cit.*, pp. 63–75 (63).

[77] Popovic, Petar, "Reading Finnis and Aquinas on Justice as the Evaluative Standard for Positive Law", *cit.*, pp. 63–75 (63).

[78] See: Alexy, Robert, "Some Reflections on the Ideal Dimension of Law and on the Legal Philosophy of John Finnis", *The American Journal of Jurisprudence*, Volume 58, Issue 2, December 2013, Pages 97–110 (108) ("This article defends a non-positivist theory of law, that is, a theory that accepts the necessary connection between legal validity and moral correctness by reference to the work of John Finnis. It begins with the *dual nature of law as comprising both a real or factual dimension and an ideal dimension.* Important examples show that at least some kinds of moral defect can deprive law of validity from the perspective of a participant in the legal system. The nature of the connection between moral defectiveness and legal defectiveness is specified in terms of three possibilities: exclusive non-positivism, in which all cases of moral defect render law invalid; inclusive non-positivism, in which moral defect renders law invalid in some cases; and super-inclusive non-positivism, in which legal validity is not affected by moral defect at all. *The paper argues for inclusive non-positivism as exemplified by the Radbruch Formula, according to which extreme injustice is not law, and which strikes the right balance between the ideal and real dimensions of law*, against John Finnis's account, which can be seen as an example of super-inclusive non-positivism, although his most recent work has tended towards the inclusive version"). Italics added.

[79] Popovic, Petar, "Reading Finnis and Aquinas on Justice as the Evaluative Standard for Positive Law", *cit.*, pp. 63–75 (64).

[80] See: Alexy, Robert, "The Dual Nature of Law," *Ratio Juris*, Volume 23, 2010, pp. 176–177. See also: Alexy, Robert, *The Argument from Injustice: A Reply to Legal Positivism*, Paulson, Stanley L. and Paulson, Bonnie Litschewski (Translators), Oxford, Clarendon Press, 2002, p. 28 ("Legal character is forfeited when norms or systems of norms cross a certain threshold of justice").

[81] Finnis, John, *Natural Law and Natural Rights*, 2nd edition, Oxford, Oxford University Press, 2011, p. 3 ("There are **human goods** that can be *secured only through the institutions of human law, and requirements of practical reasonableness that only those institutions can satisfy.* It is the object of this book to identify those goods, and those requirements *of practical reasonableness, and thus to show how and on what conditions such institutions are justified and the ways in which they*

At first blush, it seems as though Alexy blends the **human goods** of **«equality»** and **«freedom»** as the foundational values that lie at the heart of his conception of human rights,[82] which, in turn, embodies the theoretical centrepiece of his concept[83] of justice.[84]

§§ In addition to that, in Robert Alexy's offering, justice lends itself to a neatly moral criterion, a standard of morality that is underpinned by a **dual «descriptive-evaluative» nature of law**.[85] Relatedly, the intrinsic linkage between law and morality to a moral-evaluative frame of reference inheres and permeates the very nature or concept of law.[86] As a result, morality or moral goodness pervades, and runs through, the crux of the concept of law.[87] Strikingly, *Algorithmic Common Good* embraces the central tenets of **moral goodness** that must characterize algorithmic decision-making.

---

can be (and often are) defective"). Italics and bold added; Popovic, Peter, "The Three Levels of Law's Goodness and Then One More: Exploring John Finnis's Account of Good Juridical Reasons for Action," *Persona y Derecho*, Volume 83, 2020, pp. 521–552, later reprinted in Popovic, Peter, *The Goodness of Rights and the Juridical Domain of the Good: Essays in Thomistic Juridical Realism*, Roma: EDUSC, 2021, 125–156 (delves into the multifarious levels of practical goodness in Finnis's blueprint).

[82] Alexy, Robert, *Begriff und Geltung des Rechts*, 4th edition, Frankfurt am Main, Suhrkamp, 1992, pp. 64–70 (noting that the laws, rights, and the legal system in which the former rests upon must be as rational as they can be).

[83] Popovic, Petar, "Reading Finnis and Aquinas on Justice as the Evaluative Standard for Positive Law", *cit.*, pp. 63–75 (64).

[84] Alexy, Robert, "Law, Morality, and the Existence of Human Rights," *Ratio Juris*, Volume 25, 2012, p. 11; Alexy, Robert, "The Dual Nature of Law," *cit.*, p. 178.

[85] Alexy, Robert, The Dual Nature of Law," *cit.*, pp. 168, 171 ("*Law necessarily raises a claim to … moral correctness [which] is the source of the necessary relation between law and morality…* Questions of correct distribution and compensation are questions of justice, for justice is nothing other than correctness in distribution and compensation. Questions of justice are, however, moral questions"). Italics added. See also: Alexy, Robert, "Some Reflections on the Ideal Dimension of Law," *cit.*, p. 108 (arguing that human rights are fundamentally moral rights).

[86] Alexy, Robert, *The Argument from Injustice, A Reply to Legal Positivism*, Oxford, Oxford University Press, 2002, pp. 1–160 (70 ff) (arguing that there is a "necessary connection between law and morality by way of three theses: the "incorporation thesis"; "the morality thesis" and the "correctness thesis""). ("*At the heart of this book is the age-old question of how law and morality are related. The legal positivist, insisting on the separation of the two, explicates the concept of law independently of morality*. The author challenges this view, arguing that there are, first, conceptually necessary connections between law and morality and, second, normative reasons for including moral elements in the concept of law. *While the conceptual argument alone is too limited to establish a sufficiently strong connection between law and morality, and the normative argument alone fails to address the nature of law, the two arguments together support a nonpositivistic concept of law, toppling legal positivism qua comprehensive theory of law*. The author arrives at a concept of law that systematically links classical elements of legal positivism - authoritative issuance and social efficacy - with the desideratum of nonpositivistic legal theory, correctness of content"). Italics added.

[87] Popovic, Petar, "Reading Finnis and Aquinas on Justice as the Evaluative Standard for Positive Law", *cit.*, pp. 63–75 (64).

§§ Importantly, Robert Alexy's non-positivist, minimalist, and fundamentally moral nature of justice[88] therefore bestows upon stakeholders a particularly clear window on the pivotal role that justice plays in the broader theoretical apparatus within which the very concept of law[89] operates. Algorithmic decision-making, to embody Justice concerns, must therefore abide by the core features of fairness that propel forward *Algorithmic Common Good*.

5.1.1.4 «Practical Reasonableness» That Embodies Human Good (John Finnis) and Spurs *Algorithmic Common Good*

§§ Aside from Robert Alexy, John Finnis is one of the most outspoken/staunch/ bulwark supporters of the overriding claim according to which the nature of law is dual or twofold[90] within the purview of the Thomistic natural-law theory.[91]

§§ Finnis avers that law consists of **(i)** source-laden social facts (or *artifacts*)—i.e., the descriptive aspect of law's nature—and, concomitantly, of **(ii)** the law's practical-reasonable standpoint—i.e., the **individual** and **collective** evaluative standpoint from which it is feasible to gauge whether and to what extent legal norms amount to **good**

[88] Robert Alexy leverages on the theoretical underpinnings laid down by Gustav Radbruch in three instances: **(i)** allots to justice an evaluative nature that forms parts of a broader apparatus within which the nature of law operates; **(ii)** pinpoints cases of egregious infringement of human rights as the threshold at which the legal validity, and legal vitality, of unjust laws are no longer morally acceptable and are therefore is derailed/sullied/besmirched, and, lastly **(iii)** fleshes out justice in terms of a minimalist or deliberately thin evaluative frame of reference, which neatly encapsulates, hands-in-glove, the prototypical value of *human good* of equality. The groundwork outlined by Professor Gustav Radbruch can be found in: Radbruch, Gustav, "Statutory Lawlessness and Supra-Statutory Law," *Oxford Journal of Legal Studies*, Volume 26, 2006, pp. 7–8; Radbruch, Gustav, "Five Minutes of Legal Philosophy," *Oxford Journal of Legal Studies*, Volume 26, 2006, p. 14. Popovic, Petar, "Reading Finnis and Aquinas on Justice as the Evaluative Standard for Positive Law", *cit.*, pp. 63–75.

[89] Popovic, Petar, "Reading Finnis and Aquinas on Justice as the Evaluative Standard for Positive Law", *cit.*, pp. 63–75 (64).

[90] Finnis, John, "Coexisting Normative Orders? Yes, but no," *The American Journal of Jurisprudence*, Volume 57, 2012.

[91] Popovic, Petar, "Reading Finnis and Aquinas on Justice as the Evaluative Standard for Positive Law", *cit.*, pp. 63–75 (64).

juridical reasons for action.[92] Taken together,[93] both aspects morph law into «what it is.»[94] Finnis thereupon pores over the theoretical underpinnings of the evaluative aspect of law's nature with a sharper focus on **practical reasonableness**[95] paired with its manifold ties with law's descriptive nature.[96]

§§ Finnis[97] accordingly contends that idea of justice[98] is deeply woven into the fabric of evaluative features of law's nature to the extent that the latter is tightly interlocked with[99] **practical**[100] **reasonableness.**[101]

---

[92] See: Finnis, John, "Aquinas and Natural Law Jurisprudence", Duke, George/George, Robert P. (Editors), *The Cambridge Companion to Natural Law Jurisprudence*, Cambridge, Cambridge University Press, 2017, pp. 1–56 (pp. 47–48); Finnis, John, "The Nature of Law", Tasioulas, John (Editors), *The Cambridge Companion to the Philosophy of Law*, Cambridge, Cambridge University Press, 2020, pp. 38–58; Finnis, John, *Natural Law and Natural Rights*, 2nd edition, Oxford, Oxford University Press, 2011, pp. 3–22, 426–435. See also: Finnis, John, "A Grand Tour of Legal Theory," *Philosophy of Law, Collected Essays*, Volume 4, Oxford, Oxford University Press, 2011, pp. 101–102, 107; Finnis, John, "Adjudication and Legal Change", *Philosophy of Law, Collected Essays*, Volume 4, Oxford, Oxford University Press, 2011, pp. 397, 402; Finnis, John, "Reflections and Responses," *Reason, Morality and Law: The Philosophy of John Finnis*, Keown, John/George, Robert P. (Editors), Oxford: Oxford University Press, 2013, p. 547; Finnis, John, "Law as Fact and as Reason for Action," *The American Journal of Jurisprudence*, Volume 59, 2014, pp. 95–96.

[93] Popovic, Petar, "Reading Finnis and Aquinas on Justice as the Evaluative Standard for Positive Law", *cit.*, pp. 63–75 (64).

[94] Finnis, John, "Reflections and Responses," *Reason, Morality and Law: The Philosophy of John Finnis, cit.*, p. 552.

[95] Finnis, John, *Aquinas: Moral, Political, and Legal Theory, cit.*, p. 225 ("The law of the state cannot rightly regulate the full range of choices required by practical reasonableness").

[96] Popovic, Petar, "Reading Finnis and Aquinas on Justice as the Evaluative Standard for Positive Law", *cit.*, pp. 63–75 (64).

[97] Gardner, John, "Finnis on Justice," *Reason, Morality and Law: The Philosophy of John Finnis*, Keown, John/George, Robert P. (Editors), Oxford: Oxford University Press, 2013, pp. 151–166 (John Gardner seeks to parse justice as a moral virtue of one's character, irrespective of its role in the conceptualization of law).

[98] Conly, Sarah, *Against Autonomy: Justifying Coercive Paternalism*, Cambridge, United Cambridge University Press, (2012): 1–216 (*passim*) (stating that autonomy is not to be deemed unbending and unyielding. Rather, autonomy must be bent (oftentimes limited) for the sake of the community welfare on the heels of soft paternalism). But see: Wright, Joshua D./Ginsburg, Douglas H., "Behavioral Law and Economics: Its Origins, Fatal Flaws, and Implications for Liberty", *New York University Law Review*, Volume 106, 2012, pp. 1032 ff (decrying the limitation of autonomy for the sake of community welfare on the heels of soft paternalism). But see also: Sen, Amartya, *Development as Freedom*, New York, Alfred A. Knopf, 1999, pp. 1–366 (73–76) (according to this acclaimed economist, welfare boils down to awarding people the choice for a life which they deeply care about).

[99] Popovic, Petar, "Reading Finnis and Aquinas on Justice as the Evaluative Standard for Positive Law", *cit.*, pp. 63–75 (64).

[100] Finnis, John, "Practical Reason's Foundations," *Collected Essays, Volume 1, Reason in Action*, 21n2.

[101] Finnis, John, *Natural Law and Natural Rights, cit.*, p. 280 (posits that "natural law" or "the set of principles of practical reasonableness in ordering human life and human community" amounts to "only analogically law"). Finnis, John, "The Nature of Law", Tasioulas, John (Editors), *The Cambridge Companion to the Philosophy of Law, cit.*, p. 57 (Finnis elaborates on the ways in which

§§ With this context in place, **justice** forms part of broad thematic apparatus that encompasses: **(i)** the principles of **practical reasonableness**[102] that single out the elementary **human goods**[103] as **good reasons for action**[104] **(i.e. secure algorithmic fairness in algorithmic decision-making)** to be pursued as they strive to achieve **human good**[105] **(i.e. Algorithmic Common Good)**, subsequently **(ii)** rele-

---

positive exists and comes into being. Pivotally, positive law exists "in" practical reasoning of a cohort of persons whom are tasked with the duty to apply and interpret it. It therefore dwells "in" the *minds of lawmakers, legal officials, and law-abiding citizens*). Finnis, John, *Natural Law and Natural Rights*, *cit.*, p. 290 (on Finnis's seminal distinction between positive law and moral or principles, rules, and norms that amount to "practical reasonableness") Finnis, John, "Natural Law,'", *Reason in Action, Collected Essays*, Volume 1, Oxford, Oxford University Press, 2011, 205; Finnis, John, "Legal Reasoning as Practical Reason," *Reason in Action, Collected Essays*, p. 214; Finnis, John, "Natural Law,", *Reason in Action, Collected Essays*, Volume 1, Oxford, Oxford University Press, 2011, 205; Finnis, John, "Legal Reasoning as Practical Reason," *Reason in Action, Collected Essays*, p. 214.

[102] Finnis, John, *Natural Law and Natural Rights*, *cit.*, p. 290 (on Finnis's seminal distinction between positive law and moral or principles, rules, and norms that amount to "practical reasonableness"). Finnis, John, *Aquinas: Moral, Political, and Legal Theory*, *cit.*, p. 225 ("The law of the state cannot rightly regulate the full range of choices required by practical reasonableness").

[103] Finnis, John, *Natural Law and Natural Rights*, *cit.*, p. 3 ("There are **human goods** that can be *secured only through the institutions of human law, and requirements of practical reasonableness that only those institutions can satisfy*. It is the object of this book to identify those goods, and those requirements *of practical reasonableness, and thus to show how and on what conditions such institutions are justified and the ways in which they can be (and often are) defective*"). Italics and bold added; Popovic, Peter, "The Three Levels of Law's Goodness and Then One More: Exploring John Finnis's Account of Good Juridical Reasons for Action," *Persona y Derecho*, Volume 83, 2020, pp. 521–552, later reprinted in Popovic, Peter, *The Goodness of Rights and the Juridical Domain of the Good: Essays in Thomistic Juridical Realism*, Roma: EDUSC, 2021, 125–156 (delves into the multifarious levels of practical goodness in Finnis's blueprint).

[104] See: Finnis, John, "A Grand Tour of Legal Theory," *Philosophy of Law, Collected Essays*, Volume 4, *cit.*, p. 123 ("apart from the existence of laws and legal institutions in the minds and dispositions of particular persons and communities, the only reality of laws and legal institutions—but this is also their primary reality—is as *reasons for action which are good because intelligibly related to (albeit usually not deducible from!) the basic reasons for action, the basic goods, the intrinsic values at stake in human action*, and *to their integral unfolding in moral standards*"). Italics added.

[105] Finnis, John, "Aquinas and Natural Law Jurisprudence," *cit.*, pp. 20–21 ("*Insofar as one actualizes this good* [i.e., *the good of being practically reasonable*] *in one's deliberations, choices and conduct (carrying out of choices), one acts with prudentia, practical reasonableness*. As actualized, it is a virtue—a morally good disposition to have—and indeed it is the master virtue, without which one cannot really have any of the others (notably, justice ...). Prudentia presides over the identification of and compliance with the moral precepts or norms, *the propositions that state the implications of pursuing the basic goods integrally (including reasonable concern for their actualization in the lives of other people*"). Italics added. For instance, the purview of justice, which consists of the other-directed actualization of the elementary goods in a cohort, and thicket, of selves (the **common good** in a broader social apparatus within which justice operates) through one's external operations and with regard to external things or realities (*res*), domain in which, according to Finnis, *prudential* can, and should, be exercised. Popovic, Petar, "Reading Finnis and Aquinas on Justice as the Evaluative Standard for Positive Law", *cit.*, pp. 63–75.

vant stakeholders[106] operating in the camp of algorithmic decision-making endeavour to partake in the process of striving for **Algorithmic Common Good**. To the extent that this conceptual matrix reflects principles bolstering natural moral law,[107] hardly any surprise stems from the fact that justice[108] therefore embodies the central tenets of **natural moral law**.[109]

§§ All things considered, Finnis[110] sets forth an ensemble of **good reasons for action** (v.g. achieve both **algorithmic justice**[111] and **algorithmic fairness**[112] to spur **Algorithmic Common Good**). Note, though, that the good reasons for action are only valid insofar resonate with, and tune into, the core features of natural law

[106] Popovic, Petar, "Reading Finnis and Aquinas on Justice as the Evaluative Standard for Positive Law", *cit.*, pp. 63–75 (65).

[107] Finnis, John, *Natural Law and Natural Rights*, *cit.*, p. 290 (on Finnis's seminal distinction between positive law and moral or principles, rules, and norms that amount to "practical reasonableness") Finnis, John, "Natural Law,", *Reason in Action, Collected Essays*, Volume 1, Oxford, Oxford University Press, 2011, 205; Finnis, John, "Legal Reasoning as Practical Reason," *Reason in Action, Collected Essays*, p. 214.

[108] Finnis, John, *Natural Law and Natural Rights*, *cit.*, p. 225 (Finnis tackles head-on the deemed "**absolute human rights**," which forms part of a broader theoretical apparatus within which the concept of rights as objects of justice operates. In this vein, Finnis fleshes out the latter from the angle of justice while emphasizing that justice is inextricably linked with *practical reasonableness*: "it is always unreasonable to choose directly against any basic value, whether in oneself or in one's own fellow human beings."

[109] Popovic, Petar, "Reading Finnis and Aquinas on Justice as the Evaluative Standard for Positive Law", *cit.*, pp. 63–75 (66).

[110] Finnis, John, *Aquinas: Moral, Political and Legal Theory*, *cit.*, pp. 133–138, 170; Finnis, John, "Aquinas on Ius and Hart on Rights: A Response to Tierney," *The Review of Politics*, Volume 64, 2002, pp. 407–410; Finnis, John, *Natural Law and Natural Rights*, *cit.*, pp. 423–424, 459–460; Finnis, John, "Natural Law," *cit.*, p. 207; Finnis, John, "A Grand Tour of Legal Theory," *cit.*; Finnis, John, "Grounding Human Rights in Natural Law," *cit.*, pp. 213–221; Finnis, John, "On Moyn's Christian Human Rights," *King's Law Journal*, Volume 28, 2017.

[111] Finnis, John, *Natural Law and Natural Rights*, *cit.*, pp. 352–354 (provides a brief (thumbnail) sketch on the four types of injustice enshrined in law) See also: Finnis, John, A*quinas: Moral, Political, and Legal Theory*, *cit.*, pp. 272–273.

[112] Hellman, Deborah, "Measuring Algorithmic Fairness", *Virginia Law Review*, 106 (4), 2020, pp. 811–866. On the dire need to achieve algorithmic fairness through both the creation of race-aware algorithms and trade-offs to attain fairer risk scores: Kim, Pauline, "Race-Aware Algorithms: Fairness, Non-discrimination and Affirmative Action", *California Law Review*, 2022, passim; Kleinberg, Jon/S. Mullainathan/M. Raghavan, "Inherent Trade-offs in the Fair Determination of Risk Scores", *Proceedings of the 8th Conference on Innovations in Theoretical Computer Science (ITCS)*, 2017; Kroll, Joshua A./J. Huey/S. Barocas/E. W. Felten/J. R. Reidenberg/D. G. Robinson/and H. Yu, "Accountable Algorithms", *University of Pennsylvania Law Review*, 165 (3), 2017, pp. 633–705.

coupled with its underpinning **human goods**[113] **and common good.**[114] Amongst which stands *Algorithmic Common Good* that wishes algorithmic evil (*Algorithmic Dictatorship*)[115] away.

§§ Put simply, justice[116]—as a theoretical underpinning of **practical reasonableness**—boasts a normative nature that forms part of a broader theoretical apparatus within which the evaluative aspect of the dual nature of law operates.[117]

---

113 See: Finnis, John, "A Grand Tour of Legal Theory," *Philosophy of Law, Collected Essays*, Volume 4, *cit.*, p. 123 ("apart from the existence of laws and legal institutions in the minds and dispositions of particular persons and communities, the only reality of laws and legal institutions—but this is also their primary reality—is as *reasons for action which are good because intelligibly related to (albeit usually not deducible from!) the basic reasons for action, the basic goods, the intrinsic values at stake in human action*, and *to their integral unfolding in moral standards*"). Italics added.

114 Finnis, John, "Reflections and Responses," *cit.*, p. 538 ("Being for the **common good, including justice and human rights, is central to law—is at the core of law as an idea").** Bold added. See also: Finnis, John, "Reflections and Responses," *cit.*, p. 552 ("What makes social facts so utterly central to law? **Human needs, vulnerabilities, scarcities, and ways of flourishing or losing out. One of the most important of our needs is the need for justice in human responses to these problems. So justice is a necessary condition for law's counting as an adequate response to them**"). Bold added. See also: Finnis, John, "The Nature of Law," *cit.*, p. 51.

115 See: Part IV, Chap. 4, Sects. 4.1–4.1.10.6 of this book (on Algorithmic Dictatorship and its chilling effect on democracy).

116 Finnis, John, *Aquinas: Moral, Political, and Legal Theory*, Oxford: Oxford University Press, 1998, pp. 1–408, 137, 188; Finnis, John, "Grounding Human Rights in Natural Law," *The American Journal of Jurisprudence*, Volume 60, 2015, p. 208 (emphasizing **outwardness** as an intrinsic feature of justice).

117 Popovic, Petar, "Reading Finnis and Aquinas on Justice as the Evaluative Standard for Positive Law", *cit.*, pp. 63–75 (66); Finnis, John, *Natural Law and Natural Rights*, *cit.*, pp. 161–165, 459; Finnis, John, *Aquinas: Moral, Political, and Legal Theory*, *cit.*, p. 132; Finnis, John, "Grounding Human Rights in Natural Law," cit., p. 214n51; Finnis, John, "Aquinas and Natural Law Jurisprudence," *cit.*, p. 46; Finnis, John, "The Nature of Law," *cit.*, p. 51 (On Finnis's conception of justice paired with an ensemble of principles of practical reasonableness).

5.1.1.5 The Fundamental Shift Away from a Human-Centred Artificial Intelligence That Propels Forward a Pull Towards a Thing-Centred Artificial Intelligence That Secures *Algorithmic Common Good*

5.1.1.5.1 Foundations: Philosophy of Law

5.1.1.5.2 Thomas Aquinas' Concept of ius *Underpinning a Fair Algorithmic Decision-Making Conducive to* Algorithmic Common Good

§§ Thomas Aquinas's overriding claim[118] is one in which justice[119] plays a pivotal role in the evaluative piece that inheres and permeates in law's[120] backbone.[121]

§§ Thomas Aquinas expounds on the interplay between Justice and *Ius*. The classical definition of justice—comprised in the undying and unfaltering goal to allot to each person his or her own *ius*[122]—can be laid bare by grasping the very nature of law.[123]

§§ Notwithstanding, to drill into Thomas Aquinas's offering on the legal relevance of justice, light must be primarily cast upon the term «law». The latter has a far wider outreach in that comprises realities that narrower approaches often overlook/forsake. For instance, according to Finnis, «law» straddles with human positive law.[124] In the

[118] Popovic, Petar, "Reading Finnis and Aquinas on Justice as the Evaluative Standard for Positive Law", *cit.*, pp. 63–75 (69).

[119] Aquinas's following claim: "The aforesaid definition of justice [constans et perpetua voluntas ius suum unicuique tribuens] is fitting." Summa Theologica II-II, q. 58, a. 1 (hereafter: S.T.). For the English translation of the texts from Aquinas's Summa Theologica, we will be using Thomas Aquinas, Summa Theologiae: First Complete American Edition in Three Volumes, trans. Fathers of the English Dominican Province (New York: Benziger Brothers, 1947–1948). See: Popovic, Petar, "Reading Finnis and Aquinas on Justice as the Evaluative Standard for Positive Law", *cit.*, pp. 63–75, whose research I have been following.

[120] This finding (*pactum subjectionis*) chimes in with the Thomistic Philosophy background according to which King's supremacy derived from the dubbed *pactum subjectionis*: all power derived from a greater source (God Almighty), which was subsequently ascribed to the people and thereafter to the ruling monarch; Thomas Aquinas, *Summa Theologica*, V Volumes, Christian Classics; English Dominican Province Translation edition (June 1, 1981), (1981): passim (on these astounding essays a detailed account on Christian thought is provided—a book which has had a paramount and ground-breaking impact on philosophy and religion since the thirteenth century, sending ripples across the navigable eternity). This book will focus on Volume II.

[121] Finnis, John, *Natural Law and Natural Rights*, *cit.*, p. 460.

[122] *Summa Theologica*, II-II, q. 58, a. 1. See also: Popovic, Petar, *Natural Law and Thomistic Juridical Realism: Prospects for a Dialogue with Contemporary Legal Theory*, Washington, D.C.: The Catholic University of America Press, 2022, pp. 107–146 (deep dives on Aquinas's definition of justice, with a sharper focus on Aristotle and a handful of Roman jurists).

[123] Popovic, Petar, "Reading Finnis and Aquinas on Justice as the Evaluative Standard for Positive Law", *cit.*, pp. 63–75 (69).

[124] This idea becomes both clear-cut and straighforward just by reading Finnis's protracted/wearisome/long-winded delineation of both law in Natural Law and Natural Rights: Finnis, John, *Natural Law and Natural Rights*, 2nd edition, Oxford, Oxford University Press, 2011, pp. 276–277

opposite pole, Aquinas, the concept of *ius*, which stands for a juridical phenomenon in an overarching sense, is neither amenable to be hardened into binding norms nor it can be bogged down to mere legal practices.[125]

§§ Instead, in Aquina's account, «law» extends far beyond the positive law.[126] «Law» (*ius* in the classical tradition) accordingly identifies itself with the cardinal virtue of justice, according to[127] Aquinas.[128]

§§ Antithetically, Finnis conflates justice with rights.[129] The latter—rights—unfold itself into subjective rights inasmuch they embody a form of benefit or advantage of persons. Finnis accordingly relies upon a blueprint in view of which subjective rights are actionable insofar **(i)** it pertain to certain individuals, **(ii)** the latter are fundamentally entitled to dispose them, and **(iii)** they are credited with those rights inasmuch other persons are dubbed as their debtors.[130]

(“*throughout this chapter, the term ‘law’ has been used with a focal meaning so as to refer primarily to rules made, in accordance with regulative legal rules, by a determinate and effective authority* (itself identified and, standardly, constituted as an institution by legal rules) for a ‘complete’ community, and *buttressed by sanctions in accordance with the rule-guided stipulations of adjudicative institutions, this ensemble of rules being directed to reasonably resolving any of the community's co-ordination problems ... for the common good of that community*”). Italics added. Petar Popovic, “Prendere le norme sul serio nel giusnaturalismo tomista: la necessità della legge positiva secondo John Finnis e il giusrealismo tomista,” *Ius Ecclesiae*, Volume 35, 2023, passim (provides a granular and nuanced analysis on Finnis's theories in which the latter avowedly contends that positivity is a sorely needed aspect of law's essence, thereby forming part of one of the two “lives” in law's dual nature); Finnis, John, *Natural Law and Natural Rights*, *cit.*, p. 290 (on Finnis's seminal distinction between positive law and moral or principles, rules, and norms that amount to “practical reasonableness”) Finnis, John, “Natural Law,’”, *Reason in Action, Collected Essays*, Volume 1, Oxford, Oxford University Press, 2011, 205; Finnis, John, “Legal Reasoning as Practical Reason,” *Reason in Action, Collected Essays*, p. 214.

125 Popovic, Petar, “Reading Finnis and Aquinas on Justice as the Evaluative Standard for Positive Law”, *cit.*, pp. 63–75 (69).

126 Popovic, Petar, “Reading Finnis and Aquinas on Justice as the Evaluative Standard for Positive Law”, *cit.*, pp. 63–75 (69).

127 Popovic, Petar, “Reading Finnis and Aquinas on Justice as the Evaluative Standard for Positive Law”, *cit.*, pp. 63–75 (69).

128 *Summa Theologica*, II-II, q. 57, a. 1.

129 Finnis, John, “The Nature of Law”, Tasioulas, John (Editors), *The Cambridge Companion to the Philosophy of Law*, *cit.*, p. 57 (Finnis elaborates on the ways in which positive exists and comes into being. Pivotally, positive law exists “in” practical reasoning of a cohort of persons whom are tasked with the duty to apply and interpret it. It therefore dwells “in” the *minds of lawmakers, legal officials, and law-abiding citizens*). Notwithstanding, in Finnis's groundwork, the foregoing requirement is the seventh requirement of **practical reasonableness (“respect for every basic value in every act”)**, which is far cry from the requirement of justice (classified by Finnis as the eighth requirement of practical reasonableness). As a result, the underlying normative matrix of imperativeness of **absolute human rights** amounts to a foundational value of practical reasonableness, which, however, is anything but justice-charged. See: Finnis, John, *Natural Law and Natural Rights*, *cit.*, pp. 118–125. See Finnis, *Aquinas: Moral, Political, and Legal Theory*, *cit.*, p. 132 (“The basic good of ***practical reasonableness* (*bonum prudentiae*) summons one to treat *the good of other people as a reason for action in one's own practical deliberation and choosing***”). Italics and bold added.

130 Popovic, Petar, “Reading Finnis and Aquinas on Justice as the Evaluative Standard for Positive Law”, *cit.*, pp. 63–75 (69).

§§ Against this background, Finnis' account on law is conspicuously narrower in breadth and scope than Aquinas' concept of *ius*.[131] Aquinas, on the other hand, laid down the groundwork underpinning his concept of *ius* considering the affordances of justice in an overarching sense. Pivotally, *ius* loosely means that the **just thing itself** (*ipsa res iusta*)[132] or that **thing that is neatly just** (*iustum*)[133] occupies the higher echelon of justice. Bearing this backdrop very firmly in mind, this book therefore asserts that **algorithmic decision-making (a thing itself)** must be fundamentally **neatly just** and **fair** to embody the core features of **Algorithmic Common Good**.

§§ Put otherwise, for Aquinas, «law» (*ius*) is neatly identifiable with a tangible reality or thing (*res*). Aquinas tackles head-on the juridical phenomenon from a **thing-centred (or rei-centric) standpoint**, against the backdrop of which a concrete thing or reality (*res*) becomes juridical insofar is seen as the centrepiece of the important relations of[134] justice.[135] This assertion neatly encapsulates, hands-in-glove, the gist of natural right championed by Thomas Aquinas.[136]

---

[131] Finnis, John, *Natural Law and Natural Rights*, cit., p. 460.

[132] Whilst Villey points out that Aquinas's primordial meaning of *ius* is markedly objectivist and **thing-centered (*ius as ipsa res iusta*)**, the former refrained himself from systematically intertwine this meaning with either the vexing question of justice as the evaluative benchmark for positive law or with the matrixial structure of subjective rights. See: Villey, Michel, "Droit subjectif I (La genèse du droit subjectif chez Guillaume d'Occam)", *Seize Essais de philosophie du droit dont un sur la crise universitaire*, Paris, Dalloz, 1969, pp. 140–178; Villey, Michel, "Si la théorie générale du droit, pour Saint Thomas, est une théorie de la loi," *Archives de philosophie du droit*, Volume 17, 1972, pp. 427–431; Prados, Alfredo Cruz, *Sobre la realidad del Derecho. Filosofia Jurıdica*, Pamplona, EUNSA, 2021, 58–64, 142–145, 207–231, 243–250 (adopts the great bulk of Villey's stances). See also: Popovic, Petar, *Natural Law and Thomistic Juridical Realism*, pp. 105–36, 164–168, 171–188; Finnis, John, "Un ouvrage recent sur Bentham," Archives de philosophie du droit, Volume 17, 1972, pp. 423–427 (a rejoinder to Villey); Finnis, John, "Aquinas on Ius and Hart on Rights: A Response to Tierney," cit., pp. 407–410; Finnis, John, *Natural Law and Natural Rights, cit.*, pp. 245, 465–466; Finnis, John, "Natural Law", *cit.*, pp. 206–207; Finnis, John, "Grounding Human Rights in Natural Law", *cit.*, p. 214.

[133] *Summa Theologica*, II-II, q. 57, a. 1, ad 1. *Summa Theologica* II-II, q. 57, a. 3 ("*Ius* or *iustum* depends on its commensuration with another person." In the textual locus where he defines *ius*, after describing some aspects of the properties of *other-directedness* ("a man's work is said to be *just* [*iustum*] when it is related to some other"), *Summa Theologica* II-II, q. 57, a. 1 (Aquinas avers: "For this reason [*et propter hoc*] justice has its own special proper object over and above other virtues, and this object is called the just, which is the same as ius". See also: *Summa Theologica* II-II, q. 57, a. 2. "*Ius* or the just is a work [*opus*] that is adjusted to another person." S.T. II-II, q. 57, a. 2. Popovic, Petar, "Reading Finnis and Aquinas on Justice as the Evaluative Standard for Positive Law", *cit.*, pp. 63–75.

[134] Popovic, Petar, "Reading Finnis and Aquinas on Justice as the Evaluative Standard for Positive Law", *cit.*, pp. 63–75 (69).

[135] *Summa Theologica* II-II, q. 58, a. 8; II-II, q. 58, a. 10; II-II, q. 58, a. 11 (Aquinas's refers to things themselves or *res* (ranging from material objects, aspects of reality, acts, speech acts, to a wide range of states of affairs) that are tightly interlocked with, and deeply woven into the fabric of, the relations of justice that seek to furnish baselines to buttress the matrix of juridical phenomenon (*ius*).

[136] See: Hervada, Javier, "Critical Introduction to Natural Right", trans. Mindy Emmons (Montréal: Wilson & Lafleur Ltée, 2006, pp. 22–24; Hervada, Javier, *Lecciones propedéuticas de filosofia del derecho*, 4th ed, Pamplona: EUNSA, 2008, pp. 201–204; Hervada, Javier, "What is Law? The

§§ The juridical phenomenon («law») therefore becomes juridically relevant insofar manifests itself in a broader context of human relations of justice. Put simply, that **concrete thing (i.e. algorithmic decision-making)** is «caught» in the middle of an ensemble of variegated, chequered, and multilayered relations of (algorithmic) justice.[137]

§§ With this context in place, I adamantly propound a seismic shift in algorithmic decision-making. The piecemeal and haphazard concept of **human-centred Artificial Intelligence**—which, as stated earlier in this book,[138] lacks befitted, if any, theoretical underpinnings to begin with—must be accordingly abandoned.

§§ Instead, drawing on Aquinas' concept of *ius*, I propound the adoption of a **thing-centred Artificial Intelligence** that should bolster a fairness-fraught algorithmic decision-making which, in turn, will propel forward **Algorithmic Common Good**. If algorithmic decision-making achieves algorithmic fairness,[139] citizens' fundamental rights will enjoy a far greater protection than they would have enjoyed

---

Modern Response of Juridical Realism", trans. W. L. Daniel (Montréal: Wilson & Lafleur Ltée, 2009, pp. 49–51. It is important to note, though, that Hervada's axe of reasoning on the two cumulative constitutional moments of the juridical phenomenon bears a striking resemblance with Aquinas's theoretical matrix, against the backdrop of which the latter: **(i)** builds on Ulpian's definition of justice and *ius* as its direct object (*ius suum cuique tribuens*, enshrined in *Summa Theologica* II-II, q. 57, a. 4, ad 1; II-II, q. 58, a. 1), **(ii)** emphasizes that primordial meaning of *ius* is the ***just thing itself*** (*Summa Theologica* II-II, q. 57, a. 1), and **(iii)** views justice as the propelling force behind the difference between *suum and non suum* (or the definitional boundaries of what is *yours* that stand in stark contrast of what is *mine*) that pervades one's intervention in the outer world (*Summa Theologica* I-II, q. 66, a. 4, ad 1). Popovic, Petar, "Reading Finnis and Aquinas on Justice as the Evaluative Standard for Positive Law", *cit.*, pp. 63–75.

[137] Popovic, Petar, "Reading Finnis and Aquinas on Justice as the Evaluative Standard for Positive Law", *cit.*, pp. 63–75 (70).

[138] See: Part V, this chapter, Sects. 5.1.2–5.1.6.2.1 of this book (on the thing-centred algorithmic decision-making propelled by a *Controllable* and *Interpretable* Machine Learning that weeds out *Algorithmic Dictatorship* and secures *Algorithmic Common Good*. It is worth recalling that the **thing-centred algorithmic decision-making** seeks to unwind the perils arising out of the lack of theoretical underpinnings facing the **human-centred algorithmic decision-making**, as extensively fleshed out Part III, Chap. 3, Sects. 3.1.4.3–3.1.4.4 of this book).

[139] Mitchell, S./E. Potash/S. Barocas/A D'Amour/K. Lum, "Algorithmic Fairness: Choices, Assumptions, and Definitions", *Annual Review of Statistics and Its Applications* 2021 (8), 2021, pp. 141–63; Mullainathan, S., "Biased Algorithms Are Easier to fix Than Biased People." New York Times December 6, 2019, https://www.nytimes.com/2019/12/06/business/algorithm-bias-fix.html.

had they been allotted an inscrutable[140] right to explanation[141] since citizens are woefully ill-prepared to fully understand it.[142]

---

[140] See: Strandburg, Katherine J., "Rulemaking and Inscrutable Decision Tools", *Columbia Law Review*, Volume 119, 2019, passim. Note, though, that there are far more unsettling issues with which criminal justice flounders with. To begin with, the inscrutable way algorithms make their correlations and draw their inferences accordingly—which is eerily unbeknownst even for the cohort of programmers that designed them—stand out. This is deemed *black box*, that further enhances the shroud of mystery under which algorithms are cloaked. See, for a compelling account of AI black box: See: Bathaee, Yavar, "The Artificial Intelligence Black Box and the Failure of Intent and Causation", *Harvard Journal of Law and Technology*, n.° 37, 2018, p. 901 (adduces that "*one possible reason AI may be a black box to humans is that it relies on machine-learning algorithms that internalize data in ways that are not easily audited or understood by humans (…)*" "*first, a lack may arise from the complexity of the algorithm's structure, such as with deep neural network, which consists of thousands of artificial neurons working together in a diffuse way to solve a problem. This reason for AI being a black box is referred to as "complexity". Second, the lack of transparency may arise because the AI is using a machine-learning algorithm that relies on geometric relationships that humans cannot visualize, such as with support vector machines. This reason for AI being a black box is referred to as "dimensionality"*"). Italics added. See: Part V, this chapter, Sect. 5.1.7.2 of this book (on law number two to control algorithmic decision-making, which mandates that black box models must not be entrusted with the task of making high stake decisions—v.g. health and freedom).

[141] Selbst, A./Powles, J., "Meaningful information and the right to explanation", *International Data Privacy Law*, Volume 7, 2018, pp. 233 and ff and passim; Adadi, Amina/Berrada, Mohammed, "Peeking Inside the Black-Box: A Survey on Explainable Artificial Intelligence (XAI), *Institute of Electrical and Electronics Engineers*, Volume 6, 2018, passim; Miller, Tim, "Explanations in Artificial Intelligence: Insights from Social Sciences", *Artificial Intelligence*, Volume 267, 2019, pp. 1–38; Avery, Mallory/Leibbrandt, Andreas/Vecci, Joseph, "Does Artificial Intelligence Help or Hurt Gender Diversity? Evidence from Two Field Experiments on Recruitment on Tech, *Monash University, Monash Business School*, 2023, pp. 1–70. Blattner, Laura/Nelson, Scott/Spiess, Jann, *Unpacking the Black Box: Regulating Algorithmic Decisions.* See: Part V, this chapter, Sects. 5.1.7–5.1.7.5 of this book (on the five laws to control algorithmic decision-making). See: Part V, this chapter, Sects. 5.1.8–5.1.8.5 of this book (on the five laws to interpret algorithmic decision-making). See: Part V, this chapter, Sects. 5.1.2–5.1.6.2.1 of this book (on **the thing-centred algorithmic decision-making** propelled by a *Controllable* and *Interpretable* Machine Learning that weeds out *Algorithmic Dictatorship* and secures *Algorithmic Common Good*. It is worth recalling that the **thing-centred algorithmic decision-making** seeks to unwind the perils arising out of the lack of theoretical underpinnings facing the **human-centred algorithmic decision-making**, as extensively fleshed out Part III, Chap. 3, Sects. 3.1.4.3–3.1.4.4 of this book). See: Part V, this chapter, Sect. 5.1.1.7.5 of this book (on Algorithmic Common Good, with a sharper focus on the dire need of algorithmic auditing, undertaken by external auditors that must be given full access to the dataset used to train the running models). See: Part III, Chap. 3, Sects. 3.1.5.4–3.1.5.4.1.1 of this book (on Critical Artificial Intelligence Studies, with a sharper focus on the deceptive patterns evinced by Large Language Models, which has lent urgency to concerns about the trustworthiness and reliability of these tools). See: Part V, this chapter, Sect. 5.1.7.2 of this book (on law number two to control algorithmic decision-making, which mandates that black box models must not be entrusted with the task of making high stake decisions—v.g. health and freedom).

[142] Edwards, Lilian/Veale, Michael, "Slave to the Algorithm? Why a "Right to an Explanation" is Probably not the Remedy You are Looking for", *Duke Law and Technology Review*, Volume 16, 2018, pp. 18–67 (pondering whether and to what extent XAI will come in handy because citizens

§§ To cater for that, **a thing-centred Artificial Intelligence**—whose inner workings shy away from, and run counter to, algorithmic opacity[143]—must bestow upon citizens actionable[144] pathways to **challenge** and **contest**—a hallmark of **Procedural Rule of Law**[145]—the pearls of algorithmic wisdom spawned at the front end of algorithmic decision-making.

§§ To that end, a **thing-centred Artificial Intelligence**, aside from being **intrinsically fair**, must be also **controllable**[146] and **interpretable.**[147] Computer science will prove invaluable to further fortify/cement the foundations upon which stands my newly-crafted concept of **Algorithmic Common Good**.

---

are woefully ill-prepared to "make use of the kind of algorithmic explanations they are likely to be offered").

[143] For an on-point breakdown of the distinct levels of opacity arising out of machine learning algorithms in the purview of insurance policies: Selbst, Andrew D./Barocas, Solon, "The Intuitive Appeal of Explainable Machines", *Fordham Law Review*, Volume 87, 2018, pp. 1085, 1089–1099 (holding that there are plenty reasons for the insurer's ignorance. To begin with, the algorithm entails specialized knowledge to understand. That is, the insurer's employees may lack sufficient knowledge to understand the rationale behind the reasons in view of which the algorithm is producing prices for different customers—personalized pricing. Lastly, even if the insurer himself comprehends how the model operates, it may nonetheless lack expertise to comprehend why it operates the way it does. For that reason, the explainability of machines is a vital, but rather elusive, task. Thence, the famed authors deem it as the "nonintuitive" nature of algorithms. For purposes here, the insurer himself might indeed understand that its Artificial Intelligence-embedded technology formulates higher prices for those who actually access the website at hand, but may fail to come to terms with the fact that the explanation for this fact arises from the website's capacity to proxy for genetic information).

[144] See: Deeks, Ahsley, "The Judicial Demand for Explainable Artificial Intelligence", *Columbia Law Review*, Volume 119, 2019, pp. 1829 and ff and passim. See: Hacker, Phillip/Passoth, Jan-Hendrick, "Varieties of AI Explanations under the Law: From the GDPR to the AIA, and Beyond", *XxAI Beyond Explainable AI, International Workshop on Extending Explainable AI Beyond Deep Models and Classifiers*. Berlin/New York/Singapore/Beijing: Springer, 2021, pp. 343–373 ("*the quest to explain the output of artificial intelligence systems has clearly moved from a mere technical to a highly legally and politically relevant endeavor.* In this paper, we provide an overview of legal obligations to explain AI and evaluate current policy proposals. In this, we distinguish between different functional varieties of AI explanations - such as multiple forms of enabling, technical and protective transparency - and show how different legal areas engage with and mandate such different types of explanations to varying degrees. *Starting with the rights-enabling framework of the GDPR, we proceed to uncover technical and protective forms of explanations owed under contract, tort and banking law. Moreover, we discuss what the recent EU proposal for an Artificial Intelligence Act means for explainable AI, and review the proposal's strengths and limitations in this respect. Finally, from a policy perspective, we advocate for moving beyond mere explainability towards a more encompassing framework for trustworthy and responsible AI that includes actionable explanations, values-in-design and co-design methodologies, interactions with algorithmic fairness, and quality benchmarking*").

[145] See: Part V, this chapter, Sect. 5.1.1.2 of this book.

[146] See: Part V, this chapter, Sects. 5.1.7–5.1.7.5 of this book (on the five laws to control algorithmic decision-making).

[147] See: Part V, this chapter, Sects. 5.1.8–5.1.8.5 of this book (on the five laws to interpret algorithmic decision-making).

5.1.1.5.3 Foundations of Algorithmic Common Good: Computer Science and Data Science

5.1.1.5.4 «Measurement Bias» May Augment with the Exclusion, or Selection, of Input Variables (e.g. Race and Gender): How Colour-Blindness Flares Discrimination Up in Algorithmic Decision-Making

§§ There is no shortage of poignant calls arguing that the exclusion of protected markers (v.g. race and gender) to adroitly apply discrimination framework in the algorithmic setting is hardly the remedy you should look, nor hold your breath, for. Contrary to mainstream views, if one really cares about deep-seated social inequalities the inclusion of a protected markers, rather than the exclusion, could falloff disparities.[148] When a social marker should be interpreted differently for various racial lines, debarring/blackballing/excluding «race» could uptick disparities. Why? By banishing the input variable (race), we are shoehorning an identical interpretation of a given social marker for both white and non-white applicants (Blacks and Latinos).[149]

§§ When there are considerably more whites in a training[150] dataset,[151] which is extremely likely to be the case even in a representative

---

[148] Gillis, Talia B., "The Input Data Fallacy", *Minnesota Law Review*, Volume 106, 2022, pp. 1176–1263 (1229).

[149] Gillis, Talia B., "The Input Data Fallacy", *cit.*, pp. 1176–1263 (1229).

[150] Note, though, that the training of machine learning is long and tedious in that is an error-prone procedure than can ultimately impair future algorithmic decision-making: Price, W. Nicholson Price II, "Regulating Black-Box Medicine", *Michigan Law Review*, Volume 116, 2017, pp. 421–431 (leverages on Google Image's image recognition learning algorithm to shed light on the four-step process by which some algorithms are thoroughly trained. First, the algorithm is shown "a set of known images ('Here are 10,000 pictures of ducks')." Second, the algorithm "develops complex internal rules based on nonlinear processes." Third, the algorithm "tests those rules on a test set ('Which of these are ducks?')." And fourth, the algorithm accordingly adjusts its "internal rules based on the success of the test." These steps are trotted out and repeated many times "until it can accurately and consistently classify the images").

[151] It is important to note that an algorithm designed for maximum accuracy will adjust itself to the majority data, and may be less accurate for members of the underrepresented group, thus breeding *inductive bias*. See: Shellenbarger, Sue, "A Crucial Step for Avoiding AI Disasters", *Wall Street Journal*, (Feb. 13, 2019, 9:57 AM ET), https://www.wsj.com/articles/a-crucial-step-for-avoiding-ai-disasters-11550069865?ns=prod/accounts-wsj [https://perma.cc/C28U-LAAE] (discussing this issue while emphasizing how diverse development teams pay more attention to unrepresentative and underrepresented data sets). Human programmers can circumvent and bypass this problem by weighting the minority-group data more heavily, by designing different algorithms for each racial group, or by striving to contain more data to equalize group representation in the data set. See: Barua, Sukarna et al., "MWMOTE—Majority Weighted Minority Oversampling Technique for Imbalanced Data Set Learning", *IEEE Transactions on Knowledge & Data Engineering*, Volume 26, 2014, pp. 405, 405–406. See also: Hamilton, Melissa, "The Biased Algorithm: Evidence of Disparate Impact on Hispanics", *American Criminal Law Review*, Volume 56, 2019, pp. 1553 and ff and passim (which clearly demonstrates that COMPAS was significantly less accurate for Hispanic

dataset,[152] the algorithmic prediction will be shaped according to the weight ascribed to the features for white folks.[153] For instance, even if the amount of children is prognosticative of default only for white applicants as opposed to non-white applicants (e.g. Blacks and Latinos), the machine learning algorithm will attribute the feature the same weight for all racial lines when «race» is excluded.[154] This line of reasoning falls in line with, and sharply aligned with, the mounting scepticism amongst pundits about the convenience (or lack thereof) of the wide-ranging stance of debarring protected markers,[155] such as race and gender.

---

than for white defendants by several measures and suggesting that smaller numbers of Hispanic defendants might be the cause). See: Mayson, Sandra G., "Bias In, Bias Out", *cit.*, pp. 2218–2300.

[152] See: Dong et al., Qi, "Imbalanced deep learning by minority class incremental rectification, *IEEE Transactions on Pattern Analysis & Machine Intelligence*, Volume 41, 2019, p. 1367 (posit that "*most existing learning algorithms produce inductive bias (learning bias)* towards the frequent (majority) classes if training data are not balanced, *resulting in poor minority class recognition performance*"). Italics added. See: Chandler, Anupam, "The Racist Algorithm", *Michigan Law Review*, Volume 115, n.º 6, 2018, p. 1026 (on racist algorithms, noting that "the possibilities for discriminatory manipulation are legion"). But see: Altenburger, Kristen M./Ho, Daniel E., "When Algorithms Import Private Bias into Public Enforcement: The Promise and Limitations of Statistical Debiasing Solutions", *Journal of Institutional & Theoretical Economics*, Volume 175, 2019, pp. 97–98 (calls for a "debias predictive algorithms" to assuage racist and/or biased, doctored and bigoted algorithms nevertheless). See: Part V, this chapter, Sect. 5.1.7.4 of this book (on one of the law to control algorithmic decision-making, namely, law number four: data partitioning must be performed—i.e. randomly split an entire dataset into the «training dataset» and the «test dataset»—to accurately predict outcomes in the real world while forestalling «inductive bias» [learning bias]).

[153] Gillis, Talia B., "The Input Data Fallacy", *cit.*, pp. 1176–1263 (1229).

[154] Gillis, Talia B., "The Input Data Fallacy", *cit.*, pp. 1176–1263 (1229).

[155] Gillis, Talia B., "The Input Data Fallacy", *cit.*, pp. 1176–1263 (1229). See also: Hamilton, Melissa, "The Biased Algorithm: Evidence of Disparate Impact on Hispanics", *The American Criminal Law Review*, Volume 56, 2019, 2019, p. 1553 (argues that performance of the COMPAS algorithmic risk assessment on Hispanics is lacklustre insofar falls conspicuously short of matching the central tenets of fairness in that overtly discriminate Hispanics); Xiang, Alice, "Reconciling Legal and Technical Approaches to Algorithmic Bias", *Tennessee Law Review*, Volume 88, 2021, pp. 3–24 (drills into, and sheds light on, the algorithmic tool named COMPAS and the notorious case *State v. Loomis* where the court found it useful to include gender markers to propel overall accuracy); Kleinberg, Jon et al., "Algorithmic Fairness", *AEA Papers & Proceedings*, Volume 108, 2018, pp. 22–23 (discussing, anchored in a batch of national data, that including race as an input variable to a machine-learning college-admissions algorithm both "improves predicted GPAs of admitted students" and can augment "the fraction of admitted students who are black"); Kim, Pauline T., "Data-Driven Discrimination at Work", *cit.*, p. 904 ("Thus, a blanket prohibition on the explicit use of race or other prohibited characteristics does not avoid, and may even worsen, the discriminatory impact of relying on a data model"); Hamilton, Melissa, "The sexist algorithm", *Behavioral Sciences and the Law*, Volume 37, Issue 2, Special Issue: the Use of Statistics in Criminal Cases, March–April 2019, 2019, passim (argues that performance of the COMPAS algorithmic risk assessment on women falls conspicuously short of matching the central tenets of fairness in that machine learning algorithms overtly discriminate women). See: Part IV, Chap. 4, Sects. 4.1.10.1–4.1.10.6 of this book (on biased algorithmic risk assessment in criminal procedure law settings, with a sharper focus on COMPAS). See: Part IV, Chap. 4, Sects. 4.1.1–4.1.1.1 of this book (on biased predictive policing).

§§ By the same token, the inclusion of protected features might also prove pivotally important in dwindling the consumer harms[156] arising out «biased measurement» variables. To illustrate, consider a hypothetical stakeholder that forecasts a given outcome from an input bedevilled by *measurement bias.*[157] In this simple example, if the «ability»[158] is evenly distributed across racial lines, then the higher «ability» individuals (normally, white folks) default[159] considerably less,[160] since

---

[156] See: Bar-Gill, Oren/Sunstein, Cass R./Talgam-Cohen, Inbal, "Algorithmic Harm in Consumer Markets", *Journal of Legal Analysis*, Volume 15, n.º 1, 2023, pp. 1–47. See also: Lee, Nicole Turner/Resnick, Paul/Barton, Genie, *Algorithmic Bias Detection and Mitigation: Best Practices and Policies to Reduce Consumer Harms.* Washington, DC: Brookings Institution, 2019, passim; Slaughter, Rebecca Kelly, "Algorithms and Economic Justice: A Taxonomy of Harms and a Path Forward for the Federal Trade Commission", *Yale Journal of Law and Technology*, Volume 23, 2021 (on algorithmic consumer harms).

[157] But see: Corbett-Davies, Sam/Goel, Sharad, "The Measure and Mismeasure of Fairness: a critical Review of Fair Machine Learning", *Cornell University Library*, 2018, p. 18 (broaches a type of *measurement bias* coined "feature bias," which is neatly a bias in the predictors x. Note, though, that there is a second type of measurement bias deemed "label bias," which, in turn, amounts to a bias in y. The authors argue that that label bias is the worst bias there is); Kleinberg, Jon/Ludwig, Jens/Mullainathan, Sendhil/Sunstein Cass R., "Discrimination in the Age of Algorithms", *Journal of Legal Analysis*, Volume 10, 1, 2018, pp. 28–29, 33–34 (draw a distinction between "group differences in the raw data" and biases for the "choice of predictors").

[158] Gillis, Talia B., "The Input Data Fallacy", *cit.*, pp. 1176–1263 (1229).

[159] See: Barocas, Solon/Selbst, Andrew, "Big Data's Disparate Impact", *California Law Review*, Volume 104, 2016, pp. 671–678 ("in particular, by exposing so-called 'machine learning' algorithms to examples of the cases of interest (previously identified instances of fraud, spam, default, and poor health), *the algorithm 'learns' which related attributes or activities can serve as potential proxies for those qualities or outcomes of interest*"). Italics added.

[160] Chi-Jack Lin/ Sherman D. Hanna, "Racial Discrimination in the Consumer Credit Market", *Consumer Interests Annual*, Volume 56, 2010 ("*The Equal Credit Opportunity Act (ECOA), enacted in 1974, makes it unlawful for any creditors to discriminate against credit applicants because of their color, race/ethnic group, religion, national origin, sex, marital status, or age (provided the applicant has the capacity to contract)* (….) *our analyses allow for distinguishing statistical and taste discrimination. In four of five of our measures, there was discrimination against households with Black respondents, and in three out of five measures, there was discrimination against households with Hispanic respondents. Discrimination in the consumer credit market against black and Hispanic households is statistical discrimination: lenders choose to discriminate against black and Hispanic because they on average have higher default risk*"). Italics added. But see: The Use of Cash-Flow Data in Underwriting Credit: Empirical Research Findings, FINREGLAB 32, 34 (Jul. 2019), https://finreglab.org/wp-content/uploads/2019/07/FRL_Research-Report_Final.pdf [https://perma.cc/N65Q-WQML] (arguing that the use of cash flow data can underpin a prediction of default risk, thereby providing an apposite alternative to ancient credit scores. In addition to that, cash-flow data is commensurate with predictive across demographic groups). This is oft-tagged as "risk-based pricing." See: Phillipps, Robert, "Optimizing Prices for Consumer Credit", *Journal of Revenue and Pricing Management*, Volume 12, 2013, pp. 360–365 ("[A] riskier customer should pay a higher price in order to compensate for the higher probability of default and the associated cost to the lender"). See also: Staten, Michael, "Risk-Based Pricing in Consumer Lending", *Journal of Law, Economics & Policy*, Volume 11, 2015, pp. 33 and ff and passim. Gathergood, John/Guttman-Kenney, Benedict/Hunt, Stefan, "How Do Pay-day Loans Affect Borrowers? Evidence from the U.K. Market", *The Review of Financial Studies*, Volume 32, 2019, p. 496 (arguing that payday

their income[161] are exceedingly higher[162] owing to the yawning wealth[163] gap[164] between White folks and Black folks.[165]

§§ It is noteworthy that the social marker dubbed as «ability» is not directly observed by the stakeholder (say, lender, law enforcement agency, employer,

---

loans catalyse persistent increases in defaults, which, in turn, cause consumers to exceed their bank overdraft limits).

161 Morris, Darcy Steeg/Schwarcz, Daniel/Teitelbaum, Joshua C., "Do Credit-Based Insurance Scores Proxy for Income in Predicting Auto Claim Risk?", *Journal of Empirical Legal Studies*, Volume 14, 2017, pp. 397, 418–421 and ff (discussing that an insurer's use of credit-anchored insurance scores lacks a disparate impact on the basis of income and thus is not amenable to be considered as a proxy for income); Pope, Devin G. Pope/Sydnor, Justin R., "Implementing Anti-Discrimination Policies in Statistical Profiling Models", *American Economic Journal: Applied Economics*, Volume 3, 2011, pp. 206–210 (discussing how the FTC parsed credit score use in auto-insurance pricing as a proxy for race). But see: Atkinson, Abbye, "Rethinking Credit as a Social Provision", *Stanford Law Review*, Volume 71, 2019, pp. 1093–1099 (contending that credit, which shifts consumption temporally, is only beneficial insofar income ratchets up in the forthcoming future. As of now, though, "credit is fundamentally incompatible with the entrenched intergenerational poverty that plagues low-income Americans." Id. Notably, it is crucially important to come to terms with the fact that credit is not a panacea for the great bulk of economic struggles, and concretely wage stagnation. Although credit is not befitted to all consumers at all prices, affordable credit can nonetheless play a pivotal role in the creation of wealth).

162 Fryer, Roland G. Fryer/Pager, Devah/Spenkuch, Jörg L., "Racial Disparities in Job Finding and Offered Wages", *Journal of Law and Economics*, Volume 56, 2013, pp. 633–690 (contending that disparate treatment accounts for at least one third of the Black-white wage gap). See also: Burstein, Paul/Edwards, Mark Evan, "The Impact of Employment Discrimination Litigation on Racial Disparity in Earnings: Evidence and Unresolved Issues", *Law and Society Review*, Volume 28, 1994; Pager, Devah/Shepherd, Hana, "The Sociology of Discrimination: Racial Discrimination in Employment, Housing, Credit, and Consumer Markets", *Annual Review of Sociology*, Volume 34, 2008.

163 But see: Aneja/Abhay P./Avenancio-León, Carlos F., "No Credit for Time Served? Incarceration and Credit-Driven Crime Cycles", *AEA Papers and Proceedings*, Volume 109, 2019, pp. 160 and ff and passim (discusses the negative reflex of incarceration on credit scoring and income). But see: Bar-Gill/Oren/Warren, Elizabeth, "Making Credit Safer", *University of Pennsylvania Law Review*, Volume 157, 2008, pp. 1–66 (argue that Black defendants are far more likely to be incarcerated, arrested, surveilled and harassed than White folks, which leads to the conclusion that the use of credit scores and income presents another way in which credit decisions leverage on structural disadvantage).

164 Derenoncourt, Ellora/Kim, Chi Hyun/Kuhn, Moritz/Schularik, Moritz, "The Wealth of Two Nations: The U.S. Racial Wealth Gap, 1860–2020", *The Quarterly Journal of Economics*, Volume 139, Issue 2, 2024, p. 741 ("*A large class of commonly discussed policies for reducing racial wealth inequality seeks to reduce gaps in income, savings, and capital gains.* These include policies that encourage financial diversification or stock equity holdings among Black households; policies aimed at financial literacy and retirement or savings behavior; or policies aimed at improving educational and labor market outcomes of Black Americans through improved school quality or reductions in discrimination. *Yet on a realistic note, our simulation in Section IV.A shows that even if wealth accumulation conditions had been equal since 1870, the wealth gap would still be 3 to 1 today, and full convergence would be more than 200 years away. Put differently: to close the racial wealth gap in the immediate term via flow parameters, Black Americans would need a substantial positive lead over whites, not "just" more equality*""). Italics added.

165 Gillis, Talia B., "The Input Data Fallacy", *cit.*, pp. 1176–1263 (1229). See also: Saez, Emmanuel, and Gabriel Zucman, "The Rise of Income and Wealth Inequality in America: Evidence from

insurer[166] and so forth) that tasked the machine learning algorithm with the duty of making a prediction a prediction. Instead, the stakeholder has a treasure trove of information about college attendance,[167] which is highly correlated with[168] «ability».[169] It is common knowledge that racial minorities endure gruelling racial discrimination in college applications[170] and are thus less likely to attend college.[171] In this very

---

Distributional Macroeconomic Accounts," *Journal of Economic Perspectives*, Volume 34, 2020, pp. 3–26.

[166] It bears mentioning that scorching issue of whether and to what extent disparate impact alone should be actionable is different from, in that does not overlap with, the sweltering issue of proxy discrimination. See: Cohran, Matthew Jordan, "Fairness in Disparity: Challenging the Application of Disparate Impact Theory in Fair Housing Claims Against Insurers", *The George Mason University Civil Rights Law Journal*, Volume 21, 2011, pp. 159 and ff and passim (discussing the use of disparate impact theory and potential applicability to Fair Housing Act claims against insurers). For an on-point breakdown of the distinct levels of opacity arising out of machine learning algorithms in the purview of insurance policies: Selbst, Andrew D./Barocas, Solon, "The Intuitive Appeal of Explainable Machines", *Fordham Law Review*, Volume 87, 2018, pp. 1085, 1089–1099 (holding that there are plenty reasons for the insurer's ignorance. To begin with, the algorithm entails specialized knowledge to understand. That is, the insurer's employees may lack sufficient knowledge to understand the rationale behind the reasons in view of which the algorithm is producing prices for different customers—personalized pricing. Lastly, even if the insurer himself comprehends how the model operates, it may nonetheless lack expertise to comprehend why it operates the way it does. For that reason, the explainability of machines is a vital, but rather elusive, task. Thence, the famed authors deem it as the "nonintuitive" nature of algorithms. For purposes here, the insurer himself might indeed understand that its Artificial Intelligence-embedded technology formulates higher prices for those who actually access the website at hand, but may fail to come to terms with the fact that the explanation for this fact arises from the website's capacity to proxy for genetic information).

[167] McCabe, Sean Esteban McCabe et al., "Race/Ethnicity and Gender Differences in Drug Use and Abuse Among College Students", *Journal of Ethnicity Substance Abuse*, Volume 6, 2007, p. 75 (bringing to the fore compelling "evidence from one university that Hispanic and White undergraduate students were at increased risk for drug use and abuse" and discussing related literature).

[168] For example, a batch of other pieces of academic research have deftly pinpointed racial disparities with regard to access to the labour market. See: Bertrand, Marianne/Mullainathan, Sendhil, "Are Emily and Greg More Employable than Lakisha and Jamal? A Field Experiment on Labor Market Discrimination", *The American Economic Review*, Volume 94, 2004, p. 991 (reaches the conclusion according to which white-sounding names are far more likely to spark a callback than that of suitably qualified applicants with Black-sounding names); Nunley, John M./Pugh, Adam/Romero, Nicholas/Seals, R. Alan, "Racial Discrimination in the Labor Market for Recent College Graduates: Evidence from a Field Experiment", *The B.E. Journal of Economic Analysis & Policy*, Volume 15, 2015, pp. 1096 and ff and passim.

[169] Gillis, Talia B., "The Input Data Fallacy", *cit.*, pp. 1176–1263 (1229).

[170] Kleinberg, Jon et al., "Algorithmic Fairness", *AEA Papers & Proceedings*, Volume 108, 2018, pp. 22–23 (discussing, anchored in a batch of national data, that including race as an input variable to a machine-learning college-admissions algorithm both "improves predicted GPAs of admitted students" and can augment "the fraction of admitted students who are black").

[171] Pierce, C., "W.E.B. du bois and caste education: Racial capitalist schooling from reconstruction to Jim Crow", *American Educational Research Journal*, 54 (1_Suppl.), 2017, pp. 23S–47S. In education testing, for example, it is well established that the correlation between SAT scores and intelligence varies greatly by race and by a set of circumstances. See: Mayson, Sandra G., "Bias

simple example, the input variable («college attendance») is beset by *measurement bias* owing to the fact that is a noisier measurement of «ability» for members of racial minorities.[172]

5.1.1.5.5 Controllable Artificial Intelligence*: A Thing-Centred Algorithmic Decision-Making That Requires a Fundamental Shift Away from Causation and a Pull Towards Correlation*

§§ *Algorithmic fairness*, albeit a bedazzling gift, is not without sizable hurdles. This is one the main roadblocks to the uptake of Artificial Intelligence-embedded technologies. The most prominent of which is that Artificial Intelligence, to produce algorithmic fairness, must be fundamentally *interpretable* by citizens.[173] Intent and causation—agreed-upon benchmarks to gauge the extent to which the computer-generated outputs are fair and reasonable—are utterly incapable of explaining the complex world of AI-powered black box.[174]

In, Bias Out", *cit.*, pp. 2218–2300. See also: Berlak, Harold, "Race and the Achievement Gap", *Critical Social Issues in American Education: Democracy and Meaning in a Globalizing World*, 3rd edition, Shapiro, H. Svi/Purpel, David E. (Editors), 2005, pp. 223–227 (exploring the yawning racial achievement gap in other standardized tests). It is important to note, though, that a high score attained by a student who benefited from the best possible primary education and extensive SAT preparation is not as impressive as the student who attained the very same score without any extra help or additional levers. See: Mayson, Sandra G., "Bias In, Bias Out", *cit.*, pp. 2218–2300. See also: Kim, Pauline T., "Data-Driven Discrimination at Work", *William and Mary Law Review*, Volume 58, 2017, pp. 857, 863–864 (shedding a keen light on the racial effects of algorithmic prediction in the remit of employment). Converging: Zywicki, Todd J./Adamson, Joseph D., "The Law and Economics of Subprime Lending", *University of Colorado Law Review*, 2009, pp. 1–9 (contending that Black workers with roughly the same abilities and educational background earn far less than comparable white workers or have considerably fewer employment opportunities); King, Allan G./Markovich, Marko J., "Big Data" and the Risk of Employment Discrimination, *Oklahoma Law Review*, Volume 68, 2016, pp. 555–563 (on employment discrimination).

[172] Gillis, Talia B., "The Input Data Fallacy", *cit.*, pp. 1176–1263 (1230).

[173] Citron, Danielle K., "Technological Due Process", *Washington University Law Review*, Volume 85, 2008, pp. 1249–1253 ("Computer programs seamlessly combine rulemaking and individual adjudications without the critical procedural protections owed either of them"). See: Part V, this chapter, Sects. 5.1.8–5.1.8.5 of this book (on the five laws to interpret algorithmic decision-making).

[174] But see: Part V, this chapter, Sect. 5.1.7.2 of this book (on law number two to control algorithmic decision-making, which mandates that black box models must not be entrusted with the task of making high stake decisions—v.g. health and freedom). As hinted above, algorithms make their inferences and draw their conclusions in a way difficult to understand, even for the cohort of programmers that designed them. This is deemed *black box*, that further enhances the shroud of mystery under which algorithms are cloaked. See, for a compelling account of AI black box: See: Bathaee, Yavar, "The Artificial Intelligence Black Box and the Failure of Intent and Causation", *Harvard Journal of Law and Technology*, n.° 37, 2018, p. 901 (adduces that "*one possible reason AI may be a black box to humans is that it relies on machine-learning algorithms that internalize data in ways that are not easily audited or understood by humans* (...)" "*first, a lack may arise from the complexity of the algorithm's structure, such as with deep neural network, which consists of thousands of artificial neurons working together in a diffuse way to solve a problem. This reason for AI being a black box is referred to as "complexity". Second, the lack of transparency may arise because the AI is using a machine-learning algorithm that relies on geometric relationships that*

§§ For a simple reason: machine learning[175]—and, especially, deep learning[176]—is a world of hidden *correlations* embedded in the data that has been fed into the computer-generated algorithms, as opposed to a world of *causation* that currently reigns[177] in the legal arena.[178] To bypass/circumvent this perceived quandary,[179]

humans cannot visualize, such as with support vector machines. This reason for AI being a black box is referred to as "dimensionality""). Italics added. See also: Mittelstadt, B./Russell, C./Watcher, S., "Explaining explanations in AI", *Proceedings of Fairness, Accountability, and Transparency (FAT) (ACM)*, 2019, passim. But see: Pearl, Judea, *Causality*, 2nd edition, Cambridge, Cambridge University Press, 2009 (on the fundamental tenets of causality). But see: Kilbertus, Niki/Carulla, Mateo Rojas/Parascandolo, Giambattista/Hardt, Moritz/Janzing, Dominik/ Schoellkopf, Bernhard, "Avoiding Discrimination through Causal Reasoning", *Advances in Neural Information Processing Systems*, I. Guyon, U. V. Luxburg, S. Bengio, H. Wallach, R. Fergus, S. Vishwanathan, and R. Garnett (Eds.), Vol. 30. Curran Associates, Inc., 2017, pp. 656–666 (arguing that is feasible to avoiding discrimination through a granular and fine-grained causal reasoning).

175 Machine learning "involves computer algorithms *that have the ability to "learn" or improve in performance over time on some task*". Ver: Surden, Harry, "Machine Learning and Law", in: *Washington Law Review*, Volume 89, 2014, pp. 87 e ss; Murphy, Kevin P., *Machine Learning: A Probabilistic Perspective (Adaptive Computation and Machine Learning series)*, Massachusetts, The MIT Press, 2012, pp. 1–1104. Machine learning "*attempts to combine deductive, inductive, and abductive reasoning to make person-like reasoning in AI Entities possible. Machine-learning AI Entities initially learn in the same way a human child learns. First, they notice details and patterns in shapes, sounds, and behaviors*; then put them together to distinguish one person from another, or a dog from a cat. Eventually, the AI can recognize and identify" common objects. See: Hutto-Schultz, Jess, "Dicitur Ex Machina: Artificial Intelligence and the Hearsay Rule", *George Mason Law Review*, Volume 27, n.º 2, 2020, pp. 684–718 (689).

176 See: Goodfellow, Ian/Bengio, Yoshua/Courville, Aaron, *Deep Learning (Adaptive Computation and Machine Learning series)*, Massachusetts, The MIT Press, 2016, pp. 1–800 ("*Deep learning is a form of machine learning that enables computers to learn from experience and understand the world in terms of a hierarchy of concepts.* Because *the computer gathers knowledge from experience, there is no need for a human computer operator to formally specify all the knowledge that the computer needs. The hierarchy of concepts allows the computer to learn complicated concepts by building them out of simpler ones; a graph of these hierarchies would be many layers deep*"). See also: Chollet, François, *Deep Learning with Python*, Shelter Island, New York, Manning, 2017, pp. 1–384; Franceschetti, Donald R. (Editor), *Principles of Robotics and Artificial Intelligence*, New York, Salem Press, 2018, pp. 1–399. Deep learning is capable of recommending meaningful legal materials. See: Huang, Zihan/Low, Charles/Teng, Mengqiu/Zhang, Hongyi/Ho, Daniel E./ Krass, Mark S. et al., "Context-Aware Legal Citation Recommendation Using Deep Learning", *Proceedings of the 18th ACM Internationational Conference on Artificial Intelligence and Law*, 79, 2021.

177 Pearl, Judea, *Causality*, 2nd edition, Cambridge, Cambridge University Press, 2009.

178 Bibal, A., Lognoul, M/De Streel/A., Frénay B, "Legal requirements on explainability in machine learning", *Artificial Intelligence and Law*, Volume 29, 2021, pp. 149–169; Ashley, KD, *Artificial Intelligence and Legal Analytics: New Tools for Law Practice in the Digital Age*, Cambridge, Cambridge University Press, 2017.

179 See: Chap. 4 of this book.

poignant calls have been made to keep «humans in the loop»[180] as far as the emission of automated decisions is concerned.[181]

§§ Notwithstanding, the turn towards *algorithmic fairness* entails, and fundamentally requires, a shift away from a legal analysis that haphazardly seeks to unlock/unveil/unearth/unravel causal connections[182] between inputs and outputs.[183] This book therefore proposes that algorithmic decision-making must shift its gaze

---

180 Saxena, Devansh/Badillo-Urquiola, Karla/Wisniewski, Pamela J./Guha, Shion, "A Human-Centered Review of the Algorithms Used Within the U.S. Child Welfare System", *2020 Proceedings of Conference on Human Factors in Computing Systems*, Apr. 2020, 2020, passim.

181 Almada, M., "Human intervention in automated decision-making: toward the construction of contestable systems", *Proceedings of the Seventeenth International Conference on Artificial Intelligence and Law*, 2019, pp. 2–11; Williams, Rebecca, "Rethinking Administrative Law for Algorithmic Decision-Making", *Oxford Journal of Legal Studies*, Volume 42, 2021, pp. 468 e ff and passim.

182 See: Kilbertus, Niki/Carulla, Mateo Rojas/Parascandolo, Giambattista/Hardt, Moritz/Janzing, Dominik/ Schoellkopf, Bernhard, "Avoiding Discrimination through Causal Reasoning", *Advances in Neural Information Processing Systems*, I. Guyon, U. V. Luxburg, S. Bengio, H. Wallach, R. Fergus, S. Vishwanathan, and R. Garnett (Eds.), Vol. 30. Curran Associates, Inc., 2017, pp. 656–666 (arguing that is feasible to avoiding discrimination through a granular and fine-grained causal reasoning).

183 Gillis, Talia B., "The Input Data Fallacy", *Minnesota Law Review*, Volume 106, 2022, pp. 1176–1263 (p. 1257).

downstream to the algorithmic predictions[184] (outputs)[185] made by computer-generated algorithms[186] to usher in, and pave the way to, a new[187] era[188] of

[184] See: Part IV, Chap. 4 of this book.

[185] Chander, Anupam, "The Racist Algorithm?", *Michigan Law Review*, Volume 115, 2017, pp. 1023–1039 ("The focus on outcomes rather than how an algorithm operates seems especially useful as algorithms become increasingly complicated, even able to modify themselves").

[186] Gillis, Talia B., "The Input Data Fallacy", *cit.* p. 1257.

[187] In Italian doctrine, on the challenges law may face in the forthcoming future: Irti, Natalino, *Un Diritto Incalcolabile*, Torino, G. Giappichelli Editore, 2016, passim.

[188] See: Susskind, Richard, "The Future of Courts", in: *Remote Courts*, Volume 6, n.° 5, July/August 2020, 2020, pp. 1 e ss ("The uptake of various technologies, especially video, was accelerated in the justice systems of numerous countries. There remain some skeptics and critics, but in light of the experience during the crisis, there is certainly greater acceptance now than in February 2020—amongst lawyers, judges, officials, and court users—that judicial and court work might be undertaken very differently in years to come. Minds have been opened and changed over the past few months. Many assumptions have been swept aside. We remain in an era of threat, with risks of barely functioning court systems, greatly reduced access to justice, and, in turn, a potential weakening of the rule of law. We are also in an era of opportunity—the chance to build boldly on the shift of attitude and on demonstrable recent successes with technology, and to put in place improved, sustainable court services that are much more accessible than today's").

automation[189] brimming with both procedural fairness[190] and algorithmic accountability.[191]

---

[189] Weizenbaum, Joseph, *Computer Power and Human Reason: From Judgment to Calculation*, 1st edition, New York, W. H. Freeman & Co, 1976, pp. 1–300 (227) ("examines the sources of the computer's powers and offers evaluative explorations of what computers can do, cannot do, and should not be employed to do") (this founding father of Artificial Intelligence presciently noted that we should not entrust Artificial Intelligence-embedded technologies with "tasks that demand wisdom"). Italics added. The approval of rental applications is arguably one of those tasks that should never be entrusted to machines). More on this on Part IV, Chap. 4, Sects. 4.1.4–4.1.4.2.1 of this book. See: Part IV, Chap. 4, Sects. 4.1.4–4.1.4.2.1 of this book (on mortgage redlining). See: Part IV, Chap. 4, Sects. 4.1.2–4.1.4.3 of this book (on algorithmic credit scoring, consumer racism and credit card redlining). See: Part IV, Chap. 4, Sects. 4.1.4–4.1.4.2.3 of this book (on algorithmic redlining). See: Part IV, Chap. 4, Sect. 4.1.4.3 of this book (on "algorithmic redliking"). See: Part IV, Chap. 4, Sect. 4.1.3 of this book (on algorithmic prime-lining).

[190] Tyler, Tom, "What is procedural justice?", *Law and Society Review*, Volume 22, 1988, pp. 301–355; Tyler, Tom, "The Psychology of procedural justice: A test of the group value model.", in: *Journal of Personality and Social Psychology*, Volume 57, 1989, 830–838; Tyler, Tom, *Why people obey the law*, New Haven, CT, Yale University Press, 1990, 1–320 (premising his conclusions on a sound body of empirical research, the author states that "*people obey the law if they believe it's legitimate*, not because they fear punishment-this is the startling conclusion of Tom Tyler's classic study. Tyler suggests that lawmakers and law enforcers would do much better to make legal systems worthy of respect than to try to instill fear of punishment. *He finds that people obey law primarily because they believe in respecting legitimate authority*"). Italics added. Tyler, Tom, "Legitimizing unpopular public policies: Does procedure matter?", *Zeitschrift für Reichssoziologie*, Volume 14, 1993, pp. 47–54; Tyler, Tom, "Governing amid diversity: can fair decision-making procedures bridge competing public interests and values?", *Law and Society Review*, Volume 28, 1994, pp. 701–722; Tyler, Tom, "Psychological models of the justice motive", *Journal of Personality and Social Psychology*, Volume 67, 1994, 850–863; Tyler, Tom, "The relationship of the outcome and procedural fairness: How does knowing the outcome influences judgments about the procedure?", *Social Justice and Research*, Volume 9, 1996, pp. 311–325; Tyler, Tom, "Compliance with intellectual property laws", in: *Journal of International Law and Politics*, Volume 28, 1997, pp. 101–116; Tyler, Tom, "Justice and power in civil dispute processing", in: *Sociolegal studies*, Evanston, IL, Northwestern University Press, 1997; Tor, A./Gazal-Ayal, O./Garcia, S. M., "Fairness and willingness to accept plea bargain offers", *Journal of Empirical Legal Studies*, Volume 7, 2010, pp. 97–116 (drawing upon a body of empirical evidence the authors made an the interplay between overall fairness of the proceedings and the disputant's willingness to accept plea bargain offers made by the Government). But see: Guha, Neel/Henderson, Peter/Zambrano, Diego, "Vulnerabilities in Discovery Tech", *Harvard Journal of Law and Technology*, Volume 35, 2022, passim.

[191] Zarsky, Tal, "Transparency in Data Mining: From Theory to Practice", *Discrimination and Privacy in the Information Society: Data Mining and Profiling in Large Databases*, Bart Custers et al. eds., Belin, Springer, 2013; Kroll, Joshua A. et al., "Accountable Algorithms", *University of Pennsylvania Law Review*, Volume 165, 2017, passim. But see: Balkin, Jack, "Constitution in the National Surveillance State", *Minnesota Law Review*, Volume 93, 2008, p. 13 (*data mining* allows inferences not only about the direct subject of surveillance, but about other people with whom they live, work and communicate"); Pearl, Judea, "Causal inference in statistics: An overview", *Statistics Surveys*, Volume 3, 2009, pp. 96–146. But see: Pedreshi, Dino/Ruggieri, Salvatore/Turini, Franco, "Discrimination-aware Data Mining", *Proceedings of the 14th ACM SIGKDD International Conference on Knowledge Discovery and Data Mining (Las Vegas, Nevada, USA), ACM*, 2008, pp. 560–568 (arguing that one should shift its gaze downstream by putting in place discrimination-aware algorithmic tools while performing data mining).

§§ Scholars have pointed out the potential trade-offs between different concepts of fairness and accuracy paired with its relevance when endeavouring to restrict the inputs into a machine learning[192] algorithm.[193]

§§ Notwithstanding, the proposal to narrow down machine learning algorithms to inputs that instinctively hold some relevance to the outcome of interest has been met with growing reluctance, insofar the decision could be whimsical and even squander,[194] if not jeopardise, the host of advantages of big data[195] in wearing down the harm of *measurement bias.*[196]

§§ Relatedly, the selection of pre-approved[197] inputs[198] might fall short of reaching the threshold of trading off accuracy for fairness. Instead, this proposal

---

[192] Gillis, Talia B., "The Input Data Fallacy", *cit.* pp. 1176–1263.

[193] Pleiss, Geoff/Raghavan, Manish/Wu, Felix/Kleinberg, Jon/Weinberger, Kilian Q., "On Fairness and Calibration", *Proceedings of the 31st International Conference on Neural Information Processing Systems*, Association for Computing Machinery ed., 2017, 2; Prince, Anya ER/Schwarcz, Daniel, "Proxy Discrimination in the Age of Artificial Intelligence and Big Data", *cit.*, p. 1306 ("[If no solution is adopted] due to narrowly-defined notions of efficiency, then it must be acknowledged that this comes at the expense of these [anti-discrimination] laws' goals"); Corbett-Davies, Sam/Pierson, Emma/Feller, Avi/Goel, Sharad Goel/Huq, Aziz, "Algorithmic Decision Making and the Cost of Fairness", *Proceedings of the 23rd ACM SIGKDD International Conference on Knowledge Discovery and Data Mining*, Association for Computing Machinery ed., 2017, 2017, pp. 802–803.

[194] Gillis, Talia B., "The Input Data Fallacy", *cit.*, pp. 1176–1263 (1242).

[195] Big data that is in the limelight these days. See: Sivarajah, Uthayasnkar et al., "Critical Analysis of Big Data Challenges and Analytical Methods", *Journal of Business Research*, Volume 70, 2017, pp. 263 and ff and passim; Jetten, Lieke/Sharon, Stephen, "Selected Issues concerning the Ethical Use of Big Data Health Analytics", *Washington & Lee Law Review Online*, Volume 72, 2016, passim; Wachter, S./Mittelstadt. B., "A right to Reasonable Inferences: Re-thinking Data Protection Law in the Age of Big Data and AI", *Columbia Business Law Review*, 2019, pp. 1 and ff and passim; See in French doctrine: Ferey, Samuel, «Analyse économique du droit, big data et justice prédictive», *Archives de Philosophie du Droit*, Volume 60, 2018, pp. 68–81; Završnik, A. "Algorithmic justice: Algorithms and big data in criminal justice settings", *European Journal of Criminology*, 2019, passim; Joh, Elizabeth E., "The New Surveillance Discretion: Automated Suspicion, Big Data, and Policing." *Harvard Law and Policy Review*, 10 (1), 2016, pp. 15–42.

[196] Gillis, Talia B., "The Input Data Fallacy", *cit.*, pp. 1176–1263 (1243).

[197] Prince, Anya ER/Schwarcz, Daniel, "Proxy Discrimination in the Age of Artificial Intelligence and Big Data", *Iowa Law Review*, Volume 105, 2022, p. 1306 ("[i]nstead of allowing use of any variable not barred, as in the traditional anti-discrimination model, this approach would only allow actors to use pre-approved variables").

[198] See: Prince, Anya ER/Schwarcz, Daniel, "Proxy Discrimination in the Age of Artificial Intelligence and Big Data", *cit.*, p. 1316 ("[O]ne possible solution is to require those employing algorithms to convince regulators or others of causal connections between the variables utilized and the desired outcome").See also: Grimmelmann, James/Westreich, Daniel, "Incomprehensible Discrimination", *California Law Review Online*, Volume 7, 2017, p. 15 ("Where a model has a disparate impact, our test in effect requires an employer to explain why its model is not just a mathematically sophisticated proxy for a protected characteristic"); Kim, Pauline T., "Data-Driven Discrimination at Work", *William and Mary Law Review*, Volume 58, 2017, p. 921 ("*The existence of a statistical correlation should not be sufficient. Instead, because the employer's justification for using an algorithm amounts to a claim that it actually predicts something relevant to the job*, the employer should carry the burden of demonstrating that statistical bias does not plague the underlying model"). Italics added.

would most likely decrease both accuracy[199] and fairness.[200] It is worth recalling that an abridged accuracy exacts a toll on languid/feeble individuals who are outrightly prevented from achieving a desired outcome (v.g. being granted a loan; being granted a rental application; being afforded an accurate algorithmic credit scoring; being given an accurate risk assessment in criminal settings and so forth)[201] whenever the relevant stakeholder (v.g. lender, landlord, real estate agent, probation officer, employer, regulator, prosecutor, loan officer, law enforcement agent, police officer, parole officer and so forth) is unable to reliably ascertain a given[202] risk.[203]

---

[199] Goel, Sharad/Shroff, Ravi/Skeem, Jennifer/Slobogin, Christopher, *The Accuracy, Equity, and Jurisprudence of Criminal Risk Assessment* 1 (Dec. 26, 2018), 2018. But see: Hurley, Mikella/ Adebayo, Julius, "Credit Scoring in the Era of Big Data", *Yale Journal of Law and Technology*, Volume 18, 2016, p. 149 ("*recent studies have also questioned the accuracy of the data used by these tools, in some cases identifying serious flaws that have a substantial bearing on lending decisions*"). Italics added. See: Part IV, Chap. 4, Sects. 4.1.4–4.1.4.2.1 of this book (on mortgage redlining). See: Part IV, Chap. 4, Sects. 4.1.2–4.1.4.3 of this book (on algorithmic credit scoring, consumer racism and credit card redlining). See: Part IV, Chap. 4, Sects. 4.1.4–4.1.4.2.3 of this book (on algorithmic redlining). See: Part IV, Chap. 4, Sect. 4.1.4.3 of this book (on "algorithmic redliking"). See: Part IV, Chap. 4, Sect. 4.1.3 of this book (on algorithmic prime-lining).

[200] See: Simon & Schuster, Green, B., "Algorithmic realism: expanding the boundaries of algorithmic thought", *Proceedings of the 2020 Conference on Fairness Accountability and Transparency*, 2020, passim; Green, B./Hu L., "The Myth in the Methodology: Towards a Recontextualization of Fairness in Machine Learning", *Machine Learning Debates Work 35th Internation Conference of Machine Learning*, 2018, passim; Green, B., Chen Y, "Disparate interactions: An algorithm-in-the-loop analysis of fairness in risk assessments", *FAT* 2019, Proceedings of 2019 Conference of Fairness, Accountability, Transparency*, 2019, pp. 90–99 (on the central tenets of algorithmic fairness).

[201] See: Part IV, Chap. 4, Sects. 4.1.4–4.1.4.2.1 of this book (on mortgage redlining). See: Part IV, Chap. 4, Sects. 4.1.2–4.1.4.3 of this book (on algorithmic credit scoring, consumer racism and credit card redlining). See: Part IV, Chap. 4, Sects. 4.1.4–4.1.4.2.3 of this book (on algorithmic redlining). See: Part IV, Chap. 4, Sect. 4.1.4.3 of this book (on "algorithmic redliking"). See: Part IV, Chap. 4, Sect. 4.1.3 of this book (on algorithmic prime-lining). See: Part IV, Chap. 4, Sects. 4.1.10.1–4.1.10.6 of this book (on biased algorithmic risk assessment in criminal procedure law settings, with a sharper focus on COMPAS). See: Part IV, Chap. 4, Sects. 4.1.1–4.1.1.1 of this book (on biased predictive policing).

[202] Gillis, Talia B., "The Input Data Fallacy", *cit.*, pp. 1176–1263 (1243). Which, in turn, is the breedin ground for "automation bias". See: Wonyoung, So, "Which Information Matters? Measuring Landlord Assessment of Tenant Screening Reports", *Housing Policy Debate*, Volume 33, n. ° 6, 2023, pp. 1484–1510 (1484) ("*Through a behavioral experiment with landlords using simulated tenant screening reports, this study shows that landlords use blanket screening policies, that they conflate the existence of tenant records with outcomes (e.g., eviction filings with executed evictions), and that they display, on average,* ***tendencies toward automation bias that are influenced by the risk assessments and scores presented by tenant screening reports***. I argue that maintaining blanket screening policies and *automation bias*, combined with the downstream effects of creating and *using racially* ***biased eviction and criminal records, means that people of color will inevitably experience disproportionate exclusion from rental housing due to perceived "risk" on the part of landlords***"). Italics and bold added. See: Part IV, Chap. 4, Sects. 4.1.4–4.1.4.2.3 of this book.

[203] But see: Huq, Aziz Z., "Racial Equity in Algorithmic Criminal Justice", *Duke Law Journal*, Volume 68, pp. 1043, 1111–1112 (draws attention to the need to be careful on who "foots the bill" of inaccurate predictions in the context of criminal justice. Professor Huq thereupon contends

§§ It is true that pundits often aver that to ensure algorithmic accuracy tiny tweaks[204] it is all it takes, but truer still this approach is ill-fated insofar heavily relies on the causal nexus between inputs variables and the differential treatment[205] of vulnerable groups.[206] Note, though, that much more is needed to instil *algorithmic accountability*[207] onto algorithmic decision-making while ploughing ahead towards a both a *Controllable Artificial Intelligence*[208] and *Interpretable Artificial Intelligence.*[209] To that end, a fundamental shift away from causation to correlation is not only warranted but sorely needed.

§§ Compellingly, in lieu of falling prey to «input data fallacy»,[210] one must come to terms with the fact that, in the machine learning realm, it is utterly impossible to

---

that racial equity entails taking stock of who bears the inordinate harms of algorithmic errors in determining how to adroitly apply the catch-all concept of fairness).

[204] But see: Berk, Richard, "Accuracy and Fairness for Juvenile Justice Risks Assessments", *Journal of Empirical Legal Studies*, Volume 16, 2019, p. 175 (comes to the terms with the fact that tweaking/altering data to attain **statistical parity** yielded extremely high **false-negative rates**); Zachary Lipton et al., "Does Mitigating ML's Impact Disparity Require Treatment Disparity?", NIPS PROC. 1 (2018), https://arxiv.org/pdf/1711.07076.pdf [https://perma.cc/X8VF-EY53] (sets forth compelling evidence that enforced blindness to protected traits exacts a toll on the overall accuracy of the algorithmic tool); Petersilia, Joan/Turner, Susan, "Guideline-Based Justice: Prediction and Racial Minorities", *Crime and Justice*, 1987, pp. 151–174 (argues that omitting markers correlated with race from a recidivism prediction algorithm exacted a toll on the accuracy of the algorithmic tool).

[205] Loo, Rory Van, "Making Innovation More Competitive: The Case of Fintech", *UCLA Law Review*, Volume 65, 2018, pp. 232–254 (discussing how Black and Latino households are more than twice as likely to be unbanked compared to the national average).

[206] Gillis, Talia B., "The Input Data Fallacy", *cit.*, pp. 1176–1263 (1243).

[207] On algorithmic accountability: Kroll, Joshua A./J. Huey/S. Barocas/E. W. Felten/J. R. Reidenberg/D. G. Robinson/and H. Yu, "Accountable Algorithms", *University of Pennsylvania Law Review*, 165 (3), 2017, pp. 633–705; See: Katyal, Sonia, "Private Accountability in the Age of Artificial Intelligence", *UCLA Law Review*, Volume 66, 2019, pp. 54–99. See also: Williams, Rebecca, "Accountable Algorithms: Adopting the Public Law Toolbox Outside the Realm of Public Law", *Current Legal Problems,* Vol. 75, 2022, pp. 237–263; Williams, Rebecca, "Rethinking Administrative Law for Algorithmic Decision-Making", *Oxford Journal of Legal Studies*, Volume 42, 2021, pp. 468 e ff and passim; Lepri, Bruno/Oliver, Nuria/Letouzé Emmanuel/Pentland, Alex/Vinck, Patrick, "Fair, Transparent, and Accountable Algorithmic Decision-Making Processes: The Premise, the Proposed Solutions, and the Open Challenges", *Philosophy & Technology*, Volume 31, 2018, passim; Citron, Danielle Keats/Pasquale, Frank, "Network Accountability for the Domestic Intelligence Apparatus", *Hasting Law Journal*, Volume 62, 2011; Gray, David/Citron, Danielle Keats, "The Right to Quantitative Privacy", *Minnesota Law Review*, Volume 98, 2013, pp. 62–81.

[208] See: Part V, this chapter, Sects. 5.1.7–5.1.7.5 of this book (on the five laws to control algorithmic decision-making).

[209] See: Part V, this chapter, Sects. 5.1.8–5.1.8.5 of this book (on the five laws to interpret algorithmic decision-making).

[210] Gillis, Talia B., "The Input Data Fallacy", *cit.*, pp. 1176–1263 (1243).

pinpoint causal[211] relationships.[212] As extensively discussed in this book,[213] algorithmic decision-making has always been focused on causality.[214] Unsurprisingly, a cohort of polymaths still rely on this causal frame of reference to discrimination law

[211] Gillis, Talia B., "The Input Data Fallacy", *cit.*, pp. 1176–1263 (1243).

[212] See: Katz, Martin J., "The Fundamental Incoherence of Title VII: Making Sense of Causation in Disparate Treatment Law", *The Georgetown Law Journal*, Volume 94, 2006, p. 489 (shedding light on the causation requirement in the remit of anti-discrimination laws); Foster, Sheila R., "Causation in Antidiscrimination Law: Beyond Intent Versus Impact", *Houston Law Review*, Volume 41, 2005, pp. 1469, 1472 ("By definition, all discrimination claims require plaintiffs to demonstrate a causal connection between the challenged decision or outcome and a protected status characteristic"); Foster, Sheila R., "Causation in Antidiscrimination Law: Beyond Intent Versus Impact", *cit.*, p. 1472 ("The prohibition against discrimination is a prohibition against making decisions or taking actions on account of, or because of, a status characteristic singled out for protection by our civil rights laws or constitutional traditions (which generally include race, gender, nationality, religion, disability, and age")).

[213] See: Part I, Part II, Part III, and Part IV of this book.

[214] As hinted above, algorithms make their inferences and draw their conclusions in a way difficult to understand, even for the cohort of programmers that designed them. This is deemed *black box*, that further enhances the shroud of mystery under which algorithms are cloaked. See, for a compelling account of AI black box: Ver: Bathaee, Yavar, "The Artificial Intelligence Black Box and the Failure of Intent and Causation", *Harvard Journal of Law and Technology*, n.º 37, 2018, p. 901 (adduces that "*one possible reason AI may be a black box to humans is that it relies on machine-learning algorithms that internalize data in ways that are not easily audited or understood by humans* (…)" "*first, a lack may arise from the complexity of the algorithm's structure, such as with deep neural network, which consists of thousands of artificial neurons working together in a diffuse way to solve a problem. This reason for AI being a black box is referred to as "complexity". Second, the lack of transparency may arise because the AI is using a machine-learning algorithm that relies on geometric relationships that humans cannot visualize, such as with support vector machines. This reason for AI being a black box is referred to as "dimensionality""*). Italics added. See also: Mittelstadt, B./Russell, C./Watcher, S., "Explaining explanations in AI", *Proceedings of Fairness, Accountability, and Transparency (FAT) (ACM)*, 2019, passim. But see: Pearl, Judea, *Causality*, 2nd edition, Cambridge, Cambridge University Press, 2009 (on the fundamental tenets of causality). But see: Kilbertus, Niki/Carulla, Mateo Rojas/Parascandolo, Giambattista/Hardt, Moritz/Janzing, Dominik/Schoellkopf, Bernhard, "Avoiding Discrimination through Causal Reasoning", *Advances in Neural Information Processing Systems*, I. Guyon, U. V. Luxburg, S. Bengio, H. Wallach, R. Fergus, S. Vishwanathan, and R. Garnett (Eds.), Vol. 30. Curran Associates, Inc., 2017, pp. 656–666 (arguing that is feasible to avoiding discrimination through a granular and fine-grained causal reasoning).

in the algorithmic[215] field.[216] It is worth recalling that regulators themselves persist to rely on causal[217] relationships.[218]

§§ Strikingly, polyhistors believe that disparate impact's «business necessity» is not met whenever there is a mere correlation between the protected characteristics (v.g. race, age, disability, or gender) and outcome variables,[219] in spite of the fact that correlation is indeed the only meaningful/actionable relationship pinpointed by machine learning.[220]

§§ By the same token, scholars contended that, with regard to premising a disparate impact lawsuit, «there must be a nexus or causal connection between some element of institutional practices and the disparate outcome».[221] However, these causal relationships fade/falter/collapse in a machine learning world.[222] The

---

[215] Gillis, Talia B., "The Input Data Fallacy", *cit.*, pp. 1176–1263.

[216] Legal causal analysis shies away from relying upon rigorous empirical identification of causal relationships. Instead, claims of causality often focus on merely intuitive understanding of how factors and inputs are interconnected to the outcomes. For example, the National Consumer Center has timely branded this intuitive type of reasoning: "[t]here is an understandable connection between timely repayment of past obligations and the likelihood of timely repayment of future obligations, so a 'demonstrable relationship' argument can be easily made." See also: Yu, Persis/McLaughlin, Jillian/Levy, Marina, "Big Data: A Big Disappointment for Scoring Consumer Creditworthiness", National Consumer Law Center 12 (Mar. 14, 2014). Revealingly, according to the Consumer Financial Protection Bureau, Black and Latino consumers are far more likely to be credit invisible, at rates that hover around, and the vicinity of, 15% in comparison to 9% for white folks. See: Gillis, Talia B., "The Input Data Fallacy", *cit.*, pp. 1176–1263. Tantamount arguments have brought forth in the remit of employment. See: Kim, Pauline T., "Data-Driven Discrimination at Work", *cit.*, p. 881 ("If, however, the variables are merely correlated and not causally related, there is no necessary connection between them, and the correlation may not hold in the future"); King, Allan G./Mrkonich Marko J., "Big Data" and the Risk of Employment Discrimination", *Oklahoma Law Review*, Volume 68, 2016, pp. 555, 563 (broaches the impact of technology on employment discrimination, thereby arguing law's causal inquiry should be distinguished from a social science interpretation of causality). See also: Chander, Anupam, "The Racist Algorithm?", *cit.*, p. 1024 (describing the impact of algorithmic decision-making in numerous areas). It is pivotally important to note that back in September 2021, Fannie Mae announced timely rental payments would be considered in underwriting calculations. See: Ron Lieber, Always Pay the Rent? It May Help Your Mortgage Application, N.Y. TIMES (Sept. 11, 2021), https://www.nytimes.com/2021/09/11/your-money/paying-rent-mortgage.html [https://perma.cc/42DS-FS5T]. See: Gillis, Talia B., "The Input Data Fallacy", *cit.*, pp. 1176–1263.

[217] Gillis, Talia B., "The Input Data Fallacy", *cit.*, pp. 1176–1263 (1243).

[218] Gillis, Talia B., "The Input Data Fallacy", *cit.*, pp. 1176–1263 (1243).

[219] See: Grimmelmann, James/Westreich, Daniel, "Incomprehensible Discrimination", *cit.*, p. 170 ("*We believe that where a plaintiff has identified a disparate impact, the defendant's burden to show a business necessity requires it to show not just that* its model's scores are not just correlated with *job performance but explain it*"). Italics added.

[220] Gillis, Talia B., "The Input Data Fallacy", *cit.*, pp. 1176–1263 (1244).

[221] MacCarthy, Marc, "Standards of Fairness for Disparate Impact Assessment of Big Data Algorithms", *Cumberland Law Review*, Volume 48, 2018, p. 67 (wondering whether and to what extent disparate impact amounts to a moral wrong or should be considered discrimination altogether instead). See also: MacCarthy, Marc, "Standards of Fairness for Disparate Impact Assessment of Big Data Algorithms", *cit.*, p. 84.

[222] Gillis, Talia B., "The Input Data Fallacy", *cit.*, pp. 1176–1263 (1244).

host of relationships that a machine learning algorithm utilized to shape/produce a computer-anchored prediction mirrors **correlations** in the dataset,[223] as opposed to a causal connection to the outcome of interest.[224]

§§ Tellingly, when a machine learning algorithm ponders whether a borrower has a top-notch smartphone phone to forecast their creditworthiness[225] little to none regard is placed on the causal relationship between phone model and the outcome of interest (v.g. default[226]). But here is the twist: a machine learning algorithm considers

---

[223] But see: Citron, Danielle Keats/Pasquale, Frank, "The Scored Society: Due Process for Automated Predictions", *Washington Law Review*, Volume 89, 2014, pp. 1, 4–5 (highlighting how human beings programming automated systems is directly conducive to, and leads, to fundamentally inaccurate results since the source code, predictive algorithms and datasets may encompass human biases which, in turn, have a disparate impact on historically disadvantaged groups).

[224] Gillis, Talia B., "The Input Data Fallacy", *cit.*, pp. 1176–1263 (1244).

[225] Note, though, that certain types of racial discrimination may not be fully intentional. More likely than not, it can be related with the perils of big data colour-blindness that nonetheless relies on proxies to race and gender to make algorithmic decisions. Another problem is the one related with "creditworthiness by association" that causes more problems than it solves. Hurley, Mikella/Adebayo, Julius, "Credit Scoring in the Era of Big Data", *Yale Journal of Law and Technology*, Volume 18, 2016, p. 149 ("*recent studies have also questioned the accuracy of the data used by these tools, in some cases identifying serious flaws that have a substantial bearing on lending decisions. Big-data tools may also risk creating a system of "creditworthiness by association" in which consumers' familial, religious, social, and other affiliations determine their eligibility for an affordable loan. These tools may furthermore obscure discriminatory and subjective lending policies behind a single "objective" score. Such discriminatory scoring may not be intentional; instead, sophisticated algorithms may combine facially neutral data points and treat them as proxies for immutable characteristics such as race or gender, thereby circumventing existing non-discrimination laws and systematically denying credit access to certain groups. Finally, big-data tools may allow online payday lenders to target the most vulnerable consumers and lure them into debt traps*"). Italics added. See: Part IV, Chap. 4, Sects. 4.1.2–4.1.2.3 of this book.

[226] Barocas, Solon/Selbst, Andrew, "Big Data's Disparate Impact", *California Law Review*, Volume 104, pp. 2016, pp. 671–678 ("in particular, by exposing so-called 'machine learning' algorithms to examples of the cases of interest (previously identified instances of fraud, spam, default, and poor health), the algorithm 'learns' which related attributes or activities can serve as potential proxies for those qualities or outcomes of interest"). A converging stance can be found in Surden, Harry, "Machine Learning and Law", *cit.*, p. 93 ("[M]achine learning algorithms are able to automatically build accurate models of some phenomenon... without being explicitly programmed"). See also: Campisi, Natalie, From Inherent Racial Bias to Incorrect Data The Problems With Current Credit Scoring Models, Forbes (Feb. 26, 2021), https://www.forbes.com/advisor/creditcards/from-inherent-racial-bias-to-incorrect-data-the-problems-with-current-credit-scoring-models/ [https://perma.cc/EWA4-CS8E] (highlighting rampant racial bias in credit scoring systems); Oyama, Rebecca, "Do Not (Re)Enter: the Rise of Criminal Background Tenant Screening as a Violation of the Fair Housing Act", *Michigan Journal of Race and Law*, Volume 15, 2009, pp. 181, 184–193 (discussing a broad range of historical/criminal accounts as a way to screen undesirable tenants, such as Blacks and Latinos); Statement of Interest of the United States at 12, *Louis v. SafeRent Sols., LLC, No. 1:22-cv-10800* (D. Mass. Jan. 9, 2023) (holding that the Fair Housing Act liability stretches far and beyond, thus encompassing a vast assortment of entities providing housing-related services, including corporations that offer tenant screening services).

borrower's phone model as a correlation with a variable that is intrinsically/causally linked to default (v.g. income[227]) or some other sort of association.[228]

§§ Cogently, bereft of verifiable/identifiable/reliable causal relationships, input-based approaches are wholly unfit for algorithmic setting. Put differently, absent meaningful causal nexus between **input variables** (v.g. race, gender, income, age, health) and **outcomes of interests** (v.g. algorithmic risk assessment, default and so forth) machine learning algorithms are far from being effective in that it is painstakingly difficult to identify the causal nexus between input variables and outputs or outcomes of interest. This holds relevance for both disparate treatment[229] and disparate impact.[230] As far as *disparate treatment* is concerned, there is no reliable pathway to identify proxies for protected markers (e.g. race, gender, disability, age). As for *disparate impact*, blazingly new mechanisms to assess the deleterious effects, if any, of algorithmic decision-making[231] are unfit for the purpose at hand.

§§ If one endeavours to quell discrimination with fierce ambition, unrelenting resolve, and undying determination—by forestalling the discriminatory treatment of vulnerable racial lines while propelling a *Controllable Artificial Intelligence*—one must shift his gaze downstream: **outcome analysis**. Discrimination legal framework has always fought shy of focusing solely on the outcomes or consequences of an ill-based policy in a bid to pinpoint discrimination.[232] To the extent successfully scrutinizing inputs is not an actionable line of action to be taken, downstream analysis bestows upon stakeholders' avenues[233] to a *Controllable Artificial Intelligence*.

---

[227] Gillis, Talia B., "The Input Data Fallacy", *cit.*, pp. 1176–1263 (1244).

[228] Berg, Tobias/Burg, Valentin/Gombovic, Ana/Puri, Manju, "On the Rise of FinTechs: Credit Scoring Using Digital Footprints", *The Review of Financial Studies*, Volume 33, 2019, pp. 2845, 2850, 2894.

[229] See: Bornstein, Stepanhie, "Antidiscriminatory Algorithms", *Alabama Law Review*, Volume 70, 2018, p. 535 (positing that algorithmic discrimination at large could fall under the all-embracing umbrella of anti-stereotyping category within Title VII's disparate treatment). See also: Howard, Justin D Howard, "Refashioning the Disparate Treatment and Disparate Impact Doctrines in Theory and in Practice", *Howard Law Journal*, Volume 41, 1998, passim; Seiner, Joseph, "Disentangling Disparate Impact and Disparate Treatment: Adapting the Canadian Approach", *Yale Law & Policy Review*, Volume 25, 2006; Primus, Richard "The Future of Disparate Impact", *Michigan Law Review*, Volume 108, 2010, pp. 1340 and ff and passim; Stephanopoulos, Nicholas O. "Disparate Impact, Unified Law", *Yale Law Journal*, Volume 128, 2019, pp. 1566–1595.

[230] But see: Barocas, Solon/Selbst, Andrew D., "Big Data's Disparate Impact", *California Law Review*, Volume 104, 2016, p. 699 (discussing how discriminatory data mining is analogous to unintentional disparate impact analysis). See also: Sunstein, Cass R., "Algorithms, Correcting Biases", *Social Research*, Volume 86, 2019, pp. 449–506 (this famed author tagged disparate impact as "disturbing in itself, in the sense that a practice that produces such an impact helps entrench something like a caste system"). It is pivotally important to note, though, that outcome analysis forms part of a broader theoretical apparatus within which a disparate impact claim operates. Yet, seldom has outcome analysis been used as determining factor though. See, e.g., *Tex. Dep't of Hous. & Cmty. Affairs v. Inclusive Cmty. Project, Inc.*, 576 U.S., 2015, 519, 520. See: Gillis, Talia B., "The Input Data Fallacy", *cit.*, pp. 1176–1263.

[231] Gillis, Talia B., "The Input Data Fallacy", *cit.*, pp. 1176–1263 (1244).

[232] Gillis, Talia B., "The Input Data Fallacy", *cit.*, pp. 1176–1263 (1244).

[233] A cohort of pundits contend that algorithmic fairness should be dealt with in the remit of require affirmative action. See: Dwork, Cynthia/Hardt, Moritz/Pitassi, Tonian/Reingold/Zemel,

I hereby second a proposal penned by Professor Talia B. Gillis that sets forth a newfangled frame of reference for undertaking such **outcome-based analysis**.[234]

5.1.1.5.6 Corollaries of *Controllable Artificial Intelligence*

A Thing-Centred Algorithmic Decision-Making That Embraces Outcome Testing

§§ The frame of reference—which, recall, was scintillatingly designed by Professor Talia B. Gillis—that I embrace is an **outcome-based test** that stakeholders (v.g. lender, landlord, real estate agent, probation officer, employer, regulator, law enforcement agent, police officer, parole officer and so forth) must resort to gauge whether and to what extent individuals are a given **outcome of interest** (e.g. algorithmic risk assessment, default and so forth) discriminates against protected groups in infringement of the central tenets of algorithmic fairness. The test unfolds itself into three consecutive phases. At the first stage, the stakeholder (e.g. lender, landlord, real estate agent, probation officer, judge, employer, regulator, law enforcement agent, police officer, parole officer and so forth) establishes what input variables and **which machine learning algorithm** to use to forecast the outcome of interest (e.g. default and price thereupon, algorithmic risk assessment in criminal justice, grant a loan, approve a rental application, flight risk, grant bail, recidivism and so forth).[235]

§§ At the second phase, the regulator subsequently considers[236] that forecast and applies it to a dataset of individuals to assess the effects the forecast created.[237] To

---

Richard, "Fairness Through Awareness, Proceedings of the 3rd Innovations", *Theoretical Computer Science Conference*, 2012, https://dl.acm.org/doi/10.1145/2090236.2090255 [https://perma.cc/T2U3-TNQ6] (discussing an individual fairness approach to algorithmic fairness); See also: Chander, Anupam, "The Racist Algorithm?", *cit.*, p. 1040 (sets forth a template whereby unfair outcomes arising out of biased inputs should be dealt with through affirmative action). See also: Huq, Aziz Z., "Racial Equity in Algorithmic Criminal Justice", *cit.*, p. 1128 (Professor Huq brought forth a proposal to assess algorithmic criminal justice measures considering the effect on racial stratification, which neatly encapsulates an output-based frame of reference insofar it tries to grasp both the benefits and costs of the criminal justice measures). See also: Hoffmann, Anna Lauren, "Where Fairness Fails: Data, Algorithms, and the Limits of Antidiscrimination Discourse", *INFO., COMMC'N & SOC'Y*, Volume 22, 2019, p. 900 (finds that discrimination law is an insufficient framework to address the structural concerns that arise as a result of big data and algorithmic decision-making. See also: Pasquale, Frank, *The Black Box Society: The Secret Algorithms that Control Money and Information*. Cambridge, Massachusetts: Harvard University Press, 2015, 1–320 (makes a poignant call for an enhanced transparency to achieve algorithmic fairness); Dwork, Cynthia/Mulligan, Deidre K., "It's Not Privacy, and It's Not Fair", *Stanford Law Review Online*, Volume 66, 2013, pp. 35 and ff and passim (exuding some degree of scepticism on whether and to what extent transparency or privacy can address fairness concerns). See: Gillis, Talia B., "The Input Data Fallacy", *cit.*, pp. 1176–1263.

[234] Gillis, Talia B., "The Input Data Fallacy", *cit.*, pp. 1176–1263 (1245).

[235] Gillis, Talia B., "The Input Data Fallacy", *cit.*, pp. 1176–1263 (1245).

[236] Gillis, Talia B., "The Input Data Fallacy", *cit.*, pp. 1176–1263 (1245).

[237] Gillis, Talia B./Spiess, Jann L., "Big Data and Discrimination", *University of Chicago Law Review*, 2010, pp. 473–474, 485, 486 (Professor Talia B. Gillis and Professor Jann L. Spies aver that it is painstakingly difficult to parse a prediction function in the abstract. They accordingly argue that the prediction function ought to be applied to a cohort of individuals with a view to parse its

illustrate, one may look at that dataset used by the regulator as bunch of hypothetical borrowers[238] for which we aim to find out, for instance, either the price a given racial line would be charged[239] for a loan[240] or the risk score that a given racial line would be given in algorithm risk assessment.

§§ Last but not least, the regulator assesses the outcome to ascertain the degree to which the disparities produced amount to a discriminatory action.[241] I use the example of race as a protected feature, but the template is applicable to other protected features (e.g. gender, age, health, and so forth).[242] All in all, at the third stage of the test, the regulator needs to gauge whether and to what extent disparities created by a prediction amount[243] to discrimination.[244]

§§ It should come as no flabbergasting surprise that the yardstick used to gauge[245] whether and to what extent disparities amount to discrimination needs to be laid down without any reliance whatsoever to the inputs used to conduct the outcome testing. The benchmark to be used in outcome analysis is not amenable to be defined without a clear-cut definition of what discrimination legal apparatus, and disparate impact specifically, is meant to attain.[246] There are two pressing questions in dire need of

---

intrinsic properties. For data scientists, they argued, this is archetypically the ***holdout set***, which amounts to a subset of the data on which the machine learning algorithm is not trained but is instead utilized to gauge the overall accuracy of the algorithmic prediction).

[238] Gillis, Talia B., "The Input Data Fallacy", *cit.*, pp. 1176–1263 (1245).

[239] Gillis, Talia B., "The Input Data Fallacy", *cit.*, pp. 1176–1263.

[240] Gillis, Talia B., "The Input Data Fallacy", *cit.*, pp. 1176–1263.

[241] Gillis, Talia B., "The Input Data Fallacy", *cit.*, pp. 1176–1263 (1246). The overwhelming algorithmic fairness literature has poured in a staggering amount of effort on carving out multifarious definitions of fairness. Amongst which stands the concept of "classification parity", which amounts to a measure of classification error that is fundamentally equal across racial lines. See: Corbett-Davies, Sam/Goel, Sharad, "The Measure and Mismeasure of Fairness: a critical Review of Fair Machine Learning", *Cornell University Library*, 2018, 6 (noting that this category can be measured from a confusion matrix, which makes the joint distributions of a given decision and outcomes by a racial line). See also: Berk, Richard/Heidari, Hoda/Jabbari, Shahin/Kearns, Michael Kearns/Roth, Aaron, "Fairness in Criminal Justice Risk Assessments: The State of the Art", *Sociological Methods and Research*, Volume 50, 2018, p. 3. Pundits often aver that two sets of measures, the **"true positive rate" (TPR)** and **"false positive rate" (FPR),** offer a feasible pathway to thoroughly gauge the prediction accuracy. See: Gillis, Talia B., "The Input Data Fallacy", *cit.*, pp. 1176–1263. There is a segment of literature that nonetheless contends that the various classification errors are not amenable to be satisfied concomitantly. See Kleinberg, Jon/S. Mullainathan/M. Raghavan, "Inherent Trade-offs in the Fair Determination of Risk Scores", *Proceedings of the 8th Conference on Innovations in Theoretical Computer Science (ITCS)*, 2017; Chouldechova, Alexandra, "Fair Prediction with Disparate Impact: A Study of Bias in Recidivism Prediction Instruments", *Big Data*, 2017,153.

[242] Gillis, Talia B., "The Input Data Fallacy", *cit.*, pp. 1176–1263 (1246).

[243] Gillis, Talia B., "The Input Data Fallacy", *cit.*, pp. 1176–1263 (1246).

[244] Gillis, Talia B., "The Input Data Fallacy", *cit.*, pp. 1176–1263 (1246). It is pivotally important to note, though, that outcome analysis forms part of a broader theoretical apparatus within which a disparate impact claim operates. Yet, seldom has outcome analysis been used as determining factor though. See, e.g., *Tex. Dep't of Hous. & Cmty. Affairs v. Inclusive Cmty. Project, Inc.*, 576 U.S., 2015, 519, 520. See: Gillis, Talia B., "The Input Data Fallacy", *cit.*, pp. 1176–1263.

[245] Gillis, Talia B., "The Input Data Fallacy", *cit.*, pp. 1176–1263 (1246).

[246] Gillis, Talia B., "The Input Data Fallacy", *cit.*, pp. 1176–1263 (1247).

being timely, and deftly, parsed in the remit of outcome-based analysis: **(i)** whether and to what extent individuals are «**similarly situated**» and **(ii)** the degree to which the outcome of interest augments or tapers off disparities relative to some baseline.

§§ The first question is whether and to what extent individuals who are «similarly situated» are treated just the same, which would be utterly needed to parse discrimination under «discrimination as anti-classification».[247] The great bulk of the definitions of credit discrimination revolve around the understanding of discriminatory[248] intent.[249] It is oft-stated discriminatory intent might be *animus*[250] towards a protected racial line or «taste-based discrimination».[251] That is, discrimination that

---

[247] Gillis, Talia B., "The Input Data Fallacy", *cit.*, pp. 1176–1263 (1247). See also: Balkin, Jack M./ Siegel, Reva B., "The American Civil Rights Tradition: Anticlassification or Antisubordination?", *University of Miami Law Review*, Volume 58, 2003, pp. 9, 10–11 (explaining the distinction between the anticlassification and the antisubordination approaches to equality law). See: Barocas, Solon/ Selbst, Andrew, "Big Data's Disparate Impact", *cit.*, p. 723 (explaining that "[d]ata mining discrimination will force a confrontation between the two divergent principles underlying antidiscrimination law: anticlassification and antisubordination").

[248] Gillis, Talia B., "The Input Data Fallacy", *cit.*, pp. 1176–1263.

[249] In spite of the widely accepted conceptual differences between intent-based and effect-based theories of disparate impact, both approaches often dovetail seamlessly. As far as the fair lending goes, the definition of disparate impact cases is somewhat shallow, nomadic, and erratic, and dispiritingly vague. Note, though, that the loan officer's discretion leads to exceedingly higher rates of rejections for members of racial minorities. See: Ayres, Ian/Klein, Gary/West, Jeffrey, "The Rise and (Potential) Fall of Disparate Impact Lending Litigation", *Evidence and Innovation in Housing Law and Policy*, Fennell, Lee Anne/Keys, Benajmin J. (Editors), Cambridge, Cambridge University Press, 2017, pp. 231–254. However, Schwemm and Taren avowedly contend that these cases might somewhat be deemed hybrid impact/intention cases. See: Schwemm, Robert G./Taren, Jeffrey L., "Discretionary Pricing, Mortgage Discrimination, and the Fair Housing Act", *The Harvard Civil Rights-Civil Liberties Law Review*, 2010, passim. The conduct being granularly parsed is discretion ascribed to brokers—which is considered by many stakeholders a harmless neutral practice -, may nonetheless lead to brokers to intentionally discriminate against members of racial minorities. See also: Selmi, Michael, "Indirect Discrimination and the Anti-Discrimination Mandate", Oxford, Oxford University Press, *Philosophical Foundations of Discrimination Law (Philosophical Foundations of Law)*, Hellman, Deborah/Moreau, Sophia (Editors), 2013, pp. 1–304 (pp. 257 and ff and passim).

[250] See: Araiza, William D., "Animus and Its Discontents", *The Florida Law Review*, Volume 71, 2019, pp.155, 158–59 ("suggests the flexibility and portability of the animus concept").

[251] See: Chi-Jack Lin/Sherman D. Hanna, "Racial Discrimination in the Consumer Credit Market", *Consumer Interests Annual*, Volume 56, 2010 ("*The Equal Credit Opportunity Act (ECOA), enacted in 1974, makes it unlawful for any creditors to discriminate against credit applicants because of their color, race/ethnic group, religion, national origin, sex, marital status, or age (provided the applicant has the capacity to contract*). Researchers have debated the existence of discrimination within the U.S. credit market. *Many studies examine the presence of discrimination in the credit market, but none focus specifically on the effect of individuals' race or ethnic group in the consumer credit market, which we differentiate from other household credit markets, such as for home mortgages.* This research fills the research gap by examining discrimination in the consumer credit market. Using four Survey of Consumer Finance data sets from 1998 to 2007, we use five measures to assess whether there is discrimination by racial/ethnic group in the consumer credit in US, and, if present, whether the discrimination is due to statistical or taste lender motivations. *Our analyses allow for distinguishing statistical and taste discrimination. In four of five of our measures, there was discrimination against households with Black respondents, and in three out of five measures, there*

is premised on a damaging/disadvantageous preference for a given racial line[252] over the other.[253] This understanding, while interesting, fleshes out discriminatory intent under the Equal Protection clause,[254] which is hardly the best approach[255] for purposes here.[256]

---

was discrimination against households with Hispanic respondents. Discrimination in the consumer credit market against black and Hispanic households is statistical discrimination: lenders choose to discriminate against black and Hispanic because they on average have higher default risk"). Italics added.

[252] Gillis, Talia B., "The Input Data Fallacy", *cit.*, pp. 1176–1263 (1247).

[253] Gillis, Talia B., "The Input Data Fallacy", *cit.*, pp. 1176–1263 (1247).

[254] Gillis, Talia B., "The Input Data Fallacy", *cit.*, pp. 1176–1263. There are two main tools to be accounted for when it comes to entertaining discrimination claims: the Equal Protection Clause of the Federal Constitution (and analogous state constitutional regulations) and federal and state statutes that forbid discrimination on various grounds, including, but not limited to, race. A discrimination claim (lawsuit) pursuant to the Equal Protection Clause must bring forth facts to prove disparate treatment. Absent of which, the claim will not succeed; a glimpse—or a mere hint—of disparate impact alone will not suffice in this regard. Antidiscrimination statutes also allow disparate treatment claims, and some likewise allow disparate impact claims. See: Mayson, Sandra G., "Bias In, Bias Out", *cit.*, pp. 2218–2300. As Richard Primus expounds, whilst there are significant technical differences in the constitutional and statutory disparate treatment frames of references, substantive analysis of a disparate treatment claim pursuant to either is essentially the same. See: Richard Primus, "The Future of Disparate Impact", *Michigan Law Review*, Volume 108, 2010, pp. 1341, 1354–56. See: Mayson, Sandra G., "Bias In, Bias Out", *cit.*, pp. 2218–2300.

[255] Gillis, Talia B., "The Input Data Fallacy", *cit.*, pp. 1176–1263 (1247).

[256] See: Huq, Aziz Z., "Racial Equity in Algorithmic Criminal Justice", *cit.*, pp. 1088–1090 (noting that if credit discrimination is bogged down to cases of *animus*, which is neatly a human sentiment, the use of machine learning algorithms for lending decisions is highly unlikely to raise critical questions, which will according render the scrutiny of algorithmic inputs futile and useless). See also: Huq, Aziz Z., "Racial Equity in Algorithmic Criminal Justice", *cit.*, pp. 1086–1087 (argues that, as long as the machine learning algorithm was programmed to forecast the correct object, say credit risk, any way in which the data is utilized is not amenable to be motivated by *animus*, but by an earnest attempt to provide an accurate/reliable algorithmic prediction instead). It is of paramount importance to keep front of mind if the humans who designed the machine learning algorithm are motivated by *animus*, which would set in motion the legal apparatus of discrimination laws. See: Gillis, Talia B., "The Input Data Fallacy", *cit.*, pp. 1176–1263. See also: Huq, Aziz Z., "Racial Equity in Algorithmic Criminal Justice", *cit.*, p. 1089 (fleshing out intent while emphasizing that the latter can be identified when "an algorithm's designer [is] motivated by either an animosity toward a racial group, or else a prior belief that race correlates with criminality, and then deliberately design the algorithm on that basis"). See also: Barocas, Solon/Selbst, Andrew D., "Big Data's Disparate Impact", *California Law Review*, Volume 104, 2016, pp. 671–682 (discussing how data is often flawed, rigged, incomplete, imperfect and therefore algorithms inherit the prejudice of the original decision makers). But see: Citron, Danielle Keats/Pasquale, Frank, "The Scored Society: Due Process for Automated Predictions", *Washington Law Review*, Volume 89, 2014, pp. 1, 4–5 (highlighting how human beings programming automated systems is directly conducive to, and leads, to fundamentally inaccurate results since the source code, predictive algorithms and datasets may encompass human biases which, in turn, have a disparate impact on historically disadvantaged groups); Crawford, Kate/Schultz, Jason, "Big Data and Due Process: Toward a Framework to Redress Predictive Privacy Harms", *Boston College Law Review*, Volume 55, 2014, pp. 93, 99–101 (pinpointing pathways through which predictive analytic tools perpetuate discriminatory practices). But see: Bornstein, Stepanhie, "Antidiscriminatory Algorithms", *Alabama Law Review*, Volume

§§ For that reason, discriminatory intent is «anti-classification»[257] seems to be a good fit insofar focuses on whether and to what extent a protected feature (e.g. race, age, marital status, disability, gender) was the basis on which a lending[258] decision was built[259] or the rationale behind of a given risk score. Pondering whether and to what extent a «similarly situated» individuals were treated differently gives the second-best way of analysing whether and to what extent a protected feature was used as a criterion when this question is not amenable to be otherwise answered[260] in a clear and direct manner.[261] As hinted above, the second question is whether and to what extent a given prediction augments or diminishes disparities relative to

---

70, 2018, pp. 519, 524–528 (contending, however, that the tagged "facially neutral" algorithms producing discriminatory outcomes should be quashed).

[257] See: Barocas, Solon/Selbst, Andrew, "Big Data's Disparate Impact", *cit.*, p. 723 (explaining that "[d]ata mining discrimination will force a confrontation between the two divergent principles underlying antidiscrimination law: anticlassification and antisubordination").

[258] Gillis, Talia B., "The Input Data Fallacy", *cit.*, pp. 1176–1263 (1248).

[259] Huq, Aziz Z., "Racial Equity in Algorithmic Criminal Justice", *cit.*, p. 1251. See also: Siegel, Reva B., "Equality Talk: Antisubordination and Anticlassification Values in Constitutional Struggles Over Brown", *Harvard Law Review*, Volume 11, 2004, p. 1470 (discussing racial anti-classification in the context of Brown v. Board of Education).

[260] Gillis, Talia B., "The Input Data Fallacy", *cit.*, pp. 1176–1263 (1248).

[261] Xiang, Alice, "Reconciling Legal and Technical Approaches to Algorithmic Bias", *cit.*, p. 26 ("[A]nti-classification masks a history of distinguishing between benign and malicious uses of protected class attributes"); Bent, Jason R., "Is Algorithmic Affirmative Action Legal", *Georgetown Law Journal*, Volume 108, 2020, pp. 803, 809 ("Voluntary algorithmic affirmative action ought to survive a disparate treatment challenge under Ricci and under the anti-race-norming provision of Title VII"); Bent, Jason R., "Is Algorithmic Affirmative Action Legal", *cit.*, p. 852 ("[A]*nticlassificatory ideal of colorblindness is impossible in the machine-learning context, because we cannot create truly colorblind algorithms. Machines are too effective in identifying proxies*"). See also: MacCarthy, Marc, "Standards of Fairness for Disparate Impact Assessment of Big Data Algorithms", *cit.*, p. 73 ("these cases do suggest that the use of group variables in algorithms would be subject to strict scrutiny, even if their purpose is to reduce group disparities"). Hellman, Deborah, "Measuring Algorithmic Fairness", *cit.*, p. 854 (contends that separately pondering which inputs are predictive of future criminal activities may not amount to disparate treatment). See also: Gillis, Talia B., "The Input Data Fallacy", *cit.*, pp. 1176–1263 (1227–1228) ("*Figure 4 demonstrates the ability to predict "age" with a high level of accuracy from the other HMDA dataset variables. Figure 12 in Appendix B shows similar analysis for predicting "marital status" from the other HMDA variables. The two figures are a representation of how accurately I was able to predict a borrower's age and marital status from the HMDA dataset in the form of a receiver operating characteristic (ROC) curve. My prediction shows that the formal exclusion of a protected characteristic may be meaningless with respect to the ability of an algorithm to actually use the characteristics. Even if an algorithm does not seek to recover the information—that is, even if it never tries to derive race or marital status—such characteristics are available to it because they are so embedded in the rest of the data. The ability to recover a protected characteristic from other information may arguably be less of a concern when the characteristic only serves as a proxy for true characteristics of interest. This is because the protected characteristic was never of interest in and of itself, and therefore a "blind" algorithm will search for proxies of the underlying characteristics of interest rather than attempt to recover the protected characteristic.* Moreover, as the data scope and accuracy increase, there is no need to use protected characteristics, even if the algorithm was not "blind." *The concern is likely to be much greater when considering protected characteristics of direct interest. In the case of a protected characteristic that is of direct interest, changes in data scope and accuracy*

some baseline, which might be a feasible pathway to analyse[262] «discrimination as discriminatory effect».[263]

§§ This approach on disparate impact plays a pivotal role beyond identifying discriminatory intent and is meant to address policies that have a discriminatory effect even when lacking intent.[264]

§§ This approach recognizes the starring role that disparate impact plays in adjusting the benefits of accurate predictions and the interests of the stakeholders with the dire need to forestall further disparities, emphasized by inputs mirroring a biased world and *biased measurement*.[265]

§§ It is noteworthy that the orthodox benchmark against which disparate impact is gauged is the burden shifting[266] framework.[267] Note, though, that the extant burden shifting framework is wholly unfitting/unbefitting for algorithmic decision-making.[268] **Outcome testing** therefore provides a blazingly new ensemble of mechanisms to functionally carry out the same type of balancing of policy goals.[269]

A Thing-Centred Algorithmic Decision-Making That Compares Individuals Who Are Similarly Situated

§§ A pivotally important question for algorithmic decision-making is whether and to what extent individuals who are similarly situated are treated just the same.[270]

---

may only mean that algorithms will have a better ability to learn and use a protected characteristic, even when formally hidden. The wedge between what is empirically relevant and legally permissible never disappears. Eventually this could mean that there is no difference between a "blind" and "aware" algorithm, rendering the exclusion strategy meaningless. The gap between what is empirically relevant and what is normatively relevant suggests a blurring of the distinction between antidiscrimination law and affirmative action. If two people with different default risks, because they are of a different age or gender, are forced to be treated equally, there is potentially a cross-subsidization from one group (mid-aged or male borrowers) to another group (older or female lenders)"). Italics added.

262 Gillis, Talia B., "The Input Data Fallacy", *cit.*, pp. 1176–1263 (1248).

263 Gillis, Talia B., "The Input Data Fallacy", *cit.*, pp. 1176–1263 (1248).

264 Gillis, Talia B., "The Input Data Fallacy", *cit.*, pp. 1176–1263 (1248).

265 Gillis, Talia B., "The Input Data Fallacy", *cit.*, pp. 1176–1263 (1248).

266 Gillis, Talia B., "The Input Data Fallacy", *cit.*, pp. 1176–1263 (1248).

267 Gillis, Talia B./Spiess, Jann L., "Big Data and Discrimination", *cit.*, pp. 470–471. It is crucially important to ascertain how broadly or narrowly the business justification was framed. Which, in turn, will subsequently sway the weight given to those business interests over the objective of assuaging extant credit market disparities. Strikingly, to the extent that the "business justification" of the disparate impact doctrine is correlated to any business justification, then any machine learning algorithm that augments prediction's overall accuracy surely matches the threshold of business justification. See also: Gillis, Talia B., "The Input Data Fallacy", *cit.*, pp. 1176–1263.

268 Gillis, Talia B./Spiess, Jann L., "Big Data and Discrimination", *cit.*, p. 462.

269 Gillis, Talia B., "The Input Data Fallacy", *cit.*, pp. 1176–1263 (1249).

270 Golberg, Suzanne B., "Discrimination by Comparison", *Yale Law Journal*, Volume 120, 2011, p. 728 (discussing issues that arising out the judiciary's dependence on "comparators" in evaluating discrimination claims). See also: Lidge III, Ernest F., "The Courts' Misuse of the Similarly Situated Concept in Employment Discrimination Law", *Missouri Law Review*, Volume 67, 2002, pp. 831 and ff.

It has long been acknowledged that there are differences[271] that amount to a legitimate basis on which to differentiate individuals (e.g. defendants, rental applicants, and borrowers).[272] In spite of the importance of the definition of who is «similarly situated», little emphasis has been placed on the exact contours[273] of this definition though.[274]

§§ As far as algorithmic decision-making is concerned, relevant stakeholders (e.g. lender, landlord, regulator, real estate agent, probation officer, judge, employer, loan officer, prosecutor, regulator, law enforcement agent, police officer, parole officer and so forth) must pay a keen attention to the plethora of features that determines who is similarly situated. It is important to note, though, that not every differentiation amounts to discrimination. Pivotally, some differences are explained by a given ensemble of features which are not considered to be impermissible discrimination.[275] This ensemble of features can be instinctively grasped as adding control variables

[271] But see: Golberg, Suzanne B., "Discrimination by Comparison", *cit.*, p. 731 ("[E]valuating allegations of discrimination requires courts and others to see something that is not observable directly: whether an accused discriminator has acted because of a protected characteristic").

[272] Gillis, Talia B., "The Input Data Fallacy", *cit.*, pp. 1176–1263 (1250).

[273] Gillis, Talia B., "The Input Data Fallacy", *cit.*, pp. 1176–1263 (1250).

[274] In spite of the pivotal role outcome analysis plays in a disparate impact claim, chiefly in the *prima facie* case of a plaintiff, little, if any, emphasis has been placed on how exactly to conduct this cumbersome/wearisome analysis. See: Gillis, Talia B., "The Input Data Fallacy", *cit.*, pp. 1176–1263. See: Giovanna Shay, Similarly Situated, *George Mason Law Review*, 2011, pp. 581, 583 ("Although the phrase 'similarly situated' is a familiar component of equal protection case law, it has not received much scholarly attention. Constitutional law scholars have focused more on other aspects of the doctrine"). See also: Ayres, Ian/Klein, Gary/West, Jeffrey, "The Rise and (Potential) Fall of Disparate Impact Lending Litigation", *Evidence and Innovation in Housing Law and Policy*, Fennell, Lee Anne/Keys, Benajmin J. (Editors), Cambridge, Cambridge University Press, 2017, pp. 235–239. Note, though that there is some haze of ambiguity on whether and to what extent the requirement to establish that a member of a protected racial line was treated differently to someone "similarly situated" is part of the first or third phase of the burden-shifting frame of reference. See: Schwemm, Robert G., "Introduction to Mortgage Lending Discrimination Law", *The John Marshall Law Review, V*olume 28, 1995, pp. 317, 329 (poring over fair lending claim and the requirement for the plaintiff to establish that "the defendant approved loans for white applicants with qualifications similar to the plaintiff's"). See also: Schwemm, Robert G., "Introduction to Mortgage Lending Discrimination Law", *cit., pp.* 328–331 (alluding to the necessity of finding a **similarly situated individual** for duly proving intentional discrimination in mortgage discrimination lawsuits using the burden-shifting frame of reference). On this note, uncertain is the extent to which the requirement is part of a disparate treatment lawsuit likewise as a disparate impact lawsuit. See also: Gillis, Talia B., "The Input Data Fallacy", *cit.*, pp. 1176–1263. See also: Golberg, Suzanne B., "Discrimination by Comparison", *cit.*, pp. 731–733 (outlining the haze confusion hovering the comparator analysis).

[275] See: Dwork, Cynthia/Hardt, Moritz/Pitassi, Tonian/Reingold/Zemel, Richard, "Fairness Through Awareness, Proceedings of the 3rd Innovations", *Theoretical Computer Science Conference*, 2012, https://dl.acm.org/doi/10.1145/2090236.2090255 [https://perma.cc/T2U3-TNQ6], p. 214 (discussing an individual fairness approach to algorithmic fairness, against the backdrop of which a similarity metric between individuals treats the latter fairly if the classifier grants similar outcomes for similar individuals). Professor Talia B. Gillis has followed this approach. See also: Gillis, Talia B., "The Input Data Fallacy", *cit.*, pp. 1176–1263.

into a regression insofar they can explain differences between individuals.[276] The breadth, size and scope of the similarly situated set will in all likelihood have a substantial effect on whether and to what extent there is a finding of inexcusable[277] disparity[278] in algorithmic decision-making.

§§ As this set grows, more of the raw differences[279] are taken into account by the initial differences of protected racial lines. It is noteworthy that who is similarly situated is fundamentally a legal question as opposed to an empirical one, as it sharply mirrors who we believe ought to be treated[280] similarly.[281]

§§ The stark difference between the aforementioned empirical question of who is the same as opposed to who should be treated just the same becomes vividly clear when we come to terms with the fact that law forbids discrimination on the basis of protected features[282] (e.g. race, age, marital status, disability, gender) regardless if

---

[276] This is akin to the analysis undertaken in Ayres, Ian/Klein, Gary/West, Jeffrey, "The Rise and (Potential) Fall of Disparate Impact Lending Litigation", *Evidence and Innovation in Housing Law and Policy*, Fennell, Lee Anne/Keys, Benajmin J. (Editors), Cambridge, Cambridge University Press, 2017, pp. 235–239. See: Gillis, Talia B., "The Input Data Fallacy", *cit.*, pp. 1176–1263. It is oft-said said that expert report discussed in that offering brought forth different linear regression models, which, in turn, comprised different variables as controls to ponder whether and to what extent there was still a significant coefficient on "race" after manually adding the controls. See: Gillis, Talia B., "The Input Data Fallacy", *cit.*, pp. 1176–1263. Note, though, that scholars argue that controlling for covariates may engender further skewed outcomes. Those scholars accordingly suggest a method to adjust for omitted variable bias. See: Jung, Jongbin/Corbett-Davis, Sam/Shroff, Ravi/Goel, Sharad, "Omitted and Included Variable Bias in Tests for Disparate Impact", *ARXIV*, Aug. 30, 2019, at 2 https://arxiv.org/pdf/1809.05651 [https://perma.cc/57U7-LD3J], (setting forth their "risk-adjusted regression" method). See: Gillis, Talia B., "The Input Data Fallacy", *cit.*, pp. 1176–1263.

[277] Gillis, Talia B., "The Input Data Fallacy", *cit.*, pp. 1176–1263 (1250).

[278] See: Golberg, Suzanne B., "Discrimination by Comparison", *cit.*, pp. 756–757 (noting courts' deep-rooted concerns with small-scaled sample sizes when assessing comparators in discrimination claims).

[279] Kleinberg, Jon/Ludwig, Jens/Mullainathan, Sendhil/Sunstein Cass R., "Discrimination in the Age of Algorithms", *Journal of Legal Analysis*, Volume 10, 1, 2018, pp. 28–29, 33–34 (draw a distinction between "group differences in the raw data" and biases for the "choice of predictors").

[280] Gillis, Talia B., "The Input Data Fallacy", *cit.*, pp. 1176–1263 (1251).

[281] It is often pointed out that the **similarly situated** set is separate from the set of markers that is predictive of a given outcome. See: Gillis, Talia B., "The Input Data Fallacy", *cit.*, pp. 1176–1263. See: Ayres, Ian/Klein, Gary/West, Jeffrey, "The Rise and (Potential) Fall of Disparate Impact Lending Litigation", *cit.*, pp. 235–239 (creating the methodology of an expert witness in disparate impact lending litigation). Importantly, if all the social markers that are predictive of an outcome were inserted in the similarly situated dataset, then, by definition, the algorithmic credit pricing does not produce inexcusable racial disparity. **As a result, such a definition of the similarly situated test sends us back into a reality in which once the protected marker is omitted, discrimination legal apparatus ceases to be relevant at all**. See: Gillis, Talia B., "The Input Data Fallacy", *cit.*, pp. 1176–1263.

[282] Note, though, that "discriminatory intent" is anything but straightforward. See: Huq, Aziz Z., "What Is Discriminatory Intent?", *Cornell Law Review*, Volume 103, 2018, pp. 1211, 1242–1263 (drills into the various interpretations of discriminatory intent in the context of the Equal Protection Doctrine. This pundit argues that discriminatory intent is viewed as "motivation" and "animus," which are human features that has no bearing on the overall functioning of machine learning algorithms. See: Huq, Aziz Z., "What Is Discriminatory Intent?", *cit.*, pp. 1222, 1242 (describing both

they are directly related to certain outcomes of interest (e.g. flight risk,[283] grant bail, recidivism[284] or default).[285] Recall, race, gender, disability, age and marital status might indeed morph an individual's default risk. Notwithstanding, these protected features are not amenable to be used to distinguish between individuals.[286]

---

motivation and *animus* as interpretations of discriminatory intent). The basis for ascribing discriminatory intent to a machine learning algorithm might not be straightforward after all); Hellman, Deborah, "Measuring Algorithmic Fairness", *Virginia Law Review*, 106 (4), 2020, pp. 811, 820–828 (provides other examples of correlations algorithms' attempts to ferret out/identify intent, which comprises sickness and recidivism). It is worth recalling, too, that a machine learning algorithm is more befitted under an "anticlassification" interpretation of intent. See: Huq, Aziz Z., "What Is Discriminatory Intent?", *cit.,* pp. 1251–1257 (fleshing out the "anticlassification" interpretation of discriminatory intent). In the algorithmic setting the mainstream position seems to be that disparate treatment would require the exclusions of protected characteristics. See: Kleinberg, Jon/Ludwig, Jens/Mullainathan, Sendhil/Sunstein, Cass R., "Discrimination in the Age of Algorithms", *cit.*, pp. 21–22 (offers examples of disparate treatment which entail exclusions of protected markers). See also: Barocas, Solon/Selbst, Andrew, "Big Data's Disparate Impact", *cit.*, p. 723 (explaining that "[d]ata mining discrimination will force a confrontation between the two divergent principles underlying antidiscrimination law: anticlassification and antisubordination"). See also: Balkin, Jack M./ Siegel, Reva B., "The American Civil Rights Tradition: Anticlassification or Antisubordination?", *University of Miami Law Review*, Volume 58, 2003, pp. 9, 10–11 (explaining the distinction between the anticlassification and the antisubordination approaches to equality law).

283 Sunstein, Cass R., Algorithms, "Correcting Biases", *Social Research*, Volume 86, 2019, p. 507 ("Importantly, the algorithm is made blind to race. Whether a defendant is African American or Hispanic is not one of the factors that it considers in assessing flight risk").

284 But see: Rudin, Cynthia/Wang, Caroline/Coker, Beau, "The Age of Secrecy and Unfairness in Recidivism Prediction", *Harvard Data Science Review*, Issue 2.1. Winter 2020, 2020, passim; Eckhouse, L., Lum, K., Conti-Cook, C./Ciccolini, J., "Layers of bias: A unified approach for understanding problems with risk assessment", *Criminal Justice and Behavior*, Volume 46, Issue 2, 2019, pp. 185–209; Stevenson, M. T./Slobogin, C., "Algorithmic risk assessments and the double-edged sword of youth", *Washington University Law Review*, Volume 96, 2018, passim. On the challenges arising out of algorithmic risk assessment with regard to predicting criminal recidivism rates fairness wise: Johndrow, J. E./K. Lum, "An Algorithm for Removing Sensitive Information: Application to Race-Independent Recidivism Prediction", *Annals of Applied Statistics*, 13 (1), 2019, pp. 189–220; Chouldechova, A., "Fair Prediction with Disparate Impact: A Study of Bias in Recidivism Prediction Instruments", *Big data*, 5 (2), 2017, pp. 153–163; Kamiran, F./T. Calders, "Data Preprocessing Techniques for Classification Without Discrimination." Knowledge Information Systems, 2012, 33:1–33; Kearns, M/A. Roth, *The Ethical Algorithm*, Oxford, Oxford Press; Skeem, J. and C. Lowenkamp, "Using Algorithms to Address Trade-Offs Inherent in Predicting Recidivism", *Behavioural Science and Law*, Volume 38, 2020, pp. 259–278; Tonry, M., "Legal and Ethical Issues in The Prediction of Recidivism", *Federal Sentencing Reporter*, 26 (3): 2014, pp. 167–176; Zhu, Mirilla, "Jury, Using Artificial Intelligence to Predict Recidivism Rates", *Yale Scientific*, 2020, passim. See also: Chasemi et al., Medhi, "The application of Machine Learning to a General Risk-Need Assessment Instrument in the Prediction of Criminal Recidivism", *Criminal Justice and Behavior*, Volume 48, 2020, pp. 518–538.

285 But see: "The Use of Cash-Flow Data in Underwriting Credit: Empirical Research Findings", *Finreglab*, 32, 34 (Jul. 2019), available at: https://finreglab.org/wp-content/uploads/2019/07/FRL_Research-Report_Final.pdf [https://perma.cc/N65Q-WQML] (access: 19.12.2024) (arguing that the use of cash flow data can underpin a prediction of default risk, thereby providing an apposite alternative to ancient credit scores. In addition to that, cash-flow data tallies with accurate predictions across demographic groups).

286 Gillis, Talia B., "The Input Data Fallacy", *cit.*, pp. 1176–1263 (1251).

§§ Professor Talia B. Gillis rebuffs/gainsays the claim according to which the endeavour of comparing «similarly situated» individuals is commensurate with, and tantamount to, a comeback to input-based approaches, insofar heavily relies on the selection of the legitimate bases[287] for differentiation. At first blush, it looks akin to limiting a machine learning algorithm to pre-approved[288] inputs. Yet they neither straddle, nor do they conflate.

§§ Quite the opposite, though, the endeavour of comparing «similarly situated» individuals stand in stark contrast with the input-based approaches. Tellingly, limiting a machine learning algorithm's input to the similarly situated set would, while enough, not be quite necessary to successfully undertake this endeavour.[289] Strikingly, there is a myriad of inputs that enhance prediction accuracy while not producing substantial[290] disparities.[291]

§§ This is pivotally important in the case of features that would prove helpful to access to credit for protected racial lines but are highly unlikely to be inserted in the similarly situated set,[292] such as timely rental payments.[293] Furthermore, a regulator might set a threshold lenience level such that some degree disparity is tolerable when using inputs that extend beyond the «similarly situated» set.[294]

[287] Gillis, Talia B., "The Input Data Fallacy", *cit.*, pp. 1176–1263 (1251).

[288] Gillis, Talia B., "The Input Data Fallacy", *cit.*, pp. 1176–1263 (1251).

[289] Gillis, Talia B., "The Input Data Fallacy", *cit.*, pp. 1176–1263 (1251).

[290] Gillis, Talia B., "The Input Data Fallacy", *cit.*, pp. 1176–1263 (1251).

[291] Xiang, Alice, "Reconciling Legal and Technical Approaches to Algorithmic Bias", *cit.*, p. 23 ("*[I]ncluding [protected class variables] can actually improve both fairness and accuracy, depending on how they are used*"). Italics added.

[292] Gillis, Talia B., "The Input Data Fallacy", *cit.*, pp. 1176–1263 (1251).

[293] But see: Wonyoung, So, "Which Information Matters? Measuring Landlord Assessment of Tenant Screening Reports", *Housing Policy Debate*, Volume 33, n.º 6, 2023, pp. 1484–1510 (1484) ("*Through a behavioral experiment with landlords using simulated tenant screening reports, this study shows that landlords use blanket screening policies, that they conflate the existence of tenant records with outcomes (e.g., eviction filings with executed evictions), and that they display, on average, tendencies toward automation bias that are influenced by the risk assessments and scores presented by tenant screening reports.* I argue that maintaining blanket screening policies and automation bias, combined with the downstream effects of creating and *using racially biased eviction and criminal records, means that people of color will inevitably experience disproportionate exclusion from rental housing due to perceived "risk" on the part of landlords*"). Italics added. See: Part IV, Chap. 4, Sects. 4.1.4–4.1.4.2.3 of this book.

[294] Gillis, Talia B., "The Input Data Fallacy", *cit.*, pp. 1176–1263 (1251).

§§ Overall, undertaking a test that relies on similarly situated features renders the trade-off between accuracy and other policy goals clear and straightforward, as opposed to rendering it dingy/non-transparent[295] as input-based approaches do when they limit inputs to those that look instinctively relevant[296] to default. By the same token, the similarly situated set can be permanently balanced, adjusted, and tested, whereas the limitations of input-based approaches are not legible/visible, let alone ductile.[297]

A Thing-Centred Algorithmic Decision-Making That Considers Incremental Change

§§ Impermissible disparities arising out of algorithmic decision-making must consider a baseline. For instance, traditional credit pricing.[298] Rather than taking into account the absolute levels of inequalities engendered by a pricing rule, the decision-maker must pay a granular attention to the degree to which these inequalities compare to traditional credit pricing rules.[299]

§§ By the same token, a regulator could go the extra mile as to compare/juxtapose the prices created under the use of traditional lending variables with new dataset available to a given decision-maker (e.g. lender), such as consumer and payment behaviour.[300] An incremental approach to inequalities acknowledges that credit is

---

[295] See: Burrell, Jenna, "How the Machine Thinks: Understanding Opacity in Machine Learning Algorithms", *Big Data & Society*, Volume 3, 2016. But see: de Laat, Paul B. 'Algorithmic Decision-Making Based on Machine Learning from Big Data: Can Transparency Restore Accountability?", *Philosophy & Technology*, Volume 31, 2018, pp. 524 and ff and passim (broaches the plethora of limitations related with full transparency, privacy, deleterious effects, competitive edge, and the shroud of opacity under which algorithms are often wrapped).

[296] But see: Tyler, Tom, "Methodology in Legal Research", in: *Utrecht Law Review*, Volume 13, Issue 3, 2017, pp. 130–131 ("*Accurate facts plus good legal rules lead to substantive justice.* This is the normative framework of right and wrong defined by traditional legal analysis. *Risk analysis is a nice example of the benefits of empiricism because studies suggest that the use of empirical methods to assess future dangerousness is more accurate than is the use of human intuition. It is better to use a formula when making a legal decision that involves estimates of someone's likely future conduct than it is to rely upon the impressions of judges or prosecutors*" (...) "*The legal system relies on predictions about people's likely future behaviour at many points in the system*: pretrial detention; sentencing; parole and probation; etc. And it has been used with a variety of special populations, including juveniles; the mentally ill; and sexual predators. *A key reason to use such quantitative methods is that they are better able to predict future behaviour and as a consequence the many points in the system at which judgments are made – pre-trial detention; sentencing; parole – are better able to enact justice for both the innocent and the guilty. The focus by social scientists upon helping to identify and use facts in ways that produce more accurate decisions fits well with the argument that the aims of justice are best served when they are based upon accurate factual information. Accuracy, in turn is enhanced by the use of empirical methods. Facts are sought that can guide the application of normative legal principles*"). Italics added.

[297] Gillis, Talia B., "The Input Data Fallacy", *cit.*, pp. 1176–1263.

[298] Gillis, Talia B., "The Input Data Fallacy", *cit.*, pp. 1176–1263 (1252).

[299] Gillis, Talia B., "The Input Data Fallacy", *cit.*, pp. 1176–1263 (1252).

[300] Gillis, Talia B., "The Input Data Fallacy", *cit.*, pp. 1176–1263 (1252).

priced in a «biased world» but likewise aims to forestalling algorithmic pricing[301] from further entrenching structural[302] disadvantage.[303]

§§ To the extent that the ancient approach to algorithmic decision-making (e.g. computer-run algorithmic pricing) heavily relies upon biased inputs, in all likelihood it will produce outputs disparate for protected racial lines (e.g. Blacks and Latinos).[304] Therefore, this sort of test is more befitted for the effect-based interpretation of disparate impact,[305] as it strives to equipoise both the deep-rooted concern for further compounding structural disadvantage[306] with the vested interests of lenders[307] paired with the relevance of overall functioning credit markets.[308]

§§ Moreover, the **use of nontraditional datasets** could indeed soothe out/tail off the inordinate damages of *biased measurement*, which, in turn, would decrease disparities across racial lines accordingly. Compellingly, accurate algorithmic credit pricing[309] could also elongate/extend access to credit scoring,[310] which would prove incredible beneficial for vulnerable[311] racial lines.[312]

---

[301] Gillis, Talia B., "The Input Data Fallacy", *cit.*, pp. 1176–1263 (1252).

[302] Gillis, Talia B., "The Input Data Fallacy", *cit.*, pp. 1176–1263 (1252). See also: Barocas, Solon/ Selbst, Andrew, "Big Data's Disparate Impact", *California Law Review*, Volume 104, pp. 2016, p. 691 (highlighting the worrisome, and gruesome, issue of "structural disadvantage" with which racialized communities have been tussling with for centuries). See also: Powell, Richard/Porter, Jeremy, "Redlining, Concentrated Disadvantage and Crime: The Effects of Discriminatory Government Policies on Violent Crime", *American Journal of Criminal Justice*, Volume 48, 2023, pp. 1132–1156 ("*Redlining and other discriminatory government policies enacted during the first half of the Twentieth Century have had long-lasting negative effects on neighborhoods, especially those inhabited by people of color (...) The results indicate that redlining was associated with increases in both concentrated disadvantage and violent crime, and that redlining's relationship with violent crime was, indeed, partially mediated by its relationship with concentrated disadvantage*"). Italics added. See also: Gandy, Oscar H., *Coming to Terms with Chance: Engaging Rational Discrimination and Cumulative Disadvantage*, Farnham, UK: Ashgate Publishing, 2009.

[303] Gillis, Talia B., "The Input Data Fallacy", *cit.*, pp. 1176–1263 (1252).

[304] Gillis, Talia B., "The Input Data Fallacy", *cit.*, pp. 1176–1263 (1252).

[305] Gillis, Talia B., "The Input Data Fallacy", *cit.*, pp. 1176–1263 (1252).

[306] Gillis, Talia B., "The Input Data Fallacy", *cit.*, pp. 1176–1263 (1252).

[307] Gillis, Talia B., "The Input Data Fallacy", *cit.*, pp. 1176–1263 (1252).

[308] Gillis, Talia B., "The Input Data Fallacy", *cit.*, pp. 1176–1263 (1252).

[309] Gillis, Talia B., "The Input Data Fallacy", *cit.*, pp. 1176–1263 (1252).

[310] Gillis, Talia B., "The Input Data Fallacy", *cit.*, pp. 1176–1263 (1252).

[311] Gillis, Talia B., "The Input Data Fallacy", *cit.*, pp. 1176–1263 (1252).

[312] Gillis, Talia B., "The Input Data Fallacy", *cit.*, pp. 1176–1263 (1252).

§§ The key takeaway is that which there is a perceived need for an empirical-based test[313] aimed at gauging whether and to what extent there are inordinate damages to protected racial lines flowing from changes in credit pricing, as opposed to the wholesale use of biased inputs in algorithmic credit decisions.[314] This approach thereby shies away from holding machine learning algorithms to a standard that is exceedingly harsher than extant standards of fair lending are, which would undermine the incredible potential of algorithmic pricing to help consumers.[315]

A Thing-Centred Algorithmic Decision-Making That Forestalls Biased Algorithmic Decisions While Abiding by the Central Tenets of *Algorithmic Common Good*

§§ Risk-based assessment is all about distinguishing individuals. Taken together, big data and machine learning algorithms further augment the capability to distinguish, thereby enhancing the unbearable tension with algorithmic fairness that disavows differentiation of individuals on protected grounds.[316] For instance, ancient fair lending legal framework has sought to restrict pricing practices by surveying inputs.[317]

§§ However, this approach was created in a reality in which pricing heavily relied upon a handful of inputs, hinging upon human expertise, and used loan officers to determine the final terms of credit contracts.[318] Latter-day underwriting, in turn, is gradually hinging upon nontraditional inputs and advanced Artificial Intelligence-embedded technologies, thereby throwing existing discrimination doctrine[319] out of balance.[320]

§§ Compellingly, present-day approaches are unbefitting since they persist to commit the «input data fallacy»,[321] in spite of the fact that surveying decision inputs as in traditional fair lending is hardly the best course of action to be taken in the algorithmic realm.[322]

---

313 Gillis, Talia B., "The Input Data Fallacy", *cit.*, pp. 1176–1263 (1252).

314 Gillis, Talia B., "The Input Data Fallacy", *cit.*, pp. 1176–1263 (1252).

315 Gillis, Talia B., "The Input Data Fallacy", *cit.*, pp. 1176–1263 (1253).

316 Gillis, Talia B., "The Input Data Fallacy", *cit.*, pp. 1176–1263 (1253).

317 Gillis, Talia B., "The Input Data Fallacy", *cit.*, pp. 1176–1263 (1253).

318 Gillis, Talia B., "The Input Data Fallacy", *cit.*, pp. 1176–1263 (1253).

319 Gillis, Talia B., "The Input Data Fallacy", *cit.*, pp. 1176–1263 (1256).

320 See: Berk, Richard/Heidari, Hoda/Jabbari, Shahin/Kearns, Michael Kearns/Roth, Aaron, "Fairness in Criminal Justice Risk Assessments: The State of the Art", *cit.*, p. 31 ("At the same time, the benchmark is current practice. *By that standard, even small steps, imperfect as they may be, can in principle lead to meaningful improvements in criminal justice decisions. They just need to be accurately characterized*"). Italics added.

321 Gillis, Talia B., "The Input Data Fallacy", *cit.*, pp. 1176–1263 (1256).

322 Gillis, Talia B., "The Input Data Fallacy", *cit.*, pp. 1176–1263 (1257).

§§ It is crucially important to note, though, that algorithmic decision-making begs for a fundamental shift away from analysis that aims to unravel causal connections between inputs and outcomes of interest. I hereby second Professor Talia B. Gillis' proposal in view of which algorithmic decision-making, to be *controllable*,[323] *interpretable*,[324] accurate, reliable and fair, requires that relevant stakeholders (e.g. lenders, loan officers, tool developers, engineers, data scientists, statisticians, prosecutors, landlords, regulators, real estate agents, probation officers, judges, employers, loan officers, prosecutors, regulators, law enforcement agents, police officers, parole officers and so forth) shift their gaze downstream to the *outputs* of a machine learning algorithm,[325] as opposed to the *inputs*.

§§ Pivotally, regulators should employ staggering efforts to come up with tests for gauging whether and to what extent the **outputs** a machine learning algorithm produces are inexcusable on the basis of agreed-upon regulatory policy goals. Regulators should therefore commence by asking relevant questions that can be duly answered by scrutinizing **algorithmic outcomes**, such as whether and to what extent similarly situated individuals are treated differently or the degree to which a fundamental shift away from ancient decision-making to algorithmic decision-making has enhanced, rather than decreased, inequalities.[326]

§§ Relevant stakeholders ought to be chary of the warped/shoddy beliefs they cling to in a bid to carve through the chaos of *Algorithmic Dictatorship*[327] with razor sharp clarity while toiling towards a sought-after *Algorithmic Common Good* of which citizens are bound to be fond of.

5.1.2 Setting the Stage: A Thing-Centred Algorithmic Decision-Making Propelled by a Controllable and Interpretable Machine Learning That Weeds Out Algorithmic Dictatorship and Secures Algorithmic Common Good

§§ Machine learning, so scholars say, is not amenable to the considered a monolith.[328] Machine learning is therefore a dynamic body of science, as

---

323 See: Part V, this chapter, Sects. 5.1.7–5.1.7.5 of this book (on the five laws to control algorithmic decision-making).

324 See: Part V, this chapter, Sects. 5.1.8–5.1.8.5 of this book (on the five laws to interpret algorithmic decision-making).

325 Gillis, Talia B., "The Input Data Fallacy", *cit.*, pp. 1176–1263 (1257).

326 Gillis, Talia B., "The Input Data Fallacy", *cit.*, pp. 1176–1263 (1257).

327 See: Part IV, Chap. 4, Sects. 4.1–4.1.10.6 of this book (on Algorithmic Dictatorship and its chilling effect on democracy).

328 Lehr, David/Ohm, Paul, "Playing with the Data: What Legal Scholars Should Learn About Machine Learning", *University of California, Davis*, Volume 51, 2017, pp. 653–718.

opposed to a static one. Note, though, that more often than not stakeholders use «algorithms»,[329] «machine learning[330]», «artificial intelligence»,[331] «big data[332]

[329] Chabert, J.L. et al., *A History of Algorithms: From the Pebble to the Microchip.* New York/ Heidelberg: Springer, 2013; McCorduck, P., *Machines who think: A personal inquiry into the history and prospects of artificial intelligence*, Cleveland, CRC Press Books, 2004; Graeber, D., & Wengrow, D., *The dawn of everything: A new history of humanity*, London, United Kingdom, Allen Lane, 2021. But see: O'Neil, Cathy, *Weapons of Math Destruction. How Big Data Increases Inequality and Threatens Democracy*, London, Penguin Random House, 2016, passim (showing how algorithms utilized in modern societies are amenable to perpetuate racial discrimination, partially through perpetuation of social disadvantage and wealth divides). See also: O'Neil, Cathy, "When Not to Trust the Algorithm", *Interview published in the Harvard Business Review's Ideacast*, 2016, passim; O' Neil, Cathy, "Amazon's Gender-Biased Algorithm Is Not Alone", 2018, accessed 2 January 2025 (on gender-related algorithmic biases).

[330] See: Murphy, Kevin P., *Machine Learning: A Probabilistic Perspective (Adaptive Computation and Machine Learning series).* Massachusetts: The MIT Press, 2012, pp. 1–1104 (states avowedly that "machine Learning attempts to combine deductive, inductive, and abductive reasoning to make person-like reasoning in AI Entities possible. Machine-learning AI Entities initially learn in the same way a human child learns. First, they notice details and patterns in shapes, sounds, and behaviors; then put them together to distinguish one person from another, or a dog from a cat. Eventually, the AI can recognize and identify" common objects). See also: Hutto-Schultz, Jess, "Dicitur Ex Machina: Artificial Intelligence and the Hearsay Rule", *George Mason Law Review*, Volume 27, Issue 2, 2020, pp. 684–718 (689). See: Chollet, François, *Deep Learning with Python.* Shelter Island, Nova Iorque: Manning, 2018, pp. 1–384 (passim). *Deep Learning* stands as a byproduct of *Machine Learning. Machine Learning*, a subset of Artificial Intelligence, unfolds itself in *Deep Learning*, which "involves computer algorithms that have the ability to "learn" or improve in performance over time on some task". See also: Surden, Harry, "Machine Learning and Law", *Washington Law Review*, Volume 89, 2015, pp. 87 and ff. See also: Barocas, Solon/Selbst, Andrew, "Big Data's Disparate Impact", *California Law Review*, Volume 104, 2016, pp. 671–678 ("in particular, by exposing so-called 'machine learning' algorithms to examples of the cases of interest (previously identified instances of fraud, spam, default, and poor health), *the algorithm 'learns' which related attributes or activities can serve as potential proxies for those qualities or outcomes of interest*"). Italics added. See also: Chen, C./Rudin, C., "An optimization approach to learning falling rule lists", *Proceedings of Machine Learning Research, Artificial Intelligence and Statistics*, Volume 84, 2018, pp. 604–612; Sokolovska, N./Chevaleyre, Y./Zucker, J.D., "A provable algorithm for learning interpretable scoring systems", *Proceedings of Machine Learning Research, Artificial Intelligence and Statistics*, Volume 84, pp. 566–574; Rudin, Cynthia/Ustun, B., "Optimized scoring systems: toward trust in machine learning for healthcare and criminal justice", *Interfaces*, Volume 48, 2018, pp. 399–486.

[331] See: Tegmark, Max, *Life 3.0: Being Human in the Age of Artificial Intelligence.* New York: Knopf, 2018, pp. 1–384 (pp. 24 and ff) (charts the path ahead for a wide range of intelligences, including artificial intelligence in the digital age). There is a handful of authors that wonder if artificial intelligence can mimic not only human intelligence but, and foremost, human behaviour. Amongst whom stands: Russell, Stuart/Norvig, Peter, *Artificial Intelligence: A Modern Approach.* London: United Kingdom, Pearson, 2018, passim; Boden, Margaret A., *Artificial Intelligence: A Very Short Introduction.* Oxford: Oxford University Press, 2018, passim.

[332] Big data has taken algorithmic decision-making by storm. See: Sivarajah, Uthayasnkar et al., "Critical Analysis of Big Data Challenges and Analytical Methods", *Journal of Business Research*, Volume 70, 2017, pp. 263 and ff and passim; Jetten, Lieke/Sharon, Stephen, "Selected Issues concerning the Ethical Use of Big Data Health Analytics", *Washington & Lee Law Review Online*,

analytics»,[333] «biometric algorithmic surveillance»[334] and «data mining»[335] interchangeably as if the same thing they were. They are not. To name just a few, «machine learning» is what propels

Volume 72, 2016, passim; Wachter, S./Mittelstadt. B., "A right to Reasonable Inferences: Re-thinking Data Protection Law in the Age of Big Data and AI", *Columbia Business Law Review*, 2019, pp. 1 and ff and passim; See in French doctrine: Ferey, Samuel, «Analyse économique du droit, big data et justice prédictive», *Archives de Philosophie du Droit*, Volume 60, 2018, pp. 68–81; Završnik, A. "Algorithmic justice: Algorithms and big data in criminal justice settings", *European Journal of Criminology*, 2019, passim; Joh, Elizabeth E., "The New Surveillance Discretion: Automated Suspicion, Big Data, and Policing." *Harvard Law and Policy Review*, 10 (1), 2016, pp. 15–42.

[333] See: Tene, Omer/Polonetsky, Jules, "Big Data for All: Privacy and User Control in the Age of Analytics", *Northwestern Journal of Technology and Intellectual Property*, Volume 11, 2013, pp. 239 and ff and passim. Department of Justice Letter to U.S.S.C., 2017, passim (warning that the widespread use of risk assessment at sentencing "ultimately raises constitutional questions because of the use of group-based characteristics and suspect classifications in the analytics"). See also: Ashley, KD, *Artificial Intelligence and Legal Analytics: New Tools for Law Practice in the Digital Age*, Cambridge, Cambridge University Press, 2017.

[334] Hu, Margaret, "From the National Surveillance State to the Cybersurveillance State", *The Annual Review of Law and Social Science*, Volume 13, 2017, p. 169 ("*the potential for mass surveillance is part of the problematic nature of biometric credentialing and identification practices. Like most digital data, biometric identification data are not restricted to the purpose for which they were originally collected*. Biometric data can be repurposed for secondary uses, such as identification of potential suspects or victims through real-time analytics, assessment of threats of terrorism, tactical decisionmaking, or behavioral and genetic research (Duster 2003). Beyond secondary—and tertiary, quaternary, and quinary—uses, biometric data become a part of population-wide *risk assessments that incorporate bureaucratized surveillance into governing decisions, policing, and threat assessments. Through big data tools, precrime governance models are increasingly reflected in collect-it-all cybersurveillance systems. In these systems, biometric data is a surveillance axis that can be used to track, identify, and isolate suspicious persons, digital data, or devices*"). Italics added.

[335] But see: Barocas, Solon/Selbst, Andrew, "Big Data's Disparate Impact", *California Law Review*, Volume 104, 2016, pp. 671, 677–687 (showing how data mining may mirror deep-seated racial biases of society). See: Balkin, Jack, "Constitution in the National Surveillance State", *Minnesota Law Review*, Volume 93, 2008, p. 13 (*data mining* allows inferences not only about the direct subject of surveillance, but about other people with whom they live, work and communicate"); Zarsky, Tal, "Transparency in Data Mining: From Theory to Practice", *Discrimination and Privacy in the Information Society: Data Mining and Profiling in Large Databases*, Bart Custers et al. eds., Belin, Springer, 2013; Schermer, Bart W., "The Limits of Privacy in Automated Profiling and Data Mining", *Computer Law & Security Review*, Volume 27, 2011, pp. 45 and ff and passim. But see: Barocas, Solon/Selbst, Andrew D., "Big Data's Disparate Impact", *California Law Review*, Volume 104, 2016, p. 699 (discussing how discriminatory data mining is analogous to unintentional disparate impact analysis); Bornstein, Stepanhie, "Antidiscriminatory Algorithms", *Alabama Law Review*, Volume 70, 2018, p. 535 (positing that algorithmic discrimination at large could fall under the all-embracing umbrella of anti-stereotyping category within Title VII's disparate treatment). But see: Pedreshi, Dino/Ruggieri, Salvatore/Turini, Franco, "Discrimination-aware Data Mining", *Proceedings of the 14th ACM SIGKDD International Conference on Knowledge Discovery and Data Mining (Las Vegas, Nevada, USA), ACM*, 2008, pp. 560–568 (arguing that one should shift its gaze downstream by putting in place discrimination-aware algorithmic tools while performing data mining).

forward Netflix's suitably tailored recommendations,[336] predictive[337] policing,[338] and self-driving cars,[339] facial recognition,[340] bail

---

[336] Alvino, Chris/Basilico, Justin, "Learning a Personalized Homepage", *Netflix Technological Blog* (Apr. 9, 2015), https://medium.com/netflix-techblog/learning-a-personalizedhomepage-aa8ec670359a [https://perma.cc/X43V-R3S6]; Amatriain, Xavier/Basilico, Justin, "Netflix Recommendations: Beyond the 5 Stars (Part 1)", *Netflix Technology Blog* (Apr. 6, 2012), https://medium.com/netflix-techblog/netflix-recommendations-beyond-the-5-starspart-1-55838468f429 [https://perma.cc/DHD5-F2Q2]; Amatriain, Xavier/Basilico, Justin, "Netflix Recommendations: Beyond the 5 Stars (Part 2)", *Netflix Technology Blog* (June 20, 2012), https://medium.com/netflix-techblog/netflix-recommendations-beyond-the-5-stars-part-2d9b96aa399f5 [https://perma.cc/3T9U-5E22].

[337] See: Part IV, Chap. 4, Sects. 4.1.1–4.1.1.1 of this book (on biased predictive policing). See: Shapiro, Aaron, "Reform Predictive Policing", *Nature*, 2017, pp. 541, 458, 459 ("HunchLab applies machine-learning and artificial-intelligence algorithms to predict the spread of crime types"); "What PredPol Is and What PredPol Is NOT", *Predpol Blog* (Nov. 19, 2015), http://www.predpol.com/whatispredpol [https://perma.cc/F5G5 FYW9] ("Predictive Policing's forecasting technology includes high-level mathematics, machine learning, and proven theories of crime behavior, that take a forward-looking approach to crime prevention"). But see: Selbst, Andrew D., "Disparate Impact in Big Data Policing", *Georgia Law Review*, Volume 52, 2017, p. 109 (arguing that law enforcement agencies should carry out "algorithmic impact statements" with a view to measure the potential discriminatory impact of computer-run predictive policing technologies). But see: Lum, Kristian/Isaac, William, To Predict and Serve?", *Significance*, 2016, pp. 14, 19 (discussing bigoted predictive policing that target primarily members of racialized communities).

[338] Ferguson, Andrew Guthrie, "Policing Predictive Policing", *Washington Law Review*, Volume 94, 2017, pp. 1113 and ff; Ferguson, Andrew Guthrie, "Predictive Policing and Reasonable Suspicion", *Emory Law Journal*, Volume 62, 2012, pp. 259 and ff; Joh, Elizabeth E., Policing by the Numbers: Big Data and the Fourth Amendment, *Washington Law Review*, Volume 89, 2014, pp. 35 and ff. But see: Kirkpatrick, Keith, "It's not the Algorithm, it's the Data", *Communications of the ACM*, February 2017, Volume 60, n.º 2, 2017 ("critics, however, say tools such as PredPol and CommandCentral *are inherently biased since they rely heavily on reported crimes data, which is often concentrated in areas that are heavily policed, thereby skewing statistics to overrepresent poor or minority communities.* "*We know that we have a history of racially biased policing in the United States, and that has fed into all the data that we have on where arrests have occurred, which crimes are more likely to occur in specific communities, and at which particular times*," says Jennifer Lynch, senior staff attorney at the Electronic Frontier Foundation. "*That's the data that's being fed into predictive policing algorithms*"). Italics added. See also: Kirkpatrick, Keith, "Battling Algorithmic Bias: How Do We Ensure Algorithms Treat Us Fairly?" *Commun. ACM 59*, Volume 10, 2016, pp. 1 and ff and passim. See: Part IV, Chap. 4, Sects. 4.1.1–4.1.1.1 of this book (on biased predictive policing).

[339] See: Part III, Chap. 3, Sects. 3.1.5.9–3.1.5.9.3 of this book (on Critical Artificial Intelligence Studies, with a sharper focus on the functional shortcomings facing self-driving vehicles). See: Surden, Harry Surden/Williams, Mary-Anne, "Technological Opacity, Predictability, and Self-Driving Cars", *Cardozo Law Review*, Volume 38, 2016, pp. 121 and ff (arguing that self-driving cars are mostly controlled by Artificial Intelligence-technologies). See: Smith, Bryant Walker, "Proximity-Driven Liability", *The Georgetown Law Journal*, Volume 102, 2014, pp. 1777 and ff (discussing the implications arising out of the uptick of vehicle automation in decades to come).

[340] See: Part III, Chap. 3, Sects. 3.1.5.7–3.1.5.8.1 of this book (on the functional aspects of Critical Artificial Intelligence Studies, with a sharper focus on the perils concerning the deployment of facial recognition technology). See: Garvie, Clare et al., *The Perpetual Line-up: Unregulated Police Face Recognition in America*, Georgetown University. Center on Privacy and Technology, Georgetown

decision-making,[341] pretrial risk assessment,[342] amongst many other applications.[343]

§§ Notwithstanding, each of the aforementioned applications have different affordances. More to the point, each of the previously mentioned applications hinge upon different types of algorithms. Pundits are therefore adamant in averring that if we lose sight of its underlying differences its policy and legal implications are doomed to fall by the wayside. Crucially, if we persist in walking through that warped path, inordinate harms are shaping up to be overlooked while actionable pathways for assuaging those harms will most likely remain lost in the unheeded buck of oblivion.[344]

University. Law Center. Center on Privacy & Technology Georgetown Law, Center on Privacy & Technology, 2016, pp. 1–145 ("*Across the country, state and local police departments are building their own face recognition systems, many of them more advanced than the FBI's.* We know very little about these systems. We don't know how they impact privacy and civil liberties. We don't know how they address accuracy problems. And we don't know how any of these systems—local, state, or federal—affect racial and ethnic minorities. This report closes these gaps. The result of a year-long investigation and over 100 records requests to police departments around the country, it is the most comprehensive survey to date of law enforcement face recognition and the risks that it poses to privacy, civil liberties, and civil rights. *Combining FBI data with new information we obtained about state and local systems, we find that law enforcement face recognition affects over 117 million American adults. It is also unregulated. A few agencies have instituted meaningful protections to prevent the misuse of the technology. In many more cases, it is out of control*"). Italics added. See also: Fretty, Douglas A., "Face-Recognition Surveillance: A Moment of Truth for Fourth Amendment Rights in Public Places", *The Virginia Journal of Law and Technology*, Volume 16, 2011, pp. 429 and ff and.

[341] Mayson, Sandra G., "Dangerous Defendants", *Yale Law Journal*, Volume 127, 2018, p. 490 ("Bail reform is gaining momentum nationwide"); Dewan, Shaila, "Judges Replacing Conjecture with Formula for Bail", New York Times (June 26, 2015), https://www.nytimes.com/2015/06/27/us/turning-the-granting-of-bail-into-a-science.html [https://perma.cc/Y86J-GHU4] (emphasizing the mounting groundswell of support for algorithmic risk assessments in bail decision-making across jurisdictions).

[342] See: Part IV, Chap. 4, Sects. 4.1.10.1–4.1.10.6 of this book (on biased algorithmic risk assessment in criminal procedure law settings, with a sharper focus on COMPAS). See: Stevenson, Megan, "Assessing Risk Assessment in Action", *Minnesota Law Review*, Volume 103, 2018, p. 303 (discussing the burgeoning use of pretrial risk assessment as a mandatory component of bail decisions in Kentucky).

[343] Lehr, David/Ohm, Paul, "Playing with the Data: What Legal Scholars Should Learn About Machine Learning", *cit.*, pp. 653–718.

[344] Lehr, David/Ohm, Paul, "Playing with the Data: What Legal Scholars Should Learn About Machine Learning", *cit.*, pp. 653–718.

§§ Machine learning and deep learning are kindred[345] in that they are somewhat algorithmic brothers.[346] Deep learning,[347] which, as stated earlier in this book,[348] originally mirrored the neural matrix of the human brain,[349] morphs the way input

[345] See: Hutto-Schultz, Jess, "Dicitur Ex Machina: Artificial Intelligence and the Hearsay Rule", *George Mason Law Review*, Volume 27, Issue 2, 2020, pp. 684–718 (689). See: Chollet, François, *Deep Learning with Python*. Shelter Island, Nova Iorque: Manning, 2018, pp. 1–384 (passim). *Deep Learning* stands as a byproduct of *Machine Learning*. *Machine Learning*, a subset of Artificial Intelligence, unfolds itself in *Deep Learning*, which "involves computer algorithms that have the ability to "learn" or improve in performance over time on some task". See also: Surden, Harry, "Machine Learning and Law", *Washington Law Review*, Volume 89, 2015, pp. 87 and ff. See also: Barocas, Solon/Selbst, Andrew, "Big Data's Disparate Impact", *California Law Review*, Volume 104, pp. 2016, pp. 671–678 ("in particular, by exposing so-called 'machine learning' algorithms to examples of the cases of interest (previously identified instances of fraud, spam, default, and poor health), *the algorithm 'learns' which related attributes or activities can serve as potential proxies for those qualities or outcomes of interest*"). Italics added. See also: Chen, C./Rudin, C., "An optimization approach to learning falling rule lists", *Proceedings of Machine Learning Research, Artificial Intelligence and Statistics*, Volume 84, 2018, pp. 604–612; Sokolovska, N./Chevaleyre, Y./Zucker, J.D., "A provable algorithm for learning interpretable scoring systems", *Proceedings of Machine Learning Research, Artificial Intelligence and Statistics*, Volume 84, pp. 566–574; Rudin, Cynthia/Ustun, B., "Optimized scoring systems: toward trust in machine learning for healthcare and criminal justice", *Interfaces*, Volume 48, 2018, pp. 399–486.

[346] See: Goodfellow, Ian/Bengio, Yoshua/Courville, Aaron, *Deep Learning (Adaptive Computation and Machine Learning series)*, Massachusetts, The MIT Press, 2016, pp. 1–800 ("*Deep learning is a form of machine learning that enables computers to learn from experience and understand the world in terms of a hierarchy of concepts.* Because *the computer gathers knowledge from experience, there is no need for a human computer operator to formally specify all the knowledge that the computer needs. The hierarchy of concepts allows the computer to learn complicated concepts by building them out of simpler ones; a graph of these hierarchies would be many layers deep*"). See also: Chollet, François, *Deep Learning with Python*, Shelter Island, New York, Manning, 2017, pp. 1–384; Franceschetti, Donald R. (Editor), *Principles of Robotics and Artificial Intelligence*, New York, Salem Press, 2018, pp. 1–399. Deep learning is capable of recommending meaningful legal materials. See: Huang, Zihan/Low, Charles/Teng, Mengqiu/Zhang, Hongyi/Ho, Daniel E./Krass, Mark S. et al., "Context-Aware Legal Citation Recommendation Using Deep Learning", *Proceedings of the 18th ACM Internationational Conference on Artificial Intelligence and Law*, 79, 2021.

[347] Aggarwal, C. C., *Neural networks and deep learning*, Heidelberg, Springer, 2018, passim; Agrawal, A., Gans, J., & Goldfarb, A., "Prediction machines (updated and expanded): The simple economics of artificial intelligence", *Harvard Business Review Press*, 2022; Agrawal, A., Gans, J., & Goldfarb, A., "Power and prediction: The disruptive economics of artificial intelligence", *Harvard Business Review Press*, 2022; Bengio, Y., Hinton, G., Yao, A., Song, D., Abbeel, P., Harari, Y. N., Hadfield, G., Russell, S., Kahneman, D., & Mindermann, S., *Managing ai risks in an era of rapid progress*, arXiv preprint arXiv:2310.17688, 2023, passim (on neural networks and deep learning that operate jointly in the age of Artificial Intelligence-embedded technologies).

[348] See: Part II, Chap. 2, Sect. 2.1.1 of this book (undertakes a brief historical account of Artificial Intelligence).

[349] See: Part II, Chap. 2, Sects. 2.1 and 2.1.1 of this book (for further insights on how the human brain and deep neural network function, respectively).

variables[350] are regarded. Deep learning therefore weaves input variables together to produce predictions[351] or forecasts[352] in a nonlinear manner.

§§ I hereby follow the approach of Professors Lehr and Ohm in that there are eight key steps often underlying machine learning, which can be broken down into two workflows: **(i)** «playing with the data» and **(ii)** the «running model».[353]

§§ At one end of the spectrum, playing with the data comprises one meaningful step: problem definition through model training.[354] This the stage in which the great bulk of the data scientist's work comes into play. At the other end of the spectrum—deploying the model in the outer world—the «running model» workflow[355] amounts to a capstone of a thoroughgoing template that seeks to render Artificial Intelligence-embedded technologies (in general) and Machine Learning Algorithms (in particular) both *Controllable* and *Interpretable* to secure *Algorithmic Common Good*.

5.1.2.1 Computer Science: What Is Machine Learning? How Does the Training Stage Unfolds? What Is Objective Function? What Are Algorithmic Rules Developed During the Training Stage? The Examples of Stock Trading, Fraud Detection and Loan Default

§§ Prior to drilling into, and shedding a keen light on, the phases of machine learning, a faint light must be cast upon the definition—and usefulness[356]—of

---

[350] Kleinberg, Jon et al., "Algorithmic Fairness", *AEA Papers & Proceedings*, Volume 108, 2018, pp. 22–23 (discussing, anchored in a batch of national data, that including race as an input variable to a machine-learning college-admissions algorithm both "improves predicted GPAs of admitted students" and can augment "the fraction of admitted students who are black").

[351] Lehr, David/Ohm, Paul, "Playing with the Data: What Legal Scholars Should Learn About Machine Learning", *cit.*, pp. 653–718, whose stellar research I will follow closely.

[352] See: Goodfellow, Ian/Bengio, Youshua/Courville, Aaron, *Deep Learning (Adaptive Computation and Machine Learning Series)*, Massachusetts, MIT Press, 2016, pp. 1–800 (8).

[353] Lehr, David/Ohm, Paul, "Playing with the Data: What Legal Scholars Should Learn About Machine Learning", *cit.*, pp. 653–718.

[354] See: Part V, this chapter, Sects. 5.1.3–5.1.3.1.6 of this book (on the fundamental tenets of model selection). See: Part V, this chapter, Sect. 5.1.3.1.5 of this book (on the central tenets of model tuning). See: Part V, this chapter, Sects. 5.1.4–5.1.4.1.1 of this book (on the central tenets of model training).

[355] Lehr, David/Ohm, Paul, "Playing with the Data: What Legal Scholars Should Learn About Machine Learning", *cit.*, pp. 653–718.

[356] A cohort of scientists, for instance, is using machine learning to pinpoint adjectives tightly interlocked with different ethnic groups across the nineteenth and twentieth centuries to shed a keen light on the history of discrimination. See: Garg, Nikhil et al., "Word Embeddings Quantify 100 Years of Gender and Ethnic Stereotypes", *Proceedings of the National Academy of Sciences of the United States of America*, Volume 115, 2018, E3635. See: Part IV, Chap. 4, Sect. 4.1.8 of this book (on biased word embeddings with an entrenched presence on search engines run by tech moguls). See also: Berk, R. A, *Machine Learning Forecasts of Risk in Criminal Justice Settings*, New York: Springer, 2018; Berk, R. A., H. Heirdari, S. Jabbari, M. Kearns, and A. Roth, "Fairness in Criminal Justice Risk Assessments: The State of the Art." Sociological Methods and Research, 2018; Berk, R. A./A. A. Elzarka, "Almost Politically Acceptable Criminal Justice Risk Assessment", *Criminology and Public Policy*, 2020, pp. 1–28; Berk, R. A./A. K. Kuchibhotla/E. Tchetgen, "Fair

machine learning. Concisely, machine learning amounts to an automated process that seeks to discover **correlations** (interchangeably known as relationships or patterns[357] with a deeply entrenched presence in the dataset) between input variables in a given dataset[358] with a view to make predictions of some[359] outcome of interest.[360]

§§ The whole machine-learning process refers to an ensemble of mathematical steps aimed at attaining the learning stage when exposed to historical or example

---

Risk Algorithms", *Annual Review of Statistics and Its Applications*, 2022. For instance, scholars deployed a machine learning algorithm to challenge the conventional wisdom according to which there are only a limited number of legal traditions (common law and civil law) and a few legal families (the German-Romanic legal family, the francophone legal family, the lusophone legal family and so forth). See: Han-wei Ho/Huang, Patrick Chung-Chia/Garoupa, Nuno/Wells, Martin T./Chang, Yun-chien/Ginsburg, Tom, "Machine-Learning Human Rights", *Journal of Law and Empirical Analysis*, July-December 2024, 2024, pp. 1–19 (1) ("*utilizing a comprehensive panel dataset spanning from 1900 to 2020, this study introduces an innovative methodology for the analysis and categorization of legal documents, specifically national constitutions.* Contrary to the predominant reliance on unsupervised methods within the field, this research incorporates a supervised machine-learning approach, notably the SEMMS method, alongside traditional unsupervised algorithms. This dual approach facilitates a nuanced analysis of the human rights provisions contained within national constitutions, resulting in the identification of both traditional and novel constitutional groupings. *Broadly speaking, the more traditional common law-civil law divide does not seem particularly relevant in this context*") Italics added.

[357] Machine learning "involves computer algorithms *that have the ability to "learn" or improve in performance over time on some task*". Ver: Surden, Harry, "Machine Learning and Law", in: *Washington Law Review*, Volume 89, 2014, pp. 87 e ss; Murphy, Kevin P., *Machine Learning: A Probabilistic Perspective (Adaptive Computation and Machine Learning series)*, Massachusetts, The MIT Press, 2012, pp. 1–1104. Machine learning "*attempts to combine deductive, inductive, and abductive reasoning to make person-like reasoning in AI Entities possible. Machine-learning AI Entities initially learn in the same way a human child learns. First, they notice details and patterns in shapes, sounds, and behaviors*; then put them together to distinguish one person from another, or a dog from a cat. Eventually, the AI can recognize and identify" common objects. See: Hutto-Schultz, Jess, "Dicitur Ex Machina: Artificial Intelligence and the Hearsay Rule", *George Mason Law Review*, Volume 27, n.º 2, 2020, pp. 684–718 (689). See: Part V, this chapter, Sects. 5.1.1.5.2.2–5.1.1.5.2.2.1.4 of this book (on the fundamental shift away from causation to correlations in algorithmic decision-making).

[358] See: Part V, this chapter, Sects. 5.1.1.5.2.2–5.1.1.5.2.2.1.4 of this book (on the fundamental shift away from causation to correlations in algorithmic decision-making). But see: Allen, James, "The Color of Algorithms: An Analysis and Proposed Research Agenda Deterring Algorithmic Redlining", *Fordham Urban Law Journal*, Volume 46, 2019, pp. 219–234 (229–234) (discussing how historical mortgage redlining greatly swayed modern algorithms generated by massive batches of datasets that consist of decades of information built on exclusion and racial discrimination in the purview of financing, marketing, and housing). See: Part IV, Chap. 4, Sects. 4.1.4–4.1.4.2.3 of this book.

[359] Lehr, David/Ohm, Paul, "Playing with the Data: What Legal Scholars Should Learn About Machine Learning", *cit.*, pp. 653–718.

[360] Murphy, Kevin Patrick, *Machine Learning: A Probabilistic Perspective*, Massachusetts, MIT Press, 2012, pp. 1–24 (1) ("[*W*]*e define machine learning as a set of methods that can automatically detect patterns in data, and then use the uncovered patterns to predict future data*, or to perform *other kinds of decision making under uncertainty* (such as planning how to collect more data!)"). Italics added.

data.[361] More often than not, the data is «dirty»[362] or is a rigged[363] data[364] insofar suffers from biases inherited from past decision-making.[365] This process is routinely baptized as «training»[366] the algorithm.[367]

§§ It is important to note that—in pretty much all algorithms, aside from their mathematical technicalities—training takes place through the **optimization of objective function**[368] or **loss function.**[369] Let us briefly break it down. On one hand, what

[361] Lehr, David/Ohm, Paul, "Playing with the Data: What Legal Scholars Should Learn About Machine Learning", *cit.*, pp. 653–718.

[362] Richardson, Rashida, et al., "Dirty Data, Bad Predictions: How Civil Rights Violations Impact Police Data, Predictive Policing Systems, and Justice", *New York University Law Review Online*, Volume 94, 2019, passim.

[363] But see: Barocas, Solon/Selbst, Andrew D., "Big Data's Disparate Impact", *California Law Review*, Volume 104, 2016, pp. 671–682 (discussing how data is often flawed, rigged, incomplete, imperfect and therefore algorithms inherit the prejudice of the original decision makers); Crawford, Kate/Schultz, Jason, "Big Data and Due Process: Toward a Framework to Redress Predictive Privacy Harms", *Boston College Law Review*, Volume 55, 2014, pp. 93, 99–101 (pinpointing pathways through which predictive analytic tools perpetuate discriminatory practices). But see: Bornstein, Stepanhie, "Antidiscriminatory Algorithms", *Alabama Law Review*, Volume 70, 2018, pp. 519, 524–528 (contending, however, that the tagged "facially neutral" algorithms producing discriminatory outcomes should be quashed).

[364] Barocas, Solon/Selbst, Andrew D., "Big Data's Disparate Impact", *California Law Review*, Volume 104, 2016, pp. 671–682 (671) (talk about the role of bias in data and what can be done to unwind its noxious effects).

[365] See, e.g., Eaglin, Jessica M., "Constructing Recidivism Risk", *Emory Law Journal*, Volume 67, 59, 2017, 61 n.1 (arguing that "[p]redictive technologies are spreading through the criminal justice system like wildfire"). None of this is to suggest, nor is to say, that actuarial risk assessment is blazingly new to criminal justice system. Parole boards have long relied on risk-assessment instruments since the 1930s. By the same token, some jurisdictions used algorithms to forecast certain types of crimes, such as sex offenses, for decades past. See: Mason, Sandra G., "Bias in, Bias Out", *Yale Law Journal*, Volume 128 Volume 8, 2019, pp. 2219–2298. But see: Citron, Danielle Keats/Pasquale, Frank, "The Scored Society: Due Process for Automated Predictions", *Washington Law Review*, Volume 89, 2014, pp. 1, 4–5 (highlighting how human beings programming automated systems is directly conducive to, and leads, to fundamentally inaccurate results since the source code, predictive algorithms and datasets may encompass human biases which, in turn, have a disparate impact on historically disadvantaged groups).

[366] Lehr, David/Ohm, Paul, "Playing with the Data: What Legal Scholars Should Learn About Machine Learning", *cit.*, pp. 653–718.

[367] See: Murphy, Kevin Patrick, *Machine Learning: A Probabilistic Perspective*, *cit.*, pp. 1–24 (2).

[368] Lehr, David/Ohm, Paul, "Playing with the Data: What Legal Scholars Should Learn About Machine Learning", *cit.*, pp. 653–718.

[369] See: Alpaydin, Ethem, Introduction to Machine Leaning, Massachusetts, MIT Press, 2nd edition, 2010 ("*The goal of machine learning is to program computers to use example data or past experience to solve a given problem. Many successful applications of machine learning exist already, including systems that analyze past sales data to predict customer behavior, recognize faces or spoken speech, optimize robot behavior so that a task can be completed using minimum resources, and extract knowledge from bioinformatics data.* "Introduction to Machine Learning" is a comprehensive textbook on the subject, covering a broad array of topics not usually included in introductory machine learning texts. It discusses many methods based in different fields, including statistics, pattern recognition, neural networks, artificial intelligence, signal processing, control, and data mining, in order to present a unified treatment of machine learning problems and solutions. All

is an **objective function**? It is neatly a mathematical repercussion of the algorithm's overriding goal. More often than not, there is a dash of accuracy,[370] or inaccuracy, involved in this process.[371] Take, for instance, an algorithm that forecasts whether and to what extent a stock trade has all the trappings of insider trading.[372]

§§ The **objective function** therefore reflects the percentage of transactions the machine algorithm mistakenly flags. Sometimes, the algorithm signals legitimate trades as fraudulent. Sometimes is the other way around since the algorithm routinely

---

learning algorithms are explained so that the student can easily move from the equations in the book to a computer program. The book can be used by advanced undergraduates and graduate students who have completed courses in computer programming, probability, calculus, and linear algebra. It will also be of interest to engineers in the field who are concerned with the application of machine learning methods. After an introduction that defines machine learning and gives examples of machine learning applications, the book covers supervised learning, *Bayesian decision theory, parametric methods, multivariate methods, dimensionality reduction, clustering, nonparametric methods, decision trees, linear discrimination, multilayer perceptrons, local models, hidden Markov models, assessing and comparing classification algorithms, combining multiple learners, and reinforcement learning*"). Italics added. See: Alpaydin, Ethem, *Introduction to Machine Leaning*, cit., pp. 41–42 (discussing a loss function as a dimension of supervised machine-learning algorithms); Berk, Richard A., *Statistical Learning from a Regression Perspective*, Berlin/New York, Springer, 1st Edition, 2008, p. 14 ("Usual practice is to minimize a loss function with [the disparities between the observed response variable values and the fitted response variable values] as inputs"); Becker, Suzanna/Zemel, Richard S., "Unsupervised Learning with Global Objective Functions", *The Handbook of Brain Theory and Neural Networks*, 1st edition, Arbib, Michael A., Massachusetts, MIT Press, pp. 1–1134 (997) ("*The main problem in unsupervised learning research is to formulate a performance measure or cost function for the learning*, to generate this internal supervisory signal. The cost function is also known as an objective function, since it sets the objective for the learning process"). Italics added.

370 But see: Stevenson, Megan/Mayson, Sandra G., "Pretrial Detention and Bail", Luna, Erik, (Editor), *Reforming Criminal Justice: A Report of the Academy for Justice, Bridging the Gap between Scholarship and Reform*, pp. 21, 34–39 (assessing the risk of pretrial risk assessments while highlighting a slew of deep-rooted concerns regarding accuracy, racial-equality, and procedure); See: Chandler, Anupam, "The Racist Algorithm", *Michigan Law Review*, Volume 115, n.º 6, 2018, pp. 1023–1025 (arguing that the real-world facts on which algorithms used in criminal justice risk assessment are based are "deeply suffused with invidious discrimination"); Eaglin, Jessica M., "Constructing Recidivism Risk", *cit.*, pp. 94–99 (argues that risk assessment has every chance to "compromise[e] equality"); Mayson, Sandra G., "Dangerous Defendants", *cit.*, pp. 494–96; Selbst, Andrew D., "Disparate Impact in Big Data Policing", *cit.*, *passim*; Kim, Pauline T., "Data-Driven Discrimination at Work", *William and Mary Law Review*, Volume 58, 2017, pp. 857, 863–64 (shedding a keen light on the racial effects of algorithmic prediction in the remit of employment). Converging: Zywicki, Todd J./Adamson, Joseph D., "The Law and Economics of Subprime Lending", *University of Colorado Law Review*, 2009, pp. 1–9 (contending that Black workers with roughly the same abilities and educational background earn far less than comparable white workers or have considerably fewer employment opportunities); King, Allan G./Markovich, Marko J., "Big Data" and the Risk of Employment Discrimination, *Oklahoma Law Review*, Volume 68, 2016, pp. 555–563 (on employment discrimination). Dobbie, Will, Jacob Goldin, and Crystal S. Yang, "The Effects of Pretrial Detention on Conviction, Future Crime, and Employment: Evidence from Randomly Assigned Judges," *American Economic Review*, Volume 108, 2018, 201–240.

371 Berk, Richard A., *Statistical Learning from a Regression Perspective*, *cit.*, passim; Becker, Suzanna/Zemel, Richard S., "Unsupervised Learning with Global Objective Functions", *cit.*, passim.

372 Lehr, David/Ohm, Paul, "Playing with the Data: What Legal Scholars Should Learn About Machine Learning", *cit.*, pp. 653–718.

flags fraudulent[373] trades as legitimate.[374] With this context in place, what is the meaning of training that occurs through the **optimization of objective function**? It loosely means that the machine algorithm will learn[375] to make predictions[376] such that the pinpointed **objective function** is either minimized or maximized, hinging on how it is concretely identified.[377]

§§ In the stock trading example, the **objective function** was specified in terms of inaccuracy insofar it would be minimized to attain the overriding goal of a reliable, functional, and accurate forecast. To that end, the machine learning algorithm would engage in several possible **optimal predictive rules**, ultimately picking out those that would pave the way to the **minimization** of the **objective function**.[378] Note, though, that after training, «algorithm» and «model» acquire slightly different meanings.[379] In that juncture, they refer to a whole new set of predictively meaningful correlations, routinely deemed as post-training as «rules»,[380] identified during training sessions. Take now, for example, a machine learning algorithm tasked with the chore of forecasting whether and to what extent loan applicants are tagged to default[381] on a loan.[382]

---

[373] See also: Barocas, Solon/Selbst, Andrew, "Big Data's Disparate Impact", *California Law Review*, Volume 104, pp. 2016, pp. 671–678 ("in particular, by exposing so-called 'machine learning' algorithms to examples of the cases of interest (previously identified instances of fraud, spam, default, and poor health), *the algorithm 'learns' which related attributes or activities can serve as potential proxies for those qualities or outcomes of interest*").

[374] Lehr, David/Ohm, Paul, "Playing with the Data: What Legal Scholars Should Learn About Machine Learning", *cit.*, pp. 653–718.

[375] Machine-learning algorithms "*are capable of making intuitive decisions based in newly learned information, much like humans.* The new wave of AI developments will generate powerful AI that is capable of improvising itself, *perhaps even by rewriting its own algorithms, advancing its intelligence beyond that of humans*". Italics added. See: Hutto-Schultz, Jess, "Dicitur Ex Machina: Artificial Intelligence and the Hearsay Rule", *George Mason Law Review*, Volume 27, n.º 2, 2020, pp. 684–718 (684).

[376] Lehr, David/Ohm, Paul, "Playing with the Data: What Legal Scholars Should Learn About Machine Learning", *cit.*, pp. 653–718.

[377] Lehr, David/Ohm, Paul, "Playing with the Data: What Legal Scholars Should Learn About Machine Learning", *cit.*, pp. 653–718.

[378] Lehr, David/Ohm, Paul, "Playing with the Data: What Legal Scholars Should Learn About Machine Learning", *cit.*, pp. 653–718.

[379] Lehr, David/Ohm, Paul, "Playing with the Data: What Legal Scholars Should Learn About Machine Learning", *cit.*, pp. 653–718.

[380] See: Barocas, Solon/Selbst, Andrew, "Big Data's Disparate Impact", *cit.*, passim (referring throughout to a batch of predictive "rules" inferred by a trained machine learning algorithm).

[381] But see: The Use of Cash-Flow Data in Underwriting Credit: Empirical Research Findings, FINREGLAB 32, 34 (Jul. 2019), https://finreglab.org/wp-content/uploads/2019/07/FRL_Research-Report_Final.pdf [https://perma.cc/N65Q-WQML] (arguing that the use of cash flow data can underpin a prediction of default risk, thereby providing an apposite alternative to ancient credit scores. In addition to that, cash-flow data is commensurate with predictive across demographic groups).

[382] Lehr, David/Ohm, Paul, "Playing with the Data: What Legal Scholars Should Learn About Machine Learning", *cit.*, pp. 653–718.

§§ During the training stage, the machine learning algorithm may have come to terms with the fact that individuals with over twenty thousand dollars in credit card debt, can't keep a job, and have three to five offsprings will in all likelihood default in the forthcoming future. This algorithmic rule could subsequently be deployed by the trained machine learning algorithm when it is tasked with the functional duty to make forecasts in the real world. As a result, persons with twenty-thousand dollars in credit card debt, no job, and three to five offsprings would be forecasted as defaulting on a loan.[383]

5.1.2.2 Supervised Machine Learning Algorithms: The Example of Self-Driving Cars

§§ It is worth recalling that machine learning algorithms seek to forecast or predict something. It is therefore pivotally important to shed a keen light on its inner workings and how it should be estimated. Broadly speaking, algorithms can be broken down between *unsupervised machine learning algorithms* and *supervised machine learning algorithms*. Let us bring supervised machine learning algorithms into a sharper focus. Supervised machine learning algorithms are ascribed a labelled outcome variable (coined interchangeably as *output* or *response variable*)[384] reflecting the true values to be forecasted based on input data.[385] By and large, supervised machine learning algorithms[386] and the definition of outcome variable are intertwined to the extent that they are woven of the same cloth.[387] It is important to note, though, that outcome variables can acquire many shapes.[388]

§§ Tellingly, outcome variables can be framed as binary indicators—True/False, Yes/No, and so forth—and machine learning algorithms forecasting binary outcomes are routinely baptized as «classification» algorithms.[389] **Classification algorithms**

---

[383] Lehr, David/Ohm, Paul, "Playing with the Data: What Legal Scholars Should Learn About Machine Learning", *cit.*, pp. 653–718.

[384] Lehr, David/Ohm, Paul, "Playing with the Data: What Legal Scholars Should Learn About Machine Learning", *cit.*, pp. 653–718.

[385] Murphy, Kevin Patrick, *Machine Learning: A Probabilistic Perspective*, *cit.*, pp. 1–24 (2–4).

[386] See: Hardt, M., Price E, Srebro N, "Equality of opportunity in supervised learning", ArXiv ID: 1610.02413v1, 2016; Friston, K. J., Da Costa, L., Tschantz, A., Kiefer, A., Salvatori, T., Neacsu, V., & Buckley, C. L. "Supervised structure learning", arXiv preprint arXiv:2311.10300, 2023. See also: Friedman, J. H., & Popescu, B. E., "Predictive learning via rule ensembles", *Annals of Applied Statistics*, Volume 2, Issue 3, pp. 2008, pp. 916–954; Friston, K., & Kiebel, S., "Predictive coding under the free-energy principle", *Philosophical Transactions of the Royal Society B: Biological Sciences*, 364 (1521), 2009, pp. 1211–1221.

[387] See: Barocas, Solon/Selbst, Andrew, "Big Data's Disparate Impact", *cit.*, pp. 677–680 (drilling into, and shedding light on, the process and perceived difficulties of crafting the outcome variable for supervised machine learning algorithms).

[388] Lehr, David/Ohm, Paul, "Playing with the Data: What Legal Scholars Should Learn About Machine Learning", *cit.*, pp. 653–718.

[389] Murphy, Kevin Patrick, *Machine Learning: A Probabilistic Perspective*, *cit.*, p. 2.

unfold itself in either «multiple classification» or «multi-label classification» algorithms, which are tasked with the duty to forecast indicators with more than two classes. Examples range from Pedestrian/Cyclist/Tree, Red/ to Green/Blue,[390] etc.[391]

§§ Aside from classification algorithms, machine learning algorithms applied to «regression» problems forecast an ever-lasting quantitative outcome—one that can take shape of, and acquire, any given numeric[392] value.[393]

§§ It bears mentioning that conceptually kindred to both classification and regression machine learning algorithms are those that fundamentally measure ordinal outcomes. Meaning, outcomes with multifarious classes that, although not falling within a continuous number line, have some inherent ordering, such as Cold/Warm/Hot or 1/2/3 or First/[394] Second/Third.[395] Which begs the vexing question: How do programmers determine an outcome variable? Essentially, undertaking such a task amount to a translating exercise whereby abstract goals are converted into fully measurable outcomes.[396] A couple of meaningful steps deserve to be remarked upon[397] in this regard.[398]

---

[390] Lehr, David/Ohm, Paul, "Playing with the Data: What Legal Scholars Should Learn About Machine Learning", *cit.*, pp. 653–718.

[391] Murphy, Kevin Patrick, *Machine Learning: A Probabilistic Perspective*, *cit.*, p. 3.

[392] Lehr, David/Ohm, Paul, "Playing with the Data: What Legal Scholars Should Learn About Machine Learning", *cit.*, pp. 653–718.

[393] See: Murphy, Kevin Patrick, *Machine Learning: A Probabilistic Perspective*, *cit.*, pp. 8–9. It is noteworthy that the use of the term "regression" here is not meant to imply anything about the math of a machine-learning algorithm applied to predict a continuous outcome variable. Whilst there are some machine-learning methods that use a least squares-based **objective function or loss function** and, thus, resemble a general linear model mathematically, others bear less of a resemblance. See: Lehr, David/Ohm, Paul, "Playing with the Data: What Legal Scholars Should Learn About Machine Learning", *University of California, Davis*, Volume 51, 2017, pp. 653–718, which, recall, I will follow closely. See also: Berk, Richard A., *Statistical Learning from a Regression Perspective*, *cit.*, p. 301 ("Support vector machines (SVM) will seem somewhat far afield from the [regression-related] statistical learning procedures discussed to this point... [but] [*s*]*upport vector machines now can have more the look and feel of regression*"). Italics added.

[394] Lehr, David/Ohm, Paul, "Playing with the Data: What Legal Scholars Should Learn About Machine Learning", *cit.*, pp. 653–718.

[395] Murphy, Kevin Patrick, *Machine Learning: A Probabilistic Perspective*, *cit.*, p. 2.

[396] Lehr, David/Ohm, Paul, "Playing with the Data: What Legal Scholars Should Learn About Machine Learning", *cit.*, pp. 653–718.

[397] Lehr, David/Ohm, Paul, "Playing with the Data: What Legal Scholars Should Learn About Machine Learning", *cit.*, pp. 653–718.

[398] Scholars assume throughout this section that the data scientist in question has the practical ability to glean his/her own dataset, thereby creating *ex novo* the outcome variable in the algorithmic decision-making. Note, though, that there may be instances in which this is not entirely possible. Corporations at large might have pre-existing databases, and data to be fed into a machine-learning algorithm may, in practical terms, have to be curled from the foregoing databases. Lehr, David/Ohm, Paul, "Playing with the Data: What Legal Scholars Should Learn About Machine Learning", *cit.*, pp. 653–718.

§§ Firstly, and to begin with, the abstract goal must be converted into a decision about what, concretely, to[399] forecast.[400] On this note, a self-driving car programmer might set the overriding goal of producing a car that reduces human casualties. Part of attaining this overriding goal might entail the creation of a machine learning algorithm embedded within the self-driving vehicle[401] that equips it to forecast whether and to what extent objects in its surroundings are, for instance, obstacles of some sort, pedestrians, physical barriers, animals,[402] or trees,[403] and the list goes on.

§§ Strikingly, in the previous example, a developer has travelled all way from an abstract goal to a predictive goal. Secondly, the developer must convert the predictive goal to a clearly determined outcome variable. Note, though, that the ease with which

---

399 Lehr, David/Ohm, Paul, "Playing with the Data: What Legal Scholars Should Learn About Machine Learning", *cit.*, pp. 653–718.

400 See: Berk, Richard A. et al., "Forecasting Domestic Violence: A Machine Learning Approach to Help Inform Arraignment Decisions", *Journal of Empirical Legal Studies*, Volume 13, 2016, pp. 94, 94–96 (drilling into, and shedding light on, how, when devising a machine learning algorithm to inform courts' decisions of whether to release those arrested for domestic violence between their arraignments and court hearings—the sweeping goal is to falloff the looming threat to public safety, as enshrined in the Bail Reform Act of 1984, which pundits translate into the predictive goal of foretelling whether those arrested will engage in future domestic violence if released). Lehr, David/Ohm, Paul, "Playing with the Data: What Legal Scholars Should Learn About Machine Learning", *cit.*, pp. 653–718. It is worth recalling that Sam Corbett-Davies and peers, parsing the same Broward County data that *ProPublica* did, concluded that attaining parity in **false-positive rates** while still optimizing for public safety (and without detaining any other defendants) would beget a 7% uptick in violent crime. See: Corbett-Davies, Sam/Pierson, Emma/Feller, Avi/Goel, Sharad Goel/Huq, Aziz, "Algorithmic Decision Making and the Cost of Fairness", *Proceedings of the 23rd ACM SIGKDD International Conference on Knowledge Discovery and Data Mining* (Ass'n for Computing Machinery ed., 2017), 2017, p. 802. Moreover, 17% of those detained would be low-risk people for whom detention was either unwarranted or uncalled for. Mayson, Sandra G., "Bias In, Bias Out", *cit.*, pp. 2218–2300.

401 The worrisome challenges posed by the up-and-coming and rough around the edges self-driving cars. See: Teoh, Eric/Kidd, David G., "Rage Against the Machine? Google's Self-Driving Versus Human Drivers", *Journal of Safety Research*, Volume 63, 2019, pp. 57–59 and passim (on the legal quandaries laid bare by the self-driving cars). See also: Cracking the Code: the Black Box Problem of Ai, available at: https://scads.ai/cracking-the-code-the-black-box-problem-of-ai/ (access: 21.09.2024) ("Artificial intelligence (AI) is increasingly becoming integrated into our daily lives, from virtual assistants to self-driving cars. Despite AI having the potential to revolutionize the way we live and work, it also presents unique challenges. One of the most significant challenges is the "black box" problem. *The black box problem refers to the lack of transparency and interpretability of AI algorithms. As a matter of fact, it is difficult to understand how an AI system arrives at its conclusions or predictions. This poses a significant challenge. Decisions made by AI can have serious consequences, such as in healthcare or financial sectors*"). Italics added.

402 Lehr, David/Ohm, Paul, "Playing with the Data: What Legal Scholars Should Learn About Machine Learning", *cit.*, pp. 653–718.

403 It goes without saying that this an overly simplistic example of how object recognition—within the remit of computer vision—transpires in autonomous vehicles, but it is illustrative nonetheless. Lehr, David/Ohm, Paul, "Playing with the Data: What Legal Scholars Should Learn About Machine Learning", *cit.*, pp. 653–718. See: Part III, Chap. 3, Sects. 3.1.5.9–3.1.5.9.3 of this book (on Critical Artificial Intelligence Studies, with a sharper focus on the functional shortcomings facing self-driving vehicles).

this meaningful step can be swiftly achieved hinges on how distant the predictive goal is from a clearly determined outcome variable.[404]

§§ To illustrate, take the self-driving car for example. In this regard, the predictive goal—specifying whether and to what extent an object is a pedestrian, a physical barrier, an obstacle, a traffic sign, animal, or a tree—shapes the form of that output variable; it will most likely be a categorical variable with three classes, and each of the classes will be immediately codable by a human developer to produce training data.[405]

§§ However, this isn't all always the case. Take a prison altercation for example. Here, the overriding predictive goal is forecasting individuals' potentials for routinely engaging in acts of violence. Which prompts the question: what type of outcome variable could faithfully embody this concept? There are several possibilities: **(i)** a binary variable strongly suggesting an individual's participation in a violent altercation within his/her first year of incarceration; **(ii)** a continuous variable strongly suggesting how many times a given individual is embroiled in a violent altercation during the aggregate time of his/her incarceration[406]; **(iii)** a continuous variable strongly suggesting the average number of altercations in which an inmate partook per year of his[407]/her incarceration.[408]

§§ But things can get even more difficult. Imagine, if you will, that an employer is a decisionmaker whose predictive goal is pinpoint excellent employees.[409] What type of outcome variable reliably measures the «goodness»[410] of an employee or

---

[404] Lehr, David/Ohm, Paul, "Playing with the Data: What Legal Scholars Should Learn About Machine Learning", *cit.*, pp. 653–718.

[405] Lehr, David/Ohm, Paul, "Playing with the Data: What Legal Scholars Should Learn About Machine Learning", *cit.*, pp. 653–718.

[406] Lehr, David/Ohm, Paul, "Playing with the Data: What Legal Scholars Should Learn About Machine Learning", *cit.*, pp. 653–718.

[407] Lehr, David/Ohm, Paul, "Playing with the Data: What Legal Scholars Should Learn About Machine Learning", *cit.*, pp. 653–718.

[408] See: Berk, Richard A. et al., "Forecasting Domestic Violence: A Machine Learning Approach to Help Inform Arraignment Decisions", cit., pp. 98–99 (discussing how stakeholder input factored into deciding the type of the outcome variable reflecting future domestic violence, both in terms of specifying it as a three-class variable forecasting future arrest after arraignment and assessing that arrest two years after arraignment). Lehr, David/Ohm, Paul, "Playing with the Data: What Legal Scholars Should Learn About Machine Learning", *cit.*, pp. 653–718.

[409] See: Barocas, Solon/Selbst, Andrew, "Big Data's Disparate Impact", *cit.*, *passim.*

[410] Finnis, John, *Natural Law and Natural Rights*, *cit.*, p. 3 ("There are **human goods** that can be *secured only through the institutions of human law, and requirements of practical reasonableness that only those institutions can satisfy*. It is the object of this book to identify those goods, and those requirements *of practical reasonableness, and thus to show how and on what conditions such institutions are justified and the ways in which they can be (and often are) defective*"). Italics and bold added; Popovic, Peter, "The Three Levels of Law's Goodness and Then One More: Exploring John Finnis's Account of Good Juridical Reasons for Action," *Persona y Derecho*, Volume 83, 2020, pp. 521–552, later reprinted in Popovic, Peter, *The Goodness of Rights and the Juridical Domain of the Good: Essays in Thomistic Juridical Realism*, Roma: EDUSC, 2021, 125–156 (delves into the multifarious levels of practical goodness in Finnis's blueprint).

even the «suitability»[411] of a «good tenant»[412] or an «undesirable tenant»[413]? Is that the promotion of the employee? Is that the span of time the employee stays with

---

[411] But see: *Tech, Bias and Housing Initiative, the Promise and Perils of Residential Proptech, Year 1, Research Summary Report, April 2023, TechEquity Collaborative*, p. 10, available at: https://techequity.us/wp-content/uploads/2023/04/TBHI-Y1-Research-Summary-Report.pdf (28.11.2024). ("**Opaque, Predictive Algorithms Determine Who Gets What Housing Unlike Analog Models**, *Algorithmic Tenant Screening Tools Predict Future Behavior To Determine Housing Access As landlord tech took hold, more property managers of all sizes came to rely on it to interface with tenants. One key feature of landlord tech is the use of algorithms to screen rental applicants and assess their suitability as tenants. The tenant screening industry, which pulls a wide array of information about potential tenants to inform landlords' decisions, is now valued at $1.3 billion with as many as two thousand screening companies vying for market share.*10 11 *Such companies include Equifax, TransUnion, and Experian (commonly known as "The Big Three"), as well as smaller startup companies that apply algorithms to make those determinations faster*"). Italics added. See: Part IV, Chap. 4, Sects. 4.1.4–4.1.4.2.3 of this book. See also: *Tech, Bias and Housing Initiative, the Promise and Perils of Residential Proptech, Year 1, Research Summary Report, April 2023, TechEquity Collaborative*, p. 11, available at: https://techequity.us/wp-content/uploads/2023/04/TBHI-Y1-Research-Summary-Report.pdf (28.11.2024). ("*From information on company websites, it is not clear what analysis or data is behind subjective determinations like "suitability" to a unit or what the nexus between an individual's characteristics and a unit's characteristics is that indicates the likelihood for property damage. Based on sample reports, even landlords are not privy to how the determinations are made. Instead, they receive a risk score out of 100 simplified into green, yellow, and red recommendations.* What companies withhold in terms of how it works, they make up for with the extent to which they tell landlords it works: Naborly claims their predictions reduce lease defaults by up to 89%. 15 *As Naborly's sample report demonstrates, its property damage assessment is then used as an input to determine its projected eviction outcomes; its early vacancy prediction, in turn, is based on "all assessment factors"*"). Italics added.

[412] See: Power, Emma R., and Charles Gillon, "Performing the 'Good Tenant'", *Housing Studies*, Volume 37, Issue 3, 2020, pp. 459–82 (459) ("*Renters in homeowner societies like Australia, the United States and United Kingdom occupy a complex moral landscape, maligned for failure to achieve homeownership but pivotal to the value of investment properties. Identification of 'good' and 'risky' tenants is an important landlord practice (…) The good tenant demonstrates responsibility through paying rent on time and property stewardship (reporting repairs, making home). However, these practices are made necessary and risky through limited tenure security. The emotional and financial risks attending performances of the good tenant drive paradoxical relations; a good tenant is also acquiescent and silent, not reporting property repairs or lapsed leases to avoid rent increases and/or evictions.* Variegated performances of the '*good tenant' reflect cultural property norms and valorize the investment function of housing yet could also productively unsettle tenant-landlord relations*"). Italics added. See: Part IV, Chap. 4, Sects. 4.1.4–4.1.4.2.3 of this book.

[413] But see: Wonyoung, So, "Which Information Matters? Measuring Landlord Assessment of Tenant Screening Reports", *Housing Policy Debate*, Volume 33, n.° 6, 2023, pp. 1484–1510 (1500) (arguing that many landlords file evictions (eviction fillings) with no intention whatsoever of proceeding with its execution (executed evictions) only to purposefully harm an undesirable tenant, which casts a shady shadow on the eviction records, which, in turn, lack accuracy. "*With regards to eviction records, one of the most noticeable harms this study identifies is that during the tenant screening process, landlords do not distinguish between eviction filings and actually executed evictions. This is particularly alarming given that many landlords file numerous evictions without the intention of or a sound rationale for actually evicting tenants* (Garboden and Rosen 2019). *Furthermore, this study replicates the finding of "professional solidarity" among landlords* (Garboden and Rosen 2019, p. 647). *Eviction filings are a tacit tenant screening measure meant to issue a warning*

the corporation?[414] Is that the amount of overtime hours the employee works? But here is the deeper truth: more often than not, the true value of the **predictive goal**—i.e. happiness, overall satisfaction, job performance,[415] sadness, human dignity,[416] reliability, human flourishing, dexterity, ambition, stamina—is not amenable to be gauged at all. To offset such a perceived shortcoming, the best that the developers are able to do is to ferret out a decent proxy.[417] All too often, though, developers and

---

to other landlords against taking on the tenant in question (Garboden and Rosen 2019; Leung et al. 2021). *Furthermore, landlords often file multiple evictions on the same tenant—this is frequently called "serial filing"* (Immergluck et al. 2020; Leung et al. 2021). *As a result, in Washington, DC, for example, among all eviction records, only 5.5% of evictions filed in 2018 were executed* (McCabe and Rosen 2020). *This means that 94.5% of filed evictions were not executed. As this study has shown, those records may be interpreted, erroneously, as evictions by landlords and will likely still negatively affect tenants' future housing search* (Phillips, 2020)"). Italics added. See: Part IV, Chap. 4, Sects. 4.1.4–4.1.4.2.3 of this book. See: Part IV, Chap. 4, Sects. 4.1.4–4.1.4.2.1 of this book (on mortgage redlining). See: Part IV, Chap. 4, Sects. 4.1.2–4.1.4.3 of this book (on algorithmic credit scoring, consumer racism and credit card redlining). See: Part IV, Chap. 4, Sects. 4.1.4–4.1.4.2.3 of this book (on algorithmic redlining). See: Part IV, Chap. 4, Sects. 4.1.4.3 of this book (on "algorithmic redliking"). See: Part IV, Chap. 4, Sect. 4.1.3 of this book (on algorithmic prime-lining).

414 But see: King, Allan G./Markovich, Marko J., "Big Data" and the Risk of Employment Discrimination, *Oklahoma Law Review*, Volume 68, 2016, pp. 555–563 (on employment discrimination).

415 See: Grimmelmann, James/Westreich, Daniel, "Incomprehensible Discrimination", *California Law Review Online*, Volume 7, 2017, pp. 170 and ff and passim. This exciting piece of research revolves around as a vignette and mock judicial opinion, focusing on fictional case (an employment-based AI employed in the fictional universe of the movie Zootopia) under a specific legal regime (Title VII). It ultimately solves this fictional case by drawing a difference between *proxy discrimination* and *disparate impact* p. 70 ("The problem is that there is no explanation in the record as to which of these two correlations, if either, is causal. It may be that the factors directly measure applicant characteristics that determine success in the challenging and dangerous field of police work, and that those characteristics happen to be unequally distributed in our diverse society. It may also be that these factors are instead measuring applicants' species and that they measure likely job performance only because they are identifying species in an applicant pool where the relevant characteristics are unequally distributed"); Citron, Danielle Keats/Pasquale, Frank, "The Scored Society: Due Process for Automated Predictions", *Washington Law Review*, Volume 89, 2014, pp. 1, 4–5 (highlighting how human beings programming automated systems is directly conducive to, and leads, to fundamentally inaccurate results since the source code, predictive algorithms and datasets may encompass human biases which, in turn, have a disparate impact on historically disadvantaged groups).

416 Human dignity is a Kantian-inspired notion, which were to send ripples across cultures of dignity, mainly from the fundamental rights standpoint. In German doctrine: Ramm, Thilo, "Die sozialen Grundrechte im Verfassungsgefüge", in: *Soziale Grundrechte – 5. Rechtspolitischer Kongress der SPD vom 29. Februar bis 2. März 1980 in Saarbrüchen*, Heidelberg/Karlsruhe, 1981, pp. 28–32; in Portuguese doctrine, Botelho, Catarina Santos, "40 anos de Direitos Sociais: uma reflexão sobre o papel dos Direitos Fundamentais Sociais no Sèculo XXI", *Julgar*, 29, 2016, pp. 197 ff. In French doctrine: Fierens, Jacques, "La dignitè humaine comme concept juridique", *Journal des tribunaux*, 121, 2002, pp. 578–580; Carvalho, Natalia Brigagão Ferrer Alves, "Catholic Social Thought, Politics and Human Dignity in the Brazilian Constitutional Assembly of 1987–1988", *The American Journal of Legal History*, 1, 2019, 1–30; Taekema, Sanne, "The Procedural Rule of Law: Examining Waldron's Argument on Dignity and Agency", cit.: 140 ff (arguing that the «Rule of Law serves the value of human dignity»).

417 But see: Prince, Anya E. R./Schwarcz, Daniel, "Proxy Discrimination in the Age of Artificial Intelligence and Big Data", *Iowa Law Review*, Volume 105, 1257, 2020, pp. 1279–1281 ("*[P]roxy*

stakeholders[418] alike engage in an activity commonly known as «evidence[419]-based policymaking» while losing sight of the unbreakable ceiling limit capping targeting

---

discrimination will tend to occur when a suspect variable is predictive of a desired outcome only because it proxies for another, quantifiable and potentially available, *variable that causes the desired outcome but that is not included in the AI's training data*"). Italics added. See: Part IV, Chap. 4, Sect. 4.1.6.3 of this book (on proxy discrimination).

[418] See: Kim, Pauline T., "Data-Driven Discrimination at Work", *William & Mary Law Review*, Volume 58, 2017, 857–860 ("Employers are increasingly relying on data analytic tools to make personnel decisions"). See: Prince, Anya ER/Schwarcz, Daniel, "Proxy Discrimination in the Age of Artificial Intelligence and Big Data", *cit.*, p. 1316 ("[O]ne possible solution is to require those employing algorithms to convince regulators or others of causal connections between the variables utilized and the desired outcome"). See also: Grimmelmann, James/Westreich, Daniel, "Incomprehensible Discrimination", *California Law Review Online*, Volume 7, 2017, p. 15 ("Where a model has a disparate impact, our test in effect requires an employer to explain why its model is not just a mathematically sophisticated proxy for a protected characteristic"); Kim, Pauline T., "Data-Driven Discrimination at Work", *cit.*, p. 921 ("*The existence of a statistical correlation should not be sufficient. Instead, because the employer's justification for using an algorithm amounts to a claim that it actually predicts something relevant to the job*, the employer should carry the burden of demonstrating that statistical bias does not plague the underlying model"). Italics added. See also: Roberts, Jessica L./Weeks Elizabeth, *Healthism: Health Status Discrimination and the Law*, Cambridge, Cambridge University Press, 2019, pp. 1–230 (pp. 110 and ff and passim) ("*Can an employer refuse to hire someone who tests positive for nicotine or alcohol? Can an airline or movie theatre require overweight customers to purchase two seats? Can a health insurance company refuse to sell policies to those most in need of medical care? Can the government condition public assistance on wellness program participation or work activity*? In this illuminating book, Jessica L. Roberts and Elizabeth Weeks consider these and similar questions, offering readers a nuanced analysis of when and why discrimination based on health status - or 'healthism' - should be allowed, and when it should not. *They provide a methodology to distinguish desirable health-based classifications from the undesirable, and propose law and policy solutions to encourage the former and limit the latter. This work should be read by anyone concerned with how government does - and does not - regulate based on health*"). Italics added.

[419] But see: Tyler, Tom, "Methodology in Legal Research", in: *Utrecht Law Review*, Volume 13, Issue 3, 2017, pp. 130–131 ("*Accurate facts plus good legal rules lead to substantive justice.* This is the normative framework of right and wrong defined by traditional legal analysis. *Risk analysis is a nice example of the benefits of empiricism because studies suggest that the use of empirical methods to assess future dangerousness is more accurate than is the use of human intuition. It is better to use a formula when making a legal decision that involves estimates of someone's likely future conduct than it is to rely upon the impressions of judges or prosecutors*" (…) "*The legal system relies on predictions about people's likely future behaviour at many points in the system*: pretrial detention; sentencing; parole and probation; etc. And it has been used with a variety of special populations, including juveniles; the mentally ill; and sexual predators. *A key reason to use such quantitative methods is that they are better able to predict future behaviour and as a consequence the many points in the system at which judgments are made – pre-trial detention; sentencing; parole – are better able to enact justice for both the innocent and the guilty. The focus by social scientists upon helping to identify and use facts in ways that produce more accurate decisions fits well with the argument that the aims of justice are best served when they are based upon accurate factual information. Accuracy, in turn is enhanced by the use of empirical methods. Facts are sought that can guide the application of normative legal principles*"). Italics added.

policy that dictates that predictive goals should be geared towards something tangible that can be reliably measured.[420]

§§ Of note, there is a cluster of different factors that come into play in this regard. To begin with, data scientists must abide by an agreed-upon quality benchmark before determining the true value of a predictive goal. A few consecutives steps must be followed to ensure accuracy. Firstly, it is pivotally important that the data scientists have a high degree of knowledge on a given area.[421]

§§ Crucially, those with a deeply entrenched presence in a specific context may possess institutional knowledge that would bestow upon them solid reasons to believe that, for instance, employee tenure is the primal indicator of quality employee, as opposed to promotion. Secondly, there are quite a few technical steps to be mindful of and to be keenly cognizant of. To name just the most prominent one, different machine learning algorithms have the ability to work with different outcome variable forms and creating different kinds of supplementary output for different outcome variable[422] forms.

§§ Therefore, there should a strategic alignment between a bespoke machine-learning algorithm to accomplish the predictive goal at hand, a specific type of algorithmic output and the choice for a suitably tailored specified outcome variable.[423] Failing which, the room for disparate impact,[424] with a sharper focus on discrimination,[425] is humongous. And that is something stakeholders should shy

[420] Lehr, David/Ohm, Paul, "Playing with the Data: What Legal Scholars Should Learn About Machine Learning", *cit.*, pp. 653–718.

[421] Lehr, David/Ohm, Paul, "Playing with the Data: What Legal Scholars Should Learn About Machine Learning", *cit.*, pp. 653–718.

[422] Lehr, David/Ohm, Paul, "Playing with the Data: What Legal Scholars Should Learn About Machine Learning", *cit.*, pp. 653–718.

[423] Lehr, David/Ohm, Paul, "Playing with the Data: What Legal Scholars Should Learn About Machine Learning", *cit.*, pp. 653–718.

[424] See: Prince, Anya ER/Schwarcz, Daniel, "Proxy Discrimination in the Age of Artificial Intelligence and Big Data", *cit.*, p. 1316 ("[O]ne possible solution is to require those employing algorithms to convince regulators or others of causal connections between the variables utilized and the desired outcome"). Grimmelmann, James/Westreich, Daniel, "Incomprehensible Discrimination", *California Law Review Online*, Volume 7, 2017, p. 15 ("Where a model has *a disparate impact*, our test in effect requires an employer to explain why its model is not just a mathematically sophisticated proxy for a protected characteristic"). Italics added. Kim, Pauline T., "Data-Driven Discrimination at Work", *William and Mary Law Review*, Volume 58, 2017, p. 921 ("*The existence of a statistical correlation should not be sufficient. Instead, because the employer's justification for using an algorithm amounts to a claim that it actually predicts something relevant to the job*, the employer should carry the burden of demonstrating *that statistical bias does not plague the underlying model*"). Italics added.

[425] But see: Kilbertus, Niki/Carulla, Mateo Rojas/Parascandolo, Giambattista/Hardt, Moritz/Janzing, Dominik/ Schoellkopf, Bernhard, "Avoiding Discrimination through Causal Reasoning", *Advances in Neural Information Processing Systems*, I. Guyon, U. V. Luxburg, S. Bengio, H. Wallach, R. Fergus, S. Vishwanathan, and R. Garnett (Eds.), Vol. 30. Curran Associates, Inc., 2017, pp. 656–666 (arguing that is feasible to avoiding discrimination through a granular and fine-grained causal reasoning).

away from. These deep-rooted concerns on the entropies caused by technology are neither unwarranted nor uncalled for.

§§ Compellingly, certain outcome variable specifications, including ones purportedly profiling good employees, can[426] indeed exacerbate[427] both historical societal biases[428] and structural disadvantage.[429]

---

[426] Lehr, David/Ohm, Paul, "Playing with the Data: What Legal Scholars Should Learn About Machine Learning", *cit.*, pp. 653–718.

[427] See also: Hellman, Deborah, "Indirect Discrimination and the Duty to Avoid Compounding Injustice", *Foundations of Indirect Discrimination Law*, Collins, Hugh/Khaitan, Tarunabh (Editors), Oxford, Hart Publishing; Reprint edition (June 25, 2020), 2020, p. 107 (Professor Deborah Hellman coined this expression to depict a decision that "exacerbates the harm caused by the prior injustice because it entrenches the harm or carries it into another domain." This book deals with the sweltering topic of indirect discrimination ("*indirect discrimination (or disparate impact) concerns the application of the same rule to everyone, even though that rule significantly disadvantages one particular group in society*"). Italics added.

[428] See: Barocas, Solon/Selbst, Andrew, "Big Data's Disparate Impact", *cit.*, pp. 681–84. But see: Benjamin, Ruha, *Race After Technology: Abolitionist Tools for the New Jim Code*, New York, Polity, 2019, pp. 1–172 (7) (discussing that Artificial Intelligence-embedded technologies are viewed as iron-clad tools of objectivity and devoid of any biases whatsoever). Ruha Benjamin accordingly contends that "the employment of new technologies that reflect and reproduce existing inequities but that are promoted and perceived as more objective or progressive than the discriminatory systems of a previous era"). But see also: Hurley, Mikella/Adebayo, Julius, "Credit Scoring in the Era of Big Data", *Yale Journal of Law and Technology*, Volume 18, 2016, p. 149 ("*these tools may furthermore obscure discriminatory and subjective lending policies behind a single "objective" score (…) sophisticated algorithms may combine facially neutral data points and treat them as proxies for immutable characteristics such as race or gender, thereby circumventing existing non-discrimination laws and systematically denying credit access to certain groups. Finally, big-data tools may allow online payday lenders to target the most vulnerable consumers and lure them into debt traps*"). Italics added. But see also: Bornstein, Stepanhie, "Antidiscriminatory Algorithms", *Alabama Law Review*, Volume 70, 2018, pp. 519, 524–528 (contending, however, that the tagged "facially neutral" algorithms producing discriminatory outcomes should be quashed). See also: Farina, M./Lavazza, A., *Philosophy, expertise, and the myth of* neutrality, Routledge Studies in Contemporary Philosophy, London, Routledge, 2024. See also: Areheart, Bradley A./Roberts, Jessica L., "GINA, Big Data, and the Future of Employee Privacy", *Yale Law Journal*, Volume 128, 2019, pp. 710–716 (fleshing out the fundamental tenets of the GINA law).

[429] See: Kim, Pauline T., "Data-Driven Discrimination at Work", *cit.*, p. 866 ("classification bias occurs when employers rely on classification schemes, such as data algorithms, to sort or score workers in ways that worsen inequality or disadvantage along the lines of race, sex, or other protected characteristics"). These two uses of the word "bias" correspond to the notions of irrational versus rational **(or statistical) discrimination.** See: Mayson, Sandra G., "Bias In, Bias Out", *cit.*, pp. 2218–2300. See also: *Tech, Bias and Housing Initiative, the Promise and Perils of Residential Proptech, Year 1, Research Summary Report, April 2023, TechEquity Collaborative*, p. 11, available at: https://techequity.us/wp-content/uploads/2023/04/TBHI-Y1-Research-Summary-Report.pdf (28.11.2024) ("*Once bad data enters the analysis of one factor, it gets baked into the subsequent process, multiplying the effect that one disadvantageous data point can have on someone's overall housing determination*"). Italics added. See: Part IV, Chap. 4, Sects. 4.4–4.4.2.3 of this book. See: Part IV, Chap. 4, Sects. 4.1.4–4.4.2.1 of this book (on mortgage redlining). See: Part IV, Chap. 4, Sects. 4.1.2–4.1.4.3 of this book (on algorithmic credit scoring, consumer racism and credit card redlining). See: Part IV, Chap. 4, Sects. 4.1.4–4.1.4.2.3 of this book (on algorithmic redlining). See: Part IV, Chap. 4, Sect. 4.1.4.3 of this book (on "algorithmic redliking"). See: Part IV, Chap. 4, Sect. 4.1.3 of this book (on algorithmic prime-lining).

5.1.2.3 Unsupervised Machine Learning Algorithms That Clusters Subjects Based on How Similar Its Input Data Values Are

§§ Machine learning goes way beyond supervised learning.[430] Unlike supervised machine learning algorithms, unsupervised learning algorithms shy away from forecasting outcome variables labelled with ground truth. Quite the opposite, they amass or weave subjects together based, casts broadly, on the degree to which they evince similarities[431] with their underlying input data values.[432] Note, though, that the groups arising out of an unsupervised machine learning algorithm can serve as classes forecasted by a supervised[433] algorithm.[434] As far as unsupervised machine learning algorithm is concerned, the **problem definition** requires choosing a specific mathematical measure of similarity.[435]

§§ It is noteworthy that the overwhelming majority of literature mostly fleshed out supervised machine algorithms owing to the fact that these algorithms underpin the great bulk of consequential decisions made in the real world—ranging from

---

[430] In addition to that, there is yet another type of machine learning—reinforcement learning. See: Murphy, Kevin Patrick, *Machine Learning: A Probabilistic Perspective*, *cit.*, p. 2. Concisely, in reinforcement learning, an agent is placed in a given model environment and figures out the best course of action to be taken to attain a particular goal. See: Alpaydin, Ethem, *Introduction to Machine Leaning*, *cit.*, pp. 13–14. It bears mentioning that such agent and the environment in which it is placed can be sometimes physical. This typically takes place when a robot endeavours to navigate a maze, or entirely mathematically modelled landscape. The same happens when a program learns how to play Go. See: Silver, David et al., "Mastering the Game of Go with Deep Neural Networks and Tree Search", Volume 529, pp. 484, 484–487 (pointing out that Google DeepMind's AlphaGo machine learning algorithm is a blend of supervised learning and reinforcement learning). In either circumstance, it is of paramount importance to both define the problem and the "reward" that spur the agent's actions. Which is nothing but formulaic: the agent will learn to take a set of optimal actions that maximize its reward. In the case of a maze-navigating robot, for example, the reward may be distance to the end of the maze. Therefore, for reinforcement learning, problem definition can be regarded as a mixture of modelling the environment and clearly identifying the reward on the basis of the objective manifested in the environment. Lehr, David/Ohm, Paul, "Playing with the Data: What Legal Scholars Should Learn About Machine Learning", *cit.*, pp. 653–718.

[431] Lehr, David/Ohm, Paul, "Playing with the Data: What Legal Scholars Should Learn About Machine Learning", *cit.*, pp. 653–718.

[432] Murphy, Kevin Patrick, *Machine Learning: A Probabilistic Perspective*, *cit.*, pp. 9–13.

[433] Lehr, David/Ohm, Paul, "Playing with the Data: What Legal Scholars Should Learn About Machine Learning", *cit.*, pp. 653–718.

[434] In such instances, the machine-learning systems are oft-regarded as "semi supervised." See: Chapelle, Olivier/Bernhard Schölkopf/Alexander Zien, *Semi-supervised learning, Adaptive Computation and Machine Learning Series*, Massachusetts, MIT Press, 2010, passim.

[435] Murphy, Kevin Patrick, *Machine Learning: A Probabilistic Perspective*, *cit.*, pp. 877–78.

risk assessment,[436] predictive policing,[437] credit scoring,[438] to employment[439] processes.[440] Although supervised machine learning algorithms are to be brought into a sharper focus in the following sections of this book, its central tenets may be just as applicable to unsupervised machine learning algorithms.[441]

---

[436] See: Part IV, Chap. 4, Sects. 4.1.10.1–4.1.10.6 of this book (on biased algorithmic risk assessment in criminal procedure law settings, with a sharper focus on COMPAS). See: Berk, Richard A. et al., "Forecasting Domestic Violence: A Machine Learning Approach to Help Inform Arraignment Decisions", *cit.*, passim.

[437] See: Part IV, Chap. 4, Sects. 4.1.1–4.1.1.1 of this book (on biased predictive policing). See: Wang et al., "Learning to Detect Patterns of Crime", *Machine Learning and Knowledge Discovery in Databases, Machine Learning and Knowledge Discovery in Databases: European Conference,* ECML PKDD 2013, Prague, Czech Republic, September 23–27, 2013, Blockeel, Henrik/Kersting, Kristian/Nijssen, Siegfried, Železný, Filip (Editors), Berlin/Heidelberg, Springer, 2013, pp. 1–691 (pp. 517–518) (fleshing out their approach to pinpointing recurrent patterns of crime as a supervised machine learning algorithm method). See also: Koutra, Danai/Claudia Plant Gomez Rodriguez Bar alis Bonchi, *Machine Learning and Knowledge Discovery in Databases: Research track, European Conference, ECML PKDD 2023, Turin, Italy, September 18–22, 2023, Proceedings*, Part II, Berlin/Heidelberg, Springer, 2023, pp. 1–275.

[438] See: Part IV, Chap. 4, Sects. 4.1.4–4.1.4.2.1 of this book (on mortgage redlining). See: Part IV, Chap. 4, Sects. 4.1.2–4.1.4.3 of this book (on algorithmic credit scoring, consumer racism and credit card redlining). See: Part IV, Chap. 4, Sects. 4.1.4–4.1.4.2.3 of this book (on algorithmic redlining). See: Part IV, Chap. 4, Sect. 4.1.4.3 of this book (on "algorithmic redliking"). See: Part IV, Chap. 4, Sect. 4.1.3 of this book (on algorithmic prime-lining). See: Khandani, Amir E., et al., "Consumer Credit-Risk Models via Machine Learning Algorithms", *Journal of Banking and Finance*, Volume 34, 2010, pp. 2767, 2775–2777 (classifying their credit-risk model as a supervised machine algorithm, a classification tree). But see: Bar-Gill/Oren/Warren, Elizabeth, "Making Credit Safer", *University of Pennsylvania Law Review*, Volume 157, 2008, pp. 1–66 (argue that Black defendants are far more likely to be incarcerated, arrested, surveilled and harassed than White folks, which leads to the conclusion that the use of credit scores and income presents another way in which credit decisions leverage on structural disadvantage).

[439] But see: Kim, Pauline T., "Data-Driven Discrimination at Work", *William and Mary Law Review*, Volume 58, 2017, pp. 857, 863–864 (shedding a keen light on the racial effects of algorithmic prediction in the remit of employment). Converging: Zywicki, Todd J./Adamson, Joseph D., "The Law and Economics of Subprime Lending", *University of Colorado Law Review*, 2009, pp. 1–9 (contending that Black workers with roughly the same abilities and educational background earn far less than comparable white workers or have considerably fewer employment opportunities); King, Allan G./Markovich, Marko J., "Big Data" and the Risk of Employment Discrimination, *Oklahoma Law Review*, Volume 68, 2016, pp. 555–563 (on employment discrimination); Dobbie, Will, Jacob Goldin, and Crystal S. Yang, "The Effects of Pretrial Detention on Conviction, Future Crime, and Employment: Evidence from Randomly Assigned Judges," *American Economic Review*, Volume 108, 2018, 201–240.

[440] Lehr, David/Ohm, Paul, "Playing with the Data: What Legal Scholars Should Learn About Machine Learning", *cit.*, pp. 653–718. See: Qasem A. Al-Radaideh/Eman Al Nagi, "Using Data Mining Techniques to Build a Classification Model for Predicting Employees Performance", *International Journal of Advanced Computer Science and Applications*, Volume 3, 2012, pp. 144, 145–146 (shedding light on a supervised classification tree deployed for predicting employee performance).

[441] Lehr, David/Ohm, Paul, "Playing with the Data: What Legal Scholars Should Learn About Machine Learning", *cit.*, pp. 653–718.

5.1.2.4 Data Science—«Where the Rubber Hits the Road»: After Framing the Goal Underpinning the Machine Learning System, and Pursuant to the Specification of the Outcome Variable, the Data Scientist Should Proceed to the Stage of Data Collection

§§ Once data scientists have framed the goal of the machine learning system and narrowed down that overriding goal to a determined outcome variable, the data itself have to be amassed—both for the **outcome variable** and the plethora of **input variables**.[442] This stage is critically important insofar the machine learning algorithm is only as good as the data[443] it leverages on after all.[444]

---

[442] It is important to note that there is another form of data collection, of sorts, that pundits have refrained themselves from taking up in greater detail. Pivotally, stakeholders can use a portmanteau of techniques to glean from raw, often unstructured input information more actionable information that can then play the role of input variables. Revealingly, such techniques are highly diverse and are often deemed interchangeably as "feature extraction," "feature generation," "feature engineering," "feature construction," "feature processing," or "feature transformation." See: Huan Liu/ Hiroshi Motoda, *Feature Extraction, Construction and Selection: Data Mining Perspective*, 1998, pp. 3 and ff; Amazon Web Services, Amazon Machine Learning: Developer Guide, 2017, pp. 12 and ff, http://docs.aws.amazon.com/machine-learning/latest/dg/machinelearning-dg.pdf [https:// perma.cc/49JC-P8E9]; Severtson, Brad et al., "Feature Selection in the Team Data Science Process (TDSP)", *Microsoft Azure* (Mar. 24, 2017), https://docs.microsoft.com/en-us/azure/machine-learning/machine-learning-data-science-select-features [https://perma.cc/C9PNYXAF]. Scholars often aver that what lies within the essence of these techniques is sometimes difficult to fathom. In addition to that, the underlying meaning of these techniques differs greatly across context. Take the taking natural language processing as an example. Crucially, **feature extraction** may mean harvesting the frequencies of words or groupings of words in essays, two pieces of information that could subsequently be used as inputs to a given machine learning algorithm. See: Feature Extraction, SCIKIT-LEARN, http://scikitlearn.org/stable/modules/feature_extraction.html [https:// perma.cc/62WB-5F5R] (last visited Sept. 16, 2017). See: Part IV, Chap. 4, Sect. 4.1.8 of this book (on biased word embeddings with an entrenched presence on search engines run by tech moguls). By the same token, in the realm of facial recognition integrated systems, **feature extraction** could very well entail harvesting grayscale values of pixels and surrounding regions from faces of publicly available photos. See: Sarfaz, M. Saquib et al., Feature Extraction and Representation for Face Recognition", *Face Recognition*, Oravec, Milos (Editor), London, Intechopen, 2010, pp. 1–414 (pp. 1–15). In this vein, the amount of choices taken by an analyst in this type of data collection boast behemoth repercussions on the quality (or lack thereof) of the end-product machine learning algorithm. See: Lehr, David/Ohm, Paul, "Playing with the Data: What Legal Scholars Should Learn About Machine Learning", *cit.*, pp. 653–718. See also: Kleinberg, Jon/Ludwig, Jens/Mullainathan, Sendhil/Sunstein Cass R., "Discrimination in the Age of Algorithms", *Journal of Legal Analysis*, Volume 10, 1, 2018, pp. 28–29, 33–34 (draw a distinction between "group differences in the raw data" and biases for the "choice of predictors"). See: Part III, Chap. 3, Sects. 3.1.5.7–3.1.5.8.1 of this book (on the functional aspects of Critical Artificial Intelligence Studies, with a sharper focus on the perils concerning the deployment of facial recognition technology).

[443] See: Surden, Harry, "Machine Learning and Law", *Washington Law Review*, Volume 89, 2014, pp. 87, 106 ("In general, *machine learning algorithms are only as good as the data that they are given to analyze*"). Italics added.

[444] See: Barocas, Solon/Selbst, Andrew D., "Big Data's Disparate Impact", *California Law Review*, Volume 104, 2016, pp. 671–682 (discussing how data is often flawed, rigged, incomplete, imperfect and therefore algorithms inherit the prejudice of the original decision makers). But see: Citron, Danielle Keats/Pasquale, Frank, "The Scored Society: Due Process for Automated Predictions",

§§ Broadly speaking, there are two different stances of data collection: gleaning and blending data that have already been thoroughly measured,[445] and measuring data.[446] Pundits aver that the foregoing approaches are not mutually exclusive to the extent that they can be used within the same algorithmic undertaking. Either way, some factors linger on the data scientists' minds when assessing the quality of collected[447] data.[448]

§§ On the one hand, and at the shallowest level, data scientists are entrusted with the duty of ensuring that they have collated enough data for the purpose at hand. Whilst there is no technological bar to carrying out machine learning algorithms on small-scaled datasets, the task itself is ripe for misfire. Crucially, a sheer amount of machine learning algorithms have proven to operate better than orthodox techniques, «but this property is asymptotic»[449]; it transpires only as the amount of observations in a dataset grows exponentially towards[450] an unmeasurable infinity.[451]

§§ It is pivotally important to note, though, that to harvest the predictive perks arising out of the deployment of machine learning algorithms, a whopping amount

---

Washington Law Review, Volume 89, 2014, pp. 1, 4–5 (highlighting how human beings programming automated systems is directly conducive to, and leads, to fundamentally inaccurate results since the source code, predictive algorithms and datasets may encompass human biases which, in turn, have a disparate impact on historically disadvantaged groups); Crawford, Kate/Schultz, Jason, "Big Data and Due Process: Toward a Framework to Redress Predictive Privacy Harms", *Boston College Law Review*, Volume 55, 2014, pp. 93, 99–101 (pinpointing pathways through which predictive analytic tools perpetuate discriminatory practices). But see: Bornstein, Stepanhie, "Antidiscriminatory Algorithms", *Alabama Law Review*, Volume 70, 2018, pp. 519, 524–528 (contending, however, that the tagged "facially neutral" algorithms producing discriminatory outcomes should be quashed).

445 Lehr, David/Ohm, Paul, "Playing with the Data: What Legal Scholars Should Learn About Machine Learning", *cit.*, pp. 653–718.

446 Lehr, David/Ohm, Paul, "Playing with the Data: What Legal Scholars Should Learn About Machine Learning", *cit.*, pp. 653–718.

447 Lehr, David/Ohm, Paul, "Playing with the Data: What Legal Scholars Should Learn About Machine Learning", *cit.*, pp. 653–718.

448 It is oft-said that social sciences, specifically psychology, have allotted multifarious "validity" and "reliability" labels to multitudinous concepts of data quality pundits routinely discuss. See: Nunnally, Jum/Bernstein, Ira H., Psychometric Theory, 3rd edition, Belser, James R. Belser/Vaicunas, Jane Vaicunas (Editors), New York, McGraw-Hill, 1994, pp. 83–114 (discussing different main meanings of validity in the purview of psychology). It is noteworthy that some scholars fight shy of using those labels. On one hand, those labels often straddle or overlap and a haze of ambiguity usually ensues. On the other hand, a bevy of the labels, such as "internal validity," bear on statistical methods that strive to yield causal inferences. Machine learning has very little to say, or to do, about that. See: Lehr, David/Ohm, Paul, "Playing with the Data: What Legal Scholars Should Learn About Machine Learning", *cit.*, pp. 653–718.

449 Lehr, David/Ohm, Paul, "Playing with the Data: What Legal Scholars Should Learn About Machine Learning", *cit.*, pp. 653–718.

450 Lehr, David/Ohm, Paul, "Playing with the Data: What Legal Scholars Should Learn About Machine Learning", *cit.*, pp. 653–718.

451 See: Koltchinskii, V./Panchenko, D. "Empirical Margin Distributions and Bounding the Generalization Error of Combined Classifiers", *The Annals of Statistics*, Volume 30, 2002, pp. 1–2 2002 (fleshed out an asymptotic convergence for combined classifiers, such as those that enshrine both the processes commonly known as *bagging* and *boosting*).

of observations is not only required, but, and foremost, sorely needed. There is no such thing as a «one size fits all» formula on how many observations would be enough to get the job done. Notwithstanding, a few hundred, or even a few thousand observations, may fall noticeably short of ticking enough boxes, sufficiency wise.[452]

§§ Apart from that, tens of thousands could be more than enough for some applications, whereas other applications operate flawlessly on hundreds of thousands or even millions of observations. Again, a «catch-all» formula would run counter to machine learning algorithm's overall accuracy which, in turn, would prove detrimental to the accomplishment of the overriding goal at hand. Besides collating enough data, data scientists also strive to ensure that the variables for which data are collated indeed estimate what they are seemingly measuring.[453]

§§ This sort-of inquiry takes place at two consecutive degrees. Firstly, there is the vexing question of whether and to what extent the specific techniques that seek to estimate a variable possess the ability to measure accurately and reliably what the variable indicates on its face.[454] For example, if a variable in a violence risk assessment machine learning algorithm purportedly indicates whether a defendant has ever been previously indicted with gun-related violence, then it is more than

[452] Lehr, David/Ohm, Paul, "Playing with the Data: What Legal Scholars Should Learn About Machine Learning", *cit.*, pp. 653–718.

[453] Lehr, David/Ohm, Paul, "Playing with the Data: What Legal Scholars Should Learn About Machine Learning", *cit.*, pp. 653–718.

[454] Lehr, David/Ohm, Paul, "Playing with the Data: What Legal Scholars Should Learn About Machine Learning", *cit.*, pp. 653–718.

reasonable to conclude that the source of the data—extant court records or priors[455]—accurately reflect criminal charges.[456] On the flip side, if a dating website is building an algorithm to which one input is a user's self-reported age, there is a every reason to believe that most of the users, if not all, have bluntly lied about their[457] ages.

§§ In that case, the variable would not as reliably measure what, clearly, it purportedly does. The overriding idea of **«faithful measurement»**[458] also raises critical questions. One which is measurements must sharply portray not just what a variable clearly indicates, but, and foremost, to what **underlying architecture**—also tagged as **latent construct**—the developer reckons it reliably reflects.[459]

§§ This leads us to the reason why a data scientist sought to collate data for that variable to begin with. To illustrate, let us focus on the two examples brought to the fore in previous paragraphs. When building the theoretical risk assessment algorithm,

---

[455] See: Hancock, Jeffrey T. et al., "The Truth About Lying in Online Dating Profiles", *Proceedings of SIGCHI Conference on Human Factors in Computing Systems*, New York, Association for Computing Machinery, 2007, pp. 449, 451–452 (discussing the ease with which deception occurs in dating profiles). On the quality—or lack thereof—of training data in the remit of real estate and beyond, with regard to criminal records and priors. See: Wonyoung, So, "Which Information Matters? Measuring Landlord Assessment of Tenant Screening Reports", *Housing Policy Debate*, Volume 33, n.º 6, 2023, pp. 1484–1510 (1501–1502) ("*Algorithmic scoring using criminal records is problematic because training data—a data set that is used to train a machine learning model—is inaccurate and the outcome variable ("desirable tenants") is unclear. For instance, the tenant screening company RealPage produces 11,000 reports using "abbreviated" criminal records, which are cheaper to acquire than full criminal records but do not include details of the resolution* (Kirchner and Goldstein 2020). *An inaccurate model is highly likely to result from tenant screening services using these kinds of abbreviated data, given that it is important to include the final resolution of criminal justice procedures for proper assessment. Moreover, it would be challenging to set an outcome variable for developing this kind of algorithm because it is hard to project a certain criminal outcome into "good" tenant behaviors*"). Italics added. For further developments: Part IV, Chap. 4, Sects. 4.1.4–4.1.4.2.2 of this book. But see: Crow, M. S., "The complexities of prior record, race, ethnicity, and policy: Interactive effects in sentencing", *Criminal Justice Review*, Volume 33, Issue 4, 2008, pp. 502–523; Harris, Grant T./Rice, Marnie E., "Bayes and Base Rates: What Is an Informative Prior for Actuarial Violence Risk Assessment?", *Behavioural Science and Law*, Volume 31, 2013, pp. 103, 121 ("What is not axiomatic is the straightforward application of assumptions about priors... to violence risk assessment—that remains a set of important empirical matters").

[456] Lehr, David/Ohm, Paul, "Playing with the Data: What Legal Scholars Should Learn About Machine Learning", *cit.*, pp. 653–718.

[457] Lehr, David/Ohm, Paul, "Playing with the Data: What Legal Scholars Should Learn About Machine Learning", *cit.*, pp. 653–718.

[458] Lehr, David/Ohm, Paul, "Playing with the Data: What Legal Scholars Should Learn About Machine Learning", *cit.*, pp. 653–718.

[459] Lehr, David/Ohm, Paul, "Playing with the Data: What Legal Scholars Should Learn About Machine Learning", *cit.*, pp. 653–718.

data scientists might have sought out the gun-related—or drug-related arrests[460]—criminal charges variables since it could indicate the proclivity/proneness evinced by a given individual to engage in flagitious activities.[461]

§§ Note, though, that, as extensively discussed earlier in this book,[462] criminal charges for gun-related violence are a conspicuously warped/shoddy/watered down indicator of penchant for violence. Relatedly, one should be mindful of the fact that there is a cohort of individuals that routinely perpetrate violence for which they are never arrested, charged, and convicted, whereas other individuals are charged for violent crimes they never perpetrated.[463] The whopping amount of wrongful convictions[464] lends weight, and adds further plausibility, to this main contention.

[460] Saunders, J., Hunt, P., & Hollywood, J. S., "Predictions put into practice: A quasi-experimental evaluation of Chicago's predictive policing pilot", *Journal of Experimental Criminology*, 12 (3), 2016, pp. 347–371. Beckett, Katherine, Kris Nyrop, Lori Pfingst, and Melissa Bowen, "Drug Use, Drug Possession Arrests, and the Question of Race: Lessons from Seattle", *Social Problems*, (52) 3, 2005, pp. 419–441; Duster, Troy, "Pattern, Purpose and Race in the Drug War.", Crack in America: Demon Drugs and Social Justice, edited by C. Reinarman and H. G. Levine. Berkeley: University of California Press, 1997, pp. 206–287; Mitchell, O., & Caudy, M. S., Examining racial disparities in drug arrests", *Justice Quarterly*, 32 (2), 2015, pp. 288–313.

[461] Lehr, David/Ohm, Paul, "Playing with the Data: What Legal Scholars Should Learn About Machine Learning", *cit.*, pp. 653–718.

[462] See: Part IV, Chap. 4, Sects. 4.1.10.1–4.1.10.6 of this book (on biased algorithmic risk assessment in criminal procedure law settings, with a sharper focus on COMPAS). See: Part IV, Chap. 4, Sects. 4.1.1–4.1.1.1 of this book (on biased predictive policing).

[463] Lehr, David/Ohm, Paul, "Playing with the Data: What Legal Scholars Should Learn About Machine Learning", *cit.*, pp. 653–718.

[464] Jefferson, B., *Digitize and Punish: Racial Criminalization in the Digital Age*, Minnesota, University of Minnesota Press, 2020; Gross, Samuel R., Maurice Possley, and Kalara Stephens, "Race and Wrongful Convictions in the United States." National Registry of Exonerations, Newkirk Center for Science and Society, University of California-Irvine, 2017.

§§ Thence, whilst this variable might be measured on its face, it likely is not when taking stock of its **underlying construct**. The opposite could hold true of the age variable embedded in the dating website's algorithm.[465] Often, users lie egregiously about their ages.[466] Note, however, that ascertaining the users' exact ages is not definitely the underlying reason for the website to include this particular input variable.[467]

§§ Contrary to popular belief, the website truly cares about what general age ranges clients fall in[468]; being twenty-eight in lieu of twenty-six is implausible to have[469] a direct bearing on one's responsiveness to a cluster of ads, yet being twenty-eight in lieu of being forty might[470] just have a direct bearing on the user's responsiveness to certain ads. Accuracy is key in this regard. To the extent it is rarer for users to fudge their ages and, therefore, jettison themselves in the unsuitable «age trash bin» important for advertising ends, this variable could be validly measured when pondering its **underlying construct**, even though if it is not when pondering it on its face.[471]

§§ Lastly, in addition to the dimension of the dataset and variables' measurement underlying validities (or lack thereof), data scientists are fundamentally preoccupied with **generalizability**. The latter—**generalizability**—amounts to the ability of a machine learning algorithm trained on a specific dataset to produce valid, accurate, and reliable forecasts when deployed[472] on a different dataset.[473]

---

[465] Lehr, David/Ohm, Paul, "Playing with the Data: What Legal Scholars Should Learn About Machine Learning", *cit.*, pp. 653–718.

[466] Id. at Hancock, Jeffrey T. et al., "The Truth About Lying in Online Dating Profiles", *Proceedings of SIGCHI Conference on Human Factors in Computing Systems*, cit., p. 451 (noting that subjects actual ages ranged from three years younger to nine years older than they actually reported, with an average deviation hovering around 0.44 years). See: Lehr, David/Ohm, Paul, "Playing with the Data: What Legal Scholars Should Learn About Machine Learning", *cit.*, pp. 653–718.

[467] Lehr, David/Ohm, Paul, "Playing with the Data: What Legal Scholars Should Learn About Machine Learning", *cit.*, pp. 653–718.

[468] Lehr, David/Ohm, Paul, "Playing with the Data: What Legal Scholars Should Learn About Machine Learning", *cit.*, pp. 653–718.

[469] Lehr, David/Ohm, Paul, "Playing with the Data: What Legal Scholars Should Learn About Machine Learning", *cit.*, pp. 653–718.

[470] Lehr, David/Ohm, Paul, "Playing with the Data: What Legal Scholars Should Learn About Machine Learning", *cit.*, pp. 653–718.

[471] Lehr, David/Ohm, Paul, "Playing with the Data: What Legal Scholars Should Learn About Machine Learning", *cit.*, pp. 653–718.

[472] Lehr, David/Ohm, Paul, "Playing with the Data: What Legal Scholars Should Learn About Machine Learning", *cit.*, pp. 653–718.

[473] See: Murphy, Kevin Patrick, *Machine Learning: A Probabilistic Perspective*, *cit.*, p. 3 ("*Our main goal is to make predictions on novel inputs, meaning ones that we have not seen before (this is called generalization)*, since predicting the response on the training set is easy (we can just look up the answer"). Italics added.

5.1.2.4.1 Generalizability: The Ability of a Machine Learning Algorithm Trained on a Given Dataset to Create Accurate and Reliable Forecasts When Deployed on Different Basket of Data

§§ To achieve **generalizability**, the collated data used for training purposes should faithfully mirror, and be representative[474] of, the real-world data on which the machine learning algorithm will subsequently be deployed. Failing which, **inductive bias**[475] is slated to occur. When collating/amassing data requires going out into a populace and estimating data once again, data scientists should endeavour to attain representative data by randomly[476] sampling the persons of the populace for whom they estimate data.[477] Roughly speaking, random sampling from the populace

[474] See also: Dong et al., Qi, "Imbalanced deep learning by minority class incremental rectification, *IEEE Transactions on Pattern Analysis & Machine Intelligence*, Volume 41, 2019, p. 1367 (posit that "*most existing learning algorithms produce inductive bias (learning bias)* towards the frequent (majority) classes if training data are not balanced, *resulting in poor minority class recognition performance*"). Italics added. See: Chandler, Anupam, "The Racist Algorithm", *Michigan Law Review*, Volume 115, n.º 6, 2018, p. 1026 (on racist algorithms, noting that "the possibilities for discriminatory manipulation are legion"). See: Part V, this chapter, Sect. 5.1.7.4 of this book (on one of the law to control algorithmic decision-making, namely, law number four: data partitioning must be performed—i.e. randomly split an entire dataset into the «training dataset» and the «test dataset»—to accurately predict outcomes in the real world while forestalling «inductive bias» [learning bias]).

[475] It is important to note that an algorithm designed for maximum accuracy will adjust itself to the majority data, and may be less accurate for members of the underrepresented group, thus breeding *inductive bias*. See: Shellenbarger, Sue, "A Crucial Step for Avoiding AI Disasters", *Wall Street Journal*, (Feb. 13, 2019, 9:57 AM ET), https://www.wsj.com/articles/a-crucial-step-for-avoiding-ai-disasters-11550069865?ns=prod/accounts-wsj [https://perma.cc/C28U-LAAE] (discussing this issue while emphasizing how diverse development teams pay more attention to unrepresentative and underrepresented data sets). Human programmers can circumvent and bypass this problem by weighting the minority-group data more heavily, by designing different algorithms for each racial group, or by striving to contain more data to equalize group representation in the data set. See: Barua, Sukarna et al., "MWMOTE—Majority Weighted Minority Oversampling Technique for Imbalanced Data Set Learning", *IEEE Transactions on Knowledge & Data Engineering*, Volume 26, 2014, pp. 405, 405–406. See also: Hamilton, Melissa, "The Biased Algorithm: Evidence of Disparate Impact on Hispanics", *American Criminal Law Review*, Volume 56, 2019, pp. 1553 and ff and passim (which clearly demonstrates that COMPAS was significantly less accurate for Hispanic than for white defendants by several measures and suggesting that smaller numbers of Hispanic defendants might be the cause). See: Mayson, Sandra G., "Bias In, Bias Out", *cit.*, pp. 2218–2300. But see: Altenburger, Kristen M./Ho, Daniel E., "When Algorithms Import Private Bias into Public Enforcement: The Promise and Limitations of Statistical Debiasing Solutions", *Journal of Institutional & Theoretical Economics*, Volume 175, 2019, pp. 97–98 (calls for a "debias predictive algorithms" to assuage racist and/or biased, doctored and bigoted algorithms nevertheless).

[476] Vovk, V./A. Gammerman/and G. Shafer, *Algorithmic Learning in a Random World*, New York: Springer, 2005.

[477] See: Kruskal, William/Mosteller, Federick, "Representative Sampling, III: The Current Statistical Literature", *The International Statistical Review*, Volume 47, 1979, pp. 245 and ff and (parsing extant use of the expression "representative sampling" in modern statistical literature); Kruskal, William/Mosteller, Federick, "Representative Sampling, IV: The History of the Concept in Statistics", 1895–1939, *48 The International Statistical Review*, Volume 48, 1980, p. 169 (parsing the history of representative sampling in contemporary statistics).

of interest grants a decent likelihood of acquiring representative data. Much to our dismay, though, true **random sampling** seldom, if ever, happens in practical terms.[478]

§§ To illustrate, take a financial corporation building a credit-scoring algorithm[479] for example. If the outcome variable happens to be some metric of whether and to what extent an individual defaulted on a loan, then the training data[480] should be in all likelihood comprised of individuals who applied for and were indeed granted a loan. But this is hardly the population of interest—that is, the group of individuals who ever applied for a loan.[481]

---

[478] Lehr, David/Ohm, Paul, "Playing with the Data: What Legal Scholars Should Learn About Machine Learning", *cit.*, pp. 653–718.

[479] Lehr, David/Ohm, Paul, "Playing with the Data: What Legal Scholars Should Learn About Machine Learning", *cit.*, pp. 653–718.

[480] See: Barocas, Solon/Selbst, Andrew D., "Big Data's Disparate Impact", *California Law Review*, Volume 104, 2016, pp. 677–678 (arguing that predictive data is predictive of a given/specific target variable with training data which is both correctly "labelled" and "collected"). It is often contended that machine learning algorithms engender their own models to forecast future outcomes on the basis of analysis of training data. See: Mittelstadt, Brent Daniel/Taddeo, Patrick Allo, Mariarosaria/Wachter, Sandra/Floridi, Luciano, "The Ethics of Algorithms: Mapping the Debate", *Big Data & Society*, July-Dec. 2016, 2016, p. 3. But see: Wonyoung, So, "Which Information Matters? Measuring Landlord Assessment of Tenant Screening Reports", *Housing Policy Debate*, Volume 33, n.º 6, 2023, pp. 1484–1510 (1501–1502) ("*Algorithmic scoring using criminal records is problematic because training data—a data set that is used to train a machine learning model—is inaccurate and the outcome variable ("desirable tenants") is unclear. For instance, the tenant screening company RealPage produces 11,000 reports using "abbreviated" criminal records, which are cheaper to acquire than full criminal records but do not include details of the resolution* (Kirchner and Goldstein 2020). *An inaccurate model is highly likely to result from tenant screening services using these kinds of abbreviated data, given that it is important to include the final resolution of criminal justice procedures for proper assessment. Moreover, it would be challenging to set an outcome variable for developing this kind of algorithm because it is hard to project a certain criminal outcome into "good" tenant behaviors*"). Italics added.

[481] It is crucially important to note, though, that the very fact that only certain types of behaviours are assessed and gauged by credit scores leads to the conclusion some borrowers are not scored at all. The overwhelming majority of consumers boast meagre, if any, credit files owing to the fact that the likelihood to access to the sort of financial services that actually report to the orthodox credit bureaus scattered across modern economies is exceedingly low, which, in turn, morphs them into credit invisible persons. See: Yu, Persis/McLaughlin, Jilian/Levy, Marina, "Big Data: A Big Disappointment for Scoring Consumer Creditworthiness," *The National Consumer Law Center,* 2 (Mar. 14, 2014), available at: https://www.nclc.org/images/pdf/pr-reports/report-big-data.pdf [https://perma.cc/W4SK-NXD5] (access: 21.12.2024).

§§ It should not therefore come as a bewildering surprise that such a machine learning algorithm is likely to be far less predictive on individuals like those who, in the past, applied for a loan but were outrightly rejected on biased grounds.[482] This also has a direct bearing on the tremendous potential discriminatory effects arising out of machine learning.[483] To the extent that those who were downrightly rebuffed for loans in the past were inordinately minority applicants (Blacks and Latinos),[484] then the resulting machine learning algorithm may perform considerably worse on precisely those[485] applicants,[486] thereby perpetuating[487] a

[482] See: Allen, James, "The Color of Algorithms: An Analysis and Proposed Research Agenda Deterring Algorithmic Redlining", *Fordham Urban Law Journal*, Volume 46, 2019, pp. 219–234 (229–234) (discussing how historical mortgage redlining greatly swayed modern algorithms generated by massive batches of datasets that consist of decades of information built on exclusion and racial discrimination in the purview of financing, marketing, and housing). See: Part IV, Chap. 4, Sects. 4.1.4–4.1.4.2.3 of this book.

[483] See: Part IV, Chap. 4, Sects. 4.1.4–4.1.4.2.1 of this book (on mortgage redlining). See: Part IV, Chap. 4, Sects. 4.1.2–4.1.4.3 of this book (on algorithmic credit scoring, consumer racism and credit card redlining). See: Part IV, Chap. 4, Sects. 4.1.4–4.1.4.2.3 of this book (on algorithmic redlining). See: Part IV, Chap. 4, Sect. 4.1.4.3 of this book (on "algorithmic redliking"). See: Part IV, Chap. 4, Sect. 4.1.3 of this book (on algorithmic prime-lining). In spite of its deep-seated racial bias, decision-makers continue to deploy redlining tactics through big data and may even justify such unlawful practices by claiming that the latter abide by cost-effectiveness. See: Humber, Nadiyah J., "A Home for Digital Equity: Algorithmic Redlining and Property Technology", *California Law Review*, Volume 111, Issue 5, 2023, pp. 1421–1484. See: Part IV, Chap. 4, Sects. 4.1.4–4.1.4.2.3 of this book.

[484] But see: Hurley, Mikella/Adebayo, Julius, "Credit Scoring in the Era of Big Data", *Yale Journal of Law and Technology*, Volume 18, 2016, pp. 148, 151–156, 172 (averring that FICO scoring boasts a redoubtable capacity to routinely weed out some populations that have been historically and systematically underrepresented or grossly unfairly represented in the credit industry market). Tellingly, by 2016, ten states had disavowed the unlawful practice of employers using shady algorithmic credit scores due to their perceived disparate impact on low-income applicants and members of racialized communities (mostly Black folks). See: O'Neill, Cathy, *Weapons of Math Destruction. How Big Data Increases Inequality and Threatens Democracy*. London: Penguin Random House, 2016, pp. 128 and ff and passim. See: Part IV, Chap. 4, Sects. 4.1.4–4.1.4.2.3 of this book.

[485] Lehr, David/Ohm, Paul, "Playing with the Data: What Legal Scholars Should Learn About Machine Learning", *cit.*, pp. 653–718.

[486] Many scholars have offered excellent explanations on both this and other data-related sources of discriminatory impacts. See: Barocas, Solon/Selbst, Andrew, "Big Data's Disparate Impact", *cit.*, 677–694 (offering on-point explanations on this alongside data-related sources of disparate impact on protected groups); Crawford, Kate, "Think Again: Big Data", *Foreign Policy* (May 10, 2013), http://foreignpolicy.com/2013/05/10/think-again-big-data [https://perma.cc/8VH6-PKVP]. We do not wish to reel off, nor trot out, its findings here and instead direct the reader towards this existing literature. See: Lehr, David/Ohm, Paul, "Playing with the Data: What Legal Scholars Should Learn About Machine Learning", *cit.*, pp. 653–718.

[487] Note, though, that certain types of racial discrimination may not be fully intentional. More likely than not, it can be related with the perils of big data colour-blindness that nonetheless relies on proxies to race and gender to make algorithmic decisions. Another problem is the one related with "creditworthiness by association" that causes more problems than it solves. Hurley, Mikella/Adebayo, Julius, "Credit Scoring in the Era of Big Data", *Yale Journal of Law and Technology*, Volume 18, 2016, p. 149 ("*recent studies have also questioned the accuracy of the data used by these tools, in some cases identifying serious flaws that have a substantial bearing on lending decisions. Big-data*

vicious cycle of systemic racism,[488] White Supremacy[489] and White privilege[490] that still resonates today.[491]

---

tools may also risk creating a system of "creditworthiness by association" in which consumers' familial, religious, social, and other affiliations determine their eligibility for an affordable loan. These tools may furthermore obscure discriminatory and subjective lending policies behind a single "objective" score. Such discriminatory scoring may not be intentional; instead, sophisticated algorithms may combine facially neutral data points and treat them as proxies for immutable characteristics such as race or gender, thereby circumventing existing non-discrimination laws and systematically denying credit access to certain groups. Finally, big-data tools may allow online payday lenders to target the most vulnerable consumers and lure them into debt traps"). Italics added. See: Part IV, Chap. 4, Sects. 4.1.2–4.1.2.3 of this book.

488 See: Feagin, J. R., *Systemic racism: a theory of oppression*, New York: Routledge, 2006. See also: Fiske, John, "Surveilling the City: Whiteness, the Black Man and Democratic Totalitarianism", *Theory, Culture and Society*, 15 (2), 1998, pp. 67–88 (on the overhyped surveillance on black people as a byproduct of systemic racism).

489 See: Perea, Juan F., "Doctrines of Delusion: How the History of the G.I. Bill and Other Inconvenient Truths Undermind the Supreme Court's Affirmative Action Jurisprudence", *University of Pittsburgh Law Review*, Volume 75, 1995, pp. 583, 586–589 (establishes a liaison between Jim Crow laws, the G.I. Bill, and the Social Security Act and White supremacy); Milligan, Joy, "Protecting Disfavored Minorities: Towards Institutional Realism", *UCLA Law Review*, Volume 63, 2016, pp. 894, pp. 918–21 (shedding a keen light on racial inequality in U.S. Department of Agriculture farm assistance); Robinson, Reginald Leamon, "The Racial Limits of the Fair Housing Act: The Intersection of Dominant White Images, the Violence of Neighborhood Purity, and the Master Narrative of Black Inferiority", *William & Mary Law Review*, Volume 37, 1995, pp. 69, 71–74 (establishes a connection between the failures of the FHA and White supremacy). But see: Wormser, Richard, *The Rise and Fall of Jim Crow*, Manhattan, New York City, St Martin's Press, 2014, pp. 1–222 ("*White supremacy prevailed, but it did not destroy the spirit of the black community*"). Italics added.

490 Jackson, E. K., *Scandinavians in Chicago: The Origins of White Privilege in Modern America*, Chicago, Illinois, University of Illinois Press, 2019; Rothenberg, P. S., *White Privilege*, 2015, Google Books. See: Part IV, Chap. 4, Sects. 4.1.4–4.1.4.2.1 of this book (on mortgage redlining). See: Part IV, Chap. 4, Sects. 4.1.2–4.1.4.3 of this book (on algorithmic credit scoring, consumer racism and credit card redlining). See: Part IV, Chap. 4, Sects. 4.1.4–4.1.4.2.3 of this book (on algorithmic redlining). See: Part IV, Chap. 4, Sect. 4.1.4.3 of this book (on "algorithmic redliking"). See: Part IV, Chap. 4, Sect. 4.1.3 of this book (on algorithmic prime-lining).

491 See: Roithmayr, Daria, *Reproducing Racism: How everyday choices lock in White Advantage*, New York, New York University Press, 2014, pp. 1–272 ("*Argues that racial inequality reproduces itself automatically over time because early unfair advantage for whites has paved the way for continuing advantage. This book is designed to change the way we think about racial inequality (…) Legal scholar Daria Roithmayr provocatively argues that racial inequality lives on because white advantage functions as a powerful self-reinforcing monopoly, reproducing itself automatically from generation to generation even in the absence of intentional discrimination. Drawing on work in antitrust law and a range of other disciplines, Roithmayr brilliantly compares the dynamics of white advantage to the unfair tactics of giants like AT&T and Microsoft.* With penetrating insight, Roithmayr *locates the engine of white monopoly in positive feedback loops that connect the dramatic disparity of Jim Crow to modern racial gaps in jobs, housing and education. Wealthy white neighborhoods fund public schools that then turn out wealthy white neighbors. Whites with lucrative jobs informally refer their friends, who refer their friends, and so on. Roithmayr concludes that racial inequality might now be locked in place, unless policymakers immediately take drastic steps*

5.1.2.5 «Deciphering» Data Cleaning

§§ As adumbrated, collating data eyeing **quantity**, **validity**, and **generalizability** is only one facet of preparing the data.[492]

§§ Datasets are seldom, if ever, free from missing values. Albeit these quandaries are not roadblocks that stand in the way of algorithmic decision-making—analysts seldom, if ever, relinquish control over a project simply because they grapple with data—they can significantly impact the quality of algorithmic predictions. The data cleaning phase seeks to unwind, and ideally smooth out, this looming threat. For a number of reasons, subjects within a given dataset may be missing values for one or more input variables.[493] And that is something that we should keenly worry about.

§§ For that reason, it is oft-averred that mistakes tend to happen in the begrimed/ convoluted world of data in a regular basis. What can be done about these missing values? One option might be to simply erase the subjects with missing values from the dataset altogether; if a person is missing a value for his/her age, simply delete him or her entirely from object of analysis might be a go-to solution. Note, though, having enough observations is pivotally important to machine learning's **overall accuracy**.[494] It should therefore come as no surprise that this solution may seem troublesome.[495]

§§ How problematic can this situation be? It depends. If the dataset is considerably large, erasing some, perhaps even several, subjects might not hinder, let alone derail, the ability of the data to accommodate all possible variations between subjects. To

---

to dismantle this oppressive system"). Italics added. This book points out how White privilege is perpetuated throughout generations through residential segregation (*mortgage redlining*), abhorrent nepotism, and other bemoaning social practices that pester modern societies). See: Part IV, Chap. 4, Sects. 4.1.4–4.1.4.2.3 of this book. See: Part IV, Chap. 4, Sects. 4.1.4–4.1.4.2.1 of this book (on mortgage redlining). See: Part IV, Chap. 4, Sects. 4.1.2–4.1.4.3 of this book (on algorithmic credit scoring, consumer racism and credit card redlining). See: Part IV, Chap. 4, Sects. 4.1.4–4.1.4.2.3 of this book (on algorithmic redlining). See: Part IV, Chap. 4, Sect. 4.1.4.3 of this book (on "algorithmic redliking"). See: Part IV, Chap. 4, Sect. 4.1.3 of this book (on algorithmic prime-lining).

492 Lehr, David/Ohm, Paul, "Playing with the Data: What Legal Scholars Should Learn About Machine Learning", *cit.*, pp. 653–718.

493 Lehr, David/Ohm, Paul, "Playing with the Data: What Legal Scholars Should Learn About Machine Learning", *cit.*, pp. 653–718.

494 But see: Berk, Richard, "Accuracy and Fairness for Juvenile Justice Risks Assessments", *Journal of Empirical Legal Studies*, Volume 16, 2019, p. 175 (comes to the terms with the fact that tweaking/ altering data to attain statistical parity yielded extremely high false-negative rates, thereby taking a toll on the algorithm's overall accuracy); Zachary Lipton et al., "Does Mitigating ML's Impact Disparity Require Treatment Disparity?", NIPS PROC. 1 (2018), https://arxiv.org/pdf/1711.07076.pdf [https://perma.cc/X8VF-EY53] (sets forth compelling evidence that enforced blindness to protected traits exacts a toll on the overall accuracy of the algorithmic tool); Petersilia, Joan/ Turner, Susan, "Guideline-Based Justice: Prediction and Racial Minorities", *Crime and Justice*, 1987, pp. 151–174 (argues that omitting markers correlated with race from a recidivism prediction algorithm exacted a toll on the overall accuracy of the algorithmic tool).

495 Lehr, David/Ohm, Paul, "Playing with the Data: What Legal Scholars Should Learn About Machine Learning", *cit.*, pp. 653–718.

illustrate, erasing one hundred from a dataset of one million is highly unlikely to be harmful.[496]

§§ Another consideration is whether and to what extent the subject with the missing data has other data values which are not sufficiently represented in other subjects. **Representative data**[497] are pivotally important to achieve **generalizability**. For that reason, if there are few subjects with certain features, erasing even a seemingly tiny number of them could decrease **generalizability** altogether. If, for example, a dataset of one million people contains only one thousand[498] individuals of a given race, then erasing one hundred of them could very well undermine a sought-after generalizability,[499] which are hardly elating news.

§§ As with several of the trade-offs, there is no such thing as a set-in-stone mathematical «sweet spot» for making these hard choices. Pundits aver that there is

---

[496] Lehr, David/Ohm, Paul, "Playing with the Data: What Legal Scholars Should Learn About Machine Learning", *cit.*, pp. 653–718.

[497] It is important to recall that an algorithm designed for maximum accuracy will adjust itself to the **majority data**, and may be less accurate for members of the underrepresented group, thus breeding inductive bias. See: Shellenbarger, Sue, "A Crucial Step for Avoiding AI Disasters", *Wall Street Journal*, (Feb. 13, 2019, 9:57 AM ET), https://www.wsj.com/articles/a-crucial-step-for-avoiding-ai-disasters-11550069865?ns=prod/accounts-wsj [https://perma.cc/C28U-LAAE] (discussing this issue while emphasizing how diverse development teams pay more attention to unrepresentative and underrepresented data sets). Human programmers can circumvent and bypass this problem by weighting the minority-group data more heavily, by designing different algorithms for each racial group, or by striving to contain more data to equalize group representation in the data set. See: Barua, Sukarna et al., "MWMOTE—Majority Weighted Minority Oversampling Technique for Imbalanced Data Set Learning", *IEEE Transactions on Knowledge & Data Engineering*, Volume 26, 2014, pp. 405, 405–406. See also: Hamilton, Melissa, "The Biased Algorithm: Evidence of Disparate Impact on Hispanics", *American Criminal Law Review*, Volume 56, 2019, pp. 1553 and ff and passim (which clearly demonstrates that COMPAS was significantly less accurate for Hispanic than for white defendants by several measures and suggesting that smaller numbers of Hispanic defendants might be the cause). See: Mayson, Sandra G., "Bias In, Bias Out", *cit.*, pp. 2218–2300. See also: Dong et al., Qi,, "Imbalanced deep learning by minority class incremental rectification, *IEEE Transactions on Pattern Analysis & Machine Intelligence*, Volume 41, 2019, p. 1367 (posit that "*most existing learning algorithms produce inductive bias (learning bias)* towards the frequent (majority) classes if training data are not balanced, *resulting in poor minority class recognition performance*"). Italics added. See: Chandler, Anupam, "The Racist Algorithm", *Michigan Law Review*, Volume 115, n.º 6, 2018, p. 1026 (on racist algorithms, noting that "the possibilities for discriminatory manipulation are legion"). But see: Altenburger, Kristen M./Ho, Daniel E., "When Algorithms Import Private Bias into Public Enforcement: The Promise and Limitations of Statistical Debiasing Solutions", *Journal of Institutional & Theoretical Economics*, Volume 175, 2019, pp. 97–98 (calls for a "debias predictive algorithms" to assuage racist and/or biased, doctored and bigoted algorithms nevertheless).

[498] Lehr, David/Ohm, Paul, "Playing with the Data: What Legal Scholars Should Learn About Machine Learning", *cit.*, pp. 653–718.

[499] Lehr, David/Ohm, Paul, "Playing with the Data: What Legal Scholars Should Learn About Machine Learning", *cit.*, pp. 653–718.

another way of fine-tuning missing values is to attribute them. This can be attained in different ways.[500]

§§ A tool developer could make an educated guess. For instance, a toll developer may set missing values of a given input variable as the mode value for that input variable.[501] Let us say that, for instance, fifty-five out of one hundred individuals in a dataset are males, and one of the one hundred individuals is missing an observation for the gender variable, that missing value would be accordingly attributed as male.[502]

§§ On a cautionary note, there are problems associated with attributing the mistaken values for several individuals, even though some machine learning algorithms may have room for much more granular guessing processes. Tellingly, in these cases, the machine learning algorithm will pinpoint other individuals in the dataset that are akin to those with missing values, and attribution values that tend to be displayed by the **similar-situated individuals**.[503] Unsurprisingly, choosing to implement these techniques often requires a trade-off.[504]

§§ Compellingly, the data scientists would likely be adding some values that turn out to be mistaken, and this issue, in turn, is likely to render the machine learning algorithm considerably less accurate and considerably less generalizable. Beyond of missing values, data scientists also scrub out inaccurate values. One immediate quandary emerges though: what can the scientist do to identify inaccurate values? Identifying, and interpreting, missing values is not a walk in the park. For instance, when reviewing the data in tabular form, cells may be blank or filled up with a

---

[500] Lehr, David/Ohm, Paul, "Playing with the Data: What Legal Scholars Should Learn About Machine Learning", *cit.*, pp. 653–718.

[501] See: Breiman, Leo et al., *Package Random Forest: Breiman and Cutlers Random Forests for Classification and Regression*, 10–11 (Oct. 7, 2015), https://cran.rproject.org/web/packages/randomForest/randomForest.pdf [https://perma.cc/JY9N-LYBY] (discussing how the random Forest package for R contains the "na.roughfix" function, which allows for the attribution of missing values on the basis of median or mode); Meyer, David et al., *Package 'E1071': Misc Functions of the Department of Statistics, Probability Theory Group (Formerly: E1071)*, Tu Wien 25 (Feb. 2, 2017), https://cran.rproject.org/web/packages/e1071/e1071.pdf [https://perma.cc/BD82-7UK7] (discussing how the e1071 package for R, which implements a bunch machine-learning algorithms, such as support vector machines, which contains the "impute" function. Impute function, in turn, allows for the attribution of missing values based on median or mode). See: Lehr, David/Ohm, Paul, "Playing with the Data: What Legal Scholars Should Learn About Machine Learning", *cit.*, pp. 653–718.

[502] Lehr, David/Ohm, Paul, "Playing with the Data: What Legal Scholars Should Learn About Machine Learning", *cit.*, pp. 653–718.

[503] See: Breiman, Leo et al., *Package 'Random Forest': Breiman and Cutler's Random Forests for Classification and Regression*, 10–11 (Oct. 7, 2015), 23–24 (describing how the random Forest package for R contains the "rfImpute" function, which initially substitutes missing values with the median or mode using "na.roughfix," and subsequently runs the random forest algorithm on the data to generate proximity measures, which, in turn, update the previously roughly imputed values). See: Lehr, David/Ohm, Paul, "Playing with the Data: What Legal Scholars Should Learn About Machine Learning", *cit.*, pp. 653–718. See: Part V, this chapter, Sect. 5.1.1.5.2.2.1.2 of this book (on one of the foundations underpinning a thing-centred artificial intelligence: the comparison of similarly situated individuals).

[504] Lehr, David/Ohm, Paul, "Playing with the Data: What Legal Scholars Should Learn About Machine Learning", *cit.*, pp. 653–718.

seemingly inscrutable indicator such «NA». In stark contrast, inaccurate values might appear legitimate.[505]

§§ Bereft of some external clue that a value may be inaccurate, such as knowledge that a measurement technique was inadequately used, data scientists may be either led astray or stay otherwise stranded in shallow waters. It is true that values could be so exorbitant that they are most likely inaccurate, but truer still this is hardly the solace the data scientists are looking for. For instance, an allegedly ten-year-old person in a dataset with actionable and meaningful information on credit card usage amounts to a smoking gun evidence, and thereupon reeks, of a mistake in the same way a corporation with a trillion dollars in annual turnover[506] would.

§§ Data scientists must be keenly wary of these warped types of **outliers**, an endeavour that can be accomplished by the tools fleshed out in the next section. If data scientists manage to identify probable inaccurate values, they will most likely face fundamentally the same choices as when coming across a missing value. Unless they are to successfully track down the primal source of the data and obtain or estimate the true value, they ought to either erase the corresponding subject or attribute a more likely value.[507] It is a crucially important decision.[508]

5.1.2.6 Summary Statistics Review That Lies Beyond, But Intertwines with, the Problem Definition of Prediction Goal, Data Collection and Data Cleaning

§§ Pundits often aver that the extant literature has lent new urgency to concerns about playing with the data. This endeavour—playing with data—has typically three meaningful stages: **problem definition**, **data collection**, and **data cleaning**. Note, though, that much lies beyond those three stages. Compellingly, before any machine learning algorithm itself can be devised, created, and subsequently deployed, a data scientist must carefully **review summary statistics** of every single variable—input and output[509]—in the dataset.[510]

---

[505] Lehr, David/Ohm, Paul, "Playing with the Data: What Legal Scholars Should Learn About Machine Learning", *cit.*, pp. 653–718.

[506] Lehr, David/Ohm, Paul, "Playing with the Data: What Legal Scholars Should Learn About Machine Learning", *cit.*, pp. 653–718.

[507] Lehr, David/Ohm, Paul, "Playing with the Data: What Legal Scholars Should Learn About Machine Learning", *cit.*, pp. 653–718.

[508] Lehr, David/Ohm, Paul, "Playing with the Data: What Legal Scholars Should Learn About Machine Learning", *cit.*, pp. 653–718.

[509] Lehr, David/Ohm, Paul, "Playing with the Data: What Legal Scholars Should Learn About Machine Learning", *cit.*, pp. 653–718.

[510] See: Berk, Richard A., *Statistical Learning from a Regression Perspective*, *cit.*, pp. 337–338 ("All data explorations must start with an effort to get 'close' to the data. This requires a careful inspection of elementary descriptive statistics: means, standard deviations, histograms, cross-tabulations, scatterplots and the like"); Witten, Ian H. e al, *Data Mining: Practical Machine Learning Tools and*

§§ With **summary statistics review**, the data scientist accurately describes the values a particular variable takes on. As far as quantitative variables are concerned, analysing summary statistics may require, for each variable, establishing its minimum, twenty-fifth percentile, median, mean, seventy-fifth percentile, and maximum. On the flip side, class variables, in turn, may require establishing what percentage of cases are in each class.[511]

5.1.2.6.1 «Pulling Back the Curtain» of Summary Statistics Review: The Phenomenon of «Overfitting»

§§ What is the purpose of summary statistics review? One reason stands out from the crowd: cast off, and sweep aside, **outliers**. Recall, **outliers** are nothing but values that fall very much below or very much above markers like[512] the twenty-fifth and seventy-fifth percentiles, respectively. **Outliers** are hardly uplifting news for data scientists. **Outliers** are indeed bad news for the latter. And for two reasons. Firstly, several (yet definitely not all) machine learning algorithms routinely grapple with a phenomenon coined as **«overfitting»**.[513]

§§ **Outliers** arise from **noise**, or unfathomable randomness,[514] which has an entrenched presence in all datasets. To add to the data scientists' woes, if a given statistical method has a penchant for, and is fond of, finding correlations in data, chances are that such tool will identify as legitimate correlations via unfathomable

---

Techniques, Heidelberg, Springer, 2016, p. 65 ("Simple tools that show histograms of the distribution of values of nominal attributes, and graphs of the values of numeric attributes... are very helpful.... [They] make it easy to identify outliers, which may very well represent errors in the data file.... Domain experts need to be consulted to explain anomalies, missing values, the significance of integers that represent categories rather than numeric quantities, and so on. Pairwise plots of one attribute against another, or each attribute against the class value, can be extremely revealing").

511 Lehr, David/Ohm, Paul, "Playing with the Data: What Legal Scholars Should Learn About Machine Learning", *cit.*, pp. 653–718.

512 Lehr, David/Ohm, Paul, "Playing with the Data: What Legal Scholars Should Learn About Machine Learning", *cit.*, pp. 653–718.

513 See: Berk, Richard A., *Statistical Learning from a Regression Perspective*, *cit.*, p. 42; Murphy, Kevin Patrick, *Machine Learning: A Probabilistic Perspective*, *cit.*, p. 22; Domingos, Pedro, "A Few Useful Things to Know About Machine Learning", *COMM. ACM*, Volume 55, 2012, pp. 81–82.

514 Teigena, Halvor/Kanten, Alf Børre, "Out of the blue: on the suddenness of perceived chance events", *Thinking & Reasoning*, Volume 29, n.º 1, 2023, pp. 137–175 (137) ("*people commonly use terms like 'random', 'by chance', or 'accidentally' when they describe occurrences that sidestep the normal course of events, with no apparent causal link to ongoing activities. Such intrusive events are typically perceived as happening all of a sudden.* This was demonstrated in seven experiments (N ¼ 1299) by asking people to identify statements they believed belonged to stories about chance events, and by comparing chance vs. nonchance events from their own life and from the lives of others. Suddenness also appeared to be more strongly associated with beginnings than with endings of an episode. Thus, statements about sudden beginnings of a career or a relationship were more readily believed to happen 'by chance' than 'not by chance'. *But life-changing events did not become more accidental simply by being placed in the beginning of a 'life chapter'. These studies highlight a central but neglected feature of perceived randomness*"). Italics added.

randomness, including outliers, in the training data. That unfathomable randomness, in turn, will most likely not be the same in the real-world data to which the machine learning algorithm is to be deployed/applied.[515]

§§ Other cause for concern over **outliers** is its perceived **lack of generalizability**—a machine learning algorithm may fail to perform as well on real-world data as it did on training data. Note, though, that has nothing to do with **overfitting**. For instance, if certain input variables take on non-randomly exceedingly high or extremely low values in the **training dataset** and **test dataset**, yet not in real world data, the algorithmic rules a machine learning algorithm learns to create algorithmic predictions in the former might bluntly fail on the latter.[516]

§§ It is true that data analysts must be on the lookout for outliers, but truer still there is another reason for analysts to carefully perform summary statistics review, with a sharper focus on those related with the outcome variable. Pivotally, a quality benchmark, as well as a paradigm, of machine learning analysis is training a algorithm on one random sample of the complete dataset and assessing—or testing[517]—it on another sample.

§§ Under this quality benchmark/paradigm, a noticeably flawed outcome variable—i.e. one with relatively few high and/or low values — might need sampling a bigger percentage of the complete dataset for the **training dataset** and a smaller percentage for the **test dataset**.[518]

5.1.2.6.2 «Decoding» Data Partitioning: Randomly Split an Entire Dataset into the «Training Dataset» and the «Test Dataset» to Ensure Overall Accuracy

§§ Having the very same data scientist designing a machine learning algorithm and subsequently assessing it entirely on the very same data[519] is as rare as hen's teeth. That happens for a good reason: a predictive undertaking of any kind seeks to create a tool that forecasts—validly, accurately, and reliably—in the real world. Dispiritingly,

---

[515] Lehr, David/Ohm, Paul, "Playing with the Data: What Legal Scholars Should Learn About Machine Learning", *cit.*, pp. 653–718.

[516] Lehr, David/Ohm, Paul, "Playing with the Data: What Legal Scholars Should Learn About Machine Learning", *cit.*, pp. 653–718.

[517] Lehr, David/Ohm, Paul, "Playing with the Data: What Legal Scholars Should Learn About Machine Learning", *cit.*, pp. 653–718.

[518] Lehr, David/Ohm, Paul, "Playing with the Data: What Legal Scholars Should Learn About Machine Learning", *cit.*, pp. 653–718.

[519] See: Murphy, Kevin Patrick, *Machine Learning: A Probabilistic Perspective*, *cit.*, p. 23 ("Unfortunately, when training the model, we don't have access to the test set (by assumption)."); Domingos, Pedro, "A Few Useful Things to Know About Machine Learning", *cit.*, p. 80 ("The most common mistake among machine learning beginners is to test on the training data and have the illusion of success").

though, there is a plethora of reasons why the data a data scientist collates may not reflect the real world.[520]

§§ Why that happens in the first place? To begin with, the dataset could have been in all likelihood harvested in a non-representative[521] manner.[522] In addition to that, relevant changes could have occurred in the population or in the system from which data were collated between when data collection took place and when a machine learning algorithm is applied.[523]

[520] Lehr, David/Ohm, Paul, "Playing with the Data: What Legal Scholars Should Learn About Machine Learning", *cit.*, pp. 653–718.

[521] But see: Kim, Pauline T., "Data-Driven Discrimination at Work", *William and Mary Law Review*, Volume 58, 2017, p. 918 ("If the goal is to reduce biased outcomes, then a simple prohibition on using data about race or sex could be either wholly ineffective or actually counterproductive due to the existence of class proxies and the risk of omitted variable bias"); Lipton, Zachary et al., "Does Mitigating ML's Impact Disparity Require Treatment Disparity?", NIPS Proceedings 1, 2018, https://arxiv.org/pdf/1711.07076.pdf [https://perma.cc/X8VF-EY53] (arguing, premised on statistical examples, that a prohibition on race or sex data is rather counterproductive indeed); Corbett-Davies, Sam/Goel, Sharad, "The Measure and Mismeasure of Fairness: a critical Review of Fair Machine Learning", *Cornell University Library*, 2018, passim (discussing the "[l]imitations of anti-classification" as a fairness metric). See also: Kim, Pauline T., "Data-Driven Discrimination at Work", *cit.*, p. 867 ("[I]f the goal is to discourage classification bias, then the law should not forbid the inclusion of race, sex, or other sensitive information as variables, but seek to preserve these variables, and perhaps even include them in some complex models"); Kroll, Joshua A., et al., "Accountable Algorithms", *University of Pennsylvania Law Review*, Volume 165, 2017, pp. 633, 693–695. See also: Kim, Pauline T., "Data-Driven Discrimination at Work", *cit.*, p. 866 ("**classification bias** occurs when employers rely on classification schemes, such as data algorithms, to sort or score workers in ways that worsen inequality or disadvantage along the lines of race, sex, or other protected characteristics"). These two uses of the word "bias" correspond to the notions of irrational versus rational **(or statistical) discrimination.** Mayson, Sandra G., "Bias In, Bias Out", *cit.*, pp. 2218–2300. See also: Kleinberg, Jon et al., "Algorithmic Fairness", *AEA Papers & Proceedings*, Volume 108, 2018, pp. 22–23 (discussing, anchored in a batch of national data, that including race as an input variable to a machine-learning college-admissions algorithm both "improves predicted GPAs of admitted students" and can augment "the fraction of admitted students who are black").

[522] See: Lavrakas, Paul J., *Encyclopedia of Survey Research Methods*, Los Angeles/Washington D. C./New York/London, Sage, 2008, pp. 1–1000 (254–255) ("In order to avoid [threatening external validity], the researcher should make certain that the sampling design leads to the selection of a sample that is representative of the population"). See also: Kukull, Walter A./Ganguli, Mary, "Generalizability: The Trees, the Forest, and the Low-Hanging Fruit", *Neurology*, Volume 78, 2012, p. 1886 (drilling into, and shedding light on, the concept of generalizability and how representative sampling factors into it, especially in the purview of clinical and epidemiological studies). See: Lehr, David/Ohm, Paul, "Playing with the Data: What Legal Scholars Should Learn About Machine Learning", *cit.*, pp. 653–718.

[523] See: Lavrakas, Paul J., *Encyclopedia of Survey Research Methods*, *cit.*, p. 255 ("In order for a survey to be characterized as externally valid, the results should be generalizable and essentially remain invariant across different points in time"). Pundits have contended this mismatch could pose a serious problem for machine learning algorithms underpinning judges' decisions to release individuals on bail. Strikingly, if the training data were gleaned/collated before the implementation of bail reforms, but the machine learning algorithms were used after the foregoing implementation, they could forecast individuals as riskier than they indeed would be. See: Koepke, John Logan/Robinson, David G., *Zombie Predictions and the Future of Bail Reform*, https://ssrn.com/abstract=3041622 [https://perma.cc/Z8AH-3HWC]. See: Lehr, David/Ohm, Paul,

Last but not least, there is always a perceived degree of randomness[524] in the system that should be accounted for. Such a dollop of randomness might explain why a data collected at one point in time was representative and non-representative of the system at a later stage.[525] The ground truth is that which always exists a degree of uncertainty that haunts, and might hinder the work of, a data scientist in developing a machine learning algorithm.

§§ To forestall such a gruesome scenario, data scientists have been pouring in staggering efforts to develop methods of gauging, with some inevitable dash of uncertainty, how well a machine learning algorithm trained on a given dataset will perform on another dataset. One mainstream method that has been widely used is to randomly split, or partition, an entire dataset into two segments: **a «training» dataset**[526] and a **«test» dataset**.

§§ It is noteworthy that a machine learning algorithm is highly trained and learns the **optimal predictive rules** during model training. Afterwards, the machine learning algorithm's accuracy and other relevant performance metrics are painstakingly evaluated by enquiring it to forecast the outcomes of the subjects in the latter. In this vein, a machine learning algorithm is compelled to forecast data it has not dealt with before. In this way, data scientists nurture the undying hope to forecast outcomes in the «real world»[527] performance. To the extent randomness in the real

---

"Playing with the Data: What Legal Scholars Should Learn About Machine Learning", *cit.*, pp. 653–718.

[524] Teigena, Halvor/Kanten, Alf Børre, "Out of the blue: on the suddenness of perceived chance events", *Thinking & Reasoning*, Volume 29, n. ° 1, 2023, pp. 137–175 (137) ("*people commonly use terms like 'random', 'by chance', or 'accidentally' when they describe occurrences that sidestep the normal course of events, with no apparent causal link to ongoing activities. Such intrusive events are typically perceived as happening all of a sudden.* This was demonstrated in seven experiments (N ¼ 1299) by asking people to identify statements they believed belonged to stories about chance events, and by comparing chance vs. nonchance events from their own life and from the lives of others. Suddenness also appeared to be more strongly associated with beginnings than with endings of an episode. Thus, statements about sudden beginnings of a career or a relationship were more readily believed to happen 'by chance' than 'not by chance'. *But life-changing events did not become more accidental simply by being placed in the beginning of a 'life chapter'. These studies highlight a central but neglected feature of perceived randomness*"). Italics added.

[525] Lavrakas, Paul J., *Encyclopedia of Survey Research Methods*, *cit.*, p. 255 ("The major concern with this threat [of setting characteristics] to the external validity is that the findings of a particular survey research study may be influenced by some unique circumstances and conditions, and, if so, then the results are not generalizable to other survey research studies with different settings"). Randomness is amounts to a factor that could effectively render the setting of a specific body of evidence different than that of another body of evidence at a different juncture. See: Lehr, David/ Ohm, Paul, "Playing with the Data: What Legal Scholars Should Learn About Machine Learning", *cit.*, pp. 653–718.

[526] Lehr, David/Ohm, Paul, "Playing with the Data: What Legal Scholars Should Learn About Machine Learning", *cit.*, pp. 653–718.

[527] Lehr, David/Ohm, Paul, "Playing with the Data: What Legal Scholars Should Learn About Machine Learning", *cit.*, pp. 653–718.

world will, in all likelihood, be starkly different than that of the training data, so will that of the **test dataset**.[528]

§§ **Partitioning data** into **training dataset** and **test dataset** ranks is one of the most reliable and trustworthy methods for measuring an algorithm's real-world performance.[529] When a data scientist partitions the data, the former faces, and most likely will be met with, a conundrum: **(i)** what is the exact amount of data that should be assigned to successfully carry out both the **«training dataset»** and the **«test dataset»**? **(ii)** What is the specific metric underpinning both: seventy-five percent of subjects should be allocated to the training dataset whereas twenty-five should be assigned the test dataset? **(iii)** if so, would that metric suffice to ensure overall accuracy? **(iv)** Would a fifty-fifty split suffice instead? Pundits often aver that if more data are allocated to the **training dataset**, a machine learning algorithm may fare better in learning **optimal predictive rules** since it has a larger amount and a greater variety of subjects from which to adroitly learn.[530] But here is the twist: if the test dataset is too tiny, a data scientist will get a shoddy, watered-down and tapered off sense of how well the machine leaning algorithm operates. More to the point, a data scientist may also fail to realize how well the machine learning algorithm would perform and the extent to which the latter could **generalize** to a dataset other than those on which it was[531] previously trained.[532]

§§ Importantly, this decision can be steered by three considerations: **(i)** the size of the whole package (i.e. the entire starting dataset), **(ii)** the **summary statistics review** carried out on the outcome variable, and **(iii)** subject matter knowledge about the field to which a machine learning algorithm is applied. Bearing the first consideration very firmly in mind, a bigger dataset tends to tilt towards a more equal-footed split between **«training dataset»** and **test**[533] **datasets**.[534] But much more lies beyond that.

---

[528] Lehr, David/Ohm, Paul, "Playing with the Data: What Legal Scholars Should Learn About Machine Learning", *cit.*, pp. 653–718.

[529] Lehr, David/Ohm, Paul, "Playing with the Data: What Legal Scholars Should Learn About Machine Learning", *cit.*, pp. 653–718.

[530] Lehr, David/Ohm, Paul, "Playing with the Data: What Legal Scholars Should Learn About Machine Learning", *cit.*, pp. 653–718.

[531] Lehr, David/Ohm, Paul, "Playing with the Data: What Legal Scholars Should Learn About Machine Learning", *cit.*, pp. 653–718.

[532] See: Witten, Ian H., *Data Mining: Practical Machine Learning Tools and Techniques*, *cit.*, p. 164 ("There's a dilemma [in deciding how to partition data]: to find a good classifier, we want to use as much of the data as possible for training; to obtain a good error estimate, we want to use as much of it as possible for testing").

[533] Lehr, David/Ohm, Paul, "Playing with the Data: What Legal Scholars Should Learn About Machine Learning", *cit.*, pp. 653–718.

[534] See: Witten, Ian H., *Data Mining: Practical Machine Learning Tools and Techniques*, *cit.*, ("If lots of data are available, there is no problem: we take a large sample and use it for training; then another, independent large sample of different data and use it for testing"). Whilst this quote considers separately sampling the test data from the population of interest, in lieu of partitioning already sampled data, the central thrust of the quote holds in the latter context. Pivotally, if there is a whopping amount of data, an analyst should not be worried about ensuring enough training data at

§§ Crucially, getting a hold of a properly trained machine learning algorithm is of paramount importance in this regard. If there are hundreds of thousands or millions of observations, it is highly unlikely that, by assigning half to the test dataset, the training dataset would be stripped away of, and would be likewise prevented from gaining access to, meaningful examples from which the machine learning algorithm could successfully and reliably learn. Put otherwise, the likelihood of existence of an irksome redundancy in behemoth datasets[535] is exceedingly high.

§§ It is worth recalling that if the dataset is substantially shorter, caution must be accordingly exercised. For a reason that should not be baffling at this juncture: to make meaningful steps towards the development of a properly trained algorithm, a data scientist can, and should, ponder randomly allocating a larger proportion of observations to the training dataset. There is no such thing as set-in-stone mathematical directive mandating how data should be partitioned, yet this somewhat qualitative accounting of dataset dimension[536] is critically important[537] to ensure the algorithm's overall accuracy.

§§ Even if there are several observations in a given dataset, nevertheless, the second consideration previously made—the outcome variable's summary statistics review—could prime the data scientist to partition lopsidedly in favour of a bigger training dataset. Pivotally, this could result if a cluster of outcomes is very[538] rare.[539]

---

the expense of the dimension of the test data. See: Lehr, David/Ohm, Paul, "Playing with the Data: What Legal Scholars Should Learn About Machine Learning", *cit.*, pp. 653–718.

535 Lehr, David/Ohm, Paul, "Playing with the Data: What Legal Scholars Should Learn About Machine Learning", *cit.*, pp. 653–718.

536 Lehr, David/Ohm, Paul, "Playing with the Data: What Legal Scholars Should Learn About Machine Learning", *cit.*, pp. 653–718.

537 Whilst there is no rule applicable in every possible scenario, common splitting ratios for training to test data typically range from 70:30 to 80:20. See: *Amazon Web Services*, 2017, p. 14 ("A common strategy is to take all available labelled data, and split it into training and evaluation subsets, usually with a ratio of 70-80 percent for training and 20-30 percent for evaluation"); Suthaharan, Shan, *Machine Learning Models and Algorithms for Big Data Classification: Thinking with Examples for Effective Learning*, Integrated Systems in Information 36, Sharda, Ramesh/Voß, Stefan (Series Editors), Heidelberg, Springer, 2015, p. 196 ("The commonly used ratio is 80:20 for training and test data sets, based on the Pareto principle") (citations omitted). See: Schrage, Michael, "AI Is Going to Change the 80/20 Rule", Harvard Business Review (Feb. 28, 2017), 2017, https://hbr.org/2017/02/ai-is-going-to-change-the-8020-rule [https://perma.cc/MMU3-RXUB] (fleshing out the Pareto principle and how might be overhauled by artificial intelligence).

538 See: Lehr, David/Ohm, Paul, "Playing with the Data: What Legal Scholars Should Learn About Machine Learning", *cit.*, pp. 653–718.

539 See: Murphy, Kevin Patrick, *Machine Learning: A Probabilistic Perspective*, *cit.*, p. 2 ("[E]ven when one has an apparently massive data set, the effective number of data points for certain cases of interest might be quite small. In fact, data across a variety of domains exhibits a property known as the long tail, which means that a few things... are very common, but most things are quite rare.... *One consequence of the long tail is that understanding or predicting the behavior of most items requires learning from small amounts of data, even if the total amount of data is large*"). Italics added.

§§ More often than not, machine learning algorithm is deployed to forecast precisely these types of unheard of, and unforeseen, events, but even-handedly partitioning a dataset into training dataset and test dataset could imperil some of these observations ending up in the training data. Imagine, if you will, a dataset of five hundred thousand observations, of which only one percent, or five thousand, evince/ display a given **outcome of interest**.[540]

§§ Understandably, the data scientist might be tempted to timely ensure—by **randomly sampling** more than half of her data for training purposes- that the machine learning algorithm possess the ability to learn how to forecast this exceedingly rare outcome of interest.[541]

§§ On this note, it is pivotally important to measure the machine learning algorithm's ability to learn **optimal predictive rules** against the ability to evaluate the algorithm's performance on «unseen», or untested, data. If a data scientist keenly believes that the system is somewhat stable and trustworthy—insofar its inner workings[542] do not change swiftly and unexpectedly—trust can be accordingly placed upon the possibility that unseen, untested, real-world data will bear a striking resemblance with the data previously collected.[543]

§§ On the flip side, if the data scientist eagerly believes that the system itself is erratic, unstable, built in shaky foundations that are slated to wobble sometime soon, a machine learning algorithm, no matter how well-trained, will be of scarce predictive value when applied in the real[544] world.[545]

---

540 Lehr, David/Ohm, Paul, "Playing with the Data: What Legal Scholars Should Learn About Machine Learning", *cit.*, pp. 653–718.

541 Lehr, David/Ohm, Paul, "Playing with the Data: What Legal Scholars Should Learn About Machine Learning", *cit.*, pp. 653–718.

542 Lehr, David/Ohm, Paul, "Playing with the Data: What Legal Scholars Should Learn About Machine Learning", *cit.*, pp. 653–718.

543 Lehr, David/Ohm, Paul, "Playing with the Data: What Legal Scholars Should Learn About Machine Learning", *cit.*, pp. 653–718.

544 Lehr, David/Ohm, Paul, "Playing with the Data: What Legal Scholars Should Learn About Machine Learning", *cit.*, pp. 653–718.

545 See: Berk, Richard A., *Statistical Learning from a Regression Perspective*, *cit.*, p. 336 ("[T]he forecasting tool developed [to predict which high school students are at risk of dropping out] would be applied to new cohorts of students that would likely differ from the training and test samples by more than random sampling error. One might well expect a gradual drift in the background of incoming freshmen and the mix of incentives to remain in school"). Drawing on this example, if it were the case that the primitive dataset had been collated over multifarious actors, meaning that some of this drift in backdrop and incentives was captured across the training and test datasets. Which means that the analyst may be tempted to partition a larger amount of data to the test dataset for the reason pointed out in text.

5.1.3 *Model Selection: The Type of Machine Learning Algorithm (i.e. Random Forests, Decision Trees and So Forth) to Be Built and Deployed to Better Accomplish the Task at Hand. Brief Analysis of Deep «Neural Networks» and Layers of Digital Neurons (Nodes)*

§§ The stage of problem definition has been passed muster. Data on which the machine learning algorithm will operate upon have been successfully collated, cleaned, and partitioned. By the same token, summary statistics review has been fruitfully undertaken. Note, though, there is something missing in this important equation: the machine learning algorithm itself.[546]

§§ Having meaningfully reached this stage, and awash with an undying hope to build a state-of-the-art algorithm, the good data scientist then strolls to stage where he/she needs to choose the type, class, model of algorithm to implement.

§§ A data scientist could either choose a machine learning algorithm by merely implementing a pre-designed algorithm made publicly available as a cluster of code in a body of statistical software or a programming[547] language.[548] On the other hand, the data scientist could build program her own machine learning algorithm from scratch. This book broaches both possibilities, leveraging on a scintillating body of legal research that have been steering us all along.[549]

---

[546] Lehr, David/Ohm, Paul, "Playing with the Data: What Legal Scholars Should Learn About Machine Learning", *cit.*, pp. 653–718.

[547] Lehr, David/Ohm, Paul, "Playing with the Data: What Legal Scholars Should Learn About Machine Learning", *cit.*, pp. 653–718.

[548] Examples of such packages available for R, a very popular statistical programming language, can be found in: see Breiman, Leo et al., *Package 'Random Forest': Breiman and Cutler's Random Forests for Classification and Regression*, 10–11 (Oct. 7, 2015), https://cran.rproject.org/web/packages/randomForest/randomForest.pdf [https://perma.cc/JY9N-LYBY]; Meyer, David et al., *Package 'E1071': Misc Functions of the Department of Statistics, Probability Theory Group (Formerly: E1071)*, Tu Wien 25 (Feb. 2, 2017), https://cran.rproject.org/web/packages/e1071/e1071.pdf [https://perma.cc/BD82-7UK7] (discussing the implementation of support vector machines); Ridgeway, Greg, Package GBM: Generalized Boosted Regression Models (Mar. 21, 2017), https://cran.rproject.org/web/packages/gbm/gbm.pdf [https://perma.cc/UW79-3QTQ] (fleshing out the implementation of AdaBoost and stochastic gradient boosting). By the same token, the scikit learn library for the Python programming language lays down a wide range of machine learning algorithms. See: *Scikit-Learn*, http://scikit-learn.org [https://perma.cc/8MDA4EXF]. It is important to note, though, that laying down any of these "pre-programmed algorithms" will still require the programmer to make very important choices on how they should be "tuned". See: Lehr, David/Ohm, Paul, "Playing with the Data: What Legal Scholars Should Learn About Machine Learning", *cit.*, pp. 653–718.

[549] Lehr, David/Ohm, Paul, "Playing with the Data: What Legal Scholars Should Learn About Machine Learning", *cit.*, pp. 653–718.

§§ With regard to the «a kind of model», as adumbrated earlier in this book, the overwhelming majority, if not all, of machine learning algorithms operate essentially by optimizing—i.e. either minimizing or maximizing[550]—an **objective function.**[551]

§§ For instance, what renders **random forests models** all part of the same class is their construction of a «forest» of several classification or **regression trees**, accompanied by some kind of averaging of predictions across[552] trees.[553]

§§ It bears mentioning that different implementations of random forests algorithms can optimize different types of objective functions[554] and build different numbers of trees,[555] yet, at this core, they are all the same when it comes to their use of the forest.[556]

§§ By the same token, in spite of the vast assortment of pathways to build and implement a deep neural network,[557] one can meld, and accordingly cobble

---

[550] Lehr, David/Ohm, Paul, "Playing with the Data: What Legal Scholars Should Learn About Machine Learning", *cit.*, pp. 653–718.

[551] It oft-averred that the standard for classes of models may fall short of initial expectations, especially for more advanced readers. Revealingly, machine learning algorithms mechanisms produce predictions that can be ultimately "similar" or "dissimilar" along a wide range of dimensions. Moreover, these dimensions work at distinct degrees of generality. For instance, a random forests model could be deemed its own class since it uniquely deploys classification and regression trees, but it could alternatively be bundled together into a broader technological apparatus within which a class of set of machine-learning techniques operate upon. See: Lehr, David/Ohm, Paul, "Playing with the Data: What Legal Scholars Should Learn About Machine Learning", *cit.*, pp. 653–718.

[552] Lehr, David/Ohm, Paul, "Playing with the Data: What Legal Scholars Should Learn About Machine Learning", *cit.*, pp. 653–718.

[553] See: Breiman, Leo, "Random Forests", *Machine Learning*, Volume 45, 2001, pp. 5–32 (5) (providing a granular and fine-grained description of random forest models and their construction). See also: Breiman, Leo, "Random Forests", *cit.*, pp. 5–32 (5) ("*Random forests are a combination of tree predictors such that each tree depends on the values of a random vector sampled independently and with the same distribution for all trees in the forest. The generalization error for forests converges a.s. to a limit as the number of trees in the forest becomes large. The generalization error of a forest of tree classifiers depends on the strength of the individual trees in the forest and the correlation between them.* Using a random selection of features to split each node yields error rates that compare favorably to Adaboost (Y. Freund & R. Schapire, *Machine Learning*: *Proceedings of the Thirteenth International conference*, ***, 148–156), but are more robust with respect to noise. Internal estimates monitor error, strength, and correlation and these are used to show the response to increasing the number of features used in the splitting. *Internal estimates are also used to measure variable importance. These ideas are also applicable to regression*"). Italics added.

[554] See: Berk, Richard A., *Statistical Learning from a Regression Perspective*, *cit.*, p. 201 (fleshing out how, when using random forests for classification, a "1-0 loss" function and the deviance of forecasted probabilities amount to two possible loss functions).

[555] See: Breiman, Leo, "Random Forests", *Machine Learning*, cit., pp. 17–18 (arguing that the "ntree" argument for the "randomForest" function bestows upon the user the possibility to set the number of trees built). See: Lehr, David/Ohm, Paul, "Playing with the Data: What Legal Scholars Should Learn About Machine Learning", *cit.*, pp. 653–718.

[556] Lehr, David/Ohm, Paul, "Playing with the Data: What Legal Scholars Should Learn About Machine Learning", *cit.*, pp. 653–718.

[557] Recall, algorithms make their inferences and draw their conclusions in a manner eerily unknown, even for the cohort of programmers that designed them. This is deemed *black box*, that further enhances the shroud of mystery under which algorithms are cloaked. See, for a compelling account

together, such implementations into the broad scope category of «neural network» class of models. Recall,[558] deep neural networks are models that pass on information between «layers» of digital neurons (widely tagged as nodes),[559] which entails some mathematical[560] processing.[561]

---

of AI black box: Ver: Bathaee, Yavar, "The Artificial Intelligence Black Box and the Failure of Intent and Causation", *Harvard Journal of Law and Technology*, n.º 37, 2018, p. 901 (adduces that "*one possible reason AI may be a black box to humans is that it relies on machine-learning algorithms that internalize data in ways that are not easily audited or understood by humans (…)*" "*first, a lack may arise from the complexity of the algorithm's structure, such as with deep neural network, which consists of thousands of artificial neurons working together in a diffuse way to solve a problem. This reason for AI being a black box is referred to as "complexity". Second, the lack of transparency may arise because the AI is using a machine-learning algorithm that relies on geometric relationships that humans cannot visualize, such as with support vector machines. This reason for AI being a black box is referred to as "dimensionality"*"). Italics added. But see: Pearl, Judea, *Causality*, 2nd edition, Cambridge, Cambridge University Press, 2009 (on the fundamental tenets of causality). But see: Kilbertus, Niki/Carulla, Mateo Rojas/Parascandolo, Giambattista/Hardt, Moritz/Janzing, Dominik/Schoellkopf, Bernhard, "Avoiding Discrimination through Causal Reasoning", *Advances in Neural Information Processing Systems*, I. Guyon, U. V. Luxburg, S. Bengio, H. Wallach, R. Fergus, S. Vishwanathan, and R. Garnett (Eds.), Vol. 30. Curran Associates, Inc., 2017, pp. 656–666 (arguing that is feasible to avoiding discrimination through a granular and fine-grained causal reasoning). But see: Part V, this chapter, Sect. 5.1.7.2 of this book (on law number two to control algorithmic decision-making, which mandates that black box models must not be entrusted with the task of making high stake decisions—v.g. health and freedom). See: Part V, this chapter, Sects. 5.1.1.5.2.2–5.1.1.5.2.2.1.4 of this book (on the fundamental shift away from causation to correlations in algorithmic decision-making).

558 See: Part II, Chap. 2, Sects. 2.1 and 2.1.1 of this book (for further insights on how the human brain and deep neural network function, respectively).

559 Lehr, David/Ohm, Paul, "Playing with the Data: What Legal Scholars Should Learn About Machine Learning", *cit.*, pp. 653–718.

560 See: Aggarwal, C. C., *Neural networks and deep learning*, Heidelberg, Springer, 2018, passim; Agrawal, A., Gans, J., & Goldfarb, A., "Prediction machines (updated and expanded): The simple economics of artificial intelligence", *Harvard Business Review Press*, 2022; Agrawal, A., Gans, J., & Goldfarb, A., "Power and prediction: The disruptive economics of artificial intelligence", *Harvard Business Review Press*, 2022; Bengio, Y., Hinton, G., Yao, A., Song, D., Abbeel, P., Harari, Y. N., Hadfield, G., Russell, S., Kahneman, D., & Mindermann, S., *Managing ai risks in an era of rapid progress*, arXiv preprint arXiv:2310.17688, 2023 (on neural networks and deep learning that operate in the age of Artificial Intelligence-embedded technologies).

561 See: Murphy, Kevin Patrick, *Machine Learning: A Probabilistic Perspective*, *cit.*, pp. 565–572 (fleshing out the implementation in the neural network of models).

5.1.3.1 Factors That Influence the Model Selection: The Type of Output Variable, the Ability (or Lack Thereof) to Implement an «Asymmetric Cost Ratio», the Ability to Provide Interpretable Reasons for the Predictions (Interpretable Machine Learning), the Likelihood of Overfitting, Meaningful Opportunities for Fine-Tuning Parameters and Some Practical Resource Limitations

§§ Picking out a model can be either straightforward or cumbersome, depending on the backdrop and the task at hand. Six considerations sway **model selection**: **(i)** the type of output variable, **(ii)** the ability (or lack thereof) to implement an **«asymmetric cost ratio,»**[562] **(iii)** the ability to provide interpretable reasons for the predictions (a kernel of **interpretable machine learning**[563]), **(iv)** the likelihood of **overfitting**, **(v)** meaningful opportunities for tuning, and **(vi)** some practical resource limitations.[564] A brief (thumbnail) sketch overview will be given on each, with a view to bestow upon data scientists a wide range of possibilities to choose from.[565]

5.1.3.1.1 The Type of Output Variable (Strands of Support Vector Machines and Original Random Forest Algorithms)

§§ The data scientist's choices could be effortlessly narrowed down by the type of outcome variable with which the former is working. Several machine learning

---

[562] Lehr, David/Ohm, Paul, "Playing with the Data: What Legal Scholars Should Learn About Machine Learning", *cit.*, pp. 653–718. Note, though, that when Richard Berk trained the algorithm only to maximize for **overall accuracy**, it predicted rearrest for 17% of the white subgroup and 33% of the black subgroup (a 16 percentage-point difference). Strikingly, the false-positive rates were 16% for the white subgroup whereas for the black groups was 28% (a 12 percentage-point difference). See: Berk, Richard, "Accuracy and Fairness for Juvenile Justice Risks Assessments", *cit.*, p. 180. Notably, when Richard Berk changed the algorithm to equalize the *cost ratios*, it predicted rearrest for 10% of the white subgroup and 29% of the black subgroup (a 19 percentage-point difference). Relatedly, the false-positive rates were 8% for the white subset and 22% for the black subset (a 14 percentage-point difference). See: Berk, Richard, "Accuracy and Fairness for Juvenile Justice Risks Assessments", *cit.*, p. 185. See: Mayson, Sandra G., "Bias In, Bias Out", *cit.*, pp. 2218–2300.

[563] See: Part V, this chapter, Sects. 5.1.7–5.1.7.5 of this book (on the five laws to control algorithmic decision-making). See: Part V, this chapter, Sects. 5.1.8–5.1.8.5 of this book (on the five laws to interpret algorithmic decision-making).

[564] Lehr, David/Ohm, Paul, "Playing with the Data: What Legal Scholars Should Learn About Machine Learning", *cit.*, pp. 653–718.

[565] Lehr, David/Ohm, Paul, "Playing with the Data: What Legal Scholars Should Learn About Machine Learning", *cit.*, pp. 653–718.

algorithms are fully equipped to forecast binary classes and perpetual numeric[566] variables.[567]

§§ It is important to note that although computer scientists and statisticians alike are permanently fine-tuning extant machine learning algorithms, a cluster of algorithms have not yet been deployed to measure certain types of responses.[568] In other instances, algorithms that have been originally built to undertake certain tasks were extended to other purposes with little to none success though.

§§ For instance, variants of **support vector machines**,[569] which were initially programmed for **binary classification**, can be successfully deployed to multifarious classification problems, but failed nonetheless to retain some theoretical properties that developers cherish the most.[570] By the same token, the original **random forest algorithm** does not allow for predicting ordinal responses,[571] and earnest attempts have been made to extend it to other domains. But to no avail.[572] Consequently, if the

566 Lehr, David/Ohm, Paul, "Playing with the Data: What Legal Scholars Should Learn About Machine Learning", *cit.*, pp. 653–718.

567 See: Ericson, Gary et al., "How to Choose Algorithms for Microsoft Azure Machine Learning", *Microsoft Azure* (Apr. 25, 2017), https://docs.microsoft.com/enus/azure/machine-learning/machine-learning-algorithm-choice [https://perma.cc/2C8L-FZSH] (discussing the extent to which there is an overlap between, amongst other machine learning algorithms, decision forests, boosted decision trees, and deep neural networks with a sharper focus on their skillset/capabilities to engage in both classification and regression).

568 Lehr, David/Ohm, Paul, "Playing with the Data: What Legal Scholars Should Learn About Machine Learning", *cit.*, pp. 653–718.

569 See: Bathaee, Yavar, "The Artificial Intelligence Black Box and the Failure of Intent and Causation", *Harvard Journal of Law and Technology*, n.º 37, 2018, p. 901 (adduces that "*one possible reason AI may be a black box to humans is that it relies on machine-learning algorithms that internalize data in ways that are not easily audited or understood by humans* (…)" "*first, a lack may arise from the complexity of the algorithm's structure, such as with deep neural network, which consists of thousands of artificial neurons working together in a diffuse way to solve a problem. This reason for AI being a black box is referred to as "complexity". Second, the lack of transparency may arise because the AI is using a machine-learning algorithm that relies on geometric relationships that humans cannot visualize, such as with support vector machines. This reason for AI being a black box is referred to as "dimensionality"*"). Italics added.

570 See: Ürün Doğan et al., "A Unified View on Multi-Class Support Vector Classification", *Journal of Machine Learning Research*, Volume 17, 2016, p. 1 (discussing several ramifications of support vector machines to multifarious classification problems and their intrinsic properties); Chih-Wei Hsu & Chih-Jen Lin, "Comparison of Methods for Multi-Class Support Vector Machines", *IEEE Transactions Neural Networks*, Volume 13, 2002, p. 415 (bestowing upon lay readers an offering of issues similar to those taken up by Doğan et al.).

571 Silka Janitza et al., "Random Forest for Ordinal Responses: Prediction and Variable Selection", *Computational Statistics & Data Analysis*, Volume 2016, pp. 57, 70 ("The use of the ordering in the levels of an *ordinal response variable in tree construction is not supported by the classical [random forests] version of Breiman*"). Italics added.

572 See: Silka Janitza et al., "Random Forest for Ordinal Responses: Prediction and Variable Selection", *cit.*, p. 71 ("[O]rdinal regression trees are a reasonable alternative to classification trees if the response is ordinal. However, the differences were only small and their practical relevance is questionable").

outcome variable has multifarious classes or ordinal classes, a data scientist might have less algorithms to choose from.[573]

5.1.3.1.2 The Ability (or Lack Thereof) to Implement an «Asymmetric Cost Ratio» (the Cost Ratio for False Positives to False Negatives)

§§ The ability (or lack thereof) to code in, and successfully implement, an **«asymmetric cost ratio»**[574] is pivotally important. In any predictive endeavour,[575] no matter how small, there are different types of errors, or inaccurate,[576] predictions.[577]

§§ When tasked with the duty to accurately estimating a binary outcome, the algorithm can produce a wide range of **false positives**[578] (forecasting something when that something failed to happen as predicted in the real world) and **false negatives**[579] (failure to predict a given scenario that actually happened in the real world). When

---

[573] Lehr, David/Ohm, Paul, "Playing with the Data: What Legal Scholars Should Learn About Machine Learning", *cit.*, pp. 653–718.

[574] Berk, Richard A., *Statistical Learning from a Regression Perspective*, 2nd edition, Heidelberg, Springer, 2016, p. 253 ("[I]f for policy or subject matter reasons one needs to tune to approximate a target *asymmetric cost ratio* in a confusion table, *model selection is in play once again*"). Italics added. See also: Berk, Richard, "Accuracy and Fairness for Juvenile Justice Risks Assessments", *cit.*, pp. 185–186 (positing that that, to equalize **cost ratios** across racial groups in a juvenile risk-assessment context, the author "separate[d] forecasting exercises" for white and black juveniles, respectively, and that the machine-learning forecasting algorithms the data produced were different for each racial group).

[575] It is bears mentioning that **predictive parity (calibration)** can likewise be despairingly inconsistent with a **single-threshold rule**. At the very least, it does not ensure or necessarily indicate a single threshold for risk classification. See: Mayson, Sandra G., "Bias In, Bias Out", *cit.*, pp. 2218–2300.

[576] Lehr, David/Ohm, Paul, "Playing with the Data: What Legal Scholars Should Learn About Machine Learning", *cit.*, pp. 653–718.

[577] See: Witten, Ian H., *Data Mining: Practical Machine Learning Tools and Techniques*, *cit.*, pp. 179–183 (highlighting the different types of errors and how, in broadly speaking, machine-learning algorithms can be swayed by *asymmetric cost ratios*).

[578] The question of the relative cost of a false positive and false negative in the algorithmic risk assessment context evokes the prominent Blackstone ratio, which stresses the relative costs of false negatives and false positives in the context of criminal conviction and punishment. See: Blackstone, William, *Commentaries on the Laws of England*, 4 volumes, Oxford, Clarendon Press, 1765–1769, p. 352 ("[T]he law holds, that it is better that ten guilty persons escape, than that one innocent suffer"). See: Mayson, Sandra G., "Bias In, Bias Out", *cit.*, pp. 2218–2300. Angwin, Julia et al., "Machine Bias", *ProPublica* (May 23, 2016), https://www.propublica.org/article/machine-bias-risk-assessments-in-criminal-sentencing [https://perma.cc/4G83-MDAS] (harshly criticizing disparity in false-positive rates as a purely unjustified bias). See also: Freeman, Katherine, "Algorithmic Injustice: How the Wisconsin Supreme Court Failed to Protect Due Process Rights in State v. Loomis", *North Carolina Journal of Law and Technology*, Volume 18, 2016, pp. 75–86 (echoing the very same views).

[579] According to Richard Berk's research on juvenile data, tweaking the algorithm to attain statistical parity spawned a lower **false positive** rate for the black subset than the white (4% versus 9%) yet a higher **false negative** rate (50% versus 40%). See: Berk, Richard, "Accuracy and Fairness for Juvenile Justice Risks Assessments", *cit.*, p. 189. In addition to that, Berk further concluded that for

predicting a continuous outcome, overestimates[580] and underestimates,[581] however small on either end, are part of the «plot».

§§ It is noteworthy that different types of errors are routinely viewed by relevant stakeholders as having different normative valences.[582] Seldom, if ever, a relevant stakeholder to consider being wrong in one manner as likewise harmful as being wrong in the opposite manner[583] Note, though, that many,[584] albeit not all,[585] machine

---

white folks, the algorithm generated 5.25 **false positives** for every **false negative**; whilst for black folks, the algorithm generated 1.85 false negatives for every false positive. See: Berk, Richard, "Accuracy and Fairness for Juvenile Justice Risks Assessments", *cit.*, p. 189.

[580] But see: Dieterich, William et al., "COMPAS Risk Scales: Demonstrating Accuracy Equity and Predictive Parity", *Northpointe Inc.* 1, 2–3, 8–13 (July 8, 2016), http://go.volarisgroup.com/rs/430-MBX-989/images/ProPublica_Commentary_Final_070616.pdf [https://perma.cc/K4GM-RBQY] (stating that a predictive instrument is bigoted/flawed only if a certain score, or a given classification, means a starkly likelihood of the forecasted outcome for members of one racial group than members of the other group). See also: Flores: Anthony W. et al., "False Positives, False Negatives, and False Analyses: A Rejoinder to "Machine Bias: There's Software Used Across the Country to Predict Future Criminals. And It's Biased Against Blacks," *Federal Probation*, Volume 80, 2016, pp. 38–40 (positing that "well-established and accepted standards exist to test for bias in risk assessment"); Skeem, Jennifer L./Lowenkamp, Christopher T., "Risk, Race, and Recidivism: Predictive Bias and Disparate Impact", *cit.*, p. 685 (asserting that if "a given score [has] the same meaning regardless of group membership," the instrument is "unbiased").

[581] See: Kriegler, Brian/Berk, Richard A., "Small Area Estimation of the Homeless in Los Angeles: An Application of Cost-Sensitive Stochastic Gradient Boosting", *Annals of Applied Statistics*, Volume 4, 2010, pp. 1234, 1241 (discussing how stakeholders tend to analyse **underestimates**—measuring that there are fewer homeless individuals in a given county/parish/state than there indeed are—as **more costly than overestimates**—measuring that there are more homeless individuals in a given county/parish/state than there indeed are). See: Lehr, David/Ohm, Paul, "Playing with the Data: What Legal Scholars Should Learn About Machine Learning", *cit.*, pp. 653–718.

[582] Lehr, David/Ohm, Paul, "Playing with the Data: What Legal Scholars Should Learn About Machine Learning", *cit.*, pp. 653–718.

[583] See: Witten, Ian H., *Data Mining: Practical Machine Learning Tools and Techniques*, *cit.*, p. 180 ("In truth, you'd be hard pressed to find an application in which the costs of different kinds of errors were the same"). Bringing forth examples machine-learning applications where estimation of **asymmetric costs** was paramount: Berk, Richard A. et al., "Forecasting Domestic Violence: A Machine Learning Approach to Help Inform Arraignment Decisions", *cit.*, pp. 103–04 (discussing how **false negatives**—forecasting that arrestees will not perpetrate future domestic violence when they indeed do—were regarded by stakeholders as ten times more harmful than **false positives**—forecasting that arrestees will indeed perpetrate future domestic violence when they indeed do not).

[584] See: Berk, Richard A., *Statistical Learning from a Regression Perspective*, *cit.*, pp. 210–213 (describing how to implement asymmetric costs with random forests); Kriegler, Brian/Berk, Richard A., "Small Area Estimation of the Homeless in Los Angeles: An Application of Cost-Sensitive Stochastic Gradient Boosting", *Annals of Applied Statistics*, cit., passim (laying down the groundwork for asymmetric costs with stochastic gradient boosting). See also: Zhi Hua Zhou/Xu-Ying Liu, "Training Cost-Sensitive Neural Networks with Methods Addressing the Class Imbalance Problem", *IEEE Transactions Knowledge & Data Engineering*, Volume 18, 2006, p. 63 (laying down asymmetric costs with deep neural networks).

[585] See: Berk, Richard A., *Statistical Learning from a Regression Perspective*, *cit.*, p. 325 ("A final difficulty with the software [implementing support vector machines in R] is that there is no direct way to address the relative costs of false negatives and false positives"). Scholars have proposed other

learning algorithms bestow upon the data scientist the possibility to determine[586] an **asymmetric cost ratio.**[587] Crucially, data scientist foists mathematical limitations on the machine learning algorithm that force it to make certain types of errors (for example, false positives in the binary classification purview or overestimates in the regression purview) more often than others.[588]

§§ For instance, a **cost ratio** of 5:1 for false positives to false negatives would grant that, for every false negative[589] created, there are five false positives.[590]

---

methods for producing effective cost-sensitive support vector machines. See: Shuichi Katsumata/ Akiko Takeda, "Robust Cost Sensitive Support Vector Machine", *Proceedings of Machine Learning Research*, Volume 38, 2015, p. 434. It is worth recalling that the foregoing methods have not yet been vetted and thoroughly assessed, let alone validated by other stakeholders. See: Lehr, David/ Ohm, Paul, "Playing with the Data: What Legal Scholars Should Learn About Machine Learning", *cit.*, pp. 653–718.

[586] Lehr, David/Ohm, Paul, "Playing with the Data: What Legal Scholars Should Learn About Machine Learning", *cit.*, pp. 653–718.

[587] But see: Mayson, Sandra G., "Bias In, Bias Out", *cit.*, pp. 2218–2300 (arguing that equalizing false-positive rates will beget fewer false positives—**"law abiders"** mistakenly predict for rearrest—for the high-base-rate group than the low-base-rate group because there are fewer "law abiders" in the high-base-rate group in the first place). But see also: Sam Corbett-Davies and peers, parsing the same Broward County data that ProPublica did, concluded that attaining parity in **false-positive rates** while still optimizing for public safety (and without detaining any other defendants) would beget a 7% uptick in violent crime. See: Corbett-Davies, Sam/Pierson, Emma/Feller, Avi/Goel, Sharad Goel/Huq, Aziz, "Algorithmic Decision Making and the Cost of Fairness", *Proceedings of the 23rd ACM SIGKDD International Conference on Knowledge Discovery and Data Mining* (Ass'n for Computing Machinery ed., 2017), 2017, p. 802. Moreover, 17% of those detained would be low-risk people for whom detention was either unwarranted or uncalled for. According to Richard Berk's research on juvenile data, tweaking the algorithm to attain statistical parity spawned a lower false-positive rate for the black subset than the white (4% versus 9%) yet a higher false-negative rate (50% versus 40%). See: Berk, Richard, "Accuracy and Fairness for Juvenile Justice Risks Assessments", *cit.*, p. 189. In addition to that, Berk further concluded that for white folks, the algorithm generated 5.25 false positives for every false negative; whilst for black folks, the algorithm generated 1.85 false negatives for every false positive. See: Berk, Richard, "Accuracy and Fairness for Juvenile Justice Risks Assessments", *cit.*, p. 189.

[588] Lehr, David/Ohm, Paul, "Playing with the Data: What Legal Scholars Should Learn About Machine Learning", *cit.*, pp. 653–718.

[589] But see: Berk, Richard, "Accuracy and Fairness for Juvenile Justice Risks Assessments", *Journal of Empirical Legal Studies*, Volume 16, 2019, p. 175 (comes to the terms with the fact that tweaking/altering data to attain **statistical parity** yielded extremely high **false-negative rates**); Zachary Lipton et al., "Does Mitigating ML's Impact Disparity Require Treatment Disparity?", NIPS PROC. 1 (2018), https://arxiv.org/pdf/1711.07076.pdf [https://perma.cc/X8VF-EY53] (sets forth compelling evidence that enforced blindness to protected traits exacts a toll on the overall accuracy of the algorithmic tool); Petersilia, Joan/Turner, Susan, "Guideline-Based Justice: Prediction and Racial Minorities", *Crime and Justice*, 1987, pp. 151–174 (argues that omitting markers correlated with race from a recidivism prediction algorithm exacted a toll on the accuracy of the algorithmic tool).

[590] Lehr, David/Ohm, Paul, "Playing with the Data: What Legal Scholars Should Learn About Machine Learning", *cit.*, pp. 653–718.

§§ No surprise stems from the fact that implementing **asymmetric cost ratios** is a remarkable tool indeed[591]; it seamlessly, and meaningfully, translates purely normative values of relevant stakeholders into purely, and meaningfully, actionable math. In addition to that, of the machine learning algorithms that can implement **asymmetric cost ratios**,[592] how precisely implementation unfolds hinges on the type of **output variable**.[593]

[591] It is worth recalling, though, that according to Richard Berk's research on juvenile data, tweaking the algorithm to attain **statistical parity** spawned a lower false-positive rate for the black subset than the white (4% versus 9%) yet a higher false-negative rate (50% versus 40%). See: Berk, Richard, "Accuracy and Fairness for Juvenile Justice Risks Assessments", *cit.*, p. 189. In addition to that, Berk further concluded that for white folks, the algorithm generated 5.25 false positives for every false negative; whilst for black folks, the algorithm generated 1.85 false negatives for every false positive. See: Berk, Richard, "Accuracy and Fairness for Juvenile Justice Risks Assessments", *cit.*, p. 189. See also: Angwin, Julia et al., "Machine Bias", *ProPublica* (May 23, 2016), https://www.propublica.org/article/machine-bias-risk-assessments-in-criminal-sentencing [https://perma.cc/4G83-MDAS] (harshly criticizing disparity in false-positive rates as a purely unjustified bias). See also: Freeman, Katherine, "Algorithmic Injustice: How the Wisconsin Supreme Court Failed to Protect Due Process Rights in State v. Loomis", *North Carolina Journal of Law and Technology*, Volume 18, 2016, pp. 75–86 (echoing the very same views).

[592] See: Berk, Richard A., *Statistical Learning from a Regression Perspective*, *cit.*, pp. 266–271 (discussing that, in the purview of **stochastic gradient boosting**, classification problems are regarded as regression problems, estimating probabilities, with thresholds applied to morph probabilities to forecasted classes). Pivotally, the consequence of this situation is that, if **asymmetric costs** are applied by overhauling these thresholds at the very end of the machine algorithm's mathematical processing, predictor relevance and partial dependence plots will not sharply mirror this ***asymmetric cost ratio***. Put differently, it will reflect input variables' relevance and the functional types of relationships between input variables and the output variable embodying symmetric costs. Lehr, David/Ohm, Paul, "Playing with the Data: What Legal Scholars Should Learn About Machine Learning", *cit.*, pp. 653–718.

[593] Lehr, David/Ohm, Paul, "Playing with the Data: What Legal Scholars Should Learn About Machine Learning", *cit.*, pp. 653–718.

5.1.3.1.3 «Make Up Your Mind: Either You Choose Accuracy or Interpretability, You Can't Have Both»! The Ability to Provide Interpretable Reasons for the Algorithmic Predictions (Interpretable Machine Learning) Comes with a Catch Because Simpler Algorithms (e.g. Random Forests, Decision Trees, and Regression Trees) Are Far Easier to Interpret But Far Less Accurate Nonetheless

§§ At this juncture it should not come as a bewildering surprise that different means of implementation equals different types of advantages for the explainability[594] or interpretability[595] of the algorithmic[596] predictions.[597]

---

[594] See: Deeks, Ahsley, "The Judicial Demand for Explainable Artificial Intelligence", *Columbia Law Review*, Volume 119, 2019, pp. 1829 and ff and passim. See: Hacker, Phillip/Passoth, Jan-Hendrick, "Varieties of AI Explanations under the Law: From the GDPR to the AIA, and Beyond", *XxAI Beyond Explainable AI, International Workshop on Extending Explainable AI Beyond Deep Models and Classifiers*. Berlin/New York/Singapore/Beijing: Springer, 2021, pp. 343–373 ("*the quest to explain the output of artificial intelligence systems has clearly moved from a mere technical to a highly legally and politically relevant endeavor.* In this paper, we provide an overview of legal obligations to explain AI and evaluate current policy proposals. In this, we distinguish between different functional varieties of AI explanations - such as multiple forms of enabling, technical and protective transparency - and show how different legal areas engage with and mandate such different types of explanations to varying degrees. *Starting with the rights-enabling framework of the GDPR, we proceed to uncover technical and protective forms of explanations owed under contract, tort and banking law. Moreover, we discuss what the recent EU proposal for an Artificial Intelligence Act means for explainable AI, and review the proposal's strengths and limitations in this respect. Finally, from a policy perspective, we advocate for moving beyond mere explainability towards a more encompassing framework for trustworthy and responsible AI that includes actionable explanations, values-in-design and co-design methodologies, interactions with algorithmic fairness, and quality benchmarking*"). Italics added. See: Part V, this chapter, Sects. 5.1.7–5.1.7.5 of this book (on the five laws to control algorithmic decision-making). See: Part V, this chapter, Sects. 5.1.8–5.1.8.5 of this book (on the five laws to interpret algorithmic decision-making). See: Part V, this chapter, Sect. 5.1.7.2 of this book (on law number two to control algorithmic decision-making, which mandates that black box models must not be entrusted with the task of making high stake decisions—v.g. health and freedom).

[595] Citron, Danielle K., "Technological Due Process", *Washington University Law Review*, Volume 85, 2008, pp. 1249–1253 ("Computer programs seamlessly combine rulemaking and individual adjudications without the critical procedural protections owed either of them"). See also: Turek, Matt, "Explainable Artificial Intelligence (XAI)", The *Defense Advanced Research Projects Agency* (DARPA), https://www.darpa.mil/program/explainable-artificial-intelligence [https://perma.cc/2DS4-ZMNB] (shedding light on the oft-labelled interpretability of algorithms); *Making Computers Explain Themselves*, MIT's Computer Science and Artificial Intelligence Laboratory (Oct. 27, 2016), 2016, www.csail.mit.edu/making_computers_explainthemselves [https://perma.cc/C97B-PGUR] (explaining the importance of grasping the complex trappings of algorithm decision-making).

[596] Lehr, David/Ohm, Paul, "Playing with the Data: What Legal Scholars Should Learn About Machine Learning", *cit.*, pp. 653–718.

[597] See on the dire need to attain algorithmic fairness: Zajko, M, "Conservative AI and social inequality: conceptualizing alternatives to bias through social theory", *Artificial Intelligence and Society*, Volume 36, 2021, pp. 1047–1056; Dwork, Cynthia/Hardt, Moritz/Pitassi, Tonian/Reingold/Zemel, Richard, "Fairness Through Awareness, Proceedings of the 3rd Innovations",

§§ Burgeoningly, propelled by an unquenchable quest for accountable[598] and transparent[599] machine learning algorithms, a set of poignant calls have been made for meaningful pathways of grasping the inner workings[600] of black[601] boxes.[602]

§§ It is painstakingly difficult to translate into intuitive, apprehensible, reader-friendly, easy-to-understand text how precisely a machine learning algorithm

---

Theoretical Computer Science Conference, 2012, https://dl.acm.org/doi/10.1145/2090236.2090255 [https://perma.cc/T2U3-TNQ6] (discussing an individual fairness approach to algorithmic fairness); Meharabi, Ninareh/Morstatter, Fred/Saxena, Nripsuta/Lerman, Kristina/Galstyan, Aram, "A Survey on Bias and Fairness in Machine Learning", *ACM Computing Survey*, Jul. 2022; Fuster, Andreas/Goldsmith-Pinkham, Paul/Tarun Ramadorai/Walther, Angsar, "Predictably Unequal? The Effects of Machine Learning on Credit Markets", *Journal of Finance*, Volume 76, 2022, passim (providing a description of the variation in interest rates across racial groups carried out by machine learning algorithms); Zarsky, Tal, "Transparency in Data Mining: From Theory to Practice", *Discrimination and Privacy in the Information Society: Data Mining and Profiling in Large Databases*, Bart Custers et al. eds., Belin, Springer, 2013; Kroll, Joshua A. et al., "Accountable Algorithms", *University of Pennsylvania Law Review*, Volume 165, 2017, passim; Green, B./Hu L., "The Myth in the Methodology: Towards a Recontextualization of Fairness in Machine Learning", *Machine Learning Debates Work 35th Internation Conference of Machine Learning*, 2018, passim; West, SM./Whittaker, M./Crawford, K., "Discriminating systems gender, race, and power in AI", AI Now Institute, 2019; Xu, K./Nosek, B./Greenwald, AG., "Data from the race implicit association test on the project implicit demo website", *Journal of Open Psychology* Data 2:e3, 2014.

598 See: Katyal, Sonia, "Private Accountability in the Age of Artificial Intelligence", *UCLA Law Review*, Volume 66, 2019, pp. 54–99. See also: Williams, Rebecca, "Accountable Algorithms: Adopting the Public Law Toolbox Outside the Realm of Public Law", *Current Legal Problems*, Vol. 75, 2022, pp. 237–263; Williams, Rebecca, "Rethinking Administrative Law for Algorithmic Decision-Making", *Oxford Journal of Legal Studies*, Volume 42, 2021, pp. 468 e ff and passim.

599 Lepri, Bruno/Oliver, Nuria/Letouzé Emmanuel/Pentland, Alex/Vinck, Patrick, "Fair, Transparent, and Accountable Algorithmic Decision-Making Processes: The Premise, the Proposed Solutions, and the Open Challenges", *Philosophy & Technology*, Volume 31, 2018, passim.

600 See: Scherer, Matthew U. Scherer, "Regulating Artificial Intelligence Systems: Risks, Challenges, Competencies, and Strategies", *Harvard Journal of Law and Technology*, Volume 29, 2016, pp. 353–369 (frames the crippling problem of opacity as "the possibility that the inner workings of an AI system may be kept secret and may not be susceptible to reverse engineering"). See: Part V, this chapter, Sects. 5.1.7–5.1.7.5 of this book (on the five laws to control algorithmic decision-making). See: Part V, this chapter, Sects. 5.1.8–5.1.8.5 of this book (on the five laws to interpret algorithmic decision-making).

601 See; Lehr, David/Ohm, Paul, "Playing with the Data: What Legal Scholars Should Learn About Machine Learning", *cit.*, pp. 653–718. But see: Havard, Cassandra Jones, "On the Take": The Black Box of Credit Scoring and Mortgage Discrimination", *Boston University Public Interest Law Journal*, 2011, pp. 239 and ff and passim (discussing that subprime lending was undoubtably geared toward minority communities, aiming to enmesh them on the trap of excessive debt); Johnson, Creola, "The Magic of Group Identity: How Predatory Lenders Use Minorities to Target Communities of Color", *Georgetown Journal on Poverty Law and Policy*, 2010, pp. 165–169 (fleshing out several aggressive marketing tactics used by unprincipled/unscrupulous lenders to target primarily minorities for eerily predatory loans).

602 See: Citron, Danielle Keats/Pasquale, Frank A., "The Scored Society: Due Process for Automated Predictions", *cit.*, pp. 1–34. But see: Part V, this chapter, Sect. 5.1.7.2 of this book (on law number two to control algorithmic decision-making, which mandates that black box models must not be entrusted with the task of making high stake decisions—v.g. health and freedom).

produces, for each subject, an algorithmic prediction from all the subject's input variable values.[603] It is pivotally important to note, though, that there are feasible ways to render machine learning algorithms more **interpretable**.[604] Tellingly, a data scientist can choose a class of models with a simpler, easier, less complex optimization process to enable enhanced **interpretability** of algorithmic predictions. **Random forests**[605] and **decision trees** fall well within this category.[606]

§§ It bears mentioning that machine learning algorithmic class's general optimization process is the creation of a **forest of classification or regression trees**. Of course, there other alternatives. But here is the kicker: more complex models are more accurate but far less interpretable nonetheless.

§§ The data scientist therefore faces a standoff/stalemate/dilemma very difficult to untie: if the data scientist employs, for instance, a **deep neural network**[607]—which is, roughly speaking, considered to be a very complex, intricate, convoluted,

---

603 Breiman, Leo, "Statistical Modeling: The Two Cultures", *cit.*, p. 209 ("my biostatistician friends tell me, 'Doctors can interpret logistic regression.' There is no way they can interpret a black box containing fifty trees hooked together." See: Part V, this chapter, Sect. 5.1.7.2 of this book (on law number two to control algorithmic decision-making, which mandates that black box models must not be entrusted with the task of making high stake decisions—v.g. health and freedom).

604 See: Part V, this chapter, Sects. 5.1.8–5.1.8.5 of this book (on the five laws to interpret algorithmic decision-making). See: Rudin, Cynthia, "Please stop explaining black box models for high stakes decisions", *Proceedings of NeurIPS 2018 Workshop on Critiquing and Correcting Trends in Machine Learning (NIPS 2018)*, 2018, passim; Rudin, C., & Radin, J., "Why are we using black box models in AI when we don't need to? A lesson from an explainable AI competition", *Harvard Data Science Review*, 2019, Volume 1, Issue 2, passim; Tan, S., Caruana, R., Hooker, G., and Lou, Y., "Distill-and-compare: Auditing blackbox models using transparent model distillation". *Proceedings of the 2018 AAAI/ACM Conference on AI, Ethics, and Society, Association for Computing Machinery*, 2018, pp. 303–310 (arguing that explainable models are too complex and fiddly to be understood by laypeople. As a result, interpretable models should be used instead). See: Part V, this chapter, Sect. 5.1.7.2 of this book (on law number two to control algorithmic decision-making, which mandates that black box models must not be entrusted with the task of making high stake decisions—v.g. health and freedom).

605 Wyner, A. J./M. Olson/J. Bleich/D. Mease, "Explaining the Success of AdaBoost and Random Forests as Interpolating Classifiers", *Journal of Machine Learning Research*, 18 (1), 2015, pp. 1–33.

606 Lehr, David/Ohm, Paul, "Playing with the Data: What Legal Scholars Should Learn About Machine Learning", *cit.*, pp. 653–718.

607 See: Bathaee, Yavar, "The Artificial Intelligence Black Box and the Failure of Intent and Causation", *Harvard Journal of Law and Technology*, n.º 37, 2018, p. 901 (adduces that "*one possible reason AI may be a black box to humans is that it relies on machine-learning algorithms that internalize data in ways that are not easily audited or understood by humans* (…)" "*first, a lack may arise from the complexity of the algorithm's structure, such as with deep neural network, which consists of thousands of artificial neurons working together in a diffuse way to solve a problem. This reason for AI being a black box is referred to as "complexity". Second, the lack of transparency may arise because the AI is using a machine-learning algorithm that relies on geometric relationships that humans cannot visualize, such as with support vector machines. This reason for AI being a black box is referred to as "dimensionality"*"). Italics added.

and labyrinthic tool—the **black box model** will be very accurate, but far less interpretable, and more of a mathematical[608] process, very hard to follow,[609] let alone easy to interpret.[610] Note, though, that such a choice will come with a hefty cost: it will exact a toll on the interpretability of algorithmic predictions, which will be far more difficult to interpret and understand.

§§ Compellingly, a **interpretability-aware data scientist** may ended up choosing an easier, simpler, less complex type of model, such **random forests** or **decision trees**, being fully aware that a simpler model may be far less accurate one (Additionally, even the easier and simpler model may not be interpretable as the same manner as, for instance, a **regression model** is).[611] Alternatively, a data scientist can create **graphical plots** that clear identify the weight/importance that different input variables had on the algorithmic predictions. In addition to that, those **graphical plots** would also indicate how the changes in the values of input variables have every chance to be reflected into changes in the outcome[612] variable. But here is the kicker: a data scientist can only create these **graphical plots** for a limited number of machine learning[613] algorithms.[614]

[608] Lehr, David/Ohm, Paul, "Playing with the Data: What Legal Scholars Should Learn About Machine Learning", *cit.*, pp. 653–718.

[609] See: Part V, this chapter, Sect. 5.1.7.2 of this book (on law number two to control algorithmic decision-making, which mandates that black box models must not be entrusted with the task of making high stake decisions—v.g. health and freedom).

[610] See: Krakovna, Viktoriya/Doshi-Velez, Finale, "Increasing the Interpretability of Recurrent Neural Networks Using Hidden Markov Models", ARXIV:1606.05320V2, Sept. 30, 2016, at 46, https://arxiv.org/pdf/1606.05320.pdf [https://perma.cc/XJ6T-MYKD] ("[A]doption [of recurrent neural networks] has been slow in applications such as health care, where practitioners are reluctant to let an opaque expert system make crucial decisions"); Wisdom, Scott et al., "Interpretable Recurrent Neural Networks Using Sequential Sparse Recovery", ARXIV:1611.07252, Nov. 22, 2016, at 1, https://arxiv.org/pdf/1611.07252.pdf [https://perma.cc/TL24-M94R] ("*Interpreting the learned features and outputs of machine learning models is problematic. This difficulty is especially significant for deep learning approaches [like neural networks], which are able to learn effective and useful function maps due to their high complexity*"). Italics added.

[611] Lehr, David/Ohm, Paul, "Playing with the Data: What Legal Scholars Should Learn About Machine Learning", *cit.*, pp. 653–718.

[612] Lehr, David/Ohm, Paul, "Playing with the Data: What Legal Scholars Should Learn About Machine Learning", *cit.*, pp. 653–718.

[613] Lehr, David/Ohm, Paul, "Playing with the Data: What Legal Scholars Should Learn About Machine Learning", *cit.*, pp. 653–718.

[614] See: Berk, Richard A., *Statistical Learning from a Regression Perspective*, *cit.*, p. 324 ("[I]t is not easy to learn from SVM how inputs are related to outputs.... There is also no direct help in determining predictor importance"); Berk, Richard A., *Statistical Learning from a Regression Perspective*, *cit.*, p. 336 ("If one needs to examine response functions and evaluate predictor importance, an implementation of support vector machines may not have what is needed").

5.1.3.1.4 Bagging Algorithms, the Likelihood of Overfitting and the Dire Need to Create an «Overfitting-Resistant Model» (Lehr/Ohm)

§§ More often than not, data scientists have deep-rooted concerns with **overfitting** when choosing a kind of model.[615] As adumbrated when fleshing out **summary statistics review**, randomness[616] can be a quagmire for tools, like machine learning, that swiftly identify granular **correlations** in training data.[617] It is important to note, however, that some machine learning algorithms are less prone to suffer from **overfitting** than others. Crucially, some machine learning algorithms comprise a process coined as **«bagging»**.[618]

§§ **Bagging algorithms**, broadly speaking, make algorithmic predictions on multifarious, tangentially overlapping random samples of training data and subsequently, for each subject, make an educated call on a «final» algorithmic prediction by averaging or otherwise reconciling the algorithmic predictions that resulted for that subject in the entirety of the[619] samples in which it was contained.[620]

§§ As a corollary of this operation called **averaging or reconciliation**, the machine learning algorithms are less likely to **fit bogus correlations in training**

[615] See: Berk, Richard A., *Statistical Learning from a Regression Perspective, cit.*, p. 42 ("A major difficulty in statistical learning is **overfitting**. *Very flexible fitting procedures will tend to respond to idiosyncratic features of the data, producing results that do not generalize well to new data*"). Italics and bold added.

[616] On randomness: Teigena, Halvor/Kanten, Alf Børre, "Out of the blue: on the suddenness of perceived chance events", *Thinking & Reasoning*, Volume 29, n. ° 1, 2023, pp. 137–175 (137) ("*people commonly use terms like 'random', 'by chance', or 'accidentally' when they describe occurrences that sidestep the normal course of events, with no apparent causal link to ongoing activities. Such intrusive events are typically perceived as happening all of a sudden.* This was demonstrated in seven experiments (N ¼ 1299) by asking people to identify statements they believed belonged to stories about chance events, and by comparing chance vs. nonchance events from their own life and from the lives of others. Suddenness also appeared to be more strongly associated with beginnings than with endings of an episode. Thus, statements about sudden beginnings of a career or a relationship were more readily believed to happen 'by chance' than 'not by chance'. *But life-changing events did not become more accidental simply by being placed in the beginning of a 'life chapter'. These studies highlight a central but neglected feature of perceived randomness*"). Italics added.

[617] See: Part V, this chapter, Sects. 5.1.1.5.2.2–5.1.1.5.2.2.1.4 of this book (on the fundamental shift away from causation to correlations in algorithmic decision-making).

[618] Lehr, David/Ohm, Paul, "Playing with the Data: What Legal Scholars Should Learn About Machine Learning", *cit.*, pp. 653–718.

[619] Lehr, David/Ohm, Paul, "Playing with the Data: What Legal Scholars Should Learn About Machine Learning", *cit.*, pp. 653–718.

[620] See: Berk, Richard A., *Statistical Learning from a Regression Perspective, cit.*, pp. 169–174.

data.[621] Consequently, if a data scientist is performing in an exceedingly high dimensional context—one crammed with input variables—likely to facilitate **overfitting** in vulnerable models, the former should choose an **overfitting-resistant model**.[622]

5.1.3.1.5 Opportunities for Fine-Tuning Parameters

§§ It oft-contended that building a full-fledged framework comprising machine learning algorithms lends itself to a cloak-and-dagger operation teeming with algorithmic hiccups. More to the point, building machine learning algorithms is far from being a light-hearted point-and-shoot exercise of simply cracking open a computer program such as Microsoft Excel, fill in some data, and eventually find and click, for instance, the «Run Random Forests» button.[623] Whilst models within a class might well share a general optimization method, facets of that method qualified as parameters can be **adroitly controlled**, or **deftly fine-tuned**, by the data scientist.[624] Unsurprisingly, this advanced technique also points towards the direction of a **Controllable and Interpretable Artificial Intelligence (in general)**[625] and of a **Controllable and Interpretable Machine Learning (in particular).**[626]

§§ Crucially, such fine-tuning parameters confer flexibility in a sheer number of regards. It is worth recalling that has been the theme of preceding paragraphs, algorithms differ greatly across categories. A wide range of machine learning algorithms offer a greater diversity of fine-tuning parameters, whereas others have parameters

[621] See: Berk, Richard A., *Statistical Learning from a Regression Perspective, cit.*, p. 169 ("Averaging over a collection of fitted values can help compensate for *overfitting. That is, the averaging tends to cancel out results shaped by idiosyncratic features of the data.* One can then obtain more stable fitted values and more honest assessments of how good the fit really is"). Italics added.

[622] A cohort of statisticians go at lengths as to contend that certain **bagging algorithms** are not only resistant to **overfitting**, but, and foremost, fundamentally immune from it. See: Leo Breiman and Adele Cutler have contended that **random forests** "does not overfit." See: Breiman, Leo/Cutler, Adele, "Random Forests", https://www.stat.berkeley.edu/~breiman/RandomForests/cc_home.htm (last visited March. 4, 2025). See also: Breiman, "Random Forests", *cit.*, p. 7 ("*This result explains why random forests do not overfit as more trees are added*, but produce a limiting value of the generalization error"). Italics added.

[623] Lehr, David/Ohm, Paul, "Playing with the Data: What Legal Scholars Should Learn About Machine Learning", *cit.*, pp. 653–718.

[624] See: Berk, Richard A., *Statistical Learning from a Regression Perspective, cit.*, p. 42 ("for all of the statistical learning procedures examined, there are choices to be made about 'tuning parameters.'... They are parameters, much like dials on a machine, that determine how a procedure functions").

[625] See: Part V, this chapter, Sect. 5.1.1.2 of this book (on the central tenets of Procedural Rule of Law that bestows upon citizens the fundamental right to challenge the pearls of algorithmic wisdom—outputs—offered by algorithmic decision-making).

[626] See: Part V, this chapter, Sect. 5.1.7.2 of this book (on law number two to control algorithmic decision-making, which mandates that black box models must not be entrusted with the task of making high stake decisions—v.g. health and freedom). See: Part V, this chapter, Sects. 5.1.7–5.1.7.5 of this book (on the five laws to control algorithmic decision-making).

that are exceedingly more influential.[627] This could bestow upon the data scientist enhanced flexibility and greater ductility, which is yet another factor a data scientist ponders when picking out a type of model.[628]

5.1.3.1.6 Resource Limitations (Processing Power, Time, and Memory Space) That Bear on the Overall Accuracy of Machine Learning Algorithms: The Selection of Algorithms Should Be Customized to the Environments in Which They Will Be Deployed

§§ It is pivotally important to stress that not only factors set forth above—eminently mathematical concerns—bear on the overall accuracy of machine learning algorithms. Cogently, practical considerations, too, weigh on how smooth this whole process will be. Recall, machine learning algorithms possess a remarkable processing power. Processing power, which, in turn, is a time-consuming and energy-draining process that requires a humongous memory space to ensure completion of the task at hand. Understandably, and perhaps not laudably, more complex, state-of-the-art, cutting-edge, top-notch, far-fetched, and advanced machine learning algorithms[629] tend to absorb more of these.[630]

§§ For that reason, when, and if, deployed, the running model will produce algorithmic predictions for a somewhat tiny dataset on a single end-stakeholder personal machine, then maybe, just maybe, a more advanced model could be chosen. Yet this is not amenable to be overgeneralized as the existing running models burgeoningly steering automation incessantly generate algorithmic predictions[631] for whopping amounts of subjects.[632]

---

[627] See: Berk, Richard A., *Statistical Learning from a Regression Perspective*, *cit.*, p. 308 ("[S]*omewhat in contrast to random forests and stochastic gradient boosting*, variation across a set of reasonable values for the tuning parameters can have a large impact on the results"). Italics added. See also: Ericson, Gary et al., "How to Choose Algorithms for Microsoft Azure Machine Learning", *cit.*, p. 5 ("The upside is that having many parameters typically indicates that an algorithm has greater flexibility. It can often achieve very good accuracy"). Lehr, David/Ohm, Paul, "Playing with the Data: What Legal Scholars Should Learn About Machine Learning", *cit.*, pp. 653–718.

[628] Lehr, David/Ohm, Paul, "Playing with the Data: What Legal Scholars Should Learn About Machine Learning", *cit.*, pp. 653–718.

[629] Lehr, David/Ohm, Paul, "Playing with the Data: What Legal Scholars Should Learn About Machine Learning", *cit.*, pp. 653–718.

[630] See: Ericson, Gary et al., "How to Choose Algorithms for Microsoft Azure Machine Learning", (establishing a comparison between machine-learning algorithms based on of their memory footprints and training times).

[631] Lehr, David/Ohm, Paul, "Playing with the Data: What Legal Scholars Should Learn About Machine Learning", *cit.*, pp. 653–718.

[632] For instance, Amazon leverages on machine-learning systems "at incredible scale and speed" to create video recommendations for its staggering amount of clients. See: SDE – Amazon Video Recommendations: Machine Learning and Distributed Systems, Amazon Jobs, https://www.amazon.jobs/en/jobs/546401 (last visited Jan. 16, 2025).

§§ In such high-stake realms,[633] the tool developers are to perform internal cost benefit analyses[634] and choose bespoke machine learning algorithms eyeing its customization to the environments in which they will be deployed.[635]

§§ Whilst it is true that accuracy is key in algorithmic decision-making, it is truer still that some algorithms are more accurate[636] than others.[637] But here is the deeper truth: that much-acclaimed goal—of overall accuracy in the purview of algorithmic decision-making—is painstakingly difficult to forecast[638] at the inception.[639]

§§ Determining which class of model performs best is a task that is closely related to the peculiarities of a specific dataset. For that reason, the data scientist often chooses more than one type of algorithm.[640] This vast array of choices of

---

633 But see: Part V, this chapter, Sect. 5.1.7.2 of this book (on law number two to control algorithmic decision-making, which mandates that black box models must not be entrusted with the task of making high stake decisions—v.g. health and freedom). See: Part V, this chapter, Sects. 5.1.7–5.1.7.5 of this book (on the five laws to control algorithmic decision-making).

634 *Cost-benefit Analysis* is in the limelight. Its development falls conspicuously outside the scope and aim of this thesis though. See: Sunstein, Cass R., "The Real World of Cost-Benefits Analysis: Thirty-Six Questions (and almost as many answers)", *Columbia Law Review*, 114 (1), 2014, 177; Bayefsky, Rachel, "Dignity as a value in Agency Cost-Benefit Analysis", *Yale Law Journal,* 123 (2014): 1740; Sunstein, Cass R., *Valuing Life: Humanizing the Regulatory State*, 2014, 8 ff; Gordon, Jeffrey, "The Empty Call for Cost-Benefits Analysis for Financial Regulators", *Journal of Legal Studies*, 43, 2014, 351; Sunstein, Cass R., "The Limits of Quantification", *California Law Review*, 103, 2014, 1369; Adler, Mathew/Posner, Eric A., "New Foundations of Cost-Benefit Analysis", *Regulation & Governance*, 3, 2006, 72; Thomas J. Miles/Sunstein, Cass R., "The Real World of Arbitrariness Review", *University of Chicago Law Review*, 75 2008, 761; Coates, John C. IV, "Cost-Benefit Analysis of Financial Regulation: Case Studies and Implications", *Yale Law Journal*, 124, 2015, pp. 882–911; Posner, Eric A./Weyl E. Glen, "Cost-Benefit Analysis of Financial Regulations: Response to Criticisms", *Yale Law Journal*, 124, 2015, pp. 246–265 (parsing the relationship between agency cost-benefit analysis and human dignity).

635 Lehr, David/Ohm, Paul, "Playing with the Data: What Legal Scholars Should Learn About Machine Learning", *cit.*, pp. 653–718.

636 Lehr, David/Ohm, Paul, "Playing with the Data: What Legal Scholars Should Learn About Machine Learning", *cit.*, pp. 653–718.

637 See: Ericson, Gary et al., "How to Choose Algorithms for Microsoft Azure Machine Learning", *cit.*, p. 8 (differentiating some machine learning algorithms as typically showcasing "excellent accuracy" and others as archetypically showcasing "good accuracy").

638 Lehr, David/Ohm, Paul, "Playing with the Data: What Legal Scholars Should Learn About Machine Learning", *cit.*, pp. 653–718.

639 See: Berk, Richard A., *Statistical Learning from a Regression Perspective, cit.*, p. 335 ("*Random forests, boosting, and support vector machines can all perform well.* It is not yet clear which perform better for which kinds of datasets, or even if the differences in performance are likely to matter a great deal in practice"). Italics added.

640 See: Witten, Ian H., *Data Mining: Practical Machine Learning Tools and Techniques, cit.*, p. 172 ("We often need to compare two different learning schemes on the same problem to see which is the better one to use").

suitably tailored algorithms that perform best is often taken through the next step—**model training**—to establish which performs optimally and, therefore, should be deployed.[641]

5.1.4 Model Training (Machine Learning Algorithm Tuning Parameters, Machine Learning Algorithm Assessment, and Feature Selection)

§§ At this juncture, the training data is ready and a type of model (or multiple machine learning algorithms as suitably tailored candidates to optimally perform the task at hand) has been timely, and meaningfully, selected. The time is now ripe for the data scientist to set in motion the learning part of machine learning. Recall, a machine learning algorithm is applied on the training dataset[642] and, in so doing, learns **predictive optimal rules** for forecasting the **outcome of interest**.[643]

§§ Importantly, albeit sometimes left unsaid, «model training» is much more than a standalone, single, inconspicuous instance of running a machine learning algorithm on **training dataset**. Crucially, and not to be forgotten, **model training** also comprises a few supplementary chores: **(i) tuning**, **(ii) assessment**, and **(iii) feature selection**. Adroitly training a machine learning algorithm pace back and forth across these chores, thereby traversing between them runs of the model[644] on the training data.[645]

---

641 Lehr, David/Ohm, Paul, "Playing with the Data: What Legal Scholars Should Learn About Machine Learning", *cit.*, pp. 653–718.

642 But see: Citron, Danielle Keats/Pasquale, Frank, "The Scored Society: Due Process for Automated Predictions", *Washington Law Review*, Volume 89, 2014, pp. 1, 4–5 (highlighting how human beings programming automated systems is directly conducive to, and leads, to fundamentally inaccurate results since the source code, predictive algorithms and datasets may encompass human biases which, in turn, have a disparate impact on historically disadvantaged groups); Crawford, Kate/Schultz, Jason, "Big Data and Due Process: Toward a Framework to Redress Predictive Privacy Harms", *Boston College Law Review*, Volume 55, 2014, pp. 93, 99–101 (pinpointing pathways through which predictive analytic tools perpetuate discriminatory practices). But see: Bornstein, Stepanhie, "Antidiscriminatory Algorithms", *Alabama Law Review*, Volume 70, 2018, pp. 519, 524–528 (contending, however, that the tagged "facially neutral" algorithms producing discriminatory outcomes should be quashed).

643 Lehr, David/Ohm, Paul, "Playing with the Data: What Legal Scholars Should Learn About Machine Learning", *cit.*, pp. 653–718.

644 Lehr, David/Ohm, Paul, "Playing with the Data: What Legal Scholars Should Learn About Machine Learning", *cit.*, pp. 653–718.

645 See Chapman, Pete et al., CRISP-DM 1.0, 2000, p. 25, https://www.themodeling-agency.com/crisp-dm.pdf [https://perma.cc/QAJ8-6HSP] ("According to the model assessment, revise parameter settings and tune them for the next run in the Build Model task. Iterate model building and assessment until you strongly believe that you have found the best model(s)") (emphasis in original).

5.1.4.1 Machine Learning Algorithms' Categories of Fine-Tuning Parameters That Afford the Tool Developer Enhanced *Control* Over Pivotally Important Aspects of Machine Learning (Objective Function («the Goal» of Machine Learning Algorithms), Bias Variance Trade-Off, Asymmetric Cost Ratio and Assessment) That Further Buttress a *Controllable* and *Interpretable* Algorithmic Decision-Making That Trounces *Algorithmic Dictatorship*

§§ At this juncture, it should not come as a flabbergasting finding that machine learning algorithms **exhibit tuning parameters—i.e. a functional crowbar a tool developer can pull anytime to overhaul the inner workings of the machine learning algorithms.**[646] These can vary greatly hinging on the specific algorithm implemented.[647] Tellingly, and roughly speaking, machine learning algorithms allot the user **control** over the following aspects of the learning process: the **objective function**[648]; the **bias-variance trade-off**; the **cost ratio**; and **assessment**, or validation, methods.[649]

§§ These steps alone can pave the way to, and usher in, a both **Controllable and a Interpretable Artificial Intelligence (in general)** and a **Controllable**

---

[646] But see: Scherer, Matthew U. Scherer, "Regulating Artificial Intelligence Systems: Risks, Challenges, Competencies, and Strategies", *Harvard Journal of Law and Technology*, Volume 29, 2016, pp. 353–369 (frames the crippling problem of opacity as "the possibility that the inner workings of an AI system may be kept secret and may not be susceptible to reverse engineering"). See also: Turek, Matt, "Explainable Artificial Intelligence (XAI)", The *Defense Advanced Research Projects Agency* (DARPA), https://www.darpa.mil/program/explainable-artificial-intelligence [https://perma.cc/2DS4-ZMNB] (shedding light on the oft-labelled interpretability of algorithms); *Making Computers Explain Themselves*, MIT's Computer Science and Artificial Intelligence Laboratory (Oct. 27, 2016), 2016, www.csail.mit.edu/making_computers_explainthemselves [https://perma.cc/C97B-PGUR] (explaining the importance of grasping the complex trappings of algorithm decision-making).

[647] Lehr, David/Ohm, Paul, "Playing with the Data: What Legal Scholars Should Learn About Machine Learning", *cit.*, pp. 653–718.

[648] Pundits acknowledge that many advanced readers may be unwilling to regard the objective function as a tuning parameter—which seems warranted. Mind you, the objective function plays a pivotal role in defining what is to be optimized, as opposed to the other parameters that have nothing to «say», or «to do», about any of that. See: Lehr, David/Ohm, Paul, "Playing with the Data: What Legal Scholars Should Learn About Machine Learning", *cit.*, pp. 653–718.

[649] Lehr, David/Ohm, Paul, "Playing with the Data: What Legal Scholars Should Learn About Machine Learning", *cit.*, pp. 653–718.

and Interpretable algorithmic decision-making (in particular)[650] that trounces **Algorithmic Dictatorship**.[651]

§§ If you **control** the process of algorithmic decision-making, you will therefore **control** the **algorithmic predictions** while minimizing the damages arising out of **Algorithmic Dictatorship** accordingly. Hence the overriding importance of a **thing-centred algorithmic decision-making**, as opposed to a shoddy, porous, botched, warped, dangerously indetermined, shallow, hollow, nomadic, and watered down **human-centred Artificial Intelligence**[652] that, given the lack of theoretical underpinnings, creates more problems than it solves.

§§ As adumbrated, all machine learning algorithms have a «goal». It is worth recalling, too, that such a goal is specified in an **objective function**. This **objective function** mirrors mathematical values of what concretely should be **optimized**—either minimized or maximized—when **optimizing predictive rules**. Often, the **objective function** is intertwined with, and deeply woven into the fabric of, deep-seated conceptions[653] of **overall accuracy**[654] of which tool developers should not lose sight of.

§§ Roughly speaking, there are multifarious pathways to mathematically mirror overall accuracy, with distinct mathematical assumptions and trade-offs[655] hinging

---

[650] See: Part V, this chapter, Sects. 5.1.2–5.1.6.2.1 of this book (on **the thing-centred algorithmic decision-making** propelled by a *Controllable* and *Interpretable* Machine Learning that weeds out *Algorithmic Dictatorship* and secures *Algorithmic Common Good*. It is worth recalling that the **thing-centred algorithmic decision-making** seeks to unwind the perils arising out of the lack of theoretical underpinnings facing the **human-centred algorithmic decision-making**, as extensively fleshed out Part III, Chap. 3, Sects. 3.1.4.3–3.1.4.4 of this book). See: Part V, this chapter, Sects. 5.1.7–5.1.7.5 of this book (on the five laws to control algorithmic decision-making). See: Part V, this chapter, Sects. 5.1.8–5.1.8.5 of this book (on the five laws to interpret algorithmic decision-making).

[651] See: Part IV, Chap. 4, Sects. 4.1–4.1.10.6 of this book (on Algorithmic Dictatorship and its chilling effect on democracy).

[652] See: Part V, this chapter, Sects. 5.1.2–5.1.6.2.1 of this book (on the **thing-centred algorithmic decision-making** propelled by a *Controllable* and *Interpretable* Machine Learning that weeds out *Algorithmic Dictatorship* and secures *Algorithmic Common Good*. It is worth recalling that the **thing-centred algorithmic decision-making** seeks to unwind the perils arising out of the lack of theoretical underpinnings facing the **human-centred algorithmic decision-making**, as extensively fleshed out Part III, Chap. 3, Sects. 3.1.4.3–3.1.4.4 of this book).

[653] Lehr, David/Ohm, Paul, "Playing with the Data: What Legal Scholars Should Learn About Machine Learning", *cit.*, pp. 653–718.

[654] The **objective function** could well be a **Gaussian loss function**, thereby representing the residuals between the **forecasted quantitative outcomes** and the **true outcomes of interest**. See: Berk, Richard A., *Statistical Learning from a Regression Perspective*, *cit.*, p. 270 (arguing the Gaussian loss function is one possibility for stochastic gradient boosting). It could also be the homogeneity of outcomes of interest in a cluster, or node, of observations forecasted by the machine learning algorithm to all have the very same outcome. See: Berk, Richard A., *Statistical Learning from a Regression Perspective*, *cit.*, pp. 113–117 (poring over homogeneity, or downright purity, in the purview of classification and regression trees).

[655] Lehr, David/Ohm, Paul, "Playing with the Data: What Legal Scholars Should Learn About Machine Learning", *cit.*, pp. 653–718.

on a given context.[656] At the end of the day, it boils down to the decision made by the tool developer when fine-tuning the model. Importantly, **objective function** offers invaluable opportunities to **mitigate discriminatory outcomes**[657] of machine learning algorithms while paving the way to a sought-after **Algorithmic Common Good**.

§§ Besides from the **objective function**, machine learning algorithms boast a sheer number of fine-tuning parameters that impact the **«bias-variance tradeoff»**.[658] This expression sharply mirrors a common phenomenon in statistics—**tweaking** a machine learning algorithm[659] to have **less bias** (i.e., how far away the forecasts are, on average, from the ground truth)[660] augments the **variance** (i.e., how inaccurate

---

[656] See: Berk, Richard A., *Statistical Learning from a Regression Perspective*, *cit.*, pp. 270–271 (fleshing out different possible loss functions for stochastic gradient boosting and arguing that putting in place asymmetric costs could be attained through a Laplace loss function). See: Lehr, David/Ohm, Paul, "Playing with the Data: What Legal Scholars Should Learn About Machine Learning", *cit.*, pp. 653–718.

[657] Lehr, David/Ohm, Paul, "Playing with the Data: What Legal Scholars Should Learn About Machine Learning", *cit.*, pp. 653–718.

[658] See: Alpaydin, Ethem, *Introduction to Machine Leaning*, *cit.*, pp. 76–80; Berk, Richard A., *Statistical Learning from a Regression Perspective*, *cit.*, pp. 55–56.

[659] But see: Berk, Richard, "Accuracy and Fairness for Juvenile Justice Risks Assessments", *Journal of Empirical Legal Studies*, Volume 16, 2019, p. 175 (comes to the terms with the fact that tweaking/altering data to attain statistical parity yielded extremely high false-negative rates); Zachary Lipton et al., "Does Mitigating ML's Impact Disparity Require Treatment Disparity?", NIPS PROC. 1 (2018), https://arxiv.org/pdf/1711.07076.pdf [https://perma.cc/X8VF-EY53] (sets forth compelling evidence that enforced blindness to protected traits exacts a toll on the overall accuracy of the algorithmic tool); Petersilia, Joan/Turner, Susan, "Guideline-Based Justice: Prediction and Racial Minorities", *Crime and Justice*, 1987, pp. 151–174 (argues that omitting markers correlated with race from a recidivism prediction algorithm exacted a toll on the accuracy of the algorithmic tool). But see: Mayson, Sandra G., "Bias In, Bias Out", *cit.*, pp. 2218–2300 (arguing that equalizing false-positive rates will beget fewer false positives—"law abiders" mistakenly predict for rearrest—for the high-base-rate group than the low-base-rate group because there are fewer "law abiders" in the high-base-rate group in the first place). But see also: Sam Corbett-Davies and peers, parsing the same Broward County data that ProPublica did, concluded that attaining parity in false-positive rates while still optimizing for public safety (and without detaining any other defendants) would beget a 7% uptick in violent crime. See: Corbett-Davies, Sam/Pierson, Emma/Feller, Avi/Goel, Sharad Goel/Huq, Aziz, "Algorithmic Decision Making and the Cost of Fairness", *Proceedings of the 23rd ACM SIGKDD International Conference on Knowledge Discovery and Data Mining* (Ass'n for Computing Machinery ed., 2017), 2017, p. 802. Moreover, 17% of those detained would be low-risk people for whom detention was either unwarranted or uncalled for. According to Richard Berk's research on juvenile data, for example, tweaking the algorithm to attain statistical parity spawned a lower false-positive rate for the black subset than the white (4% versus 9%) yet a higher false-negative rate (50% versus 40%). See: Berk, Richard, "Accuracy and Fairness for Juvenile Justice Risks Assessments", *cit.*, p. 189. In addition to that, Berk further concluded that for white folks, the algorithm generated 5.25 false positives for every false negative; whilst for black folks, the algorithm generated 1.85 false negatives for every false positive. See: Berk, Richard, "Accuracy and Fairness for Juvenile Justice Risks Assessments", *cit.*, p. 189.

[660] Briefly, bias is related with how close the expected value of the forecasts is to the true value of what is being forecasted over several/repeated/iterative realizations of the data. See: Lehr, David/Ohm, Paul, "Playing with the Data: What Legal Scholars Should Learn About Machine Learning", *cit.*, pp. 653–718. See: Berk, Richard A., *Statistical Learning from a Regression Perspective*, *cit.*,

predictions for a particular subject's outcome would be if, say, the machine learning algorithm were retrained several times on different training datasets), and the other way around.[661]

§§ Tellingly, fine-tuning parameters are sprang into action in this trade-off since they frequently impact the complexity, and the rate and pace at which the algorithm learns. Relatedly, more advanced, more complex, and therefore slower learning algorithms will most likely yield **less bias**, yet **more variance**.[662] Relatedly, a data scientist possessing a behemoth dataset will be more than comfortable to build a more advanced, more complex, slower-learning[663] machine learning algorithm, as being in possession of such a massive batch of data can itself falloff **variance**,[664] but a tool developer with fewer data may fine-tune for a simpler, easier, expedited-learning algorithm. A third category of fine-tuning parameters can be deployed to impact **asymmetric cost**[665] **ratio**.[666]

---

p. 56. It is important to note that **"Repeated realizations"** amounts to a hypothetical scenario in which the training data are re-created several times and the machine learning algorithm is re-trained on each of those brand-new training datasets. The expected value of something equals to the result of summing together all of that something's possible values or outcomes, each multiplied by its probability of transpiring over repeated realizations. See: Lehr, David/Ohm, Paul, "Playing with the Data: What Legal Scholars Should Learn About Machine Learning", *cit.*, pp. 653–718. For instance, imagine a coin flipping game whereby the player happens to flip a coin once; the player gets to win two dollars if the coin lands on heads, but nonetheless loses one dollar if it lands on tails. Put another way, if a player were to play this game in a repeated manner (hence **"repeated realizations"** of the game itself), the former had an expectation of winning, give it, or take it, fifty cents. See: Lehr, David/Ohm, Paul, "Playing with the Data: What Legal Scholars Should Learn About Machine Learning", *cit.*, pp. 653–718.

661 Lehr, David/Ohm, Paul, "Playing with the Data: What Legal Scholars Should Learn About Machine Learning", *cit.*, pp. 653–718.

662 It bears mentioning that there are multiple parameters that can sway this for multiple machine learning algorithms. To name a few, a lower terminal node size in random forests decreases bias; variance may be augmented accordingly, while random forests' bagging may counteract some of this. See: Lehr, David/Ohm, Paul, "Playing with the Data: What Legal Scholars Should Learn About Machine Learning", *cit.*, pp. 653–718. See also: Berk, Richard A., *Statistical Learning from a Regression Perspective*, *cit.*, p. 235. Stochastic gradient boosting also has this tuning parameter, likewise another—the depth (e.g., two-way or three way) of permitted interactions effects; higher order interaction effects can indeed decrease bias but augment variance nonetheless. See also: Berk, Richard A., *Statistical Learning from a Regression Perspective*, *cit.*, 271–273. Last but not least, in deep neural networks, a staggering number of hidden layers is very likely to taper off bias, but uptick variance, and vice versa. See: Stuart Geman et al., "Neural Networks and the Bias/Variance Dilemma", *Neural Computation*, Volume 4, 1992, pp. 1, 12.

663 Lehr, David/Ohm, Paul, "Playing with the Data: What Legal Scholars Should Learn About Machine Learning", *cit.*, pp. 653–718.

664 See: Berk, Richard A., *Statistical Learning from a Regression Perspective*, *cit.*, p. 56 ("[L]arger samples in general provide estimates with a smaller variance").

665 Lehr, David/Ohm, Paul, "Playing with the Data: What Legal Scholars Should Learn About Machine Learning", *cit.*, pp. 653–718.

666 To name a just few parameters, in **random forests**, for instance, the technician can implicitly change the prior distribution, engage in stratified bootstrap sampling when building each tree, or alter the overwhelming majority voting scheme for tree nodes to a voting scheme on the basis of some threshold other than fifty percent. See: Berk, Richard A., *Statistical Learning from a Regression*

§§ There is no shortage of mathematical diversity in techniques deployed to implement **asymmetric cost ratios**, and **cost ratios**[667] can even be applied by tweaking[668] the **objective function's**[669] specification.

§§ Lastly, fine-tuning parameters can impact how a machine learning algorithm is evaluated and assessed. It should come as no surprise that algorithms can «self-evaluate» during training through a handful of seasoned procedures, including one frequently coined as **cross validation**. Tool developers can thereupon set these fine-tuning parameters with a view to **control** how these processes unfold.[670]

§§ It is noteworthy that seldom a machine learning algorithm run once on a training dataset achieves overall accuracy. That is, rare are the times in which the tool developer is entirely satisfied with the machine learning algorithm's performance and the latter is immediately deployed accordingly. Instead, the learning curve of an

---

Perspective, *cit.*, p. 211. Morphing the prior distribution is likewise applicable in support vector machines. Berk, Richard A., *Statistical Learning from a Regression Perspective*, *cit.*, pp. 321–322. See: Lehr, David/Ohm, Paul, "Playing with the Data: What Legal Scholars Should Learn About Machine Learning", *cit.*, pp. 653–718.

667 When Richard Berk trained the machine learning algorithm only to maximize for **overall accuracy**, it predicted rearrest for 17% of the white subgroup and 33% of the black subgroup (a 16 percentage-point difference). Strikingly, the **false-positive rates** were 16% for the white subgroup whereas for the black groups was 28% (a 12 percentage-point difference). See: Berk, Richard, "Accuracy and Fairness for Juvenile Justice Risks Assessments", *cit.*, p. 180. Notably, when Richard Berk changed the algorithm to equalize the cost ratios, it predicted rearrest for 10% of the white subgroup and 29% of the black subgroup (a 19 percentage-point difference). Relatedly, the false-positive rates were 8% for the white subset and 22% for the black subset (a 14 percentage-point difference). See: Berk, Richard, "Accuracy and Fairness for Juvenile Justice Risks Assessments", *cit.*, p. 185. See: Mayson, Sandra G., "Bias In, Bias Out", *cit.*, pp. 2218–2300. See also: Berk, Richard, "Accuracy and Fairness for Juvenile Justice Risks Assessments", *cit.*, pp. 185–186 (positing that that, to **equalize cost ratios** across racial groups in a juvenile risk-assessment context, the author "separate[d] forecasting exercises" for white and black juveniles, respectively, and that the machine-learning forecasting algorithms the data produced were different for each racial group).

668 But see: Berk, Richard, "Accuracy and Fairness for Juvenile Justice Risks Assessments", *Journal of Empirical Legal Studies*, Volume 16, 2019, p. 175 (comes to the terms with the fact that tweaking/altering data to attain statistical parity yielded extremely high false-negative rates); Zachary Lipton et al., "Does Mitigating ML's Impact Disparity Require Treatment Disparity?", NIPS PROC. 1 (2018), https://arxiv.org/pdf/1711.07076.pdf [https://perma.cc/X8VF-EY53] (sets forth compelling evidence that enforced blindness to protected traits exacts a toll on the overall accuracy of the algorithmic tool); Petersilia, Joan/Turner, Susan, "Guideline-Based Justice: Prediction and Racial Minorities", *Crime and Justice*, 1987, pp. 151–174 (argues that omitting markers correlated with race from a recidivism prediction algorithm exacted a toll on the accuracy of the algorithmic tool).

669 Lehr, David/Ohm, Paul, "Playing with the Data: What Legal Scholars Should Learn About Machine Learning", *cit.*, pp. 653–718.

670 Lehr, David/Ohm, Paul, "Playing with the Data: What Legal Scholars Should Learn About Machine Learning", *cit.*, pp. 653–718. But see: Part III, Chap. 3, Sects. 3.1.5.4–3.1.5.4.1 of this book (on Critical Artificial Intelligence Studies, with a sharper focus on the deceptive patterns evinced by Large Language Models, which has lent urgency to concerns about the trustworthiness and reliability of these tools).

algorithm neatly encapsulates, hands-in-glove, **trial and error procedure**.[671] Unsurprisingly, after a fine-tuned algorithm[672] is run on a given training dataset,[673] a data scientist provisionally evaluates and assesses its overall performance. Three things can occur afterwards: either the tool developer decides to **re-tune the algorithm**, **re-train it**, or **re-asses it**.[674] Such an ever-lasting cycle can occur several times. Either way, pivotal to the unfolding of the cycle are befitted assessment methods.

§§ Recall, the overriding goal of **test dataset** is to allow assessment of how the algorithm performs on mostly **unseen data**. Meaning, data that did not, in any way, bear on how the machine learning algorithm was trained.[675]

§§ Importantly, the dataset must not be used for the type of iterative assessment cycle previously mentioned. In spite of the fact that doing so would not cause the machine learning algorithm to «see» the test data in the same manner it «sees» (i.e., directly parses and learns from) the training data. On the flip side, re-running a machine learning algorithm after carefully observing its performance in a **test dataset**

---

[671] See: Berk, Richard A., *Statistical Learning from a Regression Perspective*, *cit.*, p. 275 ("[O]ne has no choice but to experiment with different sets of tuning parameter values. Unfortunately, this can be at best a trial-and error process with too often no definitive resolution"); Witten, Ian H., *Data Mining: Practical Machine Learning Tools and Techniques*, *cit.*, p. 295 ("As in many machine learning situations, **trial and error** using your own particular source of data is the final arbiter").

[672] But see: Citron, Danielle Keats/Pasquale, Frank A., "The Scored Society: Due Process for Automated Predictions", *Washington Law Review*, Volume 89, 2014, pp. 1–34 (arguing that "[a]*dvocates applaud the removal of human beings and their flaws from the assessment process*," but arguing that bias remains "[*b*]*ecause human beings program predictive algorithms, their biases and values are embedded into the software's instructions*"). Italics added.

[673] But see: Barocas, Solon/Selbst, Andrew D., "Big Data's Disparate Impact", *California Law Review*, Volume 104, 2016, pp. 671–682 (discussing how data is often flawed, rigged, incomplete, imperfect and therefore algorithms inherit the prejudice of the original decision makers). But see: Citron, Danielle Keats/Pasquale, Frank, "The Scored Society: Due Process for Automated Predictions", *Washington Law Review*, Volume 89, 2014, pp. 1, 4–5 (highlighting how human beings programming automated systems is directly conducive to, and leads, to fundamentally inaccurate results since the source code, predictive algorithms and datasets may encompass human biases which, in turn, have a disparate impact on historically disadvantaged groups); Crawford, Kate/Schultz, Jason, "Big Data and Due Process: Toward a Framework to Redress Predictive Privacy Harms", *Boston College Law Review*, Volume 55, 2014, pp. 93, 99–101 (pinpointing pathways through which predictive analytic tools perpetuate discriminatory practices). But see: Bornstein, Stepanhie, "Antidiscriminatory Algorithms", *Alabama Law Review*, Volume 70, 2018, pp. 519, 524–528 (contending, however, that the tagged "facially neutral" algorithms producing discriminatory outcomes should be quashed).

[674] Lehr, David/Ohm, Paul, "Playing with the Data: What Legal Scholars Should Learn About Machine Learning", *cit.*, pp. 653–718.

[675] Lehr, David/Ohm, Paul, "Playing with the Data: What Legal Scholars Should Learn About Machine Learning", *cit.*, pp. 653–718.

catalyses just about the very same **statistical harm**[676] as assessing a machine learning algorithm in the very same dataset on which[677] it was previously trained.[678]

§§ For that reason alone, tool developers often seek alternative pathways. Again, there is no shortfall of feasible ways that enable machine learning algorithms to measure their own set of accuracies during the training process. Casts broadly, they routinely require additional randomly **partitioning** of the **training dataset**. Crucially, running each iteration of a machine learning algorithm (e.g., **each tree in a random forest**) on a specific partition enshrined in training data. Subsequently, assessing/evaluating the machine learning algorithm's accuracy by forecasting an outcome for each subject based upon the iterations that were run on a subsection of the dataset excluding that subject—iterations that did not «see», in that it was not exposed to, that[679] subject[680] at all.

§§ Overall, such assessment pathways—of which a pivotally important procedure deemed as **cross-validation** stands as a flagship or capstone—serve a crucially invaluable function.[681]

§§ Taken together, they afford an actionable baseline of overall accuracy that can be deployed to recalibrating an algorithm's training without falling prey to the trap of either evaluating the overall accuracy of an entire machine learning algorithm or the whole training data itself. Importantly, this procedure shies aways from desecrating the sacrosanct nature of the **test dataset**.[682]

---

[676] See: Chi-Jack Lin/ Sherman D. Hanna, "Racial Discrimination in the Consumer Credit Market", *Consumer Interests Annual*, Volume 56, 2010 ("*The Equal Credit Opportunity Act (ECOA), enacted in 1974, makes it unlawful for any creditors to discriminate against credit applicants because of their color, race/ethnic group, religion, national origin, sex, marital status, or age (provided the applicant has the capacity to contract)* (....) *our analyses allow for distinguishing* ***statistical and taste discrimination****. In four of five of our measures, there was discrimination against households with Black respondents, and in three out of five measures, there was discrimination against households with Hispanic respondents. Discrimination in the consumer credit market against black and Hispanic households is statistical discrimination: lenders choose to discriminate against black and Hispanic because they on average have higher default risk*"). Italics and bold added.

[677] Lehr, David/Ohm, Paul, "Playing with the Data: What Legal Scholars Should Learn About Machine Learning", *cit.*, pp. 653–718.

[678] See: Witten, Ian H., *Data Mining: Practical Machine Learning Tools and Techniques*, *cit.*, p. 164 ("*It is important that the test data is not used in any way to create the classifier. For example, some learning schemes involve two stages, one to come up with a basic structure and the second to optimize parameters involved in that structure, and separate sets of data may be needed in the two stages.* Or you might try out several learning schemes on the training data and then evaluate them — on a fresh dataset, of course — to see which one works best. But none of this data may be used to determine an estimate of the future error rate"). Italics added.

[679] Lehr, David/Ohm, Paul, "Playing with the Data: What Legal Scholars Should Learn About Machine Learning", *cit.*, pp. 653–718.

[680] See: Witten, Ian H., *Data Mining: Practical Machine Learning Tools and Techniques*, *cit.*, pp. 167–172.

[681] Lehr, David/Ohm, Paul, "Playing with the Data: What Legal Scholars Should Learn About Machine Learning", *cit.*, pp. 653–718.

[682] Lehr, David/Ohm, Paul, "Playing with the Data: What Legal Scholars Should Learn About Machine Learning", *cit.*, pp. 653–718.

5.1.4.1.1 Feature Selection: The Unquenchable Quest to Tackle Head-on Both Dimensionality and Overfitting While Preserving Machine Learning Algorithm's Overall Accuracy

§§ One key aspect of model training is **feature selection**[683]—i.e. tamping down the machine learning algorithm's set of input variables during burdensome, cumbersome, energy-draining, and time-consuming cycles of ever-lasting training, assessment, and re-tuning.[684] Such an operation of trimming down the set of variables can be somewhat beneficial for a number of reasons. Weeding out the **«curse of dimensionality»**[685] stands arguably amongst them.[686]

§§ Cutting to the chase, if a machine learning algorithm is entrusted with the task of analysing more input variables with an entrenched presence in the dataset, a data scientist will accordingly need an astronomically larger amount of training data to adroitly cover all possible combinations of values across those input variables and,

683 One must proceed with extreme care in this regard in that this terminology should be handled with proper care. There are multiple "feature"-related steps in machine-learning algorithms workflows, but they have glaringly different meanings, and how they are employed/deployed can vary greatly between machine learning practitioners. Pivotally, one is not using **"feature selection"** here to mean the production of inputs, often by gleaning some information from **unstructured data** or by overhauling existing input variables. Such types of procedures are often deemed as **"feature extraction"** or **"feature processing"** or **"feature construction"** or **"feature transformation"** or **"feature engineering."** In addition to that, this part may be less applicable to a bunch of well-known deep learning techniques, which, more often than not, do not even need an clear feature selection step since its effect is attained implicitly in deep learning's overhauling of how input features are represented during **training data stage**. See: Lehr, David/Ohm, Paul, "Playing with the Data: What Legal Scholars Should Learn About Machine Learning", *cit.*, pp. 653–718.

684 See: Alpaydin, Ethem, *Introduction to Machine Leaning, cit.*, pp. 110–112.

685 See: Friedman, Jerome H., "On Bias, Variance, 0/1-Loss, and the Curse-of Dimensionality", *Data Mining & Knowledge Discovery*, Volume 1, 1997, pp. 55–65; Domingos, Pedro, "A Few Useful Things to Know About Machine Learning", *cit.*, pp. 82–83. See also: Bathaee, Yavar, "The Artificial Intelligence Black Box and the Failure of Intent and Causation", *Harvard Journal of Law and Technology*, n.° 37, 2018, p. 901 (adduces that "*one possible reason AI may be a black box to humans is that it relies on machine-learning algorithms that internalize data in ways that are not easily audited or understood by humans (…)*" "*first, a lack may arise from the complexity of the algorithm's structure, such as with deep neural network, which consists of thousands of artificial neurons working together in a diffuse way to solve a problem. This reason for AI being a black box is referred to as "complexity". Second, the lack of transparency may arise because the AI is using a machine-learning algorithm that relies on geometric relationships that humans cannot visualize, such as with support vector machines. This reason for AI being a black box is referred to as "dimensionality"*"). Italics added.

686 But see: Sam Corbett-Davies and Sharad Goel refer to colour-blindness—a form of feature selection—as "anti-classification." Corbett-Davies, Sam/Gaebler, Johann D./Nilforoshan, Hamed/Shrof, Ravi/Goel, Sharad, "The Measure and Mismeasure of Fairness", *Journal of Machine Learning Research*, Volume 24, 2023, pp. 1–117 (p. 36). See also: Balkin, Jack M./Siegel, Reva B., "The American Civil Rights Tradition: Anticlassification or Antisubordination?", *University of Miami Law Review*, Volume 58, 2003, pp. 9, 10–11 (explaining the distinction between the anticlassification and the antisubordination approaches to equality law).

therefore, to generate both reliable and accurate algorithmic forecasts.[687] **Feature selection** can thus provide a feasible way around this perceived quandary.[688] **Feature selection** also decreases the perceived risk of **overfitting**, as there is an exceedingly lower likelihood of producing relevant noise in less[689] variables.[690]

§§ In practical terms, **feature selection** routinely occurs «within the iterative assessment-tuning cycles mentioned above».[691] Why? There is something that relevant stakeholders should be mindful of: the overriding goal of **feature selection** is not just to eschew the plight of **dimensionality** and decrease **overfitting**, but, and foremost, doing so without undermining the algorithm's **overall accuracy**. Importantly, if too many input variables are trimmed down, then the sought-after **predictive power** is poised to fizzle out accordingly.[692] Not less importantly, a machine learning algorithm may well be trained once, have its performance regularly, and accurately, assessed through a pertinent **cross-validation**, have its features crammed, be re-trained, re-assessed and so forth. Compellingly, this perpetual cycle keeps going until pruning in input variables start exacting a toll on overall accuracy.[693]

5.1.5 Model Deployment

§§ Having successfully reached this stage, the machine learning algorithm is all set to be immediately deployed, and consequently morphed it into a «**running model**». It is likewise to ready start making forecasts in the real world. Never a dull moment to

---

687 Lehr, David/Ohm, Paul, "Playing with the Data: What Legal Scholars Should Learn About Machine Learning", *cit.*, pp. 653–718.

688 See Guyon, Isabelle Guyon/Elisseef, André, "An Introduction to Variable and Feature Selection", *Journal of Machine Learning Research*, Volume 3, 2003, pp. 1157, 1158 ("There are many potential benefits of variable and *feature selection:... defying the curse of dimensionality to improve prediction performance*"). Italics added. See also: Alpaydin, Ethem, *Introduction to Machine Leaning, cit.*, pp. 110–112 (discussing how feature selection is routinely deployed for dimensionality decrease).

689 Lehr, David/Ohm, Paul, "Playing with the Data: What Legal Scholars Should Learn About Machine Learning", *cit.*, pp. 653–718.

690 Saeys, Yvan et al., "A Review of Feature Selection Techniques in Bioinformatics", *Bioinformatics*, Volume 23, 2007, p. 2507 ("The objectives of feature selection are manifold, the most important ones being: (a) *to avoid overfitting and improve model performance....*"). Italics added.

691 See: Alpaydin, Ethem, *Introduction to Machine Leaning, cit.*, pp. 110–112 (fleshing out the processes of either manually inserting or weeding out input variables, retraining the model on the training data, and subsequently evaluating error in a validation set).

692 See: Alpaydin, Ethem, *Introduction to Machine Leaning, cit.*, pp. 111 ("We stop [adding features in sequential forward selection] if adding any feature does not decrease [the error assessed in a validation set]"); Alpaydin, Ethem, *Introduction to Machine Leaning, cit.*, pp. ("We stop [removing features in sequential backward selection] if removing a feature does not decrease the error").

693 Lehr, David/Ohm, Paul, "Playing with the Data: What Legal Scholars Should Learn About Machine Learning", *cit.*, pp. 653–718.

recall that these forecasts carry both danger and promises[694] as these are algorithmic decisions that are poised to impact[695] the outer world.

§§ Fast forward to its usefulness in the real world, building machine learning algorithms on a rolling basis entails designing programs that incessantly feed new data into the trained algorithm, as well as building a sturdy back-end data infrastructure to ensure overall accuracy. Pivotally, machine learning algorithms running at scale might also be converted into online learning systems. Note that these are systems in which the machine learning algorithms are routinely and automatically re-trained upon the collection[696] of new data.[697]

§§ A pressing challenge facing tool developers is converting the algorithm into end-user-friendly one. It is worth recalling the example of the hypothetical machine learning algorithm forecasting whether and to what extent new inmates will be embroiled in violent altercations during the time served in prison. Tool developers must therefore bear very firmly in mind that the end user of that specific algorithm might very well be a prison warden who might have to, when coming across a new prisoner, feed/bake the new inmate data into the machine learning algorithm, obtain a forecast, and subsequently make a binding decision based on,[698] at least partially, that very algorithmic prediction.[699]

§§ The relevant stakeholder (e.g. prison warden, landlord, loan officer, police officer, parole officer, probation officer, law enforcement agent and so forth) would not need to be a seasoned data scientist and could not take those meaningful steps by dealing directly with the source code[700] of the machine learning algorithm. More to the point, and to ensure a widespread usability of the machine learning algorithm, the latter must be conveniently packaged into some sort of user-friendly interface,

---

[694] Witten, Ian H., *Data Mining: Practical Machine Learning Tools and Techniques*, *cit.*, p. 30 ("[Deploying a model] normally involves integrating it into a larger software system, so the model needs to be handed over to the project's software engineers. This is the stage where the implementation details of the modeling techniques matter. For example, to slot the model into the software system it may be necessary to reimplement it in a different programming language").

[695] Lehr, David/Ohm, Paul, "Playing with the Data: What Legal Scholars Should Learn About Machine Learning", *cit.*, pp. 653–718.

[696] Lehr, David/Ohm, Paul, "Playing with the Data: What Legal Scholars Should Learn About Machine Learning", *cit.*, pp. 653–718.

[697] See: Fontenla-Romero, Óscar, et al., "Online Machine Learning", *Efficiency & Scalability Methods for Computational Intellect*, Igelnik, Boris (Editor), Hershey, Information Science Reference, 2013, pp. 27–28.

[698] Lehr, David/Ohm, Paul, "Playing with the Data: What Legal Scholars Should Learn About Machine Learning", *cit.*, pp. 653–718.

[699] Lehr, David/Ohm, Paul, "Playing with the Data: What Legal Scholars Should Learn About Machine Learning", *cit.*, pp. 653–718.

[700] See: Deeks, Ahsley, "Secret Reason-Giving", *Yale Law Journal*, Volume 129, 2019, passim; Katyal, Sonia K, "The Paradox of Source Code Secrecy", *Cornell Law Review*, Volume 104, 2019, pp. 1183–1236. But see: Citron, Danielle Keats/Pasquale, Frank, "The Scored Society: Due Process for Automated Predictions", *Washington Law Review*, Volume 89, 2014, pp. 1, 4–5 (highlighting how human beings programming automated systems is directly conducive to, and leads, to fundamentally inaccurate results since the source code, predictive algorithms and datasets may encompass human biases which, in turn, have a disparate impact on historically disadvantaged groups).

and it would be the duty of the tool developers to generating this interface and any underpinning infrastructure.[701]

§§ Understandably, ensuring that the machine learning algorithm performs at scale, preferably online, conveniently packaged and easily accessible in a user-friendly interface is pivotally important to avoid mishaps and hiccups along the line. From time to time, and if help is needed to navigate these complex environments, a hand should be lent to ensure a smooth transition from theory to practice. Especially, albeit not exclusively, in running models entrusted with the task of making high-stake decisions[702] such as predictive policing,[703] rental applications,[704] credit

---

[701] Lehr, David/Ohm, Paul, "Playing with the Data: What Legal Scholars Should Learn About Machine Learning", *cit.*, pp. 653–718.

[702] But see: Part V, this chapter, Sect. 5.1.7.2 of this book (on law number two to control algorithmic decision-making, which mandates that black box models must not be entrusted with the task of making high stake decisions—v.g. health and freedom). But see: Rudin, Cynthia, "Please stop explaining black box models for high stakes decisions", *Proceedings of NeurIPS 2018 Workshop on Critiquing and Correcting Trends in Machine Learning (NIPS 2018)*, 2018, passim; Rudin, C., & Radin, J., "Why are we using black box models in AI when we don't need to? A lesson from an explainable AI competition", *Harvard Data Science Review*, 2019, Volume 1, Issue 2, passim; Tan, S., Caruana, R., Hooker, G., and Lou, Y., "Distill-and-compare: Auditing blackbox models using transparent model distillation". *Proceedings of the 2018 AAAI/ACM Conference on AI, Ethics, and Society, Association for Computing Machinery*, 2018, pp. 303–310 (arguing that explainable models are too complex and fiddly to be understood by laypeople. As a result, interpretable models should be used instead). But see: Weizenbaum, Joseph, *Computer Power and Human Reason: From Judgment to Calculation*, 1st edition, New York, W. H. Freeman & Co, 1976, pp. 1–300 (227) ("examines the sources of the computer's powers and offers evaluative explorations of what computers can do, cannot do, and should not be employed to do") (this founding father of Artificial Intelligence presciently noted that we should not entrust Artificial Intelligence-embedded technologies with "tasks that demand wisdom"). Italics added. The approval of rental applications is arguably one of those tasks that should never be entrusted to machines). More on this on Part IV, Chap. 4, Sects. 4.1.4–4.1.4.2.1 of this book. See also: Kleinberg, Jon/Lakkaraju, Himabindu/Leskovec, Jure/Ludwig, Jens/Mullainathan, Sendhil, "Human Decisions and Machine Predictions", *Quarterly Journal of Economics*, Volume 133, 2018, passim; Pasquale, Frank, "A Rule of Persons, Not Machines: The Limits of Legal Automation", *George Washington Law Review*, Volume 87, 2019, pp. 1 and ff and passim.

[703] See: Selbst, Andrew D., "Disparate Impact in Big Data Policing", *Georgia Law Review*, Volume 52, 2017, p. 109 (arguing that law enforcement agencies should carry out "algorithmic impact statements" with a view to measure the potential discriminatory impact of computer-run predictive policing technologies). But see: Kirkpatrick, Keith, "It's not the Algorithm, it's the Data", *Communications of the ACM*, February 2017, Volume 60, n. ° 2, 2017 ("critics, however, say tools such as PredPol and CommandCentral *are inherently biased since they rely heavily on reported crimes data, which is often concentrated in areas that are heavily policed, thereby skewing statistics to overrepresent poor or minority communities.* "*We know that we have a history of racially biased policing in the United States, and that has fed into all the data that we have on where arrests have occurred, which crimes are more likely to occur in specific communities, and at which particular times*," says Jennifer Lynch, senior staff attorney at the Electronic Frontier Foundation. "*That's the data that's being fed into predictive policing algorithms*"). Italics added. See also: Kirkpatrick, Keith, "Battling Algorithmic Bias: How Do We Ensure Algorithms Treat Us Fairly?" *Commun. ACM 59*, Volume 10, 2016, pp. 1 and ff and passim. See: Part IV, Chap. 4, Sects. 4.1.1–4.1.1.1 of this book (on biased predictive policing).

[704] See: Part IV, Chap. 4, Sects. 4.1.4–4.1.4.2.3 of this book.

scoring[705] algorithms,[706] fair lending algorithms,[707] algorithmic risk assessment in criminal settings[708] and so forth.

---

[705] But see: Havard, Cassandra Jones, ""On The Take": The Black Box of Credit Scoring and Mortgage Discrimination", *Boston University Public Interest Law Journal*, Volume 20, 2011, pp. 241–247 (highlighting that algorithmic credit scoring, if left unchecked, is an intrinsic, encroached, deep-rooted form of racial discrimination akin to mortgage redlining); Pasquale, Frank, *The Black Box Society: The Secret Algorithms that Control Money and Information*. Cambridge, Massachusetts: Harvard University Press, 2015, 1–320 (passim).

[706] The approval of credit/rental applications is arguably one of those tasks that should never be entrusted to machines). More on this on Part IV, Chap. 4, Sects. 4.1.4–4.1.4.2.1 of this book. See: Part IV, Chap. 4, Sects. 4.1.4–4.1.4.2.1 of this book (on mortgage redlining). See: Part IV, Chap. 4, Sects. 4.1.2–4.1.4.3 of this book (on algorithmic credit scoring, consumer racism and credit card redlining).

[707] In spite of the widely accepted conceptual differences between intent-based and effect-based theories of disparate impact, both approaches often dovetail seamlessly. As far as the fair lending goes, the definition of disparate impact cases is somewhat shallow, nomadic, and erratic, and dispiritingly vague. Note, though, that the loan officer's discretion is directly conducive to exceedingly higher rates of rejections for members of racial minorities. See: Ayres, Ian/Klein, Gary/West, Jeffrey, "The Rise and (Potential) Fall of Disparate Impact Lending Litigation", *Evidence and Innovation in Housing Law and Policy*, Fennell, Lee Anne/Keys, Benajmin J. (Editors), Cambridge, Cambridge University Press, 2017, pp. 231–254. However, Schwemm and Taren avowedly contend that these cases might somewhat be deemed hybrid impact/intention cases. See: Schwemm, Robert G./Taren, Jeffrey L., "Discretionary Pricing, Mortgage Discrimination, and the Fair Housing Act", *The Harvard Civil Rights-Civil Liberties Law Review*, 2010, passim. The conduct being granularly parsed is discretion ascribed to brokers—which is considered by many stakeholders a harmless neutral practice -, may nonetheless lead to brokers to intentionally discriminate against members of racial minorities. See also: Selmi, Michael, "Indirect Discrimination and the Anti-Discrimination Mandate", Oxford, Oxford University Press, *Philosophical Foundations of Discrimination Law (Philosophical Foundations ofLaw)*, Hellman, Deborah/Moreau, Sophia (Editors), 2013, pp. 1–304 (pp. 257 and ff and passim).

[708] See, e.g., Eaglin, Jessica M., "Constructing Recidivism Risk", *Emory Law Journal*, Volume 67, 59, 2017, 61 n.1 (arguing that "[p]redictive technologies are spreading through the criminal justice system like wildfire"). None of this is to suggest, nor is to say, that actuarial risk assessment is blazingly new to criminal justice system. Parole boards have long relied on risk-assessment instruments since the 1930s. By the same token, some jurisdictions used algorithms to forecast certain types of crimes, such as sex offenses, for decades past. See: Mason, Sandra G., "Bias in, Bias Out", *Yale Law Journal*, Volume 128 Volume 8, 2019, pp. 2219–2298. 128. See, e.g., Model Penal Code § 1.02(2), Reporters' Note 31 (American Law Institute, Proposed Final Draft 2017) (arguing that racial disparities in sentencing often arise from racial skew in law enforcement "are largest for crimes at the low end of the seriousness scale—especially drug offenses," and collecting sources); Gase, Lauren Nichol et al., "Understanding Racial and Ethnic Disparities in Arrest: The Role of Individual, Home, School, and Community Characteristics", *Race and Social Problems*, Volume 8, 2016, pp. 296, 304–08 (coming up with the conclusion according to which "that racial/ethnic differences in arrest were not explained by differences in individual-level delinquent behaviors," but were explained by "neighbourhood racial composition"); Lum, Kristian/Isaac, William, To Predict and Serve?", *Significance*, 2016, pp. 14, 19 (discussing bigoted predictive policing that target primarily members of racialized communities). See: Part IV, Chap. 4, Sects. 4.1.10.1–4.1.10.6 of this book (on biased algorithmic risk assessment in criminal procedure law settings, with a sharper focus on COMPAS).

5.1.6 Statistical Effects Arising Out of Algorithmic Decision-Making

§§ It is oft-said that the reason why a legal scholar might take up machine learning in the first place is to harshly decry, and rebuke, its perceived harms or to lavish undeterred praise on its potential benefits. Note, though, the lack of a nuanced attention to the technical details of machine learning renders analysis piecemeal and ultimately haphazard.[709]

§§ The stellar, and sterling, work undertaken by such scholars the likes of Professor Lehr and Professor Ohm therefore allows relevant stakeholders to perform their work with the befitted rigor. In this section, three types of legal harms or benefits arising out of multiple statistical effects of machine learning will be brought to the fore and accordingly brought into a sharper focus.[710]

§§ Light will be cast upon a deeper understanding of the machine learning workflows that greatly ameliorates debates of those harms and benefits thereupon. First, discrimination—or disparate impacts[711]—will be broached. Second, the «reason-giving» or interpretability potential of machine learning algorithms will be parsed. In other words, the latter amounts to the ability to interpret the machine learning

[709] Lehr, David/Ohm, Paul, "Playing with the Data: What Legal Scholars Should Learn About Machine Learning", *cit.*, pp. 653–718.

[710] Lehr, David/Ohm, Paul, "Playing with the Data: What Legal Scholars Should Learn About Machine Learning", *cit.*, pp. 653–718.

[711] A feted scholar (Bernard Harcourt) adamantly contends that (1) predictive crime control efforts may produce more harm than good; (2) they may engender a "ratchet effect" in which the disparate impact of forecast on black folks worsens over time; and (3) the technological allure of prediction can both besmirch and mar deep-rooted moral conceptions of justice. See: Harcourt, Bernard E., *Against Prediction: Profiling, Policing, and Punishing in An Actuarial Age*, Chicago, Illinois, University of Chicago Press, 2007, pp. 7–18 and passim. Converging: Ensign, Danielle, "Runaway Feedback Loops in Predictive Policing", *Proceedings of Machine Learning Research*, Volume 81, 2018, p. 1; Starr, Sonja B., "Evidence-Based Sentencing and the Scientific Rationalization of Discrimination", *Stanford Law Review*, Volume 66, 2014, pp. 804–806 (arguing that that risk assessment during sentencing may derail deep-seated concepts of justice that we hold so dear). In addition to this line of reasoning, Professor Sandra Mayson avers that, since any extant racial disparity in crime risk is the byproduct of a long-haul historical oppression, it is therefore an unfitting basis for coercive state action. To put it bluntly, it is unfair for the state to condition coercion on crime risk that modern societies has unjustly created. Put another way, one may be led to believe that the data are simply warped and that the risk at hand is fundamentally uniform across racial lines. Understandably, though not laudably, one may be also led to believe that crime risk is a fundamentally haphazard and incoherent concept, owing to the fact that all people who are self-determining agents have an equal capacity to either eschew flagitious behaviour or engaging in criminal activities. See: Mayson, Sandra G., "Bias In, Bias Out", *cit.*, pp. 2218–2300.

algorithm's decision. Lastly, due process will be fleshed out, with a sharper focus[712] on **overall accuracy**[713] (or lack thereof).[714]

5.1.6.1 Algorithmic Discrimination (Outcome Variables Disadvantageously Framed; Data Collated in a Non-representative Manner; Data That Has a Deeply Entrenched Presence of Human Biases; Input Variables That Are More Predictive for One Group Than Another; Overfitting Algorithms That Produce Less Accurate Optimizing Predictive Rules for Members of Protected Groups)

§§ Algorithmic decision-making has received a great deal of attention from legal scholars, so too has algorithmic discrimination,[715] which, broadly speaking, consists

---

[712] Lehr, David/Ohm, Paul, "Playing with the Data: What Legal Scholars Should Learn About Machine Learning", *cit.*, pp. 653–718.

[713] When Richard Berk trained the algorithm only to maximize for **overall accuracy**, it predicted rearrest for 17% of the white subgroup and 33% of the black subgroup (a 16 percentage-point difference). Strikingly, the false-positive rates were 16% for the white subgroup whereas for the black groups was 28% (a 12 percentage-point difference). See: Berk, Richard, "Accuracy and Fairness for Juvenile Justice Risks Assessments", *cit.*, p. 180. Notably, when Richard Berk changed the algorithm to equalize the cost ratios, it predicted rearrest for 10% of the white subgroup and 29% of the black subgroup (a 19 percentage-point difference). Relatedly, the false-positive rates were 8% for the white subset and 22% for the black subset (a 14 percentage-point difference). See: Berk, Richard, "Accuracy and Fairness for Juvenile Justice Risks Assessments", *cit.*, p. 185. See: Mayson, Sandra G., "Bias In, Bias Out", *cit.*, pp. 2218–2300.

[714] As Professors Danielle Citron and Frank Pasquale presciently put it, the legal concept of due process comprises a whole lot more than just **overall accuracy**. Rather, its underpinning values also encompass transparency, accountability, participation, and fairness. See: Citron, Danielle Keats/ Pasquale, Frank A., "The Scored Society: Due Process for Automated Predictions", *cit.*, p. 20. Note, though, that should be clear-cut that the great bulk of these cherished values—with a sharper focus on fairness and accountability—are poised to dovetail seamlessly, and straddle significantly, with deep-rooted concerns on both the controllability and interpretability of pearls of algorithmic wisdom, respectively. Therefore, pundits have chosen to break off accuracy as primal focus when taking stock of due process. This thought-through choice is further bolstered/cemented by the extent to which legal tests for due process are tied to the accuracy (or lack thereof) of a decision-making process, especially in the administrative field. See: Coglianese, Cary/Lehr, David, "Transparency and Algorithmic Governance", *Administrative Law Review*, Volume 71, 2019, pp. 1184–1191 (highlights the overriding importance of transparency to propel algorithmic governance).

[715] See on algorithmic discrimination: Kleinberg, Jon, et al., "Discrimination in the Age of Algorithms", *Journal of Legal Analysis*, 2018, pp. 114–174; See: Kleinberg, Jon, et al., "Algorithms as Discrimination Detectors", *Proceeds of the National Academy of Science*, Volume 117, 2020, pp. 30096–30110; Griemmelmann, James/Westreich, Daniel, "Incomprehensible Discrimination", *California Law Review Online*, Volume 7, 2018, pp. 164–171; Xiang, Alice, "Reconciling Legal and Technical Approaches to Algorithmic Bias", *Tennessee Law Review*, Volume 88, 2021, passim; Karnow, Curtis E. A., "The Opinion of Machines", *The Cambridge Handbook of the Law of Algorithms*, Bartfield, Woodrow (Editor), Cambridge, United Kingdom: Cambridge University Press,

of a differential accuracy of a machine learning algorithm on different groups[716] of individuals. The long-winded Part IV, Chap. 4 of this book discusses algorithmic discrimination—an offspring of **Algorithmic Dictatorship**—with fine-grained detail.

§§ In this vein, **algorithmic discrimination** unfolds itself into: **(i)** outcome variables can be disadvantageously[717] framed[718]; **(ii)** data can be collated in a nonrepresentative[719] way[720]; **(iii)** data can have spuriously baked into them preexisting[721] human[722] biases[723]; **(iv)** and a whole set of input variables can be more predictive[724] for one racial line than another.[725]

2021, pp. 15 and ff and passim; Strandburg, Katherine J., "Rulemaking and Inscrutable Decision Tools", *Columbia Law Review*, Volume 119, 2019, passim; Cofone, Ignacio N., "Algorithmic Discrimination is an Information Problem", *Hastings Law Journal*, Volume 70, 2019, passim.

[716] Lehr, David/Ohm, Paul, "Playing with the Data: What Legal Scholars Should Learn About Machine Learning", *cit.*, pp. 653–718. See: Part III, Chap. 3, Sect. 3.1.1 of this book (that discusses the issue of "inequality in application" facing Artificial Intelligence-embedded technologies). See: Part IV, Chap. 4, Sects. 4.1–4.1.10.6 of this book (on Algorithmic Dictatorship and its chilling effect on democracy).

[717] See: O'Neil, Cathy, *Weapons of Math Destruction. How Big Data Increases Inequality and Threatens Democracy*, London, Penguin Random House, 2016, passim (showing how algorithms utilized in modern societies are amenable to perpetuate racial discrimination, partially through perpetuation of social disadvantage and wealth divides); O'Neil, Cathy, "When Not to Trust the Algorithm", *Interview published in the Harvard Business Review's Ideacast*, 2016, passim; O' Neil, Cathy, "Amazon's Gender-Biased Algorithm Is Not Alone", 2018, accessed 2 January 2025.

[718] See: Barocas, Solon/Selbst, Andrew, "Big Data's Disparate Impact", *cit.*, pp. 677–680; Crawford, Kate/Schultz, Jason, "Big Data and Due Process: Toward a Framework to Redress Predictive Privacy Harms", *Boston College Law Review*, Volume 55, 2014, pp. 93, 99–101 (pinpointing pathways through which predictive analytic tools perpetuate discriminatory practices).

[719] See: Dong et al., Qi,, "Imbalanced deep learning by minority class incremental rectification, *IEEE Transactions on Pattern Analysis & Machine Intelligence*, Volume 41, 2019, p. 1367 (posit that "*most existing learning algorithms produce inductive bias (learning bias)* towards the frequent (majority) *classes if training data are not balanced, resulting in poor minority class recognition performance*"). Italics added.

[720] See: Barocas, Solon/Selbst, Andrew, "Big Data's Disparate Impact", *cit.*, pp. 684–687.

[721] But see: Barocas, Solon/Selbst, Andrew D., "Big Data's Disparate Impact", *California Law Review*, Volume 104, 2016, pp. 671–682 (discussing how data is often flawed, rigged, incomplete, imperfect and therefore algorithms inherit the prejudice of the original decision makers).

[722] But see: Citron, Danielle Keats/Pasquale, Frank, "The Scored Society: Due Process for Automated Predictions", *Washington Law Review*, Volume 89, 2014, pp. 1, 4–5 (highlighting how human beings programming automated systems is directly conducive to, and leads, to fundamentally inaccurate results since the source code, predictive algorithms and datasets may encompass human biases which, in turn, have a disparate impact on historically disadvantaged groups).

[723] See: Barocas, Solon/Selbst, Andrew, "Big Data's Disparate Impact", *cit.*, 681–684; See: Citron, Danielle Keats/Pasquale, Frank A., "The Scored Society: Due Process for Automated Predictions", *cit.*, pp. 13–16; Kun, Jeremy, "Big Data Algorithms Can Discriminate, and It's not Clear What to Do About It", *Conversation* (Aug. 13, 2015), http://theconversation.com/big-data-algorithmscan-discriminate-and-its-not-clear-what-to-do-about-it-45849 [https://perma.cc/7R5NKHH8].

[724] Lehr, David/Ohm, Paul, "Playing with the Data: What Legal Scholars Should Learn About Machine Learning", *cit.*, pp. 653–718.

[725] Barocas, Solon/Selbst, Andrew, "Big Data's Disparate Impact", *cit.*, pp. 688–690.

§§ Algorithmic discrimination is mostly data-related.[726] Unsurprisingly, what usually produces inequities/inequalities in algorithmic predictions[727] is specific

[726] Interim Report - Fall 2016: A Shift from Re-Entry to Pre-Entry, Philadelphia City Council Special Committee on Criminal Justice Reform 12 (Fall 2016), http://phlcouncil.com/wp-content/uploads/2016/11/SCFall2016InterimReport.pdf [https://perma.cc/W5HX-D9PY] ("During prior public hearings, members of the Special Committee raised concerns that the data used in a risk assessment tool's calculations may be inherently biased, because of the decades of disparate impact and racial imbalance within the criminal justice system").

[727] See: Starr, Sonja B., "Evidence-Based Sentencing and the Scientific Rationalization of Discrimination", *Stanford Law Review*, Volume 66, 2014, pp. 804–806 (arguing that that risk assessment during sentencing may derail deep-seated concepts of justice that we hold so dear). In addition to this line of reasoning, Professor Sandra Mayson avers that, since any extant racial disparity in crime risk is the byproduct of a long-haul historical oppression, it is therefore an unfitting basis for coercive state action. To put it bluntly, it is unfair for the state to condition coercion on crime risk that modern societies has unjustly created. Put another way, one may be led to believe that the data are simply warped and that the risk at hand is fundamentally uniform across racial lines. Understandably, though not laudably, one may be also led to believe that crime risk is a fundamentally haphazard and incoherent concept, owing to the fact that all people who are self-determining agents have an equal capacity to either eschew flagitious behaviour or engaging in criminal activities. See: Mayson, Sandra G., "Bias In, Bias Out", *cit.*, pp. 2218–2300. See: Part IV, Chap. 4, Sects. 4.1.10.1–4.1.10.6 of this book (on biased algorithmic risk assessment in criminal procedure law settings, with a sharper focus on COMPAS).

features of the underlying dataset[728] on which a machine learning algorithm operates[729] upon.[730]

§§ With this context in place, there is one important aspect of how algorithms work that is important to keep front of mind owing to the fact that, if left unchecked and unnoticed, it can boost the conversion of data inequalities into prediction disparities—the kernel of **overfitting**. Pundits have neither been coy nor bashful in emphasizing how data, especially **survey data**, can often be considerably **noisier** for racial

[728] It is important to note that an algorithm designed for **maximum accuracy** will adjust itself to the majority data, and may be less accurate for members of the underrepresented group, thus breeding *inductive bias*. See: Shellenbarger, Sue, "A Crucial Step for Avoiding AI Disasters", *Wall Street Journal*, (Feb. 13, 2019, 9:57 AM ET), https://www.wsj.com/articles/a-crucial-step-for-avoiding-ai-disasters-11550069865?ns=prod/accounts-wsj [https://perma.cc/C28U-LAAE] (discussing this issue while emphasizing how diverse development teams pay more attention to unrepresentative and underrepresented data sets). Human programmers can circumvent and bypass this problem by weighting the minority-group data more heavily, by designing different algorithms for each racial group, or by striving to contain more data to equalize group representation in the data set. See: Barua, Sukarna et al., "MWMOTE—Majority Weighted Minority Oversampling Technique for Imbalanced Data Set Learning", *IEEE Transactions on Knowledge & Data Engineering*, Volume 26, 2014, pp. 405, 405–406. See also: Hamilton, Melissa, "The Biased Algorithm: Evidence of Disparate Impact on Hispanics", *American Criminal Law Review*, Volume 56, 2019, pp. 1553 and ff and passim (which clearly demonstrates that COMPAS was significantly less accurate for Hispanic than for white defendants by several measures and suggesting that smaller numbers of Hispanic defendants might be the cause). See: Mayson, Sandra G., "Bias In, Bias Out", *cit.*, pp. 2218–2300. See also: Dong et al., Qi, "Imbalanced deep learning by minority class incremental rectification, *IEEE Transactions on Pattern Analysis & Machine Intelligence*, Volume 41, 2019, p. 1367 (posit that "*most existing learning algorithms produce inductive bias (learning bias)* towards the frequent (majority) classes if training data are not balanced, *resulting in poor minority class recognition performance*"). Italics added. See: Chandler, Anupam, "The Racist Algorithm", *Michigan Law Review*, Volume 115, n. ° 6, 2018, p. 1026 (on racist algorithms, noting that "the possibilities for discriminatory manipulation are legion").

[729] See: Kirkpatrick, Keith, "It's not the Algorithm, it's the Data", *Communications of the ACM*, February 2017, Volume 60, n. ° 2, 2017 ("critics, however, say tools such as PredPol and Command-Central *are inherently biased since they rely heavily on reported crimes data, which is often concentrated in areas that are heavily policed, thereby skewing statistics to overrepresent poor or minority communities.* "*We know that we have a history of racially biased policing in the United States, and that has fed into all the data that we have on where arrests have occurred, which crimes are more likely to occur in specific communities, and at which particular times*," says Jennifer Lynch, senior staff attorney at the Electronic Frontier Foundation. "*That's the data that's being fed into predictive policing algorithms*"). Italics added. See also: Kirkpatrick, Keith, "Battling Algorithmic Bias: How Do We Ensure Algorithms Treat Us Fairly?" *Commun. ACM 59*, Volume 10, 2016, pp. 1 and ff and passim.

[730] Lehr, David/Ohm, Paul, "Playing with the Data: What Legal Scholars Should Learn About Machine Learning", *cit.*, pp. 653–718.

minorities than for others.[731] Compellingly, a machine learning algorithm that **overfits** has every chance of unduly capitalizing on this **noise** much more than a machine learning algorithm that refrains itself from[732] doing so (i.e. **overfitting**) would.

§§ Tellingly, an **overfitting algorithm** could produce less accurate predictive rules for minorities than for others. This is yet another reason why data scientists should seriously take stock of the proneness for **overfitting** when choosing a type of model. The need to ferret out feasible ways of soothing out disparate impacts[733] is dire. For that reason alone, the harmfulness arising out of extant ignorance of machine learning's stages[734] could not be stressed vigorously enough.

5.1.6.1.1 Can «Regularization» (Toshihiro Kamishima et al.) Reduce Algorithmic Discrimination Through the Change of Objective Function (i.e. Goal of the Deployment of Machine Learning Algorithm) During the Stages of Model Tuning and Model Training?

§§ There is a strand of literature championing for the allayment of algorithmic discrimination. But here is the twist: some changes are needed in earlier stages of the construction of a machine learning algorithm. Pivotally, some of these sorely needed changes entail meaningful intervention during both the stages of **model tuning**[735] and **model training**.[736] Crucially, Toshihiro Kamishima and his fellow co-authors,

---

[731] See: Kappelhof, Joost, *Survey Research and the Quality of Survey Data Among Ethnic Minorities, Total Survey Error in Practice (Wiley Series in Survey Methodology)*, Biemer, Paul P. et al. (Editors), 2017, pp. 235, 242–243 (noting that "*measurement error can seriously bias the accuracy of estimates and can differentially affect the responses of ethnic minorities*"). Italics added.

[732] Lehr, David/Ohm, Paul, "Playing with the Data: What Legal Scholars Should Learn About Machine Learning", *cit.*, pp. 653–718.

[733] None of this is to suggest, nor is to say, that mere disparate impact alone is of scant importance in that is not a relevant issue raised by both big data and algorithms. See, e.g.: Bartlett, Robert/Morse, Adair/Stanton, Richard/Wallace, Nancy, "Consumer-Lending Discrimination in the FinTech Era 4 (Nat'l Bureau of Econ. Research, Working Paper No. 25943"), 2019, passim (concludes that disparate impact extracts as much rents as face-to-face discrimination). It bears mentioning that scorching issue of whether and to what extent disparate impact alone should be actionable is different from, in that does not overlap with, the sweltering issue of proxy discrimination. See: Cohran, Matthew Jordan, "Fairness in Disparity: Challenging the Application of Disparate Impact Theory in Fair Housing Claims Against Insurers", *The George Mason University Civil Rights Law Journal*, Volume 21, 2011, pp. 159 and ff and passim (discussing the use of disparate impact theory and potential applicability to Fair Housing Act claims against insurers).

[734] Lehr, David/Ohm, Paul, "Playing with the Data: What Legal Scholars Should Learn About Machine Learning", *cit.*, pp. 653–718. See: Part V, this chapter, Sects. 5.1.3–5.1.3.1.6 of this book (on the fundamental tenets of model selection). See: Part V, this chapter, Sect. 5.1.3.1.5 of this book (on the central tenets of model tuning). See: Part V, this chapter, Sects. 5.1.4–5.1.4.1.1 of this book (on the central tenets of model training).

[735] See: Part V, this chapter, Sect. 5.1.3.1.5 of this book.

[736] See: Part V, this chapter, Sects. 5.1.4–5.1.4.1.1 of this book.

for example, set forth a helpful proposal for mitigating disparate impacts[737] during **model tuning** through a painstaking process baptized as **«regularization»**.[738]

§§ Concisely, **«regularization»** entails changing a machine learning algorithm's **objective or loss function** to chastise it if it produces exceedingly high disparate classifications.[739] Strikingly, Google researchers have meaningfully shown that, during

---

[737] See: Hellman, Deborah, "Indirect Discrimination and the Duty to Avoid Compounding Injustice", *Foundations of Indirect Discrimination Law*, Collins, Hugh/Khaitan, Tarunabh (Editors), Oxford, Hart Publishing; Reprint edition (June 25, 2020), 2020, p. 107 (Professor Deborah Hellman coined this expression to depict a decision that "exacerbates the harm caused by the prior injustice because it entrenches the harm or carries it into another domain." This book deals with the sweltering topic of indirect discrimination ("*indirect discrimination (or disparate impact) concerns the application of the same rule to everyone, even though that rule significantly disadvantages one particular group in society*"). Italics added. See also: Sunstein, Cass R., "Algorithms, Correcting Biases", *Social Research*, Volume 86, 2019, pp. 449–506 (this famed author tagged **disparate impact** as "disturbing in itself, in the sense that a practice that produces such an impact helps entrench something like a caste system"). This famed scholar furthermore avers that empirical evidence on the accuracy of machine versus human predictions suggests the existence of a "current offense bias" that saps ulterior/subsequent judicial assessments). But see: McIntyre, Frank/Baradaran, Shima, "Race, Prediction, and Pretrial Detention", *Journal Empirical Legal Studies*, Volume 10, 2013, pp. 742–759 (mentions black defendants' exceedingly high likelihood of being arrested on drug-related charges as a potential cause of the race gap); Skeem, Jennifer L./Lowenkamp, Christopher T., "Risk, Race, and Recidivism: Predictive Bias and Disparate Impact", *Criminology*, Volume 54, 2024, pp. 680, 683–84, 704–06 (argues that criminal history correlates with race in their respective data set). See also: Pager, Devah, *Marked: Race, Crime, and Finding Work in an Era of Mass Incarceration*, Chicago: University of Chicago Press, 2007; Fornili, K. S., "Racialized mass incarceration and the war on drugs: A critical race theory appraisal", *Journal of Addictions Nursing*, Volume 29, Issue 1, 2018, 65–72; Jacoby, S. F., Dong, B., Beard, J. H., Wiebe, D. J., & Morrison, C. N., "The enduring impact of historical and structural racism on urban violence in Philadelphia", *Social Science & Medicine*, 1982/2018, 199, 2018, pp. 87–95; Travis, Jeremy, Bruce Western, and Steve Redburn (Eds.), *Growth of Incarceration in the United States: Exploring Causes and Consequences*, Washington, DC: National Academy of Science, 2014. See: Mayson, Sandra G., "Bias In, Bias Out", *Yale Law Journal*, Volume 128, 2019, pp. 2218–2300.

[738] Lehr, David/Ohm, Paul, "Playing with the Data: What Legal Scholars Should Learn About Machine Learning", *cit.*, pp. 653–718.

[739] See: Kamishima, Toshihiro et al., "Fairness-Aware Classifier with Prejudice Remove Regularizer", *Machine Learning & Knowledge Discovery in Databases*, Flach, Peter A./Tijl De Bie/Nello Cristianini (Editors) 2012, pp. 35, 35–50. The regularizer grows exponentially when a class is forecasted chiefly based on sensitive features in the data, Unsurprisingly, sensitive features lose influence in the final classifications. This regularizer is under the control of a shrinkage parameter, whose tuning procedure keeps an eye on the extent to which the machine learning algorithm is deftly regularized. See: Lehr, David/Ohm, Paul, "Playing with the Data: What Legal Scholars Should Learn About Machine Learning", *cit.*, pp. 653–718.

the stage of **model training**, one can successfully modify the threshold at which forecasted probabilities are converted into classifications to impose forecasts to match a bevy of definitions[740] of **algorithmic**[741] **fairness**.[742]

§§ Hardly any bewildering surprise stems from the fact that overlooking these intermediate stages of the machine learning process equals forsaking feasible ways of mitigating **algorithmic discrimination**.[743] Whilst legal scholars have been paying a nuanced attention on how algorithmic discrimination arises during the stage of **data collection**,[744] they have nonetheless overlooked novel methods for curtailing it at that stage. Compellingly, a budding, yet exciting, body of research has clearly shown that a string of algorithmic discrimination can be dwindled by simply **adding noise**[745] to the dataset.[746] Overall, assuaging algorithmic discrimination is completely possible, but it nonetheless entails meaningful intervention at a number of key, often forsaken/disregarded/overlooked, stages of the

---

[740] Lehr, David/Ohm, Paul, "Playing with the Data: What Legal Scholars Should Learn About Machine Learning", *cit.*, pp. 653–718.

[741] Hellman, Deborah, "Measuring Algorithmic Fairness", *Virginia Law Review*, 106 (4), 2020, pp. 811–866. On the dire need to achieve algorithmic fairness through both the creation of race-aware algorithms and trade-offs to attain fairer risk scores: Kim, Pauline, "Race-Aware Algorithms: Fairness, Non-discrimination and Affirmative Action", *California Law Review*, 2022, passim; Kleinberg, Jon/S. Mullainathan/M. Raghavan, "Inherent Trade-offs in the Fair Determination of Risk Scores", *Proceedings of the 8th Conference on Innovations in Theoretical Computer Science (ITCS)*, 2017; Kroll, Joshua A./J. Huey/S. Barocas/E. W. Felten/J. R. Reidenberg/D. G. Robinson/and H. Yu, "Accountable Algorithms", *University of Pennsylvania Law Review*, 165 (3), 2017, pp. 633–705.

[742] See: Hardt, Moritz et al., "Equality of Opportunity in Supervised Learning", *Arxiv*:1610.02413, Oct. 11, 2016, pp. 8–10, https://arxiv.org/pdf/1610.02413.pdf [https://perma.cc/9D8U-3DBH].

[743] It is worth recalling, too, that there are different possible mathematical conceptions of fairness. Pivotally, and as adumbrated earlier in this book, optimizing one metric of fairness often forestalls achieving another. See: Berk, Richard et al., "Fairness in Criminal Justice Risk Assessments: The State of the Art", *Sociological Methods & Research*, 2018, pp. 1–10; Kleinberg, Jon, et al., "Inherent Trade-offs in the Fair Determination of Risk Scores", *Leibniz International Proceedings in Informatics*, Jan. 2017, 2017, at 43:1, 43:4; pp. 3–4 (talking about "balance for the negative class"). With this context in place, at the machine learning phases discussed here, not only do programmers have to ponder technical methods for attaining fairness, but, and foremost, they have to grapple with extremely relevant normative questions of what sort of fairness matters most in a given purview. Lehr, David/Ohm, Paul, "Playing with the Data: What Legal Scholars Should Learn About Machine Learning", *cit.*, pp. 653–718. See: Part V, this chapter, Sects. 5.1.3–5.1.3.1.6 of this book (on the fundamental tenets of model selection). See: Part V, this chapter, Sect. 5.1.3.1.5 of this book (on the central tenets of model tuning). See: Part V, this chapter, Sects. 5.1.4–5.1.4.1.1 of this book (on the central tenets of model training).

[744] See: Part V, this chapter, Sects. 5.1.2.4–5.1.2.4.1 of this book.

[745] Lehr, David/Ohm, Paul, "Playing with the Data: What Legal Scholars Should Learn About Machine Learning", *cit.*, pp. 653–718.

[746] See: Feldman, Michael et al., Certifying and Removing Disparate Impact, ARXIV:1412.3756V3, July 16, 2015, at 11–15, https://arxiv.org/pdf/1412.3756.pdf [https://perma.cc/48PZ-EW48]. This stance pass muster since it renders it less considerably likely to forecast an individual's protected group membership from values of their other input variables.

learning curve of a machine learning.[747] Something that relevant stakeholders should be mindful of or inordinate harms are otherwise slated to continually occur.

5.1.6.1.2 The Interpretability of «Pearls of Algorithmic Wisdom»

§§ There has been an onslaught/downpour of work on what is routinely coined as «explainability».[748] The latter amounts to the ability of machine learning to offer a

---

[747] Lehr, David/Ohm, Paul, "Playing with the Data: What Legal Scholars Should Learn About Machine Learning", *cit.*, pp. 653–718.

[748] See: Samek, Wojciech/Müller, Klaus-Robert, "Explainable AI: interpreting, explaining and visualizing deep learning", *Towards Explainable Artificial Intelligence*, Samek, Wojciech/Montavon, Grégoire/Vedaldi, Andrea/Hansen, Lars Kai/Müller, Klaus-Robert (Editors). Heidelberg/Berlin/New York: Springer, 2019, pp. 5–22 ("*in recent years, machine learning (ML) has become a key enabling technology for the sciences and industry.* Especially through improvements in methodology, the availability of large databases and increased computational power, *today's ML algorithms are able to achieve excellent performance (at times even exceeding the human level) on an increasing number of complex tasks. Deep learning models are at the forefront of this development. However, due to their nested non-linear structure, these powerful models have been generally considered "black boxes", not providing any information about what exactly makes them arrive at their predictions.* Since in many applications, e.g., in the medical domain, *such lack of transparency may be not acceptable, the development of methods for visualizing, explaining and interpreting deep learning models has recently attracted increasing attention. This introductory paper presents recent developments and applications in this field and makes a plea for a wider use of explainable learning algorithms in practice*"). Italics added. But see: Segran, G., "The complexity of artificial intelligence", *Singapore Management University*, 2021, passim (on the elaborate and complex trappings of Artificial Intelligence); Adadi, Amina/Berrada, Mohammed, "Peeking Inside the Black-Box: A Survey on Explainable Artificial Intelligence (XAI), *Institute of Electrical and Electronics Engineers*, Volume 6, 2018, passim. But see: Edwards, Lilian/Veale, Michael, "Slave to the Algorithm? Why a "Right to an Explanation" is Probably not the Remedy You are Looking for", *Duke Law and Technology Review*, Volume 16, 2018, pp. 18–67 (pondering whether and to what extent XAI will come in handy because citizens are woefully ill-prepared to "make use of the kind of algorithmic explanations they are likely to be offered"); Miller, Tim, "Explanations in Artificial Intelligence: Insights from Social Sciences", *Artificial Intelligence*, Volume 267, 2019, pp. 1–38. See also: Bibal, A., Lognoul, M/De Streel/A., Frénay B, "Legal requirements on explainability in machine learning", *Artificial Intelligence and Law*, Volume 29, 2021, pp. 149–169; Ashley, KD, *Artificial Intelligence and Legal Analytics: New Tools for Law Practice in the Digital Age*, Cambridge, Cambridge University Press, 2017.

set of reasons for its predictions.[749] Fourth Amendment pundits, like Michael Rich, for whom the ability to provide articulable suspicion[750] is of paramount importance, and European scholars[751] have been focusing on the General Data Protection Regulation's right to «meaningful information about the logic involved»[752] in

---

[749] See: Burrell, Jenna, "How the Machine 'Thinks': Understanding Opacity in Machine Learning Algorithms", *Big Data & Society*, Volume 3, 2016, pp. 1, 1–2; Ribeiro, Marco Tulio Ribeiro et al., "Why Should I Trust You?": Explaining the Predictions of Any Classifier", Proceedings of the 22nd Proceedings ACM SIGKDD International Conference on Knowledge Discovery & Data Mining, 2016, pp. 1135, 1135; Tutt, Andrew, "An FDA for Algorithms", *Administrative Law Review*, Volume 69, 2017, pp. 83, 101–111; 2017 Papers, FAT/ML (July 4, 2017), http://www.fatml.org/schedule/2017/page/papers-2017 [https://perma.cc/U2PF-MFXT] (identifying, ferreting out and pinpointing essays that geared towards "interpretable," "explorable," and "transparent" machine learning algorithms).

[750] Rich, Michael L., Machine Learning, "Automated Suspicion Algorithms, and the Fourth Amendment", *The University of Pennsylvania Law Review*, Volume 164, 2016, pp. 871 and ff. See: Ferguson, Andrew Guthrie, "Big Data and Predictive Reasonable Suspicion", *The University of Pennsylvania Law Review*, Volume 163, 2015, passim; Joh, Elizabeth E., "The New Surveillance Discretion: Automated Suspicion, Big Data, and Policing", *The Harvard Law & Policy Review*, Volume 10, 2016, pp. 15 and ff.

[751] See: Goodman, Bryce/Flaxman, Seth, "European Union Regulations on Algorithmic Decision-Making and a "Right to Explanation," Arxiv:1606.08813V3, Aug. 31, 2016, at 6–7, https://arxiv.org/pdf/1606.08813.pdf [https://perma.cc/2NEQ-JD9Y]; Edwards, Lilian/Veale, Michael, "Slave to the Algorithm? Why a "Right to an Explanation" is Probably not the Remedy You are Looking for", *Duke Law and Technology Review*, Volume 16, 2018, pp. 18–67 (pondering whether and to what extent XAI will come in handy because citizens are woefully ill-prepared to "make use of the kind of algorithmic explanations they are likely to be offered"); Miller, Tim, "Explanations in Artificial Intelligence: Insights from Social Sciences", *Artificial Intelligence*, Volume 267, 2019, pp. 1–38.

[752] Council Regulation 2016/679 of Apr. 27, 2016, General Data Protection Regulation, art. 13–14, 2016 O.J. (L 119/1) 40, 40–42. See: Watcher, Sandra/Mittelstadt, B./Russell, C., "Counterfactual explanations without opening the black box: automated decisions and the GDPR", *Harvard Journal of Law & Technology*, Volume 1, 2018, passim. Mittelstadt, B./Russell, C./Watcher, Sandra, "Explaining explanations in AI", *Proceedings of Fairness, Accountability, and Transparency (FAT) (ACM)*, 2019, passim.

algorithmic decision-making.[753] In addition to that, renowned European scholars have also brought EU AI Act into a sharper focus while casting a keen light upon its perceived shortcomings, drawbacks, and legal loopholes[754] alike.

[753] Lehr, David/Ohm, Paul, "Playing with the Data: What Legal Scholars Should Learn About Machine Learning", *cit.*, pp. 653–718.

[754] See: Watcher, Sandra, "Limitations and Loopholes in the EU AI Act and AI Liability Directives: What This Means for the European Union, the United States, and Beyond", *Yale Journal of Law & Technology*, Volume 26, Issue 3, 2024, pp. 671–672 ("*Predictive and generative artificial intelligence (AI) have both become integral parts of our lives through their use in making highly impactful decisions.* AI systems are already deployed widely—for example, in employment, healthcare, insurance, finance, education, public administration, and criminal justice. Yet severe ethical issues, such as bias and discrimination, privacy invasiveness, opaqueness, and environmental costs of these systems, are well known. *Generative AI (GAI) creates hallucinations and inaccurate or harmful information, which can lead to misinformation, disinformation, and the erosion of scientific knowledge. The Artificial Intelligence Act (AIA), Product Liability Directive, and the Artificial Intelligence Liability Directive reflect Europe's attempt to curb some of these issues. With the legal reach of these policies going far beyond Europe, their impact on the United States and the rest of the world cannot be overstated.* In this Essay, I show how the strong lobbying efforts of big tech companies and member states were unfortunately *able to water down much of the AIA. An overreliance on self-regulation, self-certification, weak oversight and investigatory mechanisms, and far-reaching exceptions for both the public and private sectors are the product of this lobbying. Next, I reveal the similar enforcement limitations of the liability frameworks, which focus on material harm while ignoring harm that is immaterial, monetary, and societal, such as bias, hallucinations, and financial losses due to faulty AI products. Lastly, I explore how these loopholes can be closed to create a framework that effectively guards against novel risks caused by AI in the European Union, the United States, and beyond*"). Italics added.

§§ Pivotally, scholars have not been slow to deem machine learning as a both inscrutable[755] and unfathomable «black box»,[756] whose inner

---

[755] See: Strandburg, Katherine J., "Rulemaking and Inscrutable Decision Tools", *Columbia Law Review*, Volume 119, 2019, passim; Burrell, Jenna, "How the Machine Thinks: Understanding Opacity in Machine Learning Algorithms", *Big Data & Society*, Volume 3, 2016 (on inscrutable algorithmic decision-making). It is important to note, though, that the rise of digital justice—or algorithmic justice—is set to beget the absolute power of algorithms, which will make judges' life considerably easier. Soon enough, judges will blindly follow the pearls of wisdom breed by inscrutable algorithms which will—keenly and promptly—point out to them the best course of action to be taken in a given procedure. See: Millar, Jason/Kerr, Ian, "Delegation, Relinquishment and Responsibility: The Prospect of Expert Robots", *Robot Law*, Ryan Calo/Froomkin, A. Michael/ Kerr, Ian. Cheltenham: Edward Elgar Publishing, 2016, pp. 102, 106–107 (as these authors aptly put it "*We will rely on robots without really knowing why – simply because their algorithms provide the greatest number of successful outcomes.* We have already seen this in Google's search approach. Neither Larry (Page) nor Sergey (Brin) (nor any other Google employee) knowns exactly why one particular web page is a better result than another. *When the click patterns say it is, that's good enough.* No semantic or causal analysis is required…*Like the ancients, we will, quite rationally, come to rely upon them, knowing full well that we cannot necessarily explain the reasons for their decisions*"). Italics added. Converging: Casey, Anthony J./Niblett, Anthony, "Self-driving Laws", *University of Toronto Law Journal*, Volume 66, 2016, pp. 429–435 (contend that "as more information is generated, and the evolutionary algorithm updates and become a better forecaster, we imagine that judges will increasingly rely on the advice of the algorithm"). See: Part V, this chapter, Sect. 5.1.8.5 of this book (on law number five to interpret algorithmic decision-making, which mandates that robot-judges, robot-prosecutors and robot-lawyers must not enter the courtroom for they are utterly incapable of making sound and interpretable value judgements).

[756] See: Roth, Andrea, "Machine Testimony", *Yale Law Journal*, Volume 126, 2017, pp. 1972–1977; Citron, Danielle Keats/Pasquale, Frank A., "The Scored Society: Due Process for Automated Predictions", *cit.*, p. 6; Price II, Nicholson, "Black-Box Medicine", *Harvard Journal of Law and Technology*, Volume 28, 2015, pp. 419, 421; Pasquale, Frank, *The Black Box Society: The Secret Algorithms that Control Money and Information.* Cambridge, Massachusetts: Harvard University Press, 2015, 1–320 (passim). See, for a compelling account of AI black box: Ver: Bathaee, Yavar, "The Artificial Intelligence Black Box and the Failure of Intent and Causation", *Harvard Journal of Law and Technology*, n.º 37, 2018, p. 901 (adduces that "*one possible reason AI may be a black box to humans is that it relies on machine-learning algorithms that internalize data in ways that are not easily audited or understood by humans (…)*" "*first, a lack may arise from the complexity of the algorithm's structure, such as with deep neural network, which consists of thousands of artificial neurons working together in a diffuse way to solve a problem. This reason for AI being a black box is referred to as "complexity". Second, the lack of transparency may arise because the AI is using a machine-learning algorithm that relies on geometric relationships that humans cannot visualize, such as with support vector machines. This reason for AI being a black box is referred to as "dimensionality"*""). Italics added. See also: Mittelstadt, B./Russell, C./Watcher, S., "Explaining explanations in AI", *Proceedings of Fairness, Accountability, and Transparency (FAT) (ACM)*, 2019, passim. But see: Pearl, Judea, *Causality*, 2nd edition, Cambridge, Cambridge University Press, 2009 (on the fundamental tenets of causality). But see: Kilbertus, Niki/Carulla, Mateo Rojas/Parascandolo, Giambattista/Hardt, Moritz/Janzing, Dominik/ Schoellkopf, Bernhard, "Avoiding Discrimination through Causal Reasoning", *Advances in Neural Information Processing Systems*, I. Guyon, U. V. Luxburg, S. Bengio, H. Wallach, R. Fergus, S. Vishwanathan, and R. Garnett (Eds.), Vol. 30. Curran Associates, Inc., 2017, pp. 656–666 (arguing that is feasible to avoiding discrimination through a granular and fine-grained causal reasoning). See: Part V, this chapter, Sect. 5.1.7.2 of this book (on law number two to control algorithmic decision-making,

workings[757] remain conveniently wrapped in opaqueness.[758] The shroud of opacity[759] under which algorithmic decision-making is often wrapped therefore heralded the emergence of grandiloquent sentences like[760] «even the programmers of an algorithm do not know how it makes its predictions».[761]

§§ It is noteworthy that something relevant has been missing from this cryptic equation: to grasp machine learning algorithms' inner workings a deep dive on the different technical pathways underpinning machine learning algorithms is paramount. Absent of which, the relevant stakeholder would be deprived from a treasure trove of information on how such reasons could be given paired with the

---

which mandates that black box models must not be entrusted with the task of making high stake decisions—v.g. health and freedom). See: Part V, this chapter, Sects. 5.1.7–5.1.7.5 of this book (on the five laws to control algorithmic decision-making).

[757] Scherer, Matthew U. Scherer, "Regulating Artificial Intelligence Systems: Risks, Challenges, Competencies, and Strategies", *Harvard Journal of Law and Technology*, Volume 29, 2016, pp. 353–369 (frames the crippling problem of opacity as "the possibility that the inner workings of an AI system may be kept secret and may not be susceptible to reverse engineering"). See: Part V, this chapter, Sects. 5.1.7–5.1.7.5 of this book (on the five laws to control algorithmic decision-making). See: Part V, this chapter, Sects. 5.1.8–5.1.8.5 of this book (on the five laws to interpret algorithmic decision-making). See: Part V, this chapter, Sects. 5.1.2–5.1.6.2.1 of this book (on **the thing-centred algorithmic decision-making** propelled by a *Controllable* and *Interpretable* Machine Learning that weeds out *Algorithmic Dictatorship* and secures *Algorithmic Common Good*. It is worth recalling that the **thing-centred algorithmic decision-making** seeks to unwind the perils arising out of the lack of theoretical underpinnings facing the **human-centred algorithmic decision-making**, as extensively fleshed out Part III, Chap. 3, Sects. 3.1.4.3–3.1.4.4 of this book).

[758] But see: de Laat, Paul B. 'Algorithmic Decision-Making Based on Machine Learning from Big Data: Can Transparency Restore Accountability?", *Philosophy & Technology*, Volume 31, 2018, pp. 524 and ff and passim (broaches the plethora of limitations related with full transparency, privacy, deleterious effects, competitive edge, and the shroud of opacity under which algorithms are often wrapped).

[759] For an on-point breakdown of the distinct levels of opacity arising out of machine learning algorithms in the purview of insurance policies: Selbst, Andrew D./Barocas, Solon, "The Intuitive Appeal of Explainable Machines", *Fordham Law Review*, Volume 87, 2018, pp. 1085, 1089–1099 (holding that there are plenty reasons for the insurer's ignorance. To begin with, the algorithm entails specialized knowledge to understand. That is, the insurer's employees may lack sufficient knowledge to understand the rationale behind the reasons in view of which the algorithm is producing prices for different customers—personalized pricing. Lastly, even if the insurer himself comprehends how the model operates, it may nonetheless lack expertise to comprehend why it operates the way it does. For that reason, the explainability of machines is a vital, but rather elusive, task. Thence, the famed authors deem it as the "nonintuitive" nature of algorithms. For purposes here, the insurer himself might indeed understand that its Artificial Intelligence-embedded technology formulates higher prices for those who actually access the website at hand, but may fail to come to terms with the fact that the explanation for this fact arises from the website's capacity to proxy for genetic information).

[760] Lehr, David/Ohm, Paul, "Playing with the Data: What Legal Scholars Should Learn About Machine Learning", *cit.*, pp. 653–718.

[761] See: Rich, Michael L., "Machine Learning, Automated Suspicion Algorithms, and the Fourth Amendment", *The University of Pennsylvania Law Review*, Volume 164, 2016, p. 886 ("*[E]ven the original programmers of the algorithm have little idea exactly how or why the generated model creates accurate predictions*"). Italics added.

extant advanced methods to exponentially augment the **interpretability** of pearls of algorithmic wisdom offered by algorithmic decision-making. But here is the deeper truth that no one is talking about: reducing disparate impact[762] entails paying a keen attention to the oft-overlooked stages of machine learning, alongside feasible methods for exponentially increasing[763] the **interpretability** of estimations arising out of algorithmic decision-making.

5.1.6.1.3 Pathways Conducive to an Interpretable Algorithmic Decision-Making That Weeds Out Both Automation Bias and Classification Bias: The Examples of Algorithmic Risk Assessment in Criminal Justice and Algorithmic Credit Scoring

§§ I hereby second the framework carefully built by Professor Lehr and Professor Ohm. According to these polymaths, that there are four feasible ways in which a machine learning algorithm can be **interpretable**.[764]

§§ The first one is the ability to say, for each individual on which a running model is applied, precisely what about that given individual or subject caused its algorithmic prediction. Put differently, it is the ability to say precisely how modifications in specific input variable's values for that individual would have yielded a different algorithmic prediction, holding all the subject's other input variable values constant and steady.[765]

§§ For instance, this level of **interpretability** in a risk assessment algorithm in criminal justice might entail being able to aver that a convicted felon was forecasted as perpetrating a very violent criminal activity if released on probation owing to the

[762] See: Barocas, Solon/Selbst, Andrew, "Big Data's Disparate Impact", *California Law Review*, Volume 104, pp. 2016, p. 691 (highlighting the worrisome, and gruesome, issue of "structural disadvantage" with which racialized communities have been tussling with for centuries). See also: Powell, Richard/Porter, Jeremy, "Redlining, Concentrated Disadvantage and Crime: The Effects of Discriminatory Government Policies on Violent Crime", *American Journal of Criminal Justice*, Volume 48, 2023, pp. 1132–1156. But see: Citron, Danielle Keats/Pasquale, Frank, "The Scored Society: Due Process for Automated Predictions", *Washington Law Review*, Volume 89, 2014, pp. 1, 4–5 (highlighting how human beings programming automated systems is directly conducive to, and leads, to fundamentally inaccurate results since the source code, predictive algorithms and datasets may encompass human biases which, in turn, have a **disparate impact** on historically disadvantaged groups).

[763] Lehr, David/Ohm, Paul, "Playing with the Data: What Legal Scholars Should Learn About Machine Learning", *cit.*, pp. 653–718. See: Part V, this chapter, Sects. 5.1.3–5.1.3.1.6 of this book (on the fundamental tenets of model selection). See: Part V, this chapter, Sect. 5.1.3.1.5 of this book (on the central tenets of model tuning). See: Part V, this chapter, Sects. 5.1.4–5.1.4.1.1 of this book (on the central tenets of model training). See: Part V, this chapter, Sects. 5.1.2.4–5.1.2.4.1 of this book (fleshes out the stage of data collection).

[764] Lehr, David/Ohm, Paul, "Playing with the Data: What Legal Scholars Should Learn About Machine Learning", *cit.*, pp. 653–718.

[765] Lehr, David/Ohm, Paul, "Playing with the Data: What Legal Scholars Should Learn About Machine Learning", *cit.*, pp. 653–718.

fact that he is/was male and twenty-three years old.[766] On the flip side, imagine, if you will, if he had instead been, say, **female**[767] and thirty-six years old, holding all of the subject's other input variable values constant and steady. In this case, he would have been forecasted as not perpetrating a very violent criminal activity while on probation.[768]

§§ But here is the kicker: demanding this **heightened level of interpretability**, though, is that one can never lawfully pose such ***ceteris paribus*** type[769] of questions.[770] Importantly, one is utterly unable to ask how the hypothetical felon's forecast would be different if he were instead a thirty-seven year-old female, holding everything else about that individual constant and steady, since it is not indeed feasible to hold everything else constant and steady beyond of a true body of scientific experiment. On the flip side, if this man had instead been born nineteen years earlier and woman, then pretty much every other attribute of her would by be completely different from those same attributes of the twenty-two year-old male.[771]

---

766 Lehr, David/Ohm, Paul, "Playing with the Data: What Legal Scholars Should Learn About Machine Learning", *cit.*, pp. 653–718. See: Part IV, Chap. 4, Sects. 4.1.10.1–4.1.10.6 of this book (on biased algorithmic risk assessment in criminal procedure law settings, with a sharper focus on COMPAS).

767 But see: Hamilton, Melissa, "The sexist algorithm", *Behavioral Sciences and the Law*, Volume 37, Issue 2, Special Issue: the Use of Statistics in Criminal Cases, March–April 2019, 2019, pp. 1 and ff ("*Algorithmic risk assessment tools are informed by scientific research concerning which factors are predictive of recidivism and thus support the evidence-based practice movement in criminal justice.* Automated assessments of individualized risk (low, medium, high) *permit officials to make more effective management decisions. Computer-generated algorithms appear to be objective and neutral. But are these algorithms actually fair? The focus herein is on gender equity.* Studies confirm that women typically have far lower recidivism rates than men. *This differential raises the question of how well algorithmic outcomes fare in terms of predictive parity by gender.* This essay reports original research using a large dataset of offenders who were scored on the popular risk assessment tool COMPAS. *Findings indicate that COMPAS performs reasonably well at discriminating between recidivists and non-recidivists for men and women. Nonetheless, COMPAS algorithmic outcomes systemically overclassify women in higher risk groupings. Multiple measures of algorithmic equity and predictive accuracy are provided to support the conclusion that this algorithm is sexist*"). Italics added.

768 Lehr, David/Ohm, Paul, "Playing with the Data: What Legal Scholars Should Learn About Machine Learning", *cit.*, pp. 653–718.

769 Lehr, David/Ohm, Paul, "Playing with the Data: What Legal Scholars Should Learn About Machine Learning", *cit.*, pp. 653–718.

770 Lehr, David/Ohm, Paul, "Playing with the Data: What Legal Scholars Should Learn About Machine Learning", *cit.*, pp. 653–718. Collins, John et al., "Counterfactuals and Causation: History, Problems, and Prospects", *Causation and Counterfactuals (Representation and Mind Series)*, Collins, John/Hall, Ned/Paul, L. A. (Editors), Massachusetts, MIT Press, 2004, pp. 1–480 (undertakes a thorough review of some of the most enthralling philosophical debates centred around causation and counterfactuals in an overarching sense). See: Part V, this chapter, Sects. 5.1.1.5.2.2–5.1.1.5.2.2.1.4 of this book (on the fundamental shift away from causation to correlations in algorithmic decision-making).

771 Lehr, David/Ohm, Paul, "Playing with the Data: What Legal Scholars Should Learn About Machine Learning", *cit.*, pp. 653–718.

§§ Therefore, asking this type of reason-giving is good as useless. On the other end of the interpretability spectrum, critical is to ask why a machine learning algorithm generates forecasts the way it does. A go-to response is that the machine learning algorithm's forecasts are related with forecasts that optimize the algorithm's **objective function.**[772]

§§ Put otherwise, the type of the **objective function**—what was indeed optimized is what counts the most. Note, though, that, in many legal contexts, such as risk assessment in criminal justice settings,[773] property technologies,[774] algorithmic credit scoring[775] or financial services, this type of reason-giving will not suffice insofar is largely unsatisfactory.[776] By and large, this type of reason-giving[777] is not much more than «because the algorithm said so».[778] A strand of both **automation**

---

[772] Lehr, David/Ohm, Paul, "Playing with the Data: What Legal Scholars Should Learn About Machine Learning", *cit.*, pp. 653–718. See: Part V, this chapter, Sects. 5.1.3–5.1.3.1.6 of this book (on the fundamental tenets of model selection). See: Part V, this chapter, Sect. 5.1.3.1.5 of this book (on the central tenets of model tuning). See: Part V, this chapter, Sects. 5.1.4–5.1.4.1.1 of this book (on the central tenets of model training). See: Part V, this chapter, Sects. 5.1.2.4–5.1.2.4.1 of this book (fleshes out the stage of data collection).

[773] See: Rich, Michael L., Machine Learning, "Automated Suspicion Algorithms, and the Fourth Amendment", *cit.*, pp. 893–895 (drilling into, and shedding light on, how, in the Fourth Amendment context, individualized suspicion is absolutely required—a host of reasons ought to be given in respect to why a particular individual was searched or seized). See: Part IV, Chap. 4, Sects. 4.1.10.1–4.1.10.6 of this book (on biased algorithmic risk assessment in criminal procedure law settings, with a sharper focus on COMPAS). See: Part IV, Chap. 4, Sects. 4.1.1–4.1.1.1 of this book (on biased predictive policing).

[774] The approval of rental applications is arguably one of those tasks that should never be entrusted to machines. More on this on Part IV, Chap. 4, Sects. 4.1.4–4.1.4.2.1 of this book. See also: Part V, this chapter, Sect. 5.1.1.7.2 of this book (on law number two to control algorithmic decision-making, which mandates that black box models must not be entrusted with the task of making high stake decisions—v.g. health and freedom).

[775] See: Part IV, Chap. 4, Sects. 4.1.4–4.1.4.2.1 of this book (on mortgage redlining). See: Part IV, Chap. 4, Sects. 4.1.2–4.1.4.3 of this book (on algorithmic credit scoring, consumer racism and credit card redlining). See: Part IV, Chap. 4, Sects. 4.1.4–4.1.4.2.3 of this book (on algorithmic redlining). See: Part IV, Chap. 4, Sect. 4.1.4.3 of this book (on "algorithmic redliking"). See: Part IV, Chap. 4, Sect. 4.1.3 of this book (on algorithmic prime-lining).

[776] Lehr, David/Ohm, Paul, "Playing with the Data: What Legal Scholars Should Learn About Machine Learning", *cit.*, pp. 653–718.

[777] See: Deeks, Ahsley, "Secret Reason-Giving", *Yale Law Journal*, Volume 129, 2019, passim.

[778] See: Lehr, David/Ohm, Paul, "Playing with the Data: What Legal Scholars Should Learn About Machine Learning", *cit.*, pp. 653–718. But see: Millar, Jason/Kerr, Ian, "Delegation, Relinquishment and Responsibility: The Prospect of Expert Robots", *Robot Law*, Calo, Ryan/Froomkin, A. Michael/Kerr, Ian (Editors), Cheltenham, Edward Elgar Publishing, 2016, pp. 102, 106–107 (as these authors aptly put it "*we will rely on robots without really knowing why – simply because their algorithms provide the greatest number of successful outcomes.* We have already seen this in Google's search approach. Neither Larry (Page) nor Sergey (Brin) (nor any other Google employee) knowns exactly why one particular web page is a better result than another. *When the click patterns say it is, that's good enough.* No semantic or causal analysis is required…*Like the ancients, we will, quite rationally, come to rely upon them, knowing full well that we cannot necessarily explain the reasons for their decisions*"). Italics added. Converging: Casey, Anthony J./Niblett, Anthony, "Self-driving

bias[779] and **classification bias**[780] that deserves both vitriolic remarks and trenchant criticism.

5.1.6.1.4 «Peeking Inside the Black Box» Entails Tough Choices at the Model Selection and Model Training Stages to Enable an Interpretable Algorithmic Decision-Making That Abides by the Central Tenets of Procedural Rule of Law

§§ Against this background, asking a machine learning algorithm to provide reasons why each individual estimation resulted it is largely impossible—if not downrightly unfeasible. By the same token, explaining the algorithmic predictions just by trotting

---

Laws", *University of Toronto Law Journal*, Volume 66, 2016, pp. 429–435 (contend that "as more information is generated, and the evolutionary algorithm updates and become a better forecaster, *we imagine that judges will increasingly rely on the advice of the algorithm*"). But see: Weizenbaum, Joseph, *Computer Power and Human Reason: From Judgment to Calculation*, 1st edition, New York, W. H. Freeman & Co, 1976, pp. 1–300 (227) ("examines the sources of the computer's powers and offers evaluative explorations of what computers can do, cannot do, and should not be employed to do") (this founding father of Artificial Intelligence presciently noted that we should not entrust Artificial Intelligence-embedded technologies with "tasks that demand wisdom"). Italics added. The approval of rental applications is arguably one of those tasks that should never be entrusted to machines). More on this on Part IV, Chap. 4, Sects. 4.1.4–4.1.4.2.1 of this book. See: Part V, this chapter, Sect. 5.1.8.5 of this book (on law number five to interpret algorithmic decision-making, which mandates that robot-judges, robot-prosecutors and robot-lawyers must not enter the courtroom for they are utterly incapable of making sound and interpretable value judgements).

[779] See: Wonyoung, So, "Which Information Matters? Measuring Landlord Assessment of Tenant Screening Reports", *Housing Policy Debate*, Volume 33, n. ° 6, 2023, pp. 1484–1510 (1484) ("*Through a behavioral experiment with landlords using simulated tenant screening reports, this study shows that landlords use blanket screening policies, that they conflate the existence of tenant records with outcomes (e.g., eviction filings with executed evictions), and that they display, on average, tendencies toward automation bias that are influenced by the risk assessments and scores presented by tenant screening reports.* I argue that maintaining blanket screening policies and *automation bias*, combined with the downstream effects of creating and *using racially biased eviction and criminal records, means that people of color will inevitably experience disproportionate exclusion from rental housing due to perceived "risk" on the part of landlords*"). Italics added. See: Part IV, Chap. 4, Sects. 4.1.4–4.1.4.2.3 of this book.

[780] See: Kim, Pauline T., "Data-Driven Discrimination at Work", *cit.*, p. 867 ("[I]f the goal is to discourage **classification bias**, then the law should not forbid the inclusion of race, sex, or other sensitive information as variables, but seek to preserve these variables, and perhaps even include them in some complex models"); Kroll, Joshua A., et al., "Accountable Algorithms", *University of Pennsylvania Law Review*, Volume 165, 2017, pp. 633, 693–695. See also: Kim, Pauline T., "Data-Driven Discrimination at Work", *cit.*, p. 866 ("**classification bias** occurs when employers rely on classification schemes, such as data algorithms, to sort or score workers in ways that worsen inequality or disadvantage along the lines of race, sex, or other protected characteristics"). These two uses of the word "bias" correspond to the notions of irrational versus rational **(or statistical) discrimination.** Italics and bod added. See also: Mayson, Sandra G., "Bias In, Bias Out", *cit.*, pp. 2218–2300. Kleinberg, Jon et al., "Algorithmic Fairness", *AEA Papers & Proceedings*, Volume 108, 2018, pp. 22–23 (discussing, anchored in a batch of national data, that including race as an input variable to a machine-learning college-admissions algorithm both "improves predicted GPAs of admitted students" and can augment "the fraction of admitted students who are black").

out/reeling off an optimization process falls noticeably short of matching the fundamental tenets of an **interpretable algorithmic decision-making**. Another approach is utterly needed. Pundits rightly aver that there are neatly two different types of approaches to «peeking inside the black box» that are useful. But there is catch: to successfully implement these approaches different choices ought to be made at both the stage of **model selection**[781] and **model training**.[782]

§§ One strand of approaches essentially attempts to highlight how important different input variables are to the resulting algorithmic predictions. Within this strand, a cluster of methods perform on a wide-scale, or «algorithm wide», level.[783] They do not, however, ask how relevant certain input variables are to producing a forecast for a given subject on which a running model is applied. Instead, they ask how relevant they were to the machine learning algorithm's **overall accuracy**[784] during training across many[785] subjects/individuals.[786] But more much lies beyond that, as further shown below.

5.1.6.1.5 «Understanding Correlations Between Input Variables and Output Variables»: The Dire Need of Widespread Implementation of Variable Importance Plots and Individual Conditional Expectation Plots to All Running Models (Ranging from Random Forests, Decision Trees, Stochastic Gradient Boosting Algorithms, Standard Neural Networks to Convolutional Deep Learning Neural

---

[781] See: Part V, this chapter, Sects. 5.1.3–5.1.3.1.6 of this book (on the fundamental tenets of model selection).

[782] Lehr, David/Ohm, Paul, "Playing with the Data: What Legal Scholars Should Learn About Machine Learning", *cit.*, pp. 653–718. See: Part V, this chapter, Sects. 5.1.4–5.1.4.1.1 of this book (on the central tenets of model training). See: Part V, this chapter, Sect. 5.1.3.1.5 of this book (on the central tenets of model tuning).

[783] Lehr, David/Ohm, Paul, "Playing with the Data: What Legal Scholars Should Learn About Machine Learning", *cit.*, pp. 653–718.

[784] When Richard Berk trained the algorithm only to maximize for **overall accuracy**, it predicted rearrest for 17% of the white subgroup and 33% of the black subgroup (a 16 percentage-point difference). Strikingly, the false-positive rates were 16% for the white subgroup whereas for the black groups was 28% (a 12 percentage-point difference). See: Berk, Richard, "Accuracy and Fairness for Juvenile Justice Risks Assessments", *cit.*, p. 180. Notably, when Richard Berk changed the algorithm to equalize the cost ratios, it predicted rearrest for 10% of the white subgroup and 29% of the black subgroup (a 19 percentage-point difference). Relatedly, the false-positive rates were 8% for the white subset and 22% for the black subset (a 14 percentage-point difference). See: Berk, Richard, "Accuracy and Fairness for Juvenile Justice Risks Assessments", *cit.*, p. 185. See: Mayson, Sandra G., "Bias In, Bias Out", *cit.*, pp. 2218–2300.

[785] Lehr, David/Ohm, Paul, "Playing with the Data: What Legal Scholars Should Learn About Machine Learning", *cit.*, pp. 653–718.

[786] See: Berk, Richard A., *Statistical Learning from a Regression Perspective*, *cit.*, pp. 213–222 (providing a nuanced explanation of such plots for the random forests machine learning algorithm); Berk, Richard A., *Statistical Learning from a Regression Perspective*, *cit.*, p. 274 (providing a nuanced explanation such plots for **stochastic gradient boosting**, yet coupled with the caveat that, unlike **random forests' plots**, they are not built based on out-of-bag observations insofar that they do not as faithfully recount insights of input variables to predicting overall accuracy). See: Lehr, David/Ohm, Paul, "Playing with the Data: What Legal Scholars Should Learn About Machine Learning", *cit.*, pp. 653–718.

Networks) with a View to Ensure an Interpretable Algorithmic Decision-Making That Abides by the Central Tenets of Procedure Rule of Law §§ Adherence to the central tenets of Procedural Rule of Law[787] depends on the widespread implementation of **variable importance plots,** which highlights graphically the relative importances of the different input variables.[788] Although identical plots have been hitherto deployed for «standard» neural networks»,[789] they are yet to be fully extended to **stochastic**[790] **gradient boosting** and advanced forms of «deep learning»,[791] such as convolutional neural[792] networks.[793] At its core, these tools amount to feasible ways to **meaningfully challenge** the algorithmic predictions spawned by algorithmic decision-making while abiding by the central tenets of Procedural Rule of Law.[794]

§§ Others approaches are also possible. Such as explaining what the most relevant variables were for a given subject's predictions.[795] Critical to its success, though,

---

[787] See: Part V, this chapter, Sect. 5.1.1.1 of this book (on the central tenets of Rule of Law that lends itself to a beacon of justice amidst the sepulchral darkness that is about to take hold). See: Part V, this chapter, Sect. 5.1.1.2 of this book (on the central tenets of Procedural Rule of Law that lends itself to a lighthouse of justice that allows citizens to challenge the pearls of algorithmic wisdom in a court of law).

[788] See: Berk, Richard A., *Statistical Learning from a Regression Perspective*, *cit.*, pp. 218–221, 279, 284.

[789] See: Garson, David G., "Interpreting Neural-Network Connection Weights", *AI Expert*, Apr. 1991, pp. 47–48; Goh, A. T. C., "Back-Propagation Neural Networks for Modelling Complex Systems", *Artificial Intelligence Engineering*, Volume 9, 1995, pp. 143, 146–149 (drawing on Garson's approach).

[790] Lehr, David/Ohm, Paul, "Playing with the Data: What Legal Scholars Should Learn About Machine Learning", *cit.*, pp. 653–718.

[791] Witten, Ian H., *Data Mining: Practical Machine Learning Tools and Techniques*, *cit.*, 464–466 (providing a brief (thumbnail sketch) overview on the realm of deep learning).

[792] See: Lehr, David/Ohm, Paul, "Playing with the Data: What Legal Scholars Should Learn About Machine Learning", *cit.*, pp. 653–718.

[793] See: Aggarwal, C. C., *Neural networks and deep learning*, Heidelberg, Springer, 2018, passim; Agrawal, A., Gans, J., & Goldfarb, A., "Prediction machines (updated and expanded): The simple economics of artificial intelligence", *Harvard Business Review Press*, 2022; Agrawal, A., Gans, J., & Goldfarb, A., "Power and prediction: The disruptive economics of artificial intelligence", *Harvard Business Review Press*, 2022; Bengio, Y., Hinton, G., Yao, A., Song, D., Abbeel, P., Harari, Y. N., Hadfield, G., Russell, S., Kahneman, D., & Mindermann, S., *Managing ai risks in an era of rapid progress*, arXiv preprint arXiv:2310.17688, 2023, passim (on neural networks and deep learning that operate jointly in the age of Artificial Intelligence-embedded technologies). See: Part II, Chap. 2, Sects. 2.1 and 2.1.1 of this book (for further insights on how the human brain and deep neural network function, respectively).

[794] See: Part V, this chapter, Sect. 5.1.1.1 of this book (on the central tenets of Procedural Rule of Law).

[795] See: Datta, Anupam et al., "Algorithmic Transparency via Quantitative Input Influence: Theory and Experiments with Learning Systems", *IEEE Symposium on Security & Privacy*, 2016, pp. 598, 601, 608–609.

is the extent to which these approaches can be fully extended to more advanced algorithms like deep neural[796] networks.[797]

§§ To ensure the seamless implementation of **variance importance plots**, changes need to be made at the stage of **model training.**[798] In addition to that, given that these methods are not always available for different types of machine learning algorithms, a tool developer is entrusted with the task of making tough choices at the **model selection**[799] stage either.[800]

---

[796] Lehr, David/Ohm, Paul, "Playing with the Data: What Legal Scholars Should Learn About Machine Learning", *cit.*, pp. 653–718.

[797] Datta, Anupam et al., "Algorithmic Transparency via Quantitative Input Influence: Theory and Experiments with Learning Systems", *cit.*, p. 614 ("We have not considered situations where inputs do not have well understood semantics... *With the proliferation of immense processing power, complex machine learning models such as deep neural networks have become ubiquitous in these domains.* Defining transparency and developing analysis techniques in such settings is important future work"). Italics added.

[798] See: Part V, this chapter, Sects. 5.1.4–5.1.4.1.1 of this book (on the central tenets of model training).

[799] Lehr, David/Ohm, Paul, "Playing with the Data: What Legal Scholars Should Learn About Machine Learning", *cit.*, pp. 653–718. See: Part V, this chapter, Sects. 5.1.3–5.1.3.1.6 of this book (on the fundamental tenets of model selection).

[800] It bears mentioning that the suitably tailored model is crucially important not just to get one over the threshold of being able to deploy a relevance-assessing method, but, and foremost, also to deploy highly interpretable methods. More often than not, a group of methods implemented for some machine learning algorithms afford mildly interpretable relevance measures. For instance, in a random forest algorithm used to binary classification an importance value of 0.2 for a given variable for the "True" class can be translated, or interpreted as, signifying that, if that variable was weeded out from the machine learning algorithm, the latter would produce twenty percent more errors when forecasting the "True" class. See: Berk, Richard A., *Statistical Learning from a Regression Perspective*, *cit.*, pp. 214–222. It is pivotally important to note, though, that easily interpretable numbers are not without hurdles. Every now and then, proposed metrics are nothing but simple measures of relevance. Other times, in turn, there is simply no easy way to translating into simple, readable, understandable manner what an importance value suggests. See: Garson, David G., "Interpreting Neural-Network Connection Weights", *cit.*, passim. Tellingly, it goes without saying that choosing a bespoke machine learning algorithm can prove crucially important. See: Lehr, David/ Ohm, Paul, "Playing with the Data: What Legal Scholars Should Learn About Machine Learning", *cit.*, pp. 653–718. Suffice to say that the choice of any given importance-measuring method will prove detrimental in the long run in that can run counter to the sough-after *algorithmic transparency* of which citizens are so keenly fond of. No surprise stems from the fact that stakeholders should employ their best efforts to deploy a particularly **interpretable model** to ensure the much-acclaimed, and sorely needed, ***algorithmic interpretation*** that allow citizens to meaningfully challenge the pearls of algorithmic wisdom produced by machine learning algorithms. See: Part V, this chapter, Sect. 5.1.1.1 of this book (on the central tenets of Rule of Law that lends itself to a beacon of justice amidst the sepulchral darkness that is about to take hold). See: Part V, this chapter, Sect. 5.1.1.2 of this book (on the central tenets of Procedural Rule of Law that lends itself to a lighthouse of justice that allows citizens to challenge the pearls of algorithmic wisdom in a court of law).

§§ Furthermore, there is yet another type of approach that seeks to analyse how increases or decreases in the multiple input variables convert into changes in the outcome[801] variable.[802]

§§ Put differently, these methods unravel the «functional form» of the **correlations between an input variable and the outcome variable**. This functional form can bestow upon relevant stakeholders a meaningful/helpful/actionable pathway of intuitively grasping what **correlations**[803] the machine learning algorithm is doing when generating its algorithmic predictions.[804]

§§ More to the point, they generate **actionable plots**—often dubbed as **partial dependence or individual conditional expectation plots**—that map/graph/depict the **outcome variable** as a function of a given **input variable**.[805] These methods are in dire need of being made widely available for all types of algorithms. They have hitherto been implemented for certain types of machine learning algorithms—e.g. **random forests**,[806] **gradient boosting algorithms**,[807] and «**standard**» **neural networks**[808]—but they are yet to be fully extended to more advanced techniques of deep learning,[809] which is something in dire need of changing.

5.1.6.1.6 Procedural Rule of Law in Algorithmic Decision-Making: Overall Accuracy Does Not Derive from the Data Quality (or Lack Thereof) Alone, But Also From the Surgical Intervention (or Lack Thereof) in Middle Stages (i.e. Model Selection and Model Training) of the Machine Learning Process §§

---

[801] Lehr, David/Ohm, Paul, "Playing with the Data: What Legal Scholars Should Learn About Machine Learning", *cit.*, pp. 653–718.

[802] See: Berk, Richard A., *Statistical Learning from a Regression Perspective, cit.*, pp. 222–229 (shedding light on these plots that underpin random forests algorithm); Berk, Richard A., *Statistical Learning from a Regression Perspective, cit.*, pp. 273–274 (poring over these plots for stochastic gradient boosting while providing some caveats about correctly interpreting them).

[803] See: Part V, this chapter, Sects. 5.1.1.5.2.2–5.1.1.5.2.2.1.4 of this book (on the fundamental shift away from causation to correlations in algorithmic decision-making).

[804] Lehr, David/Ohm, Paul, "Playing with the Data: What Legal Scholars Should Learn About Machine Learning", *cit.*, pp. 653–718.

[805] See: Berk, Richard A., *Statistical Learning from a Regression Perspective, cit.*, pp. 226–229, See: Berk, Richard A., *Statistical Learning from a Regression Perspective, cit.*, pp. 277–292.

[806] See: Berk, Richard A., *Statistical Learning from a Regression Perspective, cit.*, pp. 222–229.

[807] See: Berk, Richard A., *Statistical Learning from a Regression Perspective, cit.*, pp. 273–274.

[808] See: Goldstein, Alex et al., "Peeking Inside the Black Box: Visualizing Statistical Learning with Plots of Individual Conditional Expectation", *Arxiv*:1309.6392V2, Mar. 20, 2014, at 1–12, https://arxiv.org/pdf/1309.6392.pdf [https://perma.cc/6XMK-PZ3S].

[809] Lehr, David/Ohm, Paul, "Playing with the Data: What Legal Scholars Should Learn About Machine Learning", *cit.*, pp. 653–718.

The undying quest for overall accuracy[810] plays a pivotal role in algorithmic decision-making. Put coarsely, at the shallowest level, machine learning algorithms perform significantly more accurately than «bread and butter» predictive[811] techniques. There is a strand of literature that awards primacy to due process concerns insofar inaccurate algorithms can exact a toll on due process.[812]

§§ If only these pundits turned their attention to prior stages in the machine learning procedure beyond data collection, they would have come across, and be met with, blazingly new, gruesome, burdensome, cumbersome, and worrisome sources of algorithmic inaccuracy but, and foremost, they would have been able to find out where surgical interventions could have been made[813] to forestall it accordingly.

§§ As claimed earlier, machine learning is not monolith. For that reason, accuracy is not a monolith either. Consequently, overall accuracy (or lack thereof) does not derive from data quality alone. It is true that data quality is key to accuracy, but truer still there are also avenues to create a more or less accurate machine learning algorithm at later, non-data-related stages of the machine-learning process. Without acknowledging these nuances, legal scholars are accordingly deprived from important tools for ensuring algorithmic accuracy.[814] Procedural Rule of Law[815] in turn,

---

[810] See: Scharpire, Rob, COS 511: Theoretical Machine Learning Lecture #1, p. 2 (Feb. 4, 2008), https://www.cs.princeton.edu/courses/archive/spr08/cos511/scribe_notes/0204.pdf [https://perma.cc/E58K-UG5R] ("What is the advantage of machine learning over direct programming? First, the results of using machine learning are often more accurate than what can be created through direct programming"); Machine Learning: What It Is and Why It Matters, SAS (July 4, 2017, 2:28 PM), https://www.sas.com/en_us/insights/analytics/machine-learning.html [https://perma.cc/T9WW-BM5L] ("[I]t's possible to quickly and automatically produce [machine-learning] models that can analyze bigger, more complex data and deliver faster, more accurate results — even on a very large scale"); Pyle, Dorian/San Jose, Cristina, "An Executive's Guide to Machine Learning", Mckinsey Q., June 2015, http://www.mckinsey.com/industries/high-tech/our-insights/anexecutives-guide-to-machine-learning [https://perma.cc/CU9N-BWU8] ("As a result, [machine learning] *can yield insights that human analysts do not see on their own and make predictions with ever-higher degrees of accuracy*"). Italics added.

[811] Lehr, David/Ohm, Paul, "Playing with the Data: What Legal Scholars Should Learn About Machine Learning", *cit.*, pp. 653–718.

[812] Citron, Danielle Keats/Pasquale, Frank, "The Scored Society: Due Process for Automated Predictions", *cit.*, p. 19 ("Protections could draw insights from what one of has called 'technological due process' —*procedures enduring that predictive algorithms live up to some standard of review and revision to ensure their fairness and accuracy*"). Italics added.

[813] Lehr, David/Ohm, Paul, "Playing with the Data: What Legal Scholars Should Learn About Machine Learning", *cit.*, pp. 653–718. See: Part V, this chapter, Sects. 5.1.3–5.1.3.1.6 of this book (on the fundamental tenets of model selection). See: Part V, this chapter, Sect. 5.1.3.1.5 of this book (on the central tenets of model tuning). See: Part V, this chapter, Sects. 5.1.4–5.1.4.1.1 of this book (on the central tenets of model training). See: Part V, this chapter, Sects. 5.1.2.4–5.1.2.4.1 of this book (fleshes out the stage of data collection).

[814] Lehr, David/Ohm, Paul, "Playing with the Data: What Legal Scholars Should Learn About Machine Learning", *cit.*, pp. 653–718.

[815] See: Part V, this chapter, Sect. 5.1.1.1 of this book (on the central tenets of Procedural Rule of Law). See: Part V, this chapter, Sects. 5.1.3–5.1.3.1.6 of this book (on the fundamental tenets of model selection). See: Part V, this chapter, Sect. 5.1.3.1.5 of this book (on the central tenets of model tuning). See: Part V, this chapter, Sects. 5.1.4–5.1.4.1.1 of this book (on the central tenets of

will accordingly flounder with lacklustre approaches to algorithmic accuracy, which will most likely fray its fabric.

Algorithms Should Not Falter When Deployed in the Real World or the Procedural Rule of Law Will Otherwise Decay: The Cases in Which the Algorithm Fails to Fit the Dataset Well (Noisy Dataset and Bias-Variance Trade-Off)

§§ Data scientists spare no efforts, and go to great lengths, to evaluate how their machine learning algorithms perform when confronted with real-world data.[816]

§§ Crucially, a machine learning algorithm that evinces iron-clad/air-tight accuracy in the training data is completely useless if it falters when it counts the most: its deployment in the real world. There are, broadly speaking, two types of reasons why a machine learning algorithm can falter. Firstly, a running model can simply fail to fit adroitly any type of data—either the **training dataset** or **test dataset**—seamlessly. In such a case, even if the **training dataset** and **test dataset** were indeed representative of real-world data, the running model would be bluntly inaccurate when effectively deployed. Secondly, a machine learning algorithm indeed fit its training dataset and, maybe, test dataset very well, but nonetheless fails to generalize and perform likewise well in real-world[817] data.

§§ The first possibility demonstrated that failure to fit can result from choices made at different stages of machine learning. The second possibility (failure to generalize) is related with the moment in which the model is selected and trained. Here, choices made when creating a dataset can prevent the model from **fitting** the data seamlessly. Crucially, choices that result in a **noisy dataset** can forestall good[818] fits.[819]

§§ Put it bluntly, a **noisy dataset** is one in which the great bulk of the variation between individuals is spurious/bogus and unrepresentative of the real variation that a machine learning algorithm should explore to accurately distinguish between individuals. If this **noise** has an entrenched presence in both the **training dataset** and **test dataset**, then the algorithm's accuracy will be impaired in those datasets and, naturally, the real world.[820]

§§ What catalyses a **noisy dataset**? Two sources stand out from the crowd. On one hand, when collating data, the tool developer can mistakenly/erroneously measure

---

model training). See: Part V, this chapter, Sects. 5.1.2.4–5.1.2.4.1 of this book (fleshes out the stage of data collection).

[816] Lehr, David/Ohm, Paul, "Playing with the Data: What Legal Scholars Should Learn About Machine Learning", *cit.*, pp. 653–718.

[817] Lehr, David/Ohm, Paul, "Playing with the Data: What Legal Scholars Should Learn About Machine Learning", *cit.*, pp. 653–718.

[818] Lehr, David/Ohm, Paul, "Playing with the Data: What Legal Scholars Should Learn About Machine Learning", *cit.*, pp. 653–718.

[819] Witten, Ian H., *Data Mining: Practical Machine Learning Tools and Techniques*, *cit.*, p. 7 ("[O]ften, because of errors or noise in the data, misclassifications occur even on the data that is used to create the classifier").

[820] Lehr, David/Ohm, Paul, "Playing with the Data: What Legal Scholars Should Learn About Machine Learning", *cit.*, pp. 653–718.

input variables and/or output variables. Imagine, for instance, that a projected input variable to a machine algorithm is the number of years of education an individual has received/undergone.[821]

§§ Also imagine, if you will, that the tool developer has access to official education records accurately mirroring this information, and to studies of subjects in which they accurately self-report their years of official education. If that study has other actionable information a tool developer would like to add into input variables, then the tool developer might just choose to glean the education information from the self-report surveys in lieu of analysing the official education records.[822]

§§ Note, though, that self-report data are often incomplete at best or outright inaccurate at worst. Understandably, though not laudably, the overreliance on self-report data endangers introducing **measurement error**—a **type of noise**—into the dataset, which can, in turn, hamper/derail/jeopardize/undermine the algorithm's ability to fit the data seamlessly. In addition to adding noise himself through measurement error, a tool developer can fail to deftly stave off[823] «naturally occurring» randomness.[824]

§§ As adumbrated earlier, randomness inheres and permeates all data. This randomness can be a big problem if takes into consideration the generation of **outliers**. A well-adjusted and seasoned tool developer will readily spot, and promptly weed out, these outliers by reviewing summary statistics. A lousy tool developer who decides to waive this review and deep dives right into **model selection** and model training endangers overlooking this **data noise**. **Noisy data** can be a main cause to an algorithm's failure to fit. It is worth recalling that the machine learning algorithm is only as good as its data,[825] after all.[826]

---

[821] Lehr, David/Ohm, Paul, "Playing with the Data: What Legal Scholars Should Learn About Machine Learning", *cit.*, pp. 653–718.

[822] Lehr, David/Ohm, Paul, "Playing with the Data: What Legal Scholars Should Learn About Machine Learning", *cit.*, pp. 653–718.

[823] Lehr, David/Ohm, Paul, "Playing with the Data: What Legal Scholars Should Learn About Machine Learning", *cit.*, pp. 653–718.

[824] Lehr, David/Ohm, Paul, "Playing with the Data: What Legal Scholars Should Learn About Machine Learning", *cit.*, pp. 653–718.

[825] Lehr, David/Ohm, Paul, "Playing with the Data: What Legal Scholars Should Learn About Machine Learning", *cit.*, pp. 653–718.

[826] See: Surden, Harry, "Machine Learning and Law", *Washington Law Review*, Volume 89, 2014, pp. 87, 106 ("In general, *machine learning algorithms are only as good as the data that they are given to analyze*"). Italics added. See also: Kirkpatrick, Keith, "It's not the Algorithm, it's the Data", *Communications of the ACM*, February 2017, Volume 60, n. ° 2, 2017 ("critics, however, say tools such as PredPol and CommandCentral *are inherently biased since they rely heavily on reported crimes data, which is often concentrated in areas that are heavily policed, thereby skewing statistics to overrepresent poor or minority communities.* "*We know that we have a history of racially biased policing in the United States, and that has fed into all the data that we have on where arrests have occurred, which crimes are more likely to occur in specific communities, and at which particular times*," says Jennifer Lynch, senior staff attorney at the Electronic Frontier Foundation. "*That's the data that's being fed into predictive policing algorithms*"). Italics added. See also: Kirkpatrick, Keith, "Battling Algorithmic Bias: How Do We Ensure Algorithms Treat Us Fairly?" *Commun. ACM 59*, Volume 10, 2016, pp. 1 and ff and passim.

§§ In addition to that, failure to fit can also be catalysed by poor choices made when training—particularly, when fine-tuning parameters—a machine learning algorithm. As adumbrated in Sect. 5.1.3.1.5 of this book, several tuning choices impact a machine learning algorithm's **bias-variance trade-off**. If a tool developer fine-tunes some parameters to optimize more for **low variance** than for **low bias**, the former imperils programming an algorithm that fails to fit the data well enough. It is worth recalling, too, that the **bias-variance trade-off** is related with a trade-off insofar one cannot optimize for both **low variance** and **low bias** at the same[827] time.[828]

§§ Pivotally, a tool developer optimizing for **low variance** might be making a estimation that the risk of failure to generalize, pored over in the following section, is bigger than the risk of failure to fit. If this estimation is accurate, then any resulting failure to fit is not as worrisome. On the flip side, if the estimation is inaccurate, then an impossibility to fit has been unduly, and spuriously, created.[829] Crucially, this points to dire need of a tool developer pouring in staggering efforts into avoiding the perceived pitfalls of both **failure to fit** and **failure to generalize**. Caution must be accordingly exercised to carefully evaluate how different the **real-world data** are likely to be from both the **training dataset** and **test dataset.**[830]

Failure to Generalize When the Dataset Is Non-representative of the True Population of Interest (Overfitting, Primacy to Low Bias in the Bias-Variance Trade-Off, Inappropriately Evaluating Accuracy During Model Training): The Importance of Bagging Algorithms to Forestall Failure to Generalize

§§ It is not easy to recover from failure to fit at all. Relatedly, if a machine learning algorithm is unable to forecast accurately in its **training dataset** and **test dataset**, then the likelihood that the algorithm will forecast inaccurately in the **real world**[831] is exceedingly high.

§§ Tool developers must therefore pour in whopping efforts to ensure that a model is truly generalizable. Inasmuch **noisy data** can beget a failure to fit, other data flaws can likewise breed a **failure to generalize.**[832] Crucially, if data fails to represent the true population of interest, then generalizability is inevitably undermined; the algorithm will have produced **optimal predictive rules** to forecast the outcome of

---

[827] See: Part IV, Chap. 4 of this book.

[828] Lehr, David/Ohm, Paul, "Playing with the Data: What Legal Scholars Should Learn About Machine Learning", *cit.*, pp. 653–718.

[829] Lehr, David/Ohm, Paul, "Playing with the Data: What Legal Scholars Should Learn About Machine Learning", *cit.*, pp. 653–718.

[830] Lehr, David/Ohm, Paul, "Playing with the Data: What Legal Scholars Should Learn About Machine Learning", *cit.*, pp. 653–718.

[831] Lehr, David/Ohm, Paul, "Playing with the Data: What Legal Scholars Should Learn About Machine Learning", *cit.*, pp. 653–718.

[832] Lehr, David/Ohm, Paul, "Playing with the Data: What Legal Scholars Should Learn About Machine Learning", *cit.*, pp. 653–718.

interest in a starkly different group of people than that to which it is eventually deployed.[833]

§§ To the extent nonrepresentative data can arise from non-random sampling from the population of interest, tool developers should engage in **random sampling**. Note, though, that tool developers might not always have the true population of interest—from which to **randomly sample**—at their disposal.[834] Imagine, if you will, that a corporation is creating an algorithm to choose whom to hire and that the corporation is on the verge of modifying its job advertising practices; «it will soon post more on job boards than on industry blogs, which is where it had formerly targeted most of its advertising».[835]

§§ The training dataset and test dataset might include applicants hired in the past who had mostly accessed industry blogs, whilst the population of interest when the machine learning algorithm is applied will be subjects who mostly access job boards. It is quite possible that those two types of applicants differ greatly in relevant, job-related manner.[836]

§§ Unsurprisingly, an algorithm designed to forecast the job performance of one may not generalize when deployed to the other. This is exactly the kind of quandary a tool developer must be sharply attuned to. In that case, the analyst may come up with ways of boosting **generalizability**; if he possessed data on, for example, where each formerly hired applicant had visited the job listing, he could engage in non-random sampling to primarily include in the training dataset and test dataset applicants who had visited the job listing on a job board.[837]

§§ Beyond of data-related issues emerging during the early stages of our machine-learning workflows, three other issues arising at later stages that can beget failure to generalize: succumbing to **overfitting**, **primacy to low bias in the bias-variance trade-off**, and **inappropriately evaluating accuracy during model training**.[838]

§§ As hinted above, **overfitting** happens when an algorithm builds on patterns embedded in a dataset, thereby creating **optimal predictive rules** to fit them accordingly. By virtue of these patterns arising out of randomness, they will not be the just the same in the real-world data. Relatedly, **optimal predictive rules** generated to fit them will not **generalizable** to the outer world; **overall accuracy** will shrink

[833] Lehr, David/Ohm, Paul, "Playing with the Data: What Legal Scholars Should Learn About Machine Learning", *cit.*, pp. 653–718.

[834] Lehr, David/Ohm, Paul, "Playing with the Data: What Legal Scholars Should Learn About Machine Learning", *cit.*, pp. 653–718.

[835] Lehr, David/Ohm, Paul, "Playing with the Data: What Legal Scholars Should Learn About Machine Learning", *cit.*, pp. 653–718.

[836] Lehr, David/Ohm, Paul, "Playing with the Data: What Legal Scholars Should Learn About Machine Learning", *cit.*, pp. 653–718.

[837] Lehr, David/Ohm, Paul, "Playing with the Data: What Legal Scholars Should Learn About Machine Learning", *cit.*, pp. 653–718.

[838] Lehr, David/Ohm, Paul, "Playing with the Data: What Legal Scholars Should Learn About Machine Learning", *cit.*, pp. 653–718.

accordingly. Note, though, that some machine learning algorithms—e.g., those that embody **bagging algorithms**—are not as prone[839] to be affected by **overfitting**.[840]

§§ Importantly, during the **model selection** stage, tool developer could often tail off the damage of **failure to generalize** by opting for a **bagging algorithm**. When tuning the model, tool developers must not lose sight of the **bias variance trade-off**. Here, crucially, affording primacy to low bias over low variance is poised to create problems. Strikingly, a less biased, but highly variant, running model could fail to generalize if there are substantial discrepancies between the **training dataset** and **test dataset** and the **outer/real world**.[841] To offset such a perceived pitfall, the tool developer must not deploy an algorithm in the real world without, during **model training stage**, paying a nuanced attention on how generalizable the machine learning algorithm seems to be.[842]

§§ As extensively discussed earlier in this book, a key step in model training is the algorithmic assessment/evaluation—i.e. striving to gauge how well the algorithm will likely perform in the outer/real world. This process usually entails measuring algorithm's **overall accuracy** either with some sort of cross-validation or with test dataset. Whilst such testing is an important step of the whole machine learning procedure, a lousy tool developer could forgo that meaningful step instead of evaluating overall accuracy in the training dataset themselves.[843]

§§ Such a lacklustre performance would be conducive to a flawed, rigged, watered-down, shoddy, botched, warped, doctored, and ultimately costly misstep, which, in

---

[839] Lehr, David/Ohm, Paul, "Playing with the Data: What Legal Scholars Should Learn About Machine Learning", *cit.*, pp. 653–718.

[840] See: Berk, Richard A., *Statistical Learning from a Regression Perspective*, *cit.*, p. 42 ("A major difficulty in statistical learning is **overfitting**. *Very flexible fitting procedures will tend to respond to idiosyncratic features of the data, producing results that do not generalize well to new data*"). Italics and bold added. See: Berk, Richard A., *Statistical Learning from a Regression Perspective*, *cit.*, p. 169 ("Averaging over a collection of fitted values can help compensate for *overfitting. That is, the averaging tends to cancel out results shaped by idiosyncratic features of the data.* One can then obtain more stable fitted values and more honest assessments of how good the fit really is"). Italics added. A cohort of statisticians go at lengths as to contend that certain **bagging algorithms** are not only resistant to **overfitting**, but, and foremost, fundamentally immune from it. See: Leo Breiman and Adele Cutler have contended that **random forests** "does not overfit." See: Breiman, Leo/Cutler, Adele, "Random Forests", https://www.stat.berkeley.edu/~breiman/RandomForests/cc_home.htm (last visited March. 4, 2025). See also: Breiman, "Random Forests", *cit.*, p. 7 ("*This result explains why random forests do not overfit as more trees are added*, but produce a limiting value of the generalization error"). Italics added.

[841] Lehr, David/Ohm, Paul, "Playing with the Data: What Legal Scholars Should Learn About Machine Learning", *cit.*, pp. 653–718.

[842] Lehr, David/Ohm, Paul, "Playing with the Data: What Legal Scholars Should Learn About Machine Learning", *cit.*, pp. 653–718. See: Part V, this chapter, Sects. 5.1.3–5.1.3.1.6 of this book (on the fundamental tenets of model selection). See: Part V, this chapter, Sect. 5.1.3.1.5 of this book (on the central tenets of model tuning). See: Part V, this chapter, Sects. 5.1.4–5.1.4.1.1 of this book (on the central tenets of model training). See: Part V, this chapter, Sects. 5.1.2.4–5.1.2.4.1 of this book (fleshes out the stage of data collection).

[843] Lehr, David/Ohm, Paul, "Playing with the Data: What Legal Scholars Should Learn About Machine Learning", *cit.*, pp. 653–718.

turn, would lead to an overblown optimistic sense on the machine learning algorithm's ability to generalize, most likely priming the tool developer to deploy a machine learning algorithm that will, in all likelihood, fail to generalize well at all.[844] As a result, a tool developer should, if feasible, use a **test dataset**[845] to ensure generalizability.

5.1.6.2 The Overriding Importance of Paying a Nuanced Attention to the Middle Stages of Machine Learning (i.e. Model Training and Model Selection) to Unwind Algorithmic Dictatorship While Propelling Algorithmic Common Good: Why Advanced Forms of Algorithmic Decision-Making (e.g. Convolutional Neural Networks) Should Not Be Entrusted with Making High-Stake Decisions (i.e. Algorithmic Risk Assessment in Criminal Settings and Medical Settings)

§§ Scholars keenly believe that a granular attention must be paid to the middle stages of machine learning (i.e. **model training** and **model selection**).[846] Failure to do so, will unduly narrow down the scourge of (dynamic) **Algorithmic Dictatorship**[847] to (static) algorithmic discrimination. Much lies beyond piecemeal proposals to uproot biases with an entrenched presence in input[848] data.[849]

§§ Part V, this chapter of this book, if nothing else, has abundantly shown that while proposals to weed out biases deeply steeped in training datasets retain validity, meaningful steps must be taken beyond that. As captioned, a nuanced attention to the intermediate stages of machine learning is a go-to response to ensure overall accuracy of algorithmic decision-making. Enhanced **algorithmic transparency**[850]

---

[844] Lehr, David/Ohm, Paul, "Playing with the Data: What Legal Scholars Should Learn About Machine Learning", *cit.*, pp. 653–718.

[845] Lehr, David/Ohm, Paul, "Playing with the Data: What Legal Scholars Should Learn About Machine Learning", *cit.*, pp. 653–718.

[846] See: Part V, this chapter, Sects. 5.1.3–5.1.3.1.6 of this book (on the fundamental tenets of model selection). See: Part V, this chapter, Sect. 5.1.3.1.5 of this book (on the central tenets of model tuning). See: Part V, this chapter, Sects. 5.1.4–5.1.4.1.1 of this book (on the central tenets of model training). See: Part V, this chapter, Sects. 5.1.2.4–5.1.2.4.1 of this book (fleshes out the stage of data collection).

[847] See: Part IV, Chap. 4, Sects. 4.1–4.1.10.6 of this book (on Algorithmic Dictatorship and its chilling effect on democracy).

[848] Lehr, David/Ohm, Paul, "Playing with the Data: What Legal Scholars Should Learn About Machine Learning", *cit.*, pp. 653–718.

[849] See: Citron, Danielle Keats/Pasquale, Frank, "The Scored Society: Due Process for Automated Predictions", *cit.*, 13–16; Barocas, Solon/Selbst, Andrew D., "Big Data's Disparate Impact", *cit.*, pp. 677–688.

[850] See: Binns, R., "On the Apparent Conflict between Individual and Group Fairness." *FAT*'20: Proceedings of the 2020 Conference on Fairness, Accountability, and Transparency*, January 2020, Chicago, 2020, pp. 514–524; Coglianese, C. and D. Lehr, "Transparency and Algorithmic Governance." Faculty Scholarship at Penn Law, 2020; Madras, D./E. Creager/T. Pitassi/R.Zemel,

and **discriminatory impact tests,**[851] are not the answers you are looking for to tackle head-on the underlying problems[852] of machine learning.

§§ By focusing on the several overlooked middle stages of machine learning (e.g. model selection and model training), not only tracking and ameliorating harm is far easier, but, and foremost, trouncing **Algorithmic Dictatorship** while securing **Algorithmic Common Good** also is.

§§ As adumbrated earlier, **Algorithmic Common Good** cares about *how* and *why* algorithmic decision-making affects citizens' fundamental rights; most importantly, what can be done to soothe out its harmful effects.[853] It follows that algorithmic decision-making,[854] given its complexities[855] and deleterious effects,[856] should not

---

"Fairness through Causal Awareness: Learning Causal Latent-Variable Models for Biased Data", *FAT*'19: Proceedings of the Conference on Fairness, Accountability, and Transparency*, New York, NY, 2019, pp. 349–358; See also: Mittelstadt, B./Russell, C./Watcher, S., "Explaining explanations in AI", *Proceedings of Fairness, Accountability, and Transparency (FAT) (ACM)*, 2019, passim.

[851] See: Selbst, Andrew D., "Disparate Impact in Big Data Policing", *Georgia Law Review*, Volume 52, 2017, pp. 109 and ff and passim.

[852] Lehr, David/Ohm, Paul, "Playing with the Data: What Legal Scholars Should Learn About Machine Learning", *cit.*, pp. 653–718.

[853] That is why **algorithmic accountability**—a strand of **Procedural Rule of Law**—is key when it comes to challenge the algorithmic predictions arising out of algorithmic decision-making. On algorithmic accountability: Almada, M., "Human intervention in automated decision-making: toward the construction of contestable systems", *Proceedings of the Seventeenth International Conference on Artificial Intelligence and Law*, 2019, pp. 2–11; Williams, Rebecca, "Rethinking Administrative Law for Algorithmic Decision-Making", *Oxford Journal of Legal Studies*, Volume 42, 2021, pp. 468 e ff and passim. See: Part V, this chapter, Sect. 5.1.1.1 of this book (on the central tenets of Rule of Law that lends itself to a beacon of justice amidst the sepulchral darkness that is about to take hold). See: Part V, this chapter, Sect. 5.1.1.2 of this book (on the central tenets of Procedural Rule of Law that lends itself to a lighthouse of justice that allows citizens to challenge the pearls of algorithmic wisdom in a court of law).

[854] But see: Cohen, Julien E., *Between Truth and Power: The Legal Constructions of Informational Capitalism*. Oxford: Oxford University Press, 2019, pp. 1–376 (p. 192) (contends presciently that "*automated processes* have obvious efficiency advantages, *but such processes may not align well (or well at all) with applicable legal requirements that are couched in shades of gray*"). Italics added. See also: Citron, Danielle K., "Technological Due Process", *Washington University Law Review*, Volume 85, 2008, pp. 1249–1253 ("Computer programs seamlessly combine rulemaking and individual adjudications without the critical procedural protections owed either of them").

[855] See: Segran, G., "The complexity of artificial intelligence", *Singapore Management University*, 2021, passim (on the elaborate and complex trappings of Artificial Intelligence).

[856] But see: Millar, Jason/Kerr, Ian, "Delegation, Relinquishment and Responsibility: The Prospect of Expert Robots", *Robot Law*, Calo, Ryan/Froomkin, A. Michael/Kerr, Ian (Editors), Cheltenham, Edward Elgar Publishing, 2016, pp. 102, 106–107 (as these authors aptly put it "*we will rely on robots without really knowing why – simply because their algorithms provide the greatest number of successful outcomes.* We have already seen this in Google's search approach. Neither Larry (Page) nor Sergey (Brin) (nor any other Google employee) knowns exactly why one particular web page is a better result than another. *When the click patterns say it is, that's good enough.* No semantic or causal analysis is required…*Like the ancients, we will, quite rationally, come to rely upon them, knowing full well that we cannot necessarily explain the reasons for their decisions*"). Italics added. Converging: Casey, Anthony J./Niblett, Anthony, "Self-driving Laws", *University of Toronto Law Journal*, Volume 66, 2016, pp. 429–435 (contend that "as more information is

be entrusted[857] with making high-stake decisions[858] that may be conducive to either imprisonment (algorithm risk assessment in criminal[859] justice[860]) or the loss of

generated, and the evolutionary algorithm updates and become a better forecaster, *we imagine that judges will increasingly rely on the advice of the algorithm*"). Italics added. See: Part V, this chapter, Sect. 5.1.8.5 of this book (on law number five to interpret algorithmic decision-making, which mandates that robot-judges, robot-prosecutors and robot-lawyers must not enter the courtroom for they are utterly incapable of making sound and interpretable value judgements).

[857] See: Weizenbaum, Joseph, *Computer Power and Human Reason: From Judgment to Calculation*, 1st edition, New York, W. H. Freeman & Co, 1976, pp. 1–300 (227) ("examines the sources of the computer's powers and offers evaluative explorations of what computers can do, cannot do, and should not be employed to do") (this founding father of Artificial Intelligence presciently noted that we should not entrust Artificial Intelligence-embedded technologies with "tasks that demand wisdom"). Italics added. The approval of rental applications is arguably one of those tasks that should never be entrusted to machines). More on this on Part IV, Chap. 4, Sects. 4.1.4–4.1.4.2.1 of this book. See also: Kleinberg, Jon/Lakkaraju, Himabindu/Leskovec, Jure/Ludwig, Jens/Mullainathan, Sendhil, "Human Decisions and Machine Predictions", *Quarterly Journal of Economics*, Volume 133, 2018, passim; Pasquale, Frank, "A Rule of Persons, Not Machines: The Limits of Legal Automation", *George Washington Law Review*, Volume 87, 2019, pp. 1 and ff and passim.

[858] See: Part V, this chapter, Sect. 5.1.7.2 of this book (on law number two to control algorithmic decision-making, which mandates that black box models must not be entrusted with the task of making high stake decisions—v.g. health and freedom). See: Part V, this chapter, Sects. 5.1.7–5.1.7.5 of this book (on the five laws to control algorithmic decision-making). See also: Rudin, Cynthia, "Please stop explaining black box models for high stakes decisions", *Proceedings of NeurIPS 2018 Workshop on Critiquing and Correcting Trends in Machine Learning (NIPS 2018)*, 2018, passim; Rudin, C., & Radin, J., "Why are we using black box models in AI when we don't need to? A lesson from an explainable AI competition", *Harvard Data Science Review*, 2019, Volume 1, Issue 2, passim; Tan, S., Caruana, R., Hooker, G., and Lou, Y., "Distill-and-compare: Auditing blackbox models using transparent model distillation". *Proceedings of the 2018 AAAI/ACM Conference on AI, Ethics, and Society, Association for Computing Machinery*, 2018, pp. 303–310 (arguing that explainable models are too complex and fiddly to be understood by laypeople. As a result, interpretable models should be used instead).

[859] See: Part IV, Chap. 4, Sects. 4.1.10.1–4.1.10.6 of this book (on biased algorithmic risk assessment in criminal procedure law settings, with a sharper focus on COMPAS). See: Part IV, Chap. 4, Sects. 4.1.1–4.1.1.1 of this book (on biased predictive policing). On the challenges arising out of algorithmic risk assessment with regard to predicting criminal recidivism rates, fairness wise: Johndrow, J. E./K. Lum, "An Algorithm for Removing Sensitive Information: Application to Race-Independent Recidivism Prediction", *Annals of Applied Statistics*, 13 (1), 2019, pp. 189–220; Chouldechova, A., "Fair Prediction with Disparate Impact: A Study of Bias in Recidivism Prediction Instruments", *Big data*, 5 (2), 2017, pp. 153–163; Kamiran, F./T. Calders, "Data Preprocessing Techniques for Classification Without Discrimination." Knowledge Information Systems, 2012, 33:1–33; Kearns, M/A. Roth, *The Ethical Algorithm*, Oxford, Oxford Press; Skeem, J. and C. Lowenkamp, "Using Algorithms to Address Trade-Offs Inherent in Predicting Recidivism", *Behavioural Science and Law*, Volume 38, 2020, pp. 259–278; Tonry, M., "Legal and Ethical Issues in The Prediction of Recidivism", *Federal Sentencing Reporter*, 26 (3): 2014, pp. 167–176; Zhu, Mirilla, "Jury, Using Artificial Intelligence to Predict Recidivism Rates", *Yale Scientific*, 2020, passim. See also: Chasemi et al., Medhi, "The application of Machine Learning to a General Risk-Need Assessment Instrument in the Prediction of Criminal Recidivism", *Criminal Justice and Behavior*, Volume 48, 2020, pp. 518–538.

[860] Rudin, Cynthia/Wang, Caroline/Coker, Beau, "The Age of Secrecy and Unfairness in Recidivism Prediction", *Harvard Data Science Review*, Issue 2.1. Winter 2020, 2020, passim; Eckhouse,

life (algorithmic risk assessment in medical cases).[861] Especially, albeit not exclusively, relevant stakeholders should refrain themselves from resorting to particularly uninterpretable forms of algorithmic decision-making, such as convolutional neural networks.[862]

5.1.6.2.1 The Importance of «Keeping a Thorough Paper Trail» (e.g. the Implementation of *Asymmetric Cost Ratio*) Amidst a Looming Algorithmic Disparate Impact Litigation, Which Is a Byproduct of Procedural Accountability Introduced by Procedural Rule of Law

§§ Algorithmic decision-making, if nothing else, is set to give rise to a groundswell of disparate impact litigation. Understandably, and laudably, relevant stakeholders (i.e. tool developers, analysts, data scientists, engineers, programmers) should keep a thorough paper trail as to document *whether* and[863] *how* they implemented an ***asymmetric cost ratio***.

L., Lum, K., Conti-Cook, C./Ciccolini, J., "Layers of bias: A unified approach for understanding problems with risk assessment", *Criminal Justice and Behavior*, Volume 46, Issue 2, 2019, pp. 185–209; Stevenson, M. T./Slobogin, C., "Algorithmic risk assessments and the double-edged sword of youth", *Washington University Law Review*, Volume 96, 2018, passim.

[861] See: Part III, Chap. 3, Sects. 3.1.5.6–3.1.5.6.1 of this book (on Critical Artificial Intelligence Studies, with a sharper focus on the harmful effects of Large Language Models' medical hallucinations that are poised to undermine its overall trustworthiness). See: Watcher, Sandra, "Limitations and Loopholes in the EU AI Act and AI Liability Directives: What This Means for the European Union, the United States, and Beyond", *Yale Journal of Law & Technology*, Volume 26, Issue 3, 2024, pp. 671–672 ("*Predictive and generative artificial intelligence (AI) have both become integral parts of our lives through their use in making highly impactful decisions.* AI systems are already deployed widely—for example, in employment, healthcare, insurance, finance, education, public administration, and criminal justice. Yet severe ethical issues, such as bias and discrimination, privacy invasiveness, opaqueness, and environmental costs of these systems, are well known. *Generative AI (GAI) creates hallucinations and inaccurate or harmful information, which can lead to misinformation, disinformation, and the erosion of scientific knowledge. The Artificial Intelligence Act (AIA), Product Liability Directive, and the Artificial Intelligence Liability Directive reflect Europe's attempt to curb some of these issues. With the legal reach of these policies going far beyond Europe, their impact on the United States and the rest of the world cannot be overstated.* In this Essay, I show how the strong lobbying efforts of big tech companies and member states were unfortunately *able to water down much of the AIA. An overreliance on self-regulation, self-certification, weak oversight and investigatory mechanisms, and far-reaching exceptions for both the public and private sectors are the product of this lobbying. Next, I reveal the similar enforcement limitations of the liability frameworks, which focus on material harm while ignoring harm that is immaterial, monetary, and societal, such as bias, hallucinations, and financial losses due to faulty AI products. Lastly, I explore how these loopholes can be closed to create a framework that effectively guards against novel risks caused by AI in the European Union, the United States, and beyond*"). Italics added.

[862] Lehr, David/Ohm, Paul, "Playing with the Data: What Legal Scholars Should Learn About Machine Learning", *cit.*, pp. 653–718.

[863] Lehr, David/Ohm, Paul, "Playing with the Data: What Legal Scholars Should Learn About Machine Learning", *cit.*, pp. 653–718.

§§ As extensively shown earlier in this book, ***asymmetric cost ratio*** carries both promise and danger in that it can significantly shift the balance of **measurement errors** in ways that could generate disparate[864] impacts.[865] This step is key to ensure the much-needed procedural accountability sought by **Procedural Rule of Law**.[866]

§§ Another oft-heard line of reasoning is that which playing with the data entails keeping[867] a «human in the loop».[868] Deep-rooted concerns have been accordingly

---

[864] See: Hurley, Mikella/Adebayo, Julius, "Credit Scoring in the Era of Big Data", *Yale Journal of Law and Technology*, Volume 18, 2016, pp. 148, 151–156, 172 (averring that FICO scoring boasts a redoubtable capacity to routinely weed out some populations that have been historically and systematically underrepresented or grossly unfairly represented in the credit industry market). Tellingly, by 2016, ten states had disavowed the unlawful practice of employers using shady algorithmic credit scores due to their perceived **disparate impact** on low-income applicants and members of racialized communities (mostly Black folks). See: O'Neill, Cathy, *Weapons of Math Destruction. How Big Data Increases Inequality and Threatens Democracy.* London: Penguin Random House, 2016, pp. 128 and ff and passim. See: Part IV, Chap. 4, Sects. 4.1.4–4.1.4.2.3 of this book. See: Part IV, Chap. 4, Sects. 4.1.4–4.1.4.2.1 of this book (on mortgage redlining). See: Part IV, Chap. 4, Sects. 4.1.2–4.1.4.3 of this book (on algorithmic credit scoring, consumer racism and credit card redlining). See: Part IV, Chap. 4, Sects. 4.1.4–4.1.4.2.3 of this book (on algorithmic redlining). See: Part IV, Chap. 4, Sect. 4.1.4.3 of this book (on "algorithmic redliking"). See: Part IV, Chap. 4, Sect. 4.1.3 of this book (on algorithmic prime-lining).

[865] Lehr, David/Ohm, Paul, "Playing with the Data: What Legal Scholars Should Learn About Machine Learning", *cit.*, pp. 653–718.

[866] See: Part V, this chapter, Sect. 5.1.1.1 of this book (on the central tenets of Procedural Rule of Law).

[867] Lehr, David/Ohm, Paul, "Playing with the Data: What Legal Scholars Should Learn About Machine Learning", *cit.*, pp. 653–718.

[868] Arguing that humans should remain "in the loop" at the output-end of algorithmic decision-making: Saxena, Devansh/Badillo-Urquiola, Karla/Wisniewski, Pamela J./Guha, Shion, "A Human-Centered Review of the Algorithms Used Within the U.S. Child Welfare System", *2020 Proceedings of Conference on Human Factors in Computing Systems*, Apr. 2020, 2020, passim. See: Salloch, S., & Eriksen, A., "What are humans doing in the Loop? Co-reasoning and practical Judgment when using machine learning-driven decision aids", *The American Journal of Bioethics*, 2024, pp. 1–12; Binns, Reuben, "Human Judgment in Algorithmic Loops: Individual Justice and Automated Decision-Making", *Regulation & Governance*, Volume 16, 2022, passim; Simon & Schuster, Green, B., "Algorithmic realism: expanding the boundaries of algorithmic thought", *Proceedings of the 2020 Conference on Fairness Accountability and Transparency*, 2020, passim; Green, B./Hu L., "The Myth in the Methodology: Towards a Recontextualization of Fairness in Machine Learning", *Machine Learning Debates Work 35th Internation Conference of Machine Learning*, 2018, passim; Green, B., Chen Y, "Disparate interactions: An algorithm-in-the-loop analysis of fairness in risk assessments", *FAT* 2019, Proceedings of 2019 Conference of Fairness, Accountability, Transparency*, 2019, pp. 90–99 (on the central tenets of algorithmic fairness). See also: Alimardani, Armin/Jane, Emma A., "Human Hallucinations: GenAI and the Mirage of Personalised Learning for All", 2024, p. 13 ("*The output generated by GenAI models includes an inherent randomness and the same prompt may result in various outputs. Therefore, it is likely that the outputs of GenAI models are never entirely accurate and reliable. In other words, we contend that existing GenAI systems represent a technology that requires a 'human in/on the loop' to verify outputs before they reach the end user. When incorporating GenAI into an educational chatbot, students are the end users, making it challenging to identify and rectify these errors promptly*"). Italics added.

voiced with regard to the risk of trusting too much on machines.[869] Note, though, that even if we thrust the human at the output end of the running model, seldom, if anything, can be done to uproot deep seated biases.[870]

§§ It is true that some aspects of machine learning are[871] «more art than science»,[872] and tough decisions made during the training stage surely embody some form[873] of art of «building statistical models»,[874] but truer still humans must be eagerly awakened to avoid falling into the trap of «automation bias»[875] while

[869] The rise of digital justice—or algorithmic justice—is set to beget the absolute power of algorithms, which will make judges' life considerably easier. Soon enough, judges will blindly follow the pearls of wisdom breed by inscrutable algorithms which will—keenly and promptly—point out to them the best course of action to be taken in a given procedure. See: Millar, Jason/Kerr, Ian, "Delegation, Relinquishment and Responsibility: The Prospect of Expert Robots", *Robot Law*, Ryan Calo/ Froomkin, A. Michael/Kerr, Ian. Cheltenham: Edward Elgar Publishing, 2016, pp. 102, 106–107 (as these authors aptly put it "*We will rely on robots without really knowing why – simply because their algorithms provide the greatest number of successful outcomes.* We have already seen this in Google's search approach. Neither Larry (Page) nor Sergey (Brin) (nor any other Google employee) knowns exactly why one particular web page is a better result than another. *When the click patterns say it is, that's good enough.* No semantic or causal analysis is required...*Like the ancients, we will, quite rationally, come to rely upon them, knowing full well that we cannot necessarily explain the reasons for their decisions*"). Italics added. Converging: Casey, Anthony J./Niblett, Anthony, "Self-driving Laws", *University of Toronto Law Journal*, Volume 66, 2016, pp. 429–435 (contend that "as more information is generated, and the evolutionary algorithm updates and become a better forecaster, we imagine that judges will increasingly rely on the advice of the algorithm"). See: Part V, this chapter, Sect. 5.1.8.5 of this book (on law number five to interpret algorithmic decision-making, which mandates that robot-judges, robot-prosecutors and robot-lawyers must not enter the courtroom for they are utterly incapable of making sound and interpretable value judgements).

[870] Lehr, David/Ohm, Paul, "Playing with the Data: What Legal Scholars Should Learn About Machine Learning", *cit.*, pp. 653–718.

[871] Lehr, David/Ohm, Paul, "Playing with the Data: What Legal Scholars Should Learn About Machine Learning", *cit.*, pp. 653–718.

[872] Lehr, David/Ohm, Paul, "Playing with the Data: What Legal Scholars Should Learn About Machine Learning", *cit.*, pp. 653–718.

[873] Lehr, David/Ohm, Paul, "Playing with the Data: What Legal Scholars Should Learn About Machine Learning", *cit.*, pp. 653–718.

[874] Lehr, David/Ohm, Paul, "Playing with the Data: What Legal Scholars Should Learn About Machine Learning", *cit.*, pp. 653–718.

[875] See: Wonyoung, So, "Which Information Matters? Measuring Landlord Assessment of Tenant Screening Reports", *Housing Policy Debate*, Volume 33, n. ° 6, 2023, pp. 1484–1510 (1502) (arguing that landlords display automation bias as the "*study finds that landlords tend to rely more on the automated system's judgment: when a report noted that a tenant was either medium or high risk, landlords showed a higher tendency toward rejection, or, if conditionally accepted, they imposed a higher security deposit. This indicates that tenant screening services' risk scoring may critically affect landlords' decision-making.* Given that there is no regulation pertaining to producing and deploying such algorithms, and 1502 W. SO given the inherent inaccuracies of eviction data (Porton et al. 2021) and widespread, serial eviction filings (Garboden and Rosen 2019), particularly automatic eviction filings activated by digitized property management systems and large, corporate landlords (Fields 2022; Gomory 2022; Immergluck et al. 2020), *tenant screening services very likely contribute to perpetuating algorithmic inequality* (Eubanks, 2018) *by denying qualified applicants—disproportionately from protected groups—access to housing*"). Italics added.

placidly accepting the pearls of algorithmic wisdom without questioning it. If that happens, *Algorithmic Dictatorship* vanquishes *Algorithmic Common Good*. Thence, we will all perish.

5.1.7 Five Laws to Control Algorithmic Decision-Making

5.1.7.1 Law Number One: Whoever Develops and/or Deploys Running Models Must Be Held Criminally Accountable for Hard Artificial Intelligent Crimes (Hard-AI Crimes)

§§ Machines powered by redoubtable artificial intelligence-embedded technologies are gradually taking over chores previously undertaken by humans alone.[876] In attaining such time-consuming and energy-draining tasks, Artificial Intelligence may wilfully, intentionally, and knowingly engage in flagitious/criminal activities: this is the kernel of Artificial Intelligence Crimes (Hard AI Crimes). Put simply, Hard AI crime is a flagitious behaviour that would be labelled a crime (either felony or misdemeanour) if it were carried out by human beings.[877]

§§ For instance, a state-of-the-art machine learning algorithm may intentionally manipulate stock exchange markets[878] or whimsically activate weapons of mass destruction.[879] In such instances (hard AI crimes) the criminal responsibility should be ascribed to whoever developed and/or deployed the running model. This book therefore marks a plot twist in this regard.

---

[876] Nerantzi, Elina/Sartor, Giovanni, "Hard-AI Crimes: The Deterrence Turn", *Oxford Journal of Legal Studies*, Volume XX, Number XX, 2024, pp. 1–29 (1).

[877] Nerantzi, Elina/Sartor, Giovanni, "Hard-AI Crimes: The Deterrence Turn", *cit.*, pp. 1–29 (1).

[878] Nerantzi, Elina/Sartor, Giovanni, "Hard-AI Crimes: The Deterrence Turn", *cit.*, pp. 1–29 (1).

[879] About this: Acquavica, Guido, "Autonomous weapons systems controlled by Artificial Intelligence: a conceptual roadmap for international criminal responsibility", *Edward Elgar online*, Volume 60, Issue 1, 2022, pp. 89–121 ("The article explores a conceptual roadmap for considering autonomous weapons systems (AWS) not just in the framework of international humanitarian law (IHL), but also in terms of individual responsibility under international criminal law (ICL). After setting the stage with some preliminary and terminological considerations, the author considers the different perspectives through which IHL and ICL look at Artificial Intelligence as applied to weapons systems. Within this framework, the article then hones in on certain essential aspects of the contemporary understanding of ICL – a system aimed at protecting certain interests (or goods) based on individual agency as demonstrated by its approach to modes of responsibility, and sentencing. On the basis of these reflections, three main theoretical possibilities are explored: that humans remain the only subject capable of being considered criminally responsible for harm to interests protected by ICL; that AWS come to be considered 'persons' subject to (a form of) individual criminal responsibility; or, a hybrid new system combining aspects of the two. The author considers that, while the second option appears implausible and unrealistic under the present circumstances, the challenges faced by the other two options remain daunting, posing potentially irresolvable issues within the current ICL framework"). Italics added.

§§ Recall, a **thing-centred algorithmic decision-making**[880] vests the relevant stakeholders (v.g. companies, tool developers, data scientists, engineers, statisticians, public entities, law enforcement agencies, regulators, real estate agents, probation officers, judges, employers, loan officers, prosecutors, regulators, law enforcement agents, police officers, parole officers and so forth) with the **binding obligation** to **control** not only the model used to perform **algorithmic decision-making** (recall: simpler models, like **random forests**, **decision trees**[881] or **regression trees**, are far

[880] See: Part V, this chapter, Sects. 5.1.2–5.1.6.2.1 of this book (on the fundamental tenets of a thing-centred algorithmic decision-making). See: Part V, this chapter, Sects. 5.1.3–5.1.3.1.6 of this book (on the fundamental tenets of model selection). See: Part V, this chapter, Sect. 5.1.3.1.5 of this book (on the central tenets of model tuning). See: Part V, this chapter, Sects. 5.1.4–5.1.4.1.1 of this book (on the central tenets of model training). See: Part V, this chapter, Sects. 5.1.2.4–5.1.2.4.1 of this book (fleshes out the stage of data collection).

[881] See: Meert, Wannes/De Laet, Tinne/De Raedt, Luc, "Artificial Intelligence A Perspective from the Field", *The Cambridge Handbook of the Law, Ethics and Policy of Artificial Intelligence*, Smuha, Nathalie A. (Editor), Cambridge, Cambridge University Press, 2025, pp. 57–58 ("*As an example of a supervised learning technique, we discuss how decision trees can be derived from examples. Decision trees are useful for classification problems, which appear in numerous applications. The goal is to learn, in case of supervised learning, a function from a dataset with examples that are already categorized (or labeled) such that we can apply this function to predict the class of new, not yet classified examples.* A good example concerns the classification of emails as spam or not spam. Closely related with classification problems are regression problems where we want to predict a numerical value instead of a class. This is, for example, the case when the system is learning how to drive a car, and we want to predict the angle of the steering wheel and the desired speed that the car should maintain. There is vast literature on supervised classification and regression tasks as it is the most studied problem in machine learning. The techniques cover all possible types of functions we have introduced before and combinations thereof. Here we use a simple but popular technique for classification that uses decision trees. In this example, we start from a table of examples, where each row is an example, and each column is an attribute (or feature) of an example. The class of each example can be found in a special column in that table. Take for example the table in Figure 1.4 containing (simplified) data about comic books. Each example expresses the properties of a comic book series: language, length, genre, and historical. The goal is to predict whether this customer would buy an album from a particular series. A *decision tree is a tree-shaped structure where each node in the tree represents a decision made based on the value of a particular attribute. The branches emerging from a node represent the possible outcomes based on the values of that attribute. The leaves of this tree represent the predicted classification, in this example buy or not buy. When a new example is given, we traverse the tree following the branch that corresponds to the value that the attribute has in the example. Suppose there exists a series that the customer has not yet bought, with attribute values (NL/FR, Strip, Humor, Historical). When we traverse the tree, we follow the left branch (Strip) for the top node that splits on length. The next node selects based on language and we follow the left branch (NL/FR) ending in the prediction that the customer will buy this new series. The algorithm to learn a decision tree works as follows: we start with a single node and all available examples.* Next, we estimate by means of a heuristic which attrib ute differentiates best between the different classes. A simple heuristic would be to choose the attribute where, if we split the examples based on the possible values for this attribute, this split is most similar to when we would have split the examples based on their class values (buy or not buy). Once the attribute is decided, we create a branch and a new node per value of that attribute. The examples are split over the branches according to their value for that attribute. In each node we check if this new node contains (almost) only once class. If this is the case, we stop and make the node a leaf with as class the majority class. If not, we repeat the procedure on this smaller set of examples. *An advantage of decision trees is that they are easy and fast to learn and that they often deliver accurate predictions,*

easier to **control** than advanced models like **deep neural convolutional networks**), but, and foremost, the **outputs generated by the model**.

§§ In addition to that, relevant stakeholders must **fully control the algorithmic decision-making in its entirety and** introduce the **necessary tweaks at the intermediate stages of algorithmic decision-making** (v.g. **model selection**[882] and **model training**[883]) to ensure reliability, accuracy, and, to the extent possible, fairness of the outputs generated by the running model. If anything goes sideways, whoever developed and/or deployed the running model should bear the criminal liability (*sibi imputet*) accordingly (*ubi commoda, ibi incommoda*).

§§ It is worth recalling, too, that **algorithmic decision-making** begs for a fundamental shift away from analysis that seeks to unpick causal connections between inputs and outcomes of interest. I hereby second Professor Talia B. Gillis' proposal in view of which **algorithmic decision-making**, to be accurate, reliable and fair, requires that relevant stakeholders (e.g. lenders, landlords, companies, regulators, governments, real estate agents, probation officers, judges, employers, loan officers, prosecutors, regulators, law enforcement agents, police officers, parole officers and so forth) shift their gaze downstream to the *outputs* of a machine learning algorithm,[884] as opposed to the *inputs*.

§§ Relevant stakeholders ought to be wary of the warped/shoddy beliefs they cling to in a bid to carve through the chaos of **Algorithmic Dictatorship**[885] with razor sharp clarity while toiling towards a sought-after **Algorithmic Common Good** of which citizens are bound to be fond of.

---

especially if multiple trees are learned in an ensemble where each tree of the ensemble "votes" for a particular classification outcome. The accuracy of the predictions can be estimated from the data and is crucial for a user to decide whether the model is good enough to be used. Furthermore, decision trees are interpretable by users, which increases the user's trust in the model. In general, their accuracy increases when more data is available and when the quality of this data increases"). Italics added.

[882] See: Part V, this chapter, Sects. 5.1.3–5.1.3.1.6 of this book (on the fundamental tenets of model selection). See: Part V, this chapter, Sect. 5.1.3.1.5 of this book (on the central tenets of model tuning). See: Part V, this chapter, Sects. 5.1.4–5.1.4.1.1 of this book (on the central tenets of model training). See: Part V, this chapter, Sects. 5.1.2.4–5.1.2.4.1 of this book (fleshes out the stage of data collection).

[883] See: Part V, this chapter, Sects. 5.1.4–5.1.4.1.1 of this book (on the fundamental tenets of model training).

[884] Gillis, Talia B., "The Input Data Fallacy", *cit.*, pp. 1176–1263 (1257). See: Part V, this chapter, Sects. 5.1.1.5.2.2–5.1.1.5.2.2.1.4 of this book (on the fundamental shift away from causation to correlations in algorithmic decision-making).

[885] See: Part IV, Chap. 4, Sects. 4.1–4.1.10.6 of this book (on Algorithmic Dictatorship and its chilling effect on democracy).

5.1.7.2 Law Number Two: Black Box Models Must Never Be Entrusted with the Task of Making High Stake Decisions (v.g. Regarding Citizens' Freedom or Health)

§§ To the extent **black box models** are not trustworthy,[886] reliable, and fair, they should not be entrusted with the task of making stake decisions in the domains of health and freedom. More to the point, machine learning algorithms are incapable to reflect agreed-upon «human values such as fairness, accountability, and transparency («FAT»)»,[887] which are vital in making decisions[888] about citizens' life, health, liberty, and financial affairs.[889] For that reason, **white box models**—far easier to assess and far easier to interpret—should be used instead.

---

[886] But see: W. Russell Neuman et al., "Auditing the Ethical Logic of Generative AI Models" available at: https://arxiv.org/pdf/2504.17544, April 25th ("*As generative AI models become increasingly integrated into high-stakes domain*s, the need for robust methods to evaluate their ethical reasoning becomes increasingly important. This paper introduces a five-dimensional audit model—assessing *Analytic Quality, Breadth of Ethical Considerations, Depth of Explanation, Consistency, and Decisiveness—to evaluate the ethical logic of leading large language models (LLMs). Drawing on traditions from applied ethics and higher-order thinking, we present a multi-battery prompt approach, including novel ethical dilemmas, to probe the models' reasoning across diverse contexts. We benchmark seven major LLMs finding that while models generally converge on ethical decisions, they vary in explanatory rigor and moral prioritization. Chain-ofThought prompting and reasoning-optimized models significantly enhance performance on our audit metrics. This study introduces a scalable methodology for ethical benchmarking of AI systems and highlights the potential for AI to complement human moral reasoning in complex decision-making contexts*"). Italics added.

[887] Calo, Ryan, "Artificial Intelligence Policy: Primer and Roadmap", *University of California*, Davis, Volume 51, 2017, pp. 399–435 (411).

[888] Candent challenges that come under the yoke of intelligent automation, which is shaping up to morph the legal arena in an overarching sense. See: Bornet, Pascal/Barkin, Ian/Wirtz, Jochen, *Intelligent Automation: Learn how to harness Artificial Intelligence to boost business and make out world more human*, 2020, pp. 1–432.

[889] Calo, Ryan, "Artificial Intelligence Policy: Primer and Roadmap", *cit.*, pp. 399–435 (411).

§§ Inasmuch black box[890] models,[891] albeit a cutting-edge tool that excels in performing certain tasks, are fundamentally incapable of explaining themselves, they should not be deployed to make high stake decisions in the domains of health[892] and freedom accordingly. Hence the dire need to use simpler running models (e.g.

---

[890] As hinted above, algorithms make their inferences and draw their conclusions in a way difficult to understand, even for the cohort of programmers that designed them. This is deemed *black box*, that further enhances the shroud of mystery under which algorithms are cloaked. See, for a compelling account of AI black box: Ver: Bathaee, Yavar, "The Artificial Intelligence Black Box and the Failure of Intent and Causation", *Harvard Journal of Law and Technology*, n.º 37, 2018, p. 901 (adduces that "*one possible reason AI may be a black box to humans is that it relies on machine-learning algorithms that internalize data in ways that are not easily audited or understood by humans* (...)" "*first, a lack may arise from the complexity of the algorithm's structure, such as with deep neural network, which consists of thousands of artificial neurons working together in a diffuse way to solve a problem. This reason for AI being a black box is referred to as "complexity". Second, the lack of transparency may arise because the AI is using a machine-learning algorithm that relies on geometric relationships that humans cannot visualize, such as with support vector machines. This reason for AI being a black box is referred to as "dimensionality"*"). Italics added. See also: Mittelstadt, B./Russell, C./Watcher, S., "Explaining explanations in AI", *Proceedings of Fairness, Accountability, and Transparency (FAT) (ACM)*, 2019, passim. But see: Pearl, Judea, *Causality*, 2nd edition, Cambridge, Cambridge University Press, 2009 (on the fundamental tenets of causality). But see: Kilbertus, Niki/Carulla, Mateo Rojas/Parascandolo, Giambattista/Hardt, Moritz/Janzing, Dominik/ Schoellkopf, Bernhard, "Avoiding Discrimination through Causal Reasoning", *Advances in Neural Information Processing Systems*, I. Guyon, U. V. Luxburg, S. Bengio, H. Wallach, R. Fergus, S. Vishwanathan, and R. Garnett (Eds.), Vol. 30. Curran Associates, Inc., 2017, pp. 656–666 (arguing that is feasible to avoiding discrimination through a granular and fine-grained causal reasoning).

[891] See: Citron, Danielle Keats/Pasquale, Frank A., "The Scored Society: Due Process for Automated Predictions", *Washington Law Review*, Volume 89, 2014, pp. 1–34 (defining black boxes, which morph inputs into outputs without lifting the veil on its inner workings, nor revealing the way they reached the correlations underpinning the outcomes of interest/outputs). Citron, Danielle K., "Technological Due Process", *Washington University Law Review*, Volume 85, 2008, pp. 1249–1253 ("Computer programs seamlessly combine rulemaking and individual adjudications without the critical procedural protections owed either of them").

[892] For that reason, scholars have set forth guidelines for choosing the adroit use of running models – i.e. interpretable models take precedence over black box models in high stake decisions in spite of the fact that the latter is more accurate than the former. See: Petch, Jeremy/Di, Shuang/Nelson, Walter, "Opening the black box: the promise and limitations of explainable machine learning in cardiology", *Canadian Journal of Cardiology*, 2021, passim ("*data scientists should train models using both interpretable and blackbox methods to assess whether there is, in fact, an accuracy vs interpretability tradeoff in the specific case on which they are working. If there is no meaningful difference in accuracy between an interpretable model and a black box, an interpretable method should be used. However, if a black-box model does provide a higher degree of accuracy, the stakes of the decision should be considered. If the decision that will be informed by the model is a relatively low stake, a small improvement in accuracy may justify the use of a black box. However, if the stakes are high, it is reasonable to require a greater improvement in accuracy before sacrificing interpretability. Ideally, gains in accuracy from black-box methods should be sufficient to translate into meaningful improvements in clinical outcomes such as reduced morbidity or mortality.* If the use of a black box model can be justified, explainability techniques should be employed to make the model and its predictions as transparent as possible, *but clinicians should be aware of their limitations and be cautious of overinterpreting, which can lead to narrative fallacies*"). Italics added.

decision trees[893]) that often deliver accurate predictions while being fundamentally interpretable by relevant stakeholders.

---

[893] See: Meert, Wannes/De Laet, Tinne/De Raedt, Luc, "Artificial Intelligence A Perspective from the Field", *The Cambridge Handbook of the Law, Ethics and Policy of Artificial Intelligence*, Smuha, Nathalie A. (Editor), Cambridge, Cambridge University Press, 2025, pp. 57–58 ("*As an example of a supervised learning technique, we discuss how decision trees can be derived from examples. Decision trees are useful for classification problems, which appear in numerous applications. The goal is to learn, in case of supervised learning, a function from a dataset with examples that are already categorized (or labeled) such that we can apply this function to predict the class of new, not yet classified examples.* A good example concerns the classification of emails as spam or not spam. Closely related with classification problems are regression problems where we want to predict a numerical value instead of a class. This is, for example, the case when the system is learning how to drive a car, and we want to predict the angle of the steering wheel and the desired speed that the car should maintain. There is vast literature on supervised classification and regression tasks as it is the most studied problem in machine learning. The techniques cover all possible types of functions we have introduced before and combinations thereof. Here we use a simple but popular technique for classification that uses decision trees. In this example, we start from a table of examples, where each row is an example, and each column is an attribute (or feature) of an example. The class of each example can be found in a special column in that table. Take for example the table in Figure 1.4 containing (simplified) data about comic books. Each example expresses the properties of a comic book series: language, length, genre, and historical. The goal is to predict whether this customer would buy an album from a particular series. A *decision tree is a tree-shaped structure where each node in the tree represents a decision made based on the value of a particular attribute. The branches emerging from a node represent the possible outcomes based on the values of that attribute. The leaves of this tree represent the predicted classification, in this example buy or not buy. When a new example is given, we traverse the tree following the branch that corresponds to the value that the attribute has in the example. Suppose there exists a series that the customer has not yet bought, with attribute values (NL/FR, Strip, Humor, Historical). When we traverse the tree, we follow the left branch (Strip) for the top node that splits on length. The next node selects based on language and we follow the left branch (NL/FR) ending in the prediction that the customer will buy this new series. The algorithm to learn a decision tree works as follows: we start with a single node and all available examples.* Next, we estimate by means of a heuristic which attrib ute differentiates best between the different classes. A simple heuristic would be to choose the attribute where, if we split the examples based on the possible values for this attribute, this split is most similar to when we would have split the examples based on their class values (buy or not buy). Once the attribute is decided, we create a branch and a new node per value of that attribute. The examples are split over the branches according to their value for that attribute. In each node we check if this new node contains (almost) only once class. If this is the case, we stop and make the node a leaf with as class the majority class. If not, we repeat the procedure on this smaller set of examples. *An advantage of decision trees is that they are easy and fast to learn and that they often deliver accurate predictions, especially if multiple trees are learned in an ensemble where each tree of the ensemble "votes" for a particular classification outcome. The accuracy of the predictions can be estimated from the data and is crucial for a user to decide whether the model is good enough to be used. Furthermore, decision trees are interpretable by users, which increases the user's trust in the model. In general, their accuracy increases when more data is available and when the quality of this data increases*"). Italics added.

5.1.7.3 Law Number Three: The Outputs Generated by Running Models Must Be Routinely Audited Through Race-Aware Machine Learning Algorithms to Ensure the Trade-Off Between Overall Accuracy and Algorithmic Common Good

§§ To the extent that the deployment of machine learning algorithms routinely mirrors gross racial inequalities[894] in the dataset from which they are leverage on,[895] they can likewise be deployed in reverse: race-aware machine learning algorithms[896] suitably

---

[894] Eaglin, Jessica M., "When Critical Race Theory Enters the Law and Technology Frame", *Michigan Journal of Race and Law*, Volume 25, 2021, pp. 151–168 ("*[W]e built this world through legal constructions around social ideas of race; we must find novel ways to confront the social production of race through law if we are going to change it*"). Italics added.

[895] See: Barocas, Solon/Selbst, Andrew D., "Big Data's Disparate Impact", *California Law Review*, Volume 104, 2016, pp. 671–682 (discussing how data is often flawed, rigged, incomplete, imperfect and therefore algorithms inherit the prejudice of the original decision makers). But see: Citron, Danielle Keats/Pasquale, Frank, "The Scored Society: Due Process for Automated Predictions", *Washington Law Review*, Volume 89, 2014, pp. 1, 4–5 (highlighting how human beings programming automated systems is directly conducive to, and leads, to fundamentally inaccurate results since the source code, predictive algorithms and datasets may encompass human biases which, in turn, have a disparate impact on historically disadvantaged groups). But see: Bornstein, Stepanhie, "Antidiscriminatory Algorithms", *Alabama Law Review*, Volume 70, 2018, pp. 519, 524–528 (contending, however, that the tagged "facially neutral" algorithms producing discriminatory outcomes should be quashed).

[896] See: Kim, Pauline T., "Race-Aware Algorithms: Fairness, Nondiscrimination and Affirmative Action", *California Law Review*, Volume 110, 2022, pp. 1539–1596 (1596) ("*Despite rhetoric about colorblindness, the law does not in fact prohibit all forms of race consciousness in private and governmental decision-making. Entities are permitted to take account of race in order to design fair procedures so long as they do not use racial classifications to determine the outcome of individual decisions. As a result, many, although not all, race-conscious model building strategies do not amount to disparate treatment in the first place, and therefore do not require special legal justification. This observation matters because recognizing that many de-biasing strategies are non-discriminatory not only lowers the legal risk for designers exploring these strategies, it lowers the temperature as well. The rhetoric surrounding affirmative action suggests that special justification is needed because these programs harm others. However, when race-conscious strategies work to remove unfair bias from these systems, no one is unfairly harmed. Algorithms reflect the myriad choices of their creators, and not some objective, underlying truth about who deserves what. Understanding the contingency of this process undermines claims that anyone is legally entitled to maintain a pre existing system of advantage*"). Italics added.

tailored to identify the sources[897] of racial inequity[898] in algorithmic decision-making settings.[899] Crucially, if machine learning algorithms are deployed in this manner, relevant stakeholders are therefore vested with the functional duty to **audit** the pearls of **algorithmic wisdom (outputs generated by machine learning algorithms)** to identify racial inequality. Should such inequality indeed arise, by any meaningful equality metric, the next meaningful move is to determine why.[900]

§§ That can happen for two reasons: **(I)** the machine learning algorithm is far less predictive for one racial line than for another (as is turned out to entirely true for Hispanic defendants in Melissa Hamilton's body of empirical evidence of COMPAS)[901]; or, alternatively, **(II)** the machine learning algorithm is equally

---

[897] Eaglin, Jessica E., "Racializing Algorithms", *California Law Review*, Volume 111, 2023, p. 792 ("*This perspective centers racism at its juncture with law, technology, and criminal legal reform. Such an approach underscores a critical point often obscured at the intersection of race, technology, and criminal law. Criminal law is a human practice, and so it is "partly what we make it." The algorithm is a human practice that we make in and for criminal law's administration.191 Racism is a human practice that transforms, survives, and thrives in society, in part, through law. When viewed in this way, resisting algorithms as criminal legal practice is not a sufficient solution. Destabilizing racism means locating the problem not in technology or law, but in all of us, and in the way we think about and act through the intersection of law and technology with a race-colored lens*"). Italics added.

[898] But see: Kim, Pauline T., "Data-Driven Discrimination at Work", *William and Mary Law Review*, Volume 58, 2017, p. 918 ("If the goal is to reduce biased outcomes, then a simple prohibition on using data about race or sex could be either wholly ineffective or actually counterproductive due to the existence of class proxies and the risk of omitted variable bias"); Lipton, Zachary et al., "Does Mitigating ML's Impact Disparity Require Treatment Disparity?", NIPS Proceedings 1, 2018, https://arxiv.org/pdf/1711.07076.pdf [https://perma.cc/X8VF-EY53] (arguing, premised on statistical examples, that a prohibition on race or sex data is rather counterproductive indeed); Corbett-Davies, Sam/Goel, Sharad, "The Measure and Mismeasure of Fairness: a critical Review of Fair Machine Learning", *Cornell University Library*, 2018, passim (discussing the "[l]imitations of anti-classification" as a fairness metric). See also: Kim, Pauline T., "Data-Driven Discrimination at Work", *cit.*, p. 867 ("[I]f the goal is to discourage classification bias, then the law should not forbid the inclusion of race, sex, or other sensitive information as variables, but seek to preserve these variables, and perhaps even include them in some complex models"); Kroll, Joshua A., et al., "Accountable Algorithms", *University of Pennsylvania Law Review*, Volume 165, 2017, pp. 633, 693–695. See also: Kim, Pauline T., "Data-Driven Discrimination at Work", *cit.*, p. 866 ("classification bias occurs when employers rely on classification schemes, such as data algorithms, to sort or score workers in ways that worsen inequality or disadvantage along the lines of race, sex, or other protected characteristics"). These two uses of the word "bias" correspond to the notions of irrational versus rational **(or statistical) discrimination.** Mayson, Sandra G., "Bias In, Bias Out", *cit.*, pp. 2218–2300.

[899] See: Selbst, Andrew D., "Disparate Impact in Big Data Policing", *Georgia Law Review*, Volume 52, 2017, pp. 110, 169–80 (suggesting "algorithmic impact statements" which "would require police departments to evaluate the efficacy and potential discriminatory effects of all available choices for predictive policing technologies").

[900] Mayson, Sandra G., "Bias In, Bias Out", *cit.*, pp. 2218–2300 (2284).

[901] See: Hamilton, Melissa, "The Biased Algorithm: Evidence of Disparate Impact on Hispanics", *American Criminal Law Review*, Volume 56, 2019, passim (noting the likelihood that risk-assessment tools will underperform for Hispanic Americans unless they integrate cultural and situational factors that moderate risk, and concluding that it is "quite likely" that poorer performance of COMPAS for Hispanic defendants was due to failure to integrate "cultural differences"

predictive across racial groups and the perceived racial inequality arises directly from a difference in the base rate of the forecasted event (as is turned out to be entirely true for black versus white defendants in the *ProPublica* body of empirical[902] evidence).

§§ If the machine learning algorithm is consciously/conspicuously less predictive for one racial line, relevant stakeholders should employ staggering efforts to ascertain why. It may be that the data are more limited or of lower quality for one racial group.[903] This stands as one feasible pathway to ensure the trade-off between **overall accuracy** and **Algorithmic Common Good** in algorithmic decision-making.

§§ In either case, relevant stakeholders must **track** the quality of the dataset (or lack thereof)[904] from which machine learning algorithms were built to foster *algorithmic fairness* in criminal justice settings. This is the kernel of *Algorithmic Common Good* of which relevant stakeholders should not shy away from.

---

that moderate risk". See also: Shepherd, Stephane M./Lewis-Fernandez, Roberto, "Forensic Risk Assessment and Cultural Diversity: Contemporary Challenges and Future Directions", *Psychology Public Policy, and Law*, Volume 22, 2016, pp. 427–498.

902 Mayson, Sandra G., "Bias In, Bias Out", *cit.*, pp. 2218–2300 (2284). See also: Angwin J, Larson J, Mattu S, et al., "Machine bias: There's software used across the country to predict future criminals. And it's biased against blacks", 2016, passim. Available at. https://www.propublica.org/article/machine-bias-risk-assessments-in-criminal-sentencing (accessed 26 October 2024). Sun, R. (Ed.), *The Cambridge Handbook of Computational Cognitive Sciences*, Cambridge, Cambridge University Press, 2023.

903 Mayson, Sandra G., "Bias In, Bias Out", *cit.*, pp. 2218–2300 (2284).

904 See: Part V, this chapter, Sects. 5.1.2.4–5.1.2.4.1 of this book (fleshes out the stage of data collection). See: Part V, this chapter, Sect. 5.1.7.4 of this book (on one of the law to control algorithmic decision-making, namely, law number four: data partitioning must be performed—i.e. randomly split an entire dataset into the «training dataset» and the «test dataset»—to accurately predict outcomes in the real world while forestalling «inductive bias» [learning bias]).

5.1.7.4 Law Number Four: Data Partitioning Must Be Performed—i.e. Randomly Split an Entire Dataset into the «Training Dataset» and the «Test Dataset»—To Accurately Predict Outcomes in the Real World While Forestalling «Inductive Bias» (Learning Bias)

§§ The relationship between skewed data (*inputs*) and inferences (*outputs*) has shown to be reciprocal.[905] Put simply, the relationship that a given machine learning algorithm uses to make a prediction reflects hidden correlations in the data as opposed to a causal connection to the outcome/prediction.[906]

§§ A vicious cycle inevitably unfolds: biased data that feeds into the algorithm begets equally biased predictions thus further compounding a wearying tapestry of racial discrimination that besets modern societies.[907] This is epiphenomenon has been tagged as «runaway feedback loops»[908] that re-entrenches existing biases in predic-

[905] *Tech, Bias and Housing Initiative, the Promise and Perils of Residential Proptech, Year 1, Research Summary Report, April 2023, TechEquity Collaborative*, p. 11, available at: https://techequity.us/wp-content/uploads/2023/04/TBHI-Y1-Research-Summary-Report.pdf (28.11.2024). ("*Once bad data enters the analysis of one factor, it gets baked into the subsequent process, multiplying the effect that one disadvantageous data point can have on someone's overall housing determination*"). Italics added.

[906] Gillis, Talia B., "The Input Data Fallacy", *Minnesota Law Review*, Volume 106, 2022, pp. 1176–1263 (1244).

[907] *Tech, Bias and Housing Initiative, the Promise and Perils of Residential Proptech, Year 1, Research Summary Report, April 2023, TechEquity Collaborative*, p. 5 available at: https://techequity.us/wp-content/uploads/2023/04/TBHI-Y1-Research-Summary-Report.pdf (28.11.2024). ("*Residential Proptech also has the potential to exacerbate the bias inherent in our housing system. Its rise is due, in part, to the desperation felt by average home seekers. With a severely constrained housing supply, companies offering an easier pathway to homeownership may exploit communities that have been harmed by housing discrimination in the past. Opaque algorithms incorporate biased data into their decision-making processes, making it harder to enforce fair housing laws.* Residential Proptech companies often operate in a regulatory gray area, leaving consumers without the protections they would have from traditional housing regulatory systems. *As unprecedented capital investment flows into this space, venture-backed companies' winner-take-all approach to growth has the potential to exacerbate inequality rather than combat it*"). Italics added.

[908] Ensign, Danielle/Friedler, Sorelle A./Neville, Scott/Scheidegger, Carlos/ Venkatasubramanian, Suresh, "Runaway Feedback Loops in Predictive Policing", *Proceedings of Machine Learning Research, Conference on Fairness, Accountability, and Transparency*, Volume 81, 2018, pp. 1–12 (1) ("Predictive policing systems are increasingly used to determine how to allocate police across a city in order to best prevent crime. *Discovered crime data (e.g., arrest counts) are used to help update the model, and the process is repeated. Such systems have been empirically shown to be susceptible to runaway feedback loops, where police are repeatedly sent back to the same neighborhoods regardless of the true crime rate*"). Italics added.

tive policing, which primarily targets racial minorities.[909] This gruesome scenario is very common when the database is overrepresented with one group.[910]

§§ To pre-empt this loathsome scenario from coming to fruition, staggering efforts must be poured in to ensure that the dataset reflects the real world. To that end, the dataset must be representative of the real world.

§§ A predictive undertaking of any kind seeks to create a tool that forecasts—validly, accurately, and reliably—in the real world. Dispiritingly, though, there is a plethora of reasons why the data a data scientist collates may not reflect the real world.[911]

---

[909] Mayson, Sandra G., "Bias In, Bias Out", *Yale Law Journal*, Volume 128, 2019, passim. See: Part IV, Chap. 4, Sects. 4.1.10.1–4.1.10.6 of this book (on biased algorithmic risk assessment in criminal procedure law settings, with a sharper focus on COMPAS). See: Part IV, Chap. 4, Sects. 4.1.1–4.1.1.1 of this book (on biased predictive policing).

[910] It is important to note that an algorithm designed for **maximum accuracy** will adjust itself to the majority data, and may be less accurate for members of the underrepresented group, thus breeding *inductive bias*. See: Shellenbarger, Sue, "A Crucial Step for Avoiding AI Disasters", *Wall Street Journal*, (Feb. 13, 2019, 9:57 AM ET), https://www.wsj.com/articles/a-crucial-step-for-avoiding-ai-disasters-11550069865?ns=prod/accounts-wsj [https://perma.cc/C28U-LAAE] (discussing this issue while emphasizing how diverse development teams pay more attention to unrepresentative and underrepresented data sets). Human programmers can circumvent and bypass this problem by weighting the minority-group data more heavily, by designing different algorithms for each racial group, or by striving to contain more data to equalize group representation in the data set. See: Barua, Sukarna et al., "MWMOTE—Majority Weighted Minority Oversampling Technique for Imbalanced Data Set Learning", *IEEE Transactions on Knowledge & Data Engineering*, Volume 26, 2014, pp. 405, 405–406. See also: Hamilton, Melissa, "The Biased Algorithm: Evidence of Disparate Impact on Hispanics", *American Criminal Law Review*, Volume 56, 2019, pp. 1553 and ff and passim (which clearly demonstrates that COMPAS was significantly less accurate for Hispanic than for white defendants by several measures and suggesting that smaller numbers of Hispanic defendants might be the cause). See: Mayson, Sandra G., "Bias In, Bias Out", *cit.*, pp. 2218–2300.

[911] Lehr, David/Ohm, Paul, "Playing with the Data: What Legal Scholars Should Learn About Machine Learning", *cit.*, pp. 653–718.

§§ Why that happens in the first place? To begin with, the dataset could have been in all likelihood collated in a non-representative[912] manner.[913] In addition to that, relevant changes could have occurred in the population or system from which data were collated between when data collection took place and when a machine learning algorithm is applied.[914] Last but not least, there is always a perceived degree of

---

[912] But see: Kim, Pauline T., "Data-Driven Discrimination at Work", *William and Mary Law Review*, Volume 58, 2017, p. 918 ("If the goal is to reduce biased outcomes, then a simple prohibition on using data about race or sex could be either wholly ineffective or actually counterproductive due to the existence of class proxies and the risk of omitted variable bias"); Lipton, Zachary et al., "Does Mitigating ML's Impact Disparity Require Treatment Disparity?", NIPS Proceedings 1, 2018, https://arxiv.org/pdf/1711.07076.pdf [https://perma.cc/X8VF-EY53] (arguing, premised on statistical examples, that a prohibition on race or sex data is rather counterproductive indeed); Corbett-Davies, Sam/Goel, Sharad, "The Measure and Mismeasure of Fairness: a critical Review of Fair Machine Learning", *Cornell University Library*, 2018, passim (discussing the "[l]imitations of anti-classification" as a fairness metric). See also: Kim, Pauline T., "Data-Driven Discrimination at Work", *cit.*, p. 867 ("[I]f the goal is to discourage classification bias, then the law should not forbid the inclusion of race, sex, or other sensitive information as variables, but seek to preserve these variables, and perhaps even include them in some complex models"); Kroll, Joshua A., et al., "Accountable Algorithms", *University of Pennsylvania Law Review*, Volume 165, 2017, pp. 633, 693–695. See also: Kim, Pauline T., "Data-Driven Discrimination at Work", *cit.*, p. 866 ("**classification bias** occurs when employers rely on classification schemes, such as data algorithms, to sort or score workers in ways that worsen inequality or disadvantage along the lines of race, sex, or other protected characteristics"). These two uses of the word "bias" correspond to the notions of irrational versus rational **(or statistical) discrimination.** Mayson, Sandra G., "Bias In, Bias Out", *cit.*, pp. 2218–2300. See also: Kleinberg, Jon et al., "Algorithmic Fairness", *AEA Papers & Proceedings*, Volume 108, 2018, pp. 22–23 (discussing, anchored in a batch of national data, that including race as an input variable to a machine-learning college-admissions algorithm both "improves predicted GPAs of admitted students" and can augment "the fraction of admitted students who are black").

[913] See: Lavrakas, Paul J., *Encyclopedia of Survey Research Methods*, Los Angeles/Washington D. C./New York/London, Sage, 2008, pp. 1–1000 (254–255) ("In order to avoid [threatening external validity], the researcher should make certain that the sampling design leads to the selection of a sample that is representative of the population"). See also: Kukull, Walter A./Ganguli, Mary, "Generalizability: The Trees, the Forest, and the Low-Hanging Fruit", *Neurology*, Volume 78, 2012, p. 1886 (drilling into, and shedding light on, the concept of generalizability and how representative sampling factors into it, especially in the purview of clinical and epidemiological studies). See: Lehr, David/Ohm, Paul, "Playing with the Data: What Legal Scholars Should Learn About Machine Learning", *cit.*, pp. 653–718.

[914] See: Lavrakas, Paul J., *Encyclopedia of Survey Research Methods*, *cit.*, p. 255 ("In order for a survey to be characterized as externally valid, the results should be generalizable and essentially remain invariant across different points in time"). Pundits have contended this mismatch could pose a serious problem for machine learning algorithms underpinning judges' decisions to release individuals on bail. Strikingly, if the training data were gleaned/collated before the implementation of bail reforms, but the machine learning algorithms were used after the foregoing implementation, they could forecast individuals as riskier than they indeed would be. See: Koepke, John Logan/Robinson, David G., *Zombie Predictions and the Future of Bail Reform*, https://ssrn.com/abstract=3041622 [https://perma.cc/Z8AH-3HWC]. See: Lehr, David/Ohm, Paul, "Playing with the Data: What Legal Scholars Should Learn About Machine Learning", *cit.*, pp. 653–718.

randomness[915] in the system that should be accounted for. Such a dollop of randomness might explain why a data collected at one point in time was representative and non-representative of the system at a later stage.[916] The ground truth is that which always exists a degree of uncertainty that haunts, and might hinder the work of, a data scientist in developing a machine learning algorithm.

§§ To forestall such a gruesome scenario, data scientists have been pouring in staggering efforts to develop methods of gauging, with some inevitable dash of uncertainty, how well a machine learning algorithm trained on a given dataset will perform on another dataset. One mainstream method that has been widely used is to **randomly split**, or **partition**, an entire dataset into two segments: **a «training» dataset**[917] and a **«test» dataset**.

§§ It is noteworthy that a machine learning algorithm is highly trained and learns the **optimal predictive rules** during model training stage. Afterwards, the machine learning algorithm's accuracy and other relevant performance metrics are painstakingly evaluated by enquiring it to forecast the outcomes of the subjects in the latter. In this vein, a machine learning algorithm is compelled to forecast data it has not dealt with before. In this way, data scientists nurture the undying hope to forecast outcomes in the «real world»[918] performance. To the extent randomness in the real world will, in all likelihood, be starkly different than that of the **training dataset**, so will that of the **test dataset**.[919]

---

[915] Teigena, Halvor/Kanten, Alf Børre, "Out of the blue: on the suddenness of perceived chance events", *Thinking & Reasoning*, Volume 29, n. ° 1, 2023, pp. 137–175 (137) ("*people commonly use terms like 'random', 'by chance', or 'accidentally' when they describe occurrences that sidestep the normal course of events, with no apparent causal link to ongoing activities. Such intrusive events are typically perceived as happening all of a sudden.* This was demonstrated in seven experiments (N ¼ 1299) by asking people to identify statements they believed belonged to stories about chance events, and by comparing chance vs. nonchance events from their own life and from the lives of others. Suddenness also appeared to be more strongly associated with beginnings than with endings of an episode. Thus, statements about sudden beginnings of a career or a relationship were more readily believed to happen 'by chance' than 'not by chance'. *But life-changing events did not become more accidental simply by being placed in the beginning of a 'life chapter'. These studies highlight a central but neglected feature of perceived randomness*"). Italics added.

[916] Lavrakas, Paul J., *Encyclopedia of Survey Research Methods*, *cit.*, p. 255 ("The major concern with this threat [of setting characteristics] to the external validity is that the findings of a particular survey research study may be influenced by some unique circumstances and conditions, and, if so, then the results are not generalizable to other survey research studies with different settings"). Randomness is amounts to a factor that could effectively render the setting of a specific body of evidence different than that of another body of evidence at a different juncture. See: Lehr, David/ Ohm, Paul, "Playing with the Data: What Legal Scholars Should Learn About Machine Learning", *cit.*, pp. 653–718.

[917] Lehr, David/Ohm, Paul, "Playing with the Data: What Legal Scholars Should Learn About Machine Learning", *cit.*, pp. 653–718.

[918] Lehr, David/Ohm, Paul, "Playing with the Data: What Legal Scholars Should Learn About Machine Learning", *cit.*, pp. 653–718.

[919] Lehr, David/Ohm, Paul, "Playing with the Data: What Legal Scholars Should Learn About Machine Learning", *cit.*, pp. 653–718.

§§ **Partitioning data** into training dataset and test dataset ranks is one of the most reliable and trustworthy methods for measuring an algorithm's real-world performance.[920] In addition to that, **partitioning data** ensures that the **dataset** is representative of the real world while forestalling **«inductive bias» (learning bias)**.[921]

5.1.7.5 Law Number Five: The Running Model Must Be Externally Audited

§§ As fleshed out in A *Global AI Auditing Framework* (SR2024.3), running models must be regularly, and as a well externally, audited. Pivotally, the external auditor must be entrusted with the task of gauging the extent to which the running model was deftly designed, deployed, operated, and managed[922] while abiding by the central tenets of **Algorithmic Common Good**.

§§ To that end, algorithmic auditors must be given full access[923] to the complete datasets (i.e. **training datasets** and **test datasets**) paired with all the necessary tools to perform a sweeping, full-blown, full-fledged, and comprehensive algorithmic audit.

---

920 Lehr, David/Ohm, Paul, "Playing with the Data: What Legal Scholars Should Learn About Machine Learning", *cit.*, pp. 653–718.

921 See: Dong et al., Qi,, "Imbalanced deep learning by minority class incremental rectification, *IEEE Transactions on Pattern Analysis & Machine Intelligence*, Volume 41, 2019, p. 1367 (posit that "*most existing learning algorithms produce inductive bias (learning bias)* towards the frequent (majority) classes if training data are not balanced, *resulting in poor minority class recognition performance*"). Italics added. See: Chandler, Anupam, "The Racist Algorithm", *Michigan Law Review*, Volume 115, n. ° 6, 2018, p. 1026 (on racist algorithms, noting that "the possibilities for discriminatory manipulation are legion"). But see: Altenburger, Kristen M./Ho, Daniel E., "When Algorithms Import Private Bias into Public Enforcement: The Promise and Limitations of Statistical Debiasing Solutions", *Journal of Institutional & Theoretical Economics*, Volume 175, 2019, pp. 97–98 (calls for a "debias predictive algorithms" to assuage racist and/or biased, doctored, and bigoted algorithms nevertheless).

922 International Panel on the Information Environment, *Recommendations for a Global AI Auditing Framework Summary of Standards and Features, Summary for Policymakers 2024.2*, 2024, p. 3.

923 See: Zaccour, Juliette/Binns, Reuben /Rocher, Luc, Access Denied: Meaningful Data Access for Quantitative Algorithm Audits arXiv:2502.00428v1 [cs.HC] 1 Feb 2025, 2025, p. 1 ("*Independent algorithm audits hold the promise of bringing account ability to automated decision-making. However, third-party audits are commonly deployed without external and independent over sight. In the past few years, researchers and journalists have investigated high-stakes yet highly secretive algorithmic decisions are often hindered by access restrictions, forcing auditors to rely on limited, low-quality data.* To study how these limitations impact re search integrity, we conduct audit simulations on two realistic case studies for recidivism and healthcare coverage prediction. *We ex amine the accuracy of estimating group parity metrics across three levels of access: (a) aggregated statistics, (b) individual-level data with model outputs, and (c) individual-level data without model outputs. Despite selecting one of the simplest tasks for algorithmic auditing, we find that data minimization and anonymization practices can strongly increase error rates on individual-level data, leading to unreliable assessments. We discuss implications for independent auditors, as well as potential avenues for HCI researchers and regulators to improve data access and enable both reliable and holistic evaluations*"). Italics added.

Failing which, the effectiveness of pivotally important legal regulations that prove instrumental to ensure the thoroughness of algorithmic audit (e.g. art. º 10.º (5) of EU AI Act,[924] which applies to high-risk AI systems only, according to art.º 6.º of EU AI Act) not only hangs on the balance, but, and foremost, are slated to be frontally belied.

[924] See: van Bekkum, Marvin, "Using sensitive data to de-bias AI systems: Article 10(5) of the EU AI act", *Computer Law & Security Review: The International Journal of Technology Law and Practice*, 56 (2025), 2025, p. 1 ("In June 2024, the EU AI Act came into force. *The AI Act includes obligations for the provider of an AI system. Article 10 of the AI Act includes a new obligation for providers to evaluate whether their training, validation and testing datasets meet certain quality criteria, including an appropriate examination of biases in the datasets and correction measures. With the obligation comes a new provision in Article 10(5) AI Act, allowing providers to collect sensitive data to fulfil the obligation. Article 10(5) AI Act aims to prevent discrimination*"). It bears mentioning that art.º 10 (5) of EU AI Act, art.º 6.º, of GPPR and art.º 9.º of EU AI Act are not to be interpreted separately. Instead, they are stacked on top of each other. See: de Luca, Stefano/ Federico, Marina, "Algorithmic discrimination under the AI Act and the GDPR", *Digital Issues in focus, EPRS | European Parliamentary Research Service*, PE 769.509 - February 2025, 2025, pp. 1–2 ("*Article 10(5) AI Act applies to high-risk systems only. The act adopts a 'risk-based approach', in that it classifies AI systems according to the degree of risk they pose to individuals' fundamental rights and freedoms. When determining whether a system is qualified as high-risk (Article 6 AI Act), the emphasis is on a given system's scope and the specific task it performed.* To *process special categories of personal data, the specific grounds listed in Article 9 GDPR must be respected (e.g. the data subject's explicit consent). These grounds must also be respected when applying Article 10(5) AI Act, which falls within the scope of Article 9 GDPR. The act clarifies that, when the AI Act and the GDPR collide, the GDPR prevails, and states explicitly that its provisions must not affect the GDPR's application* (…) In addition to the special categories of data listed in Article 9 GDPR, discrimination may arise as a result of the processing of personal data revealing other factors, such as disability, age or gender. *These are not special categories of data pursuant to EU law, but 'merely' personal data. Therefore, the legal grounds for processing these data will be those listed in Article 6 GDPR. Article 6 GDPR is broader in content than Article 9 GDPR, providing for a larger number of legal bases for the processing of personal data (e.g. legitimate interest).* This means that, when discrimination arises with respect to factors that are not considered as special categories of personal data, the processing of data to mitigate bias can occur pursuant to the grounds of Article 6, which are more lenient and easier to prove than public interest or specific consent. In general terms, shared uncertainty appears to prevail as to how the AI Act's provision on the processing of special categories of personal data for avoiding discrimination should be interpreted. *The GDPR, which imposes limits on the processing of special categories of personal data, might prove restrictive in a context dominated by the use of AI in many sectors of the economy, and faced with the mass processing of personal and non-personal data. A reform of the GDPR or further guidelines on its interplay with the AI Act might help address these issues*"), Italics added.

§§ Notably, an algorithmic audit to be stellar, accurate, sterling, flawless, effective, and trustworthy, external algorithmic auditors must be granted access to full-fledged and comprehensive evidence[925] concerning the running model.[926] Ideally, the running model must pass muster all the stages underpinning the creation of a functional framework, ready to be deployed and to make accurate predictions in the real world.[927]

§§ It bears mentioning that, as contended in **law number one to control algorithmic decision-making,**[928] whoever developed and/or deployed the running model must be held criminally accountable for any harm[929] their models may externalize onto innocent others.[930]

§§ It is worth recalling, too, that **law number five**—which covers all the stages concerning the creation of a running model ready to be deployed in the real world, regardless of the degree of risk[931]—therefore extends far beyond the breadth

---

[925] Clavell, Galdon Gemma, AI Auditing Checklist for AI Auditing, Support Pool of Experts Programme, 2025, pp. 1–21 (5) ("*The E2EST/AA process is designed to inspect algorithmic systems used in ranking, image recognition and natural language processing. It works with systems that make decisions on individuals or groups based on known data sources, regardless of whether they use machine learning or classic computing. This definition includes most systems used by the public and private sectors to make decisions on resource allocation, categorization and identification/verification in sectors such as health, education, security, finance and for applications like fraud detection, hiring, operations management, or prediction/risk assessment. The E2EST/AA is focused on bias assessment, but not limited to it. The methodology to carry out an E2EST/AA incorporates questions related to broader social impact and desirability, as well as the incorporation of end-users in the design process and the existence of recourse mechanisms for those impacted by algorithmic systems. For a system to pass an algorithmic audit, issues of impact, proportionality, participation and resource must be tackled*"). Italics added.

[926] International Panel on the Information Environment (IPIE), *Recommendations for a Global AI Auditing Framework Summary of Standards and Features, Summary for Policymakers 2024.2*, 2024, p. 4.

[927] See: Part V, this chapter, Sects. 5.1.3–5.1.3.1.6 of this book (on the fundamental tenets of model selection). See: Part V, this chapter, Sect. 5.1.3.1.5 of this book (on the central tenets of model tuning). See: Part V, this chapter, Sects. 5.1.4–5.1.4.1.1 of this book (on the central tenets of model training). See: Part V, this chapter, Sects. 5.1.2.4–5.1.2.4.1 of this book (fleshes out the stage of data collection). See also: Part V, this chapter, Sects. 5.1.2–5.1.6.2.1 of this book (on the thing-centred algorithmic decision-making propelled by a *Controllable* and *Interpretable* Machine Learning that weeds out *Algorithmic Dictatorship* and secures *Algorithmic Common Good*).

[928] See: Part V, this chapter, Sect. 5.1.7.1 of this book (on the central tenets of law number one to control Artificial Intelligence-embedded technologies).

[929] See: Part III, Chap. 3, Sect. 3.1.1 of this book (that discusses the issue of "inequality in application" facing Artificial Intelligence-embedded technologies).

[930] International Panel on the Information Environment (IPIE), *Recommendations for a Global AI Auditing Framework Summary of Standards and Features, Summary for Policymakers 2024.2*, 2024, p. 4.

[931] See: Part V, this chapter, Sects. 5.1.3–5.1.3.1.6 of this book (on the fundamental tenets of model selection). See: Part V, this chapter, Sect. 5.1.3.1.5 of this book (on the central tenets of model tuning). See: Part V, this chapter, Sects. 5.1.4–5.1.4.1.1 of this book (on the central tenets of model training). See: Part V, this chapter, Sects. 5.1.2.4–5.1.2.4.1 of this book (fleshes out the stage of data collection).

and scope of Article 14.º of EU AI Act,[932] which generally refers to a «human oversight»[933] with regard to high-risk Artificial Intelligence systems only.

5.1.8 Five Laws to Interpret Algorithmic Decision-Making

5.1.8.1 Law Number One: The Adoption of a Thing-Centred Algorithmic Decision-Making That Requires a Fundamental Shift Away from Causation and a Pull Towards Correlation

§§ *Algorithmic fairness,* albeit a bedazzling gift, is not without sizable hurdles. This is one the main roadblocks to the uptake of Artificial Intelligence-embedded

---

[932] See: Fink, Melanie, "Human Oversight under Article 14 of the EU AI Act, Gianclaudio Malgieri, Gloria González Fuster, Alessandro Mantelero, and Gabriela Zanfir-Fortuna (Editors), AI Act Commentary: A Thematic Analysis, Hart-Bloomsbury, forthcoming 2026, 2026, p. 1 ("*Born out of the goal to ensure human-centric AI, Article 14 AI Act requires that high-risk AI systems can be 'effectively overseen by natural persons'. It sets out detailed obligations for providers of AI systems to create the conditions for effective human oversight during the period in which they are in use. This is complemented by Article 26(2) AI Act, which requires deployers of high-risk AI systems to assign human oversight.* The following first defines what Article 14 means with 'human oversight' (Section 2). Section 3 then provides the context for Article 14's applicability, elaborating on its role within the AI Act's network of risk management obligations (Section 3.1), and its relationship with human oversight requirements outside the AI Act (Section 3.2). Section 4 discusses the purpose human oversight is designed to fulfil in AI governance in general (Section 4.1) and in the AI Act in particular (Section 4.2). *Section 5 then elaborates on the concrete human oversight obligations for providers and deployers respectively, distributing them across the three key markers for effectiveness in human oversight: authority (Section 5.1), comprehension (Sect. 5.2), and environment (Sect. 5.3). Section 6 provides a look ahead, focusing on how to apply Article 14 against the background of the limits of human oversight mechanisms. Section 7 concludes*"). Italics added.

[933] But see: Fink, Melanie, "Human Oversight under Article 14 of the EU AI Act, *cit.*, pp. 13–14 ("*is safe to say that high expectations are placed on human oversight requirements in general, and on Article 14 in particular. However, research has shown that human involvement does not always meet these expectations. Empirical evidence suggests that human overseers often do not spot wrong or undesirable suggestions made by an AI system.* Human overseers may even correct perfectly good outputs, thus not only failing to improve decision-making quality, but actively undermining it.73 *A number of reasons have been identified that account for this problem, including the biases that influence human interaction with AI systems, and the practical circumstances under which human overseers operate.74 As discussed in more detail in Section 5, Article 14(4) recognises and attempts to address these issues by placing additional obligations on providers and deployers. However, not all challenges can be resolved through additional obligations.* Some limitations, particularly those inherent in human cognitive capacity, cannot be overcome *through regulatory requirements alone and need to be taken into account when designing oversight mechanisms*"). Italics added. See also: Walter, Johannes, "Human oversight done right: The AI Act should use humans to monitor AI only when effective", *ZEW policy brief* 02/2023, 2023 (on the drawbacks and pitfalls on human oversight). See also: Alon-Barkat, Saar/Busuioc, Madalina, "Human–AI Interactions in Public Sector Decision Making: "Automation Bias" and "Selective Adherence" to Algorithmic Advice", *Journal of Public Administration Research and Theory*, Volume 33, 2023, pp. 153–155 (arguing that human oversight might engender either "automation bias" or "selective adherence" to certain outputs).

technologies. The most prominent of which is that Artificial Intelligence, to produce algorithmic fairness, must be fundamentally *interpretable* by citizens.[934] Intent and causation—agreed-upon benchmarks to gauge the extent to which the computer-generated outputs are fair and reasonable—are utterly incapable of explaining the complex world of AI-powered black box.[935] Hence the dire need to use simpler

[934] Citron, Danielle K., "Technological Due Process", *Washington University Law Review*, Volume 85, 2008, pp. 1249–1253 ("Computer programs seamlessly combine rulemaking and individual adjudications without the critical procedural protections owed either of them").

[935] As hinted above, algorithms make their inferences and draw their conclusions in a way difficult to understand, even for the cohort of programmers that designed them. This is deemed *black box*, that further enhances the shroud of mystery under which algorithms are cloaked. See, for a compelling account of AI black box: Ver: Bathaee, Yavar, "The Artificial Intelligence Black Box and the Failure of Intent and Causation", *Harvard Journal of Law and Technology*, n.º 37, 2018, p. 901 (adduces that "*one possible reason AI may be a black box to humans is that it relies on machine-learning algorithms that internalize data in ways that are not easily audited or understood by humans* (...)" "*first, a lack may arise from the complexity of the algorithm's structure, such as with deep neural network, which consists of thousands of artificial neurons working together in a diffuse way to solve a problem. This reason for AI being a black box is referred to as "complexity". Second, the lack of transparency may arise because the AI is using a machine-learning algorithm that relies on geometric relationships that humans cannot visualize, such as with support vector machines. This reason for AI being a black box is referred to as "dimensionality"*"). Italics added. See also: Mittelstadt, B./Russell, C./Watcher, S., "Explaining explanations in AI", *Proceedings of Fairness, Accountability, and Transparency (FAT) (ACM)*, 2019, passim. But see: Pearl, Judea, *Causality*, 2nd edition, Cambridge, Cambridge University Press, 2009 (on the fundamental tenets of causality). But see: Kilbertus, Niki/Carulla, Mateo Rojas/Parascandolo, Giambattista/Hardt, Moritz/Janzing, Dominik/Schoellkopf, Bernhard, "Avoiding Discrimination through Causal Reasoning", *Advances in Neural Information Processing Systems*, I. Guyon, U. V. Luxburg, S. Bengio, H. Wallach, R. Fergus, S. Vishwanathan, and R. Garnett (Eds.), Vol. 30. Curran Associates, Inc., 2017, pp. 656–666 (arguing that is feasible to avoiding discrimination through a granular and fine-grained causal reasoning).

running models (e.g. **decision trees**[936]) that often deliver accurate predictions while being fundamentally interpretable by the citizens.

---

[936] See: Meert, Wannes/De Laet, Tinne/De Raedt, Luc, "Artificial Intelligence A Perspective from the Field", *The Cambridge Handbook of the Law, Ethics and Policy of Artificial Intelligence*, Smuha, Nathalie A. (Editor), Cambridge, Cambridge University Press, 2025, pp. 57–58 ("*As an example of a supervised learning technique, we discuss how decision trees can be derived from examples. Decision trees are useful for classification problems, which appear in numerous applications. The goal is to learn, in case of supervised learning, a function from a dataset with examples that are already categorized (or labeled) such that we can apply this function to predict the class of new, not yet classified examples.* A good example concerns the classification of emails as spam or not spam. Closely related with classification problems are regression problems where we want to predict a numerical value instead of a class. This is, for example, the case when the system is learning how to drive a car, and we want to predict the angle of the steering wheel and the desired speed that the car should maintain. There is vast literature on supervised classification and regression tasks as it is the most studied problem in machine learning. The techniques cover all possible types of functions we have introduced before and combinations thereof. Here we use a simple but popular technique for classification that uses decision trees. In this example, we start from a table of examples, where each row is an example, and each column is an attribute (or feature) of an example. The class of each example can be found in a special column in that table. Take for example the table in Figure 1.4 containing (simplified) data about comic books. Each example expresses the properties of a comic book series: language, length, genre, and historical. The goal is to predict whether this customer would buy an album from a particular series. A *decision tree is a tree-shaped structure where each node in the tree represents a decision made based on the value of a particular attribute. The branches emerging from a node represent the possible outcomes based on the values of that attribute. The leaves of this tree represent the predicted classification, in this example buy or not buy. When a new example is given, we traverse the tree following the branch that corresponds to the value that the attribute has in the example. Suppose there exists a series that the customer has not yet bought, with attribute values (NL/FR, Strip, Humor, Historical). When we traverse the tree, we follow the left branch (Strip) for the top node that splits on length. The next node selects based on language and we follow the left branch (NL/FR) ending in the prediction that the customer will buy this new series. The algorithm to learn a decision tree works as follows: we start with a single node and all available examples.* Next, we estimate by means of a heuristic which attrib ute differentiates best between the different classes. A simple heuristic would be to choose the attribute where, if we split the examples based on the possible values for this attribute, this split is most similar to when we would have split the examples based on their class values (buy or not buy). Once the attribute is decided, we create a branch and a new node per value of that attribute. The examples are split over the branches according to their value for that attribute. In each node we check if this new node contains (almost) only once class. If this is the case, we stop and make the node a leaf with as class the majority class. If not, we repeat the procedure on this smaller set of examples. *An advantage of decision trees is that they are easy and fast to learn and that they often deliver accurate predictions, especially if multiple trees are learned in an ensemble where each tree of the ensemble "votes" for a particular classification outcome. The accuracy of the predictions can be estimated from the data and is crucial for a user to decide whether the model is good enough to be used. Furthermore, decision trees are interpretable by users, which increases the user's trust in the model. In general, their accuracy increases when more data is available and when the quality of this data increases*"). Italics added.

§§ For a simple reason: machine learning[937]—and, especially, deep learning[938]—is a world of hidden *correlations* embedded in the data that has been fed into the computer-generated algorithms, as opposed to a world of *causation* that currently reigns[939] in the legal arena.[940] To bypass/circumvent this perceived quandary,[941]

[937] Machine learning "involves computer algorithms *that have the ability to "learn" or improve in performance over time on some task*". Ver: Surden, Harry, "Machine Learning and Law", in: *Washington Law Review*, Volume 89, 2014, pp. 87 e ss; Murphy, Kevin P., *Machine Learning: A Probabilistic Perspective (Adaptive Computation and Machine Learning series)*, Massachusetts, The MIT Press, 2012, pp. 1–1104. Machine learning "*attempts to combine deductive, inductive, and abductive reasoning to make person-like reasoning in AI Entities possible. Machine-learning AI Entities initially learn in the same way a human child learns. First, they notice details and patterns in shapes, sounds, and behaviors*; then put them together to distinguish one person from another, or a dog from a cat. Eventually, the AI can recognize and identify" common objects. See: Hutto-Schultz, Jess, "Dicitur Ex Machina: Artificial Intelligence and the Hearsay Rule", *George Mason Law Review*, Volume 27, n. ° 2, 2020, pp. 684–718 (689).

[938] See: Goodfellow, Ian/Bengio, Yoshua/Courville, Aaron, *Deep Learning (Adaptive Computation and Machine Learning series)*, Massachusetts, The MIT Press, 2016, pp. 1–800 ("*Deep learning is a form of machine learning that enables computers to learn from experience and understand the world in terms of a hierarchy of concepts.* Because *the computer gathers knowledge from experience, there is no need for a human computer operator to formally specify all the knowledge that the computer needs. The hierarchy of concepts allows the computer to learn complicated concepts by building them out of simpler ones; a graph of these hierarchies would be many layers deep*"). See also: Chollet, François, *Deep Learning with Python*, Shelter Island, New York, Manning, 2017, pp. 1–384; Franceschetti, Donald R. (Editor), *Principles of Robotics and Artificial Intelligence*, New York, Salem Press, 2018, pp. 1–399. Deep learning is capable of recommending meaningful legal materials. See: Huang, Zihan/Low, Charles/Teng, Mengqiu/Zhang, Hongyi/Ho, Daniel E./Krass, Mark S. et al., "Context-Aware Legal Citation Recommendation Using Deep Learning", *Proceedings of the 18th ACM Internationational Conference on Artificial Intelligence and Law*, 79, 2021. See: Part V, this chapter, Sects. 5.1.1.5.2.2–5.1.1.5.2.2.1.4 of this book (on the fundamental shift away from causation to correlations in algorithmic decision-making).

[939] Pearl, Judea, *Causality*, 2nd edition, Cambridge, Cambridge University Press, 2009. See: Part V, this chapter, Sects. 5.1.1.5.2.2–5.1.1.5.2.2.1.4 of this book (on the fundamental shift away from causation to correlations in algorithmic decision-making).

[940] Bibal, A., Lognoul, M/De Streel/A., Frénay B, "Legal requirements on explainability in machine learning", *Artificial Intelligence and Law*, Volume 29, 2021, pp. 149–169; Ashley, KD, *Artificial Intelligence and Legal Analytics: New Tools for Law Practice in the Digital Age*, Cambridge, Cambridge University Press, 2017. See: Part V, this chapter, Sects. 5.1.1.5.2.2–5.1.1.5.2.2.1.4 of this book (on the fundamental shift away from causation to correlations in algorithmic decision-making).

[941] See: Chap. 4 of this book.

poignant calls have been made to keep «humans in the loop»[942] as far as the emission of automated decisions is concerned.[943]

§§ Notwithstanding, the turn towards *algorithmic fairness* entails, and fundamentally requires, a shift away from a legal analysis that haphazardly seeks to unlock/unveil/unearth/unravel causal connections[944] between inputs and outputs.[945] This book therefore proposes that algorithmic decision-making must shift its gaze downstream to the algorithmic predictions[946] (outputs)[947] made by computer-generated

---

[942] Saxena, Devansh/Badillo-Urquiola, Karla/Wisniewski, Pamela J./Guha, Shion, "A Human-Centered Review of the Algorithms Used Within the U.S. Child Welfare System", *2020 Proceedings of Conference on Human Factors in Computing Systems*, Apr. 2020, 2020, passim. See: Part V, this chapter, Sects. 5.1.1.5.2.2–5.1.1.5.2.2.1.4 of this book (on the fundamental shift away from causation to correlations in algorithmic decision-making).

[943] Almada, M., "Human intervention in automated decision-making: toward the construction of contestable systems", *Proceedings of the Seventeenth International Conference on Artificial Intelligence and Law*, 2019, pp. 2–11; Williams, Rebecca, "Rethinking Administrative Law for Algorithmic Decision-Making", *Oxford Journal of Legal Studies*, Volume 42, 2021, pp. 468 e ff and passim.

[944] See: Kilbertus, Niki/Carulla, Mateo Rojas/Parascandolo, Giambattista/Hardt, Moritz/Janzing, Dominik/ Schoellkopf, Bernhard, "Avoiding Discrimination through Causal Reasoning", *Advances in Neural Information Processing Systems*, I. Guyon, U. V. Luxburg, S. Bengio, H. Wallach, R. Fergus, S. Vishwanathan, and R. Garnett (Eds.), Vol. 30. Curran Associates, Inc., 2017, pp. 656–666 (arguing that is feasible to avoiding discrimination through a granular and fine-grained causal reasoning).

[945] Gillis, Talia B., "The Input Data Fallacy", *Minnesota Law Review*, Volume 106, 2022, pp. 1176–1263 (p. 1257).

[946] See: Part IV, Chap. 4 of this book.

[947] Chander, Anupam, "The Racist Algorithm?", *Michigan Law Review*, Volume 115, 2017, pp. 1023–1039 ("The focus on outcomes rather than how an algorithm operates seems especially useful as algorithms become increasingly complicated, even able to modify themselves").

algorithms[948] to usher in, and pave the way to, a new[949] era[950] of automation[951] brimming with both procedural fairness[952] and algorithmic accountability.[953]

---

[948] Gillis, Talia B., "The Input Data Fallacy", *cit.* p. 1257.

[949] In Italian doctrine, on the challenges law may face in the forthcoming future: Irti, Natalino, *Un Diritto Incalcolabile*, Torino, G. Giappichelli Editore, 2016, passim.

[950] See: Susskind, Richard, "The Future of Courts", in: *Remote Courts*, Volume 6, n. ° 5, July/August 2020, 2020, pp. 1 e ss ("The uptake of various technologies, especially video, was accelerated in the justice systems of numerous countries. There remain some skeptics and critics, but in light of the experience during the crisis, there is certainly greater acceptance now than in February 2020—amongst lawyers, judges, officials, and court users—that judicial and court work might be undertaken very differently in years to come. Minds have been opened and changed over the past few months. Many assumptions have been swept aside. We remain in an era of threat, with risks of barely functioning court systems, greatly reduced access to justice, and, in turn, a potential weakening of the rule of law. We are also in an era of opportunity—the chance to build boldly on the shift of attitude and on demonstrable recent successes with technology, and to put in place improved, sustainable court services that are much more accessible than today's").

[951] Weizenbaum, Joseph, *Computer Power and Human Reason: From Judgment to Calculation*, 1st edition, New York, W. H. Freeman & Co, 1976, pp. 1–300 (227) ("examines the sources of the computer's powers and offers evaluative explorations of what computers can do, cannot do, and should not be employed to do") (this founding father of Artificial Intelligence presciently noted that we should not entrust Artificial Intelligence-embedded technologies with "tasks that demand wisdom"). Italics added. The approval of rental applications is arguably one of those tasks that should never be entrusted to machines). More on this on Part IV, Chap. 4, Sects. 4.1.4–4.1.4.2.1 of this book.

[952] Tyler, Tom, "What is procedural justice?", *Law and Society Review*, Volume 22, 1988, pp. 301–355; Tyler, Tom, "The Psychology of procedural justice: A test of the group value model.", in: *Journal of Personality and Social Psychology*, Volume 57, 1989, 830–838; Tyler, Tom, *Why people obey the law*, New Haven, CT, Yale University Press, 1990, 1–320 (premising his conclusions on a sound body of empirical research, the author states that "*people obey the law if they believe it's legitimate*, not because they fear punishment-this is the startling conclusion of Tom Tyler's classic study. Tyler suggests that lawmakers and law enforcers would do much better to make legal systems worthy of respect than to try to instill fear of punishment. *He finds that people obey law primarily because they believe in respecting legitimate authority*"). Italics added. Tyler, Tom, "Legitimizing unpopular public policies: Does procedure matter?", *Zeitschrift für Reichssoziologie*, Volume 14, 1993, pp. 47–54; Tyler, Tom, "Governing amid diversity: can fair decision-making procedures bridge competing public interests and values?", *Law and Society Review*, Volume 28, 1994, pp. 701–722; Tyler, Tom, "Psychological models of the justice motive", *Journal of Personality and Social Psychology*, Volume 67, 1994, 850–863; Tyler, Tom, "The relationship of the outcome and procedural fairness: How does knowing the outcome influences judgments about the procedure?", *Social Justice and Research*, Volume 9, 1996, pp. 311–325; Tyler, Tom, "Compliance with intellectual property laws", in: *Journal of International Law and Politics*, Volume 28, 1997, pp. 101–116; Tyler, Tom, "Justice and power in civil dispute processing", in: *Sociolegal studies*, Evanston, IL, Northwestern University Press, 1997; Tor, A./GAZAL-AYAL, O./GARCIA, S. M., "Fairness and willingness to accept plea bargain offers", *Journal of Empirical Legal Studies*, Volume 7, 2010, pp. 97–116 (drawing upon a body of empirical evidence the authors made an the interplay between overall fairness of the proceedings and the disputant's willingness to accept plea bargain offers made by the Government). But see: Guha, Neel/Henderson, Peter/Zambrano, Diego, "Vulnerabilities in Discovery Tech", *Harvard Journal of Law and Technology*, Volume 35, 2022, passim. See: Part V, this chapter, Sects. 5.1.1.5.2.2–5.1.1.5.2.2.1.4 of this book (on the fundamental shift away from causation to correlations in algorithmic decision-making).

[953] Zarsky, Tal, "Transparency in Data Mining: From Theory to Practice", *Discrimination and Privacy in the Information Society: Data Mining and Profiling in Large Databases*, Bart Custers

5.1.8.2 Law Number Two: Relevant Stakeholders Must Be Given the Chance to «Understand the Correlations Between Input Variables and Output Variables»: Variable Importance Plots Must Be Used with a View to Ensure an Interpretable Algorithmic Decision-Making That Abides by the Central Tenets of Procedure Rule of Law

§§ Adherence to the central tenets of **Procedural Rule of Law**[954] depends on the widespread implementation of **variable importance plots**, which highlights graphically the relative importances of the different input variables.[955] Although identical plots have been hitherto deployed for «standard» neural networks,[956] they are yet to be fully extended to stochastic[957] gradient boosting and advanced forms of «deep learning»,[958] such as convolutional neural networks.[959] Compellingly, **variable importance plots** amount to feasible ways to **meaningfully challenge** the algorithmic predictions spawned by algorithmic decision-making while abiding by the central tenets of **Procedural Rule of Law.**[960]

---

et al. eds., Belin, Springer, 2013; Kroll, Joshua A. et al., "Accountable Algorithms", *University of Pennsylvania Law Review*, Volume 165, 2017, passim. But see: Balkin, Jack, "Constitution in the National Surveillance State", *Minnesota Law Review*, Volume 93, 2008, p. 13 (*data mining* allows inferences not only about the direct subject of surveillance, but about other people with whom they live, work and communicate"); Pearl, Judea, "Causal inference in statistics: An overview", *Statistics Surveys*, Volume 3, 2009, pp. 96–146. But see: Pedreshi, Dino/Ruggieri, Salvatore/Turini, Franco, "Discrimination-aware Data Mining", *Proceedings of the 14th ACM SIGKDD International Conference on Knowledge Discovery and Data Mining (Las Vegas, Nevada, USA), ACM*, 2008, pp. 560–568 (arguing that one should shift its gaze downstream by putting in place discrimination-aware algorithmic tools while performing data mining). See: Part V, this chapter, Sect. 5.1.1.1 of this book (on the central tenets of Rule of Law that lends itself to a beacon of justice amidst the sepulchral darkness that is about to take hold). See: Part V, this chapter, Sect. 5.1.1.2 of this book (on the central tenets of Procedural Rule of Law that lends itself to a lighthouse of justice that allows citizens to challenge the pearls of algorithmic wisdom in a court of law). See: Part V, this chapter, Sects. 5.1.1.5.2.2–5.1.1.5.2.2.1.4 of this book (on the fundamental shift away from causation to correlations in algorithmic decision-making).

954 See: Part V, this chapter, Sect. 5.1.1.2 of this book (on the central tenets of Procedural Rule Law).

955 See: Berk, Richard A., *Statistical Learning from a Regression Perspective, cit.*, pp. 218–221, 279, 284.

956 See: Garson, David G., "Interpreting Neural-Network Connection Weights", *AI Expert*, Apr. 1991, pp. 47–48; Goh, A. T. C., "Back-Propagation Neural Networks for Modelling Complex Systems", *Artificial Intelligence Engineering*, Volume 9, 1995, pp. 143, 146–149 (drawing on Garson's approach).

957 Lehr, David/Ohm, Paul, "Playing with the Data: What Legal Scholars Should Learn About Machine Learning", *cit.*, pp. 653–718, whose research we have following closely.

958 Witten, Ian H., *Data Mining: Practical Machine Learning Tools and Techniques, cit.*, 464–466 (providing a brief (thumbnail sketch) overview on the realm of deep learning).

959 Buckner, Cameron, "Empiricism without Magic: Transformational Abstraction in Deep Convolutional Neural Networks", *Synthese*, Volume 195, 2018, 5339.

960 See: Part V, this chapter, Sect. 5.1.1.1 of this book (on the central tenets of Procedural Rule of Law).

§§ Others approaches are also possible. Such as explaining what the most relevant variables were for a given subject's predictions.[961] Critical to its success, though, is the extent to which these approaches can be fully extended to more advanced algorithms like deep neural[962] networks.[963]

§§ To ensure the seamless implementation of **variance importance plots**, changes need to be made at the stage of **model training.**[964] In addition to that, given that these methods are not always available for different types of machine learning algorithms, a tool developer is entrusted with the task of making tough choices at the **model selection**[965] stage either.[966]

---

[961] See: Datta, Anupam et al., "Algorithmic Transparency via Quantitative Input Influence: Theory and Experiments with Learning Systems", *IEEE Symposium on Security & Privacy*, 2016, pp. 598, 601, 608–609.

[962] Lehr, David/Ohm, Paul, "Playing with the Data: What Legal Scholars Should Learn About Machine Learning", *cit.*, pp. 653–718.

[963] Datta, Anupam et al., "Algorithmic Transparency via Quantitative Input Influence: Theory and Experiments with Learning Systems", *cit.*, p. 614 ("We have not considered situations where inputs do not have well understood semantics... *With the proliferation of immense processing power, complex machine learning models such as deep neural networks have become ubiquitous in these domains*. Defining transparency and developing analysis techniques in such settings is important future work"). Italics added.

[964] See: Part V, this chapter, Sects. 5.1.4–5.1.4.1.1 of this book (on the fundamental tenets of model training).

[965] Lehr, David/Ohm, Paul, "Playing with the Data: What Legal Scholars Should Learn About Machine Learning", *cit.*, pp. 653–718. See: Part V, this chapter, Sects. 5.1.3–5.1.3.1.6 of this book (on the fundamental tenets of model selection).

[966] It bears mentioning that the suitably tailored model is crucially important not just to get one over the threshold of being able to deploy a relevance-assessing method, but, and foremost, also to deploy highly interpretable methods. More often than not, a group of methods implemented for some machine learning algorithms afford mildly interpretable relevance measures. For instance, in a random forest algorithm used to binary classification an importance value of 0.2 for a given variable for the "True" class can be translated, or interpreted as, signifying that, if that variable was weeded out from the machine learning algorithm, the latter would produce twenty percent more errors when forecasting the "True" class. See: Berk, Richard A., *Statistical Learning from a Regression Perspective*, *cit.*, pp. 214–222. It is pivotally important to note, though, that easily interpretable numbers are not without hurdles. Every now and then, proposed metrics are nothing but simple measures of relevance. Other times, in turn, there is simply no easy way to translating into simple, readable, understandable manner what an importance value suggests. See: Garson, David G., "Interpreting Neural-Network Connection Weights", *cit.*, passim. Tellingly, it goes without saying that choosing a bespoke machine learning algorithm can prove to be crucially important. See: Lehr, David/Ohm, Paul, "Playing with the Data: What Legal Scholars Should Learn About Machine Learning", *cit.*, pp. 653–718. Suffice to say that the choice of any given importance-measuring method will prove detrimental in the long run in that can run counter to the sough-after *algorithmic transparency* of which citizens are so keenly fond of. No surprise stems from the fact that stakeholders should employ their best efforts to deploy a particularly **interpretable model** to ensure the much-acclaimed, and sorely needed, ***algorithmic interpretation*** that allow citizens to meaningfully challenge the pearls of algorithmic wisdom produced by machine learning algorithms. See: Part V, this chapter, Sect. 5.1.1.1 of this book (on the central tenets of Rule of Law that lends itself to a beacon of justice amidst the sepulchral darkness that is about to take hold). See: Part V, this chapter, Sect. 5.1.1.2 of this book (on the central tenets of Procedural Rule of Law that lends

§§ Furthermore, there is yet another type of approach that aims to analyse how increases or decreases in the multiple input variables convert into changes in the outcome[967] variable.[968]

§§ Put differently, these methods unravel the «functional form» of the **correlations between an input variable and the outcome variable**. This functional form can bestow upon relevant stakeholders a meaningful/helpful/actionable pathway of intuitively grasping what **correlations**[969] the machine learning algorithm is doing when generating its algorithmic predictions.[970]

§§ More to the point, they generate **actionable plots**—often dubbed as **partial dependence or individual conditional expectation plots**—that map/graph/depict the outcome variable as a function of a given input variable.[971] These methods are in dire need of being made widely available for all types of algorithms. They have hitherto been implemented for certain types of machine learning algorithms—e.g. **random forests**,[972] **gradient boosting algorithms**,[973] and **«standard» neural networks**[974]—but they are yet to be fully extended to more advanced techniques of deep learning,[975] which is something in dire need of changing.

§§ All in all, **law number two** upholds the «right to technical interpretability»[976]—which is far cry from a cumbersome «explainability»[977]—that draws on

---

itself to a lighthouse of justice that allows citizens to challenge the pearls of algorithmic wisdom in a court of law).

967 Lehr, David/Ohm, Paul, "Playing with the Data: What Legal Scholars Should Learn About Machine Learning", *cit.*, pp. 653–718.

968 See: Berk, Richard A., *Statistical Learning from a Regression Perspective, cit.*, pp. 222–229 (shedding light on these plots that underpin random forests algorithm); Berk, Richard A., *Statistical Learning from a Regression Perspective, cit.*, pp. 273–274 (poring over these plots for stochastic gradient boosting while providing some caveats about correctly interpreting them).

969 See: Part V, this chapter, Sects. 5.1.1.5.2.2–5.1.1.5.2.2.1.4 of this book (on the fundamental shift away from causation to correlations in algorithmic decision-making).

970 Lehr, David/Ohm, Paul, "Playing with the Data: What Legal Scholars Should Learn About Machine Learning", *cit.*, pp. 653–718.

971 See: Berk, Richard A., *Statistical Learning from a Regression Perspective, cit.*, pp. 226–29, See: Berk, Richard A., *Statistical Learning from a Regression Perspective, cit.*, pp. 277–292.

972 See: Berk, Richard A., *Statistical Learning from a Regression Perspective, cit.*, pp. 222–229.

973 See: Berk, Richard A., *Statistical Learning from a Regression Perspective, cit.*, pp. 273–274.

974 See: Goldstein, Alex et al., "Peeking Inside the Black Box: Visualizing Statistical Learning with Plots of Individual Conditional Expectation", *Arxiv*:1309.6392V2, Mar. 20, 2014, at 1–12, https://arxiv.org/pdf/1309.6392.pdf [https://perma.cc/6XMK-PZ3S].

975 Lehr, David/Ohm, Paul, "Playing with the Data: What Legal Scholars Should Learn About Machine Learning", *cit.*, pp. 653–718.

976 Gallesse, Chiara, "The AI Act proposal: a new right to technical interpretability?", *Internet Law and Digital Society: An International Overview*, Kowalicka, Paulina (Editor), Milano, Milano University Press, 2025, pp. 1–10 (passim).

977 Rudin, Cynthia et al. "Interpretable machine learning: Fundamental principles and 10 grand challenges", *Statistics Surveys*, 16, 2022, pp. 1–85; Rudin, Cynthia, "Stop explaining black box machine learning models for high stakes decisions and use interpretable models instead", Nature Machine Intelligence 1.5, 2019, pp. 206–215 (argues that "explainability" occurs when "a second (post hoc) model is created to explain the first black box model"). See also: Chazette, Larissa/

the central tenets of **interpretable Artificial Intelligence**. For that reason, we are better off keeping «interpretability» and «explainability» separate[978] for they are poles apart.

§§ Whilst «explainability» seeks to explain[979] the pearls of algorithmic wisdom (outputs) offered by black box models,[980] «interpretability»,[981] on the other hand, seeks to offer actionable cues on the rationale behind the production of pearls of algorithmic wisdom (outputs) in ways that are fundamentally human-friendly. The former is inscrutable *to* humans, whereas the latter is interpretable *to* humans. **Law number two** therefore embraces the latter («interpretability») while abhorring the «transparency fallacy»[982] associated to the former («explainability»).

§§ This is the kernel of **Procedural Rule of Law**,[983] which seeks to **challenge** the **interpretable outputs** generated by running models.[984]

Brunotte, Wasja/Speith, Timo, "Exploring explainability: A definition, a model, and a knowledge catalogue", *2021 IEEE 29th International Requirements Engineering Conference (RE)*, IEEE, 2021, pp. 197–208; Köhl, Maximilian A et al. "Explainability as a non-functional requirement", *2019 IEEE 27th International Requirements Engineering Conference (RE)*, IEEE, 2019, pp. 363–368 (on the functional shortcomings of "explainability").

[978] Rudin, Cynthia et al. "Interpretable machine learning: Fundamental principles and 10 grand challenges", *Statistics Surveys*, 16, 2022, pp. 1–85.

[979] Gallesse, Chiara, "The AI Act proposal: a new right to technical interpretability?", *cit.*, pp. 1–10 (7) ("*in certain circumstances explainability may not be a reliable method, because explainable machine learning techniques offer explanations that are not accurate representations of what the original model computes, and therefore suggest an incorrect explanation. In fact, continues the author, they are unable to accurately reconstruct the original model. If the explanation accurately described what the original model computed, it would be identical to the original model*, negating the very necessity for the original model in the first place: in other words, *the second model would be interpretable*"). Italics added.

[980] See: Rudin, Cynthia et al. "Interpretable machine learning: Fundamental principles and 10 grand challenges", arXiv:2103.11251v2 [cs.LG] 10 Jul 2021, 2021, p. 1 ("*with widespread use of machine learning (ML), the importance of interpretability has become clear in avoiding catastrophic consequences. Black box predictive models, which by definition are inscrutable, have led to serious societal problems that deeply affect health, freedom, racial bias, and safety*"). Italics added. See also: Christodoulou, Evangelia et al. "A systematic review shows no performance benefit of machine learning over logistic regression for clinical prediction models", *Journal of clinical epidemiology*, 110, 2019, pp. 12–22 (arguing that whilst black boxes are more accurate than interpretable models, there are instances where the latter can attain greater accuracy than the former).

[981] Rudin, Cynthia et al. "Interpretable machine learning: Fundamental principles and 10 grand challenges", arXiv:2103.11251v2 [cs.LG] 10 Jul 2021, 2021, p. 1 ("*Interpretable predictive models, which are constrained so that their reasoning processes are more understandable to humans, are much easier to troubleshoot and to use in practice*"). Italics added.

[982] Edwards, Lilian/Veale, Michael, "Slave to the Algorithm? Why a "Right to an Explanation" is Probably not the Remedy You are Looking for", *Duke Law and Technology Review*, Volume 16, 2018, pp. 1–67 (2) ("based on our analysis, we fear that the search for a "right to an explanation" in the GDPR may be at best distracting, *and at worst nurture a new kind of "transparency fallacy"*"). Italics added.

[983] See: Part V, this chapter, Sect. 5.1.1.2 of this book (on the central tenets of Procedural Rule of Law).

[984] See: Judgment of the Court of Justice of the European Union in Case C-203/22 (Dun & Bradstreet Austria - *Automated credit assessment*), Press Release n.º 22/25, Luxembourg, 27th February of

5.1.8.3 Law Number Three: «Asymmetric Cost Ratios» (the Cost Ratio for False Positives to False Negatives) Must Be Timely Implemented

§§ The ability (or lack thereof) to code in, and successfully implement, an **«asymmetric cost ratio»** is critically important.[985] In any predictive endeavour,[986] no matter how small, there are different types of errors, or inaccurate,[987] predictions.[988]

2025, 2025, p. 1 ("*the data subject is entitled to an explanation as to how the decision was taken in respect of him or her The explanation provided must enable the data subject to understand and challenge the automated decision In Austria, a mobile telephone operator refused to allow a customer to conclude a contract on the ground that her credit standing was insufficient. The operator relied in that regard on an assessment of the customer's credit standing carried out by automated means by Dun & Bradstreet Austria, an undertaking specialising in the provision of such assessments.* The contract would have involved a monthly payment of €10. In the ensuing dispute, an Austrian court found, by final decision, that Dun & Bradstreet had infringed the General Data Protection Regulation (GDPR). 1 Dun & Bradstreet had failed to provide *the customer with 'meaningful information about the logic involved' in the automated decision-making in question.* At the very least, the undertaking had failed to give a sufficient statement of reasons as to why it was unable to provide that information. *The court before which the customer brought the matter for the purposes of the enforcement of that judicial decision wonders what Dun & Bradstreet must do in practice in that regard. That court therefore referred the matter to the Court of Justice, seeking guidance on the interpretation of the GDPR and the directive on the protection of trade secrets. 2 According to the Court, the controller must describe the procedure and principles actually applied in such a way that the data subject can understand which of his or her personal data have been used in the automated decision-making. In order to meet the requirements of transparency and intelligibility, it could in particular be appropriate to inform the data subject of the extent to which a variation in the personal data taken into account would have led to a different result.* By contrast, the *mere communication of an algorithm does not constitute a sufficiently concise and intelligible explanation*"). Italics added.

[985] Berk, Richard A., *Statistical Learning from a Regression Perspective*, 2nd edition, Heidelberg, Springer, 2016, p. 253 ("[I]f for policy or subject matter reasons one needs to tune to approximate a target *asymmetric cost ratio* in a confusion table, *model selection is in play once again*"). Italics added. See also: Berk, Richard, "Accuracy and Fairness for Juvenile Justice Risks Assessments", *cit.*, pp. 185–186 (positing that that, to equalize **cost ratios** across racial groups in a juvenile risk-assessment context, the author "separate[d] forecasting exercises" for white and black juveniles, respectively, and that the machine-learning forecasting algorithms the data produced were different for each racial group).

[986] It is bears mentioning that **predictive parity (calibration)** can likewise be despairingly inconsistent with a **single-threshold rule**. At the very least, it does not ensure or necessarily indicate a **single-threshold rule** for risk classification. See: Mayson, Sandra G., "Bias In, Bias Out", *cit.*, pp. 2218–2300.

[987] Lehr, David/Ohm, Paul, "Playing with the Data: What Legal Scholars Should Learn About Machine Learning", *cit.*, pp. 653–718.

[988] See: Witten, Ian H., *Data Mining: Practical Machine Learning Tools and Techniques*, *cit.*, pp. 179–183 (highlighting the different types of errors and how, in broadly speaking, machine-learning algorithms and the extent to which the latter can be swayed by *asymmetric cost ratios*).

§§ When tasked with the duty of accurately estimating a binary outcome, the algorithm can produce a wide range of **false positives**[989] (forecasting something when that something failed to happen as predicted in the real world) and **false negatives**[990] (failure to predict a given scenario that actually happened in the real world). When predicting a continuous outcome, overestimates[991] and underestimates,[992] however small on either end, are part of the «plot».

§§ It is noteworthy that different types of errors are routinely viewed by relevant stakeholders as having different normative valences.[993] Seldom, if ever, a relevant stakeholder to consider being wrong in one manner as likewise harmful as being

[989] The question of the relative cost of a false positive and false negative in the algorithmic risk assessment context evokes the prominent Blackstone ratio, which stresses the relative costs of false negatives and false positives in the context of criminal conviction and punishment. See: Blackstone, William, *Commentaries on the Laws of England*, 4 volumes, Oxford, Clarendon Press, 1765–1769, p. 352 ("[T]he law holds, that it is better that ten guilty persons escape, than that one innocent suffer"). See: Mayson, Sandra G., "Bias In, Bias Out", *cit.*, pp. 2218–2300. Angwin, Julia et al., "Machine Bias", *ProPublica* (May 23, 2016), https://www.propublica.org/article/machine-bias-risk-assessments-in-criminal-sentencing [https://perma.cc/4G83-MDAS] (harshly criticizing disparity in false-positive rates as a purely unjustified bias). See also: Freeman, Katherine, "Algorithmic Injustice: How the Wisconsin Supreme Court Failed to Protect Due Process Rights in State v. Loomis", *North Carolina Journal of Law and Technology*, Volume 18, 2016, pp. 75–86 (echoing the very same views).

[990] According to Richard Berk's research on juvenile data, for example, tweaking the algorithm to attain statistical parity spawned a lower **false positive** rate for the black subset than the white (4% versus 9%) yet a higher **false negative** rate (50% versus 40%). See: Berk, Richard, "Accuracy and Fairness for Juvenile Justice Risks Assessments", *cit.*, p. 189. In addition to that, Berk further concluded that for white folks, the algorithm generated 5.25 **false positives** for every **false negative**; whilst for black folks, the algorithm generated 1.85 false negatives for every false positive. See: Berk, Richard, "Accuracy and Fairness for Juvenile Justice Risks Assessments", *cit.*, p. 189.

[991] But see: Dieterich, William et al., "COMPAS Risk Scales: Demonstrating Accuracy Equity and Predictive Parity", *Northpointe Inc.* 1, 2–3, 8–13 (July 8, 2016), http://go.volarisgroup.com/rs/430-MBX-989/images/ProPublica_Commentary_Final_070616.pdf [https://perma.cc/K4GM -RBQY] (stating that a predictive instrument is bigoted/flawed only if a certain score, or a given classification, means a starkly likelihood of the forecasted outcome for members of one racial group than members of the other group). See also: Flores: Anthony W. et al., "False Positives, False Negatives, and False Analyses: A Rejoinder to "Machine Bias: There's Software Used Across the Country to Predict Future Criminals. And It's Biased Against Blacks," *Federal Probation*, Volume 80, 2016, pp. 38–40 (positing that "well-established and accepted standards exist to test for bias in risk assessment"); Skeem, Jennifer L./Lowenkamp, Christopher T., "Risk, Race, and Recidivism: Predictive Bias and Disparate Impact", *cit.*, p. 685 (asserting that if "a given score [has] the same meaning regardless of group membership," the instrument is "unbiased").

[992] See: Kriegler, Brian/Berk, Richard A., "Small Area Estimation of the Homeless in Los Angeles: An Application of Cost-Sensitive Stochastic Gradient Boosting", *Annals of Applied Statistics*, Volume 4, 2010, pp. 1234, 1241 (discussing how stakeholders tend to analyse **underestimates**—measuring that there are fewer homeless individuals in a given county/parish/state than there indeed are—as **more costly than overestimates**—measuring that there are more homeless individuals in a given county/parish/state than there indeed are). See: Lehr, David/Ohm, Paul, "Playing with the Data: What Legal Scholars Should Learn About Machine Learning", *cit.*, pp. 653–718.

[993] Lehr, David/Ohm, Paul, "Playing with the Data: What Legal Scholars Should Learn About Machine Learning", *cit.*, pp. 653–718.

wrong in the opposite manner[994] Note, though, that many,[995] albeit not all,[996] machine learning algorithms bestow upon the data scientist the possibility to determine[997] an **asymmetric cost ratio.**[998] Crucially, data scientist foists mathematical limitations on the machine learning algorithm that force it to make certain types of errors (for

---

[994] See: Witten, Ian H., *Data Mining: Practical Machine Learning Tools and Techniques*, *cit.*, p. 180 ("In truth, you'd be hard pressed to find an application in which the costs of different kinds of errors were the same"). Bringing forth examples machine-learning applications where estimation of **asymmetric costs** was paramount: Berk, Richard A. et al., "Forecasting Domestic Violence: A Machine Learning Approach to Help Inform Arraignment Decisions", *cit.*, pp. 103–04 (discussing how **false negatives**—forecasting that arrestees will not perpetrate future domestic violence when they indeed do—were regarded by stakeholders as ten times more harmful than **false positives**—forecasting that arrestees will indeed perpetrate future domestic violence when they indeed do not).

[995] See: Berk, Richard A., *Statistical Learning from a Regression Perspective*, *cit.*, pp. 210–213 (describing how to implement asymmetric costs with random forests); Kriegler, Brian/Berk, Richard A., "Small Area Estimation of the Homeless in Los Angeles: An Application of Cost-Sensitive Stochastic Gradient Boosting", *Annals of Applied Statistics*, cit., passim (laying down the groundwork for asymmetric costs with stochastic gradient boosting). See also: Zhi Hua Zhou & Xu-Ying Liu, "Training Cost-Sensitive Neural Networks with Methods Addressing the Class Imbalance Problem", *IEEE Transactions Knowledge & Data Engineering*, Volume 18, 2006, p. 63 (laying down asymmetric costs with deep neural networks).

[996] See: Berk, Richard A., *Statistical Learning from a Regression Perspective*, *cit.*, p. 325 ("A final difficulty with the software [implementing support vector machines in R] is that there is no direct way to address the relative costs of false negatives and false positives"). Scholars have proposed other methods for producing effective cost-sensitive support vector machines. See: Shuichi Katsumata/Akiko Takeda, "Robust Cost Sensitive Support Vector Machine", *Proceedings of Machine Learning Research*, Volume 38, 2015, p. 434. It is worth recalling that the foregoing methods have not yet been vetted and thoroughly assessed, let alone validated by other stakeholders. See: Lehr, David/Ohm, Paul, "Playing with the Data: What Legal Scholars Should Learn About Machine Learning", *cit.*, pp. 653–718.

[997] Lehr, David/Ohm, Paul, "Playing with the Data: What Legal Scholars Should Learn About Machine Learning", *cit.*, pp. 653–718.

[998] But see: Mayson, Sandra G., "Bias In, Bias Out", *cit.*, pp. 2218–2300 (arguing that equalizing false-positive rates will beget fewer false positives—**"law abiders"** mistakenly predict for rearrest - for the high-base-rate group than the low-base-rate group because there are fewer "law abiders" in the high-base-rate group in the first place). But see also: Sam Corbett-Davies and peers, parsing the same Broward County data that ProPublica did, concluded that attaining parity in **false-positive rates** while still optimizing for public safety (and without detaining any other defendants) would beget a 7% uptick in violent crime. See: Corbett-Davies, Sam/Pierson, Emma/Feller, Avi/Goel, Sharad Goel/Huq, Aziz, "Algorithmic Decision Making and the Cost of Fairness", *Proceedings of the 23rd ACM SIGKDD International Conference on Knowledge Discovery and Data Mining* (Ass'n for Computing Machinery ed., 2017), 2017, p. 802. Moreover, 17% of those detained would be low-risk people for whom detention was either unwarranted or uncalled for. According to Richard Berk's research on juvenile data, for example, tweaking the algorithm to attain statistical parity spawned a lower false-positive rate for the black subset than the white (4% versus 9%) yet a higher false-negative rate (50% versus 40%). See: Berk, Richard, "Accuracy and Fairness for Juvenile Justice Risks Assessments", *cit.*, p. 189. In addition to that, Berk further concluded that for white folks, the algorithm generated 5.25 false positives for every false negative; whilst for black folks, the algorithm generated 1.85 false negatives for every false positive. See: Berk, Richard, "Accuracy and Fairness for Juvenile Justice Risks Assessments", *cit.*, p. 189.

example, false positives in the binary classification purview or overestimates in the regression purview) more often than others.[999]

§§ For instance, a **cost ratio** of 5:1 for false positives to false negatives would grant that, for every false negative[1000] created, there are five false positives.[1001]

§§ As extensively shown earlier in this book, ***asymmetric cost ratio*** carries both promise and danger in that it can significantly shift the balance of **measurement errors** in ways that could generate disparate[1002] impacts.[1003] This step is key to ensure the much-needed procedural accountability sought by **Procedural Rule of Law.**[1004]

§§ No surprise stems from the fact that implementing **asymmetric cost ratios** is a remarkable tool indeed[1005]; it seamlessly, and meaningfully, translates purely

---

[999] Lehr, David/Ohm, Paul, "Playing with the Data: What Legal Scholars Should Learn About Machine Learning", *cit.*, pp. 653–718.

[1000] But see: Berk, Richard, "Accuracy and Fairness for Juvenile Justice Risks Assessments", *Journal of Empirical Legal Studies*, Volume 16, 2019, p. 175 (comes to the terms with the fact that tweaking/altering data to attain **statistical parity** yielded extremely high **false-negative rates**); Zachary Lipton et al., "Does Mitigating ML's Impact Disparity Require Treatment Disparity?", NIPS PROC. 1 (2018), https://arxiv.org/pdf/1711.07076.pdf [https://perma.cc/X8VF-EY53] (sets forth compelling evidence that enforced blindness to protected traits exacts a toll on the overall accuracy of the algorithmic tool); Petersilia, Joan/Turner, Susan, "Guideline-Based Justice: Prediction and Racial Minorities", *Crime and Justice*, 1987, pp. 151–174 (argues that omitting markers correlated with race from a recidivism prediction algorithm exacted a toll on the accuracy of the algorithmic tool).

[1001] Lehr, David/Ohm, Paul, "Playing with the Data: What Legal Scholars Should Learn About Machine Learning", *cit.*, pp. 653–718.

[1002] See: Hurley, Mikella/Adebayo, Julius, "Credit Scoring in the Era of Big Data", *Yale Journal of Law and Technology*, Volume 18, 2016, pp. 148, 151–156, 172 (averring that FICO scoring boasts a redoubtable capacity to routinely weed out some populations that have been historically and systematically underrepresented or grossly unfairly represented in the credit industry market). Tellingly, by 2016, ten states had disavowed the unlawful practice of employers using shady algorithmic credit scores due to their perceived **disparate impact** on low-income applicants and members of racialized communities (mostly Black folks). See: O'Neill, Cathy, *Weapons of Math Destruction. How Big Data Increases Inequality and Threatens Democracy*. London: Penguin Random House, 2016, pp. 128 and ff and passim. See: Part IV, Chap. 4, Sects. 4.1.4–4.1.4.2.3 of this book.

[1003] Lehr, David/Ohm, Paul, "Playing with the Data: What Legal Scholars Should Learn About Machine Learning", *cit.*, pp. 653–718.

[1004] See: Part V, this chapter, Sect. 5.1.1.1 of this book (on the central tenets of Procedural Rule of Law).

[1005] It is worth recalling, though, that according to Richard Berk's research on juvenile data, for example, tweaking the algorithm to attain **statistical parity** spawned a lower false-positive rate for the black subset than the white (4% versus 9%) yet a higher false-negative rate (50% versus 40%). See: Berk, Richard, "Accuracy and Fairness for Juvenile Justice Risks Assessments", *cit.*, p. 189. In addition to that, Berk further concluded that for white folks, the algorithm generated 5.25 false positives for every false negative; whilst for black folks, the algorithm generated 1.85 false negatives for every false positive. See: Berk, Richard, "Accuracy and Fairness for Juvenile Justice Risks Assessments", *cit.*, p. 189. See also: Angwin, Julia et al., "Machine Bias", *ProPublica* (May 23, 2016), https://www.propublica.org/article/machine-bias-risk-assessments-in-criminal-sentencing [https://perma.cc/4G83-MDAS] (harshly criticizing disparity in false-positive rates as a purely unjustified bias). See also: Freeman, Katherine, "Algorithmic Injustice: How the Wisconsin Supreme Court

normative values of relevant stakeholders into purely, and meaningfully, actionable math. In addition to that, of the machine learning algorithms that can implement **asymmetric cost ratios,**[1006] how precisely implementation unfolds hinges on the type of output variable.[1007]

5.1.8.4 Law Number Four: «Regularization» Must Be Timely Implemented to Assuage *Algorithmic Dictatorship*—During the Stages of Model Tuning and Model Training—While Increasing *Algorithmic Common Good*

§§ There is a strand of literature championing for the allayment of algorithmic discrimination. But here is the twist: some changes are needed in earlier stages of the construction of a machine learning algorithm. Pivotally, some of these sorely needed changes entail meaningful intervention during both the stages of **model tuning**[1008] and **model training.**[1009] Crucially, Toshihiro Kamishima and his fellow co-authors,

---

Failed to Protect Due Process Rights in State v. Loomis", *North Carolina Journal of Law and Technology*, Volume 18, 2016, pp. 75–86 (echoing the very same views).

[1006] See: Berk, Richard A., *Statistical Learning from a Regression Perspective*, *cit.*, pp. 266–271 (discussing that, in the purview of **stochastic gradient boosting**, classification problems are regarded as regression problems, estimating probabilities, with thresholds applied to morph probabilities to forecasted classes). Pivotally, the consequence of this situation is that, if **asymmetric costs** are applied by overhauling these thresholds at the very end of the machine algorithm's mathematical processing, predictor relevance and partial dependence plots will not sharply mirror this ***asymmetric cost ratio***. Put differently, it will reflect input variables' relevance and the functional types of relationships between input variables and the output variable embodying symmetric costs. Lehr, David/Ohm, Paul, "Playing with the Data: What Legal Scholars Should Learn About Machine Learning", *cit.*, pp. 653–718.

[1007] Lehr, David/Ohm, Paul, "Playing with the Data: What Legal Scholars Should Learn About Machine Learning", *cit.*, pp. 653–718.

[1008] See: Part V, this chapter, Sect. 5.1.3.1.5 of this book (on the central tenets of model tuning).

[1009] See: Part V, this chapter, Sects. 5.1.4–5.1.4.1.1 of this book (on the central tenets of model training).

for example, have set forth a helpful proposal for mitigating disparate impacts[1010] during model tuning through a painstaking process baptized as **«regularization»**.[1011]

§§ Concisely, **«regularization»** entails changing a machine learning algorithm's **objective or loss function** to chastise it if it produces exceedingly high disparate classifications.[1012] Strikingly, Google researchers have meaningfully shown that, during the stage of **model training**, one can successfully modify the threshold at

---

[1010] See: Hellman, Deborah, "Indirect Discrimination and the Duty to Avoid Compounding Injustice", *Foundations of Indirect Discrimination Law*, Collins, Hugh/Khaitan, Tarunabh (Editors), Oxford, Hart Publishing; Reprint edition (June 25, 2020), 2020, p. 107 (Professor Deborah Hellman coined this expression to depict a decision that "exacerbates the harm caused by the prior injustice because it entrenches the harm or carries it into another domain." This book deals with the sweltering topic of indirect discrimination ("*indirect discrimination (or disparate impact) concerns the application of the same rule to everyone, even though that rule significantly disadvantages one particular group in society*"). Italics added. See also: Sunstein, Cass R., "Algorithms, Correcting Biases", *Social Research*, Volume 86, 2019, pp. 449–506 (this famed author tagged **disparate impact** as "disturbing in itself, in the sense that a practice that produces such an impact helps entrench something like a caste system"). This famed scholar furthermore avers that empirical evidence on the accuracy of machine versus human predictions suggests the existence of a "current offense bias" that saps ulterior/subsequent judicial assessments). But see: McIntyre, Frank/Baradaran, Shima, "Race, Prediction, and Pretrial Detention", *Journal Empirical Legal Studies*, Volume 10, 2013, pp. 742–759 (mentions black defendants' exceedingly high likelihood of being arrested on drug-related charges as a potential cause of the race gap); Skeem, Jennifer L./Lowenkamp, Christopher T., "Risk, Race, and Recidivism: Predictive Bias and Disparate Impact", *Criminology*, Volume 54, 2024, pp. 680, 683–84, 704–06 (argues that criminal history correlates with race in their respective data set). See also: Pager, Devah, *Marked: Race, Crime, and Finding Work in an Era of Mass Incarceration*, Chicago: University of Chicago Press, 2007; Fornili, K. S., "Racialized mass incarceration and the war on drugs: A critical race theory appraisal", *Journal of Addictions Nursing*, Volume 29, Issue 1, 2018, 65–72; Jacoby, S. F., Dong, B., Beard, J. H., Wiebe, D. J., & Morrison, C. N., "The enduring impact of historical and structural racism on urban violence in Philadelphia", *Social Science & Medicine*, 1982/2018, 199, 2018, pp. 87–95; Travis, Jeremy, Bruce Western, and Steve Redburn (Eds.), *Growth of Incarceration in the United States: Exploring Causes and Consequences*, Washington, DC: National Academy of Science, 2014. See: Mayson, Sandra G., "Bias In, Bias Out", *Yale Law Journal*, Volume 128, 2019, pp. 2218–2300.

[1011] Lehr, David/Ohm, Paul, "Playing with the Data: What Legal Scholars Should Learn About Machine Learning", *cit.*, pp. 653–718.

[1012] See: Kamishima, Toshihiro et al., "Fairness-Aware Classifier with Prejudice Remove Regularizer", *Machine Learning & Knowledge Discovery in Databases*, Flach, Peter A./Tijl De Bie/ Nello Cristianini (Editors) 2012, pp. 35, 35–50. The regularizer grows exponentially when a class is forecasted chiefly based on sensitive features in the data, Unsurprisingly, sensitive features lose influence in the final classifications. This regularizer is under the control of a shrinkage parameter, whose tuning procedure keeps an eye the extent to which the machine learning algorithm is deftly regularized. See: Lehr, David/Ohm, Paul, "Playing with the Data: What Legal Scholars Should Learn About Machine Learning", *cit.*, pp. 653–718.

which forecasted probabilities are converted into classifications to impose forecasts to match a bevy of definitions[1013] of **algorithmic**[1014] **fairness.**[1015]

§§ Hardly any bewildering surprise stems from the fact that overlooking these intermediate stages of the machine learning process equals forsaking feasible ways of mitigating **algorithmic discrimination**[1016] while trouncing **Algorithmic Dictatorship**[1017] Whilst legal scholars have been paying a nuanced attention on how algorithmic discrimination arises during the stage of **data collection,**[1018] they have nonetheless overlooked novel methods for curtailing it at that stage. Compellingly, a budding, yet exciting, body of research has clearly shown that a string of algorithmic discrimination can be dwindled by simply **adding noise**[1019] to the dataset.[1020] Overall, assuaging algorithmic discrimination is completely possible, but it nonetheless entails meaningful intervention at a number of key, often forsaken/disregarded/overlooked, stages of the learning curve of a machine learning.[1021]

[1013] Lehr, David/Ohm, Paul, "Playing with the Data: What Legal Scholars Should Learn About Machine Learning", *cit.*, pp. 653–718.

[1014] Hellman, Deborah, "Measuring Algorithmic Fairness", *Virginia Law Review*, 106 (4), 2020, pp. 811–866. On the dire need to achieve algorithmic fairness through both the creation of race-aware algorithms and trade-offs to attain fairer risk scores: Kim, Pauline, "Race-Aware Algorithms: Fairness, Non-discrimination and Affirmative Action", *California Law Review*, 2022, passim; Kleinberg, Jon/S. Mullainathan/M. Raghavan, "Inherent Trade-offs in the Fair Determination of Risk Scores", *Proceedings of the 8th Conference on Innovations in Theoretical Computer Science (ITCS)*, 2017; Kroll, Joshua A./J. Huey/S. Barocas/E. W. Felten/J. R. Reidenberg/D. G. Robinson/and H. Yu, "Accountable Algorithms", *University of Pennsylvania Law Review*, 165 (3), 2017, pp. 633–705.

[1015] See: Hardt, Moritz et al., "Equality of Opportunity in Supervised Learning", *Arxiv*:1610.02413, Oct. 11, 2016, pp. 8–10, https://arxiv.org/pdf/1610.02413.pdf [https://perma.cc/9D8U-3DBH].

[1016] It is worth recalling, too, that there are different possible mathematical conceptions of fairness. Pivotally, and as adumbrated earlier in this book, optimizing one metric of fairness often forestalls achieving another. See: Berk, Richard et al., "Fairness in Criminal Justice Risk Assessments: The State of the Art", *Sociological Methods & Research*, 2018, pp. 1–10; Kleinberg, Jon, et al., "Inherent Trade-offs in the Fair Determination of Risk Scores", *Leibniz International Proceedings in Informatics*, Jan. 2017, 2017, at 43:1, 43:4; pp. 3–4 (talking about "balance for the negative class"). With this context in place, at the machine learning phases discussed here, not only do programmers have to ponder technical methods for attaining fairness, but, and foremost, they have to grapple with extremely relevant normative questions of what sort of fairness matters most in a given purview.

[1017] See: Part IV, Chap. 4, Sects. 4.1–4.1.10.6 of this book (on Algorithmic Dictatorship and its chilling effect on democracy).

[1018] See: Part V, this chapter, Sects. 5.1.2.4–5.1.2.4.1 of this book.

[1019] Lehr, David/Ohm, Paul, "Playing with the Data: What Legal Scholars Should Learn About Machine Learning", *cit.*, pp. 653–718.

[1020] See: Feldman, Michael et al., Certifying and Removing Disparate Impact, ARXIV:1412.3756V3, July 16, 2015, at 11–15, https://arxiv.org/pdf/1412.3756.pdf [https://perma.cc/48PZ-EW48]. This stance pass muster since it renders it less considerably likely to forecast an individual's protected group membership from values of their other input variables.

[1021] Lehr, David/Ohm, Paul, "Playing with the Data: What Legal Scholars Should Learn About Machine Learning", *cit.*, pp. 653–718. See: Part V, this chapter, Sects. 5.1.3–5.1.3.1.6 of this book (on the fundamental tenets of model selection). See: Part V, this chapter, Sect. 5.1.3.1.5 of this book (on the central tenets of model tuning). See: Part V, this chapter, Sects. 5.1.4–5.1.4.1.1 of this book (on the central tenets of model training).

5.1.8.5 Law Number Five: Robot-Judges Must Not Enter the Courtroom as the Latter—Much Like Robot-Prosecutors and Robot-Lawyers—Are Utterly Incapable of Making Interpretable Value Judgments in Judicial Decisions

§§ It is often ventured that, in the forthcoming future, robot judges will write better judicial decisions[1022] than human judges.[1023] But know this: human judges,[1024] unlike robot-judges, are fully equipped to make sound value judgments.[1025] No surprise stems from the fact that value judgments inhere and permeate judicial decision-making.[1026] But here is the twist: Artificial Intelligence, if ever enters

[1022] Kozlov, Yuri/Shutova, Maria/Bajwa, Taaha, *Automated Judge is Not a Task For LegalTech But For DeepTech*, 24th February of 2025, 2025, p. 1 ("*Artificial intelligence is increasingly used in law, but current AI predictors face serious limitations in judicial processes. Most LegalTech tools rely on precedent-based statistical analysis, which cannot replicate true legal reasoning—rooted in logic, justice, and adaptability. Automating justice requires more than predictions. It demands deterministic, rule-based reasoning through strict algorithmization of legal norms and procedures. This shifts the challenge from LegalTech to DeepTech, involving formal logic, math modeling, and legal theory. This article explores the limitations of predictive AI in legal disputes and presents an alternative: JudgeAI. Unlike predictors, JudgeAI replicates legal reasoning with 96% accuracy in real cases*, offering transparent, *logic-driven decisions through algorithmic evidence analysis and behavior modelling*"). Italics added.

[1023] Volokh, Eugene, "Chief Justice Robots", *Duke Law Journal*, Volume 68, 2019, pp. 1135 and ff and passim ("*Say an AI program someday passes a Turing test, because it can converse in a way indistinguishable from a human. And say that its developers can then teach it to converse—and even present an extended persuasive argument—in a way indistinguishable from the sort of human we call a "lawyer."* The program could thus become an AI briefwriter, capable of regularly winning brief-writing competitions against human lawyers. *Once that happens (if it ever happens), this Essay argues, the same technology can be used to create AI judges, judges that we should accept as no less reliable (and more cost-effective) than human judges. If the software can create persuasive opinions, capable of regularly winning opinion-writing competitions against human judges—and if it can be adequately protected against hacking and similar attacks—we should in principle accept it as a judge, even if the opinions do not stem from human judgment*"). Italics added.

[1024] See: Zou, Mimi/Leffley, Ellen, "Generative Artificial Intelligence and Article 6 of the European Convention on Human Rights: The Right to a Human Judge?", Mimi Zou, Martin Ebers, Cristina Poncibò and Ryan Calo (Editors), *The Cambridge Handbook of Generative AI and the* Law, Cambridge, Cambridge University Press 2025, passim (championing for a "right to a human judge").

[1025] See: Davis, Joshua P., "Of Robolawyers and robojudges", *Hastings Law Journal*, Volume 73, Issue 5, 2022, pp. 1176–1201 (1198). See also: Davis, Joshua P., *Unnatural Law: AI, Consciousness, Ethics, and Legal Theory*. Cambridge: Cambridge University Press, 2023.

[1026] Davis, Joshua P., "Of Robolawyers and robojudges", *cit.*, pp. 1176–1201 (1198).

the courtroom,[1027] must rely on human value judgments embedded in past judicial decisions[1028] to generate outputs.[1029] And these are hardly uplifting news.

[1027] See: Grimm, Paul V./Grossman, Maura R./Gless, Sabine/Hildebrant, Mireille, "Artificial Justice: The Quandary of AI in the Courtroom", *Judicature International*, September 2022, Bolch Judicial Institute at Duke Law, Duke University School of Law, 2022, p. 1 ("*Commonplace as the technology is, AI can be so complex that even the most sophisticated computer scientists can have difficulty explaining it, much less unraveling the difficult ethical questions that arise when humans and algorithms are inextricably linked. And what happens when machine learned and AI-generated data enter the courtroom*? Should that evidence be considered reliable?"). Italics added. See on the multifarious issues arising out of evidence produced by Artificial Intelligence-powered devices in criminal trials: Gless, Sabine/Lederer, Fredric/Weigend, Thomas, "AI-Based Evidence in Criminal Trials? AI-Based Evidence in Criminal Trials?", *Tulsa Law Review*, Volume 59, Issue 1, 2024, p. 35 ("*The amount and importance of device evidence in criminal cases is bound to increase with the digital turn that has led to profound changes in transportation, medicine, and other important areas of human life. This development has been accompanied by an extensive monitoring of the human-robot-interaction, necessary to ensure safety (as in driving automation).* While device evidence gains impetus, it presents significant legal questions in adversarial as well as inquisitorial legal systems. *This is true especially when the devices that generate data proffered as evidence in a criminal case were not developed with criminal evidence law in mind. Criminal courts therefore face the question of whether to admit various kinds of device data offered as evidence*"). Italics added.

[1028] Davis, Joshua P., "Of Robolawyers and robojudges", *cit.*, pp. 1176–1201 (1198).

[1029] But see: Schwarcz, Daniel/Sam Manning/Patrick Barry/David R. Cleveland/JJ Prescott/Beverly Rich, "AI-Powered Lawyering: AI Reasoning Models, Retrieval Augmented Generation, and the Future of Legal practice", 2025, pp. 1–2 ("*This article examines two emerging AI innovations that may mitigate these lingering issues: Retrieval Augmented Generation (RAG), which grounds AI-powered analysis in legal sources, and AI reasoning models, which structure complex reasoning before generating output. We conducted the first randomized controlled trial assessing these technologies, assigning upper-level law students to complete six legal tasks using a RAG-powered legal AI tool (Vincent AI), an AI reasoning model (OpenAI's o1-preview), or no AI. We find that both AI tools significantly enhanced legal work quality, a marked contrast with previous research examining older large language models like GPT-4*"). Italics added.

§§ Worryingly, rigged past data[1030] may contain deep-rooted human biases that we may not wish to re-entrench into computer-generated algorithms[1031] that will decide our future.[1032] But much more lies beyond that.[1033]

§§ It bears mentioning that circumstances tend to change dramatically in judicial settings. Often, human beings may find themselves hemmed in, and their very lives are often budged by, fortunate strokes of serendipity. But here is the kicker: to be remotely

1030 Barocas, Solon/Selbst, Andrew D., "Big Data's Disparate Impact", *California Law Review*, Volume 104, 2016, pp. 671–682 (discussing how data is often flawed, rigged, incomplete, imperfect, and therefore algorithms inherit the prejudice of the original decision makers). But see: Citron, Danielle Keats/Pasquale, Frank, "The Scored Society: Due Process for Automated Predictions", *Washington Law Review*, Volume 89, 2014, pp. 1, 4–5 (highlighting how human beings programming automated systems is directly conducive to, and leads, to fundamentally inaccurate results since the source code, predictive algorithms and datasets may encompass human biases which, in turn, have a disparate impact on historically disadvantaged groups). But see: Bornstein, Stepanhie, "Antidiscriminatory Algorithms", *Alabama Law Review*, Volume 70, 2018, pp. 519, 524–528 (contending, however, that the tagged "facially neutral" algorithms producing discriminatory outcomes should be quashed).

1031 Balkin, Jack M., "The Three Laws of Robotics in the Age of Big Data", *Ohio State Law Journal*, Volume 78, Issue 5, 2017, pp. 1217–1241.

1032 *Tech, Bias and Housing Initiative, the Promise and Perils of Residential Proptech, Year 1, Research Summary Report, April 2023, TechEquity Collaborative*, p. 11, available at: https://techequity.us/wp-content/uploads/2023/04/TBHI-Y1-Research-Summary-Report.pdf (28.11.2024). ("*Once bad data enters the analysis of one factor, it gets baked into the subsequent process, multiplying the effect that one disadvantageous data point can have on someone's overall housing determination*"). Italics added.

1033 For instance, Artificial Intelligence, with the right settings, can classify relevant case law. See: Sargeant Holli/Izzidien, Ahmed/Steffek, Felix, "Topic classification of case law using a large language model and a new taxonomy for UK law: AI insights into summary judgment", *Artificial Intelligence and Law*, 2025, p. 1 ("*This paper addresses a critical gap in legal analytics by developing and applying a novel taxonomy for topic classification of summary judgment cases in the United Kingdom. Using a curated dataset of summary judgment cases, we use the Large Language Model Claude 3 Opus to explore functional topics and trends. We find that Claude 3 Opus correctly classified the topic with an accuracy of 87.13% and an F1 score of 0.87. The analysis reveals distinct patterns in the application of summary judgments across various legal domains. As case law in the United Kingdom is not originally labelled with keywords or a topic filtering option, the findings not only refine our understanding of the thematic underpinnings of summary judgments but also illustrate the potential of combining traditional and AI-driven approaches in legal classification.* Therefore, this paper provides a new and general taxonomy for UK law. The implications of this work serve as a foundation for further research and policy discussions in the field of judicial administration and computational legal research methodologies"). Italics added.

functional and tangentially accurate,[1034] Artificial Intelligence will need new data[1035] from humans to deftly capture the fundamental changes in circumstances to make new judgments.[1036] Compellingly, Artificial Intelligence, unlike humans, evince a lacklustre performance when met with the shifting narrative of uncertainty.[1037]

[1034] Judges are still looking for feasible pathways to deftly harness Artificial Intelligence in judicial settings. Unsurprisingly, definitional quandaries persist. See: Golobardes, Mireia Artigot i/ Gianluca Grasso/ Paola Iamiceli/Maria Rosaria Maugeri, "Artificial intelligence and justice: what challenges for courts and judicial decision-making?", *Artificial Intelligence, Judicial Decision-Making and Fundamental Rights, JuLIA ("Justice, fundamental rights and Artificial intelligence")*, Scuola Superiore della Magistratura, University of Trento, European Union, 2024, p. 9 ("*Although the use of AI in the field of justice has not (yet) entered the ordinary practice of judicial decision-making, its impact is real and bears consideration well before its actualization. In fact, critical challenges are posed by existing experiments that seek to empower search engines through AI and machine learning and by testing tools for online dispute resolution based on the use of AI technologies. How are these tools designed, and by whom? What data, i.a., past judicial decisions, feed machine learning*? Who should select this data and be responsible for feeding the system at time of development and, later, during its use? How and to what extent could this data be anonymized and by whom? What is an adequate amount of data needed for machine learning? How are biases prevented? *Does AI reduce the limits of human rationality in judicial decision-making, its errors and its biases, or does it generate new errors and biases? How can due process and a fair trial be ensured when AI is involved? To what extent can the algorithm be "explained" and support a sufficiently motivated decision? What is the expected output of a given AI-based tool due that is to be used in the field of judicial decision-making?*"). Italics added.

[1035] Davis, Joshua P., "Of Robolawyers and robojudges", *cit.*, pp. 1176–1201 (1198).

[1036] Davis, Joshua P., "Of Robolawyers and robojudges", *cit.*, pp. 1176–1201 (1198).

[1037] Fellin, Teppo/Hollweg, Mathias, *Theory Is All You Need: AI, Human Cognition, and Decision Making*, Oxford, 2025, pp. 1–53 (43) ("*We anticipate that AI will help humans make better decisions across many domains, especially in settings that are conducive to routine, repetition, and computation. However, decisions under uncertainty—given the emphasis on unpredictability, surprise, and the new—provide a realm that is not readily amenable to data- or frequency-based prediction and associated computation. Thus we question the idea that AI will (or should) replace human decision making* (e.g., Kahneman, 2018)"). Italics added.

§§ Case in point, Artificial Intelligence fails to grasp, let alone replicate,[1038] human cognition[1039] in judicial settings,[1040] which is firmly rooted in justice concerns[1041] and human values. On one hand, human cognition is two-fold. It is both **backward-looking** (as it can delve into the past to portend the future with a human touch)

[1038] But see: Li, Yuran et al., "Leveraging LLMs as Meta-Judges: A Multi-Agent Framework for Evaluating LLM Judgments", available at: arXiv:2504.17087v1 [cs.AI] 23 Apr 2025, p. 1 ("*Large language models (LLMs) are being widely applied across various fields, but as tasks become more complex, evaluating their responses is increasingly challenging. Compared to human evaluators, the use of LLMs to support performance evaluation offers a more efficient alternative. However, most studies focus mainly on aligning LLMs' judgments with human preferences, overlooking the existence of biases and mistakes in human judgment.* Furthermore, how to select suitable LLM judgments given multiple potential LLM responses remains underexplored. To address these two aforementioned issues, we propose a three-stage meta-judge selection pipeline: 1) developing a comprehensive rubric with GPT4 and human experts, 2) using three advanced LLM agents to score judgments, and 3) applying a threshold to filter out low-scoring judgments. *Compared to methods using a single LLM as both judge and meta-judge, our pipeline introduces multi-agent collaboration and a more comprehensive rubric. Experimental results on the JudgeBench dataset show about 15.55% improvement compared to raw judgments and about 8.37% improvement over the single-agent baseline. Our work demonstrates the potential of LLMs as meta-judges and lays the foundation for future research on constructing preference datasets for LLM-as-a-judge reinforcement learning*"). Italics added.

[1039] Fellin, Teppo/Hollweg, Mathias, *Theory Is All You Need: AI, Human Cognition, and Decision Making, cit.*, pp. 1–53 (43) ("*While AI inspired models of cognition continue to emphasize the similarities between machines and humans, we argue that AI's data and prediction-orientation does not capture human cognition*"). Italics added.

[1040] But see: Hodge, Samuel D., "Revolutionizing Justice: Unleashing the Power of Artificial Intelligence", *SMU Science and Technology Law Review*, Volume 26, 2023, p. 217 ("*Linking artificial intelligence and the law, however, is a natural progression. Both operate in similar fashions:* each examines and applies "historical examples in order to infer rules to apply to new situations"). Italics added. Internal citations omitted. See also: Sourdin, Tania, "Judge V Robot? Artificial Intelligence and Judicial Decision-Making", *UNSW Law Journal*, Volume 41, Issue 4, 2018, p. 1123 ("*does this mean that judges will be replaced by technology? Arguably not, or at least not initially. This is partly because there are so many factors that impact on judicial decision-making. The Australian Law Reform Commission has noted that such factors include induction and intuition, as well as the capacity to assess the social impact of decisions*"). Italics added.

[1041] See: Chen, Benjamin/Hermstrüwer, Yoan/Pascal Langenbach/Alexander Stremitzer/Tobia, Kevin, "Mitigating the Judicial Human-AI Fairness Gap", *Center for Law & Economics Working Paper Series*, Working Paper Series Number 07/2025, ETH Zürich, Switzerland, April 2025, 2025, pp. 1–27 (1) ("Are robot judges perceived as less fair than human judges? If so, how can this perceived judicial human-AI fairness gap be mitigated? We conduct a large online experiment with more than 4,800 observations to explore whether delegating judicial tasks to algorithms affects perceived procedural fairness and how human-in-the-loop interventions might offset any fairness gap. Participants are randomly assigned to assess one of the following conditions: a pure robot court (no human oversight), a pure human court (no algorithmic decision aids), or a hybrid court (a human judge assisted by algorithmic decision aids). Within the human and the hybrid conditions, we further vary whether the human judge conducts a thorough (high involvement) or brief (low involvement) review. *Confirming prior research, we find robust evidence of a judicial human-AI fairness gap: participants perceive robot courts as less fair than human courts. Crucially, even low human involvement fully closes this gap. Although the fairness gap persists among Black participants, it is significantly smaller than the gap seen among White participants, highlighting an ethnic disparity. Overall, our results suggest that delegating judicial tasks to algorithmic systems may not*

and **forward-looking**[1042] (as it can create blazingly new theoretical underpinnings to chart the path ahead for new judicial trends while addressing the underlying intricacies of the lawsuit at hand).

§§ On the other hand, algorithmic decision-making is mostly **backward-looking** (in that is utterly unable to accurately forecast the future as it heavily relies upon past[1043] data[1044] in which patterns are embedded to come up with a decision that nonetheless fails to tackle the nuances of the topic at hand).

§§ Whilst Artificial Intelligence excels in some time-consuming legal tasks[1045] and performs uncannily well in a sheer number of recreational chores,[1046] it nonetheless falls noticeably short of capturing the nuances underpinning each lawsuit[1047] that

---

undermine perceived procedural fairness if they remain subject to human review. However, our findings also raise the concern that nominal human oversight could be used to legitimize substantively unfair algorithmic procedures in the eyes of ordinary citizens"). Italics added.

[1042] Fellin, Teppo/Hollweg, Mathias, *Theory Is All You Need: AI, Human Cognition, and Decision Making, cit.*, pp. 1–53 (43) ("*We argue that humans—compared to computers and AI—have unique cognitive capacities that center on forward-looking beliefs and theorizing*: the *ability to engage in novel causal reasoning, problem solving, and experimentation*"). Italics added.

[1043] Di Stefano, Stephania et al., "European Journal of Legal Studies Symposium Editorial: is fairness in digital governance a trap?", *European Journal of Legal Studies, Special Issue on Law and Technology*, February 2025, 2025, p. 11 ("*Since machine learning algorithms operate on the expectation that the future will look similar to the past (and that anything which falls outside this backward-looking pattern raises suspicion*"). Italics added.

[1044] Fellin, Teppo/Hollweg, Mathias, *Theory Is All You Need: AI, Human Cognition, and Decision Making, cit.*, pp. 1–53 (43) ("AI cannot causally map and project into or anticipate the future, as illustrated by LLMs which are delimited by past data").

[1045] Nielsen, Aileen/Stavroula Skylaki/Milda Norkute/Alexander Stremitzer, "Building a better lawyer: Experimental evidence that artificial intelligence can increase legal work efficiency", *Journal of Empirical Legal Studies*, Volume 21, 2024, pp. 979–1022 (979) ("*Our results show that AI support can dramatically increase the efficiency of legal task completion*, but finding the optimal form of AI assistance is a fine-tuning exercise"). Italics added.

[1046] Fellin, Teppo/Hollweg, Mathias, Theory Is All You Need: AI, Human Cognition, and Decision Making, *cit.*, pp. 1–53 (3) ("*Artificial intelligence (AI) now matches or outperforms humans in any number of games, standardized tests, and cognitive tasks that involve high-level thinking and strategic reasoning. For example, AI engines can readily beat humans in chess, which for decades served as a key benchmark of AI capability* (Bory 2019; Simon 1985). *AI systems also now perform extremely well in complex games (like Diplomacy or Stratego) that involve sophisticated negotiation, complex interaction with others, alliances, deception, and understanding other players' intentions* (e.g., Ananthaswamy 2022). *Current AI models also outperform over 90% of humans in various professional qualification exams, like the Bar exam in law and the CPA exam in accounting* (Achiam et al. 2023). *AI has also made radical strides in medical diagnosis, beating highly-trained medical professionals in diagnosing some illnesses* (e.g., Zhou et al. 2023). These rapid advances have led some AI scholars to argue that even the most human of traits, like consciousness, will in principle soon be replicable by machines (e.g., Butlin et al. 2023; Goyal and Bengio 2022). In all, AI is rapidly devising algorithms that "think humanly," "think rationally," "act humanly," and "act rationally" (Csaszar and Steinberger 2022"). Italics added.

[1047] Scholars have not been slow to identify the perceived challenges arising out from the deployment of Artificial Intelligence in the courtroom. See: Gless, Sabine, "AI in the Courtroom: A Comparative Analysis of Machine Learning in Criminal Trials", *Georgetown Journal of International Law*, Volume 51, 2020, p. 250 ("*Where machine evidence is proffered as evidence in a criminal trial, it*

find its way to the courtroom. Compellingly, there is no such thing as two identical lawsuits in judicial settings (except made, perhaps, to class actions).

§§ Unable to grasp this ground truth, and bereft of an entrenched pattern to build upon, robot-judges, robot-prosecutors[1048] or robot-lawyers[1049] will either provide a downright bogus opinion[1050] or a plausible, yet inaccurate, one. Which brings me

---

must be adequately contextualized and tested for reliability. Such evidence—just like human testimony—is not infallible. Especially where the digital output of an opaque device, initially produced as technology for a consumer need, is accepted as a conduit of fact or circumstantial evidence, legislatures and courts must address this issue both open- mindedly and critically. With the rise of AI in all areas of human life, it seems especially important that legal scholarship point out that our presumptions of regularity and impartiality in machine workings are often inaccurate. Many factors have to be taken into account. Research conducted across a variety of fields has demonstrated that the *physical shape and cognitive capacity of an AI-driven device directly affects our perception of its reliability, soundness, and overall "character." We seldom realize this fact and even more rarely question what features of any device should trigger confidence or doubt in the reliability of is findings. From a legal perspective, the use of AI-generated evidence in criminal proceedings remains an enigma. Laws do not provide rules around scrutinizing "intelligent machines" for credibility*"). Italics added.

[1048] Anderson, Stephen E., "Should Robots Prosecute and Defend?", *Oklahoma Law Review*, Volume 72, Number 1, 2019, pp. 1–20 (1) ("*Even when we achieve the 'holy grail' of artificial intelligence—machine intelligence that is at least as smart as a human being in every area of thought—there may be classes of decisions for which it is intrinsically important to retain a human in the loop. On the common account of American criminal adjudication, the role of prosecutor seems to include such decisions given the largely unreviewable declination authority, whereas the role of defense counsel would seem fully susceptible of automation. And even for the prosecutor, the benefits of automation might outweigh the intrinsic decision-making loss, given that the ultimate decision—by judge or jury—should remain a human (or at least role reversible) one*"). Italics added.

[1049] Anderson, Stephen E., "Should Robots Prosecute and Defend?", *cit*., pp. 1–20 (1) "*Thus, while many details need to be worked out, we might within decades have a criminal justice system consisting of robo-defense lawyers and robo-prosecutors.* And even if we never do, their consideration *provides another lens through which to consider these roles and, ultimately, our criminal justice system*"). Italics added.

[1050] See: Part III, Chap. 3, Sects. 3.1.5.4–3.1.5.4.1.1 of this book (on the functional aspects of Critical Artificial Intelligence Studies, with a sharper focus on the harmful effects of Artificial Intelligence-embedded technologies, namely Large Language Models and its multifarious downsides and shortcomings). See also: Part IV, Chap. 4, Sects. 4.1.9.1–4.1.9.2 (on ChatGPT's functional abilities). See also: Part IV, Chap. 4, Sects. 4.1.9–4.1.9.7 (on ChatGPT's functional drawbacks and pitfalls, including, but no limited to, "hallucinations"). See: Part III, Chap. 3, Sects. 3.1.5.6–3.1.5.6.1 of this book (on Critical Artificial Intelligence Studies, with a sharper focus on the harmful effects of Large Language Models' medical hallucinations that are poised to undermine its overall trustworthiness). See: Part III, Chap. 3, Sects. 3.1.5.6–3.1.5.6.1 of this book (on Critical Artificial Intelligence Studies, with a sharper focus on the harmful effects of Large Language Models' medical hallucinations that are poised to undermine its overall trustworthiness). See: Watcher, Sandra, "Limitations and Loopholes in the EU AI Act and AI Liability Directives: What This Means for the European Union, the United States, and Beyond", *Yale Journal of Law & Technology*, Volume 26, Issue 3, 2024, pp. 671–672 ("*Predictive and generative artificial intelligence (AI) have both become integral parts of our lives through their use in making highly impactful decisions.* AI systems are already deployed widely—for example, in employment, healthcare, insurance, finance, education, public administration, and criminal justice. Yet severe ethical issues, such as bias and discrimination, privacy invasiveness, opaqueness, and environmental costs of these systems, are well known. *Generative AI (GAI) creates hallucinations and inaccurate or harmful information, which can lead*

to the second line of reasoning against the deployment of robot-judges to decide lawsuits in judicial courts.

§§ It is pivotally important to aver that **human behaviour is shaped by underlying values, whereas machines' predictions are shaped by patterns with an entrenched presence in the dataset**. Which prompts the vexing question: why must not machines be entrusted with the task of making high stake decisions in judicial settings? Machines, unlike human beings, have no human values[1051] (e.g. sympathy, empathy, judicial independence, forbearance, lenience). Instead, they operate through deep-seated patterns and entrenched **optimal predictive rules**. To illustrate, take a hard look on how Artificial Intelligence mechanically operates[1052] through the lens of **overfitting**.

§§ As noted above, **overfitting** occurs when a machine learning algorithm builds on patterns embedded in a dataset, thereby creating **optimal predictive rules** to fit them accordingly. By virtue of these patterns arising out of randomness, they will not be the just the same in the real-world data. Relatedly, **optimal predictive rules** generated to fit them will not **generalizable** to the outer world; **overall accuracy** will shrink accordingly. Note, though, that some machine learning algorithms—e.g., those that embody **bagging algorithms**—are not as prone[1053] to be affected by **overfitting**.[1054]

---

to misinformation, disinformation, and the erosion of scientific knowledge. The Artificial Intelligence Act (AIA), Product Liability Directive, and the Artificial Intelligence Liability Directive reflect Europe's attempt to curb some of these issues. With the legal reach of these policies going far beyond Europe, their impact on the United States and the rest of the world cannot be overstated. In this Essay, I show how the strong lobbying efforts of big tech companies and member states were unfortunately *able to water down much of the AIA. An overreliance on self-regulation, self-certification, weak oversight and investigatory mechanisms, and far-reaching exceptions for both the public and private sectors are the product of this lobbying. Next, I reveal the similar enforcement limitations of the liability frameworks, which focus on material harm while ignoring harm that is immaterial, monetary, and societal, such as bias, hallucinations, and financial losses due to faulty AI products. Lastly, I explore how these loopholes can be closed to create a framework that effectively guards against novel risks caused by AI in the European Union, the United States, and beyond*"). Italics added.

[1051] See: Sourdin, Tania, *Judges, Technology and Artificial Intelligence: The Artificial Judge*, Cheltenham: Edward Elgar, 2021, p. 257 ("*it is inevitable that a values-based approach must be incorporated into such a framework ... this should reflect the values underpinning the judicial system within a particular jurisdiction*").

[1052] Note, though, that "current AI systems have significant limitations and require human oversight; there are no fully autonomous AI systems capable of operating independently within courts". See: European Commission for the Efficiency of Justice (CEPEJ), *Working Group on Cyberjustice and Artificial Intelligence (CEPEJ-GT-CYBERJUST), Advisory Board on Artificial Intelligence (CEPEJ-AIAB), 1st AIAB Report on the use of Artificial Intelligence (AI) in the Judiciary based on the information contained in the resource centre on Cyberjustice and AI*, European Commission for Efficiency of Justice, Strasburg, 28th February of 2025, 2025, p. 4.

[1053] Lehr, David/Ohm, Paul, "Playing with the Data: What Legal Scholars Should Learn About Machine Learning", *cit.*, pp. 653–718.

[1054] See: Berk, Richard A., *Statistical Learning from a Regression Perspective*, *cit.*, p. 42 ("A major difficulty in statistical learning is **overfitting**. *Very flexible fitting procedures will tend to respond to idiosyncratic features of the data, producing results that do not generalize well to new data*").

§§ It doesn't take much to understand that human judges operate quite differently from machines. Human judges, unlike robot-judges, will not generalize the patterns with an entrenched presence in a given dataset. Instead, human judges will carefully review the evidence pertaining to each lawsuit and render a judicial decision accordingly. But, again, much more lies beyond that.

§§ One should not lose sight of the fact that Artificial Intelligence-embedded Natural Language Processing (NLP) systems have traditionally floundered with understanding the whopping variety of syntactical fluctuation, linguistic fluidity, semantic ambivalence, semantic vagueness, use of words to convey empathy, and abstract obscurity that forms part of a broader linguistic apparatus within which human written and spoken communication[1055] operates. Which may undermine the principle of respect for fundamental rights.[1056]

§§ Besides, a piece of empirical evidence used **«prompt engineering»** to gauge whether and to what extent ChatGPT could engage in legal reasoning[1057] while assuming the role of an appellate judge and accordingly render a judicial decision based on the materials timely provided.[1058] Pundits sought to ascertain the degree

---

Italics and bold added. See: Berk, Richard A., *Statistical Learning from a Regression Perspective, cit.*, p. 169 ("Averaging over a collection of fitted values can help compensate for *overfitting. That is, the averaging tends to cancel out results shaped by idiosyncratic features of the data.* One can then obtain more stable fitted values and more honest assessments of how good the fit really is"). Italics added. A cohort of statisticians go at lengths as to contend that certain **bagging algorithms** are not only resistant to **overfitting**, but, and foremost, fundamentally immune from it. See: Leo Breiman and Adele Cutler have contended that **random forests** "does not overfit." See: Breiman, Leo/Cutler, Adele, "Random Forests", https://www.stat.berkeley.edu/~breiman/RandomForests/cc_home.htm (last visited March. 4, 2025). See also: Breiman, "Random Forests", *cit.*, p. 7 ("*This result explains why random forests do not overfit as more trees are added*, but produce a limiting value of the generalization error"). Italics added.

[1055] Surden, Harry, "ChatGPT, AI Large Language Models, and Law", *cit.*, pp. 1941–1972 (1947).

[1056] European Commission for the Efficiency of Justice (CEPEJ), *European ethical Charter on the use of Artificial Intelligence in judicial systems and their environment*, Adopted at the 31st plenary meeting of the CEPEJ (Strasbourg, 3–4 December 2018), Council of Europe, European Commission for the Efficiency of Justice (CEPEJ), 2018, p. 9.

[1057] But see: Schwarcz, Daniel/Sam Manning/Patrick Barry/David R. Cleveland/JJ Prescott/Beverly Rich, "AI-Powered Lawyering: AI Reasoning Models, Retrieval Augmented Generation, and the Future of Legal practice", 2025, pp. 1–2 ("*This article examines two emerging AI innovations that may mitigate these lingering issues: Retrieval Augmented Generation (RAG), which grounds AI-powered analysis in legal sources, and AI reasoning models, which structure complex reasoning before generating output. We conducted the first randomized controlled trial assessing these technologies, assigning upper-level law students to complete six legal tasks using a RAG-powered legal AI tool (Vincent AI), an AI reasoning model (OpenAI's o1-preview), or no AI. We find that both AI tools significantly enhanced legal work quality, a marked contrast with previous research examining older large language models like GPT-4*"). Italics added.

[1058] Posner, Eric A./Saran, Shivam, "Judge AI: Assessing Large Language Models in Judicial Decision-Making", *The University of Chicago, Coase-Sandor Institute for Law and Economics, The Law School, Coase-Sandor Institute for Law and Economics Research Paper n. º 25–03*, January 2025, 2025, pp. 1–41 (25–26).

to which ChatGPT's decision-making could be shaped through a few targeted interventions.[1059] A broad a range of *prompt-engineering* techniques aimed at steering ChatGPT towards decision-making patterns akin to that of human judges were empirically experimented.[1060] But to no avail.

§§ Compellingly, the cluster of findings arising out of a budding piece of empirical evidence bestow upon the public the vividly clear impression that ChatGPT is, above else, a legal formalist[1061] that pays little to none regard for non-legal factors.[1062] In stark contrast, human judges are swayed by non-legal factors.[1063] Such

---

[1059] Posner, Eric A./Saran, Shivam, "Judge AI: Assessing Large Language Models in Judicial Decision-Making", *cit.*, pp. 1–41 (25–26).

[1060] Posner, Eric A./Saran, Shivam, "Judge AI: Assessing Large Language Models in Judicial Decision-Making", *cit.*, pp. 1–41 (25–26).

[1061] But see: Schwarcz, Daniel/Sam Manning/Patrick Barry/David R. Cleveland/JJ Prescott/Beverly Rich, "AI-Powered Lawyering: AI Reasoning Models, Retrieval Augmented Generation, and the Future of Legal practice", 2025, pp. 1–2 ("*Moreover, we find that these models maintain the efficiency benefits associated with use of older AI technologies. Our findings show that AI assistance significantly boosts productivity in five out of six tested legal tasks, with Vincent yielding statistically significant gains of approximately 38% to 115% and o1- preview increasing productivity by 34% to 140%, with particularly strong effects in complex tasks like drafting persuasive letters and analyzing complaints.* ***Notably, o1-preview improved the analytical depth of participants' work product but resulted in some hallucinations, whereas Vincent AI-aided participants produced roughly the same amount of hallucinations as participants who did not use AI at all.*** *These findings suggest that integrating domain-specific RAG capabilities with reasoning models could yield synergistic improvements, shaping the next generation of AI-powered legal tools and the future of lawyering more generally*"). Italics and bold added. See: Watcher, Sandra, "Limitations and Loopholes in the EU AI Act and AI Liability Directives: What This Means for the European Union, the United States, and Beyond", *Yale Journal of Law & Technology*, Volume 26, Issue 3, 2024, pp. 671–672 ("*Predictive and generative artificial intelligence (AI) have both become integral parts of our lives through their use in making highly impactful decisions.* AI systems are already deployed widely—for example, in employment, healthcare, insurance, finance, education, public administration, and criminal justice. Yet severe ethical issues, such as bias and discrimination, privacy invasiveness, opaqueness, and environmental costs of these systems, are well known. *Generative AI (GAI) creates hallucinations and inaccurate or harmful information, which can lead to misinformation, disinformation, and the erosion of scientific knowledge. The Artificial Intelligence Act (AIA), Product Liability Directive, and the Artificial Intelligence Liability Directive reflect Europe's attempt to curb some of these issues. With the legal reach of these policies going far beyond Europe, their impact on the United States and the rest of the world cannot be overstated.* In this Essay, I show how the strong lobbying efforts of big tech companies and member states were unfortunately *able to water down much of the AIA. An overreliance on self-regulation, self-certification, weak oversight and investigatory mechanisms, and far-reaching exceptions for both the public and private sectors are the product of this lobbying. Next, I reveal the similar enforcement limitations of the liability frameworks, which focus on material harm while ignoring harm that is immaterial, monetary, and societal, such as bias, hallucinations, and financial losses due to faulty AI products. Lastly, I explore how these loopholes can be closed to create a framework that effectively guards against novel risks caused by AI in the European Union, the United States, and beyond*"). Italics added.

[1062] Posner, Eric A./Saran, Shivam, "Judge AI: Assessing Large Language Models in Judicial Decision-Making", *cit.*, pp. 1–41 (25–26).

[1063] Posner, Eric A./Saran, Shivam, "Judge AI: Assessing Large Language Models in Judicial Decision-Making", *cit.*, pp. 1–41 (25–26).

as empathy,[1064] sympathy,[1065] and so forth. ChatGPT is therefore a legal formalist, as opposed to a decision-maker.[1066]

§§ Compellingly, no amount of *prompt engineering* can budge ChatGPT from deeply-rooted ideas it has ingested from reams of data and billions of texts[1067] harvested from the internet. The key takeaway is that, at its best, ChatGPT is a decent predictor.[1068] At its worst, ChatGPT is a lousy decision-maker whose lacklustre performance should keep us eagerly awaken at night.

5.1.9 Concluding Remarks

§§ Artificial Intelligence-embedded technologies represent a blazingly new path, a foray into uncharted territory that holds a wealth, and a treasure trove, of scorching

---

[1064] See: Newell, Lauren A., "Rebooting Empathy for the Digital Generation Lawyer", *Ohio State Journal on Dispute Resolution*, Volume 34, Issue 1, 2019, 1–96 (4–6) (contending that empathy is now needed more than ever amidst a digital world in which people somewhere along the line ceased to communicate "face to face". Rebooting empathy in the remit of administration of justice is the way forward in this scholar's insightful view).

[1065] Posner, Eric A./Saran, Shivam, "Judge AI: Assessing Large Language Models in Judicial Decision-Making", *cit.*, pp. 1–41 (25–26). See also: Putnam, Robert D., *Bowling Alone: The Collapse and Revival of American Community*, Touchstone Books by Simon & Schuster; 1st edition (August 7, 2001), 2001, pp. 19 ff (stating that "*The definitions and understanding of social capital are by no means univocal. The term "social capital" was first coined in 1916 by L.J. Hanifan, the supervisor of rural schools in West Virginia, who argued that the strengthening of social networks ultimately benefited the entire community. The individual is helpless socially, if left to himself.... If he comes into contact with his neighbors, and they with other neighbors, there will be an accumulation of social capital,* which may immediately satisfy his social needs and which may bear a social potentiality sufficient to the substantial improvement of living conditions in the whole community. *The community as a whole will benefit by the cooperation of all its parts, while the individual will find in his associations the advantages of the help,* ***the sympathy****, and the fellowship of his neighbors*"). Italics and bolds added. See also: Ludwig, Bernd, "Sympathy for the Devil (s)? Personality and Legal Coercion in Kant's Doctrine of Law", *Jurisprudence*, 6, 2015, pp. 34 ff (arguing that human beings have certain moral duties to abide by, such as treating others, including legal officials, with utmost respect); Correia, Vasco, "Bias and Fallacies: The Role of Motivated Irrationality in Fallacious Reasoning", *Cogency*, 3, 2011, pp. 108 ff (emphasizes that oftentimes people tend to jump into conclusions and are prone to make steadfast judgments with little to none regard for its intrinsic accuracy. Which amounts to either conscious or unconscious biases. This is acutely important with regard of lawyer's actions in a court of law or (in an overarching sense) in dispute resolution settings. As it is an utterly impossible task to ascertain as to whether and to what extent a "lawyer is deliberately trying to manipulate the audience, or whether the desire to win the case (*or sympathy towards the client*, etc.) unconsciously affects her judgment…"). Italics added.

[1066] Posner, Eric A./Saran, Shivam, "Judge AI: Assessing Large Language Models in Judicial Decision-Making", *cit.*, pp. 1–41 (25–26).

[1067] Posner, Eric A./Saran, Shivam, "Judge AI: Assessing Large Language Models in Judicial Decision-Making", *cit.*, pp. 1–41 (25–26).

[1068] Agrawal, Ajay/Gans, Joshua/Goldfarb, Avi, *Prediction Machines: The Simple Economics of Artificial Intelligence*, 2nd Edition. Massachusetts: Harvard Business Review Press, 2022, pp. 1–304.

challenges that should not leave anyone lukewarm. When it comes to cutting-edge technology, you better not try your luck and the let the chips fall where they may.

§§ Artificial Intelligence-embedded technology, albeit a seemingly bedazzling gift to humankind, is not without multifarious caveats. This has been a fodder for thought ever since the Darthmouth Proposal for Artificial Intelligence was brought forth back in 1956, which has blazed a new trail for the heated debate around which the sough-after fusion between humans and machines revolves, which still resonates today.

§§ Artificial Intelligence-embedded technology is not an ordinary taxonomy. It holds the blueprint of our destiny and the disruptive power it carries. This is about the unfolding of newer and higher forms of intrusiveness in our daily lives that extend beyond our collective grasp. The newly-crafted concept of *Critical Artificial Intelligence Studies* holds nothing short of an assertion.

§§ *Critical Artificial Intelligence Studies* (CAIS) seeks to set out a broad roadmap for the safe use of technology in an overarching sense. To cater for that, CAIS charts a course, and maps out a pathway, forward with a view to anticipating how Artificial Intelligence-embedded technologies may fare in the long-term. CAIS accordingly queries how central are the principles underpinning the brawny exercise of authority to secure *Algorithmic Common Good* (ACG).

§§ The great bulk of issues concerning Artificial Intelligence-embedded technologies are familiar, well-worn, and well-canvassed in, which yields further insights on the potential of advanced technology (or lack thereof) to contribute exponentially to the overall betterment of humankind.

§§ However, whilst the legal community is rallying around the idea according to which technology *must* be timely regulated, it remains nonetheless deeply divided and unclear on *how* should technology be regulated. This is a pressing issue that is in dire need of being shrewdly addressed or inordinate harms may otherwise occur. Spoiler alert: piecemeal, patchwork and haphazard measures (such the right to explanation) will not suffice in this regard. Which is nothing but formulaic: citizens are woefully ill-equipped to understand the multiple correlations made by machine learning algorithms.

§§ Citizens will most likely shy away from promptly accepting pearls of algorithmic wisdom that they are utterly unable to understand, which will accordingly undermine the much-needed legitimacy of algorithmic decision-making. As a result, the lack of trust on algorithmic decision-making will beget an abridged law abidingness. For that reason, the outputs generated by machine learning algorithms should be *interpretable*, rather than merely *explainable.*

§§ *Critical Artificial Intelligence Studies* (CAIS) therefore seeks to shine a keen light on the harmful effects arising out of state-of-the-art technology and the extent to which the latter degrade, rather than enhance, human flourishing.

§§ *Critical Artificial Intelligence Studies* (CAIS) aims to propel forward a *safe* and *controllable* environment whereby humans can *trust* and *interpret* the pearls of algorithmic wisdom produced by Artificial Intelligence-embedded technologies. This is the gist of *Interpretable* and *Controllable* Artificial Intelligence, which forms part of a broader technological apparatus within which *Algorithmic Common Good* (ACG) operates.

§§ *Critical Artificial Intelligence Studies* (CAIS) thereupon frames Artificial Intelligence-embedded technologies as an *interpretable* and *controllable* environment against the backdrop of which *Algorithmic Dictatorship*-borne racial disparities are to be both dwindled and brushed aside while paving the way for *Algorithmic Common Good*.

§§ *Critical Artificial Intelligence Studies* sharply contends that Artificial Intelligence-embedded technologies are on the cusp of spinning into the realm of pervasiveness, thereby hurling human beings into a dystopian reality whereby truths and lies dovetail seamlessly. The darndest effects arising out of deepfakes and the LLM's hallucinations neatly encapsulate, hands-in-glove, this loathsome reality that sidesteps the normal course of events.

§§ Artificial Intelligence-embedded technologies therefore bestows upon humankind a particularly clear window on the battle between light and darkness that is poised to overhaul our lives beyond recognition. Oddly, human beings are increasingly losing sight of the fact that their fundamental rights are wearing down/tailing off amidst the hustle and bustle of daily life.

§§ Human beings are so buoyed and enthralled by the perks of technology that they are utterly unable to grasp the unvarnished truth that lies beneath both the shapeless stream of foam and the smokescreen of distractions: Artificial Intelligence-embedded technologies speak of things in the same wavelength of mayhem.

§§ Although Artificial Intelligence-embedded technologies carry a vibe of ambition (piercing into every single aspect of our daily lives), little emphasis has nonetheless been placed on where the inordinate costs of that lofty ambition may fall.

§§ It is true that Artificial Intelligence-anchored technologies provide a hint towards breaking ground in ventures leading to global blossoming, but truer still the boundaries between *benign* leaps forward (that carries forwards an overhyped promise to make humankind better-off) and *malicious* breakthroughs (that make humankind worse-off while hastening the demise of the Rule of Law) are on the brink of becoming increasingly blurred, if not outright dispelled.

§§ Aside from this odd quandary, the geographic spread of Artificial Intelligence-embedded technologies connects the information society along umpteenth digital routes. Whilst Artificial Intelligence-anchored technologies are spearheading policy transformation while enjoying global blossoming, citizens tend to harbour the propensity to distrust the mighty power it wields nonetheless.

§§ This deep-seated distrust is shaping up to lurch algorithmic decision-making into a legitimacy crisis that may be rendered impossible to unwind somewhere along the line. Relatedly, the unbridled rise of Artificial Intelligence-embedded technologies and the robust protection of fundamental rights must not be poles apart. We are better off keeping them together accordingly.

§§ That is the only way forward with a view to build a tangible roadmap that ensures that the gist of citizens' fundamental rights retain vitality amidst the age of *Algorithmic Dictatorship*. To cater for that, policymakers and lawmakers must not shy away from pouring in whopping efforts to chart the path ahead for *human flourishing* amidst the age of *Algorithmic Dictatorship* that is upon us. This is a place to dwell permanently.

§§ *Algorithmic Dictatorship* has an entrenched presence in algorithmic decision-making. Distorting this ground truth by either turning a blind eye to it, or simply looking the other way, would amount to a dereliction of our duty to throw the algorithmic injustice out of balance. Which prompts the vexing question: what gets us past this gruesome situation? For now, suffice to say that the consequences of a fallout at the border of algorithmic fairness would be steep. We must credit *Algorithmic Dictatorship* with that level of sophistication and deleterious power.

§§ Strikingly, algorithmic injustice does not need a reason to wreak havoc in algorithmic decision-making, nor does need an excuse. Compellingly, algorithmic injustice, if not deftly tackled heads-on, is set to leave algorithmic decision-making in shambles and torn into pieces thereupon. If pundits refrain themselves from toiling towards the protection of swiftly fading fundamental rights amidst the age of *Algorithmic Dictatorship*, they will most likely have their fingerprints on it.

§§ Pundits should accordingly fight shy of, and keep aloof from, having algorithmic decision-making out in a storm without an umbrella. Before you, dear reader, start firing off questions while urging to be clued in, bear this assertion very firmly in mind instead: *Algorithmic Dictatorship* is in dire need of quashing, which would be the best of all outcomes for mankind. Failing which, an ominous portent for the future lies before us. So, now you, dear reader, know that not only *Algorithmic Dictatorship* needs to be trounced, but, and foremost, *Algorithmic Common Good* must be firmly rooted in both the *Rule of Law* and *Procedural Rule of Law*.

§§ Bearing this background very firmly in mind, a spate of vexing questions emerges: to what extent is the ongoing war waged by darkness against light—that rages unseen at the outskirts of our variegated reality—worth taking part of? Are the mental throes arising out of an ever-evolving technology worth coming to blows over? Is the quest to find out what's under the hood of the complex trappings, and the beneath the surface of infallibility, of Artificial Intelligence-embedded technologies worth taking part of? Are the inner workings of Artificial Intelligence-anchored technologies intrinsically benign or fundamentally malign; even mischievous? Is the action of returning to a former or less developed state of Artificial Intelligence a scenario worth taking stock of? Is the endless regress to a state of pure mental privacy worth fighting for?

§§ On the flip side, what can be done to soothe out, and fundamentally allay, the harmful effects of an ever-present technology that is bound to *control* our thoughts, emotions, likes and dislikes that we collectively hold so dear? Does that feel too close to home? Does that hit home? If so, what can be done about it?

§§ Dear reader, there is no point in nursing hold wounds on *how* far back the jaw-dropping achievements of advanced technology go and *what* we could, and should have, done about it. Nor should you hold grudges on *who* should have done something about it. We have long passed that first critical stage.

§§ All too often human beings refrain themselves from shifting their gaze inward in pursuit of actionable lines of action to be taken envisioning an inevitable coexistence between human beings and cutting-edge technology in decades to come. This is an all-too-common pattern in dire need of quashing. A key takeaway jumps out as ripe in this juncture: we must learn from the lessons arising out of the steep learning curve of our lives. Hardly any surprise flows from the fact that the virulent effects of advanced technology on your quotidian lies at its heart.

§§ This finding sits easily with the discourse around which the coexistence between human beings and state-of-the-art technology revolves. Such a coexistence is not amenable to be reasoned away by our brains though. Human beings must therefore come to terms with the fact that Artificial Intelligence-embedded technologies are not only upon us, but, and foremost, are a suitably tailored vessel to navigate the uncharted waters of the *new world order* whereby human beings and machines are bound to conflate.

§§ The emergence of *Brain-Computer Interfaces* stands as a living testament of such an overriding goal. When that day comes, and it will, human beings should bid a fond farewell to their beloved *mental privacy.*

§§ Artificial Intelligence-embedded technologies propel forward the gruelling process towards the *in-humanization* of human beings amidst the age of unfettered technological achievements that are narrowing down the once yawning gap between human beings and machines. To illustrate, take a hard look at the pathways through which Brain-Computer Interfaces, an offspring of disembodied agency, pledges to gear human beings toward.

§§ It is worth recalling that Brain-Computer Interfaces neatly encapsulates, hands-in-glove, the lens through which the harrowing **process of in-humanization** can be seen: if a computer can read your thoughts, you are no longer a human being, but an extension of a machine instead. Put otherwise, human beings are framed as «connected minds» that operate as an extension of an ever-recording machine—the kernel of the «extended mind thesis».

§§ Brain-Computer Interfaces spearhead staggering efforts to decode citizens' minds at granular levels. Governments—and tech moguls alike—have doubled down their whopping efforts to decipher citizens' minds. As a result, the perils for citizens' *right to be left alone and unaccounted for* soared accordingly. But not just that though. Freedom of thought and free will—of which human beings are so fond of—hangs on the balance as well.

§§ Mankind is sitting at the cusp of the greatest technological achievements ever recorded in history. Such technological advancements carry both danger (to the freedom of thought and to the free will) and promise (to restoring sight to the blind and affording mobility enhancement to those who have been unfortunately deprived from it).

§§ Strikingly, the interplay between Brain-Computer Interfaces and Artificial Intelligence-embedded technologies is poised to further blur the boundaries between human beings and machines. It bears mentioning that such an interplay is not only harmful to the freedom of thought, but, and foremost, to the free will. That is exactly the rationale behind the blend between Brain-Computer Interfaces and Artificial

Intelligence-embedded technologies: read your thoughts, *control* your mind while shaping your current and future behavioural patterns, thereby morphing you into an obedient individual unable to question the dystopian reality that is upon us.

§§ Before long, the interplay between Brain-Computer Interfaces and Artificial Intelligence-embedded technologies will not only allow machines to gain access to your deep-rooted memories but, and foremost, will be able to implant false memories of events that never occurred. Before long, criminal procedure law will be met be with scorching challenges that, if not deftly addressed, may topple its brawny foundations.

§§ Long story short, it boils down to a simple question: should prosecutors gain access to the memories of a crime etched on the defendant's brain only to convict him/her in a court of law? The answer is a resounding «no». The privilege against self-incrimination—a building block of Rule of Law—should stand tall amidst the mayhem of ubiquitous and pervasive Artificial Intelligence-embedded technologies that will reverberate through the corridors of modern societies.

§§ Yet a burning question remains unanswered: will the remnants of the best of the decaying *old world order*—that attached great importance to the citizens' fundamental rights—leave something behind? Put it coarsely, in spite of the withering series of attacks that fundamental rights have been enduring lately, can we nurture the unshattered hope that something can still be done to ensure that they will not vanish into thin air as time inexorably goes by amidst the age of *Algorithmic Dictatorship*? The answer is a resounding «yes». Here lies the pivotal importance of *Algorithmic Common Good*, which has been purposefully framed to throw *Algorithmic Dictatorship* out of balance.

§§ But know this: any hopes of either *understand* or *pin down* Artificial Intelligence-embedded technologies are fundamentally dashed by its unsustainable murkiness, its unfathomable ubiquity, and its unbearable opacity that forestalls any endeavour, no matter how earnest, to grasp both its inner workings and complex trappings.

§§ All we can do is *control*, rather than *understand*, Artificial Intelligence-embedded technologies or inordinate harms will otherwise occur. To cater for that, *Algorithmic Common Good* should stand tall in the midst of the storm of *Algorithmic Dictatorship* in a bid to taper off its nefarious effects.

§§ Against this background, this book proposes a major shift in conceptualizing the problems Artificial Intelligence-embedded technologies present in society at the intersection of law and technology. An initial step lies in shifting the gravitational centre of the legal discourse.

§§ This book accordingly proposes a legal perspective that critically centres *Algorithmic Dictatorship* and *Critical Artificial Intelligence Studies* at its intersection with Artificial Intelligence-embedded technologies and *Algorithmic Common Good* going forward. *Algorithmic Common Good* must be as fluid and capacious in approach as *Algorithmic Dictatorship* is in producing algorithmic discrimination.

§§ Building upon this, this book rebuffs altogether the firmly established notion that tinkering around or facilitating the eradication of machine learning algorithms present the only viable way to uproot deep-seated biases with an entrenched presence in datasets. This approach centres racial discrimination at its juncture with law and algorithmic risk assessment in criminal justice. This book therefore sides squarely with these budding doctrinal instalments in an earnest attempt to furnish baselines for *Algorithmic Common Good*.

§§ Holding all else constant, my stance therefore falls neatly into line with a bigger and sharper picture: uphold *Algorithmic Common Good* amidst the rise of Artificial Intelligence-embedded technologies whirlwind, which is playing havoc with our ability to deftly portend a future for algorithmic fairness. To that end, the definitional quandaries facing algorithmic risk assessment are in dire need of being tackled head-on.

§§ Compellingly, algorithmic risk assessment has garnered widespread attention. Algorithmic risk assessment has accordingly been received as a lightning bolt of great significance in the purview of criminal justice. Which caused algorithmic decision-making to swell. It is true that algorithmic risk assessment has aroused heated controversy lately, but truer still police, prosecutors, judges, and other criminal justice stakeholders are increasingly relying upon algorithmic risk assessment to predict if a defendant will engage in flagitious activities in the forthcoming future. The vexing question that this book sought to adroitly address, and deftly tackle, is: should they?

§§ These deep-rooted concerns are neither unwarranted, nor uncalled for, nor are they statistically unsound. It hardly amounts to a flabbergasting finding that these cutting-edge tools are not without humongous drawbacks. Tellingly, artificial intelligence-embedded technologies—which forms part of a broader technological apparatus within which algorithm risk assessment operates—often evince the devilishly harmful virus of algorithmic bias, which, I may venture to add, is wholly unbecoming in the purview of criminal procedure law.

§§ To further compound our functional woes and mental throes, machine learning algorithms, if nothing else, tend to be beset by racial skew, which falls inordinately on members of racialized communities. Contrary to popular belief, machine learning algorithms reflect the plethora of choices of their developers, and not some impervious goal, underlying truth on who deserves to be afforded *what* and *when*.

§§ It is true that Artificial Intelligence lies at the crossroads between the perennial quest for the overall betterment of society and the undeterred yearn to grasp algorithmic fairness measures, but truer still Artificial Intelligence-entrenched technologies exacerbate longstanding implicit biases with which modern societies have been grappling with.

§§ A key takeaway accordingly jumps out as ripe in this regard: AI-embedded technologies, if nothing else, are prone to reify, compound and exacerbate deep-seated social and ethnic concerns with which modern societies have been scuffling with for a long-haul, such as misogyny, racism, xenophobe, and political hatred which, taken together, are rife for misfire, social outcry, uproar, and a plethora of grievances alike. *Algorithmic Dictatorship* is a living testament of such gruesome reality.

§§ *Algorithmic Common Good* is therefore sorely needed—paired with tools like race-aware algorithms—to assuage the darkest patterns of Artificial Intelligence-embedded technologies arising out of the dingiest corners of the digital reality.

§§ But here is a much deeper truth: Artificial Intelligence-embedded technologies should not get to decide who should live and who should die; who should get appropriate medical care and who should not; who should get expedited access to credit and who should be prevented from gaining access to credit; which neighbourhoods should constantly be targeted by law enforcement agencies and which ones should not. Concisely, machines should not be entrusted with the task of making high stake decisions.

§§ To prevent that gruesome scenario from coming to fruition, society should roll up its collective sleeves in a bid to chart the path ahead for the implementation of a *Controllable Artificial Intelligence* amenable to be *interpretable*, *controllable*, *accountable*, and *fair*. Lest we endeavour to eschew the labyrinthic rule of machines, this is the pathway forward that prospective lawmakers and policymakers should choose to pursue.

§§ Bearing this backdrop very firmly in mind, the general furore over Artificial Intelligence-embedded technologies must be halted. Some tools—a robot-judge or a robot-prosecutor that can carry underlying racial biases against members of certain groups—must be accordingly pulled from use until they are duly tested and adroitly calibrated. That's the very least prominent industry stakeholders can do.

§§ Herculean efforts have been made to, and most of the academic community is burgeoningly rallying around the idea of, pinning down, weeding out, unwinding, and uprooting multiple forms of firmly rooted racial inequality with an entrenched presence on skewed datasets baked into machine learning algorithms. But, despite the good intentions with which those laudable initiatives are suffused by, to no avail. It is important to note, though, that our frame of reference does not lend itself to a misdiagnosis.

§§ Artificial Intelligence is leaving an indelible mark, and a unique fingerprint, on our daily lives. Nevertheless, Artificial Intelligence is a barren desert of murkiness, as opposed to a lush oasis of transparency. Notably, Artificial Intelligence is not a space of unwavering peace, infallibility, and transparency in that we must become acutely aware that one of its outgrowths—Generative Artificial Intelligence—may catalyse metamorphic shifts in the communications channels through which humans interact amidst the *age of permanent deception.*

§§ The speck of algorithmic lust underpinning Generative Artificial Intelligence is becoming visible. The audience—by definition, all of us—is accordingly besotted by the headways, and rapid strides, made by a Generative Artificial Intelligence that never ceases to amaze. Generative Artificial Intelligence is accordingly holding the audience spellbound.

§§ It is important to note, though, the audience's curiosity often laces with awe and discomfort insofar acts of meaningful communication were hitherto carried out by humans and humans only. Which prompts the burning questions: how did we get here? Foremost, what lies ahead? Will Generative Artificial disrupt old communication patterns while presenting new paradigms of communication? Will these new paradigms of communications involve encountering, and stumbling upon, unpleasant hurdles (v.g. ChatGPT hallucinations that sully the trustworthiness of Generative

Artificial Intelligence)? Is Generative Artificial Intelligence a stinging reminder that a fast-paced technology is bound to overhaul the system of justice beyond recognition?

§§ Let's take a step back to state the threadbare: there have been colossal breakthroughs in the purview of Artificial Intelligence-embedded technologies in recent years. Amongst these significant advancements stands arguably Large Language Models (hereinafter LLMs).

§§ Note, though, that the central thrust to equip machines with an ability to meaningfully communicate in a manner tantamount to that of humans is anything but new in that is an endeavour that is somewhat hackneyed.

§§ As noted above, chatbot Eliza was created by Joseph Weizenbaum back in 1964. Chatbot Eliza, just like ChatGPT, was fully capable of engaging in meaningful conversation with human beings. Eliza's behaviour was akin to that of humans insofar she could behave in a way a human would. Eliza was fully equipped to deftly use expressions, mannerisms, emotions, and archaisms that a human would. Hardly any surprise stems from the fact that Eliza was designed to mimic human behaviour while appearing to be one. Eliza would have passed the Turing Test with flying colours.

§§ Relatedly, finding number 4 enshrined in the Proposal for the Dartmouth Summer Research Project on Artificial Intelligence set forth in 1956 (*how can a computer be programmed to use a language*) bears a striking resemblance with the basic tenets of Large Language Models against the backdrop of which ChatGPT unfolds.

§§ On this note, it is noteworthy that the risks posed by LLMs (Large Language Models within which ChatGPT operates) hallucinations to the legal field comprise providing lawyers and scholars with misleading information, bedraggled information, phony cases, fictitious sources, and bogus statutory law, which, in turn, might be eventually used in written briefs, written motions, appeals, and court submissions, as in *Mata v. Avianca, Inc.*

§§ This finding should not come as a bewildering surprise, nor should strike you, dear reader, as odd. A body of empirical evidence has shown that ChatGPT amounts to an algorithmic-anchored tool prone to hallucinations in that its «large legal fictions» are anything but accurate, trustworthy, and reliable.

§§ Crucially, and perhaps disturbingly, «large legal fictions» are upon us in that they boast an exceedingly high degree of inevitability in the legal field. The leading case *Mata v. Avianca* therefore lends weight, and adds plausibility to, this main contention.

§§ In *Mata v. Avianca* the lawyers representing plaintiffs filed documents with the judicial court that comprised phony judicial opinions littered with fabricated quotes and fictitious citations generated by an Artificial Intelligence-embedded tool, thereby resulting in a finding of bad faith, sanctions, and a express request to apologize to, and atone for, all the judges whose names were unceremoniously, albeit unjustifiably, included in the groundless LLM output.

§§ This judicial decision has reverberated across the United States of America. Magistrates have accordingly begun issuing orders demanding lawyers/scholars who appear before them to vouchsafe whether and to what extent they have relied upon Generative Artificial Intelligence (ChatGPT) in drafting briefs, injunction reliefs, motions, appeals they file while strongly urging them to pay a nuanced attention to the reliability of the sources before those legal documents are formally submitted to a court of law.

§§ Lawyers, scholars, judges, and legal actors alike must realise that ChatGPT, as an AI tool, is a work in progress in that its legal-related outputs are mostly inaccurate, unreliable, and somewhat bedraggled. The former must therefore employ staggering efforts in carefully reviewing the *pearls of algorithmic wisdom* generated by LLM systems. Failing which, the Rule of Law will be irreparably lurched into abeyance. Worse still, Rule of Law will most likely careen into the chaos of lack of legitimacy whereby AI hallucinations soar and judicial legitimacy falters.

§§ Against this well-trodden background, ChatGPT is woefully ill-prepared to undertake legal-related tasks, such as fact-finding, discovery, writing briefs, written motions, affidavits, subpoenas, indictments, or court decisions. The relinquishment of human-related legal tasks to machines accordingly runs counter to basic tenets of truthfulness/accountability that may cost us dearly along the line. That is why *Algorithmic Common Good* is sorely needed.

§§ *Algorithmic Common Good*, to be fully operational, requires a *procedural accountability to the Rule of Law*. In addition to that, relevant stakeholders must abide by a responsible agency theory. Both concepts have been gleaned in the realm of Philosophy of Law and seek to instil both trust and trustworthiness upon algorithmic decision-making.

§§ Taken together, Professor Jeremy Waldron's procedural approach to the Rule of Law and Professor Lon. L. Fuller's responsible agency theory should steer relevant stakeholders' demeanours in algorithmic decision-making. Professor Joseph Raz's somewhat seconds the responsible agency theory.

§§ Professor Jeremy Waldron's procedural approach to the Rule of Law (Procedural Rule of Law) is two-fold. On one hand, means that the Rule of Law is inextricably linked to procedural concerns. Citizens must be bestowed upon the procedural opportunity to not only be part of a «technological due process», but also be awarded the chance to **challenge** the legal decisions issued therein. On the other hand, *Procedural Rule of Law* seeks to fizzle out both algorithmic biases and human biases that feed into machine learning algorithms, thereby impairing a sought-after *Algorithmic Common Good*.

§§ *Procedural Rule of Law* thus plays a pivotal role in keeping *Algorithmic Dictatorship* at bay. It accordingly seeks to allay algorithmic decision-making's deficiencies. Procedural Rule of Law therefore amounts to a beacon of algorithmic fairness suitably tailored to keep citizens' human dignity unscathed.

§§ Procedural Rule of Law lends itself to a lighthouse of legality and fairness befitted to peter out the harmful effects of *Algorithmic Dictatorship* while shielding citizens' human dignity.

§§ This book further contends that there must be a fundamental shift away from a **human-centred algorithmic decision-making** to a **thing-centred algorithmic decision-making**. Pivotally, relevant stakeholders must **control** the whole process of algorithmic decision-making from top to bottom.

§§ A **thing-centred algorithmic decision-making** accordingly vests relevant stakeholders (v.g. companies, public entities, law enforcement agencies, regulators, real estate agents, probation officers, judges, employers, loan officers, prosecutors, regulators, law enforcement agents, police officers, parole officers, engineers, programmers, tool developers, statisticians, data scientists, and so forth) with the **binding obligation** to **control** not only the model used to perform **algorithmic decision-making** (recall: simpler models, like random forests, decision trees or regression trees, are far easier to **control** than advanced models like deep neural convolutional networks), but, and foremost, the **outputs generated by the running model**.

§§ In so doing (i.e. **controlling the outputs generated by the running model**) algorithmic decision-making must embrace a fundamental shift away from analysis that aims to unravel causal connections between inputs and outcomes of interest.

§§ Compellingly, algorithmic decision-making, to be **controllable**, **interpretable**, accurate, reliable, and fair, requires that relevant stakeholders **shift their gaze downstream to the *outputs* of a machine learning algorithm, as opposed to the *inputs*.** This requires a fundamental shift away from **causation** and a pull towards **correlations**.

§§ The thematic underpinning of this main contention is simple: if relevant stakeholders deftly **control** the process of creation of algorithmic outputs, not only harms can be timely mitigated but, and foremost, citizens can adroitly **interpret** the pearls of algorithmic wisdom spawned by the running model and **challenge** them accordingly. This is the kernel of **Procedural Rule of Law**, that bestows upon citizens the chance to **challenge** the outputs generated by running models **(i.e. the correlations embedded in the dataset that paved the way to the production of outputs by the running model).**

§§ To cater for that, this book thereupon proposes **five laws to control Artificial algorithmic decision-making** and **five laws to interpret Artificial Intelligence-algorithmic decision-making.**

§§ The five laws to **control** algorithmic decision-making read as follows:

§§ **Law number one:** Whoever develops and/or deploys running models must be held criminally accountable for Hard Artificial Intelligent Crimes (Hard-AI crimes).

§§ **Law number two:** Black box models must never be entrusted with the task of making high stake decisions (v.g. regarding citizens' freedom or health).

§§ **Law number three:** The outputs generated by running models must be routinely audited through race-aware machine learning algorithms to ensure the trade-off between overall accuracy and fairness.

§§ **Law number four:** data partitioning must be performed—i.e. randomly split an entire dataset into the «training dataset» and the «test dataset»—to accurately predict outcomes in the real world while forestalling «inductive bias» (learning bias).

§§ **Law number five:** The running model must be externally audited.

§§ Fast forward to the thematic underpinnings of the **five laws to interpret algorithmic decision-making**, it should be noted from the outset that *algorithmic fairness*, albeit a bedazzling gift, is not without sizable hurdles. This is one the main roadblocks to the uptake of Artificial Intelligence-embedded technologies. The most prominent of which is that Artificial Intelligence, to produce algorithmic fairness, must be fundamentally *interpretable* by citizens. Intent and causation—agreed-upon benchmarks to gauge the extent to which the computer-generated outputs are fair and reasonable—are utterly incapable of explaining the complex world of AI-powered black box.

§§ For a simple reason: machine learning—and, especially, deep learning—is a world of hidden *correlations* embedded in the data that has been fed into the computer-generated algorithms, as opposed to a world of *causation* that currently reigns in the legal arena. To bypass/circumvent this perceived quandary, poignant calls have been made to keep «humans in the loop» as far as the emission of automated decisions is concerned.

§§ Notwithstanding, the turn towards *algorithmic fairness* entails, and fundamentally requires, a shift away from a legal analysis that haphazardly seeks to unlock/unveil/unearth/unravel causal connections between inputs and outputs. This book therefore proposes that algorithmic decision-making must shift its gaze downstream to the **algorithmic predictions (outputs)** made by computer-generated algorithms to usher in, and pave the way to, a new era of automation brimming with both procedural fairness and algorithmic accountability.

§§ To that end, **five laws to interpret algorithmic decision-making** must be kept front of mind.

§§ **Law number one:** The adoption of a **thing-centred algorithmic decision-making** that requires a fundamental shift away from **causation** and a pull towards **correlation**.

§§ **Law number two:** Relevant stakeholders must be given the chance to «understand the correlations between input variables and output variables»: **variable importance plots** must be used with a view to ensure an **interpretable** algorithmic decision-making that abides by the central tenets of Procedure Rule of Law.

§§ **Law number three: «Asymmetric Cost Ratios»** (the *cost ratio* for false positives to false negatives) must be timely implemented.

§§ **Law number four:** «Regularization» must be timely implemented to assuage *Algorithmic Dictatorship*—during the stages of model tuning and model training—while increasing *Algorithmic Common Good*.

§§ **Law number five:** robot-judges must not enter the courtroom as the latter—much like robot-prosecutors and robot-lawyers—are utterly incapable of making sound and interpretable value judgments in judicial decisions.

§§ Against this background, humankind is sitting at the cusp of a Great Technological Reset that marks the demise of the *old order* and the emergence of a *new world order*. Humankind is therefore standing at the crosspoint of infinite potential of Artificial Intelligence-embedded technologies.

§§ But know this: dear reader, your inner compass is the gatekeeper—and it has been constantly asking you: should you credulously rely on Artificial Intelligence-anchored technologies that will ultimately drag you to the limbic stage between humanism and transhumanism? If so, isn't humankind swiftly heading towards a **causal finitism** that will most likely wipe out humanity as we know? This is the kernel of **causal finitism** which, if left unaddressed, unchecked, and unaccounted for, is bound to throw humankind out of balance amidst the unbridled rise of **General Artificial Intelligence** equipped with a cognitive performance beyond that of humans.

§§ Whilst it is true that algorithmic justice concerns must be balanced against the need to ensure that technological innovation thrives, it is truer still that the latter must not come to the expense of the former. This assertion raises critical questions on how to strike a delicate balance between both.

§§ My take on this straightforward: Artificial Intelligence-embedded technology, while clustered in the shady hands of a handful of tech moguls, must generally work to the advantage of humankind. Technological breakthroughs must neither come the expense of human dignity nor harbour particularly malevolent attitudes towards the individuals affected. To illustrate, technological leaps must shy away from further compounding algorithmic injustice facing members of racialized communities.

§§ As we trudge through the desert of *Algorithmic Dictatorship*, staggering efforts must be thereupon poured in to achieve a magnificent oasis (*Algorithmic Common Good*) that lies before us. *Algorithmic Common Good* therefore lends a new urgency to concerns that beckons the dire need to vanquish *Algorithmic Dictatorship*. To cater for that, justice concerns must be kept front of mind.

§§ Pivotally, justice concerns must trump unfairness. Crucially, *Algorithmic Common Good* boast a mammoth and unrivalled advantage over Algorithmic Dictatorship: it provides a solace to those in throes with a wailing algorithmic grief. And that is a redoubtable force with which to reckon in algorithmic settings.

Index

H. L. dos Santos, *Controllable Artificial Intelligence and the Future of Law*, Artificial Intelligence and the Rule of Law, https://doi.org/10.1007/978-981-95-0508-1

GPSR Compliance

The European Union's (EU) General Product Safety Regulation (GPSR) is a set of rules that requires consumer products to be safe and our obligations to ensure this.

If you have any concerns about our products, you can contact us on ProductSafety@springernature.com

In case Publisher is established outside the EU, the EU authorized representative is:

Springer Nature Customer Service Center GmbH
Europaplatz 3
69115 Heidelberg, Germany

Batch number: 10725818

Printed by Printforce, the Netherlands